Weiss Ratings' Investment Research Guide to Bond & Money Market Mutual Funds

Weiss Ratings
4400 Northcorp Parkway
Palm Beach Gardens, FL 33410
561-627-3300

WeissRatings
Independent. Unbiased. Accurate. Trusted.

Published by Grey House Publishing, Inc., located at 4919 Route 22, Amenia, NY 12501; telephone 518-789-8700. Grey House Publishing neither guarantees the accuracy of the data contained herein nor assumes any responsibility for errors, omissions or discrepancies. Grey House Publishing accepts no payment for listing; inclusion in the publication of any organization, agency, institution, publication, service or individual does not imply endorsement of the publisher.

Grey House Publishing

Edition #13, Summer 2020

ISBN: 978-1-64265-569-8

Weiss Ratings' Investment Research Guide to Bond & Money Market Mutual Funds

Summer 2020

GREY HOUSE PUBLISHING

Contents

Terms and Conditions

Date of Data Analyzed: June 30, 2020

Welcome to Weiss Ratings' Investment Research Guide to Bond & Money Market Mutual Funds

With investing such a complex subject and the enormous popularity of mutual funds as a simple way to enter the markets it is no surprise that consumers need assistance. It is a complex subject and consumers want unbiased, independent guidance in helping them find a path to investing that is focused on their needs.

This is where Weiss Ratings comes in. We take all the data and process it, daily, to ensure that you receive not only the most up-to-date rating possible but also data that you may not easily find elsewhere. We publish this data in guides, and on our website so that you can feel empowered to make decisions about your investing future. Our focus is on balance and our ratings reflect this. No matter how strong a return has been if the level of risk taken is too high, in our opinion, then the overall rating will be reduced.

Weiss Ratings' Mission Statement

Weiss Ratings' mission is to empower consumers, professionals, and institutions with high quality advisory information for selecting or monitoring a financial services company or financial investment.

In doing so, Weiss Ratings will adhere to the highest ethical standards by maintaining our independent, unbiased outlook and approach for our customers.

Why rely on Weiss Ratings?

Weiss Ratings are fundamentally incomparable to nearly all other ratings available in America today. Here's why ...

Complete Independence

We are America's only 100% independent rating agency covering stocks, ETFs, mutual funds, insurance companies, banks, and credit unions; and our independence is grounded in a very critical difference in the way we do business: Unlike most other rating agencies,

- we never accept compensation from any company for its rating;
- we never allow companies to influence our analysis or conclusions (although they are always free to provide us with supplemental data that's not publicly available);
- we reserve the right to publish our ratings based exclusively on publicly available data;
- we never suppress publication of our ratings at a company's request; and
- we are always dedicated to providing our analysis and opinions with complete objectivity.

Dedication to End Users -- Investors and Consumers

Other rating agencies derive most of their revenues from the very same companies that they cover.

In contrast, our primary source of revenues is the end user – investors seeking the best combination of risk and reward, plus consumers seeking the best deals with the most safety.

Unmatched Accuracy and Performance

Our independence and objectivity help explain why the U.S. Government Accountability Office (GAO) concluded that Weiss was first in warning consumers about future insurance company failures three times more often than our closest competitor (A.M. Best) and why, in comparison to S&P or Moody's, there was no contest.

It's the reason why The New York Times wrote "Weiss was the first to warn of dangers and say so unambiguously."

And it's also why The Wall Street Journal was able to report that the Weiss Stock Ratings outperformed all Wall Street investment banks, brokers and independent research organizations in a third-party study of stock ratings.

Broader Coverage

While other rating agencies focus mostly on larger companies that can afford to pay them large fees, Weiss Ratings covers all companies, large or small, as long as they report sufficient data for us to analyze. This allows us to provide far broader coverage, including nearly all U.S.-traded stocks, ETFs and mutual funds plus nearly all U.S. banks, credit unions and insurance companies.

Overall ...

Weiss Ratings gives you more accuracy, more choices, and better wealth-building potential – all with stronger risk protection and safety.

How to Use This Guide

The purpose of the *Weiss Ratings' Investment Research Guide to Bond & Money Market Mutual Funds* is to provide investors with a reliable source of investment ratings and analyses on a timely basis. We realize that past performance is an important factor to consider when making the decision to purchase shares in a mutual fund. The ratings and analyses in this Guide can make that evaluation easier when you are considering Bond & Money Market Mutual funds. The rating for a particular fund indicates our opinion regarding that fund's past risk-adjusted performance.

When evaluating a specific mutual fund, we recommend you follow these steps:

Step 1 Confirm the fund name and ticker symbol. To ensure you evaluate the correct mutual fund, verify the fund's exact name and ticker symbol as it was given to you in its prospectus or appears on your account statement. Many funds have similar names, so you want to make sure the fund you look up is really the one you are interested in evaluating.

Step 2 Check the fund's Investment Rating. Turn to Section I, the *Index to Bond & Money Market Mutual Funds*, and locate the fund you are evaluating. This section contains all bond and money market mutual funds analyzed by Weiss Ratings, including those that did not receive an Investment Rating. All funds are listed in alphabetical order by the name of the fund with the ticker symbol following the name for additional verification. Once you have located your specific fund, the fourth column after the ticker symbol under the Ratings header shows its overall Investment Rating. Turn to *About Weiss Investment Ratings* for information about what this rating means.

Step 3 Analyze the supporting data. In addition to the Weiss Mutual Fund Rating are some of the various measures we have used in rating the fund. Refer to the Section I introduction to see what each of these factors measures. In most cases, lower rated funds will have a low reward rating and/or a low risk rating (i.e., high volatility). Bear in mind, however, that the Weiss Mutual Fund Rating is the result of a complex proprietary computer-generated analysis which cannot be reproduced using only the data provided here.

Step 4 When looking to identify a mutual fund that achieves your specific investing goals, we recommend the following:

- **Check the listing of the Largest funds.** If your priority is to stick with large funds because you believe that the size of the fund matters then these funds should be looked at. In this listing of the 100 largest funds you can also be assured that the Weiss Mutual Fund Rating is just as important as for the smallest fund.

- **Check the listing of the Best All-Around funds.** If your priority is to achieve a balanced return with the amount of risk being taken then check out this listing. We have selected what we believe provides a better return for those funds with over $1 billion in assets and with a maximum initial investment of $5,000 or less required.

- **Check the High Performance funds.** If your priority is to achieve the highest return, balanced with the amount of risk we have chosen the top mutual funds with the best financial performance. Not just "Buy" rated these funds have hit our demanding criteria of being in the top 25% of total returns for funds over a number of time-periods. Keep in mind that past performance alone is not always a guide to future performance.

- **Check the funds with Low Volatility.** On the other hand, if ultimate safety is your top priority, check out our list of the top recommended mutual funds with the lowest volatility. These funds may have lower performance ratings than some other funds, but can provide a safe place for your savings.

- **Check out the Top-Rated Funds by Fund Type.** If you are looking to invest in a particular type of mutual fund turn to our listing of "Buy" rated Mutual Funds by Fund Type. There you will find the top mutual funds with the highest performance rating in each category.

Step 5 Refer back to Section I. Once you have identified a particular fund that interests you, refer back to Section I, the *Index of Bond & Money Market Mutual Funds*, for a more thorough analysis.

Step 6 Always remember:

- **Read our warnings and cautions.** In order to use Weiss Investment Ratings most effectively, we strongly recommend you consult the Important Warnings and Cautions. These are more than just "standard disclaimers." They are very important factors you should be aware of before using this guide.

- **Stay up to date.** Periodically review the latest Weiss Mutual Fund Ratings for the funds that you own to make sure they are still in line with your investment goals and level of risk tolerance. You can find more detailed information and receive automated updates on ratings through www.weissratings.com

Data Source: Weiss Ratings
Morningstar, Inc.

Date of data analyzed: June 30, 2020

About Weiss Investment Ratings

Weiss Investment Ratings of stocks, ETFs and mutual funds are in the same realm as "buy," "sell" and "hold" ratings. They are designed to help investors make more informed decisions with the goal of maximizing gains and minimizing risk. Safety is also an important consideration. The higher the rating, the more likely the investment will be profitable. But when using our investment ratings, you should always remember that, by definition, all investments involve some element of risk.

A	Strong Buy
B	Buy
C	Hold or Avoid
D	Sell
E	Strong Sell

Our **Overall Rating** is measured on a scale from A to E based on each fund's risk and performance. The funds are analyzed using the latest daily data available and the quarterly filings with the SEC. Weiss takes thousands of pieces of fund data and, based on its own model, balances reward against the amount of risk to assign a rating. The results provide a simple and understandable opinion as to whether we think the fund is a BUY, SELL, or HOLD.

Our **Reward Rating** is based on the total return over a period of up to five years, including net asset value and price growth. The total return figure is stated net of the expenses and fees charged by the fund. Based on proprietary modeling the individual components of the risk and reward ratings are calculated and weighted and the final rating is generated.

Our **Risk Rating** includes the risk ratings of component stocks where applicable and also includes the financial stability of the fund, turnover where applicable, together with the level of volatility as measured by the fund's daily returns over a period of up to five years. Funds with greater stability are considered less risky and receive a higher risk rating. Funds with greater volatility are considered riskier, and will receive a lower risk rating. In addition to considering the fund's volatility, the risk rating also considers an assessment of the valuation and quality of a fund's holdings.

In order to help guarantee our objectivity, we reserve the right to publish ratings expressing our opinion of an investment reward and risk based exclusively on publicly available data and our own proprietary standards for safety. But when using our investment ratings, you should always remember that, by definition, all investments involve some element of risk.

Current Weiss Ratings Distribution of Bond & Money Market Mutual Funds

as of June 30, 2020

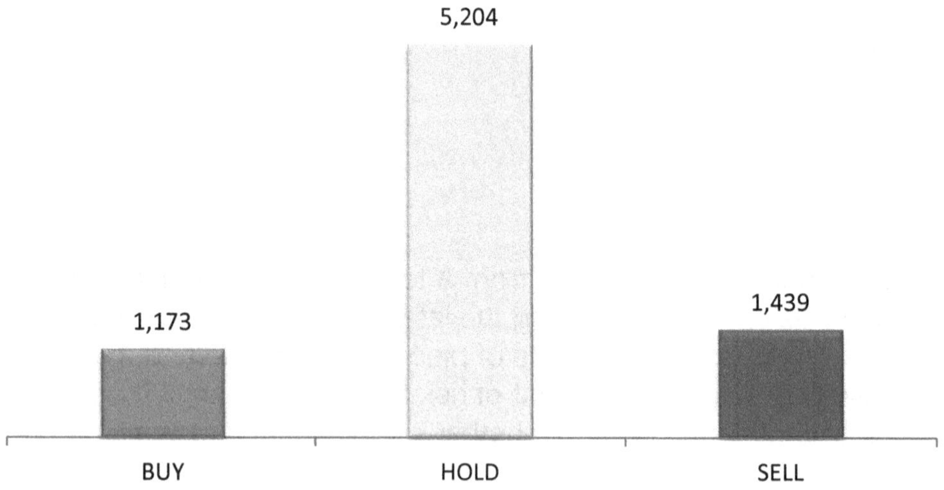

What Our Ratings Mean

Weiss Mutual Funds, Closed-End Funds, and Exchange Traded Funds Ratings represent a completely independent, unbiased opinion of funds—now, and in the future. The funds are analyzed using the latest daily data available and the quarterly filings with the SEC. Weiss takes thousands of pieces of fund data and, based on its own model, balances reward against the amount of risk to assign a rating. The results provide a simple and understandable opinion as to whether we think the fund is a BUY, SELL, or HOLD.

In order to help guarantee our objectivity, we reserve the right to publish ratings expressing our opinion of an investment reward and risk based exclusively on publicly available data and our own proprietary standards for safety. But when using our investment ratings, you should always remember that, by definition, all investments involve some element of risk.

Strong Buy

A **Excellent.** The fund has an excellent track record for maximizing performance while minimizing risk, thus delivering the best possible combination of total return on investment and reduced volatility. It has made the most of the recent economic environment to maximize risk-adjusted returns compared to other mutual funds. Although even the best funds can decline in a down market, our "A" rating can generally be considered the equivalent of a "Strong Buy".

Buy

B **Good.** The fund has a good track record for balancing performance with risk. Compared to other mutual funds, it has achieved above-average returns given the level of risk in its underlying investments. Although even good funds can decline in a down market, our "B" rating is considered the equivalent of a "Buy".

Hold or Avoid

C **Fair.** In the trade-off between performance and risk, the fund has a track record which is about average. It is neither significantly better nor significantly worse than most other funds. With some funds in this category, the total return may be better than average, but this can be misleading if the higher return was achieved with higher than average risk. With other funds, the risk may be lower than average, but the returns are also lower. Although funds can be driven higher or lower by general market trends, our "C" rating can generally be considered the equivalent of a "Hold" or "Avoid."

Sell

D **Weak.** The fund has underperformed the universe of other funds given the level of risk in its underlying investments, resulting in a weak risk-adjusted performance. Thus, its investment strategy and/or management has not been attuned to capitalize on the recent economic environment. Even weak funds can rise in an up market. However, our "D" rating can generally be considered equivalent to a "Sell."

Strong Sell

E **Very Weak.** The fund has significantly underperformed most other funds given the level of risk in its underlying investments, resulting in a very weak risk-adjusted performance. Thus, its investment strategy and/or management has done just the opposite of what was needed to maximize returns in the recent economic environment. Even some of the weakest funds can rise in certain market conditions. However, our "E" rating can generally be considered the equivalent of a "Strong Sell."

\+ The plus sign is an indication that the fund is in the upper third of the letter grade.

\- The minus sign is an indication that the fund is in the lower third of the letter grade.

U Unrated. The fund is unrated because it is too new to make a reliable assessment of its risk-adjusted performance. Typically, a fund must be established for at least one year before it is eligible to receive a Weiss Investment Rating.

Important Warnings & Cautions

1. A rating alone cannot tell the whole story. Please read the explanatory information contained here, in the section introductions and in the appendix. It is provided in order to give you an understanding of our rating methodology as well as to paint a more complete picture of a mutual fund's strengths and weaknesses.

2. Investment ratings shown in this directory were current as of the publication date. In the meantime, the rating may have been updated based on more recent data. Weiss Ratings offers a notification service for ratings changes on companies that you specify. For more information visit www.weissratings.com.

3. When deciding to invest in or sell holdings in a specific mutual fund, your decision must be based on a wide variety of factors in addition to the Weiss Mutual Fund Rating. These include any charges you may incur from switching funds, to what degree it meets your long-term planning needs, and what other choices are available to you. Weiss Ratings recommends that you should always consult an independent financial advisor over your investment decisions.

4. Weiss Mutual Fund Ratings represent our opinion of a mutual fund's past risk adjusted performance. As such, a high rating means we feel that the mutual fund has at least achieved above-average returns at the same time as it has balanced risk and returns. A high rating is not a guarantee that a fund will continue to perform well, nor is a low rating a prediction of continued weak performance. Any references to "Buy", "Hold", or "Sell" correlate with our opinion of a particular fund and Weiss Mutual Fund Ratings are not deemed to be a recommendation concerning the purchase or sale of any mutual fund.

5. All funds that have the same Weiss Investment Rating should be considered to be essentially equal from a risk/reward perspective. This is true regardless of any differences in the underlying numbers which might appear to indicate greater strengths.

6. Our rating standards are more consumer-oriented than those used by other rating agencies. We make more conservative assumptions about the amortization of loads and other fees as we attempt to identify those funds that have historically provided superior returns with only little or moderate risk.

7. We are an independent rating agency and do not depend on the cooperation of the managers operating the mutual funds we rate. Our data is obtained from a data aggregator. Data is input daily, as available, into our proprietary models where a complex series of algorithms provide us with ratings based on quantitative analysis. We do not grant mutual fund managers the right to stop or influence publication of the ratings. This policy stems from the fact that this Guide is designed for the information of the consumer.

Mutual Funds vs. Exchange-Traded Funds… Which is Right For You?

Both ETF's and Mutual Funds give you an inexpensive and easy way to diversify your investments and allow you to gain access to different asset classes with a single purchase. Ultimately, you'll need to consider a variety of factors including your tax strategy, the amount of money available to invest, and your overall investment strategy in order to determine which option is right for you.

Mutual Funds

Pros

- Mutual Funds are typically actively managed compared to ETF's which are typically tracking an index. Some of the better fund managers can regularly beat an index, although they will mostly have higher fees associated with them.
- Bigger Universe: There are over 28,000 Mutual Funds vs. less than 2,000 ETF's. You'll have more choices if you choose mutual funds, though the gap is narrowing every year.

Cons

- Mutual funds can only be purchased or sold at the end of the trading day after the market closes and their price is based on Net Asset Value (NAV), the value of fund assets minus liabilities divided by the number of shares.
- Mutual Fund holders can only see the holding of the Funds on a semi-annual basis.
- They are more tax prone- because the buying and selling within the fund by the Portfolio Manager creates more taxable events.
- Higher Minimum Investments

Stock Mutual Funds vs. Bond Mutual Funds

- Primarily, investors purchase stock mutual funds for appreciation or growth from within the companies inside the mutual fund itself. Conversely, bond mutual funds are primarily targeted for income reasons, since the entities inside a bond mutual fund give off income in the form of a coupon payment. Bonds and stocks frequently have an inverse relationship in market cycles, bonds will do well in down markets and stocks will do well in bull markets. For this reason, and for other diversification principles, it's important to have both bond and stock mutual funds in a long term retirement portfolio.
- It's important to note that there are exceptions to this rule, some stocks funds will give off an income in the form of dividend payments and many bond funds seek appreciation as well as income.
- There are risks associated with both bond and stock mutual funds. The risks in stock funds are primarily "market risk" meaning if the overall market is trending lower many stock funds will follow. The risks associated with bond funds are mostly associated with interest rates. In an environment with interest rates rising bond prices will follow and vice versa.

Exchange-Traded Funds (ETFs)

Pros

- ETFs offer much more flexibility. ETFs trade like stocks. They are priced on what Investors believe is Fair Market Value and you can buy and sell shares throughout the day.
- ETFs offer much more transparency, which means that investors can typically see the fund's holdings on a daily basis
- ETFs are more tax efficient than Mutual Funds. Because they are based off an index, there are fewer taxable events. Keep in mind, however, that capital gains and dividends are taxed the same as a Mutual Fund.
- ETFs have a lower expense ratio. In 2016, the average was .23 vs .82 of actively managed funds according to the Investment Company Institute.
- ETFs typically require lower minimum investments. Most of the time you can buy just a single share of the fund.
- You are typically paying a commission on buying and selling an exchange-traded fund. You'll pay a front or back end load when you purchase regular Mutual Funds.

Cons

- Some ETFs have limited choices in their asset class. Mutual Funds typically have more options.
- Given that an ETF trades like a stock, every purchase or sale requires paying a commission.

Section I:
Index of Bond & Money Market Mutual Funds

Investment Ratings and analysis of all rated and unrated Bond & Money Market Mutual Funds. Funds are listed in alphabetical order.

Section I: Contents

This section contains Weiss Investment Ratings, key rating factors, and summary financial data for over 8,000 Bond & Money Market Mutual funds. Funds are listed in alphabetical order.

Left Pages

Fund Name

Describes the fund's assets, regions of investments and investment strategies. Many funds have similar names, so you want to make sure the fund you look up is really the one you are interested in evaluating. In many cases, the Fund Name indicates the Class of the fund.

The most common Classes are:

Class A: This class of Mutual Fund typically has a front-end sales load and a loaded fee structure. Although the fees for Class A may typically be lower, because they normally charge front end fees, your initial amount invested will be lower and your overall return will be affected. An annual asset based fee may well be levied, although this is typically lower than other classes.

Class B: This class of shares, instead of a front-end or back-end sales load normally charges fees called a contingent deferred sales charge (CDSC). This fee is paid if you sell the shares within a certain period of time and may well decline after each year. An annual asset based fee is likely to be levied. Often a Class B share will convert to Class A within a couple of years of reaching the end of the CDSC expiry at which point Class A fees will be initiated.

Class C: A C-share is a class of mutual fund with a level load. They typically don’t have front-end loads, but do sometimes have back-end loads. They are usually around 1% but are sometimes eliminated after the shares are held for over a year. Annual asset based fees are normal for this class of share.

Class I: This class is sold to institutional shareholders. Also called Y-Shares, these have different fees and do not charge traditional loads.

Class R: R share funds, Also known as K shares, are for retirement accounts, and the R share class mutual funds are only available through employer-sponsored retirement plans. R share mutual funds do not have any loads, but they do have annual asset based fees typically of around 0.25% to 0.50%.

MARKET

Ticker Symbol

An arrangement of characters (usually letters) representing a particular security listed on an exchange or otherwise traded publicly. When a company issues securities to the public marketplace, it selects an available ticker symbol for its securities which investors use to place trade orders. Every listed security has a unique ticker symbol, facilitating the vast array of trade orders that flow through the financial markets every day. If a ticker symbol is not assigned to a particular fund, the International Securities Identification Number (ISIN) is displayed.

Traded On (Exchange)

The stock exchange on which the fund is listed. The core function of a stock exchange is to ensure fair and orderly trading, as well as efficient dissemination of price information. Exchanges such as: NYSE (New York Stock Exchange), AMEX (American Stock Exchange), NNM (NASDAQ National Market), and NASQ (NASDAQ Small Cap) give companies, governments and other groups a platform to sell securities to the investing public.

FUND TYPE, CATEGORY & OBJECTIVE

Fund Type

Describes the fund's assets, regions of investments and investment strategies.

Open End Fund

A type of mutual fund that does not have restrictions on the amount of shares the fund will issue. If demand is high enough, the fund will continue to issue shares no matter how many investors there are. Open-end funds also buy back shares when investors wish to sell.

Closed End Fund

They are launched through an Initial Public Offering in order to raise money and then trade in the open market just like a stock or an ETF. They only issue a set amount of shares and, although their value is also based on the Net Asset Value, the actual price of the fund is affected by supply and demand, allowing it to trade at prices above or below its real value.

Money Market Fund

Mutual fund that invests primarily in low-risk, short-term investments such as treasury bills, government securities, certificates of deposit and other highly liquid, safe securities.

Category

Identifies funds according to their actual investment styles as measured by their portfolio holdings. This categorization allows investors to spread their money around in a mix of funds with a variety of risk and return characteristics.

Prospectus Objective
Gives a general idea of a fund's overall investment approach and goals.

RATINGS

Overall Rating
The Weiss rating measured on a scale from A to E based on each fund's risk and performance. See the preceding section, "What Our Ratings Mean," for an explanation of each letter grade rating.

Reward Rating
This is based on the total return over a period of up to five years, including net asset value and price growth. The total return figure is stated net of the expenses and fees charged by the fund. Based on proprietary modeling the individual components of the risk and reward ratings are calculated and weighted and the final rating is generated.

Risk Rating
This is includes the risk ratings of component stocks where applicable and also includes the financial stability of the fund, turnover where applicable, together with the level of volatility as measured by the fund's daily returns over a period of up to five years. Funds with greater stability are considered less risky and receive a higher risk rating. Funds with greater volatility are considered riskier, and will receive a lower risk rating. In addition to considering the fund's volatility, the risk rating also considers an assessment of the valuation and quality of a fund's holdings.

Recent Upgrade/Downgrade
An "Up" or "Down" indicates that the Weiss Mutual Fund rating has changed since the publication of the last print edition. If a fund has had a rating change since March 31, 2020, the change is identified with an "Up" or "Down."

NEW INVESTORS

Open to New Investors
Indicates whether the fund accepts investments from those who are not existing investors. A "Y" in this column identifies that the fund accepts new investors. No data in this column indicates that the fund is closed to new investors. The fund may be closed to new investors because the fund's asset base is getting too large to effectively execute its investing style. Although, the fund may be closed, in most cases, existing investors are able to add to their holdings.

Telephone
The company's phone number.

Right Pages

RETURNS & PERFORMANCE

3-Month Total Return
The rate of return on an investment over three months that includes interest, capital gains, dividends and distributions realized.

6-Month Total Return
The rate of return on an investment over six months that includes interest, capital gains, dividends and distributions realized.

1-Year Total Return
The rate of return on an investment over one year that includes interest, capital gains, dividends and distributions realized.

3-Year Total Return
The rate of return on an investment over three years that includes interest, capital gains, dividends and distributions realized.

5-Year Total Return
The rate of return on an investment over five years that includes interest, capital gains, dividends and distributions realized.

Dividend Yield (TTM)
Trailing twelve months dividends paid out relative to the share price. Expressed as a percentage and measures how much cash flow an investor is getting for each invested dollar. **Trailing Twelve Months** (TTM) is a representation of a fund's financial performance over the most recent 12 months. TTM uses the latest available financial data from a company's interim, quarterly or annual reports.

Expense Ratio
A measure of what it costs an investment company to operate a mutual fund. An expense ratio is determined through an annual calculation, where a fund's operating expenses are divided by the average dollar value of its assets under management. Operating expenses may include money spent on administration and management of the fund, advertising, etc. An expense ratio of 1 percent per annum means that each year 1 percent of the fund's total assets will be used to cover expenses.

3-Year Standard Deviation
A statistical measurement of dispersion about an average, which depicts how widely the returns varied over the past three years. Investors use the standard deviation of historical performance to try to predict the range of returns that are most likely for a given fund. When a fund has a high standard deviation, the predicted range of performance is wide, implying greater volatility. Standard deviation is most appropriate for measuring risk if it is for a fund that is an investor's only holding. The figure cannot be combined for more than one fund

because the standard deviation for a portfolio of multiple funds is a function of not only the individual standard deviations, but also of the degree of correlation among the funds' returns. If a fund's returns follow a normal distribution, then approximately 68 percent of the time they will fall within one standard deviation of the mean return for the fund, and 95 percent of the time within two standard deviations.

Effective Duration

Effective duration for all long fixed income positions in a portfolio. This value gives a better estimation of how the price of bonds with embedded options, which are common in many mutual funds, will change as a result of changes in interest rates. Effective duration takes into account expected mortgage prepayment or the likelihood that embedded options will be exercised if a fund holds futures, other derivative securities, or other funds as assets, the aggregate effective duration should include the weighted impact of those exposures.

ASSETS

NAV (Net Asset Value)

A fund's price per share. The value is calculated by dividing the total value of all the securities in the portfolio, less any liabilities, by the number of fund shares outstanding.

Total Assets (MIL)

The total of all assets listed on the institution's balance sheet. This figure primarily consists of loans, investments, and fixed assets. Total Assets are displayed in millions.

ASSET ALLOCATION & TURNOVER

Asset Allocation

Indicates the percentage of assets in each category. Used as an investment strategy that attempts to balance risk versus reward by adjusting the percentage of each asset in an investment portfolio according to the investor's risk tolerance, goals and investment time frame. Allocation percentages may not add up to 100%. Negative values reflect short positions.

%Cash

The percentage of the fund's assets invested in short-term obligations, usually less than 90 days, that provide a return in the form of interest payments. This type of investment generally offers a low return compared to other investments but has a low risk level.

%Government Bonds

The percentage of the fund's assets invested in government bonds. A government bond is issued by a national government.

%Municipal Bonds

The percentage of the fund's assets invested in municipal bonds. A municipal bond is issued by or on behalf of a local authority.

%Corporate Bonds
The percentage of the fund's assets invested in corporate bonds. A corporate bond is issued by a corporation.

%Other
The percentage of the fund's assets invested in other financial instruments.

Turnover Ratio
The percentage of a mutual fund or other investment vehicle's holdings that have been replaced with other holdings in a given year. Generally, low turnover ratio is favorable, because high turnover equates to higher brokerage transaction fees, which reduce fund returns.

Average Coupon Rate
The annual interest rate of a debt/bond security that the issuer promises to pay to the holder until maturity.

MINIMUMS

Minimum Initial Investment
The smallest investment amount a fund will accept to establish a new account. This amount could be $0 or any other number set by the fund.

Minimum Additional Investment
The smallest additional investment amount a fund will accept in an existing account.

FEES

Front End Fee (%)
A commission or sales charge applied at the time of the initial purchase of an investment. The fee percentage is generally based on the amount of the investment. Larger investments, both initial and cumulative, generally receive percentage discounts based on the dollar value invested. Fees are displayed as a percent.

Back End Fee (%)
A fee that investors pay when withdrawing money from an investment within a specified number of years, usually five to 10 years. The back-end load is designed to discourage withdrawals and typically declines for each year that a shareholder remains in a fund. The fee is a percentage of the value of the share being sold. Fees are displayed as a percent.

Inception Date
The date on which the fund began its operations. The commencement date indicates when a fund began investing in the market. Many investors prefer funds with longer operating histories. Funds with longer histories have longer track records and can thereby provide investors with a more long-standing picture of their performance.

	MARKET		FUND TYPE, CATEGORY & OBJECTIVE		RATINGS				NEW INVESTORS	
Fund Name	Ticker Symbol	Traded On	Fund Type	Category and (Prospectus Objective)	Overall Rating	Reward Rating	Risk Rating	Recent Up/ Downgrade	Open to New Investors	Telephone
1290 Diversified Bond Fund Class A	TNUAX	NAS CM	Open End	Fixed Inc Misc (Income)	B-	C	B+	Up	Y	212-554-1234
1290 Diversified Bond Fund Class I	TNUIX	NAS CM	Open End	Fixed Inc Misc (Income)	B-	C	B+	Up	Y	212-554-1234
1290 Diversified Bond Fund Class R	TNURX	NAS CM	Open End	Fixed Inc Misc (Income)	B-	C	B	Up	Y	212-554-1234
1290 High Yield Bond Fund Class A	TNHAX	NAS CM	Open End	US Fixed Inc (Corp Bond - High Yield)	C-	D+	C	Down	Y	212-554-1234
1290 High Yield Bond Fund Class I	TNHIX	NAS CM	Open End	US Fixed Inc (Corp Bond - High Yield)	C-	D+	C	Down	Y	212-554-1234
1290 High Yield Bond Fund Class R	TNHRX	NAS CM	Open End	US Fixed Inc (Corp Bond - High Yield)	C-	D+	C		Y	212-554-1234
1290 High Yield Bond Fund Class T	TNHCX	NAS CM	Open End	US Fixed Inc (Corp Bond - High Yield)	C-	D+	C	Down	Y	212-554-1234
1290 VT DoubleLine Opportunistic Bond Portfolio Class IB			Open End	US Fixed Inc (Income)	U	U	U		Y	877-222-2144
1290 VT DoubleLine Opportunistic Bond Portfolio Class K			Open End	US Fixed Inc (Income)	U	U	U		Y	877-222-2144
1290 VT High Yield Bond Portfolio Class IB			Open End	US Fixed Inc (Corp Bond - High Yield)	U	U	U		Y	877-222-2144
1290 VT High Yield Bond Portfolio Class K			Open End	US Fixed Inc (Corp Bond - High Yield)	U	U	U		Y	877-222-2144
1919 Maryland Tax-Free Income Fund Class A	LMMDX	NAS CM	Open End	US Muni Fixed Inc (Muni Bond - Single State)	C	C	B-		Y	
1919 Maryland Tax-Free Income Fund Class C	LMMCX	NAS CM	Open End	US Muni Fixed Inc (Muni Bond - Single State)	C	C-	C+		Y	
1919 Maryland Tax-Free Income Fund Class I	LMMIX	NAS CM	Open End	US Muni Fixed Inc (Muni Bond - Single State)	C	C	B-		Y	
1WS Credit Income Fund Beneficial Interest			Closed End	US Fixed Inc (Growth & Income)	D	D	D	Up	Y	
A3 Alternative Credit Fund			Closed End	US Fixed Inc (Growth & Income)	U	U	U		Y	303-997-9010
AAAMCO Ultrashort Financing Fund Class I	REPOX	NAS CM	Open End	US Fixed Inc (Income)	C	C-	C+		Y	305-379-6656
AAAMCO Ultrashort Financing Fund Class Y	REPYX	NAS CM	Open End	US Fixed Inc (Income)	C	C-	C+		Y	305-379-6656
AAM/HIMCO Short Duration Fund Class A	ASDAX	NAS CM	Open End	US Fixed Inc (Income)	C	C-	C+		Y	800-617-0004
AAM/HIMCO Short Duration Fund Class C	ASDCX	NAS CM	Open End	US Fixed Inc (Income)	C-	D+	C		Y	800-617-0004
AAM/HIMCO Short Duration Fund Class I	ASDIX	NAS CM	Open End	US Fixed Inc (Income)	C	C-	C+		Y	800-617-0004
AAM/Insight Select Income Fund Class A	CPUAX	NAS CM	Open End	US Fixed Inc (Income)	C+	C	B	Up	Y	800-617-0004
AAM/Insight Select Income Fund Class C	CPUCX	NAS CM	Open End	US Fixed Inc (Income)	C	C	B-		Y	800-617-0004
AAM/Insight Select Income Fund Class I	CPUIX	NAS CM	Open End	US Fixed Inc (Income)	C+	C	B	Up	Y	800-617-0004
AAM/Insight Select Income Fund Class Y	CPUYX	NAS CM	Open End	US Fixed Inc (Income)	C+	C	B	Up	Y	800-617-0004
AAMA Income Fund	AMFIX	NAS CM	Open End	US Fixed Inc (Income)	C	C-	B-		Y	
AB Bond Inflation Strategy Advisor Class	ABNYX	NAS CM	Open End	US Fixed Inc (Govt Bond - Treasury)	C	C	B-		Y	212-969-1000
AB Bond Inflation Strategy Class 1	ABNOX	NAS CM	Open End	US Fixed Inc (Govt Bond - Treasury)	C	C-	B-		Y	212-969-1000
AB Bond Inflation Strategy Class 2	ABNTX	NAS CM	Open End	US Fixed Inc (Govt Bond - Treasury)	C	C	B-		Y	212-969-1000
AB Bond Inflation Strategy Class A	ABNAX	NAS CM	Open End	US Fixed Inc (Govt Bond - Treasury)	C	C-	B-		Y	212-969-1000
AB Bond Inflation Strategy Class C	ABNCX	NAS CM	Open End	US Fixed Inc (Govt Bond - Treasury)	C	C-	C+	Up	Y	212-969-1000
AB Bond Inflation Strategy Class I	ANBIX	NAS CM	Open End	US Fixed Inc (Govt Bond - Treasury)	C	C	B-		Y	212-969-1000
AB Bond Inflation Strategy Class K	ABNKX	NAS CM	Open End	US Fixed Inc (Govt Bond - Treasury)	C	C-	B-		Y	212-969-1000
AB Bond Inflation Strategy Class R	ABNRX	NAS CM	Open End	US Fixed Inc (Govt Bond - Treasury)	C	C-	B-		Y	212-969-1000
AB Bond Inflation Strategy Fund Class Z	ABNZX	NAS CM	Open End	US Fixed Inc (Govt Bond - Treasury)	C	C	B-		Y	212-969-1000
AB Corporate Income Shares	ACISX	NAS CM	Open End	US Fixed Inc (Income)	C+	C	B	Up	Y	212-969-1000
AB Diversified Municipal Portfolio	SNDPX	NAS CM	Open End	US Muni Fixed Inc (Muni Bond - Natl)	C	C-	C+		Y	212-969-1000
AB FlexFee High Yield Portfolio Advisor Class	HIYYX	NAS CM	Open End	US Fixed Inc (Corp Bond - High Yield)	C-	D+	C		Y	212-969-1000
AB FlexFee International Bond Portfolio Advisor Class	FFIYX	NAS CM	Open End	Global Fixed Inc (Income)	C	C-	C+		Y	212-969-1000
AB Global Bond Fund Advisor Class	ANAYX	NAS CM	Open End	Global Fixed Inc (Worldwide Bond)	C	C	B-		Y	212-969-1000
AB Global Bond Fund Class A	ANAGX	NAS CM	Open End	Global Fixed Inc (Worldwide Bond)	C	C	B-		Y	212-969-1000
AB Global Bond Fund Class C	ANACX	NAS CM	Open End	Global Fixed Inc (Worldwide Bond)	C	C-	C+		Y	212-969-1000
AB Global Bond Fund Class I	ANAIX	NAS CM	Open End	Global Fixed Inc (Worldwide Bond)	C	C	B-		Y	212-969-1000
AB Global Bond Fund Class K	ANAKX	NAS CM	Open End	Global Fixed Inc (Worldwide Bond)	C	C	B-		Y	212-969-1000
AB Global Bond Fund Class R	ANARX	NAS CM	Open End	Global Fixed Inc (Worldwide Bond)	C	C-	B-		Y	212-969-1000
AB Global Bond Fund Class Z	ANAZX	NAS CM	Open End	Global Fixed Inc (Worldwide Bond)	C	C	B		Y	212-969-1000
AB Government Money Market Portfolio Advisor Class	AEYXX	NAS CM	Money Mkt	US Money Mkt (Money Mkt - Govt)	C	C-	C+		Y	212-969-1000
AB Government Money Market Portfolio Class 1	AGRXX	NAS CM	Money Mkt	US Money Mkt (Money Mkt - Govt)	C	C-	C+		Y	212-969-1000
AB Government Money Market Portfolio Class A	AEAXX	NAS CM	Money Mkt	US Money Mkt (Money Mkt - Govt)	C	C-	C+		Y	212-969-1000
AB Government Money Market Portfolio Class AB	MYMXX	NAS CM	Money Mkt	US Money Mkt (Money Mkt - Govt)	C	C	C+		Y	212-969-1000
AB Government Money Market Portfolio Class C	AECXX	NAS CM	Money Mkt	US Money Mkt (Money Mkt - Govt)	C	C-	C+		Y	212-969-1000
AB Government Money Market Portfolio Class I	AIEXX	NAS CM	Money Mkt	US Money Mkt (Money Mkt - Govt)	C	C-	C+		Y	212-969-1000

★ Expanded analysis of this fund is included in Section II.

TOTAL RETURNS & PERFORMANCE									ASSETS		ASSET ALLOCATION & TURNOVER							MINIMUMS		FEES		
3-Month Total Return	6-Month Total Return	1-Year Total Return	3-Year Total Return	5-Year Total Return	Dividend Yield (TTM)	Expense Ratio	3-Yr Std Deviation	Effective Duration	NAV	Total Assets (ML)	%Cash	%Government Bonds	%Municipal Bonds	%Corporate Bonds	%Other	Turnover Ratio	Average Coupon Rate	Min Initial Investment	Min Additional Investment	Front End Fee (%)	Back End Fee (%)	Inception Date
11.18	5.68	8.34	20.24	27.57	2.97	0.75	5.23	8.63	10.5248	110.0	5	33	0	46	0	194	4.93	1,000	50	4.50		Jul-15
11.29	5.89	8.67	21.29	29.33	3.1	0.5	5.25	8.63	10.5614	110.0	5	33	0	46	0	194	4.93	1,000,000				Jul-15
11.20	5.66	8.11	19.54	26.20	2.82	1	5.23	8.63	10.5071	110.0	5	33	0	46	0	194	4.93	0				Jul-15
8.87	-2.23	1.09	9.65	21.06	5.35	1	7.32	3.40	8.7445	37.8	3	0	0	97	0	54	6.58	1,000	50	4.50		Nov-14
9.00	-2.11	1.35	10.59	22.69	5.6	0.75	7.34	3.40	8.7509	37.8	3	0	0	97	0	54	6.58	1,000,000		2.50		Nov-14
8.85	-2.35	0.85	8.98	19.62	5.09	1.25	7.29	3.40	8.7416	37.8	3	0	0	97	0	54	6.58	0				Nov-14
9.02	-2.11	1.46	10.59	22.70	5.6	1	7.34	3.40	8.7491	37.8	3	0	0	97	0	54	6.58	1,000	50	2.50	1.00	Nov-14
-0.99	-0.09	-1.84	6.24		1.59	1.05	2.46	4.85		334.6	2	35	0	30	0	120	3.77	0				Apr-15
-0.99	0.01	-1.58	6.96		1.84	0.8	2.49	4.85		334.6	2	35	0	30	0	120	3.77	0				Apr-15
-1.83	-0.10	-0.06	15.69	17.69	4.88	1.1	3.58	3.80		203.9	3	0	0	97	0	61	6.45	0				Feb-13
-1.83	0.00	0.19	16.48	19.10	5.13	0.85	3.63	3.80		203.9	3	0	0	97	0	61	6.45	0				Feb-13
1.28	1.55	2.93	7.96	13.06	2.37	0.75	2.49		15.74	84.3	1	0	99	0	0	21	3.87	1,000	50	4.25		Apr-91
1.14	1.28	2.37	6.20	10.00	1.82	1.3	2.5		15.74	84.3	1	0	99	0	0	21	3.87	1,000	50		1.00	Feb-09
1.38	1.63	3.08	8.52	13.91	2.52	0.6	2.5		15.75	84.3	1	0	99	0	0	21	3.87	1,000,000				Jul-08
10.40	-7.22	-3.69			6.81	2.95			18.38	--						26		1,000,000				Mar-19
0.79	5.24					3.3			10.42	--	49	0	0	0	-8		2.17	100,000				Oct-19
0.20	0.48	1.57	5.92		1.75	0.35			9.9992	507.5	90	0	0	0	0	258	0.89	25,000				Jun-17
0.22	0.52	1.63	6.09		1.8	0.3			10.0002	507.5	90	0	0	0	0	258	0.89	10,000,000				Jun-17
4.49	0.02	1.52	6.63	11.59	2.24	0.84	3.29	0.86	9.98	288.4	12	5	0	54	-1	33	2.64	2,500	500	2.50		Jun-14
4.25	-0.28	0.83	4.31	7.58	1.48	1.59	3.29	0.86	9.96	288.4	12	5	0	54	-1	33	2.64	2,500	500		1.00	Jun-14
4.53	0.13	1.75	7.42	13.04	2.48	0.59	3.34	0.86	9.99	288.4	12	5	0	54	-1	33	2.64	25,000	5,000			Jun-14
11.11	3.63	8.03	17.46	29.32	2.82	0.84	7.59	7.78	10.87	174.6	1	3	1	80	-1	155	4.55	2,500	500	3.00		Apr-13
10.99	3.32	7.22	14.96	24.80	2.12	1.56	7.62	7.78	10.86	174.6	1	3	1	80	-1	155	4.55	2,500	500		1.00	Apr-13
11.27	3.75	8.32	18.46	31.14	3.11	0.53	7.66	7.78	10.88	174.6	1	3	1	80	-1	155	4.55	25,000	5,000			Apr-13
11.29	3.78	8.37	18.47	31.15	3.16	0.5	7.69	7.78	10.87	174.6	1	3	1	80	-1	155	4.55	1,000,000	100,000			Oct-17
0.02	2.52	3.20	5.86		1.08	0.93			25.58	153.0	16	84	0	0	0	20	2.18	10,000				Jun-17
7.53	2.23	4.44	11.20	18.09	2.5	0.97	4.81	2.90	11.23	579.6	-5	53	0	8	0	40	1.58	0				Jan-10
7.48	2.10	4.29	10.90	17.51	2.6	1.07	4.84	2.90	11.02	579.6	-5	53	0	8	0	40	1.58	5,000				Jan-10
7.51	2.14	4.40	11.14	17.94	2.71	0.96	4.85	2.90	11.01	579.6	-5	53	0	8	0	40	1.58	5,000,000				Jan-10
7.39	2.02	4.09	10.36	16.50	2.23	1.25	4.86	2.90	11.21	579.6	-5	53	0	8	0	40	1.58	2,500	50	4.25		Jan-10
7.27	1.68	3.35	7.88	12.26	1.59	1.99	4.85	2.90	10.91	579.6	-5	53	0	8	0	40	1.58	2,500	50		1.00	Jan-10
7.54	2.18	4.46	11.21	18.13	2.58	0.95	4.85	2.90	11.1	579.6	-5	53	0	8	0	40	1.58	2,000,000				Jan-10
7.50	2.04	4.19	10.36	16.60	2.23	1.28	4.84	2.90	11.19	579.6	-5	53	0	8	0	40	1.58	0				Jan-10
7.43	1.97	3.94	9.68	15.33	1.87	1.47	4.83	2.90	11.21	579.6	-5	53	0	8	0	40	1.58	0				Jan-10
7.48	2.13	4.38	11.18	18.08	2.69	0.96	4.84	2.90	11.05	579.6	-5	53	0	8	0	40	1.58	2,000,000				Dec-14
11.72	4.82	10.07	21.58	33.10	3.77	0	7.85	8.54	12.1	120.3	-13	15	0	79	0	140	4.41	0				Dec-06
2.82	1.00	2.38	8.29	12.96	2.32	0.47	3.52	4.40	14.56	6,074	1	1	97	1	0	22	4.81	25,000				Jan-89
11.71	-3.93	0.14	10.04	22.13	6.56	0.3	9.5	4.63	8.98	36.1	-22	22	0	58	8	40	5.35	0				Jul-16
3.76	1.06	2.40	11.96		3.1	0.2		8.18	10.05	48.4	-11	33	0	8	0	96	2.63	0	0			Jun-17
5.15	1.94	3.53	10.95	21.43	3.3	0.56	4.28	7.57	8.57	6,699	-18	31	0	13	0	126	2.99	0				Nov-07
5.21	1.81	3.27	10.11	20.02	3.05	0.81	4.37	7.57	8.58	6,699	-18	31	0	13	0	126	2.99	2,500	50	4.25		Mar-92
4.87	1.43	2.49	7.63	15.43	2.29	1.56	4.35	7.57	8.6	6,699	-18	31	0	13	0	126	2.99	2,500	50		1.00	May-93
5.13	1.93	3.53	10.99	21.63	3.3	0.55	4.27	7.57	8.57	6,699	-18	31	0	13	0	126	2.99	2,000,000				Nov-07
5.04	1.73	3.13	9.76	19.29	2.91	0.93	4.33	7.57	8.57	6,699	-18	31	0	13	0	126	2.99	0				Nov-07
4.96	1.58	2.81	8.75	17.42	2.6	1.24	4.27	7.57	8.57	6,699	-18	31	0	13	0	126	2.99	0				Nov-07
5.15	1.95	3.57	11.15	21.77	3.34	0.5	4.28	7.57	8.57	6,699	-18	31	0	13	0	126	2.99	2,000,000				Oct-13
0.04	0.36	1.30	4.44	5.06	1.47	0.26			1	15,472	69	31	0	0	0			0				Nov-17
0.06	0.39	1.35	4.69	5.10	1.52	0.22			1	15,472	69	31	0	0	0			100,000				Nov-17
0.05	0.37	1.31	4.33	4.44	1.47	0.5			1	15,472	69	31	0	0	0			2,500	50	4.25		Nov-17
0.06	0.39	1.36	4.75	5.37	1.53	0.11	0.18		1	15,472	69	31	0	0	0							Dec-06
0.05	0.37	1.31	4.11	3.17	1.47	1.02			1	15,472	69	31	0	0	0			2,500	50		1.00	Nov-17
0.05	0.37	1.33	4.68	5.30	1.5	0.13			1	15,472	69	31	0	0	0			5,000,000				Nov-17

	MARKET			FUND TYPE, CATEGORY & OBJECTIVE	RATINGS				NEW INVESTORS	
Fund Name	Ticker Symbol	Traded On	Fund Type	Category and (Prospectus Objective)	Overall Rating	Reward Rating	Risk Rating	Recent Up/ Downgrade	Open to New Investors	Telephone
AB Government Money Market Portfolio Class K	AEKXX	NAS CM	Money Mkt	US Money Mkt (Money Mkt - Govt)	C	C-	C+		Y	212-969-1000
AB Government Money Market Portfolio Institutional Class	GMOXX	NAS CM	Money Mkt	US Money Mkt (Money Mkt - Govt)	C	C-	C+		Y	212-969-1000
AB Government Money Market Portfolio Investor Class	GMNXX	NAS CM	Money Mkt	US Money Mkt (Money Mkt - Govt)	C	C-	C+		Y	212-969-1000
AB Government Money Market Portfolio Premium Class	GMPXX	NAS CM	Money Mkt	US Money Mkt (Money Mkt - Govt)	C	C-	C+		Y	212-969-1000
AB Government Money Market Portfolio Select Class			Money Mkt	US Money Mkt (Money Mkt - Govt)	C	C-	C+		Y	212-969-1000
AB High Income Fund Advisor Class	AGDYX	NAS CM	Open End	US Fixed Inc (Worldwide Bond)	D	D	D+	Down	Y	212-969-1000
AB High Income Fund Class A	AGDAX	NAS CM	Open End	US Fixed Inc (Worldwide Bond)	D	D	D+	Down	Y	212-969-1000
AB High Income Fund Class C	AGDCX	NAS CM	Open End	US Fixed Inc (Worldwide Bond)	D	D	D	Down	Y	212-969-1000
AB High Income Fund Class I	AGDIX	NAS CM	Open End	US Fixed Inc (Worldwide Bond)	D	D	D+	Down	Y	212-969-1000
AB High Income Fund Class K	AGDKX	NAS CM	Open End	US Fixed Inc (Worldwide Bond)	D	D	D+	Down	Y	212-969-1000
AB High Income Fund Class R	AGDRX	NAS CM	Open End	US Fixed Inc (Worldwide Bond)	D	D	D	Down	Y	212-969-1000
AB High Income Fund Class Z	AGDZX	NAS CM	Open End	US Fixed Inc (Worldwide Bond)	D	D	D+	Down	Y	212-969-1000
AB High Income Municipal Portfolio Advisor Class	ABTYX	NAS CM	Open End	US Muni Fixed Inc (Muni Bond - Natl)	C-	D+	C	Down	Y	212-969-1000
AB High Income Municipal Portfolio Class A	ABTHX	NAS CM	Open End	US Muni Fixed Inc (Muni Bond - Natl)	C-	D+	C	Down	Y	212-969-1000
AB High Income Municipal Portfolio Class C	ABTFX	NAS CM	Open End	US Muni Fixed Inc (Muni Bond - Natl)	C-	D+	C	Down	Y	212-969-1000
AB High Income Municipal Portfolio Class Z	ABTZX	NAS CM	Open End	US Muni Fixed Inc (Muni Bond - Natl)	C-	D+	C	Down	Y	212-969-1000
AB Impact Municipal Income Shares	ABIMX	NAS CM	Open End	US Muni Fixed Inc (Muni Bond - Natl)	C	C-	C+		Y	212-969-1000
AB Income Fund Advisor Class	ACGYX	NAS CM	Open End	US Fixed Inc (Income)	C	C-	C+		Y	212-969-1000
AB Income Fund Class A	AKGAX	NAS CM	Open End	US Fixed Inc (Income)	C	C-	C+		Y	212-969-1000
AB Income Fund Class C	AKGCX	NAS CM	Open End	US Fixed Inc (Income)	C	C-	C		Y	212-969-1000
AB Income Fund Class Z	ACGZX	NAS CM	Open End	US Fixed Inc (Income)	C	C-	C+		Y	212-969-1000
AB Intermediate California Muni Portfolio Advisor Class	AICYX	NAS CM	Open End	US Muni Fixed Inc (Muni Bond - Single State)	C	C-	C+		Y	212-969-1000
AB Intermediate California Municipal Portfolio Class A	AICAX	NAS CM	Open End	US Muni Fixed Inc (Muni Bond - Single State)	C	C-	C+		Y	212-969-1000
AB Intermediate California Municipal Portfolio Class C	ACMCX	NAS CM	Open End	US Muni Fixed Inc (Muni Bond - Single State)	C	C-	C		Y	212-969-1000
AB Intermediate Diversified Muni Portfolio Advisor Class	AIDYX	NAS CM	Open End	US Muni Fixed Inc (Muni Bond - Natl)	C	C-	C+		Y	212-969-1000
AB Intermediate Diversified Municipal Portfolio Class A	AIDAX	NAS CM	Open End	US Muni Fixed Inc (Muni Bond - Natl)	C	C-	C+		Y	212-969-1000
AB Intermediate Diversified Municipal Portfolio Class C	AIMCX	NAS CM	Open End	US Muni Fixed Inc (Muni Bond - Natl)	C	C-	C		Y	212-969-1000
AB Intermediate Diversified Municipal Portfolio Class Z	AIDZX	NAS CM	Open End	US Muni Fixed Inc (Muni Bond - Natl)	C	C-	C+		Y	212-969-1000
AB Intermediate Duration Portfolio A	IDPAX	NAS CM	Open End	US Fixed Inc (Corp Bond - High Quality)	C+	C	B	Up	Y	212-969-1000
AB Intermediate Duration Portfolio Advisor Class	IDPYX	NAS CM	Open End	US Fixed Inc (Corp Bond - High Quality)	B-	C	B	Up	Y	212-969-1000
AB Intermediate Duration Portfolio Class Z	IDPZX	NAS CM	Open End	US Fixed Inc (Corp Bond - High Quality)	B-	C	B	Up	Y	212-969-1000
AB Intermediate New York Municipal Portfolio Advisor Class	ANIYX	NAS CM	Open End	US Muni Fixed Inc (Muni Bond - Single State)	C	C-	C		Y	212-969-1000
AB Intermediate New York Municipal Portfolio Class A	ANIAX	NAS CM	Open End	US Muni Fixed Inc (Muni Bond - Single State)	C-	D+	C	Down	Y	212-969-1000
AB Intermediate New York Municipal Portfolio Class C	ANMCX	NAS CM	Open End	US Muni Fixed Inc (Muni Bond - Single State)	C-	D+	C	Down	Y	212-969-1000
AB Limited Duration High Income Portfolio Advisor Class	ALHYX	NAS CM	Open End	US Fixed Inc (Income)	D+	D	C-	Down	Y	212-969-1000
AB Limited Duration High Income Portfolio Class A	ALHAX	NAS CM	Open End	US Fixed Inc (Income)	D+	D	C-	Down	Y	212-969-1000
AB Limited Duration High Income Portfolio Class C	ALHCX	NAS CM	Open End	US Fixed Inc (Income)	D	D	C-	Down	Y	212-969-1000
AB Limited Duration High Income Portfolio Class I	ALIHX	NAS CM	Open End	US Fixed Inc (Income)	D+	D	C-	Down	Y	212-969-1000
AB Limited Duration High Income Portfolio Class K	ALHKX	NAS CM	Open End	US Fixed Inc (Income)	D+	D	C-	Down	Y	212-969-1000
AB Limited Duration High Income Portfolio Class R	ALHRX	NAS CM	Open End	US Fixed Inc (Income)	D+	D	C-	Down	Y	212-969-1000
AB Municipal Bond Inflation Strategy Advisor Class	AUNYX	NAS CM	Open End	US Muni Fixed Inc (Muni Bond - Natl)	C-	D+	C		Y	212-969-1000
AB Municipal Bond Inflation Strategy Class 1	AUNOX	NAS CM	Open End	US Muni Fixed Inc (Muni Bond - Natl)	C-	D+	C		Y	212-969-1000
AB Municipal Bond Inflation Strategy Class 2	AUNTX	NAS CM	Open End	US Muni Fixed Inc (Muni Bond - Natl)	C-	D+	C		Y	212-969-1000
AB Municipal Bond Inflation Strategy Class A	AUNAX	NAS CM	Open End	US Muni Fixed Inc (Muni Bond - Natl)	D+	D	C	Down	Y	212-969-1000
AB Municipal Bond Inflation Strategy Class C	AUNCX	NAS CM	Open End	US Muni Fixed Inc (Muni Bond - Natl)	D+	D	C	Down	Y	212-969-1000
AB Muni Income Fund California Portfolio Advisor Class	ALCVX	NAS CM	Open End	US Muni Fixed Inc (Muni Bond - Single State)	C	C-	C+		Y	212-969-1000
AB Municipal Income Fund California Portfolio Class A	ALCAX	NAS CM	Open End	US Muni Fixed Inc (Muni Bond - Single State)	C	C-	C+		Y	212-969-1000
AB Municipal Income Fund California Portfolio Class C	ACACX	NAS CM	Open End	US Muni Fixed Inc (Muni Bond - Single State)	C-	D+	C	Down	Y	212-969-1000
AB Municipal Income Fund II Arizona Portfolio Class A	AAZAX	NAS CM	Open End	US Muni Fixed Inc (Muni Bond - Single State)	C	C-	C+		Y	212-969-1000
AB Municipal Income Fund II Arizona Portfolio Class C	AAZCX	NAS CM	Open End	US Muni Fixed Inc (Muni Bond - Single State)	C-	D+	C	Down	Y	212-969-1000
AB Muni Income II Massachusetts Portfolio Advisor Cl	AMAYX	NAS CM	Open End	US Muni Fixed Inc (Muni Bond - Single State)	C	C-	B-		Y	212-969-1000
AB Muni Income Fund II Massachusetts Portfolio Class A	AMAAX	NAS CM	Open End	US Muni Fixed Inc (Muni Bond - Single State)	C	C-	C+		Y	212-969-1000

★ Expanded analysis of this fund is included in Section II.

TOTAL RETURNS & PERFORMANCE									ASSETS		ASSET ALLOCATION & TURNOVER							MINIMUMS		FEES		
3-Month Total Return	6-Month Total Return	1-Year Total Return	3-Year Total Return	5-Year Total Return	Dividend Yield (TTM)	Expense Ratio	3-Yr Std Deviation	Effective Duration	NAV	Total Assets (MIL)	%Cash	%Government Bonds	%Municipal Bonds	%Corporate Bonds	%Other	Turnover Ratio	Average Coupon Rate	Min Initial Investment	Min Additional Investment	Front End Fee (%)	Back End Fee (%)	Inception Date
0.05	0.37	1.31	4.48	4.59	1.47	0.41			1	15,472	69	31	0	0	0			0				Nov-17
0.06	0.39	1.35	4.75	5.39	1.52	0.11	0.18		1	15,472	69	31	0	0	0			20,000,000				Jun-16
0.05	0.35	1.25	4.10	4.20		0.27			1	15,472	69	31	0	0	0			100,000				Jul-19
0.06	0.38	1.34	4.61	5.14		0.16			1	15,472	69	31	0	0	0			5,000,000				Jul-19
0.05	0.37	1.29	4.25	4.45		0.21			1	15,472	69	31	0	0	0			1,000,000				Jul-19
11.95	-9.06	-5.24	0.25	15.76	7.33	0.62	11.93	3.81	7.32	4,940	-19	15	0	39	1	49	6.06	0				Jan-08
11.72	-9.19	-5.49	-0.49	14.30	7.06	0.87	11.86	3.81	7.31	4,940	-19	15	0	39	1	49	6.06	2,500	50	4.25		Feb-94
11.69	-9.54	-6.25	-2.93	9.69	6.16	1.62	11.93	3.81	7.4	4,940	-19	15	0	39	1	49	6.06	2,500	50		1.00	Feb-94
11.90	-9.07	-5.11	0.35	15.95	7.34	0.6	11.85	3.81	7.33	4,940	-19	15	0	39	1	49	6.06	2,000,000				Jan-08
11.82	-9.23	-5.45	-0.57	14.13	6.98	0.94	11.87	3.81	7.32	4,940	-19	15	0	39	1	49	6.06	0				Jan-08
11.75	-9.40	-5.90	-1.73	12.04	6.59	1.28	11.93	3.81	7.31	4,940	-19	15	0	39	1	49	6.06	0				Jan-08
11.91	-9.04	-5.18	0.49	16.17	7.41	0.54	11.86	3.81	7.33	4,940	-19	15	0	39	1	49	6.06	2,000,000				Oct-13
4.06	-2.82	0.40	13.50	26.06	4.24	0.62	7.62	9.46	11.29	2,760	2	0	98	0	0	23	5.27	0				Jan-10
3.99	-2.85	0.23	12.64	24.59	3.97	0.87	7.62	9.46	11.3	2,760	2	0	98	0	0	23	5.27	2,500	50	3.00		Jan-10
3.81	-3.30	-0.59	10.06	19.94	3.17	1.62	7.59	9.46	11.29	2,760	2	0	98	0	0	23	5.27	2,500	50		1.00	Jan-10
4.08	-2.79	0.52	13.55	26.12	4.27	0.62	7.63	9.46	11.3	2,760	2	0	98	0	0	23	5.27	0				Sep-18
2.53	0.56	3.56			3.22	0		6.81	10.45	271.3	8	0	88	5	0	23	4.78	0				Sep-17
7.69	1.18	4.56	12.04	23.38	4.06	0.52	6.12	5.51	7.93	4,321	-39	41	0	19	0	270	4.75	0				Aug-87
7.64	1.06	4.31	11.21	21.70	3.82	0.77	6.12	5.51	7.92	4,321	-39	41	0	19	0	270	4.75	2,500	50	4.25		Apr-16
7.43	0.68	3.53	8.74	17.33	3.05	1.52	6.11	5.51	7.93	4,321	-39	41	0	19	0	270	4.75	2,500	50		1.00	Apr-16
7.72	1.22	4.61	12.09	23.43		0.5	6.09	5.51	7.93	4,321	-39	41	0	19	0	270	4.75	2,000,000				Nov-19
3.16	0.71	2.18	7.78	12.38	2.12	0.48	3.52	4.22	14.42	1,357	2	0	98	0	0	24	4.86	0				Jul-16
3.10	0.58	1.92	6.97	11.12	1.87	0.73	3.52	4.22	14.42	1,357	2	0	98	0	0	24	4.86	2,500	50	3.00		Feb-02
2.91	0.27	1.16	4.60	7.03	1.11	1.49	3.52	4.22	14.42	1,357	2	0	98	0	0	24	4.86	2,500	50		1.00	Feb-02
2.83	1.03	2.50	8.37	13.01	2.44	0.43	3.53	4.40	14.55	6,074	1	1	97	1	0	22	4.81	0				Jun-15
2.76	0.90	2.24	7.54	11.65	2.19	0.66	3.52	4.40	14.57	6,074	1	1	97	1	0	22	4.81	2,500	50	3.00		Feb-02
2.58	0.45	1.47	5.08	7.47	1.43	1.43	3.51	4.40	14.56	6,074	1	1	97	1	0	22	4.81	2,500	50		1.00	Feb-02
2.83	0.97	2.46	8.31	12.98	2.4	0.38	3.52	4.40	14.57	6,074	1	1	97	1	0	22	4.81	2,000,000				Jul-18
4.77	4.32	5.90	12.65	20.64		0.71	3.88	6.50	13.93	3,490	-45	47	0	19	0	62	3.00	2,500	50	4.25		Jul-19
4.84	4.37	6.09	13.42	22.07		0.46	3.91	6.50	13.92	3,490	-45	47	0	19	0	62	3.00	0	0			Jul-19
4.91	4.66	6.93	14.32	23.04		0.5	3.91	6.50	13.92	3,490	-45	47	0	19	0	62	3.00	2,000,000	0			Jul-19
2.40	-0.16	1.18	6.77	12.02	2.29	0.49	3.74	4.75	14	1,743	0	0	99	0	0	18	4.87	0				Jul-16
2.27	-0.29	0.93	5.97	10.75	2.03	0.74	3.74	4.75	14	1,743	0	0	99	0	0	18	4.87	2,500	50	3.00		Feb-02
2.15	-0.59	0.24	3.61	6.75	1.27	1.49	3.75	4.75	14.01	1,743	0	0	99	0	0	18	4.87	2,500	50		1.00	Feb-02
12.31	-4.39	-1.74	6.55	16.32	4.92	0.7	9.69	4.02	9.71	262.6	-27	21	0	61	3	37	5.13	0				Dec-11
12.23	-4.50	-1.98	5.75	14.83	4.65	0.95	9.69	4.02	9.72	262.6	-27	21	0	61	3	37	5.13	2,500	50	4.25		Dec-11
12.02	-4.77	-2.71	3.41	10.65	3.86	1.7	9.68	4.02	9.72	262.6	-27	21	0	61	3	37	5.13	2,500	50		1.00	Dec-11
12.29	-4.37	-1.72	6.44	16.34	4.93	0.75	9.7	4.02	9.72	262.6	-27	21	0	61	3	37	5.13	2,000,000				Dec-11
12.23	-4.49	-1.96	5.77	14.84	4.67	1	9.7	4.02	9.72	262.6	-27	21	0	61	3	37	5.13	0				Dec-11
12.16	-4.61	-2.20	4.98	13.42	4.41	1.25	9.7	4.02	9.72	262.6	-27	21	0	61	3	37	5.13	0				Dec-11
4.46	-2.41	-0.71	5.07	9.99	2.58	0.5	4.88	2.51	9.99	908.4	3	1	96	0	0	12	4.69	0				Jan-10
4.37	-2.46	-0.77	4.72	9.38	2.54	0.6	4.86	2.51	9.93	908.4	3	1	96	0	0	12	4.69	5,000				Jan-10
4.39	-2.41	-0.67	5.03	10.03	2.63	0.5	4.87	2.51	9.94	908.4	3	1	96	0	0	12	4.69	0				Jan-10
4.29	-2.54	-0.96	4.17	8.62	2.33	0.75	4.88	2.51	9.98	908.4	3	1	96	0	0	12	4.69	2,500	50	3.00		Jan-10
4.08	-2.92	-1.73	1.85	4.61	1.53	1.5	4.82	2.51	9.97	908.4	3	1	96	0	0	12	4.69	2,500	50		1.00	Jan-10
3.87	0.30	2.36	10.19	18.05	3.23	0.51	4.83	6.04	11.14	916.9	3	0	97	0	0	13	4.92	0				Aug-08
3.81	0.17	2.11	9.38	16.59	2.98	0.76	4.83	6.04	11.14	916.9	3	0	97	0	0	13	4.92	2,500	50	3.00		Dec-86
3.62	-0.19	1.35	6.95	12.31	2.21	1.51	4.77	6.04	11.14	916.9	3	0	97	0	0	13	4.92	2,500	50		1.00	May-93
2.49	-0.30	1.66	9.08	17.95	2.7	0.78	4.26	5.52	11.14	114.1	3	0	97	0	0	12	5.00	2,500	50	3.00		Jun-94
2.31	-0.76	0.91	6.67	13.54	1.94	1.53	4.26	5.52	11.12	114.1	3	0	97	0	0	12	5.00	2,500	50		1.00	Jun-94
2.54	1.12	3.06	10.08	17.28	3.1	0.53	4.02	5.67	11.3	199.1	4	0	96	0	0	12	5.00	0				Jul-16
2.47	0.91	2.80	9.25	16.11	2.84	0.78	4.05	5.67	11.3	199.1	4	0	96	0	0	12	5.00	2,500	50	3.00		Mar-94

	MARKET			FUND TYPE, CATEGORY & OBJECTIVE	RATINGS				NEW INVESTORS	
Fund Name	Ticker Symbol	Traded On	Fund Type	Category and (Prospectus Objective)	Overall Rating	Reward Rating	Risk Rating	Recent Up/ Downgrade	Open to New Investors	Telephone
AB Muni Income Fund II Massachusetts Portfolio Class C	AMACX	NAS CM	Open End	US Muni Fixed Inc (Muni Bond - Single State)	C	C-	C+		Y	212-969-1000
AB Municipal Income Fund II Minnesota Portfolio Class A	AMNAX	NAS CM	Open End	US Muni Fixed Inc (Muni Bond - Single State)	C	C-	B-		Y	212-969-1000
AB Municipal Income Fund II Minnesota Portfolio Class C	AMNCX	NAS CM	Open End	US Muni Fixed Inc (Muni Bond - Single State)	C	C-	C+		Y	212-969-1000
AB Municipal Income Fund II New Jersey Portfolio Class A	ANJAX	NAS CM	Open End	US Muni Fixed Inc (Muni Bond - Single State)	C	C-	C		Y	212-969-1000
AB Municipal Income Fund II New Jersey Portfolio Class C	ANJCX	NAS CM	Open End	US Muni Fixed Inc (Muni Bond - Single State)	C-	D+	C	Down	Y	212-969-1000
AB Municipal Income Fund II Ohio Portfolio Class A	AOHAX	NAS CM	Open End	US Muni Fixed Inc (Muni Bond - Single State)	C	C-	C+		Y	212-969-1000
AB Municipal Income Fund II Ohio Portfolio Class C	AOHCX	NAS CM	Open End	US Muni Fixed Inc (Muni Bond - Single State)	C	C-	C		Y	212-969-1000
AB Municipal Income Fund II Pennsylvania Portfolio Class A	APAAX	NAS CM	Open End	US Muni Fixed Inc (Muni Bond - Single State)	C	C-	C+		Y	212-969-1000
AB Muni Income II Pennsylvania Portfolio Cl Cl C	APACX	NAS CM	Open End	US Muni Fixed Inc (Muni Bond - Single State)	C	C-	C+		Y	212-969-1000
AB Muni Income Fund II Virginia Portfolio Advisor Class	AVAYX	NAS CM	Open End	US Muni Fixed Inc (Muni Bond - Single State)	C	C-	B-		Y	212-969-1000
AB Municipal Income Fund II Virginia Portfolio Class A	AVAAX	NAS CM	Open End	US Muni Fixed Inc (Muni Bond - Single State)	C	C-	C+		Y	212-969-1000
AB Municipal Income Fund II Virginia Portfolio Class C	AVACX	NAS CM	Open End	US Muni Fixed Inc (Muni Bond - Single State)	C	C-	C		Y	212-969-1000
AB Municipal Income Fund National Portfolio Advisor Class	ALTVX	NAS CM	Open End	US Muni Fixed Inc (Muni Bond - Natl)	C	C-	C+		Y	212-969-1000
AB Municipal Income Fund National Portfolio Class A	ALTHX	NAS CM	Open End	US Muni Fixed Inc (Muni Bond - Natl)	C	C-	C+		Y	212-969-1000
AB Municipal Income Fund National Portfolio Class C	ALNCX	NAS CM	Open End	US Muni Fixed Inc (Muni Bond - Natl)	C-	D+	C	Down	Y	212-969-1000
AB Municipal Income Fund New York Portfolio Advisor Class	ALNVX	NAS CM	Open End	US Muni Fixed Inc (Muni Bond - Single State)	C-	D+	C	Down	Y	212-969-1000
AB Municipal Income Fund New York Portfolio Class A	ALNYX	NAS CM	Open End	US Muni Fixed Inc (Muni Bond - Single State)	C-	D+	C	Down	Y	212-969-1000
AB Municipal Income Fund New York Portfolio Class C	ANYCX	NAS CM	Open End	US Muni Fixed Inc (Muni Bond - Single State)	C-	D+	C	Down	Y	212-969-1000
AB Municipal Income Shares	MISHX	NAS CM	Open End	US Muni Fixed Inc (Muni Bond - Natl)	C-	D+	C	Down	Y	212-969-1000
AB Short Duration Income Portfolio Advisor Class	SHUYX	NAS CM	Open End	US Fixed Inc (Income)	D	D+	C		Y	212-969-1000
AB Short Duration Income Portfolio Class A	SHUAX	NAS CM	Open End	US Fixed Inc (Income)	D	D	C-		Y	212-969-1000
AB Short Duration Income Portfolio Class C	SHUCX	NAS CM	Open End	US Fixed Inc (Income)	D	D	C		Y	212-969-1000
AB Short Duration Plus Portfolio	SNSDX	NAS CM	Open End	US Fixed Inc (Corp Bond - High Quality)	C	C-	B-		Y	212-969-1000
AB Short Duration Portfolio Class A	ADPAX	NAS CM	Open End	US Fixed Inc (Corp Bond - High Quality)	C	C-	C+		Y	212-969-1000
AB Short Duration Portfolio Class C	ADPCX	NAS CM	Open End	US Fixed Inc (Corp Bond - High Quality)	C	C-	C+		Y	212-969-1000
AB Taxable Multi-Sector Income Shares	CSHTX	NAS CM	Open End	US Fixed Inc (Multisector Bond)	C	C	B-		Y	212-969-1000
AB Tax-Aware Fixed Income Opportunities Portfol Advisor Cl	ATTYX	NAS CM	Open End	US Muni Fixed Inc (Income)	C-	D+	C	Down	Y	212-969-1000
AB Tax-Aware Fixed Income Opportunities Portfolio Class A	ATTAX	NAS CM	Open End	US Muni Fixed Inc (Income)	D+	D+	C-	Down	Y	212-969-1000
AB Tax-Aware Fixed Income Opportunities Portfolio Class C	ATCCX	NAS CM	Open End	US Muni Fixed Inc (Income)	D+	D	C-	Down	Y	212-969-1000
AB Total Return Bond Portfolio Advisor Class	ABQYX	NAS CM	Open End	US Fixed Inc (Corp Bond - General)	C	C-	B-		Y	212-969-1000
AB Total Return Bond Portfolio Class A	ABQUX	NAS CM	Open End	US Fixed Inc (Corp Bond - General)	C	C-	B-		Y	212-969-1000
AB Total Return Bond Portfolio Class C	ABQCX	NAS CM	Open End	US Fixed Inc (Corp Bond - General)	C	C-	C+		Y	212-969-1000
AB Total Return Bond Portfolio Class I	ABQIX	NAS CM	Open End	US Fixed Inc (Corp Bond - General)	C	C-	B-		Y	212-969-1000
AB Total Return Bond Portfolio Class K	ABQKX	NAS CM	Open End	US Fixed Inc (Corp Bond - General)	C	C-	B-		Y	212-969-1000
AB Total Return Bond Portfolio Class R	ABQRX	NAS CM	Open End	US Fixed Inc (Corp Bond - General)	C	C-	B-		Y	212-969-1000
AB Total Return Bond Portfolio Class Z	ABQZX	NAS CM	Open End	US Fixed Inc (Corp Bond - General)	C	C-	B-		Y	212-969-1000
AB Unconstrained Bond Fund Advisor Class	AGSIX	NAS CM	Open End	Fixed Inc Misc (Worldwide Bond)	D	D	C-		Y	212-969-1000
AB Unconstrained Bond Fund Class A	AGSAX	NAS CM	Open End	Fixed Inc Misc (Worldwide Bond)	D	D-	C-		Y	212-969-1000
AB Unconstrained Bond Fund Class C	AGCCX	NAS CM	Open End	Fixed Inc Misc (Worldwide Bond)	D	D-	C-		Y	212-969-1000
AB Unconstrained Bond Fund Class I	AGLIX	NAS CM	Open End	Fixed Inc Misc (Worldwide Bond)	D	D	C-		Y	212-969-1000
AB Unconstrained Bond Fund Class K	AGSKX	NAS CM	Open End	Fixed Inc Misc (Worldwide Bond)	D	D-	C-		Y	212-969-1000
AB Unconstrained Bond Fund Class R	AGSRX	NAS CM	Open End	Fixed Inc Misc (Worldwide Bond)	D	D-	C-		Y	212-969-1000
Aberdeen Asia-Pacific Income Fund Inc	FAX	AMEX	Closed End	Global Fixed Inc (Worldwide Bond)	D+	D	C-	Down	Y	866-667-9231
Aberdeen Emerging Markets Debt Fund Class A	AKFAX	NAS CM	Open End	Emerg Mkts Fixed Inc (Growth & Income)	D	D	C-	Down	Y	866-667-9231
Aberdeen Emerging Markets Debt Fund Class C	AKFCX	NAS CM	Open End	Emerg Mkts Fixed Inc (Growth & Income)	D	D	D+	Down	Y	866-667-9231
Aberdeen Emerging Markets Debt Fund Class R	AKFRX	NAS CM	Open End	Emerg Mkts Fixed Inc (Growth & Income)	D	D	D+	Down	Y	866-667-9231
Aberdeen Emerging Markets Debt Fund Institutional Class	AKFIX	NAS CM	Open End	Emerg Mkts Fixed Inc (Growth & Income)	D	D	C-	Down	Y	866-667-9231
Aberdeen Emerg Mkts Debt Fund Institutional Service Class	AKFSX	NAS CM	Open End	Emerg Mkts Fixed Inc (Growth & Income)	D	D	C-	Down	Y	866-667-9231
Aberdeen Global Absolute Return Strategies Fund Class A	CUGAX	NAS CM	Open End	Global Fixed Inc (Growth & Income)	C	C-	C+		Y	866-667-9231
Aberdeen Global Absolute Return Strategies Fund Class C	CGBCX	NAS CM	Open End	Global Fixed Inc (Growth & Income)	C	C-	C		Y	866-667-9231
Aberdeen Global Absolute Return Strategies Inst Cl	AGCIX	NAS CM	Open End	Global Fixed Inc (Growth & Income)	C	C-	C+		Y	866-667-9231
Aberdeen Global Absolute Return Strategies Inst Service Cl	CGFIX	NAS CM	Open End	Global Fixed Inc (Growth & Income)	C	C-	C+		Y	866-667-9231

★Expanded analysis of this fund is included in Section II.

TOTAL RETURNS & PERFORMANCE									ASSETS		ASSET ALLOCATION & TURNOVER							MINIMUMS		FEES		
3-Month Total Return	6-Month Total Return	1-Year Total Return	3-Year Total Return	5-Year Total Return	Dividend Yield (TTM)	Expense Ratio	3-Yr Std Deviation	Effective Duration	NAV	Total Assets (MIL)	%Cash	%Government Bonds	%Municipal Bonds	%Corporate Bonds	%Other	Turnover Ratio	Average Coupon Rate	Min Initial Investment	Min Additional Investment	Front End Fee (%)	Back End Fee (%)	Inception Date
2.29	0.54	2.04	6.85	11.88	2.09	1.53	3.98	5.67	11.28	199.1	4	0	96	0	0	12	5.00	2,500	50		1.00	Mar-94
1.72	0.91	2.69	9.61	16.18	2.58	0.87	3.68	5.58	10.37	54.6	5	0	95	0	0	14	4.79	2,500	50	3.00		Jun-93
1.54	0.54	1.92	7.16	11.89	1.83	1.62	3.67	5.58	10.38	54.6	5	0	95	0	0	14	4.79	2,500	50		1.00	Jun-93
3.22	-0.39	1.86	9.91	19.28	3.14	0.84	4.86	6.24	9.74	74.3	1	0	99	0	0	8	5.05	2,500	50	3.00		Jun-93
3.03	-0.76	0.99	7.36	14.76	2.37	1.59	4.86	6.24	9.74	74.3	1	0	99	0	0	8	5.05	2,500	50		1.00	Jun-93
2.98	0.40	2.37	8.90	17.35	2.78	0.81	4.28	5.68	10.01	72.2	0	0	100	0	0	8	4.94	2,500	50	3.00		Jun-93
2.90	0.13	1.71	6.60	13.17	2.02	1.56	4.37	5.68	10.01	72.2	0	0	100	0	0	8	4.94	2,500	50		1.00	Jun-93
2.38	0.58	2.70	9.97	18.12	2.91	0.86	3.99	5.94	10.55	70.7	0	0	100	0	0	9	4.95	2,500	50	3.00		Jun-93
2.28	0.31	1.94	7.52	13.88	2.15	1.61	4.01	5.94	10.56	70.7	0	0	100	0	0	9	4.95	2,500	50		1.00	Jun-93
2.68	0.73	2.93	10.26	18.67	2.87	0.56	4.22	5.69	11.23	210.4	3	0	97	0	0	6	4.78	0				Jul-16
2.71	0.61	2.67	9.54	17.50	2.62	0.81	4.17	5.69	11.23	210.4	3	0	97	0	0	6	4.78	2,500	50	3.00		Apr-94
2.53	0.24	1.92	7.14	13.24	1.87	1.56	4.2	5.69	11.2	210.4	3	0	97	0	0	6	4.78	2,500	50		1.00	Apr-94
3.41	0.43	2.51	10.73	19.84	2.84	0.5	4.81	5.95	10.37	1,614	3	0	97	0	0	19	4.80	0				Aug-08
3.34	0.31	2.26	9.90	18.36	2.58	0.75	4.82	5.95	10.37	1,614	3	0	97	0	0	19	4.80	2,500	50	3.00		Dec-86
3.06	-0.15	1.40	7.38	13.93	1.82	1.5	4.83	5.95	10.35	1,614	3	0	97	0	0	19	4.80	2,500	50		1.00	May-93
2.39	-1.05	1.04	8.54	17.00	2.95	0.51	4.96	6.18	9.88	603.2	1	0	99	0	0	15	4.93	0				Aug-08
2.33	-1.27	0.69	7.62	15.44	2.7	0.76	4.94	6.18	9.87	603.2	1	0	99	0	0	15	4.93	2,500	50	3.00		Dec-86
2.14	-1.54	-0.05	5.35	11.32	1.93	1.51	4.93	6.18	9.87	603.2	1	0	99	0	0	15	4.93	2,500	50		1.00	May-93
5.33	-2.39	0.88	14.38	28.83	3.9	0.01	8.06	8.04	11.6	4,885	1	1	98	0	0	14	4.98	0				Sep-10
4.55	-1.21	1.45			4.07	0.49		2.38	9.9	42.8	-8	34	0	10	1	181	3.31	0				Dec-18
4.46	-2.67	-0.12			3.99	0.7		2.38	9.76	42.8	-8	34	0	10	1	181	3.31	2,500	50	4.25		Dec-18
4.29	-1.63	0.54			3.15	1.49		2.38	9.9	42.8	-8	34	0	10	1	181	3.31	2,500	50		1.00	Dec-18
0.79	1.23	2.40	6.17	7.62	1.95	0.56	1.03	2.12	11.8	242.6	-39	75	0	5	0	39	2.20	25,000				Dec-88
0.58	0.88	1.82	4.63	5.40	1.48	0.97	1.07	2.12	11.8	242.6	-39	75	0	5	0	39	2.20	2,500	50	4.25		May-03
0.53	0.86	1.71	4.10	4.35	1.27	1.73	1.04	2.12	11.78	242.6	-39	75	0	5	0	39	2.20	2,500	50		1.00	May-03
3.34	1.69	3.58	9.45	13.05	2.6	0	2.24	1.57	10	211.8	13	7	6	61	0	45	2.92	0				Sep-10
5.10	-3.59	-1.10	7.64	15.65	3.29	0.51	7.64	7.07	10.57	74.9	1	3	90	1	0	52	4.66	0				Dec-13
5.03	-3.71	-1.34	6.85	14.23	3.02	0.76	7.64	7.07	10.57	74.9	1	3	90	1	0	52	4.66	2,500	50	3.00		Dec-13
4.84	-4.07	-2.08	4.48	10.03	2.22	1.51	7.64	7.07	10.57	74.9	1	3	90	1	0	52	4.66	2,500	50		1.00	Dec-13
8.03	2.73	5.41	13.11	21.49	3.24	0.52	5.86	7.15	11.45	358.2	-74	50	0	16	0	74	3.28	0				Oct-00
7.98	2.60	5.15	12.28	20.02	3	0.77	5.88	7.15	11.44	358.2	-74	50	0	16	0	74	3.28	2,500	50	4.25		Jul-99
7.80	2.23	4.38	9.83	15.65	2.25	1.52	5.85	7.15	11.42	358.2	-74	50	0	16	0	74	3.28	2,500	50		1.00	Jul-99
8.03	2.72	5.40	13.10	21.48	3.23	0.52	5.86	7.15	11.46	358.2	-74	50	0	16	0	74	3.28	2,000,000				Mar-05
7.96	2.51	5.05	12.27	19.99	2.99	0.77	5.86	7.15	11.45	358.2	-74	50	0	16	0	74	3.28	0				Mar-05
7.90	2.47	4.89	11.45	18.53	2.74	1.02	5.86	7.15	11.44	358.2	-74	50	0	16	0	74	3.28	0				Nov-03
8.02	2.72	5.40	13.20	21.47	3.24	0.52	5.85	7.15	11.47	358.2	-74	50	0	16	0	74	3.28	2,000,000				Apr-14
0.06	-2.18	-2.73	-6.69	1.58	6.08	0.65	4.04		7.33	75.5	2,218	7	0	1	0	59	1.48	0				Dec-97
0.00	-2.43	-2.98	-7.52	0.26	5.8	0.9	4.05		7.34	75.5	2,218	7	0	1	0	59	1.48	2,500	50	4.25		Jan-96
-0.18	-2.67	-3.72	-9.51	-3.33	5.01	1.65	4.09		7.35	75.5	2,218	7	0	1	0	59	1.48	2,500	50		1.00	Mar-96
0.19	-2.17	-2.69	-6.68	1.57	6.13	0.65	4.03		7.32	75.5	2,218	7	0	1	0	59	1.48	2,000,000				Mar-05
0.08	-2.36	-2.96	-7.49	0.21	5.63	0.9	4.02		7.4	75.5	2,218	7	0	1	0	59	1.48	0				Mar-05
0.01	-2.51	-3.27	-8.16	-1.02	5.29	1.15	4.08		7.4	75.5	2,218	7	0	1	0	59	1.48	0				Mar-05
11.83	-3.02	-0.70	3.95	14.24	3.69		10.06		4.56	1,092	4	50	0	46	0	46	5.21					Apr-86
12.67	-5.53	-3.11	3.33	19.85	3.2	1.05	11.91	6.91	9.1	50.3	6	80	0	15	0	71	6.19	1,000	50	3.00		Nov-12
12.40	-5.90	-3.71	1.48	16.07	2.56	1.66	11.87	6.91	9.06	50.3	6	80	0	15	0	71	6.19	1,000	50		1.00	Nov-12
12.51	-5.70	-3.27	2.54	18.37	3.11	1.3	11.84	6.91	9.06	50.3	6	80	0	15	0	71	6.19	0				Nov-12
12.74	-5.38	-2.64	4.58	22.05	3.74	0.66	11.86	6.91	9.12	50.3	6	80	0	15	0	71	6.19	1,000,000				Nov-12
12.75	-5.36	-2.71	4.62	22.10	3.77	0.66	11.87	6.91	9.12	50.3	6	80	0	15	0	71	6.19	1,000,000				Nov-12
0.90	-0.99	2.69	7.08	18.65	2.94	0.97	2.67		9.99	22.0	47	23	0	0	0	53		1,000	50	3.00		Nov-01
0.71	-1.30	1.92	4.86	14.55	0.48	1.65	2.72		9.83	22.0	47	23	0	0	0	53		1,000	50		1.00	Apr-05
0.99	-0.78	2.75	7.79	20.12	3.45	0.65	2.7		10.12	22.0	47	23	0	0	0	53		1,000,000				Jul-09
0.90	-0.88	2.85	7.59	19.55	3.34	0.79	2.7		10.04	22.0	47	23	0	0	0	53		1,000,000				Nov-90

Fund Name	MARKET Ticker Symbol	MARKET Traded On	FUND TYPE, CATEGORY & OBJECTIVE Fund Type	Category and (Prospectus Objective)	RATINGS Overall Rating	Reward Rating	Risk Rating	Recent Up/ Downgrade	NEW INVESTORS Open to New Investors	Telephone
Aberdeen Global High Income Fund Class A	BJBHX	NAS CM	Open End	Global Fixed Inc (Income)	D+	D	C	Down	Y	866-667-9231
Aberdeen Global High Income Fund Class I	JHYIX	NAS CM	Open End	Global Fixed Inc (Income)	C-	D+	C		Y	866-667-9231
Aberdeen Global Income Fund Inc.	FCO	AMEX	Closed End	Global Fixed Inc (Worldwide Bond)	D	D	D	Down	Y	866-667-9231
Aberdeen Income Credit Strategies Fund	ACP	NYSE	Closed End	US Fixed Inc (Income)	D	D-	D		Y	215-405-5700
Aberdeen Intermediate Municipal Income Fund Class A	NTFAX	NAS CM	Open End	US Muni Fixed Inc (Muni Bond - Natl)	C	C-	C		Y	866-667-9231
Aberdeen Intermediate Municipal Income Fund Class C	GTICX	NAS CM	Open End	US Muni Fixed Inc (Muni Bond - Natl)	C-	D+	C	Down	Y	866-667-9231
Aberdeen Intermediate Muni Income Fund Institutional Class	ABEIX	NAS CM	Open End	US Muni Fixed Inc (Muni Bond - Natl)	C	C-	C		Y	866-667-9231
Aberdeen Intermed Muni Income Inst Services Cl	ABESX	NAS CM	Open End	US Muni Fixed Inc (Muni Bond - Natl)	C	C-	C		Y	866-667-9231
Aberdeen Short Duration High Yield Municipal Fund Class A	AAHMX	NAS CM	Open End	US Muni Fixed Inc (Muni Bond - Natl)	C-	D+	C	Down	Y	866-667-9231
Aberdeen Short Duration High Yield Muni Institutional Cl	AHYMX	NAS CM	Open End	US Muni Fixed Inc (Muni Bond - Natl)	C	C-	C		Y	866-667-9231
Aberdeen Total Return Bond Fund Class A	BJBGX	NAS CM	Open End	US Fixed Inc (Corp Bond - General)	B	B-	B+	Up	Y	866-667-9231
Aberdeen Total Return Bond Fund Class I	JBGIX	NAS CM	Open End	US Fixed Inc (Corp Bond - General)	B	B-	B+	Up	Y	866-667-9231
Aberdeen Ultra Short Municipal Income Fund Class A	ATOAX	NAS CM	Open End	US Muni Fixed Inc (Muni Bond - Natl)	C	C-	C+		Y	866-667-9231
Aberdeen Ultra Short Municipal Income Fund Class A1	ATOBX	NAS CM	Open End	US Muni Fixed Inc (Muni Bond - Natl)	C	C-	C+		Y	866-667-9231
Aberdeen Ultra Short Muni Income Fund Institutional Class	ATOIX	NAS CM	Open End	US Muni Fixed Inc (Muni Bond - Natl)	C	C-	C+		Y	866-667-9231
Access Capital Community Investment Fund Class A	ACASX	NAS CM	Open End	US Fixed Inc (Corp Bond - High Quality)	C+	C	B-		Y	800-422-2766
Access Capital Community Investment Fund Class IS	ACATX	NAS CM	Open End	US Fixed Inc (Corp Bond - High Quality)	C+	C	B-		Y	800-422-2766
Access Capital Community Investment Institutional Cl	ACCSX	NAS CM	Open End	US Fixed Inc (Corp Bond - High Quality)	C+	C	B-		Y	800-422-2766
Access Flex High Yield Fund Investor Class	FYAIX	NAS CM	Open End	US Fixed Inc (Corp Bond - High Yield)	C-	D+	C	Down	Y	614-470-8626
Access Flex High Yield Fund Service Class	FYASX	NAS CM	Open End	US Fixed Inc (Corp Bond - High Yield)	D+	D+	C-	Down	Y	614-470-8626
ACM Tactical Income Fund Class A	TINAX	NAS CM	Open End	Fixed Inc Misc (Income)	D	D+	C+		Y	
ACM Tactical Income Fund Class I	TINIX	NAS CM	Open End	Fixed Inc Misc (Income)	D	D+	C+		Y	
AdvisorOne CLS Flexible Income Fund Class N	CLFLX	NAS CM	Open End	US Fixed Inc (Growth & Income)	C	C-	C+		Y	
AdvisorOne CLS Flexible Income Fund Class T	FLEIX	NAS CM	Open End	US Fixed Inc (Growth & Income)	C	C-	C+		Y	
Aegon Emerging Markets Debt Fund Institutional Shares	AMMIX	NAS CM	Open End	Emerg Mkts Fixed Inc (Diversified Emerg Mkts)	D-	D	D		Y	
Aegon Emerging Markets Debt Fund Investor Shares	AMMVX	NAS CM	Open End	Emerg Mkts Fixed Inc (Diversified Emerg Mkts)	D-	D	D		Y	
Aegon Short Duration High Yield Fund Institutional Shares	ADHIX	NAS CM	Open End	US Fixed Inc (Corp Bond - High Yield)	D-	D	D			
Aegon Short Duration High Yield Fund Investor Shares	ADHVX	NAS CM	Open End	US Fixed Inc (Corp Bond - High Yield)	D-	D	D			
AIG Flexible Credit Fund Class A	SHNAX	NAS CM	Open End	US Fixed Inc (Growth & Income)	D+	D	C-	Down	Y	800-858-8850
AIG Flexible Credit Fund Class C	SHNCX	NAS CM	Open End	US Fixed Inc (Growth & Income)	D	D	C-	Down	Y	800-858-8850
AIG Flexible Credit Fund Class W	SHNWX	NAS CM	Open End	US Fixed Inc (Growth & Income)	D+	D	C-	Down	Y	800-858-8850
AIG Government Money Market Fund Class A	SMAXX	NAS CM	Money Mkt	US Money Mkt (Money Mkt - Govt)	C	C-	C		Y	800-858-8850
AIG Government Money Market Fund Class I	NAIXX	NAS CM	Money Mkt	US Money Mkt (Money Mkt - Govt)	C	C-	C		Y	800-858-8850
AIG Senior Floating Rate Fund Class A	SASFX	NAS CM	Open End	US Fixed Inc (Income)	D+	D	C-	Down	Y	800-858-8850
AIG Senior Floating Rate Fund Class C	NFRCX	NAS CM	Open End	US Fixed Inc (Income)	D+	D	C-	Down	Y	800-858-8850
AIG Senior Floating Rate Fund Class W	NFRWX	NAS CM	Open End	US Fixed Inc (Income)	D+	D	C-	Down	Y	800-858-8850
AIG Strategic Bond Fund Class A	SDIAX	NAS CM	Open End	US Fixed Inc (Multisector Bond)	C	C-	C+		Y	800-858-8850
AIG Strategic Bond Fund Class B	SDIBX	NAS CM	Open End	US Fixed Inc (Multisector Bond)	C	C-	C		Y	800-858-8850
AIG Strategic Bond Fund Class C	NAICX	NAS CM	Open End	US Fixed Inc (Multisector Bond)	C	C-	C+		Y	800-858-8850
AIG Strategic Bond Fund Class W	SDIWX	NAS CM	Open End	US Fixed Inc (Multisector Bond)	C	C-	C+		Y	800-858-8850
AIG U.S. Government Securities Fund Class A	SGTAX	NAS CM	Open End	US Fixed Inc (Govt Bond - General)	B	B-	B	Up	Y	800-858-8850
AIG U.S. Government Securities Fund Class C	NASBX	NAS CM	Open End	US Fixed Inc (Govt Bond - General)	B-	C+	B		Y	800-858-8850
Alight Money Market Fund Administrative Class	HEWXX	NAS CM	Money Mkt	US Money Mkt (Money Mkt - Govt)	C	C-	C		Y	
AllianceBernstein Global High Income Fund Inc.	AWF	NYSE	Closed End	US Fixed Inc (Worldwide Bond)	D	D	D+	Down	Y	212-969-1000
AllianceBernstein National Municipal Income Fund	AFB	NYSE	Closed End	US Muni Fixed Inc (Muni Bond - Natl)	C-	C-	C-		Y	212-969-1000
AllianzGI Core Bond Fund Class P	AOBPX	NAS CM	Open End	US Fixed Inc (Income)	C	D+	B+	Up	Y	800-498-5413
AllianzGI Core Bond Fund Class R6	AOBSX	NAS CM	Open End	US Fixed Inc (Income)	C	D+	B+	Up	Y	800-498-5413
AllianzGI Core Bond Fund Institutional Class	AOBIX	NAS CM	Open End	US Fixed Inc (Income)	C	D+	B+	Up	Y	800-498-5413
AllianzGI Core Plus Bond Fund Class P	ACKPX	NAS CM	Open End	US Fixed Inc (Growth & Income)	C	D+	B	Up	Y	800-498-5413
AllianzGI Core Plus Bond Fund Class R6	ACOSX	NAS CM	Open End	US Fixed Inc (Growth & Income)	C	D+	B	Up	Y	800-498-5413
AllianzGI Core Plus Bond Fund Institutional Class	ACKIX	NAS CM	Open End	US Fixed Inc (Growth & Income)	C	D+	B	Up	Y	800-498-5413
AllianzGI Emerging Markets SRI Debt Fund Class A	AGMAX	NAS CM	Open End	Emerg Mkts Fixed Inc (Growth & Income)	C-	D+	C	Down	Y	800-498-5413

★ Expanded analysis of this fund is included in Section II.

TOTAL RETURNS & PERFORMANCE									ASSETS		ASSET ALLOCATION & TURNOVER							MINIMUMS		FEES		
3-Month Total Return	6-Month Total Return	1-Year Total Return	3-Year Total Return	5-Year Total Return	Dividend Yield (TTM)	Expense Ratio	3-Yr Std Deviation	Effective Duration	NAV	Total Assets (MIL)	%Cash	%Government Bonds	%Municipal Bonds	%Corporate Bonds	%Other	Turnover Ratio	Average Coupon Rate	Min Initial Investment	Min Additional Investment	Front End Fee (%)	Back End Fee (%)	Inception Date
12.44	-4.92	-0.56	8.28	12.11	4.65	1.02	10.35	3.92	8.23	160.5	4	2	0	94	0	98	6.11	1,000	50			Dec-02
12.50	-4.92	-0.43	9.06	13.43	5.35	0.77	10.36	3.92	7.61	160.5	4	2	0	94	0	98	6.11	1,000,000				Jan-03
12.44	-13.22	-10.06	-3.85	5.70	5.69		13.99		6.52	55.6	8	41	0	51	0	59	6.21					Feb-92
27.24	-13.20	-13.30	-10.41	2.09	14.53	3.02	21.82		9.85	120.7	4	3	0	89	0	93	7.29					Jan-11
1.85	-0.78	1.08	6.73	11.00	2.77	0.76	4.11	4.84	9.71	67.8	2	0	98	0	0	58	4.68	1,000	50	2.50		May-98
1.77	-1.04	0.44	4.48	6.99	2.01	1.5	4.13	4.84	9.7	67.8	2	0	98	0	0	58	4.68	1,000	50		1.00	Sep-03
1.91	-0.55	1.20	7.39	12.30	3.04	0.5	4.05	4.84	9.72	67.8	2	0	98	0	0	58	4.68	1,000,000				Mar-86
1.91	-0.55	1.44	7.57	12.36	3.03	0.5	4	4.84	9.72	67.8	2	0	98	0	0	58	4.68	1,000,000				Feb-13
1.63	-1.24	0.53	6.40	12.80	2.98	0.9	3.11	3.16	9.97	237.7	2	0	98	0	0	105	4.84	1,000	50	2.50		May-13
1.69	-1.12	0.78	7.10	14.11	3.23	0.65	3.12	3.16	9.97	237.7	2	0	98	0	0	105	4.84	1,000,000				May-13
6.14	7.37	9.88	17.21	25.07	2.54	0.69	4	6.45	14.38	192.3	-9	15	6	35	0	141	3.45	1,000	50			Jul-92
6.25	7.59	10.19	18.16	26.67	2.93	0.44	4.01	6.45	14.14	192.3	-9	15	6	35	0	141	3.45	1,000,000				Nov-99
0.25	0.46	0.95	3.34	4.28	1.12	0.7	0.17	0.10	10.09	975.2	6	0	94	0	0	231	1.99	1,000	50	0.50		Mar-04
0.25	0.56	1.05	3.45	4.38	1.12	0.7	0.18	0.10	10.1	975.2	6	0	94	0	0	231	1.99	1,000	50	0.50	0.25	Feb-19
0.22	0.59	1.21	3.97	5.43	1.37	0.45	0.13	0.10	10.03	975.2	6	0	94	0	0	231	1.99	1,000,000				Dec-02
0.95	3.21	4.83	8.97	12.23	2.3	0.88	2.17	2.53	9.16	557.8	2	0	4	0	0	12	3.51	2,500		3.75		Jan-09
1.02	3.22	5.02	9.92	13.91	0	0.4	2.16	2.53	9.14	557.8	2	0	4	0	0	12	3.51	2,500				Mar-19
1.04	3.27	5.20	10.08	14.07	2.64	0.53	2.16	2.53	9.15	557.8	2	0	4	0	0	12	3.51	1,000,000				Jun-98
2.52	-7.20	-4.55	6.33	17.71	2.77	1.78	6.68		31.49	45.3	31	69	0	0	0	1,362	1.38	15,000				Dec-04
2.27	-7.63	-5.48	3.25	12.11	2.02	2.78	6.68		31.21	45.3	31	69	0	0	0	1,362	1.38	15,000				Dec-04
3.92	1.58	2.45			3.29	2.58		8.48	10.22	23.6	63	12	10	6	0	645	3.67	2,000	500	5.75		Dec-18
4.18	1.79	2.79			3.52	2.33		8.48	10.23	23.6	63	12	10	6	0	645	3.67	10,000	500			Dec-18
6.63	-0.42	2.38	9.51	15.79	2.65	1.19	5.21	5.29	10.39	193.0	5	27	0	47	0	22	3.68	2,500	250			Oct-09
6.63	-0.42	2.37	9.48	15.76	2.64	1.06	5.21	5.29	10.39	193.0	5	27	0	47	0	22	3.68	2,500	250			Dec-18
13.75	-3.90	-0.71				0.75			9.62	43.8	2	69	0	30	0		5.81	250,000				Jun-19
13.70	-4.00	-0.94				1			9.62	43.8	2	69	0	30	0		5.81	2,000	50			Jun-19
6.95	-5.07	-2.38				0.7			9.3822	19.4	3	0	0	96	0		5.61	250,000				Jun-19
8.13	-4.08	-1.40				0.95			9.511	19.4	3	0	0	96	0		5.61	2,000	50			Jun-19
10.52	-5.74	-2.68	4.48	13.39	5.46	1.05	9.43	2.40	3.08	265.8	4	0	0	95	0	67	3.62	500	100	4.75		Nov-98
10.67	-6.02	-3.60	2.46	9.77	4.7	1.71	9.69	2.40	3.1	265.8	4	0	0	95	0	67	3.62	500	100		1.00	Aug-00
10.59	-5.65	-2.80	5.09	14.20	5.63	0.84	9.57	2.40	3.08	265.8	4	0	0	95	0	67	3.62	50,000				Oct-14
0.00	0.12	0.66	2.13	2.17	0.77	1.1	0.15		1	190.1	66	34	0	0	0			500	100			Oct-84
0.00	0.15	0.72	2.67	2.72	0.85	0.8	0.16		1	190.1	66	34	0	0	0			0				Nov-01
7.52	-5.00	-3.03	3.79	11.57	4.78	1.03	7.66	0.30	7.36	159.5	6	0	0	94	0	34	1.49	500	100	3.75		Oct-06
7.42	-5.32	-3.54	2.52	9.55	4.36	1.43	7.68	0.30	7.35	159.5	6	0	0	94	0	34	1.49	500	100		1.00	Aug-98
7.55	-5.00	-2.90	4.43	11.69	4.86	0.83	7.7	0.30	7.38	159.5	6	0	0	94	0	34	1.49	50,000				Apr-17
7.86	0.98	3.80	10.44	19.49	3.54	1.1	5.7	4.53	3.38	300.1	2	13	0	58	0	85	4.41	500	100	4.75		Nov-93
7.34	0.61	2.70	7.74	15.02	2.75	1.82	5.7	4.53	3.37	300.1	2	13	0	58	0	85	4.41	500	100		4.00	Mar-94
7.66	0.66	3.08	8.24	15.29	2.83	1.77	5.71	4.53	3.39	300.1	2	13	0	58	0	85	4.41	500	100		1.00	Mar-94
7.93	1.07	4.02	10.84	20.38	3.75	0.9	5.75	4.53	3.37	300.1	2	13	0	58	0	85	4.41	50,000				Jan-15
0.24	7.19	8.32	12.67	12.20	1.55	0.99	3.17	6.34	9.81	136.5	0	75	0	0	0	40	2.93	500	100	4.75		Oct-93
0.08	6.74	7.64	10.41	8.52	0.93	1.64	3.19	6.34	9.8	136.5	0	75	0	0	0	40	2.93	500	100		1.00	Jun-99
0.00	0.18	0.86	3.15	3.25	1.02	0.85	0.17		1	760.6	100	0	0	0	0			10,000	1,000			Dec-00
11.37	-9.27	-5.24	1.43	20.05	6.83		11.76	3.91	11.75	991.6	-40	16	0	33	1	32	5.77					Jul-93
3.81	-0.21	2.47	12.23	28.24	3.79	0	7.82	5.04	14.9	417.4	1	0	99	0	0	14	5.16					Jan-02
5.06	7.88	10.81			2.56	0.3			16.15	46.6	2	28	0	28	0	902	2.69	1,000,000	0			May-18
5.09	7.97	10.94			2.67	0.2			16.14	46.6	2	28	0	28	0	902	2.69	0				May-18
5.01	7.94	10.82			2.62	0.25			16.14	46.6	2	28	0	28	0	902	2.69	1,000,000	0			May-18
5.82	6.58	9.64			2.52	0.35			16.18	55.9	3	24	0	29	0	864	3.00	1,000,000	0			May-18
5.91	6.70	9.81			2.61	0.25			16.18	55.9	3	24	0	29	0	864	3.00	0				May-18
5.83	6.67	9.69			2.56	0.3			16.18	55.9	3	24	0	29	0	864	3.00	1,000,000	0			May-18
8.82	-2.48	-0.44	5.71	20.13	3.41	1.05	9.16		13.67	24.3	6	94	0	1	0	176	4.83	1,000	50	3.75		Sep-14

Fund Name	MARKET Ticker Symbol	Traded On	FUND TYPE, CATEGORY & OBJECTIVE Fund Type	Category and (Prospectus Objective)	RATINGS Overall Rating	Reward Rating	Risk Rating	Recent Up/ Downgrade	NEW INVESTORS Open to New Investors	Telephone
AllianzGI Emerging Markets SRI Debt Fund Class C	AGMCX	NAS CM	Open End	Emerg Mkts Fixed Inc (Growth & Income)	D+	D	C-	Down	Y	800-498-5413
AllianzGI Emerg Mkts SRI Debt Fund Class Institutional	AGMIX	NAS CM	Open End	Emerg Mkts Fixed Inc (Growth & Income)	C-	D+	C	Down	Y	800-498-5413
AllianzGI Emerging Markets SRI Debt Fund Class P	AGMPX	NAS CM	Open End	Emerg Mkts Fixed Inc (Growth & Income)	C-	D+	C	Down	Y	800-498-5413
AllianzGI Floating Rate Note Fund Class P	AREPX	NAS CM	Open End	Global Fixed Inc (Growth & Income)	D+	D	C	Down	Y	800-498-5413
AllianzGI Floating Rate Note Fund Institutional Class	ARIEX	NAS CM	Open End	Global Fixed Inc (Growth & Income)	C-	D+	C		Y	800-498-5413
AllianzGI Global High Yield Fund Class P	AGHPX	NAS CM	Open End	Global Fixed Inc (Corp Bond - High Yield)	D+	D	C-	Down		800-498-5413
AllianzGI Global High Yield Fund Institutional Class	AGIHX	NAS CM	Open End	Global Fixed Inc (Corp Bond - High Yield)	D+	D	C-	Down		800-498-5413
AllianzGI Green Bond Fund Class A	AGBFX	NAS CM	Open End	US Fixed Inc (Growth)	D+	D+	C	Up	Y	800-498-5413
AllianzGI Green Bond Fund Class P	AGBPX	NAS CM	Open End	US Fixed Inc (Growth)	D+	D+	C	Up	Y	800-498-5413
AllianzGI Green Bond Fund Institutional Class	ABGTX	NAS CM	Open End	US Fixed Inc (Growth)	D+	D+	C	Up	Y	800-498-5413
AllianzGI High Yield Bond Fund Administrative Class	AYBVX	NAS CM	Open End	US Fixed Inc (Corp Bond - High Yield)	D+	D+	C-	Down	Y	800-498-5413
AllianzGI High Yield Bond Fund Class A	AYBAX	NAS CM	Open End	US Fixed Inc (Corp Bond - High Yield)	D+	D+	C-	Down	Y	800-498-5413
AllianzGI High Yield Bond Fund Class C	AYBCX	NAS CM	Open End	US Fixed Inc (Corp Bond - High Yield)	D+	D	C-	Down	Y	800-498-5413
AllianzGI High Yield Bond Fund Class P	AYBPX	NAS CM	Open End	US Fixed Inc (Corp Bond - High Yield)	D+	D+	C-	Down	Y	800-498-5413
AllianzGI High Yield Bond Fund Class R	AYBRX	NAS CM	Open End	US Fixed Inc (Corp Bond - High Yield)	D+	D	C-	Down	Y	800-498-5413
AllianzGI High Yield Bond Fund Institutional Class	AYBIX	NAS CM	Open End	US Fixed Inc (Corp Bond - High Yield)	D+	D+	C-	Down	Y	800-498-5413
AllianzGI Short Duration High Income Fund Class A	ASHAX	NAS CM	Open End	US Fixed Inc (Income)	D+	D	C-	Down	Y	800-498-5413
AllianzGI Short Duration High Income Fund Class C	ASHCX	NAS CM	Open End	US Fixed Inc (Income)	D	D	C-	Down	Y	800-498-5413
AllianzGI Short Duration High Income Fund Class P	ASHPX	NAS CM	Open End	US Fixed Inc (Income)	D+	D	C-	Down	Y	800-498-5413
AllianzGI Short Duration High Income Fund Class R6	ASHSX	NAS CM	Open End	US Fixed Inc (Income)	D+	D	C-	Down	Y	800-498-5413
AllianzGI Short Duration High Income Institutional Cl	ASHIX	NAS CM	Open End	US Fixed Inc (Income)	D+	D	C-	Down	Y	800-498-5413
AllianzGI Short Term Bond Fund Class A	ASTHX	NAS CM	Open End	US Fixed Inc (Income)	C-	D+	B	Up	Y	800-498-5413
AllianzGI Short Term Bond Fund Class P	ASTJX	NAS CM	Open End	US Fixed Inc (Income)	C-	D+	B	Up	Y	800-498-5413
AllianzGI Short Term Bond Fund Institutional Class	ASTKX	NAS CM	Open End	US Fixed Inc (Income)	C-	D+	B	Up	Y	800-498-5413
AlphaCentric Income Opportunities Fund Class A	IOFAX	NAS CM	Open End	US Fixed Inc (Income)	D-	D-	D	Down	Y	
AlphaCentric Income Opportunities Fund Class C	IOFCX	NAS CM	Open End	US Fixed Inc (Income)	D-	D-	D	Down	Y	
AlphaCentric Income Opportunities Fund Class I	IOFIX	NAS CM	Open End	US Fixed Inc (Income)	D	D-	D	Down	Y	
AlphaCentric Municipal Opportunities Fund Class A	MUNAX	NAS CM	Open End	US Muni Fixed Inc (Muni Bond - Natl)	U	U	U		Y	
AlphaCentric Municipal Opportunities Fund Class C	MUNCX	NAS CM	Open End	US Muni Fixed Inc (Muni Bond - Natl)	U	U	U		Y	
AlphaCentric Municipal Opportunities Fund Class I	MUNIX	NAS CM	Open End	US Muni Fixed Inc (Muni Bond - Natl)	U	U	U		Y	
AlphaCentric Prime Meridian Income Fund			Closed End	US Fixed Inc (Income)	U	U	U		Y	
ALPS/Smith Short Duration Bond Fund Class A	SMASX	NAS CM	Open End	US Fixed Inc (Income)	C-	D+	B	Up	Y	866-759-5679
ALPS/Smith Short Duration Bond Fund Class C	SMCMX	NAS CM	Open End	US Fixed Inc (Income)	C-	D+	B	Up	Y	866-759-5679
ALPS/Smith Short Duration Bond Fund Class I	SMDSX	NAS CM	Open End	US Fixed Inc (Income)	C-	D+	B	Up	Y	866-759-5679
ALPS/Smith Short Duration Bond Fund Investor Shares	SMRSX	NAS CM	Open End	US Fixed Inc (Income)	C-	D+	B	Up	Y	866-759-5679
ALPS/Smith Total Return Bond Fund Class A	SMAMX	NAS CM	Open End	US Fixed Inc (Growth & Income)	C-	D+	B	Up	Y	866-759-5679
ALPS/Smith Total Return Bond Fund Class C	SMCHX	NAS CM	Open End	US Fixed Inc (Growth & Income)	C-	D+	B	Up	Y	866-759-5679
ALPS/Smith Total Return Bond Fund Class I	SMTHX	NAS CM	Open End	US Fixed Inc (Growth & Income)	C-	D+	B	Up	Y	866-759-5679
ALPS/Smith Total Return Bond Fund Investor Shares	SMTRX	NAS CM	Open End	US Fixed Inc (Growth & Income)	C-	D+	B	Up	Y	866-759-5679
Amana Participation Fund Institutional Shares	AMIPX	NAS CM	Open End	Emerg Mkts Fixed Inc (Growth)	C	C-	C+		Y	888-732-6262
Amana Participation Fund Investor Shares	AMAPX	NAS CM	Open End	Emerg Mkts Fixed Inc (Growth)	C	C-	C+		Y	888-732-6262
American Beacon Apollo Total Return Fund Y Class	ATRYX	NAS CM	Closed End	US Fixed Inc (Growth & Income)	D+	D+	C	Up		800-658-5811
American Beacon Crescent Short Duration High Income A Cl	ACHAX	NAS CM	Open End	US Fixed Inc (Corp Bond - High Yield)	D	D	C-	Down	Y	800-658-5811
American Beacon Crescent Short Duration High Income C Cl	ACHCX	NAS CM	Open End	US Fixed Inc (Corp Bond - High Yield)	D	D	C-	Down	Y	800-658-5811
American Beacon Crescent Short Duration High Inc Inv Cl	ACHPX	NAS CM	Open End	US Fixed Inc (Corp Bond - High Yield)	D+	D	C-	Down	Y	800-658-5811
American Beacon Crescent Short Duration High Income R5 Cl	ACHIX	NAS CM	Open End	US Fixed Inc (Corp Bond - High Yield)	D+	D	C-	Down	Y	800-658-5811
American Beacon Crescent Short Duration High Income Y Cl	ACHYX	NAS CM	Open End	US Fixed Inc (Corp Bond - High Yield)	D+	D	C-	Down	Y	800-658-5811
American Beacon Frontier Markets Income Fund A Class	AGUAX	NAS CM	Open End	Emerg Mkts Fixed Inc (Growth & Income)	D+	D	C-	Down	Y	800-658-5811
American Beacon Frontier Markets Income Fund C Class	AGECX	NAS CM	Open End	Emerg Mkts Fixed Inc (Growth & Income)	D+	D	C-	Down	Y	800-658-5811
American Beacon Frontier Markets Income Investor Cl	AGEPX	NAS CM	Open End	Emerg Mkts Fixed Inc (Growth & Income)	D+	D	C	Down	Y	800-658-5811
American Beacon Frontier Markets Income Fund R5 Class	AGEIX	NAS CM	Open End	Emerg Mkts Fixed Inc (Growth & Income)	D+	D	C	Down	Y	800-658-5811
American Beacon Frontier Markets Income Fund Y Class	AGEYX	NAS CM	Open End	Emerg Mkts Fixed Inc (Growth & Income)	D+	D	C	Down	Y	800-658-5811

★Expanded analysis of this fund is included in Section II.

TOTAL RETURNS & PERFORMANCE									ASSETS		ASSET ALLOCATION & TURNOVER							MINIMUMS		FEES		
3-Month Total Return	6-Month Total Return	1-Year Total Return	3-Year Total Return	5-Year Total Return	Dividend Yield (TTM)	Expense Ratio	3-Yr Std Deviation	Effective Duration	NAV	Total Assets (MIL)	%Cash	%Government Bonds	%Municipal Bonds	%Corporate Bonds	%Other	Turnover Ratio	Average Coupon Rate	Min Initial Investment	Min Additional Investment	Front End Fee (%)	Back End Fee (%)	Inception Date
8.66	-2.92	-1.25	3.30	15.65	2.62	1.8	9.15		13.76	24.3	6	94	0	1	0	176	4.83	1,000	50		1.00	Sep-14
8.86	-2.41	-0.25	6.59	21.65	3.73	0.8	9.14		13.45	24.3	6	94	0	1	0	176	4.83	1,000,000				Sep-14
8.83	-2.45	-0.33	6.20	21.02	3.63	0.9	9.11		13.4	24.3	6	94	0	1	0	176	4.83	1,000,000				Sep-14
6.07	-1.99	0.06			1.75	0.4			14.59	14.0	5	6	0	71	0	161	2.45	1,000,000				Dec-17
6.11	-1.88	0.15			1.85	0.3			14.57	14.0	5	6	0	71	0	161	2.45	1,000,000				Dec-17
-3.28	-7.29	-2.85	5.21		4.18	0.8	8.07			21.5	4	0	0	94	0	112	5.77	1,000,000				May-17
-3.25	-7.24	-2.74	5.46		4.3	0.7	8.11			21.5	4	0	0	94	0	112	5.77	1,000,000				May-17
7.19	2.18	3.45			1.37	0.75			16.52	28.5	4	38	0	59	0	121	2.11	1,000	50	3.75		Nov-18
7.18	2.27	3.64			1.55	0.55			16.51	28.5	4	38	0	59	0	121	2.11	1,000,000				Nov-18
7.25	2.29	3.76			1.59	0.5			16.53	28.5	4	38	0	59	0	121	2.11	1,000,000				Nov-18
5.37	-6.64	-3.64	3.09	11.41	5.39	0.94	8.02	3.40	7.81	107.1	7	0	0	93	0	70	6.47	1,000,000				Apr-10
5.34	-6.79	-3.29	2.15	11.15	5.31	1.07	7.88	3.40	8.17	107.1	7	0	0	93	0	70	6.47	1,000	50	3.75		Apr-10
5.17	-7.03	-3.85	0.22	7.50	4.58	1.76	7.88	3.40	8.16	107.1	7	0	0	93	0	70	6.47	1,000	50		1.00	Apr-10
5.43	-6.57	-2.91	3.31	13.31	5.98	0.73	7.85	3.40	7.8	107.1	7	0	0	93	0	70	6.47	1,000,000				Apr-10
5.10	-6.93	-3.64	0.96	8.67	5.22	1.48	7.87	3.40	7.78	107.1	7	0	0	93	0	70	6.47	0				Apr-10
5.41	-6.55	-2.95	3.17	13.00	5.9	0.79	7.89	3.40	7.83	107.1	7	0	0	93	0	70	6.47	1,000,000				Jul-96
9.26	-3.91	-0.71	3.80	13.09	4.91	0.86	7.83	2.10	13.8	868.6	5	0	0	95	0	47	5.38	1,000	50	2.25		Oct-11
9.20	-4.03	-0.97	3.08	11.71	4.63	1.11	7.84	2.10	13.79	868.6	5	0	0	95	0	47	5.38	1,000	50		1.00	Oct-11
9.22	-3.82	-0.55	4.52	14.43	5.11	0.65	7.79	2.10	13.71	868.6	5	0	0	95	0	47	5.38	1,000,000				Oct-11
9.24	-3.78	-0.40	4.82	14.98	5.26	0.55	7.8	2.10	13.7	868.6	5	0	0	95	0	47	5.38	0				Feb-17
9.23	-3.81	-0.53	4.59	14.65	5.2	0.6	7.8	2.10	13.7	868.6	5	0	0	95	0	47	5.38	1,000,000				Oct-11
8.39	4.87	7.26			3.5	0.64			15.74	21.8	6	5	0	89	0	46	4.82	1,000	50	2.25		Aug-18
8.43	4.98	7.45			3.52	0.49			15.78	21.8	6	5	0	89	0	46	4.82	1,000,000				Aug-18
8.45	5.05	7.60			3.71	0.39			15.76	21.8	6	5	0	89	0	46	4.82	1,000,000				Aug-18
20.92	-22.87	-18.38	-4.36	16.87	6.07	1.75	23.38		9.73	2,585	6	0	0	0	0	54	1.72	2,500	100	4.75		May-15
20.65	-23.18	-18.98	-6.58	12.56	5.16	2.5	23.37		9.69	2,585	6	0	0	0	0	54	1.72	2,500	100			May-15
20.96	-22.80	-18.21	-3.71	18.37	6.4	1.5	23.38		9.74	2,585	6	0	0	0	0	54	1.72	2,500	100			May-15
10.31	1.93					1.58			10.16	0.44	12	0	80	0	0	314	5.01	2,500	100	4.75		Dec-19
1.72	2.02					2.33			10.17	0.44	12	0	80	0	0	314	5.01	2,500	100			Dec-19
1.93	2.24					1.33			10.17	0.44	12	0	80	0	0	314	5.01	2,500	100			Dec-19
2.01	2.99					2.97			9.85	--								2,500	1,000			Dec-19
4.63	4.25	5.94			1.78	0.79			10.53	82.3	8	31	0	47	0	639	2.72	2,500		5.50		Jun-18
4.45	3.99	5.29			1.08	1.49			10.53	82.3	8	31	0	47	0	639	2.72	2,500			1.00	Jun-18
4.69	4.38	6.23			2.04	0.49			10.54	82.3	8	31	0	47	0	639	2.72	100,000				Jun-18
4.73	4.35	6.05			1.79	0.79			10.54	82.3	8	31	0	47	0	639	2.72	2,500				Jun-18
5.69	5.72	8.51			1.62	0.97			11.39	1,022	5	31	0	49	0	489	3.08	2,500		5.50		Jun-18
5.42	5.37	7.71			1.01	1.67			11.37	1,022	5	31	0	49	0	489	3.08	2,500			1.00	Jun-18
5.67	5.78	8.81			1.89	0.67			11.38	1,022	5	31	0	49	0	489	3.08	100,000				Jun-18
5.50	5.64	8.40			1.62	0.97			11.38	1,022	5	31	0	49	0	489	3.08	2,500				Jun-18
5.50	1.87	3.96	9.98		2.55	0.64	3.64	3.14	10.24	116.6	9	29	0	66	0		3.92	100,000	25			Sep-15
5.34	1.75	3.72	9.11		2.31	0.88	3.57	3.14	10.2	116.6	9	29	0	66	0		3.92	5,000	25			Sep-15
6.20	-2.83	1.74			3.41	2.09			9.77	--	12	0	0	88	0		2.52	100,000				Sep-18
3.79	-7.51	-4.72	0.87	9.73	4.33	1.15	6.61		8.54	49.4	20	0	0	80	0	91	5.00	2,500	50	2.50		Oct-14
3.78	-7.79	-5.27	-1.16	5.98	3.51	1.95	6.61		8.56	49.4	20	0	0	80	0	91	5.00	1,000	50		1.00	Oct-14
3.91	-7.39	-4.57	1.22	10.17	4.35	1.11	6.58		8.57	49.4	20	0	0	80	0	91	5.00	2,500	50			Oct-14
4.10	-7.21	-4.23	2.39	12.30	4.76	0.86	6.64		8.57	49.4	20	0	0	80	0	91	5.00	250,000	50			Oct-14
3.96	-7.39	-4.45	2.09	11.87	4.65	0.96	6.63		8.55	49.4	20	0	0	80	0	91	5.00	100,000	50			Oct-14
11.03	-5.07	-0.93	8.91	24.43	8.84	1.5	10.46		8.04	362.7	11	78	0	11	0	39	10.11	2,500	50	4.75		Feb-14
11.02	-5.15	-1.42	6.81	20.46	8.11	2.2	10.42		8.02	362.7	11	78	0	11	0	39	10.11	1,000	50		1.00	Feb-14
11.18	-4.85	-0.75	9.30	25.00	8.88	1.48	10.42		8.05	362.7	11	78	0	11	0	39	10.11	2,500	50			Feb-14
11.13	-4.82	-0.59	10.26	27.08	9.2	1.17	10.42		8.05	362.7	11	78	0	11	0	39	10.11	250,000	50			Feb-14
11.25	-4.73	-0.51	10.17	26.46	9.14	1.23	10.45		8.06	362.7	11	78	0	11	0	39	10.11	100,000	50			Feb-14

	MARKET			FUND TYPE, CATEGORY & OBJECTIVE	RATINGS				NEW INVESTORS	
Fund Name	Ticker Symbol	Traded On	Fund Type	Category and (Prospectus Objective)	Overall Rating	Reward Rating	Risk Rating	Recent Up/ Downgrade	Open to New Investors	Telephone
American Beacon Garcia Hamilton Quality Bond Investor Cl	GHQPX	NAS CM	Open End	US Fixed Inc (Income)	C+	C	B	Up	Y	800-658-5811
American Beacon Garcia Hamilton Quality Bond Fund R5 Class	GHQIX	NAS CM	Open End	US Fixed Inc (Income)	C+	C	B	Up	Y	800-658-5811
American Beacon Garcia Hamilton Quality Bond Fund R6 Class	GHQRX	NAS CM	Open End	US Fixed Inc (Income)	C+	C	B	Up		800-658-5811
American Beacon Garcia Hamilton Quality Bond Fund Y Class	GHQYX	NAS CM	Open End	US Fixed Inc (Income)	C+	C	B	Up	Y	800-658-5811
American Beacon GLG Total Return Fund A Class	GLGAX	NAS CM	Open End	Fixed Inc Misc (Growth & Income)	C+	C	B	Up	Y	800-658-5811
American Beacon GLG Total Return Fund C Class	GLRCX	NAS CM	Open End	Fixed Inc Misc (Growth & Income)	C	C	B-	Up	Y	800-658-5811
American Beacon GLG Total Return Fund Investor Class	GLGPX	NAS CM	Open End	Fixed Inc Misc (Growth & Income)	C+	C	B	Up	Y	800-658-5811
American Beacon GLG Total Return Fund R5 Class	GLGIX	NAS CM	Open End	Fixed Inc Misc (Growth & Income)	C+	C	B	Up	Y	800-658-5811
American Beacon GLG Total Return Fund Ultra Class	GLGUX	NAS CM	Open End	Fixed Inc Misc (Growth & Income)	C+	C	B	Up	Y	800-658-5811
American Beacon GLG Total Return Fund Y Class	GLGYX	NAS CM	Open End	Fixed Inc Misc (Growth & Income)	C+	C	B	Up	Y	800-658-5811
American Beacon SiM High Yield Opportunities Fund A Class	SHOAX	NAS CM	Open End	US Fixed Inc (Corp Bond - High Yield)	D	D	D+	Down	Y	800-658-5811
American Beacon SiM High Yield Opportunities Fund C Class	SHOCX	NAS CM	Open End	US Fixed Inc (Corp Bond - High Yield)	D	D	D+	Down	Y	800-658-5811
American Beacon SiM High Yield Opportunities Investor Cl	SHYPX	NAS CM	Open End	US Fixed Inc (Corp Bond - High Yield)	D	D	D+	Down	Y	800-658-5811
American Beacon SiM High Yield Opportunities Fund R5 Class	SHOIX	NAS CM	Open End	US Fixed Inc (Corp Bond - High Yield)	D	D	D+	Down	Y	800-658-5811
American Beacon SiM High Yield Opportunities Fund Y Class	SHOYX	NAS CM	Open End	US Fixed Inc (Corp Bond - High Yield)	D	D	D+	Down	Y	800-658-5811
American Beacon Sound Point Enhanced Income Cl Y Shares	SPEYX	NAS CM	Closed End	Fixed Inc Misc (Income)	D	D	C-	Down		800-658-5811
American Beacon Sound Point Floating Rate Income A Cl	SOUAX	NAS CM	Open End	US Fixed Inc (Income)	D	D	D+	Down	Y	800-658-5811
American Beacon Sound Point Floating Rate Income C Cl	SOUCX	NAS CM	Open End	US Fixed Inc (Income)	D	D	D		Y	800-658-5811
American Beacon Sound Point Floating Rate Inc Inv Cl	SPFPX	NAS CM	Open End	US Fixed Inc (Income)	D	D	D+	Down	Y	800-658-5811
American Beacon Sound Point Floating Rate Income R5 Cl	SPFLX	NAS CM	Open End	US Fixed Inc (Income)	D	D	D+	Down	Y	800-658-5811
American Beacon Sound Point Floating Rate Income SP Cl	SPFRX	NAS CM	Open End	US Fixed Inc (Income)	D	D	D+	Down	Y	800-658-5811
American Beacon Sound Point Floating Rate Income Y Cl	SPFYX	NAS CM	Open End	US Fixed Inc (Income)	D	D	D+	Down	Y	800-658-5811
American Beacon TwentyFour Short Term Bond Fund A Class	TFBAX	NAS CM	Open End	US Fixed Inc (Income)	U	U	U		Y	800-658-5811
American Beacon TwentyFour Short Term Bond Fund C Class	TFBCX	NAS CM	Open End	US Fixed Inc (Income)	U	U	U		Y	800-658-5811
American Beacon TwentyFour Short Term Bond Fund R6 Class	TFBRX	NAS CM	Open End	US Fixed Inc (Income)	U	U	U		Y	800-658-5811
American Beacon TwentyFour Short Term Bond Fund Y Class	TFBYX	NAS CM	Open End	US Fixed Inc (Income)	U	U	U		Y	800-658-5811
American Beacon TwentyFour Strategic Income Fund A Class	TFSAX	NAS CM	Open End	US Fixed Inc (Multisector Bond)	C	C-	C		Y	800-658-5811
American Beacon TwentyFour Strategic Income Fund C Class	TFGCX	NAS CM	Open End	US Fixed Inc (Multisector Bond)	C-	C-	C	Down	Y	800-658-5811
American Beacon TwentyFour Strategic Income Investor Cl	TFGPX	NAS CM	Open End	US Fixed Inc (Multisector Bond)	C	C-	C+		Y	800-658-5811
American Beacon TwentyFour Strategic Income Fund R5 Class	TFGIX	NAS CM	Open End	US Fixed Inc (Multisector Bond)	C	C-	C+		Y	800-658-5811
American Beacon TwentyFour Strategic Income Ultra Cl	TFGUX	NAS CM	Open End	US Fixed Inc (Multisector Bond)	C	C-	C+		Y	800-658-5811
American Beacon TwentyFour Strategic Income Fund Y Class	TFGYX	NAS CM	Open End	US Fixed Inc (Multisector Bond)	C	C-	C+		Y	800-658-5811
American Beacon U.S. Government Money Market Select Fund	AAOXX	NAS CM	Money Mkt	US Money Mkt (Money Mkt - Govt)	C	C-	C+		Y	800-658-5811
American Century California High Yield Muni Fund A Class	CAYAX	NAS CM	Open End	US Muni Fixed Inc (Muni Bond - Single State)	C	C-	C		Y	800-444-4015
American Century California High Yield Muni Fund Class C	CAYCX	NAS CM	Open End	US Muni Fixed Inc (Muni Bond - Single State)	C-	D+	C	Down	Y	800-444-4015
American Century California High Yield Muni Fund I Class	BCHIX	NAS CM	Open End	US Muni Fixed Inc (Muni Bond - Single State)	C	C-	C+		Y	800-444-4015
American Century California High Yield Muni Investor Cl	BCHYX	NAS CM	Open End	US Muni Fixed Inc (Muni Bond - Single State)	C	C-	C		Y	800-444-4015
American Century California High Yield Muni Fund Y Class	ACYHX	NAS CM	Open End	US Muni Fixed Inc (Muni Bond - Single State)	C	C-	C+		Y	800-444-4015
American Century Calif Intermed-Term Tax-Free Bond A Cl	BCIAX	NAS CM	Open End	US Muni Fixed Inc (Muni Bond - Single State)	C	C-	C+		Y	800-444-4015
American Century Calif Intermed-Term Tax-Free Bond C Cl	BCIYX	NAS CM	Open End	US Muni Fixed Inc (Muni Bond - Single State)	C	C-	C		Y	800-444-4015
American Century Calif Intermed-Term Tax-Free Bond I Cl	BCTIX	NAS CM	Open End	US Muni Fixed Inc (Muni Bond - Single State)	C	C-	B-		Y	800-444-4015
American Century Calif Intermed-Term Tax-Free Bond Inv Cl	BCITX	NAS CM	Open End	US Muni Fixed Inc (Muni Bond - Single State)	C	C-	B-		Y	800-444-4015
American Century Calif Intermed-Term Tax-Free Bond Y Cl	ACYTX	NAS CM	Open End	US Muni Fixed Inc (Muni Bond - Single State)	C	C-	B-		Y	800-444-4015
American Century Capital Preservation Fund Investor Class	CPFXX	NAS CM	Money Mkt	US Money Mkt (Money Mkt - Treasury)	C	C-	C+		Y	800-444-4015
American Century Core Plus Fund Class A	ACCQX	NAS CM	Open End	US Fixed Inc (Growth)	B-	C	B	Up	Y	800-444-4015
American Century Core Plus Fund Class C	ACCKX	NAS CM	Open End	US Fixed Inc (Growth)	C+	C	B	Up	Y	800-444-4015
American Century Core Plus Fund Class R	ACCPX	NAS CM	Open End	US Fixed Inc (Growth)	C+	C	B	Up	Y	800-444-4015
American Century Core Plus Fund I Class	ACCTX	NAS CM	Open End	US Fixed Inc (Growth)	B-	C	B	Up	Y	800-444-4015
American Century Core Plus Fund Investor Class	ACCNX	NAS CM	Open End	US Fixed Inc (Growth)	B-	C	B	Up	Y	800-444-4015
American Century Core Plus Fund R5 Class	ACCUX	NAS CM	Open End	US Fixed Inc (Growth)	B-	C	B	Up	Y	800-444-4015
American Century Diversified Bond Fund A Class	ADFAX	NAS CM	Open End	US Fixed Inc (Income)	B-	C+	B	Up	Y	800-444-4015
American Century Diversified Bond Fund C Class	CDBCX	NAS CM	Open End	US Fixed Inc (Income)	C+	C+	B	Up	Y	800-444-4015

★Expanded analysis of this fund is included in Section II.

TOTAL RETURNS & PERFORMANCE									ASSETS		ASSET ALLOCATION & TURNOVER							MINIMUMS		FEES		
3-Month Total Return	6-Month Total Return	1-Year Total Return	3-Year Total Return	5-Year Total Return	Dividend Yield (TTM)	Expense Ratio	3-Yr Std Deviation	Effective Duration	NAV	Total Assets (MIL)	%Cash	%Government Bonds	%Municipal Bonds	%Corporate Bonds	%Other	Turnover Ratio	Average Coupon Rate	Min Initial Investment	Min Additional Investment	Front End Fee (%)	Back End Fee (%)	Inception Date
4.53	3.15	4.52	8.88		1.83	0.84	2.67		10.25	348.0	5	7	0	68	0	58	2.68	2,500	50			Apr-16
4.60	3.34	4.91	10.11		2.1	0.46	2.69		10.26	348.0	5	7	0	68	0	58	2.68	250,000	50			Apr-16
4.51	3.35	4.95	10.05		2.13	0.42	2.62		10.25	348.0	5	7	0	68	0	58	2.68	0	50			Feb-19
4.57	3.28	4.91	9.78		2	0.56	2.67		10.26	348.0	5	7	0	68	0	58	2.68	100,000	50			Apr-16
-0.46	8.62	7.00	3.57		0	1.24	4.59		10.7	20.1	85	29	0	0	0	19	1.00	2,500	50	4.75		May-16
-0.66	8.19	6.21	1.25		0	2	4.59		10.43	20.1	85	29	0	0	0	19	1.00	1,000	50		1.00	May-16
-0.37	9.02	7.39	4.04		0	1.46	4.7		10.75	20.1	85	29	0	0	0	19	1.00	2,500	50			May-16
-0.45	8.68	7.39	4.94		0	0.98	4.62		10.89	20.1	85	29	0	0	0	19	1.00	250,000	50			May-16
-0.27	9.28	7.98	5.61		0	0.99	4.7		10.95	20.1	85	29	0	0	0	19	1.00	500,000,000	50			May-16
-0.46	8.44	7.04	4.17		0	1.1	4.57		10.79	20.1	85	29	0	0	0	19	1.00	100,000	50			May-16
15.35	-7.13	-4.56	5.62	18.08	6.45	1.17	12.17		8.55	1,202	-4	0	0	100	2	44	5.89	2,500	50	4.75		Feb-11
15.17	-7.40	-5.20	3.66	14.24	5.64	1.89	12.12		8.62	1,202	-4	0	0	100	2	44	5.89	1,000	50		1.00	Feb-11
15.47	-7.04	-4.48	6.11	18.75	6.41	1.15	12.15		8.56	1,202	-4	0	0	100	2	44	5.89	2,500	50			Feb-11
15.37	-6.84	-4.12	7.05	20.65	6.77	0.84	12.04		8.59	1,202	-4	0	0	100	2	44	5.89	250,000	50			Feb-11
15.50	-6.78	-4.08	6.99	20.44	6.71	0.91	12.1		8.59	1,202	-4	0	0	100	2	44	5.89	100,000	50			Feb-11
8.74	-3.81	-4.45			5.34	2.14			8.99	--	0	0	0	100	0		1.36	100,000				Jul-18
9.75	-7.90	-8.05	-1.22	8.42	7.18	1.14	10.14		8.61	632.6	3	0	0	97	0	58	1.62	2,500	50	2.50		Dec-15
9.37	-8.23	-8.73	-3.48	4.46	6.29	1.91	10.04		8.64	632.6	3	0	0	97	0	58	1.62	1,000	50		1.00	Dec-15
9.62	-7.87	-8.11	-1.22	8.75	7.04	1.23	10.06		8.58	632.6	3	0	0	97	0	58	1.62	2,500	50			Dec-15
9.70	-7.70	-7.71	-0.17	10.40	7.48	0.85	10.01		8.6	632.6	3	0	0	97	0	58	1.62	250,000	50			Dec-12
9.72	-7.88	-8.04	-1.42	8.55	7.02	1.16	10.07		8.64	632.6	3	0	0	97	0	58	1.62	1,000	50			May-14
9.68	-7.81	-7.87	-0.48	9.90	7.41	0.91	10.04		8.6	632.6	3	0	0	97	0	58	1.62	100,000	50			Dec-15
3.27						0.87			9.89	10.1	6	0	0	89	0		5.35	2,500	250	2.50		Feb-20
2.97						1.62			9.85	10.1	6	0	0	89	0		5.35	1,000	250		1.00	Feb-20
3.38						0.47			9.91	10.1	6	0	0	89	0		5.35	0	50			Feb-20
3.27						0.57			9.9	10.1	6	0	0	89	0		5.35	100,000	50			Feb-20
9.65	-0.32	3.33	14.32		3.51	1.12	7.04		10.16	120.9	17	18	0	56	0	198	4.90	2,500	50	3.75		Oct-18
9.38	-0.69	2.51	11.83		2.95	1.87	6.98		10.13	120.9	17	18	0	56	0	198	4.90	1,000	50		1.00	Oct-18
9.67	-0.29	3.38	14.08		3.55	1.09	6.97		10.16	120.9	17	18	0	56	0	198	4.90	2,500	50			Apr-17
9.72	-0.14	3.71	15.24		3.56	0.72	6.99		10.27	120.9	17	18	0	56	0	198	4.90	250,000	50			Apr-17
9.69	-0.13	3.79	15.55		3.54	0.67	6.98		10.3	120.9	17	18	0	56	0	198	4.90	350,000,000	50			Apr-17
9.74	-0.14	3.61	15.04		3.57	0.82	6.98		10.25	120.9	17	18	0	56	0	198	4.90	100,000	50			Apr-17
0.05	0.36	1.29	4.53	5.16	1.46	0.13	0.17		1	929.1	67	33	0	0	0			1,000,000				Dec-01
2.93	-1.24	1.58	11.64	23.03	3.02	0.75	5.98	8.55	10.72	1,369	0	0	100	0	0	39	4.99	5,000	50	4.50		Jan-03
2.65	-1.59	0.83	9.17	18.53	2.24	1.5	5.94	8.55	10.72	1,369	0	0	100	0	0	39	4.99	5,000	50		1.00	Jan-03
2.94	-1.03	1.94	13.14	25.82	3.48	0.3	5.96	8.55	10.71	1,369	0	0	100	0	0	39	4.99	5,000,000	50			Mar-10
2.99	-1.12	1.83	12.47	24.57	3.27	0.5	5.98	8.55	10.72	1,369	0	0	100	0	0	39	4.99	5,000	50			Dec-86
3.04	-0.92	2.07	13.22	25.44	3.52	0.27	6.02	8.55	10.72	1,369	0	0	100	0	0	39	4.99	0				Apr-17
2.17	0.64	2.43	8.70	14.40	2.06	0.72	3.91	5.60	12.06	1,971	1	0	99	0	0	54	4.80	5,000	50	4.50		Mar-10
1.99	0.27	1.68	6.30	10.21	1.31	1.47	3.91	5.60	12.07	1,971	1	0	99	0	0	54	4.80	5,000	50		1.00	Mar-10
2.28	0.85	2.88	10.16	16.98	2.51	0.27	3.91	5.60	12.06	1,971	1	0	99	0	0	54	4.80	5,000,000	50			Mar-10
2.23	0.76	2.68	9.52	15.83	2.31	0.47	3.92	5.60	12.06	1,971	1	0	99	0	0	54	4.80	5,000	50			Nov-83
2.28	0.87	2.91	10.27	16.67	2.54	0.24	3.92	5.60	12.06	1,971	1	0	99	0	0	54	4.80	0				Apr-17
0.00	0.23	1.00	3.72	3.84	1.15	0.48	0.17		1	2,219	80	20	0	0	0			2,500	50			Oct-72
4.55	3.82	5.90	12.50	19.77	1.92	0.8	3.98	5.88	11.23	148.3	6	34	2	26	0	129	3.10	2,500	50	4.50		Nov-06
4.45	3.45	5.13	10.11	15.38	1.19	1.55	4.03	5.88	11.23	148.3	6	34	2	26	0	129	3.10	2,500	50		1.00	Nov-06
4.49	3.70	5.64	11.77	18.29	1.67	1.05	4.01	5.88	11.23	148.3	6	34	2	26	0	129	3.10	2,500	50			Nov-06
4.64	3.99	6.27	13.78	21.75	2.26	0.45	4	5.88	11.23	148.3	6	34	2	26	0	129	3.10	5,000,000	50			Apr-17
4.61	3.94	6.16	13.42	21.26	2.16	0.55	4	5.88	11.23	148.3	6	34	2	26	0	129	3.10	2,500	50			Nov-06
4.67	3.95	6.37	14.02	22.36	2.36	0.35	4.06	5.88	11.22	148.3	6	34	2	26	0	129	3.10	0				Nov-06
3.88	5.75	7.81	13.31	19.32	1.86	0.85	3.58	5.91	11.5	2,349	9	28	2	26	0	82	3.01	2,500	50	4.50		Dec-01
3.70	5.38	7.12	10.80	14.95	1.14	1.6	3.55	5.91	11.49	2,349	9	28	2	26	0	82	3.01	2,500	50		1.00	Jan-03

	MARKET			FUND TYPE, CATEGORY & OBJECTIVE	RATINGS				NEW INVESTORS	
Fund Name	Ticker Symbol	Traded On	Fund Type	Category and (Prospectus Objective)	Overall Rating	Reward Rating	Risk Rating	Recent Up/ Downgrade	Open to New Investors	Telephone
American Century Diversified Bond Fund I Class	ACBPX	NAS CM	Open End	US Fixed Inc (Income)	B	C+	B+	Up	Y	800-444-4015
American Century Diversified Bond Fund Investor Class	ADFIX	NAS CM	Open End	US Fixed Inc (Income)	B	C+	B	Up	Y	800-444-4015
American Century Diversified Bond Fund R Class	ADVRX	NAS CM	Open End	US Fixed Inc (Income)	B-	C+	B	Up	Y	800-444-4015
American Century Diversified Bond Fund R5 Class	ADRVX	NAS CM	Open End	US Fixed Inc (Income)	B	C+	B+	Up	Y	800-444-4015
American Century Diversified Bond Fund R6 Class	ADDVX	NAS CM	Open End	US Fixed Inc (Income)	B	C+	B+	Up	Y	800-444-4015
American Century Diversified Bond Fund Y Class	ADVYX	NAS CM	Open End	US Fixed Inc (Income)	B	C+	B+	Up	Y	800-444-4015
American Century Emerging Markets Debt Fund A Class	AEDQX	NAS CM	Open End	Emerg Mkts Fixed Inc (Growth & Income)	C-	D+	C		Y	800-444-4015
American Century Emerging Markets Debt Fund C Class	AEDHX	NAS CM	Open End	Emerg Mkts Fixed Inc (Growth & Income)	C-	D+	C		Y	800-444-4015
American Century Emerging Markets Debt Fund G CLASS	AEDGX	NAS CM	Open End	Emerg Mkts Fixed Inc (Growth & Income)	C-	D+	C	Down	Y	800-444-4015
American Century Emerging Markets Debt Fund I Class	AEHDX	NAS CM	Open End	Emerg Mkts Fixed Inc (Growth & Income)	C-	D+	C	Down	Y	800-444-4015
American Century Emerging Markets Debt Fund Investor Class	AEDVX	NAS CM	Open End	Emerg Mkts Fixed Inc (Growth & Income)	C-	D+	C	Down	Y	800-444-4015
American Century Emerging Markets Debt Fund R Class	AEDWX	NAS CM	Open End	Emerg Mkts Fixed Inc (Growth & Income)	C-	D+	C		Y	800-444-4015
American Century Emerging Markets Debt Fund R5 Class	AEDJX	NAS CM	Open End	Emerg Mkts Fixed Inc (Growth & Income)	C-	D+	C	Down	Y	800-444-4015
American Century Emerging Markets Debt Fund R6 Class	AEXDX	NAS CM	Open End	Emerg Mkts Fixed Inc (Growth & Income)	C-	D+	C	Down	Y	800-444-4015
American Century Emerging Markets Debt Fund Y Class	AEYDX	NAS CM	Open End	Emerg Mkts Fixed Inc (Growth & Income)	C-	D+	C	Down	Y	800-444-4015
American Century Ginnie Mae Fund A Class	BGNAX	NAS CM	Open End	US Fixed Inc (Govt Bond - Mortgage)	C+	C+	B		Y	800-444-4015
American Century Ginnie Mae Fund I Class	AGMHX	NAS CM	Open End	US Fixed Inc (Govt Bond - Mortgage)	C+	C+	B-		Y	800-444-4015
American Century Ginnie Mae Fund Investor Class	BGNMX	NAS CM	Open End	US Fixed Inc (Govt Bond - Mortgage)	C+	C+	B-		Y	800-444-4015
American Century Ginnie Mae Fund R Class	AGMWX	NAS CM	Open End	US Fixed Inc (Govt Bond - Mortgage)	C+	C	B-	Up	Y	800-444-4015
American Century Ginnie Mae Fund R5 Class	AGMNX	NAS CM	Open End	US Fixed Inc (Govt Bond - Mortgage)	B-	C+	B-	Up	Y	800-444-4015
American Century Global Bond Fund A Class	AGBAX	NAS CM	Open End	Global Fixed Inc (Worldwide Bond)	C	C-	B-		Y	800-444-4015
American Century Global Bond Fund C Class	AGBTX	NAS CM	Open End	Global Fixed Inc (Worldwide Bond)	C	C-	C+		Y	800-444-4015
American Century Global Bond Fund G CLASS	AGBGX	NAS CM	Open End	Global Fixed Inc (Worldwide Bond)	C	C	B		Y	800-444-4015
American Century Global Bond Fund I Class	AGBHX	NAS CM	Open End	Global Fixed Inc (Worldwide Bond)	C	C	B-		Y	800-444-4015
American Century Global Bond Fund Investor Class	AGBVX	NAS CM	Open End	Global Fixed Inc (Worldwide Bond)	C	C	B-		Y	800-444-4015
American Century Global Bond Fund R Class	AGBRX	NAS CM	Open End	Global Fixed Inc (Worldwide Bond)	C	C-	C+		Y	800-444-4015
American Century Global Bond Fund R5 Class	AGBNX	NAS CM	Open End	Global Fixed Inc (Worldwide Bond)	C	C	B-		Y	800-444-4015
American Century Global Bond Fund R6 Class	AGBDX	NAS CM	Open End	Global Fixed Inc (Worldwide Bond)	C	C	B-		Y	800-444-4015
American Century Global Bond Fund Y Class	AGBWX	NAS CM	Open End	Global Fixed Inc (Worldwide Bond)	C	C	B-		Y	800-444-4015
American Century Government Bond Fund A Class	ABTAX	NAS CM	Open End	US Fixed Inc (Govt Bond - General)	B	B-	B	Up	Y	800-444-4015
American Century Government Bond Fund C Class	ABTCX	NAS CM	Open End	US Fixed Inc (Govt Bond - General)	B-	C+	B		Y	800-444-4015
American Century Government Bond Fund I Class	ABHTX	NAS CM	Open End	US Fixed Inc (Govt Bond - General)	B	B-	B		Y	800-444-4015
American Century Government Bond Fund Investor Class	CPTNX	NAS CM	Open End	US Fixed Inc (Govt Bond - General)	B	B-	B		Y	800-444-4015
American Century Government Bond Fund R Class	ABTRX	NAS CM	Open End	US Fixed Inc (Govt Bond - General)	B	B-	B	Up	Y	800-444-4015
American Century Government Bond Fund R5 Class	ABTIX	NAS CM	Open End	US Fixed Inc (Govt Bond - General)	B	B-	B+		Y	800-444-4015
American Century High Income Fund A Class	AHIAX	NAS CM	Open End	US Fixed Inc (Corp Bond - High Yield)	C-	D+	C		Y	800-444-4015
American Century High Income Fund I Class	AHIIX	NAS CM	Open End	US Fixed Inc (Corp Bond - High Yield)	C-	D+	C		Y	800-444-4015
American Century High Income Fund Investor Class	AHIVX	NAS CM	Open End	US Fixed Inc (Corp Bond - High Yield)	C-	D+	C		Y	800-444-4015
American Century High Income Fund R5 Class	AHIEX	NAS CM	Open End	US Fixed Inc (Corp Bond - High Yield)	C-	D+	C		Y	800-444-4015
American Century High Income Fund R6 Class	AHIDX	NAS CM	Open End	US Fixed Inc (Corp Bond - High Yield)	C-	D+	C		Y	800-444-4015
American Century High Income Fund Y Class	NPHIX	NAS CM	Open End	US Fixed Inc (Corp Bond - High Yield)	C-	D+	C		Y	800-444-4015
American Century High Yield Municipal Fund Class A	AYMAX	NAS CM	Open End	US Muni Fixed Inc (Muni Bond - Natl)	C-	D+	C	Down	Y	800-444-4015
American Century High Yield Municipal Fund Class C	AYMCX	NAS CM	Open End	US Muni Fixed Inc (Muni Bond - Natl)	C-	D+	C	Down	Y	800-444-4015
American Century High Yield Municipal Fund I Class	AYMIX	NAS CM	Open End	US Muni Fixed Inc (Muni Bond - Natl)	C-	D+	C	Down	Y	800-444-4015
American Century High Yield Municipal Fund Investor Class	ABHYX	NAS CM	Open End	US Muni Fixed Inc (Muni Bond - Natl)	C-	D+	C	Down	Y	800-444-4015
American Century High-Yield Fund A Class	AHYVX	NAS CM	Open End	US Fixed Inc (Corp Bond - High Yield)	C-	D+	C		Y	800-444-4015
American Century High-Yield Fund C Class	AHDCX	NAS CM	Open End	US Fixed Inc (Corp Bond - High Yield)	C-	D+	C		Y	800-444-4015
American Century High-Yield Fund I Class	AHYHX	NAS CM	Open End	US Fixed Inc (Corp Bond - High Yield)	C-	D+	C		Y	800-444-4015
American Century High-Yield Fund Investor Class	ABHIX	NAS CM	Open End	US Fixed Inc (Corp Bond - High Yield)	C-	D+	C		Y	800-444-4015
American Century High-Yield Fund R Class	AHYRX	NAS CM	Open End	US Fixed Inc (Corp Bond - High Yield)	C-	D+	C		Y	800-444-4015
American Century High-Yield Fund R5 Class	ACYIX	NAS CM	Open End	US Fixed Inc (Corp Bond - High Yield)	C-	D+	C		Y	800-444-4015
American Century High-Yield Fund R6 Class	AHYDX	NAS CM	Open End	US Fixed Inc (Corp Bond - High Yield)	C-	D+	C		Y	800-444-4015

★ Expanded analysis of this fund is included in Section II.

TOTAL RETURNS & PERFORMANCE									ASSETS		ASSET ALLOCATION & TURNOVER							MINIMUMS		FEES		
3-Month Total Return	6-Month Total Return	1-Year Total Return	3-Year Total Return	5-Year Total Return	Dividend Yield (TTM)	Expense Ratio	3-Yr Std Deviation	Effective Duration	NAV	Total Assets (MIL)	%Cash	%Government Bonds	%Municipal Bonds	%Corporate Bonds	%Other	Turnover Ratio	Average Coupon Rate	Min Initial Investment	Min Additional Investment	Front End Fee (%)	Back End Fee (%)	Inception Date
3.89	5.98	8.28	14.78	21.96	2.3	0.4	3.52	5.91	11.5	2,349	9	28	2	26	0	82	3.01	5,000,000	50			Apr-93
3.94	5.88	8.17	14.12	20.78	2.11	0.6	3.53	5.91	11.5	2,349	9	28	2	26	0	82	3.01	2,500	50			Dec-01
3.81	5.63	7.64	12.50	17.88	1.63	1.1	3.53	5.91	11.5	2,349	9	28	2	26	0	82	3.01	2,500	50			Jul-05
3.98	5.98	8.28	14.80	21.99	2.3	0.4	3.58	5.91	11.5	2,349	9	28	2	26	0	82	3.01	0				Apr-17
3.99	6.00	8.43	15.05	22.36	2.35	0.35	3.6	5.91	11.51	2,349	9	28	2	26	0	82	3.01	0				Jul-13
3.90	6.00	8.31	14.88	22.07	2.33	0.37	3.53	5.91	11.5	2,349	9	28	2	26	0	82	3.01	0				Apr-17
12.30	-2.36	0.88	8.32	21.82	3.75	1.22	9.48	4.57	10.09	339.4	8	16	0	58	0	75	4.30	2,500	50	4.50		Jul-14
12.01	-2.72	0.14	5.93	17.38	2.99	1.97	9.46	4.57	10.07	339.4	8	16	0	58	0	75	4.30	2,500	50		1.00	Jul-14
12.61	-1.78	2.09	12.17	27.28	5	0.01	9.46	4.57	10.1	339.4	8	16	0	58	0	75	4.30	0				Nov-17
12.38	-2.19	1.23	9.58	23.97	4.12	0.87	9.47	4.57	10.1	339.4	8	16	0	58	0	75	4.30	5,000,000	50			Apr-17
12.36	-2.24	1.13	9.24	23.47	4.01	0.97	9.47	4.57	10.1	339.4	8	16	0	58	0	75	4.30	2,500	50			Jul-14
12.24	-2.48	0.64	7.63	20.45	3.51	1.47	9.46	4.57	10.09	339.4	8	16	0	58	0	75	4.30	2,500	50			Jul-14
12.41	-2.14	1.36	9.95	24.77	4.25	0.77	9.45	4.57	10.1	339.4	8	16	0	58	0	75	4.30	0				Jul-14
12.42	-2.12	1.38	10.05	24.88	4.27	0.72	9.48	4.57	10.1	339.4	8	16	0	58	0	75	4.30	0				Jul-14
12.41	-2.14	1.33	9.88	24.55	4.22	0.77	9.46	4.57	10.1	339.4	8	16	0	58	0	75	4.30	0				Apr-17
0.64	3.30	4.91	10.10	12.41	2.21	0.8	2.29	2.92	10.78	1,042	8	0	0	0	0	270	3.35	2,500	50	4.50		Oct-97
0.72	3.47	5.17	11.25	14.18	2.55	0.45	2.29	2.92	10.78	1,042	8	0	0	0	0	270	3.35	5,000,000	50			Apr-17
0.79	3.42	5.17	10.92	13.82	2.46	0.55	2.28	2.92	10.78	1,042	8	0	0	0	0	270	3.35	2,500	50			Sep-85
0.67	3.28	4.66	9.28	11.02	1.97	1.05	2.29	2.92	10.78	1,042	8	0	0	0	0	270	3.35	2,500	50			Sep-07
0.83	3.52	5.38	11.58	14.95	2.65	0.35	2.27	2.92	10.78	1,042	8	0	0	0	0	270	3.35	0				Sep-07
4.21	0.80	2.08	10.09	17.70	1.74	1.09	4.37	7.25	10.22	1,186	8	50	1	25	0	46	3.23	2,500	50	4.50		Jan-12
3.93	0.45	1.26	7.62	13.29	0.83	1.84	4.33	7.25	10.14	1,186	8	50	1	25	0	46	3.23	2,500	50		1.00	Jan-12
4.38	1.29	3.07	13.65	22.52	3.02	0.01	4.34	7.25	10.28	1,186	8	50	1	25	0	46	3.23	0				Jul-17
4.29	0.96	2.39	11.13	19.70	2.15	0.74	4.37	7.25	10.27	1,186	8	50	1	25	0	46	3.23	5,000,000	50			Apr-17
4.27	1.01	2.34	10.91	19.18	2.03	0.84	4.38	7.25	10.25	1,186	8	50	1	25	0	46	3.23	2,500	50			Jan-12
4.16	0.69	1.81	9.27	16.23	1.44	1.34	4.38	7.25	10.19	1,186	8	50	1	25	0	46	3.23	2,500	50			Jan-12
4.32	1.01	2.44	11.55	20.26	2.27	0.64	4.4	7.25	10.26	1,186	8	50	1	25	0	46	3.23	0				Jan-12
4.34	1.03	2.52	11.64	20.58	2.33	0.59	4.4	7.25	10.26	1,186	8	50	1	25	0	46	3.23	0				Jul-13
4.31	1.10	2.54	11.58	20.41	2.27	0.64	4.38	7.25	10.28	1,186	8	50	1	25	0	46	3.23	0				Apr-17
0.66	6.32	7.75	13.50	16.80	1.9	0.72	3.18	5.31	11.72	898.1	5	45	2	0	0	103	2.98	2,500	50	4.50		Oct-97
0.48	5.94	7.06	11.00	12.53	1.18	1.47	3.17	5.31	11.72	898.1	5	45	2	0	0	103	2.98	2,500	50		1.00	Mar-10
0.74	6.50	8.22	14.59	18.63	2.24	0.37	3.12	5.31	11.71	898.1	5	45	2	0	0	103	2.98	5,000,000	50			Apr-17
0.63	6.44	8.01	14.35	18.26	2.14	0.47	3.2	5.31	11.72	898.1	5	45	2	0	0	103	2.98	2,500	50			May-80
0.60	6.19	7.58	12.66	15.36	1.66	0.97	3.17	5.31	11.72	898.1	5	45	2	0	0	103	2.98	2,500	50			Mar-10
0.76	6.55	8.32	15.03	19.44	2.33	0.27	3.15	5.31	11.72	898.1	5	45	2	0	0	103	2.98	0				Mar-10
9.10	-4.65	-1.55	6.99	19.80	5.27	1.04	8.49	4.13	8.78	618.2	1	0	0	99	0	55	6.17	2,500	50	4.50		Oct-17
9.07	-4.49	-1.33	7.99	21.77	5.63	0.69	8.48	4.13	8.77	618.2	1	0	0	99	0	55	6.17	5,000,000				Oct-17
9.17	-4.53	-1.31	7.79	21.31	5.53	0.79	8.49	4.13	8.78	618.2	1	0	0	99	0	55	6.17	2,500	50			Oct-17
9.09	-4.55	-1.21	8.31	22.38	5.76	0.59	8.49	4.13	8.77	618.2	1	0	0	99	0	55	6.17	0				Oct-17
9.11	-4.42	-1.18	8.45	22.54	5.8	0.54	8.42	4.13	8.77	618.2	1	0	0	99	0	55	6.17	0				Oct-17
9.09	-4.55	-1.23	8.30	22.37	5.74	0.59	8.49	4.13	8.77	618.2	1	0	0	99	0	55	6.17	0				Dec-12
4.16	-1.87	0.99	12.20	23.57	3.34	0.85	6.96	8.92	9.64	668.9	0	0	100	0	0	57	5.01	5,000	50	4.50		Jan-03
3.98	-2.23	0.35	9.85	19.18	2.56	1.6	6.99	8.92	9.64	668.9	0	0	100	0	0	57	5.01	5,000	50		1.00	Jul-02
4.27	-1.66	1.44	13.71	26.35	3.81	0.4	6.96	8.92	9.64	668.9	0	0	100	0	0	57	5.01	5,000,000	50			Mar-10
4.33	-1.65	1.34	13.17	25.25	3.6	0.6	6.95	8.92	9.65	668.9	0	0	100	0	0	57	5.01	5,000	50			Mar-98
7.27	-3.97	-1.03	6.62	16.87	4.46	1.04	7.27	3.89	5.33	127.2	6	0	0	94	0	38	5.53	2,500	50	4.50		Mar-02
7.09	-4.31	-1.75	4.45	12.60	3.69	1.79	7.28	3.89	5.33	127.2	6	0	0	94	0	38	5.53	2,500	50		1.00	Dec-01
7.15	-3.80	-0.68	7.74	18.50	4.82	0.69	7.17	3.89	5.33	127.2	6	0	0	94	0	38	5.53	5,000,000	50			Apr-17
7.13	-3.86	-0.79	7.40	18.11	4.72	0.79	7.21	3.89	5.32	127.2	6	0	0	94	0	38	5.53	2,500	50			Sep-97
7.21	-4.08	-1.27	5.83	15.43	4.2	1.29	7.29	3.89	5.33	127.2	6	0	0	94	0	38	5.53	2,500	50			Jul-05
7.39	-3.76	-0.59	8.02	19.49	4.93	0.59	7.28	3.89	5.33	127.2	6	0	0	94	0	38	5.53	0				Aug-04
7.20	-3.75	-0.54	8.18	19.79	4.99	0.54	7.22	3.89	5.32	127.2	6	0	0	94	0	38	5.53	0				Jul-13

	MARKET		FUND TYPE, CATEGORY & OBJECTIVE		RATINGS				NEW INVESTORS	
Fund Name	Ticker Symbol	Traded On	Fund Type	Category and (Prospectus Objective)	Overall Rating	Reward Rating	Risk Rating	Recent Up/ Downgrade	Open to New Investors	Telephone
American Century High-Yield Fund Y Class	AHYLX	NAS CM	Open End	US Fixed Inc (Corp Bond - High Yield)	C-	D+	C		Y	800-444-4015
American Century High-Yield Municipal Fund Y Class	AYMYX	NAS CM	Open End	US Muni Fixed Inc (Muni Bond - Natl)	C-	D+	C	Down	Y	800-444-4015
American Century Inflation Adjusted Bond Fund A Class	AIAVX	NAS CM	Open End	US Fixed Inc (Govt Bond - General)	B-	C+	B+	Up	Y	800-444-4015
American Century Inflation Adjusted Bond Fund C Class	AINOX	NAS CM	Open End	US Fixed Inc (Govt Bond - General)	C+	C	B	Up	Y	800-444-4015
American Century Inflation Adjusted Bond Fund I Class	AIAHX	NAS CM	Open End	US Fixed Inc (Govt Bond - General)	B-	C+	B+	Up	Y	800-444-4015
American Century Inflation Adjusted Bond Investor Cl	ACITX	NAS CM	Open End	US Fixed Inc (Govt Bond - General)	B-	C+	B+	Up	Y	800-444-4015
American Century Inflation Adjusted Bond Fund R Class	AIARX	NAS CM	Open End	US Fixed Inc (Govt Bond - General)	B-	C	B	Up	Y	800-444-4015
American Century Inflation Adjusted Bond Fund R5 Class	AIANX	NAS CM	Open End	US Fixed Inc (Govt Bond - General)	B	C+	B+	Up	Y	800-444-4015
American Century Inflation Adjusted Bond Fund Y Class	AIAYX	NAS CM	Open End	US Fixed Inc (Govt Bond - General)	B-	C+	B+	Up	Y	800-444-4015
American Century Inflation-Adjusted Bond Fund G Class	AINGX	NAS CM	Open End	US Fixed Inc (Govt Bond - General)	B	C+	B+	Up	Y	800-444-4015
American Century Inflation-Adjusted Bond Fund R6 Class	AIADX	NAS CM	Open End	US Fixed Inc (Govt Bond - General)	B	C+	B+	Up	Y	800-444-4015
American Century Intermediate Term Tax-Free Bond Cl A	TWWOX	NAS CM	Open End	US Muni Fixed Inc (Muni Bond - Natl)	C	C-	C+		Y	800-444-4015
American Century Intermediate Term Tax-Free Bond Cl C	TWTCX	NAS CM	Open End	US Muni Fixed Inc (Muni Bond - Natl)	C	C-	C+		Y	800-444-4015
American Century Intermediate Term Tax-Free Bond I Cl	AXBIX	NAS CM	Open End	US Muni Fixed Inc (Muni Bond - Natl)	C	C-	B-		Y	800-444-4015
American Century Intermed Term Tax-Free Bond Investor Cl	TWTIX	NAS CM	Open End	US Muni Fixed Inc (Muni Bond - Natl)	C	C-	B-		Y	800-444-4015
American Century Intermediate-Term Tax-Free Bond Y Cl	ATBYX	NAS CM	Open End	US Muni Fixed Inc (Muni Bond - Natl)	C	C-	B-		Y	800-444-4015
American Century International Bond Fund A Class	AIBDX	NAS CM	Open End	Global Fixed Inc (Corp Bond - General)	D+	D	C	Down	Y	800-444-4015
American Century International Bond Fund C Class	AIQCX	NAS CM	Open End	Global Fixed Inc (Corp Bond - General)	D+	D	C	Down	Y	800-444-4015
American Century International Bond Fund G Class	AIBGX	NAS CM	Open End	Global Fixed Inc (Corp Bond - General)	C-	D	C		Y	800-444-4015
American Century International Bond Fund I Class	AIBHX	NAS CM	Open End	Global Fixed Inc (Corp Bond - General)	D+	D	C	Down	Y	800-444-4015
American Century International Bond Fund Investor Class	BEGBX	NAS CM	Open End	Global Fixed Inc (Corp Bond - General)	D+	D	C	Down	Y	800-444-4015
American Century International Bond Fund R Class	AIBRX	NAS CM	Open End	Global Fixed Inc (Corp Bond - General)	D+	D	C	Down	Y	800-444-4015
American Century International Bond Fund R5 Class	AIDIX	NAS CM	Open End	Global Fixed Inc (Corp Bond - General)	D+	D	C	Down	Y	800-444-4015
American Century International Bond Fund R6 Class	AIDDX	NAS CM	Open End	Global Fixed Inc (Corp Bond - General)	D+	D	C	Down	Y	800-444-4015
American Century International Bond Fund Y Class	AIBYX	NAS CM	Open End	Global Fixed Inc (Corp Bond - General)	D+	D	C	Down	Y	800-444-4015
American Century Inv Trust Prime Money Mkt Investor Cl	ARCXX	NAS CM	Money Mkt	US Money Mkt (Money Mkt - Taxable)	C	C-	C		Y	800-444-4015
American Century Inv Trust Prime Money Mkt Investor Cl	BPRXX	NAS CM	Money Mkt	US Money Mkt (Money Mkt - Taxable)	C	C-	C+		Y	800-444-4015
American Century Inv Calif Tax-Free Money Mkt Investor Cl	BCTXX	NAS CM	Money Mkt	US Money Mkt (Money Mkt - Single State)	C	C-	C		Y	800-444-4015
American Century Investments Ginnie Mae Fund C Class	BGNCX	NAS CM	Open End	US Fixed Inc (Govt Bond - Mortgage)	C+	C	B-	Up	Y	800-444-4015
American Century Investments Prime Money Mkt Fund Class A	ACAXX	NAS CM	Money Mkt	US Money Mkt (Money Mkt - Taxable)	C	C-	C		Y	800-444-4015
American Century Inv Tax-Free Money Mkt Investor Cl	BNTXX	NAS CM	Money Mkt	US Money Mkt (Money Mkt - Fed Tax Exmpt)	C	C-	C		Y	800-444-4015
American Century NT Diversified Bond Fund G Class	ACLDX	NAS CM	Open End	US Fixed Inc (Corp Bond - General)	B	C+	B+	Up	Y	800-444-4015
American Century NT High Income Fund G Class	AHGNX	NAS CM	Open End	US Fixed Inc (Corp Bond - High Yield)	D+	D	C-	Down	Y	800-444-4015
American Century NT High Income Fund Investor Class	AHGVX	NAS CM	Open End	US Fixed Inc (Corp Bond - High Yield)	D	D	C-	Down	Y	800-444-4015
American Century Short Duration Fund A Class	ACSQX	NAS CM	Open End	US Fixed Inc (Growth & Income)	C	C	C+		Y	800-444-4015
American Century Short Duration Fund C Class	ACSKX	NAS CM	Open End	US Fixed Inc (Growth & Income)	C	C-	C+	Up	Y	800-444-4015
American Century Short Duration Fund I Class	ASHHX	NAS CM	Open End	US Fixed Inc (Growth & Income)	C	C	B-		Y	800-444-4015
American Century Short Duration Fund Investor Class	ACSNX	NAS CM	Open End	US Fixed Inc (Growth & Income)	C	C	B-		Y	800-444-4015
American Century Short Duration Fund R Class	ACSPX	NAS CM	Open End	US Fixed Inc (Growth & Income)	C	C	C+		Y	800-444-4015
American Century Short Duration Fund R5 Class	ACSUX	NAS CM	Open End	US Fixed Inc (Growth & Income)	C	C	B-		Y	800-444-4015
American Century Short Duration Fund R6 CLASS	ASDDX	NAS CM	Open End	US Fixed Inc (Growth & Income)	C	C	B-		Y	800-444-4015
American Century Short Duration Inflat Protect Bond A Cl	APOAX	NAS CM	Open End	US Fixed Inc (Growth & Income)	C	C-	B-		Y	800-444-4015
American Century Short Duration Inflat Protect Bond C Cl	APOCX	NAS CM	Open End	US Fixed Inc (Growth & Income)	C	C-	C+	Up	Y	800-444-4015
American Century Short Duration Inflat Protect Bond G Cl	APOGX	NAS CM	Open End	US Fixed Inc (Growth & Income)	C	C	B-		Y	800-444-4015
American Century Short Duration Inflat Protect Bond I Cl	APOHX	NAS CM	Open End	US Fixed Inc (Growth & Income)	C	C	B-		Y	800-444-4015
American Century Short Duration Inflat Protect Bond Inv Cl	APOIX	NAS CM	Open End	US Fixed Inc (Growth & Income)	C	C	B-		Y	800-444-4015
American Century Short Duration Inflat Protect Bond R Cl	APORX	NAS CM	Open End	US Fixed Inc (Growth & Income)	C	C-	C+		Y	800-444-4015
American Century Short Duration Inflat Protect Bond R5 Cl	APISX	NAS CM	Open End	US Fixed Inc (Growth & Income)	C	C	B-		Y	800-444-4015
American Century Short Duration Inflat Protect Bond R6 Cl	APODX	NAS CM	Open End	US Fixed Inc (Growth & Income)	C	C	B-		Y	800-444-4015
American Century Short Duration Inflat Protect Bond Y Cl	APOYX	NAS CM	Open End	US Fixed Inc (Growth & Income)	C	C	B-		Y	800-444-4015
American Century Short Duration Strategic Income A Cl	ASADX	NAS CM	Open End	US Fixed Inc (Income)	C	C-	C+		Y	800-444-4015
American Century Short Duration Strategic Income C Cl	ASCDX	NAS CM	Open End	US Fixed Inc (Income)	C	C-	C	Up	Y	800-444-4015

★ Expanded analysis of this fund is included in Section II.

TOTAL RETURNS & PERFORMANCE									ASSETS		ASSET ALLOCATION & TURNOVER							MINIMUMS		FEES		
3-Month Total Return	6-Month Total Return	1-Year Total Return	3-Year Total Return	5-Year Total Return	Dividend Yield (TTM)	Expense Ratio	3-Yr Std Deviation	Effective Duration	NAV	Total Assets (MIL)	%Cash	%Government Bonds	%Municipal Bonds	%Corporate Bonds	%Other	Turnover Ratio	Average Coupon Rate	Min Initial Investment	Min Additional Investment	Front End Fee (%)	Back End Fee (%)	Inception Date
7.39	-3.76	-0.59	8.02	18.85	4.92	0.59	7.31	3.89	5.33	127.2	6	0	0	94	0	38	5.53	0				Apr-17
4.28	-1.65	1.47	13.94	26.16	3.84	0.37	6.99	8.92	9.64	668.9	0	0	100	0	0	57	5.01	0				Apr-17
4.89	4.98	6.65	12.08	15.95	2.12	0.72	4.04	7.85	12.05	2,414	2	87	0	0	0	24	1.19	2,500	50	4.50		Jun-98
4.69	4.60	5.93	9.56	11.71	1.39	1.47	4	7.85	12.08	2,414	2	87	0	0	0	24	1.19	2,500	50		1.00	Mar-10
4.96	5.14	7.02	13.15	17.67	2.46	0.37	4	7.85	12.06	2,414	2	87	0	0	0	24	1.19	5,000,000	50			Apr-17
4.90	5.08	7.00	12.90	17.38	2.36	0.47	3.99	7.85	12.08	2,414	2	87	0	0	0	24	1.19	2,500	50			Feb-97
4.74	4.83	6.35	11.18	14.42	1.87	0.97	3.99	7.85	12.11	2,414	2	87	0	0	0	24	1.19	2,500	50			Mar-10
5.00	5.19	7.22	13.59	18.59	2.55	0.27	3.96	7.85	12.07	2,414	2	87	0	0	0	24	1.19	0				Oct-02
4.92	5.19	7.13	13.49	18.05	2.55	0.27	3.99	7.85	12.06	2,414	2	87	0	0	0	24	1.19	0				Apr-17
5.04	5.31	7.49	14.41	18.96	2.8	0.01	3.95	7.85	12.07	2,414	2	87	0	0	0	24	1.19	0				Jul-17
5.03	5.21	7.27	13.67	18.18	2.6	0.22	4	7.85	12.06	2,414	2	87	0	0	0	24	1.19	0	50			Jul-17
2.54	0.94	2.84	9.84	15.37	2.18	0.72	3.96	5.71	11.6	3,997	1	0	99	0	0	40	4.67	5,000	50	4.50		Mar-10
2.36	0.58	2.09	7.41	11.15	1.43	1.47	3.96	5.71	11.59	3,997	1	0	99	0	0	40	4.67	5,000	50		1.00	Mar-10
2.65	1.16	3.30	11.32	17.98	2.63	0.27	3.98	5.71	11.6	3,997	1	0	99	0	0	40	4.67	5,000,000	50			Apr-03
2.51	1.06	3.01	10.55	16.70	2.43	0.47	4	5.71	11.59	3,997	1	0	99	0	0	40	4.67	5,000	50			Mar-87
2.65	1.18	3.24	11.32	17.54	2.66	0.24	4	5.71	11.59	3,997	1	0	99	0	0	40	4.67	0				Apr-17
4.00	-1.77	-1.69	2.17	8.31	0	1.06	6.22	8.32	12.74	588.1	8	72	0	14	0	46	3.11	2,500	50	4.50		Oct-98
3.89	-2.07	-2.38	-0.02	4.34	0	1.81	6.28	8.32	12.28	588.1	8	72	0	14	0	46	3.11	2,500	50		1.00	Sep-07
4.27	-1.20	-0.67	5.36	12.25	0	0.02	6.25	8.32	13.16	588.1	8	72	0	14	0	46	3.11	0				Jul-17
4.17	-1.51	-1.29	3.38	10.13	0	0.71	6.27	8.32	12.98	588.1	8	72	0	14	0	46	3.11	5,000,000	50			Apr-17
4.19	-1.52	-1.37	3.04	9.78	0	0.81	6.24	8.32	12.93	588.1	8	72	0	14	0	46	3.11	2,500	50			Jan-92
3.95	-1.78	-1.86	1.53	7.03	0	1.31	6.24	8.32	12.62	588.1	8	72	0	14	0	46	3.11	2,500	50			Sep-07
4.16	-1.51	-1.21	3.64	10.80	0	0.61	6.25	8.32	13.01	588.1	8	72	0	14	0	46	3.11	0				Aug-04
4.15	-1.51	-1.21	3.77	11.09	0	0.56	6.26	8.32	13.02	588.1	8	72	0	14	0	46	3.11	0				Jul-13
4.16	-1.51	-1.21	3.55	10.49	0	0.61	6.22	8.32	13.01	588.1	8	72	0	14	0	46	3.11	0				Apr-17
0.00	0.12	0.53	2.18	2.50	0.63	1.33	0.12		1	1,663	69	9	12	10	0			2,500	50		1.00	May-02
0.08	0.38	1.18	4.17	4.51	1.33	0.58	0.15		1	1,663	69	9	12	10	0			2,500	50			Nov-93
0.03	0.28	0.66	2.44	2.75	0.75	0.5	0.11		1	137.9	23	0	77	0	0			2,500	50			Nov-83
0.46	2.93	4.14	7.66	8.29	1.48	1.55	2.32	2.92	10.78	1,042	8	0	0	0	0	270	3.35	2,500	50		1.00	Mar-10
0.04	0.28	0.95	3.49	3.82	1.08	0.83	0.14		1	1,663	69	9	12	10	0			2,500	50			Aug-98
0.03	0.34	0.79	2.69	3.03	0.9	0.5	0.12		1	159.5	2	0	98	0	0			2,500	50			Jul-84
3.63	6.24	8.75	16.21	23.41	2.72	0.01	3.48	5.89	11.5	2,213	10	32	1	23	0	128	2.98	0				May-06
10.13	-5.48	-1.78	8.10		6.78	0.01	9.44	4.17	8.92	593.5	1	0	0	98	0	58	6.14	0				May-17
9.93	-5.83	-2.52	5.69		5.96	0.79	9.46	4.17	8.92	593.5	1	0	0	98	0	58	6.14	0				May-17
3.00	1.85	2.82	6.94	9.58	1.82	0.84	1.91	2.51	10.32	408.5	3	35	0	39	0	156	2.85	2,500	50	2.25		Nov-06
2.92	1.48	2.07	4.57	5.67	1.08	1.59	1.95	2.51	10.33	408.5	3	35	0	39	0	156	2.85	2,500	50		1.00	Nov-06
3.08	2.02	3.18	8.06	11.52	2.17	0.49	1.91	2.51	10.32	408.5	3	35	0	39	0	156	2.85	5,000,000				Apr-17
3.06	1.97	2.97	7.74	10.95	2.07	0.59	1.92	2.51	10.32	408.5	3	35	0	39	0	156	2.85	2,500	50			Nov-06
2.94	1.73	2.57	6.15	8.34	1.58	1.09	1.91	2.51	10.33	408.5	3	35	0	39	0	156	2.85	2,500	50			Nov-06
3.11	2.07	3.28	8.38	12.06	2.27	0.39	1.91	2.51	10.32	408.5	3	35	0	39	0	156	2.85	0				Nov-06
3.12	2.10	3.23	8.42	12.11	2.32	0.34	1.97	2.51	10.31	408.5	3	35	0	39	0	156	2.85	0				Jul-17
3.49	1.34	2.31	6.08	7.74	1.45	0.82	2.34	3.19	10.24	1,755	8	85	0	0	0	50	0.69	2,500	50	2.25		May-05
3.33	0.91	1.63	3.70	3.73	0.71	1.57	2.36	3.19	9.91	1,755	8	85	0	0	0	50	0.69	2,500	50		1.00	May-05
3.71	1.59	3.08	8.48	11.22	2.23	0.01	2.38	3.19	10.42	1,755	8	85	0	0	0	50	0.69	0				Jul-17
3.59	1.48	2.69	7.19	9.60	1.78	0.47	2.33	3.19	10.42	1,755	8	85	0	0	0	50	0.69	5,000,000				Apr-17
3.57	1.44	2.66	6.92	9.09	1.69	0.57	2.33	3.19	10.34	1,755	8	85	0	0	0	50	0.69	2,500	50			May-05
3.40	1.10	2.09	5.17	6.37	1.17	1.07	2.32	3.19	10.45	1,755	8	85	0	0	0	50	0.69	2,500	50			May-05
3.54	1.43	2.74	7.40	10.11	1.88	0.37	2.33	3.19	10.41	1,755	8	85	0	0	0	50	0.69	0				May-05
3.56	1.45	2.82	7.56	10.41	1.93	0.32	2.31	3.19	10.41	1,755	8	85	0	0	0	50	0.69	0				Jul-13
3.64	1.53	2.74	7.51	10.15	1.88	0.37	2.38	3.19	10.42	1,755	8	85	0	0	0	50	0.69	0				Apr-17
4.83	1.21	2.67	6.89	11.82	2.2	0.77	3.26	2.53	9.6	188.9	0	23	0	51	0	98	3.10	2,500	50	2.25		Jul-14
4.65	0.85	1.93	4.54	7.63	1.47	1.52	3.27	2.53	9.6	188.9	0	23	0	51	0	98	3.10	2,500	50		1.00	Jul-14

Fund Name	MARKET Ticker Symbol	Traded On	Fund Type	FUND TYPE, CATEGORY & OBJECTIVE Category and (Prospectus Objective)	RATINGS Overall Rating	Reward Rating	Risk Rating	Recent Up/ Downgrade	NEW INVESTORS Open to New Investors	Telephone
American Century Short Duration Strategic Income I Cl	ASDHX	NAS CM	Open End	US Fixed Inc (Income)	C	C	B-		Y	800-444-4015
American Century Short Duration Strat Income Investor Cl	ASDVX	NAS CM	Open End	US Fixed Inc (Income)	C	C	B-		Y	800-444-4015
American Century Short Duration Strategic Income R Cl	ASDRX	NAS CM	Open End	US Fixed Inc (Income)	C	C-	C+		Y	800-444-4015
American Century Short Duration Strategic Income R5 Cl	ASDJX	NAS CM	Open End	US Fixed Inc (Income)	C	C	B-		Y	800-444-4015
American Century Short Duration Strategic Income R6 Cl	ASXDX	NAS CM	Open End	US Fixed Inc (Income)	C	C	B-		Y	800-444-4015
American Century Short Duration Strategic Income Y Cl	ASYDX	NAS CM	Open End	US Fixed Inc (Income)	C	C-	B-		Y	800-444-4015
American Century Short-Term Government Fund A Class	TWAVX	NAS CM	Open End	US Fixed Inc (Govt Bond - General)	C+	C	B	Up	Y	800-444-4015
American Century Short-Term Government Fund C Class	TWACX	NAS CM	Open End	US Fixed Inc (Govt Bond - General)	C	C	B-		Y	800-444-4015
American Century Short-Term Government Fund I Class	ASGHX	NAS CM	Open End	US Fixed Inc (Govt Bond - General)	C+	C	B	Up	Y	800-444-4015
American Century Short-Term Government Fund Investor Class	TWUSX	NAS CM	Open End	US Fixed Inc (Govt Bond - General)	C+	C	B	Up	Y	800-444-4015
American Century Short-Term Government Fund R Class	TWARX	NAS CM	Open End	US Fixed Inc (Govt Bond - General)	C+	C	B-	Up	Y	800-444-4015
American Century Short-Term Government Fund R5 Class	TWUOX	NAS CM	Open End	US Fixed Inc (Govt Bond - General)	C+	C	B	Up	Y	800-444-4015
American Century Strategic Income Fund A Class	ASIQX	NAS CM	Open End	US Fixed Inc (Income)	C	C-	C+		Y	800-444-4015
American Century Strategic Income Fund C Class	ASIHX	NAS CM	Open End	US Fixed Inc (Income)	C	C-	C+		Y	800-444-4015
American Century Strategic Income Fund I Class	ASIGX	NAS CM	Open End	US Fixed Inc (Income)	C	C-	B-		Y	800-444-4015
American Century Strategic Income Fund Investor Class	ASIEX	NAS CM	Open End	US Fixed Inc (Income)	C	C-	B-		Y	800-444-4015
American Century Strategic Income Fund R Class	ASIWX	NAS CM	Open End	US Fixed Inc (Income)	C	C-	C+		Y	800-444-4015
American Century Strategic Income Fund R5 Class	ASIJX	NAS CM	Open End	US Fixed Inc (Income)	C	C-	B-		Y	800-444-4015
American Century Strategic Income Fund R6 Class	ASIPX	NAS CM	Open End	US Fixed Inc (Income)	C	C-	B-		Y	800-444-4015
American Century Strategic Income Fund Y Class	ASYIX	NAS CM	Open End	US Fixed Inc (Income)	C	C-	B-		Y	800-444-4015
American Century U.S. Government Money Market Fund A Class	AGQXX	NAS CM	Money Mkt	US Money Mkt (Money Mkt - Govt)	C	C-	C		Y	800-444-4015
American Century U.S. Government Money Market Fund C Class	AGHXX	NAS CM	Money Mkt	US Money Mkt (Money Mkt - Govt)	C	C-	C		Y	800-444-4015
American Century U.S. Government Money Market Fund G CLASS	AGGXX	NAS CM	Money Mkt	US Money Mkt (Money Mkt - Govt)	C	C-	C+		Y	800-444-4015
American Century U.S. Govt Money Mkt Fund Investor Class	TCRXX	NAS CM	Money Mkt	US Money Mkt (Money Mkt - Govt)	C	C-	C+		Y	800-444-4015
American Century Zero Coupon 2020 Fund Advisor Class	ACTEX	NAS CM	Open End	US Fixed Inc (Govt Bond - Treasury)	C	C-	C+		Y	800-444-4015
American Century Zero Coupon 2020 Fund Investor Class	BTTTX	NAS CM	Open End	US Fixed Inc (Govt Bond - Treasury)	C	C	C+		Y	800-444-4015
American Century Zero Coupon 2025 Fund Advisor Class	ACTVX	NAS CM	Open End	US Fixed Inc (Govt Bond - Treasury)	B	B	B		Y	800-444-4015
American Century Zero Coupon 2025 Fund Investor Class	BTTRX	NAS CM	Open End	US Fixed Inc (Govt Bond - Treasury)	B	B	B		Y	800-444-4015
American Funds American High-Income Trust® Class 529-A	CITAX	NAS CM	Open End	US Fixed Inc (Corp Bond - High Yield)	D+	D	C-	Down	Y	800-421-4225
American Funds American High-Income Trust® Class 529-C	CITCX	NAS CM	Open End	US Fixed Inc (Corp Bond - High Yield)	D+	D	C-	Down	Y	800-421-4225
American Funds American High-Income Trust® Class 529-E	CITEX	NAS CM	Open End	US Fixed Inc (Corp Bond - High Yield)	D+	D	C-	Down	Y	800-421-4225
American Funds American High-Income Trust® Class 529-F-1	CITFX	NAS CM	Open End	US Fixed Inc (Corp Bond - High Yield)	D+	D+	C-	Down	Y	800-421-4225
American Funds American High-Income Trust® Class A	AHITX	NAS CM	Open End	US Fixed Inc (Corp Bond - High Yield)	D+	D	C-	Down	Y	800-421-4225
American Funds American High-Income Trust® Class C	AHTCX	NAS CM	Open End	US Fixed Inc (Corp Bond - High Yield)	D+	D	C-	Down	Y	800-421-4225
American Funds American High-Income Trust® Class F-1	AHTFX	NAS CM	Open End	US Fixed Inc (Corp Bond - High Yield)	D+	D	C-	Down	Y	800-421-4225
American Funds American High-Income Trust® Class F-2	AHIFX	NAS CM	Open End	US Fixed Inc (Corp Bond - High Yield)	D+	D+	C-	Down	Y	800-421-4225
American Funds American High-Income Trust® Class F-3	HIGFX	NAS CM	Open End	US Fixed Inc (Corp Bond - High Yield)	D+	D+	C-	Down	Y	800-421-4225
American Funds American High-Income Trust® Class R-1	RITAX	NAS CM	Open End	US Fixed Inc (Corp Bond - High Yield)	D+	D	C-	Down	Y	800-421-4225
American Funds American High-Income Trust® Class R-2	RITBX	NAS CM	Open End	US Fixed Inc (Corp Bond - High Yield)	D+	D	C-	Down	Y	800-421-4225
American Funds American High-Income Trust® Class R-2E	RTEHX	NAS CM	Open End	US Fixed Inc (Corp Bond - High Yield)	D+	D	C-	Down	Y	800-421-4225
American Funds American High-Income Trust® Class R-3	RITCX	NAS CM	Open End	US Fixed Inc (Corp Bond - High Yield)	D+	D	C-	Down	Y	800-421-4225
American Funds American High-Income Trust® Class R-5	RITFX	NAS CM	Open End	US Fixed Inc (Corp Bond - High Yield)	D+	D+	C-	Down	Y	800-421-4225
American Funds American High-Income Trust® Class R-5E	RITHX	NAS CM	Open End	US Fixed Inc (Corp Bond - High Yield)	D+	D+	C-	Down	Y	800-421-4225
American Funds American High-Income Trust® Class R-6	RITGX	NAS CM	Open End	US Fixed Inc (Corp Bond - High Yield)	D+	D+	C-	Down	Y	800-421-4225
American Funds Capital World Bond Fund® Class 529-A	CCWAX	NAS CM	Open End	Global Fixed Inc (Worldwide Bond)	C	C	B-		Y	800-421-4225
American Funds Capital World Bond Fund® Class 529-C	CCWCX	NAS CM	Open End	Global Fixed Inc (Worldwide Bond)	C	C	B-		Y	800-421-4225
American Funds Capital World Bond Fund® Class 529-E	CCWEX	NAS CM	Open End	Global Fixed Inc (Worldwide Bond)	C	C	B-		Y	800-421-4225
American Funds Capital World Bond Fund® Class 529-F	CCWFX	NAS CM	Open End	Global Fixed Inc (Worldwide Bond)	C	C	B-		Y	800-421-4225
American Funds Capital World Bond Fund® Class A	CWBFX	NAS CM	Open End	Global Fixed Inc (Worldwide Bond)	C	C	B-		Y	800-421-4225
American Funds Capital World Bond Fund® Class C	CWBCX	NAS CM	Open End	Global Fixed Inc (Worldwide Bond)	C	C	B-		Y	800-421-4225
American Funds Capital World Bond Fund® Class F-1	WBFFX	NAS CM	Open End	Global Fixed Inc (Worldwide Bond)	C	C	B-		Y	800-421-4225
American Funds Capital World Bond Fund® Class F-2	BFWFX	NAS CM	Open End	Global Fixed Inc (Worldwide Bond)	C+	C	B-	Up	Y	800-421-4225

★ Expanded analysis of this fund is included in Section II.

TOTAL RETURNS & PERFORMANCE									ASSETS		ASSET ALLOCATION & TURNOVER							MINIMUMS		FEES		
3-Month Total Return	6-Month Total Return	1-Year Total Return	3-Year Total Return	5-Year Total Return	Dividend Yield (TTM)	Expense Ratio	3-Yr Std Deviation	Effective Duration	NAV	Total Assets (MIL)	%Cash	%Government Bonds	%Municipal Bonds	%Corporate Bonds	%Other	Turnover Ratio	Average Coupon Rate	Min Initial Investment	Min Additional Investment	Front End Fee (%)	Back End Fee (%)	Inception Date
4.92	1.49	3.14	8.01	13.65	2.56	0.42	3.27	2.53	9.6	188.9	0	23	0	51	0	98	3.10	5,000,000				Apr-17
4.89	1.34	2.93	7.70	13.23	2.46	0.52	3.27	2.53	9.6	188.9	0	23	0	51	0	98	3.10	2,500	50			Jul-14
4.77	1.09	2.43	6.11	10.34	1.96	1.02	3.31	2.53	9.6	188.9	0	23	0	51	0	98	3.10	0				Jul-14
4.94	1.54	3.25	8.46	14.37	2.67	0.32	3.26	2.53	9.61	188.9	0	23	0	51	0	98	3.10	0				Jul-14
5.06	1.56	3.30	8.62	14.65	2.72	0.27	3.34	2.53	9.61	188.9	0	23	0	51	0	98	3.10	0				Jul-14
4.94	1.42	3.13	8.28	14.17	2.66	0.32	3.32	2.53	9.6	188.9	0	23	0	51	0	98	3.10	0				Apr-17
0.44	2.87	3.56	6.32	6.35	1.13	0.8	1.09	1.95	9.79	251.2	1	76	8	0	0	206	1.75	2,500	50	2.25		Jul-98
0.31	2.50	2.80	4.01	2.47	0.4	1.55	1.11	1.95	9.6	251.2	1	76	8	0	0	206	1.75	2,500	50		1.00	Mar-10
0.52	3.05	3.81	7.44	8.02	1.47	0.45	1.15	1.95	9.78	251.2	1	76	8	0	0	206	1.75	5,000,000	50			Apr-17
0.50	3.00	3.71	7.01	7.57	1.37	0.55	1.12	1.95	9.78	251.2	1	76	8	0	0	206	1.75	2,500	50			Dec-82
0.39	2.77	3.33	5.56	5.05	0.88	1.05	1.14	1.95	9.75	251.2	1	76	8	0	0	206	1.75	2,500	50			Mar-10
0.54	2.99	3.91	7.65	8.64	1.57	0.35	1.08	1.95	9.78	251.2	1	76	8	0	0	206	1.75	0				Mar-10
8.07	0.98	3.07	10.56	20.62	2.37	1.01	5.92	4.64	9.97	30.5	7	15	0	59	0	88	4.13	2,500	50	4.50		Jul-14
7.77	0.51	2.32	8.01	16.09	1.62	1.76	5.89	4.64	9.96	30.5	7	15	0	59	0	88	4.13	2,500	50		1.00	Jul-14
8.05	1.05	3.43	11.72	22.61	2.72	0.66	5.86	4.64	9.96	30.5	7	15	0	59	0	88	4.13	5,000,000				Apr-17
8.13	1.10	3.32	11.37	22.11	2.62	0.76	5.93	4.64	9.97	30.5	7	15	0	59	0	88	4.13	2,500	50			Jul-14
7.89	0.75	2.82	9.74	19.14	2.12	1.26	5.86	4.64	9.97	30.5	7	15	0	59	0	88	4.13	2,500	50			Jul-14
8.18	1.19	3.53	12.05	23.35	2.82	0.56	5.93	4.64	9.97	30.5	7	15	0	59	0	88	4.13	0				Jul-14
8.08	1.12	3.47	12.11	23.53	2.87	0.51	5.9	4.64	9.96	30.5	7	15	0	59	0	88	4.13	0				Jul-14
8.08	1.12	3.57	12.08	23.25	2.86	0.56	5.89	4.64	9.96	30.5	7	15	0	59	0	88	4.13	0				Apr-17
0.00	0.20	0.86	3.17	3.21	1	0.71	0.15		1	1,615	55	31	5	9	0	0		2,500	50			Dec-15
0.00	0.08	0.49	1.93	1.72	0.59	1.21	0.12		1	1,615	55	31	5	9	0	0		2,500	50			Dec-15
0.06	0.44	1.46	5.14	5.32	1.64	0.01			1	1,615	55	31	5	9	0	0		0				Jul-17
0.00	0.27	1.06	3.82	3.99	1.21	0.46	0.17		1	1,615	55	31	5	9	0	0		2,500	50			Apr-93
-0.07	0.89	1.49	3.20	6.34	3.79	0.8	1.01	0.55	102.57	135.7	1	99	0	0	0	13		2,500	50			Oct-98
0.00	1.02	1.74	3.98	7.67	3.84	0.55	1.02	0.55	108.2	135.7	1	99	0	0	0	13		2,500	50			Dec-89
1.71	8.25	9.25	15.65	23.87	3.13	0.8	4.29	5.58	109.27	140.0	1	99	0	0	0	21		2,500	50			Jun-98
1.78	8.38	9.51	16.51	25.42	3.19	0.55	4.29	5.58	115.41	140.0	1	99	0	0	0	21		2,500	50			Feb-96
8.56	-5.36	-3.43	6.02	16.59	6.59	0.77	8.66	3.60	9.25	15,653	9	0	0	90	0	52	6.71	250	50	3.75		Feb-02
8.36	-5.71	-4.14	3.68	12.29	5.8	1.53	8.66	3.60	9.25	15,653	9	0	0	90	0	52	6.71	250	50		1.00	Feb-02
8.51	-5.45	-3.60	5.43	15.49	6.4	0.96	8.66	3.60	9.25	15,653	9	0	0	90	0	52	6.71	250	50			Mar-02
8.62	-5.26	-3.20	6.76	17.93	6.83	0.52	8.66	3.60	9.25	15,653	9	0	0	90	0	52	6.71	250	50			Sep-02
8.56	-5.35	-3.41	6.20	16.98	6.61	0.73	8.66	3.60	9.25	15,653	9	0	0	90	0	52	6.71	250	50	3.75		Feb-88
8.37	-5.70	-4.11	3.79	12.53	5.83	1.48	8.66	3.60	9.25	15,653	9	0	0	90	0	52	6.71	250	50		1.00	Mar-01
8.57	-5.35	-3.40	6.11	16.80	6.61	0.73	8.66	3.60	9.25	15,653	9	0	0	90	0	52	6.71	250	50			Mar-01
8.64	-5.21	-3.13	7.01	18.42	6.92	0.44	8.66	3.60	9.25	15,653	9	0	0	90	0	52	6.71	250	50			Aug-08
8.67	-5.17	-3.02	7.34	18.40	7.03	0.34	8.66	3.60	9.25	15,653	9	0	0	90	0	52	6.71	1,000,000	50			Jan-17
8.36	-5.71	-4.12	3.77	12.53	5.81	1.47	8.66	3.60	9.25	15,653	9	0	0	90	0	52	6.71	250	50			Jul-02
8.37	-5.69	-4.10	3.84	12.58	5.84	1.45	8.66	3.60	9.25	15,653	9	0	0	90	0	52	6.71	250	50			Jun-02
8.45	-5.56	-3.82	4.74	14.41	6.15	1.16	8.66	3.60	9.25	15,653	9	0	0	90	0	52	6.71	250	50			Aug-14
8.50	-5.48	-3.66	5.25	15.19	6.33	1	8.66	3.60	9.25	15,653	9	0	0	90	0	52	6.71	250	50			Jun-02
8.66	-5.19	-3.07	7.19	18.76	6.98	0.39	8.66	3.60	9.25	15,653	9	0	0	90	0	52	6.71	250	50			May-02
8.63	-5.24	-3.18	6.92	18.13	6.86	0.48	8.66	3.60	9.25	15,653	9	0	0	90	0	52	6.71	250	50			Nov-15
8.67	-5.16	-3.02	7.36	19.08	7.04	0.34	8.66	3.60	9.25	15,653	9	0	0	90	0	52	6.71	250	50			May-09
5.13	2.25	3.64	10.42	17.39	1.91	0.97	4.62	6.88	20.56	13,123	6	66	0	24	0	163	2.96	250	50	3.75		Feb-02
4.89	1.88	2.88	8.00	13.04	1.18	1.74	4.62	6.88	20.31	13,123	6	66	0	24	0	163	2.96	250	50		1.00	Feb-02
5.03	2.20	3.52	9.92	16.45	1.78	1.13	4.6	6.88	20.42	13,123	6	66	0	24	0	163	2.96	250	50			May-02
5.17	2.39	3.92	11.28	18.83	2.17	0.73	4.6	6.88	20.43	13,123	6	66	0	24	0	163	2.96	250	50			Sep-02
5.10	2.27	3.68	10.62	17.81	1.96	0.95	4.6	6.88	20.5	13,123	6	66	0	24	0	163	2.96	250	50	3.75		Aug-87
4.95	1.92	2.96	8.12	13.35	1.24	1.69	4.62	6.88	20.15	13,123	6	66	0	24	0	163	2.96	250	50		1.00	Mar-01
5.11	2.28	3.70	10.66	17.85	1.97	0.92	4.61	6.88	20.45	13,123	6	66	0	24	0	163	2.96	250	50			Mar-01
5.20	2.46	4.03	11.71	19.68	2.27	0.62	4.62	6.88	20.47	13,123	6	66	0	24	0	163	2.96	250	50			Aug-08

Fund Name	Ticker Symbol	Traded On	Fund Type	Category and (Prospectus Objective)	Overall Rating	Reward Rating	Risk Rating	Recent Up/ Downgrade	Open to New Investors	Telephone
American Funds Capital World Bond Fund® Class F-3	WFBFX	NAS CM	Open End	Global Fixed Inc (Worldwide Bond)	C+	C	B	Up	Y	800-421-4225
American Funds Capital World Bond Fund® Class R-1	RCWAX	NAS CM	Open End	Global Fixed Inc (Worldwide Bond)	C	C	B-		Y	800-421-4225
American Funds Capital World Bond Fund® Class R-2	RCWBX	NAS CM	Open End	Global Fixed Inc (Worldwide Bond)	C	C	B-		Y	800-421-4225
American Funds Capital World Bond Fund® Class R-2E	RCEBX	NAS CM	Open End	Global Fixed Inc (Worldwide Bond)	C	C	B-		Y	800-421-4225
American Funds Capital World Bond Fund® Class R-3	RCWCX	NAS CM	Open End	Global Fixed Inc (Worldwide Bond)	C	C	B-		Y	800-421-4225
American Funds Capital World Bond Fund® Class R-5	RCWFX	NAS CM	Open End	Global Fixed Inc (Worldwide Bond)	C+	C	B-	Up	Y	800-421-4225
American Funds Capital World Bond Fund® Class R-5E	RCWHX	NAS CM	Open End	Global Fixed Inc (Worldwide Bond)	C+	C	B-	Up	Y	800-421-4225
American Funds Capital World Bond Fund® Class R-6	RCWGX	NAS CM	Open End	Global Fixed Inc (Worldwide Bond)	C+	C	B	Up	Y	800-421-4225
American Funds College Enrollment Fund Class 529-A	CENAX	NAS CM	Open End	US Fixed Inc (Growth & Income)	B-	C+	B	Up	Y	800-421-4225
American Funds College Enrollment Fund Class 529-C	CENCX	NAS CM	Open End	US Fixed Inc (Growth & Income)	C+	C	B-	Up	Y	800-421-4225
American Funds College Enrollment Fund Class 529-E	CENEX	NAS CM	Open End	US Fixed Inc (Growth & Income)	B-	C	B	Up	Y	800-421-4225
American Funds College Enrollment Fund Class 529-F-1	CENFX	NAS CM	Open End	US Fixed Inc (Growth & Income)	B-	C+	B	Up	Y	800-421-4225
American Funds Corporate Bond Fund Class 529-A	COBAX	NAS CM	Open End	US Fixed Inc (Income)	B	B	B	Up	Y	800-421-4225
American Funds Corporate Bond Fund Class 529-C	COBCX	NAS CM	Open End	US Fixed Inc (Income)	B	B	B	Up	Y	800-421-4225
American Funds Corporate Bond Fund Class 529-E	COBEX	NAS CM	Open End	US Fixed Inc (Income)	B	B	B	Up	Y	800-421-4225
American Funds Corporate Bond Fund Class 529-F-1	COBFX	NAS CM	Open End	US Fixed Inc (Income)	B	B	B+	Up	Y	800-421-4225
American Funds Corporate Bond Fund Class A	BFCAX	NAS CM	Open End	US Fixed Inc (Income)	B	B	B	Up	Y	800-421-4225
American Funds Corporate Bond Fund Class C	BFCCX	NAS CM	Open End	US Fixed Inc (Income)	B	B	B	Up	Y	800-421-4225
American Funds Corporate Bond Fund Class F-1	BFCFX	NAS CM	Open End	US Fixed Inc (Income)	B	B	B	Up	Y	800-421-4225
American Funds Corporate Bond Fund Class F-2	BFCGX	NAS CM	Open End	US Fixed Inc (Income)	B	B	B+	Up	Y	800-421-4225
American Funds Corporate Bond Fund Class F-3	CFBFX	NAS CM	Open End	US Fixed Inc (Income)	B	B	B+	Up	Y	800-421-4225
American Funds Corporate Bond Fund Class R-1	RCBAX	NAS CM	Open End	US Fixed Inc (Income)	B	B	B	Up	Y	800-421-4225
American Funds Corporate Bond Fund Class R-2	RCBBX	NAS CM	Open End	US Fixed Inc (Income)	B	B	B	Up	Y	800-421-4225
American Funds Corporate Bond Fund Class R-2E	RCBGX	NAS CM	Open End	US Fixed Inc (Income)	B	B	B	Up	Y	800-421-4225
American Funds Corporate Bond Fund Class R-3	RCBCX	NAS CM	Open End	US Fixed Inc (Income)	B	B	B	Up	Y	800-421-4225
American Funds Corporate Bond Fund Class R-4	RCBDX	NAS CM	Open End	US Fixed Inc (Income)	B	B	B	Up	Y	800-421-4225
American Funds Corporate Bond Fund Class R-5	RCBEX	NAS CM	Open End	US Fixed Inc (Income)	B	B	B+	Up	Y	800-421-4225
American Funds Corporate Bond Fund Class R-5E	RCBHX	NAS CM	Open End	US Fixed Inc (Income)	B	B	B+	Up	Y	800-421-4225
American Funds Corporate Bond Fund Class R-6	RCBFX	NAS CM	Open End	US Fixed Inc (Income)	B	B	B+	Up	Y	800-421-4225
American Funds Emerging Markets Bond Fund Class 529-A	CBNAX	NAS CM	Open End	Emerg Mkts Fixed Inc (Diversified Emerg Mkts)	C-	D+	C	Down	Y	800-421-4225
American Funds Emerging Markets Bond Fund Class 529-C	CBNCX	NAS CM	Open End	Emerg Mkts Fixed Inc (Diversified Emerg Mkts)	D+	D	C-	Down	Y	800-421-4225
American Funds Emerging Markets Bond Fund Class 529-E	CBNEX	NAS CM	Open End	Emerg Mkts Fixed Inc (Diversified Emerg Mkts)	C-	D+	C	Down	Y	800-421-4225
American Funds Emerging Markets Bond Fund Class 529-F-1	CBNFX	NAS CM	Open End	Emerg Mkts Fixed Inc (Diversified Emerg Mkts)	C-	D+	C	Down	Y	800-421-4225
American Funds Emerging Markets Bond Fund Class A	EBNAX	NAS CM	Open End	Emerg Mkts Fixed Inc (Diversified Emerg Mkts)	C-	D+	C	Down	Y	800-421-4225
American Funds Emerging Markets Bond Fund Class C	EBNCX	NAS CM	Open End	Emerg Mkts Fixed Inc (Diversified Emerg Mkts)	D+	D	C-	Down	Y	800-421-4225
American Funds Emerging Markets Bond Fund Class F-1	EBNEX	NAS CM	Open End	Emerg Mkts Fixed Inc (Diversified Emerg Mkts)	C-	D+	C	Down	Y	800-421-4225
American Funds Emerging Markets Bond Fund Class F-2	EBNFX	NAS CM	Open End	Emerg Mkts Fixed Inc (Diversified Emerg Mkts)	C-	D+	C	Down	Y	800-421-4225
American Funds Emerging Markets Bond Fund Class F-3	EBNGX	NAS CM	Open End	Emerg Mkts Fixed Inc (Diversified Emerg Mkts)	C-	D+	C	Down	Y	800-421-4225
American Funds Emerging Markets Bond Fund Class R-1	REGAX	NAS CM	Open End	Emerg Mkts Fixed Inc (Diversified Emerg Mkts)	D+	D+	C-	Down	Y	800-421-4225
American Funds Emerging Markets Bond Fund Class R-2	REGBX	NAS CM	Open End	Emerg Mkts Fixed Inc (Diversified Emerg Mkts)	D+	D	C-	Down	Y	800-421-4225
American Funds Emerging Markets Bond Fund Class R-2E	REGHX	NAS CM	Open End	Emerg Mkts Fixed Inc (Diversified Emerg Mkts)	C-	D+	C	Down	Y	800-421-4225
American Funds Emerging Markets Bond Fund Class R-3	REGCX	NAS CM	Open End	Emerg Mkts Fixed Inc (Diversified Emerg Mkts)	C-	D+	C	Down	Y	800-421-4225
American Funds Emerging Markets Bond Fund Class R-4	REGEX	NAS CM	Open End	Emerg Mkts Fixed Inc (Diversified Emerg Mkts)	C-	D+	C	Down	Y	800-421-4225
American Funds Emerging Markets Bond Fund Class R-5	REGFX	NAS CM	Open End	Emerg Mkts Fixed Inc (Diversified Emerg Mkts)	C-	D+	C	Down	Y	800-421-4225
American Funds Emerging Markets Bond Fund Class R-5E	REGJX	NAS CM	Open End	Emerg Mkts Fixed Inc (Diversified Emerg Mkts)	C-	D+	C	Down	Y	800-421-4225
American Funds Emerging Markets Bond Fund Class R-6	REGGX	NAS CM	Open End	Emerg Mkts Fixed Inc (Diversified Emerg Mkts)	C-	D+	C	Down	Y	800-421-4225
American Funds Inflation Linked Bond Fund Class 529-A	CNLAX	NAS CM	Open End	US Fixed Inc (Growth & Income)	B	B	B+	Up	Y	800-421-4225
American Funds Inflation Linked Bond Fund Class 529-C	CNLCX	NAS CM	Open End	US Fixed Inc (Growth & Income)	B	B-	B	Up	Y	800-421-4225
American Funds Inflation Linked Bond Fund Class 529-E	CNLEX	NAS CM	Open End	US Fixed Inc (Growth & Income)	B	B	B+	Up	Y	800-421-4225
American Funds Inflation Linked Bond Fund Class 529-F-1	CNLFX	NAS CM	Open End	US Fixed Inc (Growth & Income)	B	B	B+	Up	Y	800-421-4225
American Funds Inflation Linked Bond Fund Class A	BFIAX	NAS CM	Open End	US Fixed Inc (Growth & Income)	B	B	B+	Up	Y	800-421-4225
American Funds Inflation Linked Bond Fund Class C	BFICX	NAS CM	Open End	US Fixed Inc (Growth & Income)	B	B-	B	Up	Y	800-421-4225

★ Expanded analysis of this fund is included in Section II.

TOTAL RETURNS & PERFORMANCE									ASSETS		ASSET ALLOCATION & TURNOVER							MINIMUMS		FEES		
3-Month Total Return	6-Month Total Return	1-Year Total Return	3-Year Total Return	5-Year Total Return	Dividend Yield (TTM)	Expense Ratio	3-Yr Std Deviation	Effective Duration	NAV	Total Assets (MIL)	%Cash	%Government Bonds	%Municipal Bonds	%Corporate Bonds	%Other	Turnover Ratio	Average Coupon Rate	Min Initial Investment	Min Additional Investment	Front End Fee (%)	Back End Fee (%)	Inception Date
5.26	2.55	4.14	12.02	19.51	2.39	0.5	4.63	6.88	20.49	13,123	6	66	0	24	0	163	2.96	1,000,000	50			Jan-17
4.92	1.92	2.93	8.24	13.62	1.27	1.65	4.61	6.88	20.29	13,123	6	66	0	24	0	163	2.96	250	50			Jun-02
4.94	1.96	3.03	8.40	13.71	1.32	1.6	4.61	6.88	20.27	13,123	6	66	0	24	0	163	2.96	250	50			Jul-02
5.03	2.09	3.32	9.33	15.75	1.61	1.32	4.6	6.88	20.45	13,123	6	66	0	24	0	163	2.96	250	50			Aug-14
5.06	2.17	3.47	9.86	16.35	1.75	1.15	4.61	6.88	20.47	13,123	6	66	0	24	0	163	2.96	250	50			Jul-02
5.20	2.48	4.10	11.87	19.95	2.34	0.54	4.59	6.88	20.51	13,123	6	66	0	24	0	163	2.96	250	50			May-02
5.19	2.43	4.00	11.44	19.13	2.25	0.64	4.61	6.88	20.47	13,123	6	66	0	24	0	163	2.96	250	50			Nov-15
5.22	2.51	4.17	12.08	20.32	2.41	0.49	4.59	6.88	20.5	13,123	6	66	0	24	0	163	2.96	250	50			May-09
1.66	4.86	5.77	9.79	12.69	2.2	0.7	1.71	3.07	10.35	1,113	10	42	0	10	0	5		250	50	2.50		Sep-12
1.47	4.45	4.95	7.32	8.57	1.34	1.46	1.74	3.07	10.32	1,113	10	42	0	10	0	5		250	50		1.00	Sep-12
1.57	4.66	5.52	9.07	11.57	1.96	0.93	1.71	3.07	10.32	1,113	10	42	0	10	0	5		250	50			Sep-12
1.66	4.95	6.02	10.52	14.04	2.44	0.47	1.7	3.07	10.38	1,113	10	42	0	10	0	5		250	50			Sep-12
9.15	9.42	13.20	23.30	37.84	2.08	0.9	5.37	7.65	11.69	1,181	5	6	0	88	0	203	3.43	250	50	3.75		Jul-16
8.95	9.00	12.36	20.50	32.89	1.37	1.62	5.37	7.65	11.69	1,181	5	6	0	88	0	203	3.43	250	50		1.00	Jul-16
9.10	9.31	13.00	22.60	36.63	1.91	1.05	5.37	7.65	11.69	1,181	5	6	0	88	0	203	3.43	250	50			Jul-16
9.22	9.54	13.47	24.15	39.16	2.3	0.62	5.37	7.65	11.69	1,181	5	6	0	88	0	203	3.43	250	50			Jul-16
9.15	9.41	13.20	23.41	38.09	2.08	0.86	5.37	7.65	11.69	1,181	5	6	0	88	0	203	3.43	250	50	3.75		Dec-12
8.96	9.03	12.42	20.70	33.14	1.42	1.57	5.37	7.65	11.69	1,181	5	6	0	88	0	203	3.43	250	50		1.00	Jul-16
9.16	9.43	13.23	23.36	37.97	2.11	0.84	5.37	7.65	11.69	1,181	5	6	0	88	0	203	3.43	250	50			Jul-16
9.23	9.57	13.54	24.39	39.49	2.36	0.56	5.37	7.65	11.69	1,181	5	6	0	88	0	203	3.43	250	50			Jul-16
9.26	9.62	13.65	24.75	39.79	2.45	0.46	5.37	7.65	11.69	1,181	5	6	0	88	0	203	3.43	1,000,000	50			Jan-17
8.99	9.09	12.52	21.17	34.52	1.5	1.53	5.36	7.65	11.69	1,181	5	6	0	88	0	203	3.43	250	50			Jul-16
8.98	9.05	12.45	20.87	34.17	1.45	1.55	5.37	7.65	11.69	1,181	5	6	0	88	0	203	3.43	250	50			Jul-16
9.05	9.20	12.78	22.28	36.71	1.72	1.26	5.36	7.65	11.69	1,181	5	6	0	88	0	203	3.43	250	50			Jul-16
9.09	9.28	12.93	22.43	36.60	1.85	1.09	5.37	7.65	11.69	1,181	5	6	0	88	0	203	3.43	250	50			Jul-16
9.17	9.44	13.26	23.47	38.32	2.13	0.8	5.37	7.65	11.69	1,181	5	6	0	88	0	203	3.43	250	50			Jul-16
9.25	9.60	13.60	24.58	39.71	2.41	0.5	5.37	7.65	11.69	1,181	5	6	0	88	0	203	3.43	250	50			Jul-16
9.22	9.54	13.48	24.36	39.52	2.31	0.58	5.37	7.65	11.69	1,181	5	6	0	88	0	203	3.43	250	50			Jul-16
9.26	9.62	13.65	24.71	39.79	2.45	0.46	5.37	7.65	11.69	1,181	5	6	0	88	0	203	3.43	250	50			Jul-16
13.18	-2.90	-0.24	9.33		6.28	1.03	11.42	6.35	9.38	849.9	11	81	0	8	0	54	6.33	250	50	3.75		Jul-16
12.97	-3.26	-0.99	6.94		5.49	1.81	11.42	6.35	9.38	849.9	11	81	0	8	0	54	6.33	250	50		1.00	Jul-16
13.12	-3.00	-0.45	8.70		6.06	1.26	11.42	6.35	9.38	849.9	11	81	0	8	0	54	6.33	250	50			Jul-16
13.24	-2.78	-0.02	10.10		6.51	0.81	11.42	6.35	9.38	849.9	11	81	0	8	0	54	6.33	250	50			Jul-16
13.18	-2.90	-0.25	9.52		6.28	1.01	11.42	6.35	9.38	849.9	11	81	0	8	0	54	6.33	250	50	3.75		Apr-16
12.98	-3.24	-0.96	7.03		5.52	1.76	11.42	6.35	9.38	849.9	11	81	0	8	0	54	6.33	250	50		1.00	Jul-16
13.18	-2.89	-0.24	9.39		6.28	1.03	11.42	6.35	9.38	849.9	11	81	0	8	0	54	6.33	250	50			Jul-16
13.26	-2.76	0.02	10.30		6.56	0.77	11.42	6.35	9.38	849.9	11	81	0	8	0	54	6.33	250	50			Jul-16
13.29	-2.71	0.12	10.49		6.67	0.65	11.42	6.35	9.38	849.9	11	81	0	8	0	54	6.33	1,000,000	50			Jan-17
13.04	-3.14	-0.73	7.81		5.77	1.76	11.42	6.35	9.38	849.9	11	81	0	8	0	54	6.33	250	50			Jul-16
12.99	-3.22	-0.91	7.41		5.57	1.71	11.41	6.35	9.38	849.9	11	81	0	8	0	54	6.33	250	50			Jul-16
13.10	-3.06	-0.61	8.72		5.88	1.44	11.43	6.35	9.38	849.9	11	81	0	8	0	54	6.33	250	50			Jul-16
13.12	-3.01	-0.48	8.61		6.02	1.28	11.42	6.35	9.38	849.9	11	81	0	8	0	54	6.33	250	50			Jul-16
13.19	-2.87	-0.21	9.52		6.32	1.01	11.42	6.35	9.38	849.9	11	81	0	8	0	54	6.33	250	50			Jul-16
13.28	-2.73	0.08	10.46		6.63	0.7	11.42	6.35	9.38	849.9	11	81	0	8	0	54	6.33	250	50			Jul-16
13.32	-2.71	0.13	10.49		6.71	0.77	11.44	6.35	9.38	849.9	11	81	0	8	0	54	6.33	250	50			Jul-16
13.29	-2.70	0.14	10.57		6.69	0.64	11.42	6.35	9.38	849.9	11	81	0	8	0	54	6.33	250	50			Jul-16
5.16	9.43	10.92	17.35	21.92	0.88	0.71	3.35	7.62	10.79	6,297	1	95	0	4	3	78	0.84	250	50	2.50		Jan-15
4.99	9.05	10.17	14.85	17.22	0.19	1.48	3.31	7.62	10.72	6,297	1	95	0	4	3	78	0.84	250	50		1.00	Jan-15
5.19	9.36	10.75	16.58	20.30	0.79	0.92	3.31	7.62	10.74	6,297	1	95	0	4	3	78	0.84	250	50			Jan-15
5.25	9.51	11.21	18.11	22.88	1.05	0.48	3.31	7.62	10.82	6,297	1	95	0	4	3	78	0.84	250	50			Jan-15
5.16	9.43	10.91	17.41	21.73	0.87	0.73	3.32	7.62	10.79	6,297	1	95	0	4	3	78	0.84	250	50	2.50		Dec-12
5.09	9.05	10.32	14.89	17.46	0.12	1.43	3.32	7.62	10.72	6,297	1	95	0	4	3	78	0.84	250	50		1.00	Jan-15

	MARKET			FUND TYPE, CATEGORY & OBJECTIVE	RATINGS				NEW INVESTORS	
Fund Name	Ticker Symbol	Traded On	Fund Type	Category and (Prospectus Objective)	Overall Rating	Reward Rating	Risk Rating	Recent Up/ Downgrade	Open to New Investors	Telephone
American Funds Inflation Linked Bond Fund Class F-1	BFIFX	NAS CM	Open End	US Fixed Inc (Growth & Income)	B	B	B+	Up	Y	800-421-4225
American Funds Inflation Linked Bond Fund Class F-2	BFIGX	NAS CM	Open End	US Fixed Inc (Growth & Income)	B	B	B+	Up	Y	800-421-4225
American Funds Inflation Linked Bond Fund Class F-3	FILBX	NAS CM	Open End	US Fixed Inc (Growth & Income)	B	B	B+	Up	Y	800-421-4225
American Funds Inflation Linked Bond Fund Class R-1	RILAX	NAS CM	Open End	US Fixed Inc (Growth & Income)	B	B-	B	Up	Y	800-421-4225
American Funds Inflation Linked Bond Fund Class R-2	RILBX	NAS CM	Open End	US Fixed Inc (Growth & Income)	B	B-	B	Up	Y	800-421-4225
American Funds Inflation Linked Bond Fund Class R-2E	RILGX	NAS CM	Open End	US Fixed Inc (Growth & Income)	B	B	B	Up	Y	800-421-4225
American Funds Inflation Linked Bond Fund Class R-3	RILCX	NAS CM	Open End	US Fixed Inc (Growth & Income)	B	B	B+	Up	Y	800-421-4225
American Funds Inflation Linked Bond Fund Class R-4	RILDX	NAS CM	Open End	US Fixed Inc (Growth & Income)	B	B	B+	Up	Y	800-421-4225
American Funds Inflation Linked Bond Fund Class R-5	RILEX	NAS CM	Open End	US Fixed Inc (Growth & Income)	B	B	B+	Up	Y	800-421-4225
American Funds Inflation Linked Bond Fund Class R-5E	RILHX	NAS CM	Open End	US Fixed Inc (Growth & Income)	B	B	B+	Up	Y	800-421-4225
American Funds Inflation Linked Bond Fund Class R-6	RILFX	NAS CM	Open End	US Fixed Inc (Growth & Income)	B	B	B+	Up	Y	800-421-4225
American Funds Intermediate Bond of America® Cl 529-A	CBOAX	NAS CM	Open End	US Fixed Inc (Income)	B-	C+	B	Up	Y	800-421-4225
American Funds Intermediate Bond of America® Cl 529-C	CBOCX	NAS CM	Open End	US Fixed Inc (Income)	C+	C	B		Y	800-421-4225
American Funds Intermediate Bond of America® Cl 529-E	CBOEX	NAS CM	Open End	US Fixed Inc (Income)	B-	C+	B	Up	Y	800-421-4225
American Funds Intermediate Bond of America® Cl 529-F	CBOFX	NAS CM	Open End	US Fixed Inc (Income)	B-	C+	B	Up	Y	800-421-4225
American Funds Intermediate Bond Fund of America® Class A	AIBAX	NAS CM	Open End	US Fixed Inc (Income)	B-	C+	B	Up	Y	800-421-4225
American Funds Intermediate Bond Fund of America® Class C	IBFCX	NAS CM	Open End	US Fixed Inc (Income)	C+	C	B		Y	800-421-4225
American Funds Intermediate Bond of America® Cl F-1	IBFFX	NAS CM	Open End	US Fixed Inc (Income)	B-	C+	B	Up	Y	800-421-4225
American Funds Intermediate Bond of America® Cl F-2	IBAFX	NAS CM	Open End	US Fixed Inc (Income)	B-	C+	B	Up	Y	800-421-4225
American Funds Intermediate Bond of America® Cl F-3	IFBFX	NAS CM	Open End	US Fixed Inc (Income)	B-	C+	B	Up	Y	800-421-4225
American Funds Intermediate Bond of America® Cl R-1	RBOAX	NAS CM	Open End	US Fixed Inc (Income)	C+	C	B		Y	800-421-4225
American Funds Intermediate Bond of America® Cl R-2	RBOBX	NAS CM	Open End	US Fixed Inc (Income)	C+	C	B		Y	800-421-4225
American Funds Intermediate Bond of America® Cl R-2E	REBBX	NAS CM	Open End	US Fixed Inc (Income)	C+	C+	B		Y	800-421-4225
American Funds Intermediate Bond of America® Cl R-3	RBOCX	NAS CM	Open End	US Fixed Inc (Income)	B-	C+	B	Up	Y	800-421-4225
American Funds Intermediate Bond of America® Cl R-4	RBOEX	NAS CM	Open End	US Fixed Inc (Income)	B-	C+	B	Up	Y	800-421-4225
American Funds Intermediate Bond of America® Cl R-5	RBOFX	NAS CM	Open End	US Fixed Inc (Income)	B-	C+	B	Up	Y	800-421-4225
American Funds Intermediate Bond of America® Cl R-5E	RBOHX	NAS CM	Open End	US Fixed Inc (Income)	B-	C+	B	Up	Y	800-421-4225
American Funds Intermediate Bond of America® Cl R-6	RBOGX	NAS CM	Open End	US Fixed Inc (Income)	B-	C+	B	Up	Y	800-421-4225
American Funds Limited Term Tax Exempt Bond Fund® Class A	LTEBX	NAS CM	Open End	US Muni Fixed Inc (Muni Bond - Natl)	C	C	B-		Y	800-421-4225
American Funds Limited Term Tax Exempt Bond Fund® Class C	LTXCX	NAS CM	Open End	US Muni Fixed Inc (Muni Bond - Natl)	C	C	C+		Y	800-421-4225
American Funds Limited Term Tax Exempt Bond Fund® Class F1	LTXFX	NAS CM	Open End	US Muni Fixed Inc (Muni Bond - Natl)	C	C	B-		Y	800-421-4225
American Funds Limited Term Tax Exempt Bond Fund® Class F2	LTEFX	NAS CM	Open End	US Muni Fixed Inc (Muni Bond - Natl)	C	C	B-		Y	800-421-4225
American Funds Limited Term Tax-Exempt Bond Fund® Cl F-3	FLTEX	NAS CM	Open End	US Muni Fixed Inc (Muni Bond - Natl)	C	C	B-		Y	800-421-4225
American Funds Mortgage Fund® Class 529-A	CMFAX	NAS CM	Open End	US Fixed Inc (Govt Bond - Mortgage)	B-	C+	B	Up	Y	800-421-4225
American Funds Mortgage Fund® Class 529-C	CMFCX	NAS CM	Open End	US Fixed Inc (Govt Bond - Mortgage)	C+	C	B		Y	800-421-4225
American Funds Mortgage Fund® Class 529-E	CMFEX	NAS CM	Open End	US Fixed Inc (Govt Bond - Mortgage)	B-	C+	B	Up	Y	800-421-4225
American Funds Mortgage Fund® Class 529-F-1	CMFFX	NAS CM	Open End	US Fixed Inc (Govt Bond - Mortgage)	B-	B-	B		Y	800-421-4225
American Funds Mortgage Fund® Class A	MFAAX	NAS CM	Open End	US Fixed Inc (Govt Bond - Mortgage)	B-	C+	B	Up	Y	800-421-4225
American Funds Mortgage Fund® Class C	MFACX	NAS CM	Open End	US Fixed Inc (Govt Bond - Mortgage)	C+	C+	B		Y	800-421-4225
American Funds Mortgage Fund® Class F-1	MFAEX	NAS CM	Open End	US Fixed Inc (Govt Bond - Mortgage)	B-	C+	B	Up	Y	800-421-4225
American Funds Mortgage Fund® Class F-2	MFAFX	NAS CM	Open End	US Fixed Inc (Govt Bond - Mortgage)	B-	B-	B		Y	800-421-4225
American Funds Mortgage Fund® Class F-3	AFFMX	NAS CM	Open End	US Fixed Inc (Govt Bond - Mortgage)	B	B-	B	Up	Y	800-421-4225
American Funds Mortgage Fund® Class R-1	RMAAX	NAS CM	Open End	US Fixed Inc (Govt Bond - Mortgage)	C+	C+	B-	Up	Y	800-421-4225
American Funds Mortgage Fund® Class R-2	RMABX	NAS CM	Open End	US Fixed Inc (Govt Bond - Mortgage)	C+	C+	B		Y	800-421-4225
American Funds Mortgage Fund® Class R-2E	RMBEX	NAS CM	Open End	US Fixed Inc (Govt Bond - Mortgage)	B-	C+	B	Up	Y	800-421-4225
American Funds Mortgage Fund® Class R-3	RMACX	NAS CM	Open End	US Fixed Inc (Govt Bond - Mortgage)	B-	C+	B	Up	Y	800-421-4225
American Funds Mortgage Fund® Class R-4	RMAEX	NAS CM	Open End	US Fixed Inc (Govt Bond - Mortgage)	B-	C+	B	Up	Y	800-421-4225
American Funds Mortgage Fund® Class R-5	RMAFX	NAS CM	Open End	US Fixed Inc (Govt Bond - Mortgage)	B-	B-	B	Up	Y	800-421-4225
American Funds Mortgage Fund® Class R-5E	RMAHX	NAS CM	Open End	US Fixed Inc (Govt Bond - Mortgage)	B-	B-	B		Y	800-421-4225
American Funds Mortgage Fund® Class R-6	RMAGX	NAS CM	Open End	US Fixed Inc (Govt Bond - Mortgage)	B-	B-	B	Up	Y	800-421-4225
American Funds Multi-Sector Income Fund Class 529-A	CMBKX	NAS CM	Open End	US Fixed Inc (Corp Bond - General)	D	D+	C		Y	800-421-4225
American Funds Multi-Sector Income Fund Class 529-C	CMBLX	NAS CM	Open End	US Fixed Inc (Corp Bond - General)	D	D+	C		Y	800-421-4225

★ Expanded analysis of this fund is included in Section II.

TOTAL RETURNS & PERFORMANCE									ASSETS		ASSET ALLOCATION & TURNOVER							MINIMUMS		FEES		
3-Month Total Return	6-Month Total Return	1-Year Total Return	3-Year Total Return	5-Year Total Return	Dividend Yield (TTM)	Expense Ratio	3-Yr Std Deviation	Effective Duration	NAV	Total Assets (ML)	%Cash	%Government Bonds	%Municipal Bonds	%Corporate Bonds	%Other	Turnover Ratio	Average Coupon Rate	Min Initial Investment	Min Additional Investment	Front End Fee (%)	Back End Fee (%)	Inception Date
5.16	9.42	10.98	17.37	21.71	0.84	0.7	3.36	7.62	10.8	6,297	1	95	0	4	3	78	0.84	250	50			Jan-15
5.24	9.60	11.38	18.34	23.38	1.11	0.43	3.35	7.62	10.84	6,297	1	95	0	4	3	78	0.84	250	50			Jan-15
5.35	9.62	11.41	18.68	23.18	1.22	0.33	3.35	7.62	10.82	6,297	1	95	0	4	3	78	0.84	1,000,000	50			Jan-17
4.98	9.03	10.22	14.78	17.31	0.06	1.48	3.29	7.62	10.74	6,297	1	95	0	4	3	78	0.84	250	50			Jan-15
4.94	9.03	10.20	14.85	17.25	0.32	1.43	3.33	7.62	10.62	6,297	1	95	0	4	3	78	0.84	250	50			Jan-15
5.07	9.23	10.50	15.81	19.80	0.6	1.15	3.33	7.62	10.76	6,297	1	95	0	4	3	78	0.84	250	50			Jan-15
5.10	9.28	10.69	16.38	19.97	0.71	0.98	3.32	7.62	10.71	6,297	1	95	0	4	3	78	0.84	250	50			Jan-15
5.17	9.44	11.03	17.37	21.75	0.97	0.68	3.31	7.62	10.78	6,297	1	95	0	4	3	78	0.84	250	50			Jan-15
5.24	9.60	11.35	18.54	23.62	1.18	0.38	3.34	7.62	10.84	6,297	1	95	0	4	3	78	0.84	250	50			Jan-15
5.26	9.53	11.23	18.18	22.97	1.14	0.46	3.32	7.62	10.8	6,297	1	95	0	4	3	78	0.84	250	50			Nov-15
5.34	9.59	11.39	18.66	23.93	1.22	0.32	3.34	7.62	10.85	6,297	1	95	0	4	3	78	0.84	250	50			Nov-13
2.50	5.92	6.89	11.44	14.18	1.63	0.67	1.9	3.51	14.14	23,949	7	26	0	19	0	168	2.77	250	50	2.50		Feb-02
2.25	5.46	6.06	8.99	10.04	0.94	1.43	1.84	3.51	14.13	23,949	7	26	0	19	0	168	2.77	250	50		1.00	Feb-02
2.45	5.82	6.70	10.83	13.10	1.46	0.86	1.9	3.51	14.14	23,949	7	26	0	19	0	168	2.77	250	50			Mar-02
2.56	6.04	7.15	12.24	15.53	1.86	0.43	1.9	3.51	14.14	23,949	7	26	0	19	0	168	2.77	250	50			Sep-02
2.50	5.91	6.89	11.59	14.53	1.64	0.64	1.9	3.51	14.14	23,949	7	26	0	19	0	168	2.77	250	50	2.50		Feb-88
2.26	5.48	6.09	9.07	10.22	0.97	1.37	1.88	3.51	14.13	23,949	7	26	0	19	0	168	2.77	250	50		1.00	Mar-01
2.50	5.92	6.90	11.47	14.27	1.64	0.67	1.91	3.51	14.14	23,949	7	26	0	19	0	168	2.77	250	50			Mar-01
2.57	6.07	7.21	12.46	15.94	1.92	0.35	1.9	3.51	14.14	23,949	7	26	0	19	0	168	2.77	250	50			Aug-08
2.53	6.05	7.25	12.73	15.84	2.02	0.26	1.85	3.51	14.13	23,949	7	26	0	19	0	168	2.77	1,000,000	50			Jan-17
2.25	5.48	6.06	9.03	10.22	0.94	1.38	1.86	3.51	14.13	23,949	7	26	0	19	0	168	2.77	250	50			Jun-02
2.26	5.49	6.09	9.11	10.29	0.97	1.35	1.84	3.51	14.13	23,949	7	26	0	19	0	168	2.77	250	50			May-02
2.32	5.63	6.39	10.00	12.05	1.24	1.08	1.87	3.51	14.12	23,949	7	26	0	19	0	168	2.77	250	50			Aug-14
2.44	5.79	6.63	10.64	12.83	1.39	0.91	1.9	3.51	14.14	23,949	7	26	0	19	0	168	2.77	250	50			Jun-02
2.52	5.95	6.95	11.65	14.55	1.69	0.61	1.91	3.51	14.14	23,949	7	26	0	19	0	168	2.77	250	50			Jun-02
2.59	6.10	7.27	12.65	16.27	1.98	0.31	1.91	3.51	14.14	23,949	7	26	0	19	0	168	2.77	250	50			May-02
2.57	6.05	7.16	12.40	15.69	1.88	0.41	1.9	3.51	14.14	23,949	7	26	0	19	0	168	2.77	250	50			Nov-15
2.53	6.06	7.25	12.75	16.51	2.03	0.25	1.9	3.51	14.13	23,949	7	26	0	19	0	168	2.77	250	50			May-09
2.46	2.10	3.41	8.67	12.29	1.68	0.62	2.47	3.39	16.09	4,512	1	0	97	0	0	42	4.28	250	50	2.50		Oct-93
2.28	1.75	2.69	6.33	8.25	0.98	1.32	2.47	3.39	16.09	4,512	1	0	97	0	0	42	4.28	250	50		1.00	Mar-01
2.45	2.08	3.38	8.47	11.91	1.64	0.65	2.47	3.39	16.09	4,512	1	0	97	0	0	42	4.28	250	50			Mar-01
2.52	2.22	3.65	9.34	13.37	1.91	0.38	2.47	3.39	16.09	4,512	1	0	97	0	0	42	4.28	250	50			Aug-08
2.54	2.27	3.75	9.67	13.46	2.01	0.28	2.47	3.39	16.09	4,512	1	0	97	0	0	42	4.28	1,000,000	50			Jan-17
1.31	5.69	6.80	11.00	16.44	1.76	0.74	2.43	3.47	10.56	7,229	3	6	0	0	0	605	3.11	250	50	3.75		Nov-10
1.16	5.26	5.99	8.51	12.08	1.06	1.51	2.44	3.47	10.51	7,229	3	6	0	0	0	605	3.11	250	50		1.00	Nov-10
1.16	5.48	6.60	10.32	15.15	1.57	0.95	2.44	3.47	10.56	7,229	3	6	0	0	0	605	3.11	250	50			Nov-10
1.37	5.71	7.06	11.78	17.74	1.99	0.5	2.44	3.47	10.56	7,229	3	6	0	0	0	605	3.11	250	50			Nov-10
1.31	5.71	6.85	11.31	16.92	1.8	0.71	2.43	3.47	10.57	7,229	3	6	0	0	0	605	3.11	250	50	3.75		Nov-10
1.06	5.27	6.01	8.63	12.34	1.09	1.46	2.47	3.47	10.52	7,229	3	6	0	0	0	605	3.11	250	50		1.00	Nov-10
1.32	5.72	6.88	11.20	16.90	1.83	0.67	2.41	3.47	10.57	7,229	3	6	0	0	0	605	3.11	250	50			Nov-10
1.39	5.86	7.17	12.14	18.52	2.09	0.38	2.49	3.47	10.57	7,229	3	6	0	0	0	605	3.11	250	50			Nov-10
1.42	5.92	7.28	12.49	19.14	2.19	0.29	2.48	3.47	10.57	7,229	3	6	0	0	0	605	3.11	1,000,000	50			Jan-17
1.06	5.28	6.02	8.57	12.45	1.11	1.44	2.46	3.47	10.52	7,229	3	6	0	0	0	605	3.11	250	50			Nov-10
1.17	5.40	6.17	8.92	12.51	1.13	1.39	2.45	3.47	10.51	7,229	3	6	0	0	0	605	3.11	250	50			Nov-10
1.22	5.52	6.45	9.90	15.16	1.43	1.13	2.45	3.47	10.55	7,229	3	6	0	0	0	605	3.11	250	50			Aug-14
1.25	5.58	6.56	10.08	14.86	1.53	0.98	2.44	3.47	10.55	7,229	3	6	0	0	0	605	3.11	250	50			Nov-10
1.33	5.73	6.89	11.28	17.05	1.84	0.65	2.41	3.47	10.57	7,229	3	6	0	0	0	605	3.11	250	50			Nov-10
1.40	5.88	7.20	12.28	18.75	2.12	0.34	2.44	3.47	10.57	7,229	3	6	0	0	0	605	3.11	250	50			Nov-10
1.37	5.73	7.11	12.06	18.40	2.04	0.45	2.42	3.47	10.56	7,229	3	6	0	0	0	605	3.11	250	50			Nov-15
1.42	5.92	7.29	12.51	19.17	2.2	0.28	2.41	3.47	10.57	7,229	3	6	0	0	0	605	3.11	250	50			Nov-10
8.59	1.66	5.08				0.97		5.83	10.13	156.0	7	10	2	64	0	115	5.11	250	50	3.75		May-20
8.43	1.34	4.39				1.67		5.83	10.13	156.0	7	10	2	64	0	115	5.11	250	50		1.00	May-20

	MARKET			FUND TYPE, CATEGORY & OBJECTIVE	RATINGS				NEW INVESTORS	
Fund Name	Ticker Symbol	Traded On	Fund Type	Category and (Prospectus Objective)	Overall Rating	Reward Rating	Risk Rating	Recent Up/ Downgrade	Open to New Investors	Telephone
American Funds Multi-Sector Income Fund Class 529-E	CMBMX	NAS CM	Open End	US Fixed Inc (Corp Bond - General)	D	D+	C		Y	800-421-4225
American Funds Multi-Sector Income Fund Class 529-F-1	CMBOX	NAS CM	Open End	US Fixed Inc (Corp Bond - General)	D	D+	C		Y	800-421-4225
American Funds Multi-Sector Income Fund Class A	MIAQX	NAS CM	Open End	US Fixed Inc (Corp Bond - General)	D	D+	C		Y	800-421-4225
American Funds Multi-Sector Income Fund Class C	MIAUX	NAS CM	Open End	US Fixed Inc (Corp Bond - General)	D	D+	C		Y	800-421-4225
American Funds Multi-Sector Income Fund Class F-1	MIAWX	NAS CM	Open End	US Fixed Inc (Corp Bond - General)	D	D+	C		Y	800-421-4225
American Funds Multi-Sector Income Fund Class F-2	MIAYX	NAS CM	Open End	US Fixed Inc (Corp Bond - General)	D	D+	C		Y	800-421-4225
American Funds Multi-Sector Income Fund Class F-3	MIAZX	NAS CM	Open End	US Fixed Inc (Corp Bond - General)	D	D+	C		Y	800-421-4225
American Funds Multi-Sector Income Fund Class R-1	RMDNX	NAS CM	Open End	US Fixed Inc (Corp Bond - General)	D	D+	C		Y	800-421-4225
American Funds Multi-Sector Income Fund Class R-2	RMDOX	NAS CM	Open End	US Fixed Inc (Corp Bond - General)	D	D+	C		Y	800-421-4225
American Funds Multi-Sector Income Fund Class R-2E	RMDPX	NAS CM	Open End	US Fixed Inc (Corp Bond - General)	D	D+	C		Y	800-421-4225
American Funds Multi-Sector Income Fund Class R-3	RMDQX	NAS CM	Open End	US Fixed Inc (Corp Bond - General)	D	D+	C		Y	800-421-4225
American Funds Multi-Sector Income Fund Class R-4	RMDRX	NAS CM	Open End	US Fixed Inc (Corp Bond - General)	D	D+	C		Y	800-421-4225
American Funds Multi-Sector Income Fund Class R-5	RMDTX	NAS CM	Open End	US Fixed Inc (Corp Bond - General)	D	D+	C		Y	800-421-4225
American Funds Multi-Sector Income Fund Class R-5E	RMDSX	NAS CM	Open End	US Fixed Inc (Corp Bond - General)	D	D+	C		Y	800-421-4225
American Funds Multi-Sector Income Fund Class R-6	RMDUX	NAS CM	Open End	US Fixed Inc (Corp Bond - General)	D	D+	C		Y	800-421-4225
American Funds Preservation Portfolio Class 529-A	CPPAX	NAS CM	Open End	US Fixed Inc (Corp Bond - High Quality)	B-	C+	B	Up	Y	800-421-4225
American Funds Preservation Portfolio Class 529-C	CPPCX	NAS CM	Open End	US Fixed Inc (Corp Bond - High Quality)	C+	C	B-	Up	Y	800-421-4225
American Funds Preservation Portfolio Class 529-E	CPPEX	NAS CM	Open End	US Fixed Inc (Corp Bond - High Quality)	C+	C	B		Y	800-421-4225
American Funds Preservation Portfolio Class 529-F-1	CPPFX	NAS CM	Open End	US Fixed Inc (Corp Bond - High Quality)	B-	C+	B	Up	Y	800-421-4225
American Funds Preservation Portfolio Class A	PPVAX	NAS CM	Open End	US Fixed Inc (Corp Bond - High Quality)	B-	C+	B	Up	Y	800-421-4225
American Funds Preservation Portfolio Class ABLE-A	CPPGX	NAS CM	Open End	US Fixed Inc (Corp Bond - High Quality)	B-	C+	B	Up	Y	800-421-4225
American Funds Preservation Portfolio Class C	PPVCX	NAS CM	Open End	US Fixed Inc (Corp Bond - High Quality)	C+	C	B-	Up	Y	800-421-4225
American Funds Preservation Portfolio Class F-1	PPVFX	NAS CM	Open End	US Fixed Inc (Corp Bond - High Quality)	B-	C+	B	Up	Y	800-421-4225
American Funds Preservation Portfolio Class F-2	PPEFX	NAS CM	Open End	US Fixed Inc (Corp Bond - High Quality)	B-	C+	B	Up	Y	800-421-4225
American Funds Preservation Portfolio Class F-3	PPFFX	NAS CM	Open End	US Fixed Inc (Corp Bond - High Quality)	B-	C+	B	Up	Y	800-421-4225
American Funds Preservation Portfolio Class R-1	RPPVX	NAS CM	Open End	US Fixed Inc (Corp Bond - High Quality)	C+	C	B-	Up	Y	800-421-4225
American Funds Preservation Portfolio Class R-2	RPPBX	NAS CM	Open End	US Fixed Inc (Corp Bond - High Quality)	C+	C	B-	Up	Y	800-421-4225
American Funds Preservation Portfolio Class R-2E	RPBEX	NAS CM	Open End	US Fixed Inc (Corp Bond - High Quality)	C+	C	B-	Up	Y	800-421-4225
American Funds Preservation Portfolio Class R-3	RPPCX	NAS CM	Open End	US Fixed Inc (Corp Bond - High Quality)	C+	C	B		Y	800-421-4225
American Funds Preservation Portfolio Class R-4	RPPEX	NAS CM	Open End	US Fixed Inc (Corp Bond - High Quality)	B-	C+	B	Up	Y	800-421-4225
American Funds Preservation Portfolio Class R-5	RPPFX	NAS CM	Open End	US Fixed Inc (Corp Bond - High Quality)	B-	C+	B	Up	Y	800-421-4225
American Funds Preservation Portfolio Class R-5E	RGMFX	NAS CM	Open End	US Fixed Inc (Corp Bond - High Quality)	B-	C+	B	Up	Y	800-421-4225
American Funds Preservation Portfolio Class R-6	RPPGX	NAS CM	Open End	US Fixed Inc (Corp Bond - High Quality)	B-	C+	B	Up	Y	800-421-4225
American Funds Short-Term Bond of America® Cl 529-A	CAAFX	NAS CM	Open End	US Fixed Inc (Income)	C+	C	B	Up	Y	800-421-4225
American Funds Short-Term Bond of America® Cl 529-C	CCAMX	NAS CM	Open End	US Fixed Inc (Income)	C	C	B-		Y	800-421-4225
American Funds Short-Term Bond of America® Cl 529-E	CEAMX	NAS CM	Open End	US Fixed Inc (Income)	C+	C	B	Up	Y	800-421-4225
American Funds Short-Term Bond of America® Cl 529-F-1	CFAMX	NAS CM	Open End	US Fixed Inc (Income)	C+	C	B	Up	Y	800-421-4225
American Funds Short-Term Bond Fund of America® Class A	ASBAX	NAS CM	Open End	US Fixed Inc (Income)	C+	C	B	Up	Y	800-421-4225
American Funds Short-Term Bond Fund of America® Class C	ASBCX	NAS CM	Open End	US Fixed Inc (Income)	C	C	B-		Y	800-421-4225
American Funds Short-Term Bond Fund of America® Class F-1	ASBFX	NAS CM	Open End	US Fixed Inc (Income)	C+	C	B	Up	Y	800-421-4225
American Funds Short-Term Bond Fund of America® Class F-2	SBFFX	NAS CM	Open End	US Fixed Inc (Income)	C+	C	B	Up	Y	800-421-4225
American Funds Short-Term Bond Fund of America® Class F-3	FSBTX	NAS CM	Open End	US Fixed Inc (Income)	C+	C	B	Up	Y	800-421-4225
American Funds Short-Term Bond Fund of America® Class R-1	RAMAX	NAS CM	Open End	US Fixed Inc (Income)	C	C	B-		Y	800-421-4225
American Funds Short-Term Bond Fund of America® Class R-2	RAMBX	NAS CM	Open End	US Fixed Inc (Income)	C	C	B-		Y	800-421-4225
American Funds Short-Term Bond Fund of America® Class R-2E	RAAEX	NAS CM	Open End	US Fixed Inc (Income)	C	C	B-		Y	800-421-4225
American Funds Short-Term Bond Fund of America® Class R-3	RAMCX	NAS CM	Open End	US Fixed Inc (Income)	C+	C	B	Up	Y	800-421-4225
American Funds Short-Term Bond Fund of America® Class R-4	RAMEX	NAS CM	Open End	US Fixed Inc (Income)	C+	C	B	Up	Y	800-421-4225
American Funds Short-Term Bond Fund of America® Class R-5	RAMFX	NAS CM	Open End	US Fixed Inc (Income)	C+	C	B	Up	Y	800-421-4225
American Funds Short-Term Bond Fund of America® Class R-5E	RAAGX	NAS CM	Open End	US Fixed Inc (Income)	C+	C	B	Up	Y	800-421-4225
American Funds Short-Term Bond Fund of America® Class R-6	RMMGX	NAS CM	Open End	US Fixed Inc (Income)	C+	C	B		Y	800-421-4225
American Funds Short-Term Tax Exempt Bond Fund® Class F-3	SFTEX	NAS CM	Open End	US Muni Fixed Inc (Muni Bond - Natl)	C	C	B-		Y	800-421-4225
American Funds Short-Term Tax-Exempt Bond Fund® Class A	ASTEX	NAS CM	Open End	US Muni Fixed Inc (Muni Bond - Natl)	C	C	B-		Y	800-421-4225

★Expanded analysis of this fund is included in Section II.

TOTAL RETURNS & PERFORMANCE									ASSETS		ASSET ALLOCATION & TURNOVER							MINIMUMS		FEES		
3-Month Total Return	6-Month Total Return	1-Year Total Return	3-Year Total Return	5-Year Total Return	Dividend Yield (TTM)	Expense Ratio	3-Yr Std Deviation	Effective Duration	NAV	Total Assets (MIL)	%Cash	%Government Bonds	%Municipal Bonds	%Corporate Bonds	%Other	Turnover Ratio	Average Coupon Rate	Min Initial Investment	Min Additional Investment	Front End Fee (%)	Back End Fee (%)	Inception Date
8.57	1.60	4.92				1.12		5.83	10.13	156.0	7	10	2	64	0	115	5.11	250	50			May-20
8.61	1.68	5.10				0.67		5.83	10.13	156.0	7	10	2	64	0	115	5.11	250	50			May-20
8.59	1.67	5.09			4.48	0.91		5.83	10.13	156.0	7	10	2	64	0	115	5.11	250	50	3.75		Mar-19
8.39	1.30	4.35				1.61		5.83	10.13	156.0	7	10	2	64	0	115	5.11	250	50		1.00	May-20
8.59	1.66	5.09				0.9		5.83	10.13	156.0	7	10	2	64	0	115	5.11	250	50			May-20
8.60	1.67	5.09			4.46	0.63		5.83	10.13	156.0	7	10	2	64	0	115	5.11	250	50			Mar-19
8.62	1.69	5.09			4.45	0.52		5.83	10.13	156.0	7	10	2	64	0	115	5.11	1,000,000	50			Mar-19
8.48	1.39	4.44				1.75		5.83	10.13	156.0	7	10	2	64	0	115	5.11	250	50			May-20
8.51	1.47	4.66				1.81		5.83	10.13	156.0	7	10	2	64	0	115	5.11	250	50			May-20
8.55	1.55	4.81				1.46		5.83	10.13	156.0	7	10	2	64	0	115	5.11	250	50			May-20
8.57	1.59	4.91				1.25		5.83	10.13	156.0	7	10	2	64	0	115	5.11	250	50			May-20
8.61	1.68	5.11				0.86		5.83	10.13	156.0	7	10	2	64	0	115	5.11	250	50			May-20
8.61	1.68	5.11				0.57		5.83	10.13	156.0	7	10	2	64	0	115	5.11	250	50			May-20
8.61	1.68	5.10				0.7		5.83	10.13	156.0	7	10	2	64	0	115	5.11	250	50			May-20
8.63	1.70	5.09			4.45	0.52		5.83	10.13	156.0	7	10	2	64	0	115	5.11	250	50			Mar-19
1.94	4.74	5.64	9.74	12.39	1.77	0.69	1.54	3.02	10.37	2,119	7	52	0	16	0	4		250	50	2.50		May-12
1.66	4.28	4.74	7.26	8.09	1.04	1.45	1.59	3.02	10.36	2,119	7	52	0	16	0	4		250	50		1.00	May-12
1.89	4.63	5.41	9.03	11.16	1.55	0.91	1.53	3.02	10.37	2,119	7	52	0	16	0	4		250	50			May-12
2.00	4.85	5.78	10.52	13.60	2	0.45	1.59	3.02	10.37	2,119	7	52	0	16	0	4		250	50			May-12
1.84	4.74	5.53	9.76	12.40	1.77	0.68	1.56	3.02	10.37	2,119	7	52	0	16	0	4		250	50	2.50		May-12
1.84	4.74	5.64	9.76	12.53	1.77	0.63	1.59	3.02	10.37	2,119	7	52	0	16	0	4		250	50	2.50		Jul-18
1.77	4.42	4.91	7.45	8.56	1.09	1.39	1.58	3.02	10.36	2,119	7	52	0	16	0	4		250	50		1.00	May-12
1.85	4.65	5.54	9.77	12.39	1.78	0.68	1.53	3.02	10.37	2,119	7	52	0	16	0	4		250	50			May-12
1.91	4.87	5.82	10.66	13.90	2.03	0.4	1.57	3.02	10.37	2,119	7	52	0	16	0	4		250	50			May-12
2.03	4.91	6.02	10.99	14.37	2.12	0.32	1.59	3.02	10.37	2,119	7	52	0	16	0	4		1,000,000	50			Jan-17
1.66	4.26	4.71	7.22	8.24	1.02	1.46	1.56	3.02	10.37	2,119	7	52	0	16	0	4		250	50			May-12
1.67	4.31	4.78	7.33	8.36	1.07	1.41	1.54	3.02	10.34	2,119	7	52	0	16	0	4		250	50			May-12
1.75	4.46	5.09	8.28	10.28	1.35	1.13	1.54	3.02	10.37	2,119	7	52	0	16	0	4		250	50			Aug-14
1.78	4.52	5.24	8.77	10.85	1.5	0.95	1.54	3.02	10.36	2,119	7	52	0	16	0	4		250	50			May-12
1.95	4.75	5.66	9.87	12.67	1.8	0.65	1.53	3.02	10.38	2,119	7	52	0	16	0	4		250	50			May-12
2.02	4.88	5.96	10.79	14.26	2.07	0.37	1.53	3.02	10.38	2,119	7	52	0	16	0	4		250	50			May-12
1.90	4.84	5.75	10.55	13.83	1.98	0.46	1.58	3.02	10.38	2,119	7	52	0	16	0	4		250	50			Nov-15
2.03	4.90	6.01	10.96	14.56	2.12	0.32	1.53	3.02	10.38	2,119	7	52	0	16	0	4		250	50			May-12
1.15	3.10	3.77	7.36	8.85	1.66	0.71	1.06	2.28	10.18	8,924	18	47	0	8	0	153	2.20	250	50	2.50		Nov-06
0.99	2.67	2.97	4.94	4.64	0.96	1.47	1.02	2.28	10.02	8,924	18	47	0	8	0	153	2.20	250	50		1.00	Nov-06
1.10	2.99	3.55	6.66	7.47	1.45	0.93	1.04	2.28	10.17	8,924	18	47	0	8	0	153	2.20	250	50			Dec-06
1.21	3.22	4.01	8.12	9.94	1.89	0.47	1.08	2.28	10.18	8,924	18	47	0	8	0	153	2.20	250	50			Nov-06
1.15	3.09	3.76	7.43	9.02	1.65	0.71	1.06	2.28	10.18	8,924	18	47	0	8	0	153	2.20	250	50	2.50		Oct-06
0.99	2.68	3.00	5.02	4.87	0.99	1.41	1.01	2.28	10.05	8,924	18	47	0	8	0	153	2.20	250	50		1.00	Nov-06
1.15	3.10	3.77	7.36	8.71	1.66	0.71	1.06	2.28	10.18	8,924	18	47	0	8	0	153	2.20	250	50			Nov-06
1.22	3.24	4.05	8.26	10.21	1.93	0.42	1.04	2.28	10.18	8,924	18	47	0	8	0	153	2.20	250	50			Aug-08
1.24	3.29	4.15	8.55	10.29	2.03	0.33	1.07	2.28	10.18	8,924	18	47	0	8	0	153	2.20	1,000,000	50			Jan-17
0.89	2.67	2.97	4.96	4.80	0.96	1.43	1.08	2.28	10.04	8,924	18	47	0	8	0	153	2.20	250	50			Dec-06
0.99	2.67	2.98	5.10	4.88	0.97	1.41	1.1	2.28	10.04	8,924	18	47	0	8	0	153	2.20	250	50			Dec-06
1.03	2.76	3.30	5.79	6.50	1.2	1.16	1.01	2.28	10.17	8,924	18	47	0	8	0	153	2.20	250	50			Aug-14
0.99	2.86	3.39	6.40	7.16	1.39	0.97	1.11	2.28	10.16	8,924	18	47	0	8	0	153	2.20	250	50			Nov-06
1.16	3.11	3.80	7.48	8.90	1.69	0.67	1.06	2.28	10.18	8,924	18	47	0	8	0	153	2.20	250	50			Jan-07
1.23	3.26	4.10	8.41	10.47	1.98	0.38	1.06	2.28	10.18	8,924	18	47	0	8	0	153	2.20	250	50			Jan-07
1.21	3.21	3.99	8.21	9.98	1.87	0.47	1.06	2.28	10.18	8,924	18	47	0	8	0	153	2.20	250	50			Nov-15
1.25	3.29	4.16	8.60	10.80	2.03	0.32	1.08	2.28	10.18	8,924	18	47	0	8	0	153	2.20	250	50			May-09
1.80	2.07	3.10	6.71	8.87	1.53	0.41	1.42	2.11	10.32	1,172	1	0	97	0	0	34	4.01	1,000,000	50			Jan-17
1.75	1.98	2.91	6.20	8.29	1.35	0.59	1.41	2.11	10.32	1,172	1	0	97	0	0	34	4.01	250	50	2.50		Aug-09

	MARKET			FUND TYPE, CATEGORY & OBJECTIVE	RATINGS				NEW INVESTORS	
Fund Name	Ticker Symbol	Traded On	Fund Type	Category and (Prospectus Objective)	Overall Rating	Reward Rating	Risk Rating	Recent Up/ Downgrade	Open to New Investors	Telephone
American Funds Short-Term Tax-Exempt Bond Fund® Class F-1	FSTTX	NAS CM	Open End	US Muni Fixed Inc (Muni Bond - Natl)	C	C	B-		Y	800-421-4225
American Funds Short-Term Tax-Exempt Bond Fund® Class F-2	ASTFX	NAS CM	Open End	US Muni Fixed Inc (Muni Bond - Natl)	C	C	B-		Y	800-421-4225
American Funds Strategic Bond Fund Class 529-A	CANAX	NAS CM	Open End	US Fixed Inc (Corp Bond - General)	B	B	B	Up	Y	800-421-4225
American Funds Strategic Bond Fund Class 529-C	CANCX	NAS CM	Open End	US Fixed Inc (Corp Bond - General)	B	B	B		Y	800-421-4225
American Funds Strategic Bond Fund Class 529-E	CANEX	NAS CM	Open End	US Fixed Inc (Corp Bond - General)	B	B	B	Up	Y	800-421-4225
American Funds Strategic Bond Fund Class 529-F-1	CANFX	NAS CM	Open End	US Fixed Inc (Corp Bond - General)	B	B	B	Up	Y	800-421-4225
American Funds Strategic Bond Fund Class A	ANBAX	NAS CM	Open End	US Fixed Inc (Corp Bond - General)	B	B	B+		Y	800-421-4225
American Funds Strategic Bond Fund Class C	ANBCX	NAS CM	Open End	US Fixed Inc (Corp Bond - General)	B	B	B	Up	Y	800-421-4225
American Funds Strategic Bond Fund Class F-1	ANBEX	NAS CM	Open End	US Fixed Inc (Corp Bond - General)	B	B	B+		Y	800-421-4225
American Funds Strategic Bond Fund Class F-2	ANBFX	NAS CM	Open End	US Fixed Inc (Corp Bond - General)	B	B	B	Up	Y	800-421-4225
American Funds Strategic Bond Fund Class F-3	ANBGX	NAS CM	Open End	US Fixed Inc (Corp Bond - General)	B	B	B	Up	Y	800-421-4225
American Funds Strategic Bond Fund Class R-1	RANAX	NAS CM	Open End	US Fixed Inc (Corp Bond - General)	B	B	B		Y	800-421-4225
American Funds Strategic Bond Fund Class R-2	RANBX	NAS CM	Open End	US Fixed Inc (Corp Bond - General)	B	B	B		Y	800-421-4225
American Funds Strategic Bond Fund Class R-2E	RANHX	NAS CM	Open End	US Fixed Inc (Corp Bond - General)	B	B	B+		Y	800-421-4225
American Funds Strategic Bond Fund Class R-3	RANCX	NAS CM	Open End	US Fixed Inc (Corp Bond - General)	B	B	B	Up	Y	800-421-4225
American Funds Strategic Bond Fund Class R-4	RANEX	NAS CM	Open End	US Fixed Inc (Corp Bond - General)	B	B	B	Up	Y	800-421-4225
American Funds Strategic Bond Fund Class R-5	RANFX	NAS CM	Open End	US Fixed Inc (Corp Bond - General)	B	B	B	Up	Y	800-421-4225
American Funds Strategic Bond Fund Class R-5E	RANJX	NAS CM	Open End	US Fixed Inc (Corp Bond - General)	B	B	B	Up	Y	800-421-4225
American Funds Strategic Bond Fund Class R-6	RANGX	NAS CM	Open End	US Fixed Inc (Corp Bond - General)	B	B	B+		Y	800-421-4225
American Funds Tax Exempt Bond Fund® Class F-3	TFEBX	NAS CM	Open End	US Muni Fixed Inc (Muni Bond - Natl)	C	C-	B		Y	800-421-4225
American Funds Tax-Exempt Bond Fund® Class A	AFTEX	NAS CM	Open End	US Muni Fixed Inc (Muni Bond - Natl)	C	C-	B-		Y	800-421-4225
American Funds Tax-Exempt Bond Fund® Class C	TEBCX	NAS CM	Open End	US Muni Fixed Inc (Muni Bond - Natl)	C	C-	B-		Y	800-421-4225
American Funds Tax-Exempt Bond Fund® Class F1	AFTFX	NAS CM	Open End	US Muni Fixed Inc (Muni Bond - Natl)	C	C-	B-		Y	800-421-4225
American Funds Tax-Exempt Bond Fund® Class F2	TEAFX	NAS CM	Open End	US Muni Fixed Inc (Muni Bond - Natl)	C	C-	B		Y	800-421-4225
American Funds Tax-Exempt Fund of California® Class A	TAFTX	NAS CM	Open End	US Muni Fixed Inc (Muni Bond - Single State)	C	C-	B-		Y	800-421-4225
American Funds Tax-Exempt Fund of California® Class C	TECCX	NAS CM	Open End	US Muni Fixed Inc (Muni Bond - Single State)	C	C-	C+		Y	800-421-4225
American Funds Tax-Exempt Fund of California® Class F-1	TECFX	NAS CM	Open End	US Muni Fixed Inc (Muni Bond - Single State)	C	C-	B-		Y	800-421-4225
American Funds Tax-Exempt Fund of California® Class F-2	TEFEX	NAS CM	Open End	US Muni Fixed Inc (Muni Bond - Single State)	C	C-	B-		Y	800-421-4225
American Funds Tax-Exempt Fund of California® Class F-3	EXCAX	NAS CM	Open End	US Muni Fixed Inc (Muni Bond - Single State)	C	C-	B-		Y	800-421-4225
American Funds Tax-Exempt Fund of New York® Class A	NYAAX	NAS CM	Open End	US Muni Fixed Inc (Muni Bond - Single State)	C	C-	C+		Y	800-421-4225
American Funds Tax-Exempt Fund of New York® Class C	NYACX	NAS CM	Open End	US Muni Fixed Inc (Muni Bond - Single State)	C	C-	C		Y	800-421-4225
American Funds Tax-Exempt Fund of New York® Class F-1	NYAEX	NAS CM	Open End	US Muni Fixed Inc (Muni Bond - Single State)	C	C-	C+		Y	800-421-4225
American Funds Tax-Exempt Fund of New York® Class F-2	NYAFX	NAS CM	Open End	US Muni Fixed Inc (Muni Bond - Single State)	C	C-	C+		Y	800-421-4225
American Funds Tax-Exempt Fund of New York® Class F-3	TFNYX	NAS CM	Open End	US Muni Fixed Inc (Muni Bond - Single State)	C	C-	C+		Y	800-421-4225
American Funds Tax-Exempt Preservation Portfolio Class A	TEPAX	NAS CM	Open End	US Muni Fixed Inc (Corp Bond - High Quality)	C	C	B-		Y	800-421-4225
American Funds Tax-Exempt Preservation Portfolio Class C	TEPCX	NAS CM	Open End	US Muni Fixed Inc (Corp Bond - High Quality)	C	C	C+		Y	800-421-4225
American Funds Tax-Exempt Preservation Portfolio Class F-1	TEPFX	NAS CM	Open End	US Muni Fixed Inc (Corp Bond - High Quality)	C	C	B-		Y	800-421-4225
American Funds Tax-Exempt Preservation Portfolio Class F-2	TXEFX	NAS CM	Open End	US Muni Fixed Inc (Corp Bond - High Quality)	C	C	B-		Y	800-421-4225
American Funds Tax-Exempt Preservation Portfolio Class F-3	TYEFX	NAS CM	Open End	US Muni Fixed Inc (Corp Bond - High Quality)	C	C	B-		Y	800-421-4225
★ American Funds The Bond Fund of America® Class 529-A	CFAAX	NAS CM	Open End	US Fixed Inc (Income)	B	B	B	Up	Y	800-421-4225
★ American Funds The Bond Fund of America® Class 529-C	CFACX	NAS CM	Open End	US Fixed Inc (Income)	B	B-	B	Up	Y	800-421-4225
★ American Funds The Bond Fund of America® Class 529-E	CFAEX	NAS CM	Open End	US Fixed Inc (Income)	B	B	B	Up	Y	800-421-4225
★ American Funds The Bond Fund of America® Class 529-F	CFAFX	NAS CM	Open End	US Fixed Inc (Income)	B	B	B		Y	800-421-4225
★ American Funds The Bond Fund of America® Class A	ABNDX	NAS CM	Open End	US Fixed Inc (Income)	B	B	B		Y	800-421-4225
★ American Funds The Bond Fund of America® Class C	BFACX	NAS CM	Open End	US Fixed Inc (Income)	B	B-	B	Up	Y	800-421-4225
★ American Funds The Bond Fund of America® Class F-1	BFAFX	NAS CM	Open End	US Fixed Inc (Income)	B	B	B	Up	Y	800-421-4225
★ American Funds The Bond Fund of America® Class F-2	ABNFX	NAS CM	Open End	US Fixed Inc (Income)	B	B	B+		Y	800-421-4225
American Funds The Bond Fund of America® Class F-3	BFFAX	NAS CM	Open End	US Fixed Inc (Income)	B	B	B+		Y	800-421-4225
★ American Funds The Bond Fund of America® Class R-1	RBFAX	NAS CM	Open End	US Fixed Inc (Income)	B	B-	B	Up	Y	800-421-4225
★ American Funds The Bond Fund of America® Class R-2	RBFBX	NAS CM	Open End	US Fixed Inc (Income)	B	B-	B	Up	Y	800-421-4225
★ American Funds The Bond Fund of America® Class R-2E	RBEBX	NAS CM	Open End	US Fixed Inc (Income)	B	B	B	Up	Y	800-421-4225
★ American Funds The Bond Fund of America® Class R-3	RBFCX	NAS CM	Open End	US Fixed Inc (Income)	B	B	B	Up	Y	800-421-4225

★ Expanded analysis of this fund is included in Section II.

TOTAL RETURNS & PERFORMANCE									ASSETS		ASSET ALLOCATION & TURNOVER							MINIMUMS		FEES		
3-Month Total Return	6-Month Total Return	1-Year Total Return	3-Year Total Return	5-Year Total Return	Dividend Yield (TTM)	Expense Ratio	3-Yr Std Deviation	Effective Duration	NAV	Total Assets (MIL)	%Cash	%Government Bonds	%Municipal Bonds	%Corporate Bonds	%Other	Turnover Ratio	Average Coupon Rate	Min Initial Investment	Min Additional Investment	Front End Fee (%)	Back End Fee (%)	Inception Date
1.70	1.88	2.71	5.52	7.11	1.16	0.78	1.41	2.11	10.32	1,172	1	0	97	0	0	34	4.01	250	50			Aug-09
1.78	2.04	3.04	6.46	8.61	1.47	0.46	1.42	2.11	10.32	1,172	1	0	97	0	0	34	4.01	250	50			Aug-09
6.34	14.54	15.85	24.54		0.97	0.9	3.6	8.62	11.68	2,132	10	42	1	29	0	428	2.45	250	50	3.75		Mar-16
6.17	14.16	15.02	21.73		0.37	1.68	3.56	8.62	11.64	2,132	10	42	1	29	0	428	2.45	250	50		1.00	Mar-16
6.29	14.40	15.59	23.87		0.79	1.11	3.59	8.62	11.69	2,132	10	42	1	29	0	428	2.45	250	50			Mar-16
6.39	14.64	16.10	25.40		1.18	0.68	3.58	8.62	11.69	2,132	10	42	1	29	0	428	2.45	250	50			Mar-16
6.34	14.52	15.83	24.71		0.97	0.92	3.6	8.62	11.69	2,132	10	42	1	29	0	428	2.45	250	50	3.75		Mar-16
6.13	14.06	14.95	21.85		0.46	1.62	3.58	8.62	11.63	2,132	10	42	1	29	0	428	2.45	250	50		1.00	Mar-16
6.30	14.52	15.84	24.56		1.02	0.9	3.59	8.62	11.68	2,132	10	42	1	29	0	428	2.45	250	50			Mar-16
6.41	14.67	16.14	25.74		1.22	0.62	3.58	8.62	11.7	2,132	10	42	1	29	0	428	2.45	250	50			Mar-16
6.43	14.72	16.26	25.97		1.3	0.52	3.59	8.62	11.69	2,132	10	42	1	29	0	428	2.45	1,000,000	50			Jan-17
6.23	14.17	15.11	22.29		0.42	1.6	3.6	8.62	11.68	2,132	10	42	1	29	0	428	2.45	250	50			Mar-16
6.11	14.14	15.05	22.11		0.48	1.59	3.57	8.62	11.65	2,132	10	42	1	29	0	428	2.45	250	50			Mar-16
6.21	14.35	15.41	24.11		0.77	1.35	3.51	8.62	11.69	2,132	10	42	1	29	0	428	2.45	250	50			Mar-16
6.29	14.41	15.60	23.84		0.78	1.14	3.59	8.62	11.68	2,132	10	42	1	29	0	428	2.45	250	50			Mar-16
6.35	14.56	15.92	24.83		1.03	0.84	3.59	8.62	11.69	2,132	10	42	1	29	0	428	2.45	250	50			Mar-16
6.41	14.68	16.19	25.77		1.26	0.57	3.58	8.62	11.7	2,132	10	42	1	29	0	428	2.45	250	50			Mar-16
6.39	14.64	16.09	25.57		1.19	0.67	3.6	8.62	11.7	2,132	10	42	1	29	0	428	2.45	250	50			Mar-16
6.51	14.80	16.34	26.05		1.3	0.52	3.58	8.62	11.71	2,132	10	42	1	29	0	428	2.45	250	50			Mar-16
2.19	1.43	3.64	12.88	20.52	2.81	0.26	4.02	5.96	13.34	23,607	1	0	99	0	0	20	4.61	1,000,000	50			Jan-17
2.12	1.29	3.35	12.02	19.50	2.53	0.54	4.02	5.96	13.34	23,607	1	0	99	0	0	20	4.61	250	50	3.75		Oct-79
1.93	0.91	2.59	9.46	14.95	1.79	1.29	4.02	5.96	13.34	23,607	1	0	99	0	0	20	4.61	250	50		1.00	Mar-01
2.10	1.25	3.26	11.66	18.79	2.45	0.63	4.02	5.96	13.34	23,607	1	0	99	0	0	20	4.61	250	50			Mar-01
2.17	1.38	3.53	12.52	20.35	2.71	0.36	4.02	5.96	13.34	23,607	1	0	99	0	0	20	4.61	250	50			Aug-08
2.23	1.02	3.08	11.89	19.37	2.48	0.61	4.14	6.23	18.02	2,830	2	0	98	0	0	27	4.63	1,000	50	3.75		Oct-86
2.04	0.64	2.31	9.32	14.81	1.72	1.36	4.14	6.23	18.02	2,830	2	0	98	0	0	27	4.63	1,000	50		1.00	Mar-01
2.21	0.97	2.98	11.50	18.65	2.38	0.7	4.14	6.23	18.02	2,830	2	0	98	0	0	27	4.63	1,000	50			Mar-01
2.28	1.11	3.27	12.39	20.19	2.66	0.43	4.14	6.23	18.02	2,830	2	0	98	0	0	27	4.63	1,000	50			Aug-08
2.30	1.15	3.35	12.71	20.36	2.75	0.34	4.14	6.23	18.02	2,830	2	0	98	0	0	27	4.63	1,000,000	50			Jan-17
1.80	0.28	2.16	9.72	17.11	2.49	0.64	4.56	6.31	10.94	282.6	1	0	99	0	0	16	4.81	1,000	50	3.75		Nov-10
1.61	-0.08	1.40	7.20	12.63	1.72	1.39	4.56	6.31	10.94	282.6	1	0	99	0	0	16	4.81	1,000	50		1.00	Nov-10
1.80	0.28	2.15	9.59	17.06	2.48	0.7	4.56	6.31	10.94	282.6	1	0	99	0	0	16	4.81	1,000	50			Nov-10
1.84	0.37	2.34	10.23	17.96	2.67	0.44	4.57	6.31	10.94	282.6	1	0	99	0	0	16	4.81	1,000	50			Nov-10
1.87	0.42	2.44	10.55	18.38	2.77	0.35	4.56	6.31	10.94	282.6	1	0	99	0	0	16	4.81	1,000,000	50			Jan-17
2.18	1.97	3.20	7.51	11.61	1.65	0.67	2.15	3.01	10	483.6	3	0	96	0	0	15		250	50	2.50		May-12
2.11	1.65	2.48	5.36	7.75	0.96	1.37	2.13	3.01	9.99	483.6	3	0	96	0	0	15		250	50		1.00	May-12
2.27	2.06	3.15	7.50	11.54	1.61	0.72	2.14	3.01	10.01	483.6	3	0	96	0	0	15		250	50			May-12
2.24	2.18	3.44	8.32	13.08	1.88	0.43	2.15	3.01	10	483.6	3	0	96	0	0	15		250	50			May-12
2.26	2.13	3.55	8.65	13.46	1.98	0.34	2.14	3.01	10	483.6	3	0	96	0	0	15		1,000,000	50			Jan-17
4.10	8.02	10.15	17.14	23.95	2.1	0.65	3.11	6.27	13.99	56,642	7	30	1	28	0	286	3.09	250	50	3.75		Feb-02
3.91	7.63	9.35	14.56	19.40	1.4	1.41	3.11	6.27	13.99	56,642	7	30	1	28	0	286	3.09	250	50		1.00	Feb-02
4.06	7.92	9.95	16.48	22.75	1.93	0.85	3.11	6.27	13.99	56,642	7	30	1	28	0	286	3.09	250	50			Mar-02
4.17	8.15	10.41	17.98	25.41	2.33	0.41	3.11	6.27	13.99	56,642	7	30	1	28	0	286	3.09	250	50			Sep-02
4.12	8.05	10.20	17.38	24.42	2.15	0.61	3.11	6.27	13.99	56,642	7	30	1	28	0	286	3.09	250	50	3.75		May-74
3.93	7.65	9.39	14.71	19.67	1.44	1.36	3.11	6.27	13.99	56,642	7	30	1	28	0	286	3.09	250	50		1.00	Mar-01
4.11	8.03	10.17	17.23	24.17	2.12	0.63	3.11	6.27	13.99	56,642	7	30	1	28	0	286	3.09	250	50			Mar-01
4.18	8.18	10.48	18.29	26.00	2.39	0.34	3.11	6.27	13.99	56,642	7	30	1	28	0	286	3.09	250	50			Aug-08
4.21	8.24	10.60	18.60	25.89	2.49	0.24	3.11	6.27	13.99	56,642	7	30	1	28	0	286	3.09	1,000,000	50			Jan-17
3.92	7.64	9.38	14.74	19.79	1.43	1.35	3.11	6.27	13.99	56,642	7	30	1	28	0	286	3.09	250	50			Jun-02
3.93	7.66	9.39	14.78	19.85	1.44	1.34	3.11	6.27	13.99	56,642	7	30	1	28	0	286	3.09	250	50			May-02
4.01	7.81	9.72	15.80	21.81	1.73	1.04	3.11	6.27	13.99	56,642	7	30	1	28	0	286	3.09	250	50			Aug-14
4.04	7.89	9.89	16.33	22.55	1.87	0.89	3.11	6.27	13.99	56,642	7	30	1	28	0	286	3.09	250	50			Jun-02

	MARKET		FUND TYPE, CATEGORY & OBJECTIVE		RATINGS				NEW INVESTORS	
Fund Name	Ticker Symbol	Traded On	Fund Type	Category and (Prospectus Objective)	Overall Rating	Reward Rating	Risk Rating	Recent Up/ Downgrade	Open to New Investors	Telephone
★ American Funds The Bond Fund of America® Class R-4	RBFEX	NAS CM	Open End	US Fixed Inc (Income)	B	B	B		Y	800-421-4225
★ American Funds The Bond Fund of America® Class R-5	RBFFX	NAS CM	Open End	US Fixed Inc (Income)	B	B	B+		Y	800-421-4225
★ American Funds The Bond Fund of America® Class R-5E	RBFHX	NAS CM	Open End	US Fixed Inc (Income)	B	B	B		Y	800-421-4225
★ American Funds The Bond Fund of America® Class R-6	RBFGX	NAS CM	Open End	US Fixed Inc (Income)	B	B	B	Up	Y	800-421-4225
American Funds U.S. Govt Money Mkt Fund Class 529-A	AAFXX	NAS CM	Money Mkt	US Money Mkt (Money Mkt - Govt)	C	C-	C+		Y	800-421-4225
American Funds U.S. Govt Money Mkt Fund Class 529-C	CCFXX	NAS CM	Money Mkt	US Money Mkt (Money Mkt - Govt)	C	C-	C+		Y	800-421-4225
American Funds U.S. Govt Money Mkt Fund Class 529-E	EAFXX	NAS CM	Money Mkt	US Money Mkt (Money Mkt - Govt)	C	C-	C+		Y	800-421-4225
American Funds U.S. Govt Money Mkt Fund Class 529-F-1	FARXX	NAS CM	Money Mkt	US Money Mkt (Money Mkt - Govt)	C	C-	C+		Y	800-421-4225
American Funds U.S. Government Money Market Fund Class A	AFAXX	NAS CM	Money Mkt	US Money Mkt (Money Mkt - Govt)	C	C-	C+		Y	800-421-4225
American Funds U.S. Govt Money Mkt Fund Class ABLE-A	AAZXX	NAS CM	Money Mkt	US Money Mkt (Money Mkt - Govt)	C	C-	C+		Y	800-421-4225
American Funds U.S. Government Money Market Fund Class C	AFCXX	NAS CM	Money Mkt	US Money Mkt (Money Mkt - Govt)	C	C-	C+		Y	800-421-4225
American Funds U.S. Government Money Market Fund Class F-1	AFFXX	NAS CM	Money Mkt	US Money Mkt (Money Mkt - Govt)	C	C-	C+		Y	800-421-4225
American Funds U.S. Government Money Market Fund Class F-2	AFGXX	NAS CM	Money Mkt	US Money Mkt (Money Mkt - Govt)	C	C-	C+		Y	800-421-4225
American Funds U.S. Government Money Market Fund Class F-3	USGXX	NAS CM	Money Mkt	US Money Mkt (Money Mkt - Govt)	C	C-	C+		Y	800-421-4225
American Funds U.S. Government Money Market Fund Class R-1	RAAXX	NAS CM	Money Mkt	US Money Mkt (Money Mkt - Govt)	C	C-	C+		Y	800-421-4225
American Funds U.S. Government Money Market Fund Class R-2	RABXX	NAS CM	Money Mkt	US Money Mkt (Money Mkt - Govt)	C	C-	C		Y	800-421-4225
American Funds U.S. Govt Money Mkt Fund Class R-2E	RBEXX	NAS CM	Money Mkt	US Money Mkt (Money Mkt - Govt)	C	C-	C		Y	800-421-4225
American Funds U.S. Government Money Market Fund Class R-3	RACXX	NAS CM	Money Mkt	US Money Mkt (Money Mkt - Govt)	C	C-	C		Y	800-421-4225
American Funds U.S. Government Money Market Fund Class R-4	RADXX	NAS CM	Money Mkt	US Money Mkt (Money Mkt - Govt)	C	C-	C+		Y	800-421-4225
American Funds U.S. Government Money Market Fund Class R-5	RAEXX	NAS CM	Money Mkt	US Money Mkt (Money Mkt - Govt)	C	C-	C+		Y	800-421-4225
American Funds U.S. Govt Money Mkt Fund Class R-5E	RAGXX	NAS CM	Money Mkt	US Money Mkt (Money Mkt - Govt)	C	C-	C+		Y	800-421-4225
American Funds U.S. Government Money Market Fund Class R-6	RAFXX	NAS CM	Money Mkt	US Money Mkt (Money Mkt - Govt)	C	C-	C+		Y	800-421-4225
American Funds U.S. Govt Securities Fund® Class 529-A	CGTAX	NAS CM	Open End	US Fixed Inc (Govt Bond - General)	B	B	B		Y	800-421-4225
American Funds U.S. Govt Securities Fund® Class 529-C	CGTCX	NAS CM	Open End	US Fixed Inc (Govt Bond - General)	B-	B-	B		Y	800-421-4225
American Funds U.S. Govt Securities Fund® Class 529-E	CGTEX	NAS CM	Open End	US Fixed Inc (Govt Bond - General)	B	B	B	Up	Y	800-421-4225
American Funds U.S. Govt Securities Fund® Class 529-F-1	CGTFX	NAS CM	Open End	US Fixed Inc (Govt Bond - General)	B	B	B		Y	800-421-4225
American Funds U.S. Government Securities Fund® Class A	AMUSX	NAS CM	Open End	US Fixed Inc (Govt Bond - General)	B	B	B		Y	800-421-4225
American Funds U.S. Government Securities Fund® Class C	UGSCX	NAS CM	Open End	US Fixed Inc (Govt Bond - General)	B-	B-	B		Y	800-421-4225
American Funds U.S. Government Securities Fund® Class F-1	UGSFX	NAS CM	Open End	US Fixed Inc (Govt Bond - General)	B	B	B		Y	800-421-4225
American Funds U.S. Government Securities Fund® Class F-2	GVTFX	NAS CM	Open End	US Fixed Inc (Govt Bond - General)	B	B	B		Y	800-421-4225
American Funds U.S. Government Securities Fund® Class F-3	USGFX	NAS CM	Open End	US Fixed Inc (Govt Bond - General)	B	B	B		Y	800-421-4225
American Funds U.S. Government Securities Fund® Class R-1	RGVAX	NAS CM	Open End	US Fixed Inc (Govt Bond - General)	B-	B-	B		Y	800-421-4225
American Funds U.S. Government Securities Fund® Class R-2	RGVBX	NAS CM	Open End	US Fixed Inc (Govt Bond - General)	B	B-	B	Up	Y	800-421-4225
American Funds U.S. Government Securities Fund® Class R-2E	RGEVX	NAS CM	Open End	US Fixed Inc (Govt Bond - General)	B	B-	B	Up	Y	800-421-4225
American Funds U.S. Government Securities Fund® Class R-3	RGVCX	NAS CM	Open End	US Fixed Inc (Govt Bond - General)	B	B	B	Up	Y	800-421-4225
American Funds U.S. Government Securities Fund® Class R-4	RGVEX	NAS CM	Open End	US Fixed Inc (Govt Bond - General)	B	B	B		Y	800-421-4225
American Funds U.S. Government Securities Fund® Class R-5	RGVFX	NAS CM	Open End	US Fixed Inc (Govt Bond - General)	B	B	B		Y	800-421-4225
American Funds U.S. Government Securities Fund® Class R-5E	RGVJX	NAS CM	Open End	US Fixed Inc (Govt Bond - General)	B	B	B		Y	800-421-4225
American Funds U.S. Government Securities Fund® Class R-6	RGVGX	NAS CM	Open End	US Fixed Inc (Govt Bond - General)	B	B	B		Y	800-421-4225
American High-Income Municipal Bond Fund® Class A	AMHIX	NAS CM	Open End	US Muni Fixed Inc (Muni Bond - Natl)	C-	D+	C	Down	Y	800-421-4225
American High-Income Municipal Bond Fund® Class C	AHICX	NAS CM	Open End	US Muni Fixed Inc (Muni Bond - Natl)	C-	D+	C	Down	Y	800-421-4225
American High-Income Municipal Bond Fund® Class F-1	ABHFX	NAS CM	Open End	US Muni Fixed Inc (Muni Bond - Natl)	C-	D+	C	Down	Y	800-421-4225
American High-Income Municipal Bond Fund® Class F-2	AHMFX	NAS CM	Open End	US Muni Fixed Inc (Muni Bond - Natl)	C-	D+	C	Down	Y	800-421-4225
American High-Income Municipal Bond Fund® Class F-3	HIMFX	NAS CM	Open End	US Muni Fixed Inc (Muni Bond - Natl)	C-	D+	C	Down	Y	800-421-4225
AMG GW&K Core Bond ESG Fund - Class I	MBDFX	NAS CM	Open End	US Fixed Inc (Corp Bond - General)	B-	C+	B	Up	Y	800-835-3879
AMG GW&K Core Bond ESG Fund - Class N	MBGVX	NAS CM	Open End	US Fixed Inc (Corp Bond - General)	B-	C+	B	Up	Y	800-835-3879
AMG GW&K Core Bond ESG Fund - Class Z	MBDLX	NAS CM	Open End	US Fixed Inc (Corp Bond - General)	B-	C+	B+	Up	Y	800-835-3879
AMG GW&K Enhanced Core Bond ESG Fund - Class I	MFDSX	NAS CM	Open End	US Fixed Inc (Corp Bond - General)	B-	C+	B	Up	Y	800-835-3879
AMG GW&K Enhanced Core Bond ESG Fund - Class N	MFDAX	NAS CM	Open End	US Fixed Inc (Corp Bond - General)	B-	C+	B	Up	Y	800-835-3879
AMG GW&K Enhanced Core Bond ESG Fund - Class Z	MFDYX	NAS CM	Open End	US Fixed Inc (Corp Bond - General)	B-	C+	B+	Up	Y	800-835-3879
AMG GW&K Municipal Bond Fund Class I	GWMIX	NAS CM	Open End	US Muni Fixed Inc (Muni Bond - Natl)	C+	C	B	Up	Y	800-835-3879
AMG GW&K Municipal Bond Fund Class N	GWMTX	NAS CM	Open End	US Muni Fixed Inc (Muni Bond - Natl)	C	C	B		Y	800-835-3879

★ Expanded analysis of this fund is included in Section II.

TOTAL RETURNS & PERFORMANCE									ASSETS		ASSET ALLOCATION & TURNOVER							MINIMUMS		FEES		
3-Month Total Return	6-Month Total Return	1-Year Total Return	3-Year Total Return	5-Year Total Return	Dividend Yield (TTM)	Expense Ratio	3-Yr Std Deviation	Effective Duration	NAV	Total Assets (MIL)	%Cash	%Government Bonds	%Municipal Bonds	%Corporate Bonds	%Other	Turnover Ratio	Average Coupon Rate	Min Initial Investment	Min Additional Investment	Front End Fee (%)	Back End Fee (%)	Inception Date
4.12	8.06	10.22	17.40	24.45	2.16	0.58	3.11	6.27	13.99	56,642	7	30	1	28	0	286	3.09	250	50			May-02
4.20	8.21	10.55	18.45	26.31	2.45	0.28	3.11	6.27	13.99	56,642	7	30	1	28	0	286	3.09	250	50			May-02
4.17	8.16	10.44	18.10	25.51	2.36	0.37	3.12	6.27	13.99	56,642	7	30	1	28	0	286	3.09	250	50			Nov-15
4.21	8.24	10.60	18.64	26.64	2.5	0.23	3.11	6.27	13.99	56,642	7	30	1	28	0	286	3.09	250	50			May-09
0.00	0.26	1.02	3.72	3.83	1.17	0.45	0.17		1	24,763	82	17	0	0	0			1,000	50			May-09
0.00	0.26	1.02	3.72	3.82	1.17	0.45	0.17		1	24,763	82	17	0	0	0			1,000	50		1.00	May-09
0.00	0.26	1.03	3.75	3.86	1.18	0.44	0.17		1	24,763	82	17	0	0	0			1,000	50			May-09
0.00	0.26	1.02	3.72	3.83	1.17	0.45	0.17		1	24,763	82	17	0	0	0			1,000	50			May-09
0.00	0.26	1.05	3.97	4.15	1.23	0.38	0.17		1	24,763	82	17	0	0	0			1,000	50			May-09
0.00	0.27	1.08	3.87	3.96	1.23	0.36			1	24,763	82	17	0	0	0			1,000	50			Jul-18
0.01	0.27	1.06	3.90	4.04	1.23	0.39	0.17		1	24,763	82	17	0	0	0			1,000	50		1.00	May-09
0.00	0.19	0.84	3.07	3.10	0.98	0.68	0.16		1	24,763	82	17	0	0	0			1,000	50			May-09
0.00	0.26	1.07	3.90	4.02	1.24	0.37	0.17		1	24,763	82	17	0	0	0			1,000	50			May-09
0.01	0.29	1.13	4.12	4.28	1.3	0.32	0.17		1	24,763	82	17	0	0	0			1,000,000	50			Jan-17
0.00	0.26	1.03	3.83	3.96	1.2	0.41	0.17		1	24,763	82	17	0	0	0			1,000	50			May-09
0.00	0.02	0.29	1.19	1.23	0.38	1.41	0.12		1	24,763	82	17	0	0	0			1,000	50			May-09
0.00	0.08	0.51	1.91	1.91	0.62	1.13	0.15		1	24,763	82	17	0	0	0			1,000	50			Aug-14
0.00	0.12	0.61	2.24	2.28	0.74	0.97	0.16		1	24,763	82	17	0	0	0			1,000	50			May-09
0.00	0.18	0.84	3.10	3.16	0.98	0.67	0.16		1	24,763	82	17	0	0	0			1,000	50			May-09
0.00	0.27	1.07	3.96	4.11	1.24	0.37	0.17		1	24,763	82	17	0	0	0			1,000	50			May-09
0.00	0.24	1.00	3.68	3.74	1.16	0.46	0.17		1	24,763	82	17	0	0	0			1,000	50			Nov-15
0.01	0.29	1.12	4.12	4.32	1.29	0.32	0.17		1	24,763	82	17	0	0	0			1,000	50			May-09
0.97	8.80	9.86	14.89	19.07	1.58	0.68	3.56	5.67	14.91	17,998	3	39	0	0	0	350	2.59	250	50	3.75		Feb-02
0.74	8.39	8.98	12.32	14.69	0.91	1.45	3.56	5.67	14.85	17,998	3	39	0	0	0	350	2.59	250	50		1.00	Feb-02
0.91	8.69	9.63	14.16	17.77	1.38	0.9	3.56	5.67	14.91	17,998	3	39	0	0	0	350	2.59	250	50			Mar-02
1.02	8.92	10.11	15.69	20.42	1.8	0.45	3.55	5.67	14.91	17,998	3	39	0	0	0	350	2.59	250	50			Oct-02
0.96	8.79	9.84	14.91	19.34	1.57	0.67	3.54	5.67	14.91	17,998	3	39	0	0	0	350	2.59	250	50	3.75		Oct-85
0.81	8.39	9.07	12.46	14.91	0.93	1.4	3.54	5.67	14.87	17,998	3	39	0	0	0	350	2.59	250	50		1.00	Mar-01
0.97	8.81	9.89	15.03	19.34	1.61	0.63	3.56	5.67	14.91	17,998	3	39	0	0	0	350	2.59	250	50			Mar-01
1.04	8.96	10.19	15.89	20.95	1.87	0.36	3.55	5.67	14.91	17,998	3	39	0	0	0	350	2.59	250	50			Aug-08
1.07	8.94	10.23	16.26	20.91	1.97	0.26	3.54	5.67	14.91	17,998	3	39	0	0	0	350	2.59	1,000,000	50			Jan-17
0.75	8.39	9.08	12.44	15.02	0.93	1.37	3.55	5.67	14.87	17,998	3	39	0	0	0	350	2.59	250	50			Jun-02
0.82	8.41	9.09	12.59	15.13	0.95	1.35	3.54	5.67	14.87	17,998	3	39	0	0	0	350	2.59	250	50			May-02
0.87	8.59	9.43	13.52	17.03	1.2	1.07	3.56	5.67	14.91	17,998	3	39	0	0	0	350	2.59	250	50			Aug-14
0.84	8.59	9.51	13.94	17.51	1.34	0.93	3.54	5.67	14.9	17,998	3	39	0	0	0	350	2.59	250	50			Jun-02
0.98	8.75	9.85	15.05	19.52	1.64	0.61	3.54	5.67	14.91	17,998	3	39	0	0	0	350	2.59	250	50			May-02
1.06	8.91	10.17	16.08	21.29	1.92	0.31	3.54	5.67	14.91	17,998	3	39	0	0	0	350	2.59	250	50			May-02
1.03	8.87	10.07	15.81	20.58	1.83	0.41	3.52	5.67	14.9	17,998	3	39	0	0	0	350	2.59	250	50			Nov-15
1.07	9.02	10.31	16.36	21.64	1.97	0.25	3.55	5.67	14.91	17,998	3	39	0	0	0	350	2.59	250	50			May-09
3.07	-1.68	1.06	12.87	24.66	3.53	0.7	6.02	7.11	15.89	6,927	2	0	98	0	0	20	4.81	250	50	3.75		Sep-94
2.89	-2.02	0.36	10.44	20.15	2.79	1.4	6.01	7.11	15.89	6,927	2	0	98	0	0	20	4.81	250	50		1.00	Mar-01
3.06	-1.70	1.04	12.70	24.28	3.5	0.73	6.02	7.11	15.89	6,927	2	0	98	0	0	20	4.81	250	50			Mar-01
3.13	-1.57	1.30	13.58	25.89	3.78	0.46	6.02	7.11	15.89	6,927	2	0	98	0	0	20	4.81	250	50			Aug-08
3.16	-1.52	1.41	13.94	25.97	3.89	0.36	6.02	7.11	15.89	6,927	2	0	98	0	0	20	4.81	1,000,000	50			Jan-17
4.99	5.36	8.20	15.85	22.59	2.24	0.55	4.11	6.08	10.94	210.6	3	9	8	50	0	48	3.94	100,000	100			Apr-93
4.91	5.09	7.76	14.72	20.46	1.93	0.88	4.14	6.08	10.93	210.6	3	9	8	50	0	48	3.94	2,000	100			May-15
5.01	5.40	8.29	16.02	22.93	2.31	0.48	4.17	6.08	10.93	210.6	3	9	8	50	0	48	3.94	5,000,000	1,000			May-15
5.61	5.42	8.47	16.52	20.36	2.4	0.55	4.2	6.19	10.62	34.6	3	5	8	55	0	71	4.31	100,000	100			Nov-12
5.68	5.45	8.30	16.06	19.47	2.23	0.73	4.2	6.19	10.59	34.6	3	5	8	55	0	71	4.31	2,000	100			Jan-97
5.63	5.56	8.54	16.87	20.92	2.46	0.48	4.18	6.19	10.62	34.6	3	5	8	55	0	71	4.31	5,000,000	1,000			Jan-97
2.73	2.16	4.05	11.78	20.04	1.79	0.39	4.06	4.67	12.34	1,116	10	0	90	0	0	18	5.00	100,000	100			Jun-09
2.58	1.93	3.75	10.70	17.89	1.49	0.71	4.04	4.67	12.27	1,116	10	0	90	0	0	18	5.00	2,000	100			Jun-09

	MARKET			FUND TYPE, CATEGORY & OBJECTIVE	RATINGS				NEW INVESTORS	
Fund Name	Ticker Symbol	Traded On	Fund Type	Category and (Prospectus Objective)	Overall Rating	Reward Rating	Risk Rating	Recent Up/ Downgrade	Open to New Investors	Telephone
AMG GW&K Municipal Enhanced Yield Fund Class I	GWMEX	NAS CM	Open End	US Muni Fixed Inc (Muni Bond - Natl)	C	C-	C+		Y	800-835-3879
AMG GW&K Municipal Enhanced Yield Fund Class N	GWMNX	NAS CM	Open End	US Muni Fixed Inc (Muni Bond - Natl)	C	C-	C+		Y	800-835-3879
AMG GW&K Municipal Enhanced Yield Fund Class Z	GWMZX	NAS CM	Open End	US Muni Fixed Inc (Muni Bond - Natl)	C	C-	C+		Y	800-835-3879
AMG Managers DoubleLine Core Plus Bond Fund Class I	ADLIX	NAS CM	Open End	US Fixed Inc (Multisector Bond)	C	C-	C+		Y	800-835-3879
AMG Managers DoubleLine Core Plus Bond Fund Class N	ADBLX	NAS CM	Open End	US Fixed Inc (Multisector Bond)	C	C-	C+		Y	800-835-3879
AMG Managers DoubleLine Core Plus Bond Fund Class Z	ADZIX	NAS CM	Open End	US Fixed Inc (Multisector Bond)	C	C-	C+		Y	800-835-3879
AMG Managers Global Income Opportunity Fund Class N	MGGBX	NAS CM	Open End	Global Fixed Inc (Worldwide Bond)	C+	C	B-	Up	Y	800-835-3879
AMG Managers Loomis Sayles Bond Fund Class I	MGBIX	NAS CM	Open End	US Fixed Inc (Income)	C	C-	B-		Y	800-835-3879
AMG Managers Loomis Sayles Bond Fund Class N	MGFIX	NAS CM	Open End	US Fixed Inc (Income)	C	C-	B-		Y	800-835-3879
Anchor Risk Managed Muni Strategies Institutional Cl	ATMSX	NAS CM	Open End	US Fixed Inc (Muni Bond - Natl)	C-	D+	C	Down	Y	
Ancora Income Fund Class I	AAIIX	NAS CM	Open End	US Fixed Inc (Income)	D+	D+	C-	Down	Y	
Anfield Universal Fixed Income Fund Class A	AFLEX	NAS CM	Open End	Fixed Inc Misc (Income)	D+	D	C	Down	Y	
Anfield Universal Fixed Income Fund Class C	AFLKX	NAS CM	Open End	Fixed Inc Misc (Income)	D	D	C-	Down	Y	
Anfield Universal Fixed Income Fund Class I	AFLIX	NAS CM	Open End	Fixed Inc Misc (Income)	D+	D	C	Down	Y	
Angel Oak Financial Strats Income Term	FINS	NYSE	Closed End	US Fixed Inc (Income)	D	D	D+		Y	404-953-4397
Angel Oak Financials Income Fund Class A	ANFLX	NAS CM	Open End	US Fixed Inc (Income)	D+	D+	C-	Down	Y	404-953-4900
Angel Oak Financials Income Fund Class C	AFLCX	NAS CM	Open End	US Fixed Inc (Income)	D+	D	C-	Down	Y	404-953-4900
Angel Oak Financials Income Fund Institutional Class	ANFIX	NAS CM	Open End	US Fixed Inc (Income)	D+	D+	C-	Down	Y	404-953-4900
Angel Oak High Yield Opportunities Fund Class A	ANHAX	NAS CM	Open End	US Fixed Inc (Corp Bond - High Yield)	D+	D	C-	Down	Y	404-953-4900
Angel Oak High Yield Opportunities Cl Institutional	ANHIX	NAS CM	Open End	US Fixed Inc (Corp Bond - High Yield)	C-	D+	C		Y	404-953-4900
Angel Oak Multi-Strategy Income Fund A Shares	ANGLX	NAS CM	Open End	US Fixed Inc (Income)	D	D	D+	Down	Y	404-953-4900
Angel Oak Multi-Strategy Income Fund Class C	ANGCX	NAS CM	Open End	US Fixed Inc (Income)	D	D	D+	Down	Y	404-953-4900
Angel Oak Multi-Strategy Income Fund Institutional Shares	ANGIX	NAS CM	Open End	US Fixed Inc (Income)	D	D	C-	Down	Y	404-953-4900
Angel Oak Strategic Credit Fund	ASCIX	NAS CM	Closed End	Fixed Inc Misc (Growth & Income)	D	D	D	Down	Y	404-953-4397
Angel Oak UltraShort Income Fund Class A	AOUAX	NAS CM	Open End	US Fixed Inc (Income)	C-	D+	C		Y	404-953-4900
Angel Oak UltraShort Income Fund Institutional Class	AOUIX	NAS CM	Open End	US Fixed Inc (Income)	C-	D+	C		Y	404-953-4900
Aperture New World Opportunities Fund Institutional Shares	ANWOX	NAS CM	Open End	Emerg Mkts Fixed Inc (Growth & Income)	D	D	C	Up	Y	
Aperture New World Opportunities Fund X	ANWRX	NAS CM	Open End	Emerg Mkts Fixed Inc (Growth & Income)	D	D+	C	Up	Y	
Apollo Senior Floating Rate Fund	AFT	NYSE	Closed End	US Fixed Inc (Income)	D	D	D	Down	Y	
Apollo Tactical Income Fund Inc.	AIF	NYSE	Closed End	US Fixed Inc (Income)	D	D	D	Down	Y	
AQR Core Plus Bond Fund Class I	QCPIX	NAS CM	Open End	US Fixed Inc (Growth & Income)	C	C-	B	Up	Y	203-742-3600
AQR Core Plus Bond Fund Class N	QCPNX	NAS CM	Open End	US Fixed Inc (Growth & Income)	C	C-	B	Up	Y	203-742-3600
AQR Core Plus Bond Fund Class R6	QCPRX	NAS CM	Open End	US Fixed Inc (Growth & Income)	C	C-	B	Up	Y	203-742-3600
Aquila Churchill Tax Free Fund of Kentucky Class A	CHTFX	NAS CM	Open End	US Muni Fixed Inc (Muni Bond - Single State)	C	C	B-		Y	800-437-1020
Aquila Churchill Tax Free Fund of Kentucky Class C	CHKCX	NAS CM	Open End	US Muni Fixed Inc (Muni Bond - Single State)	C	C-	C+		Y	800-437-1020
Aquila Churchill Tax Free Fund of Kentucky Class I	CHKIX	NAS CM	Open End	US Muni Fixed Inc (Muni Bond - Single State)	C	C	B-		Y	800-437-1020
Aquila Churchill Tax Free Fund of Kentucky Class Y	CHKYX	NAS CM	Open End	US Muni Fixed Inc (Muni Bond - Single State)	C	C	B-		Y	800-437-1020
Aquila Narragansett Tax-Free Income Fund Class A	NITFX	NAS CM	Open End	US Muni Fixed Inc (Muni Bond - Single State)	C+	C	B	Up	Y	800-437-1020
Aquila Narragansett Tax-Free Income Fund Class C	NITCX	NAS CM	Open End	US Muni Fixed Inc (Muni Bond - Single State)	C	C	B-		Y	800-437-1020
Aquila Narragansett Tax-Free Income Fund Class F	NIFFX	NAS CM	Open End	US Muni Fixed Inc (Muni Bond - Single State)	C+	C	B	Up	Y	800-437-1020
Aquila Narragansett Tax-Free Income Cl Institutional	NITIX	NAS CM	Open End	US Muni Fixed Inc (Muni Bond - Single State)	C+	C	B	Up	Y	800-437-1020
Aquila Narragansett Tax-Free Income Fund Class Y	NITYX	NAS CM	Open End	US Muni Fixed Inc (Muni Bond - Single State)	C+	C	B	Up	Y	800-437-1020
Aquila Tax-Free Fund For Utah Class A	UTAHX	NAS CM	Open End	US Muni Fixed Inc (Muni Bond - Single State)	C+	C	B	Up	Y	800-437-1020
Aquila Tax-Free Fund For Utah Class C	UTACX	NAS CM	Open End	US Muni Fixed Inc (Muni Bond - Single State)	C	C	B-		Y	800-437-1020
Aquila Tax-Free Fund For Utah Class F	UTAFX	NAS CM	Open End	US Muni Fixed Inc (Muni Bond - Single State)	C+	C	B	Up	Y	800-437-1020
Aquila Tax-Free Fund For Utah Class Y	UTAYX	NAS CM	Open End	US Muni Fixed Inc (Muni Bond - Single State)	C+	C	B	Up	Y	800-437-1020
Aquila Tax-Free Fund of Colorado Class A	COTFX	NAS CM	Open End	US Muni Fixed Inc (Muni Bond - Single State)	C+	C	B-	Up	Y	800-437-1020
Aquila Tax-Free Fund of Colorado Class C	COTCX	NAS CM	Open End	US Muni Fixed Inc (Muni Bond - Single State)	C	C	C+		Y	800-437-1020
Aquila Tax-Free Fund of Colorado Class Y	COTYX	NAS CM	Open End	US Muni Fixed Inc (Muni Bond - Single State)	C+	C	B-	Up	Y	800-437-1020
Aquila Tax-Free Trust of Arizona Class A	AZTFX	NAS CM	Open End	US Muni Fixed Inc (Muni Bond - Single State)	C	C	B-		Y	800-437-1020
Aquila Tax-Free Trust of Arizona Class C	AZTCX	NAS CM	Open End	US Muni Fixed Inc (Muni Bond - Single State)	C	C-	C+		Y	800-437-1020
Aquila Tax-Free Trust of Arizona Class Y	AZTYX	NAS CM	Open End	US Muni Fixed Inc (Muni Bond - Single State)	C	C	B		Y	800-437-1020

★Expanded analysis of this fund is included in Section II.

TOTAL RETURNS & PERFORMANCE									ASSETS		ASSET ALLOCATION & TURNOVER							MINIMUMS		FEES		
3-Month Total Return	6-Month Total Return	1-Year Total Return	3-Year Total Return	5-Year Total Return	Dividend Yield (TTM)	Expense Ratio	3-Yr Std Deviation	Effective Duration	NAV	Total Assets (MIL)	%Cash	%Government Bonds	%Municipal Bonds	%Corporate Bonds	%Other	Turnover Ratio	Average Coupon Rate	Min Initial Investment	Min Additional Investment	Front End Fee (%)	Back End Fee (%)	Inception Date
4.79	0.17	3.23	16.19	29.12	2.76	0.64	7.61	8.53	10.04	289.4	6	0	94	0	0	40	4.99	100,000	100			Dec-05
4.69	-0.01	2.86	14.84	26.43	2.31	0.99	7.64	8.53	10.31	289.4	6	0	94	0	0	40	4.99	2,000	100			Jul-09
4.80	0.19	3.38	16.40	29.37	2.81	0.59	7.65	8.53	10.04	289.4	6	0	94	0	0	40	4.99	5,000,000	1,000			Feb-17
6.94	1.48	3.33	11.16	18.80	3.48	0.72	5.45	5.02	10.69	494.8	1	20	0	35	0	47	3.64	100,000	100			Jul-11
6.87	1.26	2.97	10.20	17.19	3.22	0.97	5.5	5.02	10.69	494.8	1	20	0	35	0	47	3.64	2,000	100			Jul-11
6.95	1.52	3.41	11.48	19.15	3.56	0.64	5.44	5.02	10.7	494.8	1	20	0	35	0	47	3.64	5,000,000	1,000			Sep-17
7.06	4.23	5.58	10.80	19.62	0.3	0.89	5.16	7.10	22.42	8.8	-4	36	0	31	0	52	3.91	2,000	100			Mar-94
6.22	0.72	4.27	12.49	22.74	3.58	0.5	5.13	7.74	26.86	1,109	1	30	1	64	0	20	4.48	100,000	100			Apr-13
6.16	0.62	4.09	11.99	21.96	3.38	0.71	5.1	7.74	26.86	1,109	1	30	1	64	0	20	4.48	2,000	100			Jun-84
3.41	-4.81	-2.25	7.45		1.75	3.33	7.41	11.35	9.94	26.0	1	0	96	0	0	183	5.70	1,000	100			Sep-16
10.10	-6.05	-2.42	4.66	18.70	4.36	1.64	9.96	1.72	7.2	20.7	11	29	0	54	0	103	2.29	5,000	1,000			Jan-04
2.44	-2.85	-2.88	1.32	7.09	2.59	1.41	3.99		9.5	221.6	15	0	0	47	0	37	4.87	2,500	500	5.75		Jun-13
2.36	-3.10	-3.51	-0.84	3.37	1.82	2.16	4		9.51	221.6	15	0	0	47	0	37	4.87	2,500	500		1.00	Jun-13
2.51	-2.72	-2.63	2.07	8.50	2.85	1.16	3.96		9.51	221.6	15	0	0	47	0	37	4.87	100,000	1,000			Jun-13
-0.03	-6.14	-2.02			6.72	3.62			18.39	212.5	5	0	0	73	0	21	5.86					May-19
-0.85	-7.00	-4.47	4.82	5.76	4.48	1.11	5.02	3.58	8.67	152.7	0	0	0	88	0	36	5.67	1,000	100	2.25		Nov-14
-1.04	-7.30	-5.07	2.61	1.94	3.76	1.86	5.01	3.58	8.59	152.7	0	0	0	88	0	36	5.67	1,000	100		1.00	Aug-15
-0.79	-6.90	-4.14	5.69	7.09	4.75	0.86	5.02	3.58	8.66	152.7	0	0	0	88	0	36	5.67	1,000,000	100			Nov-14
11.53	-5.42	-1.93	7.98	24.25	5.77	0.91	9.82	3.87	10.9	68.5	7	0	0	88	0	36	6.44	1,000	100	2.25		Jul-12
11.54	-5.33	-1.71	8.80	25.74	6.05	0.66	9.82	3.87	10.85	68.5	7	0	0	88	0	36	6.44	1,000,000	100			Mar-09
7.23	-6.36	-4.62	2.65	9.13	4.87	1.37	8.52	2.07	10.11	5,895	10	0	0	7	0	63	3.19	1,000	100	2.25		Jun-11
7.00	-6.76	-5.36	0.32	5.12	4.13	2.12	8.53	2.07	10.01	5,895	10	0	0	7	0	63	3.19	1,000	100		1.00	Aug-15
7.20	-6.35	-4.49	3.30	10.44	5.15	1.12	8.57	2.07	10.08	5,895	10	0	0	7	0	63	3.19	1,000,000	100			Aug-12
13.01	-10.04	-7.18			8.48	1.01			21.19	--	18	0	0	9	-6	73	6.27	50,000				Dec-17
4.03	0.00	1.60			2.72	0.75		0.91	9.98	439.0	17	0	0	1	0	156	3.00	1,000	100	2.25		Apr-18
4.10	0.23	1.95			2.97	0.5		0.91	9.99	439.0	17	0	0	1	0	156	3.00	1,000,000	100			Apr-18
9.66	1.28	2.59			4.27	1.33			9.92	346.5	9	30	0	60	-1	78	5.02	500				Mar-19
9.66	1.28	2.60				1.48			9.92	346.5	9	30	0	60	-1	78	5.02	500				Sep-19
12.89	-10.07	-6.33	0.63	12.17	7.93	2.63	12.74		14.7388	225.1	7	0	0	92	0	101	5.32					Feb-11
13.16	-10.54	-6.86	3.92	16.61	8.3	2.94	13.27		14.5352	205.9	4	0	0	91	0	112	5.58					Feb-13
2.91	5.33	8.20			2.76	0.48			10.78	115.7	15	39	0	4	14	1,004	2.48	5,000,000				Apr-18
2.94	5.19	8.02			2.51	0.73			10.78	115.7	15	39	0	4	14	1,004	2.48	1,000,000				Apr-18
3.02	5.36	8.28			2.83	0.38			10.78	115.7	15	39	0	4	14	1,004	2.48	50,000,000				Apr-18
0.64	0.91	2.53	8.98	13.99	2.25	0.79	2.97	4.11	10.8	176.4	1	0	99	0	0	6	4.64	1,000		4.00		May-87
0.52	0.58	1.76	6.35	9.38	1.4	1.64	2.94	4.11	10.8	176.4	1	0	99	0	0	6	4.64	1,000			1.00	Apr-96
0.70	0.93	2.48	8.61	13.30	2.11	0.99	2.93	4.11	10.8	176.4	1	0	99	0	0	6	4.64	0				Aug-01
0.68	0.99	2.68	9.47	14.87	2.4	0.64	2.91	4.11	10.8	176.4	1	0	99	0	0	6	4.64	0				Apr-96
1.81	2.27	3.99	10.53	17.64	2.2	0.85	2.89	4.80	11.05	244.9	1	0	99	0	0	6	4.13	1,000		4.00		Sep-92
1.60	1.85	3.12	7.77	12.79	1.36	1.7	2.89	4.80	11.05	244.9	1	0	99	0	0	6	4.13	1,000			1.00	May-96
1.86	2.27	4.08	10.72	17.84	2.37	0.7		4.80	11.03	244.9	1	0	99	0	0	6	4.13	0				Nov-18
1.86	2.29	3.93	10.36	17.07	2.05	1.06	2.85	4.80	11.06	244.9	1	0	99	0	0	6	4.13	0				Nov-98
1.85	2.35	4.15	11.02	18.57	2.35	0.7	2.86	4.80	11.05	244.9	1	0	99	0	0	6	4.13	0				May-96
2.24	2.50	4.28	10.86	17.14	2.23	0.87	3.05	4.89	10.68	428.1	2	0	98	0	0	8	4.67	1,000		4.00		Jul-92
2.13	2.19	3.56	8.34	12.73	1.44	1.66	3.03	4.89	10.68	428.1	2	0	98	0	0	8	4.67	1,000			1.00	May-96
2.28	2.80	4.61	11.32	17.63	2.45	0.66		4.89	10.72	428.1	2	0	98	0	0	8	4.67	0				Nov-18
2.38	2.59	4.38	11.52	18.31	2.43	0.67	3.14	4.89	10.71	428.1	2	0	98	0	0	8	4.67	0				May-96
2.15	2.43	3.68	8.48	13.76	1.94	0.71	2.65	4.35	10.74	274.9	2	0	98	0	0	13	4.84	1,000		4.00		May-87
1.91	1.96	2.81	5.46	8.55	1.01	1.66	2.7	4.35	10.72	274.9	2	0	98	0	0	13	4.84	1,000			1.00	Apr-96
2.16	2.36	3.73	8.55	13.93	1.99	0.66	2.68	4.35	10.76	274.9	2	0	98	0	0	13	4.84	0				Apr-96
1.99	1.63	3.34	10.09	15.94	2.4	0.73	3.05	4.56	10.83	265.0	2	0	98	0	0	21	4.55	1,000		4.00		Mar-86
1.78	1.20	2.48	7.25	11.05	1.55	1.58	3.05	4.56	10.82	265.0	2	0	98	0	0	21	4.55	1,000			1.00	Apr-96
2.02	1.70	3.49	10.46	16.69	2.54	0.59	3.01	4.56	10.84	265.0	2	0	98	0	0	21	4.55	0				Apr-96

	MARKET			FUND TYPE, CATEGORY & OBJECTIVE	RATINGS				NEW INVESTORS	
Fund Name	Ticker Symbol	Traded On	Fund Type	Category and (Prospectus Objective)	Overall Rating	Reward Rating	Risk Rating	Recent Up/ Downgrade	Open to New Investors	Telephone
Aquila Tax-Free Trust of Oregon Class A	ORTFX	NAS CM	Open End	US Muni Fixed Inc (Muni Bond - Single State)	C+	C	B	Up	Y	800-437-1020
Aquila Tax-Free Trust of Oregon Class C	ORTCX	NAS CM	Open End	US Muni Fixed Inc (Muni Bond - Single State)	C	C	B-		Y	800-437-1020
Aquila Tax-Free Trust of Oregon Class F	ORFFX	NAS CM	Open End	US Muni Fixed Inc (Muni Bond - Single State)	C+	C	B	Up	Y	800-437-1020
Aquila Tax-Free Trust of Oregon Class Y	ORTYX	NAS CM	Open End	US Muni Fixed Inc (Muni Bond - Single State)	C+	C	B	Up	Y	800-437-1020
Aquila Three Peaks High Income Fund Class A	ATPAX	NAS CM	Open End	US Fixed Inc (Corp Bond - High Yield)	C	C-	C+		Y	800-437-1020
Aquila Three Peaks High Income Fund Class C	ATPCX	NAS CM	Open End	US Fixed Inc (Corp Bond - High Yield)	C	C-	C	Up	Y	800-437-1020
Aquila Three Peaks High Income Fund Class Institutional	ATIPX	NAS CM	Open End	US Fixed Inc (Corp Bond - High Yield)	C	C-	C+		Y	800-437-1020
Aquila Three Peaks High Income Fund Class Y	ATPYX	NAS CM	Open End	US Fixed Inc (Corp Bond - High Yield)	C	C-	C+		Y	800-437-1020
Archer Income Fund	ARINX	NAS CM	Open End	US Fixed Inc (Multisector Bond)	C	C-	C+		Y	
Ares Dynamic Credit Allocation Fund, Inc.	ARDC	NYSE	Closed End	US Fixed Inc (Growth & Income)	D	D	D	Down	Y	310-201-4100
Aristotle Strategic Credit Fund	ARSSX	NAS CM	Open End	US Fixed Inc (Growth & Income)	C	C-	B-		Y	
Arrow Dynamic Income Fund Class A	ASFFX	NAS CM	Open End	Fixed Inc Misc (Growth & Income)	D-	D-	D-	Down	Y	877-277-6933
Arrow Dynamic Income Fund Class C	ASFTX	NAS CM	Open End	Fixed Inc Misc (Growth & Income)	D-	D-	D-	Down	Y	877-277-6933
Arrow Dynamic Income Fund Institutional Class	ASFNX	NAS CM	Open End	Fixed Inc Misc (Growth & Income)	D-	D-	D-	Down	Y	877-277-6933
Artisan High Income Fund Advisor Shares	APDFX	NAS CM	Open End	US Fixed Inc (Corp Bond - High Yield)	C-	D+	C		Y	800-344-1770
Artisan High Income Fund Institutional Shares	APHFX	NAS CM	Open End	US Fixed Inc (Corp Bond - High Yield)	C-	D+	C		Y	800-344-1770
Artisan High Income Fund Investor Shares	ARTFX	NAS CM	Open End	US Fixed Inc (Corp Bond - High Yield)	C-	D+	C		Y	800-344-1770
Ascendant Tactical Yield Fund Class A	ATYAX	NAS CM	Open End	Fixed Inc Misc (Income)	D	D	D	Down	Y	
Ascendant Tactical Yield Fund Class I	ATYIX	NAS CM	Open End	Fixed Inc Misc (Income)	D	D	D	Down	Y	
Ashmore Emerging Markets Corporate Income Fund Class A	ECDAX	NAS CM	Open End	Emerg Mkts Fixed Inc (Income)	D	D	D+	Down	Y	866-876-8294
Ashmore Emerging Markets Corporate Income Fund Class C	ECDCX	NAS CM	Open End	Emerg Mkts Fixed Inc (Income)	D	D	D+	Down	Y	866-876-8294
Ashmore Emerg Mkts Corp Income Fund Institutional Class	EMCIX	NAS CM	Open End	Emerg Mkts Fixed Inc (Income)	D	D	D+	Down	Y	866-876-8294
Ashmore Emerging Markets Local Currency Bond Fund Class A	ELBAX	NAS CM	Open End	Emerg Mkts Fixed Inc (Income)	D	D	D+	Down	Y	866-876-8294
Ashmore Emerging Markets Local Currency Bond Fund Class C	ELBCX	NAS CM	Open End	Emerg Mkts Fixed Inc (Income)	D	D	D+	Down	Y	866-876-8294
Ashmore Emerg Mkts Local Currency Bond Fund Institutional	ELBIX	NAS CM	Open End	Emerg Mkts Fixed Inc (Income)	D	D	D+	Down	Y	866-876-8294
Ashmore Emerging Markets Short Duration Fund Class A	ESFAX	NAS CM	Open End	Emerg Mkts Fixed Inc (Income)	D-	D-	D	Down	Y	866-876-8294
Ashmore Emerging Markets Short Duration Fund Class C	ESFCX	NAS CM	Open End	Emerg Mkts Fixed Inc (Income)	D-	D-	D	Down	Y	866-876-8294
Ashmore Emerg Mkts Short Duration Fund Institutional Class	ESFIX	NAS CM	Open End	Emerg Mkts Fixed Inc (Income)	D-	D-	D	Down	Y	866-876-8294
Ashmore Emerging Markets Total Return Fund A Class	EMKAX	NAS CM	Open End	Emerg Mkts Fixed Inc (Income)	D	D	D	Down	Y	866-876-8294
Ashmore Emerging Markets Total Return Fund C Class	EMKCX	NAS CM	Open End	Emerg Mkts Fixed Inc (Income)	D	D	D	Down	Y	866-876-8294
Ashmore Emerg Mkts Total Return Fund Institutional Class	EMKIX	NAS CM	Open End	Emerg Mkts Fixed Inc (Income)	D	D	D	Down	Y	866-876-8294
Aspiriant Risk-Managed Municipal Bond Fund	RMMBX	NAS CM	Open End	US Muni Fixed Inc (Muni Bond - Natl)	C	C-	B-		Y	877-997-9971
Aspiriant Risk-Managed Taxable Bond Fund	RMTBX	NAS CM	Open End	US Fixed Inc (Growth & Income)	C	C-	B-	Up	Y	877-997-9971
AST Government Money Market Portfolio	US00767H5928		Money Mkt	US Money Mkt (Money Mkt - Govt)	U	U	U		Y	
Axonic Alternative Income Fund	AAIDX	NAS CM	Closed End	Fixed Inc Misc (Income)	D	D	D		Y	212-259-0430
Axonic Strategic Income Fund Class I Shares	AXSIX	NAS CM	Open End	US Fixed Inc (Income)	U	U	U		Y	
Azzad Wise Capital Fund	WISEX	NAS CM	Open End	US Fixed Inc (Growth & Income)	C	C-	C+		Y	
Baird Aggregate Bond Fund Class Institutional	BAGIX	NAS CM	Open End	US Fixed Inc (Income)	B	C+	B+	Up	Y	800-792-2473
Baird Aggregate Bond Fund Class Investor	BAGSX	NAS CM	Open End	US Fixed Inc (Income)	B	C+	B+	Up	Y	800-792-2473
Baird Core Intermediate Muni Bond Fund Institutional Class	BMNIX	NAS CM	Open End	US Muni Fixed Inc (Muni Bond - Natl)	C+	C	B	Up	Y	800-792-2473
Baird Core Intermediate Municipal Bond Fund Investor Class	BMNSX	NAS CM	Open End	US Muni Fixed Inc (Muni Bond - Natl)	C+	C	B	Up	Y	800-792-2473
Baird Core Plus Bond Fund Class Institutional	BCOIX	NAS CM	Open End	US Fixed Inc (Income)	B	C+	B+	Up	Y	800-792-2473
Baird Core Plus Bond Fund Class Investor	BCOSX	NAS CM	Open End	US Fixed Inc (Income)	B	C+	B+	Up	Y	800-792-2473
Baird Intermediate Bond Fund Class Institutional	BIMIX	NAS CM	Open End	US Fixed Inc (Income)	B	C+	B+	Up	Y	800-792-2473
Baird Intermediate Bond Fund Class Investor	BIMSX	NAS CM	Open End	US Fixed Inc (Income)	B-	C+	B+	Up	Y	800-792-2473
Baird Municipal Bond Fund Institutional	BMQIX	NAS CM	Open End	US Muni Fixed Inc (Muni Bond - Natl)	U	U	U		Y	800-792-2473
Baird Municipal Bond Fund Investor	BMQSX	NAS CM	Open End	US Muni Fixed Inc (Muni Bond - Natl)	U	U	U		Y	800-792-2473
Baird Quality Intermediate Muni Bond Cl Institutional	BMBIX	NAS CM	Open End	US Muni Fixed Inc (Muni Bond - Natl)	C+	C	B	Up	Y	800-792-2473
Baird Quality Intermediate Muni Bond Fund Class Investor	BMBSX	NAS CM	Open End	US Muni Fixed Inc (Muni Bond - Natl)	C+	C	B	Up	Y	800-792-2473
Baird Short-Term Bond Fund Institutional Class	BSBIX	NAS CM	Open End	US Fixed Inc (Income)	C+	C	B-	Up	Y	800-792-2473
Baird Short-Term Bond Fund Investor Class	BSBSX	NAS CM	Open End	US Fixed Inc (Income)	C	C	B-		Y	800-792-2473
Baird Short-Term Municipal Bond Fund Institutional Class	BTMIX	NAS CM	Open End	US Muni Fixed Inc (Muni Bond - Natl)	C	C	B-		Y	800-792-2473

★ Expanded analysis of this fund is included in Section II.

TOTAL RETURNS & PERFORMANCE									ASSETS		ASSET ALLOCATION & TURNOVER							MINIMUMS		FEES		
3-Month Total Return	6-Month Total Return	1-Year Total Return	3-Year Total Return	5-Year Total Return	Dividend Yield (TTM)	Expense Ratio	3-Yr Std Deviation	Effective Duration	NAV	Total Assets (MIL)	%Cash	%Government Bonds	%Municipal Bonds	%Corporate Bonds	%Other	Turnover Ratio	Average Coupon Rate	Min Initial Investment	Min Additional Investment	Front End Fee (%)	Back End Fee (%)	Inception Date
2.59	2.95	4.38	9.39	14.12	1.8	0.7	2.89	4.55	11.37	646.7	2	0	98	0	0	12	4.81	1,000		4.00		Jun-86
2.37	2.52	3.51	6.67	9.41	0.97	1.55	2.88	4.55	11.36	646.7	2	0	98	0	0	12	4.81	1,000			1.00	Apr-96
2.63	3.13	4.57	9.68	14.42	1.97	0.55		4.55	11.35	646.7	2	0	98	0	0	12	4.81	0				Nov-18
2.63	3.03	4.54	9.89	14.99	1.95	0.55	2.9	4.55	11.36	646.7	2	0	98	0	0	12	4.81	0				Apr-96
4.63	-0.09	1.86	7.26	18.41	3.65	1.21	3.66	3.66	8.23	167.4	9	0	0	91	0	124	5.63	1,000		4.00		Jun-06
4.43	-0.48	1.05	4.71	13.70	2.84	2	3.65	3.66	8.23	167.4	9	0	0	91	0	124	5.63	1,000			1.00	Jun-06
4.62	-0.12	1.79	7.14	17.89	3.57	1.31	3.67	3.66	8.23	167.4	9	0	0	91	0	124	5.63	0				Jun-06
4.56	-0.23	1.94	7.77	19.28	3.85	1.01	3.68	3.66	8.22	167.4	9	0	0	91	0	124	5.63	0				Jun-06
4.40	0.56	2.21	8.15	14.30	2.65	0.98	3.36		19.26	11.7	5	0	28	66	0	12	4.72	2,500	100			Mar-11
20.94	-12.47	-9.74	0.56	16.53	9.41	2.73	17.42		14.26	309.1	5	0	0	64	0	12	7.73					Nov-12
9.56	1.29	4.54	13.01	23.38	3.66	0.62	6.46		10.03	7.1	4	0	0	96	0	54	4.89	2,500	100			Dec-14
2.10	-22.65	-19.30	-21.38	-10.89	7.74	2.02	14.24		5.81	3.1	50	2	0	12	0	307	2.98	5,000	250	5.75		Oct-07
1.85	-22.91	-19.84	-23.09	-14.15	7.46	2.77	14.22		5.48	3.1	50	2	0	12	0	307	2.98	5,000	250			Oct-07
2.25	-22.39	-18.85	-20.60	-9.48	7.9	1.77	14.26		5.89	3.1	50	2	0	12	0	307	2.98	1,000,000				Mar-12
12.18	-3.28	1.17	12.21	31.72	6.77	0.84	9.79	2.59	9.16	4,093	19	0	0	82	0	75	7.12	250,000				Mar-14
12.21	-3.22	1.28	12.63	31.58	6.88	0.74	9.79	2.59	9.16	4,093	19	0	0	82	0	75	7.12	1,000,000				Oct-16
12.12	-3.32	1.12	11.80	30.75	6.6	0.99	9.78	2.59	9.17	4,093	19	0	0	82	0	75	7.12	1,000				Mar-14
0.44	-10.97	-10.05	-3.32	2.23	3.01	3.82	8.32	7.27	8.92	13.1	54	5	0	30	-1	145	4.96	1,000	100	5.75	1.00	May-15
0.33	-10.96	-9.97	-2.75	3.27	3.33	3.57	8.27	7.27	8.93	13.1	54	5	0	30	-1	145	4.96	1,000,000	25,000			May-15
16.29	-5.59	-3.14	6.21	24.25	6.68	1.42	13.42		7.3	298.5	3	6	0	90	-1	96	6.82	1,000	50	4.00		May-11
16.13	-5.91	-3.84	3.90	19.69	5.89	2.17	13.43		7.29	298.5	3	6	0	90	-1	96	6.82	1,000	50		1.00	May-11
16.36	-5.50	-2.91	7.12	25.93	6.94	1.17	13.4		7.61	298.5	3	6	0	90	-1	96	6.82	1,000,000	5,000			Dec-10
11.11	-8.57	-5.86	-0.71	9.09	1.62	1.22	13.76		6.8	37.0	13	46	0	3	0	56	6.95	1,000	50	4.00		May-11
10.92	-8.93	-6.42	-2.82	5.15	1.24	1.97	13.76		6.7	37.0	13	46	0	3	0	56	6.95	1,000	50		1.00	May-11
11.11	-8.44	-5.65	0.05	10.51	1.66	0.97	13.76		7.1	37.0	13	46	0	3	0	56	6.95	1,000,000	5,000			Dec-10
19.19	-17.50	-21.62	-12.46	13.49	9.77	0.92	18.26		7.23	564.1	9	27	0	65	-1	53	7.62	1,000	50	2.25		Sep-14
18.99	-17.78	-22.19	-16.00	7.35	8.96	1.67	18.16		6.95	564.1	9	27	0	65	-1	53	7.62	1,000	50		1.00	Jun-17
19.38	-17.30	-21.29	-11.80	14.98	10.14	0.67	18.24		7.11	564.1	9	27	0	65	-1	53	7.62	1,000,000	5,000			Jun-14
14.92	-10.28	-10.43	-2.81	13.91	5.89	1.27	14.28		6.69	1,327	7	50	0	9	0	49	6.79	1,000	50	4.00		May-11
14.82	-10.58	-11.07	-4.97	9.72	5.11	2.02	14.28		6.67	1,327	7	50	0	9	0	49	6.79	1,000	50		1.00	May-11
14.93	-10.15	-10.15	-2.12	15.26	6.15	1.02	14.26		6.79	1,327	7	50	0	9	0	49	6.79	1,000,000	5,000			Dec-10
2.12	0.68	3.09	12.22	19.97	3.54	0.45	4		10.25	1,525	2	0	98	0	13		4.76	0				Jul-15
4.14	3.71	5.75			3.32	0.69		4.16	10.48	299.9	2	25	0	15	0		3.35	0				Mar-18
0.01	0.01	0.01	0.01	0.02	0	0.57	0			989.3	76				2	0		0				Nov-92
-0.25	-17.63	-14.93			5.32	2.56			20.45	--						48		50,000				Dec-18
3.83	-5.20					1.1			9.48	335.6								25,000	1,000			Dec-19
4.09	0.42	2.21	6.90	9.41	1.68	1.29	2.68		10.65	145.3	34	23	0	40	0	39	3.68	4,000	300			Apr-10
4.78	6.35	9.34	17.76	26.34	2.59	0.3	3.69	5.69	11.78	25,882	3	22	1	38	0	31	3.47	25,000				Sep-00
4.72	6.27	9.01	16.84	24.70	2.26	0.55	3.68	5.69	12.2	25,882	3	22	1	38	0	31	3.47	2,500	100			Sep-00
2.26	2.32	4.53	12.76		2.3	0.3	3.15	4.50	10.78	555.1	1	0	99	0	0	38	4.29	25,000				Aug-15
2.30	2.31	4.38	11.95		2.07	0.55	3.14	4.50	10.78	555.1	1	0	99	0	0	38	4.29	2,500	100			Aug-15
5.75	5.79	8.92	17.76	27.38	2.79	0.3	3.98	5.56	12.07	26,008	2	17	1	47	0	26	3.65	25,000				Sep-00
5.70	5.68	8.62	16.78	25.66	2.43	0.55	3.99	5.56	12.59	26,008	2	17	1	47	0	26	3.65	2,500	100			Sep-00
4.40	5.55	7.50	14.45	20.39	2.42	0.3	2.78	3.93	11.76	4,546	3	41	1	43	0	26	3.08	25,000				Sep-00
4.39	5.43	7.33	13.67	18.93	2.06	0.55	2.76	3.93	12.32	4,546	3	41	1	43	0	26	3.08	2,500	100			Sep-00
3.25	4.98					0.3		5.62	10.5	12.7	3	0	97	0	0		4.19	25,000				Nov-19
3.20	4.87					0.55		5.62	10.5	12.7	3	0	97	0	0		4.19	2,500	100			Nov-19
2.40	2.75	4.38	10.17	15.32	2.18	0.3	2.82	4.19	11.95	1,359	3	0	97	0	0	20	4.78	25,000				Mar-01
2.36	2.64	4.18	9.36	13.88	1.88	0.55	2.83	4.19	12.25	1,359	3	0	97	0	0	20	4.78	2,500	100			Mar-01
3.42	2.92	4.46	9.80	13.65	2.37	0.3	1.84	1.87	9.95	7,437	4	27	1	54	0	64	2.96	25,000				Aug-04
3.36	2.80	4.31	8.99	12.26	2.12	0.55	1.8	1.87	9.95	7,437	4	27	1	54	0	64	2.96	2,500	100			Sep-12
2.00	1.61	2.94	8.27		1.77	0.3	1.84	2.50	10.34	1,100	3	0	97	0	0	34	3.79	25,000				Aug-15

	MARKET		FUND TYPE, CATEGORY & OBJECTIVE		RATINGS				NEW INVESTORS	
Fund Name	Ticker Symbol	Traded On	Fund Type	Category and (Prospectus Objective)	Overall Rating	Reward Rating	Risk Rating	Recent Up/ Downgrade	Open to New Investors	Telephone
Baird Short-Term Municipal Bond Fund Investor Class	BTMSX	NAS CM	Open End	US Muni Fixed Inc (Muni Bond - Natl)	C	C	B-		Y	800-792-2473
Baird Strategic Municipal Bond Fund Institutional	BSNIX	NAS CM	Open End	US Muni Fixed Inc (Muni Bond - Natl)	U	U	U		Y	800-792-2473
Baird Strategic Municipal Bond Fund Investor	BSNSX	NAS CM	Open End	US Muni Fixed Inc (Muni Bond - Natl)	U	U	U		Y	800-792-2473
Baird Ultra Short Bond Fund Institutional Class	BUBIX	NAS CM	Open End	US Fixed Inc (Income)	C	C-	B-		Y	800-792-2473
Baird Ultra Short Bond Fund Investor Class	BUBSX	NAS CM	Open End	US Fixed Inc (Income)	C	C	B-		Y	800-792-2473
Barings Active Short Duration Bond Fund Class A	BXDAX	NAS CM	Open End	US Fixed Inc (Income)	D+	D	C-	Down	Y	
Barings Active Short Duration Bond Fund Class C	BXDCX	NAS CM	Open End	US Fixed Inc (Income)	D	D	C-	Down	Y	
Barings Active Short Duration Bond Fund Class I	BXDIX	NAS CM	Open End	US Fixed Inc (Income)	D+	D	C	Down	Y	
Barings Active Short Duration Bond Fund Class L	BXDLX	NAS CM	Open End	US Fixed Inc (Income)	D+	D	C-		Y	
Barings Active Short Duration Bond Fund Class Y	BXDYX	NAS CM	Open End	US Fixed Inc (Income)	D+	D	C-	Down	Y	
Barings Corporate Investors	MCI	NYSE	Closed End	US Fixed Inc (Corp Bond - High Yield)	C-	C-	C-	Down	Y	
Barings Diversified Income Fund Class A	BXTAX	NAS CM	Open End	US Fixed Inc (Income)	D	D	D	Down	Y	
Barings Diversified Income Fund Class C	BXTCX	NAS CM	Open End	US Fixed Inc (Income)	D	D	D	Down	Y	
Barings Diversified Income Fund Class I	BXTIX	NAS CM	Open End	US Fixed Inc (Income)	D	D	D	Down	Y	
Barings Diversified Income Fund Class Y	BXTYX	NAS CM	Open End	US Fixed Inc (Income)	D	D	D	Down	Y	
Barings Emerg Mkts Debt Blended Total Return Fund Class A	BXEAX	NAS CM	Open End	Emerg Mkts Fixed Inc (Growth & Income)	C	C-	C		Y	
Barings Emerg Mkts Debt Blended Total Return Fund Class C	BXECX	NAS CM	Open End	Emerg Mkts Fixed Inc (Growth & Income)	C	C-	C		Y	
Barings Emerg Mkts Debt Blended Total Return Fund Class I	BXEIX	NAS CM	Open End	Emerg Mkts Fixed Inc (Growth & Income)	C	C-	C		Y	
Barings Emerg Mkts Debt Blended Total Return Fund Class Y	BXEYX	NAS CM	Open End	Emerg Mkts Fixed Inc (Growth & Income)	C	C-	C		Y	
Barings Global Credit Income Opportunities Fund Class A	BXIAX	NAS CM	Open End	Global Fixed Inc (Growth & Income)	D	D	D+	Down	Y	
Barings Global Credit Income Opportunities Fund Class C	BXICX	NAS CM	Open End	Global Fixed Inc (Growth & Income)	D	D	D+	Down	Y	
Barings Global Credit Income Opportunities Fund Class I	BXITX	NAS CM	Open End	Global Fixed Inc (Growth & Income)	D	D	D+	Down	Y	
Barings Global Credit Income Opportunities Fund Class Y	BXIYX	NAS CM	Open End	Global Fixed Inc (Growth & Income)	D	D	D+	Down	Y	
Barings Global Floating Rate Fund Class A	BXFAX	NAS CM	Open End	US Fixed Inc (Income)	D	D	C-	Down	Y	
Barings Global Floating Rate Fund Class C	BXFCX	NAS CM	Open End	US Fixed Inc (Income)	D	D	D+	Down	Y	
Barings Global Floating Rate Fund Class I	BXFIX	NAS CM	Open End	US Fixed Inc (Income)	D+	D	C-	Down	Y	
Barings Global Floating Rate Fund Class Y	BXFYX	NAS CM	Open End	US Fixed Inc (Income)	D+	D	C-	Down	Y	
Barings Global Short Duration High Yield Fund	BGH	NYSE	Closed End	Global Fixed Inc (Income)	D	D-	D		Y	
Barings U.S. High Yield Fund Class A	BXHAX	NAS CM	Open End	US Fixed Inc (Corp Bond - High Yield)	D+	D	C-	Down	Y	
Barings U.S. High Yield Fund Class C	BXHCX	NAS CM	Open End	US Fixed Inc (Corp Bond - High Yield)	D	D	D+	Down	Y	
Barings U.S. High Yield Fund Class I	BXHIX	NAS CM	Open End	US Fixed Inc (Corp Bond - High Yield)	D+	D	C-	Down	Y	
Barings U.S. High Yield Fund Class Y	BXHYX	NAS CM	Open End	US Fixed Inc (Corp Bond - High Yield)	D+	D	C-	Down	Y	
BBH Income Fund Class I Shares	BBNIX	NAS CM	Open End	US Fixed Inc (Growth & Income)	C-	D+	B	Up	Y	800-575-1265
BBH Intermediate Municipal Bond Fund Class I	BBIIX	NAS CM	Open End	US Muni Fixed Inc (Muni Bond - Natl)	C+	C	B	Up	Y	800-575-1265
BBH Intermediate Municipal Bond Fund Class N	BBINX	NAS CM	Open End	US Muni Fixed Inc (Muni Bond - Natl)	C+	C	B	Up	Y	800-575-1265
BBH Limited Duration Fund Class Institutional	BBBIX	NAS CM	Open End	US Fixed Inc (Corp Bond - General)	C	C-	C+		Y	800-575-1265
BBH Limited Duration Fund Class N	BBBMX	NAS CM	Open End	US Fixed Inc (Corp Bond - General)	C	C-	C+		Y	800-575-1265
BBH U.S. Government Money Market Fund Institutional Shares	BBSXX	NAS CM	Money Mkt	US Money Mkt (Money Mkt - Govt)	C	C-	C+		Y	800-575-1265
BBH U.S. Government Money Market Fund Regular Shares	BBMXX	NAS CM	Money Mkt	US Money Mkt (Money Mkt - Govt)	C	C-	C+		Y	800-575-1265
Bernstein Intermediate Duration Institutional Portfolio	SIIDX	NAS CM	Open End	US Fixed Inc (Corp Bond - High Quality)	B-	C+	B+	Up	Y	212-969-1000
Bernstein Short Duration Diversified Municipal Portfolio	SDDMX	NAS CM	Open End	US Muni Fixed Inc (Muni Bond - Natl)	C	C-	C+		Y	212-969-1000
BIF Treasury Fund	CMTXX	NAS CM	Money Mkt	US Money Mkt (Money Mkt - Treasury)	U	U	U		Y	800-441-7762
Bishop Street Hawaii Municipal Bond Fund Class A	BHIAX	NAS CM	Open End	US Muni Fixed Inc (Muni Bond - Single State)	C	C	B-		Y	
Bishop Street Hawaii Muni Bond Fund Class Institutional	BSHIX	NAS CM	Open End	US Muni Fixed Inc (Muni Bond - Single State)	C	C	B-		Y	
Bishop Street High Grade Income Fund Class Institutional	BSHGX	NAS CM	Open End	US Fixed Inc (Growth & Income)	B	B-	B	Up	Y	
BlackRock 2022 Global Income Opportunity Trust	BGIO	NYSE	Closed End	Global Fixed Inc (World Stock)	D	D	D+	Down	Y	800-441-7762
BlackRock Allocation Target Shares Series A Portfolio	BATAX	NAS CM	Open End	US Fixed Inc (Income)	C-	D+	C	Down	Y	800-441-7762
BlackRock Allocation Target Shares Series C Portfolio	BRACX	NAS CM	Open End	US Fixed Inc (Multisector Bond)	B-	C+	B+	Up	Y	800-441-7762
BlackRock Allocation Target Shares Series E Portfolio	BATEX	NAS CM	Open End	US Muni Fixed Inc (Multisector Bond)	C-	D+	C	Down	Y	800-441-7762
BlackRock Allocation Target Shares Series M Portfolio	BRAMX	NAS CM	Open End	US Fixed Inc (Multisector Bond)	B-	C+	B+	Up	Y	800-441-7762
BlackRock Allocation Target Shares Series P Portfolio	BATPX	NAS CM	Open End	Fixed Inc Misc (Multisector Bond)	D	D	D		Y	800-441-7762
BlackRock Allocation Target Shares Series S Portfolio	BRASX	NAS CM	Open End	US Fixed Inc (Multisector Bond)	C	C	B-		Y	800-441-7762

★ Expanded analysis of this fund is included in Section II.

TOTAL RETURNS & PERFORMANCE									ASSETS		ASSET ALLOCATION & TURNOVER							MINIMUMS		FEES		
3-Month Total Return	6-Month Total Return	1-Year Total Return	3-Year Total Return	5-Year Total Return	Dividend Yield (TTM)	Expense Ratio	3-Yr Std Deviation	Effective Duration	NAV	Total Assets (MIL)	%Cash	%Government Bonds	%Municipal Bonds	%Corporate Bonds	%Other	Turnover Ratio	Average Coupon Rate	Min Initial Investment	Min Additional Investment	Front End Fee (%)	Back End Fee (%)	Inception Date
1.94	1.49	2.69	7.51		1.52	0.55	1.8	2.50	10.33	1,100	3	0	97	0	0	34	3.79	2,500	100			Aug-15
3.67	4.80					0.3		4.54	10.46	33.8	1	0	97	2	0		3.97	25,000				Nov-19
3.53	4.61					0.55		4.54	10.45	33.8	1	0	97	2	0		3.97	2,500	100			Nov-19
1.69	1.18	2.50	7.07	9.27	2.26	0.15	0.84	0.48	10.09	2,327	13	22	1	39	0	70	2.75	25,000				Dec-13
1.97	1.40	2.50	6.54	8.22	1.96	0.4	0.96	0.48	10.12	2,327	13	22	1	39	0	70	2.75	2,500	100			Dec-13
4.90	-3.19	-1.73	2.83	6.62	2.99	0.65	4.79	0.25		771.2	6	1	0	39	0	43	3.57	1,000	250			Jul-15
4.82	-3.33	-2.01	1.99	5.33	2.72	0.9	4.79	0.25		771.2	6	1	0	39	0	43	3.57	1,000	250		0.50	Jul-15
4.94	-3.10	-1.50	3.62	7.93	3.25	0.4	4.79	0.25		771.2	6	1	0	39	0	43	3.57	500,000	250			Jul-15
5.16	-2.96	-1.48	3.10	6.47		0.65	4.79	0.25		771.2	6	1	0	39	0	43	3.57	0		2.00		Apr-20
4.90	-3.14	-1.54	3.55	7.82	3.21	0.4	4.79	0.25		771.2	6	1	0	39	0	43	3.57	100,000	250			Jul-15
0.00	-5.64	-0.16	17.35	37.87	8.06		6.61		14.14	396.7	15	0	0	84	0	21	9.10					Sep-71
9.54	-10.20	-8.11	-4.76	1.30	3.65	0.8	10.7	0.53		41.0	12	0	0	38	0	193	3.96	1,000	250	4.00		Jul-15
9.34	-10.54	-8.79	-6.88	-2.31	2.82	1.55	10.7	0.53		41.0	12	0	0	38	0	193	3.96	1,000	250		1.00	Jul-15
9.60	-10.09	-7.87	-4.06	2.52	3.92	0.55	10.7	0.53		41.0	12	0	0	38	0	193	3.96	500,000	250			Jul-15
9.60	-10.10	-7.88	-4.06	2.52	3.92	0.55	10.7	0.53		41.0	12	0	0	38	0	193	3.96	100,000	250			Jul-15
24.50	4.43	9.76	20.84		6.1	1.2	14.31	5.85		58.3	17	56	0	28	0	90	7.82	1,000	250	4.00		Oct-15
24.28	4.00	8.94	18.24		5.41	1.95	14.31	5.85		58.3	17	56	0	28	0	90	7.82	1,000	250		1.00	Oct-15
24.60	4.58	10.04	21.78		6.32	0.95	14.32	5.85		58.3	17	56	0	28	0	90	7.82	500,000	250			Oct-15
24.57	4.52	9.97	21.71		6.33	0.95	14.31	5.85		58.3	17	56	0	28	0	90	7.82	100,000	250			Oct-15
14.09	-6.92	-3.82	1.78	15.53	5.9	1.2	11.54	1.83	8.1435	160.8	5	0	0	87	0	59	5.58	1,000	250	4.00		Sep-13
13.88	-7.27	-4.53	-0.49	11.26	5.08	1.95	11.53	1.83	8.1334	160.8	5	0	0	87	0	59	5.58	1,000	250		1.00	Sep-13
14.16	-6.81	-3.58	2.52	16.94	6.17	0.95	11.54	1.83	8.1417	160.8	5	0	0	87	0	59	5.58	500,000	250			Sep-13
14.16	-6.80	-3.57	2.54	16.96	6.17	0.95	11.54	1.83	8.141	160.8	5	0	0	87	0	59	5.58	100,000	250			Sep-13
11.53	-5.68	-2.85	3.87	13.53	5	1	9.76	0.29	8.5607	211.7	6	0	0	94	0	47	4.46	1,000	250	3.00		Sep-13
11.33	-6.03	-3.57	1.58	9.50	4.2	1.75	9.76	0.29	8.5288	211.7	6	0	0	94	0	47	4.46	1,000	250		1.00	Sep-13
11.60	-5.56	-2.53	4.78	15.25	5.28	0.75	9.77	0.29	8.5839	211.7	6	0	0	94	0	47	4.46	500,000	250			Sep-13
11.60	-5.56	-2.60	4.68	15.11	5.27	0.75	9.77	0.29	8.5743	211.7	6	0	0	94	0	47	4.46	100,000	250			Sep-13
16.33	-19.24	-16.63	-12.95	2.52	12.23	1.98	18.8		14.06	270.3	2	0	0	67	0	52	8.61					Oct-12
7.96	-7.20	-3.69	3.26		6.06	1	8.78	4.60		46.0	2	0	0	98	0	56	6.11	1,000	250	4.00		Oct-15
7.29	-7.53	-4.66	0.98		5.26	1.75	8.78	4.60	8.91	46.0	2	0	0	98	0	56	6.11	1,000	250		1.00	Oct-15
8.02	-7.07	-3.46	4.05		6.33	0.75	8.78	4.60		46.0	2	0	0	98	0	56	6.11	500,000	250			Oct-15
8.02	-7.07	-3.45	4.06		6.33	0.75	8.78	4.60		46.0	2	0	0	98	0	56	6.11	100,000	250			Oct-15
6.33	5.13	7.76			3.1	0.5		5.70	10.63	441.1	2	23	0	53	0	77	3.50	25,000	5,000			Jun-18
2.61	2.43	4.45	13.75	23.18	1.96	0.5	3.16	4.50	10.88	591.4	0	0	100	0	0	104	3.51	50,000	5,000			Apr-14
2.55	2.33	4.37	13.21	22.23	1.8	0.65	3.15	4.50	10.89	591.4	0	0	100	0	0	104	3.51	5,000	500			Apr-14
4.00	0.59	2.15	8.41	12.51	2.84	0.28	2.76	0.86	10.18	6,797	15	0	2	44	0	53	3.27	50,000	5,000			Jul-00
3.98	0.56	1.98	8.06	11.81	2.77	0.35	2.76	0.86	10.18	6,797	15	0	2	44	0	53	3.27	5,000	1,000			Jul-00
0.04	0.34	1.21	4.37	4.62	1.38	0.24	0.17		1	3,199	93	7	0	0	0			5,000,000				Jan-07
0.01	0.25	1.01	3.63	3.73	1.16	0.47	0.16		1	3,199	93	7	0	0	0			100,000				Dec-83
5.32	5.19	7.75	15.36	24.36	2.92	0.45	3.92	6.60	15.92	837.8	-47	48	0	19	0	70	2.95	3,000,000				May-02
1.87	1.14	1.96	4.58	5.85	1.27	0.5	1.41	2.13	12.72	210.7	10	0	90	0	0	57	4.43	25,000				Oct-94
0.36	0.70	1.16	1.43	1.44	1.16	0.59	0.16			1.4	95	5	0	0	0			5,000	1,000			Apr-91
1.87	1.74	3.39	8.47	13.60	1.83	0.8	3.08		10.84	124.5	1	0	99	0	0	36	4.76	1,000		3.00		Jun-99
1.93	1.96	3.65	9.41	15.17	2.1	0.55	3.12		10.84	124.5	1	0	99	0	0	36	4.76	1,000,000				Feb-95
3.60	6.24	8.84	15.69	21.44	2.06	0.76	3.95		10.41	34.2	5	35	5	50	0	16	3.65	1,000,000				Jan-97
13.84	-9.82	-6.07	4.76		7.19	1.59	13.53		8.54	184.4	-24	6	0	61	0	41	5.41					Feb-17
8.54	-1.22	0.58	11.37		4.52	0.01	7.07	2.02	9.73	1,084	7	0	0	7	0	48	3.25	0				Sep-15
8.83	6.50	10.94	21.87	33.98	3.37	0	5.83	7.36	11.33	509.6	2	4	2	93	0	83	3.88	0				Sep-04
4.47	-1.82	1.69	15.95	34.12	4.12	0.09	7.72	9.50	10.89	301.9	3	0	95	4	0	54	4.97	0				Aug-14
2.37	3.72	6.00	13.51	19.37	3.27	0	2.26	1.42	9.96	1,017	1	0	0	0	0	1,316	3.56	0				Sep-04
0.25	-10.07	-10.11	-12.08	-15.36	1.47	0.16	6.12	-7.95	7.94	34.1	77	2	0	14	0	15	2.99	0				Mar-13
5.48	1.82	3.92	10.66	16.13	3.27	0.57	3.81	2.83	9.66	189.6	-31	0	0	44	0	144	3.11	0				Sep-04

	MARKET		FUND TYPE, CATEGORY & OBJECTIVE		RATINGS				NEW INVESTORS	
Fund Name	Ticker Symbol	Traded On	Fund Type	Category and (Prospectus Objective)	Overall Rating	Reward Rating	Risk Rating	Recent Up/ Downgrade	Open to New Investors	Telephone
BlackRock California Municipal Income Trust	BFZ	NYSE	Closed End	US Muni Fixed Inc (Muni Bond - Single State)	C-	C-	C-		Y	800-441-7762
BlackRock California Municipal Opportunities Fund Class K	MKCMX	NAS CM	Open End	US Muni Fixed Inc (Muni Bond - Single State)	C-	D+	C	Down	Y	800-441-7762
BlackRock California Muni Opportunities Inst shares	MACMX	NAS CM	Open End	US Muni Fixed Inc (Muni Bond - Single State)	C-	D+	C	Down	Y	800-441-7762
BlackRock California Muni Opportunities Investor A Shares	MECMX	NAS CM	Open End	US Muni Fixed Inc (Muni Bond - Single State)	C-	D+	C	Down	Y	800-441-7762
BlackRock California Muni Opportunities Investor A1 Shares	MDCMX	NAS CM	Open End	US Muni Fixed Inc (Muni Bond - Single State)	C-	D+	C	Down		800-441-7762
BlackRock California Muni Opportunities Investor C Shares	MFCMX	NAS CM	Open End	US Muni Fixed Inc (Muni Bond - Single State)	D+	D	C	Down	Y	800-441-7762
BlackRock Cash Funds Institutional SL Agency Shares	BISXX	NAS CM	Money Mkt	US Money Mkt (Money Mkt - Taxable)	C	C	B-		Y	800-441-7762
BlackRock Cash Funds Treasury Institutional Shares	BRIXX	NAS CM	Money Mkt	US Money Mkt (Money Mkt - Treasury)	C	C-	C+		Y	800-441-7762
BlackRock Cash Funds Treasury SL Agency Shares	XTSLA	NAS CM	Money Mkt	US Money Mkt (Money Mkt - Treasury)	C	C-	C+		Y	800-441-7762
BlackRock Core Bond Portfolio Class K	CCBBX	NAS CM	Open End	US Fixed Inc (Income)	B-	C+	B	Up	Y	800-441-7762
BlackRock Core Bond Portfolio Class R Shares	BCBRX	NAS CM	Open End	US Fixed Inc (Income)	B-	C+	B	Up	Y	800-441-7762
BlackRock Core Bond Portfolio Institutional Shares	BFMCX	NAS CM	Open End	US Fixed Inc (Income)	B-	C+	B	Up	Y	800-441-7762
BlackRock Core Bond Portfolio Investor A Shares	BCBAX	NAS CM	Open End	US Fixed Inc (Income)	B-	C+	B	Up	Y	800-441-7762
BlackRock Core Bond Portfolio Investor C Shares	BCBCX	NAS CM	Open End	US Fixed Inc (Income)	B-	C+	B	Up	Y	800-441-7762
BlackRock Core Bond Portfolio Service Shares	CMCBX	NAS CM	Open End	US Fixed Inc (Income)	B-	C+	B	Up	Y	800-441-7762
BlackRock Core Bond Trust	BHK	NYSE	Closed End	US Fixed Inc (Corp Bond - General)	C	C	C+		Y	800-441-7762
BlackRock CoreAlpha Bond Fund Class K	BCRKX	NAS CM	Open End	US Fixed Inc (Govt Bond - General)	B	C+	B+	Up	Y	800-441-7762
BlackRock CoreAlpha Bond Fund Institutional Shares	BCRIX	NAS CM	Open End	US Fixed Inc (Govt Bond - General)	B	C+	B+	Up	Y	800-441-7762
BlackRock CoreAlpha Bond Fund Investor A Shares	BCRAX	NAS CM	Open End	US Fixed Inc (Govt Bond - General)	B	C+	B+	Up	Y	800-441-7762
BlackRock CoreAlpha Bond Fund Investor C Shares	BCRCX	NAS CM	Open End	US Fixed Inc (Govt Bond - General)	B-	C+	B	Up	Y	800-441-7762
BlackRock Corporate High Yield Fund, Inc	HYT	NYSE	Closed End	US Fixed Inc (Corp Bond - High Yield)	D+	D+	C-	Down	Y	800-441-7762
BlackRock Credit Allocation Income Trust	BTZ	NYSE	Closed End	US Fixed Inc (Growth & Income)	C	C-	C+		Y	800-441-7762
BlackRock Credit Strategies Fund Class A			Closed End	US Fixed Inc (Income)	U	U	U		Y	800-441-7762
BlackRock Credit Strategies Fund Institutional Shares			Closed End	US Fixed Inc (Income)	D	D	C-		Y	800-441-7762
BlackRock Debt Strategies Fund Inc	DSU	NYSE	Closed End	US Fixed Inc (Corp Bond - General)	D	D	D+	Down	Y	800-441-7762
BlackRock Emerging Markets Bond Fund Class K Shares	BEHKX	NAS CM	Open End	Emerg Mkts Fixed Inc (Growth & Income)	D+	D	C-	Down	Y	800-441-7762
BlackRock Emerging Markets Bond Fund Institutional Shares	BEHIX	NAS CM	Open End	Emerg Mkts Fixed Inc (Growth & Income)	D+	D	C-	Down	Y	800-441-7762
BlackRock Emerg Mkts Flexible Dynamic Bond Portfolio Cl K	BREDX	NAS CM	Open End	Emerg Mkts Fixed Inc (Growth & Income)	C	C-	C	Up	Y	800-441-7762
BlackRock Emerg Mkts Flex Dynamic Bond Port Inst Shares	BEDIX	NAS CM	Open End	Emerg Mkts Fixed Inc (Growth & Income)	C	C-	C	Up	Y	800-441-7762
BlackRock Emerg Mkts Flex Dynamic Bond Port Inv A Shares	BAEDX	NAS CM	Open End	Emerg Mkts Fixed Inc (Growth & Income)	C-	D+	C	Up	Y	800-441-7762
BlackRock Emerg Mkts Flex Dynamic Bond Port Inv C Shares	BCEDX	NAS CM	Open End	Emerg Mkts Fixed Inc (Growth & Income)	C-	D+	C	Up	Y	800-441-7762
BlackRock Enhanced Government Fund Inc.	EGF	NYSE	Closed End	US Fixed Inc (Govt Bond - General)	C-	C	D+	Down	Y	800-441-7762
BlackRock Financial Inst Ser Trust Summit Cash Res Inst	MSIXX	NAS CM	Money Mkt	US Money Mkt (Money Mkt - Govt)	C	C-	C+		Y	800-441-7762
BlackRock Fin Inst Ser Trust Summit Cash Res Inv A Shares	MSAXX	NAS CM	Money Mkt	US Money Mkt (Money Mkt - Govt)	C	C-	C+		Y	800-441-7762
BlackRock Fin Inst Ser Trust Summit Cash Res Inv C Shares	MCBXX	NAS CM	Money Mkt	US Money Mkt (Money Mkt - Govt)	C	C-	C		Y	800-441-7762
BlackRock Floating Rate Income Fund Class K	BFRKX	NAS CM	Open End	US Fixed Inc (Income)	D+	D	C	Down	Y	800-441-7762
BlackRock Floating Rate Income Fund Institutional shares	BFRIX	NAS CM	Open End	US Fixed Inc (Income)	D+	D	C	Down	Y	800-441-7762
BlackRock Floating Rate Income Fund Investor C shares	BFRCX	NAS CM	Open End	US Fixed Inc (Income)	D+	D	C-	Down	Y	800-441-7762
BlackRock Floating Rate Income Portfolio Investor A Shares	BFRAX	NAS CM	Open End	US Fixed Inc (Income)	D+	D	C-	Down	Y	800-441-7762
BlackRock Floating Rate Income Strategies Fund Inc	FRA	NYSE	Closed End	US Fixed Inc (Corp Bond - General)	D	D	D+	Down	Y	800-441-7762
BlackRock Floating Rate Income Trust Fund	BGT	NYSE	Closed End	US Fixed Inc (Corp Bond - High Yield)	D	D	D+	Down	Y	800-441-7762
BlackRock Florida Municipal 2020 Term Trust	BFO	NYSE	Closed End	US Muni Fixed Inc (Muni Bond - Single State)	C-	C	D+		Y	800-441-7762
BlackRock Funds For Institutions Series Treasury Fund	MLTXX	NAS CM	Money Mkt	US Money Mkt (Money Mkt - Govt)	C	C-	C+			800-441-7762
BlackRock GNMA Portfolio Class K	BBGPX	NAS CM	Open End	US Fixed Inc (Govt Bond - Mortgage)	B-	C+	B-	Up	Y	800-441-7762
BlackRock GNMA Portfolio Institutional Shares	BGNIX	NAS CM	Open End	US Fixed Inc (Govt Bond - Mortgage)	B-	C+	B	Up	Y	800-441-7762
BlackRock GNMA Portfolio Investor A Shares	BGPAX	NAS CM	Open End	US Fixed Inc (Govt Bond - Mortgage)	B-	C+	B	Up	Y	800-441-7762
BlackRock GNMA Portfolio Investor C Shares	BGPCX	NAS CM	Open End	US Fixed Inc (Govt Bond - Mortgage)	C+	C	B-	Up	Y	800-441-7762
BlackRock GNMA Portfolio Service Shares	BGPSX	NAS CM	Open End	US Fixed Inc (Govt Bond - Mortgage)	B-	C+	B	Up	Y	800-441-7762
BlackRock High Yield Bond Portfolio Class K	BRHYX	NAS CM	Open End	US Fixed Inc (Corp Bond - High Yield)	C-	D+	C		Y	800-441-7762
BlackRock High Yield Bond Portfolio Class R Shares	BHYRX	NAS CM	Open End	US Fixed Inc (Corp Bond - High Yield)	C-	D+	C		Y	800-441-7762
BlackRock High Yield Bond Portfolio Institutional Shares	BHYIX	NAS CM	Open End	US Fixed Inc (Corp Bond - High Yield)	C-	D+	C		Y	800-441-7762
BlackRock High Yield Bond Portfolio Investor A Shares	BHYAX	NAS CM	Open End	US Fixed Inc (Corp Bond - High Yield)	C-	D+	C		Y	800-441-7762

★ Expanded analysis of this fund is included in Section II.

TOTAL RETURNS & PERFORMANCE									ASSETS		ASSET ALLOCATION & TURNOVER							MINIMUMS		FEES		
3-Month Total Return	6-Month Total Return	1-Year Total Return	3-Year Total Return	5-Year Total Return	Dividend Yield (TTM)	Expense Ratio	3-Yr Std Deviation	Effective Duration	NAV	Total Assets (MIL)	%Cash	%Government Bonds	%Municipal Bonds	%Corporate Bonds	%Other	Turnover Ratio	Average Coupon Rate	Min Initial Investment	Min Additional Investment	Front End Fee (%)	Back End Fee (%)	Inception Date
5.20	1.65	5.20	14.16	23.20	3.18	0	7.71		15.4	481.7	-36	0	99	0	0	51	5.17					Jul-01
2.89	-2.77	-0.94	8.27	17.36	2.28	0.58	5.16	7.16	12.34	3,287	11	0	89	0	0	126	4.85	5,000,000				Jan-18
2.88	-2.80	-0.91	8.14	17.22	2.22	0.63	5.15	7.16	12.34	3,287	11	0	89	0	0	126	4.85	2,000,000				Oct-88
2.82	-2.92	-1.16	7.33	15.80	1.96	0.88	5.14	7.16	12.33	3,287	11	0	89	0	0	126	4.85	1,000	50	4.25		Oct-06
2.86	-2.84	-0.99	7.84	16.67	2.14	0.73	5.14	7.16	12.34	3,287	11	0	89	0	0	126	4.85	1,000	50	4.00		Oct-94
2.63	-3.28	-1.90	4.94	11.53	1.18	1.63	5.15	7.16	12.34	3,287	11	0	89	0	0	126	4.85	1,000	50		1.00	Oct-06
0.35	0.71	1.78	6.00	7.35	1.85	0.09	0.17		1.0013	55,723	100	0	0	0	0			100,000,000				Feb-09
0.04	0.36	1.29	4.80	5.43	1.48	0.12	0.18		1	14,643	100	0	0	0	0			100,000,000				Sep-04
0.05	0.37	1.32	4.89	5.56	1.51	0.09	0.18		1	14,643	100	0	0	0	0			100,000,000				Feb-09
5.11	5.72	8.69	16.77	23.54	2.47	0.44	3.84	5.98	10.39	4,127	-4	18	3	28	0	684	3.47	5,000,000				May-97
4.97	5.44	8.11	14.87	20.07	1.94	0.99	3.84	5.98	10.38	4,127	-4	18	3	28	0	684	3.47	100				Oct-06
5.11	5.71	8.66	16.50	23.26	2.42	0.49	3.85	5.98	10.36	4,127	-4	18	3	28	0	684	3.47	2,000,000				Dec-92
5.04	5.57	8.27	15.63	21.47	2.18	0.74	3.88	5.98	10.37	4,127	-4	18	3	28	0	684	3.47	1,000	50	4.00		Jan-96
4.86	5.20	7.49	13.10	17.06	1.45	1.49	3.84	5.98	10.33	4,127	-4	18	3	28	0	684	3.47	1,000	50		1.00	Feb-97
5.04	5.58	8.28	15.63	21.61	2.18	0.74	3.85	5.98	10.36	4,127	-4	18	3	28	0	684	3.47	5,000				Jan-96
9.51	6.07	11.78	26.39	46.66	5.04	0	8.23		15.9	841.4	-30	23	2	50	0	21	4.82					Nov-01
5.45	6.48	9.22	18.71	25.69	2.69	0.24	3.91	5.39	11.09	1,675	9	0	1	40	0	263	3.36	5,000,000				Mar-16
5.54	6.45	9.17	18.55	25.43	2.64	0.29	3.93	5.39	11.09	1,675	9	0	1	40	0	263	3.36	2,000,000				Feb-11
5.47	6.32	8.90	17.51	23.35	2.4	0.54	3.93	5.39	11.09	1,675	9	0	1	40	0	263	3.36	1,000	50	4.00		Apr-12
5.18	5.93	8.10	14.89	18.93	1.69	1.29	3.96	5.39	11.09	1,675	9	0	1	40	0	263	3.36	1,000	50		1.00	Apr-12
14.61	-6.30	-1.10	10.67	26.56	8.37	0	12.64		10.76	1,312	1	0	0	99	0	20	6.04					May-03
14.73	0.02	6.26	17.69	34.12	6.51	1.22	11.21		14.54	1,349	-40	2	1	90	0	2	5.91					Dec-06
15.81						3.7			9.7	--						43		2,500		2.50		Apr-20
14.44	-2.53	1.14			5.25	2.95			9.69	--						43		250,000				Feb-19
12.52	-8.66	-4.37	5.10	19.46	7.77	1.24	12.18		10.83	534.7	0	0	0	100	0	53	4.94					Mar-98
13.93	-3.60	-1.75	5.23		4.97	0.6			9.04	21.9	2	84	0	10	0	68	5.69	5,000,000				Jul-17
13.91	-3.64	-1.83	4.98		4.88	0.69			9.04	21.9	2	84	0	10	0	68	5.69	2,000,000				Jul-17
10.01	5.51	2.55	4.84	24.39	5	0.63	9.76	3.71	8.31	107.8	0	77	0	14	0	118	6.58	5,000,000				Feb-08
10.11	5.60	2.62	4.94	24.30	4.95	0.68	9.74	3.71	8.33	107.8	0	77	0	14	0	118	6.58	2,000,000				Feb-08
10.07	5.48	2.36	4.02	22.55	4.71	0.93	9.8	3.71	8.31	107.8	0	77	0	14	0	118	6.58	1,000	50	4.00		Feb-08
9.72	4.96	1.48	1.71	17.92	3.97	1.68	9.76	3.71	8.31	107.8	0	77	0	14	0	118	6.58	1,000	50		1.00	Feb-08
1.51	1.45	3.01	6.97	11.96	2.57		1.77		13.51	64.3	-12	43	0	2	0	17	3.30					Oct-05
0.00	0.25	1.09	3.06	3.07		0.42			1	490.4	71	29	0	0	0			2,000,000	0			Jul-19
0.00	0.25	1.08	3.04	3.05	1.23	0.42	0.21		1	490.4	71	29	0	0	0			1,000	50			Dec-82
0.00	0.09	0.54	0.99	-0.48	0.64	1.17			1	490.4	71	29	0	0	0			1,000			1.00	Aug-18
8.23	-4.34	-1.39	5.76	13.86	4.9	0.65	7.5	0.01	9.38	2,400	4	0	0	96	0	52	4.28	5,000,000				Mar-16
8.21	-4.37	-1.43	5.63	13.83	4.85	0.71	7.54	0.01	9.38	2,400	4	0	0	96	0	52	4.28	2,000,000				Mar-11
7.94	-4.86	-2.44	2.44	8.25	3.78	1.73	7.51	0.01	9.38	2,400	4	0	0	96	0	52	4.28	1,000	50		1.00	Mar-11
8.14	-4.49	-1.70	4.73	12.13	4.57	0.99	7.51	0.01	9.38	2,400	4	0	0	96	0	52	4.28	1,000	50	2.50		Nov-89
11.59	-8.13	-4.42	3.34	13.71	6.78		11.25		12.97	466.0	0	0	0	100	0	16	4.74					Oct-03
11.81	-7.98	-4.40	3.37	14.04	6.79	0	11.26		12.59	289.2	0	0	0	100	0	6	4.75					Aug-04
0.32	1.61	2.51	3.85	7.61	1.03		1.13		14.82	81.1	16	0	84	0	0	20	3.17					Sep-03
0.02	0.29	0.99	3.97	4.27	1.11	0	0.16		1	95.4	100	0	0	0	0			100,000				Dec-89
1.55	3.51	5.49	11.66	15.70	3.35	0.9	2.22	1.16	9.55	559.1	13	0	0	0	0	1,482	4.16	5,000,000				Dec-02
1.53	3.48	5.43	11.37	15.33	3.3	0.95	2.2	1.16	9.58	559.1	13	0	0	0	0	1,482	4.16	2,000,000				May-98
1.47	3.35	5.16	10.55	13.79	3.06	1.2	2.18	1.16	9.62	559.1	13	0	0	0	0	1,482	4.16	1,000	50	4.00		May-98
1.28	2.97	4.50	8.21	9.70	2.32	1.95	2.2	1.16	9.58	559.1	13	0	0	0	0	1,482	4.16	1,000	50		1.00	May-98
1.36	3.36	5.17	10.55	13.76	3.06	1.2	2.16	1.16	9.56	559.1	13	0	0	0	0	1,482	4.16	5,000				May-98
9.57	-5.12	-0.76	10.12	23.38	5.99	0.51	9.08	2.83	7.17	22,195	-1	0	0	98	0	102	5.95	5,000,000				Nov-98
9.40	-5.45	-1.45	7.76	19.00	5.27	1.24	9.18	2.83	7.16	22,195	-1	0	0	98	0	102	5.95	100				Oct-06
9.71	-5.05	-0.75	9.90	22.93	5.87	0.62	9.14	2.83	7.17	22,195	-1	0	0	98	0	102	5.95	2,000,000				Nov-98
9.47	-5.33	-1.19	8.71	20.83	5.55	0.94	9.17	2.83	7.16	22,195	-1	0	0	98	0	102	5.95	1,000	50	4.00		Nov-98

	MARKET		FUND TYPE, CATEGORY & OBJECTIVE		RATINGS				NEW INVESTORS	
Fund Name	Ticker Symbol	Traded On	Fund Type	Category and (Prospectus Objective)	Overall Rating	Reward Rating	Risk Rating	Recent Up/ Downgrade	Open to New Investors	Telephone
BlackRock High Yield Bond Portfolio Investor C Shares	BHYCX	NAS CM	Open End	US Fixed Inc (Corp Bond - High Yield)	C-	D+	C		Y	800-441-7762
BlackRock High Yield Bond Portfolio Service Shares	BHYSX	NAS CM	Open End	US Fixed Inc (Corp Bond - High Yield)	C-	D+	C		Y	800-441-7762
BlackRock High Yield Municipal Fund Class K	MKYHX	NAS CM	Open End	US Muni Fixed Inc (Muni Bond - Natl)	C-	D+	C	Down	Y	800-441-7762
BlackRock High Yield Municipal Fund Institutional Shares	MAYHX	NAS CM	Open End	US Muni Fixed Inc (Muni Bond - Natl)	C-	D+	C	Down	Y	800-441-7762
BlackRock High Yield Municipal Fund Investor A Shares	MDYHX	NAS CM	Open End	US Muni Fixed Inc (Muni Bond - Natl)	D+	D+	C-	Down	Y	800-441-7762
BlackRock High Yield Municipal Fund Investor C Shares	MCYHX	NAS CM	Open End	US Muni Fixed Inc (Muni Bond - Natl)	D+	D+	C-	Down	Y	800-441-7762
BlackRock Income Fund Class K Shares	BMSKX	NAS CM	Open End	US Fixed Inc (Multisector Bond)	C	C-	C+		Y	800-441-7762
BlackRock Income Fund Institutional Shares	BMSIX	NAS CM	Open End	US Fixed Inc (Multisector Bond)	C	C-	C		Y	800-441-7762
BlackRock Income Fund Investor A Shares	BMSAX	NAS CM	Open End	US Fixed Inc (Multisector Bond)	C-	D+	C	Down	Y	800-441-7762
BlackRock Income Fund Investor C Shares	BMSCX	NAS CM	Open End	US Fixed Inc (Multisector Bond)	C-	D+	C		Y	800-441-7762
BlackRock Income Trust	BKT	NYSE	Closed End	US Fixed Inc (Govt Bond - General)	C+	C	C+	Up	Y	800-441-7762
BlackRock Inflation Protected Bond Fund Class K	BPLBX	NAS CM	Open End	US Fixed Inc (Growth & Income)	B	C+	A-	Up	Y	800-441-7762
BlackRock Inflation Protected Bond Institutional Shares	BPRIX	NAS CM	Open End	US Fixed Inc (Growth & Income)	B	C+	A-	Up	Y	800-441-7762
BlackRock Inflation Protected Bond Fund Investor A Shares	BPRAX	NAS CM	Open End	US Fixed Inc (Growth & Income)	B	C+	B+	Up	Y	800-441-7762
BlackRock Inflation Protected Bond Fund Investor C Shares	BPRCX	NAS CM	Open End	US Fixed Inc (Growth & Income)	B-	C+	B	Up	Y	800-441-7762
BlackRock Inflation Protected Bond Fund Service Shares	BPRSX	NAS CM	Open End	US Fixed Inc (Growth & Income)	B	C+	B+	Up	Y	800-441-7762
BlackRock Investment Quality Municipal	BKN	NYSE	Closed End	US Muni Fixed Inc (Muni Bond - Natl)	C-	C-	C-		Y	800-441-7762
BlackRock Limited Duration Income	BLW	NYSE	Closed End	US Fixed Inc (Corp Bond - General)	C-	D+	C		Y	800-441-7762
BlackRock Liquid Environmentally Aware Fund Direct	LEDXX	NAS CM	Money Mkt	US Money Mkt (Income)	D	D	C+		Y	800-441-7762
BlackRock Liquid Environmentally Aware Fund Institutional	LEFXX	NAS CM	Money Mkt	US Money Mkt (Income)	D	D	C+		Y	800-441-7762
BlackRock Liquid Environmentally Aware Fund Investor A	LEAXX	NAS CM	Money Mkt	US Money Mkt (Income)	D	D	C+		Y	800-441-7762
★ BlackRock Liquidity FedFund Fund Capital			Money Mkt	US Money Mkt (Money Mkt - Govt)	C	C-	C+		Y	800-441-7762
BlackRock Liquidity Funds California Money Admin Shares	BLCXX	NAS CM	Money Mkt	US Money Mkt (Money Mkt - Single State)	U	U	U		Y	800-441-7762
BlackRock Liquidity Funds California Money Dollar Shares	MUDXX	NAS CM	Money Mkt	US Money Mkt (Money Mkt - Single State)	U	U	U		Y	800-441-7762
BlackRock Liquidity Funds California Money Inst Shares	MUCXX	NAS CM	Money Mkt	US Money Mkt (Money Mkt - Single State)	C	C-	C		Y	800-441-7762
BlackRock Liquidity Funds California Money Premier Shares	BLBXX	NAS CM	Money Mkt	US Money Mkt (Money Mkt - Single State)	C	C-	C+		Y	800-441-7762
BlackRock Liq Funds Calif Money Private Client Shares	BCAXX	NAS CM	Money Mkt	US Money Mkt (Money Mkt - Single State)	U	U	U		Y	800-441-7762
BlackRock Liquidity Funds California Money Select Shares	BCBXX	NAS CM	Money Mkt	US Money Mkt (Money Mkt - Single State)	U	U	U		Y	800-441-7762
BlackRock Liquidity Funds Federal Trust Fund Admin Shares	BFTXX	NAS CM	Money Mkt	US Money Mkt (Money Mkt - Govt)	C	C-	C+		Y	800-441-7762
BlackRock Liquidity Funds Federal Trust Cash Management Cl	BFMXX	NAS CM	Money Mkt	US Money Mkt (Money Mkt - Govt)	C	C-	C+		Y	800-441-7762
BlackRock Liquidity Funds Federal Trust Fund Cash Reserve	BFDXX	NAS CM	Money Mkt	US Money Mkt (Money Mkt - Govt)	C	C-	C+		Y	800-441-7762
BlackRock Liquidity Funds Federal Trust Fund Dollar Shares	TSDXX	NAS CM	Money Mkt	US Money Mkt (Money Mkt - Govt)	C	C-	C+		Y	800-441-7762
BlackRock Liquidity Funds Fed Trust Inst Shares	TFFXX	NAS CM	Money Mkt	US Money Mkt (Money Mkt - Govt)	C	C-	C+		Y	800-441-7762
BlackRock Liquidity Funds Federal Trust Premier Shares	FPXXX	NAS CM	Money Mkt	US Money Mkt (Money Mkt - Govt)	C	C-	C+		Y	800-441-7762
★ BlackRock Liquidity Funds FedFund Administration Shares	BLFXX	NAS CM	Money Mkt	US Money Mkt (Money Mkt - Govt)	C	C-	C+		Y	800-441-7762
★ BlackRock Liquidity Funds FedFund Cash Management Shares	BFFXX	NAS CM	Money Mkt	US Money Mkt (Money Mkt - Govt)	C	C-	C+		Y	800-441-7762
★ BlackRock Liquidity Funds FedFund Cash Reserve Shares	BFRXX	NAS CM	Money Mkt	US Money Mkt (Money Mkt - Govt)	C	C-	C+		Y	800-441-7762
★ BlackRock Liquidity Funds FedFund Dollar Shares	TDDXX	NAS CM	Money Mkt	US Money Mkt (Money Mkt - Govt)	C	C-	C+		Y	800-441-7762
BlackRock Liquidity Funds FedFund Institutional Shares	TFDXX	NAS CM	Money Mkt	US Money Mkt (Money Mkt - Govt)	C	C-	C+		Y	800-441-7762
BlackRock Liquidity Funds FedFund Premier Shares	BUPXX	NAS CM	Money Mkt	US Money Mkt (Money Mkt - Govt)	C	C-	C		Y	800-441-7762
★ BlackRock Liquidity Funds FedFund Select Shares	BFBXX	NAS CM	Money Mkt	US Money Mkt (Money Mkt - Govt)	C	C-	C		Y	800-441-7762
BlackRock Liquidity Funds MuniCash Dollar Shares	MCDXX	NAS CM	Money Mkt	US Money Mkt (Money Mkt - Fed Tax Exmpt)	C	C-	C+		Y	800-441-7762
BlackRock Liquidity Funds MuniCash Institutional Shares	MCSXX	NAS CM	Money Mkt	US Money Mkt (Money Mkt - Fed Tax Exmpt)	C	C-	C+		Y	800-441-7762
BlackRock Liquidity Funds MuniFund Administration Shares	BIAXX	NAS CM	Money Mkt	US Money Mkt (Money Mkt - Fed Tax Exmpt)	C	C-	C		Y	800-441-7762
BlackRock Liquidity Funds MuniFund Cash Management Shares	BCMXX	NAS CM	Money Mkt	US Money Mkt (Money Mkt - Fed Tax Exmpt)	U	U	U		Y	800-441-7762
BlackRock Liquidity Funds MuniFund Dollar Shares	MFDXX	NAS CM	Money Mkt	US Money Mkt (Money Mkt - Fed Tax Exmpt)	C	C-	C		Y	800-441-7762
BlackRock Liquidity Funds MuniFund Institutional Shares	MFTXX	NAS CM	Money Mkt	US Money Mkt (Money Mkt - Fed Tax Exmpt)	C	C-	C+		Y	800-441-7762
BlackRock Liquidity Funds MuniFund Premier Shares	BLSXX	NAS CM	Money Mkt	US Money Mkt (Money Mkt - Fed Tax Exmpt)	C	C-	C+		Y	800-441-7762
BlackRock Liquidity Funds MuniFund Private Client Shares	BMPXX	NAS CM	Money Mkt	US Money Mkt (Money Mkt - Fed Tax Exmpt)	C	C-	C+		Y	800-441-7762
BlackRock Liquidity Funds MuniFund Select Shares	BMBXX	NAS CM	Money Mkt	US Money Mkt (Money Mkt - Fed Tax Exmpt)	C	C-	C		Y	800-441-7762
BlackRock Liquidity Funds New York Money Fund Admin Shares	BLNXX	NAS CM	Money Mkt	US Money Mkt (Money Mkt - Single State)	U	U	U		Y	800-441-7762
BlackRock Liquidity Funds New York Money Cash Mgmt Shares	BLYXX	NAS CM	Money Mkt	US Money Mkt (Money Mkt - Single State)	U	U	U		Y	800-441-7762

★ Expanded analysis of this fund is included in Section II.

TOTAL RETURNS & PERFORMANCE									ASSETS		ASSET ALLOCATION & TURNOVER							MINIMUMS		FEES		
3-Month Total Return	6-Month Total Return	1-Year Total Return	3-Year Total Return	5-Year Total Return	Dividend Yield (TTM)	Expense Ratio	3-Yr Std Deviation	Effective Duration	NAV	Total Assets (MIL)	%Cash	%Government Bonds	%Municipal Bonds	%Corporate Bonds	%Other	Turnover Ratio	Average Coupon Rate	Min Initial Investment	Min Additional Investment	Front End Fee (%)	Back End Fee (%)	Inception Date
9.27	-5.65	-1.88	6.44	16.53	4.81	1.66	9.17	2.83	7.17	22,195	-1	0	0	98	0	102	5.95	1,000	50		1.00	Nov-98
9.46	-5.30	-1.13	9.00	21.03	5.6	0.89	9.05	2.83	7.17	22,195	-1	0	0	98	0	102	5.95	5,000				Nov-98
4.95	-3.06	0.12	12.71	26.38	4	0.66	8.27	9.15	9.54	1,231	8	0	92	0	0	14	5.27	5,000,000				Jan-18
4.94	-3.08	0.08	12.62	26.27	3.96	0.71	8.27	9.15	9.54	1,231	8	0	92	0	0	14	5.27	2,000,000				Aug-06
4.88	-3.11	-0.16	11.75	24.69	3.68	0.96	8.24	9.15	9.52	1,231	8	0	92	0	0	14	5.27	1,000	50	4.25		Aug-06
4.68	-3.46	-0.90	9.25	20.20	2.87	1.71	8.26	9.15	9.55	1,231	8	0	92	0	0	14	5.27	1,000	50		1.00	Aug-06
9.97	-1.31	2.28	12.28	22.70	4.81	0.61	7.54	2.81	9.98	1,319	8	1	0	80	0	77	5.24	5,000,000				Aug-16
9.96	-1.33	2.23	12.12	22.47	4.76	0.66	7.54	2.81	9.98	1,319	8	1	0	80	0	77	5.24	2,000,000				Feb-10
9.89	-1.45	1.98	11.39	20.96	4.51	0.91	7.53	2.81	9.98	1,319	8	1	0	80	0	77	5.24	1,000	50	2.50		Feb-10
9.69	-1.82	1.22	8.82	16.52	3.74	1.66	7.53	2.81	9.98	1,319	8	1	0	80	0	77	5.24	1,000	50		1.00	Feb-10
1.80	3.07	5.19	12.36	17.35	4.55		3.25		6.32	405.1	-41	2	0	0	0	255	4.46					Jul-88
5.35	6.08	8.64	15.24	18.95	1.53	0.6	3.88	8.00	11.24	1,814	-25	93	0	3	0	252	1.11	5,000,000				Jun-04
5.37	6.08	8.70	15.11	18.64	1.51	0.65	3.89	8.00	11.42	1,814	-25	93	0	3	0	252	1.11	2,000,000				Jun-04
5.28	6.01	8.40	14.28	17.03	1.41	0.9	3.85	8.00	11.13	1,814	-25	93	0	3	0	252	1.11	1,000	50	4.00		Jun-04
5.11	5.56	7.63	11.74	12.80	1.15	1.65	3.87	8.00	10.69	1,814	-25	93	0	3	0	252	1.11	1,000	50		1.00	Jun-04
5.32	5.95	8.42	14.29	17.05	1.41	0.9	3.86	8.00	11.25	1,814	-25	93	0	3	0	252	1.11	5,000				Jun-04
4.61	0.43	4.14	17.95	33.31	4.38		8.1		16.07	270.5	-46	0	100	0	0	29	5.02					Feb-93
12.83	-5.27	-0.93	10.92	26.50	7.13		10.79		15.65	554.3	-42	5	0	86	0	14	5.30					Jul-03
0.29	0.61	1.65			1.71	0.14			1.0011	992.9	85	10	2	3	0			1,000,000				Apr-19
0.27	0.58	1.55			1.61	0.2			1.0011	992.9	85	10	2	3	0			2,000,000				Apr-19
0.20	0.44	1.29			1.36	0.45			1.0011	992.9	85	10	2	3	0			1,000	50			Apr-19
0.02	0.32	1.25	4.62	5.24	1.43	0.22			1	168,607	71	28	0	0	0	0		50,000				Nov-17
0.00	0.10	0.18	0.23	0.25	0.08	0.3	0.06			45.8	2	0	94	4	0	0		5,000				Jun-04
0.00	0.10	0.14	0.16	0.18	0.04	0.45	0.06			45.8	2	0	94	4	0	0		5,000				Feb-83
0.03	0.32	0.76	2.79	3.45	0.87	0.2	0.1		1.0001	830.5	16	0	84	0	0	0		3,000,000				Feb-83
0.02	0.31	0.76	2.79	3.45		0.2			1.0001	830.5	16	0	84	0	0	0		3,000,000				Mar-04
0.23	0.38	0.61	0.81	0.83	0.49	0.68	0.09			494.7	4	0	96	0	0	0		0				Mar-04
0.10	0.16	0.24	0.35	0.38	0.2	1	0.07			494.7	4	0	96	0	0	0		0				May-02
0.02	0.32	1.19	4.35	4.69	1.37	0.27	0.17		1	5,328	74	24	0	0	0	0		5,000				Apr-09
0.00	0.20	0.86	3.18	3.23	1.01	0.67	0.16		1	5,328	74	24	0	0	0	0		5,000				Sep-10
0.04	0.37	1.29	5.12	5.26	1.47	0.57	0.7		1	5,328	74	24	0	0	0	0		5,000				Apr-16
0.00	0.26	1.06	3.91	4.07	1.23	0.42	0.17		1	5,328	74	24	0	0	0	0		5,000				Dec-90
0.05	0.37	1.29	4.67	5.17	1.47	0.17	0.17		1	5,328	74	24	0	0	0	0		3,000,000				Dec-90
0.04	0.36	1.29	4.66	5.16		0.17			1	5,328	74	24	0	0	0	0		3,000,000				Jul-19
0.01	0.30	1.19	4.42	4.88	1.38	0.27	0.17		1	168,607	71	28	0	0	0	0		5,000				Nov-04
0.00	0.19	0.88	3.26	3.38	1.03	0.67	0.16		1	168,607	71	28	0	0	0	0		5,000				Aug-08
0.00	0.21	0.95	3.55	3.70	1.11	0.57	0.17		1	168,607	71	28	0	0	0	0		5,000				Apr-03
0.00	0.25	1.06	4.01	4.25	1.23	0.42	0.18		1	168,607	71	28	0	0	0	0		5,000				Mar-84
0.04	0.35	1.29	4.74	5.36	1.48	0.17	0.17		1	168,607	71	28	0	0	0	0		3,000,000				Feb-80
0.04	0.36	1.11	1.12	1.14	1.12	0.17			1	168,607	71	28	0	0	0	0		3,000,000				Mar-04
0.00	0.12	0.64	2.33	2.38	0.77	1	0.15		1	168,607	71	28	0	0	0	0		0				May-02
0.03	0.30	0.75	2.70	3.13	0.84	0.45	0.13		1.0002	6,932	16	0	82	0	0	0		5,000				Feb-84
0.06	0.38	0.95	3.33	4.07	1.07	0.2	0.11		1.0002	6,932	16	0	82	0	0	0		3,000,000				Nov-85
0.03	0.32	0.87	3.11	3.59	1	0.3	0.11		1	317.3	21	0	79	0	0	0		5,000				Apr-02
0.00	0.16	0.48	0.64	0.70	0.48	0.7	0.08			255.3	15	0	79	0	0	0		5,000				Jun-99
0.02	0.27	0.75	2.66	2.97	0.86	0.45	0.11		1	317.3	21	0	79	0	0	0		5,000				Jan-86
0.05	0.37	0.97	3.40	4.02	1.1	0.2	0.11		1	317.3	21	0	79	0	0	0		3,000,000				Feb-80
0.05	0.36	0.98	3.40	4.03		0.2			1	317.3	21	0	79	0	0	0		3,000,000				Mar-05
0.01	0.21	0.57	1.99	2.10	0.66	0.68	0.1		1	317.3	21	0	79	0	0	0		0				Mar-04
0.00	0.11	0.31	1.15	1.18	0.39	1	0.09		1	317.3	21	0	79	0	0	0		0				May-02
0.12	0.12	0.35	0.40	0.41	0.09	0.3	0.12			19.1	1	0	96	3	0	0		5,000				Jun-04
0.00	0.00	0.14	0.16	0.18	0	0.7	0.08			19.1	1	0	96	3	0	0		5,000				Mar-05

Fund Name	MARKET Ticker Symbol	MARKET Traded On	FUND TYPE, CATEGORY & OBJECTIVE Fund Type	Category and (Prospectus Objective)	RATINGS Overall Rating	Reward Rating	Risk Rating	Recent Up/ Downgrade	NEW INVESTORS Open to New Investors	Telephone
BlackRock Liquidity Funds New York Money Inst Shares	MUNXX	NAS CM	Money Mkt	US Money Mkt (Money Mkt - Single State)	C	C-	C+		Y	800-441-7762
BlackRock Liquidity Funds New York Money Premier Shares	BNBXX	NAS CM	Money Mkt	US Money Mkt (Money Mkt - Single State)	C	C-	C+		Y	800-441-7762
BlackRock Liq Funds New York Money Private Client Shares	BYPXX	NAS CM	Money Mkt	US Money Mkt (Money Mkt - Single State)	U	U	U		Y	800-441-7762
BlackRock Liquidity Funds New York Money Select Shares	BIBXX	NAS CM	Money Mkt	US Money Mkt (Money Mkt - Single State)	U	U	U		Y	800-441-7762
BlackRock Liquidity Funds TempCash Administration Shares	BLAXX	NAS CM	Money Mkt	US Money Mkt (Money Mkt - Taxable)	U	U	U		Y	800-441-7762
BlackRock Liquidity Funds TempCash Capital Shares	TPCXX	NAS CM	Money Mkt	US Money Mkt (Money Mkt - Taxable)	U	U	U		Y	800-441-7762
BlackRock Liquidity Funds TempCash Institutional Shares	TMCXX	NAS CM	Money Mkt	US Money Mkt (Money Mkt - Taxable)	C	C-	C+		Y	800-441-7762
BlackRock Liquidity Funds TempCash Premier Shares	TCPXX	NAS CM	Money Mkt	US Money Mkt (Money Mkt - Taxable)	C	C-	C+		Y	800-441-7762
BlackRock Liquidity Funds TempFund Administration Shares	BTMXX	NAS CM	Money Mkt	US Money Mkt (Money Mkt - Taxable)	C	C-	C+		Y	800-441-7762
BlackRock Liquidity Funds TempFund Cash Management Shares	BRTXX	NAS CM	Money Mkt	US Money Mkt (Money Mkt - Taxable)	C	C-	C+		Y	800-441-7762
BlackRock Liquidity Funds TempFund Cash Reserve Shares	BRRXX	NAS CM	Money Mkt	US Money Mkt (Money Mkt - Taxable)	C	C	C+		Y	800-441-7762
BlackRock Liquidity Funds TempFund Dollar Shares	TDOXX	NAS CM	Money Mkt	US Money Mkt (Money Mkt - Taxable)	C	C-	C+		Y	800-441-7762
BlackRock Liquidity Funds TempFund Institutional Shares	TMPXX	NAS CM	Money Mkt	US Money Mkt (Money Mkt - Taxable)	C	C-	C+		Y	800-441-7762
BlackRock Liquidity Funds TempFund Premier Shares	BFPXX	NAS CM	Money Mkt	US Money Mkt (Money Mkt - Taxable)	U	U	U		Y	800-441-7762
BlackRock Liquidity Funds TempFund Private Client Shares	BTVXX	NAS CM	Money Mkt	US Money Mkt (Money Mkt - Taxable)	C	C-	C+		Y	800-441-7762
★ BlackRock Liquidity Funds T-Fund Administration Shares	BTAXX	NAS CM	Money Mkt	US Money Mkt (Money Mkt - Treasury)	C	C-	C+		Y	800-441-7762
★ BlackRock Liquidity Funds T-Fund Cash Management Shares	BPTXX	NAS CM	Money Mkt	US Money Mkt (Money Mkt - Treasury)	C	C-	C+		Y	800-441-7762
★ BlackRock Liquidity Funds T-Fund Dollar Shares	TFEXX	NAS CM	Money Mkt	US Money Mkt (Money Mkt - Treasury)	C	C-	C+		Y	800-441-7762
BlackRock Liquidity Funds T-Fund Institutional Shares	TSTXX	NAS CM	Money Mkt	US Money Mkt (Money Mkt - Treasury)	C	C-	C+		Y	800-441-7762
BlackRock Liquidity Funds T-Fund Premier Shares	BEMXX	NAS CM	Money Mkt	US Money Mkt (Money Mkt - Treasury)	C	C-	C+		Y	800-441-7762
★ BlackRock Liquidity Funds T-Fund Select Shares	BSLXX	NAS CM	Money Mkt	US Money Mkt (Money Mkt - Treasury)	C	C-	C		Y	800-441-7762
★ BlackRock Liquidity Funds Treasury Trust Fund Admin Shares	BITXX	NAS CM	Money Mkt	US Money Mkt (Money Mkt - Treasury)	C	C-	C+		Y	800-441-7762
BlackRock Liquidity Funds Treasury Trust Capital Shares	BUCXX	NAS CM	Money Mkt	US Money Mkt (Money Mkt - Treasury)	U	U	U		Y	800-441-7762
★ BlackRock Liquidity Funds Treas Trust Cash Reserve Shares	BTFXX	NAS CM	Money Mkt	US Money Mkt (Money Mkt - Treasury)	C	C	C+		Y	800-441-7762
★ BlackRock Liquidity Funds Treasury Trust Dollar Shares	TTDXX	NAS CM	Money Mkt	US Money Mkt (Money Mkt - Treasury)	C	C-	C+		Y	800-441-7762
BlackRock Liquidity Funds Treas Trust Inst Shares	TTTXX	NAS CM	Money Mkt	US Money Mkt (Money Mkt - Treasury)	C	C-	C+		Y	800-441-7762
BlackRock Liquidity Funds Treasury Trust Premier Shares	TPTXX	NAS CM	Money Mkt	US Money Mkt (Money Mkt - Treasury)	C	C-	C+		Y	800-441-7762
★ BlackRock Liquidity Funds Treasury Trust Select Shares	TSLXX	NAS CM	Money Mkt	US Money Mkt (Money Mkt - Treasury)	C	C-	C		Y	800-441-7762
BlackRock Liquidity MuniCash Fund Capital Shares	MCPXX	NAS CM	Money Mkt	US Money Mkt (Money Mkt - Fed Tax Exmpt)	U	U	U		Y	800-441-7762
BlackRock Liquidity MuniCash Fund Premier Class	MPPXX	NAS CM	Money Mkt	US Money Mkt (Money Mkt - Fed Tax Exmpt)	C	C-	C+		Y	800-441-7762
BlackRock Liquidity TempFund Capital Shares	TFCXX	NAS CM	Money Mkt	US Money Mkt (Money Mkt - Taxable)	U	U	U		Y	800-441-7762
★ BlackRock Liquidity T-Fund Capital Shares	BCHXX	NAS CM	Money Mkt	US Money Mkt (Money Mkt - Treasury)	C	C-	C+		Y	800-441-7762
BlackRock Long-Term Municipal Advantage Trust	BTA	NYSE	Closed End	US Muni Fixed Inc (Muni Bond - Natl)	D+	D+	C-	Down	Y	800-441-7762
BlackRock Low Duration Bond Portfolio Class K	CLDBX	NAS CM	Open End	US Fixed Inc (Income)	C	C-	C+		Y	800-441-7762
BlackRock Low Duration Bond Portfolio Class R	BLDPX	NAS CM	Open End	US Fixed Inc (Income)	C	C-	C+		Y	800-441-7762
BlackRock Low Duration Bond Portfolio Institutional Shares	BFMSX	NAS CM	Open End	US Fixed Inc (Income)	C	C-	C+		Y	800-441-7762
BlackRock Low Duration Bond Portfolio Investor A Shares	BLDAX	NAS CM	Open End	US Fixed Inc (Income)	C	C-	C+		Y	800-441-7762
BlackRock Low Duration Bond Portfolio Investor A1 Shares	CMGAX	NAS CM	Open End	US Fixed Inc (Income)	C	C-	C+			800-441-7762
BlackRock Low Duration Bond Portfolio Investor C Shares	BLDCX	NAS CM	Open End	US Fixed Inc (Income)	C	C-	C	Up	Y	800-441-7762
BlackRock Low Duration Bond Portfolio Service Shares	CMGBX	NAS CM	Open End	US Fixed Inc (Income)	C	C-	C+		Y	800-441-7762
BlackRock Maryland Municipal Bond	BZM	AMEX	Closed End	US Muni Fixed Inc (Muni Bond - Single State)	D+	D+	D+	Down	Y	800-441-7762
BlackRock Money Market Portfolio Institutional Shares	PNIXX	NAS CM	Money Mkt	US Money Mkt (Money Mkt - Taxable)	C	C-	C+		Y	800-441-7762
BlackRock Money Market Portfolio Investor A Shares	PINXX	NAS CM	Money Mkt	US Money Mkt (Money Mkt - Taxable)	C	C-	C+		Y	800-441-7762
BlackRock Money Market Portfolio Investor C Shares	BMCXX	NAS CM	Money Mkt	US Money Mkt (Money Mkt - Taxable)	C	C-	C		Y	800-441-7762
BlackRock Money Market Portfolio Premier	BMMXX	NAS CM	Money Mkt	US Money Mkt (Money Mkt - Taxable)	C	C-	C+		Y	800-441-7762
BlackRock Money Market Portfolio Service Shares	PNPXX	NAS CM	Money Mkt	US Money Mkt (Money Mkt - Taxable)	C	C-	C+		Y	800-441-7762
BlackRock Multi-Sector Income Trust	BIT	NYSE	Closed End	US Fixed Inc (Multisector Bond)	D	D	D+		Y	800-441-7762
BlackRock Multi-Sector Opportunities Trust	XMSOX	NAS CM	Closed End	Global Fixed Inc (Growth & Income)	D	D	D	Down	Y	800-441-7762
BlackRock Multi-Sector Opportunities Trust II			Closed End	US Fixed Inc (Growth & Income)	D	D	D-		Y	800-441-7762
BlackRock Muni Intermediate Duration Income	MUI	NYSE	Closed End	US Muni Fixed Inc (Muni Bond - Natl)	C-	C-	C-		Y	800-441-7762
BlackRock Muni NY Intermediate Duration Fund	MNE	NYSE	Closed End	US Muni Fixed Inc (Muni Bond - Single State)	D+	D+	D+	Down	Y	800-441-7762
BlackRock MuniAssets Fund	MUA	NYSE	Closed End	US Muni Fixed Inc (Muni Bond - Natl)	D+	D+	C-	Down	Y	800-441-7762

★ Expanded analysis of this fund is included in Section II.

TOTAL RETURNS & PERFORMANCE									ASSETS		ASSET ALLOCATION & TURNOVER							MINIMUMS		FEES		
3-Month Total Return	6-Month Total Return	1-Year Total Return	3-Year Total Return	5-Year Total Return	Dividend Yield (TTM)	Expense Ratio	3-Yr Std Deviation	Effective Duration	NAV	Total Assets (MIL)	%Cash	%Government Bonds	%Municipal Bonds	%Corporate Bonds	%Other	Turnover Ratio	Average Coupon Rate	Min Initial Investment	Min Additional Investment	Front End Fee (%)	Back End Fee (%)	Inception Date
0.03	0.36	0.92	3.23	4.08	1.05	0.2	0.12		1	237.5	3	0	97	0	0	0		3,000,000				Aug-83
0.02	0.36	0.92	3.23	4.08		0.2			1	237.5	3	0	97	0	0	0		3,000,000				Mar-04
0.00	0.18	0.51	0.91	0.93	0.51	0.68	0.14			130.4	2	0	98	0	0	0		0				Mar-04
0.06	0.13	0.29	0.57	0.59	0.28	1	0.12			130.4	2	0	98	0	0	0		0				May-02
0.01	0.01	0.10	0.21	0.40	0.09	0.28	0.03			771.9	96	0	0	2	3	0		5,000				Nov-05
0.14	0.27	0.45	0.70	0.91		0.23				771.9	96	0	0	2	3	0		50,000				Apr-17
0.25	0.56	1.57	5.54	6.38	1.69	0.18	0.18		1.0012	10,265	97	3	0	1	0	0		3,000,000				Feb-84
0.25	0.56	1.57	5.54	6.37		0.18			1.0012	10,265	97	3	0	1	0	0		3,000,000				Jul-19
0.21	0.49	1.45	5.21	6.14	1.59	0.28	0.18		1.001	10,148	96	3	0	1	0	0		5,000				Apr-02
0.13	0.31	1.06	3.98	4.34	1.19	0.68	0.18		1.001	10,148	96	3	0	1	0	0		5,000				Jun-99
0.16	0.37	1.23	4.66	5.10	1.38	0.58	0.25		1.001	10,148	96	3	0	1	0	0		5,000				May-00
0.18	0.42	1.29	4.82	5.49	1.44	0.43	0.19		1.001	10,148	96	3	0	1	0	0		5,000				Oct-73
0.23	0.54	1.54	5.51	6.65	1.69	0.18	0.18		1.001	10,148	96	3	0	1	0	0		3,000,000				Oct-73
0.00	0.03	0.08	0.10	0.12	0	0.68	0.02			13,460	90	0	0	1	9	0		0				Mar-05
0.12	0.31	1.06	3.97	4.32	1.19	0.68	0.18		1.001	10,148	96	3	0	1	0	0		0				Mar-04
0.00	0.29	1.16	4.37	4.73	1.34	0.27	0.18		1	85,954	64	36	0	0	0	0		5,000				Apr-02
0.00	0.18	0.86	3.24	3.31	1.01	0.67	0.16		1	85,954	64	36	0	0	0	0		5,000				May-99
0.00	0.24	1.04	3.93	4.12	1.21	0.42	0.17		1	85,954	64	36	0	0	0	0		5,000				Jan-86
0.03	0.33	1.26	4.68	5.21	1.44	0.17	0.18		1	85,954	64	36	0	0	0	0		3,000,000				Mar-80
0.02	0.33	1.27	4.68	5.21		0.17			1	85,954	64	36	0	0	0	0		3,000,000				Oct-07
0.00	0.11	0.62	2.30	2.31	0.75	1	0.15		1	85,954	64	36	0	0	0	0		0				Mar-08
0.02	0.32	1.17	4.34	4.65	1.34	0.27	0.17		1	68,611	72	25	0	0	0	0		5,000				May-02
0.00	0.09	0.22	0.33	0.34		0.22				24,539	76	15	0	0	0	0		50,000				Apr-17
0.00	0.21	0.91	3.45	3.53	1.07	0.57	0.16		1	68,611	72	25	0	0	0	0		5,000				Jan-03
0.01	0.27	1.05	3.99	4.16	1.22	0.42	0.18		1	68,611	72	25	0	0	0	0		5,000				Jun-89
0.03	0.36	1.26	4.64	5.10	1.44	0.17	0.17		1	68,611	72	25	0	0	0	0		3,000,000				May-89
0.03	0.36	1.26	4.64	5.10		0.17			1	68,611	72	25	0	0	0	0		3,000,000				Jul-19
0.00	0.11	0.60	2.24	2.14	0.72	1	0.15		1	68,611	72	25	0	0	0	0		0				Oct-15
0.08	0.15	0.34	0.37	0.38		0.25				3,763	12	0	85	2	0	0		50,000				Apr-17
0.05	0.37	0.93	2.88	3.31		0.2			1.0002	6,932	16	0	82	0	0	0		3,000,000				Jul-19
0.13	0.36	0.64	0.95	1.12		0.23				13,460	90	0	0	1	9	0		50,000				Apr-17
0.02	0.31	1.22	4.57	5.10	1.4	0.22			1	85,954	64	36	0	0	0	0		50,000				Nov-17
5.59	-2.04	1.48	14.36	29.49	5.11	0	9		12.26	159.2	0	0	100	0	0	31	5.44					Feb-06
4.47	1.26	2.75	8.02	11.55	2.47	0.44	2.95	1.89	9.64	6,955	1	4	0	44	0	182	3.03	5,000,000				Jun-97
4.33	0.88	2.08	6.16	8.42	1.92	0.99	3.01	1.89	9.64	6,955	1	4	0	44	0	182	3.03	100				Jul-11
4.45	1.24	2.70	7.87	11.28	2.42	0.49	2.94	1.89	9.65	6,955	1	4	0	44	0	182	3.03	2,000,000				Jul-92
4.39	1.11	2.44	7.07	9.90	2.17	0.74	2.92	1.89	9.65	6,955	1	4	0	44	0	182	3.03	1,000	50	2.25		Jan-96
4.53	1.19	2.59	7.54	10.76	2.32	0.59	3	1.89	9.66	6,955	1	4	0	44	0	182	3.03	1,000	50	1.00		Oct-06
4.20	0.74	1.68	4.68	5.75	1.42	1.49	2.97	1.89	9.64	6,955	1	4	0	44	0	182	3.03	1,000	50		1.00	Feb-97
4.50	1.11	2.44	7.07	9.92	2.17	0.74	3	1.89	9.65	6,955	1	4	0	44	0	182	3.03	5,000				Jan-96
1.72	-1.88	0.91	9.46	22.29	3.18	0	6.4		14.87	30.5	1	0	99	0	0	16	4.76					Apr-02
0.13	0.49	1.49	5.30	6.38	1.65	0.2	0.15		1	3,366	96	3	1	0	0	0		2,000,000				Aug-93
0.06	0.34	1.18	4.28	4.83	1.35	0.55	0.15		1	3,366	96	3	1	0	0	0		1,000	50			Jan-93
0.04	0.14	0.58	2.13	2.37	0.69	1.3	0.13		1	3,366	96	3	1	0	0	0		1,000	50		1.00	Oct-96
0.13	0.49	1.47	4.69	5.32		0.2			1	3,366	96	3	1	0	0	0		2,000,000	0			Jul-19
0.06	0.34	1.19	4.39	5.03	1.35	0.5	0.16		1	3,366	96	3	1	0	0	0		5,000				Oct-89
20.46	-4.21	-7.33	3.43	25.49	8.87	2.1	14.22		15.92	584.8	-49	5	0	58	0	32	5.25					Feb-13
18.36	-13.05	-9.03			9.56	3.65			79.95	--						47		0		1.00		Feb-18
16.71	-15.85	-12.48			7.9	3.28			81.33	--						29		0				Apr-19
3.80	-0.13	2.53	13.37	24.85	3.52	0	6.43		15.55	581.7	0	0	100	0	0	24	5.08					Aug-03
-2.35	-4.20	-2.35	5.55	15.81	3.04	0	5.51			62.1	0	0	100	0	0	15	5.17					Aug-03
4.14	-1.96	0.99	11.63	25.88	4.73		6.94		13.76	481.2	1	0	99	0	0	19	5.86					Jun-93

	MARKET		FUND TYPE, CATEGORY & OBJECTIVE		RATINGS				NEW INVESTORS	
Fund Name	Ticker Symbol	Traded On	Fund Type	Category and (Prospectus Objective)	Overall Rating	Reward Rating	Risk Rating	Recent Up/ Downgrade	Open to New Investors	Telephone
BlackRock Municipal 2020 Term Trust	BKK	NYSE	Closed End	US Muni Fixed Inc (Muni Bond - Natl)	C-	C-	C-		Y	800-441-7762
BlackRock Municipal 2030 Target Term	BTT	NYSE	Closed End	US Muni Fixed Inc (Income)	C-	C-	C-	Down	Y	800-441-7762
BlackRock Municipal Bond Trust	BBK	NYSE	Closed End	US Muni Fixed Inc (Muni Bond - Natl)	C-	C-	C-		Y	800-441-7762
BlackRock Municipal Income Investment Quality Trust	BAF	NYSE	Closed End	US Muni Fixed Inc (Muni Bond - Single State)	C-	C-	C-		Y	800-441-7762
BlackRock Municipal Income Investment Trust	BBF	NYSE	Closed End	US Muni Fixed Inc (Muni Bond - Single State)	D+	D+	C-	Down	Y	800-441-7762
BlackRock Municipal Income Quality Trust	BYM	NYSE	Closed End	US Muni Fixed Inc (Muni Bond - Natl)	C-	C-	C-		Y	800-441-7762
BlackRock Municipal Income Trust	BFK	NYSE	Closed End	US Muni Fixed Inc (Muni Bond - Natl)	D+	D+	C-	Down	Y	800-441-7762
BlackRock Municipal Income Trust II	BLE	AMEX	Closed End	US Muni Fixed Inc (Muni Bond - Natl)	C-	D+	C-		Y	800-441-7762
BlackRock MuniEnhanced Fund, Inc.	MEN	NYSE	Closed End	US Muni Fixed Inc (Muni Bond - Natl)	C-	C-	C-		Y	800-441-7762
BlackRock MuniHoldings California Quality Fund, Inc.	MUC	NYSE	Closed End	US Muni Fixed Inc (Muni Bond - Single State)	C-	C-	C-		Y	800-441-7762
BlackRock MuniHoldings Fund II	MUH	NYSE	Closed End	US Muni Fixed Inc (Muni Bond - Natl)	C-	C-	C-		Y	800-441-7762
BlackRock MuniHoldings Fund Inc	MHD	NYSE	Closed End	US Muni Fixed Inc (Muni Bond - Natl)	C-	D+	C-		Y	800-441-7762
BlackRock MuniHoldings Investment Quality Fund	MFL	NYSE	Closed End	US Muni Fixed Inc (Muni Bond - Single State)	C-	C-	C-		Y	800-441-7762
BlackRock MuniHoldings New Jersey Quality Fund, Inc.	MUJ	NYSE	Closed End	US Muni Fixed Inc (Muni Bond - Single State)	C-	D+	C-		Y	800-441-7762
BlackRock MuniHoldings New York Quality Fund, Inc.	MHN	NYSE	Closed End	US Muni Fixed Inc (Muni Bond - Single State)	C-	C-	C-		Y	800-441-7762
BlackRock MuniHoldings Quality Fund II, Inc.	MUE	NYSE	Closed End	US Muni Fixed Inc (Muni Bond - Natl)	C-	C-	C-		Y	800-441-7762
BlackRock MuniHoldings Quality Fund, Inc.	MUS	NYSE	Closed End	US Muni Fixed Inc (Muni Bond - Natl)	C-	C-	C-		Y	800-441-7762
BlackRock MuniVest	MVF	AMEX	Closed End	US Muni Fixed Inc (Muni Bond - Natl)	C-	D+	C-	Down	Y	800-441-7762
BlackRock MuniVest Fund II	MVT	NYSE	Closed End	US Muni Fixed Inc (Muni Bond - Natl)	D+	D+	C-	Down	Y	800-441-7762
BlackRock MuniYield	MYD	NYSE	Closed End	US Muni Fixed Inc (Muni Bond - Natl)	C-	D+	C		Y	800-441-7762
BlackRock MuniYield Arizona	MZA	AMEX	Closed End	US Muni Fixed Inc (Muni Bond - Single State)	D+	C-	D+	Down	Y	800-441-7762
BlackRock MuniYield CA Fund	MYC	NYSE	Closed End	US Muni Fixed Inc (Muni Bond - Single State)	C-	C-	C-		Y	800-441-7762
BlackRock MuniYield California Quality Fund, Inc.	MCA	NYSE	Closed End	US Muni Fixed Inc (Muni Bond - Single State)	C-	C-	C-		Y	800-441-7762
BlackRock MuniYield Investment Fund	MYF	NYSE	Closed End	US Muni Fixed Inc (Muni Bond - Single State)	C-	C-	C-		Y	800-441-7762
BlackRock MuniYield Investment Quality Fund	MFT	NYSE	Closed End	US Muni Fixed Inc (Muni Bond - Single State)	C-	D+	C-		Y	800-441-7762
BlackRock MuniYield Michigan Quality Fund, Inc.	MIY	NYSE	Closed End	US Muni Fixed Inc (Muni Bond - Single State)	C-	C-	C-		Y	800-441-7762
BlackRock MuniYield New Jersey	MYJ	NYSE	Closed End	US Muni Fixed Inc (Muni Bond - Single State)	C-	D+	C-		Y	800-441-7762
BlackRock MuniYield New York Quality Fund, Inc.	MYN	NYSE	Closed End	US Muni Fixed Inc (Muni Bond - Single State)	C-	C-	C-		Y	800-441-7762
BlackRock MuniYield Pennsylvania Quality Fund	MPA	NYSE	Closed End	US Muni Fixed Inc (Muni Bond - Single State)	C-	C-	C-		Y	800-441-7762
BlackRock MuniYield Quality	MQY	NYSE	Closed End	US Muni Fixed Inc (Muni Bond - Natl)	C-	C-	C-		Y	800-441-7762
BlackRock MuniYield Quality Fund III, Inc.	MYI	NYSE	Closed End	US Muni Fixed Inc (Muni Bond - Natl)	C-	C-	C-	Down	Y	800-441-7762
BlackRock MuniYield Quality II	MQT	NYSE	Closed End	US Muni Fixed Inc (Muni Bond - Natl)	C-	C-	C-		Y	800-441-7762
BlackRock National Municipal Fund Institutional Shares	MANLX	NAS CM	Open End	US Muni Fixed Inc (Muni Bond - Natl)	C	C-	B-		Y	800-441-7762
BlackRock National Municipal Fund Investor A Shares	MDNLX	NAS CM	Open End	US Muni Fixed Inc (Muni Bond - Natl)	C	C-	C+		Y	800-441-7762
BlackRock National Municipal Fund Investor C Shares	MFNLX	NAS CM	Open End	US Muni Fixed Inc (Muni Bond - Natl)	C	D+	C		Y	800-441-7762
BlackRock National Municipal Fund K Share	BNMLX	NAS CM	Open End	US Muni Fixed Inc (Muni Bond - Natl)	C	C-	B-		Y	800-441-7762
BlackRock National Municipal Fund Service Share	BNMSX	NAS CM	Open End	US Muni Fixed Inc (Muni Bond - Natl)	C	C-	C+		Y	800-441-7762
BlackRock New Jersey Municipal Bond Fund Class K	MKNJX	NAS CM	Open End	US Muni Fixed Inc (Muni Bond - Single State)	C-	D+	C	Down	Y	800-441-7762
BlackRock New Jersey Muni Bond Fund Institutional Shares	MANJX	NAS CM	Open End	US Muni Fixed Inc (Muni Bond - Single State)	C-	D+	C	Down	Y	800-441-7762
BlackRock New Jersey Municipal Bond Fund Investor A Shares	MENJX	NAS CM	Open End	US Muni Fixed Inc (Muni Bond - Single State)	C-	D+	C	Down	Y	800-441-7762
BlackRock New Jersey Muni Bond Fund Investor A1 Shares	MDNJX	NAS CM	Open End	US Muni Fixed Inc (Muni Bond - Single State)	C-	D+	C	Down		800-441-7762
BlackRock New Jersey Municipal Bond Fund Investor C Shares	MFNJX	NAS CM	Open End	US Muni Fixed Inc (Muni Bond - Single State)	C-	D+	C	Down	Y	800-441-7762
BlackRock New Jersey Municipal Bond Fund Service Shares	MSNJX	NAS CM	Open End	US Muni Fixed Inc (Muni Bond - Single State)	C-	D+	C	Down	Y	800-441-7762
BlackRock New York Municipal Bond Trust	BQH	NYSE	Closed End	US Muni Fixed Inc (Muni Bond - Single State)	D+	C-	D+	Down	Y	800-441-7762
BlackRock New York Municipal Income Quality Trust	BSE	NYSE	Closed End	US Muni Fixed Inc (Muni Bond - Single State)	C-	C-	C-		Y	800-441-7762
BlackRock New York Municipal Income Trust	BNY	NYSE	Closed End	US Muni Fixed Inc (Muni Bond - Single State)	C-	C-	C-		Y	800-441-7762
BlackRock New York Municipal Income Trust II	BFY	AMEX	Closed End	US Muni Fixed Inc (Muni Bond - Single State)	C-	C-	C-		Y	800-441-7762
BlackRock New York Municipal Opportunities Fund Class K	MKNKX	NAS CM	Open End	US Muni Fixed Inc (Muni Bond - Single State)	C-	D+	C	Down	Y	800-441-7762
BlackRock New York Muni Opportunities Institutional Shares	MANKX	NAS CM	Open End	US Muni Fixed Inc (Muni Bond - Single State)	C-	D+	C	Down	Y	800-441-7762
BlackRock New York Muni Opportunities Investor A Shares	MENKX	NAS CM	Open End	US Muni Fixed Inc (Muni Bond - Single State)	D+	D+	C	Down	Y	800-441-7762
BlackRock New York Muni Opportunities Investor A1 Shares	MDNKX	NAS CM	Open End	US Muni Fixed Inc (Muni Bond - Single State)	D+	D+	C	Down		800-441-7762
BlackRock New York Muni Opportunities Investor C Shares	MFNKX	NAS CM	Open End	US Muni Fixed Inc (Muni Bond - Single State)	D+	D	C-	Down	Y	800-441-7762

★Expanded analysis of this fund is included in Section II.

TOTAL RETURNS & PERFORMANCE									ASSETS		ASSET ALLOCATION & TURNOVER							MINIMUMS		FEES		
3-Month Total Return	6-Month Total Return	1-Year Total Return	3-Year Total Return	5-Year Total Return	Dividend Yield (TTM)	Expense Ratio	3-Yr Std Deviation	Effective Duration	NAV	Total Assets (MIL)	%Cash	%Government Bonds	%Municipal Bonds	%Corporate Bonds	%Other	Turnover Ratio	Average Coupon Rate	Min Initial Investment	Min Additional Investment	Front End Fee (%)	Back End Fee (%)	Inception Date
0.33	0.46	1.21	4.03	7.75	1.69		0.94		15.09	305.4	26	0	74	0	0	6	3.31					Sep-03
3.53	0.30	4.09	19.45	37.01	2.99	1.34	7.23		25.65	1,765	1	0	100	0	0	21	4.69					Aug-12
4.40	-0.46	3.07	15.06	29.42	4.16	0	7.76		16.15	166.6	-48	0	100	0	0	19	5.07					Apr-02
3.71	-0.19	2.89	11.49	22.91	4.24	0	6.89		15.06	129.0	-33	0	100	0	0	36	5.41					Oct-02
4.11	-1.57	1.74	10.35	19.39	4.74	0	8.28		13.68	136.3	0	0	100	0	0	36	5.29					Jul-01
4.32	0.60	3.90	14.49	27.36	3.88	0	7.29		15.26	394.8	-34	0	99	0	0	15	5.37					Oct-02
4.94	-0.75	2.45	13.17	25.80	4.76		8.19		14.06	609.7	-43	0	99	0	0	19	5.36					Jul-01
4.86	-0.15	2.74	12.20	25.00	4.93	0	7.43		14.54	332.4	-45	0	100	0	0	18	5.41					Jul-02
4.36	0.51	4.09	15.96	28.78	4.04		8.25		11.96	347.6	1	0	100	0	0	22	5.08					Mar-89
3.88	0.89	4.18	13.01	23.37	3.47		6.63		15.55	629.8	-39	0	99	0	0	24	5.07					Feb-98
4.69	-0.14	3.27	14.56	26.42	4.57		8.33		15.4	169.7	-32	0	100	0	0	30	5.20					Feb-98
4.96	-0.29	2.74	13.14	25.48	4.68		8.28		16.51	226.8	-35	0	98	0	0	17	5.34					May-97
4.95	0.53	3.68	12.56	23.73	3.91		7.76		14.5	536.2	3	0	98	0	0	52	5.07					Sep-97
2.91	-1.13	1.29	13.42	26.51	4.25		7.01		15.39	453.8	1	0	99	0	0	8	5.05					Mar-98
3.41	0.31	3.06	12.86	25.79	3.65		6.64		14.81	455.5	0	0	100	0	0	23	4.99					Sep-97
4.37	0.46	3.34	11.39	22.55	3.96		6.81		13.75	303.1	-43	0	100	0	0	26	5.25					Feb-99
4.03	0.34	3.26	11.42	22.42	4.01		7.12		13.62	173.5	1	0	99	0	0	27	5.29					May-98
4.91	-0.78	2.37	12.63	23.51	4.6		8.07		9.39	591.3	-41	0	100	0	0	31	5.29					Sep-88
5.14	-0.39	2.75	13.40	24.83	4.68		8.24		14.84	305.8	-44	0	99	0	0	25	5.20					Mar-93
4.96	-0.24	2.92	13.67	26.97	4.8		8.13		14.52	659.7	3	0	98	0	0	17	5.34					Nov-91
5.22	-0.33	2.86	13.52	25.61	3.72		7.75		14.5	66.0	3	0	98	0	0	25	4.98					Oct-93
6.31	2.39	5.94	16.33	27.52	3.35		7.87		15.75	331.6	1	0	100	0	0	45	5.26					Feb-92
3.87	0.17	3.42	12.95	23.10	3.63		7.17		15.62	529.5	1	0	99	0	0	27	5.30					Jun-92
3.72	-0.33	2.70	11.40	21.48	4.92		7.45		14.14	189.5	1	0	99	0	0	27	5.18					Feb-92
3.77	-0.54	2.70	11.23	22.33	4.49		7.46		13.92	115.0	-48	0	100	0	0	39	5.27					Oct-92
2.83	0.57	3.38	14.22	27.56	3.85		6.11		15.53	453.7	1	0	100	0	0	15	4.96					Oct-92
2.94	-1.33	1.35	13.59	26.82	4.81		7.03		15.46	892.1	2	0	99	0	0	14	5.20					May-92
3.41	0.50	3.29	12.71	25.82	3.62		6.53		14.22	557.0	0	0	100	0	0	19	5.10					Feb-92
2.73	-0.26	1.64	13.16	25.16	3.63		7.25		15.65	205.8	3	0	98	0	0	21	5.16					Oct-92
4.41	0.81	4.17	16.36	30.02	4.1		7.9		15.96	479.7	0	0	100	0	0	21	5.12					Jun-92
3.74	-1.20	2.56	15.44	26.83	3.81		8.74		14.52	964.1	2	0	99	0	0	23	5.27					Apr-92
4.21	0.59	4.01	15.46	28.73	3.88		7.82		14.02	309.3	-37	0	100	0	0	22	5.07					Aug-92
3.56	0.52	2.51	10.85	18.35	2.47	0.49	4.56	6.59	11.07	12,991	18	0	82	0	0	77	4.73	2,000,000				Nov-79
3.49	0.40	2.26	10.12	17.03	2.22	0.74	4.56	6.59	11.08	12,991	18	0	82	0	0	77	4.73	1,000	50	4.25		Oct-94
3.30	0.03	1.50	7.59	12.75	1.46	1.49	4.56	6.59	11.08	12,991	18	0	82	0	0	77	4.73	1,000	50		1.00	Oct-06
3.57	0.55	2.65	11.12	18.84	2.52	0.44	4.59	6.59	11.08	12,991	18	0	82	0	0	77	4.73	5,000,000				Jul-11
3.59	0.49	2.36	10.16	17.11	2.23	0.74	4.54	6.59	11.07	12,991	18	0	82	0	0	77	4.73	5,000				Jul-11
2.25	-0.92	1.25	11.71	20.87	3.45	0.6	5.29	8.30	11.07	353.1	3	0	97	0	0	15	4.74	5,000,000				Jan-18
2.14	-0.95	1.11	11.57	20.72	3.39	0.65	5.28	8.30	11.07	353.1	3	0	97	0	0	15	4.74	2,000,000				Aug-90
2.08	-1.06	0.86	10.84	19.42	3.14	0.9	5.27	8.30	11.08	353.1	3	0	97	0	0	15	4.74	1,000	50	4.25		Oct-06
2.12	-0.99	1.02	11.25	20.29	3.3	0.75	5.29	8.30	11.08	353.1	3	0	97	0	0	15	4.74	1,000	50	4.00		Oct-94
1.89	-1.44	0.20	8.39	15.01	2.36	1.65	5.27	8.30	11.07	353.1	3	0	97	0	0	15	4.74	1,000	50		1.00	Oct-06
2.08	-1.07	0.86	10.74	19.42	3.13	0.9	5.27	8.30	11.07	353.1	3	0	97	0	0	15	4.74	5,000				Oct-06
3.48	0.35	3.16	12.10	25.80	3.63	0	7.2		15.94	44.4	4	0	97	0	0	24	5.08					Apr-02
2.62	0.02	2.52	10.72	23.34	3.31	0	6.21		14.82	95.7	0	0	100	0	0	24	5.23					Oct-02
3.67	-0.26	2.34	11.22	24.45	3.78	0	6.71		14.78	189.3	-50	0	100	0	0	23	5.18					Jul-01
3.91	-0.38	2.48	11.02	24.18	3.93	0	7.15		15.26	75.4	0	0	100	0	0	26	5.04					Jul-02
1.76	-4.46	-2.45	6.57	16.90	2.71	0.61	5.82	7.68	10.83	1,613	7	0	92	1	0	43	4.69	5,000,000				Jan-18
1.75	-4.48	-2.50	6.45	16.76	2.66	0.66	5.85	7.68	10.83	1,613	7	0	92	1	0	43	4.69	2,000,000				Oct-88
1.69	-4.51	-2.73	5.75	15.43	2.4	0.91	5.82	7.68	10.84	1,613	7	0	92	1	0	43	4.69	1,000	50	4.25		Oct-06
1.72	-4.44	-2.59	6.23	16.25	2.56	0.76	5.82	7.68	10.84	1,613	7	0	92	1	0	43	4.69	1,000	50	4.00		Oct-94
1.50	-4.96	-3.46	3.31	11.09	1.61	1.66	5.82	7.68	10.83	1,613	7	0	92	1	0	43	4.69	1,000	50		1.00	Oct-06

	MARKET		FUND TYPE, CATEGORY & OBJECTIVE		RATINGS				NEW INVESTORS	
Fund Name	Ticker Symbol	Traded On	Fund Type	Category and (Prospectus Objective)	Overall Rating	Reward Rating	Risk Rating	Recent Up/ Downgrade	Open to New Investors	Telephone
BlackRock Pennsylvania Municipal Bond Fund Class K	MKPYX	NAS CM	Open End	US Muni Fixed Inc (Muni Bond - Single State)	C	C-	C+		Y	800-441-7762
BlackRock Pennsylvania Muni Bond Fund Institutional Shares	MAPYX	NAS CM	Open End	US Muni Fixed Inc (Muni Bond - Single State)	C	D+	C		Y	800-441-7762
BlackRock Pennsylvania Muni Bond Fund Investor A Shares	MEPYX	NAS CM	Open End	US Muni Fixed Inc (Muni Bond - Single State)	C-	D+	C	Down	Y	800-441-7762
BlackRock Pennsylvania Muni Bond Fund Investor A1 Shares	MDPYX	NAS CM	Open End	US Muni Fixed Inc (Muni Bond - Single State)	C-	D+	C	Down		800-441-7762
BlackRock Pennsylvania Muni Bond Fund Investor C Shares	MFPYX	NAS CM	Open End	US Muni Fixed Inc (Muni Bond - Single State)	C-	D+	C	Down	Y	800-441-7762
BlackRock Pennsylvania Municipal Bond Fund Service Shares	MSPYX	NAS CM	Open End	US Muni Fixed Inc (Muni Bond - Single State)	C-	D+	C	Down	Y	800-441-7762
BlackRock Ready Assets Government Liquidity Fund	MRAXX	NAS CM	Money Mkt	US Money Mkt (Money Mkt - Govt)	C	C-	C			800-441-7762
BlackRock Retmnt Res Money of Retmnt Ser Trust I Shares	MRRXX	NAS CM	Money Mkt	US Money Mkt (Money Mkt - Govt)	C	C-	C			800-441-7762
BlackRock Retmnt Res Money of Retmnt Ser Trust II Shares	MBIXX	NAS CM	Money Mkt	US Money Mkt (Money Mkt - Govt)	C	C-	C			800-441-7762
BlackRock Short Obligations Fund Class K	BBSOX	NAS CM	Open End	US Fixed Inc (Income)	C	C	B-		Y	800-441-7762
BlackRock Short Obligations Fund Institutional Shares	BISOX	NAS CM	Open End	US Fixed Inc (Income)	C	C-	B-		Y	800-441-7762
BlackRock Short Obligations Fund Investor A Shares	BASOX	NAS CM	Open End	US Fixed Inc (Income)	C	C-	B-		Y	800-441-7762
BlackRock Short-Term Municipal Fund Class K	MPLMX	NAS CM	Open End	US Muni Fixed Inc (Muni Bond - Natl)	C	C-	C+		Y	800-441-7762
BlackRock Short-Term Municipal Fund Institutional Shares	MALMX	NAS CM	Open End	US Muni Fixed Inc (Muni Bond - Natl)	C	C-	C+		Y	800-441-7762
BlackRock Short-Term Municipal Fund Investor A Shares	MELMX	NAS CM	Open End	US Muni Fixed Inc (Muni Bond - Natl)	C	C-	C+		Y	800-441-7762
BlackRock Short-Term Municipal Fund Investor A1 Shares	MDLMX	NAS CM	Open End	US Muni Fixed Inc (Muni Bond - Natl)	C	C-	C+		Y	800-441-7762
BlackRock Short-Term Municipal Fund Investor C Shares	MFLMX	NAS CM	Open End	US Muni Fixed Inc (Muni Bond - Natl)	C-	C-	C		Y	800-441-7762
BlackRock Strategic Global Bond Fund, Inc. Class K	MKWIX	NAS CM	Open End	Global Fixed Inc (Income)	C+	C	B	Up	Y	800-441-7762
BlackRock Strategic Global Bond Fund Institutional Shares	MAWIX	NAS CM	Open End	Global Fixed Inc (Income)	C+	C	B	Up	Y	800-441-7762
BlackRock Strategic Global Bond Fund Investor A Shares	MDWIX	NAS CM	Open End	Global Fixed Inc (Income)	C+	C	B	Up	Y	800-441-7762
BlackRock Strategic Global Bond Fund Investor C Shares	MHWIX	NAS CM	Open End	Global Fixed Inc (Income)	C	C	B-		Y	800-441-7762
BlackRock Strategic Income Opportunities Portfolio Class K	BSIKX	NAS CM	Open End	Fixed Inc Misc (Income)	C	C-	C+		Y	800-441-7762
BlackRock Strategic Income Opp Portfol Inst Shares	BSIIX	NAS CM	Open End	Fixed Inc Misc (Income)	C	C-	C+		Y	800-441-7762
BlackRock Strategic Income Opp Portfol Investor A Shares	BASIX	NAS CM	Open End	Fixed Inc Misc (Income)	C	C-	C+		Y	800-441-7762
BlackRock Strategic Income Opp Portfol Investor C Shares	BSICX	NAS CM	Open End	Fixed Inc Misc (Income)	C	C-	C		Y	800-441-7762
Blackrock Strat Muni Opp Fd Of Blackrock Muni Ser Tr Cl K	MKMTX	NAS CM	Open End	US Muni Fixed Inc (Muni Bond - Natl)	D+	D	C-	Down	Y	800-441-7762
Blackrock Strat Muni Opp Fd Of Blackrock Muni Ser Tr Inst	MAMTX	NAS CM	Open End	US Muni Fixed Inc (Muni Bond - Natl)	D+	D	C-	Down	Y	800-441-7762
Blackrock Strat Muni Opp Fd Of Blackrock Muni Ser Tr Inv A	MEMTX	NAS CM	Open End	US Muni Fixed Inc (Muni Bond - Natl)	D+	D	C-	Down	Y	800-441-7762
Blackrock Strat Muni Opp Fd Of Blackrock Muni Ser Tr Inv A	MDMTX	NAS CM	Open End	US Muni Fixed Inc (Muni Bond - Natl)	D+	D	C-	Down		800-441-7762
Blackrock Strat Muni Opp Fd Of Blackrock Muni Ser Tr Inv C	MFMTX	NAS CM	Open End	US Muni Fixed Inc (Muni Bond - Natl)	D+	D	C-	Down	Y	800-441-7762
BlackRock Strategic Municipal Trust	BSD	NYSE	Closed End	US Muni Fixed Inc (Muni Bond - Natl)	C-	D+	C-		Y	800-441-7762
BlackRock Systematic ESG Bond Fund Class K	BIAKX	NAS CM	Open End	US Fixed Inc (Corp Bond - General)	B	B-	B	Up	Y	800-441-7762
BlackRock Systematic ESG Bond Fund Institutional	BIIIX	NAS CM	Open End	US Fixed Inc (Corp Bond - General)	B	B-	B	Up	Y	800-441-7762
BlackRock Systematic ESG Bond Fund Investor A	BIAAX	NAS CM	Open End	US Fixed Inc (Corp Bond - General)	B	B-	B	Up	Y	800-441-7762
BlackRock Systematic ESG Bond Fund Investor C	BIACX	NAS CM	Open End	US Fixed Inc (Corp Bond - General)	B-	B-	B		Y	800-441-7762
BlackRock Taxable Municipal Bond Trust	BBN	NYSE	Closed End	US Fixed Inc (Muni Bond - Natl)	C	C-	C+	Down	Y	800-441-7762
BlackRock Total Return Fund Class K Shares	MPHQX	NAS CM	Open End	US Fixed Inc (Income)	B-	C+	B+	Up	Y	800-441-7762
BlackRock Total Return Fund Class R Shares	MRCBX	NAS CM	Open End	US Fixed Inc (Income)	B-	C+	B	Up	Y	800-441-7762
BlackRock Total Return Fund Institutional Shares	MAHQX	NAS CM	Open End	US Fixed Inc (Income)	B-	C+	B+	Up	Y	800-441-7762
BlackRock Total Return Fund Investor A Shares	MDHQX	NAS CM	Open End	US Fixed Inc (Income)	B-	C+	B	Up	Y	800-441-7762
BlackRock Total Return Fund Investor A1 Shares	MEHQX	NAS CM	Open End	US Fixed Inc (Income)	B-	C+	B+	Up		800-441-7762
BlackRock Total Return Fund Investor C Shares	MFHQX	NAS CM	Open End	US Fixed Inc (Income)	B-	C	B	Up	Y	800-441-7762
BlackRock Total Return Fund Service Shares	MSHQX	NAS CM	Open End	US Fixed Inc (Income)	B-	C+	B	Up	Y	800-441-7762
BlackRock Treasury Strategies Institutional Fund	MLIXX	NAS CM	Money Mkt	US Money Mkt (Money Mkt - Govt)	C	C-	C+		Y	800-441-7762
BlackRock U.S. Government Bond Portfolio Class K	BIGLX	NAS CM	Open End	US Fixed Inc (Govt Bond - General)	B	B-	B		Y	800-441-7762
BlackRock U.S. Government Bond Portfolio Class R	BGBRX	NAS CM	Open End	US Fixed Inc (Govt Bond - General)	B	B-	B	Up	Y	800-441-7762
BlackRock U.S. Govt Bond Portfolio Institutional Shares	PNIGX	NAS CM	Open End	US Fixed Inc (Govt Bond - General)	B	B-	B		Y	800-441-7762
BlackRock U.S. Government Bond Portfolio Investor A Shares	CIGAX	NAS CM	Open End	US Fixed Inc (Govt Bond - General)	B	B-	B	Up	Y	800-441-7762
BlackRock U.S. Government Bond Portfolio Investor C Shares	BIGCX	NAS CM	Open End	US Fixed Inc (Govt Bond - General)	B-	C+	B		Y	800-441-7762
BlackRock U.S. Government Bond Portfolio Service Shares	PIGSX	NAS CM	Open End	US Fixed Inc (Govt Bond - General)	B	B-	B	Up	Y	800-441-7762
BlackRock US Mortgage Portfolio Institutional Shares	MSUMX	NAS CM	Open End	US Fixed Inc (Govt Bond - Mortgage)	C	C	B-		Y	800-441-7762
BlackRock US Mortgage Portfolio Investor A Shares	BMPAX	NAS CM	Open End	US Fixed Inc (Govt Bond - Mortgage)	C	C	B-		Y	800-441-7762

★ Expanded analysis of this fund is included in Section II.

TOTAL RETURNS & PERFORMANCE									ASSETS		ASSET ALLOCATION & TURNOVER							MINIMUMS		FEES		
3-Month Total Return	6-Month Total Return	1-Year Total Return	3-Year Total Return	5-Year Total Return	Dividend Yield (TTM)	Expense Ratio	3-Yr Std Deviation	Effective Duration	NAV	Total Assets (MIL)	%Cash	%Government Bonds	%Municipal Bonds	%Corporate Bonds	%Other	Turnover Ratio	Average Coupon Rate	Min Initial Investment	Min Additional Investment	Front End Fee (%)	Back End Fee (%)	Inception Date
2.08	-0.30	1.09	9.23	17.79	3.58	0.79	4.74	8.04	10.87	547.6	4	0	96	0	0	23	4.87	5,000,000				Jan-18
2.07	-0.33	1.04	9.10	17.64	3.53	0.84	4.75	8.04	10.87	547.6	4	0	96	0	0	23	4.87	2,000,000				Aug-90
2.00	-0.45	0.79	8.19	16.30	3.28	1.09	4.72	8.04	10.88	547.6	4	0	96	0	0	23	4.87	1,000	50	4.25		Oct-06
2.14	-0.37	0.94	8.78	17.29	3.43	0.94	4.77	8.04	10.89	547.6	4	0	96	0	0	23	4.87	10,000		4.00		Oct-94
1.81	-0.82	0.04	5.89	11.98	2.51	1.84	4.73	8.04	10.88	547.6	4	0	96	0	0	23	4.87	1,000	50		1.00	Oct-06
2.10	-0.36	0.88	8.29	16.40	3.28	1.09	4.72	8.04	10.89	547.6	4	0	96	0	0	23	4.87	5,000				Oct-06
0.00	0.17	0.78	2.90	2.93	0.92	0.78	0.15		1	449.3	92	8	0	0	0			5,000	1			Feb-75
0.01	0.17	0.75	2.87	2.92	0.88	0	0.15		1	25.8	100	0	0	0	0			0				Apr-82
0.01	0.19	0.75	2.61	2.66	0.91	0	0.16		1	25.8	100	0	0	0	0			0				Oct-98
1.54	1.22	2.41	7.00	9.48	2.11	0.3	0.82	0.41	10.08	3,874	59	1	0	39	0	18	2.25	5,000,000				Nov-12
1.52	1.07	2.31	6.64	9.03	2.02	0.35	0.82	0.41	10.06	3,874	59	1	0	39	0	18	2.25	2,000,000				Jul-13
1.47	1.08	2.11	6.13	8.04	1.83	0.6	0.81	0.41	10.06	3,874	59	1	0	39	0	18	2.25	1,000	50			Mar-18
1.40	0.61	1.51	4.71	6.04	1.57	0.31	1.15	1.10	10.15	579.9	14	0	84	0	0	129	3.23	5,000,000				Oct-06
1.29	0.58	1.46	4.56	5.86	1.52	0.36	1.1	1.10	10.15	579.9	14	0	84	0	0	129	3.23	2,000,000				Nov-79
1.33	0.56	1.32	3.81	4.64	1.27	0.61	1.14	1.10	10.16	579.9	14	0	84	0	0	129	3.23	1,000	50	3.00		Oct-06
1.36	0.53	1.36	4.25	5.32	1.42	0.46	1.14	1.10	10.16	579.9	14	0	84	0	0	129	3.23	0		1.00		Oct-94
1.07	0.08	0.45	1.42	0.65	0.52	1.36	1.12	1.10	9.89	579.9	14	0	84	0	0	129	3.23	1,000	50		1.00	Oct-06
5.75	2.99	4.50	13.24	25.06	2.24	0.59	4.67	6.03	6.26	518.6	0	41	0	26	0	373	3.83	5,000,000				Nov-15
5.73	2.97	4.45	13.07	24.78	2.19	0.64	4.73	6.03	6.26	518.6	0	41	0	26	0	373	3.83	2,000,000				Sep-88
5.85	3.01	4.19	12.23	23.25	1.95	0.89	4.74	6.03	6.26	518.6	0	41	0	26	0	373	3.83	1,000	50	4.00		Oct-94
5.48	2.46	3.42	9.56	18.53	1.21	1.64	4.7	6.03	6.25	518.6	0	41	0	26	0	373	3.83	1,000	50		1.00	Oct-06
6.42	0.22	2.63	10.13	15.64	3.25	0.76	4.74	3.00	9.87	30,922	-25	15	3	21	0	1,805	4.28	5,000,000				Mar-16
6.29	0.18	2.54	9.85	15.24	3.16	0.84	4.7	3.00	9.86	30,922	-25	15	3	21	0	1,805	4.28	2,000,000				Feb-08
6.33	0.03	2.25	8.91	13.59	2.87	1.14	4.76	3.00	9.86	30,922	-25	15	3	21	0	1,805	4.28	1,000	50	4.00		Feb-08
6.04	-0.32	1.51	6.55	9.48	2.13	1.87	4.7	3.00	9.85	30,922	-25	15	3	21	0	1,805	4.28	1,000	50		1.00	Feb-08
2.80	-4.81	-2.92	6.24	16.84	2.74	0.72	6.47	8.53	11.07	9,153	5	0	95	0	0	68	4.58	5,000,000				Jan-18
2.79	-4.84	-2.98	6.07	16.66	2.67	0.78	6.47	8.53	11.07	9,153	5	0	95	0	0	68	4.58	2,000,000				Oct-88
2.73	-4.95	-3.20	5.37	15.39	2.43	1.01	6.48	8.53	11.06	9,153	5	0	95	0	0	68	4.58	1,000	50	4.25		Oct-06
2.77	-4.80	-3.05	5.85	16.35	2.6	0.86	6.45	8.53	11.07	9,153	5	0	95	0	0	68	4.58	1,000	0	1.00		Oct-94
2.54	-5.23	-3.92	3.00	11.09	1.63	1.77	6.46	8.53	11.07	9,153	5	0	95	0	0	68	4.58	1,000	50		1.00	Oct-06
4.19	-1.20	1.97	13.03	25.87	4.87	0	8.08		14.01	99.4	-43	0	100	0	0	28	5.42					Aug-99
3.47	7.00	9.61	17.78		2.09	0.37	3.39		10.65	49.8	22	14	0	35	0	202	3.90	5,000,000				Aug-16
3.46	6.98	9.57	17.65		2.05	0.42	3.38		10.65	49.8	22	14	0	35	0	202	3.90	2,000,000				Aug-16
3.39	6.84	9.29	16.73		1.8	0.67	3.4		10.65	49.8	22	14	0	35	0	202	3.90	1,000	50	4.00		Aug-16
3.20	6.45	8.48	14.15		1.08	1.42	3.42		10.65	49.8	22	14	0	35	0	202	3.90	1,000	50		1.00	Aug-16
8.23	3.51	7.30	26.65	54.08	5.71	1.59	10.64		24.56	1,349	-47	0	90	7	0	7	6.36					Aug-10
5.64	5.12	8.02	16.19	24.29	2.86	0.44	4.14	6.09	12.39	17,266	-11	11	3	27	0	574	3.78	5,000,000				Dec-01
5.47	4.78	7.40	13.93	20.33	2.21	1.1	4.14	6.09	12.4	17,266	-11	11	3	27	0	574	3.78	100				Oct-06
5.62	5.09	7.94	15.96	23.89	2.78	0.51	4.16	6.09	12.39	17,266	-11	11	3	27	0	574	3.78	2,000,000				Sep-07
5.63	4.92	7.67	14.80	21.83	2.46	0.85	4.16	6.09	12.4	17,266	-11	11	3	27	0	574	3.78	1,000	50	4.00		Sep-07
5.68	5.01	7.87	15.45	22.98	2.64	0.66	4.19	6.09	12.39	17,266	-11	11	3	27	0	574	3.78	1,000	50	1.00		Sep-07
5.45	4.57	6.96	12.55	17.90	1.81	1.51	4.18	6.09	12.39	17,266	-11	11	3	27	0	574	3.78	1,000	50		1.00	Dec-01
5.63	5.02	7.71	15.01	22.08	2.5	0.81	4.18	6.09	12.4	17,266	-11	11	3	27	0	574	3.78	5,000				Sep-07
0.00	0.31	1.03	3.94	4.29	1.07	0.35	0.16		1	116.9	100	0	0	0	0			3,000,000				Dec-74
1.29	6.16	8.26	14.45	19.22	2.2	0.91	3.01	4.74	11.11	818.1	11	42	0	0	0	837	2.68	5,000,000				Jan-18
1.15	5.96	7.75	12.71	16.11	1.67	1.46	3	4.74	11.14	818.1	11	42	0	0	0	837	2.68	100				Jul-11
1.28	6.13	8.20	14.31	19.08	2.15	0.96	3	4.74	11.11	818.1	11	42	0	0	0	837	2.68	2,000,000				Apr-92
1.21	6.09	7.92	13.56	17.60	1.91	1.21	3	4.74	11.14	818.1	11	42	0	0	0	837	2.68	1,000	50	4.00		May-92
1.03	5.71	7.13	11.06	13.15	1.19	1.96	3.02	4.74	11.12	818.1	11	42	0	0	0	837	2.68	1,000	50		1.00	Oct-96
1.21	6.01	7.84	13.48	17.71	1.91	1.21	3	4.74	11.1	818.1	11	42	0	0	0	837	2.68	5,000				Jul-93
4.47	1.63	3.81	10.57	16.96	3.26	1.44	3.46	1.36	10.24	247.7	-8	0	0	1	0	1,580	3.47	2,000,000				Jul-05
4.41	1.51	3.55	9.74	15.44	3.01	1.69	3.46	1.36	10.22	247.7	-8	0	0	1	0	1,580	3.47	1,000	50	4.00		Dec-10

	MARKET		FUND TYPE, CATEGORY & OBJECTIVE		RATINGS				NEW INVESTORS	
Fund Name	Ticker Symbol	Traded On	Fund Type	Category and (Prospectus Objective)	Overall Rating	Reward Rating	Risk Rating	Recent Up/ Downgrade	Open to New Investors	Telephone
BlackRock US Mortgage Portfolio Investor C Shares	BMPCX	NAS CM	Open End	US Fixed Inc (Govt Bond - Mortgage)	C	C-	C+		Y	800-441-7762
BlackRock Virginia Municipal Bond Trust	BHV	AMEX	Closed End	US Muni Fixed Inc (Muni Bond - Single State)	D+	C-	D+	Down	Y	800-441-7762
Blackstone / GSO Floating Rate Enhanced Inc Advisory Cl D	BGFDX	NAS CM	Closed End	US Fixed Inc (Income)	D	D	D		Y	
Blackstone / GSO Floating Rate Enhanced Inc Brokerage Cl T	BGFTX	NAS CM	Closed End	US Fixed Inc (Income)	D	D	D	Down	Y	
Blackstone / GSO Floating Rate Enhanced Inc Brokerage Cl T			Closed End	US Fixed Inc (Income)	D	D	D		Y	
Blackstone / GSO Floating Rate Enhanced Income Inst Cl I	BGFLX	NAS CM	Closed End	US Fixed Inc (Income)	D	D	D+	Down	Y	
Blackstone / GSO Strategic Credit Fund	BGB	NYSE	Closed End	US Fixed Inc (Income)	D	D	D	Down	Y	
Blackstone/GSO Long-Short Credit Income Fund	BGX	NYSE	Closed End	US Fixed Inc (Growth & Income)	D	D	D	Down	Y	
Blackstone/GSO Senior Floating Rate Term Fund	BSL	NYSE	Closed End	US Fixed Inc (Growth & Income)	D	D	D	Down	Y	
Bluestone Community Development Fund			Closed End	US Fixed Inc (Income)	C+	C	B-	Up	Y	
BMO Core Plus Bond Fund Class A	BATCX	NAS CM	Open End	US Fixed Inc (Multisector Bond)	B-	C+	B+	Up	Y	800-236-3863
BMO Core Plus Bond Fund Class I	MCBIX	NAS CM	Open End	US Fixed Inc (Multisector Bond)	B-	C+	B+	Up	Y	800-236-3863
BMO Core Plus Bond Fund Class Y	MCYBX	NAS CM	Open End	US Fixed Inc (Multisector Bond)	B-	C+	B+	Up	Y	800-236-3863
BMO Corporate Income Fund Class A	BATIX	NAS CM	Open End	US Fixed Inc (Corp Bond - General)	C+	C	B	Up	Y	800-236-3863
BMO Corporate Income Fund Class I	MCIIX	NAS CM	Open End	US Fixed Inc (Corp Bond - General)	C+	C	B	Up	Y	800-236-3863
BMO Corporate Income Fund Class Y	MCIYX	NAS CM	Open End	US Fixed Inc (Corp Bond - General)	C+	C	B	Up	Y	800-236-3863
BMO Government Money Market Fund Class Premier	MGNXX	NAS CM	Money Mkt	US Money Mkt (Money Mkt - Govt)	C	C-	C+		Y	800-236-3863
BMO Government Money Market Fund Class Y	MGYXX	NAS CM	Money Mkt	US Money Mkt (Money Mkt - Govt)	C	C-	C+		Y	800-236-3863
BMO High Yield Bond Fund Class A	BMHAX	NAS CM	Open End	US Fixed Inc (Corp Bond - High Yield)	D+	D+	C-	Down	Y	800-236-3863
BMO High Yield Bond Fund Class I	MHBNX	NAS CM	Open End	US Fixed Inc (Corp Bond - High Yield)	D+	D+	C-	Down	Y	800-236-3863
BMO Institutional Prime Money Market Fund Investor Class	BYFXX	NAS CM	Money Mkt	US Money Mkt (Money Mkt - General)	C	C-	C+		Y	800-236-3863
BMO Institutional Prime Money Market Fund Premier Class	BPFXX	NAS CM	Money Mkt	US Money Mkt (Money Mkt - General)	C	C-	C+		Y	800-236-3863
BMO Intermediate Tax Free Fund Class Y	MITFX	NAS CM	Open End	US Muni Fixed Inc (Muni Bond - Natl)	C	C-	C+		Y	800-236-3863
BMO Intermediate Tax-Free Fund Class A	BITAX	NAS CM	Open End	US Muni Fixed Inc (Muni Bond - Natl)	C	C-	C+		Y	800-236-3863
BMO Intermediate Tax-Free Fund Class I	MIITX	NAS CM	Open End	US Muni Fixed Inc (Muni Bond - Natl)	C	C-	C+		Y	800-236-3863
BMO Prime Money Market Fund Class Premier	MAIXX	NAS CM	Money Mkt	US Money Mkt (Money Mkt - Taxable)	C	C	C+		Y	800-236-3863
BMO Prime Money Market Fund Class Y	MARXX	NAS CM	Money Mkt	US Money Mkt (Money Mkt - Taxable)	C	C-	C+		Y	800-236-3863
BMO Short Tax-Free Fund Class A	BASFX	NAS CM	Open End	US Muni Fixed Inc (Muni Bond - Natl)	C	C-	C+		Y	800-236-3863
BMO Short Tax-Free Fund Class I	MTFIX	NAS CM	Open End	US Muni Fixed Inc (Muni Bond - Natl)	C	C-	C+		Y	800-236-3863
BMO Short Term Income Advisor Fund Class I	MSIFX	NAS CM	Open End	US Fixed Inc (Multisector Bond)	C+	C	B	Up	Y	800-236-3863
BMO Short-Term Income Fund Class A	BTMAX	NAS CM	Open End	US Fixed Inc (Multisector Bond)	C	C	B-		Y	800-236-3863
BMO Strategic Income Fund Class A	BMTAX	NAS CM	Open End	US Fixed Inc (Worldwide Bond)	C-	D+	C	Down	Y	800-236-3863
BMO Strategic Income Fund Class I	MGIIX	NAS CM	Open End	US Fixed Inc (Worldwide Bond)	C-	D+	C	Down	Y	800-236-3863
BMO Strategic Income Fund Class Y	MRGIX	NAS CM	Open End	US Fixed Inc (Worldwide Bond)	C-	D+	C	Down	Y	800-236-3863
BMO Tax-Free Money Market Fund Class Premier	MFIXX	NAS CM	Money Mkt	US Money Mkt (Money Mkt - Fed Tax Exmpt)	C	C-	C+		Y	800-236-3863
BMO Tax-Free Money Market Fund Class Y	MTFXX	NAS CM	Money Mkt	US Money Mkt (Money Mkt - Fed Tax Exmpt)	C	C-	C		Y	800-236-3863
BMO Ultra Short Tax-Free Fund Class A	BAUSX	NAS CM	Open End	US Muni Fixed Inc (Muni Bond - Natl)	C	C-	C		Y	800-236-3863
BMO Ultra Short Tax-Free Fund Class I	MUISX	NAS CM	Open End	US Muni Fixed Inc (Muni Bond - Natl)	C	C-	C+		Y	800-236-3863
BNY Mellon Alcentra Global Credit Inc 2024 Target Term Fun	DCF	NYSE	Closed End	Global Fixed Inc (Income)	D	D	D	Down	Y	
BNY Mellon Alcentra Global Multi-Strategy Credit Fund			Closed End	Fixed Inc Misc (Income)	U	U	U		Y	
BNY Mellon AMT-Free Municipal Bond Fund - Class A	DMUAX	NAS CM	Open End	US Muni Fixed Inc (Muni Bond - Natl)	C	C-	B-		Y	
BNY Mellon AMT-Free Municipal Bond Fund - Class C	DMUCX	NAS CM	Open End	US Muni Fixed Inc (Muni Bond - Natl)	C	C-	C+		Y	
BNY Mellon AMT-Free Municipal Bond Fund - Class I	DMBIX	NAS CM	Open End	US Muni Fixed Inc (Muni Bond - Natl)	C	C-	B-		Y	
BNY Mellon AMT-Free Municipal Bond Fund - Class Y	DMUYX	NAS CM	Open End	US Muni Fixed Inc (Muni Bond - Natl)	C	C-	B-		Y	
BNY Mellon AMT-Free Municipal Bond Fund - Class Z	DRMBX	NAS CM	Open End	US Muni Fixed Inc (Muni Bond - Natl)	C	C-	B-			
BNY Mellon Bond Fund Class Investor	MIBDX	NAS CM	Open End	US Fixed Inc (Corp Bond - General)	B	C+	B+	Up	Y	800-645-6561
BNY Mellon Bond Fund Class M	MPBFX	NAS CM	Open End	US Fixed Inc (Corp Bond - General)	B	C+	B+	Up	Y	800-645-6561
BNY Mellon Bond Market Index Fund - Class I	DBIRX	NAS CM	Open End	US Fixed Inc (Corp Bond - General)	B	B-	B+		Y	
BNY Mellon Bond Market Index Fund - Investor Shares	DBMIX	NAS CM	Open End	US Fixed Inc (Corp Bond - General)	B	B-	B	Up	Y	
BNY Mellon California AMT-Free Muni Bond Fund - Cl A	DCAAX	NAS CM	Open End	US Muni Fixed Inc (Muni Bond - Single State)	C	C-	C+		Y	
BNY Mellon California AMT-Free Muni Bond Fund - Cl C	DCACX	NAS CM	Open End	US Muni Fixed Inc (Muni Bond - Single State)	C	C-	C		Y	
BNY Mellon California AMT-Free Muni Bond Fund - Cl I	DCMIX	NAS CM	Open End	US Muni Fixed Inc (Muni Bond - Single State)	C	C-	B-		Y	

★ Expanded analysis of this fund is included in Section II.

TOTAL RETURNS & PERFORMANCE									ASSETS		ASSET ALLOCATION & TURNOVER							MINIMUMS		FEES		
3-Month Total Return	6-Month Total Return	1-Year Total Return	3-Year Total Return	5-Year Total Return	Dividend Yield (TTM)	Expense Ratio	3-Yr Std Deviation	Effective Duration	NAV	Total Assets (MIL)	%Cash	%Government Bonds	%Municipal Bonds	%Corporate Bonds	%Other	Turnover Ratio	Average Coupon Rate	Min Initial Investment	Min Additional Investment	Front End Fee (%)	Back End Fee (%)	Inception Date
4.22	1.03	2.69	7.33	11.12	2.26	2.44	3.46	1.36	10.22	247.7	-8	0	0	1	0	1,580	3.47	1,000	50		1.00	Dec-10
4.51	0.37	2.97	10.54	21.50	3.71	0	6.46		15.17	24.0	4	0	97	0	0	17	4.96					Apr-02
16.83	-7.62	-4.19			6.92	3.19			21.87	--	0	0	0	95	0	72		10,000	1,000			Sep-18
16.82	-7.88	-4.53			6.66	3.44			21.8	--	0	0	0	95	0	72		10,000	1,000	2.50		May-18
15.09	-10.67	-10.20			0	3.44			22.26	--	0	0	0	95	0	72		10,000	1,000	3.50		Apr-19
16.92	-7.67	-4.07			7.2	2.94			21.84	--	0	0	0	95	0	72		1,000,000	1,000			Jan-18
16.88	-10.82	-8.23	-0.47	9.27	10.16		15.29		13.07	569.0	1	0	0	99	0	40						Sep-12
19.57	-9.81	-6.13	4.13	16.03	10.59	2.19	16.19		13.61	167.9	2	0	0	96	0	40						Jan-11
17.16	-8.68	-6.23	2.90	13.63	8.85	2.04	14.5		14.47	215.8	-1	0	0	99	0	40						May-10
7.58	4.40	5.87	14.46	20.94	3.51	1.75	4.15		10.02	--	6	0	0	94	1		5.83	10,000	10,000	1.00		Dec-13
4.62	4.54	7.28	14.66	23.62	2.88	0.58	3.4	6.09	12.28	1,117	5	23	0	35	0	51	3.37	1,000	50	3.50		May-14
4.78	4.75	7.54	15.61	25.16	3.13	0.33	3.46	6.09	12.28	1,117	5	23	0	35	0	51	3.37	1,000,000				Dec-08
4.71	4.62	7.27	14.75	23.71	2.88	0.58	3.4	6.09	12.29	1,117	5	23	0	35	0	51	3.37	1,000	50			Dec-08
9.95	4.12	8.76	18.10	33.32	3.13	0.59	6.7	7.72	14	347.7	6	1	0	92	0	37	3.87	1,000	50	3.50		May-14
10.00	4.29	8.96	18.66	34.39	3.32	0.42	6.72	7.72	13.99	347.7	6	1	0	92	0	37	3.87	1,000,000				Dec-08
9.95	4.12	8.76	18.09	33.31	3.13	0.59	6.7	7.72	14	347.7	6	1	0	92	0	37	3.87	1,000	50			Dec-08
0.00	0.30	1.21	4.52	4.95	1.39	0.21	0.18		1	4,009	66	34	0	0	0			10,000,000				May-04
0.00	0.23	1.02	3.79	3.94	1.18	0.46	0.17		1	4,009	66	34	0	0	0			1,000	50			May-04
9.95	-4.93	-2.47	5.54	15.42	5.25	0.91	8.96	4.15	8.63	10.4	2	0	0	97	0	24	5.88	1,000	50	3.50		May-14
10.03	-4.83	-2.24	6.29	16.68	5.49	0.66	8.98	4.15	8.62	10.4	2	0	0	97	0	24	5.88	1,000,000				Dec-11
0.01	0.31	1.17	4.39		1.36	0.45	0.17		1	483.9	97	1	2	0	0			1,000	50			Jun-16
0.06	0.42	1.41	5.15		1.6	0.2	0.17		1	483.9	97	1	2	0	0			10,000,000				Jun-16
2.19	0.25	2.19	9.35	15.59	2.68	0.54	4	5.64	11.37	1,817	1	0	99	0	0	64	4.65	1,000	50			Feb-94
2.28	0.25	2.19	9.35	15.60	2.69	0.54	4	5.64	11.37	1,817	1	0	99	0	0	64	4.65	1,000	50	3.50		May-14
2.34	0.36	2.44	10.18	17.02	2.94	0.3	4.01	5.64	11.36	1,817	1	0	99	0	0	64	4.65	1,000,000				Dec-10
0.04	0.39	1.37	5.05	5.80	1.56	0.2	0.17		1	631.0	97	2	1	0	0			10,000,000				Apr-00
0.01	0.29	1.14	4.29	4.63	1.32	0.45	0.17		1	631.0	97	2	1	0	0			1,000	50			Nov-92
1.68	0.61	1.75	5.39	7.99	1.68	0.55	1.54	1.80	10.24	130.6	5	0	95	0	0	94	3.83	1,000	50	2.00		May-14
1.82	0.79	1.90	5.97	8.91	1.83	0.4	1.5	1.80	10.25	130.6	5	0	95	0	0	94	3.83	1,000,000				Nov-12
2.56	2.16	3.66	9.09	12.70	2.38	0.35	1.53	1.71	9.55	252.4	7	18	0	44	0	53	2.75	1,000,000				May-07
2.50	2.14	3.51	8.39	11.43	2.13	0.6	1.46	1.71	9.54	252.4	7	18	0	44	0	53	2.75	1,000	50	2.00		May-14
12.85	-0.32	2.95	12.26	20.51	5.38	0.8	8.67	5.37	9.11	65.6	5	4	0	73	0	39	5.23	1,000	50	3.50		May-14
12.79	-0.21	3.09	13.10	22.01	5.64	0.55	8.66	5.37	9.1	65.6	5	4	0	73	0	39	5.23	1,000,000				May-07
12.85	-0.32	2.95	12.26	20.51	5.38	0.8	8.68	5.37	9.11	65.6	5	4	0	73	0	39	5.23	1,000	50			Dec-92
0.13	0.46	1.07	3.53	4.24	1.18	0.2	0.11		1	354.7	24	0	76	0	0	27,434		10,000,000				Jun-05
0.06	0.34	0.83	2.75	3.13	0.93	0.45	0.11		1	354.7	24	0	76	0	0	27,434		1,000	50			Sep-04
0.51	0.40	1.04	3.56	4.72	1.18	0.55	0.58	0.65	10.08	533.8	13	0	87	0	0	155	1.67	1,000	50	2.00		May-14
0.57	0.53	1.29	4.34	6.04	1.43	0.3	0.58	0.65	10.07	533.8	13	0	87	0	0	155	1.67	1,000,000				Sep-09
23.06	-8.48	-5.85			8.35	2.44		0.71	8.17	115.4	2	0	0	64	0	55	6.19					Oct-17
28.59	-7.75					3.57			90.28	--	3	0	0	46	0	34	6.28	25,000				Aug-19
2.64	1.15	3.35	11.42	19.31	2.38	0.7	4.35	5.17	14.44	1,081	1	0	99	0	0	18	4.78	1,000	100	4.50		Mar-03
2.45	0.78	2.58	8.95	14.92	1.62	1.45	4.32	5.17	14.44	1,081	1	0	99	0	0	18	4.78	1,000	100		1.00	Mar-03
2.63	1.27	3.53	12.18	20.72	2.63	0.45	4.37	5.17	14.44	1,081	1	0	99	0	0	18	4.78	1,000	100			Dec-08
2.70	1.23	3.62	12.53	21.46	2.72	0.45	4.37	5.17	14.44	1,081	1	0	99	0	0	18	4.78	1,000,000				Jul-13
2.69	1.26	3.57	12.18	20.64	2.6	0.47	4.35	5.17	14.45	1,081	1	0	99	0	0	18	4.78	1,000	100			May-94
3.93	5.58	7.99	15.19	21.42	2.45	0.8	3.34	5.68	13.51	1,201	1	25	6	37	0	80	3.43	10,000	100			Jul-01
3.99	5.71	8.26	16.07	22.97	2.71	0.55	3.32	5.68	13.54	1,201	1	25	6	37	0	80	3.43	10,000	100			Oct-00
2.64	6.24	8.73	16.38	22.84	2.58	0.15	3.25	5.85	11.09	1,118	5	42	1	25	0	126	3.27	1,000	100			Nov-93
2.57	6.21	8.46	15.62	21.33	2.34	0.4	3.23	5.85	11.09	1,118	5	42	1	25	0	126	3.27	2,500	100			Apr-94
2.13	0.66	2.79	9.09	16.75	2.61	0.98	4.35	5.43	14.96	852.8	0	0	100	0	0	23	5.14	1,000	100	4.50		Oct-04
1.87	0.28	1.94	6.63	12.32	1.84	1.75	4.34	5.43	14.95	852.8	0	0	100	0	0	23	5.14	1,000	100		1.00	Oct-04
2.12	0.78	3.04	9.90	18.21	2.86	0.73	4.33	5.43	14.95	852.8	0	0	100	0	0	23	5.14	1,000	100			Dec-08

Fund Name	MARKET Ticker Symbol	Traded On	FUND TYPE, CATEGORY & OBJECTIVE Fund Type	Category and (Prospectus Objective)	RATINGS Overall Rating	Reward Rating	Risk Rating	Recent Up/ Downgrade	NEW INVESTORS Open to New Investors	Telephone
BNY Mellon California AMT-Free Muni Bond Fund - Cl Y	DCAYX	NAS CM	Open End	US Muni Fixed Inc (Muni Bond - Single State)	C	C-	B-		Y	
BNY Mellon California AMT-Free Muni Bond Fund - Cl Z	DRCAX	NAS CM	Open End	US Muni Fixed Inc (Muni Bond - Single State)	C	C-	B-			
BNY Mellon Connecticut Fund Class A	PSCTX	NAS CM	Open End	US Muni Fixed Inc (Muni Bond - Single State)	C	C-	C+		Y	
BNY Mellon Connecticut Fund Class C	PMCCX	NAS CM	Open End	US Muni Fixed Inc (Muni Bond - Single State)	C	C-	C+		Y	
BNY Mellon Connecticut Fund Class I	DTCIX	NAS CM	Open End	US Muni Fixed Inc (Muni Bond - Single State)	C	C-	B-		Y	
BNY Mellon Connecticut Fund Class Y	DPMYX	NAS CM	Open End	US Muni Fixed Inc (Muni Bond - Single State)	C	C-	B-		Y	
BNY Mellon Connecticut Fund Class Z	DPMZX	NAS CM	Open End	US Muni Fixed Inc (Muni Bond - Single State)	C	C-	B-			
BNY Mellon Core Plus Fund Class A	DCPAX	NAS CM	Open End	US Fixed Inc (Income)	B-	C+	B+	Up	Y	
BNY Mellon Core Plus Fund Class C	DCPCX	NAS CM	Open End	US Fixed Inc (Income)	B-	C	B	Up	Y	
BNY Mellon Core Plus Fund Class I	DCPIX	NAS CM	Open End	US Fixed Inc (Income)	B-	C+	B+	Up	Y	
BNY Mellon Core Plus Fund Class Y	DCPYX	NAS CM	Open End	US Fixed Inc (Income)	B-	C+	B+	Up	Y	
BNY Mellon Corporate Bond Fund Class M Shares	BYMMX	NAS CM	Open End	US Fixed Inc (Corp Bond - General)	C	C-	B		Y	800-645-6561
BNY Mellon Corporate Bond Fund Investor Shares	BYMIX	NAS CM	Open End	US Fixed Inc (Corp Bond - General)	C	C-	B		Y	800-645-6561
BNY Mellon Floating Rate Income Fund - Class A	DFLAX	NAS CM	Open End	US Fixed Inc (Income)	D	D	C-	Down	Y	
BNY Mellon Floating Rate Income Fund - Class C	DFLCX	NAS CM	Open End	US Fixed Inc (Income)	D	D	C-	Down	Y	
BNY Mellon Floating Rate Income Fund - Class I	DFLIX	NAS CM	Open End	US Fixed Inc (Income)	D+	D	C-	Down	Y	
BNY Mellon Floating Rate Income Fund - Class Y	DFLYX	NAS CM	Open End	US Fixed Inc (Income)	D+	D	C-	Down	Y	
BNY Mellon Funds Trust Natl Muni Money Mkt Fund Class M	MOMXX	NAS CM	Money Mkt	US Money Mkt (Money Mkt - Fed Tax Exmpt)	C	C-	C+		Y	800-645-6561
BNY Mellon Funds Trust Natl Muni Money Mkt Investor Cl	MNTXX	NAS CM	Money Mkt	US Money Mkt (Money Mkt - Fed Tax Exmpt)	C	C-	C+		Y	800-645-6561
BNY Mellon Global Dynamic Bond Income Fund - Class A	DGDAX	NAS CM	Open End	Fixed Inc Misc (Worldwide Bond)	C	C-	C+		Y	
BNY Mellon Global Dynamic Bond Income Fund - Class C	DGDCX	NAS CM	Open End	Fixed Inc Misc (Worldwide Bond)	C	C-	C		Y	
BNY Mellon Global Dynamic Bond Income Fund - Class I	DGDIX	NAS CM	Open End	Fixed Inc Misc (Worldwide Bond)	C	C-	C+		Y	
BNY Mellon Global Dynamic Bond Income Fund - Class Y	DGDYX	NAS CM	Open End	Fixed Inc Misc (Worldwide Bond)	C	C-	B-		Y	
BNY Mellon Global Fixed Income Fund - Class A	DHGAX	NAS CM	Open End	Global Fixed Inc (Worldwide Bond)	C+	C	B	Up	Y	
BNY Mellon Global Fixed Income Fund - Class C	DHGCX	NAS CM	Open End	Global Fixed Inc (Worldwide Bond)	C	C	B-		Y	
BNY Mellon Global Fixed Income Fund - Class I	SDGIX	NAS CM	Open End	Global Fixed Inc (Worldwide Bond)	C+	C	B	Up	Y	
BNY Mellon Global Fixed Income Fund - Class Y	DSDYX	NAS CM	Open End	Global Fixed Inc (Worldwide Bond)	C+	C	B	Up	Y	
BNY Mellon Government Money Market Fund Class Investor	MLOXX	NAS CM	Money Mkt	US Money Mkt (Money Mkt - Govt)	C	C	C+		Y	800-645-6561
BNY Mellon Government Money Market Fund Class M	MLMXX	NAS CM	Money Mkt	US Money Mkt (Money Mkt - Govt)	C	C-	C+		Y	800-645-6561
BNY Mellon High Yield Fund - Class A	DPLTX	NAS CM	Open End	US Fixed Inc (Corp Bond - High Yield)	C-	D+	C		Y	
BNY Mellon High Yield Fund - Class C	PTHIX	NAS CM	Open End	US Fixed Inc (Corp Bond - High Yield)	C-	D+	C		Y	
BNY Mellon High Yield Fund - Class I	DLHRX	NAS CM	Open End	US Fixed Inc (Corp Bond - High Yield)	C-	D+	C		Y	
BNY Mellon High Yield Municipal Bond Fund - Class A	DHYAX	NAS CM	Open End	US Muni Fixed Inc (Muni Bond - Natl)	C-	D+	C	Down	Y	
BNY Mellon High Yield Municipal Bond Fund - Class C	DHYCX	NAS CM	Open End	US Muni Fixed Inc (Muni Bond - Natl)	D+	D	C-	Down	Y	
BNY Mellon High Yield Municipal Bond Fund - Class Y	DHYYX	NAS CM	Open End	US Muni Fixed Inc (Muni Bond - Natl)	C-	D+	C	Down	Y	
BNY Mellon High Yield Municipal Bond Fund - Class Z	DHMBX	NAS CM	Open End	US Muni Fixed Inc (Muni Bond - Natl)	C-	D+	C	Down		
BNY Mellon High Yield Municipal Bond Fund- Class I	DYBIX	NAS CM	Open End	US Muni Fixed Inc (Muni Bond - Natl)	C-	D+	C	Down	Y	
BNY Mellon High Yield Strategies Fund	DHF	NYSE	Closed End	US Fixed Inc (Corp Bond - High Yield)	D	D	D+	Down	Y	
BNY Mellon Inflation Adjusted Securities Fund Class I	DIASX	NAS CM	Open End	US Fixed Inc (Income)	B-	C	B	Up	Y	
BNY Mellon Inflation Adjusted Securities Cl Investor	DIAVX	NAS CM	Open End	US Fixed Inc (Income)	C+	C	B	Up	Y	
BNY Mellon Inflation Adjusted Securities Fund Class Y	DAIYX	NAS CM	Open End	US Fixed Inc (Income)	B-	C	B	Up	Y	
BNY Mellon Intermediate Bond Fund Class Investor	MIIDX	NAS CM	Open End	US Fixed Inc (Corp Bond - General)	C+	C	B	Up	Y	800-645-6561
BNY Mellon Intermediate Bond Fund Class M	MPIBX	NAS CM	Open End	US Fixed Inc (Corp Bond - General)	B-	C	B	Up	Y	800-645-6561
BNY Mellon Intermediate Municipal Bond Fund	DITEX	NAS CM	Open End	US Muni Fixed Inc (Muni Bond - Natl)	C	C-	B-		Y	
BNY Mellon International Bond Fund Class A	DIBAX	NAS CM	Open End	Global Fixed Inc (Worldwide Bond)	D	D	C-	Down	Y	
BNY Mellon International Bond Fund Class C	DIBCX	NAS CM	Open End	Global Fixed Inc (Worldwide Bond)	D	D	C-	Down	Y	
BNY Mellon International Bond Fund Class I	DIBRX	NAS CM	Open End	Global Fixed Inc (Worldwide Bond)	D	D	C-	Down	Y	
BNY Mellon International Bond Fund Class Y	DIBYX	NAS CM	Open End	Global Fixed Inc (Worldwide Bond)	D	D	C-	Down	Y	
BNY Mellon MA Intermediate Muni Bond Fund Class Investor	MMBIX	NAS CM	Open End	US Muni Fixed Inc (Muni Bond - Single State)	C	C-	B-		Y	800-645-6561
BNY Mellon MA Intermediate Municipal Bond Fund Class M	MMBMX	NAS CM	Open End	US Muni Fixed Inc (Muni Bond - Single State)	C	C-	B-		Y	800-645-6561
BNY Mellon Massachusetts Fund Class A	PSMAX	NAS CM	Open End	US Muni Fixed Inc (Muni Bond - Single State)	C	C-	C+		Y	
BNY Mellon Massachusetts Fund Class C	PCMAX	NAS CM	Open End	US Muni Fixed Inc (Muni Bond - Single State)	C	C-	C		Y	

★Expanded analysis of this fund is included in Section II.

TOTAL RETURNS & PERFORMANCE									ASSETS		ASSET ALLOCATION & TURNOVER							MINIMUMS		FEES		
3-Month Total Return	6-Month Total Return	1-Year Total Return	3-Year Total Return	5-Year Total Return	Dividend Yield (TTM)	Expense Ratio	3-Yr Std Deviation	Effective Duration	NAV	Total Assets (MIL)	%Cash	%Government Bonds	%Municipal Bonds	%Corporate Bonds	%Other	Turnover Ratio	Average Coupon Rate	Min Initial Investment	Min Additional Investment	Front End Fee (%)	Back End Fee (%)	Inception Date
2.13	0.79	3.07	9.99	18.36	2.89	0.7	4.36	5.43	14.95	852.8	0	0	100	0	0	23	5.14	1,000,000				Jul-13
2.18	0.77	3.02	9.80	18.02	2.84	0.76	4.34	5.43	14.96	852.8	0	0	100	0	0	23	5.14	1,000	100			Jul-83
1.96	0.90	2.88	8.71	15.06	2.37	0.85	3.95	4.64	11.85	199.2	0	0	100	0	0	5	4.84	1,000	100	4.50		May-87
1.76	0.50	1.98	6.07	10.66	1.57	1.65	3.92	4.64	11.83	199.2	0	0	100	0	0	5	4.84	1,000	100		1.00	Aug-95
2.02	1.02	3.04	9.49	16.45	2.62	0.62	3.95	4.64	11.85	199.2	0	0	100	0	0	5	4.84	1,000	100			Dec-08
2.02	1.04	3.07	9.51	16.55	2.66	0.58	3.96	4.64	11.84	199.2	0	0	100	0	0	5	4.84	1,000,000				Sep-13
2.02	1.11	3.12	9.44	16.42	2.59	0.65	3.95	4.64	11.85	199.2	0	0	100	0	0	5	4.84	1,000	100			May-07
6.78	4.99	7.97	17.43	27.02	2.56	0.7	4.33	5.68	10.87	1,182	1	17	1	53	0	185	3.65	1,000	100	4.50		Feb-18
6.57	4.60	7.26	14.91	22.45	1.83	1.45	4.31	5.68	10.88	1,182	1	17	1	53	0	185	3.65	1,000	100		1.00	Feb-18
6.84	5.12	8.23	18.15	27.80	2.81	0.45	4.33	5.68	10.87	1,182	1	17	1	53	0	185	3.65	1,000	100			Feb-18
6.95	5.24	8.48	18.26	27.91	2.84	0.45	4.31	5.68	10.88	1,182	1	17	1	53	0	185	3.65	1,000,000				Dec-10
8.87	2.66	6.42	16.15	27.51	3.6	0.56	6.22	5.14	13.46	899.6	1	2	5	90	0	31	4.28	10,000	100			Mar-12
8.80	2.44	6.05	15.24	25.93	3.33	0.81	6.27	5.14	13.46	899.6	1	2	5	90	0	31	4.28	10,000	100			Mar-12
10.16	-4.36	-2.11	3.04	8.45	5.44	1.03	8.48	0.13	10.89	617.8	4	0	0	91	0	86	4.85	1,000	100	2.50		Sep-13
9.94	-4.69	-2.88	0.73	4.48	4.63	1.78	8.48	0.13	10.88	617.8	4	0	0	91	0	86	4.85	1,000	100		1.00	Sep-13
10.22	-4.21	-1.87	3.89	10.01	5.76	0.78	8.45	0.13	10.87	617.8	4	0	0	91	0	86	4.85	1,000	100			Sep-13
10.16	-4.18	-1.84	3.96	10.02	5.79	0.74	8.45	0.13	10.85	617.8	4	0	0	91	0	86	4.85	1,000,000				Sep-13
0.05	0.37	0.90	3.08	3.48	1.03	0.3	0.11		1	520.7	17	0	83	0	0	0		10,000	100			Jun-03
0.03	0.29	0.70	2.35	2.51	0.8	0.55	0.11		1	520.7	17	0	83	0	0	0		10,000	100			Jun-03
5.34	0.09	1.96	10.03	15.14	4.07	1.08	4.44	5.61	12.16	133.6	4	24	0	20	0	84	3.97	1,000	100	4.50		Mar-11
5.20	-0.27	1.21	7.63	10.82	3.26	1.83	4.45	5.61	12	133.6	4	24	0	20	0	84	3.97	1,000	100		1.00	Mar-11
5.46	0.22	2.23	10.94	16.50	4.24	0.81	4.44	5.61	12.22	133.6	4	24	0	20	0	84	3.97	1,000	100			Mar-11
5.46	0.22	2.23	10.97	16.59	4.24	0.71	4.44	5.61	12.22	133.6	4	24	0	20	0	84	3.97	1,000,000				Jul-13
6.14	3.58	5.30	12.23	17.58	0.5	0.78	4.26	7.47	22.64	2,919	3	36	0	25	0	157	2.88	1,000	100	2.50		Dec-09
5.95	3.20	4.55	9.79	13.35	0.23	1.53	4.23	7.47	22.25	2,919	3	36	0	25	0	157	2.88	1,000	100		1.00	Dec-09
6.19	3.71	5.56	13.16	19.29	0.64	0.51	4.24	7.47	22.72	2,919	3	36	0	25	0	157	2.88	1,000	100			Dec-93
6.20	3.74	5.61	13.38	19.64	0.67	0.45	4.23	7.47	22.74	2,919	3	36	0	25	0	157	2.88	1,000,000				Jul-13
0.00	0.22	0.96	3.58	3.69	1.12	0.55	0.17		1	565.8	65	35	0	0	0	0		10,000	100			Jun-03
0.02	0.30	1.16	4.32	4.63	1.34	0.3	0.17		1	565.8	65	35	0	0	0	0		10,000	100			Jun-03
8.96	-4.79	-1.32	7.25	17.42	5.48	0.95	8.5	2.45	5.73	878.2	5	0	0	91	0	68	6.22	1,000	100	4.50		Jun-97
8.76	-5.14	-2.05	4.86	13.11	4.7	1.7	8.5	2.45	5.73	878.2	5	0	0	91	0	68	6.22	1,000	100		1.00	Jun-97
9.21	-4.66	-0.90	8.07	18.91	5.74	0.7	8.57	2.45	5.74	878.2	5	0	0	91	0	68	6.22	1,000	100			Jun-97
4.80	-4.23	-1.16	11.49	27.03	3.63	0.84	8.67	8.54	12.08	269.1	0	0	100	0	0	40	5.27	1,000	100	4.50		Mar-07
4.70	-4.60	-1.91	8.98	22.23	2.8	1.61	8.64	8.54	12.08	269.1	0	0	100	0	0	40	5.27	1,000	100		1.00	Mar-07
4.96	-4.04	-0.83	12.41	28.63	3.89	0.57	8.63	8.54	12.08	269.1	0	0	100	0	0	40	5.27	1,000,000				Jul-13
4.85	-4.16	-1.01	11.96	27.79	3.78	0.69	8.65	8.54	12.06	269.1	0	0	100	0	0	40	5.27	1,000	100			Sep-05
4.87	-4.13	-0.93	12.31	28.51	3.88	0.6	8.64	8.54	12.06	269.1	0	0	100	0	0	40	5.27	1,000	100			Dec-08
16.58	-9.18	-4.41	5.52	21.17	8.84	1.36	14.39	3.54	2.95	212.3	1	0	0	92	0	71	7.07					Apr-98
3.53	3.88	5.27	10.65	13.49	1.4	0.53	2.53	4.91	13.17	69.1	2	98	0	0	0	92	1.16	1,000	100			Oct-02
3.39	3.76	4.93	9.78	12.03	1.15	0.8	2.54	4.91	13.13	69.1	2	98	0	0	0	92	1.16	10,000	100			Oct-02
3.46	3.91	5.34	10.86	13.88	1.46	0.47	2.51	4.91	13.18	69.1	2	98	0	0	0	92	1.16	1,000,000				Jul-13
3.20	3.74	5.26	10.14	13.69	1.88	0.8	2.09	3.19	13.04	949.8	1	52	4	41	0	33	2.58	10,000	100			Jul-01
3.35	3.89	5.56	10.94	15.18	2.15	0.55	2.13	3.19	13.03	949.8	1	52	4	41	0	33	2.58	10,000	100			Oct-00
2.33	1.02	2.95	10.11	17.27	2.23	0.75	3.85	4.77	13.75	569.6	1	0	99	0	0	17	4.90	2,500	100			Aug-83
5.77	-4.04	-3.79	-2.07	3.98	0	1.02	7.93	8.76	14.46	448.7	4	43	0	18	0	108	2.20	1,000	100	4.50		Dec-05
5.60	-4.38	-4.45	-3.91	0.99	0	1.68	7.91	8.76	13.95	448.7	4	43	0	18	0	108	2.20	1,000	100		1.00	Dec-05
5.91	-3.86	-3.41	-0.91	6.33	0	0.66	7.96	8.76	14.69	448.7	4	43	0	18	0	108	2.20	1,000	100			Dec-05
5.97	-3.85	-3.35	-0.62	6.76	0	0.57	7.94	8.76	14.71	448.7	4	43	0	18	0	108	2.20	1,000,000				Jul-13
2.51	1.06	2.71	9.36	14.93	1.86	0.78	3.88	4.67	13	310.0	0	0	100	0	0	81	4.64	10,000	100			Sep-85
2.49	1.11	2.96	10.18	16.36	2.11	0.53	3.88	4.67	13	310.0	0	0	100	0	0	81	4.64	10,000	100			Feb-93
2.01	0.89	2.79	8.85	14.96	2.2	0.99	4.14	4.85	11.74	127.0	0	0	100	0	0	5	4.81	1,000	100	4.50		May-87
1.66	0.18	1.67	5.66	9.81	1.14	1.93	4.17	4.85	11.74	127.0	0	0	100	0	0	5	4.81	1,000	100		1.00	Aug-95

	MARKET			FUND TYPE, CATEGORY & OBJECTIVE	RATINGS				NEW INVESTORS	
Fund Name	Ticker Symbol	Traded On	Fund Type	Category and (Prospectus Objective)	Overall Rating	Reward Rating	Risk Rating	Recent Up/ Downgrade	Open to New Investors	Telephone
BNY Mellon Massachusetts Fund Class Z	PMAZX	NAS CM	Open End	US Muni Fixed Inc (Muni Bond - Single State)	C	C-	B-			
BNY Mellon Municipal Bond Fund	DRTAX	NAS CM	Open End	US Muni Fixed Inc (Muni Bond - Natl)	C	C-	C+		Y	
BNY Mellon Municipal Bond Infrastructure Fund, Inc.	DMB	NYSE	Closed End	US Muni Fixed Inc (Muni Bond - Natl)	D+	D+	C-	Down	Y	
BNY Mellon Municipal Income	DMF	AMEX	Closed End	US Muni Fixed Inc (Muni Bond - Natl)	D+	D+	C-	Down	Y	
BNY Mellon Municipal Opportunities Fund Class Investor	MOTIX	NAS CM	Open End	US Muni Fixed Inc (Muni Bond - Natl)	C	D+	C+			800-645-6561
BNY Mellon Municipal Opportunities Fund Class M	MOTMX	NAS CM	Open End	US Muni Fixed Inc (Muni Bond - Natl)	C	D+	C+			800-645-6561
BNY Mellon Natl Intermediate Muni Bond Fund Class Investor	MINMX	NAS CM	Open End	US Muni Fixed Inc (Muni Bond - Natl)	C	C-	B-		Y	800-645-6561
BNY Mellon Natl Intermediate Muni Bond Fund Class M	MPNIX	NAS CM	Open End	US Muni Fixed Inc (Muni Bond - Natl)	C	C	B-		Y	800-645-6561
BNY Mellon Natl Short Term Muni Bond Fund Class Investor	MINSX	NAS CM	Open End	US Muni Fixed Inc (Muni Bond - Natl)	C	C-	C+		Y	800-645-6561
BNY Mellon National Short Term Municipal Bond Fund Class M	MPSTX	NAS CM	Open End	US Muni Fixed Inc (Muni Bond - Natl)	C	C-	C+		Y	800-645-6561
BNY Mellon New Jersey Municipal Bond Fund, Inc. Class A	DRNJX	NAS CM	Open End	US Muni Fixed Inc (Muni Bond - Single State)	C	C-	C+		Y	
BNY Mellon New Jersey Municipal Bond Fund, Inc. Class C	DCNJX	NAS CM	Open End	US Muni Fixed Inc (Muni Bond - Single State)	C	C-	C		Y	
BNY Mellon New Jersey Municipal Bond Fund, Inc. Class I	DNMIX	NAS CM	Open End	US Muni Fixed Inc (Muni Bond - Single State)	C	C-	C+		Y	
BNY Mellon New Jersey Municipal Bond Fund, Inc. Class Y	DNJYX	NAS CM	Open End	US Muni Fixed Inc (Muni Bond - Single State)	C	C-	C+		Y	
BNY Mellon New Jersey Municipal Bond Fund, Inc. Class Z	DZNJX	NAS CM	Open End	US Muni Fixed Inc (Muni Bond - Single State)	C	C-	C+			
BNY Mellon New York AMT-Free Municipal Bond Fund Class A	PSNYX	NAS CM	Open End	US Muni Fixed Inc (Muni Bond - Single State)	C	C-	C+		Y	
BNY Mellon New York AMT-Free Municipal Bond Fund Class C	PNYCX	NAS CM	Open End	US Muni Fixed Inc (Muni Bond - Single State)	C	C-	C		Y	
BNY Mellon New York AMT-Free Municipal Bond Fund Class I	DNYIX	NAS CM	Open End	US Muni Fixed Inc (Muni Bond - Single State)	C	C-	C+		Y	
BNY Mellon New York AMT-Free Municipal Bond Fund Class Y	DNYYX	NAS CM	Open End	US Muni Fixed Inc (Muni Bond - Single State)	C	C-	C+		Y	
BNY Mellon New York Intermediate Tax-Exempt Bond Cl M	MNYMX	NAS CM	Open End	US Muni Fixed Inc (Muni Bond - Single State)	C	C-	C+		Y	800-645-6561
BNY Mellon New York Intermed Tax-Ex Bond Investor Shares	MNYIX	NAS CM	Open End	US Muni Fixed Inc (Muni Bond - Single State)	C	C-	C+		Y	800-645-6561
BNY Mellon New York Tax Exempt Bond Fund, Inc.	DRNYX	NAS CM	Open End	US Muni Fixed Inc (Muni Bond - Single State)	C	C-	C+		Y	
BNY Mellon Opportunistic Municipal Securities Fund Class A	PTEBX	NAS CM	Open End	US Muni Fixed Inc (Muni Bond - Natl)	C	C-	B-		Y	
BNY Mellon Opportunistic Municipal Securities Fund Class C	DMBCX	NAS CM	Open End	US Muni Fixed Inc (Muni Bond - Natl)	C	C-	C+		Y	
BNY Mellon Opportunistic Municipal Securities Fund Class I	DMBVX	NAS CM	Open End	US Muni Fixed Inc (Muni Bond - Natl)	C	C-	B-		Y	
BNY Mellon Opportunistic Municipal Securities Fund Class Y	DMBYX	NAS CM	Open End	US Muni Fixed Inc (Muni Bond - Natl)	C	C-	B-		Y	
BNY Mellon Opportunistic Municipal Securities Fund Class Z	DMBZX	NAS CM	Open End	US Muni Fixed Inc (Muni Bond - Natl)	C	C-	B-			
BNY Mellon Pennsylvania Fund Class A	PTPAX	NAS CM	Open End	US Muni Fixed Inc (Muni Bond - Single State)	C	C-	C+		Y	
BNY Mellon Pennsylvania Fund Class C	PPACX	NAS CM	Open End	US Muni Fixed Inc (Muni Bond - Single State)	C	C-	C+		Y	
BNY Mellon Pennsylvania Fund Class Z	DPENX	NAS CM	Open End	US Muni Fixed Inc (Muni Bond - Single State)	C	C-	B-			
BNY Mellon Pennsylvania Intermediate Muni Bond Cl Investor	MIPAX	NAS CM	Open End	US Muni Fixed Inc (Muni Bond - Single State)	C	C	B-		Y	800-645-6561
BNY Mellon Pennsylvania Intermediate Muni Bond Cl M	MPPIX	NAS CM	Open End	US Muni Fixed Inc (Muni Bond - Single State)	C	C	B		Y	800-645-6561
BNY Mellon Short Term Income Fund Class D	DSTIX	NAS CM	Open End	US Fixed Inc (Growth & Income)	C	C	B-		Y	
BNY Mellon Short Term Income Fund Class P	DSHPX	NAS CM	Open End	US Fixed Inc (Growth & Income)	C	C	B-		Y	
BNY Mellon Short Term U.S. Govt Securities Cl Investor	MISTX	NAS CM	Open End	US Fixed Inc (Govt Bond - General)	C	C	B-		Y	800-645-6561
BNY Mellon Short Term U.S. Govt Securities Fund Class M	MPSUX	NAS CM	Open End	US Fixed Inc (Govt Bond - General)	C+	C	B-	Up	Y	800-645-6561
BNY Mellon Short-Intermediate Municipal Bond Fund Class A	DMBAX	NAS CM	Open End	US Muni Fixed Inc (Muni Bond - Natl)	C	C-	C+		Y	
BNY Mellon Short-Intermediate Municipal Bond Fund Class D	DSIBX	NAS CM	Open End	US Muni Fixed Inc (Muni Bond - Natl)	C	C-	C+		Y	
BNY Mellon Short-Intermediate Municipal Bond Fund Class I	DIMIX	NAS CM	Open End	US Muni Fixed Inc (Muni Bond - Natl)	C	C-	C+		Y	
BNY Mellon Short-Intermediate Municipal Bond Fund Class Y	DMYBX	NAS CM	Open End	US Muni Fixed Inc (Muni Bond - Natl)	C	C-	C+		Y	
BNY Mellon Strategic Municipal Bond	DSM	NYSE	Closed End	US Muni Fixed Inc (Muni Bond - Natl)	C-	D+	C	Down	Y	
BNY Mellon Strategic Municipals Inc.	LEO	NYSE	Closed End	US Muni Fixed Inc (Muni Bond - Natl)	C-	D+	C	Down	Y	
BNY Mellon Tax Sensitive Total Return Bond Fund Class A	DSDAX	NAS CM	Open End	US Muni Fixed Inc (Muni Bond - Natl)	C	C-	C+		Y	
BNY Mellon Tax Sensitive Total Return Bond Fund Class C	DSDCX	NAS CM	Open End	US Muni Fixed Inc (Muni Bond - Natl)	C	C-	C		Y	
BNY Mellon Tax Sensitive Total Return Bond Fund Class I	SDITX	NAS CM	Open End	US Muni Fixed Inc (Muni Bond - Natl)	C	C-	C+		Y	
BNY Mellon Tax Sensitive Total Return Bond Fund Class Y	SDYTX	NAS CM	Open End	US Muni Fixed Inc (Muni Bond - Natl)	C	C-	C+		Y	
BNY Mellon U.S. Mortgage Fund Class A	GPGAX	NAS CM	Open End	US Fixed Inc (Govt Bond - Mortgage)	C+	C	B-	Up	Y	
BNY Mellon U.S. Mortgage Fund Class C	GPNCX	NAS CM	Open End	US Fixed Inc (Govt Bond - Mortgage)	C	C	B-		Y	
BNY Mellon U.S. Mortgage Fund Class I	GPNIX	NAS CM	Open End	US Fixed Inc (Govt Bond - Mortgage)	C+	C	B-		Y	
BNY Mellon U.S. Mortgage Fund Class Y	GPNYX	NAS CM	Open End	US Fixed Inc (Govt Bond - Mortgage)	C+	C	B-		Y	
BNY Mellon U.S. Mortgage Fund Class Z	DRGMX	NAS CM	Open End	US Fixed Inc (Govt Bond - Mortgage)	C+	C	B-			
BNY Mellon Ultra Short Income Fund Class D	DSDDX	NAS CM	Open End	US Fixed Inc (Govt Bond - General)	C	C-	C+		Y	

★ Expanded analysis of this fund is included in Section II.

TOTAL RETURNS & PERFORMANCE									ASSETS		ASSET ALLOCATION & TURNOVER							MINIMUMS		FEES		
3-Month Total Return	6-Month Total Return	1-Year Total Return	3-Year Total Return	5-Year Total Return	Dividend Yield (TTM)	Expense Ratio	3-Yr Std Deviation	Effective Duration	NAV	Total Assets (MIL)	%Cash	%Government Bonds	%Municipal Bonds	%Corporate Bonds	%Other	Turnover Ratio	Average Coupon Rate	Min Initial Investment	Min Additional Investment	Front End Fee (%)	Back End Fee (%)	Inception Date
2.08	1.02	3.12	9.60	16.26	2.43	0.76	4.14	4.85	11.74	127.0	0	0	100	0	0	5	4.81	1,000	100			Oct-04
2.64	0.61	2.88	10.95	19.29	2.64	0.73	4.65	5.00	11.86	1,196	0	0	100	0	0	14	4.88	2,500	100			Oct-76
5.49	-1.48	2.10	13.80	32.61	4.72	1.72	8.18		13.96	247.9	0	0	100	0	0	23	6.06					Apr-13
3.18	-2.27	0.70	9.88	21.41	4.44	0	7.39		8.93	179.9	0	0	100	0	0	32	7.35					Oct-88
3.55	-0.40	1.83	12.35	20.11	2.89	0.98	5.44	5.47	13.34	1,999	0	0	99	1	0	73	4.84	10,000	100			Oct-08
3.61	-0.35	2.07	13.10	21.50	3.14	0.73	5.43	5.47	13.33	1,999	0	0	99	1	0	73	4.84	10,000	100			Oct-08
2.76	1.23	3.04	10.14	16.17	1.94	0.75	4.01	4.73	13.93	2,520	0	0	100	0	0	62	4.67	10,000	100			Jul-01
2.89	1.43	3.37	10.95	17.70	2.19	0.5	4.04	4.73	13.95	2,520	0	0	100	0	0	62	4.67	10,000	100			Oct-00
1.75	0.69	1.52	4.19	5.31	1.15	0.75	1.64	2.06	12.89	1,051	2	0	98	0	0	129	3.60	10,000	100			Jul-01
1.81	0.82	1.77	4.97	6.62	1.4	0.5	1.64	2.06	12.9	1,051	2	0	98	0	0	129	3.60	10,000	100			Oct-00
1.83	0.03	1.97	10.34	18.71	2.67	0.85	4.27	5.19	12.77	418.9	2	0	98	0	0	17	4.90	1,000	100	4.50		Nov-87
1.57	-0.33	1.13	7.83	14.29	1.92	1.6	4.28	5.19	12.75	418.9	2	0	98	0	0	17	4.90	1,000	100		1.00	Jan-03
1.89	0.15	2.22	11.10	20.22	2.93	0.6	4.26	5.19	12.77	418.9	2	0	98	0	0	17	4.90	1,000	100			Dec-08
1.81	0.15	2.23	11.59	20.65	2.93	0.6	4.27	5.19	12.82	418.9	2	0	98	0	0	17	4.90	1,000,000				Jul-13
1.80	0.14	2.20	10.99	19.97	2.9	0.65	4.22	5.19	12.77	418.9	2	0	98	0	0	17	4.90	1,000	100			Jun-07
1.64	0.38	2.45	9.09	16.91	2.53	0.88	4.43	5.20	15.01	302.9	0	0	100	0	0	9	5.18	1,000	100	4.50		Dec-86
1.45	0.00	1.67	6.64	12.56	1.76	1.65	4.4	5.20	15.01	302.9	0	0	100	0	0	9	5.18	1,000	100		1.00	Sep-95
1.70	0.50	2.69	9.88	18.33	2.78	0.65	4.43	5.20	15.01	302.9	0	0	100	0	0	9	5.18	1,000	100			Dec-08
1.63	0.44	2.70	9.83	18.27	2.77	0.65	4.42	5.20	15.01	302.9	0	0	100	0	0	9	5.18	1,000,000				Jul-13
2.25	0.33	2.16	9.46	16.26	2.15	0.59	4.19	4.63	11.26	157.0	0	0	100	0	0	90	4.56	10,000	100			Aug-92
2.18	0.30	1.99	8.64	14.92	1.9	0.84	4.23	4.63	11.27	157.0	0	0	100	0	0	90	4.56	10,000	100			Aug-92
2.10	0.79	2.79	9.44	17.85	2.75	0.78	4.23	5.03	14.93	996.7	1	0	99	0	0	10	5.14	2,500	100			Jul-83
2.68	0.79	3.19	11.59	19.42	2.76	0.73	4.6	5.21	13.18	384.6	0	0	100	0	0	27	4.86	1,000	100	4.50		Nov-86
2.48	0.40	2.31	9.01	14.93	1.97	1.52	4.59	5.21	13.21	384.6	0	0	100	0	0	27	4.86	1,000	100		1.00	Jul-95
2.83	0.92	3.45	12.41	20.62	3.01	0.49	4.58	5.21	13.19	384.6	0	0	100	0	0	27	4.86	1,000	100			Aug-16
2.75	0.92	3.44	12.28	20.07	3.01	0.49	4.58	5.21	13.18	384.6	0	0	100	0	0	27	4.86	1,000,000				Aug-16
2.70	0.82	3.24	11.77	19.74	2.81	0.68	4.59	5.21	13.18	384.6	0	0	100	0	0	27	4.86	1,000	100			Oct-04
1.73	0.54	2.57	10.68	19.43	2.49	0.9	4.15	4.85	16.2	120.7	0	0	100	0	0	9	4.81	1,000	100	4.50		Jul-87
1.52	0.06	1.72	7.96	14.72	1.65	1.72	4.16	4.85	16.2	120.7	0	0	100	0	0	9	4.81	1,000	100		1.00	Aug-95
1.80	0.59	2.80	11.32	20.65	2.71	0.72	4.16	4.85	16.19	120.7	0	0	100	0	0	9	4.81	1,000	100			Nov-07
2.43	1.58	3.42	10.57	16.21	1.91	0.95	3.65	4.66	12.53	185.2	0	0	100	0	0	70	4.61	10,000	100			Jul-01
2.57	1.71	3.68	11.48	17.66	2.16	0.7	3.66	4.66	12.55	185.2	0	0	100	0	0	70	4.61	10,000	100			Oct-00
5.18	2.53	3.80	7.17	8.81	2.28	0.65	3.13	2.64	10.3	123.6	2	23	0	33	0	144	3.15	2,500	100			Aug-92
5.16	2.50	3.74	7.06	8.50	2.23	0.7	3.11	2.64	10.32	123.6	2	23	0	33	0	144	3.15	100,000	100			Nov-02
0.38	2.52	3.31	5.81	5.94	1.72	0.8	1.09	1.56	11.82	240.1	2	14	6	0	0	120	2.57	10,000	100			Jul-01
0.37	2.50	3.44	6.52	7.17	2.02	0.55	1.08	1.56	11.82	240.1	2	14	6	0	0	120	2.57	10,000	100			Oct-00
1.66	1.19	2.06	4.66	6.34	1.23	0.64	1.68	2.17	13.09	291.0	8	0	92	0	0	47	4.59	1,000	100	2.50		Aug-09
1.62	1.19	2.14	5.05	7.06	1.38	0.49	1.66	2.17	13.08	291.0	8	0	92	0	0	47	4.59	2,500	100			Apr-87
1.73	1.24	2.32	5.43	7.66	1.48	0.39	1.68	2.17	13.09	291.0	8	0	92	0	0	47	4.59	1,000	100			Dec-08
1.65	1.24	2.36	5.14	7.36	1.51	0.39	1.67	2.17	13.05	291.0	8	0	92	0	0	47	4.59	1,000,000				Jul-13
4.31	-2.24	0.79	10.04	23.89	4.66	0	7.54		7.97	381.9	0	0	100	0	0	41	7.49					Nov-89
4.89	-2.65	0.65	11.17	25.13	4.84	0	8.4		8.25	495.2	0	0	100	0	0	33	7.53					Sep-87
2.85	0.72	2.42	9.14	15.21	2.15	0.7	3.9	4.41	22.66	117.3	1	0	90	5	0	29	4.51	1,000	100	4.50		Mar-09
2.66	0.35	1.66	6.70	11.02	1.41	1.45	3.92	4.41	22.67	117.3	1	0	90	5	0	29	4.51	1,000	100		1.00	Mar-09
2.91	0.85	2.72	9.96	16.71	2.4	0.45	3.9	4.41	22.68	117.3	1	0	90	5	0	29	4.51	1,000	100			Nov-92
2.86	0.85	2.68	9.96	16.71	2.4	0.45	3.91	4.41	22.67	117.3	1	0	90	5	0	29	4.51	1,000,000				Jul-13
1.14	2.81	4.33	8.72	11.50	2.09	0.9	1.88	3.30	15.24	304.7	2	0	0	0	0	46	3.40	1,000	100	4.50		May-07
0.95	2.41	3.50	6.06	7.05	1.29	1.65	1.88	3.30	15.25	304.7	2	0	0	0	0	46	3.40	1,000	100		1.00	May-07
1.20	2.91	4.55	9.43	12.43	2.31	0.65	1.87	3.30	15.23	304.7	2	0	0	0	0	46	3.40	1,000	100			Aug-16
1.27	2.99	4.56	9.54	12.93	2.33	0.65	1.87	3.30	15.24	304.7	2	0	0	0	0	46	3.40	1,000,000				Sep-15
1.16	2.86	4.37	9.07	12.04	2.2	0.8	1.89	3.30	15.24	304.7	2	0	0	0	0	46	3.40	1,000	100			May-85
0.12	0.32	1.16	4.36	3.98	1.33	0.6	0.2		10.07	87.4	100	0	0	0	0	52		100,000	100			Nov-13

	MARKET			FUND TYPE, CATEGORY & OBJECTIVE	RATINGS				NEW INVESTORS	
Fund Name	Ticker Symbol	Traded On	Fund Type	Category and (Prospectus Objective)	Overall Rating	Reward Rating	Risk Rating	Recent Up/ Downgrade	Open to New Investors	Telephone
BNY Mellon Ultra Short Income Fund Class Z	DSIGX	NAS CM	Open End	US Fixed Inc (Govt Bond - General)	C	C-	C+			
BNY Mellon Ultra Short Income Fund Institutional Shares	DSYDX	NAS CM	Open End	US Fixed Inc (Govt Bond - General)	C	C-	C+		Y	
BNY Mellon Yield Enhancement Strategy Fund - Class I	DABKX	NAS CM	Open End	US Fixed Inc (Income)	C-	D+	C	Down	Y	
BNY Mellon Yield Enhancement Strategy Fund - Class Y	DABJX	NAS CM	Open End	US Fixed Inc (Income)	C-	D+	C	Down	Y	
BNY Mellon Yield Enhancement Strategy Fund Class A	DABMX	NAS CM	Open End	US Fixed Inc (Income)	C-	D+	C	Down	Y	
BNY Mellon Yield Enhancement Strategy Fund Class C	DABLX	NAS CM	Open End	US Fixed Inc (Income)	C-	D+	C		Y	
Boyd Watterson Limited Duration Enhanced Inc Cl A Shares	BWDAX	NAS CM	Open End	US Fixed Inc (Income)	C	C-	C+		Y	
Boyd Watterson Limited Duration Enhanced Inc Cl C Shares	BWDCX	NAS CM	Open End	US Fixed Inc (Income)	C	C-	C	Up	Y	
Boyd Watterson Limited Duration Enhanced Income Cl I	BWDIX	NAS CM	Open End	US Fixed Inc (Income)	C	C-	C+		Y	
Boyd Watterson Limited Duration Enhanced Income Cl I2	BWDTX	NAS CM	Open End	US Fixed Inc (Income)	C	C-	C+		Y	
Braddock Multi-Strategy Income Fund Class A Shares	BDKAX	NAS CM	Open End	US Fixed Inc (Income)	D-	E+	D-	Down	Y	800-207-7108
Braddock Multi-Strategy Income Fund Class C Shares	BDKCX	NAS CM	Open End	US Fixed Inc (Income)	D-	E+	D-	Down	Y	800-207-7108
Braddock Multi-Strategy Income Institutional Cl Shares	BDKNX	NAS CM	Open End	US Fixed Inc (Income)	D-	E+	D-	Down	Y	800-207-7108
Bramshill Income Performance Fund Institutional Class	BRMSX	NAS CM	Open End	Fixed Inc Misc (Income)	C	D+	C+	Up	Y	
Brandes Core Plus Fixed Income Fund Class A	BCPAX	NAS CM	Open End	US Fixed Inc (Growth & Income)	C+	C	B		Y	800-331-2979
Brandes Core Plus Fixed Income Fund Class I	BCPIX	NAS CM	Open End	US Fixed Inc (Growth & Income)	B-	C+	B	Up	Y	800-331-2979
Brandes Core Plus Fixed Income Fund Class R6	BCPRX	NAS CM	Open End	US Fixed Inc (Growth & Income)	B-	C+	B+	Up	Y	800-331-2979
Brandes Separately Managed Account Reserve Trust	SMARX	NAS CM	Open End	US Fixed Inc (Growth & Income)	C+	C	B	Up	Y	800-331-2979
BrandywineGLOBAL - Global Flexible Income Fund Class A	LFLAX	NAS CM	Open End	US Fixed Inc (Income)	B-	C+	B+	Up	Y	877-721-1926
BrandywineGLOBAL - Global Flexible Income Fund Class I	LFLIX	NAS CM	Open End	US Fixed Inc (Income)	B	C+	B+	Up	Y	877-721-1926
BrandywineGLOBAL - Global Flexible Income Fund Class IS	LFLSX	NAS CM	Open End	US Fixed Inc (Income)	B	C+	B+	Up	Y	877-721-1926
BrandywineGLOBAL - Global High Yield Fund Class A	LBHAX	NAS CM	Open End	Global Fixed Inc (Corp Bond - High Yield)	C-	D+	C		Y	877-721-1926
BrandywineGLOBAL - Global High Yield Fund Class C	LBHCX	NAS CM	Open End	Global Fixed Inc (Corp Bond - High Yield)	D+	D	C	Down	Y	877-721-1926
BrandywineGLOBAL - Global High Yield Fund Class FI	LBHFX	NAS CM	Open End	Global Fixed Inc (Corp Bond - High Yield)	C-	D+	C		Y	877-721-1926
BrandywineGLOBAL - Global High Yield Fund Class I	LMYIX	NAS CM	Open End	Global Fixed Inc (Corp Bond - High Yield)	C-	D+	C		Y	877-721-1926
BrandywineGLOBAL - Global High Yield Fund Class IS	LMZIX	NAS CM	Open End	Global Fixed Inc (Corp Bond - High Yield)	C-	D+	C		Y	877-721-1926
BrandywineGLOBAL – Global Income Opportunities Fund	BWG	NYSE	Closed End	Global Fixed Inc (Income)	C-	C-	C-		Y	877-721-1926
BrandywineGLOBAL - Global Opp Bond (USD Hedged) Cl I	GBUSX	NAS CM	Open End	Global Fixed Inc (Income)	D	D+	B-	Up	Y	877-721-1926
BrandywineGLOBAL - Global Opp Bond (USD Hedged) Cl IS	GLOBX	NAS CM	Open End	Global Fixed Inc (Income)	D	D+	B-	Up	Y	877-721-1926
BrandywineGLOBAL - Global Opportunities Bond Fund Class A	GOBAX	NAS CM	Open End	Global Fixed Inc (Worldwide Bond)	D+	D	C	Down	Y	877-721-1926
BrandywineGLOBAL - Global Opportunities Bond Fund Class A2	LOBAX	NAS CM	Open End	Global Fixed Inc (Worldwide Bond)	D+	D	C	Down	Y	877-721-1926
BrandywineGLOBAL - Global Opportunities Bond Fund Class C	LGOCX	NAS CM	Open End	Global Fixed Inc (Worldwide Bond)	D+	D	C-	Down	Y	877-721-1926
BrandywineGLOBAL - Global Opportunities Bond Fund Class C1	GOBCX	NAS CM	Open End	Global Fixed Inc (Worldwide Bond)	D+	D	C	Down	Y	877-721-1926
BrandywineGLOBAL - Global Opportunities Bond Fund Class FI	GOBFX	NAS CM	Open End	Global Fixed Inc (Worldwide Bond)	D+	D	C	Down	Y	877-721-1926
BrandywineGLOBAL - Global Opportunities Bond Fund Class I	GOBIX	NAS CM	Open End	Global Fixed Inc (Worldwide Bond)	D+	D	C	Down	Y	877-721-1926
BrandywineGLOBAL - Global Opportunities Bond Fund Class IS	GOBSX	NAS CM	Open End	Global Fixed Inc (Worldwide Bond)	D+	D	C	Down	Y	877-721-1926
BrandywineGLOBAL - Global Opportunities Bond Fund Class R	LBORX	NAS CM	Open End	Global Fixed Inc (Worldwide Bond)	D+	D	C	Down	Y	877-721-1926
BrandywineGLOBAL - Global Unconstrained Bond Fund Class A	LROAX	NAS CM	Open End	Fixed Inc Misc (Growth)	D+	D	C	Down	Y	877-721-1926
BrandywineGLOBAL - Global Unconstrained Bond Fund Class C	LAOCX	NAS CM	Open End	Fixed Inc Misc (Growth)	D+	D	C	Down	Y	877-721-1926
BrandywineGLOBAL - Global Unconstrained Bond Fund Class C1	LROCX	NAS CM	Open End	Fixed Inc Misc (Growth)	D+	D	C	Down		877-721-1926
BrandywineGLOBAL - Global Unconstrained Bond Fund Class FI	LBAFX	NAS CM	Open End	Fixed Inc Misc (Growth)	D+	D	C	Down	Y	877-721-1926
BrandywineGLOBAL - Global Unconstrained Bond Fund Class I	LROIX	NAS CM	Open End	Fixed Inc Misc (Growth)	D+	D	C	Down	Y	877-721-1926
BrandywineGLOBAL - Global Unconstrained Bond Fund Class IS	LROSX	NAS CM	Open End	Fixed Inc Misc (Growth)	D+	D	C	Down	Y	877-721-1926
BrandywineGLOBAL - Global Unconstrained Bond Fund Class R	LBARX	NAS CM	Open End	Fixed Inc Misc (Growth)	D+	D	C	Down	Y	877-721-1926
BrandywineGLOBAL - InterNatl Opportunities Bond Cl A	LWOAX	NAS CM	Open End	Global Fixed Inc (Worldwide Bond)	D	D	D+	Down	Y	877-721-1926
BrandywineGLOBAL - InterNatl Opportunities Bond Cl C	LIOCX	NAS CM	Open End	Global Fixed Inc (Worldwide Bond)	D	D	D+	Down	Y	877-721-1926
BrandywineGLOBAL - InterNatl Opportunities Bond Cl FI	LWOFX	NAS CM	Open End	Global Fixed Inc (Worldwide Bond)	D	D	D+	Down	Y	877-721-1926
BrandywineGLOBAL - InterNatl Opportunities Bond Cl I	LWOIX	NAS CM	Open End	Global Fixed Inc (Worldwide Bond)	D	D	D+	Down	Y	877-721-1926
BrandywineGLOBAL - InterNatl Opportunities Bond Cl IS	LMOTX	NAS CM	Open End	Global Fixed Inc (Worldwide Bond)	D	D	D+	Down	Y	877-721-1926
BrandywineGLOBAL - InterNatl Opportunities Bond Cl R	LWORX	NAS CM	Open End	Global Fixed Inc (Worldwide Bond)	D	D	D+	Down	Y	877-721-1926
Bridge Builder Core Bond Fund	BBTBX	NAS CM	Open End	US Fixed Inc (Income)	B	C+	B+	Up	Y	
Bridge Builder Core Plus Bond Fund	BBCPX	NAS CM	Open End	US Fixed Inc (Income)	B	C+	B+	Up	Y	

★ Expanded analysis of this fund is included in Section II.

TOTAL RETURNS & PERFORMANCE									ASSETS		ASSET ALLOCATION & TURNOVER							MINIMUMS		FEES		
3-Month Total Return	6-Month Total Return	1-Year Total Return	3-Year Total Return	5-Year Total Return	Dividend Yield (TTM)	Expense Ratio	3-Yr Std Deviation	Effective Duration	NAV	Total Assets (MIL)	%Cash	%Government Bonds	%Municipal Bonds	%Corporate Bonds	%Other	Turnover Ratio	Average Coupon Rate	Min Initial Investment	Min Additional Investment	Front End Fee (%)	Back End Fee (%)	Inception Date
0.15	0.40	1.30	4.79	4.73	1.48	0.44	0.16		10.07	87.4	100	0	0	0	0	52		0				Apr-87
0.22	0.51	1.56	5.94	6.17	1.72	0.2	0.28		10.09	87.4	100	0	0	0	0	52		10,000,000				Nov-13
6.89	-1.75	0.87	9.64	18.03	4.27	0.68	6.17	3.91	11.91	374.5	5	7	34	43	0	21	4.89	1,000	100			Mar-14
6.90	-1.73	0.84	9.67	18.32	4.32	0.65	6.18	3.91	11.9	374.5	5	7	34	43	0	21	4.89	1,000,000				Mar-14
6.80	-1.99	0.42	8.47	16.23	3.89	1.06	6.19	3.91	11.88	374.5	5	7	34	43	0	21	4.89	1,000	100	4.50		Mar-14
6.73	-2.24	0.05	6.19	11.95	3.39	1.71	6.2	3.91	11.88	374.5	5	7	34	43	0	21	4.89	1,000	100		1.00	Mar-14
6.47	0.39	2.34	8.92		3.19	0.84	4.62	2.09	9.89	245.2	6	0	0	57	0	47	4.64	1,000	100	2.25		Feb-19
6.26	0.06	1.55	6.81		2.56	1.59	4.61	2.09	9.9	245.2	6	0	0	57	0	47	4.64	1,000	100			Feb-19
6.65	0.56	2.57	9.56		3.48	0.61	4.65	2.09	9.89	245.2	6	0	0	57	0	47	4.64	100,000	100			Apr-17
6.61	0.66	2.77	10.07		3.46	0.41	4.62	2.09	9.95	245.2	6	0	0	57	0	47	4.64	5,000,000	1,000			Jul-16
33.76	-33.76	-32.16	-25.49	-17.39	5.65	1.77	31.21		6.74	820.6	37	0	0	1	-7	27	4.40	2,500	100	4.25		Dec-15
33.39	-34.03	-32.67	-27.20	-20.47	4.53	2.52	31.17		6.72	820.6	37	0	0	1	-7	27	4.40	2,500	100		1.00	Dec-15
33.83	-33.74	-32.05	-25.02	-16.41	6.02	1.52	31.24		6.74	820.6	37	0	0	1	-7	27	4.40	1,000,000	100,000			Jul-09
7.92	-0.60	1.43	8.95		3.09	1.47	6.54		9.85	540.8	25	24	3	47	1	134	3.98	100,000	5,000			Apr-16
2.41	4.20	5.49	10.61	16.56	2.2	0.7	2.62	4.82	9.44	86.5	4	55	0	26	0	19	3.34	2,500	500	3.75		Jan-13
2.42	4.35	5.75	11.33	17.96	2.38	0.5	2.56	4.82	9.52	86.5	4	55	0	26	0	19	3.34	100,000	500			Dec-07
2.53	4.57	6.26	13.27	20.02	3.01	0.35	2.62	4.82	9.52	86.5	4	55	0	26	0	19	3.34	1,000,000	0			Oct-17
3.70	2.73	4.35	11.17	22.89	3.57	0	3.28	5.07	8.8	182.5	7	35	0	43	0	36	4.35	0				Oct-05
6.54	5.77	8.08	17.70	30.77	4.67	1.11	4.51	6.79	10.46	15.9	15	10	0	52	0	356	3.39	1,000	50	4.25		May-16
6.45	5.68	8.25	18.43	32.34	4.89	0.76	4.46	6.79	10.46	15.9	15	10	0	52	0	356	3.39	1,000,000				May-16
6.55	5.80	8.28	18.53	32.64	4.92	0.66	4.58	6.79	10.47	15.9	15	10	0	52	0	356	3.39	1,000,000				May-16
7.86	-2.99	1.10	6.31	16.63	5.32	1.16	7.06	3.45	8.33	35.7	9	1	0	77	0	104	5.72	1,000	50	4.25		Feb-14
7.65	-3.34	0.35	3.96	12.49	4.54	1.91	7.03	3.45	8.34	35.7	9	1	0	77	0	104	5.72	1,000	50		1.00	Feb-14
7.97	-2.86	1.11	6.33	17.14	5.31	1.16	7.06	3.45	8.36	35.7	9	1	0	77	0	104	5.72	0				Feb-14
7.92	-2.84	1.40	7.39	18.72	5.62	0.86	7.03	3.45	8.35	35.7	9	1	0	77	0	104	5.72	1,000,000				Feb-14
7.95	-2.80	1.50	7.58	19.09	5.72	0.76	7.06	3.45	8.34	35.7	9	1	0	77	0	104	5.72	1,000,000				Nov-12
10.34	-3.62	3.10	8.55	16.49	2.15		11.03		13.52	277.9	9	24	0	28	0	55	5.85					Mar-12
7.14	5.24	7.95			3.56	0.74		6.80	10.55	151.9	16	30	0	17	0	86	4.72	1,000,000				Mar-19
6.78	4.90	7.62			3.58	0.65		6.80	10.55	151.9	16	30	0	17	0	86	4.72	1,000,000				Mar-19
10.68	-1.89	0.59	3.53	13.41	1.12	1	9.43	6.91	10.46	2,375	8	31	0	14	0	103	4.44	1,000	50	4.25		Mar-10
10.61	-1.97	0.41	3.02	12.52	1.02	1.11	9.43	6.91	10.42	2,375	8	31	0	14	0	103	4.44	1,000	50	4.25		Oct-12
10.35	-2.29	-0.15	1.17	9.18	0.61	1.73	9.36	6.91	10.23	2,375	8	31	0	14	0	103	4.44	1,000	50		1.00	Aug-12
10.48	-2.17	0.11	2.20	11.06	0.76	1.39	9.45	6.91	10.33	2,375	8	31	0	14	0	103	4.44	1,000	50		1.00	Mar-10
10.61	-1.93	0.49	3.39	13.24	1.14	0.98	9.45	6.91	10.32	2,375	8	31	0	14	0	103	4.44	0				Feb-09
10.75	-1.83	0.86	4.37	14.91	1.46	0.68	9.45	6.91	10.4	2,375	8	31	0	14	0	103	4.44	1,000,000				Mar-09
10.62	-1.77	0.93	4.65	15.48	1.56	0.58	9.39	6.91	10.41	2,375	8	31	0	14	0	103	4.44	1,000,000				Nov-06
10.54	-2.07	0.27	2.56	11.72	0.85	1.25	9.45	6.91	10.38	2,375	8	31	0	14	0	103	4.44	0				Sep-11
7.00	-1.77	0.50	-0.19	5.08	0.4	1.1	7.93	4.23	11.61	741.1	13	7	0	12	0	44	4.00	1,000	50	2.25		Feb-11
6.89	-2.00	-0.04	-1.97	1.91	0.12	1.84	7.95	4.23	11.47	741.1	13	7	0	12	0	44	4.00	1,000	50		1.00	Aug-12
6.87	-1.99	0.05	-1.38	2.88	0.13	1.6	7.89	4.23	11.51	741.1	13	7	0	12	0	44	4.00	1,000	50			Feb-11
7.01	-1.72	1.13	0.47	5.61	0.42	1.2	7.89	4.23	11.75	741.1	13	7	0	12	0	44	4.00	0				Oct-11
7.05	-1.58	0.94	0.84	6.97	0.57	0.85	7.89	4.23	11.69	741.1	13	7	0	12	0	44	4.00	1,000,000				Feb-11
7.12	-1.45	1.07	1.24	7.61	0.61	0.75	7.91	4.23	11.73	741.1	13	7	0	12	0	44	4.00	1,000,000				Mar-13
6.93	-1.77	0.34	-0.80	3.87	0.33	1.43	7.89	4.23	11.57	741.1	13	7	0	12	0	44	4.00	0				Oct-11
11.14	-5.02	-2.93	-2.39	5.43	0.37	1.01	10.46	3.47	10.97	62.8	10	29	0	12	0	90	4.36	1,000	50	4.25		Oct-11
10.85	-5.43	-3.63	-4.51	1.49	0	1.76	10.43	3.47	10.62	62.8	10	29	0	12	0	90	4.36	1,000	50		1.00	Aug-12
11.13	-5.01	-2.92	-2.32	5.50	0.4	1.01	10.44	3.47	10.98	62.8	10	29	0	12	0	90	4.36	0				Oct-11
11.24	-4.89	-2.58	-1.57	6.75	0.59	0.76	10.42	3.47	11.08	62.8	10	29	0	12	0	90	4.36	1,000,000				Oct-11
11.32	-4.79	-2.55	-1.29	7.23	0.66	0.66	10.44	3.47	11.11	62.8	10	29	0	12	0	90	4.36	1,000,000				Dec-09
11.05	-5.15	-3.19	-3.13	4.00	0.22	1.26	10.39	3.47	10.85	62.8	10	29	0	12	0	90	4.36	0				Oct-11
4.44	6.23	8.98	17.73	26.05	2.96	0.14	3.63	5.71	10.91	13,593	5	17	1	30	0	153	3.50	0				Oct-13
5.69	5.58	7.91	17.48	24.02	3.43	0.24	3.82	5.69	10.56	18,564	5	26	0	29	0	242	3.17	0				Jul-15

	MARKET		FUND TYPE, CATEGORY & OBJECTIVE		RATINGS				NEW INVESTORS	
Fund Name	Ticker Symbol	Traded On	Fund Type	Category and (Prospectus Objective)	Overall Rating	Reward Rating	Risk Rating	Recent Up/ Downgrade	Open to New Investors	Telephone
Bridge Builder Municipal Bond Fund	BBMUX	NAS CM	Open End	US Muni Fixed Inc (Muni Bond - Natl)	C	C-	B-		Y	
Brighthouse Funds Trust I JPMorgan Core Bond Portfol Cl A			Open End	US Fixed Inc (Growth & Income)	U	U	U		Y	
Brookfield Real Assets Income Fund Inc.	RA	NYSE	Closed End	US Fixed Inc (Growth & Income)	D	D	D	Down	Y	312-377-8300
Brown Advisory Intermediate Income Advisor Shares	BAIAX	NAS CM	Open End	US Fixed Inc (Income)	C+	C	B	Up	Y	800-540-6807
Brown Advisory Intermediate Income Fund Investor Shares	BIAIX	NAS CM	Open End	US Fixed Inc (Income)	C+	C	B	Up	Y	800-540-6807
Brown Advisory Maryland Bond Fund Investor Shares	BIAMX	NAS CM	Open End	US Muni Fixed Inc (Muni Bond - Single State)	C	C-	C		Y	800-540-6807
Brown Advisory Mortgage Securities Institutional Shares	BAFZX	NAS CM	Open End	US Fixed Inc (Income)	C+	C+	B		Y	800-540-6807
Brown Advisory Mortgage Securities Fund Investor Shares	BIAZX	NAS CM	Open End	US Fixed Inc (Income)	C+	C+	B		Y	800-540-6807
Brown Advisory Strategic Bond Fund Institutional Shares	BIABX	NAS CM	Open End	US Fixed Inc (Growth & Income)	C-	D+	C		Y	800-540-6807
Brown Advisory Strategic Bond Fund Investor Shares	BATBX	NAS CM	Open End	US Fixed Inc (Growth & Income)	C-	D+	C		Y	800-540-6807
Brown Advisory Sustainable Bond Fund Institutional Shares	BAISX	NAS CM	Open End	US Fixed Inc (Growth & Income)	C+	C	B	Up	Y	800-540-6807
Brown Advisory Sustainable Bond Fund Investor Shares	BASBX	NAS CM	Open End	US Fixed Inc (Growth & Income)	C	C	B		Y	800-540-6807
Brown Advisory Tax Exempt Bond Fund Institutional Shares	BTEIX	NAS CM	Open End	US Muni Fixed Inc (Muni Bond - Natl)	C	C-	C+		Y	800-540-6807
Brown Advisory Tax Exempt Bond Fund Investor Shares	BIAEX	NAS CM	Open End	US Muni Fixed Inc (Muni Bond - Natl)	C	C-	C+		Y	800-540-6807
Brown Advisory Tax-Exempt Sustainable Bond Investor Shares	BITEX	NAS CM	Open End	US Muni Fixed Inc (Govt Bond - General)	U	U	U		Y	800-540-6807
Brown Advisory Total Return Fund Institutional Shares	BAFTX	NAS CM	Open End	US Fixed Inc (Growth & Income)	C+	C	B	Up	Y	800-540-6807
Brown Advisory Total Return Fund Investor Shares	BIATX	NAS CM	Open End	US Fixed Inc (Growth & Income)	C+	C	B	Up	Y	800-540-6807
BTS Managed Income Fund Class I Shares	BTSIX	NAS CM	Open End	Fixed Inc Misc (Income)	D	D+	B-		Y	877-287-9820
BTS Managed Income Fund Class R Shares	BTSRX	NAS CM	Open End	Fixed Inc Misc (Income)	D	D+	B-		Y	877-287-9820
BTS Tactical Fixed Income Fund Class A	BTFAX	NAS CM	Open End	Fixed Inc Misc (Growth & Income)	C	C-	C		Y	877-287-9820
BTS Tactical Fixed Income Fund Class C	BTFCX	NAS CM	Open End	Fixed Inc Misc (Growth & Income)	C-	C-	C		Y	877-287-9820
BTS Tactical Fixed Income Fund Class I	BTFIX	NAS CM	Open End	Fixed Inc Misc (Growth & Income)	C	C-	C		Y	877-287-9820
BTS Tactical Fixed Income Fund Class R	BTFRX	NAS CM	Open End	Fixed Inc Misc (Growth & Income)	C-	C-	C		Y	877-287-9820
Buffalo High Yield Fund	BUFHX	NAS CM	Open End	US Fixed Inc (Corp Bond - High Yield)	C-	D+	C		Y	800-492-8332
Buffalo High Yield Fund Institutional Class	BUIHX	NAS CM	Open End	US Fixed Inc (Corp Bond - High Yield)	C-	D+	C		Y	800-492-8332
Calamos Global Funds PLC - Calamos Short-Term Bond Cl A	CSTBX	NAS CM	Open End	US Fixed Inc (Income)	D+	D+	C+	Up	Y	800-582-6959
Calamos Global Funds PLC - Calamos Short-Term Bond Cl I	CSTIX	NAS CM	Open End	US Fixed Inc (Income)	D+	D+	B-	Up	Y	800-582-6959
Calamos High Income Opportunities Fund Class A	CHYDX	NAS CM	Open End	US Fixed Inc (Corp Bond - High Yield)	D+	D	C-	Down	Y	800-582-6959
Calamos High Income Opportunities Fund Class C	CCHYX	NAS CM	Open End	US Fixed Inc (Corp Bond - High Yield)	D	D	D+	Down	Y	800-582-6959
Calamos High Income Opportunities Fund Class I	CIHYX	NAS CM	Open End	US Fixed Inc (Corp Bond - High Yield)	D+	D	C-	Down	Y	800-582-6959
Calamos Total Return Bond Fund Class A	CTRAX	NAS CM	Open End	US Fixed Inc (Income)	B-	C+	B	Up	Y	800-582-6959
Calamos Total Return Bond Fund Class C	CTRCX	NAS CM	Open End	US Fixed Inc (Income)	C+	C	B-	Up	Y	800-582-6959
Calamos Total Return Bond Fund Class I	CTRIX	NAS CM	Open End	US Fixed Inc (Income)	B-	C+	B	Up	Y	800-582-6959
Calvert Bond Fund Class A	CSIBX	NAS CM	Open End	US Fixed Inc (Income)	C+	C	B	Up	Y	202-238-2200
Calvert Bond Fund Class C	CSBCX	NAS CM	Open End	US Fixed Inc (Income)	C	C	B-		Y	202-238-2200
Calvert Bond Fund Class I	CBDIX	NAS CM	Open End	US Fixed Inc (Income)	C+	C	B	Up	Y	202-238-2200
Calvert Bond Fund Class R6	CBORX	NAS CM	Open End	US Fixed Inc (Income)	C+	C	B	Up	Y	202-238-2200
Calvert Flexible Bond Fund Class A	CUBAX	NAS CM	Open End	Fixed Inc Misc (Income)	D+	D	C	Down	Y	202-238-2200
Calvert Flexible Bond Fund Class C	CUBCX	NAS CM	Open End	Fixed Inc Misc (Income)	D	D	C-	Down	Y	202-238-2200
Calvert Flexible Bond Fund Class I	CUBIX	NAS CM	Open End	Fixed Inc Misc (Income)	D+	D+	C	Down	Y	202-238-2200
Calvert Flexible Bond Fund Class R6	CUBRX	NAS CM	Open End	Fixed Inc Misc (Income)	D+	D+	C	Down	Y	202-238-2200
Calvert Floating-Rate Advantage Fund Class A	CFOAX	NAS CM	Open End	US Fixed Inc (Income)	D	D	C-	Down	Y	202-238-2200
Calvert Floating-Rate Advantage Fund Class I	CFOIX	NAS CM	Open End	US Fixed Inc (Income)	D	D	C-	Down	Y	202-238-2200
Calvert Floating-Rate Advantage Fund Class R6	CFORX	NAS CM	Open End	US Fixed Inc (Income)	D	D	C-	Down	Y	202-238-2200
Calvert Green Bond Fund Class A	CGAFX	NAS CM	Open End	US Fixed Inc (Income)	C+	C	B	Up	Y	202-238-2200
Calvert Green Bond Fund Class I	CGBIX	NAS CM	Open End	US Fixed Inc (Income)	C+	C	B	Up	Y	202-238-2200
Calvert Green Bond Fund Class R6	CBGRX	NAS CM	Open End	US Fixed Inc (Income)	C+	C	B	Up	Y	202-238-2200
Calvert High Yield Bond Fund Class A	CYBAX	NAS CM	Open End	US Fixed Inc (Corp Bond - High Yield)	C-	D+	C	Down	Y	202-238-2200
Calvert High Yield Bond Fund Class C	CHBCX	NAS CM	Open End	US Fixed Inc (Corp Bond - High Yield)	C-	D+	C		Y	202-238-2200
Calvert High Yield Bond Fund Class I	CYBIX	NAS CM	Open End	US Fixed Inc (Corp Bond - High Yield)	C-	D+	C	Down	Y	202-238-2200
Calvert High Yield Bond Fund Class R6	CYBRX	NAS CM	Open End	US Fixed Inc (Corp Bond - High Yield)	C-	D+	C	Down	Y	202-238-2200
Calvert Income Fund Class A	CFICX	NAS CM	Open End	US Fixed Inc (Corp Bond - General)	C	C-	C+		Y	202-238-2200

★Expanded analysis of this fund is included in Section II.

TOTAL RETURNS & PERFORMANCE									ASSETS		ASSET ALLOCATION & TURNOVER							MINIMUMS		FEES		
3-Month Total Return	6-Month Total Return	1-Year Total Return	3-Year Total Return	5-Year Total Return	Dividend Yield (TTM)	Expense Ratio	3-Yr Std Deviation	Effective Duration	NAV	Total Assets (MIL)	%Cash	%Government Bonds	%Municipal Bonds	%Corporate Bonds	%Other	Turnover Ratio	Average Coupon Rate	Min Initial Investment	Min Additional Investment	Front End Fee (%)	Back End Fee (%)	Inception Date
2.76	0.65	2.68	11.17		2.52	0.17	3.9	4.61	10.49	6,101	4	0	96	0	0	42	4.43	0				Sep-15
2.47	5.49	6.26	6.62	13.10	2.93	0.44	2.87	5.84		1,773	1	26	0	25	0	24	3.72	0				Feb-13
12.80	-13.82	-11.22	0.68		8.51	2.23	14.9		18.83	690.3	13	0	0	43	0	46	4.43					Dec-16
5.56	3.63	5.41	11.22	15.75	2.02	0.82	3.96	3.25	10.82	147.3	5	19	1	39	0	82	2.72	100	100			May-91
5.60	3.68	5.65	11.99	17.15	2.22	0.57	3.96	3.25	11.06	147.3	5	19	1	39	0	82	2.72	100	100			Nov-95
1.26	-0.68	1.42	8.54	14.02	2.73	0.49	4.06	4.96	10.67	173.4	3	0	97	0	0	33	4.37	100	100			Dec-00
2.13	4.23	6.19	13.40	17.91	1.61	0.47	2.54	2.53	10.46	245.9	4	4	1	6	0	200	3.44	1,000,000	100			May-14
2.12	4.21	6.14	13.34	17.67	1.56	0.52	2.55	2.53	10.47	245.9	4	4	1	6	0	200	3.44	100	100			Dec-13
8.70	-2.25	0.26	6.49	11.98	3.48	0.61	6.88	2.16	9.29	149.9	16	0	2	43	0	115	3.81	1,000,000	100			Oct-14
8.68	-2.08	0.31	6.22	11.14	3.41	0.66	6.77	2.16	9.3	149.9	16	0	2	43	0	115	3.81	100	100			Sep-11
6.55	5.76	8.24			2.69	0.52		5.64	10.54	151.2	-9	29	11	38	0	66	3.34	1,000,000	100			Jul-18
6.54	5.73	8.19			2.64	0.57		5.64	10.54	151.2	-9	29	11	38	0	66	3.34	100	100			Aug-17
2.41	-0.83	1.57	11.24	17.62	2.89	0.43	4.96	5.13	10.08	1,104	1	0	99	0	0	53	3.91	1,000,000	100			Jul-18
2.49	-0.75	1.62	11.24	17.62	2.84	0.48	4.96	5.13	10.09	1,104	1	0	99	0	0	53	3.91	100	100			Jun-12
1.07	-0.56					0.58			9.88	119.3	4	0	96	0	0		4.15	100	100			Dec-19
8.29	5.10	8.00	17.13	26.07	2.69	0.49	5.84	5.78	10.51	394.7	-13	29	2	44	0	106	3.25	1,000,000	100			Oct-14
8.28	5.07	7.95	16.96	25.88	2.64	0.54	5.85	5.78	10.51	394.7	-13	29	2	44	0	106	3.25	100	100			Oct-14
5.85	4.75	6.60			2.08	1.71		10.53	10.61	3.5	44	21	0	30	0	163	3.59	100,000	1,000			Dec-18
5.85	4.75	6.60			2.08	2.21		10.53	10.61	3.5	44	21	0	30	0	163	3.59	1,000	100			Dec-18
0.20	1.33	1.86	-1.55	12.54	2.42	1.91	3.42		9.58	530.8	100	0	0	0	0	493		1,000	100	5.00		May-13
0.10	0.95	1.09	-3.67	8.46	1.8	2.66	3.42		9.51	530.8	100	0	0	0	0	493		1,000	100			May-13
0.31	1.39	2.06	-0.80	13.98	2.69	1.66	3.42		9.55	530.8	100	0	0	0	0	493		100,000	1,000			May-15
0.10	1.18	1.57	-2.31	11.17	2.2	2.16	3.47		9.55	530.8	100	0	0	0	0	493		1,000	100			May-15
9.99	-3.76	0.15	7.80	16.44	4.43	1.02	8.28	3.44	10.57	202.3	2	0	0	98	0	36	5.25	2,500	100			May-95
10.09	-3.66	0.24	7.99	16.65		0.87	8.31	3.44	10.56	202.3	2	0	0	98	0	36	5.25	250,000	100			Jul-19
3.09	1.84	3.38			2.61	0.65		1.80	10.18	175.7	4	14	1	62	0	132	3.16	2,500	50	2.25		Sep-18
3.15	1.96	3.64			2.86	0.4		1.80	10.19	175.7	4	14	1	62	0	132	3.16	1,000,000				Sep-18
10.14	-6.57	-3.40	4.23	12.63	6.51	1.01	10.2	3.76	7.7	37.6	5	0	0	95	0	46	5.48	2,500	50	2.25		Aug-99
9.86	-6.92	-4.10	2.04	8.57	5.29	1.76	10.18	3.76	8.17	37.6	5	0	0	95	0	46	5.48	2,500	50		1.00	Dec-00
10.20	-6.45	-3.16	5.00	14.05	6.78	0.76	10.23	3.76	7.7	37.6	5	0	0	95	0	46	5.48	1,000,000				Mar-02
3.56	4.69	6.97	13.42	20.17	2.26	0.9	3.47	5.68	10.86	78.6	4	18	0	48	0	64	3.21	2,500	50	2.25		Jun-07
3.37	4.31	6.18	10.92	15.89	1.53	1.65	3.45	5.68	10.86	78.6	4	18	0	48	0	64	3.21	2,500	50		1.00	Jun-07
3.62	4.82	7.23	14.27	21.79	2.51	0.65	3.46	5.68	10.86	78.6	4	18	0	48	0	64	3.21	1,000,000				Jun-07
5.11	3.22	5.63	13.11	21.94	2.37	0.73	4.22	5.74	16.8	1,802	3	10	4	40	0	75	3.20	1,000		3.75		Aug-87
4.88	2.78	4.76	10.40	16.93	1.58	1.53	4.19	5.74	16.68	1,802	3	10	4	40	0	75	3.20	1,000			1.00	Jun-98
5.16	3.33	5.84	13.98	23.86	2.57	0.53	4.22	5.74	16.83	1,802	3	10	4	40	0	75	3.20	250,000				Mar-00
5.18	3.36	5.92	13.92	22.81	2.64	0.46	4.22	5.74	16.82	1,802	3	10	4	40	0	75	3.20	1,000,000				Oct-17
6.50	-3.34	-1.42	4.30	12.30	3.07	0.94	6.08	2.50	14.44	204.8	12	6	0	33	0	87	3.70	1,000		3.75		Sep-14
6.30	-3.70	-2.09	1.96	8.17	2.28	1.69	6.07	2.50	14.45	204.8	12	6	0	33	0	87	3.70	1,000			1.00	Sep-14
6.58	-3.23	-1.19	5.18	14.21	3.33	0.69	6.1	2.50	14.4	204.8	12	6	0	33	0	87	3.70	250,000				Sep-14
6.37	-3.34	-1.26	5.10	14.12	3.39	0.65	6.05	2.50	14.41	204.8	12	6	0	33	0	87	3.70	1,000,000				May-19
7.30	-6.13	-3.15			4.85	1.98		0.25	9.01	66.0	4	0	0	96	0	44	3.75	1,000		3.75		Oct-17
7.37	-6.12	-3.04			5.09	1.73		0.25	9	66.0	4	0	0	96	0	44	3.75	250,000				Oct-17
7.37	-6.11	-2.94			5.09	1.73		0.25	9	66.0	4	0	0	96	0	44	3.75	1,000,000				Oct-17
5.76	3.40	5.65	12.90	20.02	2.14	0.73	4.8	6.03	16.11	488.7	5	16	6	53	0	21	2.82	1,000		3.75		Oct-13
5.82	3.46	5.84	13.93	22.11	2.38	0.48	4.77	6.03	16.13	488.7	5	16	6	53	0	21	2.82	250,000				Oct-13
5.83	3.55	5.96	14.08	22.27	2.44	0.43	4.79	6.03	16.14	488.7	5	16	6	53	0	21	2.82	1,000,000				Feb-19
7.32	-3.60	0.03	7.30	18.68	4.85	1.02	6.95	3.84	25.8	256.8	7	0	0	93	0	39	5.72	1,000		3.75		Feb-07
7.11	-3.94	-0.71	4.90	14.18	4.08	1.77	6.95	3.84	26.2	256.8	7	0	0	93	0	39	5.72	1,000			1.00	Oct-11
7.38	-3.46	0.24	8.20	20.54	5.1	0.77	6.98	3.84	25.43	256.8	7	0	0	93	0	39	5.72	250,000				Jul-01
7.41	-3.42	0.35	8.36	20.71	5.17	0.71	6.98	3.84	25.44	256.8	7	0	0	93	0	39	5.72	1,000,000				Feb-19
8.32	0.44	4.83	13.65	25.21	3.36	0.95	7.44		17	576.4	4	0	0	70	0	57	4.18	1,000		3.75		Oct-82

	MARKET			FUND TYPE, CATEGORY & OBJECTIVE	RATINGS				NEW INVESTORS	
Fund Name	Ticker Symbol	Traded On	Fund Type	Category and (Prospectus Objective)	Overall Rating	Reward Rating	Risk Rating	Recent Up/ Downgrade	Open to New Investors	Telephone
Calvert Income Fund Class C	CIFCX	NAS CM	Open End	US Fixed Inc (Corp Bond - General)	C	C-	C+		Y	202-238-2200
Calvert Income Fund Class I	CINCX	NAS CM	Open End	US Fixed Inc (Corp Bond - General)	C	C-	C+		Y	202-238-2200
Calvert Long-Term Income Fund Class A	CLDAX	NAS CM	Open End	US Fixed Inc (Income)	B-	C+	B		Y	202-238-2200
Calvert Long-Term Income Fund Class I	CLDIX	NAS CM	Open End	US Fixed Inc (Income)	B-	C+	B		Y	202-238-2200
Calvert Responsible Municipal Income Fund Class A	CTTLX	NAS CM	Open End	US Muni Fixed Inc (Muni Bond - Natl)	C+	C	B	Up	Y	202-238-2200
Calvert Responsible Municipal Income Fund Class C	CTTCX	NAS CM	Open End	US Muni Fixed Inc (Muni Bond - Natl)	C	C	B-		Y	202-238-2200
Calvert Responsible Municipal Income Fund Class I	CTTIX	NAS CM	Open End	US Muni Fixed Inc (Muni Bond - Natl)	C+	C	B	Up	Y	202-238-2200
Calvert Short Duration Income Fund Class A	CSDAX	NAS CM	Open End	US Fixed Inc (Corp Bond - General)	C	C-	C		Y	202-238-2200
Calvert Short Duration Income Fund Class C	CDICX	NAS CM	Open End	US Fixed Inc (Corp Bond - General)	C-	D+	C		Y	202-238-2200
Calvert Short Duration Income Fund Class I	CDSIX	NAS CM	Open End	US Fixed Inc (Corp Bond - General)	C	C-	C+		Y	202-238-2200
Calvert Short Duration Income Fund Class R6	CDSRX	NAS CM	Open End	US Fixed Inc (Corp Bond - General)	C	C-	C+		Y	202-238-2200
Calvert Ultra-Short Duration Income Fund Class A	CULAX	NAS CM	Open End	US Fixed Inc (Income)	C-	D	C		Y	202-238-2200
Calvert Ultra-Short Duration Income Fund Class I	CULIX	NAS CM	Open End	US Fixed Inc (Income)	C-	D+	C		Y	202-238-2200
Calvert Ultra-Short Duration Income Fund Class R6	CULRX	NAS CM	Open End	US Fixed Inc (Income)	C-	D+	C		Y	202-238-2200
Capital Group California Core Municipal Fund	CCCMX	NAS CM	Open End	US Muni Fixed Inc (Muni Bond - Single State)	C	C	B-		Y	213-486-9257
Capital Group California Short-Term Municipal Fund	CCSTX	NAS CM	Open End	US Muni Fixed Inc (Muni Bond - Single State)	C	C	B-		Y	213-486-9257
Capital Group Core Bond Fund	CCBPX	NAS CM	Open End	US Fixed Inc (Corp Bond - High Quality)	B-	C+	B	Up	Y	213-486-9257
Capital Group Core Municipal Fund	CCMPX	NAS CM	Open End	US Muni Fixed Inc (Muni Bond - Natl)	C+	C	B	Up	Y	213-486-9257
Capital Group Short-Term Municipal Fund	CSTMX	NAS CM	Open End	US Muni Fixed Inc (Muni Bond - Natl)	C	C	B-		Y	213-486-9257
Capstone Church Capital Fund	XCBFX	NAS CM	Closed End	US Fixed Inc (Income)	C	C-	B-	Down	Y	800-262-6631
Carillon Reams Core Bond Fund Class A	CRCBX	NAS CM	Open End	US Fixed Inc (Corp Bond - General)	B	B	B+		Y	800-421-4184
Carillon Reams Core Bond Fund Class C	CRCDX	NAS CM	Open End	US Fixed Inc (Corp Bond - General)	B	B	B	Up	Y	800-421-4184
Carillon Reams Core Bond Fund Class I	SCCIX	NAS CM	Open End	US Fixed Inc (Corp Bond - General)	B	B	B+		Y	800-421-4184
Carillon Reams Core Bond Fund Class R-3	CRCQX	NAS CM	Open End	US Fixed Inc (Corp Bond - General)	B	B	B+	Up	Y	800-421-4184
Carillon Reams Core Bond Fund Class R-5	CRCSX	NAS CM	Open End	US Fixed Inc (Corp Bond - General)	B	B	B+		Y	800-421-4184
Carillon Reams Core Bond Fund Class R-6	CRCUX	NAS CM	Open End	US Fixed Inc (Corp Bond - General)	B	B	B+		Y	800-421-4184
Carillon Reams Core Bond Fund Class Y	SCCYX	NAS CM	Open End	US Fixed Inc (Corp Bond - General)	B	B	B+		Y	800-421-4184
Carillon Reams Core Plus Bond Fund Class A	SCPDX	NAS CM	Open End	US Fixed Inc (Multisector Bond)	B	B	B+	Up	Y	800-421-4184
Carillon Reams Core Plus Bond Fund Class C	SCPEX	NAS CM	Open End	US Fixed Inc (Multisector Bond)	B	B	B	Up	Y	800-421-4184
Carillon Reams Core Plus Bond Fund Class I	SCPZX	NAS CM	Open End	US Fixed Inc (Multisector Bond)	B	B	B+	Up	Y	800-421-4184
Carillon Reams Core Plus Bond Fund Class R-3	SCPUX	NAS CM	Open End	US Fixed Inc (Multisector Bond)	B	B	B	Up	Y	800-421-4184
Carillon Reams Core Plus Bond Fund Class R-5	SCPVX	NAS CM	Open End	US Fixed Inc (Multisector Bond)	B	B	B+	Up	Y	800-421-4184
Carillon Reams Core Plus Bond Fund Class R-6	SCPWX	NAS CM	Open End	US Fixed Inc (Multisector Bond)	B	B	B+	Up	Y	800-421-4184
Carillon Reams Core Plus Bond Fund Class Y	SCPYX	NAS CM	Open End	US Fixed Inc (Multisector Bond)	B	B	B+	Up	Y	800-421-4184
Carillon Reams Unconstrained Bond Fund Class A	SUBDX	NAS CM	Open End	Fixed Inc Misc (Multisector Bond)	B-	C	B	Up	Y	800-421-4184
Carillon Reams Unconstrained Bond Fund Class C	SUBEX	NAS CM	Open End	Fixed Inc Misc (Multisector Bond)	C+	C	B-	Up	Y	800-421-4184
Carillon Reams Unconstrained Bond Fund Class I	SUBFX	NAS CM	Open End	Fixed Inc Misc (Multisector Bond)	B-	C+	B+	Up	Y	800-421-4184
Carillon Reams Unconstrained Bond Fund Class R-3	SUBRX	NAS CM	Open End	Fixed Inc Misc (Multisector Bond)	B-	C	B	Up	Y	800-421-4184
Carillon Reams Unconstrained Bond Fund Class R-5	SUBSX	NAS CM	Open End	Fixed Inc Misc (Multisector Bond)	B-	C+	B+	Up	Y	800-421-4184
Carillon Reams Unconstrained Bond Fund Class R-6	SUBTX	NAS CM	Open End	Fixed Inc Misc (Multisector Bond)	B-	C+	B+	Up	Y	800-421-4184
Carillon Reams Unconstrained Bond Fund Class Y	SUBYX	NAS CM	Open End	Fixed Inc Misc (Multisector Bond)	B-	C	B	Up	Y	800-421-4184
Carret Kansas Tax - Exempt Bond Fund Institutional Class	SEKSX	NAS CM	Open End	US Muni Fixed Inc (Muni Bond - Single State)	C+	C	B	Up		
Carret Kansas Tax - Exempt Bond FundClass A	IKSTX	NAS CM	Open End	US Muni Fixed Inc (Muni Bond - Single State)	C+	C	B	Up	Y	
Catalyst Enhanced Income Strategy Fund Class A	EIXAX	NAS CM	Open End	Fixed Inc Misc (Income)	D	D+	C		Y	866-447-4228
Catalyst Enhanced Income Strategy Fund Class C	EIXCX	NAS CM	Open End	Fixed Inc Misc (Income)	D	D	C		Y	866-447-4228
Catalyst Enhanced Income Strategy Fund Class I	EIXIX	NAS CM	Open End	Fixed Inc Misc (Income)	D	D+	C		Y	866-447-4228
Catalyst Floating Rate Income Fund Class A	CFRAX	NAS CM	Open End	US Fixed Inc (Growth & Income)	C-	D+	C		Y	866-447-4228
Catalyst Floating Rate Income Fund Class C	CFRCX	NAS CM	Open End	US Fixed Inc (Growth & Income)	D+	D	C	Down	Y	866-447-4228
Catalyst Floating Rate Income Fund Class I	CFRIX	NAS CM	Open End	US Fixed Inc (Growth & Income)	C-	D+	C		Y	866-447-4228
Catalyst Insider Income Fund Class A	IIXAX	NAS CM	Open End	US Fixed Inc (Income)	C	C-	C+		Y	866-447-4228
Catalyst Insider Income Fund Class C	IIXCX	NAS CM	Open End	US Fixed Inc (Income)	C	D+	C	Up	Y	866-447-4228
Catalyst Insider Income Fund Class I	IIXIX	NAS CM	Open End	US Fixed Inc (Income)	C	C-	C+		Y	866-447-4228

★ Expanded analysis of this fund is included in Section II.

TOTAL RETURNS & PERFORMANCE									ASSETS		ASSET ALLOCATION & TURNOVER							MINIMUMS		FEES		
3-Month Total Return	6-Month Total Return	1-Year Total Return	3-Year Total Return	5-Year Total Return	Dividend Yield (TTM)	Expense Ratio	3-Yr Std Deviation	Effective Duration	NAV	Total Assets (MIL)	%Cash	%Government Bonds	%Municipal Bonds	%Corporate Bonds	%Other	Turnover Ratio	Average Coupon Rate	Min Initial Investment	Min Additional Investment	Front End Fee (%)	Back End Fee (%)	Inception Date
8.07	0.07	4.00	11.06	20.49	2.6	1.7	7.44		16.98	576.4	4	0	0	70	0	57	4.18	1,000			1.00	Jul-00
8.38	0.57	5.03	14.73	27.39	3.62	0.7	7.45		17.04	576.4	4	0	0	70	0	57	4.18	250,000				Feb-99
9.95	8.02	14.21	26.89	45.20	2.78	0.92	8.67	13.26	19.64	92.6	4	7	4	79	0	43	3.99	1,000		3.75		Dec-04
10.01	8.15	14.49	27.97	48.06	3.02	0.67	8.66	13.26	19.66	92.6	4	7	4	79	0	43	3.99	250,000				Jan-15
2.23	2.12	4.27	11.89	19.04	1.86	0.75	3.84	5.29	16.57	243.9	11	0	86	3	0	18	4.48	1,000		3.75		Aug-83
2.04	1.75	3.49	9.37	14.68	1.12	1.5	3.84	5.29	16.57	243.9	11	0	86	3	0	18	4.48	1,000			1.00	Jul-15
2.35	2.31	4.52	12.99	21.01	2.11	0.5	3.84	5.29	16.62	243.9	11	0	86	3	0	18	4.48	250,000				Jul-15
5.06	0.51	2.07	7.45	12.17	2.55	0.76	3.83	2.56	16.04	1,604	6	2	1	51	0	80	3.11	1,000		2.75		Jan-02
4.82	0.14	1.31	5.07	8.07	1.78	1.51	3.8	2.56	15.98	1,604	6	2	1	51	0	80	3.11	1,000			1.00	Oct-02
5.10	0.65	2.33	8.41	14.13	2.8	0.51	3.8	2.56	16.15	1,604	6	2	1	51	0	80	3.11	250,000				Apr-06
5.11	0.67	2.36	7.92	12.66	2.83	0.46	3.81	2.56	16.15	1,604	6	2	1	51	0	80	3.11	1,000,000				Feb-19
3.90	-0.61	0.56	4.49	7.21	2.04	0.72	3.06	0.78	9.85	876.8	14	4	0	41	0	85	2.15	1,000		1.25		Oct-06
3.97	-0.48	0.81	5.37	8.85	2.3	0.47	3.07	0.78	9.85	876.8	14	4	0	41	0	85	2.15	250,000				Jan-14
3.87	-0.46	0.85	5.21	7.95	2.34	0.43	3.02	0.78	9.84	876.8	14	4	0	41	0	85	2.15	1,000,000				Oct-17
2.16	2.11	3.43	9.08	14.30	1.69	0.28	2.42	3.63	10.87	599.8	2	0	98	0	0	22	4.39	25,000				Apr-10
1.73	1.59	2.48	5.99	8.17	1.32	0.3	1.61	2.30	10.39	179.6	0	0	100	0	0	39	4.30	25,000				Apr-10
2.74	5.76	7.17	12.91	17.15	1.99	0.28	2.22	3.97	10.71	525.4	5	54	0	22	0	151	2.39	25,000				Apr-10
2.51	2.68	4.13	10.09	14.36	1.87	0.28	2.34	3.39	10.73	611.2	-1	0	99	0	0	38	4.22	25,000				Apr-10
1.78	2.36	3.39	7.59	10.30	1.62	0.3	1.46	2.19	10.31	201.2	-1	0	99	0	0	50	4.07	25,000				Apr-10
1.79	3.22	-0.39	12.76	11.17	0.08	1.93	4.68		12.49	37.4	4	14	0	78	20	29	5.25	2,000	100	3.25		Oct-05
6.34	12.62	14.83	23.54	29.84	1.61	0.8	3.86	5.50	13.07	246.3	3	6	0	56	0		3.44	1,000		4.75		Nov-17
6.17	12.22	13.98	20.81	25.09	0.93	1.55	3.87	5.50	13.06	246.3	3	6	0	56	0		3.44	1,000			1.00	Nov-17
6.52	12.88	15.32	25.01	32.04	1.96	0.4	3.87	5.50	13.09	246.3	3	6	0	56	0		3.44	10,000				Feb-01
6.26	12.49	14.55	22.63	28.24	1.37	1.05	3.86	5.50	13.08	246.3	3	6	0	56	0		3.44	0				Nov-17
6.40	12.74	15.21	24.69	31.70	1.87	0.5	3.84	5.50	13.09	246.3	3	6	0	56	0		3.44	0				Nov-17
6.43	12.88	15.31	25.01	32.04	1.96	0.4	3.88	5.50	13.09	246.3	3	6	0	56	0		3.44	0				Nov-17
6.35	12.63	14.82	23.48	29.47	1.61	0.8	3.85	5.50	13.08	246.3	3	6	0	56	0		3.44	1,000				Apr-11
8.58	12.27	14.56	22.90	29.22	1.87	0.8	4.27	5.10	36.15	754.8	2	5	0	64	0		3.40	1,000		4.75		Nov-17
8.51	11.99	13.85	20.30	24.62	1.15	1.55	4.32	5.10	36.16	754.8	2	5	0	64	0		3.40	1,000			1.00	Nov-17
8.79	12.61	15.17	24.43	31.49	2.22	0.4	4.31	5.10	36.23	754.8	2	5	0	64	0		3.40	10,000				Nov-96
8.68	12.32	14.46	22.17	27.81	1.62	1.05	4.33	5.10	36.22	754.8	2	5	0	64	0		3.40	0				Nov-17
8.82	12.60	15.10	24.15	31.19	2.13	0.5	4.32	5.10	36.24	754.8	2	5	0	64	0		3.40	0				Nov-17
8.82	12.64	15.20	24.47	31.52	2.22	0.4	4.31	5.10	36.24	754.8	2	5	0	64	0		3.40	0				Nov-17
8.71	12.43	14.71	22.95	28.95	1.87	0.8	4.31	5.10	36.2	754.8	2	5	0	64	0		3.40	1,000				Nov-09
8.23	5.62	7.71	12.55	19.29	2.17	0.8	3.6	-0.50	12.62	880.2	86	0	0	31	0		3.37	1,000		4.75		Nov-17
8.06	5.29	6.99	10.01	14.88	1.43	1.55	3.62	-0.50	12.6	880.2	86	0	0	31	0		3.37	1,000			1.00	Nov-17
8.39	5.83	8.16	13.47	20.87	2.44	0.5	3.64	-0.50	12.62	880.2	86	0	0	31	0		3.37	10,000				Sep-11
8.16	5.51	7.53	11.59	17.69	1.91	1.05	3.63	-0.50	12.61	880.2	86	0	0	31	0		3.37	0				Nov-17
8.39	5.83	8.16	13.47	20.87	2.44	0.5	3.64	-0.50	12.62	880.2	86	0	0	31	0		3.37	0				Nov-17
8.42	5.88	8.26	13.76	21.18	2.54	0.4	3.64	-0.50	12.62	880.2	86	0	0	31	0		3.37	0				Nov-17
8.26	5.67	7.81	12.48	19.14	2.14	0.8	3.61	-0.50	12.68	880.2	86	0	0	31	0		3.37	1,000				Dec-12
2.18	3.12	4.93	11.05	16.23	2.25	0.48	2.94		11.14	177.3	1	0	99	0	0		4.37	3,000,000	5,000			Dec-90
2.12	2.90	4.67	10.04	14.32	2.01	0.73	2.94		11.14	177.3	1	0	99	0	0		4.37	5,000	250	4.25		Aug-02
8.97	1.51	4.41			4.86	1.75			11.11	129.7	4	0	0	0	0		3.27	2,500	50	4.75		Dec-18
8.72	1.07	3.63			4.2	2.5			11.07	129.7	4	0	0	0	0		3.27	2,500	50			Dec-18
9.03	1.63	4.74			5.08	1.5			11.11	129.7	4	0	0	0	0		3.27	2,500	50			Dec-18
9.10	-2.98	0.27	12.44	15.03	5.15	1.18	7.73		9.17	87.0	5	0	0	89	0	178	5.95	2,500	50	4.75		Dec-12
9.00	-3.29	-0.42	9.91	10.89	4.39	1.93	7.73		9.14	87.0	5	0	0	89	0	178	5.95	2,500	50			Dec-12
9.15	-2.86	0.51	13.27	16.72	5.41	0.93	7.82		9.18	87.0	5	0	0	89	0	178	5.95	2,500	50			Dec-12
6.59	0.86	2.68	10.35	11.05	2.81	1	4.04		9.5	50.7	14	0	0	86	0	126	5.64	2,500	50	4.75		Jul-14
6.30	0.47	1.92	8.16	7.29	2.03	1.75	4.03		9.5	50.7	14	0	0	86	0	126	5.64	2,500	50			Jul-14
6.61	0.92	2.86	11.41	12.65	2.99	0.75	4.02		9.51	50.7	14	0	0	86	0	126	5.64	2,500	50			Jul-14

	MARKET			FUND TYPE, CATEGORY & OBJECTIVE	RATINGS				NEW INVESTORS	
Fund Name	Ticker Symbol	Traded On	Fund Type	Category and (Prospectus Objective)	Overall Rating	Reward Rating	Risk Rating	Recent Up/ Downgrade	Open to New Investors	Telephone
Catalyst/SMH High Income Fund Class A	HIIFX	NAS CM	Open End	US Fixed Inc (Corp Bond - High Yield)	D+	D	C-	Down	Y	866-447-4228
Catalyst/SMH High Income Fund Class C	HIICX	NAS CM	Open End	US Fixed Inc (Corp Bond - High Yield)	D+	D	C-	Down	Y	866-447-4228
Catalyst/SMH High Income Fund Class I	HIIIX	NAS CM	Open End	US Fixed Inc (Corp Bond - High Yield)	D+	D	C-	Down	Y	866-447-4228
Catalyst/Stone Beach Income Opportunity Fund Class A	IOXAX	NAS CM	Open End	Fixed Inc Misc (Growth & Income)	B-	C	A-		Y	866-447-4228
Catalyst/Stone Beach Income Opportunity Fund Class C	IOXCX	NAS CM	Open End	Fixed Inc Misc (Growth & Income)	B-	C	B		Y	866-447-4228
Catalyst/Stone Beach Income Opportunity Fund Class I	IOXIX	NAS CM	Open End	Fixed Inc Misc (Growth & Income)	B	C	A-	Up	Y	866-447-4228
Cavalier Adaptive Income Fund C Class	CADAX	NAS CM	Open End	US Fixed Inc (Growth & Income)	D+	D+	C	Down	Y	800-773-3863
Cavalier Adaptive Income Fund Institutional Class	CADTX	NAS CM	Open End	US Fixed Inc (Growth & Income)	C-	D+	C	Down	Y	800-773-3863
Cavalier Hedged High Income Fund C Class	CAHIX	NAS CM	Open End	US Fixed Inc (Income)	C-	D+	C		Y	800-773-3863
Cavalier Hedged High Income Fund Institutional Class	CHIIX	NAS CM	Open End	US Fixed Inc (Income)	C	C-	C		Y	800-773-3863
Cavanal Hill Bond Fund Class A	AABOX	NAS CM	Open End	US Fixed Inc (Corp Bond - High Quality)	B-	C+	B	Up	Y	
Cavanal Hill Bond Fund Institutional Class	AIBNX	NAS CM	Open End	US Fixed Inc (Corp Bond - High Quality)	B-	C+	B+		Y	
Cavanal Hill Bond Fund Investor Class	APBDX	NAS CM	Open End	US Fixed Inc (Corp Bond - High Quality)	B-	C+	B	Up	Y	
Cavanal Hill Govt Securities Money Mkt Administrative Cl	APCXX	NAS CM	Money Mkt	US Money Mkt (Money Mkt - Govt)	C	C-	C+			
Cavanal Hill Govt Securities Money Mkt Institutional Cl	APHXX	NAS CM	Money Mkt	US Money Mkt (Money Mkt - Govt)	C	C-	C+		Y	
Cavanal Hill Govt Securities Money Mkt Fund Premier Class	APPXX	NAS CM	Money Mkt	US Money Mkt (Money Mkt - Govt)	C	C-	C+			
Cavanal Hill Govt Securities Money Mkt Fund Select Class	APSXX	NAS CM	Money Mkt	US Money Mkt (Money Mkt - Govt)	C	C-	C+			
Cavanal Hill Limited Duration Fund Class A	AASTX	NAS CM	Open End	US Fixed Inc (Corp Bond - High Quality)	C+	C	B		Y	
Cavanal Hill Limited Duration Fund Institutional Class	AISTX	NAS CM	Open End	US Fixed Inc (Corp Bond - High Quality)	C+	C	B		Y	
Cavanal Hill Limited Duration Fund Investor Class	APSTX	NAS CM	Open End	US Fixed Inc (Corp Bond - High Quality)	C+	C	B		Y	
Cavanal Hill Moderate Duration Fund Class A	AAIBX	NAS CM	Open End	US Fixed Inc (Corp Bond - High Quality)	C	C	B		Y	
Cavanal Hill Moderate Duration Fund Institutional Class	AIFBX	NAS CM	Open End	US Fixed Inc (Corp Bond - High Quality)	C+	C	B	Up	Y	
Cavanal Hill Moderate Duration Fund Investor Class	APFBX	NAS CM	Open End	US Fixed Inc (Corp Bond - High Quality)	C	C	B		Y	
Cavanal Hill Strategic Enhanced Yield Fund Class A	AAENX	NAS CM	Open End	US Fixed Inc (Growth & Income)	C	C	B		Y	
Cavanal Hill Strategic Enhanced Yield Fund Institutional	AIENX	NAS CM	Open End	US Fixed Inc (Growth & Income)	C	C	B		Y	
Cavanal Hill Strategic Enhanced Yield Fund Investor	APENX	NAS CM	Open End	US Fixed Inc (Growth & Income)	C	C	B		Y	
Cavanal Hill U.S. Treasury Fund Administrative Class	APGXX	NAS CM	Money Mkt	US Money Mkt (Money Mkt - Treasury)	C	C-	C			
Cavanal Hill U.S. Treasury Fund Institutional Class	APKXX	NAS CM	Money Mkt	US Money Mkt (Money Mkt - Treasury)	C	C-	C+		Y	
Cavanal Hill U.S. Treasury Fund Select Class	APNXX	NAS CM	Money Mkt	US Money Mkt (Money Mkt - Treasury)	C	C-	C			
Cavanal Hill U.S. Treasury Fund Service Class	APJXX	NAS CM	Money Mkt	US Money Mkt (Money Mkt - Treasury)	C	C-	C+		Y	
Cavanal Hill Ultra Short Tax-Free Income Fund Class A	AAUSX	NAS CM	Open End	US Muni Fixed Inc (Muni Bond - Natl)	C	C-	C		Y	
Cavanal Hill Ultra Short Tax-Free Income Fund Investor	APUSX	NAS CM	Open End	US Muni Fixed Inc (Muni Bond - Natl)	C	C-	C		Y	
Cavanal HillUltra Short Tax-Free Income Fund Institutional	AIUSX	NAS CM	Open End	US Muni Fixed Inc (Muni Bond - Natl)	C	C-	C+		Y	
Centre Active U.S. Treasury Fund Institutional Class	DHTUX	NAS CM	Open End	US Fixed Inc (Govt Bond - Treasury)	C-	D+	C	Down	Y	855-298-4236
Centre Active U.S. Treasury Fund Investor Class	DHTRX	NAS CM	Open End	US Fixed Inc (Govt Bond - Treasury)	D+	D	C	Down	Y	855-298-4236
Changing Parameters Fund	CPMPX	NAS CM	Open End	US Fixed Inc (Growth & Income)	C+	C	B	Up	Y	
Charter Multi-Sector Bond Portfolio Class A			Open End	US Fixed Inc (Multisector Bond)	E-	E-	E-	Down	Y	877-222-2144
Charter Multi-Sector Bond Portfolio Class B			Open End	US Fixed Inc (Multisector Bond)	E-	E-	E-	Down	Y	877-222-2144
Charter Multi-Sector Bond Portfolio Class K			Open End	US Fixed Inc (Multisector Bond)	E-	E-	E-	Down	Y	877-222-2144
Chartwell Short Duration High Yield Fund	CWFIX	NAS CM	Open End	US Fixed Inc (Corp Bond - High Yield)	C	D+	C		Y	610-296-1400
CION Ares Diversified Credit Fund A Share	CADEX	NAS CM	Closed End	US Fixed Inc (Multisector Bond)	D+	D	C-	Down	Y	212-418-4700
CION Ares Diversified Credit Fund C Share	CADCX	NAS CM	Closed End	US Fixed Inc (Multisector Bond)	D+	D	C-	Down	Y	212-418-4700
CION Ares Diversified Credit Fund Class L Shares			Closed End	US Fixed Inc (Multisector Bond)	D	D	D		Y	212-418-4700
CION Ares Diversified Credit Fund Class U			Closed End	US Fixed Inc (Multisector Bond)	U	U	U		Y	212-418-4700
CION Ares Diversified Credit Fund Class W	CADFX	NAS CM	Closed End	US Fixed Inc (Multisector Bond)	D	D	D		Y	212-418-4700
CION Ares Diversified Credit Fund I Share	CADUX	NAS CM	Closed End	US Fixed Inc (Multisector Bond)	D+	D	C-	Down	Y	212-418-4700
City Natl Rochdale California Tax-Exempt Bond Fund Class N	CCTEX	NAS CM	Open End	US Muni Fixed Inc (Muni Bond - Single State)	C	C	C+		Y	
City Natl Rochdale California Tax-Exempt Bond Cl Servicing	CNTIX	NAS CM	Open End	US Muni Fixed Inc (Muni Bond - Single State)	C	C	B-		Y	
City National Rochdale Corporate Bond Fund Class N	CCBAX	NAS CM	Open End	US Fixed Inc (Corp Bond - General)	C+	C	B	Up	Y	
City National Rochdale Corporate Bond Fund Class Servicing	CNCIX	NAS CM	Open End	US Fixed Inc (Corp Bond - General)	C+	C	B	Up	Y	
City Natl Rochdale Fixed Income Opportunities Fund Class N	RIMOX	NAS CM	Open End	US Fixed Inc (Corp Bond - High Yield)	D	D	D+	Down	Y	
City National Rochdale Government Bond Fund Class N	CGBAX	NAS CM	Open End	US Fixed Inc (Govt Bond - General)	C+	C	B		Y	

★ Expanded analysis of this fund is included in Section II.

TOTAL RETURNS & PERFORMANCE									ASSETS		ASSET ALLOCATION & TURNOVER							MINIMUMS		FEES		
3-Month Total Return	6-Month Total Return	1-Year Total Return	3-Year Total Return	5-Year Total Return	Dividend Yield (TTM)	Expense Ratio	3-Yr Std Deviation	Effective Duration	NAV	Total Assets (MIL)	%Cash	%Government Bonds	%Municipal Bonds	%Corporate Bonds	%Other	Turnover Ratio	Average Coupon Rate	Min Initial Investment	Min Additional Investment	Front End Fee (%)	Back End Fee (%)	Inception Date
8.84	-4.53	-1.76	7.66	14.50	5.47	1.48	9.08		3.53	16.9	17	0	0	83	0	28	5.52	2,500	50	4.75		May-08
8.63	-4.89	-2.77	5.24	10.25	4.66	2.23	8.98		3.53	16.9	17	0	0	83	0	28	5.52	2,500	50			May-08
8.90	-4.42	-1.78	8.46	15.94	5.74	1.23	9.02		3.53	16.9	17	0	0	83	0	28	5.52	2,500	50			Jul-13
1.72	4.09	6.77	13.81	16.06	5.18	1.58	2.41		9.63	27.0	20	0	0	0	0	242	5.76	2,500	50	4.75		Nov-14
1.55	3.76	6.01	11.44	11.75	4.47	2.33	2.43		9.6	27.0	20	0	0	0	0	242	5.76	2,500	50			Nov-14
1.78	4.22	7.04	14.33	17.25	5.43	1.33	2.45		9.6	27.0	20	0	0	0	0	242	5.76	2,500	50			Nov-14
4.72	-3.35	-2.66	5.10	11.77	2.43	2.26	5.5		9.43	46.5	8	4	0	1	0	28	3.68	1,000	50		1.00	Feb-11
5.03	-2.90	-1.60	8.31	17.46	3.45	1.26	5.48		9.8	46.5	8	4	0	1	0	28	3.68	1,000	50			Oct-09
5.94	-3.62	-0.09	3.24	13.66	2.38	2.55	6.5	3.65	9.51	17.9	15	1	0	84	0	82		1,000	50		1.00	Sep-12
6.28	-3.16	0.83	6.47	19.56	3.51	1.55	6.65	3.65	9.59	17.9	15	1	0	84	0	82		1,000	50			Sep-12
2.90	5.13	7.29	13.65	17.52	2.07	0.74	3.34		10.07	92.8	5	25	9	20	0	33	3.01	0		2.00		May-11
2.86	5.16	7.46	14.40	18.76	2.31	0.49	3.34		10.04	92.8	5	25	9	20	0	33	3.01	1,000				Dec-05
2.90	5.13	7.17	13.47	17.54	2.06	0.77	3.41		10.07	92.8	5	25	9	20	0	33	3.01	100				Sep-90
-0.05	0.14	0.85	3.34	3.43	1.06	0.58	0.17		1	2,220	61	39	0	0	0			1,000				Sep-90
-0.02	0.23	1.09	4.18	4.50	1.32	0.29	0.18		1	2,220	61	39	0	0	0			1,000				Jan-07
0.01	0.29	1.16	4.32	4.68	1.35	0.26	0.18		1	2,220	61	39	0	0	0			1,000				Sep-12
0.01	0.30	1.19	4.46	4.80	1.4	0.21	0.18		1	2,220	61	39	0	0	0			1,000,000				Sep-16
1.59	3.02	4.27	8.92	11.15	1.96	0.73	1.32		9.79	134.4	9	29	1	11	0	34	2.88	0		2.00		May-11
1.65	3.15	4.53	9.62	12.54	2.21	0.49	1.32		9.78	134.4	9	29	1	11	0	34	2.88	1,000				Dec-05
1.59	3.13	4.27	8.82	11.06	1.96	0.75	1.34		9.79	134.4	9	29	1	11	0	34	2.88	100				Oct-94
2.56	2.27	3.47	9.18	11.77	2	0.74	2.31		10.76	30.4	5	17	11	19	0	25	2.85	0		2.00		May-11
2.62	2.40	3.73	10.00	13.08	2.25	0.49	2.32		10.76	30.4	5	17	11	19	0	25	2.85	1,000				Dec-05
2.56	2.37	3.57	9.13	11.64	2	0.74	2.31		10.75	30.4	5	17	11	19	0	25	2.85	100				Sep-90
1.99	5.31	7.38			2.12	1.02			10.65	16.3	6	47	0	4	0	59	3.63	0		2.00		Dec-17
2.05	5.53	7.74			2.36	0.77			10.66	16.3	6	47	0	4	0	59	3.63	1,000				Dec-17
1.96	5.34	7.41			2.12	1.02			10.8	16.3	6	47	0	4	0	59	3.63	100				Dec-17
0.00	0.17	0.81	3.05	3.09	0.95	0.67	0.16		1	1,274	67	33	0	0	0			1,000				Sep-90
-0.04	0.21	1.07	4.18	4.44	1.3	0.25	0.17		1	1,274	67	33	0	0	0			1,000				Jan-07
0.03	0.31	1.21	4.23	4.27	1.38	0.17			1	1,274	67	33	0	0	0			1,000,000				Dec-17
-0.04	0.19	0.98	3.84	3.99	1.19	0.37	0.17		1	1,274	67	33	0	0	0			10,000				Jan-07
0.10	0.33	0.81			0.9	0.6			10.01	31.9	8	0	92	0	0	135	1.61	0		1.00		Dec-17
0.20	0.43	1.01			0.9	0.6			10.01	31.9	8	0	92	0	0	135	1.61	100				Dec-17
0.26	0.56	1.16			1.15	0.35			10.02	31.9	8	0	92	0	0	135	1.61	1,000				Dec-17
-1.90	-3.42	-2.60	1.90	3.07	1.96	0.67	2.1		9.16	29.1	12	88	0	6	0	9	3.99	1,000,000	10,000			Jan-14
-2.04	-3.60	-3.02	0.58	1.23	1.47	1.1	2.09		9.1	29.1	12	88	0	6	0	9	3.99	5,000	1,000			Jan-14
5.44	4.10	6.13	11.75	24.07	2.79	2.53	2.66	3.31	10.66	70.8	3	8	15	70	2	260	5.52	2,500	100			Oct-06
2.09	4.27	5.85	5.35	9.92	2.21	1.1	2.05	4.37		179.6	2	56	0	33	0	5	3.15	0				Jan-87
2.09	4.28	5.87	5.63	9.92	2.21	1.1	2.09	4.37		179.6	2	56	0	33	0	5	3.15	0				Oct-96
2.35	4.53	6.36	6.39	11.29	2.42	0.85	2.17	4.37		179.6	2	56	0	33	0	5	3.15	0				Aug-11
6.05	-0.76	1.23	8.31	14.96	3.58	0.49	4.47	1.36	9.47	107.0	11	0	0	89	0	41	5.37	1,000	100			Jul-14
8.53	-7.77	-4.83	9.84		6.12	4.81	9.43		23.24	--	0	0	0	77	1			2,500	100	5.75		Jan-17
8.55	-7.78	-4.95	9.70		6.13	4.6			23.21	--	0	0	0	77	1			2,500			1.00	Jul-17
8.41	-7.78	-7.43			0	3.74			23.23	--	0	0	0	77	1			2,500				Nov-17
8.61	-7.54					3.87			23.3	--	0	0	0	77	1			2,500	100			Jul-19
8.74	-7.31	-4.39			6.09	3.6			23.35	--	0	0	0	77	1			25,000	10,000	3.00		Dec-18
8.81	-7.53	-4.59	10.12		6.11	3.61			23.3	--	0	0	0	77	1			1,000,000				Jul-17
2.02	1.38	2.29	6.43	9.55	1.19	1.06	2.67		10.91	79.3	1	0	99	0	0	24	4.40	0				Apr-00
2.09	1.60	2.64	7.35	10.93	1.45	0.81	2.63		10.88	79.3	1	0	99	0	0	24	4.40	0				Jan-00
4.33	3.20	4.52	8.84	11.84	1.95	1.12	2.61		10.77	131.2	12	0	16	70	0	21	3.47	0				Apr-00
4.39	3.32	4.88	9.65	13.30	2.21	0.87	2.55		10.76	131.2	12	0	16	70	0	21	3.47	0				Jan-00
14.57	-5.75	-3.80	3.29	14.92	6.62	1.15	11.71		22.21	3,247	5	18	0	71	1	180	6.11	0				Jul-09
0.18	3.70	4.52	6.87	7.26	0.91	1.35	1.69		10.93	41.6	0	82	2	0	0	60	2.53	0				Apr-00

	MARKET			FUND TYPE, CATEGORY & OBJECTIVE	RATINGS				NEW INVESTORS	
Fund Name	Ticker Symbol	Traded On	Fund Type	Category and (Prospectus Objective)	Overall Rating	Reward Rating	Risk Rating	Recent Up/ Downgrade	Open to New Investors	Telephone
City Natl Rochdale Govt Bond Fund Class Servicing	CNBIX	NAS CM	Open End	US Fixed Inc (Govt Bond - General)	C+	C	B		Y	
City Natl Rochdale Govt Money Mkt Fund Class N	CNGXX	NAS CM	Money Mkt	US Money Mkt (Money Mkt - Govt)	C	C-	C+		Y	
City Natl Rochdale Govt Money Mkt Fund Class S	CNFXX	NAS CM	Money Mkt	US Money Mkt (Money Mkt - Govt)	C	C-	C		Y	
City Natl Rochdale Govt Money Mkt Fund Class Servicing	CNIXX	NAS CM	Money Mkt	US Money Mkt (Money Mkt - Govt)	C	C-	C+		Y	
City Natl Rochdale Intermediate Fixed Income Fund Class N	RIMCX	NAS CM	Open End	US Fixed Inc (Corp Bond - General)	C+	C	B-	Up	Y	
City Natl Rochdale Intermed Fixed Income Inst Cl	CNRIX	NAS CM	Open End	US Fixed Inc (Corp Bond - General)	B-	C	B	Up	Y	
City National Rochdale Municipal High Income Fund Class N	CNRNX	NAS CM	Open End	US Muni Fixed Inc (Muni Bond - Natl)	C-	D+	C	Down	Y	
City Natl Rochdale Muni High Income Fund Class Servicing	CNRMX	NAS CM	Open End	US Muni Fixed Inc (Muni Bond - Natl)	C-	D+	C	Down	Y	
City Natl Rochdale Short Term Emerg Mkts Debt Fund Class Y	CNRGX	NAS CM	Open End	Emerg Mkts Fixed Inc (Growth & Income)	D	D	D		Y	
Cliffwater Corporate Lending Fund Class I Shares			Closed End	US Fixed Inc (Growth & Income)	D	D+	C+	Up	Y	310-448-5015
CM Advisors Fixed Income Fund	CMFIX	NAS CM	Open End	US Fixed Inc (Income)	C	C-	C+		Y	888-859-5856
CMG Tactical Bond Fund Class A	CHYAX	NAS CM	Open End	Fixed Inc Misc (Corp Bond - High Yield)	C	C-	C		Y	
CMG Tactical Bond Fund Class I	CHYOX	NAS CM	Open End	Fixed Inc Misc (Corp Bond - High Yield)	C	C-	C		Y	
Colorado Bond Shares A Tax Exempt Fund	HICOX	NAS CM	Open End	US Muni Fixed Inc (Muni Bond - Single State)	C	C-	C+		Y	800-572-0069
Columbia Bond Fund Advisor Class	CNDRX	NAS CM	Open End	US Fixed Inc (Income)	B-	C	B	Up	Y	800-345-6611
Columbia Bond Fund Class A	CNDAX	NAS CM	Open End	US Fixed Inc (Income)	B-	C	B	Up	Y	800-345-6611
Columbia Bond Fund Class C	CNDCX	NAS CM	Open End	US Fixed Inc (Income)	C+	C	B	Up	Y	800-345-6611
Columbia Bond Fund Class R	CBFRX	NAS CM	Open End	US Fixed Inc (Income)	C+	C	B	Up	Y	800-345-6611
Columbia Bond Fund Class V	CNDTX	NAS CM	Open End	US Fixed Inc (Income)	B-	C	B	Up		800-345-6611
Columbia Bond Fund Institutional 2 Class	CNFRX	NAS CM	Open End	US Fixed Inc (Income)	B-	C	B+	Up	Y	800-345-6611
Columbia Bond Fund Institutional 3 Class	CBFYX	NAS CM	Open End	US Fixed Inc (Income)	B-	C	B+	Up	Y	800-345-6611
Columbia Bond Fund Institutional Class	UMMGX	NAS CM	Open End	US Fixed Inc (Income)	B-	C	B	Up	Y	800-345-6611
Columbia California Intermediate Muni Bond Advisor Cl	CCMRX	NAS CM	Open End	US Muni Fixed Inc (Muni Bond - Single State)	C	C-	B-		Y	800-345-6611
Columbia California Intermediate Muni Bond Fund Class A	NACMX	NAS CM	Open End	US Muni Fixed Inc (Muni Bond - Single State)	C	C-	C+		Y	800-345-6611
Columbia California Intermediate Muni Bond Fund Class C	CCICX	NAS CM	Open End	US Muni Fixed Inc (Muni Bond - Single State)	C	C-	C+		Y	800-345-6611
Columbia California Intermed Muni Bond Inst 2 Cl	CNBRX	NAS CM	Open End	US Muni Fixed Inc (Muni Bond - Single State)	C	C-	B-		Y	800-345-6611
Columbia California Intermed Muni Bond Inst 3 Cl	CCBYX	NAS CM	Open End	US Muni Fixed Inc (Muni Bond - Single State)	C	C-	B-		Y	800-345-6611
Columbia California Intermed Muni Bond Inst Cl	NCMAX	NAS CM	Open End	US Muni Fixed Inc (Muni Bond - Single State)	C	C-	B-		Y	800-345-6611
Columbia Connecticut Intermediate Muni Bond Advisor Cl	CCTMX	NAS CM	Open End	US Muni Fixed Inc (Muni Bond - Single State)	C	C	B-		Y	800-345-6611
Columbia Connecticut Intermediate Muni Bond Fund Class A	LCTAX	NAS CM	Open End	US Muni Fixed Inc (Muni Bond - Single State)	C	C	B-		Y	800-345-6611
Columbia Connecticut Intermediate Muni Bond Fund Class C	LCTCX	NAS CM	Open End	US Muni Fixed Inc (Muni Bond - Single State)	C	C-	B-		Y	800-345-6611
Columbia Connecticut Intermediate Muni Bond Fund Class V	GCBAX	NAS CM	Open End	US Muni Fixed Inc (Muni Bond - Single State)	C	C	B-			800-345-6611
Columbia Connecticut Intermed Muni Bond Inst 3 Cl	CCTYX	NAS CM	Open End	US Muni Fixed Inc (Muni Bond - Single State)	C	C	B		Y	800-345-6611
Columbia Connecticut Intermed Muni Bond Inst Cl	SCTEX	NAS CM	Open End	US Muni Fixed Inc (Muni Bond - Single State)	C	C	B-		Y	800-345-6611
Columbia Corporate Income Fund Advisor Class	CIFRX	NAS CM	Open End	US Fixed Inc (Corp Bond - General)	B-	C+	B	Up	Y	800-345-6611
Columbia Corporate Income Fund Class A	LIIAX	NAS CM	Open End	US Fixed Inc (Corp Bond - General)	B-	C+	B	Up	Y	800-345-6611
Columbia Corporate Income Fund Class C	CIOCX	NAS CM	Open End	US Fixed Inc (Corp Bond - General)	B-	C+	B	Up	Y	800-345-6611
Columbia Corporate Income Fund Institutional 2 Class	CPIRX	NAS CM	Open End	US Fixed Inc (Corp Bond - General)	B-	C+	B	Up	Y	800-345-6611
Columbia Corporate Income Fund Institutional 3 Class	CRIYX	NAS CM	Open End	US Fixed Inc (Corp Bond - General)	B-	C+	B	Up	Y	800-345-6611
Columbia Corporate Income Fund Institutional Class	SRINX	NAS CM	Open End	US Fixed Inc (Corp Bond - General)	B-	C+	B	Up	Y	800-345-6611
Columbia Emerging Markets Bond Fund Advisor Class	CEBSX	NAS CM	Open End	Emerg Mkts Fixed Inc (Growth & Income)	D	D	C-	Down	Y	800-345-6611
Columbia Emerging Markets Bond Fund Class A	REBAX	NAS CM	Open End	Emerg Mkts Fixed Inc (Growth & Income)	D	D	C-	Down	Y	800-345-6611
Columbia Emerging Markets Bond Fund Class C	REBCX	NAS CM	Open End	Emerg Mkts Fixed Inc (Growth & Income)	D	D	D+	Down	Y	800-345-6611
Columbia Emerging Markets Bond Fund Class R	CMBRX	NAS CM	Open End	Emerg Mkts Fixed Inc (Growth & Income)	D	D	C-	Down	Y	800-345-6611
Columbia Emerging Markets Bond Fund Institutional 2 Class	CEBRX	NAS CM	Open End	Emerg Mkts Fixed Inc (Growth & Income)	D+	D	C-	Down	Y	800-345-6611
Columbia Emerging Markets Bond Fund Institutional 3 Class	CEBYX	NAS CM	Open End	Emerg Mkts Fixed Inc (Growth & Income)	D+	D	C-	Down	Y	800-345-6611
Columbia Emerging Markets Bond Fund Institutional Class	CMBZX	NAS CM	Open End	Emerg Mkts Fixed Inc (Growth & Income)	D	D	C-	Down	Y	800-345-6611
Columbia Floating Rate Fund Advisor Class	CFLRX	NAS CM	Open End	US Fixed Inc (Growth & Income)	D+	D	C-	Down	Y	800-345-6611
Columbia Floating Rate Fund Class A	RFRAX	NAS CM	Open End	US Fixed Inc (Growth & Income)	D	D	C-	Down	Y	800-345-6611
Columbia Floating Rate Fund Class C	RFRCX	NAS CM	Open End	US Fixed Inc (Growth & Income)	D	D	D+	Down	Y	800-345-6611
Columbia Floating Rate Fund Class R	CFRRX	NAS CM	Open End	US Fixed Inc (Growth & Income)	D	D	C-	Down	Y	800-345-6611
Columbia Floating Rate Fund Institutional 2 Class	RFRFX	NAS CM	Open End	US Fixed Inc (Growth & Income)	D+	D	C-	Down	Y	800-345-6611

★Expanded analysis of this fund is included in Section II.

TOTAL RETURNS & PERFORMANCE									ASSETS		ASSET ALLOCATION & TURNOVER							MINIMUMS		FEES		
3-Month Total Return	6-Month Total Return	1-Year Total Return	3-Year Total Return	5-Year Total Return	Dividend Yield (TTM)	Expense Ratio	3-Yr Std Deviation	Effective Duration	NAV	Total Assets (MIL)	%Cash	%Government Bonds	%Municipal Bonds	%Corporate Bonds	%Other	Turnover Ratio	Average Coupon Rate	Min Initial Investment	Min Additional Investment	Front End Fee (%)	Back End Fee (%)	Inception Date
0.24	3.83	4.78	7.67	8.64	1.15	1.11	1.68		10.91	41.6	0	82	2	0	0	60	2.53	0				Jan-00
0.00	0.15	0.76	2.70	2.76	0.9	0.76	0.18		1	4,572	81	19	0	0	0			0				Jun-99
0.00	0.13	0.66	2.40	2.45	0.79	0.91	0.16		1	4,572	81	19	0	0	0			0				Oct-99
0.00	0.22	0.98	3.71	3.77	1.14	0.46	0.18		1	4,572	81	19	0	0	0			0				Apr-00
5.23	4.87	6.53	11.38	16.44	2.04	1.14	3.32		27.46	110.9	7	1	42	44	1	35	3.45	0				Dec-99
5.36	5.14	7.08	13.07	19.44	2.55	0.64	3.3		27.46	110.9	7	1	42	44	1	35	3.45	1,000,000				Dec-13
3.83	-2.71	-0.11	8.82	17.99	3.57	1.08	6.86		10.46	1,489	7	0	92	1	0	33	5.12	0				Dec-13
3.88	-2.59	0.12	9.74	19.62	3.83	0.83	6.83		10.47	1,489	7	0	92	1	0	33	5.12	0				Dec-13
20.77	-6.87	-3.79			9.8	1			8.67	255.1	4	23	0	73	0	121	7.43	0				May-19
3.93	2.29	5.30				2.63			10.21	--	17	0	0	54	30		6.95	10,000,000	5,000			Jun-19
1.40	1.00	1.40	2.93	9.90	1.96	0.92	1.8		10.82	39.6	9	47	0	44	0	20	3.06	2,500				Mar-06
-3.31	-4.81	-3.40	1.00	4.10	2.21	2.19	2.61	0.41	9.32	38.7	78	22	0	0	0	433	2.02	5,000	1,000	5.75		May-15
-3.22	-4.64	-3.02	2.26	6.17	2.55	1.77	2.57	0.41	9.3	38.7	78	22	0	0	0	433	2.02	15,000	1,000			Oct-14
3.77	0.43	2.75	14.58	25.49	4.16	0.55	3.4		9.123	1,408	33	0	67	1	0	10	5.25	500		4.75		Jun-87
7.18	5.39	7.86	16.04	24.62	2.66	0.56	4.91	5.86	8.99	438.1	-20	21	0	12	0	236	3.44	2,000				Nov-12
7.11	5.25	7.71	15.17	23.07	2.42	0.81	4.92	5.86	9	438.1	-20	21	0	12	0	236	3.44	2,000		4.75		Mar-08
6.92	4.87	6.92	12.62	18.57	1.69	1.56	4.9	5.86	8.99	438.1	-20	21	0	12	0	236	3.44	2,000			1.00	Mar-08
7.04	5.13	7.45	14.31	21.54	2.18	1.06	4.89	5.86	9	438.1	-20	21	0	12	0	236	3.44	0				Nov-11
7.15	5.19	7.70	15.53	23.56	2.52	0.71	4.91	5.86	8.98	438.1	-20	21	0	12	0	236	3.44	2,000		4.75		Mar-11
7.22	5.44	7.96	16.40	25.14	2.75	0.46	4.93	5.86	8.97	438.1	-20	21	0	12	0	236	3.44	0				Nov-12
7.32	5.45	8.12	16.68	25.69	2.81	0.4	4.95	5.86	9.02	438.1	-20	21	0	12	0	236	3.44	1,000,000				Jul-09
7.17	5.38	7.98	16.02	24.60	2.67	0.56	4.91	5.86	9	438.1	-20	21	0	12	0	236	3.44	2,000				Jan-86
2.05	0.65	2.51	10.10	17.24	2.54	0.5	3.86	5.04	10.57	451.3	0	0	100	0	0	17	4.88	2,000				Mar-13
1.98	0.52	2.26	9.27	15.78	2.29	0.75	3.81	5.04	10.6	451.3	0	0	100	0	0	17	4.88	2,000		3.00		Sep-02
1.79	0.15	1.40	6.84	11.42	1.53	1.5	3.88	5.04	10.59	451.3	0	0	100	0	0	17	4.88	2,000			1.00	Sep-02
2.17	0.77	2.57	10.30	17.68	2.6	0.44	3.87	5.04	10.55	451.3	0	0	100	0	0	17	4.88	0				Nov-12
2.08	0.70	2.62	10.45	17.66	2.65	0.39	3.82	5.04	10.57	451.3	0	0	100	0	0	17	4.88	1,000,000				Mar-17
2.14	0.74	2.51	10.20	17.24	2.54	0.5	3.88	5.04	10.58	451.3	0	0	100	0	0	17	4.88	2,000				Aug-02
1.95	1.65	3.52	10.56	15.21	2.66	0.56	3.37	5.11	10.7	96.6	0	0	100	0	0	12	4.74	0				Mar-13
1.98	1.53	3.26	9.73	13.77	2.41	0.81	3.37	5.11	10.72	96.6	0	0	100	0	0	12	4.74	2,000		3.00		Nov-02
1.87	1.40	2.89	8.26	11.24	1.96	1.56	3.37	5.11	10.72	96.6	0	0	100	0	0	12	4.74	2,000			1.00	Nov-02
1.91	1.58	3.36	10.06	14.34	2.51	0.71	3.33	5.11	10.7	96.6	0	0	100	0	0	12	4.74	2,000		4.75		Jun-00
2.07	1.70	3.62	10.90	15.59	2.76	0.45	3.34	5.11	10.74	96.6	0	0	100	0	0	12	4.74	0				Mar-17
1.95	1.65	3.52	10.56	15.09	2.66	0.56	3.35	5.11	10.71	96.6	0	0	100	0	0	12	4.74	2,000				Aug-94
10.31	5.52	9.97	20.22	32.02	2.85	0.65	6.62	7.62	11.18	1,124	1	13	0	86	0	65	3.93	2,000				Nov-12
10.13	5.28	9.69	19.32	30.37	2.61	0.9	6.6	7.62	11.19	1,124	1	13	0	86	0	65	3.93	2,000		4.75		Jul-00
10.08	5.07	9.04	17.20	26.53	2.03	1.65	6.62	7.62	11.19	1,124	1	13	0	86	0	65	3.93	2,000			1.00	Jul-02
10.34	5.57	10.08	20.69	32.83	2.95	0.55	6.58	7.62	11.18	1,124	1	13	0	86	0	65	3.93	0				Nov-12
10.35	5.59	10.14	20.76	33.03	3	0.49	6.62	7.62	11.19	1,124	1	13	0	86	0	65	3.93	1,000,000				Nov-12
10.20	5.51	9.96	20.21	32.00	2.85	0.65	6.58	7.62	11.19	1,124	1	13	0	86	0	65	3.93	2,000				Mar-86
12.86	-2.62	-2.19	4.99	23.14	3.46	0.86	11.35	7.97	10.85	323.1	7	63	0	22	0	106	5.45	2,000				Mar-13
12.92	-2.66	-2.36	4.30	21.69	3.2	1.11	11.36	7.97	10.84	323.1	7	63	0	22	0	106	5.45	2,000		4.75		Feb-06
12.58	-3.05	-3.11	1.90	17.15	2.43	1.86	11.31	7.97	10.76	323.1	7	63	0	22	0	106	5.45	2,000			1.00	Feb-06
12.74	-2.78	-2.61	3.52	20.13	2.94	1.36	11.32	7.97	10.83	323.1	7	63	0	22	0	106	5.45	0				Nov-11
12.90	-2.48	-2.00	5.40	24.11	3.58	0.74	11.31	7.97	10.84	323.1	7	63	0	22	0	106	5.45	0				Nov-12
13.02	-2.45	-1.94	5.66	24.53	3.63	0.69	11.35	7.97	10.85	323.1	7	63	0	22	0	106	5.45	1,000,000				Nov-12
12.87	-2.62	-2.20	4.99	23.16	3.46	0.86	11.35	7.97	10.84	323.1	7	63	0	22	0	106	5.45	2,000				Sep-10
9.34	-6.24	-3.91	4.09	12.47	5.43	0.77	8.94	0.23	8.17	654.2	4	0	0	96	0	32	5.12	2,000				Feb-13
9.26	-6.34	-4.13	3.22	10.96	5.16	1.02	8.93	0.23	8.18	654.2	4	0	0	96	0	32	5.12	2,000		3.00		Feb-06
8.92	-6.69	-4.96	0.92	6.89	4.36	1.77	8.85	0.23	8.18	654.2	4	0	0	96	0	32	5.12	2,000			1.00	Feb-06
9.18	-6.45	-4.36	2.45	9.60	4.89	1.27	8.92	0.23	8.19	654.2	4	0	0	96	0	32	5.12	0				Sep-10
9.31	-6.28	-3.94	4.14	12.61	5.47	0.73	8.92	0.23	8.21	654.2	4	0	0	96	0	32	5.12	0				Aug-08

Fund Name	MARKET Ticker Symbol	MARKET Traded On	FUND TYPE, CATEGORY & OBJECTIVE Fund Type	Category and (Prospectus Objective)	RATINGS Overall Rating	Reward Rating	Risk Rating	Recent Up/ Downgrade	NEW INVESTORS Open to New Investors	Telephone
Columbia Floating Rate Fund Institutional 3 Class	CFRYX	NAS CM	Open End	US Fixed Inc (Growth & Income)	D+	D	C-	Down	Y	800-345-6611
Columbia Floating Rate Fund Institutional Class	CFRZX	NAS CM	Open End	US Fixed Inc (Growth & Income)	D+	D	C-	Down	Y	800-345-6611
Columbia Georgia Intermediate Muni Bond Fund Advisor Class	CGIMX	NAS CM	Open End	US Muni Fixed Inc (Muni Bond - Single State)	C+	C	B	Up	Y	800-345-6611
Columbia Georgia Intermediate Municipal Bond Fund Class A	NGIMX	NAS CM	Open End	US Muni Fixed Inc (Muni Bond - Single State)	C	C	B-		Y	800-345-6611
Columbia Georgia Intermediate Municipal Bond Fund Class C	NGINX	NAS CM	Open End	US Muni Fixed Inc (Muni Bond - Single State)	C	C	C+		Y	800-345-6611
Columbia Georgia Intermediate Muni Bond Institutional 3 Cl	CGIYX	NAS CM	Open End	US Muni Fixed Inc (Muni Bond - Single State)	C+	C	B	Up	Y	800-345-6611
Columbia Georgia Intermediate Muni Bond Institutional Cl	NGAMX	NAS CM	Open End	US Muni Fixed Inc (Muni Bond - Single State)	C+	C	B	Up	Y	800-345-6611
Columbia Government Money Market Fund Class A	IDSXX	NAS CM	Money Mkt	US Money Mkt (Money Mkt - Govt)	C	C-	C+		Y	800-345-6611
Columbia Government Money Market Fund Class C	RCCXX	NAS CM	Money Mkt	US Money Mkt (Money Mkt - Govt)	C	C-	C+		Y	800-345-6611
Columbia Government Money Market Fund Class R	RVRXX	NAS CM	Money Mkt	US Money Mkt (Money Mkt - Govt)	C	C-	C+		Y	800-345-6611
Columbia Govt Money Mkt Fund Institutional 2 Class	CMRXX	NAS CM	Money Mkt	US Money Mkt (Money Mkt - Govt)	C	C-	C+		Y	800-345-6611
Columbia Govt Money Mkt Fund Institutional 3 Class	CGMXX	NAS CM	Money Mkt	US Money Mkt (Money Mkt - Govt)	C	C-	C+		Y	800-345-6611
Columbia Government Money Market Fund Institutional Class	IDYXX	NAS CM	Money Mkt	US Money Mkt (Money Mkt - Govt)	C	C-	C+		Y	800-345-6611
Columbia High Yield Bond Fund Advisor Class	CYLRX	NAS CM	Open End	US Fixed Inc (Corp Bond - High Yield)	C-	D+	C		Y	800-345-6611
Columbia High Yield Bond Fund Class A	INEAX	NAS CM	Open End	US Fixed Inc (Corp Bond - High Yield)	C-	D+	C		Y	800-345-6611
Columbia High Yield Bond Fund Class C	APECX	NAS CM	Open End	US Fixed Inc (Corp Bond - High Yield)	C-	D+	C		Y	800-345-6611
Columbia High Yield Bond Fund Class R	CHBRX	NAS CM	Open End	US Fixed Inc (Corp Bond - High Yield)	C-	D+	C		Y	800-345-6611
Columbia High Yield Bond Fund Institutional 2 Class	RSHRX	NAS CM	Open End	US Fixed Inc (Corp Bond - High Yield)	C-	D+	C	Down	Y	800-345-6611
Columbia High Yield Bond Fund Institutional 3 Class	CHYYX	NAS CM	Open End	US Fixed Inc (Corp Bond - High Yield)	C-	D+	C	Down	Y	800-345-6611
Columbia High Yield Bond Fund Institutional Class	CHYZX	NAS CM	Open End	US Fixed Inc (Corp Bond - High Yield)	C-	D+	C		Y	800-345-6611
Columbia High Yield Municipal Fund Advisor Class	CHIYX	NAS CM	Open End	US Muni Fixed Inc (Muni Bond - Natl)	C-	D+	C	Down	Y	800-345-6611
Columbia High Yield Municipal Fund Class A	LHIAX	NAS CM	Open End	US Muni Fixed Inc (Muni Bond - Natl)	C-	D+	C	Down	Y	800-345-6611
Columbia High Yield Municipal Fund Class C	CHMCX	NAS CM	Open End	US Muni Fixed Inc (Muni Bond - Natl)	C-	D+	C	Down	Y	800-345-6611
Columbia High Yield Municipal Fund Institutional 2 Class	CHMYX	NAS CM	Open End	US Muni Fixed Inc (Muni Bond - Natl)	C-	D+	C	Down	Y	800-345-6611
Columbia High Yield Municipal Fund Institutional 3 Class	CHHYX	NAS CM	Open End	US Muni Fixed Inc (Muni Bond - Natl)	C-	D+	C	Down	Y	800-345-6611
Columbia High Yield Municipal Fund Institutional Class	SRHMX	NAS CM	Open End	US Muni Fixed Inc (Muni Bond - Natl)	C-	D+	C	Down	Y	800-345-6611
Columbia Income Opportunities Fund Advisor Class	CPPRX	NAS CM	Open End	US Fixed Inc (Growth & Income)	C-	D+	C		Y	800-345-6611
Columbia Income Opportunities Fund Class A	AIOAX	NAS CM	Open End	US Fixed Inc (Growth & Income)	C-	D+	C		Y	800-345-6611
Columbia Income Opportunities Fund Class C	RIOCX	NAS CM	Open End	US Fixed Inc (Growth & Income)	D+	D+	C-	Down	Y	800-345-6611
Columbia Income Opportunities Fund Class R	CIORX	NAS CM	Open End	US Fixed Inc (Growth & Income)	D+	D+	C-	Down	Y	800-345-6611
Columbia Income Opportunities Fund Institutional 2 Class	CEPRX	NAS CM	Open End	US Fixed Inc (Growth & Income)	C-	D+	C		Y	800-345-6611
Columbia Income Opportunities Fund Institutional 3 Class	CIOYX	NAS CM	Open End	US Fixed Inc (Growth & Income)	C-	D+	C		Y	800-345-6611
Columbia Income Opportunities Fund Institutional Class	CIOZX	NAS CM	Open End	US Fixed Inc (Growth & Income)	C-	D+	C		Y	800-345-6611
Columbia Intermediate Municipal Bond Fund Advisor Class	CIMRX	NAS CM	Open End	US Muni Fixed Inc (Muni Bond - Natl)	C	C-	C+		Y	800-345-6611
Columbia Intermediate Municipal Bond Fund Class A	LITAX	NAS CM	Open End	US Muni Fixed Inc (Muni Bond - Natl)	C	C-	C+		Y	800-345-6611
Columbia Intermediate Municipal Bond Fund Class C	LITCX	NAS CM	Open End	US Muni Fixed Inc (Muni Bond - Natl)	C	C-	C		Y	800-345-6611
Columbia Intermediate Municipal Bond Fund Class V	GIMAX	NAS CM	Open End	US Muni Fixed Inc (Muni Bond - Natl)	C	C-	C+			800-345-6611
Columbia Intermediate Muni Bond Fund Institutional 2 Class	CTMRX	NAS CM	Open End	US Muni Fixed Inc (Muni Bond - Natl)	C	C-	C+		Y	800-345-6611
Columbia Intermediate Muni Bond Fund Institutional 3 Class	CIMYX	NAS CM	Open End	US Muni Fixed Inc (Muni Bond - Natl)	C	C-	C+		Y	800-345-6611
Columbia Intermediate Muni Bond Fund Institutional Class	SETMX	NAS CM	Open End	US Muni Fixed Inc (Muni Bond - Natl)	C	C-	C+		Y	800-345-6611
Columbia Limited Duration Credit Fund Advisor Class	CDLRX	NAS CM	Open End	US Fixed Inc (Corp Bond - General)	C+	C	B	Up	Y	800-345-6611
Columbia Limited Duration Credit Fund Class A	ALDAX	NAS CM	Open End	US Fixed Inc (Corp Bond - General)	C+	C	B	Up	Y	800-345-6611
Columbia Limited Duration Credit Fund Class C	RDCLX	NAS CM	Open End	US Fixed Inc (Corp Bond - General)	C	C	B-		Y	800-345-6611
Columbia Limited Duration Credit Institutional 2 Cl	CTLRX	NAS CM	Open End	US Fixed Inc (Corp Bond - General)	C+	C	B	Up	Y	800-345-6611
Columbia Limited Duration Credit Institutional 3 Cl	CLDYX	NAS CM	Open End	US Fixed Inc (Corp Bond - General)	C+	C	B	Up	Y	800-345-6611
Columbia Limited Duration Credit Fund Institutional Class	CLDZX	NAS CM	Open End	US Fixed Inc (Corp Bond - General)	C+	C	B	Up	Y	800-345-6611
Columbia Maryland Intermediate Muni Bond Advisor Cl	CMDMX	NAS CM	Open End	US Muni Fixed Inc (Muni Bond - Single State)	C	C	B-		Y	800-345-6611
Columbia Maryland Intermediate Municipal Bond Fund Class A	NMDMX	NAS CM	Open End	US Muni Fixed Inc (Muni Bond - Single State)	C	C-	B-		Y	800-345-6611
Columbia Maryland Intermediate Municipal Bond Fund Class C	NMINX	NAS CM	Open End	US Muni Fixed Inc (Muni Bond - Single State)	C	C-	C+		Y	800-345-6611
Columbia Maryland Intermed Muni Bond Inst 3 Cl	CMYYX	NAS CM	Open End	US Muni Fixed Inc (Muni Bond - Single State)	C	C	B-		Y	800-345-6611
Columbia Maryland Intermediate Muni Bond Institutional Cl	NMDBX	NAS CM	Open End	US Muni Fixed Inc (Muni Bond - Single State)	C	C	B-		Y	800-345-6611
Columbia Massachusetts Intermediate Muni Bond Advisor Cl	CMANX	NAS CM	Open End	US Muni Fixed Inc (Muni Bond - Single State)	C	C-	B-		Y	800-345-6611

★ Expanded analysis of this fund is included in Section II.

TOTAL RETURNS & PERFORMANCE									ASSETS		ASSET ALLOCATION & TURNOVER							MINIMUMS		FEES		
3-Month Total Return	6-Month Total Return	1-Year Total Return	3-Year Total Return	5-Year Total Return	Dividend Yield (TTM)	Expense Ratio	3-Yr Std Deviation	Effective Duration	NAV	Total Assets (MIL)	%Cash	%Government Bonds	%Municipal Bonds	%Corporate Bonds	%Other	Turnover Ratio	Average Coupon Rate	Min Initial Investment	Min Additional Investment	Front End Fee (%)	Back End Fee (%)	Inception Date
9.36	-6.18	-3.81	4.26	12.87	5.52	0.68	8.94	0.23	8.18	654.2	4	0	0	96	0	32	5.12	1,000,000				Jun-15
9.34	-6.24	-3.91	3.98	12.34	5.43	0.77	8.94	0.23	8.17	654.2	4	0	0	96	0	32	5.12	2,000				Sep-10
2.32	2.15	4.14	10.31	15.64	2.49	0.56	3.18	4.89	10.62	40.7	1	0	99	1	0	3	4.61	2,000				Mar-13
2.26	2.03	3.88	9.38	14.20	2.24	0.81	3.16	4.89	10.63	40.7	1	0	99	1	0	3	4.61	2,000		3.00		May-92
2.07	1.74	3.10	7.05	10.00	1.49	1.56	3.12	4.89	10.64	40.7	1	0	99	1	0	3	4.61	2,000			1.00	Jun-92
2.35	2.30	4.24	10.65	16.02	2.59	0.46	3.12	4.89	10.66	40.7	1	0	99	1	0	3	4.61	1,000,000				Mar-17
2.32	2.15	4.14	10.31	15.63	2.49	0.56	3.18	4.89	10.63	40.7	1	0	99	1	0	3	4.61	2,000				Feb-92
0.00	0.24	1.05	3.70	3.75	1.17	0.48	0.18		1	603.1	83	17	0	0	0			2,000				Oct-75
0.00	0.25	1.05	3.72	3.78	1.17	0.48	0.17		1	603.1	83	17	0	0	0			2,000			1.00	Jun-00
0.00	0.24	1.04	3.70	3.78	1.17	0.48	0.17		1	603.1	83	17	0	0	0			0				Aug-09
0.01	0.29	1.13	4.15	4.39	1.26	0.34	0.17		1	603.1	83	17	0	0	0			0				Dec-06
0.00	0.29	1.19	4.25	4.43	1.33	0.29	0.18		1	603.1	83	17	0	0	0			1,000,000				Mar-17
0.00	0.24	1.05	3.71	3.78	1.17	0.48	0.17		1	603.1	83	17	0	0	0			2,000				Apr-10
9.06	-4.50	0.29	9.04	22.39	5.33	0.78	8.6	4.45	2.81	1,332	4	0	0	96	0	41	6.09	2,000				Dec-06
9.44	-4.32	0.37	8.57	20.86	5.06	1.03	8.72	4.45	2.8	1,332	4	0	0	96	0	41	6.09	2,000		4.75		Dec-83
8.88	-4.73	-0.40	6.10	16.37	4.29	1.78	8.77	4.45	2.78	1,332	4	0	0	96	0	41	6.09	2,000			1.00	Jun-00
8.95	-4.76	-0.21	7.40	18.96	4.79	1.28	8.64	4.45	2.8	1,332	4	0	0	96	0	41	6.09	0				Dec-06
9.14	-4.19	0.67	9.59	22.84	5.39	0.71	8.48	4.45	2.79	1,332	4	0	0	96	0	41	6.09	0				Dec-06
9.15	-4.17	0.38	9.76	23.14	5.45	0.66	8.8	4.45	2.79	1,332	4	0	0	96	0	41	6.09	1,000,000				Nov-12
9.12	-4.54	0.26	9.35	22.34	5.31	0.78	8.7	4.45	2.79	1,332	4	0	0	96	0	41	6.09	2,000				Sep-10
3.07	-2.76	-0.15	11.36	21.45	4.55	0.66	7.11	9.64	10.29	711.4	0	0	100	0	0	35	5.11	0				Mar-13
3.02	-2.86	-0.26	10.69	20.24	4.34	0.86	7.1	9.64	10.28	711.4	0	0	100	0	0	35	5.11	2,000		3.00		Jul-00
2.85	-3.18	-0.90	8.56	16.41	3.64	1.61	7.1	9.64	10.28	711.4	0	0	100	0	0	35	5.11	2,000			1.00	Jul-02
3.08	-2.84	-0.12	11.49	21.80	4.6	0.62	7.07	9.64	10.27	711.4	0	0	100	0	0	35	5.11	100,000				Nov-12
3.09	-2.80	-0.05	11.57	21.83	4.65	0.57	7.08	9.64	10.3	711.4	0	0	100	0	0	35	5.11	0				Mar-17
3.07	-2.77	-0.15	11.36	21.45	4.55	0.66	7.12	9.64	10.28	711.4	0	0	100	0	0	35	5.11	2,000				Mar-84
8.42	-6.23	-1.90	6.92	18.94	4.97	0.78	9.12	4.04	9.28	1,502	7	0	0	78	0	43	5.74	2,000				Nov-12
8.38	-6.37	-2.16	6.10	17.44	4.7	1.03	9.13	4.04	9.25	1,502	7	0	0	78	0	43	5.74	2,000		4.75		Jun-03
8.19	-6.73	-2.90	3.73	13.12	3.92	1.78	9.11	4.04	9.24	1,502	7	0	0	78	0	43	5.74	2,000			1.00	Jun-03
8.31	-6.49	-2.41	5.30	15.98	4.44	1.28	9.11	4.04	9.25	1,502	7	0	0	78	0	43	5.74	0				Sep-10
8.57	-6.10	-1.83	7.16	19.49	5.04	0.71	9.16	4.04	9.28	1,502	7	0	0	78	0	43	5.74	0				Nov-12
8.48	-6.19	-1.79	7.20	19.65	5.1	0.66	9.14	4.04	9.26	1,502	7	0	0	78	0	43	5.74	1,000,000				Mar-11
8.43	-6.24	-1.90	6.92	18.94	4.97	0.78	9.12	4.04	9.27	1,502	7	0	0	78	0	43	5.74	2,000				Sep-10
2.00	0.50	2.42	9.41	16.10	3.02	0.53	3.82	4.84	10.44	1,138	0	0	100	0	0	14	4.98	0				Mar-13
2.05	0.40	2.22	8.87	15.07	2.82	0.73	3.88	4.84	10.45	1,138	0	0	100	0	0	14	4.98	2,000		3.00		Nov-02
1.78	0.07	1.56	6.76	11.39	2.16	1.38	3.81	4.84	10.45	1,138	0	0	100	0	0	14	4.98	2,000			1.00	Nov-02
2.06	0.42	2.36	9.03	15.35	2.87	0.68	3.88	4.84	10.45	1,138	0	0	100	0	0	14	4.98	2,000		4.75		Jun-00
2.02	0.53	2.49	9.64	16.56	3.09	0.46	3.82	4.84	10.43	1,138	0	0	100	0	0	14	4.98	100,000				Nov-12
2.03	0.56	2.54	9.79	16.54	3.13	0.41	3.8	4.84	10.46	1,138	0	0	100	0	0	14	4.98	0				Mar-17
2.00	0.50	2.42	9.41	16.11	3.02	0.53	3.79	4.84	10.45	1,138	0	0	100	0	0	14	4.98	2,000				Jun-93
7.17	3.15	5.41	11.70	17.85	2.24	0.54	4.36	2.74	10.28	772.4	8	17	0	76	0	99	3.03	2,000				Feb-13
7.11	3.02	5.15	10.98	16.38	2	0.79	4.33	2.74	10.28	772.4	8	17	0	76	0	99	3.03	2,000		3.00		Jun-03
7.02	2.64	4.37	8.51	12.11	1.26	1.54	4.35	2.74	10.28	772.4	8	17	0	76	0	99	3.03	2,000			1.00	Jun-03
7.29	3.18	5.47	11.99	18.17	2.3	0.48	4.35	2.74	10.29	772.4	8	17	0	76	0	99	3.03	0				Nov-12
7.30	3.20	5.52	12.16	18.46	2.35	0.43	4.35	2.74	10.29	772.4	8	17	0	76	0	99	3.03	1,000,000				Mar-13
7.28	3.15	5.41	11.81	17.84	2.24	0.54	4.35	2.74	10.29	772.4	8	17	0	76	0	99	3.03	2,000				Sep-10
1.28	1.05	2.76	9.06	15.33	2.59	0.56	3.01	4.37	10.6	49.7	0	0	100	0	0	4	4.83	2,000				Mar-13
1.31	0.92	2.60	8.25	13.89	2.34	0.81	3.06	4.37	10.6	49.7	0	0	100	0	0	4	4.83	2,000		3.00		Aug-90
1.03	0.55	1.74	5.84	9.60	1.58	1.56	3.01	4.37	10.6	49.7	0	0	100	0	0	4	4.83	2,000			1.00	Jun-92
1.30	1.10	2.86	9.39	15.60	2.68	0.47	3	4.37	10.63	49.7	0	0	100	0	0	4	4.83	1,000,000				Mar-17
1.38	1.14	2.86	9.05	15.21	2.59	0.56	3.02	4.37	10.6	49.7	0	0	100	0	0	4	4.83	2,000				Aug-90
1.66	0.87	2.76	9.23	14.56	2.75	0.56	3.51	5.10	10.58	228.6	0	0	100	0	0	15	5.00	0				Mar-13

	MARKET			FUND TYPE, CATEGORY & OBJECTIVE	RATINGS				NEW INVESTORS	
Fund Name	Ticker Symbol	Traded On	Fund Type	Category and (Prospectus Objective)	Overall Rating	Reward Rating	Risk Rating	Recent Up/ Downgrade	Open to New Investors	Telephone
Columbia Massachusetts Intermediate Muni Bond Fund Class A	LMIAX	NAS CM	Open End	US Muni Fixed Inc (Muni Bond - Single State)	C	C-	C+		Y	800-345-6611
Columbia Massachusetts Intermediate Muni Bond Fund Class C	LMICX	NAS CM	Open End	US Muni Fixed Inc (Muni Bond - Single State)	C	C-	C+		Y	800-345-6611
Columbia Massachusetts Intermediate Muni Bond Fund Class V	GMBAX	NAS CM	Open End	US Muni Fixed Inc (Muni Bond - Single State)	C	C-	B-			800-345-6611
Columbia Massachusetts Intermed Muni Bond Inst 2 Cl	CMAUX	NAS CM	Open End	US Muni Fixed Inc (Muni Bond - Single State)	C	C-	B-		Y	800-345-6611
Columbia Massachusetts Intermed Muni Bond Inst 3 Cl	CMMYX	NAS CM	Open End	US Muni Fixed Inc (Muni Bond - Single State)	C	C-	B-		Y	800-345-6611
Columbia Massachusetts Intermed Muni Bond Inst Cl	SEMAX	NAS CM	Open End	US Muni Fixed Inc (Muni Bond - Single State)	C	C-	B-		Y	800-345-6611
Columbia Minnesota Tax-Exempt Fund Advisor Class	CLONX	NAS CM	Open End	US Muni Fixed Inc (Muni Bond - Single State)	C	C-	B-		Y	800-345-6611
Columbia Minnesota Tax-Exempt Fund Class A	IMNTX	NAS CM	Open End	US Muni Fixed Inc (Muni Bond - Single State)	C	C-	B-		Y	800-345-6611
Columbia Minnesota Tax-Exempt Fund Class C	RMTCX	NAS CM	Open End	US Muni Fixed Inc (Muni Bond - Single State)	C	C-	C+		Y	800-345-6611
Columbia Minnesota Tax-Exempt Fund Institutional 2 Class	CADOX	NAS CM	Open End	US Muni Fixed Inc (Muni Bond - Single State)	C	C-	B-		Y	800-345-6611
Columbia Minnesota Tax-Exempt Fund Institutional 3 Class	CMNYX	NAS CM	Open End	US Muni Fixed Inc (Muni Bond - Single State)	C	C-	B-		Y	800-345-6611
Columbia Minnesota Tax-Exempt Fund Institutional Class	CMNZX	NAS CM	Open End	US Muni Fixed Inc (Muni Bond - Single State)	C	C-	B-		Y	800-345-6611
Columbia Mortgage Opportunities Fund Advisor Class	CLMFX	NAS CM	Open End	Fixed Inc Misc (Govt Bond - Mortgage)	C-	D+	C	Down	Y	800-345-6611
Columbia Mortgage Opportunities Fund Class A	CLMAX	NAS CM	Open End	Fixed Inc Misc (Govt Bond - Mortgage)	C-	D+	C	Down	Y	800-345-6611
Columbia Mortgage Opportunities Fund Class C	CLMCX	NAS CM	Open End	Fixed Inc Misc (Govt Bond - Mortgage)	C-	D+	C	Down	Y	800-345-6611
Columbia Mortgage Opportunities Fund Institutional 2 Class	CLMVX	NAS CM	Open End	Fixed Inc Misc (Govt Bond - Mortgage)	C-	D+	C	Down	Y	800-345-6611
Columbia Mortgage Opportunities Fund Institutional 3 Class	CMOYX	NAS CM	Open End	Fixed Inc Misc (Govt Bond - Mortgage)	C-	D+	C	Down	Y	800-345-6611
Columbia Mortgage Opportunities Fund Institutional Class	CLMZX	NAS CM	Open End	Fixed Inc Misc (Govt Bond - Mortgage)	C-	D+	C	Down	Y	800-345-6611
Columbia New York Intermediate Muni Bond Advisor Cl	CNYIX	NAS CM	Open End	US Muni Fixed Inc (Muni Bond - Single State)	C	C-	B-		Y	800-345-6611
Columbia New York Intermediate Municipal Bond Fund Class A	LNYAX	NAS CM	Open End	US Muni Fixed Inc (Muni Bond - Single State)	C	C-	C+		Y	800-345-6611
Columbia New York Intermediate Municipal Bond Fund Class C	LNYCX	NAS CM	Open End	US Muni Fixed Inc (Muni Bond - Single State)	C	C-	C+		Y	800-345-6611
Columbia New York Intermediate Municipal Bond Fund Class V	GANYX	NAS CM	Open End	US Muni Fixed Inc (Muni Bond - Single State)	C	C-	C+			800-345-6611
Columbia New York Intermed Muni Bond Inst 2 Cl	CNYUX	NAS CM	Open End	US Muni Fixed Inc (Muni Bond - Single State)	C	C-	B-		Y	800-345-6611
Columbia New York Intermed Muni Bond Inst 3 Cl	CNYYX	NAS CM	Open End	US Muni Fixed Inc (Muni Bond - Single State)	C	C-	B-		Y	800-345-6611
Columbia New York Intermediate Muni Bond Institutional Cl	GNYTX	NAS CM	Open End	US Muni Fixed Inc (Muni Bond - Single State)	C	C-	B-		Y	800-345-6611
Columbia North Carolina Intermediate Muni Bond Advisor Cl	CNCEX	NAS CM	Open End	US Muni Fixed Inc (Muni Bond - Single State)	C	C	B-		Y	800-345-6611
Columbia North Carolina Intermediate Muni Bond Cl A	NNCIX	NAS CM	Open End	US Muni Fixed Inc (Muni Bond - Single State)	C	C	B-		Y	800-345-6611
Columbia North Carolina Intermediate Muni Bond Cl C	NNINX	NAS CM	Open End	US Muni Fixed Inc (Muni Bond - Single State)	C	C-	C+		Y	800-345-6611
Columbia North Carolina Intermed Muni Bond Inst 3 Cl	CNCYX	NAS CM	Open End	US Muni Fixed Inc (Muni Bond - Single State)	C	C	B-		Y	800-345-6611
Columbia North Carolina Intermed Muni Bond Inst Cl	NNIBX	NAS CM	Open End	US Muni Fixed Inc (Muni Bond - Single State)	C	C	B-		Y	800-345-6611
Columbia Oregon Intermediate Muni Bond Fund Advisor Class	CORMX	NAS CM	Open End	US Muni Fixed Inc (Muni Bond - Single State)	C+	C	B	Up	Y	800-345-6611
Columbia Oregon Intermediate Municipal Bond Fund Class A	COEAX	NAS CM	Open End	US Muni Fixed Inc (Muni Bond - Single State)	C+	C	B	Up	Y	800-345-6611
Columbia Oregon Intermediate Municipal Bond Fund Class C	CORCX	NAS CM	Open End	US Muni Fixed Inc (Muni Bond - Single State)	C	C	B-		Y	800-345-6611
Columbia Oregon Intermediate Muni Bond Institutional 2 Cl	CODRX	NAS CM	Open End	US Muni Fixed Inc (Muni Bond - Single State)	C+	C	B	Up	Y	800-345-6611
Columbia Oregon Intermediate Muni Bond Institutional 3 Cl	CORYX	NAS CM	Open End	US Muni Fixed Inc (Muni Bond - Single State)	C+	C	B	Up	Y	800-345-6611
Columbia Oregon Intermediate Muni Bond Institutional Cl	CMBFX	NAS CM	Open End	US Muni Fixed Inc (Muni Bond - Single State)	C+	C	B	Up	Y	800-345-6611
Columbia Quality Income Fund Advisor Class	CUVRX	NAS CM	Open End	US Fixed Inc (Govt Bond - Mortgage)	C	C	B		Y	800-345-6611
Columbia Quality Income Fund Class A	AUGAX	NAS CM	Open End	US Fixed Inc (Govt Bond - Mortgage)	C	C	B		Y	800-345-6611
Columbia Quality Income Fund Class C	AUGCX	NAS CM	Open End	US Fixed Inc (Govt Bond - Mortgage)	C	C-	C+		Y	800-345-6611
Columbia Quality Income Fund Class R	CUGUX	NAS CM	Open End	US Fixed Inc (Govt Bond - Mortgage)	C	C-	B-		Y	800-345-6611
Columbia Quality Income Fund Institutional 2 Class	CGVRX	NAS CM	Open End	US Fixed Inc (Govt Bond - Mortgage)	C	C	B		Y	800-345-6611
Columbia Quality Income Fund Institutional 3 Class	CUGYX	NAS CM	Open End	US Fixed Inc (Govt Bond - Mortgage)	C	C	B		Y	800-345-6611
Columbia Quality Income Fund Institutional Class	CUGZX	NAS CM	Open End	US Fixed Inc (Govt Bond - Mortgage)	C	C	B		Y	800-345-6611
Columbia Short Term Bond Fund Advisor Class	CMDRX	NAS CM	Open End	US Fixed Inc (Income)	C	C-	C		Y	800-345-6611
Columbia Short Term Bond Fund Class A	NSTRX	NAS CM	Open End	US Fixed Inc (Income)	C-	D+	C		Y	800-345-6611
Columbia Short Term Bond Fund Class C	NSTIX	NAS CM	Open End	US Fixed Inc (Income)	C-	D+	C		Y	800-345-6611
Columbia Short Term Bond Fund Class R	CSBRX	NAS CM	Open End	US Fixed Inc (Income)	C-	D+	C		Y	800-345-6611
Columbia Short Term Bond Fund Institutional 2 Class	CCBRX	NAS CM	Open End	US Fixed Inc (Income)	C	C-	C		Y	800-345-6611
Columbia Short Term Bond Fund Institutional 3 Class	CSBYX	NAS CM	Open End	US Fixed Inc (Income)	C	C-	C		Y	800-345-6611
Columbia Short Term Bond Fund Institutional Class	NSTMX	NAS CM	Open End	US Fixed Inc (Income)	C-	D+	C	Down	Y	800-345-6611
Columbia Short Term Municipal Bond Fund Advisor Class	CSMTX	NAS CM	Open End	US Muni Fixed Inc (Muni Bond - Natl)	C	C-	C+		Y	800-345-6611
Columbia Short Term Municipal Bond Fund Class A	NSMMX	NAS CM	Open End	US Muni Fixed Inc (Muni Bond - Natl)	C	C-	C+		Y	800-345-6611

★ Expanded analysis of this fund is included in Section II.

TOTAL RETURNS & PERFORMANCE									ASSETS		ASSET ALLOCATION & TURNOVER							MINIMUMS		FEES		
3-Month Total Return	6-Month Total Return	1-Year Total Return	3-Year Total Return	5-Year Total Return	Dividend Yield (TTM)	Expense Ratio	3-Yr Std Deviation	Effective Duration	NAV	Total Assets (MIL)	%Cash	%Government Bonds	%Municipal Bonds	%Corporate Bonds	%Other	Turnover Ratio	Average Coupon Rate	Min Initial Investment	Min Additional Investment	Front End Fee (%)	Back End Fee (%)	Inception Date
1.60	0.74	2.51	8.42	13.14	2.5	0.81	3.48	5.10	10.59	228.6	0	0	100	0	0	15	5.00	2,000		3.00		Dec-02
1.49	0.43	1.95	6.86	10.52	2.04	1.56	3.53	5.10	10.58	228.6	0	0	100	0	0	15	5.00	2,000			1.00	Dec-02
1.63	0.79	2.61	8.74	13.70	2.6	0.71	3.48	5.10	10.59	228.6	0	0	100	0	0	15	5.00	2,000		4.75		Jun-00
1.77	0.90	2.82	9.42	14.88	2.8	0.5	3.55	5.10	10.61	228.6	0	0	100	0	0	15	5.00	100,000				Mar-16
1.69	0.93	2.87	9.59	14.96	2.86	0.45	3.49	5.10	10.64	228.6	0	0	100	0	0	15	5.00	0				Mar-17
1.66	0.87	2.76	9.23	14.56	2.75	0.56	3.48	5.10	10.59	228.6	0	0	100	0	0	15	5.00	2,000				Jun-93
2.33	0.96	3.16	11.50	19.27	2.83	0.53	4.66	8.29	5.55	695.7	0	0	100	0	0	18	4.36	2,000				Mar-13
2.27	0.83	2.90	10.67	17.79	2.58	0.78	4.79	8.29	5.55	695.7	0	0	100	0	0	18	4.36	2,000		3.00		Aug-86
2.08	0.46	2.14	8.21	13.46	1.82	1.53	4.78	8.29	5.55	695.7	0	0	100	0	0	18	4.36	2,000			1.00	Jun-00
2.33	0.77	3.15	11.26	19.02	2.82	0.54	4.65	8.29	5.54	695.7	0	0	100	0	0	18	4.36	0				Dec-13
2.34	0.80	3.20	11.43	18.90	2.87	0.49	4.7	8.29	5.55	695.7	0	0	100	0	0	18	4.36	1,000,000				Mar-17
2.15	0.78	3.16	11.30	19.05	2.83	0.53	4.64	8.29	5.54	695.7	0	0	100	0	0	18	4.36	2,000				Sep-10
8.72	-1.21	0.65	15.25	26.60	3.56	0.75	7.1	-1.39	9.8	1,452	23	43	0	1	0	528	3.29	2,000				Apr-14
8.76	-1.24	0.40	14.49	25.13	3.29	1	7.13	-1.39	9.81	1,452	23	43	0	1	0	528	3.29	2,000		3.00		Apr-14
8.56	-1.61	-0.25	11.94	20.52	2.49	1.75	7.07	-1.39	9.81	1,452	23	43	0	1	0	528	3.29	2,000			1.00	Apr-14
8.85	-1.09	0.70	15.41	27.00	3.61	0.71	7.1	-1.39	9.8	1,452	23	43	0	1	0	528	3.29	0				Apr-14
8.85	-1.07	0.85	15.70	27.20	3.66	0.66	7.07	-1.39	9.81	1,452	23	43	0	1	0	528	3.29	1,000,000				Mar-17
8.83	-1.11	0.76	15.36	26.72	3.56	0.75	7.07	-1.39	9.81	1,452	23	43	0	1	0	528	3.29	2,000				Apr-14
1.26	0.52	2.21	9.37	15.25	2.49	0.5	3.7	5.00	11.97	225.0	0	0	100	0	0	19	4.94	0				Mar-13
1.20	0.40	2.04	8.55	13.83	2.24	0.75	3.66	5.00	11.99	225.0	0	0	100	0	0	19	4.94	2,000		3.00		Nov-02
1.08	0.17	1.58	7.09	11.38	1.78	1.5	3.66	5.00	11.99	225.0	0	0	100	0	0	19	4.94	2,000			1.00	Nov-02
1.22	0.45	2.14	8.87	14.48	2.34	0.65	3.67	5.00	11.99	225.0	0	0	100	0	0	19	4.94	2,000		4.75		Dec-91
1.27	0.56	2.36	9.60	15.53	2.56	0.43	3.67	5.00	12.01	225.0	0	0	100	0	0	19	4.94	100,000				Mar-16
1.28	0.58	2.32	9.73	15.36	2.6	0.39	3.71	5.00	12.03	225.0	0	0	100	0	0	19	4.94	0				Mar-17
1.26	0.52	2.29	9.36	15.34	2.49	0.5	3.67	5.00	11.99	225.0	0	0	100	0	0	19	4.94	2,000				Dec-91
2.27	1.73	3.39	9.65	14.86	2.22	0.56	3.31	5.10	10.57	195.3	0	0	100	0	0	23	4.82	2,000				Mar-13
2.10	1.51	3.03	8.72	13.33	1.97	0.81	3.32	5.10	10.58	195.3	0	0	100	0	0	23	4.82	2,000		3.00		Dec-92
1.92	1.23	2.36	6.41	9.26	1.23	1.56	3.29	5.10	10.58	195.3	0	0	100	0	0	23	4.82	2,000			1.00	Dec-92
2.19	1.68	3.37	9.81	15.06	2.3	0.48	3.31	5.10	10.6	195.3	0	0	100	0	0	23	4.82	1,000,000				Mar-17
2.17	1.64	3.39	9.54	14.75	2.22	0.56	3.32	5.10	10.57	195.3	0	0	100	0	0	23	4.82	2,000				Dec-92
2.26	2.46	4.32	10.93	16.80	2.45	0.56	3	4.76	12.67	346.4	3	0	97	0	0	8	4.85	2,000				Mar-13
2.20	2.34	3.97	10.10	15.35	2.2	0.81	3	4.76	12.67	346.4	3	0	97	0	0	8	4.85	2,000		3.00		Nov-02
2.09	2.11	3.59	8.62	12.78	1.76	1.56	2.98	4.76	12.67	346.4	3	0	97	0	0	8	4.85	2,000			1.00	Oct-03
2.28	2.48	4.27	11.03	17.02	2.48	0.53	3	4.76	12.65	346.4	3	0	97	0	0	8	4.85	0				Nov-12
2.28	2.50	4.40	11.28	17.10	2.53	0.48	3.03	4.76	12.69	346.4	3	0	97	0	0	8	4.85	1,000,000				Mar-17
2.26	2.47	4.32	10.92	16.79	2.45	0.56	2.99	4.76	12.67	346.4	3	0	97	0	0	8	4.85	2,000				Jul-84
5.33	2.54	4.49	12.58	18.12	2.67	0.66	4.08	2.03	5.64	1,857	6	29	0	1	0	302	3.45	2,000				Nov-12
5.27	2.41	4.23	11.74	16.65	2.42	0.91	4.15	2.03	5.64	1,857	6	29	0	1	0	302	3.45	2,000		3.00		Feb-02
5.06	2.03	3.46	9.25	12.36	1.66	1.66	4.16	2.03	5.65	1,857	6	29	0	1	0	302	3.45	2,000			1.00	Feb-02
5.20	2.29	3.98	11.12	15.22	2.17	1.16	4.1	2.03	5.64	1,857	6	29	0	1	0	302	3.45	0				Mar-16
5.35	2.59	4.60	12.92	18.92	2.76	0.55	4.1	2.03	5.64	1,857	6	29	0	1	0	302	3.45	0				Nov-12
5.38	2.62	4.65	13.31	19.23	2.81	0.51	4.09	2.03	5.62	1,857	6	29	0	1	0	302	3.45	1,000,000				Oct-14
5.33	2.54	4.49	12.79	18.33	2.66	0.66	4.08	2.03	5.64	1,857	6	29	0	1	0	302	3.45	2,000				Sep-10
6.47	0.42	1.92	6.54	8.97	3.53	0.54	4.65	1.94	9.9	1,042	-15	20	0	27	0	169	3.32	2,000				Nov-12
6.40	0.29	1.57	5.75	7.51	3.27	0.79	4.65	1.94	9.91	1,042	-15	20	0	27	0	169	3.32	2,000		1.00		Oct-92
6.25	0.00	1.06	3.86	4.36	2.66	1.54	4.66	1.94	9.89	1,042	-15	20	0	27	0	169	3.32	2,000			1.00	Oct-92
6.33	0.17	1.32	4.85	6.18	3.02	1.04	4.64	1.94	9.91	1,042	-15	20	0	27	0	169	3.32	0				Sep-10
6.39	0.35	1.90	6.72	9.26	3.61	0.44	4.65	1.94	9.88	1,042	-15	20	0	27	0	169	3.32	0				Nov-12
6.40	0.48	1.96	6.99	9.65	3.67	0.39	4.58	1.94	9.89	1,042	-15	20	0	27	0	169	3.32	1,000,000				Jul-09
6.47	0.41	1.92	6.54	8.97	3.53	0.54	4.64	1.94	9.9	1,042	-15	20	0	27	0	169	3.32	2,000				Sep-92
1.25	0.60	1.59	5.54	7.46	1.73	0.42	1.52	1.76	10.41	744.3	11	0	89	0	0	55	3.46	2,000				Mar-13
1.19	0.38	1.34	4.55	5.93	1.47	0.67	1.56	1.76	10.39	744.3	11	0	89	0	0	55	3.46	2,000		1.00		Nov-93

	MARKET			FUND TYPE, CATEGORY & OBJECTIVE	RATINGS				NEW INVESTORS	
Fund Name	Ticker Symbol	Traded On	Fund Type	Category and (Prospectus Objective)	Overall Rating	Reward Rating	Risk Rating	Recent Up/ Downgrade	Open to New Investors	Telephone
Columbia Short Term Municipal Bond Fund Class C	NSMUX	NAS CM	Open End	US Muni Fixed Inc (Muni Bond - Natl)	C	C-	C		Y	800-345-6611
Columbia Short Term Muni Bond Fund Institutional 2 Class	CNNRX	NAS CM	Open End	US Muni Fixed Inc (Muni Bond - Natl)	C	C-	C+		Y	800-345-6611
Columbia Short Term Muni Bond Fund Institutional 3 Class	CSMYX	NAS CM	Open End	US Muni Fixed Inc (Muni Bond - Natl)	C	C-	C+		Y	800-345-6611
Columbia Short Term Muni Bond Fund Institutional Class	NSMIX	NAS CM	Open End	US Muni Fixed Inc (Muni Bond - Natl)	C	C-	C+		Y	800-345-6611
Columbia South Carolina Intermediate Muni Bond Advisor Cl	CSICX	NAS CM	Open End	US Muni Fixed Inc (Muni Bond - Single State)	C	C	B-		Y	800-345-6611
Columbia South Carolina Intermediate Muni Bond Cl A	NSCIX	NAS CM	Open End	US Muni Fixed Inc (Muni Bond - Single State)	C	C	B-		Y	800-345-6611
Columbia South Carolina Intermediate Muni Bond Cl C	NSICX	NAS CM	Open End	US Muni Fixed Inc (Muni Bond - Single State)	C	C-	C+		Y	800-345-6611
Columbia South Carolina Intermed Muni Bond Inst 3 Cl	CSOYX	NAS CM	Open End	US Muni Fixed Inc (Muni Bond - Single State)	C	C	B		Y	800-345-6611
Columbia South Carolina Intermed Muni Bond Inst Cl	NSCMX	NAS CM	Open End	US Muni Fixed Inc (Muni Bond - Single State)	C	C	B-		Y	800-345-6611
Columbia Strategic California Muni Income Advisor Cl	CCARX	NAS CM	Open End	US Muni Fixed Inc (Muni Bond - Single State)	C	C-	B-		Y	800-345-6611
Columbia Strategic California Muni Income Fund Class A	CLMPX	NAS CM	Open End	US Muni Fixed Inc (Muni Bond - Single State)	C	C-	B-		Y	800-345-6611
Columbia Strategic California Muni Income Fund Class C	CCAOX	NAS CM	Open End	US Muni Fixed Inc (Muni Bond - Single State)	C	C-	B-		Y	800-345-6611
Columbia Strategic California Muni Income Inst 2 Cl	CCAUX	NAS CM	Open End	US Muni Fixed Inc (Muni Bond - Single State)	C	C-	B-		Y	800-345-6611
Columbia Strategic California Muni Income Inst 3 Cl	CCXYX	NAS CM	Open End	US Muni Fixed Inc (Muni Bond - Single State)	C	C-	B-		Y	800-345-6611
Columbia Strategic California Muni Income Institutional Cl	CCAZX	NAS CM	Open End	US Muni Fixed Inc (Muni Bond - Single State)	C	C-	B-		Y	800-345-6611
Columbia Strategic Income Fund Advisor Class	CMNRX	NAS CM	Open End	Fixed Inc Misc (Multisector Bond)	C-	D+	C	Down	Y	800-345-6611
Columbia Strategic Income Fund Class A	COSIX	NAS CM	Open End	Fixed Inc Misc (Multisector Bond)	C-	D+	C	Down	Y	800-345-6611
Columbia Strategic Income Fund Class C	CLSCX	NAS CM	Open End	Fixed Inc Misc (Multisector Bond)	C-	D+	C		Y	800-345-6611
Columbia Strategic Income Fund Class R	CSNRX	NAS CM	Open End	Fixed Inc Misc (Multisector Bond)	C-	D+	C		Y	800-345-6611
Columbia Strategic Income Fund Institutional 2 Class	CTIVX	NAS CM	Open End	Fixed Inc Misc (Multisector Bond)	C-	D+	C	Down	Y	800-345-6611
Columbia Strategic Income Fund Institutional 3 Class	CPHUX	NAS CM	Open End	Fixed Inc Misc (Multisector Bond)	C-	D+	C	Down	Y	800-345-6611
Columbia Strategic Income Fund Institutional Class	LSIZX	NAS CM	Open End	Fixed Inc Misc (Multisector Bond)	C-	D+	C	Down	Y	800-345-6611
Columbia Strategic Municipal Income Fund Advisor Class	CATRX	NAS CM	Open End	US Muni Fixed Inc (Muni Bond - Natl)	C	C-	B-		Y	800-345-6611
Columbia Strategic Municipal Income Fund Class A	INTAX	NAS CM	Open End	US Muni Fixed Inc (Muni Bond - Natl)	C	C-	C+		Y	800-345-6611
Columbia Strategic Municipal Income Fund Class C	RTCEX	NAS CM	Open End	US Muni Fixed Inc (Muni Bond - Natl)	C	C-	C+		Y	800-345-6611
Columbia Strategic Muni Income Fund Institutional 2 Class	CADNX	NAS CM	Open End	US Muni Fixed Inc (Muni Bond - Natl)	C	C-	B-		Y	800-345-6611
Columbia Strategic Muni Income Fund Institutional 3 Class	CATYX	NAS CM	Open End	US Muni Fixed Inc (Muni Bond - Natl)	C	C-	B-		Y	800-345-6611
Columbia Strategic Muni Income Fund Institutional Class	CATZX	NAS CM	Open End	US Muni Fixed Inc (Muni Bond - Natl)	C	C-	B-		Y	800-345-6611
Columbia Strategic New York Muni Income Fund Advisor Class	CNYEX	NAS CM	Open End	US Muni Fixed Inc (Muni Bond - Single State)	C	C-	C+		Y	800-345-6611
Columbia Strategic New York Municipal Income Fund Class A	COLNX	NAS CM	Open End	US Muni Fixed Inc (Muni Bond - Single State)	C	C-	C+		Y	800-345-6611
Columbia Strategic New York Municipal Income Fund Class C	CNYCX	NAS CM	Open End	US Muni Fixed Inc (Muni Bond - Single State)	C	C-	C+		Y	800-345-6611
Columbia Strategic New York Muni Income Institutional 2 Cl	CNYRX	NAS CM	Open End	US Muni Fixed Inc (Muni Bond - Single State)	C	C-	C+		Y	800-345-6611
Columbia Strategic New York Muni Income Institutional 3 Cl	CNTYX	NAS CM	Open End	US Muni Fixed Inc (Muni Bond - Single State)	C	C-	B-		Y	800-345-6611
Columbia Strategic New York Muni Income Institutional Cl	CNYZX	NAS CM	Open End	US Muni Fixed Inc (Muni Bond - Single State)	C	C-	C+		Y	800-345-6611
Columbia Tax-Exempt Fund Advisor Class	CTERX	NAS CM	Open End	US Muni Fixed Inc (Muni Bond - Natl)	C	C-	C		Y	800-345-6611
Columbia Tax-Exempt Fund Class A	COLTX	NAS CM	Open End	US Muni Fixed Inc (Muni Bond - Natl)	C	C-	C		Y	800-345-6611
Columbia Tax-Exempt Fund Class C	COLCX	NAS CM	Open End	US Muni Fixed Inc (Muni Bond - Natl)	C-	D+	C	Down	Y	800-345-6611
Columbia Tax-Exempt Fund Institutional 2 Class	CADMX	NAS CM	Open End	US Muni Fixed Inc (Muni Bond - Natl)	C	C-	C+		Y	800-345-6611
Columbia Tax-Exempt Fund Institutional 3 Class	CTEYX	NAS CM	Open End	US Muni Fixed Inc (Muni Bond - Natl)	C	C-	C+		Y	800-345-6611
Columbia Tax-Exempt Fund Institutional Class	CTEZX	NAS CM	Open End	US Muni Fixed Inc (Muni Bond - Natl)	C	C-	C		Y	800-345-6611
Columbia Total Return Bond Fund Advisor Class	CBNRX	NAS CM	Open End	US Fixed Inc (Growth & Income)	B-	C	B+	Up	Y	800-345-6611
Columbia Total Return Bond Fund Class A	LIBAX	NAS CM	Open End	US Fixed Inc (Growth & Income)	B-	C	B+	Up	Y	800-345-6611
Columbia Total Return Bond Fund Class C	LIBCX	NAS CM	Open End	US Fixed Inc (Growth & Income)	C+	C	B	Up	Y	800-345-6611
Columbia Total Return Bond Fund Class R	CIBRX	NAS CM	Open End	US Fixed Inc (Growth & Income)	B-	C	B	Up	Y	800-345-6611
Columbia Total Return Bond Fund Institutional 2 Class	CTBRX	NAS CM	Open End	US Fixed Inc (Growth & Income)	B-	C	B+	Up	Y	800-345-6611
Columbia Total Return Bond Fund Institutional 3 Class	CTBYX	NAS CM	Open End	US Fixed Inc (Growth & Income)	B-	C	B+	Up	Y	800-345-6611
Columbia Total Return Bond Fund Institutional Class	SRBFX	NAS CM	Open End	US Fixed Inc (Growth & Income)	B-	C	B+	Up	Y	800-345-6611
Columbia U.S. Social Bond Fund Advisor Class	CONFX	NAS CM	Open End	US Muni Fixed Inc (Growth & Income)	C	C	B		Y	800-345-6611
Columbia U.S. Social Bond Fund Class A	CONAX	NAS CM	Open End	US Muni Fixed Inc (Growth & Income)	C	C	B		Y	800-345-6611
Columbia U.S. Social Bond Fund Class C	CONCX	NAS CM	Open End	US Muni Fixed Inc (Growth & Income)	C	C-	B-		Y	800-345-6611
Columbia U.S. Social Bond Fund Institutional 2 Class	COVNX	NAS CM	Open End	US Muni Fixed Inc (Growth & Income)	C	C	B		Y	800-345-6611
Columbia U.S. Social Bond Fund Institutional 3 Class	CONYX	NAS CM	Open End	US Muni Fixed Inc (Growth & Income)	C	C	B		Y	800-345-6611

★Expanded analysis of this fund is included in Section II.

TOTAL RETURNS & PERFORMANCE									ASSETS		ASSET ALLOCATION & TURNOVER							MINIMUMS		FEES		
3-Month Total Return	6-Month Total Return	1-Year Total Return	3-Year Total Return	5-Year Total Return	Dividend Yield (TTM)	Expense Ratio	3-Yr Std Deviation	Effective Duration	NAV	Total Assets (MIL)	%Cash	%Government Bonds	%Municipal Bonds	%Corporate Bonds	%Other	Turnover Ratio	Average Coupon Rate	Min Initial Investment	Min Additional Investment	Front End Fee (%)	Back End Fee (%)	Inception Date
0.90	0.01	0.49	2.21	2.05	0.72	1.42	1.52	1.76	10.38	744.3	11	0	89	0	0	55	3.46	2,000			1.00	May-94
1.26	0.53	1.64	5.57	7.62	1.77	0.37	1.52	1.76	10.39	744.3	11	0	89	0	0	55	3.46	0				Nov-12
1.28	0.55	1.69	5.62	7.60	1.82	0.32	1.51	1.76	10.39	744.3	11	0	89	0	0	55	3.46	1,000,000				Mar-17
1.25	0.50	1.60	5.32	7.25	1.73	0.42	1.52	1.76	10.39	744.3	11	0	89	0	0	55	3.46	2,000				Oct-93
1.65	1.54	3.35	10.20	16.24	2.47	0.56	3.17	4.61	10.38	111.8	0	0	100	0	0	9	4.94	2,000				Mar-13
1.58	1.42	3.10	9.38	14.80	2.22	0.81	3.17	4.61	10.38	111.8	0	0	100	0	0	9	4.94	2,000		3.00		May-92
1.39	1.04	2.33	6.94	10.59	1.47	1.56	3.18	4.61	10.39	111.8	0	0	100	0	0	9	4.94	2,000			1.00	Jun-92
1.67	1.60	3.46	10.56	16.66	2.58	0.46	3.17	4.61	10.42	111.8	0	0	100	0	0	9	4.94	1,000,000				Mar-17
1.75	1.64	3.35	10.20	16.24	2.47	0.56	3.23	4.61	10.39	111.8	0	0	100	0	0	9	4.94	2,000				Jan-92
2.87	1.32	3.93	12.81	21.73	3.11	0.54	5.04	8.29	7.7	573.7	0	0	100	0	0	37	4.78	0				Mar-13
2.81	1.32	3.80	11.97	20.22	2.86	0.79	5.03	8.29	7.7	573.7	0	0	100	0	0	37	4.78	2,000		3.00		Jun-86
2.69	1.10	3.34	10.47	17.55	2.41	1.54	5.05	8.29	7.7	573.7	0	0	100	0	0	37	4.78	2,000			1.00	Aug-97
2.87	1.33	3.94	12.87	21.46	3.13	0.52	5.01	8.29	7.71	573.7	0	0	100	0	0	37	4.78	100,000				Mar-16
2.88	1.49	3.99	13.04	21.28	3.18	0.47	5.02	8.29	7.74	573.7	0	0	100	0	0	37	4.78	0				Mar-17
2.87	1.45	3.93	12.82	21.73	3.11	0.54	5.05	8.29	7.7	573.7	0	0	100	0	0	37	4.78	2,000				Sep-05
10.32	-0.76	1.92	10.91	20.91	4.07	0.69	7.08	3.55	5.79	4,920	7	25	0	29	0	179	4.57	2,000				Nov-12
10.05	-1.04	1.63	10.07	19.44	3.73	0.94	6.98	3.55	5.9	4,920	7	25	0	29	0	179	4.57	2,000		4.75		Apr-77
9.85	-1.40	0.87	7.47	15.07	2.97	1.69	6.97	3.55	5.9	4,920	7	25	0	29	0	179	4.57	2,000			1.00	Jul-97
10.29	-0.99	1.37	9.38	18.03	3.46	1.19	7.04	3.55	5.95	4,920	7	25	0	29	0	179	4.57	0				Sep-10
10.31	-0.74	1.79	11.04	21.27	4.1	0.65	7.09	3.55	5.8	4,920	7	25	0	29	0	179	4.57	0				Mar-11
10.37	-0.72	2.02	11.06	21.65	4.17	0.6	7.08	3.55	5.78	4,920	7	25	0	29	0	179	4.57	1,000,000				Jun-13
10.31	-0.76	1.92	10.90	21.10	4.06	0.69	6.99	3.55	5.8	4,920	7	25	0	29	0	179	4.57	2,000				Jan-99
2.98	0.21	2.78	13.95	24.45	3.04	0.55	5.58	8.37	4.08	2,199	2	0	98	0	0	30	4.66	2,000				Mar-13
2.66	0.08	2.52	12.82	22.60	2.78	0.8	5.64	8.37	4.08	2,199	2	0	98	0	0	30	4.66	2,000		3.00		Nov-76
2.72	-0.28	2.01	10.58	18.38	2.02	1.55	5.6	8.37	4.09	2,199	2	0	98	0	0	30	4.66	2,000			1.00	Jun-00
2.99	0.45	3.04	13.96	24.14	3.05	0.54	5.61	8.37	4.08	2,199	2	0	98	0	0	30	4.66	0				Dec-13
2.74	0.24	2.84	13.85	23.49	3.1	0.49	5.69	8.37	4.08	2,199	2	0	98	0	0	30	4.66	1,000,000				Mar-17
2.98	0.45	3.03	13.95	24.45	3.04	0.55	5.61	8.37	4.08	2,199	2	0	98	0	0	30	4.66	2,000				Sep-10
1.96	0.63	2.97	11.16	20.06	2.98	0.55	5.06	8.12	7.42	187.8	0	0	100	0	0	46	4.70	0				Mar-13
1.90	0.50	2.71	10.33	18.57	2.73	0.8	5.05	8.12	7.43	187.8	0	0	100	0	0	46	4.70	2,000		3.00		Sep-86
1.92	0.28	2.25	8.99	16.09	2.27	1.55	5.15	8.12	7.43	187.8	0	0	100	0	0	46	4.70	2,000			1.00	Aug-97
2.11	0.63	3.12	11.35	20.35	3	0.53	5.13	8.12	7.41	187.8	0	0	100	0	0	46	4.70	100,000				Nov-12
1.98	0.66	3.03	11.49	19.91	3.05	0.49	5.11	8.12	7.43	187.8	0	0	100	0	0	46	4.70	0				Mar-17
2.10	0.63	3.10	11.30	20.22	2.98	0.55	5.07	8.12	7.43	187.8	0	0	100	0	0	46	4.70	2,000				Sep-11
1.80	-0.81	1.59	11.07	18.69	3.66	0.53	5.42	8.05	13.27	3,207	0	0	100	0	0	20	4.80	2,000				Mar-13
1.67	-0.91	1.31	10.41	17.52	3.46	0.73	5.36	8.05	13.27	3,207	0	0	100	0	0	20	4.80	2,000		3.00		Nov-78
1.59	-1.23	0.74	8.28	13.77	2.78	1.48	5.41	8.05	13.27	3,207	0	0	100	0	0	20	4.80	2,000			1.00	Aug-97
1.80	-0.73	1.60	11.18	18.92	3.67	0.52	5.41	8.05	13.28	3,207	0	0	100	0	0	20	4.80	0				Dec-13
1.81	-0.77	1.66	11.27	18.51	3.73	0.47	5.4	8.05	13.31	3,207	0	0	100	0	0	20	4.80	1,000,000				Mar-17
1.72	-0.81	1.52	10.99	18.69	3.66	0.53	5.34	8.05	13.27	3,207	0	0	100	0	0	20	4.80	2,000				Sep-05
9.10	6.33	8.70	18.07	27.64	2.87	0.5	5.19	5.51	9.67	2,186	-28	19	0	14	1	262	3.67	2,000				Nov-12
9.02	6.30	8.42	17.18	26.04	2.62	0.75	5.2	5.51	9.68	2,186	-28	19	0	14	1	262	3.67	2,000		3.00		Jul-00
8.82	5.80	7.62	14.58	21.41	1.9	1.5	5.18	5.51	9.68	2,186	-28	19	0	14	1	262	3.67	2,000			1.00	Feb-02
8.96	6.06	8.15	16.31	24.48	2.38	1	5.18	5.51	9.68	2,186	-28	19	0	14	1	262	3.67	0				Jan-06
9.12	6.48	8.78	18.32	28.06	2.94	0.42	5.14	5.51	9.67	2,186	-28	19	0	14	1	262	3.67	0				Nov-12
9.23	6.49	8.94	18.60	28.50	2.99	0.37	5.19	5.51	9.69	2,186	-28	19	0	14	1	262	3.67	1,000,000				Nov-12
9.09	6.32	8.69	18.05	27.62	2.87	0.5	5.16	5.51	9.68	2,186	-28	19	0	14	1	262	3.67	2,000				Dec-78
2.38	1.58	3.87	13.28	21.38	2.68	0.45	4.26	7.20	10.57	58.7	0	0	87	13	0	11	4.37	0				Mar-15
2.32	1.46	3.62	12.44	19.78	2.43	0.7	4.31	7.20	10.57	58.7	0	0	87	13	0	11	4.37	2,000		3.00		Mar-15
2.13	1.08	2.85	9.94	15.49	1.67	1.45	4.27	7.20	10.57	58.7	0	0	87	13	0	11	4.37	2,000			1.00	Mar-15
2.38	1.59	3.88	13.41	21.44	2.69	0.44	4.24	7.20	10.58	58.7	0	0	87	13	0	11	4.37	100,000				Mar-15
2.49	1.61	3.92	13.49	21.60	2.73	0.39	4.29	7.20	10.61	58.7	0	0	87	13	0	11	4.37	0				Mar-17

Fund Name	MARKET: Ticker Symbol	MARKET: Traded On	FUND TYPE, CATEGORY & OBJECTIVE: Fund Type	Category and (Prospectus Objective)	RATINGS: Overall Rating	Reward Rating	Risk Rating	Recent Up/ Downgrade	NEW INVESTORS: Open to New Investors	Telephone
Columbia U.S. Social Bond Fund Institutional Class	CONZX	NAS CM	Open End	US Muni Fixed Inc (Growth & Income)	C	C	B		Y	800-345-6611
Columbia U.S. Treasury Index Fund Class A	LUTAX	NAS CM	Open End	US Fixed Inc (Govt Bond - Treasury)	B	B	B		Y	800-345-6611
Columbia U.S. Treasury Index Fund Class C	LUTCX	NAS CM	Open End	US Fixed Inc (Govt Bond - Treasury)	B	B	B		Y	800-345-6611
Columbia U.S. Treasury Index Fund Institutional 2 Class	CUTRX	NAS CM	Open End	US Fixed Inc (Govt Bond - Treasury)	B	B	B		Y	800-345-6611
Columbia U.S. Treasury Index Fund Institutional 3 Class	CUTYX	NAS CM	Open End	US Fixed Inc (Govt Bond - Treasury)	B	B	B		Y	800-345-6611
Columbia U.S. Treasury Index Fund Institutional Class	IUTIX	NAS CM	Open End	US Fixed Inc (Govt Bond - Treasury)	B	B	B		Y	800-345-6611
Columbia Ultra Short Term Bond Fund Advisor Class	CUSHX	NAS CM	Open End	US Fixed Inc (Income)	C	C-	C+		Y	800-345-6611
Columbia Ultra Short Term Bond Fund Class A	CUSOX	NAS CM	Open End	US Fixed Inc (Income)	C	C-	C+		Y	800-345-6611
Columbia Ultra Short Term Bond Fund Institutional Class	CUSBX	NAS CM	Open End	US Fixed Inc (Income)	C	C-	C+		Y	800-345-6611
Columbia Ultra Short Term Bond Fund Institutional Class3	CMGUX	NAS CM	Open End	US Fixed Inc (Income)	C	C-	C+		Y	800-345-6611
Columbia Virginia Intermediate Muni Bond Advisor Cl	CAIVX	NAS CM	Open End	US Muni Fixed Inc (Muni Bond - Single State)	C	C	B-		Y	800-345-6611
Columbia Virginia Intermediate Municipal Bond Fund Class A	NVAFX	NAS CM	Open End	US Muni Fixed Inc (Muni Bond - Single State)	C	C	B-		Y	800-345-6611
Columbia Virginia Intermediate Municipal Bond Fund Class C	NVRCX	NAS CM	Open End	US Muni Fixed Inc (Muni Bond - Single State)	C	C-	C+		Y	800-345-6611
Columbia Virginia Intermed Muni Bond Inst 3 Cl	CVAYX	NAS CM	Open End	US Muni Fixed Inc (Muni Bond - Single State)	C	C	B-		Y	800-345-6611
Columbia Virginia Intermediate Muni Bond Institutional Cl	NVABX	NAS CM	Open End	US Muni Fixed Inc (Muni Bond - Single State)	C	C	B-		Y	800-345-6611
Commerce Bond Fund	CFBNX	NAS CM	Open End	US Fixed Inc (Income)	B-	C	B	Up	Y	
Commerce Kansas Tax Free Intermediate Bond Fund	KTXIX	NAS CM	Open End	US Muni Fixed Inc (Muni Bond - Single State)	C+	C	B	Up	Y	
Commerce Missouri Tax Free Intermediate Bond Fund	CFMOX	NAS CM	Open End	US Muni Fixed Inc (Muni Bond - Single State)	C+	C	B	Up	Y	
Commerce National Tax Free Intermediate Bond Fund	CFNLX	NAS CM	Open End	US Muni Fixed Inc (Muni Bond - Natl)	C+	C	B	Up	Y	
Commerce Short Term Government Fund	CFSTX	NAS CM	Open End	US Fixed Inc (Govt Bond - General)	C+	C	B	Up	Y	
Cornerstone Advisors Core Plus Bond Institutional Shares	CACTX	NAS CM	Open End	US Fixed Inc (Worldwide Bond)	C+	C	B	Up	Y	
Counterpoint Tactical Income Fund Class A	CPATX	NAS CM	Open End	Fixed Inc Misc (Growth & Income)	C	C	B-		Y	
Counterpoint Tactical Income Fund Class C	CPCTX	NAS CM	Open End	Fixed Inc Misc (Growth & Income)	C	C-	C+		Y	
Counterpoint Tactical Income Fund Class I	CPITX	NAS CM	Open End	Fixed Inc Misc (Growth & Income)	C	C	B-		Y	
Counterpoint Tactical Municipal Fund Class A	TMNAX	NAS CM	Open End	US Muni Fixed Inc (Muni Bond - Natl)	C-	D+	B-	Up	Y	
Counterpoint Tactical Municipal Fund Class C	TMNCX	NAS CM	Open End	US Muni Fixed Inc (Muni Bond - Natl)	C-	D+	C+	Up	Y	
Counterpoint Tactical Municipal Fund Class I	TMNIX	NAS CM	Open End	US Muni Fixed Inc (Muni Bond - Natl)	C-	D+	B-	Up	Y	
CRA Qualified Investment CRA Shares	CRAIX	NAS CM	Open End	US Fixed Inc (Income)	C+	C	B-		Y	877-272-1977
CRA Qualified Investment Institutional Shares	CRANX	NAS CM	Open End	US Fixed Inc (Income)	C+	C	B-		Y	877-272-1977
CRA Qualified Investment Retail Shares	CRATX	NAS CM	Open End	US Fixed Inc (Income)	C+	C	B-		Y	877-272-1977
Credit Suisse Asset Management Income Fund, Inc	CIK	AMEX	Closed End	US Fixed Inc (Corp Bond - High Yield)	D	D	D+	Down	Y	
Credit Suisse Floating Rate High Income Fund A	CHIAX	NAS CM	Open End	US Fixed Inc (Corp Bond - High Yield)	D	D	C-	Down	Y	877-870-2874
Credit Suisse Floating Rate High Income Fund C	CHICX	NAS CM	Open End	US Fixed Inc (Corp Bond - High Yield)	D	D	D+	Down	Y	877-870-2874
Credit Suisse Floating Rate High Income Institutional Cl	CSHIX	NAS CM	Open End	US Fixed Inc (Corp Bond - High Yield)	D	D	C-	Down	Y	877-870-2874
Credit Suisse High Yield Bond	DHY	AMEX	Closed End	US Fixed Inc (Corp Bond - High Yield)	D	D	D+	Down	Y	
Credit Suisse Strategic Income Fund Class A Shares	CSOAX	NAS CM	Open End	US Fixed Inc (Growth & Income)	D+	D	C-	Down	Y	877-870-2874
Credit Suisse Strategic Income Fund Class C Shares	CSOCX	NAS CM	Open End	US Fixed Inc (Growth & Income)	D	D	C-	Down	Y	877-870-2874
Credit Suisse Strategic Income Fund Class I Shares	CSOIX	NAS CM	Open End	US Fixed Inc (Growth & Income)	D+	D	C-	Down	Y	877-870-2874
CrossingBridge Low Duration High Yield Inst Cl Shares	CBLDX	NAS CM	Open End	US Fixed Inc (Corp Bond - High Yield)	C-	D	C		Y	
Crossmark Steward Select Bond Fund Class A	SEAKX	NAS CM	Open End	US Fixed Inc (Income)	C+	C	B	Up	Y	800-262-6631
Crossmark Steward Select Bond Fund Class C	SEAAX	NAS CM	Open End	US Fixed Inc (Income)	C	C	C+	Down	Y	800-262-6631
Crossmark Steward Select Bond Fund Class Institutional	SEACX	NAS CM	Open End	US Fixed Inc (Income)	B-	C	B	Up	Y	800-262-6631
Crossmark Steward Select Bond Fund Class R6	SEABX	NAS CM	Open End	US Fixed Inc (Income)	C	C	C+	Down	Y	800-262-6631
Crow Point Alternative Income Institutional Cl Shares	AIIFX	NAS CM	Open End	Fixed Inc Misc (Income)	D	D	C-	Down	Y	
Davis Government Bond Fund Class A	RFBAX	NAS CM	Open End	US Fixed Inc (Govt Bond - General)	C	C	B-		Y	800-279-0279
Davis Government Bond Fund Class C	DGVCX	NAS CM	Open End	US Fixed Inc (Govt Bond - General)	C	C	C+		Y	800-279-0279
Davis Government Bond Fund Class Y	DGVYX	NAS CM	Open End	US Fixed Inc (Govt Bond - General)	C	C	B-		Y	800-279-0279
Davis Government Money Market Fund Class A	RPGXX	NAS CM	Money Mkt	US Money Mkt (Money Mkt - Govt)	C	C-	C+		Y	800-279-0279
Davis Government Money Market Fund Class C			Money Mkt	US Money Mkt (Money Mkt - Govt)	C	C-	C+		Y	800-279-0279
DAVIS GOVERNMENT MONEY MARKET FUND CLASS Y			Money Mkt	US Money Mkt (Money Mkt - Govt)	C	C-	C+		Y	800-279-0279
DDJ Opportunistic High Yield Fund Class I	DDJCX	NAS CM	Open End	US Fixed Inc (Corp Bond - High Yield)	D	D	D+	Down	Y	
DDJ Opportunistic High Yield Fund Class II	DDJRX	NAS CM	Open End	US Fixed Inc (Corp Bond - High Yield)	D	D	D+	Down	Y	

★ Expanded analysis of this fund is included in Section II.

TOTAL RETURNS & PERFORMANCE									ASSETS		ASSET ALLOCATION & TURNOVER							MINIMUMS		FEES		
3-Month Total Return	6-Month Total Return	1-Year Total Return	3-Year Total Return	5-Year Total Return	Dividend Yield (TTM)	Expense Ratio	3-Yr Std Deviation	Effective Duration	NAV	Total Assets (MIL)	%Cash	%Government Bonds	%Municipal Bonds	%Corporate Bonds	%Other	Turnover Ratio	Average Coupon Rate	Min Initial Investment	Min Additional Investment	Front End Fee (%)	Back End Fee (%)	Inception Date
2.38	1.58	3.87	13.28	21.37	2.68	0.45	4.31	7.20	10.57	58.7	0	0	87	13	0	11	4.37	2,000				Mar-15
0.44	8.50	10.20	16.31	20.33	1.69	0.42	4.14	6.85	12.24	1,134	0	100	0	0	0	50	2.40	2,000				Nov-02
0.27	8.13	9.53	13.91	16.32	1.03	1.17	4.16	6.85	12.24	1,134	0	100	0	0	0	50	2.40	2,000			1.00	Nov-02
0.48	8.60	10.38	16.86	21.37	1.84	0.17	4.15	6.85	12.22	1,134	0	100	0	0	0	50	2.40	0				Nov-12
0.48	8.63	10.49	16.97	21.36	1.84	0.17	4.19	6.85	12.32	1,134	0	100	0	0	0	50	2.40	1,000,000				Mar-17
0.48	8.58	10.45	16.93	21.44	1.84	0.17	4.18	6.85	12.25	1,134	0	100	0	0	0	50	2.40	2,000				Jun-91
2.35	0.96	2.18	6.57	8.56	2.26	0.35	1.38	0.53	9.04	1,647	17	5	0	44	0	95	2.77	2,000				Dec-18
2.43	1.00	2.04	6.13	7.79	2.12	0.5	1.46	0.53	9.04	1,647	17	5	0	44	0	95	2.77	2,000				Feb-19
2.36	0.96	2.19	6.59	8.58	2.27	0.35	1.4	0.53	9.04	1,647	17	5	0	44	0	95	2.77	2,000				Dec-18
2.48	1.09	2.33	6.79	8.79	2.3	0.25	1.47	0.53	9.05	1,647	17	5	0	44	0	95	2.77	1,000,000				Mar-04
1.97	1.59	3.37	9.27	14.65	2.7	0.56	3.28	4.98	10.73	143.2	3	0	97	0	0	13	4.64	2,000				Mar-13
2.01	1.56	3.12	8.37	13.13	2.46	0.81	3.26	4.98	10.73	143.2	3	0	97	0	0	13	4.64	2,000		3.00		Dec-89
1.82	1.19	2.35	6.05	9.07	1.7	1.56	3.28	4.98	10.74	143.2	3	0	97	0	0	13	4.64	2,000			1.00	Jun-92
1.99	1.64	3.37	9.47	14.90	2.79	0.47	3.27	4.98	10.75	143.2	3	0	97	0	0	13	4.64	1,000,000				Mar-17
1.98	1.59	3.28	9.07	14.44	2.71	0.56	3.24	4.98	10.72	143.2	3	0	97	0	0	13	4.64	2,000				Sep-89
5.54	3.96	6.44	14.57	22.65	3.02	0.62	4.48	5.60	20.84	1,233	2	12	10	42	0	16	3.72	1,000	250			Dec-94
2.12	2.92	4.46	11.19	16.32	1.97	0.7	2.9	4.63	20.15	172.1	1	0	99	0	0	14	4.09	1,000	250			Dec-00
1.93	2.45	4.07	10.97	17.00	2.01	0.64	2.87	4.37	20.18	377.0	3	0	97	0	0	25	4.04	1,000	250			Feb-95
2.19	2.74	4.57	11.97	19.09	1.96	0.59	3.23	4.92	20.42	439.4	7	0	92	1	0	29	4.15	1,000	250			Feb-95
0.85	2.93	3.68	7.52	9.16	2.39	0.68	1.3	2.14	17.34	72.3	2	39	0	0	0	30	2.50	1,000	250			Dec-94
2.96	2.65	4.20	10.96		2.96	0.5	2.73		10.08	353.8	12	30	2	27	0	150	3.45	2,000				Aug-16
1.02	-0.29	2.39	7.05	26.93	2.69	2.35	3.21	3.47	10.83	418.3	15	1	0	79	6	353	6.24	5,000	250	4.50		Dec-14
0.84	-0.63	1.64	4.69	22.33	2.09	3.1	3.23	3.47	10.78	418.3	15	1	0	79	6	353	6.24	5,000	250			Dec-14
1.12	-0.11	2.67	7.91	28.49	2.89	2.1	3.22	3.47	10.83	418.3	15	1	0	79	6	353	6.24	100,000	10,000			Dec-14
0.86	1.31	3.51			1.92	1.72		6.54	10.52	36.1	6	0	93	0	0	125	5.23	5,000	250	4.50		Jun-18
0.67	0.86	2.69			1.54	2.47		6.54	10.46	36.1	6	0	93	0	0	125	5.23	5,000	250			Jun-18
0.95	1.45	3.79			2.11	1.47		6.54	10.53	36.1	6	0	93	0	0	125	5.23	100,000	10,000			Jun-18
1.30	3.46	4.95	9.78	13.55	2.16	0.92	2.22		10.88	2,480	3	4	16	4	0	23	3.29	500,000				Aug-99
1.51	3.69	5.53	11.28	16.15	2.6	0.48	2.22		10.87	2,480	3	4	16	4	0	23	3.29	100,000				Mar-07
1.42	3.61	5.16	10.22	14.25	2.26	0.82	2.26		10.87	2,480	3	4	16	4	0	23	3.29	2,500	1,000			Mar-07
14.19	-8.21	-3.98	8.18	24.77	8.99	0	13.01		3.08	156.9	4	0	0	95	0	35	6.65					Mar-87
9.19	-5.63	-3.32	2.46	11.45	5.29	0.95	8.54	0.43	6.16	1,746	7	0	0	88	0	23	4.79	2,500	100	4.75		Mar-99
8.96	-5.96	-4.01	0.22	7.40	4.48	1.7	8.51	0.43	6.18	1,746	7	0	0	88	0	23	4.79	2,500	100		1.00	Feb-00
9.29	-5.56	-3.11	3.32	12.95	5.55	0.7	8.58	0.43	6.13	1,746	7	0	0	88	0	23	4.79	250,000	100,000			Aug-00
13.65	-9.53	-5.87	5.74	27.38	9.2	1.95	13.3		2.26	228.7	4	0	0	95	0	32	6.68					Jul-98
10.26	-5.19	-2.29	5.68	20.61	5.55	1.04	8.96	1.87	9.26	264.0	6	0	0	89	0	37	5.94	2,500	100	4.75		Sep-12
10.05	-5.55	-3.12	3.33	16.18	4.74	1.79	8.99	1.87	9.26	264.0	6	0	0	89	0	37	5.94	2,500	100		1.00	Sep-12
10.20	-5.18	-2.16	6.36	22.12	5.81	0.79	8.94	1.87	9.25	264.0	6	0	0	89	0	37	5.94	250,000	100,000			Sep-12
4.36	-0.91	-0.07			3.07	0.91			9.7454	135.9	26	0	0	70	0	199	5.55	250,000	1,000			Jan-18
4.05	3.48	5.57	10.14	14.13	1.86	0.97	2.81		25.58	153.3	9	17	1	67	0	25	3.67	1,000				Oct-04
3.61	2.46	2.75	3.54	5.90	4.06	1.68	2.72		29.07	153.3	9	17	1	67	0	25	3.67	1,000				Dec-17
4.17	3.69	5.94	11.19	16.01	2.16	0.68	2.81		25.47	153.3	9	17	1	67	0	25	3.67	100,000	50,000			Oct-04
3.66	2.77	3.90	5.30	9.87	5.16	0.58	2.76		28.92	153.3	9	17	1	67	0	25	3.67	0				Dec-17
5.29	-4.89	-3.41	0.69	-0.18	1.53	2.36			8.16	0.01	18	13	0	58	3	169	4.29	1,000				Jan-12
0.23	1.91	2.95	5.18	5.57	1.48	1.05	0.97		5.44	33.0	18	0	0	0	0	13	3.13	1,000	25	4.75		Dec-94
-0.13	1.35	1.81	2.55	1.41	0.74	1.8	1.01		5.42	33.0	18	0	0	0	0	13	3.13	1,000	25		1.00	Aug-97
0.29	2.02	3.01	5.93	6.96	1.73	0.8	1.04		5.48	33.0	18	0	0	0	0	13	3.13	5,000,000	25			Sep-98
0.00	0.22	0.99	3.57	3.73	1.14	0.53	0.17		1	136.6	57	43	0	0	0			1,000	25			Oct-89
0.00	0.22	0.99	3.57	3.74	1.14	0.53	0.17		1	136.6	57	43	0	0	0			1,000	25			Mar-95
0.00	0.22	0.99	3.57	3.74	1.14	0.53	0.17		1	136.6	57	43	0	0	0			5,000,000	25			Jul-06
9.84	-7.59	-6.86	1.24	19.73	8.63	0.89	10.09		7.81	76.8	6	0	0	88	0	43	7.37	1,000,000	50,000			Jul-15
9.71	-7.83	-7.19	0.14	17.86	8.21	1.14	10.1		7.83	76.8	6	0	0	88	0	43	7.37	5,000	2,500			Jul-15

	MARKET			FUND TYPE, CATEGORY & OBJECTIVE	RATINGS				NEW INVESTORS	
Fund Name	Ticker Symbol	Traded On	Fund Type	Category and (Prospectus Objective)	Overall Rating	Reward Rating	Risk Rating	Recent Up/ Downgrade	Open to New Investors	Telephone
DDJ Opportunistic High Yield Fund Institutional Class	DDJIX	NAS CM	Open End	US Fixed Inc (Corp Bond - High Yield)	D	D	D+	Down	Y	
Deer Park Total Return Credit Fund Class A	DPFAX	NAS CM	Open End	US Fixed Inc (Growth & Income)	D	D	D+	Down	Y	888-868-9501
Deer Park Total Return Credit Fund Class C	DPFCX	NAS CM	Open End	US Fixed Inc (Growth & Income)	D	D	D+	Down	Y	888-868-9501
Deer Park Total Return Credit Fund Class I	DPFNX	NAS CM	Open End	US Fixed Inc (Growth & Income)	D+	D	C-	Down	Y	888-868-9501
Delaware Corporate Bond Fund Class A	DGCAX	NAS CM	Open End	US Fixed Inc (Corp Bond - General)	B-	C	B	Up	Y	
Delaware Corporate Bond Fund Class C	DGCCX	NAS CM	Open End	US Fixed Inc (Corp Bond - General)	C+	C	B	Up	Y	
Delaware Corporate Bond Fund Class R	DGCRX	NAS CM	Open End	US Fixed Inc (Corp Bond - General)	C+	C	B	Up	Y	
Delaware Corporate Bond Fund Class R6	DGCZX	NAS CM	Open End	US Fixed Inc (Corp Bond - General)	B-	C	B	Up	Y	
Delaware Corporate Bond Fund Institutional Class	DGCIX	NAS CM	Open End	US Fixed Inc (Corp Bond - General)	B-	C	B	Up	Y	
Delaware Diversified Income Fund Class A	DPDFX	NAS CM	Open End	US Fixed Inc (Multisector Bond)	B-	C+	B+	Up	Y	
Delaware Diversified Income Fund Class C	DPCFX	NAS CM	Open End	US Fixed Inc (Multisector Bond)	B-	C	B	Up	Y	
Delaware Diversified Income Fund Class R	DPRFX	NAS CM	Open End	US Fixed Inc (Multisector Bond)	B-	C+	B+	Up	Y	
Delaware Diversified Income Fund Class R6	DPZRX	NAS CM	Open End	US Fixed Inc (Multisector Bond)	B-	C+	B+	Up	Y	
Delaware Diversified Income Fund Institutional Class	DPFFX	NAS CM	Open End	US Fixed Inc (Multisector Bond)	B-	C+	B+	Up	Y	
Delaware Emerging Markets Debt Corporate Fund Class A	DEDAX	NAS CM	Open End	Emerg Mkts Fixed Inc (Diversified Emerg Mkts)	C-	D+	C	Down	Y	
Delaware Emerging Markets Debt Corporate Fund Class C	DEDCX	NAS CM	Open End	Emerg Mkts Fixed Inc (Diversified Emerg Mkts)	D+	D+	C-	Down	Y	
Delaware Emerg Mkts Debt Corp Fund Class Institutional	DEDIX	NAS CM	Open End	Emerg Mkts Fixed Inc (Diversified Emerg Mkts)	C-	D+	C	Down	Y	
Delaware Emerging Markets Debt Corporate Fund Class R	DEDRX	NAS CM	Open End	Emerg Mkts Fixed Inc (Diversified Emerg Mkts)	C-	D+	C	Down	Y	
Delaware Extended Duration Bond Fund Class A	DEEAX	NAS CM	Open End	US Fixed Inc (Corp Bond - General)	C+	C	B		Y	
Delaware Extended Duration Bond Fund Class C	DEECX	NAS CM	Open End	US Fixed Inc (Corp Bond - General)	C+	C	B-	Up	Y	
Delaware Extended Duration Bond Fund Class Institutional	DEEIX	NAS CM	Open End	US Fixed Inc (Corp Bond - General)	C+	C	B		Y	
Delaware Extended Duration Bond Fund Class R	DEERX	NAS CM	Open End	US Fixed Inc (Corp Bond - General)	C+	C	B-		Y	
Delaware Extended Duration Bond Fund Class R6	DEZRX	NAS CM	Open End	US Fixed Inc (Corp Bond - General)	C+	C	B		Y	
Delaware Floating Rate Fund Class A	DDFAX	NAS CM	Open End	Fixed Inc Misc (Growth & Income)	C-	D+	C		Y	
Delaware Floating Rate Fund Class C	DDFCX	NAS CM	Open End	Fixed Inc Misc (Growth & Income)	D+	D	C-	Down	Y	
Delaware Floating Rate Fund Class R	DDFFX	NAS CM	Open End	Fixed Inc Misc (Growth & Income)	D+	D	C	Down	Y	
Delaware Floating Rate Fund Institutional Class	DDFLX	NAS CM	Open End	Fixed Inc Misc (Growth & Income)	C-	D+	C		Y	
Delaware Floating Rate II Fund Class A	FRFDX	NAS CM	Open End	US Fixed Inc (Income)	D+	D	C	Down	Y	
Delaware Floating Rate II Fund Class R6	FRFNX	NAS CM	Open End	US Fixed Inc (Income)	C-	D+	C		Y	
Delaware Floating Rate II Fund Institutional Class	FRFEX	NAS CM	Open End	US Fixed Inc (Income)	D+	D	C	Down	Y	
Delaware Fund for Income Class A	FIFIX	NAS CM	Open End	US Fixed Inc (Corp Bond - High Yield)	C-	D+	C		Y	
Delaware Fund for Income Class R6	FIFLX	NAS CM	Open End	US Fixed Inc (Corp Bond - High Yield)	C-	D+	C		Y	
Delaware Fund for Income Institutional Class	FIFKX	NAS CM	Open End	US Fixed Inc (Corp Bond - High Yield)	C-	D+	C		Y	
Delaware Government Cash Management Fund Class A	FICXX	NAS CM	Money Mkt	US Money Mkt (Money Mkt - Govt)	C	C-	C+		Y	
Delaware Government Cash Management Fund Class R6	FIFXX	NAS CM	Money Mkt	US Money Mkt (Money Mkt - Govt)	C	C-	C		Y	
Delaware High-Yield Opportunities Fund Class A	DHOAX	NAS CM	Open End	US Fixed Inc (Corp Bond - High Yield)	C-	D+	C		Y	
Delaware High-Yield Opportunities Fund Class C	DHOCX	NAS CM	Open End	US Fixed Inc (Corp Bond - High Yield)	C-	D+	C		Y	
Delaware High-Yield Opportunities Fund Class R	DHIRX	NAS CM	Open End	US Fixed Inc (Corp Bond - High Yield)	C-	D+	C		Y	
Delaware High-Yield Opportunities Fund Institutional Class	DHOIX	NAS CM	Open End	US Fixed Inc (Corp Bond - High Yield)	C-	D+	C		Y	
Delaware International Opportunities Bond Fund Class A	FIOBX	NAS CM	Open End	Global Fixed Inc (Corp Bond - General)	D	D	C-	Down	Y	
Delaware International Opportunities Bond Fund Class R6	FIOEX	NAS CM	Open End	Global Fixed Inc (Corp Bond - General)	D+	D	C		Y	
Delaware InterNatl Opportunities Bond Institutional Cl	FIODX	NAS CM	Open End	Global Fixed Inc (Corp Bond - General)	D	D	C-	Down	Y	
Delaware Investment Grade Fund Class A	FIIGX	NAS CM	Open End	US Fixed Inc (Corp Bond - General)	C+	C	B	Up	Y	
Delaware Investment Grade Fund Class R6	FIIKX	NAS CM	Open End	US Fixed Inc (Corp Bond - General)	B-	C	B	Up	Y	
Delaware Investment Grade Fund Institutional Class	FIIJX	NAS CM	Open End	US Fixed Inc (Corp Bond - General)	B-	C	B	Up	Y	
Delaware Investments Colorado Municipal Income Fund	VCF	AMEX	Closed End	US Muni Fixed Inc (Muni Bond - Single State)	D+	C-	D+	Down	Y	
Delaware Investments National Municipal Income Fund	VFL	AMEX	Closed End	US Muni Fixed Inc (Muni Bond - Natl)	D+	D+	C-	Down	Y	
Delaware Investments Ultrashort Fund Class A	DLTAX	NAS CM	Open End	US Fixed Inc (Growth & Income)	C	C-	C+		Y	
Delaware Investments Ultrashort Fund Class C	DLTCX	NAS CM	Open End	US Fixed Inc (Growth & Income)	C	C-	C+		Y	
Delaware Investments Ultrashort Fund Class L	DLTLX	NAS CM	Open End	US Fixed Inc (Growth & Income)	C	C-	C+			
Delaware Investments Ultrashort Fund Institutional Class	DULTX	NAS CM	Open End	US Fixed Inc (Growth & Income)	C	C-	C+		Y	
Delaware Limited Duration Bond Fund Class A	FLDKX	NAS CM	Open End	US Fixed Inc (Corp Bond - General)	C	C	C+		Y	

★ Expanded analysis of this fund is included in Section II.

TOTAL RETURNS & PERFORMANCE									ASSETS		ASSET ALLOCATION & TURNOVER							MINIMUMS		FEES		
3-Month Total Return	6-Month Total Return	1-Year Total Return	3-Year Total Return	5-Year Total Return	Dividend Yield (TTM)	Expense Ratio	3-Yr Std Deviation	Effective Duration	NAV	Total Assets (MIL)	%Cash	%Government Bonds	%Municipal Bonds	%Corporate Bonds	%Other	Turnover Ratio	Average Coupon Rate	Min Initial Investment	Min Additional Investment	Front End Fee (%)	Back End Fee (%)	Inception Date
9.83	-7.70	-6.91	1.07	19.53	8.46	0.79	10.15		7.81	76.8	6	0	0	88	0	43	7.37	5,000,000				Jul-15
10.58	-5.09	-2.84	6.61		6.04	2.15	10.11		10.07	590.9	9	0	0	0	0	29	2.61	2,500	100	5.75		Oct-15
10.32	-5.55	-3.65	4.19		5.3	2.9	10.1		10.03	590.9	9	0	0	0	0	29	2.61	2,500	100			Apr-17
10.63	-4.96	-2.58	7.50		6.31	1.9	10.08		10.08	590.9	9	0	0	0	0	29	2.61	100,000	100			Oct-15
10.45	4.91	9.27	19.56	29.84	3.08	0.82	7.25	8.09	6.31	1,096	-2	5	0	92	0	173	3.98	1,000	100	4.50		Sep-98
10.26	4.54	8.47	16.92	25.10	2.34	1.57	7.25	8.09	6.31	1,096	-2	5	0	92	0	173	3.98	1,000	100		1.00	Sep-98
10.37	4.78	8.99	18.66	28.22	2.83	1.07	7.2	8.09	6.32	1,096	-2	5	0	92	0	173	3.98	0				Jun-03
10.54	5.08	9.64	20.60	31.63	3.41	0.48	7.22	8.09	6.31	1,096	-2	5	0	92	0	173	3.98	0				Jan-19
10.52	5.04	9.53	20.45	31.46	3.32	0.57	7.25	8.09	6.31	1,096	-2	5	0	92	0	173	3.98	0				Sep-98
6.72	5.07	7.80	15.67	22.50	2.99	0.7	4.54	5.94	9.13	3,446	-3	24	0	41	0	167	3.86	1,000	100	4.50		Dec-97
6.53	4.70	7.01	13.13	18.03	2.26	1.45	4.51	5.94	9.13	3,446	-3	24	0	41	0	167	3.86	1,000	100		1.00	Oct-02
6.54	4.96	7.42	14.82	20.85	2.74	0.95	4.45	5.94	9.12	3,446	-3	24	0	41	0	167	3.86	0				Jun-03
6.79	5.36	8.14	16.94	24.06	3.31	0.36	4.45	5.94	9.14	3,446	-3	24	0	41	0	167	3.86	0				May-16
6.77	5.31	8.05	16.66	24.02	3.23	0.45	4.49	5.94	9.14	3,446	-3	24	0	41	0	167	3.86	0				Oct-02
13.39	-3.44	0.08	10.89	27.09	3.95	1.04	10.95	5.05	8.3	64.1	2	9	0	88	1	74	5.06	1,000	100	4.50		Sep-13
13.19	-3.80	-0.63	8.35	23.92	3.2	1.79	10.96	5.05	8.29	64.1	2	9	0	88	1	74	5.06	1,000	100		1.00	Sep-13
13.48	-3.43	0.23	11.54	28.06	4.23	0.79	10.99	5.05	8.29	64.1	2	9	0	88	1	74	5.06	0				Sep-13
13.48	-3.32	0.35	11.68	28.09	4.24	1.29	10.96	5.05	8.29	64.1	2	9	0	88	1	74	5.06	0				Sep-13
12.02	5.64	12.74	24.94	43.19	3.21	0.82	10.88	14.60	7.24	542.5	-2	3	3	90	0	133	4.52	1,000	100	4.50		Sep-98
11.68	5.12	11.76	22.21	38.00	2.48	1.57	10.81	14.60	7.23	542.5	-2	3	3	90	0	133	4.52	1,000	100		1.00	Sep-98
12.11	5.77	13.03	26.08	45.01	3.45	0.57	10.87	14.60	7.23	542.5	-2	3	3	90	0	133	4.52	0				Sep-98
11.94	5.51	12.45	24.18	41.38	2.97	1.07	10.87	14.60	7.25	542.5	-2	3	3	90	0	133	4.52	0				Oct-05
11.95	5.66	13.11	26.19	45.25	3.52	0.49	10.79	14.60	7.23	542.5	-2	3	3	90	0	133	4.52	0				May-16
7.55	-4.68	-1.62	6.67	10.20	5.2	0.94	7.29	1.11	7.74	112.5	3	0	0	95	-2	143	4.28	1,000	100	2.75		Feb-10
7.36	-4.91	-2.22	4.32	6.18	4.4	1.69	7.28	1.11	7.74	112.5	3	0	0	95	-2	143	4.28	1,000	100		1.00	Feb-10
7.63	-4.68	-1.74	5.88	8.83	4.94	1.19	7.35	1.11	7.74	112.5	3	0	0	95	-2	143	4.28	0				Feb-10
7.61	-4.57	-1.38	7.47	11.57	5.46	0.69	7.28	1.11	7.74	112.5	3	0	0	95	-2	143	4.28	0				Feb-10
7.15	-3.48	-1.40	5.18	10.80	4.62	1.05	6.61	1.15	9.05	64.9	0	0	0	99	0	49	4.12	1,000	100	2.75		Oct-13
7.10	-3.33	-0.96	6.45	13.05	4.97	0.74	6.53	1.15	9.06	64.9	0	0	0	99	0	49	4.12	0				Oct-13
7.20	-3.41	-1.27	5.63	11.74	4.8	0.89	6.63	1.15	9.04	64.9	0	0	0	99	0	49	4.12	0				Oct-13
9.30	-3.65	-0.42	7.90	18.19	5.24	1.15	8.05	4.28	2.32	421.5	4	0	0	96	-1	47	6.07	1,000	100	4.50		Dec-70
9.36	-3.45	-0.02	9.11	20.69	5.63	0.8	8	4.28	2.33	421.5	4	0	0	96	-1	47	6.07	0				Apr-13
9.44	-3.59	-0.20	7.77	18.68	5.48	0.9	8.18	4.28	2.3	421.5	4	0	0	96	-1	47	6.07	0				Apr-13
0.00	0.20	0.89	3.30	3.30	1.04	0.55	0.17		1	188.6	90	10	0	0	0			1,000	100		1.00	Oct-78
0.01	0.20	0.90	3.33	3.33	1.05	0.6	0.18		1	188.6	90	10	0	0	0			0				Apr-13
9.82	-3.55	0.33	9.32	17.63	5.53	0.94	8.51	4.06	3.58	167.8	4	0	0	96	1	76	6.24	1,000	100	4.50		Dec-96
9.30	-3.90	-0.66	6.64	13.04	4.75	1.69	8.43	4.06	3.58	167.8	4	0	0	96	1	76	6.24	1,000	100		1.00	Feb-98
9.73	-3.65	-0.16	8.54	15.91	5.27	1.19	8.56	4.06	3.59	167.8	4	0	0	96	1	76	6.24	0				Jun-03
9.58	-3.71	0.30	9.84	18.76	5.79	0.69	8.52	4.06	3.57	167.8	4	0	0	96	1	76	6.24	0				Dec-96
2.12	1.00	-3.17	-3.16	3.22	0.22	1.39	6.81	9.76	8.47	45.8	4	96	0	1	3	61	1.74	1,000	100	4.50		Aug-12
2.32	1.23	-2.77	-1.89	5.51	0.52	0.94	6.86	9.76	8.67	45.8	4	96	0	1	3	61	1.74	0				Apr-13
2.31	1.16	-2.79	-2.19	4.78	0.43	1.09	6.86	9.76	8.58	45.8	4	96	0	1	3	61	1.74	0				Apr-13
10.97	4.63	8.19	17.32	25.63	2.85	1.03	7.39	8.15	9.9	290.5	-4	5	0	94	0	36	3.96	1,000	100	4.50		Feb-91
11.15	4.91	8.68	18.79	28.38	3.21	0.66	7.36	8.15	9.94	290.5	-4	5	0	94	0	36	3.96	0				Apr-13
11.11	4.75	8.66	18.53	27.72	3.2	0.74	7.43	8.15	9.96	290.5	-4	5	0	94	0	36	3.96	0				Apr-13
4.35	0.14	2.43	11.32	22.88	3.81		6.6	5.73	14.81	69.9	-45	0	100	0	4	7	5.10					Jul-93
4.39	-2.09	0.46	10.25	21.83	3.87		8.5	6.99	14.18	61.9	-51	0	100	0	3	33	4.99					Feb-93
2.73	0.21	1.53	5.84	7.38	2.04	0.4	2.02	0.35	9.99	73.0	2	0	0	41	9	82	1.91	1,000	100	2.00		Mar-88
2.73	0.21	1.53	5.84	7.38	2.04	0.4	2.02	0.35	9.99	73.0	2	0	0	41	9	82	1.91	1,000	100		1.00	Nov-95
2.83	0.31	1.64	5.94	7.49	2.04	0.4	2.08	0.35	10	73.0	2	0	0	41	9	82	1.91	1,000	100			Jun-78
2.83	0.21	1.53	5.95	7.50	2.04	0.4	2.08	0.35	10	73.0	2	0	0	41	9	82	1.91	0				Jan-16
3.01	2.62	3.63	7.37	8.89	2.45	0.74	1.9	2.19	9.42	191.1	3	19	0	36	0	57	2.83	1,000	100	2.75		May-14

	MARKET			FUND TYPE, CATEGORY & OBJECTIVE	RATINGS				NEW INVESTORS	
Fund Name	Ticker Symbol	Traded On	Fund Type	Category and (Prospectus Objective)	Overall Rating	Reward Rating	Risk Rating	Recent Up/ Downgrade	Open to New Investors	Telephone
Delaware Limited Duration Bond Fund Class R6	FLDMX	NAS CM	Open End	US Fixed Inc (Corp Bond - General)	C	C	B-		Y	
Delaware Limited Duration Bond Fund Institutional Class	FLDLX	NAS CM	Open End	US Fixed Inc (Corp Bond - General)	C	C	B-		Y	
Delaware Limited-Term Diversified Income Fund Class A	DTRIX	NAS CM	Open End	US Fixed Inc (Growth & Income)	C	C	B-		Y	
Delaware Limited-Term Diversified Income Fund Class C	DTICX	NAS CM	Open End	US Fixed Inc (Growth & Income)	C	C	C+		Y	
Delaware Limited-Term Diversified Income Fund Class R	DLTRX	NAS CM	Open End	US Fixed Inc (Growth & Income)	C	C	B-		Y	
Delaware Limited-Term Diversified Income Fund Class R6	DLTZX	NAS CM	Open End	US Fixed Inc (Growth & Income)	C	C	B-		Y	
Delaware Limited-Term Diversified Income Institutional Cl	DTINX	NAS CM	Open End	US Fixed Inc (Growth & Income)	C	C	B-		Y	
Delaware Minnesota High-Yield Municipal Bond Fund Class A	DVMHX	NAS CM	Open End	US Muni Fixed Inc (Muni Bond - Single State)	C-	D+	C	Down	Y	
Delaware Minnesota High-Yield Municipal Bond Fund Class C	DVMMX	NAS CM	Open End	US Muni Fixed Inc (Muni Bond - Single State)	C-	D+	C	Down	Y	
Delaware Minnesota High-Yield Muni Bond Institutional Cl	DMHIX	NAS CM	Open End	US Muni Fixed Inc (Muni Bond - Single State)	C-	D+	C	Down	Y	
Delaware Minnesota Municipal Income II	VMM	AMEX	Closed End	US Muni Fixed Inc (Muni Bond - Single State)	C-	C-	C-		Y	
Delaware National High Yield Municipal Bond Fund Class A	CXHYX	NAS CM	Open End	US Muni Fixed Inc (Muni Bond - Natl)	C-	D+	C	Down	Y	
Delaware National High Yield Municipal Bond Fund Class C	DVHCX	NAS CM	Open End	US Muni Fixed Inc (Muni Bond - Natl)	C-	D+	C	Down	Y	
Delaware Natl High Yield Muni Bond Institutional Cl	DVHIX	NAS CM	Open End	US Muni Fixed Inc (Muni Bond - Natl)	C-	D+	C	Down	Y	
Delaware Strategic Income Fund Class A	DEGGX	NAS CM	Open End	US Fixed Inc (Growth & Income)	C	C-	C		Y	
Delaware Strategic Income Fund Class C	DUGCX	NAS CM	Open End	US Fixed Inc (Growth & Income)	C-	C-	C		Y	
Delaware Strategic Income Fund Class R	DUGRX	NAS CM	Open End	US Fixed Inc (Growth & Income)	C	C-	C	Up	Y	
Delaware Strategic Income Fund Institutional Class	DUGIX	NAS CM	Open End	US Fixed Inc (Growth & Income)	C	C-	C		Y	
Delaware Strategic Income II Fund Class A	FSIFX	NAS CM	Open End	US Fixed Inc (Income)	C-	D+	C		Y	
Delaware Strategic Income II Fund Institutional Class	FSIHX	NAS CM	Open End	US Fixed Inc (Income)	C-	D+	C		Y	
Delaware Tax Free Minnesota Fund Institutional Class	DMNIX	NAS CM	Open End	US Muni Fixed Inc (Muni Bond - Single State)	C	C-	C+		Y	
Delaware Tax-Exempt Income Fund Class A	FITAX	NAS CM	Open End	US Muni Fixed Inc (Muni Bond - Natl)	C	C-	C+		Y	
Delaware Tax-Exempt Income Fund Class R6	FITEX	NAS CM	Open End	US Muni Fixed Inc (Muni Bond - Natl)	C	C-	B-		Y	
Delaware Tax-Exempt Income Fund Institutional Class	FITDX	NAS CM	Open End	US Muni Fixed Inc (Muni Bond - Natl)	C	C-	C+		Y	
Delaware Tax-Exempt Opportunities Fund Class A	EIITX	NAS CM	Open End	US Muni Fixed Inc (Muni Bond - Natl)	C	C-	C+		Y	
Delaware Tax-Exempt Opportunities Fund Class R6	EIINX	NAS CM	Open End	US Muni Fixed Inc (Muni Bond - Natl)	C	C-	C+		Y	
Delaware Tax-Exempt Opportunities Fund Institutional Class	EIIAX	NAS CM	Open End	US Muni Fixed Inc (Muni Bond - Natl)	C	C-	C+		Y	
Delaware Tax-Free Arizona Fund Class A	VAZIX	NAS CM	Open End	US Muni Fixed Inc (Muni Bond - Single State)	C	C-	C+		Y	
Delaware Tax-Free Arizona Fund Class C	DVACX	NAS CM	Open End	US Muni Fixed Inc (Muni Bond - Single State)	C	C-	C		Y	
Delaware Tax-Free Arizona Fund Institutional Class	DAZIX	NAS CM	Open End	US Muni Fixed Inc (Muni Bond - Single State)	C	C-	C+		Y	
Delaware Tax-Free California Fund Class A	DVTAX	NAS CM	Open End	US Muni Fixed Inc (Muni Bond - Single State)	C	C-	C+		Y	
Delaware Tax-Free California Fund Class C	DVFTX	NAS CM	Open End	US Muni Fixed Inc (Muni Bond - Single State)	C	C-	C		Y	
Delaware Tax-Free California Fund Institutional Class	DCTIX	NAS CM	Open End	US Muni Fixed Inc (Muni Bond - Single State)	C	C-	C+		Y	
Delaware Tax-Free California II Fund Class A	FICAX	NAS CM	Open End	US Muni Fixed Inc (Muni Bond - Single State)	C	C-	C		Y	
Delaware Tax-Free California II Fund Class R6	FICLX	NAS CM	Open End	US Muni Fixed Inc (Muni Bond - Single State)	C	C-	C+		Y	
Delaware Tax-Free California II Fund Institutional Class	FICJX	NAS CM	Open End	US Muni Fixed Inc (Muni Bond - Single State)	C	C-	C+		Y	
Delaware Tax-Free Colorado Fund Class A	VCTFX	NAS CM	Open End	US Muni Fixed Inc (Muni Bond - Single State)	C	C-	C+		Y	
Delaware Tax-Free Colorado Fund Class C	DVCTX	NAS CM	Open End	US Muni Fixed Inc (Muni Bond - Single State)	C	C-	C		Y	
Delaware Tax-Free Colorado Fund Institutional Class	DCOIX	NAS CM	Open End	US Muni Fixed Inc (Muni Bond - Single State)	C	C-	C+		Y	
Delaware Tax-Free Idaho Fund Class A	VIDAX	NAS CM	Open End	US Muni Fixed Inc (Muni Bond - Single State)	C	C-	C+		Y	
Delaware Tax-Free Idaho Fund Class C	DVICX	NAS CM	Open End	US Muni Fixed Inc (Muni Bond - Single State)	C	C-	C		Y	
Delaware Tax-Free Idaho Fund Institutional Class	DTIDX	NAS CM	Open End	US Muni Fixed Inc (Muni Bond - Single State)	C	C-	B-		Y	
Delaware Tax-Free Minnesota Fund Class A	DEFFX	NAS CM	Open End	US Muni Fixed Inc (Muni Bond - Single State)	C	C-	C+		Y	
Delaware Tax-Free Minnesota Fund Class C	DMOCX	NAS CM	Open End	US Muni Fixed Inc (Muni Bond - Single State)	C	C-	C		Y	
Delaware Tax-Free Minnesota Intermediate Fund Class A	DXCCX	NAS CM	Open End	US Muni Fixed Inc (Muni Bond - Single State)	C	C-	C+		Y	
Delaware Tax-Free Minnesota Intermediate Fund Class C	DVSCX	NAS CM	Open End	US Muni Fixed Inc (Muni Bond - Single State)	C	C-	C		Y	
Delaware Tax-Free Minnesota Intermediate Institutional Cl	DMIIX	NAS CM	Open End	US Muni Fixed Inc (Muni Bond - Single State)	C	C-	C+		Y	
Delaware Tax-Free New Jersey Fund Class A	FINJX	NAS CM	Open End	US Muni Fixed Inc (Muni Bond - Single State)	C	C-	C+		Y	
Delaware Tax-Free New Jersey Fund Class R6	FINNX	NAS CM	Open End	US Muni Fixed Inc (Muni Bond - Single State)	C	C-	B-		Y	
Delaware Tax-Free New Jersey Fund Institutional Class	FINLX	NAS CM	Open End	US Muni Fixed Inc (Muni Bond - Single State)	C	C-	C+		Y	
Delaware Tax-Free New York Fund Class A	FTNYX	NAS CM	Open End	US Muni Fixed Inc (Muni Bond - Single State)	C	C-	C+		Y	
Delaware Tax-Free New York Fund Class C	DVFNX	NAS CM	Open End	US Muni Fixed Inc (Muni Bond - Single State)	C	C-	C		Y	

★Expanded analysis of this fund is included in Section II.

TOTAL RETURNS & PERFORMANCE									ASSETS		ASSET ALLOCATION & TURNOVER							MINIMUMS		FEES		
3-Month Total Return	6-Month Total Return	1-Year Total Return	3-Year Total Return	5-Year Total Return	Dividend Yield (TTM)	Expense Ratio	3-Yr Std Deviation	Effective Duration	NAV	Total Assets (MIL)	%Cash	%Government Bonds	%Municipal Bonds	%Corporate Bonds	%Other	Turnover Ratio	Average Coupon Rate	Min Initial Investment	Min Additional Investment	Front End Fee (%)	Back End Fee (%)	Inception Date
2.99	2.70	4.04	8.73	11.33	2.85	0.36	1.81	2.19	9.46	191.1	3	19	0	36	0	57	2.83	0				May-14
3.06	2.73	4.00	8.23	10.39	2.71	0.51	1.89	2.19	9.45	191.1	3	19	0	36	0	57	2.83	0				May-14
3.28	2.57	3.94	6.70	10.93	2.58	0.54	2.18	2.74	8.39	402.0	9	19	0	33	0	123	2.72	1,000	100	2.75		Nov-85
2.95	2.03	2.96	3.92	6.34	1.74	1.39	2.1	2.74	8.38	402.0	9	19	0	33	0	123	2.72	1,000	100		1.00	Nov-95
3.20	2.27	3.59	5.60	9.01	2.23	0.89	2.17	2.74	8.39	402.0	9	19	0	33	0	123	2.72	0				Jun-03
3.33	2.55	4.04	7.40	11.54	2.8	0.32	2.19	2.74	8.38	402.0	9	19	0	33	0	123	2.72	0				May-17
3.32	2.64	4.10	7.18	11.76	2.73	0.39	2.14	2.74	8.39	402.0	9	19	0	33	0	123	2.72	0				Jun-92
2.64	-1.08	1.26	9.43	16.73	2.8	0.89	5.37	7.08	10.84	195.4	0	0	100	0	1	12	4.95	1,000	100	4.50		Jun-96
2.46	-1.43	0.53	7.02	12.36	2.03	1.64	5.36	7.08	10.86	195.4	0	0	100	0	1	12	4.95	1,000	100		1.00	Jun-96
2.70	-0.96	1.51	10.35	18.19	3.06	0.64	5.32	7.08	10.84	195.4	0	0	100	0	1	12	4.95	0				Dec-13
2.65	-0.24	2.05	9.99	19.25	3.14		5.84	5.45	14.58	164.9	-47	0	100	0	3	13	4.97					Feb-93
5.08	-1.79	1.68	12.98	24.90	4.27	0.85	8.11	10.16	10.94	1,249	0	0	100	0	1	33	5.54	1,000	100	4.50		Sep-86
4.89	-2.16	0.91	10.36	20.28	3.44	1.6	8.11	10.16	10.98	1,249	0	0	100	0	1	33	5.54	1,000	100		1.00	May-97
5.20	-1.64	1.95	13.83	26.43	4.54	0.6	8.09	10.16	11.04	1,249	0	0	100	0	1	33	5.54	0				Dec-08
10.54	-0.08	3.62	9.02	15.21	4.09	0.84	7.66	6.11	8.03	40.5	-3	18	2	52	3	106	4.73	1,000	100	4.50		Aug-85
10.48	-0.34	2.83	6.60	10.98	3.3	1.59	7.73	6.11	8.04	40.5	-3	18	2	52	3	106	4.73	1,000	100		1.00	Nov-95
10.58	-0.10	3.34	8.33	13.77	3.81	1.09	7.72	6.11	8.06	40.5	-3	18	2	52	3	106	4.73	0				Jun-03
10.74	0.15	3.87	9.85	16.66	4.35	0.59	7.72	6.11	8.04	40.5	-3	18	2	52	3	106	4.73	0				Jun-92
12.44	-0.78	1.78	6.89	12.88	3.42	1.11	8.82	5.01	9.16	104.8	4	8	0	54	2	40	4.64	1,000	100	4.50		Apr-13
12.39	-0.76	2.02	7.85	15.02	3.67	0.86	8.74	5.01	9.15	104.8	4	8	0	54	2	40	4.64	0				Apr-13
2.30	0.19	2.23	9.60	16.64	2.89	0.6	4.39	6.05	12.36	565.4	0	0	100	0	1	13	4.97	0				Dec-13
3.31	1.28	3.05	8.69	13.48	2.95	0.8	4.35	5.93	9.35	507.3	0	0	100	0	1	39	5.13	1,000	100	4.00	1.00	Aug-77
3.25	1.38	3.23	9.71	14.65	3.13	0.62	4.41	5.93	9.34	507.3	0	0	100	0	1	39	5.13	0				May-13
3.24	1.35	3.21	9.39	15.03	3.12	0.65	4.38	5.93	9.35	507.3	0	0	100	0	1	39	5.13	0				May-13
4.46	0.92	3.00	9.46	15.82	2.89	0.95	5.9	8.11	16.6	347.9	0	0	100	0	1	60	5.05	1,000	100	4.50	1.00	Jul-90
4.48	1.08	3.18	9.50	16.49	3.19	0.65	5.86	8.11	16.57	347.9	0	0	100	0	1	60	5.05	0				May-13
4.47	1.01	3.15	10.18	16.89	3.15	0.66	5.88	8.11	16.62	347.9	0	0	100	0	1	60	5.05	0				May-13
3.30	0.15	2.82	10.27	18.06	3.22	0.84	5.11	6.50	11.43	78.3	0	0	100	0	3	31	4.92	1,000	100	4.50		Apr-91
3.11	-0.11	2.06	7.83	13.73	2.44	1.59	5.1	6.50	11.46	78.3	0	0	100	0	3	31	4.92	1,000	100		1.00	May-94
3.36	0.28	3.07	11.09	19.54	3.47	0.59	5.11	6.50	11.43	78.3	0	0	100	0	3	31	4.92	0				Dec-13
4.04	0.38	3.08	10.77	20.12	3.25	0.82	5.54	7.01	12.09	79.5	0	0	100	0	1	32	5.12	1,000	100	4.50		Mar-95
3.86	0.03	2.33	8.37	15.77	2.49	1.57	5.53	7.01	12.11	79.5	0	0	100	0	1	32	5.12	1,000	100		1.00	Apr-96
4.02	0.42	3.24	11.55	21.56	3.51	0.57	5.57	7.01	12.08	79.5	0	0	100	0	1	32	5.12	0				Dec-13
3.24	-0.12	1.93	8.60	15.51	2.68	0.92	5.48	6.74	12.66	37.0	0	0	100	0	2	40	5.03	1,000	100	4.50	1.00	Feb-87
3.31	0.01	2.20	9.55	17.05	2.96	0.65	5.51	6.74	12.63	37.0	0	0	100	0	2	40	5.03	0				May-13
3.31	0.01	2.20	9.57	17.25	2.96	0.64	5.46	6.74	12.63	37.0	0	0	100	0	2	40	5.03	0				May-13
2.77	0.39	2.64	10.35	18.72	3.05	0.84	4.66	6.10	11.24	216.2	0	0	100	0	2	16	5.03	1,000	100	4.50		Apr-87
2.68	0.04	1.89	7.92	14.37	2.29	1.59	4.68	6.10	11.27	216.2	0	0	100	0	2	16	5.03	1,000	100		1.00	May-94
2.83	0.54	2.92	11.20	20.23	3.33	0.59	4.68	6.10	11.24	216.2	0	0	100	0	2	16	5.03	0				Dec-13
2.44	0.48	2.78	9.84	16.76	2.97	0.86	4.24	5.80	11.45	100.3	0	0	100	0	1	14	4.87	1,000	100	4.50		Jan-95
2.36	0.21	2.12	7.42	12.49	2.21	1.61	4.22	5.80	11.45	100.3	0	0	100	0	1	14	4.87	1,000	100		1.00	Jan-95
2.59	0.68	3.12	10.66	18.21	3.23	0.61	4.23	5.80	11.46	100.3	0	0	100	0	1	14	4.87	0				Dec-13
2.24	0.15	2.06	8.79	15.29	2.64	0.85	4.36	6.05	12.37	565.4	0	0	100	0	1	13	4.97	1,000	100	4.50		Feb-84
2.06	-0.19	1.32	6.40	11.08	1.88	1.6	4.34	6.05	12.41	565.4	0	0	100	0	1	13	4.97	1,000	100		1.00	May-94
1.92	0.02	1.73	7.95	13.60	2.59	0.71	4.02	5.22	11	85.4	0	0	100	0	2	19	4.69	1,000	100	2.75		Oct-85
1.71	-0.46	0.80	5.26	8.91	1.73	1.56	4.01	5.22	11.02	85.4	0	0	100	0	2	19	4.69	1,000	100		1.00	May-94
1.95	0.09	1.87	8.53	14.45	2.75	0.56	4.04	5.22	11.01	85.4	0	0	100	0	2	19	4.69	0				Dec-13
2.69	0.96	2.71	9.53	16.15	2.49	0.9	4.65	5.91	12.85	35.8	0	0	100	0	4	47	4.92	1,000	100	4.50	1.00	Sep-88
2.67	0.99	2.96	10.37	17.69	2.74	0.66	4.63	5.91	12.81	35.8	0	0	100	0	4	47	4.92	0				May-13
2.66	0.99	2.91	10.30	17.71	2.7	0.68	4.64	5.91	12.83	35.8	0	0	100	0	4	47	4.92	0				May-13
2.52	0.40	3.13	10.25	18.81	2.98	0.8	5.21	6.78	11.57	86.2	0	0	100	0	1	21	4.85	1,000	100	4.50		Nov-87
2.35	0.04	2.28	7.82	14.47	2.22	1.55	5.22	6.78	11.54	86.2	0	0	100	0	1	21	4.85	1,000	100		1.00	Apr-95

	MARKET		FUND TYPE, CATEGORY & OBJECTIVE		RATINGS				NEW INVESTORS	
Fund Name	Ticker Symbol	Traded On	Fund Type	Category and (Prospectus Objective)	Overall Rating	Reward Rating	Risk Rating	Recent Up/ Downgrade	Open to New Investors	Telephone
Delaware Tax-Free New York Fund Institutional Class	DTNIX	NAS CM	Open End	US Muni Fixed Inc (Muni Bond - Single State)	C	C-	C+		Y	
Delaware Tax-Free New York II Fund Class A	FNYFX	NAS CM	Open End	US Muni Fixed Inc (Muni Bond - Single State)	C	C-	B-		Y	
Delaware Tax-Free New York II Fund Class R6	FNYJX	NAS CM	Open End	US Muni Fixed Inc (Muni Bond - Single State)	C	C-	B-		Y	
Delaware Tax-Free New York II Fund Institutional Class	FNYHX	NAS CM	Open End	US Muni Fixed Inc (Muni Bond - Single State)	C	C-	B-		Y	
Delaware Tax-Free Oregon Fund Class A	FTORX	NAS CM	Open End	US Muni Fixed Inc (Muni Bond - Single State)	C	C-	B-		Y	
Delaware Tax-Free Oregon Fund Class R6	FTOUX	NAS CM	Open End	US Muni Fixed Inc (Muni Bond - Single State)	C	C	B-		Y	
Delaware Tax-Free Oregon Fund Institutional Class	FTOTX	NAS CM	Open End	US Muni Fixed Inc (Muni Bond - Single State)	C	C	B-		Y	
Delaware Tax-Free Pennsylvania Fund Class A	DELIX	NAS CM	Open End	US Muni Fixed Inc (Muni Bond - Single State)	C	C-	C		Y	
Delaware Tax-Free Pennsylvania Fund Class C	DPTCX	NAS CM	Open End	US Muni Fixed Inc (Muni Bond - Single State)	C	C-	C		Y	
Delaware Tax-Free Pennsylvania Fund Institutional Class	DTPIX	NAS CM	Open End	US Muni Fixed Inc (Muni Bond - Single State)	C	C-	C+		Y	
Delaware Tax-Free USA Fund Class A	DMTFX	NAS CM	Open End	US Muni Fixed Inc (Muni Bond - Natl)	C	C-	C+		Y	
Delaware Tax-Free USA Fund Class C	DUSCX	NAS CM	Open End	US Muni Fixed Inc (Muni Bond - Natl)	C	C-	C+		Y	
Delaware Tax-Free USA Fund Institutional Class	DTFIX	NAS CM	Open End	US Muni Fixed Inc (Muni Bond - Natl)	C	C-	B-		Y	
Delaware Tax-Free USA Intermediate Fund Class A	DMUSX	NAS CM	Open End	US Muni Fixed Inc (Muni Bond - Natl)	C	C-	B-		Y	
Delaware Tax-Free USA Intermediate Fund Class C	DUICX	NAS CM	Open End	US Muni Fixed Inc (Muni Bond - Natl)	C	C-	C+		Y	
Delaware Tax-Free USA Intermediate Institutional Cl	DUSIX	NAS CM	Open End	US Muni Fixed Inc (Muni Bond - Natl)	C	C-	B-		Y	
Destinations Core Fixed Income Fund Class I	DCFFX	NAS CM	Open End	US Fixed Inc (Income)	C+	C	B	Up	Y	
Destinations Core Fixed Income Fund Class Z	DCFZX	NAS CM	Open End	US Fixed Inc (Income)	C+	C	B	Up	Y	
Destinations Global Fixed Income Opportunities Cl I	DGFFX	NAS CM	Open End	Global Fixed Inc (Income)	D+	D+	C	Down	Y	
Destinations Global Fixed Income Opportunities Cl Z	DGFZX	NAS CM	Open End	Global Fixed Inc (Income)	C-	D+	C		Y	
Destinations Low Duration Fixed Income Fund Class I	DLDFX	NAS CM	Open End	US Fixed Inc (Income)	D+	D	C	Down	Y	
Destinations Low Duration Fixed Income Fund Class Z	DLDZX	NAS CM	Open End	US Fixed Inc (Income)	D+	D	C	Down	Y	
Destinations Municipal Fixed Income Fund Class I	DMFFX	NAS CM	Open End	US Muni Fixed Inc (Income)	C	C	B-		Y	
Destinations Municipal Fixed Income Fund Class Z	DMFZX	NAS CM	Open End	US Muni Fixed Inc (Income)	C	C	B-		Y	
Destra InterNatl & Event-Driven Credit Fund Class A Shares	CEDAX	NAS CM	Closed End	Misc (Growth & Income)	D	D	D+		Y	877-855-3434
Destra InterNatl & Event-Driven Credit Fund Class I Shares	CEDIX	NAS CM	Closed End	Misc (Growth & Income)	D	D	D+	Down	Y	877-855-3434
Destra InterNatl & Event-Driven Credit Fund Class L Shares	CEDLX	NAS CM	Closed End	Misc (Growth & Income)	D	D	D+		Y	877-855-3434
Destra InterNatl & Event-Driven Credit Fund Class T Shares	CEDTX	NAS CM	Closed End	Misc (Growth & Income)	D	D	D		Y	877-855-3434
DFA Calif Intermed-Term Muni Bond Portfol Inst Cl Shares	DCIBX	NAS CM	Open End	US Muni Fixed Inc (Muni Bond - Single State)	C	C	B-		Y	512-306-7400
DFA California Muni Real Return Portfolio Institutional Cl	DCARX	NAS CM	Open End	US Muni Fixed Inc (Muni Bond - Single State)	C-	D+	C		Y	512-306-7400
DFA California Short Term Muni Bond Portfol Inst Cl	DFCMX	NAS CM	Open End	US Muni Fixed Inc (Muni Bond - Single State)	C	C-	C+		Y	512-306-7400
DFA Diversified Fixed Income PortfolioInstitutional Class	DFXIX	NAS CM	Open End	US Fixed Inc (Worldwide Bond)	B-	C+	B		Y	512-306-7400
DFA Five-Year Global Fixed Income Portfol Inst Cl	DFGBX	NAS CM	Open End	Global Fixed Inc (Worldwide Bond)	C	C	B-		Y	512-306-7400
DFA Global Core Plus Fixed Income Portfol Inst Cl	DGCFX	NAS CM	Open End	Global Fixed Inc (Worldwide Bond)	C	C	B-		Y	512-306-7400
DFA Global Sustainability Fixed Income Portfol Inst Cl	DGSFX	NAS CM	Open End	Global Fixed Inc (Growth & Income)	D+	D+	B-	Up	Y	512-306-7400
DFA Inflation-Protected Securities Portfol Inst Cl	DIPSX	NAS CM	Open End	US Fixed Inc (Growth & Income)	B	B-	B+	Up	Y	512-306-7400
DFA Intermed Govt Fixed Income Portfol Inst Cl	DFIGX	NAS CM	Open End	US Fixed Inc (Govt Bond - General)	B	B	B		Y	512-306-7400
DFA Intermed-Term Extended Quality Portfol Inst Cl Shares	DFTEX	NAS CM	Open End	US Fixed Inc (Corp Bond - High Quality)	B-	C	B	Up	Y	512-306-7400
DFA Intermediate-Term Muni Bond Portfolio Institutional Cl	DFTIX	NAS CM	Open End	US Muni Fixed Inc (Muni Bond - Natl)	C+	C	B	Up	Y	512-306-7400
DFA Investment Grade Portfolio Institutional Class Shares	DFAPX	NAS CM	Open End	US Fixed Inc (Corp Bond - General)	B	B-	B	Up	Y	512-306-7400
DFA LTIP Portfolio Institutional Class	DRXIX	NAS CM	Open End	US Fixed Inc (Growth & Income)	B	B	B		Y	512-306-7400
DFA MN Municipal Bond Portfolio Institutional Class	DMNBX	NAS CM	Open End	US Muni Fixed Inc (Muni Bond - Single State)	C	C-	C+		Y	512-306-7400
DFA Municipal Bond Portfolio Institutional Class	DFMPX	NAS CM	Open End	US Muni Fixed Inc (Muni Bond - Natl)	C	C	B-		Y	512-306-7400
DFA Municipal Real Return Portfolio Institutional Class	DMREX	NAS CM	Open End	US Muni Fixed Inc (Muni Bond - Natl)	C-	D+	C		Y	512-306-7400
DFA NY Municipal Bond Portfolio Institutional Class	DNYMX	NAS CM	Open End	US Muni Fixed Inc (Muni Bond - Single State)	C	C-	C+		Y	512-306-7400
DFA One-Year Fixed Income Portfolio Institutional Class	DFIHX	NAS CM	Open End	US Fixed Inc (Corp Bond - High Quality)	C	C-	C+		Y	512-306-7400
DFA Oregon Municipal Bond Portfolio Institutional Class	DOGMX	NAS CM	Open End	US Muni Fixed Inc (Muni Bond - Single State)	U	U	U		Y	512-306-7400
DFA Selectively Hedged Global Fixed Income Portfol Inst Cl	DFSHX	NAS CM	Open End	Global Fixed Inc (Worldwide Bond)	C	C-	B-		Y	512-306-7400
DFA Short Term Muni Bond Portfolio Institutional Class	DFSMX	NAS CM	Open End	US Muni Fixed Inc (Muni Bond - Natl)	C	C-	C+		Y	512-306-7400
DFA Short-Duration Real Return Portfolio Institutional Cl	DFAIX	NAS CM	Open End	US Fixed Inc (Multisector Bond)	C	C-	C+		Y	512-306-7400
DFA Short-Term Extended Quality Portfolio Institutional Cl	DFEQX	NAS CM	Open End	US Fixed Inc (Corp Bond - High Quality)	C	C	B-		Y	512-306-7400
DFA Short-Term Government Portfolio Institutional Class	DFFGX	NAS CM	Open End	US Fixed Inc (Govt Bond - General)	C	C-	C+		Y	512-306-7400

★Expanded analysis of this fund is included in Section II.

TOTAL RETURNS & PERFORMANCE									ASSETS		ASSET ALLOCATION & TURNOVER							MINIMUMS		FEES		
3-Month Total Return	6-Month Total Return	1-Year Total Return	3-Year Total Return	5-Year Total Return	Dividend Yield (TTM)	Expense Ratio	3-Yr Std Deviation	Effective Duration	NAV	Total Assets (MIL)	%Cash	%Government Bonds	%Municipal Bonds	%Corporate Bonds	%Other	Turnover Ratio	Average Coupon Rate	Min Initial Investment	Min Additional Investment	Front End Fee (%)	Back End Fee (%)	Inception Date
2.59	0.44	3.29	11.07	20.29	3.23	0.55	5.23	6.78	11.56	86.2	0	0	100	0	1	21	4.85	0				Dec-13
2.49	1.16	3.20	9.66	15.78	2.72	0.86	4.67	6.24	14.31	128.4	0	0	100	0	1	27	5.08	1,000	100	4.50	1.00	Jun-84
2.54	1.28	3.45	10.54	17.31	2.96	0.62	4.67	6.24	14.33	128.4	0	0	100	0	1	27	5.08	0				May-13
2.48	1.22	3.37	10.46	17.39	2.96	0.6	4.65	6.24	14.31	128.4	0	0	100	0	1	27	5.08	0				May-13
2.71	1.95	3.66	9.31	14.82	2.43	0.91	3.93	5.30	13.52	43.8	0	0	100	0	1	50	4.89	1,000	100	4.50	1.00	May-92
2.67	1.97	3.80	9.95	16.21	2.56	0.67	3.91	5.30	13.49	43.8	0	0	100	0	1	50	4.89	0				May-13
2.85	2.08	3.98	10.19	16.54	2.67	0.66	3.9	5.30	13.5	43.8	0	0	100	0	1	50	4.89	0				May-13
2.67	0.10	2.62	10.00	17.88	3.19	0.83	5.08	6.36	7.97	423.9	0	0	100	0	1	23	5.05	1,000	100	4.50		Mar-77
2.49	-0.25	1.87	7.56	13.38	2.41	1.59	5.09	6.36	7.97	423.9	0	0	100	0	1	23	5.05	1,000	100		1.00	Nov-95
2.73	0.08	2.87	10.80	19.15	3.44	0.59	5.07	6.36	7.96	423.9	0	0	100	0	1	23	5.05	0				Dec-13
5.16	1.67	4.41	12.86	20.73	3.34	0.81	6.37	8.93	11.76	571.4	0	0	100	0	1	43	5.18	1,000	100	4.50		Jan-84
4.98	1.31	3.65	10.27	16.29	2.57	1.56	6.34	8.93	11.76	571.4	0	0	100	0	1	43	5.18	1,000	100		1.00	Nov-95
5.28	1.82	4.69	13.70	22.23	3.62	0.56	6.34	8.93	11.85	571.4	0	0	100	0	1	43	5.18	0				Dec-08
3.67	1.13	3.37	11.01	17.18	2.94	0.65	4.8	5.84	12.12	544.2	0	0	100	0	1	25	4.98	1,000	100	2.75		Jan-93
3.47	0.73	2.51	8.15	12.34	2.07	1.5	4.8	5.84	12.11	544.2	0	0	100	0	1	25	4.98	1,000	100		1.00	Nov-95
3.68	1.21	3.43	11.39	17.95	3.09	0.5	4.81	5.84	12.23	544.2	0	0	100	0	1	25	4.98	0				Dec-08
3.56	3.02	4.80	11.44		2.58	0.81	3.31		10.35	2,069	10	26	0	20	0	43	3.09	0				Mar-17
3.60	3.12	4.92	11.84		2.65	0.66	3.3		10.62	2,069	10	26	0	20	0	43	3.09	0				Jul-18
7.61	-2.27	-0.82	5.16		4.28	0.98	6.03		9.46	706.8	15	7	0	74	1	84	5.33	0				Mar-17
7.64	-2.26	-0.76	5.27		4.37	0.83	6.06		9.61	706.8	15	7	0	74	1	84	5.33	0				Jul-18
3.92	-1.92	-1.21	4.46		3.77	0.93	3.69		9.41	361.5	25	4	0	55	0	138	4.86	0				Mar-17
3.99	-1.91	-1.04	4.60		3.85	0.78	3.73		9.6	361.5	25	4	0	55	0	138	4.86	0				Jul-18
2.60	1.79	3.36	9.10		1.88	0.8	3.38		10.46	869.7	8	0	92	0	0	38	4.50	0				Mar-17
2.63	1.86	3.50	9.55		2.02	0.65	3.39		10.49	869.7	8	0	92	0	0	38	4.50	0				Jul-18
8.36	-8.07	-3.13			6.11	2.52			22.79	--	11	16	0	64	7	124	5.90	2,500		5.75		Dec-18
8.38	-7.99	-2.93			6.39	2.27			22.78	--	11	16	0	64	7	124	5.90	100,000				May-18
8.30	-8.20	-3.38			5.83	2.77			22.79	--	11	16	0	64	7	124	5.90	2,500		4.25		Dec-18
8.22	-8.33	-3.59			5.57	3.02			22.78	--	11	16	0	64	7	124	5.90	2,500		3.00		Dec-18
2.82	1.91	3.11	7.27	12.38	1.45	0.23	2.59	3.44	10.86	541.4	6	0	94	0	0	19	4.81	0				Nov-11
4.73	-1.51	0.00			1.32	0.3		3.23	9.93	147.1	8	48	48	0	0	12	2.94	0				Nov-17
0.77	0.62	1.24	3.30	5.52	1.14	0.22	0.77	0.80	10.31	1,100	29	0	71	0	0	97	4.77	0				Apr-07
1.25	5.53	6.87	12.85		2.1	0.15	2.48	5.21	10.39	1,177	15	70	0	4	0	3	2.64	0				Aug-16
0.93	1.11	2.01	7.40	11.77	2.28	0.26	1.28	1.72	10.85	13,457	26	27	0	16	0	46	1.02	0				Nov-90
7.38	3.10	5.58			1.89	0.29		7.05	10.62	1,760	15	11	0	43	0	14	3.22	0				Jan-18
5.56	4.47	6.63			2.69	0.28		7.47	11.2	405.9	23	22	0	30	0	7	3.00	0				Nov-18
4.58	6.32	8.04	16.21	21.12	2.12	0.11	3.76	8.00	12.78	5,056	1	99	0	0	0	28	1.68	0				Sep-06
0.97	9.62	11.14	18.72	24.29	2.04	0.12	4.31	6.96	13.88	5,344	1	99	0	0	0	25	3.47	0				Oct-90
8.77	6.00	9.68	19.81	31.25	2.9	0.22	6.06	7.05	11.74	1,870	1	10	0	88	0	19	4.12	0				Jul-10
2.59	2.73	3.99	8.61	13.81	1.48	0.21	2.44	3.62	10.59	2,030	4	0	96	0	0	12	4.84	0				Mar-12
4.90	7.34	9.88	18.64	26.49	2.53	0.22	3.73	5.73	11.97	9,643	1	42	0	53	0	21	3.62	0				Mar-11
6.53	18.63	26.74	40.45	54.16	2.17	0.15	11.69	24.74	11.9	240.5	1	99	0	0	0	38	0.96	0				Mar-12
1.55	1.64	2.62	4.84		1.09	0.32		2.01	10.17	70.8	0	0	100	0	0	14	4.46	0				Jul-17
2.40	2.42	3.56	7.57	12.68	1.44	0.23	2.2	3.28	10.51	496.4	5	0	95	0	0	13	4.83	0				Mar-15
5.25	-0.43	1.33	5.90	10.16	1.6	0.24	4.38	3.95	10	765.8	6	49	48	0	0	6	2.88	0				Nov-14
1.06	1.04	1.78	4.44	9.45	1.29	0.25	1.17	1.36	10.31	106.6	12	0	88	0	0	27	4.37	0				Jun-15
0.19	0.55	1.63	5.28	6.78	1.76	0.17	0.36	0.17	10.3	7,217	72	22	0	6	0	30	1.03	0				Jul-83
2.50	2.30					0.32		3.37	10.2	33.6	10	0	90	0	0	0	4.93	0				Sep-19
2.43	0.93	2.30	7.69	12.76	2.51	0.17	1.82	1.67	9.67	1,120	19	17	0	36	0	62	1.53	0				Jan-08
0.57	0.77	1.34	3.50	5.72	1.12	0.22	0.6	0.66	10.2	2,562	29	0	71	0	0	90	4.51	0				Aug-02
3.56	-0.30	1.40	6.68	10.72	2.56	0.22	2.83	1.35	9.87	1,304	10	55	0	32	0	42	1.57	0				Nov-13
2.10	1.13	2.42	7.55	11.97	2.18	0.22	1.5	1.19	10.9	6,103	25	19	0	40	0	51	1.80	0				Mar-09
-0.04	0.38	1.33	3.87	5.75	1.69	0.19	1.05	0.19	10.56	2,621	43	57	0	0	0	58		0				Jun-87

	MARKET			FUND TYPE, CATEGORY & OBJECTIVE	RATINGS				NEW INVESTORS	
Fund Name	Ticker Symbol	Traded On	Fund Type	Category and (Prospectus Objective)	Overall Rating	Reward Rating	Risk Rating	Recent Up/ Downgrade	Open to New Investors	Telephone
DFA Social Fixed Income Portfolio Institutional Class	DSFIX	NAS CM	Open End	US Fixed Inc (Income)	B	B-	B	Up	Y	512-306-7400
DFA Targeted Credit Portfolio Institutional Class	DTCPX	NAS CM	Open End	US Fixed Inc (Growth & Income)	C	C-	C+		Y	512-306-7400
DFA Two Year Global Fixed Income Portfol Inst Cl	DFGFX	NAS CM	Open End	Global Fixed Inc (Worldwide Bond)	C	C-	B-		Y	512-306-7400
DFA Two-Year Fixed Income Portfolio Institutional Class	DFCFX	NAS CM	Open End	US Fixed Inc (Corp Bond - General)	C	C-	C+			512-306-7400
DFA Two-Year Government Portfolio Institutional Class	DFYGX	NAS CM	Open End	US Fixed Inc (Govt Bond - General)	C	C-	C+			512-306-7400
DFA World ex U.S. Govt Fixed Income Portfol Inst Cl Shares	DWFIX	NAS CM	Open End	Global Fixed Inc (Govt Bond - General)	B-	C	B+		Y	512-306-7400
Diamond Hill Core Bond Fund Class A	DHRAX	NAS CM	Open End	US Fixed Inc (Growth & Income)	B	C+	B+	Up	Y	888-226-5595
Diamond Hill Core Bond Fund Class I	DHRIX	NAS CM	Open End	US Fixed Inc (Growth & Income)	B	C+	A-	Up	Y	888-226-5595
Diamond Hill Core Bond Fund Class Y	DHRYX	NAS CM	Open End	US Fixed Inc (Growth & Income)	B	C+	A-	Up	Y	888-226-5595
Diamond Hill Corporate Credit Fund Class A	DSIAX	NAS CM	Open End	US Fixed Inc (Income)	C-	D+	C	Down	Y	888-226-5595
Diamond Hill Corporate Credit Fund Class I	DHSTX	NAS CM	Open End	US Fixed Inc (Income)	C-	D+	C	Down	Y	888-226-5595
Diamond Hill Corporate Credit Fund Class Y	DSIYX	NAS CM	Open End	US Fixed Inc (Income)	C-	D+	C	Down	Y	888-226-5595
Diamond Hill High Yield Fund Class A	DHHAX	NAS CM	Open End	US Fixed Inc (Corp Bond - High Yield)	C	C-	C		Y	888-226-5595
Diamond Hill High Yield Fund Class I	DHHIX	NAS CM	Open End	US Fixed Inc (Corp Bond - High Yield)	C	C-	C+		Y	888-226-5595
Diamond Hill High Yield Fund Class Y	DHHYX	NAS CM	Open End	US Fixed Inc (Corp Bond - High Yield)	C	C-	B-		Y	888-226-5595
Diamond Hill Short Duration Total Return Fund Class A	DHEAX	NAS CM	Open End	US Fixed Inc (Growth & Income)	D+	D	C-	Down	Y	888-226-5595
Diamond Hill Short Duration Total Return Fund Class I	DHEIX	NAS CM	Open End	US Fixed Inc (Growth & Income)	D+	D	C-	Down	Y	888-226-5595
Diamond Hill Short Duration Total Return Fund Class Y	DHEYX	NAS CM	Open End	US Fixed Inc (Growth & Income)	D+	D	C-	Down	Y	888-226-5595
Dodge & Cox Global Bond Fund	DODLX	NAS CM	Open End	Global Fixed Inc (Worldwide Bond)	C+	C	B	Up	Y	415-981-1710
★ Dodge & Cox Income Fund	DODIX	NAS CM	Open End	US Fixed Inc (Income)	B	C+	B+	Up	Y	415-981-1710
Domini Impact Bond Fund Institutional Shares	DSBIX	NAS CM	Open End	US Fixed Inc (Corp Bond - General)	B	B-	B+	Up	Y	800-582-6757
Domini Impact Bond Fund Investor Shares	DSBFX	NAS CM	Open End	US Fixed Inc (Corp Bond - General)	B	B-	B+	Up	Y	800-582-6757
DoubleLine Core Fixed Income Fund Class I	DBLFX	NAS CM	Open End	US Fixed Inc (Growth & Income)	C	C	B-		Y	877-354-6311
DoubleLine Core Fixed Income Fund Class N	DLFNX	NAS CM	Open End	US Fixed Inc (Growth & Income)	C	C-	B-		Y	877-354-6311
DoubleLine Core Fixed Income Fund Class R6	DDCFX	NAS CM	Open End	US Fixed Inc (Growth & Income)	C	C	B-		Y	877-354-6311
DoubleLine Emerging Markets Fixed Income Fund Class I	DBLEX	NAS CM	Open End	Emerg Mkts Fixed Inc (Growth & Income)	D+	D+	C-	Down	Y	877-354-6311
DoubleLine Emerging Markets Fixed Income Fund Class N	DLENX	NAS CM	Open End	Emerg Mkts Fixed Inc (Growth & Income)	D+	D	C-	Down	Y	877-354-6311
DoubleLine Emerg Mkts Local Currency Bond Fund Class I	DBELX	NAS CM	Open End	Emerg Mkts Fixed Inc (Diversified Emerg Mkts)	D-	D	D		Y	877-354-6311
DoubleLine Emerg Mkts Local Currency Bond Fund Class N	DLELX	NAS CM	Open End	Emerg Mkts Fixed Inc (Diversified Emerg Mkts)	D-	D	D		Y	877-354-6311
DoubleLine Flexible Income Fund Class I	DFLEX	NAS CM	Open End	Fixed Inc Misc (Income)	D+	D	C-	Down	Y	877-354-6311
DoubleLine Flexible Income Fund Class N	DLINX	NAS CM	Open End	Fixed Inc Misc (Income)	D	D	C-	Down	Y	877-354-6311
DoubleLine Flexible Income Fund Class R6	DFFLX	NAS CM	Open End	Fixed Inc Misc (Income)	D+	D	C-	Down	Y	877-354-6311
DoubleLine Floating Rate Fund Class I Shares	DBFRX	NAS CM	Open End	US Fixed Inc (Income)	D+	D	C	Down	Y	877-354-6311
DoubleLine Floating Rate Fund Class N Shares	DLFRX	NAS CM	Open End	US Fixed Inc (Income)	D+	D	C-	Down	Y	877-354-6311
DoubleLine Global Bond Fund Class I	DBLGX	NAS CM	Open End	Global Fixed Inc (Growth & Income)	C	C-	C		Y	877-354-6311
DoubleLine Global Bond Fund Class N	DLGBX	NAS CM	Open End	Global Fixed Inc (Growth & Income)	C	C-	C		Y	877-354-6311
DoubleLine Income Fund Class I	DBLIX	NAS CM	Open End	US Fixed Inc (Income)	U	U	U		Y	877-354-6311
DoubleLine Income Fund Class N	DBLNX	NAS CM	Open End	US Fixed Inc (Income)	U	U	U		Y	877-354-6311
DoubleLine Income Solutions Fund	DSL	NYSE	Closed End	Global Fixed Inc (Multisector Bond)	D	D-	D	Down	Y	877-354-6311
DoubleLine Infrastructure Income Fund Class I	BILDX	NAS CM	Open End	US Fixed Inc (Income)	C	C-	C		Y	877-354-6311
DoubleLine Infrastructure Income Fund Class N	BILTX	NAS CM	Open End	US Fixed Inc (Income)	C	C-	C+		Y	877-354-6311
DoubleLine Long Duration Total Return Bond Fund Class I	DBLDX	NAS CM	Open End	US Fixed Inc (Growth & Income)	B	B	B		Y	877-354-6311
DoubleLine Long Duration Total Return Bond Fund Class N	DLLDX	NAS CM	Open End	US Fixed Inc (Growth & Income)	B	B	B-		Y	877-354-6311
DoubleLine Low Duration Bond Fund Class I	DBLSX	NAS CM	Open End	US Fixed Inc (Income)	C-	D+	C	Down	Y	877-354-6311
DoubleLine Low Duration Bond Fund Class N	DLSNX	NAS CM	Open End	US Fixed Inc (Income)	C-	D+	C	Down	Y	877-354-6311
DoubleLine Low Duration Bond Fund Class R6	DDLDX	NAS CM	Open End	US Fixed Inc (Income)	C-	D+	C	Down	Y	877-354-6311
DoubleLine Low Duration Emerg Mkts Fixed Income Cl I	DBLLX	NAS CM	Open End	Emerg Mkts Fixed Inc (Diversified Emerg Mkts)	C	C-	C+		Y	877-354-6311
DoubleLine Low Duration Emerg Mkts Fixed Income Cl N	DELNX	NAS CM	Open End	Emerg Mkts Fixed Inc (Diversified Emerg Mkts)	C	C-	C+		Y	877-354-6311
Doubleline Opportunistic Credit Fund	DBL	NYSE	Closed End	US Fixed Inc (Multisector Bond)	D+	D+	C-	Down	Y	877-354-6311
Doubleline Selective Credit Fund Class I	DBSCX	NAS CM	Open End	US Fixed Inc (Growth)	D+	D	C-	Down	Y	877-354-6311
DoubleLine Total Return Bond Fund Class I	DBLTX	NAS CM	Open End	US Fixed Inc (Govt Bond - General)	C	C	B		Y	877-354-6311
★ DoubleLine Total Return Bond Fund Class N	DLTNX	NAS CM	Open End	US Fixed Inc (Govt Bond - General)	C	C	B-		Y	877-354-6311

★Expanded analysis of this fund is included in Section II.

TOTAL RETURNS & PERFORMANCE									ASSETS		ASSET ALLOCATION & TURNOVER							MINIMUMS		FEES		
3-Month Total Return	6-Month Total Return	1-Year Total Return	3-Year Total Return	5-Year Total Return	Dividend Yield (TTM)	Expense Ratio	3-Yr Std Deviation	Effective Duration	NAV	Total Assets (MIL)	%Cash	%Government Bonds	%Municipal Bonds	%Corporate Bonds	%Other	Turnover Ratio	Average Coupon Rate	Min Initial Investment	Min Additional Investment	Front End Fee (%)	Back End Fee (%)	Inception Date
4.92	7.42	9.81	18.49		2.34	0.27	3.83	5.78	10.89	373.1	1	41	0	54	0	15	3.53	0				Apr-16
4.14	0.41	2.19	8.48	14.08	3.08	0.2	3.19	2.00	10.04	766.7	5	3	0	66	0	17	2.50	0				May-15
0.40	0.70	1.82	5.81	7.57	2.05	0.17	0.52	0.47	9.98	5,227	49	23	0	12	0	59	1.79	0				Feb-96
0.31	0.58	1.63	5.27	6.95	2.1	0.21	0.5	0.18	9.96	99.2	64	28	0	8	0	50	1.21	0				Jun-96
0.04	0.48	1.36	4.19	5.03	1.67	0.2	0.51	0.22	9.78	193.4	27	73	0	0	0	57		0				Jun-96
2.39	4.29	4.86	19.40	30.26	3.08	0.2	4.5	9.93	10.68	1,500	29	40	0	2	0	49	2.37	0				Dec-11
4.02	6.15	8.11	17.04		2.22	0.76	3.69	5.81	10.7	200.3	4	22	0	17	0	29	3.28	2,500		3.50		Jul-16
4.09	6.30	8.41	17.97		2.5	0.47	3.7	5.81	10.7	200.3	4	22	0	17	0	29	3.28	2,500				Jul-16
4.12	6.35	8.53	18.40		2.6	0.35	3.63	5.81	10.71	200.3	4	22	0	17	0	29	3.28	500,000				Jul-16
11.11	-1.16	2.33	14.59	31.09	5.02	0.92	8.3	5.08	11.07	1,253	8	0	0	88	0	132	5.73	2,500		3.50		Sep-02
11.12	-1.12	2.62	15.59	32.97	5.32	0.63	8.26	5.08	11.03	1,253	8	0	0	88	0	132	5.73	2,500				Jan-05
11.26	-0.98	2.75	16.11	33.87	5.45	0.51	8.26	5.08	11.03	1,253	8	0	0	88	0	132	5.73	500,000				Dec-11
13.21	0.60	4.72	20.45	40.82	5.29	0.96	8.79	5.94	10.81	343.1	9	0	0	88	0	164	5.60	2,500		3.50		Dec-15
13.38	0.75	5.10	21.55	42.81	5.57	0.67	8.86	5.94	10.82	343.1	9	0	0	88	0	164	5.60	2,500				Dec-14
13.29	0.79	5.21	21.93	43.54	5.67	0.55	8.8	5.94	10.82	343.1	9	0	0	88	0	164	5.60	500,000				Dec-14
5.18	-2.82	-1.48	6.20		3.97	0.81	5.51	1.37	9.66	734.3	5	0	0	2	0	54	3.80	2,500		2.25		Jul-16
5.25	-2.77	-1.21	7.13		4.26	0.52	5.55	1.37	9.66	734.3	5	0	0	2	0	54	3.80	2,500				Jul-16
5.27	-2.62	-1.10	7.44		4.38	0.4	5.55	1.37	9.67	734.3	5	0	0	2	0	54	3.80	500,000				Jul-16
11.41	2.88	6.60	16.48	28.57	3.36	0.45	6.98	3.20	11.42	568.0	2	26	3	59	0	60	5.01	2,500	100			May-14
6.01	5.27	8.38	17.02	26.26	2.87	0.42	3.41	4.20	14.53	63,192	2	9	3	39	0	49	4.21	2,500	100			Jan-89
4.91	7.07	9.93	18.24	27.15	2.26	0.57	3.39		12.2	182.0	21	18	5	16	0	319	3.22	500,000				Nov-11
4.81	6.88	9.65	17.18	25.40	1.97	0.87	3.36		12.28	182.0	21	18	5	16	0	319	3.22	2,500	100			Jun-00
5.41	1.93	3.87	11.79	19.68	3.33	0.48	4.58	4.81	11.11	11,587	3	30	0	30	0	43	3.40	100,000	100			Jun-10
5.34	1.71	3.61	10.96	18.10	3.08	0.73	4.59	4.81	11.1	11,587	3	30	0	30	0	43	3.40	2,000	100			Jun-10
5.41	1.95	3.90	11.82	19.71		0.43	4.57	4.81	11.11	11,587	3	30	0	30	0	43	3.40	0				Jul-19
14.79	-3.33	-1.43	7.11	21.00	5.01	0.89	11.24	4.78	10.01	901.7	2	18	0	80	0	37	5.42	100,000	100			Apr-10
14.71	-3.46	-1.71	6.27	19.45	4.73	1.14	11.23	4.78	10.01	901.7	2	18	0	80	0	37	5.42	2,000	100			Apr-10
7.98	-6.36	-5.53				0.91			9.33	9.4	10	85	0	5	0		5.46	100,000	100			Jun-19
7.98	-6.43	-5.72				1.16			9.33	9.4	10	85	0	5	0		5.46	2,000	100			Jun-19
9.85	-3.94	-2.38	5.14	12.16	4.55	0.76	8.52	1.62	9.13	1,104	6	11	0	26	0	41	4.27	100,000	100			Apr-14
9.78	-4.08	-2.63	4.36	10.68	4.29	1.01	8.53	1.62	9.12	1,104	6	11	0	26	0	41	4.27	2,000	100			Apr-14
9.86	-3.92	-2.34	5.18	12.20		0.71	8.53	1.62	9.13	1,104	6	11	0	26	0	41	4.27	0				Jul-19
7.87	-3.89	-1.97	4.83	10.38	5.07	0.65	7.13	0.54	9.01	186.6	0	0	0	99	0	58	4.38	100,000	100			Feb-13
7.78	-4.12	-2.34	4.00	8.74	4.79	0.89	7.17	0.54	9.02	186.6	0	0	0	99	0	58	4.38	2,000	100			Feb-13
2.05	-0.38	0.02	3.71		1.11	0.55	4.16	5.64	10.42	1,184	7	86	0	0	0	21	2.38	100,000	100			Dec-15
2.05	-0.38	-0.14	2.99		0.72	0.8	4.12	5.64	10.42	1,184	7	86	0	0	0	21	2.38	2,000	100			Dec-15
6.65	-12.27					0.66		1.53	8.51	68.3	1	17	0	0	0	33	3.86	100,000	100			Sep-19
6.60	-12.38					0.91		1.53	8.51	68.3	1	17	0	0	0	33	3.86	2,000	100			Sep-19
25.27	-15.80	-14.73	-3.17	12.19	12.23	2.28	21.64		15.62	1,467	3	3	0	71	0	40	7.47					Apr-13
8.69	0.86	3.24	11.70		3.26	0.59	6.74	3.42	10.31	565.2	5	1	0	54	0	10	3.95	100,000	100			Apr-16
8.62	0.73	3.00	10.85		3.02	0.84	6.72	3.42	10.31	565.2	5	1	0	54	0	10	3.95	2,000	100			Apr-16
1.14	17.14	20.17	31.91	45.98	2.21	0.65	10.41	16.42	11.82	105.2	-12	54	0	0	0	40	2.84	100,000	100			Dec-14
0.99	16.90	19.77	30.82	44.05	1.98	0.9	10.39	16.42	11.81	105.2	-12	54	0	0	0	40	2.84	2,000	100			Dec-14
4.33	-0.25	1.10	6.93	11.67	3.04	0.43	3.34	0.93	9.86	6,727	5	11	0	23	0	60	2.66	100,000	100			Sep-11
4.27	-0.38	0.84	6.14	10.19	2.79	0.68	3.36	0.93	9.85	6,727	5	11	0	23	0	60	2.66	2,000	100			Sep-11
4.34	-0.24	1.12	6.96	11.70		0.38	3.34	0.93	9.86	6,727	5	11	0	23	0	60	2.66	0				Jul-19
5.12	0.17	1.79	8.98	15.25	3.15	0.59	3.82	1.79	9.77	215.8	9	19	0	71	0	65	4.46	100,000	100			Apr-14
4.94	0.04	1.53	8.13	13.77	2.89	0.84	3.78	1.79	9.78	215.8	9	19	0	71	0	65	4.46	2,000	100			Apr-14
12.39	-3.69	-0.90	10.05	26.26	4.76		11.6		19.07	274.1	2	3	0	6	0	26	5.68					Jan-12
8.11	-3.17	-1.59	9.09	22.83	5.61	0.64	7.46		8.23	1,011	8	0	0	0	0	34	3.48	100,000				Aug-14
3.40	2.63	4.14	11.93	18.91	3.61	0.48	3.46	3.23	10.72	50,032	0	11	0	1	0	31	3.23	100,000	100			Apr-10
3.24	2.40	3.78	10.99	17.32	3.36	0.73	3.4	3.23	10.71	50,032	0	11	0	1	0	31	3.23	2,000	100			Apr-10

	MARKET		FUND TYPE, CATEGORY & OBJECTIVE		RATINGS				NEW INVESTORS	
Fund Name	Ticker Symbol	Traded On	Fund Type	Category and (Prospectus Objective)	Overall Rating	Reward Rating	Risk Rating	Recent Up/ Downgrade	Open to New Investors	Telephone
★ DoubleLine Total Return Bond Fund Class R6	DDTRX	NAS CM	Open End	US Fixed Inc (Govt Bond - General)	C	C	C+		Y	877-354-6311
DoubleLine Ultra Short Bond Fund Class I	DBULX	NAS CM	Open End	US Fixed Inc (Income)	C	C-	C+		Y	877-354-6311
DoubleLine Ultra Short Bond Fund Class N	DLUSX	NAS CM	Open End	US Fixed Inc (Income)	C	C-	C+		Y	877-354-6311
DoubleLine Yield Opportunities Fund	DLY	NYSE	Closed End	US Fixed Inc (Growth & Income)	U	U	U		Y	877-354-6311
Dreyfus AMT-Free Muni Cash Management Plus Inst Shares	DIMXX	NAS CM	Money Mkt	US Money Mkt (Money Mkt - Fed Tax Exmpt)	C	C-	C+		Y	800-645-6561
Dreyfus AMT-Free Muni Cash Management Plus Investor Shares	DVMXX	NAS CM	Money Mkt	US Money Mkt (Money Mkt - Fed Tax Exmpt)	C	C-	C		Y	800-645-6561
Dreyfus AMT-Free New York Muni Cash Management Inst Shares	DIYXX	NAS CM	Money Mkt	US Money Mkt (Money Mkt - Single State)	C	C-	C+		Y	800-645-6561
Dreyfus AMT-Free New York Muni Cash Mgmt Investor Shares	DVYXX	NAS CM	Money Mkt	US Money Mkt (Money Mkt - Single State)	C	C-	C		Y	800-645-6561
Dreyfus AMT-Free Tax Exempt Cash Mgmt Investor Shares	DEVXX	NAS CM	Money Mkt	US Money Mkt (Money Mkt - Fed Tax Exmpt)	C	C-	C		Y	800-645-6561
Dreyfus AMT-Free Tax Exempt Cash Mgmt Particip Shares	DEIXX	NAS CM	Money Mkt	US Money Mkt (Money Mkt - Fed Tax Exmpt)	C	C-	C+		Y	800-645-6561
Dreyfus Basic Money Market Fund	DBAXX	NAS CM	Money Mkt	US Money Mkt (Money Mkt - Taxable)	C	C-	C+		Y	800-645-6561
Dreyfus Cash Management Fund Administrative Class	DACXX	NAS CM	Money Mkt	US Money Mkt (Money Mkt - Taxable)	C	C-	C+		Y	800-645-6561
Dreyfus Cash Management Fund Institutional Class	DICXX	NAS CM	Money Mkt	US Money Mkt (Money Mkt - Taxable)	C	C-	C+		Y	800-645-6561
Dreyfus Cash Management Fund Investor Class	DVCXX	NAS CM	Money Mkt	US Money Mkt (Money Mkt - Taxable)	C	C-	C+		Y	800-645-6561
Dreyfus General Govt Securities Money Mkt Fund Brex Shares	GGBXX	NAS CM	Money Mkt	US Money Mkt (Money Mkt - Govt)	C	C-	C		Y	800-645-6561
Dreyfus General Govt Securities Money Mkt Dreyfus Cl	GGDXX	NAS CM	Money Mkt	US Money Mkt (Money Mkt - Govt)	C	C-	C+		Y	800-645-6561
Dreyfus General Money Market Fund, Inc. Class A	GMMXX	NAS CM	Money Mkt	US Money Mkt (Money Mkt - General)	C	C-	C+		Y	800-645-6561
Dreyfus General Money Market Fund, Inc. Class B	GMBXX	NAS CM	Money Mkt	US Money Mkt (Money Mkt - General)	C	C-	C			800-645-6561
Dreyfus General Money Market Fund, Inc. Dreyfus Class	GMGXX	NAS CM	Money Mkt	US Money Mkt (Money Mkt - General)	C	C-	C+		Y	800-645-6561
Dreyfus Govt Cash Management Fund Administrative Shares	DAGXX	NAS CM	Money Mkt	US Money Mkt (Money Mkt - Govt)	C	C-	C+		Y	800-645-6561
Dreyfus Govt Cash Management Fund Institutional Shares	DGCXX	NAS CM	Money Mkt	US Money Mkt (Money Mkt - Govt)	C	C-	C+		Y	800-645-6561
Dreyfus Government Cash Management Fund Investor Shares	DGVXX	NAS CM	Money Mkt	US Money Mkt (Money Mkt - Govt)	C	C-	C+		Y	800-645-6561
Dreyfus Government Cash Management Fund Participant Shares	DPGXX	NAS CM	Money Mkt	US Money Mkt (Money Mkt - Govt)	C	C-	C		Y	800-645-6561
Dreyfus Govt Securities Cash Mgmt Administrative Shares	DAPXX	NAS CM	Money Mkt	US Money Mkt (Money Mkt - Govt)	C	C-	C+		Y	800-645-6561
Dreyfus Govt Securities Cash Management Inst Shares	DIPXX	NAS CM	Money Mkt	US Money Mkt (Money Mkt - Govt)	C	C-	C+		Y	800-645-6561
Dreyfus Govt Securities Cash Management Investor Shares	DVPXX	NAS CM	Money Mkt	US Money Mkt (Money Mkt - Govt)	C	C-	C+		Y	800-645-6561
Dreyfus Govt Securities Cash Management Participant Shares	DGPXX	NAS CM	Money Mkt	US Money Mkt (Money Mkt - Govt)	C	C-	C+		Y	800-645-6561
Dreyfus Inst Preferred Govt Money Mkt Hamilton Shares	DSHXX	NAS CM	Money Mkt	US Money Mkt (Money Mkt - Govt)	C	C-	C+		Y	800-645-6561
Dreyfus Inst Preferred Govt Money Mkt Inst Shares	DSVXX	NAS CM	Money Mkt	US Money Mkt (Money Mkt - Govt)	C	C-	C+		Y	800-645-6561
Dreyfus Inst Preferred Govt Money Mkt Premier Shares	DERXX	NAS CM	Money Mkt	US Money Mkt (Money Mkt - Govt)	C	C-	C+		Y	800-645-6561
Dreyfus Institutional Preferred Govt Plus Money Mkt Fund	US26200T2087		Money Mkt	US Money Mkt (Money Mkt - Govt)	U	U	U		Y	800-645-6561
Dreyfus Institutional Preferred Money Mkt Hamilton Shares	DRSXX	NAS CM	Money Mkt	US Money Mkt (Money Mkt - Taxable)	C	C-	C+		Y	800-645-6561
Dreyfus Inst Preferred Money Mkt Inst Shares	DIQXX	NAS CM	Money Mkt	US Money Mkt (Money Mkt - Taxable)	C	C-	C+		Y	800-645-6561
Dreyfus Inst Pref Treas Sec Money Mkt Hamilton Shares	CEAXX	NAS CM	Money Mkt	US Money Mkt (Money Mkt - Govt)	C	C-	C+		Y	800-645-6561
Dreyfus Inst Pref Treas Sec Money Mkt Inst Shares	CEIXX	NAS CM	Money Mkt	US Money Mkt (Money Mkt - Govt)	C	C-	C+		Y	800-645-6561
Dreyfus Inst Pref Treas Sec Money Mkt Prem Shares	CEBXX	NAS CM	Money Mkt	US Money Mkt (Money Mkt - Govt)	C	C-	C+			800-645-6561
Dreyfus Inst Treas Oblig Cash Advantage Hamilton Shares	DHLXX	NAS CM	Money Mkt	US Money Mkt (Money Mkt - Treasury)	C	C-	C+		Y	800-645-6561
Dreyfus Inst Treas Obligations Cash Advantage Inst Shares	DNSXX	NAS CM	Money Mkt	US Money Mkt (Money Mkt - Treasury)	C	C-	C+		Y	800-645-6561
Dreyfus Inst Treas Oblig Cash Advantage Premier Shares	DRRXX	NAS CM	Money Mkt	US Money Mkt (Money Mkt - Treasury)	C	C-	C+		Y	800-645-6561
Dreyfus Inst Treas Sec Cash Adv Hamilton Shares	DHMXX	NAS CM	Money Mkt	US Money Mkt (Money Mkt - Govt)	C	C-	C+		Y	800-645-6561
Dreyfus Inst Treas Securities Cash Advantage Inst Shares	DUPXX	NAS CM	Money Mkt	US Money Mkt (Money Mkt - Govt)	C	C-	C+		Y	800-645-6561
Dreyfus Inst Treas Sec Cash Adv Prem Shares	DMEXX	NAS CM	Money Mkt	US Money Mkt (Money Mkt - Govt)	C	C-	C		Y	800-645-6561
Dreyfus Liquid Assets, Inc. Class 1	DLAXX	NAS CM	Money Mkt	US Money Mkt (Money Mkt - Taxable)	C	C-	C+		Y	800-645-6561
Dreyfus Liquid Assets, Inc. Class 2	DLBXX	NAS CM	Money Mkt	US Money Mkt (Money Mkt - Taxable)	C	C	C+		Y	800-645-6561
Dreyfus Liquid Assets, Inc. Class Z	DLZXX	NAS CM	Money Mkt	US Money Mkt (Money Mkt - Taxable)	C	C-	C+		Y	800-645-6561
Dreyfus Prime Money Market Fund Class A	CZEXX	NAS CM	Money Mkt	US Money Mkt (Money Mkt - Taxable)	C	C-	C+		Y	800-645-6561
Dreyfus Treasury and Agency Liquidity Money Market Fund	DTLXX	NAS CM	Money Mkt	US Money Mkt (Money Mkt - Treasury)	C	C-	C		Y	800-645-6561
Dreyfus Treas Oblig Cash Management Administrative Shares	DTAXX	NAS CM	Money Mkt	US Money Mkt (Money Mkt - Govt)	C	C-	C+		Y	800-645-6561
Dreyfus Treas Obligations Cash Management Inst Shares	DTRXX	NAS CM	Money Mkt	US Money Mkt (Money Mkt - Govt)	C	C-	C+		Y	800-645-6561
Dreyfus Treas Obligations Cash Management Investor Shares	DTVXX	NAS CM	Money Mkt	US Money Mkt (Money Mkt - Govt)	C	C-	C+		Y	800-645-6561
Dreyfus Treas Obligations Cash Management Particip Shares	DTPXX	NAS CM	Money Mkt	US Money Mkt (Money Mkt - Govt)	C	C-	C+		Y	800-645-6561
Dreyfus Treas Securities Cash Mgmt Administrative Shares	DARXX	NAS CM	Money Mkt	US Money Mkt (Money Mkt - Govt)	C	C-	C+		Y	800-645-6561

★ Expanded analysis of this fund is included in Section II.

TOTAL RETURNS & PERFORMANCE									ASSETS		ASSET ALLOCATION & TURNOVER							MINIMUMS		FEES		
3-Month Total Return	6-Month Total Return	1-Year Total Return	3-Year Total Return	5-Year Total Return	Dividend Yield (TTM)	Expense Ratio	3-Yr Std Deviation	Effective Duration	NAV	Total Assets (MIL)	%Cash	%Government Bonds	%Municipal Bonds	%Corporate Bonds	%Other	Turnover Ratio	Average Coupon Rate	Min Initial Investment	Min Additional Investment	Front End Fee (%)	Back End Fee (%)	Inception Date
3.42	2.55	4.19	11.98	18.96		0.43	3.44	3.23	10.72	50,032	0	11	0	1	0	31	3.23	0				Jul-19
2.36	0.38	1.57	5.74		1.9	0.22	1.65	0.12	10.02	237.9	39	6	0	55	0	60	1.46	100,000	100			Jun-16
2.29	0.25	1.41	5.15		1.65	0.47	1.57	0.12	10.04	237.9	39	6	0	55	0	60	1.46	2,000	100			Jun-16
6.76						2.91			18.46	842.8	25	1	0	36	0		6.04					Feb-20
0.04	0.32	0.77	2.92	3.76	0.88	0.58	0.1		1	78.0	17	0	83	0	0			10,000,000				Oct-90
0.02	0.24	0.58	2.22	2.89	0.66	0.78	0.1		1	78.0	17	0	83	0	0			10,000,000				Sep-93
0.09	0.39	0.92	3.10	3.53	1	0.35	0.11		1	141.0	15	0	85	0	0			10,000,000				Nov-91
0.06	0.30	0.71	2.39	2.55	0.76	0.59	0.11		1	141.0	15	0	85	0	0			10,000,000				Jan-94
0.06	0.29	0.77	2.61	2.83	0.89	0.49	0.11		0.9999	888.7	19	0	81	0	0			10,000,000				Jan-94
0.07	0.39	0.98	3.33	3.84	1.12	0.26	0.12		0.9999	888.7	19	0	81	0	0			10,000,000				Mar-85
0.04	0.34	1.19	4.45	4.93	1.37	0.45	0.16		1	140.7	100	0	0	0	0			25,000	100			May-92
0.14	0.52	1.49	5.36	6.02	1.58	0.31	0.16		1.0013	6,065	100	0	0	0	0			10,000,000				Nov-96
0.16	0.56	1.59	5.68	6.51	1.68	0.21	0.16		1.0013	6,065	100	0	0	0	0			10,000,000				Mar-85
0.10	0.43	1.35	4.88	5.30	1.43	0.46	0.16		1.0013	6,065	100	0	0	0	0			10,000,000				Jan-94
0.00	0.05	0.53	2.08	1.59		1.19			1	3,394	70	30	0	0	0			2,500	0			Dec-19
0.00	0.21	0.95	3.52	3.63	1.1	0.58	0.17		1	3,394	70	30	0	0	0			2,500	100			Sep-15
0.00	0.17	0.81	3.39	3.57	0.96	0.87	0.16		1	3,198	100	0	0	0	0			2,500	100			Feb-82
0.00	0.15	0.72	2.82	2.87	0.86	1.07	0.15		1	3,198	100	0	0	0	0			2,500	100			Mar-95
0.00	0.25	1.02	4.02	4.25	1.19	0.56	0.17		1	3,198	100	0	0	0	0			2,500	100			Sep-15
0.01	0.30	1.18	4.40	4.81	1.36	0.31	0.18		1	85,714	69	31	0	0	0			10,000,000				Nov-96
0.03	0.34	1.28	4.71	5.30	1.46	0.21	0.18		1	85,714	69	31	0	0	0			10,000,000				Mar-85
0.00	0.25	1.06	3.96	4.18	1.23	0.46	0.17		1	85,714	69	31	0	0	0			10,000,000				Jan-94
0.00	0.21	0.95	3.54	3.66	1.1	0.62	0.17		1	85,714	69	31	0	0	0			10,000,000				Nov-96
0.01	0.30	1.14	4.26	4.57	1.31	0.32	0.17		1	6,043	69	31	0	0	0			10,000,000				Feb-98
0.04	0.35	1.24	4.57	5.05	1.41	0.22	0.17		1	6,043	69	31	0	0	0			10,000,000				Feb-98
0.00	0.25	1.01	3.82	3.98	1.17	0.47	0.16		1	6,043	69	31	0	0	0			10,000,000				Feb-98
0.00	0.21	0.90	3.40	3.48	1.04	0.62	0.16		1	6,043	69	31	0	0	0			10,000,000				Feb-98
0.02	0.34	1.27	4.73	5.31	1.46	0.19	0.18		1	10,027	64	36	0	0	0			250,000,000				Aug-92
0.04	0.36	1.32	4.88	5.56	1.51	0.14	0.18		1	10,027	64	36	0	0	0			1 Billion				Nov-05
0.00	0.25	1.06	3.99	4.19	1.23	0.44	0.17		1	10,027	64	36	0	0	0			250,000,000				Aug-94
0.26	0.52	0.84	1.28	1.45	0.84	0.1	0.1			1,730	100	0	0	0	0			1 Billion				Oct-00
0.13	0.46	1.44	5.19	5.96	1.59	0.16	0.17		1.0002	3,895	100	0	0	0	0			250,000,000				Dec-07
0.14	0.49	1.50	5.37	6.28	1.65	0.1	0.17		1.0002	3,895	100	0	0	0	0			1 Billion				Jun-97
0.02	0.34	1.24	4.65	5.07	1.42	0.15	0.17		1	154.6	79	21	0	0	0			250,000,000				May-02
0.03	0.37	1.29	4.82	5.39	1.47	0.1	0.17		1	154.6	79	21	0	0	0			1 Billion				Mar-16
0.00	0.28	1.08	4.07	4.25	1.24	0.35	0.17		1	154.6	79	21	0	0	0			250,000,000				May-02
0.01	0.29	1.19	4.54	5.01	1.37	0.19	0.18		1	692.3	63	37	0	0	0			250,000,000				Apr-97
0.03	0.33	1.24	4.70	5.26	1.42	0.14	0.18		1	692.3	63	37	0	0	0			250,000,000				Nov-05
0.00	0.22	0.99	3.81	3.98	1.15	0.44	0.17		1	692.3	63	37	0	0	0			250,000,000				Apr-97
0.00	0.30	1.18	4.43	4.79	1.36	0.2	0.18		1	795.1	78	22	0	0	0			250,000,000				Mar-07
0.00	0.32	1.21	4.55	4.97	1.39	0.16	0.18		1	795.1	78	22	0	0	0			250,000,000				Nov-06
0.00	0.23	0.98	3.72	3.84	1.15	0.45	0.17		1	795.1	78	22	0	0	0			250,000,000				Dec-06
0.00	0.25	1.00	3.47	3.58	1.16	0.64	0.17		1	509.6	100	0	0	0	0			2,500	100			Jan-74
0.02	0.30	1.13	4.21	4.55	1.3	0.6	0.17		1	509.6	100	0	0	0	0			0				Apr-05
0.00	0.24	0.97	3.28	3.34	1.13	0.68	0.18		1	509.6	100	0	0	0	0			1,000	50			Sep-15
0.08	0.42	1.40	5.17	5.92	1.58	0.2	0.16		1	169.5	100	0	0	0	0			1,000,000				Mar-16
0.00	0.00	0.00			0	0.09			1	7,162	89	11	0	0	0			3 Billion				Dec-17
0.00	0.27	1.13	4.33	4.67	1.32	0.31	0.18		1	25,302	68	32	0	0	0			10,000,000				Nov-96
0.03	0.32	1.24	4.64	5.15	1.41	0.21	0.18		1	25,302	68	32	0	0	0			10,000,000				Sep-86
0.00	0.23	1.01	3.89	4.08	1.18	0.46	0.17		1	25,302	68	32	0	0	0			10,000,000				Jan-94
0.00	0.20	0.91	3.47	3.57	1.06	0.61	0.17		1	25,302	68	32	0	0	0			10,000,000				Nov-96
0.01	0.30	1.14	4.28	4.56	1.32	0.31	0.17		1	40,344	67	33	0	0	0			10,000,000				Nov-96

Fund Name	MARKET Ticker Symbol	Traded On	FUND TYPE, CATEGORY & OBJECTIVE Fund Type	Category and (Prospectus Objective)	RATINGS Overall Rating	Reward Rating	Risk Rating	Recent Up/ Downgrade	NEW INVESTORS Open to New Investors	Telephone
Dreyfus Treas Securities Cash Management Inst Shares	DIRXX	NAS CM	Money Mkt	US Money Mkt (Money Mkt - Govt)	C	C-	C+		Y	800-645-6561
Dreyfus Treas Securities Cash Management Investor Shares	DVRXX	NAS CM	Money Mkt	US Money Mkt (Money Mkt - Govt)	C	C-	C+		Y	800-645-6561
Dreyfus Treas Securities Cash Management Particip Shares	DPRXX	NAS CM	Money Mkt	US Money Mkt (Money Mkt - Govt)	C	C-	C+		Y	800-645-6561
Duff & Phelps Tax-free Income	DTF	NYSE	Closed End	US Muni Fixed Inc (Muni Bond - Natl)	C-	C-	D+		Y	212-871-2549
Duff & Phelps Utility & Corporate Bond	DUC	NYSE	Closed End	US Fixed Inc (Corp Bond - General)	C	C	C-		Y	212-871-2549
Dunham Corporate/Government Bond Fund Class A	DACGX	NAS CM	Open End	US Fixed Inc (Growth & Income)	C+	C	B-	Up	Y	800-442-4358
Dunham Corporate/Government Bond Fund Class C	DCCGX	NAS CM	Open End	US Fixed Inc (Growth & Income)	C	C	B-		Y	800-442-4358
Dunham Corporate/Government Bond Fund Class N	DNCGX	NAS CM	Open End	US Fixed Inc (Growth & Income)	C+	C	B	Up	Y	800-442-4358
Dunham Floating Rate Bond Fund Class A	DAFRX	NAS CM	Open End	US Fixed Inc (Income)	D	D	C-	Down	Y	800-442-4358
Dunham Floating Rate Bond Fund Class C	DCFRX	NAS CM	Open End	US Fixed Inc (Income)	D	D	C-	Down	Y	800-442-4358
Dunham Floating Rate Bond Fund Class N	DNFRX	NAS CM	Open End	US Fixed Inc (Income)	D	D	C-	Down	Y	800-442-4358
Dunham High-Yield Bond Fund Class A	DAHYX	NAS CM	Open End	US Fixed Inc (Corp Bond - High Yield)	C-	D+	C		Y	800-442-4358
Dunham High-Yield Bond Fund Class C	DCHYX	NAS CM	Open End	US Fixed Inc (Corp Bond - High Yield)	C-	D+	C		Y	800-442-4358
Dunham High-Yield Bond Fund Class N	DNHYX	NAS CM	Open End	US Fixed Inc (Corp Bond - High Yield)	C-	D+	C		Y	800-442-4358
Dunham International Opportunity Bond Fund Class A	DAIOX	NAS CM	Open End	Global Fixed Inc (Income)	D	D	D+	Down	Y	800-442-4358
Dunham International Opportunity Bond Fund Class C	DCIOX	NAS CM	Open End	Global Fixed Inc (Income)	D	D	D+		Y	800-442-4358
Dunham International Opportunity Bond Fund Class N	DNIOX	NAS CM	Open End	Global Fixed Inc (Income)	D	D	D+	Down	Y	800-442-4358
DuPont Capital Emerging Markets Debt Fund Class I	DCDEX	NAS CM	Open End	Emerg Mkts Fixed Inc (Diversified Emerg Mkts)	D	D	D+	Down	Y	888-447-0014
Dupree Mutual Fund Alabama Tax-Free Income Fund	DUALX	NAS CM	Open End	US Muni Fixed Inc (Muni Bond - Single State)	B-	C	B+	Up	Y	
Dupree Mutual Fund Intermediate Government Bond Fund	DPIGX	NAS CM	Open End	US Fixed Inc (Govt Bond - General)	C+	C	B		Y	
Dupree Mutual Fund Kentucky Tax-Free Income Fund	KYTFX	NAS CM	Open End	US Muni Fixed Inc (Muni Bond - Single State)	C	C	B-		Y	
Dupree Mutual Fund Kentucky Tax-Free Short-To-Medium Fund	KYSMX	NAS CM	Open End	US Muni Fixed Inc (Muni Bond - Single State)	C	C	B-		Y	
Dupree Mutual Fund Mississippi Tax-Free Income Fund	DUMSX	NAS CM	Open End	US Muni Fixed Inc (Muni Bond - Single State)	C+	C	B	Up	Y	
Dupree Mutual Fund North Carolina Tax-Free Income Fund	NTFIX	NAS CM	Open End	US Muni Fixed Inc (Muni Bond - Single State)	C+	C	B	Up	Y	
Dupree Mutual North Carolina Tax-Free Short-To-Medium Fund	NTSMX	NAS CM	Open End	US Muni Fixed Inc (Muni Bond - Single State)	C	C	B-		Y	
Dupree Mutual Fund Tennessee Tax-Free Income Fund	TNTIX	NAS CM	Open End	US Muni Fixed Inc (Muni Bond - Single State)	C+	C	B	Up	Y	
Dupree Mutual Fund Tennessee Tax-Free Short-To-Medium Fund	TTSMX	NAS CM	Open End	US Muni Fixed Inc (Muni Bond - Single State)	C	C	B-		Y	
Dupree Taxable Municipal Bond Series	DUTMX	NAS CM	Open End	US Muni Fixed Inc (Govt Bond - General)	B-	C	B+		Y	
DWS California Tax-Free Income Fund - Class A	KCTAX	NAS CM	Open End	US Muni Fixed Inc (Muni Bond - Single State)	C	C-	C+		Y	
DWS California Tax-Free Income Fund - Class C	KCTCX	NAS CM	Open End	US Muni Fixed Inc (Muni Bond - Single State)	C	C-	C		Y	
DWS California Tax-Free Income Fund - Class S	SDCSX	NAS CM	Open End	US Muni Fixed Inc (Muni Bond - Single State)	C	C-	C+		Y	
DWS Emerging Markets Fixed Income Fund - Class A	SZEAX	NAS CM	Open End	Emerg Mkts Fixed Inc (Diversified Emerg Mkts)	D	D	C-	Down	Y	
DWS Emerging Markets Fixed Income Fund - Class C	SZECX	NAS CM	Open End	Emerg Mkts Fixed Inc (Diversified Emerg Mkts)	D	D	C-	Down	Y	
DWS Emerging Markets Fixed Income Fund - Class Inst	SZEIX	NAS CM	Open End	Emerg Mkts Fixed Inc (Diversified Emerg Mkts)	D+	D	C-	Down	Y	
DWS Emerging Markets Fixed Income Fund - Class S	SCEMX	NAS CM	Open End	Emerg Mkts Fixed Inc (Diversified Emerg Mkts)	D+	D	C-	Down	Y	
DWS ESG Global Bond Fund - Class A	SZGAX	NAS CM	Open End	Global Fixed Inc (Worldwide Bond)	C+	C	B	Up	Y	
DWS ESG Global Bond Fund - Class C	SZGCX	NAS CM	Open End	Global Fixed Inc (Worldwide Bond)	C	C	B-		Y	
DWS ESG Global Bond Fund - Class S	SSTGX	NAS CM	Open End	Global Fixed Inc (Worldwide Bond)	C+	C	B	Up	Y	
DWS ESG Liquidity Fund - Capital Shares	ESIXX	NAS CM	Money Mkt	US Money Mkt (Money Mkt - Taxable)	C	C-	C+		Y	
DWS ESG Liquidity Fund - Institutional Shares	ESGXX	NAS CM	Money Mkt	US Money Mkt (Money Mkt - Taxable)	C	C-	C+		Y	
DWS ESG Liquidity Fund Institutional Reserved Shares	ESRXX	NAS CM	Money Mkt	US Money Mkt (Money Mkt - Taxable)	C	C-	C+		Y	
DWS Floating Rate Fund - Class A	DFRAX	NAS CM	Open End	US Fixed Inc (Income)	D+	D	C-	Down	Y	
DWS Floating Rate Fund - Class C	DFRCX	NAS CM	Open End	US Fixed Inc (Income)	D	D	C-	Down	Y	
DWS Floating Rate Fund - Class Inst	DFRTX	NAS CM	Open End	US Fixed Inc (Income)	D+	D	C-	Down	Y	
DWS Floating Rate Fund - Class R6	DFRRX	NAS CM	Open End	US Fixed Inc (Income)	D+	D	C-	Down	Y	
DWS Floating Rate Fund - Class S	DFRPX	NAS CM	Open End	US Fixed Inc (Income)	D+	D	C-	Down	Y	
DWS Global High Income Fund - Class A	SGHAX	NAS CM	Open End	Global Fixed Inc (Income)	C-	D+	C		Y	
DWS Global High Income Fund - Class C	SGHCX	NAS CM	Open End	Global Fixed Inc (Income)	C-	D+	C		Y	
DWS Global High Income Fund - Class Inst	MGHYX	NAS CM	Open End	Global Fixed Inc (Income)	C-	D+	C	Down	Y	
DWS Global High Income Fund - Class R6	SGHRX	NAS CM	Open End	Global Fixed Inc (Income)	C-	D+	C	Down	Y	
DWS Global High Income Fund - Class S	SGHSX	NAS CM	Open End	Global Fixed Inc (Income)	C-	D+	C		Y	
DWS Global High Income Fund - Class T	SGHTX	NAS CM	Open End	Global Fixed Inc (Income)	C-	D+	C		Y	

★ Expanded analysis of this fund is included in Section II.

TOTAL RETURNS & PERFORMANCE									ASSETS		ASSET ALLOCATION & TURNOVER							MINIMUMS		FEES		
3-Month Total Return	6-Month Total Return	1-Year Total Return	3-Year Total Return	5-Year Total Return	Dividend Yield (TTM)	Expense Ratio	3-Yr Std Deviation	Effective Duration	NAV	Total Assets (MIL)	%Cash	%Government Bonds	%Municipal Bonds	%Corporate Bonds	%Other	Turnover Ratio	Average Coupon Rate	Min Initial Investment	Min Additional Investment	Front End Fee (%)	Back End Fee (%)	Inception Date
0.04	0.35	1.24	4.59	5.03	1.42	0.21	0.17		1	40,344	67	33	0	0	0			10,000,000				Dec-88
0.00	0.25	1.02	3.84	3.99	1.18	0.46	0.17		1	40,344	67	33	0	0	0			10,000,000				Jan-94
0.00	0.21	0.90	3.41	3.48	1.05	0.61	0.16		1	40,344	67	33	0	0	0			10,000,000				Nov-96
2.60	1.87	4.03	12.15	21.46	2.95		5.6		15.75	133.0	-48	0	100	0	2	10	4.95					Nov-91
10.12	5.06	7.40	14.81	22.15	3.45	0	6.14		9.69	263.9	8	2	0	92	-35	21	4.80					Jan-93
5.89	3.46	6.08	11.20	16.18	2.14	1.45	4.43		14.29	49.7	5	13	7	41	0	76	4.00	5,000	100	4.50		Jan-07
5.63	3.18	5.53	9.57	13.22	1.68	1.95	4.41		14.18	49.7	5	13	7	41	0	76	4.00	5,000	100			Dec-04
5.94	3.59	6.33	12.09	17.60	2.38	1.2	4.41		14.31	49.7	5	13	7	41	0	76	4.00	100,000				Dec-04
6.91	-6.29	-4.27	0.83	6.60	4.48	1.27	7.75		8.68	159.6	5	0	0	90	0	44	5.07	5,000	100	4.50		Nov-13
6.65	-6.61	-4.75	-0.65	3.98	3.94	1.77	7.72		8.68	159.6	5	0	0	90	0	44	5.07	5,000	100			Nov-13
6.97	-6.16	-4.02	1.58	7.94	4.74	1.02	7.74		8.69	159.6	5	0	0	90	0	44	5.07	100,000				Nov-13
9.02	-3.04	-0.25	8.22	18.48	4.61	1.38	8.02		8.69	90.8	2	0	0	98	0	70	5.99	5,000	100	4.50		Jan-07
9.03	-3.23	-0.77	6.73	15.77	4.15	1.88	8.07		8.56	90.8	2	0	0	98	0	70	5.99	5,000	100			Jul-05
9.19	-2.95	0.00	8.99	19.90	4.93	1.13	8.08		8.6	90.8	2	0	0	98	0	70	5.99	100,000				Jul-05
13.68	-4.20	-4.49	-2.30	2.75	0.89	1.86	11.26		8.79	34.8	6	18	0	34	0	109	4.80	5,000	100	4.50		Nov-13
13.54	-4.39	-4.79	-3.57	0.29	0.71	2.36	11.29		8.57	34.8	6	18	0	34	0	109	4.80	5,000	100			Nov-13
13.72	-4.06	-4.25	-1.52	4.05	0.98	1.61	11.21		8.88	34.8	6	18	0	34	0	109	4.80	100,000				Nov-13
12.30	-8.09	-8.78	-0.16	22.04	7.83	0.89	12.68		7.72	6.7	8	69	0	22	0	10	6.69	1,000,000	100,000			Sep-13
2.29	3.19	5.48	13.00	19.65	2.55	0.84	3.21	4.47	12.78	27.0	0	0	100	0	0	17	4.73	100				Dec-99
0.56	3.84	4.97	9.09	14.39	2.3	0.61	2.2	2.89	10.37	15.6	0	100	0	0	0	0	5.22	100				Jul-92
0.78	1.05	3.07	10.50	16.88	2.68	0.57	3.69	5.00	7.86	953.1	0	0	100	0	0	10	4.75	100				Jul-79
1.74	1.41	2.65	6.99	10.65	1.69	0.77	2.55	3.25	5.41	47.2	0	0	100	0	0	5	4.82	100				Sep-87
2.00	2.38	4.08	10.59	18.59	2.52	0.97	3.12	4.42	12.37	10.5	0	0	100	0	0	5	4.86	100				Dec-99
2.08	2.65	4.47	11.82	18.15	2.28	0.71	3.76	5.01	11.93	159.5	0	0	100	0	0	13	4.63	100				Nov-95
1.95	1.89	3.23	8.10	10.63	1.54	0.88	2.65	4.11	11.2	12.9	0	0	100	0	0	14	4.81	100				Nov-95
1.63	1.97	3.76	10.11	16.14	2.41	0.71	3.27	4.24	11.66	95.0	0	0	100	0	0	6	4.72	100				Dec-93
2.15	2.28	3.58	7.94	10.98	1.59	1.08	2.41	3.74	11.02	6.7	0	0	100	0	0	11	4.55	100				Nov-94
1.99	3.48	5.28	15.16	27.31	5.07	0.86	3.35	4.82	10.4	13.4	0	0	100	0	0	4	6.14	100				Nov-10
2.18	-0.13	2.06	9.39	16.22	2.83	0.79	4.68		7.51	696.0	0	0	100	0	0	48	4.78	1,000	50	2.75		Feb-83
1.86	-0.50	1.32	6.85	11.98	2.07	1.54	4.68		7.46	696.0	0	0	100	0	0	48	4.78	1,000	50		1.00	May-94
2.24	-0.02	2.31	10.20	17.67	3.08	0.54	4.63		7.5	696.0	0	0	100	0	0	48	4.78	2,500	50			Jun-01
17.53	-3.58	-0.29	6.09	14.71	4.34	1.13	13.03	3.83	8.93	69.9	2	71	0	27	0	13	6.01	1,000	50	4.50		Jun-01
17.27	-4.02	-1.13	3.62	10.37	3.56	1.88	13.02	3.83	8.95	69.9	2	71	0	27	0	13	6.01	1,000	50		1.00	Jun-01
17.50	-3.57	-0.16	6.82	16.31	4.6	0.88	13.01	3.83	8.91	69.9	2	71	0	27	0	13	6.01	1,000,000				Mar-08
17.47	-3.57	-0.07	6.80	16.07	4.57	0.88	12.96	3.83	8.92	69.9	2	71	0	27	0	13	6.01	2,500	50			Dec-93
4.06	2.87	5.11	11.39	19.98	1.8	0.95	4.29	7.25	9.59	55.9	6	38	0	47	0	167	2.59	1,000	50	4.50		Jun-01
3.87	2.49	4.33	8.92	15.57	1.06	1.7	4.27	7.25	9.59	55.9	6	38	0	47	0	167	2.59	1,000	50		1.00	Jun-01
4.02	3.00	5.39	12.12	21.38	2.05	0.7	4.23	7.25	9.57	55.9	6	38	0	47	0	167	2.59	2,500	50			Mar-91
0.25	0.56	1.61	5.60	7.06	1.74	0.1	0.19		1.0003	387.5	82	0	18	0	0			25,000,000				Apr-11
0.24	0.55	1.60	5.42	6.77	1.74	0.12	0.19		1.0002	387.5	82	0	18	0	0			10,000,000				Dec-13
0.24	0.55	1.58	5.62	7.07	1.72	0.17			1.0014	387.5	82	0	18	0	0			1,000,000				Oct-18
6.18	-5.59	-2.64	2.33	2.16	4.67	1.01	6.88		7.52	165.5	2	0	0	98	0	26		1,000	50	2.75		Jun-07
5.95	-5.91	-3.45	0.10	-1.61	3.89	1.76	6.84		7.56	165.5	2	0	0	98	0	26		1,000	50		1.00	Jun-07
6.24	-5.36	-2.40	3.10	3.45	4.93	0.76	6.85		7.52	165.5	2	0	0	98	0	26		1,000,000				Jun-07
6.09	-5.47	-2.52	3.10	3.47	4.93	0.76	6.8		7.52	165.5	2	0	0	98	0	26		0				Oct-14
6.07	-5.53	-2.50	2.78	2.91	4.82	0.86	6.81		7.51	165.5	2	0	0	98	0	26		2,500	50			Jun-07
8.38	-4.54	-0.73	10.02	24.35	4.89	0.85	8.11	4.88	6.47	512.4	4	0	0	95	0	74	5.58	1,000	50	4.50		May-05
7.98	-5.01	-1.60	7.62	19.83	4.1	1.6	8.1	4.88	6.49	512.4	4	0	0	95	0	74	5.58	1,000	50		1.00	May-05
8.47	-4.44	-0.56	10.93	26.14	5.08	0.6	8.13	4.88	6.45	512.4	4	0	0	95	0	74	5.58	1,000,000				Mar-98
8.32	-4.42	-0.52	10.90	26.05	5.14	0.55	8.11	4.88	6.44	512.4	4	0	0	95	0	74	5.58	0				Nov-16
8.22	-4.55	-0.58	10.61	25.54	5.01	0.65	8.11	4.88	6.5	512.4	4	0	0	95	0	74	5.58	2,500	50			May-05
8.20	-4.54	-0.80	9.98	24.44	4.82	0.85	8.06	4.88	6.47	512.4	4	0	0	95	0	74	5.58	1,000	50	2.50		Jun-17

	MARKET		FUND TYPE, CATEGORY & OBJECTIVE		RATINGS				NEW INVESTORS	
Fund Name	Ticker Symbol	Traded On	Fund Type	Category and (Prospectus Objective)	Overall Rating	Reward Rating	Risk Rating	Recent Up/ Downgrade	Open to New Investors	Telephone
DWS GNMA Fund - Class A	GGGGX	NAS CM	Open End	US Fixed Inc (Govt Bond - Mortgage)	C+	C	B-		Y	
DWS GNMA Fund - Class C	GCGGX	NAS CM	Open End	US Fixed Inc (Govt Bond - Mortgage)	C	C	B-		Y	
DWS GNMA Fund - Class Inst	GIGGX	NAS CM	Open End	US Fixed Inc (Govt Bond - Mortgage)	C+	C	B		Y	
DWS GNMA Fund - Class R	GRGGX	NAS CM	Open End	US Fixed Inc (Govt Bond - Mortgage)	C	C	B-		Y	
DWS GNMA Fund - Class R6	GRRGX	NAS CM	Open End	US Fixed Inc (Govt Bond - Mortgage)	C+	C	B		Y	
DWS GNMA Fund - Class S	SGINX	NAS CM	Open End	US Fixed Inc (Govt Bond - Mortgage)	C+	C	B		Y	
DWS GNMA Fund - Class T	GIGTX	NAS CM	Open End	US Fixed Inc (Govt Bond - Mortgage)	C+	C	B-		Y	
DWS Govt & Agency Sec Port: DWS Govt & Agency Money Fund	DTGXX	NAS CM	Money Mkt	US Money Mkt (Money Mkt - Govt)	C	C-	C+		Y	
DWS Govt & Agency Securities Portfol: DWS Gov't Cash Inst	DBBXX	NAS CM	Money Mkt	US Money Mkt (Money Mkt - Govt)	C	C-	C+		Y	
DWS Govt & Agency Securities Portfolio: Gov't Cash Managed	DCMXX	NAS CM	Money Mkt	US Money Mkt (Money Mkt - Govt)	C	C-	C+		Y	
DWS Govt & Agency Securities Portfolio: Service Shares	CAGXX	NAS CM	Money Mkt	US Money Mkt (Money Mkt - Govt)	C	C-	C		Y	
DWS Government Cash Management Fund	BICXX	NAS CM	Money Mkt	US Money Mkt (Money Mkt - Govt)	C	C-	C+		Y	
DWS Government Cash Reserves Fund Institutional	BIRXX	NAS CM	Money Mkt	US Money Mkt (Money Mkt - Govt)	C	C-	C+		Y	
DWS Government Money Market Series - Institutional Shares	ICAXX	NAS CM	Money Mkt	US Money Mkt (Money Mkt - Govt)	C	C-	C+		Y	
DWS High Income Fund - Class A	KHYAX	NAS CM	Open End	US Fixed Inc (Corp Bond - High Yield)	C-	D+	C		Y	
DWS High Income Fund - Class C	KHYCX	NAS CM	Open End	US Fixed Inc (Corp Bond - High Yield)	C-	D+	C		Y	
DWS High Income Fund - Class Inst	KHYIX	NAS CM	Open End	US Fixed Inc (Corp Bond - High Yield)	C-	D+	C		Y	
DWS High Income Fund - Class R	KHYRX	NAS CM	Open End	US Fixed Inc (Corp Bond - High Yield)	C-	D+	C		Y	
DWS High Income Fund - Class R6	KHYQX	NAS CM	Open End	US Fixed Inc (Corp Bond - High Yield)	C-	D+	C		Y	
DWS High Income Fund - Class S	KHYSX	NAS CM	Open End	US Fixed Inc (Corp Bond - High Yield)	C-	D+	C		Y	
DWS High Income Fund - Class T	KHYTX	NAS CM	Open End	US Fixed Inc (Corp Bond - High Yield)	C-	D+	C		Y	
DWS Intermediate Tax-Free Fund - Class A	SZMAX	NAS CM	Open End	US Muni Fixed Inc (Muni Bond - Natl)	C	C-	B-		Y	
DWS Intermediate Tax-Free Fund - Class C	SZMCX	NAS CM	Open End	US Muni Fixed Inc (Muni Bond - Natl)	C	C-	C+		Y	
DWS Intermediate Tax-Free Fund - Class Inst	SZMIX	NAS CM	Open End	US Muni Fixed Inc (Muni Bond - Natl)	C	C	B-		Y	
DWS Intermediate Tax-Free Fund - Class S	SCMTX	NAS CM	Open End	US Muni Fixed Inc (Muni Bond - Natl)	C	C	B-		Y	
DWS Managed Municipal Bond Fund - Class A	SMLAX	NAS CM	Open End	US Muni Fixed Inc (Muni Bond - Natl)	C	C-	C+		Y	
DWS Managed Municipal Bond Fund - Class C	SMLCX	NAS CM	Open End	US Muni Fixed Inc (Muni Bond - Natl)	C-	D+	C	Down	Y	
DWS Managed Municipal Bond Fund - Class Inst	SMLIX	NAS CM	Open End	US Muni Fixed Inc (Muni Bond - Natl)	C	C-	C+		Y	
DWS Managed Municipal Bond Fund - Class S	SCMBX	NAS CM	Open End	US Muni Fixed Inc (Muni Bond - Natl)	C	C-	C+		Y	
DWS Massachusetts Tax Free Fund - Class A	SQMAX	NAS CM	Open End	US Muni Fixed Inc (Muni Bond - Single State)	C	C	B-		Y	
DWS Massachusetts Tax Free Fund - Class C	SQMCX	NAS CM	Open End	US Muni Fixed Inc (Muni Bond - Single State)	C	C-	C+		Y	
DWS Massachusetts Tax Free Fund - Class S	SCMAX	NAS CM	Open End	US Muni Fixed Inc (Muni Bond - Single State)	C	C	B-		Y	
DWS Money Mkt Prime Ser - DWS Cash Investment Trust - Cl A	DOAXX	NAS CM	Money Mkt	US Money Mkt (Money Mkt - Taxable)	C	C-	C+		Y	
DWS Money Mkt Prime Ser - DWS Cash Investment Trust - Cl C	DOCXX	NAS CM	Money Mkt	US Money Mkt (Money Mkt - Taxable)	C	C-	C		Y	
DWS Money Mkt Prime Ser - DWS Cash Investment Trust - Cl S	DOSXX	NAS CM	Money Mkt	US Money Mkt (Money Mkt - Taxable)	C	C-	C+		Y	
DWS Money Market Prime Series - DWS Money Market Fund	KMMXX	NAS CM	Money Mkt	US Money Mkt (Money Mkt - Taxable)	C	C-	C+		Y	
DWS Municipal Income Trust	KTF	NYSE	Closed End	US Muni Fixed Inc (Muni Bond - Natl)	C-	C-	C-	Down	Y	
DWS New York Tax-Free Income Fund - Class A	KNTAX	NAS CM	Open End	US Muni Fixed Inc (Muni Bond - Single State)	C	C-	C+		Y	
DWS New York Tax-Free Income Fund - Class C	KNTCX	NAS CM	Open End	US Muni Fixed Inc (Muni Bond - Single State)	C	C-	C+		Y	
DWS New York Tax-Free Income Fund - Class S	SNWYX	NAS CM	Open End	US Muni Fixed Inc (Muni Bond - Single State)	C	C-	B-		Y	
DWS Short Duration Fund - Class A	PPIAX	NAS CM	Open End	US Fixed Inc (Corp Bond - General)	C	C-	C+		Y	
DWS Short Duration Fund - Class C	PPLCX	NAS CM	Open End	US Fixed Inc (Corp Bond - General)	C	C-	C	Up	Y	
DWS Short Duration Fund - Class Inst	PPILX	NAS CM	Open End	US Fixed Inc (Corp Bond - General)	C	C-	C+		Y	
DWS Short Duration Fund - Class R6	PPLZX	NAS CM	Open End	US Fixed Inc (Corp Bond - General)	C	C-	C+		Y	
DWS Short Duration Fund - Class S	DBPIX	NAS CM	Open End	US Fixed Inc (Corp Bond - General)	C	C-	C+		Y	
DWS Short Duration Fund - Class T	PPITX	NAS CM	Open End	US Fixed Inc (Corp Bond - General)	C	C-	C+		Y	
DWS Short Term Municipal Bond Fund - Class A	SRMAX	NAS CM	Open End	US Muni Fixed Inc (Muni Bond - Natl)	C	C-	C+		Y	
DWS Short Term Municipal Bond Fund - Class C	SRMCX	NAS CM	Open End	US Muni Fixed Inc (Muni Bond - Natl)	C	C-	C		Y	
DWS Short Term Municipal Bond Fund - Class Inst	MGSMX	NAS CM	Open End	US Muni Fixed Inc (Muni Bond - Natl)	C	C-	C+		Y	
DWS Short Term Municipal Bond Fund - Class S	SRMSX	NAS CM	Open End	US Muni Fixed Inc (Muni Bond - Natl)	C	C-	C+		Y	
DWS Strategic High Yield Tax-Free Fund - Class A	NOTAX	NAS CM	Open End	US Muni Fixed Inc (Muni Bond - Natl)	C-	D+	C	Down	Y	
DWS Strategic High Yield Tax-Free Fund - Class C	NOTCX	NAS CM	Open End	US Muni Fixed Inc (Muni Bond - Natl)	D+	D+	C	Down	Y	

★ Expanded analysis of this fund is included in Section II.

TOTAL RETURNS & PERFORMANCE									ASSETS		ASSET ALLOCATION & TURNOVER							MINIMUMS		FEES		
3-Month Total Return	6-Month Total Return	1-Year Total Return	3-Year Total Return	5-Year Total Return	Dividend Yield (TTM)	Expense Ratio	3-Yr Std Deviation	Effective Duration	NAV	Total Assets (MIL)	%Cash	%Government Bonds	%Municipal Bonds	%Corporate Bonds	%Other	Turnover Ratio	Average Coupon Rate	Min Initial Investment	Min Additional Investment	Front End Fee (%)	Back End Fee (%)	Inception Date
1.10	2.38	4.46	9.67	11.93	2.43	0.79	2.01	3.03	13.96	1,473	14	1	0	0	0	317	3.45	1,000	50	2.75		Feb-09
0.90	2.06	3.63	7.13	7.71	1.65	1.57	2.02	3.03	13.97	1,473	14	1	0	0	0	317	3.45	1,000	50		1.00	Feb-09
1.17	2.51	4.71	10.48	13.34	2.67	0.54	2.01	3.03	13.97	1,473	14	1	0	0	0	317	3.45	1,000,000				Feb-09
1.02	2.21	4.11	8.52	10.08	2.1	1.17	2.02	3.03	13.98	1,473	14	1	0	0	0	317	3.45	0				May-12
1.18	2.61	4.86	10.62	13.40	2.74	0.48	2.03	3.03	13.98	1,473	14	1	0	0	0	317	3.45	0				Feb-15
1.16	2.57	4.78	10.46	13.36	2.66	0.56	2.02	3.03	13.99	1,473	14	1	0	0	0	317	3.45	2,500	50			Jul-00
1.10	2.44	4.51	9.61	11.93	2.4	0.82	2.06	3.03	13.97	1,473	14	1	0	0	0	317	3.45	1,000	50	2.50		Jun-17
0.01	0.32	1.21	4.35	4.83	1.37	0.28	0.21		1	3,015	53	47	0	0	0			1,000	50			Mar-07
0.03	0.35	1.28	4.53	5.16	1.43	0.18	0.21		1	3,015	53	47	0	0	0			1,000,000				Feb-07
0.00	0.27	1.10	3.97	4.23	1.25	0.42	0.2		1	3,015	53	47	0	0	0			100,000	1,000			Feb-07
0.00	0.13	0.63	2.25	2.27	0.74	1.05	0.16		1	3,015	53	47	0	0	0			1,000	100			Dec-90
0.00	0.27	1.12	4.12	4.52	1.28	0.3	0.21		1	201.0	48	52	0	0	0			1,000,000				Jul-90
0.01	0.30	1.18	4.29	4.81	1.35	0.21	0.21		1	329.6	100	0	0	0	0	2		10,000,000				Jan-94
0.04	0.36	1.31	4.75	5.46	1.48	0.14	0.19		1	17,198	100	0	0	0	0			1,000,000				Aug-97
8.72	-4.12	-0.56	10.05	22.40	4.96	0.96	8.17	4.61	4.49	721.8	2	0	0	98	0	77	5.79	1,000	50	4.50		Jan-78
8.49	-4.47	-1.13	7.51	17.97	4.14	1.74	8.09	4.61	4.5	721.8	2	0	0	98	0	77	5.79	1,000	50		1.00	May-94
8.76	-4.00	-0.31	10.84	24.11	5.21	0.73	8.01	4.61	4.5	721.8	2	0	0	98	0	77	5.79	1,000,000				Aug-02
8.63	-4.27	-0.88	8.92	20.28	4.63	1.27	8.02	4.61	4.49	721.8	2	0	0	98	0	77	5.79	0				May-12
9.04	-3.97	-0.05	10.94	24.03	5.25	0.69	8.16	4.61	4.5	721.8	2	0	0	98	0	77	5.79	0				Aug-14
8.75	-4.01	-0.36	10.61	23.46	5.15	0.76	8.01	4.61	4.5	721.8	2	0	0	98	0	77	5.79	2,500	50			May-12
8.70	-4.11	-0.34	10.14	22.48	4.95	0.98	8.08	4.61	4.5	721.8	2	0	0	98	0	77	5.79	1,000	50	2.50		Jun-17
2.44	1.54	3.18	9.15	14.70	2.53	0.77	3.56		11.89	964.0	1	0	99	0	0	61	4.62	1,000	50	2.75		Jun-01
2.25	1.22	2.51	6.74	10.48	1.78	1.52	3.57		11.89	964.0	1	0	99	0	0	61	4.62	1,000	50		1.00	Jun-01
2.51	1.72	3.43	9.96	16.13	2.78	0.52	3.58		11.89	964.0	1	0	99	0	0	61	4.62	1,000,000				Dec-04
2.59	1.80	3.52	10.04	16.19	2.78	0.52	3.57		11.9	964.0	1	0	99	0	0	61	4.62	2,500	50			Apr-83
2.65	0.05	2.12	9.71	16.99	3.05	0.77	5.02		9.13	3,865	0	0	100	0	0	39	4.99	1,000	50	2.75		Jun-01
2.46	-0.32	1.34	7.18	12.51	2.25	1.56	5.02		9.13	3,865	0	0	100	0	0	39	4.99	1,000	50		1.00	Jun-01
2.69	0.03	2.22	10.30	18.29	3.27	0.55	5.1		9.13	3,865	0	0	100	0	0	39	4.99	1,000,000				Aug-02
2.70	0.04	2.21	10.24	18.16	3.25	0.56	5.06		9.14	3,865	0	0	100	0	0	39	4.99	2,500	50			Oct-76
2.27	1.42	3.42	10.39	16.81	2.29	0.89	4.15		14.63	359.8	1	0	99	0	0	43	4.85	1,000	50	2.75		Jun-01
2.09	1.06	2.67	7.90	12.56	1.55	1.64	4.17		14.62	359.8	1	0	99	0	0	43	4.85	1,000	50		1.00	Jun-01
2.34	1.54	3.67	11.20	18.26	2.53	0.64	4.15		14.63	359.8	1	0	99	0	0	43	4.85	2,500	50			May-87
0.08	0.35	1.03	3.50	3.66	1.2	0.82	0.14		1	705.2	63	0	32	5	0	0		1,000	50			Mar-07
0.05	0.14	0.47	1.57	1.60	0.58	1.54	0.12		1	705.2	63	0	32	5	0	0		1,000	50		1.00	Mar-07
0.10	0.44	1.26	4.20	4.54	1.44	0.57	0.14		1	705.2	63	0	32	5	0	0		2,500	50			Mar-07
0.11	0.45	1.27	4.23	4.61	1.46	0.55	0.15		1	705.2	63	0	32	5	0	0		1,000	50			Nov-74
3.08	0.19	2.83	11.93	20.64	4.06	0	6.84		12.37	478.0	0	0	100	0	0	18	5.62					Oct-88
2.17	0.68	2.62	9.61	17.04	2.59	0.85	4.4		10.79	276.1	0	0	100	0	0	41	4.75	1,000	50	2.75		Dec-85
1.98	0.32	1.88	7.22	12.78	1.85	1.6	4.39		10.79	276.1	0	0	100	0	0	41	4.75	1,000	50		1.00	May-94
2.23	0.80	2.87	10.42	18.50	2.85	0.6	4.41		10.79	276.1	0	0	100	0	0	41	4.75	2,500	50			Jun-01
5.45	1.22	2.78	7.96	10.49	2.58	0.77	3.63	2.31	8.69	1,041	3	15	1	47	0	51	3.29	1,000	50	2.75		Dec-02
5.14	0.85	2.03	5.58	6.43	1.85	1.52	3.56	2.31	8.68	1,041	3	15	1	47	0	51	3.29	1,000	50		1.00	Feb-03
5.51	1.35	3.03	8.77	11.88	2.83	0.52	3.62	2.31	8.7	1,041	3	15	1	47	0	51	3.29	1,000,000				Aug-08
5.51	1.35	3.03	8.76	11.75	2.82	0.52	3.62	2.31	8.7	1,041	3	15	1	47	0	51	3.29	0				Aug-14
5.38	1.35	3.02	8.76	11.88	2.82	0.52	3.57	2.31	8.71	1,041	3	15	1	47	0	51	3.29	2,500	50			Dec-98
5.33	1.22	2.78	7.96	10.50	2.58	0.77	3.55	2.31	8.69	1,041	3	15	1	47	0	51	3.29	1,000	50	2.50		Jun-17
1.91	1.02	1.95	5.25	7.29	1.31	0.72	1.65		10.18	314.4	2	0	98	0	0	109	3.68	1,000	50	2.00		Feb-03
1.72	0.64	1.21	3.04	3.37	0.57	1.47	1.63		10.18	314.4	2	0	98	0	0	109	3.68	1,000	50		1.00	Feb-03
1.87	1.15	2.20	6.02	8.63	1.56	0.47	1.63		10.18	314.4	2	0	98	0	0	109	3.68	1,000,000				Mar-95
1.95	1.20	2.10	5.72	8.10	1.46	0.57	1.64		10.17	314.4	2	0	98	0	0	109	3.68	2,500	50			Feb-05
3.22	-2.45	-0.01	8.03	16.96	3.87	0.9	6.63		11.72	991.0	4	0	96	0	0	47	5.39	1,000	50	2.75		May-00
3.12	-2.81	-0.75	5.61	12.54	3.07	1.65	6.66		11.73	991.0	4	0	96	0	0	47	5.39	1,000	50		1.00	May-00

	MARKET		FUND TYPE, CATEGORY & OBJECTIVE		RATINGS				NEW INVESTORS	
Fund Name	Ticker Symbol	Traded On	Fund Type	Category and (Prospectus Objective)	Overall Rating	Reward Rating	Risk Rating	Recent Up/ Downgrade	Open to New Investors	Telephone
DWS Strategic High Yield Tax-Free Fund - Class Inst	NOTIX	NAS CM	Open End	US Muni Fixed Inc (Muni Bond - Natl)	C-	D+	C	Down	Y	
DWS Strategic High Yield Tax-Free Fund - Class S	SHYTX	NAS CM	Open End	US Muni Fixed Inc (Muni Bond - Natl)	C-	D+	C	Down	Y	
DWS Strategic Municipal Income Trust	KSM	NYSE	Closed End	US Muni Fixed Inc (Muni Bond - Natl)	D+	D+	C-	Down	Y	
DWS Tax Exempt Portfolio: Cash Premier Shares	SCIXX	NAS CM	Money Mkt	US Money Mkt (Money Mkt - Fed Tax Exmpt)	C	C-	C+		Y	
DWS Tax Exempt Portfolio: DWS Tax-Exempt Money Fund	DTBXX	NAS CM	Money Mkt	US Money Mkt (Money Mkt - Fed Tax Exmpt)	C	C-	C+		Y	
DWS Tax Exempt Portfolio: DWS Tax-Free Money - Cl S	DTCXX	NAS CM	Money Mkt	US Money Mkt (Money Mkt - Fed Tax Exmpt)	C	C	C+		Y	
DWS Tax Exempt Portfolio: Service Shares	CHSXX	NAS CM	Money Mkt	US Money Mkt (Money Mkt - Fed Tax Exmpt)	C	C-	C		Y	
DWS Tax Exempt Portfolio: Tax Exempt Cash Managed Shares	TXMXX	NAS CM	Money Mkt	US Money Mkt (Money Mkt - Fed Tax Exmpt)	C	C-	C		Y	
DWS Tax Exempt Portfolio: Tax Free Investment Class	DTDXX	NAS CM	Money Mkt	US Money Mkt (Money Mkt - Fed Tax Exmpt)	C	C-	C		Y	
DWS Total Return Bond Fund - Class A	SZIAX	NAS CM	Open End	US Fixed Inc (Income)	B-	C	B	Up	Y	
DWS Total Return Bond Fund - Class C	SZICX	NAS CM	Open End	US Fixed Inc (Income)	C+	C	B	Up	Y	
DWS Total Return Bond Fund - Class Inst	SZIIX	NAS CM	Open End	US Fixed Inc (Income)	B-	C	B+	Up	Y	
DWS Total Return Bond Fund - Class R	SZIRX	NAS CM	Open End	US Fixed Inc (Income)	B-	C	B	Up	Y	
DWS Total Return Bond Fund - Class S	SCSBX	NAS CM	Open End	US Fixed Inc (Income)	B-	C	B+	Up	Y	
DWS Total Return Bond Fund Class R6	SZIWX	NAS CM	Open End	US Fixed Inc (Income)	B-	C	B+	Up	Y	
DWS Treasury Portfolio - Capital Shares	ICGXX	NAS CM	Money Mkt	US Money Mkt (Money Mkt - Treasury)	C	C-	C+		Y	
DWS Treasury Portfolio - DWS U.S. Treasury Money Cl S	IUSXX	NAS CM	Money Mkt	US Money Mkt (Money Mkt - Treasury)	C	C-	C+		Y	
DWS Treasury Portfolio - Institutional Shares	ICTXX	NAS CM	Money Mkt	US Money Mkt (Money Mkt - Treasury)	C	C-	C+		Y	
DWS Treasury Portfolio - Investment Class	ITVXX	NAS CM	Money Mkt	US Money Mkt (Money Mkt - Treasury)	C	C-	C		Y	
Eagle Point Credit Co LLC	ECC	NYSE	Closed End	US Fixed Inc (Income)	D	D	D		Y	
Eagle Point Income Co Inc	EIC	NYSE	Closed End	US Fixed Inc (Income)	U	U	U		Y	
Eagle Rock Floating Rate Fund Investor Class	ERFAX	NAS CM	Open End	US Fixed Inc (Income)	U	U	U		Y	
Eaton Vance AMT-Free Municipal Income Fund Class A	ETMBX	NAS CM	Open End	US Muni Fixed Inc (Muni Bond - Natl)	C	C	B		Y	
Eaton Vance AMT-Free Municipal Income Fund Class C	ECMBX	NAS CM	Open End	US Muni Fixed Inc (Muni Bond - Natl)	C	C-	B-		Y	
Eaton Vance Amt-Free Municipal Income Fund Class I	EVMBX	NAS CM	Open End	US Muni Fixed Inc (Muni Bond - Natl)	C	C	B	Down	Y	
Eaton Vance Arizona Municipal Income Fund Class A	ETAZX	NAS CM	Open End	US Muni Fixed Inc (Muni Bond - Single State)	C	C	B		Y	
Eaton Vance Arizona Municipal Income Fund Class C	ECAZX	NAS CM	Open End	US Muni Fixed Inc (Muni Bond - Single State)	C	C	B-		Y	
Eaton Vance Arizona Municipal Income Fund Class I	EIAZX	NAS CM	Open End	US Muni Fixed Inc (Muni Bond - Single State)	C+	C	B	Up	Y	
Eaton Vance California Municipal Bond Fund	EVM	AMEX	Closed End	US Muni Fixed Inc (Muni Bond - Single State)	C	C	C-	Up	Y	
Eaton Vance California Municipal Income Trust	CEV	AMEX	Closed End	US Muni Fixed Inc (Muni Bond - Single State)	C-	C-	C-		Y	
Eaton Vance California Muni Opportunities Fund Class A	EACAX	NAS CM	Open End	US Muni Fixed Inc (Muni Bond - Single State)	C	C	B		Y	
Eaton Vance California Muni Opportunities Fund Class C	ECCAX	NAS CM	Open End	US Muni Fixed Inc (Muni Bond - Single State)	C	C-	B-		Y	
Eaton Vance California Muni Opportunities Fund Class I	EICAX	NAS CM	Open End	US Muni Fixed Inc (Muni Bond - Single State)	C+	C	B	Up	Y	
Eaton Vance Connecticut Municipal Income Fund Class A	ETCTX	NAS CM	Open End	US Muni Fixed Inc (Muni Bond - Single State)	C	C	B-		Y	
Eaton Vance Connecticut Municipal Income Fund Class C	ECCTX	NAS CM	Open End	US Muni Fixed Inc (Muni Bond - Single State)	C	C-	C+		Y	
Eaton Vance Connecticut Municipal Income Fund Class I	EICTX	NAS CM	Open End	US Muni Fixed Inc (Muni Bond - Single State)	C	C	B-		Y	
Eaton Vance Core Bond Fund Class A	EAGIX	NAS CM	Open End	US Fixed Inc (Growth & Income)	C+	C	B	Up	Y	
Eaton Vance Core Bond Fund Institutional Class	EIGIX	NAS CM	Open End	US Fixed Inc (Growth & Income)	C+	C	B	Up	Y	
Eaton Vance Core Plus Bond Fund Class A	EBABX	NAS CM	Open End	US Fixed Inc (Income)	C-	D+	C	Down	Y	
Eaton Vance Core Plus Bond Fund Class C	ECBAX	NAS CM	Open End	US Fixed Inc (Income)	C-	D+	C		Y	
Eaton Vance Core Plus Bond Fund Class I	EIBAX	NAS CM	Open End	US Fixed Inc (Income)	C-	D+	C	Down	Y	
Eaton Vance Emerging Markets Debt Fund Class I	EEIDX	NAS CM	Open End	Emerg Mkts Fixed Inc (Diversified Emerg Mkts)	D	D	D+	Down	Y	
Eaton Vance Emerg Mkts Debt Opportunities Fund Class A	EADOX	NAS CM	Open End	Emerg Mkts Fixed Inc (Diversified Emerg Mkts)	C	C-	C		Y	
Eaton Vance Emerg Mkts Debt Opportunities Fund Class I	EIDOX	NAS CM	Open End	Emerg Mkts Fixed Inc (Diversified Emerg Mkts)	C	C-	C		Y	
Eaton Vance Emerg Mkts Debt Opportunities Fund Class R6	EELDX	NAS CM	Open End	Emerg Mkts Fixed Inc (Diversified Emerg Mkts)	C	C-	C		Y	
Eaton Vance Emerging Markets Local Income Fund Class A	EEIAX	NAS CM	Open End	Emerg Mkts Fixed Inc (Income)	C-	C-	C-	Down	Y	
Eaton Vance Emerging Markets Local Income Fund Class C	EEICX	NAS CM	Open End	Emerg Mkts Fixed Inc (Income)	C-	C-	C-	Down	Y	
Eaton Vance Emerging Markets Local Income Fund Class I	EEIIX	NAS CM	Open End	Emerg Mkts Fixed Inc (Income)	C-	C-	C	Down	Y	
Eaton Vance Floating - Rate Fund Advisor Class	EABLX	NAS CM	Open End	US Fixed Inc (Income)	D+	D	C-	Down	Y	
Eaton Vance Floating - Rate Fund Class A	EVBLX	NAS CM	Open End	US Fixed Inc (Income)	D+	D	C-	Down	Y	
Eaton Vance Floating - Rate Fund Class C	ECBLX	NAS CM	Open End	US Fixed Inc (Income)	D	D	C-	Down	Y	
Eaton Vance Floating - Rate Fund Institutional Class	EIBLX	NAS CM	Open End	US Fixed Inc (Income)	D+	D	C-	Down	Y	

★ Expanded analysis of this fund is included in Section II.

TOTAL RETURNS & PERFORMANCE									ASSETS		ASSET ALLOCATION & TURNOVER							MINIMUMS		FEES		
3-Month Total Return	6-Month Total Return	1-Year Total Return	3-Year Total Return	5-Year Total Return	Dividend Yield (TTM)	Expense Ratio	3-Yr Std Deviation	Effective Duration	NAV	Total Assets (MIL)	%Cash	%Government Bonds	%Municipal Bonds	%Corporate Bonds	%Other	Turnover Ratio	Average Coupon Rate	Min Initial Investment	Min Additional Investment	Front End Fee (%)	Back End Fee (%)	Inception Date
3.37	-2.24	0.23	8.99	18.58	4.14	0.64	6.69		11.74	991.0	4	0	96	0	0	47	5.39	1,000,000				Aug-02
3.28	-2.32	0.23	8.89	18.48	4.14	0.65	6.62		11.73	991.0	4	0	96	0	0	47	5.39	2,500	50			Jan-87
4.16	-2.47	0.81	12.33	23.58	4.55	0	9.09		12.15	131.5	0	0	100	0	0	28	5.71					Mar-89
0.09	0.45	1.02	3.40	4.11	1.12	0.2	0.14		1	243.2	13	0	87	0	0			1,000,000				Nov-99
0.10	0.44	1.01	3.34	3.98	1.1	0.38	0.14		1	243.2	13	0	87	0	0			1,000	50			Mar-07
0.08	0.43	0.97	3.24	3.83	1.08	0.4	0.14		1	243.2	13	0	87	0	0			2,500	50			Mar-07
0.01	0.18	0.34	0.98	1.11	0.39	1.18	0.1		1	243.2	13	0	87	0	0			1,000	100			May-05
0.05	0.38	0.85	2.75	3.16	0.95	0.54	0.14		1	243.2	13	0	87	0	0			100,000	1,000			Nov-99
0.05	0.31	0.69	2.21	2.39	0.77	0.72	0.14		1	243.2	13	0	87	0	0			2,000				Mar-07
5.79	4.65	6.41	14.45	22.33	2.68	0.84	4.26	6.01	11.24	442.4	4	17	0	43	0	211	3.40	1,000	50	2.75		Jun-01
5.59	4.26	5.61	11.90	17.82	1.94	1.59	4.28	6.01	11.25	442.4	4	17	0	43	0	211	3.40	1,000	50		1.00	Jun-01
5.97	4.89	6.70	15.44	23.91	2.92	0.59	4.33	6.01	11.2	442.4	4	17	0	43	0	211	3.40	1,000,000				Jun-01
5.72	4.52	6.15	13.60	20.82	2.43	1.09	4.27	6.01	11.24	442.4	4	17	0	43	0	211	3.40	0				Oct-17
5.86	4.78	6.68	15.32	23.87	2.92	0.59	4.26	6.01	11.24	442.4	4	17	0	43	0	211	3.40	2,500	50			Apr-28
5.78	4.70	6.69	15.32	23.88		0.59	4.26	6.01	11.19	442.4	4	17	0	43	0	211	3.40	0				Aug-19
0.01	0.32	1.23	4.43	5.10	1.38	0.2	0.21		1	903.6	27	73	0	0	0			10,000,000				Feb-16
0.00	0.29	1.14	4.18	4.57	1.29	0.33	0.2		1	903.6	27	73	0	0	0			2,500	50			May-07
0.02	0.34	1.26	4.53	5.07	1.41	0.25	0.2		1	903.6	27	73	0	0	0			1,000,000				Dec-91
0.00	0.22	0.93	3.21	3.30	1.06	0.73	0.18		1	903.6	27	73	0	0	0			2,000				May-07
0.00	3.70	-15.65	-9.89	13.56	15.09	9.53	19.23		9.41	271.7	7	0	0	14	0	35						Oct-14
0.00	0.00					4.35			18.2344	22.0												Jul-19
0.00	0.00					1.39				3.8	38	0	0	55	0	94		1,000	100			Aug-18
1.62	1.84	3.98	12.89	21.01	3.23	1.04	4.12	5.82	9.24	319.0	5	0	96	0	0	33	5.43	1,000		4.75		Jan-98
1.55	1.47	3.22	10.40	16.58	2.48	1.79	4.14	5.82	9.19	319.0	5	0	96	0	0	33	5.43	1,000			1.00	May-06
1.72	1.94	4.17	13.69	22.44	3.48	0.79	4.15	5.82	10.09	319.0	5	0	96	0	0	33	5.43	250,000				Mar-78
2.25	1.89	3.62	11.46	19.15	2.63	0.7	3.7	5.36	9.79	64.2	1	0	99	0	0	6	4.88	1,000		4.75		Dec-93
2.01	1.49	2.88	8.95	14.71	1.9	1.45	3.71	5.36	10.88	64.2	1	0	99	0	0	6	4.88	1,000			1.00	Dec-05
2.31	2.00	3.83	12.14	20.36	2.84	0.49	3.7	5.36	9.79	64.2	1	0	99	0	0	6	4.88	250,000				Aug-10
4.29	2.59	5.23	14.05	25.01	3.6	0	6.06	1.90	12.6	314.4	-1	0	100	0	0	17	9.52					Aug-02
4.06	2.37	5.41	14.46	26.38	3.73	0	7.2	4.20	14.36	101.5	1	0	99	0	0	8	9.06					Jan-99
3.10	1.91	4.40	12.62	22.33	2.16	0.8	4.29	4.40	10.84	432.6	3	0	97	0	0	235	4.33	1,000		4.75		May-94
2.92	1.50	3.61	10.10	17.81	1.41	1.55	4.27	4.40	10.02	432.6	3	0	97	0	0	235	4.33	1,000			1.00	Aug-04
3.15	1.92	4.55	13.34	23.72	2.4	0.55	4.27	4.40	10.84	432.6	3	0	97	0	0	235	4.33	250,000				Mar-08
1.77	1.44	3.18	9.88	17.04	2.79	0.73	3.21	4.85	10.22	76.5	1	0	99	0	0	16	4.65	1,000		4.75		Apr-94
1.69	1.07	2.52	7.44	12.74	2.03	1.47	3.22	4.85	10.19	76.5	1	0	99	0	0	16	4.65	1,000			1.00	Feb-06
1.92	1.65	3.49	10.54	18.22	2.99	0.53	3.25	4.85	10.23	76.5	1	0	99	0	0	16	4.65	250,000				Mar-08
6.14	3.10	5.69	13.35	18.77	2.64	0.74	4.71	5.96	10.19	150.7	4	4	2	44	0	89	3.35	1,000		4.75		Jan-09
6.10	3.23	5.85	14.10	20.27	2.89	0.49	4.72	5.96	10.17	150.7	4	4	2	44	0	89	3.35	250,000				Mar-07
8.57	-2.92	-0.36	8.94	20.15	3.74	0.74	7.99	5.57	11.5	789.4	6	7	0	43	0	75	4.06	1,000		4.75		Nov-09
8.48	-3.28	-1.02	6.62	15.76	2.95	1.49	8.03	5.57	11.5	789.4	6	7	0	43	0	75	4.06	1,000	100		1.00	Nov-09
8.65	-2.80	-0.12	9.76	21.56	4	0.49	8	5.57	11.49	789.4	6	7	0	43	0	75	4.06	250,000				Nov-09
10.76	-6.75	-1.48			6.95	0.85			9.49	7.9	-111	81	0	6	0	187		250,000				May-18
13.90	-2.28	5.88	16.18	30.40	8.91	1.15	10.35		8.66	292.7	-28	57	0	8	0	85		1,000		4.75		Sep-15
13.95	-2.25	6.03	16.96	32.35	9.18	0.9	10.4		8.68	292.7	-28	57	0	8	0	85		250,000				Sep-15
13.86	-2.25	6.08	17.11	32.20	9.22	0.85	10.36		8.65	292.7	-28	57	0	8	0	85		1,000,000				Feb-13
14.13	-4.48	4.25	12.05	27.57	14.75	1.2	13.61		5.16	1,143	0	78	0	1	100	46		1,000		4.75		Jun-07
14.03	-4.88	3.58	9.73	23.24	13.94	1.9	13.7		5.22	1,143	0	78	0	1	100	46		1,000			1.00	Aug-10
14.22	-4.33	4.75	13.06	29.45	15.07	0.9	13.64		5.16	1,143	0	78	0	1	100	46		250,000				Nov-09
8.33	-4.70	-2.71	4.20	13.36	4.62	1.03	7.79	0.17	8.27	5,163	8	0	0	89	1	16	4.02	1,000				Feb-01
8.33	-4.70	-2.60	4.25	13.40	4.62	1.02	7.73	0.17	8.56	5,163	8	0	0	89	1	16	4.02	1,000		2.25		May-03
8.27	-4.94	-3.32	2.00	9.33	3.83	1.78	7.79	0.17	8.27	5,163	8	0	0	89	1	16	4.02	1,000			1.00	Feb-01
8.38	-4.57	-2.35	4.99	14.80	4.89	0.77	7.74	0.17	8.28	5,163	8	0	0	89	1	16	4.02	250,000				Jan-01

Fund Name	MARKET Ticker Symbol	Traded On	FUND TYPE, CATEGORY & OBJECTIVE Fund Type	Category and (Prospectus Objective)	RATINGS Overall Rating	Reward Rating	Risk Rating	Recent Up/ Downgrade	NEW INVESTORS Open to New Investors	Telephone
Eaton Vance Floating Rate Fund Class R6	ESBLX	NAS CM	Open End	US Fixed Inc (Income)	D+	D	C-	Down	Y	
Eaton Vance Floating-Rate & High Income Advisers Cl	EAFHX	NAS CM	Open End	US Fixed Inc (Income)	D+	D	C-	Down	Y	
Eaton Vance Floating-Rate & High Income Fund Class A	EVFHX	NAS CM	Open End	US Fixed Inc (Income)	D+	D	C-	Down	Y	
Eaton Vance Floating-Rate & High Income Fund Class C	ECFHX	NAS CM	Open End	US Fixed Inc (Income)	D	D	C-	Down	Y	
Eaton Vance Floating-Rate & High Income Fund Class I	EIFHX	NAS CM	Open End	US Fixed Inc (Income)	D+	D	C-	Down	Y	
Eaton Vance Floating-Rate & High Income Fund R6 Class	ESFHX	NAS CM	Open End	US Fixed Inc (Income)	D+	D	C-	Down	Y	
Eaton Vance Floating-Rate Advantage Fund Class A	EAFAX	NAS CM	Open End	US Fixed Inc (Income)	D	D	D+	Down	Y	
Eaton Vance Floating-Rate Advantage Fund Class Advisers	EVFAX	NAS CM	Open End	US Fixed Inc (Income)	D	D	D+	Down	Y	
Eaton Vance Floating-Rate Advantage Fund Class C	ECFAX	NAS CM	Open End	US Fixed Inc (Income)	D	D	D+	Down	Y	
Eaton Vance Floating-Rate Advantage Fund Class I	EIFAX	NAS CM	Open End	US Fixed Inc (Income)	D+	D	D+	Down	Y	
Eaton Vance Floating-Rate Advantage Fund Class R6	EFRRX	NAS CM	Open End	US Fixed Inc (Income)	D+	D	D+	Down	Y	
Eaton Vance Floating-Rate Income Plus Fund	EFF	NYSE	Closed End	US Fixed Inc (Growth & Income)	D	D	D	Down	Y	
Eaton Vance Floating-Rate Income Trust	EFT	NYSE	Closed End	US Fixed Inc (Corp Bond - High Yield)	D	D	D	Down	Y	
Eaton Vance Floating-Rate Municipal Income Fund Class A	EXFLX	NAS CM	Open End	US Muni Fixed Inc (Muni Bond - Natl)	C-	D+	C	Down	Y	
Eaton Vance Floating-Rate Municipal Income Fund Class I	EILMX	NAS CM	Open End	US Muni Fixed Inc (Muni Bond - Natl)	C-	C-	C	Down	Y	
Eaton Vance Float-Rate 2022 Target Term	EFL	NYSE	Closed End	US Fixed Inc (Income)	D	D	D+	Down	Y	617-672-8277
Eaton Vance Georgia Municipal Income Fund Class A	ETGAX	NAS CM	Open End	US Muni Fixed Inc (Muni Bond - Single State)	C+	C	B	Up	Y	
Eaton Vance Georgia Municipal Income Fund Class C	ECGAX	NAS CM	Open End	US Muni Fixed Inc (Muni Bond - Single State)	C	C	B-		Y	
Eaton Vance Georgia Municipal Income Fund Class I	EIGAX	NAS CM	Open End	US Muni Fixed Inc (Muni Bond - Single State)	C+	C	B	Up	Y	
Eaton Vance Global Bond Fund Class A	EAIIX	NAS CM	Open End	US Fixed Inc (Growth & Income)	C	C-	C+		Y	
Eaton Vance Global Bond Fund Class C	ECIMX	NAS CM	Open End	US Fixed Inc (Growth & Income)	C	C-	C		Y	
Eaton Vance Global Bond Fund Class I	EIIMX	NAS CM	Open End	US Fixed Inc (Growth & Income)	C	C-	C+		Y	
Eaton Vance Global Macro Absolute Return Advantage Cl A	EGRAX	NAS CM	Open End	Fixed Inc Misc (Growth & Income)	C-	C-	C	Down	Y	
Eaton Vance Global Macro Absolute Return Advantage Cl C	EGRCX	NAS CM	Open End	Fixed Inc Misc (Growth & Income)	C-	C-	C	Down	Y	
Eaton Vance Global Macro Absolute Return Advantage Cl I	EGRIX	NAS CM	Open End	Fixed Inc Misc (Growth & Income)	C	C-	C		Y	
Eaton Vance Global Macro Absolute Return Advantage Cl R	EGRRX	NAS CM	Open End	Fixed Inc Misc (Growth & Income)	C-	C-	C	Down	Y	
Eaton Vance Global Macro Absolute Return Advantage Cl R6	EGRSX	NAS CM	Open End	Fixed Inc Misc (Growth & Income)	C	C-	C		Y	
Eaton Vance Global Macro Absolute Return Fund Class A	EAGMX	NAS CM	Open End	Fixed Inc Misc (Growth & Income)	C	C-	C+		Y	
Eaton Vance Global Macro Absolute Return Fund Class C	ECGMX	NAS CM	Open End	Fixed Inc Misc (Growth & Income)	C	C-	C		Y	
Eaton Vance Global Macro Absolute Return Fund Class I	EIGMX	NAS CM	Open End	Fixed Inc Misc (Growth & Income)	C	C-	C+		Y	
Eaton Vance Global Macro Absolute Return Fund Class R	ERGMX	NAS CM	Open End	Fixed Inc Misc (Growth & Income)	C	C-	C		Y	
Eaton Vance Global Macro Absolute Return Fund Class R6	EGMSX	NAS CM	Open End	Fixed Inc Misc (Growth & Income)	C	C-	C+		Y	
Eaton Vance Government Opportunities Fund Class A	EVGOX	NAS CM	Open End	US Fixed Inc (Govt Bond - General)	C+	C	B	Up	Y	
Eaton Vance Government Opportunities Fund Class C	ECGOX	NAS CM	Open End	US Fixed Inc (Govt Bond - General)	C	C	B-		Y	
Eaton Vance Government Opportunities Fund Class I	EIGOX	NAS CM	Open End	US Fixed Inc (Govt Bond - General)	C+	C	B	Up	Y	
Eaton Vance Government Opportunities Fund Class R	ERGOX	NAS CM	Open End	US Fixed Inc (Govt Bond - General)	C+	C	B	Up	Y	
Eaton Vance High Income 2021 Target Term Trust	EHT	NYSE	Closed End	US Fixed Inc (Income)	D+	D+	C-	Down	Y	
Eaton Vance High Income Opportunities Fund Class A	ETHIX	NAS CM	Open End	US Fixed Inc (Corp Bond - High Yield)	C-	D+	C		Y	
Eaton Vance High Income Opportunities Fund Class C	ECHIX	NAS CM	Open End	US Fixed Inc (Corp Bond - High Yield)	D+	D	C-	Down	Y	
Eaton Vance High Income Opportunities Fund Class I	EIHIX	NAS CM	Open End	US Fixed Inc (Corp Bond - High Yield)	C-	D+	C		Y	
Eaton Vance High Yield Municipal Income Fund Class I	EIHYX	NAS CM	Open End	US Muni Fixed Inc (Muni Bond - Natl)	C	C-	C+		Y	
Eaton Vance High-Yield Municipal Income Fund Class A	ETHYX	NAS CM	Open End	US Muni Fixed Inc (Muni Bond - Natl)	C	C-	C		Y	
Eaton Vance High-Yield Municipal Income Fund Class C	ECHYX	NAS CM	Open End	US Muni Fixed Inc (Muni Bond - Natl)	C-	D+	C	Down	Y	
Eaton Vance Income Fund of Boston Class A	EVIBX	NAS CM	Open End	US Fixed Inc (Corp Bond - High Yield)	C-	D+	C		Y	
Eaton Vance Income Fund of Boston Class C	ECIBX	NAS CM	Open End	US Fixed Inc (Corp Bond - High Yield)	C-	D+	C		Y	
Eaton Vance Income Fund of Boston Class I	EIBIX	NAS CM	Open End	US Fixed Inc (Corp Bond - High Yield)	C-	D+	C		Y	
Eaton Vance Income Fund of Boston Class R	ERIBX	NAS CM	Open End	US Fixed Inc (Corp Bond - High Yield)	C-	D+	C		Y	
Eaton Vance Income Fund of Boston Class R6	EIBRX	NAS CM	Open End	US Fixed Inc (Corp Bond - High Yield)	C-	D+	C		Y	
Eaton Vance Limited Duration Income Fund	EVV	AMEX	Closed End	US Fixed Inc (Multisector Bond)	D	D	D+	Down	Y	
Eaton Vance Maryland Municipal Income Fund Class A	ETMDX	NAS CM	Open End	US Muni Fixed Inc (Muni Bond - Single State)	C	C-	C+		Y	
Eaton Vance Maryland Municipal Income Fund Class C	ECMDX	NAS CM	Open End	US Muni Fixed Inc (Muni Bond - Single State)	C	C-	C+		Y	
Eaton Vance Maryland Municipal Income Fund Class I	EIMDX	NAS CM	Open End	US Muni Fixed Inc (Muni Bond - Single State)	C	C-	B-		Y	

★ Expanded analysis of this fund is included in Section II.

TOTAL RETURNS & PERFORMANCE									ASSETS		ASSET ALLOCATION & TURNOVER							MINIMUMS		FEES		
3-Month Total Return	6-Month Total Return	1-Year Total Return	3-Year Total Return	5-Year Total Return	Dividend Yield (TTM)	Expense Ratio	3-Yr Std Deviation	Effective Duration	NAV	Total Assets (MIL)	%Cash	%Government Bonds	%Municipal Bonds	%Corporate Bonds	%Other	Turnover Ratio	Average Coupon Rate	Min Initial Investment	Min Additional Investment	Front End Fee (%)	Back End Fee (%)	Inception Date
8.53	-4.53	-2.28	5.28	15.02	4.95	0.72	7.76	0.17	8.29	5,163	8	0	0	89	1	16	4.02	1,000,000				Dec-16
8.52	-4.93	-2.57	4.35	14.09	4.76	1.04	7.96	0.76	8.13	911.7	7	0	0	90	1	5	4.37	1,000				Sep-00
8.57	-4.95	-2.61	4.31	14.14	4.75	1.04	7.94	0.76	8.65	911.7	7	0	0	90	1	5	4.37	1,000		2.25		May-03
8.35	-5.29	-3.42	2.01	9.88	3.97	1.79	7.95	0.76	8.11	911.7	7	0	0	90	1	5	4.37	1,000			1.00	Sep-00
8.59	-4.92	-2.44	5.02	15.52	5.03	0.79	7.95	0.76	8.13	911.7	7	0	0	90	1	5	4.37	250,000				Sep-00
8.61	-4.89	-2.39	5.30	14.63	5.09	0.73	7.95	0.76	8.13	911.7	7	0	0	90	1	5	4.37	1,000,000				Jun-16
10.66	-6.81	-4.25	3.73	14.30	5.43	1.87	10.1	0.16	9.77	5,488	2	0	0	95	0	17	3.98	1,000		2.25		Mar-08
10.66	-6.72	-4.16	3.74	14.40	5.42	1.87	10.12	0.16	9.77	5,488	2	0	0	95	0	17	3.98	1,000				Mar-08
10.43	-7.05	-4.74	2.17	11.56	4.89	2.37	10.04	0.16	9.75	5,488	2	0	0	95	0	17	3.98	1,000			1.00	Mar-08
10.73	-6.69	-3.92	4.52	15.83	5.69	1.62	10.12	0.16	9.77	5,488	2	0	0	95	0	17	3.98	250,000				Mar-08
10.64	-6.67	-3.95	4.50	15.80	5.77	1.56	10.07	0.16	9.76	5,488	2	0	0	95	0	17	3.98	1,000,000				May-19
14.04	-8.68	-6.34	0.21	11.99	6.43	2.24	13.04		15.18	114.1	1	0	0	94	0	24	4.14					Jun-13
14.96	-9.16	-6.32	2.34	15.81	7.08	0	13.38		13.24	519.4	1	0	0	95	0	24	4.23					Jun-04
-0.71	-0.87	-0.02	2.82	3.97	1.24	0.6	0.86	0.09	9.72	502.7	3	0	97	0	0	49	0.79	1,000		2.25		Jun-96
-0.57	-0.69	0.12	3.39	4.76	1.4	0.45	0.86	0.09	9.73	502.7	3	0	97	0	0	49	0.79	250,000				Aug-10
11.05	-7.30	-4.03	2.32		6.23	2.66			8.61	202.1	3	0	0	97	0	22	4.04					Jul-17
2.28	2.03	3.73	10.85	18.40	2.32	0.7	3.45	5.02	8.75	94.0	4	0	96	0	0	12	4.75	1,000		4.75		Dec-93
2.09	1.70	2.98	8.34	14.09	1.57	1.45	3.44	5.02	9.36	94.0	4	0	96	0	0	12	4.75	1,000			1.00	Apr-06
2.21	2.13	3.81	11.38	19.44	2.51	0.49	3.45	5.02	8.77	94.0	4	0	96	0	0	12	4.75	250,000				Mar-08
3.64	0.27	2.51	5.50	13.62	6.53	1.01	3.67	0.27	8.3	56.3	0	27	0	4	100	92		1,000		4.75		Jun-07
3.46	-0.07	1.80	3.30	9.69	5.8	1.71	3.68	0.27	8.3	56.3	0	27	0	4	100	92		1,000			1.00	Mar-11
3.72	0.29	2.81	6.42	15.30	6.83	0.71	3.74	0.27	8.27	56.3	0	27	0	4	100	92		250,000				Mar-11
11.21	-0.19	7.89	5.41	16.95	4.09	1.57	8.42		10.31	2,756	0	75	0	4	100	71		1,000		4.75		Aug-10
11.06	-0.49	7.17	3.25	13.01	3.07	2.29	8.41		10.04	2,756	0	75	0	4	100	71		1,000			1.00	Aug-10
11.28	-0.09	8.18	6.35	18.73	4.22	1.29	8.42		10.45	2,756	0	75	0	4	100	71		250,000				Aug-10
11.23	-0.29	7.73	4.76	15.86	3.78	1.79	8.46		10.2	2,756	0	75	0	4	100	71		1,000				Dec-10
11.38	0.00	8.28	6.71	19.24	4.31	1.26	8.46		10.47	2,756	0	75	0	4	100	71		1,000,000				May-17
6.61	-0.39	4.44	6.62	13.55	5.39	1.04	5.14	2.20	8.64	3,175	0	65	0	6	100	61		1,000		4.75		Jun-07
6.41	-0.73	3.72	4.42	9.54	4.67	1.76	5.12	2.20	8.67	3,175	0	65	0	6	100	61		1,000	100		1.00	Oct-09
6.58	-0.24	4.76	7.58	15.21	5.7	0.75	5.08	2.20	8.62	3,175	0	65	0	6	100	61		250,000				Jun-07
6.55	-0.48	4.36	6.00	12.42	5.19	1.26	5.15	2.20	8.66	3,175	0	65	0	6	100	61		1,000				Apr-10
6.73	-0.21	4.83	7.77	15.41	5.76	0.69	5.17	2.20	8.62	3,175	0	65	0	6	100	61		1,000,000				May-17
1.90	3.80	4.60	7.45	8.76	2.95	1.12	1.16	1.61	6.19	356.8	-3	0	0	0	0	90	3.46	1,000		2.25		Aug-84
1.55	3.42	3.83	5.06	4.75	2.21	1.87	1.11	1.61	6.18	356.8	-3	0	0	0	0	90	3.46	1,000			1.00	Nov-93
1.80	3.93	4.69	8.07	9.94	3.19	0.87	1.07	1.61	6.18	356.8	-3	0	0	0	0	90	3.46	250,000				Apr-09
1.68	3.68	4.18	6.46	7.21	2.7	1.37	1.12	1.61	6.16	356.8	-3	0	0	0	0	90	3.46	1,000				Aug-05
5.26	-0.91	1.31	9.60		4.35	1.61	4.56		9.74	207.3	0	0	0	100	0	38	5.36					May-16
9.48	-6.05	-2.17	5.58	18.15	5.82	0.91	9.21	3.79	4.09	772.5	3	0	0	96	0	32	6.10	1,000		4.75		Mar-04
9.26	-6.43	-2.93	3.18	13.74	5	1.67	9.22	3.79	4.09	772.5	3	0	0	96	0	32	6.10	1,000			1.00	Jun-94
9.53	-5.91	-1.91	6.37	19.90	6.09	0.66	9.17	3.79	4.1	772.5	3	0	0	96	0	32	6.10	250,000				Oct-09
2.66	-1.08	1.65	14.47	27.27	4.2	0.64	5.77	5.44	8.97	1,240	3	1	95	1	0	23	5.30	250,000				May-07
2.71	-1.10	1.51	13.76	25.72	3.95	0.89	5.78	5.44	8.97	1,240	3	1	95	1	0	23	5.30	1,000		4.75		Aug-95
2.42	-1.46	0.73	11.16	21.08	3.2	1.64	5.81	5.44	8.29	1,240	3	1	95	1	0	23	5.30	1,000			1.00	Jun-97
8.37	-4.80	-1.36	6.81	18.59	6.08	1	8.01	3.80	5.22	5,261	7	0	0	92	0	38	6.08	1,000		4.75		Jun-72
8.13	-5.17	-2.13	4.36	14.32	5.25	1.75	8.02	3.80	5.23	5,261	7	0	0	92	0	38	6.08	1,000			1.00	Jun-02
8.44	-4.67	-1.11	7.42	20.08	6.35	0.75	8.01	3.80	5.22	5,261	7	0	0	92	0	38	6.08	250,000				Jul-99
8.29	-4.93	-1.63	5.94	17.04	5.8	1.25	8.02	3.80	5.22	5,261	7	0	0	92	0	38	6.08	1,000				Jan-04
8.46	-4.63	-1.02	7.71	20.61	6.45	0.66	8.02	3.80	5.22	5,261	7	0	0	92	0	38	6.08	1,000,000				Jul-14
12.36	-6.77	-3.94	3.98	16.35	7.06	1.12	11.03		12.9	1,480	1	0	0	66	0	49	4.98					May-03
1.50	0.82	2.68	9.15	15.24	2.36	0.73	4.04	5.38	8.94	67.4	1	0	99	0	0	21	4.46	1,000		4.75		Dec-93
1.35	0.48	1.89	6.76	11.04	1.61	1.49	4.07	5.38	9.75	67.4	1	0	99	0	0	21	4.46	1,000			1.00	May-06
1.55	1.03	2.88	9.80	16.38	2.56	0.52	4.05	5.38	8.96	67.4	1	0	99	0	0	21	4.46	250,000				Mar-08

	MARKET			FUND TYPE, CATEGORY & OBJECTIVE	RATINGS				NEW INVESTORS	
Fund Name	Ticker Symbol	Traded On	Fund Type	Category and (Prospectus Objective)	Overall Rating	Reward Rating	Risk Rating	Recent Up/ Downgrade	Open to New Investors	Telephone
Eaton Vance Massachusetts Municipal Income Fund Class A	ETMAX	NAS CM	Open End	US Muni Fixed Inc (Muni Bond - Single State)	C	C	B-		Y	
Eaton Vance Massachusetts Municipal Income Fund Class C	ECMMX	NAS CM	Open End	US Muni Fixed Inc (Muni Bond - Single State)	C	C-	B-		Y	
Eaton Vance Massachusetts Municipal Income Fund Class I	EIMAX	NAS CM	Open End	US Muni Fixed Inc (Muni Bond - Single State)	C	C	B		Y	
Eaton Vance Minnesota Municipal Income Fund Class A	ETMNX	NAS CM	Open End	US Muni Fixed Inc (Muni Bond - Single State)	C+	C	B	Up	Y	
Eaton Vance Minnesota Municipal Income Fund Class C	ECMNX	NAS CM	Open End	US Muni Fixed Inc (Muni Bond - Single State)	C	C	B-		Y	
Eaton Vance Minnesota Municipal Income Fund Class I	EIMNX	NAS CM	Open End	US Muni Fixed Inc (Muni Bond - Single State)	C+	C	B	Up	Y	
Eaton Vance Missouri Municipal Income Fund Class A	ETMOX	NAS CM	Open End	US Muni Fixed Inc (Muni Bond - Single State)	C+	C	B	Up	Y	
Eaton Vance Missouri Municipal Income Fund Class C	ECMOX	NAS CM	Open End	US Muni Fixed Inc (Muni Bond - Single State)	C+	C	B	Up	Y	
Eaton Vance Missouri Municipal Income Fund Class I	EIMOX	NAS CM	Open End	US Muni Fixed Inc (Muni Bond - Single State)	C+	C	B	Up	Y	
Eaton Vance Multi-Asset Credit Fund Class A	EAAMX	NAS CM	Open End	US Fixed Inc (Income)	D+	D	C-	Down	Y	
Eaton Vance Multi-Asset Credit Fund Class C	ECAMX	NAS CM	Open End	US Fixed Inc (Income)	D+	D	C-	Down	Y	
Eaton Vance Multi-Asset Credit Fund Class I	EIAMX	NAS CM	Open End	US Fixed Inc (Income)	D+	D	C-	Down	Y	
Eaton Vance Multi-Asset Credit Fund Class R6	ERAMX	NAS CM	Open End	US Fixed Inc (Income)	D+	D	C-	Down	Y	
Eaton Vance Municipal Bond Fund	EIM	AMEX	Closed End	US Muni Fixed Inc (Muni Bond - Natl)	C	C-	C+		Y	
Eaton Vance Municipal Income 2028 Term Trust	ETX	NYSE	Closed End	US Muni Fixed Inc (Muni Bond - Natl)	C-	C-	C-		Y	
Eaton Vance Municipal Income Trust	EVN	NYSE	Closed End	US Muni Fixed Inc (Muni Bond - Natl)	C-	C-	C-	Down	Y	
Eaton Vance Municipal Opportunities Fund Class A	EMOAX	NAS CM	Open End	US Muni Fixed Inc (Income)	C-	D+	C	Down	Y	
Eaton Vance Municipal Opportunities Fund Class C	EMOCX	NAS CM	Open End	US Muni Fixed Inc (Income)	C-	D+	C	Down	Y	
Eaton Vance Municipal Opportunities Fund Class I	EMOIX	NAS CM	Open End	US Muni Fixed Inc (Income)	C-	D+	C	Down	Y	
Eaton Vance Natl Limited Maturity Muni Income Fund Class A	EXNAX	NAS CM	Open End	US Muni Fixed Inc (Muni Bond - Natl)	C	C-	C+		Y	
Eaton Vance Natl Limited Maturity Muni Income Fund Class C	EZNAX	NAS CM	Open End	US Muni Fixed Inc (Muni Bond - Natl)	C	C-	C		Y	
Eaton Vance Natl Limited Maturity Muni Income Fund Class I	EINAX	NAS CM	Open End	US Muni Fixed Inc (Muni Bond - Natl)	C	C-	C+		Y	
Eaton Vance National Municipal Income Fund Class A	EANAX	NAS CM	Open End	US Muni Fixed Inc (Muni Bond - Natl)	C	C	B		Y	
Eaton Vance National Municipal Income Fund Class C	ECHMX	NAS CM	Open End	US Muni Fixed Inc (Muni Bond - Natl)	C	C-	B-		Y	
Eaton Vance National Municipal Income Fund Class I	EIHMX	NAS CM	Open End	US Muni Fixed Inc (Muni Bond - Natl)	C+	C	B		Y	
Eaton Vance National Municipal Opportunities Trust	EOT	NYSE	Closed End	US Muni Fixed Inc (Muni Bond - Natl)	C-	C-	C-		Y	
Eaton Vance New Jersey Municipal Income Fund Class A	ETNJX	NAS CM	Open End	US Muni Fixed Inc (Muni Bond - Single State)	C	C-	B	Down	Y	
Eaton Vance New Jersey Municipal Income Fund Class C	ECNJX	NAS CM	Open End	US Muni Fixed Inc (Muni Bond - Single State)	C	C-	B-		Y	
Eaton Vance New Jersey Municipal Income Fund Class I	EINJX	NAS CM	Open End	US Muni Fixed Inc (Muni Bond - Single State)	C	C-	B	Down	Y	
Eaton Vance New York Municipal Bond Fund	ENX	AMEX	Closed End	US Muni Fixed Inc (Muni Bond - Single State)	C-	C-	C-		Y	800-836-2414
Eaton Vance New York Municipal Income Fund Class A	ETNYX	NAS CM	Open End	US Muni Fixed Inc (Muni Bond - Single State)	C	C	B		Y	
Eaton Vance New York Municipal Income Fund Class C	ECNYX	NAS CM	Open End	US Muni Fixed Inc (Muni Bond - Single State)	C	C-	B-		Y	
Eaton Vance New York Municipal Income Fund Class I	EINYX	NAS CM	Open End	US Muni Fixed Inc (Muni Bond - Single State)	C+	C	B		Y	
Eaton Vance New York Municipal Income Trust	EVY	AMEX	Closed End	US Muni Fixed Inc (Muni Bond - Single State)	C-	C-	D+		Y	
Eaton Vance New York Municipal Opportunities Fund Class A	EXNYX	NAS CM	Open End	US Muni Fixed Inc (Muni Bond - Single State)	C	C-	C+		Y	
Eaton Vance New York Municipal Opportunities Fund Class C	EZNYX	NAS CM	Open End	US Muni Fixed Inc (Muni Bond - Single State)	C	C-	C		Y	
Eaton Vance New York Municipal Opportunities Fund Class I	ENYIX	NAS CM	Open End	US Muni Fixed Inc (Muni Bond - Single State)	C	C-	C+		Y	
Eaton Vance North Carolina Municipal Income Fund Class A	ETNCX	NAS CM	Open End	US Muni Fixed Inc (Muni Bond - Single State)	C	C	B-		Y	
Eaton Vance North Carolina Municipal Income Fund Class C	ECNCX	NAS CM	Open End	US Muni Fixed Inc (Muni Bond - Single State)	C	C-	C+		Y	
Eaton Vance North Carolina Municipal Income Fund Class I	EINCX	NAS CM	Open End	US Muni Fixed Inc (Muni Bond - Single State)	C	C	B-		Y	
Eaton Vance Ohio Municipal Income Fund Class A	ETOHX	NAS CM	Open End	US Muni Fixed Inc (Muni Bond - Single State)	C+	C	B	Up	Y	
Eaton Vance Ohio Municipal Income Fund Class C	ECOHX	NAS CM	Open End	US Muni Fixed Inc (Muni Bond - Single State)	C+	C	B	Up	Y	
Eaton Vance Ohio Municipal Income Fund Class I	EIOHX	NAS CM	Open End	US Muni Fixed Inc (Muni Bond - Single State)	C+	C	B	Up	Y	
Eaton Vance Oregon Municipal Income Fund Class A	ETORX	NAS CM	Open End	US Muni Fixed Inc (Muni Bond - Single State)	C+	C	B	Up	Y	
Eaton Vance Oregon Municipal Income Fund Class C	ECORX	NAS CM	Open End	US Muni Fixed Inc (Muni Bond - Single State)	C+	C	B	Up	Y	
Eaton Vance Oregon Municipal Income Fund Class I	EIORX	NAS CM	Open End	US Muni Fixed Inc (Muni Bond - Single State)	B-	C	B	Up	Y	
Eaton Vance Pennsylvania Municipal Income Fund Class A	ETPAX	NAS CM	Open End	US Muni Fixed Inc (Muni Bond - Single State)	C	C	B-		Y	
Eaton Vance Pennsylvania Municipal Income Fund Class C	ECPAX	NAS CM	Open End	US Muni Fixed Inc (Muni Bond - Single State)	C	C-	B-		Y	
Eaton Vance Pennsylvania Municipal Income Fund Class I	EIPAX	NAS CM	Open End	US Muni Fixed Inc (Muni Bond - Single State)	C	C	B		Y	
Eaton Vance Senior Floating-Rate Trust	EFR	NYSE	Closed End	US Fixed Inc (Corp Bond - High Yield)	D	D	D+	Down	Y	
Eaton Vance Senior Income Trust	EVF	NYSE	Closed End	US Fixed Inc (Corp Bond - High Yield)	D	D	D	Down	Y	
Eaton Vance Short Duration Government Income Fund Class A	EALDX	NAS CM	Open End	US Fixed Inc (Govt Bond - General)	C	C	B-		Y	

★ Expanded analysis of this fund is included in Section II.

TOTAL RETURNS & PERFORMANCE									ASSETS		ASSET ALLOCATION & TURNOVER							MINIMUMS		FEES		
3-Month Total Return	6-Month Total Return	1-Year Total Return	3-Year Total Return	5-Year Total Return	Dividend Yield (TTM)	Expense Ratio	3-Yr Std Deviation	Effective Duration	NAV	Total Assets (MIL)	%Cash	%Government Bonds	%Municipal Bonds	%Corporate Bonds	%Other	Turnover Ratio	Average Coupon Rate	Min Initial Investment	Min Additional Investment	Front End Fee (%)	Back End Fee (%)	Inception Date
2.01	1.88	3.46	10.48	17.10	2.67	0.76	3.9	5.39	8.99	185.7	2	0	98	0	0	49	4.79	1,000		4.75		Dec-93
1.83	1.41	2.71	8.05	12.83	1.93	1.51	3.86	5.39	8.99	185.7	2	0	98	0	0	49	4.79	1,000			1.00	May-06
2.16	1.97	3.66	11.14	18.40	2.87	0.56	3.8	5.39	8.99	185.7	2	0	98	0	0	49	4.79	250,000				Jun-93
2.14	1.99	3.92	10.36	16.13	2.01	0.7	3.46	4.85	9.73	182.6	1	0	99	0	0	21	4.45	1,000		4.75		Dec-93
2.03	1.64	3.22	8.01	11.92	1.27	1.46	3.48	4.85	10.47	182.6	1	0	99	0	0	21	4.45	1,000			1.00	Dec-05
2.19	2.09	4.13	11.02	17.29	2.21	0.5	3.47	4.85	9.73	182.6	1	0	99	0	0	21	4.45	250,000				Aug-10
2.18	2.48	4.52	12.22	20.40	2.86	0.71	3.39	5.16	9.65	76.0	2	0	98	0	0	19	4.51	1,000		4.75		Dec-93
2.05	2.10	3.68	9.71	15.85	2.12	1.46	3.35	5.16	10.65	76.0	2	0	98	0	0	19	4.51	1,000			1.00	Feb-06
2.22	2.57	4.70	12.75	21.45	3.05	0.5	3.38	5.16	9.66	76.0	2	0	98	0	0	19	4.51	250,000				Aug-10
9.12	-5.82	-2.43	6.56	17.46	4.99	0.96	8.94	2.17	10.04	398.2	11	2	0	76	0	96	4.84	1,000		4.75		Oct-11
8.91	-6.17	-3.13	4.77	13.77	4.24	1.71	8.95	2.17	10.05	398.2	11	2	0	76	0	96	4.84	1,000			1.00	Oct-11
9.16	-5.78	-2.19	7.87	19.52	5.24	0.71	8.95	2.17	10.06	398.2	11	2	0	76	0	96	4.84	250,000				Oct-11
9.08	-5.76	-2.14	7.92	19.58		0.66	8.9	2.17	10.06	398.2	11	2	0	76	0	96	4.84	1,000,000				Sep-19
3.94	2.78	5.76	15.45	28.26	3.87	0	6.42	0.90	14	1,050	0	1	99	0	0	18	9.77					Aug-02
3.47	0.93	3.67	15.83	36.53	4.03	1.86	5.75	10.10	21.23	227.2	1	0	99	0	0	1	7.19					Mar-13
4.03	1.81	5.07	17.84	40.89	4.14	0	7.62	9.00	13.74	535.5	0	1	98	1	0	17	8.72					Jan-99
2.77	-0.70	1.04	8.92	18.55	2.17	0.96	5.19	5.81	12.13	1,328	2	0	97	1	0	34	4.44	1,000		4.75		May-11
2.58	-1.07	0.29	6.50	14.20	1.4	1.71	5.23	5.81	12.12	1,328	2	0	97	1	0	34	4.44	1,000			1.00	Aug-14
2.83	-0.58	1.29	9.64	20.03	2.43	0.71	5.24	5.81	12.14	1,328	2	0	97	1	0	34	4.44	250,000				May-11
1.98	0.75	2.25	7.29	12.57	2.59	0.68	2.82	3.21	9.83	488.4	2	0	98	0	0	40	4.46	1,000		2.25		Jun-96
1.77	0.34	1.47	4.84	8.42	1.84	1.43	2.78	3.21	9.22	488.4	2	0	98	0	0	40	4.46	1,000			1.00	Dec-93
2.01	0.82	2.30	7.67	13.41	2.74	0.53	2.78	3.21	9.83	488.4	2	0	98	0	0	40	4.46	250,000				Oct-09
2.91	2.18	4.52	14.09	25.05	2.91	0.8	4.45	5.51	10.19	3,215	5	0	95	0	0	89	4.86	1,000		4.75		Apr-94
2.72	1.80	3.66	11.58	20.49	2.17	1.55	4.44	5.51	10.19	3,215	5	0	95	0	0	89	4.86	1,000			1.00	Dec-93
2.97	2.30	4.77	14.93	26.60	3.15	0.55	4.45	5.51	10.19	3,215	5	0	95	0	0	89	4.86	250,000				Jul-99
2.88	-0.54	2.08	11.25	19.93	4.23	0.91	6.26	19.10	20.93	312.5	2	1	95	2	0	44	5.41					May-09
2.11	1.22	3.69	13.39	21.97	2.82	0.72	4.53	6.08	9.5	171.0	3	0	97	0	0	39	4.47	1,000		4.75		Apr-94
1.86	0.76	2.89	10.85	17.46	2.07	1.47	4.53	6.08	9.91	171.0	3	0	97	0	0	39	4.47	1,000			1.00	Dec-05
2.04	1.20	3.88	14.04	23.17	3.01	0.52	4.52	6.08	9.5	171.0	3	0	97	0	0	39	4.47	250,000				Mar-08
3.48	0.83	2.89	9.94	19.96	3.61	0	6.55	2.50	13.26	237.9	1	1	99	0	0	25	7.70					Aug-02
2.03	2.11	4.07	12.32	20.63	2.29	0.73	4.45	5.88	10.45	422.8	3	1	97	0	0	114	4.52	1,000		4.75		Apr-94
1.84	1.84	3.40	9.83	16.21	1.55	1.48	4.46	5.88	10.46	422.8	3	1	97	0	0	114	4.52	1,000			1.00	Sep-03
2.08	2.21	4.37	12.98	21.83	2.49	0.53	4.44	5.88	10.45	422.8	3	1	97	0	0	114	4.52	250,000				Mar-08
2.86	1.50	4.21	14.38	26.26	3.55	0	7.26	13.70	14.69	78.4	2	1	95	2	0	25	8.72					Jan-99
2.55	0.65	2.60	9.53	14.47	2.12	0.79	4.37	5.97	10.09	74.0	6	0	95	0	0	102	4.50	1,000		4.75		Jun-96
2.25	0.25	1.76	7.11	10.23	1.36	1.54	4.31	5.97	9.59	74.0	6	0	95	0	0	102	4.50	1,000			1.00	Dec-93
2.59	0.72	2.76	10.02	15.33	2.27	0.64	4.38	5.97	10.09	74.0	6	0	95	0	0	102	4.50	250,000				Aug-10
2.06	1.79	3.71	9.57	16.67	2.46	0.74	3.54	5.42	9.13	132.5	1	0	98	0	0	37	4.76	1,000		4.75		Dec-93
1.88	1.38	2.96	7.19	12.34	1.71	1.49	3.51	5.42	9.82	132.5	1	0	98	0	0	37	4.76	1,000			1.00	May-06
2.10	1.77	3.91	10.22	17.69	2.65	0.53	3.53	5.42	9.15	132.5	1	0	98	0	0	37	4.76	250,000				Mar-08
2.63	2.54	4.46	13.04	21.16	2.86	0.84	3.97	5.77	9.28	172.0	1	0	99	0	0	11	5.18	1,000		4.75		Dec-93
2.55	2.17	3.80	10.53	16.72	2.11	1.59	3.98	5.77	9.28	172.0	1	0	99	0	0	11	5.18	1,000			1.00	Feb-06
2.79	2.64	4.78	13.71	22.37	3.06	0.64	4	5.77	9.29	172.0	1	0	99	0	0	11	5.18	250,000				Aug-10
2.61	3.07	5.13	12.33	21.37	2.61	0.77	3.22	5.26	8.87	138.5	3	0	97	0	0	36	4.84	1,000		4.75		Dec-93
2.36	2.64	4.35	9.85	16.87	1.86	1.52	3.23	5.26	9.71	138.5	3	0	97	0	0	36	4.84	1,000			1.00	Mar-06
2.66	3.16	5.33	12.99	22.58	2.8	0.56	3.24	5.26	8.86	138.5	3	0	97	0	0	36	4.84	250,000				Aug-10
2.06	1.67	3.33	10.28	16.84	3.23	0.82	3.16	4.69	8.64	184.7	6	0	94	0	0	18	5.17	1,000		4.75		Jun-94
1.82	1.41	2.68	7.87	12.66	2.47	1.57	3.14	4.69	8.95	184.7	6	0	94	0	0	18	5.17	1,000			1.00	Jan-06
2.10	1.77	3.54	10.94	18.02	3.43	0.61	3.11	4.69	8.67	184.7	6	0	94	0	0	18	5.17	250,000				Mar-08
15.59	-8.69	-5.68	3.92	18.97	7.26	0	13.5	0.11	13.02	472.0	1	0	0	95	0	28	4.21					Nov-03
15.13	-9.33	-6.49	2.42	17.22	6.84	0	13.59		6.2	231.4	2	0	0	94	0	26	4.24					Oct-98
0.90	1.93	2.43	6.32	8.68	2.74	0.85	0.61	0.64	8.14	5,226	11	0	0	0	0	59	2.96	1,000		2.25		Sep-02

	MARKET		FUND TYPE, CATEGORY & OBJECTIVE		RATINGS				NEW INVESTORS	
Fund Name	Ticker Symbol	Traded On	Fund Type	Category and (Prospectus Objective)	Overall Rating	Reward Rating	Risk Rating	Recent Up/ Downgrade	Open to New Investors	Telephone
Eaton Vance Short Duration Government Income Fund Class C	ECLDX	NAS CM	Open End	US Fixed Inc (Govt Bond - General)	C	C	B-		Y	
Eaton Vance Short Duration Government Income Fund Class I	EILDX	NAS CM	Open End	US Fixed Inc (Govt Bond - General)	C	C	B-		Y	
Eaton Vance Short Duration High Income Fund Class A	ESHAX	NAS CM	Open End	US Fixed Inc (Corp Bond - High Yield)	C-	D+	C		Y	
Eaton Vance Short Duration High Income Fund Class I	ESHIX	NAS CM	Open End	US Fixed Inc (Corp Bond - High Yield)	C-	D+	C		Y	
Eaton Vance Short Duration Inflation-Protected Income Cl A	EARRX	NAS CM	Open End	US Fixed Inc (Growth)	C-	D+	C		Y	
Eaton Vance Short Duration Inflation-Protected Income Cl C	ECRRX	NAS CM	Open End	US Fixed Inc (Growth)	D+	D	C	Down	Y	
Eaton Vance Short Duration Inflation-Protected Income Cl I	EIRRX	NAS CM	Open End	US Fixed Inc (Growth)	C-	D+	C		Y	
Eaton Vance Short Duration Muni Opportunities Fund Class A	EXMAX	NAS CM	Open End	US Muni Fixed Inc (Muni Bond - Natl)	C-	D+	C	Down	Y	
Eaton Vance Short Duration Muni Opportunities Fund Class C	EZMAX	NAS CM	Open End	US Muni Fixed Inc (Muni Bond - Natl)	C-	D+	C	Down	Y	
Eaton Vance Short Duration Muni Opportunities Fund Class I	EMAIX	NAS CM	Open End	US Muni Fixed Inc (Muni Bond - Natl)	C-	D+	C	Down	Y	
Eaton Vance Short Duration Strategic Income Fund Class A	ETSIX	NAS CM	Open End	Fixed Inc Misc (Growth & Income)	C	C-	B-		Y	
Eaton Vance Short Duration Strategic Income Fund Class C	ECSIX	NAS CM	Open End	Fixed Inc Misc (Growth & Income)	C	C-	C+		Y	
Eaton Vance Short Duration Strategic Income Fund Class I	ESIIX	NAS CM	Open End	Fixed Inc Misc (Growth & Income)	C	C-	B-		Y	
Eaton Vance Short Duration Strategic Income Fund Class R	ERSIX	NAS CM	Open End	Fixed Inc Misc (Growth & Income)	C	C-	B-		Y	
Eaton Vance South Carolina Municipal Income Fund Class A	EASCX	NAS CM	Open End	US Muni Fixed Inc (Muni Bond - Single State)	C	C	B		Y	
Eaton Vance South Carolina Municipal Income Fund Class C	ECSCX	NAS CM	Open End	US Muni Fixed Inc (Muni Bond - Single State)	C	C	B-		Y	
Eaton Vance South Carolina Municipal Income Fund Class I	EISCX	NAS CM	Open End	US Muni Fixed Inc (Muni Bond - Single State)	C	C	B		Y	
Eaton Vance Virginia Municipal Income Fund Class A	ETVAX	NAS CM	Open End	US Muni Fixed Inc (Muni Bond - Single State)	C	C	B		Y	
Eaton Vance Virginia Municipal Income Fund Class C	ECVAX	NAS CM	Open End	US Muni Fixed Inc (Muni Bond - Single State)	C	C	C+		Y	
Eaton Vance Virginia Municipal Income Fund Class I	EVAIX	NAS CM	Open End	US Muni Fixed Inc (Muni Bond - Single State)	C+	C	B	Up	Y	
Edward Jones Money Market Fund Investor Class	JNSXX	NAS CM	Money Mkt	US Money Mkt (Money Mkt - Govt)	C	C-	C		Y	
Edward Jones Money Market Fund Retirement Shares	JRSXX	NAS CM	Money Mkt	US Money Mkt (Money Mkt - Govt)	C	C-	C		Y	
Elfun Government Money Market Fund	ELMXX	NAS CM	Money Mkt	US Money Mkt (Money Mkt - Govt)	C	C-	C+		Y	617-664-7338
Elfun Income Fund	EINFX	NAS CM	Open End	US Fixed Inc (Income)	B-	C+	B+	Up	Y	617-664-7338
Elfun Tax-Exempt Income Fund	ELFTX	NAS CM	Open End	US Muni Fixed Inc (Muni Bond - Natl)	C	C	B		Y	617-664-7338
Ellington Income Opportunities Fund Class A Shares			Closed End	Alternative Misc (Income)	U	U	U		Y	
Ellington Income Opportunities Fund Class M Shares			Closed End	Alternative Misc (Income)	D	D	D		Y	
EQ/AB Short Duration Government Bond Portfolio Class IB			Open End	US Fixed Inc (Govt Bond - General)	U	U	U		Y	877-222-2144
EQ/AB Short Duration Government Bond Portfolio Class K			Open End	US Fixed Inc (Govt Bond - General)	U	U	U		Y	877-222-2144
EQ/Core Bond Index Portfolio Class IA			Open End	US Fixed Inc (Growth & Income)	U	U	U		Y	877-222-2144
EQ/Core Bond Index Portfolio Class IB			Open End	US Fixed Inc (Growth & Income)	U	U	U		Y	877-222-2144
EQ/Core Bond Index Portfolio Class K			Open End	US Fixed Inc (Growth & Income)	U	U	U		Y	877-222-2144
EQ/Franklin Strategic Income Portfolio Class IB			Open End	US Fixed Inc (Income)	U	U	U		Y	877-222-2144
EQ/Global Bond PLUS Portfolio Class IA			Open End	US Fixed Inc (Worldwide Bond)	U	U	U		Y	877-222-2144
EQ/Global Bond PLUS Portfolio Class IB			Open End	US Fixed Inc (Worldwide Bond)	U	U	U		Y	877-222-2144
EQ/Global Bond PLUS Portfolio Class K			Open End	US Fixed Inc (Worldwide Bond)	U	U	U		Y	877-222-2144
EQ/Intermediate Government Bond Portfolio Class IA			Open End	US Fixed Inc (Govt Bond - General)	U	U	U		Y	877-222-2144
EQ/Intermediate Government Bond Portfolio Class IB			Open End	US Fixed Inc (Govt Bond - General)	U	U	U		Y	877-222-2144
EQ/Intermediate Government Bond Portfolio Class K			Open End	US Fixed Inc (Govt Bond - General)	U	U	U		Y	877-222-2144
EQ/Money Market Portfolio Class IA			Money Mkt	US Money Mkt (Money Mkt - Govt)	U	U	U		Y	877-222-2144
EQ/Money Market Portfolio Class IB			Money Mkt	US Money Mkt (Money Mkt - Govt)	U	U	U		Y	877-222-2144
EQ/PIMCO Global Real Return Portfolio Class IB			Open End	US Fixed Inc (Growth & Income)	U	U	U		Y	877-222-2144
EQ/PIMCO Global Real Return Portfolio Class K			Open End	US Fixed Inc (Growth & Income)	U	U	U		Y	877-222-2144
EQ/PIMCO Real Return Portfolio Class IB			Open End	US Fixed Inc (Income)	U	U	U		Y	877-222-2144
EQ/PIMCO Total Return Portfolio Class IB			Open End	US Fixed Inc (Income)	U	U	U		Y	877-222-2144
EQ/PIMCO Ultra Short Bond Portfolio Class IA			Open End	US Fixed Inc (Corp Bond - General)	U	U	U		Y	877-222-2144
EQ/PIMCO Ultra Short Bond Portfolio Class IB			Open End	US Fixed Inc (Corp Bond - General)	U	U	U		Y	877-222-2144
EQ/PIMCO Ultra Short Bond Portfolio Class K			Open End	US Fixed Inc (Corp Bond - General)	U	U	U		Y	877-222-2144
EQ/Quality Bond PLUS Portfolio Class IA			Open End	US Fixed Inc (Corp Bond - General)	U	U	U		Y	877-222-2144
EQ/Quality Bond PLUS Portfolio Class IB			Open End	US Fixed Inc (Corp Bond - General)	U	U	U		Y	877-222-2144
EQ/Quality Bond PLUS Portfolio Class K			Open End	US Fixed Inc (Corp Bond - General)	U	U	U		Y	877-222-2144
EuroPac International Bond Fund Class A	EPIBX	NAS CM	Open End	Global Fixed Inc (Growth)	D+	D	C	Down	Y	

★Expanded analysis of this fund is included in Section II.

TOTAL RETURNS & PERFORMANCE									ASSETS		ASSET ALLOCATION & TURNOVER							MINIMUMS		FEES		
3-Month Total Return	6-Month Total Return	1-Year Total Return	3-Year Total Return	5-Year Total Return	Dividend Yield (TTM)	Expense Ratio	3-Yr Std Deviation	Effective Duration	NAV	Total Assets (MIL)	%Cash	%Government Bonds	%Municipal Bonds	%Corporate Bonds	%Other	Turnover Ratio	Average Coupon Rate	Min Initial Investment	Min Additional Investment	Front End Fee (%)	Back End Fee (%)	Inception Date
0.75	1.63	1.81	4.43	5.35	2.13	1.45	0.63	0.64	8.15	5,226	11	0	0	0	0	59	2.96	1,000			1.00	Sep-02
0.96	2.06	2.68	7.12	9.90	2.99	0.6	0.62	0.64	8.13	5,226	11	0	0	0	0	59	2.96	250,000				May-09
5.53	-4.04	-1.60	5.06	14.88	4.74	0.9	5.82	1.74	9	52.1	2	0	0	97	0	63	5.48	1,000		2.25		Nov-13
5.71	-4.01	-1.45	5.75	16.34	5.01	0.65	5.9	1.74	9.01	52.1	2	0	0	97	0	63	5.48	250,000				Nov-13
6.13	-1.11	0.32	5.00	9.19	2.99	0.95	4.64	2.14	9.61	176.6	7	44	0	31	0	36	2.20	1,000		2.25	1.00	Apr-10
5.84	-1.64	-0.52	2.55	5.00	2.14	1.7	4.65	2.14	9.52	176.6	7	44	0	31	0	36	2.20	1,000			1.00	Apr-10
6.13	-1.05	0.63	5.75	10.59	3.25	0.7	4.61	2.14	9.61	176.6	7	44	0	31	0	36	2.20	250,000				Apr-10
1.54	-0.99	0.39	7.29	13.48	1.93	0.7	3.23	3.19	10.01	807.9	3	0	97	0	0	52	3.30	1,000		2.25		Jun-96
1.40	-1.34	-0.30	4.94	9.39	1.16	1.45	3.2	3.19	9.59	807.9	3	0	97	0	0	52	3.30	1,000			1.00	Dec-93
1.68	-0.82	0.64	7.88	14.43	2.08	0.55	3.22	3.19	10.02	807.9	3	0	97	0	0	52	3.30	250,000				Aug-10
10.09	1.95	5.48	10.35	16.07	6.99	1.21	6.27	3.21	7.11	1,618	21	27	1	12	1	11	5.13	1,000		2.25		Jan-98
9.94	1.55	4.75	7.90	11.91	6.4	1.96	6.31	3.21	6.7	1,618	21	27	1	12	1	11	5.13	1,000			1.00	May-94
10.17	2.08	5.75	11.18	17.52	7.25	0.94	6.28	3.21	7.1	1,618	21	27	1	12	1	11	5.13	250,000				Apr-09
10.01	1.83	5.22	9.53	14.62	6.74	1.47	6.26	3.21	7.12	1,618	21	27	1	12	1	11	5.13	1,000				Aug-09
2.44	2.08	3.71	10.14	18.99	2.51	0.75	3	4.54	9.39	141.6	0	0	100	0	0	19	4.49	1,000		4.75		Feb-94
2.15	1.75	2.87	7.63	14.58	1.76	1.5	2.88	4.54	9.96	141.6	0	0	100	0	0	19	4.49	1,000			1.00	Jan-06
2.49	2.18	3.92	10.80	20.17	2.71	0.55	2.93	4.54	9.4	141.6	0	0	100	0	0	19	4.49	250,000				Mar-08
3.00	2.38	4.25	10.19	18.47	2.67	0.82	3.58	5.55	8.01	69.3	0	0	100	0	0	22	5.01	1,000		4.75		Dec-93
2.70	1.90	3.44	7.70	14.08	1.92	1.57	3.6	5.55	8.87	69.3	0	0	100	0	0	22	5.01	1,000			1.00	Feb-06
2.92	2.35	4.33	10.75	19.55	2.87	0.61	3.58	5.55	8.02	69.3	0	0	100	0	0	22	5.01	250,000				Mar-08
0.00	0.13	0.70	2.47	2.54	0.8	0.69	0.14		1	30,894	66	34	0	0	0			0				May-80
0.00	0.12	0.69	2.43	2.49	0.79	0.72	0.14		1	30,894	66	34	0	0	0			0				May-01
0.03	0.32	1.22	4.31	4.65	1.38	0.26	0.17		1	147.9	65	35	0	0	0			500				Jun-90
4.76	5.11	7.82	15.65	23.68	2.67	0.29	3.5		12.16	239.3	10	33	0	30	0	107	3.15	500				Dec-84
2.24	1.64	3.81	11.80	19.63	3.7	0.2	3.84		11.52	1,358	0	0	100	0	0	25	4.90	500				Jan-80
5.87	-10.01					3.26			9.11	--								2,500	100	5.75		Dec-19
6.21	-9.66	-7.51			6.04	2.61			9.03	--								10,000,000	100,000	0.00		Nov-18
0.71	1.43	2.05	2.45	1.72	1.31	0.8	0.4	0.92		1,567	15	71	0	7	0	48	2.44	0				May-13
0.70	1.57	2.29	3.20	2.99	1.55	0.55	0.4	0.92		1,567	15	71	0	7	0	48	2.44	0				May-13
1.84	4.16	5.03	3.65	6.96	1.9	0.67	2.18	3.92		7,721	2	63	0	35	0	36	2.59	0				Mar-02
1.84	4.15	5.02	3.64	6.95	1.9	0.67	2.19	3.92		7,721	2	63	0	35	0	36	2.59	0				Jan-98
1.94	4.31	5.29	4.43	8.31	2.14	0.42	2.16	3.92		7,721	2	63	0	35	0	36	2.59	0				Aug-11
1.80	4.50					0.93		3.29		116.0	3	14	1	51	0	22	4.70	0				Oct-18
1.00	3.93	2.77	1.32	-0.22	1.36	0.95	4.28	5.28		274.8	2	75	0	22	0	45	3.32	0				Oct-05
1.01	3.94	2.77	1.32	-0.23	1.36	0.95	4.3	5.28		274.8	2	75	0	22	0	45	3.32	0				Oct-05
1.11	4.05	2.94	2.00	0.92	1.65	0.7	4.21	5.28		274.8	2	75	0	22	0	45	3.32	0				Aug-11
1.37	3.10	4.03	1.85	4.20	1.28	0.68	1.77	3.16		7,605	2	98	0	0	0	70	2.17	0				Apr-91
1.38	3.12	4.05	1.85	4.21	1.29	0.68	1.74	3.16		7,605	2	98	0	0	0	70	2.17	0				May-97
1.47	3.26	4.29	2.61	5.51	1.52	0.43	1.77	3.16		7,605	2	98	0	0	0	70	2.17	0				Aug-11
0.37	0.78	1.47	2.26	2.26	1.45	0.71	0.18			1,242	76	24	0	0	0			0				Jul-81
0.36	0.77	1.46	2.26	2.26	1.45	0.71	0.18			1,242	76	24	0	0	0			0				Oct-96
2.59	4.98	4.98	13.07	17.80	2.45	1.54	4.49	11.88		97.5	2	86	0	2	1	66	1.39	0				Feb-13
2.68	5.21	5.21	13.96	19.31	2.69	1.29	4.49	11.88		97.5	2	86	0	2	1	66	1.39	0				Feb-13
2.16	4.37					1.38		7.04		86.9	6	80	0	3	0	25	1.55	0				Oct-18
2.23	5.17					1.39		3.74		264.1	4	34	0	25	0	122	3.42	0				Oct-18
0.40	0.69	1.40	5.65	5.51	1.99	0.81	0.61	-0.04		1,393	5	54	1	26	0	77	2.90	0				Mar-07
0.50	0.69	1.40	5.74	5.50	1.99	0.81	0.61	-0.04		1,393	5	54	1	26	0	77	2.90	0				Jan-02
0.50	0.85	1.65	6.44	6.83	2.24	0.56	0.62	-0.04		1,393	5	54	1	26	0	77	2.90	0				Aug-11
1.78	3.94	4.70	3.03	6.35	1.71	0.84	2.18	3.90		1,618	1	74	0	11	0	204	2.65	0				Oct-93
1.67	3.83	4.59	2.91	6.23	1.72	0.84	2.22	3.90		1,618	1	74	0	11	0	204	2.65	0				Jul-98
1.78	3.95	4.96	3.68	7.69	1.96	0.59	2.26	3.90		1,618	1	74	0	11	0	204	2.65	0				Apr-14
7.46	-1.27	-1.04	2.28	3.71	0	1.15	7.21		8.49	41.2	11	69	0	19	1	26	5.58	2,500	250	4.50		Nov-10

	MARKET			FUND TYPE, CATEGORY & OBJECTIVE	RATINGS				NEW INVESTORS	
Fund Name	Ticker Symbol	Traded On	Fund Type	Category and (Prospectus Objective)	Overall Rating	Reward Rating	Risk Rating	Recent Up/ Downgrade	Open to New Investors	Telephone
EuroPac International Bond Fund Class I	EPBIX	NAS CM	Open End	Global Fixed Inc (Growth)	D+	D	C	Down	Y	
Eventide Limited-Term Bond Fund Class A	ETABX	NAS CM	Open End	US Fixed Inc (Multisector Bond)	C+	C	B	Up	Y	
Eventide Limited-Term Bond Fund Class C	ETCBX	NAS CM	Open End	US Fixed Inc (Multisector Bond)	C	C	B-		Y	
Eventide Limited-Term Bond Fund Class I	ETIBX	NAS CM	Open End	US Fixed Inc (Multisector Bond)	C+	C	B	Up	Y	
Eventide Limited-Term Bond Fund Class N	ETNBX	NAS CM	Open End	US Fixed Inc (Multisector Bond)	C+	C	B	Up	Y	
Fairholme Focused Income Fund	FOCIX	NAS CM	Open End	US Fixed Inc (Income)	D	D	D+	Down		866-202-2263
FCI Bond Fund	FCIZX	NAS CM	Open End	US Fixed Inc (Growth & Income)	B-	C+	B	Up	Y	
Federated for U.S. Govt Securities Cl Institutional Shares	FCBRX	NAS CM	Open End	US Fixed Inc (Govt Bond - Mortgage)	C+	C+	B-		Y	800-341-7400
Federated Govt Income Securities Fund Institutional Shares	GISIX	NAS CM	Open End	US Fixed Inc (Govt Bond - General)	B-	C+	B		Y	800-341-7400
Federated Hermes Adjustable Rate Fund Institutional Shares	FEUNX	NAS CM	Open End	US Fixed Inc (Govt Bond - ARM)	C	C-	C+		Y	800-341-7400
Federated Hermes Adjustable Rate Fund Service Shares	FEUGX	NAS CM	Open End	US Fixed Inc (Govt Bond - ARM)	C	C-	C+		Y	800-341-7400
Federated Hermes CA Muni Cash Capital	CCCXX	NAS CM	Money Mkt	US Money Mkt (Money Mkt - Single State)	C	C-	C		Y	800-341-7400
Federated Hermes CA Muni Cash Cash II	CALXX	NAS CM	Money Mkt	US Money Mkt (Money Mkt - Single State)	C	C-	C		Y	800-341-7400
Federated Hermes CA Muni Cash Cash Srs	CCSXX	NAS CM	Money Mkt	US Money Mkt (Money Mkt - Single State)	C	C-	C		Y	800-341-7400
Federated Hermes CA Muni Cash Wealth	CAIXX	NAS CM	Money Mkt	US Money Mkt (Money Mkt - Single State)	C	C-	C+		Y	800-341-7400
Federated Hermes CA Municipal Cash Svc	CACXX	NAS CM	Money Mkt	US Money Mkt (Money Mkt - Single State)	C	C-	C		Y	800-341-7400
Federated Hermes Capital Reserves	FRFXX	NAS CM	Money Mkt	US Money Mkt (Money Mkt - Taxable)	C	C-	C		Y	800-341-7400
Federated Hermes Corporate Bond Fund Class A Shares	FDBAX	NAS CM	Open End	US Fixed Inc (Corp Bond - General)	C+	C	B	Up	Y	800-341-7400
Federated Hermes Corporate Bond Fund Class B Shares	FDBBX	NAS CM	Open End	US Fixed Inc (Corp Bond - General)	C	C	B-			800-341-7400
Federated Hermes Corporate Bond Fund Class C Shares	FDBCX	NAS CM	Open End	US Fixed Inc (Corp Bond - General)	C	C	B-		Y	800-341-7400
Federated Hermes Corporate Bond Fund Class F Shares	ISHIX	NAS CM	Open End	US Fixed Inc (Corp Bond - General)	C+	C	B	Up	Y	800-341-7400
Federated Hermes Corp Bond Fund Class Institutional Shares	FDBIX	NAS CM	Open End	US Fixed Inc (Corp Bond - General)	C+	C	B	Up	Y	800-341-7400
Federated Hermes Corporate Bond Fund Class R6 Shares	FDBLX	NAS CM	Open End	US Fixed Inc (Corp Bond - General)	C+	C	B	Up	Y	800-341-7400
Federated Hermes Corporate Bond Strategy Portfolio	FCSPX	NAS CM	Open End	US Fixed Inc (Income)	B-	C	B	Up	Y	800-341-7400
Federated Hermes Emerging Market Debt Fund Class A Shares	IHIAX	NAS CM	Open End	Emerg Mkts Fixed Inc (Income)	D+	D+	C-	Down	Y	800-341-7400
Federated Hermes Emerging Market Debt Fund Class C Shares	IHICX	NAS CM	Open End	Emerg Mkts Fixed Inc (Income)	D	D	C-	Down	Y	800-341-7400
Federated Hermes Emerging Market Debt Institutional Shares	EMDIX	NAS CM	Open End	Emerg Mkts Fixed Inc (Income)	D+	D+	C-	Down	Y	800-341-7400
Federated Hermes Floating Rate Strategic Income Cl A	FRSAX	NAS CM	Open End	US Fixed Inc (Income)	D+	D	C-	Down	Y	800-341-7400
Federated Hermes Floating Rate Strategic Income Cl C	FRICX	NAS CM	Open End	US Fixed Inc (Income)	D	D	C-	Down	Y	800-341-7400
Federated Hermes Floating Rate Strat Income Cl R6 Shares	FFRLX	NAS CM	Open End	US Fixed Inc (Income)	D+	D	C-	Down	Y	800-341-7400
Federated Hermes Floating Rate Strat Income Inst Shares	FFRSX	NAS CM	Open End	US Fixed Inc (Income)	D+	D	C-	Down	Y	800-341-7400
Federated Hermes for U.S. Govt Securities Cl A shares	FUSGX	NAS CM	Open End	US Fixed Inc (Govt Bond - Mortgage)	C+	C+	B		Y	800-341-7400
Federated Hermes for U.S. Govt Securities Cl B shares	FUSBX	NAS CM	Open End	US Fixed Inc (Govt Bond - Mortgage)	C+	C	B-	Up		800-341-7400
Federated Hermes for U.S. Govt Securities Cl C shares	FUSCX	NAS CM	Open End	US Fixed Inc (Govt Bond - Mortgage)	C+	C	B-	Up	Y	800-341-7400
Federated Hermes GA Muni Cash	GAMXX	NAS CM	Money Mkt	US Money Mkt (Money Mkt - Single State)	C	C-	C+		Y	800-341-7400
Federated Hermes Global Total Return Bond Cl A Shares	FTIIX	NAS CM	Open End	Global Fixed Inc (Worldwide Bond)	C	C-	C		Y	800-341-7400
Federated Hermes Global Total Return Bond Cl C Shares	FTIBX	NAS CM	Open End	Global Fixed Inc (Worldwide Bond)	C	C-	C	Up	Y	800-341-7400
Federated Hermes Global Total Return Bond Inst Shares	FGTBX	NAS CM	Open End	Global Fixed Inc (Worldwide Bond)	C	C-	C+		Y	800-341-7400
Federated Hermes Govt Income Fund Institutional Shares	FICMX	NAS CM	Open End	US Fixed Inc (Govt Bond - Mortgage)	B-	C+	B	Up	Y	800-341-7400
Federated Hermes Government Income Fund Service Shares	FITSX	NAS CM	Open End	US Fixed Inc (Govt Bond - Mortgage)	B-	C	B	Up	Y	800-341-7400
Federated Hermes Govt Income Securities Class C Shares	FGOCX	NAS CM	Open End	US Fixed Inc (Govt Bond - General)	B-	C+	B	Up	Y	800-341-7400
Federated Hermes Govt Income Securities Inc Class A Shares	FGOAX	NAS CM	Open End	US Fixed Inc (Govt Bond - General)	B-	C+	B		Y	800-341-7400
Federated Hermes Govt Income Securities Inc Class F Shares	FGOIX	NAS CM	Open End	US Fixed Inc (Govt Bond - General)	B-	C+	B		Y	800-341-7400
Federated Hermes Government Reserves A	GRAXX	NAS CM	Money Mkt	US Money Mkt (Money Mkt - Govt)	C	C-	C+		Y	800-341-7400
Federated Hermes Government Reserves B	GRBXX	NAS CM	Money Mkt	US Money Mkt (Money Mkt - Govt)	C	C-	C		Y	800-341-7400
Federated Hermes Government Reserves C	GRCXX	NAS CM	Money Mkt	US Money Mkt (Money Mkt - Govt)	C	C-	C		Y	800-341-7400
Federated Hermes Government Reserves F	GRGXX	NAS CM	Money Mkt	US Money Mkt (Money Mkt - Govt)	C	C-	C+		Y	800-341-7400
Federated Hermes Government Reserves P	GRFXX	NAS CM	Money Mkt	US Money Mkt (Money Mkt - Govt)	C	C-	C		Y	800-341-7400
Federated Hermes Government Ultrashort Fund Class A	FGUAX	NAS CM	Open End	US Fixed Inc (Govt Bond - General)	C	C-	C+		Y	800-341-7400
Federated Hermes Government Ultrashort Fund Class R6	FGULX	NAS CM	Open End	US Fixed Inc (Govt Bond - General)	C	C-	B-		Y	800-341-7400
Federated Hermes Govt Ultrashort Fund Institutional Class	FGUSX	NAS CM	Open End	US Fixed Inc (Govt Bond - General)	C	C-	B-		Y	800-341-7400
Federated Hermes Government Ultrashort Fund Service Class	FEUSX	NAS CM	Open End	US Fixed Inc (Govt Bond - General)	C	C-	C+		Y	800-341-7400

★ Expanded analysis of this fund is included in Section II.

TOTAL RETURNS & PERFORMANCE									ASSETS		ASSET ALLOCATION & TURNOVER							MINIMUMS		FEES		
3-Month Total Return	6-Month Total Return	1-Year Total Return	3-Year Total Return	5-Year Total Return	Dividend Yield (TTM)	Expense Ratio	3-Yr Std Deviation	Effective Duration	NAV	Total Assets (MIL)	%Cash	%Government Bonds	%Municipal Bonds	%Corporate Bonds	%Other	Turnover Ratio	Average Coupon Rate	Min Initial Investment	Min Additional Investment	Front End Fee (%)	Back End Fee (%)	Inception Date
7.50	-1.26	-0.80	2.90	4.96	0	0.9	7.2		8.6	41.2	11	69	0	19	1	26	5.58	15,000	2,500			Jul-13
2.54	2.55	4.30	8.57	12.97	1.98	0.81	2.22	2.82	10.65	66.6	6	38	2	37	0		2.68	1,000	50	5.75		Jul-10
2.38	2.22	3.50	6.10	8.76	1.3	1.56	2.24	2.82	10.6	66.6	6	38	2	37	0		2.68	1,000	50			Dec-18
2.73	2.72	4.67	9.42	12.38	2.2	0.56	2.18	2.82	10.89	66.6	6	38	2	37	0		2.68	100,000	50		1.00	Jul-10
2.56	2.59	4.37	8.61	13.01	2.04	0.76	2.21	2.82	10.62	66.6	6	38	2	37	0		2.68	1,000	50			Dec-18
3.35	-6.50	-8.15	-3.53	15.56	2.55	1.02	8.46		9.56	175.3	79	5	0	9	0	17		10,000	1,000			Dec-09
4.71	5.00	6.94	13.08	18.00	2	0.8	2.99	3.92	11.03	37.8	1	35	0	60	0	18	3.03	250,000	100			Oct-05
0.90	3.12	5.08	9.91	13.37		0.72	2.2	2.10	7.55	216.4	5	0	0	0	0	82	3.54	1,000,000				May-20
1.00	5.31	6.85	12.09	15.44		0.76	2.74	4.20	9.24	157.1	6	24	0	0	0	71	3.19	1,000,000				Apr-20
1.70	0.55	1.66	5.26	5.37		0.31	1.36	1.00	9.63	126.3	1	0	0	0	0	35	2.55	1,000,000				Aug-19
1.66	0.45	1.47	5.07	5.18	2	0.56	1.39	1.00	9.63	126.3	1	0	0	0	0	35	2.55	1,000,000				Dec-85
0.06	0.32	0.79	2.84	3.57	0.88	0.38	0.1		1	1,316	30	0	70	0	0			25,000				Jan-05
0.03	0.20	0.53	1.96	2.40	0.6	0.68	0.09		1	1,316	30	0	70	0	0			10,000				Dec-00
0.02	0.11	0.26	1.03	1.36	0.3	1.03	0.08		1	1,316	30	0	70	0	0			1,000				Jan-05
0.09	0.36	0.88	3.15	4.01	0.98	0.28	0.1		1	1,316	30	0	70	0	0			25,000				Mar-96
0.04	0.26	0.66	2.40	2.97	0.74	0.53	0.1		1	1,316	30	0	70	0	0			10,000				Apr-89
0.00	0.19	0.80	3.07	3.13	0.94	1.02	0.15		1	4,385	90	0	3	7	0			500	100			Feb-05
9.22	3.07	7.05	16.23	29.02	3.55	0.86	6.51	6.30	9.65	1,356	1	5	0	94	0	18	4.71	1,500	100	4.50		Jun-95
8.92	2.60	6.20	13.43	23.63	2.69	1.73	6.45	6.30	9.72	1,356	1	5	0	94	0	18	4.71	1,500	100		5.50	Jun-95
8.93	2.63	6.14	13.42	23.78	2.74	1.7	6.47	6.30	9.72	1,356	1	5	0	94	0	18	4.71	1,500	100		1.00	Jun-95
9.13	3.04	7.10	16.32	28.95	3.52	0.86	6.44	6.30	9.74	1,356	1	5	0	94	0	18	4.71	1,500	100	1.00		May-87
9.16	3.09	7.32	17.10	30.39	3.8	0.61	6.43	6.30	9.65	1,356	1	5	0	94	0	18	4.71	1,000,000				Jan-08
9.27	3.20	7.44	17.24	30.29	3.82	0.59	6.45	6.30	9.67	1,356	1	5	0	94	0	18	4.71	0				Sep-16
11.66	5.38	10.44	23.06	38.35	3.85	0	7.49	7.70	11.87	110.3	1	18	0	82	0	18	4.32	0				Jun-06
13.53	-3.94	-1.13	5.83	14.30	2.44	1.19	11.45	5.10	8.3	32.2	0	57	0	42	0	91	6.51	1,500	100	4.50		Oct-96
13.26	-4.33	-1.89	3.48	10.00	1.67	1.94	11.44	5.10	8.25	32.2	0	57	0	42	0	91	6.51	1,500	100		1.00	Oct-96
13.42	-3.92	-1.00	6.49	15.72	2.7	0.94	11.4	5.10	8.31	32.2	0	57	0	42	0	91	6.51	1,000,000				Mar-12
6.29	-5.27	-3.44	2.19	9.66	4.2	0.99	6.86	0.71	9.07	632.5	10	0	0	84	10	21	5.09	1,500	100	1.00		Feb-11
6.07	-5.64	-4.16	0.12	6.08	3.41	1.81	6.86	0.71	9.08	632.5	10	0	0	84	10	21	5.09	1,500	100		1.00	Sep-13
6.48	-5.15	-3.15	3.24	11.57	4.53	0.73	6.91	0.71	9.07	632.5	10	0	0	84	10	21	5.09	0				Dec-16
6.36	-5.15	-3.16	3.21	11.53	4.52	0.74	6.85	0.71	9.07	632.5	10	0	0	84	10	21	5.09	1,000,000				Dec-10
1.08	3.30	5.27	10.10	13.56	2.32	0.97	2.2	2.10	7.55	216.4	5	0	0	0	0	82	3.54	1,500	100	4.50		Oct-69
0.88	3.03	4.46	7.61	9.45	1.57	1.72	2.23	2.10	7.56	216.4	5	0	0	0	0	82	3.54	1,500	100		5.50	Jul-94
1.02	3.05	4.47	7.76	9.62	1.58	1.72	2.14	2.10	7.56	216.4	5	0	0	0	0	82	3.54	1,500	100		1.00	Apr-93
0.04	0.35	0.80	2.64	2.96	0.91	0.53	0.12		1	118.9	5	0	95	0	0			10,000				Aug-95
3.87	0.50	1.20	4.82	11.03	1.41	1.04	4.35	6.85	9.93	39.8	10	68	0	15	10	80	2.78	1,500	100	4.50		Jun-91
3.72	0.21	0.48	2.51	6.91	0.49	1.79	4.34	6.85	9.46	39.8	10	68	0	15	10	80	2.78	1,500	100		1.00	Apr-93
3.97	0.60	1.40	5.61	11.98	1.71	0.79	4.38	6.85	9.94	39.8	10	68	0	15	10	80	2.78	1,000,000				Dec-16
1.25	3.40	5.46	10.87	14.57	1.87	0.64	2.07	1.90	10.51	276.0	4	0	0	0	0	302	3.15	1,000,000				Mar-82
1.20	3.30	5.25	10.21	13.43	1.67	0.84	2.1	1.90	10.51	276.0	4	0	0	0	0	302	3.15	1,000,000				Jun-92
0.78	4.94	6.06	9.42	11.35	1.26	1.77	2.8	4.20	9.27	157.1	6	24	0	0	0	71	3.19	1,500	100		1.00	Aug-96
0.98	5.34	6.87	11.96	15.68	2	1.01	2.76	4.20	9.26	157.1	6	24	0	0	0	71	3.19	1,500	100	4.50		Aug-96
0.99	5.23	6.89	12.00	15.74	2	1.01	2.74	4.20	9.24	157.1	6	24	0	0	0	71	3.19	1,500	100	1.00		Apr-86
0.00	0.15	0.74	2.68	2.70	0.87	0.87	0.16		1	11,135	67	33	0	0	0			1,500	100			Jul-15
0.00	0.06	0.45	1.67	1.64	0.56	1.27	0.13		1	11,135	67	33	0	0	0			1,500	100		5.50	Jul-15
0.00	0.06	0.47	1.69	1.66	0.57	1.27	0.13		1	11,135	67	33	0	0	0			1,500	100		1.00	Jul-15
0.00	0.14	0.73	2.67	2.69	0.87	0.87	0.16		1	11,135	67	33	0	0	0			1,500	100			Jul-15
0.00	0.12	0.63	2.27	2.27	0.76	1.02	0.15		1	11,135	67	33	0	0	0			500	100			Feb-05
0.94	1.05	1.77	4.52	4.20	1.39	0.41	0.51	0.70	9.88	1,125	31	14	0	0	0	31	1.42	1,500	100	2.00		Mar-03
0.97	1.13	2.07	5.80	6.56	1.7	0.24	0.45	0.70	9.94	1,125	31	14	0	0	0	31	1.42	0				Mar-16
0.97	1.12	2.15	5.74	6.47	1.68	0.26	0.46	0.70	9.94	1,125	31	14	0	0	0	31	1.42	1,000,000				Jul-97
0.94	1.07	2.06	5.54	5.95	1.59	0.36	0.44	0.70	9.94	1,125	31	14	0	0	0	31	1.42	1,000,000				Sep-99

Fund Name	MARKET Ticker Symbol	MARKET Traded On	FUND TYPE, CATEGORY & OBJECTIVE Fund Type	FUND TYPE, CATEGORY & OBJECTIVE Category and (Prospectus Objective)	RATINGS Overall Rating	RATINGS Reward Rating	RATINGS Risk Rating	RATINGS Recent Up/ Downgrade	NEW INVESTORS Open to New Investors	NEW INVESTORS Telephone
Federated Hermes Govt Obl Admin	GOEXX	NAS CM	Money Mkt	US Money Mkt (Money Mkt - Govt)	C	C-	C+		Y	800-341-7400
Federated Hermes Govt Obl Advisor	GOVXX	NAS CM	Money Mkt	US Money Mkt (Money Mkt - Govt)	C	C-	C+		Y	800-341-7400
Federated Hermes Govt Obl Capital	GOCXX	NAS CM	Money Mkt	US Money Mkt (Money Mkt - Govt)	C	C-	C+		Y	800-341-7400
★ Federated Hermes Govt Obl Cash II	GFYXX	NAS CM	Money Mkt	US Money Mkt (Money Mkt - Govt)	C	C-	C		Y	800-341-7400
★ Federated Hermes Govt Obl Cash Srs	GFSXX	NAS CM	Money Mkt	US Money Mkt (Money Mkt - Govt)	C	C-	C		Y	800-341-7400
Federated Hermes Govt Obl IS	GOIXX	NAS CM	Money Mkt	US Money Mkt (Money Mkt - Govt)	C	C-	C+		Y	800-341-7400
Federated Hermes Govt Obl Premier	GOFXX	NAS CM	Money Mkt	US Money Mkt (Money Mkt - Govt)	C	C-	C+		Y	800-341-7400
★ Federated Hermes Govt Obl Select	GRTXX	NAS CM	Money Mkt	US Money Mkt (Money Mkt - Govt)	C	C	C+		Y	800-341-7400
Federated Hermes Govt Obl Svc	GOSXX	NAS CM	Money Mkt	US Money Mkt (Money Mkt - Govt)	C	C-	C+		Y	800-341-7400
Federated Hermes Govt Obl Trust	GORXX	NAS CM	Money Mkt	US Money Mkt (Money Mkt - Govt)	C	C-	C		Y	800-341-7400
Federated Hermes Govt Obl Tx-Mgd Atmtd	GOAXX	NAS CM	Money Mkt	US Money Mkt (Money Mkt - Govt)	C	C-	C+		Y	800-341-7400
Federated Hermes Govt Obl Tx-Mgd IS	GOTXX	NAS CM	Money Mkt	US Money Mkt (Money Mkt - Govt)	C	C-	C+		Y	800-341-7400
Federated Hermes Govt Obl Tx-Mgd Svc	GTSXX	NAS CM	Money Mkt	US Money Mkt (Money Mkt - Govt)	C	C-	C+		Y	800-341-7400
Federated Hermes High Income Bond Fund Class IS Shares	FHISX	NAS CM	Open End	US Fixed Inc (Corp Bond - High Yield)	C-	D+	C		Y	800-341-7400
Federated Hermes High Income Bond Fund Class R6 Shares	FHBRX	NAS CM	Open End	US Fixed Inc (Corp Bond - High Yield)	C-	D+	C		Y	800-341-7400
Federated Hermes High-Income Bond Fund Class A Shares	FHIIX	NAS CM	Open End	US Fixed Inc (Corp Bond - High Yield)	C-	D+	C		Y	800-341-7400
Federated Hermes High-Income Bond Fund Class B Shares	FHBBX	NAS CM	Open End	US Fixed Inc (Corp Bond - High Yield)	C-	D+	C			800-341-7400
Federated Hermes High-Income Bond Fund Class C Shares	FHICX	NAS CM	Open End	US Fixed Inc (Corp Bond - High Yield)	C-	D+	C		Y	800-341-7400
Federated Hermes High-Yield Strategy Portfolio	FHYSX	NAS CM	Open End	US Fixed Inc (Corp Bond - High Yield)	C-	D+	C		Y	800-341-7400
Federated Hermes Inst Money Mkt Mgmt Cap	MMLXX	NAS CM	Money Mkt	US Money Mkt (Money Mkt - Taxable)	C	C-	C+		Y	800-341-7400
Federated Hermes Inst Money Mkt Mgmt Eag	MMMXX	NAS CM	Money Mkt	US Money Mkt (Money Mkt - Taxable)	C	C-	C+			800-341-7400
Federated Hermes Inst Money Mkt Mgmt IS	MMPXX	NAS CM	Money Mkt	US Money Mkt (Money Mkt - Taxable)	C	C-	C+		Y	800-341-7400
Federated Hermes Inst Money Mkt Mgmt Svc	MMSXX	NAS CM	Money Mkt	US Money Mkt (Money Mkt - Taxable)	C	C-	C+		Y	800-341-7400
Federated Hermes Inst Prime Obl Capital	POPXX	NAS CM	Money Mkt	US Money Mkt (Money Mkt - Taxable)	C	C-	C+		Y	800-341-7400
Federated Hermes Inst Prime Val Obl Cap	PVCXX	NAS CM	Money Mkt	US Money Mkt (Money Mkt - Taxable)	C	C-	C+		Y	800-341-7400
Federated Hermes Inst Prime Val Obl IS	PVOXX	NAS CM	Money Mkt	US Money Mkt (Money Mkt - Taxable)	C	C-	B-		Y	800-341-7400
Federated Hermes Inst Prime Val Obl Svc	PVSXX	NAS CM	Money Mkt	US Money Mkt (Money Mkt - Taxable)	C	C-	C+		Y	800-341-7400
Federated Hermes Institutional High Yield Bond Cl R6	FIHLX	NAS CM	Open End	US Fixed Inc (Corp Bond - High Yield)	C-	D+	C		Y	800-341-7400
Federated Hermes Inst High Yield Bond Inst Shares	FIHBX	NAS CM	Open End	US Fixed Inc (Corp Bond - High Yield)	C-	D+	C		Y	800-341-7400
Federated Hermes Instl Prime Obl IS	POIXX	NAS CM	Money Mkt	US Money Mkt (Money Mkt - Taxable)	C	C-	C+		Y	800-341-7400
Federated Hermes Instl Prime Obl Svc	PRSXX	NAS CM	Money Mkt	US Money Mkt (Money Mkt - Taxable)	C	C-	C+		Y	800-341-7400
Federated Hermes Instl T-F Cash IS	FFTXX	NAS CM	Money Mkt	US Money Mkt (Money Mkt - Fed Tax Exmpt)	C	C-	C+		Y	800-341-7400
Federated Hermes Instl T-F Cash Premier	FTFXX	NAS CM	Money Mkt	US Money Mkt (Money Mkt - Fed Tax Exmpt)	C	C-	C+		Y	800-341-7400
Federated Hermes Intermed Corp Bond Inst Shares	FIIFX	NAS CM	Open End	US Fixed Inc (Corp Bond - General)	B-	C	B	Up	Y	800-341-7400
Federated Hermes Intermediate Corp Bond Service Shares	INISX	NAS CM	Open End	US Fixed Inc (Corp Bond - General)	C+	C	B	Up	Y	800-341-7400
Federated Hermes Intermediate Muni Institutional Shares	FIMYX	NAS CM	Open End	US Muni Fixed Inc (Muni Bond - Natl)	C	C	B		Y	800-341-7400
Federated Hermes Intermediate Muni Fund Service Shares	FIMTX	NAS CM	Open End	US Muni Fixed Inc (Muni Bond - Natl)	C	C	B-		Y	800-341-7400
Federated Hermes International Bond Strategy Portfolio	FIBPX	NAS CM	Open End	Global Fixed Inc (Worldwide Bond)	C	C-	C		Y	800-341-7400
Federated Hermes MA Muni Cash Cash Srs	FMCXX	NAS CM	Money Mkt	US Money Mkt (Money Mkt - Single State)	C	C-	C		Y	800-341-7400
Federated Hermes MA Muni Cash Svc	MMCXX	NAS CM	Money Mkt	US Money Mkt (Money Mkt - Single State)	C	C-	C		Y	800-341-7400
Federated Hermes MA Muni Cash Wealth	MAWXX	NAS CM	Money Mkt	US Money Mkt (Money Mkt - Single State)	C	C-	C+		Y	800-341-7400
Federated Hermes Michigan Intermediate Muni Cl A Shares	MMIFX	NAS CM	Open End	US Muni Fixed Inc (Muni Bond - Single State)	C+	C	B	Up	Y	800-341-7400
Federated Hermes Michigan Intermed Muni Inst Shares	MMFIX	NAS CM	Open End	US Muni Fixed Inc (Muni Bond - Single State)	C+	C	B		Y	800-341-7400
Federated Hermes Mortgage Strategy Portfolio	FMBPX	NAS CM	Open End	US Fixed Inc (Income)	B-	C+	B	Up	Y	800-341-7400
Federated Hermes Muni Obl Automated	MOTXX	NAS CM	Money Mkt	US Money Mkt (Money Mkt - Fed Tax Exmpt)	C	C-	C			800-341-7400
Federated Hermes Municipal Bond Fund Class A Shares	LMSFX	NAS CM	Open End	US Muni Fixed Inc (Muni Bond - Natl)	C	C-	B-		Y	800-341-7400
Federated Hermes Municipal Bond Fund Class B Shares	LMSBX	NAS CM	Open End	US Muni Fixed Inc (Muni Bond - Natl)	C	C-	C+			800-341-7400
Federated Hermes Municipal Bond Fund Class C Shares	LMSCX	NAS CM	Open End	US Muni Fixed Inc (Muni Bond - Natl)	C	C-	C+		Y	800-341-7400
Federated Hermes Municipal Bond Fund Class F Shares	LMFFX	NAS CM	Open End	US Muni Fixed Inc (Muni Bond - Natl)	C	C-	B-		Y	800-341-7400
Federated Hermes Muni Bond Fund Class Institutional Shares	LMBIX	NAS CM	Open End	US Muni Fixed Inc (Muni Bond - Natl)	C	C-	B-		Y	800-341-7400
Federated Hermes Muni High Yield Advantage Cl A Shares	FMOAX	NAS CM	Open End	US Muni Fixed Inc (Muni Bond - Natl)	C-	D+	C	Down	Y	800-341-7400
Federated Hermes Muni High Yield Advantage Cl B Shares	FMOBX	NAS CM	Open End	US Muni Fixed Inc (Muni Bond - Natl)	C-	D+	C	Down		800-341-7400

★ Expanded analysis of this fund is included in Section II.

TOTAL RETURNS & PERFORMANCE									ASSETS		ASSET ALLOCATION & TURNOVER							MINIMUMS		FEES		
3-Month Total Return	6-Month Total Return	1-Year Total Return	3-Year Total Return	5-Year Total Return	Dividend Yield (TTM)	Expense Ratio	3-Yr Std Deviation	Effective Duration	NAV	Total Assets (MIL)	%Cash	%Government Bonds	%Municipal Bonds	%Corporate Bonds	%Other	Turnover Ratio	Average Coupon Rate	Min Initial Investment	Min Additional Investment	Front End Fee (%)	Back End Fee (%)	Inception Date
0.00	0.25	1.05	3.88	3.91	1.21	0.45			1	155,932	66	34	0	0	0			500,000				Sep-17
0.04	0.37	1.32	4.71	5.26	1.49	0.15			1	155,932	66	34	0	0	0			1,000,000				Jan-19
0.01	0.30	1.17	4.30	4.67	1.34	0.3	0.18		1	155,932	66	34	0	0	0			500,000				Jan-05
0.00	0.16	0.76	2.77	2.81	0.89	0.85	0.16		1	155,932	66	34	0	0	0			25,000				Jun-15
0.00	0.12	0.65	2.28	2.31	0.78	1.05	0.16		1	155,932	66	34	0	0	0			10,000	250			Jun-15
0.03	0.34	1.27	4.65	5.20	1.45	0.2	0.18		1	155,932	66	34	0	0	0			500,000				Mar-90
0.05	0.38	1.32	4.77	5.40	1.49	0.15	0.18		1	155,932	66	34	0	0	0			5,000,000				Jan-15
0.04	0.36	1.22	2.67	2.73	1.31	0.17	0.18		1	155,932	66	34	0	0	0			0				Feb-16
0.00	0.26	1.07	3.97	4.17	1.24	0.45	0.17		1	155,932	66	34	0	0	0			500,000				Jul-94
0.00	0.19	0.87	3.21	3.28	1.01	0.7	0.16		1	155,932	66	34	0	0	0			500,000				Feb-03
0.00	0.24	0.99	3.65	3.78	1.14	0.55	0.17		1	8,516	66	34	0	0	0			25,000				Jul-15
0.03	0.35	1.27	4.59	5.11	1.45	0.2	0.17		1	8,516	66	34	0	0	0			500,000				Jun-95
0.00	0.25	1.04	3.84	4.00	1.21	0.45	0.17		1	8,516	66	34	0	0	0			500,000				May-95
9.40	-3.77	0.02	9.09	23.16	5.85	0.65	8.37	4.00	7.05	576.1	4	0	0	96	0	26	6.22	1,000,000				Jan-17
9.40	-3.76	0.03	9.11	23.08	5.87	0.64	8.35	4.00	7.05	576.1	4	0	0	96	0	26	6.22	0				Jan-17
9.33	-4.01	-0.22	8.11	22.09	5.59	0.9	8.41	4.00	7.05	576.1	4	0	0	96	0	26	6.22	1,500	100	4.50		Nov-77
9.14	-4.29	-1.03	5.46	17.29	4.75	1.76	8.38	4.00	7.03	576.1	4	0	0	96	0	26	6.22	1,500	100		5.50	Sep-94
9.15	-4.28	-1.01	5.54	17.41	4.78	1.72	8.38	4.00	7.03	576.1	4	0	0	96	0	26	6.22	1,500	100		1.00	Apr-93
9.57	-4.03	-0.06	10.48	27.88	6.61	0.03	8.5		12.27	38.2	6	0	0	94	0	25	6.35	0				Dec-08
0.24	0.56	1.53	5.30	6.06	1.65	0.25	0.16		1.0002	1,307	99	0	0	1	0			500,000				Jan-05
0.21	0.50	1.43	4.99	5.49	1.55	0.4	0.16		1.0002	1,307	99	0	0	1	0			1,500	100			Jul-14
0.25	0.59	1.63	5.62	6.60	1.75	0.15	0.16		1.0002	1,307	99	0	0	1	0			500,000				Aug-04
0.21	0.48	1.39	4.82	5.31	1.5	0.4	0.16		1.0001	1,307	99	0	0	1	0			500,000				Jan-05
0.25	0.54	1.53	5.43	6.22	1.66	0.25	0.18		1.0009	22,906	96	0	0	4	0			500,000				Jun-12
0.24	0.51	1.48	5.26	6.10	1.61	0.3	0.18		1.0007	16,439	100	0	0	0	0			500,000				Feb-93
0.27	0.56	1.58	5.57	6.63	1.71	0.2	0.18		1.0007	16,439	100	0	0	0	0			500,000				Feb-93
0.20	0.43	1.33	4.78	5.36	1.46	0.45	0.18		1.0007	16,439	100	0	0	0	0			500,000				Sep-93
9.40	-3.83	0.07	9.58	25.82	5.98	0.49	8.42	4.10	9.29	7,903	3	0	0	97	0	26	6.22	0				Jun-16
9.53	-3.74	0.17	9.66	25.77	5.97	0.5	8.47	4.10	9.29	7,903	3	0	0	97	0	26	6.22	1,000,000				Nov-02
0.25	0.55	1.58	5.57	6.48	1.71	0.2	0.18		1.0008	22,906	96	0	0	4	0			500,000				Mar-90
0.20	0.43	1.33	4.86	5.34	1.47	0.45	0.18		1.0007	22,906	96	0	0	4	0			500,000				Jul-94
0.06	0.43	1.00	3.39	3.99	1.13	0.2	0.14		1	1,412	2	0	99	0	0			500,000				Feb-16
0.06	0.45	1.04	3.54	4.21	1.18	0.15	0.14		1	1,412	2	0	99	0	0			5,000,000				Mar-79
7.84	4.05	7.12	14.89	22.43	2.74	0.58	4.85	4.10	9.6	154.1	4	6	0	90	0	23	3.74	1,000,000				Dec-93
7.77	3.92	6.85	13.92	20.79	2.5	0.83	4.85	4.10	9.6	154.1	4	6	0	90	0	23	3.74	1,000,000				Dec-93
2.45	1.88	3.81	11.39	19.45	2.15	0.48	3.74	5.60	10.38	106.0	0	0	100	0	0	25	4.52	1,000,000				Oct-03
2.29	1.66	3.56	10.60	18.18	1.91	0.73	3.71	5.60	10.38	106.0	0	0	100	0	0	25	4.52	1,000,000				Dec-85
8.47	-0.34	1.62	9.73	20.65	3.54	0.04	7.05	7.83	14.46	23.9	8	81	0	2	49	52	2.59	0				Dec-08
0.02	0.17	0.41	1.26	1.35	0.43	1.02	0.1		1	41.1	23	0	77	0	0			1,000				Jan-05
0.02	0.28	0.74	2.39	2.62	0.8	0.61	0.11		1	41.1	23	0	77	0	0			10,000				May-90
0.07	0.39	0.96	3.01	3.24	1.03	0.36			1	41.1	23	0	77	0	0			25,000				Nov-17
1.96	2.18	3.82	9.54	15.05	2.26	0.77	3.24	5.00	11.4	75.3	0	0	100	0	0	21	4.72	1,500	100	3.00		Sep-91
1.55	2.22	3.85	9.57	14.99		0.52	3.27	5.00	11.4	75.3	0	0	100	0	0	21	4.72	1,000,000				Apr-20
1.24	3.94	5.98	12.98	19.00	2.96	0.03	2.2	1.40	10.23	133.8	5	0	0	0	0	7	3.34	0				Dec-07
0.07	0.35	0.81	2.73	3.05	0.91	0.56	0.11		1	3,462	16	0	84	0	0			25,000				Jun-15
2.24	0.83	3.05	11.15	18.56	2.51	0.84	4.54	7.60	10.63	317.9	0	0	100	0	0	9	4.81	1,500	100	4.50		Oct-76
2.05	0.37	2.29	8.67	14.10	1.75	1.59	4.54	7.60	10.64	317.9	0	0	100	0	0	9	4.81	1,500	100		5.50	Jul-94
2.05	0.46	2.29	8.67	14.10	1.75	1.59	4.56	7.60	10.64	317.9	0	0	100	0	0	9	4.81	1,500	100		1.00	Apr-93
2.34	0.84	3.06	11.15	18.56	2.51	0.84	4.59	7.60	10.63	317.9	0	0	100	0	0	9	4.81	1,500	100	1.00		May-07
2.31	0.58	3.02	11.28	18.69	2.77	0.59	4.62	7.60	10.59	317.9	0	0	100	0	0	9	4.81	1,000,000				Jul-17
3.23	-3.20	-0.40	10.16	20.61	3.85	0.89	6.9	9.10	8.76	528.2	0	0	100	0	0	11	5.18	1,500	100	4.50		Aug-96
3.05	-3.46	-1.14	7.70	16.17	3.06	1.64	6.95	9.10	8.75	528.2	0	0	100	0	0	11	5.18	1,500	100		5.50	Aug-96

Fund Name	MARKET Ticker Symbol	Traded On	FUND TYPE, CATEGORY & OBJECTIVE Fund Type	Category and (Prospectus Objective)	RATINGS Overall Rating	Reward Rating	Risk Rating	Recent Up/ Downgrade	NEW INVESTORS Open to New Investors	Telephone
Federated Hermes Muni High Yield Advantage Cl C Shares	FMNCX	NAS CM	Open End	US Muni Fixed Inc (Muni Bond - Natl)	C-	D+	C	Down	Y	800-341-7400
Federated Hermes Muni High Yield Advantage Cl F Shares	FHTFX	NAS CM	Open End	US Muni Fixed Inc (Muni Bond - Natl)	C-	D+	C	Down	Y	800-341-7400
Federated Hermes Muni High Yield Advantage Cl Inst	FMYIX	NAS CM	Open End	US Muni Fixed Inc (Muni Bond - Natl)	C-	D+	C	Down	Y	800-341-7400
Federated Hermes Municipal Obl Capital	MFCXX	NAS CM	Money Mkt	US Money Mkt (Money Mkt - Fed Tax Exmpt)	C	C-	C+		Y	800-341-7400
Federated Hermes Municipal Obl Cash II	MODXX	NAS CM	Money Mkt	US Money Mkt (Money Mkt - Fed Tax Exmpt)	C	C-	C		Y	800-341-7400
Federated Hermes Municipal Obl Cash Srs	MFSXX	NAS CM	Money Mkt	US Money Mkt (Money Mkt - Fed Tax Exmpt)	C	C-	C		Y	800-341-7400
Federated Hermes Municipal Obl Invsmt	MOIXX	NAS CM	Money Mkt	US Money Mkt (Money Mkt - Fed Tax Exmpt)	C	C-	C		Y	800-341-7400
Federated Hermes Municipal Obl Svc	MOSXX	NAS CM	Money Mkt	US Money Mkt (Money Mkt - Fed Tax Exmpt)	C	C-	C		Y	800-341-7400
Federated Hermes Municipal Obl Wealth	MOFXX	NAS CM	Money Mkt	US Money Mkt (Money Mkt - Fed Tax Exmpt)	C	C-	C+		Y	800-341-7400
Federated Hermes Municipal Ultrashort Fund Class A Shares	FMUUX	NAS CM	Open End	US Muni Fixed Inc (Income)	C	C-	C		Y	800-341-7400
Federated Hermes Municipal UltraShort Fund Class R6 Shares	FMULX	NAS CM	Open End	US Muni Fixed Inc (Income)	C	C-	C+		Y	800-341-7400
Federated Hermes Muni Ultrashort Fund Institutional Shares	FMUSX	NAS CM	Open End	US Muni Fixed Inc (Income)	C	C-	C+		Y	800-341-7400
Federated Hermes NY Muni Cash Cash II	NYCXX	NAS CM	Money Mkt	US Money Mkt (Muni Bond - Single State)	C	C-	C		Y	800-341-7400
Federated Hermes NY Muni Cash Cash Srs	FNCXX	NAS CM	Money Mkt	US Money Mkt (Muni Bond - Single State)	C	C-	C		Y	800-341-7400
Federated Hermes NY Muni Cash Wealth	NISXX	NAS CM	Money Mkt	US Money Mkt (Muni Bond - Single State)	C	C-	C+		Y	800-341-7400
Federated Hermes NY Municipal Cash Svc	FNTXX	NAS CM	Money Mkt	US Money Mkt (Muni Bond - Single State)	C	C-	C+		Y	800-341-7400
Federated Hermes Ohio Municipal Income Fund Class A Shares	OMIAX	NAS CM	Open End	US Muni Fixed Inc (Muni Bond - Single State)	C	C	B-		Y	800-341-7400
Federated Hermes Ohio Municipal Income Fund Class F Shares	OMIFX	NAS CM	Open End	US Muni Fixed Inc (Muni Bond - Single State)	C	C	B-		Y	800-341-7400
Federated Hermes Opportunistic High Yield Bond Cl A	FHYAX	NAS CM	Open End	US Fixed Inc (Corp Bond - High Yield)	D+	D+	C-	Down	Y	800-341-7400
Federated Hermes Opportunistic High Yield Bond Cl C	FHYCX	NAS CM	Open End	US Fixed Inc (Corp Bond - High Yield)	D+	D	C-	Down	Y	800-341-7400
Federated Hermes Opportunistic High Yield Bond Cl R6 Sh	FHYLX	NAS CM	Open End	US Fixed Inc (Corp Bond - High Yield)	C-	D+	C		Y	800-341-7400
Federated Hermes Opportunistic High Yield Bond Inst Shares	FHTIX	NAS CM	Open End	US Fixed Inc (Corp Bond - High Yield)	C-	D+	C		Y	800-341-7400
Federated Hermes Opportunistic High Yield Bond Service Sh	FHYTX	NAS CM	Open End	US Fixed Inc (Corp Bond - High Yield)	D+	D+	C-	Down	Y	800-341-7400
Federated Hermes PA Muni Cash Cash Srs	PACXX	NAS CM	Money Mkt	US Money Mkt (Money Mkt - Single State)	C	C-	C		Y	800-341-7400
Federated Hermes PA Muni Cash Wealth	PAMXX	NAS CM	Money Mkt	US Money Mkt (Money Mkt - Single State)	C	C-	C		Y	800-341-7400
Federated Hermes PA Municipal Cash Svc	FPAXX	NAS CM	Money Mkt	US Money Mkt (Money Mkt - Single State)	C	C-	C		Y	800-341-7400
Federated Hermes Pennsylvania Muni Income Cl A Shares	PAMFX	NAS CM	Open End	US Muni Fixed Inc (Muni Bond - Single State)	C	C	B-		Y	800-341-7400
Federated Hermes Premier Municipal Inc	FMN	NYSE	Closed End	US Muni Fixed Inc (Muni Bond - Natl)	C-	C-	C-		Y	
Federated Hermes Prime Cash Obl Advisor	PCVXX	NAS CM	Money Mkt	US Money Mkt (Money Mkt - Taxable)	C	C	B-		Y	800-341-7400
Federated Hermes Prime Cash Obl Automtd	PTAXX	NAS CM	Money Mkt	US Money Mkt (Money Mkt - Taxable)	C	C-	C+		Y	800-341-7400
Federated Hermes Prime Cash Obl Capital	PCCXX	NAS CM	Money Mkt	US Money Mkt (Money Mkt - Taxable)	C	C-	C+		Y	800-341-7400
Federated Hermes Prime Cash Obl Cash II	PCDXX	NAS CM	Money Mkt	US Money Mkt (Money Mkt - Taxable)	C	C-	C		Y	800-341-7400
Federated Hermes Prime Cash Obl Cash Srs	PTSXX	NAS CM	Money Mkt	US Money Mkt (Money Mkt - Taxable)	C	C-	C+		Y	800-341-7400
Federated Hermes Prime Cash Obl R	PTRXX	NAS CM	Money Mkt	US Money Mkt (Money Mkt - Taxable)	C	C-	C+		Y	800-341-7400
Federated Hermes Prime Cash Obl Svc	PRCXX	NAS CM	Money Mkt	US Money Mkt (Money Mkt - Taxable)	C	C-	C+		Y	800-341-7400
Federated Hermes Prime Cash Obl Trust	PTTXX	NAS CM	Money Mkt	US Money Mkt (Money Mkt - Taxable)	C	C-	C+		Y	800-341-7400
Federated Hermes Prime Cash Obl Wealth	PCOXX	NAS CM	Money Mkt	US Money Mkt (Money Mkt - Taxable)	C	C-	C+		Y	800-341-7400
Federated Hermes Project and Trade Finance Tender Fund	XPTFX	NAS CM	Closed End	US Fixed Inc (Growth & Income)	C	C-	C+		Y	800-341-7400
Federated Hermes Real Return Bond Fund Class A Shares	RRFAX	NAS CM	Open End	US Fixed Inc (Income)	B	C+	A-	Up	Y	800-341-7400
Federated Hermes Real Return Bond Fund Class C Shares	RRFCX	NAS CM	Open End	US Fixed Inc (Income)	B-	C+	B+	Up	Y	800-341-7400
Federated Hermes Real Return Bond Institutional Shares	RRFIX	NAS CM	Open End	US Fixed Inc (Income)	B	C+	A-	Up	Y	800-341-7400
Federated Hermes SDG Engagement High Yield Credit Inst Sh	FHHIX	NAS CM	Open End	Global Fixed Inc (Corp Bond - High Yield)	U	U	U		Y	800-341-7400
Federated Hermes Select Total Return Bond Inst Shares	FGFIX	NAS CM	Open End	US Fixed Inc (Govt Bond - Mortgage)	C	C-	C+		Y	800-341-7400
Federated Hermes Select Total Return Bond Service Shares	FGFSX	NAS CM	Open End	US Fixed Inc (Govt Bond - Mortgage)	C	C-	C+		Y	800-341-7400
Federated Hermes Short Term Income Fund Class R6 Shares	FSILX	NAS CM	Open End	US Fixed Inc (Corp Bond - General)	C	C	B-		Y	800-341-7400
Federated Hermes Short-Intermed Duration Muni Trust Cl A S	FMTAX	NAS CM	Open End	US Muni Fixed Inc (Muni Bond - Natl)	C-	C-	C	Down	Y	800-341-7400
Federated Hermes Short-Intermed Duration Muni Trust Inst S	FSHIX	NAS CM	Open End	US Muni Fixed Inc (Muni Bond - Natl)	C	C-	C		Y	800-341-7400
Federated Hermes Short-Intermed Duration Muni Trust Servic	FSHSX	NAS CM	Open End	US Muni Fixed Inc (Muni Bond - Natl)	C-	C-	C	Down	Y	800-341-7400
Federated Hermes Short-Intermediate Govt Fund Class R	FIGKX	NAS CM	Open End	US Fixed Inc (Govt Bond - General)	C+	C	B		Y	800-341-7400
Federated Hermes Short-Intermed Govt Inst Shares	FIGTX	NAS CM	Open End	US Fixed Inc (Govt Bond - General)	B-	C+	B		Y	800-341-7400
Federated Hermes Short-Intermediate Govt Service Shares	FIGIX	NAS CM	Open End	US Fixed Inc (Govt Bond - General)	B-	C+	B	Up	Y	800-341-7400
Federated Hermes Short-Intermediate Total Return Bond Cl A	FGCAX	NAS CM	Open End	US Fixed Inc (Income)	C+	C	B		Y	800-341-7400

★Expanded analysis of this fund is included in Section II.

TOTAL RETURNS & PERFORMANCE									ASSETS		ASSET ALLOCATION & TURNOVER							MINIMUMS		FEES		
3-Month Total Return	6-Month Total Return	1-Year Total Return	3-Year Total Return	5-Year Total Return	Dividend Yield (TTM)	Expense Ratio	3-Yr Std Deviation	Effective Duration	NAV	Total Assets (MIL)	%Cash	%Government Bonds	%Municipal Bonds	%Corporate Bonds	%Other	Turnover Ratio	Average Coupon Rate	Min Initial Investment	Min Additional Investment	Front End Fee (%)	Back End Fee (%)	Inception Date
3.05	-3.56	-1.14	7.74	16.07	3.06	1.64	6.89	9.10	8.75	528.2	0	0	100	0	0	11	5.18	1,500	100		1.00	Aug-96
3.23	-3.10	-0.40	10.16	20.61	3.85	0.89	6.95	9.10	8.76	528.2	0	0	100	0	0	11	5.18	1,500	100	1.00		Apr-87
3.18	-3.09	-0.26	10.88	22.02	4.12	0.64	6.91	9.10	8.74	528.2	0	0	100	0	0	11	5.18	1,000,000				Jun-13
0.11	0.45	1.05	3.49	4.20	1.16	0.31	0.1		1	3,462	16	0	84	0	0			500,000				Feb-93
0.03	0.22	0.52	1.73	1.90	0.59	0.91	0.1		1	3,462	16	0	84	0	0			25,000				Jun-15
0.03	0.19	0.42	1.40	1.54	0.49	1.02	0.1		1	3,462	16	0	84	0	0			10,000	250			Jun-15
0.03	0.26	0.61	2.07	2.29	0.7	0.78	0.1		1	3,462	16	0	84	0	0			1,500	100			Jun-15
0.08	0.38	0.90	3.01	3.53	1.01	0.46	0.1		1	3,462	16	0	84	0	0			500,000				Feb-93
0.13	0.50	1.14	3.79	4.64	1.26	0.21	0.1		1	3,462	16	0	84	0	0			500,000				Feb-93
0.72	0.23	0.87	3.12	3.88	1.13	0.51	0.81	0.75	9.99	2,216	6	0	94	0	0	83	2.02	1,500	100	2.00		Oct-00
0.76	0.32	1.17	4.26	5.97	1.46	0.34	0.83	0.75	9.99	2,216	6	0	94	0	0	83	2.02	0				May-19
0.76	0.21	1.15	4.34	6.06	1.44	0.36	0.81	0.75	9.99	2,216	6	0	94	0	0	83	2.02	1,000,000				Oct-00
0.03	0.22	0.56	1.89	1.98	0.63	0.77	0.09		1	554.3	20	0	80	0	0			10,000				Apr-91
0.01	0.14	0.35	1.20	1.23	0.42	1.02	0.09		1	554.3	20	0	80	0	0			10,000				Jan-05
0.09	0.39	0.95	3.22	3.74	1.06	0.32	0.1		1	554.3	20	0	80	0	0			10,000				Jan-05
0.04	0.29	0.74	2.55	2.82	0.84	0.54	0.1		1	554.3	20	0	80	0	0			10,000				Nov-82
1.90	1.58	3.39	10.07	17.34	2.34	0.77	3.52	6.70	11.33	145.3	0	0	100	0	0	15	4.91	1,500	100	4.50		Nov-08
1.86	1.42	3.23	9.57	16.46	2.19	0.92	3.5	6.70	11.33	145.3	0	0	100	0	0	15	4.91	1,500	100	1.00		Oct-90
10.80	-5.86	-2.00	5.88	18.87	5.31	0.98	10	4.20	6.21	608.1	3	0	0	96	0	31	6.25	1,500	100	4.50		Apr-14
10.57	-6.25	-2.80	3.45	14.61	4.46	1.81	9.97	4.20	6.21	608.1	3	0	0	96	0	31	6.25	1,500	100		1.00	Apr-14
11.08	-5.61	-1.76	6.84	20.02	5.58	0.72	10.02	4.20	6.2	608.1	3	0	0	96	0	31	6.25	0				Apr-17
10.89	-5.77	-1.78	6.79	20.51	5.57	0.73	9.96	4.20	6.19	608.1	3	0	0	96	0	31	6.25	1,000,000				Jun-13
11.01	-5.74	-1.87	6.02	19.04	5.31	0.98	10.08	4.20	6.2	608.1	3	0	0	96	0	31	6.25	1,000,000				Aug-84
0.02	0.18	0.35	1.19	1.26	0.42	1.06	0.1		1	67.3	6	0	94	0	0			10,000				Dec-90
0.05	0.34	0.82	2.81	3.18	0.93	0.47	0.12		1	67.3	6	0	94	0	0			10,000				Jul-95
0.03	0.28	0.65	2.24	2.43	0.75	0.67	0.12		1	67.3	6	0	94	0	0			10,000				Nov-89
1.53	1.51	3.53	10.90	18.56	2.52	0.76	3.6	7.10	11.01	154.6	0	3	97	0	0	16	4.89	1,500	100	4.50		Oct-90
4.42	0.13	3.32	14.53	27.75	4.08	0	7.27	7.00	15.07	169.0	0	4	96	0	0	15	4.99					Dec-02
0.13	0.50	1.51	5.39	6.37	1.68	0.2			1	29,720	98	0	0	2	0			250,000				Jan-19
0.05	0.34	1.17	4.38	4.83	1.34	0.55	0.16		1	29,720	98	0	0	2	0			25,000				Jun-15
0.11	0.45	1.41	5.07	5.85	1.58	0.3	0.16		1	29,720	98	0	0	2	0			500,000				Oct-94
0.00	0.21	0.86	3.26	3.41	1	0.9	0.15		1	29,720	98	0	0	2	0			25,000				Jun-15
0.00	0.16	0.74	2.90	2.97	0.87	1.05	0.15		1	29,720	98	0	0	2	0			10,000	250			Jun-15
0.00	0.14	0.67	2.57	2.62	0.79	1.15	0.15		1	29,720	98	0	0	2	0			0				Jun-15
0.07	0.38	1.26	4.60	5.13	1.43	0.45	0.16		1	29,720	98	0	0	2	0			500,000				Sep-93
0.02	0.27	1.02	3.84	4.10	1.18	0.7	0.16		1	29,720	98	0	0	2	0			500,000				Jun-15
0.13	0.50	1.51	5.39	6.37	1.68	0.2	0.16		1	29,720	98	0	0	2	0			500,000				Feb-93
1.90	-0.12	1.84	10.26		3.86	0.71	1.62		9.8	--	37	1	0	60	4	73	1.69	100,000	25,000			Feb-17
4.38	5.33	7.46	15.02	17.48	1.86	0.75	3.27	7.90	11.19	45.9	2	98	0	0	0	35	0.83	1,500	100	4.50		Oct-06
4.17	4.97	6.61	12.36	13.14	1.19	1.5	3.34	7.90	10.98	45.9	2	98	0	0	0	35	0.83	1,500	100		1.00	Oct-06
4.35	5.46	7.71	15.84	19.00	2.09	0.5	3.29	7.90	11.26	45.9	2	98	0	0	0	35	0.83	1,000,000				Oct-06
12.13	-3.74					0.63		5.50	9.74	29.4	3	2	0	96	0		5.02	1,000,000				Sep-19
5.27	2.53	3.98	10.02	15.35	2.87	0.35	4.84	5.70	9.69	30.4	12	29	0	0	0	391	2.86	1,000,000				May-97
5.30	2.38	3.78	9.15	13.64	2.57	0.65	4.9	5.70	9.69	30.4	12	29	0	0	0	391	2.86	1,000,000				May-97
3.23	1.66	3.22	8.91	11.90	2.43	0.35	2.12	1.90	8.63	1,566	4	14	0	30	0	40	2.50	0				Jan-17
2.20	-0.11	0.80	3.63	4.88	1.33	0.71	2.49	2.30	10.25	783.3	0	0	100	0	0	39	3.00	1,500	100	1.00		Dec-06
2.16	-0.08	1.06	5.05	7.38	1.71	0.46	2.48	2.30	10.24	783.3	0	0	100	0	0	39	3.00	1,000,000				Aug-81
2.20	-0.10	0.91	4.39	6.20	1.46	0.71	2.53	2.30	10.25	783.3	0	0	100	0	0	39	3.00	1,000,000				Sep-93
0.40	5.16	5.83	8.64	8.47	1.22	1.33	2.52	3.80	11.4	289.3	2	81	0	0	0	33	2.25	0				Apr-03
0.58	5.54	6.50	10.93	12.30	1.93	0.6	2.53	3.80	11.4	289.3	2	81	0	0	0	33	2.25	1,000,000				Feb-83
0.53	5.42	6.25	10.17	11.12	1.71	0.83	2.54	3.80	11.4	289.3	2	81	0	0	0	33	2.25	1,000,000				Jun-92
2.16	3.53	4.90	9.55	13.19	1.91	0.63	1.52	2.60	10.68	559.5	4	51	0	26	4	33	2.43	1,500	100	1.00		Jan-14

Fund Name	Ticker Symbol	Traded On	Fund Type	Category and (Prospectus Objective)	Overall Rating	Reward Rating	Risk Rating	Recent Up/ Downgrade	Open to New Investors	Telephone
	MARKET		FUND TYPE, CATEGORY & OBJECTIVE		RATINGS				NEW INVESTORS	
Federated Hermes Short-Intermed Total Return Bond Cl R6 Sh	SRBRX	NAS CM	Open End	US Fixed Inc (Income)	C+	C	B		Y	800-341-7400
Federated Hermes Short-Intermed Total Return Bond Inst Sh	FGCIX	NAS CM	Open End	US Fixed Inc (Income)	C+	C	B		Y	800-341-7400
Federated Hermes Short-Intermed Total Return Bond Service	FGCSX	NAS CM	Open End	US Fixed Inc (Income)	C+	C	B		Y	800-341-7400
Federated Hermes Short-Term Government Fund Class Y Shares	FSGTX	NAS CM	Open End	US Fixed Inc (Govt Bond - Treasury)	C+	C	B	Up	Y	800-341-7400
Federated Hermes Short-Term Govt Fund Institutional Shares	FSGVX	NAS CM	Open End	US Fixed Inc (Govt Bond - Treasury)	C+	C	B	Up	Y	800-341-7400
Federated Hermes Short-Term Government Fund Service Shares	FSGIX	NAS CM	Open End	US Fixed Inc (Govt Bond - Treasury)	C+	C	B-	Up	Y	800-341-7400
Federated Hermes Short-Term Income Fund Class A Shares	FTIAX	NAS CM	Open End	US Fixed Inc (Corp Bond - General)	C	C	B-		Y	800-341-7400
Federated Hermes Short-Term Income Institutional Shares	FSTYX	NAS CM	Open End	US Fixed Inc (Corp Bond - General)	C	C	B-		Y	800-341-7400
Federated Hermes Short-Term Income Fund Service Shares	FSTIX	NAS CM	Open End	US Fixed Inc (Corp Bond - General)	C	C	B-		Y	800-341-7400
Federated Hermes Strategic Income Fund Class A Shares	STIAX	NAS CM	Open End	US Fixed Inc (Multisector Bond)	C-	D+	C		Y	800-341-7400
Federated Hermes Strategic Income Fund Class B Shares	SINBX	NAS CM	Open End	US Fixed Inc (Multisector Bond)	C-	D+	C			800-341-7400
Federated Hermes Strategic Income Fund Class C Shares	SINCX	NAS CM	Open End	US Fixed Inc (Multisector Bond)	C-	D+	C		Y	800-341-7400
Federated Hermes Strategic Income Fund Class F Shares	STFSX	NAS CM	Open End	US Fixed Inc (Multisector Bond)	C-	D+	C		Y	800-341-7400
Federated Hermes Strategic Income Fund Class IS Shares	STISX	NAS CM	Open End	US Fixed Inc (Multisector Bond)	C-	D+	C		Y	800-341-7400
Federated Hermes Strategic Income Fund Class R6 Shares	STILX	NAS CM	Open End	US Fixed Inc (Multisector Bond)	C-	D+	C		Y	800-341-7400
Federated Hermes Tax-Free Obl Advisor	TBVXX	NAS CM	Money Mkt	US Money Mkt (Money Mkt - Fed Tax Exmpt)	C	C	C+		Y	800-341-7400
Federated Hermes Tax-Free Obl Svc	TBSXX	NAS CM	Money Mkt	US Money Mkt (Money Mkt - Fed Tax Exmpt)	C	C-	C+		Y	800-341-7400
Federated Hermes Tax-Free Obl Wealth	TBIXX	NAS CM	Money Mkt	US Money Mkt (Money Mkt - Fed Tax Exmpt)	C	C-	C+		Y	800-341-7400
Federated Hermes Total Return Bond Fund Class A Shares	TLRAX	NAS CM	Open End	US Fixed Inc (Growth & Income)	B-	C+	B+	Up	Y	800-341-7400
Federated Hermes Total Return Bond Fund Class B Shares	TLRBX	NAS CM	Open End	US Fixed Inc (Growth & Income)	B-	C+	B	Up	Y	800-341-7400
Federated Hermes Total Return Bond Fund Class C Shares	TLRCX	NAS CM	Open End	US Fixed Inc (Growth & Income)	B-	C+	B	Up	Y	800-341-7400
Federated Hermes Total Return Bond Fund Class R Shares	FTRKX	NAS CM	Open End	US Fixed Inc (Growth & Income)	B-	C+	B	Up	Y	800-341-7400
Federated Hermes Total Return Bond Fund Class R6 Shares	FTRLX	NAS CM	Open End	US Fixed Inc (Growth & Income)	B	C+	B+	Up	Y	800-341-7400
Federated Hermes Total Return Bond Institutional Shares	FTRBX	NAS CM	Open End	US Fixed Inc (Growth & Income)	B	C+	B+	Up	Y	800-341-7400
Federated Hermes Total Return Bond Fund Service Shares	FTRFX	NAS CM	Open End	US Fixed Inc (Growth & Income)	B	C+	B+	Up	Y	800-341-7400
Federated Hermes Total Return Govt Bond Fund Class R6	FTGLX	NAS CM	Open End	US Fixed Inc (Govt Bond - Treasury)	B	B	B+		Y	800-341-7400
Federated Hermes Total Return Govt Bond Inst Shares	FTRGX	NAS CM	Open End	US Fixed Inc (Govt Bond - Treasury)	B	B	B+		Y	800-341-7400
Federated Hermes Total Return Govt Bond Service Shares	FTGSX	NAS CM	Open End	US Fixed Inc (Govt Bond - Treasury)	B	B	B		Y	800-341-7400
Federated Hermes Tr for US Trs Obl IS	TTOXX	NAS CM	Money Mkt	US Money Mkt (Money Mkt - Treasury)	C	C-	C+		Y	800-341-7400
Federated Hermes Tr US Trs Obl Cash II	TTIXX	NAS CM	Money Mkt	US Money Mkt (Money Mkt - Treasury)	C	C-	C+		Y	800-341-7400
Federated Hermes Tr US Trs Obl Cash Srs	TCSXX	NAS CM	Money Mkt	US Money Mkt (Money Mkt - Treasury)	C	C-	C		Y	800-341-7400
★ Federated Hermes Treasury Obl Automated	TOAXX	NAS CM	Money Mkt	US Money Mkt (Money Mkt - Treasury)	C	C-	C+		Y	800-341-7400
Federated Hermes Treasury Obl Capital	TOCXX	NAS CM	Money Mkt	US Money Mkt (Money Mkt - Treasury)	C	C-	C+		Y	800-341-7400
Federated Hermes Treasury Obl IS	TOIXX	NAS CM	Money Mkt	US Money Mkt (Money Mkt - Treasury)	C	C-	C+		Y	800-341-7400
Federated Hermes Treasury Obl Svc	TOSXX	NAS CM	Money Mkt	US Money Mkt (Money Mkt - Treasury)	C	C-	C+		Y	800-341-7400
Federated Hermes Treasury Obl Trust	TOTXX	NAS CM	Money Mkt	US Money Mkt (Money Mkt - Treasury)	C	C-	C+		Y	800-341-7400
Federated Hermes Ultrashort Bond Fund Class A Shares	FULAX	NAS CM	Open End	US Fixed Inc (Income)	C	C-	C+		Y	800-341-7400
Federated Hermes UltraShort Bond Fund Class R6 Shares	FULLX	NAS CM	Open End	US Fixed Inc (Income)	C	C-	C+		Y	800-341-7400
Federated Hermes Ultrashort Bond Fund Institutional Shares	FULIX	NAS CM	Open End	US Fixed Inc (Income)	C	C-	C+		Y	800-341-7400
Federated Hermes Ultrashort Bond Fund Service Shares	FULBX	NAS CM	Open End	US Fixed Inc (Income)	C	C-	C+		Y	800-341-7400
Federated Hermes US Treas Cash Res IS	UTIXX	NAS CM	Money Mkt	US Money Mkt (Money Mkt - Govt)	C	C-	C+		Y	800-341-7400
Federated Hermes US Treas Cash Res Svc	TISXX	NAS CM	Money Mkt	US Money Mkt (Money Mkt - Govt)	C	C-	C+		Y	800-341-7400
Federated Hermes VA Muni Cash Cash Srs	VCSXX	NAS CM	Money Mkt	US Money Mkt (Money Mkt - Single State)	C	C-	C		Y	800-341-7400
Federated Hermes VA Muni Cash Svc	VACXX	NAS CM	Money Mkt	US Money Mkt (Money Mkt - Single State)	C	C-	C		Y	800-341-7400
Federated Ohio Municipal Income Fund Institutional Shares	OMIIX	NAS CM	Open End	US Muni Fixed Inc (Muni Bond - Single State)	C	C-	B-		Y	800-341-7400
Federated Pennsylvania Muni Income Institutional Shares	PAMIX	NAS CM	Open End	US Muni Fixed Inc (Muni Bond - Single State)	C	C	B-		Y	800-341-7400
Fidelity Advisor® California Municipal Income Fund Class A	FCMAX	NAS CM	Open End	US Muni Fixed Inc (Muni Bond - Natl)	C	C	B-		Y	617-563-7000
Fidelity Advisor® California Municipal Income Fund Class C	FCMKX	NAS CM	Open End	US Muni Fixed Inc (Muni Bond - Natl)	C	C-	C+		Y	617-563-7000
Fidelity Advisor® California Municipal Income Fund Class I	FCMQX	NAS CM	Open End	US Muni Fixed Inc (Muni Bond - Natl)	C	C	B-		Y	617-563-7000
Fidelity Advisor® California Municipal Income Fund Class M	FCMTX	NAS CM	Open End	US Muni Fixed Inc (Muni Bond - Natl)	C	C	B-		Y	617-563-7000
Fidelity Advisor® California Municipal Income Fund Class Z	FIJBX	NAS CM	Open End	US Muni Fixed Inc (Muni Bond - Natl)	C	C	B		Y	617-563-7000
Fidelity Advisor® Corporate Bond Fund Class A	FCBAX	NAS CM	Open End	US Fixed Inc (Corp Bond - General)	B-	C	B	Up	Y	617-563-7000

★ Expanded analysis of this fund is included in Section II.

TOTAL RETURNS & PERFORMANCE									ASSETS		ASSET ALLOCATION & TURNOVER							MINIMUMS		FEES		
3-Month Total Return	6-Month Total Return	1-Year Total Return	3-Year Total Return	5-Year Total Return	Dividend Yield (TTM)	Expense Ratio	3-Yr Std Deviation	Effective Duration	NAV	Total Assets (MIL)	%Cash	%Government Bonds	%Municipal Bonds	%Corporate Bonds	%Other	Turnover Ratio	Average Coupon Rate	Min Initial Investment	Min Additional Investment	Front End Fee (%)	Back End Fee (%)	Inception Date
2.33	3.67	5.17	10.40	13.66	2.16	0.37	1.48	2.60	10.68	559.5	4	51	0	26	4	33	2.43	0				Jan-14
2.32	3.66	5.16	10.37	14.61	2.15	0.38	1.49	2.60	10.68	559.5	4	51	0	26	4	33	2.43	1,000,000				Sep-05
2.17	3.54	4.90	9.56	13.21	1.91	0.63	1.47	2.60	10.67	559.5	4	51	0	26	4	33	2.43	1,000,000				Sep-05
0.43	2.86	3.71	7.25	8.10	1.9	0.37	1.13	1.80	10.45	187.2	4	80	0	0	0	110	1.73	100,000				Aug-01
0.51	2.82	3.72	7.07	7.63	1.82	0.54	1.12	1.80	10.46	187.2	4	80	0	0	0	110	1.73	1,000,000				Mar-84
0.30	2.51	3.20	5.68	5.49	1.41	0.87	1.13	1.80	10.44	187.2	4	80	0	0	0	110	1.73	1,000,000				May-92
3.15	1.62	2.80	7.02	8.56	2.01	0.71	2.13	1.90	8.63	1,566	4	14	0	30	0	40	2.50	1,500	100	1.00		Aug-04
3.10	1.64	3.06	8.71	11.94	2.4	0.38	2.12	1.90	8.62	1,566	4	14	0	30	0	40	2.50	100,000				Aug-04
3.16	1.50	2.78	8.04	10.93	2.12	0.66	2.14	1.90	8.62	1,566	4	14	0	30	0	40	2.50	1,000,000				Jul-86
9.00	-2.84	0.00	8.05	18.09	3.21	0.97	7.86	3.60	8.78	657.3	5	15	0	50	25	58	4.49	1,500	100	4.50		May-94
8.68	-3.24	-0.78	5.47	13.56	2.43	1.76	7.84	3.60	8.76	657.3	5	15	0	50	25	58	4.49	1,500	100		5.50	Jul-95
8.81	-3.22	-0.75	5.63	13.61	2.44	1.74	7.91	3.60	8.77	657.3	5	15	0	50	25	58	4.49	1,500	100		1.00	May-94
8.94	-2.97	0.00	7.99	17.97	3.24	0.97	7.91	3.60	8.71	657.3	5	15	0	50	25	58	4.49	1,500	100	1.00		May-94
9.01	-2.81	0.32	9.02	19.72	3.55	0.65	7.85	3.60	8.72	657.3	5	15	0	50	25	58	4.49	1,000,000				Jan-08
9.09	-2.79	0.33	9.11	17.81	3.55	0.64	7.9	3.60	8.78	657.3	5	15	0	50	25	58	4.49	0				Jan-17
0.11	0.46	1.06	3.55	4.40	1.17	0.21			1	4,391	14	0	86	0	0			250,000				Jan-19
0.06	0.34	0.82	2.78	3.31	0.92	0.46	0.11		1	4,391	14	0	86	0	0			500,000				Jul-94
0.11	0.45	1.07	3.55	4.40	1.17	0.21	0.11		1	4,391	14	0	86	0	0			500,000				Dec-89
5.46	5.18	7.69	14.70	22.19	2.57	0.94	3.56	5.70	11.51	8,906	2	32	1	35	7	43	3.60	1,500	100	4.50		Aug-01
5.32	4.98	7.12	12.86	18.80	2.05	1.51	3.58	5.70	11.51	8,906	2	32	1	35	7	43	3.60	1,500	100		5.50	Aug-01
5.33	4.92	7.16	12.98	19.01	2.09	1.49	3.57	5.70	11.51	8,906	2	32	1	35	7	43	3.60	1,500	100		1.00	Aug-01
5.32	5.08	7.50	14.02	21.05	2.4	1.13	3.52	5.70	11.51	8,906	2	32	1	35	7	43	3.60	0				Apr-03
5.61	5.56	8.29	16.63	25.52	3.12	0.38	3.5	5.70	11.51	8,906	2	32	1	35	7	43	3.60	0				Apr-15
5.51	5.46	8.28	16.49	25.46	3.11	0.39	3.52	5.70	11.51	8,906	2	32	1	35	7	43	3.60	1,000,000				Oct-96
5.43	5.31	7.96	15.46	23.60	2.82	0.69	3.52	5.70	11.51	8,906	2	32	1	35	7	43	3.60	1,000,000				Oct-96
0.65	8.38	10.12	17.35	22.08	2.17	0.32	3.85	2.70	11.82	467.7	13	53	0	0	0	56	2.73	0				Jun-16
0.56	8.37	10.11	17.21	22.03	2.16	0.33	3.86	2.70	11.82	467.7	13	53	0	0	0	56	2.73	1,000,000				Oct-95
0.56	8.19	9.74	16.03	19.98	1.84	0.67	3.83	2.70	11.82	467.7	13	53	0	0	0	56	2.73	1,000,000				Oct-95
0.03	0.33	1.24	4.60	5.11	1.42	0.2	0.18		1	3,958	73	27	0	0	0			25,000				Nov-79
0.00	0.14	0.70	2.59	2.61	0.83	0.9	0.16		1	3,958	73	27	0	0	0			25,000				Jun-15
0.00	0.11	0.61	2.22	2.22	0.73	1.05	0.15		1	3,958	73	27	0	0	0			10,000	250			Jun-15
0.00	0.23	1.00	3.84	3.97	1.16	0.55	0.17		1	54,381	75	25	0	0	0			25,000				Jun-14
0.01	0.30	1.17	4.35	4.69	1.34	0.3	0.18		1	54,381	75	25	0	0	0			500,000				Apr-97
0.03	0.34	1.26	4.66	5.16	1.44	0.2	0.18		1	54,381	75	25	0	0	0			500,000				Dec-89
0.00	0.25	1.05	3.91	4.08	1.21	0.45	0.17		1	54,381	75	25	0	0	0			500,000				Jul-94
0.00	0.19	0.86	3.20	3.26	1.01	0.7	0.16		1	54,381	75	25	0	0	0			500,000				Feb-03
3.45	0.55	1.55	5.52	7.16	1.96	0.52	2.51	1.00	9.12	3,844	2	1	1	34	0	36	2.22	1,500	100	2.00		Oct-02
3.36	0.52	1.88	5.99	7.85	2.33	0.36	2.42	1.00	9.11	3,844	2	1	1	34	0	36	2.22	0	0			May-19
3.48	0.63	1.99	7.02	9.88	2.32	0.37	2.42	1.00	9.12	3,844	2	1	1	34	0	36	2.22	1,000,000				Feb-00
3.46	0.58	1.74	5.81	7.66	2.04	0.47	2.42	1.00	9.12	3,844	2	1	1	34	0	36	2.22	1,000,000				May-97
0.03	0.34	1.25	4.59	5.04	1.43	0.2	0.17		1	47,385	74	26	0	0	0			500,000				Jun-91
0.00	0.25	1.03	3.85	3.99	1.19	0.45	0.17		1	47,385	74	26	0	0	0			500,000				Oct-94
0.03	0.19	0.37	1.19	1.31	0.42	1.05	0.1		1	183.9	7	0	93	0	0			1,000				Jan-05
0.04	0.29	0.67	2.23	2.45	0.75	0.66	0.12		1	183.9	7	0	93	0	0			10,000				Sep-93
1.92	1.47	3.29	9.62	16.52		0.52	3.48	6.70	11.33	145.3	0	0	100	0	0	15	4.91	1,000,000				Apr-20
0.82	1.54	3.56	10.83	18.26		0.53	3.61	7.10	11	154.6	0	3	97	0	0	16	4.89	1,000,000				Apr-20
2.17	1.18	3.15	10.91	18.15	2.29	0.79	4.3	6.51	13.26	2,130	0	0	100	0	0	11	4.77	0		4.00		Aug-02
1.98	0.80	2.39	8.44	13.80	1.54	1.54	4.32	6.51	13.24	2,130	0	0	100	0	0	11	4.77	0			1.00	Aug-02
2.23	1.30	3.40	11.72	19.60	2.53	0.55	4.3	6.51	13.27	2,130	0	0	100	0	0	11	4.77	0				Aug-02
2.17	1.27	3.18	11.11	18.36	2.33	0.75	4.26	6.51	13.3	2,130	0	0	100	0	0	11	4.77	0		4.00		Aug-02
2.26	1.36	3.52	12.06	20.19	2.65	0.43	4.32	6.51	13.27	2,130	0	0	100	0	0	11	4.77	0				Oct-18
10.15	5.76	9.70	19.87	31.53	2.69	0.79	6.89	7.79	12.68	2,855	3	6	0	90	0	28	3.67	0		4.00		May-10

Fund Name	MARKET Ticker Symbol	Traded On	Fund Type	FUND TYPE, CATEGORY & OBJECTIVE Category and (Prospectus Objective)	RATINGS Overall Rating	Reward Rating	Risk Rating	Recent Up/ Downgrade	NEW INVESTORS Open to New Investors	Telephone
Fidelity Advisor® Corporate Bond Fund Class C	FCCCX	NAS CM	Open End	US Fixed Inc (Corp Bond - General)	B-	C	B	Up	Y	617-563-7000
Fidelity Advisor® Corporate Bond Fund Class M	FCBTX	NAS CM	Open End	US Fixed Inc (Corp Bond - General)	B-	C	B	Up	Y	617-563-7000
Fidelity Advisor® Corporate Bond Fund Class Z	FIKOX	NAS CM	Open End	US Fixed Inc (Corp Bond - General)	B-	C	B	Up	Y	617-563-7000
Fidelity Advisor® Corporate Bond Fund I Class	FCBIX	NAS CM	Open End	US Fixed Inc (Corp Bond - General)	B-	C	B	Up	Y	617-563-7000
Fidelity Advisor® Floating Rate High Income Fund Class A	FFRAX	NAS CM	Open End	US Fixed Inc (Income)	D+	D	C-	Down	Y	617-563-7000
Fidelity Advisor® Floating Rate High Income Fund Class C	FFRCX	NAS CM	Open End	US Fixed Inc (Income)	D	D	C-	Down	Y	617-563-7000
Fidelity Advisor® Floating Rate High Income Fund Class M	FFRTX	NAS CM	Open End	US Fixed Inc (Income)	D+	D	C-	Down	Y	617-563-7000
Fidelity Advisor® Floating Rate High Income Fund Class Z	FIQSX	NAS CM	Open End	US Fixed Inc (Income)	D+	D	C-	Down	Y	617-563-7000
Fidelity Advisor® Floating Rate High Income Fund I Class	FFRIX	NAS CM	Open End	US Fixed Inc (Income)	D+	D	C-	Down	Y	617-563-7000
Fidelity Advisor® Global Credit Fund Class A	FGBZX	NAS CM	Open End	Global Fixed Inc (Worldwide Bond)	C	C-	B-		Y	617-563-7000
Fidelity Advisor® Global Credit Fund Class C	FGBYX	NAS CM	Open End	Global Fixed Inc (Worldwide Bond)	C	C-	B-		Y	617-563-7000
Fidelity Advisor® Global Credit Fund Class M	FGBWX	NAS CM	Open End	Global Fixed Inc (Worldwide Bond)	C	C-	B-		Y	617-563-7000
Fidelity Advisor® Global Credit Fund Class Z	FIQYX	NAS CM	Open End	Global Fixed Inc (Worldwide Bond)	C	C-	B		Y	617-563-7000
Fidelity Advisor® Global Credit Fund I Class	FGBIX	NAS CM	Open End	Global Fixed Inc (Worldwide Bond)	C	C-	B		Y	617-563-7000
Fidelity Advisor® Global High Income Fund Class A	FGHAX	NAS CM	Open End	Global Fixed Inc (Income)	D+	D	C-	Down	Y	617-563-7000
Fidelity Advisor® Global High Income Fund Class C	FGHCX	NAS CM	Open End	Global Fixed Inc (Income)	D+	D	C-	Down	Y	617-563-7000
Fidelity Advisor® Global High Income Fund Class M	FGHTX	NAS CM	Open End	Global Fixed Inc (Income)	D+	D	C-	Down	Y	617-563-7000
Fidelity Advisor® Global High Income Fund I Class	FGHIX	NAS CM	Open End	Global Fixed Inc (Income)	D+	D	C-	Down	Y	617-563-7000
Fidelity Advisor® Government Income Fund Class A	FVIAX	NAS CM	Open End	US Fixed Inc (Govt Bond - General)	B	B	B		Y	617-563-7000
Fidelity Advisor® Government Income Fund Class C	FVICX	NAS CM	Open End	US Fixed Inc (Govt Bond - General)	B-	B-	B		Y	617-563-7000
Fidelity Advisor® Government Income Fund Class I	FVIIX	NAS CM	Open End	US Fixed Inc (Govt Bond - General)	B	B	B		Y	617-563-7000
Fidelity Advisor® Government Income Fund Class M	FVITX	NAS CM	Open End	US Fixed Inc (Govt Bond - General)	B	B	B		Y	617-563-7000
Fidelity Advisor® Government Income Fund Class Z	FIKPX	NAS CM	Open End	US Fixed Inc (Govt Bond - General)	B	B	B		Y	617-563-7000
Fidelity Advisor® High Income Advantage Fund Class A	FAHDX	NAS CM	Open End	US Fixed Inc (Income)	D	D	D+	Down	Y	617-563-7000
Fidelity Advisor® High Income Advantage Fund Class C	FAHEX	NAS CM	Open End	US Fixed Inc (Income)	D	D	D+	Down	Y	617-563-7000
Fidelity Advisor® High Income Advantage Fund Class M	FAHYX	NAS CM	Open End	US Fixed Inc (Income)	D	D	D+	Down	Y	617-563-7000
Fidelity Advisor® High Income Advantage Fund Class Z	FIQTX	NAS CM	Open End	US Fixed Inc (Income)	D+	D	D+	Down	Y	617-563-7000
Fidelity Advisor® High Income Advantage Fund I Class	FAHCX	NAS CM	Open End	US Fixed Inc (Income)	D+	D	D+	Down	Y	617-563-7000
Fidelity Advisor® High Income Fund Class A	FGQMX	NAS CM	Open End	US Fixed Inc (Growth & Income)	C-	D+	C		Y	617-563-7000
Fidelity Advisor® High Income Fund Class C	FGSMX	NAS CM	Open End	US Fixed Inc (Growth & Income)	D+	D	C-	Down	Y	617-563-7000
Fidelity Advisor® High Income Fund Class I	FGTMX	NAS CM	Open End	US Fixed Inc (Growth & Income)	C-	D+	C		Y	617-563-7000
Fidelity Advisor® High Income Fund Class M	FGRMX	NAS CM	Open End	US Fixed Inc (Growth & Income)	C-	D+	C		Y	617-563-7000
Fidelity Advisor® High Income Fund Class Z	FGUMX	NAS CM	Open End	US Fixed Inc (Growth & Income)	C-	D+	C		Y	617-563-7000
Fidelity Advisor® Intermediate Muni Income Fund Class A	FZIAX	NAS CM	Open End	US Muni Fixed Inc (Muni Bond - Natl)	C	C-	B-		Y	617-563-7000
Fidelity Advisor® Intermediate Muni Income Fund Class C	FZICX	NAS CM	Open End	US Muni Fixed Inc (Muni Bond - Natl)	C	C-	C+		Y	617-563-7000
Fidelity Advisor® Intermediate Muni Income Fund Class I	FZIIX	NAS CM	Open End	US Muni Fixed Inc (Muni Bond - Natl)	C	C	B-		Y	617-563-7000
Fidelity Advisor® Intermediate Muni Income Fund Class M	FZITX	NAS CM	Open End	US Muni Fixed Inc (Muni Bond - Natl)	C	C-	B-		Y	617-563-7000
Fidelity Advisor® Intermediate Muni Income Fund Class Z	FIQZX	NAS CM	Open End	US Muni Fixed Inc (Muni Bond - Natl)	C	C	B-		Y	617-563-7000
Fidelity Advisor® Investment Grade Bond Fund Class A	FGBAX	NAS CM	Open End	US Fixed Inc (Income)	B	B-	B+	Up	Y	617-563-7000
Fidelity Advisor® Investment Grade Bond Fund Class C	FGBCX	NAS CM	Open End	US Fixed Inc (Income)	B-	B-	B	Up	Y	617-563-7000
Fidelity Advisor® Investment Grade Bond Fund Class I	FGBPX	NAS CM	Open End	US Fixed Inc (Income)	B	B-	B+	Up	Y	617-563-7000
Fidelity Advisor® Investment Grade Bond Fund Class M	FGBTX	NAS CM	Open End	US Fixed Inc (Income)	B	B-	B+	Up	Y	617-563-7000
Fidelity Advisor® Investment Grade Bond Fund Class Z	FIKQX	NAS CM	Open End	US Fixed Inc (Income)	B	B-	B+	Up	Y	617-563-7000
Fidelity Advisor® Limited Term Bond Fund Class A	FDIAX	NAS CM	Open End	US Fixed Inc (Income)	C+	C	B	Up	Y	617-563-7000
Fidelity Advisor® Limited Term Bond Fund Class C	FNBCX	NAS CM	Open End	US Fixed Inc (Income)	C	C	B-		Y	617-563-7000
Fidelity Advisor® Limited Term Bond Fund Class I	EFIPX	NAS CM	Open End	US Fixed Inc (Income)	C+	C	B	Up	Y	617-563-7000
Fidelity Advisor® Limited Term Bond Fund Class M	FTBRX	NAS CM	Open End	US Fixed Inc (Income)	C+	C	B	Up	Y	617-563-7000
Fidelity Advisor® Limited Term Bond Fund Class Z	FIKRX	NAS CM	Open End	US Fixed Inc (Income)	C+	C	B	Up	Y	617-563-7000
Fidelity Advisor® Limited Term Muni Income Fund - Class M	FTSHX	NAS CM	Open End	US Muni Fixed Inc (Muni Bond - Natl)	C	C-	C+		Y	617-563-7000
Fidelity Advisor® Limited Term Muni Income Fund Class A	FASHX	NAS CM	Open End	US Muni Fixed Inc (Muni Bond - Natl)	C	C-	C+		Y	617-563-7000
Fidelity Advisor® Limited Term Muni Income Fund Class C	FCSHX	NAS CM	Open End	US Muni Fixed Inc (Muni Bond - Natl)	C	C-	C		Y	617-563-7000
Fidelity Advisor® Limited Term Muni Income Fund Class I	FISHX	NAS CM	Open End	US Muni Fixed Inc (Muni Bond - Natl)	C	C-	C+		Y	617-563-7000

★Expanded analysis of this fund is included in Section II.

TOTAL RETURNS & PERFORMANCE									ASSETS		ASSET ALLOCATION & TURNOVER							MINIMUMS		FEES		
3-Month Total Return	6-Month Total Return	1-Year Total Return	3-Year Total Return	5-Year Total Return	Dividend Yield (TTM)	Expense Ratio	3-Yr Std Deviation	Effective Duration	NAV	Total Assets (MIL)	%Cash	%Government Bonds	%Municipal Bonds	%Corporate Bonds	%Other	Turnover Ratio	Average Coupon Rate	Min Initial Investment	Min Additional Investment	Front End Fee (%)	Back End Fee (%)	Inception Date
9.85	5.27	8.78	17.07	26.54	1.93	1.55	6.81	7.79	12.67	2,855	3	6	0	90	0	28	3.67	0			1.00	May-10
10.13	5.73	9.64	19.61	31.03	2.63	0.87	6.89	7.79	12.68	2,855	3	6	0	90	0	28	3.67	0		4.00		May-10
10.17	5.89	10.06	21.08	33.62	3.09	0.36	6.84	7.79	12.67	2,855	3	6	0	90	0	28	3.67	0				Oct-18
10.22	5.90	10.00	20.90	33.42	2.95	0.49	6.9	7.79	12.68	2,855	3	6	0	90	0	28	3.67	0				May-10
8.42	-5.83	-3.53	3.61	11.09	4.89	0.98	8.25		8.76	7,048	4	0	0	96	0	22	4.48	0		2.75		Aug-00
8.09	-6.29	-4.26	1.20	6.99	4.1	1.73	8.24		8.75	7,048	4	0	0	96	0	22	4.48	0			1.00	Aug-00
8.30	-5.95	-3.56	3.46	10.88	4.88	0.99	8.24		8.74	7,048	4	0	0	96	0	22	4.48	0		2.75		Aug-00
8.53	-5.68	-3.21	4.08	11.54	5.26	0.63	8.31		8.74	7,048	4	0	0	96	0	22	4.48	0				Oct-18
8.51	-5.72	-3.20	4.35	12.40	5.17	0.74	8.26		8.74	7,048	4	0	0	96	0	22	4.48	0				Aug-00
9.75	2.67	7.12	16.21	24.71	2.14	1	7.42	7.14	9.81	88.6	-77	4	0	87	0	85	4.07	0		4.00		May-12
9.56	2.38	6.35	13.70	20.19	1.44	1.75	7.43	7.14	9.8	88.6	-77	4	0	87	0	85	4.07	0			1.00	May-12
9.74	2.76	7.22	16.31	24.73	2.13	1	7.41	7.14	9.81	88.6	-77	4	0	87	0	85	4.07	0		4.00		May-12
9.79	2.93	7.58	17.28	26.45	2.37	0.66	7.43	7.14	9.83	88.6	-77	4	0	87	0	85	4.07	0				Oct-18
9.80	2.83	7.47	17.16	26.32	2.37	0.75	7.42	7.14	9.82	88.6	-77	4	0	87	0	85	4.07	0				May-12
12.57	-5.15	-2.35	6.11	18.89	4.81	1.25	10.27		8.9	92.1	4	2	0	93	0	54	6.10	0		4.00		May-11
12.36	-5.51	-3.08	3.76	14.53	4.02	2	10.27		8.9	92.1	4	2	0	93	0	54	6.10	0			1.00	May-11
12.57	-5.15	-2.35	6.22	18.89	4.81	1.25	10.27		8.9	92.1	4	2	0	93	0	54	6.10	0		4.00		May-11
12.76	-4.93	-2.00	7.03	20.52	5.07	1	10.29		8.91	92.1	4	2	0	93	0	54	6.10	0				May-11
0.34	7.12	8.60	14.21	17.75	1.38	0.78	3.63	5.46	11.19	4,665	23	50	0	0	-1	246	2.31	0		4.00		Oct-06
0.18	6.84	7.82	11.77	13.46	0.65	1.54	3.7	5.46	11.19	4,665	23	50	0	0	-1	246	2.31	0			1.00	Oct-06
0.41	7.37	8.91	15.30	19.39	1.65	0.49	3.68	5.46	11.19	4,665	23	50	0	0	-1	246	2.31	0				Oct-06
0.35	7.23	8.62	14.37	17.92	1.39	0.76	3.68	5.46	11.19	4,665	23	50	0	0	-1	246	2.31	0		4.00		Oct-06
0.45	7.43	9.14	15.58	19.91	1.77	0.36	3.62	5.46	11.2	4,665	23	50	0	0	-1	246	2.31	0				Oct-18
13.24	-7.05	-3.28	8.25	21.68	4.34	1.01	12.26		10.44	1,459	3	0	0	96	0	53	6.15	0		4.00		Jan-87
13.05	-7.43	-4.03	5.80	17.15	3.53	1.77	12.27		10.42	1,459	3	0	0	96	0	53	6.15	0			1.00	Nov-97
13.17	-7.17	-3.33	8.09	21.61	4.34	1	12.23		10.49	1,459	3	0	0	96	0	53	6.15	0		4.00		Jan-87
13.23	-7.01	-3.03	8.69	22.29	4.73	0.65	12.27		9.77	1,459	3	0	0	96	0	53	6.15	0				Oct-18
13.21	-7.06	-3.03	8.97	23.03	4.63	0.76	12.24		9.77	1,459	3	0	0	96	0	53	6.15	0				Jul-95
8.18	-6.31	-3.04	7.22	19.94	5.19	0.99	8.76		8.19	5,033	4	0	0	96	0	44	6.20	0		4.00		Dec-18
7.96	-6.67	-3.67	4.94	15.65	4.37	1.77	8.72		8.2	5,033	4	0	0	96	0	44	6.20	0			1.00	Dec-18
8.25	-6.19	-2.80	8.00	21.42	5.45	0.78	8.76		8.19	5,033	4	0	0	96	0	44	6.20	0				Dec-18
8.18	-6.32	-3.05	7.20	19.92	5.18	1.01	8.76		8.19	5,033	4	0	0	96	0	44	6.20	0		4.00		Dec-18
8.28	-6.15	-2.70	8.19	21.63	5.56	0.64	8.76		8.19	5,033	4	0	0	96	0	44	6.20	0				Dec-18
2.48	1.23	2.93	10.14	15.27	1.99	0.67	3.62	4.85	10.67	8,025	3	0	97	0	0	14	4.68	0		4.00		Oct-05
2.39	0.86	2.27	7.81	11.16	1.25	1.42	3.66	4.85	10.68	8,025	3	0	97	0	0	14	4.68	0			1.00	Oct-05
2.55	1.36	3.18	10.94	16.69	2.23	0.43	3.63	4.85	10.68	8,025	3	0	97	0	0	14	4.68	0				Oct-05
2.59	1.34	3.05	10.34	15.57	2.02	0.64	3.69	4.85	10.67	8,025	3	0	97	0	0	14	4.68	0		4.00		Oct-05
2.67	1.51	3.40	11.37	17.33	2.36	0.3	3.69	4.85	10.69	8,025	3	0	97	0	0	14	4.68	0				Oct-18
5.52	7.33	9.96	18.18	25.11	2.11	0.77	3.44	5.60	8.7	7,365	2	46	1	31	-1	59	3.37	0		4.00		Aug-02
5.31	6.91	9.11	15.47	20.40	1.36	1.54	3.51	5.60	8.71	7,365	2	46	1	31	-1	59	3.37	0			1.00	Aug-02
5.58	7.47	10.12	18.98	26.80	2.38	0.5	3.55	5.60	8.71	7,365	2	46	1	31	-1	59	3.37	0				Aug-02
5.52	7.34	9.83	18.00	24.99	2.12	0.77	3.55	5.60	8.7	7,365	2	46	1	31	-1	59	3.37	0		4.00		Aug-02
5.61	7.53	10.38	19.27	27.08	2.49	0.36	3.47	5.60	8.72	7,365	2	46	1	31	-1	59	3.37	0				Oct-18
4.50	3.13	4.77	9.74	13.38	2.05	0.75	2.73	2.58	11.89	2,971	6	9	1	62	0	29	3.09	0		2.75		Sep-96
4.30	2.73	3.87	7.21	8.97	1.27	1.54	2.74	2.58	11.86	2,971	6	9	1	62	0	29	3.09	0			1.00	Nov-97
4.55	3.26	5.03	10.58	14.84	2.3	0.5	2.73	2.58	11.92	2,971	6	9	1	62	0	29	3.09	0				Feb-84
4.58	3.13	4.76	9.81	13.34	2.05	0.76	2.78	2.58	11.9	2,971	6	9	1	62	0	29	3.09	0		2.75		Sep-92
4.59	3.33	5.17	10.83	15.10	2.44	0.36	2.74	2.58	11.92	2,971	6	9	1	62	0	29	3.09	0				Oct-18
2.45	1.31	2.41	6.46	8.86	1.43	0.65	2.31	2.84	10.76	2,869	4	0	96	0	0	43	4.38	0		2.75		Jul-03
2.44	1.30	2.38	6.34	8.65	1.4	0.66	2.3	2.84	10.78	2,869	4	0	96	0	0	43	4.38	0		2.75		Jul-03
2.26	0.94	1.66	4.03	4.72	0.68	1.38	2.3	2.84	10.76	2,869	4	0	96	0	0	43	4.38	0			1.00	Jul-03
2.52	1.36	2.67	7.10	9.99	1.68	0.37	2.3	2.84	10.76	2,869	4	0	96	0	0	43	4.38	0				Jul-03

	MARKET			FUND TYPE, CATEGORY & OBJECTIVE	RATINGS				NEW INVESTORS	
Fund Name	Ticker Symbol	Traded On	Fund Type	Category and (Prospectus Objective)	Overall Rating	Reward Rating	Risk Rating	Recent Up/ Downgrade	Open to New Investors	Telephone
Fidelity Advisor® Limited Term Muni Income Fund Class Z	FIWAX	NAS CM	Open End	US Muni Fixed Inc (Muni Bond - Natl)	C	C-	C+		Y	617-563-7000
Fidelity Advisor® Mortgage Securities Fund Class A	FMGAX	NAS CM	Open End	US Fixed Inc (Govt Bond - Mortgage)	B-	C+	B	Up	Y	617-563-7000
Fidelity Advisor® Mortgage Securities Fund Class C	FOMCX	NAS CM	Open End	US Fixed Inc (Govt Bond - Mortgage)	C+	C	B-	Up	Y	617-563-7000
Fidelity Advisor® Mortgage Securities Fund Class I	FMSCX	NAS CM	Open End	US Fixed Inc (Govt Bond - Mortgage)	C+	C+	B-		Y	617-563-7000
Fidelity Advisor® Mortgage Securities Fund Class M	FMSAX	NAS CM	Open End	US Fixed Inc (Govt Bond - Mortgage)	B-	C+	B	Up	Y	617-563-7000
Fidelity Advisor® Mortgage Securities Fund Class Z	FIKUX	NAS CM	Open End	US Fixed Inc (Govt Bond - Mortgage)	B-	C+	B	Up	Y	617-563-7000
Fidelity Advisor® Municipal Income Fund Class A	FHUGX	NAS CM	Open End	US Muni Fixed Inc (Muni Bond - Natl)	C	C-	C+		Y	617-563-7000
Fidelity Advisor® Municipal Income Fund Class C	FKISX	NAS CM	Open End	US Muni Fixed Inc (Muni Bond - Natl)	C	C-	C+		Y	617-563-7000
Fidelity Advisor® Municipal Income Fund Class I	FROGX	NAS CM	Open End	US Muni Fixed Inc (Muni Bond - Natl)	C	C-	B-		Y	617-563-7000
Fidelity Advisor® Municipal Income Fund Class M	FLUVX	NAS CM	Open End	US Muni Fixed Inc (Muni Bond - Natl)	C	C-	C+		Y	617-563-7000
Fidelity Advisor® Municipal Income Fund Class Z	FIWEX	NAS CM	Open End	US Muni Fixed Inc (Muni Bond - Natl)	C	C-	B-		Y	617-563-7000
Fidelity Advisor® New Markets Income Fund Class A	FGVMX	NAS CM	Open End	Emerg Mkts Fixed Inc (Diversified Emerg Mkts)	D	D	D+	Down	Y	617-563-7000
Fidelity Advisor® New Markets Income Fund Class C	FGYMX	NAS CM	Open End	Emerg Mkts Fixed Inc (Diversified Emerg Mkts)	D	D	D+	Down	Y	617-563-7000
Fidelity Advisor® New Markets Income Fund Class I	FGZMX	NAS CM	Open End	Emerg Mkts Fixed Inc (Diversified Emerg Mkts)	D	D	D+	Down	Y	617-563-7000
Fidelity Advisor® New Markets Income Fund Class M	FGWMX	NAS CM	Open End	Emerg Mkts Fixed Inc (Diversified Emerg Mkts)	D	D	D+	Down	Y	617-563-7000
Fidelity Advisor® New Markets Income Fund Class Z	FGBMX	NAS CM	Open End	Emerg Mkts Fixed Inc (Diversified Emerg Mkts)	D	D	D+	Down	Y	617-563-7000
Fidelity Advisor® New York Municipal Income Fund Class A	FNMAX	NAS CM	Open End	US Muni Fixed Inc (Muni Bond - Single State)	C	C-	C+		Y	617-563-7000
Fidelity Advisor® New York Municipal Income Fund Class C	FNYCX	NAS CM	Open End	US Muni Fixed Inc (Muni Bond - Single State)	C	C-	C+		Y	617-563-7000
Fidelity Advisor® New York Municipal Income Fund Class I	FEMIX	NAS CM	Open End	US Muni Fixed Inc (Muni Bond - Single State)	C	C-	B-		Y	617-563-7000
Fidelity Advisor® New York Municipal Income Fund Class M	FNYPX	NAS CM	Open End	US Muni Fixed Inc (Muni Bond - Single State)	C	C-	C+		Y	617-563-7000
Fidelity Advisor® New York Municipal Income Fund Class Z	FIJAX	NAS CM	Open End	US Muni Fixed Inc (Muni Bond - Single State)	C	C-	B-		Y	617-563-7000
Fidelity Advisor® Short Duration High Income Fund Class A	FSBHX	NAS CM	Open End	US Fixed Inc (Income)	C-	D+	C		Y	617-563-7000
Fidelity Advisor® Short Duration High Income Fund Class C	FSDHX	NAS CM	Open End	US Fixed Inc (Income)	C-	D+	C		Y	617-563-7000
Fidelity Advisor® Short Duration High Income Fund Class M	FSEHX	NAS CM	Open End	US Fixed Inc (Income)	C-	D+	C		Y	617-563-7000
Fidelity Advisor® Short Duration High Income Fund Class Z	FIJWX	NAS CM	Open End	US Fixed Inc (Income)	C-	D+	C		Y	617-563-7000
Fidelity Advisor® Short Duration High Income Fund I Class	FSFHX	NAS CM	Open End	US Fixed Inc (Income)	C-	D+	C		Y	617-563-7000
Fidelity Advisor® Short-Term Bond Fund Class A	FBNAX	NAS CM	Open End	US Fixed Inc (Income)	C	C	B-		Y	617-563-7000
Fidelity Advisor® Short-Term Bond Fund Class C	FANCX	NAS CM	Open End	US Fixed Inc (Income)	C	C	B-		Y	617-563-7000
Fidelity Advisor® Short-Term Bond Fund Class I	FBNIX	NAS CM	Open End	US Fixed Inc (Income)	C+	C	B-	Up	Y	617-563-7000
Fidelity Advisor® Short-Term Bond Fund Class M	FBNTX	NAS CM	Open End	US Fixed Inc (Income)	C	C	B-		Y	617-563-7000
Fidelity Advisor® Short-Term Bond Fund Class Z	FIKTX	NAS CM	Open End	US Fixed Inc (Income)	C+	C	B-	Up	Y	617-563-7000
Fidelity Advisor® Strategic Income Fund Class A	FSTAX	NAS CM	Open End	US Fixed Inc (Multisector Bond)	C	D+	C		Y	617-563-7000
Fidelity Advisor® Strategic Income Fund Class C	FSRCX	NAS CM	Open End	US Fixed Inc (Multisector Bond)	C-	D+	C		Y	617-563-7000
Fidelity Advisor® Strategic Income Fund Class I	FSRIX	NAS CM	Open End	US Fixed Inc (Multisector Bond)	C	C-	C+		Y	617-563-7000
Fidelity Advisor® Strategic Income Fund Class M	FSIAX	NAS CM	Open End	US Fixed Inc (Multisector Bond)	C	D+	C		Y	617-563-7000
Fidelity Advisor® Strategic Income Fund Class Z	FIWDX	NAS CM	Open End	US Fixed Inc (Multisector Bond)	C	C-	C+		Y	617-563-7000
Fidelity Advisor® Total Bond Fund Class A	FEPAX	NAS CM	Open End	US Fixed Inc (Income)	B-	C+	B+	Up	Y	617-563-7000
Fidelity Advisor® Total Bond Fund Class C	FCEPX	NAS CM	Open End	US Fixed Inc (Income)	B-	C	B	Up	Y	617-563-7000
Fidelity Advisor® Total Bond Fund Class I	FEPIX	NAS CM	Open End	US Fixed Inc (Income)	B	C+	B+	Up	Y	617-563-7000
Fidelity Advisor® Total Bond Fund Class M	FEPTX	NAS CM	Open End	US Fixed Inc (Income)	B-	C+	B+	Up	Y	617-563-7000
Fidelity Advisor® Total Bond Fund Class Z	FBKWX	NAS CM	Open End	US Fixed Inc (Income)	B	C+	B+	Up	Y	617-563-7000
Fidelity Arizona Municipal Money Market Fund	FSAXX	NAS CM	Money Mkt	US Money Mkt (Money Mkt - Single State)	C	C-	C+		Y	617-563-7000
Fidelity California AMT Tax-Free Money Market Fund	FSPXX	NAS CM	Money Mkt	US Money Mkt (Money Mkt - Single State)	C	C-	C+		Y	617-563-7000
Fidelity California AMT Tax-Free Money Market Fund Class S	FSSXX	NAS CM	Money Mkt	US Money Mkt (Money Mkt - Single State)	C	C-	C		Y	617-563-7000
Fidelity California AMT Tax-Free Money Mkt Inst Cl	FSBXX	NAS CM	Money Mkt	US Money Mkt (Money Mkt - Single State)	C	C-	C+		Y	617-563-7000
Fidelity California Municipal Money Market Fund	FCFXX	NAS CM	Money Mkt	US Money Mkt (Money Mkt - Single State)	C	C-	C		Y	617-563-7000
Fidelity Flex Conservative Income Bond Fund	FJTDX	NAS CM	Open End	US Fixed Inc (Income)	C	D+	B-	Up	Y	617-563-7000
Fidelity Flex Conservative Income Municipal Bond Fund	FUEMX	NAS CM	Open End	US Muni Fixed Inc (Muni Bond - Natl)	C	C-	C+		Y	617-563-7000
Fidelity Flex Municipal Income Fund	FUENX	NAS CM	Open End	US Muni Fixed Inc (Muni Bond - Natl)	C	C-	C		Y	617-563-7000
Fidelity Massachusetts AMT Tax-Free Money Market Fund	FMSXX	NAS CM	Money Mkt	US Money Mkt (Money Mkt - Single State)	C	C-	C		Y	617-563-7000
Fidelity Massachusetts AMT Tax-Free Money Mkt Fund Class S	FMHXX	NAS CM	Money Mkt	US Money Mkt (Money Mkt - Single State)	C	C-	C+		Y	617-563-7000
Fidelity Massachusetts AMT Tax-Free Money Mkt Inst Cl	FMAXX	NAS CM	Money Mkt	US Money Mkt (Money Mkt - Single State)	C	C-	C		Y	617-563-7000

★Expanded analysis of this fund is included in Section II.

TOTAL RETURNS & PERFORMANCE									ASSETS		ASSET ALLOCATION & TURNOVER							MINIMUMS		FEES		
3-Month Total Return	6-Month Total Return	1-Year Total Return	3-Year Total Return	5-Year Total Return	Dividend Yield (TTM)	Expense Ratio	3-Yr Std Deviation	Effective Duration	NAV	Total Assets (MIL)	%Cash	%Government Bonds	%Municipal Bonds	%Corporate Bonds	%Other	Turnover Ratio	Average Coupon Rate	Min Initial Investment	Min Additional Investment	Front End Fee (%)	Back End Fee (%)	Inception Date
2.53	1.39	2.75	7.37	10.43	1.76	0.31	2.31	2.84	10.76	2,869	4	0	96	0	0	43	4.38	0				Oct-18
1.19	3.31	5.11	10.85	15.18	1.99	0.8	2.16	0.40	11.62	870.3	15	5	0	0	-2	680	3.40	0		4.00		Mar-97
1.00	2.91	4.31	8.38	10.95	1.22	1.54	2.22	0.40	11.6	870.3	15	5	0	0	-2	680	3.40	0			1.00	Aug-01
1.27	3.46	5.44	11.89	17.05	2.3	0.49	2.13	0.40	11.61	870.3	15	5	0	0	-2	680	3.40	0				Mar-97
1.19	3.30	5.10	10.81	15.13	1.98	0.81	2.22	0.40	11.64	870.3	15	5	0	0	-2	680	3.40	0		4.00		Mar-97
1.22	3.54	5.47	12.19	17.47	2.41	0.36	2.18	0.40	11.61	870.3	15	5	0	0	-2	680	3.40	0				Oct-18
1.98	0.19	2.38	11.89	19.50	2.45	0.79	5.09	7.06	13.25	4,781	4	0	96	0	0	16	4.93	0		4.00		Mar-18
1.79	-0.17	1.63	9.43	15.14	1.69	1.53	5.08	7.06	13.25	4,781	4	0	96	0	0	16	4.93	0			1.00	Mar-18
2.05	0.32	2.64	12.73	21.00	2.71	0.53	5.09	7.06	13.25	4,781	4	0	96	0	0	16	4.93	0				Mar-18
1.98	0.20	2.40	11.93	19.54	2.47	0.77	5.07	7.06	13.26	4,781	4	0	96	0	0	16	4.93	0		4.00		Mar-18
2.07	0.38	2.67	12.90	21.18	2.82	0.42	5.06	7.06	13.25	4,781	4	0	96	0	0	16	4.93	0				Oct-18
11.90	-4.08	-3.12	0.58	19.94	4.71	1.12	11.23		14.15	7,261	8	76	0	16	0	79	6.15	0		4.00		Dec-18
11.70	-4.44	-3.83	-1.61	15.58	3.93	1.86	11.22		14.15	7,261	8	76	0	16	0	79	6.15	0			1.00	Dec-18
11.99	-4.00	-2.91	1.40	21.53	5.01	0.83	11.25		14.15	7,261	8	76	0	16	0	79	6.15	0				Dec-18
11.90	-4.15	-3.19	0.58	19.94	4.7	1.13	11.25		14.15	7,261	8	76	0	16	0	79	6.15	0		4.00		Dec-18
12.01	-3.95	-2.80	1.56	21.71	5.13	0.73	11.25		14.15	7,261	8	76	0	16	0	79	6.15	0				Dec-18
1.13	0.26	2.19	9.60	16.59	2.1	0.79	4.62	7.08	13.37	1,701	0	0	100	0	0	15	4.87	0		4.00		Aug-02
0.94	-0.09	1.45	7.21	12.35	1.37	1.53	4.62	7.08	13.37	1,701	0	0	100	0	0	15	4.87	0			1.00	Aug-02
1.19	0.39	2.44	10.44	18.07	2.36	0.53	4.63	7.08	13.36	1,701	0	0	100	0	0	15	4.87	0				Aug-02
1.14	0.28	2.15	9.75	16.87	2.15	0.74	4.62	7.08	13.38	1,701	0	0	100	0	0	15	4.87	0		4.00		Aug-02
1.22	0.44	2.55	10.74	18.57	2.46	0.43	4.6	7.08	13.36	1,701	0	0	100	0	0	15	4.87	0				Oct-18
7.07	-2.08	-0.23	7.08	13.93	3.72	1.05	6.2		9.09	88.7	3	0	0	97	0	77	5.66	0		4.00		Nov-13
6.87	-2.45	-0.97	4.71	9.75	2.96	1.8	6.2		9.09	88.7	3	0	0	97	0	77	5.66	0			1.00	Nov-13
7.07	-2.08	-0.23	7.08	13.93	3.72	1.05	6.19		9.09	88.7	3	0	0	97	0	77	5.66	0		4.00		Nov-13
7.16	-2.02	0.10	7.93	15.40	4.07	0.71	6.23		9.09	88.7	3	0	0	97	0	77	5.66	0				Oct-18
7.14	-1.96	0.01	7.89	15.36	3.98	0.8	6.2		9.09	88.7	3	0	0	97	0	77	5.66	0				Nov-13
2.93	2.66	3.94	7.97	10.22	1.84	0.65	1.64	1.99	8.86	5,482	5	23	0	48	0	46	2.59	0		1.50		Jul-16
2.59	2.23	2.94	5.11	5.55	0.99	1.51	1.63	1.99	8.85	5,482	5	23	0	48	0	46	2.59	0			1.00	Jul-16
2.97	2.74	4.09	8.45	11.03	1.99	0.51	1.63	1.99	8.86	5,482	5	23	0	48	0	46	2.59	0				Jul-16
2.93	2.66	3.93	7.94	10.16	1.83	0.67	1.63	1.99	8.86	5,482	5	23	0	48	0	46	2.59	0		1.50		Jul-16
3.36	2.82	4.24	8.79	11.44	2.13	0.36	1.64	1.99	8.86	5,482	5	23	0	48	0	46	2.59	0				Oct-18
8.23	-1.09	1.33	9.54	20.36	2.88	0.98	6.52	5.08	12.01	14,613	-2	35	0	52	0	138	4.59	0		4.00		Sep-96
8.05	-1.46	0.58	7.13	15.99	2.13	1.73	6.53	5.08	11.98	14,613	-2	35	0	52	0	138	4.59	0			1.00	Nov-97
8.28	-0.93	1.60	10.35	21.88	3.14	0.72	6.53	5.08	12.18	14,613	-2	35	0	52	0	138	4.59	0				Jul-95
8.14	-1.09	1.25	9.47	20.39	2.89	0.97	6.52	5.08	12	14,613	-2	35	0	52	0	138	4.59	0		4.00		Oct-94
8.30	-0.96	1.62	10.13	21.12	3.23	0.62	6.55	5.08	12.18	14,613	-2	35	0	52	0	138	4.59	0				Oct-18
5.80	5.25	7.86	15.69	24.09	2.42	0.75	3.78	5.16	11.35	28,185	3	37	1	33	0	170	3.48	0		4.00		Jun-04
5.60	4.76	6.95	12.97	19.44	1.67	1.52	3.8	5.16	11.35	28,185	3	37	1	33	0	170	3.48	0			1.00	Jun-04
5.97	5.39	8.14	16.59	25.68	2.66	0.5	3.84	5.16	11.33	28,185	3	37	1	33	0	170	3.48	0				Jun-04
5.81	5.26	7.87	15.70	24.06	2.42	0.75	3.79	5.16	11.33	28,185	3	37	1	33	0	170	3.48	0		4.00		Jun-04
5.91	5.47	8.29	17.07	26.55	2.8	0.36	3.79	5.16	11.33	28,185	3	37	1	33	0	170	3.48	0				Dec-14
0.03	0.32	0.76	2.72	3.07	0.87	0.5	0.12		1	87.2	10	0	90	0	0	13		0				Oct-94
0.05	0.32	0.82	2.96	3.44	0.93	0.3	0.1		1	3,876	21	0	77	0	10	0		25,000				Nov-89
0.04	0.28	0.69	2.52	2.81	0.78	0.45	0.1		1	3,876	21	0	77	0	10	0		1,000,000				Apr-07
0.07	0.37	0.91	3.26	3.87	1.03	0.2	0.1		1	3,876	21	0	77	0	10	0		1,000,000				Apr-07
0.05	0.34	0.83	2.68	2.97	0.88	0.5	0.12		1	1,573	21	0	79	0	0	0		0				Jul-84
1.75	0.94	2.28			2.22	0		0.31	10.03	103.2	33	6	0	61	0	12	1.82	0				May-18
0.83	0.80	1.74			1.77	0		0.71	10.02	58.2	6	0	94	0	0	52	2.72	0				Oct-17
2.20	-0.33	2.00			2.62	0		6.00	10.19	207.4	11	0	89	0	0	18	4.79	0				Oct-17
0.06	0.37	0.89	3.05	3.60	1.01	0.3	0.11		1	1,759	13	0	86	0	11	0		25,000				Mar-91
0.04	0.30	0.74	2.59	2.96	0.86	0.45	0.11		1	1,759	13	0	86	0	11	0		1,000,000				Apr-07
0.09	0.42	0.99	3.35	4.04	1.11	0.2	0.11		1	1,759	13	0	86	0	11	0		1,000,000				Apr-07

	MARKET		FUND TYPE, CATEGORY & OBJECTIVE		RATINGS				NEW INVESTORS	
Fund Name	Ticker Symbol	Traded On	Fund Type	Category and (Prospectus Objective)	Overall Rating	Reward Rating	Risk Rating	Recent Up/ Downgrade	Open to New Investors	Telephone
Fidelity Massachusetts Municipal Money Market Fund	FDMXX	NAS CM	Money Mkt	US Money Mkt (Money Mkt - Single State)	C	C-	C		Y	617-563-7000
Fidelity Michigan Municipal Money Market Fund	FMIXX	NAS CM	Money Mkt	US Money Mkt (Money Mkt - Single State)	C	C-	C		Y	617-563-7000
Fidelity Municipal Money Market Fund	FTEXX	NAS CM	Money Mkt	US Money Mkt (Money Mkt - Fed Tax Exmpt)	C	C-	C+		Y	617-563-7000
Fidelity New Jersey AMT Tax-Free Money Market Fund	FSJXX	NAS CM	Money Mkt	US Money Mkt (Money Mkt - Single State)	C	C-	C+		Y	617-563-7000
Fidelity New Jersey Municipal Money Market Fund	FNJXX	NAS CM	Money Mkt	US Money Mkt (Money Mkt - Single State)	C	C-	C+		Y	617-563-7000
Fidelity New York AMT Tax-Free Money Market Fund	FSNXX	NAS CM	Money Mkt	US Money Mkt (Money Mkt - Single State)	C	C-	C+		Y	617-563-7000
Fidelity New York AMT Tax-Free Money Market Fund Class S	FNOXX	NAS CM	Money Mkt	US Money Mkt (Money Mkt - Single State)	C	C-	C+		Y	617-563-7000
Fidelity New York AMT Tax-Free Money Mkt Institutional Cl	FNKXX	NAS CM	Money Mkt	US Money Mkt (Money Mkt - Single State)	C	C-	C		Y	617-563-7000
Fidelity New York Municipal Money Market Fund	FNYXX	NAS CM	Money Mkt	US Money Mkt (Money Mkt - Single State)	C	C-	C+		Y	617-563-7000
Fidelity Ohio Municipal Money Market Fund	FOMXX	NAS CM	Money Mkt	US Money Mkt (Money Mkt - Single State)	C	C-	C		Y	617-563-7000
Fidelity Pennsylvania Municipal Money Market Fund	FPTXX	NAS CM	Money Mkt	US Money Mkt (Money Mkt - Single State)	C	C-	C		Y	617-563-7000
Fidelity SAI Total Bond Fund	FSMTX	NAS CM	Open End	US Fixed Inc (Income)	D+	D+	B	Up	Y	617-563-7000
Fidelity Treasury Only Money Market Fund	FDLXX	NAS CM	Money Mkt	US Money Mkt (Money Mkt - Treasury)	C	C-	C+			617-563-7000
Fidelity® Arizona Municipal Income Fund	FSAZX	NAS CM	Open End	US Muni Fixed Inc (Muni Bond - Single State)	C	C	B		Y	617-563-7000
Fidelity® California Limited Term Tax-Free Bond Fund	FCSTX	NAS CM	Open End	US Muni Fixed Inc (Muni Bond - Natl)	C	C	C+		Y	617-563-7000
Fidelity® California Municipal Income Fund	FCTFX	NAS CM	Open End	US Muni Fixed Inc (Muni Bond - Natl)	C	C	B		Y	617-563-7000
Fidelity® Capital & Income Fund	FAGIX	NAS CM	Open End	US Fixed Inc (Growth & Income)	D+	D	C-	Down	Y	617-563-7000
Fidelity® Connecticut Municipal Income Fund	FICNX	NAS CM	Open End	US Muni Fixed Inc (Muni Bond - Single State)	C	C	B-		Y	617-563-7000
Fidelity® Connecticut Municipal Money Market Fund	FCMXX	NAS CM	Money Mkt	US Money Mkt (Money Mkt - Single State)	C	C-	C		Y	617-563-7000
Fidelity® Conservative Income Bond Fund	FCONX	NAS CM	Open End	US Fixed Inc (Income)	C	C-	C+		Y	617-563-7000
Fidelity® Conservative Income Bond Institutional Class	FCNVX	NAS CM	Open End	US Fixed Inc (Income)	C	C-	B-		Y	617-563-7000
Fidelity® Conservative Income Municipal Bond Fund	FCRDX	NAS CM	Open End	US Muni Fixed Inc (Muni Bond - Natl)	C	C-	C+		Y	617-563-7000
Fidelity® Conservative Income Muni Bond Institutional Cl	FMNDX	NAS CM	Open End	US Muni Fixed Inc (Muni Bond - Natl)	C	C-	C+		Y	617-563-7000
Fidelity® Corporate Bond Fund	FCBFX	NAS CM	Open End	US Fixed Inc (Corp Bond - General)	B-	C	B	Up	Y	617-563-7000
Fidelity® Flex Core Bond Fund	FLXCX	NAS CM	Open End	US Fixed Inc (Corp Bond - General)	B	C+	B+	Up	Y	617-563-7000
Fidelity® Flex Government Money Market Fund	FLGXX	NAS CM	Money Mkt	US Money Mkt (Money Mkt - Govt)	C	C-	C+		Y	617-563-7000
Fidelity® Flex Inflation-Protected Bond Index Fund	FBUIX	NAS CM	Open End	US Fixed Inc (Income)	B	B-	A-	Up	Y	617-563-7000
Fidelity® Flex Short-Term Bond Fund	FBSTX	NAS CM	Open End	US Fixed Inc (Income)	C+	C	B	Up	Y	617-563-7000
Fidelity® Flex U.S. Bond Index Fund	FIBUX	NAS CM	Open End	US Fixed Inc (Corp Bond - General)	B-	B-	B	Up	Y	617-563-7000
Fidelity® Floating Rate High Income Fund	FFRHX	NAS CM	Open End	US Fixed Inc (Income)	D+	D	C-	Down	Y	617-563-7000
Fidelity® Focused High Income Fund	FHIFX	NAS CM	Open End	US Fixed Inc (Growth & Income)	C	C-	C+		Y	617-563-7000
Fidelity® Global Credit Fund	FGBFX	NAS CM	Open End	Global Fixed Inc (Worldwide Bond)	C	C-	B		Y	617-563-7000
Fidelity® Global High Income Fund	FGHNX	NAS CM	Open End	Global Fixed Inc (Income)	D+	D	C-	Down	Y	617-563-7000
Fidelity® GNMA Fund	FGMNX	NAS CM	Open End	US Fixed Inc (Govt Bond - Mortgage)	B-	C+	B	Up	Y	617-563-7000
★ Fidelity® Government Cash Reserves	FDRXX	NAS CM	Money Mkt	US Money Mkt (Money Mkt - Taxable)	C	C-	C+		Y	617-563-7000
Fidelity® Government Income Fund	FGOVX	NAS CM	Open End	US Fixed Inc (Govt Bond - General)	B	B	B		Y	617-563-7000
★ Fidelity® Government Money Market Fund	SPAXX	NAS CM	Money Mkt	US Money Mkt (Money Mkt - Govt)	C	C-	C+		Y	617-563-7000
★ Fidelity® Government Money Market Fund Advisor M Class	FZGXX	NAS CM	Money Mkt	US Money Mkt (Money Mkt - Govt)	C	C-	C+		Y	617-563-7000
★ Fidelity® Govt Money Mkt Fund Capital Reserves Class	FZAXX	NAS CM	Money Mkt	US Money Mkt (Money Mkt - Govt)	C	C-	C+		Y	617-563-7000
★ Fidelity® Government Money Market Fund Class K6	FNBXX	NAS CM	Money Mkt	US Money Mkt (Money Mkt - Govt)	C	C-	C		Y	617-563-7000
★ Fidelity® Government Money Market Fund Daily Money Class	FZBXX	NAS CM	Money Mkt	US Money Mkt (Money Mkt - Govt)	C	C-	C+		Y	617-563-7000
Fidelity® Government Money Market Fund Premium Class	FZCXX	NAS CM	Money Mkt	US Money Mkt (Money Mkt - Govt)	C	C	C+		Y	617-563-7000
Fidelity® High Income Fund	SPHIX	NAS CM	Open End	US Fixed Inc (Growth & Income)	C-	D+	C		Y	617-563-7000
Fidelity® Inflation-Protected Bond Index Fund	FIPDX	NAS CM	Open End	US Fixed Inc (Govt Bond - Treasury)	B	B-	A-	Up	Y	617-563-7000
Fidelity® Inst Money Mkt Funds Prime Reserves Portfol Cl I	FDPXX	NAS CM	Money Mkt	US Money Mkt (Money Mkt - General)	C	C-	C+		Y	617-563-7000
Fidelity® Inst Money Mkt Funds Prime Res Portfol Cl II	FEPXX	NAS CM	Money Mkt	US Money Mkt (Money Mkt - General)	C	C	B-		Y	617-563-7000
Fidelity® Inst Money Mkt Funds Prime Res Portfol Cl III	FFPXX	NAS CM	Money Mkt	US Money Mkt (Money Mkt - General)	C	C-	C+		Y	617-563-7000
Fidelity® Inst Money Mkt Funds Prime Res Portfol Inst Cl	FHPXX	NAS CM	Money Mkt	US Money Mkt (Money Mkt - General)	C	C-	C+		Y	617-563-7000
Fidelity® Inst Money Mkt Funds Prime Res Portfol Select Cl	FGPXX	NAS CM	Money Mkt	US Money Mkt (Money Mkt - General)	C	C-	C+		Y	617-563-7000
Fidelity® Intermediate Bond Fund	FTHRX	NAS CM	Open End	US Fixed Inc (Income)	B-	C+	B	Up	Y	617-563-7000
Fidelity® Intermediate Government Income Fund	FSTGX	NAS CM	Open End	US Fixed Inc (Govt Bond - General)	B-	C+	B		Y	617-563-7000
Fidelity® Intermediate Municipal Income Fund	FLTMX	NAS CM	Open End	US Muni Fixed Inc (Muni Bond - Natl)	C	C	B-		Y	617-563-7000

★ Expanded analysis of this fund is included in Section II.

TOTAL RETURNS & PERFORMANCE									ASSETS		ASSET ALLOCATION & TURNOVER							MINIMUMS		FEES		
3-Month Total Return	6-Month Total Return	1-Year Total Return	3-Year Total Return	5-Year Total Return	Dividend Yield (TTM)	Expense Ratio	3-Yr Std Deviation	Effective Duration	NAV	Total Assets (MIL)	%Cash	%Government Bonds	%Municipal Bonds	%Corporate Bonds	%Other	Turnover Ratio	Average Coupon Rate	Min Initial Investment	Min Additional Investment	Front End Fee (%)	Back End Fee (%)	Inception Date
0.04	0.37	0.82	2.73	3.09	0.86	0.49	0.14		1	1,388	20	0	80	0	0	0		0				Nov-83
0.04	0.33	0.74	2.57	2.87	0.84	0.55	0.13		1	228.2	5	0	95	0	0	0		0				Jan-90
0.07	0.37	0.94	3.06	3.44	0.99	0.42	0.12		1	5,738	22	0	78	0	0			0				Jan-80
0.06	0.36	0.86	3.04	3.51	0.98	0.3	0.1		1	430.8	14	0	84	0	11			25,000				May-90
0.04	0.32	0.81	2.76	3.02	0.88	0.51	0.12		1	515.2	20	0	80	0	0	0		0				Mar-88
0.07	0.38	0.91	3.13	3.67	1.01	0.3	0.11		1	2,140	18	0	80	0	9	0		25,000				Feb-90
0.04	0.31	0.76	2.67	2.99	0.86	0.45	0.11		1	2,140	18	0	80	0	9	0		1,000,000				Apr-07
0.10	0.44	1.01	3.43	4.07	1.11	0.2	0.11		1	2,140	18	0	80	0	9	0		1,000,000				Apr-07
0.07	0.35	0.79	2.77	3.11	0.86	0.49	0.12		1	1,204	18	0	82	0	0	0		0				Jul-84
0.04	0.31	0.77	2.72	2.99	0.88	0.53	0.12		1	226.3	13	0	87	0	0	0		0				Aug-89
0.08	0.36	0.83	2.66	2.92	0.88	0.5	0.12		1	191.4	10	0	90	0	0	0		0				Aug-86
5.99	4.73	7.58			3.02	0.32		5.47	10.84	15,696	4	26	1	45	0	209	3.65	0				Oct-18
0.00	0.25	1.04	3.92	4.07	1.21	0.42	0.17		1	4,882	68	32	0	0	0			0				Jan-88
2.29	1.53	3.67	11.48	19.43	2.27	0.55	3.94	6.08	12.45	173.2	0	0	100	0	0	13	4.94	0				Oct-94
2.12	1.38	2.61	6.87	10.30	1.63	0.47	2.29	3.14	10.81	688.9	1	0	99	0	0	31	4.21	0				Oct-05
2.34	1.43	3.58	12.12	20.26	2.63	0.45	4.29	6.51	13.25	2,130	0	0	100	0	0	11	4.77	0				Jul-84
14.40	-5.63	-1.03	11.04	24.10	4.48	0.69	12.08		9.45	10,587	3	0	0	96	0	46	6.21	0				Nov-77
2.09	1.23	3.52	12.06	18.63	2.5	0.48	3.96	5.96	11.79	339.2	0	0	100	0	0	20	4.88	0				Oct-87
0.04	0.32	0.78	2.78	3.05	0.9	0.49	0.12		1	371.4	13	0	87	0	0	16		0				Aug-89
1.87	0.79	1.96	6.16	8.05	1.91	0.35	1.13	0.31	10.06	12,239	31	6	0	62	0	36	1.77	0				Mar-11
1.90	0.84	2.06	6.48	8.59	2.01	0.25	1.13	0.31	10.06	12,239	31	6	0	62	0	36	1.77	1,000,000				Mar-11
0.62	0.48	1.15	4.07	5.33	1.32	0.35	0.63	0.62	10.04	2,090	13	0	87	0	0	63	2.58	0				Oct-13
0.64	0.43	1.25	4.39	5.85	1.42	0.25	0.63	0.62	10.04	2,090	13	0	87	0	0	63	2.58	1,000,000				Oct-13
10.24	5.93	10.05	21.07	33.74	3	0.45	6.89	7.79	12.68	2,855	3	6	0	90	0	28	3.67	0				May-10
6.92	6.54	9.60	19.10		3.08	0	3.96	5.21	10.87	63.5	7	38	0	31	0	102	3.41	0				Mar-17
0.05	0.40	1.42	5.23		1.61	0	0.18		1	56.4	75	23	0	2	0			0				Mar-17
4.06	6.07	8.38	15.87		0.41	0	3.53	5.68	10.99	6.5	1	99	0	0	0	40	0.76	0				Mar-17
2.25	3.29	4.64	10.00		2.21	0	1.19	2.02	10.33	6.6	3	42	0	43	0	62	2.41	0				Mar-17
2.89	6.52	9.01	17.03		2.51	0	3.3	5.48	10.95	477.1	6	42	0	26	0	85	2.88	0				Mar-17
8.39	-5.80	-3.26	4.41	12.69	5.21	0.68	8.25		8.74	7,048	4	0	0	96	0	22	4.48	0				Sep-02
7.20	-2.89	0.86	11.60	23.33	4.27	0.79	6.93		8.48	393.3	7	0	0	93	0	43	5.51	0				Sep-04
9.80	2.83	7.47	17.16	26.32	2.37	0.75	7.41	7.14	9.82	88.6	-77	4	0	87	0	85	4.07	0				May-12
12.75	-4.93	-2.00	7.02	20.51	5.07	1	10.28		8.91	92.1	4	2	0	93	0	54	6.10	0				May-11
1.02	3.20	4.77	10.59	14.98	2.24	0.45	2.03	0.07	11.8	4,204	20	0	0	0	0	420	3.62	0				Nov-85
0.00	0.26	1.10	4.11	4.40	1.28	0.38	0.18		1	201,168	63	36	0	1	0	0		0				May-79
0.51	7.40	9.06	15.45	19.77	1.68	0.45	3.62	5.46	11.18	4,665	23	50	0	0	-1	246	2.31	0				Apr-79
0.00	0.25	1.06	3.96	4.18	1.23	0.42	0.17		1	189,478	65	34	0	1	0	0		0				Feb-90
0.00	0.19	0.86	3.20	2.91	1.02	0.7			1	189,478	65	34	0	1	0	0		0				Jul-17
0.00	0.13	0.68	2.48	2.51	0.81	0.95	0.16		1	189,478	65	34	0	1	0	0		0				Apr-15
0.01	0.31	1.20	4.37	4.58	1.39	0.25			1	189,478	65	34	0	1	0	0		0				Jan-18
0.00	0.19	0.85	3.17	3.24	1.01	0.7	0.16		1	189,478	65	34	0	1	0	0		0				Apr-15
0.00	0.27	1.14	4.25	4.62	1.33	0.32	0.18		1	189,478	65	34	0	1	0	0		100,000				Apr-15
8.26	-6.17	-2.76	8.10	21.52	5.49	0.7	8.78		8.19	5,033	4	0	0	96	0	44	6.20	0				Aug-90
4.17	6.13	8.42	15.85	20.72	0.37	0.05	3.55	5.68	10.68	7,433	0	100	0	0	0	33	0.77	0				May-12
0.14	0.48	1.47	5.39		1.62	0.18	0.17		1.0007	8,091	94	4	0	1	0			1,000,000				Jun-16
0.12	0.41	1.33	4.93		1.47	0.33	0.17		1.0008	8,091	94	4	0	1	0			1,000,000				Jun-16
0.09	0.37	1.23	4.61		1.37	0.43	0.17		1.0007	8,091	94	4	0	1	0			1,000,000				Jun-16
0.16	0.50	1.51	5.51		1.66	0.14	0.17		1.0008	8,091	94	4	0	1	0			10,000,000				Jun-16
0.13	0.45	1.42	5.23		1.57	0.23	0.17		1.0007	8,091	94	4	0	1	0			1,000,000				Jun-16
4.65	4.97	6.95	13.50	19.11	2.36	0.45	3.05	3.91	11.49	2,860	4	33	0	43	0	34	3.08	0				May-75
0.48	5.74	6.75	11.96	14.49	1.58	0.45	2.61	3.82	11.16	578.1	11	77	0	0	0	244	1.95	0				May-88
2.66	1.49	3.35	11.29	17.25	2.31	0.35	3.7	4.85	10.67	8,025	3	0	97	0	0	14	4.68	0				Apr-77

	MARKET		FUND TYPE, CATEGORY & OBJECTIVE		RATINGS				NEW INVESTORS	
Fund Name	Ticker Symbol	Traded On	Fund Type	Category and (Prospectus Objective)	Overall Rating	Reward Rating	Risk Rating	Recent Up/ Downgrade	Open to New Investors	Telephone
Fidelity® Intermediate Treasury Bond Index Fund	FUAMX	NAS CM	Open End	US Fixed Inc (Govt Bond - Treasury)	B	B	B		Y	617-563-7000
Fidelity® International Bond Index Fund	FBIIX	NAS CM	Open End	Global Fixed Inc (Income)	U	U	U		Y	617-563-7000
Fidelity® Investment Grade Bond Fund	FBNDX	NAS CM	Open End	US Fixed Inc (Income)	B	B-	B+	Up	Y	617-563-7000
Fidelity® Investments Money Mkt Funds Govt Portfolio Cl I	FIGXX	NAS CM	Money Mkt	US Money Mkt (Money Mkt - Govt)	C	C-	C+		Y	617-563-7000
Fidelity® Investments Money Mkt Funds Govt Portfolio Cl II	FCVXX	NAS CM	Money Mkt	US Money Mkt (Money Mkt - Govt)	C	C-	C+		Y	617-563-7000
Fidelity® Inv Money Mkt Funds Govt Portfol Cl III	FCGXX	NAS CM	Money Mkt	US Money Mkt (Money Mkt - Govt)	C	C-	C+		Y	617-563-7000
Fidelity® Inv Money Mkt Funds Govt Portfol Inst Cl	FRGXX	NAS CM	Money Mkt	US Money Mkt (Money Mkt - Govt)	C	C-	C+		Y	617-563-7000
Fidelity® Inv Money Mkt Funds Govt Portfol Select Cl	FGEXX	NAS CM	Money Mkt	US Money Mkt (Money Mkt - Govt)	C	C-	C+		Y	617-563-7000
Fidelity® Inv Money Mkt Funds Money Mkt Portfol Cl I	FMPXX	NAS CM	Money Mkt	US Money Mkt (Money Mkt - General)	C	C-	C+		Y	617-563-7000
Fidelity® Inv Money Mkt Funds Money Mkt Portfol Cl II	FCIXX	NAS CM	Money Mkt	US Money Mkt (Money Mkt - General)	C	C-	C+		Y	617-563-7000
Fidelity® Inv Money Mkt Funds Money Mkt Portfol Cl III	FCOXX	NAS CM	Money Mkt	US Money Mkt (Money Mkt - General)	C	C-	C+		Y	617-563-7000
Fidelity® Inv Money Mkt Funds Money Mkt Portfol Inst Cl	FNSXX	NAS CM	Money Mkt	US Money Mkt (Money Mkt - General)	C	C-	C+		Y	617-563-7000
Fidelity® Inv Money Mkt Funds Money Mkt Portfol Select Cl	FMYXX	NAS CM	Money Mkt	US Money Mkt (Money Mkt - General)	C	C-	C+		Y	617-563-7000
Fidelity® Inv Money Mkt Funds Prime Money Mkt Portfol Cl I	FIDXX	NAS CM	Money Mkt	US Money Mkt (Money Mkt - General)	C	C-	C+		Y	617-563-7000
Fidelity® Inv Money Mkt Funds Prime Money Mkt Port Cl II	FDOXX	NAS CM	Money Mkt	US Money Mkt (Money Mkt - General)	C	C-	C+		Y	617-563-7000
Fidelity® Inv Money Mkt Funds Prime Money Mkt Port Cl III	FCDXX	NAS CM	Money Mkt	US Money Mkt (Money Mkt - General)	C	C-	C+		Y	617-563-7000
Fidelity® Inv Money Mkt Funds Prime Money Mkt Port Cl IV	FDVXX	NAS CM	Money Mkt	US Money Mkt (Money Mkt - General)	C	C-	C		Y	617-563-7000
Fidelity® Inv Money Mkt Funds Prime Money Mkt Port Inst Cl	FIPXX	NAS CM	Money Mkt	US Money Mkt (Money Mkt - General)	C	C-	C+		Y	617-563-7000
Fidelity® Inv Money Mkt Funds Prime Money Mkt Port Select	FDIXX	NAS CM	Money Mkt	US Money Mkt (Money Mkt - General)	C	C-	C+		Y	617-563-7000
Fidelity® Inv Money Mkt Funds Tax Exempt Portfol Cl I	FTCXX	NAS CM	Money Mkt	US Money Mkt (Money Mkt - Fed Tax Exmpt)	C	C-	C+		Y	617-563-7000
Fidelity® Inv Money Mkt Funds Tax Exempt Portfol Cl II	FEXXX	NAS CM	Money Mkt	US Money Mkt (Money Mkt - Fed Tax Exmpt)	C	C-	C+		Y	617-563-7000
Fidelity® Inv Money Mkt Funds Tax Exempt Portfol Cl III	FETXX	NAS CM	Money Mkt	US Money Mkt (Money Mkt - Fed Tax Exmpt)	C	C-	C+		Y	617-563-7000
Fidelity® Inv Money Mkt Funds Tax Exempt Portfol Select Cl	FSXXX	NAS CM	Money Mkt	US Money Mkt (Money Mkt - Fed Tax Exmpt)	C	C-	C+		Y	617-563-7000
Fidelity® Inv Money Mkt Funds Treas Only Portfol Cl I	FSIXX	NAS CM	Money Mkt	US Money Mkt (Money Mkt - Treasury)	C	C-	C+		Y	617-563-7000
Fidelity® Inv Money Mkt Funds Treas Only Portfol Cl II	FOXXX	NAS CM	Money Mkt	US Money Mkt (Money Mkt - Treasury)	C	C-	C+		Y	617-563-7000
Fidelity® Inv Money Mkt Funds Treas Only Portfol Cl III	FOIXX	NAS CM	Money Mkt	US Money Mkt (Money Mkt - Treasury)	C	C-	C+		Y	617-563-7000
Fidelity® Inv Money Mkt Funds Treas Only Portfol Cl IV	FOPXX	NAS CM	Money Mkt	US Money Mkt (Money Mkt - Treasury)	C	C-	C+		Y	617-563-7000
Fidelity® Inv Money Mkt Funds Treas Only Portfol Inst Cl	FRSXX	NAS CM	Money Mkt	US Money Mkt (Money Mkt - Treasury)	C	C-	C+		Y	617-563-7000
Fidelity® Inv Money Mkt Funds Treas Only Portfol Select Cl	FTYXX	NAS CM	Money Mkt	US Money Mkt (Money Mkt - Treasury)	C	C-	C+		Y	617-563-7000
Fidelity® Inv Money Mkt Funds Treas Portfol Cl I	FISXX	NAS CM	Money Mkt	US Money Mkt (Money Mkt - Treasury)	C	C-	C+		Y	617-563-7000
Fidelity® Inv Money Mkt Funds Treas Portfol Cl II	FCEXX	NAS CM	Money Mkt	US Money Mkt (Money Mkt - Treasury)	C	C-	C+		Y	617-563-7000
Fidelity® Inv Money Mkt Funds Treas Portfol Cl III	FCSXX	NAS CM	Money Mkt	US Money Mkt (Money Mkt - Treasury)	C	C-	C+		Y	617-563-7000
Fidelity® Inv Money Mkt Funds Treas Portfol Cl IV	FTVXX	NAS CM	Money Mkt	US Money Mkt (Money Mkt - Treasury)	C	C-	C+		Y	617-563-7000
Fidelity® Inv Money Mkt Funds Treas Portfol Inst Cl	FRBXX	NAS CM	Money Mkt	US Money Mkt (Money Mkt - Treasury)	C	C-	C+		Y	617-563-7000
Fidelity® Inv Money Mkt Funds Treas Portfol Select Cl	FTUXX	NAS CM	Money Mkt	US Money Mkt (Money Mkt - Treasury)	C	C-	C+		Y	617-563-7000
Fidelity® Limited Term Bond Fund	FJRLX	NAS CM	Open End	US Fixed Inc (Income)	C	C	B-		Y	617-563-7000
Fidelity® Limited Term Government Fund	FFXSX	NAS CM	Open End	US Fixed Inc (Govt Bond - General)	B-	C	B	Up	Y	617-563-7000
Fidelity® Limited Term Municipal Income Fund	FSTFX	NAS CM	Open End	US Muni Fixed Inc (Muni Bond - Natl)	C	C-	C+		Y	617-563-7000
Fidelity® Long-Term Treasury Bond Index Fund	FNBGX	NAS CM	Open End	US Fixed Inc (Govt Bond - Treasury)	B	B	B		Y	617-563-7000
Fidelity® Maryland Municipal Income Fund	SMDMX	NAS CM	Open End	US Muni Fixed Inc (Muni Bond - Single State)	C	C-	B-		Y	617-563-7000
Fidelity® Massachusetts Municipal Income Fund	FDMMX	NAS CM	Open End	US Muni Fixed Inc (Muni Bond - Single State)	C	C	B-		Y	617-563-7000
Fidelity® Michigan Municipal Income Fund	FMHTX	NAS CM	Open End	US Muni Fixed Inc (Muni Bond - Single State)	C+	C	B	Up	Y	617-563-7000
Fidelity® Minnesota Municipal Income Fund	FIMIX	NAS CM	Open End	US Muni Fixed Inc (Muni Bond - Single State)	C+	C	B	Up	Y	617-563-7000
★ Fidelity® Money Market Fund	SPRXX	NAS CM	Money Mkt	US Money Mkt (Money Mkt - Taxable)	C	C-	C+		Y	617-563-7000
Fidelity® Money Market Fund Premium Class	FZDXX	NAS CM	Money Mkt	US Money Mkt (Money Mkt - Taxable)	C	C-	C+		Y	617-563-7000
Fidelity® Mortgage Securities Fund	FMSFX	NAS CM	Open End	US Fixed Inc (Govt Bond - Mortgage)	B-	C+	B		Y	617-563-7000
Fidelity® Municipal Bond Index Fund	FMBIX	NAS CM	Open End	US Muni Fixed Inc (Muni Bond - Natl)	U	U	U		Y	617-563-7000
Fidelity® Municipal Income Fund	FHIGX	NAS CM	Open End	US Muni Fixed Inc (Muni Bond - Natl)	C	C-	B-		Y	617-563-7000
Fidelity® New Jersey AMT Tax-Free Money Mkt Fund Class S	FNNXX	NAS CM	Money Mkt	US Money Mkt (Money Mkt - Single State)	C	C-	C+		Y	617-563-7000
Fidelity® New Jersey AMT Tax-Free Money Mkt Inst Cl	FSKXX	NAS CM	Money Mkt	US Money Mkt (Money Mkt - Single State)	C	C-	C		Y	617-563-7000
Fidelity® New Jersey Municipal Income Fund	FNJHX	NAS CM	Open End	US Muni Fixed Inc (Muni Bond - Single State)	C	C-	C+		Y	617-563-7000
Fidelity® New Markets Income Fund	FNMIX	NAS CM	Open End	Emerg Mkts Fixed Inc (Diversified Emerg Mkts)	D	D	D+	Down	Y	617-563-7000

★ Expanded analysis of this fund is included in Section II.

TOTAL RETURNS & PERFORMANCE									ASSETS		ASSET ALLOCATION & TURNOVER							MINIMUMS		FEES		
3-Month Total Return	6-Month Total Return	1-Year Total Return	3-Year Total Return	5-Year Total Return	Dividend Yield (TTM)	Expense Ratio	3-Yr Std Deviation	Effective Duration	NAV	Total Assets (MIL)	%Cash	%Government Bonds	%Municipal Bonds	%Corporate Bonds	%Other	Turnover Ratio	Average Coupon Rate	Min Initial Investment	Min Additional Investment	Front End Fee (%)	Back End Fee (%)	Inception Date
0.74	9.71	11.25	19.05	24.88	1.88	0.03	4.61	6.47	12.04	3,960	6	94	0	0	0	58	2.25	0				Oct-17
2.32	2.10					0.06		7.95	10.05	38.4	2	40	0	7	0		1.71	0				Oct-19
5.72	7.49	10.29	19.29	27.09	2.41	0.45	3.49	5.60	8.71	7,365	2	46	1	31	-1	59	3.37	0				Aug-71
0.02	0.34	1.26	4.68	5.24	1.46	0.18	0.18		1	185,466	64	35	0	1	0	0		1,000,000				Jul-85
0.00	0.28	1.13	4.23	4.55	1.31	0.33	0.18		1	185,466	64	35	0	1	0	0		1,000,000				Nov-95
0.00	0.24	1.05	3.93	4.12	1.22	0.43	0.17		1	185,466	64	35	0	1	0	0		1,000,000				Apr-94
0.03	0.36	1.31	4.81	5.44	1.5	0.14	0.18		1	185,466	64	35	0	1	0	0		10,000,000				May-14
0.01	0.31	1.21	4.52	5.01	1.41	0.23	0.18		1	185,466	64	35	0	1	0	0		1,000,000				Jan-02
0.11	0.49	1.50	5.47	6.58	1.68	0.18	0.16		1	66,381	87	13	0	0	0			1,000,000				Jul-85
0.07	0.41	1.35	5.00	5.80	1.53	0.33	0.16		1	66,381	87	13	0	0	0			1,000,000				Nov-95
0.05	0.36	1.24	4.69	5.32	1.43	0.43	0.16		1	66,381	87	13	0	0	0			1,000,000				Nov-93
0.12	0.51	1.54	5.60	6.80	1.72	0.14	0.16		1	66,381	87	13	0	0	0			10,000,000				Dec-07
0.09	0.46	1.45	5.31	6.32	1.63	0.23	0.16		1	66,381	87	13	0	0	0			1,000,000				Jan-02
0.12	0.45	1.45	5.30	6.40	1.61	0.18	0.16		1.0008	5,778	97	2	0	1	0			1,000,000				Nov-89
0.09	0.38	1.29	4.84	5.64	1.46	0.33	0.17		1.0007	5,778	97	2	0	1	0			1,000,000				Nov-95
0.08	0.35	1.20	4.54	5.16	1.36	0.43	0.17		1.0007	5,778	97	2	0	1	0			1,000,000				Jul-94
0.05	0.26	0.99	3.79	4.15	1.13	0.68	0.16		1.0015	5,778	97	2	0	1	0			1,000,000				Dec-07
0.14	0.47	1.48	5.43	6.60	1.65	0.14	0.17		1.0007	5,778	97	2	0	1	0			10,000,000				Dec-07
0.12	0.43	1.39	5.15	6.13	1.56	0.23	0.17		1.0008	5,778	97	2	0	1	0			1,000,000				Jan-02
0.09	0.44	1.05	3.54	4.33	1.16	0.18	0.11		1	7,136	15	0	84	0	10			1,000,000				Jul-85
0.06	0.37	0.89	3.08	3.66	1.01	0.33	0.11		1	7,136	15	0	84	0	10			1,000,000				Nov-95
0.04	0.33	0.80	2.79	3.24	0.92	0.43	0.11		1	7,136	15	0	84	0	10			1,000,000				Nov-95
0.09	0.42	1.00	3.39	4.10	1.11	0.23	0.11		1	7,136	15	0	84	0	10			1,000,000				Jan-02
0.02	0.34	1.25	4.62	5.07	1.43	0.18	0.17		1	43,912	70	30	0	0	0			1,000,000				Oct-90
0.00	0.28	1.11	4.17	4.39	1.29	0.33	0.17		1	43,912	70	30	0	0	0			1,000,000				Nov-95
0.00	0.25	1.03	3.88	4.03	1.2	0.43	0.17		1	43,912	70	30	0	0	0			1,000,000				Nov-95
0.00	0.19	0.84	3.17	3.21	0.99	0.68	0.16		1	43,912	70	30	0	0	0			1,000,000				Dec-07
0.03	0.37	1.28	4.75	5.26	1.47	0.14	0.17		1	43,912	70	30	0	0	0			10,000,000				May-14
0.02	0.33	1.20	4.47	4.84	1.38	0.23	0.17		1	43,912	70	30	0	0	0			1,000,000				Jan-02
0.03	0.34	1.26	4.67	5.17	1.45	0.18	0.18		1	42,781	66	34	0	0	0			1,000,000				Feb-87
0.00	0.28	1.12	4.21	4.47	1.3	0.33	0.18		1	42,781	66	34	0	0	0			1,000,000				Nov-95
0.00	0.24	1.04	3.92	4.08	1.21	0.43	0.17		1	42,781	66	34	0	0	0			1,000,000				Oct-93
0.00	0.19	0.86	3.21	3.27	1.01	0.68	0.16		1	42,781	66	34	0	0	0			1,000,000				Dec-07
0.04	0.36	1.30	4.79	5.36	1.49	0.14	0.18		1	42,781	66	34	0	0	0			10,000,000				May-14
0.02	0.32	1.22	4.51	4.93	1.4	0.23	0.18		1	42,781	66	34	0	0	0			1,000,000				Jan-02
4.56	3.28	5.08	10.74	15.11	2.35	0.45	2.73	2.58	11.92	2,971	6	9	1	62	0	29	3.09	0				Nov-13
0.34	4.05	4.99	8.94	10.34	1.59	0.45	1.81	2.75	10.37	469.4	11	81	0	0	0	160	1.77	0				Nov-86
2.52	1.45	2.70	7.40	10.46	1.71	0.37	2.33	2.84	10.76	2,869	4	0	96	0	0	43	4.38	0				Dec-86
-0.54	21.58	25.69	40.23	57.64	2.15	0.03	12.15	19.18	16.96	2,895	2	98	0	0	0	54	3.15	0				Oct-17
1.17	0.59	2.67	9.91	18.14	2.25	0.55	4.12	6.21	11.6	217.6	0	0	100	0	0	10	4.89	0				Apr-93
1.99	1.37	3.44	11.14	18.72	2.48	0.45	3.97	6.33	12.44	2,230	0	0	100	0	0	12	4.92	0				Nov-83
2.28	2.28	4.26	12.94	20.40	2.38	0.48	3.71	6.30	12.6	669.0	0	0	100	0	0	14	4.73	0				Nov-85
2.07	1.96	4.00	11.59	18.34	2.28	0.49	3.73	5.94	12.01	604.6	0	0	100	0	0	9	4.73	0				Nov-85
0.04	0.35	1.24	4.69	5.47	1.42	0.42	0.16		1	56,039	89	10	0	0	0			0				Jan-89
0.06	0.41	1.35	5.07	6.07	1.54	0.3	0.16		1	56,039	89	10	0	0	0			100,000				Apr-15
1.28	3.48	5.46	11.99	17.26	2.32	0.45	2.15	0.40	11.65	870.3	15	5	0	0	-2	680	3.40	0				Dec-84
0.68	0.33					0.07		6.14	19.97	51.5	0	0	100	0	0		4.65	0				Jul-19
2.06	0.36	2.72	12.93	21.22	2.79	0.45	5.1	7.06	13.26	4,781	4	0	96	0	0	16	4.93	10,000				Dec-77
0.03	0.28	0.72	2.59	2.88	0.83	0.45	0.1		1	430.8	14	0	84	0	11			1,000,000				Apr-07
0.09	0.41	0.96	3.36	3.96	1.08	0.2	0.1		1	430.8	14	0	84	0	11			1,000,000				Apr-07
1.66	-0.37	1.87	13.43	22.08	2.66	0.47	4.87	6.48	12.07	546.0	1	0	99	0	0	12	4.95	0				Dec-87
11.99	-3.93	-2.88	1.43	21.56	5.04	0.82	11.25		14.15	7,261	8	76	0	16	0	79	6.15	0				May-93

	MARKET			FUND TYPE, CATEGORY & OBJECTIVE	RATINGS				NEW INVESTORS	
Fund Name	Ticker Symbol	Traded On	Fund Type	Category and (Prospectus Objective)	Overall Rating	Reward Rating	Risk Rating	Recent Up/ Downgrade	Open to New Investors	Telephone
Fidelity® New York Municipal Income Fund	FTFMX	NAS CM	Open End	US Muni Fixed Inc (Muni Bond - Single State)	C	C-	B-		Y	617-563-7000
Fidelity® Ohio Municipal Income Fund	FOHFX	NAS CM	Open End	US Muni Fixed Inc (Muni Bond - Single State)	C	C-	B-		Y	617-563-7000
Fidelity® Pennsylvania Municipal Income Fund	FPXTX	NAS CM	Open End	US Muni Fixed Inc (Muni Bond - Single State)	C	C-	B-		Y	617-563-7000
Fidelity® Real Estate High Income Fund			Open End	US Fixed Inc (Specialty - Real Estate)	D	D	D	Down	Y	617-563-7000
Fidelity® SAI Long-Term Treasury Bond Index Fund	FBLTX	NAS CM	Open End	US Fixed Inc (Govt Bond - Treasury)	B	B	B		Y	617-563-7000
Fidelity® SAI Municipal Bond Index Fund	FSABX	NAS CM	Open End	US Muni Fixed Inc (Muni Bond - Natl)	U	U	U		Y	617-563-7000
Fidelity® SAI Municipal Income Fund	FSMNX	NAS CM	Open End	US Muni Fixed Inc (Income)	D+	D+	C	Up	Y	617-563-7000
Fidelity® SAI Municipal Money Market Fund	FMQXX	NAS CM	Money Mkt	US Money Mkt (Money Mkt - Fed Tax Exmpt)	C	C-	C	Up	Y	617-563-7000
Fidelity® SAI Tax-Free Bond Fund	FSAJX	NAS CM	Open End	US Muni Fixed Inc (Income)	D+	D+	C	Up	Y	617-563-7000
Fidelity® SAI U.S. Treasury Bond Index Fund	FUTBX	NAS CM	Open End	US Fixed Inc (Income)	B	B	B		Y	617-563-7000
Fidelity® Series Bond Index Fund	FIFZX	NAS CM	Open End	US Fixed Inc (Income)	D	D+	B		Y	617-563-7000
Fidelity® Series Corporate Bond Fund	FHMFX	NAS CM	Open End	US Fixed Inc (Corp Bond - General)	C-	D+	B	Up	Y	617-563-7000
Fidelity® Series Emerging Markets Debt Fund	FEDCX	NAS CM	Open End	Emerg Mkts Fixed Inc (Growth & Income)	D	D	C-	Down		617-563-7000
Fidelity® Series Floating Rate High Income Fund	FFHCX	NAS CM	Open End	US Fixed Inc (Income)	D+	D+	C-	Down		617-563-7000
Fidelity® Series Government Bond Index Fund	FHNFX	NAS CM	Open End	US Fixed Inc (Govt Bond - General)	C-	C-	B+	Up	Y	617-563-7000
Fidelity® Series Government Money Market Fund	FGNXX	NAS CM	Money Mkt	US Money Mkt (Money Mkt - Govt)	C	C	B-		Y	617-563-7000
Fidelity® Series High Income Fund	FSHNX	NAS CM	Open End	US Fixed Inc (Income)	C-	D+	C			617-563-7000
Fidelity® Series Inflation-Protected Bond Index Fund	FSIPX	NAS CM	Open End	US Fixed Inc (Growth & Income)	B-	C	B+	Up		617-563-7000
Fidelity® Series International Credit Fund	FCDSX	NAS CM	Open End	Global Fixed Inc (Income)	C	C-	C+		Y	617-563-7000
Fidelity® Series Investment Grade Bond Fund	FSIGX	NAS CM	Open End	US Fixed Inc (Income)	B	C+	B+	Up		617-563-7000
Fidelity® Series Investment Grade Securitized Fund	FHPFX	NAS CM	Open End	US Fixed Inc (Corp Bond - High Quality)	C-	D+	B	Up	Y	617-563-7000
Fidelity® Series Long-Term Treasury Bond Index Fund	FTLTX	NAS CM	Open End	US Fixed Inc (Income)	B	B	B		Y	617-563-7000
Fidelity® Series Short-Term Credit Fund	FYBTX	NAS CM	Open End	US Fixed Inc (Corp Bond - General)	C	C	B-		Y	617-563-7000
Fidelity® Series Treasury Bill Index Fund	FHQFX	NAS CM	Open End	US Fixed Inc (Govt Bond - Treasury)	C-	D+	C+	Up	Y	617-563-7000
Fidelity® Short Duration High Income Fund	FSAHX	NAS CM	Open End	US Fixed Inc (Income)	C-	D+	C		Y	617-563-7000
Fidelity® Short-Term Bond Fund	FSHBX	NAS CM	Open End	US Fixed Inc (Income)	C+	C	B-	Up	Y	617-563-7000
Fidelity® Short-Term Bond Index Fund	FNSOX	NAS CM	Open End	US Fixed Inc (Income)	C+	C	B	Up	Y	617-563-7000
Fidelity® Short-Term Treasury Bond Index Fund	FUMBX	NAS CM	Open End	US Fixed Inc (Govt Bond - Treasury)	B-	C+	B	Up	Y	617-563-7000
Fidelity® Strategic Income Fund	FADMX	NAS CM	Open End	US Fixed Inc (Multisector Bond)	C	C-	C+		Y	617-563-7000
Fidelity® Sustainability Bond Index Fund	FNDSX	NAS CM	Open End	US Fixed Inc (Growth & Income)	C-	D+	B	Up	Y	617-563-7000
Fidelity® Tax-Exempt Money Market Fund	FMOXX	NAS CM	Money Mkt	US Money Mkt (Money Mkt - Fed Tax Exmpt)	C	C-	C+		Y	617-563-7000
Fidelity® Tax-Exempt Money Mkt Fund Capital Reserves Class	FERXX	NAS CM	Money Mkt	US Money Mkt (Money Mkt - Fed Tax Exmpt)	C	C-	C		Y	617-563-7000
Fidelity® Tax-Exempt Money Market Fund Daily Money Class	FDEXX	NAS CM	Money Mkt	US Money Mkt (Money Mkt - Fed Tax Exmpt)	C	C-	C		Y	617-563-7000
Fidelity® Tax-Exempt Money Market Fund Premium Class	FZEXX	NAS CM	Money Mkt	US Money Mkt (Money Mkt - Fed Tax Exmpt)	C	C	C+		Y	617-563-7000
Fidelity® Tax-Free Bond Fund	FTABX	NAS CM	Open End	US Muni Fixed Inc (Muni Bond - Natl)	C	C-	B-		Y	617-563-7000
Fidelity® Total Bond Fund	FTBFX	NAS CM	Open End	US Fixed Inc (Income)	B	C+	B+	Up	Y	617-563-7000
Fidelity® Total Bond K6 Fund	FTKFX	NAS CM	Open End	US Fixed Inc (Income)	C+	C	B	Up	Y	617-563-7000
Fidelity® Treasury Money Market Fund	FZFXX	NAS CM	Money Mkt	US Money Mkt (Money Mkt - Treasury)	C	C-	C+		Y	617-563-7000
Fidelity® Treasury Money Market Fund Advisor C Class	FDCXX	NAS CM	Money Mkt	US Money Mkt (Money Mkt - Treasury)	C	C-	C		Y	617-563-7000
Fidelity® Treasury Money Mkt Fund Capital Reserves Class	FSRXX	NAS CM	Money Mkt	US Money Mkt (Money Mkt - Treasury)	C	C-	C		Y	617-563-7000
Fidelity® Treasury Money Market Fund Daily Money Class	FDUXX	NAS CM	Money Mkt	US Money Mkt (Money Mkt - Treasury)	C	C-	C+		Y	617-563-7000
★ Fidelity® U.S. Bond Index Fund	FXNAX	NAS CM	Open End	US Fixed Inc (Multisector Bond)	B	B-	B+		Y	617-563-7000
Fidelity® Variable Insur Products Bond Ind Port Service Cl	FVISX	NAS CM	Open End	US Fixed Inc (Growth & Income)	U	U	U		Y	617-563-7000
★ First American Government Obligations Fund Class A	FAAXX	NAS CM	Money Mkt	US Money Mkt (Money Mkt - Govt)	C	C-	C+		Y	800-677-3863
★ First American Government Obligations Fund Class D	FGDXX	NAS CM	Money Mkt	US Money Mkt (Money Mkt - Govt)	C	C-	C		Y	800-677-3863
★ First American Government Obligations Fund Class P	FPPXX	NAS CM	Money Mkt	US Money Mkt (Money Mkt - Govt)	C	C-	C+		Y	800-677-3863
★ First American Government Obligations Fund Class U	FGUXX	NAS CM	Money Mkt	US Money Mkt (Money Mkt - Govt)	C	C-	C+		Y	800-677-3863
First American Government Obligations Fund Class V	FVIXX	NAS CM	Money Mkt	US Money Mkt (Money Mkt - Govt)	C	C-	C+		Y	800-677-3863
First American Government Obligations Fund Class X	FGXXX	NAS CM	Money Mkt	US Money Mkt (Money Mkt - Govt)	C	C-	C+		Y	800-677-3863
★ First American Government Obligations Fund Class Y	FGVXX	NAS CM	Money Mkt	US Money Mkt (Money Mkt - Govt)	C	C-	C+		Y	800-677-3863
First American Government Obligations Fund Class Z	FGZXX	NAS CM	Money Mkt	US Money Mkt (Money Mkt - Govt)	C	C-	C+		Y	800-677-3863
First American Institutional Prime Obligations Cl T	FIUXX	NAS CM	Money Mkt	US Money Mkt (Money Mkt - Taxable)	C	C	C+		Y	800-677-3863

★Expanded analysis of this fund is included in Section II.

TOTAL RETURNS & PERFORMANCE									ASSETS		ASSET ALLOCATION & TURNOVER							MINIMUMS		FEES		
3-Month Total Return	6-Month Total Return	1-Year Total Return	3-Year Total Return	5-Year Total Return	Dividend Yield (TTM)	Expense Ratio	3-Yr Std Deviation	Effective Duration	NAV	Total Assets (ML)	%Cash	%Government Bonds	%Municipal Bonds	%Corporate Bonds	%Other	Turnover Ratio	Average Coupon Rate	Min Initial Investment	Min Additional Investment	Front End Fee (%)	Back End Fee (%)	Inception Date
1.21	0.50	2.52	10.77	18.60	2.44	0.46	4.61	7.08	13.38	1,701	0	0	100	0	0	15	4.87	0				Jul-84
1.67	0.90	2.96	10.85	19.90	2.55	0.48	4.04	6.23	12.34	665.1	0	0	100	0	0	10	4.80	0				Nov-85
1.34	0.91	3.13	11.80	19.49	2.6	0.48	4.09	6.74	11.34	501.5	1	0	99	0	0	20	4.67	0				Aug-86
3.86	-15.34	-13.25	-2.68	4.03	5.51	0.8	12.38		7.26	653.9	0	0	0	10	0	26	4.31	1,000,000				Jan-95
-0.60	22.13	26.43	41.88		1.83	0.03	12.5	19.78	13.3	1,108	1	99	0	0	0	18	2.99	0				Oct-15
1.76	1.77					0.07		6.12	20.26	51.1	1	0	99	0	0		4.68	0				Jul-19
2.18	0.11	2.44			2.73	0.36		6.69	10.57	1,371	9	0	91	0	0	21	4.88	0				Oct-18
0.11	0.49	1.13			1.21	0.14			1.0005	190.7	22	0	78	0	0			0				Jan-18
2.66	-0.15	2.10			2.22	0.25		6.56	10.57	1,506	1	0	99	0	3	12	4.66	0				Oct-18
0.26	8.82	10.51	17.56		1.92	0.03	4.26	7.00	10.88	3,961	3	97	0	0	0	23	2.34	0				Mar-16
3.02	6.26	8.94			2.46	0		5.48	10.88	11,142	4	43	0	25	0	20	3.05	0				Apr-19
10.63	5.73	9.99			3.36	0.1		7.71	11.15	160.1	4	6	0	90	0	32	3.82	0				Aug-18
12.88	-3.86	-2.70	5.31	26.87	6.14	0.01	11.42		8.97	1,326	8	73	0	19	0	61	6.18	0				Mar-11
8.49	-4.90	-2.11	8.14	15.21	5.91	0.01	8.02		8.62	263.5	7	0	0	93	0	33	4.68	0				Oct-11
0.23	8.70	10.39			1.94	0		6.90	11.27	195.7	3	97	0	0	0	59	2.28	0				Aug-18
0.06	0.40	1.42	5.22		1.62	0	0.18		1	13,856	67	32	0	1	0			0				Apr-16
8.72	-5.14	-1.34	10.98	24.89	6.7	0	8.63		8.83	1,537	3	0	0	97	0	41	6.20	0				Mar-11
3.72	4.11	5.84	12.31	15.68	0.33	0	2.62	3.29	10.45	11,830	0	100	0	0	0	18	0.69	0				Sep-09
7.91	2.34	6.60	17.16		2.77	0.01		6.43	10.24	113.2	-203	6	0	88	0	88	3.85	0				Jul-17
5.94	6.32	9.26	18.53	27.13	2.9	0	3.87	5.56	12.13	32,265	4	22	1	43	-1	175	3.49	0				Oct-08
1.17	4.20	6.13			2.54	0.01		0.75	10.62	152.7	21	7	0	0	0	1,434	3.36	0				Aug-18
-0.54	21.34	25.52	40.11		2.09	0	12.09	19.19	10.39	6,050	1	99	0	0	0	33	3.08	0				Jul-16
4.05	2.63	4.45	10.11	13.06	2.62	0	2.33	1.75	10.22	2,352	4	10	0	60	0	67	2.76	0				Mar-15
0.06	0.83	1.87			1.55	0		0.29	10.01	2,228	38	62	0	0	0			0				Aug-18
7.14	-1.96	0.01	7.89	15.36	3.98	0.8	6.2		9.09	88.7	3	0	0	97	0	77	5.66	0				Nov-13
2.98	2.77	4.14	8.63	11.27	2.04	0.45	1.62	1.99	8.86	5,482	5	23	0	48	0	46	2.59	0				Sep-86
1.57	4.08	5.51			2.03	0.03		2.59	10.39	836.5	0	77	0	22	0	83	2.06	0				Oct-17
0.23	4.20	5.37	10.04	11.98	1.71	0.03	1.85	2.61	10.89	3,467	0	100	0	0	0	46	1.87	0				Oct-17
8.20	-0.99	1.56	10.15	21.14	3.18	0.68	6.49	5.08	12.17	14,613	-2	35	0	52	0	138	4.59	0				Apr-18
2.53	6.47	8.84			2.37	0.1		5.35	11.08	121.0	5	45	0	24	0	89	2.93	0				Jun-18
0.05	0.34	0.85	2.84	3.20	0.92	0.45	0.11		1	3,309	16	0	83	0	4	0		0				Jun-01
0.03	0.19	0.46	1.43	1.54	0.48	0.95	0.1		1	3,309	16	0	83	0	4	0		0				Oct-97
0.04	0.26	0.65	2.12	2.29	0.7	0.7	0.11		1	3,309	16	0	83	0	4	0		0				Nov-83
0.07	0.39	1.00	3.24	3.75	1.04	0.33	0.12		1	3,309	16	0	83	0	4	0		100,000				Apr-15
2.34	0.56	3.01	13.16	21.83	2.84	0.25	5.08	6.94	11.81	3,966	0	0	100	0	2	8	4.85	25,000				Apr-01
5.88	5.32	8.08	16.64	25.86	2.71	0.45	3.84	5.16	11.34	28,185	3	37	1	33	0	170	3.48	0				Oct-02
6.23	5.36	8.25	16.67		2.83	0.3	3.96	5.15	10.65	1,492	6	39	0	31	0	83	3.44	0				May-17
0.00	0.25	1.05	3.97	4.15	1.23	0.42	0.18		1	29,731	65	34	0	1	0	0		0				Apr-15
0.00	0.03	0.33	1.31	1.33	0.42	1.45	0.12		1	29,731	65	34	0	1	0	0		0			1.00	Nov-97
0.00	0.13	0.67	2.48	2.50	0.81	0.95	0.16		1	29,731	65	34	0	1	0	0		0				Oct-97
0.00	0.18	0.85	3.18	3.23	1.01	0.7	0.16		1	29,731	65	34	0	1	0	0		0				Aug-83
2.77	6.54	9.01	17.02	23.88	2.46	0.03	3.29	5.48	12.54	50,694	3	45	0	24	0	35	3.06	0				May-11
4.33	6.57	8.86				0.24		5.54		171.5	2	49	0	23	0	168	3.24	0				Apr-19
0.00	0.17	0.81	3.00	3.04	0.95	0.75	0.16		1	66,790	70	30	0	0	0			1,000				Sep-01
0.00	0.21	0.92	3.42	3.51	1.08	0.6	0.17		1	66,790	70	30	0	0	0			0				Jan-95
0.03	0.35	1.30	4.58	4.76	1.48	0.18			1	66,790	70	30	0	0	0			0				Dec-17
0.04	0.37	1.33	4.62	4.79	1.51	0.12			1	66,790	70	30	0	0	0			0				Feb-18
0.01	0.30	1.16	4.29	4.65	1.34	0.3	0.18		1	66,790	70	30	0	0	0			0				Mar-06
0.03	0.36	1.30	4.78	5.31	1.49	0.14	0.18		1	66,790	70	30	0	0	0			50,000,000				Apr-16
0.00	0.24	1.03	3.85	4.02	1.2	0.45	0.17		1	66,790	70	30	0	0	0			0				Mar-90
0.03	0.34	1.27	4.65	5.20	1.45	0.18	0.18		1	66,790	70	30	0	0	0			10,000,000				Dec-03
0.10	0.34	1.22	4.60	5.01	1.39	0.4	0.17		1.0002	1,176	96	0	4	0	0			0				Sep-01

	MARKET		FUND TYPE, CATEGORY & OBJECTIVE		RATINGS				NEW INVESTORS	
Fund Name	Ticker Symbol	Traded On	Fund Type	Category and (Prospectus Objective)	Overall Rating	Reward Rating	Risk Rating	Recent Up/ Downgrade	Open to New Investors	Telephone
First American Institutional Prime Obligations Cl V	FPIXX	NAS CM	Money Mkt	US Money Mkt (Money Mkt - Taxable)	C	C	C+		Y	800-677-3863
First American Institutional Prime Obligations Cl Y	FAIXX	NAS CM	Money Mkt	US Money Mkt (Money Mkt - Taxable)	C	C-	C+		Y	800-677-3863
First American Institutional Prime Obligations Cl Z	FPZXX	NAS CM	Money Mkt	US Money Mkt (Money Mkt - Taxable)	C	C-	C+		Y	800-677-3863
First American Retail Prime Obligations Fund Class A	FAPXX	NAS CM	Money Mkt	US Money Mkt (Money Mkt - General)	C	C-	C+		Y	800-677-3863
First American Retail Prime Obligations Fund Class T	FEIXX	NAS CM	Money Mkt	US Money Mkt (Money Mkt - General)	C	C-	C+		Y	800-677-3863
First American Retail Prime Obligations Fund Class V	FPUXX	NAS CM	Money Mkt	US Money Mkt (Money Mkt - General)	C	C	B-		Y	800-677-3863
First American Retail Prime Obligations Fund Class X	FXRXX	NAS CM	Money Mkt	US Money Mkt (Money Mkt - General)	C	C-	C+		Y	800-677-3863
First American Retail Prime Obligations Fund Class Y	FYRXX	NAS CM	Money Mkt	US Money Mkt (Money Mkt - General)	C	C-	C+		Y	800-677-3863
First American Retail Prime Obligations Fund Class Z	FZRXX	NAS CM	Money Mkt	US Money Mkt (Money Mkt - General)	C	C-	C+		Y	800-677-3863
First American Retail Tax Free Obligations Fund Class A	FTAXX	NAS CM	Money Mkt	US Money Mkt (Money Mkt - Fed Tax Exmpt)	C	C-	C		Y	800-677-3863
First American Retail Tax Free Obligations Fund Class V	FHIXX	NAS CM	Money Mkt	US Money Mkt (Money Mkt - Fed Tax Exmpt)	C	C-	C+		Y	800-677-3863
First American Retail Tax Free Obligations Fund Class Y	FFCXX	NAS CM	Money Mkt	US Money Mkt (Money Mkt - Fed Tax Exmpt)	C	C-	C		Y	800-677-3863
First American Retail Tax Free Obligations Fund Class Z	FTZXX	NAS CM	Money Mkt	US Money Mkt (Money Mkt - Fed Tax Exmpt)	C	C-	C		Y	800-677-3863
First American Treasury Obligations Fund Class A	FATXX	NAS CM	Money Mkt	US Money Mkt (Money Mkt - Treasury)	C	C-	C		Y	800-677-3863
First American Treasury Obligations Fund Class D	FTDXX	NAS CM	Money Mkt	US Money Mkt (Money Mkt - Treasury)	C	C-	C+		Y	800-677-3863
First American Treasury Obligations Fund Class P	FUPXX	NAS CM	Money Mkt	US Money Mkt (Money Mkt - Treasury)	C	C-	C+		Y	800-677-3863
First American Treasury Obligations Fund Class V	FLIXX	NAS CM	Money Mkt	US Money Mkt (Money Mkt - Treasury)	C	C-	C+		Y	800-677-3863
First American Treasury Obligations Fund Class X	FXFXX	NAS CM	Money Mkt	US Money Mkt (Money Mkt - Treasury)	C	C-	C+		Y	800-677-3863
First American Treasury Obligations Fund Class Y	FOCXX	NAS CM	Money Mkt	US Money Mkt (Money Mkt - Treasury)	C	C-	C+		Y	800-677-3863
First American Treasury Obligations Fund Class Z	FUZXX	NAS CM	Money Mkt	US Money Mkt (Money Mkt - Treasury)	C	C	C+		Y	800-677-3863
First American U.S. Treasury Money Market Fund Class A	FOEXX	NAS CM	Money Mkt	US Money Mkt (Money Mkt - Treasury)	C	C-	C		Y	800-677-3863
First American U.S. Treasury Money Market Fund Class D	FODXX	NAS CM	Money Mkt	US Money Mkt (Money Mkt - Treasury)	C	C-	C		Y	800-677-3863
First American U.S. Treasury Money Market Fund Class Y	FOYXX	NAS CM	Money Mkt	US Money Mkt (Money Mkt - Treasury)	C	C-	C+		Y	800-677-3863
First American U.S. Treasury Money Market Fund Class Z	FOZXX	NAS CM	Money Mkt	US Money Mkt (Money Mkt - Treasury)	C	C-	C+		Y	800-677-3863
First Eagle High Income Fund Class A	FEHAX	NAS CM	Open End	US Fixed Inc (Corp Bond - High Yield)	D+	D	C	Down	Y	800-334-2143
First Eagle High Income Fund Class C	FEHCX	NAS CM	Open End	US Fixed Inc (Corp Bond - High Yield)	D	D	C-	Down	Y	800-334-2143
First Eagle High Income Fund Class I	FEHIX	NAS CM	Open End	US Fixed Inc (Corp Bond - High Yield)	D+	D	C	Down	Y	800-334-2143
First Eagle High Income Fund Class R3	EARHX	NAS CM	Open End	US Fixed Inc (Corp Bond - High Yield)	D+	D	C	Down	Y	800-334-2143
First Eagle High Income Fund Class R4	FIHRX	NAS CM	Open End	US Fixed Inc (Corp Bond - High Yield)	D+	D	C	Down	Y	800-334-2143
First Eagle High Income Fund Class R5	FERHX	NAS CM	Open End	US Fixed Inc (Corp Bond - High Yield)	D+	D	C	Down	Y	800-334-2143
First Eagle High Income Fund Class R6	FEHRX	NAS CM	Open End	US Fixed Inc (Corp Bond - High Yield)	D+	D	C	Down	Y	800-334-2143
First Eagle Senior Loan Fund	FSLF	NYSE	Closed End	US Fixed Inc (Income)	D	D	D	Down	Y	212-701-4500
First Investors Fund For Income Class B	FIFJX	NAS CM	Open End	US Fixed Inc (Corp Bond - High Yield)	U	U	U		Y	800-423-4026
First Investors Investment Grade Series Class B	FIIHX	NAS CM	Open End	US Fixed Inc (Corp Bond - General)	U	U	U		Y	800-423-4026
First Investors Tax Exempt Income Fund Class B	FITCX	NAS CM	Open End	US Muni Fixed Inc (Muni Bond - Natl)	U	U	U		Y	800-423-4026
First Investors Tax Exempt New Jersey Fund Class B	FINKX	NAS CM	Open End	US Muni Fixed Inc (Muni Bond - Single State)	U	U	U		Y	800-423-4026
First Investors Tax Exempt Oregon Fund Class B	FTOBX	NAS CM	Open End	US Muni Fixed Inc (Muni Bond - Single State)	U	U	U		Y	800-423-4026
First Trust High Inc Long/Short Fund	FSD	NYSE	Closed End	US Fixed Inc (World Stock)	D+	D+	C-	Down	Y	866-848-9727
First Trust Mortgage Income Fund	FMY	NYSE	Closed End	US Fixed Inc (Govt Bond - Mortgage)	C-	C-	D+		Y	866-848-9727
First Trust Senior Floating Rate Income Fund II	FCT	NYSE	Closed End	US Fixed Inc (Corp Bond - High Yield)	D	D	D+	Down	Y	866-848-9727
First Trust Senior FR 2022 Target Term	FIV	NYSE	Closed End	US Fixed Inc (Income)	D+	D	D+	Down	Y	866-848-9727
First Trust Short Duration High Income Fund Class A	FDHAX	NAS CM	Open End	US Fixed Inc (Corp Bond - High Yield)	D+	D	C	Down	Y	800-621-1675
First Trust Short Duration High Income Fund Class C	FDHCX	NAS CM	Open End	US Fixed Inc (Corp Bond - High Yield)	D+	D	C	Down	Y	800-621-1675
First Trust Short Duration High Income Fund Class I	FDHIX	NAS CM	Open End	US Fixed Inc (Corp Bond - High Yield)	C-	D+	C		Y	800-621-1675
First Trust/Aberdeen Global Opportunity Income Fund	FAM	NYSE	Closed End	Global Fixed Inc (Worldwide Bond)	D+	D	C-	Down	Y	866-848-9727
First Western Fixed Income Fund	FWFIX	NAS CM	Open End	US Fixed Inc (Income)	C+	C+	B		Y	310-229-2940
First Western Short Duration Bond Fund	FWSBX	NAS CM	Open End	US Fixed Inc (Corp Bond - General)	C	C	B-		Y	310-229-2940
First Western Short Duration High Yield Credit Inst Shares	FWSHX	NAS CM	Open End	US Fixed Inc (Corp Bond - High Yield)	C-	D+	C		Y	310-229-2940
Fisher Inv Inst Group ESG Fixed Income for Retmnt Plans	QDVBX	NAS CM	Open End	US Fixed Inc (Income)	U	U	U		Y	415-851-3334
Fisher Inv Inst Group Fixed Income for Retmnt Plans	QDIBX	NAS CM	Open End	US Fixed Inc (Income)	U	U	U		Y	415-851-3334
Forefront Income Trust	BFITX	NAS CM	Closed End	US Fixed Inc (Income)	C	C	C		Y	
FPA Flexible Fixed Income Fund	FPFIX	NAS CM	Open End	Fixed Inc Misc (Multisector Bond)	D	D+	C+		Y	800-982-4372

★ Expanded analysis of this fund is included in Section II.

TOTAL RETURNS & PERFORMANCE									ASSETS		ASSET ALLOCATION & TURNOVER							MINIMUMS		FEES		
3-Month Total Return	6-Month Total Return	1-Year Total Return	3-Year Total Return	5-Year Total Return	Dividend Yield (TTM)	Expense Ratio	3-Yr Std Deviation	Effective Duration	NAV	Total Assets (MIL)	%Cash	%Government Bonds	%Municipal Bonds	%Corporate Bonds	%Other	Turnover Ratio	Average Coupon Rate	Min Initial Investment	Min Additional Investment	Front End Fee (%)	Back End Fee (%)	Inception Date
0.13	0.40	1.33	4.93	5.49	1.49	0.3	0.17		1.0003	1,176	96	0	4	0	0			0				Mar-06
0.10	0.33	1.18	4.46	4.81	1.34	0.45	0.17		1.0003	1,176	96	0	4	0	0			0				Mar-90
0.15	0.46	1.47	5.38	6.15	1.64	0.2	0.17		1.0002	1,176	96	0	4	0	0			1,000,000				Aug-03
0.00	0.26	1.05	3.88		1.22	0.75	0.18		1	2,860	96	0	4	0	0			1,000				Jul-16
0.04	0.36	1.25	4.65		1.42	0.4	0.16		1	2,860	96	0	4	0	0			0				Jul-16
0.06	0.39	1.34	4.97		1.52	0.3	0.16		1	2,860	96	0	4	0	0			0				Jul-16
0.11	0.49	1.51	5.47		1.68	0.14	0.16		1	2,860	96	0	4	0	0			50,000,000				Sep-16
0.03	0.33	1.19	4.50		1.37	0.45	0.16		1	2,860	96	0	4	0	0			0				Jul-16
0.09	0.45	1.45	5.28		1.62	0.2	0.16		1	2,860	96	0	4	0	0			10,000,000				Jul-16
0.01	0.22	0.52	1.75	1.79	0.61	0.75	0.11		1	555.7	13	0	87	0	0			1,000				Sep-01
0.06	0.38	0.91	3.06	3.50	1.02	0.3	0.11		1	555.7	13	0	87	0	0			0				Mar-06
0.04	0.31	0.76	2.61	2.87	0.87	0.45	0.11		1	555.7	13	0	87	0	0			0				Jan-95
0.08	0.42	0.99	3.37	3.94	1.12	0.2	0.11		1	555.7	13	0	87	0	0			10,000,000				Dec-03
0.00	0.17	0.81	3.01	3.03	0.94	0.75	0.16		1	18,361	73	27	0	0	0			1,000				Sep-01
0.00	0.20	0.91	3.42	3.50	1.06	0.6	0.17		1	18,361	73	27	0	0	0			0				Oct-93
0.03	0.34	1.28	4.49	4.57	1.46	0.18			1	18,361	73	27	0	0	0			0				Dec-17
0.00	0.27	1.13	4.28	4.60	1.31	0.3	0.18		1	18,361	73	27	0	0	0			0				Mar-06
0.03	0.35	1.29	4.77	5.26	1.47	0.14	0.18		1	18,361	73	27	0	0	0			50,000,000				Apr-16
0.00	0.23	1.02	3.84	4.00	1.19	0.45	0.17		1	18,361	73	27	0	0	0			0				Jan-95
0.02	0.32	1.24	4.64	5.15	1.43	0.18	0.18		1	18,361	73	27	0	0	0			10,000,000				Dec-03
0.00	0.16	0.76	2.90	2.92	0.9	0.75	0.16		1	3,144	81	19	0	0	0			1,000				Oct-04
0.00	0.19	0.87	3.31	3.38	1.02	0.6	0.16		1	3,144	81	19	0	0	0			0				Oct-04
0.00	0.23	0.99	3.75	3.88	1.15	0.45	0.17		1	3,144	81	19	0	0	0			0				Oct-04
0.03	0.33	1.21	4.50	4.89	1.38	0.2	0.17		1	3,144	81	19	0	0	0			10,000,000				Oct-04
9.80	-3.56	-1.34	5.94	13.53	4.48	1.24	7.62		8.3	215.4	13	0	0	86	0	24	5.58	2,500	100	4.50		Jan-12
9.61	-3.93	-2.20	3.47	9.37	3.69	2	7.67		8.29	215.4	13	0	0	86	0	24	5.58	2,500	100		1.00	Jan-12
9.88	-3.42	-1.18	6.73	15.15	4.78	0.95	7.66		8.3	215.4	13	0	0	86	0	24	5.58	1,000,000	100			Nov-07
9.62	-3.74	-1.52	5.50	13.03	4.39	1.34	7.62		8.3	215.4	13	0	0	86	0	24	5.58	0				May-18
9.67	-3.76	-1.68	5.98	14.11		1.6	7.67		8.3	215.4	13	0	0	86	0	24	5.58	0				Jul-19
9.83	-3.50	-1.39	6.50	14.90		1.49	7.67		8.3	215.4	13	0	0	86	0	24	5.58	0				Jul-19
9.89	-3.40	-1.14	6.69	14.98	4.82	0.92	7.65		8.3	215.4	13	0	0	86	0	24	5.58	0				Mar-17
6.22	-14.25	-13.27	-8.17	5.59	7.88	2.46	11.86		14	104.6	7	0	0	93	0	65	5.63					Sep-13
1.12	5.28	4.09	14.75	11.92	4.46	2.04	4	3.00		535.0	2	0	0	98	0	47	6.46	1,000			4.00	Jan-95
3.74	7.23	7.14	5.71	10.65	2.56	1.97	3.28	6.41		507.7	3	7	0	90	0	58	4.62	1,000			4.00	Jan-95
2.22	4.07	3.90	2.29	9.22	2.52	1.79	2.37	5.43		640.1	1	0	99	0	0	11	5.37	1,000			4.00	Jan-95
2.74	4.60	4.81	3.32	11.40	2.31	1.71	2.96	6.26		48.6	-1	0	100	0	0	30	5.07	1,000			4.00	Jan-95
2.42	3.79	3.50	-0.84	6.90	0.54	3.35	3.12	5.47		52.5	1	0	99	0	0	25	4.91	1,000			4.00	Jan-95
10.65	-8.38	-3.79	5.56	20.30	6.11		11.01		15.13	521.5	-6	0	0	97	0	33	6.29					Sep-10
3.37	0.55	1.30	8.42	14.17	2.69	2.45	3.59		14.6	61.5	2	0	0	0	0	69	4.11					May-05
9.30	-7.72	-3.54	3.25	13.58	6.85	0	10.02		12.31	332.6	2	0	0	98	0	58						May-04
8.49	-6.90	-3.45	2.80		3.68	2.08	9.47		8.83	319.6	3	0	0	97	0	61						Dec-16
6.97	-3.40	-0.32	4.23	12.64	4.55	1.23	6.72		18.59	132.8	6	0	0	94	0	37		2,500	50	3.50		Nov-12
6.83	-3.72	-1.01	2.28	8.90	3.78	1.98	6.72		18.59	132.8	6	0	0	94	0	37		2,500	50		1.00	Nov-12
7.08	-3.23	-0.02	6.67	15.85	4.81	0.98	6.7		18.61	132.8	6	0	0	94	0	37		1,000,000				Nov-12
11.09	-4.96	-0.89	6.12	23.36	6.21	1.21	11.86		10.93	137.6	6	65	0	11	0	42	5.82					Nov-04
3.85	4.59	6.52	14.75	22.89	2.5	0.6	2.87		10.33	90.6	2	30	2	22	0	36	3.54	100,000	1,000			Nov-12
2.70	1.57	2.69	7.84	12.37	2.75	0.6	1.75		9.93	105.4	4	11	3	31	0	47	3.58	100,000	1,000			Apr-13
9.36	-3.99	-1.75	6.44		5.64	0.95	7.95		9.31	36.3	4	0	0	92	0	86	6.66	100,000	1,000			Oct-15
4.64	3.70					0.02			10.36	3.1								0	0			Dec-19
4.64	3.70					0.05			10.36	3.1								0	0			Dec-19
0.00	-0.18	2.10	0.66	20.74	0	1.75	9.37		10.67	--	56				0			1,000		3.00		Dec-14
3.30	1.87	3.01			2.79	0.39		1.52	10.18	186.9	11	0	0	10	0	30	3.42	100,000	100			Dec-18

	MARKET			FUND TYPE, CATEGORY & OBJECTIVE	RATINGS				NEW INVESTORS	
Fund Name	Ticker Symbol	Traded On	Fund Type	Category and (Prospectus Objective)	Overall Rating	Reward Rating	Risk Rating	Recent Up/ Downgrade	Open to New Investors	Telephone
FPA New Income Fund	FPNIX	NAS CM	Open End	US Fixed Inc (Growth & Income)	C	C-	B-		Y	800-982-4372
Franklin Adjustable U.S. Govt Securities Advisor Cl	FAUZX	NAS CM	Open End	US Fixed Inc (Govt Bond - Mortgage)	C	C-	C+		Y	650-312-2000
Franklin Adjustable U.S. Govt Securities Fund Class A	FISAX	NAS CM	Open End	US Fixed Inc (Govt Bond - Mortgage)	C	C-	C+		Y	650-312-2000
Franklin Adjustable U.S. Govt Securities Fund Class A1	FAUGX	NAS CM	Open End	US Fixed Inc (Govt Bond - Mortgage)	C	C-	C+		Y	650-312-2000
Franklin Adjustable U.S. Govt Securities Fund Class C	FCSCX	NAS CM	Open End	US Fixed Inc (Govt Bond - Mortgage)	C	C-	C		Y	650-312-2000
Franklin Adjustable U.S. Govt Securities Fund Class R6	FAURX	NAS CM	Open End	US Fixed Inc (Govt Bond - Mortgage)	C	C-	C+		Y	650-312-2000
Franklin Alabama Tax Free Income Fund Advisor Class	FALZX	NAS CM	Open End	US Muni Fixed Inc (Muni Bond - Single State)	C+	C	B	Up	Y	650-312-2000
Franklin Alabama Tax Free Income Fund Class A	FALQX	NAS CM	Open End	US Muni Fixed Inc (Muni Bond - Single State)	C+	C	B	Up	Y	650-312-2000
Franklin Alabama Tax Free Income Fund Class A1	FRALX	NAS CM	Open End	US Muni Fixed Inc (Muni Bond - Single State)	C+	C	B	Up	Y	650-312-2000
Franklin Alabama Tax Free Income Fund Class C	FALEX	NAS CM	Open End	US Muni Fixed Inc (Muni Bond - Single State)	C	C	B		Y	650-312-2000
Franklin Alabama Tax Free Income Fund Class R6	FALRX	NAS CM	Open End	US Muni Fixed Inc (Muni Bond - Single State)	C+	C	B	Up	Y	650-312-2000
Franklin Arizona Tax Free Income Fund Advisor Class	FAZZX	NAS CM	Open End	US Muni Fixed Inc (Muni Bond - Single State)	C	C	B-		Y	650-312-2000
Franklin Arizona Tax Free Income Fund Class A	FAZQX	NAS CM	Open End	US Muni Fixed Inc (Muni Bond - Single State)	C	C	B-		Y	650-312-2000
Franklin Arizona Tax Free Income Fund Class A1	FTAZX	NAS CM	Open End	US Muni Fixed Inc (Muni Bond - Single State)	C	C	B-		Y	650-312-2000
Franklin Arizona Tax Free Income Fund Class C	FAZIX	NAS CM	Open End	US Muni Fixed Inc (Muni Bond - Single State)	C	C-	B-		Y	650-312-2000
Franklin Arizona Tax Free Income Fund Class R6	FAZRX	NAS CM	Open End	US Muni Fixed Inc (Muni Bond - Single State)	C	C	B		Y	650-312-2000
Franklin California High Yield Muni Fund Advisor Class	FVCAX	NAS CM	Open End	US Muni Fixed Inc (Muni Bond - Single State)	C	C-	C+		Y	650-312-2000
Franklin California High Yield Municipal Fund Class A	FCQAX	NAS CM	Open End	US Muni Fixed Inc (Muni Bond - Single State)	C	C-	C+		Y	650-312-2000
Franklin California High Yield Municipal Fund Class A1	FCAMX	NAS CM	Open End	US Muni Fixed Inc (Muni Bond - Single State)	C	C-	C+		Y	650-312-2000
Franklin California High Yield Municipal Fund Class C	FCAHX	NAS CM	Open End	US Muni Fixed Inc (Muni Bond - Single State)	C	C-	C		Y	650-312-2000
Franklin California High Yield Municipal Fund Class R6	FCAQX	NAS CM	Open End	US Muni Fixed Inc (Muni Bond - Single State)	C	C-	C+		Y	650-312-2000
Franklin Calif Intermed-Term Tax-Free Income Advisor Cl	FRCZX	NAS CM	Open End	US Muni Fixed Inc (Muni Bond - Single State)	C	C-	B-		Y	650-312-2000
Franklin California Intermediate-Term Tax-Free Income Cl A	FCCQX	NAS CM	Open End	US Muni Fixed Inc (Muni Bond - Single State)	C	C-	C+		Y	650-312-2000
Franklin California Intermed-Term Tax-Free Income Cl A1	FKCIX	NAS CM	Open End	US Muni Fixed Inc (Muni Bond - Single State)	C	C-	B-		Y	650-312-2000
Franklin California Intermediate-Term Tax-Free Income Cl C	FCCIX	NAS CM	Open End	US Muni Fixed Inc (Muni Bond - Single State)	C	C-	C+		Y	650-312-2000
Franklin California Intermed-Term Tax-Free Income Cl R6	FCCRX	NAS CM	Open End	US Muni Fixed Inc (Muni Bond - Single State)	C	C-	B-		Y	650-312-2000
Franklin California Tax Free Income Fund Advisor Class	FCAVX	NAS CM	Open End	US Muni Fixed Inc (Muni Bond - Single State)	C	C-	B	Down	Y	650-312-2000
Franklin California Tax Free Income Fund Class A	FTFQX	NAS CM	Open End	US Muni Fixed Inc (Muni Bond - Single State)	C	C-	B-		Y	650-312-2000
Franklin California Tax Free Income Fund Class A1	FKTFX	NAS CM	Open End	US Muni Fixed Inc (Muni Bond - Single State)	C	C-	B		Y	650-312-2000
Franklin California Tax Free Income Fund Class C	FRCTX	NAS CM	Open End	US Muni Fixed Inc (Muni Bond - Single State)	C	C-	B-		Y	650-312-2000
Franklin California Tax Free Income Fund Class R6	FKTQX	NAS CM	Open End	US Muni Fixed Inc (Muni Bond - Single State)	C	C-	B	Down	Y	650-312-2000
Franklin Colorado Tax Free Income Fund Advisor Class	FCOZX	NAS CM	Open End	US Muni Fixed Inc (Muni Bond - Single State)	C	C	B		Y	650-312-2000
Franklin Colorado Tax Free Income Fund Class A	FCOQX	NAS CM	Open End	US Muni Fixed Inc (Muni Bond - Single State)	C	C	B		Y	650-312-2000
Franklin Colorado Tax Free Income Fund Class A1	FRCOX	NAS CM	Open End	US Muni Fixed Inc (Muni Bond - Single State)	C	C	B		Y	650-312-2000
Franklin Colorado Tax Free Income Fund Class C	FCOIX	NAS CM	Open End	US Muni Fixed Inc (Muni Bond - Single State)	C	C	B-		Y	650-312-2000
Franklin Colorado Tax Free Income Fund Class R6	FKTLX	NAS CM	Open End	US Muni Fixed Inc (Muni Bond - Single State)	C	C	B		Y	650-312-2000
Franklin Connecticut Tax-Free Income Fund Advisor Class	FCNZX	NAS CM	Open End	US Muni Fixed Inc (Muni Bond - Single State)	C	C-	B-		Y	650-312-2000
Franklin Connecticut Tax-Free Income Fund Class A	FQCTX	NAS CM	Open End	US Muni Fixed Inc (Muni Bond - Single State)	C	C-	B-		Y	650-312-2000
Franklin Connecticut Tax-Free Income Fund Class A1	FXCTX	NAS CM	Open End	US Muni Fixed Inc (Muni Bond - Single State)	C	C-	B-		Y	650-312-2000
Franklin Connecticut Tax-Free Income Fund Class C	FCTIX	NAS CM	Open End	US Muni Fixed Inc (Muni Bond - Single State)	C	C-	C+		Y	650-312-2000
Franklin Connecticut Tax-Free Income Fund Class R6	FCTQX	NAS CM	Open End	US Muni Fixed Inc (Muni Bond - Single State)	C	C-	B-		Y	650-312-2000
Franklin Emerging Market Debt Opportunities Fund	FEMDX	NAS CM	Open End	Emerg Mkts Fixed Inc (Growth & Income)	D	D	D+	Down	Y	650-312-2000
Franklin Fed Intermed-Term Tax-Free Income Advisor Cl	FITZX	NAS CM	Open End	US Muni Fixed Inc (Muni Bond - Natl)	C	C	B-		Y	650-312-2000
Franklin Federal Intermediate-Term Tax-Free Income Cl A	FKQTX	NAS CM	Open End	US Muni Fixed Inc (Muni Bond - Natl)	C	C	B-		Y	650-312-2000
Franklin Federal Intermediate-Term Tax-Free Income Cl A1	FKITX	NAS CM	Open End	US Muni Fixed Inc (Muni Bond - Natl)	C	C	B-		Y	650-312-2000
Franklin Federal Intermediate-Term Tax-Free Income Cl C	FCITX	NAS CM	Open End	US Muni Fixed Inc (Muni Bond - Natl)	C	C	C+		Y	650-312-2000
Franklin Federal Intermediate-Term Tax-Free Income Cl R6	FITQX	NAS CM	Open End	US Muni Fixed Inc (Muni Bond - Natl)	C	C	B-		Y	650-312-2000
Franklin Federal Limited-Term Tax-Free Income Advisor Cl	FTFZX	NAS CM	Open End	US Muni Fixed Inc (Muni Bond - Natl)	C	C	B-		Y	650-312-2000
Franklin Federal Limited-Term Tax-Free Income Fund Class A	FFLQX	NAS CM	Open End	US Muni Fixed Inc (Muni Bond - Natl)	C	C	B-		Y	650-312-2000
Franklin Federal Limited-Term Tax-Free Income Cl A1	FFTFX	NAS CM	Open End	US Muni Fixed Inc (Muni Bond - Natl)	C	C	B-		Y	650-312-2000
Franklin Federal Limited-Term Tax-Free Income Cl R6	FFTRX	NAS CM	Open End	US Muni Fixed Inc (Muni Bond - Natl)	C	C	B-		Y	650-312-2000
Franklin Federal Tax Free Income Fund Advisor Class	FAFTX	NAS CM	Open End	US Muni Fixed Inc (Muni Bond - Natl)	C	C	B		Y	650-312-2000

★Expanded analysis of this fund is included in Section II.

TOTAL RETURNS & PERFORMANCE									ASSETS		ASSET ALLOCATION & TURNOVER							MINIMUMS		FEES		
3-Month Total Return	6-Month Total Return	1-Year Total Return	3-Year Total Return	5-Year Total Return	Dividend Yield (TTM)	Expense Ratio	3-Yr Std Deviation	Effective Duration	NAV	Total Assets (MIL)	%Cash	%Government Bonds	%Municipal Bonds	%Corporate Bonds	%Other	Turnover Ratio	Average Coupon Rate	Min Initial Investment	Min Additional Investment	Front End Fee (%)	Back End Fee (%)	Inception Date
2.65	1.23	2.53	9.06	12.34	2.55	0.5	1.76	1.35	9.98	7,449	8	1	0	5	0	25	3.13	1,500	100			Jul-84
2.47	1.11	1.81	4.49	4.24	2.91	0.7	1.62	1.28	7.99	764.6	10	0	0	0	0	13	3.41	100,000				May-08
2.41	0.86	1.56	3.70	2.93	2.66	0.95	1.6	1.28	7.98	764.6	10	0	0	0	0	13	3.41	1,000		2.25		Oct-87
2.45	1.06	1.71	4.18	3.72	2.81	0.8	1.62	1.28	7.98	764.6	10	0	0	0	0	13	3.41	1,000		2.25		Jun-14
2.44	0.79	1.28	2.60	1.02	2.26	1.35	1.66	1.28	7.98	764.6	10	0	0	0	0	13	3.41	1,000			1.00	Jul-03
2.63	1.17	2.05	5.01	5.00	3.02	0.59	1.66	1.28	8	764.6	10	0	0	0	0	13	3.41	1,000,000				Sep-13
1.69	2.23	4.30	11.26	17.23	2.87	0.66	3.04	4.16	11.23	241.4	1	0	99	0	0	5	4.92	100,000				Sep-16
1.63	2.11	4.04	10.42	15.92	2.62	0.91	3.06	4.16	11.24	241.4	1	0	99	0	0	5	4.92	1,000		3.75		Sep-18
1.67	2.19	4.20	10.93	16.80	2.77	0.76	3.01	4.16	11.23	241.4	1	0	99	0	0	5	4.92	1,000		3.75		Sep-87
1.51	1.89	3.61	9.00	13.55	2.23	1.31	3.08	4.16	11.38	241.4	1	0	99	0	0	5	4.92	1,000			1.00	May-95
1.70	2.25	4.33	11.32	17.20	2.9	0.63	3.05	4.16	11.23	241.4	1	0	99	0	0	5	4.92	0				Aug-17
2.10	1.41	3.65	11.45	18.06	2.9	0.56	4	5.19	10.94	962.1	0	0	100	0	0	11	4.84	100,000				Jul-08
2.04	1.28	3.39	10.75	16.75	2.65	0.81	3.93	5.19	10.93	962.1	0	0	100	0	0	11	4.84	1,000		3.75		Sep-18
2.08	1.36	3.55	11.16	17.54	2.8	0.66	3.95	5.19	10.91	962.1	0	0	100	0	0	11	4.84	1,000		3.75		Sep-87
1.91	1.08	2.96	9.28	14.29	2.24	1.21	3.91	5.19	11.1	962.1	0	0	100	0	0	11	4.84	1,000			1.00	May-95
2.11	1.42	3.68	11.62	18.02	2.93	0.53	3.99	5.19	10.94	962.1	0	0	100	0	0	11	4.84	0				Aug-17
3.12	-0.47	2.27	12.99	25.66	3.43	0.58	6.08	7.19	11	2,886	0	0	100	0	0	14	4.89	100,000				Nov-06
3.06	-0.59	1.92	12.28	24.17	3.17	0.83	6.05	7.19	10.99	2,886	0	0	100	0	0	14	4.89	1,000		3.75		Sep-18
3.10	-0.52	2.07	12.69	25.00	3.33	0.68	6.05	7.19	10.97	2,886	0	0	100	0	0	14	4.89	1,000		3.75		May-93
2.85	-0.86	1.52	10.78	21.56	2.77	1.23	6.03	7.19	11.05	2,886	0	0	100	0	0	14	4.89	1,000			1.00	May-96
3.13	-0.44	2.31	13.17	25.53	3.47	0.55	6.06	7.19	11.01	2,886	0	0	100	0	0	14	4.89	1,000,000				Aug-17
2.64	1.32	2.94	9.13	15.74	2.52	0.49	3.56	4.35	12.12	1,707	0	0	100	0	0	15	4.74	100,000				Oct-08
2.59	1.19	2.60	8.34	14.36	2.27	0.74	3.56	4.35	12.09	1,707	0	0	100	0	0	15	4.74	1,000		2.25		Sep-18
2.63	1.27	2.76	8.74	15.13	2.42	0.59	3.6	4.35	12.08	1,707	0	0	100	0	0	15	4.74	1,000		2.25		Sep-92
2.48	0.99	2.19	6.93	12.04	1.87	1.14	3.56	4.35	12.13	1,707	0	0	100	0	0	15	4.74	1,000			1.00	Jul-03
2.65	1.42	2.97	9.20	15.61	2.55	0.46	3.61	4.35	12.12	1,707	0	0	100	0	0	15	4.74	1,000,000				Aug-17
3.20	1.81	4.52	14.23	24.72	3.15	0.51	5.24	6.50	7.66	16,309	1	0	99	0	0	16	4.76	100,000				Oct-01
3.13	1.69	4.26	13.22	23.18	2.9	0.76	5.26	6.50	7.68	16,309	1	0	99	0	0	16	4.76	1,000		3.75		Sep-18
3.17	1.76	4.42	13.75	24.13	3.05	0.61	5.27	6.50	7.67	16,309	1	0	99	0	0	16	4.76	1,000		3.75		Jan-77
3.04	1.48	3.85	11.89	20.64	2.5	1.16	5.32	6.50	7.65	16,309	1	0	99	0	0	16	4.76	1,000			1.00	Apr-95
3.21	1.83	4.56	14.28	24.71	3.19	0.47	5.26	6.50	7.66	16,309	1	0	99	0	0	16	4.76	0				Aug-17
2.15	1.87	3.83	10.84	17.48	2.85	0.59	3.74	5.12	11.7	710.2	0	0	100	0	0	15	4.88	100,000				Jul-09
2.09	1.83	3.66	10.12	16.14	2.6	0.84	3.74	5.12	11.71	710.2	0	0	100	0	0	15	4.88	1,000		3.75		Sep-18
2.12	1.91	3.73	10.52	16.92	2.75	0.69	3.76	5.12	11.7	710.2	0	0	100	0	0	15	4.88	1,000		3.75		Sep-87
2.05	1.62	3.23	8.79	13.75	2.2	1.24	3.78	5.12	11.85	710.2	0	0	100	0	0	15	4.88	1,000			1.00	May-95
2.16	1.98	3.86	11.01	17.44	2.88	0.55	3.75	5.12	11.71	710.2	0	0	100	0	0	15	4.88	0				Aug-17
1.82	1.46	3.00	9.12	14.30	3.01	0.67	2.84	3.73	10.18	201.5	0	0	100	0	0	12	4.83	100,000				Jul-09
1.86	1.44	2.85	8.42	13.12	2.76	0.92	2.91	3.73	10.2	201.5	0	0	100	0	0	12	4.83	1,000		3.75		Sep-18
1.90	1.51	3.00	8.80	13.86	2.91	0.77	2.93	3.73	10.19	201.5	0	0	100	0	0	12	4.83	1,000		3.75		Oct-88
1.75	1.23	2.43	7.07	10.78	2.36	1.32	2.89	3.73	10.28	201.5	0	0	100	0	0	12	4.83	1,000			1.00	May-95
1.93	1.58	3.14	9.32	14.40	3.05	0.63	2.92	3.73	10.19	201.5	0	0	100	0	0	12	4.83	0				Aug-17
8.43	-8.23	-6.50	5.00	19.75	8.26	0.98	10.97	3.33	10.03	208.0	10	51	0	27	2	14	7.89	1,000,000				May-06
2.34	2.01	3.45	8.68	14.34	2.43	0.46	2.98	4.19	12.27	3,665	0	0	99	0	0	15	4.85	100,000				Dec-08
2.28	1.89	3.19	7.88	12.86	2.18	0.71	3.03	4.19	12.25	3,665	0	0	99	0	0	15	4.85	1,000		2.25		Sep-18
2.32	1.96	3.35	8.38	13.72	2.33	0.56	3.01	4.19	12.24	3,665	0	0	99	0	0	15	4.85	1,000		2.25		Sep-92
2.18	1.68	2.78	6.50	10.60	1.78	1.11	3.06	4.19	12.27	3,665	0	0	99	0	0	15	4.85	1,000			1.00	Jul-03
2.36	2.04	3.51	8.85	14.21	2.48	0.4	3	4.19	12.27	3,665	0	0	99	0	0	15	4.85	0				Aug-17
1.66	1.60	2.75	6.73	8.33	1.6	0.4	1.62	2.55	10.58	1,117	3	0	97	0	0	10	3.22	100,000				Feb-11
1.69	1.57	2.49	5.95	7.00	1.36	0.65	1.64	2.55	10.58	1,117	3	0	97	0	0	10	3.22	1,000		2.25		Sep-18
1.72	1.62	2.69	6.26	7.54	1.45	0.55	1.64	2.55	10.59	1,117	3	0	97	0	0	10	3.22	1,000		2.25		Sep-03
1.77	1.71	2.79	6.81	8.09	1.64	0.36	1.64	2.55	10.58	1,117	3	0	97	0	0	10	3.22	0				Aug-17
2.21	1.87	3.94	11.36	17.95	3.17	0.53	3.99	5.08	12.05	10,625	0	0	100	0	0	15	4.81	100,000				Mar-02

	MARKET			FUND TYPE, CATEGORY & OBJECTIVE	RATINGS				NEW INVESTORS	
Fund Name	Ticker Symbol	Traded On	Fund Type	Category and (Prospectus Objective)	Overall Rating	Reward Rating	Risk Rating	Recent Up/ Downgrade	Open to New Investors	Telephone
Franklin Federal Tax Free Income Fund Class A	FFQAX	NAS CM	Open End	US Muni Fixed Inc (Muni Bond - Natl)	C	C	B-		Y	650-312-2000
Franklin Federal Tax Free Income Fund Class A1	FKTIX	NAS CM	Open End	US Muni Fixed Inc (Muni Bond - Natl)	C	C	B-		Y	650-312-2000
Franklin Federal Tax Free Income Fund Class C	FRFTX	NAS CM	Open End	US Muni Fixed Inc (Muni Bond - Natl)	C	C-	B-		Y	650-312-2000
Franklin Federal Tax Free Income Fund Class R6	FFTQX	NAS CM	Open End	US Muni Fixed Inc (Muni Bond - Natl)	C	C	B		Y	650-312-2000
Franklin Floating Rate Daily Access Fund Advisor Class	FDAAX	NAS CM	Open End	US Fixed Inc (Corp Bond - General)	D	D	D+	Down	Y	650-312-2000
Franklin Floating Rate Daily Access Fund Class A	FAFRX	NAS CM	Open End	US Fixed Inc (Corp Bond - General)	D	D	D+	Down	Y	650-312-2000
Franklin Floating Rate Daily Access Fund Class C	FCFRX	NAS CM	Open End	US Fixed Inc (Corp Bond - General)	D	D	D		Y	650-312-2000
Franklin Floating Rate Daily Access Fund Class R6	FFRDX	NAS CM	Open End	US Fixed Inc (Corp Bond - General)	D	D	D+	Down	Y	650-312-2000
Franklin Florida Tax Free Income Fund Advisor Class	FFTZX	NAS CM	Open End	US Muni Fixed Inc (Muni Bond - Single State)	C	C-	B-		Y	650-312-2000
Franklin Florida Tax Free Income Fund Class A	FQFLX	NAS CM	Open End	US Muni Fixed Inc (Muni Bond - Single State)	C	C-	B-		Y	650-312-2000
Franklin Florida Tax Free Income Fund Class A1	FRFLX	NAS CM	Open End	US Muni Fixed Inc (Muni Bond - Single State)	C	C-	B-		Y	650-312-2000
Franklin Florida Tax Free Income Fund Class C	FRFIX	NAS CM	Open End	US Muni Fixed Inc (Muni Bond - Single State)	C	C-	C+		Y	650-312-2000
Franklin Florida Tax Free Income Fund Class R6	FRFQX	NAS CM	Open End	US Muni Fixed Inc (Muni Bond - Single State)	C	C-	B-		Y	650-312-2000
Franklin Georgia Tax Free Income Fund Advisor Class	FGFZX	NAS CM	Open End	US Muni Fixed Inc (Muni Bond - Single State)	C	C	B-		Y	650-312-2000
Franklin Georgia Tax Free Income Fund Class A	FGAQX	NAS CM	Open End	US Muni Fixed Inc (Muni Bond - Single State)	C	C-	B-		Y	650-312-2000
Franklin Georgia Tax Free Income Fund Class A1	FTGAX	NAS CM	Open End	US Muni Fixed Inc (Muni Bond - Single State)	C	C-	B-		Y	650-312-2000
Franklin Georgia Tax Free Income Fund Class C	FGAIX	NAS CM	Open End	US Muni Fixed Inc (Muni Bond - Single State)	C	C-	B-		Y	650-312-2000
Franklin Georgia Tax Free Income Fund Class R6	FGFQX	NAS CM	Open End	US Muni Fixed Inc (Muni Bond - Single State)	C	C	B-		Y	650-312-2000
Franklin High Income Fund Advisor Class	FVHIX	NAS CM	Open End	US Fixed Inc (Corp Bond - High Yield)	C-	D+	C		Y	650-312-2000
Franklin High Income Fund Class A	FHQRX	NAS CM	Open End	US Fixed Inc (Corp Bond - High Yield)	C-	D+	C		Y	650-312-2000
Franklin High Income Fund Class A1	FHAIX	NAS CM	Open End	US Fixed Inc (Corp Bond - High Yield)	C-	D+	C		Y	650-312-2000
Franklin High Income Fund Class C	FCHIX	NAS CM	Open End	US Fixed Inc (Corp Bond - High Yield)	C-	D+	C		Y	650-312-2000
Franklin High Income Fund Class R	FHIRX	NAS CM	Open End	US Fixed Inc (Corp Bond - High Yield)	C-	D+	C		Y	650-312-2000
Franklin High Income Fund Class R6	FHRRX	NAS CM	Open End	US Fixed Inc (Corp Bond - High Yield)	C-	D+	C		Y	650-312-2000
Franklin High Yield Tax Free Income Fund Advisor Class	FHYVX	NAS CM	Open End	US Muni Fixed Inc (Muni Bond - Natl)	C	C-	C+		Y	650-312-2000
Franklin High Yield Tax Free Income Fund Class A	FHYQX	NAS CM	Open End	US Muni Fixed Inc (Muni Bond - Natl)	C	C-	C+		Y	650-312-2000
Franklin High Yield Tax Free Income Fund Class A1	FRHIX	NAS CM	Open End	US Muni Fixed Inc (Muni Bond - Natl)	C	C-	C+		Y	650-312-2000
Franklin High Yield Tax Free Income Fund Class C	FHYIX	NAS CM	Open End	US Muni Fixed Inc (Muni Bond - Natl)	C-	D+	C	Down	Y	650-312-2000
Franklin High Yield Tax Free Income Fund Class R6	FHYRX	NAS CM	Open End	US Muni Fixed Inc (Muni Bond - Natl)	C	C-	C+		Y	650-312-2000
Franklin IFT Money Market Portfolio	INFXX	NAS CM	Money Mkt	US Money Mkt (Money Mkt - Govt)	C	C-	C+		Y	650-312-2000
Franklin Kentucky Tax Free Income Fund Advisor Class	FKTZX	NAS CM	Open End	US Muni Fixed Inc (Muni Bond - Single State)	C	C	B-		Y	650-312-2000
Franklin Kentucky Tax Free Income Fund Class A	FRKQX	NAS CM	Open End	US Muni Fixed Inc (Muni Bond - Single State)	C	C-	B-		Y	650-312-2000
Franklin Kentucky Tax Free Income Fund Class A1	FRKYX	NAS CM	Open End	US Muni Fixed Inc (Muni Bond - Single State)	C	C-	B-		Y	650-312-2000
Franklin Kentucky Tax Free Income Fund Class R6	FKTRX	NAS CM	Open End	US Muni Fixed Inc (Muni Bond - Single State)	C	C	B-		Y	650-312-2000
Franklin Limited Duration Income Trust	FTF	AMEX	Closed End	US Fixed Inc (Corp Bond - High Yield)	D	D	C-	Down	Y	954-527-7500
Franklin Louisiana Tax Free Income Fund Advisor Class	FLTZX	NAS CM	Open End	US Muni Fixed Inc (Muni Bond - Single State)	C	C	B-		Y	650-312-2000
Franklin Louisiana Tax Free Income Fund Class A	FQLAX	NAS CM	Open End	US Muni Fixed Inc (Muni Bond - Single State)	C	C	B-		Y	650-312-2000
Franklin Louisiana Tax Free Income Fund Class A1	FKLAX	NAS CM	Open End	US Muni Fixed Inc (Muni Bond - Single State)	C	C	B-		Y	650-312-2000
Franklin Louisiana Tax Free Income Fund Class C	FLAIX	NAS CM	Open End	US Muni Fixed Inc (Muni Bond - Single State)	C	C-	B-		Y	650-312-2000
Franklin Louisiana Tax Free Income Fund Class R6	FLAQX	NAS CM	Open End	US Muni Fixed Inc (Muni Bond - Single State)	C	C	B-		Y	650-312-2000
Franklin Low Duration Total Return Fund Advisor Class	FLDZX	NAS CM	Open End	US Fixed Inc (Income)	C-	D+	C		Y	650-312-2000
Franklin Low Duration Total Return Fund Class A	FLDAX	NAS CM	Open End	US Fixed Inc (Income)	C-	D+	C		Y	650-312-2000
Franklin Low Duration Total Return Fund Class C	FLDCX	NAS CM	Open End	US Fixed Inc (Income)	C-	D+	C		Y	650-312-2000
Franklin Low Duration Total Return Fund Class R	FLDRX	NAS CM	Open End	US Fixed Inc (Income)	C-	D+	C		Y	650-312-2000
Franklin Low Duration Total Return Fund Class R6	FLRRX	NAS CM	Open End	US Fixed Inc (Income)	C-	D+	C		Y	650-312-2000
Franklin Maryland Tax Free Income Fund Advisor Class	FMDZX	NAS CM	Open End	US Muni Fixed Inc (Muni Bond - Single State)	C	C-	B-		Y	650-312-2000
Franklin Maryland Tax Free Income Fund Class A	FQMDX	NAS CM	Open End	US Muni Fixed Inc (Muni Bond - Single State)	C	C-	B-		Y	650-312-2000
Franklin Maryland Tax Free Income Fund Class A1	FMDTX	NAS CM	Open End	US Muni Fixed Inc (Muni Bond - Single State)	C	C-	B-		Y	650-312-2000
Franklin Maryland Tax Free Income Fund Class C	FMDIX	NAS CM	Open End	US Muni Fixed Inc (Muni Bond - Single State)	C	C-	C+		Y	650-312-2000
Franklin Maryland Tax Free Income Fund Class R6	FMDQX	NAS CM	Open End	US Muni Fixed Inc (Muni Bond - Single State)	C	C-	B-		Y	650-312-2000
Franklin Massachusetts Tax-Free Income Fund Advisor Class	FMAHX	NAS CM	Open End	US Muni Fixed Inc (Muni Bond - Single State)	C+	C	B	Up	Y	650-312-2000
Franklin Massachusetts Tax-Free Income Fund Class A	FMAQX	NAS CM	Open End	US Muni Fixed Inc (Muni Bond - Single State)	C	C	B		Y	650-312-2000

★Expanded analysis of this fund is included in Section II.

TOTAL RETURNS & PERFORMANCE									ASSETS		ASSET ALLOCATION & TURNOVER							MINIMUMS		FEES		
3-Month Total Return	6-Month Total Return	1-Year Total Return	3-Year Total Return	5-Year Total Return	Dividend Yield (TTM)	Expense Ratio	3-Yr Std Deviation	Effective Duration	NAV	Total Assets (MIL)	%Cash	%Government Bonds	%Municipal Bonds	%Corporate Bonds	%Other	Turnover Ratio	Average Coupon Rate	Min Initial Investment	Min Additional Investment	Front End Fee (%)	Back End Fee (%)	Inception Date
2.15	1.66	3.69	10.36	16.32	2.92	0.78	4.01	5.08	12.03	10,625	0	0	100	0	0	15	4.81	1,000		3.75		Sep-18
2.18	1.74	3.84	10.95	17.30	3.07	0.63	4	5.08	12.03	10,625	0	0	100	0	0	15	4.81	1,000		3.75		Oct-83
2.13	1.55	3.28	9.13	14.16	2.52	1.18	3.97	5.08	12.03	10,625	0	0	100	0	0	15	4.81	1,000			1.00	Apr-95
2.22	1.81	3.98	11.37	17.74	3.21	0.49	3.99	5.08	12.04	10,625	0	0	100	0	0	15	4.81	1,000,000				Aug-17
3.10	-8.83	-8.37	-4.00	4.08	5.87	0.64	7.08	0.79	7.32	1,484	8	0	0	86	4	23		100,000				May-01
3.04	-9.07	-8.72	-4.84	2.77	5.59	0.89	7.13	0.79	7.31	1,484	8	0	0	86	4	23		1,000		2.25		May-01
2.80	-9.25	-9.09	-5.96	0.76	5.15	1.29	7.09	0.79	7.31	1,484	8	0	0	86	4	23		1,000			1.00	May-01
3.12	-8.77	-8.27	-3.61	4.78	5.97	0.56	7.09	0.79	7.33	1,484	8	0	0	86	4	23		1,000,000				May-13
1.20	0.98	2.60	9.29	15.23	3.39	0.6	3.03	3.86	10.58	536.4	0	0	100	0	0	9	4.84	100,000				Sep-16
1.23	0.95	2.34	8.40	13.86	3.14	0.85	3.03	3.86	10.57	536.4	0	0	100	0	0	9	4.84	1,000		3.75		Sep-18
1.27	1.03	2.50	8.89	14.72	3.29	0.7	3.03	3.86	10.56	536.4	0	0	100	0	0	9	4.84	1,000		3.75		Sep-87
1.03	0.67	1.96	7.09	11.57	2.75	1.25	3.01	3.86	10.79	536.4	0	0	100	0	0	9	4.84	1,000			1.00	May-95
1.30	1.10	2.73	9.37	15.22	3.43	0.56	3	3.86	10.59	536.4	0	0	100	0	0	9	4.84	0				Aug-17
1.98	1.65	3.51	10.22	15.88	2.91	0.62	3.7	4.79	11.92	464.2	0	0	100	0	0	13	4.71	100,000				Sep-16
1.92	1.44	3.17	9.32	14.49	2.66	0.87	3.67	4.79	11.91	464.2	0	0	100	0	0	13	4.71	1,000		3.75		Sep-18
1.96	1.52	3.32	9.81	15.36	2.81	0.72	3.67	4.79	11.91	464.2	0	0	100	0	0	13	4.71	1,000		3.75		Sep-87
1.71	1.23	2.74	7.99	12.22	2.26	1.27	3.68	4.79	12.09	464.2	0	0	100	0	0	13	4.71	1,000			1.00	May-95
1.91	1.59	3.46	10.22	15.79	2.95	0.57	3.72	4.79	11.91	464.2	0	0	100	0	0	13	4.71	0				Aug-17
8.83	-3.79	-0.55	8.68	19.30	5.87	0.61	8.21	3.77	1.74	2,757	3	0	0	97	0	25	6.25	100,000				Dec-96
8.83	-3.93	-0.80	7.96	17.97	5.63	0.86	8.25	3.77	1.73	2,757	3	0	0	97	0	25	6.25	1,000		3.75		Sep-18
8.79	-3.88	-0.72	8.21	18.47	5.69	0.76	8.1	3.77	1.74	2,757	3	0	0	97	0	25	6.25	1,000		3.75		Dec-69
9.16	-4.04	-0.67	7.04	15.92	5.07	1.26	8.46	3.77	1.77	2,757	3	0	0	97	0	25	6.25	1,000			1.00	May-95
9.14	-3.95	-0.51	7.49	16.66	5.2	1.11	8.4	3.77	1.78	2,757	3	0	0	97	0	25	6.25	1,000				Jan-02
8.87	-3.74	0.09	9.68	20.15	5.98	0.51	8.32	3.77	1.74	2,757	3	0	0	97	0	25	6.25	1,000,000				May-13
3.10	-0.14	1.94	10.65	19.75	4.14	0.56	4.96	6.11	10	6,108	0	0	100	0	0	12	5.40	100,000				Jan-06
2.94	-0.27	1.68	9.85	18.35	3.88	0.81	4.96	6.11	9.96	6,108	0	0	100	0	0	12	5.40	1,000		3.75		Sep-18
3.09	-0.10	1.93	10.36	19.25	4.04	0.66	5	6.11	9.96	6,108	0	0	100	0	0	12	5.40	1,000		3.75		Mar-86
2.89	-0.44	1.30	8.52	16.04	3.46	1.21	4.94	6.11	10.16	6,108	0	0	100	0	0	12	5.40	1,000			1.00	May-95
3.11	-0.02	2.08	10.86	19.79	4.18	0.52	4.95	6.11	10.01	6,108	0	0	100	0	0	12	5.40	0				Aug-17
0.00	0.26	1.09	4.00	4.16	1.27	0.35	0.17		1	14,250	100	0	0	0	0			100,000				Jul-85
0.96	1.08	2.72	9.76	14.80	2.82	0.71	3.12	4.35	10.95	144.9	0	0	100	0	0	14	4.67	100,000				Sep-16
0.90	1.04	2.55	9.14	13.63	2.57	0.96	3.08	4.35	10.96	144.9	0	0	100	0	0	14	4.67	1,000		3.75		Sep-18
0.93	1.12	2.71	9.54	14.39	2.72	0.81	3.09	4.35	10.95	144.9	0	0	100	0	0	14	4.67	1,000		3.75		Oct-91
0.88	1.10	2.75	9.95	14.81	2.86	0.67	3.1	4.35	10.95	144.9	0	0	100	0	0	14	4.67	0				Aug-17
7.75	-5.05	-3.06	0.55	8.22	5.68	0	8.06		9.02	271.2	-2	0	0	62	0	113	5.47					Aug-03
0.34	1.04	2.89	10.58	16.69	2.91	0.63	3.37	4.69	11.21	377.1	2	0	98	0	0	5	4.99	100,000				Sep-16
0.27	0.92	2.64	9.77	15.40	2.66	0.88	3.4	4.69	11.21	377.1	2	0	98	0	0	5	4.99	1,000		3.75		Sep-18
0.40	0.99	2.88	10.26	16.27	2.81	0.73	3.41	4.69	11.21	377.1	2	0	98	0	0	5	4.99	1,000		3.75		Sep-87
0.17	0.72	2.22	8.43	13.09	2.25	1.28	3.39	4.69	11.39	377.1	2	0	98	0	0	5	4.99	1,000			1.00	May-95
0.34	1.06	2.93	10.66	16.69	2.94	0.59	3.38	4.69	11.21	377.1	2	0	98	0	0	5	4.99	0				Aug-17
6.08	-0.66	0.55	5.29	8.50	3.5	0.46	4.71	1.81	9.49	3,058	-18	25	2	22	0	52	3.61	100,000				May-08
6.07	-0.76	0.32	4.45	7.24	3.27	0.71	4.73	1.81	9.44	3,058	-18	25	2	22	0	52	3.61	1,000		2.25		Nov-04
6.04	-0.92	-0.03	3.32	5.14	2.9	1.11	4.76	1.81	9.4	3,058	-18	25	2	22	0	52	3.61	1,000			1.00	Oct-12
5.92	-0.85	0.11	3.72	5.95		0.96	4.67	1.81	9.44	3,058	-18	25	2	22	0	52	3.61	1,000				Oct-19
6.09	-0.61	0.66	5.71	9.24	3.62	0.32	4.7	1.81	9.5	3,058	-18	25	2	22	0	52	3.61	1,000,000				May-13
0.90	0.52	2.30	9.61	15.89	2.88	0.63	3.57	4.15	11	410.4	0	0	100	0	0	8	4.68	100,000				Jul-09
0.83	0.39	1.95	8.90	14.48	2.63	0.88	3.5	4.15	10.98	410.4	0	0	100	0	0	8	4.68	1,000		3.75		Sep-18
0.96	0.47	2.20	9.39	15.34	2.78	0.73	3.51	4.15	10.99	410.4	0	0	100	0	0	8	4.68	1,000		3.75		Oct-88
0.81	0.20	1.64	7.56	12.25	2.22	1.28	3.47	4.15	11.22	410.4	0	0	100	0	0	8	4.68	1,000			1.00	May-95
0.91	0.54	2.25	9.71	15.67	2.92	0.58	3.5	4.15	11	410.4	0	0	100	0	0	8	4.68	0				Aug-17
1.76	1.92	3.90	11.17	19.31	2.76	0.61	3.94	5.09	11.91	439.1	-1	0	100	0	0	13	4.62	100,000				Jul-09
1.69	1.87	3.73	10.34	17.85	2.51	0.86	4	5.09	11.92	439.1	-1	0	100	0	0	13	4.62	1,000		3.75		Sep-18

Fund Name	Ticker Symbol	Traded On	Fund Type	Category and (Prospectus Objective)	Overall Rating	Reward Rating	Risk Rating	Recent Up/ Downgrade	Open to New Investors	Telephone
	MARKET			FUND TYPE, CATEGORY & OBJECTIVE	RATINGS				NEW INVESTORS	
Franklin Massachusetts Tax-Free Income Fund Class A1	FMISX	NAS CM	Open End	US Muni Fixed Inc (Muni Bond - Single State)	C	C	B		Y	650-312-2000
Franklin Massachusetts Tax-Free Income Fund Class C	FMAIX	NAS CM	Open End	US Muni Fixed Inc (Muni Bond - Single State)	C	C	B-		Y	650-312-2000
Franklin Massachusetts Tax-Free Income Fund Class R6	FKTMX	NAS CM	Open End	US Muni Fixed Inc (Muni Bond - Single State)	C+	C	B	Up	Y	650-312-2000
Franklin Michigan Tax-Free Income Fund Class A	FMQTX	NAS CM	Open End	US Muni Fixed Inc (Muni Bond - Single State)	C+	C	B	Up	Y	650-312-2000
Franklin Michigan Tax-Free Income Fund Class A1	FTTMX	NAS CM	Open End	US Muni Fixed Inc (Muni Bond - Single State)	C+	C	B	Up	Y	650-312-2000
Franklin Michigan Tax-Free Income Fund Class Adv	FMTFX	NAS CM	Open End	US Muni Fixed Inc (Muni Bond - Single State)	C+	C	B	Up	Y	650-312-2000
Franklin Michigan Tax-Free Income Fund Class C	FRMTX	NAS CM	Open End	US Muni Fixed Inc (Muni Bond - Single State)	C+	C	B	Up	Y	650-312-2000
Franklin Michigan Tax-Free Income Fund Class R6	FKTNX	NAS CM	Open End	US Muni Fixed Inc (Muni Bond - Single State)	C+	C	B		Y	650-312-2000
Franklin Minnesota Tax-Free Income Fund Advisor Class	FMNZX	NAS CM	Open End	US Muni Fixed Inc (Muni Bond - Single State)	C+	C	B	Up	Y	650-312-2000
Franklin Minnesota Tax-Free Income Fund Class A	FMNQX	NAS CM	Open End	US Muni Fixed Inc (Muni Bond - Single State)	C+	C	B	Up	Y	650-312-2000
Franklin Minnesota Tax-Free Income Fund Class A1	FMINX	NAS CM	Open End	US Muni Fixed Inc (Muni Bond - Single State)	C+	C	B	Up	Y	650-312-2000
Franklin Minnesota Tax-Free Income Fund Class C	FMNIX	NAS CM	Open End	US Muni Fixed Inc (Muni Bond - Single State)	C+	C	B	Up	Y	650-312-2000
Franklin Minnesota Tax-Free Income Fund Class R6	FKTDX	NAS CM	Open End	US Muni Fixed Inc (Muni Bond - Single State)	C+	C	B	Up	Y	650-312-2000
Franklin Missouri Tax Free Income Fund Advisor Class	FRMZX	NAS CM	Open End	US Muni Fixed Inc (Muni Bond - Single State)	C	C	B		Y	650-312-2000
Franklin Missouri Tax Free Income Fund Class A	FMQOX	NAS CM	Open End	US Muni Fixed Inc (Muni Bond - Single State)	C	C	B-		Y	650-312-2000
Franklin Missouri Tax Free Income Fund Class A1	FRMOX	NAS CM	Open End	US Muni Fixed Inc (Muni Bond - Single State)	C	C	B		Y	650-312-2000
Franklin Missouri Tax Free Income Fund Class C	FMOIX	NAS CM	Open End	US Muni Fixed Inc (Muni Bond - Single State)	C	C-	C+		Y	650-312-2000
Franklin Missouri Tax Free Income Fund Class R6	FMOQX	NAS CM	Open End	US Muni Fixed Inc (Muni Bond - Single State)	C	C	B		Y	650-312-2000
Franklin Municipal Green Bond Fund Advisor Class	FGBKX	NAS CM	Open End	US Muni Fixed Inc (Income)	U	U	U		Y	650-312-2000
Franklin New Jersey Tax Free Income Fund Advisor Class	FNJZX	NAS CM	Open End	US Muni Fixed Inc (Muni Bond - Single State)	C	C-	C+		Y	650-312-2000
Franklin New Jersey Tax Free Income Fund Class A	FNJQX	NAS CM	Open End	US Muni Fixed Inc (Muni Bond - Single State)	C	C-	C+		Y	650-312-2000
Franklin New Jersey Tax Free Income Fund Class A1	FRNJX	NAS CM	Open End	US Muni Fixed Inc (Muni Bond - Single State)	C	C-	C+		Y	650-312-2000
Franklin New Jersey Tax Free Income Fund Class C	FNIIX	NAS CM	Open End	US Muni Fixed Inc (Muni Bond - Single State)	C	C-	C		Y	650-312-2000
Franklin New Jersey Tax Free Income Fund Class R6	FNJRX	NAS CM	Open End	US Muni Fixed Inc (Muni Bond - Single State)	C	C-	C+		Y	650-312-2000
Franklin New York Intermediate Tax-Free Income Advisor Cl	FNYZX	NAS CM	Open End	US Muni Fixed Inc (Muni Bond - Natl)	C	C-	C+		Y	650-312-2000
Franklin New York Intermediate Tax-Free Income Cl A	FKNQX	NAS CM	Open End	US Muni Fixed Inc (Muni Bond - Natl)	C	C-	C+		Y	650-312-2000
Franklin New York Intermediate Tax-Free Income Cl A1	FKNIX	NAS CM	Open End	US Muni Fixed Inc (Muni Bond - Natl)	C	C-	C+		Y	650-312-2000
Franklin New York Intermediate Tax-Free Income Cl C	FKNCX	NAS CM	Open End	US Muni Fixed Inc (Muni Bond - Natl)	C	C-	C+		Y	650-312-2000
Franklin New York Intermediate Tax-Free Income Cl R6	FKNRX	NAS CM	Open End	US Muni Fixed Inc (Muni Bond - Natl)	C	C-	C+		Y	650-312-2000
Franklin New York Tax Free Income Fund Advisor Class	FNYAX	NAS CM	Open End	US Muni Fixed Inc (Muni Bond - Single State)	C	C-	B-		Y	650-312-2000
Franklin New York Tax Free Income Fund Class A	FNYQX	NAS CM	Open End	US Muni Fixed Inc (Muni Bond - Single State)	C	C-	B-		Y	650-312-2000
Franklin New York Tax Free Income Fund Class A1	FNYTX	NAS CM	Open End	US Muni Fixed Inc (Muni Bond - Single State)	C	C-	B-		Y	650-312-2000
Franklin New York Tax Free Income Fund Class C	FNYIX	NAS CM	Open End	US Muni Fixed Inc (Muni Bond - Single State)	C	C-	B-		Y	650-312-2000
Franklin New York Tax Free Income Fund Class R6	FKTJX	NAS CM	Open End	US Muni Fixed Inc (Muni Bond - Single State)	C	C-	B-		Y	650-312-2000
Franklin North Carolina Tax-Free Income Fund Advisor Class	FNCZX	NAS CM	Open End	US Muni Fixed Inc (Muni Bond - Single State)	C	C	B-		Y	650-312-2000
Franklin North Carolina Tax-Free Income Fund Class A	FQNCX	NAS CM	Open End	US Muni Fixed Inc (Muni Bond - Single State)	C	C	B-		Y	650-312-2000
Franklin North Carolina Tax-Free Income Fund Class A1	FXNCX	NAS CM	Open End	US Muni Fixed Inc (Muni Bond - Single State)	C	C	B-		Y	650-312-2000
Franklin North Carolina Tax-Free Income Fund Class C	FNCIX	NAS CM	Open End	US Muni Fixed Inc (Muni Bond - Single State)	C	C	C+		Y	650-312-2000
Franklin North Carolina Tax-Free Income Fund Class R6	FNCQX	NAS CM	Open End	US Muni Fixed Inc (Muni Bond - Single State)	C	C	B-		Y	650-312-2000
Franklin Ohio Tax-Free Income Fund Class A	FOHQX	NAS CM	Open End	US Muni Fixed Inc (Muni Bond - Single State)	C+	C	B	Up	Y	650-312-2000
Franklin Ohio Tax-Free Income Fund Class A1	FTOIX	NAS CM	Open End	US Muni Fixed Inc (Muni Bond - Single State)	C+	C	B	Up	Y	650-312-2000
Franklin Ohio Tax-Free Income Fund Class Adv	FROZX	NAS CM	Open End	US Muni Fixed Inc (Muni Bond - Single State)	B-	C	B	Up	Y	650-312-2000
Franklin Ohio Tax-Free Income Fund Class C	FOITX	NAS CM	Open End	US Muni Fixed Inc (Muni Bond - Single State)	C+	C	B	Up	Y	650-312-2000
Franklin Ohio Tax-Free Income Fund Class R6	FKTOX	NAS CM	Open End	US Muni Fixed Inc (Muni Bond - Single State)	B-	C	B	Up	Y	650-312-2000
Franklin Oregon Tax Free Income Fund Advisor Class	FOFZX	NAS CM	Open End	US Muni Fixed Inc (Muni Bond - Single State)	C+	C	B	Up	Y	650-312-2000
Franklin Oregon Tax Free Income Fund Class A	FOFQX	NAS CM	Open End	US Muni Fixed Inc (Muni Bond - Single State)	C	C	B		Y	650-312-2000
Franklin Oregon Tax Free Income Fund Class A1	FRORX	NAS CM	Open End	US Muni Fixed Inc (Muni Bond - Single State)	C+	C	B	Up	Y	650-312-2000
Franklin Oregon Tax Free Income Fund Class C	FORIX	NAS CM	Open End	US Muni Fixed Inc (Muni Bond - Single State)	C	C	B-		Y	650-312-2000
Franklin Oregon Tax Free Income Fund Class R6	FOFRX	NAS CM	Open End	US Muni Fixed Inc (Muni Bond - Single State)	C+	C	B	Up	Y	650-312-2000
Franklin Pennsylvania Tax-Free Income Fund Advisor Class	FPFZX	NAS CM	Open End	US Muni Fixed Inc (Muni Bond - Single State)	C	C	B-		Y	650-312-2000
Franklin Pennsylvania Tax-Free Income Fund Class A	FPAQX	NAS CM	Open End	US Muni Fixed Inc (Muni Bond - Single State)	C	C-	B-		Y	650-312-2000
Franklin Pennsylvania Tax-Free Income Fund Class A1	FRPAX	NAS CM	Open End	US Muni Fixed Inc (Muni Bond - Single State)	C	C-	B-		Y	650-312-2000

★ Expanded analysis of this fund is included in Section II.

TOTAL RETURNS & PERFORMANCE									ASSETS		ASSET ALLOCATION & TURNOVER							MINIMUMS		FEES		
3-Month Total Return	6-Month Total Return	1-Year Total Return	3-Year Total Return	5-Year Total Return	Dividend Yield (TTM)	Expense Ratio	3-Yr Std Deviation	Effective Duration	NAV	Total Assets (MIL)	%Cash	%Government Bonds	%Municipal Bonds	%Corporate Bonds	%Other	Turnover Ratio	Average Coupon Rate	Min Initial Investment	Min Additional Investment	Front End Fee (%)	Back End Fee (%)	Inception Date
1.73	1.95	3.80	10.85	18.74	2.67	0.71	4.01	5.09	11.91	439.1	-1	0	100	0	0	13	4.62	1,000		3.75		Apr-85
1.58	1.66	3.30	9.02	15.51	2.12	1.26	3.94	5.09	12.06	439.1	-1	0	100	0	0	13	4.62	1,000			1.00	May-95
1.77	2.02	4.03	11.34	19.27	2.8	0.57	3.99	5.09	11.92	439.1	-1	0	100	0	0	13	4.62	0				Aug-17
1.95	2.49	4.67	12.50	17.81	2.44	0.83	3.49	4.69	11.87	947.0	1	0	99	0	0	4	4.80	1,000		3.75		Sep-18
2.08	2.65	4.83	12.91	18.60	2.59	0.68	3.5	4.69	11.86	947.0	1	0	99	0	0	4	4.80	1,000		3.75		Apr-85
2.10	2.70	4.92	13.21	19.22	2.69	0.58	3.47	4.69	11.9	947.0	1	0	99	0	0	4	4.80	100,000				Jul-08
1.91	2.34	4.21	10.99	15.32	2.04	1.23	3.5	4.69	12.05	947.0	1	0	99	0	0	4	4.80	1,000			1.00	May-95
2.11	2.71	4.96	13.39	19.10	2.72	0.54	3.48	4.69	11.91	947.0	1	0	99	0	0	4	4.80	0				Aug-17
2.10	2.71	4.73	11.73	17.70	2.5	0.58	3.73	5.30	12.69	1,035	-1	0	100	0	0	16	4.23	100,000				Jul-09
2.12	2.58	4.47	11.01	16.36	2.25	0.83	3.74	5.30	12.68	1,035	-1	0	100	0	0	16	4.23	1,000		3.75		Sep-18
2.15	2.66	4.63	11.42	17.14	2.4	0.68	3.76	5.30	12.68	1,035	-1	0	100	0	0	16	4.23	1,000		3.75		Apr-85
1.99	2.36	4.03	9.57	13.88	1.86	1.23	3.79	5.30	12.82	1,035	-1	0	100	0	0	16	4.23	1,000			1.00	May-95
2.19	2.73	4.78	11.86	17.61	2.55	0.53	3.74	5.30	12.7	1,035	-1	0	100	0	0	16	4.23	0				Aug-17
1.86	1.85	3.64	11.03	17.14	2.77	0.59	3.57	4.58	11.85	998.8	0	0	99	0	0	15	4.79	100,000				Jul-09
1.80	1.73	3.38	10.32	15.80	2.53	0.84	3.58	4.58	11.85	998.8	0	0	99	0	0	15	4.79	1,000		3.75		Sep-18
1.84	1.81	3.54	10.72	16.58	2.68	0.69	3.62	4.58	11.84	998.8	0	0	99	0	0	15	4.79	1,000		3.75		Sep-87
1.68	1.52	3.05	8.91	13.45	2.12	1.24	3.59	4.58	11.97	998.8	0	0	99	0	0	15	4.79	1,000			1.00	May-95
1.87	1.78	3.67	11.13	17.00	2.81	0.54	3.59	4.58	11.85	998.8	0	0	99	0	0	15	4.79	0				Aug-17
2.85	3.09					0.46			10.25	5.1	7	0	93	0	0		4.20	100,000				Oct-19
1.15	-0.12	1.83	9.84	16.14	2.87	0.58	4.2	5.15	11.28	848.8	-1	0	100	0	0	18	4.80	100,000				Jul-08
1.00	-0.33	1.57	8.93	14.63	2.61	0.83	4.15	5.15	11.28	848.8	-1	0	100	0	0	18	4.80	1,000		3.75		Sep-18
1.12	-0.17	1.73	9.52	15.60	2.77	0.68	4.21	5.15	11.27	848.8	-1	0	100	0	0	18	4.80	1,000		3.75		May-88
0.97	-0.51	1.09	7.64	12.39	2.21	1.23	4.19	5.15	11.42	848.8	-1	0	100	0	0	18	4.80	1,000			1.00	May-95
1.16	-0.10	1.87	9.94	16.03	2.91	0.54	4.2	5.15	11.28	848.8	-1	0	100	0	0	18	4.80	0				Aug-17
0.77	0.86	2.47	8.52	14.21	2.48	0.59	3.9	4.98	11.67	915.7	0	0	100	0	0	16	4.66	100,000				Dec-08
0.72	0.74	2.22	7.74	12.86	2.23	0.84	3.89	4.98	11.63	915.7	0	0	100	0	0	16	4.66	1,000		2.25		Sep-18
0.67	0.81	2.29	8.13	13.61	2.38	0.69	3.87	4.98	11.63	915.7	0	0	100	0	0	16	4.66	1,000		2.25		Sep-92
0.61	0.54	1.82	6.43	10.58	1.83	1.24	3.86	4.98	11.68	915.7	0	0	100	0	0	16	4.66	1,000			1.00	Jul-03
0.79	0.89	2.53	8.57	14.06	2.54	0.53	3.87	4.98	11.67	915.7	0	0	100	0	0	16	4.66	1,000,000				Aug-17
2.08	1.49	3.58	10.50	15.27	2.84	0.53	4.4	5.25	11.19	3,785	0	0	100	0	0	20	4.85	100,000				Oct-01
1.93	1.37	3.23	9.70	13.88	2.59	0.78	4.4	5.25	11.17	3,785	0	0	100	0	0	20	4.85	1,000		3.75		Sep-18
2.06	1.44	3.48	10.19	14.74	2.74	0.63	4.36	5.25	11.18	3,785	0	0	100	0	0	20	4.85	1,000		3.75		Sep-82
1.92	1.16	2.92	8.38	11.65	2.19	1.18	4.36	5.25	11.17	3,785	0	0	100	0	0	20	4.85	1,000			1.00	May-95
2.09	1.51	3.62	10.68	15.24	2.87	0.5	4.37	5.25	11.2	3,785	0	0	100	0	0	20	4.85	1,000,000				Aug-17
2.03	2.15	3.72	10.22	15.53	2.64	0.58	3.18	4.49	11.68	846.4	0	0	100	0	0	15	4.54	100,000				Jul-09
2.05	2.11	3.56	9.40	14.10	2.4	0.83	3.21	4.49	11.69	846.4	0	0	100	0	0	15	4.54	1,000		3.75		Sep-18
2.00	2.10	3.71	9.90	14.97	2.55	0.68	3.21	4.49	11.68	846.4	0	0	100	0	0	15	4.54	1,000		3.75		Sep-87
1.92	1.89	3.12	8.15	11.84	2	1.23	3.26	4.49	11.88	846.4	0	0	100	0	0	15	4.54	1,000			1.00	May-95
2.04	2.26	3.85	10.30	15.39	2.68	0.54	3.26	4.49	11.68	846.4	0	0	100	0	0	15	4.54	0				Aug-17
1.94	2.67	4.61	12.07	19.40	2.58	0.8	3.24	4.61	13.06	1,593	0	0	100	0	0	5	4.78	1,000		3.75		Sep-18
2.06	2.75	4.85	12.58	20.30	2.73	0.65	3.25	4.61	13.06	1,593	0	0	100	0	0	5	4.78	1,000		3.75		Apr-85
2.00	2.80	4.95	12.89	20.86	2.83	0.55	3.26	4.61	13.07	1,593	0	0	100	0	0	5	4.78	100,000				Jul-08
1.89	2.44	4.25	10.68	16.97	2.19	1.2	3.21	4.61	13.24	1,593	0	0	100	0	0	5	4.78	1,000			1.00	May-95
2.01	2.82	4.91	12.99	20.74	2.87	0.51	3.25	4.61	13.07	1,593	0	0	100	0	0	5	4.78	0				Aug-17
2.02	2.43	4.49	11.29	18.60	2.71	0.55	3.62	4.98	11.81	1,276	-1	0	100	0	0	15	4.71	100,000				Jul-09
2.04	2.30	4.23	10.57	17.16	2.46	0.8	3.62	4.98	11.81	1,276	-1	0	100	0	0	15	4.71	1,000		3.75		Sep-18
2.08	2.38	4.38	11.07	18.05	2.61	0.65	3.61	4.98	11.8	1,276	-1	0	100	0	0	15	4.71	1,000		3.75		Sep-87
1.92	2.08	3.87	9.21	14.80	2.06	1.2	3.62	4.98	11.99	1,276	-1	0	100	0	0	15	4.71	1,000			1.00	May-95
2.11	2.45	4.52	11.46	18.46	2.74	0.52	3.63	4.98	11.81	1,276	-1	0	100	0	0	15	4.71	0				Aug-17
1.34	1.39	3.00	9.56	16.17	3.12	0.58	2.97	3.80	9.91	1,081	-2	0	100	0	0	14	4.63	100,000				Jul-09
1.28	1.38	2.86	8.76	14.77	2.88	0.83	2.96	3.80	9.9	1,081	-2	0	100	0	0	14	4.63	1,000		3.75		Sep-18
1.42	1.45	3.00	9.24	15.63	3.02	0.68	2.95	3.80	9.9	1,081	-2	0	100	0	0	14	4.63	1,000		3.75		Dec-86

	MARKET			FUND TYPE, CATEGORY & OBJECTIVE	RATINGS				NEW INVESTORS	
Fund Name	Ticker Symbol	Traded On	Fund Type	Category and (Prospectus Objective)	Overall Rating	Reward Rating	Risk Rating	Recent Up/ Downgrade	Open to New Investors	Telephone
Franklin Pennsylvania Tax-Free Income Fund Class C	FRPTX	NAS CM	Open End	US Muni Fixed Inc (Muni Bond - Single State)	C	C-	C+		Y	650-312-2000
Franklin Pennsylvania Tax-Free Income Fund Class R6	FRPRX	NAS CM	Open End	US Muni Fixed Inc (Muni Bond - Single State)	C	C	B-		Y	650-312-2000
Franklin Strategic Income Fund Advisor Class	FKSAX	NAS CM	Open End	US Fixed Inc (Multisector Bond)	C-	D+	C		Y	650-312-2000
Franklin Strategic Income Fund Class A	FRSTX	NAS CM	Open End	US Fixed Inc (Multisector Bond)	D+	D+	C	Down	Y	650-312-2000
Franklin Strategic Income Fund Class C	FSGCX	NAS CM	Open End	US Fixed Inc (Multisector Bond)	D+	D	C-	Down	Y	650-312-2000
Franklin Strategic Income Fund Class R	FKSRX	NAS CM	Open End	US Fixed Inc (Multisector Bond)	D+	D	C-	Down	Y	650-312-2000
Franklin Strategic Income Fund Class R6	FGKNX	NAS CM	Open End	US Fixed Inc (Multisector Bond)	C-	D+	C		Y	650-312-2000
Franklin Strategic Mortgage Fund Class A	FSMFX	NAS CM	Open End	US Fixed Inc (Govt Bond - Mortgage)	C+	C	B	Up	Y	650-312-2000
Franklin Strategic Mortgage Fund Class A1	FSMIX	NAS CM	Open End	US Fixed Inc (Govt Bond - Mortgage)	C+	C	B	Up		650-312-2000
Franklin Strategic Mortgage Portfolio Advisor Class	FSMZX	NAS CM	Open End	US Fixed Inc (Govt Bond - Mortgage)	C+	C	B	Up	Y	650-312-2000
Franklin Strategic Mortgage Portfolio Class C	FSMHX	NAS CM	Open End	US Fixed Inc (Govt Bond - Mortgage)	C+	C	B-	Up	Y	650-312-2000
Franklin Strategic Mortgage Portfolio Class R6	FSMQX	NAS CM	Open End	US Fixed Inc (Govt Bond - Mortgage)	C+	C	B	Up	Y	650-312-2000
Franklin Templeton SMACS: Series CH Advisor Class	FQCHX	NAS CM	Open End	US Muni Fixed Inc (Muni Bond - Natl)	D-	D	D+		Y	650-312-2000
Franklin Templeton SMACS: Series H Advisor Class	FQTHX	NAS CM	Open End	US Muni Fixed Inc (Muni Bond - Natl)	D-	D	D		Y	650-312-2000
Franklin Templeton SMACS: Series I Advisor Class	FQTIX	NAS CM	Open End	US Fixed Inc (Income)	D-	D	D		Y	650-312-2000
Franklin Tennessee Municipal Bond Fund Advisor Class	FTMZX	NAS CM	Open End	US Muni Fixed Inc (Muni Bond - Single State)	C	C-	B-		Y	650-312-2000
Franklin Tennessee Municipal Bond Fund Class A	FTQMX	NAS CM	Open End	US Muni Fixed Inc (Muni Bond - Single State)	C	C-	B-		Y	650-312-2000
Franklin Tennessee Municipal Bond Fund Class A1	FRTIX	NAS CM	Open End	US Muni Fixed Inc (Muni Bond - Single State)	C	C-	B-		Y	650-312-2000
Franklin Tennessee Municipal Bond Fund Class R6	FTMQX	NAS CM	Open End	US Muni Fixed Inc (Muni Bond - Single State)	C	C	B-		Y	650-312-2000
Franklin Total Return Fund Advisor Class	FBDAX	NAS CM	Open End	US Fixed Inc (Income)	C	C	B-		Y	650-312-2000
Franklin Total Return Fund Class A	FKBAX	NAS CM	Open End	US Fixed Inc (Income)	C	C	B-		Y	650-312-2000
Franklin Total Return Fund Class C	FCTLX	NAS CM	Open End	US Fixed Inc (Income)	C	C	C+		Y	650-312-2000
Franklin Total Return Fund Class R	FTRRX	NAS CM	Open End	US Fixed Inc (Income)	C	C	B-		Y	650-312-2000
Franklin Total Return Fund Class R6	FRERX	NAS CM	Open End	US Fixed Inc (Income)	C	C	B-		Y	650-312-2000
Franklin U.S. Government Money Fund Class A	FMFXX	NAS CM	Money Mkt	US Money Mkt (Money Mkt - Govt)	C	C-	C+		Y	650-312-2000
Franklin U.S. Government Money Fund Class C	FTQXX	NAS CM	Money Mkt	US Money Mkt (Money Mkt - Govt)	C	C-	C		Y	650-312-2000
Franklin U.S. Government Money Fund Class R	FRQXX	NAS CM	Money Mkt	US Money Mkt (Money Mkt - Govt)	C	C-	C		Y	650-312-2000
Franklin U.S. Government Money Fund Class R6			Money Mkt	US Money Mkt (Money Mkt - Govt)	C	C-	C+		Y	650-312-2000
Franklin U.S. Government Securities Fund Advisor Class	FUSAX	NAS CM	Open End	US Fixed Inc (Govt Bond - Mortgage)	C+	C+	B-		Y	650-312-2000
Franklin U.S. Government Securities Fund Class A	FKFSX	NAS CM	Open End	US Fixed Inc (Govt Bond - Mortgage)	C+	C	B-	Up	Y	650-312-2000
Franklin U.S. Government Securities Fund Class A1	FKUSX	NAS CM	Open End	US Fixed Inc (Govt Bond - Mortgage)	C+	C	B		Y	650-312-2000
Franklin U.S. Government Securities Fund Class C	FRUGX	NAS CM	Open End	US Fixed Inc (Govt Bond - Mortgage)	C+	C	B-	Up	Y	650-312-2000
Franklin U.S. Government Securities Fund Class R	FUSRX	NAS CM	Open End	US Fixed Inc (Govt Bond - Mortgage)	C+	C	B-	Up	Y	650-312-2000
Franklin U.S. Government Securities Fund Class R6	FGORX	NAS CM	Open End	US Fixed Inc (Govt Bond - Mortgage)	C+	C+	B-		Y	650-312-2000
Franklin Virginia Tax Free Income Fund Advisor Class	FRVZX	NAS CM	Open End	US Muni Fixed Inc (Muni Bond - Single State)	C	C	B-		Y	650-312-2000
Franklin Virginia Tax Free Income Fund Class A	FVAQX	NAS CM	Open End	US Muni Fixed Inc (Muni Bond - Single State)	C	C-	B-		Y	650-312-2000
Franklin Virginia Tax Free Income Fund Class A1	FRVAX	NAS CM	Open End	US Muni Fixed Inc (Muni Bond - Single State)	C	C	B-		Y	650-312-2000
Franklin Virginia Tax Free Income Fund Class C	FVAIX	NAS CM	Open End	US Muni Fixed Inc (Muni Bond - Single State)	C	C-	C+		Y	650-312-2000
Franklin Virginia Tax Free Income Fund Class R6	FRVRX	NAS CM	Open End	US Muni Fixed Inc (Muni Bond - Single State)	C	C	B-		Y	650-312-2000
Frost Credit Fund A Class Shares	FCFBX	NAS CM	Open End	US Fixed Inc (Growth & Income)	D+	D	C	Down	Y	
Frost Credit Fund Institutional Class	FCFIX	NAS CM	Open End	US Fixed Inc (Growth & Income)	C-	D+	C	Down	Y	
Frost Credit Fund Investor Class	FCFAX	NAS CM	Open End	US Fixed Inc (Growth & Income)	D+	D	C	Down	Y	
Frost Low Duration Bond Fund Class Institutional	FILDX	NAS CM	Open End	US Fixed Inc (Growth & Income)	C	C	B-		Y	
Frost Low Duration Bond Fund Investor Class Shares	FADLX	NAS CM	Open End	US Fixed Inc (Growth & Income)	C	C	C+		Y	
Frost Municipal Bond Fund Class Institutional	FIMUX	NAS CM	Open End	US Muni Fixed Inc (Muni Bond - Natl)	C	C	B-		Y	
Frost Municipal Bond Fund Investor Class Shares	FAUMX	NAS CM	Open End	US Muni Fixed Inc (Muni Bond - Natl)	C	C	B-		Y	
Frost Total Return Bond Fund A Class Shares	FAJEX	NAS CM	Open End	US Fixed Inc (Growth & Income)	C-	D+	C	Down	Y	
Frost Total Return Bond Fund Class Institutional	FIJEX	NAS CM	Open End	US Fixed Inc (Growth & Income)	C-	D+	C	Down	Y	
Frost Total Return Bond Fund Investor Class	FATRX	NAS CM	Open End	US Fixed Inc (Growth & Income)	C-	D+	C	Down	Y	
FS Credit Income Fund Class A Share	FCREX	NAS CM	Closed End	Fixed Inc Misc (Growth & Income)	D	D	D	Down	Y	877-628-8575
FS Credit Income Fund Class I Share	FCRIX	NAS CM	Closed End	Fixed Inc Misc (Growth & Income)	D	D	D+	Down	Y	877-628-8575
FS Credit Income Fund T			Closed End	Fixed Inc Misc (Growth & Income)	D	D	D	Down	Y	877-628-8575

★ Expanded analysis of this fund is included in Section II.

TOTAL RETURNS & PERFORMANCE									ASSETS		ASSET ALLOCATION & TURNOVER							MINIMUMS		FEES		
3-Month Total Return	6-Month Total Return	1-Year Total Return	3-Year Total Return	5-Year Total Return	Dividend Yield (TTM)	Expense Ratio	3-Yr Std Deviation	Effective Duration	NAV	Total Assets (MIL)	%Cash	%Government Bonds	%Municipal Bonds	%Corporate Bonds	%Other	Turnover Ratio	Average Coupon Rate	Min Initial Investment	Min Additional Investment	Front End Fee (%)	Back End Fee (%)	Inception Date
1.17	1.16	2.33	7.47	12.43	2.46	1.23	2.96	3.80	10.03	1,081	-2	0	100	0	0	14	4.63	1,000			1.00	May-95
1.35	1.41	3.04	9.65	16.06	3.16	0.54	2.95	3.80	9.91	1,081	-2	0	100	0	0	14	4.63	0				Aug-17
7.45	-2.87	-1.55	5.24	12.12	4.85	0.64	6.95	4.97	9.12	4,022	-21	23	2	27	3	116	4.33	100,000				Aug-99
7.39	-2.89	-1.81	4.46	10.74	4.59	0.89	6.95	4.97	9.11	4,022	-21	23	2	27	3	116	4.33	1,000		3.75		May-94
7.28	-3.09	-2.21	3.18	8.62	4.16	1.29	6.94	4.97	9.11	4,022	-21	23	2	27	3	116	4.33	1,000			1.00	May-98
7.36	-3.13	-2.06	3.68	9.40	4.35	1.14	6.96	4.97	9.07	4,022	-21	23	2	27	3	116	4.33	1,000				Jan-02
7.48	-2.82	-1.44	5.67	12.90	4.96	0.51	7.01	4.97	9.12	4,022	-21	23	2	27	3	116	4.33	1,000,000				May-13
1.64	2.53	3.95	9.15	13.80	2.77	1.01	2.36	2.15	9.31	63.6	3	7	0	0	0	223	3.63	1,000		3.75		Feb-12
1.69	2.54	4.09	9.85	15.22	3.01	0.76	2.4	2.15	9.31	63.6	3	7	0	0	0	223	3.63	1,000		3.75		Feb-93
1.69	2.54	4.20	9.86	15.22	3.01	0.76	2.33	2.15	9.3	63.6	3	7	0	0	0	223	3.63	100,000				Feb-12
1.54	2.22	3.54	7.75	11.57	2.37	1.41	2.38	2.15	9.31	63.6	3	7	0	0	0	223	3.63	1,000			1.00	Feb-12
1.84	2.72	4.34	10.28	15.66	3.15	0.63	2.42	2.15	9.3	63.6	3	7	0	0	0	223	3.63	1,000,000				Aug-17
2.34	-3.13	0.22				0			9.61	2.9	3	0	97	0	0		4.53	0				Jun-19
3.15	-3.41	-1.98				0			9.53	2.8	3	0	97	0	0		4.53	0				Jun-19
5.76	-10.47	-9.77				0		3.08	8.53	3.3	6	0	0	86	0		6.42	0				Jun-19
1.43	1.47	3.15	9.46	15.16	2.86	0.68	3.28	4.30	11.01	199.9	0	0	100	0	0	3	4.75	100,000				Sep-16
1.37	1.35	2.89	8.54	13.77	2.61	0.93	3.3	4.30	11.01	199.9	0	0	100	0	0	3	4.75	1,000		3.75		Sep-18
1.41	1.42	3.04	9.04	14.64	2.76	0.78	3.28	4.30	11	199.9	0	0	100	0	0	3	4.75	1,000		3.75		May-94
1.35	1.49	3.18	9.43	15.05	2.89	0.65	3.32	4.30	11	199.9	0	0	100	0	0	3	4.75	1,000,000				Aug-17
7.27	2.93	4.96	12.13	17.60	3.67	0.63	5.42	6.77	10.05	5,091	-40	27	3	27	0	170	3.75	100,000				Aug-98
7.26	2.83	4.73	11.32	16.14	3.42	0.88	5.49	6.77	9.99	5,091	-40	27	3	27	0	170	3.75	1,000		3.75		Aug-98
7.11	2.55	4.25	9.98	13.79	3.04	1.28	5.5	6.77	9.91	5,091	-40	27	3	27	0	170	3.75	1,000			1.00	Mar-02
7.23	2.71	4.49	10.51	14.80	3.18	1.13	5.5	6.77	9.95	5,091	-40	27	3	27	0	170	3.75	1,000				Jan-02
7.29	2.99	5.08	12.49	18.33	3.78	0.51	5.45	6.77	10.06	5,091	-40	27	3	27	0	170	3.75	1,000,000				May-13
0.00	0.20	0.94	3.40	3.46	1.09	0.55	0.17		1	4,002	100	0	0	0	0	0		1,000				Apr-76
0.00	0.07	0.49	1.61	0.37		1.2			1	4,002	100	0	0	0	0	0		1,000			1.00	Oct-19
0.00	0.09	0.59	2.01	1.06		1.05			1	4,002	100	0	0	0	0	0		1,000				Oct-19
0.00	0.22	1.00	3.63	3.74	1.16	0.48	0.17		1	4,002	100	0	0	0	0	0		1,000,000				May-13
0.37	3.29	4.67	9.96	12.06	2.9	0.64	2.13	1.38	6.16	4,905	2	0	0	0	0	41	3.90	100,000				Dec-96
0.48	3.19	4.63	9.05	10.59	2.69	0.89	2.13	1.38	6.14	4,905	2	0	0	0	0	41	3.90	1,000		3.75		Sep-18
0.34	3.23	4.53	9.50	11.27	2.77	0.79	2.13	1.38	6.14	4,905	2	0	0	0	0	41	3.90	1,000		3.75		May-70
0.38	3.00	4.22	7.93	8.59	2.3	1.29	2.1	1.38	6.1	4,905	2	0	0	0	0	41	3.90	1,000			1.00	May-95
0.41	3.05	4.34	8.37	9.35	2.43	1.14	2.14	1.38	6.14	4,905	2	0	0	0	0	41	3.90	1,000				Jan-02
0.56	3.34	4.96	10.53	12.95	3.02	0.51	2.1	1.38	6.17	4,905	2	0	0	0	0	41	3.90	0				May-13
2.04	1.60	3.45	9.31	16.05	2.64	0.59	3.23	4.36	11.21	611.5	1	0	99	0	0	14	4.43	100,000				Jul-09
1.89	1.38	3.19	8.50	14.53	2.39	0.84	3.19	4.36	11.2	611.5	1	0	99	0	0	14	4.43	1,000		3.75		Sep-18
2.02	1.55	3.35	8.99	15.40	2.54	0.69	3.24	4.36	11.2	611.5	1	0	99	0	0	14	4.43	1,000		3.75		Sep-87
1.85	1.26	2.76	7.28	12.34	1.99	1.24	3.21	4.36	11.4	611.5	1	0	99	0	0	14	4.43	1,000			1.00	May-95
2.05	1.62	3.49	9.40	15.83	2.68	0.55	3.25	4.36	11.21	611.5	1	0	99	0	0	14	4.43	0				Aug-17
8.67	-1.76	0.19	8.64	20.78	4.39	1.11	6.8		9.33	194.8	11	0	0	36	0	33	5.07	1,000	500	2.50		Jun-18
8.60	-1.74	0.34	9.58	22.43	4.66	0.7	6.78		9.34	194.8	11	0	0	36	0	33	5.07	1,000,000				Dec-12
8.54	-1.77	0.09	8.88	20.95	4.4	0.95	6.75		9.33	194.8	11	0	0	36	0	33	5.07	2,500	500			Dec-12
3.30	2.39	3.50	8.37	11.26	2.01	0.45	1.88		10.44	421.3	8	24	0	19	0	20	2.55	1,000,000				Apr-08
3.24	2.17	3.24	7.56	9.78	1.76	0.7	1.88		10.44	421.3	8	24	0	19	0	20	2.55	2,500	500			Jun-08
2.00	1.73	3.18	9.20	13.80	2.5	0.53	2.45		10.53	68.4	5	0	95	0	0	3	4.64	1,000,000				Apr-08
2.03	1.69	3.02	8.56	12.46	2.24	0.78	2.46		10.54	68.4	5	0	95	0	0	3	4.64	2,500	500			Aug-08
4.21	-1.71	-0.78	5.78	13.27	3.64	0.88	4.59		9.98	3,327	1	16	1	23	0		4.15	1,000	500	2.50		Jun-18
4.27	-1.58	-0.61	6.62	14.74	3.93	0.48	4.65		9.98	3,327	1	16	1	23	0		4.15	1,000,000				Apr-08
4.21	-1.71	-0.77	5.94	13.34	3.66	0.73	4.6		9.98	3,327	1	16	1	23	0		4.15	2,500	500			Jun-08
13.80	-7.02	-4.68			6.24	2.1			11.79	--						126		2,500	100	5.75		Jun-18
13.87	-7.00	-4.56			6.48	1.85			11.82	--						126		1,000,000				Nov-17
15.54	-5.78	-3.49			6.01	2.35			11.82	--						126		2,500	100	3.50		Aug-18

	MARKET			FUND TYPE, CATEGORY & OBJECTIVE	RATINGS				NEW INVESTORS	
Fund Name	Ticker Symbol	Traded On	Fund Type	Category and (Prospectus Objective)	Overall Rating	Reward Rating	Risk Rating	Recent Up/ Downgrade	Open to New Investors	Telephone
FundX Flexible Income Fund	INCMX	NAS CM	Open End	US Fixed Inc (Income)	C-	D+	C		Y	866-455-3863
Gabelli U.S. Treasury Money Market Fund Class A	GBAXX	NAS CM	Money Mkt	US Money Mkt (Money Mkt - Treasury)	C	C	C+			914-921-5135
Gabelli U.S. Treasury Money Market Fund Class AAA	GABXX	NAS CM	Money Mkt	US Money Mkt (Money Mkt - Treasury)	C	C-	C+		Y	914-921-5135
Gabelli U.S. Treasury Money Market Fund Class C	GBCXX	NAS CM	Money Mkt	US Money Mkt (Money Mkt - Treasury)	C	C	C+			914-921-5135
GE RSP Income Fund	GESLX	NAS CM	Open End	US Fixed Inc (Income)	B	C+	B+	Up	Y	617-664-7338
General California Municipal Money Market Fund Class A	GCAXX	NAS CM	Money Mkt	US Money Mkt (Money Mkt - Single State)	C	C-	C		Y	800-645-6561
General California Municipal Money Market Fund Class B	GENXX	NAS CM	Money Mkt	US Money Mkt (Money Mkt - Single State)	C	C-	C			800-645-6561
General Government Securities Money Markets Fund Class A	GGSXX	NAS CM	Money Mkt	US Money Mkt (Money Mkt - Govt)	C	C-	C		Y	800-645-6561
General Government Securities Money Markets Fund Class B	GSBXX	NAS CM	Money Mkt	US Money Mkt (Money Mkt - Govt)	C	C-	C			800-645-6561
General Municipal Money Market Fund Class A	GTMXX	NAS CM	Money Mkt	US Money Mkt (Money Mkt - Fed Tax Exmpt)	C	C-	C		Y	800-645-6561
General Municipal Money Market Fund Class B	GBMXX	NAS CM	Money Mkt	US Money Mkt (Money Mkt - Fed Tax Exmpt)	C	C-	C			800-645-6561
General New Jersey Municipal Money Market Fund Class A	DNJXX	NAS CM	Money Mkt	US Money Mkt (Money Mkt - Single State)	C	C-	C		Y	800-645-6561
General New York AMT-Free Muni Money Mkt Fund Class A	GNMXX	NAS CM	Money Mkt	US Money Mkt (Money Mkt - Single State)	C	C-	C		Y	800-645-6561
General New York AMT-Free Muni Money Mkt Fund Class B	GNYXX	NAS CM	Money Mkt	US Money Mkt (Money Mkt - Single State)	C	C-	C			800-645-6561
General Treasury & Agency Money Market Fund Class A	DUIXX	NAS CM	Money Mkt	US Money Mkt (Money Mkt - Govt)	C	C-	C+		Y	
General Treasury & Agency Money Market Fund Class B	DABXX	NAS CM	Money Mkt	US Money Mkt (Money Mkt - Govt)	C	C-	C		Y	
General Treasury & Agency Money Market Fund Dreyfus Class	DUTXX	NAS CM	Money Mkt	US Money Mkt (Money Mkt - Govt)	C	C-	C+		Y	
General Treasury Securities Money Market Fund Class A	GTAXX	NAS CM	Money Mkt	US Money Mkt (Money Mkt - Govt)	C	C-	C		Y	800-645-6561
General Treasury Securities Money Market Fund Class B	GTBXX	NAS CM	Money Mkt	US Money Mkt (Money Mkt - Govt)	C	C-	C			800-645-6561
General Treasury Securities Money Mkt Fund Dreyfus Class	GTFXX	NAS CM	Money Mkt	US Money Mkt (Money Mkt - Govt)	C	C-	C		Y	800-645-6561
GL Beyond Income Fund	GLBFX	NAS CM	Closed End	US Fixed Inc (Income)	D+	D+	D	Up	Y	
Glenmede Fund Core Fixed Income Portfolio	GTCGX	NAS CM	Open End	US Fixed Inc (Govt Bond - General)	B	B-	B		Y	800-442-8299
Glenmede High Yield Municipal Portfolio	GHYMX	NAS CM	Open End	US Muni Fixed Inc (Muni Bond - Natl)	C-	D+	C	Down	Y	800-442-8299
Glenmede Municipal Intermediate Portfolio	GTCMX	NAS CM	Open End	US Muni Fixed Inc (Muni Bond - Single State)	C+	C	B	Up	Y	800-442-8299
Glenmede Short Term Tax Aware Fixed Income Portfolio	GTAWX	NAS CM	Open End	US Muni Fixed Inc (Growth & Income)	C	C-	C+		Y	800-442-8299
GMO Asset Allocation Bond Fund Class III	GMOBX	NAS CM	Open End	US Fixed Inc (Multisector Bond)	B	B-	A-	Up	Y	617-330-7500
GMO Asset Allocation Bond Fund Class VI	GABFX	NAS CM	Open End	US Fixed Inc (Multisector Bond)	B	B-	A-	Up	Y	617-330-7500
GMO Core Plus Bond Fund Class III	GUGAX	NAS CM	Open End	US Fixed Inc (Corp Bond - General)	B	C+	B+	Up	Y	617-330-7500
GMO Core Plus Bond Fund Class IV	GPBFX	NAS CM	Open End	US Fixed Inc (Corp Bond - General)	B	C+	B+	Up	Y	617-330-7500
GMO Emerging Country Debt Fund Class III	GMCDX	NAS CM	Open End	Emerg Mkts Fixed Inc (Worldwide Bond)	D+	D+	C-	Down	Y	617-330-7500
GMO Emerging Country Debt Fund Class IV	GMDFX	NAS CM	Open End	Emerg Mkts Fixed Inc (Worldwide Bond)	D+	D+	C-	Down	Y	617-330-7500
GMO High Yield Fund Class VI	GHVIX	NAS CM	Open End	US Fixed Inc (Corp Bond - High Yield)	D	D	C-	Down	Y	617-330-7500
GMO Opportunistic Income Fund Class I	GMOLX	NAS CM	Open End	Fixed Inc Misc (Growth)	C-	D+	C	Down	Y	617-330-7500
GMO Opportunistic Income Fund Class VI	GMODX	NAS CM	Open End	Fixed Inc Misc (Growth)	C-	D+	C	Down	Y	617-330-7500
GMO U.S. Treasury Fund	GUSTX	NAS CM	Open End	US Fixed Inc (Govt Bond - Treasury)	C	C	B-		Y	617-330-7500
Goldman Sachs Bond Fund Class A Shares	GSFAX	NAS CM	Open End	US Fixed Inc (Growth & Income)	B-	B-	B	Up	Y	800-526-7384
Goldman Sachs Bond Fund Class C Shares	GSFCX	NAS CM	Open End	US Fixed Inc (Growth & Income)	B-	C+	B	Up	Y	800-526-7384
Goldman Sachs Bond Fund Class P	GMVPX	NAS CM	Open End	US Fixed Inc (Growth & Income)	B	B-	B	Up	Y	800-526-7384
Goldman Sachs Bond Fund Class R Shares	GSNRX	NAS CM	Open End	US Fixed Inc (Growth & Income)	B-	C+	B	Up	Y	800-526-7384
Goldman Sachs Bond Fund Class R6 Shares	GSFUX	NAS CM	Open End	US Fixed Inc (Growth & Income)	B	B-	B	Up	Y	800-526-7384
Goldman Sachs Bond Fund Institutional Shares	GSNIX	NAS CM	Open End	US Fixed Inc (Growth & Income)	B	B-	B	Up	Y	800-526-7384
Goldman Sachs Bond Fund Investor Shares	GSNTX	NAS CM	Open End	US Fixed Inc (Growth & Income)	B-	B-	B	Up	Y	800-526-7384
Goldman Sachs Bond Fund Service Shares	GSNSX	NAS CM	Open End	US Fixed Inc (Growth & Income)	B-	B-	B	Up	Y	800-526-7384
Goldman Sachs Core Fixed Income Fund Class A	GCFIX	NAS CM	Open End	US Fixed Inc (Growth & Income)	B	B-	B	Up	Y	800-526-7384
Goldman Sachs Core Fixed Income Fund Class C	GCFCX	NAS CM	Open End	US Fixed Inc (Growth & Income)	B-	B-	B	Up	Y	800-526-7384
Goldman Sachs Core Fixed Income Fund Class P	GAKPX	NAS CM	Open End	US Fixed Inc (Growth & Income)	B	B-	B	Up	Y	800-526-7384
Goldman Sachs Core Fixed Income Fund Class R6	GCFUX	NAS CM	Open End	US Fixed Inc (Growth & Income)	B	B-	B	Up	Y	800-526-7384
Goldman Sachs Core Fixed Income Fund Institutional Class	GSFIX	NAS CM	Open End	US Fixed Inc (Growth & Income)	B	B-	B	Up	Y	800-526-7384
Goldman Sachs Core Fixed Income Fund Service Class	GSCSX	NAS CM	Open End	US Fixed Inc (Growth & Income)	B	B-	B	Up	Y	800-526-7384
Goldman Sachs Core Fixed-Income Fund Class R	GDFRX	NAS CM	Open End	US Fixed Inc (Growth & Income)	B	B-	B	Up	Y	800-526-7384
Goldman Sachs Core Fixed-Income Fund Investor Class	GDFTX	NAS CM	Open End	US Fixed Inc (Growth & Income)	B	B-	B	Up	Y	800-526-7384
Goldman Sachs Dynamic Municipal Income Fund Class A	GSMIX	NAS CM	Open End	US Muni Fixed Inc (Muni Bond - Natl)	C-	D+	C	Down	Y	800-526-7384

★Expanded analysis of this fund is included in Section II.

TOTAL RETURNS & PERFORMANCE									ASSETS		ASSET ALLOCATION & TURNOVER							MINIMUMS		FEES		
3-Month Total Return	6-Month Total Return	1-Year Total Return	3-Year Total Return	5-Year Total Return	Dividend Yield (TTM)	Expense Ratio	3-Yr Std Deviation	Effective Duration	NAV	Total Assets (MIL)	%Cash	%Government Bonds	%Municipal Bonds	%Corporate Bonds	%Other	Turnover Ratio	Average Coupon Rate	Min Initial Investment	Min Additional Investment	Front End Fee (%)	Back End Fee (%)	Inception Date
2.07	-4.43	-1.63	2.88	11.06	2.18	1.63	4.68	5.73	26.57	86.3	4	57	0	26	4	180	2.84	1,000	100			Jul-02
0.11	0.47	1.44	4.78	5.26	1.61	0.08	0.18		1	3,007	84	16	0	0	0			3,000			1.00	Nov-08
0.11	0.47	1.44	4.97	5.53	1.61	0.08	0.16		1	3,007	84	16	0	0	0			10,000				Oct-92
0.11	0.47	1.45	4.78	5.27	1.61	0.08	0.18		1	3,007	84	16	0	0	0			3,000			1.00	Nov-08
4.79	5.22	7.94	15.78	23.76	2.66	0.17	3.46	5.72	12.29	2,057	12	32	0	28	0	422	3.20	0				Jan-80
0.03	0.29	0.58	1.82	2.13	0.66	0.81	0.12		1	93.8	7	0	93	0	0			2,500	100			Mar-87
0.03	0.24	0.43	1.33	1.61	0.5	1.24	0.12		1	93.8	7	0	93	0	0			2,500	100			Aug-95
0.00	0.14	0.73	2.80	2.82	0.87	0.85	0.16		1	3,394	70	30	0	0	0			2,500	100			Feb-83
0.00	0.10	0.59	2.22	2.23	0.72	1.04	0.15		1	3,394	70	30	0	0	0			2,500	100			Mar-95
0.03	0.30	0.69	2.31	2.47	0.8	0.61	0.11		1	727.4	12	0	88	0	0			2,500	100			Dec-83
0.02	0.18	0.34	1.13	1.16	0.4	1.06	0.1		1	727.4	12	0	88	0	0			2,500	100			Mar-95
0.01	0.14	0.42	1.68	1.86	0.51	0.79	0.09		1	53.4	30	0	70	0	0	0		2,500	100			Jun-88
0.02	0.23	0.54	1.87	1.94	0.63	0.75	0.11		1	155.6	16	0	84	0	0			2,500	100			Dec-86
0.01	0.14	0.25	0.90	0.92	0.31	1.14	0.09		1	155.6	16	0	84	0	0			2,500	100			Sep-95
0.00	0.17	0.80	3.11	3.17	0.95	0.7	0.16		1	254.5	76	24	0	0	0			2,500	100			Apr-94
0.00	0.12	0.63	2.41	2.17	0.75	0.95	0.15		1	254.5	76	24	0	0	0			2,500	100			Jan-16
0.00	0.21	0.95	3.67	3.81	1.11	0.5	0.17		1	254.5	76	24	0	0	0			2,500	100			Feb-91
0.00	0.16	0.75	2.88	2.90	0.89	0.82	0.16		1	2,431	70	30	0	0	0			2,500	100			Dec-99
0.00	0.11	0.58	2.18	2.20	0.69	1.06	0.15		1	2,431	70	30	0	0	0			2,500	100			Dec-99
0.00	0.20	0.87	3.35	3.41	1.03	0.61	0.16		1	2,431	70	30	0	0	0			2,500	100			Dec-15
6.14	2.59	9.09	-30.32	-53.42	0	3.01	15.13		0.94	--	11	0	0	89	0	12	13.10	1,000		5.75		Mar-12
1.83	6.13	8.45	15.17	20.50	2.25	0.53	3.04	5.80	11.81	474.5	2	36	0	24	0	36	3.57	0				Nov-88
2.74	-2.11	0.57	12.17		3.01	1	5.86	7.19	10.47	205.7	1	0	99	0	0	27	4.73	0				Dec-15
2.34	2.47	3.87	9.67	15.04	1.86	0.24	2.68	3.82	11.38	308.7	2	0	98	0	0	24	4.65	0				Jun-92
1.68	1.34	2.19	4.99		1.22	0.56	1.3	1.94	10.16	50.0	3	2	87	8	0	25	4.16	0				Jun-16
4.18	6.36	8.03	17.23	13.75	4.39	0.41	3.21		23.38	171.7	0	100	0	0	0	16	1.30	5,000,000				Mar-09
4.22	6.44	8.17	17.56	14.27	4.48	0.31	3.21		23.45	171.7	0	100	0	0	0	16	1.30	300,000,000				Mar-09
4.47	5.83	8.37	20.01	25.32	2.77	0.48	3.99		22.66	411.1	-124	48	0	5	0	215		5,000,000				Apr-97
4.45	5.86	8.39	20.22	25.68	2.8	0.43	4		22.73	411.1	-124	48	0	5	0	215		125,000,000				Jul-05
12.53	-3.75	-0.63	6.93	30.88	7.19	0.54	11.11		26.12	4,021	-12	72	0	11	0	41	5.81	5,000,000		1.50		Apr-94
12.51	-3.72	-0.59	7.09	31.18	7.25	0.49	11.12		26.08	4,021	-12	72	0	11	0	41	5.81	125,000,000		1.50		Jan-98
7.00	-4.98	-1.61			8.15	0.55			19.24	174.4	-4	3	0	42	0	105	6.03	300,000,000				Jun-18
4.51	0.19	1.50	10.30	20.90		0.68	3.85		25.71	740.8	-85	10	0	0	0	47		0				Nov-19
4.54	0.31	1.66	10.68	21.55	5.75	0.49	3.84		25.75	740.8	-85	10	0	0	0	47		300,000,000		0.40		Oct-11
0.26	1.19	2.15	6.09	6.84	1.5	0.08	0.3		5.04	407.7	0	100	0	0	0	0	0.62	5,000,000				Mar-09
5.86	5.73	8.24	14.70	21.76	2.64	0.8	4.49	6.14	10.98	462.1	-21	4	1	25	0	742	3.59	1,000	50	3.75		Nov-06
5.67	5.35	7.45	12.17	17.32	1.93	1.55	4.48	6.14	10.97	462.1	-21	4	1	25	0	742	3.59	1,000	50		1.00	Nov-06
5.95	5.81	8.52	15.86	23.71	2.98	0.45	4.53	6.14	10.98	462.1	-21	4	1	25	0	742	3.59	0				Apr-18
5.80	5.61	7.98	13.96	20.27	2.4	1.05	4.56	6.14	10.97	462.1	-21	4	1	25	0	742	3.59	0				Nov-07
5.95	5.81	8.52	15.91	23.76	2.98	0.45	4.56	6.14	10.98	462.1	-21	4	1	25	0	742	3.59	5,000,000				Jul-15
5.95	5.91	8.60	15.98	23.84	2.97	0.46	4.55	6.14	10.98	462.1	-21	4	1	25	0	742	3.59	1,000,000				Nov-06
5.94	5.77	8.42	15.58	23.32	2.89	0.55	4.54	6.14	10.94	462.1	-21	4	1	25	0	742	3.59	0				Nov-07
5.82	5.65	8.07	14.26	20.81	2.49	0.96	4.55	6.14	10.98	462.1	-21	4	1	25	0	742	3.59	0				Jun-07
5.09	6.51	9.05	16.60	23.22	2.35	0.72	3.95	5.67	11.32	1,530	-5	7	1	22	0	693	3.46	1,000	50	3.75		May-97
4.97	6.18	8.31	13.97	18.76	1.63	1.47	4.02	5.67	11.38	1,530	-5	7	1	22	0	693	3.46	1,000	50		1.00	Aug-97
5.16	6.66	9.39	17.74	25.38	2.69	0.37	3.96	5.67	11.39	1,530	-5	7	1	22	0	693	3.46	0				Apr-18
5.26	6.76	9.50	17.89	25.53	2.69	0.37	4.01	5.67	11.38	1,530	-5	7	1	22	0	693	3.46	5,000,000				Jul-15
5.26	6.76	9.49	17.74	25.38	2.68	0.38	4.01	5.67	11.37	1,530	-5	7	1	22	0	693	3.46	1,000,000				Jan-94
5.03	6.50	8.95	16.00	22.19	2.2	0.88	3.98	5.67	11.37	1,530	-5	7	1	22	0	693	3.46	0				Mar-96
5.12	6.47	8.88	15.72	21.68	2.11	0.97	4.04	5.67	11.33	1,530	-5	7	1	22	0	693	3.46	0				Nov-07
5.15	6.73	9.42	17.46	24.74	2.59	0.47	3.96	5.67	11.33	1,530	-5	7	1	22	0	693	3.46	0				Nov-07
3.39	-1.25	0.91	11.08	19.71	2.32	0.75	5.28	5.99	16.03	7,405	4	1	95	0	0	23	4.49	1,000	50	3.75		Jul-93

	MARKET		FUND TYPE, CATEGORY & OBJECTIVE		RATINGS				NEW INVESTORS	
Fund Name	Ticker Symbol	Traded On	Fund Type	Category and (Prospectus Objective)	Overall Rating	Reward Rating	Risk Rating	Recent Up/ Downgrade	Open to New Investors	Telephone
Goldman Sachs Dynamic Municipal Income Fund Class C	GSMUX	NAS CM	Open End	US Muni Fixed Inc (Muni Bond - Natl)	C-	D+	C	Down	Y	800-526-7384
Goldman Sachs Dynamic Municipal Income Fund Class P	GAJPX	NAS CM	Open End	US Muni Fixed Inc (Muni Bond - Natl)	C-	D+	C	Down	Y	800-526-7384
Goldman Sachs Dynamic Municipal Income Fund Class R6	GYISX	NAS CM	Open End	US Muni Fixed Inc (Muni Bond - Natl)	C	D+	C		Y	800-526-7384
Goldman Sachs Dynamic Muni Income Fund Institutional Class	GSMTX	NAS CM	Open End	US Muni Fixed Inc (Muni Bond - Natl)	C	D+	C		Y	800-526-7384
Goldman Sachs Dynamic Municipal Income Fund Investor Class	GUIRX	NAS CM	Open End	US Muni Fixed Inc (Muni Bond - Natl)	C-	D+	C	Down	Y	800-526-7384
Goldman Sachs Dynamic Municipal Income Fund Service Class	GSMEX	NAS CM	Open End	US Muni Fixed Inc (Muni Bond - Natl)	C-	D+	C	Down	Y	800-526-7384
Goldman Sachs Emerging Markets Debt Fund Class A	GSDAX	NAS CM	Open End	Emerg Mkts Fixed Inc (Diversified Emerg Mkts)	D	D	C-	Down	Y	800-526-7384
Goldman Sachs Emerging Markets Debt Fund Class C	GSCDX	NAS CM	Open End	Emerg Mkts Fixed Inc (Diversified Emerg Mkts)	D	D	D+	Down	Y	800-526-7384
Goldman Sachs Emerging Markets Debt Fund Class P	GAIPX	NAS CM	Open End	Emerg Mkts Fixed Inc (Diversified Emerg Mkts)	D	D	C-	Down	Y	800-526-7384
Goldman Sachs Emerging Markets Debt Fund Class R6	GSIUX	NAS CM	Open End	Emerg Mkts Fixed Inc (Diversified Emerg Mkts)	D	D	C-	Down	Y	800-526-7384
Goldman Sachs Emerg Mkts Debt Fund Institutional Class	GSDIX	NAS CM	Open End	Emerg Mkts Fixed Inc (Diversified Emerg Mkts)	D	D	C-	Down	Y	800-526-7384
Goldman Sachs Emerging Markets Debt Fund Investor Class	GSIRX	NAS CM	Open End	Emerg Mkts Fixed Inc (Diversified Emerg Mkts)	D	D	C-	Down	Y	800-526-7384
Goldman Sachs Enhanced Income Fund Class A	GEIAX	NAS CM	Open End	US Fixed Inc (Income)	C	C-	C+		Y	800-526-7384
Goldman Sachs Enhanced Income Fund Class Administration	GEADX	NAS CM	Open End	US Fixed Inc (Income)	C	C-	C+		Y	800-526-7384
Goldman Sachs Enhanced Income Fund Class P	GAEPX	NAS CM	Open End	US Fixed Inc (Income)	C	C	C+		Y	800-526-7384
Goldman Sachs Enhanced Income Fund Class R6	GEIUX	NAS CM	Open End	US Fixed Inc (Income)	C	C	C+		Y	800-526-7384
Goldman Sachs Enhanced Income Fund Institutional Class	GEIIX	NAS CM	Open End	US Fixed Inc (Income)	C	C	C+		Y	800-526-7384
Goldman Sachs Enhanced Income Fund Investor Class	GHIRX	NAS CM	Open End	US Fixed Inc (Income)	C	C	C+		Y	800-526-7384
Goldman Sachs Financial Square Fed Instrumen Admin Shares	FIOXX	NAS CM	Money Mkt	US Money Mkt (Money Mkt - Govt)	C	C-	C+		Y	800-526-7384
Goldman Sachs Fin Square Fed Instrumen Capital Shares	FIKXX	NAS CM	Money Mkt	US Money Mkt (Money Mkt - Govt)	C	C	C+		Y	800-526-7384
Goldman Sachs Fin Square Fed Instrumen Cash Mgmt Shares	FIWXX	NAS CM	Money Mkt	US Money Mkt (Money Mkt - Govt)	C	C-	C		Y	800-526-7384
Goldman Sachs Financial Square Fed Instrumen Inst Shares	FIRXX	NAS CM	Money Mkt	US Money Mkt (Money Mkt - Govt)	C	C-	C+		Y	800-526-7384
Goldman Sachs Fin Square Fed Instrumen Pref Shares	FIHXX	NAS CM	Money Mkt	US Money Mkt (Money Mkt - Govt)	C	C-	C+		Y	800-526-7384
Goldman Sachs Fin Square Fed Instrumen Prem Shares	FIQXX	NAS CM	Money Mkt	US Money Mkt (Money Mkt - Govt)	C	C-	C+		Y	800-526-7384
Goldman Sachs Financial Square Fed Instrumen Select Shares	FIJXX	NAS CM	Money Mkt	US Money Mkt (Money Mkt - Govt)	C	C-	C+		Y	800-526-7384
Goldman Sachs Fin Square Fed Instrumen Service Shares	FILXX	NAS CM	Money Mkt	US Money Mkt (Money Mkt - Govt)	C	C-	C+		Y	800-526-7384
★ Goldman Sachs Financial Square Government Fund A Shares	FSOXX	NAS CM	Money Mkt	US Money Mkt (Money Mkt - Govt)	C	C-	C+		Y	800-526-7384
Goldman Sachs Financial Square Govt Fund Admin Shares	FOAXX	NAS CM	Money Mkt	US Money Mkt (Money Mkt - Govt)	C	C-	C+		Y	800-526-7384
★ Goldman Sachs Financial Square Government Fund C Shares	FSGXX	NAS CM	Money Mkt	US Money Mkt (Money Mkt - Govt)	C	C-	C		Y	800-526-7384
Goldman Sachs Financial Square Govt Fund Capital Shares	GCGXX	NAS CM	Money Mkt	US Money Mkt (Money Mkt - Govt)	C	C-	C+		Y	800-526-7384
Goldman Sachs Financial Square Govt Fund Cash Management	GVCXX	NAS CM	Money Mkt	US Money Mkt (Money Mkt - Govt)	C	C-	C+		Y	800-526-7384
Goldman Sachs Financial Square Government Fund Class R6	FGGXX	NAS CM	Money Mkt	US Money Mkt (Money Mkt - Govt)	C	C-	C+		Y	800-526-7384
Goldman Sachs Fin Square Govt Drexel Hamilton Cl Shares	VETXX	NAS CM	Money Mkt	US Money Mkt (Money Mkt - Govt)	C	C-	C+		Y	800-526-7384
Goldman Sachs Financial Square Govt Institutional Shares	FGTXX	NAS CM	Money Mkt	US Money Mkt (Money Mkt - Govt)	C	C-	C+		Y	800-526-7384
Goldman Sachs Financial Square Govt Fund Preferred Shares	GPGXX	NAS CM	Money Mkt	US Money Mkt (Money Mkt - Govt)	C	C-	C+		Y	800-526-7384
Goldman Sachs Financial Square Government Fund Premier	GGPXX	NAS CM	Money Mkt	US Money Mkt (Money Mkt - Govt)	C	C-	C+		Y	800-526-7384
Goldman Sachs Financial Square Government Fund Resource	GVRXX	NAS CM	Money Mkt	US Money Mkt (Money Mkt - Govt)	C	C-	C		Y	800-526-7384
Goldman Sachs Financial Square Govt Fund Select Shares	GSGXX	NAS CM	Money Mkt	US Money Mkt (Money Mkt - Govt)	C	C-	C+		Y	800-526-7384
Goldman Sachs Financial Square Govt Fund Service Shares	FOSXX	NAS CM	Money Mkt	US Money Mkt (Money Mkt - Govt)	C	C-	C+		Y	800-526-7384
Goldman Sachs Financial Square Money Mkt Fund Admin Shares	FADXX	NAS CM	Money Mkt	US Money Mkt (Money Mkt - Taxable)	C	C-	C+		Y	800-526-7384
Goldman Sachs Financial Square Money Mkt Capital Shares	GCKXX	NAS CM	Money Mkt	US Money Mkt (Money Mkt - Taxable)	C	C-	C+		Y	800-526-7384
Goldman Sachs Financial Square Money Mkt Cash Mgmt Shares	GSCXX	NAS CM	Money Mkt	US Money Mkt (Money Mkt - Taxable)	C	C-	C		Y	800-526-7384
Goldman Sachs Financial Square Money Mkt Inst Shares	FSMXX	NAS CM	Money Mkt	US Money Mkt (Money Mkt - Taxable)	C	C-	C+		Y	800-526-7384
Goldman Sachs Financial Square Money Mkt Preferred Shares	GPMXX	NAS CM	Money Mkt	US Money Mkt (Money Mkt - Taxable)	C	C-	C+		Y	800-526-7384
Goldman Sachs Financial Square Money Mkt Premier Shares	GPRXX	NAS CM	Money Mkt	US Money Mkt (Money Mkt - Taxable)	C	C-	C+		Y	800-526-7384
Goldman Sachs Financial Square Money Mkt Resource Shares	GREXX	NAS CM	Money Mkt	US Money Mkt (Money Mkt - Taxable)	C	C-	C+		Y	800-526-7384
Goldman Sachs Financial Square Money Mkt Select Shares	GSMXX	NAS CM	Money Mkt	US Money Mkt (Money Mkt - Taxable)	C	C-	C+		Y	800-526-7384
Goldman Sachs Financial Square Money Mkt Service Shares	FSVXX	NAS CM	Money Mkt	US Money Mkt (Money Mkt - Taxable)	C	C-	C+		Y	800-526-7384
Goldman Sachs Financial Square Prime Oblig Admin Shares	FBAXX	NAS CM	Money Mkt	US Money Mkt (Money Mkt - Taxable)	C	C-	C+		Y	800-526-7384
Goldman Sachs Financial Square Prime Oblig Capital Shares	GCPXX	NAS CM	Money Mkt	US Money Mkt (Money Mkt - Taxable)	C	C	B-		Y	800-526-7384
Goldman Sachs Fin Square Prime Oblig Cash Mgmt Shares	GFOXX	NAS CM	Money Mkt	US Money Mkt (Money Mkt - Taxable)	C	C	C+		Y	800-526-7384
Goldman Sachs Fin Square Prime Oblig Drexel Hamilton Cl Sh	VTNXX	NAS CM	Money Mkt	US Money Mkt (Money Mkt - Taxable)	C	C-	C+		Y	800-526-7384

★ Expanded analysis of this fund is included in Section II.

TOTAL RETURNS & PERFORMANCE									ASSETS		ASSET ALLOCATION & TURNOVER							MINIMUMS		FEES		
3-Month Total Return	6-Month Total Return	1-Year Total Return	3-Year Total Return	5-Year Total Return	Dividend Yield (TTM)	Expense Ratio	3-Yr Std Deviation	Effective Duration	NAV	Total Assets (MIL)	%Cash	%Government Bonds	%Municipal Bonds	%Corporate Bonds	%Other	Turnover Ratio	Average Coupon Rate	Min Initial Investment	Min Additional Investment	Front End Fee (%)	Back End Fee (%)	Inception Date
3.20	-1.55	0.22	8.60	15.30	1.54	1.5	5.28	5.99	16.04	7,405	4	1	95	0	0	23	4.49	1,000	50		1.00	Aug-97
3.48	-1.08	1.26	11.91	20.61	2.68	0.4	5.29	5.99	16.03	7,405	4	1	95	0	0	23	4.49	0				Apr-18
3.48	-1.08	1.26	12.09	20.80	2.68	0.4	5.28	5.99	16.03	7,405	4	1	95	0	0	23	4.49	5,000,000				Nov-17
3.48	-1.08	1.25	12.14	21.68	2.67	0.41	5.28	5.99	16.02	7,405	4	1	95	0	0	23	4.49	1,000,000				Aug-97
3.46	-1.13	1.16	11.85	21.20	2.58	0.5	5.27	5.99	16.01	7,405	4	1	95	0	0	23	4.49	0				Jul-10
3.34	-1.31	0.76	10.53	18.74	2.16	0.91	5.28	5.99	16.11	7,405	4	1	95	0	0	23	4.49	0				Aug-97
14.63	-3.23	-2.32	3.58	20.79	4.39	1.16	12.4	8.20	11.76	1,234	13	64	0	20	0	87	5.71	1,000	50	4.50		Aug-03
14.32	-3.67	-3.13	1.31	16.30	3.6	1.91	12.38	8.20	11.75	1,234	13	64	0	20	0	87	5.71	1,000	50		1.00	Sep-06
14.70	-3.07	-2.00	4.56	22.74	4.74	0.84	12.36	8.20	11.77	1,234	13	64	0	20	0	87	5.71	0				Apr-18
14.70	-3.15	-2.08	4.57	22.79	4.74	0.84	12.4	8.20	11.77	1,234	13	64	0	20	0	87	5.71	5,000,000				Jul-15
14.69	-3.07	-2.00	4.62	22.82	4.72	0.85	12.36	8.20	11.78	1,234	13	64	0	20	0	87	5.71	1,000,000				Aug-03
14.67	-3.10	-2.06	4.37	22.30	4.66	0.91	12.39	8.20	11.78	1,234	13	64	0	20	0	87	5.71	0				Jul-10
3.65	1.18	2.43	6.44	8.20	1.96	0.59	2.15	0.93	9.52	413.6	10	6	1	67	0	53	2.70	1,000	50	1.50		Aug-00
3.75	1.28	2.52	6.52	8.48	1.95	0.6	2.14	0.93	9.54	413.6	10	6	1	67	0	53	2.70	0				Aug-00
3.83	1.30	2.79	7.22	9.74	2.21	0.34	2.17	0.93	9.51	413.6	10	6	1	67	0	53	2.70	0				Apr-18
3.83	1.31	2.79	7.35	9.89	2.21	0.34	2.18	0.93	9.51	413.6	10	6	1	67	0	53	2.70	5,000,000				Jul-15
3.83	1.41	2.78	7.32	9.84	2.2	0.35	2.17	0.93	9.51	413.6	10	6	1	67	0	53	2.70	1,000,000				Aug-00
3.81	1.36	2.69	7.03	9.35	2.11	0.44	2.17	0.93	9.5	413.6	10	6	1	67	0	53	2.70	0				Jul-10
0.00	0.28	1.09	3.94		1.26	0.39	0.85		1	4,157	76	24	0	0	0			10,000,000				Oct-15
0.01	0.32	1.18	4.24		1.35	0.29	0.85		1	4,157	76	24	0	0	0			10,000,000				Oct-15
0.00	0.14	0.67	2.37		0.79	0.94	0.85		1	4,157	76	24	0	0	0			10,000,000				Oct-15
0.05	0.39	1.32	4.70		1.5	0.14	0.17		1	4,157	76	24	0	0	0			10,000,000				Oct-15
0.02	0.34	1.22	4.39		1.4	0.24	0.85		1	4,157	76	24	0	0	0			10,000,000				Oct-15
0.00	0.26	1.01	3.65		1.17	0.49	0.85		1	4,157	76	24	0	0	0			10,000,000				Oct-15
0.04	0.38	1.30	4.61		1.47	0.17	0.85		1	4,157	76	24	0	0	0			10,000,000				Oct-15
0.00	0.21	0.89	3.22		1.04	0.64	0.85		1	4,157	76	24	0	0	0			10,000,000				Oct-15
0.00	0.25	1.07	4.01	4.09	1.25	0.43	0.17		1	225,345	77	22	0	1	0			1,000				Feb-16
0.00	0.26	1.08	4.01	4.22	1.25	0.43	0.17		1	225,345	77	22	0	1	0			10,000,000				Sep-93
0.00	0.09	0.53	1.94	1.51	0.65	1.18	0.14		1	225,345	77	22	0	1	0			1,000			1.00	Feb-16
0.00	0.29	1.16	4.30	4.68	1.35	0.33	0.18		1	225,345	77	22	0	1	0			10,000,000				Aug-02
0.00	0.13	0.67	2.46	2.47	0.8	0.98	0.16		1	225,345	77	22	0	1	0			10,000,000				May-10
0.05	0.37	1.32	4.79	5.42	1.5	0.18	0.18		1	225,345	77	22	0	1	0			5,000,000				Dec-15
0.04	0.36	1.31	4.78	5.41		0.18			1	225,345	77	22	0	1	0			10,000,000				Sep-19
0.05	0.36	1.31	4.78	5.41	1.5	0.18	0.18		1	225,345	77	22	0	1	0			10,000,000				Apr-93
0.02	0.32	1.22	4.47	4.92	1.4	0.28	0.18		1	225,345	77	22	0	1	0			10,000,000				May-96
0.00	0.23	1.00	3.72	3.85	1.16	0.53	0.17		1	225,345	77	22	0	1	0			10,000,000				May-10
0.00	0.17	0.79	2.88	2.90	0.92	0.83	0.16		1	225,345	77	22	0	1	0			10,000,000				May-10
0.04	0.35	1.28	4.69	5.26	1.47	0.21	0.18		1	225,345	77	22	0	1	0			10,000,000				Jan-00
0.00	0.19	0.89	3.30	3.36	1.04	0.68	0.17		1	225,345	77	22	0	1	0			10,000,000				May-95
0.27	0.46	1.38	4.95	5.54	1.49	0.43	0.2		1.0012	6,842	88	0	8	4	0			10,000,000				May-94
0.29	0.53	1.49	5.27	6.03	1.59	0.33	0.2		1.0013	6,842	88	0	8	4	0			10,000,000				Aug-02
0.19	0.26	0.89	3.32	3.43	0.98	0.98	0.2		1.0012	6,842	88	0	8	4	0			10,000,000				May-10
0.32	0.59	1.63	5.73	6.81	1.74	0.18	0.2		1.0012	6,842	88	0	8	4	0			10,000,000				May-94
0.31	0.54	1.53	5.42	6.28	1.64	0.28	0.21		1.0012	6,842	88	0	8	4	0			10,000,000				May-96
0.23	0.42	1.28	4.64	5.15	1.39	0.53	0.2		1.0013	6,842	88	0	8	4	0			10,000,000				May-10
0.21	0.30	1.00	3.74	4.04	1.11	0.83	0.2		1.0012	6,842	88	0	8	4	0			10,000,000				May-10
0.33	0.57	1.59	5.64	6.64	1.71	0.21	0.21		1.0011	6,842	88	0	8	4	0			10,000,000				Jan-00
0.23	0.36	1.13	4.14	4.42	1.25	0.68	0.2		1.0008	6,842	88	0	8	4	0			10,000,000				Jul-95
0.23	0.48	1.40	4.95	5.54	1.49	0.43	0.19		1.0014	5,321	89	0	8	3	0			10,000,000				Nov-92
0.26	0.53	1.50	5.26	6.02	1.6	0.33	0.19		1.0014	5,321	89	0	8	3	0			10,000,000				Aug-02
0.17	0.28	0.91	3.31	3.52	0.98	0.98	0.19		1.0013	5,321	89	0	8	3	0			10,000,000				May-10
0.28	0.60	1.64	5.74	6.79		0.18			1.0014	5,321	89	0	8	3	0			10,000,000				Sep-19

	MARKET		FUND TYPE, CATEGORY & OBJECTIVE		RATINGS				NEW INVESTORS	
Fund Name	Ticker Symbol	Traded On	Fund Type	Category and (Prospectus Objective)	Overall Rating	Reward Rating	Risk Rating	Recent Up/ Downgrade	Open to New Investors	Telephone
Goldman Sachs Financial Square Prime Oblig Inst Shares	FPOXX	NAS CM	Money Mkt	US Money Mkt (Money Mkt - Taxable)	C	C-	C+		Y	800-526-7384
Goldman Sachs Fin Square Prime Oblig Pref Shares	GPPXX	NAS CM	Money Mkt	US Money Mkt (Money Mkt - Taxable)	C	C-	B-		Y	800-526-7384
Goldman Sachs Financial Square Prime Obligations Premier	GOPXX	NAS CM	Money Mkt	US Money Mkt (Money Mkt - Taxable)	C	C-	C+		Y	800-526-7384
Goldman Sachs Financial Square Prime Obligations Resource	GBRXX	NAS CM	Money Mkt	US Money Mkt (Money Mkt - Taxable)	C	C-	C+		Y	800-526-7384
Goldman Sachs Financial Square Prime Oblig Select Shares	GSPXX	NAS CM	Money Mkt	US Money Mkt (Money Mkt - Taxable)	C	C	B-		Y	800-526-7384
Goldman Sachs Financial Square Prime Oblig Service Shares	FBSXX	NAS CM	Money Mkt	US Money Mkt (Money Mkt - Taxable)	C	C-	C+			800-526-7384
Goldman Sachs Fin Square Treas Instrumen Admin Shares	FRAXX	NAS CM	Money Mkt	US Money Mkt (Money Mkt - Govt)	C	C-	C+		Y	800-526-7384
Goldman Sachs Fin Square Treas Instrumen Capital Shares	GCIXX	NAS CM	Money Mkt	US Money Mkt (Money Mkt - Govt)	C	C-	C+		Y	800-526-7384
Goldman Sachs Fin Square Treas Instrumen Cash Mgmt Shares	GICXX	NAS CM	Money Mkt	US Money Mkt (Money Mkt - Govt)	C	C-	C		Y	800-526-7384
Goldman Sachs Financial Square Treas Instrumen Inst Shares	FTIXX	NAS CM	Money Mkt	US Money Mkt (Money Mkt - Govt)	C	C-	C+		Y	800-526-7384
Goldman Sachs Fin Square Treas Instrumen Pref Shares	GPIXX	NAS CM	Money Mkt	US Money Mkt (Money Mkt - Govt)	C	C-	C+		Y	800-526-7384
Goldman Sachs Fin Square Treas Instrumen Prem Shares	GIPXX	NAS CM	Money Mkt	US Money Mkt (Money Mkt - Govt)	C	C-	C+		Y	800-526-7384
Goldman Sachs Fin Square Treas Instrumen Res Shares	GIRXX	NAS CM	Money Mkt	US Money Mkt (Money Mkt - Govt)	C	C-	C		Y	800-526-7384
Goldman Sachs Fin Square Treas Instrumen Select Shares	GSIXX	NAS CM	Money Mkt	US Money Mkt (Money Mkt - Govt)	C	C-	C+		Y	800-526-7384
Goldman Sachs Fin Square Treas Instrumen Service Shares	FYSXX	NAS CM	Money Mkt	US Money Mkt (Money Mkt - Govt)	C	C-	C		Y	800-526-7384
Goldman Sachs Financial Square Treas Oblig Admin Shares	FGAXX	NAS CM	Money Mkt	US Money Mkt (Money Mkt - Govt)	C	C-	C+		Y	800-526-7384
Goldman Sachs Financial Square Treas Oblig Capital Shares	GCTXX	NAS CM	Money Mkt	US Money Mkt (Money Mkt - Govt)	C	C-	C+		Y	800-526-7384
Goldman Sachs Fin Square Treas Oblig Cash Mgmt Shares	GTOXX	NAS CM	Money Mkt	US Money Mkt (Money Mkt - Govt)	C	C-	C		Y	800-526-7384
Goldman Sachs Financial Square Treas Oblig Inst Shares	FTOXX	NAS CM	Money Mkt	US Money Mkt (Money Mkt - Govt)	C	C-	C+		Y	800-526-7384
Goldman Sachs Fin Square Treas Oblig Pref Shares	GPOXX	NAS CM	Money Mkt	US Money Mkt (Money Mkt - Govt)	C	C-	C+		Y	800-526-7384
Goldman Sachs Financial Square Treas Oblig Premier Shares	GTPXX	NAS CM	Money Mkt	US Money Mkt (Money Mkt - Govt)	C	C-	C+		Y	312-362-3000
Goldman Sachs Financial Square Treas Oblig Resource Shares	GTRXX	NAS CM	Money Mkt	US Money Mkt (Money Mkt - Govt)	C	C-	C		Y	800-526-7384
Goldman Sachs Financial Square Treas Oblig Select Shares	GSOXX	NAS CM	Money Mkt	US Money Mkt (Money Mkt - Govt)	C	C-	C+		Y	800-526-7384
Goldman Sachs Financial Square Treas Oblig Service Shares	FYAXX	NAS CM	Money Mkt	US Money Mkt (Money Mkt - Govt)	C	C-	C		Y	800-526-7384
Goldman Sachs Fin Square Treas Solutions Admin Shares	FVAXX	NAS CM	Money Mkt	US Money Mkt (Money Mkt - Treasury)	C	C-	C+		Y	800-526-7384
Goldman Sachs Fin Square Treas Solutions Capital Shares	GCFXX	NAS CM	Money Mkt	US Money Mkt (Money Mkt - Treasury)	C	C-	C+		Y	800-526-7384
Goldman Sachs Fin Square Treas Solutions Cash Mgmt Shares	GFCXX	NAS CM	Money Mkt	US Money Mkt (Money Mkt - Treasury)	C	C-	C		Y	800-526-7384
Goldman Sachs Financial Square Treas Solutions Inst Shares	FEDXX	NAS CM	Money Mkt	US Money Mkt (Money Mkt - Treasury)	C	C-	C+		Y	800-526-7384
Goldman Sachs Fin Square Treas Solutions Pref Shares	GPFXX	NAS CM	Money Mkt	US Money Mkt (Money Mkt - Treasury)	C	C-	C+		Y	800-526-7384
Goldman Sachs Fin Square Treas Solutions Prem Shares	GFPXX	NAS CM	Money Mkt	US Money Mkt (Money Mkt - Treasury)	C	C-	C+		Y	800-526-7384
Goldman Sachs Fin Square Treas Solutions Res Shares	GFRXX	NAS CM	Money Mkt	US Money Mkt (Money Mkt - Treasury)	C	C-	C		Y	800-526-7384
Goldman Sachs Fin Square Treas Solutions Select Shares	GSFXX	NAS CM	Money Mkt	US Money Mkt (Money Mkt - Treasury)	C	C-	C+		Y	800-526-7384
Goldman Sachs Fin Square Treas Solutions Service Shares	FVSXX	NAS CM	Money Mkt	US Money Mkt (Money Mkt - Treasury)	C	C-	C		Y	800-526-7384
Goldman Sachs Global Core Fixed Income Fund Class A Shares	GSGIX	NAS CM	Open End	Global Fixed Inc (Worldwide Bond)	B	C+	B+	Up	Y	800-526-7384
Goldman Sachs Global Core Fixed Income Fund Class C Shares	GSLCX	NAS CM	Open End	Global Fixed Inc (Worldwide Bond)	C+	C	B	Up	Y	800-526-7384
Goldman Sachs Global Core Fixed Income Fund Class P	GGXPX	NAS CM	Open End	Global Fixed Inc (Worldwide Bond)	B	C+	B+	Up	Y	800-526-7384
Goldman Sachs Global Core Fixed Income Cl R6 Shares	GBIUX	NAS CM	Open End	Global Fixed Inc (Worldwide Bond)	B	C+	B+	Up	Y	800-526-7384
Goldman Sachs Global Core Fixed Income Inst Shares	GSGLX	NAS CM	Open End	Global Fixed Inc (Worldwide Bond)	B	C+	B+	Up	Y	800-526-7384
Goldman Sachs Global Core Fixed Income Investor Shares	GBIRX	NAS CM	Open End	Global Fixed Inc (Worldwide Bond)	B	C+	B+	Up	Y	800-526-7384
Goldman Sachs Global Core Fixed Income Fund Service Shares	GGISX	NAS CM	Open End	Global Fixed Inc (Worldwide Bond)	B-	C+	B+	Up	Y	800-526-7384
Goldman Sachs Government Income Fund Class A	GSGOX	NAS CM	Open End	US Fixed Inc (Govt Bond - General)	B	B-	B	Up	Y	800-526-7384
Goldman Sachs Government Income Fund Class C	GSOCX	NAS CM	Open End	US Fixed Inc (Govt Bond - General)	B-	C+	B		Y	800-526-7384
Goldman Sachs Government Income Fund Class P	GGTPX	NAS CM	Open End	US Fixed Inc (Govt Bond - General)	B	B-	B	Up	Y	800-526-7384
Goldman Sachs Government Income Fund Class R	GSORX	NAS CM	Open End	US Fixed Inc (Govt Bond - General)	B-	B-	B		Y	800-526-7384
Goldman Sachs Government Income Fund Class R6	GSOUX	NAS CM	Open End	US Fixed Inc (Govt Bond - General)	B	B-	B	Up	Y	800-526-7384
Goldman Sachs Government Income Fund Institutional Class	GSOIX	NAS CM	Open End	US Fixed Inc (Govt Bond - General)	B	B-	B+	Up	Y	800-526-7384
Goldman Sachs Government Income Fund Investor Class	GSOTX	NAS CM	Open End	US Fixed Inc (Govt Bond - General)	B	B-	B	Up	Y	800-526-7384
Goldman Sachs Government Income Fund Service Class	GSOSX	NAS CM	Open End	US Fixed Inc (Govt Bond - General)	B-	B-	B		Y	800-526-7384
Goldman Sachs High Quality Floating Rate Cl A Shares	GSAMX	NAS CM	Open End	US Fixed Inc (Govt Bond - ARM)	C-	D+	C		Y	800-526-7384
Goldman Sachs High Quality Floating Rate Fund Class P	GGOPX	NAS CM	Open End	US Fixed Inc (Govt Bond - ARM)	C	C-	C		Y	800-526-7384
Goldman Sachs High Quality Floating Rate Cl R6 Shares	GTAUX	NAS CM	Open End	US Fixed Inc (Govt Bond - ARM)	C	C-	C		Y	800-526-7384
Goldman Sachs High Quality Floating Rate Inst Shares	GSARX	NAS CM	Open End	US Fixed Inc (Govt Bond - ARM)	C	C-	C		Y	800-526-7384

★ Expanded analysis of this fund is included in Section II.

TOTAL RETURNS & PERFORMANCE									ASSETS		ASSET ALLOCATION & TURNOVER							MINIMUMS		FEES		
3-Month Total Return	6-Month Total Return	1-Year Total Return	3-Year Total Return	5-Year Total Return	Dividend Yield (TTM)	Expense Ratio	3-Yr Std Deviation	Effective Duration	NAV	Total Assets (MIL)	%Cash	%Government Bonds	%Municipal Bonds	%Corporate Bonds	%Other	Turnover Ratio	Average Coupon Rate	Min Initial Investment	Min Additional Investment	Front End Fee (%)	Back End Fee (%)	Inception Date
0.30	0.62	1.65	5.75	6.80	1.75	0.18	0.18		1.0015	5,321	89	0	8	3	0			10,000,000				Mar-90
0.27	0.55	1.54	5.41	6.24	1.65	0.28	0.19		1.0012	5,321	89	0	8	3	0			10,000,000				May-96
0.20	0.43	1.30	4.64	5.14	1.39	0.53	0.18		1.0013	5,321	89	0	8	3	0			10,000,000				May-10
0.18	0.32	1.03	3.75	3.93	1.11	0.83	0.19		1.0013	5,321	89	0	8	3	0			10,000,000				May-10
0.29	0.60	1.63	5.66	6.63	1.72	0.21	0.19		1.0014	5,321	89	0	8	3	0			10,000,000				Jan-00
0.13	0.32	1.11	4.12	4.41	1.25	0.68	0.19		1.0007	5,321	89	0	8	3	0			10,000,000				Jan-92
0.00	0.26	1.05	3.89	4.04	1.22	0.45	0.17		1	122,675	72	28	0	0	0			10,000,000				Apr-97
0.01	0.30	1.15	4.19	4.43	1.31	0.35	0.17		1	122,675	72	28	0	0	0			10,000,000				Aug-02
0.00	0.12	0.63	2.32	2.33	0.76	1	0.15		1	122,675	72	28	0	0	0			10,000,000				May-10
0.04	0.36	1.28	4.65	5.14	1.46	0.2	0.17		1	122,675	72	28	0	0	0			10,000,000				Mar-97
0.02	0.32	1.19	4.35	4.68	1.36	0.3	0.17		1	122,675	72	28	0	0	0			10,000,000				May-97
0.00	0.23	0.97	3.60	3.69	1.13	0.55	0.16		1	122,675	72	28	0	0	0			10,000,000				May-10
0.00	0.15	0.75	2.75	2.76	0.88	0.85	0.15		1	122,675	72	28	0	0	0			10,000,000				May-10
0.04	0.35	1.26	4.56	5.01	1.43	0.23	0.17		1	122,675	72	28	0	0	0			10,000,000				Jan-00
0.00	0.20	0.86	3.17	3.22	1	0.7	0.16		1	122,675	72	28	0	0	0			10,000,000				Mar-97
0.00	0.24	1.04	3.94	4.10	1.21	0.45	0.17		1	29,200	75	25	0	0	0			10,000,000				Jan-93
0.00	0.27	1.12	4.22	4.51	1.3	0.35	0.18		1	29,200	75	25	0	0	0			10,000,000				Aug-02
0.00	0.13	0.65	2.40	2.41	0.77	1	0.15		1	29,200	75	25	0	0	0			10,000,000				May-10
0.04	0.34	1.27	4.70	5.23	1.45	0.2	0.18		1	29,200	75	25	0	0	0			10,000,000				Apr-90
0.01	0.29	1.17	4.39	4.75	1.35	0.3	0.18		1	29,200	75	25	0	0	0			10,000,000				May-96
0.00	0.23	0.97	3.66	3.76	1.13	0.55	0.17		1	29,200	75	25	0	0	0			10,000,000				May-10
0.00	0.15	0.75	2.81	2.83	0.89	0.85	0.16		1	29,200	75	25	0	0	0			10,000,000				May-10
0.03	0.33	1.24	4.60	5.08	1.42	0.23	0.18		1	29,200	75	25	0	0	0			10,000,000				Jan-00
0.00	0.19	0.86	3.24	3.29	1.01	0.7	0.16		1	29,200	75	25	0	0	0			10,000,000				Oct-91
0.00	0.26	1.07	3.92	4.08	1.24	0.45	0.17		1	16,235	69	31	0	0	0			1,000	100			Apr-97
0.01	0.30	1.15	4.21	4.47	1.33	0.35	0.17		1	16,235	69	31	0	0	0			10,000,000				Aug-02
0.00	0.13	0.65	2.36	2.37	0.78	1	0.15		1	16,235	69	31	0	0	0			10,000,000				May-10
0.03	0.36	1.30	4.67	5.18	1.48	0.2	0.17		1	16,235	69	31	0	0	0			10,000,000				Feb-97
0.01	0.32	1.20	4.37	4.71	1.38	0.3	0.17		1	16,235	69	31	0	0	0			10,000,000				May-97
0.00	0.24	1.00	3.63	3.73	1.15	0.55	0.16		1	16,235	69	31	0	0	0			10,000,000				May-10
0.00	0.16	0.76	2.77	2.79	0.9	0.85	0.16		1	16,235	69	31	0	0	0			10,000,000				May-10
0.03	0.35	1.27	4.58	5.04	1.45	0.23	0.17		1	16,235	69	31	0	0	0			10,000,000				Jan-00
0.00	0.20	0.88	3.21	3.26	1.03	0.7	0.16		1	16,235	69	31	0	0	0			10,000,000				Mar-97
4.57	4.47	6.24	14.66	21.62	1.5	1	3.72	7.19	13.36	675.3	-5	27	0	23	0	610	3.10	1,000	50	3.75		Aug-91
4.49	4.12	5.51	12.27	17.28	0.79	1.75	3.74	7.19	13.25	675.3	-5	27	0	23	0	610	3.10	1,000	50		1.00	Aug-97
4.65	4.63	6.59	15.45	21.66	1.81	0.68	3.76	7.19	13.35	675.3	-5	27	0	23	0	610	3.10	0				Apr-18
4.73	4.72	6.59	15.93	23.76	1.81	0.68	3.74	7.19	13.34	675.3	-5	27	0	23	0	610	3.10	5,000,000				Jul-15
4.65	4.63	6.58	15.81	23.67	1.8	0.69	3.72	7.19	13.34	675.3	-5	27	0	23	0	610	3.10	1,000,000				Aug-95
4.73	4.61	6.52	15.55	23.23	1.74	0.75	3.74	7.19	13.31	675.3	-5	27	0	23	0	610	3.10	0				Jul-10
4.55	4.40	6.08	14.17	20.31	1.32	1.19	3.71	7.19	13.26	675.3	-5	27	0	23	0	610	3.10	0				Aug-91
1.04	6.01	7.54	12.83	16.46	1.74	0.88	2.98	4.84	15.68	369.9	4	25	1	0	0	943	3.33	1,000	50	3.75		Feb-93
0.79	5.62	6.74	10.34	12.19	1.01	1.63	3.02	4.84	15.68	369.9	4	25	1	0	0	943	3.33	1,000	50		1.00	Aug-97
1.12	6.12	7.89	13.67	17.32	2.05	0.56	3.02	4.84	15.65	369.9	4	25	1	0	0	943	3.33	0				Apr-18
0.92	5.82	7.28	12.01	15.03	1.49	1.13	3.03	4.84	15.66	369.9	4	25	1	0	0	943	3.33	0				Nov-07
1.06	6.12	7.82	14.00	18.39	2.05	0.56	3.01	4.84	15.65	369.9	4	25	1	0	0	943	3.33	5,000,000				Jul-15
1.06	6.11	7.81	13.97	18.35	2.04	0.57	3.04	4.84	15.65	369.9	4	25	1	0	0	943	3.33	1,000,000				Aug-97
1.04	6.07	7.73	13.68	17.92	1.98	0.63	3.02	4.84	15.67	369.9	4	25	1	0	0	943	3.33	0				Nov-07
0.93	5.86	7.28	12.21	15.45	1.56	1.07	3	4.84	15.63	369.9	4	25	1	0	0	943	3.33	0				Aug-97
2.58	-0.43	0.58	4.19	5.51	1.82	0.6	2.08	0.13	8.61	226.7	6	0	8	0	0	8	1.74	1,000	50	1.50		May-95
2.64	-0.30	0.72	5.19	7.07	2.07	0.35	2.17	0.13	8.61	226.7	6	0	8	0	0	8	1.74	0				Apr-18
2.64	-0.30	0.84	5.20	7.11	2.07	0.35	2.09	0.13	8.61	226.7	6	0	8	0	0	8	1.74	5,000,000				Jul-15
2.52	-0.43	0.71	5.05	6.93	2.06	0.36	2.09	0.13	8.6	226.7	6	0	8	0	0	8	1.74	1,000,000				Jul-91

Fund Name	Ticker Symbol	Traded On	Fund Type	Category and (Prospectus Objective)	Overall Rating	Reward Rating	Risk Rating	Recent Up/ Downgrade	Open to New Investors	Telephone
	MARKET			FUND TYPE, CATEGORY & OBJECTIVE	RATINGS				NEW INVESTORS	
Goldman Sachs High Quality Floating Rate Investor Shares	GTATX	NAS CM	Open End	US Fixed Inc (Govt Bond - ARM)	C	C-	C	Up	Y	800-526-7384
Goldman Sachs High Quality Floating Rate Service Shares	GSASX	NAS CM	Open End	US Fixed Inc (Govt Bond - ARM)	C-	D+	C		Y	800-526-7384
Goldman Sachs High Yield Floating Rate Fund Class A	GFRAX	NAS CM	Open End	US Fixed Inc (Income)	D	D	C-	Down	Y	800-526-7384
Goldman Sachs High Yield Floating Rate Fund Class C	GFRCX	NAS CM	Open End	US Fixed Inc (Income)	D	D	D+	Down	Y	800-526-7384
Goldman Sachs High Yield Floating Rate Fund Class P	GGNPX	NAS CM	Open End	US Fixed Inc (Income)	D	D	C-	Down	Y	800-526-7384
Goldman Sachs High Yield Floating Rate Fund Class R	GFRRX	NAS CM	Open End	US Fixed Inc (Income)	D	D	C-	Down	Y	800-526-7384
Goldman Sachs High Yield Floating Rate Fund Class R6	GFRSX	NAS CM	Open End	US Fixed Inc (Income)	D	D	C-	Down	Y	800-526-7384
Goldman Sachs High Yield Floating Rate Institutional Cl	GSFRX	NAS CM	Open End	US Fixed Inc (Income)	D	D	C-	Down	Y	800-526-7384
Goldman Sachs High Yield Floating Rate Fund Investor Class	GFRIX	NAS CM	Open End	US Fixed Inc (Income)	D	D	C-	Down	Y	800-526-7384
Goldman Sachs High Yield Fund Class A	GSHAX	NAS CM	Open End	US Fixed Inc (Corp Bond - High Yield)	C-	D+	C		Y	800-526-7384
Goldman Sachs High Yield Fund Class C	GSHCX	NAS CM	Open End	US Fixed Inc (Corp Bond - High Yield)	D+	D	C-	Down	Y	800-526-7384
Goldman Sachs High Yield Fund Class P	GGMPX	NAS CM	Open End	US Fixed Inc (Corp Bond - High Yield)	C-	D+	C		Y	800-526-7384
Goldman Sachs High Yield Fund Class R	GSHRX	NAS CM	Open End	US Fixed Inc (Corp Bond - High Yield)	D+	D+	C-	Down	Y	800-526-7384
Goldman Sachs High Yield Fund Class R6	GSHUX	NAS CM	Open End	US Fixed Inc (Corp Bond - High Yield)	C-	D+	C		Y	800-526-7384
Goldman Sachs High Yield Fund Institutional Shares	GSHIX	NAS CM	Open End	US Fixed Inc (Corp Bond - High Yield)	C-	D+	C		Y	800-526-7384
Goldman Sachs High Yield Fund Investor Shares	GSHTX	NAS CM	Open End	US Fixed Inc (Corp Bond - High Yield)	C-	D+	C		Y	800-526-7384
Goldman Sachs High Yield Fund Service Shares	GSHSX	NAS CM	Open End	US Fixed Inc (Corp Bond - High Yield)	D+	D+	C-	Down	Y	800-526-7384
Goldman Sachs High Yield Municipal Fund Class A	GHYAX	NAS CM	Open End	US Muni Fixed Inc (Muni Bond - Natl)	C-	D+	C	Down	Y	800-526-7384
Goldman Sachs High Yield Municipal Fund Class C	GHYCX	NAS CM	Open End	US Muni Fixed Inc (Muni Bond - Natl)	C-	D+	C	Down	Y	800-526-7384
Goldman Sachs High Yield Municipal Fund Class P	GGLPX	NAS CM	Open End	US Muni Fixed Inc (Muni Bond - Natl)	C-	D+	C	Down	Y	800-526-7384
Goldman Sachs High Yield Municipal Fund Class R6	GHYSX	NAS CM	Open End	US Muni Fixed Inc (Muni Bond - Natl)	C-	D+	C	Down	Y	800-526-7384
Goldman Sachs High Yield Muni Fund Institutional Class	GHYIX	NAS CM	Open End	US Muni Fixed Inc (Muni Bond - Natl)	C-	D+	C	Down	Y	800-526-7384
Goldman Sachs High Yield Municipal Fund Investor Class	GYIRX	NAS CM	Open End	US Muni Fixed Inc (Muni Bond - Natl)	C-	D+	C	Down	Y	800-526-7384
Goldman Sachs Income Fund Class A Shares	GSCHX	NAS CM	Open End	US Fixed Inc (Income)	U	U	U		Y	800-526-7384
Goldman Sachs Income Fund Class C Shares	GSCJX	NAS CM	Open End	US Fixed Inc (Income)	U	U	U		Y	800-526-7384
Goldman Sachs Income Fund Class P Shares	GSCUX	NAS CM	Open End	US Fixed Inc (Income)	U	U	U		Y	800-526-7384
Goldman Sachs Income Fund Class R Shares	GSCNX	NAS CM	Open End	US Fixed Inc (Income)	U	U	U		Y	800-526-7384
Goldman Sachs Income Fund Class R6 Shares	GSCRX	NAS CM	Open End	US Fixed Inc (Income)	U	U	U		Y	800-526-7384
Goldman Sachs Income Fund Institutional Shares	GSNCX	NAS CM	Open End	US Fixed Inc (Income)	U	U	U		Y	800-526-7384
Goldman Sachs Income Fund Investor Shares	GSCMX	NAS CM	Open End	US Fixed Inc (Income)	U	U	U		Y	800-526-7384
Goldman Sachs Inflation Protected Securities Cl A Shares	GSAPX	NAS CM	Open End	US Fixed Inc (Growth & Income)	B	C+	B+	Up	Y	800-526-7384
Goldman Sachs Inflation Protected Securities Cl C Shares	GSCFX	NAS CM	Open End	US Fixed Inc (Growth & Income)	B-	C+	B	Up	Y	800-526-7384
Goldman Sachs Inflation Protected Securities Fund Class P	GGJPX	NAS CM	Open End	US Fixed Inc (Growth & Income)	B	C+	A-	Up	Y	800-526-7384
Goldman Sachs Inflation Protected Securities Cl R Shares	GSRPX	NAS CM	Open End	US Fixed Inc (Growth & Income)	B-	C+	B+	Up	Y	800-526-7384
Goldman Sachs Inflation Protected Securities Cl R6 Shares	GSRUX	NAS CM	Open End	US Fixed Inc (Growth & Income)	B	C+	A-	Up	Y	800-526-7384
Goldman Sachs Inflation Protected Securities Inst Shares	GSIPX	NAS CM	Open End	US Fixed Inc (Growth & Income)	B	C+	A-	Up	Y	800-526-7384
Goldman Sachs Inflation Protected Sec Investor Shares	GSTPX	NAS CM	Open End	US Fixed Inc (Growth & Income)	B	C+	A-	Up	Y	800-526-7384
Goldman Sachs Investment Grade Credit Fund Class A	GSGAX	NAS CM	Open End	US Fixed Inc (Corp Bond - General)	C+	C	B	Up	Y	800-526-7384
Goldman Sachs Investment Grade Credit Fund Class P	GGBPX	NAS CM	Open End	US Fixed Inc (Corp Bond - General)	C+	C	B	Up	Y	800-526-7384
Goldman Sachs Investment Grade Credit Fund Class R6	GTIUX	NAS CM	Open End	US Fixed Inc (Corp Bond - General)	C+	C	B	Up	Y	800-526-7384
Goldman Sachs Inv Grade Credit Cl Separate Account Inst	GSCPX	NAS CM	Open End	US Fixed Inc (Corp Bond - General)	C+	C	B	Up	Y	800-526-7384
Goldman Sachs Investment Grade Credit Institutional Shares	GSGDX	NAS CM	Open End	US Fixed Inc (Corp Bond - General)	C+	C	B	Up	Y	800-526-7384
Goldman Sachs Investment Grade Credit Fund Investor Shares	GTIRX	NAS CM	Open End	US Fixed Inc (Corp Bond - General)	C+	C	B	Up	Y	800-526-7384
Goldman Sachs Investor Money Mkt Fund Admin Shares	FMKXX	NAS CM	Money Mkt	US Money Mkt (Money Mkt - Taxable)	C	C-	C+		Y	800-526-7384
Goldman Sachs Investor Money Mkt Cash Management Shares	FHMXX	NAS CM	Money Mkt	US Money Mkt (Money Mkt - Taxable)	C	C-	C		Y	800-526-7384
Goldman Sachs Investor Money Market Fund Class A	FMEXX	NAS CM	Money Mkt	US Money Mkt (Money Mkt - Taxable)	C	C-	C+		Y	800-526-7384
Goldman Sachs Investor Money Market Fund Class C	FMGXX	NAS CM	Money Mkt	US Money Mkt (Money Mkt - Taxable)	C	C-	C+		Y	800-526-7384
Goldman Sachs Investor Money Market Fund Class I	FMJXX	NAS CM	Money Mkt	US Money Mkt (Money Mkt - Taxable)	C	C-	C+		Y	800-526-7384
Goldman Sachs Investor Money Market Fund Resource Shares	FHRXX	NAS CM	Money Mkt	US Money Mkt (Money Mkt - Taxable)	C	C-	C+		Y	800-526-7384
Goldman Sachs Investor Money Market Fund Service Shares	FHSXX	NAS CM	Money Mkt	US Money Mkt (Money Mkt - Taxable)	C	C-	C+		Y	800-526-7384
Goldman Sachs Investor Tax-Exempt Money Mkt Fund A Shares	FKIXX	NAS CM	Money Mkt	US Money Mkt (Money Mkt - Fed Tax Exmpt)	C	C-	C+		Y	800-526-7384
Goldman Sachs Investor Tax-Exempt Money Mkt Admin Shares	FEAXX	NAS CM	Money Mkt	US Money Mkt (Money Mkt - Fed Tax Exmpt)	C	C-	C+		Y	800-526-7384

★Expanded analysis of this fund is included in Section II.

TOTAL RETURNS & PERFORMANCE									ASSETS		ASSET ALLOCATION & TURNOVER							MINIMUMS		FEES		
3-Month Total Return	6-Month Total Return	1-Year Total Return	3-Year Total Return	5-Year Total Return	Dividend Yield (TTM)	Expense Ratio	3-Yr Std Deviation	Effective Duration	NAV	Total Assets (MIL)	%Cash	%Government Bonds	%Municipal Bonds	%Corporate Bonds	%Other	Turnover Ratio	Average Coupon Rate	Min Initial Investment	Min Additional Investment	Front End Fee (%)	Back End Fee (%)	Inception Date
2.62	-0.47	0.62	4.77	6.44	1.97	0.45	2.17	0.13	8.58	226.7	6	0	8	0	0	8	1.74	0				Nov-07
2.38	-0.66	0.22	3.50	4.34	1.56	0.86	2.07	0.13	8.64	226.7	6	0	8	0	0	8	1.74	0				Mar-97
11.94	-5.40	-2.47	3.04	9.55	5.04	0.98	9.93	0.05	8.74	1,235	5	0	0	31	0	39	4.71	1,000	50	2.25		Mar-11
11.74	-5.75	-3.19	0.75	5.53	4.25	1.73	9.94	0.05	8.74	1,235	5	0	0	31	0	39	4.71	1,000	50		1.00	Mar-11
12.15	-5.22	-2.10	4.13	11.46	5.42	0.63	9.96	0.05	8.76	1,235	5	0	0	31	0	39	4.71	0				Apr-18
11.88	-5.51	-2.69	2.19	8.13	4.81	1.23	9.92	0.05	8.74	1,235	5	0	0	31	0	39	4.71	5,000,000				Mar-11
12.02	-5.23	-2.22	4.13	11.46	5.42	0.63	9.92	0.05	8.75	1,235	5	0	0	31	0	39	4.71	5,000,000				Nov-17
12.02	-5.23	-2.13	4.10	11.43	5.41	0.64	9.9	0.05	8.75	1,235	5	0	0	31	0	39	4.71	1,000,000				Mar-11
11.98	-5.27	-2.21	3.94	10.95	5.31	0.73	9.9	0.05	8.76	1,235	5	0	0	31	0	39	4.71	0				Mar-11
10.32	-5.50	-1.69	6.27	16.32	5.89	1.03	9.65	4.72	5.95	1,945	6	0	0	94	0	80	6.33	1,000	50	4.50		Aug-97
9.92	-6.00	-2.42	3.92	11.90	5.1	1.78	9.58	4.72	5.95	1,945	6	0	0	94	0	80	6.33	1,000	50		1.00	Aug-97
10.18	-5.50	-1.54	7.23	18.00	6.2	0.74	9.57	4.72	5.96	1,945	6	0	0	94	0	80	6.33	0				Apr-18
10.07	-5.78	-2.10	5.47	14.70	5.63	1.28	9.6	4.72	5.94	1,945	6	0	0	94	0	80	6.33	0				Nov-07
10.16	-5.49	-1.54	7.27	18.20	6.2	0.74	9.57	4.72	5.97	1,945	6	0	0	94	0	80	6.33	5,000,000				Jul-15
10.18	-5.51	-1.56	7.22	17.99	6.19	0.75	9.58	4.72	5.96	1,945	6	0	0	94	0	80	6.33	1,000,000				Aug-97
10.37	-5.37	-1.44	7.09	17.63	6.16	0.78	9.65	4.72	5.96	1,945	6	0	0	94	0	80	6.33	0				Nov-07
10.07	-5.62	-1.92	5.60	15.04	5.66	1.25	9.59	4.72	5.94	1,945	6	0	0	94	0	80	6.33	0				Aug-97
3.89	-2.36	1.06	16.29	32.25	3.6	0.86	7.33	7.81	9.88	7,717	2	1	96	0	0	20	4.95	1,000	50	4.50		Apr-00
3.70	-2.72	0.21	13.71	27.40	2.8	1.61	7.37	7.81	9.88	7,717	2	1	96	0	0	20	4.95	1,000	50		1.00	Apr-00
3.98	-2.21	1.28	17.22	34.07	3.93	0.54	7.38	7.81	9.87	7,717	2	1	96	0	0	20	4.95	0				Apr-18
4.08	-2.20	1.37	17.33	34.18	3.93	0.54	7.35	7.81	9.88	7,717	2	1	96	0	0	20	4.95	5,000,000				Nov-17
3.97	-2.21	1.27	17.33	34.19	3.92	0.55	7.38	7.81	9.88	7,717	2	1	96	0	0	20	4.95	1,000,000				Apr-00
3.95	-2.23	1.21	17.17	33.85	3.86	0.61	7.32	7.81	9.89	7,717	2	1	96	0	0	20	4.95	0				Jul-10
12.57	0.01					0.98			9.9	25.8	4	11	0	59	0	110	4.35	1,000	50	3.75		Dec-19
12.36	-0.35					1.73			9.9	25.8	4	11	0	59	0	110	4.35	1,000	50		1.00	Dec-19
12.55	0.08					0.63			9.89	25.8	4	11	0	59	0	110	4.35	0				Dec-19
12.39	-0.21					1.23			9.89	25.8	4	11	0	59	0	110	4.35	0				Dec-19
12.55	0.08					0.63			9.89	25.8	4	11	0	59	0	110	4.35	0				Dec-19
12.55	0.08					0.64			9.89	25.8	4	11	0	59	0	110	4.35	1,000,000				Dec-19
12.53	0.03					0.73			9.89	25.8	4	11	0	59	0	110	4.35	0				Dec-19
4.12	5.46	7.76	13.78	17.65	2.33	0.68	3.5	7.76	11.16	373.3	4	96	0	0	0	62	0.56	1,000	50	3.75		Aug-07
3.89	5.01	6.89	11.21	13.32	1.56	1.43	3.58	7.76	10.95	373.3	4	96	0	0	0	62	0.56	1,000	50		1.00	Aug-07
4.15	5.66	8.12	14.91	19.70	2.62	0.33	3.53	7.76	11.3	373.3	4	96	0	0	0	62	0.56	0				Apr-18
4.03	5.31	7.41	12.87	16.18	2.14	0.93	3.51	7.76	11.1	373.3	4	96	0	0	0	62	0.56	0				Nov-07
4.25	5.66	8.13	15.04	19.76	2.63	0.33	3.54	7.76	11.3	373.3	4	96	0	0	0	62	0.56	5,000,000				Jul-15
4.15	5.56	8.01	14.88	19.66	2.62	0.34	3.52	7.76	11.3	373.3	4	96	0	0	0	62	0.56	1,000,000				Aug-07
4.16	5.56	7.98	14.58	19.12	2.56	0.43	3.56	7.76	11.23	373.3	4	96	0	0	0	62	0.56	0				Nov-07
11.37	4.49	8.76	19.35	29.35	2.93	0.72	7.92	7.99	9.91	522.5	7	4	1	88	0	76	4.26	1,000	50	3.75		Nov-03
11.46	4.67	9.13	20.59	31.44	3.27	0.37	7.94	7.99	9.91	522.5	7	4	1	88	0	76	4.26	0				Apr-18
11.34	4.56	9.02	20.48	31.46	3.27	0.37	7.9	7.99	9.91	522.5	7	4	1	88	0	76	4.26	5,000,000				Jul-15
11.45	4.67	9.13	20.71	31.56	3.27	0.37	7.92	7.99	9.92	522.5	7	4	1	88	0	76	4.26	0				Nov-03
11.33	4.56	9.00	20.56	31.55	3.26	0.38	7.9	7.99	9.91	522.5	7	4	1	88	0	76	4.26	1,000,000				Nov-03
11.42	4.62	9.02	20.36	30.95	3.17	0.47	7.9	7.99	9.92	522.5	7	4	1	88	0	76	4.26	0				Jul-11
0.09	0.42	1.32	4.71		1.49	0.43	0.16		1	2,157	84	1	12	3	0			10,000,000				Jan-16
0.00	0.20	0.82	3.05		0.96	0.98	0.15		1	2,157	84	1	12	3	0			10,000,000				May-16
0.09	0.42	1.32	4.71		1.49	0.43	0.16		1	2,157	84	1	12	3	0			1,000				Jan-16
0.00	0.15	0.67	2.48		0.79	1.18	0.15		1	2,157	84	1	12	3	0			1,000			1.00	Jan-16
0.15	0.54	1.57	5.49		1.74	0.18	0.16		1	2,157	84	1	12	3	0			10,000,000				Jan-16
0.01	0.25	0.95	3.49		1.09	0.83	0.16		1	2,157	84	1	12	3	0			10,000,000				May-16
0.03	0.29	1.07	3.93		1.24	0.68	0.16		1	2,157	84	1	12	3	0			10,000,000				May-16
0.02	0.27	0.72	2.59	2.73	0.82	0.43	0.1		1	1,701	24	0	76	0	0			1,000				Mar-16
0.02	0.26	0.71	2.58	2.91	0.82	0.43	0.1		1	1,701	24	0	76	0	0			10,000,000				Aug-94

Fund Name	Ticker Symbol	Traded On	Fund Type	Category and (Prospectus Objective)	Overall Rating	Reward Rating	Risk Rating	Recent Up/ Downgrade	Open to New Investors	Telephone
Goldman Sachs Investor Tax-Exempt Money Mkt Fund C Shares	FCYXX	NAS CM	Money Mkt	US Money Mkt (Money Mkt - Fed Tax Exmpt)	C	C-	C		Y	800-526-7384
Goldman Sachs Investor Tax-Exempt Money Mkt Capital Shares	GCXXX	NAS CM	Money Mkt	US Money Mkt (Money Mkt - Fed Tax Exmpt)	C	C-	C		Y	800-526-7384
Goldman Sachs Investor Tax-Ex Money Mkt Cash Mgmt Shares	GXCXX	NAS CM	Money Mkt	US Money Mkt (Money Mkt - Fed Tax Exmpt)	C	C-	C		Y	800-526-7384
Goldman Sachs Investor Tax-Exempt Money Mkt Inst Shares	FTXXX	NAS CM	Money Mkt	US Money Mkt (Money Mkt - Fed Tax Exmpt)	C	C-	C+		Y	312-362-3000
Goldman Sachs Investor Tax-Ex Money Mkt Preferred Shares	GPTXX	NAS CM	Money Mkt	US Money Mkt (Money Mkt - Fed Tax Exmpt)	C	C-	C		Y	800-526-7384
Goldman Sachs Investor Tax-Exempt Money Mkt Premier Shares	GXPXX	NAS CM	Money Mkt	US Money Mkt (Money Mkt - Fed Tax Exmpt)	C	C-	C+		Y	800-526-7384
Goldman Sachs Investor Tax-Ex Money Mkt Resource Shares	GXRXX	NAS CM	Money Mkt	US Money Mkt (Money Mkt - Fed Tax Exmpt)	C	C-	C		Y	800-526-7384
Goldman Sachs Investor Tax-Exempt Money Mkt Select Shares	GSTXX	NAS CM	Money Mkt	US Money Mkt (Money Mkt - Fed Tax Exmpt)	C	C-	C+		Y	800-526-7384
Goldman Sachs Investor Tax-Exempt Money Mkt Service Shares	FESXX	NAS CM	Money Mkt	US Money Mkt (Money Mkt - Fed Tax Exmpt)	C	C-	C		Y	800-526-7384
Goldman Sachs Local Emerging Markets Debt Fund Class A	GAMDX	NAS CM	Open End	Emerg Mkts Fixed Inc (Growth & Income)	D	D	D+	Down	Y	800-526-7384
Goldman Sachs Local Emerging Markets Debt Fund Class C	GCMDX	NAS CM	Open End	Emerg Mkts Fixed Inc (Growth & Income)	D	D	D+	Down	Y	800-526-7384
Goldman Sachs Local Emerging Markets Debt Fund Class P	GMWPX	NAS CM	Open End	Emerg Mkts Fixed Inc (Growth & Income)	D	D	D+	Down	Y	800-526-7384
Goldman Sachs Local Emerging Markets Debt Fund Class R6	GIMSX	NAS CM	Open End	Emerg Mkts Fixed Inc (Growth & Income)	D	D	D+	Down	Y	800-526-7384
Goldman Sachs Local Emerg Mkts Debt Institutional Cl	GIMDX	NAS CM	Open End	Emerg Mkts Fixed Inc (Growth & Income)	D	D	D+	Down	Y	800-526-7384
Goldman Sachs Local Emerg Mkts Debt Fund Investor Class	GLIRX	NAS CM	Open End	Emerg Mkts Fixed Inc (Growth & Income)	D	D	D+	Down	Y	800-526-7384
Goldman Sachs Short Duration Government Fund Class A	GSSDX	NAS CM	Open End	US Fixed Inc (Govt Bond - General)	C+	C	B	Up	Y	800-526-7384
Goldman Sachs Short Duration Government Fund Class C	GSDCX	NAS CM	Open End	US Fixed Inc (Govt Bond - General)	C+	C	B-	Up	Y	800-526-7384
Goldman Sachs Short Duration Government Fund Class P	GMDPX	NAS CM	Open End	US Fixed Inc (Govt Bond - General)	C+	C	B	Up	Y	800-526-7384
Goldman Sachs Short Duration Government Fund Class R6	GSTUX	NAS CM	Open End	US Fixed Inc (Govt Bond - General)	C+	C	B	Up	Y	800-526-7384
Goldman Sachs Short Duration Govt Fund Institutional Class	GSTGX	NAS CM	Open End	US Fixed Inc (Govt Bond - General)	C+	C	B	Up	Y	800-526-7384
Goldman Sachs Short Duration Govt Fund Investor Class	GTDTX	NAS CM	Open End	US Fixed Inc (Govt Bond - General)	C+	C	B	Up	Y	800-526-7384
Goldman Sachs Short Duration Government Fund Service Class	GSDSX	NAS CM	Open End	US Fixed Inc (Govt Bond - General)	C+	C	B	Up	Y	800-526-7384
Goldman Sachs Short Duration Income Fund Class A	GDIAX	NAS CM	Open End	US Fixed Inc (Income)	C	C	B-		Y	800-526-7384
Goldman Sachs Short Duration Income Fund Class C	GDICX	NAS CM	Open End	US Fixed Inc (Income)	C	C	B-		Y	800-526-7384
Goldman Sachs Short Duration Income Fund Class P	GMCPX	NAS CM	Open End	US Fixed Inc (Income)	C+	C	B	Up	Y	800-526-7384
Goldman Sachs Short Duration Income Fund Class R	GIFRX	NAS CM	Open End	US Fixed Inc (Income)	C	C	B-		Y	800-526-7384
Goldman Sachs Short Duration Income Fund Class R6	GDIUX	NAS CM	Open End	US Fixed Inc (Income)	C+	C	B	Up	Y	800-526-7384
Goldman Sachs Short Duration Income Institutional Cl	GDFIX	NAS CM	Open End	US Fixed Inc (Income)	C	C	B-		Y	800-526-7384
Goldman Sachs Short Duration Income Fund Investor Class	GSSRX	NAS CM	Open End	US Fixed Inc (Income)	C+	C	B	Up	Y	800-526-7384
Goldman Sachs Short Duration Tax-Free Fund Class A	GSDTX	NAS CM	Open End	US Muni Fixed Inc (Muni Bond - Natl)	C	C-	C+		Y	800-526-7384
Goldman Sachs Short Duration Tax-Free Fund Class C	GSTCX	NAS CM	Open End	US Muni Fixed Inc (Muni Bond - Natl)	C	C-	C+		Y	800-526-7384
Goldman Sachs Short Duration Tax-Free Fund Class P	GANPX	NAS CM	Open End	US Muni Fixed Inc (Muni Bond - Natl)	C	C-	B-		Y	800-526-7384
Goldman Sachs Short Duration Tax-Free Fund Class R6	GDUSX	NAS CM	Open End	US Muni Fixed Inc (Muni Bond - Natl)	C	C-	C+		Y	800-526-7384
Goldman Sachs Short Duration Tax-Free Institutional Cl	GSDUX	NAS CM	Open End	US Muni Fixed Inc (Muni Bond - Natl)	C	C-	B-		Y	800-526-7384
Goldman Sachs Short Duration Tax-Free Fund Investor Class	GDIRX	NAS CM	Open End	US Muni Fixed Inc (Muni Bond - Natl)	C	C-	C+		Y	800-526-7384
Goldman Sachs Short Duration Tax-Free Fund Service Class	GSFSX	NAS CM	Open End	US Muni Fixed Inc (Muni Bond - Natl)	C	C-	C+		Y	800-526-7384
Goldman Sachs Short-Term Conservative Income Admin Shares	GPPAX	NAS CM	Open End	US Fixed Inc (Income)	C	C-	C+		Y	800-526-7384
Goldman Sachs Short-Term Conservative Income Fund Class A	GPAPX	NAS CM	Open End	US Fixed Inc (Income)	C	C-	C+		Y	800-526-7384
Goldman Sachs Short-Term Conservative Income Fund Class P	GMBPX	NAS CM	Open End	US Fixed Inc (Income)	C	C-	B-		Y	800-526-7384
Goldman Sachs Short-Term Conservative Income Cl R6 Shares	GPPSX	NAS CM	Open End	US Fixed Inc (Income)	C	C-	C+		Y	800-526-7384
Goldman Sachs Short-Term Conservative Income Inst Shares	GPPIX	NAS CM	Open End	US Fixed Inc (Income)	C	C-	B-		Y	800-526-7384
Goldman Sachs Short-Term Cons Income Investor Shares	GPPOX	NAS CM	Open End	US Fixed Inc (Income)	C	C-	C+		Y	800-526-7384
Goldman Sachs Short-Term Cons Income Preferred Shares	GPPPX	NAS CM	Open End	US Fixed Inc (Income)	C	C-	C+		Y	800-526-7384
Goldman Sachs Strategic Income Fund Class A	GSZAX	NAS CM	Open End	Fixed Inc Misc (Income)	C-	D+	C		Y	800-526-7384
Goldman Sachs Strategic Income Fund Class C	GSZCX	NAS CM	Open End	Fixed Inc Misc (Income)	D+	D	C		Y	800-526-7384
Goldman Sachs Strategic Income Fund Class P	GSOPX	NAS CM	Open End	Fixed Inc Misc (Income)	C	D+	C	Up	Y	800-526-7384
Goldman Sachs Strategic Income Fund Class R	GSZRX	NAS CM	Open End	Fixed Inc Misc (Income)	D+	D	C	Down	Y	800-526-7384
Goldman Sachs Strategic Income Fund Class R6	GSZUX	NAS CM	Open End	Fixed Inc Misc (Income)	C	D+	C	Up	Y	800-526-7384
Goldman Sachs Strategic Income Fund Institutional Class	GSZIX	NAS CM	Open End	Fixed Inc Misc (Income)	C-	D+	C		Y	800-526-7384
Goldman Sachs Strategic Income Fund Investor Class	GZIRX	NAS CM	Open End	Fixed Inc Misc (Income)	C-	D+	C		Y	800-526-7384
Goldman Sachs U.S. Mortgages Fund Class A Shares	GSUAX	NAS CM	Open End	US Fixed Inc (Govt Bond - Mortgage)	C+	C+	B		Y	800-526-7384
Goldman Sachs U.S. Mortgages Fund Class P	GSBPX	NAS CM	Open End	US Fixed Inc (Govt Bond - Mortgage)	B-	C+	B	Up	Y	800-526-7384

★ Expanded analysis of this fund is included in Section II.

TOTAL RETURNS & PERFORMANCE									ASSETS		ASSET ALLOCATION & TURNOVER							MINIMUMS		FEES		
3-Month Total Return	6-Month Total Return	1-Year Total Return	3-Year Total Return	5-Year Total Return	Dividend Yield (TTM)	Expense Ratio	3-Yr Std Deviation	Effective Duration	NAV	Total Assets (MIL)	%Cash	%Government Bonds	%Municipal Bonds	%Corporate Bonds	%Other	Turnover Ratio	Average Coupon Rate	Min Initial Investment	Min Additional Investment	Front End Fee (%)	Back End Fee (%)	Inception Date
0.00	0.07	0.14	0.64	0.16	0.2	1.18	0.06		1	1,701	24	0	76	0	0			1,000			1.00	Mar-16
0.04	0.30	0.80	2.88	3.32	0.92	0.33	0.1		1	1,701	24	0	76	0	0			10,000,000				Aug-02
0.00	0.11	0.28	1.07	1.16	0.35	0.98	0.08		1	1,701	24	0	76	0	0			10,000,000				May-10
0.07	0.36	0.95	3.33	3.99	1.07	0.18	0.1		1	1,701	24	0	76	0	0			10,000,000				Jul-94
0.04	0.32	0.85	3.04	3.54	0.97	0.28	0.1		1	1,701	24	0	76	0	0			10,000,000				May-96
0.01	0.22	0.62	2.29	2.53	0.73	0.53	0.1		1	1,701	24	0	76	0	0			10,000,000				May-10
0.00	0.14	0.39	1.44	1.52	0.47	0.83	0.09		1	1,701	24	0	76	0	0			10,000,000				May-10
0.06	0.35	0.91	3.24	3.84	1.04	0.21	0.1		1	1,701	24	0	76	0	0			10,000,000				Jan-00
0.01	0.18	0.51	1.87	1.99	0.6	0.68	0.1		1	1,701	24	0	76	0	0			10,000,000				Sep-94
10.36	-8.73	-6.69	-3.80	3.45	3.84	1.22	14.6	6.73	5.46	83.5	15	65	0	12	0	84	5.96	1,000	50	4.50		Feb-08
10.38	-8.92	-7.24	-5.78	-0.48	3.05	1.97	14.59	6.73	5.46	83.5	15	65	0	12	0	84	5.96	1,000	50		1.00	Feb-08
10.69	-8.45	-6.27	-2.79	4.87	4.17	0.91	14.58	6.73	5.45	83.5	15	65	0	12	0	84	5.96	0				Apr-18
10.69	-8.45	-6.27	-2.79	4.88	4.17	0.91	14.6	6.73	5.45	83.5	15	65	0	12	0	84	5.96	5,000,000				Nov-17
10.68	-8.46	-6.12	-2.80	4.87	4.16	0.92	14.66	6.73	5.45	83.5	15	65	0	12	0	84	5.96	1,000,000				Feb-08
10.45	-8.63	-6.32	-2.95	4.56	4.11	0.97	14.49	6.73	5.45	83.5	15	65	0	12	0	84	5.96	0				Jul-10
0.79	3.03	3.69	6.64	7.57	1.88	0.82	1.07	1.89	10.02	878.4	1	30	0	0	0	479	3.47	1,000	50	1.50		May-97
0.69	2.74	3.29	5.37	5.49	1.49	1.22	1.07	1.89	9.95	878.4	1	30	0	0	0	479	3.47	1,000	50		0.65	Aug-97
0.88	3.11	4.06	7.64	9.32	2.23	0.47	1.06	1.89	9.98	878.4	1	30	0	0	0	479	3.47	0				Apr-18
0.88	3.11	3.95	7.76	9.37	2.22	0.47	1.13	1.89	9.98	878.4	1	30	0	0	0	479	3.47	5,000,000				Jul-15
0.87	3.11	3.94	7.62	9.30	2.22	0.48	1.11	1.89	9.98	878.4	1	30	0	0	0	479	3.47	1,000,000				Aug-88
0.95	3.15	3.94	7.54	8.92	2.13	0.57	1.12	1.89	10.03	878.4	1	30	0	0	0	479	3.47	0				Nov-07
0.75	2.85	3.43	6.13	6.72	1.72	0.98	1.07	1.89	9.97	878.4	1	30	0	0	0	479	3.47	0				Apr-96
5.41	2.94	4.59	9.23	12.85	2.42	0.79	3.4	2.98	10.16	1,017	1	3	1	59	0	192	3.76	1,000	50	1.50		Feb-12
5.20	2.63	3.97	7.83	10.41	2.03	1.19	3.42	2.98	10.15	1,017	1	3	1	59	0	192	3.76	1,000	50		0.65	Feb-12
5.49	3.11	4.84	10.25	14.68	2.77	0.44	3.46	2.98	10.17	1,017	1	3	1	59	0	192	3.76	0				Apr-18
5.34	2.81	4.22	8.31	11.34	2.18	1.04	3.47	2.98	10.17	1,017	1	3	1	59	0	192	3.76	0				Feb-12
5.49	3.11	4.84	10.22	14.62	2.77	0.44	3.41	2.98	10.17	1,017	1	3	1	59	0	192	3.76	5,000,000				Jul-15
5.38	3.00	4.83	10.24	14.67	2.76	0.45	3.37	2.98	10.17	1,017	1	3	1	59	0	192	3.76	1,000,000				Feb-12
5.47	3.06	4.64	9.94	14.15	2.67	0.54	3.46	2.98	10.17	1,017	1	3	1	59	0	192	3.76	0				Feb-12
1.63	0.83	1.76	6.52	8.84	1.42	0.68	1.79	2.23	10.77	7,730	6	0	94	0	0	29	3.83	1,000	50	1.50		May-97
1.54	0.63	1.35	5.25	6.70	1.01	1.08	1.72	2.23	10.76	7,730	6	0	94	0	0	29	3.83	1,000	50		0.65	Aug-97
1.71	0.99	2.07	7.41	10.47	1.73	0.37	1.77	2.23	10.75	7,730	6	0	94	0	0	29	3.83	0				Apr-18
1.71	0.99	2.07	7.42	10.47	1.73	0.37	1.78	2.23	10.75	7,730	6	0	94	0	0	29	3.83	5,000,000				Nov-17
1.71	0.98	2.06	7.49	10.54	1.72	0.38	1.72	2.23	10.76	7,730	6	0	94	0	0	29	3.83	1,000,000				Oct-92
1.70	0.96	2.01	7.34	10.23	1.67	0.43	1.72	2.23	10.76	7,730	6	0	94	0	0	29	3.83	0				Jul-10
1.59	0.73	1.56	5.90	7.82	1.22	0.88	1.7	2.23	10.76	7,730	6	0	94	0	0	29	3.83	0				Sep-94
2.07	0.78	1.89	6.19	7.84	1.89	0.49	1.25	0.29	10.06	4,082	41	0	0	59	0	87	2.22	0				Feb-14
2.08	0.79	1.90	6.08	7.80	1.9	0.48	1.26	0.29	10.06	4,082	41	0	0	59	0	87	2.22	1,000	50	1.50		Oct-16
2.24	0.91	2.25	7.00	9.21	2.15	0.23	1.31	0.29	10.06	4,082	41	0	0	59	0	87	2.22	0				Apr-18
2.14	0.91	2.25	7.07	9.28	2.15	0.23	1.25	0.29	10.07	4,082	41	0	0	59	0	87	2.22	5,000,000				Nov-17
2.14	0.91	2.14	6.99	9.19	2.14	0.24	1.25	0.29	10.06	4,082	41	0	0	59	0	87	2.22	1,000,000				Feb-14
2.12	0.86	2.05	6.79	8.99	2.05	0.33	1.25	0.29	10.06	4,082	41	0	0	59	0	87	2.22	0				Aug-18
2.12	0.87	2.06	6.69	8.82	2.05	0.34	1.25	0.29	10.06	4,082	41	0	0	59	0	87	2.22	0				Oct-16
9.38	1.06	2.01	2.69	4.30	3.27	0.99	6.25	2.13	9.19	1,064	-11	2	1	24	0	491	3.82	1,000	50	3.75		Jun-10
4.91	-3.16	-2.73	-3.56	-3.41	2.51	1.74	6.3	2.13	9.17	1,064	-11	2	1	24	0	491	3.82	1,000	50		1.00	Jun-10
9.48	1.24	2.37	3.70	6.04	3.63	0.64	6.26	2.13	9.18	1,064	-11	2	1	24	0	491	3.82	0				Apr-18
9.45	1.04	1.86	1.93	3.04	3.02	1.24	6.34	2.13	9.18	1,064	-11	2	1	24	0	491	3.82	0				Jun-10
9.59	1.35	2.48	3.80	6.18	3.62	0.64	6.29	2.13	9.2	1,064	-11	2	1	24	0	491	3.82	5,000,000				Jul-15
5.18	-2.73	-1.75	-0.39	1.85	3.61	0.65	6.34	2.13	9.2	1,064	-11	2	1	24	0	491	3.82	1,000,000				Jun-10
5.16	-2.77	-1.74	-0.63	1.42	3.52	0.74	6.28	2.13	9.2	1,064	-11	2	1	24	0	491	3.82	0				Jun-10
2.33	3.84	5.73	10.96	14.97	2.71	0.79	2.26	2.09	10.72	360.2	-40	0	0	0	1	1,233	3.45	1,000	50	3.75		Nov-03
2.31	3.91	6.09	12.10	16.94	3.05	0.44	2.23	2.09	10.74	360.2	-40	0	0	0	1	1,233	3.45	0				Apr-18

Fund Name	Ticker Symbol	Traded On	Fund Type	Category and (Prospectus Objective)	Overall Rating	Reward Rating	Risk Rating	Recent Up/ Downgrade	Open to New Investors	Telephone
	MARKET		FUND TYPE, CATEGORY & OBJECTIVE		RATINGS				NEW INVESTORS	
Goldman Sachs U.S. Mortgages Fund Class R6 Shares	GGIUX	NAS CM	Open End	US Fixed Inc (Govt Bond - Mortgage)	B-	C+	B	Up	Y	800-526-7384
Goldman Sachs U.S. Mortgages Cl Sep Account Inst Shares	GSUPX	NAS CM	Open End	US Fixed Inc (Govt Bond - Mortgage)	B-	C+	B	Up	Y	800-526-7384
Goldman Sachs U.S. Mortgages Fund Institutional Shares	GSUIX	NAS CM	Open End	US Fixed Inc (Govt Bond - Mortgage)	C+	C+	B-		Y	800-526-7384
Goldman Sachs U.S. Mortgages Fund Investor Shares	GGIRX	NAS CM	Open End	US Fixed Inc (Govt Bond - Mortgage)	C+	C+	B-		Y	800-526-7384
Great Lakes Bond Fund Institutional Class Shares	GLBNX	NAS CM	Open End	US Fixed Inc (Income)	C	C	B-		Y	
Great-West Bond Index Fund Class L	MXBJX	NAS CM	Open End	US Fixed Inc (Growth)	B	B-	B	Up	Y	
Great-West Bond Index Fund Institutional Class	MXCOX	NAS CM	Open End	US Fixed Inc (Growth)	B-	B-	B		Y	
Great-West Bond Index Fund Investor Class	MXBIX	NAS CM	Open End	US Fixed Inc (Growth)	B	B-	B	Up	Y	
Great-West Core Bond Fund Institutional Class	MXIUX	NAS CM	Open End	US Fixed Inc (Growth & Income)	B	C+	B+	Up	Y	
Great-West Core Bond Fund Investor Class	MXFDX	NAS CM	Open End	US Fixed Inc (Growth & Income)	B	C+	B+	Up	Y	
Great-West Core Strategies: Flexible Bond Fund Class L	MXGAX	NAS CM	Open End	US Fixed Inc (Growth & Income)	C-	D+	B	Up	Y	
Great-West Core Strategies: Flexible Bond Institutional Cl	MXEDX	NAS CM	Open End	US Fixed Inc (Growth & Income)	C-	D+	B	Up	Y	
Great-West Core Strategies: Inflat-Protect Securities Cl L	MXGEX	NAS CM	Open End	US Fixed Inc (Income)	C-	D+	B-	Up	Y	
Great-West Core Strategies: Inflat-Protect Sec Inst Cl	MXEGX	NAS CM	Open End	US Fixed Inc (Income)	C-	D+	B	Up	Y	
Great-West Core Strategies: Short Duration Bond Cl L	MXGDX	NAS CM	Open End	US Fixed Inc (Growth & Income)	C-	D+	C+	Up	Y	
Great-West Core Strategies: Short Duration Bond Inst Cl	MXEEX	NAS CM	Open End	US Fixed Inc (Growth & Income)	C-	D+	C+	Up	Y	
Great-West Global Bond Fund Institutional Class	MXZMX	NAS CM	Open End	Global Fixed Inc (Worldwide Bond)	C-	D+	C		Y	
Great-West Global Bond Fund Investor Class	MXGBX	NAS CM	Open End	Global Fixed Inc (Worldwide Bond)	C-	D+	C		Y	
Great-West Govt Money Mkt Fund Institutional Class	MXGXX	NAS CM	Money Mkt	US Money Mkt (Money Mkt - Govt)	C	C-	C+		Y	
Great-West Government Money Market Fund Investor Class	MXMXX	NAS CM	Money Mkt	US Money Mkt (Money Mkt - Govt)	C	C-	C+		Y	
Great-West High Yield Bond Fund Institutional Class	MXFRX	NAS CM	Open End	US Fixed Inc (Corp Bond - High Yield)	C	D+	C	Up	Y	
Great-West High Yield Bond Fund Investor Class	MXHYX	NAS CM	Open End	US Fixed Inc (Corp Bond - High Yield)	C-	D+	C		Y	
Great-West Inflation-Protected Securities Fund Class L	MXIDX	NAS CM	Open End	US Fixed Inc (Income)	C	C	B-		Y	
Great-West Inflation-Protected Securities Institutional Cl	MXIOX	NAS CM	Open End	US Fixed Inc (Income)	C	C	B-		Y	
Great-West Inflation-Protected Securities Investor Cl	MXIHX	NAS CM	Open End	US Fixed Inc (Income)	C	C	B-		Y	
Great-West Multi-Sector Bond Fund Class L	MXGGX	NAS CM	Open End	US Fixed Inc (Growth & Income)	C	C-	C+		Y	
Great-West Multi-Sector Bond Fund Institutional Class	MXUGX	NAS CM	Open End	US Fixed Inc (Growth & Income)	C	C-	B-		Y	
Great-West Multi-Sector Bond Fund Investor Class	MXLMX	NAS CM	Open End	US Fixed Inc (Growth & Income)	C	C-	C+		Y	
Great-West Short Duration Bond Fund Class L	MXTDX	NAS CM	Open End	US Fixed Inc (Growth & Income)	C	C	C+		Y	
Great-West Short Duration Bond Fund Institutional Class	MXXJX	NAS CM	Open End	US Fixed Inc (Growth & Income)	C	C	B-		Y	
Great-West Short Duration Bond Fund Investor Class	MXSDX	NAS CM	Open End	US Fixed Inc (Growth & Income)	C	C	B-		Y	
Great-West U.S. Govt Securities Fund Institutional Class	MXDQX	NAS CM	Open End	US Fixed Inc (Govt Bond - Mortgage)	B	B-	B+		Y	
Great-West U.S. Government Securities Fund Investor Class	MXGMX	NAS CM	Open End	US Fixed Inc (Govt Bond - Mortgage)	B	B-	B+	Up	Y	
Green California Tax-Free Income Fund	CFNTX	NAS CM	Open End	US Muni Fixed Inc (Muni Bond - Single State)	C	C	B-		Y	800-955-9988
Griffin Institutional Access Credit Class L			Closed End	US Fixed Inc (Multisector Bond)	D	D	D+	Down	Y	310-469-6100
Griffin Institutional Access Credit Fund Class A	CRDTX	NAS CM	Closed End	US Fixed Inc (Multisector Bond)	D	D	C-	Down	Y	310-469-6100
Griffin Institutional Access Credit Fund Class C	CGCCX	NAS CM	Closed End	US Fixed Inc (Multisector Bond)	D	D	C-	Down	Y	310-469-6100
Griffin Institutional Access Credit Fund Class F	CRDFX	NAS CM	Closed End	US Fixed Inc (Multisector Bond)	D	D	C-	Down	Y	310-469-6100
Griffin Institutional Access Credit Fund Class I	CRDIX	NAS CM	Closed End	US Fixed Inc (Multisector Bond)	D	D	C-	Down	Y	310-469-6100
Guggenheim Credit Allocation Fund	GGM	NYSE	Closed End	US Fixed Inc (Growth & Income)	D	D	D+	Down	Y	212-739-0700
Guggenheim Energy & Income Fund	XGEIX	NAS CM	Closed End	US Fixed Inc (Income)	D	D	D		Y	212-518-9290
Guggenheim Floating Rate Strategies Fund Class A	GIFAX	NAS CM	Open End	US Fixed Inc (Income)	D	D	C-	Down	Y	212-518-9290
Guggenheim Floating Rate Strategies Fund Class C	GIFCX	NAS CM	Open End	US Fixed Inc (Income)	D	D	D+	Down	Y	212-518-9290
Guggenheim Floating Rate Strategies Fund Class P	GIFPX	NAS CM	Open End	US Fixed Inc (Income)	D	D	C-	Down	Y	212-518-9290
Guggenheim Floating Rate Strategies Fund Class R6	GIFSX	NAS CM	Open End	US Fixed Inc (Income)	D	D	C-	Down	Y	212-518-9290
Guggenheim Floating Rate Strategies Institutional Cl	GIFIX	NAS CM	Open End	US Fixed Inc (Income)	D	D	C-	Down	Y	212-518-9290
Guggenheim High Yield Fund Class A	SIHAX	NAS CM	Open End	US Fixed Inc (Corp Bond - High Yield)	D+	D	C-	Down	Y	212-518-9290
Guggenheim High Yield Fund Class C	SIHSX	NAS CM	Open End	US Fixed Inc (Corp Bond - High Yield)	D	D	C-	Down	Y	212-518-9290
Guggenheim High Yield Fund Class P	SIHPX	NAS CM	Open End	US Fixed Inc (Corp Bond - High Yield)	D+	D	C-	Down	Y	212-518-9290
Guggenheim High Yield Fund Class R6	SHYSX	NAS CM	Open End	US Fixed Inc (Corp Bond - High Yield)	D+	D	C-	Down	Y	212-518-9290
Guggenheim High Yield Fund Institutional Class	SHYIX	NAS CM	Open End	US Fixed Inc (Corp Bond - High Yield)	D+	D	C-	Down	Y	212-518-9290
Guggenheim Investment Grade Bond Fund Class A	SIUSX	NAS CM	Open End	US Fixed Inc (Multisector Bond)	B	B-	A-	Up	Y	212-518-9290

★ Expanded analysis of this fund is included in Section II.

TOTAL RETURNS & PERFORMANCE									ASSETS		ASSET ALLOCATION & TURNOVER							MINIMUMS		FEES		
3-Month Total Return	6-Month Total Return	1-Year Total Return	3-Year Total Return	5-Year Total Return	Dividend Yield (TTM)	Expense Ratio	3-Yr Std Deviation	Effective Duration	NAV	Total Assets (MIL)	%Cash	%Government Bonds	%Municipal Bonds	%Corporate Bonds	%Other	Turnover Ratio	Average Coupon Rate	Min Initial Investment	Min Additional Investment	Front End Fee (%)	Back End Fee (%)	Inception Date
2.41	4.01	6.09	12.12	17.10	3.05	0.44	2.25	2.09	10.75	360.2	-40	0	0	0	1	1,233	3.45	5,000,000				Jul-15
2.41	3.92	6.09	12.12	16.96	3.05	0.44	2.25	2.09	10.72	360.2	-40	0	0	0	1	1,233	3.45	0				Nov-03
2.31	3.91	5.98	11.98	16.93	3.04	0.45	2.26	2.09	10.74	360.2	-40	0	0	0	1	1,233	3.45	1,000,000				Nov-03
2.29	3.86	5.88	11.68	16.29	2.95	0.54	2.27	2.09	10.74	360.2	-40	0	0	0	1	1,233	3.45	0				Jul-11
5.38	2.17	3.89	9.49	16.93	2.47	0.58	3.66		10	104.7	2	0	7	68	0	87	4.04	100,000	100			Sep-12
2.64	6.00	8.15	14.49	19.57	2.05	0.75	3.36	5.90	9.53	1,366	1	45	1	24	0	40	3.04	0				Jul-11
2.67	6.26	8.76	16.57	23.12	2.77	0.14	3.29	5.90	10.47	1,366	1	45	1	24	0	40	3.04	0				May-15
2.68	6.12	8.42	15.31	21.03	1.05	0.5	3.28	5.90	15.31	1,366	1	45	1	24	0	40	3.04	0				Dec-92
4.86	5.85	8.46	17.25	25.22	2.97	0.35	3.35	5.55	10.49	431.7	0	20	1	33	4	180	3.36	0				May-15
4.66	5.59	8.10	15.94	22.93	2.45	0.7	3.35	5.55	11.54	431.7	0	20	1	33	4	180	3.36	0				May-03
3.84	6.72	8.61			1.68	1.05			10.79	11.2	2	41	0	23	0		3.09	0				Sep-18
3.94	6.94	9.26			1.86	0.45			11.08	11.2	2	41	0	23	0		3.09	0				Jun-18
4.56	3.43	4.66			2.15	0.95			10.54	140.3	1	69	1	0	0	59	1.01	0				Sep-18
4.71	3.80	5.24			2.53	0.35			10.65	140.3	1	69	1	0	0	59	1.01	0				Jun-18
5.18	2.07	3.49			2.05	0.85			10.34	193.1	1	2	0	82	0	105	3.02	0				Sep-18
5.31	2.33	4.07			2.53	0.25			10.51	193.1	1	2	0	82	0	105	3.02	0				Jun-18
3.29	-0.74	-1.40	3.12	4.93	3.95	0.65	5.02	-0.71	8.86	412.3	9	61	0	22	0	73	2.94	0				May-15
3.22	-0.85	-1.69	2.18	3.11	3.86	1.01	4.96	-0.71	8.01	412.3	9	61	0	22	0	73	2.94	0				Jul-99
0.06	0.40	1.39	4.84	5.39	1.56	0.11	0.16		1	2,482	87	13	0	0	0	0		0				Oct-15
0.03	0.28	1.05	3.80	3.90	1.22	0.46	0.16		1	2,482	87	13	0	0	0	0		0				Feb-82
12.42	-1.21	2.76	12.55	26.12	4.9	0.75	8.9	4.34	9.27	251.1	0	0	0	100	0	64	5.25	0				May-15
12.29	-1.45	2.42	11.41	23.95	5.51	1.1	8.93	4.34	7.56	251.1	0	0	0	100	0	64	5.25	0				May-03
4.77	2.97	4.30			1.63	0.95		5.83	10.18	365.7	0	50	1	0	0	66	0.94	0				Jan-18
4.86	3.05	4.55			2.15	0.35		5.83	10.13	365.7	0	50	1	0	0	66	0.94	0				Jan-18
4.89	2.88	4.31			1.49	0.7		5.83	10.19	365.7	0	50	1	0	0	66	0.94	0				Jan-18
9.66	1.05	3.79	10.53	21.20	2.52	1.15	6.88	6.17	10.1	581.7	0	9	2	68	0	81	4.72	0				Sep-18
9.79	1.30	4.50	12.59	24.86	2.86	0.55	6.88	6.17	9.6	581.7	0	9	2	68	0	81	4.72	0				May-15
9.80	1.16	4.09	11.42	22.78	1.63	0.9	6.91	6.17	13.83	581.7	0	9	2	68	0	81	4.72	0				Nov-94
5.30	2.80	4.44	9.37	12.58	2.36	0.85	2.95	1.67	9.79	283.7	3	1	0	88	0	136	3.11	0				Oct-12
5.51	2.94	4.81	10.80	14.82	2.9	0.25	2.99	1.67	10.1	283.7	3	1	0	88	0	136	3.11	0				May-15
5.43	2.83	4.44	9.68	12.93	2.06	0.6	2.96	1.67	10.72	283.7	3	1	0	88	0	136	3.11	0				Aug-95
0.96	6.29	7.98	15.19	20.04	2.58	0.25	2.93	4.96	10.14	361.6	0	41	0	0	0	57	2.91	0				May-15
0.88	6.03	7.64	13.95	18.07	1.4	0.6	2.91	4.96	12.97	361.6	0	41	0	0	0	57	2.91	0				Dec-92
2.74	1.78	3.04	8.38	13.39	1.81	0.77	3.11	4.59	11.7	62.9	2	0	98	0	0	4	4.71	1,000	100			Dec-85
10.61	-7.52	-4.37			5.69	2.86			22.22	--								2,500		4.25		Sep-17
10.65	-7.52	-4.40	6.76		7.63	2.61	10.22		22.23	--								2,500	100	5.75		Apr-17
10.65	-7.52	-4.40	6.76		7.63	3.36	10.22		22.23	--								2,500	100		1.00	Apr-17
10.60	-7.53	-4.41	6.71		7.61	1.85			22.23	--								0				Sep-17
10.65	-7.52	-4.39	6.77		7.63	2.36	10.22		22.23	--								1,000,000				Apr-17
14.20	-6.37	-3.20	4.65	25.28	13.12	2.74	11.91		17.01	135.1	0	0	0	99	1	52	7.13					Jun-13
25.84	-11.75	-11.34	-6.04		14.66	1.75	18.54		745.49	--	0	0	0	99	5	16	6.59	25,000				Aug-15
8.13	-6.64	-4.39	1.31	8.46	4.7	1.06	8.56	1.04	23.16	780.3	11	1	0	84	1	10	4.61	2,500	100	3.00		Nov-11
7.94	-6.99	-5.10	-0.96	4.48	3.9	1.81	8.56	1.04	23.15	780.3	11	1	0	84	1	10	4.61	2,500	100		1.00	Nov-11
8.13	-6.64	-4.39	1.27	8.47	4.7	1.06	8.55	1.04	23.17	780.3	11	1	0	84	1	10	4.61	0				May-15
8.19	-6.53	-4.15	2.00	9.76	4.95	0.82	8.56	1.04	23.18	780.3	11	1	0	84	1	10	4.61	2,000,000				Mar-19
8.19	-6.53	-4.20	1.99	9.75	4.95	0.82	8.56	1.04	23.18	780.3	11	1	0	84	1	10	4.61	2,000,000				Nov-11
9.51	-5.77	-2.73	4.67	19.34	6.27	1.28	9.02	3.75	10.03	357.7	18	0	0	98	-5	61	6.23	2,500	100	4.00		Aug-96
9.23	-6.16	-3.49	2.25	14.90	5.47	2.03	8.99	3.75	10.11	357.7	18	0	0	98	-5	61	6.23	2,500	100		1.00	May-00
9.38	-5.88	-2.83	4.48	19.41	6.27	1.28	8.99	3.75	10.03	357.7	18	0	0	98	-5	61	6.23	0				May-15
9.61	-5.61	-2.37	5.79	20.67	6.69	0.9	9.03	3.75	10.02	357.7	18	0	0	98	-5	61	6.23	2,000,000				May-17
9.42	-5.64	-2.51	5.37	21.00	6.61	1	8.95	3.75	8.17	357.7	18	0	0	98	-5	61	6.23	2,000,000				Jul-08
5.44	8.71	9.79	17.05	27.98	2.02	0.8	2.79	5.84	20.14	1,078	20	22	2	26	-3	77	2.92	2,500	100	4.00		Aug-85

	MARKET		FUND TYPE, CATEGORY & OBJECTIVE		RATINGS				NEW INVESTORS	
Fund Name	Ticker Symbol	Traded On	Fund Type	Category and (Prospectus Objective)	Overall Rating	Reward Rating	Risk Rating	Recent Up/ Downgrade	Open to New Investors	Telephone
Guggenheim Investment Grade Bond Fund Class C	SDICX	NAS CM	Open End	US Fixed Inc (Multisector Bond)	B	C+	A-	Up	Y	212-518-9290
Guggenheim Investment Grade Bond Fund Class P	SIUPX	NAS CM	Open End	US Fixed Inc (Multisector Bond)	B	B-	A-	Up	Y	212-518-9290
Guggenheim Investment Grade Bond Fund Institutional Class	GIUSX	NAS CM	Open End	US Fixed Inc (Multisector Bond)	B	B-	A-	Up	Y	212-518-9290
Guggenheim Limited Duration Fund A-Class	GILDX	NAS CM	Open End	US Fixed Inc (Income)	C	C	B-		Y	212-518-9290
Guggenheim Limited Duration Fund C-Class	GILFX	NAS CM	Open End	US Fixed Inc (Income)	C	C	B-		Y	212-518-9290
Guggenheim Limited Duration Fund Class P	GILPX	NAS CM	Open End	US Fixed Inc (Income)	C	C	B-		Y	212-518-9290
Guggenheim Limited Duration Fund Class R6	GIKRX	NAS CM	Open End	US Fixed Inc (Income)	C+	C	B	Up	Y	212-518-9290
Guggenheim Limited Duration Fund Institutional Class	GILHX	NAS CM	Open End	US Fixed Inc (Income)	C+	C	B	Up	Y	212-518-9290
Guggenheim Macro Opportunities Fund Class A	GIOAX	NAS CM	Open End	Fixed Inc Misc (Multisector Bond)	D+	D	C	Down	Y	212-518-9290
Guggenheim Macro Opportunities Fund Class C	GIOCX	NAS CM	Open End	Fixed Inc Misc (Multisector Bond)	D	D-	C	Down	Y	212-518-9290
Guggenheim Macro Opportunities Fund Class P	GIOPX	NAS CM	Open End	Fixed Inc Misc (Multisector Bond)	D+	D	C	Down	Y	212-518-9290
Guggenheim Macro Opportunities Fund Class R6	GIOSX	NAS CM	Open End	Fixed Inc Misc (Multisector Bond)	D+	D	C	Down	Y	212-518-9290
Guggenheim Macro Opportunities Fund Institutional Class	GIOIX	NAS CM	Open End	Fixed Inc Misc (Multisector Bond)	D+	D	C	Down	Y	212-518-9290
Guggenheim Municipal Income Fund Class A	GIJAX	NAS CM	Open End	US Muni Fixed Inc (Muni Bond - Natl)	C	C	B-		Y	212-518-9290
Guggenheim Municipal Income Fund Class C	GIJCX	NAS CM	Open End	US Muni Fixed Inc (Muni Bond - Natl)	C	C-	B-		Y	212-518-9290
Guggenheim Municipal Income Fund Class P	GIJPX	NAS CM	Open End	US Muni Fixed Inc (Muni Bond - Natl)	C	C	B-		Y	212-518-9290
Guggenheim Municipal Income Fund Institutional Class	GIJIX	NAS CM	Open End	US Muni Fixed Inc (Muni Bond - Natl)	C	C	B		Y	212-518-9290
Guggenheim Strategic Opportunities Fund	GOF	NYSE	Closed End	US Fixed Inc (Growth & Income)	C-	D+	C	Down	Y	312-827-0100
Guggenheim Taxable Municipal Managed Duration Trust	GBAB	NYSE	Closed End	US Fixed Inc (Govt Bond - Treasury)	C-	C	C-	Down	Y	312-827-0100
Guggenheim Total Return Bond Fund Class A	GIBAX	NAS CM	Open End	US Fixed Inc (Growth & Income)	B	B-	A-	Up	Y	212-518-9290
Guggenheim Total Return Bond Fund Class C	GIBCX	NAS CM	Open End	US Fixed Inc (Growth & Income)	B	C+	A-	Up	Y	212-518-9290
Guggenheim Total Return Bond Fund Class P	GIBLX	NAS CM	Open End	US Fixed Inc (Growth & Income)	B	B-	A-	Up	Y	212-518-9290
Guggenheim Total Return Bond Fund Class R6	GIBRX	NAS CM	Open End	US Fixed Inc (Growth & Income)	B	B-	A-	Up	Y	212-518-9290
Guggenheim Total Return Bond Fund Institutional Class	GIBIX	NAS CM	Open End	US Fixed Inc (Growth & Income)	B	B-	A-	Up	Y	212-518-9290
Guggenheim Ultra Short Duration Fund Class A	GIYAX	NAS CM	Open End	US Fixed Inc (Income)	C	C-	C+		Y	212-518-9290
Guggenheim Ultra Short Duration Fund Institutional	GIYIX	NAS CM	Open End	US Fixed Inc (Income)	C	C-	C+		Y	212-518-9290
GuideMark® Core Fixed Income Fund Institutional Shares	GICFX	NAS CM	Open End	US Fixed Inc (Corp Bond - General)	C-	D+	C		Y	603-888-5500
GuideMark® Core Fixed Income Fund Service Shares	GMCOX	NAS CM	Open End	US Fixed Inc (Corp Bond - General)	B-	B-	B	Up	Y	603-888-5500
GuideMark® Opportunistic Fixed Income Institutional Shares	GIOFX	NAS CM	Open End	Global Fixed Inc (Income)	C-	D+	C	Down	Y	603-888-5500
GuideMark® Opportunistic Fixed Income Fund Service Shares	GMIFX	NAS CM	Open End	Global Fixed Inc (Income)	D	D	C	Down	Y	603-888-5500
GuideMark® Tax-Exempt Fixed Income Fund Service Shares	GMTEX	NAS CM	Open End	US Muni Fixed Inc (Muni Bond - Natl)	C	C-	C+		Y	603-888-5500
Guidepath® Conservative Income Fund	GPICX	NAS CM	Open End	US Fixed Inc (Income)	C-	D+	C		Y	800-664-5345
Guidepath® Income Fund	GPINX	NAS CM	Open End	US Fixed Inc (Income)	C-	D+	C		Y	800-664-5345
GuideStone Funds Extended-Duration Bond Institutional Cl	GEDYX	NAS CM	Open End	US Fixed Inc (Income)	B	B-	B+	Up	Y	214-720-1171
GuideStone Funds Extended-Duration Bond Investor Cl	GEDZX	NAS CM	Open End	US Fixed Inc (Income)	B	B-	B+	Up	Y	214-720-1171
GuideStone Funds Global Bond Fund Institutional Class	GGBEX	NAS CM	Open End	Global Fixed Inc (Multisector Bond)	C-	C-	C	Down	Y	214-720-1171
GuideStone Funds Global Bond Fund Investor Class	GGBFX	NAS CM	Open End	Global Fixed Inc (Multisector Bond)	C-	D+	C	Down	Y	214-720-1171
GuideStone Funds Low-Duration Bond Institutional Cl	GLDYX	NAS CM	Open End	US Fixed Inc (Income)	C	C	B-		Y	214-720-1171
GuideStone Funds Low-Duration Bond Fund Investor Class	GLDZX	NAS CM	Open End	US Fixed Inc (Income)	C	C	B-		Y	214-720-1171
GuideStone Funds Medium-Duration Bond Institutional Cl	GMDYX	NAS CM	Open End	US Fixed Inc (Income)	B	C+	B+	Up	Y	214-720-1171
GuideStone Funds Medium-Duration Bond Fund Investor Class	GMDZX	NAS CM	Open End	US Fixed Inc (Income)	B	C+	B+	Up	Y	214-720-1171
GuideStone Funds Money Market Fund Institutional Class	GMYXX	NAS CM	Money Mkt	US Money Mkt (Money Mkt - Govt)	C	C-	C+		Y	214-720-1171
GuideStone Funds Money Market Fund Investor Class	GMZXX	NAS CM	Money Mkt	US Money Mkt (Money Mkt - Govt)	C	C-	C+		Y	214-720-1171
Guinness Atkinson Renminbi Yuan & Bond Fund	GARBX	NAS CM	Open End	Emerg Mkts Fixed Inc (Growth & Income)	C	D	B-		Y	800-915-6566
Hancock Horizon Louisiana Tax-Free Income Institutional Cl	HHLTX	NAS CM	Open End	US Muni Fixed Inc (Muni Bond - Single State)	C+	C	B	Up	Y	800-990-2434
Hancock Horizon Louisiana Tax-Free Income Investor Cl	HHLAX	NAS CM	Open End	US Muni Fixed Inc (Muni Bond - Single State)	C+	C	B	Up	Y	800-990-2434
Hancock Horizon Mississippi Tax-Free Income Inst Cl	HHMTX	NAS CM	Open End	US Muni Fixed Inc (Muni Bond - Single State)	C+	C	B	Up	Y	800-990-2434
Hancock Horizon Mississippi Tax-Free Income Investor Cl	HIMAX	NAS CM	Open End	US Muni Fixed Inc (Muni Bond - Single State)	C+	C	B	Up	Y	800-990-2434
Hanlon Managed Income Fund Class A	HANAX	NAS CM	Open End	US Fixed Inc (Income)	D	D	D+	Down	Y	
Hanlon Managed Income Fund Class C	HANCX	NAS CM	Open End	US Fixed Inc (Income)	D	D	D+	Down	Y	
Hanlon Managed Income Fund Class I	HANIX	NAS CM	Open End	US Fixed Inc (Income)	D	D	D+	Down	Y	
Hanlon Managed Income Fund Class R	HANRX	NAS CM	Open End	US Fixed Inc (Income)	D	D	D+	Down	Y	

★Expanded analysis of this fund is included in Section II.

TOTAL RETURNS & PERFORMANCE									ASSETS		ASSET ALLOCATION & TURNOVER							MINIMUMS		FEES		
3-Month Total Return	6-Month Total Return	1-Year Total Return	3-Year Total Return	5-Year Total Return	Dividend Yield (TTM)	Expense Ratio	3-Yr Std Deviation	Effective Duration	NAV	Total Assets (MIL)	%Cash	%Government Bonds	%Municipal Bonds	%Corporate Bonds	%Other	Turnover Ratio	Average Coupon Rate	Min Initial Investment	Min Additional Investment	Front End Fee (%)	Back End Fee (%)	Inception Date
5.22	8.30	8.96	14.50	23.30	1.31	1.55	2.79	5.84	20.05	1,078	20	22	2	26	-3	77	2.92	2,500	100		1.00	May-00
5.38	8.64	9.72	17.01	27.97	2.02	0.8	2.79	5.84	20.15	1,078	20	22	2	26	-3	77	2.92	0				May-15
5.47	8.87	10.06	18.06	29.77	2.3	0.51	2.82	5.84	20.11	1,078	20	22	2	26	-3	77	2.92	2,000,000				Jan-13
4.21	3.74	4.50	8.63	14.72	2.02	0.77	1.72	1.74	25.27	2,928	23	9	1	32	-3	72	2.52	2,500	100	2.25		Dec-13
3.98	3.36	3.72	6.23	10.48	1.29	1.52	1.7	1.74	25.25	2,928	23	9	1	32	-3	72	2.52	2,500	100		1.00	Dec-13
4.21	3.73	4.54	8.63	14.66	2.02	0.77	1.72	1.74	25.27	2,928	23	9	1	32	-3	72	2.52	0				May-15
4.28	3.87	4.77	9.48	16.17	2.29	0.52	1.72	1.74	25.25	2,928	23	9	1	32	-3	72	2.52	2,000,000				Mar-19
4.23	3.82	4.75	9.44	16.13	2.27	0.52	1.69	1.74	25.26	2,928	23	9	1	32	-3	72	2.52	2,000,000				Dec-13
5.56	-0.84	-0.19	3.22	13.48	2.93	1.43	4.26	0.95	25.1	4,368	31	1	1	21	0	46	3.65	2,500	100	4.00		Nov-11
5.37	-1.17	-0.94	0.99	9.36	2.16	2.18	4.23	0.95	25.09	4,368	31	1	1	21	0	46	3.65	2,500	100		1.00	Nov-11
5.56	-0.84	-0.20	3.22	13.66	2.92	1.43	4.25	0.95	25.11	4,368	31	1	1	21	0	46	3.65	0				May-15
5.66	-0.64	0.15	4.44	15.66	3.34	1.02	4.25	0.95	25.12	4,368	31	1	1	21	0	46	3.65	2,000,000				Mar-19
5.65	-0.60	0.19	4.47	15.69	3.33	1.02	4.22	0.95	25.14	4,368	31	1	1	21	0	46	3.65	2,000,000				Nov-11
1.88	1.21	3.06	11.67	18.17	2.05	0.81	4.18	6.30	13.12	59.1	9	0	91	9	-1	30	5.08	2,500	100	4.00		Apr-04
1.70	0.84	2.30	9.21	13.85	1.31	1.56	4.17	6.30	13.11	59.1	9	0	91	9	-1	30	5.08	2,500	100		1.00	Jan-12
1.88	1.13	2.97	11.57	18.12	2.05	0.81	4.17	6.30	13.11	59.1	9	0	91	9	-1	30	5.08	0				May-15
1.95	1.33	3.31	12.41	19.55	2.3	0.56	4.16	6.30	13.12	59.1	9	0	91	9	-1	30	5.08	2,000,000				Jan-12
9.94	-2.96	-0.68	12.30	46.23	5.57	1.62	8.41		15.48	603.3	5	5	5	56	0	38						Jul-07
4.85	3.20	5.60	17.93	38.25	1.08	1.2	5.24		22.46	390.7	-3	0	90	8	1	6	6.66					Oct-10
5.62	8.76	9.84	16.83	28.59	2.14	0.81	2.88	5.97	29.15	16,534	16	24	2	13	-2	68	2.95	2,500	100	4.00		Nov-11
5.46	8.40	9.06	14.29	23.95	1.42	1.56	2.86	5.97	29.16	16,534	16	24	2	13	-2	68	2.95	2,500	100		1.00	Nov-11
5.65	8.80	9.88	16.87	28.78	2.14	0.81	2.87	5.97	29.14	16,534	16	24	2	13	-2	68	2.95	0				May-15
5.68	8.90	10.14	17.89	30.66	2.42	0.52	2.87	5.97	29.19	16,534	16	24	2	13	-2	68	2.95	2,000,000				Oct-16
5.68	8.94	10.19	17.91	30.67	2.42	0.52	2.86	5.97	29.18	16,534	16	24	2	13	-2	68	2.95	2,000,000				Nov-11
1.80	0.41	1.40	5.30	7.85	1.95	0.58	1.26	0.60	9.93	468.7	45	0	0	53	-1	55	2.49	2,500	100			Dec-18
1.87	0.53	1.65	5.99	9.10	2.2	0.3	1.27	0.60	9.92	468.7	45	0	0	53	-1	55	2.49	2,000,000				Mar-14
0.00	0.00	0.00	2.47	4.61	0	0.6	0.78			139.4	-2	27	1	22	0	239	3.38	0				Apr-11
4.43	6.41	8.77	14.70	20.49	1.06	1.2	3.44		10.196	139.3	-7	29	1	25	0	279	3.25	0				Jun-01
1.40	-2.96	-4.14	2.06	6.84	5.33	0.96	4.95		7.632	38.6	12	22	0	0	0	71	4.55	0				Apr-11
1.47	-3.04	-4.50	-0.74	2.91	4.72	1.56	4.99		7.635	38.6	12	22	0	0	0	71	4.55	0				Apr-11
3.36	0.37	2.40	8.86	15.07	2.54	1.29	5.04		11.294	23.1	0	0	100	0	0	36	5.24	0				Jun-01
0.21	-0.80	0.28			1.55	0.76		1.90	9.91	9.5	35	65	0	0	0	191	1.95	0				Apr-18
1.79	-1.59	0.82			2.64	0.95		5.45	9.995	28.6	3	69	0	13	0	248	2.76	0				Apr-18
5.55	8.49	12.65	24.00	41.83	2.52	0.57	5.2	9.67	19.45	276.7	5	38	0	55	0	39	3.48	1,000,000				Aug-01
5.53	8.41	12.41	23.06	40.03	2.27	0.83	5.21	9.67	19.46	276.7	5	38	0	55	0	39	3.48	1,000	100			Aug-01
7.37	-1.72	0.63	7.04	18.89	2.93	0.55	6.49	5.14	9.75	577.1	-9	48	0	38	0	59	4.15	1,000,000				Apr-15
7.28	-1.93	0.26	6.04	17.07	2.75	0.83	6.54	5.14	9.72	577.1	-9	48	0	38	0	59	4.15	1,000	100			Dec-06
2.91	2.10	3.43	8.15	10.97	2.28	0.35	1.73	1.91	13.56	957.7	-34	45	0	25	0	525	2.37	1,000,000				Aug-01
2.84	2.05	3.22	7.36	9.55	2.01	0.62	1.7	1.91	13.57	957.7	-34	45	0	25	0	525	2.37	1,000	100			Aug-01
5.40	6.15	9.31	17.54	25.35	2.51	0.4	3.86	6.40	15.79	1,756	-10	33	0	26	0	433	3.53	1,000,000				Aug-01
5.33	5.96	8.95	16.60	23.58	2.26	0.66	3.84	6.40	15.79	1,756	-10	33	0	26	0	433	3.53	1,000	100			Aug-01
0.06	0.39	1.36	4.80	5.44	1.54	0.14	0.17		1	1,548	72	28	0	0	0			1,000,000				Aug-01
0.02	0.28	1.10	4.00	4.21	1.27	0.42	0.17		1	1,548	72	28	0	0	0			1,000	100			Aug-01
0.88	-0.34	-0.39	6.11	0.65	1.42	0.9	5.47		11.43	1.4	35	25	0	39	0	0	4.98	10,000	1,000			Jun-11
1.43	2.44	4.15	11.07	19.74	2.37	0.75	3.11		17.45	6.3	7	0	93	0	0	10	3.95	1,000	100			Feb-11
1.40	2.36	3.99	10.50	18.53	2.22	1	3.11		17.45	6.3	7	0	93	0	0	10	3.95	1,000	100	4.00		Feb-11
2.15	2.58	4.44	11.25	19.51	2.18	0.75	3.51		16.99	12.0	5	0	95	0	0	6	3.86	1,000	100			Feb-11
2.12	2.58	4.38	10.75	18.44	2.07	1	3.53		17.01	12.0	5	0	95	0	0	6	3.86	1,000	100	4.00		Feb-11
-0.23	-7.81	-5.79	-4.97		2.57	2.06	5.12	5.72	8.49	99.0	40	0	0	52	0	484	5.17	2,500	500	5.75		Sep-15
-0.35	-8.16	-6.49	-7.02		2.05	2.81	5.22	5.72	8.4	99.0	40	0	0	52	0	484	5.17	2,500	500		1.00	Sep-15
-0.11	-7.68	-5.53	-4.14		2.8	1.81	5.14	5.72	8.45	99.0	40	0	0	52	0	484	5.17	100,000	500			Sep-15
-0.23	-7.86	-5.90	-5.35		2.46	2.21	5.14	5.72	8.46	99.0	40	0	0	52	0	484	5.17	2,500	500			Sep-15

	MARKET		FUND TYPE, CATEGORY & OBJECTIVE		RATINGS				NEW INVESTORS	
Fund Name	Ticker Symbol	Traded On	Fund Type	Category and (Prospectus Objective)	Overall Rating	Reward Rating	Risk Rating	Recent Up/ Downgrade	Open to New Investors	Telephone
Harbor Bond Fund Administrative Class	HRBDX	NAS CM	Open End	US Fixed Inc (Corp Bond - General)	B	C+	B+	Up	Y	800-422-1050
Harbor Bond Fund Institutional Class	HABDX	NAS CM	Open End	US Fixed Inc (Corp Bond - General)	B	C+	B+	Up	Y	800-422-1050
Harbor Bond Fund Retirement Class	HBFRX	NAS CM	Open End	US Fixed Inc (Corp Bond - General)	B	C+	B+	Up	Y	800-422-1050
Harbor Core Bond Fund Institutional Class	HACBX	NAS CM	Open End	US Fixed Inc (Corp Bond - General)	C-	D+	B	Up	Y	800-422-1050
Harbor Core Bond Fund Retirement Class	HCBRX	NAS CM	Open End	US Fixed Inc (Corp Bond - General)	C-	D+	B	Up	Y	800-422-1050
Harbor High Yield Bond Fund Retirement Class	HNHYX	NAS CM	Open End	US Fixed Inc (Corp Bond - High Yield)	C-	D+	C		Y	800-422-1050
Harbor High-Yield Bond Fund Administrative Class	HYFRX	NAS CM	Open End	US Fixed Inc (Corp Bond - High Yield)	C-	D+	C		Y	800-422-1050
Harbor High-Yield Bond Fund Institutional Class	HYFAX	NAS CM	Open End	US Fixed Inc (Corp Bond - High Yield)	C-	D+	C		Y	800-422-1050
Harbor High-Yield Bond Fund Investor Class	HYFIX	NAS CM	Open End	US Fixed Inc (Corp Bond - High Yield)	C-	D+	C		Y	800-422-1050
Harbor High-Yield Opportunities Fund Administrative Class	HHYAX	NAS CM	Open End	US Fixed Inc (Corp Bond - High Yield)	D+	D	C-	Down	Y	800-422-1050
Harbor High-Yield Opportunities Fund Institutional Class	HHYNX	NAS CM	Open End	US Fixed Inc (Corp Bond - High Yield)	D+	D	C-	Down	Y	800-422-1050
Harbor High-Yield Opportunities Fund Investor Class	HHYVX	NAS CM	Open End	US Fixed Inc (Corp Bond - High Yield)	D+	D	C-	Down	Y	800-422-1050
Harbor High-Yield Opportunities Fund Retirement Class	HHYRX	NAS CM	Open End	US Fixed Inc (Corp Bond - High Yield)	D+	D	C-	Down	Y	800-422-1050
Harbor Money Market Fund Administrative Class	HRMXX	NAS CM	Money Mkt	US Money Mkt (Money Mkt - Govt)	C	C-	C+		Y	800-422-1050
Harbor Money Market Fund Institutional Class	HARXX	NAS CM	Money Mkt	US Money Mkt (Money Mkt - Govt)	C	C-	C+		Y	800-422-1050
Hartford Emerging Markets Local Debt Fund Class A	HLDAX	NAS CM	Open End	Emerg Mkts Fixed Inc (Diversified Emerg Mkts)	D	D	D+	Down	Y	888-843-7824
Hartford Emerging Markets Local Debt Fund Class C	HLDCX	NAS CM	Open End	Emerg Mkts Fixed Inc (Diversified Emerg Mkts)	D	D	D+	Down	Y	888-843-7824
Hartford Emerging Markets Local Debt Fund Class F	HLDFX	NAS CM	Open End	Emerg Mkts Fixed Inc (Diversified Emerg Mkts)	D	D	D+	Down	Y	888-843-7824
Hartford Emerging Markets Local Debt Fund Class I	HLDIX	NAS CM	Open End	Emerg Mkts Fixed Inc (Diversified Emerg Mkts)	D	D	D+	Down	Y	888-843-7824
Hartford Emerging Markets Local Debt Fund Class R3	HLDRX	NAS CM	Open End	Emerg Mkts Fixed Inc (Diversified Emerg Mkts)	D	D	D+	Down	Y	888-843-7824
Hartford Emerging Markets Local Debt Fund Class R4	HLDSX	NAS CM	Open End	Emerg Mkts Fixed Inc (Diversified Emerg Mkts)	D	D	D+	Down	Y	888-843-7824
Hartford Emerging Markets Local Debt Fund Class R5	HLDTX	NAS CM	Open End	Emerg Mkts Fixed Inc (Diversified Emerg Mkts)	D	D	D+	Down	Y	888-843-7824
Hartford Emerging Markets Local Debt Fund Class Y	HLDYX	NAS CM	Open End	Emerg Mkts Fixed Inc (Diversified Emerg Mkts)	D	D	D+	Down	Y	888-843-7824
Hartford Floating Rate Fund Class A	HFLAX	NAS CM	Open End	US Fixed Inc (Income)	D+	D	C-	Down	Y	888-843-7824
Hartford Floating Rate Fund Class C	HFLCX	NAS CM	Open End	US Fixed Inc (Income)	D	D	C-	Down	Y	888-843-7824
Hartford Floating Rate Fund Class F	HFLFX	NAS CM	Open End	US Fixed Inc (Income)	D+	D	C-	Down	Y	888-843-7824
Hartford Floating Rate Fund Class I	HFLIX	NAS CM	Open End	US Fixed Inc (Income)	D+	D	C-	Down	Y	888-843-7824
Hartford Floating Rate Fund Class R3	HFLRX	NAS CM	Open End	US Fixed Inc (Income)	D	D	C-	Down	Y	888-843-7824
Hartford Floating Rate Fund Class R4	HFLSX	NAS CM	Open End	US Fixed Inc (Income)	D+	D	C-	Down	Y	888-843-7824
Hartford Floating Rate Fund Class R5	HFLTX	NAS CM	Open End	US Fixed Inc (Income)	D+	D	C-	Down	Y	888-843-7824
Hartford Floating Rate Fund Class Y	HFLYX	NAS CM	Open End	US Fixed Inc (Income)	D+	D	C-	Down	Y	888-843-7824
Hartford Floating Rate High Income Fund Class A	HFHAX	NAS CM	Open End	US Fixed Inc (Corp Bond - High Yield)	D+	D	C-	Down	Y	888-843-7824
Hartford Floating Rate High Income Fund Class C	HFHCX	NAS CM	Open End	US Fixed Inc (Corp Bond - High Yield)	D	D	D+	Down	Y	888-843-7824
Hartford Floating Rate High Income Fund Class F	HFHFX	NAS CM	Open End	US Fixed Inc (Corp Bond - High Yield)	D+	D	C-	Down	Y	888-843-7824
Hartford Floating Rate High Income Fund Class I	HFHIX	NAS CM	Open End	US Fixed Inc (Corp Bond - High Yield)	D+	D	C-	Down	Y	888-843-7824
Hartford Floating Rate High Income Fund Class R3	HFHRX	NAS CM	Open End	US Fixed Inc (Corp Bond - High Yield)	D	D	C-	Down	Y	888-843-7824
Hartford Floating Rate High Income Fund Class R4	HFHSX	NAS CM	Open End	US Fixed Inc (Corp Bond - High Yield)	D+	D	C-	Down	Y	888-843-7824
Hartford Floating Rate High Income Fund Class R5	HFHTX	NAS CM	Open End	US Fixed Inc (Corp Bond - High Yield)	D+	D	C-	Down	Y	888-843-7824
Hartford Floating Rate High Income Fund Class Y	HFHYX	NAS CM	Open End	US Fixed Inc (Corp Bond - High Yield)	D+	D	C-	Down	Y	888-843-7824
Hartford High Yield Fund Class A	HAHAX	NAS CM	Open End	US Fixed Inc (Corp Bond - High Yield)	C-	D+	C		Y	888-843-7824
Hartford High Yield Fund Class C	HAHCX	NAS CM	Open End	US Fixed Inc (Corp Bond - High Yield)	C-	D+	C		Y	888-843-7824
Hartford High Yield Fund Class F	HAHFX	NAS CM	Open End	US Fixed Inc (Corp Bond - High Yield)	C-	D+	C		Y	888-843-7824
Hartford High Yield Fund Class R3	HAHRX	NAS CM	Open End	US Fixed Inc (Corp Bond - High Yield)	C-	D+	C		Y	888-843-7824
Hartford High Yield Fund Class R4	HAHSX	NAS CM	Open End	US Fixed Inc (Corp Bond - High Yield)	C-	D+	C		Y	888-843-7824
Hartford High Yield Fund Class R5	HAHTX	NAS CM	Open End	US Fixed Inc (Corp Bond - High Yield)	C-	D+	C		Y	888-843-7824
Hartford High Yield Fund Class Y	HAHYX	NAS CM	Open End	US Fixed Inc (Corp Bond - High Yield)	C-	D+	C		Y	888-843-7824
Hartford High Yield Fund Institutional	HAHIX	NAS CM	Open End	US Fixed Inc (Corp Bond - High Yield)	C-	D+	C		Y	888-843-7824
Hartford High Yield HLS Fund Class IA	HIAYX	NAS CM	Open End	US Fixed Inc (Corp Bond - High Yield)	C-	D+	C		Y	888-843-7824
Hartford High Yield HLS Fund Class IB	HBHYX	NAS CM	Open End	US Fixed Inc (Corp Bond - High Yield)	C-	D+	C		Y	888-843-7824
Hartford Inflation Plus Fund Class A	HIPAX	NAS CM	Open End	US Fixed Inc (Income)	C+	C	B	Up	Y	888-843-7824
Hartford Inflation Plus Fund Class C	HIPCX	NAS CM	Open End	US Fixed Inc (Income)	C	C	B-		Y	888-843-7824
Hartford Inflation Plus Fund Class F	HIPFX	NAS CM	Open End	US Fixed Inc (Income)	C+	C	B	Up	Y	888-843-7824

★ Expanded analysis of this fund is included in Section II.

TOTAL RETURNS & PERFORMANCE									ASSETS		ASSET ALLOCATION & TURNOVER							MINIMUMS		FEES		
3-Month Total Return	6-Month Total Return	1-Year Total Return	3-Year Total Return	5-Year Total Return	Dividend Yield (TTM)	Expense Ratio	3-Yr Std Deviation	Effective Duration	NAV	Total Assets (MIL)	%Cash	%Government Bonds	%Municipal Bonds	%Corporate Bonds	%Other	Turnover Ratio	Average Coupon Rate	Min Initial Investment	Min Additional Investment	Front End Fee (%)	Back End Fee (%)	Inception Date
4.22	6.05	8.32	15.91	22.95	2.7	1.29	3.42		12.31	1,903	-3	40	0	20	0	644	3.10	50,000				Nov-02
4.20	6.19	8.54	16.82	24.45	2.97	1.04	3.44		12.29	1,903	-3	40	0	20	0	644	3.10	1,000				Dec-87
4.22	6.24	8.64	16.92	24.56	3.05	0.96	3.43		12.28	1,903	-3	40	0	20	0	644	3.10	1,000,000				Jun-18
4.19	7.00	9.51			2.69	0.45			11.05	101.2	5	15	2	35	0	61	3.64	1,000				Jun-18
4.21	6.95	9.60			2.76	0.37			11.05	101.2	5	15	2	35	0	61	3.64	1,000,000				Jun-18
9.06	-3.88	-0.33	8.84	18.91	5.81	0.57	8.01	3.64	9.27	405.5	3	0	0	97	0	80	5.64	1,000,000				Mar-16
8.93	-4.12	-0.67	7.88	17.05	5.41	0.9	8	3.64	9.31	405.5	3	0	0	97	0	80	5.64	50,000				Nov-02
9.03	-3.92	-0.42	8.69	18.54	5.72	0.65	8.01	3.64	9.27	405.5	3	0	0	97	0	80	5.64	1,000				Nov-02
8.81	-4.19	-0.79	7.42	16.40	5.28	1.02	7.98	3.64	9.3	405.5	3	0	0	97	0	80	5.64	2,500				Nov-02
9.34	-4.65	-0.90			5.15	0.98			9.15	76.8	3	0	0	97	0	94	6.12	50,000				Nov-17
9.40	-4.62	-0.70			5.36	0.73			9.15	76.8	3	0	0	97	0	94	6.12	1,000				Nov-17
9.31	-4.70	-1.07			4.97	1.1			9.15	76.8	3	0	0	97	0	94	6.12	2,500				Nov-17
9.43	-4.49	-0.62			5.44	0.65			9.15	76.8	3	0	0	97	0	94	6.12	1,000,000				Nov-17
0.04	0.29	1.00	3.97	4.76	1.15	0.53	0.12		1	102.1	100	0	0	0	0			50,000				Nov-02
0.07	0.37	1.21	4.43	5.19	1.38	0.28	0.14		1	102.1	100	0	0	0	0			1,000				Dec-87
12.92	-8.14	-4.52	0.32	8.80	4.96	1.19	13.98	5.58	5.36	79.4	4	84	0	13	0	110	4.23	5,000	50	4.50		May-11
12.89	-8.50	-5.32	-1.91	4.86	4.07	1.94	14.08	5.58	5.37	79.4	4	84	0	13	0	110	4.23	5,000	50		1.00	May-11
13.09	-7.98	-4.32	1.32	10.61	5.4	0.84	13.97	5.58	5.34	79.4	4	84	0	13	0	110	4.23	1,000,000				Feb-17
13.07	-8.03	-4.25	1.08	10.24	5.3	0.94	14.04	5.58	5.34	79.4	4	84	0	13	0	110	4.23	5,000	50			May-11
12.99	-8.12	-4.50	0.21	7.77	5.03	1.49	14	5.58	5.34	79.4	4	84	0	13	0	110	4.23	0				May-11
13.21	-8.16	-4.54	0.35	8.80	4.98	1.19	14.17	5.58	5.34	79.4	4	84	0	13	0	110	4.23	0				May-11
13.19	-8.01	-4.22	1.19	10.04	5.56	0.89	14.06	5.58	5.12	79.4	4	84	0	13	0	110	4.23	0				May-11
13.18	-8.06	-4.22	1.30	10.63	5.41	0.89	14.05	5.58	5.3	79.4	4	84	0	13	0	110	4.23	250,000				May-11
9.70	-5.48	-2.96	3.60	11.84	4.22	1	8.94	0.23	7.88	2,020	13	0	0	87	0	46	2.64	2,000	50	3.00		Apr-05
9.57	-5.76	-3.59	1.39	7.98	3.45	1.74	8.91	0.23	7.96	2,020	13	0	0	87	0	46	2.64	2,000	50		1.00	Apr-05
9.51	-5.46	-2.65	4.63	13.82	4.58	0.65	8.84	0.23	7.86	2,020	13	0	0	87	0	46	2.64	1,000,000				Feb-17
9.77	-5.38	-2.60	4.46	13.39	4.51	0.72	8.95	0.23	7.87	2,020	13	0	0	87	0	46	2.64	2,000	50			Aug-06
9.58	-5.55	-3.16	2.84	10.45	3.96	1.26	8.89	0.23	7.93	2,020	13	0	0	87	0	46	2.64	0				Dec-06
9.70	-5.37	-2.85	3.65	12.00	4.22	1.01	8.84	0.23	7.88	2,020	13	0	0	87	0	46	2.64	0				Dec-06
9.77	-5.27	-2.64	4.43	13.52	4.46	0.77	8.92	0.23	7.87	2,020	13	0	0	87	0	46	2.64	0				Dec-06
9.68	-5.38	-2.65	4.44	13.63	4.6	0.73	8.87	0.23	7.84	2,020	13	0	0	87	0	46	2.64	250,000				Apr-05
11.08	-6.03	-3.09	4.10	13.37	4.49	1.06	9.99	0.38	9.04	348.3	12	0	0	88	0	78	2.78	2,000	50	3.00		Sep-11
10.92	-6.30	-3.84	1.88	9.30	3.7	1.81	9.97	0.38	9.12	348.3	12	0	0	88	0	78	2.78	2,000	50		1.00	Sep-11
11.19	-5.91	-2.92	5.10	14.99	4.81	0.76	10.02	0.38	9.01	348.3	12	0	0	88	0	78	2.78	1,000,000				Feb-17
11.07	-6.24	-3.19	4.65	14.42	4.76	0.81	10.11	0.38	8.99	348.3	12	0	0	88	0	78	2.78	2,000	50			Sep-11
10.98	-6.15	-3.36	3.29	11.92	4.17	1.36	9.96	0.38	9.06	348.3	12	0	0	88	0	78	2.78	0				Sep-11
11.10	-5.95	-3.10	4.18	13.52	4.49	1.06	9.96	0.38	9.02	348.3	12	0	0	88	0	78	2.78	0				Sep-11
11.08	-5.84	-2.84	5.18	16.31	4.8	0.76	9.92	0.38	8.99	348.3	12	0	0	88	0	78	2.78	0				Sep-11
11.20	-5.84	-2.76	5.16	15.22	4.77	0.79	9.97	0.38	9	348.3	12	0	0	88	0	78	2.78	250,000				Sep-11
10.16	-3.76	0.12	9.36	20.24	4.85	1.06	8.94	4.14	7.03	328.8	2	0	0	97	0	36	5.41	2,000	50	4.50		Sep-98
10.00	-4.12	-0.61	6.87	15.91	4.08	1.81	8.88	4.14	7.01	328.8	2	0	0	97	0	36	5.41	2,000	50		1.00	Sep-98
10.08	-3.60	0.42	10.43	21.87	5.32	0.71	8.85	4.14	7.03	328.8	2	0	0	97	0	36	5.41	1,000,000				Feb-17
9.92	-3.90	-0.16	8.32	18.55	4.54	1.36	8.82	4.14	7.03	328.8	2	0	0	97	0	36	5.41	0				Dec-06
10.15	-3.75	0.13	9.36	20.36	4.85	1.06	8.92	4.14	7.04	328.8	2	0	0	97	0	36	5.41	0				Dec-06
10.27	-3.51	0.59	10.44	22.31	5.22	0.76	8.85	4.14	7.01	328.8	2	0	0	97	0	36	5.41	0				Dec-06
10.28	-3.70	0.44	10.11	22.07	5.08	0.8	8.98	4.14	6.98	328.8	2	0	0	97	0	36	5.41	250,000				Sep-98
10.20	-3.63	0.39	10.26	21.98	5.12	0.81	8.87	4.14	7.05	328.8	2	0	0	97	0	36	5.41	2,000	50			May-07
10.47	-4.22	0.00	9.62	21.99	6.75	0.78	9.18	4.07	7.7	222.6	2	0	0	97	0	41	5.41	0				Sep-98
10.54	-4.30	-0.29	8.86	20.43	6.58	1.03	9.3	4.07	7.55	222.6	2	0	0	97	0	41	5.41	0				Sep-98
5.16	3.34	5.13	9.88	13.48	1.69	0.85	3.35	5.01	10.8	479.0	6	81	0	4	0	77	1.06	2,000	50	4.50		Oct-02
5.03	2.96	4.38	7.55	9.34	0.57	1.59	3.37	5.01	10.43	479.0	6	81	0	4	0	77	1.06	2,000	50		1.00	Oct-02
5.25	3.57	5.45	10.91	14.66	1.96	0.45	3.37	5.01	11.01	479.0	6	81	0	4	0	77	1.06	1,000,000				Feb-17

	MARKET		FUND TYPE, CATEGORY & OBJECTIVE		RATINGS				NEW INVESTORS	
Fund Name	Ticker Symbol	Traded On	Fund Type	Category and (Prospectus Objective)	Overall Rating	Reward Rating	Risk Rating	Recent Up/ Downgrade	Open to New Investors	Telephone
Hartford Inflation Plus Fund Class I	HIPIX	NAS CM	Open End	US Fixed Inc (Income)	C+	C	B	Up	Y	888-843-7824
Hartford Inflation Plus Fund Class R3	HIPRX	NAS CM	Open End	US Fixed Inc (Income)	C+	C	B-	Up	Y	888-843-7824
Hartford Inflation Plus Fund Class R4	HIPSX	NAS CM	Open End	US Fixed Inc (Income)	C+	C	B	Up	Y	888-843-7824
Hartford Inflation Plus Fund Class R5	HIPTX	NAS CM	Open End	US Fixed Inc (Income)	C+	C	B	Up	Y	888-843-7824
Hartford Inflation Plus Fund Class Y	HIPYX	NAS CM	Open End	US Fixed Inc (Income)	C+	C	B	Up	Y	888-843-7824
Hartford Municipal Income Fund Class A	HMKAX	NAS CM	Open End	US Muni Fixed Inc (Income)	C	C-	B-		Y	888-843-7824
Hartford Municipal Income Fund Class C	HMKCX	NAS CM	Open End	US Muni Fixed Inc (Income)	C	C-	B-		Y	888-843-7824
Hartford Municipal Income Fund Class F	HMKFX	NAS CM	Open End	US Muni Fixed Inc (Income)	C	C-	B		Y	888-843-7824
Hartford Municipal Income Fund Class I	HMKIX	NAS CM	Open End	US Muni Fixed Inc (Income)	C	C-	B		Y	888-843-7824
Hartford Municipal Opportunities Fund Class A	HHMAX	NAS CM	Open End	US Muni Fixed Inc (Muni Bond - Natl)	C	C-	B-		Y	888-843-7824
Hartford Municipal Opportunities Fund Class C	HHMCX	NAS CM	Open End	US Muni Fixed Inc (Muni Bond - Natl)	C	C-	C+		Y	888-843-7824
Hartford Municipal Opportunities Fund Class F	HHMFX	NAS CM	Open End	US Muni Fixed Inc (Muni Bond - Natl)	C	C-	B-		Y	888-843-7824
Hartford Municipal Opportunities Fund Class I	HHMIX	NAS CM	Open End	US Muni Fixed Inc (Muni Bond - Natl)	C	C-	B-		Y	888-843-7824
Hartford Municipal Opportunities Fund Class Y	HHMYX	NAS CM	Open End	US Muni Fixed Inc (Muni Bond - Natl)	C	C-	B-		Y	888-843-7824
Hartford Municipal Short Duration Fund Class A	HMJAX	NAS CM	Open End	US Muni Fixed Inc (Income)	C	C-	C+		Y	888-843-7824
Hartford Municipal Short Duration Fund Class C	HMJCX	NAS CM	Open End	US Muni Fixed Inc (Income)	C	C-	C		Y	888-843-7824
Hartford Municipal Short Duration Fund Class F	HMJFX	NAS CM	Open End	US Muni Fixed Inc (Income)	C	C-	C+		Y	888-843-7824
Hartford Municipal Short Duration Fund Class I	HMJIX	NAS CM	Open End	US Muni Fixed Inc (Income)	C	C-	C+		Y	888-843-7824
Hartford Quality Bond Fund Class A	HQBAX	NAS CM	Open End	US Fixed Inc (Corp Bond - High Quality)	B	B-	B+	Up	Y	888-843-7824
Hartford Quality Bond Fund Class C	HQBCX	NAS CM	Open End	US Fixed Inc (Corp Bond - High Quality)	B-	C+	B		Y	888-843-7824
Hartford Quality Bond Fund Class F	HQBFX	NAS CM	Open End	US Fixed Inc (Corp Bond - High Quality)	B	B-	B+	Up	Y	888-843-7824
Hartford Quality Bond Fund Class I	HQBIX	NAS CM	Open End	US Fixed Inc (Corp Bond - High Quality)	B	B-	B+	Up	Y	888-843-7824
Hartford Quality Bond Fund Class R3	HQBRX	NAS CM	Open End	US Fixed Inc (Corp Bond - High Quality)	B-	C+	B		Y	888-843-7824
Hartford Quality Bond Fund Class R4	HQBSX	NAS CM	Open End	US Fixed Inc (Corp Bond - High Quality)	B	B-	B+	Up	Y	888-843-7824
Hartford Quality Bond Fund Class R5	HQBTX	NAS CM	Open End	US Fixed Inc (Corp Bond - High Quality)	B	B-	B+	Up	Y	888-843-7824
Hartford Quality Bond Fund Class Y	HQBYX	NAS CM	Open End	US Fixed Inc (Corp Bond - High Quality)	B	B-	B+	Up	Y	888-843-7824
Hartford Schroders Emerg Mkts Multi-Sector Bond Cl A	SMSVX	NAS CM	Open End	Emerg Mkts Fixed Inc (Diversified Emerg Mkts)	D	D	D	Down	Y	888-843-7824
Hartford Schroders Emerg Mkts Multi-Sector Bond Cl C	HFZCX	NAS CM	Open End	Emerg Mkts Fixed Inc (Diversified Emerg Mkts)	D	D	D	Down	Y	888-843-7824
Hartford Schroders Emerg Mkts Multi-Sector Bond Cl F	HFZFX	NAS CM	Open End	Emerg Mkts Fixed Inc (Diversified Emerg Mkts)	D	D	D	Down	Y	888-843-7824
Hartford Schroders Emerg Mkts Multi-Sector Bond Cl I	SMSNX	NAS CM	Open End	Emerg Mkts Fixed Inc (Diversified Emerg Mkts)	D	D	D	Down	Y	888-843-7824
Hartford Schroders Emerg Mkts Multi-Sector Bond Cl R3	HFZRX	NAS CM	Open End	Emerg Mkts Fixed Inc (Diversified Emerg Mkts)	D	D	D	Down	Y	888-843-7824
Hartford Schroders Emerg Mkts Multi-Sector Bond Cl R4	HFZSX	NAS CM	Open End	Emerg Mkts Fixed Inc (Diversified Emerg Mkts)	D	D	D	Down	Y	888-843-7824
Hartford Schroders Emerg Mkts Multi-Sector Bond Cl R5	HFZTX	NAS CM	Open End	Emerg Mkts Fixed Inc (Diversified Emerg Mkts)	D	D	D	Down	Y	888-843-7824
Hartford Schroders Emerg Mkts Multi-Sector Bond Cl SDR	SMSRX	NAS CM	Open End	Emerg Mkts Fixed Inc (Diversified Emerg Mkts)	D	D	D	Down	Y	888-843-7824
Hartford Schroders Emerg Mkts Multi-Sector Bond Cl Y	HFZYX	NAS CM	Open End	Emerg Mkts Fixed Inc (Diversified Emerg Mkts)	D	D	D	Down	Y	888-843-7824
Hartford Schroders Opportunistic Income Fund Class A			Closed End	US Fixed Inc (Growth & Income)	U	U	U		Y	
Hartford Schroders Opportunistic Income Fund Class A2			Closed End	US Fixed Inc (Growth & Income)	U	U	U		Y	
Hartford Schroders Opportunistic Income Fund Class I			Closed End	US Fixed Inc (Growth & Income)	U	U	U		Y	
Hartford Schroders Opportunistic Income Fund Class SDR			Closed End	US Fixed Inc (Growth & Income)	U	U	U		Y	
Hartford Schroders Securitized Income Fund Class A	HITAX	NAS CM	Open End	US Fixed Inc (Growth & Income)	D	D	C-		Y	888-843-7824
Hartford Schroders Securitized Income Fund Class C	HITCX	NAS CM	Open End	US Fixed Inc (Growth & Income)	D	D	D+		Y	888-843-7824
Hartford Schroders Securitized Income Fund Class F	HITFX	NAS CM	Open End	US Fixed Inc (Growth & Income)	D	D	C-		Y	888-843-7824
Hartford Schroders Securitized Income Fund Class I	HITIX	NAS CM	Open End	US Fixed Inc (Growth & Income)	D	D	C-		Y	888-843-7824
Hartford Schroders Securitized Income Fund Class SDR	HITSX	NAS CM	Open End	US Fixed Inc (Growth & Income)	D	D	C-		Y	888-843-7824
Hartford Schroders Securitized Income Fund Class Y	HITYX	NAS CM	Open End	US Fixed Inc (Growth & Income)	D	D	C-		Y	888-843-7824
Hartford Schroders Tax-Aware Bond Fund Class A	STWVX	NAS CM	Open End	US Fixed Inc (Income)	B-	C	B+	Up	Y	888-843-7824
Hartford Schroders Tax-Aware Bond Fund Class C	HFKCX	NAS CM	Open End	US Fixed Inc (Income)	C+	C	B	Up	Y	888-843-7824
Hartford Schroders Tax-Aware Bond Fund Class F	HFKFX	NAS CM	Open End	US Fixed Inc (Income)	B-	C	B+	Up	Y	888-843-7824
Hartford Schroders Tax-Aware Bond Fund Class I	STWTX	NAS CM	Open End	US Fixed Inc (Income)	B-	C	B+	Up	Y	888-843-7824
Hartford Schroders Tax-Aware Bond Fund Class SDR	HFKVX	NAS CM	Open End	US Fixed Inc (Income)	B-	C	B+	Up	Y	888-843-7824
Hartford Schroders Tax-Aware Bond Fund Class Y	HFKYX	NAS CM	Open End	US Fixed Inc (Income)	B-	C	B+	Up	Y	888-843-7824
Hartford Short Duration Fund Class A	HSDAX	NAS CM	Open End	US Fixed Inc (Multisector Bond)	C	C-	C+		Y	888-843-7824

★ Expanded analysis of this fund is included in Section II.

TOTAL RETURNS & PERFORMANCE									ASSETS		ASSET ALLOCATION & TURNOVER							MINIMUMS		FEES		
3-Month Total Return	6-Month Total Return	1-Year Total Return	3-Year Total Return	5-Year Total Return	Dividend Yield (TTM)	Expense Ratio	3-Yr Std Deviation	Effective Duration	NAV	Total Assets (MIL)	%Cash	%Government Bonds	%Municipal Bonds	%Corporate Bonds	%Other	Turnover Ratio	Average Coupon Rate	Min Initial Investment	Min Additional Investment	Front End Fee (%)	Back End Fee (%)	Inception Date
5.35	3.57	5.49	10.85	15.04	1.91	0.55	3.38	5.01	11.02	479.0	6	81	0	4	0	77	1.06	2,000	50			Aug-06
5.05	3.21	4.75	8.74	11.46	1.36	1.17	3.34	5.01	10.59	479.0	6	81	0	4	0	77	1.06	0				Dec-06
5.15	3.34	5.14	9.78	13.22	1.61	0.87	3.3	5.01	10.81	479.0	6	81	0	4	0	77	1.06	0				Dec-06
5.27	3.58	5.49	10.76	14.87	1.89	0.57	3.36	5.01	10.98	479.0	6	81	0	4	0	77	1.06	0				Dec-06
5.34	3.56	5.50	10.96	15.21	1.92	0.56	3.37	5.01	11.04	479.0	6	81	0	4	0	77	1.06	250,000				Nov-03
2.93	1.23	3.69	13.29	22.09	2.18	0.7	4.51	5.87	10.76	59.5	8	0	92	0	0	47	4.48	2,000	50	4.50		May-15
2.75	0.88	2.93	12.43	19.75	1.52	1.45	4.51	5.87	10.76	59.5	8	0	92	0	0	47	4.48	2,000	50		1.00	May-15
2.81	1.38	4.00	14.15	23.65	2.48	0.4	4.45	5.87	10.73	59.5	8	0	92	0	0	47	4.48	1,000,000				Feb-17
2.99	1.34	3.94	14.09	23.58	2.42	0.47	4.5	5.87	10.73	59.5	8	0	92	0	0	47	4.48	2,000	50			May-15
2.68	0.79	2.86	11.24	19.13	2.25	0.7	4.14	5.26	8.87	1,241	7	0	93	0	0	15	4.49	2,000	50	4.50		May-07
2.50	0.42	2.10	8.87	14.72	1.49	1.46	4.14	5.26	8.88	1,241	7	0	93	0	0	15	4.49	2,000	50		1.00	May-07
2.75	0.94	3.18	12.29	20.69	2.57	0.39	4.17	5.26	8.86	1,241	7	0	93	0	0	15	4.49	1,000,000				Feb-17
2.73	1.02	3.22	12.28	20.69	2.5	0.46	4.12	5.26	8.88	1,241	7	0	93	0	0	15	4.49	2,000	50			May-07
2.73	0.89	3.08	12.12	20.52	2.48	0.47	4.16	5.26	8.87	1,241	7	0	93	0	0	15	4.49	250,000				May-18
2.00	0.30	1.52	5.85	8.54	1.72	0.7	2.29	2.73	10.09	23.8	10	0	90	0	0	73	4.54	2,000	50	4.50		May-15
1.82	-0.05	0.89	5.16	6.41	1.16	1.45	2.29	2.73	10.09	23.8	10	0	90	0	0	73	4.54	2,000	50		1.00	May-15
2.07	0.45	1.83	6.78	9.93	2.03	0.4	2.34	2.73	10.09	23.8	10	0	90	0	0	73	4.54	1,000,000				Feb-17
2.05	0.41	1.77	6.57	9.81	1.99	0.47	2.32	2.73	10.08	23.8	10	0	90	0	0	73	4.54	2,000	50			May-15
2.51	6.24	8.25	14.47	19.83	2.19	0.86	3.18	5.01	10.65	140.3	18	25	0	0	0	59	3.22	2,000	50	4.50		Nov-12
2.20	5.85	7.47	11.80	15.20	1.48	1.61	3.19	5.01	10.57	140.3	18	25	0	0	0	59	3.22	2,000	50		1.00	Nov-12
2.58	6.43	8.62	15.77	21.80	2.72	0.45	3.26	5.01	10.6	140.3	18	25	0	0	0	59	3.22	1,000,000				Feb-17
2.57	6.40	8.62	15.38	21.35	2.61	0.61	3.19	5.01	10.61	140.3	18	25	0	0	0	59	3.22	2,000	50			Nov-12
2.36	6.12	7.74	13.18	18.23	1.89	1.2	3.25	5.01	10.63	140.3	18	25	0	0	0	59	3.22	0				Nov-12
2.54	6.44	8.50	15.11	21.16	2.42	0.95	3.21	5.01	10.64	140.3	18	25	0	0	0	59	3.22	0				Nov-12
2.55	6.47	8.52	15.47	22.17	2.54	0.65	3.22	5.01	10.63	140.3	18	25	0	0	0	59	3.22	0				Nov-12
2.55	6.44	8.88	15.86	22.07	3.08	0.55	3.18	5.01	10.68	140.3	18	25	0	0	0	59	3.22	250,000				Nov-12
14.20	-8.36	-8.32	-0.86	12.40	5.74	1.15	14.25	6.75	8.13	60.0	5	48	0	41	0	240	5.90	5,000	50	4.50		Jun-13
14.02	-8.65	-8.91	-3.11	8.20	4.92	1.9	14.26	6.75	8.11	60.0	5	48	0	41	0	240	5.90	5,000	50		1.00	Oct-16
14.11	-8.33	-8.11	0.08	14.01	11.87	0.75	14.24	6.75	7.64	60.0	5	48	0	41	0	240	5.90	1,000,000				Feb-17
14.33	-8.08	-7.91	0.09	14.01	6.11	0.9	14.22	6.75	8.12	60.0	5	48	0	41	0	240	5.90	5,000	50			Jun-13
14.16	-8.35	-8.13	-0.53	12.29	6.02	1.45	14.24	6.75	8.14	60.0	5	48	0	41	0	240	5.90	0				Oct-16
14.15	-8.24	-8.03	-0.19	13.17	6.08	1.15	14.23	6.75	8.12	60.0	5	48	0	41	0	240	5.90	0				Oct-16
14.18	-8.21	-8.01	0.00	13.89	6.13	0.85	14.22	6.75	8.11	60.0	5	48	0	41	0	240	5.90	0				Oct-16
14.35	-8.14	-7.94	0.28	14.46	6.19	0.75	14.27	6.75	8.12	60.0	5	48	0	41	0	240	5.90	5,000,000				Dec-14
14.21	-8.16	-7.96	0.16	14.16	6.18	0.85	14.19	6.75	8.11	60.0	5	48	0	41	0	240	5.90	250,000				Oct-16
7.66	-2.87					2.48			24.2	--	-4	0	0	5	0		2.64	5,000	250	3.00		Nov-19
7.69						2.98			24.17	--	-4	0	0	5	0		2.64	5,000	250			Jan-20
7.79	-2.74					2.18			24.24	--	-4	0	0	5	0		2.64	5,000				Nov-19
7.89	-2.63					1.98			24.26	--	-4	0	0	5	0		2.64	5,000,000				Nov-19
6.56	-2.78	-1.73			2.44	1.3		1.89	9.63	71.9	-15	0	0	3	0	35	2.99	2,000	50	3.00		Feb-19
6.27	-3.18	-2.49				2.15		1.89	9.63	71.9	-15	0	0	3	0	35	2.99	2,000	50		1.00	Feb-20
6.51	-2.82	-1.73			2.55	0.9		1.89	9.62	71.9	-15	0	0	3	0	35	2.99	1,000,000				Feb-19
6.46	-2.79	-1.74			2.45	1.05		1.89	9.63	71.9	-15	0	0	3	0	35	2.99	2,000	50			Feb-19
6.64	-2.68	-1.55			2.62	0.9		1.89	9.63	71.9	-15	0	0	3	0	35	2.99	5,000,000				Feb-19
6.58	-2.75	-1.57			2.52	1		1.89	9.63	71.9	-15	0	0	3	0	35	2.99	250,000				Feb-19
3.98	3.64	5.28	13.27	21.99	1.74	0.71	3.05	4.29	11.41	395.3	8	7	59	27	0	161	3.45	2,000	50	4.50		Dec-14
3.73	3.27	4.42	10.49	17.27	0.87	1.59	3.05	4.29	11.42	395.3	8	7	59	27	0	161	3.45	2,000	50		1.00	Oct-16
3.95	3.77	5.55	14.03	23.48	2	0.46	3.03	4.29	11.42	395.3	8	7	59	27	0	161	3.45	1,000,000				Feb-17
4.04	3.85	5.52	14.01	23.46	1.97	0.49	3.07	4.29	11.42	395.3	8	7	59	27	0	161	3.45	2,000	50			Oct-11
3.96	3.78	5.56	14.07	23.52	2	0.46	3.05	4.29	11.41	395.3	8	7	59	27	0	161	3.45	5,000,000				Oct-16
3.92	3.72	5.43	13.83	23.37	1.89	0.56	3.04	4.29	11.42	395.3	8	7	59	27	0	161	3.45	250,000				Oct-16
5.75	0.82	2.72	8.15	12.21	2.48	0.81	3.94	1.70	9.91	1,414	3	19	0	57	0	30	2.86	2,000	50	2.00		Oct-02

	MARKET			FUND TYPE, CATEGORY & OBJECTIVE	RATINGS				NEW INVESTORS	
Fund Name	Ticker Symbol	Traded On	Fund Type	Category and (Prospectus Objective)	Overall Rating	Reward Rating	Risk Rating	Recent Up/ Downgrade	Open to New Investors	Telephone
Hartford Short Duration Fund Class C	HSDCX	NAS CM	Open End	US Fixed Inc (Multisector Bond)	C	C-	C+	Up	Y	888-843-7824
Hartford Short Duration Fund Class F	HSDFX	NAS CM	Open End	US Fixed Inc (Multisector Bond)	C	C-	B-		Y	888-843-7824
Hartford Short Duration Fund Class I	HSDIX	NAS CM	Open End	US Fixed Inc (Multisector Bond)	C	C-	B-		Y	888-843-7824
Hartford Short Duration Fund Class R3	HSDRX	NAS CM	Open End	US Fixed Inc (Multisector Bond)	C	C-	C+		Y	888-843-7824
Hartford Short Duration Fund Class R4	HSDSX	NAS CM	Open End	US Fixed Inc (Multisector Bond)	C	C-	C+		Y	888-843-7824
Hartford Short Duration Fund Class R5	HSDTX	NAS CM	Open End	US Fixed Inc (Multisector Bond)	C	C-	B-		Y	888-843-7824
Hartford Short Duration Fund Class R6	HSDVX	NAS CM	Open End	US Fixed Inc (Multisector Bond)	C	C-	B-		Y	888-843-7824
Hartford Short Duration Fund Class Y	HSDYX	NAS CM	Open End	US Fixed Inc (Multisector Bond)	C	C-	B-		Y	888-843-7824
Hartford Total Return Bond HLS Fund Class IA	HIABX	NAS CM	Open End	US Fixed Inc (Corp Bond - General)	B-	C+	B+	Up	Y	888-843-7824
Hartford Total Return Bond HLS Fund Class IB	HBNBX	NAS CM	Open End	US Fixed Inc (Corp Bond - General)	B-	C+	B+	Up	Y	888-843-7824
Hartford U.S. Government Securities HLS Fund Class IA	HAUSX	NAS CM	Open End	US Fixed Inc (Govt Bond - General)	B-	C+	B		Y	888-843-7824
Hartford U.S. Government Securities HLS Fund Class IB	HBUSX	NAS CM	Open End	US Fixed Inc (Govt Bond - General)	B-	C+	B	Up	Y	888-843-7824
Hartford Ultrashort Bond HLS Fund Class IA	HUBAX	NAS CM	Open End	US Fixed Inc (Income)	C	C-	B-		Y	888-843-7824
Hartford Ultrashort Bond HLS Fund Class IB	HUBBX	NAS CM	Open End	US Fixed Inc (Income)	C	C-	C+		Y	888-843-7824
Harvest Asian Bond Fund A Shares	HXIAX	NAS CM	Open End	Emerg Mkts Fixed Inc (Income)	C-	D+	C	Down	Y	
Harvest Asian Bond Fund Institutional Shares	HXIIX	NAS CM	Open End	Emerg Mkts Fixed Inc (Income)	C-	D+	C	Down	Y	
Hawaii Municipal Fund Class Investor	SURFX	NAS CM	Open End	US Muni Fixed Inc (Muni Bond - Single State)	C	C	B-		Y	
Hawaiian Tax-Free Trust Class A	HULAX	NAS CM	Open End	US Muni Fixed Inc (Muni Bond - Single State)	C	C	B-		Y	800-437-1020
Hawaiian Tax-Free Trust Class C	HULCX	NAS CM	Open End	US Muni Fixed Inc (Muni Bond - Single State)	C	C	C+		Y	800-437-1020
Hawaiian Tax-Free Trust Class F	HULFX	NAS CM	Open End	US Muni Fixed Inc (Muni Bond - Single State)	C	C	B-		Y	800-437-1020
Hawaiian Tax-Free Trust Class Y	HULYX	NAS CM	Open End	US Muni Fixed Inc (Muni Bond - Single State)	C	C	B-		Y	800-437-1020
HC The Inflation Protected Sec Port HC Strat Shares	HCPBX	NAS CM	Open End	Inflation Linked (Income)	U	U	U		Y	
Highland Fixed Income Fund Class A	HFBAX	NAS CM	Open End	US Fixed Inc (Corp Bond - General)	C	C	B-		Y	877-665-1287
Highland Fixed Income Fund Class C	HFBCX	NAS CM	Open End	US Fixed Inc (Corp Bond - General)	C	C-	C+		Y	877-665-1287
Highland Fixed Income Fund Class Y	HFBYX	NAS CM	Open End	US Fixed Inc (Corp Bond - General)	C	C	B-		Y	877-665-1287
Highland Income Fund	HFRO	NYSE	Closed End	US Fixed Inc (Income)	D	D	D+	Down	Y	877-665-1287
Holbrook Income Fund Class I	HOBIX	NAS CM	Open End	US Fixed Inc (Income)	D	D	D+	Down	Y	
Holbrook Income Fund Investor Class	HOBEX	NAS CM	Open End	US Fixed Inc (Income)	D	D	D+	Down	Y	
Homestead Funds Daily Income Fund	HDIXX	NAS CM	Money Mkt	US Money Mkt (Money Mkt - Taxable)	C	C-	C		Y	
Homestead Funds Short-Term Bond Fund	HOSBX	NAS CM	Open End	US Fixed Inc (Corp Bond - High Quality)	B-	C	B	Up	Y	
Homestead Funds Short-Term Government Securities Fund	HOSGX	NAS CM	Open End	US Fixed Inc (Govt Bond - General)	C+	C	B		Y	
Homestead Intermediate Bond Fund	HOIBX	NAS CM	Open End	US Fixed Inc (Multisector Bond)	D	D+	B		Y	
Horizon Active Income Fund Class A	AIHAX	NAS CM	Open End	US Fixed Inc (Income)	C	C	B-		Y	
Horizon Active Income Fund Class I	AIRIX	NAS CM	Open End	US Fixed Inc (Income)	C	C	B-		Y	
Horizon Active Income Fund Investor Class	AIMNX	NAS CM	Open End	US Fixed Inc (Income)	C	C	B-		Y	
Hotchkis & Wiley High Yield Fund Class A	HWHAX	NAS CM	Open End	US Fixed Inc (Corp Bond - High Yield)	D	D	D+	Down	Y	866-493-8637
Hotchkis & Wiley High Yield Fund Class C	HWHCX	NAS CM	Open End	US Fixed Inc (Corp Bond - High Yield)	D	D	D	Down	Y	866-493-8637
Hotchkis & Wiley High Yield Fund Class I	HWHIX	NAS CM	Open End	US Fixed Inc (Corp Bond - High Yield)	D	D	D+	Down	Y	866-493-8637
Hotchkis & Wiley High Yield Fund Class Z	HWHZX	NAS CM	Open End	US Fixed Inc (Corp Bond - High Yield)	D	D	D+	Down	Y	866-493-8637
HSBC High Yield Fund A	HBYAX	NAS CM	Open End	Global Fixed Inc (Corp Bond - High Yield)	C-	D+	C		Y	888-936-4722
HSBC High Yield Fund I	HBYIX	NAS CM	Open End	Global Fixed Inc (Corp Bond - High Yield)	C-	D+	C		Y	888-936-4722
HSBC Strategic Income Fund A	HBIAX	NAS CM	Open End	US Fixed Inc (Income)	C	C-	B-		Y	888-936-4722
HSBC Strategic Income Fund I	HBIIX	NAS CM	Open End	US Fixed Inc (Income)	C	C-	B-		Y	888-936-4722
HSBC U.S. Government Money Market Fund Class A	FTRXX	NAS CM	Money Mkt	US Money Mkt (Money Mkt - Govt)	C	C-	C+		Y	888-936-4722
HSBC U.S. Government Money Market Fund Class D	HGDXX	NAS CM	Money Mkt	US Money Mkt (Money Mkt - Govt)	C	C-	C		Y	888-936-4722
HSBC U.S. Government Money Market Fund Class I	HGIXX	NAS CM	Money Mkt	US Money Mkt (Money Mkt - Govt)	C	C-	C+		Y	888-936-4722
HSBC U.S. Government Money Market Fund Class Y	RGYXX	NAS CM	Money Mkt	US Money Mkt (Money Mkt - Govt)	C	C-	C+		Y	888-936-4722
HSBC U.S. Government Money Market Fund Intermediary Class	HGGXX	NAS CM	Money Mkt	US Money Mkt (Money Mkt - Govt)	C	C-	C+		Y	888-936-4722
HSBC U.S. Govt Money Mkt Fund Intermediary Service Class	HGFXX	NAS CM	Money Mkt	US Money Mkt (Money Mkt - Govt)	C	C-	C+		Y	888-936-4722
HSBC U.S. Treasury Money Market Fund Class D	HTDXX	NAS CM	Money Mkt	US Money Mkt (Money Mkt - Govt)	C	C-	C+		Y	888-936-4722
HSBC U.S. Treasury Money Market Fund Class I	HBIXX	NAS CM	Money Mkt	US Money Mkt (Money Mkt - Govt)	C	C	C+		Y	888-936-4722
HSBC U.S. Treasury Money Market Fund Class Y	HTYXX	NAS CM	Money Mkt	US Money Mkt (Money Mkt - Govt)	C	C-	C+		Y	888-936-4722

★Expanded analysis of this fund is included in Section II.

TOTAL RETURNS & PERFORMANCE									ASSETS		ASSET ALLOCATION & TURNOVER							MINIMUMS		FEES		
3-Month Total Return	6-Month Total Return	1-Year Total Return	3-Year Total Return	5-Year Total Return	Dividend Yield (TTM)	Expense Ratio	3-Yr Std Deviation	Effective Duration	NAV	Total Assets (MIL)	%Cash	%Government Bonds	%Municipal Bonds	%Corporate Bonds	%Other	Turnover Ratio	Average Coupon Rate	Min Initial Investment	Min Additional Investment	Front End Fee (%)	Back End Fee (%)	Inception Date
5.67	0.57	2.08	5.84	8.20	1.74	1.56	3.94	1.70	9.92	1,414	3	19	0	57	0	30	2.86	2,000	50		1.00	Oct-02
5.84	1.10	3.17	9.40	13.63	3.03	0.45	3.88	1.70	9.89	1,414	3	19	0	57	0	30	2.86	1,000,000				Feb-17
5.92	1.05	3.12	9.14	13.87	2.88	0.53	3.95	1.70	9.9	1,414	3	19	0	57	0	30	2.86	2,000	50			Feb-10
5.67	0.76	2.47	7.50	10.79	2.12	1.17	3.85	1.70	9.9	1,414	3	19	0	57	0	30	2.86	0				Sep-11
5.73	0.93	2.81	8.21	12.26	2.57	0.87	3.84	1.70	9.9	1,414	3	19	0	57	0	30	2.86	0				Sep-11
5.82	1.04	3.07	9.18	14.06	2.84	0.57	3.87	1.70	9.88	1,414	3	19	0	57	0	30	2.86	0				Sep-11
5.87	1.10	3.16	8.79	12.88	3.02	0.45	3.84	1.70	9.85	1,414	3	19	0	57	0	30	2.86	0				Feb-19
5.83	1.05	3.08	9.28	14.04	2.84	0.54	3.82	1.70	9.86	1,414	3	19	0	57	0	30	2.86	250,000				Nov-03
6.53	5.41	8.85	17.74	27.05	3.82	0.51	4.15	5.79	12.06	1,998	2	20	1	27	0	61	3.22	0				Aug-77
6.48	5.27	8.52	16.78	25.53	3.58	0.76	4.15	5.79	11.98	1,998	2	20	1	27	0	61	3.22	0				Apr-98
1.68	5.33	6.58	11.61	15.88	2.46	0.52	2.25	3.74	10.86	335.5	6	47	0	0	0	44	2.64	0				Mar-87
1.59	5.24	6.30	10.76	14.45	2.19	0.77	2.23	3.74	10.84	335.5	6	47	0	0	0	44	2.64	0				May-02
1.57	1.27	2.40	6.29	7.78	1.88	0.45	0.79		10.32	437.4	4	33	0	23	0	70		0				Oct-13
1.47	1.17	2.13	5.49	6.39	1.61	0.7	0.79		10.3	437.4	4	33	0	23	0	70		0				Apr-98
9.75	-1.75	-0.68	11.36	23.36	4.98	1.13	8.39		9.45	13.4	2	14	0	84	0	659	4.57	2,500	100	4.25		Feb-13
9.85	-1.58	-0.38	12.19	24.63	5.32	0.88	8.4		9.42	13.4	2	14	0	84	0	659	4.57	1,000,000				Feb-13
2.24	1.65	3.24	8.73	13.66	2.01	0.98	3.35		11.3	161.4						24		10,000	100			Nov-88
2.19	2.10	3.34	7.47	12.26	1.79	0.85	2.66	4.04	11.56	651.2	0	0	100	0	0	12	4.70	1,000		4.00		Feb-85
1.90	1.61	2.51	4.89	7.88	0.99	1.65	2.63	4.04	11.55	651.2	0	0	100	0	0	12	4.70	1,000			1.00	Apr-96
2.24	2.21	3.74	7.90	12.71	2	0.67		4.04	11.59	651.2	0	0	100	0	0	12	4.70	0				Nov-18
2.15	2.20	3.53	8.17	13.40	1.98	0.65	2.63	4.04	11.58	651.2	0	0	100	0	0	12	4.70	0				Apr-96
-0.50	-2.64	-1.99			0	0.16				--						27		0				Apr-14
4.86	1.69	3.76	9.09	17.55	2.83	0.95	4.07		13.06	189.1	0	22	5	30	0	53	3.31	1,000	1,000	4.25		Feb-93
4.68	1.33	3.08	6.70	13.37	2.07	1.7	4.03		13.08	189.1	0	22	5	30	0	53	3.31	1,000	1,000		1.00	Sep-99
4.92	1.81	4.10	9.91	19.03	3.09	0.7	4.08		13.05	189.1	0	22	5	30	0	53	3.31	0				Nov-93
1.77	-5.42	-6.96	-0.08	3.49	7.59	1.18	8.48		12.52	873.7	39	0	0	54	10	18	7.28					Jan-00
13.24	-4.89	-2.33	6.11		4.22	1.31	10.04		9.56	121.5	3	3	0	84	0	78	4.76	100,000	500			Jul-16
13.14	-5.18	-2.76	4.54		3.72	1.81	10.04		9.56	121.5	3	3	0	84	0	78	4.76	2,500	100			Jul-16
0.00	0.17	0.77	2.87	2.90	0.92	0.79	0.15		1	178.4	100	0	0	0	0	0		500				Nov-90
2.84	4.14	5.20	10.51	13.91	1.38	0.79	1.28		5.41	533.6	5	49	0	34	0	276	2.07	500				Nov-91
0.91	3.50	4.45	8.40	9.65	1.16	0.75	1.3		5.37	76.3	4	58	0	33	0	237	1.56	500				May-95
4.01	6.28	8.50			1.59	0.81			5.41	53.7	6	28	0	33	0	395	2.77	500				May-19
3.22	1.80	3.87	5.73	8.55	2.1	1.47	3.44	7.62	9.58	257.9	3	42	1	30	0	167	3.31	2,500	250	5.75		Feb-16
3.31	2.06	4.09	6.41	8.81	2.74	1.23	3.46	7.62	9.49	257.9	3	42	1	30	0	167	3.31	10,000,000				Sep-16
3.16	2.01	4.09	6.29	8.48	2.64	1.31	3.39	7.62	9.52	257.9	3	42	1	30	0	167	3.31	2,500	250			Sep-13
10.41	-8.85	-7.51	-1.30	10.25	6.22	0.95	10.55	3.83	10.13	1,610	6	0	0	94	1	41	6.24	2,500	100	3.75		May-09
10.27	-8.91	-7.96	-3.29	6.52	5.45	1.65	10.44	3.83	10.21	1,610	6	0	0	94	1	41	6.24	2,500	100		1.00	Dec-12
10.52	-8.48	-7.01	-0.32	11.90	6.49	0.7	10.42	3.83	10.22	1,610	6	0	0	94	1	41	6.24	250,000	100			Mar-09
10.42	-8.51	-6.99	-0.10	12.16	6.6	0.6	10.42	3.83	10.22	1,610	6	0	0	94	1	41	6.24	1,000,000	100			Mar-18
10.62	-3.40	0.24	8.00	21.16	5.56	0.93	8.32		9.31	31.9	8	4	0	89	0	76	6.40	1,000	100	3.75		Jul-15
10.79	-3.22	0.58	9.13	23.23	5.88	0.58	8.32		9.35	31.9	8	4	0	89	0	76	6.40	1,000,000	0	0.00		Jul-15
12.29	1.51	4.48	12.90	24.51	4.47	1.05	7.62		10.16	29.7	14	3	0	82	0	104	5.35	1,000	100	3.75		Jul-15
12.49	1.76	4.94	14.18	26.81	4.71	0.7	7.64		10.24	29.7	14	3	0	82	0	104	5.35	1,000,000	0			Jul-15
0.00	0.19	0.88	3.31	3.40	1.03	0.66	0.16		1	36,186	67	33	0	0	0			1,000	100			May-90
0.01	0.23	1.00	3.74	3.90	1.15	0.51	0.17		1	36,186	67	33	0	0	0			1,000	100			Apr-99
0.04	0.35	1.29	4.79	5.41	1.48	0.14	0.18		1	36,186	67	33	0	0	0			50,000,000	5,000,000			Dec-03
0.01	0.30	1.19	4.46	4.90	1.37	0.26	0.18		1	36,186	67	33	0	0	0			5,000,000	0			Jul-96
0.02	0.33	1.27	4.66	5.13	1.45	0.18	0.18		1	36,186	67	33	0	0	0			20,000,000	0			Jul-16
0.02	0.32	1.24	4.60	5.04	1.42	0.2	0.18		1	36,186	67	33	0	0	0			10,000,000	0			Jul-16
0.00	0.23	0.96	3.61	3.73	1.11	0.53	0.16		1	4,145	71	29	0	0	0			1,000	100			May-01
0.04	0.35	1.26	4.67	5.16	1.44	0.14	0.17		1	4,145	71	29	0	0	0			50,000,000	5,000,000			Dec-03
0.01	0.29	1.15	4.33	4.65	1.33	0.28	0.17		1	4,145	71	29	0	0	0			5,000,000	0			May-01

	MARKET		FUND TYPE, CATEGORY & OBJECTIVE		RATINGS				NEW INVESTORS	
Fund Name	Ticker Symbol	Traded On	Fund Type	Category and (Prospectus Objective)	Overall Rating	Reward Rating	Risk Rating	Recent Up/ Downgrade	Open to New Investors	Telephone
HSBC U.S. Treasury Money Market Fund Intermediary Class	HTGXX	NAS CM	Money Mkt	US Money Mkt (Money Mkt - Govt)	C	C-	C+		Y	888-936-4722
HSBC U.S. Treasury Money Mkt Intermediary Service Cl	HTFXX	NAS CM	Money Mkt	US Money Mkt (Money Mkt - Govt)	C	C-	C+		Y	888-936-4722
ICON Flexible Bond Fund Class A	IOBAX	NAS CM	Open End	US Fixed Inc (Income)	C-	D+	C		Y	303-790-1600
ICON Flexible Bond Fund Class C	IOBCX	NAS CM	Open End	US Fixed Inc (Income)	C-	D+	C		Y	303-790-1600
ICON Flexible Bond Fund Class S	IOBZX	NAS CM	Open End	US Fixed Inc (Income)	C-	D+	C		Y	303-790-1600
Idaho Tax-Exempt Fund	NITEX	NAS CM	Open End	US Muni Fixed Inc (Muni Bond - Single State)	C+	C	B	Up	Y	
iM Dolan McEniry Corporate Bond Fund Advisor Shares	IDMAX	NAS CM	Open End	US Fixed Inc (Corp Bond - High Quality)	D+	D+	C	Up	Y	888-898-1041
iM Dolan McEniry Corporate Bond Fund Institutional Shares	IDMIX	NAS CM	Open End	US Fixed Inc (Corp Bond - High Quality)	D+	D+	C+	Up	Y	888-898-1041
Insight Select Income Fund	INSI	NYSE	Closed End	US Fixed Inc (Corp Bond - General)	C-	C-	C-		Y	212-527-1800
Integrity High Income Fund Class A	IHFAX	NAS CM	Open End	US Fixed Inc (Income)	C-	D+	C		Y	800-276-1262
Integrity High Income Fund Class C	IHFCX	NAS CM	Open End	US Fixed Inc (Income)	C-	D+	C		Y	800-276-1262
Integrity High Income Fund Class I	IHFIX	NAS CM	Open End	US Fixed Inc (Income)	C-	D+	C		Y	800-276-1262
Integrity Short Term Government Fund Class A	MDSAX	NAS CM	Open End	US Fixed Inc (Govt Bond - Mortgage)	C	C	B-		Y	
Integrity Short Term Government Fund Class I	MDSIX	NAS CM	Open End	US Fixed Inc (Govt Bond - Mortgage)	C	C	B		Y	
Intrepid Income Fund Institutional Class	ICMUX	NAS CM	Open End	US Fixed Inc (Growth & Income)	C-	D+	C		Y	
Invesco Advantage Municipal Income Trust II	VKI	AMEX	Closed End	US Muni Fixed Inc (Muni Bond - Natl)	C-	C-	C-	Down	Y	404-892-0896
Invesco Bond Fund	VBF	NYSE	Closed End	US Fixed Inc (Corp Bond - General)	C	C	C-	Up	Y	404-892-0896
Invesco California Value Municipal Income Trust	VCV	NYSE	Closed End	US Muni Fixed Inc (Muni Bond - Single State)	C-	C-	C-		Y	404-892-0896
Invesco Conservative Income Fund Class A	ICIVX	NAS CM	Open End	US Fixed Inc (Income)	C	C	B-		Y	800-659-1005
Invesco Conservative Income Fund Class R6	ICIRX	NAS CM	Open End	US Fixed Inc (Income)	C	C	B-			800-659-1005
Invesco Conservative Income Fund Class Y	ICIYX	NAS CM	Open End	US Fixed Inc (Income)	C	C	B-		Y	800-659-1005
Invesco Conservative Income Fund Institutional Class	ICIFX	NAS CM	Open End	US Fixed Inc (Income)	C	C	B-		Y	800-659-1005
Invesco Core Plus Bond Fund Class A	ACPSX	NAS CM	Open End	US Fixed Inc (Income)	C+	C	B	Up	Y	800-659-1005
Invesco Core Plus Bond Fund Class C	CPCFX	NAS CM	Open End	US Fixed Inc (Income)	C+	C	B	Up	Y	800-659-1005
Invesco Core Plus Bond Fund Class R	CPBRX	NAS CM	Open End	US Fixed Inc (Income)	C+	C	B	Up	Y	800-659-1005
Invesco Core Plus Bond Fund Class R6	CPBFX	NAS CM	Open End	US Fixed Inc (Income)	B-	C	B	Up	Y	800-659-1005
Invesco Core Plus Bond Fund Class Y	CPBYX	NAS CM	Open End	US Fixed Inc (Income)	B-	C	B	Up	Y	800-659-1005
Invesco Core Plus Bond Fund R5 Class	CPIIX	NAS CM	Open End	US Fixed Inc (Income)	B-	C	B	Up	Y	800-659-1005
Invesco Corporate Bond Fund Class A	ACCBX	NAS CM	Open End	US Fixed Inc (Corp Bond - General)	C	C	B-		Y	800-659-1005
Invesco Corporate Bond Fund Class C	ACCEX	NAS CM	Open End	US Fixed Inc (Corp Bond - General)	C	C	B-		Y	800-659-1005
Invesco Corporate Bond Fund Class R	ACCZX	NAS CM	Open End	US Fixed Inc (Corp Bond - General)	C	C	B-		Y	800-659-1005
Invesco Corporate Bond Fund Class R6	ICBFX	NAS CM	Open End	US Fixed Inc (Corp Bond - General)	C	C	B		Y	800-659-1005
Invesco Corporate Bond Fund Class Y	ACCHX	NAS CM	Open End	US Fixed Inc (Corp Bond - General)	C	C	B		Y	800-659-1005
Invesco Corporate Bond Fund R5 Class	ACCWX	NAS CM	Open End	US Fixed Inc (Corp Bond - General)	C	C	B		Y	800-659-1005
Invesco Dynamic Credit Opportunities Fund	VTA	NYSE	Closed End	US Fixed Inc (Worldwide Bond)	D	D	D	Down	Y	404-892-0896
Invesco Floating Rate Fund Class A	AFRAX	NAS CM	Open End	US Fixed Inc (Growth & Income)	D+	D	C-	Down	Y	800-659-1005
Invesco Floating Rate Fund Class C	AFRCX	NAS CM	Open End	US Fixed Inc (Growth & Income)	D	D	C-	Down	Y	800-659-1005
Invesco Floating Rate Fund Class R	AFRRX	NAS CM	Open End	US Fixed Inc (Growth & Income)	D	D	C-	Down	Y	800-659-1005
Invesco Floating Rate Fund Class R6	AFRFX	NAS CM	Open End	US Fixed Inc (Growth & Income)	D+	D	C-	Down	Y	800-659-1005
Invesco Floating Rate Fund Class Y	AFRYX	NAS CM	Open End	US Fixed Inc (Growth & Income)	D+	D	C-	Down	Y	800-659-1005
Invesco Floating Rate Fund R5 Class	AFRIX	NAS CM	Open End	US Fixed Inc (Growth & Income)	D+	D	C-	Down	Y	800-659-1005
Invesco Government Money Market Fund Class A	ADAXX	NAS CM	Money Mkt	US Money Mkt (Money Mkt - Govt)	C	C-	C+			800-659-1005
Invesco Government Money Market Fund Class AX	ACZXX	NAS CM	Money Mkt	US Money Mkt (Money Mkt - Govt)	C	C-	C+		Y	800-659-1005
Invesco Government Money Market Fund Class C			Money Mkt	US Money Mkt (Money Mkt - Govt)	C	C-	C		Y	800-659-1005
Invesco Government Money Market Fund Class CX	ACXXX	NAS CM	Money Mkt	US Money Mkt (Money Mkt - Govt)	C	C-	C		Y	800-659-1005
Invesco Government Money Market Fund Class R			Money Mkt	US Money Mkt (Money Mkt - Govt)	C	C-	C		Y	800-659-1005
Invesco Government Money Market Fund Class R6	INVXX	NAS CM	Money Mkt	US Money Mkt (Money Mkt - Govt)	C	C-	C+		Y	800-659-1005
Invesco Government Money Market Fund Class Y			Money Mkt	US Money Mkt (Money Mkt - Govt)	C	C-	C+		Y	800-659-1005
Invesco Govt Money Mkt Fund Invesco Cash Reserves Class	AIMXX	NAS CM	Money Mkt	US Money Mkt (Money Mkt - Govt)	C	C-	C+		Y	800-659-1005
Invesco Government Money Market Fund Investor Class	INAXX	NAS CM	Money Mkt	US Money Mkt (Money Mkt - Govt)	C	C-	C+			800-659-1005
Invesco High Income Trust II	VLT	NYSE	Closed End	US Fixed Inc (Corp Bond - High Yield)	D	D	D	Down	Y	404-892-0896
Invesco High Yield Bond Factor Fund Class A	OGYAX	NAS CM	Open End	Global Fixed Inc (Corp Bond - High Yield)	C-	D+	C		Y	800-659-1005

★Expanded analysis of this fund is included in Section II.

TOTAL RETURNS & PERFORMANCE									ASSETS		ASSET ALLOCATION & TURNOVER							MINIMUMS		FEES		
3-Month Total Return	6-Month Total Return	1-Year Total Return	3-Year Total Return	5-Year Total Return	Dividend Yield (TTM)	Expense Ratio	3-Yr Std Deviation	Effective Duration	NAV	Total Assets (MIL)	%Cash	%Government Bonds	%Municipal Bonds	%Corporate Bonds	%Other	Turnover Ratio	Average Coupon Rate	Min Initial Investment	Min Additional Investment	Front End Fee (%)	Back End Fee (%)	Inception Date
0.03	0.34	1.24	4.48	4.86	1.42	0.18	0.19		1	4,145	71	29	0	0	0			20,000,000	0			Jul-16
0.03	0.33	1.23	4.55	4.96	1.4	0.2	0.17		1	4,145	71	29	0	0	0			10,000,000	0			Jul-16
8.12	-2.76	-0.43	6.37	15.77	4.79	1.17	7.11	1.68	8.85	154.8	7	2	1	88	-1	144	6.14	1,000	100	4.75		Sep-10
7.90	-3.11	-0.97	4.50	12.46	4.18	1.77	7.06	1.68	8.92	154.8	7	2	1	88	-1	144	6.14	1,000	100		0.85	Oct-02
8.01	-2.73	-0.17	7.15	17.34	5.05	0.92	7	1.68	8.89	154.8	7	2	1	88	-1	144	6.14	1,000	100			May-04
1.90	2.35	4.11	10.99	15.71	1.87	0.69	2.86	4.82	5.63	14.1	4	0	96	0	0	4	4.20	1,000	25			Sep-87
7.60	1.53	4.66			2.36	1.06			10.64	31.5	21	0	0	79	0	16	4.39	2,000				May-19
7.69	1.70	4.92			2.71	0.71			10.65	31.5	21	0	0	79	0	16	4.39	10,000				Sep-18
10.31	2.20	6.83	15.40	29.38	3.91	0.81	7.71		21.48	225.1	0	3	1	79	0	60	5.40					Jun-71
8.46	-3.98	-0.81	9.36	22.65	5.02	0.99	8.05		7.36	35.1	1	0	0	99	0	28	6.11	1,000	50	4.25		Apr-04
8.24	-4.32	-1.41	7.09	18.17	4.24	1.74	8.02		7.38	35.1	1	0	0	99	0	28	6.11	1,000	50		1.00	Apr-04
8.53	-3.74	-0.44	10.33	23.97	5.28	0.74	7.96		7.36	35.1	1	0	0	99	0	28	6.11	1,000	50			Aug-16
0.60	1.46	2.56	7.01	7.79		0.82	1.08		9.21	21.0	2	6	0	0	0		2.60	1,000	50	2.00		Jan-20
0.56	1.58	2.81	7.81	9.14	4.2	0.57	1.06		9.2	21.0	2	6	0	0	0		2.60	1,000	50			Jun-11
4.79	-2.17	-0.79	4.65	11.68	3.83	0.91	4.48	1.04	8.78	87.8	19	0	0	79	0	104	5.41	2,500	100			Jul-07
4.23	0.37	2.74	11.98	24.60	4.63		6.69	10.34	11.76	510.1	2	0	98	0	0	9	6.21					Aug-93
8.92	3.43	8.53	18.15	34.18	3.86		6.73	7.84	20.79	231.3	1	4	0	89	0	158	4.50					Oct-70
4.60	1.82	4.47	13.10	26.62	4.08		6.46	10.30	13.34	629.9	0	0	100	0	0	8	6.11					Apr-93
1.94	1.29	2.42	6.99	8.87	2.03	0.4	1.02	0.44	10.09	2,825	35	0	0	50	0		2.18	1,000	50			Apr-18
1.98	1.36	2.55	7.34	9.44		0.25	1.01	0.44	10.1	2,825	35	0	0	50	0		2.18	1,000,000				May-20
1.97	1.25	2.43	7.22	9.32		0.25	1.09	0.44	10.08	2,825	35	0	0	50	0		2.18	1,000	50			Dec-19
1.98	1.36	2.55	7.34	9.44	2.15	0.3	1.01	0.44	10.09	2,825	35	0	0	50	0		2.18	1,000				Jul-14
7.36	4.80	8.15	14.98	25.28	2.94	0.75	4.96	5.92	11.42	4,582	-7	10	0	41	0	250	3.49	1,000	50	4.25		Jun-09
7.17	4.32	7.36	12.43	20.70	2.21	1.5	5	5.92	11.41	4,582	-7	10	0	41	0	250	3.49	1,000	50		1.00	Jun-09
7.40	4.67	7.98	14.23	23.84	2.7	1	4.98	5.92	11.42	4,582	-7	10	0	41	0	250	3.49	0				Jun-09
7.45	4.96	8.48	16.04	27.30	3.23	0.45	4.97	5.92	11.41	4,582	-7	10	0	41	0	250	3.49	1,000,000				Sep-12
7.52	4.92	8.41	15.92	26.83	3.18	0.5	5	5.92	11.43	4,582	-7	10	0	41	0	250	3.49	1,000	50			Jun-09
7.43	4.93	8.42	15.84	26.91	3.18	0.5	5.01	5.92	11.41	4,582	-7	10	0	41	0	250	3.49	1,000,000				Jun-09
10.24	3.54	8.32	17.33	31.83	3.43	0.83	7.28	7.69	7.73	2,120	1	5	0	86	0	192	4.23	1,000	50	4.25		Sep-71
9.97	3.02	7.50	14.91	27.18	2.7	1.53	7.31	7.69	7.79	2,120	1	5	0	86	0	192	4.23	1,000	50		1.00	Aug-93
10.02	3.27	7.91	16.51	30.25	3.18	1.08	7.3	7.69	7.73	2,120	1	5	0	86	0	192	4.23	0				Jun-11
10.32	3.74	8.74	18.85	34.67	3.84	0.43	7.27	7.69	7.75	2,120	1	5	0	86	0	192	4.23	1,000,000				Sep-12
10.14	3.53	8.44	18.21	33.47	3.69	0.58	7.28	7.69	7.74	2,120	1	5	0	86	0	192	4.23	1,000	50			Aug-05
10.31	3.69	8.64	18.63	34.04	3.74	0.49	7.27	7.69	7.74	2,120	1	5	0	86	0	192	4.23	1,000,000				Jun-10
13.97	-12.32	-9.38	0.37	12.37	6.8	0	14.58		10.6	648.7	9	0	0	87	1	83	5.24					Jun-07
7.03	-5.85	-4.13	3.01	10.68	5.7	1.09	7.52		6.76	1,624	13	0	0	86	1	55	4.65	1,000	50	2.50		May-97
6.93	-6.12	-4.64	1.44	7.88	5.18	1.59	7.58		6.73	1,624	13	0	0	86	1	55	4.65	1,000	50		1.00	Mar-00
7.11	-5.94	-4.22	2.41	9.32	5.43	1.34	7.53		6.78	1,624	13	0	0	86	1	55	4.65	0				Apr-06
7.13	-5.70	-3.80	4.08	12.40	6.09	0.75	7.53		6.75	1,624	13	0	0	86	1	55	4.65	1,000,000				Sep-12
7.11	-5.74	-3.90	3.77	12.01	5.97	0.84	7.53		6.75	1,624	13	0	0	86	1	55	4.65	1,000	50			Oct-08
7.26	-5.72	-3.74	3.86	12.09	5.98	0.84	7.56		6.77	1,624	13	0	0	86	1	55	4.65	1,000,000				Apr-06
0.00	0.24	0.99	3.54	3.71		0.43			1	3,844	58	42	0	0	0			1,000	50			May-20
0.00	0.24	1.00	3.54	3.72	1.16	0.58	0.18		1	3,844	58	42	0	0	0			1,000	50			Jun-10
0.00	0.07	0.45	1.84	2.00	0.55	0.43	0.11		1	3,844	58	42	0	0	0			1,000	50		1.00	Aug-97
0.00	0.06	0.45	1.84	2.00	0.55	1.33	0.11		1	3,844	58	42	0	0	0			1,000	50		1.00	Jun-10
0.00	0.17	0.81	2.88	2.99	0.95	0.43	0.16		1	3,844	58	42	0	0	0			0				Jun-02
0.02	0.30	1.16	4.29	4.49	1.33	0.36	0.17		1	3,844	58	42	0	0	0			1,000,000				Apr-17
0.00	0.28	1.11	3.97	4.18	1.29	0.43	0.18		1	3,844	58	42	0	0	0			1,000	50			Oct-08
0.00	0.24	0.99	3.53	3.71	1.16	0.58	0.18		1	3,844	58	42	0	0	0			1,000	50			Oct-93
0.01	0.28	1.12	3.98	4.19	1.29	0.43	0.18		1	3,844	58	42	0	0	0			1,000	50			Sep-03
16.80	-11.11	-7.13	1.96	15.81	7.29		14.54	3.89	13.44	85.2	-35	0	0	94	0	41	6.62					Apr-89
9.62	-4.24	-1.44	6.47	15.89	5.35	0.64	8.71		8.57	30.9	-7	19	0	79	0	127	6.23	1,000	50	4.25		Nov-13

Fund Name	Ticker Symbol	Traded On	Fund Type	Category and (Prospectus Objective)	Overall Rating	Reward Rating	Risk Rating	Recent Up/ Downgrade	Open to New Investors	Telephone
	MARKET			**FUND TYPE, CATEGORY & OBJECTIVE**	**RATINGS**				**NEW INVESTORS**	
Invesco High Yield Bond Factor Fund Class C	**OGYCX**	NAS CM	Open End	Global Fixed Inc (Corp Bond - High Yield)	**D+**	D	C-	Down	Y	800-659-1005
Invesco High Yield Bond Factor Fund Class R	**OGYNX**	NAS CM	Open End	Global Fixed Inc (Corp Bond - High Yield)	**D+**	D	C	Down	Y	800-659-1005
Invesco High Yield Bond Factor Fund Class R5	**GBHYX**	NAS CM	Open End	Global Fixed Inc (Corp Bond - High Yield)	**C-**	D+	C		Y	800-659-1005
Invesco High Yield Bond Factor Fund Class R6	**OGYIX**	NAS CM	Open End	Global Fixed Inc (Corp Bond - High Yield)	**C-**	D+	C		Y	800-659-1005
Invesco High Yield Bond Factor Fund Class Y	**OGYYX**	NAS CM	Open End	Global Fixed Inc (Corp Bond - High Yield)	**C-**	D+	C		Y	800-659-1005
Invesco High Yield Fund Class A	**AMHYX**	NAS CM	Open End	US Fixed Inc (Corp Bond - High Yield)	**D**	D	D+	Down	Y	800-659-1005
Invesco High Yield Fund Class C	**AHYCX**	NAS CM	Open End	US Fixed Inc (Corp Bond - High Yield)	**D**	D	D+	Down	Y	800-659-1005
Invesco High Yield Fund Class R6	**HYIFX**	NAS CM	Open End	US Fixed Inc (Corp Bond - High Yield)	**D**	D	D+	Down	Y	800-659-1005
Invesco High Yield Fund Class Y	**AHHYX**	NAS CM	Open End	US Fixed Inc (Corp Bond - High Yield)	**D**	D	D+	Down	Y	800-659-1005
Invesco High Yield Fund Investor Class	**HYINX**	NAS CM	Open End	US Fixed Inc (Corp Bond - High Yield)	**D**	D	D+	Down		800-659-1005
Invesco High Yield Fund R5 Class	**AHIYX**	NAS CM	Open End	US Fixed Inc (Corp Bond - High Yield)	**D**	D	D+	Down	Y	800-659-1005
Invesco High Yield Municipal Fund Class A	**ACTHX**	NAS CM	Open End	US Muni Fixed Inc (Muni Bond - Natl)	**C-**	D+	C	Down		800-659-1005
Invesco High Yield Municipal Fund Class C	**ACTFX**	NAS CM	Open End	US Muni Fixed Inc (Muni Bond - Natl)	**C-**	D+	C	Down		800-659-1005
Invesco High Yield Municipal Fund Class R5	**ACTNX**	NAS CM	Open End	US Muni Fixed Inc (Muni Bond - Natl)	**C-**	D+	C	Down	Y	800-659-1005
Invesco High Yield Municipal Fund Class R6	**ACTSX**	NAS CM	Open End	US Muni Fixed Inc (Muni Bond - Natl)	**C-**	D+	C	Down	Y	800-659-1005
Invesco High Yield Municipal Fund Class Y	**ACTDX**	NAS CM	Open End	US Muni Fixed Inc (Muni Bond - Natl)	**C-**	D+	C	Down		800-659-1005
Invesco Income Fund Class A	**AGOVX**	NAS CM	Open End	US Fixed Inc (Govt Bond - General)	**D**	D-	D	Down	Y	800-659-1005
Invesco Income Fund Class C	**AGVCX**	NAS CM	Open End	US Fixed Inc (Govt Bond - General)	**D**	D-	D	Down	Y	800-659-1005
Invesco Income Fund Class R	**AGVRX**	NAS CM	Open End	US Fixed Inc (Govt Bond - General)	**D**	D-	D	Down	Y	800-659-1005
Invesco Income Fund Class R5	**AGOIX**	NAS CM	Open End	US Fixed Inc (Govt Bond - General)	**D**	D-	D	Down	Y	800-659-1005
Invesco Income Fund Class R6	**AGVSX**	NAS CM	Open End	US Fixed Inc (Govt Bond - General)	**D**	D-	D	Down	Y	800-659-1005
Invesco Income Fund Class Y	**AGVYX**	NAS CM	Open End	US Fixed Inc (Govt Bond - General)	**D**	D-	D	Down	Y	800-659-1005
Invesco Income Fund Investor Class	**AGIVX**	NAS CM	Open End	US Fixed Inc (Govt Bond - General)	**D**	D-	D	Down		800-659-1005
Invesco Insured Municipal Income Trust	**IIM**	NYSE	Closed End	US Muni Fixed Inc (Muni Bond - Natl)	**C-**	C-	C-	Down	Y	404-892-0896
Invesco Intermediate Bond Factor Fund Class A	**OFIAX**	NAS CM	Open End	US Fixed Inc (Growth & Income)	**B-**	C+	B	Up	Y	800-659-1005
Invesco Intermediate Bond Factor Fund Class C	**OFICX**	NAS CM	Open End	US Fixed Inc (Growth & Income)	**C+**	C	B	Up	Y	800-659-1005
Invesco Intermediate Bond Factor Fund Class R	**OFINX**	NAS CM	Open End	US Fixed Inc (Growth & Income)	**B-**	C	B	Up	Y	800-659-1005
Invesco Intermediate Bond Factor Fund Class R5	**IOTEX**	NAS CM	Open End	US Fixed Inc (Growth & Income)	**B-**	C+	B	Up	Y	800-659-1005
Invesco Intermediate Bond Factor Fund Class R6	**OFIIX**	NAS CM	Open End	US Fixed Inc (Growth & Income)	**B-**	C+	B	Up	Y	800-659-1005
Invesco Intermediate Bond Factor Fund Class Y	**OFIYX**	NAS CM	Open End	US Fixed Inc (Growth & Income)	**B-**	C+	B	Up	Y	800-659-1005
Invesco Intermediate Term Municipal Income Fund Class A	**VKLMX**	NAS CM	Open End	US Muni Fixed Inc (Muni Bond - Natl)	**C-**	D+	C	Down	Y	800-659-1005
Invesco Intermediate Term Municipal Income Fund Class C	**VKLCX**	NAS CM	Open End	US Muni Fixed Inc (Muni Bond - Natl)	**C-**	D+	C	Down	Y	800-659-1005
Invesco Intermediate Term Municipal Income Fund Class R6	**VKLSX**	NAS CM	Open End	US Muni Fixed Inc (Muni Bond - Natl)	**C**	C-	C		Y	800-659-1005
Invesco Intermediate Term Municipal Income Fund Class Y	**VKLIX**	NAS CM	Open End	US Muni Fixed Inc (Muni Bond - Natl)	**C**	C-	C		Y	800-659-1005
Invesco Limited Term Municipal Income Fund Class A	**ATFAX**	NAS CM	Open End	US Muni Fixed Inc (Muni Bond - Natl)	**C**	C-	C+		Y	800-659-1005
Invesco Limited Term Municipal Income Fund Class A2	**AITFX**	NAS CM	Open End	US Muni Fixed Inc (Muni Bond - Natl)	**C**	C-	C+			800-659-1005
Invesco Limited Term Municipal Income Fund Class C	**ATFCX**	NAS CM	Open End	US Muni Fixed Inc (Muni Bond - Natl)	**C**	C-	C		Y	800-659-1005
Invesco Limited Term Municipal Income Fund Class R5	**ATFIX**	NAS CM	Open End	US Muni Fixed Inc (Muni Bond - Natl)	**C**	C-	B-		Y	800-659-1005
Invesco Limited Term Municipal Income Fund Class R6	**ATFSX**	NAS CM	Open End	US Muni Fixed Inc (Muni Bond - Natl)	**C**	C-	B-		Y	800-659-1005
Invesco Limited Term Municipal Income Fund Class Y	**ATFYX**	NAS CM	Open End	US Muni Fixed Inc (Muni Bond - Natl)	**C**	C-	C+		Y	800-659-1005
Invesco Municipal Income Fund Class A	**VKMMX**	NAS CM	Open End	US Muni Fixed Inc (Muni Bond - Natl)	**C**	C-	C		Y	800-659-1005
Invesco Municipal Income Fund Class C	**VMICX**	NAS CM	Open End	US Muni Fixed Inc (Muni Bond - Natl)	**C-**	D+	C	Down	Y	800-659-1005
Invesco Municipal Income Fund Class R6	**VKMSX**	NAS CM	Open End	US Muni Fixed Inc (Muni Bond - Natl)	**C**	C-	C+		Y	800-659-1005
Invesco Municipal Income Fund Class Y	**VMIIX**	NAS CM	Open End	US Muni Fixed Inc (Muni Bond - Natl)	**C**	C-	C+		Y	800-659-1005
Invesco Municipal Income Fund Investor Class	**VMINX**	NAS CM	Open End	US Muni Fixed Inc (Muni Bond - Natl)	**C**	C-	C		Y	800-659-1005
Invesco Municipal Income Opportunities Trust	**OIA**	NYSE	Closed End	US Muni Fixed Inc (Muni Bond - Natl)	**D+**	D+	C-	Down	Y	404-892-0896
Invesco Municipal Opportunity Trust	**VMO**	NYSE	Closed End	US Muni Fixed Inc (Muni Bond - Natl)	**C**	C-	C+		Y	404-892-0896
Invesco Municipal Trust	**VKQ**	NYSE	Closed End	US Muni Fixed Inc (Muni Bond - Natl)	**C**	C-	C+		Y	404-892-0896
Invesco Oppenheimer Emerg Mkts Local Debt Fund Class A	**OEMAX**	NAS CM	Open End	Emerg Mkts Fixed Inc (Diversified Emerg Mkts)	**D+**	D	C-	Down	Y	800-659-1005
Invesco Oppenheimer Emerg Mkts Local Debt Fund Class C	**OEMCX**	NAS CM	Open End	Emerg Mkts Fixed Inc (Diversified Emerg Mkts)	**D**	D	C-	Down	Y	800-659-1005
Invesco Oppenheimer Emerg Mkts Local Debt Fund Class R	**OEMNX**	NAS CM	Open End	Emerg Mkts Fixed Inc (Diversified Emerg Mkts)	**D**	D	C-	Down	Y	800-659-1005
Invesco Oppenheimer Emerg Mkts Local Debt Fund Class R5	**EMLDX**	NAS CM	Open End	Emerg Mkts Fixed Inc (Diversified Emerg Mkts)	**D+**	D	C-	Down	Y	800-659-1005

★ Expanded analysis of this fund is included in Section II.

TOTAL RETURNS & PERFORMANCE									ASSETS		ASSET ALLOCATION & TURNOVER							MINIMUMS		FEES		
3-Month Total Return	6-Month Total Return	1-Year Total Return	3-Year Total Return	5-Year Total Return	Dividend Yield (TTM)	Expense Ratio	3-Yr Std Deviation	Effective Duration	NAV	Total Assets (MIL)	%Cash	%Government Bonds	%Municipal Bonds	%Corporate Bonds	%Other	Turnover Ratio	Average Coupon Rate	Min Initial Investment	Min Additional Investment	Front End Fee (%)	Back End Fee (%)	Inception Date
9.42	-4.49	-2.14	4.36	12.03	4.61	1.39	8.65		8.57	30.9	-7	19	0	79	0	127	6.23	1,000	50	4.25	1.00	Nov-13
9.55	-4.36	-1.69	5.68	14.47	5.1	0.89	8.69		8.57	30.9	-7	19	0	79	0	127	6.23	0		4.25		Nov-13
9.68	-4.11	-1.16	7.60	17.81	5.65	0.39	8.74		8.57	30.9	-7	19	0	79	0	127	6.23	1,000,000		4.25		May-19
9.67	-4.10	-1.13	7.76	17.99	5.69	0.39	8.7		8.58	30.9	-7	19	0	79	0	127	6.23	1,000,000		4.25		Nov-13
9.68	-4.12	-1.17	7.41	17.74	5.66	0.39	8.68		8.57	30.9	-7	19	0	79	0	127	6.23	1,000	50	4.25		Nov-13
10.35	-7.33	-4.60	3.26	12.64	6.52	1.17	9.89	4.07	3.68	980.7	2	1	0	91	0	62	6.41	1,000	50	4.25		Jul-78
10.46	-7.46	-5.10	1.18	8.73	5.67	1.92	10	4.07	3.68	980.7	2	1	0	91	0	62	6.41	1,000	50		1.00	Aug-97
10.78	-7.14	-3.98	4.76	15.24	6.95	0.77	9.97	4.07	3.68	980.7	2	1	0	91	0	62	6.41	1,000,000				Sep-12
10.39	-7.19	-4.34	3.80	14.06	6.78	0.92	9.88	4.07	3.69	980.7	2	1	0	91	0	62	6.41	1,000	50			Oct-08
10.35	-7.33	-4.61	3.33	12.80	6.51	1.17	9.92	4.07	3.68	980.7	2	1	0	91	0	62	6.41	1,000	50			Sep-03
10.79	-7.20	-4.04	4.37	14.62	6.97	0.86	10.06	4.07	3.67	980.7	2	1	0	91	0	62	6.41	1,000,000				Apr-04
2.67	-3.76	-0.89	10.81	24.82	4.75	1.22	7.47	9.36	9.69	9,177	5	0	95	0	0	10	6.54	1,000	50	4.25		Jan-86
2.48	-4.14	-1.55	8.37	20.33	3.93	1.97	7.43	9.36	9.66	9,177	5	0	95	0	0	10	6.54	1,000	50		1.00	Dec-93
2.73	-3.66	-0.65	11.52	26.18	5.03	0.99	7.47	9.36	9.68	9,177	5	0	95	0	0	10	6.54	1,000,000				Apr-12
2.75	-3.60	-0.47	11.85	26.17	5.11	0.92	7.39	9.36	9.68	9,177	5	0	95	0	0	10	6.54	1,000,000				Apr-17
2.73	-3.63	-0.63	11.65	26.51	5.02	0.97	7.43	9.36	9.71	9,177	5	0	95	0	0	10	6.54	1,000	50			Mar-06
13.63	-14.65	-11.91	-8.40	-5.50	5.42	1.08	15.06	4.25	7.28	407.3	-10	1	0	9	0	50	4.08	1,000	50	4.25		Apr-87
13.56	-14.88	-12.46	-10.24	-8.77	4.5	1.83	15.05	4.25	7.29	407.3	-10	1	0	9	0	50	4.08	1,000	50		1.00	Aug-97
13.54	-14.75	-12.12	-9.07	-6.66	5.12	1.33	15.06	4.25	7.29	407.3	-10	1	0	9	0	50	4.08	0				Jun-02
13.73	-14.49	-11.59	-7.43	-3.82	5.86	0.73	15.09	4.25	7.28	407.3	-10	1	0	9	0	50	4.08	1,000,000				Apr-05
13.58	-14.51	-11.70	-7.62	-4.82	5.88	0.7	15.04	4.25	7.27	407.3	-10	1	0	9	0	50	4.08	1,000,000				Apr-17
13.84	-14.40	-11.64	-7.55	-4.14	5.73	0.83	15.08	4.25	7.3	407.3	-10	1	0	9	0	50	4.08	1,000	50			Oct-08
13.63	-14.61	-11.84	-8.24	-5.28	5.48	1.02	15.08	4.25	7.29	407.3	-10	1	0	9	0	50	4.08	1,000	50			Sep-03
4.08	0.75	3.38	14.02	28.01	4.36		6.97	10.34	16.2	748.7	2	0	98	0	-1	6	6.58					Feb-93
4.77	4.67	7.56	14.04	23.80	2.67	0.52	3.94	5.59	11.38	192.8	-4	38	0	38	0	64	2.96	1,000	50	4.25		Aug-10
4.49	4.26	6.61	11.26	18.99	1.77	1.27	3.93	5.59	11.37	192.8	-4	38	0	38	0	64	2.96	1,000	50		1.00	Aug-10
4.61	4.51	7.13	12.94	22.00	2.25	0.77	3.88	5.59	11.38	192.8	-4	38	0	38	0	64	2.96	0				Aug-10
4.84	4.80	7.78	14.85	25.31	2.87	0.27	3.91	5.59	11.38	192.8	-4	38	0	38	0	64	2.96	1,000,000				May-19
4.84	4.81	7.89	15.39	26.37	2.98	0.27	3.93	5.59	11.38	192.8	-4	38	0	38	0	64	2.96	1,000,000				Nov-12
4.74	4.81	7.93	15.02	25.49	3.01	0.27	3.92	5.59	11.37	192.8	-4	38	0	38	0	64	2.96	1,000	50			Aug-10
2.39	-0.85	1.05	8.90	15.53	2.77	0.88	4.7	5.30	11.13	1,846	5	0	95	0	0	11	4.87	1,000	50	2.50		May-93
2.29	-1.23	0.38	6.48	11.32	1.99	1.63	4.68	5.30	11.1	1,846	5	0	95	0	0	11	4.87	1,000	50		1.00	Oct-93
2.47	-0.70	1.42	9.76	16.49	3.05	0.63	4.69	5.30	11.12	1,846	5	0	95	0	0	11	4.87	1,000,000				Apr-17
2.45	-0.73	1.30	9.72	16.99	3.03	0.63	4.7	5.30	11.12	1,846	5	0	95	0	0	11	4.87	1,000	50			Aug-05
2.25	1.30	2.61	6.73	9.89	2.1	0.63	2.32	3.15	11.43	2,232	0	0	100	0	0	26	4.37	1,000	50	2.50		Oct-02
2.31	1.51	2.95	7.53	11.27	2.35	0.38	2.37	3.15	11.44	2,232	0	0	100	0	0	26	4.37	1,000	50	1.00		May-87
2.15	1.01	1.94	4.44	5.85	1.35	1.38	2.39	3.15	11.43	2,232	0	0	100	0	0	26	4.37	1,000	50		1.00	Jun-13
2.33	1.46	2.94	7.62	11.32	2.42	0.38	2.33	3.15	11.42	2,232	0	0	100	0	0	26	4.37	1,000,000				Jul-04
2.42	1.55	3.03	7.86	11.45	2.42	0.3	2.32	3.15	11.43	2,232	0	0	100	0	0	26	4.37	1,000,000				Apr-17
2.40	1.51	2.95	7.62	11.36	2.35	0.38	2.39	3.15	11.43	2,232	0	0	100	0	0	26	4.37	1,000	50			Oct-08
3.07	-0.39	2.14	10.73	19.32	3.28	1.01	5.79	8.22	13.29	3,361	4	0	96	0	0	9	5.34	1,000	50	4.25		Aug-90
2.89	-0.78	1.38	8.35	15.01	2.5	1.76	5.8	8.22	13.23	3,361	4	0	96	0	0	9	5.34	1,000	50		1.00	Aug-93
3.15	-0.23	2.47	11.74	20.46	3.62	0.69	5.8	8.22	13.29	3,361	4	0	96	0	0	9	5.34	1,000,000				Apr-17
3.06	-0.34	2.32	11.45	20.78	3.55	0.76	5.82	8.22	13.28	3,361	4	0	96	0	0	9	5.34	1,000	50			Aug-05
3.09	-0.35	2.24	11.06	19.93	3.38	0.88	5.8	8.22	13.3	3,361	4	0	96	0	0	9	5.34	1,000	50			Jul-13
3.62	-2.59	0.49	12.89	28.00	5.35		8.12	11.12	7.29	337.2	2	0	98	0	0	19	7.48					Sep-88
4.13	0.48	2.98	12.25	24.98	4.6		6.66	10.39	13.17	867.0	2	0	98	0	0	9	6.19					Apr-92
4.07	0.36	2.87	12.48	24.89	4.66		6.76	10.55	13.16	710.3	2	0	98	0	0	11	6.37					Sep-91
11.80	-5.53	-2.52	3.79	18.55	5.12	1.15	12.65	5.84	6.53	187.2	17	44	0	2	0		7.34	1,000	50	4.25		Jun-10
11.57	-5.93	-3.48	1.19	13.84	4.24	2	12.71	5.84	6.53	187.2	17	44	0	2	0		7.34	1,000	50	4.25	1.00	Jun-10
11.70	-5.70	-2.86	2.85	16.86	4.75	1.5	12.63	5.84	6.53	187.2	17	44	0	2	0		7.34	0		4.25		Jun-10
12.07	-5.41	-2.26	4.65	20.37	5.4	0.9	12.78	5.84	6.53	187.2	17	44	0	2	0		7.34	1,000,000		4.25		May-19

	MARKET		FUND TYPE, CATEGORY & OBJECTIVE		RATINGS				NEW INVESTORS	
Fund Name	Ticker Symbol	Traded On	Fund Type	Category and (Prospectus Objective)	Overall Rating	Reward Rating	Risk Rating	Recent Up/ Downgrade	Open to New Investors	Telephone
Invesco Oppenheimer Emerg Mkts Local Debt Fund Class R6	OEMIX	NAS CM	Open End	Emerg Mkts Fixed Inc (Diversified Emerg Mkts)	D+	D	C-	Down	Y	800-659-1005
Invesco Oppenheimer Emerg Mkts Local Debt Fund Class Y	OEMYX	NAS CM	Open End	Emerg Mkts Fixed Inc (Diversified Emerg Mkts)	D+	D	C-	Down	Y	800-659-1005
Invesco Oppenheimer Global Strategic Income Class A	OPSIX	NAS CM	Open End	US Fixed Inc (Multisector Bond)	D	D	D+	Down	Y	800-659-1005
Invesco Oppenheimer Global Strategic Income Class C	OSICX	NAS CM	Open End	US Fixed Inc (Multisector Bond)	D	D	D+	Down	Y	800-659-1005
Invesco Oppenheimer Global Strategic Income Class R	OSINX	NAS CM	Open End	US Fixed Inc (Multisector Bond)	D	D	D+	Down	Y	800-659-1005
Invesco Oppenheimer Global Strategic Income Class R6	OSIIX	NAS CM	Open End	US Fixed Inc (Multisector Bond)	D	D	D+	Down	Y	800-659-1005
Invesco Oppenheimer Global Strategic Income Class Y	OSIYX	NAS CM	Open End	US Fixed Inc (Multisector Bond)	D	D	D+	Down	Y	800-659-1005
Invesco Oppenheimer Global Strategic Income Fund Class R5	GLSSX	NAS CM	Open End	US Fixed Inc (Multisector Bond)	D	D	D+	Down	Y	800-659-1005
Invesco Oppenheimer Government Money Market Fund Class C	GMCXX	NAS CM	Money Mkt	US Money Mkt (Money Mkt - Govt)	C	C-	C		Y	800-659-1005
Invesco Oppenheimer Government Money Market Fund Class R	GMLXX	NAS CM	Money Mkt	US Money Mkt (Money Mkt - Govt)	C	C-	C		Y	800-659-1005
Invesco Oppenheimer Government Money Market Fund Class R6	GMRXX	NAS CM	Money Mkt	US Money Mkt (Money Mkt - Govt)	C	C-	C		Y	800-659-1005
Invesco Oppenheimer Government Money Market Fund Class Y	OMBXX	NAS CM	Money Mkt	US Money Mkt (Money Mkt - Govt)	C	C-	C		Y	800-659-1005
Invesco Oppenheimer Govt Money Mkt Invesco Cash Reserve	GMQXX	NAS CM	Money Mkt	US Money Mkt (Money Mkt - Govt)	C	C-	C		Y	800-659-1005
Invesco Oppenheimer International Bond Fund Class A	OIBAX	NAS CM	Open End	Global Fixed Inc (Worldwide Bond)	D	D	D+	Down	Y	800-659-1005
Invesco Oppenheimer International Bond Fund Class C	OIBCX	NAS CM	Open End	Global Fixed Inc (Worldwide Bond)	D	D	D+	Down	Y	800-659-1005
Invesco Oppenheimer International Bond Fund Class R	OIBNX	NAS CM	Open End	Global Fixed Inc (Worldwide Bond)	D	D	D+	Down	Y	800-659-1005
Invesco Oppenheimer International Bond Fund Class R5	INBQX	NAS CM	Open End	Global Fixed Inc (Worldwide Bond)	D	D	D+	Down	Y	800-659-1005
Invesco Oppenheimer International Bond Fund Class R6	OIBIX	NAS CM	Open End	Global Fixed Inc (Worldwide Bond)	D	D	D+	Down	Y	800-659-1005
Invesco Oppenheimer International Bond Fund Class Y	OIBYX	NAS CM	Open End	Global Fixed Inc (Worldwide Bond)	D	D	D+	Down	Y	800-659-1005
Invesco Oppenheimer Municipal Fund Class A	OPAMX	NAS CM	Open End	US Muni Fixed Inc (Muni Bond - Single State)	C	C-	B		Y	800-659-1005
Invesco Oppenheimer Municipal Fund Class C	OPCMX	NAS CM	Open End	US Muni Fixed Inc (Muni Bond - Single State)	C	C-	B-		Y	800-659-1005
Invesco Oppenheimer Municipal Fund Class R6	IOMUX	NAS CM	Open End	US Muni Fixed Inc (Muni Bond - Single State)	C	C-	B	Down	Y	800-659-1005
Invesco Oppenheimer Municipal Fund Class Y	OPYMX	NAS CM	Open End	US Muni Fixed Inc (Muni Bond - Single State)	C	C-	B		Y	800-659-1005
Invesco Oppenheimer Rochester AMT-Free Muni Fund Class A	OPTAX	NAS CM	Open End	US Muni Fixed Inc (Muni Bond - Natl)	C	C-	B	Down	Y	800-659-1005
Invesco Oppenheimer Rochester AMT-Free Muni Fund Class C	OMFCX	NAS CM	Open End	US Muni Fixed Inc (Muni Bond - Natl)	C	C-	B	Down	Y	800-659-1005
Invesco Oppenheimer Rochester AMT-Free Muni Fund Class R6	IORAX	NAS CM	Open End	US Muni Fixed Inc (Muni Bond - Natl)	C+	C-	B+	Down	Y	800-659-1005
Invesco Oppenheimer Rochester AMT-Free Muni Fund Class Y	OMFYX	NAS CM	Open End	US Muni Fixed Inc (Muni Bond - Natl)	C+	C-	B	Down	Y	800-659-1005
Invesco Oppenheimer Rochester AMT-Free New York Muni Cl A	OPNYX	NAS CM	Open End	US Muni Fixed Inc (Muni Bond - Single State)	C	C-	C+		Y	800-659-1005
Invesco Oppenheimer Rochester AMT-Free New York Muni Cl C	ONYCX	NAS CM	Open End	US Muni Fixed Inc (Muni Bond - Single State)	C	D+	C		Y	800-659-1005
Invesco Oppenheimer Rochester AMT-Free New York Muni Cl R6	IORNX	NAS CM	Open End	US Muni Fixed Inc (Muni Bond - Single State)	C	C-	B-		Y	800-659-1005
Invesco Oppenheimer Rochester AMT-Free New York Muni Cl Y	ONYYX	NAS CM	Open End	US Muni Fixed Inc (Muni Bond - Single State)	C	C-	B-		Y	800-659-1005
Invesco Oppenheimer Rochester California Muni Class R6	IORCX	NAS CM	Open End	US Muni Fixed Inc (Muni Bond - Single State)	C+	C-	B		Y	800-659-1005
Invesco Oppenheimer Rochester California Muni Fund Class A	OPCAX	NAS CM	Open End	US Muni Fixed Inc (Muni Bond - Single State)	C	C-	B	Down	Y	800-659-1005
Invesco Oppenheimer Rochester California Muni Fund Class C	OCACX	NAS CM	Open End	US Muni Fixed Inc (Muni Bond - Single State)	C	C-	B		Y	800-659-1005
Invesco Oppenheimer Rochester California Muni Fund Class Y	OCAYX	NAS CM	Open End	US Muni Fixed Inc (Muni Bond - Single State)	C	C-	B	Down	Y	800-659-1005
Invesco Oppenheimer Rochester High Yield Muni Fund Class A	ORNAX	NAS CM	Open End	US Muni Fixed Inc (Muni Bond - Natl)	C	C-	B-	Down	Y	800-659-1005
Invesco Oppenheimer Rochester High Yield Muni Fund Class C	ORNCX	NAS CM	Open End	US Muni Fixed Inc (Muni Bond - Natl)	C	C-	C+		Y	800-659-1005
Invesco Oppenheimer Rochester High Yield Muni Cl R5	IORHX	NAS CM	Open End	US Muni Fixed Inc (Muni Bond - Natl)	C	C-	B-	Down	Y	800-659-1005
Invesco Oppenheimer Rochester High Yield Muni Cl R6	IORYX	NAS CM	Open End	US Muni Fixed Inc (Muni Bond - Natl)	C	C-	B-	Down	Y	800-659-1005
Invesco Oppenheimer Rochester High Yield Muni Fund Class Y	ORNYX	NAS CM	Open End	US Muni Fixed Inc (Muni Bond - Natl)	C	C-	B-	Down	Y	800-659-1005
Invesco Oppenheimer Rochester Limited Term Calif Muni Cl A	OLCAX	NAS CM	Open End	US Muni Fixed Inc (Muni Bond - Single State)	C	C-	B-		Y	800-659-1005
Invesco Oppenheimer Rochester Limited Term Calif Muni Cl C	OLCCX	NAS CM	Open End	US Muni Fixed Inc (Muni Bond - Single State)	C	C-	B-		Y	800-659-1005
Invesco Oppenheimer Rochester Limited Term Calif Muni Cl R	IORLX	NAS CM	Open End	US Muni Fixed Inc (Muni Bond - Single State)	C	C-	C+		Y	800-659-1005
Invesco Oppenheimer Rochester Limited Term Calif Muni Cl Y	OLCYX	NAS CM	Open End	US Muni Fixed Inc (Muni Bond - Single State)	C	C-	C+		Y	800-659-1005
Invesco Oppenheimer Rochester Limited Term NY Muni Cl A	LTNYX	NAS CM	Open End	US Muni Fixed Inc (Muni Bond - Single State)	C	C-	C+		Y	800-659-1005
Invesco Oppenheimer Rochester Limited Term NY Muni Cl R6	IORMX	NAS CM	Open End	US Muni Fixed Inc (Muni Bond - Single State)	C	C-	C+		Y	800-659-1005
Invesco Oppenheimer Rochester New Jersey Muni Cl R6	IORJX	NAS CM	Open End	US Muni Fixed Inc (Muni Bond - Single State)	C	C-	B-		Y	800-659-1005
Invesco Oppenheimer Rochester New York Munis Fund Class A	RMUNX	NAS CM	Open End	US Muni Fixed Inc (Muni Bond - Single State)	C	C-	B	Down	Y	800-659-1005
Invesco Oppenheimer Rochester New York Munis Fund Class C	RMUCX	NAS CM	Open End	US Muni Fixed Inc (Muni Bond - Single State)	C	C-	B-		Y	800-659-1005
Invesco Oppenheimer Rochester New York Munis Fund Class R6	IORUX	NAS CM	Open End	US Muni Fixed Inc (Muni Bond - Single State)	C	C-	B	Down	Y	800-659-1005
Invesco Oppenheimer Rochester New York Munis Fund Class Y	RMUYX	NAS CM	Open End	US Muni Fixed Inc (Muni Bond - Single State)	C	C-	B	Down	Y	800-659-1005
Invesco Oppenheimer Rochester Pennsylvania Muni Cl R6	IORPX	NAS CM	Open End	US Muni Fixed Inc (Muni Bond - Single State)	C	C-	B	Down	Y	800-659-1005

★Expanded analysis of this fund is included in Section II.

TOTAL RETURNS & PERFORMANCE									ASSETS		ASSET ALLOCATION & TURNOVER							MINIMUMS		FEES		
3-Month Total Return	6-Month Total Return	1-Year Total Return	3-Year Total Return	5-Year Total Return	Dividend Yield (TTM)	Expense Ratio	3-Yr Std Deviation	Effective Duration	NAV	Total Assets (MIL)	%Cash	%Government Bonds	%Municipal Bonds	%Corporate Bonds	%Other	Turnover Ratio	Average Coupon Rate	Min Initial Investment	Min Additional Investment	Front End Fee (%)	Back End Fee (%)	Inception Date
12.07	-5.26	-2.23	4.86	20.70	5.42	0.85	12.76	5.84	6.53	187.2	17	44	0	2	0		7.34	1,000,000		4.25		Sep-12
12.03	-5.29	-2.31	4.58	20.29	5.32	0.95	12.73	5.84	6.54	187.2	17	44	0	2	0		7.34	1,000	50	4.25		Jun-10
15.04	-4.66	-3.07	2.73	9.00	4.1	1	11.21	3.58	3.54	2,754	-17	31	0	16	6		5.21	1,000	50	4.25		Oct-89
14.87	-5.04	-3.82	0.38	4.91	3.29	1.76	11.18	3.58	3.53	2,754	-17	31	0	16	6		5.21	1,000	50		1.00	May-95
14.97	-5.03	-3.32	1.93	7.61	3.82	1.26	11.34	3.58	3.54	2,754	-17	31	0	16	6		5.21	0				Mar-01
14.86	-4.52	-2.74	3.85	11.13	4.5	0.62	11.15	3.58	3.52	2,754	-17	31	0	16	6		5.21	1,000,000				Jan-12
15.11	-4.55	-2.58	3.72	10.58	4.36	0.76	11.17	3.58	3.54	2,754	-17	31	0	16	6		5.21	1,000	50			Jan-98
14.78	-4.72	-2.71	3.13	9.43	4.48	0.67	11.14	3.58	3.54	2,754	-17	31	0	16	6		5.21	1,000,000				May-19
0.00	0.00	0.23	0.74	-1.16	0.33	1.58			1	1,617	66	32	0	0	0			1,000	50			May-19
0.00	0.09	0.56	2.07	1.14	0.7	1.08			1	1,617	66	32	0	0	0			0				May-19
0.00	0.22	1.00	3.55	3.62	1.17	0.48			1	1,617	66	32	0	0	0			1,000,000				May-19
0.00	0.20	0.93	3.46	3.54	1.14	0.58	0.17		1	1,617	66	32	0	0	0			1,000	50			Apr-74
0.00	0.16	0.83	3.05	2.83	0.98	0.73			1	1,617	66	32	0	0	0			1,000	50			May-19
15.69	-3.84	-2.49	2.69	13.72	4.67	1.01	11.91	5.12	5.26	2,916	-2	32	0	5	0		6.50	1,000	50	4.25		Jun-95
15.29	-4.22	-3.24	0.36	9.50	3.88	1.76	11.82	5.12	5.24	2,916	-2	32	0	5	0		6.50	1,000	50		1.00	Jun-95
15.65	-3.97	-2.75	2.08	12.30	4.41	1.26	11.9	5.12	5.25	2,916	-2	32	0	5	0		6.50	0				Mar-01
15.54	-3.68	-2.20	3.02	14.09	4.98	0.67	11.82	5.12	5.26	2,916	-2	32	0	5	0		6.50	1,000,000				May-19
15.80	-3.65	-2.10	4.10	16.09	5.08	0.62	11.9	5.12	5.26	2,916	-2	32	0	5	0		6.50	1,000,000				Jan-12
15.76	-3.72	-2.25	3.45	15.13	4.93	0.76	11.88	5.12	5.26	2,916	-2	32	0	5	0		6.50	1,000	50			Sep-04
2.59	0.52	2.90	15.40	22.92	3.46	0.9	5.22	8.30	13.31	136.3	3	0	97	0	0	14	4.99	1,000	50	4.25		Nov-06
2.45	0.17	2.31	13.22	18.73	2.86	1.45	5.26	8.30	13.3	136.3	3	0	97	0	0	14	4.99	1,000	50		1.00	Nov-06
2.68	0.70	3.26	15.83	23.38	3.81	0.55	5.22	8.30	13.31	136.3	3	0	97	0	0	14	4.99	0				May-19
2.65	0.57	3.08	16.00	23.64	3.71	0.65	5.25	8.30	13.3	136.3	3	0	97	0	0	14	4.99	1,000	50			Jul-11
3.64	2.47	6.23	21.42	41.87	3.96	1.01	6.29	7.45	7.63	2,161	4	0	96	0	0	8	5.40	1,000	50	4.25		Oct-76
3.40	2.16	5.40	18.79	36.69	3.16	1.76	6.3	7.45	7.57	2,161	4	0	96	0	0	8	5.40	1,000	50		1.00	Aug-95
3.61	2.66	6.56	21.82	42.34	4.27	0.72	6.26	7.45	7.63	2,161	4	0	96	0	0	8	5.40	1,000,000				May-19
3.60	2.62	6.38	22.22	43.56	4.23	0.76	6.35	7.45	7.6	2,161	4	0	96	0	0	8	5.40	1,000	50			Nov-10
2.27	-1.26	1.27	12.76	27.70	3.16	1.15	6.55	8.56	11.62	855.3	-3	0	100	0	0	11	5.40	1,000	50	4.25		Aug-84
1.99	-1.72	0.41	10.10	22.80	2.37	1.91	6.55	8.56	11.62	855.3	-3	0	100	0	0	11	5.40	1,000	50		1.00	Aug-95
2.27	-1.17	1.59	13.14	28.13	3.48	0.81	6.52	8.56	11.62	855.3	-3	0	100	0	0	11	5.40	1,000,000				May-19
2.24	-1.22	1.43	13.44	29.18	3.4	0.91	6.52	8.56	11.63	855.3	-3	0	100	0	0	11	5.40	1,000	50			Jan-11
3.86	2.21	5.20	18.25	35.71	3.68	0.85	5.49	7.98	8.98	1,887	-2	0	98	0	0	11	5.40	1,000,000				May-19
3.93	1.93	4.90	17.89	35.29	3.38	1.11	5.5	7.98	8.97	1,887	-2	0	98	0	0	11	5.40	1,000	50	4.25		Nov-88
3.64	1.55	4.02	15.20	30.15	2.64	1.86	5.51	7.98	8.92	1,887	-2	0	98	0	0	11	5.40	1,000	50		1.00	Nov-95
3.88	2.06	5.16	18.74	36.93	3.63	0.86	5.51	7.98	8.97	1,887	-2	0	98	0	0	11	5.40	1,000	50			Nov-10
5.31	-0.94	3.04	21.11	46.05	5.16	1.19	8.35	10.04	7.63	6,492	-2	0	99	0	0	9	6.33	1,000	50	4.25		Oct-93
5.10	-1.21	2.45	18.80	41.07	4.44	1.84	8.29	10.04	7.6	6,492	-2	0	99	0	0	9	6.33	1,000	50		1.00	Aug-95
5.28	-0.49	3.78	21.84	46.92	5.93	0.94	8.38	10.04	7.62	6,492	-2	0	99	0	0	9	6.33	1,000,000				May-19
5.28	-0.76	3.50	21.53	46.55	5.49	0.92	8.28	10.04	7.63	6,492	-2	0	99	0	0	9	6.33	0				May-19
5.26	-0.80	3.32	22.07	47.70	5.45	0.94	8.29	10.04	7.62	6,492	-2	0	99	0	0	9	6.33	1,000	50			Nov-10
2.81	0.42	2.57	13.75	19.04	2.58	0.93	4.26	5.05	3.31	582.4	-4	0	100	0	0	13	4.84	1,000	50	2.50		Feb-04
2.94	0.35	1.81	11.26	14.72	1.83	1.68	4.26	5.05	3.3	582.4	-4	0	100	0	0	13	4.84	1,000	50		1.00	Feb-04
2.88	0.88	2.88	14.12	19.43	2.88	0.6	4.16	5.05	3.31	582.4	-4	0	100	0	0	13	4.84	1,000,000				May-19
2.86	0.55	2.81	14.54	20.44	2.82	0.68	4.22	5.05	3.32	582.4	-4	0	100	0	0	13	4.84	1,000	50			Nov-10
1.71	0.13	2.13	13.34	16.14	3.49	0.89	4.24	4.29	3.02	1,685	-2	0	99	0	0	1	5.23	1,000	50	2.50		Sep-91
1.78	0.27	2.09	13.69	16.50	3.78	0.61	4.13	4.29	3.02	1,685	-2	0	99	0	0	1	5.23	0				May-19
2.63	-0.91	2.07	17.70	24.03	4.64	0.99	6.56	6.26	9.57	236.9	1	0	99	0	0	12	5.63	0				May-19
3.08	0.36	3.31	20.73	40.81	3.4	0.91	7.15	8.98	16.55	5,298	-1	0	100	0	0	2	5.18	1,000	50	4.25		May-86
2.83	-0.01	2.47	18.01	35.31	2.63	1.67	7.14	8.98	16.5	5,298	-1	0	100	0	0	2	5.18	1,000	50		1.00	Mar-97
3.09	0.51	3.54	21.03	41.15	3.68	0.64	7.14	8.98	16.55	5,298	-1	0	100	0	0	2	5.18	0				May-19
3.08	0.49	3.50	21.61	42.27	3.64	0.67	7.14	8.98	16.55	5,298	-1	0	100	0	0	2	5.18	1,000	50			Apr-00
2.92	1.08	4.03	19.24	34.60	3.68	0.9	6.01	7.11	11.19	812.5	0	0	100	0	0	6	5.47	1,000,000				May-19

	MARKET		FUND TYPE, CATEGORY & OBJECTIVE		RATINGS				NEW INVESTORS	
Fund Name	Ticker Symbol	Traded On	Fund Type	Category and (Prospectus Objective)	Overall Rating	Reward Rating	Risk Rating	Recent Up/ Downgrade	Open to New Investors	Telephone
Invesco Oppenheimer Rochester® Limited Term NY Muni Cl C	LTNCX	NAS CM	Open End	US Muni Fixed Inc (Muni Bond - Single State)	C	C-	C+		Y	800-659-1005
Invesco Oppenheimer Rochester® Limited Term NY Muni Cl Y	LTBYX	NAS CM	Open End	US Muni Fixed Inc (Muni Bond - Single State)	C	C-	C+		Y	800-659-1005
Invesco Oppenheimer Rochester® New Jersey Muni Cl A	ONJAX	NAS CM	Open End	US Muni Fixed Inc (Muni Bond - Single State)	C	C-	B-		Y	800-659-1005
Invesco Oppenheimer Rochester® New Jersey Muni Cl C	ONJCX	NAS CM	Open End	US Muni Fixed Inc (Muni Bond - Single State)	C	C-	B-		Y	800-659-1005
Invesco Oppenheimer Rochester® New Jersey Muni Cl Y	ONJYX	NAS CM	Open End	US Muni Fixed Inc (Muni Bond - Single State)	C	C-	B-		Y	800-659-1005
Invesco Oppenheimer Rochester® Pennsylvania Muni Cl A	OPATX	NAS CM	Open End	US Muni Fixed Inc (Muni Bond - Single State)	C	C-	B	Down	Y	800-659-1005
Invesco Oppenheimer Rochester® Pennsylvania Muni Cl C	OPACX	NAS CM	Open End	US Muni Fixed Inc (Muni Bond - Single State)	C	C-	B		Y	800-659-1005
Invesco Oppenheimer Rochester® Pennsylvania Muni Cl Y	OPAYX	NAS CM	Open End	US Muni Fixed Inc (Muni Bond - Single State)	C	C-	B	Down	Y	800-659-1005
Invesco Oppenheimer Senior Floating Rate Fund Class A	OOSAX	NAS CM	Open End	US Fixed Inc (Corp Bond - General)	D	D-	D		Y	800-659-1005
Invesco Oppenheimer Senior Floating Rate Fund Class C	OOSCX	NAS CM	Open End	US Fixed Inc (Corp Bond - General)	D	D-	D		Y	800-659-1005
Invesco Oppenheimer Senior Floating Rate Fund Class R	OOSNX	NAS CM	Open End	US Fixed Inc (Corp Bond - General)	D	D-	D		Y	800-659-1005
Invesco Oppenheimer Senior Floating Rate Fund Class R5	SFRRX	NAS CM	Open End	US Fixed Inc (Corp Bond - General)	D	D-	D		Y	800-659-1005
Invesco Oppenheimer Senior Floating Rate Fund Class R6	OOSIX	NAS CM	Open End	US Fixed Inc (Corp Bond - General)	D	D-	D		Y	800-659-1005
Invesco Oppenheimer Senior Floating Rate Fund Class Y	OOSYX	NAS CM	Open End	US Fixed Inc (Corp Bond - General)	D	D-	D		Y	800-659-1005
Invesco Oppenheimer Senior Floating Rate Plus Fund Class A	OSFAX	NAS CM	Open End	US Fixed Inc (Income)	D	D-	D		Y	800-659-1005
Invesco Oppenheimer Senior Floating Rate Plus Fund Class C	OSFCX	NAS CM	Open End	US Fixed Inc (Income)	D	D-	D		Y	800-659-1005
Invesco Oppenheimer Senior Floating Rate Plus Fund Class R	SFRPX	NAS CM	Open End	US Fixed Inc (Income)	D	D-	D		Y	800-659-1005
Invesco Oppenheimer Senior Floating Rate Plus Cl R5	SFPPX	NAS CM	Open End	US Fixed Inc (Income)	D	D	D		Y	800-659-1005
Invesco Oppenheimer Senior Floating Rate Plus Cl R6	OSFIX	NAS CM	Open End	US Fixed Inc (Income)	D	D-	D		Y	800-659-1005
Invesco Oppenheimer Senior Floating Rate Plus Fund Class Y	OSFYX	NAS CM	Open End	US Fixed Inc (Income)	D	D-	D		Y	800-659-1005
Invesco Oppenheimer Short Term Municipal Fund Class A	ORSTX	NAS CM	Open End	US Muni Fixed Inc (Muni Bond - Natl)	C	C	B-		Y	800-659-1005
Invesco Oppenheimer Short Term Municipal Fund Class C	ORSCX	NAS CM	Open End	US Muni Fixed Inc (Muni Bond - Natl)	C	C-	C+		Y	800-659-1005
Invesco Oppenheimer Short Term Municipal Fund Class R6	STMUX	NAS CM	Open End	US Muni Fixed Inc (Muni Bond - Natl)	C	C	B-		Y	800-659-1005
Invesco Oppenheimer Short Term Municipal Fund Class Y	ORSYX	NAS CM	Open End	US Muni Fixed Inc (Muni Bond - Natl)	C	C	B-		Y	800-659-1005
Invesco Oppenheimer Total Return Bond Fund Class A	OPIGX	NAS CM	Open End	US Fixed Inc (Growth & Income)	B	C+	B+	Up	Y	800-659-1005
Invesco Oppenheimer Total Return Bond Fund Class C	OPBCX	NAS CM	Open End	US Fixed Inc (Growth & Income)	B-	C+	B	Up	Y	800-659-1005
Invesco Oppenheimer Total Return Bond Fund Class R	OPBNX	NAS CM	Open End	US Fixed Inc (Growth & Income)	B	C+	B	Up	Y	800-659-1005
Invesco Oppenheimer Total Return Bond Fund Class R5	TRTMX	NAS CM	Open End	US Fixed Inc (Growth & Income)	B	C+	B+	Up	Y	800-659-1005
Invesco Oppenheimer Total Return Bond Fund Class R6	OPBIX	NAS CM	Open End	US Fixed Inc (Growth & Income)	B	C+	B+	Up	Y	800-659-1005
Invesco Oppenheimer Total Return Bond Fund Class Y	OPBYX	NAS CM	Open End	US Fixed Inc (Growth & Income)	B	C+	B+	Up	Y	800-659-1005
Invesco Pennsylvania Value Municipal Income Trust	VPV	NYSE	Closed End	US Muni Fixed Inc (Muni Bond - Single State)	C-	C-	C-		Y	404-892-0896
Invesco Premier U.S. Govt Money Portfolio Institutional Cl	IUGXX	NAS CM	Money Mkt	US Money Mkt (Money Mkt - Govt)	C	C	C+		Y	800-659-1005
Invesco Premier U.S. Govt Money Portfolio Investor Class	FUGXX	NAS CM	Money Mkt	US Money Mkt (Money Mkt - Govt)	C	C-	C+		Y	800-659-1005
Invesco Quality Income Fund Class A	VKMGX	NAS CM	Open End	US Fixed Inc (Govt Bond - Mortgage)	C+	C	B-	Up	Y	800-659-1005
Invesco Quality Income Fund Class C	VUSCX	NAS CM	Open End	US Fixed Inc (Govt Bond - Mortgage)	C	C	B-		Y	800-659-1005
Invesco Quality Income Fund Class R	VUSRX	NAS CM	Open End	US Fixed Inc (Govt Bond - Mortgage)	C+	C	B-		Y	800-659-1005
Invesco Quality Income Fund Class R6	VUSSX	NAS CM	Open End	US Fixed Inc (Govt Bond - Mortgage)	C+	C	B	Up	Y	800-659-1005
Invesco Quality Income Fund Class Y	VUSIX	NAS CM	Open End	US Fixed Inc (Govt Bond - Mortgage)	C+	C	B	Up	Y	800-659-1005
Invesco Quality Income Fund R5 Class	VUSJX	NAS CM	Open End	US Fixed Inc (Govt Bond - Mortgage)	C+	C	B	Up	Y	800-659-1005
Invesco Quality Municipal Income Trust	IQI	NYSE	Closed End	US Muni Fixed Inc (Muni Bond - Natl)	C-	C-	C-	Down	Y	404-892-0896
Invesco Senior Income Trust	VVR	NYSE	Closed End	US Fixed Inc (Corp Bond - General)	D	D	D	Down	Y	404-892-0896
Invesco Senior Loan Fund Class A	VSLAX	NAS CM	Closed End	US Fixed Inc (Income)	D	D	D+	Down	Y	800-659-1005
Invesco Senior Loan Fund Class C	VSLCX	NAS CM	Closed End	US Fixed Inc (Income)	D	D	D+	Down	Y	800-659-1005
Invesco Senior Loan Fund Class IB	XPRTX	NAS CM	Closed End	US Fixed Inc (Income)	D	D	D+	Down		800-659-1005
Invesco Senior Loan Fund Class IC	XSLCX	NAS CM	Closed End	US Fixed Inc (Income)	D	D	D+	Down		800-659-1005
Invesco Senior Loan Fund Class Y	VSLYX	NAS CM	Closed End	US Fixed Inc (Income)	D	D	D+	Down	Y	800-659-1005
Invesco Short Duration High Yield Municipal Fund Class A	ISHAX	NAS CM	Open End	US Muni Fixed Inc (Muni Bond - Natl)	D+	D+	C-	Down	Y	800-659-1005
Invesco Short Duration High Yield Municipal Fund Class C	ISHCX	NAS CM	Open End	US Muni Fixed Inc (Muni Bond - Natl)	D+	D	C-	Down	Y	800-659-1005
Invesco Short Duration High Yield Municipal Fund Class R5	ISHFX	NAS CM	Open End	US Muni Fixed Inc (Muni Bond - Natl)	D+	D+	C-	Down	Y	800-659-1005
Invesco Short Duration High Yield Municipal Fund Class R6	ISHSX	NAS CM	Open End	US Muni Fixed Inc (Muni Bond - Natl)	D+	D+	C-	Down	Y	800-659-1005
Invesco Short Duration High Yield Municipal Fund Class Y	ISHYX	NAS CM	Open End	US Muni Fixed Inc (Muni Bond - Natl)	D+	D+	C-	Down	Y	800-659-1005
Invesco Short Duration Inflation Protected Fund Class A	LMTAX	NAS CM	Open End	US Fixed Inc (Growth & Income)	C	C	B-		Y	800-659-1005

★ Expanded analysis of this fund is included in Section II.

TOTAL RETURNS & PERFORMANCE									ASSETS		ASSET ALLOCATION & TURNOVER							MINIMUMS		FEES		
3-Month Total Return	6-Month Total Return	1-Year Total Return	3-Year Total Return	5-Year Total Return	Dividend Yield (TTM)	Expense Ratio	3-Yr Std Deviation	Effective Duration	NAV	Total Assets (MIL)	%Cash	%Government Bonds	%Municipal Bonds	%Corporate Bonds	%Other	Turnover Ratio	Average Coupon Rate	Min Initial Investment	Min Additional Investment	Front End Fee (%)	Back End Fee (%)	Inception Date
1.53	0.08	1.38	11.26	12.32	2.75	1.65	4.09	4.29	3.01	1,685	-2	0	99	0	0	1	5.23	1,000	50		1.00	May-97
2.10	0.58	2.72	14.55	17.95	3.74	0.65	4.14	4.29	3.03	1,685	-2	0	99	0	0	1	5.23	1,000	50			Mar-11
2.51	-1.12	1.70	17.26	23.56	4.28	1.33	6.54	6.26	9.57	236.9	1	0	99	0	0	12	5.63	1,000	50	4.25		Mar-94
2.40	-1.39	1.14	15.07	19.47	3.59	1.98	6.54	6.26	9.59	236.9	1	0	99	0	0	12	5.63	1,000	50		1.00	Aug-95
2.59	-1.07	1.96	18.11	24.84	4.55	1.09	6.53	6.26	9.58	236.9	1	0	99	0	0	12	5.63	1,000	50			Nov-10
2.86	0.94	3.75	19.00	34.32	3.4	1.19	6	7.11	11.2	812.5	0	0	100	0	0	6	5.47	1,000	50	4.25		Sep-89
2.70	0.70	3.17	16.62	29.75	2.74	1.84	5.98	7.11	11.17	812.5	0	0	100	0	0	6	5.47	1,000	50		1.00	Aug-95
2.91	1.06	4.09	19.85	35.83	3.65	0.94	5.97	7.11	11.21	812.5	0	0	100	0	0	6	5.47	1,000	50			Nov-10
5.09	-11.54	-13.13	-8.22	0.89	5.58	1.11	8.55		6.47	4,515	0	0	0	100	1		4.86	1,000	50	3.25		Sep-99
4.72	-12.00	-13.89	-10.38	-2.93	4.73	1.86	8.52		6.47	4,515	0	0	0	100	1		4.86	1,000	50		1.00	Sep-99
4.86	-11.67	-13.37	-8.94	-0.50	5.3	1.36	8.5		6.46	4,515	0	0	0	100	1		4.86	0				Oct-12
5.17	-11.40	-12.85	-8.02	1.12	5.94	0.8	8.58		6.47	4,515	0	0	0	100	1		4.86	1,000,000				May-19
5.19	-11.42	-12.86	-7.30	2.55	5.99	0.75	8.6		6.45	4,515	0	0	0	100	1		4.86	1,000,000				Oct-12
4.99	-11.47	-12.96	-7.60	1.96	5.86	0.86	8.5		6.45	4,515	0	0	0	100	1		4.86	1,000	50			Nov-05
5.94	-11.83	-13.34	-7.76	0.12	5.99	1.59	9.35		7.46	42.5	0	0	0	100	1	77	4.75	1,000	50	3.25		Aug-13
5.70	-12.23	-14.02	-10.00	-3.95	4.96	2.49	9.36		7.46	42.5	0	0	0	100	1	77	4.75	1,000	50		1.00	Aug-13
6.02	-11.94	-13.45	-8.29	-0.52	5.71	1.84	9.39		7.46	42.5	0	0	0	100	1	77	4.75	0				May-19
6.00	-11.73	-13.04	-6.94	1.95	6.24	1.37	9.37		7.46	42.5	0	0	0	100	1	77	4.75	1,000,000				May-19
6.00	-11.88	-13.15	-6.95	1.94	6.3	1.32	9.41		7.48	42.5	0	0	0	100	1	77	4.75	0				Aug-13
6.14	-11.71	-13.01	-6.94	1.41	6.27	1.34	9.37		7.47	42.5	0	0	0	100	1	77	4.75	1,000	50			Aug-13
1.47	1.61	2.21	6.36	10.60	1.68	0.82	0.98	1.51	3.78	1,663	-4	0	97	0	0		3.63	1,000	50	2.50		Dec-10
1.29	1.22	1.44	3.98	6.50	0.93	1.57	1.01	1.51	3.78	1,663	-4	0	97	0	0		3.63	1,000	50		1.00	Dec-10
1.82	1.73	2.76	7.47	12.30	1.95	0.5	1.14	1.51	3.79	1,663	-4	0	97	0	0		3.63	0				May-19
1.53	1.71	2.44	7.12	11.94	1.9	0.57	1.01	1.51	3.78	1,663	-4	0	97	0	0		3.63	1,000	50			Dec-10
5.73	6.94	9.58	17.47	24.81	2.41	0.75	3.74	5.66	7.37	1,856	-17	23	0	34	0		3.41	1,000	50	5.50		Apr-88
5.67	6.67	8.71	14.67	20.06	1.64	1.56	3.7	5.66	7.38	1,856	-17	23	0	34	0		3.41	1,000	50		1.00	Jul-95
5.80	6.79	9.26	16.41	23.10	2.13	1.05	3.7	5.66	7.37	1,856	-17	23	0	34	0		3.41	0				Mar-01
5.81	7.11	9.90	17.85	25.22	2.7	0.43	3.74	5.66	7.37	1,856	-17	23	0	34	0		3.41	1,000,000				May-19
5.84	7.15	9.83	18.75	27.05	2.77	0.38	3.76	5.66	7.36	1,856	-17	23	0	34	0		3.41	1,000,000				Apr-12
5.84	7.14	9.94	18.58	26.83	2.7	0.45	3.66	5.66	7.33	1,856	-17	23	0	34	0		3.41	1,000	50			Apr-98
2.73	0.16	2.92	12.57	23.34	4.43		6.36	10.51	13.73	320.5	0	0	100	0	-1	5	5.84					Apr-93
0.04	0.36	1.28	4.73	5.31	1.46	0.18	0.17		1	13,123	61	39	0	0	0			1,000				Jun-06
0.04	0.35	1.28	4.72	5.31	1.46	0.18	0.17		1	13,123	61	39	0	0	0			1,000	50			Apr-91
2.56	3.16	4.82	10.07	15.48	3.69	0.81	2.46	2.80	11.87	1,624	-50	1	0	0	0	448	3.22	1,000	50	4.25		May-84
2.46	2.86	4.12	7.67	11.34	2.94	1.61	2.48	2.80	11.8	1,624	-50	1	0	0	0	448	3.22	1,000	50		1.00	Aug-93
2.49	3.02	4.54	9.21	13.99		1.11	2.46	2.80	11.86	1,624	-50	1	0	0	0	448	3.22	0				May-20
2.73	3.34	5.29	11.41	16.97	4.07	0.47	2.48	2.80	11.92	1,624	-50	1	0	0	0	448	3.22	1,000,000				Apr-17
2.70	3.28	5.16	10.87	17.00	3.93	0.51	2.47	2.80	11.92	1,624	-50	1	0	0	0	448	3.22	1,000	50			Sep-06
2.64	3.34	5.21	11.32	17.61	4.07	0.47	2.46	2.80	11.91	1,624	-50	1	0	0	0	448	3.22	1,000,000				Jun-10
4.32	0.94	3.51	13.23	27.88	4.54		6.69	10.05	13.37	693.8	3	0	97	0	-1	12	6.42					Sep-92
8.72	-10.72	-8.38	-0.30	10.30	6.96	0	11.17		4.09	619.8	7	0	0	92	1	63	2.57					Jun-98
8.27	-8.34	-6.84	0.97	11.08	5.43	2.46	9.56		5.81	1,296	4	0	0	95	2	55	4.71	1,000	50	3.25		Feb-05
7.86	-8.82	-7.67	-1.32	6.95	4.59	3.21	9.52		5.82	1,296	4	0	0	95	2	55	4.71	1,000	50		1.00	Feb-05
8.34	-8.36	-6.60	1.76	12.35	5.71	2.21	9.61		5.81	1,296	4	0	0	95	2	55	4.71	1,000	50			Oct-89
8.30	-8.30	-6.74	1.30	11.68	5.54	2.36	9.56		5.81	1,296	4	0	0	95	2	55	4.71	1,000	50			Jun-03
8.34	-8.22	-6.60	1.76	12.52	5.7	2.21	9.59		5.81	1,296	4	0	0	95	2	55	4.71	1,000	50			Nov-13
1.58	-5.44	-3.11	7.22		3.53	0.86	6.31	4.59	10.05	1,277	13	0	88	0	0		5.06	1,000	50	2.50		Sep-15
1.39	-5.82	-3.95	4.82		2.71	1.61	6.32	4.59	10.03	1,277	13	0	88	0	0		5.06	1,000	50		1.00	Sep-15
1.65	-5.31	-2.95	8.03		3.8	0.56	6.36	4.59	10.06	1,277	13	0	88	0	0		5.06	1,000,000				Sep-15
1.55	-5.41	-2.96	8.02		3.8	0.56	6.32	4.59	10.06	1,277	13	0	88	0	0		5.06	1,000,000				Apr-17
1.55	-5.41	-2.96	8.03		3.81	0.61	6.32	4.59	10.05	1,277	13	0	88	0	0		5.06	1,000	50			Sep-15
2.92	2.09	3.29	6.86	9.31	1.79	0.55	1.82	3.05	10.49	512.3	0	100	0	0	0	45	0.44	1,000	50	2.50		Oct-02

	MARKET		FUND TYPE, CATEGORY & OBJECTIVE		RATINGS				NEW INVESTORS	
Fund Name	Ticker Symbol	Traded On	Fund Type	Category and (Prospectus Objective)	Overall Rating	Reward Rating	Risk Rating	Recent Up/ Downgrade	Open to New Investors	Telephone
Invesco Short Duration Inflation Protected Fund Class A2	SHTIX	NAS CM	Open End	US Fixed Inc (Growth & Income)	C	C	B-			800-659-1005
Invesco Short Duration Inflation Protected Fund Class R5	ALMIX	NAS CM	Open End	US Fixed Inc (Growth & Income)	C	C	B		Y	800-659-1005
Invesco Short Duration Inflation Protected Fund Class R6	SDPSX	NAS CM	Open End	US Fixed Inc (Growth & Income)	C	C	B		Y	800-659-1005
Invesco Short Duration Inflation Protected Fund Class Y	LMTYX	NAS CM	Open End	US Fixed Inc (Growth & Income)	C	C	B		Y	800-659-1005
Invesco Short Term Bond Fund Class A	STBAX	NAS CM	Open End	US Fixed Inc (Income)	C	C-	C+		Y	800-659-1005
Invesco Short Term Bond Fund Class C	STBCX	NAS CM	Open End	US Fixed Inc (Income)	C	C-	C+		Y	800-659-1005
Invesco Short Term Bond Fund Class R	STBRX	NAS CM	Open End	US Fixed Inc (Income)	C	C-	C+		Y	800-659-1005
Invesco Short Term Bond Fund Class R6	ISTFX	NAS CM	Open End	US Fixed Inc (Income)	C	C-	C+		Y	800-659-1005
Invesco Short Term Bond Fund Class Y	STBYX	NAS CM	Open End	US Fixed Inc (Income)	C	C-	C+		Y	800-659-1005
Invesco Short Term Bond Fund R5 Class	ISTBX	NAS CM	Open End	US Fixed Inc (Income)	C	C-	C+		Y	800-659-1005
Invesco Short-Term Inv Trust Govt & Agency Port Cash Mgmt			Money Mkt	US Money Mkt (Money Mkt - Govt)	C	C-	C+		Y	800-659-1005
Invesco Short-Term Inv Trust Govt & Agency Portfol Corp Cl	AGCXX	NAS CM	Money Mkt	US Money Mkt (Money Mkt - Govt)	C	C-	C+		Y	800-659-1005
Invesco Short-Term Inv Trust Govt & Agency Portfol Inst Cl	AGPXX	NAS CM	Money Mkt	US Money Mkt (Money Mkt - Govt)	C	C-	C+		Y	800-659-1005
Invesco Short-Term Inv Trust Govt & Agency Port Pers Inv C			Money Mkt	US Money Mkt (Money Mkt - Govt)	C	C-	C		Y	800-659-1005
Invesco Short-Term Inv Trust Govt & Agency Port Private In	GPVXX	NAS CM	Money Mkt	US Money Mkt (Money Mkt - Govt)	C	C-	C+		Y	800-659-1005
Invesco Short-Term Inv Trust Govt & Agency Portfol Res Cl			Money Mkt	US Money Mkt (Money Mkt - Govt)	C	C-	C		Y	800-659-1005
Invesco Short-Term Inv Trust Govt & Agency Port Res Cl			Money Mkt	US Money Mkt (Money Mkt - Govt)	C	C-	C+		Y	800-659-1005
Invesco Short-Term Inv Trust Liq Assets Port Cash Mgmt Cl			Money Mkt	US Money Mkt (Money Mkt - General)	C	C-	C+		Y	800-659-1005
Invesco Short-Term Inv Trust Liquid Assets Portfol Corp Cl	LPCXX	NAS CM	Money Mkt	US Money Mkt (Money Mkt - General)	C	C-	C+		Y	800-659-1005
Invesco Short-Term Inv Trust Liquid Assets Portfol Inst Cl	LAPXX	NAS CM	Money Mkt	US Money Mkt (Money Mkt - General)	C	C-	C+		Y	800-659-1005
Invesco Short-Term Inv Trust Liq Assets Port Pers Inv Cl			Money Mkt	US Money Mkt (Money Mkt - General)	C	C-	C+		Y	800-659-1005
Invesco Short-Term Inv Trust Liq Assets Port Private Inv C	LPVXX	NAS CM	Money Mkt	US Money Mkt (Money Mkt - General)	C	C-	C+		Y	800-659-1005
Invesco Short-Term Inv Trust Liquid Assets Portfol Res Cl			Money Mkt	US Money Mkt (Money Mkt - General)	C	C-	C		Y	800-659-1005
Invesco Short-Term Inv Trust Liq Assets Port Res Cl			Money Mkt	US Money Mkt (Money Mkt - General)	C	C-	B-		Y	800-659-1005
Invesco Short-Term Inv Trust STIC Prime Port Cash Mgmt Cl			Money Mkt	US Money Mkt (Money Mkt - General)	C	C-	C+		Y	800-659-1005
Invesco Short-Term Inv Trust STIC Prime Portfol Corp Cl	SSCXX	NAS CM	Money Mkt	US Money Mkt (Money Mkt - General)	C	C-	C+		Y	800-659-1005
Invesco Short-Term Inv Trust STIC Prime Portfol Inst Cl	SRIXX	NAS CM	Money Mkt	US Money Mkt (Money Mkt - General)	C	C-	C+		Y	800-659-1005
Invesco Short-Term Inv Trust STIC Prime Portfol Pers Cl			Money Mkt	US Money Mkt (Money Mkt - General)	C	C-	C+		Y	800-659-1005
Invesco Short-Term Inv Trust STIC Prime Portfol Private Cl	SPVXX	NAS CM	Money Mkt	US Money Mkt (Money Mkt - General)	C	C-	C+		Y	800-659-1005
Invesco Short-Term Inv Trust STIC Prime Portfol Reserve Cl			Money Mkt	US Money Mkt (Money Mkt - General)	C	C-	C		Y	800-659-1005
Invesco Short-Term Inv Trust STIC Prime Port Res Cl			Money Mkt	US Money Mkt (Money Mkt - General)	C	C-	C+		Y	800-659-1005
Invesco Short-Term Inv Trust Tax-Free Cash Res Port Cash M			Money Mkt	US Money Mkt (Money Mkt - Fed Tax Exmpt)	C	C-	C+		Y	800-659-1005
Invesco Short-Term Inv Trust Tax-Free Cash Res Port Corp C	TFOXX	NAS CM	Money Mkt	US Money Mkt (Money Mkt - Fed Tax Exmpt)	C	C-	C+		Y	800-659-1005
Invesco Short-Term Inv Trust Tax-Free Cash Res Port Inst C	TFPXX	NAS CM	Money Mkt	US Money Mkt (Money Mkt - Fed Tax Exmpt)	C	C-	C		Y	800-659-1005
Invesco Short-Term Inv Trust Tax-Free Cash Res Port Pers I			Money Mkt	US Money Mkt (Money Mkt - Fed Tax Exmpt)	C	C-	C		Y	800-659-1005
Invesco Short-Term Inv Trust Tax-Free Cash Res Port Priv I	TRCXX	NAS CM	Money Mkt	US Money Mkt (Money Mkt - Fed Tax Exmpt)	C	C-	C		Y	800-659-1005
Invesco Short-Term Inv Trust Tax-Free Cash Res Port Res Cl			Money Mkt	US Money Mkt (Money Mkt - Fed Tax Exmpt)	C	C-	C		Y	800-659-1005
Invesco Short-Term Inv Trust Tax-Free Cash Res Port Res Cl			Money Mkt	US Money Mkt (Money Mkt - Fed Tax Exmpt)	C	C-	C		Y	800-659-1005
Invesco Short-Term Inv Trust Treas Oblig Port Cash Mgmt Cl			Money Mkt	US Money Mkt (Money Mkt - Treasury)	C	C-	C+		Y	800-659-1005
Invesco Short-Term Inv Trust Treas Oblig Portfol Corp Cl	TACXX	NAS CM	Money Mkt	US Money Mkt (Money Mkt - Treasury)	C	C-	C+		Y	800-659-1005
Invesco Short-Term Inv Trust Treas Oblig Portfol Inst Cl	TSPXX	NAS CM	Money Mkt	US Money Mkt (Money Mkt - Treasury)	C	C-	C+		Y	800-659-1005
Invesco Short-Term Inv Trust Treas Oblig Port Pers Inv Cl			Money Mkt	US Money Mkt (Money Mkt - Treasury)	C	C-	C		Y	800-659-1005
Invesco Short-Term Inv Trust Treas Oblig Port Private Inv	TXPXX	NAS CM	Money Mkt	US Money Mkt (Money Mkt - Treasury)	C	C-	C+		Y	800-659-1005
Invesco Short-Term Inv Trust Treas Oblig Portfol Res Cl			Money Mkt	US Money Mkt (Money Mkt - Treasury)	C	C-	C+		Y	800-659-1005
Invesco Short-Term Inv Trust Treas Oblig Port Res Cl			Money Mkt	US Money Mkt (Money Mkt - Treasury)	C	C-	C+		Y	800-659-1005
Invesco Short-Term Inv Trust Treas Portfol Cash Mgmt Cl			Money Mkt	US Money Mkt (Money Mkt - Treasury)	C	C-	C+		Y	800-659-1005
Invesco Short-Term Inv Trust Treas Portfol Corp Cl	TYCXX	NAS CM	Money Mkt	US Money Mkt (Money Mkt - Treasury)	C	C	C+		Y	800-659-1005
Invesco Short-Term Inv Trust Treas Portfol Inst Cl	TRPXX	NAS CM	Money Mkt	US Money Mkt (Money Mkt - Treasury)	C	C-	C+		Y	800-659-1005
Invesco Short-Term Inv Trust Treas Portfol Personal Inv Cl			Money Mkt	US Money Mkt (Money Mkt - Treasury)	C	C-	C		Y	800-659-1005
Invesco Short-Term Inv Trust Treas Portfol Private Inv Cl	TPFXX	NAS CM	Money Mkt	US Money Mkt (Money Mkt - Treasury)	C	C-	C+		Y	800-659-1005
Invesco Short-Term Inv Trust Treas Portfol Reserve Cl			Money Mkt	US Money Mkt (Money Mkt - Treasury)	C	C-	C		Y	800-659-1005
Invesco Short-Term Inv Trust Treas Portfol Resource Cl			Money Mkt	US Money Mkt (Money Mkt - Treasury)	C	C-	C+		Y	800-659-1005

★ Expanded analysis of this fund is included in Section II.

TOTAL RETURNS & PERFORMANCE									ASSETS		ASSET ALLOCATION & TURNOVER							MINIMUMS		FEES		
3-Month Total Return	6-Month Total Return	1-Year Total Return	3-Year Total Return	5-Year Total Return	Dividend Yield (TTM)	Expense Ratio	3-Yr Std Deviation	Effective Duration	NAV	Total Assets (MIL)	%Cash	%Government Bonds	%Municipal Bonds	%Corporate Bonds	%Other	Turnover Ratio	Average Coupon Rate	Min Initial Investment	Min Additional Investment	Front End Fee (%)	Back End Fee (%)	Inception Date
2.94	2.14	3.39	7.19	9.91	1.89	0.45	1.86	3.05	10.5	512.3	0	100	0	0	0	45	0.44	1,000	50	1.00		Dec-87
2.99	2.12	3.47	7.64	10.56	2.08	0.28	1.89	3.05	10.49	512.3	0	100	0	0	0	45	0.44	1,000,000				Jul-87
2.99	2.33	3.59	7.80	10.64	2.09	0.27	1.83	3.05	10.5	512.3	0	100	0	0	0	45	0.44	1,000,000				Dec-15
2.98	2.22	3.55	7.67	10.65	2.04	0.3	1.82	3.05	10.5	512.3	0	100	0	0	0	45	0.44	1,000	50			Oct-08
4.77	1.05	2.54	7.26	11.40	2.69	0.64	3.28	1.94	8.58	2,937	8	11	0	51	0	155	2.92	1,000	50	2.50		Apr-04
4.91	1.09	2.41	6.38	9.72	2.34	0.99	3.36	1.94	8.59	2,937	8	11	0	51	0	155	2.92	1,000	50			Aug-02
4.91	1.10	2.42	6.39	9.73	2.34	0.99	3.36	1.94	8.61	2,937	8	11	0	51	0	155	2.92	0				Apr-04
4.83	1.18	2.81	8.12	13.02	2.96	0.36	3.27	1.94	8.59	2,937	8	11	0	51	0	155	2.92	1,000,000				Sep-12
4.93	1.24	2.82	7.88	12.38	2.84	0.45	3.28	1.94	8.59	2,937	8	11	0	51	0	155	2.92	1,000	50			Oct-08
4.95	1.26	2.88	8.04	12.80	2.91	0.36	3.34	1.94	8.57	2,937	8	11	0	51	0	155	2.92	1,000,000				Apr-04
0.02	0.32	1.21	4.52	5.02	1.39	0.24	0.17		1	37,258	64	36	0	0	0			1,000				Sep-98
0.03	0.34	1.26	4.68	5.26	1.44	0.19	0.17		1	37,258	64	36	0	0	0			1,000				Jun-05
0.03	0.35	1.29	4.76	5.39	1.47	0.16	0.18		1	37,258	64	36	0	0	0			1,000				Sep-98
0.00	0.18	0.83	3.12	3.35	0.99	0.71	0.16		1	37,258	64	36	0	0	0			1,000				Jan-00
0.00	0.24	1.02	3.86	4.18	1.19	0.46	0.17		1	37,258	64	36	0	0	0			1,000				Sep-98
0.00	0.11	0.61	2.49	2.75	0.73	1.03	0.12		1	37,258	64	36	0	0	0			1,000				Jan-00
0.00	0.28	1.13	4.27	4.66	1.31	0.32	0.17		1	37,258	64	36	0	0	0			1,000				Sep-98
0.11	0.47	1.44	5.19	6.08	1.61	0.26	0.16		1	2,270	89	0	6	5	0			1,000				Jan-96
0.11	0.49	1.49	5.35	6.34	1.66	0.21	0.16		1	2,270	89	0	6	5	0			1,000				Mar-05
0.12	0.51	1.52	5.45	6.51	1.69	0.18	0.16		1	2,270	89	0	6	5	0			1,000				Nov-93
0.01	0.26	0.99	3.74	4.08	1.15	0.73	0.16		1	2,270	89	0	6	5	0			1,000				Jan-99
0.05	0.36	1.22	4.51	5.01	1.39	0.48	0.16		1	2,270	89	0	6	5	0			1,000				Feb-96
0.00	0.16	0.74	2.90	3.19	0.87	1.05	0.14		1	2,270	89	0	6	5	0			1,000				Jan-00
0.07	0.41	1.32	4.82	5.48	1.49	0.38	0.16		1	2,270	89	0	6	5	0			1,000				Sep-96
0.08	0.41	1.33	4.89	5.58	1.52	0.26	0.16		1	395.1	84	0	13	4	0			1,000				Jun-94
0.09	0.43	1.39	5.03	5.80	1.57	0.21	0.16		1	395.1	84	0	13	4	0			1,000				Mar-05
0.09	0.44	1.41	5.14	5.96	1.6	0.18	0.16		1	395.1	84	0	13	4	0			1,000				Nov-80
0.01	0.23	0.91	3.48	3.88	1.06	0.73	0.15		1	395.1	84	0	13	4	0			1,000				Aug-91
0.04	0.31	1.13	4.22	4.70	1.3	0.48	0.16		1	395.1	84	0	13	4	0			1,000				Jul-93
0.00	0.14	0.66	2.74	3.14	0.79	1.05	0.12		1	395.1	84	0	13	4	0			1,000				Jan-99
0.06	0.37	1.26	4.64	5.22	1.44	0.34	0.16		1	395.1	84	0	13	4	0			1,000				Jan-96
0.04	0.36	0.88	3.06	3.54	1	0.28	0.12		1	222.0	13	0	87	0	0			1,000				Jan-99
0.04	0.38	0.92	3.20	3.74	1.05	0.23	0.12		1	222.0	13	0	87	0	0			1,000				Sep-05
0.05	0.39	0.95	3.30	3.87	1.08	0.2	0.12		1	222.0	13	0	87	0	0			1,000				Apr-83
0.02	0.23	0.51	1.85	2.17	0.59	0.75	0.1		1	222.0	13	0	87	0	0			1,000				Dec-00
0.03	0.31	0.74	2.57	2.93	0.85	0.45	0.12		1	222.0	13	0	87	0	0			1,000				Apr-92
0.00	0.15	0.28	1.22	1.55	0.33	1.07	0.08		1	222.0	13	0	87	0	0			1,000				Jun-99
0.03	0.34	0.82	2.83	3.23	0.93	0.36	0.12		1	222.0	13	0	87	0	0			1,000				Apr-99
0.02	0.32	1.18	4.41	4.77	1.37	0.26	0.17		1	1,405	63	36	0	0	0			1,000				Dec-99
0.03	0.35	1.24	4.46	4.81	1.42	0.21	0.18		1	1,405	63	36	0	0	0			1,000				Feb-06
0.05	0.36	1.27	4.66	5.12	1.45	0.18	0.17		1	1,405	63	36	0	0	0			1,000				Aug-90
0.00	0.18	0.80	3.04	3.26	0.95	0.73	0.16		1	1,405	63	36	0	0	0			1,000				May-01
0.00	0.26	1.04	3.90	4.17	1.21	0.43	0.17		1	1,405	63	36	0	0	0			1,000				Dec-94
0.00	0.11	0.57	2.40	2.65	0.69	1.05	0.12		1	1,405	63	36	0	0	0			1,000				Jun-03
0.01	0.29	1.12	4.17	4.48	1.29	0.34	0.17		1	1,405	63	36	0	0	0			1,000				Dec-99
0.00	0.29	1.16	4.45	4.87	1.35	0.26	0.18		1	21,781	71	29	0	0	0			1,000				Aug-93
0.02	0.31	1.22	4.60	5.09	1.4	0.21	0.18		1	21,781	71	29	0	0	0			1,000				Aug-05
0.02	0.33	1.25	4.70	5.25	1.43	0.18	0.18		1	21,781	71	29	0	0	0			1,000				Apr-84
0.00	0.18	0.81	3.13	3.33	0.96	0.73	0.16		1	21,781	71	29	0	0	0			1,000				Aug-91
0.00	0.23	1.00	3.81	4.05	1.16	0.48	0.17		1	21,781	71	29	0	0	0			1,000				Nov-91
0.00	0.11	0.58	2.39	2.57	0.7	1.05	0.13		1	21,781	71	29	0	0	0			1,000				Jan-99
0.00	0.27	1.10	4.21	4.53	1.28	0.34	0.17		1	21,781	71	29	0	0	0			1,000				Mar-96

	MARKET		FUND TYPE, CATEGORY & OBJECTIVE		RATINGS				NEW INVESTORS	
Fund Name	Ticker Symbol	Traded On	Fund Type	Category and (Prospectus Objective)	Overall Rating	Reward Rating	Risk Rating	Recent Up/ Downgrade	Open to New Investors	Telephone
Invesco Treasurer's Ser Trust Premier Portfol Inst Cl	IPPXX	NAS CM	Money Mkt	US Money Mkt (Money Mkt - General)	C	C-	C+		Y	800-659-1005
Invesco Treasurer's Ser Trust Premier Portfol Investor Cl	IMRXX	NAS CM	Money Mkt	US Money Mkt (Money Mkt - General)	C	C-	C+		Y	800-659-1005
Invesco Treasurer's Ser Trust Premier Portfol Pers Inv Cl	IPVXX	NAS CM	Money Mkt	US Money Mkt (Money Mkt - General)	C	C-	C+		Y	800-659-1005
Invesco Treasurer's Ser Trust Prem Port Private Inv Cl	IPTXX	NAS CM	Money Mkt	US Money Mkt (Money Mkt - General)	C	C-	C+		Y	800-659-1005
Invesco Treasurer's Ser Trust Premier Portfolio Reserve Cl	IRVXX	NAS CM	Money Mkt	US Money Mkt (Money Mkt - General)	C	C-	C		Y	800-659-1005
Invesco Treasurer's Ser Trust Premier Portfol Resource Cl	IRCXX	NAS CM	Money Mkt	US Money Mkt (Money Mkt - General)	C	C-	C+		Y	800-659-1005
Invesco Treasurer's Ser Trust Prem Tax-Ex Port Inst Cl	PEIXX	NAS CM	Money Mkt	US Money Mkt (Money Mkt - Fed Tax Exmpt)	C	C-	C+		Y	800-659-1005
Invesco Treasurer's Ser Trust Prem Tax-Ex Port Investor Cl	ITTXX	NAS CM	Money Mkt	US Money Mkt (Money Mkt - Fed Tax Exmpt)	C	C-	C+		Y	800-659-1005
Invesco Trust for Investment Grade Municipals	VGM	NYSE	Closed End	US Muni Fixed Inc (Muni Bond - Natl)	C-	C-	C-	Down	Y	404-892-0896
Invesco Trust for New York Investment Grade Municipals	VTN	NYSE	Closed End	US Muni Fixed Inc (Muni Bond - Single State)	C-	D+	C-		Y	404-892-0896
Invesco World Bond Factor Fund Class A	AUBAX	NAS CM	Open End	Global Fixed Inc (Growth & Income)	C+	C	B	Up	Y	800-659-1005
Invesco World Bond Factor Fund Class C	AUBCX	NAS CM	Open End	Global Fixed Inc (Growth & Income)	C	C	B-		Y	800-659-1005
Invesco World Bond Factor Fund Class R5	AUBIX	NAS CM	Open End	Global Fixed Inc (Growth & Income)	C+	C	B	Up	Y	800-659-1005
Invesco World Bond Factor Fund Class R6	AUBFX	NAS CM	Open End	Global Fixed Inc (Growth & Income)	C+	C	B	Up	Y	800-659-1005
Invesco World Bond Factor Fund Class Y	AUBYX	NAS CM	Open End	Global Fixed Inc (Growth & Income)	C+	C	B	Up	Y	800-659-1005
InvestEd Fixed Income Portfolio	WFXPX	NAS CM	Open End	US Fixed Inc (Multisector Bond)	C	C	B		Y	888-923-3355
Iron Strategic Income Fund Institutional Class	IFUNX	NAS CM	Open End	Fixed Inc Misc (Income)	D	D	C-	Down	Y	877-322-0575
Iron Strategic Income Fund Investor Class	IRNIX	NAS CM	Open End	Fixed Inc Misc (Income)	D	D	C-	Down	Y	877-322-0575
iShares Municipal Bond Index Fund Class K	BIDKX	NAS CM	Open End	US Muni Fixed Inc (Muni Bond - Natl)	C+	C	B	Up	Y	800-441-7762
iShares Municipal Bond Index Fund Institutional	BIDIX	NAS CM	Open End	US Muni Fixed Inc (Muni Bond - Natl)	C+	C	B	Up	Y	800-441-7762
iShares Municipal Bond Index Fund Investor A Shares	BIDAX	NAS CM	Open End	US Muni Fixed Inc (Muni Bond - Natl)	C	C	B			800-441-7762
iShares Municipal Bond Index Fund Investor P Shares	BIDPX	NAS CM	Open End	US Muni Fixed Inc (Muni Bond - Natl)	C	C	B		Y	800-441-7762
iShares Short-Term TIPS Bond Index Fund Class K	BKIPX	NAS CM	Open End	US Fixed Inc (Growth & Income)	C	C	B		Y	800-441-7762
iShares Short-Term TIPS Bond Ind Institutional Shares	BIIPX	NAS CM	Open End	US Fixed Inc (Growth & Income)	C	C	B-		Y	800-441-7762
iShares Short-Term TIPS Bond Index Fund Investor A Shares	BAIPX	NAS CM	Open End	US Fixed Inc (Growth & Income)	C	C	B-		Y	800-441-7762
iShares U.S. Aggregate Bond Index Fund Class K	WFBIX	NAS CM	Open End	US Fixed Inc (Income)	B	B-	B+		Y	800-441-7762
iShares U.S. Aggregate Bond Ind Institutional Shares	BMOIX	NAS CM	Open End	US Fixed Inc (Income)	B	B-	B+		Y	800-441-7762
iShares U.S. Aggregate Bond Index Fund Investor A Shares	BMOAX	NAS CM	Open End	US Fixed Inc (Income)	B	B-	B	Up	Y	800-441-7762
iShares U.S. Aggregate Bond Index Fund Investor P Shares	BMOPX	NAS CM	Open End	US Fixed Inc (Income)	B	B-	B	Up	Y	800-441-7762
Ivy Apollo Strategic Income Fund Class A	IAPOX	NAS CM	Open End	US Fixed Inc (Income)	C-	D+	C		Y	
Ivy Apollo Strategic Income Fund Class C	ICPOX	NAS CM	Open End	US Fixed Inc (Income)	C-	D+	C		Y	
Ivy Apollo Strategic Income Fund Class I	IIPOX	NAS CM	Open End	US Fixed Inc (Income)	C-	D+	C	Down	Y	
Ivy Apollo Strategic Income Fund Class N	IRPOX	NAS CM	Open End	US Fixed Inc (Income)	C-	D+	C	Down	Y	
Ivy Apollo Strategic Income Fund Class Y	IYPOX	NAS CM	Open End	US Fixed Inc (Income)	C-	D+	C		Y	
Ivy California Municipal High Income Fund Class A	IMHAX	NAS CM	Open End	US Muni Fixed Inc (Muni Bond - Single State)	C	C-	C		Y	
Ivy California Municipal High Income Fund Class C	IMHCX	NAS CM	Open End	US Muni Fixed Inc (Muni Bond - Single State)	C-	D+	C	Down	Y	
Ivy California Municipal High Income Fund Class I	IMHIX	NAS CM	Open End	US Muni Fixed Inc (Muni Bond - Single State)	C	C-	C+		Y	
Ivy California Municipal High Income Fund Class Y	IMHYX	NAS CM	Open End	US Muni Fixed Inc (Muni Bond - Single State)	C	C-	C+		Y	
Ivy Cash Management Fund Class A	IAAXX	NAS CM	Money Mkt	US Money Mkt (Money Mkt - Taxable)	C	C-	C+			
Ivy Cash Management Fund Class B	IABXX	NAS CM	Money Mkt	US Money Mkt (Money Mkt - Taxable)	C	C-	C			
Ivy Cash Management Fund Class C	IACXX	NAS CM	Money Mkt	US Money Mkt (Money Mkt - Taxable)	C	C-	C			
Ivy Corporate Bond Fund Class A	IBJAX	NAS CM	Open End	US Fixed Inc (Corp Bond - General)	B-	C+	B	Up	Y	
Ivy Corporate Bond Fund Class B	IBJBX	NAS CM	Open End	US Fixed Inc (Corp Bond - General)	C	C	C+			
Ivy Corporate Bond Fund Class C	IBJCX	NAS CM	Open End	US Fixed Inc (Corp Bond - General)	C+	C	B-	Up	Y	
Ivy Corporate Bond Fund Class I	IBJIX	NAS CM	Open End	US Fixed Inc (Corp Bond - General)	B-	C+	B	Up	Y	
Ivy Corporate Bond Fund Class N	IBJNX	NAS CM	Open End	US Fixed Inc (Corp Bond - General)	B-	C+	B	Up	Y	
Ivy Corporate Bond Fund Class Y	IBJYX	NAS CM	Open End	US Fixed Inc (Corp Bond - General)	B-	C+	B	Up		
Ivy Crossover Credit Fund Class A	ICKAX	NAS CM	Open End	US Fixed Inc (Multisector Bond)	C+	C	B	Up	Y	
Ivy Crossover Credit Fund Class I	ICKIX	NAS CM	Open End	US Fixed Inc (Multisector Bond)	C+	C	B	Up	Y	
Ivy Crossover Credit Fund Class N	ICKNX	NAS CM	Open End	US Fixed Inc (Multisector Bond)	C+	C	B	Up	Y	
Ivy Crossover Credit Fund Class Y	ICKYX	NAS CM	Open End	US Fixed Inc (Multisector Bond)	C+	C	B	Up	Y	
Ivy Global Bond Fund Class A	IVSAX	NAS CM	Open End	Global Fixed Inc (Worldwide Bond)	C	C-	B-		Y	

★Expanded analysis of this fund is included in Section II.

TOTAL RETURNS & PERFORMANCE									ASSETS		ASSET ALLOCATION & TURNOVER							MINIMUMS		FEES		
3-Month Total Return	6-Month Total Return	1-Year Total Return	3-Year Total Return	5-Year Total Return	Dividend Yield (TTM)	Expense Ratio	3-Yr Std Deviation	Effective Duration	NAV	Total Assets (MIL)	%Cash	%Government Bonds	%Municipal Bonds	%Corporate Bonds	%Other	Turnover Ratio	Average Coupon Rate	Min Initial Investment	Min Additional Investment	Front End Fee (%)	Back End Fee (%)	Inception Date
0.13	0.52	1.55	5.47	6.41	1.72	0.18	0.16		1	1,734	90	0	6	3	0			1,000				Feb-05
0.13	0.52	1.55	5.47	6.41	1.72	0.18	0.16		1	1,734	90	0	6	3	0			1,000	50			Apr-88
0.02	0.27	1.02	3.79	3.61	1.18	0.73	0.15		1	1,734	90	0	6	3	0			1,000				Sep-16
0.06	0.38	1.25	4.54	4.85	1.42	0.48	0.15		1	1,734	90	0	6	3	0			1,000				Sep-16
0.00	0.19	0.77	2.85	2.13	0.9	1.05	0.15		1	1,734	90	0	6	3	0			1,000				Sep-16
0.09	0.44	1.39	4.98	5.59	1.56	0.34	0.15		1	1,734	90	0	6	3	0			1,000				Sep-16
0.04	0.39	0.99	3.45	4.03	1.12	0.2	0.12		1	93.4	12	0	88	0	0			1,000				Feb-05
0.03	0.38	0.99	3.45	4.02	1.12	0.2	0.12		1	93.4	12	0	88	0	0			1,000	50			Apr-88
4.11	0.45	2.87	11.86	24.02	4.6		6.63	10.43	13.58	719.6	3	0	97	0	0	9	6.41					Jan-92
2.77	-1.27	1.17	9.13	20.27	4.24		7.11	11.00	13.96	268.0	0	0	100	0	0	12	6.18					Mar-92
4.41	2.72	5.96	11.78	23.77	2.4	0.54	5.39	7.38	10.74	28.5	9	34	0	29	0		2.80	1,000	50	4.25		Mar-06
4.13	2.39	5.14	9.25	19.08	1.72	1.29	5.4	7.38	10.71	28.5	9	34	0	29	0		2.80	1,000	50		1.00	Mar-06
4.40	2.75	5.93	12.08	24.60	2.64	0.29	5.39	7.38	10.68	28.5	9	34	0	29	0		2.80	1,000,000				Mar-06
4.38	2.83	6.11	12.60	25.30	2.63	0.29	5.38	7.38	10.74	28.5	9	34	0	29	0		2.80	1,000,000				Sep-12
4.38	2.83	6.11	12.60	25.31	2.63	0.29	5.4	7.38	10.73	28.5	9	34	0	29	0		2.80	1,000	50			Oct-08
2.51	3.21	4.40			1.7	0.76		2.70	10.6	57.8	17	43	0	24	0	27	2.83	250		2.50		Sep-17
3.30	-6.59	-4.92	-1.34	1.95	4.14	1.25	6.04		9.39	39.0	12	17	0	70	0	216	4.89	10,000	1,000			Oct-06
3.13	-6.75	-5.26	-2.39	0.19	3.71	1.6	6.03		9.48	39.0	12	17	0	70	0	216	4.89	10,000	1,000			Feb-09
2.32	1.93	4.00	12.12	19.25	2.48	0.21	3.86		12.1	348.0	2	0	98	0	0	24	4.85	5,000,000				Nov-18
2.39	1.91	3.96	12.06	19.18	2.45	0.25	3.88		12.1	348.0	2	0	98	0	0	24	4.85	2,000,000				Nov-18
2.33	1.78	3.69	11.60	18.69	2.19	0.51	3.87		12.1	348.0	2	0	98	0	0	24	4.85	1,000	50	3.00		Dec-00
2.24	1.78	3.69	11.60	18.69	2.19	0.48	3.86		12.1	348.0	2	0	98	0	0	24	4.85	1,000	50	4.00		Nov-18
2.51	1.80	3.26	7.92		2.07	0.06	1.64		10.1	24.4	6	91	0	0	0	45	0.41	5,000,000				Feb-16
2.61	1.88	3.31	7.89		2.01	0.11	1.71		10.11	24.4	6	91	0	0	0	45	0.41	2,000,000				Feb-16
2.49	1.70	3.00	7.02		1.79	0.36	1.68		10.09	24.4	6	91	0	0	0	45	0.41	1,000	50			Feb-16
2.91	6.30	9.01	16.79	23.54	2.72	0.05	3.26	5.50	10.91	2,215	7	40	1	25	0	158	3.12	5,000,000				Jul-93
2.90	6.28	8.97	16.51	23.13	2.67	0.1	3.33	5.50	10.9	2,215	7	40	1	25	0	158	3.12	2,000,000				Mar-11
2.84	6.15	8.69	15.76	21.63	2.43	0.35	3.26	5.50	10.9	2,215	7	40	1	25	0	158	3.12	1,000	50			Mar-11
2.84	6.16	8.72	15.75	21.84	2.46	0.35	3.29	5.50	10.9	2,215	7	40	1	25	0	158	3.12	1,000	50	4.00		Aug-18
8.70	-1.71	0.28	7.90		4.58	1.05	6.96	3.40	9.63	410.2	11	11	0	74	0	45	5.26	750		5.75		Oct-15
8.61	-2.09	-0.39	5.51		3.77	1.82	6.96	3.40	9.63	410.2	11	11	0	74	0	45	5.26	750			1.00	Oct-15
8.91	-1.52	0.76	9.06		4.97	0.67	6.96	3.40	9.64	410.2	11	11	0	74	0	45	5.26	0				Oct-15
8.91	-1.52	0.76	9.16		4.97	0.67	6.96	3.40	9.64	410.2	11	11	0	74	0	45	5.26	1,000,000				Oct-15
8.82	-1.71	0.29	7.99		4.59	1.05	7.03	3.40	9.63	410.2	11	11	0	74	0	45	5.26	0				Oct-15
2.85	-0.93	1.29	10.73		2.17	0.8	5.34	6.70	10.37	34.3	8	0	92	0	0	10	4.69	750		4.25		Oct-16
2.63	-1.36	0.41	7.98		1.27	1.66	5.34	6.70	10.37	34.3	8	0	92	0	0	10	4.69	750			1.00	Oct-16
2.90	-0.84	1.49	11.39		2.37	0.6	5.34	6.70	10.37	34.3	8	0	92	0	0	10	4.69	0				Oct-16
2.85	-0.93	1.28	10.67		2.17	0.8	5.34	6.70	10.37	34.3	8	0	92	0	0	10	4.69	0				Oct-16
0.07	0.34	1.12	3.86	4.03	1.3	0.71	0.16		1	1,565	73	22	2	4	0	0		750		5.75	1.00	Aug-79
0.00	0.08	0.48	1.55	1.59	0.57	1.51	0.13		1	1,565	73	22	2	4	0	0		750			5.00	Sep-99
0.00	0.04	0.36	1.31	1.36	0.45	1.65	0.11		1	1,565	73	22	2	4	0	0		750			1.00	Sep-99
9.12	6.05	9.52	17.63	26.03	2.38	1.02	5.88	7.50	6.83	856.7	3	2	2	88	0	63	3.86	750		5.75		Mar-64
8.73	5.21	7.68	12.24	17.10	0.85	2.61	5.95	7.50	6.82	856.7	3	2	2	88	0	63	3.86	750			5.00	Sep-99
8.92	5.61	8.42	14.57	20.64	1.54	1.92	5.91	7.50	6.82	856.7	3	2	2	88	0	63	3.86	750			1.00	Sep-99
9.20	6.05	9.69	18.74	27.96	2.67	0.7	5.97	7.50	6.83	856.7	3	2	2	88	0	63	3.86	0				Jun-95
9.24	6.29	10.01	19.30	27.83	2.83	0.55	5.83	7.50	6.83	856.7	3	2	2	88	0	63	3.86	1,000,000				Oct-17
9.15	6.10	9.59	18.05	26.49	2.45	0.93	5.85	7.50	6.83	856.7	3	2	2	88	0	63	3.86	0				Oct-17
14.80	6.06	10.42	20.20		2.66	0.9	8.65	6.20	11.07	50.1	4	0	0	96	0	94	4.08	750		5.75		Apr-17
14.87	6.19	10.70	21.11		2.91	0.65	8.65	6.20	11.07	50.1	4	0	0	96	0	94	4.08	0				Apr-17
14.87	6.19	10.70	21.11		2.91	0.65	8.65	6.20	11.07	50.1	4	0	0	96	0	94	4.08	1,000,000				Apr-17
14.80	6.06	10.42	20.20		2.66	0.9	8.65	6.20	11.07	50.1	4	0	0	96	0	94	4.08	0				Apr-17
9.39	2.17	3.47	12.00	18.59	2.01	0.96	6.03	4.20	10.08	426.5	2	27	0	71	0	38	4.42	750		5.75		Apr-08

	MARKET			FUND TYPE, CATEGORY & OBJECTIVE	RATINGS				NEW INVESTORS	
Fund Name	Ticker Symbol	Traded On	Fund Type	Category and (Prospectus Objective)	Overall Rating	Reward Rating	Risk Rating	Recent Up/ Downgrade	Open to New Investors	Telephone
Ivy Global Bond Fund Class B	IVSBX	NAS CM	Open End	Global Fixed Inc (Worldwide Bond)	C	C-	C+			
Ivy Global Bond Fund Class C	IVSCX	NAS CM	Open End	Global Fixed Inc (Worldwide Bond)	C	C-	C+		Y	
Ivy Global Bond Fund Class I	IVSIX	NAS CM	Open End	Global Fixed Inc (Worldwide Bond)	C	C-	B-		Y	
Ivy Global Bond Fund Class N	IVBDX	NAS CM	Open End	Global Fixed Inc (Worldwide Bond)	C	C-	B-		Y	
Ivy Global Bond Fund Class R	IYGOX	NAS CM	Open End	Global Fixed Inc (Worldwide Bond)	C	C-	B-		Y	
Ivy Global Bond Fund Class Y	IVSYX	NAS CM	Open End	Global Fixed Inc (Worldwide Bond)	C	C-	B-		Y	
Ivy Government Money Market Fund Class A	WRAXX	NAS CM	Money Mkt	US Money Mkt (Money Mkt - Govt)	C	C-	C+		Y	
Ivy Government Money Market Fund Class B	WRBXX	NAS CM	Money Mkt	US Money Mkt (Money Mkt - Govt)	C	C-	C			
Ivy Government Money Market Fund Class C	WRCXX	NAS CM	Money Mkt	US Money Mkt (Money Mkt - Govt)	C	C-	C		Y	
Ivy Government Money Market Fund Class E	IVEXX	NAS CM	Money Mkt	US Money Mkt (Money Mkt - Govt)	C	C-	C+		Y	
Ivy Government Money Market Fund Class N	WRNXX	NAS CM	Money Mkt	US Money Mkt (Money Mkt - Govt)	C	C-	C+		Y	
Ivy Government Securities Fund Class A	IGJAX	NAS CM	Open End	US Fixed Inc (Govt Bond - General)	B-	C+	B		Y	
Ivy Government Securities Fund Class B	IGJBX	NAS CM	Open End	US Fixed Inc (Govt Bond - General)	C+	C	B-			
Ivy Government Securities Fund Class C	IGJCX	NAS CM	Open End	US Fixed Inc (Govt Bond - General)	C+	C+	B-		Y	
Ivy Government Securities Fund Class I	IGJIX	NAS CM	Open End	US Fixed Inc (Govt Bond - General)	B-	B-	B		Y	
Ivy Government Securities Fund Class N	IGJNX	NAS CM	Open End	US Fixed Inc (Govt Bond - General)	B-	B-	B		Y	
Ivy High Income Fund Class A	WHIAX	NAS CM	Open End	US Fixed Inc (Growth & Income)	D	D	D+	Down	Y	
Ivy High Income Fund Class B	WHIBX	NAS CM	Open End	US Fixed Inc (Growth & Income)	D	D	D+	Down		
Ivy High Income Fund Class C	WRHIX	NAS CM	Open End	US Fixed Inc (Growth & Income)	D	D	D+	Down	Y	
Ivy High Income Fund Class E	IVHEX	NAS CM	Open End	US Fixed Inc (Growth & Income)	D	D	D+	Down	Y	
Ivy High Income Fund Class I	IVHIX	NAS CM	Open End	US Fixed Inc (Growth & Income)	D	D	D+	Down	Y	
Ivy High Income Fund Class N	IHIFX	NAS CM	Open End	US Fixed Inc (Growth & Income)	D	D	D+	Down	Y	
Ivy High Income Fund Class R	IYHIX	NAS CM	Open End	US Fixed Inc (Growth & Income)	D	D	D+	Down	Y	
Ivy High Income Fund Class Y	WHIYX	NAS CM	Open End	US Fixed Inc (Growth & Income)	D	D	D+	Down	Y	
Ivy High Income Opportunities Fund	IVH	NYSE	Closed End	US Fixed Inc (Corp Bond - High Yield)	D	D	D	Down	Y	
Ivy Limited-Term Bond Fund Class A	WLTAX	NAS CM	Open End	US Fixed Inc (Corp Bond - General)	C+	C	B-	Up	Y	
Ivy Limited-Term Bond Fund Class B	WLTBX	NAS CM	Open End	US Fixed Inc (Corp Bond - General)	C	C	B-			
Ivy Limited-Term Bond Fund Class C	WLBCX	NAS CM	Open End	US Fixed Inc (Corp Bond - General)	C	C	B-		Y	
Ivy Limited-Term Bond Fund Class E	IVLEX	NAS CM	Open End	US Fixed Inc (Corp Bond - General)	C	C	B-		Y	
Ivy Limited-Term Bond Fund Class I	ILTIX	NAS CM	Open End	US Fixed Inc (Corp Bond - General)	C+	C	B-	Up	Y	
Ivy Limited-Term Bond Fund Class N	ILMDX	NAS CM	Open End	US Fixed Inc (Corp Bond - General)	C+	C	B-	Up	Y	
Ivy Limited-Term Bond Fund Class R	IYLTX	NAS CM	Open End	US Fixed Inc (Corp Bond - General)	C	C	B-		Y	
Ivy Limited-Term Bond Fund Class Y	WLTYX	NAS CM	Open End	US Fixed Inc (Corp Bond - General)	C+	C	B-	Up	Y	
Ivy Municipal Bond Fund Class A	WMBAX	NAS CM	Open End	US Muni Fixed Inc (Muni Bond - Natl)	C	C-	B-		Y	
Ivy Municipal Bond Fund Class B	WMBBX	NAS CM	Open End	US Muni Fixed Inc (Muni Bond - Natl)	C	C-	C+			
Ivy Municipal Bond Fund Class C	WMBCX	NAS CM	Open End	US Muni Fixed Inc (Muni Bond - Natl)	C	C-	C+		Y	
Ivy Municipal Bond Fund Class I	IMBIX	NAS CM	Open End	US Muni Fixed Inc (Muni Bond - Natl)	C	C-	B-		Y	
Ivy Municipal Bond Fund Class N	IMBNX	NAS CM	Open End	US Muni Fixed Inc (Muni Bond - Natl)	C	C-	B-		Y	
Ivy Municipal Bond Fund Class Y	WMBYX	NAS CM	Open End	US Muni Fixed Inc (Muni Bond - Natl)	C	C-	B-			
Ivy Municipal High Income Fund Class A	IYIAX	NAS CM	Open End	US Muni Fixed Inc (Muni Bond - Natl)	C	C-	C		Y	
Ivy Municipal High Income Fund Class B	IYIBX	NAS CM	Open End	US Muni Fixed Inc (Muni Bond - Natl)	C-	D+	C	Down		
Ivy Municipal High Income Fund Class C	IYICX	NAS CM	Open End	US Muni Fixed Inc (Muni Bond - Natl)	C-	D+	C	Down	Y	
Ivy Municipal High Income Fund Class I	WYMHX	NAS CM	Open End	US Muni Fixed Inc (Muni Bond - Natl)	C	C-	C		Y	
Ivy Municipal High Income Fund Class N	IYINX	NAS CM	Open End	US Muni Fixed Inc (Muni Bond - Natl)	C	C-	C		Y	
Ivy Municipal High Income Fund Class Y	IYIYX	NAS CM	Open End	US Muni Fixed Inc (Muni Bond - Natl)	C	C-	C		Y	
Ivy Pictet Emerg Mkts Local Currency Debt Fund Class A	IECAX	NAS CM	Open End	Emerg Mkts Fixed Inc (Diversified Emerg Mkts)	D	D	D+	Down	Y	
Ivy Pictet Emerg Mkts Local Currency Debt Fund Class C	IECCX	NAS CM	Open End	Emerg Mkts Fixed Inc (Diversified Emerg Mkts)	D	D	D+	Down	Y	
Ivy Pictet Emerg Mkts Local Currency Debt Fund Class I	IECIX	NAS CM	Open End	Emerg Mkts Fixed Inc (Diversified Emerg Mkts)	D	D	D+	Down	Y	
Ivy Pictet Emerg Mkts Local Currency Debt Fund Class N	IMMCX	NAS CM	Open End	Emerg Mkts Fixed Inc (Diversified Emerg Mkts)	D	D	D+	Down	Y	
Ivy Pictet Emerg Mkts Local Currency Debt Fund Class Y	IECYX	NAS CM	Open End	Emerg Mkts Fixed Inc (Diversified Emerg Mkts)	D	D	D+	Down	Y	
Ivy Pictet Targeted Return Bond Fund Class A	IRBAX	NAS CM	Open End	Fixed Inc Misc (Growth & Income)	C	C-	C+		Y	
Ivy Pictet Targeted Return Bond Fund Class C	IRBCX	NAS CM	Open End	Fixed Inc Misc (Growth & Income)	C	C-	C		Y	

★ Expanded analysis of this fund is included in Section II.

TOTAL RETURNS & PERFORMANCE									ASSETS		ASSET ALLOCATION & TURNOVER							MINIMUMS		FEES		
3-Month Total Return	6-Month Total Return	1-Year Total Return	3-Year Total Return	5-Year Total Return	Dividend Yield (TTM)	Expense Ratio	3-Yr Std Deviation	Effective Duration	NAV	Total Assets (MIL)	%Cash	%Government Bonds	%Municipal Bonds	%Corporate Bonds	%Other	Turnover Ratio	Average Coupon Rate	Min Initial Investment	Min Additional Investment	Front End Fee (%)	Back End Fee (%)	Inception Date
9.09	1.81	2.72	9.62	14.36	1.28	1.68	6.04	4.20	10.07	426.5	2	27	0	71	0	38	4.42	750			5.00	Apr-08
9.19	1.79	2.69	9.52	14.25	1.26	1.72	6.01	4.20	10.08	426.5	2	27	0	71	0	38	4.42	750			1.00	Apr-08
9.44	2.29	3.72	12.83	20.06	2.25	0.74	6.04	4.20	10.08	426.5	2	27	0	71	0	38	4.42	0				Apr-08
9.44	2.30	3.73	12.90	20.10	2.26	0.71	6.04	4.20	10.08	426.5	2	27	0	71	0	38	4.42	1,000,000				Jul-14
9.27	1.93	2.99	10.44	15.76	1.54	1.45	6.07	4.20	10.06	426.5	2	27	0	71	0	38	4.42	0				Dec-12
9.39	2.17	3.47	11.99	18.58	2.01	0.99	6.1	4.20	10.08	426.5	2	27	0	71	0	38	4.42	0				Apr-08
0.03	0.26	0.94	3.32	3.39	1.09	0.78	0.14		1	224.2	40	60	0	0	0			750		5.75		Jun-00
0.00	0.06	0.31	0.98	1.02	0.39	1.7	0.09		1	224.2	40	60	0	0	0			750			5.00	Jun-00
0.00	0.04	0.28	1.10	1.13	0.34	1.54	0.1		1	224.2	40	60	0	0	0			750			1.00	Jun-00
0.05	0.34	1.15	3.70	3.76	1.32	0.51	0.16		1	224.2	40	60	0	0	0			250		2.50		Apr-07
0.04	0.33	1.14	3.97	4.05	1.31	0.5			1	224.2	40	60	0	0	0			1,000,000				Jul-17
0.32	5.56	6.54	11.27	14.36	1.36	0.97	3.06	4.70	5.8	355.6	2	56	0	0	0	12	2.64	750		4.25		Apr-84
0.05	5.01	5.36	7.81	8.28	0.28	2.02	3.05	4.70	5.8	355.6	2	56	0	0	0	12	2.64	750			5.00	Oct-99
0.10	5.10	5.61	8.41	9.48	0.51	1.85	3.06	4.70	5.8	355.6	2	56	0	0	0	12	2.64	750			1.00	Oct-99
0.38	5.69	6.82	12.16	15.97	1.62	0.72	3.06	4.70	5.8	355.6	2	56	0	0	0	12	2.64	0				Sep-95
0.41	5.74	6.94	12.47	15.60	1.73	0.61	3.07	4.70	5.8	355.6	2	56	0	0	0	12	2.64	1,000,000				Oct-17
8.54	-8.64	-6.36	1.44	13.03	7.65	0.95	10.31	2.80	6.3	3,912	6	0	0	94	0	30	7.27	750		5.75		Jul-00
8.34	-8.99	-7.07	-0.86	8.82	6.81	1.71	10.31	2.80	6.3	3,912	6	0	0	94	0	30	7.27	750			5.00	Jul-00
8.35	-8.96	-7.02	-0.69	9.09	6.87	1.66	10.31	2.80	6.3	3,912	6	0	0	94	0	30	7.27	750			1.00	Jul-97
8.52	-8.68	-6.45	0.99	12.01	7.53	1.08	10.31	2.80	6.3	3,912	6	0	0	94	0	30	7.27	250		2.50		Apr-07
8.60	-8.53	-6.15	2.15	14.40	7.9	0.72	10.31	2.80	6.3	3,912	6	0	0	94	0	30	7.27	0				Apr-07
8.64	-8.46	-6.00	2.63	15.32	8.07	0.56	10.32	2.80	6.3	3,912	6	0	0	94	0	30	7.27	1,000,000				Jul-14
8.44	-8.80	-6.70	0.35	11.05	7.25	1.3	10.31	2.80	6.3	3,912	6	0	0	94	0	30	7.27	0				Dec-12
8.54	-8.63	-6.35	1.46	13.04	7.66	0.95	10.31	2.80	6.3	3,912	6	0	0	94	0	30	7.27	0				Dec-98
11.46	-11.83	-9.32	0.70	16.24	9.43	2.13	13.72		12.73	210.1	8	0	0	95	0	34	7.29					May-13
2.35	2.78	3.85	8.18	11.80	1.82	0.91	1.59	2.00	11.08	1,130	6	49	0	30	0	61	2.78	750		2.50		Aug-00
2.12	2.32	2.89	5.32	6.99	0.9	1.77	1.59	2.00	11.08	1,130	6	49	0	30	0	61	2.78	750			5.00	Jul-00
2.16	2.40	3.06	5.77	7.69	1.06	1.65	1.59	2.00	11.08	1,130	6	49	0	30	0	61	2.78	750			1.00	Sep-92
2.35	2.76	3.82	8.01	11.39	1.78	0.95	1.6	2.00	11.08	1,130	6	49	0	30	0	61	2.78	250		2.50		Apr-07
2.41	2.89	4.09	8.93	13.12	2.04	0.67	1.6	2.00	11.08	1,130	6	49	0	30	0	61	2.78	0				Apr-07
2.45	2.97	4.25	9.44	13.99	2.19	0.51	1.6	2.00	11.08	1,130	6	49	0	30	0	61	2.78	1,000,000				Jul-14
2.26	2.59	3.47	7.01	9.79	1.45	1.26	1.59	2.00	11.08	1,130	6	49	0	30	0	61	2.78	0				Dec-12
2.35	2.78	3.85	8.17	11.79	1.81	0.91	1.6	2.00	11.08	1,130	6	49	0	30	0	61	2.78	0				Dec-95
1.59	1.11	2.71	8.59	14.37	2.75	0.84	3.03	5.00	11.79	764.4	2	0	98	0	0	18	5.02	750		4.25		Sep-00
1.36	0.67	1.79	5.91	9.86	1.85	1.74	3.02	5.00	11.79	764.4	2	0	98	0	0	18	5.02	750			5.00	Aug-00
1.36	0.68	1.82	5.88	9.84	1.88	1.71	3.02	5.00	11.79	764.4	2	0	98	0	0	18	5.02	750			1.00	Sep-92
1.62	1.17	2.85	9.08	15.32	2.89	0.7	3.03	5.00	11.79	764.4	2	0	98	0	0	18	5.02	0				Nov-09
1.65	1.23	2.96	9.43	13.53	3	0.59	3.04	5.00	11.79	764.4	2	0	98	0	0	18	5.02	1,000,000				Jul-17
1.59	1.11	2.71	8.61	14.38	2.75	0.84	3.03	5.00	11.79	764.4	2	0	98	0	0	18	5.02	0				Dec-95
2.81	0.05	1.90	9.35	16.84	3.83	0.87	4.41	7.20	4.96	1,013	2	0	98	0	0	18	5.32	750		4.25		May-09
2.62	-0.32	1.15	7.00	12.60	3.05	1.6	4.4	7.20	4.96	1,013	2	0	98	0	0	18	5.32	750			5.00	May-09
2.63	-0.29	1.19	7.08	12.78	3.1	1.58	4.4	7.20	4.96	1,013	2	0	98	0	0	18	5.32	750			1.00	May-09
2.87	0.17	2.18	10.18	18.16	4.1	0.61	4.4	7.20	4.96	1,013	2	0	98	0	0	18	5.32	0				Dec-98
2.88	0.19	2.21	10.50	18.51	4.14	0.57	4.41	7.20	4.96	1,013	2	0	98	0	0	18	5.32	1,000,000				Jul-17
2.81	0.05	1.90	9.39	16.86	3.83	0.87	4.4	7.20	4.96	1,013	2	0	98	0	0	18	5.32	0				May-09
11.02	-7.31	-4.75	-6.44	-0.20	1.24	1.21	12.63		8.36	105.2	18	77	0	0	0	111	6.14	750		5.75		Apr-14
10.91	-7.50	-5.32	-8.04	-3.48	1.15	1.85	12.58		8.13	105.2	18	77	0	0	0	111	6.14	750			1.00	Apr-14
11.02	-7.13	-4.41	-5.28	1.45	1.31	0.8	12.61		8.46	105.2	18	77	0	0	0	111	6.14	0				Apr-14
11.02	-7.13	-4.41	-5.27	1.45	1.31	0.8	12.59		8.46	105.2	18	77	0	0	0	111	6.14	1,000,000				Jan-15
11.00	-7.30	-4.74	-6.33	-0.09	1.24	1.21	12.62		8.37	105.2	18	77	0	0	0	111	6.14	0				Apr-14
3.37	0.19	2.07	8.68		1.59	1.22	3.42		10.11	188.5	10	72	0	19	0	121	3.36	750		5.75		Jan-16
3.19	-0.19	1.32	6.30		1.05	1.92	3.42		10	188.5	10	72	0	19	0	121	3.36	750			1.00	Jan-16

	MARKET			FUND TYPE, CATEGORY & OBJECTIVE	RATINGS				NEW INVESTORS	
Fund Name	Ticker Symbol	Traded On	Fund Type	Category and (Prospectus Objective)	Overall Rating	Reward Rating	Risk Rating	Recent Up/ Downgrade	Open to New Investors	Telephone
Ivy Pictet Targeted Return Bond Fund Class I	IRBIX	NAS CM	Open End	Fixed Inc Misc (Growth & Income)	C	C-	C+		Y	
Ivy Pictet Targeted Return Bond Fund Class N	IRBRX	NAS CM	Open End	Fixed Inc Misc (Growth & Income)	C	C-	B-		Y	
Ivy Pictet Targeted Return Bond Fund Class Y	IRBYX	NAS CM	Open End	Fixed Inc Misc (Growth & Income)	C	C-	C+		Y	
Ivy PineBridge High Yield Fund Class A	IPNAX	NAS CM	Open End	US Fixed Inc (Corp Bond - High Yield)	D+	D	C	Down	Y	
Ivy PineBridge High Yield Fund Class I	IPNIX	NAS CM	Open End	US Fixed Inc (Corp Bond - High Yield)	D+	D+	C	Down	Y	
Ivy PineBridge High Yield Fund Class N	IPNNX	NAS CM	Open End	US Fixed Inc (Corp Bond - High Yield)	D+	D	C	Down	Y	
Ivy ProShares Interest Rate Hedged High Yield Ind Cl A	IAIRX	NAS CM	Open End	US Fixed Inc (Corp Bond - High Yield)	D	D	D+	Down	Y	
Ivy ProShares Interest Rate Hedged High Yield Ind Cl E	IIREX	NAS CM	Open End	US Fixed Inc (Corp Bond - High Yield)	D	D	D+	Down	Y	
Ivy ProShares Interest Rate Hedged High Yield Ind Cl I	IIIRX	NAS CM	Open End	US Fixed Inc (Corp Bond - High Yield)	D	D	D+	Down	Y	
Ivy ProShares Interest Rate Hedged High Yield Ind Cl N	IIRNX	NAS CM	Open End	US Fixed Inc (Corp Bond - High Yield)	D	D	D+	Down	Y	
Ivy ProShares Interest Rate Hedged High Yield Ind Cl R	IIRRX	NAS CM	Open End	US Fixed Inc (Corp Bond - High Yield)	D	D	D+	Down	Y	
Ivy ProShares S&P 500 Bond Index Fund Class A	IAPRX	NAS CM	Open End	US Fixed Inc (Corp Bond - General)	C+	C	B-	Up	Y	
Ivy ProShares S&P 500 Bond Index Fund Class E	IPREX	NAS CM	Open End	US Fixed Inc (Corp Bond - General)	C+	C	B-	Up	Y	
Ivy ProShares S&P 500 Bond Index Fund Class I	IPRIX	NAS CM	Open End	US Fixed Inc (Corp Bond - General)	C+	C	B-	Up	Y	
Ivy ProShares S&P 500 Bond Index Fund Class N	IPRNX	NAS CM	Open End	US Fixed Inc (Corp Bond - General)	C+	C	B-	Up	Y	
Ivy ProShares S&P 500 Bond Index Fund Class R	IPRRX	NAS CM	Open End	US Fixed Inc (Corp Bond - General)	C	C	B-		Y	
Ivy Securian Core Bond Fund Class A	IBOAX	NAS CM	Open End	US Fixed Inc (Income)	C+	C	B	Up	Y	
Ivy Securian Core Bond Fund Class B	IBOBX	NAS CM	Open End	US Fixed Inc (Income)	C	C	B-			
Ivy Securian Core Bond Fund Class C	IBOCX	NAS CM	Open End	US Fixed Inc (Income)	C	C	B-		Y	
Ivy Securian Core Bond Fund Class E	IVBEX	NAS CM	Open End	US Fixed Inc (Income)	C+	C	B	Up	Y	
Ivy Securian Core Bond Fund Class I	IVBIX	NAS CM	Open End	US Fixed Inc (Income)	C+	C	B	Up	Y	
Ivy Securian Core Bond Fund Class N	IBNDX	NAS CM	Open End	US Fixed Inc (Income)	C+	C	B	Up	Y	
Ivy Securian Core Bond Fund Class R	IYBDX	NAS CM	Open End	US Fixed Inc (Income)	C	C	B		Y	
Ivy Securian Core Bond Fund Class Y	IBOYX	NAS CM	Open End	US Fixed Inc (Income)	C+	C	B	Up	Y	
James Alpha Structured Credit Value Portfolio Class A	JASVX	NAS CM	Open End	Fixed Inc Misc (Growth & Income)	C-	D+	B	Up	Y	
James Alpha Structured Credit Value Portfolio Class C	JSVCX	NAS CM	Open End	Fixed Inc Misc (Growth & Income)	C-	D+	B	Up	Y	
James Alpha Structured Credit Value Portfolio Class I	JSVIX	NAS CM	Open End	Fixed Inc Misc (Growth & Income)	C-	D+	B	Up	Y	
James Alpha Structured Credit Value Portfolio Class S	JASSX	NAS CM	Open End	Fixed Inc Misc (Growth & Income)	C-	D+	B	Up	Y	
Janus Henderson Absolute Return Income Opp - A Shares	JUCAX	NAS CM	Open End	Fixed Inc Misc (Multisector Bond)	C	C	C		Y	877-335-2687
Janus Henderson Absolute Return Income Opp - C Shares	JUCCX	NAS CM	Open End	Fixed Inc Misc (Multisector Bond)	C-	C-	C	Down	Y	877-335-2687
Janus Henderson Absolute Return Income Opp - D Shares	JUCDX	NAS CM	Open End	Fixed Inc Misc (Multisector Bond)	C	C	C		Y	877-335-2687
Janus Henderson Absolute Return Income Opp - I Shares	JUCIX	NAS CM	Open End	Fixed Inc Misc (Multisector Bond)	C	C	C		Y	877-335-2687
Janus Henderson Absolute Return Income Opp - N Shares	JUCNX	NAS CM	Open End	Fixed Inc Misc (Multisector Bond)	C	C	C		Y	877-335-2687
Janus Henderson Absolute Return Income Opp - R Shares	JUCRX	NAS CM	Open End	Fixed Inc Misc (Multisector Bond)	C	C-	C		Y	877-335-2687
Janus Henderson Absolute Return Income Opp - S Shares	JUCSX	NAS CM	Open End	Fixed Inc Misc (Multisector Bond)	C	C	C		Y	877-335-2687
Janus Henderson Absolute Return Income Opp - T Shares	JUCTX	NAS CM	Open End	Fixed Inc Misc (Multisector Bond)	C	C	C		Y	877-335-2687
Janus Henderson Developed World Bond Fund Class A	HFAAX	NAS CM	Open End	Global Fixed Inc (Multisector Bond)	B-	C	B+	Up	Y	877-335-2687
Janus Henderson Developed World Bond Fund Class C	HFACX	NAS CM	Open End	Global Fixed Inc (Multisector Bond)	C+	C	B	Up	Y	877-335-2687
Janus Henderson Developed World Bond Fund Class D	HFADX	NAS CM	Open End	Global Fixed Inc (Multisector Bond)	B-	C	B+	Up	Y	877-335-2687
Janus Henderson Developed World Bond Fund Class I	HFAIX	NAS CM	Open End	Global Fixed Inc (Multisector Bond)	B-	C	B+	Up	Y	877-335-2687
Janus Henderson Developed World Bond Fund Class N	HFARX	NAS CM	Open End	Global Fixed Inc (Multisector Bond)	B-	C	B+	Up	Y	877-335-2687
Janus Henderson Developed World Bond Fund Class S	HFASX	NAS CM	Open End	Global Fixed Inc (Multisector Bond)	B-	C	B	Up	Y	877-335-2687
Janus Henderson Developed World Bond Fund Class T	HFATX	NAS CM	Open End	Global Fixed Inc (Multisector Bond)	B-	C	B+	Up	Y	877-335-2687
Janus Henderson Flexible Bond Fund Class A	JDFAX	NAS CM	Open End	US Fixed Inc (Multisector Bond)	B-	C+	B	Up	Y	877-335-2687
Janus Henderson Flexible Bond Fund Class C	JFICX	NAS CM	Open End	US Fixed Inc (Multisector Bond)	B-	C+	B	Up	Y	877-335-2687
Janus Henderson Flexible Bond Fund Class D	JANFX	NAS CM	Open End	US Fixed Inc (Multisector Bond)	B	C+	B+	Up		877-335-2687
Janus Henderson Flexible Bond Fund Class I	JFLEX	NAS CM	Open End	US Fixed Inc (Multisector Bond)	B	C+	B+	Up	Y	877-335-2687
Janus Henderson Flexible Bond Fund Class N	JDFNX	NAS CM	Open End	US Fixed Inc (Multisector Bond)	B	C+	B+	Up	Y	877-335-2687
Janus Henderson Flexible Bond Fund Class R	JDFRX	NAS CM	Open End	US Fixed Inc (Multisector Bond)	B-	C+	B	Up	Y	877-335-2687
Janus Henderson Flexible Bond Fund Class S	JADFX	NAS CM	Open End	US Fixed Inc (Multisector Bond)	B-	C+	B	Up	Y	877-335-2687
Janus Henderson Flexible Bond Fund Class T	JAFIX	NAS CM	Open End	US Fixed Inc (Multisector Bond)	B	C+	B	Up	Y	877-335-2687
Janus Henderson Global Bond Fund Class A	JGBAX	NAS CM	Open End	Global Fixed Inc (Worldwide Bond)	B-	C+	B	Up	Y	877-335-2687

★ Expanded analysis of this fund is included in Section II.

TOTAL RETURNS & PERFORMANCE									ASSETS		ASSET ALLOCATION & TURNOVER							MINIMUMS		FEES		
3-Month Total Return	6-Month Total Return	1-Year Total Return	3-Year Total Return	5-Year Total Return	Dividend Yield (TTM)	Expense Ratio	3-Yr Std Deviation	Effective Duration	NAV	Total Assets (MIL)	%Cash	%Government Bonds	%Municipal Bonds	%Corporate Bonds	%Other	Turnover Ratio	Average Coupon Rate	Min Initial Investment	Min Additional Investment	Front End Fee (%)	Back End Fee (%)	Inception Date
3.46	0.29	2.29	9.30		1.77	1	3.46		10.14	188.5	10	72	0	19	0	121	3.36	0				Jan-16
3.46	0.29	2.41	9.81		1.86	0.87	3.41		10.16	188.5	10	72	0	19	0	121	3.36	1,000,000				Jan-16
3.37	0.19	2.17	8.68		1.59	1.22	3.39		10.11	188.5	10	72	0	19	0	121	3.36	0				Jan-16
9.38	-3.30	-0.16	9.64		5.2	0.99	8.36	4.30	9.41	118.0	8	0	0	92	0	69	5.89	750		5.75		May-17
9.45	-3.17	0.01	10.57		5.48	0.72	8.4	4.30	9.41	118.0	8	0	0	92	0	69	5.89	0				May-17
9.46	-3.17	0.00	10.45		5.49	0.72	8.39	4.30	9.4	118.0	8	0	0	92	0	69	5.89	1,000,000				May-17
5.66	-9.14	-6.73	0.06		6.17	0.9	8.87		8.47	41.6	3	0	0	99	0	50	6.29	750		2.50		Apr-17
5.66	-9.14	-6.73	0.06		6.17	0.89	8.86		8.47	41.6	3	0	0	99	0	50	6.29	250		2.50		Apr-17
5.72	-9.12	-6.49	0.81		6.44	0.65	8.89		8.47	41.6	3	0	0	99	0	50	6.29	0				Apr-17
5.84	-8.80	-6.16	1.16		6.43	0.65	8.82		8.5	41.6	3	0	0	99	0	50	6.29	1,000,000				Apr-17
5.52	-9.40	-7.22	-1.42		5.6	1.39	8.82		8.47	41.6	3	0	0	99	0	50	6.29	0				Apr-17
7.55	5.83	9.86	18.54		2.56	0.65	5.7	8.50	11	134.4	1	0	0	99	0	33	3.83	750		2.50		Apr-17
7.56	5.76	9.92	18.71		2.62	0.59	5.72	8.50	11	134.4	1	0	0	99	0	33	3.83	250		2.50		Apr-17
7.61	5.86	10.14	19.31		2.81	0.4	5.71	8.50	11	134.4	1	0	0	99	0	33	3.83	0				Apr-17
7.61	5.86	10.14	19.32		2.81	0.4	5.71	8.50	11	134.4	1	0	0	99	0	33	3.83	1,000,000				Apr-17
7.41	5.56	9.40	16.75		2.07	1.15	5.69	8.50	11	134.4	1	0	0	99	0	33	3.83	0				Apr-17
6.28	3.08	5.23	12.90	21.23	2.44	0.93	5.14	6.90	11.09	1,168	3	33	1	29	0	118	3.48	750		5.75		Aug-87
6.04	2.64	4.25	9.95	15.83	1.51	1.74	5.13	6.90	11.09	1,168	3	33	1	29	0	118	3.48	750			5.00	Dec-03
6.08	2.68	4.44	10.47	16.92	1.69	1.62	5.14	6.90	11.09	1,168	3	33	1	29	0	118	3.48	750			1.00	Dec-03
6.26	3.06	5.22	12.92	21.23	2.44	0.95	5.14	6.90	11.09	1,168	3	33	1	29	0	118	3.48	250		2.50		Apr-07
6.39	3.30	5.70	14.51	23.83	2.89	0.45	5.14	6.90	11.09	1,168	3	33	1	29	0	118	3.48	0				Apr-07
6.39	3.29	5.70	14.51	24.11	2.89	0.45	5.14	6.90	11.09	1,168	3	33	1	29	0	118	3.48	1,000,000				Jul-14
6.19	2.91	4.90	11.98	19.57	2.14	1.21	5.14	6.90	11.09	1,168	3	33	1	29	0	118	3.48	0				Dec-12
6.29	3.09	5.26	13.11	21.64	2.47	0.86	5.14	6.90	11.09	1,168	3	33	1	29	0	118	3.48	0				Dec-03
11.68	6.63	8.91			4.64	1.75			10.89	104.3	21	3	0	17	0	111	4.94	2,500		5.75		Aug-18
11.51	6.24	8.18			3.9	2.5			10.67	104.3	21	3	0	17	0	111	4.94	2,500			1.00	Aug-18
11.77	6.86	9.32			4.93	1.51			10.67	104.3	21	3	0	17	0	111	4.94	1,000,000				Aug-18
11.92	7.02	9.68			4.89	1.13			10.74	104.3	21	3	0	17	0	111	4.94	0				Aug-18
1.12	1.92	3.62	1.26	7.36	2.78	0.96	3.48	1.34	9.01	107.3	4	1	0	64	0	170	2.99	2,500		4.75		May-14
0.83	1.44	2.90	-0.90	3.50	2.08	1.77	3.42	1.34	9	107.3	4	1	0	64	0	170	2.99	2,500			1.00	May-14
1.16	1.89	3.78	1.60	7.76	2.97	0.84	3.5	1.34	9.01	107.3	4	1	0	64	0	170	2.99	2,500	100			May-14
1.18	1.92	3.87	1.89	8.59	3.03	0.72	3.44	1.34	9	107.3	4	1	0	64	0	170	2.99	1,000,000				May-14
1.20	2.07	3.93	2.14	8.93	3.08	0.68	3.48	1.34	9.01	107.3	4	1	0	64	0	170	2.99	1,000,000				May-14
1.01	1.69	3.27	-0.05	5.09	2.33	1.43	3.45	1.34	9.02	107.3	4	1	0	64	0	170	2.99	2,500				Feb-15
1.07	1.82	3.43	0.62	6.27	2.59	1.18	3.5	1.34	9.02	107.3	4	1	0	64	0	170	2.99	2,500				May-14
1.02	1.84	3.69	1.45	7.70	2.85	0.93	3.4	1.34	9	107.3	4	1	0	64	0	170	2.99	2,500				May-14
6.80	3.87	5.95	16.20	28.88	2.97	0.83	4.49		9.94	1,504	0	22	0	78	0	42	3.27	2,500		4.75		Sep-03
6.55	3.53	5.14	13.61	24.08	2.31	1.58	4.47		9.87	1,504	0	22	0	78	0	42	3.27	2,500			1.00	Sep-03
6.86	3.98	6.05	16.84	29.59	3.15	0.7	4.56		9.93	1,504	0	22	0	78	0	42	3.27	2,500	100			Jun-17
6.90	4.02	6.24	17.12	30.57	3.22	0.58	4.5		9.91	1,504	0	22	0	78	0	42	3.27	1,000,000				Apr-11
6.91	4.05	6.20	17.21	30.67	3.29	0.58	4.56		9.91	1,504	0	22	0	78	0	42	3.27	1,000,000				Nov-15
6.76	3.78	5.82	15.81	28.46	2.91	1.08	4.51		9.93	1,504	0	22	0	78	0	42	3.27	2,500				Jun-17
6.82	3.91	6.05	16.81	29.57	3.06	0.83	4.5		9.93	1,504	0	22	0	78	0	42	3.27	2,500				Jun-17
6.82	6.73	9.89	16.05	21.35	2.43	0.91	4.08	5.68	11.14	3,779	4	16	0	44	0	219	3.46	2,500		4.75		Jul-09
6.55	6.40	9.11	13.96	17.57	1.83	1.54	3.99	5.68	11.14	3,779	4	16	0	44	0	219	3.46	2,500			1.00	Jul-09
6.90	6.88	10.21	17.11	23.01	2.71	0.59	4.07	5.68	11.14	3,779	4	16	0	44	0	219	3.46	2,500	100			Jul-87
6.81	6.92	10.18	17.40	23.42	2.79	0.52	4	5.68	11.14	3,779	4	16	0	44	0	219	3.46	1,000,000				Jul-09
6.93	7.06	10.37	17.64	24.08	2.85	0.45	4.04	5.68	11.14	3,779	4	16	0	44	0	219	3.46	1,000,000				May-12
6.63	6.56	9.44	15.02	19.39	2.12	1.2	3.99	5.68	11.14	3,779	4	16	0	44	0	219	3.46	2,500				Jul-09
6.70	6.69	9.71	15.88	20.90	2.36	0.95	3.98	5.68	11.14	3,779	4	16	0	44	0	219	3.46	2,500				Jul-09
6.87	6.83	10.10	16.80	22.60	2.62	0.7	4.07	5.68	11.14	3,779	4	16	0	44	0	219	3.46	2,500				Jul-87
3.79	5.47	6.52	11.41	15.34	1.22	0.96	4.25	8.64	10.1	219.3	8	58	0	12	0	248	2.96	2,500		4.75		Dec-10

	MARKET		FUND TYPE, CATEGORY & OBJECTIVE		RATINGS				NEW INVESTORS	
Fund Name	Ticker Symbol	Traded On	Fund Type	Category and (Prospectus Objective)	Overall Rating	Reward Rating	Risk Rating	Recent Up/ Downgrade	Open to New Investors	Telephone
Janus Henderson Global Bond Fund Class C	JGBCX	NAS CM	Open End	Global Fixed Inc (Worldwide Bond)	C+	C	B	Up	Y	877-335-2687
Janus Henderson Global Bond Fund Class D	JGBDX	NAS CM	Open End	Global Fixed Inc (Worldwide Bond)	B-	C+	B	Up	Y	877-335-2687
Janus Henderson Global Bond Fund Class I	JGBIX	NAS CM	Open End	Global Fixed Inc (Worldwide Bond)	B-	C+	B	Up	Y	877-335-2687
Janus Henderson Global Bond Fund Class N	JGLNX	NAS CM	Open End	Global Fixed Inc (Worldwide Bond)	B-	C+	B	Up	Y	877-335-2687
Janus Henderson Global Bond Fund Class S	JGBSX	NAS CM	Open End	Global Fixed Inc (Worldwide Bond)	B-	C+	B	Up	Y	877-335-2687
Janus Henderson Global Bond Fund Class T	JHBTX	NAS CM	Open End	Global Fixed Inc (Worldwide Bond)	B-	C+	B	Up	Y	877-335-2687
Janus Henderson Government Money Market Fund Class D	JGVXX	NAS CM	Money Mkt	US Money Mkt (Money Mkt - Govt)	C	C-	C+			877-335-2687
Janus Henderson Government Money Market Fund Class T	JAGXX	NAS CM	Money Mkt	US Money Mkt (Money Mkt - Govt)	C	C-	C+		Y	877-335-2687
Janus Henderson High-Yield Fund Class A	JHYAX	NAS CM	Open End	US Fixed Inc (Corp Bond - High Yield)	C-	D+	C		Y	877-335-2687
Janus Henderson High-Yield Fund Class C	JDHCX	NAS CM	Open End	US Fixed Inc (Corp Bond - High Yield)	D+	D+	C-	Down	Y	877-335-2687
Janus Henderson High-Yield Fund Class D	JNHYX	NAS CM	Open End	US Fixed Inc (Corp Bond - High Yield)	C-	D+	C			877-335-2687
Janus Henderson High-Yield Fund Class I	JHYFX	NAS CM	Open End	US Fixed Inc (Corp Bond - High Yield)	C-	D+	C		Y	877-335-2687
Janus Henderson High-Yield Fund Class N	JHYNX	NAS CM	Open End	US Fixed Inc (Corp Bond - High Yield)	C-	D+	C		Y	877-335-2687
Janus Henderson High-Yield Fund Class R	JHYRX	NAS CM	Open End	US Fixed Inc (Corp Bond - High Yield)	D+	D+	C-	Down	Y	877-335-2687
Janus Henderson High-Yield Fund Class S	JDHYX	NAS CM	Open End	US Fixed Inc (Corp Bond - High Yield)	D+	D+	C-	Down	Y	877-335-2687
Janus Henderson High-Yield Fund Class T	JAHYX	NAS CM	Open End	US Fixed Inc (Corp Bond - High Yield)	C-	D+	C		Y	877-335-2687
Janus Henderson Money Market Fund Class D	JNMXX	NAS CM	Money Mkt	US Money Mkt (Money Mkt - Taxable)	C	C-	C+			877-335-2687
Janus Henderson Money Market Fund Class T	JAMXX	NAS CM	Money Mkt	US Money Mkt (Money Mkt - Taxable)	C	C-	C+		Y	877-335-2687
Janus Henderson Multi-Sector Income Fund Class A	JMUAX	NAS CM	Open End	US Fixed Inc (Multisector Bond)	C-	D+	C	Down	Y	877-335-2687
Janus Henderson Multi-Sector Income Fund Class C	JMUCX	NAS CM	Open End	US Fixed Inc (Multisector Bond)	C-	D+	C		Y	877-335-2687
Janus Henderson Multi-Sector Income Fund Class D	JMUDX	NAS CM	Open End	US Fixed Inc (Multisector Bond)	C-	D+	C	Down	Y	877-335-2687
Janus Henderson Multi-Sector Income Fund Class I	JMUIX	NAS CM	Open End	US Fixed Inc (Multisector Bond)	C-	D+	C	Down	Y	877-335-2687
Janus Henderson Multi-Sector Income Fund Class N	JMTNX	NAS CM	Open End	US Fixed Inc (Multisector Bond)	C-	D+	C	Down	Y	877-335-2687
Janus Henderson Multi-Sector Income Fund Class S	JMUSX	NAS CM	Open End	US Fixed Inc (Multisector Bond)	C-	D+	C	Down	Y	877-335-2687
Janus Henderson Multi-Sector Income Fund Class T	JMUTX	NAS CM	Open End	US Fixed Inc (Multisector Bond)	C-	D+	C	Down	Y	877-335-2687
Janus Henderson Short-Term Bond Fund Class A	JSHAX	NAS CM	Open End	US Fixed Inc (Corp Bond - General)	C	C	C+		Y	877-335-2687
Janus Henderson Short-Term Bond Fund Class C	JSHCX	NAS CM	Open End	US Fixed Inc (Corp Bond - General)	C	C-	C+	Up	Y	877-335-2687
Janus Henderson Short-Term Bond Fund Class D	JNSTX	NAS CM	Open End	US Fixed Inc (Corp Bond - General)	C	C	C+			877-335-2687
Janus Henderson Short-Term Bond Fund Class I	JSHIX	NAS CM	Open End	US Fixed Inc (Corp Bond - General)	C	C	C+		Y	877-335-2687
Janus Henderson Short-Term Bond Fund Class N	JSHNX	NAS CM	Open End	US Fixed Inc (Corp Bond - General)	C	C	C+		Y	877-335-2687
Janus Henderson Short-Term Bond Fund Class S	JSHSX	NAS CM	Open End	US Fixed Inc (Corp Bond - General)	C	C	C+		Y	877-335-2687
Janus Henderson Short-Term Bond Fund Class T	JASBX	NAS CM	Open End	US Fixed Inc (Corp Bond - General)	C	C	C+		Y	877-335-2687
Janus Henderson VIT Flexible Bond Portfol Inst Cl	JAFLX	NAS CM	Open End	US Fixed Inc (Income)	B	C+	B	Up	Y	877-335-2687
Janus Henderson VIT Flexible Bond Portfolio Service Class			Open End	US Fixed Inc (Income)	B-	C+	B	Up	Y	877-335-2687
JHancock Short Duration Bond Fund Class A	JSNAX	NAS CM	Open End	US Fixed Inc (Multisector Bond)	U	U	U		Y	800-225-5291
JHancock Short Duration Bond Fund Class C	JSNCX	NAS CM	Open End	US Fixed Inc (Multisector Bond)	U	U	U		Y	800-225-5291
JHancock Short Duration Bond Fund Class I	JSNIX	NAS CM	Open End	US Fixed Inc (Multisector Bond)	U	U	U		Y	800-225-5291
JHancock Short Duration Bond Fund Class R6	JSNRX	NAS CM	Open End	US Fixed Inc (Multisector Bond)	U	U	U		Y	800-225-5291
JNL/American Funds Capital World Bond Fund Class A			Open End	Global Fixed Inc (Multisector Bond)	C	C	B-		Y	
JNL/American Funds Capital World Bond Fund Class I			Open End	Global Fixed Inc (Multisector Bond)	C	C	B-		Y	
JNL/DoubleLine Core Fixed Income Fund Class A			Open End	US Fixed Inc (Corp Bond - General)	C	C-	B-		Y	
JNL/DoubleLine Core Fixed Income Fund Class I			Open End	US Fixed Inc (Corp Bond - General)	C	C-	B-		Y	
JNL/DoubleLine Emerging Markets Fixed Income Fund Class A			Open End	Emerg Mkts Fixed Inc (Income)	D+	D	C-	Down	Y	
JNL/DoubleLine Emerging Markets Fixed Income Fund Class I			Open End	Emerg Mkts Fixed Inc (Income)	D+	D+	C-	Down	Y	
JNL/DoubleLine® Total Return Fund Class A			Open End	US Fixed Inc (Growth & Income)	C	C-	B-		Y	
JNL/DoubleLine® Total Return Fund Class I			Open End	US Fixed Inc (Growth & Income)	C	C-	B-		Y	
JNL/Fidelity Inst Asset Management® Total Bond Cl A			Open End	US Fixed Inc (Worldwide Bond)	B-	C	B	Up	Y	
JNL/Fidelity Inst Asset Management® Total Bond Cl I			Open End	US Fixed Inc (Worldwide Bond)	B-	C+	B	Up	Y	
JNL/Franklin Templeton Global Multisector Bond Cl A			Open End	Fixed Inc Misc (Multisector Bond)	D	D	D+	Down	Y	
JNL/Franklin Templeton Global Multisector Bond Cl I			Open End	Fixed Inc Misc (Multisector Bond)	D	D	C-	Down	Y	
JNL/JPMorgan U.S. Government & Quality Bond Fund Class A			Open End	US Fixed Inc (Govt Bond - General)	B	B-	B+	Up	Y	
JNL/JPMorgan U.S. Government & Quality Bond Fund Class I			Open End	US Fixed Inc (Govt Bond - General)	B	B-	B+		Y	

★Expanded analysis of this fund is included in Section II.

TOTAL RETURNS & PERFORMANCE									ASSETS		ASSET ALLOCATION & TURNOVER							MINIMUMS		FEES		
3-Month Total Return	6-Month Total Return	1-Year Total Return	3-Year Total Return	5-Year Total Return	Dividend Yield (TTM)	Expense Ratio	3-Yr Std Deviation	Effective Duration	NAV	Total Assets (MIL)	%Cash	%Government Bonds	%Municipal Bonds	%Corporate Bonds	%Other	Turnover Ratio	Average Coupon Rate	Min Initial Investment	Min Additional Investment	Front End Fee (%)	Back End Fee (%)	Inception Date
3.68	5.09	5.73	9.12	11.20	0.5	1.69	4.32	8.64	10.11	219.3	8	58	0	12	0	248	2.96	2,500			1.00	Dec-10
3.85	5.59	6.75	12.11	16.38	1.42	0.75	4.31	8.64	10.09	219.3	8	58	0	12	0	248	2.96	2,500	100			Dec-10
3.86	5.61	6.79	12.28	16.69	1.47	0.69	4.31	8.64	10.09	219.3	8	58	0	12	0	248	2.96	1,000,000				Dec-10
3.99	5.66	6.90	12.73	17.38	1.56	0.59	4.29	8.64	10.09	219.3	8	58	0	12	0	248	2.96	1,000,000				Oct-13
3.74	5.38	6.24	11.09	15.04	1.06	1.1	4.34	8.64	10.1	219.3	8	58	0	12	0	248	2.96	2,500				Dec-10
3.81	5.53	6.64	11.92	15.87	1.33	0.84	4.31	8.64	10.1	219.3	8	58	0	12	0	248	2.96	2,500				Dec-10
0.01	0.24	0.95	3.50	3.55	1.1	0.59	0.16		1	337.1	79	10	1	8	0			2,500	100			Feb-10
0.01	0.23	0.93	3.43	3.47	1.08	0.61	0.16		1	337.1	79	10	1	8	0			2,500	100			Feb-95
9.81	-6.15	-2.08	7.04	19.04	5.34	1.04	9.51	2.79	7.77	1,112	6	1	0	92	0	110	6.42	2,500		4.75		Jul-09
9.61	-6.49	-2.76	4.91	15.01	4.61	1.73	9.52	2.79	7.77	1,112	6	1	0	92	0	110	6.42	2,500			1.00	Jul-09
9.86	-6.05	-1.86	7.80	20.39	5.58	0.8	9.52	2.79	7.77	1,112	6	1	0	92	0	110	6.42	2,500	100			Dec-95
9.88	-6.03	-1.94	7.98	20.67	5.62	0.73	9.57	2.79	7.77	1,112	6	1	0	92	0	110	6.42	1,000,000				Jul-09
9.90	-5.98	-1.72	8.27	21.15	5.73	0.65	9.52	2.79	7.77	1,112	6	1	0	92	0	110	6.42	1,000,000				May-12
9.70	-6.38	-2.65	5.64	16.43	4.86	1.45	9.57	2.79	7.76	1,112	6	1	0	92	0	110	6.42	2,500				Jul-09
9.74	-6.24	-2.38	6.50	18.03	5.13	1.2	9.55	2.79	7.78	1,112	6	1	0	92	0	110	6.42	2,500				Jul-09
9.84	-6.10	-1.95	7.50	19.72	5.48	0.89	9.54	2.79	7.77	1,112	6	1	0	92	0	110	6.42	2,500				Dec-95
0.01	0.27	1.04	3.81	3.97	1.19	0.57	0.16		1	1,179	83	3	3	11	0	0		2,500	100			Feb-10
0.01	0.27	1.02	3.74	3.77	1.17	0.59	0.16		1	1,179	83	3	3	11	0	0		2,500	100			Feb-95
9.64	-2.87	0.70	11.20	22.57	4.54	0.95	8.15	3.79	9.47	2,348	6	0	0	42	0	142	4.46	2,500		4.75		Feb-14
9.31	-3.25	-0.08	8.55	18.12	3.72	1.73	8.08	3.79	9.47	2,348	6	0	0	42	0	142	4.46	2,500			1.00	Feb-14
9.56	-2.80	0.85	11.63	23.61	4.7	0.78	8.08	3.79	9.47	2,348	6	0	0	42	0	142	4.46	2,500	100			Feb-14
9.58	-2.77	0.91	11.98	24.18	4.76	0.71	8.08	3.79	9.47	2,348	6	0	0	42	0	142	4.46	1,000,000				Feb-14
9.49	-2.83	0.88	11.96	24.33	4.83	0.64	8.07	3.79	9.46	2,348	6	0	0	42	0	142	4.46	1,000,000				Feb-14
9.47	-2.95	0.48	11.08	22.63	4.43	1.14	8.11	3.79	9.46	2,348	6	0	0	42	0	142	4.46	2,500				Feb-14
9.55	-2.85	0.65	11.28	22.96	4.6	0.89	8.15	3.79	9.46	2,348	6	0	0	42	0	142	4.46	2,500				Feb-14
4.64	2.42	3.56	7.78	9.56	2.22	0.75	2.52	1.65	3.06	1,094	9	11	0	57	0	79	3.12	2,500		2.50		Jul-09
4.45	2.04	2.82	5.07	5.64	1.52	1.52	2.66	1.65	3.05	1,094	9	11	0	57	0	79	3.12	2,500			1.00	Jul-09
4.68	2.50	3.73	7.94	10.44	2.38	0.58	2.49	1.65	3.06	1,094	9	11	0	57	0	79	3.12	2,500	100			Sep-92
4.35	2.17	3.41	8.07	10.39	2.41	0.54	2.48	1.65	3.05	1,094	9	11	0	57	0	79	3.12	1,000,000				Jul-09
4.73	2.57	3.88	8.39	10.86	2.52	0.44	2.48	1.65	3.05	1,094	9	11	0	57	0	79	3.12	1,000,000				May-12
4.60	2.32	3.38	6.86	8.74	2.04	0.94	2.5	1.65	3.05	1,094	9	11	0	57	0	79	3.12	2,500				Jul-09
4.65	2.44	3.62	7.60	9.88	2.28	0.69	2.47	1.65	3.06	1,094	9	11	0	57	0	79	3.12	2,500				Sep-92
6.81	6.72	10.00	16.94	22.85	3.15	0.57	4.06	5.64	12.46	557.9	4	17	0	43	0	177	3.44	0				Sep-93
6.70	6.62	9.68	16.07	21.35	2.68	0.82	4.07	5.64	13.65	557.9	4	17	0	43	0	177	3.44	0				Dec-99
3.72	1.06					0.65			9.97	162.7	1	10	2	45	0		3.32	1,000		2.25		Jul-19
3.57	0.73					1.4			9.97	162.7	1	10	2	45	0		3.32	1,000			1.00	Jul-19
3.76	1.16					0.4			9.97	162.7	1	10	2	45	0		3.32	250,000				Jul-19
3.78	1.21					0.29			9.97	162.7	1	10	2	45	0		3.32	1,000,000				Jul-19
5.01	1.85	3.22	9.50	16.10	0	1.07	4.61	6.61	11.52	454.6	7	66	0	19	0		3.22	0				May-10
5.04	2.01	3.45	10.43	17.61	0	0.77	4.62	6.61	11.67	454.6	7	66	0	19	0		3.22	0				May-10
5.27	1.51	3.35	10.69	18.34	2.71	0.77	4.6	4.72	13.37	3,753	2	32	0	27	0		3.33	0				Mar-98
5.31	1.61	3.69	11.66	19.81	2.81	0.47	4.58	4.72	14.47	3,753	2	32	0	27	0		3.33	0				Mar-04
13.34	-4.56	-3.17	5.24		0	1.08	11.19	3.79	11.3	672.1	9	5	0	86	0		5.67	0				Apr-16
13.31	-4.45	-2.95	6.14		0	0.78	11.14	3.79	11.15	672.1	9	5	0	86	0		5.67	0				Sep-17
2.70	1.06	2.52	10.10	16.80	0	0.83	3.6	3.36	11.39	2,807	3	5	0	0	0	25	3.54	0				Sep-13
2.78	1.24	2.78	11.02	17.78	0	0.53	3.58	3.36	11.43	2,807	3	5	0	0	0	25	3.54	0				Sep-17
5.88	4.82	7.30	13.24	19.58	1.69	0.8	4.25	5.77	12.59	1,122	3	28	1	38	0		3.65	0				May-95
6.02	4.98	7.65	14.23	21.11	1.95	0.5	4.27	5.77	12.85	1,122	3	28	1	38	0		3.65	0				Mar-04
-0.10	-6.99	-9.46	-5.67	-2.68	11.33	1.05	6.93	2.49	9.17	622.5	30	23	0	0	0		5.39	0				Dec-11
0.10	-6.82	-9.12	-4.74	-1.37	11.6	0.75	6.95	2.49	9.28	622.5	30	23	0	0	0		5.39	0				Dec-11
1.40	6.43	8.11	14.57	18.98	0	0.71	3.27	5.13	14.39	2,169	10	37	0	3	0		2.97	0				May-95
1.40	6.51	8.33	15.55	20.44	0	0.41	3.26	5.13	15.2	2,169	10	37	0	3	0		2.97	0				Mar-04

	MARKET		FUND TYPE, CATEGORY & OBJECTIVE		RATINGS				NEW INVESTORS	
Fund Name	Ticker Symbol	Traded On	Fund Type	Category and (Prospectus Objective)	Overall Rating	Reward Rating	Risk Rating	Recent Up/ Downgrade	Open to New Investors	Telephone
JNL/Mellon Bond Index Fund Class A			Open End	US Fixed Inc (Corp Bond - General)	B	B-	B	Up	Y	
JNL/Mellon Bond Index Fund Class I			Open End	US Fixed Inc (Corp Bond - General)	B	B-	B	Up	Y	
JNL/Neuberger Berman Strategic Income Fund Class A			Open End	US Fixed Inc (Income)	C-	D+	C		Y	
JNL/Neuberger Berman Strategic Income Fund Class I			Open End	US Fixed Inc (Income)	C-	D+	C		Y	
JNL/PIMCO Income Fund Class A			Open End	US Fixed Inc (Income)	C-	D+	C	Down	Y	
JNL/PIMCO Income Fund Class I			Open End	US Fixed Inc (Income)	C-	D+	C	Down	Y	
JNL/PIMCO Investment Grade Credit Bond A			Open End	US Fixed Inc (Income)	B-	C+	B	Up	Y	
JNL/PIMCO Investment Grade Credit Bond I			Open End	US Fixed Inc (Income)	B-	C+	B+	Up	Y	
JNL/PIMCO Real Return Fund Class A			Open End	US Fixed Inc (Income)	B	C+	B+	Up	Y	
JNL/PIMCO Real Return Fund Class I			Open End	US Fixed Inc (Income)	B	C+	B+	Up	Y	
JNL/PPM America Floating Rate Income Fund Class A			Open End	US Fixed Inc (Income)	D+	D	C-	Down	Y	
JNL/PPM America Floating Rate Income Fund Class I			Open End	US Fixed Inc (Income)	D+	D	C-	Down	Y	
JNL/PPM America High Yield Bond Fund Class A			Open End	US Fixed Inc (Corp Bond - High Yield)	D+	D	C-	Down	Y	
JNL/PPM America High Yield Bond Fund Class I			Open End	US Fixed Inc (Corp Bond - High Yield)	C-	D+	C		Y	
JNL/PPM America Low Duration Bond Fund Class A			Open End	US Fixed Inc (Growth & Income)	C	C	B-		Y	
JNL/PPM America Low Duration Bond Fund Class I			Open End	US Fixed Inc (Growth & Income)	C	C	B-		Y	
JNL/PPM America Total Return Fund Class A			Open End	US Fixed Inc (Growth & Income)	B	B-	B+	Up	Y	
JNL/PPM America Total Return Fund Class I			Open End	US Fixed Inc (Growth & Income)	B	B-	B+	Up	Y	
JNL/T. Rowe Price Short-Term Bond Fund Class A			Open End	US Fixed Inc (Income)	C	C	B-		Y	
JNL/T. Rowe Price Short-Term Bond Fund Class I			Open End	US Fixed Inc (Income)	C	C	B-		Y	
JNL/T. Rowe Price U.S. High Yield Fund Class A			Open End	US Fixed Inc (Corp Bond - High Yield)	D+	D	C-	Down	Y	
JNL/T. Rowe Price U.S. High Yield Fund Class I			Open End	US Fixed Inc (Corp Bond - High Yield)	D+	D	C-	Down	Y	
JNL/Vanguard Global Bond Market Index Fund Class A			Open End	Global Fixed Inc (Worldwide Bond)	C+	C	B	Up	Y	
JNL/Vanguard Global Bond Market Index Fund Class I			Open End	Global Fixed Inc (Worldwide Bond)	C+	C	B	Up	Y	
JNL/WMC Government Money Market Fund Class A			Money Mkt	US Money Mkt (Money Mkt - Govt)	C	C-	C+		Y	
JNL/WMC Government Money Market Fund Class I			Money Mkt	US Money Mkt (Money Mkt - Govt)	C	C-	C+		Y	
John Hancock Bond Fund Class A	JHNBX	NAS CM	Open End	US Fixed Inc (Income)	B-	C	B	Up	Y	800-225-5291
John Hancock Bond Fund Class B	JHBBX	NAS CM	Open End	US Fixed Inc (Income)	C+	C	B	Up		800-225-5291
John Hancock Bond Fund Class C	JHCBX	NAS CM	Open End	US Fixed Inc (Income)	C+	C	B	Up	Y	800-225-5291
John Hancock Bond Fund Class I	JHBIX	NAS CM	Open End	US Fixed Inc (Income)	B-	C	B+	Up	Y	800-225-5291
John Hancock Bond Fund Class NAV			Open End	US Fixed Inc (Income)	B-	C	B+	Up	Y	800-225-5291
John Hancock Bond Fund Class R2	JHRBX	NAS CM	Open End	US Fixed Inc (Income)	B-	C	B	Up	Y	800-225-5291
John Hancock Bond Fund Class R4	JBFRX	NAS CM	Open End	US Fixed Inc (Income)	B-	C	B+	Up	Y	800-225-5291
John Hancock Bond Fund Class R6	JHBSX	NAS CM	Open End	US Fixed Inc (Income)	B-	C	B+	Up	Y	800-225-5291
John Hancock California Tax Free Income Fund Class I	JCAFX	NAS CM	Open End	US Muni Fixed Inc (Muni Bond - Single State)	C	C-	C+		Y	800-225-5291
John Hancock California Tax Free Income Fund Class R6	JCSRX	NAS CM	Open End	US Muni Fixed Inc (Muni Bond - Single State)	C	C-	C+		Y	800-225-5291
John Hancock California Tax-Free Income Fund Class A	TACAX	NAS CM	Open End	US Muni Fixed Inc (Muni Bond - Single State)	C	C-	C+		Y	800-225-5291
John Hancock California Tax-Free Income Fund Class B	TSCAX	NAS CM	Open End	US Muni Fixed Inc (Muni Bond - Single State)	C	C-	C			800-225-5291
John Hancock California Tax-Free Income Fund Class C	TCCAX	NAS CM	Open End	US Muni Fixed Inc (Muni Bond - Single State)	C	C-	C		Y	800-225-5291
John Hancock ESG Core Bond Fund Class A	JBOAX	NAS CM	Open End	US Fixed Inc (Multisector Bond)	B-	C+	B	Up	Y	800-225-5291
John Hancock ESG Core Bond Fund Class I	JBOIX	NAS CM	Open End	US Fixed Inc (Multisector Bond)	B-	C+	B	Up	Y	800-225-5291
John Hancock ESG Core Bond Fund Class R6	JBORX	NAS CM	Open End	US Fixed Inc (Multisector Bond)	B-	C+	B	Up	Y	800-225-5291
John Hancock Funds Absolute Return Currency Fund Class A	JCUAX	NAS CM	Open End	Currency (Growth & Income)	C	C	C+		Y	800-225-5291
John Hancock Funds Absolute Return Currency Fund Class C	JCUCX	NAS CM	Open End	Currency (Growth & Income)	C	C	C+		Y	800-225-5291
John Hancock Funds Absolute Return Currency Fund Class I	JCUIX	NAS CM	Open End	Currency (Growth & Income)	C	C	C+		Y	800-225-5291
John Hancock Funds Absolute Return Currency Fund Class NAV	JCUNX	NAS CM	Open End	Currency (Growth & Income)	C+	C	C+	Up	Y	800-225-5291
John Hancock Funds Absolute Return Currency Fund Class R2	JHCCX	NAS CM	Open End	Currency (Growth & Income)	C	C	C+		Y	800-225-5291
John Hancock Funds Absolute Return Currency Fund Class R6	JCURX	NAS CM	Open End	Currency (Growth & Income)	C+	C	C+	Up	Y	800-225-5291
John Hancock Funds Emerging Markets Debt Fund Class A	JMKAX	NAS CM	Open End	Emerg Mkts Fixed Inc (Diversified Emerg Mkts)	D+	D	C-	Down	Y	800-225-5291
John Hancock Funds Emerging Markets Debt Fund Class C	JMKCX	NAS CM	Open End	Emerg Mkts Fixed Inc (Diversified Emerg Mkts)	D	D	C-	Down	Y	800-225-5291
John Hancock Funds Emerging Markets Debt Fund Class I	JMKIX	NAS CM	Open End	Emerg Mkts Fixed Inc (Diversified Emerg Mkts)	D+	D+	C-	Down	Y	800-225-5291
John Hancock Funds Emerging Markets Debt Fund Class NAV			Open End	Emerg Mkts Fixed Inc (Diversified Emerg Mkts)	D+	D+	C-	Down	Y	800-225-5291

★Expanded analysis of this fund is included in Section II.

TOTAL RETURNS & PERFORMANCE									ASSETS		ASSET ALLOCATION & TURNOVER							MINIMUMS		FEES		
3-Month Total Return	6-Month Total Return	1-Year Total Return	3-Year Total Return	5-Year Total Return	Dividend Yield (TTM)	Expense Ratio	3-Yr Std Deviation	Effective Duration	NAV	Total Assets (MIL)	%Cash	%Government Bonds	%Municipal Bonds	%Corporate Bonds	%Other	Turnover Ratio	Average Coupon Rate	Min Initial Investment	Min Additional Investment	Front End Fee (%)	Back End Fee (%)	Inception Date
2.65	5.97	8.13	14.78	20.17	2.17	0.57	3.22	5.67	12.78	1,295	5	46	1	24	0	62	3.19	0				Jan-02
2.70	6.06	8.52	15.87	21.73	2.35	0.27	3.27	5.67	13.29	1,295	5	46	1	24	0	62	3.19	0				Mar-04
10.45	-0.62	1.65	8.12	17.32	2.68	0.94	7.21	3.87	11.2	813.2	2	21	0	51	0	95	4.19	0				Apr-12
10.44	-0.44	1.95	9.22	19.01	2.96	0.64	7.16	3.87	11.31	813.2	2	21	0	51	0	95	4.19	0				Apr-12
5.27	-1.33	0.00			2.83	0.94		1.32	10.37	1,548	14	13	0	29	0	365	3.66	0				Sep-17
5.44	-1.13	0.32			2.95	0.64		1.32	10.45	1,548	14	13	0	29	0	365	3.66	0				Sep-17
8.38	5.38	9.46	20.06	32.21	2.32	0.92	5.8	7.51	12.92	1,580	9	19	0	64	0	183	3.79	0				Feb-12
8.53	5.61	9.79	21.09	33.34	2.48	0.62	5.84	7.51	12.97	1,580	9	19	0	64	0	183	3.79	0				Sep-17
5.63	5.63	7.90	14.11	18.29	0	1.67	3.95	8.10	11.06	1,335	1	69	0	6	0	225	1.37	0				Jan-07
5.74	5.84	8.29	15.10	19.83	0	1.37	3.95	8.10	11.23	1,335	1	69	0	6	0	225	1.37	0				Jan-07
7.94	-5.57	-3.00	2.72	9.75	0	0.93	7.98		10.33	1,123	6	0	0	93	0	36	4.35	0				Jan-11
8.00	-5.45	-2.71	3.53	10.61	0	0.63	8		10.39	1,123	6	0	0	93	0	36	4.35	0				Sep-17
8.57	-6.18	-2.54	4.97	15.76	0	0.76	9.16	4.29	13.04	1,787	3	0	0	96	0	75	5.92	0				Mar-98
8.56	-6.06	-2.29	5.89	17.10	0	0.46	9.15	4.29	15.34	1,787	3	0	0	96	0	75	5.92	0				Mar-04
2.90	2.01	3.20	7.64	10.38	0	0.74	1.82	1.80	10.64	509.7	6	7	0	52	0	116	2.91	0				Sep-13
2.97	2.19	3.57	8.45	11.21	0	0.44	1.85	1.80	10.72	509.7	6	7	0	52	0	116	2.91	0				Sep-17
5.97	6.30	9.05	17.48	25.81	0	0.81	3.78	5.70	13.49	1,548	2	12	0	46	0	95	3.57	0				Dec-08
6.03	6.54	9.38	18.57	26.98	0	0.51	3.77	5.70	13.52	1,548	2	12	0	46	0	95	3.57	0				Sep-17
3.99	2.26	3.58	7.86	10.09	0	0.71	2.34	2.06	10.4	1,557	4	17	0	47	0	71	2.92	0				May-06
4.14	2.52	3.93	8.97	11.65	0	0.41	2.32	2.06	10.56	1,557	4	17	0	47	0	71	2.92	0				May-06
3.32	-6.89	-4.02	2.02		0	0.98	6.59	3.51	10.26	540.1	42	0	0	58	0		5.99	0				Apr-16
3.44	-6.66	-3.67	2.89		0	0.68	6.58	3.51	10.22	540.1	42	0	0	58	0		5.99	0				Sep-17
2.43	4.12	5.87			0	0.66		7.19	11.36	151.6	2	64	0	21	0		2.61	0				Sep-17
2.50	4.18	6.11			0	0.36		7.19	11.46	151.6	2	64	0	21	0		2.61	0				Sep-17
0.02	0.21	0.88	3.02	3.02	0.99	0.57	0.17		1	2,222	80	20	0	0	0			0				May-95
0.00	0.26	1.14	4.29	4.29	1.3	0.27	0.2		1	2,222	80	20	0	0	0			0				Mar-04
5.96	4.56	7.31	15.44	23.87	2.96	0.78	4.31	5.94	16.58	18,214	3	14	0	45	0	106	3.84	1,000		4.00		Nov-73
5.79	4.13	6.51	12.98	19.56	2.28	1.48	4.34	5.94	16.57	18,214	3	14	0	45	0	106	3.84	1,000			5.00	Nov-93
5.78	4.20	6.57	13.05	19.63	2.28	1.48	4.31	5.94	16.58	18,214	3	14	0	45	0	106	3.84	1,000			1.00	Oct-98
6.04	4.64	7.56	16.45	25.74	3.26	0.48	4.3	5.94	16.58	18,214	3	14	0	45	0	106	3.84	250,000				Sep-01
6.08	4.72	7.70	16.88	26.43	3.38	0.36	4.29	5.94	16.6	18,214	3	14	0	45	0	106	3.84	0				Aug-15
6.00	4.51	7.22	15.10	23.26	2.88	0.88	4.35	5.94	16.6	18,214	3	14	0	45	0	106	3.84	0				Mar-12
6.00	4.57	7.42	15.97	24.96	3.13	0.63	4.3	5.94	16.6	18,214	3	14	0	45	0	106	3.84	0				Mar-15
6.13	4.76	7.74	16.82	26.50	3.37	0.38	4.35	5.94	16.61	18,214	3	14	0	45	0	106	3.84	1,000,000				Aug-11
2.69	0.10	2.28	10.79	19.66	3.3	0.7	4.85	6.49	10.78	210.9	1	0	99	0	0	22	5.08	250,000				Feb-17
2.79	0.11	2.40	10.97	19.80	3.33	0.67	4.84	6.49	10.79	210.9	1	0	99	0	0	22	5.08	1,000,000				Aug-17
2.75	0.02	2.22	10.40	19.18	3.15	0.85	4.87	6.49	10.78	210.9	1	0	99	0	0	22	5.08	1,000		4.00		Dec-89
2.56	-0.33	1.47	8.05	14.91	2.39	1.6	4.8	6.49	10.79	210.9	1	0	99	0	0	22	5.08	1,000			5.00	Dec-91
2.56	-0.33	1.46	7.95	14.81	2.38	1.6	4.87	6.49	10.78	210.9	1	0	99	0	0	22	5.08	1,000			1.00	Apr-99
2.92	5.16	6.64	11.80		1.95	0.87	2.4		10.69	64.6	3	23	11	44	0	37	2.91	1,000		4.00		Dec-16
2.97	5.26	6.89	12.60		2.2	0.62	2.42		10.69	64.6	3	23	11	44	0	37	2.91	250,000				Dec-16
2.99	5.31	7.00	12.95		2.3	0.51	2.4		10.69	64.6	3	23	11	44	0	37	2.91	1,000,000				Dec-16
0.10	17.17	16.99	4.51	23.78	2.43	1.36	9.54		9.89	380.3	100	0	0	0	0	0		1,000		3.00		Aug-10
-0.10	16.84	16.07	2.36	19.52	1.79	2.06	9.55		9.85	380.3	100	0	0	0	0	0		1,000			1.00	Aug-14
0.19	17.47	17.38	5.52	25.83	2.62	1.06	9.54		10.22	380.3	100	0	0	0	0	0		250,000				Aug-10
0.19	17.45	17.51	5.90	26.58	2.69	0.94	9.51		10.36	380.3	100	0	0	0	0	0		0				Aug-10
0.09	17.33	17.19	4.88	24.59	2.38	1.45	9.56		10.22	380.3	100	0	0	0	0	0		0				Mar-15
0.19	17.51	17.56	5.91	26.52	2.69	0.95	9.53		10.33	380.3	100	0	0	0	0	0		1,000,000				Nov-11
13.12	-5.09	-2.50	6.52	24.21	4.97	1.18	11.98	7.30	8.88	970.3	5	50	0	45	0	7	5.84	1,000		4.00		Dec-09
12.64	-5.67	-3.42	3.96	19.62	4.23	1.88	11.94	7.30	8.87	970.3	5	50	0	45	0	7	5.84	1,000			1.00	Aug-14
13.33	-4.94	-2.09	7.48	26.27	5.29	0.88	12.01	7.30	8.89	970.3	5	50	0	45	0	7	5.84	250,000				Dec-09
13.40	-4.87	-1.96	7.89	27.04	5.43	0.76	12.02	7.30	8.88	970.3	5	50	0	45	0	7	5.84	0				Jun-13

Fund Name	MARKET Ticker Symbol	Traded On	FUND TYPE, CATEGORY & OBJECTIVE Fund Type	Category and (Prospectus Objective)	RATINGS Overall Rating	Reward Rating	Risk Rating	Recent Up/ Downgrade	NEW INVESTORS Open to New Investors	Telephone
John Hancock Funds Emerging Markets Debt Fund Class R2	JHEMX	NAS CM	Open End	Emerg Mkts Fixed Inc (Diversified Emerg Mkts)	D+	D+	C-	Down	Y	800-225-5291
John Hancock Funds Emerging Markets Debt Fund Class R6	JEMIX	NAS CM	Open End	Emerg Mkts Fixed Inc (Diversified Emerg Mkts)	D+	D+	C-	Down	Y	800-225-5291
John Hancock Funds Floating Rate Income Fund Class 1	JFIHX	NAS CM	Open End	US Fixed Inc (Income)	D+	D	C-	Down	Y	800-225-5291
John Hancock Funds Floating Rate Income Fund Class A	JFIAX	NAS CM	Open End	US Fixed Inc (Income)	D+	D	C-	Down	Y	800-225-5291
John Hancock Funds Floating Rate Income Fund Class B	JFIBX	NAS CM	Open End	US Fixed Inc (Income)	D	D	C-	Down		800-225-5291
John Hancock Funds Floating Rate Income Fund Class C	JFIGX	NAS CM	Open End	US Fixed Inc (Income)	D	D	C-	Down	Y	800-225-5291
John Hancock Funds Floating Rate Income Fund Class I	JFIIX	NAS CM	Open End	US Fixed Inc (Income)	D+	D	C-	Down	Y	800-225-5291
John Hancock Funds Floating Rate Income Fund Class NAV	JFIDX	NAS CM	Open End	US Fixed Inc (Income)	D+	D	C-	Down	Y	800-225-5291
John Hancock Funds Floating Rate Income Fund Class R6	JFIRX	NAS CM	Open End	US Fixed Inc (Income)	D+	D	C-	Down	Y	800-225-5291
John Hancock Funds II Asia Pacific Total Return Bond Cl NA			Open End	Global Fixed Inc (Income)	C	C-	C+		Y	800-225-5291
John Hancock Funds II Core Bond Fund Class 1	JICDX	NAS CM	Open End	US Fixed Inc (Income)	B	B-	B	Up	Y	800-225-5291
John Hancock Funds II Core Bond Fund Class NAV	JHCDX	NAS CM	Open End	US Fixed Inc (Income)	B	B-	B	Up	Y	800-225-5291
John Hancock Funds II Global Bond Fund Class NAV	JHGDX	NAS CM	Open End	Global Fixed Inc (Worldwide Bond)	U	U	U		Y	800-225-5913
John Hancock Funds II High Yield Fund Class 1	JIHDX	NAS CM	Open End	US Fixed Inc (Corp Bond - High Yield)	C-	D+	C		Y	800-225-5291
John Hancock Funds II Opportunistic Fixed Income Cl 1	JIGDX	NAS CM	Open End	Global Fixed Inc (Worldwide Bond)	B-	C+	B	Up	Y	800-225-5291
John Hancock Funds II U.S. High Yield Bond Fund Class 1	JIHLX	NAS CM	Open End	US Fixed Inc (Corp Bond - High Yield)	C-	D+	C		Y	800-225-5291
John Hancock Funds II U.S. High Yield Bond Fund Class NAV	JHHLX	NAS CM	Open End	US Fixed Inc (Corp Bond - High Yield)	C-	D+	C		Y	800-225-5291
John Hancock Funds Short Duration Credit Opp Cl A	JMBAX	NAS CM	Open End	US Fixed Inc (Multisector Bond)	C-	D+	C		Y	800-225-5291
John Hancock Funds Short Duration Credit Opp Cl C	JMBCX	NAS CM	Open End	US Fixed Inc (Multisector Bond)	D+	D	C	Down	Y	800-225-5291
John Hancock Funds Short Duration Credit Opp Cl I	JMBIX	NAS CM	Open End	US Fixed Inc (Multisector Bond)	C-	D+	C		Y	800-225-5291
John Hancock Funds Short Duration Credit Opp Cl NAV	JMBNX	NAS CM	Open End	US Fixed Inc (Multisector Bond)	C-	D+	C		Y	800-225-5291
John Hancock Funds Short Duration Credit Opp Cl R6	JSDEX	NAS CM	Open End	US Fixed Inc (Multisector Bond)	C-	D+	C		Y	800-225-5291
John Hancock Funds Strategic Income Opportunities Cl A	JIPAX	NAS CM	Open End	US Fixed Inc (Income)	C	C-	C	Up	Y	800-225-5291
John Hancock Funds Strategic Income Opportunities Cl C	JIPCX	NAS CM	Open End	US Fixed Inc (Income)	C-	C-	C		Y	800-225-5291
John Hancock Funds Strategic Income Opportunities Cl I	JIPIX	NAS CM	Open End	US Fixed Inc (Income)	C	C-	C		Y	800-225-5291
John Hancock Funds Strategic Income Opportunities Cl NAV	JHSEX	NAS CM	Open End	US Fixed Inc (Income)	C	C-	C		Y	800-225-5291
John Hancock Funds Strategic Income Opportunities Cl R2	JIPPX	NAS CM	Open End	US Fixed Inc (Income)	C	C-	C	Up	Y	800-225-5291
John Hancock Funds Strategic Income Opportunities Cl R6	JIPRX	NAS CM	Open End	US Fixed Inc (Income)	C	C-	C		Y	800-225-5291
John Hancock Government Income Fund Class A	JHGIX	NAS CM	Open End	US Fixed Inc (Govt Bond - General)	B	B	B		Y	800-225-5291
John Hancock Government Income Fund Class B	TSGIX	NAS CM	Open End	US Fixed Inc (Govt Bond - General)	B-	C+	B			800-225-5291
John Hancock Government Income Fund Class C	TCGIX	NAS CM	Open End	US Fixed Inc (Govt Bond - General)	B-	C+	B		Y	800-225-5291
John Hancock Government Income Fund Class I	JGIFX	NAS CM	Open End	US Fixed Inc (Govt Bond - General)	B	B	B		Y	800-225-5291
John Hancock Government Income Fund Class R6	JTSRX	NAS CM	Open End	US Fixed Inc (Govt Bond - General)	B	B	B		Y	800-225-5291
John Hancock High Yield Fund Class A	JHHBX	NAS CM	Open End	US Fixed Inc (Corp Bond - High Yield)	D+	D+	C-	Down	Y	800-225-5291
John Hancock High Yield Fund Class B	TSHYX	NAS CM	Open End	US Fixed Inc (Corp Bond - High Yield)	D+	D	C-	Down		800-225-5291
John Hancock High Yield Fund Class C	JHYCX	NAS CM	Open End	US Fixed Inc (Corp Bond - High Yield)	D+	D	C-	Down	Y	800-225-5291
John Hancock High Yield Fund Class I	JYHIX	NAS CM	Open End	US Fixed Inc (Corp Bond - High Yield)	C-	D+	C		Y	800-225-5291
John Hancock High Yield Fund Class NAV			Open End	US Fixed Inc (Corp Bond - High Yield)	C-	D+	C		Y	800-225-5291
John Hancock High Yield Fund Class R6	JFHYX	NAS CM	Open End	US Fixed Inc (Corp Bond - High Yield)	C-	D+	C		Y	800-225-5291
John Hancock High Yield Municipal Bond Fund Class A	JHTFX	NAS CM	Open End	US Muni Fixed Inc (Muni Bond - Natl)	C-	D+	C	Down	Y	800-225-5291
John Hancock High Yield Municipal Bond Fund Class B	TSHTX	NAS CM	Open End	US Muni Fixed Inc (Muni Bond - Natl)	C-	D+	C	Down		800-225-5291
John Hancock High Yield Municipal Bond Fund Class C	JCTFX	NAS CM	Open End	US Muni Fixed Inc (Muni Bond - Natl)	C-	D+	C	Down	Y	800-225-5291
John Hancock High Yield Municipal Bond Fund Class I	JHYMX	NAS CM	Open End	US Muni Fixed Inc (Muni Bond - Natl)	C-	D+	C	Down	Y	800-225-5291
John Hancock High Yield Municipal Bond Fund Class R6	JCTRX	NAS CM	Open End	US Muni Fixed Inc (Muni Bond - Natl)	C-	D+	C	Down	Y	800-225-5291
John Hancock Income Fund Class A	JHFIX	NAS CM	Open End	US Fixed Inc (Multisector Bond)	C	C-	C+		Y	800-225-5291
John Hancock Income Fund Class B	STIBX	NAS CM	Open End	US Fixed Inc (Multisector Bond)	C	C-	C			800-225-5291
John Hancock Income Fund Class C	JSTCX	NAS CM	Open End	US Fixed Inc (Multisector Bond)	C	C-	C		Y	800-225-5291
John Hancock Income Fund Class I	JSTIX	NAS CM	Open End	US Fixed Inc (Multisector Bond)	C	C-	C+		Y	800-225-5291
John Hancock Income Fund Class R1	JSTRX	NAS CM	Open End	US Fixed Inc (Multisector Bond)	C	C-	C+		Y	800-225-5291
John Hancock Income Fund Class R2	JSNSX	NAS CM	Open End	US Fixed Inc (Multisector Bond)	C	C-	C+		Y	800-225-5291
John Hancock Income Fund Class R3	JSNHX	NAS CM	Open End	US Fixed Inc (Multisector Bond)	C	C-	C+		Y	800-225-5291
John Hancock Income Fund Class R4	JSNFX	NAS CM	Open End	US Fixed Inc (Multisector Bond)	C	C-	C+		Y	800-225-5291

★ Expanded analysis of this fund is included in Section II.

TOTAL RETURNS & PERFORMANCE									ASSETS		ASSET ALLOCATION & TURNOVER							MINIMUMS		FEES		
3-Month Total Return	6-Month Total Return	1-Year Total Return	3-Year Total Return	5-Year Total Return	Dividend Yield (TTM)	Expense Ratio	3-Yr Std Deviation	Effective Duration	NAV	Total Assets (MIL)	%Cash	%Government Bonds	%Municipal Bonds	%Corporate Bonds	%Other	Turnover Ratio	Average Coupon Rate	Min Initial Investment	Min Additional Investment	Front End Fee (%)	Back End Fee (%)	Inception Date
13.12	-5.19	-2.49	6.67	24.85	5.01	1.27	11.98	7.30	8.87	970.3	5	50	0	45	0	7	5.84	0				Mar-15
13.38	-4.89	-2.09	7.79	26.85	5.42	0.77	12	7.30	8.88	970.3	5	50	0	45	0	7	5.84	1,000,000				Mar-15
10.18	-4.90	-2.37	4.95	10.87	6.08	0.71	8.96	0.52	7.66	719.5	7	0	0	93	0	120	1.88	0				Jan-08
10.09	-5.03	-2.66	4.01	9.07	5.76	1.01	8.95	0.52	7.67	719.5	7	0	0	93	0	120	1.88	1,000		2.50		Jan-08
10.03	-5.38	-3.25	1.83	5.31	4.97	1.76	8.96	0.52	7.68	719.5	7	0	0	93	0	120	1.88	1,000			5.00	Jan-08
9.99	-5.35	-3.23	1.87	5.25	4.97	1.76	8.98	0.52	7.71	719.5	7	0	0	93	0	120	1.88	1,000			1.00	Jan-08
10.30	-4.92	-2.44	4.87	10.53	6	0.78	9.03	0.52	7.67	719.5	7	0	0	93	0	120	1.88	250,000				Jan-08
9.93	-5.09	-2.55	4.87	10.90	5.86	0.67	8.93	0.52	7.67	719.5	7	0	0	93	0	120	1.88	0				Jan-08
10.18	-4.87	-2.33	5.08	11.12	6.12	0.67	8.95	0.52	7.67	719.5	7	0	0	93	0	120	1.88	1,000,000				Sep-11
10.60	0.30	2.88	11.16	21.91	4.02	0.81	7.38		9.8	207.1	1	49	0	50	0	60	4.90	0				Jan-13
4.28	6.28	8.66	15.57	21.84	2.38	0.65	3.48	5.49	13.83	2,621	1	15	0	29	0	447	3.30	0				Oct-05
4.30	6.32	8.81	15.77	22.09	2.43	0.6	3.47	5.49	13.81	2,621	1	15	0	29	0	447	3.30	0				Oct-05
1.76	2.79	-1.29	5.75	7.44	1.38	0.8	5.23	6.45		75.0	-8	71	0	10	2	31	2.26	0				Oct-05
11.72	-5.49	-1.42	8.30	18.71	6.14	0.81	10.49	4.07	7.44	198.1	1	11	0	83	0	51	5.97	0				Oct-05
8.52	5.22	6.68	14.06	24.66	3.44	1.14	5.78	5.96	13.49	67.4	12	37	0	11	0	53	2.74	0				Oct-05
10.95	-3.33	0.09	9.87	22.70	5.63	0.86	8.64	3.74	10.53	226.3	5	0	0	95	0	41	5.59	0				Oct-05
10.98	-3.22	0.15	10.05	23.04	5.69	0.81	8.6	3.74	10.52	226.3	5	0	0	95	0	41	5.59	0				Oct-05
9.67	-1.34	0.35	6.32	12.01	3.29	1.2	7.14	2.50	9.31	693.4	3	25	0	40	0	59	3.20	1,000		2.50		Nov-09
9.49	-1.68	-0.33	4.17	8.25	2.58	1.9	7.14	2.50	9.31	693.4	3	25	0	40	0	59	3.20	1,000			1.00	Jun-14
9.76	-1.20	0.76	7.30	13.79	3.6	0.9	7.15	2.50	9.3	693.4	3	25	0	40	0	59	3.20	250,000				Nov-09
9.79	-1.12	0.90	7.71	14.60	3.73	0.78	7.07	2.50	9.32	693.4	3	25	0	40	0	59	3.20	0				Nov-09
9.78	-1.14	0.87	7.66	14.47	3.72	0.79	7.14	2.50	9.31	693.4	3	25	0	40	0	59	3.20	1,000,000				Mar-15
7.14	-0.43	2.14	5.90	13.62	2.13	1.08	5.89	5.09	10.57	4,494	3	33	1	54	0	84	4.01	1,000		4.00		Jan-10
6.96	-0.78	1.44	3.71	9.73	1.42	1.78	5.89	5.09	10.57	4,494	3	33	1	54	0	84	4.01	1,000			1.00	Jan-10
7.22	-0.29	2.45	6.84	15.35	2.43	0.78	5.89	5.09	10.57	4,494	3	33	1	54	0	84	4.01	250,000				Jan-10
7.16	-0.31	2.58	7.13	16.03	2.56	0.66	5.87	5.09	10.56	4,494	3	33	1	54	0	84	4.01	0				Apr-06
7.11	-0.47	2.06	5.63	13.13	2.04	1.17	5.87	5.09	10.58	4,494	3	33	1	54	0	84	4.01	0				Mar-12
7.24	-0.23	2.66	7.19	15.97	2.54	0.67	5.87	5.09	10.58	4,494	3	33	1	54	0	84	4.01	1,000,000				Sep-11
0.39	7.50	8.95	14.19	17.28	1.49	0.98	3.9	6.69	10.07	316.5	0	66	0	0	1	87	2.40	1,000		4.00		Sep-94
0.20	7.08	7.99	11.41	12.78	0.73	1.78	3.82	6.69	10.06	316.5	0	66	0	0	1	87	2.40	1,000			5.00	Feb-88
0.20	7.19	8.10	11.53	12.78	0.73	1.78	3.91	6.69	10.07	316.5	0	66	0	0	1	87	2.40	1,000			1.00	Apr-99
0.54	7.71	9.17	14.88	17.30	1.69	0.78	3.82	6.69	10.08	316.5	0	66	0	0	1	87	2.40	250,000				Sep-16
0.57	7.77	9.28	15.04	16.46	1.79	0.67	3.83	6.69	10.08	316.5	0	66	0	0	1	87	2.40	1,000,000				Aug-17
10.63	-5.07	-2.01	6.16	18.81	5.58	0.94	9.35		3.19	1,088	6	0	0	93	0	59	5.96	1,000		4.00		Jun-93
10.43	-5.70	-3.03	3.80	14.38	4.78	1.69	9.54		3.19	1,088	6	0	0	93	0	59	5.96	1,000			5.00	Oct-87
10.43	-5.42	-2.74	3.81	14.78	4.79	1.69	9.33		3.19	1,088	6	0	0	93	0	59	5.96	1,000			1.00	May-98
10.73	-5.25	-2.08	6.91	20.28	5.84	0.69	9.57		3.18	1,088	6	0	0	93	0	59	5.96	250,000				Aug-07
10.78	-5.18	-1.66	7.29	21.03	5.97	0.57	9.57		3.18	1,088	6	0	0	93	0	59	5.96	0				Oct-13
10.76	-5.20	-1.69	7.25	19.08	5.95	0.58	9.46		3.18	1,088	6	0	0	93	0	59	5.96	1,000,000				Oct-16
3.92	-2.63	0.12	10.55	19.63	4.4	0.96	7.28	8.08	7.63	141.6	-1	0	100	0	1	41	5.18	1,000		4.00		Dec-93
3.73	-2.99	-0.74	8.10	15.24	3.6	1.71	7.3	8.08	7.63	141.6	-1	0	100	0	1	41	5.18	1,000			5.00	Aug-86
3.73	-2.99	-0.61	8.10	15.24	3.6	1.71	7.28	8.08	7.63	141.6	-1	0	100	0	1	41	5.18	1,000			1.00	Apr-99
3.96	-2.67	0.15	10.91	18.74	4.56	0.81	7.29	8.08	7.64	141.6	-1	0	100	0	1	41	5.18	250,000				Feb-17
3.96	-2.66	0.17	10.99	18.32	4.58	0.78	7.26	8.08	7.64	141.6	-1	0	100	0	1	41	5.18	1,000,000				Aug-17
6.06	0.36	3.45	8.52	14.98	2.68	0.82	4.84	4.89	6.44	1,776	4	33	1	51	0	58	3.96	1,000		4.00		Aug-86
5.88	0.01	2.73	6.27	11.03	1.97	1.52	4.84	4.89	6.44	1,776	4	33	1	51	0	58	3.96	1,000			5.00	Oct-93
5.88	0.02	2.74	6.27	11.04	1.97	1.52	4.84	4.89	6.44	1,776	4	33	1	51	0	58	3.96	1,000			1.00	May-98
6.15	0.51	3.76	9.48	16.72	2.98	0.52	4.86	4.89	6.43	1,776	4	33	1	51	0	58	3.96	250,000				Sep-01
5.97	0.21	3.12	7.42	13.03	2.35	1.16	4.85	4.89	6.46	1,776	4	33	1	51	0	58	3.96	0				Aug-03
5.88	0.32	3.20	8.21	14.45	2.6	0.91	4.78	4.89	6.43	1,776	4	33	1	51	0	58	3.96	0				Mar-12
6.00	0.24	3.21	7.74	13.62	2.45	1.06	4.83	4.89	6.44	1,776	4	33	1	51	0	58	3.96	0				May-09
6.10	0.44	3.63	9.03	15.88	2.85	0.66	4.86	4.89	6.44	1,776	4	33	1	51	0	58	3.96	0				May-09

	MARKET			FUND TYPE, CATEGORY & OBJECTIVE	RATINGS				NEW INVESTORS	
Fund Name	Ticker Symbol	Traded On	Fund Type	Category and (Prospectus Objective)	Overall Rating	Reward Rating	Risk Rating	Recent Up/ Downgrade	Open to New Investors	Telephone
John Hancock Income Fund Class R5	JSNVX	NAS CM	Open End	US Fixed Inc (Multisector Bond)	C	C-	B-		Y	800-225-5291
John Hancock Income Fund Class R6	JSNWX	NAS CM	Open End	US Fixed Inc (Multisector Bond)	C	C-	B-		Y	800-225-5291
John Hancock Income Securities Trust	JHS	NYSE	Closed End	US Fixed Inc (Corp Bond - General)	C	C	C-	Up	Y	800-225-5291
John Hancock Investment Grade Bond Fund Class A	TAUSX	NAS CM	Open End	US Fixed Inc (Income)	B-	C+	B+	Up	Y	800-225-5291
John Hancock Investment Grade Bond Fund Class B	TSUSX	NAS CM	Open End	US Fixed Inc (Income)	B-	C+	B	Up		800-225-5291
John Hancock Investment Grade Bond Fund Class C	TCUSX	NAS CM	Open End	US Fixed Inc (Income)	B-	C+	B	Up	Y	800-225-5291
John Hancock Investment Grade Bond Fund Class I	TIUSX	NAS CM	Open End	US Fixed Inc (Income)	B	C+	B+	Up	Y	800-225-5291
John Hancock Investment Grade Bond Fund Class R2	JIGBX	NAS CM	Open End	US Fixed Inc (Income)	B-	C+	B+	Up	Y	800-225-5291
John Hancock Investment Grade Bond Fund Class R4	JIGMX	NAS CM	Open End	US Fixed Inc (Income)	B	C+	B+	Up	Y	800-225-5291
John Hancock Investment Grade Bond Fund Class R6	JIGEX	NAS CM	Open End	US Fixed Inc (Income)	B	C+	B+	Up	Y	800-225-5291
John Hancock Investors Trust	JHI	NYSE	Closed End	US Fixed Inc (Corp Bond - General)	D+	D+	C-	Down	Y	800-225-5291
John Hancock Managed Account Sh Inv-Grade Corp Bond Port	JMABX	NAS CM	Open End	US Fixed Inc (Corp Bond - High Quality)	U	U	U		Y	800-225-5291
John Hancock Managed Account Sh Non-Inv-Grade Corp Bond Po	JMADX	NAS CM	Open End	US Fixed Inc (Corp Bond - High Yield)	U	U	U		Y	800-225-5291
John Hancock Managed Account Shares Securitized Debt Port	JMAEX	NAS CM	Open End	US Fixed Inc (Income)	U	U	U		Y	800-225-5291
John Hancock Money Market Fund Class A	JHMXX	NAS CM	Money Mkt	US Money Mkt (Money Mkt - Govt)	C	C-	C+		Y	800-225-5291
John Hancock Money Market Fund Class B	TSMXX	NAS CM	Money Mkt	US Money Mkt (Money Mkt - Govt)	C	C-	C+			800-225-5291
John Hancock Money Market Fund Class C	JMCXX	NAS CM	Money Mkt	US Money Mkt (Money Mkt - Govt)	C	C-	C+			800-225-5291
John Hancock Tax-Free Bond Fund Class A	TAMBX	NAS CM	Open End	US Muni Fixed Inc (Income)	C	C-	C		Y	800-225-5291
John Hancock Tax-Free Bond Fund Class B	TSMBX	NAS CM	Open End	US Muni Fixed Inc (Income)	C-	D+	C	Down		800-225-5291
John Hancock Tax-Free Bond Fund Class C	TBMBX	NAS CM	Open End	US Muni Fixed Inc (Income)	C-	D+	C	Down	Y	800-225-5291
John Hancock Tax-Free Bond Fund Class I	JTBDX	NAS CM	Open End	US Muni Fixed Inc (Income)	C	C-	C+		Y	800-225-5291
John Hancock Tax-Free Bond Fund Class R6	JTMRX	NAS CM	Open End	US Muni Fixed Inc (Income)	C	C-	C+		Y	800-225-5291
John Hancock Variable Insur Trust Money Mkt Trust Ser I	JHOXX	NAS CM	Money Mkt	US Money Mkt (Money Mkt - Govt)	U	U	U		Y	800-225-5913
John Hancock Var Insur Trust Strat Inc Opp Trust Ser I	JESNX	NAS CM	Open End	US Fixed Inc (Multisector Bond)	U	U	U		Y	800-225-5913
John Hancock Var Insur Trust Total Bond Mkt Trust B Ser I	JTBMX	NAS CM	Open End	US Fixed Inc (Govt Bond - General)	U	U	U		Y	800-225-5913
Johnson Fixed Income Fund	JFINX	NAS CM	Open End	US Fixed Inc (Income)	B	B-	B+	Up	Y	
Johnson Institutional Core Bond Fund	JIBFX	NAS CM	Open End	US Fixed Inc (Income)	B	B	B+		Y	
Johnson Institutional Core Bond Fund Class F	JIMFX	NAS CM	Open End	US Fixed Inc (Income)	B	B	B+		Y	
Johnson Institutional Intermediate Bond Fund	JIBEX	NAS CM	Open End	US Fixed Inc (Income)	B	B-	B+	Up	Y	
Johnson Institutional Intermediate Bond Fund Class F	JIMEX	NAS CM	Open End	US Fixed Inc (Income)	B	C+	B+	Up	Y	
Johnson Institutional Short Duration Bond Fund Class F	JIMDX	NAS CM	Open End	US Fixed Inc (Income)	C+	C	B	Up	Y	
Johnson Institutional Short Duration Bond Fund Class I	JIBDX	NAS CM	Open End	US Fixed Inc (Income)	C+	C	B	Up	Y	
Johnson Municipal Income Fund	JMUNX	NAS CM	Open End	US Muni Fixed Inc (Muni Bond - Single State)	C+	C	B	Up	Y	
JPMorgan 100% U.S. Treasury Securities Money Mkt Agency Cl	VPIXX	NAS CM	Money Mkt	US Money Mkt (Money Mkt - Treasury)	C	C-	C+		Y	800-480-4111
JPMorgan 100% U.S. Treas Securities Money Mkt Capital Cl	CJTXX	NAS CM	Money Mkt	US Money Mkt (Money Mkt - Treasury)	C	C-	C+		Y	800-480-4111
JPMorgan 100% U.S. Treasury Securities Money Mkt IM Cl	JSMXX	NAS CM	Money Mkt	US Money Mkt (Money Mkt - Treasury)	C	C-	C		Y	800-480-4111
JPMorgan 100% U.S. Treas Securities Money Mkt Inst Cl	JTSXX	NAS CM	Money Mkt	US Money Mkt (Money Mkt - Treasury)	C	C-	C+		Y	800-480-4111
★ JPMorgan 100% U.S. Treasury Securities Money Mkt Morgan Cl	HTSXX	NAS CM	Money Mkt	US Money Mkt (Money Mkt - Treasury)	C	C-	C+		Y	800-480-4111
JPMorgan 100% U.S. Treas Securities Money Mkt Premier Cl	VHPXX	NAS CM	Money Mkt	US Money Mkt (Money Mkt - Treasury)	C	C-	C+		Y	800-480-4111
JPMorgan 100% U.S. Treas Securities Money Mkt Reserve Cl	RJTXX	NAS CM	Money Mkt	US Money Mkt (Money Mkt - Treasury)	C	C-	C		Y	800-480-4111
JPMorgan California Muni Money Mkt Fund Agency Share	JOYXX	NAS CM	Money Mkt	US Money Mkt (Money Mkt - Single State)	C	C-	C		Y	800-480-4111
JPMorgan California Muni Money Mkt Fund E*Trade Class	JCEXX	NAS CM	Money Mkt	US Money Mkt (Money Mkt - Single State)	U	U	U		Y	800-480-4111
JPMorgan California Muni Money Mkt Institutional Share	JGCXX	NAS CM	Money Mkt	US Money Mkt (Money Mkt - Single State)	C	C-	C		Y	800-480-4111
JPMorgan California Muni Money Mkt Fund Morgan Class	VCAXX	NAS CM	Money Mkt	US Money Mkt (Money Mkt - Single State)	C	C-	C		Y	800-480-4111
JPMorgan California Muni Money Mkt Fund Premier Class	JCRXX	NAS CM	Money Mkt	US Money Mkt (Money Mkt - Single State)	C	C-	C+		Y	800-480-4111
JPMorgan California Muni Money Mkt Fund Service Class	JCVXX	NAS CM	Money Mkt	US Money Mkt (Money Mkt - Single State)	C	C-	C		Y	800-480-4111
JPMorgan California Tax Free Bond Fund Class A	JCBAX	NAS CM	Open End	US Muni Fixed Inc (Muni Bond - Single State)	C	C	B-		Y	800-480-4111
JPMorgan California Tax Free Bond Fund Class C	JCBCX	NAS CM	Open End	US Muni Fixed Inc (Muni Bond - Single State)	C	C	B-		Y	800-480-4111
JPMorgan California Tax Free Bond Fund Class R6	JCBSX	NAS CM	Open End	US Muni Fixed Inc (Muni Bond - Single State)	C+	C	B	Up	Y	800-480-4111
JPMorgan Core Bond Fund Class A	PGBOX	NAS CM	Open End	US Fixed Inc (Growth & Income)	B	C+	B+	Up	Y	800-480-4111
JPMorgan Core Bond Fund Class C	OBOCX	NAS CM	Open End	US Fixed Inc (Growth & Income)	B-	C+	B	Up	Y	800-480-4111
JPMorgan Core Bond Fund Class I	WOBDX	NAS CM	Open End	US Fixed Inc (Growth & Income)	B	C+	B+	Up	Y	800-480-4111

★Expanded analysis of this fund is included in Section II.

TOTAL RETURNS & PERFORMANCE									ASSETS		ASSET ALLOCATION & TURNOVER							MINIMUMS		FEES		
3-Month Total Return	6-Month Total Return	1-Year Total Return	3-Year Total Return	5-Year Total Return	Dividend Yield (TTM)	Expense Ratio	3-Yr Std Deviation	Effective Duration	NAV	Total Assets (MIL)	%Cash	%Government Bonds	%Municipal Bonds	%Corporate Bonds	%Other	Turnover Ratio	Average Coupon Rate	Min Initial Investment	Min Additional Investment	Front End Fee (%)	Back End Fee (%)	Inception Date
6.16	0.54	3.82	9.67	17.03	3.04	0.46	4.85	4.89	6.43	1,776	4	33	1	51	0	58	3.96	0				May-09
6.17	0.72	3.88	9.84	17.36	3.09	0.41	4.86	4.89	6.44	1,776	4	33	1	51	0	58	3.96	1,000,000				Sep-11
10.96	3.56	7.07	17.22	31.69	4.32		7.19		15.64	179.5	1	2	0	65	0	50	4.25					Feb-73
4.91	5.65	8.09	15.53	22.36	2.63	0.75	3.7	5.97	11.15	2,069	4	14	1	37	0	111	3.42	1,000		4.00		Dec-91
4.72	5.26	7.29	12.98	17.88	1.89	1.5	3.71	5.97	11.15	2,069	4	14	1	37	0	111	3.42	1,000			5.00	Dec-91
4.72	5.26	7.29	12.98	17.88	1.89	1.5	3.71	5.97	11.15	2,069	4	14	1	37	0	111	3.42	1,000			1.00	Apr-99
4.88	5.78	8.25	16.38	23.90	2.87	0.5	3.65	5.97	11.15	2,069	4	14	1	37	0	111	3.42	250,000				Jul-03
4.87	5.58	7.96	15.03	21.79	2.51	0.89	3.71	5.97	11.15	2,069	4	14	1	37	0	111	3.42	0				Mar-15
4.84	5.71	8.10	15.92	23.18	2.74	0.64	3.65	5.97	11.15	2,069	4	14	1	37	0	111	3.42	0				Mar-15
4.91	5.84	8.37	16.75	24.59	2.98	0.39	3.69	5.97	11.15	2,069	4	14	1	37	0	111	3.42	1,000,000				Mar-15
18.51	-7.98	-2.92	9.41	30.08	7.74	0	15.08		16.34	141.7	1	3	0	93	0	40	5.88					Jan-71
10.50	2.47	6.39				0			10.25	8.2	2	5	1	85	0		4.05	0				Jul-19
11.83	-5.11	-1.98				0			9.21	7.3	1	1	0	99	0		6.31	0				Jul-19
5.21	1.14	2.63				0			10.11	8.1	1	0	0	0	0		3.17	0				Jul-19
0.00	0.23	0.97	3.56	3.67	1.12	0.58	0.16		1	864.5	65	35	0	0	0			1,000				Sep-95
0.00	0.22	0.97	3.52	3.54	1.12	0.58	0.18		1	864.5	65	35	0	0	0			1,000			5.00	Dec-94
0.00	0.23	0.97	3.56	3.67	1.12	0.58	0.16		1	864.5	65	35	0	0	0			1,000			1.00	May-98
2.43	-0.47	1.82	9.74	16.76	3.08	0.82	5.01	6.48	9.73	469.1	0	0	100	0	0	33	4.90	1,000		4.00		Jan-90
2.13	-0.94	0.96	7.30	12.48	2.3	1.57	4.97	6.48	9.73	469.1	0	0	100	0	0	33	4.90	1,000			5.00	Dec-91
2.14	-0.94	0.96	7.20	12.36	2.31	1.57	4.97	6.48	9.72	469.1	0	0	100	0	0	33	4.90	1,000			1.00	Apr-99
2.35	-0.50	1.87	10.23	17.46	3.23	0.67	4.98	6.48	9.74	469.1	0	0	100	0	0	33	4.90	250,000				Feb-17
2.36	-0.49	1.90	10.31	17.37	3.26	0.64	5	6.48	9.74	469.1	0	0	100	0	0	33	4.90	1,000,000				Aug-17
0.11	0.18	0.23	0.25	0.26	0.22	0.33	0.04			2,135	72				0			0				Jun-85
2.22	4.87	5.07	14.93	32.13	2.43	0.75	2.6	4.28		613.4	6				3	49	4.44	0				May-04
2.18	3.67	5.64	13.26	15.93	2.68	0.3	2.81	5.45		598.7	7				0	67	3.52	0				Nov-12
3.07	7.31	9.58	16.88	23.81	2	0.85	3.43	5.99	18.48	872.3	2	24	3	49	0		3.22	2,000	100			Jan-93
3.31	8.53	11.06	20.02	28.46	2.38	0.25	3.47	6.28	17.61	328.0	2	25	2	47	0	29	3.20	1,000,000	100			Aug-00
3.27	8.51	10.82	18.92	26.65	2.21	0.4	3.48	6.28	17.73	328.0	2	25	2	47	0	29	3.20	500,000	100			May-18
3.19	6.00	8.13	15.73	22.58	2.4	0.25	2.42	4.29	16.75	160.7	3	37	3	45	0	33	3.09	1,000,000	100			Aug-00
3.18	5.90	7.94	14.81	21.00	2.21	0.4	2.42	4.29	16.89	160.7	3	37	3	45	0	33	3.09	500,000	100			May-18
2.49	3.10	4.51	8.89	11.52	2.02	0.4	1.38	2.12	15.55	171.1	5	18	6	52	0	48	3.04	500,000	100			May-18
2.55	3.17	4.73	9.73	12.94	2.21	0.25	1.39	2.12	15.44	171.1	5	18	6	52	0	48	3.04	1,000,000	100			Aug-00
2.25	3.02	4.62	10.73	16.04	1.79	0.66	3.24	5.58	18.1	237.8	3	0	97	1	0	11	4.36	2,000	100			May-94
0.01	0.32	1.17	4.37	4.72	1.35	0.26	0.17		1	139,126	71	29	0	0	0			5,000,000				Jun-96
0.03	0.35	1.25	4.62	5.09	1.43	0.18	0.17		1	139,126	71	29	0	0	0			50,000,000				Feb-05
0.04	0.34	1.02	3.54	3.61		0.15			1	139,126	71	29	0	0	0			50,000,000				Jan-20
0.03	0.33	1.22	4.53	4.95	1.4	0.21	0.17		1	139,126	71	29	0	0	0			10,000,000				Sep-01
0.00	0.21	0.90	3.41	3.48	1.05	0.59	0.16		1	139,126	71	29	0	0	0			1,000	50			Nov-91
0.00	0.25	1.01	3.81	3.95	1.17	0.45	0.17		1	139,126	71	29	0	0	0			1,000,000				Jun-96
0.00	0.19	0.83	3.10	3.13	0.96	0.7	0.16		1	139,126	71	29	0	0	0			10,000,000				Feb-05
0.05	0.34	0.87	2.46	2.65	0.96	0.26			1	724.3	34	0	66	0	0	1		5,000,000				Mar-19
0.00	0.00	0.00	0.03	0.07	0	1	0.01			1,413	15	0	85	0	0	1		0				Jan-06
0.06	0.37	0.92	2.52	2.71	1.01	0.21			1	724.3	34	0	66	0	0	1		10,000,000				Mar-19
0.02	0.23	0.59	2.10	2.28	0.66	0.59	0.1		1	724.3	34	0	66	0	0	1		1,000	50			Mar-92
0.03	0.27	0.70	2.50	2.81	0.78	0.45	0.1		1	724.3	34	0	66	0	0	1		1,000,000				Mar-16
0.00	0.11	0.24	0.91	0.97	0.28	1.05	0.08		1	724.3	34	0	66	0	0	1		10,000,000				Jul-09
2.74	2.16	3.87	9.93	15.24	1.95	0.6	3.5	5.00	11.14	369.9	5	0	95	0	0	8	4.98	1,000	50	3.75		Sep-01
2.54	1.83	3.29	8.27	12.29	1.46	1.1	3.47	5.00	11.04	369.9	5	0	95	0	0	8	4.98	1,000	50		1.00	Feb-05
2.66	2.22	3.98	10.30	15.89	2.19	0.4	3.48	5.00	10.88	369.9	5	0	95	0	0	8	4.98	15,000,000				Oct-18
3.41	5.74	8.01	15.45	21.58	2.32	0.75	3.55	5.91	12.37	33,035	5	28	0	24	0	29	3.53	1,000	50	3.75		May-92
3.23	5.47	7.30	13.43	17.95	1.71	1.35	3.5	5.91	12.46	33,035	5	28	0	24	0	29	3.53	1,000	50		1.00	Mar-99
3.39	5.87	8.29	16.34	23.02	2.57	0.5	3.51	5.91	12.36	33,035	5	28	0	24	0	29	3.53	1,000,000				May-91

	MARKET		FUND TYPE, CATEGORY & OBJECTIVE		RATINGS				NEW INVESTORS	
Fund Name	Ticker Symbol	Traded On	Fund Type	Category and (Prospectus Objective)	Overall Rating	Reward Rating	Risk Rating	Recent Up/ Downgrade	Open to New Investors	Telephone
JPMorgan Core Bond Fund Class R2	**JCBZX**	NAS CM	Open End	US Fixed Inc (Growth & Income)	**B-**	C+	B	Up	Y	800-480-4111
JPMorgan Core Bond Fund Class R3	**JCBPX**	NAS CM	Open End	US Fixed Inc (Growth & Income)	**B**	C+	B+	Up	Y	800-480-4111
JPMorgan Core Bond Fund Class R4	**JCBQX**	NAS CM	Open End	US Fixed Inc (Growth & Income)	**B**	C+	B+	Up	Y	800-480-4111
JPMorgan Core Bond Fund Class R5	**JCBRX**	NAS CM	Open End	US Fixed Inc (Growth & Income)	**B**	C+	B+	Up	Y	800-480-4111
JPMorgan Core Bond Fund Class R6	**JCBUX**	NAS CM	Open End	US Fixed Inc (Growth & Income)	**B**	C+	B+	Up	Y	800-480-4111
JPMorgan Core Focus SMA Fund SMA	**JCKUX**	NAS CM	Open End	US Fixed Inc (Corp Bond - General)	**C**	C	B-	Up	Y	800-480-4111
JPMorgan Core Plus Bond Fund Class A	**ONIAX**	NAS CM	Open End	US Fixed Inc (Income)	**B-**	C	B+	Up	Y	800-480-4111
JPMorgan Core Plus Bond Fund Class C	**OBDCX**	NAS CM	Open End	US Fixed Inc (Income)	**C+**	C	B	Up	Y	800-480-4111
JPMorgan Core Plus Bond Fund Class I	**HLIPX**	NAS CM	Open End	US Fixed Inc (Income)	**B-**	C	B+	Up	Y	800-480-4111
JPMorgan Core Plus Bond Fund Class R2	**JCPZX**	NAS CM	Open End	US Fixed Inc (Income)	**B-**	C	B	Up	Y	800-480-4111
JPMorgan Core Plus Bond Fund Class R3	**JCPPX**	NAS CM	Open End	US Fixed Inc (Income)	**B-**	C	B	Up	Y	800-480-4111
JPMorgan Core Plus Bond Fund Class R4	**JCPQX**	NAS CM	Open End	US Fixed Inc (Income)	**B-**	C	B+	Up	Y	800-480-4111
JPMorgan Core Plus Bond Fund Class R5	**JCPYX**	NAS CM	Open End	US Fixed Inc (Income)	**B-**	C	B+	Up	Y	800-480-4111
JPMorgan Core Plus Bond Fund Class R6	**JCPUX**	NAS CM	Open End	US Fixed Inc (Income)	**B-**	C	B+	Up	Y	800-480-4111
JPMorgan Corporate Bond Fund Class A	**CBRAX**	NAS CM	Open End	US Fixed Inc (Corp Bond - General)	**B-**	C	B	Up	Y	800-480-4111
JPMorgan Corporate Bond Fund Class C	**CBRCX**	NAS CM	Open End	US Fixed Inc (Corp Bond - General)	**B-**	C	B	Up	Y	800-480-4111
JPMorgan Corporate Bond Fund Class I	**CBFSX**	NAS CM	Open End	US Fixed Inc (Corp Bond - General)	**B-**	C	B	Up	Y	800-480-4111
JPMorgan Corporate Bond Fund Class R6	**CBFVX**	NAS CM	Open End	US Fixed Inc (Corp Bond - General)	**B-**	C	B	Up	Y	800-480-4111
JPMorgan Emerging Markets Debt Fund Class A	**JEDAX**	NAS CM	Open End	Emerg Mkts Fixed Inc (Diversified Emerg Mkts)	**D**	D	D+	Down	Y	800-480-4111
JPMorgan Emerging Markets Debt Fund Class C	**JEDCX**	NAS CM	Open End	Emerg Mkts Fixed Inc (Diversified Emerg Mkts)	**D**	D	D+	Down	Y	800-480-4111
JPMorgan Emerging Markets Debt Fund Class I	**JEMDX**	NAS CM	Open End	Emerg Mkts Fixed Inc (Diversified Emerg Mkts)	**D**	D	D+	Down	Y	800-480-4111
JPMorgan Emerging Markets Debt Fund Class R5	**JEMRX**	NAS CM	Open End	Emerg Mkts Fixed Inc (Diversified Emerg Mkts)	**D**	D	C-	Down	Y	800-480-4111
JPMorgan Emerging Markets Debt Fund Class R6	**JEMVX**	NAS CM	Open End	Emerg Mkts Fixed Inc (Diversified Emerg Mkts)	**D**	D	C-	Down	Y	800-480-4111
JPMorgan Emerging Markets Strategic Debt Fund Class A	**JECAX**	NAS CM	Open End	Emerg Mkts Fixed Inc (Diversified Emerg Mkts)	**D**	D	C-	Down	Y	800-480-4111
JPMorgan Emerging Markets Strategic Debt Fund Class C	**JECCX**	NAS CM	Open End	Emerg Mkts Fixed Inc (Diversified Emerg Mkts)	**D**	D	D+	Down	Y	800-480-4111
JPMorgan Emerging Markets Strategic Debt Fund Class I	**JECSX**	NAS CM	Open End	Emerg Mkts Fixed Inc (Diversified Emerg Mkts)	**D**	D	C-	Down	Y	800-480-4111
JPMorgan Emerging Markets Strategic Debt Fund Class R2	**JECZX**	NAS CM	Open End	Emerg Mkts Fixed Inc (Diversified Emerg Mkts)	**D**	D	C-	Down	Y	800-480-4111
JPMorgan Emerging Markets Strategic Debt Fund Class R5	**JECRX**	NAS CM	Open End	Emerg Mkts Fixed Inc (Diversified Emerg Mkts)	**D**	D	C-	Down	Y	800-480-4111
JPMorgan Emerging Markets Strategic Debt Fund Class R6	**JECUX**	NAS CM	Open End	Emerg Mkts Fixed Inc (Diversified Emerg Mkts)	**D**	D	C-	Down	Y	800-480-4111
JPMorgan Federal Money Market Fund Agency Class	**VFIXX**	NAS CM	Money Mkt	US Money Mkt (Money Mkt - Treasury)	**C**	C-	C+		Y	800-480-4111
JPMorgan Federal Money Market Fund Institutional Class	**JFMXX**	NAS CM	Money Mkt	US Money Mkt (Money Mkt - Treasury)	**C**	C-	C+		Y	800-480-4111
JPMorgan Federal Money Market Fund Morgan Class	**VFVXX**	NAS CM	Money Mkt	US Money Mkt (Money Mkt - Treasury)	**C**	C-	C+		Y	800-480-4111
JPMorgan Federal Money Market Fund Premier Class	**VFPXX**	NAS CM	Money Mkt	US Money Mkt (Money Mkt - Treasury)	**C**	C-	C+		Y	800-480-4111
JPMorgan Floating Rate Income Fund Class A	**JPHAX**	NAS CM	Open End	US Fixed Inc (Income)	**D**	D	C-	Down	Y	800-480-4111
JPMorgan Floating Rate Income Fund Class C	**JPHCX**	NAS CM	Open End	US Fixed Inc (Income)	**D**	D	C-	Down	Y	800-480-4111
JPMorgan Floating Rate Income Fund Class I	**JPHSX**	NAS CM	Open End	US Fixed Inc (Income)	**D+**	D	C-	Down	Y	800-480-4111
JPMorgan Floating Rate Income Fund Class R6	**JPHRX**	NAS CM	Open End	US Fixed Inc (Income)	**D+**	D	C-	Down	Y	800-480-4111
JPMorgan Global Bond Opportunities Fund Class A	**GBOAX**	NAS CM	Open End	US Fixed Inc (Worldwide Bond)	**C**	C-	C+		Y	800-480-4111
JPMorgan Global Bond Opportunities Fund Class C	**GBOCX**	NAS CM	Open End	US Fixed Inc (Worldwide Bond)	**C**	C-	C+		Y	800-480-4111
JPMorgan Global Bond Opportunities Fund Class I	**GBOSX**	NAS CM	Open End	US Fixed Inc (Worldwide Bond)	**C**	C-	B-		Y	800-480-4111
JPMorgan Global Bond Opportunities Fund Class R6	**GBONX**	NAS CM	Open End	US Fixed Inc (Worldwide Bond)	**C**	C-	B-		Y	800-480-4111
JPMorgan Government Bond Fund Class A	**OGGAX**	NAS CM	Open End	US Fixed Inc (Govt Bond - General)	**B**	B-	B	Up	Y	800-480-4111
JPMorgan Government Bond Fund Class C	**OGVCX**	NAS CM	Open End	US Fixed Inc (Govt Bond - General)	**B-**	B-	B		Y	800-480-4111
JPMorgan Government Bond Fund Class I	**HLGAX**	NAS CM	Open End	US Fixed Inc (Govt Bond - General)	**B**	B-	B		Y	800-480-4111
JPMorgan Government Bond Fund Class R2	**JGBZX**	NAS CM	Open End	US Fixed Inc (Govt Bond - General)	**B-**	B-	B		Y	800-480-4111
JPMorgan Government Bond Fund Class R3	**OGGPX**	NAS CM	Open End	US Fixed Inc (Govt Bond - General)	**B**	B-	B	Up	Y	800-480-4111
JPMorgan Government Bond Fund Class R4	**OGGQX**	NAS CM	Open End	US Fixed Inc (Govt Bond - General)	**B**	B-	B		Y	800-480-4111
JPMorgan Government Bond Fund Class R6	**OGGYX**	NAS CM	Open End	US Fixed Inc (Govt Bond - General)	**B**	B-	B+		Y	800-480-4111
JPMorgan High Yield Fund Class A	**OHYAX**	NAS CM	Open End	US Fixed Inc (Corp Bond - High Yield)	**D+**	D	C-	Down	Y	800-480-4111
JPMorgan High Yield Fund Class C	**OGHCX**	NAS CM	Open End	US Fixed Inc (Corp Bond - High Yield)	**D+**	D	C-	Down	Y	800-480-4111
JPMorgan High Yield Fund Class I	**OHYFX**	NAS CM	Open End	US Fixed Inc (Corp Bond - High Yield)	**D+**	D+	C-	Down	Y	800-480-4111
JPMorgan High Yield Fund Class R2	**JHYZX**	NAS CM	Open End	US Fixed Inc (Corp Bond - High Yield)	**D+**	D	C-	Down	Y	800-480-4111

★ Expanded analysis of this fund is included in Section II.

TOTAL RETURNS & PERFORMANCE									ASSETS		ASSET ALLOCATION & TURNOVER							MINIMUMS		FEES		
3-Month Total Return	6-Month Total Return	1-Year Total Return	3-Year Total Return	5-Year Total Return	Dividend Yield (TTM)	Expense Ratio	3-Yr Std Deviation	Effective Duration	NAV	Total Assets (MIL)	%Cash	%Government Bonds	%Municipal Bonds	%Corporate Bonds	%Other	Turnover Ratio	Average Coupon Rate	Min Initial Investment	Min Additional Investment	Front End Fee (%)	Back End Fee (%)	Inception Date
3.24	5.56	7.55	14.27	19.76	1.98	1.1	3.5	5.91	12.35	33,035	5	28	0	24	0	29	3.53	0				Nov-08
3.32	5.62	7.85	15.10	20.89	2.24	0.85	3.53	5.91	12.33	33,035	5	28	0	24	0	29	3.53	0				Sep-16
3.38	5.79	8.15	15.98	22.44	2.44	0.6	3.48	5.91	12.35	33,035	5	28	0	24	0	29	3.53	0				Sep-16
3.49	5.91	8.36	16.53	23.50	2.62	0.45	3.48	5.91	12.35	33,035	5	28	0	24	0	29	3.53	0				May-06
3.51	5.94	8.44	16.94	24.16	2.72	0.35	3.48	5.91	12.38	33,035	5	28	0	24	0	29	3.53	15,000,000				Feb-05
4.35	3.54	5.66			3.33	0			10.56	28.2	14	3	0	22	0	25	3.87	0				Mar-18
3.85	4.52	6.57	14.45	21.77	2.78	0.75	3.62	5.80	8.71	14,071	9	19	0	24	0	36	3.88	1,000	50	3.75		Mar-93
3.66	4.28	5.96	12.39	17.96	2.12	1.4	3.61	5.80	8.77	14,071	9	19	0	24	0	36	3.88	1,000	50		1.00	May-00
3.92	4.68	6.88	15.45	23.54	3.07	0.46	3.61	5.80	8.71	14,071	9	19	0	24	0	36	3.88	1,000,000				Mar-93
3.75	4.32	6.14	13.21	19.47	2.38	1.15	3.61	5.80	8.71	14,071	9	19	0	24	0	36	3.88	0				Nov-08
3.82	4.45	6.42	13.96	21.08	2.63	0.9	3.61	5.80	8.7	14,071	9	19	0	24	0	36	3.88	0				Sep-16
3.88	4.58	6.56	14.82	22.54	2.88	0.65	3.6	5.80	8.7	14,071	9	19	0	24	0	36	3.88	0				Sep-16
3.92	4.66	6.84	15.33	23.37	3.03	0.5	3.6	5.80	8.71	14,071	9	19	0	24	0	36	3.88	0				Sep-16
3.94	4.70	6.94	15.79	24.04	3.13	0.4	3.61	5.80	8.72	14,071	9	19	0	24	0	36	3.88	15,000,000				Feb-05
8.54	4.79	8.91	20.44	33.02	2.28	0.75	6.32	7.99	10.66	2,630	4	0	0	96	0	86	3.62	1,000	50	3.75		Mar-13
8.42	4.64	8.50	18.72	29.79	1.79	1.25	6.29	7.99	10.65	2,630	4	0	0	96	0	86	3.62	1,000	50		1.00	Mar-13
8.59	4.91	9.28	21.33	34.81	2.51	0.5	6.28	7.99	10.68	2,630	4	0	0	96	0	86	3.62	1,000,000				Mar-13
8.72	5.06	9.38	21.80	35.61	2.6	0.4	6.3	7.99	10.69	2,630	4	0	0	96	0	86	3.62	15,000,000				Mar-13
14.65	-5.15	-3.14	5.30	19.26	4.99	1.1	12.15	7.18	7.6	545.1	8	72	0	20	0	106	5.97	1,000	50	3.75		Jun-06
14.55	-5.26	-3.60	3.82	16.30	4.5	1.6	12.14	7.18	7.57	545.1	8	72	0	20	0	106	5.97	1,000	50		1.00	Jun-06
14.85	-5.00	-2.87	6.10	20.74	5.27	0.85	12.18	7.18	7.61	545.1	8	72	0	20	0	106	5.97	1,000,000				Apr-97
14.86	-4.89	-2.82	6.56	21.76	5.38	0.8	12.18	7.18	7.69	545.1	8	72	0	20	0	106	5.97	0				May-06
14.70	-4.88	-2.75	6.75	22.09	5.53	0.7	12.17	7.18	7.62	545.1	8	72	0	20	0	106	5.97	15,000,000				Jul-12
11.80	-4.94	-2.80	3.86	7.48	5.13	1.2	10.85	8.10	7.51	260.8	10	75	0	15	0	164	5.67	1,000	50	3.75		Jun-12
11.64	-5.28	-3.32	2.17	4.81	4.74	1.7	10.84	8.10	7.34	260.8	10	75	0	15	0	164	5.67	1,000	50		1.00	Jun-12
11.78	-4.78	-2.56	4.50	8.80	5.32	0.95	10.8	8.10	7.56	260.8	10	75	0	15	0	164	5.67	1,000,000				Jun-12
11.73	-4.99	-3.06	3.11	6.27	4.94	1.45	10.84	8.10	7.42	260.8	10	75	0	15	0	164	5.67	0				Jun-12
11.72	-4.80	-2.49	4.99	9.81	5.49	0.8	10.81	8.10	7.62	260.8	10	75	0	15	0	164	5.67	0				Jun-12
11.87	-4.74	-2.38	5.38	10.25	5.58	0.7	10.82	8.10	7.64	260.8	10	75	0	15	0	164	5.67	15,000,000				Jun-12
0.02	0.32	1.19	4.41	4.83	1.37	0.26	0.17		1	3,874	61	39	0	0	0			5,000,000				Apr-94
0.03	0.35	1.25	4.56	5.06	1.42	0.21	0.17		1	3,874	61	39	0	0	0			10,000,000				Sep-01
0.00	0.22	0.92	3.44	3.55	1.08	0.59	0.16		1	3,874	61	39	0	0	0			1,000	50			May-94
0.01	0.26	1.04	3.85	4.03	1.2	0.45	0.17		1	3,874	61	39	0	0	0			1,000,000				Apr-94
9.22	-5.14	-3.34	2.29	6.79	4.9	1	8.4	0.73	8.44	757.6	5	0	0	95	0	46	4.98	1,000	50	2.25		Jun-11
8.85	-5.51	-3.95	0.66	4.04	4.38	1.5	8.35	0.73	8.4	757.6	5	0	0	95	0	46	4.98	1,000	50		1.00	Jun-11
9.16	-5.13	-3.21	2.95	8.02	5.16	0.75	8.39	0.73	8.43	757.6	5	0	0	95	0	46	4.98	1,000,000				Jun-11
9.18	-5.09	-3.11	3.26	8.56	5.27	0.65	8.4	0.73	8.43	757.6	5	0	0	95	0	46	4.98	15,000,000				Oct-13
6.91	0.61	2.83	11.34	22.28	4.43	0.9	4.99	5.91	10.04	2,573	5	24	0	49	0	72	4.15	1,000	50	3.75		Sep-12
6.75	0.44	2.46	9.98	19.92	4.03	1.3	4.98	5.91	10	2,573	5	24	0	49	0	72	4.15	1,000	50		1.00	Sep-12
6.94	0.71	3.06	12.12	23.75	4.67	0.65	5.04	5.91	10.06	2,573	5	24	0	49	0	72	4.15	1,000,000				Sep-12
7.07	0.77	3.31	12.61	24.74	4.83	0.5	5.01	5.91	10.07	2,573	5	24	0	49	0	72	4.15	15,000,000				Sep-12
0.87	6.49	8.08	14.37	18.41	1.8	0.75	3.37	5.25	11.35	3,245	9	32	0	0	0	12	3.02	1,000	50	3.75		Mar-93
0.65	6.11	7.38	12.26	14.68	1.24	1.4	3.36	5.25	11.31	3,245	9	32	0	0	0	12	3.02	1,000	50		1.00	Mar-99
0.85	6.64	8.38	15.32	19.96	2.06	0.48	3.37	5.25	11.34	3,245	9	32	0	0	0	12	3.02	1,000,000				Feb-93
0.79	6.31	7.72	13.20	16.61	1.46	1.1	3.33	5.25	11.34	3,245	9	32	0	0	0	12	3.02	0				Nov-08
0.77	6.44	7.99	14.07	17.97	1.71	0.85	3.36	5.25	11.34	3,245	9	32	0	0	0	12	3.02	0				Sep-16
0.83	6.58	8.26	14.93	19.40	1.95	0.6	3.35	5.25	11.34	3,245	9	32	0	0	0	12	3.02	0				Sep-16
0.89	6.70	8.53	15.77	20.66	2.19	0.35	3.35	5.25	11.34	3,245	9	32	0	0	0	12	3.02	15,000,000				Aug-16
7.85	-6.71	-3.74	4.69	14.89	5.84	1	8.93	3.99	6.57	7,624	2	0	0	98	0	60	6.23	1,000	50	3.75		Nov-98
7.53	-7.07	-4.36	2.95	11.88	5.29	1.5	8.92	3.99	6.58	7,624	2	0	0	98	0	60	6.23	1,000	50		1.00	Mar-99
7.86	-6.68	-3.48	5.44	16.21	6.07	0.75	8.95	3.99	6.61	7,624	2	0	0	98	0	60	6.23	1,000,000				Nov-98
7.60	-6.88	-4.09	3.60	13.03	5.47	1.35	8.86	3.99	6.56	7,624	2	0	0	98	0	60	6.23	0				Nov-08

	MARKET		FUND TYPE, CATEGORY & OBJECTIVE		RATINGS				NEW INVESTORS	
Fund Name	Ticker Symbol	Traded On	Fund Type	Category and (Prospectus Objective)	Overall Rating	Reward Rating	Risk Rating	Recent Up/ Downgrade	Open to New Investors	Telephone
JPMorgan High Yield Fund Class R3	JRJYX	NAS CM	Open End	US Fixed Inc (Corp Bond - High Yield)	D+	D	C-	Down	Y	800-480-4111
JPMorgan High Yield Fund Class R4	JRJKX	NAS CM	Open End	US Fixed Inc (Corp Bond - High Yield)	D+	D	C-	Down	Y	800-480-4111
JPMorgan High Yield Fund Class R5	JYHRX	NAS CM	Open End	US Fixed Inc (Corp Bond - High Yield)	D+	D+	C-	Down	Y	800-480-4111
JPMorgan High Yield Fund Class R6	JHYUX	NAS CM	Open End	US Fixed Inc (Corp Bond - High Yield)	D+	D+	C-	Down	Y	800-480-4111
JPMorgan High Yield Municipal Fund Class A Shares	JTIAX	NAS CM	Open End	US Muni Fixed Inc (Muni Bond - Natl)	C-	D+	C	Down	Y	800-480-4111
JPMorgan High Yield Municipal Fund Class C Shares	JTICX	NAS CM	Open End	US Muni Fixed Inc (Muni Bond - Natl)	D+	D+	C	Down	Y	800-480-4111
JPMorgan High Yield Municipal Fund Class I Shares	JTISX	NAS CM	Open End	US Muni Fixed Inc (Muni Bond - Natl)	C-	D+	C	Down	Y	800-480-4111
JPMorgan High Yield Municipal Fund Class R6 Shares	JTIRX	NAS CM	Open End	US Muni Fixed Inc (Muni Bond - Natl)	C-	D+	C	Down	Y	800-480-4111
JPMorgan Income Fund Class A	JGIAX	NAS CM	Open End	US Fixed Inc (Income)	C-	D+	C	Down	Y	800-480-4111
JPMorgan Income Fund Class C	JGCGX	NAS CM	Open End	US Fixed Inc (Income)	C-	D+	C	Down	Y	800-480-4111
JPMorgan Income Fund Class I	JMSIX	NAS CM	Open End	US Fixed Inc (Income)	C-	D+	C	Down	Y	800-480-4111
JPMorgan Income Fund Class R6	JMSFX	NAS CM	Open End	US Fixed Inc (Income)	C-	D+	C	Down	Y	800-480-4111
JPMorgan Inflation Managed Bond Fund Class A Shares	JIMAX	NAS CM	Open End	US Fixed Inc (Growth & Income)	C	C	B-		Y	800-480-4111
JPMorgan Inflation Managed Bond Fund Class C Shares	JIMCX	NAS CM	Open End	US Fixed Inc (Growth & Income)	C	C-	C+		Y	800-480-4111
JPMorgan Inflation Managed Bond Fund Class I Shares	JRBSX	NAS CM	Open End	US Fixed Inc (Growth & Income)	C	C	B-		Y	800-480-4111
JPMorgan Inflation Managed Bond Fund Class R5 Shares	JIMRX	NAS CM	Open End	US Fixed Inc (Growth & Income)	C	C	B-		Y	800-480-4111
JPMorgan Inflation Managed Bond Fund Class R6 Shares	JIMMX	NAS CM	Open End	US Fixed Inc (Growth & Income)	C	C	B-		Y	800-480-4111
JPMorgan Institutional Tax Free Money Market Fund Agency	JOAXX	NAS CM	Money Mkt	US Money Mkt (Money Mkt - Fed Tax Exmpt)	C	C-	C+	Up	Y	800-480-4111
JPMorgan Institutional Tax Free Money Market Fund Capital	JOCXX	NAS CM	Money Mkt	US Money Mkt (Money Mkt - Fed Tax Exmpt)	C	C-	C+	Up	Y	800-480-4111
JPMorgan Institutional Tax Free Money Market Fund IM	JOIXX	NAS CM	Money Mkt	US Money Mkt (Money Mkt - Fed Tax Exmpt)	C	C-	C+	Up	Y	800-480-4111
JPMorgan Institutional Tax Free Money Mkt Institutional Cl	JOFXX	NAS CM	Money Mkt	US Money Mkt (Money Mkt - Fed Tax Exmpt)	C	C-	C+	Up	Y	800-480-4111
JPMorgan Insurance Trust Core Bond Portfolio Class 1			Open End	US Fixed Inc (Multisector Bond)	B-	C+	B+		Y	800-480-4111
JPMorgan Insurance Trust Core Bond Portfolio Class 2			Open End	US Fixed Inc (Multisector Bond)	B-	C+	B+	Up	Y	800-480-4111
JPMorgan Intermediate Tax Free Bond Fund Class A	JITAX	NAS CM	Open End	US Muni Fixed Inc (Muni Bond - Natl)	C	C	B-		Y	800-480-4111
JPMorgan Intermediate Tax Free Bond Fund Class C	JITCX	NAS CM	Open End	US Muni Fixed Inc (Muni Bond - Natl)	C	C	B-		Y	800-480-4111
JPMorgan Intermediate Tax Free Bond Fund Class R6	JITZX	NAS CM	Open End	US Muni Fixed Inc (Muni Bond - Natl)	C	C	B		Y	800-480-4111
JPMorgan Limited Duration Bond Fund Class A	ONUAX	NAS CM	Open End	US Fixed Inc (Govt Bond - General)	C	C-	C+		Y	800-480-4111
JPMorgan Limited Duration Bond Fund Class C	OGUCX	NAS CM	Open End	US Fixed Inc (Govt Bond - General)	C	C-	C+		Y	800-480-4111
JPMorgan Limited Duration Bond Fund Class I	HLGFX	NAS CM	Open End	US Fixed Inc (Govt Bond - General)	C	C-	C+		Y	800-480-4111
JPMorgan Limited Duration Bond Fund Class R6	JUSUX	NAS CM	Open End	US Fixed Inc (Govt Bond - General)	C	C-	C+		Y	800-480-4111
JPMorgan Liquid Assets Money Market Fund Agency Class	AJLXX	NAS CM	Money Mkt	US Money Mkt (Money Mkt - Taxable)	C	C-	C+		Y	800-480-4111
JPMorgan Liquid Assets Money Market Fund Capital Class	CJLXX	NAS CM	Money Mkt	US Money Mkt (Money Mkt - Taxable)	C	C-	C+		Y	800-480-4111
JPMorgan Liquid Assets Money Market Fund Class C	OPCXX	NAS CM	Money Mkt	US Money Mkt (Money Mkt - Taxable)	C	C-	C		Y	800-480-4111
JPMorgan Liquid Assets Money Market Fund E*Trade Class	JLEXX	NAS CM	Money Mkt	US Money Mkt (Money Mkt - Taxable)	U	U	U		Y	800-480-4111
JPMorgan Liquid Assets Money Mkt Fund Institutional Class	IJLXX	NAS CM	Money Mkt	US Money Mkt (Money Mkt - Taxable)	C	C	B-		Y	800-480-4111
JPMorgan Liquid Assets Money Market Fund Investor Class	HLPXX	NAS CM	Money Mkt	US Money Mkt (Money Mkt - Taxable)	C	C-	C+		Y	800-480-4111
JPMorgan Liquid Assets Money Market Fund Morgan Class	MJLXX	NAS CM	Money Mkt	US Money Mkt (Money Mkt - Taxable)	C	C-	C+		Y	800-480-4111
JPMorgan Liquid Assets Money Market Fund Premier Class	PJLXX	NAS CM	Money Mkt	US Money Mkt (Money Mkt - Taxable)	C	C-	C+		Y	800-480-4111
JPMorgan Liquid Assets Money Market Fund Reserve Class	HPIXX	NAS CM	Money Mkt	US Money Mkt (Money Mkt - Taxable)	C	C-	C+		Y	800-480-4111
JPMorgan Managed Income Fund Class I	JMGLX	NAS CM	Open End	US Fixed Inc (Income)	C	C-	C+		Y	800-480-4111
JPMorgan Managed Income Fund L Class Shares	JMGIX	NAS CM	Open End	US Fixed Inc (Income)	C	C-	B-		Y	800-480-4111
JPMorgan Mortgage Backed Securities Fund Class C	OBBCX	NAS CM	Open End	US Fixed Inc (Govt Bond - Mortgage)	C+	C	B		Y	800-480-4111
JPMorgan Mortgage-Backed Securities Fund Class A	OMBAX	NAS CM	Open End	US Fixed Inc (Govt Bond - Mortgage)	B-	C	B	Up	Y	800-480-4111
JPMorgan Mortgage-Backed Securities Fund Class I	OMBIX	NAS CM	Open End	US Fixed Inc (Govt Bond - Mortgage)	B-	C	B+	Up	Y	800-480-4111
JPMorgan Mortgage-Backed Securities Fund Class R6	JMBUX	NAS CM	Open End	US Fixed Inc (Govt Bond - Mortgage)	B-	C	B+	Up	Y	800-480-4111
JPMorgan Municipal Income Fund Class A	OTBAX	NAS CM	Open End	US Muni Fixed Inc (Muni Bond - Natl)	C	C	B-		Y	800-480-4111
JPMorgan Municipal Income Fund Class C	OMICX	NAS CM	Open End	US Muni Fixed Inc (Muni Bond - Natl)	C	C	B-		Y	800-480-4111
JPMorgan Municipal Income Fund Class I	HLTAX	NAS CM	Open End	US Muni Fixed Inc (Muni Bond - Natl)	C+	C	B-	Up	Y	800-480-4111
JPMorgan Municipal Income Fund Class R6	HLTZX	NAS CM	Open End	US Muni Fixed Inc (Muni Bond - Natl)	C+	C	B	Up	Y	800-480-4111
JPMorgan Municipal Money Market Fund Agency Class	JMAXX	NAS CM	Money Mkt	US Money Mkt (Money Mkt - General)	C	C-	C		Y	800-480-4111
JPMorgan Municipal Money Market Fund E*Trade Class	JMEXX	NAS CM	Money Mkt	US Money Mkt (Money Mkt - General)	U	U	U		Y	800-480-4111
JPMorgan Municipal Money Market Fund Institutional Class	IJMXX	NAS CM	Money Mkt	US Money Mkt (Money Mkt - General)	C	C-	C+		Y	800-480-4111

★Expanded analysis of this fund is included in Section II.

TOTAL RETURNS & PERFORMANCE									ASSETS		ASSET ALLOCATION & TURNOVER							MINIMUMS		FEES		
3-Month Total Return	6-Month Total Return	1-Year Total Return	3-Year Total Return	5-Year Total Return	Dividend Yield (TTM)	Expense Ratio	3-Yr Std Deviation	Effective Duration	NAV	Total Assets (MIL)	%Cash	%Government Bonds	%Municipal Bonds	%Corporate Bonds	%Other	Turnover Ratio	Average Coupon Rate	Min Initial Investment	Min Additional Investment	Front End Fee (%)	Back End Fee (%)	Inception Date
7.77	-6.84	-3.94	4.36	14.45	5.7	1.1	8.97	3.99	6.61	7,624	2	0	0	98	0	60	6.23	0				Aug-17
7.84	-6.73	-3.58	5.15	15.89	5.96	0.85	8.99	3.99	6.61	7,624	2	0	0	98	0	60	6.23	0				Aug-17
7.69	-6.65	-3.56	5.59	16.45	6.11	0.7	8.88	3.99	6.62	7,624	2	0	0	98	0	60	6.23	0				May-06
7.90	-6.61	-3.33	5.92	16.97	6.23	0.6	8.97	3.99	6.61	7,624	2	0	0	98	0	60	6.23	15,000,000				Feb-05
2.89	-3.78	-0.77	9.19	15.74	2.99	0.65	7.56	8.67	10.92	444.2	2	0	98	0	0		4.67	1,000	50	3.75		Sep-07
2.77	-4.02	-1.26	7.59	12.92	2.47	1.15	7.51	8.67	10.9	444.2	2	0	98	0	0		4.67	1,000	50		1.00	Sep-07
2.92	-3.73	-0.67	9.52	16.33	3.09	0.55	7.56	8.67	10.92	444.2	2	0	98	0	0		4.67	1,000,000				Sep-07
2.94	-3.68	-0.57	9.60	16.42	3.2	0.45	7.56	8.67	10.92	444.2	2	0	98	0	0		4.67	15,000,000				Nov-18
8.81	-3.69	-0.64	10.82	20.94	5.14	0.65	8.14	4.45	9.06	5,716	10	3	0	33	0	77	4.79	1,000	50	3.75		Jun-14
8.65	-3.96	-1.18	9.01	17.81	4.55	1.2	8.13	4.45	9.06	5,716	10	3	0	33	0	77	4.79	1,000	50		1.00	Jun-14
8.76	-3.57	-0.38	11.58	22.55	5.42	0.4	8.13	4.45	9.05	5,716	10	3	0	33	0	77	4.79	1,000,000				Jun-14
8.90	-3.56	-0.26	11.62	22.79	5.43	0.4	8.15	4.45	9.05	5,716	10	3	0	33	0	77	4.79	15,000,000				Jun-14
5.41	1.51	3.60	8.16	11.56	1.96	0.75	3.82	3.60	10.41	1,233	3	22	0	32	0	146	2.73	1,000	50	3.75		Mar-10
5.23	1.25	2.90	6.06	8.10	1.31	1.4	3.81	3.60	10.35	1,233	3	22	0	32	0	146	2.73	1,000	50		1.00	Mar-10
5.47	1.62	3.70	8.57	12.38	2.15	0.55	3.85	3.60	10.4	1,233	3	22	0	32	0	146	2.73	1,000,000				Mar-10
5.47	1.66	3.88	8.86	12.77	2.22	0.45	3.86	3.60	10.45	1,233	3	22	0	32	0	146	2.73	0				Mar-10
5.51	1.72	3.99	9.17	13.28	2.33	0.35	3.87	3.60	10.42	1,233	3	22	0	32	0	146	2.73	15,000,000				Nov-10
0.07	0.43	0.99			1.03	0.26			1.0007	1,973	21	0	79	0	0			5,000,000				Mar-18
0.07	0.45	1.05			1.1	0.18			1.0007	1,973	21	0	79	0	0			50,000,000				Mar-18
0.07	0.45	1.07			1.12	0.16			1.0007	1,973	21	0	79	0	0			50,000,000				Mar-18
0.07	0.43	1.03			1.08	0.21			1.0007	1,973	21	0	79	0	0			10,000,000				Mar-18
3.45	5.57	7.97	15.63	21.85	2.03	0.58	3.55	5.97	11.63	460.2	9	28	0	19	0	20	3.56	0				May-97
3.42	5.56	7.70	14.78	20.41	1.89	0.83	3.57	5.97	11.49	460.2	9	28	0	19	0	20	3.56	0				Aug-06
2.64	1.95	3.77	9.76	14.61	2.05	0.65	3.67	5.26	11.34	6,026	6	0	94	0	0	20	4.78	1,000	50	3.75		Dec-03
2.49	1.63	3.21	7.94	11.43	1.55	1.2	3.63	5.26	11.05	6,026	6	0	94	0	0	20	4.78	1,000	50		1.00	Dec-03
2.79	2.17	4.22	11.03	16.62	2.44	0.3	3.69	5.26	11.13	6,026	6	0	94	0	0	20	4.78	15,000,000				Nov-17
3.54	1.43	2.43	7.35	9.31	2.01	0.7	2.28	1.64	10.14	1,232	11	0	0	8	0	27	2.45	1,000	50	2.25		Mar-93
3.35	1.10	1.85	5.71	6.59	1.54	1.2	2.3	1.64	10.02	1,232	11	0	0	8	0	27	2.45	1,000	50		1.00	Nov-01
3.60	1.56	2.69	8.15	10.68	2.26	0.45	2.29	1.64	10.14	1,232	11	0	0	8	0	27	2.45	1,000,000				Feb-93
3.54	1.56	2.89	8.68	11.80	2.46	0.25	2.28	1.64	10.15	1,232	11	0	0	8	0	27	2.45	15,000,000				Feb-05
0.12	0.49	1.48	5.24	6.12	1.64	0.26	0.16		1	11,942	94	3	0	2	0			5,000,000				Feb-05
0.14	0.53	1.55	5.48	6.54	1.72	0.18	0.16		1	11,942	94	3	0	2	0			50,000,000				Feb-05
0.00	0.19	0.82	3.08	3.20	0.95	0.97	0.15		1	11,942	94	3	0	2	0			1,000	50		1.00	May-00
0.00	0.00	0.00	0.01	0.12	0	1	0			1,049	100	0	0	1	0			0				Jan-09
0.14	0.52	1.53	5.40	6.37	1.69	0.21	0.16		1	11,942	94	3	0	2	0			10,000,000				Feb-05
0.06	0.36	1.23	4.45	4.93	1.39	0.51	0.16		1	11,942	94	3	0	2	0			1,000,000				Jan-87
0.04	0.33	1.15	4.21	4.59	1.31	0.59	0.16		1	11,942	94	3	0	2	0			1,000	50			Feb-05
0.08	0.40	1.29	4.64	5.19	1.45	0.45	0.16		1	11,942	94	3	0	2	0			1,000,000				Feb-05
0.03	0.28	1.04	3.87	4.17	1.2	0.7	0.16		1	11,942	94	3	0	2	0			10,000,000				Feb-92
1.76	0.91	2.08	6.44	8.45	2.04	0.4	1.07	0.97	10.04	11,754	28	1	0	64	0	82	2.32	1,000,000				Jul-17
1.80	0.99	2.13	6.91	8.92	2.19	0.25	1.08	0.97	10.05	11,754	28	1	0	64	0	82	2.32	3,000,000				Sep-10
2.65	3.41	4.87	11.24	15.58	2.27	1.15	2.57	2.91	11.55	2,998	4	0	0	1	0	23	3.94	1,000	50		1.00	Jul-12
2.78	3.63	5.40	12.89	18.40	2.67	0.65	2.57	2.91	11.9	2,998	4	0	0	1	0	23	3.94	1,000	50	3.75		Aug-00
2.92	3.78	5.73	13.74	19.94	3	0.4	2.6	2.91	11.58	2,998	4	0	0	1	0	23	3.94	1,000,000				Aug-00
2.87	3.76	5.80	14.15	20.77	3.15	0.25	2.64	2.91	11.57	2,998	4	0	0	1	0	23	3.94	15,000,000				Feb-05
2.19	1.83	3.47	9.23	15.26	1.91	0.7	3.22	4.78	9.91	283.0	5	0	95	0	0		4.59	1,000	50	3.75		Feb-93
2.08	1.56	2.93	7.41	12.23	1.38	1.25	3.18	4.78	9.81	283.0	5	0	95	0	0		4.59	1,000	50		1.00	Nov-97
2.27	1.86	3.75	10.01	16.71	2.18	0.45	3.2	4.78	9.83	283.0	5	0	95	0	0		4.59	1,000,000				Feb-93
2.30	1.92	3.86	10.30	17.01	2.28	0.35	3.22	4.78	9.83	283.0	5	0	95	0	0		4.59	15,000,000				Nov-17
0.07	0.42	0.97	3.30	3.86	1.09	0.26	0.12		1	1,377	22	0	78	0	0			5,000,000				Feb-05
0.00	0.00	0.00	0.02	0.05	0	1	0			3,869	7	0	91	0	1			0				Jan-06
0.10	0.45	1.04	3.46	4.09	1.14	0.21	0.12		1	1,377	22	0	78	0	0			10,000,000				Feb-05

	MARKET		FUND TYPE, CATEGORY & OBJECTIVE		RATINGS				NEW INVESTORS	
Fund Name	Ticker Symbol	Traded On	Fund Type	Category and (Prospectus Objective)	Overall Rating	Reward Rating	Risk Rating	Recent Up/ Downgrade	Open to New Investors	Telephone
JPMorgan Municipal Money Market Fund Morgan Class	MJMXX	NAS CM	Money Mkt	US Money Mkt (Money Mkt - General)	C	C-	C		Y	800-480-4111
JPMorgan Municipal Money Market Fund Premier Class	HTOXX	NAS CM	Money Mkt	US Money Mkt (Money Mkt - General)	C	C-	C		Y	800-480-4111
JPMorgan Municipal Money Market Fund Service Class	SJMXX	NAS CM	Money Mkt	US Money Mkt (Money Mkt - General)	C	C-	C		Y	800-480-4111
JPMorgan New York Municipal Money Market Fund Agency Share	JONXX	NAS CM	Money Mkt	US Money Mkt (Money Mkt - Single State)	C	C-	C		Y	800-480-4111
JPMorgan New York Muni Money Mkt Fund E*Trade Class	JNEXX	NAS CM	Money Mkt	US Money Mkt (Money Mkt - Single State)	U	U	U		Y	800-480-4111
JPMorgan New York Muni Money Mkt Fund Institutional Share	JGNXX	NAS CM	Money Mkt	US Money Mkt (Money Mkt - Single State)	C	C-	C		Y	800-480-4111
JPMorgan New York Municipal Money Market Fund Morgan Class	VNYXX	NAS CM	Money Mkt	US Money Mkt (Money Mkt - Single State)	C	C-	C		Y	800-480-4111
JPMorgan New York Muni Money Mkt Fund Premier Class	JNPXX	NAS CM	Money Mkt	US Money Mkt (Money Mkt - Single State)	C	C-	C+		Y	800-480-4111
JPMorgan New York Muni Money Mkt Fund Reserve Class	JNYXX	NAS CM	Money Mkt	US Money Mkt (Money Mkt - Single State)	C	C-	C		Y	800-480-4111
JPMorgan New York Muni Money Mkt Fund Service Class	JNVXX	NAS CM	Money Mkt	US Money Mkt (Money Mkt - Single State)	C	C-	C		Y	800-480-4111
JPMorgan New York Tax Free Bond Fund Class A	VANTX	NAS CM	Open End	US Muni Fixed Inc (Muni Bond - Single State)	C	C-	C+		Y	800-480-4111
JPMorgan New York Tax Free Bond Fund Class C	JCNTX	NAS CM	Open End	US Muni Fixed Inc (Muni Bond - Single State)	C	C-	C+		Y	800-480-4111
JPMorgan New York Tax Free Bond Fund Class R6	VINRX	NAS CM	Open End	US Muni Fixed Inc (Muni Bond - Single State)	C	C-	B-		Y	800-480-4111
JPMorgan Prime Money Market Fund Academy	JPAXX	NAS CM	Money Mkt	US Money Mkt (Money Mkt - Taxable)	C	C-	C+		Y	800-480-4111
JPMorgan Prime Money Market Fund Agency Class	VMIXX	NAS CM	Money Mkt	US Money Mkt (Money Mkt - Taxable)	C	C-	C+		Y	800-480-4111
JPMorgan Prime Money Market Fund Capital Class	CJPXX	NAS CM	Money Mkt	US Money Mkt (Money Mkt - Taxable)	C	C-	C+		Y	800-480-4111
★ JPMorgan Prime Money Market Fund Class C	JXCXX	NAS CM	Money Mkt	US Money Mkt (Money Mkt - Taxable)	C	C-	C+		Y	800-480-4111
JPMorgan Prime Money Market Fund Class IM	JIMXX	NAS CM	Money Mkt	US Money Mkt (Money Mkt - Taxable)	U	U	U		Y	800-480-4111
JPMorgan Prime Money Market Fund Institutional Class	JINXX	NAS CM	Money Mkt	US Money Mkt (Money Mkt - Taxable)	C	C-	C+		Y	800-480-4111
★ JPMorgan Prime Money Market Fund Morgan Class	VMVXX	NAS CM	Money Mkt	US Money Mkt (Money Mkt - Taxable)	C	C-	C+		Y	800-480-4111
JPMorgan Prime Money Market Fund Premier Class	VPMXX	NAS CM	Money Mkt	US Money Mkt (Money Mkt - Taxable)	C	C-	C+		Y	800-480-4111
JPMorgan Prime Money Market Reserves Fund Reserve Class	JRVXX	NAS CM	Money Mkt	US Money Mkt (Money Mkt - Taxable)	C	C	C+		Y	800-480-4111
JPMorgan Securities Lending Money Mkt Fund Agency SL Class	VSLXX	NAS CM	Money Mkt	US Money Mkt (Money Mkt - General)	D+	D+	B-	Up	Y	800-480-4111
JPMorgan Short Duration Bond Fund Class A	OGLVX	NAS CM	Open End	US Fixed Inc (Multisector Bond)	C+	C	B-	Up	Y	800-480-4111
JPMorgan Short Duration Bond Fund Class C	OSTCX	NAS CM	Open End	US Fixed Inc (Multisector Bond)	C	C	B-		Y	800-480-4111
JPMorgan Short Duration Bond Fund Class I	HLLVX	NAS CM	Open End	US Fixed Inc (Multisector Bond)	C+	C	B-	Up	Y	800-480-4111
JPMorgan Short Duration Bond Fund Class R6	JSDUX	NAS CM	Open End	US Fixed Inc (Multisector Bond)	C+	C	B	Up	Y	800-480-4111
JPMorgan Short Duration Core Plus Fund Class A	JSDHX	NAS CM	Open End	US Fixed Inc (Multisector Bond)	C	C	C+		Y	800-480-4111
JPMorgan Short Duration Core Plus Fund Class C	JSDCX	NAS CM	Open End	US Fixed Inc (Multisector Bond)	C	C-	C+		Y	800-480-4111
JPMorgan Short Duration Core Plus Fund Class I	JSDSX	NAS CM	Open End	US Fixed Inc (Multisector Bond)	C	C	C+		Y	800-480-4111
JPMorgan Short Duration Core Plus Fund Class R6	JSDRX	NAS CM	Open End	US Fixed Inc (Multisector Bond)	C	C	C+		Y	800-480-4111
JPMorgan Short-Intermediate Municipal Bond Fund Class A	OSTAX	NAS CM	Open End	US Muni Fixed Inc (Muni Bond - Natl)	C	C	C+		Y	800-480-4111
JPMorgan Short-Intermediate Municipal Bond Fund Class C	STMCX	NAS CM	Open End	US Muni Fixed Inc (Muni Bond - Natl)	C	C-	C+		Y	800-480-4111
JPMorgan Short-Intermediate Municipal Bond Fund Class R6	OSTSX	NAS CM	Open End	US Muni Fixed Inc (Muni Bond - Natl)	C	C	B-		Y	800-480-4111
JPMorgan Strategic Income Opportunities Cl A Shares	JSOAX	NAS CM	Open End	Fixed Inc Misc (Income)	C-	D+	C		Y	800-480-4111
JPMorgan Strategic Income Opportunities Cl C Shares	JSOCX	NAS CM	Open End	Fixed Inc Misc (Income)	C-	D+	C		Y	800-480-4111
JPMorgan Strategic Income Opportunities Cl I Shares	JSOSX	NAS CM	Open End	Fixed Inc Misc (Income)	C-	D+	C		Y	800-480-4111
JPMorgan Strategic Income Opportunities Cl R5 Shares	JSORX	NAS CM	Open End	Fixed Inc Misc (Income)	C-	D+	C	Down	Y	800-480-4111
JPMorgan Strategic Income Opportunities Fund Class R6	JSOZX	NAS CM	Open End	Fixed Inc Misc (Income)	C	D+	C		Y	800-480-4111
JPMorgan Tax Aware Real Return Fund Class A	TXRAX	NAS CM	Open End	US Muni Fixed Inc (Muni Bond - Natl)	D	D	C-	Down	Y	800-480-4111
JPMorgan Tax Aware Real Return Fund Class C	TXRCX	NAS CM	Open End	US Muni Fixed Inc (Muni Bond - Natl)	D	D	C-	Down	Y	800-480-4111
JPMorgan Tax Aware Real Return Fund Class R6	TXRRX	NAS CM	Open End	US Muni Fixed Inc (Muni Bond - Natl)	D+	D	C	Down	Y	800-480-4111
JPMorgan Tax Free Bond Fund Class A	PMBAX	NAS CM	Open End	US Muni Fixed Inc (Muni Bond - Natl)	C	C-	B-		Y	800-480-4111
JPMorgan Tax Free Bond Fund Class C	JTFCX	NAS CM	Open End	US Muni Fixed Inc (Muni Bond - Natl)	C	C-	B-		Y	800-480-4111
JPMorgan Tax Free Bond Fund Class I	PRBIX	NAS CM	Open End	US Muni Fixed Inc (Muni Bond - Natl)	C	C-	B-		Y	800-480-4111
JPMorgan Tax Free Bond Fund Class R6	RUNFX	NAS CM	Open End	US Muni Fixed Inc (Muni Bond - Natl)	C	C-	B-		Y	800-480-4111
JPMorgan Tax Free Money Market Fund Reserve Class	RTJXX	NAS CM	Money Mkt	US Money Mkt (Money Mkt - Fed Tax Exmpt)	C	C-	C+		Y	800-480-4111
JPMorgan Tax-Free Money Market Fund Agency Class	VTIXX	NAS CM	Money Mkt	US Money Mkt (Money Mkt - Fed Tax Exmpt)	C	C-	C+		Y	800-480-4111
JPMorgan Tax-Free Money Market Fund Morgan Class	VTMXX	NAS CM	Money Mkt	US Money Mkt (Money Mkt - Fed Tax Exmpt)	C	C-	C		Y	800-480-4111
JPMorgan Tax-Free Money Market Fund Premier Class	VXPXX	NAS CM	Money Mkt	US Money Mkt (Money Mkt - Fed Tax Exmpt)	C	C-	C+		Y	800-480-4111
JPMorgan Tax-Free Money Market Institutional Class	JTFXX	NAS CM	Money Mkt	US Money Mkt (Money Mkt - Fed Tax Exmpt)	C	C-	C+		Y	800-480-4111
JPMorgan Total Return Fund Class A Shares	JMTAX	NAS CM	Open End	US Fixed Inc (Growth & Income)	B	C+	B+	Up	Y	800-480-4111

★Expanded analysis of this fund is included in Section II.

TOTAL RETURNS & PERFORMANCE									ASSETS		ASSET ALLOCATION & TURNOVER							MINIMUMS		FEES		
3-Month Total Return	6-Month Total Return	1-Year Total Return	3-Year Total Return	5-Year Total Return	Dividend Yield (TTM)	Expense Ratio	3-Yr Std Deviation	Effective Duration	NAV	Total Assets (MIL)	%Cash	%Government Bonds	%Municipal Bonds	%Corporate Bonds	%Other	Turnover Ratio	Average Coupon Rate	Min Initial Investment	Min Additional Investment	Front End Fee (%)	Back End Fee (%)	Inception Date
0.02	0.28	0.67	2.31	2.51	0.78	0.59	0.11		1	1,377	22	0	78	0	0			1,000	50			Feb-05
0.03	0.32	0.79	2.72	3.04	0.9	0.45	0.12		1	1,377	22	0	78	0	0			1,000,000				Jun-87
0.02	0.17	0.33	1.10	1.14	0.39	1.05	0.09		1	1,377	22	0	78	0	0			10,000,000				Jul-05
0.06	0.39	0.92	2.57	2.72	1.04	0.26			1	1,709	22	0	78	0	0			5,000,000				Mar-19
0.00	0.00	0.00	0.02	0.05	0	1	0			869.7	4	0	91	5	1			0				Jan-06
0.08	0.42	0.97	2.63	2.78	1.09	0.21			1	1,709	22	0	78	0	0			10,000,000				Mar-19
0.02	0.27	0.64	2.20	2.35	0.74	0.59	0.11		1	1,709	22	0	78	0	0			1,000	50			Sep-87
0.03	0.32	0.75	2.60	2.87	0.86	0.45	0.11		1	1,709	22	0	78	0	0			1,000,000				Mar-16
0.02	0.24	0.55	1.89	1.97	0.64	0.7	0.11		1	1,709	22	0	78	0	0			10,000,000				Jul-00
0.02	0.15	0.29	0.99	1.02	0.35	1.05	0.09		1	1,709	22	0	78	0	0			10,000,000				Jul-09
1.79	1.05	2.61	8.05	12.61	1.89	0.75	3.56	4.61	6.91	411.9	2	0	98	0	0	13	4.95	1,000	50	3.75		Feb-01
1.66	0.79	2.09	6.58	9.66	1.37	1.25	3.6	4.61	6.91	411.9	2	0	98	0	0	13	4.95	1,000	50		1.00	Jan-03
1.86	1.22	2.95	8.63	13.21	2.23	0.4	3.54	4.61	6.94	411.9	2	0	98	0	0	13	4.95	15,000,000				Oct-18
0.19	0.56	1.59	5.00	5.62	1.72	0.18			1.001	70,465	91	4	0	3	0			5,000,000				May-19
0.20	0.54	1.53	5.32	6.26	1.64	0.26	0.16		1.0012	70,465	91	4	0	3	0			5,000,000				Apr-94
0.20	0.56	1.58	5.53	6.66	1.72	0.18	0.16		1.0009	70,465	91	4	0	3	0			50,000,000				Feb-05
0.12	0.33	0.94	3.23	3.38	1.03	0.97	0.15		1.0009	70,465	91	4	0	3	0			1,000	50		1.00	May-98
0.36	0.90	1.78	3.45	3.65	1.89	0.15	0.18			43,805	97	0	0	2	1			50,000,000				May-12
0.19	0.53	1.54	5.43	6.49	1.69	0.21	0.16		1.0009	70,465	91	4	0	3	0			10,000,000				Sep-01
0.17	0.47	1.32	4.59	5.09	1.39	0.52	0.16		1.0015	70,465	91	4	0	3	0			1,000	50			Oct-98
0.15	0.45	1.34	4.72	5.34	1.45	0.45	0.16		1.001	70,465	91	4	0	3	0			1,000,000				Nov-93
0.13	0.36	1.12	3.99	4.32	1.2	0.7	0.16		1.0013	70,465	91	4	0	3	0			10,000,000				Jul-00
0.19	0.56	1.64			1.81	0.06			1.0004	3,632	97	3	0	0	0			100,000,000				Sep-18
3.10	3.12	4.37	8.18	9.39	2.09	0.59	1.61	1.79	11.11	3,032	5	16	0	33	0	88	2.92	1,000	50	2.25		Feb-92
3.04	2.84	3.81	6.56	6.67	1.57	1.09	1.63	1.79	11.19	3,032	5	16	0	33	0	88	2.92	1,000	50		1.00	Nov-01
3.16	3.14	4.62	8.88	10.65	2.33	0.34	1.58	1.79	11.12	3,032	5	16	0	33	0	88	2.92	1,000,000				Sep-90
3.17	3.18	4.68	9.60	11.85	2.41	0.28	1.61	1.79	11.12	3,032	5	16	0	33	0	88	2.92	15,000,000				Feb-05
4.47	1.97	3.47	9.32	17.96	2.2	0.64	2.96	2.59	9.7	3,434	1	13	0	43	0	157	3.15	1,000	50	2.25		Mar-13
4.35	1.74	2.96	7.72	15.02	1.71	1.14	2.98	2.59	9.68	3,434	1	13	0	43	0	157	3.15	1,000	50		1.00	Mar-13
4.53	2.10	3.72	10.22	19.46	2.44	0.39	2.97	2.59	9.7	3,434	1	13	0	43	0	157	3.15	1,000,000				Mar-13
4.55	2.13	3.89	10.44	19.93	2.5	0.33	2.97	2.59	9.7	3,434	1	13	0	43	0	157	3.15	15,000,000				Mar-13
1.94	1.35	2.58	6.62	9.33	1.48	0.7	2.5	3.65	10.77	1,577	4	0	96	0	0		4.25	1,000	50	2.25		May-98
1.80	1.08	2.13	5.09	6.65	0.96	1.2	2.47	3.65	10.87	1,577	4	0	96	0	0		4.25	1,000	50		1.00	Nov-01
2.06	1.68	3.17	7.66	10.40	1.96	0.2	2.5	3.65	10.83	1,577	4	0	96	0	0		4.25	15,000,000				Oct-18
3.53	-0.37	0.39	4.70	12.80	2.02	1.04	2.87	0.65	11.32	11,054	44	0	0	40	0	53	2.76	1,000	50	3.75		Oct-08
3.41	-0.62	-0.11	3.13	10.02	1.51	1.54	2.89	0.65	11.29	11,054	44	0	0	40	0	53	2.76	1,000	50		1.00	Oct-08
3.59	-0.25	0.64	5.48	14.22	2.27	0.79	2.87	0.65	11.35	11,054	44	0	0	40	0	53	2.76	1,000,000				Oct-08
3.62	-0.26	0.79	5.99	15.25	2.42	0.64	2.91	0.65	11.36	11,054	44	0	0	40	0	53	2.76	0				Oct-08
3.64	-0.12	0.89	6.24	15.52	2.52	0.54	2.89	0.65	11.37	11,054	44	0	0	40	0	53	2.76	15,000,000				Nov-17
4.74	-3.75	-1.81	1.68	5.28	2.36	0.75	5.75	4.86	8.93	388.6	2	0	98	0	0	4	4.97	1,000	50	3.75		Aug-05
4.63	-4.00	-2.31	0.23	2.43	1.81	1.25	5.7	4.86	8.91	388.6	2	0	98	0	0	4	4.97	1,000	50		1.00	Aug-05
4.71	-3.78	-1.57	2.63	7.01	2.72	0.4	5.78	4.86	8.94	388.6	2	0	98	0	0	4	4.97	15,000,000				Aug-13
2.51	1.47	3.90	11.75	19.03	2.41	0.67	4.73	7.28	12.29	511.6	5	0	95	0	0		4.59	1,000	50	3.75		Mar-88
2.38	1.19	3.24	9.83	15.43	1.84	1.25	4.73	7.28	12.18	511.6	5	0	95	0	0		4.59	1,000	50		1.00	Jul-08
2.57	1.51	4.05	12.45	20.19	2.64	0.45	4.74	7.28	12.23	511.6	5	0	95	0	0		4.59	1,000,000				Feb-95
2.59	1.62	4.11	12.21	19.52	2.69	0.4	4.75	7.28	12.23	511.6	5	0	95	0	0		4.59	15,000,000				Oct-18
0.02	0.24	0.56	1.90	2.00	0.65	0.7	0.11		1	12,994	24	0	76	0	0			10,000,000				Feb-05
0.07	0.39	0.94	3.18	3.69	1.05	0.26	0.11		1	12,994	24	0	76	0	0			5,000,000				Nov-93
0.02	0.26	0.64	2.21	2.37	0.74	0.59	0.11		1	12,994	24	0	76	0	0			1,000	50			Sep-87
0.04	0.31	0.76	2.62	2.90	0.87	0.45	0.11		1	12,994	24	0	76	0	0			1,000,000				Oct-90
0.07	0.41	0.98	3.33	3.90	1.1	0.21	0.11		1	12,994	24	0	76	0	0			10,000,000				Sep-01
4.43	5.35	7.88	15.74	24.27	2.27	0.67	3.63	5.58	10.68	501.5	28	5	0	37	0	420	3.47	1,000	50	3.75		Jun-08

	MARKET		FUND TYPE, CATEGORY & OBJECTIVE		RATINGS				NEW INVESTORS	
Fund Name	Ticker Symbol	Traded On	Fund Type	Category and (Prospectus Objective)	Overall Rating	Reward Rating	Risk Rating	Recent Up/ Downgrade	Open to New Investors	Telephone
JPMorgan Total Return Fund Class C Shares	JMTCX	NAS CM	Open End	US Fixed Inc (Growth & Income)	B-	C+	B	Up	Y	800-480-4111
JPMorgan Total Return Fund Class I Shares	JMTSX	NAS CM	Open End	US Fixed Inc (Growth & Income)	B	C+	B+	Up	Y	800-480-4111
JPMorgan Total Return Fund Class R2 Shares	JMTTX	NAS CM	Open End	US Fixed Inc (Growth & Income)	B-	C+	B	Up	Y	800-480-4111
JPMorgan Total Return Fund Class R5 Shares	JMTRX	NAS CM	Open End	US Fixed Inc (Growth & Income)	B	C+	B+	Up	Y	800-480-4111
JPMorgan Total Return Fund Class R6 Shares	JMTIX	NAS CM	Open End	US Fixed Inc (Growth & Income)	B	C+	B+	Up	Y	800-480-4111
JPMorgan U.S. Government Money Market Fund Academy	JGAXX	NAS CM	Money Mkt	US Money Mkt (Money Mkt - Govt)	C	C	C+		Y	800-480-4111
JPMorgan U.S. Government Money Market Fund Agency Class	OGAXX	NAS CM	Money Mkt	US Money Mkt (Money Mkt - Govt)	C	C-	C+		Y	800-480-4111
JPMorgan U.S. Government Money Market Fund Capital Shares	OGVXX	NAS CM	Money Mkt	US Money Mkt (Money Mkt - Govt)	C	C-	C+		Y	800-480-4111
JPMorgan U.S. Government Money Market Fund Class IM	MGMXX	NAS CM	Money Mkt	US Money Mkt (Money Mkt - Govt)	C	C-	C+		Y	800-480-4111
★ JPMorgan U.S. Government Money Market Fund E*TRADE Class	JUSXX	NAS CM	Money Mkt	US Money Mkt (Money Mkt - Govt)	C	C-	C		Y	800-480-4111
JPMorgan U.S. Govt Money Mkt Fund Institutional Class	IJGXX	NAS CM	Money Mkt	US Money Mkt (Money Mkt - Govt)	C	C	C+		Y	800-480-4111
JPMorgan U.S. Government Money Market Fund Investor Class	JGMXX	NAS CM	Money Mkt	US Money Mkt (Money Mkt - Govt)	C	C-	C+		Y	800-480-4111
★ JPMorgan U.S. Government Money Market Fund Morgan Class	MJGXX	NAS CM	Money Mkt	US Money Mkt (Money Mkt - Govt)	C	C-	C+		Y	800-480-4111
JPMorgan U.S. Government Money Market Fund Premier Class	OGSXX	NAS CM	Money Mkt	US Money Mkt (Money Mkt - Govt)	C	C-	C+		Y	800-480-4111
JPMorgan U.S. Government Money Market Fund Reserve Class	RJGXX	NAS CM	Money Mkt	US Money Mkt (Money Mkt - Govt)	C	C-	C+		Y	800-480-4111
JPMorgan U.S. Government Money Market Fund Service Class	SJGXX	NAS CM	Money Mkt	US Money Mkt (Money Mkt - Govt)	C	C-	C		Y	800-480-4111
JPMorgan U.S. Treasury Plus Money Market Fund Agency Class	AJTXX	NAS CM	Money Mkt	US Money Mkt (Money Mkt - Treasury)	C	C-	C+		Y	800-480-4111
JPMorgan U.S. Treasury Plus Money Mkt Fund Capital Shares	JTCXX	NAS CM	Money Mkt	US Money Mkt (Money Mkt - Treasury)	C	C-	C+		Y	800-480-4111
JPMorgan U.S. Treasury Plus Money Market Fund Class C	OTCXX	NAS CM	Money Mkt	US Money Mkt (Money Mkt - Treasury)	C	C-	C		Y	800-480-4111
JPMorgan U.S. Treasury Plus Money Market Fund Class IM	MJPXX	NAS CM	Money Mkt	US Money Mkt (Money Mkt - Treasury)	C	C-	C+		Y	800-480-4111
JPMorgan U.S. Treasury Plus Money Mkt Institutional Cl	IJTXX	NAS CM	Money Mkt	US Money Mkt (Money Mkt - Treasury)	C	C	C+		Y	800-480-4111
JPMorgan U.S. Treasury Plus Money Mkt Fund Investor Class	HGOXX	NAS CM	Money Mkt	US Money Mkt (Money Mkt - Treasury)	C	C-	C+		Y	800-480-4111
JPMorgan U.S. Treasury Plus Money Market Fund Morgan Class	MJTXX	NAS CM	Money Mkt	US Money Mkt (Money Mkt - Treasury)	C	C-	C+		Y	800-480-4111
JPMorgan U.S. Treasury Plus Money Mkt Fund Premier Class	PJTXX	NAS CM	Money Mkt	US Money Mkt (Money Mkt - Treasury)	C	C-	C+		Y	800-480-4111
JPMorgan U.S. Treasury Plus Money Mkt Fund Reserve Shares	HTIXX	NAS CM	Money Mkt	US Money Mkt (Money Mkt - Treasury)	C	C-	C+		Y	800-480-4111
JPMorgan Ultra-Short Municipal Fund Class A	USMSX	NAS CM	Open End	US Muni Fixed Inc (Muni Bond - Natl)	C	C-	C+		Y	800-480-4111
JPMorgan Ultra-Short Municipal Fund Class I	USMTX	NAS CM	Open End	US Muni Fixed Inc (Muni Bond - Natl)	C	C-	C+		Y	800-480-4111
JPMorgan Unconstrained Debt Fund Class A Shares	JSIAX	NAS CM	Open End	Fixed Inc Misc (Growth & Income)	C	C-	C+		Y	800-480-4111
JPMorgan Unconstrained Debt Fund Class C Shares	JINCX	NAS CM	Open End	Fixed Inc Misc (Growth & Income)	C	C-	C		Y	800-480-4111
JPMorgan Unconstrained Debt Fund Class I Shares	JSISX	NAS CM	Open End	Fixed Inc Misc (Growth & Income)	C	C-	C+		Y	800-480-4111
JPMorgan Unconstrained Debt Fund Class R2 Shares	JISZX	NAS CM	Open End	Fixed Inc Misc (Growth & Income)	C	C-	C		Y	800-480-4111
JPMorgan Unconstrained Debt Fund Class R5 Shares	JSIRX	NAS CM	Open End	Fixed Inc Misc (Growth & Income)	C	C-	C+		Y	800-480-4111
JPMorgan Unconstrained Debt Fund Class R6	JSIMX	NAS CM	Open End	Fixed Inc Misc (Growth & Income)	C	C-	C+		Y	800-480-4111
Kansas Municipal Fund Class A	KSMUX	NAS CM	Open End	US Muni Fixed Inc (Muni Bond - Single State)	C+	C	B	Up	Y	800-276-1262
Kansas Municipal Fund Class I	KSITX	NAS CM	Open End	US Muni Fixed Inc (Muni Bond - Single State)	C+	C	B	Up	Y	800-276-1262
Kensington Managed Income Fund Class A Shares	KAMAX	NAS CM	Open End	Alternative Misc (Income)	D	D	C		Y	
Kensington Managed Income Fund Class C Shares	KAMCX	NAS CM	Open End	Alternative Misc (Income)	D	D	C		Y	
Kensington Managed Income Fund Institutional Class Shares	KAMIX	NAS CM	Open End	Alternative Misc (Income)	D	D	C		Y	
Kinetics Alternative Income Fund Advisor Class A	KWIAX	NAS CM	Open End	US Fixed Inc (Income)	C	C	B-		Y	800-930-3828
Kinetics Alternative Income Fund Advisor Class C	KWICX	NAS CM	Open End	US Fixed Inc (Income)	C	C	C+		Y	800-930-3828
Kinetics Alternative Income Fund Institutional Class	KWIIX	NAS CM	Open End	US Fixed Inc (Income)	C	C	B-		Y	800-930-3828
Kinetics Alternative Income Fund No Load Class	KWINX	NAS CM	Open End	US Fixed Inc (Income)	C	C	B-		Y	800-930-3828
Kinetics Multi-Disciplinary Income Fund Class Advisor A	KMDAX	NAS CM	Open End	US Fixed Inc (Income)	D+	D+	C-	Down	Y	800-930-3828
Kinetics Multi-Disciplinary Income Fund Class Advisor C	KMDCX	NAS CM	Open End	US Fixed Inc (Income)	D+	D	C-	Down	Y	800-930-3828
Kinetics Multi-Disciplinary Income Cl Institutional	KMDYX	NAS CM	Open End	US Fixed Inc (Income)	D+	D+	C	Down	Y	800-930-3828
Kinetics Multi-Disciplinary Income Fund Class No Load	KMDNX	NAS CM	Open End	US Fixed Inc (Income)	D+	D+	C	Down	Y	800-930-3828
KKR Credit Opportunities Portfolio Class I			Closed End	Global Fixed Inc (Income)	U	U	U		Y	
KKR Income Opportunities Fund	KIO	NYSE	Closed End	US Fixed Inc (Income)	D	D	D	Down	Y	212-750-8300
Knights of Columbus Core Bond Fund Class S Shares	KCCSX	NAS CM	Open End	US Fixed Inc (Growth & Income)	B-	C	B	Up	Y	203-772-2130
Knights of Columbus Core Bond Fund I Shares	KCCIX	NAS CM	Open End	US Fixed Inc (Growth & Income)	B-	C	B	Up	Y	203-772-2130
Knights of Columbus Core Bond Fund Investor Shares	KCCVX	NAS CM	Open End	US Fixed Inc (Growth & Income)	C+	C	B		Y	203-772-2130
Knights of Columbus Limited Duration Fund Class S	KCLSX	NAS CM	Open End	US Fixed Inc (Growth & Income)	C	C	C+		Y	203-772-2130

★ Expanded analysis of this fund is included in Section II.

TOTAL RETURNS & PERFORMANCE									ASSETS		ASSET ALLOCATION & TURNOVER							MINIMUMS		FEES		
3-Month Total Return	6-Month Total Return	1-Year Total Return	3-Year Total Return	5-Year Total Return	Dividend Yield (TTM)	Expense Ratio	3-Yr Std Deviation	Effective Duration	NAV	Total Assets (MIL)	%Cash	%Government Bonds	%Municipal Bonds	%Corporate Bonds	%Other	Turnover Ratio	Average Coupon Rate	Min Initial Investment	Min Additional Investment	Front End Fee (%)	Back End Fee (%)	Inception Date
4.27	5.02	7.10	13.54	20.28	1.64	1.32	3.69	5.58	10.65	501.5	28	5	0	37	0	420	3.47	1,000	50		1.00	Jun-08
4.54	5.47	7.95	16.16	24.96	2.36	0.57	3.66	5.58	10.71	501.5	28	5	0	37	0	420	3.47	1,000,000				Jun-08
4.38	5.15	7.29	14.04	21.15	1.74	1.17	3.68	5.58	10.7	501.5	28	5	0	37	0	420	3.47	0				Mar-14
4.46	5.43	7.97	16.40	25.42	2.46	0.47	3.65	5.58	10.7	501.5	28	5	0	37	0	420	3.47	0				Jun-08
4.58	5.56	8.13	16.58	25.76	2.51	0.42	3.7	5.58	10.7	501.5	28	5	0	37	0	420	3.47	15,000,000				Mar-14
0.04	0.35	1.28	4.69	5.31	1.46	0.18			1	218,802	65	33	0	1	0			5,000,000				May-19
0.02	0.32	1.20	4.45	4.90	1.38	0.26	0.17		1	218,802	65	33	0	1	0			5,000,000				Nov-01
0.04	0.35	1.28	4.69	5.31	1.46	0.18	0.17		1	218,802	65	33	0	1	0			50,000,000				Jun-93
0.05	0.37	1.32	4.78	5.42	1.5	0.15	0.17		1	218,802	65	33	0	1	0			50,000,000				May-12
	0.18	0.76	2.31	1.89	0.76	1	0.15			218,802	65	33	0	1	0			0				Mar-16
0.04	0.35	1.26	4.61	5.17	1.43	0.21	0.17		1	218,802	65	33	0	1	0			10,000,000				Feb-05
0.00	0.23	1.00	3.73	3.88	1.16	0.49	0.17		1	218,802	65	33	0	1	0			1,000,000				Jul-09
0.00	0.21	0.94	3.48	3.60	1.09	0.59	0.17		1	218,802	65	33	0	1	0			1,000	50			Feb-05
0.00	0.25	1.04	3.89	4.09	1.21	0.45	0.17		1	218,802	65	33	0	1	0			1,000,000				Apr-00
0.00	0.20	0.86	3.18	3.25	1	0.7	0.16		1	218,802	65	33	0	1	0			10,000,000				Feb-05
0.00	0.12	0.60	2.20	2.23	0.72	1.04	0.15		1	218,802	65	33	0	1	0			10,000,000				Jul-05
0.01	0.30	1.18	4.44	4.83	1.36	0.26	0.17		1	28,924	68	32	0	0	0			5,000,000				Feb-05
0.04	0.35	1.26	4.61	4.74	1.44	0.18			1	28,924	68	32	0	0	0			50,000,000				Sep-17
0.00	0.12	0.64	2.42	2.42	0.76	0.97	0.15		1	28,924	68	32	0	0	0			1,000	50		1.00	Feb-98
0.04	0.37	1.29	4.78	5.33	1.48	0.14	0.18		1	28,924	68	32	0	0	0			50,000,000				May-12
0.03	0.33	1.24	4.60	5.07	1.41	0.21	0.17		1	28,924	68	32	0	0	0			10,000,000				Feb-05
0.00	0.22	0.98	3.72	3.84	1.14	0.5	0.17		1	28,924	68	32	0	0	0			1,000,000				Jan-87
0.00	0.20	0.91	3.48	3.55	1.07	0.59	0.17		1	28,924	68	32	0	0	0			1,000	50			Feb-05
0.00	0.24	1.02	3.88	4.04	1.19	0.44	0.17		1	28,924	68	32	0	0	0			1,000,000				Feb-05
0.00	0.19	0.84	3.17	3.22	0.98	0.7	0.16		1	28,924	68	32	0	0	0			10,000,000				Feb-92
0.50	0.48	1.19	3.55		1.18	0.45	0.53	0.92	10.06	3,852	28	3	69	0	0		2.33	1,000	50	2.25		May-16
0.53	0.57	1.37	4.17		1.36	0.25	0.51	0.92	10.05	3,852	28	3	69	0	0		2.33	1,000,000				May-16
4.77	1.15	2.82	8.04	14.82	3.2	0.9	3.63	3.50	9.81	918.6	12	8	0	18	0	74	3.67	1,000	50	3.75		Dec-10
4.62	0.85	2.26	6.42	12.00	2.71	1.4	3.59	3.50	9.74	918.6	12	8	0	18	0	74	3.67	1,000	50		1.00	Dec-10
4.74	1.19	2.98	8.83	16.22	3.45	0.65	3.63	3.50	9.82	918.6	12	8	0	18	0	74	3.67	1,000,000				Dec-10
4.73	1.01	2.48	6.92	13.12	2.84	1.25	3.63	3.50	9.79	918.6	12	8	0	18	0	74	3.67	0				Dec-10
4.85	1.31	3.13	9.14	17.00	3.5	0.6	3.63	3.50	9.84	918.6	12	8	0	18	0	74	3.67	0				Dec-10
4.88	1.36	3.24	9.27	17.36	3.6	0.5	3.65	3.50	9.83	918.6	12	8	0	18	0	74	3.67	15,000,000				Nov-11
2.23	2.82	4.41	10.53	16.33	2.15	0.98	3.06		11.03	68.8	0	0	100	0	0	29	4.35	1,000	50	2.50		Nov-90
2.20	2.95	4.58	11.14	16.97	2.4	0.73	3.07		11.03	68.8	0	0	100	0	0	29	4.35	1,000	50			Nov-17
2.03	-0.83	0.84			1.35	2.76			10.07	127.7								1,000	250	4.75		May-19
1.92	-1.16	0.14				3.74			10.05	127.7								1,000	250		1.00	Aug-19
2.08	-0.73	1.01			1.48	2.26			10.08	127.7								25,000	250			May-19
1.64	1.74	2.43	5.58	10.85	1	1.25	0.99	2.29	98.73	14.6	62	0	0	36	0	0	3.24	2,500		5.75		Jun-07
1.52	1.46	1.91	3.99	8.08	0.65	1.75	0.99	2.29	94.77	14.6	62	0	0	36	0	0	3.24	2,500			1.00	Jun-07
1.75	1.95	2.87	7.00	13.35	1.55	0.8	1	2.29	101.22	14.6	62	0	0	36	0	0	3.24	1,000,000				Jun-07
1.70	1.84	2.67	6.36	12.27	1.36	1	0.99	2.29	99.89	14.6	62	0	0	36	0	0	3.24	2,500				Jun-07
6.65	-4.70	-3.04	3.46	13.01	4.07	2.02	6.81		10.19	29.3	17	3	1	66	0	0	5.11	2,500		5.75		Feb-08
6.45	-5.00	-3.47	1.89	10.22	3.64	2.52	6.81		10.07	29.3	17	3	1	66	0	0	5.11	2,500			1.00	Feb-08
6.69	-4.55	-2.55	4.91	15.61	4.57	1.57	6.78		10.26	29.3	17	3	1	66	0	0	5.11	1,000,000				Feb-08
6.63	-4.58	-2.77	4.28	14.38	4.38	1.77	6.81		10.24	29.3	17	3	1	66	0	0	5.11	2,500				Feb-08
11.41						2.99			25.09	--								1,000,000	500			Mar-20
21.75	-10.08	-8.08	2.25	26.09	11.08	2.65	16.92		13.69	264.4	2	0	0	98	0	62	7.57					Jul-13
4.43	3.71	6.74	14.57	22.67	2.8	0.6	4.16		10.5	104.2	1	19	1	33	0	47	3.62	0				Jul-15
4.45	3.76	6.84	14.78	23.09	2.89	0.5	4.16		10.51	104.2	1	19	1	33	0	47	3.62	25,000	250			Feb-15
4.41	3.65	6.59	13.96	21.39	2.64	0.75	4.19		10.5	104.2	1	19	1	33	0	47	3.62	1,000				Jun-16
3.58	1.61	3.01	7.49	9.88	2.3	0.6	2.33		10.03	108.3	4	25	0	49	0	76	2.98	0				Jul-15

	MARKET			FUND TYPE, CATEGORY & OBJECTIVE	RATINGS				NEW INVESTORS	
Fund Name	Ticker Symbol	Traded On	Fund Type	Category and (Prospectus Objective)	Overall Rating	Reward Rating	Risk Rating	Recent Up/ Downgrade	Open to New Investors	Telephone
Knights of Columbus Limited Duration Fund I Shares	KCLIX	NAS CM	Open End	US Fixed Inc (Growth & Income)	C	C	C+		Y	203-772-2130
Knights of Columbus Limited Duration Fund Investor Shares	KCLVX	NAS CM	Open End	US Fixed Inc (Growth & Income)	C	C	C+		Y	203-772-2130
KP Fixed Income Fund Institutional Shares	KPFIX	NAS CM	Open End	US Fixed Inc (Income)	B-	C	B+	Up	Y	
Lazard Emerg Mkts Debt Portfolio Institutional Shares	LEDIX	NAS CM	Open End	Emerg Mkts Fixed Inc (Growth & Income)	D	D	C-	Down	Y	800-823-6300
Lazard Emerging Markets Debt Portfolio Open Shares	LEDOX	NAS CM	Open End	Emerg Mkts Fixed Inc (Growth & Income)	D	D	C-	Down	Y	800-823-6300
Lazard Emerging Markets Debt Portfolio R6 Shares	RLEDX	NAS CM	Open End	Emerg Mkts Fixed Inc (Growth & Income)	D	D	C-	Down	Y	800-823-6300
Lazard Enhanced Opportunities Portfol Inst Shares	LEOIX	NAS CM	Open End	Fixed Inc Misc (Growth & Income)	D+	D	C	Down	Y	800-823-6300
Lazard Enhanced Opportunities Portfolio Open Shares	LEOOX	NAS CM	Open End	Fixed Inc Misc (Growth & Income)	D+	D	C	Down	Y	800-823-6300
Lazard Global Fixed Income Portfolio Institutional Shares	LZGIX	NAS CM	Open End	Global Fixed Inc (Worldwide Bond)	C+	C	B	Up	Y	800-823-6300
Lazard Global Fixed Income Portfolio Open Shares	LZGOX	NAS CM	Open End	Global Fixed Inc (Worldwide Bond)	C	C	B-		Y	800-823-6300
Lazard US Corporate Income Portfolio Institutional Shares	LZHYX	NAS CM	Open End	US Fixed Inc (Corp Bond - High Yield)	C-	D+	C	Down	Y	800-823-6300
Lazard US Corporate Income Portfolio Open Shares	LZHOX	NAS CM	Open End	US Fixed Inc (Corp Bond - High Yield)	C-	D+	C		Y	800-823-6300
Lazard US Corporate Income Portfolio R6 Shares	RLCIX	NAS CM	Open End	US Fixed Inc (Corp Bond - High Yield)	C-	D+	C		Y	800-823-6300
Lazard US Short Duration Fixed Income Portfol Inst Shares	UMNIX	NAS CM	Open End	US Fixed Inc (Income)	C+	C	B-	Up	Y	800-823-6300
Lazard US Short Duration Fixed Income Portfol Open Shares	UMNOX	NAS CM	Open End	US Fixed Inc (Income)	C	C	B-		Y	800-823-6300
Leader Capital Leader Total Return Fund Class A Shares	LCATX	NAS CM	Open End	US Fixed Inc (Multisector Bond)	D+	D	C-		Y	800-711-9164
Leader Capital Leader Total Return Fund Class C	LCCTX	NAS CM	Open End	US Fixed Inc (Multisector Bond)	D+	D	C-		Y	800-711-9164
Leader Capital Leader Total Return Institutional Shares	LCTIX	NAS CM	Open End	US Fixed Inc (Multisector Bond)	C-	D+	C-	Up	Y	800-711-9164
Leader Capital Leader Total Return Fund Investor Shares	LCTRX	NAS CM	Open End	US Fixed Inc (Multisector Bond)	D+	D	C-		Y	800-711-9164
Leader High Quality Low Duration Bond InstitutionalShares	LFIFX	NAS CM	Open End	US Fixed Inc (Income)	D	D	D+	Down	Y	800-711-9164
Leader High Quality Low Duration Bond Fund InvestorShares	LFVFX	NAS CM	Open End	US Fixed Inc (Income)	D	D-	D+	Down	Y	800-711-9164
Leader Short Term High Yield Bond Fund Class A Shares	LCAMX	NAS CM	Open End	US Fixed Inc (Income)	D	D	D		Y	800-711-9164
Leader Short Term High Yield Bond Fund Class C	LCMCX	NAS CM	Open End	US Fixed Inc (Income)	D	D	D		Y	800-711-9164
Leader Short Term High Yield Bond Fund Institutional Class	LCCIX	NAS CM	Open End	US Fixed Inc (Income)	D	D	D+		Y	800-711-9164
Leader Short Term High Yield Bond Fund Investor Class	LCCMX	NAS CM	Open End	US Fixed Inc (Income)	D	D	D		Y	800-711-9164
Lebenthal Ultra Short Tax-Free Income Fund Class A Shares	LEAAX	NAS CM	Open End	US Muni Fixed Inc (Muni Bond - Natl)	U	U	U		Y	
Lebenthal Ultra Short Tax-Free Income Fund Class I Shares	LETAX	NAS CM	Open End	US Muni Fixed Inc (Muni Bond - Natl)	U	U	U		Y	
Legg Mason BW InterNatl Opportunities Bond Fund Class C1	LWOCX	NAS CM	Open End	Global Fixed Inc (Worldwide Bond)	U	U	U		Y	877-721-1926
LKCM Fixed Income Fund	LKFIX	NAS CM	Open End	US Fixed Inc (Income)	C+	C	B-	Up	Y	800-688-5526
Loomis Sayles Bond Fund Admin Class	LBFAX	NAS CM	Open End	US Fixed Inc (Corp Bond - General)	D+	D	C-	Down	Y	800-633-3330
Loomis Sayles Bond Fund Class N	LSBNX	NAS CM	Open End	US Fixed Inc (Corp Bond - General)	D+	D	C-	Down	Y	800-633-3330
Loomis Sayles Bond Fund Institutional Class	LSBDX	NAS CM	Open End	US Fixed Inc (Corp Bond - General)	D+	D	C-	Down	Y	800-633-3330
Loomis Sayles Bond Fund Retail Class	LSBRX	NAS CM	Open End	US Fixed Inc (Corp Bond - General)	D+	D	C-	Down	Y	800-633-3330
Loomis Sayles Core Plus Bond Fund Class A	NEFRX	NAS CM	Open End	US Fixed Inc (Corp Bond - General)	B	C+	B+	Up	Y	800-862-4863
Loomis Sayles Core Plus Bond Fund Class C	NECRX	NAS CM	Open End	US Fixed Inc (Corp Bond - General)	B	C+	B+	Up	Y	800-862-4863
Loomis Sayles Core Plus Bond Fund Class N	NERNX	NAS CM	Open End	US Fixed Inc (Corp Bond - General)	B	B-	B+	Up	Y	800-862-4863
Loomis Sayles Core Plus Bond Fund Class Y	NERYX	NAS CM	Open End	US Fixed Inc (Corp Bond - General)	B	C+	B+	Up	Y	800-862-4863
Loomis Sayles Fixed Income Fund	LSFIX	NAS CM	Open End	US Fixed Inc (Corp Bond - General)	C-	D+	C		Y	800-633-3330
Loomis Sayles Global Bond Fund Class N	LSGNX	NAS CM	Open End	Global Fixed Inc (Worldwide Bond)	C+	C	B	Up	Y	800-633-3330
Loomis Sayles Global Bond Fund Institutional Class	LSGBX	NAS CM	Open End	Global Fixed Inc (Worldwide Bond)	C+	C	B	Up	Y	800-633-3330
Loomis Sayles Global Bond Fund Retail Class	LSGLX	NAS CM	Open End	Global Fixed Inc (Worldwide Bond)	C+	C	B-	Up	Y	800-633-3330
Loomis Sayles High Income Fund Class A	NEFHX	NAS CM	Open End	US Fixed Inc (Corp Bond - High Yield)	D+	D	C-	Down	Y	800-862-4863
Loomis Sayles High Income Fund Class C	NEHCX	NAS CM	Open End	US Fixed Inc (Corp Bond - High Yield)	D	D	C-	Down	Y	800-862-4863
Loomis Sayles High Income Fund Class Y	NEHYX	NAS CM	Open End	US Fixed Inc (Corp Bond - High Yield)	D+	D	C-	Down	Y	800-862-4863
Loomis Sayles High Income Opportunities Institutional Cl	LSIOX	NAS CM	Open End	US Fixed Inc (Income)	C-	D+	C		Y	800-633-3330
Loomis Sayles Inflation Protected Securities Cl Inst	LSGSX	NAS CM	Open End	US Fixed Inc (Govt Bond - General)	B	B	A-	Up	Y	800-633-3330
Loomis Sayles Inflation Protected Securities Fund Class N	LIPNX	NAS CM	Open End	US Fixed Inc (Govt Bond - General)	B	B	A-	Up	Y	800-633-3330
Loomis Sayles Inflation Protected Securities Retail Cl	LIPRX	NAS CM	Open End	US Fixed Inc (Govt Bond - General)	B	B	A-	Up	Y	800-633-3330
Loomis Sayles Institutional High Income Fund	LSHIX	NAS CM	Open End	US Fixed Inc (Corp Bond - High Yield)	D	D	D+	Down	Y	800-633-3330
Loomis Sayles Intermediate Duration Bond Fund A Class	LSDRX	NAS CM	Open End	US Fixed Inc (Corp Bond - General)	B-	C+	B	Up	Y	800-862-4863
Loomis Sayles Intermediate Duration Bond Fund C Class	LSCDX	NAS CM	Open End	US Fixed Inc (Corp Bond - General)	C+	C	B	Up	Y	800-862-4863
Loomis Sayles Intermediate Duration Bond Fund Class N	LSDNX	NAS CM	Open End	US Fixed Inc (Corp Bond - General)	B-	C+	B+	Up	Y	800-862-4863

★ Expanded analysis of this fund is included in Section II.

TOTAL RETURNS & PERFORMANCE									ASSETS		ASSET ALLOCATION & TURNOVER							MINIMUMS		FEES		
3-Month Total Return	6-Month Total Return	1-Year Total Return	3-Year Total Return	5-Year Total Return	Dividend Yield (TTM)	Expense Ratio	3-Yr Std Deviation	Effective Duration	NAV	Total Assets (MIL)	%Cash	%Government Bonds	%Municipal Bonds	%Corporate Bonds	%Other	Turnover Ratio	Average Coupon Rate	Min Initial Investment	Min Additional Investment	Front End Fee (%)	Back End Fee (%)	Inception Date
3.59	1.65	3.10	7.77	10.21	2.4	0.5	2.35		10.03	108.3	4	25	0	49	0	76	2.98	25,000	250			Feb-15
3.64	1.63	2.85	7.01	8.80	2.15	0.75	2.37		10.03	108.3	4	25	0	49	0	76	2.98	1,000				Jun-16
5.32	4.49	7.30	15.58	23.67	3.04	0.29	3.8		10.69	2,255	4	32	1	33	0		3.58	0				Jan-14
11.39	-6.70	-3.43	3.48	13.93	4.84	0.95	12.32	7.11	7.38	35.0	5	91	0	4	0	106	6.41	10,000	50			Feb-11
11.56	-6.69	-3.53	3.02	12.61	4.62	1.15	12.39	7.11	7.46	35.0	5	91	0	4	0	106	6.41	2,500	50			Feb-11
11.54	-6.55	-3.09	4.10	14.54	4.76	0.9	12.36	7.11	7.93	35.0	5	91	0	4	0	106	6.41	1,000,000				Jul-16
4.99	-2.48	-1.06	5.19	9.59	0	2.79	5.24		8.62	11.2	4	0	0	97	0	354	2.09	10,000	50			Dec-14
4.76	-2.72	-1.29	3.63	8.19	0	3.04	5.21		8.58	11.2	4	0	0	97	0	354	2.09	2,500	50			Dec-14
4.08	2.97	4.60	10.47	15.76	1.94	0.7	4.23	5.36	9.27	8.2	9	57	2	32	0	65	3.17	10,000	50			Mar-12
3.90	2.85	4.34	9.60	14.05	1.69	0.95	4.25	5.36	9.27	8.2	9	57	2	32	0	65	3.17	2,500	50			Mar-12
7.79	-2.77	0.36	9.15	19.86	4.47	0.58	7.04	3.78	4.68	271.0	8	0	0	92	0	21	5.22	10,000	50			Jan-98
7.70	-2.87	0.12	8.03	18.16	4.2	0.83	6.98	3.78	4.7	271.0	8	0	0	92	0	21	5.22	2,500	50			Feb-98
8.00	-2.76	0.60	6.72	17.02	4.5	0.58	7.12	3.78	4.7	271.0	8	0	0	92	0	21	5.22	1,000,000				Nov-16
0.76	2.50	3.64	6.87	8.22	1.82	0.4	0.72	1.21	9.94	99.3	8	53	0	29	0	175	2.39	10,000	50			Feb-11
0.60	2.27	3.27	5.85	7.63	1.56	0.65	0.71	1.21	9.94	99.3	8	53	0	29	0	175	2.39	2,500	50			Feb-11
11.32	-4.19	-5.82	3.88	2.00	2.97	2.31	9.11	3.85	9.24	12.8	28	0	0	71	0	398	5.69	2,500	100	1.50		Mar-12
11.24	-4.46	-6.32	2.36	-0.38	2.51	2.81	9.1	3.85	9.29	12.8	28	0	0	71	0	398	5.69	2,500	100		1.00	Aug-12
11.49	-3.89	-5.37	5.44	4.67	3.62	1.81	9.12	3.85	9.22	12.8	28	0	0	71	0	398	5.69	100,000				Jul-10
11.30	-4.19	-5.90	3.91	2.15	3.06	2.31	9.08	3.85	9.26	12.8	28	0	0	71	0	398	5.69	2,500	100			Jul-10
-1.93	-7.63	-6.66	-0.92		2.46	1.01	5.14	0.70	9.21	115.5	1	0	0	0	0	248	2.46	2,000,000				Dec-16
-2.02	-7.88	-7.05	-2.15		2.03	1.39	5.09	0.70	9.2	115.5	1	0	0	0	0	248	2.46	2,500	100			Dec-16
11.60	-9.15	-10.49	-6.07	-9.50	3.41	1.65	9.88	2.56	7.77	46.8	47	0	0	52	0	496	5.73	2,500	100	1.50		Mar-12
11.44	-9.33	-10.90	-7.42	-11.74	2.83	2.16	9.92	2.56	7.78	46.8	47	0	0	52	0	496	5.73	2,500	100		1.00	Aug-12
11.90	-8.86	-9.97	-4.59	-7.13	3.91	1.16	9.95	2.56	7.86	46.8	47	0	0	52	0	496	5.73	2,000,000				Oct-08
11.72	-9.13	-10.47	-5.95	-9.46	3.38	1.66	9.93	2.56	7.79	46.8	47	0	0	52	0	496	5.73	2,500	100			Jul-05
0.03	0.24					0.74			10	9.3	22	0	78	0	0		4.57	1,500	50	0.50		Dec-19
0.13	0.41					0.49			10.01	9.3	22	0	78	0	0		4.57	250,000				Dec-19
-4.27	-8.62	-11.06	-7.07	3.02	0.98	1.45	6.84	7.64		231.8	4				1	43	4.64	1,000	50		1.00	Oct-11
3.87	3.08	4.84	10.88	16.41	2.21	0.5	2.72		11.15	289.7	4	23	0	71	0	37	3.01	2,000	1,000			Dec-97
6.58	-6.01	-3.28	2.05	10.86	3.15	1.17	7.3	3.92	12.72	9,082	10	39	1	48	0	17	4.90	0				Jan-98
6.77	-5.76	-2.69	3.82	14.09	3.74	0.59	7.35	3.92	12.83	9,082	10	39	1	48	0	17	4.90	1,000,000				Feb-13
6.74	-5.79	-2.76	3.59	13.58	3.66	0.67	7.35	3.92	12.84	9,082	10	39	1	48	0	17	4.90	100,000	50			May-91
6.62	-5.94	-3.03	2.81	12.20	3.41	0.92	7.31	3.92	12.77	9,082	10	39	1	48	0	17	4.90	2,500	50			Dec-96
5.14	6.63	9.11	17.13	25.20	2.31	0.73	3.47	6.18	13.94	8,216	15	23	0	34	0	297	3.50	2,500	50	4.25		Nov-73
4.94	6.32	8.36	14.58	20.69	1.58	1.48	3.42	6.18	13.95	8,216	15	23	0	34	0	297	3.50	2,500	50		1.00	Dec-94
5.26	6.90	9.55	18.34	27.51	2.61	0.39	3.47	6.18	14.07	8,216	15	23	0	34	0	297	3.50	1,000,000				Feb-13
5.24	6.86	9.46	18.04	26.85	2.53	0.48	3.47	6.18	14.06	8,216	15	23	0	34	0	297	3.50	100,000	50			Dec-94
9.14	-5.03	-0.91	7.12	19.03	4.55	0.57	8.59	4.89	12.65	662.1	1	22	1	74	0	14	5.08	3,000,000	50,000			Jan-95
7.31	4.16	5.42	12.14	21.26	0.49	0.65	4.88	7.08	17.76	632.1	3	38	0	45	0	215	3.38	1,000,000				Feb-13
7.26	4.11	5.38	11.98	20.77	0.44	0.7	4.89	7.08	17.71	632.1	3	38	0	45	0	215	3.38	100,000	50			May-91
7.20	4.00	5.14	11.17	19.37	0.19	0.95	4.86	7.08	17.4	632.1	3	38	0	45	0	215	3.38	2,500	50			Dec-96
11.59	-4.26	-2.14	5.89	16.31	5.32	1	9.55	4.66	3.96	111.2	5	0	0	93	0	48	5.85	2,500	50	4.25		Feb-84
11.04	-4.84	-3.12	3.46	11.90	4.5	1.75	9.37	4.66	3.97	111.2	5	0	0	93	0	48	5.85	2,500	50		1.00	Mar-98
11.38	-4.38	-2.13	6.72	17.86	5.61	0.75	9.41	4.66	3.95	111.2	5	0	0	93	0	48	5.85	100,000	50			Feb-08
9.86	-3.37	-0.59	10.23	25.64	5.81	0	8.32		9.96	257.5	15	5	0	67	0	48	5.46	0				Apr-04
5.23	8.10	10.29	17.80	22.31	2.01	0.4	3.94	8.71	11.45	64.8	5	87	0	8	0	246	0.75	100,000	50			May-91
5.23	8.10	10.43	18.06	22.61	2.06	0.35	3.89	8.71	11.46	64.8	5	87	0	8	0	246	0.75	1,000,000				Feb-17
5.24	8.01	10.19	17.09	20.74	1.71	0.65	3.92	8.71	11.44	64.8	5	87	0	8	0	246	0.75	2,500	50			May-10
11.00	-9.45	-7.72	-1.20	11.71	6.58	0.68	11.04	3.88	5.65	503.3	3	25	0	71	0	23	5.52	3,000,000	50,000			Jun-96
5.05	5.46	7.42	14.15	18.99	2.04	0.65	2.93	3.95	10.91	277.6	4	23	0	49	0	135	2.49	2,500	50	4.25		May-10
4.76	4.99	6.63	11.48	14.42	1.34	1.4	2.9	3.95	10.93	277.6	4	23	0	49	0	135	2.49	2,500	50		1.00	Aug-16
5.13	5.62	7.74	15.10	20.47	2.33	0.35	2.9	3.95	10.9	277.6	4	23	0	49	0	135	2.49	1,000,000				Feb-19

	MARKET		FUND TYPE, CATEGORY & OBJECTIVE		RATINGS				NEW INVESTORS	
Fund Name	Ticker Symbol	Traded On	Fund Type	Category and (Prospectus Objective)	Overall Rating	Reward Rating	Risk Rating	Recent Up/ Downgrade	Open to New Investors	Telephone
Loomis Sayles Intermediate Duration Bond Fund Y Class	LSDIX	NAS CM	Open End	US Fixed Inc (Corp Bond - General)	B-	C+	B+	Up	Y	800-862-4863
Loomis Sayles Intermediate Municipal Bond Fund Class A	MIMAX	NAS CM	Open End	US Muni Fixed Inc (Muni Bond - Natl)	C	C	B-		Y	800-862-4863
Loomis Sayles Intermediate Municipal Bond Fund Class C	MIMCX	NAS CM	Open End	US Muni Fixed Inc (Muni Bond - Natl)	C	C-	C+		Y	800-862-4863
Loomis Sayles Intermediate Municipal Bond Fund Class Y	MIMYX	NAS CM	Open End	US Muni Fixed Inc (Muni Bond - Natl)	C	C	B-		Y	800-862-4863
Loomis Sayles Investment Grade Bond Fund Admin Class	LIGAX	NAS CM	Open End	US Fixed Inc (Corp Bond - General)	B-	C	B	Up	Y	800-862-4863
Loomis Sayles Investment Grade Bond Fund Class A	LIGRX	NAS CM	Open End	US Fixed Inc (Corp Bond - General)	B-	C	B+	Up	Y	800-862-4863
Loomis Sayles Investment Grade Bond Fund Class C	LGBCX	NAS CM	Open End	US Fixed Inc (Corp Bond - General)	C+	C	B	Up	Y	800-862-4863
Loomis Sayles Investment Grade Bond Fund Class N	LGBNX	NAS CM	Open End	US Fixed Inc (Corp Bond - General)	B-	C	B+	Up	Y	800-862-4863
Loomis Sayles Investment Grade Bond Fund Class Y	LSIIX	NAS CM	Open End	US Fixed Inc (Corp Bond - General)	B-	C	B+	Up	Y	800-862-4863
Loomis Sayles Investment Grade Fixed Income Fund	LSIGX	NAS CM	Open End	US Fixed Inc (Income)	C-	D+	C	Down	Y	800-633-3330
Loomis Sayles Limited Term Govt & Agency Fund Class A	NEFLX	NAS CM	Open End	US Fixed Inc (Govt Bond - General)	C+	C	B	Up	Y	800-862-4863
Loomis Sayles Limited Term Govt & Agency Fund Class C	NECLX	NAS CM	Open End	US Fixed Inc (Govt Bond - General)	C	C	B-		Y	800-862-4863
Loomis Sayles Limited Term Govt & Agency Fund Class N	LGANX	NAS CM	Open End	US Fixed Inc (Govt Bond - General)	C+	C	B		Y	800-862-4863
Loomis Sayles Limited Term Govt & Agency Fund Class Y	NELYX	NAS CM	Open End	US Fixed Inc (Govt Bond - General)	C+	C	B		Y	800-862-4863
Loomis Sayles Securitized Asset Fund	LSSAX	NAS CM	Open End	US Fixed Inc (Income)	C+	C	B	Up	Y	800-633-3330
Loomis Sayles Senior Floating Rate & Fixed Income Cl A	LSFAX	NAS CM	Open End	US Fixed Inc (Income)	D	D	D+	Down	Y	800-862-4863
Loomis Sayles Senior Floating Rate & Fixed Income Cl C	LSFCX	NAS CM	Open End	US Fixed Inc (Income)	D	D	D+		Y	800-862-4863
Loomis Sayles Senior Floating Rate & Fixed Income Cl N	LSFNX	NAS CM	Open End	US Fixed Inc (Income)	D	D	D+	Down	Y	800-862-4863
Loomis Sayles Senior Floating Rate & Fixed Income Cl Y	LSFYX	NAS CM	Open End	US Fixed Inc (Income)	D	D	D+	Down	Y	800-862-4863
Loomis Sayles Strategic Alpha Fund Class A	LABAX	NAS CM	Open End	Fixed Inc Misc (Growth & Income)	C	D+	C+	Up	Y	800-862-4863
Loomis Sayles Strategic Alpha Fund Class C	LABCX	NAS CM	Open End	Fixed Inc Misc (Growth & Income)	C-	D	C		Y	800-862-4863
Loomis Sayles Strategic Alpha Fund Class N	LASNX	NAS CM	Open End	Fixed Inc Misc (Growth & Income)	C	D+	C+	Up	Y	800-862-4863
Loomis Sayles Strategic Alpha Fund Class Y	LASYX	NAS CM	Open End	Fixed Inc Misc (Growth & Income)	C	D+	C+	Up	Y	800-862-4863
Loomis Sayles Strategic Income Fund Admin Class	NEZAX	NAS CM	Open End	US Fixed Inc (Growth & Income)	D	D	C-	Down	Y	800-862-4863
Loomis Sayles Strategic Income Fund Class A	NEFZX	NAS CM	Open End	US Fixed Inc (Growth & Income)	D	D	C-	Down	Y	800-862-4863
Loomis Sayles Strategic Income Fund Class C	NECZX	NAS CM	Open End	US Fixed Inc (Growth & Income)	D	D	D+	Down	Y	800-862-4863
Loomis Sayles Strategic Income Fund Class N	NEZNX	NAS CM	Open End	US Fixed Inc (Growth & Income)	D+	D	C-	Down	Y	800-862-4863
Loomis Sayles Strategic Income Fund Class Y	NEZYX	NAS CM	Open End	US Fixed Inc (Growth & Income)	D+	D	C-	Down	Y	800-862-4863
Lord Abbett Bond Debenture Fund Class A	LBNDX	NAS CM	Open End	US Fixed Inc (Corp Bond - High Yield)	C-	D+	C		Y	201-827-2000
Lord Abbett Bond Debenture Fund Class C	BDLAX	NAS CM	Open End	US Fixed Inc (Corp Bond - High Yield)	C-	D+	C		Y	201-827-2000
Lord Abbett Bond Debenture Fund Class F3	LBNOX	NAS CM	Open End	US Fixed Inc (Corp Bond - High Yield)	C-	D+	C		Y	201-827-2000
Lord Abbett Bond Debenture Fund Class I	LBNYX	NAS CM	Open End	US Fixed Inc (Corp Bond - High Yield)	C-	D+	C		Y	201-827-2000
Lord Abbett Bond Debenture Fund Class P	LBNPX	NAS CM	Open End	US Fixed Inc (Corp Bond - High Yield)	C-	D+	C			201-827-2000
Lord Abbett Bond Debenture Fund Class R4	LBNSX	NAS CM	Open End	US Fixed Inc (Corp Bond - High Yield)	C-	D+	C		Y	201-827-2000
Lord Abbett Bond Debenture Fund Class R5	LBNTX	NAS CM	Open End	US Fixed Inc (Corp Bond - High Yield)	C-	D+	C		Y	201-827-2000
Lord Abbett Bond Debenture Fund Class R6	LBNVX	NAS CM	Open End	US Fixed Inc (Corp Bond - High Yield)	C-	D+	C		Y	201-827-2000
Lord Abbett Bond-Debenture Fund Class F	LBDFX	NAS CM	Open End	US Fixed Inc (Corp Bond - High Yield)	C-	D+	C		Y	201-827-2000
Lord Abbett Bond-Debenture Fund Class R2	LBNQX	NAS CM	Open End	US Fixed Inc (Corp Bond - High Yield)	C-	D+	C		Y	201-827-2000
Lord Abbett Bond-Debenture Fund Class R3	LBNRX	NAS CM	Open End	US Fixed Inc (Corp Bond - High Yield)	C-	D+	C		Y	201-827-2000
Lord Abbett California Tax Free Fund Class A	LCFIX	NAS CM	Open End	US Muni Fixed Inc (Muni Bond - Natl)	C	C-	B-		Y	201-827-2000
Lord Abbett California Tax Free Fund Class C	CALAX	NAS CM	Open End	US Muni Fixed Inc (Muni Bond - Natl)	C	C-	C+		Y	201-827-2000
Lord Abbett California Tax Free Fund Class F	LCFFX	NAS CM	Open End	US Muni Fixed Inc (Muni Bond - Natl)	C	C-	B-		Y	201-827-2000
Lord Abbett California Tax Free Fund Class F3	LCFOX	NAS CM	Open End	US Muni Fixed Inc (Muni Bond - Natl)	C	C-	B-		Y	201-827-2000
Lord Abbett California Tax Free Fund Class I	CAILX	NAS CM	Open End	US Muni Fixed Inc (Muni Bond - Natl)	C	C-	B-		Y	201-827-2000
Lord Abbett Core Fixed Income Fund Class A	LCRAX	NAS CM	Open End	US Fixed Inc (Corp Bond - General)	B-	C+	B	Up	Y	201-827-2000
Lord Abbett Core Fixed Income Fund Class C	LCRCX	NAS CM	Open End	US Fixed Inc (Corp Bond - General)	B-	C	B	Up	Y	201-827-2000
Lord Abbett Core Fixed Income Fund Class F	LCRFX	NAS CM	Open End	US Fixed Inc (Corp Bond - General)	B-	C+	B+	Up	Y	201-827-2000
Lord Abbett Core Fixed Income Fund Class F3	LCROX	NAS CM	Open End	US Fixed Inc (Corp Bond - General)	B	C+	B+	Up	Y	201-827-2000
Lord Abbett Core Fixed Income Fund Class I	LCRYX	NAS CM	Open End	US Fixed Inc (Corp Bond - General)	B-	C+	B+	Up	Y	201-827-2000
Lord Abbett Core Fixed Income Fund Class P	LCRPX	NAS CM	Open End	US Fixed Inc (Corp Bond - General)	B	C+	B+	Up		201-827-2000
Lord Abbett Core Fixed Income Fund Class R2	LCRQX	NAS CM	Open End	US Fixed Inc (Corp Bond - General)	B-	C+	B	Up	Y	201-827-2000
Lord Abbett Core Fixed Income Fund Class R3	LCRRX	NAS CM	Open End	US Fixed Inc (Corp Bond - General)	B-	C+	B	Up	Y	201-827-2000

★Expanded analysis of this fund is included in Section II.

TOTAL RETURNS & PERFORMANCE									ASSETS		ASSET ALLOCATION & TURNOVER							MINIMUMS		FEES		
3-Month Total Return	6-Month Total Return	1-Year Total Return	3-Year Total Return	5-Year Total Return	Dividend Yield (TTM)	Expense Ratio	3-Yr Std Deviation	Effective Duration	NAV	Total Assets (MIL)	%Cash	%Government Bonds	%Municipal Bonds	%Corporate Bonds	%Other	Turnover Ratio	Average Coupon Rate	Min Initial Investment	Min Additional Investment	Front End Fee (%)	Back End Fee (%)	Inception Date
5.02	5.50	7.69	15.02	20.39	2.28	0.4	2.88	3.95	10.9	277.6	4	23	0	49	0	135	2.49	100,000	50			Jan-98
2.04	1.24	3.07	9.49	15.39	2.24	0.71	3.6		10.4	25.1	5	0	95	0	0	11	4.83	2,500	50	3.00		Dec-12
1.86	0.87	2.31	7.06	11.17	1.49	1.46	3.58		10.4	25.1	5	0	95	0	0	11	4.83	2,500	50		1.00	Dec-12
2.10	1.27	3.33	10.31	16.94	2.48	0.46	3.58		10.41	25.1	5	0	95	0	0	11	4.83	100,000	50			Dec-12
8.50	5.36	7.89	15.22	23.69	2.85	1.01	5.16	3.56	11.67	5,463	6	10	0	58	0	44	4.09	0				Feb-10
8.54	5.47	8.14	15.95	24.97	3.09	0.76	5.15	3.56	11.7	5,463	6	10	0	58	0	44	4.09	2,500	50	4.25		Dec-96
8.35	5.05	7.32	13.35	20.42	2.38	1.51	5.19	3.56	11.56	5,463	6	10	0	58	0	44	4.09	2,500	50		1.00	Sep-03
8.62	5.62	8.46	17.01	27.18	3.38	0.46	5.16	3.56	11.7	5,463	6	10	0	58	0	44	4.09	1,000,000				Feb-13
8.60	5.59	8.40	16.90	26.63	3.33	0.51	5.15	3.56	11.71	5,463	6	10	0	58	0	44	4.09	100,000	50			Dec-96
6.35	-1.10	0.80	8.23	19.44	2.41	0.5	5.39	5.96	12.11	223.6	12	41	1	44	0	11	3.94	3,000,000	50,000			Jul-94
0.63	2.93	3.65	7.50	8.66	1.73	0.8	1.3	1.99	11.54	948.0	9	33	0	0	0	527	2.29	2,500	50	2.25		Jan-89
0.45	2.55	2.89	5.12	4.68	0.99	1.55	1.28	1.99	11.55	948.0	9	33	0	0	0	527	2.29	2,500	50		1.00	Dec-94
0.71	3.10	4.08	8.69	10.07	2.06	0.46	1.29	1.99	11.58	948.0	9	33	0	0	0	527	2.29	1,000,000				Feb-17
0.69	3.05	3.99	8.30	10.02	1.97	0.55	1.26	1.99	11.58	948.0	9	33	0	0	0	527	2.29	100,000	50			Mar-94
3.83	2.33	4.34	13.39	20.66	5.56	0	3.26		9.79	1,472	10	7	0	0	0	369	3.29	0				Mar-06
10.86	-7.31	-6.33	0.09	8.51	6.42	1.06	10.14	0.21	8.35	1,307	7	0	0	93	0	52		2,500	50	3.50		Sep-11
10.69	-7.69	-6.98	-2.16	4.51	5.6	1.81	10.17	0.21	8.32	1,307	7	0	0	93	0	52		2,500	50		1.00	Sep-11
10.79	-7.27	-6.15	0.88	10.04	6.75	0.76	10.13	0.21	8.35	1,307	7	0	0	93	0	52		1,000,000				Mar-17
10.91	-7.18	-6.08	0.85	9.99	6.69	0.81	10.14	0.21	8.36	1,307	7	0	0	93	0	52		100,000	50			Sep-11
7.97	2.00	2.43	8.10	13.07	2.59	0.99	4.58	2.85	9.78	1,086	14	3	0	41	0	414	4.35	2,500	50	4.25		Dec-10
7.92	1.64	1.76	5.71	8.93	1.83	1.74	4.66	2.85	9.75	1,086	14	3	0	41	0	414	4.35	2,500	50		1.00	Dec-10
8.07	2.19	2.79	9.13	14.78	2.94	0.67	4.62	2.85	9.76	1,086	14	3	0	41	0	414	4.35	1,000,000				May-17
8.07	2.05	2.73	8.83	14.45	2.87	0.74	4.63	2.85	9.75	1,086	14	3	0	41	0	414	4.35	100,000	50			Dec-10
6.29	-6.91	-3.66	0.87	8.24	3.13	1.2	7.68	3.51	13.25	6,178	12	39	2	46	0	13	4.87	0				Feb-10
6.34	-6.77	-3.40	1.56	9.61	3.38	0.96	7.67	3.51	13.3	6,178	12	39	2	46	0	13	4.87	2,500	50	4.25		May-95
6.15	-7.13	-4.19	-0.73	5.49	2.53	1.71	7.7	3.51	13.43	6,178	12	39	2	46	0	13	4.87	2,500	50		1.00	May-95
6.52	-6.55	-3.08	2.65	11.47	3.74	0.63	7.73	3.51	13.29	6,178	12	39	2	46	0	13	4.87	1,000,000				Feb-13
6.41	-6.66	-3.23	2.33	10.94	3.66	0.71	7.72	3.51	13.28	6,178	12	39	2	46	0	13	4.87	100,000	50			Dec-99
10.08	-3.01	-0.77	10.23	23.70	4.19	0.79	8.96	5.95	7.72	16,417	0	3	4	85	0	217	4.98	1,000		2.25		Apr-71
9.88	-3.42	-1.38	8.16	19.88	3.53	1.42	8.92	5.95	7.74	16,417	0	3	4	85	0	217	4.98	1,000			1.00	Jul-96
10.19	-2.91	-0.41	11.23	24.88	4.45	0.52	8.92	5.95	7.69	16,417	0	3	4	85	0	217	4.98	0				Apr-17
10.18	-2.94	-0.48	10.99	24.91	4.39	0.59	8.94	5.95	7.68	16,417	0	3	4	85	0	217	4.98	1,000,000				Mar-98
10.09	-3.13	-1.02	9.69	22.92	3.93	1.04	8.93	5.95	7.9	16,417	0	3	4	85	0	217	4.98	0				Aug-98
10.07	-3.15	-0.81	10.07	22.95	4.14	0.84	8.94	5.95	7.72	16,417	0	3	4	85	0	217	4.98	0				Jun-15
10.17	-2.93	-0.46	11.02	24.64	4.4	0.59	8.92	5.95	7.69	16,417	0	3	4	85	0	217	4.98	0				Jun-15
10.05	-2.90	-0.53	11.12	24.89	4.47	0.52	8.93	5.95	7.68	16,417	0	3	4	85	0	217	4.98	0				Jun-15
10.11	-2.97	-0.68	10.54	24.28	4.29	0.69	8.92	5.95	7.71	16,417	0	3	4	85	0	217	4.98	0				Sep-07
9.97	-3.20	-1.16	8.92	21.28	3.78	1.19	8.94	5.95	7.72	16,417	0	3	4	85	0	217	4.98	0				Sep-07
10.01	-3.16	-1.06	9.39	21.90	3.88	1.09	8.92	5.95	7.71	16,417	0	3	4	85	0	217	4.98	0				Sep-07
3.29	0.29	3.16	12.74	22.55	2.67	0.79	5.84	9.04	11.3	489.9	0	0	100	0	0	15	4.71	1,000		2.25		Sep-85
3.21	-0.03	2.59	10.74	18.74	2.02	1.4	5.81	9.04	11.31	489.9	0	0	100	0	0	15	4.71	1,000			1.00	Jul-96
3.31	0.34	3.25	13.06	23.14	2.77	0.69	5.83	9.04	11.3	489.9	0	0	100	0	0	15	4.71	0				Sep-07
3.34	0.39	3.37	13.48	23.40	2.88	0.56	5.76	9.04	11.3	489.9	0	0	100	0	0	15	4.71	0				Apr-17
3.43	0.48	3.45	13.51	23.75	2.87	0.59	5.83	9.04	11.3	489.9	0	0	100	0	0	15	4.71	1,000,000				Jan-11
3.61	5.30	7.31	14.24	20.06	2.2	0.64	3.44	5.47	11.52	1,929	6	36	1	32	0	836	2.95	1,500		2.25		Aug-00
3.46	4.99	6.68	12.18	16.44	1.59	1.25	3.46	5.47	11.47	1,929	6	36	1	32	0	836	2.95	1,500			1.00	Aug-00
3.63	5.44	7.51	14.58	20.64	2.28	0.54	3.46	5.47	11.52	1,929	6	36	1	32	0	836	2.95	0				Sep-07
3.68	5.42	7.59	15.21	21.57	2.45	0.36	3.46	5.47	11.52	1,929	6	36	1	32	0	836	2.95	0				Apr-17
3.66	5.51	7.65	15.02	21.35	2.42	0.4	3.45	5.47	11.52	1,929	6	36	1	32	0	836	2.95	1,000,000				Mar-98
3.96	5.90	8.44	17.65	23.46	2.75	0.89	3.48	5.47	11.75	1,929	6	36	1	32	0	836	2.95	0				Aug-00
3.51	5.09	6.89	12.79	17.70	1.81	1.04	3.45	5.47	11.52	1,929	6	36	1	32	0	836	2.95	0				Sep-07
3.53	5.14	6.99	13.13	18.31	1.9	0.94	3.45	5.47	11.52	1,929	6	36	1	32	0	836	2.95	0				Sep-07

	MARKET		FUND TYPE, CATEGORY & OBJECTIVE		RATINGS				NEW INVESTORS	
Fund Name	Ticker Symbol	Traded On	Fund Type	Category and (Prospectus Objective)	Overall Rating	Reward Rating	Risk Rating	Recent Up/ Downgrade	Open to New Investors	Telephone
Lord Abbett Core Fixed Income Fund Class R4	LCRSX	NAS CM	Open End	US Fixed Inc (Corp Bond - General)	B-	C+	B	Up	Y	201-827-2000
Lord Abbett Core Fixed Income Fund Class R5	LCRTX	NAS CM	Open End	US Fixed Inc (Corp Bond - General)	B-	C+	B+	Up	Y	201-827-2000
Lord Abbett Core Fixed Income Fund Class R6	LCRVX	NAS CM	Open End	US Fixed Inc (Corp Bond - General)	B	C+	B+	Up	Y	201-827-2000
Lord Abbett Core Plus Bond Fund Class A	LAPLX	NAS CM	Open End	US Fixed Inc (Growth & Income)	C	C	B		Y	201-827-2000
Lord Abbett Core Plus Bond Fund Class C	LAPCX	NAS CM	Open End	US Fixed Inc (Growth & Income)	C	C-	B-		Y	201-827-2000
Lord Abbett Core Plus Bond Fund Class F	LPLFX	NAS CM	Open End	US Fixed Inc (Growth & Income)	C	C	B		Y	201-827-2000
Lord Abbett Core Plus Bond Fund Class F3	LOPLX	NAS CM	Open End	US Fixed Inc (Growth & Income)	C	C	B		Y	201-827-2000
Lord Abbett Core Plus Bond Fund Class I	LAPIX	NAS CM	Open End	US Fixed Inc (Growth & Income)	C	C	B		Y	201-827-2000
Lord Abbett Core Plus Bond Fund Class R2	LAPTX	NAS CM	Open End	US Fixed Inc (Growth & Income)	C	C-	C+		Y	201-827-2000
Lord Abbett Core Plus Bond Fund Class R3	LAPQX	NAS CM	Open End	US Fixed Inc (Growth & Income)	C	C	B-		Y	201-827-2000
Lord Abbett Core Plus Bond Fund Class R4	LAPUX	NAS CM	Open End	US Fixed Inc (Growth & Income)	C	C	B-		Y	201-827-2000
Lord Abbett Core Plus Bond Fund Class R5	LAPVX	NAS CM	Open End	US Fixed Inc (Growth & Income)	C	C	B		Y	201-827-2000
Lord Abbett Core Plus Bond Fund Class R6	LAPWX	NAS CM	Open End	US Fixed Inc (Growth & Income)	C	C	B		Y	201-827-2000
Lord Abbett Corporate Bond Fund Class A	LBCAX	NAS CM	Open End	US Fixed Inc (Corp Bond - General)	C	C-	C+		Y	201-827-2000
Lord Abbett Corporate Bond Fund Class C	LBCCX	NAS CM	Open End	US Fixed Inc (Corp Bond - General)	C	C-	C+		Y	201-827-2000
Lord Abbett Corporate Bond Fund Class F	LCCFX	NAS CM	Open End	US Fixed Inc (Corp Bond - General)	C	C-	C+		Y	201-827-2000
Lord Abbett Corporate Bond Fund Class F3	LBCOX	NAS CM	Open End	US Fixed Inc (Corp Bond - General)	C	C-	C+		Y	201-827-2000
Lord Abbett Corporate Bond Fund Class I	LICIX	NAS CM	Open End	US Fixed Inc (Corp Bond - General)	C	C-	C+		Y	201-827-2000
Lord Abbett Corporate Bond Fund Class R2	LCBQX	NAS CM	Open End	US Fixed Inc (Corp Bond - General)	C	C-	C+		Y	201-827-2000
Lord Abbett Corporate Bond Fund Class R3	LRCBX	NAS CM	Open End	US Fixed Inc (Corp Bond - General)	C	C-	C+		Y	201-827-2000
Lord Abbett Corporate Bond Fund Class R4	LBCSX	NAS CM	Open End	US Fixed Inc (Corp Bond - General)	C	C-	C+		Y	201-827-2000
Lord Abbett Corporate Bond Fund Class R5	LBCUX	NAS CM	Open End	US Fixed Inc (Corp Bond - General)	C	C-	C+		Y	201-827-2000
Lord Abbett Corporate Bond Fund Class R6	LBCVX	NAS CM	Open End	US Fixed Inc (Corp Bond - General)	C	C-	C+		Y	201-827-2000
Lord Abbett Credit Opportunities Fund Class A			Closed End	US Fixed Inc (Income)	U	U	U		Y	201-827-2000
Lord Abbett Credit Opportunities Fund Institutional Class			Closed End	US Fixed Inc (Income)	D	D	D		Y	201-827-2000
Lord Abbett Emerging Markets Bond Fund Class A	LDMAX	NAS CM	Open End	Emerg Mkts Fixed Inc (Growth & Income)	D+	D	C-	Down	Y	201-827-2000
Lord Abbett Emerging Markets Bond Fund Class C	LDMCX	NAS CM	Open End	Emerg Mkts Fixed Inc (Growth & Income)	D+	D	C-	Down	Y	201-827-2000
Lord Abbett Emerging Markets Bond Fund Class F	LDMFX	NAS CM	Open End	Emerg Mkts Fixed Inc (Growth & Income)	D+	D	C-	Down	Y	201-827-2000
Lord Abbett Emerging Markets Bond Fund Class F3	LODMX	NAS CM	Open End	Emerg Mkts Fixed Inc (Growth & Income)	D+	D	C-	Down	Y	201-827-2000
Lord Abbett Emerging Markets Bond Fund Class I	LDMYX	NAS CM	Open End	Emerg Mkts Fixed Inc (Growth & Income)	D+	D	C-	Down	Y	201-827-2000
Lord Abbett Emerging Markets Bond Fund Class R2	LDMQX	NAS CM	Open End	Emerg Mkts Fixed Inc (Growth & Income)	D+	D	C-	Down	Y	201-827-2000
Lord Abbett Emerging Markets Bond Fund Class R3	LDMRX	NAS CM	Open End	Emerg Mkts Fixed Inc (Growth & Income)	D+	D	C-	Down	Y	201-827-2000
Lord Abbett Emerging Markets Bond Fund Class R4	LDMSX	NAS CM	Open End	Emerg Mkts Fixed Inc (Growth & Income)	D+	D	C-	Down	Y	201-827-2000
Lord Abbett Emerging Markets Bond Fund Class R5	LDMTX	NAS CM	Open End	Emerg Mkts Fixed Inc (Growth & Income)	D+	D	C-	Down	Y	201-827-2000
Lord Abbett Emerging Markets Bond Fund Class R6	LDMVX	NAS CM	Open End	Emerg Mkts Fixed Inc (Growth & Income)	D+	D	C-	Down	Y	201-827-2000
Lord Abbett Emerging Markets Corporate Debt Fund Class A	LCDAX	NAS CM	Open End	Emerg Mkts Fixed Inc (Diversified Emerg Mkts)	C-	D+	C	Down	Y	201-827-2000
Lord Abbett Emerging Markets Corporate Debt Fund Class C	LEDCX	NAS CM	Open End	Emerg Mkts Fixed Inc (Diversified Emerg Mkts)	C-	D+	C	Down	Y	201-827-2000
Lord Abbett Emerging Markets Corporate Debt Fund Class F	LCDFX	NAS CM	Open End	Emerg Mkts Fixed Inc (Diversified Emerg Mkts)	C-	D+	C	Down	Y	201-827-2000
Lord Abbett Emerging Markets Corporate Debt Fund Class F3	LCDOX	NAS CM	Open End	Emerg Mkts Fixed Inc (Diversified Emerg Mkts)	C-	D+	C	Down	Y	201-827-2000
Lord Abbett Emerging Markets Corporate Debt Fund Class I	LCDIX	NAS CM	Open End	Emerg Mkts Fixed Inc (Diversified Emerg Mkts)	C-	D+	C	Down	Y	201-827-2000
Lord Abbett Emerging Markets Corporate Debt Fund Class R2	LCDQX	NAS CM	Open End	Emerg Mkts Fixed Inc (Diversified Emerg Mkts)	C-	D+	C	Down	Y	201-827-2000
Lord Abbett Emerging Markets Corporate Debt Fund Class R3	LCDRX	NAS CM	Open End	Emerg Mkts Fixed Inc (Diversified Emerg Mkts)	C-	D+	C	Down	Y	201-827-2000
Lord Abbett Emerging Markets Corporate Debt Fund Class R4	LCDSX	NAS CM	Open End	Emerg Mkts Fixed Inc (Diversified Emerg Mkts)	C-	D+	C	Down	Y	201-827-2000
Lord Abbett Emerging Markets Corporate Debt Fund Class R5	LCDTX	NAS CM	Open End	Emerg Mkts Fixed Inc (Diversified Emerg Mkts)	C-	D+	C	Down	Y	201-827-2000
Lord Abbett Emerging Markets Corporate Debt Fund Class R6	LCDVX	NAS CM	Open End	Emerg Mkts Fixed Inc (Diversified Emerg Mkts)	C-	D+	C	Down	Y	201-827-2000
Lord Abbett Floating Rate Fund Class A	LFRAX	NAS CM	Open End	US Fixed Inc (Income)	D	D	D+	Down	Y	201-827-2000
Lord Abbett Floating Rate Fund Class C	LARCX	NAS CM	Open End	US Fixed Inc (Income)	D	D	D+	Down	Y	201-827-2000
Lord Abbett Floating Rate Fund Class F	LFRFX	NAS CM	Open End	US Fixed Inc (Income)	D	D	D+	Down	Y	201-827-2000
Lord Abbett Floating Rate Fund Class F3	LFROX	NAS CM	Open End	US Fixed Inc (Income)	D	D	D+	Down	Y	201-827-2000
Lord Abbett Floating Rate Fund Class I	LFRIX	NAS CM	Open End	US Fixed Inc (Income)	D	D	D+	Down	Y	201-827-2000
Lord Abbett Floating Rate Fund Class R2	LFRRX	NAS CM	Open End	US Fixed Inc (Income)	D	D	D+	Down	Y	201-827-2000
Lord Abbett Floating Rate Fund Class R3	LRRRX	NAS CM	Open End	US Fixed Inc (Income)	D	D	D+	Down	Y	201-827-2000

★Expanded analysis of this fund is included in Section II.

TOTAL RETURNS & PERFORMANCE									ASSETS		ASSET ALLOCATION & TURNOVER							MINIMUMS		FEES		
3-Month Total Return	6-Month Total Return	1-Year Total Return	3-Year Total Return	5-Year Total Return	Dividend Yield (TTM)	Expense Ratio	3-Yr Std Deviation	Effective Duration	NAV	Total Assets (MIL)	%Cash	%Government Bonds	%Municipal Bonds	%Corporate Bonds	%Other	Turnover Ratio	Average Coupon Rate	Min Initial Investment	Min Additional Investment	Front End Fee (%)	Back End Fee (%)	Inception Date
3.60	5.37	7.36	14.08	19.82	2.15	0.69	3.45	5.47	11.52	1,929	6	36	1	32	0	836	2.95	0				Jun-15
3.66	5.40	7.52	14.93	21.34	2.39	0.44	3.45	5.47	11.52	1,929	6	36	1	32	0	836	2.95	0				Jun-15
3.68	5.53	7.70	15.22	21.87	2.46	0.36	3.45	5.47	11.52	1,929	6	36	1	32	0	836	2.95	0				Jun-15
5.50	1.87	4.20	12.67		3.12	0.68	4.74	4.77	15.31	262.1	5	13	1	44	0	598	3.82	1,500		2.25		Dec-15
5.39	1.53	3.58	10.45		2.46	1.32	4.76	4.77	15.32	262.1	5	13	1	44	0	598	3.82	1,500			1.00	Dec-15
5.60	1.92	4.30	12.92		3.22	0.58	4.77	4.77	15.3	262.1	5	13	1	44	0	598	3.82	0				Dec-15
5.63	1.92	4.37	13.52		3.35	0.39	4.78	4.77	15.31	262.1	5	13	1	44	0	598	3.82	0				Apr-17
5.62	1.97	4.39	13.36		3.31	0.48	4.78	4.77	15.31	262.1	5	13	1	44	0	598	3.82	1,000,000				Dec-15
-2.45	0.69	4.30	9.90		2.75	1.08	4.78	4.77		262.1	5	13	1	44	0	598	3.82	0				Dec-15
5.49	1.73	3.92	11.72		2.85	0.98	4.78	4.77	15.31	262.1	5	13	1	44	0	598	3.82	0				Dec-15
5.56	1.85	4.16	12.54		3.09	0.73	4.74	4.77	15.31	262.1	5	13	1	44	0	598	3.82	0				Dec-15
5.62	1.98	4.42	13.37		3.34	0.48	4.78	4.77	15.31	262.1	5	13	1	44	0	598	3.82	0				Dec-15
5.64	2.08	4.54	13.58		3.38	0.39	4.75	4.77	15.32	262.1	5	13	1	44	0	598	3.82	0				Dec-15
10.20	3.33	7.31	16.41		3.59	0.68	7.52	8.39	10.39	8.9	1	0	2	96	0	54	4.78	1,500		2.25		Apr-17
10.14	3.08	6.59	13.98		2.91	1.33	7.58	8.39	10.39	8.9	1	0	2	96	0	54	4.78	1,500			1.00	Apr-17
10.33	3.38	7.40	16.97		3.68	0.58	7.55	8.39	10.41	8.9	1	0	2	96	0	54	4.78	0				Apr-17
10.27	3.45	7.56	17.38		3.83	0.45	7.51	8.39	10.39	8.9	1	0	2	96	0	54	4.78	0				Apr-17
10.38	3.53	7.52	17.09		3.78	0.48	7.54	8.39	10.39	8.9	1	0	2	96	0	54	4.78	1,000,000				Apr-17
10.22	3.13	6.88	15.04		3.19	1.08	7.58	8.39	10.39	8.9	1	0	2	96	0	54	4.78	0				Apr-17
10.25	3.18	6.99	15.37		3.29	0.98	7.59	8.39	10.39	8.9	1	0	2	96	0	54	4.78	0				Apr-17
10.20	3.31	7.25	16.25		3.54	0.73	7.51	8.39	10.39	8.9	1	0	2	96	0	54	4.78	0				Apr-17
10.27	3.43	7.41	17.12		3.79	0.48	7.51	8.39	10.39	8.9	1	0	2	96	0	54	4.78	0				Apr-17
10.27	3.45	7.56	17.38		3.83	0.45	7.51	8.39	10.39	8.9	1	0	2	96	0	54	4.78	0				Apr-17
13.81	-6.57					2.25			8.96	--	2	0	0	83	0		6.31	2,500	100	2.50	1.50	Sep-19
13.31	-6.23	-4.12			8.68	1.5			8.96	--	2	0	0	83	0		6.31	1,000,000				Feb-19
13.99	-3.57	-0.64	8.19	14.76	5.19	0.96	11.94	7.24	4.98	188.5	0	71	0	28	0	47	5.36	1,000		2.25		Sep-88
13.73	-4.02	-1.41	6.25	11.35	4.52	1.58	11.87	7.24	5.01	188.5	0	71	0	28	0	47	5.36	1,000			1.00	Jul-96
14.04	-3.48	-0.47	8.64	15.46	5.36	0.76	11.86	7.24	4.98	188.5	0	71	0	28	0	47	5.36	0				Sep-07
13.82	-3.67	-0.64	8.83	15.48	5.4	0.75	11.82	7.24	4.97	188.5	0	71	0	28	0	47	5.36	0				Apr-17
13.82	-3.49	-0.45	8.82	15.89	5.4	0.76	11.8	7.24	4.97	188.5	0	71	0	28	0	47	5.36	1,000,000				Oct-04
13.88	-3.72	-1.18	6.95	12.55	4.77	1.36	11.89	7.24	4.99	188.5	0	71	0	28	0	47	5.36	0				Sep-07
13.68	-3.72	-0.94	7.22	13.07	4.87	1.26	11.81	7.24	4.97	188.5	0	71	0	28	0	47	5.36	0				Sep-07
13.75	-3.78	-0.88	7.82	14.31	5.15	1.01	11.86	7.24	4.97	188.5	0	71	0	28	0	47	5.36	0				Jun-15
13.82	-3.49	-0.44	8.85	15.99	5.4	0.76	11.78	7.24	4.97	188.5	0	71	0	28	0	47	5.36	0				Jun-15
13.82	-3.66	-0.63	8.87	16.19	5.42	0.75	11.82	7.24	4.97	188.5	0	71	0	28	0	47	5.36	0				Jun-15
12.01	-2.52	1.08	10.13	24.43	4.48	1.05	9.46	5.79	14.83	56.1	0	8	0	92	0	64	5.26	1,000		2.25		Dec-13
11.83	-2.84	0.43	7.99	20.37	3.81	1.68	9.46	5.79	14.83	56.1	0	8	0	92	0	64	5.26	1,000			1.00	Dec-13
12.03	-2.48	1.16	10.42	24.94	4.57	0.95	9.46	5.79	14.83	56.1	0	8	0	92	0	64	5.26	0				Dec-13
12.10	-2.36	1.41	11.30	26.32	4.82	0.68	9.46	5.79	14.83	56.1	0	8	0	92	0	64	5.26	0				Apr-17
12.14	-2.45	1.24	10.67	25.57	4.65	0.85	9.5	5.79	14.82	56.1	0	8	0	92	0	64	5.26	1,000,000				Dec-13
-0.50	-1.23	3.07	9.94	24.97	4.07	1.45	9.49	5.79		56.2	0	8	0	92	0	64	5.26	0				Dec-13
12.01	-2.67	0.85	10.05	24.79	4.17	1.35	9.49	5.79	14.83	56.1	0	8	0	92	0	64	5.26	0				Dec-13
12.00	-2.55	1.04	9.91	23.59	4.43	1.1	9.46	5.79	14.82	56.1	0	8	0	92	0	64	5.26	0				Jun-15
12.06	-2.42	1.29	10.81	25.20	4.69	0.85	9.46	5.79	14.83	56.1	0	8	0	92	0	64	5.26	0				Jun-15
12.10	-2.35	1.43	11.31	25.97	4.83	0.68	9.46	5.79	14.83	56.1	0	8	0	92	0	64	5.26	0				Jun-15
7.53	-9.41	-7.49	-0.58	8.03	5.77	0.81	9.38	0.47	7.81	6,295	0	0	0	98	0	58		1,500		2.25		Dec-07
7.35	-9.57	-8.05	-2.44	4.81	5.08	1.45	9.37	0.47	7.82	6,295	0	0	0	98	0	58		1,500			1.00	Dec-07
7.56	-9.38	-7.41	-0.32	8.52	5.88	0.71	9.39	0.47	7.8	6,295	0	0	0	98	0	58		0				Dec-07
7.58	-9.29	-7.25	0.09	9.33	6.04	0.54	9.38	0.47	7.82	6,295	0	0	0	98	0	58		0				Apr-17
7.43	-9.32	-7.31	-0.11	9.08	5.98	0.61	9.32	0.47	7.81	6,295	0	0	0	98	0	58		1,000,000				Dec-07
7.41	-9.57	-7.84	-1.74	5.94	5.34	1.21	9.38	0.47	7.82	6,295	0	0	0	98	0	58		0				Dec-07
7.45	-9.54	-7.76	-1.56	6.46	5.44	1.11	9.41	0.47	7.81	6,295	0	0	0	98	0	58		0				Dec-07

Fund Name	Ticker Symbol	Traded On	Fund Type	Category and (Prospectus Objective)	Overall Rating	Reward Rating	Risk Rating	Recent Up/ Downgrade	Open to New Investors	Telephone
	MARKET			**FUND TYPE, CATEGORY & OBJECTIVE**	**RATINGS**				**NEW INVESTORS**	
Lord Abbett Floating Rate Fund Class R4	LRRKX	NAS CM	Open End	US Fixed Inc (Income)	D	D	D+	Down	Y	201-827-2000
Lord Abbett Floating Rate Fund Class R5	LRRTX	NAS CM	Open End	US Fixed Inc (Income)	D	D	D+	Down	Y	201-827-2000
Lord Abbett Floating Rate Fund Class R6	LRRVX	NAS CM	Open End	US Fixed Inc (Income)	D	D	D+	Down	Y	201-827-2000
Lord Abbett Global Bond Fund Class A	LAGGX	NAS CM	Open End	Global Fixed Inc (Income)	D+	D	C		Y	201-827-2000
Lord Abbett Global Bond Fund Class C	LGFCX	NAS CM	Open End	Global Fixed Inc (Income)	D+	D	C		Y	201-827-2000
Lord Abbett Global Bond Fund Class F	LGBFX	NAS CM	Open End	Global Fixed Inc (Income)	D+	D	C		Y	201-827-2000
Lord Abbett Global Bond Fund Class F3	LGBOX	NAS CM	Open End	Global Fixed Inc (Income)	D+	D	C		Y	201-827-2000
Lord Abbett Global Bond Fund Class I	LGBYX	NAS CM	Open End	Global Fixed Inc (Income)	D+	D	C		Y	201-827-2000
Lord Abbett Global Bond Fund Class R3	LGBRX	NAS CM	Open End	Global Fixed Inc (Income)	D+	D	C		Y	201-827-2000
Lord Abbett Global Bond Fund Class R4	LGBUX	NAS CM	Open End	Global Fixed Inc (Income)	D+	D	C		Y	201-827-2000
Lord Abbett Global Bond Fund Class R5	LGBVX	NAS CM	Open End	Global Fixed Inc (Income)	D+	D	C		Y	201-827-2000
Lord Abbett Global Bond Fund Class R6	LGBWX	NAS CM	Open End	Global Fixed Inc (Income)	D+	D	C		Y	201-827-2000
Lord Abbett High Yield Fund Class A	LHYAX	NAS CM	Open End	US Fixed Inc (Corp Bond - High Yield)	D	D	D+	Down	Y	201-827-2000
Lord Abbett High Yield Fund Class C	LHYCX	NAS CM	Open End	US Fixed Inc (Corp Bond - High Yield)	D	D	D+	Down	Y	201-827-2000
Lord Abbett High Yield Fund Class F	LHYFX	NAS CM	Open End	US Fixed Inc (Corp Bond - High Yield)	D	D	D+	Down	Y	201-827-2000
Lord Abbett High Yield Fund Class F3	LHYOX	NAS CM	Open End	US Fixed Inc (Corp Bond - High Yield)	D+	D	C-	Down	Y	201-827-2000
Lord Abbett High Yield Fund Class I	LAHYX	NAS CM	Open End	US Fixed Inc (Corp Bond - High Yield)	D+	D	C-	Down	Y	201-827-2000
Lord Abbett High Yield Fund Class P	LHYPX	NAS CM	Open End	US Fixed Inc (Corp Bond - High Yield)	D	D	D+	Down		201-827-2000
Lord Abbett High Yield Fund Class R2	LHYQX	NAS CM	Open End	US Fixed Inc (Corp Bond - High Yield)	D	D	D+	Down	Y	201-827-2000
Lord Abbett High Yield Fund Class R3	LHYRX	NAS CM	Open End	US Fixed Inc (Corp Bond - High Yield)	D	D	D+	Down	Y	201-827-2000
Lord Abbett High Yield Fund Class R4	LHYSX	NAS CM	Open End	US Fixed Inc (Corp Bond - High Yield)	D	D	D+	Down	Y	201-827-2000
Lord Abbett High Yield Fund Class R5	LHYTX	NAS CM	Open End	US Fixed Inc (Corp Bond - High Yield)	D+	D	C-	Down	Y	201-827-2000
Lord Abbett High Yield Fund Class R6	LHYVX	NAS CM	Open End	US Fixed Inc (Corp Bond - High Yield)	D+	D	C-	Down	Y	201-827-2000
Lord Abbett High Yield Municipal Bond Fund Class A	HYMAX	NAS CM	Open End	US Muni Fixed Inc (Muni Bond - Natl)	C-	D+	C	Down	Y	201-827-2000
Lord Abbett High Yield Municipal Bond Fund Class C	HYMCX	NAS CM	Open End	US Muni Fixed Inc (Muni Bond - Natl)	C-	D+	C	Down	Y	201-827-2000
Lord Abbett High Yield Municipal Bond Fund Class F	HYMFX	NAS CM	Open End	US Muni Fixed Inc (Muni Bond - Natl)	C-	D+	C	Down	Y	201-827-2000
Lord Abbett High Yield Municipal Bond Fund Class F3	HYMOX	NAS CM	Open End	US Muni Fixed Inc (Muni Bond - Natl)	C-	D+	C	Down	Y	201-827-2000
Lord Abbett High Yield Municipal Bond Fund Class I	HYMIX	NAS CM	Open End	US Muni Fixed Inc (Muni Bond - Natl)	C-	D+	C	Down	Y	201-827-2000
Lord Abbett Income Fund Class A	LAGVX	NAS CM	Open End	US Fixed Inc (Income)	C	C-	C+		Y	201-827-2000
Lord Abbett Income Fund Class C	LAUSX	NAS CM	Open End	US Fixed Inc (Income)	C	C-	C+		Y	201-827-2000
Lord Abbett Income Fund Class F	LAUFX	NAS CM	Open End	US Fixed Inc (Income)	C	C-	C+		Y	201-827-2000
Lord Abbett Income Fund Class F3	LOGVX	NAS CM	Open End	US Fixed Inc (Income)	C	C-	C+		Y	201-827-2000
Lord Abbett Income Fund Class I	LAUYX	NAS CM	Open End	US Fixed Inc (Income)	C	C-	B-		Y	201-827-2000
Lord Abbett Income Fund Class R2	LAUQX	NAS CM	Open End	US Fixed Inc (Income)	C	C-	C+		Y	201-827-2000
Lord Abbett Income Fund Class R3	LAURX	NAS CM	Open End	US Fixed Inc (Income)	C	C-	C+		Y	201-827-2000
Lord Abbett Inflation Focused Fund Class A	LIFAX	NAS CM	Open End	US Fixed Inc (Growth & Income)	D	D	C-		Y	201-827-2000
Lord Abbett Inflation Focused Fund Class C	LIFCX	NAS CM	Open End	US Fixed Inc (Growth & Income)	D	D	D+		Y	201-827-2000
Lord Abbett Inflation Focused Fund Class F	LIFFX	NAS CM	Open End	US Fixed Inc (Growth & Income)	D	D	C-	Down	Y	201-827-2000
Lord Abbett Inflation Focused Fund Class F3	LIFOX	NAS CM	Open End	US Fixed Inc (Growth & Income)	D	D	C-	Down	Y	201-827-2000
Lord Abbett Inflation Focused Fund Class I	LIFIX	NAS CM	Open End	US Fixed Inc (Growth & Income)	D	D	C-	Down	Y	201-827-2000
Lord Abbett Inflation Focused Fund Class R2	LIFQX	NAS CM	Open End	US Fixed Inc (Growth & Income)	D	D	D+		Y	201-827-2000
Lord Abbett Inflation Focused Fund Class R3	LIFRX	NAS CM	Open End	US Fixed Inc (Growth & Income)	D	D	C-		Y	201-827-2000
Lord Abbett Inflation Focused Fund Class R4	LIFKX	NAS CM	Open End	US Fixed Inc (Growth & Income)	D	D	C-		Y	201-827-2000
Lord Abbett Inflation Focused Fund Class R5	LIFTX	NAS CM	Open End	US Fixed Inc (Growth & Income)	D	D	C-	Down	Y	201-827-2000
Lord Abbett Inflation Focused Fund Class R6	LIFVX	NAS CM	Open End	US Fixed Inc (Growth & Income)	D	D	C-	Down	Y	201-827-2000
Lord Abbett Intermediate Tax Free Fund Class A	LISAX	NAS CM	Open End	US Muni Fixed Inc (Muni Bond - Natl)	C	C-	C+		Y	201-827-2000
Lord Abbett Intermediate Tax Free Fund Class C	LISCX	NAS CM	Open End	US Muni Fixed Inc (Muni Bond - Natl)	C	C-	C		Y	201-827-2000
Lord Abbett Intermediate Tax Free Fund Class F3	LOISX	NAS CM	Open End	US Muni Fixed Inc (Muni Bond - Natl)	C	C-	C+		Y	201-827-2000
Lord Abbett Intermediate Tax Free Fund Class I	LAIIX	NAS CM	Open End	US Muni Fixed Inc (Muni Bond - Natl)	C	C-	C+		Y	201-827-2000
Lord Abbett Intermediate Tax-Free Fund Class F	LISFX	NAS CM	Open End	US Muni Fixed Inc (Muni Bond - Natl)	C	C-	C+		Y	201-827-2000
Lord Abbett Investment Trust - Lord Abbett Income Cl R4	LAUKX	NAS CM	Open End	US Fixed Inc (Income)	C	C-	C+		Y	201-827-2000
Lord Abbett Investment Trust - Lord Abbett Income Cl R5	LAUTX	NAS CM	Open End	US Fixed Inc (Income)	C	C-	B-		Y	201-827-2000

★ Expanded analysis of this fund is included in Section II.

TOTAL RETURNS & PERFORMANCE									ASSETS		ASSET ALLOCATION & TURNOVER							MINIMUMS		FEES		
3-Month Total Return	6-Month Total Return	1-Year Total Return	3-Year Total Return	5-Year Total Return	Dividend Yield (TTM)	Expense Ratio	3-Yr Std Deviation	Effective Duration	NAV	Total Assets (MIL)	%Cash	%Government Bonds	%Municipal Bonds	%Corporate Bonds	%Other	Turnover Ratio	Average Coupon Rate	Min Initial Investment	Min Additional Investment	Front End Fee (%)	Back End Fee (%)	Inception Date
7.51	-9.44	-7.55	-0.83	7.90	5.71	0.86	9.38	0.47	7.81	6,295	0	0	0	98	0	58		0				Jun-15
7.57	-9.31	-7.30	-0.06	9.32	5.98	0.61	9.37	0.47	7.82	6,295	0	0	0	98	0	58		0				Jun-15
7.59	-9.29	-7.25	0.18	9.57	6.03	0.54	9.36	0.47	7.82	6,295	0	0	0	98	0	58		0				Jun-15
6.40	-1.85	-0.21			3.28	0.78			9.78	10.6	4	19	0	59	0	315	3.85	1,000		2.25		Jul-18
6.24	-2.14	-0.89			2.56	1.56			9.78	10.6	4	19	0	59	0	315	3.85	1,000			1.00	Jul-18
6.45	-1.75	-0.01			3.49	0.58			9.78	10.6	4	19	0	59	0	315	3.85	0				Jul-18
6.47	-1.70	0.08			3.6	0.53			9.78	10.6	4	19	0	59	0	315	3.85	0				Jul-18
6.45	-1.75	-0.01			3.49	0.58			9.78	10.6	4	19	0	59	0	315	3.85	1,000,000				Jul-18
6.32	-1.99	-0.51			2.97	1.08			9.78	10.6	4	19	0	59	0	315	3.85	0				Jul-18
6.38	-1.87	-0.26			3.23	0.83			9.78	10.6	4	19	0	59	0	315	3.85	0				Jul-18
6.45	-1.75	-0.01			3.49	0.58			9.78	10.6	4	19	0	59	0	315	3.85	0				Jul-18
6.47	-1.70	0.08			3.6	0.53			9.78	10.6	4	19	0	59	0	315	3.85	0				Jul-18
10.70	-7.72	-5.09	4.20	18.85	6.03	0.91	10.94	4.74	6.72	7,492	0	0	0	99	0	86	5.91	1,500		2.25		Dec-98
10.76	-7.93	-5.59	2.32	15.21	5.36	1.54	11	4.74	6.69	7,492	0	0	0	99	0	86	5.91	1,500			1.00	Dec-98
10.74	-7.69	-5.01	4.48	19.39	6.13	0.81	10.97	4.74	6.71	7,492	0	0	0	99	0	86	5.91	0				Sep-07
10.74	-7.55	-4.78	5.03	20.00	6.33	0.62	10.93	4.74	6.75	7,492	0	0	0	99	0	86	5.91	0				Apr-17
10.88	-7.59	-4.86	4.86	20.09	6.24	0.71	11	4.74	6.75	7,492	0	0	0	99	0	86	5.91	1,000,000				May-99
10.84	-7.69	-5.17	3.51	17.48	5.77	1.16	10.98	4.74	6.82	7,492	0	0	0	99	0	86	5.91	0				Dec-02
10.71	-7.84	-5.40	3.07	16.51	5.61	1.31	10.99	4.74	6.76	7,492	0	0	0	99	0	86	5.91	0				Sep-07
10.74	-7.80	-5.31	3.37	17.23	5.71	1.21	10.99	4.74	6.76	7,492	0	0	0	99	0	86	5.91	0				Sep-07
10.87	-7.63	-5.14	4.07	18.65	5.96	0.96	10.98	4.74	6.72	7,492	0	0	0	99	0	86	5.91	0				Jun-15
10.89	-7.60	-4.86	4.91	20.18	6.23	0.71	10.97	4.74	6.75	7,492	0	0	0	99	0	86	5.91	0				Jun-15
10.92	-7.55	-4.77	5.05	20.69	6.34	0.62	11.02	4.74	6.75	7,492	0	0	0	99	0	86	5.91	0				Jun-15
4.34	-3.40	0.19	14.64	27.66	3.97	0.79	8.34	11.44	11.96	2,927	0	0	100	0	0	11	5.20	1,000		2.25		Dec-04
4.18	-3.70	-0.51	12.51	23.64	3.29	1.42	8.29	11.44	11.96	2,927	0	0	100	0	0	11	5.20	1,000			1.00	Dec-04
4.36	-3.35	0.29	14.96	28.27	4.07	0.69	8.34	11.44	11.97	2,927	0	0	100	0	0	11	5.20	0				Sep-07
4.41	-3.22	0.40	15.42	28.58	4.2	0.55	8.36	11.44	11.94	2,927	0	0	100	0	0	11	5.20	0				Apr-17
4.40	-3.24	0.37	15.30	28.74	4.17	0.59	8.36	11.44	11.94	2,927	0	0	100	0	0	11	5.20	1,000,000				Jul-10
11.00	0.90	4.58	13.64	25.26	3.89	0.77	8.21	5.92	2.88	2,629	2	2	0	86	0	108	4.90	1,500		2.25		Jan-82
10.79	0.59	3.58	11.55	21.43	3.25	1.39	8.25	5.92	2.89	2,629	2	2	0	86	0	108	4.90	1,500			1.00	Jul-96
11.03	0.94	4.31	13.96	25.85	3.98	0.67	8.2	5.92	2.88	2,629	2	2	0	86	0	108	4.90	0				Sep-07
11.08	1.03	4.86	14.59	25.94	4.15	0.49	8.21	5.92	2.88	2,629	2	2	0	86	0	108	4.90	0				Apr-17
11.05	1.00	4.42	14.31	26.50	4.09	0.57	8.21	5.92	2.88	2,629	2	2	0	86	0	108	4.90	1,000,000				Oct-04
10.82	0.71	3.80	12.28	22.76	3.48	1.17	8.16	5.92	2.9	2,629	2	2	0	86	0	108	4.90	0				Jul-08
10.88	0.75	4.27	12.63	23.41	3.58	1.07	8.16	5.92	2.89	2,629	2	2	0	86	0	108	4.90	0				Jul-08
10.53	-5.81	-4.15	-0.40	-0.31	4.14	0.69	8.73	2.65	10.54	640.7	0	20	0	40	0	43	3.63	1,500		2.25		Apr-11
10.25	-6.17	-4.73	-2.28	-3.46	3.47	1.33	8.66	2.65	10.55	640.7	0	20	0	40	0	43	3.63	1,500			1.00	Apr-11
10.55	-5.84	-4.05	-0.10	0.17	4.24	0.59	8.73	2.65	10.55	640.7	0	20	0	40	0	43	3.63	0				Apr-11
10.50	-5.78	-3.99	0.45	0.88	4.42	0.42	8.72	2.65	10.53	640.7	0	20	0	40	0	43	3.63	0				Apr-17
10.47	-5.80	-3.96	0.19	0.68	4.36	0.49	8.69	2.65	10.54	640.7	0	20	0	40	0	43	3.63	1,000,000				Apr-11
10.26	-6.17	-4.70	-1.76	-2.44	3.74	1.09	8.72	2.65	10.51	640.7	0	20	0	40	0	43	3.63	0				Apr-11
10.45	-6.03	-4.43	-1.19	-1.76	3.82	0.99	8.74	2.65	10.54	640.7	0	20	0	40	0	43	3.63	0				Apr-11
10.41	-5.93	-4.20	-0.54	-0.56	4.08	0.74	8.67	2.65	10.54	640.7	0	20	0	40	0	43	3.63	0				Jun-15
10.48	-5.82	-4.06	0.20	0.61	4.35	0.49	8.74	2.65	10.53	640.7	0	20	0	40	0	43	3.63	0				Jun-15
10.61	-5.69	-3.89	0.56	1.33	4.42	0.42	8.73	2.65	10.54	640.7	0	20	0	40	0	43	3.63	0				Jun-15
3.32	0.15	2.25	10.58	17.28	2.6	0.7	5.06	6.13	11.04	4,963	0	0	100	0	0	19	4.70	1,000		2.25		Jun-03
3.08	-0.24	1.53	8.57	13.60	1.97	1.31	5.04	6.13	11.02	4,963	0	0	100	0	0	19	4.70	1,000			1.00	Jun-03
3.29	0.17	2.39	11.35	18.03	2.83	0.46	5.03	6.13	11.04	4,963	0	0	100	0	0	19	4.70	0				Apr-17
3.37	0.24	2.45	11.24	18.44	2.8	0.5	5.08	6.13	11.04	4,963	0	0	100	0	0	19	4.70	1,000,000				Jan-11
3.35	0.19	2.35	11.01	17.85	2.7	0.6	5.02	6.13	11.04	4,963	0	0	100	0	0	19	4.70	0				Sep-07
10.99	0.86	4.16	13.48	24.96	3.83	0.82	8.22	5.92	2.88	2,629	2	2	0	86	0	108	4.90	0				Jun-15
11.05	0.99	4.42	14.31	26.51	4.08	0.57	8.18	5.92	2.88	2,629	2	2	0	86	0	108	4.90	0				Jun-15

Fund Name	MARKET Ticker Symbol	MARKET Traded On	FUND TYPE, CATEGORY & OBJECTIVE Fund Type	FUND TYPE, CATEGORY & OBJECTIVE Category and (Prospectus Objective)	RATINGS Overall Rating	RATINGS Reward Rating	RATINGS Risk Rating	RATINGS Recent Up/ Downgrade	NEW INVESTORS Open to New Investors	NEW INVESTORS Telephone
Lord Abbett Investment Trust - Lord Abbett Income Cl R6	LAUVX	NAS CM	Open End	US Fixed Inc (Income)	C	C-	B-		Y	201-827-2000
Lord Abbett National Tax Free Fund Class A	LANSX	NAS CM	Open End	US Muni Fixed Inc (Muni Bond - Natl)	C	C-	C+		Y	201-827-2000
Lord Abbett National Tax Free Fund Class C	LTNSX	NAS CM	Open End	US Muni Fixed Inc (Muni Bond - Natl)	C	C-	C		Y	201-827-2000
Lord Abbett National Tax Free Fund Class F	LANFX	NAS CM	Open End	US Muni Fixed Inc (Muni Bond - Natl)	C	C-	C+		Y	201-827-2000
Lord Abbett National Tax Free Fund Class F3	LONSX	NAS CM	Open End	US Muni Fixed Inc (Muni Bond - Natl)	C	C-	C+		Y	201-827-2000
Lord Abbett National Tax Free Fund Class I	LTNIX	NAS CM	Open End	US Muni Fixed Inc (Muni Bond - Natl)	C	C-	C+		Y	201-827-2000
Lord Abbett New Jersey Tax Free Fund Class A	LANJX	NAS CM	Open End	US Muni Fixed Inc (Muni Bond - Natl)	C	C-	C+		Y	201-827-2000
Lord Abbett New Jersey Tax Free Fund Class F	LNJFX	NAS CM	Open End	US Muni Fixed Inc (Muni Bond - Natl)	C	C-	C+		Y	201-827-2000
Lord Abbett New Jersey Tax Free Fund Class F3	LONJX	NAS CM	Open End	US Muni Fixed Inc (Muni Bond - Natl)	C	C-	C+		Y	201-827-2000
Lord Abbett New Jersey Tax Free Fund Class I	LINJX	NAS CM	Open End	US Muni Fixed Inc (Muni Bond - Natl)	C	C-	C+		Y	201-827-2000
Lord Abbett New York Tax Free Fund Class A	LANYX	NAS CM	Open End	US Muni Fixed Inc (Muni Bond - Natl)	C	C-	C+		Y	201-827-2000
Lord Abbett New York Tax Free Fund Class C	NYLAX	NAS CM	Open End	US Muni Fixed Inc (Muni Bond - Natl)	C	C-	C		Y	201-827-2000
Lord Abbett New York Tax Free Fund Class F	LNYFX	NAS CM	Open End	US Muni Fixed Inc (Muni Bond - Natl)	C	C-	C+		Y	201-827-2000
Lord Abbett New York Tax Free Fund Class F3	LONYX	NAS CM	Open End	US Muni Fixed Inc (Muni Bond - Natl)	C	C-	C+		Y	201-827-2000
Lord Abbett New York Tax Free Fund Class I	NYLIX	NAS CM	Open End	US Muni Fixed Inc (Muni Bond - Natl)	C	C-	C+		Y	201-827-2000
Lord Abbett Short Duration Core Bond Fund Class A	LDCAX	NAS CM	Open End	US Fixed Inc (Income)	C	C-	C+		Y	201-827-2000
Lord Abbett Short Duration Core Bond Fund Class C	LDCCX	NAS CM	Open End	US Fixed Inc (Income)	C	C-	C		Y	201-827-2000
Lord Abbett Short Duration Core Bond Fund Class F	LDCFX	NAS CM	Open End	US Fixed Inc (Income)	C	C-	C+		Y	201-827-2000
Lord Abbett Short Duration Core Bond Fund Class F3	LSCOX	NAS CM	Open End	US Fixed Inc (Income)	C	C-	C+		Y	201-827-2000
Lord Abbett Short Duration Core Bond Fund Class I	LSCIX	NAS CM	Open End	US Fixed Inc (Income)	C	C-	C+		Y	201-827-2000
Lord Abbett Short Duration Core Bond Fund Class R3	LDCRX	NAS CM	Open End	US Fixed Inc (Income)	C	C-	C+		Y	201-827-2000
Lord Abbett Short Duration Core Bond Fund Class R4	LSCSX	NAS CM	Open End	US Fixed Inc (Income)	C	C-	C+		Y	201-827-2000
Lord Abbett Short Duration Core Bond Fund Class R5	LSCUX	NAS CM	Open End	US Fixed Inc (Income)	C	C-	C+		Y	201-827-2000
Lord Abbett Short Duration Core Bond Fund Class R6	LDCVX	NAS CM	Open End	US Fixed Inc (Income)	C	C-	C+		Y	201-827-2000
Lord Abbett Short Duration High Yield Muni Bond Cl A	SDHAX	NAS CM	Open End	US Muni Fixed Inc (Muni Bond - Natl)	C-	D+	C	Down	Y	201-827-2000
Lord Abbett Short Duration High Yield Muni Bond Cl C	SDHCX	NAS CM	Open End	US Muni Fixed Inc (Muni Bond - Natl)	D+	D+	C	Down	Y	201-827-2000
Lord Abbett Short Duration High Yield Muni Bond Cl F	SDHFX	NAS CM	Open End	US Muni Fixed Inc (Muni Bond - Natl)	C-	D+	C	Down	Y	201-827-2000
Lord Abbett Short Duration High Yield Muni Bond Cl F3	HYMQX	NAS CM	Open End	US Muni Fixed Inc (Muni Bond - Natl)	C-	D+	C	Down	Y	201-827-2000
Lord Abbett Short Duration High Yield Muni Bond Cl I	SDHIX	NAS CM	Open End	US Muni Fixed Inc (Muni Bond - Natl)	C-	D+	C	Down	Y	201-827-2000
★ Lord Abbett Short Duration Income Fund Class A	LALDX	NAS CM	Open End	US Fixed Inc (Income)	C	C-	C		Y	201-827-2000
★ Lord Abbett Short Duration Income Fund Class C	LDLAX	NAS CM	Open End	US Fixed Inc (Income)	C-	D+	C		Y	201-827-2000
★ Lord Abbett Short Duration Income Fund Class F	LDLFX	NAS CM	Open End	US Fixed Inc (Income)	C	C-	C		Y	201-827-2000
★ Lord Abbett Short Duration Income Fund Class F3	LOLDX	NAS CM	Open End	US Fixed Inc (Income)	C	C-	C		Y	201-827-2000
Lord Abbett Short Duration Income Fund Class I	LLDYX	NAS CM	Open End	US Fixed Inc (Income)	C	C-	C		Y	201-827-2000
★ Lord Abbett Short Duration Income Fund Class R2	LDLQX	NAS CM	Open End	US Fixed Inc (Income)	C-	D+	C	Down	Y	201-827-2000
★ Lord Abbett Short Duration Income Fund Class R3	LDLRX	NAS CM	Open End	US Fixed Inc (Income)	C-	D+	C	Down	Y	201-827-2000
★ Lord Abbett Short Duration Income Fund Class R4	LDLKX	NAS CM	Open End	US Fixed Inc (Income)	C	C-	C		Y	201-827-2000
★ Lord Abbett Short Duration Income Fund Class R5	LDLTX	NAS CM	Open End	US Fixed Inc (Income)	C	C-	C		Y	201-827-2000
★ Lord Abbett Short Duration Income Fund Class R6	LDLVX	NAS CM	Open End	US Fixed Inc (Income)	C	C-	C		Y	201-827-2000
Lord Abbett Short Duration Tax Free Fund Class A	LSDAX	NAS CM	Open End	US Muni Fixed Inc (Muni Bond - Natl)	C	C-	C		Y	201-827-2000
Lord Abbett Short Duration Tax Free Fund Class C	LSDCX	NAS CM	Open End	US Muni Fixed Inc (Muni Bond - Natl)	C-	C-	C	Down	Y	201-827-2000
Lord Abbett Short Duration Tax Free Fund Class F	LSDFX	NAS CM	Open End	US Muni Fixed Inc (Muni Bond - Natl)	C	C-	C		Y	201-827-2000
Lord Abbett Short Duration Tax Free Fund Class F3	LSDOX	NAS CM	Open End	US Muni Fixed Inc (Muni Bond - Natl)	C	C-	C+		Y	201-827-2000
Lord Abbett Short Duration Tax Free Fund Class I	LISDX	NAS CM	Open End	US Muni Fixed Inc (Muni Bond - Natl)	C	C-	C+		Y	201-827-2000
Lord Abbett Total Return Fund Class A	LTRAX	NAS CM	Open End	US Fixed Inc (Growth & Income)	C+	C	B	Up	Y	201-827-2000
Lord Abbett Total Return Fund Class C	LTRCX	NAS CM	Open End	US Fixed Inc (Growth & Income)	C+	C	B	Up	Y	201-827-2000
Lord Abbett Total Return Fund Class F	LTRFX	NAS CM	Open End	US Fixed Inc (Growth & Income)	C+	C	B	Up	Y	201-827-2000
Lord Abbett Total Return Fund Class F3	LTROX	NAS CM	Open End	US Fixed Inc (Growth & Income)	C+	C	B	Up	Y	201-827-2000
Lord Abbett Total Return Fund Class I	LTRYX	NAS CM	Open End	US Fixed Inc (Growth & Income)	C+	C	B	Up	Y	201-827-2000
Lord Abbett Total Return Fund Class P	LTRPX	NAS CM	Open End	US Fixed Inc (Growth & Income)	C+	C	B	Up		201-827-2000
Lord Abbett Total Return Fund Class R2	LTRQX	NAS CM	Open End	US Fixed Inc (Growth & Income)	C+	C	B	Up	Y	201-827-2000
Lord Abbett Total Return Fund Class R3	LTRRX	NAS CM	Open End	US Fixed Inc (Growth & Income)	C+	C	B	Up	Y	201-827-2000

★Expanded analysis of this fund is included in Section II.

TOTAL RETURNS & PERFORMANCE									ASSETS		ASSET ALLOCATION & TURNOVER							MINIMUMS		FEES		
3-Month Total Return	6-Month Total Return	1-Year Total Return	3-Year Total Return	5-Year Total Return	Dividend Yield (TTM)	Expense Ratio	3-Yr Std Deviation	Effective Duration	NAV	Total Assets (MIL)	%Cash	%Government Bonds	%Municipal Bonds	%Corporate Bonds	%Other	Turnover Ratio	Average Coupon Rate	Min Initial Investment	Min Additional Investment	Front End Fee (%)	Back End Fee (%)	Inception Date
11.08	1.03	4.86	14.61	27.10	4.16	0.49	8.18	5.92	2.88	2,629	2	2	0	86	0	108	4.90	0				Jun-15
3.32	-0.17	2.52	13.22	22.36	3.05	0.77	5.97	9.00	11.6	3,373	0	0	100	0	0	11	4.69	1,000		2.25		Apr-84
3.06	-0.48	1.88	11.12	18.61	2.4	1.39	5.97	9.00	11.61	3,373	0	0	100	0	0	11	4.69	1,000			1.00	Jul-96
3.35	-0.12	2.62	13.54	22.94	3.15	0.67	5.99	9.00	11.59	3,373	0	0	100	0	0	11	4.69	0				Sep-07
3.29	-0.07	2.74	13.98	23.24	3.27	0.53	5.98	9.00	11.59	3,373	0	0	100	0	0	11	4.69	0				Apr-17
3.28	-0.07	2.72	13.88	23.42	3.25	0.57	5.98	9.00	11.59	3,373	0	0	100	0	0	11	4.69	1,000,000				Jul-10
2.63	-0.30	1.93	12.66	22.20	2.6	0.82	5.51	8.39	5.12	123.0	0	0	100	0	0	4	4.63	1,000		2.25		Jan-91
2.66	-0.25	2.03	12.99	22.79	2.7	0.72	5.52	8.39	5.12	123.0	0	0	100	0	0	4	4.63	0				Sep-07
2.49	-0.39	1.95	13.21	23.09	2.82	0.59	5.43	8.39	5.12	123.0	0	0	100	0	0	4	4.63	0				Apr-17
2.48	-0.39	1.93	13.09	23.42	2.81	0.62	5.37	8.39	5.12	123.0	0	0	100	0	0	4	4.63	1,000,000				Jan-11
2.62	0.13	2.25	10.60	19.21	2.39	0.79	5.44	8.46	11.62	476.7	0	0	100	0	0	7	4.69	1,000		2.25		Apr-84
2.46	-0.27	1.52	8.46	15.42	1.74	1.4	5.37	8.46	11.6	476.7	0	0	100	0	0	7	4.69	1,000			1.00	Jul-96
2.65	0.18	2.35	10.93	19.78	2.49	0.69	5.44	8.46	11.63	476.7	0	0	100	0	0	7	4.69	0				Sep-07
2.68	0.24	2.47	11.34	20.15	2.62	0.56	5.42	8.46	11.63	476.7	0	0	100	0	0	7	4.69	0				Apr-17
2.67	0.23	2.45	11.26	20.38	2.6	0.59	5.41	8.46	11.63	476.7	0	0	100	0	0	7	4.69	1,000,000				Jan-11
4.05	0.82	2.31	7.61		2.93	0.6	2.93	1.56	9.84	59.9	1	12	0	43	0	136	2.98	1,500		2.25		Apr-17
3.77	0.38	1.51	5.18		2.23	1.29	2.85	1.56	9.83	59.9	1	12	0	43	0	136	2.98	1,500			1.00	Apr-17
3.96	0.76	2.29	7.81		3.01	0.5	2.84	1.56	9.83	59.9	1	12	0	43	0	136	2.98	0				Apr-17
4.13	0.96	2.47	8.40		3.18	0.34	2.92	1.56	9.83	59.9	1	12	0	43	0	136	2.98	0				Apr-17
4.10	0.92	2.51	8.25		3.12	0.4	2.92	1.56	9.84	59.9	1	12	0	43	0	136	2.98	1,000,000				Apr-17
3.87	0.58	1.92	6.58		2.64	0.9	2.85	1.56	9.83	59.9	1	12	0	43	0	136	2.98	0				Apr-17
4.03	0.79	2.26	7.47		2.87	0.65	2.86	1.56	9.84	59.9	1	12	0	43	0	136	2.98	0				Apr-17
4.09	0.92	2.51	8.28		3.13	0.4	2.92	1.56	9.84	59.9	1	12	0	43	0	136	2.98	0				Apr-17
4.02	0.86	2.47	8.41		3.18	0.34	2.84	1.56	9.83	59.9	1	12	0	43	0	136	2.98	0				Apr-17
3.02	-2.73	-0.37	7.80	15.05	2.86	0.65	5.42	4.52	15.04	438.1	2	0	98	0	0	29	4.42	1,000		2.25		Jun-15
2.79	-3.05	-1.02	5.68	11.05	2.17	1.31	5.37	4.52	15.04	438.1	2	0	98	0	0	29	4.42	1,000			1.00	Jun-15
3.05	-2.68	-0.28	8.12	15.60	2.96	0.55	5.42	4.52	15.04	438.1	2	0	98	0	0	29	4.42	0				Jun-15
3.02	-2.61	-0.12	8.62	16.38	3.12	0.39	5.37	4.52	15.04	438.1	2	0	98	0	0	29	4.42	0				Apr-17
3.00	-2.64	-0.18	8.44	16.17	3.06	0.45	5.37	4.52	15.04	438.1	2	0	98	0	0	29	4.42	1,000,000				Jun-15
5.88	0.14	1.62	7.78	12.75	3.42	0.6	4.31	1.58	4.15	51,496	3	4	0	51	0	57	3.42	1,500		2.25		Nov-93
5.42	-0.40	0.99	5.54	9.04	2.78	1.22	4.21	1.58	4.17	51,496	3	4	0	51	0	57	3.42	1,500			1.00	Jul-96
5.65	-0.05	1.72	7.83	13.02	3.52	0.5	4.27	1.58	4.14	51,496	3	4	0	51	0	57	3.42	0				Sep-07
5.68	0.02	1.88	8.60	13.66	3.68	0.34	4.24	1.58	4.15	51,496	3	4	0	51	0	57	3.42	0				Apr-17
5.67	0.00	1.82	8.16	13.58	3.62	0.4	4.27	1.58	4.14	51,496	3	4	0	51	0	57	3.42	1,000,000				Oct-04
5.51	-0.05	1.22	6.51	10.55	3.02	1	4.27	1.58	4.15	51,496	3	4	0	51	0	57	3.42	0				Jul-09
5.53	0.00	1.32	6.59	10.87	3.12	0.9	4.25	1.58	4.15	51,496	3	4	0	51	0	57	3.42	0				Jul-09
5.60	-0.12	1.57	7.39	12.24	3.36	0.65	4.27	1.58	4.15	51,496	3	4	0	51	0	57	3.42	0				Jun-15
5.67	0.22	1.81	8.44	13.62	3.62	0.4	4.29	1.58	4.14	51,496	3	4	0	51	0	57	3.42	0				Jun-15
5.69	0.02	1.88	8.37	13.98	3.68	0.34	4.27	1.58	4.14	51,496	3	4	0	51	0	57	3.42	0				Jun-15
1.85	0.15	1.41	5.34	7.08	1.73	0.65	2.37	2.75	15.7	1,653	1	0	99	0	0	33	3.12	1,000		2.25		Dec-08
1.70	-0.14	0.79	3.43	3.85	1.11	1.26	2.37	2.75	15.7	1,653	1	0	99	0	0	33	3.12	1,000			1.00	Dec-08
1.81	0.20	1.51	5.64	7.59	1.83	0.55	2.36	2.75	15.7	1,653	1	0	99	0	0	33	3.12	0				Dec-08
1.91	0.26	1.63	6.10	8.28	1.95	0.42	2.37	2.75	15.71	1,653	1	0	99	0	0	33	3.12	0				Apr-17
1.83	0.18	1.54	5.96	8.13	1.93	0.45	2.36	2.75	15.7	1,653	1	0	99	0	0	33	3.12	1,000,000				Dec-08
4.51	3.29	5.23	12.18	19.24	2.68	0.68	3.93	5.41	10.67	4,055	6	24	1	41	0	736	3.52	1,500		2.25		Aug-00
4.36	2.98	4.59	10.12	15.55	2.07	1.3	3.93	5.41	10.66	4,055	6	24	1	41	0	736	3.52	1,500			1.00	Aug-00
4.44	3.24	5.23	12.40	19.69	2.78	0.58	3.94	5.41	10.66	4,055	6	24	1	41	0	736	3.52	0				Sep-07
4.59	3.33	5.53	13.20	20.83	2.97	0.37	3.96	5.41	10.67	4,055	6	24	1	41	0	736	3.52	0				Apr-17
4.56	3.41	5.47	12.94	20.53	2.92	0.44	3.93	5.41	10.69	4,055	6	24	1	41	0	736	3.52	1,000,000				Dec-98
4.43	3.15	4.96	11.34	17.75	2.43	0.93	3.92	5.41	10.72	4,055	6	24	1	41	0	736	3.52	0				Aug-00
4.31	2.99	4.71	10.74	16.78	2.28	1.08	3.95	5.41	10.66	4,055	6	24	1	41	0	736	3.52	0				Sep-07
4.34	3.04	4.82	11.08	17.37	2.38	0.98	3.95	5.41	10.66	4,055	6	24	1	41	0	736	3.52	0				Sep-07

Fund Name	Ticker Symbol	Traded On	Fund Type	Category and (Prospectus Objective)	Overall Rating	Reward Rating	Risk Rating	Recent Up/ Downgrade	Open to New Investors	Telephone
	MARKET		FUND TYPE, CATEGORY & OBJECTIVE		RATINGS				NEW INVESTORS	
Lord Abbett Total Return Fund Class R4	LTRKX	NAS CM	Open End	US Fixed Inc (Growth & Income)	C+	C	B	Up	Y	201-827-2000
Lord Abbett Total Return Fund Class R5	LTRTX	NAS CM	Open End	US Fixed Inc (Growth & Income)	C+	C	B	Up	Y	201-827-2000
Lord Abbett Total Return Fund Class R6	LTRHX	NAS CM	Open End	US Fixed Inc (Growth & Income)	C+	C	B	Up	Y	201-827-2000
Lord Abbett U.S. Govt & Govt Spons Enterpr Money Mkt Cl A	LACXX	NAS CM	Money Mkt	US Money Mkt (Money Mkt - Govt)	C	C-	C+		Y	201-827-2000
Lord Abbett U.S. Govt & Govt Spons Enterpr Money Mkt Cl C	LCCXX	NAS CM	Money Mkt	US Money Mkt (Money Mkt - Govt)	C	C-	C+		Y	201-827-2000
Lord Abbett U.S. Govt & Govt Spons Enterpr Money Mkt Cl I	LAYXX	NAS CM	Money Mkt	US Money Mkt (Money Mkt - Govt)	C	C-	C+		Y	201-827-2000
Lord Abbett Ultra Short Bond Fund Class A	LUBAX	NAS CM	Open End	US Fixed Inc (Income)	C	C-	C+		Y	201-827-2000
Lord Abbett Ultra Short Bond Fund Class A1	LUSNX	NAS CM	Open End	US Fixed Inc (Income)	C	C-	C+		Y	201-827-2000
Lord Abbett Ultra Short Bond Fund Class F	LUBFX	NAS CM	Open End	US Fixed Inc (Income)	C	C-	C+		Y	201-827-2000
Lord Abbett Ultra Short Bond Fund Class F3	LUBOX	NAS CM	Open End	US Fixed Inc (Income)	C	C-	C+		Y	201-827-2000
Lord Abbett Ultra Short Bond Fund Class I	LUBYX	NAS CM	Open End	US Fixed Inc (Income)	C	C-	C+		Y	201-827-2000
Lord Abbett Ultra Short Bond Fund Class R5	LUBVX	NAS CM	Open End	US Fixed Inc (Income)	C	C-	C+		Y	201-827-2000
Lord Abbett Ultra Short Bond Fund Class R6	LUBWX	NAS CM	Open End	US Fixed Inc (Income)	C	C-	B-		Y	201-827-2000
Macquarie Pooled Trust Core Plus Bond Portfolio	DCPFX	NAS CM	Open End	US Fixed Inc (Multisector Bond)	B	C+	B+	Up	Y	215-255-2300
Macquarie Pooled Trust High Yield Bond Portfolio	DPHYX	NAS CM	Open End	US Fixed Inc (Corp Bond - High Yield)	C-	D+	C		Y	215-255-2300
Madison Core Bond Fund Class A	MBOAX	NAS CM	Open End	US Fixed Inc (Corp Bond - General)	B	B-	B	Up	Y	800-767-0300
Madison Core Bond Fund Class B	MBOBX	NAS CM	Open End	US Fixed Inc (Corp Bond - General)	B-	C+	B	Up	Y	800-767-0300
Madison Core Bond Fund Class Y	MBOYX	NAS CM	Open End	US Fixed Inc (Corp Bond - General)	B	B-	B+	Up	Y	800-767-0300
Madison Corporate Bond Fund Class Y	COINX	NAS CM	Open End	US Fixed Inc (Corp Bond - General)	B-	C+	B	Up	Y	800-767-0300
Madison Government Money Market Fund Class A	MFAXX	NAS CM	Money Mkt	US Money Mkt (Money Mkt - Govt)	C	C-	C+		Y	800-767-0300
Madison Government Money Market Fund Class B	MFBXX	NAS CM	Money Mkt	US Money Mkt (Money Mkt - Govt)	C	C-	C		Y	800-767-0300
Madison High Income Fund Class A	MHNAX	NAS CM	Open End	US Fixed Inc (Corp Bond - High Yield)	D+	D	C-	Down	Y	800-767-0300
Madison High Income Fund Class B	MHNBX	NAS CM	Open End	US Fixed Inc (Corp Bond - High Yield)	D	D	C-	Down	Y	800-767-0300
Madison High Income Fund Class Y	MHNYX	NAS CM	Open End	US Fixed Inc (Corp Bond - High Yield)	D+	D	C-	Down	Y	800-767-0300
Madison High Quality Bond Fund Class Y	MIIBX	NAS CM	Open End	US Fixed Inc (Corp Bond - High Quality)	C+	C+	B		Y	800-767-0300
Madison Tax-Free National Fund Class Y	GTFHX	NAS CM	Open End	US Muni Fixed Inc (Muni Bond - Natl)	C+	C	B	Up	Y	800-767-0300
Madison Tax-Free Virginia Fund Class Y	GTVAX	NAS CM	Open End	US Muni Fixed Inc (Muni Bond - Single State)	C+	C	B	Up	Y	800-767-0300
Maine Municipal Fund Class A	MEMUX	NAS CM	Open End	US Muni Fixed Inc (Muni Bond - Single State)	C	C	B-		Y	800-276-1262
Maine Municipal Fund Class I	MEIMX	NAS CM	Open End	US Muni Fixed Inc (Muni Bond - Single State)	C	C	B-		Y	800-276-1262
MainStay Candriam Emerging Markets Debt Fund Class A	MGHAX	NAS CM	Open End	Emerg Mkts Fixed Inc (Worldwide Bond)	D	D	D+	Down	Y	800-624-6782
MainStay Candriam Emerging Markets Debt Fund Class B	MGHBX	NAS CM	Open End	Emerg Mkts Fixed Inc (Worldwide Bond)	D	D	D+	Down		800-624-6782
MainStay Candriam Emerging Markets Debt Fund Class C	MHYCX	NAS CM	Open End	Emerg Mkts Fixed Inc (Worldwide Bond)	D	D	D+	Down	Y	800-624-6782
MainStay Candriam Emerging Markets Debt Fund Class I	MGHIX	NAS CM	Open End	Emerg Mkts Fixed Inc (Worldwide Bond)	D	D	D+	Down	Y	800-624-6782
MainStay Candriam Emerg Mkts Debt Fund Investor Class	MGHHX	NAS CM	Open End	Emerg Mkts Fixed Inc (Worldwide Bond)	D	D	D+	Down	Y	800-624-6782
MainStay Floating Rate Fund Class A	MXFAX	NAS CM	Open End	US Fixed Inc (Income)	D+	D	C-	Down	Y	800-624-6782
MainStay Floating Rate Fund Class B	MXFBX	NAS CM	Open End	US Fixed Inc (Income)	D	D	C-	Down		800-624-6782
MainStay Floating Rate Fund Class C	MXFCX	NAS CM	Open End	US Fixed Inc (Income)	D	D	C-	Down	Y	800-624-6782
MainStay Floating Rate Fund Class I	MXFIX	NAS CM	Open End	US Fixed Inc (Income)	D+	D	C-	Down	Y	800-624-6782
MainStay Floating Rate Fund Class R3	MXFHX	NAS CM	Open End	US Fixed Inc (Income)	D+	D	C-	Down	Y	800-624-6782
MainStay Floating Rate Fund Class R6	MXFEX	NAS CM	Open End	US Fixed Inc (Income)	D+	D	C	Down	Y	800-624-6782
MainStay Floating Rate Fund Investor Class	MXFNX	NAS CM	Open End	US Fixed Inc (Income)	D+	D	C-	Down	Y	800-624-6782
MainStay MacKay California Tax Free Opportunities Cl A	MSCAX	NAS CM	Open End	US Muni Fixed Inc (Muni Bond - Natl)	C	C-	B-		Y	800-624-6782
MainStay MacKay California Tax Free Opportunities Cl C	MSCCX	NAS CM	Open End	US Muni Fixed Inc (Muni Bond - Natl)	C	C-	B-		Y	800-624-6782
MainStay MacKay California Tax Free Opportunities Cl I	MCOIX	NAS CM	Open End	US Muni Fixed Inc (Muni Bond - Natl)	C	C-	B-		Y	800-624-6782
MainStay MacKay California Tax Free Opportunities Cl R6	MSODX	NAS CM	Open End	US Muni Fixed Inc (Muni Bond - Natl)	C	C-	B			800-624-6782
MainStay MacKay California Tax Free Opp Investor Cl	MSCVX	NAS CM	Open End	US Muni Fixed Inc (Muni Bond - Natl)	C	C-	B-		Y	800-624-6782
MainStay MacKay DefinedTerm Municipal Opportunities Fund	MMD	NYSE	Closed End	US Muni Fixed Inc (Income)	C-	C-	C-		Y	212-938-6500
MainStay MacKay High Yield Corporate Bond Fund Class A	MHCAX	NAS CM	Open End	US Fixed Inc (Corp Bond - High Yield)	C-	D+	C		Y	800-624-6782
MainStay MacKay High Yield Corporate Bond Fund Class B	MKHCX	NAS CM	Open End	US Fixed Inc (Corp Bond - High Yield)	C-	D+	C			800-624-6782
MainStay MacKay High Yield Corporate Bond Fund Class C	MYHCX	NAS CM	Open End	US Fixed Inc (Corp Bond - High Yield)	C-	D+	C		Y	800-624-6782
MainStay MacKay High Yield Corporate Bond Fund Class I	MHYIX	NAS CM	Open End	US Fixed Inc (Corp Bond - High Yield)	C-	D+	C		Y	800-624-6782
MainStay MacKay High Yield Corporate Bond Fund Class R1	MHHRX	NAS CM	Open End	US Fixed Inc (Corp Bond - High Yield)	C-	D+	C		Y	800-624-6782

★Expanded analysis of this fund is included in Section II.

TOTAL RETURNS & PERFORMANCE									ASSETS		ASSET ALLOCATION & TURNOVER							MINIMUMS		FEES		
3-Month Total Return	6-Month Total Return	1-Year Total Return	3-Year Total Return	5-Year Total Return	Dividend Yield (TTM)	Expense Ratio	3-Yr Std Deviation	Effective Duration	NAV	Total Assets (MIL)	%Cash	%Government Bonds	%Municipal Bonds	%Corporate Bonds	%Other	Turnover Ratio	Average Coupon Rate	Min Initial Investment	Min Additional Investment	Front End Fee (%)	Back End Fee (%)	Inception Date
4.50	3.26	5.17	12.02	18.42	2.62	0.73	3.93	5.41	10.67	4,055	6	24	1	41	0	736	3.52	0				Jun-15
4.56	3.38	5.43	12.86	19.66	2.87	0.48	3.94	5.41	10.67	4,055	6	24	1	41	0	736	3.52	0				Jun-15
4.49	3.34	5.43	13.11	20.86	2.97	0.37	3.92	5.41	10.67	4,055	6	24	1	41	0	736	3.52	0				Jun-15
0.00	0.23	1.04	3.40	3.47	1.22	0.31	0.18		1	734.3	79	21	0	0	0			1,000			1.00	Jun-79
0.00	0.23	1.05	3.41	3.46	1.22	0.31	0.18		1	734.3	79	21	0	0	0			1,000			1.00	Jul-96
0.00	0.23	1.05	3.40	3.46	1.22	0.31	0.18		1	734.3	79	21	0	0	0			0				Oct-04
2.13	0.76	1.97	6.32		2	0.45	1.25	0.18	10.03	18,933	35	0	0	48	0	46	1.75	1,500				Oct-16
2.01	0.71	1.85	6.17			0.52	1.24	0.18	10.03	18,933	35	0	0	48	0	46	1.75	1,500	0	1.50	0.50	Jul-19
2.15	0.78	1.92	6.48		2.05	0.4	1.25	0.18	10.03	18,933	35	0	0	48	0	46	1.75	0				Oct-16
2.18	0.85	2.06	6.93		2.19	0.25	1.25	0.18	10.03	18,933	35	0	0	48	0	46	1.75	0		1.50		Apr-17
2.07	0.73	2.02	6.69		2.15	0.3	1.24	0.18	10.02	18,933	35	0	0	48	0	46	1.75	1,000,000				Oct-16
2.17	0.84	2.03	6.86		2.16	0.3	1.24	0.18	10.03	18,933	35	0	0	48	0	46	1.75	0				Oct-16
2.08	0.86	2.07	6.93		2.2	0.25	1.25	0.18	10.03	18,933	35	0	0	48	0	46	1.75	0				Oct-16
6.96	5.47	8.45	17.06	24.24	4.73	0.45	4.54	5.94	10.59	140.0	-4	21	0	43	0	177	3.83	1,000,000				Jun-02
9.42	-3.14	0.66	9.60	20.38	5.54	0.59	8.28	4.06	7.08	98.6	6	0	0	94	0	82	6.21	1,000,000				Dec-96
4.57	6.64	8.82	15.55	22.01	2	0.9	3.36	6.07	10.77	120.1	2	23	1	35	0	36	3.49	1,000	50	4.50		Dec-97
4.37	6.12	8.00	12.87	17.53	1.28	1.65	3.3	6.07	10.78	120.1	2	23	1	35	0	36	3.49	1,000	150		4.50	Dec-97
4.66	6.81	9.17	16.40	23.60	2.47	0.65	3.3	6.07	10.71	120.1	2	23	1	35	0	36	3.49	25,000	50			Jun-06
11.42	5.85	10.04	20.03	31.35	2.77	0.65	6.89	7.31	12.57	14.2	3	0	0	97	0	20	3.93	25,000	50			Jul-07
0.02	0.25	0.98	3.47	3.50	1.13	0.55	0.16		1	17.5	80	20	0	0	0	33		1,000	50			Dec-97
0.00	0.05	0.40	1.48	1.48	0.49	1.3	0.12		1	17.5	80	20	0	0	0	33		1,000	150		4.50	Dec-97
8.69	-3.59	-2.42	3.28	13.16	4.95	1.01	7.41	3.22	5.47	16.6	3	0	0	96	0	16	5.94	1,000	50	4.50		Dec-97
8.61	-3.84	-3.07	0.95	9.01	4.02	1.76	7.45	3.22	5.65	16.6	3	0	0	96	0	16	5.94	1,000	150		4.50	Dec-97
8.77	-3.37	-2.14	4.09	14.71	5.61	0.76	7.42	3.22	5.34	16.6	3	0	0	96	0	16	5.94	25,000	50			Jun-06
1.65	4.38	5.66	10.18	12.78	1.69	0.49	1.78	2.65	11.44	167.0	15	50	0	36	0	20	2.27	0				May-00
2.13	2.50	4.43	10.28	17.08	2	0.75	3.2	4.95	11.08	23.5	2	0	98	0	0	26	4.76	25,000	50			Dec-82
2.65	2.87	4.56	10.10	15.60	1.73	0.85	3.02	5.00	11.92	22.3	2	0	98	0	0	22	4.66	25,000	50			Oct-87
1.04	1.52	2.65	7.26	11.76	2.01	0.98	2.57		10.89	15.5	3	0	97	0	0	8	4.26	1,000	50	2.50		Dec-91
1.10	1.64	2.90	7.95	12.48	2.26	0.73	2.58		10.89	15.5	3	0	97	0	0	8	4.26	1,000	50			Nov-17
15.20	-6.46	-4.75	4.04	24.94	5.16	1.18	13.31		9.7	110.7	2	77	0	21	6	102	5.91	15,000		4.50		Jun-98
14.84	-7.01	-5.77	0.97	18.89	4.11	2.23	13.3		9.5	110.7	2	77	0	21	6	102	5.91	1,000	50		5.00	Jun-98
14.94	-6.90	-5.76	0.97	18.99	4.1	2.23	13.31		9.52	110.7	2	77	0	21	6	102	5.91	1,000	50		1.00	Sep-98
15.27	-6.30	-4.44	4.89	26.57	5.51	0.86	13.31		9.71	110.7	2	77	0	21	6	102	5.91	1,000,000				Aug-07
15.06	-6.63	-5.01	3.29	23.50	4.77	1.48	13.27		9.8	110.7	2	77	0	21	6	102	5.91	1,000	50	4.50		Feb-08
8.49	-4.37	-1.92	4.91	12.23	4.38	1.09	7.8	0.90	8.6	927.2	6	0	0	94	0	19	1.29	15,000		3.00		May-04
8.42	-4.71	-2.52	2.70	8.10	3.62	1.83	7.78	0.90	8.61	927.2	6	0	0	94	0	19	1.29	1,000	50		3.00	May-04
8.29	-4.71	-2.64	2.58	7.97	3.62	1.83	7.77	0.90	8.6	927.2	6	0	0	94	0	19	1.29	1,000	50		1.00	May-04
8.56	-4.25	-1.68	5.70	13.51	4.64	0.84	7.78	0.90	8.6	927.2	6	0	0	94	0	19	1.29	1,000,000				May-04
8.40	-4.53	-2.27	3.80	10.26	4.01	1.44	7.78	0.90	8.6	927.2	6	0	0	94	0	19	1.29	0				Feb-16
8.62	-4.13	-1.46	6.00	13.84	4.87	0.64	7.78	0.90	8.6	927.2	6	0	0	94	0	19	1.29	0				Feb-19
8.49	-4.36	-1.91	4.91	12.20	4.39	1.08	7.79	0.90	8.6	927.2	6	0	0	94	0	19	1.29	1,000	50	3.00		Feb-08
2.86	0.83	3.55	13.59	25.17	2.61	0.75	5.14	6.81	10.73	932.3	6	0	94	0	0	47	4.67	15,000		4.50		Feb-13
2.79	0.69	3.27	12.65	23.41	2.33	1.02	5.17	6.81	10.73	932.3	6	0	94	0	0	47	4.67	2,500	50		1.00	Feb-13
2.92	0.95	3.81	14.44	26.75	2.86	0.5	5.18	6.81	10.73	932.3	6	0	94	0	0	47	4.67	1,000,000				Feb-13
2.93	0.97	3.83	14.46	26.78		0.49	5.18	6.81	10.73	932.3	6	0	94	0	0	47	4.67	0				Nov-19
2.85	0.82	3.53	13.50	24.97	2.59	0.77	5.19	6.81	10.73	932.3	6	0	94	0	0	47	4.67	2,500	50	4.50		Feb-13
5.14	1.51	4.01	18.02	41.69	5.15		5.63		20.25	547.1	0	0	100	0	0	27	7.07					Jun-12
9.42	-4.39	-0.79	8.87	23.63	6.03	0.99	8.16	3.88	5.27	10,964	6	0	0	94	0	30	6.10	15,000		4.50		Jan-95
9.00	-4.84	-1.82	6.17	18.59	5.16	1.8	8.1	3.88	5.24	10,964	6	0	0	94	0	30	6.10	1,000	50		5.00	May-86
9.21	-4.82	-1.64	6.37	18.80	5.16	1.8	8.17	3.88	5.25	10,964	6	0	0	94	0	30	6.10	1,000	50		1.00	Sep-98
9.50	-4.25	-0.68	9.75	25.04	6.33	0.74	8.16	3.88	5.27	10,964	6	0	0	94	0	30	6.10	1,000,000				Jan-04
9.49	-4.31	-0.62	9.22	24.41	6.23	0.84	8.16	3.88	5.26	10,964	6	0	0	94	0	30	6.10	0				Jun-12

	MARKET			FUND TYPE, CATEGORY & OBJECTIVE	RATINGS				NEW INVESTORS	
Fund Name	Ticker Symbol	Traded On	Fund Type	Category and (Prospectus Objective)	Overall Rating	Reward Rating	Risk Rating	Recent Up/ Downgrade	Open to New Investors	Telephone
MainStay MacKay High Yield Corporate Bond Fund Class R2	MHYRX	NAS CM	Open End	US Fixed Inc (Corp Bond - High Yield)	C-	D+	C		Y	800-624-6782
MainStay MacKay High Yield Corporate Bond Fund Class R3	MHYTX	NAS CM	Open End	US Fixed Inc (Corp Bond - High Yield)	C-	D+	C		Y	800-624-6782
MainStay MacKay High Yield Corporate Bond Fund Class R6	MHYSX	NAS CM	Open End	US Fixed Inc (Corp Bond - High Yield)	C-	D+	C		Y	800-624-6782
MainStay MacKay High Yield Corp Bond Fund Investor Class	MHHIX	NAS CM	Open End	US Fixed Inc (Corp Bond - High Yield)	C-	D+	C		Y	800-624-6782
MainStay MacKay High Yield Municipal Bond Fund Class A	MMHAX	NAS CM	Open End	US Muni Fixed Inc (Muni Bond - Natl)	C-	D+	C	Down	Y	800-624-6782
MainStay MacKay High Yield Municipal Bond Fund Class C	MMHDX	NAS CM	Open End	US Muni Fixed Inc (Muni Bond - Natl)	C-	D+	C	Down	Y	800-624-6782
MainStay MacKay High Yield Municipal Bond Fund Class I	MMHIX	NAS CM	Open End	US Muni Fixed Inc (Muni Bond - Natl)	C	D+	C		Y	800-624-6782
MainStay MacKay High Yield Municipal Bond Fund Class R6	MMHEX	NAS CM	Open End	US Muni Fixed Inc (Muni Bond - Natl)	C-	D+	C	Down		800-624-6782
MainStay MacKay High Yield Muni Bond Fund Investor Class	MMHVX	NAS CM	Open End	US Muni Fixed Inc (Muni Bond - Natl)	C-	D+	C	Down	Y	800-624-6782
MainStay MacKay Infrastructure Bond Fund Class A	MGVAX	NAS CM	Open End	US Fixed Inc (Govt Bond - General)	C	C	B-	Down	Y	800-624-6782
MainStay MacKay Infrastructure Bond Fund Class B	MCSGX	NAS CM	Open End	US Fixed Inc (Govt Bond - General)	C	C-	C+			800-624-6782
MainStay MacKay Infrastructure Bond Fund Class C	MGVCX	NAS CM	Open End	US Fixed Inc (Govt Bond - General)	C	C-	C+		Y	800-624-6782
MainStay MacKay Infrastructure Bond Fund Class I	MGOIX	NAS CM	Open End	US Fixed Inc (Govt Bond - General)	C+	C	B		Y	800-624-6782
MainStay MacKay Infrastructure Bond Fund Class Investor	MGVNX	NAS CM	Open End	US Fixed Inc (Govt Bond - General)	C	C	C+		Y	800-624-6782
MainStay MacKay Infrastructure Bond R6	MGVDX	NAS CM	Open End	US Fixed Inc (Govt Bond - General)	C	C	C+		Y	800-624-6782
MainStay MacKay Intermediate Tax Free Bond Fund Class A	MTFDX	NAS CM	Open End	US Muni Fixed Inc (Muni Bond - Natl)	D-	D	C		Y	800-624-6782
MainStay MacKay Intermediate Tax Free Bond Fund Class C	MTFFX	NAS CM	Open End	US Muni Fixed Inc (Muni Bond - Natl)	D-	D	C		Y	800-624-6782
MainStay MacKay Intermediate Tax Free Bond Fund Class I	MTFGX	NAS CM	Open End	US Muni Fixed Inc (Muni Bond - Natl)	D-	D	C		Y	800-624-6782
MainStay MacKay Intermediate Tax Free Bond Fund Class R6	MTFHX	NAS CM	Open End	US Muni Fixed Inc (Muni Bond - Natl)	D-	D	C		Y	800-624-6782
MainStay MacKay Intermediate Tax Free Bond Investor Cl	MTFEX	NAS CM	Open End	US Muni Fixed Inc (Muni Bond - Natl)	D-	D	C		Y	800-624-6782
MainStay MacKay New York Tax Free Opportunities Cl A	MNOAX	NAS CM	Open End	US Muni Fixed Inc (Muni Bond - Single State)	C	C-	B-		Y	800-624-6782
MainStay MacKay New York Tax Free Opportunities Cl C	MNOCX	NAS CM	Open End	US Muni Fixed Inc (Muni Bond - Single State)	C	C-	B-		Y	800-624-6782
MainStay MacKay New York Tax Free Opportunities Cl I	MNOIX	NAS CM	Open End	US Muni Fixed Inc (Muni Bond - Single State)	C	C-	B-		Y	800-624-6782
MainStay MacKay New York Tax Free Opportunities Cl R6	MNODX	NAS CM	Open End	US Muni Fixed Inc (Muni Bond - Single State)	C	C-	B-			800-624-6782
MainStay MacKay New York Tax Free Opp Investor Cl	MNOVX	NAS CM	Open End	US Muni Fixed Inc (Muni Bond - Single State)	C	C-	B-		Y	800-624-6782
MainStay MacKay Short Duration High Yield Fund Class A	MDHAX	NAS CM	Open End	US Fixed Inc (Corp Bond - High Yield)	C-	D+	C		Y	800-624-6782
MainStay MacKay Short Duration High Yield Fund Class C	MDHCX	NAS CM	Open End	US Fixed Inc (Corp Bond - High Yield)	D+	D	C-	Down	Y	800-624-6782
MainStay MacKay Short Duration High Yield Fund Class I	MDHIX	NAS CM	Open End	US Fixed Inc (Corp Bond - High Yield)	C-	D+	C		Y	800-624-6782
MainStay MacKay Short Duration High Yield Fund Class R2	MDHRX	NAS CM	Open End	US Fixed Inc (Corp Bond - High Yield)	C-	D+	C		Y	800-624-6782
MainStay MacKay Short Duration High Yield Fund Class R3	MDHTX	NAS CM	Open End	US Fixed Inc (Corp Bond - High Yield)	D+	D	C	Down	Y	800-624-6782
MainStay MacKay Short Duration High Yield Investor Cl	MDHVX	NAS CM	Open End	US Fixed Inc (Corp Bond - High Yield)	C-	D+	C		Y	800-624-6782
MainStay MacKay Short Term Municipal Fund A	MSTAX	NAS CM	Open End	US Muni Fixed Inc (Growth & Income)	C	C-	C+		Y	800-624-6782
MainStay MacKay Short Term Municipal Fund I	MSTIX	NAS CM	Open End	US Muni Fixed Inc (Growth & Income)	C	C-	C+		Y	800-624-6782
MainStay MacKay Short Term Municipal Fund Investor	MYTBX	NAS CM	Open End	US Muni Fixed Inc (Growth & Income)	C	C-	C+		Y	800-624-6782
MainStay MacKay Tax Free Bond Fund Class A	MTBAX	NAS CM	Open End	US Muni Fixed Inc (Muni Bond - Natl)	C+	C	B	Up	Y	800-624-6782
MainStay MacKay Tax Free Bond Fund Class B	MKTBX	NAS CM	Open End	US Muni Fixed Inc (Muni Bond - Natl)	C	C	B			800-624-6782
MainStay MacKay Tax Free Bond Fund Class C	MTFCX	NAS CM	Open End	US Muni Fixed Inc (Muni Bond - Natl)	C	C	B		Y	800-624-6782
MainStay MacKay Tax Free Bond Fund Class I	MTBIX	NAS CM	Open End	US Muni Fixed Inc (Muni Bond - Natl)	C+	C	B		Y	800-624-6782
MainStay MacKay Tax Free Bond Fund Class R6	MTBDX	NAS CM	Open End	US Muni Fixed Inc (Muni Bond - Natl)	C+	C	B	Up		800-624-6782
MainStay MacKay Tax Free Bond Fund Investor Class	MKINX	NAS CM	Open End	US Muni Fixed Inc (Muni Bond - Natl)	C+	C	B	Up	Y	800-624-6782
MainStay MacKay Total Return Bond Fund Class A	MTMAX	NAS CM	Open End	US Fixed Inc (Corp Bond - General)	B-	C+	B	Up	Y	800-624-6782
MainStay MacKay Total Return Bond Fund Class B	MTMBX	NAS CM	Open End	US Fixed Inc (Corp Bond - General)	C+	C	B	Up		800-624-6782
MainStay MacKay Total Return Bond Fund Class C	MTMCX	NAS CM	Open End	US Fixed Inc (Corp Bond - General)	C+	C	B	Up	Y	800-624-6782
MainStay MacKay Total Return Bond Fund Class I	MTMIX	NAS CM	Open End	US Fixed Inc (Corp Bond - General)	B-	C+	B+	Up	Y	800-624-6782
MainStay MacKay Total Return Bond Fund Class R1	MTMRX	NAS CM	Open End	US Fixed Inc (Corp Bond - General)	B-	C+	B	Up	Y	800-624-6782
MainStay MacKay Total Return Bond Fund Class R2	MTRTX	NAS CM	Open End	US Fixed Inc (Corp Bond - General)	B-	C+	B	Up	Y	800-624-6782
MainStay MacKay Total Return Bond Fund Class R3	MTRVX	NAS CM	Open End	US Fixed Inc (Corp Bond - General)	B-	C+	B	Up	Y	800-624-6782
MainStay MacKay Total Return Bond Fund Class R6	MTRDX	NAS CM	Open End	US Fixed Inc (Corp Bond - General)	B-	C+	B+	Up	Y	800-624-6782
MainStay MacKay Total Return Bond Fund Investor Class	MTMNX	NAS CM	Open End	US Fixed Inc (Corp Bond - General)	B-	C+	B	Up	Y	800-624-6782
MainStay MacKay Unconstrained Fund Class A	MASAX	NAS CM	Open End	Fixed Inc Misc (Multisector Bond)	C-	D+	C		Y	800-624-6782
MainStay MacKay Unconstrained Fund Class B	MASBX	NAS CM	Open End	Fixed Inc Misc (Multisector Bond)	D+	D	C	Down		800-624-6782
MainStay MacKay Unconstrained Fund Class C	MSICX	NAS CM	Open End	Fixed Inc Misc (Multisector Bond)	D+	D	C	Down	Y	800-624-6782

★Expanded analysis of this fund is included in Section II.

3-Month Total Return	6-Month Total Return	1-Year Total Return	3-Year Total Return	5-Year Total Return	Dividend Yield (TTM)	Expense Ratio	3-Yr Std Deviation	Effective Duration	NAV	Total Assets (MIL)	%Cash	%Government Bonds	%Municipal Bonds	%Corporate Bonds	%Other	Turnover Ratio	Average Coupon Rate	Min Initial Investment	Min Additional Investment	Front End Fee (%)	Back End Fee (%)	Inception Date
9.39	-4.43	-0.88	8.57	23.02	5.94	1.09	8.15	3.88	5.27	10,964	6	0	0	94	0	30	6.10	0				May-08
9.11	-4.57	-1.32	7.57	21.12	5.67	1.34	8.06	3.88	5.26	10,964	6	0	0	94	0	30	6.10	0				Feb-16
9.56	-4.19	-0.37	10.03	25.80	6.48	0.59	8.13	3.88	5.26	10,964	6	0	0	94	0	30	6.10	0				Jun-13
9.34	-4.36	-0.96	8.80	23.32	5.99	1.05	8.1	3.88	5.31	10,964	6	0	0	94	0	30	6.10	1,000	50	4.50		Feb-08
3.38	-1.20	1.47	14.00	29.27	3.71	0.86	6.49	8.50	12.62	6,637	2	0	99	0	0	27	4.80	15,000		4.50		Mar-10
3.19	-1.50	0.71	11.44	24.44	2.91	1.62	6.5	8.50	12.59	6,637	2	0	99	0	0	27	4.80	2,500	50		1.00	Mar-10
3.44	-1.08	1.73	14.86	30.78	3.97	0.61	6.53	8.50	12.62	6,637	2	0	99	0	0	27	4.80	1,000,000				Mar-10
3.39	-1.12	1.69	14.82	30.73		0.56	6.51	8.50	12.61	6,637	2	0	99	0	0	27	4.80	0				Nov-19
3.38	-1.21	1.46	13.96	29.06	3.7	0.87	6.5	8.50	12.6	6,637	2	0	99	0	0	27	4.80	2,500	50	4.50		Mar-10
2.33	3.13	5.11	12.28	15.05	2.33	0.85	4.96	6.23	8.73	495.6	18	0	73	11	0	124	3.53	15,000		4.50		Jan-95
2.06	2.59	4.01	8.74	9.20	1.26	1.93	4.97	6.23	8.73	495.6	18	0	73	11	0	124	3.53	1,000	50		5.00	May-86
2.06	2.59	4.01	8.73	9.19	1.26	1.93	4.92	6.23	8.73	495.6	18	0	73	11	0	124	3.53	1,000	50		1.00	Sep-98
2.49	3.35	5.45	13.14	16.49	2.58	0.6	4.96	6.23	8.83	495.6	18	0	73	11	0	124	3.53	1,000,000				Jan-04
2.24	2.96	4.76	11.15	13.29	2.01	1.18	4.92	6.23	8.77	495.6	18	0	73	11	0	124	3.53	1,000	50	4.50		Feb-08
2.39	3.40	5.11	9.89	10.35		0.53	4.96	6.23	8.83	495.6	18	0	73	11	0	124	3.53	0				Nov-19
3.24	0.64	3.05				0.77		4.31	10.07	52.5	5	0	96	0	0		4.37	15,000		4.50		Jun-19
3.28	0.52	2.78				1.17		4.31	10.07	52.5	5	0	96	0	0		4.37	1,000	50		1.00	Jun-19
3.30	0.66	3.20				0.52		4.31	10.06	52.5	5	0	96	0	0		4.37	1,000,000				Jun-19
3.31	0.68	3.23				0.5		4.31	10.06	52.5	5	0	96	0	0		4.37	0				Jun-19
3.24	0.54	2.93				0.92		4.31	10.06	52.5	5	0	96	0	0		4.37	1,000	50	4.50		Jun-19
2.70	0.98	3.26	12.56	22.46	2.9	0.76	4.88	7.70	10.63	839.8	1	0	99	0	0	28	4.43	15,000		4.50		May-12
2.63	0.85	2.99	11.65	20.77	2.63	1.03	4.83	7.70	10.63	839.8	1	0	99	0	0	28	4.43	2,500	50		1.00	May-12
2.76	1.11	3.52	13.41	24.00	3.15	0.51	4.83	7.70	10.63	839.8	1	0	99	0	0	28	4.43	1,000,000				May-12
2.78	1.12	3.54	13.43	24.03		0.51	4.82	7.70	10.63	839.8	1	0	99	0	0	28	4.43	0				Nov-19
2.69	0.97	3.24	12.49	22.31	2.88	0.78	4.9	7.70	10.63	839.8	1	0	99	0	0	28	4.43	2,500	50	4.50		May-12
9.29	-3.94	-1.38	6.69	17.21	4.84	1.05	7.59	2.25	9.3	1,323	5	0	0	95	0	32	5.24	15,000		3.00		Dec-12
8.94	-4.35	-2.21	4.11	12.34	3.97	1.87	7.58	2.25	9.3	1,323	5	0	0	95	0	32	5.24	2,500	50		1.00	Dec-12
9.23	-3.83	-1.13	7.50	18.56	5.1	0.8	7.52	2.25	9.3	1,323	5	0	0	95	0	32	5.24	1,000,000				Dec-12
9.26	-3.89	-1.37	6.48	16.64	4.75	1.15	7.58	2.25	9.3	1,323	5	0	0	95	0	32	5.24	0				Dec-12
8.96	-4.21	-1.82	5.46	15.01	4.48	1.4	7.52	2.25	9.3	1,323	5	0	0	95	0	32	5.24	0				Feb-16
9.14	-3.99	-1.46	6.60	16.63	4.75	1.12	7.52	2.25	9.3	1,323	5	0	0	95	0	32	5.24	2,500	50	3.00		Dec-12
1.38	1.00	1.84	4.90	7.11	1.44	0.7	1.04	1.69	9.66	654.9	15	0	85	0	0	96	4.18	15,000		1.00	1.00	Jan-04
1.56	1.25	2.12	5.93	8.61	1.73	0.4	1.09	1.69	9.66	654.9	15	0	85	0	0	96	4.18	1,000,000				Jan-91
1.40	1.01	1.52	3.69	5.01	1.12	1.3	1.1	1.69	9.69	654.9	15	0	85	0	0	96	4.18	1,000	50	1.00	1.00	Feb-08
2.95	2.13	4.35	14.18	23.14	2.75	0.78	4.28	5.45	10.42	6,395	1	0	99	0	0	38	4.61	15,000		4.50		Jan-95
2.89	2.00	4.19	13.36	21.68	2.49	1.02	4.32	5.45	10.42	6,395	1	0	99	0	0	38	4.61	1,000	50		5.00	May-86
2.88	1.99	4.18	13.35	21.80	2.49	1.02	4.26	5.45	10.43	6,395	1	0	99	0	0	38	4.61	1,000	50		1.00	Sep-98
3.01	2.35	4.71	15.03	24.80	3	0.53	4.28	5.45	10.43	6,395	1	0	99	0	0	38	4.61	1,000,000				Dec-09
3.03	2.29	4.56	13.76	22.12		0.45	4.27	5.45	10.43	6,395	1	0	99	0	0	38	4.61	0				Nov-19
2.94	2.12	4.44	14.18	23.18	2.74	0.77	4.32	5.45	10.47	6,395	1	0	99	0	0	38	4.61	1,000	50	4.50		Feb-08
5.94	5.18	7.99	14.55	21.62	2.42	0.88	4.28	5.92	11.28	1,323	1	22	0	49	2	100	3.62	15,000		4.50		Jan-04
5.59	4.68	6.97	11.46	16.74	1.49	1.8	4.26	5.92	11.29	1,323	1	22	0	49	2	100	3.62	1,000	50		5.00	Jan-04
5.58	4.68	6.87	11.45	16.73	1.49	1.8	4.24	5.92	11.3	1,323	1	22	0	49	2	100	3.62	1,000	50		1.00	Jan-04
5.90	5.31	8.28	15.53	23.66	2.68	0.6	4.26	5.92	11.28	1,323	1	22	0	49	2	100	3.62	1,000,000				Jan-91
5.98	5.26	8.16	15.17	23.03	2.57	0.73	4.25	5.92	11.28	1,323	1	22	0	49	2	100	3.62	0				Jun-12
5.82	5.13	7.81	14.23	21.29	2.34	0.98	4.24	5.92	11.27	1,323	1	22	0	49	2	100	3.62	0				Jun-12
5.85	5.00	7.64	13.48	20.07	2.1	1.23	4.28	5.92	11.28	1,323	1	22	0	49	2	100	3.62	0				Feb-16
6.02	5.34	8.35	15.79	24.08	2.75	0.54	4.29	5.92	11.28	1,323	1	22	0	49	2	100	3.62	0				Dec-14
5.85	5.04	7.74	13.93	21.12	2.22	1.05	4.26	5.92	11.34	1,323	1	22	0	49	2	100	3.62	1,000	50	4.50		Feb-08
7.26	-0.72	1.24	5.65	11.76	2.61	1.27	5.36	2.16	8.59	716.3	3	15	0	60	2	50	3.77	15,000		4.50		Feb-97
6.97	-1.22	0.46	3.12	7.56	1.83	2.04	5.31	2.16	8.54	716.3	3	15	0	60	2	50	3.77	1,000	50		5.00	Feb-97
6.97	-1.22	0.35	3.13	7.45	1.83	2.04	5.34	2.16	8.53	716.3	3	15	0	60	2	50	3.77	1,000	50		1.00	Sep-98

	MARKET			FUND TYPE, CATEGORY & OBJECTIVE	RATINGS				NEW INVESTORS	
Fund Name	Ticker Symbol	Traded On	Fund Type	Category and (Prospectus Objective)	Overall Rating	Reward Rating	Risk Rating	Recent Up/ Downgrade	Open to New Investors	Telephone
MainStay MacKay Unconstrained Fund Class I	MSDIX	NAS CM	Open End	Fixed Inc Misc (Multisector Bond)	C-	D+	C		Y	800-624-6782
MainStay MacKay Unconstrained Fund Class R2	MSIRX	NAS CM	Open End	Fixed Inc Misc (Multisector Bond)	C-	D+	C		Y	800-624-6782
MainStay MacKay Unconstrained Fund Class R3	MSDJX	NAS CM	Open End	Fixed Inc Misc (Multisector Bond)	C-	D+	C		Y	800-624-6782
MainStay MacKay Unconstrained Fund Class R6	MSYEX	NAS CM	Open End	Fixed Inc Misc (Multisector Bond)	C-	D+	C		Y	800-624-6782
MainStay MacKay Unconstrained Fund Investor Class	MSYDX	NAS CM	Open End	Fixed Inc Misc (Multisector Bond)	C-	D+	C		Y	800-624-6782
MainStay Money Market Class C	MSCXX	NAS CM	Money Mkt	US Money Mkt (Money Mkt - Taxable)	C	C-	C+		Y	800-624-6782
MainStay Money Market Fund Class A	MMAXX	NAS CM	Money Mkt	US Money Mkt (Money Mkt - Taxable)	C	C-	C+		Y	800-624-6782
MainStay Money Market Fund Class B	MKMXX	NAS CM	Money Mkt	US Money Mkt (Money Mkt - Taxable)	C	C-	C			800-624-6782
MainStay Money Market Fund Investor Class	MKTXX	NAS CM	Money Mkt	US Money Mkt (Money Mkt - Taxable)	C	C-	C+		Y	800-624-6782
MainStay Short Term Bond Fund Class A	MIXAX	NAS CM	Open End	US Fixed Inc (Corp Bond - General)	C	C	B-		Y	800-624-6782
MainStay Short Term Bond Fund Class I	MIXIX	NAS CM	Open End	US Fixed Inc (Corp Bond - General)	C	C	B-		Y	800-624-6782
MainStay Short Term Bond Fund Class Investor	MIXNX	NAS CM	Open End	US Fixed Inc (Corp Bond - General)	C	C	C+		Y	800-624-6782
Manning & Napier Core Bond Series Class I	EXCIX	NAS CM	Open End	US Fixed Inc (Corp Bond - High Quality)	B	C+	B	Up	Y	585-325-6880
Manning & Napier Core Bond Series Class S	EXCRX	NAS CM	Open End	US Fixed Inc (Corp Bond - High Quality)	B-	C+	B	Up	Y	585-325-6880
Manning & Napier Core Bond Series Class W	MCBWX	NAS CM	Open End	US Fixed Inc (Corp Bond - High Quality)	B	C+	B	Up	Y	585-325-6880
Manning & Napier Core Bond Series Class Z	MCBZX	NAS CM	Open End	US Fixed Inc (Corp Bond - High Quality)	B-	C+	B	Up	Y	585-325-6880
Manning & Napier Diversified Tax Exempt Ser Cl A	EXDVX	NAS CM	Open End	US Muni Fixed Inc (Muni Bond - Natl)	C+	C	B	Up	Y	585-325-6880
Manning & Napier Diversified Tax Exempt Ser Cl W	MNDWX	NAS CM	Open End	US Muni Fixed Inc (Muni Bond - Natl)	C+	C	B	Up	Y	585-325-6880
Manning & Napier High Yield Bond Series Class I	MNHAX	NAS CM	Open End	US Fixed Inc (Corp Bond - High Yield)	D+	D+	C-	Down	Y	585-325-6880
Manning & Napier High Yield Bond Series Class S	MNHYX	NAS CM	Open End	US Fixed Inc (Corp Bond - High Yield)	D+	D+	C-	Down	Y	585-325-6880
Manning & Napier High Yield Bond Series Class W	MHYWX	NAS CM	Open End	US Fixed Inc (Corp Bond - High Yield)	C-	D+	C		Y	585-325-6880
Manning & Napier High Yield Bond Series Class Z	MHYZX	NAS CM	Open End	US Fixed Inc (Corp Bond - High Yield)	D+	D+	C-	Down	Y	585-325-6880
Manning & Napier New York Tax Exempt Series Fund Class A	EXNTX	NAS CM	Open End	US Muni Fixed Inc (Muni Bond - Single State)	C	C	B-		Y	585-325-6880
Manning & Napier New York Tax Exempt Series Fund Class W	MNNWX	NAS CM	Open End	US Muni Fixed Inc (Muni Bond - Single State)	C	C	B-		Y	585-325-6880
Manning & Napier Unconstrained Bond Series Class I	MNCPX	NAS CM	Open End	Fixed Inc Misc (Growth & Income)	C	C-	C+		Y	585-325-6880
Manning & Napier Unconstrained Bond Series Class S	EXCPX	NAS CM	Open End	Fixed Inc Misc (Growth & Income)	C	C-	C+		Y	585-325-6880
Manning & Napier Unconstrained Bond Series Class W	MUBWX	NAS CM	Open End	Fixed Inc Misc (Growth & Income)	C	C-	C+		Y	585-325-6880
Manor Investment Funds Bond Fund	MNRBX	NAS CM	Open End	US Fixed Inc (Govt Bond - General)	B-	C+	B		Y	
Massachusetts Tax-Exempt Trust	MHE	AMEX	Closed End	US Muni Fixed Inc (Muni Bond - Single State)	D+	C-	D+	Down	Y	800-441-7762
MassMutual Participation Investors	MPV	NYSE	Closed End	US Fixed Inc (Corp Bond - High Yield)	C-	C-	C-	Down	Y	
MassMutual Premier Core Bond Fund Administrative Class	MCBLX	NAS CM	Open End	US Fixed Inc (Corp Bond - General)	C+	C	B	Up	Y	
MassMutual Premier Core Bond Fund Class A	MMCBX	NAS CM	Open End	US Fixed Inc (Corp Bond - General)	C	C	B		Y	
MassMutual Premier Core Bond Fund Class I	MCZZX	NAS CM	Open End	US Fixed Inc (Corp Bond - General)	C+	C	B	Up	Y	
MassMutual Premier Core Bond Fund Class R3	MCBNX	NAS CM	Open End	US Fixed Inc (Corp Bond - General)	C	C	B		Y	
MassMutual Premier Core Bond Fund Class R4	MCZRX	NAS CM	Open End	US Fixed Inc (Corp Bond - General)	C	C	B		Y	
MassMutual Premier Core Bond Fund Class R5	MCBDX	NAS CM	Open End	US Fixed Inc (Corp Bond - General)	C+	C	B	Up	Y	
MassMutual Premier Core Bond Fund Service Class	MCBYX	NAS CM	Open End	US Fixed Inc (Corp Bond - General)	C+	C	B	Up	Y	
MassMutual Premier Diversified Bond Administrative Cl	MDBLX	NAS CM	Open End	US Fixed Inc (Multisector Bond)	C	C-	B-		Y	
MassMutual Premier Diversified Bond Fund Class A	MDVAX	NAS CM	Open End	US Fixed Inc (Multisector Bond)	C	C-	C+		Y	
MassMutual Premier Diversified Bond Fund Class I	MDBZX	NAS CM	Open End	US Fixed Inc (Multisector Bond)	C	C-	B-		Y	
MassMutual Premier Diversified Bond Fund Class R3	MDBRX	NAS CM	Open End	US Fixed Inc (Multisector Bond)	C	C-	C+		Y	
MassMutual Premier Diversified Bond Fund Class R4	MDBFX	NAS CM	Open End	US Fixed Inc (Multisector Bond)	C	C-	B-		Y	
MassMutual Premier Diversified Bond Fund Class R5	MDBSX	NAS CM	Open End	US Fixed Inc (Multisector Bond)	C	C-	B-		Y	
MassMutual Premier Diversified Bond Fund Service Class	MDBYX	NAS CM	Open End	US Fixed Inc (Multisector Bond)	C	C-	B-		Y	
MassMutual Premier High Yield Fund Administrative Class	MPHLX	NAS CM	Open End	US Fixed Inc (Corp Bond - High Yield)	D+	D	C-	Down	Y	
MassMutual Premier High Yield Fund Class A	MPHAX	NAS CM	Open End	US Fixed Inc (Corp Bond - High Yield)	D+	D	C-	Down	Y	
MassMutual Premier High Yield Fund Class I	MPHZX	NAS CM	Open End	US Fixed Inc (Corp Bond - High Yield)	D+	D+	C-	Down	Y	
MassMutual Premier High Yield Fund Class R3	MPHNX	NAS CM	Open End	US Fixed Inc (Corp Bond - High Yield)	D+	D	C-	Down	Y	
MassMutual Premier High Yield Fund Class R4	MPHRX	NAS CM	Open End	US Fixed Inc (Corp Bond - High Yield)	D+	D	C-	Down	Y	
MassMutual Premier High Yield Fund Class R5	MPHSX	NAS CM	Open End	US Fixed Inc (Corp Bond - High Yield)	D+	D+	C-	Down	Y	
MassMutual Premier High Yield Fund Service Class	DLHYX	NAS CM	Open End	US Fixed Inc (Corp Bond - High Yield)	D+	D	C-	Down	Y	
MassMutual Prem Inflat-Protect & Income Administrative Cl	MIPLX	NAS CM	Open End	US Fixed Inc (Growth & Income)	B-	C	B+	Up	Y	

★Expanded analysis of this fund is included in Section II.

TOTAL RETURNS & PERFORMANCE									ASSETS		ASSET ALLOCATION & TURNOVER							MINIMUMS		FEES		
3-Month Total Return	6-Month Total Return	1-Year Total Return	3-Year Total Return	5-Year Total Return	Dividend Yield (TTM)	Expense Ratio	3-Yr Std Deviation	Effective Duration	NAV	Total Assets (MIL)	%Cash	%Government Bonds	%Municipal Bonds	%Corporate Bonds	%Other	Turnover Ratio	Average Coupon Rate	Min Initial Investment	Min Additional Investment	Front End Fee (%)	Back End Fee (%)	Inception Date
7.19	-0.71	1.38	6.32	13.15	2.86	1.02	5.3	2.16	8.59	716.3	3	15	0	60	2	50	3.77	1,000,000				Jan-04
7.24	-0.88	1.14	5.22	11.08	2.51	1.37	5.36	2.16	8.58	716.3	3	15	0	60	2	50	3.77	0				Feb-14
7.16	-1.00	0.89	4.44	9.92	2.25	1.62	5.35	2.16	8.59	716.3	3	15	0	60	2	50	3.77	0				Feb-16
7.75	-0.26	1.93	6.98	13.16	3.05	0.85	5.42	2.16	8.62	716.3	3	15	0	60	2	50	3.77	0				Feb-18
7.19	-0.84	1.21	5.53	11.67	2.56	1.29	5.33	2.16	8.66	716.3	3	15	0	60	2	50	3.77	1,000	50	4.50		Feb-08
0.00	0.17	0.81	3.05	3.15	0.95	0.8	0.16		1	478.6	83	16	0	1	0			1,000	50			Sep-98
0.01	0.25	1.00	3.72	3.90	1.16	0.56	0.16		1	478.6	83	16	0	1	0			25,000				Jan-95
0.00	0.17	0.81	3.05	3.15	0.95	0.8	0.16		1	478.6	83	16	0	1	0			1,000	50			May-86
0.00	0.18	0.81	3.05	3.15	0.95	0.8	0.16		1	478.6	83	16	0	1	0			1,000	50			Feb-08
5.43	1.09	3.45	9.54	14.46	2.12	0.74	4.52	1.87	10.65	128.8	5	32	0	45	0	75	2.84	15,000		1.00		Jan-04
5.58	1.30	3.79	10.41	16.19	2.36	0.4	4.54	1.87	10.67	128.8	5	32	0	45	0	75	2.84	1,000,000				Jan-91
5.42	1.03	3.23	8.68	13.05	1.82	0.92	4.57	1.87	10.72	128.8	5	32	0	45	0	75	2.84	1,000	50	1.00		Feb-08
4.14	6.07	8.47	15.43	21.53	2.58	0.45	3.53	5.69	10.58	315.6	1	26	0	32	0	66	3.17	1,000,000				Aug-15
4.03	5.86	8.25	14.62	20.02	2.01	0.7	3.52	5.69	11.5	315.6	1	26	0	32	0	66	3.17	2,000				Apr-05
4.13	6.17	8.87	15.52	20.97	2.66	0.05	3.51	5.69	11.49	315.6	1	26	0	32	0	66	3.17	0				Mar-19
4.14	6.09	8.62	15.24	20.68	2.63	0.3	3.51	5.69	10.6	315.6	1	26	0	32	0	66	3.17	1,000,000				Mar-19
2.35	3.88	5.43	9.84	13.14	1.64	0.58	2.87	4.76	11.52	252.1	2	0	98	0	0	29	4.53	2,000				Feb-94
2.38	4.07	5.96	10.62	13.96	2.12	0.11	2.88	4.76	11.53	252.1	2	0	98	0	0	29	4.53	0				Mar-19
10.64	-5.85	-1.31	9.47	23.31	8.7	0.66	9.36	3.54	7.94	131.6	5	0	0	94	0	143	6.63	1,000,000				Aug-12
10.64	-5.95	-1.57	8.76	21.85	7.05	0.91	9.38	3.54	9.33	131.6	5	0	0	94	0	143	6.63	2,000				Sep-09
10.87	-5.64	-0.78	9.85	23.08	8.05	0.11	9.41	3.54	9.31	131.6	5	0	0	94	0	143	6.63	0				Mar-19
10.81	-5.80	-1.09	9.33	22.49	8.81	0.51	9.35	3.54	7.95	131.6	5	0	0	94	0	143	6.63	1,000,000				Mar-19
1.91	2.76	3.99	8.15	11.62	1.63	0.63	3.06	5.01	10.73	105.3	4	0	96	0	0	24	4.25	2,000				Jan-94
2.03	3.06	4.53	8.84	12.33	2.13	0.16	3.13	5.01	10.74	105.3	4	0	96	0	0	24	4.25	0				Mar-19
5.97	1.27	3.47	8.48	14.21	3.34	0.5	3.24	3.30	9.25	622.0	10	5	0	46	0	75	4.32	1,000,000				Aug-13
5.92	1.19	3.17	7.63	12.82	2.65	0.76	3.24	3.30	10.45	622.0	10	5	0	46	0	75	4.32	2,000				Apr-05
6.12	1.51	3.91	8.50	13.74	3.38	0.06	3.21	3.30	10.42	622.0	10	5	0	46	0	75	4.32	0				Mar-19
0.26	6.74	7.66	11.54	10.21	0.81	0.95	2.86		11.24	1.5	11	89	0	0	0	21	1.80	1,000	25			Jun-99
2.52	-1.12	1.61	9.52	21.52	3.61		6.73		13.49	31.7	-58	0	99	0	0	10	4.92					Jul-93
0.00	-5.79	-0.55	13.35	34.03	7.89		6.7		12.8	189.3	15	0	0	84	0	22	8.99					Oct-88
6.54	3.12	5.82	13.68	18.98	3.15	0.73	5.09	5.46	11.23	1,344	11	22	0	24	0	261	3.94	0				May-99
6.50	2.96	5.47	12.72	17.38	2.89	0.98	5.11	5.46	11.13	1,344	11	22	0	24	0	261	3.94	0		4.25		Jan-98
6.67	3.27	6.07	14.69	20.69	3.41	0.43	5.14	5.46	11.35	1,344	11	22	0	24	0	261	3.94	0				Dec-10
6.46	2.89	5.41	12.36	16.61	2.89	1.13	5.07	5.46	11.36	1,344	11	22	0	24	0	261	3.94	0				Dec-02
6.55	2.97	5.57	13.11	17.94	3.06	0.88	5.15	5.46	11.06	1,344	11	22	0	24	0	261	3.94	0				Apr-14
6.64	3.17	6.04	14.38	20.08	3.31	0.53	5.09	5.46	11.39	1,344	11	22	0	24	0	261	3.94	0				Sep-94
6.59	3.09	5.84	14.00	19.54	3.19	0.63	5.09	5.46	11.32	1,344	11	22	0	24	0	261	3.94	0				Jan-98
7.23	1.26	4.33	12.10	18.94	3.25	0.85	6	5.40	10.38	231.1	10	21	0	31	0	236	4.26	0				May-99
7.13	1.17	4.10	11.22	17.48	2.92	1.1	6.03	5.40	10.36	231.1	10	21	0	31	0	236	4.26	0		4.25		May-99
7.31	1.45	4.73	13.04	20.74	3.34	0.55	5.98	5.40	11.15	231.1	10	21	0	31	0	236	4.26	0				Dec-10
7.12	1.08	3.94	10.74	16.56	2.75	1.25	6.05	5.40	10.22	231.1	10	21	0	31	0	236	4.26	0				Apr-14
7.21	1.28	4.28	11.61	18.17	3.18	1	6	5.40	10.25	231.1	10	21	0	31	0	236	4.26	0				Apr-14
7.21	1.38	4.53	12.76	20.09	3.53	0.65	6.01	5.40	10.25	231.1	10	21	0	31	0	236	4.26	0				May-99
7.21	1.36	4.43	12.38	19.54	3.35	0.75	5.99	5.40	10.4	231.1	10	21	0	31	0	236	4.26	0				May-99
7.21	-6.52	-3.36	4.49	20.19	6.53	0.84	8.46	4.60	8.17	491.9	1	0	0	99	0	54	5.92	0				Nov-04
7.10	-6.65	-3.62	3.70	18.74	6.4	1.09	8.44	4.60	8.14	491.9	1	0	0	99	0	54	5.92	0		5.50		Nov-04
7.27	-6.34	-3.08	5.40	22.04	6.87	0.54	8.46	4.60	8.26	491.9	1	0	0	99	0	54	5.92	0				Mar-11
7.14	-6.67	-3.72	3.23	17.89	6.02	1.24	8.46	4.60	8.25	491.9	1	0	0	99	0	54	5.92	0				Nov-04
7.19	-6.51	-3.48	4.02	19.37	6.68	0.99	8.43	4.60	8.04	491.9	1	0	0	99	0	54	5.92	0				Apr-14
7.22	-6.41	-3.17	5.14	21.40	6.7	0.64	8.42	4.60	8.31	491.9	1	0	0	99	0	54	5.92	0				Nov-04
7.22	-6.41	-3.25	4.85	20.80	6.61	0.74	8.44	4.60	8.31	491.9	1	0	0	99	0	54	5.92	0				Sep-00
6.04	4.93	7.21	13.71	18.78	1.73	0.78	4.6	5.82	11.05	323.4	24	29	0	0	1	42	2.12	0				Dec-03

	MARKET		FUND TYPE, CATEGORY & OBJECTIVE		RATINGS				NEW INVESTORS	
Fund Name	Ticker Symbol	Traded On	Fund Type	Category and (Prospectus Objective)	Overall Rating	Reward Rating	Risk Rating	Recent Up/ Downgrade	Open to New Investors	Telephone
MassMutual Premier Inflation-Protected & Income Cl A	MPSAX	NAS CM	Open End	US Fixed Inc (Growth & Income)	B-	C	B	Up	Y	
MassMutual Premier Inflation-Protected & Income Cl I	MIPZX	NAS CM	Open End	US Fixed Inc (Growth & Income)	B-	C	B+	Up	Y	
MassMutual Premier Inflation-Protected & Income Cl R3	MIPNX	NAS CM	Open End	US Fixed Inc (Growth & Income)	B-	C	B	Up	Y	
MassMutual Premier Inflation-Protected & Income Cl R4	MIPRX	NAS CM	Open End	US Fixed Inc (Growth & Income)	B-	C	B	Up	Y	
MassMutual Premier Inflation-Protected & Income Cl R5	MIPSX	NAS CM	Open End	US Fixed Inc (Growth & Income)	B-	C	B+	Up	Y	
MassMutual Premier Inflation-Protected & Income Service Cl	MIPYX	NAS CM	Open End	US Fixed Inc (Growth & Income)	B-	C	B+	Up	Y	
MassMutual Premier Short-Duration Bond Administrative Cl	MSTLX	NAS CM	Open End	US Fixed Inc (Corp Bond - General)	D+	D	C	Down	Y	
MassMutual Premier Short-Duration Bond Fund Class A	MSHAX	NAS CM	Open End	US Fixed Inc (Corp Bond - General)	D+	D	C	Down	Y	
MassMutual Premier Short-Duration Bond Fund Class I	MSTZX	NAS CM	Open End	US Fixed Inc (Corp Bond - General)	D+	D	C	Down	Y	
MassMutual Premier Short-Duration Bond Fund Class R3	MSDNX	NAS CM	Open End	US Fixed Inc (Corp Bond - General)	D	D	C-	Down	Y	
MassMutual Premier Short-Duration Bond Fund Class R4	MPSDX	NAS CM	Open End	US Fixed Inc (Corp Bond - General)	D+	D	C	Down	Y	
MassMutual Premier Short-Duration Bond Fund Class R5	MSTDX	NAS CM	Open End	US Fixed Inc (Corp Bond - General)	D+	D	C	Down	Y	
MassMutual Premier Short-Duration Bond Fund Service Class	MSBYX	NAS CM	Open End	US Fixed Inc (Corp Bond - General)	D+	D	C	Down	Y	
MassMutual Premier U.S. Govt Money Mkt Fund Class R5	MKSXX	NAS CM	Money Mkt	US Money Mkt (Money Mkt - Govt)	C	C-	C+		Y	
MassMutual Select Strategic Bond Fund Administrative Class	MSBLX	NAS CM	Open End	US Fixed Inc (Multisector Bond)	C+	C	B	Up	Y	
MassMutual Select Strategic Bond Fund Class A	MSBAX	NAS CM	Open End	US Fixed Inc (Multisector Bond)	C+	C	B	Up	Y	
MassMutual Select Strategic Bond Fund Class I	MSBZX	NAS CM	Open End	US Fixed Inc (Multisector Bond)	C+	C	B	Up	Y	
MassMutual Select Strategic Bond Fund Class R3	MSBNX	NAS CM	Open End	US Fixed Inc (Multisector Bond)	C+	C	B	Up	Y	
MassMutual Select Strategic Bond Fund Class R4	MSBRX	NAS CM	Open End	US Fixed Inc (Multisector Bond)	C+	C	B	Up	Y	
MassMutual Select Strategic Bond Fund Class R5	MBSSX	NAS CM	Open End	US Fixed Inc (Multisector Bond)	C+	C	B	Up	Y	
MassMutual Select Strategic Bond Fund Service Class	MBSYX	NAS CM	Open End	US Fixed Inc (Multisector Bond)	C+	C	B	Up	Y	
MassMutual Select T. Rowe Price Bond Asset Fund Class I	MMBEX	NAS CM	Open End	Global Fixed Inc (Multisector Bond)	C	C	B-		Y	
MassMutual Select T. Rowe Price Emerg Mkts Bond Cl I	MMEMX	NAS CM	Open End	Emerg Mkts Fixed Inc (Diversified Emerg Mkts)	D	D	D+	Down	Y	
MassMutual Select T. Rowe Price Lim Dur Inflat Foc Bond Cl	MMLDX	NAS CM	Open End	US Fixed Inc (Income)	C	C-	B-		Y	
MassMutual Select T. Rowe Price U.S. Treas Long-Term Cl I	MMUTX	NAS CM	Open End	US Fixed Inc (Income)	C	C	B		Y	
MassMutual Select Total Return Bond Administrative Cl	MSPLX	NAS CM	Open End	US Fixed Inc (Growth)	B	B-	B+	Up	Y	
MassMutual Select Total Return Bond Fund Class A	MPTRX	NAS CM	Open End	US Fixed Inc (Growth)	B	C+	B	Up	Y	
MassMutual Select Total Return Bond Fund Class I	MSPZX	NAS CM	Open End	US Fixed Inc (Growth)	B	B-	B+	Up	Y	
MassMutual Select Total Return Bond Fund Class R3	MSPNX	NAS CM	Open End	US Fixed Inc (Growth)	B	C+	B	Up	Y	
MassMutual Select Total Return Bond Fund Class R4	MSPGX	NAS CM	Open End	US Fixed Inc (Growth)	B	B-	B	Up	Y	
MassMutual Select Total Return Bond Fund Class R5	MSPSX	NAS CM	Open End	US Fixed Inc (Growth)	B	B-	B+	Up	Y	
MassMutual Select Total Return Bond Fund Service Class	MSPHX	NAS CM	Open End	US Fixed Inc (Growth)	B	B-	B+	Up	Y	
Matthews Asia Credit Opportunities Institutional Cl Shares	MICPX	NAS CM	Open End	Emerg Mkts Fixed Inc (Growth & Income)	C-	D+	C	Down	Y	800-789-2742
Matthews Asia Credit Opportunities Investor Cl Shares	MCRDX	NAS CM	Open End	Emerg Mkts Fixed Inc (Growth & Income)	C-	D+	C	Down	Y	800-789-2742
Matthews Asia Total Return Bond Institutional Cl Shares	MINCX	NAS CM	Open End	Emerg Mkts Fixed Inc (Income)	C-	D+	C	Down	Y	800-789-2742
Matthews Asia Total Return Bond Fund Investor Class Shares	MAINX	NAS CM	Open End	Emerg Mkts Fixed Inc (Income)	D+	D	C	Down	Y	800-789-2742
Meeder Institutional Prime Money Market Fund	FLPXX	NAS CM	Money Mkt	US Money Mkt (Money Mkt - Taxable)	C	C-	B-		Y	
Meeder Prime Money Market Fund Retail Class	FFMXX	NAS CM	Money Mkt	US Money Mkt (Money Mkt - Taxable)	C	C-	C+		Y	
Meeder Total Return Bond Fund Adviser Class	BNDAX	NAS CM	Open End	US Fixed Inc (Growth & Income)	B-	C	B	Up	Y	
Meeder Total Return Bond Fund Institutional Class	BNDIX	NAS CM	Open End	US Fixed Inc (Growth & Income)	B-	C	B	Up	Y	
Meeder Total Return Bond Fund Retail Class	FLBDX	NAS CM	Open End	US Fixed Inc (Growth & Income)	C+	C	B	Up	Y	
Mercer Core Fixed Income Fund Class Y3	MCFIX	NAS CM	Open End	US Fixed Inc (Income)	B	C+	B+	Up	Y	
Mercer Opportunistic Fixed Income Fund Class Y-3	MOFIX	NAS CM	Open End	US Fixed Inc (Income)	C-	D	C		Y	
Merk Hard Currency Fund Class Investor	MERKX	NAS CM	Open End	Global Fixed Inc (Income)	D	D	C-		Y	866-637-5386
Merk Hard Currency Fund Institutional Class	MHCIX	NAS CM	Open End	Global Fixed Inc (Income)	D	D	C-		Y	866-637-5386
Mesirow Financial Enhanced Core Plus Institutional Shares	MFBIX	NAS CM	Open End	US Fixed Inc (Growth & Income)	U	U	U		Y	
Mesirow Financial Enhanced Core Plus Fund Investor Shares	MFBVX	NAS CM	Open End	US Fixed Inc (Growth & Income)	U	U	U		Y	
Mesirow Financial High Yield Fund Institutional Shares	MFHIX	NAS CM	Open End	US Fixed Inc (Income)	D	D	D		Y	
Mesirow Financial High Yield Fund Investor Shares	MFHVX	NAS CM	Open End	US Fixed Inc (Income)	D	D	D		Y	
MetLife Core Plus Fund I Class	LPCIX	NAS CM	Open End	US Fixed Inc (Growth & Income)	B	C+	B+	Up	Y	
MetLife Core Plus Fund R Class	LPCYX	NAS CM	Open End	US Fixed Inc (Growth & Income)	C+	C	B	Up	Y	
Metropolitan West Corporate Bond Fund Class I	MWCBX	NAS CM	Open End	US Fixed Inc (Growth & Income)	C-	C-	B+	Up	Y	800-241-4671

★ Expanded analysis of this fund is included in Section II.

TOTAL RETURNS & PERFORMANCE									ASSETS		ASSET ALLOCATION & TURNOVER							MINIMUMS		FEES		
3-Month Total Return	6-Month Total Return	1-Year Total Return	3-Year Total Return	5-Year Total Return	Dividend Yield (TTM)	Expense Ratio	3-Yr Std Deviation	Effective Duration	NAV	Total Assets (MIL)	%Cash	%Government Bonds	%Municipal Bonds	%Corporate Bonds	%Other	Turnover Ratio	Average Coupon Rate	Min Initial Investment	Min Additional Investment	Front End Fee (%)	Back End Fee (%)	Inception Date
6.00	4.76	6.85	12.86	17.27	1.55	1.03	4.56	5.82	10.77	323.4	24	29	0	0	1	42	2.12	0		4.25		Dec-03
6.19	5.17	7.60	14.89	20.61	2.05	0.48	4.56	5.82	10.97	323.4	24	29	0	0	1	42	2.12	0				Mar-11
6.03	4.78	6.82	12.53	16.53	1.4	1.18	4.54	5.82	10.72	323.4	24	29	0	0	1	42	2.12	0				Dec-03
6.14	4.89	7.13	13.32	18.09	1.68	0.93	4.57	5.82	10.71	323.4	24	29	0	0	1	42	2.12	0				Apr-14
6.19	4.97	7.40	14.43	19.99	1.96	0.58	4.56	5.82	10.97	323.4	24	29	0	0	1	42	2.12	0				Dec-03
6.21	4.98	7.40	14.19	19.39	1.84	0.68	4.59	5.82	10.94	323.4	24	29	0	0	1	42	2.12	0				Dec-03
4.30	-2.80	-1.21	3.46	7.25	3.34	0.73	4.26	0.32	9.7	433.5	10	10	0	33	0	55	3.59	0				May-99
4.22	-2.92	-1.45	2.74	5.94	3.11	0.98	4.26	0.32	9.63	433.5	10	10	0	33	0	55	3.59	0		2.50		Jan-98
4.37	-2.68	-0.99	4.41	8.89	3.64	0.43	4.29	0.32	9.78	433.5	10	10	0	33	0	55	3.59	0				Dec-10
4.19	-3.00	-1.61	2.19	5.04	2.9	1.13	4.29	0.32	9.69	433.5	10	10	0	33	0	55	3.59	0				Dec-02
4.27	-2.88	-1.35	3.09	6.57	3.16	0.88	4.28	0.32	9.76	433.5	10	10	0	33	0	55	3.59	0				Apr-14
4.36	-2.77	-1.08	4.05	8.30	3.53	0.53	4.28	0.32	9.81	433.5	10	10	0	33	0	55	3.59	0				Sep-94
4.28	-2.79	-1.15	3.74	7.74	3.39	0.63	4.3	0.32	9.74	433.5	10	10	0	33	0	55	3.59	0				Jan-98
0.00	0.22	0.97	3.62	3.73	1.12	0.52	0.17		1	282.7	66	34	0	0	0			0				Sep-94
7.26	3.55	7.53	14.89	25.93	2.53	0.79	5.34	6.90	11.06	712.3	3	37	0	22	0	262	3.85	0				Dec-04
7.08	3.37	7.21	13.93	24.31	2.32	1.04	5.34	6.90	11.03	712.3	3	37	0	22	0	262	3.85	0		4.25		Dec-04
7.24	3.64	7.83	15.73	27.81	2.82	0.49	5.36	6.90	11.1	712.3	3	37	0	22	0	262	3.85	0				Apr-14
7.17	3.31	7.16	13.49	23.44	2.13	1.19	5.37	6.90	10.89	712.3	3	37	0	22	0	262	3.85	0				Dec-04
7.11	3.38	7.32	14.21	24.90	2.4	0.94	5.36	6.90	10.99	712.3	3	37	0	22	0	262	3.85	0				Apr-14
7.23	3.63	7.70	15.47	27.14	2.7	0.59	5.33	6.90	11.11	712.3	3	37	0	22	0	262	3.85	0				Dec-04
7.33	3.63	7.66	15.15	26.50	2.58	0.69	5.41	6.90	11.11	712.3	3	37	0	22	0	262	3.85	0				Dec-04
5.95	2.33	4.96			3	0.4			10.5	624.5	5	39	0	24	0	287	3.02	0				Feb-18
13.51	-4.74	-3.53			5.65	0.7			9.24	101.5	4	69	0	26	0	39	6.02	0				Feb-18
4.20	1.96	3.49			1.88	0.15			10.4	172.8	3	79	0	8	0	135	1.24	0				Feb-18
-0.15	20.79	25.51			2.29	0.15			13.13	45.1	2	85	0	0	0	155	2.69	0				Feb-18
3.90	6.19	8.71	16.42	22.71	2.45	0.66	3.44	5.32	10.63	882.0	11	24	1	18	0	217	3.16	0				Jul-10
3.82	6.00	8.47	15.57	21.24	2.41	0.91	3.43	5.32	10.59	882.0	11	24	1	18	0	217	3.16	0		4.25		Apr-14
3.99	6.38	9.09	17.56	24.61	2.9	0.36	3.41	5.32	10.66	882.0	11	24	1	18	0	217	3.16	0				Jul-10
3.81	5.99	8.35	15.07	20.38	2.22	1.06	3.4	5.32	10.61	882.0	11	24	1	18	0	217	3.16	0				Jul-10
3.88	6.15	8.55	15.97	21.91	2.44	0.81	3.41	5.32	10.7	882.0	11	24	1	18	0	217	3.16	0				Jul-10
4.00	6.39	8.97	17.28	24.07	2.78	0.46	3.4	5.32	10.65	882.0	11	24	1	18	0	217	3.16	0				Jul-10
3.98	6.36	8.85	16.87	23.42	2.69	0.56	3.5	5.32	10.69	882.0	11	24	1	18	0	217	3.16	0				Jul-10
9.23	-4.62	-1.27	8.15		5.34	0.9	8.92		9.88	93.2	6	7	0	88	0	81	5.29	100,000	100			Apr-16
9.15	-4.73	-1.48	7.35		5.07	1.12	8.9		9.88	93.2	6	7	0	88	0	81	5.29	2,500	100			Apr-16
10.39	-3.54	0.42	8.88	24.54	5.07	0.9	9.15		10.54	100.7	7	20	0	51	0	84	5.06	100,000	100			Nov-11
10.31	-3.65	0.26	8.14	23.09	4.87	1.07	9.13		10.54	100.7	7	20	0	51	0	84	5.06	2,500	100			Nov-11
0.25	0.53	1.55	5.39		1.69	0.51	0.19		1.0005	287.1	76	16	2	7	0			500,000	2,500			Oct-16
0.09	0.42	1.36	4.55	5.18	1.52	0.97	0.17		1	36.2	81	12	1	6	0			2,500	100			Mar-85
4.24	4.37	6.09	11.77	18.15	2.36	1.22	3.16	5.59	9.79	62.0	6	41	1	30	0	95	3.71	2,500	100			Oct-16
4.23	4.38	6.12	12.30	18.68	2.39	1.1	3.14	5.59	9.79	62.0	6	41	1	30	0	95	3.71	1,000,000	100			Oct-16
4.16	4.20	5.79	10.94	16.86	2	1.48	3.13	5.59	9.78	62.0	6	41	1	30	0	95	3.71	2,500	100			Jun-11
4.58	6.30	9.36	17.72	25.50	2.73	0.18	3.46	5.64	10.96	1,025	0	26	1	34	0	158	3.30	0				Aug-05
9.57	-1.48	1.07	5.32	12.91	2.42	0.44	8.06	4.87	9.27	1,058	5	47	0	41	0	148	5.15	0				Aug-13
5.86	-2.48	-1.63	-5.68	-4.60	0	1.38	6.56		9.02	58.2	33	48	0	0	5	53	3.42	2,500	100			May-05
6.01	-2.34	-1.39	-4.98	-3.42	0	1.13	6.56		9.17	58.2	33	48	0	0	5	53	3.42	250,000				Apr-10
7.42	2.40					0.54			10.09	15.7	10	10	1	67	0		4.19	100,000			1.00	Oct-19
7.38	2.41					0.79			10.09	15.7	10	10	1	67	0		4.19	5,000			1.00	Oct-19
10.94	-7.70	-4.62			8.05	0.77			8.91	35.7	4	0	0	96	0		7.48	1,000,000				Dec-18
10.89	-7.91	-4.95			7.8	1.02			8.9	35.7	4	0	0	96	0		7.48	5,000				Dec-18
4.82	5.60	8.40	16.81	26.05	2.64	0.45	3.82		10.41	49.3	7	19	1	31	0	356	3.52	5,000,000				Dec-14
4.07	3.62	4.33	9.48	17.89	2.76	0.7	3.52		9.71	49.3	7	19	1	31	0	356	3.52	500,000				Dec-14
7.52	7.49	11.86			8.39	0.5			10.91	4.4	11	9	2	65	0	65	3.50	3,000,000	50,000			Jun-18

Fund Name	Ticker Symbol	Traded On	Fund Type	Category and (Prospectus Objective)	Overall Rating	Reward Rating	Risk Rating	Recent Up/ Downgrade	Open to New Investors	Telephone
	MARKET			**FUND TYPE, CATEGORY & OBJECTIVE**	**RATINGS**				**NEW INVESTORS**	
Metropolitan West Corporate Bond Fund Class M	**MWCSX**	NAS CM	Open End	US Fixed Inc (Growth & Income)	**C-**	C-	B	Up	Y	800-241-4671
Metropolitan West Flexible Income Fund Class I	**MWFEX**	NAS CM	Open End	US Fixed Inc (Income)	**D+**	C-	B+	Up	Y	800-241-4671
Metropolitan West Flexible Income Fund Class M	**MWFSX**	NAS CM	Open End	US Fixed Inc (Income)	**D+**	C-	B+	Up	Y	800-241-4671
Metropolitan West Floating Rate Income Fund Class I Shares	**MWFLX**	NAS CM	Open End	US Fixed Inc (Income)	**C-**	D+	C		Y	800-241-4671
Metropolitan West Floating Rate Income Fund Class M	**MWFRX**	NAS CM	Open End	US Fixed Inc (Income)	**C-**	D+	C		Y	800-241-4671
Metropolitan West High Yield Bond Fund Class Institutional	**MWHIX**	NAS CM	Open End	US Fixed Inc (Corp Bond - High Yield)	**B-**	C	B	Up	Y	800-241-4671
Metropolitan West High Yield Bond Fund Class M	**MWHYX**	NAS CM	Open End	US Fixed Inc (Corp Bond - High Yield)	**B-**	C	B	Up	Y	800-241-4671
Metropolitan West Intermediate Bond Cl Institutional	**MWIIX**	NAS CM	Open End	US Fixed Inc (Worldwide Bond)	**B-**	C+	B+	Up	Y	800-241-4671
Metropolitan West Intermediate Bond Fund Class M	**MWIMX**	NAS CM	Open End	US Fixed Inc (Worldwide Bond)	**B-**	C+	B	Up	Y	800-241-4671
Metropolitan West Investment Grade Credit Fund Class I	**MWIGX**	NAS CM	Open End	US Fixed Inc (Growth & Income)	**C-**	D+	B	Up	Y	800-241-4671
Metropolitan West Investment Grade Credit Fund Class M	**MWISX**	NAS CM	Open End	US Fixed Inc (Growth & Income)	**C-**	D+	B	Up	Y	800-241-4671
Metropolitan West Low Duration Bond Administrative Cl	**MWLNX**	NAS CM	Open End	US Fixed Inc (Corp Bond - General)	**C**	C	B-		Y	800-241-4671
Metropolitan West Low Duration Bond Fund Class I	**MWLIX**	NAS CM	Open End	US Fixed Inc (Corp Bond - General)	**C**	C	B-		Y	800-241-4671
Metropolitan West Low Duration Bond Fund Class M	**MWLDX**	NAS CM	Open End	US Fixed Inc (Corp Bond - General)	**C**	C	B-		Y	800-241-4671
Metropolitan West Strategic Income Cl Institutional	**MWSIX**	NAS CM	Open End	Fixed Inc Misc (Corp Bond - General)	**C-**	D+	C	Down	Y	800-241-4671
Metropolitan West Strategic Income Fund Class M	**MWSTX**	NAS CM	Open End	Fixed Inc Misc (Corp Bond - General)	**C-**	D+	C	Down	Y	800-241-4671
★ Metropolitan West Total Return Bond Administrative Cl	**MWTNX**	NAS CM	Open End	US Fixed Inc (Corp Bond - General)	**B**	B-	B	Up	Y	800-241-4671
Metropolitan West Total Return Bond Fund Class I	**MWTIX**	NAS CM	Open End	US Fixed Inc (Corp Bond - General)	**B**	B-	B+	Up	Y	800-241-4671
Metropolitan West Total Return Bond Fund Class I-2	**MWTTX**	NAS CM	Open End	US Fixed Inc (Corp Bond - General)	**B**	B-	B+		Y	800-241-4671
★ Metropolitan West Total Return Bond Fund Class M	**MWTRX**	NAS CM	Open End	US Fixed Inc (Corp Bond - General)	**B**	B-	B+	Up	Y	800-241-4671
Metropolitan West Total Return Bond Fund Plan Class	**MWTSX**	NAS CM	Open End	US Fixed Inc (Corp Bond - General)	**B**	B-	B+	Up	Y	800-241-4671
Metropolitan West Ultra Short Bond Cl Institutional	**MWUIX**	NAS CM	Open End	US Fixed Inc (Corp Bond - General)	**C**	C-	B-		Y	800-241-4671
Metropolitan West Ultra Short Bond Fund Class M	**MWUSX**	NAS CM	Open End	US Fixed Inc (Corp Bond - General)	**C**	C-	C+		Y	800-241-4671
Metropolitan West Unconstrained Bond Fund Class I	**MWCIX**	NAS CM	Open End	Fixed Inc Misc (Worldwide Bond)	**C**	C-	C		Y	800-241-4671
Metropolitan West Unconstrained Bond Fund Class M	**MWCRX**	NAS CM	Open End	Fixed Inc Misc (Worldwide Bond)	**C**	C-	C		Y	800-241-4671
Metropolitan West Unconstrained Bond Fund Plan Class	**MWCPX**	NAS CM	Open End	Fixed Inc Misc (Worldwide Bond)	**C**	C-	C		Y	800-241-4671
MFS Alabama Municipal Bond Fund Class A	**MFALX**	NAS CM	Open End	US Muni Fixed Inc (Muni Bond - Single State)	**C**	C-	B-		Y	877-960-6077
MFS Alabama Municipal Bond Fund Class B	**MBABX**	NAS CM	Open End	US Muni Fixed Inc (Muni Bond - Single State)	**C**	C-	C+		Y	877-960-6077
MFS Alabama Municipal Bond Fund Class I	**MLALX**	NAS CM	Open End	US Muni Fixed Inc (Muni Bond - Single State)	**C**	C-	B-		Y	877-960-6077
MFS Alabama Municipal Bond Fund Class R6	**MPOLX**	NAS CM	Open End	US Muni Fixed Inc (Muni Bond - Single State)	**C**	C-	B-		Y	877-960-6077
MFS Arkansas Municipal Bond Fund Class A	**MFARX**	NAS CM	Open End	US Muni Fixed Inc (Muni Bond - Single State)	**C**	C-	B-		Y	877-960-6077
MFS Arkansas Municipal Bond Fund Class B	**MBARX**	NAS CM	Open End	US Muni Fixed Inc (Muni Bond - Single State)	**C**	C-	C+		Y	877-960-6077
MFS Arkansas Municipal Bond Fund Class I	**MARLX**	NAS CM	Open End	US Muni Fixed Inc (Muni Bond - Single State)	**C**	C-	B-		Y	877-960-6077
MFS Arkansas Municipal Bond Fund Class R6	**MPRAX**	NAS CM	Open End	US Muni Fixed Inc (Muni Bond - Single State)	**C**	C-	B-		Y	877-960-6077
MFS California Municipal Bond Fund Class A	**MCFTX**	NAS CM	Open End	US Muni Fixed Inc (Muni Bond - Single State)	**C**	C-	C+		Y	877-960-6077
MFS California Municipal Bond Fund Class B	**MBCAX**	NAS CM	Open End	US Muni Fixed Inc (Muni Bond - Single State)	**C**	C-	C		Y	877-960-6077
MFS California Municipal Bond Fund Class C	**MCCAX**	NAS CM	Open End	US Muni Fixed Inc (Muni Bond - Single State)	**C**	C-	C		Y	877-960-6077
MFS California Municipal Bond Fund Class I	**MCAVX**	NAS CM	Open End	US Muni Fixed Inc (Muni Bond - Single State)	**C**	C-	C+		Y	877-960-6077
MFS California Municipal Bond Fund Class R6	**MPOAX**	NAS CM	Open End	US Muni Fixed Inc (Muni Bond - Single State)	**C**	C-	C+		Y	877-960-6077
MFS Corporate Bond Fund Class A	**MFBFX**	NAS CM	Open End	US Fixed Inc (Corp Bond - General)	**B-**	C+	B	Up	Y	877-960-6077
MFS Corporate Bond Fund Class B	**MFBBX**	NAS CM	Open End	US Fixed Inc (Corp Bond - General)	**B-**	C	B	Up	Y	877-960-6077
MFS Corporate Bond Fund Class C	**MFBCX**	NAS CM	Open End	US Fixed Inc (Corp Bond - General)	**B-**	C	B	Up	Y	877-960-6077
MFS Corporate Bond Fund Class I	**MBDIX**	NAS CM	Open End	US Fixed Inc (Corp Bond - General)	**B-**	C+	B	Up	Y	877-960-6077
MFS Corporate Bond Fund Class R1	**MFBGX**	NAS CM	Open End	US Fixed Inc (Corp Bond - General)	**B-**	C+	B	Up	Y	877-960-6077
MFS Corporate Bond Fund Class R2	**MBRRX**	NAS CM	Open End	US Fixed Inc (Corp Bond - General)	**B-**	C+	B	Up	Y	877-960-6077
MFS Corporate Bond Fund Class R3	**MFBHX**	NAS CM	Open End	US Fixed Inc (Corp Bond - General)	**B-**	C+	B	Up	Y	877-960-6077
MFS Corporate Bond Fund Class R4	**MFBJX**	NAS CM	Open End	US Fixed Inc (Corp Bond - General)	**B-**	C+	B	Up	Y	877-960-6077
MFS Corporate Bond Fund Class R6	**MFBKX**	NAS CM	Open End	US Fixed Inc (Corp Bond - General)	**B-**	C+	B	Up	Y	877-960-6077
MFS Emerging Markets Debt Fund Class A	**MEDAX**	NAS CM	Open End	Emerg Mkts Fixed Inc (Diversified Emerg Mkts)	**C-**	D+	C	Down	Y	877-960-6077
MFS Emerging Markets Debt Fund Class B	**MEDBX**	NAS CM	Open End	Emerg Mkts Fixed Inc (Diversified Emerg Mkts)	**C-**	D+	C	Down	Y	877-960-6077
MFS Emerging Markets Debt Fund Class C	**MEDCX**	NAS CM	Open End	Emerg Mkts Fixed Inc (Diversified Emerg Mkts)	**C-**	D+	C	Down	Y	877-960-6077
MFS Emerging Markets Debt Fund Class I	**MEDIX**	NAS CM	Open End	Emerg Mkts Fixed Inc (Diversified Emerg Mkts)	**C-**	D+	C	Down	Y	877-960-6077

★ Expanded analysis of this fund is included in Section II.

TOTAL RETURNS & PERFORMANCE									ASSETS		ASSET ALLOCATION & TURNOVER							MINIMUMS		FEES		
3-Month Total Return	6-Month Total Return	1-Year Total Return	3-Year Total Return	5-Year Total Return	Dividend Yield (TTM)	Expense Ratio	3-Yr Std Deviation	Effective Duration	NAV	Total Assets (MIL)	%Cash	%Government Bonds	%Municipal Bonds	%Corporate Bonds	%Other	Turnover Ratio	Average Coupon Rate	Min Initial Investment	Min Additional Investment	Front End Fee (%)	Back End Fee (%)	Inception Date
7.46	7.36	11.58			8.14	0.75			10.91	4.4	11	9	2	65	0	65	3.50	5,000				Jun-18
6.14	7.49	12.08			20.83	0.57			9.99	11.1	17	7	1	25	0	122	3.32	3,000,000	50,000			Nov-18
6.34	7.64	12.14			20.85	0.82			9.99	11.1	17	7	1	25	0	122	3.32	5,000	0			Nov-18
7.03	-2.34	-0.14	7.71	15.10	4.32	0.7	6.06	0.47	9.53	271.5	3	2	0	95	0	51	3.80	3,000,000	50,000			Jun-13
6.98	-2.53	-0.34	6.95	13.84	4.12	0.9	6.05	0.47	9.53	271.5	3	2	0	95	0	51	3.80	5,000				Jun-13
8.65	2.42	5.30	16.67	27.85	4.16	0.6	5.59	3.49	9.96	565.3	7	0	1	86	0	181	4.83	3,000,000	50,000			Mar-03
8.58	2.39	5.14	15.92	26.39	3.91	0.85	5.55	3.49	9.97	565.3	7	0	1	86	0	181	4.83	5,000	0			Sep-02
3.84	5.23	6.97	13.89	18.01	2.45	0.47	2.58	3.41	11.01	740.2	6	24	1	38	0	393	2.54	3,000,000	50,000			Jun-02
3.88	5.21	6.84	13.22	16.73	2.23	0.69	2.59	3.41	11.02	740.2	6	24	1	38	0	393	2.54	5,000	0			Jun-03
5.60	4.63	7.32			10.59	0.49			10	10.1	13	10	2	50	0	76	3.20	3,000,000	50,000			Jun-18
5.54	4.52	7.10			10.37	0.7			10	10.1	13	10	2	50	0	76	3.20	5,000				Jun-18
2.60	1.88	3.00	7.39	9.25	2	0.72	1.74	1.14	11.43	1,976	15	6	0	31	0	233	2.89	2,500	0			Sep-09
2.76	2.00	3.41	8.47	11.07	2.31	0.41	1.74	1.14	8.85	1,976	15	6	0	31	0	233	2.89	3,000,000	50,000			Mar-00
2.71	1.90	3.20	7.80	9.90	2.11	0.62	1.74	1.14	8.85	1,976	15	6	0	31	0	233	2.89	5,000	0			Mar-97
7.32	-0.15	1.63	8.85	14.33	4.65	1.53	5.21	1.67	7.71	60.8	6	4	1	36	0	50	3.58	3,000,000	50,000			Mar-04
7.29	-0.24	1.28	8.06	12.86	4.42	1.84	5.29	1.67	7.71	60.8	6	4	1	36	0	50	3.58	5,000	0			Jun-03
3.97	6.30	8.79	16.54	21.95	2.01	0.78	3.48	5.32	11.53	83,642	2	18	1	30	0	405	3.04	2,500	0			Dec-09
4.06	6.48	9.16	17.73	24.04	2.33	0.44	3.44	5.32	11.52	83,642	2	18	1	30	0	405	3.04	3,000,000	50,000			Mar-00
4.07	6.34	8.99	16.91	22.73		0.49	3.44	5.32	11.52	83,642	2	18	1	30	0	405	3.04	3,000,000	50,000			Mar-20
4.00	6.26	8.92	16.83	22.65	2.12	0.67	3.43	5.32	11.52	83,642	2	18	1	30	0	405	3.04	5,000	0			Mar-97
4.11	6.46	9.27	17.94	24.54	2.4	0.37	3.43	5.32	10.84	83,642	2	18	1	30	0	405	3.04	25,000,000	50,000			Jul-11
0.97	0.82	1.98	6.19	8.00	2.41	0.34	0.92	0.17	4.26	176.3	34	28	0	10	0	303	2.05	3,000,000	50,000			Jul-04
0.93	0.74	1.81	5.68	7.14	2.24	0.5	0.8	0.17	4.26	176.3	34	28	0	10	0	303	2.05	5,000	0			Jun-03
6.31	0.09	1.97	9.22	15.69	3.65	0.75	4.57	1.68	11.73	3,043	0	5	2	37	0	85	3.26	3,000,000	50,000			Sep-11
6.33	-0.03	1.69	8.28	14.00	3.37	1.03	4.66	1.68	11.74	3,043	0	5	2	37	0	85	3.26	5,000	0			Sep-11
6.08	-0.13	1.75	8.98	15.43		0.69	4.58	1.68	11.72	3,043	0	5	2	37	0	85	3.26	25,000,000	50,000			Mar-20
2.07	0.79	2.96	10.56	17.57	2.5	0.9	4.14	6.82	10.33	78.0	6	0	95	0	-3	30	4.80	1,000		4.25		Feb-90
1.99	0.52	2.31	8.13	13.28	1.76	1.65	4.17	6.82	10.34	78.0	6	0	95	0	-3	30	4.80	1,000			4.00	Sep-93
2.21	0.99	3.23	11.31	18.85	2.75	0.65	4.1	6.82	9.85	78.0	6	0	95	0	-3	30	4.80	0				Apr-16
2.23	1.03	3.31	11.69	18.76	2.82	0.59	4.12	6.82	9.85	78.0	6	0	95	0	-3	30	4.80	0				Aug-17
2.40	1.21	3.03	10.18	16.84	2.74	0.78	3.63	6.12	9.92	157.6	0	0	99	0	0	20	4.75	1,000		4.25		Feb-92
2.21	0.84	2.27	7.75	12.55	1.99	1.53	3.64	6.12	9.93	157.6	0	0	99	0	0	20	4.75	1,000			4.00	Sep-93
2.44	1.36	3.13	10.51	17.41	2.84	0.68	3.61	6.12	9.85	157.6	0	0	99	0	0	20	4.75	0				Apr-16
2.46	1.29	3.20	10.72	17.42	2.91	0.6	3.63	6.12	9.85	157.6	0	0	99	0	0	20	4.75	0				Aug-17
2.90	-0.25	2.18	11.42	22.05	2.94	0.72	5.48	8.06	6.1	566.1	2	0	98	0	0	22	4.86	1,000		4.25		Jun-85
2.71	-0.62	1.43	8.96	17.35	2.18	1.47	5.45	8.06	6.1	566.1	2	0	98	0	0	22	4.86	1,000			4.00	Sep-93
2.66	-0.69	1.27	8.45	16.67	2.02	1.62	5.44	8.06	6.12	566.1	2	0	98	0	0	22	4.86	1,000			1.00	Jan-94
3.01	-0.27	2.33	11.79	22.52	3.04	0.62	5.45	8.06	9.93	566.1	2	0	98	0	0	22	4.86	0				Apr-16
3.03	-0.13	2.40	11.99	22.67	3.12	0.54	5.4	8.06	9.93	566.1	2	0	98	0	0	22	4.86	0				Aug-17
9.82	5.86	10.04	19.78	31.53	2.82	0.78	6.58	8.10	15.37	5,159	2	8	1	90	5	38	3.85	1,000		4.25		May-74
9.56	5.48	9.25	17.16	26.76	2.1	1.53	6.55	8.10	15.34	5,159	2	8	1	90	5	38	3.85	1,000			4.00	Sep-93
9.58	5.48	9.26	17.09	26.68	2.1	1.53	6.57	8.10	15.32	5,159	2	8	1	90	5	38	3.85	1,000			1.00	Jan-94
9.89	5.99	10.39	20.68	33.09	3.06	0.53	6.58	8.10	15.36	5,159	2	8	1	90	5	38	3.85	0				Jan-97
9.64	5.55	9.32	17.16	26.76	2.1	1.53	6.57	8.10	15.34	5,159	2	8	1	90	5	38	3.85	0				Apr-05
9.68	5.73	9.77	18.90	29.91	2.58	1.03	6.54	8.10	15.37	5,159	2	8	1	90	5	38	3.85	0				Oct-03
9.82	5.86	10.04	19.78	31.53	2.82	0.78	6.58	8.10	15.37	5,159	2	8	1	90	5	38	3.85	0				Apr-05
9.88	6.05	10.38	20.75	33.16	3.06	0.53	6.57	8.10	15.38	5,159	2	8	1	90	5	38	3.85	0				Apr-05
9.92	6.04	10.49	21.04	33.76	3.16	0.43	6.57	8.10	15.36	5,159	2	8	1	90	5	38	3.85	0				Jun-12
11.87	-1.34	1.42	10.12	23.19	4.46	1.06	9.54	6.58	14.39	5,943	6	61	0	31	1	94	5.27	1,000		4.25		Mar-98
11.70	-1.70	0.67	7.62	18.68	3.68	1.81	9.56	6.58	14.45	5,943	6	61	0	31	1	94	5.27	1,000			4.00	May-02
11.71	-1.71	0.67	7.61	18.59	3.69	1.81	9.59	6.58	14.43	5,943	6	61	0	31	1	94	5.27	1,000			1.00	May-02
11.96	-1.23	1.73	10.85	24.63	4.71	0.81	9.58	6.58	14.35	5,943	6	61	0	31	1	94	5.27	0				Mar-98

	MARKET			FUND TYPE, CATEGORY & OBJECTIVE	RATINGS				NEW INVESTORS	
Fund Name	Ticker Symbol	Traded On	Fund Type	Category and (Prospectus Objective)	Overall Rating	Reward Rating	Risk Rating	Recent Up/ Downgrade	Open to New Investors	Telephone
MFS Emerging Markets Debt Fund Class R1	**MEDDX**	NAS CM	Open End	Emerg Mkts Fixed Inc (Diversified Emerg Mkts)	**C-**	D+	C	Down	Y	877-960-6077
MFS Emerging Markets Debt Fund Class R2	**MEDEX**	NAS CM	Open End	Emerg Mkts Fixed Inc (Diversified Emerg Mkts)	**C-**	D+	C	Down	Y	877-960-6077
MFS Emerging Markets Debt Fund Class R3	**MEDFX**	NAS CM	Open End	Emerg Mkts Fixed Inc (Diversified Emerg Mkts)	**C-**	D+	C	Down	Y	877-960-6077
MFS Emerging Markets Debt Fund Class R4	**MEDGX**	NAS CM	Open End	Emerg Mkts Fixed Inc (Diversified Emerg Mkts)	**C-**	D+	C	Down	Y	877-960-6077
MFS Emerging Markets Debt Fund Class R6	**MEDHX**	NAS CM	Open End	Emerg Mkts Fixed Inc (Diversified Emerg Mkts)	**C-**	D+	C	Down	Y	877-960-6077
MFS Emerging Markets Debt Local Currency Fund Class A	**EMLAX**	NAS CM	Open End	Emerg Mkts Fixed Inc (Income)	**D**	D	D+	Down	Y	877-960-6077
MFS Emerging Markets Debt Local Currency Fund Class B	**EMLBX**	NAS CM	Open End	Emerg Mkts Fixed Inc (Income)	**D**	D	D+	Down	Y	877-960-6077
MFS Emerging Markets Debt Local Currency Fund Class C	**EMLCX**	NAS CM	Open End	Emerg Mkts Fixed Inc (Income)	**D**	D	D+	Down	Y	877-960-6077
MFS Emerging Markets Debt Local Currency Fund Class I	**EMLIX**	NAS CM	Open End	Emerg Mkts Fixed Inc (Income)	**D**	D	D+	Down	Y	877-960-6077
MFS Emerging Markets Debt Local Currency Fund Class R1	**EMLJX**	NAS CM	Open End	Emerg Mkts Fixed Inc (Income)	**D**	D	D+	Down	Y	877-960-6077
MFS Emerging Markets Debt Local Currency Fund Class R2	**EMLKX**	NAS CM	Open End	Emerg Mkts Fixed Inc (Income)	**D**	D	D+	Down	Y	877-960-6077
MFS Emerging Markets Debt Local Currency Fund Class R3	**EMLLX**	NAS CM	Open End	Emerg Mkts Fixed Inc (Income)	**D**	D	D+	Down	Y	877-960-6077
MFS Emerging Markets Debt Local Currency Fund Class R4	**EMLMX**	NAS CM	Open End	Emerg Mkts Fixed Inc (Income)	**D**	D	D+	Down	Y	877-960-6077
MFS Emerging Markets Debt Local Currency Fund Class R6	**EMLNX**	NAS CM	Open End	Emerg Mkts Fixed Inc (Income)	**D**	D	D+	Down	Y	877-960-6077
MFS Georgia Municipal Bond Fund Class A	**MMGAX**	NAS CM	Open End	US Muni Fixed Inc (Muni Bond - Single State)	**C**	C-	C+		Y	877-960-6077
MFS Georgia Municipal Bond Fund Class B	**MBGAX**	NAS CM	Open End	US Muni Fixed Inc (Muni Bond - Single State)	**C**	C-	C		Y	877-960-6077
MFS Georgia Municipal Bond Fund Class I	**MGATX**	NAS CM	Open End	US Muni Fixed Inc (Muni Bond - Single State)	**C**	C-	C+		Y	877-960-6077
MFS Georgia Municipal Bond Fund Class R6	**MPGOX**	NAS CM	Open End	US Muni Fixed Inc (Muni Bond - Single State)	**C**	C-	B-		Y	877-960-6077
MFS Global Bond Fund Class A	**MGBAX**	NAS CM	Open End	Global Fixed Inc (Worldwide Bond)	**C**	C	B-		Y	877-960-6077
MFS Global Bond Fund Class B	**MGBBX**	NAS CM	Open End	Global Fixed Inc (Worldwide Bond)	**C**	C	C+		Y	877-960-6077
MFS Global Bond Fund Class C	**MGBDX**	NAS CM	Open End	Global Fixed Inc (Worldwide Bond)	**C**	C	C+		Y	877-960-6077
MFS Global Bond Fund Class I	**MGBJX**	NAS CM	Open End	Global Fixed Inc (Worldwide Bond)	**C**	C	B-		Y	877-960-6077
MFS Global Bond Fund Class R1	**MGBKX**	NAS CM	Open End	Global Fixed Inc (Worldwide Bond)	**C**	C	C+		Y	877-960-6077
MFS Global Bond Fund Class R2	**MGBLX**	NAS CM	Open End	Global Fixed Inc (Worldwide Bond)	**C**	C	B-		Y	877-960-6077
MFS Global Bond Fund Class R3	**MGBMX**	NAS CM	Open End	Global Fixed Inc (Worldwide Bond)	**C**	C	B-		Y	877-960-6077
MFS Global Bond Fund Class R4	**MGBNX**	NAS CM	Open End	Global Fixed Inc (Worldwide Bond)	**C**	C	B-		Y	877-960-6077
MFS Global Bond Fund Class R6	**MGBOX**	NAS CM	Open End	Global Fixed Inc (Worldwide Bond)	**C**	C	B-		Y	877-960-6077
MFS Global High Yield Fund Class A	**MHOAX**	NAS CM	Open End	Global Fixed Inc (Corp Bond - High Yield)	**C-**	D+	C		Y	877-960-6077
MFS Global High Yield Fund Class B	**MHOBX**	NAS CM	Open End	Global Fixed Inc (Corp Bond - High Yield)	**C-**	D+	C		Y	877-960-6077
MFS Global High Yield Fund Class C	**MHOCX**	NAS CM	Open End	Global Fixed Inc (Corp Bond - High Yield)	**C-**	D+	C		Y	877-960-6077
MFS Global High Yield Fund Class I	**MHOIX**	NAS CM	Open End	Global Fixed Inc (Corp Bond - High Yield)	**C-**	D+	C		Y	877-960-6077
MFS Global High Yield Fund Class R1	**MHORX**	NAS CM	Open End	Global Fixed Inc (Corp Bond - High Yield)	**C-**	D+	C		Y	877-960-6077
MFS Global High Yield Fund Class R2	**MHOSX**	NAS CM	Open End	Global Fixed Inc (Corp Bond - High Yield)	**C-**	D+	C		Y	877-960-6077
MFS Global High Yield Fund Class R3	**MHOTX**	NAS CM	Open End	Global Fixed Inc (Corp Bond - High Yield)	**C-**	D+	C		Y	877-960-6077
MFS Global High Yield Fund Class R4	**MHOUX**	NAS CM	Open End	Global Fixed Inc (Corp Bond - High Yield)	**C-**	D+	C		Y	877-960-6077
MFS Global High Yield Fund Class R6	**MHOVX**	NAS CM	Open End	Global Fixed Inc (Corp Bond - High Yield)	**C-**	D+	C		Y	877-960-6077
MFS Government Securities Fund Class A	**MFGSX**	NAS CM	Open End	US Fixed Inc (Govt Bond - General)	**B**	B-	B	Up	Y	877-960-6077
MFS Government Securities Fund Class B	**MFGBX**	NAS CM	Open End	US Fixed Inc (Govt Bond - General)	**B-**	C+	B		Y	877-960-6077
MFS Government Securities Fund Class C	**MFGDX**	NAS CM	Open End	US Fixed Inc (Govt Bond - General)	**B-**	C+	B		Y	877-960-6077
MFS Government Securities Fund Class I	**MGSIX**	NAS CM	Open End	US Fixed Inc (Govt Bond - General)	**B**	B-	B	Up	Y	877-960-6077
MFS Government Securities Fund Class R1	**MFGGX**	NAS CM	Open End	US Fixed Inc (Govt Bond - General)	**B-**	C+	B		Y	877-960-6077
MFS Government Securities Fund Class R2	**MGVSX**	NAS CM	Open End	US Fixed Inc (Govt Bond - General)	**B-**	B-	B		Y	877-960-6077
MFS Government Securities Fund Class R3	**MFGHX**	NAS CM	Open End	US Fixed Inc (Govt Bond - General)	**B**	B-	B	Up	Y	877-960-6077
MFS Government Securities Fund Class R4	**MFGJX**	NAS CM	Open End	US Fixed Inc (Govt Bond - General)	**B**	B-	B	Up	Y	877-960-6077
MFS Government Securities Fund Class R6	**MFGKX**	NAS CM	Open End	US Fixed Inc (Govt Bond - General)	**B**	B-	B		Y	877-960-6077
MFS High Income Fund Class 529A	**EAHIX**	NAS CM	Open End	US Fixed Inc (Corp Bond - High Yield)	**C-**	D+	C	Down	Y	877-960-6077
MFS High Income Fund Class 529B	**EMHBX**	NAS CM	Open End	US Fixed Inc (Corp Bond - High Yield)	**C-**	D+	C		Y	877-960-6077
MFS High Income Fund Class 529C	**EMHCX**	NAS CM	Open End	US Fixed Inc (Corp Bond - High Yield)	**C-**	D+	C		Y	877-960-6077
MFS High Income Fund Class A	**MHITX**	NAS CM	Open End	US Fixed Inc (Corp Bond - High Yield)	**C-**	D+	C	Down	Y	877-960-6077
MFS High Income Fund Class B	**MHIBX**	NAS CM	Open End	US Fixed Inc (Corp Bond - High Yield)	**C-**	D+	C		Y	877-960-6077
MFS High Income Fund Class C	**MHICX**	NAS CM	Open End	US Fixed Inc (Corp Bond - High Yield)	**C-**	D+	C		Y	877-960-6077
MFS High Income Fund Class I	**MHIIX**	NAS CM	Open End	US Fixed Inc (Corp Bond - High Yield)	**C-**	D+	C	Down	Y	877-960-6077

★Expanded analysis of this fund is included in Section II.

TOTAL RETURNS & PERFORMANCE									ASSETS		ASSET ALLOCATION & TURNOVER							MINIMUMS		FEES		
3-Month Total Return	6-Month Total Return	1-Year Total Return	3-Year Total Return	5-Year Total Return	Dividend Yield (TTM)	Expense Ratio	3-Yr Std Deviation	Effective Duration	NAV	Total Assets (MIL)	%Cash	%Government Bonds	%Municipal Bonds	%Corporate Bonds	%Other	Turnover Ratio	Average Coupon Rate	Min Initial Investment	Min Additional Investment	Front End Fee (%)	Back End Fee (%)	Inception Date
11.70	-1.70	0.67	7.62	18.59	3.68	1.81	9.55	6.58	14.45	5,943	6	61	0	31	1	94	5.27	0				Dec-08
11.92	-1.39	1.24	9.31	21.66	4.2	1.31	9.58	6.58	14.45	5,943	6	61	0	31	1	94	5.27	0				Dec-08
11.94	-1.28	1.48	10.12	23.18	4.46	1.06	9.58	6.58	14.4	5,943	6	61	0	31	1	94	5.27	0				Dec-08
12.01	-1.15	1.74	10.94	24.72	4.71	0.81	9.59	6.58	14.4	5,943	6	61	0	31	1	94	5.27	0				Dec-08
11.97	-1.17	1.77	11.16	25.21	4.82	0.72	9.54	6.58	14.38	5,943	6	61	0	31	1	94	5.27	0				May-06
11.82	-9.34	-5.11	2.48	7.51	4.96	1.1	13.96	7.48	6.27	335.2	11	59	0	5	0	136	5.66	1,000		4.25		Sep-11
11.42	-9.82	-5.96	0.06	3.38	4.16	1.85	14	7.48	6.27	335.2	11	59	0	5	0	136	5.66	1,000			4.00	Sep-11
11.62	-9.69	-5.82	0.20	3.56	4.16	1.85	13.98	7.48	6.27	335.2	11	59	0	5	0	136	5.66	1,000			1.00	Sep-11
11.93	-9.26	-4.90	3.22	8.66	5.23	0.85	14.04	7.48	6.25	335.2	11	59	0	5	0	136	5.66	0				Sep-11
11.60	-9.80	-5.94	0.22	3.58	4.16	1.85	13.98	7.48	6.28	335.2	11	59	0	5	0	136	5.66	0				Sep-11
11.56	-9.59	-5.48	1.72	6.18	4.69	1.35	13.97	7.48	6.27	335.2	11	59	0	5	0	136	5.66	0				Sep-11
11.78	-9.31	-5.22	2.66	7.70	4.96	1.1	13.93	7.48	6.29	335.2	11	59	0	5	0	136	5.66	0				Sep-11
11.83	-9.31	-4.97	3.74	9.38	5.23	0.85	14.05	7.48	6.3	335.2	11	59	0	5	0	136	5.66	0				Sep-11
11.92	-9.31	-4.93	3.53	9.35	5.32	0.84	14.03	7.48	6.27	335.2	11	59	0	5	0	136	5.66	0				Dec-12
2.05	0.18	2.22	9.32	16.27	2.38	0.9	4.31	6.91	10.86	121.9	7	0	93	0	-2	28	4.77	1,000		4.25		Jun-88
1.87	-0.16	1.50	6.95	12.06	1.65	1.65	4.32	6.91	10.9	121.9	7	0	93	0	-2	28	4.77	1,000			4.00	Sep-93
2.06	0.31	2.46	10.08	17.33	2.63	0.65	4.33	6.91	9.84	121.9	7	0	93	0	-2	28	4.77	0				Apr-16
2.18	0.33	2.51	10.25	17.26	2.68	0.6	4.32	6.91	9.85	121.9	7	0	93	0	-2	28	4.77	0				Aug-17
5.83	2.44	3.87	11.07	19.03	1.85	1.05	5.01	6.60	9.28	626.6	28	28	1	23	0	126	2.93	1,000		4.25		Jun-10
5.67	1.96	3.11	8.52	14.73	1.11	1.8	5.04	6.60	9.23	626.6	28	28	1	23	0	126	2.93	1,000			4.00	Jun-10
5.67	1.96	3.11	8.52	14.59	1.11	1.8	5.05	6.60	9.23	626.6	28	28	1	23	0	126	2.93	1,000			1.00	Jun-10
5.92	2.46	4.13	11.93	20.57	2.1	0.8	5.05	6.60	9.24	626.6	28	28	1	23	0	126	2.93	0				Jun-10
5.55	1.96	3.11	8.52	14.73	1.11	1.8	4.97	6.60	9.23	626.6	28	28	1	23	0	126	2.93	0				Jun-10
5.79	2.32	3.62	10.28	17.48	1.61	1.3	5.05	6.60	9.23	626.6	28	28	1	23	0	126	2.93	0				Jun-10
5.74	2.34	3.88	10.98	18.95	1.85	1.05	5	6.60	9.23	626.6	28	28	1	23	0	126	2.93	0				Jun-10
5.80	2.46	4.13	11.80	20.42	2.1	0.8	5.02	6.60	9.23	626.6	28	28	1	23	0	126	2.93	0				Jun-10
5.94	2.61	4.22	12.28	21.29	2.19	0.74	5.04	6.60	9.23	626.6	28	28	1	23	0	126	2.93	0				Oct-12
8.91	-4.52	-0.97	7.96	19.01	4.71	1.06	8.24	3.25	5.88	280.5	5	1	0	83	0	26	5.67	1,000		4.25		Jul-98
8.70	-4.87	-1.70	5.57	14.66	3.92	1.81	8.26	3.25	5.89	280.5	5	1	0	83	0	26	5.67	1,000			4.00	Jul-98
8.73	-5.04	-1.87	5.55	14.62	3.92	1.81	8.38	3.25	5.87	280.5	5	1	0	83	0	26	5.67	1,000			1.00	Jul-98
8.98	-4.40	-0.72	8.77	20.50	4.97	0.81	8.28	3.25	5.88	280.5	5	1	0	83	0	26	5.67	0				Jul-98
8.72	-4.88	-1.71	5.39	14.46	3.92	1.81	8.29	3.25	5.88	280.5	5	1	0	83	0	26	5.67	0				Jun-08
8.84	-4.78	-1.21	7.16	17.55	4.44	1.31	8.27	3.25	5.89	280.5	5	1	0	83	0	26	5.67	0				Jun-08
8.87	-4.64	-1.10	8.50	19.61	4.7	1.06	8.29	3.25	5.91	280.5	5	1	0	83	0	26	5.67	0				Jun-08
8.95	-4.53	-0.86	8.62	20.15	4.97	0.81	8.34	3.25	5.9	280.5	5	1	0	83	0	26	5.67	0				Jun-08
9.03	-4.36	-0.63	9.10	20.91	5.08	0.74	8.26	3.25	5.87	280.5	5	1	0	83	0	26	5.67	0				Jun-08
0.98	6.10	7.65	13.49	16.55	2.03	0.86	3.15	5.16	10.45	2,270	-5	37	2	2	-2	113	3.17	1,000		4.25		Jul-84
0.89	5.83	6.97	10.99	12.29	1.31	1.61	3.12	5.16	10.44	2,270	-5	37	2	2	-2	113	3.17	1,000			4.00	Aug-93
0.89	5.81	6.95	10.97	12.27	1.31	1.61	3.11	5.16	10.47	2,270	-5	37	2	2	-2	113	3.17	1,000			1.00	Apr-96
1.14	6.24	7.92	14.35	17.90	2.28	0.61	3.08	5.16	10.44	2,270	-5	37	2	2	-2	113	3.17	0				Jan-97
0.89	5.83	6.97	10.99	12.29	1.31	1.61	3.13	5.16	10.44	2,270	-5	37	2	2	-2	113	3.17	0				Apr-05
0.92	5.98	7.39	12.66	15.12	1.79	1.11	3.12	5.16	10.44	2,270	-5	37	2	2	-2	113	3.17	0				Oct-03
1.08	6.21	7.76	13.49	16.55	2.03	0.86	3.11	5.16	10.45	2,270	-5	37	2	2	-2	113	3.17	0				Apr-05
1.04	6.23	7.91	14.34	18.01	2.28	0.61	3.12	5.16	10.45	2,270	-5	37	2	2	-2	113	3.17	0				Apr-05
1.07	6.29	8.02	14.71	18.67	2.37	0.5	3.15	5.16	10.44	2,270	-5	37	2	2	-2	113	3.17	0				Jul-12
7.14	-4.13	-0.24	8.20	19.30	4.74	0.99	7.24	3.24	3.24	1,623	4	0	0	96	0	58	5.84	250		4.25		Jul-02
6.93	-4.20	-0.68	5.79	15.21	3.96	1.74	7.16	3.24	3.25	1,623	4	0	0	96	0	58	5.84	250			4.00	Jul-02
6.93	-4.48	-0.68	5.78	14.88	3.96	1.74	7.16	3.24	3.25	1,623	4	0	0	96	0	58	5.84	250			1.00	Jul-02
6.80	-4.11	-0.19	8.02	19.53	4.79	0.94	7.2	3.24	3.24	1,623	4	0	0	96	0	58	5.84	1,000		4.25		Feb-78
6.94	-4.45	-0.64	5.94	15.16	4.02	1.69	7.15	3.24	3.25	1,623	4	0	0	96	0	58	5.84	1,000			4.00	Sep-93
6.94	-4.45	-0.92	5.64	15.16	4.01	1.69	7.32	3.24	3.25	1,623	4	0	0	96	0	58	5.84	1,000			1.00	Jan-94
6.89	-4.01	0.03	8.81	20.64	5.05	0.69	7.16	3.24	3.23	1,623	4	0	0	96	0	58	5.84	0				Jan-97

	MARKET			FUND TYPE, CATEGORY & OBJECTIVE	RATINGS				NEW INVESTORS	
Fund Name	Ticker Symbol	Traded On	Fund Type	Category and (Prospectus Objective)	Overall Rating	Reward Rating	Risk Rating	Recent Up/ Downgrade	Open to New Investors	Telephone
MFS High Income Fund Class R1	**MHIGX**	NAS CM	Open End	US Fixed Inc (Corp Bond - High Yield)	**C-**	D+	C		Y	877-960-6077
MFS High Income Fund Class R2	**MIHRX**	NAS CM	Open End	US Fixed Inc (Corp Bond - High Yield)	**C-**	D+	C		Y	877-960-6077
MFS High Income Fund Class R3	**MHIHX**	NAS CM	Open End	US Fixed Inc (Corp Bond - High Yield)	**C-**	D+	C	Down	Y	877-960-6077
MFS High Income Fund Class R4	**MHIJX**	NAS CM	Open End	US Fixed Inc (Corp Bond - High Yield)	**C-**	D+	C	Down	Y	877-960-6077
MFS High Income Fund Class R6	**MHIKX**	NAS CM	Open End	US Fixed Inc (Corp Bond - High Yield)	**C-**	D+	C	Down	Y	877-960-6077
MFS High Income Municipal Trust	**CXE**	NYSE	Closed End	US Muni Fixed Inc (Muni Bond - Natl)	**D+**	D+	C-	Down	Y	877-960-6077
MFS High Yield Pooled Portfolio Fund Shares	**HYPPX**	NAS CM	Open End	US Fixed Inc (Corp Bond - High Yield)	**C-**	D+	C	Down	Y	877-960-6077
MFS Inflation-Adjusted Bond Fund Class A	**MIAAX**	NAS CM	Open End	US Fixed Inc (Govt Bond - Treasury)	**B**	C+	B+	Up	Y	877-960-6077
MFS Inflation-Adjusted Bond Fund Class B	**MIABX**	NAS CM	Open End	US Fixed Inc (Govt Bond - Treasury)	**B-**	C+	B	Up	Y	877-960-6077
MFS Inflation-Adjusted Bond Fund Class C	**MIACX**	NAS CM	Open End	US Fixed Inc (Govt Bond - Treasury)	**B-**	C+	B	Up	Y	877-960-6077
MFS Inflation-Adjusted Bond Fund Class I	**MIAIX**	NAS CM	Open End	US Fixed Inc (Govt Bond - Treasury)	**B**	C+	B+	Up	Y	877-960-6077
MFS Inflation-Adjusted Bond Fund Class R1	**MIALX**	NAS CM	Open End	US Fixed Inc (Govt Bond - Treasury)	**C+**	C+	B		Y	877-960-6077
MFS Inflation-Adjusted Bond Fund Class R2	**MIATX**	NAS CM	Open End	US Fixed Inc (Govt Bond - Treasury)	**B-**	C+	B+	Up	Y	877-960-6077
MFS Inflation-Adjusted Bond Fund Class R3	**MIAHX**	NAS CM	Open End	US Fixed Inc (Govt Bond - Treasury)	**B**	C+	B+	Up	Y	877-960-6077
MFS Inflation-Adjusted Bond Fund Class R4	**MIAJX**	NAS CM	Open End	US Fixed Inc (Govt Bond - Treasury)	**B**	C+	B+	Up	Y	877-960-6077
MFS Inflation-Adjusted Bond Fund Class R6	**MIAKX**	NAS CM	Open End	US Fixed Inc (Govt Bond - Treasury)	**B**	C+	B+	Up	Y	877-960-6077
MFS Limited Maturity Fund Class 529A	**EALMX**	NAS CM	Open End	US Fixed Inc (Corp Bond - General)	**C**	C	C+		Y	877-960-6077
MFS Limited Maturity Fund Class 529B	**EBLMX**	NAS CM	Open End	US Fixed Inc (Corp Bond - General)	**C**	C-	C+		Y	877-960-6077
MFS Limited Maturity Fund Class 529C	**ELDCX**	NAS CM	Open End	US Fixed Inc (Corp Bond - General)	**C**	C-	C+		Y	877-960-6077
MFS Limited Maturity Fund Class A	**MQLFX**	NAS CM	Open End	US Fixed Inc (Corp Bond - General)	**C**	C	C+		Y	877-960-6077
MFS Limited Maturity Fund Class B	**MQLBX**	NAS CM	Open End	US Fixed Inc (Corp Bond - General)	**C**	C-	C+			877-960-6077
MFS Limited Maturity Fund Class C	**MQLCX**	NAS CM	Open End	US Fixed Inc (Corp Bond - General)	**C**	C-	C+		Y	877-960-6077
MFS Limited Maturity Fund Class I	**MQLIX**	NAS CM	Open End	US Fixed Inc (Corp Bond - General)	**C**	C	C+		Y	877-960-6077
MFS Limited Maturity Fund Class R1	**MQLGX**	NAS CM	Open End	US Fixed Inc (Corp Bond - General)	**C**	C-	C+		Y	877-960-6077
MFS Limited Maturity Fund Class R2	**MLMRX**	NAS CM	Open End	US Fixed Inc (Corp Bond - General)	**C**	C	C+		Y	877-960-6077
MFS Limited Maturity Fund Class R3	**MQLHX**	NAS CM	Open End	US Fixed Inc (Corp Bond - General)	**C**	C	C+		Y	877-960-6077
MFS Limited Maturity Fund Class R4	**MQLJX**	NAS CM	Open End	US Fixed Inc (Corp Bond - General)	**C**	C	C+		Y	877-960-6077
MFS Limited Maturity Fund Class R6	**MQLKX**	NAS CM	Open End	US Fixed Inc (Corp Bond - General)	**C**	C	C+		Y	877-960-6077
MFS Maryland Municipal Bond Fund Class A	**MFSMX**	NAS CM	Open End	US Muni Fixed Inc (Muni Bond - Single State)	**C**	C-	C+		Y	877-960-6077
MFS Maryland Municipal Bond Fund Class B	**MBMDX**	NAS CM	Open End	US Muni Fixed Inc (Muni Bond - Single State)	**C**	C-	C		Y	877-960-6077
MFS Maryland Municipal Bond Fund Class I	**MMDIX**	NAS CM	Open End	US Muni Fixed Inc (Muni Bond - Single State)	**C**	C-	C+		Y	877-960-6077
MFS Maryland Municipal Bond Fund Class R6	**MPMDX**	NAS CM	Open End	US Muni Fixed Inc (Muni Bond - Single State)	**C**	C-	C+		Y	877-960-6077
MFS Massachusetts Municipal Bond Fund Class A	**MFSSX**	NAS CM	Open End	US Muni Fixed Inc (Muni Bond - Single State)	**C**	C-	C+		Y	877-960-6077
MFS Massachusetts Municipal Bond Fund Class B	**MBMAX**	NAS CM	Open End	US Muni Fixed Inc (Muni Bond - Single State)	**C-**	D+	C	Down	Y	877-960-6077
MFS Massachusetts Municipal Bond Fund Class I	**MTALX**	NAS CM	Open End	US Muni Fixed Inc (Muni Bond - Single State)	**C**	C-	C+		Y	877-960-6077
MFS Massachusetts Municipal Bond Fund Class R6	**MPMAX**	NAS CM	Open End	US Muni Fixed Inc (Muni Bond - Single State)	**C**	C-	C+		Y	877-960-6077
MFS Mississippi Municipal Bond Fund Class A	**MISSX**	NAS CM	Open End	US Muni Fixed Inc (Muni Bond - Single State)	**C**	C-	B-		Y	877-960-6077
MFS Mississippi Municipal Bond Fund Class B	**MBMSX**	NAS CM	Open End	US Muni Fixed Inc (Muni Bond - Single State)	**C**	C-	C+		Y	877-960-6077
MFS Mississippi Municipal Bond Fund Class I	**MMSTX**	NAS CM	Open End	US Muni Fixed Inc (Muni Bond - Single State)	**C**	C	B-		Y	877-960-6077
MFS Mississippi Municipal Bond Fund Class R6	**MPMSX**	NAS CM	Open End	US Muni Fixed Inc (Muni Bond - Single State)	**C**	C	B-		Y	877-960-6077
MFS Multi-Market Income Fund	**MMT**	NYSE	Closed End	US Fixed Inc (Multisector Bond)	**C**	C-	C+		Y	877-960-6077
MFS Municipal High Income Fund Class A	**MMHYX**	NAS CM	Open End	US Muni Fixed Inc (Muni Bond - Natl)	**C-**	D+	C	Down	Y	877-960-6077
MFS Municipal High Income Fund Class B	**MMHBX**	NAS CM	Open End	US Muni Fixed Inc (Muni Bond - Natl)	**C-**	D+	C	Down	Y	877-960-6077
MFS Municipal High Income Fund Class C	**MMHCX**	NAS CM	Open End	US Muni Fixed Inc (Muni Bond - Natl)	**C-**	D+	C	Down	Y	877-960-6077
MFS Municipal High Income Fund Class I	**MMIIX**	NAS CM	Open End	US Muni Fixed Inc (Muni Bond - Natl)	**C-**	D+	C	Down	Y	877-960-6077
MFS Municipal High Income Fund Class R6	**MMHKX**	NAS CM	Open End	US Muni Fixed Inc (Muni Bond - Natl)	**C-**	D+	C	Down	Y	877-960-6077
MFS Municipal Income Fund Class A	**MFIAX**	NAS CM	Open End	US Muni Fixed Inc (Growth & Income)	**C**	C-	C+		Y	877-960-6077
MFS Municipal Income Fund Class A1	**MMIDX**	NAS CM	Open End	US Muni Fixed Inc (Growth & Income)	**C**	C-	C+			877-960-6077
MFS Municipal Income Fund Class B	**MMIBX**	NAS CM	Open End	US Muni Fixed Inc (Growth & Income)	**C**	C-	C		Y	877-960-6077
MFS Municipal Income Fund Class B1	**MMIGX**	NAS CM	Open End	US Muni Fixed Inc (Growth & Income)	**C**	C-	C			877-960-6077
MFS Municipal Income Fund Class C	**MMICX**	NAS CM	Open End	US Muni Fixed Inc (Growth & Income)	**C**	C-	C		Y	877-960-6077
MFS Municipal Income Fund Class I	**MIMIX**	NAS CM	Open End	US Muni Fixed Inc (Growth & Income)	**C**	C-	C+		Y	877-960-6077

★Expanded analysis of this fund is included in Section II.

TOTAL RETURNS & PERFORMANCE									ASSETS		ASSET ALLOCATION & TURNOVER							MINIMUMS		FEES		
3-Month Total Return	6-Month Total Return	1-Year Total Return	3-Year Total Return	5-Year Total Return	Dividend Yield (TTM)	Expense Ratio	3-Yr Std Deviation	Effective Duration	NAV	Total Assets (MIL)	%Cash	%Government Bonds	%Municipal Bonds	%Corporate Bonds	%Other	Turnover Ratio	Average Coupon Rate	Min Initial Investment	Min Additional Investment	Front End Fee (%)	Back End Fee (%)	Inception Date
6.94	-4.18	-0.63	5.94	15.16	4.02	1.69	7.14	3.24	3.25	1,623	4	0	0	96	0	58	5.84	0				Apr-05
7.09	-4.23	-0.45	7.52	18.04	4.53	1.19	7.35	3.24	3.24	1,623	4	0	0	96	0	58	5.84	0				Oct-03
7.15	-4.11	0.08	8.33	19.52	4.78	0.94	7.29	3.24	3.24	1,623	4	0	0	96	0	58	5.84	0				Apr-05
7.20	-3.70	0.35	9.16	21.39	5.05	0.69	7.21	3.24	3.25	1,623	4	0	0	96	0	58	5.84	0				Apr-05
7.25	-3.94	0.16	9.19	21.66	5.16	0.58	7.35	3.24	3.24	1,623	4	0	0	96	0	58	5.84	0				Jun-12
3.44	-5.14	-2.24	9.38	23.50	5.01	0	8.52	12.27	5.04	153.5	1	0	99	0	0	17	5.11					Feb-89
7.62	-4.22	0.28	10.57	25.00	5.72	0.02	7.43	3.24	8.73	1,180	4	0	0	96	0	59	5.84	0				Mar-13
4.07	5.71	7.79	13.95	16.96	1.96	0.8	3.95	3.32	10.95	1,174	4	85	2	3	0	38	1.54	1,000		4.25		Sep-03
3.86	5.41	6.99	11.42	12.74	1.24	1.55	3.9	3.32	10.9	1,174	4	85	2	3	0	38	1.54	1,000			4.00	Sep-04
3.84	5.27	6.79	11.10	12.09	1.14	1.65	3.96	3.32	10.9	1,174	4	85	2	3	0	38	1.54	1,000			1.00	Sep-04
4.09	5.87	7.93	14.44	17.80	2.11	0.65	3.95	3.32	10.96	1,174	4	85	2	3	0	38	1.54	0				Sep-03
3.85	5.28	6.80	11.01	12.11	1.14	1.65	3.92	3.32	10.88	1,174	4	85	2	3	0	38	1.54	0				Apr-05
3.92	5.57	7.36	12.81	14.91	1.63	1.15	3.93	3.32	10.93	1,174	4	85	2	3	0	38	1.54	0				Sep-04
4.05	5.77	7.69	13.62	16.40	1.87	0.9	3.94	3.32	10.95	1,174	4	85	2	3	0	38	1.54	0				Apr-05
4.09	5.88	7.94	14.34	17.81	2.11	0.65	3.95	3.32	10.95	1,174	4	85	2	3	0	38	1.54	0				Apr-05
4.19	6.00	8.10	14.82	18.39	2.19	0.6	3.94	3.32	10.99	1,174	4	85	2	3	0	38	1.54	0				Mar-13
4.72	2.17	3.64	8.45	10.91	2.45	0.67	2.74	1.97	6.07	1,879	-4	17	1	51	0	55	2.88	250		2.50		Jul-02
4.54	1.79	2.86	6.00	6.76	1.68	1.42	2.86	1.97	6.05	1,879	-4	17	1	51	0	55	2.88	250			4.00	Jul-02
4.50	1.75	2.77	5.75	6.33	1.61	1.52	2.76	1.97	6.07	1,879	-4	17	1	51	0	55	2.88	250			1.00	Jul-02
4.73	2.20	3.69	8.61	11.19	2.5	0.62	2.76	1.97	6.07	1,879	-4	17	1	51	0	55	2.88	1,000		2.50		Feb-92
4.55	1.65	2.75	6.02	6.91	1.75	1.37	2.84	1.97	6.05	1,879	-4	17	1	51	0	55	2.88	1,000			4.00	Sep-93
4.52	1.60	2.65	5.88	6.39	1.65	1.47	2.84	1.97	6.06	1,879	-4	17	1	51	0	55	2.88	1,000			1.00	Jul-94
4.79	2.28	3.85	9.10	11.84	2.65	0.47	2.88	1.97	6.04	1,879	-4	17	1	51	0	55	2.88	0				Jan-97
4.53	1.77	2.82	5.88	6.39	1.65	1.47	2.87	1.97	6.05	1,879	-4	17	1	51	0	55	2.88	0				Apr-05
4.67	2.07	3.43	7.79	9.80	2.25	0.87	2.76	1.97	6.07	1,879	-4	17	1	51	0	55	2.88	0				Oct-03
4.70	2.15	3.59	8.28	10.45	2.4	0.72	2.87	1.97	6.07	1,879	-4	17	1	51	0	55	2.88	0				Apr-05
4.93	2.27	3.84	9.45	12.39	2.65	0.47	2.88	1.97	6.09	1,879	-4	17	1	51	0	55	2.88	0				Apr-05
4.80	2.14	3.74	9.14	12.23	2.71	0.4	2.86	1.97	6.05	1,879	-4	17	1	51	0	55	2.88	0				Sep-12
2.37	0.11	2.01	9.30	16.45	2.84	0.83	4.4	7.11	10.8	105.5	6	0	94	0	-3	27	4.75	1,000		4.25		Oct-84
2.09	-0.34	1.26	6.77	12.06	2.08	1.58	4.36	7.11	10.79	105.5	6	0	94	0	-3	27	4.75	1,000			4.00	Sep-93
2.40	0.20	2.28	10.02	17.56	3.09	0.58	4.38	7.11	9.74	105.5	6	0	94	0	-3	27	4.75	0				Apr-16
2.42	0.14	2.34	10.30	17.52	3.15	0.53	4.38	7.11	9.74	105.5	6	0	94	0	-3	27	4.75	0				Aug-17
2.22	-0.32	1.67	9.54	17.16	2.86	0.85	5.01	7.59	11.07	357.2	3	0	97	0	-2	29	4.88	1,000		4.25		Apr-85
2.03	-0.69	0.91	7.07	12.77	2.08	1.6	5	7.59	11.09	357.2	3	0	97	0	-2	29	4.88	1,000			4.00	Sep-93
2.29	-0.13	1.95	10.29	18.24	3.09	0.6	5.04	7.59	9.69	357.2	3	0	97	0	-2	29	4.88	0				Apr-16
2.31	-0.09	2.02	10.59	18.28	3.16	0.53	5.03	7.59	9.7	357.2	3	0	97	0	-2	29	4.88	0				Aug-17
2.41	1.27	3.16	10.12	17.15	2.79	0.85	3.94	6.44	9.8	100.5	1	0	97	0	-2	30	4.90	1,000		4.25		Aug-92
2.25	0.95	2.50	8.00	13.36	2.14	1.5	3.96	6.44	9.81	100.5	1	0	97	0	-2	30	4.90	1,000			4.00	Sep-93
2.44	1.31	3.26	10.30	17.58	2.89	0.75	3.98	6.44	9.78	100.5	1	0	97	0	-2	30	4.90	0				Apr-16
2.45	1.34	3.31	10.48	17.53	2.94	0.68	3.99	6.44	9.78	100.5	1	0	97	0	-2	30	4.90	0				Aug-17
11.73	-1.40	3.25	14.89	28.58	4.74		8.84	5.19	6.06	374.7	0	10	0	61	0	65	4.97					Mar-87
2.72	-2.80	0.13	11.68	24.16	3.88	0.67	6.53	9.16	8.13	5,240	2	0	98	0	0	12	5.22	1,000		4.25		Feb-84
2.53	-3.03	-0.59	9.22	19.70	3.09	1.42	6.51	9.16	8.14	5,240	2	0	98	0	0	12	5.22	1,000			4.00	Sep-93
2.47	-3.16	-0.84	8.40	18.27	2.82	1.67	6.52	9.16	8.14	5,240	2	0	98	0	0	12	5.22	1,000			1.00	Sep-98
2.59	-2.81	0.01	11.53	24.13	3.88	0.67	6.57	9.16	8.12	5,240	2	0	98	0	0	12	5.22	0				Jun-11
2.75	-2.76	0.21	11.77	24.26	3.97	0.59	6.54	9.16	8.12	5,240	2	0	98	0	0	12	5.22	0				Jun-17
2.42	-0.55	1.90	10.86	19.98	2.92	0.76	5.22	7.97	8.83	4,814	2	0	97	0	0	23	4.82	1,000		4.25		Sep-93
2.48	-0.31	2.16	11.83	21.63	3.18	0.51	5.24	7.97	8.84	4,814	2	0	97	0	0	23	4.82	1,000		4.25		Jun-07
2.23	-0.91	1.04	8.43	15.60	2.16	1.51	5.2	7.97	8.84	4,814	2	0	97	0	0	23	4.82	1,000			4.00	Dec-86
2.41	-0.68	1.41	9.36	17.12	2.41	1.26	5.21	7.97	8.85	4,814	2	0	97	0	0	23	4.82	1,000			4.00	Jun-07
2.22	-0.91	1.15	8.41	15.55	2.15	1.51	5.2	7.97	8.86	4,814	2	0	97	0	0	23	4.82	1,000			1.00	Jan-94
2.48	-0.43	2.04	11.81	21.47	3.17	0.51	5.21	7.97	8.82	4,814	2	0	97	0	0	23	4.82	0				Aug-11

	MARKET		FUND TYPE, CATEGORY & OBJECTIVE		RATINGS				NEW INVESTORS	
Fund Name	Ticker Symbol	Traded On	Fund Type	Category and (Prospectus Objective)	Overall Rating	Reward Rating	Risk Rating	Recent Up/ Downgrade	Open to New Investors	Telephone
MFS Municipal Income Fund Class R6	MPMNX	NAS CM	Open End	US Muni Fixed Inc (Growth & Income)	C	C-	C+		Y	877-960-6077
MFS Municipal Income Trust	MFM	NYSE	Closed End	US Muni Fixed Inc (Muni Bond - Natl)	D+	D+	C-	Down	Y	877-960-6077
MFS Municipal Limited Maturity Fund Class A	MTLFX	NAS CM	Open End	US Muni Fixed Inc (Muni Bond - Natl)	C	C-	C+		Y	877-960-6077
MFS Municipal Limited Maturity Fund Class B	MTLBX	NAS CM	Open End	US Muni Fixed Inc (Muni Bond - Natl)	C	C-	C			877-960-6077
MFS Municipal Limited Maturity Fund Class C	MTLCX	NAS CM	Open End	US Muni Fixed Inc (Muni Bond - Natl)	C	C-	C		Y	877-960-6077
MFS Municipal Limited Maturity Fund Class I	MTLIX	NAS CM	Open End	US Muni Fixed Inc (Muni Bond - Natl)	C	C-	C+		Y	877-960-6077
MFS Municipal Limited Maturity Fund Class R6	MTLRX	NAS CM	Open End	US Muni Fixed Inc (Muni Bond - Natl)	C	C-	C+		Y	877-960-6077
MFS New York Municipal Bond Fund Class A	MSNYX	NAS CM	Open End	US Muni Fixed Inc (Muni Bond - Single State)	C	C-	C+		Y	877-960-6077
MFS New York Municipal Bond Fund Class B	MBNYX	NAS CM	Open End	US Muni Fixed Inc (Muni Bond - Single State)	C	C-	C		Y	877-960-6077
MFS New York Municipal Bond Fund Class C	MCNYX	NAS CM	Open End	US Muni Fixed Inc (Muni Bond - Single State)	C	C-	C		Y	877-960-6077
MFS New York Municipal Bond Fund Class I	MNYLX	NAS CM	Open End	US Muni Fixed Inc (Muni Bond - Single State)	C	C-	C+		Y	877-960-6077
MFS New York Municipal Bond Fund Class R6	MPNYX	NAS CM	Open End	US Muni Fixed Inc (Muni Bond - Single State)	C	C-	C+		Y	877-960-6077
MFS North Carolina Municipal Bond Fund Class A	MSNCX	NAS CM	Open End	US Muni Fixed Inc (Muni Bond - Single State)	C	C-	C+		Y	877-960-6077
MFS North Carolina Municipal Bond Fund Class B	MBNCX	NAS CM	Open End	US Muni Fixed Inc (Muni Bond - Single State)	C	C-	C		Y	877-960-6077
MFS North Carolina Municipal Bond Fund Class C	MCNCX	NAS CM	Open End	US Muni Fixed Inc (Muni Bond - Single State)	C	C-	C		Y	877-960-6077
MFS North Carolina Municipal Bond Fund Class I	MNCLX	NAS CM	Open End	US Muni Fixed Inc (Muni Bond - Single State)	C	C-	C+		Y	877-960-6077
MFS North Carolina Municipal Bond Fund Class R6	MPNCX	NAS CM	Open End	US Muni Fixed Inc (Muni Bond - Single State)	C	C-	C+		Y	877-960-6077
MFS Pennsylvania Municipal Bond Fund Class A	MFPAX	NAS CM	Open End	US Muni Fixed Inc (Muni Bond - Single State)	C	C-	B-		Y	877-960-6077
MFS Pennsylvania Municipal Bond Fund Class B	MBPAX	NAS CM	Open End	US Muni Fixed Inc (Muni Bond - Single State)	C	C-	C+		Y	877-960-6077
MFS Pennsylvania Municipal Bond Fund Class I	MPALX	NAS CM	Open End	US Muni Fixed Inc (Muni Bond - Single State)	C	C-	B-		Y	877-960-6077
MFS Pennsylvania Municipal Bond Fund Class R6	MPPAX	NAS CM	Open End	US Muni Fixed Inc (Muni Bond - Single State)	C	C-	B-		Y	877-960-6077
MFS South Carolina Municipal Bond Fund Class A	MFSCX	NAS CM	Open End	US Muni Fixed Inc (Muni Bond - Single State)	C	C-	C+		Y	877-960-6077
MFS South Carolina Municipal Bond Fund Class B	MBSCX	NAS CM	Open End	US Muni Fixed Inc (Muni Bond - Single State)	C	C-	C+		Y	877-960-6077
MFS South Carolina Municipal Bond Fund Class I	MTSCX	NAS CM	Open End	US Muni Fixed Inc (Muni Bond - Single State)	C	C-	B-		Y	877-960-6077
MFS South Carolina Municipal Bond Fund Class R6	MPOCX	NAS CM	Open End	US Muni Fixed Inc (Muni Bond - Single State)	C	C-	B-		Y	877-960-6077
MFS Strategic Income Fund Class A	MFIOX	NAS CM	Open End	US Fixed Inc (Multisector Bond)	C+	C	B	Up	Y	877-960-6077
MFS Strategic Income Fund Class B	MIOBX	NAS CM	Open End	US Fixed Inc (Multisector Bond)	C	C	B-		Y	877-960-6077
MFS Strategic Income Fund Class C	MIOCX	NAS CM	Open End	US Fixed Inc (Multisector Bond)	C	C	B-		Y	877-960-6077
MFS Strategic Income Fund Class I	MFIIX	NAS CM	Open End	US Fixed Inc (Multisector Bond)	C+	C	B	Up	Y	877-960-6077
MFS Strategic Income Fund Class R6	MFIWX	NAS CM	Open End	US Fixed Inc (Multisector Bond)	C+	C	B	Up	Y	877-960-6077
MFS Tennessee Municipal Bond Fund Class A	MSTNX	NAS CM	Open End	US Muni Fixed Inc (Muni Bond - Single State)	C	C-	C+		Y	877-960-6077
MFS Tennessee Municipal Bond Fund Class B	MBTNX	NAS CM	Open End	US Muni Fixed Inc (Muni Bond - Single State)	C-	D+	C	Down	Y	877-960-6077
MFS Tennessee Municipal Bond Fund Class I	MTNLX	NAS CM	Open End	US Muni Fixed Inc (Muni Bond - Single State)	C	C-	C+		Y	877-960-6077
MFS Tennessee Municipal Bond Fund Class R6	MPONX	NAS CM	Open End	US Muni Fixed Inc (Muni Bond - Single State)	C	C-	C+		Y	877-960-6077
MFS Total Return Bond Fund Class 529A	EARBX	NAS CM	Open End	US Fixed Inc (Corp Bond - General)	B-	C	B	Up	Y	877-960-6077
MFS Total Return Bond Fund Class 529B	EBRBX	NAS CM	Open End	US Fixed Inc (Corp Bond - General)	C+	C	B	Up	Y	877-960-6077
MFS Total Return Bond Fund Class 529C	ECRBX	NAS CM	Open End	US Fixed Inc (Corp Bond - General)	C+	C	B	Up	Y	877-960-6077
MFS Total Return Bond Fund Class A	MRBFX	NAS CM	Open End	US Fixed Inc (Corp Bond - General)	B-	C	B	Up	Y	877-960-6077
MFS Total Return Bond Fund Class B	MRBBX	NAS CM	Open End	US Fixed Inc (Corp Bond - General)	C+	C	B	Up	Y	877-960-6077
MFS Total Return Bond Fund Class C	MRBCX	NAS CM	Open End	US Fixed Inc (Corp Bond - General)	C+	C	B	Up	Y	877-960-6077
MFS Total Return Bond Fund Class I	MRBIX	NAS CM	Open End	US Fixed Inc (Corp Bond - General)	B-	C	B	Up	Y	877-960-6077
MFS Total Return Bond Fund Class R1	MRBGX	NAS CM	Open End	US Fixed Inc (Corp Bond - General)	C+	C	B	Up	Y	877-960-6077
MFS Total Return Bond Fund Class R2	MRRRX	NAS CM	Open End	US Fixed Inc (Corp Bond - General)	B-	C	B	Up	Y	877-960-6077
MFS Total Return Bond Fund Class R3	MRBHX	NAS CM	Open End	US Fixed Inc (Corp Bond - General)	B-	C	B	Up	Y	877-960-6077
MFS Total Return Bond Fund Class R4	MRBJX	NAS CM	Open End	US Fixed Inc (Corp Bond - General)	B-	C	B	Up	Y	877-960-6077
MFS Total Return Bond Fund Class R6	MRBKX	NAS CM	Open End	US Fixed Inc (Corp Bond - General)	B-	C	B+	Up	Y	877-960-6077
MFS Virginia Municipal Bond Fund Class A	MSVAX	NAS CM	Open End	US Muni Fixed Inc (Muni Bond - Single State)	C	C-	B-		Y	877-960-6077
MFS Virginia Municipal Bond Fund Class B	MBVAX	NAS CM	Open End	US Muni Fixed Inc (Muni Bond - Single State)	C	C-	C+		Y	877-960-6077
MFS Virginia Municipal Bond Fund Class C	MVACX	NAS CM	Open End	US Muni Fixed Inc (Muni Bond - Single State)	C	C-	C+		Y	877-960-6077
MFS Virginia Municipal Bond Fund Class I	MIVAX	NAS CM	Open End	US Muni Fixed Inc (Muni Bond - Single State)	C	C-	B-		Y	877-960-6077
MFS Virginia Municipal Bond Fund Class R6	MPVOX	NAS CM	Open End	US Muni Fixed Inc (Muni Bond - Single State)	C	C-	B-		Y	877-960-6077
MFS West Virginia Municipal Bond Fund Class A	MFWVX	NAS CM	Open End	US Muni Fixed Inc (Muni Bond - Single State)	C	C-	B-		Y	877-960-6077

★ Expanded analysis of this fund is included in Section II.

TOTAL RETURNS & PERFORMANCE									ASSETS		ASSET ALLOCATION & TURNOVER							MINIMUMS		FEES		
3-Month Total Return	6-Month Total Return	1-Year Total Return	3-Year Total Return	5-Year Total Return	Dividend Yield (TTM)	Expense Ratio	3-Yr Std Deviation	Effective Duration	NAV	Total Assets (MIL)	%Cash	%Government Bonds	%Municipal Bonds	%Corporate Bonds	%Other	Turnover Ratio	Average Coupon Rate	Min Initial Investment	Min Additional Investment	Front End Fee (%)	Back End Fee (%)	Inception Date
2.50	-0.28	2.23	11.74	19.12	3.25	0.44	5.23	7.97	8.82	4,814	2	0	97	0	0	23	4.82	0				Aug-17
3.15	-3.70	-0.78	9.82	23.63	4.65	0	7.68	11.33	7.01	280.1	0	0	100	0	0	18	5.10					Nov-86
2.19	0.68	2.21	8.11	12.66	2	0.68	2.93	3.72	8.27	2,596	5	0	95	0	0	32	4.39	1,000		2.50		Mar-92
2.00	0.20	1.46	5.72	8.56	1.25	1.43	2.91	3.72	8.26	2,596	5	0	95	0	0	32	4.39	1,000			4.00	Sep-93
1.85	0.14	1.23	5.40	7.86	1.14	1.53	2.99	3.72	8.27	2,596	5	0	95	0	0	32	4.39	1,000			1.00	Jul-94
2.23	0.63	2.36	8.59	13.36	2.15	0.53	2.98	3.72	8.26	2,596	5	0	95	0	0	32	4.39	0				Aug-10
2.13	0.68	2.31	8.66	13.24	2.23	0.45	2.93	3.72	8.25	2,596	5	0	95	0	0	32	4.39	0				Sep-17
2.04	-0.23	1.92	9.82	18.58	2.72	0.89	4.94	7.49	11.08	272.2	0	0	99	0	0	25	4.88	1,000		4.25		Jun-88
1.86	-0.60	1.16	7.38	14.23	1.95	1.64	4.93	7.49	11.05	272.2	0	0	99	0	0	25	4.88	1,000			4.00	Sep-93
1.95	-0.60	1.16	7.38	14.21	1.95	1.64	4.9	7.49	11.07	272.2	0	0	99	0	0	25	4.88	1,000			1.00	Dec-00
2.18	-0.11	2.17	10.63	19.87	2.97	0.64	4.95	7.49	9.8	272.2	0	0	99	0	0	25	4.88	0				Apr-16
2.20	-0.07	2.24	10.78	19.61	3.04	0.58	4.93	7.49	9.8	272.2	0	0	99	0	0	25	4.88	0				Aug-17
2.55	0.04	1.95	9.08	15.98	2.72	0.84	4.6	7.53	11.67	484.1	4	0	96	0	-3	28	4.75	1,000		4.25		Oct-84
2.28	-0.40	1.19	6.57	11.63	1.96	1.59	4.56	7.53	11.65	484.1	4	0	96	0	-3	28	4.75	1,000			4.00	Sep-93
2.28	-0.32	1.19	6.64	11.70	1.95	1.59	4.57	7.53	11.66	484.1	4	0	96	0	-3	28	4.75	1,000			1.00	Jan-94
2.47	0.02	2.16	9.81	17.19	2.97	0.59	4.61	7.53	9.72	484.1	4	0	96	0	-3	28	4.75	0				Apr-16
2.49	0.06	2.23	9.96	16.92	3.04	0.52	4.6	7.53	9.72	484.1	4	0	96	0	-3	28	4.75	0				Aug-17
2.09	0.47	2.75	11.49	20.39	3.12	0.81	4.39	7.41	10.38	159.1	2	0	98	0	0	17	4.84	1,000		4.25		Feb-93
1.80	0.01	1.99	8.93	15.96	2.36	1.56	4.38	7.41	10.4	159.1	2	0	98	0	0	17	4.84	1,000			4.00	Sep-93
1.98	0.47	2.83	11.74	20.89	3.22	0.71	4.4	7.41	9.88	159.1	2	0	98	0	0	17	4.84	0				Apr-16
2.10	0.51	2.90	12.00	20.94	3.29	0.64	4.37	7.41	9.89	159.1	2	0	98	0	0	17	4.84	0				Aug-17
2.02	0.62	2.47	9.60	16.43	2.62	0.84	4.13	6.78	12.11	242.3	1	0	99	0	0	22	4.72	1,000		4.25		Oct-84
1.83	0.25	1.71	7.08	12.17	1.86	1.59	4.1	6.78	12.1	242.3	1	0	99	0	0	22	4.72	1,000			4.00	Sep-93
2.10	0.71	2.70	10.30	17.55	2.87	0.59	4.08	6.78	9.81	242.3	1	0	99	0	0	22	4.72	0				Apr-16
2.12	0.74	2.75	10.56	17.46	2.92	0.53	4.11	6.78	9.81	242.3	1	0	99	0	0	22	4.72	0				Aug-17
8.33	3.78	6.78	14.78	25.39	2.94	0.79	5.91	5.87	6.94	381.7	-2	22	1	53	0	103	3.78	1,000		4.25		Oct-87
8.19	3.41	5.86	12.19	20.75	2.2	1.54	5.97	5.87	6.89	381.7	-2	22	1	53	0	103	3.78	1,000			4.00	Sep-93
8.05	3.42	5.88	12.13	20.70	2.2	1.54	5.95	5.87	6.87	381.7	-2	22	1	53	0	103	3.78	1,000			1.00	Sep-94
8.41	3.91	6.89	15.48	26.78	3.19	0.54	5.91	5.87	6.93	381.7	-2	22	1	53	0	103	3.78	0				Jan-97
8.41	3.95	7.12	15.81	26.51	3.26	0.45	5.91	5.87	6.94	381.7	-2	22	1	53	0	103	3.78	0				Mar-18
2.54	-0.13	1.70	8.52	15.66	2.96	0.86	4.51	7.05	10.36	98.4	3	0	97	0	-2	34	4.85	1,000		4.25		Aug-88
2.25	-0.59	0.86	6.13	11.44	2.21	1.61	4.47	7.05	10.35	98.4	3	0	97	0	-2	34	4.85	1,000			4.00	Sep-93
2.52	-0.11	1.87	9.25	16.87	3.22	0.61	4.45	7.05	9.68	98.4	3	0	97	0	-2	34	4.85	0				Apr-16
2.54	-0.07	1.94	9.40	16.59	3.29	0.54	4.51	7.05	9.67	98.4	3	0	97	0	-2	34	4.85	0				Aug-17
6.36	4.81	7.55	15.24	22.24	2.7	0.73	4.6	5.99	11.37	6,991	-1	13	2	45	0	60	3.62	250		4.25		Jul-02
6.32	4.75	7.02	12.68	17.48	1.9	1.58	4.56	5.99	11.43	6,991	-1	13	2	45	0	60	3.62	250			4.00	Jul-02
6.12	4.35	6.61	12.25	17.04	1.85	1.58	4.57	5.99	11.4	6,991	-1	13	2	45	0	60	3.62	250			1.00	Jul-02
6.26	4.82	7.57	15.32	22.29	2.72	0.68	4.52	5.99	11.38	6,991	-1	13	2	45	0	60	3.62	1,000		4.25		Jan-99
6.15	4.43	6.77	12.76	17.91	1.99	1.43	4.56	5.99	11.4	6,991	-1	13	2	45	0	60	3.62	1,000			4.00	Dec-00
6.13	4.47	6.66	12.42	17.32	1.89	1.53	4.57	5.99	11.4	6,991	-1	13	2	45	0	60	3.62	1,000			1.00	Dec-00
6.39	4.99	7.72	15.82	23.31	2.87	0.53	4.55	5.99	11.39	6,991	-1	13	2	45	0	60	3.62	0				Jan-99
6.13	4.38	6.66	12.42	17.32	1.89	1.53	4.58	5.99	11.4	6,991	-1	13	2	45	0	60	3.62	0				Apr-05
6.17	4.64	7.20	14.12	20.29	2.38	1.03	4.53	5.99	11.38	6,991	-1	13	2	45	0	60	3.62	0				Oct-03
6.23	4.77	7.46	14.97	21.80	2.62	0.78	4.52	5.99	11.38	6,991	-1	13	2	45	0	60	3.62	0				Apr-05
6.39	4.99	7.72	15.82	23.31	2.87	0.53	4.58	5.99	11.39	6,991	-1	13	2	45	0	60	3.62	0				Apr-05
6.42	5.04	7.83	16.18	23.97	2.96	0.42	4.56	5.99	11.39	6,991	-1	13	2	45	0	60	3.62	0				May-06
2.79	1.00	3.00	10.33	17.79	2.84	0.85	4.28	7.01	11.3	343.8	4	0	96	0	-3	24	4.82	1,000		4.25		Oct-84
2.61	0.63	2.24	7.88	13.37	2.08	1.6	4.25	7.01	11.29	343.8	4	0	96	0	-3	24	4.82	1,000			4.00	Sep-93
2.61	0.54	2.14	7.77	13.34	2.07	1.6	4.27	7.01	11.29	343.8	4	0	96	0	-3	24	4.82	1,000			1.00	Jan-94
2.86	1.07	3.17	11.14	18.93	3.08	0.6	4.23	7.01	9.82	343.8	4	0	96	0	-3	24	4.82	0				Apr-16
2.87	1.11	3.35	11.35	18.88	3.16	0.53	4.28	7.01	9.83	343.8	4	0	96	0	-3	24	4.82	0				Aug-17
2.05	1.14	2.92	9.69	16.69	2.96	0.87	3.46	6.32	11.1	108.2	0	0	97	0	2	19	4.86	1,000		4.25		Oct-84

	MARKET			FUND TYPE, CATEGORY & OBJECTIVE	RATINGS				NEW INVESTORS	
Fund Name	Ticker Symbol	Traded On	Fund Type	Category and (Prospectus Objective)	Overall Rating	Reward Rating	Risk Rating	Recent Up/ Downgrade	Open to New Investors	Telephone
MFS West Virginia Municipal Bond Fund Class B	MBWVX	NAS CM	Open End	US Muni Fixed Inc (Muni Bond - Single State)	C	C-	C+		Y	877-960-6077
MFS West Virginia Municipal Bond Fund Class I	MWVIX	NAS CM	Open End	US Muni Fixed Inc (Muni Bond - Single State)	C	C-	B-		Y	877-960-6077
MFS West Virginia Municipal Bond Fund Class R6	MPWVX	NAS CM	Open End	US Muni Fixed Inc (Muni Bond - Single State)	C	C	B-		Y	877-960-6077
MFS® Charter Income	MCR	NYSE	Closed End	US Fixed Inc (Multisector Bond)	C	C-	C+		Y	877-960-6077
MFS® Government Markets Income	MGF	NYSE	Closed End	US Fixed Inc (Multisector Bond)	B-	B-	C+	Up	Y	877-960-6077
MFS® High Yield Municipal Trust	CMU	NYSE	Closed End	US Muni Fixed Inc (Muni Bond - Natl)	D+	D+	C-	Down	Y	877-960-6077
MFS® Intermediate High Income Fund	CIF	NYSE	Closed End	US Fixed Inc (Corp Bond - High Yield)	D+	D+	C-	Down	Y	877-960-6077
MFS® Intermediate Income Fund	MIN	NYSE	Closed End	US Fixed Inc (Multisector Bond)	C+	C+	C+	Up	Y	877-960-6077
MFS® Investment Grade Municipal Trust	CXH	NYSE	Closed End	US Muni Fixed Inc (Muni Bond - Natl)	C-	C-	C-		Y	877-960-6077
MFS® U.S. Government Cash Reserve Fund Class 529A	MACXX	NAS CM	Money Mkt	US Money Mkt (Money Mkt - Govt)	C	C-	C			877-960-6077
MFS® U.S. Government Cash Reserve Fund Class 529B	MRBXX	NAS CM	Money Mkt	US Money Mkt (Money Mkt - Govt)	C	C-	C			877-960-6077
MFS® U.S. Government Cash Reserve Fund Class 529C	MRCXX	NAS CM	Money Mkt	US Money Mkt (Money Mkt - Govt)	C	C-	C			877-960-6077
MFS® U.S. Government Cash Reserve Fund Class A	MSRXX	NAS CM	Money Mkt	US Money Mkt (Money Mkt - Govt)	C	C-	C+		Y	877-960-6077
MFS® U.S. Government Cash Reserve Fund Class B	MCRXX	NAS CM	Money Mkt	US Money Mkt (Money Mkt - Govt)	C	C-	C+		Y	877-960-6077
MFS® U.S. Government Cash Reserve Fund Class C	MCCXX	NAS CM	Money Mkt	US Money Mkt (Money Mkt - Govt)	C	C-	C		Y	877-960-6077
MFS® U.S. Government Cash Reserve Fund Class I	CRHXX	NAS CM	Money Mkt	US Money Mkt (Money Mkt - Govt)	C	C-	C+			877-960-6077
MFS® U.S. Government Cash Reserve Fund Class R1	CRVXX	NAS CM	Money Mkt	US Money Mkt (Money Mkt - Govt)	C	C-	C+		Y	877-960-6077
MFS® U.S. Government Cash Reserve Fund Class R2	CRMXX	NAS CM	Money Mkt	US Money Mkt (Money Mkt - Govt)	C	C-	C+		Y	877-960-6077
MFS® U.S. Government Cash Reserve Fund Class R3	CRJXX	NAS CM	Money Mkt	US Money Mkt (Money Mkt - Govt)	C	C-	C+		Y	877-960-6077
MFS® U.S. Government Cash Reserve Fund Class R4	CRKXX	NAS CM	Money Mkt	US Money Mkt (Money Mkt - Govt)	C	C-	C		Y	877-960-6077
MFS® U.S. Government Cash Reserve Fund Class R6	CRRXX	NAS CM	Money Mkt	US Money Mkt (Money Mkt - Govt)	C	C-	C+		Y	877-960-6077
MFS® U.S. Government Money Market Fund	MCMXX	NAS CM	Money Mkt	US Money Mkt (Money Mkt - Govt)	C	C-	C+			877-960-6077
MH Elite Income Fund of Funds	MHEIX	NAS CM	Open End	US Fixed Inc (Income)	C-	D+	C		Y	
Milestone Funds Treas Obligations Portfol Inst Cl	MTIXX	NAS CM	Money Mkt	US Money Mkt (Money Mkt - Treasury)	C	C-	C+		Y	
Milestone Funds Treasury Obligations Portfolio Investor Cl	MTOXX	NAS CM	Money Mkt	US Money Mkt (Money Mkt - Treasury)	C	C-	C+		Y	
Miller Intermediate Bond Fund Class I	MIFIX	NAS CM	Open End	US Fixed Inc (Multisector Bond)	C-	D+	C		Y	877-441-4434
Mirova Global Green Bond Fund Class A	MGGAX	NAS CM	Open End	Global Fixed Inc (Multisector Bond)	C+	C	B	Up	Y	800-862-4863
Mirova Global Green Bond Fund Class N	MGGNX	NAS CM	Open End	Global Fixed Inc (Multisector Bond)	C+	C	B	Up	Y	800-862-4863
Mirova Global Green Bond Fund Class Y	MGGYX	NAS CM	Open End	Global Fixed Inc (Multisector Bond)	C+	C	B	Up	Y	800-862-4863
Mondrian International Government Fixed Income Fund	MPIFX	NAS CM	Open End	Global Fixed Inc (Worldwide Bond)	C+	C	B-	Up	Y	888-832-4386
Monteagle Fixed Income Fund Class I	MFHRX	NAS CM	Open End	US Fixed Inc (Multisector Bond)	C+	C	B-		Y	
Morgan Stanley California Tax-Free Daily Income Trust R Cl	DSCXX	NAS CM	Money Mkt	US Money Mkt (Money Mkt - Taxable)	C	C-	C		Y	855-332-5306
Morgan Stanley California Tax-Free Daily Income Trust S Cl	DFSXX	NAS CM	Money Mkt	US Money Mkt (Money Mkt - Taxable)	C	C-	C		Y	855-332-5306
Morgan Stanley Emerging Markets Domestic Fund	EDD	NYSE	Closed End	Emerg Mkts Fixed Inc (Worldwide Bond)	D	D	D+	Down	Y	855-332-5306
Morgan Stanley Global Fixed Income Opportunities Cl A	DINAX	NAS CM	Open End	US Fixed Inc (Growth & Income)	C	D+	C		Y	855-332-5306
Morgan Stanley Global Fixed Income Opportunities Cl C	MSIPX	NAS CM	Open End	US Fixed Inc (Growth & Income)	C-	D+	C	Down	Y	855-332-5306
Morgan Stanley Global Fixed Income Opportunities Cl I	DINDX	NAS CM	Open End	US Fixed Inc (Growth & Income)	C	C-	C+		Y	855-332-5306
Morgan Stanley Global Fixed Income Opportunities Cl IR	MFIRX	NAS CM	Open End	US Fixed Inc (Growth & Income)	C	C-	C+		Y	855-332-5306
Morgan Stanley Global Fixed Income Opportunities Cl IS	MGFOX	NAS CM	Open End	US Fixed Inc (Growth & Income)	C	C-	C+		Y	855-332-5306
Morgan Stanley Global Fixed Income Opportunities Cl L	DINCX	NAS CM	Open End	US Fixed Inc (Growth & Income)	C-	D+	C	Down		855-332-5306
Morgan Stanley Inst Trust Core Plus Fixed Inc Portfol Cl A	MFXAX	NAS CM	Open End	US Fixed Inc (Corp Bond - General)	C+	C	B	Up	Y	855-332-5306
Morgan Stanley Inst Trust Core Plus Fixed Inc Portfol Cl C	MSCKX	NAS CM	Open End	US Fixed Inc (Corp Bond - General)	C+	C	B	Up	Y	855-332-5306
Morgan Stanley Inst Trust Core Plus Fixed Inc Port Cl Inst	MPFIX	NAS CM	Open End	US Fixed Inc (Corp Bond - General)	B-	C	B	Up	Y	855-332-5306
Morgan Stanley Inst Trust Core Plus Fixed Inc Port Cl IS	MPLRX	NAS CM	Open End	US Fixed Inc (Corp Bond - General)	B-	C	B	Up	Y	855-332-5306
Morgan Stanley Inst Trust Core Plus Fixed Inc Portfol Cl L	MSIOX	NAS CM	Open End	US Fixed Inc (Corp Bond - General)	C+	C	B	Up		855-332-5306
Morgan Stanley Inst Trust Corp Bond Portfol Cl A	MIGAX	NAS CM	Open End	US Fixed Inc (Corp Bond - General)	C+	C	B	Up	Y	855-332-5306
Morgan Stanley Inst Trust Corp Bond Portfol Cl C	MSBOX	NAS CM	Open End	US Fixed Inc (Corp Bond - General)	C+	C	B	Up	Y	855-332-5306
Morgan Stanley Inst Trust Corp Bond Portfol Cl I	MPFDX	NAS CM	Open End	US Fixed Inc (Corp Bond - General)	C+	C	B	Up	Y	855-332-5306
Morgan Stanley Inst Trust Corp Bond Portfol Cl L	MGILX	NAS CM	Open End	US Fixed Inc (Corp Bond - General)	C+	C	B	Up		855-332-5306
Morgan Stanley Inst Trust High Yield Portfol Cl A	MSYPX	NAS CM	Open End	US Fixed Inc (Corp Bond - High Yield)	D	D	C-	Down	Y	855-332-5306
Morgan Stanley Inst Trust High Yield Portfol Cl C	MSHDX	NAS CM	Open End	US Fixed Inc (Corp Bond - High Yield)	D	D	D+	Down	Y	855-332-5306
Morgan Stanley Inst Trust High Yield Portfol Cl I	MSYIX	NAS CM	Open End	US Fixed Inc (Corp Bond - High Yield)	D+	D	C-	Down	Y	855-332-5306

★Expanded analysis of this fund is included in Section II.

TOTAL RETURNS & PERFORMANCE									ASSETS		ASSET ALLOCATION & TURNOVER							MINIMUMS		FEES		
3-Month Total Return	6-Month Total Return	1-Year Total Return	3-Year Total Return	5-Year Total Return	Dividend Yield (TTM)	Expense Ratio	3-Yr Std Deviation	Effective Duration	NAV	Total Assets (MIL)	%Cash	%Government Bonds	%Municipal Bonds	%Corporate Bonds	%Other	Turnover Ratio	Average Coupon Rate	Min Initial Investment	Min Additional Investment	Front End Fee (%)	Back End Fee (%)	Inception Date
1.86	0.76	2.16	7.33	12.39	2.2	1.62	3.49	6.32	11.1	108.2	0	0	97	0	2	19	4.86	1,000			4.00	Sep-93
2.09	1.32	3.16	10.45	17.86	3.19	0.62	3.47	6.32	9.77	108.2	0	0	97	0	2	19	4.86	0				Apr-16
2.22	1.36	3.23	10.57	17.63	3.26	0.55	3.53	6.32	9.77	108.2	0	0	97	0	2	19	4.86	0				Aug-17
8.67	-0.29	3.65	16.62	30.91	4.22		6.97	5.28	8.59	385.6	11	17	0	44	1	94	4.68					Jul-89
2.67	6.99	8.88	15.79	20.57	2.3		3.31	5.84	4.85	158.1	-2	33	3	14	-9	48	3.46					May-87
3.43	-5.38	-2.45	9.11	23.95	4.92	0	8.74	12.47	4.54	124.3	2	0	98	0	0	17	5.09					Mar-87
10.41	-5.99	-1.05	8.77	24.62	5.83	0	10.37	4.82	2.32	45.8	-40	0	0	100	0	56	5.82					Jul-88
4.99	5.65	7.82	14.17	19.71	2.5		3.07	4.07	4.03	468.8	1	32	4	59	0	18	3.19					Mar-88
3.69	0.04	2.61	12.91	26.35	4.06	0	6.53	10.99	10.5	93.8	-1	0	100	0	0	15	5.10					May-89
0.00	0.15	0.74	2.81	2.83	0.88	0.78	0.16		1	302.2	100	0	0	0	0			250				Jul-02
0.00	0.15	0.74	2.81	2.83	0.88	0.78	0.16		1	302.2	100	0	0	0	0			250			4.00	Jul-02
0.00	0.15	0.74	2.81	2.82	0.88	0.78	0.16		1	302.2	100	0	0	0	0			250			1.00	Jul-02
0.00	0.16	0.78	2.95	2.98	0.92	0.73	0.16		1	302.2	100	0	0	0	0			1,000				Sep-93
0.00	0.16	0.78	2.95	2.98	0.92	0.73	0.16		1	302.2	100	0	0	0	0			1,000			4.00	Dec-86
0.00	0.16	0.78	2.95	2.98	0.92	0.73	0.16		1	302.2	100	0	0	0	0			1,000			1.00	Apr-96
0.00	0.16	0.78	2.96	2.98	0.92	0.73			1	302.2	100	0	0	0	0			0				Sep-18
0.00	0.16	0.78	2.95	2.98	0.92	0.73	0.16		1	302.2	100	0	0	0	0			0				Apr-05
0.00	0.16	0.78	2.94	2.97	0.92	0.73	0.16		1	302.2	100	0	0	0	0			0				Apr-05
0.00	0.16	0.78	2.94	2.98	0.92	0.73	0.16		1	302.2	100	0	0	0	0			0				Apr-05
0.00	0.16	0.78	2.95	2.98	0.92	0.73	0.16		1	302.2	100	0	0	0	0			0				Apr-05
0.00	0.17	0.82	3.05	3.08	0.97	0.66			1	302.2	100	0	0	0	0			0				Sep-18
0.00	0.19	0.87	3.22	3.33	1.02	0.62	0.17		1	544.4	100	0	0	0	0			1,000				Dec-75
8.27	-2.92	-0.14	6.39	13.65	2.51	1.9	7.2	5.98	5.1	7.5	12	17	0	40	0	16	3.99	10,000	1,000			Aug-11
0.00	0.28	1.19	4.48	4.91	1.36	0.2	0.18		1	266.6	95	5	0	0	0			10,000,000				Dec-94
0.00	0.20	1.00	3.86	4.27	1.15	0.45	0.16		1	266.6	95	5	0	0	0			1,000,000				Dec-94
11.63	-0.19	3.01	9.40	18.46	2.94	0.95	7.98	1.48	15.98	83.7	6	18	0	76	0	77	2.37	1,000,000	100			Dec-14
5.12	2.73	3.99	14.17		0.85	0.96	4.84		10.59	35.2	5	30	0	65	0	25	2.20	2,500	50	4.25		Feb-17
5.18	2.77	4.24	15.04		1.1	0.66	4.86		10.61	35.2	5	30	0	65	0	25	2.20	1,000,000				Feb-17
5.18	2.85	4.19	14.92		1.06	0.71	4.91		10.6	35.2	5	30	0	65	0	25	2.20	100,000	50			Feb-17
3.40	2.61	3.34	11.62	20.59	3.66	0.6	5.61		9.83	25.0	-1	97	0	3	0	42	2.56	50,000	100			Nov-07
2.76	3.71	5.09	9.81	12.84	1.49	1.07	2.36			8.0	1	35	0	64	0	13	2.88	50,000				Dec-99
0.02	0.33	0.81	2.44	2.65	0.9	0.6	0.12		1	35.6	12	0	88	0	0			5,000	100			Jul-88
0.02	0.33	0.81	2.34	2.49	0.9	0.6	0.13		1	35.6	12	0	88	0	0			5,000	100			Jun-16
8.50	-10.27	-7.72	-6.18	-3.07	7.87	0	14.19	5.77	6.76	453.4	5	93	0	1	0	36	6.63					Apr-07
8.05	-0.43	1.70	12.29	20.47	3.62	0.87	5.98	4.40	5.61	849.7	12	24	0	35	0	94	3.95	1,000	100	3.25		Jul-97
8.07	-0.61	1.15	9.91	16.40	2.88	1.6	5.98	4.40	5.6	849.7	12	24	0	35	0	94	3.95	1,000	100		1.00	Apr-15
8.41	-0.11	2.31	13.50	22.47	3.85	0.6	6.06	4.40	5.68	849.7	12	24	0	35	0	94	3.95	5,000,000				Jul-97
8.23	-0.25	2.22	13.66	22.64	3.93	0.57	6	4.40	5.68	849.7	12	24	0	35	0	94	3.95	10,000,000				Jun-18
8.43	-0.07	2.22	13.53	22.87	3.93	0.52	6.12	4.40	5.68	849.7	12	24	0	35	0	94	3.95	10,000,000				Sep-13
8.00	-0.55	1.60	11.43	18.98	3.33	1.15	5.98	4.40	5.6	849.7	12	24	0	35	0	94	3.95	1,000	100			Jul-97
6.31	3.87	6.70	15.99	34.39	2.69	0.77	4.59	6.13	11.81	808.1	8	27	0	28	0	217	3.49	1,000		3.25		Nov-96
6.08	3.51	5.98	13.42	29.51	2.05	1.52	4.58	6.13	11.72	808.1	8	27	0	28	0	217	3.49	1,000			1.00	Apr-15
6.42	4.01	7.05	17.14	36.65	3.06	0.42	4.62	6.13	11.79	808.1	8	27	0	28	0	217	3.49	5,000,000				Nov-84
6.34	4.04	7.02	17.16	36.67	3.12	0.37	4.56	6.13	11.78	808.1	8	27	0	28	0	217	3.49	10,000,000				Jun-18
6.24	3.75	6.38	15.01	32.66	2.41	1.02	4.63	6.13	11.82	808.1	8	27	0	28	0	217	3.49	1,000				Apr-12
9.94	4.73	9.35	18.42	40.23	2.76	1.05	6.86	7.86	13.34	151.7	2	20	0	75	0	64	3.71	1,000		3.25		May-02
9.81	4.36	8.54	15.72	34.89	1.89	1.8	6.89	7.86	13.25	151.7	2	20	0	75	0	64	3.71	1,000			1.00	Apr-15
10.05	4.86	9.61	19.52	42.43	3.04	0.7	6.9	7.86	13.32	151.7	2	20	0	75	0	64	3.71	5,000,000				Aug-90
9.93	4.57	8.94	17.15	37.86	2.34	1.49	6.92	7.86	13.33	151.7	2	20	0	75	0	64	3.71	1,000				Jun-08
9.93	-7.74	-4.14	5.77	17.94	6.58	1	10.4	4.11	8.84	178.7	1	0	0	99	0	42	6.25	1,000		3.25		Feb-12
9.66	-8.10	-4.95	3.53	13.63	5.77	1.75	10.43	4.11	8.83	178.7	1	0	0	99	0	42	6.25	1,000			1.00	Apr-15
10.04	-7.57	-3.89	6.94	19.93	6.96	0.65	10.44	4.11	8.85	178.7	1	0	0	99	0	42	6.25	5,000,000				Feb-12

Fund Name	MARKET Ticker Symbol	Traded On	FUND TYPE, CATEGORY & OBJECTIVE Fund Type	Category and (Prospectus Objective)	RATINGS Overall Rating	Reward Rating	Risk Rating	Recent Up/ Downgrade	NEW INVESTORS Open to New Investors	Telephone
Morgan Stanley Inst Trust High Yield Portfol Cl IR	MRHYX	NAS CM	Open End	US Fixed Inc (Corp Bond - High Yield)	D+	D	C-	Down	Y	855-332-5306
Morgan Stanley Inst Trust High Yield Portfol Cl IS	MSHYX	NAS CM	Open End	US Fixed Inc (Corp Bond - High Yield)	D+	D	C-	Down	Y	855-332-5306
Morgan Stanley Inst Trust High Yield Portfol Cl L	MSYLX	NAS CM	Open End	US Fixed Inc (Corp Bond - High Yield)	D	D	D+	Down		855-332-5306
Morgan Stanley Inst Trust Senior Loan Portfol Cl A	MSLGX	NAS CM	Open End	US Fixed Inc (Income)	U	U	U		Y	855-332-5306
Morgan Stanley Inst Trust Senior Loan Portfol Cl C	MSLFX	NAS CM	Open End	US Fixed Inc (Income)	U	U	U		Y	855-332-5306
Morgan Stanley Inst Trust Senior Loan Portfol Cl I	MSLJX	NAS CM	Open End	US Fixed Inc (Income)	U	U	U		Y	855-332-5306
Morgan Stanley Inst Trust Senior Loan Portfol Cl IS	MSLEX	NAS CM	Open End	US Fixed Inc (Income)	U	U	U		Y	855-332-5306
Morgan Stanley Inst Trust Short Duration Income Port Cl A	MLDAX	NAS CM	Open End	US Fixed Inc (Corp Bond - General)	C	C-	C+		Y	855-332-5306
Morgan Stanley Inst Trust Short Duration Income Port Cl C	MSLDX	NAS CM	Open End	US Fixed Inc (Corp Bond - General)	C	C-	C+	Up	Y	855-332-5306
Morgan Stanley Inst Trust Short Duration Income Port Cl I	MPLDX	NAS CM	Open End	US Fixed Inc (Corp Bond - General)	C	C-	C+		Y	855-332-5306
Morgan Stanley Inst Trust Short Duration Income Port Cl IS	MSDSX	NAS CM	Open End	US Fixed Inc (Corp Bond - General)	C	C-	C+		Y	855-332-5306
Morgan Stanley Inst Trust Short Duration Income Port Cl L	MSJLX	NAS CM	Open End	US Fixed Inc (Corp Bond - General)	C	C-	C+			855-332-5306
Morgan Stanley Inst Trust Strategic Income Portfol Cl A	MSADX	NAS CM	Open End	US Fixed Inc (Growth & Income)	D+	D	C-	Down	Y	855-332-5306
Morgan Stanley Inst Trust Strategic Income Portfol Cl C	MSPDX	NAS CM	Open End	US Fixed Inc (Growth & Income)	D	D	C-	Down	Y	855-332-5306
Morgan Stanley Inst Trust Strategic Income Portfol Cl I	MSIDX	NAS CM	Open End	US Fixed Inc (Growth & Income)	D+	D	C-	Down	Y	855-332-5306
Morgan Stanley Inst Trust Strategic Income Portfol Cl IS	MSTCX	NAS CM	Open End	US Fixed Inc (Growth & Income)	D+	D	C-	Down	Y	855-332-5306
Morgan Stanley Inst Trust Ultra-Short Income Portfol Cl A	MUAIX	NAS CM	Open End	US Fixed Inc (Income)	C	C-	C+		Y	855-332-5306
Morgan Stanley Inst Trust Ultra-Short Income Portfol Cl IR	MULSX	NAS CM	Open End	US Fixed Inc (Income)	C	C-	C+		Y	855-332-5306
Morgan Stanley Inst Trust Ultra-Short Income Port Inst Cl	MUIIX	NAS CM	Open End	US Fixed Inc (Income)	C	C-	C+		Y	855-332-5306
Morgan Stanley Inst Fund Emerg Mkts Fixed Inc Opp Port A	MEAPX	NAS CM	Open End	Emerg Mkts Fixed Inc (Diversified Emerg Mkts)	D	D	C-	Down	Y	855-332-5306
Morgan Stanley Inst Fund Emerg Mkts Fixed Inc Opp Port C	MSEDX	NAS CM	Open End	Emerg Mkts Fixed Inc (Diversified Emerg Mkts)	D	D	D+	Down	Y	855-332-5306
Morgan Stanley Inst Fund Emerg Mkts Fixed Inc Opp Port I	MEAIX	NAS CM	Open End	Emerg Mkts Fixed Inc (Diversified Emerg Mkts)	D	D	C-	Down	Y	855-332-5306
Morgan Stanley Inst Fund Emerg Mkts Fixed Inc Opp Port IS	MRDPX	NAS CM	Open End	Emerg Mkts Fixed Inc (Diversified Emerg Mkts)	D	D	C-	Down	Y	855-332-5306
Morgan Stanley Inst Fund Emerg Mkts Fixed Inc Opp Port L	MEALX	NAS CM	Open End	Emerg Mkts Fixed Inc (Diversified Emerg Mkts)	D	D	C-	Down		855-332-5306
Morgan Stanley Inst Liq ESG Money Mkt Port Admin Cl	MANXX	NAS CM	Money Mkt	US Money Mkt (Money Mkt - General)	C-	C-	C		Y	855-332-5306
Morgan Stanley Inst Liq ESG Money Mkt Port Advisory Cl	MVSXX	NAS CM	Money Mkt	US Money Mkt (Money Mkt - General)	C	C-	C+		Y	855-332-5306
Morgan Stanley Inst Liq ESG Money Mkt Port Cash Mgmt Cl	MSHXX	NAS CM	Money Mkt	US Money Mkt (Money Mkt - General)	C	C-	C+		Y	855-332-5306
Morgan Stanley Inst Liq ESG Money Mkt Port Inst Cl	MPUXX	NAS CM	Money Mkt	US Money Mkt (Money Mkt - General)	C	C-	C+		Y	855-332-5306
Morgan Stanley Inst Liq ESG Money Mkt Port Inst Select Cl	MMRXX	NAS CM	Money Mkt	US Money Mkt (Money Mkt - General)	C	C-	C+		Y	855-332-5306
Morgan Stanley Inst Liq ESG Money Mkt Port Investor Cl	MIOXX	NAS CM	Money Mkt	US Money Mkt (Money Mkt - General)	C-	C-	C		Y	855-332-5306
Morgan Stanley Inst Liq ESG Money Mkt Port Particip Cl	MMNXX	NAS CM	Money Mkt	US Money Mkt (Money Mkt - General)	C-	D+	C	Down	Y	855-332-5306
Morgan Stanley Inst Liq Govt Port Administrative Cl	MGOXX	NAS CM	Money Mkt	US Money Mkt (Money Mkt - General)	C	C-	C+		Y	855-332-5306
Morgan Stanley Inst Liquidity Govt Portfol Advisor Cl	MAYXX	NAS CM	Money Mkt	US Money Mkt (Money Mkt - General)	C	C-	C+		Y	855-332-5306
Morgan Stanley Inst Liquidity Govt Portfol Cash Mgmt Cl	MSGXX	NAS CM	Money Mkt	US Money Mkt (Money Mkt - General)	C	C-	C+		Y	855-332-5306
Morgan Stanley Inst Liquidity Govt Portfol Inst Cl	MVRXX	NAS CM	Money Mkt	US Money Mkt (Money Mkt - General)	C	C-	C+		Y	855-332-5306
Morgan Stanley Inst Liquidity Govt Portfol Inst Select Cl	MGSXX	NAS CM	Money Mkt	US Money Mkt (Money Mkt - General)	C	C-	C+		Y	855-332-5306
Morgan Stanley Inst Liquidity Govt Portfol Investor Cl	MVVXX	NAS CM	Money Mkt	US Money Mkt (Money Mkt - General)	C	C-	C+		Y	855-332-5306
Morgan Stanley Inst Liquidity Govt Portfol Particip Cl	MPCXX	NAS CM	Money Mkt	US Money Mkt (Money Mkt - General)	C	C-	C+		Y	855-332-5306
★ Morgan Stanley Inst Liquidity Govt Portfol Select Cl	MSDXX	NAS CM	Money Mkt	US Money Mkt (Money Mkt - General)	C	C-	C		Y	855-332-5306
Morgan Stanley Inst Liq Govt Sec Port Administrative Cl	MGAXX	NAS CM	Money Mkt	US Money Mkt (Money Mkt - General)	C-	D+	C	Down	Y	855-332-5306
Morgan Stanley Inst Liq Govt Sec Port Advisory Cl	MVAXX	NAS CM	Money Mkt	US Money Mkt (Money Mkt - General)	C-	D+	C	Down	Y	855-332-5306
Morgan Stanley Inst Liq Govt Sec Port Cash Mgmt Cl	MCHXX	NAS CM	Money Mkt	US Money Mkt (Money Mkt - General)	C-	D+	C	Down	Y	855-332-5306
Morgan Stanley Inst Liq Govt Sec Port Inst Cl	MUIXX	NAS CM	Money Mkt	US Money Mkt (Money Mkt - General)	C	C-	C		Y	855-332-5306
Morgan Stanley Inst Liq Govt Sec Port Inst Select Cl	MSVXX	NAS CM	Money Mkt	US Money Mkt (Money Mkt - General)	C	C-	C+		Y	855-332-5306
Morgan Stanley Inst Liq Govt Sec Port Investor Cl	MVIXX	NAS CM	Money Mkt	US Money Mkt (Money Mkt - General)	C	C-	C+		Y	855-332-5306
Morgan Stanley Inst Liq Govt Sec Port Particip Cl	MGPXX	NAS CM	Money Mkt	US Money Mkt (Money Mkt - General)	C-	D+	C	Down	Y	855-332-5306
Morgan Stanley Inst Liq Prime Port Administrative Cl	MPMXX	NAS CM	Money Mkt	US Money Mkt (Money Mkt - General)	C-	C-	C		Y	855-332-5306
Morgan Stanley Inst Liquidity Prime Portfol Advisory Cl	MAVXX	NAS CM	Money Mkt	US Money Mkt (Money Mkt - General)	C	C-	C+		Y	855-332-5306
Morgan Stanley Inst Liquidity Prime Portfol Cash Mgmt Cl	MSPXX	NAS CM	Money Mkt	US Money Mkt (Money Mkt - General)	C	C-	C+		Y	855-332-5306
Morgan Stanley Inst Liquidity Prime Portfol Inst Cl	MPFXX	NAS CM	Money Mkt	US Money Mkt (Money Mkt - General)	C	C-	C+		Y	855-332-5306
Morgan Stanley Inst Liquidity Prime Portfol Inst Select Cl	MPEXX	NAS CM	Money Mkt	US Money Mkt (Money Mkt - General)	C	C-	C+		Y	855-332-5306
Morgan Stanley Inst Liquidity Prime Portfol Investor Cl	MPVXX	NAS CM	Money Mkt	US Money Mkt (Money Mkt - General)	C-	C-	C		Y	855-332-5306

★ Expanded analysis of this fund is included in Section II.

TOTAL RETURNS & PERFORMANCE									ASSETS		ASSET ALLOCATION & TURNOVER							MINIMUMS		FEES		
3-Month Total Return	6-Month Total Return	1-Year Total Return	3-Year Total Return	5-Year Total Return	Dividend Yield (TTM)	Expense Ratio	3-Yr Std Deviation	Effective Duration	NAV	Total Assets (MIL)	%Cash	%Government Bonds	%Municipal Bonds	%Corporate Bonds	%Other	Turnover Ratio	Average Coupon Rate	Min Initial Investment	Min Additional Investment	Front End Fee (%)	Back End Fee (%)	Inception Date
10.05	-7.56	-3.86	7.00	20.00	6.98	0.62	10.45	4.11	8.85	178.7	1	0	0	99	0	42	6.25	10,000,000				Jun-18
10.18	-7.46	-3.65	7.15	20.36	6.98	0.62	10.46	4.11	8.86	178.7	1	0	0	99	0	42	6.25	10,000,000				Mar-14
9.89	-7.81	-4.37	5.03	16.49	6.31	1.25	10.46	4.11	8.84	178.7	1	0	0	99	0	42	6.25	1,000				Feb-12
8.14						1.15			9.37	47.2	14	0	0	86	0		1.80	1,000		3.25		Jan-20
7.94						1.9			9.37	47.2	14	0	0	86	0		1.80	1,000			1.00	Jan-20
8.37						0.8			9.38	47.2	14	0	0	86	0		1.80	5,000,000				Jan-20
8.37						0.75			9.38	47.2	14	0	0	86	0		1.80	10,000,000				Jan-20
5.06	1.47	2.89	8.08	17.06	2.29	0.55	3.12	1.88	8.3	239.6	7	27	0	47	0	64	3.08	1,000		1.00		Sep-07
4.87	1.02	2.12	5.67	12.64	1.53	1.3	3.12	1.88	8.26	239.6	7	27	0	47	0	64	3.08	1,000			1.00	Apr-15
5.14	1.58	3.16	8.93	18.64	2.55	0.3	3.13	1.88	8.28	239.6	7	27	0	47	0	64	3.08	5,000,000				Mar-92
5.28	1.73	3.33	9.21	19.18	2.6	0.25	3.13	1.88	8.29	239.6	7	27	0	47	0	64	3.08	10,000,000				Jan-16
5.14	1.37	2.77	7.28	15.50	2.05	0.8	3.19	1.88	8.28	239.6	7	27	0	47	0	64	3.08	1,000				Apr-12
9.66	-3.84	-1.82	5.61	12.11	2.66	0.95	8.46	2.59	9.65	24.8	4	5	0	41	0	97	4.02	1,000		3.25		Dec-14
9.52	-4.17	-2.50	3.47	8.08	1.9	1.7	8.44	2.59	9.63	24.8	4	5	0	41	0	97	4.02	1,000			1.00	Apr-15
9.87	-3.60	-1.42	6.83	14.18	3.05	0.6	8.52	2.59	9.67	24.8	4	5	0	41	0	97	4.02	5,000,000				Dec-14
9.75	-3.69	-1.49	6.97	14.44	3.08	0.57	8.46	2.59	9.67	24.8	4	5	0	41	0	97	4.02	10,000,000				Dec-14
0.46	0.23	1.25	5.07		1.69	0.55	0.43	0.15	9.99	14,302	98	0	0	2	0		3.12	1,000				Apr-16
0.42	0.36	1.50	5.86		1.94	0.25	0.35	0.15	9.99	14,302	98	0	0	2	0		3.12	10,000,000				Apr-16
0.51	0.33	1.45	5.68		1.89	0.3	0.42	0.15	9.99	14,302	98	0	0	2	0		3.12	5,000,000				Apr-16
12.80	-5.75	-3.08	4.15	21.77	5.37	1.2	12.12	5.84	8.59	46.4	6	70	0	24	0	58	6.59	1,000		3.25		May-12
12.58	-6.11	-3.75	1.89	17.18	4.57	1.95	12.11	5.84	8.55	46.4	6	70	0	24	0	58	6.59	1,000			1.00	Apr-15
13.02	-5.54	-2.72	5.30	23.90	5.74	0.85	12.18	5.84	8.61	46.4	6	70	0	24	0	58	6.59	5,000,000				May-12
12.89	-5.53	-2.69	5.27	23.89	5.78	0.82	12.08	5.84	8.62	46.4	6	70	0	24	0	58	6.59	10,000,000				Sep-13
12.88	-5.82	-3.23	3.48	20.12	5.11	1.45	12.14	5.84	8.58	46.4	6	70	0	24	0	58	6.59	1,000				May-12
0.00	0.00	0.00	0.00	0.25	0	0.35	0		1	3,285	95	0	0	5	0			10,000,000				Nov-04
0.25	0.45	1.34	4.89	5.60	1.49	0.45	0.2		1.0013	3,285	95	0	0	5	0			10,000,000				Feb-04
0.28	0.50	1.46	5.21	5.75	1.59	0.35	0.19		1.0008	3,285	95	0	0	5	0			1,000,000				Aug-05
0.32	0.58	1.61	5.68	6.85	1.75	0.2	0.19		1.0011	3,285	95	0	0	5	0			10,000,000				Feb-04
0.30	0.54	1.55	5.52	6.58	1.7	0.25	0.19		1.0009	3,285	95	0	0	5	0			10,000,000				Nov-04
0.00	0.00	0.00	0.00	0.31	0	0.3	0		1	3,285	95	0	0	5	0			10,000,000				Jun-04
-3.59	-3.47	-2.74	0.07	-12.46	0.01	0.7	2.21		1.0009	3,285	95	0	0	5	0			10,000,000				Nov-04
0.00	0.27	1.13	4.26	4.61	1.31	0.35	0.18		1	109,097	66	34	0	0	0			10,000,000				Nov-04
0.00	0.24	1.05	3.98	4.17	1.23	0.45	0.18		1	109,097	66	34	0	0	0			10,000,000				Oct-04
0.00	0.28	1.15	3.04	3.19	1.31	0.35	0.68		1	109,097	66	34	0	0	0			1,000,000				Aug-08
0.03	0.33	1.28	4.72	5.30	1.46	0.2	0.18		1	109,097	66	34	0	0	0			10,000,000				Aug-04
0.01	0.31	1.22	4.56	5.08	1.41	0.25	0.18		1	109,097	66	34	0	0	0			10,000,000				Nov-04
0.00	0.28	1.17	4.40	4.83	1.36	0.3	0.18		1	109,097	66	34	0	0	0			10,000,000				Aug-04
0.00	0.19	0.87	3.26	3.33	1.02	0.7	0.17		1	109,097	66	34	0	0	0			10,000,000				Nov-04
0.00	0.12	0.64	2.41	2.09	0.77	1	0.16		1	109,097	66	34	0	0	0			0				Mar-16
-3.86	-3.61	-2.84	0.00	0.15	0	0.35	2.31		1	5,629	69	31	0	0	0			10,000,000				Mar-08
-3.60	-3.37	-2.65	0.00	0.08	0	0.45	2.15		1	5,629	69	31	0	0	0			10,000,000				Mar-08
-3.82	-3.57	-2.80	0.00	0.15	0	0.35	2.29		1	5,629	69	31	0	0	0			1,000,000				Jul-08
-1.01	-0.70	0.18	3.47	3.77	0.37	0.2	0.69		1	5,629	69	31	0	0	0			10,000,000				Mar-08
0.02	0.32	1.20	4.42	4.69	1.38	0.25	0.18		1	5,629	69	31	0	0	0			10,000,000				Mar-08
0.01	0.30	1.16	4.26	4.56	1.33	0.3	0.17		1	5,629	69	31	0	0	0			10,000,000				Mar-08
-3.60	-3.37	-2.65	0.00	0.09	0	0.45	2.16		1	5,629	69	31	0	0	0			10,000,000				Mar-08
0.00	0.00	0.00	0.00	0.21	0	0.35	0		1	16,722	95	0	0	5	0			10,000,000				Nov-04
0.23	0.37	1.27	4.79	5.09	1.48	0.45	0.21		0.9999	16,722	95	0	0	5	0			10,000,000				Apr-04
0.25	0.42	1.36	5.10	5.90	1.59	0.35	0.21		1.0001	16,722	95	0	0	5	0			1,000,000				Aug-08
0.30	0.48	1.51	5.57	6.67	1.74	0.2	0.22		1.0003	16,722	95	0	0	5	0			10,000,000				Feb-04
0.28	0.45	1.45	5.42	6.15	1.69	0.25	0.22		0.9999	16,722	95	0	0	5	0			10,000,000				Nov-04
0.00	0.00	0.00	0.00	0.22	0	0.3	0		1	16,722	95	0	0	5	0			10,000,000				Nov-04

	MARKET		FUND TYPE, CATEGORY & OBJECTIVE		RATINGS				NEW INVESTORS	
Fund Name	Ticker Symbol	Traded On	Fund Type	Category and (Prospectus Objective)	Overall Rating	Reward Rating	Risk Rating	Recent Up/ Downgrade	Open to New Investors	Telephone
Morgan Stanley Inst Liquidity Prime Portfol Particip Cl	MPNXX	NAS CM	Money Mkt	US Money Mkt (Money Mkt - General)	C-	C-	C		Y	855-332-5306
Morgan Stanley Inst Liq Tax-Ex Port Administrative Cl	MXAXX	NAS CM	Money Mkt	US Money Mkt (Money Mkt - Fed Tax Exmpt)	C-	C-	C		Y	855-332-5306
Morgan Stanley Inst Liquidity Tax-Ex Portfol Advisory Cl	MADXX	NAS CM	Money Mkt	US Money Mkt (Money Mkt - Fed Tax Exmpt)	C-	C-	C		Y	855-332-5306
Morgan Stanley Inst Liquidity Tax-Ex Portfol Cash Mgmt Cl	MTMXX	NAS CM	Money Mkt	US Money Mkt (Money Mkt - Fed Tax Exmpt)	C-	C-	C	Down	Y	855-332-5306
Morgan Stanley Inst Liquidity Tax-Exempt Portfol Inst Cl	MTXXX	NAS CM	Money Mkt	US Money Mkt (Money Mkt - Fed Tax Exmpt)	C	C-	C+		Y	855-332-5306
Morgan Stanley Inst Liq Tax-Ex Port Inst Select Cl	MXSXX	NAS CM	Money Mkt	US Money Mkt (Money Mkt - Fed Tax Exmpt)	C	C-	C+		Y	855-332-5306
Morgan Stanley Inst Liquidity Tax-Ex Portfol Investor Cl	MXIXX	NAS CM	Money Mkt	US Money Mkt (Money Mkt - Fed Tax Exmpt)	C-	C-	C		Y	855-332-5306
Morgan Stanley Inst Liquidity Tax-Ex Portfol Particip Cl	MXPXX	NAS CM	Money Mkt	US Money Mkt (Money Mkt - Fed Tax Exmpt)	C-	C-	C		Y	855-332-5306
Morgan Stanley Inst Liq Treas Port Administrative Cl	MTTXX	NAS CM	Money Mkt	US Money Mkt (Money Mkt - General)	C	C-	C+		Y	855-332-5306
Morgan Stanley Inst Liquidity Treas Portfol Advisory Cl	MAOXX	NAS CM	Money Mkt	US Money Mkt (Money Mkt - General)	C	C-	C+		Y	855-332-5306
Morgan Stanley Inst Liquidity Treas Portfol Cash Mgmt Cl	MREXX	NAS CM	Money Mkt	US Money Mkt (Money Mkt - General)	C-	D+	C	Down	Y	855-332-5306
Morgan Stanley Inst Liquidity Treas Portfol Inst Cl	MISXX	NAS CM	Money Mkt	US Money Mkt (Money Mkt - General)	C	C-	C+		Y	855-332-5306
Morgan Stanley Inst Liquidity Treas Portfol Inst Select Cl	MTSXX	NAS CM	Money Mkt	US Money Mkt (Money Mkt - General)	C	C-	C+		Y	855-332-5306
Morgan Stanley Inst Liquidity Treas Portfol Investor Cl	MTNXX	NAS CM	Money Mkt	US Money Mkt (Money Mkt - General)	C	C-	C+		Y	855-332-5306
Morgan Stanley Inst Liquidity Treas Portfol Particip Cl	MTCXX	NAS CM	Money Mkt	US Money Mkt (Money Mkt - General)	C-	D+	C	Down	Y	855-332-5306
Morgan Stanley Inst Liquidity Treas Portfol Select Cl	MSTXX	NAS CM	Money Mkt	US Money Mkt (Money Mkt - General)	C	C-	C		Y	855-332-5306
Morgan Stanley Inst Liq Treas Sec Port Administrative Cl	MAMXX	NAS CM	Money Mkt	US Money Mkt (Money Mkt - General)	C-	D+	C	Down	Y	855-332-5306
Morgan Stanley Inst Liq Treas Sec Port Advisory Cl	MVYXX	NAS CM	Money Mkt	US Money Mkt (Money Mkt - General)	C-	D+	C	Down	Y	855-332-5306
Morgan Stanley Inst Liq Treas Sec Port Cash Mgmt Cl	MHSXX	NAS CM	Money Mkt	US Money Mkt (Money Mkt - General)	C-	D+	C	Down	Y	855-332-5306
Morgan Stanley Inst Liq Treas Sec Port Inst Cl	MSUXX	NAS CM	Money Mkt	US Money Mkt (Money Mkt - General)	C	C-	C+		Y	855-332-5306
Morgan Stanley Inst Liq Treas Sec Port Inst Select Cl	MSSXX	NAS CM	Money Mkt	US Money Mkt (Money Mkt - General)	C	C-	C+		Y	855-332-5306
Morgan Stanley Inst Liq Treas Sec Port Investor Cl	MNVXX	NAS CM	Money Mkt	US Money Mkt (Money Mkt - General)	C-	D+	C	Down	Y	855-332-5306
Morgan Stanley Inst Liq Treas Sec Port Particip Cl	MPRXX	NAS CM	Money Mkt	US Money Mkt (Money Mkt - General)	C-	D+	C	Down	Y	855-332-5306
★ Morgan Stanley Inst Liq Treas Sec Port Select Cl	MSEXX	NAS CM	Money Mkt	US Money Mkt (Money Mkt - General)	C	C-	C		Y	855-332-5306
Morgan Stanley Mortgage Securities Trust Class A	MTGAX	NAS CM	Open End	US Fixed Inc (Govt Bond - Mortgage)	C-	D+	C	Down	Y	855-332-5306
Morgan Stanley Mortgage Securities Trust Class C	MSMTX	NAS CM	Open End	US Fixed Inc (Govt Bond - Mortgage)	C-	D+	C	Down	Y	855-332-5306
Morgan Stanley Mortgage Securities Trust Class I	MTGDX	NAS CM	Open End	US Fixed Inc (Govt Bond - Mortgage)	C-	D+	C	Down	Y	855-332-5306
Morgan Stanley Mortgage Securities Trust Class IS	MORGX	NAS CM	Open End	US Fixed Inc (Govt Bond - Mortgage)	C-	D+	C	Down	Y	855-332-5306
Morgan Stanley Mortgage Securities Trust Class L	MTGCX	NAS CM	Open End	US Fixed Inc (Govt Bond - Mortgage)	C-	D+	C	Down		855-332-5306
Morgan Stanley New York Muni Money Mkt Trust Reserve Class	DWNXX	NAS CM	Money Mkt	US Money Mkt (Money Mkt - Taxable)	C	C-	C		Y	855-332-5306
Morgan Stanley New York Muni Money Mkt Trust Sweep Class	AANXX	NAS CM	Money Mkt	US Money Mkt (Money Mkt - Taxable)	C	C	C		Y	855-332-5306
Morgan Stanley Pathway Funds Core Fixed Income Fund	TIIUX	NAS CM	Open End	US Fixed Inc (Corp Bond - General)	B	C+	B+	Up	Y	855-332-5306
Morgan Stanley Pathway Funds High Yield Fund	THYUX	NAS CM	Open End	US Fixed Inc (Corp Bond - High Yield)	D+	D+	C-	Down	Y	855-332-5306
Morgan Stanley Pathway Funds Inflation-Linked Fixed Inc Fu	TILUX	NAS CM	Open End	US Fixed Inc (Income)	B	B-	B+	Up	Y	855-332-5306
Morgan Stanley Pathway Funds InterNatl Fixed Income Fund	TIFUX	NAS CM	Open End	Global Fixed Inc (Worldwide Bond)	C	C	B-		Y	855-332-5306
Morgan Stanley Pathway Funds Municipal Bond Fund	TMUUX	NAS CM	Open End	US Muni Fixed Inc (Muni Bond - Natl)	C	C-	B-		Y	855-332-5306
Morgan Stanley Pathway Funds Ultra-Short Term Fixed Inc Fu	TSDUX	NAS CM	Open End	US Fixed Inc (Corp Bond - General)	C	C-	C+		Y	855-332-5306
Morgan Stanley Tax-Free Daily Income Trust R Class	DSTXX	NAS CM	Money Mkt	US Money Mkt (Money Mkt - Fed Tax Exmpt)	C	C-	C+		Y	855-332-5306
Morgan Stanley Tax-Free Daily Income Trust S Class	DFRXX	NAS CM	Money Mkt	US Money Mkt (Money Mkt - Fed Tax Exmpt)	C	C-	C+		Y	855-332-5306
Morgan Stanley U.S. Government Money Market Trust R Class	DWGXX	NAS CM	Money Mkt	US Money Mkt (Money Mkt - Govt)	C	C-	C+		Y	855-332-5306
Morgan Stanley U.S. Government Money Market Trust S Class	DGEXX	NAS CM	Money Mkt	US Money Mkt (Money Mkt - Govt)	C	C-	C+		Y	855-332-5306
Morgan Stanley U.S. Government Securities Trust Class A	USGAX	NAS CM	Open End	US Fixed Inc (Govt Bond - General)	B-	C+	B		Y	855-332-5306
Morgan Stanley U.S. Government Securities Trust Class C	MSGVX	NAS CM	Open End	US Fixed Inc (Govt Bond - General)	C+	C	B		Y	855-332-5306
Morgan Stanley U.S. Government Securities Trust Class I	USGDX	NAS CM	Open End	US Fixed Inc (Govt Bond - General)	B	C+	B+	Up	Y	855-332-5306
Morgan Stanley U.S. Government Securities Trust Class L	USGCX	NAS CM	Open End	US Fixed Inc (Govt Bond - General)	B-	C+	B			855-332-5306
Morgan Stanley Ultra-Short Muni Income Portfolio Class A	MUAMX	NAS CM	Open End	US Muni Fixed Inc (Multisector Bond)	D	D+	C		Y	855-332-5306
Morgan Stanley Ultra-Short Muni Income Portfolio Class IR	MULMX	NAS CM	Open End	US Muni Fixed Inc (Multisector Bond)	D	D+	C		Y	855-332-5306
Morgan Stanley Ultra-Short Muni Income Portfol Inst Cl	MUIMX	NAS CM	Open End	US Muni Fixed Inc (Multisector Bond)	D	D+	C		Y	855-332-5306
Morningstar Defensive Bond Fund	MSTBX	NAS CM	Open End	US Fixed Inc (Income)	D+	D+	B	Up	Y	312-616-1620
Morningstar Multisector Bond Fund	MSTMX	NAS CM	Open End	US Fixed Inc (Growth & Income)	D	D	C-		Y	312-616-1620
Morningstar Municipal Bond Fund	MSTPX	NAS CM	Open End	US Muni Fixed Inc (Muni Bond - Natl)	D+	D+	C	Up	Y	312-616-1620
Morningstar Total Return Bond Fund	MSTRX	NAS CM	Open End	US Fixed Inc (Growth & Income)	D+	D+	B	Up	Y	312-616-1620

★ Expanded analysis of this fund is included in Section II.

TOTAL RETURNS & PERFORMANCE									ASSETS		ASSET ALLOCATION & TURNOVER							MINIMUMS		FEES		
3-Month Total Return	6-Month Total Return	1-Year Total Return	3-Year Total Return	5-Year Total Return	Dividend Yield (TTM)	Expense Ratio	3-Yr Std Deviation	Effective Duration	NAV	Total Assets (MIL)	%Cash	%Government Bonds	%Municipal Bonds	%Corporate Bonds	%Other	Turnover Ratio	Average Coupon Rate	Min Initial Investment	Min Additional Investment	Front End Fee (%)	Back End Fee (%)	Inception Date
0.00	0.00	0.00	0.00	0.03	0	0.7	0		1	16,722	95	0	0	5	0			10,000,000				Nov-04
0.00	0.00	0.00	0.00	0.31	0	0.35	0		1	483.0	6	0	94	0	0			10,000,000				Nov-04
0.00	0.00	0.00	0.00	0.32	0	0.45	0		1	483.0	6	0	94	0	0			10,000,000				Jun-04
-1.25	-0.93	-0.41	1.64	2.13	0	0.35	0.8		1.0003	483.0	6	0	94	0	0			1,000,000				Aug-05
0.06	0.41	1.02	3.44	4.20	1.13	0.2	0.12		1.0002	483.0	6	0	94	0	0			10,000,000				Feb-04
0.04	0.38	0.97	3.28	3.97	1.08	0.25	0.12		1.0002	483.0	6	0	94	0	0			10,000,000				Nov-04
0.00	0.00	0.00	0.00	0.33	0	0.3	0		1	483.0	6	0	94	0	0			10,000,000				Jun-04
0.00	0.00	0.00	0.00	0.24	0	0.7	0.01		1	483.0	6	0	94	0	0			10,000,000				Nov-04
0.00	0.25	1.09	4.20	4.49	1.27	0.35	0.18		1	36,681	67	33	0	0	0			10,000,000				Nov-04
0.00	0.23	1.02	3.92	4.09	1.19	0.45	0.18		1	36,681	67	33	0	0	0			10,000,000				Aug-04
-3.92	-3.68	-2.90	0.00	0.13	0	0.35	2.33		1	36,681	67	33	0	0	0			1,000,000				Aug-05
0.01	0.30	1.22	4.64	5.16	1.4	0.2	0.18		1	36,681	67	33	0	0	0			10,000,000				Aug-04
0.00	0.28	1.17	4.49	4.94	1.35	0.25	0.18		1	36,681	67	33	0	0	0			10,000,000				Nov-04
0.00	0.26	1.13	4.34	4.71	1.31	0.3	0.18		1	36,681	67	33	0	0	0			10,000,000				Nov-04
-3.04	-2.87	-2.24	0.00	-0.04	0	0.7	1.82		1	36,681	67	33	0	0	0			10,000,000				Nov-04
0.00	0.11	0.61	2.37	2.04	0.74	1	0.15		1	36,681	67	33	0	0	0			0				Mar-16
-3.83	-3.58	-2.82	0.00	0.14	0	0.35	2.3		1	51,701	71	29	0	0	0			10,000,000				Oct-08
-3.59	-3.36	-2.64	0.00	0.07	0	0.45	2.14		1	51,701	71	29	0	0	0			10,000,000				Oct-08
-3.83	-3.58	-2.82	0.00	0.14	0	0.35	2.29		1	51,701	71	29	0	0	0			1,000,000				Oct-08
0.03	0.34	1.25	4.58	5.03	1.42	0.2	0.17		1	51,701	71	29	0	0	0			10,000,000				Oct-08
0.02	0.32	1.17	4.42	4.66	1.35	0.25	0.17		1	51,701	71	29	0	0	0			10,000,000				Oct-08
-3.96	-3.70	-2.91	0.00	0.19	0	0.3	2.37		1	51,701	71	29	0	0	0			10,000,000				Oct-08
-2.95	-2.77	-2.17	0.00	0.00	0	0.7	1.76		1	51,701	71	29	0	0	0			10,000,000				Oct-08
0.00	0.12	0.60	2.26	1.90	0.72	1	0.15		1	51,701	71	29	0	0	0			0				Mar-16
6.02	-1.15	0.89	8.97	21.58	3.84	1	5.58	1.36	8.44	161.0	7	12	0	1	0	261	3.76	1,000	100	3.25		Jul-97
6.02	-1.40	0.15	6.70	17.21	3.09	1.8	5.62	1.36	8.38	161.0	7	12	0	1	0	261	3.76	1,000	100		1.00	Apr-15
6.21	-0.90	1.23	10.33	23.60	4.24	0.7	5.61	1.36	8.3	161.0	7	12	0	1	0	261	3.76	5,000,000				Jul-97
6.24	-0.88	1.38	10.41	23.70	4.28	0.65	5.56	1.36	8.3	161.0	7	12	0	1	0	261	3.76	10,000,000				Jun-18
6.01	-1.18	0.60	8.14	20.04	3.56	1.3	5.59	1.36	8.37	161.0	7	12	0	1	0	261	3.76	1,000	100			Jul-97
0.03	0.36	0.91	2.81	2.99	1.03	0.6	0.14		1	3.2	1	0	97	0	0			5,000	100			Mar-90
0.02	0.35	0.90	2.81	3.04	1.02	0.6	0.14		1	3.2	1	0	97	0	0			5,000	100			Sep-07
4.96	5.70	8.88	16.73	24.56	2.7	0.56	3.72		8.7	965.4	5	45	0	19	0	210	3.33	1,000				Nov-91
5.66	-7.60	-4.26	4.51	13.17	5.08	1.12	8.1		3.45	269.0	4	0	0	96	0	43	6.22	1,000				Jul-98
6.17	6.70	8.79	15.35		2.07	1.3	4.14		10.7	150.4	-11	78	0	1	0	143	1.48	1,000				Mar-16
3.66	1.14	2.18	13.68	24.15	4.51	1.19	3.88		7.92	132.8	1	46	0	4	0	265	2.08	1,000				Nov-91
2.80	0.77	2.68	10.48	16.79	2.3	0.74	3.9		9.45	67.4	1	0	99	0	0	42	4.32	1,000				Nov-91
3.64	1.21	2.33	6.40		2.17	0.77	2.25		9.96	390.7	6	37	0	25	0	97	1.73	1,000				Mar-16
0.03	0.35	0.94	2.96	3.18	1.06	0.6	0.13		1	49.4	34	0	66	0	0	0		5,000	100			Feb-81
0.02	0.35	0.94	2.80	2.95	1.06	0.6	0.14		1	49.4	34	0	66	0	0	0		5,000	100			Jun-16
0.01	0.28	1.14	4.13	4.25	1.31	0.35	0.18		1	782.2	67	33	0	0	0			1,000	50			Feb-82
0.00	0.27	1.14	4.13	4.26	1.31	0.35	0.18		1	782.2	67	33	0	0	0			1,000	50			Jun-16
2.33	4.93	6.61	12.56	18.65	2.82	0.85	3.15	5.10	8.99	400.6	5	29	10	2	0	167	3.89	1,000	100	3.25		Jul-97
2.12	4.49	5.75	9.92	14.01	2.05	1.62	3.09	5.10	9.06	400.6	5	29	10	2	0	167	3.89	1,000	100		1.00	Apr-15
2.41	5.09	7.07	13.83	20.47	3.15	0.52	3.04	5.10	9	400.6	5	29	10	2	0	167	3.89	5,000,000				Jul-97
2.23	4.72	6.27	11.71	16.77	2.53	1.12	3.13	5.10	9.06	400.6	5	29	10	2	0	167	3.89	1,000	100			Jul-97
0.10	0.40	0.98			0	0.45			10	349.0	19	0	81	0	0		0.71	1,000		0.50		Dec-18
0.15	0.51	1.20			1.3	0.25			10	349.0	19	0	81	0	0		0.71	15,000,000				Dec-18
0.12	0.46	1.20			1.19	0.35			10.01	349.0	19	0	81	0	0		0.71	10,000,000				Dec-18
2.10	2.93	3.83			2.36	0.55		1.92	10.28	188.4	14	33	0	13	0		2.57	0				Nov-18
9.10	-3.22	-1.22			4.27	0.8		4.57	9.89	238.9	9	37	0	26	0		5.74	0				Nov-18
2.33	0.82	2.69			2.14	0.59		4.55	10.53	342.2	2	0	98	0	0		4.26	0				Nov-18
6.05	6.22	9.01			2.42	0.54		5.77	11.14	523.7	8	27	1	14	-6		3.34	0				Nov-18

	MARKET		FUND TYPE, CATEGORY & OBJECTIVE		RATINGS				NEW INVESTORS	
Fund Name	Ticker Symbol	Traded On	Fund Type	Category and (Prospectus Objective)	Overall Rating	Reward Rating	Risk Rating	Recent Up/ Downgrade	Open to New Investors	Telephone
MS Emerging Markets Debt Fund	MSD	NYSE	Closed End	Emerg Mkts Fixed Inc (Worldwide Bond)	D+	D	C-	Down	Y	855-332-5306
MSIFT Liquid Assets Prime Portfolio Advisory Class	MAHXX	NAS CM	Money Mkt	US Money Mkt (Money Mkt - General)	D	D	C+		Y	855-332-5306
MSIFT Liquid Assets Prime Portfolio Class A	MAEXX	NAS CM	Money Mkt	US Money Mkt (Money Mkt - General)	D	D	C		Y	855-332-5306
MSIFT Liquid Assets Prime Portfolio Wealth Class	MAJXX	NAS CM	Money Mkt	US Money Mkt (Money Mkt - General)	D	D	C+		Y	855-332-5306
Multimanager Core Bond Portfolio Class IA			Open End	US Fixed Inc (Corp Bond - General)	U	U	U		Y	877-222-2144
Multimanager Core Bond Portfolio Class IB			Open End	US Fixed Inc (Corp Bond - General)	U	U	U		Y	877-222-2144
Multimanager Core Bond Portfolio Class K			Open End	US Fixed Inc (Corp Bond - General)	U	U	U		Y	877-222-2144
Multi-Manager Total Return Bond Strategies Inst 3 Cl	CTREX	NAS CM	Open End	US Fixed Inc (Multisector Bond)	B-	C+	B	Up	Y	800-345-6611
Multi-Manager Total Return Bond Strategies Inst Cl	CTRZX	NAS CM	Open End	US Fixed Inc (Multisector Bond)	B-	C	B	Up	Y	800-345-6611
Multisector Bond SMA Completion Portfolio	MBSAX	NAS CM	Open End	US Fixed Inc (Income)	U	U	U		Y	800-345-6611
Mutual of America Institutional Funds Inc Bond Fund	MABOX	NAS CM	Open End	US Fixed Inc (Corp Bond - General)	B	B-	B+		Y	
Mutual of America Institutional Funds Inc Money Mkt Fund	MAFXX	NAS CM	Money Mkt	US Money Mkt (Money Mkt - Taxable)	C	C-	C+		Y	
Muzinich Credit Opportunities Fund Institutional Shares	MZCIX	NAS CM	Open End	US Fixed Inc (Corp Bond - High Yield)	C	C-	B-		Y	
Muzinich Credit Opportunities Supra Institutional Shares	MZCSX	NAS CM	Open End	US Fixed Inc (Corp Bond - High Yield)	C	C-	B-		Y	
Muzinich High Income Floating Rate Institutional Shares	MZFIX	NAS CM	Open End	US Fixed Inc (Income)	D+	D	C-		Y	
Muzinich Low Duration Fund Institutional Shares	MZLIX	NAS CM	Open End	US Fixed Inc (Income)	C-	D+	C	Down	Y	
Muzinich Low Duration Fund Supra Institutional Shares	MZLSX	NAS CM	Open End	US Fixed Inc (Income)	C-	D+	C		Y	
Muzinich U.S. High Yield Corp Bond Institutional Shares	MZHIX	NAS CM	Open End	US Fixed Inc (Corp Bond - High Yield)	C-	D+	C		Y	
Muzinich U.S. High Yield Corp Bond Supra Inst Shares	MZHSX	NAS CM	Open End	US Fixed Inc (Corp Bond - High Yield)	C-	D+	C		Y	
Nationwide Amundi Global High Yield Fund Class A	NWXIX	NAS CM	Open End	Global Fixed Inc (Corp Bond - High Yield)	D	D	D+	Down	Y	800-848-0920
Nationwide Amundi Global High Yield Fund Class C	NWXJX	NAS CM	Open End	Global Fixed Inc (Corp Bond - High Yield)	D	D	D+	Down	Y	800-848-0920
Nationwide Amundi Global High Yield Fund Class R6	NWXKX	NAS CM	Open End	Global Fixed Inc (Corp Bond - High Yield)	D	D	D+	Down	Y	800-848-0920
Nationwide Amundi Global High Yield Inst Service Cl	NWXLX	NAS CM	Open End	Global Fixed Inc (Corp Bond - High Yield)	D	D	D+	Down	Y	800-848-0920
Nationwide Amundi Strategic Income Fund Class A	NWXEX	NAS CM	Open End	US Fixed Inc (Income)	D	D	D+	Down	Y	800-848-0920
Nationwide Amundi Strategic Income Fund Class C	NWXFX	NAS CM	Open End	US Fixed Inc (Income)	D	D	D+	Down	Y	800-848-0920
Nationwide Amundi Strategic Income Fund Class R6	NWXGX	NAS CM	Open End	US Fixed Inc (Income)	D	D	D+	Down	Y	800-848-0920
Nationwide Amundi Strategic Income Inst Service Cl	NWXHX	NAS CM	Open End	US Fixed Inc (Income)	D	D	D+	Down	Y	800-848-0920
Nationwide Bond Fund Class A	NBDAX	NAS CM	Open End	US Fixed Inc (Multisector Bond)	B-	C+	B+	Up	Y	800-848-0920
Nationwide Bond Fund Class C	GBDCX	NAS CM	Open End	US Fixed Inc (Multisector Bond)	C+	C	B	Up	Y	800-848-0920
Nationwide Bond Fund Class R	GBDRX	NAS CM	Open End	US Fixed Inc (Multisector Bond)	B-	C	B	Up	Y	800-848-0920
Nationwide Bond Fund Class R6	NWIBX	NAS CM	Open End	US Fixed Inc (Multisector Bond)	B-	C+	B+	Up	Y	800-848-0920
Nationwide Bond Fund Institutional Service Class	MUIBX	NAS CM	Open End	US Fixed Inc (Multisector Bond)	B-	C+	B+	Up	Y	800-848-0920
Nationwide Bond Index Fund Class A	GBIAX	NAS CM	Open End	US Fixed Inc (Corp Bond - General)	B	C+	B	Up	Y	800-848-0920
Nationwide Bond Index Fund Class C	GBICX	NAS CM	Open End	US Fixed Inc (Corp Bond - General)	B-	C+	B		Y	800-848-0920
Nationwide Bond Index Fund Class R6	GBXIX	NAS CM	Open End	US Fixed Inc (Corp Bond - General)	B	C+	B+		Y	800-848-0920
Nationwide Bond Index Fund Institutional Service Class	NWXOX	NAS CM	Open End	US Fixed Inc (Corp Bond - General)	B-	C+	B	Up	Y	800-848-0920
Nationwide Core Plus Bond Fund Class A	NWCPX	NAS CM	Open End	US Fixed Inc (Growth & Income)	B-	C+	B+	Up	Y	800-848-0920
Nationwide Core Plus Bond Fund Class R6	NWCIX	NAS CM	Open End	US Fixed Inc (Growth & Income)	B-	C+	B+	Up	Y	800-848-0920
Nationwide Core Plus Bond Fund Institutional Service Class	NWCSX	NAS CM	Open End	US Fixed Inc (Growth & Income)	B-	C+	B+	Up	Y	800-848-0920
Nationwide Emerging Markets Debt Fund Class A	NWXAX	NAS CM	Open End	Emerg Mkts Fixed Inc (Income)	D+	D	C-	Down	Y	800-848-0920
Nationwide Emerging Markets Debt Fund Class C	NWXBX	NAS CM	Open End	Emerg Mkts Fixed Inc (Income)	D	D	D+	Down	Y	800-848-0920
Nationwide Emerging Markets Debt Fund Class R6	NWXCX	NAS CM	Open End	Emerg Mkts Fixed Inc (Income)	D+	D	C-	Down	Y	800-848-0920
Nationwide Emerg Mkts Debt Institutional Service Cl	NWXDX	NAS CM	Open End	Emerg Mkts Fixed Inc (Income)	D+	D	C-	Down	Y	800-848-0920
Nationwide Government Money Market Fund Class R6	GMIXX	NAS CM	Money Mkt	US Money Mkt (Money Mkt - Govt)	C	C-	C+		Y	800-848-0920
Nationwide Government Money Market Fund Investor Shares	MIFXX	NAS CM	Money Mkt	US Money Mkt (Money Mkt - Govt)	C	C-	C+		Y	800-848-0920
Nationwide Government Money Market Fund Service Class	NWSXX	NAS CM	Money Mkt	US Money Mkt (Money Mkt - Govt)	C	C-	C		Y	800-848-0920
Nationwide Inflation-Protected Securities Fund Class A	NIFAX	NAS CM	Open End	US Fixed Inc (Income)	B	C+	B+	Up	Y	800-848-0920
Nationwide Inflation-Protected Securities Fund Class R6	NIFIX	NAS CM	Open End	US Fixed Inc (Income)	B	C+	A-	Up	Y	800-848-0920
Nationwide Inflation-Protected Securities Inst Service Cl	NWXNX	NAS CM	Open End	US Fixed Inc (Income)	B	C+	B+	Up	Y	800-848-0920
Nationwide Loomis Core Bond Fund Class A	NWJGX	NAS CM	Open End	US Fixed Inc (Income)	B-	C+	B	Up	Y	800-848-0920
Nationwide Loomis Core Bond Fund Class C	NWJHX	NAS CM	Open End	US Fixed Inc (Income)	B-	C+	B	Up	Y	800-848-0920
Nationwide Loomis Core Bond Fund Class R6	NWJIX	NAS CM	Open End	US Fixed Inc (Income)	B	C+	B+	Up	Y	800-848-0920

★Expanded analysis of this fund is included in Section II.

TOTAL RETURNS & PERFORMANCE									ASSETS		ASSET ALLOCATION & TURNOVER							MINIMUMS		FEES		
3-Month Total Return	6-Month Total Return	1-Year Total Return	3-Year Total Return	5-Year Total Return	Dividend Yield (TTM)	Expense Ratio	3-Yr Std Deviation	Effective Duration	NAV	Total Assets (MIL)	%Cash	%Government Bonds	%Municipal Bonds	%Corporate Bonds	%Other	Turnover Ratio	Average Coupon Rate	Min Initial Investment	Min Additional Investment	Front End Fee (%)	Back End Fee (%)	Inception Date
10.51	-4.99	-3.17	4.29	19.37	5.28	0	10.77	7.21	9.88	196.7	7	79	0	14	0	39	5.80					Jul-93
0.00	0.37	1.35			1.54	0.23			1	51.0	98	0	0	2	0			1,000,000				May-19
0.00	0.30	1.16			1.33	0.48			1	51.0	98	0	0	2	0			1,000				May-19
0.00	0.37	1.35			1.54	0.23			1	51.0	98	0	0	2	0			1,000,000				May-19
2.12	4.66	5.17	5.88	9.92	2.63	0.96	2.38	4.24		824.8	3	38	1	23	1	312	3.28	0				Dec-01
2.01	4.54	5.16	5.76	9.79	2.62	0.96	2.34	4.24		824.8	3	38	1	23	1	312	3.28	0				Dec-01
2.18	4.78	5.54	6.67	11.36	2.87	0.71	2.33	4.24		824.8	3	38	1	23	1	312	3.28	0				Aug-11
5.68	5.26	8.16	15.06	22.35		0.46	4.18	5.80	10.65	8,344	27	21	0	24	0	219	3.60	1,000,000				Dec-19
5.69	5.15	8.05	14.95	22.23	2.74	0.49	4.23	5.80	10.63	8,344	27	21	0	24	0	219	3.60	100				Jan-17
3.06	-6.67					0			11.26	--	-17	11	0	0	0			0				Oct-19
1.67	6.66	8.55	15.73	23.69	2.57	0.45	3.03		10.5354	25.0	3	48	0	22	0	13	3.16	25,000	5,000			May-96
0.11	0.39	1.32	4.72	5.24	2.15	0.2	0.16		10.5091	18.6	92	8	0	0	0			25,000	5,000			May-97
7.66	0.59	3.94	13.61	24.13	2.53	0.66	5.5	5.52	10.83	434.7	4	4	0	70	0	293	4.17	1,000,000	100			Oct-14
7.57	0.53	4.00	13.77	24.42	2.59	0.6	5.52	5.52	10.83	434.7	4	4	0	70	0	293	4.17	5,000,000	100			Jan-13
9.66	-2.16	-0.13			4.19	0.65		0.20	9.43	10.8	5	0	0	74	0		4.40	1,000,000	100		1.00	Jun-18
7.85	-3.76	-0.01	7.89		1.18	0.47	6.67	2.02	9.88	577.1	0	3	0	60	0		3.76	1,000,000	100			Apr-19
7.85	-2.37	0.09	8.03		1.2	0.5	6.54	2.02	9.74	577.1	0	3	0	60	0		3.76	1,000,000	100			Jun-16
9.16	-3.00	0.70	9.56		5.31	0.65	7.76	3.60	9.3	56.6	4	0	0	96	0		6.04	1,000,000	100			Mar-17
9.28	-2.90	0.92	9.63		5.32	0.64	7.76	3.60	9.3	56.6	4	0	0	96	0		6.04	5,000,000	100		1.00	Mar-16
12.12	-9.85	-5.66	5.58		5.97	1.2	12.32	3.79	8.81	111.8	9	0	0	82	0	75	6.66	2,000	100	2.25		Nov-15
11.91	-10.20	-6.44	3.18		5.2	1.95	12.31	3.79	8.8	111.8	9	0	0	82	0	75	6.66	2,000	100		1.00	Nov-15
12.17	-9.72	-5.39	6.44		6.26	0.7	12.31	3.79	8.82	111.8	9	0	0	82	0	75	6.66	1,000,000				Nov-15
12.15	-9.67	-5.39	6.15		6.15	0.95	12.28	3.79	8.82	111.8	9	0	0	82	0	75	6.66	50,000				Nov-15
16.09	-5.07	-1.55	8.57		3.86	0.99	11.29	-0.01	9.82	145.1	35	2	0	35	0	94	5.33	2,000	100	2.25		Nov-15
15.88	-5.47	-2.28	6.13		3.09	1.74	11.26	-0.01	9.81	145.1	35	2	0	35	0	94	5.33	2,000	100		1.00	Nov-15
16.30	-4.91	-1.09	9.72		4.27	0.49	11.3	-0.01	9.83	145.1	35	2	0	35	0	94	5.33	1,000,000				Nov-15
16.15	-4.96	-1.29	9.51		4.17	0.74	11.29	-0.01	9.82	145.1	35	2	0	35	0	94	5.33	50,000				Nov-15
4.12	4.96	7.08	15.22	21.96	2.52	0.72	3.65	6.31	10.3	373.5	-7	35	0	22	0	39	3.45	2,000	100	2.25		May-98
3.81	4.56	6.26	12.48	17.28	1.76	1.49	3.61	6.31	10.31	373.5	-7	35	0	22	0	39	3.45	2,000	100		1.00	Sep-03
4.01	4.75	6.85	14.17	19.91	2.22	1.14	3.64	6.31	10.31	373.5	-7	35	0	22	0	39	3.45	0				Oct-03
4.18	5.10	7.47	16.18	23.69	2.79	0.44	3.64	6.31	10.32	373.5	-7	35	0	22	0	39	3.45	1,000,000				Dec-12
4.06	5.06	7.29	15.84	23.21	2.72	0.51	3.62	6.31	10.31	373.5	-7	35	0	22	0	39	3.45	50,000				Mar-80
2.63	5.62	7.95	14.29	19.56	2.08	0.66	3.29	5.52	11.82	909.3	7	40	1	25	0	98	3.21	2,000	100	2.25		Dec-99
2.46	5.27	7.22	11.98	15.60	1.42	1.34	3.31	5.52	11.82	909.3	7	40	1	25	0	98	3.21	2,000	100		1.00	Mar-06
2.75	5.85	8.41	15.75	22.09	2.49	0.24	3.3	5.52	11.8	909.3	7	40	1	25	0	98	3.21	1,000,000				Dec-99
2.77	5.72	8.15	15.07	21.18	2.25	0.49	3.28	5.52	11.8	909.3	7	40	1	25	0	98	3.21	50,000				Dec-16
5.77	4.89	7.30	14.51	22.39	2.53	0.84	3.82	5.18	10.76	1,108	3	8	1	54	0	114	3.98	2,000	100	4.25		Apr-13
5.85	5.06	7.77	15.73	24.70	2.87	0.49	3.78	5.18	10.77	1,108	3	8	1	54	0	114	3.98	1,000,000				Jul-92
5.83	5.02	7.57	15.37	23.97	2.79	0.59	3.84	5.18	10.77	1,108	3	8	1	54	0	114	3.98	50,000				Apr-13
11.90	-6.89	-3.14	6.12		2.6	1.4	11.86	6.19	9.4	67.6	2	55	0	17	0	74	6.14	2,000	100	2.25		Feb-16
11.78	-7.25	-3.80	3.73		2.07	2.15	11.91	6.19	9.33	67.6	2	55	0	17	0	74	6.14	2,000	100		1.00	Feb-16
11.96	-6.77	-2.90	6.93		2.87	0.9	11.88	6.19	9.4	67.6	2	55	0	17	0	74	6.14	1,000,000				Feb-16
12.10	-6.77	-2.80	6.95		2.87	1.15	11.92	6.19	9.4	67.6	2	55	0	17	0	74	6.14	50,000				Feb-16
0.00	0.24	1.03	3.81	4.01	1.2	0.47	0.17		1	629.5	61	39	0	0	0			1,000,000				Dec-01
0.00	0.22	0.97	3.58	3.65	1.13	0.57	0.18		1	629.5	61	39	0	0	0			2,000	100			Mar-80
0.00	0.17	0.83	3.02	3.05	0.98	0.75	0.16		1	629.5	61	39	0	0	0			50,000				Jan-99
4.26	5.63	7.93	14.09	17.87	1.42	0.66	3.93	5.33	10.51	242.9	10	85	0	0	0	15	1.42	2,000	100	2.25		Sep-12
4.22	5.72	8.21	15.05	19.40	1.81	0.3	3.86	5.33	10.58	242.9	10	85	0	0	0	15	1.42	1,000,000				Sep-12
4.29	5.74	8.19	14.78	18.91	1.65	0.42	3.91	5.33	10.58	242.9	10	85	0	0	0	15	1.42	50,000				Dec-16
4.84	6.27	9.00	16.55	23.14	2.24	0.89	3.86	5.66	11.52	516.1	9	16	0	42	0	145	2.99	2,000	100	2.25		Jun-94
4.64	5.95	8.53	15.02	20.53	1.78	1.32	3.78	5.66	11.45	516.1	9	16	0	42	0	145	2.99	2,000	100		1.00	Nov-03
4.92	6.41	9.39	17.77	25.28	2.53	0.5	3.82	5.66	11.74	516.1	9	16	0	42	0	145	2.99	1,000,000				Sep-13

Fund Name	MARKET Ticker Symbol	Traded On	FUND TYPE, CATEGORY & OBJECTIVE Fund Type	Category and (Prospectus Objective)	RATINGS Overall Rating	Reward Rating	Risk Rating	Recent Up/ Downgrade	NEW INVESTORS Open to New Investors	Telephone
Nationwide Loomis Core Bond Institutional Service Cl	NWJJX	NAS CM	Open End	US Fixed Inc (Income)	B-	C+	B	Up	Y	800-848-0920
Nationwide Loomis Short Term Bond Fund Class A	NWJSX	NAS CM	Open End	US Fixed Inc (Income)	C	C	B-		Y	800-848-0920
Nationwide Loomis Short Term Bond Fund Class C	NWJTX	NAS CM	Open End	US Fixed Inc (Income)	C	C	C+		Y	800-848-0920
Nationwide Loomis Short Term Bond Fund Class R6	NWJUX	NAS CM	Open End	US Fixed Inc (Income)	C	C	B-		Y	800-848-0920
Nationwide Loomis Short Term Bond Institutional Service Cl	NWJVX	NAS CM	Open End	US Fixed Inc (Income)	C	C	B-		Y	800-848-0920
Navigator Duration Neutral Bond Fund Class A	NDNAX	NAS CM	Open End	Fixed Inc Misc (Muni Bond - Natl)	C-	D+	C	Down	Y	
Navigator Duration Neutral Bond Fund Class C	NDNCX	NAS CM	Open End	Fixed Inc Misc (Muni Bond - Natl)	D+	D	C	Down	Y	
Navigator Duration Neutral Bond Fund Class I	NDNIX	NAS CM	Open End	Fixed Inc Misc (Muni Bond - Natl)	C-	D+	C	Down	Y	
Navigator Tactical Fixed Income Fund Class A	NTBAX	NAS CM	Open End	Fixed Inc Misc (Growth & Income)	C+	C	B	Up	Y	
Navigator Tactical Fixed Income Fund Class C	NTBCX	NAS CM	Open End	Fixed Inc Misc (Growth & Income)	C+	C	B	Up	Y	
Navigator Tactical Fixed Income Fund Class I	NTBIX	NAS CM	Open End	Fixed Inc Misc (Growth & Income)	B-	C	B	Up	Y	
Navigator Ultra Short Term Bond Fund Class A	NUSAX	NAS CM	Open End	US Fixed Inc (Income)	D	D+	C+	Up	Y	
Navigator Ultra Short Term Bond Fund Class I	NUSIX	NAS CM	Open End	US Fixed Inc (Income)	D	D+	C	Up	Y	
Nebraska Municipal Fund Class A	NEMUX	NAS CM	Open End	US Muni Fixed Inc (Muni Bond - Single State)	C+	C	B	Up	Y	800-276-1262
Nebraska Municipal Fund Class I	NEITX	NAS CM	Open End	US Muni Fixed Inc (Muni Bond - Single State)	C+	C	B	Up	Y	800-276-1262
Neuberger Berman Advisers Mgmt Trust Short Dur Bond Port C			Open End	US Fixed Inc (Income)	C	C-	C	Up	Y	212-476-9000
Neuberger Berman California Municipal Fund	NBW	AMEX	Closed End	US Muni Fixed Inc (Muni Bond - Single State)	D+	D+	C-	Down	Y	212-476-9000
Neuberger Berman Core Bond Fund Class A	NCRAX	NAS CM	Open End	US Fixed Inc (Asset Allocation)	B-	C+	B	Up	Y	212-476-9000
Neuberger Berman Core Bond Fund Class C	NCRCX	NAS CM	Open End	US Fixed Inc (Asset Allocation)	B-	C+	B	Up	Y	212-476-9000
Neuberger Berman Core Bond Fund Class R6	NRCRX	NAS CM	Open End	US Fixed Inc (Asset Allocation)	B	C+	B+	Up	Y	212-476-9000
Neuberger Berman Core Bond Fund Institutional Class	NCRLX	NAS CM	Open End	US Fixed Inc (Asset Allocation)	B	C+	B+	Up	Y	212-476-9000
Neuberger Berman Core Bond Fund Investor Class	NCRIX	NAS CM	Open End	US Fixed Inc (Asset Allocation)	B-	C+	B	Up		212-476-9000
Neuberger Berman Emerging Markets Debt Fund Class A	NERAX	NAS CM	Open End	Emerg Mkts Fixed Inc (Income)	D+	D	C-	Down	Y	212-476-9000
Neuberger Berman Emerging Markets Debt Fund Class C	NERCX	NAS CM	Open End	Emerg Mkts Fixed Inc (Income)	D	D	C-	Down	Y	212-476-9000
Neuberger Berman Emerg Mkts Debt Fund Institutional Class	NERIX	NAS CM	Open End	Emerg Mkts Fixed Inc (Income)	D+	D	C-	Down	Y	212-476-9000
Neuberger Berman Floating Rate Income Fund Class A	NFIAX	NAS CM	Open End	US Fixed Inc (Income)	D+	D	C-	Down	Y	212-476-9000
Neuberger Berman Floating Rate Income Fund Class C	NFICX	NAS CM	Open End	US Fixed Inc (Income)	D	D	C-	Down	Y	212-476-9000
Neuberger Berman Floating Rate Income Institutional Cl	NFIIX	NAS CM	Open End	US Fixed Inc (Income)	D+	D	C-	Down	Y	212-476-9000
Neuberger Berman High Income Bond Fund Class A	NHIAX	NAS CM	Open End	US Fixed Inc (Corp Bond - High Yield)	C-	D+	C		Y	212-476-9000
Neuberger Berman High Income Bond Fund Class C	NHICX	NAS CM	Open End	US Fixed Inc (Corp Bond - High Yield)	C-	D+	C		Y	212-476-9000
Neuberger Berman High Income Bond Fund Class R3	NHIRX	NAS CM	Open End	US Fixed Inc (Corp Bond - High Yield)	C-	D+	C		Y	212-476-9000
Neuberger Berman High Income Bond Fund Class R6	NRHIX	NAS CM	Open End	US Fixed Inc (Corp Bond - High Yield)	C-	D+	C		Y	212-476-9000
Neuberger Berman High Income Bond Fund Institutional Class	NHILX	NAS CM	Open End	US Fixed Inc (Corp Bond - High Yield)	C-	D+	C		Y	212-476-9000
Neuberger Berman High Income Bond Fund Investor Class	NHINX	NAS CM	Open End	US Fixed Inc (Corp Bond - High Yield)	C-	D+	C			212-476-9000
Neuberger Berman High Yield Strategies	NHS	AMEX	Closed End	US Fixed Inc (Corp Bond - High Yield)	D	D	D+	Down	Y	212-476-9000
Neuberger Berman Municipal Fund	NBH	AMEX	Closed End	US Muni Fixed Inc (Muni Bond - Natl)	D+	D+	C-	Down	Y	212-476-9000
Neuberger Berman Municipal High Income Fund Class A	NMHAX	NAS CM	Open End	US Muni Fixed Inc (Muni Bond - Natl)	C-	D+	C	Down	Y	212-476-9000
Neuberger Berman Municipal High Income Fund Class C	NMHCX	NAS CM	Open End	US Muni Fixed Inc (Muni Bond - Natl)	C-	D+	C	Down	Y	212-476-9000
Neuberger Berman Muni High Income Fund Institutional Class	NMHIX	NAS CM	Open End	US Muni Fixed Inc (Muni Bond - Natl)	C-	D+	C	Down	Y	212-476-9000
Neuberger Berman Municipal Impact Fund Class A Shares	NIMAX	NAS CM	Open End	US Muni Fixed Inc (Muni Bond - Natl)	C+	C	B-	Up	Y	212-476-9000
Neuberger Berman Municipal Impact Fund Class C Shares	NIMCX	NAS CM	Open End	US Muni Fixed Inc (Muni Bond - Natl)	C	C	C+		Y	212-476-9000
Neuberger Berman Muni Impact Institutional Cl Shares	NMIIX	NAS CM	Open End	US Muni Fixed Inc (Muni Bond - Natl)	C+	C	B	Up	Y	212-476-9000
Neuberger Berman Municipal Intermediate Bond Fund Class A	NMNAX	NAS CM	Open End	US Muni Fixed Inc (Muni Bond - Natl)	C	C-	C+		Y	212-476-9000
Neuberger Berman Municipal Intermediate Bond Fund Class C	NMNCX	NAS CM	Open End	US Muni Fixed Inc (Muni Bond - Natl)	C	C-	C		Y	212-476-9000
Neuberger Berman Muni Intermediate Bond Institutional Cl	NMNLX	NAS CM	Open End	US Muni Fixed Inc (Muni Bond - Natl)	C	C-	B-		Y	212-476-9000
Neuberger Berman Muni Intermediate Bond Investor Cl	NMUIX	NAS CM	Open End	US Muni Fixed Inc (Muni Bond - Natl)	C	C-	C+			212-476-9000
Neuberger Berman New York Municipal Fund	NBO	AMEX	Closed End	US Muni Fixed Inc (Muni Bond - Single State)	D+	D+	C-	Down	Y	212-476-9000
Neuberger Berman Short Duration Bond Fund Class A	NSHAX	NAS CM	Open End	US Fixed Inc (Corp Bond - High Quality)	C-	D+	C		Y	212-476-9000
Neuberger Berman Short Duration Bond Fund Class C	NSHCX	NAS CM	Open End	US Fixed Inc (Corp Bond - High Quality)	D+	D	C	Down	Y	212-476-9000
Neuberger Berman Short Duration Bond Institutional Cl	NSHLX	NAS CM	Open End	US Fixed Inc (Corp Bond - High Quality)	C-	D+	C		Y	212-476-9000
Neuberger Berman Short Duration Bond Fund Investor Class	NSBIX	NAS CM	Open End	US Fixed Inc (Corp Bond - High Quality)	C-	D+	C			212-476-9000
Neuberger Berman Short Duration Bond Fund Trust Class	NSBTX	NAS CM	Open End	US Fixed Inc (Corp Bond - High Quality)	C-	D+	C			212-476-9000

★ Expanded analysis of this fund is included in Section II.

TOTAL RETURNS & PERFORMANCE									ASSETS		ASSET ALLOCATION & TURNOVER							MINIMUMS		FEES		
3-Month Total Return	6-Month Total Return	1-Year Total Return	3-Year Total Return	5-Year Total Return	Dividend Yield (TTM)	Expense Ratio	3-Yr Std Deviation	Effective Duration	NAV	Total Assets (MIL)	%Cash	%Government Bonds	%Municipal Bonds	%Corporate Bonds	%Other	Turnover Ratio	Average Coupon Rate	Min Initial Investment	Min Additional Investment	Front End Fee (%)	Back End Fee (%)	Inception Date
4.85	6.28	9.02	16.78	23.79	2.28	0.75	3.78	5.66	11.74	516.1	9	16	0	42	0	145	2.99	50,000				Feb-84
5.18	2.76	4.48	9.55	11.64	2.06	0.78	2.77	1.86	10.27	210.0	11	4	0	59	0	127	2.74	2,000	100	2.25		Nov-04
5.08	2.57	4.01	7.80	8.88	1.54	1.27	2.76	1.86	10.4	210.0	11	4	0	59	0	127	2.74	2,000	100		1.00	Nov-04
5.25	2.92	4.82	10.62	13.56	2.38	0.45	2.77	1.86	10.29	210.0	11	4	0	59	0	127	2.74	1,000,000				Sep-13
5.24	2.90	4.76	10.41	13.20	2.33	0.5	2.78	1.86	10.29	210.0	11	4	0	59	0	127	2.74	50,000				Nov-04
-0.90	-3.42	-1.33	2.84	5.80	1.25	1.33	2.66		9.82	49.1	17	0	80	0	0	156	5.11	5,000	500	3.75		Sep-13
-1.02	-3.67	-2.01	0.61	1.90	0.7	2.08	2.68		9.67	49.1	17	0	80	0	0	156	5.11	5,000	500			Sep-13
-0.86	-3.23	-1.09	3.68	7.12	1.53	1.08	2.66		9.78	49.1	17	0	80	0	0	156	5.11	25,000				Sep-13
6.25	2.03	5.43	11.91	32.27	2.1	1.26	4.81		10.53	5,572	11	0	1	62	26	151	2.69	5,000	500	3.75		Mar-14
6.03	1.65	4.74	9.45	27.41	1.4	2.01	4.77		10.55	5,572	11	0	1	62	26	151	2.69	5,000	500			Mar-14
6.37	2.11	5.75	12.84	33.85	2.34	1.01	4.83		10.53	5,572	11	0	1	62	26	151	2.69	25,000				Mar-14
3.08	1.27	3.15			0.68	0.81			10.35	53.9	12	0	0	88	0		1.49	5,000	500	3.75		Mar-19
2.94	0.77	1.96			2	0.56			9.99	53.9	12	0	0	88	0		1.49	25,000				Mar-19
1.71	2.00	3.48	9.70	15.41	2.04	0.98	2.82		10.69	52.1	0	0	100	0	0	8	4.56	1,000	50	2.50		Nov-93
1.77	2.23	3.74	10.41	16.15	2.29	0.73	2.83		10.69	52.1	0	0	100	0	0	8	4.56	1,000	50			Nov-17
5.25	0.47	1.63	5.27	7.36	2.02	0.88	3.74	2.23	10.62	98.3	8	44	0	20	0	91	2.75	0				Sep-84
4.54	-1.66	1.01	10.54	22.27	3.64		7.96	5.68	15.03	82.0	1	0	99	0	0	25	4.71					Sep-02
5.54	6.23	8.44	15.11	21.25	2.95	0.79	3.61	6.78	10.94	413.4	2	26	0	25	0	147	3.29	1,000	100	4.25		Dec-07
5.24	5.84	7.64	12.55	16.80	2.23	1.54	3.58	6.78	10.95	413.4	2	26	0	25	0	147	3.29	1,000	100		1.00	Dec-07
5.65	6.47	9.07	16.74	23.83	3.44	0.29	3.61	6.78	10.98	413.4	2	26	0	25	0	147	3.29	0				Jan-19
5.62	6.42	8.85	16.58	23.66	3.34	0.39	3.63	6.78	10.98	413.4	2	26	0	25	0	147	3.29	1,000,000				Sep-95
5.43	6.22	8.33	15.10	21.12	2.95	0.79	3.65	6.78	10.95	413.4	2	26	0	25	0	147	3.29	2,000	100			Jan-97
13.13	-5.33	-1.52	5.09	16.63	4.83	1.17	12.18	6.24	8.15	137.6	6	68	0	25	0	68	5.98	1,000	100	4.25		Sep-13
12.92	-5.68	-2.37	2.87	12.35	4.04	1.91	12.16	6.24	8.15	137.6	6	68	0	25	0	68	5.98	1,000	100		1.00	Sep-13
13.21	-5.14	-1.26	6.51	18.94	5.22	0.79	12.1	6.24	8.16	137.6	6	68	0	25	0	68	5.98	1,000,000				Sep-13
11.70	-3.90	-1.36	4.83	10.45	4.67	1.09	9.16	0.44	9.15	154.7	3	0	0	96	0	60	1.92	1,000	100	4.25		Dec-09
11.37	-4.37	-2.21	2.39	6.28	3.89	1.84	9.16	0.44	9.14	154.7	3	0	0	96	0	60	1.92	2,500	100		1.00	Dec-09
11.79	-3.73	-1.00	5.99	12.50	5.05	0.72	9.16	0.44	9.15	154.7	3	0	0	96	0	60	1.92	1,000,000				Dec-09
9.81	-4.98	-1.51	6.36	16.45	5.14	1.13	8.85	4.68	8.02	1,758	8	0	0	92	0	96	5.59	1,000	100	4.25		May-09
9.75	-5.29	-2.06	4.22	12.59	4.42	1.83	8.89	4.68	8.04	1,758	8	0	0	92	0	96	5.59	2,500	100		1.00	May-09
9.74	-5.07	-1.69	5.60	15.21	4.94	1.31	8.86	4.68	8.03	1,758	8	0	0	92	0	96	5.59	0				May-09
10.08	-4.71	-0.85	8.07	19.56	5.7	0.6	8.9	4.68	8.04	1,758	8	0	0	92	0	96	5.59	0				Mar-13
9.92	-4.76	-1.07	7.67	18.92	5.59	0.7	8.84	4.68	8.03	1,758	8	0	0	92	0	96	5.59	1,000,000				May-09
9.88	-4.85	-1.24	7.14	18.05	5.42	0.86	8.87	4.68	8.02	1,758	8	0	0	92	0	96	5.59	2,000	100			Jan-92
16.73	-10.16	-5.22	3.61	17.71	9.75	0	15.46	4.90	11.11	217.7	1	0	0	99	0	89	5.80					Jul-03
4.45	-1.71	1.03	10.59	21.44	5.24		7.31	5.06	14.68	269.1	0	0	100	0	0	44	4.71					Sep-02
3.95	-2.39	0.25	10.34	20.42	3.11	0.87	6.89	6.94	10.19	112.7	1	0	99	0	0	112	4.24	1,000	100	4.25		Jun-15
3.76	-2.75	-0.48	7.99	16.11	2.31	1.62	6.9	6.94	10.2	112.7	1	0	99	0	0	112	4.24	1,000	100		1.00	Jun-15
4.15	-2.12	0.63	11.66	22.77	3.5	0.5	6.87	6.94	10.2	112.7	1	0	99	0	0	112	4.24	1,000,000				Jun-15
2.33	2.06	3.70	9.41	14.66	1.86	0.81	3.3	4.78	17.79	60.1	1	0	99	0	0	100	3.90	1,000	100	4.25		Jun-18
2.15	1.68	2.99	6.97	10.45	1.12	1.55	3.29	4.78	17.79	60.1	1	0	99	0	0	100	3.90	1,000	100		1.00	Jun-18
2.37	2.25	4.08	10.58	16.74	2.22	0.44	3.31	4.78	17.78	60.1	1	0	99	0	0	100	3.90	1,000,000				Mar-13
2.42	0.60	2.25	8.87	14.08	2.27	0.67	4.22	4.94	11.96	210.0	0	0	100	0	0	92	3.99	1,000	100	4.25		Jun-10
2.14	0.23	1.49	6.46	9.90	1.51	1.42	4.28	4.94	11.96	210.0	0	0	100	0	0	92	3.99	1,000	100		1.00	Jun-10
2.51	0.79	2.62	10.08	16.30	2.64	0.3	4.25	4.94	11.97	210.0	0	0	100	0	0	92	3.99	1,000,000				Jun-10
2.47	0.71	2.47	9.59	15.43	2.49	0.45	4.22	4.94	11.98	210.0	0	0	100	0	0	92	3.99	2,000	100			Jul-87
3.40	-1.37	0.57	6.86	16.49	3.37		6.95	5.07	13.61	67.6	0	0	100	0	0	29	4.37					Sep-02
6.49	0.07	1.45	4.90	5.95	2.82	0.72	4.63	2.24	7.32	81.0	6	43	0	23	0	131	2.92	1,000	100	2.50		Jun-10
6.14	-0.29	0.70	2.57	2.07	2.06	1.47	4.63	2.24	7.32	81.0	6	43	0	23	0	131	2.92	1,000	100		1.00	Jun-10
6.58	0.31	1.76	6.15	7.92	3.19	0.35	4.67	2.24	7.68	81.0	6	43	0	23	0	131	2.92	1,000,000				Jun-10
6.53	0.22	1.68	5.52	6.85	2.99	0.55	4.64	2.24	7.69	81.0	6	43	0	23	0	131	2.92	2,000	100			Jun-86
6.49	0.11	1.52	5.27	6.47	2.89	0.65	4.63	2.24	7.33	81.0	6	43	0	23	0	131	2.92	0				Aug-93

Fund Name	Ticker Symbol	Traded On	Fund Type	Category and (Prospectus Objective)	Overall Rating	Reward Rating	Risk Rating	Recent Up/ Downgrade	Open to New Investors	Telephone
	MARKET		FUND TYPE, CATEGORY & OBJECTIVE		RATINGS				NEW INVESTORS	
Neuberger Berman Short Duration High Income Fund Class A	NHSAX	NAS CM	Open End	US Fixed Inc (Corp Bond - High Yield)	D	D-	D	Down	Y	212-476-9000
Neuberger Berman Short Duration High Income Fund Class C	NHSCX	NAS CM	Open End	US Fixed Inc (Corp Bond - High Yield)	D	D-	D	Down	Y	212-476-9000
Neuberger Berman Short Duration High Income Inst Cl	NHSIX	NAS CM	Open End	US Fixed Inc (Corp Bond - High Yield)	D	D	D	Down	Y	212-476-9000
Neuberger Berman Strategic Income Fund Class A	NSTAX	NAS CM	Open End	US Fixed Inc (Growth & Income)	C-	D+	C		Y	212-476-9000
Neuberger Berman Strategic Income Fund Class C	NSTCX	NAS CM	Open End	US Fixed Inc (Growth & Income)	C-	D+	C		Y	212-476-9000
Neuberger Berman Strategic Income Fund Class R6	NRSIX	NAS CM	Open End	US Fixed Inc (Growth & Income)	C-	D+	C		Y	212-476-9000
Neuberger Berman Strategic Income Fund Institutional Class	NSTLX	NAS CM	Open End	US Fixed Inc (Growth & Income)	C-	D+	C		Y	212-476-9000
Neuberger Berman Strategic Income Fund Trust Class	NSTTX	NAS CM	Open End	US Fixed Inc (Growth & Income)	C-	D+	C			212-476-9000
Neuberger Berman Unconstrained Bond Fund Class A	NUBAX	NAS CM	Open End	Fixed Inc Misc (Worldwide Bond)	D	D	D+		Y	212-476-9000
Neuberger Berman Unconstrained Bond Fund Class C	NUBCX	NAS CM	Open End	Fixed Inc Misc (Worldwide Bond)	D	D	D		Y	212-476-9000
Neuberger Berman Unconstrained Bond Fund Class R6	NRUBX	NAS CM	Open End	Fixed Inc Misc (Worldwide Bond)	D	D	D+		Y	212-476-9000
Neuberger Berman Unconstrained Bond Institutional Cl	NUBIX	NAS CM	Open End	Fixed Inc Misc (Worldwide Bond)	D	D	D+		Y	212-476-9000
New America High Income Fund	HYB	NYSE	Closed End	US Fixed Inc (Corp Bond - High Yield)	D+	D+	C-	Down	Y	410-345-2000
New Covenant Income Fund	NCICX	NAS CM	Open End	US Fixed Inc (Multisector Bond)	B-	C	B	Up	Y	
Nicholas High Income Fund Class Institutional	NCINX	NAS CM	Open End	US Fixed Inc (Corp Bond - High Yield)	C-	D+	C	Down	Y	800-544-6547
Nicholas High Income Fund Class N	NNHIX	NAS CM	Open End	US Fixed Inc (Corp Bond - High Yield)	C-	D+	C			800-544-6547
NIF (Dublin) I Loomis Sayles High Income Fund Class N	LSHNX	NAS CM	Open End	US Fixed Inc (Corp Bond - High Yield)	D+	D	C-	Down	Y	800-862-4863
North Capital Treasury Money Mkt Institutional Cl Shares	NCGXX	NAS CM	Money Mkt	US Money Mkt (Money Mkt - Treasury)	U	U	U		Y	
North Country Intermediate Bond Fund	NCBDX	NAS CM	Open End	US Fixed Inc (Corp Bond - General)	B-	C+	B	Up	Y	
North Square Strategic Income Fund I	ADVNX	NAS CM	Open End	US Fixed Inc (Growth & Income)	B	C+	B+	Up	Y	855-551-5521
North Star Bond Fund Class I	NSBDX	NAS CM	Open End	Fixed Inc Misc (Income)	D	D	C-	Down	Y	312-580-0
Northeast Investors Trust	NTHEX	NAS CM	Open End	US Fixed Inc (Corp Bond - High Yield)	D	D	D+		Y	855-755-6344
Northern Arizona Tax-Exempt Fund	NOAZX	NAS CM	Open End	US Muni Fixed Inc (Muni Bond - Single State)	C	C	B		Y	800-595-9111
Northern Bond Index Fund	NOBOX	NAS CM	Open End	US Fixed Inc (Income)	B	B-	B+		Y	800-595-9111
Northern California Intermediate Tax-Exempt Fund	NCITX	NAS CM	Open End	US Muni Fixed Inc (Muni Bond - Single State)	C	C	B		Y	800-595-9111
Northern California Tax-Exempt Fund	NCATX	NAS CM	Open End	US Muni Fixed Inc (Muni Bond - Single State)	C+	C	B	Up	Y	800-595-9111
Northern Core Bond Fund	NOCBX	NAS CM	Open End	US Fixed Inc (Income)	B-	C+	B+	Up	Y	800-595-9111
Northern Fixed Income Fund	NOFIX	NAS CM	Open End	US Fixed Inc (Income)	B-	C	B	Up	Y	800-595-9111
Northern High Yield Fixed Income Fund	NHFIX	NAS CM	Open End	US Fixed Inc (Corp Bond - High Yield)	D+	D+	C-	Down	Y	800-595-9111
Northern High Yield Municipal Fund	NHYMX	NAS CM	Open End	US Muni Fixed Inc (Muni Bond - Natl)	C-	D+	C	Down	Y	800-595-9111
Northern Institutional Municipal Portfolio	NMUXX	NAS CM	Money Mkt	US Money Mkt (Money Mkt - Fed Tax Exmpt)	C	C-	C+		Y	800-595-9111
Northern Institutional Prime Obligations Portfolio Shares	NPAXX	NAS CM	Money Mkt	US Money Mkt (Money Mkt - General)	C	C-	B-		Y	800-595-9111
Northern Institutional Treasury Portfolio	NITXX	NAS CM	Money Mkt	US Money Mkt (Money Mkt - Treasury)	C	C	C+		Y	800-595-9111
★ Northern Institutional Treasury Portfolio Premier Shares	NTPXX	NAS CM	Money Mkt	US Money Mkt (Money Mkt - Treasury)	C	C-	C+		Y	800-595-9111
Northern Institutional U.S. Government Portfolio	BNGXX	NAS CM	Money Mkt	US Money Mkt (Money Mkt - Govt)	C	C-	C+		Y	800-595-9111
Northern Institutional U.S. Govt Portfolio Service Shares	BGCXX	NAS CM	Money Mkt	US Money Mkt (Money Mkt - Govt)	C	C	C+		Y	800-595-9111
Northern Institutional U.S. Government Select Portfolio	BGSXX	NAS CM	Money Mkt	US Money Mkt (Money Mkt - Govt)	C	C-	C+		Y	800-595-9111
Northern Inst U.S. Govt Select Portfol Service Shares	BSCXX	NAS CM	Money Mkt	US Money Mkt (Money Mkt - Govt)	C	C-	C+		Y	800-595-9111
Northern Inst U.S. Govt Select Port Williams Capital Sh	WCGXX	NAS CM	Money Mkt	US Money Mkt (Money Mkt - Govt)	C	C-	C+		Y	800-595-9111
Northern Intermediate Tax-Exempt Fund	NOITX	NAS CM	Open End	US Muni Fixed Inc (Muni Bond - Natl)	C+	C	B	Up	Y	800-595-9111
Northern Money Market Fund	NORXX	NAS CM	Money Mkt	US Money Mkt (Money Mkt - Taxable)	C	C-	C+		Y	800-595-9111
Northern Multi-Manager Emerg Mkts Debt Opportunity Fund	NMEDX	NAS CM	Open End	Emerg Mkts Fixed Inc (Growth & Income)	D	D	D+	Down	Y	800-595-9111
Northern Multi-Manager High Yield Opportunity Fund	NMHYX	NAS CM	Open End	US Fixed Inc (Corp Bond - High Yield)	D+	D	C-	Down	Y	800-595-9111
Northern Municipal Money Market Fund	NOMXX	NAS CM	Money Mkt	US Money Mkt (Money Mkt - Fed Tax Exmpt)	C	C-	C+		Y	800-595-9111
Northern Short Bond Fund	BSBAX	NAS CM	Open End	US Fixed Inc (Income)	C	C	B-		Y	800-595-9111
Northern Short-Intermediate Tax-Exempt Fund	NSITX	NAS CM	Open End	US Muni Fixed Inc (Muni Bond - Natl)	C	C	B-		Y	800-595-9111
Northern Short-Intermediate U.S. Government Fund	NSIUX	NAS CM	Open End	US Fixed Inc (Govt Bond - General)	B-	C	B	Up	Y	800-595-9111
Northern Tax-Advantaged Ultra-Short Fixed Income Fund	NTAUX	NAS CM	Open End	US Fixed Inc (Govt Bond - General)	C	C-	C+		Y	800-595-9111
Northern Tax-Exempt Fund	NOTEX	NAS CM	Open End	US Muni Fixed Inc (Muni Bond - Natl)	C+	C	B	Up	Y	800-595-9111
Northern U.S. Government Fund	NOUGX	NAS CM	Open End	US Fixed Inc (Govt Bond - General)	B-	C+	B		Y	800-595-9111
Northern U.S. Government Money Market Fund	NOGXX	NAS CM	Money Mkt	US Money Mkt (Money Mkt - Govt)	C	C-	C+		Y	800-595-9111
Northern U.S. Government Select Money Market Fund	NOSXX	NAS CM	Money Mkt	US Money Mkt (Money Mkt - Govt)	C	C-	C+		Y	800-595-9111

★ Expanded analysis of this fund is included in Section II.

TOTAL RETURNS & PERFORMANCE									ASSETS		ASSET ALLOCATION & TURNOVER							MINIMUMS		FEES		
3-Month Total Return	6-Month Total Return	1-Year Total Return	3-Year Total Return	5-Year Total Return	Dividend Yield (TTM)	Expense Ratio	3-Yr Std Deviation	Effective Duration	NAV	Total Assets (MIL)	%Cash	%Government Bonds	%Municipal Bonds	%Corporate Bonds	%Other	Turnover Ratio	Average Coupon Rate	Min Initial Investment	Min Additional Investment	Front End Fee (%)	Back End Fee (%)	Inception Date
3.76	-18.57	-16.65	-11.10	-5.45	4.11	1.13	12.36	1.79	7.76	7.9	82	0	0	17	0	64	5.64	1,000	100	4.25		Sep-12
3.62	-18.86	-17.26	-13.06	-8.98	3.35	1.88	12.37	1.79	7.74	7.9	82	0	0	17	0	64	5.64	1,000	100		1.00	Sep-12
3.91	-18.40	-16.33	-10.09	-3.76	4.49	0.76	12.36	1.79	7.76	7.9	82	0	0	17	0	64	5.64	1,000,000				Sep-12
10.94	-0.92	1.54	8.12	16.53	3.71	1	7.63	3.83	10.8	2,663	9	9	3	48	0	113	3.88	1,000	100	4.25		Dec-07
10.87	-1.26	0.83	5.88	12.54	2.99	1.7	7.68	3.83	10.79	2,663	9	9	3	48	0	113	3.88	1,000	100		1.00	Dec-07
11.09	-0.68	2.04	9.70	19.35	4.22	0.5	7.66	3.83	10.78	2,663	9	9	3	48	0	113	3.88	0				Mar-13
11.05	-0.73	1.94	9.42	18.87	4.12	0.6	7.64	3.83	10.79	2,663	9	9	3	48	0	113	3.88	1,000,000				Jul-03
11.07	-0.90	1.68	8.38	16.92	3.76	0.95	7.68	3.83	10.79	2,663	9	9	3	48	0	113	3.88	1,000	100			Apr-07
12.93	-6.60	-5.22	-4.15	-3.58	2.62	1.04	10.1	2.42	8.32	4.0	43	18	0	28	0	61	3.66	1,000	100	4.25		Feb-14
12.88	-6.93	-5.91	-6.36	-7.10	1.84	1.79	10.15	2.42	8.32	4.0	43	18	0	28	0	61	3.66	1,000	100		1.00	Feb-14
13.37	-6.38	-4.88	-3.05	-1.40	3.12	0.57	10.21	2.42	8.32	4.0	43	18	0	28	0	61	3.66	0				Feb-14
13.18	-6.33	-4.88	-3.20	-1.79	3.01	0.67	10.11	2.42	8.32	4.0	43	18	0	28	0	61	3.66	1,000,000				Feb-14
16.11	-7.00	-1.75	8.52	28.36	7.23	0.96	13.15		9.01	210.1	1	0	0	97	0	66	6.69					Feb-88
3.99	3.94	5.89	12.09	17.15	2.32	0.95	2.81		24.32	328.0	2	45	1	18	0	188	3.56	500	100			Jul-99
4.77	-4.38	-0.99	5.20	11.86	4.42	0.74	6.06	4.04	8.54	98.1	12	0	0	88	0	30	5.36	100,000	100			Nov-77
4.80	-4.31	-0.98	4.60	10.51	4.2	0.94	6.01	4.04	8.71	98.1	12	0	0	88	0	30	5.36	500	100			Feb-05
11.67	-4.13	-1.84	7.12	17.88	5.64	0.7	9.48	4.66	3.96	111.2	5	0	0	93	0	48	5.85	1,000,000				Nov-16
0.00	0.15					0.45			1	0.11	100	0	0	0	0			0				Jul-19
4.45	4.44	6.73	13.29	18.07	1.81	0.89	3.43	4.14	10.93	83.5	3	26	0	65	0	22	3.26	500	100			Mar-01
6.66	4.52	8.07	14.56	24.32	2.72	0.95	4.1		9.8163	65.7	3	29	0	68	1	36	4.20	1,000,000				Dec-12
6.97	-4.98	-2.83	1.73	8.30	3.73	1.64	7.52		9.11	23.9	2	0	0	98	0	33	5.50	5,000	500			Dec-14
8.07	-6.88	-8.38	-8.86	-8.26	6.23	1.56	8.02		3.71	215.3	3	0	0	96	-4	45	6.99	1,000				Mar-50
1.85	1.75	3.67	11.19	18.90	2.55	0.47	3.81	5.54	10.9	134.7	0	0	100	0	0	63	4.73	2,500	50			Oct-99
2.69	6.06	8.73	16.41	23.05	2.65	0.15	3.29	5.87	11.28	3,094	0	47	1	23	0	54	3.19	2,500	50			Feb-07
2.46	1.86	3.61	10.55	17.29	2.47	0.45	3.71	5.36	10.94	489.0	3	0	97	0	0	32	4.35	2,500	50			Oct-99
2.45	2.25	4.36	12.87	20.95	2.71	0.47	4.05	6.05	11.86	198.1	7	0	93	0	0	55	4.58	2,500	50			Apr-97
4.65	5.08	8.05	15.72	21.94	2.43	0.41	3.89	6.23	10.9	195.9	0	31	1	29	0	484	2.90	2,500	50			Mar-01
5.27	4.35	7.27	15.07	21.77	2.76	0.45	4.23	6.30	10.65	831.3	0	29	1	34	0	439	3.15	2,500	50			Mar-94
12.08	-6.09	-1.87	8.67	18.41	6.67	0.78	10.72	4.65	6.16	3,217	0	0	0	100	0	48	6.73	2,500	50			Dec-98
3.93	-2.12	0.43	9.82	18.69	4.19	0.61	6.98	8.29	8.55	472.9	0	0	100	0	0	48	5.13	2,500	50			Dec-98
0.05	0.40	0.97	3.31	3.89	1.1	0.2	0.11		1	261.7	10	0	90	0	0			5,000,000				Dec-99
0.06	0.38	1.40	5.33	6.37	1.63	0.15	0.19		0.9998	1,250	96	3	0	1	0	2		5,000,000				Aug-03
0.05	0.38	1.33	4.78	5.35	1.51	0.15	0.17		1	84,262	70	29	0	0	0			5,000,000				Nov-08
0.04	0.35	1.29	4.61	5.14	1.46	0.2	0.17		1	84,262	70	29	0	0	0			0				Aug-16
0.04	0.35	1.28	4.53	4.93	1.45	0.25	0.17		1	21,248	62	37	0	1	0	0		5,000,000				Oct-85
0.05	0.35	1.28	4.54	4.93	1.45	0.25	0.17		1	21,248	62	37	0	1	0	0		0				Apr-99
0.05	0.37	1.31	4.65	5.18	1.48	0.2	0.17		1	44,590	63	37	0	0	0			5,000,000				Nov-90
0.05	0.37	1.31	4.66	5.18	1.48	0.2	0.17		1	44,590	63	37	0	0	0			0				May-99
0.05	0.37	1.31	4.65	5.17	1.48	0.2	0.17		1	44,590	63	37	0	0	0			0				Sep-14
2.48	2.26	4.27	11.09	18.01	2.18	0.47	3.3	4.42	10.89	3,062	7	0	93	0	0	128	4.45	2,500	50			Mar-94
0.02	0.36	1.29	4.87	5.59	1.48	0.35	0.17		1	402.3	97	2	0	1	0			2,500	50			Apr-94
12.71	-8.00	-6.48	0.87	9.36	2.94	0.96	12.73	6.50	8.6	155.5	1	94	0	5	0	73	6.66	2,500	50			Dec-13
9.59	-6.24	-3.83	3.92	17.54	7.79	0.87	9.32	3.74	8.55	183.4	0	0	0	100	0	81	6.67	2,500	50			Sep-09
0.04	0.33	0.84	2.98	3.73	0.96	0.35	0.1		1	188.2	15	0	85	0	0			2,500	50			Apr-94
2.94	1.94	3.50	8.32	10.76	2.38	0.4	1.82	2.14	19.04	390.1	1	30	0	34	0	95	2.82	2,500	50			Jan-93
2.57	2.27	3.51	7.58	9.94	1.63	0.46	2.06	2.98	10.58	880.5	6	0	94	0	0	126	4.29	2,500	50			Aug-07
0.49	3.88	4.99	8.66	9.65	1.19	0.42	1.73	3.47	10.1	73.0	0	75	0	0	0	839	1.13	2,500	50			Oct-99
1.15	1.11	2.04	5.18	7.10	1.45	0.25	0.71	0.97	10.23	4,013	10	3	76	11	0	70	3.73	2,500	50			Jun-09
2.38	2.10	4.42	12.70	21.27	2.68	0.46	4.22	5.89	10.95	1,681	4	0	96	0	0	123	4.57	2,500	50			Mar-94
0.71	5.58	6.94	11.82	13.82	1.21	0.45	2.62	4.89	10.23	44.3	0	75	0	0	0	855	1.26	2,500	50			Mar-94
0.02	0.31	1.18	4.22	4.48	1.35	0.35	0.17		1	18,182	63	37	0	0	0			2,500	50			Apr-94
0.02	0.30	1.17	4.21	4.51	1.35	0.35	0.17		1	3,983	62	38	0	0	0			2,500	50			Dec-94

	MARKET		FUND TYPE, CATEGORY & OBJECTIVE		RATINGS				NEW INVESTORS	
Fund Name	Ticker Symbol	Traded On	Fund Type	Category and (Prospectus Objective)	Overall Rating	Reward Rating	Risk Rating	Recent Up/ Downgrade	Open to New Investors	Telephone
Northern U.S. Treasury Index Fund	BTIAX	NAS CM	Open End	US Fixed Inc (Govt Bond - Treasury)	B	B	B		Y	800-595-9111
Northern Ultra-Short Fixed Income Fund	NUSFX	NAS CM	Open End	US Fixed Inc (Income)	C	C	B-		Y	800-595-9111
Nuveen All-American Municipal Bond Fund Class A	FLAAX	NAS CM	Open End	US Muni Fixed Inc (Muni Bond - Natl)	C	C-	B-		Y	312-917-8146
Nuveen All-American Municipal Bond Fund Class C	FACCX	NAS CM	Open End	US Muni Fixed Inc (Muni Bond - Natl)	C	C-	C+		Y	312-917-8146
Nuveen All-American Municipal Bond Fund Class C2	FAACX	NAS CM	Open End	US Muni Fixed Inc (Muni Bond - Natl)	C	C-	C+			312-917-8146
Nuveen All-American Municipal Bond Fund Class I	FAARX	NAS CM	Open End	US Muni Fixed Inc (Muni Bond - Natl)	C	C-	B-		Y	312-917-8146
Nuveen All-American Municipal Bond Fund Class R6	FAAWX	NAS CM	Open End	US Muni Fixed Inc (Muni Bond - Natl)	C	C-	B-		Y	312-917-8146
Nuveen AMT-Free Municipal Credit Income Fund	NVG	NYSE	Closed End	US Muni Fixed Inc (Muni Bond - Natl)	C	C-	C+		Y	312-917-8146
Nuveen AMT-Free Municipal Value Fund	NUW	NYSE	Closed End	US Muni Fixed Inc (Muni Bond - Natl)	C-	C-	C-		Y	312-917-8146
Nuveen AMT-Free Quality Muni Inc	NEA	NYSE	Closed End	US Muni Fixed Inc (Muni Bond - Natl)	C	C-	C+		Y	312-917-8146
Nuveen Arizona Municipal Bond Fund Class A	FAZTX	NAS CM	Open End	US Muni Fixed Inc (Muni Bond - Single State)	C	C	B		Y	312-917-8146
Nuveen Arizona Municipal Bond Fund Class C	FZCCX	NAS CM	Open End	US Muni Fixed Inc (Muni Bond - Single State)	C	C-	B-		Y	312-917-8146
Nuveen Arizona Municipal Bond Fund Class C2	FAZCX	NAS CM	Open End	US Muni Fixed Inc (Muni Bond - Single State)	C	C-	B-			312-917-8146
Nuveen Arizona Municipal Bond Fund Class I	NMARX	NAS CM	Open End	US Muni Fixed Inc (Muni Bond - Single State)	C	C	B		Y	312-917-8146
Nuveen Arizona Quality Municipal Income Fund	NAZ	NYSE	Closed End	US Muni Fixed Inc (Muni Bond - Single State)	C-	C-	C-		Y	312-917-8146
Nuveen California AMT- Free Quality Municipal Income Fund	NKX	NYSE	Closed End	US Muni Fixed Inc (Muni Bond - Single State)	C-	C-	C-	Down	Y	312-917-8146
Nuveen California High Yield Municipal Bond Fund Class A	NCHAX	NAS CM	Open End	US Muni Fixed Inc (Muni Bond - Single State)	C	C-	C+		Y	312-917-8146
Nuveen California High Yield Municipal Bond Fund Class C	NAWSX	NAS CM	Open End	US Muni Fixed Inc (Muni Bond - Single State)	C-	D+	C	Down	Y	312-917-8146
Nuveen California High Yield Municipal Bond Fund Class C2	NCHCX	NAS CM	Open End	US Muni Fixed Inc (Muni Bond - Single State)	C	C-	C			312-917-8146
Nuveen California High Yield Municipal Bond Fund Class I	NCHRX	NAS CM	Open End	US Muni Fixed Inc (Muni Bond - Single State)	C	C-	C+		Y	312-917-8146
Nuveen California Intermediate Municipal Bond Fund Class A	NUCAX	NAS CM	Open End	US Muni Fixed Inc (Muni Bond - Single State)	C	C-	B-		Y	312-917-8146
Nuveen California Intermediate Municipal Bond Fund Class C	NUCCX	NAS CM	Open End	US Muni Fixed Inc (Muni Bond - Single State)	C	C-	C+		Y	312-917-8146
Nuveen California Intermediate Municipal Bond Fund Class I	NUCIX	NAS CM	Open End	US Muni Fixed Inc (Muni Bond - Single State)	C	C-	B-		Y	312-917-8146
Nuveen California Municipal Bond Fund Class A	NCAAX	NAS CM	Open End	US Muni Fixed Inc (Muni Bond - Single State)	C	C-	B-		Y	312-917-8146
Nuveen California Municipal Bond Fund Class C	NAKFX	NAS CM	Open End	US Muni Fixed Inc (Muni Bond - Single State)	C	C-	B-		Y	312-917-8146
Nuveen California Municipal Bond Fund Class C2	NCACX	NAS CM	Open End	US Muni Fixed Inc (Muni Bond - Single State)	C	C-	B-			312-917-8146
Nuveen California Municipal Bond Fund Class I	NCSPX	NAS CM	Open End	US Muni Fixed Inc (Muni Bond - Single State)	C	C-	B-		Y	312-917-8146
Nuveen California Municipal Value Fund	NCA	NYSE	Closed End	US Muni Fixed Inc (Muni Bond - Single State)	C-	C	C-		Y	312-917-8146
Nuveen California Municipal Value Fund 2	NCB	NYSE	Closed End	US Muni Fixed Inc (Muni Bond - Single State)	C-	C-	D+		Y	312-917-8146
Nuveen California Quality Municipal Income Fund	NAC	NYSE	Closed End	US Muni Fixed Inc (Muni Bond - Single State)	C	C-	C+		Y	312-917-8146
Nuveen California Select Tax-Free Income Portfolio	NXC	NYSE	Closed End	US Muni Fixed Inc (Muni Bond - Single State)	C-	C	D+		Y	312-917-8146
Nuveen Colorado Municipal Bond Fund Class A	FCOTX	NAS CM	Open End	US Muni Fixed Inc (Muni Bond - Single State)	C+	C	B	Up	Y	312-917-8146
Nuveen Colorado Municipal Bond Fund Class C	FAFKX	NAS CM	Open End	US Muni Fixed Inc (Muni Bond - Single State)	C	C	B-		Y	312-917-8146
Nuveen Colorado Municipal Bond Fund Class C2	FCOCX	NAS CM	Open End	US Muni Fixed Inc (Muni Bond - Single State)	C	C	B			312-917-8146
Nuveen Colorado Municipal Bond Fund Class I	FCORX	NAS CM	Open End	US Muni Fixed Inc (Muni Bond - Single State)	C+	C	B	Up	Y	312-917-8146
Nuveen Connecticut Municipal Bond Fund Class A	FCTTX	NAS CM	Open End	US Muni Fixed Inc (Muni Bond - Single State)	C	C-	B-		Y	312-917-8146
Nuveen Connecticut Municipal Bond Fund Class C	FDCDX	NAS CM	Open End	US Muni Fixed Inc (Muni Bond - Single State)	C	C-	C+		Y	312-917-8146
Nuveen Connecticut Municipal Bond Fund Class C2	FCTCX	NAS CM	Open End	US Muni Fixed Inc (Muni Bond - Single State)	C	C-	C+			312-917-8146
Nuveen Connecticut Municipal Bond Fund Class I	FCTRX	NAS CM	Open End	US Muni Fixed Inc (Muni Bond - Single State)	C	C-	B-		Y	312-917-8146
Nuveen Credit Opportunities 2022 Target Term	JCO	NYSE	Closed End	US Fixed Inc (Equity-Income)	D	D	D	Down	Y	312-917-8146
Nuveen Credit Strategies Income Fund	JQC	NYSE	Closed End	US Fixed Inc (Income)	D	D	D	Down	Y	312-917-8146
Nuveen Emerging Markets Debt 2022 Target Term Fund	JEMD	NYSE	Closed End	US Fixed Inc (Income)	D	D	D		Y	312-917-8146
Nuveen Enhanced Municipal Value Fund	NEV	NYSE	Closed End	US Muni Fixed Inc (Muni Bond - Natl)	C-	C-	C-	Down	Y	312-917-8146
Nuveen Floating Rate Income Fund	JFR	NYSE	Closed End	US Fixed Inc (Corp Bond - General)	D	D	D	Down	Y	312-917-8146
Nuveen Floating Rate Income Opportunity Fund	JRO	NYSE	Closed End	US Fixed Inc (Corp Bond - General)	D	D	D	Down	Y	312-917-8146
Nuveen Georgia Municipal Bond Fund Class A	FGATX	NAS CM	Open End	US Muni Fixed Inc (Muni Bond - Single State)	C	C	B-		Y	312-917-8146
Nuveen Georgia Municipal Bond Fund Class C	FGCCX	NAS CM	Open End	US Muni Fixed Inc (Muni Bond - Single State)	C	C-	B-		Y	312-917-8146
Nuveen Georgia Municipal Bond Fund Class C2	FGACX	NAS CM	Open End	US Muni Fixed Inc (Muni Bond - Single State)	C	C-	B-			312-917-8146
Nuveen Georgia Municipal Bond Fund Class I	FGARX	NAS CM	Open End	US Muni Fixed Inc (Muni Bond - Single State)	C	C	B		Y	312-917-8146
Nuveen Georgia Quality Municipal Income Fund	NKG	NYSE	Closed End	US Muni Fixed Inc (Muni Bond - Single State)	C-	C-	C-		Y	312-917-8146
Nuveen Global High Income Fund	JGH	NYSE	Closed End	Global Fixed Inc (Income)	D	D	D	Down	Y	312-917-8146
Nuveen High Income 2020 Target Term Fund	JHY	NYSE	Closed End	US Fixed Inc (Income)	D+	D+	C-	Down	Y	312-917-8146

★Expanded analysis of this fund is included in Section II.

TOTAL RETURNS & PERFORMANCE									ASSETS		ASSET ALLOCATION & TURNOVER							MINIMUMS		FEES		
3-Month Total Return	6-Month Total Return	1-Year Total Return	3-Year Total Return	5-Year Total Return	Dividend Yield (TTM)	Expense Ratio	3-Yr Std Deviation	Effective Duration	NAV	Total Assets (MIL)	%Cash	%Government Bonds	%Municipal Bonds	%Corporate Bonds	%Other	Turnover Ratio	Average Coupon Rate	Min Initial Investment	Min Additional Investment	Front End Fee (%)	Back End Fee (%)	Inception Date
0.21	8.62	10.49	17.07	21.51	1.87	0.17	4.25	6.89	23.75	115.8	0	100	0	0	0	50	2.22	2,500	50			Jan-93
2.77	1.80	3.20	7.79	10.46	2.23	0.25	1.55	0.89	10.34	2,515	9	11	0	70	0	76	2.37	2,500	50			Jun-09
3.26	0.59	3.06	13.50	23.17	3.39	0.73	5.59	8.48	11.77	5,882	0	0	100	0	0	14	4.99	3,000	100	4.20		Oct-88
3.14	0.18	2.24	10.84	18.31	2.57	1.53	5.61	8.48	11.77	5,882	0	0	100	0	0	14	4.99	3,000	100		1.00	Feb-14
3.20	0.30	2.49	11.67	19.79	2.82	1.28	5.61	8.48	11.78	5,882	0	0	100	0	0	14	4.99	0			1.00	Jun-93
3.30	0.60	3.26	14.14	24.34	3.58	0.53	5.62	8.48	11.82	5,882	0	0	100	0	0	14	4.99	100,000				Feb-97
3.30	0.62	3.30	14.29	24.29	3.62	0.49	5.59	8.48	11.83	5,882	0	0	100	0	0	14	4.99	1,000,000				Jun-16
4.93	-0.22	4.00	21.04	37.63	4.9	0	8.68		16.69	3,437	0	0	100	0	1	6	5.55					Mar-02
2.56	-0.19	2.93	12.72	22.83	3.32	0.73	6.12		16.67	253.7	0	0	100	0	1	31	5.16					Feb-09
3.80	1.31	4.76	17.97	33.41	4.29	0	7.14		15.42	4,193	0	0	100	0	1	8	5.21					Nov-02
2.51	1.61	3.70	12.00	20.10	2.67	0.87	4.18	6.78	11.12	148.3	2	0	98	0	0	6	4.95	3,000	100	4.20		Oct-86
2.30	1.19	2.88	9.40	15.41	1.87	1.67	4.22	6.78	11.11	148.3	2	0	98	0	0	6	4.95	3,000	100		1.00	Feb-14
2.37	1.33	3.14	10.16	16.94	2.12	1.42	4.22	6.78	11.12	148.3	2	0	98	0	0	6	4.95	0			1.00	Feb-94
2.56	1.71	3.91	12.72	21.31	2.88	0.67	4.21	6.78	11.14	148.3	2	0	98	0	0	6	4.95	100,000				Feb-97
4.42	1.55	4.53	15.13	27.01	3.57		6.63		14.92	170.6	0	0	100	0	0	6	5.45					Nov-92
4.60	2.50	6.20	18.71	34.86	3.79	0	7.82		16.46	774.6	0	0	100	0	1	11	5.31					Nov-02
4.24	-0.71	2.73	15.03	28.87	3.85	1.17	8.11	12.76	9.88	1,188	0	0	99	0	0	2	6.48	3,000	100	4.20		Mar-06
3.92	-1.12	1.90	12.29	23.66	3.01	1.97	8.07	12.76	9.87	1,188	0	0	99	0	0	2	6.48	3,000	100		1.00	Feb-14
3.99	-0.98	2.08	13.04	25.25	3.29	1.71	8.09	12.76	9.86	1,188	0	0	99	0	0	2	6.48	0			1.00	Mar-06
4.19	-0.62	2.91	15.68	30.10	4.03	0.96	8.08	12.76	9.87	1,188	0	0	99	0	0	2	6.48	100,000				Mar-06
2.74	0.99	2.47	10.61		1.6	0.77	4.22	5.95	10.55	11.9	2	0	98	0	0	2	4.89	3,000	100	3.00		Oct-16
2.54	0.49	1.56	7.94		0.79	1.56	4.18	5.95	10.53	11.9	2	0	98	0	0	2	4.89	3,000	100		1.00	Oct-16
2.78	1.08	2.64	11.19		1.77	0.58	4.23	5.95	10.56	11.9	2	0	98	0	0	2	4.89	100,000				Oct-16
3.24	1.66	4.03	12.44	23.00	2.82	0.76	4.99	7.20	11.46	1,910	0	0	100	0	0	13	5.06	3,000	100	4.20		Sep-94
3.04	1.16	3.12	9.69	18.08	2.02	1.56	4.93	7.20	11.41	1,910	0	0	100	0	0	13	5.06	3,000	100		1.00	Feb-14
3.10	1.37	3.45	10.60	19.61	2.25	1.31	4.97	7.20	11.44	1,910	0	0	100	0	0	13	5.06	0			1.00	Sep-94
3.29	1.67	4.15	13.12	24.14	3.02	0.56	4.96	7.20	11.47	1,910	0	0	100	0	0	13	5.06	100,000				Jul-86
2.96	1.83	4.55	14.34	25.38	3.16		5.13		10.71	298.9	1	0	99	0	1	8	5.04					Oct-87
2.72	1.59	4.07	12.99	22.82	3	0.78	5.36		16.29	53.5	1	0	99	0	1	25	4.93					Apr-09
4.28	1.81	4.84	16.36	32.11	4.03	0	7.19		15.92	2,277	0	0	100	0	1	11	5.21					May-99
3.06	2.34	5.20	14.98	27.14	3.34		4.9		15.77	99.6	0	0	100	0	1	10	5.17					Jun-92
2.73	1.95	4.43	13.39	21.95	2.67	0.82	4.3	7.48	11.11	453.5	2	0	98	0	0	19	4.67	3,000	100	4.20		May-87
2.62	1.64	3.61	10.75	17.28	1.88	1.62	4.33	7.48	11.09	453.5	2	0	98	0	0	19	4.67	3,000	100		1.00	Feb-14
2.59	1.68	3.78	11.44	18.64	2.13	1.37	4.35	7.48	11.08	453.5	2	0	98	0	0	19	4.67	0			1.00	Feb-97
2.78	2.06	4.55	14.01	23.16	2.87	0.62	4.34	7.48	11.1	453.5	2	0	98	0	0	19	4.67	100,000				Feb-97
1.69	1.09	3.14	10.14	17.07	2.96	0.8	3.88	6.34	10.66	250.4	1	0	99	0	0	11	4.91	3,000	100	4.20		Jul-87
1.49	0.69	2.34	7.56	12.57	2.17	1.6	3.88	6.34	10.64	250.4	1	0	99	0	0	11	4.91	3,000	100		1.00	Feb-14
1.55	0.81	2.56	8.38	13.94	2.39	1.35	3.89	6.34	10.66	250.4	1	0	99	0	0	11	4.91	0			1.00	Oct-93
1.75	1.20	3.36	10.86	18.34	3.18	0.6	3.91	6.34	10.69	250.4	1	0	99	0	0	11	4.91	100,000				Feb-97
5.90	-15.40	-13.86	-4.97		7.36	1.63	12.7		7.86	212.4	0	0	0	100	2	66	5.13					Mar-17
8.67	-10.76	-7.66	-0.73	5.67	8.24	0	10.97		6.78	922.1	-6	0	0	98	7	59	4.13					Jun-03
18.99	-12.43	-13.49			6.27	2.17			7.54	102.3	-30	65	0	34	33	14	6.33					Sep-17
5.34	1.62	4.80	16.73	28.33	4.68	1.17	8.69		15.12	364.0	-1	0	100	0	1	11	8.01					Sep-09
10.06	-13.35	-10.52	-3.72	5.96	8.02	1.1	12.85		9.18	517.4	5	0	0	94	-5	32	4.34					Mar-04
9.98	-13.33	-10.50	-3.54	5.84	8.02	1.14	12.8		9.11	365.7	6	0	0	94	-5	34	4.38					Jul-04
2.26	1.27	3.97	11.21	16.36	2.36	0.84	4.23	6.38	11	170.9	2	0	98	0	0	19	5.15	3,000	100	4.20		Mar-86
2.06	0.85	3.04	8.51	11.83	1.55	1.64	4.23	6.38	10.96	170.9	2	0	98	0	0	19	5.15	3,000	100		1.00	Feb-14
2.13	1.00	3.42	9.39	13.20	1.82	1.39	4.25	6.38	10.96	170.9	2	0	98	0	0	19	5.15	0			1.00	Jan-94
2.31	1.36	4.15	11.80	17.50	2.53	0.64	4.23	6.38	10.97	170.9	2	0	98	0	0	19	5.15	100,000				Feb-97
2.59	1.50	4.44	13.67	22.93	3.2	0	5.84		14.07	145.1	0	0	100	0	1	20	5.80					Sep-02
17.54	-13.23	-8.30	2.79	15.51	8.08	1.1	16.69		15.15	345.8	1	11	0	87	2	43	6.40					Nov-14
3.50	-2.25	-1.09	8.73	26.41	2.98	1.46	4.02		9.48	148.2	32	10	0	58	1	61	4.93					Jul-15

	MARKET			FUND TYPE, CATEGORY & OBJECTIVE	RATINGS				NEW INVESTORS	
Fund Name	Ticker Symbol	Traded On	Fund Type	Category and (Prospectus Objective)	Overall Rating	Reward Rating	Risk Rating	Recent Up/ Downgrade	Open to New Investors	Telephone
Nuveen High Income 2023 Target Term Fund	JHAA	NYSE	Closed End	US Fixed Inc (Income)	D	D	D+		Y	312-917-8146
Nuveen High Income Bond Fund Class A	FJSIX	NAS CM	Open End	US Fixed Inc (Corp Bond - High Yield)	D	D	D+	Down	Y	312-917-8146
Nuveen High Income Bond Fund Class C	FCSIX	NAS CM	Open End	US Fixed Inc (Corp Bond - High Yield)	D	D	D+	Down	Y	312-917-8146
Nuveen High Income Bond Fund Class I	FJSYX	NAS CM	Open End	US Fixed Inc (Corp Bond - High Yield)	D	D	D+	Down	Y	312-917-8146
Nuveen High Income Bond Fund Class R3	FANSX	NAS CM	Open End	US Fixed Inc (Corp Bond - High Yield)	D	D	D+	Down	Y	312-917-8146
Nuveen High Income November 2021 Target Term Fund	JHB	NYSE	Closed End	US Fixed Inc (Income)	D+	D+	C-	Down	Y	312-917-8146
Nuveen High Yield Municipal Bond Fund Class A	NHMAX	NAS CM	Open End	US Muni Fixed Inc (Muni Bond - Natl)	C-	D+	C	Down	Y	312-917-8146
Nuveen High Yield Municipal Bond Fund Class C	NHCCX	NAS CM	Open End	US Muni Fixed Inc (Muni Bond - Natl)	C-	D+	C	Down	Y	312-917-8146
Nuveen High Yield Municipal Bond Fund Class C2	NHMCX	NAS CM	Open End	US Muni Fixed Inc (Muni Bond - Natl)	C-	D+	C	Down		312-917-8146
Nuveen High Yield Municipal Bond Fund Class I	NHMRX	NAS CM	Open End	US Muni Fixed Inc (Muni Bond - Natl)	C-	D+	C	Down	Y	312-917-8146
Nuveen High Yield Municipal Bond Fund Class R6	NHMFX	NAS CM	Open End	US Muni Fixed Inc (Muni Bond - Natl)	C-	D+	C	Down	Y	312-917-8146
Nuveen Intermediate Duration Municipal Bond Fund Class A	NMBAX	NAS CM	Open End	US Muni Fixed Inc (Muni Bond - Natl)	C	C-	B-		Y	312-917-8146
Nuveen Intermediate Duration Municipal Bond Fund Class C	NNCCX	NAS CM	Open End	US Muni Fixed Inc (Muni Bond - Natl)	C	C-	C+		Y	312-917-8146
Nuveen Intermediate Duration Municipal Bond Fund Class C2	NNSCX	NAS CM	Open End	US Muni Fixed Inc (Muni Bond - Natl)	C	C-	B-			312-917-8146
Nuveen Intermediate Duration Municipal Bond Fund Class I	NUVBX	NAS CM	Open End	US Muni Fixed Inc (Muni Bond - Natl)	C	C-	B-		Y	312-917-8146
Nuveen Intermediate Duration Municipal Term Fund	NID	NYSE	Closed End	US Muni Fixed Inc (Muni Bond - Natl)	D+	D+	C-	Down	Y	312-917-8146
Nuveen Intermediate Duration Quality Municipal Term Fund	NIQ	NYSE	Closed End	US Muni Fixed Inc (Income)	C-	C-	C-		Y	312-917-8146
Nuveen Kansas Municipal Bond Fund Class A	FKSTX	NAS CM	Open End	US Muni Fixed Inc (Muni Bond - Single State)	C	C-	C+		Y	312-917-8146
Nuveen Kansas Municipal Bond Fund Class C	FAFOX	NAS CM	Open End	US Muni Fixed Inc (Muni Bond - Single State)	C-	D+	C	Down	Y	312-917-8146
Nuveen Kansas Municipal Bond Fund Class C2	FCKSX	NAS CM	Open End	US Muni Fixed Inc (Muni Bond - Single State)	C-	D+	C	Down		312-917-8146
Nuveen Kansas Municipal Bond Fund Class I	FRKSX	NAS CM	Open End	US Muni Fixed Inc (Muni Bond - Single State)	C	C-	C+		Y	312-917-8146
Nuveen Kentucky Municipal Bond Fund Class A	FKYTX	NAS CM	Open End	US Muni Fixed Inc (Muni Bond - Single State)	C	C-	B-		Y	312-917-8146
Nuveen Kentucky Municipal Bond Fund Class C	FKCCX	NAS CM	Open End	US Muni Fixed Inc (Muni Bond - Single State)	C	C-	C+		Y	312-917-8146
Nuveen Kentucky Municipal Bond Fund Class C2	FKYCX	NAS CM	Open End	US Muni Fixed Inc (Muni Bond - Single State)	C	C-	C+			312-917-8146
Nuveen Kentucky Municipal Bond Fund Class I	FKYRX	NAS CM	Open End	US Muni Fixed Inc (Muni Bond - Single State)	C	C-	B-		Y	312-917-8146
Nuveen Limited Term Municipal Bond Fund Class A	FLTDX	NAS CM	Open End	US Muni Fixed Inc (Muni Bond - Natl)	C	C	B-		Y	312-917-8146
Nuveen Limited Term Municipal Bond Fund Class C	FAFJX	NAS CM	Open End	US Muni Fixed Inc (Muni Bond - Natl)	C	C-	C+		Y	312-917-8146
Nuveen Limited Term Municipal Bond Fund Class C2	FLTCX	NAS CM	Open End	US Muni Fixed Inc (Muni Bond - Natl)	C	C-	B-			312-917-8146
Nuveen Limited Term Municipal Bond Fund Class I	FLTRX	NAS CM	Open End	US Muni Fixed Inc (Muni Bond - Natl)	C	C	B-		Y	312-917-8146
Nuveen Louisiana Municipal Bond Fund Class A	FTLAX	NAS CM	Open End	US Muni Fixed Inc (Muni Bond - Single State)	C	C-	B-		Y	312-917-8146
Nuveen Louisiana Municipal Bond Fund Class C	FAFLX	NAS CM	Open End	US Muni Fixed Inc (Muni Bond - Single State)	C	C-	C+		Y	312-917-8146
Nuveen Louisiana Municipal Bond Fund Class C2	FTLCX	NAS CM	Open End	US Muni Fixed Inc (Muni Bond - Single State)	C	C-	C+			312-917-8146
Nuveen Louisiana Municipal Bond Fund Class I	FTLRX	NAS CM	Open End	US Muni Fixed Inc (Muni Bond - Single State)	C	C-	B-		Y	312-917-8146
Nuveen Maryland Municipal Bond Fund Class A	NMDAX	NAS CM	Open End	US Muni Fixed Inc (Muni Bond - Single State)	C	C-	C+		Y	312-917-8146
Nuveen Maryland Municipal Bond Fund Class C	NACCX	NAS CM	Open End	US Muni Fixed Inc (Muni Bond - Single State)	C	C-	C		Y	312-917-8146
Nuveen Maryland Municipal Bond Fund Class C2	NMDCX	NAS CM	Open End	US Muni Fixed Inc (Muni Bond - Single State)	C	C-	C+			312-917-8146
Nuveen Maryland Municipal Bond Fund Class I	NMMDX	NAS CM	Open End	US Muni Fixed Inc (Muni Bond - Single State)	C	C-	B-		Y	312-917-8146
Nuveen Maryland Quality Municipal Income Fund	NMY	NYSE	Closed End	US Muni Fixed Inc (Muni Bond - Single State)	C-	C-	C-		Y	312-917-8146
Nuveen Massachusetts Municipal Bond Fund Class A	NMAAX	NAS CM	Open End	US Muni Fixed Inc (Muni Bond - Single State)	C	C-	B-		Y	312-917-8146
Nuveen Massachusetts Municipal Bond Fund Class C	NAAGX	NAS CM	Open End	US Muni Fixed Inc (Muni Bond - Single State)	C	C-	C+		Y	312-917-8146
Nuveen Massachusetts Municipal Bond Fund Class C2	NMACX	NAS CM	Open End	US Muni Fixed Inc (Muni Bond - Single State)	C	C-	C+			312-917-8146
Nuveen Massachusetts Municipal Bond Fund Class I	NBMAX	NAS CM	Open End	US Muni Fixed Inc (Muni Bond - Single State)	C	C-	B-		Y	312-917-8146
Nuveen Massachusetts Quality Municipal Income Fund	NMT	NYSE	Closed End	US Muni Fixed Inc (Muni Bond - Single State)	C-	C-	C-		Y	312-917-8146
Nuveen Michigan Municipal Bond Fund Class A	FMITX	NAS CM	Open End	US Muni Fixed Inc (Muni Bond - Single State)	C+	C	B	Up	Y	312-917-8146
Nuveen Michigan Municipal Bond Fund Class C	FAFNX	NAS CM	Open End	US Muni Fixed Inc (Muni Bond - Single State)	C	C	B-		Y	312-917-8146
Nuveen Michigan Municipal Bond Fund Class C2	FLMCX	NAS CM	Open End	US Muni Fixed Inc (Muni Bond - Single State)	C+	C	B	Up		312-917-8146
Nuveen Michigan Municipal Bond Fund Class I	NMMIX	NAS CM	Open End	US Muni Fixed Inc (Muni Bond - Single State)	C+	C	B	Up	Y	312-917-8146
Nuveen Michigan Quality Municipal Income Fund	NUM	NYSE	Closed End	US Muni Fixed Inc (Muni Bond - Single State)	C	C	C-	Up	Y	312-917-8146
Nuveen Minnesota Intermediate Municipal Bond Fund Class A	FAMAX	NAS CM	Open End	US Muni Fixed Inc (Muni Bond - Single State)	C	C-	B-		Y	312-917-8146
Nuveen Minnesota Intermediate Municipal Bond Fund Class C	NIBCX	NAS CM	Open End	US Muni Fixed Inc (Muni Bond - Single State)	C	C-	C+		Y	312-917-8146
Nuveen Minnesota Intermediate Municipal Bond Fund Class C1	FACMX	NAS CM	Open End	US Muni Fixed Inc (Muni Bond - Single State)	C	C-	B-		Y	312-917-8146
Nuveen Minnesota Intermediate Municipal Bond Fund Class C2	NIBMX	NAS CM	Open End	US Muni Fixed Inc (Muni Bond - Single State)	C	C-	C+			312-917-8146

★ Expanded analysis of this fund is included in Section II.

TOTAL RETURNS & PERFORMANCE									ASSETS		ASSET ALLOCATION & TURNOVER							MINIMUMS		FEES		
3-Month Total Return	6-Month Total Return	1-Year Total Return	3-Year Total Return	5-Year Total Return	Dividend Yield (TTM)	Expense Ratio	3-Yr Std Deviation	Effective Duration	NAV	Total Assets (MIL)	%Cash	%Government Bonds	%Municipal Bonds	%Corporate Bonds	%Other	Turnover Ratio	Average Coupon Rate	Min Initial Investment	Min Additional Investment	Front End Fee (%)	Back End Fee (%)	Inception Date
10.60	-7.52	-4.29			6.66	2.2			9.29	71.9	13	1	0	86	1	34	5.42					Dec-18
10.48	-9.71	-5.29	3.57	13.15	5.88	1.03	11.14	3.71	6.69	186.7	9	1	0	90	1	113	6.28	3,000	100	4.75		Aug-01
10.44	-9.96	-6.01	1.34	9.02	5.05	1.78	11.19	3.71	6.69	186.7	9	1	0	90	1	113	6.28	3,000	100		1.00	Aug-01
10.52	-9.57	-5.17	4.30	14.50	6.13	0.78	11.18	3.71	6.71	186.7	9	1	0	90	1	113	6.28	100,000				Aug-01
10.53	-9.72	-5.59	2.86	11.77	5.57	1.28	11.19	3.71	6.84	186.7	9	1	0	90	1	113	6.28	0				Sep-01
6.80	-4.56	-2.53	7.69		5.28	1.53	7.06		9.29	512.6	10	6	0	84	1	41	5.59					Aug-16
5.66	-3.46	0.09	15.69	30.34	5.18	1.12	9.26	12.65	16.94	18,466	2	0	97	1	0	21	7.04	3,000	100	4.20		Jun-99
5.45	-3.81	-0.64	13.02	25.31	4.32	1.92	9.23	12.65	16.93	18,466	2	0	97	1	0	21	7.04	3,000	100		1.00	Feb-14
5.52	-3.68	-0.44	13.80	26.81	4.6	1.68	9.27	12.65	16.93	18,466	2	0	97	1	0	21	7.04	0			1.00	Jun-99
5.72	-3.36	0.29	16.38	31.66	5.4	0.92	9.26	12.65	16.94	18,466	2	0	97	1	0	21	7.04	100,000				Jun-99
5.66	-3.34	0.29	16.51	31.80	5.46	0.89	9.26	12.65	16.95	18,466	2	0	97	1	0	21	7.04	1,000,000				Jun-16
3.01	1.35	3.32	12.03	19.28	2.58	0.67	4	5.69	9.48	8,890	1	0	99	0	0	22	4.34	3,000	100	3.00		Jun-95
2.80	0.93	2.50	9.40	14.56	1.77	1.47	3.98	5.69	9.48	8,890	1	0	99	0	0	22	4.34	3,000	100		1.00	Feb-14
2.86	1.06	2.75	10.25	16.04	2.03	1.22	3.97	5.69	9.49	8,890	1	0	99	0	0	22	4.34	0			1.00	Jun-95
3.05	1.44	3.50	12.77	20.51	2.76	0.47	3.96	5.69	9.51	8,890	1	0	99	0	0	22	4.34	100,000				Nov-76
5.71	-0.70	1.50	15.09	27.46	3.74	1.4	7.12		13.97	640.3	0	0	99	0	1	13	6.37					Dec-12
4.60	1.73	4.14	14.31	26.25	2.66	1.27	5.85		14.56	188.1	1	0	99	0	1	20	6.30					Feb-13
3.39	0.26	1.80	9.00	15.35	3.01	0.89	4.35	6.32	10.61	280.6	1	0	99	0	0	15	4.83	3,000	100	4.20		Jan-92
3.29	-0.13	1.00	6.46	10.82	2.22	1.69	4.36	6.32	10.59	280.6	1	0	99	0	0	15	4.83	3,000	100		1.00	Feb-14
3.24	-0.02	1.23	7.18	12.20	2.44	1.44	4.34	6.32	10.6	280.6	1	0	99	0	0	15	4.83	0			1.00	Feb-97
3.43	0.37	2.02	9.59	16.47	3.23	0.69	4.37	6.32	10.65	280.6	1	0	99	0	0	15	4.83	100,000				Feb-97
1.48	0.74	2.89	10.28	16.92	2.64	0.97	4.04	6.57	10.97	348.8	0	0	100	0	0	25	5.46	3,000	100	4.20		May-87
1.27	0.23	1.97	7.59	12.25	1.82	1.77	4.09	6.57	10.96	348.8	0	0	100	0	0	25	5.46	3,000	100		1.00	Feb-14
1.34	0.37	2.24	8.36	13.65	2.09	1.51	4.06	6.57	10.96	348.8	0	0	100	0	0	25	5.46	0			1.00	Oct-93
1.53	0.75	3.01	10.81	17.99	2.86	0.76	4.06	6.57	10.95	348.8	0	0	100	0	0	25	5.46	100,000				Feb-97
3.23	1.89	3.17	9.36	12.76	1.97	0.63	2.85	3.60	11.32	6,060	3	0	97	0	0	22	4.03	3,000	100	2.50		Oct-87
3.03	1.58	2.35	6.75	8.37	1.17	1.43	2.82	3.60	11.28	6,060	3	0	97	0	0	22	4.03	3,000	100		1.00	Feb-14
3.14	1.79	2.88	8.24	10.77	1.6	0.98	2.87	3.60	11.3	6,060	3	0	97	0	0	22	4.03	0			1.00	Dec-95
3.29	2.00	3.38	9.98	13.89	2.17	0.43	2.8	3.60	11.28	6,060	3	0	97	0	0	22	4.03	100,000				Feb-97
1.94	0.63	2.53	11.30	17.85	3.11	0.85	3.97	6.82	11.27	197.2	2	0	98	0	0	14	4.94	3,000	100	4.20		Sep-89
1.83	0.21	1.79	8.75	13.26	2.27	1.65	3.96	6.82	11.22	197.2	2	0	98	0	0	14	4.94	3,000	100		1.00	Feb-14
1.89	0.34	2.04	9.59	14.69	2.53	1.4	3.96	6.82	11.23	197.2	2	0	98	0	0	14	4.94	0			1.00	Feb-94
2.08	0.73	2.83	12.09	19.06	3.32	0.65	3.98	6.82	11.3	197.2	2	0	98	0	0	14	4.94	100,000				Feb-97
2.32	0.60	2.69	10.06	18.40	2.75	0.84	4.36	7.24	10.81	247.7	0	0	100	0	0	17	4.74	3,000	100	4.20		Sep-94
2.21	0.27	1.87	7.60	13.77	1.94	1.63	4.32	7.24	10.77	247.7	0	0	100	0	0	17	4.74	3,000	100		1.00	Feb-14
2.18	0.32	2.13	8.25	15.19	2.2	1.38	4.34	7.24	10.78	247.7	0	0	100	0	0	17	4.74	0			1.00	Sep-94
2.37	0.70	2.91	10.79	19.60	2.97	0.64	4.36	7.24	10.81	247.7	0	0	100	0	0	17	4.74	100,000				Feb-92
2.94	-0.82	2.55	13.48	25.11	3.71		7.5		14.72	331.9	1	0	99	0	1	17	5.29					Mar-93
2.10	1.13	3.32	10.73	19.00	2.56	0.8	4.56	7.17	10.32	522.4	2	0	98	0	0	7	4.91	3,000	100	4.20		Sep-94
1.91	0.83	2.60	8.19	14.31	1.75	1.6	4.59	7.17	10.24	522.4	2	0	98	0	0	7	4.91	3,000	100		1.00	Feb-14
1.96	0.84	2.84	8.85	15.78	1.98	1.35	4.55	7.17	10.25	522.4	2	0	98	0	0	7	4.91	0			1.00	Oct-94
2.15	1.22	3.60	11.44	20.19	2.73	0.6	4.59	7.17	10.32	522.4	2	0	98	0	0	7	4.91	100,000				Dec-86
3.61	1.52	4.25	13.70	25.78	3.38		6.75		14.89	136.6	1	0	99	0	1	16	5.19					Mar-93
2.41	2.50	4.64	12.05	20.41	2.42	0.86	3.74	6.09	11.94	281.2	2	0	98	0	0	16	5.12	3,000	100	4.20		Jun-85
2.12	2.10	3.73	9.44	15.60	1.62	1.66	3.72	6.09	11.9	281.2	2	0	98	0	0	16	5.12	3,000	100		1.00	Feb-14
2.18	2.14	3.98	10.17	17.04	1.87	1.41	3.7	6.09	11.91	281.2	2	0	98	0	0	16	5.12	0			1.00	Jun-93
2.38	2.52	4.77	12.77	21.58	2.62	0.66	3.74	6.09	11.92	281.2	2	0	98	0	0	16	5.12	100,000				Feb-97
3.41	2.90	5.65	15.49	27.57	3.36	0	5.29		15.96	321.4	1	0	99	0	1	14	5.31					Oct-91
2.24	1.05	3.01	10.04	16.71	2.65	0.81	3.48	5.30	10.55	405.4	0	0	100	0	0	20	4.37	3,000	100	3.00		Feb-94
2.05	0.65	2.11	7.46	12.09	1.86	1.61	3.45	5.30	10.48	405.4	0	0	100	0	0	20	4.37	3,000	100		1.00	Feb-14
2.11	0.91	2.53	8.61	14.13	2.19	1.26	3.46	5.30	10.59	405.4	0	0	100	0	0	20	4.37	3,000	100		1.00	Oct-09
2.10	0.76	2.34	8.19	13.46	2.09	1.36	3.44	5.30	10.51	405.4	0	0	100	0	0	20	4.37	3,000	100		1.00	Jan-11

	MARKET			FUND TYPE, CATEGORY & OBJECTIVE	RATINGS				NEW INVESTORS	
Fund Name	Ticker Symbol	Traded On	Fund Type	Category and (Prospectus Objective)	Overall Rating	Reward Rating	Risk Rating	Recent Up/ Downgrade	Open to New Investors	Telephone
Nuveen Minnesota Intermediate Municipal Bond Fund Class I	FAMTX	NAS CM	Open End	US Muni Fixed Inc (Muni Bond - Single State)	C	C	B-		Y	312-917-8146
Nuveen Minnesota Municipal Bond Fund Class A	FJMNX	NAS CM	Open End	US Muni Fixed Inc (Muni Bond - Single State)	C	C-	B-		Y	312-917-8146
Nuveen Minnesota Municipal Bond Fund Class C	NTCCX	NAS CM	Open End	US Muni Fixed Inc (Muni Bond - Single State)	C	C-	C+		Y	312-917-8146
Nuveen Minnesota Municipal Bond Fund Class C1	FCMNX	NAS CM	Open End	US Muni Fixed Inc (Muni Bond - Single State)	C	C-	C+		Y	312-917-8146
Nuveen Minnesota Municipal Bond Fund Class C2	NMBCX	NAS CM	Open End	US Muni Fixed Inc (Muni Bond - Single State)	C	C-	C+			312-917-8146
Nuveen Minnesota Municipal Bond Fund Class I	FYMNX	NAS CM	Open End	US Muni Fixed Inc (Muni Bond - Single State)	C	C-	B-		Y	312-917-8146
Nuveen Minnesota Quality Municipal Income Fund	NMS	NYSE	Closed End	US Muni Fixed Inc (Muni Bond - Single State)	D+	C-	D+	Down	Y	312-917-8146
Nuveen Missouri Municipal Bond Fund Class A	FMOTX	NAS CM	Open End	US Muni Fixed Inc (Muni Bond - Single State)	C	C	B		Y	312-917-8146
Nuveen Missouri Municipal Bond Fund Class C	FAFPX	NAS CM	Open End	US Muni Fixed Inc (Muni Bond - Single State)	C	C-	B-		Y	312-917-8146
Nuveen Missouri Municipal Bond Fund Class C2	FMOCX	NAS CM	Open End	US Muni Fixed Inc (Muni Bond - Single State)	C	C-	B-			312-917-8146
Nuveen Missouri Municipal Bond Fund Class I	FMMRX	NAS CM	Open End	US Muni Fixed Inc (Muni Bond - Single State)	C	C	B		Y	312-917-8146
Nuveen Missouri Quality Municipal Income Fund	NOM	NYSE	Closed End	US Muni Fixed Inc (Muni Bond - Single State)	C-	C-	D+		Y	312-917-8146
Nuveen Mortgage Opportunity Term	JLS	NYSE	Closed End	US Fixed Inc (Growth & Income)	D	D	D	Down	Y	312-917-8146
Nuveen Multi-Market Income Fund	JMM	NYSE	Closed End	US Fixed Inc (Govt Bond - General)	D+	D	C-	Down	Y	312-917-8146
Nuveen Municipal 2021 Target Term	NHA	NYSE	Closed End	US Muni Fixed Inc (Muni Bond - Natl)	C-	C	C-		Y	312-917-8146
Nuveen Municipal Credit Income Fund	NZF	NYSE	Closed End	US Muni Fixed Inc (Muni Bond - Natl)	C-	D+	C	Down	Y	312-917-8146
Nuveen Municipal Credit Opps Fund	NMCO	NYSE	Closed End	US Muni Fixed Inc (Income)	U	U	U		Y	312-917-8146
Nuveen Municipal High Income Opportunity Fund	NMZ	NYSE	Closed End	US Muni Fixed Inc (Muni Bond - Natl)	C-	D+	C	Down	Y	312-917-8146
Nuveen Municipal Income	NMI	NYSE	Closed End	US Muni Fixed Inc (Muni Bond - Natl)	C-	C-	C-		Y	312-917-8146
Nuveen Municipal Total Return Managed Accounts	NMTRX	NAS CM	Open End	US Muni Fixed Inc (Muni Bond - Natl)	C	C-	B	Down	Y	312-917-8146
Nuveen Municipal Value Fund	NUV	NYSE	Closed End	US Muni Fixed Inc (Muni Bond - Natl)	C	C-	C+		Y	312-917-8146
Nuveen Nebraska Municipal Bond Fund Class A	FNTAX	NAS CM	Open End	US Muni Fixed Inc (Muni Bond - Single State)	C+	C	B	Up	Y	312-917-8146
Nuveen Nebraska Municipal Bond Fund Class C	NAAFX	NAS CM	Open End	US Muni Fixed Inc (Muni Bond - Single State)	C	C	B-		Y	312-917-8146
Nuveen Nebraska Municipal Bond Fund Class C1	FNTCX	NAS CM	Open End	US Muni Fixed Inc (Muni Bond - Single State)	C+	C	B	Up	Y	312-917-8146
Nuveen Nebraska Municipal Bond Fund Class C2	NCNBX	NAS CM	Open End	US Muni Fixed Inc (Muni Bond - Single State)	C	C	B			312-917-8146
Nuveen Nebraska Municipal Bond Fund Class I	FNTYX	NAS CM	Open End	US Muni Fixed Inc (Muni Bond - Single State)	C+	C	B	Up	Y	312-917-8146
Nuveen New Jersey Municipal Bond Fund Class A	NNJAX	NAS CM	Open End	US Muni Fixed Inc (Muni Bond - Single State)	C	C-	C+		Y	312-917-8146
Nuveen New Jersey Municipal Bond Fund Class C	NJCCX	NAS CM	Open End	US Muni Fixed Inc (Muni Bond - Single State)	C	C-	C+		Y	312-917-8146
Nuveen New Jersey Municipal Bond Fund Class C2	NNJCX	NAS CM	Open End	US Muni Fixed Inc (Muni Bond - Single State)	C	C-	C+			312-917-8146
Nuveen New Jersey Municipal Bond Fund Class I	NMNJX	NAS CM	Open End	US Muni Fixed Inc (Muni Bond - Single State)	C	C-	B-		Y	312-917-8146
Nuveen New Jersey Municipal Value Fund	NJV	NYSE	Closed End	US Muni Fixed Inc (Muni Bond - Single State)	D+	C-	D+	Down	Y	312-917-8146
Nuveen New Jersey Quality Municipal Income Fund	NXJ	NYSE	Closed End	US Muni Fixed Inc (Muni Bond - Single State)	C-	C-	C-		Y	312-917-8146
Nuveen New Mexico Municipal Bond Fund Class A	FNMTX	NAS CM	Open End	US Muni Fixed Inc (Muni Bond - Single State)	C	C	B		Y	312-917-8146
Nuveen New Mexico Municipal Bond Fund Class C	FNCCX	NAS CM	Open End	US Muni Fixed Inc (Muni Bond - Single State)	C	C	B-		Y	312-917-8146
Nuveen New Mexico Municipal Bond Fund Class C2	FNMCX	NAS CM	Open End	US Muni Fixed Inc (Muni Bond - Single State)	C	C	B-			312-917-8146
Nuveen New Mexico Municipal Bond Fund Class I	FNMRX	NAS CM	Open End	US Muni Fixed Inc (Muni Bond - Single State)	C+	C	B	Up	Y	312-917-8146
Nuveen New York AMT - Free Quality Municipal Income Fund	NRK	NYSE	Closed End	US Muni Fixed Inc (Muni Bond - Single State)	C	C-	C+		Y	312-917-8146
Nuveen New York Municipal Bond Fund Class A	NNYAX	NAS CM	Open End	US Muni Fixed Inc (Muni Bond - Single State)	C	C-	C+		Y	312-917-8146
Nuveen New York Municipal Bond Fund Class C	NAJPX	NAS CM	Open End	US Muni Fixed Inc (Muni Bond - Single State)	C	C-	C		Y	312-917-8146
Nuveen New York Municipal Bond Fund Class C2	NNYCX	NAS CM	Open End	US Muni Fixed Inc (Muni Bond - Single State)	C	C-	C			312-917-8146
Nuveen New York Municipal Bond Fund Class I	NTNYX	NAS CM	Open End	US Muni Fixed Inc (Muni Bond - Single State)	C	C-	C+		Y	312-917-8146
Nuveen New York Municipal Value Fund	NNY	NYSE	Closed End	US Muni Fixed Inc (Muni Bond - Single State)	C-	C-	C-		Y	312-917-8146
Nuveen New York Municipal Value Fund 2	NYV	NYSE	Closed End	US Muni Fixed Inc (Muni Bond - Single State)	C-	C-	D+		Y	312-917-8146
Nuveen New York Quality Municipal Income Fund	NAN	NYSE	Closed End	US Muni Fixed Inc (Muni Bond - Single State)	C-	C-	C-		Y	312-917-8146
Nuveen New York Select Tax-Free Income Fund	NXN	NYSE	Closed End	US Muni Fixed Inc (Muni Bond - Single State)	C-	C-	D+		Y	312-917-8146
Nuveen North Carolina Municipal Bond Fund Class A	FLNCX	NAS CM	Open End	US Muni Fixed Inc (Muni Bond - Single State)	C	C	B		Y	312-917-8146
Nuveen North Carolina Municipal Bond Fund Class C	FDCCX	NAS CM	Open End	US Muni Fixed Inc (Muni Bond - Single State)	C	C	B-		Y	312-917-8146
Nuveen North Carolina Municipal Bond Fund Class C2	FCNCX	NAS CM	Open End	US Muni Fixed Inc (Muni Bond - Single State)	C	C	B-			312-917-8146
Nuveen North Carolina Municipal Bond Fund Class I	FCNRX	NAS CM	Open End	US Muni Fixed Inc (Muni Bond - Single State)	C+	C	B	Up	Y	312-917-8146
Nuveen Ohio Municipal Bond Fund Class A	FOHTX	NAS CM	Open End	US Muni Fixed Inc (Muni Bond - Single State)	C+	C	B	Up	Y	312-917-8146
Nuveen Ohio Municipal Bond Fund Class C	FAFMX	NAS CM	Open End	US Muni Fixed Inc (Muni Bond - Single State)	C+	C	B	Up	Y	312-917-8146
Nuveen Ohio Municipal Bond Fund Class C2	FOHCX	NAS CM	Open End	US Muni Fixed Inc (Muni Bond - Single State)	C+	C	B	Up		312-917-8146

★ Expanded analysis of this fund is included in Section II.

TOTAL RETURNS & PERFORMANCE									ASSETS		ASSET ALLOCATION & TURNOVER							MINIMUMS		FEES		
3-Month Total Return	6-Month Total Return	1-Year Total Return	3-Year Total Return	5-Year Total Return	Dividend Yield (TTM)	Expense Ratio	3-Yr Std Deviation	Effective Duration	NAV	Total Assets (MIL)	%Cash	%Government Bonds	%Municipal Bonds	%Corporate Bonds	%Other	Turnover Ratio	Average Coupon Rate	Min Initial Investment	Min Additional Investment	Front End Fee (%)	Back End Fee (%)	Inception Date
2.29	1.14	3.20	10.78	17.93	2.84	0.61	3.47	5.30	10.5	405.4	0	0	100	0	0	20	4.37	100,000				Feb-94
2.38	0.86	3.21	11.38	19.82	2.92	0.8	4.36	7.45	11.9	589.4	0	0	100	0	0	25	4.37	3,000	100	4.20		Jul-88
2.17	0.37	2.31	8.72	15.04	2.1	1.6	4.36	7.45	11.88	589.4	0	0	100	0	0	25	4.37	3,000	100		1.00	Feb-14
2.27	0.55	2.68	9.81	17.08	2.47	1.25	4.34	7.45	11.84	589.4	0	0	100	0	0	25	4.37	2,500	100		1.00	Feb-99
2.23	0.58	2.65	9.60	16.62	2.35	1.35	4.32	7.45	11.91	589.4	0	0	100	0	0	25	4.37	3,000	100		1.00	Jan-11
2.44	0.88	3.34	12.08	20.97	3.12	0.6	4.39	7.45	11.88	589.4	0	0	100	0	0	25	4.37	100,000				Aug-97
3.26	-0.29	3.08	14.67	24.13	3.88	1.69	7.12		15.11	85.6	0	0	100	0	1	30	4.48					Jun-93
1.87	1.37	3.57	12.05	21.16	3.07	0.78	3.75	6.58	11.52	633.3	1	0	99	0	0	17	4.59	3,000	100	4.20		Aug-87
1.58	0.96	2.74	9.32	16.39	2.25	1.58	3.79	6.58	11.47	633.3	1	0	99	0	0	17	4.59	3,000	100		1.00	Feb-14
1.73	1.09	3.00	10.18	17.92	2.51	1.33	3.77	6.58	11.48	633.3	1	0	99	0	0	17	4.59	0			1.00	Feb-94
1.84	1.48	3.70	12.68	22.26	3.28	0.58	3.82	6.58	11.5	633.3	1	0	99	0	0	17	4.59	100,000				Feb-97
2.23	0.65	3.02	12.14	24.99	3.57		5.3		13.8	32.0	1	0	99	0	1	23	4.79					May-93
12.41	-6.78	-5.88	3.33	19.34	5.66	2.25	12.12		20.72	109.1	-17	0	0	1	19	100	3.50					Nov-09
7.75	-4.52	-2.46	5.37	14.64	4.82		7.76		7.48	68.9	-27	1	0	16	31	159	4.56					Dec-88
2.24	1.54	2.37	9.35		1.75	1.33	1.62		9.96	85.7	16	0	83	0	1	12	4.57					Jan-16
4.62	-1.44	1.88	18.76	34.99	5	0	9.37		16	2,190	0	0	100	0	1	12	5.31					Sep-01
6.61	-12.38					3.07			12.89	636.0	2	0	98	0	1		5.34					Sep-19
5.52	-2.94	0.40	17.55	31.58	5.68	1.27	9.82		13.25	995.8	1	0	99	0	2	15	8.39					Nov-03
2.68	-0.12	2.03	10.49	21.18	3.9		4.84		11.04	99.0	0	0	100	0	1	10	5.11					Apr-88
2.34	1.16	4.01	14.90	27.07	3.13	0.12	5.08	7.18	11.52	1,285	1	0	99	0	0	20	5.44	0				May-07
2.57	0.93	3.70	14.47	25.76	3.61	0.61	5.14		10.47	2,134	0	0	100	0	0	13	5.24					Jun-87
2.43	2.66	4.74	11.57	18.63	2.45	0.88	3.67	7.20	11.02	99.2	0	0	100	0	0	20	4.34	3,000	100	4.20		Feb-01
2.22	2.34	3.90	8.97	13.98	1.66	1.68	3.69	7.20	11	99.2	0	0	100	0	0	20	4.34	3,000	100		1.00	Feb-14
2.33	2.45	4.21	10.03	15.99	2.03	1.33	3.63	7.20	10.95	99.2	0	0	100	0	0	20	4.34	2,500	100		1.00	Feb-01
2.28	2.38	4.16	9.70	15.43	1.91	1.43	3.65	7.20	11.03	99.2	0	0	100	0	0	20	4.34	3,000	100		1.00	Jan-11
2.48	2.77	4.95	12.27	19.87	2.66	0.68	3.63	7.20	11.04	99.2	0	0	100	0	0	20	4.34	100,000				Feb-01
1.59	-0.16	2.08	11.65	21.38	2.95	0.82	4.8	7.57	11.46	406.7	3	0	97	0	0	13	4.45	3,000	100	4.20		Sep-94
1.47	-0.49	1.25	9.03	16.70	2.12	1.62	4.81	7.57	11.41	406.7	3	0	97	0	0	13	4.45	3,000	100		1.00	Feb-14
1.45	-0.44	1.51	9.77	18.08	2.37	1.37	4.78	7.57	11.42	406.7	3	0	97	0	0	13	4.45	0			1.00	Sep-94
1.64	-0.05	2.28	12.31	22.57	3.15	0.62	4.8	7.57	11.5	406.7	3	0	97	0	0	13	4.45	100,000				Feb-92
1.16	-1.30	1.02	10.66	20.03	3.12	0.85	5.21		15.05	22.7	1	0	99	0	0	21	5.05					Apr-09
2.42	-0.70	2.45	16.63	33.27	4.03	0	7.07		15.97	654.6	1	0	99	0	0	8	5.55					Mar-01
2.50	2.21	4.39	11.34	18.68	2.81	0.88	3.49	6.02	10.59	90.7	3	0	97	0	0	15	4.85	3,000	100	4.20		Sep-92
2.29	1.80	3.56	8.65	13.97	2.01	1.68	3.44	6.02	10.61	90.7	3	0	97	0	0	15	4.85	3,000	100		1.00	Feb-14
2.35	1.92	3.74	9.38	15.40	2.28	1.43	3.47	6.02	10.58	90.7	3	0	97	0	0	15	4.85	0			1.00	Feb-97
2.44	2.31	4.50	11.94	19.82	3.02	0.68	3.46	6.02	10.64	90.7	3	0	97	0	0	15	4.85	100,000				Feb-97
3.94	0.51	3.54	13.61	28.54	3.74	0	6.75		14.65	1,260	0	0	100	0	1	12	5.15					Nov-02
2.11	-0.10	2.09	9.67	18.66	2.98	0.78	5.04	7.24	11.01	1,140	0	0	100	0	0	7	4.96	3,000	100	4.20		Sep-94
1.99	-0.42	1.28	7.06	14.09	2.16	1.58	5.05	7.24	11	1,140	0	0	100	0	0	7	4.96	3,000	100		1.00	Feb-14
1.97	-0.37	1.45	7.89	15.49	2.43	1.32	5.04	7.24	11	1,140	0	0	100	0	0	7	4.96	0			1.00	Sep-94
2.16	0.00	2.31	10.28	19.93	3.2	0.58	5.05	7.24	11.02	1,140	0	0	100	0	0	7	4.96	100,000				Dec-86
2.38	0.19	2.45	11.75	21.66	3.51		4.63		10.02	151.0	1	0	99	0	1	7	5.02					Oct-87
2.34	1.59	3.99	14.16	21.78	2.64	0.83	4.9		15.8	36.8	2	0	98	0	1	17	4.74					Apr-09
3.90	0.32	3.15	13.47	25.90	3.89	0	6.72		15.18	460.0	0	0	100	0	1	8	5.56					May-99
2.29	0.41	2.79	11.09	19.72	3.37		4.32		14.19	55.1	1	0	99	0	1	5	5.15					Jun-92
1.72	1.73	3.74	10.92	17.90	2.26	0.82	4.1	7.03	11.18	625.3	1	0	99	0	0	24	5.01	3,000	100	4.20		Mar-86
1.70	1.41	3.00	8.40	13.36	1.45	1.62	4.12	7.03	11.2	625.3	1	0	99	0	0	24	5.01	3,000	100		1.00	Feb-14
1.67	1.45	3.19	9.09	14.74	1.72	1.37	4.09	7.03	11.19	625.3	1	0	99	0	0	24	5.01	0			1.00	Oct-93
1.86	1.83	3.95	11.57	19.11	2.47	0.62	4.09	7.03	11.23	625.3	1	0	99	0	0	24	5.01	100,000				Feb-97
3.56	3.32	5.24	13.24	21.49	2.46	0.79	3.66	6.77	11.96	682.1	1	0	99	0	0	13	5.04	3,000	100	4.20		Jun-85
3.37	2.92	4.42	10.52	16.76	1.67	1.59	3.69	6.77	11.89	682.1	1	0	99	0	0	13	5.04	3,000	100		1.00	Feb-14
3.52	3.13	4.76	11.44	18.24	1.91	1.33	3.74	6.77	11.93	682.1	1	0	99	0	0	13	5.04	0			1.00	Aug-93

	MARKET		FUND TYPE, CATEGORY & OBJECTIVE		RATINGS				NEW INVESTORS	
Fund Name	Ticker Symbol	Traded On	Fund Type	Category and (Prospectus Objective)	Overall Rating	Reward Rating	Risk Rating	Recent Up/ Downgrade	Open to New Investors	Telephone
Nuveen Ohio Municipal Bond Fund Class I	NXOHX	NAS CM	Open End	US Muni Fixed Inc (Muni Bond - Single State)	B-	C	B	Up	Y	312-917-8146
Nuveen Ohio Quality Municipal Income Fund	NUO	NYSE	Closed End	US Muni Fixed Inc (Muni Bond - Single State)	C	C	C-	Up	Y	312-917-8146
Nuveen Oregon Intermediate Municipal Bond Fund Class A	FOTAX	NAS CM	Open End	US Muni Fixed Inc (Muni Bond - Single State)	C+	C	B	Up	Y	312-917-8146
Nuveen Oregon Intermediate Municipal Bond Fund Class C	NAFOX	NAS CM	Open End	US Muni Fixed Inc (Muni Bond - Single State)	C	C	B-		Y	312-917-8146
Nuveen Oregon Intermediate Municipal Bond Fund Class C2	NIMOX	NAS CM	Open End	US Muni Fixed Inc (Muni Bond - Single State)	C	C	B-			312-917-8146
Nuveen Oregon Intermediate Municipal Bond Fund Class I	FORCX	NAS CM	Open End	US Muni Fixed Inc (Muni Bond - Single State)	C+	C	B	Up	Y	312-917-8146
Nuveen Pennsylvania Municipal Bond Fund Class A	FPNTX	NAS CM	Open End	US Muni Fixed Inc (Muni Bond - Single State)	C	C	B		Y	312-917-8146
Nuveen Pennsylvania Municipal Bond Fund Class C	FPCCX	NAS CM	Open End	US Muni Fixed Inc (Muni Bond - Single State)	C	C-	B-		Y	312-917-8146
Nuveen Pennsylvania Municipal Bond Fund Class C2	FPMBX	NAS CM	Open End	US Muni Fixed Inc (Muni Bond - Single State)	C	C-	B-			312-917-8146
Nuveen Pennsylvania Municipal Bond Fund Class I	NBPAX	NAS CM	Open End	US Muni Fixed Inc (Muni Bond - Single State)	C	C	B		Y	312-917-8146
Nuveen Pennsylvania Municipal Value Fund	NPN	NYSE	Closed End	US Muni Fixed Inc (Muni Bond - Single State)	D+	C-	D	Down	Y	312-917-8146
Nuveen Pennsylvania Quality Municipal Income Fund	NQP	NYSE	Closed End	US Muni Fixed Inc (Muni Bond - Single State)	C-	C-	C-		Y	312-917-8146
Nuveen Quality Muni Income Fund	NAD	NYSE	Closed End	US Muni Fixed Inc (Muni Bond - Natl)	C	C-	C+		Y	312-917-8146
Nuveen Select Maturities Municipal Fund	NIM	NYSE	Closed End	US Muni Fixed Inc (Muni Bond - Natl)	C-	C-	C-		Y	312-917-8146
Nuveen Select Tax-Free Income Portfolio	NXP	NYSE	Closed End	US Muni Fixed Inc (Muni Bond - Natl)	C-	C-	C-	Down	Y	312-917-8146
Nuveen Select Tax-Free Income Portfolio 2	NXQ	NYSE	Closed End	US Muni Fixed Inc (Muni Bond - Natl)	C-	C-	C-		Y	312-917-8146
Nuveen Select Tax-Free Income Portfolio 3	NXR	NYSE	Closed End	US Muni Fixed Inc (Muni Bond - Natl)	C-	C	C-	Down	Y	312-917-8146
Nuveen Senior Income Fund	NSL	NYSE	Closed End	US Fixed Inc (Corp Bond - General)	D	D	D	Down	Y	312-917-8146
Nuveen Short Duration Credit Opportunity Fund	JSD	NYSE	Closed End	US Fixed Inc (Growth & Income)	D	D	D	Down	Y	312-917-8146
Nuveen Short Duration High Yield Muni Bond Fund Class A	NVHAX	NAS CM	Open End	US Muni Fixed Inc (Muni Bond - Natl)	C-	D+	C	Down	Y	312-917-8146
Nuveen Short Duration High Yield Muni Bond Fund Class C	NVCCX	NAS CM	Open End	US Muni Fixed Inc (Muni Bond - Natl)	D+	D+	C	Down	Y	312-917-8146
Nuveen Short Duration High Yield Muni Bond Fund Class C2	NVHCX	NAS CM	Open End	US Muni Fixed Inc (Muni Bond - Natl)	C-	D+	C	Down		312-917-8146
Nuveen Short Duration High Yield Muni Bond Fund Class I	NVHIX	NAS CM	Open End	US Muni Fixed Inc (Muni Bond - Natl)	C-	D+	C	Down	Y	312-917-8146
Nuveen Short Term Municipal Bond Fund Class A	FSHAX	NAS CM	Open End	US Muni Fixed Inc (Muni Bond - Natl)	C	C-	C+		Y	312-917-8146
Nuveen Short Term Municipal Bond Fund Class C	NAAEX	NAS CM	Open End	US Muni Fixed Inc (Muni Bond - Natl)	C	C-	C		Y	312-917-8146
Nuveen Short Term Municipal Bond Fund Class C2	NSVCX	NAS CM	Open End	US Muni Fixed Inc (Muni Bond - Natl)	C	C-	C+			312-917-8146
Nuveen Short Term Municipal Bond Fund Class I	FSHYX	NAS CM	Open End	US Muni Fixed Inc (Muni Bond - Natl)	C	C-	C+		Y	312-917-8146
Nuveen Strategic Income Fund Class A	FCDDX	NAS CM	Open End	US Fixed Inc (Multisector Bond)	C	C-	C		Y	312-917-8146
Nuveen Strategic Income Fund Class C	FCBCX	NAS CM	Open End	US Fixed Inc (Multisector Bond)	C	C-	C		Y	312-917-8146
Nuveen Strategic Income Fund Class I	FCBYX	NAS CM	Open End	US Fixed Inc (Multisector Bond)	C	C-	C+		Y	312-917-8146
Nuveen Strategic Income Fund Class R3	FABSX	NAS CM	Open End	US Fixed Inc (Multisector Bond)	C	C-	C		Y	312-917-8146
Nuveen Strategic Income Fund Class R6	FSFRX	NAS CM	Open End	US Fixed Inc (Multisector Bond)	C	C-	C+		Y	312-917-8146
Nuveen Strategic Municipal Opportunities Fund Class A	NSAOX	NAS CM	Open End	US Muni Fixed Inc (Muni Bond - Natl)	C	C-	B	Down	Y	312-917-8146
Nuveen Strategic Municipal Opportunities Fund Class C	NSCOX	NAS CM	Open End	US Muni Fixed Inc (Muni Bond - Natl)	C	C-	B-		Y	312-917-8146
Nuveen Strategic Municipal Opportunities Fund Class I	NSIOX	NAS CM	Open End	US Muni Fixed Inc (Muni Bond - Natl)	C	C-	B	Down	Y	312-917-8146
Nuveen Symphony Floating Rate Income Fund Class A	NFRAX	NAS CM	Open End	US Fixed Inc (Growth)	D	D	C-	Down	Y	312-917-8146
Nuveen Symphony Floating Rate Income Fund Class C	NFFCX	NAS CM	Open End	US Fixed Inc (Growth)	D	D	C-	Down	Y	312-917-8146
Nuveen Symphony Floating Rate Income Fund Class I	NFRIX	NAS CM	Open End	US Fixed Inc (Growth)	D+	D	C-	Down	Y	312-917-8146
Nuveen Symphony Floating Rate Income Fund Class R6	NFRFX	NAS CM	Open End	US Fixed Inc (Growth)	D+	D	C-	Down	Y	312-917-8146
Nuveen Symphony High Yield Income Fund Class A	NCOAX	NAS CM	Open End	US Fixed Inc (Corp Bond - High Yield)	D+	D	C-	Down	Y	312-917-8146
Nuveen Symphony High Yield Income Fund Class C	NCFCX	NAS CM	Open End	US Fixed Inc (Corp Bond - High Yield)	D	D	D+	Down	Y	312-917-8146
Nuveen Symphony High Yield Income Fund Class I	NCOIX	NAS CM	Open End	US Fixed Inc (Corp Bond - High Yield)	D+	D	C-	Down	Y	312-917-8146
Nuveen Symphony High Yield Income Fund Class R6	NCSRX	NAS CM	Open End	US Fixed Inc (Corp Bond - High Yield)	D+	D	C-	Down	Y	312-917-8146
Nuveen Taxable Municipal Income Fund	NBB	NYSE	Closed End	US Fixed Inc (Govt Bond - Treasury)	C-	C-	C-		Y	312-917-8146
Nuveen Tennessee Municipal Bond Fund Class A	FTNTX	NAS CM	Open End	US Muni Fixed Inc (Muni Bond - Single State)	C	C-	B-		Y	312-917-8146
Nuveen Tennessee Municipal Bond Fund Class C	FTNDX	NAS CM	Open End	US Muni Fixed Inc (Muni Bond - Single State)	C	C-	C+		Y	312-917-8146
Nuveen Tennessee Municipal Bond Fund Class C2	FTNCX	NAS CM	Open End	US Muni Fixed Inc (Muni Bond - Single State)	C	C-	C+			312-917-8146
Nuveen Tennessee Municipal Bond Fund Class I	FTNRX	NAS CM	Open End	US Muni Fixed Inc (Muni Bond - Single State)	C	C-	B-		Y	312-917-8146
Nuveen Virginia Municipal Bond Fund Class A	FVATX	NAS CM	Open End	US Muni Fixed Inc (Muni Bond - Single State)	C	C-	B-		Y	312-917-8146
Nuveen Virginia Municipal Bond Fund Class C	FVCCX	NAS CM	Open End	US Muni Fixed Inc (Muni Bond - Single State)	C	C-	C+		Y	312-917-8146
Nuveen Virginia Municipal Bond Fund Class C2	FVACX	NAS CM	Open End	US Muni Fixed Inc (Muni Bond - Single State)	C	C-	B-			312-917-8146
Nuveen Virginia Municipal Bond Fund Class I	NMVAX	NAS CM	Open End	US Muni Fixed Inc (Muni Bond - Single State)	C	C-	B-		Y	312-917-8146

★Expanded analysis of this fund is included in Section II.

TOTAL RETURNS & PERFORMANCE									ASSETS		ASSET ALLOCATION & TURNOVER							MINIMUMS		FEES		
3-Month Total Return	6-Month Total Return	1-Year Total Return	3-Year Total Return	5-Year Total Return	Dividend Yield (TTM)	Expense Ratio	3-Yr Std Deviation	Effective Duration	NAV	Total Assets (MIL)	%Cash	%Government Bonds	%Municipal Bonds	%Corporate Bonds	%Other	Turnover Ratio	Average Coupon Rate	Min Initial Investment	Min Additional Investment	Front End Fee (%)	Back End Fee (%)	Inception Date
3.63	3.43	5.47	13.94	22.77	2.67	0.59	3.66	6.77	11.92	682.1	1	0	99	0	0	13	5.04	100,000				Feb-97
4.47	3.80	6.73	17.49	29.97	2.97		5.87		17.49	318.7	0	0	100	0	1	15	5.40					Oct-91
2.71	2.44	4.25	10.40	16.18	1.98	0.82	3.48	5.15	10.65	243.0	0	0	100	0	0	18	4.80	3,000	100	3.00		Feb-99
2.52	2.04	3.35	7.78	11.62	1.19	1.62	3.49	5.15	10.59	243.0	0	0	100	0	0	18	4.80	3,000	100		1.00	Feb-14
2.57	2.15	3.57	8.61	12.99	1.42	1.37	3.51	5.15	10.63	243.0	0	0	100	0	0	18	4.80	3,000	100		1.00	Jan-11
2.75	2.52	4.42	11.07	17.40	2.14	0.62	3.49	5.15	10.67	243.0	0	0	100	0	0	18	4.80	100,000				Aug-97
2.74	1.92	3.90	13.62	21.47	2.63	0.8	4.33	7.72	11.3	483.5	2	0	98	0	0	14	4.48	3,000	100	4.20		Oct-86
2.54	1.61	3.09	10.91	16.66	1.83	1.6	4.28	7.72	11.26	483.5	2	0	98	0	0	14	4.48	3,000	100		1.00	Feb-14
2.60	1.65	3.36	11.73	18.17	2.1	1.35	4.3	7.72	11.27	483.5	2	0	98	0	0	14	4.48	0			1.00	Feb-94
2.80	2.03	4.12	14.27	22.57	2.84	0.6	4.35	7.72	11.28	483.5	2	0	98	0	0	14	4.48	100,000				Feb-97
2.85	1.12	2.98	11.72	18.81	2.94	0.89	4.66		15.19	18.3	1	0	99	0	1	20	4.88					Apr-09
4.31	2.11	4.62	18.02	28.64	3.9	0	6.64		15.76	580.6	2	0	98	0	-1	11	5.90					Feb-91
4.15	0.90	4.27	17.05	31.38	4.22	1.2	7.52		15.69	3,238	0	0	100	0	1	8	5.23					May-99
3.65	1.40	3.39	12.58	19.89	2.99		4.03		10.74	132.2	1	0	99	0	0	13	4.55					Sep-92
2.59	1.53	4.57	17.19	29.59	3.43		5.01		16.04	264.1	0	0	100	0	0	10	5.03					Mar-92
2.85	1.60	4.58	15.69	27.77	3.34		4.97		15.33	267.5	1	0	99	0	1	0	5.00					May-92
2.47	2.21	5.13	17.68	31.13	3.18		5.13		16.55	214.2	0	0	100	0	1	13	5.02					Jul-92
9.82	-14.44	-11.61	-4.01	4.58	8.19	1.32	13.26		5.41	206.6	4	0	0	96	-4	31	4.39					Oct-99
10.51	-15.21	-12.98	-5.48	3.93	8.47	0	13.91		13.66	136.0	3	0	0	97	-3	33	4.45					May-11
2.30	-4.23	-1.97	10.32	17.76	3.82	0.82	5.77	4.90	9.9	4,513	1	0	97	1	0	26	5.03	3,000	100	2.50		Feb-13
2.18	-4.53	-2.67	7.75	13.24	2.96	1.62	5.76	4.90	9.91	4,513	1	0	97	1	0	26	5.03	3,000	100		1.00	Feb-14
2.15	-4.50	-2.53	8.53	14.58	3.21	1.37	5.76	4.90	9.9	4,513	1	0	97	1	0	26	5.03	0			1.00	Feb-13
2.34	-4.13	-1.80	11.00	18.90	4	0.62	5.78	4.90	9.92	4,513	1	0	97	1	0	26	5.03	100,000				Feb-13
1.80	0.80	1.78	5.33	7.00	1.57	0.72	1.72	2.00	10.17	714.6	4	0	96	0	0	37	4.26	3,000	100	2.50		Oct-02
1.71	0.51	1.09	2.89	2.92	0.78	1.52	1.76	2.00	10.15	714.6	4	0	96	0	0	37	4.26	3,000	100		1.00	Feb-14
1.81	0.72	1.52	4.32	5.22	1.22	1.06	1.76	2.00	10.17	714.6	4	0	96	0	0	37	4.26	0			1.00	Aug-11
1.86	0.92	2.00	5.95	8.01	1.78	0.52	1.76	2.00	10.18	714.6	4	0	96	0	0	37	4.26	100,000				Oct-02
8.78	0.95	4.52	12.09	20.37	3.7	0.85	6.9	4.38	10.69	584.9	2	3	2	61	1	54	4.54	3,000	100	4.25		Feb-00
8.62	0.56	3.83	9.67	16.05	2.93	1.6	6.84	4.38	10.64	584.9	2	3	2	61	1	54	4.54	3,000	100		1.00	Feb-00
8.84	1.06	4.75	12.87	21.89	3.93	0.6	6.92	4.38	10.69	584.9	2	3	2	61	1	54	4.54	100,000				Feb-00
8.79	0.83	4.27	11.28	18.93	3.46	1.1	6.87	4.38	10.73	584.9	2	3	2	61	1	54	4.54	0				Sep-01
8.84	1.02	4.85	13.18	22.45	4.03	0.51	6.89	4.38	10.73	584.9	2	3	2	61	1	54	4.54	5,000,000				Jan-15
4.50	1.09	3.54	18.98	30.12	2.62	0.83	5.94	9.44	11.09	798.6	1	0	99	0	0	62	4.67	3,000	100	3.00		Dec-14
4.29	0.59	2.63	16.17	24.87	1.81	1.63	5.96	9.44	11.08	798.6	1	0	99	0	0	62	4.67	3,000	100		1.00	Dec-14
4.55	1.20	3.66	19.64	31.29	2.84	0.63	5.99	9.44	11.1	798.6	1	0	99	0	0	62	4.67	100,000				Dec-14
6.78	-6.34	-4.06	1.99	9.27	6.02	1.01	7.58	0.31	17.39	829.0	3	0	0	97	0	32		3,000	100	3.00		May-11
6.58	-6.75	-4.79	-0.31	5.20	5.2	1.76	7.61	0.31	17.39	829.0	3	0	0	97	0	32		3,000	100		1.00	May-11
6.84	-6.26	-3.86	2.70	10.62	6.29	0.77	7.61	0.31	17.4	829.0	3	0	0	97	0	32		100,000				May-11
6.84	-6.20	-3.79	3.15	11.18	6.4	0.67	7.59	0.31	17.47	829.0	3	0	0	97	0	32		1,000,000				Jan-15
7.93	-8.26	-5.09	5.55	15.86	6.27	1.01	9.33	2.86	17.99	472.7	5	0	0	95	0	70	6.48	3,000	100	4.75		Apr-10
7.73	-8.59	-5.82	3.20	11.60	5.44	1.76	9.33	2.86	17.97	472.7	5	0	0	95	0	70	6.48	3,000	100		1.00	Apr-10
8.05	-8.09	-4.85	6.37	17.35	6.53	0.76	9.34	2.86	18.01	472.7	5	0	0	95	0	70	6.48	100,000				Apr-10
8.06	-8.04	-4.74	6.74	17.93	6.67	0.65	9.34	2.86	18.08	472.7	5	0	0	95	0	70	6.48	1,000,000				Oct-14
11.61	2.45	5.26	17.84	37.02	5.58	1.01	10.96		21.9	567.4	-24	0	98	0	26	16	7.45					Apr-10
2.06	1.17	2.94	9.31	16.84	3.03	0.94	3.36	5.78	11.77	375.3	1	0	99	0	0	7	5.38	3,000	100	4.20		Nov-87
1.85	0.76	2.12	6.76	12.32	2.21	1.74	3.36	5.78	11.74	375.3	1	0	99	0	0	7	5.38	3,000	100		1.00	Feb-14
1.92	0.88	2.37	7.48	13.73	2.46	1.49	3.34	5.78	11.76	375.3	1	0	99	0	0	7	5.38	0			1.00	Oct-93
2.11	1.27	3.15	10.00	18.06	3.24	0.74	3.39	5.78	11.75	375.3	1	0	99	0	0	7	5.38	100,000				Feb-97
2.71	1.37	3.80	11.45	20.14	2.65	0.8	4.38	7.22	11.4	566.4	2	0	99	0	0	29	4.83	3,000	100	4.20		Mar-86
2.42	0.97	2.89	8.80	15.41	1.85	1.6	4.36	7.22	11.39	566.4	2	0	99	0	0	29	4.83	3,000	100		1.00	Feb-14
2.48	1.11	3.16	9.60	16.83	2.12	1.35	4.34	7.22	11.39	566.4	2	0	99	0	0	29	4.83	0			1.00	Oct-93
2.77	1.57	4.01	12.17	21.33	2.86	0.6	4.35	7.22	11.38	566.4	2	0	99	0	0	29	4.83	100,000				Feb-97

	MARKET		FUND TYPE, CATEGORY & OBJECTIVE		RATINGS				NEW INVESTORS	
Fund Name	Ticker Symbol	Traded On	Fund Type	Category and (Prospectus Objective)	Overall Rating	Reward Rating	Risk Rating	Recent Up/ Downgrade	Open to New Investors	Telephone
Nuveen Virginia Quality Municipal Income Fund	NPV	NYSE	Closed End	US Muni Fixed Inc (Muni Bond - Single State)	C-	C-	C-		Y	312-917-8146
Nuveen Wisconsin Municipal Bond Fund Class A	FWIAX	NAS CM	Open End	US Muni Fixed Inc (Muni Bond - Single State)	C	C-	B-			312-917-8146
Nuveen Wisconsin Municipal Bond Fund Class C	FWCCX	NAS CM	Open End	US Muni Fixed Inc (Muni Bond - Single State)	C	C-	C+		Y	312-917-8146
Nuveen Wisconsin Municipal Bond Fund Class C2	FWICX	NAS CM	Open End	US Muni Fixed Inc (Muni Bond - Single State)	C	C-	C+			312-917-8146
Nuveen Wisconsin Municipal Bond Fund Class I	FWIRX	NAS CM	Open End	US Muni Fixed Inc (Muni Bond - Single State)	C	C-	B-			312-917-8146
OFS Credit Company Inc	OCCI	NAS CM	Closed End	US Fixed Inc (Income)	D	D	D		Y	
Oklahoma Municipal Fund Class A	OKMUX	NAS CM	Open End	US Muni Fixed Inc (Muni Bond - Single State)	C	C	B-		Y	800-276-1262
Oklahoma Municipal Fund Class I	OKMIX	NAS CM	Open End	US Muni Fixed Inc (Muni Bond - Single State)	C+	C	B	Up	Y	800-276-1262
Old Westbury California Municipal Bond Fund	OWCAX	NAS CM	Open End	US Muni Fixed Inc (Growth & Income)	D	D+	C+		Y	212-708-9100
Old Westbury Fixed Income Fund	OWFIX	NAS CM	Open End	US Fixed Inc (Corp Bond - General)	B-	C+	B		Y	212-708-9100
Old Westbury Municipal Bond Fund	OWMBX	NAS CM	Open End	US Muni Fixed Inc (Muni Bond - Natl)	C+	C	B	Up	Y	212-708-9100
Old Westbury New York Municipal Bond Fund	OWNYX	NAS CM	Open End	US Muni Fixed Inc (Growth & Income)	D	D+	C+		Y	212-708-9100
Optimum Fixed Income Fund Class A	OAFIX	NAS CM	Open End	US Fixed Inc (Income)	B	C+	B+	Up	Y	
Optimum Fixed Income Fund Class C	OCFIX	NAS CM	Open End	US Fixed Inc (Income)	B-	C+	B	Up	Y	
Optimum Fixed Income Fund Institutional Class	OIFIX	NAS CM	Open End	US Fixed Inc (Income)	B	C+	B+	Up	Y	
Osterweis Strategic Income Fund	OSTIX	NAS CM	Open End	US Fixed Inc (Multisector Bond)	D+	D	C	Down	Y	866-236-0050
Osterweis Total Return Fund	OSTRX	NAS CM	Open End	US Fixed Inc (Multisector Bond)	C+	C	B-	Up	Y	866-236-0050
Oxford Lane Capital Corporation	OXLC	NAS CM	Closed End	US Fixed Inc (Income)	C-	D+	C	Down	Y	
PACE Global Fixed Income Investments Class A	PWFAX	NAS CM	Open End	Global Fixed Inc (Worldwide Bond)	C	C	B-		Y	212-882-5586
PACE Global Fixed Income Investments Class P	PCGLX	NAS CM	Open End	Global Fixed Inc (Worldwide Bond)	C	C	B-		Y	212-882-5586
PACE Global Fixed Income Investments Class Y	PWFYX	NAS CM	Open End	Global Fixed Inc (Worldwide Bond)	C	C	B-		Y	212-882-5586
PACE Government Money Market Investments Class P	PCEXX	NAS CM	Money Mkt	US Money Mkt (Money Mkt - Govt)	C	C-	C		Y	212-882-5586
PACE High Yield Investments Class A	PHIAX	NAS CM	Open End	US Fixed Inc (Corp Bond - High Yield)	D+	D	C-	Down	Y	212-882-5586
PACE High Yield Investments Class P	PHYPX	NAS CM	Open End	US Fixed Inc (Corp Bond - High Yield)	D+	D	C-	Down	Y	212-882-5586
PACE High Yield Investments Class Y	PHDYX	NAS CM	Open End	US Fixed Inc (Corp Bond - High Yield)	D+	D	C-	Down	Y	212-882-5586
PACE Intermediate Fixed Income Investments Class A	PIFAX	NAS CM	Open End	US Fixed Inc (Govt Bond - General)	B-	C+	B	Up	Y	212-882-5586
PACE Intermediate Fixed Income Investments Class P	PCIFX	NAS CM	Open End	US Fixed Inc (Govt Bond - General)	B	C+	B	Up	Y	212-882-5586
PACE Intermediate Fixed Income Investments Class Y	PIFYX	NAS CM	Open End	US Fixed Inc (Govt Bond - General)	B	C+	B	Up	Y	212-882-5586
PACE Mortgage-Backed Securities Fixed Income Inv Cl A	PFXAX	NAS CM	Open End	US Fixed Inc (Govt Bond - General)	B-	C+	B	Up	Y	212-882-5586
PACE Mortgage-Backed Securities Fixed Income Inv Cl P	PCGTX	NAS CM	Open End	US Fixed Inc (Govt Bond - General)	B-	C+	B	Up	Y	212-882-5586
PACE Mortgage-Backed Securities Fixed Income Inv Cl Y	PFXYX	NAS CM	Open End	US Fixed Inc (Govt Bond - General)	B-	C+	B	Up	Y	212-882-5586
PACE Municipal Fixed Income Investments Class A	PMUAX	NAS CM	Open End	US Muni Fixed Inc (Muni Bond - Natl)	C	C-	B-		Y	212-882-5586
PACE Municipal Fixed Income Investments Class P	PCMNX	NAS CM	Open End	US Muni Fixed Inc (Muni Bond - Natl)	C	C	B-		Y	212-882-5586
PACE Municipal Fixed Income Investments Class Y	PMUYX	NAS CM	Open End	US Muni Fixed Inc (Muni Bond - Natl)	C	C	B-		Y	212-882-5586
PACE Strategic Fixed Income Investments Class A	PBNAX	NAS CM	Open End	US Fixed Inc (Corp Bond - General)	B-	C+	B+	Up	Y	212-882-5586
PACE Strategic Fixed Income Investments Class P	PCSIX	NAS CM	Open End	US Fixed Inc (Corp Bond - General)	B-	C+	B+	Up	Y	212-882-5586
PACE Strategic Fixed Income Investments Class Y	PSFYX	NAS CM	Open End	US Fixed Inc (Corp Bond - General)	B-	C+	B+	Up	Y	212-882-5586
Pacific Capital Tax Free Securities Fund Class Y	PTXFX	NAS CM	Open End	US Muni Fixed Inc (Muni Bond - Natl)	C+	C	B	Up	Y	
Pacific Capital Tax Free Short Intermed Securities Cl Y	PTFSX	NAS CM	Open End	US Muni Fixed Inc (Muni Bond - Natl)	C	C	B-		Y	
Pacific Capital U.S. Govt Money Mkt Fund Investor Class	PCUXX	NAS CM	Money Mkt	US Money Mkt (Money Mkt - Govt)	C-	D+	C+	Up	Y	
Pacific Funds Core Income Class P			Open End	US Fixed Inc (Income)	B-	C	B	Up	Y	800-722-2333
Pacific Funds Core Income Fund Advisor Class	PLIDX	NAS CM	Open End	US Fixed Inc (Income)	B-	C	B	Up	Y	800-722-2333
Pacific Funds Core Income Fund Class A	PLIAX	NAS CM	Open End	US Fixed Inc (Income)	B-	C	B	Up	Y	800-722-2333
Pacific Funds Core Income Fund Class C	PLNCX	NAS CM	Open End	US Fixed Inc (Income)	C+	C	B	Up	Y	800-722-2333
Pacific Funds Core Income Fund Class I	PLIIX	NAS CM	Open End	US Fixed Inc (Income)	B-	C	B	Up	Y	800-722-2333
Pacific Funds Floating Rate Income Fund Advisor Class	PLFDX	NAS CM	Open End	US Fixed Inc (Income)	D+	D	C	Down	Y	800-722-2333
Pacific Funds Floating Rate Income Fund Class A	PLFLX	NAS CM	Open End	US Fixed Inc (Income)	D+	D	C	Down	Y	800-722-2333
Pacific Funds Floating Rate Income Fund Class C	PLBCX	NAS CM	Open End	US Fixed Inc (Income)	D+	D	C-	Down	Y	800-722-2333
Pacific Funds Floating Rate Income Fund Class I	PLFRX	NAS CM	Open End	US Fixed Inc (Income)	C-	D+	C		Y	800-722-2333
Pacific Funds Floating Rate Income Fund Class P Shares			Open End	US Fixed Inc (Income)	C-	D+	C		Y	800-722-2333
Pacific Funds High Income Fund Advisor Class	PLHYX	NAS CM	Open End	US Fixed Inc (Income)	C-	D+	C		Y	800-722-2333
Pacific Funds High Income Fund Class A	PLAHX	NAS CM	Open End	US Fixed Inc (Income)	C-	D+	C		Y	800-722-2333

★Expanded analysis of this fund is included in Section II.

TOTAL RETURNS & PERFORMANCE									ASSETS		ASSET ALLOCATION & TURNOVER							MINIMUMS		FEES		
3-Month Total Return	6-Month Total Return	1-Year Total Return	3-Year Total Return	5-Year Total Return	Dividend Yield (TTM)	Expense Ratio	3-Yr Std Deviation	Effective Duration	NAV	Total Assets (MIL)	%Cash	%Government Bonds	%Municipal Bonds	%Corporate Bonds	%Other	Turnover Ratio	Average Coupon Rate	Min Initial Investment	Min Additional Investment	Front End Fee (%)	Back End Fee (%)	Inception Date
3.89	1.09	4.54	15.31	26.39	3.62		7.06		14.84	259.4	-1	0	100	0	2	21	5.41					Mar-93
2.88	0.52	2.85	12.23	18.59	2.7	0.93	4.56	8.66	10.84	157.2	0	0	100	0	0	26	4.90	3,000	100	4.20		Jun-94
2.68	0.12	2.02	9.56	13.99	1.87	1.73	4.56	8.66	10.84	157.2	0	0	100	0	0	26	4.90	3,000	100		1.00	Feb-14
2.74	0.25	2.29	10.34	15.42	2.14	1.48	4.55	8.66	10.85	157.2	0	0	100	0	0	26	4.90	0			1.00	Feb-97
2.93	0.62	3.04	12.82	19.84	2.89	0.73	4.54	8.66	10.86	157.2	0	0	100	0	0	26	4.90	100,000				Feb-97
0.00	0.00	-16.40			13.37	14.34			13.4298	42.7	5	0	0	7	-44	29	8.79					Oct-18
1.39	1.53	3.12	9.23	15.97	2.12	0.98	3.26		11.94	63.7	0	0	100	0	0	18	4.21	1,000	50	2.50		Sep-96
1.45	1.66	3.37	10.03	16.81	2.37	0.73	3.27		11.95	63.7	0	0	100	0	0	18	4.21	1,000	50			Nov-17
2.51	2.70	3.83			1.19	0.57			10.58	376.5	0	8	91	0	0	41	4.65	1,000	100			Dec-18
1.71	5.58	7.23	13.03	15.68	1.84	0.57	2.48		11.88	1,553	4	76	0	16	0	34	2.26	1,000	100			Mar-98
2.51	2.83	4.19	9.26	13.35	1.3	0.58	2.8		12.53	3,928	2	9	90	0	0	26	4.64	1,000	100			Mar-98
2.02	2.21	3.33			1.25	0.58			10.56	546.2	1	10	89	0	0	29	4.67	1,000	100			Dec-18
5.17	5.38	7.38	14.65	20.31	2.26	1.08	3.6	5.61	10.17	2,575	4	27	0	29	-28	361	3.27	1,000	100	4.50		Aug-03
4.96	4.96	6.57	12.14	15.92	1.52	1.83	3.56	5.61	10.15	2,575	4	27	0	29	-28	361	3.27	1,000	100		1.00	Aug-03
5.27	5.60	7.67	15.56	21.77	2.51	0.83	3.57	5.61	10.17	2,575	4	27	0	29	-28	361	3.27	0				Aug-03
7.38	-0.31	-0.09	7.17	17.33	4.68	0.85	5.06	1.74	10.59	4,144	11	0	0	87	1	40	5.77	5,000	100			Aug-02
3.44	2.34	5.53	12.49		2.41	0.68	2.13	4.29	10.38	177.4	10	2	0	33	0	214	3.22	5,000	100			Dec-16
0.00	0.00	-4.62	6.12	26.14	26.41	12.45	18.33		6	461.2	-6	0	0	2	0	18	13.75					Jan-11
3.03	1.89	2.79	7.88	13.65	1.55	1.04	3.92	7.18	10.18	324.7	9	52	0	22	0	54	3.02	1,000	100	3.75		Dec-00
3.10	2.02	3.05	8.44	14.67	1.8	0.85	3.88	7.18	10.16	324.7	9	52	0	22	0	54	3.02	10,000	500			Aug-95
3.11	2.03	3.07	8.36	14.59	1.81	0.88	3.89	7.18	10.12	324.7	9	52	0	22	0	54	3.02	2,000,000	0			Jan-01
0.00	0.20	0.91	3.39	3.49	1.14	0.6	0.17		1	328.2	55	45	0	0	0	212	0.44	5,000	500			Aug-95
11.75	-5.39	-2.29	6.23	21.24	6.18	1.06	10	3.09	8.98	255.7	3	2	0	95	0	62	6.11	1,000	100	3.75		May-06
11.82	-5.37	-2.14	6.62	22.15	6.45	0.91	10.05	3.09	8.98	255.7	3	2	0	95	0	62	6.11	10,000	500			Apr-06
11.98	-5.18	-1.96	7.01	22.59	6.41	0.88	10.04	3.09	9.03	255.7	3	2	0	95	0	62	6.11	2,000,000	0			Dec-08
4.35	5.94	8.14	14.54	18.93	2.11	0.91	3.41	5.32	13.16	336.7	2	54	0	18	0	511	2.85	1,000	100	3.75		Jan-01
4.41	5.98	8.32	15.38	20.41	2.35	0.66	3.47	5.32	13.16	336.7	2	54	0	18	0	511	2.85	10,000	500			Aug-95
4.41	6.07	8.41	15.39	20.42	2.35	0.66	3.4	5.32	13.16	336.7	2	54	0	18	0	511	2.85	2,000,000	0			Feb-01
2.53	3.77	5.66	11.40	16.21	3.17	1.25	2.31	1.93	13	335.3	-9	4	0	0	0	905	3.38	1,000	100	3.75		Jan-01
2.67	3.90	6.01	12.24	17.66	3.41	1	2.3	1.93	13.01	335.3	-9	4	0	0	0	905	3.38	10,000	500			Aug-95
2.67	3.90	6.01	12.24	17.76	3.41	0.98	2.31	1.93	13.01	335.3	-9	4	0	0	0	905	3.38	2,000,000	0			Feb-01
2.52	1.18	2.93	9.92	16.71	2.15	0.82	3.89	4.77	13.21	321.0	0	0	100	0	0	21	4.86	1,000	100	2.25		Jan-01
2.59	1.30	3.19	10.80	18.23	2.4	0.57	3.92	4.77	13.22	321.0	0	0	100	0	0	21	4.86	10,000	500			Aug-95
2.67	1.38	3.27	10.81	18.08	2.4	0.57	3.9	4.77	13.22	321.0	0	0	100	0	0	21	4.86	2,000,000	0			Feb-01
5.38	5.46	8.17	16.13	24.61	3.09	1.48	4.19	4.76	14.61	708.9	2	51	0	22	0	308	2.92	1,000	100	3.75		Dec-00
5.37	5.59	8.37	16.93	26.14	3.34	1.2	4.13	4.76	14.6	708.9	2	51	0	22	0	308	2.92	10,000	500			Aug-95
5.38	5.60	8.39	16.96	26.00	3.35	1.21	4.12	4.76	14.58	708.9	2	51	0	22	0	308	2.92	2,000,000	0			Feb-01
2.55	2.80	4.80	11.90	18.53	2.46	0.11	3.28		10.6	271.9	1	0	99	0	0	11	4.75	0				Oct-94
1.93	1.74	2.81	6.06	8.73	1.61	0.34	1.7		10.28	52.3	4	0	96	0	0	34	4.49	0				Oct-94
0.00	0.24	1.02			1.2	0.78			1	182.7	100	0	0	0	0			0				Jun-18
6.88	4.18	7.39	16.43	24.20	2.79	0.55	4.67	6.37	11.3	1,032	1	15	0	69	0	70	3.39	0				Apr-15
6.90	4.19	7.40	16.47	24.23	2.79	0.55	4.69	6.37	11.28	1,032	1	15	0	69	0	70	3.39	0				Jun-12
6.73	3.95	7.00	15.37	22.42	2.51	0.85	4.66	6.37	11.25	1,032	1	15	0	69	0	70	3.39	1,000	50	4.25		Dec-10
6.54	3.57	6.20	12.80	17.89	1.77	1.6	4.69	6.37	11.25	1,032	1	15	0	69	0	70	3.39	1,000	50		1.00	Jun-11
6.81	4.10	7.31	16.39	24.36	2.79	0.55	4.65	6.37	11.26	1,032	1	15	0	69	0	70	3.39	500,000				Dec-10
6.80	-4.28	-1.86	6.28	16.12	4.88	0.77	6.87	0.34	9.34	1,332	6	2	0	92	0	116	4.51	0				Jun-12
6.75	-4.33	-2.08	5.49	14.70	4.59	1.02	6.87	0.34	9.31	1,332	6	2	0	92	0	116	4.51	1,000	50	3.00		Dec-11
6.46	-4.81	-2.83	3.24	10.53	3.8	1.72	6.83	0.34	9.29	1,332	6	2	0	92	0	116	4.51	1,000	50		1.00	Dec-11
6.83	-4.27	-1.82	6.45	16.32	4.94	0.72	6.89	0.34	9.32	1,332	6	2	0	92	0	116	4.51	500,000				Jun-11
6.83	-4.27	-1.82	6.43	16.25	4.94	0.72	6.86	0.34	9.32	1,332	6	2	0	92	0	116	4.51	0				Dec-12
9.86	-5.73	-2.15	8.14	19.58	5.62	0.7	9.39	3.80	9.48	136.0	3	0	0	95	0	63	6.28	0				Jun-12
9.81	-5.85	-2.40	7.24	18.11	5.37	0.95	9.38	3.80	9.47	136.0	3	0	0	95	0	63	6.28	1,000	50	4.25		Jun-12

	MARKET			FUND TYPE, CATEGORY & OBJECTIVE	RATINGS				NEW INVESTORS	
Fund Name	Ticker Symbol	Traded On	Fund Type	Category and (Prospectus Objective)	Overall Rating	Reward Rating	Risk Rating	Recent Up/ Downgrade	Open to New Investors	Telephone
Pacific Funds High Income Fund Class C	PLCHX	NAS CM	Open End	US Fixed Inc (Income)	D+	D	C-	Down	Y	800-722-2333
Pacific Funds High Income Fund Class I	PLHIX	NAS CM	Open End	US Fixed Inc (Income)	C-	D+	C		Y	800-722-2333
Pacific Funds High Income Fund Class P			Open End	US Fixed Inc (Income)	C-	D+	C		Y	800-722-2333
Pacific Funds Short Duration Income Fund Advisor Class	PLDSX	NAS CM	Open End	US Fixed Inc (Growth & Income)	C	C	B-		Y	800-722-2333
Pacific Funds Short Duration Income Fund Class A	PLADX	NAS CM	Open End	US Fixed Inc (Growth & Income)	C	C-	B-		Y	800-722-2333
Pacific Funds Short Duration Income Fund Class C	PLCSX	NAS CM	Open End	US Fixed Inc (Growth & Income)	C	C-	C+		Y	800-722-2333
Pacific Funds Short Duration Income Fund Class I	PLSDX	NAS CM	Open End	US Fixed Inc (Growth & Income)	C	C-	C+		Y	800-722-2333
Pacific Funds Strategic Income Fund Advisor Class	PLSFX	NAS CM	Open End	US Fixed Inc (Multisector Bond)	C	C-	C+		Y	800-722-2333
Pacific Funds Strategic Income Fund Class A	PLSTX	NAS CM	Open End	US Fixed Inc (Multisector Bond)	C	C-	C+	Up	Y	800-722-2333
Pacific Funds Strategic Income Fund Class C	PLCNX	NAS CM	Open End	US Fixed Inc (Multisector Bond)	C-	D+	C		Y	800-722-2333
Pacific Funds Strategic Income Fund Class I	PLSRX	NAS CM	Open End	US Fixed Inc (Multisector Bond)	C	C-	C+		Y	800-722-2333
Pacific Funds Ultra Short Income Advisor Class	PLUDX	NAS CM	Open End	US Fixed Inc (Income)	D-	D+	C		Y	800-722-2333
Pacific Funds Ultra Short Income Class I	PLUIX	NAS CM	Open End	US Fixed Inc (Income)	D-	D+	C		Y	800-722-2333
Palmer Square Income Plus Fund	PSYPX	NAS CM	Open End	US Fixed Inc (Income)	C-	D+	C		Y	866-933-9033
Palmer Square Opportunistic Income Fund	PSOIX	NAS CM	Closed End	Fixed Inc Misc (Income)	D	D	D	Down	Y	866-933-9033
Palmer Square Ultra-Short Duration Investment Grade Fund	PSDSX	NAS CM	Open End	US Fixed Inc (Income)	C	C-	C+		Y	866-933-9033
Parametric TABS 10-to-20 Year Laddered Muni Bond Cl A	EATTX	NAS CM	Open End	US Muni Fixed Inc (Muni Bond - Natl)	C+	C	B		Y	
Parametric TABS 10-to-20 Year Laddered Muni Bond Cl C	ECTTX	NAS CM	Open End	US Muni Fixed Inc (Muni Bond - Natl)	C+	C	B		Y	
Parametric TABS 10-to-20 Year Laddered Muni Bond Cl I	EITTX	NAS CM	Open End	US Muni Fixed Inc (Muni Bond - Natl)	C+	C	B		Y	
Parametric TABS 1-to-10 Year Laddered Muni Bond Cl A	EALBX	NAS CM	Open End	US Muni Fixed Inc (Muni Bond - Natl)	C	C	B-		Y	
Parametric TABS 1-to-10 Year Laddered Muni Bond Cl C	ECLBX	NAS CM	Open End	US Muni Fixed Inc (Muni Bond - Natl)	C	C-	C+		Y	
Parametric TABS 1-to-10 Year Laddered Muni Bond Cl I	EILBX	NAS CM	Open End	US Muni Fixed Inc (Muni Bond - Natl)	C	C	B-		Y	
Parametric TABS 5-to-15 Year Laddered Muni Bond Cl A	EALTX	NAS CM	Open End	US Muni Fixed Inc (Muni Bond - Natl)	C	C	B		Y	
Parametric TABS 5-to-15 Year Laddered Muni Bond Cl C	ECLTX	NAS CM	Open End	US Muni Fixed Inc (Muni Bond - Natl)	C	C	B-		Y	
Parametric TABS 5-to-15 Year Laddered Muni Bond Cl I	EILTX	NAS CM	Open End	US Muni Fixed Inc (Muni Bond - Natl)	C+	C	B	Up	Y	
Parametric TABS Intermediate-Term Muni Bond Fund Class A	EITAX	NAS CM	Open End	US Muni Fixed Inc (Muni Bond - Natl)	C+	C	B	Up	Y	
Parametric TABS Intermediate-Term Muni Bond Fund Class C	EITCX	NAS CM	Open End	US Muni Fixed Inc (Muni Bond - Natl)	C	C	B-		Y	
Parametric TABS Intermediate-Term Muni Bond Fund Class I	ETIIX	NAS CM	Open End	US Muni Fixed Inc (Muni Bond - Natl)	C+	C	B	Up	Y	
Parametric TABS Short-Term Municipal Bond Fund Class A	EABSX	NAS CM	Open End	US Muni Fixed Inc (Muni Bond - Natl)	C+	C	B	Up	Y	
Parametric TABS Short-Term Municipal Bond Fund Class C	ECBSX	NAS CM	Open End	US Muni Fixed Inc (Muni Bond - Natl)	C	C	B-		Y	
Parametric TABS Short-Term Municipal Bond Fund Class I	EIBSX	NAS CM	Open End	US Muni Fixed Inc (Muni Bond - Natl)	B-	C	B	Up	Y	
Parnassus Fixed Income Fund	PRFIX	NAS CM	Open End	US Fixed Inc (Corp Bond - General)	B	B-	B	Up	Y	999-350-5
Parnassus Fixed Income Fund Institutional Shares	PFPLX	NAS CM	Open End	US Fixed Inc (Corp Bond - General)	B	B-	B	Up	Y	999-350-5
Pax Core Bond Fund Individual Investor Class	PAXBX	NAS CM	Open End	US Fixed Inc (Multisector Bond)	B-	C+	B		Y	800-767-1729
Pax Core Bond Fund Institutional Class	PXBIX	NAS CM	Open End	US Fixed Inc (Multisector Bond)	B-	C+	B		Y	800-767-1729
Pax High Yield Bond Fund Class A	PXHAX	NAS CM	Open End	US Fixed Inc (Corp Bond - High Yield)	C	C-	C+		Y	800-767-1729
Pax High Yield Bond Fund Individual Investor Class	PAXHX	NAS CM	Open End	US Fixed Inc (Corp Bond - High Yield)	C	C-	C+		Y	800-767-1729
Pax High Yield Bond Fund Institutional Class	PXHIX	NAS CM	Open End	US Fixed Inc (Corp Bond - High Yield)	C	C-	C+		Y	800-767-1729
Payden Absolute Return Bond Fund Investor Class	PYARX	NAS CM	Open End	Fixed Inc Misc (Growth & Income)	C-	D+	C		Y	614-470-8006
Payden Absolute Return Bond Fund SI Class	PYAIX	NAS CM	Open End	Fixed Inc Misc (Growth & Income)	C-	D+	C		Y	614-470-8006
Payden California Municipal Social Impact Fund	PYCRX	NAS CM	Open End	US Muni Fixed Inc (Muni Bond - Single State)	C	C-	B	Down	Y	614-470-8006
Payden Cash Reserves Money Market Fund	PBHXX	NAS CM	Money Mkt	US Money Mkt (Money Mkt - Govt)	C	C-	C+		Y	614-470-8006
Payden Core Bond Fund Advisor Class	PYCWX	NAS CM	Open End	US Fixed Inc (Corp Bond - High Quality)	C+	C	B	Up	Y	614-470-8006
Payden Core Bond Fund Investor Class	PYCBX	NAS CM	Open End	US Fixed Inc (Corp Bond - High Quality)	C+	C	B	Up	Y	614-470-8006
Payden Core Bond Fund SI Class	PYCSX	NAS CM	Open End	US Fixed Inc (Corp Bond - High Quality)	C+	C	B	Up	Y	614-470-8006
Payden Corporate Bond Fund	PYACX	NAS CM	Open End	US Fixed Inc (Corp Bond - General)	C	C	B		Y	614-470-8006
Payden Emerging Markets Bond Fund Advisor Class	PYEWX	NAS CM	Open End	Emerg Mkts Fixed Inc (Income)	D+	D+	C-	Down	Y	614-470-8006
Payden Emerging Markets Bond Fund Investor Class	PYEMX	NAS CM	Open End	Emerg Mkts Fixed Inc (Income)	D+	D+	C-	Down	Y	614-470-8006
Payden Emerging Markets Bond Fund SI Class	PYEIX	NAS CM	Open End	Emerg Mkts Fixed Inc (Income)	D+	D+	C-	Down	Y	614-470-8006
Payden Emerging Markets Corporate Bond Fund Investor Class	PYCEX	NAS CM	Open End	Emerg Mkts Fixed Inc (Income)	C-	D+	C	Down	Y	614-470-8006
Payden Emerging Markets Corporate Bond Fund SI Class	PYCIX	NAS CM	Open End	Emerg Mkts Fixed Inc (Income)	C-	D+	C	Down	Y	614-470-8006
Payden Emerging Markets Local Bond Fund Investor Class	PYELX	NAS CM	Open End	Emerg Mkts Fixed Inc (Income)	D	D	D+	Down	Y	614-470-8006

★ Expanded analysis of this fund is included in Section II.

TOTAL RETURNS & PERFORMANCE									ASSETS		ASSET ALLOCATION & TURNOVER							MINIMUMS		FEES		
3-Month Total Return	6-Month Total Return	1-Year Total Return	3-Year Total Return	5-Year Total Return	Dividend Yield (TTM)	Expense Ratio	3-Yr Std Deviation	Effective Duration	NAV	Total Assets (MIL)	%Cash	%Government Bonds	%Municipal Bonds	%Corporate Bonds	%Other	Turnover Ratio	Average Coupon Rate	Min Initial Investment	Min Additional Investment	Front End Fee (%)	Back End Fee (%)	Inception Date
9.63	-6.18	-3.10	5.11	13.97	4.63	1.65	9.37	3.80	9.46	136.0	3	0	0	95	0	63	6.28	1,000	50		1.00	Jun-12
9.73	-5.79	-2.28	7.99	19.49	5.69	0.7	9.35	3.80	9.37	136.0	3	0	0	95	0	63	6.28	500,000				Dec-11
9.86	-5.79	-2.28	8.09	19.46	5.68	0.7	9.41	3.80	9.37	136.0	3	0	0	95	0	63	6.28	0				Jan-15
4.71	1.38	3.10	9.10	13.17	2.43	0.5	3.1	1.88	10.47	1,071	1	11	0	67	0	56	2.77	0				Jun-12
4.54	1.15	2.85	8.20	11.68	2.19	0.75	3.08	1.88	10.46	1,071	1	11	0	67	0	56	2.77	1,000	50	3.00		Jun-12
4.36	0.78	2.08	5.82	7.61	1.45	1.5	3.08	1.88	10.44	1,071	1	11	0	67	0	56	2.77	1,000	50		1.00	Jun-12
4.71	1.38	3.11	9.12	13.16	2.44	0.5	3.16	1.88	10.45	1,071	1	11	0	67	0	56	2.77	500,000				Dec-11
11.58	-0.36	3.36	13.79	24.21	4.2	0.71	8.22	4.05	10.73	687.4	2	1	0	90	0	98	4.82	0				Jun-12
11.40	-0.58	3.01	12.84	22.67	3.95	0.96	8.23	4.05	10.72	687.4	2	1	0	90	0	98	4.82	1,000	50	4.25		Jun-12
11.35	-0.92	2.30	10.55	18.34	3.26	1.66	8.28	4.05	10.7	687.4	2	1	0	90	0	98	4.82	1,000	50		1.00	Jun-12
11.56	-0.34	3.34	13.94	24.55	4.28	0.66	8.24	4.05	10.66	687.4	2	1	0	90	0	98	4.82	500,000				Dec-11
4.36	1.04	2.47				0.32		0.81	10.03	25.7	11	7	0	60	0	81	2.25	0				Jun-19
4.36	1.03	2.46				0.32		0.81	10.03	25.7	11	7	0	60	0	81	2.25	500,000				Jun-19
8.43	-0.20	1.53	8.00	13.03	3.12	0.78	5.64		9.75	568.8	17	0	0	36	7		3.19	250,000				Feb-14
24.20	-6.71	-4.24	3.67	12.01	6.89	1.86	16.78		16.63	--	5	0	0	11	4	74	7.13	250,000	2,500	3.00		Aug-14
2.44	0.79	1.90	6.49		2.41	0.51	1.62		20.01	40.8	34	0	0	21	5		2.56	250,000				Oct-16
2.95	2.77	5.61	16.71	30.18	2.32	0.65	4.92	5.80	11.39	15.3	9	0	91	0	0	33	4.33	1,000		4.75		May-15
2.76	2.48	4.82	14.11	25.48	1.57	1.4	4.91	5.80	11.4	15.3	9	0	91	0	0	33	4.33	1,000			1.00	May-15
3.01	2.98	5.96	17.58	31.96	2.57	0.4	4.92	5.80	11.4	15.3	9	0	91	0	0	33	4.33	250,000				May-15
2.95	2.05	3.34	8.17	13.79	1.53	0.65	2.75	3.34	10.64	68.8	8	0	92	0	0	41	3.58	1,000		2.25		May-15
2.76	1.67	2.57	5.78	9.56	0.78	1.4	2.8	3.34	10.64	68.8	8	0	92	0	0	41	3.58	1,000			1.00	May-15
3.01	2.08	3.60	8.99	15.34	1.78	0.4	2.74	3.34	10.65	68.8	8	0	92	0	0	41	3.58	250,000				May-15
2.91	2.47	4.13	11.10	21.46	1.8	0.65	3.94	5.21	12.89	719.9	5	0	95	0	0	28	4.66	1,000		4.75		Feb-10
2.64	2.01	3.36	8.64	16.99	1.05	1.4	3.91	5.21	12.88	719.9	5	0	95	0	0	28	4.66	1,000			1.00	Feb-10
2.98	2.51	4.39	12.03	23.00	2.05	0.4	3.94	5.21	12.88	719.9	5	0	95	0	0	28	4.66	250,000				Feb-10
3.51	3.51	5.21	11.18	18.95	1.66	0.9	3.73	5.17	12.94	501.4	9	0	91	0	0	74	4.38	1,000		4.75		Feb-10
3.24	3.05	4.43	8.63	14.49	0.93	1.65	3.67	5.17	12.93	501.4	9	0	91	0	0	74	4.38	1,000			1.00	Feb-10
3.49	3.63	5.47	12.01	20.43	1.91	0.65	3.69	5.17	12.95	501.4	9	0	91	0	0	74	4.38	250,000				Feb-10
2.57	4.25	5.42	8.79	12.02	1.3	0.82	2.26	3.87	10.92	322.2	11	0	89	0	0	51	4.68	1,000		2.25		Mar-09
2.30	3.88	4.55	6.39	7.82	0.57	1.57	2.23	3.87	10.89	322.2	11	0	89	0	0	51	4.68	1,000			1.00	Mar-09
2.54	4.38	5.58	9.61	13.42	1.54	0.57	2.22	3.87	10.92	322.2	11	0	89	0	0	51	4.68	250,000				Mar-09
3.19	6.65	8.87	16.42	23.29	1.95	0.68	3.51	6.46	18.03	293.1	4	49	0	46	0	54	2.93	2,000	50			Aug-92
3.30	6.82	9.11	17.27	24.54	2.16	0.45	3.54	6.46	18.03	293.1	4	49	0	46	0	54	2.93	100,000	50			Apr-15
3.34	5.59	7.86	14.32		2.18	0.71	3.43		10.76	687.0	4	29	4	29	0		3.09	1,000	50			Dec-16
3.40	5.72	8.13	15.17		2.43	0.46	3.42		10.76	687.0	4	29	4	29	0		3.09	250,000				Dec-16
8.81	-1.50	2.67	10.89	22.61	4.99	0.96	7.12	3.08	6.53	342.3	2	0	0	98	0		5.97	1,000	50	4.50		May-13
8.66	-1.66	2.51	10.72	22.24	4.99	0.96	7.12	3.08	6.51	342.3	2	0	0	98	0		5.97	1,000	50			Oct-99
8.75	-1.40	2.76	11.70	23.89	5.25	0.71	7.05	3.08	6.49	342.3	2	0	0	98	0		5.97	250,000				Jun-04
8.73	-1.00	0.38	6.90	13.17	3.09	0.7	6.48	1.92	9.8	722.6	-5	20	0	23	0	82	3.52	100,000	250			Nov-14
8.90	-0.88	0.61	7.66	14.18	3.33	0.47	6.48	1.92	9.81	722.6	-5	20	0	23	0	82	3.52	50,000,000	250			Nov-14
1.89	1.36	3.80	12.75	19.03	2.22	0.53	3.9	4.52	10.44	59.1	2	0	92	6	-4	132	4.56	5,000	250			Dec-98
0.02	0.30	1.19	4.39	4.76	1.37	0.25	0.18		1	340.2	60	37	0	10	0			5,000	250			Dec-97
5.34	3.38	5.64	12.87	21.04	2.61	0.78	4.36	5.96	11.05	972.2	-9	27	1	31	0	86	3.55	5,000	250			Nov-09
5.40	3.40	5.89	13.66	22.46	2.85	0.53	4.37	5.96	11.07	972.2	-9	27	1	31	0	86	3.55	100,000	250			Dec-93
5.52	3.55	6.11	13.98	22.81	2.96	0.42	4.4	5.96	11.07	972.2	-9	27	1	31	0	86	3.55	50,000,000	250			Jan-18
9.29	3.44	7.71	18.73	34.85	3.09	0.65	7.21	7.66	11.95	440.5	-1	11	2	85	0	49	4.24	5,000	250			Mar-09
13.35	-4.01	-1.38	8.65	25.05	5.42	0.97	11.82	7.26	12.9	952.6	4	63	0	16	0	73	6.11	5,000	250			Nov-09
13.34	-3.98	-1.15	9.39	26.51	5.68	0.72	11.81	7.26	12.88	952.6	4	63	0	16	0	73	6.11	100,000	250			Dec-98
13.29	-3.94	-1.16	9.49	26.84	5.75	0.69	11.82	7.26	12.86	952.6	4	63	0	16	0	73	6.11	50,000,000	250			Apr-12
11.07	-1.49	1.18	10.67	23.24	4.83	0.95	8.86	4.89	9.7	39.7	7	9	0	74	0	94	5.45	100,000	250			Nov-13
11.19	-1.35	1.39	10.99	23.82	4.93	0.85	8.93	4.89	9.72	39.7	7	9	0	74	0	94	5.45	50,000,000	250			Nov-13
10.54	-8.51	-5.09	-0.21	7.99	5.85	0.91	13.39	5.61	5.87	134.7	6	49	0	8	0	62	6.57	100,000	250			Nov-11

	MARKET			FUND TYPE, CATEGORY & OBJECTIVE	RATINGS				NEW INVESTORS	
Fund Name	Ticker Symbol	Traded On	Fund Type	Category and (Prospectus Objective)	Overall Rating	Reward Rating	Risk Rating	Recent Up/ Downgrade	Open to New Investors	Telephone
Payden Floating Rate Fund Investor Class	PYFRX	NAS CM	Open End	US Fixed Inc (Income)	D+	D	C-	Down	Y	614-470-8006
Payden Floating Rate Fund SI Class	PYFIX	NAS CM	Open End	US Fixed Inc (Income)	D+	D	C-	Down	Y	614-470-8006
Payden Global Fixed Income Fund	PYGFX	NAS CM	Open End	Global Fixed Inc (Worldwide Bond)	C	C	B		Y	614-470-8006
Payden Global Low Duration Fund	PYGSX	NAS CM	Open End	Global Fixed Inc (Worldwide Bond)	C	C-	C+		Y	614-470-8006
Payden GNMA Fund Investor Class	PYGNX	NAS CM	Open End	US Fixed Inc (Govt Bond - Mortgage)	B-	C+	B	Up	Y	614-470-8006
Payden High Income Fund Investor Class	PYHRX	NAS CM	Open End	US Fixed Inc (Corp Bond - High Yield)	C-	D+	C		Y	614-470-8006
Payden Limited Maturity Fund	PYLMX	NAS CM	Open End	US Fixed Inc (Corp Bond - High Quality)	C	C-	C+		Y	614-470-8006
Payden Low Duration Fund	PYSBX	NAS CM	Open End	US Fixed Inc (Corp Bond - High Quality)	C	C-	C+		Y	614-470-8006
Payden Strategic Income Fund Investor Class	PYSGX	NAS CM	Open End	US Fixed Inc (Income)	C	C-	C+		Y	614-470-8006
Payden Strategic Income Fund SI Class	PYSIX	NAS CM	Open End	US Fixed Inc (Income)	C	C-	C+		Y	614-470-8006
Payden U.S. Government Fund Investor Class	PYUSX	NAS CM	Open End	US Fixed Inc (Govt Bond - General)	C+	C	B		Y	614-470-8006
Payden/Kravitz Cash Balance Plan Fund Advisor Class	PKCBX	NAS CM	Open End	US Fixed Inc (Income)	D	D	C-	Down	Y	614-470-8006
Payden/Kravitz Cash Balance Plan Fund Institutional Class	PKCIX	NAS CM	Open End	US Fixed Inc (Income)	D+	D	C-	Down	Y	614-470-8006
Payden/Kravitz Cash Balance Plan Fund Retirement Class	PKCRX	NAS CM	Open End	US Fixed Inc (Income)	D	D	C-	Down	Y	614-470-8006
Payden/Kravitz Cash Balance Plan Fund SI Class	PKBIX	NAS CM	Open End	US Fixed Inc (Income)	D+	D	C-	Down	Y	614-470-8006
PCM Fund	PCM	NYSE	Closed End	US Fixed Inc (Corp Bond - General)	D	D	D	Down	Y	866-746-2602
Penn Capital Defensive Floating Rate Income Inst Cl	PFRNX	NAS CM	Open End	US Fixed Inc (Income)	D+	D	C	Down	Y	
Penn Capital Defensive Short Duration High Income Inst Cl	PSHNX	NAS CM	Open End	US Fixed Inc (Corp Bond - High Yield)	D+	D	C	Down	Y	
Penn Capital Multi-Credit High Income Institutional Cl	PHYNX	NAS CM	Open End	US Fixed Inc (Growth & Income)	D	D	D+	Down	Y	
Penn Mutual AM Strategic Income Fund I Shares	PMUBX	NAS CM	Open End	Fixed Inc Misc (Growth & Income)	C-	D+	C	Up	Y	877--
Performance Trust Municipal Bond Fund - A Class	PTRMX	NAS CM	Open End	US Muni Fixed Inc (Muni Bond - Natl)	C	C	B	Down	Y	
Performance Trust Muni Bond Fund - Institutional Class	PTIMX	NAS CM	Open End	US Muni Fixed Inc (Muni Bond - Natl)	C+	C	B		Y	
Performance Trust Strategic Bond Fund	PTIAX	NAS CM	Open End	US Fixed Inc (Growth & Income)	C	C-	B-		Y	
Performance Trust Strategic Bond Fund Class A	PTAOX	NAS CM	Open End	US Fixed Inc (Growth & Income)	C	C-	B-		Y	
Performance Trust Strategic Bond Fund Class C	PTCOX	NAS CM	Open End	US Fixed Inc (Growth & Income)	C	C-	C+		Y	
Permanent Portfolio Short-Term Treasury Portfolio Class I	PRTBX	NAS CM	Open End	US Fixed Inc (Govt Bond - Treasury)	C	C-	C+		Y	800-531-5142
Permanent Portfolio Versatile Bond Portfolio Class A	PRVDX	NAS CM	Open End	US Fixed Inc (Multisector Bond)	C	C-	C+	Up	Y	800-531-5142
Permanent Portfolio Versatile Bond Portfolio Class C	PRVHX	NAS CM	Open End	US Fixed Inc (Multisector Bond)	C	D+	C+	Up	Y	800-531-5142
Permanent Portfolio Versatile Bond Portfolio Class I	PRVBX	NAS CM	Open End	US Fixed Inc (Multisector Bond)	C	C-	B-	Up	Y	800-531-5142
PF Emerging Markets Debt Fund Class P			Open End	Emerg Mkts Fixed Inc (Diversified Emerg Mkts)	D	D	D	Down	Y	800-722-2333
PF Inflation Managed Fund Class P			Open End	US Fixed Inc (Growth & Income)	B	C+	B+	Up	Y	800-722-2333
PF Managed Bond Fund Class P			Open End	US Fixed Inc (Corp Bond - General)	B	C+	B+	Up	Y	800-722-2333
PF Short Duration Bond Fund Class P			Open End	US Fixed Inc (Growth & Income)	C	C	B-		Y	800-722-2333
PFG Active Core Bond Strategy Fund Class R	PFDOX	NAS CM	Open End	US Fixed Inc (Growth & Income)	C	C-	C+		Y	800-735-7199
PFM Multi-Manager Fixed-Income Fund Institutional Class			Open End	US Fixed Inc (Growth & Income)	C	C	B		Y	
PGIM Absolute Return Bond Fund- Class A	PADAX	NAS CM	Open End	Fixed Inc Misc (Income)	D+	D	C-	Down	Y	800-225-1852
PGIM Absolute Return Bond Fund- Class C	PADCX	NAS CM	Open End	Fixed Inc Misc (Income)	D	D	C-	Down	Y	800-225-1852
PGIM Absolute Return Bond Fund- Class R6	PADQX	NAS CM	Open End	Fixed Inc Misc (Income)	D+	D	C-	Down	Y	800-225-1852
PGIM Absolute Return Bond Fund- Class Z	PADZX	NAS CM	Open End	Fixed Inc Misc (Income)	D+	D	C-	Down	Y	800-225-1852
PGIM California Muni Income Fund-Class A	PBCAX	NAS CM	Open End	US Muni Fixed Inc (Muni Bond - Single State)	C	C-	C+		Y	800-225-1852
PGIM California Muni Income Fund-Class B	PCAIX	NAS CM	Open End	US Muni Fixed Inc (Muni Bond - Single State)	C	C-	C			800-225-1852
PGIM California Muni Income Fund-Class C	PCICX	NAS CM	Open End	US Muni Fixed Inc (Muni Bond - Single State)	C	C-	C		Y	800-225-1852
PGIM California Muni Income Fund-Class R6	PCIQX	NAS CM	Open End	US Muni Fixed Inc (Muni Bond - Single State)	C	C-	C+		Y	800-225-1852
PGIM California Muni Income Fund-Class Z	PCIZX	NAS CM	Open End	US Muni Fixed Inc (Muni Bond - Single State)	C	C-	C+		Y	800-225-1852
PGIM Core Bond Fund- Class A	TPCAX	NAS CM	Open End	US Fixed Inc (Corp Bond - General)	B-	C+	B	Up	Y	800-225-1852
PGIM Core Bond Fund- Class C	TPCCX	NAS CM	Open End	US Fixed Inc (Corp Bond - General)	C+	C	B	Up	Y	800-225-1852
PGIM Core Bond Fund- Class R	TPCRX	NAS CM	Open End	US Fixed Inc (Corp Bond - General)	B-	C+	B	Up	Y	800-225-1852
PGIM Core Bond Fund- Class R6	TPCQX	NAS CM	Open End	US Fixed Inc (Corp Bond - General)	B-	C+	B+	Up	Y	800-225-1852
PGIM Core Bond Fund- Class Z	TAIBX	NAS CM	Open End	US Fixed Inc (Corp Bond - General)	B-	C+	B+	Up	Y	800-225-1852
PGIM Core Conservative Bond Fund-Class R6	PQCNX	NAS CM	Open End	US Fixed Inc (Multisector Bond)	B	C+	B	Up	Y	800-225-1852
PGIM Core Short-Term Bond Fund			Open End	US Fixed Inc (Income)	C	C-	C+		Y	800-225-1852
PGIM Corporate Bond Fund- Class A	PCWAX	NAS CM	Open End	US Fixed Inc (Corp Bond - General)	C+	C	B	Up	Y	800-225-1852

★Expanded analysis of this fund is included in Section II.

TOTAL RETURNS & PERFORMANCE									ASSETS		ASSET ALLOCATION & TURNOVER							MINIMUMS		FEES		
3-Month Total Return	6-Month Total Return	1-Year Total Return	3-Year Total Return	5-Year Total Return	Dividend Yield (TTM)	Expense Ratio	3-Yr Std Deviation	Effective Duration	NAV	Total Assets (ML)	%Cash	%Government Bonds	%Municipal Bonds	%Corporate Bonds	%Other	Turnover Ratio	Average Coupon Rate	Min Initial Investment	Min Additional Investment	Front End Fee (%)	Back End Fee (%)	Inception Date
7.87	-4.69	-1.92	5.16	12.84	4.44	0.76	7.07	0.71	9.33	65.8	7	0	0	87	-4	29	4.53	100,000	250			Nov-13
8.02	-4.54	-1.82	5.51	13.46	4.54	0.66	7.13	0.71	9.34	65.8	7	0	0	87	-4	29	4.53	50,000,000	250			Nov-13
6.04	2.18	3.84	13.02	20.61	2.93	0.71	4.76	6.93	9.21	151.2	-3	21	0	14	0	67	3.02	5,000	250			Sep-92
4.24	1.10	2.34	7.21	9.63	2.52	0.53	2.93	1.82	10.03	103.8	-21	42	0	31	0	107	2.59	5,000	250			Sep-96
0.73	3.86	5.35	10.90	14.77	3.13	0.5	2.44	2.63	9.57	123.1	4	0	0	0	-39	18	3.30	100,000	250			Aug-99
11.88	-4.18	0.05	11.27	23.12	5.62	0.63	9.78	4.16	6.19	401.5	7	0	0	87	0	74	5.94	100,000	250			Dec-97
3.10	0.68	2.02	6.66	8.79	2.25	0.25	2.05	0.64	9.47	922.2	11	12	0	34	0	74	2.10	5,000	250			Apr-94
3.90	1.85	3.18	7.62	10.22	2.12	0.43	2.4	1.84	10.18	1,409	-16	41	0	31	0	166	2.35	5,000	250			Dec-93
8.52	0.86	2.73	10.27	17.61	3.17	0.7	5.91	3.74	10.12	131.0	0	16	4	44	0	72	3.82	100,000	250			May-14
8.57	0.84	2.79	10.51	18.29	3.33	0.55	5.99	3.74	10.11	131.0	0	16	4	44	0	72	3.82	50,000,000	250			May-14
1.61	3.76	5.22	8.88	10.21	2.64	0.43	1.45	2.73	10.58	43.4	0	0	0	0	0	49	3.09	100,000	250			Jan-95
11.08	-2.93	-1.92	4.70	8.46	3.54	1.5	8.5	1.92	9.92	158.1	-19	28	0	14	0	84	3.69	25,000				Sep-08
11.14	-2.74	-1.45	6.45	12.99	3.56	0.95	8.49	1.92	10.27	158.1	-19	28	0	14	0	84	3.69	5,000,000				Jun-16
10.95	-3.08	-2.10	3.95	7.24	3.75	1.75	8.46	1.92	9.42	158.1	-19	28	0	14	0	84	3.69	25,000				Apr-09
11.14	-2.86	-1.71	5.51	9.86	3.53	1.25	8.49	1.92	10.17	158.1	-19	28	0	14	0	84	3.69	25,000				Sep-08
14.07	-10.97	-8.18	11.64	35.32	11.65		14.66		8.46	95.7	-139	26	0	17	0	8	3.61					Sep-93
7.17	-5.02	-2.56	5.13		4.68	0.64	7.22	1.71	9.3	36.2	2	0	0	98	0	57	4.35	10,000	100			Nov-15
4.37	-4.76	-2.43	3.79		3.96	0.54		1.53	9.33	44.4	7	1	0	92	0	48	5.72	10,000	100			Jul-17
7.57	-8.64	-5.95	3.41		6.06	0.72	9.27	3.58	8.88	17.5	-1	0	0	99	0	85	5.72	10,000	100			Nov-15
5.52	0.62	2.47			2.55	0.78			10.07	113.4	11	25	6	20	0	83	3.54	25,000				Jul-18
2.87	2.21	4.65	14.00	24.26	2.45	0.8	4.89		25.35	444.0	3	0	96	1	0	35	4.84	1,000	500	2.25		Sep-12
2.94	2.32	4.90	14.86	25.78	2.69	0.55	4.9		25.33	444.0	3	0	96	1	0	35	4.84	2,500	500			Jun-11
3.91	1.30	3.12	13.75	27.11	4.08	0.81	4.52		22.68	3,670	8	0	26	7	0	41	3.91	2,500	500			Aug-10
3.80	1.15	2.85	12.98	25.62	3.86	1.06	4.51		22.68	3,670	8	0	26	7	0	41	3.91	1,000	500	2.25		Jan-19
3.63	0.78	2.08	10.44	20.98	3.2	1.81	4.52		22.61	3,670	8	0	26	7	0	41	3.91	1,000	500			Jan-19
-0.10	0.38	1.05	3.47	2.86	1.64	0.66	0.26		65.27	14.2	65	35	0	0	0	55	1.46	1,000	100			Sep-87
13.53	0.44	3.50	13.54	20.22	2.25	0.91	9.06	3.22	61.39	8.9	13	0	0	87	0	53	4.12	1,000	100	4.00		May-16
13.31	0.04	2.72	11.00	15.80	1.55	1.66	9.06	3.22	61.02	8.9	13	0	0	87	0	53	4.12	1,000	100		1.00	May-16
13.59	0.57	3.76	14.37	21.73	2.52	0.66	9.05	3.22	61.48	8.9	13	0	0	87	0	53	4.12	1,000	100			Sep-91
14.90	-8.94	-8.97	-0.18	18.76	5.98	0.93	13.87		8.25	81.2	8	55	0	11	0	73	6.82	0				Jun-12
6.02	5.90	8.43	15.55	18.90	1.22	1.07	4.08		9.68	21.5	1	67	0	4	0	249	1.34	0				Dec-02
5.53	6.39	9.18	17.64	29.06	1.24	0.63	4.01	6.84	11.64	403.5	2	22	0	31	0	512	3.51	0				Sep-01
4.40	2.51	3.95	8.77	11.19	2.59	0.55	2.4		10.2	143.4	5	1	0	54	0	109	3.18	0				Dec-03
4.82	1.99	3.19			1.94	2.51			10.22	197.1	-33	29	0	14	6	38	3.61	0				Dec-17
5.51	3.84	6.55			2.92	0.56			10.7	831.5	2	16	8	40	0	84	3.57	1,000,000	0			Dec-17
9.05	-6.10	-3.40	4.10	11.25	3.74	0.96	8.58	0.65	8.79	1,537	12	5	1	14	1	50	4.44	1,000	100	3.25		Mar-11
8.96	-6.43	-4.09	1.78	7.17	2.95	1.72	8.57	0.65	8.82	1,537	12	5	1	14	1	50	4.44	1,000	100		1.00	Mar-11
9.28	-5.95	-3.08	4.94	12.90	4.08	0.65	8.6	0.65	8.79	1,537	12	5	1	14	1	50	4.44	0				Mar-11
9.09	-5.95	-3.11	4.95	12.70	4.03	0.73	8.54	0.65	8.83	1,537	12	5	1	14	1	50	4.44	0				Mar-11
1.64	-0.03	1.91	9.56	16.78	2.93	0.69	4.26	6.61	10.6	189.3	2	0	98	0	0	61	4.81	1,000	100	3.25		Dec-90
0.83	-0.38	1.47	7.95	14.29	2.41	1.41	4.26	6.61		189.3	2	0	98	0	0	61	4.81	2,500	100		5.00	Dec-93
1.43	-0.42	1.20	6.98	12.36	2.12	1.5	4.26	6.61	10.6	189.3	2	0	98	0	0	61	4.81	1,000	100		1.00	Aug-94
1.74	0.12	2.17	10.61	17.90	3.18	0.38	4.24	6.61	10.6	189.3	2	0	98	0	0	61	4.81	0				Oct-17
1.74	0.11	2.16	10.29	18.19	3.17	0.39	4.26	6.61	10.6	189.3	2	0	98	0	0	61	4.81	0				Sep-96
5.12	5.36	7.92	15.30	22.62	2.49	0.67	4.08	5.56	10.61	1,094	4	9	1	29	0	69	3.33	1,000	100	3.25		Feb-15
4.92	4.96	7.22	12.85	18.11	1.75	1.45	4.03	5.56	10.62	1,094	4	9	1	29	0	69	3.33	1,000	100		1.00	Feb-15
5.06	5.22	7.76	14.44	21.16	2.24	0.95	4.01	5.56	10.61	1,094	4	9	1	29	0	69	3.33	0				Feb-15
5.11	5.55	8.31	16.40	24.52	2.83	0.32	4.08	5.56	10.61	1,094	4	9	1	29	0	69	3.33	0				Feb-15
5.22	5.54	8.28	16.26	24.31	2.8	0.33	4.14	5.56	10.61	1,094	4	9	1	29	0	69	3.33	0				Jan-93
3.08	5.67	8.22	15.14		2.5	0.5	3.46		10.67	51.4	5	37	1	26	0	107	3.14	0				Nov-16
2.55	0.72	2.18	7.66	11.09	2.73	0.03	1.54	0.19	9.18	2,716	-13	27	0	33	0	43	2.33	0				Nov-05
9.52	3.93	8.04	16.96	30.27	2.89	0.8	7.07	7.56	12.01	39.5	3	3	1	87	0	71	3.89	1,000	100	3.25		May-15

	MARKET			FUND TYPE, CATEGORY & OBJECTIVE	RATINGS				NEW INVESTORS	
Fund Name	Ticker Symbol	Traded On	Fund Type	Category and (Prospectus Objective)	Overall Rating	Reward Rating	Risk Rating	Recent Up/ Downgrade	Open to New Investors	Telephone
PGIM Corporate Bond Fund- Class C	PCWCX	NAS CM	Open End	US Fixed Inc (Corp Bond - General)	C	C	B-		Y	800-225-1852
PGIM Corporate Bond Fund- Class R	PCWRX	NAS CM	Open End	US Fixed Inc (Corp Bond - General)	C+	C	B	Up	Y	800-225-1852
PGIM Corporate Bond Fund- Class R6	PCWQX	NAS CM	Open End	US Fixed Inc (Corp Bond - General)	C+	C	B	Up	Y	800-225-1852
PGIM Corporate Bond Fund- Class Z	TGMBX	NAS CM	Open End	US Fixed Inc (Corp Bond - General)	C+	C	B	Up	Y	800-225-1852
PGIM Emerging Markets Debt Hard Currency Fund-Class A	PDHAX	NAS CM	Open End	Emerg Mkts Fixed Inc (Diversified Emerg Mkts)	D	D	D+	Down	Y	800-225-1852
PGIM Emerging Markets Debt Hard Currency Fund-Class C	PDHCX	NAS CM	Open End	Emerg Mkts Fixed Inc (Diversified Emerg Mkts)	D	D	D+	Down	Y	800-225-1852
PGIM Emerging Markets Debt Hard Currency Fund-Class R6	PDHQX	NAS CM	Open End	Emerg Mkts Fixed Inc (Diversified Emerg Mkts)	D	D	D+	Down	Y	800-225-1852
PGIM Emerging Markets Debt Hard Currency Fund-Class Z	PDHVX	NAS CM	Open End	Emerg Mkts Fixed Inc (Diversified Emerg Mkts)	D	D	D+	Down	Y	800-225-1852
PGIM Emerging Markets Debt Local Currency Fund-Class A	EMDAX	NAS CM	Open End	Emerg Mkts Fixed Inc (Growth & Income)	D	D	D+	Down	Y	800-225-1852
PGIM Emerging Markets Debt Local Currency Fund-Class C	EMDCX	NAS CM	Open End	Emerg Mkts Fixed Inc (Growth & Income)	D	D	D+	Down	Y	800-225-1852
PGIM Emerging Markets Debt Local Currency Fund-Class R6	EMDQX	NAS CM	Open End	Emerg Mkts Fixed Inc (Growth & Income)	D	D	D+	Down	Y	800-225-1852
PGIM Emerging Markets Debt Local Currency Fund-Class Z	EMDZX	NAS CM	Open End	Emerg Mkts Fixed Inc (Growth & Income)	D	D	D+	Down	Y	800-225-1852
PGIM Floating Rate Income Fund- Class A	FRFAX	NAS CM	Open End	US Fixed Inc (Income)	D	D	C-	Down	Y	800-225-1852
PGIM Floating Rate Income Fund- Class C	FRFCX	NAS CM	Open End	US Fixed Inc (Income)	D	D	D+	Down	Y	800-225-1852
PGIM Floating Rate Income Fund- Class R6	PFRIX	NAS CM	Open End	US Fixed Inc (Income)	D	D	C-	Down	Y	800-225-1852
PGIM Floating Rate Income Fund- Class Z	FRFZX	NAS CM	Open End	US Fixed Inc (Income)	D	D	C-	Down	Y	800-225-1852
PGIM Global Dynamic Bond Fund- Class A	PAJAX	NAS CM	Open End	Fixed Inc Misc (Growth & Income)	D+	D+	C-	Down	Y	800-225-1852
PGIM Global Dynamic Bond Fund- Class C	PAJCX	NAS CM	Open End	Fixed Inc Misc (Growth & Income)	D+	D	C-	Down	Y	800-225-1852
PGIM Global Dynamic Bond Fund- Class R6	PAJQX	NAS CM	Open End	Fixed Inc Misc (Growth & Income)	D+	D+	C-	Down	Y	800-225-1852
PGIM Global Dynamic Bond Fund- Class Z	PAJZX	NAS CM	Open End	Fixed Inc Misc (Growth & Income)	D+	D+	C-	Down	Y	800-225-1852
PGIM Global High Yield Fund, Inc.	GHY	NYSE	Closed End	Global Fixed Inc (Income)	D+	D	C-	Down	Y	800-225-1852
PGIM Global Total Return (USD Hedged) Fund- Class A	PHEAX	NAS CM	Open End	Global Fixed Inc (Worldwide Bond)	C	C	B-		Y	800-225-1852
PGIM Global Total Return (USD Hedged) Fund- Class C	PHECX	NAS CM	Open End	Global Fixed Inc (Worldwide Bond)	C	C	B-		Y	800-225-1852
PGIM Global Total Return (USD Hedged) Fund- Class R6	PHEQX	NAS CM	Open End	Global Fixed Inc (Worldwide Bond)	C	C	B		Y	800-225-1852
PGIM Global Total Return (USD Hedged) Fund- Class Z	PHEZX	NAS CM	Open End	Global Fixed Inc (Worldwide Bond)	C	C	B		Y	800-225-1852
PGIM Global Total Return Fund - Class A	GTRAX	NAS CM	Open End	Global Fixed Inc (Worldwide Bond)	C	C-	C+		Y	800-225-1852
PGIM Global Total Return Fund - Class B	PBTRX	NAS CM	Open End	Global Fixed Inc (Worldwide Bond)	C	C-	C+			800-225-1852
PGIM Global Total Return Fund - Class C	PCTRX	NAS CM	Open End	Global Fixed Inc (Worldwide Bond)	C	C-	C+		Y	800-225-1852
PGIM Global Total Return Fund - Class R2	PGTOX	NAS CM	Open End	Global Fixed Inc (Worldwide Bond)	C	C-	C+		Y	800-225-1852
PGIM Global Total Return Fund - Class R4	PGTSX	NAS CM	Open End	Global Fixed Inc (Worldwide Bond)	C	C-	C+		Y	800-225-1852
PGIM Global Total Return Fund - Class R6	PGTQX	NAS CM	Open End	Global Fixed Inc (Worldwide Bond)	C	C-	C+		Y	800-225-1852
PGIM Global Total Return Fund - Class Z	PZTRX	NAS CM	Open End	Global Fixed Inc (Worldwide Bond)	C	C-	C+		Y	800-225-1852
PGIM Government Income Fund- Class A	PGVAX	NAS CM	Open End	US Fixed Inc (Income)	B-	B-	B		Y	800-225-1852
PGIM Government Income Fund- Class B	PBGPX	NAS CM	Open End	US Fixed Inc (Income)	C+	C+	B			800-225-1852
PGIM Government Income Fund- Class C	PRICX	NAS CM	Open End	US Fixed Inc (Income)	B-	C+	B	Up	Y	800-225-1852
PGIM Government Income Fund- Class R	JDRVX	NAS CM	Open End	US Fixed Inc (Income)	B-	C+	B		Y	800-225-1852
PGIM Government Income Fund- Class R6	PGIQX	NAS CM	Open End	US Fixed Inc (Income)	B	B-	B	Up	Y	800-225-1852
PGIM Government Income Fund- Class Z	PGVZX	NAS CM	Open End	US Fixed Inc (Income)	B	B-	B	Up	Y	800-225-1852
PGIM Government Money Market Fund- Class A Exchange	MJAXX	NAS CM	Money Mkt	US Money Mkt (Money Mkt - Govt)	C	C-	C+		Y	800-225-1852
PGIM Government Money Market Fund- Class A Purchase	PBMXX	NAS CM	Money Mkt	US Money Mkt (Money Mkt - Govt)	C	C-	C+		Y	800-225-1852
PGIM Government Money Market Fund- Class B Exchange	MJBXX	NAS CM	Money Mkt	US Money Mkt (Money Mkt - Govt)	C	C-	C			800-225-1852
PGIM Government Money Market Fund- Class C Exchange	MJCXX	NAS CM	Money Mkt	US Money Mkt (Money Mkt - Govt)	C	C-	C+		Y	800-225-1852
PGIM Government Money Market Fund- Class Z Purchase	PMZXX	NAS CM	Money Mkt	US Money Mkt (Money Mkt - Govt)	C	C-	C+		Y	800-225-1852
PGIM High Yield Bond Fund, Inc.	ISD	NYSE	Closed End	US Fixed Inc (Income)	D+	D+	C-	Down	Y	800-225-1852
PGIM High Yield Fund- Class A	PBHAX	NAS CM	Open End	US Fixed Inc (Corp Bond - High Yield)	C-	D+	C		Y	800-225-1852
PGIM High Yield Fund- Class B	PBHYX	NAS CM	Open End	US Fixed Inc (Corp Bond - High Yield)	C-	D+	C			800-225-1852
PGIM High Yield Fund- Class C	PRHCX	NAS CM	Open End	US Fixed Inc (Corp Bond - High Yield)	C-	D+	C		Y	800-225-1852
PGIM High Yield Fund- Class R	JDYRX	NAS CM	Open End	US Fixed Inc (Corp Bond - High Yield)	C-	D+	C		Y	800-225-1852
PGIM High Yield Fund- Class R2	PHYEX	NAS CM	Open End	US Fixed Inc (Corp Bond - High Yield)	C-	D+	C		Y	800-225-1852
PGIM High Yield Fund- Class R4	PHYGX	NAS CM	Open End	US Fixed Inc (Corp Bond - High Yield)	C-	D+	C		Y	800-225-1852
PGIM High Yield Fund- Class R6	PHYQX	NAS CM	Open End	US Fixed Inc (Corp Bond - High Yield)	C-	D+	C	Down	Y	800-225-1852
PGIM High Yield Fund- Class Z	PHYZX	NAS CM	Open End	US Fixed Inc (Corp Bond - High Yield)	C-	D+	C		Y	800-225-1852

★Expanded analysis of this fund is included in Section II.

TOTAL RETURNS & PERFORMANCE									ASSETS		ASSET ALLOCATION & TURNOVER							MINIMUMS		FEES		
3-Month Total Return	6-Month Total Return	1-Year Total Return	3-Year Total Return	5-Year Total Return	Dividend Yield (TTM)	Expense Ratio	3-Yr Std Deviation	Effective Duration	NAV	Total Assets (MIL)	%Cash	%Government Bonds	%Municipal Bonds	%Corporate Bonds	%Other	Turnover Ratio	Average Coupon Rate	Min Initial Investment	Min Additional Investment	Front End Fee (%)	Back End Fee (%)	Inception Date
9.35	3.55	7.26	14.29	25.31	2.15	1.55	7.08	7.56	11.98	39.5	3	3	1	87	0	71	3.89	1,000	100		1.00	May-15
9.48	3.81	7.79	16.01	28.45	2.65	1.05	7.09	7.56	11.98	39.5	3	3	1	87	0	71	3.89	0				May-15
9.61	4.06	8.32	17.75	31.56	3.14	0.55	7.09	7.56	11.98	39.5	3	3	1	87	0	71	3.89	0				May-15
9.61	4.06	8.32	17.74	31.56	3.14	0.55	7.08	7.56	11.98	39.5	3	3	1	87	0	71	3.89	0				Jan-93
15.63	-5.69	-3.44			6.14	1.05		7.63	8.83	34.7	2	54	0	10	0	33	6.52	1,000	100	3.25		Dec-17
15.43	-6.03	-4.14			5.35	1.8		7.63	8.83	34.7	2	54	0	10	0	33	6.52	1,000	100		1.00	Dec-17
15.87	-5.40	-2.99			6.52	0.65		7.63	8.84	34.7	2	54	0	10	0	33	6.52	0				Dec-17
15.84	-5.45	-3.08			6.42	0.75		7.63	8.84	34.7	2	54	0	10	0	33	6.52	0				Dec-17
14.09	-6.73	-2.68	1.75	10.02	5.28	1.13	14.25	7.40	5.62	50.3	5	25	0	2	0	69	6.33	1,000	100	3.25		Mar-11
14.01	-7.17	-3.50	-0.80	5.78	4.5	1.88	14.3	7.40	5.66	50.3	5	25	0	2	0	69	6.33	1,000	100		1.00	Mar-11
14.32	-6.59	-2.40	2.55	11.66	5.65	0.65	14.26	7.40	5.67	50.3	5	25	0	2	0	69	6.33	0				Mar-11
14.50	-6.45	-2.27	2.47	11.27	5.63	0.72	14.29	7.40	5.68	50.3	5	25	0	2	0	69	6.33	0				Mar-11
12.37	-5.38	-3.41	3.77	11.97	6.23	0.97	10.16		8.8	333.6	1	1	0	85	0	66	5.33	1,000	100	2.25		Mar-11
12.16	-5.73	-4.13	1.47	7.77	5.43	1.72	10.16		8.8	333.6	1	1	0	85	0	66	5.33	1,000	100		1.00	Mar-11
12.31	-5.33	-3.22	4.59	13.42	6.54	0.67	10.18		8.8	333.6	1	1	0	85	0	66	5.33	0				Apr-15
12.29	-5.36	-3.27	4.44	13.20	6.49	0.72	10.18		8.8	333.6	1	1	0	85	0	66	5.33	0				Mar-11
14.57	-6.84	-2.29	12.59		5.74	1.2	12.07	4.71	9.32	60.3	6	7	0	11	0	33	4.55	1,000	100	3.25		Nov-15
14.26	-7.21	-3.04	9.98		4.93	1.95	12.04	4.71	9.3	60.3	6	7	0	11	0	33	4.55	1,000	100		1.00	Nov-15
14.70	-6.67	-1.90	13.75		6.18	0.8	12.12	4.71	9.31	60.3	6	7	0	11	0	33	4.55	0				Nov-15
14.67	-6.68	-1.95	13.61		6.12	0.85	12.07	4.71	9.32	60.3	6	7	0	11	0	33	4.55	0				Nov-15
19.61	-6.99	-2.83	11.30	24.93	8.6	1.49	14.24		14.9	592.6	2	10	0	52	0	96	6.49					Dec-12
7.69	3.04	7.18			4.03	0.88		8.44	10.33	37.5	-1	16	0	13	0	31	3.56	1,000	100	3.25		Dec-17
7.49	2.66	6.42			3.32	1.63		8.44	10.33	37.5	-1	16	0	13	0	31	3.56	1,000	100		1.00	Dec-17
7.76	3.19	7.53			4.35	0.58		8.44	10.33	37.5	-1	16	0	13	0	31	3.56	0				Dec-17
7.75	3.16	7.47			4.29	0.63		8.44	10.33	37.5	-1	16	0	13	0	31	3.56	0				Dec-17
8.06	0.38	3.55	15.53	29.72	3.34	0.88	7.36	8.57	6.78	3,617	5	16	0	12	0	37	3.78	1,000	100	3.25		Jul-86
8.73	0.32	2.80	12.83	24.44	2.59	1.63	7.4	8.57		3,617	5	16	0	12	0	37	3.78	2,500	100		5.00	Jan-96
7.88	0.01	2.79	13.00	25.03	2.59	1.63	7.42	8.57	6.77	3,617	5	16	0	12	0	37	3.78	1,000	100		1.00	Jan-96
8.08	0.44	3.49	15.04	29.17	3.13	1.08	7.42	8.57	6.87	3,617	5	16	0	12	0	37	3.78	0				Dec-17
8.14	0.42	3.60	15.76	29.98	3.39	0.83	7.41	8.57	6.87	3,617	5	16	0	12	0	37	3.78	0				Dec-17
8.23	0.56	3.89	16.47	31.50	3.67	0.56	7.46	8.57	6.86	3,617	5	16	0	12	0	37	3.78	0				Feb-12
8.25	0.51	3.81	16.32	31.60	3.58	0.63	7.43	8.57	6.82	3,617	5	16	0	12	0	37	3.78	0				Mar-97
0.85	5.60	7.18	12.38	16.55	1.84	0.96	3.12	4.78	10.13	778.1	6	46	0	1	0	119	3.19	1,000	100	3.25		Jan-90
0.57	5.01	6.07	9.21	11.43	0.86	2.03	3.13	4.78		778.1	6	46	0	1	0	119	3.19	2,500	100		5.00	Apr-85
0.76	5.32	6.33	9.75	12.12	1.07	1.79	3.14	4.78	10.16	778.1	6	46	0	1	0	119	3.19	1,000	100		1.00	Aug-94
0.87	5.55	6.87	11.46	15.00	1.56	1.25	3.11	4.78	10.15	778.1	6	46	0	1	0	119	3.19	0				May-04
1.06	5.95	7.69	14.04	17.65	2.29	0.47	3.16	4.78	10.11	778.1	6	46	0	1	0	119	3.19	0				Aug-16
0.96	5.84	7.63	13.58	18.37	2.23	0.48	3.13	4.78	10.11	778.1	6	46	0	1	0	119	3.19	0				Mar-96
0.00	0.20	0.90	3.32	3.37	1.04	0.64	0.17		1	1,025	56	44	0	0	0			1,000	100			Jun-76
0.00	0.20	0.90	3.32	3.37	1.04	0.64	0.17		1	1,025	56	44	0	0	0			2,500	100			Jun-76
0.00	0.17	0.79	3.07	3.15	0.92	0.77	0.16			1,025	56	44	0	0	0			2,500	100			Mar-05
0.00	0.20	0.87	3.30	3.39	1	0.65	0.17		1	1,025	56	44	0	0	0			1,000	100			Mar-05
0.00	0.25	1.07	3.91	3.98	1.23	0.43	0.18		1	1,025	56	44	0	0	0			0				Mar-96
15.55	-6.80	-1.54	11.74	24.21	8.27	1.12	12.19	3.72	15.2	500.5	2	0	0	96	0	87	6.58					Apr-12
10.36	-5.36	-1.25	10.41	26.06	6.37	0.8	9.46	3.84	5.12	15,592	8	0	0	86	0	43	6.47	1,000	100	3.25		Jan-90
12.35	-5.05	-1.01	9.26	23.95	5.86	1.28	9.45	3.84		15,592	8	0	0	86	0	43	6.47	2,500	100		5.00	Mar-79
10.41	-5.51	-1.74	8.13	21.86	5.67	1.49	9.44	3.84	5.12	15,592	8	0	0	86	0	43	6.47	1,000	100		1.00	Aug-94
10.28	-5.50	-1.54	9.46	24.36	6.08	1.09	9.36	3.84	5.12	15,592	8	0	0	86	0	43	6.47	0				Jun-05
10.55	-5.39	-1.16	9.87	24.20	6.27	0.91	9.42	3.84	5.13	15,592	8	0	0	86	0	43	6.47	0				Dec-17
10.61	-5.10	-0.92	10.59	25.01	6.53	0.66	9.44	3.84	5.13	15,592	8	0	0	86	0	43	6.47	0				Dec-17
10.47	-5.17	-0.85	11.73	28.29	6.8	0.4	9.47	3.84	5.12	15,592	8	0	0	86	0	43	6.47	0				Oct-11
10.63	-5.04	-0.79	11.30	28.02	6.65	0.54	9.41	3.84	5.14	15,592	8	0	0	86	0	43	6.47	0				Mar-96

Fund Name	MARKET Ticker Symbol	Traded On	FUND TYPE, CATEGORY & OBJECTIVE Fund Type	Category and (Prospectus Objective)	RATINGS Overall Rating	Reward Rating	Risk Rating	Recent Up/ Downgrade	NEW INVESTORS Open to New Investors	Telephone
PGIM International Bond Fund- Class A	PXBAX	NAS CM	Open End	Global Fixed Inc (Multisector Bond)	C	C-	B		Y	800-225-1852
PGIM International Bond Fund- Class C	PXBCX	NAS CM	Open End	Global Fixed Inc (Multisector Bond)	C	C-	B		Y	800-225-1852
PGIM International Bond Fund- Class R6	PXBQX	NAS CM	Open End	Global Fixed Inc (Multisector Bond)	C	C-	B		Y	800-225-1852
PGIM International Bond Fund- Class Z	PXBZX	NAS CM	Open End	Global Fixed Inc (Multisector Bond)	C	C-	B		Y	800-225-1852
PGIM Muni High Income Fund-Class A	PRHAX	NAS CM	Open End	US Muni Fixed Inc (Muni Bond - Natl)	C-	D+	C	Down	Y	800-225-1852
PGIM Muni High Income Fund-Class B	PMHYX	NAS CM	Open End	US Muni Fixed Inc (Muni Bond - Natl)	C-	D+	C	Down		800-225-1852
PGIM Muni High Income Fund-Class C	PHICX	NAS CM	Open End	US Muni Fixed Inc (Muni Bond - Natl)	C-	D+	C	Down	Y	800-225-1852
PGIM Muni High Income Fund-Class R6	PHIQX	NAS CM	Open End	US Muni Fixed Inc (Muni Bond - Natl)	C-	D+	C	Down	Y	800-225-1852
PGIM Muni High Income Fund-Class Z	PHIZX	NAS CM	Open End	US Muni Fixed Inc (Muni Bond - Natl)	C-	D+	C	Down	Y	800-225-1852
PGIM National Muni Fund - Class Z	DNMZX	NAS CM	Open End	US Muni Fixed Inc (Muni Bond - Natl)	C	C-	C+		Y	800-225-1852
PGIM National Muni Fund- Class A	PRNMX	NAS CM	Open End	US Muni Fixed Inc (Muni Bond - Natl)	C	C-	C+		Y	800-225-1852
PGIM National Muni Fund- Class B	PBHMX	NAS CM	Open End	US Muni Fixed Inc (Muni Bond - Natl)	C	C-	C			800-225-1852
PGIM National Muni Fund- Class C	PNMCX	NAS CM	Open End	US Muni Fixed Inc (Muni Bond - Natl)	C	C-	C		Y	800-225-1852
PGIM National Muni Fund- Class R6	PNMQX	NAS CM	Open End	US Muni Fixed Inc (Muni Bond - Natl)	C	C-	C+		Y	800-225-1852
PGIM Securitized Credit Fund Class A	SCFOX	NAS CM	Open End	Fixed Inc Misc (Growth & Income)	U	U	U		Y	800-225-1852
PGIM Securitized Credit Fund Class C	SCFVX	NAS CM	Open End	Fixed Inc Misc (Growth & Income)	U	U	U		Y	800-225-1852
PGIM Securitized Credit Fund Class R6	SCFQX	NAS CM	Open End	Fixed Inc Misc (Growth & Income)	U	U	U		Y	800-225-1852
PGIM Securitized Credit Fund Class Z	SCFZX	NAS CM	Open End	Fixed Inc Misc (Growth & Income)	U	U	U		Y	800-225-1852
PGIM Short Duration High Yield Income Fund- Class A	HYSAX	NAS CM	Open End	US Fixed Inc (Corp Bond - High Yield)	C-	D+	C		Y	800-225-1852
PGIM Short Duration High Yield Income Fund- Class C	HYSCX	NAS CM	Open End	US Fixed Inc (Corp Bond - High Yield)	C-	D+	C		Y	800-225-1852
PGIM Short Duration High Yield Income Fund- Class R6	HYSQX	NAS CM	Open End	US Fixed Inc (Corp Bond - High Yield)	C-	D+	C		Y	800-225-1852
PGIM Short Duration High Yield Income Fund- Class Z	HYSZX	NAS CM	Open End	US Fixed Inc (Corp Bond - High Yield)	C-	D+	C		Y	800-225-1852
PGIM Short Duration Multi-Sector Bond Fund- Class A	SDMAX	NAS CM	Open End	US Fixed Inc (Multisector Bond)	C	C-	C		Y	800-225-1852
PGIM Short Duration Multi-Sector Bond Fund- Class C	SDMCX	NAS CM	Open End	US Fixed Inc (Multisector Bond)	C	C-	C		Y	800-225-1852
PGIM Short Duration Multi-Sector Bond Fund- Class R6	SDMQX	NAS CM	Open End	US Fixed Inc (Multisector Bond)	C	C-	C+		Y	800-225-1852
PGIM Short Duration Multi-Sector Bond Fund- Class Z	SDMZX	NAS CM	Open End	US Fixed Inc (Multisector Bond)	C	C-	C+		Y	800-225-1852
PGIM Short Duration Muni Fund- Class A	PDSAX	NAS CM	Open End	US Muni Fixed Inc (Muni Bond - Natl)	C	C-	C		Y	800-225-1852
PGIM Short Duration Muni Fund- Class C	PDSCX	NAS CM	Open End	US Muni Fixed Inc (Muni Bond - Natl)	C-	D+	C	Down	Y	800-225-1852
PGIM Short Duration Muni Fund- Class R6	PDSQX	NAS CM	Open End	US Muni Fixed Inc (Muni Bond - Natl)	C	C-	C+		Y	800-225-1852
PGIM Short Duration Muni Fund- Class Z	PDSZX	NAS CM	Open End	US Muni Fixed Inc (Muni Bond - Natl)	C	C-	C+		Y	800-225-1852
PGIM Short-Term Corporate Bond Fund- Class A	PBSMX	NAS CM	Open End	US Fixed Inc (Corp Bond - General)	C	C	B-		Y	800-225-1852
PGIM Short-Term Corporate Bond Fund- Class B	PSMBX	NAS CM	Open End	US Fixed Inc (Corp Bond - General)	C	C-	C+	Up		800-225-1852
PGIM Short-Term Corporate Bond Fund- Class C	PIFCX	NAS CM	Open End	US Fixed Inc (Corp Bond - General)	C	C	C+		Y	800-225-1852
PGIM Short-Term Corporate Bond Fund- Class R	JDTRX	NAS CM	Open End	US Fixed Inc (Corp Bond - General)	C	C	B-		Y	800-225-1852
PGIM Short-Term Corporate Bond Fund- Class R2	PIFEX	NAS CM	Open End	US Fixed Inc (Corp Bond - General)	C	C	C+		Y	800-225-1852
PGIM Short-Term Corporate Bond Fund- Class R4	PIFGX	NAS CM	Open End	US Fixed Inc (Corp Bond - General)	C	C	C+		Y	800-225-1852
PGIM Short-Term Corporate Bond Fund- Class R6	PSTQX	NAS CM	Open End	US Fixed Inc (Corp Bond - General)	C	C	C+		Y	800-225-1852
PGIM Short-Term Corporate Bond Fund- Class Z	PIFZX	NAS CM	Open End	US Fixed Inc (Corp Bond - General)	C	C	C+		Y	800-225-1852
PGIM Strategic Bond Fund- Class A	PUCAX	NAS CM	Open End	US Fixed Inc (Growth & Income)	C-	D+	C	Down	Y	800-225-1852
PGIM Strategic Bond Fund- Class C	PUCCX	NAS CM	Open End	US Fixed Inc (Growth & Income)	C-	D+	C	Down	Y	800-225-1852
PGIM Strategic Bond Fund- Class R6	PUCQX	NAS CM	Open End	US Fixed Inc (Growth & Income)	C	C-	C		Y	800-225-1852
PGIM Strategic Bond Fund- Class Z	PUCZX	NAS CM	Open End	US Fixed Inc (Growth & Income)	C	C-	C		Y	800-225-1852
PGIM TIPS Fund- Class R6	PQTSX	NAS CM	Open End	US Fixed Inc (Govt Bond - Treasury)	B	C+	B+	Up	Y	800-225-1852
★ PGIM Total Return Bond Fund -Class A	PDBAX	NAS CM	Open End	US Fixed Inc (Multisector Bond)	C+	C	B		Y	800-225-1852
★ PGIM Total Return Bond Fund -Class B	PRDBX	NAS CM	Open End	US Fixed Inc (Multisector Bond)	C	C	B			800-225-1852
★ PGIM Total Return Bond Fund -Class C	PDBCX	NAS CM	Open End	US Fixed Inc (Multisector Bond)	C+	C	B	Up	Y	800-225-1852
★ PGIM Total Return Bond Fund -Class R	DTBRX	NAS CM	Open End	US Fixed Inc (Multisector Bond)	C+	C	B	Up	Y	800-225-1852
★ PGIM Total Return Bond Fund -Class R2	PDBRX	NAS CM	Open End	US Fixed Inc (Multisector Bond)	C+	C	B	Up	Y	800-225-1852
★ PGIM Total Return Bond Fund -Class R4	PDBSX	NAS CM	Open End	US Fixed Inc (Multisector Bond)	C+	C	B		Y	800-225-1852
PGIM Total Return Bond Fund -Class R6	PTRQX	NAS CM	Open End	US Fixed Inc (Multisector Bond)	C+	C	B		Y	800-225-1852
PGIM Total Return Bond Fund -Class Z	PDBZX	NAS CM	Open End	US Fixed Inc (Multisector Bond)	C+	C	B		Y	800-225-1852
PIA BBB Bond Fund	PBBBX	NAS CM	Open End	US Fixed Inc (Income)	C+	C	B		Y	800-251-1970

★ Expanded analysis of this fund is included in Section II.

TOTAL RETURNS & PERFORMANCE									ASSETS		ASSET ALLOCATION & TURNOVER							MINIMUMS		FEES		
3-Month Total Return	6-Month Total Return	1-Year Total Return	3-Year Total Return	5-Year Total Return	Dividend Yield (TTM)	Expense Ratio	3-Yr Std Deviation	Effective Duration	NAV	Total Assets (MIL)	%Cash	%Government Bonds	%Municipal Bonds	%Corporate Bonds	%Other	Turnover Ratio	Average Coupon Rate	Min Initial Investment	Min Additional Investment	Front End Fee (%)	Back End Fee (%)	Inception Date
7.26	0.66	4.67	20.99		7.38	0.99	6.45	10.51	10.1	43.7	5	17	0	7	0	49	3.45	1,000	100	3.25		Dec-16
7.06	0.37	3.97	18.28		6.59	1.74	6.45	10.51	10.1	43.7	5	17	0	7	0	49	3.45	1,000	100		1.00	Dec-16
7.37	0.87	5.03	22.00		7.72	0.58	6.45	10.51	10.1	43.7	5	17	0	7	0	49	3.45	0				Dec-16
7.35	0.84	4.99	21.97		7.69	0.63	6.44	10.51	10.1	43.7	5	17	0	7	0	49	3.45	0				Dec-16
3.97	-1.30	1.50	11.97	22.68	3.8	0.81	6.51	7.58	10.2	793.1	0	0	100	0	0	54	5.09	1,000	100	3.25		Jan-90
2.91	-1.66	0.89	10.71	20.36	3.46	1.26	6.56	7.58		793.1	0	0	100	0	0	54	5.09	2,500	100		5.00	Sep-87
3.78	-1.67	0.65	9.49	18.22	3.02	1.56	6.5	7.58	10.2	793.1	0	0	100	0	0	54	5.09	1,000	100		1.00	Aug-94
4.06	-1.16	1.67	13.12	23.35	4.07	0.49	6.52	7.58	10.19	793.1	0	0	100	0	0	54	5.09	0				Jun-17
4.04	-1.19	1.63	12.75	24.25	4.04	0.58	6.5	7.58	10.18	793.1	0	0	100	0	0	54	5.09	0				Sep-96
2.81	0.41	2.61	10.95	18.97	3.21	0.36	4.82	6.39	14.9	764.9	1	0	99	0	0	42	4.74	0				Jan-99
2.74	0.28	2.37	10.20	17.57	2.97	0.61	4.86	6.39	14.91	764.9	1	0	99	0	0	42	4.74	1,000	100	3.25		Jan-90
2.14	-0.13	1.72	8.70	15.08	2.41	1.09	4.86	6.39		764.9	1	0	99	0	0	42	4.74	2,500	100		5.00	Apr-80
2.59	-0.11	1.58	7.65	13.13	2.12	1.44	4.86	6.39	14.95	764.9	1	0	99	0	0	42	4.74	1,000	100		1.00	Aug-94
2.83	0.44	2.67	11.18	17.95	3.26	0.29	4.84	6.39	14.9	764.9	1	0	99	0	0	42	4.74	0				Dec-17
9.14	-5.09	-3.56				0.9			9.26	26.8	7	0	0	10	1	14	3.41	1,000	100	3.25	1.00	Jul-19
8.94	-5.43	-4.27				1.65			9.26	26.8	7	0	0	10	1	14	3.41	1,000	100		1.00	Jul-19
9.21	-4.95	-3.28				0.6			9.26	26.8	7	0	0	10	1	14	3.41	0				Jul-19
9.21	-4.96	-3.32				0.65			9.26	26.8	7	0	0	10	1	14	3.41	0				Jul-19
9.08	-3.90	-0.60	9.55	19.64	5.38	1	7.67	2.67	8.47	2,874	6	0	0	92	0	49	6.26	1,000	100	2.25		Oct-12
8.89	-4.26	-1.34	7.13	15.25	4.6	1.75	7.66	2.67	8.47	2,874	6	0	0	92	0	49	6.26	1,000	100		1.00	Oct-12
9.16	-3.76	-0.42	10.53	21.36	5.69	0.7	7.66	2.67	8.47	2,874	6	0	0	92	0	49	6.26	0				Oct-14
9.15	-3.78	-0.35	10.37	21.00	5.64	0.75	7.68	2.67	8.47	2,874	6	0	0	92	0	49	6.26	0				Oct-12
4.98	0.07	1.95	8.48	13.69	3.33	0.7	3.94	2.14	9.46	1,989	9	25	0	19	0	67	3.65	1,000	100	2.25		Dec-13
4.87	-0.23	1.21	5.90	9.34	2.5	1.56	4	2.14	9.47	1,989	9	25	0	19	0	67	3.65	1,000	100		1.00	Dec-13
5.18	0.34	2.41	9.66	15.51	3.69	0.32	4.01	2.14	9.47	1,989	9	25	0	19	0	67	3.65	0				Dec-13
5.15	0.31	2.32	9.40	15.57	3.59	0.39	4	2.14	9.5	1,989	9	25	0	19	0	67	3.65	0				Dec-13
2.32	-0.35	1.41	8.09	13.67	1.99	0.64	3.6	3.80	10.31	152.1	2	0	98	0	0	83	4.47	1,000	100	2.25		May-14
2.15	-0.71	0.68	5.72	9.51	1.23	1.41	3.6	3.80	10.3	152.1	2	0	98	0	0	83	4.47	1,000	100		1.00	May-14
2.51	-0.11	1.79	9.04	15.12	2.26	0.29	3.65	3.80	10.31	152.1	2	0	98	0	0	83	4.47	0				May-17
2.40	-0.12	1.68	8.92	15.11	2.26	0.32	3.57	3.80	10.31	152.1	2	0	98	0	0	83	4.47	0				May-14
6.47	2.43	4.50	9.80	14.39	2.53	0.76	4.01	2.64	11.24	10,827	7	1	0	78	0	60	3.32	1,000	100	2.25		Sep-89
7.31	1.99	3.15	5.60	8.27	1.29	1.46	4.05	2.64		10,827	7	1	0	78	0	60	3.32	2,500	100		3.00	Dec-92
6.37	2.16	3.86	7.49	10.41	1.84	1.45	4	2.64	11.25	10,827	7	1	0	78	0	60	3.32	1,000	100		1.00	Aug-94
6.39	2.28	4.17	8.70	12.78	2.22	1.08	4	2.64	11.24	10,827	7	1	0	78	0	60	3.32	0				May-04
6.50	2.45	4.45	9.55	14.13	2.41	0.88	4	2.64	11.29	10,827	7	1	0	78	0	60	3.32	0				Dec-17
6.57	2.58	4.62	10.25	14.87	2.66	0.63	4	2.64	11.29	10,827	7	1	0	78	0	60	3.32	0				Dec-17
6.64	2.70	4.88	11.02	16.48	2.91	0.38	4.05	2.64	11.28	10,827	7	1	0	78	0	60	3.32	0				Mar-12
6.62	2.57	4.78	10.67	15.87	2.81	0.47	4.05	2.64	11.27	10,827	7	1	0	78	0	60	3.32	0				Dec-96
10.08	-2.07	1.64	14.95	33.01	4.14	1.02	7.99	3.97	10.06	1,375	12	10	0	25	0	239	4.33	1,000	100	3.25		Jul-15
9.92	-2.42	0.89	12.42	27.98	3.37	1.77	8.02	3.97	10.04	1,375	12	10	0	25	0	239	4.33	1,000	100		1.00	Jul-15
10.17	-1.87	2.03	16.36	31.86	4.54	0.59	8.01	3.97	10.06	1,375	12	10	0	25	0	239	4.33	0				Apr-17
10.17	-1.89	2.00	16.15	34.93	4.52	0.62	8.02	3.97	10.05	1,375	12	10	0	25	0	239	4.33	0				Jul-15
3.97	5.55	7.97	14.48		2.24	0.4	3.64		10.44	39.0	2	98	0	0	0	40	0.57	0				Nov-16
6.66	3.54	6.55	16.15	26.33	3.08	0.76	5.49	6.01	14.75	55,453	4	18	1	29	0	45	3.83	1,000	100	3.25		Jan-95
7.70	3.15	6.10	14.38	22.89	2.6	1.26	5.46	6.01		55,453	4	18	1	29	0	45	3.83	2,500	100		5.00	Jan-95
6.40	3.11	5.80	13.65	21.69	2.39	1.48	5.47	6.01	14.73	55,453	4	18	1	29	0	45	3.83	1,000	100		1.00	Jan-95
6.51	3.34	6.28	15.27	24.65	2.84	1.01	5.46	6.01	14.77	55,453	4	18	1	29	0	45	3.83	0				Jan-08
6.56	3.48	6.42	15.79	25.94	2.96	0.89	5.46	6.01	14.71	55,453	4	18	1	29	0	45	3.83	0				Dec-17
6.62	3.54	6.69	16.52	26.72	3.21	0.64	5.47	6.01	14.71	55,453	4	18	1	29	0	45	3.83	0				Dec-17
6.76	3.73	7.02	17.43	28.56	3.45	0.39	5.49	6.01	14.72	55,453	4	18	1	29	0	45	3.83	0				Dec-10
6.75	3.68	6.85	17.09	27.95	3.35	0.49	5.5	6.01	14.7	55,453	4	18	1	29	0	45	3.83	0				Sep-96
10.25	3.51	8.77	19.94	32.32	3.67	0.19	7.53		9.96	162.7	1	12	0	87	0	20	4.76	1,000	50			Sep-03

	MARKET		FUND TYPE, CATEGORY & OBJECTIVE		RATINGS				NEW INVESTORS	
Fund Name	Ticker Symbol	Traded On	Fund Type	Category and (Prospectus Objective)	Overall Rating	Reward Rating	Risk Rating	Recent Up/ Downgrade	Open to New Investors	Telephone
PIA High Yield (MACS) Managed Account Completion Shares	PIAMX	NAS CM	Open End	US Fixed Inc (Corp Bond - High Yield)	D+	D	C-	Down	Y	800-251-1970
PIA High Yield Fund Institutional Class	PHYSX	NAS CM	Open End	US Fixed Inc (Corp Bond - High Yield)	D	D	C-	Down	Y	800-251-1970
PIA MBS Bond Fund	PMTGX	NAS CM	Open End	US Fixed Inc (Income)	B-	C+	B-	Up	Y	800-251-1970
PIA Short Term Securities Fund Advisor Class	PIASX	NAS CM	Open End	US Fixed Inc (Govt Bond - General)	C	C	B-		Y	800-251-1970
PIMCO California Intermediate Municipal Bond Fund Class A	PCMBX	NAS CM	Open End	US Muni Fixed Inc (Muni Bond - Single State)	C	C	B-		Y	866-746-2602
PIMCO California Intermediate Municipal Bond Fund Class C	PCFCX	NAS CM	Open End	US Muni Fixed Inc (Muni Bond - Single State)	C	C-	C+		Y	866-746-2602
PIMCO California Intermediate Muni Bond Fund Class I-2	PCIPX	NAS CM	Open End	US Muni Fixed Inc (Muni Bond - Single State)	C	C	B-		Y	866-746-2602
PIMCO California Intermediate Muni Bond Institutional Cl	PCIMX	NAS CM	Open End	US Muni Fixed Inc (Muni Bond - Single State)	C	C	B-		Y	866-746-2602
PIMCO California Municipal Bond Fund Class A	PCTTX	NAS CM	Open End	US Muni Fixed Inc (Muni Bond - Single State)	C+	C	B		Y	866-746-2602
PIMCO California Municipal Bond Fund Class C	PCTGX	NAS CM	Open End	US Muni Fixed Inc (Muni Bond - Single State)	C	C	B		Y	866-746-2602
PIMCO California Municipal Bond Fund Class I-2	PCTPX	NAS CM	Open End	US Muni Fixed Inc (Muni Bond - Single State)	C+	C	B		Y	866-746-2602
PIMCO California Municipal Bond Fund Institutional Class	PCTIX	NAS CM	Open End	US Muni Fixed Inc (Muni Bond - Single State)	C+	C	B		Y	866-746-2602
PIMCO California Municipal Income Fund	PCQ	NYSE	Closed End	US Muni Fixed Inc (Muni Bond - Single State)	C-	C-	C-	Down	Y	866-746-2602
PIMCO California Municipal Income Fund II	PCK	NYSE	Closed End	US Muni Fixed Inc (Muni Bond - Single State)	C-	C-	C-	Down	Y	866-746-2602
PIMCO California Municipal Income Fund III	PZC	NYSE	Closed End	US Muni Fixed Inc (Muni Bond - Single State)	C-	C-	C-	Down	Y	866-746-2602
PIMCO California Short Duration Muni Income Fund Class A	PCDAX	NAS CM	Open End	US Muni Fixed Inc (Muni Bond - Single State)	C	C-	C		Y	866-746-2602
PIMCO California Short Duration Muni Income Fund Class I-2	PCDPX	NAS CM	Open End	US Muni Fixed Inc (Muni Bond - Single State)	C	C-	C+		Y	866-746-2602
PIMCO California Short Duration Muni Income Inst Cl	PCDIX	NAS CM	Open End	US Muni Fixed Inc (Muni Bond - Single State)	C	C-	C+		Y	866-746-2602
PIMCO Climate Bond Fund Class A	PCEBX	NAS CM	Open End	US Fixed Inc (Specialty - Unaligned)	U	U	U		Y	866-746-2602
PIMCO Climate Bond Fund Class C	PCECX	NAS CM	Open End	US Fixed Inc (Specialty - Unaligned)	U	U	U		Y	866-746-2602
PIMCO Climate Bond Fund I-2	PCEPX	NAS CM	Open End	US Fixed Inc (Specialty - Unaligned)	U	U	U		Y	866-746-2602
PIMCO Climate Bond Fund I-3	PCEWX	NAS CM	Open End	US Fixed Inc (Specialty - Unaligned)	U	U	U		Y	866-746-2602
PIMCO Climate Bond Fund Institutional Class	PCEIX	NAS CM	Open End	US Fixed Inc (Specialty - Unaligned)	U	U	U		Y	866-746-2602
PIMCO Corporate & Income Strategy Fund	PCN	NYSE	Closed End	US Fixed Inc (Corp Bond - General)	D	D	D+	Down	Y	866-746-2602
PIMCO Corporate and Income Opportunity Fund	PTY	NYSE	Closed End	US Fixed Inc (Corp Bond - General)	D	D	D+	Down	Y	866-746-2602
PIMCO Diversified Income Fund Administrative Class	PDAAX	NAS CM	Open End	US Fixed Inc (Income)	C	C-	C+		Y	866-746-2602
PIMCO Diversified Income Fund Class A	PDVAX	NAS CM	Open End	US Fixed Inc (Income)	C	C-	C+		Y	866-746-2602
PIMCO Diversified Income Fund Class C	PDICX	NAS CM	Open End	US Fixed Inc (Income)	C	C-	C		Y	866-746-2602
PIMCO Diversified Income Fund Class I-2	PDVPX	NAS CM	Open End	US Fixed Inc (Income)	C	C-	C+		Y	866-746-2602
PIMCO Diversified Income Fund Class I-3	PDNIX	NAS CM	Open End	US Fixed Inc (Income)	C	C-	C+		Y	866-746-2602
PIMCO Diversified Income Fund Institutional Class	PDIIX	NAS CM	Open End	US Fixed Inc (Income)	C	C-	C+		Y	866-746-2602
PIMCO Dynamic Bond Fund Class A	PUBAX	NAS CM	Open End	Fixed Inc Misc (Growth & Income)	C	D+	C+		Y	866-746-2602
PIMCO Dynamic Bond Fund Class C	PUBCX	NAS CM	Open End	Fixed Inc Misc (Growth & Income)	C-	D+	C		Y	866-746-2602
PIMCO Dynamic Bond Fund Class I-2	PUCPX	NAS CM	Open End	Fixed Inc Misc (Growth & Income)	C	C-	C+		Y	866-746-2602
PIMCO Dynamic Bond Fund Class I-3	PFNUX	NAS CM	Open End	Fixed Inc Misc (Growth & Income)	C	C-	C+		Y	866-746-2602
PIMCO Dynamic Bond Fund Class R	PUBRX	NAS CM	Open End	Fixed Inc Misc (Growth & Income)	C	D+	C		Y	866-746-2602
PIMCO Dynamic Bond Fund Institutional Class	PFIUX	NAS CM	Open End	Fixed Inc Misc (Growth & Income)	C	C-	C+		Y	866-746-2602
PIMCO Dynamic Credit and Mortgage Income Fund	PCI	NYSE	Closed End	US Fixed Inc (Income)	D	D	D	Down	Y	866-746-2602
PIMCO Dynamic Income Fund	PDI	NYSE	Closed End	US Fixed Inc (Worldwide Bond)	D	D	D	Down	Y	866-746-2602
PIMCO Emerging Markets Bond Fund Class A	PAEMX	NAS CM	Open End	Emerg Mkts Fixed Inc (Diversified Emerg Mkts)	C-	D+	C	Down	Y	866-746-2602
PIMCO Emerging Markets Bond Fund Class C	PEBCX	NAS CM	Open End	Emerg Mkts Fixed Inc (Diversified Emerg Mkts)	C-	D+	C	Down	Y	866-746-2602
PIMCO Emerging Markets Bond Fund Class I-2	PEMPX	NAS CM	Open End	Emerg Mkts Fixed Inc (Diversified Emerg Mkts)	C-	D+	C	Down	Y	866-746-2602
PIMCO Emerging Markets Bond Fund Class I-3	PEBNX	NAS CM	Open End	Emerg Mkts Fixed Inc (Diversified Emerg Mkts)	C-	D+	C	Down	Y	866-746-2602
PIMCO Emerging Markets Bond Fund Institutional Class	PEBIX	NAS CM	Open End	Emerg Mkts Fixed Inc (Diversified Emerg Mkts)	C-	D+	C	Down	Y	866-746-2602
PIMCO Emerg Mkts Corp Bond Fund Institutional Class	PEMIX	NAS CM	Open End	Emerg Mkts Fixed Inc (Diversified Emerg Mkts)	C-	D+	C	Down	Y	866-746-2602
PIMCO Emerg Mkts Currency & Short-Term Investments Cl A	PLMAX	NAS CM	Open End	Currency (Diversified Emerg Mkts)	D	D	C-	Down	Y	866-746-2602
PIMCO Emerg Mkts Currency & Short-Term Investments Cl I-2	PLMPX	NAS CM	Open End	Currency (Diversified Emerg Mkts)	D	D	C-	Down	Y	866-746-2602
PIMCO Emerg Mkts Currency & Short-Term Inv Inst Cl	PLMIX	NAS CM	Open End	Currency (Diversified Emerg Mkts)	D	D	C-	Down	Y	866-746-2602
PIMCO Emerg Mkts Full Spectrum Bond Institutional Cl	PFSIX	NAS CM	Open End	Emerg Mkts Fixed Inc (Corp Bond - General)	D+	D	C-	Down	Y	866-746-2602
PIMCO Emerg Mkts Local Currency & Bond Fund Class A	PELAX	NAS CM	Open End	Emerg Mkts Fixed Inc (Diversified Emerg Mkts)	D	D	D+	Down	Y	866-746-2602
PIMCO Emerg Mkts Local Currency & Bond Fund Class C	PELCX	NAS CM	Open End	Emerg Mkts Fixed Inc (Diversified Emerg Mkts)	D	D	D+	Down	Y	866-746-2602
PIMCO Emerg Mkts Local Currency & Bond Fund Class I-2	PELPX	NAS CM	Open End	Emerg Mkts Fixed Inc (Diversified Emerg Mkts)	D	D	D+	Down	Y	866-746-2602

★Expanded analysis of this fund is included in Section II.

TOTAL RETURNS & PERFORMANCE									ASSETS		ASSET ALLOCATION & TURNOVER							MINIMUMS		FEES		
3-Month Total Return	6-Month Total Return	1-Year Total Return	3-Year Total Return	5-Year Total Return	Dividend Yield (TTM)	Expense Ratio	3-Yr Std Deviation	Effective Duration	NAV	Total Assets (MIL)	%Cash	%Government Bonds	%Municipal Bonds	%Corporate Bonds	%Other	Turnover Ratio	Average Coupon Rate	Min Initial Investment	Min Additional Investment	Front End Fee (%)	Back End Fee (%)	Inception Date
10.65	-4.11	-1.37			7.46	0.25			8.85	77.0	2	0	0	98	0	36	7.14	1,000	50			Dec-17
11.79	-4.93	-2.63	6.12	20.62	7.41	0.87	9.98		8.97	43.0	1	0	0	99	0	63	7.29	1,000	50			Dec-10
0.29	3.27	5.16	11.34	16.08	2.76	0.23	2.29		9.76	70.2	1	3	0	0	0	20	3.49	1,000	50			Feb-06
1.35	1.40	2.66	6.18	8.21	1.89	0.39	0.79		10.13	169.4	10	39	0	41	0	48	2.26	1,000	50			Apr-94
2.59	1.40	2.86	9.61	15.19	1.85	0.78	3.51	4.76	10.06	181.8	5	0	95	0	0	35	4.49	1,000	50	2.25		Oct-99
2.40	1.02	2.10	7.18	10.96	1.11	1.53	3.5	4.76	10.06	181.8	5	0	95	0	0	35	4.49	1,000	50		1.00	Aug-09
2.65	1.51	3.10	10.37	16.51	2.08	0.55	3.51	4.76	10.06	181.8	5	0	95	0	0	35	4.49	1,000,000				Apr-08
2.68	1.56	3.20	10.70	17.10	2.18	0.45	3.51	4.76	10.06	181.8	5	0	95	0	0	35	4.49	1,000,000				Aug-99
3.23	2.78	5.53	14.93	26.55	1.98	0.84	4.58	7.67	11.48	63.7	2	0	95	0	0	41	4.24	1,000	50	2.25		May-12
3.04	2.41	4.75	12.39	21.91	1.24	1.59	4.58	7.67	11.48	63.7	2	0	95	0	0	41	4.24	1,000	50		1.00	May-12
3.29	2.91	5.80	15.79	28.13	2.23	0.59	4.59	7.67	11.48	63.7	2	0	95	0	0	41	4.24	1,000,000				May-12
3.32	2.96	5.90	16.14	28.77	2.33	0.49	4.59	7.67	11.48	63.7	2	0	95	0	0	41	4.24	1,000,000				May-12
5.21	-0.11	4.34	18.11	36.25	6.36	0	9.15		13.79	255.6	6	0	94	0	0	16	4.97					Jun-01
5.75	-0.62	4.18	19.64	38.81	4.63	0	10.76		8.73	275.0	8	0	92	0	0	16	4.86					Jun-02
5.11	-0.39	4.02	17.94	35.79	4.94	0	9.22		9.93	218.4	5	0	94	0	0	16	4.98					Oct-02
1.23	0.48	1.26	3.84	5.19	1.1	0.73	1.41	1.78	9.94	154.8	13	0	87	0	0	69	3.45	1,000	50	2.25		Aug-06
1.31	0.63	1.57	4.77	6.77	1.4	0.43	1.41	1.78	9.94	154.8	13	0	87	0	0	69	3.45	1,000,000				May-08
1.33	0.68	1.67	5.09	7.31	1.5	0.33	1.41	1.78	9.94	154.8	13	0	87	0	0	69	3.45	1,000,000				Aug-06
7.99	2.62					0.9		5.36	10.19	5.7	4	4	4	56	0	21	3.23	1,000	50	2.25		Dec-19
7.80	2.25					1.65		5.36	10.19	5.7	4	4	4	56	0	21	3.23	1,000	50		1.00	Dec-19
8.07	2.76					0.6		5.36	10.19	5.7	4	4	4	56	0	21	3.23	1,000,000				Dec-19
8.06	2.74					0.65		5.36	10.19	5.7	4	4	4	56	0	21	3.23	1,000,000				Dec-19
8.10	2.82					0.5		5.36	10.19	5.7	4	4	4	56	0	21	3.23	1,000,000				Dec-19
12.46	-11.44	-7.68	9.56	38.73	10.92	0	14.1		12.43	481.2	-63	40	2	19	0	18	4.33					Dec-01
13.89	-12.22	-7.30	15.45	50.17	12.18	1.19	15.59		12.09	1,115	-88	40	1	20	0	22	4.26					Dec-02
7.11	-1.01	1.52	13.14	29.22	4.28	1.04	6.47	5.88	10.84	4,101	-58	32	0	24	2	127	3.63	1,000,000				Oct-04
7.07	-1.09	1.37	12.63	28.26	4.13	1.19	6.47	5.88	10.84	4,101	-58	32	0	24	2	127	3.63	1,000	50	3.75		Jul-03
6.87	-1.45	0.62	10.14	23.56	3.37	1.94	6.47	5.88	10.84	4,101	-58	32	0	24	2	127	3.63	1,000	50		1.00	Jul-03
7.15	-0.94	1.67	13.65	30.19	4.44	0.89	6.47	5.88	10.84	4,101	-58	32	0	24	2	127	3.63	1,000,000				Apr-08
7.14	-0.96	1.62	13.43	29.68	4.39	0.94	6.47	5.88	10.84	4,101	-58	32	0	24	2	127	3.63	1,000,000				Apr-18
7.17	-0.89	1.77	13.98	30.83	4.54	0.79	6.47	5.88	10.84	4,101	-58	32	0	24	2	127	3.63	1,000,000				Jul-03
6.31	0.66	1.65	8.81	15.23	4.54	1.41	3.81	0.41	10.57	3,238	-20	27	0	10	11	433	2.62	1,000	50	3.75		Jun-08
6.11	0.29	0.89	6.40	10.90	3.78	2.16	3.8	0.41	10.57	3,238	-20	27	0	10	11	433	2.62	1,000	50		1.00	Jul-08
6.38	0.81	1.95	9.79	16.97	4.84	1.11	3.81	0.41	10.57	3,238	-20	27	0	10	11	433	2.62	1,000,000				Jun-08
6.37	0.78	1.90	9.59	16.52	4.79	1.16	3.81	0.41	10.57	3,238	-20	27	0	10	11	433	2.62	1,000,000				Apr-18
6.24	0.54	1.40	8.00	13.91	4.29	1.66	3.81	0.41	10.57	3,238	-20	27	0	10	11	433	2.62	0				Jul-08
6.41	0.86	2.05	10.12	17.56	4.95	1.01	3.81	0.41	10.57	3,238	-20	27	0	10	11	433	2.62	1,000,000				Jun-08
13.41	-16.39	-13.49	7.26	33.04	14.45	2.15	17.17		18.13	2,444	-115	21	0	21	2	13	3.81					Jan-13
14.11	-12.08	-10.20	9.98	38.98	14.07	2.18	15.33		22.56	1,261	-108	22	0	20	1	12	3.96					May-12
11.74	-2.85	0.44	9.88	25.89	4.47	1.22	10.37	7.12	10.18	2,189	-29	50	0	15	0	97	4.59	1,000	50	3.75		Jul-97
11.54	-3.21	-0.29	7.45	21.28	3.69	1.97	10.37	7.12	10.18	2,189	-29	50	0	15	0	97	4.59	1,000	50		1.00	Jul-97
11.81	-2.72	0.71	10.77	27.60	4.75	0.95	10.37	7.12	10.18	2,189	-29	50	0	15	0	97	4.59	1,000,000				Apr-08
11.80	-2.74	0.66	10.54	27.08	4.7	1	10.37	7.12	10.18	2,189	-29	50	0	15	0	97	4.59	1,000,000				Apr-18
11.84	-2.67	0.81	11.10	28.23	4.85	0.85	10.37	7.12	10.18	2,189	-29	50	0	15	0	97	4.59	1,000,000				Jul-97
12.19	-1.45	1.13	13.50	24.25	4.51	0.98	9.2	5.06	10.49	129.1	-11	31	0	61	0	67	4.97	1,000,000				Jul-09
6.84	-6.87	-5.71	-2.32	2.65	3.4	1.28	8.78	0.80	7.49	1,120	85	20	0	7	4	84	4.17	1,000	50	3.75		May-05
6.91	-6.73	-5.43	-1.44	4.19	3.71	0.98	8.78	0.80	7.49	1,120	85	20	0	7	4	84	4.17	1,000,000				Apr-08
6.94	-6.68	-5.34	-1.15	4.71	3.82	0.88	8.78	0.80	7.49	1,120	85	20	0	7	4	84	4.17	1,000,000				May-05
11.97	-5.45	-1.31	7.04	16.74	5.38	0.98	11.45	6.23	7.07	273.6	-5	42	0	10	0	21	5.05	1,000,000				Feb-13
13.05	-9.57	-4.62	0.93	7.96	6.06	1.34	14.8	7.18	6.36	1,522	-19	46	0	4	0	197	4.25	1,000	50	3.75		Jul-07
12.85	-9.90	-5.33	-1.29	4.00	5.26	2.09	14.79	7.18	6.36	1,522	-19	46	0	4	0	197	4.25	1,000	50		1.00	Jul-07
13.13	-9.43	-4.33	1.84	9.66	6.38	1.04	14.8	7.18	6.36	1,522	-19	46	0	4	0	197	4.25	1,000,000				May-08

	MARKET		FUND TYPE, CATEGORY & OBJECTIVE		RATINGS				NEW INVESTORS	
Fund Name	Ticker Symbol	Traded On	Fund Type	Category and (Prospectus Objective)	Overall Rating	Reward Rating	Risk Rating	Recent Up/ Downgrade	Open to New Investors	Telephone
PIMCO Emerg Mkts Local Currency & Bond Fund Class I-3	PELNX	NAS CM	Open End	Emerg Mkts Fixed Inc (Diversified Emerg Mkts)	D	D	D+	Down	Y	866-746-2602
PIMCO Emerg Mkts Local Currency & Bond Institutional Cl	PELBX	NAS CM	Open End	Emerg Mkts Fixed Inc (Diversified Emerg Mkts)	D	D	D+	Down	Y	866-746-2602
PIMCO Extended Duration Fund Class I-2	PEDPX	NAS CM	Open End	US Fixed Inc (Growth & Income)	B	B	B		Y	866-746-2602
PIMCO Extended Duration Fund Institutional Class	PEDIX	NAS CM	Open End	US Fixed Inc (Growth & Income)	B	B	B		Y	866-746-2602
PIMCO Fixed Income SHares: Series C	FXICX	NAS CM	Open End	US Fixed Inc (Worldwide Bond)	B-	C	B+	Up	Y	866-746-2602
PIMCO Fixed Income SHares: Series LD	FXIDX	NAS CM	Open End	Fixed Inc Misc (Worldwide Bond)	C	C-	B-		Y	866-746-2602
PIMCO Fixed Income SHares: Series M	FXIMX	NAS CM	Open End	US Fixed Inc (Multisector Bond)	C+	C	B	Up	Y	866-746-2602
PIMCO Fixed Income SHares: Series R	FXIRX	NAS CM	Open End	US Fixed Inc (Worldwide Bond)	B	B	A-	Up	Y	866-746-2602
PIMCO Fixed Income SHares: Series TE	FXIEX	NAS CM	Open End	US Muni Fixed Inc (Muni Bond - Natl)	C+	C	B	Up	Y	866-746-2602
PIMCO Flexible Credit Income Fund Class A-2			Closed End	US Fixed Inc (Income)	U	U	U		Y	866-746-2602
PIMCO Flexible Credit Income Fund Class A-4	PFFLX	NAS CM	Closed End	US Fixed Inc (Income)	D	D	D		Y	866-746-2602
PIMCO Flexible Credit Income Fund Class Inst	PFLEX	NAS CM	Closed End	US Fixed Inc (Income)	D	D	D	Down	Y	866-746-2602
PIMCO Flexible Municipal Income Fund A-3 Class			Closed End	US Muni Fixed Inc (Muni Bond - Natl)	U	U	U		Y	866-746-2602
PIMCO Flexible Municipal Income Fund Institutional Class			Closed End	US Muni Fixed Inc (Muni Bond - Natl)	D	D+	C	Up	Y	866-746-2602
PIMCO Global Advantage Strategy Bond Fund Class A	PGSAX	NAS CM	Open End	Global Fixed Inc (Growth & Income)	C	C-	B-		Y	866-746-2602
PIMCO Global Advantage Strategy Bond Institutional Cl	PSAIX	NAS CM	Open End	Global Fixed Inc (Growth & Income)	C	C-	B-		Y	866-746-2602
PIMCO Global Bond Opp (U.S. Dollar-Hedged) Admin Cl	PGDAX	NAS CM	Open End	Global Fixed Inc (Worldwide Bond)	C	C	B-		Y	866-746-2602
PIMCO Global Bond Opportunities (U.S. Dollar-Hedged) Cl A	PAIIX	NAS CM	Open End	Global Fixed Inc (Worldwide Bond)	C	C	B-		Y	866-746-2602
PIMCO Global Bond Opp (U.S. Dollar-Hedged) Cl I-2	PGNPX	NAS CM	Open End	Global Fixed Inc (Worldwide Bond)	C	C	B-		Y	866-746-2602
PIMCO Global Bond Opportunities (U.S. Dollar-Hedged) CIC	PCIIX	NAS CM	Open End	Global Fixed Inc (Worldwide Bond)	C	C-	C+		Y	866-746-2602
PIMCO Global Bond Opp (U.S. Dollar-Hedged) Inst Cl	PGBIX	NAS CM	Open End	Global Fixed Inc (Worldwide Bond)	C	C	B-		Y	866-746-2602
PIMCO Global Bond Opp (Unhedged) Administrative Cl	PADMX	NAS CM	Open End	Global Fixed Inc (Worldwide Bond)	D+	D	C	Down	Y	866-746-2602
PIMCO Global Bond Opportunities Fund (Unhedged) Class A	PAGPX	NAS CM	Open End	Global Fixed Inc (Worldwide Bond)	D+	D	C	Down	Y	866-746-2602
PIMCO Global Bond Opportunities (Unhedged) Inst Cl	PIGLX	NAS CM	Open End	Global Fixed Inc (Worldwide Bond)	D+	D	C	Down	Y	866-746-2602
PIMCO GNMA and Government Securities Fund Class A	PAGNX	NAS CM	Open End	US Fixed Inc (Govt Bond - Mortgage)	B-	C+	B	Up	Y	866-746-2602
PIMCO GNMA and Government Securities Fund Class C	PCGNX	NAS CM	Open End	US Fixed Inc (Govt Bond - Mortgage)	C+	C+	B-	Up	Y	866-746-2602
PIMCO GNMA and Government Securities Fund Class I-2	PPGNX	NAS CM	Open End	US Fixed Inc (Govt Bond - Mortgage)	B-	C+	B	Up	Y	866-746-2602
PIMCO GNMA and Government Securities Fund Class I-3	PANNX	NAS CM	Open End	US Fixed Inc (Govt Bond - Mortgage)	B-	C+	B	Up	Y	866-746-2602
PIMCO GNMA & Govt Securities Fund Institutional Class	PDMIX	NAS CM	Open End	US Fixed Inc (Govt Bond - Mortgage)	B-	B-	B	Up	Y	866-746-2602
PIMCO Government Money Market Fund Class A	AMAXX	NAS CM	Money Mkt	US Money Mkt (Money Mkt - Govt)	C	C-	C+		Y	866-746-2602
PIMCO Government Money Market Fund Class Administrative	PGOXX	NAS CM	Money Mkt	US Money Mkt (Money Mkt - Govt)	C	C-	C+		Y	866-746-2602
PIMCO Government Money Market Fund Class C	AMGXX	NAS CM	Money Mkt	US Money Mkt (Money Mkt - Govt)	C	C-	C+		Y	866-746-2602
PIMCO Government Money Market Fund Class I-2	PGPXX	NAS CM	Money Mkt	US Money Mkt (Money Mkt - Govt)	C	C-	C+		Y	866-746-2602
PIMCO Government Money Market Fund Class Institutional	PGYXX	NAS CM	Money Mkt	US Money Mkt (Money Mkt - Govt)	C	C-	C+		Y	866-746-2602
PIMCO Government Money Market Fund Class M	PGFXX	NAS CM	Money Mkt	US Money Mkt (Money Mkt - Govt)	C	C-	C+		Y	866-746-2602
PIMCO Gurtin California Muni Intermed Value Inst Shares	GCMVX	NAS CM	Open End	US Muni Fixed Inc (Muni Bond - Single State)	C+	C	B	Up	Y	866-746-2602
PIMCO Gurtin Calif Muni Opportunistic Value Inst Shares	GCMFX	NAS CM	Open End	US Muni Fixed Inc (Muni Bond - Single State)	C	C	B-		Y	866-746-2602
PIMCO Gurtin Natl Muni Intermed Value Inst Shares	GNMVX	NAS CM	Open End	US Muni Fixed Inc (Muni Bond - Natl)	C+	C	B	Up	Y	866-746-2602
PIMCO Gurtin Natl Muni Opportunistic Value Inst Shares	GNMFX	NAS CM	Open End	US Muni Fixed Inc (Muni Bond - Natl)	C	C	B-		Y	866-746-2602
PIMCO High Income Fund	PHK	NYSE	Closed End	US Fixed Inc (Corp Bond - High Yield)	D	D	D	Down	Y	866-746-2602
PIMCO High Yield Fund Administrative Class	PHYAX	NAS CM	Open End	US Fixed Inc (Corp Bond - High Yield)	C-	D+	C		Y	866-746-2602
PIMCO High Yield Fund Class A	PHDAX	NAS CM	Open End	US Fixed Inc (Corp Bond - High Yield)	C-	D+	C		Y	866-746-2602
PIMCO High Yield Fund Class C	PHDCX	NAS CM	Open End	US Fixed Inc (Corp Bond - High Yield)	C-	D+	C		Y	866-746-2602
PIMCO High Yield Fund Class I-2	PHLPX	NAS CM	Open End	US Fixed Inc (Corp Bond - High Yield)	C-	D+	C	Down	Y	866-746-2602
PIMCO High Yield Fund Class R	PHYRX	NAS CM	Open End	US Fixed Inc (Corp Bond - High Yield)	C-	D+	C		Y	866-746-2602
PIMCO High Yield Fund I-3	PHNNX	NAS CM	Open End	US Fixed Inc (Corp Bond - High Yield)	C-	D+	C	Down	Y	866-746-2602
PIMCO High Yield Fund Institutional Class	PHIYX	NAS CM	Open End	US Fixed Inc (Corp Bond - High Yield)	C-	D+	C	Down	Y	866-746-2602
PIMCO High Yield Municipal Bond Fund Class A	PYMAX	NAS CM	Open End	US Muni Fixed Inc (Muni Bond - Natl)	C	C-	C+		Y	866-746-2602
PIMCO High Yield Municipal Bond Fund Class C	PYMCX	NAS CM	Open End	US Muni Fixed Inc (Muni Bond - Natl)	C	C-	C+		Y	866-746-2602
PIMCO High Yield Municipal Bond Fund Class I-2	PYMPX	NAS CM	Open End	US Muni Fixed Inc (Muni Bond - Natl)	C	C-	B-	Down	Y	866-746-2602
PIMCO High Yield Municipal Bond Fund Institutional Class	PHMIX	NAS CM	Open End	US Muni Fixed Inc (Muni Bond - Natl)	C	C-	B-	Down	Y	866-746-2602
PIMCO High Yield Spectrum Fund Class A	PHSAX	NAS CM	Open End	US Fixed Inc (Corp Bond - High Yield)	C-	D+	C		Y	866-746-2602

★Expanded analysis of this fund is included in Section II.

TOTAL RETURNS & PERFORMANCE									ASSETS		ASSET ALLOCATION & TURNOVER							MINIMUMS		FEES		
3-Month Total Return	6-Month Total Return	1-Year Total Return	3-Year Total Return	5-Year Total Return	Dividend Yield (TTM)	Expense Ratio	3-Yr Std Deviation	Effective Duration	NAV	Total Assets (MIL)	%Cash	%Government Bonds	%Municipal Bonds	%Corporate Bonds	%Other	Turnover Ratio	Average Coupon Rate	Min Initial Investment	Min Additional Investment	Front End Fee (%)	Back End Fee (%)	Inception Date
13.12	-9.46	-4.38	1.66	9.24	6.32	1.09	14.8	7.18	6.36	1,522	-19	46	0	4	0	197	4.25	1,000,000				Apr-18
13.16	-9.39	-4.24	2.14	10.20	6.48	0.94	14.8	7.18	6.36	1,522	-19	46	0	4	0	197	4.25	1,000,000				Dec-06
-0.76	29.10	34.88	53.43	82.63	2.04	1.27	17.31	27.47	10.93	1,387	23	58	0	1	0	179		1,000,000				Sep-08
-0.73	29.16	35.02	53.89	83.55	2.13	1.17	17.31	27.47	10.93	1,387	23	58	0	1	0	179		1,000,000				Aug-06
6.68	5.03	7.73	17.23	21.39	3.63	0.21	4.34		10.77	1,462	-66	13	1	24	0	533	3.34	0				Mar-00
7.06	2.92	4.32	9.14	17.27	3.99	2.98	4.52		9.52	86.2	-84	25	0	43	0	88	3.60	0				Dec-13
7.92	3.72	6.26	18.73	39.69	4.52	0.06	5.33		10.68	1,474	-97	24	2	13	0	543	2.86	0				Mar-00
7.16	8.42	11.44	21.38	25.64	2.44	1.35	4.7		10.11	128.0	-36	64	0	1	0	357	1.90	0				Apr-04
4.25	2.71	5.45	16.25	27.84	3.52	0.08	4.28		10.49	88.2	7	0	93	0	0	31	4.84	0				Jun-12
8.85	-12.37					4.41			8.19	--	-62	9	0	36	7		4.81	2,500	50	2.00		Oct-19
8.93	-12.23	-10.23			11.4	4.66			8.19	--	-62	9	0	36	7		4.81	2,500	50	3.00		Nov-18
9.17	-11.84	-9.50	5.19		12.34	3.91	12.28		8.19	--	-62	9	0	36	7		4.81	1,000,000				Feb-17
6.01	1.34					2.23			10.78	--	-16	0	93	4	1	96	4.12	2,500	50	3.00		Sep-19
6.23	1.73	6.70			3.25	1.48			10.78	--	-16	0	93	4	1	96	4.12	1,000,000				Mar-19
6.17	0.67	2.73	11.42	20.00	2.35	1.25	4.65	6.45	11.09	329.5	-19	27	0	8	1	407	2.90	1,000	50	3.75		Feb-09
6.27	0.87	3.14	12.76	22.41	2.74	0.85	4.66	6.45	11.09	329.5	-19	27	0	8	1	407	2.90	1,000,000				Feb-09
4.74	1.93	3.63	9.95	20.22	3.71	0.87	3.27	5.25	10.35	886.4	-63	34	0	6	5	469	3.03	1,000,000				Sep-03
4.71	1.88	3.53	9.62	19.62	3.61	0.97	3.27	5.25	10.35	886.4	-63	34	0	6	5	469	3.03	1,000	50	3.75		Oct-95
4.78	2.01	3.78	10.45	21.12	3.86	0.72	3.27	5.25	10.35	886.4	-63	34	0	6	5	469	3.03	1,000,000				Apr-08
4.52	1.51	2.76	7.19	15.22	2.86	1.72	3.26	5.25	10.35	886.4	-63	34	0	6	5	469	3.03	1,000	50		1.00	Oct-95
4.80	2.06	3.89	10.78	21.72	3.96	0.62	3.27	5.25	10.35	886.4	-63	34	0	6	5	469	3.03	1,000,000				Feb-98
7.34	-1.24	0.56	4.26	14.60	2.65	0.97	6.1	5.39	8.89	198.6	-30	35	0	6	2	440	2.83	1,000,000				Jul-96
7.30	-1.31	0.41	3.80	13.75	2.5	1.12	6.1	5.39	8.89	198.6	-30	35	0	6	2	440	2.83	1,000	50	3.75		Jan-18
7.40	-1.12	0.81	5.04	16.03	2.9	0.72	6.1	5.39	8.89	198.6	-30	35	0	6	2	440	2.83	1,000,000				Nov-93
1.55	4.13	6.17	11.79	15.58	2.73	1.11	2.38	1.79	11.43	1,737	-39	0	0	0	0	903	3.29	1,000	50	3.75		Nov-00
1.36	3.75	5.39	9.31	11.34	2	1.86	2.38	1.79	11.43	1,737	-39	0	0	0	0	903	3.29	1,000	50		1.00	May-01
1.62	4.29	6.49	12.79	17.32	3.02	0.81	2.38	1.79	11.43	1,737	-39	0	0	0	0	903	3.29	1,000,000				Apr-08
1.61	4.26	6.44	12.54	16.83	2.97	0.86	2.38	1.79	11.43	1,737	-39	0	0	0	0	903	3.29	1,000,000				Jan-19
1.65	4.34	6.59	13.13	17.91	3.12	0.71	2.38	1.79	11.43	1,737	-39	0	0	0	0	903	3.29	1,000,000				Jul-97
0.01	0.27	1.14	4.35	4.77	1.31	0.33	0.18		1	1,851	91	7	0	0	0			1,000	50			May-09
0.01	0.30	1.24	4.78	5.45	1.43	0.18	0.19		1	1,851	91	7	0	0	0			1,000,000				May-16
0.00	0.26	1.13	4.34	4.76	1.3	0.33	0.18		1	1,851	91	7	0	0	0			1,000	50			May-09
0.01	0.27	1.17	4.49	4.99	1.35	0.28	0.18		1	1,851	91	7	0	0	0			1,000,000				May-09
0.00	0.30	1.24	4.78	5.45	1.43	0.18	0.19		1	1,851	91	7	0	0	0			1,000,000				May-16
0.00	0.30	1.24	4.76	5.44	1.43	0.18	0.19		1	1,851	91	7	0	0	0			1,000,000				Jan-09
2.76	2.05	3.59	11.28		1.7	0.39	3.45	5.24	10.67	52.0	4	0	96	0	0	17	4.86	250,000				Dec-15
1.21	0.82	2.38	9.29	14.97	2.47	0.6	2.02	4.46	10.24	258.6	6	0	94	0	0	16	4.78	250,000				Nov-14
2.09	2.17	3.94	11.30		1.87	0.39	3.02	4.97	10.61	144.4	1	0	99	0	0	15	4.61	250,000				Dec-15
1.06	1.10	2.98	11.32	17.53	2.51	0.6	2.67	5.26	10.43	274.8	3	0	96	0	0	14	4.96	250,000				Nov-14
10.89	-15.53	-11.91	9.22	41.38	11.13	0	15.4		4.93	626.8	-145	54	2	10	0	20	3.85					Apr-03
7.91	-4.06	-0.43	9.06	22.84	4.93	0.84	7.76	3.41	8.47	10,459	0	5	0	78	2	34	5.63	1,000,000				Jan-95
7.88	-4.11	-0.52	8.74	22.23	4.82	0.94	7.76	3.41	8.47	10,459	0	5	0	78	2	34	5.63	1,000	50	3.75		Jan-97
7.68	-4.46	-1.26	6.33	17.75	4.05	1.69	7.76	3.41	8.47	10,459	0	5	0	78	2	34	5.63	1,000	50		1.00	Jan-97
7.95	-3.99	-0.28	9.55	23.76	5.08	0.69	7.76	3.41	8.47	10,459	0	5	0	78	2	34	5.63	1,000,000				Apr-08
7.82	-4.23	-0.77	7.93	20.72	4.57	1.19	7.76	3.41	8.47	10,459	0	5	0	78	2	34	5.63	0				Dec-02
7.93	-4.01	-0.33	9.35	23.28	5.03	0.74	7.77	3.41	8.47	10,459	0	5	0	78	2	34	5.63	1,000,000				Apr-18
7.97	-3.94	-0.18	9.88	24.38	5.18	0.59	7.77	3.41	8.47	10,459	0	5	0	78	2	34	5.63	1,000,000				Dec-92
3.43	-0.19	3.03	15.59	31.49	3.34	0.96	6.22	7.20	9.27	1,669	7	0	91	1	1	68	4.86	1,000	50	2.25		Jul-06
3.24	-0.56	2.27	13.03	26.67	2.57	1.71	6.22	7.20	9.27	1,669	7	0	91	1	1	68	4.86	1,000	50		1.00	Dec-06
3.48	-0.10	3.23	16.28	32.81	3.55	0.76	6.22	7.20	9.27	1,669	7	0	91	1	1	68	4.86	1,000,000				Apr-08
3.50	-0.05	3.33	16.63	33.47	3.65	0.66	6.22	7.20	9.27	1,669	7	0	91	1	1	68	4.86	1,000,000				Jul-06
8.76	-5.03	-1.22	7.75	23.23	5.55	0.98	8.55	3.37	9.21	346.9	6	3	0	73	1	27	6.38	1,000	50	3.75		Sep-10

	MARKET			FUND TYPE, CATEGORY & OBJECTIVE	RATINGS				NEW INVESTORS	
Fund Name	Ticker Symbol	Traded On	Fund Type	Category and (Prospectus Objective)	Overall Rating	Reward Rating	Risk Rating	Recent Up/ Downgrade	Open to New Investors	Telephone
PIMCO High Yield Spectrum Fund Class C	PHSCX	NAS CM	Open End	US Fixed Inc (Corp Bond - High Yield)	C-	D+	C		Y	866-746-2602
PIMCO High Yield Spectrum Fund Class I-2	PHSPX	NAS CM	Open End	US Fixed Inc (Corp Bond - High Yield)	C-	D+	C		Y	866-746-2602
PIMCO High Yield Spectrum Fund Class I-3	PHFNX	NAS CM	Open End	US Fixed Inc (Corp Bond - High Yield)	C-	D+	C		Y	866-746-2602
PIMCO High Yield Spectrum Fund Institutional Class	PHSIX	NAS CM	Open End	US Fixed Inc (Corp Bond - High Yield)	C-	D+	C		Y	866-746-2602
PIMCO Income Fund Administrative Class	PIINX	NAS CM	Open End	US Fixed Inc (Multisector Bond)	C-	D+	C	Down	Y	866-746-2602
★ PIMCO Income Fund Class A	PONAX	NAS CM	Open End	US Fixed Inc (Multisector Bond)	C-	D+	C	Down	Y	866-746-2602
★ PIMCO Income Fund Class C	PONCX	NAS CM	Open End	US Fixed Inc (Multisector Bond)	C-	D+	C	Down	Y	866-746-2602
PIMCO Income Fund Class I-2	PONPX	NAS CM	Open End	US Fixed Inc (Multisector Bond)	C-	D+	C	Down	Y	866-746-2602
PIMCO Income Fund Class I-3	PIPNX	NAS CM	Open End	US Fixed Inc (Multisector Bond)	C-	D+	C	Down	Y	866-746-2602
★ PIMCO Income Fund Class R	PONRX	NAS CM	Open End	US Fixed Inc (Multisector Bond)	C-	D+	C	Down	Y	866-746-2602
PIMCO Income Fund Institutional Class	PIMIX	NAS CM	Open End	US Fixed Inc (Multisector Bond)	C-	D+	C	Down	Y	866-746-2602
PIMCO Income Opportunity Fund	PKO	NYSE	Closed End	US Fixed Inc (Worldwide Bond)	D	D	D+	Down	Y	866-746-2602
PIMCO Income Strategy Fund	PFL	NYSE	Closed End	US Fixed Inc (Corp Bond - General)	D	D	D+	Down	Y	866-746-2602
PIMCO Income Strategy Fund II	PFN	NYSE	Closed End	US Fixed Inc (Corp Bond - General)	D	D	D+	Down	Y	866-746-2602
PIMCO InterNatl Bond (U.S. Dollar-Hedged) Admin Cl	PFRAX	NAS CM	Open End	Global Fixed Inc (Worldwide Bond)	C	C	B-		Y	866-746-2602
PIMCO International Bond Fund (U.S. Dollar-Hedged) Class A	PFOAX	NAS CM	Open End	Global Fixed Inc (Worldwide Bond)	C	C	B-		Y	866-746-2602
PIMCO International Bond Fund (U.S. Dollar-Hedged) Class C	PFOCX	NAS CM	Open End	Global Fixed Inc (Worldwide Bond)	C	C	B-		Y	866-746-2602
PIMCO InterNatl Bond Fund (U.S. Dollar-Hedged) Class I-2	PFBPX	NAS CM	Open End	Global Fixed Inc (Worldwide Bond)	C	C	B-		Y	866-746-2602
PIMCO InterNatl Bond Fund (U.S. Dollar-Hedged) Class I-3	PFONX	NAS CM	Open End	Global Fixed Inc (Worldwide Bond)	C	C	B-		Y	866-746-2602
PIMCO International Bond Fund (U.S. Dollar-Hedged) Class R	PFRRX	NAS CM	Open End	Global Fixed Inc (Worldwide Bond)	C	C	B		Y	866-746-2602
PIMCO InterNatl Bond (U.S. Dollar-Hedged) Institutional Cl	PFORX	NAS CM	Open End	Global Fixed Inc (Worldwide Bond)	C	C	B-		Y	866-746-2602
PIMCO InterNatl Bond Fund (Unhedged) Administrative Class	PFUUX	NAS CM	Open End	Global Fixed Inc (Worldwide Bond)	D+	D	C	Down	Y	866-746-2602
PIMCO International Bond Fund (Unhedged) Class A	PFUAX	NAS CM	Open End	Global Fixed Inc (Worldwide Bond)	D+	D	C	Down	Y	866-746-2602
PIMCO International Bond Fund (Unhedged) Class C	PFRCX	NAS CM	Open End	Global Fixed Inc (Worldwide Bond)	D+	D	C-	Down	Y	866-746-2602
PIMCO International Bond Fund (Unhedged) Class I-2	PFUPX	NAS CM	Open End	Global Fixed Inc (Worldwide Bond)	D+	D	C	Down	Y	866-746-2602
PIMCO International Bond Fund (Unhedged) Class I-3	PFUNX	NAS CM	Open End	Global Fixed Inc (Worldwide Bond)	D+	D	C	Down	Y	866-746-2602
PIMCO InterNatl Bond Fund (Unhedged) Institutional Class	PFUIX	NAS CM	Open End	Global Fixed Inc (Worldwide Bond)	D+	D	C	Down	Y	866-746-2602
PIMCO Investment Grade Credit Bond Administrative Cl	PGCAX	NAS CM	Open End	US Fixed Inc (Corp Bond - General)	C	C-	B-		Y	866-746-2602
PIMCO Investment Grade Credit Bond Fund Class A	PBDAX	NAS CM	Open End	US Fixed Inc (Corp Bond - General)	C	C-	B-		Y	866-746-2602
PIMCO Investment Grade Credit Bond Fund Class C	PBDCX	NAS CM	Open End	US Fixed Inc (Corp Bond - General)	C	C-	B-		Y	866-746-2602
PIMCO Investment Grade Credit Bond Fund Class I-2	PBDPX	NAS CM	Open End	US Fixed Inc (Corp Bond - General)	C	C-	B		Y	866-746-2602
PIMCO Investment Grade Credit Bond Fund Class I-3	PCNNX	NAS CM	Open End	US Fixed Inc (Corp Bond - General)	C	C-	B-		Y	866-746-2602
PIMCO Investment Grade Credit Bond Institutional Cl	PIGIX	NAS CM	Open End	US Fixed Inc (Corp Bond - General)	C	C-	B		Y	866-746-2602
PIMCO Long Duration Total Return Fund Class A	PLRAX	NAS CM	Open End	US Fixed Inc (Growth & Income)	B	B	B	Up	Y	866-746-2602
PIMCO Long Duration Total Return Fund Class C	PLRCX	NAS CM	Open End	US Fixed Inc (Growth & Income)	B	B	B	Up	Y	866-746-2602
PIMCO Long Duration Total Return Fund Class I-2	PLRPX	NAS CM	Open End	US Fixed Inc (Growth & Income)	B	B	B		Y	866-746-2602
PIMCO Long Duration Total Return Fund Institutional Class	PLRIX	NAS CM	Open End	US Fixed Inc (Growth & Income)	B	B	B		Y	866-746-2602
PIMCO Long-Term Credit Bond Fund Class I-2	PLCPX	NAS CM	Open End	US Fixed Inc (Growth & Income)	C+	C	B		Y	866-746-2602
PIMCO Long-Term Credit Bond Fund Institutional Class	PTCIX	NAS CM	Open End	US Fixed Inc (Growth & Income)	C+	C	B		Y	866-746-2602
PIMCO Long-Term Real Return Fund Class I-2	PRTPX	NAS CM	Open End	US Fixed Inc (Growth & Income)	B	B	B+		Y	866-746-2602
PIMCO Long-Term Real Return Fund Institutional Class	PRAIX	NAS CM	Open End	US Fixed Inc (Growth & Income)	B	B	B+		Y	866-746-2602
PIMCO Long-Term U.S. Government Fund Administrative Class	PLGBX	NAS CM	Open End	US Fixed Inc (Govt Bond - General)	B	B	B		Y	866-746-2602
PIMCO Long-Term U.S. Government Fund Class A	PFGAX	NAS CM	Open End	US Fixed Inc (Govt Bond - General)	B	B	B		Y	866-746-2602
PIMCO Long-Term U.S. Government Fund Class C	PFGCX	NAS CM	Open End	US Fixed Inc (Govt Bond - General)	B	B	B		Y	866-746-2602
PIMCO Long-Term U.S. Government Fund Class I-2	PLTPX	NAS CM	Open End	US Fixed Inc (Govt Bond - General)	B	B	B		Y	866-746-2602
PIMCO Long-Term U.S. Government Fund Institutional Class	PGOVX	NAS CM	Open End	US Fixed Inc (Govt Bond - General)	B	B	B		Y	866-746-2602
PIMCO Low Duration ESG Fund Class I-2	PLUPX	NAS CM	Open End	US Fixed Inc (Income)	C	C	B-		Y	866-746-2602
PIMCO Low Duration ESG Fund Institutional Class	PLDIX	NAS CM	Open End	US Fixed Inc (Income)	C	C	B-		Y	866-746-2602
PIMCO Low Duration Fund Administrative Class	PLDAX	NAS CM	Open End	US Fixed Inc (Income)	C	C	B-		Y	866-746-2602
PIMCO Low Duration Fund Class A	PTLAX	NAS CM	Open End	US Fixed Inc (Income)	C	C	B-		Y	866-746-2602
PIMCO Low Duration Fund Class C	PTLCX	NAS CM	Open End	US Fixed Inc (Income)	C	C	B-		Y	866-746-2602
PIMCO Low Duration Fund Class I-2	PLDPX	NAS CM	Open End	US Fixed Inc (Income)	C	C	B-		Y	866-746-2602

★Expanded analysis of this fund is included in Section II.

TOTAL RETURNS & PERFORMANCE									ASSETS		ASSET ALLOCATION & TURNOVER							MINIMUMS		FEES		
3-Month Total Return	6-Month Total Return	1-Year Total Return	3-Year Total Return	5-Year Total Return	Dividend Yield (TTM)	Expense Ratio	3-Yr Std Deviation	Effective Duration	NAV	Total Assets (MIL)	%Cash	%Government Bonds	%Municipal Bonds	%Corporate Bonds	%Other	Turnover Ratio	Average Coupon Rate	Min Initial Investment	Min Additional Investment	Front End Fee (%)	Back End Fee (%)	Inception Date
8.56	-5.38	-1.95	5.37	18.72	4.78	1.73	8.54	3.37	9.21	346.9	6	3	0	73	1	27	6.38	1,000	50		1.00	Sep-10
8.82	-4.91	-0.97	8.56	24.78	5.81	0.73	8.55	3.37	9.21	346.9	6	3	0	73	1	27	6.38	1,000,000				Sep-10
8.81	-4.94	-1.02	8.35	24.28	5.76	0.78	8.55	3.37	9.21	346.9	6	3	0	73	1	27	6.38	1,000,000				Apr-18
8.85	-4.87	-0.87	8.88	25.39	5.92	0.63	8.55	3.37	9.21	346.9	6	3	0	73	1	27	6.38	1,000,000				Sep-10
6.39	-1.82	0.32	9.44	24.06	5.9	1.3	5.45	0.77	11.5	116,854	-26	25	0	7	0	421	3.22	1,000,000				Mar-07
6.35	-1.89	0.18	8.95	23.13	5.75	1.45	5.45	0.77	11.5	116,854	-26	25	0	7	0	421	3.22	1,000	50	3.75		Mar-07
6.16	-2.26	-0.56	6.53	18.61	4.96	2.2	5.45	0.77	11.5	116,854	-26	25	0	7	0	421	3.22	1,000	50		1.00	Mar-07
6.43	-1.74	0.47	9.93	24.98	6.06	1.15	5.45	0.77	11.5	116,854	-26	25	0	7	0	421	3.22	1,000,000				Apr-08
6.42	-1.77	0.43	9.72	24.49	6.01	1.2	5.45	0.77	11.5	116,854	-26	25	0	7	0	421	3.22	1,000,000				Apr-18
6.29	-2.01	-0.06	8.13	21.60	5.49	1.7	5.45	0.77	11.5	116,854	-26	25	0	7	0	421	3.22	0				Mar-07
6.45	-1.69	0.58	10.26	25.61	6.17	1.05	5.45	0.77	11.5	116,854	-26	25	0	7	0	421	3.22	1,000,000				Mar-07
13.23	-8.34	-5.70	13.49	38.31	11.04	2.7	13.28		21.09	368.2	-93	23	0	31	0	18	4.29					Nov-07
14.22	-10.18	-6.57	9.25	31.50	11.41	1.81	14.25		9.24	268.4	-38	36	2	23	0	17	4.55					Aug-03
14.00	-10.16	-6.83	10.43	33.74	11.87	1.74	14.14		8.33	557.4	-27	36	2	19	0	17	4.32					Oct-04
3.71	1.65	2.90	13.93	25.19	5.9	0.8	3.29	8.70	10.8	11,230	-57	33	0	6	4	333	2.64	1,000,000				Jan-97
3.67	1.57	2.75	13.42	24.26	5.74	0.95	3.28	8.70	10.8	11,230	-57	33	0	6	4	333	2.64	1,000	50	3.75		Jan-97
3.48	1.20	1.98	10.86	19.69	4.98	1.7	3.27	8.70	10.8	11,230	-57	33	0	6	4	333	2.64	1,000	50		1.00	Jan-97
3.75	1.72	3.05	14.44	26.13	6.05	0.65	3.29	8.70	10.8	11,230	-57	33	0	6	4	333	2.64	1,000,000				Apr-08
3.74	1.70	3.00	14.23	25.65	6	0.7	3.29	8.70	10.8	11,230	-57	33	0	6	4	333	2.64	1,000,000				Apr-18
3.61	1.45	2.49	12.58	22.72	5.49	1.2	3.28	8.70	10.8	11,230	-57	33	0	6	4	333	2.64	0				Dec-02
3.77	1.77	3.15	14.78	26.76	6.15	0.55	3.29	8.70	10.8	11,230	-57	33	0	6	4	333	2.64	1,000,000				Dec-92
7.88	-1.54	-0.26	4.81	14.06	1.96	0.91	7.36	8.82	9.49	1,136	-44	30	0	6	0	325	2.63	1,000,000				Feb-06
7.84	-1.61	-0.40	4.34	13.21	1.81	1.06	7.36	8.82	9.49	1,136	-44	30	0	6	0	325	2.63	1,000	50	3.75		Jul-04
7.64	-1.97	-1.14	2.03	9.05	1.05	1.81	7.35	8.82	9.49	1,136	-44	30	0	6	0	325	2.63	1,000	50		1.00	Jul-04
7.92	-1.47	-0.11	5.28	14.91	2.11	0.76	7.36	8.82	9.49	1,136	-44	30	0	6	0	325	2.63	1,000,000				Apr-08
7.91	-1.49	-0.16	5.09	14.48	2.07	0.81	7.35	8.82	9.49	1,136	-44	30	0	6	0	325	2.63	1,000,000				Apr-18
7.94	-1.42	-0.01	5.59	15.49	2.22	0.66	7.36	8.82	9.49	1,136	-44	30	0	6	0	325	2.63	1,000,000				Apr-04
8.51	1.91	6.23	16.84	30.39	3.65	1.02	6.98	7.15	10.94	17,737	-66	17	0	41	0	213	3.17	1,000,000				Sep-02
8.47	1.83	6.08	16.32	29.43	3.5	1.17	6.98	7.15	10.94	17,737	-66	17	0	41	0	213	3.17	1,000	50	3.75		Jul-04
8.27	1.46	5.29	13.75	24.69	2.76	1.92	6.97	7.15	10.94	17,737	-66	17	0	41	0	213	3.17	1,000	50		1.00	Jul-04
8.55	1.98	6.39	17.37	31.38	3.8	0.87	6.98	7.15	10.94	17,737	-66	17	0	41	0	213	3.17	1,000,000				Apr-08
8.54	1.96	6.34	17.15	30.87	3.75	0.92	6.98	7.15	10.94	17,737	-66	17	0	41	0	213	3.17	1,000,000				Apr-18
8.58	2.03	6.50	17.72	32.03	3.9	0.77	6.98	7.15	10.94	17,737	-66	17	0	41	0	213	3.17	1,000,000				Apr-00
7.50	12.96	18.63	33.24	54.74	2.81	1.37	8.79	17.03	11.9	3,411	9	31	1	18	1	269	3.66	1,000	50	3.75		Sep-17
7.30	12.54	17.76	30.29	49.08	2.13	2.12	8.79	17.03	11.9	3,411	9	31	1	18	1	269	3.66	1,000	50		1.00	Jan-18
7.58	13.12	18.97	34.39	57.02	3.08	1.07	8.8	17.03	11.9	3,411	9	31	1	18	1	269	3.66	1,000,000				Sep-08
7.60	13.17	19.09	34.79	57.80	3.17	0.97	8.8	17.03	11.9	3,411	9	31	1	18	1	269	3.66	1,000,000				Aug-06
11.08	5.00	12.69	28.89	53.85	4.36	0.89	10.06	13.36	13.28	3,846	-53	22	1	34	0	180	3.75	1,000,000				Feb-12
11.10	5.05	12.81	29.28	54.62	4.45	0.79	10.06	13.36	13.28	3,846	-53	22	1	34	0	180	3.75	1,000,000				Mar-09
8.07	16.91	23.62	35.73	44.84	2.15	1.37	9.79	21.97	10.13	984.7	-24	66	0	0	0	250	1.85	1,000,000				Nov-10
8.09	16.97	23.74	36.14	45.56	2.24	1.27	9.79	21.97	10.13	984.7	-24	66	0	0	0	250	1.85	1,000,000				Nov-01
0.56	21.51	25.56	37.81	54.04	1.99	1.22	11.71	19.42	7.88	1,018	5	60	0	1	-2	220	3.43	1,000,000				Sep-97
0.54	21.45	25.44	37.41	53.29	1.9	1.32	11.7	19.42	7.88	1,018	5	60	0	1	-2	220	3.43	1,000	50	3.75		Jan-97
0.35	21.02	24.52	34.38	47.69	1.23	2.07	11.7	19.42	7.88	1,018	5	60	0	1	-2	220	3.43	1,000	50		1.00	Jan-97
0.60	21.60	25.74	38.42	55.19	2.12	1.07	11.71	19.42	7.88	1,018	5	60	0	1	-2	220	3.43	1,000,000				Apr-08
0.63	21.66	25.87	38.84	55.97	2.21	0.97	11.71	19.42	7.88	1,018	5	60	0	1	-2	220	3.43	1,000,000				Jul-91
1.81	2.03	3.35	7.12	9.37	1.95	0.62	1.37	2.92	9.65	315.6	-38	42	1	14	0	296	3.61	1,000,000				Nov-10
1.84	2.08	3.45	7.44	9.92	2.05	0.52	1.37	2.92	9.65	315.6	-38	42	1	14	0	296	3.61	1,000,000				Dec-96
2.29	2.15	3.46	7.53	9.93	2.58	0.96	1.57	2.54	9.91	7,860	-39	48	0	12	8	269	3.95	1,000,000				Jan-95
2.28	2.13	3.42	7.37	9.57	2.55	1	1.57	2.54	9.91	7,860	-39	48	0	12	8	269	3.95	1,000	50	2.25		Jan-97
2.19	1.95	3.06	6.29	7.81	2.2	1.35	1.57	2.54	9.91	7,860	-39	48	0	12	8	269	3.95	1,000	50		1.00	Jan-97
2.32	2.22	3.62	8.02	10.76	2.73	0.81	1.57	2.54	9.91	7,860	-39	48	0	12	8	269	3.95	1,000,000				Apr-08

	MARKET			FUND TYPE, CATEGORY & OBJECTIVE	RATINGS				NEW INVESTORS	
Fund Name	Ticker Symbol	Traded On	Fund Type	Category and (Prospectus Objective)	Overall Rating	Reward Rating	Risk Rating	Recent Up/ Downgrade	Open to New Investors	Telephone
PIMCO Low Duration Fund Class R	PLDRX	NAS CM	Open End	US Fixed Inc (Income)	C	C	B-		Y	866-746-2602
PIMCO Low Duration Fund I-3	PTLNX	NAS CM	Open End	US Fixed Inc (Income)	C	C	B-		Y	866-746-2602
PIMCO Low Duration Fund Institutional Class	PTLDX	NAS CM	Open End	US Fixed Inc (Income)	C	C	B-		Y	866-746-2602
PIMCO Low Duration II Fund Administrative Class	PDFAX	NAS CM	Open End	US Fixed Inc (Income)	C+	C	B-	Up	Y	866-746-2602
PIMCO Low Duration II Fund Institutional Class	PLDTX	NAS CM	Open End	US Fixed Inc (Income)	C+	C	B	Up	Y	866-746-2602
PIMCO Low Duration Income Fund Class A	PFIAX	NAS CM	Open End	Fixed Inc Misc (Income)	C-	D+	C	Down	Y	866-746-2602
PIMCO Low Duration Income Fund Class C	PFNCX	NAS CM	Open End	Fixed Inc Misc (Income)	C-	D+	C	Down	Y	866-746-2602
PIMCO Low Duration Income Fund Class I-2	PFTPX	NAS CM	Open End	Fixed Inc Misc (Income)	C-	D+	C	Down	Y	866-746-2602
PIMCO Low Duration Income Fund I-3	PFNIX	NAS CM	Open End	Fixed Inc Misc (Income)	C-	D+	C	Down	Y	866-746-2602
PIMCO Low Duration Income Fund Institutional Class	PFIIX	NAS CM	Open End	Fixed Inc Misc (Income)	C-	D+	C	Down	Y	866-746-2602
PIMCO Moderate Duration Fund Class I-2	PMOPX	NAS CM	Open End	US Fixed Inc (Growth & Income)	B-	C+	B	Up	Y	866-746-2602
PIMCO Moderate Duration Fund Institutional Class	PMDRX	NAS CM	Open End	US Fixed Inc (Growth & Income)	B	C+	B+	Up	Y	866-746-2602
PIMCO Mortgage Opportunities and Bond Fund Class A	PMZAX	NAS CM	Open End	Fixed Inc Misc (Growth & Income)	C	C-	C+		Y	866-746-2602
PIMCO Mortgage Opportunities and Bond Fund Class C	PMZCX	NAS CM	Open End	Fixed Inc Misc (Growth & Income)	C	C-	C		Y	866-746-2602
PIMCO Mortgage Opportunities and Bond Fund Class I-2	PMZPX	NAS CM	Open End	Fixed Inc Misc (Growth & Income)	C	C-	C+		Y	866-746-2602
PIMCO Mortgage Opportunities and Bond Fund Class I-3	PMZNX	NAS CM	Open End	Fixed Inc Misc (Growth & Income)	C	C-	C+		Y	866-746-2602
PIMCO Mortgage Opportunities & Bond Institutional Cl	PMZIX	NAS CM	Open End	Fixed Inc Misc (Growth & Income)	C	C-	C+		Y	866-746-2602
PIMCO Mortgage-Backed Securities Fund Class A	PMRAX	NAS CM	Open End	US Fixed Inc (Growth & Income)	B-	C	B	Up	Y	866-746-2602
PIMCO Mortgage-Backed Securities Fund Class C	PMRCX	NAS CM	Open End	US Fixed Inc (Growth & Income)	C+	C	B	Up	Y	866-746-2602
PIMCO Mortgage-Backed Securities Fund Class I-2	PMRPX	NAS CM	Open End	US Fixed Inc (Growth & Income)	B-	C	B	Up	Y	866-746-2602
PIMCO Mortgage-Backed Securities Fund Class I-3	PSANX	NAS CM	Open End	US Fixed Inc (Growth & Income)	B-	C	B	Up	Y	866-746-2602
PIMCO Mortgage-Backed Securities Fund Institutional Class	PTRIX	NAS CM	Open End	US Fixed Inc (Growth & Income)	B-	C	B+	Up	Y	866-746-2602
PIMCO Municipal Bond Fund Class A	PMLAX	NAS CM	Open End	US Muni Fixed Inc (Muni Bond - Natl)	C	C-	B		Y	866-746-2602
PIMCO Municipal Bond Fund Class C	PMLCX	NAS CM	Open End	US Muni Fixed Inc (Muni Bond - Natl)	C	C-	B-		Y	866-746-2602
PIMCO Municipal Bond Fund Class I-2	PMUPX	NAS CM	Open End	US Muni Fixed Inc (Muni Bond - Natl)	C	C-	B	Down	Y	866-746-2602
PIMCO Municipal Bond Fund Institutional Class	PFMIX	NAS CM	Open End	US Muni Fixed Inc (Muni Bond - Natl)	C	C-	B	Down	Y	866-746-2602
PIMCO Municipal Income Fund	PMF	NYSE	Closed End	US Muni Fixed Inc (Muni Bond - Natl)	C-	C-	C-		Y	866-746-2602
PIMCO Municipal Income Fund II	PML	NYSE	Closed End	US Muni Fixed Inc (Muni Bond - Natl)	C	C-	C+		Y	866-746-2602
PIMCO Municipal Income Fund III	PMX	NYSE	Closed End	US Muni Fixed Inc (Muni Bond - Natl)	C-	C-	C-		Y	866-746-2602
PIMCO National Intermediate Municipal Bond Fund Class A	PMNTX	NAS CM	Open End	US Muni Fixed Inc (Muni Bond - Natl)	C	C-	B-		Y	866-746-2602
PIMCO National Intermediate Municipal Bond Fund Class C	PMNNX	NAS CM	Open End	US Muni Fixed Inc (Muni Bond - Natl)	C	C-	C+		Y	866-746-2602
PIMCO National Intermediate Municipal Bond Fund Class I-2	PMNPX	NAS CM	Open End	US Muni Fixed Inc (Muni Bond - Natl)	C	C	B-		Y	866-746-2602
PIMCO Natl Intermediate Muni Bond Fund Institutional Class	PMNIX	NAS CM	Open End	US Muni Fixed Inc (Muni Bond - Natl)	C	C	B-		Y	866-746-2602
PIMCO New York Municipal Bond Fund Class A	PNYAX	NAS CM	Open End	US Muni Fixed Inc (Muni Bond - Single State)	C	C-	B-		Y	866-746-2602
PIMCO New York Municipal Bond Fund Class C	PBFCX	NAS CM	Open End	US Muni Fixed Inc (Muni Bond - Single State)	C	C-	C+		Y	866-746-2602
PIMCO New York Municipal Bond Fund Institutional Class	PNYIX	NAS CM	Open End	US Muni Fixed Inc (Muni Bond - Single State)	C	C	B		Y	866-746-2602
PIMCO New York Municipal Fund Class I-2	PNYPX	NAS CM	Open End	US Muni Fixed Inc (Muni Bond - Single State)	C	C	B		Y	866-746-2602
PIMCO New York Municipal Income Fund	PNF	NYSE	Closed End	US Muni Fixed Inc (Muni Bond - Single State)	C-	D+	C-		Y	866-746-2602
PIMCO New York Municipal Income Fund II	PNI	NYSE	Closed End	US Muni Fixed Inc (Muni Bond - Single State)	C-	C-	C-		Y	866-746-2602
PIMCO New York Municipal Income Fund III	PYN	NYSE	Closed End	US Muni Fixed Inc (Muni Bond - Single State)	D+	D+	D+	Down	Y	866-746-2602
PIMCO Real Return Fund Administrative Class	PARRX	NAS CM	Open End	US Fixed Inc (Growth & Income)	B	C+	B+	Up	Y	866-746-2602
PIMCO Real Return Fund Class A	PRTNX	NAS CM	Open End	US Fixed Inc (Growth & Income)	B	C+	B+	Up	Y	866-746-2602
PIMCO Real Return Fund Class C	PRTCX	NAS CM	Open End	US Fixed Inc (Growth & Income)	B-	C+	B+	Up	Y	866-746-2602
PIMCO Real Return Fund Class I-2	PRLPX	NAS CM	Open End	US Fixed Inc (Growth & Income)	B	C+	B+	Up	Y	866-746-2602
PIMCO Real Return Fund Class R	PRRRX	NAS CM	Open End	US Fixed Inc (Growth & Income)	B	C+	B+	Up	Y	866-746-2602
PIMCO Real Return Fund I-3	PRNPX	NAS CM	Open End	US Fixed Inc (Growth & Income)	B	C+	B+	Up	Y	866-746-2602
PIMCO Real Return Fund Institutional Class	PRRIX	NAS CM	Open End	US Fixed Inc (Growth & Income)	B	C+	B+	Up	Y	866-746-2602
PIMCO Senior Floating Rate Fund Class A	PSRZX	NAS CM	Open End	US Fixed Inc (Income)	D+	D	C-	Down	Y	866-746-2602
PIMCO Senior Floating Rate Fund Class C	PSRWX	NAS CM	Open End	US Fixed Inc (Income)	D	D	C-	Down	Y	866-746-2602
PIMCO Senior Floating Rate Fund Class I-2	PSRPX	NAS CM	Open End	US Fixed Inc (Income)	D+	D	C-	Down	Y	866-746-2602
PIMCO Senior Floating Rate Fund Institutional Class	PSRIX	NAS CM	Open End	US Fixed Inc (Income)	D+	D	C-	Down	Y	866-746-2602
PIMCO Short Asset Investment Fund Administrative Class	PAIQX	NAS CM	Open End	US Fixed Inc (Income)	C	C-	C+		Y	866-746-2602

★Expanded analysis of this fund is included in Section II.

TOTAL RETURNS & PERFORMANCE									ASSETS		ASSET ALLOCATION & TURNOVER							MINIMUMS		FEES		
3-Month Total Return	6-Month Total Return	1-Year Total Return	3-Year Total Return	5-Year Total Return	Dividend Yield (TTM)	Expense Ratio	3-Yr Std Deviation	Effective Duration	NAV	Total Assets (MIL)	%Cash	%Government Bonds	%Municipal Bonds	%Corporate Bonds	%Other	Turnover Ratio	Average Coupon Rate	Min Initial Investment	Min Additional Investment	Front End Fee (%)	Back End Fee (%)	Inception Date
2.20	1.98	3.11	6.45	8.08	2.25	1.3	1.57	2.54	9.91	7,860	-39	48	0	12	8	269	3.95	0				Dec-02
2.31	2.20	3.56	7.81	10.33	2.68	0.86	1.57	2.54	9.91	7,860	-39	48	0	12	8	269	3.95	1,000,000				Apr-18
2.35	2.27	3.72	8.34	11.31	2.83	0.71	1.57	2.54	9.91	7,860	-39	48	0	12	8	269	3.95	1,000,000				May-87
1.70	2.64	3.48	7.27	9.82	1.97	0.79	1.24	2.14	9.89	426.0	-20	41	0	9	7	234	3.84	1,000,000				Feb-98
1.76	2.76	3.74	8.07	11.20	2.22	0.54	1.24	2.14	9.89	426.0	-20	41	0	9	7	234	3.84	1,000,000				Oct-91
5.48	-1.50	0.08	7.83	19.35	4.28	0.99	4.42	0.61	8.32	5,598	-29	15	0	17	0	432	3.37	1,000	50	2.25		Jul-04
5.40	-1.64	-0.21	6.87	17.58	3.97	1.29	4.42	0.61	8.32	5,598	-29	15	0	17	0	432	3.37	1,000	50		1.00	Sep-04
5.55	-1.35	0.38	8.80	21.14	4.59	0.69	4.41	0.61	8.32	5,598	-29	15	0	17	0	432	3.37	1,000,000				Apr-08
5.54	-1.37	0.33	8.60	20.68	4.54	0.74	4.41	0.61	8.32	5,598	-29	15	0	17	0	432	3.37	1,000,000				Apr-18
5.58	-1.30	0.48	9.13	21.75	4.69	0.59	4.41	0.61	8.32	5,598	-29	15	0	17	0	432	3.37	1,000,000				Jul-04
3.83	5.91	7.50	13.85	19.11	2.37	0.7	2.41	4.84	10.85	1,427	-45	45	0	18	7	374	4.20	1,000,000				Dec-09
3.86	5.96	7.61	14.19	19.71	2.47	0.6	2.41	4.84	10.85	1,427	-45	45	0	18	7	374	4.20	1,000,000				Dec-96
4.80	0.98	2.91	8.83	17.94	4.04	1.77	3.36	0.85	10.79	5,386	14	7	0	0	-8	727	2.92	1,000	50	3.75		Oct-12
4.60	0.60	2.13	6.40	13.60	3.27	2.52	3.36	0.85	10.79	5,386	14	7	0	0	-8	727	2.92	1,000	50		1.00	Oct-12
4.88	1.13	3.22	9.81	19.68	4.35	1.47	3.36	0.85	10.79	5,386	14	7	0	0	-8	727	2.92	1,000,000				Oct-12
4.86	1.11	3.17	9.60	19.26	4.3	1.52	3.36	0.85	10.79	5,386	14	7	0	0	-8	727	2.92	1,000,000				Apr-18
4.90	1.18	3.32	10.14	20.33	4.45	1.37	3.36	0.85	10.79	5,386	14	7	0	0	-8	727	2.92	1,000,000				Oct-12
2.24	2.81	4.56	11.66	18.35	3.04	1.15	2.12	1.59	10.72	180.9	-31	8	0	0	-5	884	3.42	1,000	50	3.75		Jul-00
2.06	2.44	3.79	9.20	14.02	2.31	1.9	2.11	1.59	10.72	180.9	-31	8	0	0	-5	884	3.42	1,000	50		1.00	Jul-00
2.32	2.96	4.87	12.67	20.14	3.34	0.85	2.12	1.59	10.72	180.9	-31	8	0	0	-5	884	3.42	1,000,000				Apr-08
2.31	2.94	4.83	12.45	19.67	3.29	0.9	2.12	1.59	10.72	180.9	-31	8	0	0	-5	884	3.42	1,000,000				Apr-18
2.34	3.01	4.98	13.00	20.74	3.44	0.75	2.12	1.59	10.72	180.9	-31	8	0	0	-5	884	3.42	1,000,000				Jul-97
2.88	1.68	4.32	14.08	23.65	2.65	0.86	4.16	6.30	10.18	1,411	9	0	89	1	1	55	4.61	1,000	50	2.25		Apr-98
2.75	1.43	3.81	12.39	20.61	2.15	1.36	4.15	6.30	10.18	1,411	9	0	89	1	1	55	4.61	1,000	50		1.00	Apr-98
2.93	1.79	4.54	14.80	24.95	2.86	0.65	4.16	6.30	10.18	1,411	9	0	89	1	1	55	4.61	1,000,000				Apr-08
2.96	1.84	4.65	15.14	25.57	2.96	0.55	4.16	6.30	10.18	1,411	9	0	89	1	1	55	4.61	1,000,000				Dec-97
5.38	-2.13	1.89	17.32	35.70	5.55	0	10.35		12.75	320.0	5	0	94	0	0	16	5.00					Jun-01
5.24	-1.55	2.44	19.02	37.67	6.42	0	10		11.95	731.4	6	0	93	0	0	12	4.96					Jun-02
5.58	-1.34	2.60	19.10	40.13	5.5	0	9.94		10.91	351.5	8	0	92	0	0	14	4.90					Oct-02
3.01	1.27	3.02	10.39	17.36	1.91	0.8	3.65	4.70	10.88	145.6	10	0	89	0	0	28	4.50	1,000	50	2.25		May-12
2.88	1.02	2.51	8.76	14.47	1.41	1.3	3.65	4.70	10.88	145.6	10	0	89	0	0	28	4.50	1,000	50		1.00	May-12
3.07	1.39	3.28	11.22	18.83	2.16	0.55	3.66	4.70	10.88	145.6	10	0	89	0	0	28	4.50	1,000,000				May-12
3.10	1.44	3.38	11.55	19.43	2.26	0.45	3.66	4.70	10.88	145.6	10	0	89	0	0	28	4.50	1,000,000				May-12
2.01	1.29	3.28	10.95	18.82	1.91	0.87	3.87	5.91	11.59	610.1	14	0	86	0	0	56	4.22	1,000	50	2.25		Oct-99
1.82	0.92	2.52	8.49	14.46	1.16	1.62	3.87	5.91	11.59	610.1	14	0	86	0	0	56	4.22	1,000	50		1.00	Aug-09
2.09	1.46	3.62	12.04	20.78	2.24	0.54	3.87	5.91	11.59	610.1	14	0	86	0	0	56	4.22	1,000,000				Aug-99
2.07	1.41	3.52	11.71	20.18	2.14	0.64	3.87	5.91	11.59	610.1	14	0	86	0	0	56	4.22	1,000,000				Nov-10
4.71	-1.87	1.98	13.29	31.46	5.1	0	10.2		11.67	89.1	7	0	93	0	0	25	4.82					Jun-01
4.62	-2.15	2.01	15.13	32.36	4.45	0	10.6		11.1	120.9	7	0	93	0	0	17	4.96					Jun-02
4.18	-2.34	1.11	11.36	26.94	4.89	0	9.05		8.86	49.8	8	0	92	0	0	14	4.94					Oct-02
5.31	6.06	8.28	14.71	18.82	1.67	1.23	3.79	8.32	11.85	9,094	-23	65	0	1	21	314	2.00	1,000,000				Apr-00
5.27	5.98	8.12	14.20	17.94	1.52	1.38	3.79	8.32	11.85	9,094	-23	65	0	1	21	314	2.00	1,000	50	3.75		Jan-97
5.14	5.72	7.58	12.51	15.03	1.04	1.88	3.79	8.32	11.85	9,094	-23	65	0	1	21	314	2.00	1,000	50		1.00	Jan-97
5.35	6.14	8.44	15.22	19.71	1.81	1.08	3.79	8.32	11.85	9,094	-23	65	0	1	21	314	2.00	1,000,000				Apr-08
5.21	5.85	7.85	13.35	16.48	1.28	1.63	3.79	8.32	11.85	9,094	-23	65	0	1	21	314	2.00	0				Dec-02
5.34	6.11	8.39	15.00	19.24	1.76	1.13	3.79	8.32	11.85	9,094	-23	65	0	1	21	314	2.00	1,000,000				Apr-18
5.38	6.19	8.55	15.57	20.31	1.91	0.98	3.79	8.32	11.85	9,094	-23	65	0	1	21	314	2.00	1,000,000				Jan-97
4.87	-7.05	-4.29	2.22	8.75	4.36	1.05	7.13	0.53	8.99	662.8	6	0	0	80	2	49	4.47	1,000	50	2.25		Apr-11
4.68	-7.40	-5.01	-0.03	4.76	3.57	1.8	7.13	0.53	8.99	662.8	6	0	0	80	2	49	4.47	1,000	50		1.00	Apr-11
4.92	-6.96	-4.10	2.84	9.84	4.57	0.85	7.14	0.53	8.99	662.8	6	0	0	80	2	49	4.47	1,000,000				Apr-11
4.95	-6.91	-4.01	3.14	10.39	4.68	0.75	7.14	0.53	8.99	662.8	6	0	0	80	2	49	4.47	1,000,000				Apr-11
2.53	0.47	1.57	5.46	7.96	1.9	0.63	1.74	0.19	9.98	4,147	22	11	1	40	13	89	2.35	1,000,000				May-12

Fund Name	MARKET Ticker Symbol	MARKET Traded On	FUND TYPE, CATEGORY & OBJECTIVE Fund Type	Category and (Prospectus Objective)	RATINGS Overall Rating	Reward Rating	Risk Rating	Recent Up/ Downgrade	NEW INVESTORS Open to New Investors	Telephone
PIMCO Short Asset Investment Fund Class A	PAIAX	NAS CM	Open End	US Fixed Inc (Income)	C	C-	C+		Y	866-746-2602
PIMCO Short Asset Investment Fund Class I-2	PAIPX	NAS CM	Open End	US Fixed Inc (Income)	C	C-	C+		Y	866-746-2602
PIMCO Short Asset Investment Fund Class I-3	PANDX	NAS CM	Open End	US Fixed Inc (Income)	C	C-	C+		Y	866-746-2602
PIMCO Short Asset Investment Fund Class M	PAMSX	NAS CM	Open End	US Fixed Inc (Income)	C	C-	C+		Y	866-746-2602
PIMCO Short Asset Investment Fund Institutional Class	PAIDX	NAS CM	Open End	US Fixed Inc (Income)	C	C-	C+		Y	866-746-2602
PIMCO Short Duration Municipal Income Fund Class A	PSDAX	NAS CM	Open End	US Muni Fixed Inc (Muni Bond - Natl)	C	C-	C+		Y	866-746-2602
PIMCO Short Duration Municipal Income Fund Class C	PSDCX	NAS CM	Open End	US Muni Fixed Inc (Muni Bond - Natl)	C	C-	C+		Y	866-746-2602
PIMCO Short Duration Municipal Income Fund Class I-2	PSDPX	NAS CM	Open End	US Muni Fixed Inc (Muni Bond - Natl)	C	C	B-		Y	866-746-2602
PIMCO Short Duration Muni Income Fund Institutional Class	PSDIX	NAS CM	Open End	US Muni Fixed Inc (Muni Bond - Natl)	C	C	B-		Y	866-746-2602
PIMCO Short Term Fund I-3	PTSNX	NAS CM	Open End	US Fixed Inc (Income)	C	C-	C+		Y	866-746-2602
PIMCO Short-Term Fund Administrative Class	PSFAX	NAS CM	Open End	US Fixed Inc (Income)	C	C-	C+		Y	866-746-2602
PIMCO Short-Term Fund Class A	PSHAX	NAS CM	Open End	US Fixed Inc (Income)	C	C-	C+		Y	866-746-2602
PIMCO Short-Term Fund Class C	PFTCX	NAS CM	Open End	US Fixed Inc (Income)	C	C-	C+		Y	866-746-2602
PIMCO Short-Term Fund Class I-2	PTSPX	NAS CM	Open End	US Fixed Inc (Income)	C	C-	C+		Y	866-746-2602
PIMCO Short-Term Fund Class R	PTSRX	NAS CM	Open End	US Fixed Inc (Income)	C	C-	C+		Y	866-746-2602
PIMCO Short-Term Fund Institutional Class	PTSHX	NAS CM	Open End	US Fixed Inc (Income)	C	C-	C+		Y	866-746-2602
PIMCO Strategic Bond Fund Class A	ATMAX	NAS CM	Open End	Fixed Inc Misc (Income)	C	C-	C+		Y	866-746-2602
PIMCO Strategic Bond Fund Class C	ATMCX	NAS CM	Open End	Fixed Inc Misc (Income)	C	D+	C+		Y	866-746-2602
PIMCO Strategic Bond Fund Class I-2	PUTPX	NAS CM	Open End	Fixed Inc Misc (Income)	C	C	C+		Y	866-746-2602
PIMCO Strategic Bond Fund Institutional Class	PUTIX	NAS CM	Open End	Fixed Inc Misc (Income)	C	C	C+		Y	866-746-2602
PIMCO Strategic Income Fund	RCS	NYSE	Closed End	US Fixed Inc (Corp Bond - General)	D	D	D+	Down	Y	866-746-2602
PIMCO Total Return ESG Fund Administrative Class	PRFAX	NAS CM	Open End	US Fixed Inc (Growth & Income)	B	C+	B+	Up	Y	866-746-2602
PIMCO Total Return ESG Fund Class A	PTGAX	NAS CM	Open End	US Fixed Inc (Growth & Income)	B-	C+	B+	Up	Y	866-746-2602
PIMCO Total Return ESG Fund Class C	PTGCX	NAS CM	Open End	US Fixed Inc (Growth & Income)	B-	C+	B	Up	Y	866-746-2602
PIMCO Total Return ESG Fund Class I-2	PRAPX	NAS CM	Open End	US Fixed Inc (Growth & Income)	B	C+	B+	Up	Y	866-746-2602
PIMCO Total Return ESG Fund Institutional Class	PTSAX	NAS CM	Open End	US Fixed Inc (Growth & Income)	B	C+	B+	Up	Y	866-746-2602
PIMCO Total Return Fund Administrative Class	PTRAX	NAS CM	Open End	US Fixed Inc (Growth & Income)	B	C+	B+	Up	Y	866-746-2602
★ PIMCO Total Return Fund Class A	PTTAX	NAS CM	Open End	US Fixed Inc (Growth & Income)	B	C+	B+	Up	Y	866-746-2602
★ PIMCO Total Return Fund Class C	PTTCX	NAS CM	Open End	US Fixed Inc (Growth & Income)	B-	C+	B	Up	Y	866-746-2602
PIMCO Total Return Fund Class I-2	PTTPX	NAS CM	Open End	US Fixed Inc (Growth & Income)	B	C+	B+	Up	Y	866-746-2602
★ PIMCO Total Return Fund Class R	PTRRX	NAS CM	Open End	US Fixed Inc (Growth & Income)	B	C+	B+	Up	Y	866-746-2602
PIMCO Total Return Fund I-3	PTTNX	NAS CM	Open End	US Fixed Inc (Growth & Income)	B	C+	B+	Up	Y	866-746-2602
PIMCO Total Return Fund Institutional Class	PTTRX	NAS CM	Open End	US Fixed Inc (Growth & Income)	B	C+	B+	Up	Y	866-746-2602
PIMCO Total Return Fund IV Class A	PTUZX	NAS CM	Open End	US Fixed Inc (Growth & Income)	B-	C	B	Up	Y	866-746-2602
PIMCO Total Return Fund IV Institutional Class	PTUIX	NAS CM	Open End	US Fixed Inc (Growth & Income)	B-	C	B+	Up	Y	866-746-2602
PIMCO Total Return II Fund Administrative Class	PRADX	NAS CM	Open End	US Fixed Inc (Growth & Income)	B	C+	B+	Up	Y	866-746-2602
PIMCO Total Return II Fund Class I-2	PMTPX	NAS CM	Open End	US Fixed Inc (Growth & Income)	B	C+	B+	Up	Y	866-746-2602
PIMCO Total Return II Fund Institutional Class	PMBIX	NAS CM	Open End	US Fixed Inc (Growth & Income)	B	C+	B+	Up	Y	866-746-2602
Pioneer AMT-Free Municipal Fund Class A	PBMFX	NAS CM	Open End	US Muni Fixed Inc (Muni Bond - Natl)	B-	C	B	Up	Y	617-742-7825
Pioneer AMT-Free Municipal Fund Class C	MNBCX	NAS CM	Open End	US Muni Fixed Inc (Muni Bond - Natl)	C+	C	B	Up	Y	617-742-7825
Pioneer AMT-Free Municipal Fund Class Y	PBYMX	NAS CM	Open End	US Muni Fixed Inc (Muni Bond - Natl)	B-	C	B	Up	Y	617-742-7825
Pioneer Bond Fund Class A	PIOBX	NAS CM	Open End	US Fixed Inc (Growth & Income)	C	C-	B-		Y	617-742-7825
Pioneer Bond Fund Class C	PCYBX	NAS CM	Open End	US Fixed Inc (Growth & Income)	C	C-	C+		Y	617-742-7825
Pioneer Bond Fund Class K	PBFKX	NAS CM	Open End	US Fixed Inc (Growth & Income)	C	C-	B		Y	617-742-7825
Pioneer Bond Fund Class R	PBFRX	NAS CM	Open End	US Fixed Inc (Growth & Income)	C	C-	B-		Y	617-742-7825
Pioneer Bond Fund Class Y	PICYX	NAS CM	Open End	US Fixed Inc (Growth & Income)	C	C-	B-		Y	617-742-7825
Pioneer Corporate High Yield Fund Class A	HYCAX	NAS CM	Open End	US Fixed Inc (Corp Bond - High Yield)	D+	D+	C-	Down	Y	617-742-7825
Pioneer Corporate High Yield Fund Class C	HYCCX	NAS CM	Open End	US Fixed Inc (Corp Bond - High Yield)	D+	D	C-	Down	Y	617-742-7825
Pioneer Corporate High Yield Fund Class Y	HYCYX	NAS CM	Open End	US Fixed Inc (Corp Bond - High Yield)	D+	D+	C-	Down	Y	617-742-7825
Pioneer Diversified High Income Trust	HNW	AMEX	Closed End	US Fixed Inc (Corp Bond - High Yield)	D	D	D	Down	Y	844-693-6546
Pioneer Dynamic Credit Fund Class A	RCRAX	NAS CM	Open End	Fixed Inc Misc (Income)	D	D	D+	Down	Y	617-742-7825
Pioneer Dynamic Credit Fund Class C	RCRCX	NAS CM	Open End	Fixed Inc Misc (Income)	D	D	D+	Down	Y	617-742-7825

★ Expanded analysis of this fund is included in Section II.

TOTAL RETURNS & PERFORMANCE									ASSETS		ASSET ALLOCATION & TURNOVER							MINIMUMS		FEES		
3-Month Total Return	6-Month Total Return	1-Year Total Return	3-Year Total Return	5-Year Total Return	Dividend Yield (TTM)	Expense Ratio	3-Yr Std Deviation	Effective Duration	NAV	Total Assets (MIL)	%Cash	%Government Bonds	%Municipal Bonds	%Corporate Bonds	%Other	Turnover Ratio	Average Coupon Rate	Min Initial Investment	Min Additional Investment	Front End Fee (%)	Back End Fee (%)	Inception Date
2.50	0.43	1.47	5.22	7.50	1.81	0.73	1.74	0.19	9.98	4,147	22	11	1	40	13	89	2.35	1,000	50	2.25		May-12
2.57	0.55	1.72	6.01	8.85	2.06	0.48	1.74	0.19	9.98	4,147	22	11	1	40	13	89	2.35	1,000,000				May-12
2.55	0.53	1.67	5.80	8.43	2.01	0.53	1.74	0.19	9.98	4,147	22	11	1	40	13	89	2.35	1,000,000				Apr-18
2.59	0.60	1.83	6.34	9.41	2.16	0.38	1.74	0.19	9.98	4,147	22	11	1	40	13	89	2.35	1,000,000				Dec-15
2.59	0.60	1.82	6.32	9.40	2.16	0.38	1.74	0.19	9.98	4,147	22	11	1	40	13	89	2.35	1,000,000				May-12
1.74	1.23	2.20	5.85	7.31	1.39	0.73	1.47	2.14	8.53	299.0	12	0	88	0	0	53	3.53	1,000	50	2.25		Mar-02
1.67	1.08	1.89	4.90	5.71	1.09	1.03	1.47	2.14	8.53	299.0	12	0	88	0	0	53	3.53	1,000	50		1.00	Mar-02
1.82	1.38	2.50	6.80	8.93	1.69	0.43	1.47	2.14	8.53	299.0	12	0	88	0	0	53	3.53	1,000,000				Apr-08
1.84	1.43	2.61	7.12	9.47	1.78	0.33	1.47	2.14	8.53	299.0	12	0	88	0	0	53	3.53	1,000,000				Aug-99
3.83	1.62	2.60	6.68	10.53	2.39	0.65	2.29	0.26	9.82	13,447	22	13	0	31	13	222	2.73	1,000,000				Apr-18
3.81	1.57	2.50	6.40	10.13	2.29	0.75	2.3	0.26	9.82	13,447	22	13	0	31	13	222	2.73	1,000,000				Feb-96
3.81	1.57	2.50	6.40	10.13	2.29	0.75	2.3	0.26	9.82	13,447	22	13	0	31	13	222	2.73	1,000	50	2.25		Jan-97
3.73	1.42	2.19	5.45	8.49	1.99	1.05	2.29	0.26	9.82	13,447	22	13	0	31	13	222	2.73	1,000	50		1.00	Jan-97
3.84	1.65	2.65	6.88	10.95	2.44	0.6	2.3	0.26	9.82	13,447	22	13	0	31	13	222	2.73	1,000,000				Apr-08
3.74	1.45	2.24	5.61	8.76	2.04	1	2.3	0.26	9.82	13,447	22	13	0	31	13	222	2.73	0				Dec-02
3.87	1.70	2.75	7.20	11.51	2.54	0.5	2.3	0.26	9.82	13,447	22	13	0	31	13	222	2.73	1,000,000				Oct-87
4.41	0.32	1.93	10.88	19.58	2.85	0.94	2.87	0.61	10.69	102.3	-36	29	0	12	0	345	2.54	1,000	50	3.75		Jan-09
4.22	-0.03	1.17	8.43	15.19	2.1	1.69	2.87	0.61	10.69	102.3	-36	29	0	12	0	345	2.54	1,000	50		1.00	Jan-09
4.48	0.47	2.23	11.88	21.38	3.15	0.64	2.87	0.61	10.69	102.3	-36	29	0	12	0	345	2.54	1,000,000				Sep-09
4.51	0.52	2.33	12.21	21.98	3.25	0.54	2.88	0.61	10.69	102.3	-36	29	0	12	0	345	2.54	1,000,000				Jan-09
11.51	-9.60	-6.92	7.84	24.28	7.9	1.15	12.88		5.94	253.7	-114	9	0	9	0	655	3.93					Feb-94
4.05	5.69	8.13	15.16	21.64	3.07	1.09	3.6	6.80	9.7	1,542	-39	28	1	23	0	396	3.24	1,000,000				Apr-97
4.01	5.61	7.98	14.65	20.74		1.24	3.6	6.80	9.7	1,542	-39	28	1	23	0	396	3.24	1,000	50	2.25		Feb-20
3.94	5.34	7.30	12.26	16.47		1.99	3.6	6.80	9.7	1,542	-39	28	1	23	0	396	3.24	1,000	50		1.00	Feb-20
4.20	5.87	8.41	15.80	22.68	3.22	0.94	3.6	6.80	9.7	1,542	-39	28	1	23	0	396	3.24	1,000,000				Mar-09
4.11	5.82	8.40	16.03	23.17	3.31	0.84	3.6	6.80	9.7	1,542	-39	28	1	23	0	396	3.24	1,000,000				May-91
3.81	6.02	8.26	15.59	22.79	3.17	0.96	3.38	6.57	10.83	67,970	-54	34	0	16	7	554	3.67	1,000,000				Sep-94
3.78	5.97	8.16	15.27	22.11	3.08	1.05	3.38	6.57	10.83	67,970	-54	34	0	16	7	554	3.67	1,000	50	3.75		Jan-97
3.59	5.58	7.36	12.66	17.57	2.35	1.8	3.38	6.57	10.83	67,970	-54	34	0	16	7	554	3.67	1,000	50		1.00	Jan-97
3.85	6.09	8.42	16.11	23.71	3.32	0.81	3.38	6.57	10.83	67,970	-54	34	0	16	7	554	3.67	1,000,000				Apr-08
3.72	5.84	7.90	14.36	20.53	2.84	1.3	3.38	6.57	10.83	67,970	-54	34	0	16	7	554	3.67	0				Dec-02
3.83	6.07	8.37	15.90	23.24	3.27	0.86	3.39	6.57	10.83	67,970	-54	34	0	16	7	554	3.67	1,000,000				Apr-18
3.87	6.15	8.53	16.46	24.33	3.41	0.71	3.39	6.57	10.83	67,970	-54	34	0	16	7	554	3.67	1,000,000				May-87
3.50	4.45	7.05	14.42	20.89	2.28	1.04	3.83	6.20	11.17	438.8	-19	25	0	14	0	401	3.69	1,000	50	3.75		May-11
3.59	4.62	7.42	15.61	23.01	2.62	0.69	3.83	6.20	11.17	438.8	-19	25	0	14	0	401	3.69	1,000,000				May-11
3.63	6.26	8.39	16.69	24.13	2.59	1.1	3.5	6.46	10.29	577.6	-64	22	0	25	6	607	3.64	1,000,000				Nov-94
3.67	6.34	8.55	17.20	25.05	2.74	0.95	3.51	6.46	10.29	577.6	-64	22	0	25	6	607	3.64	1,000,000				Dec-09
3.70	6.39	8.66	17.56	25.68	2.84	0.85	3.51	6.46	10.29	577.6	-64	22	0	25	6	607	3.64	1,000,000				Dec-91
2.71	3.21	6.70	15.61	25.84	2.56	0.81	4.77	8.55	15.47	1,301	6	0	94	0	0	10	4.41	1,000	100	4.50		Sep-96
2.47	2.77	5.87	12.94	21.15	1.81	1.56	4.77	8.55	15.33	1,301	6	0	94	0	0	10	4.41	1,000	500		1.00	Oct-03
2.65	3.15	6.77	16.29	27.25	2.82	0.55	4.77	8.55	15.4	1,301	6	0	94	0	0	10	4.41	5,000,000				Nov-06
8.75	2.39	5.09	12.44	19.99	3.02	0.84	6.08	5.45	9.98	5,773	5	6	0	37	0	52	3.90	1,000	100	4.50		Oct-78
8.56	2.08	4.46	10.16	15.86	2.38	1.49	6.11	5.45	9.87	5,773	5	6	0	37	0	52	3.90	1,000	500		1.00	Jan-96
8.99	2.74	5.72	13.94	22.52	3.53	0.34	6.13	5.45	9.98	5,773	5	6	0	37	0	52	3.90	5,000,000				Dec-12
8.73	2.26	4.84	11.60	18.50	2.79	1.09	6.16	5.45	10.07	5,773	5	6	0	37	0	52	3.90	0				Apr-03
8.92	2.59	5.52	13.58	21.89	3.42	0.46	6.12	5.45	9.89	5,773	5	6	0	37	0	52	3.90	5,000,000				Sep-01
10.57	-6.96	-2.78	6.77		5.79	0.9	10.09		9.35	24.1	-1	4	0	96	0	60	6.10	1,000	100	4.50		Jan-17
10.50	-7.23	-3.40	4.51		4.99	1.65	10.1		9.35	24.1	-1	4	0	96	0	60	6.10	1,000	500		1.00	Jan-17
10.78	-6.83	-2.51	7.61		6.07	0.6	10.15		9.35	24.1	-1	4	0	96	0	60	6.10	5,000,000				Jan-17
16.36	-12.51	-8.99	-3.56	9.74	8.49		15.94		13.79	111.9	5	2	0	86	1	37	6.95					May-07
9.83	-6.24	-4.36	1.19	12.59	4.56	1.27	9.95	3.29	8.43	116.6	3	7	0	53	0	49	5.13	1,000	100	4.50		Apr-11
9.66	-6.64	-5.03	-1.13	8.36	3.7	2.07	9.96	3.29	8.4	116.6	3	7	0	53	0	49	5.13	1,000	500		1.00	Apr-11

	MARKET			FUND TYPE, CATEGORY & OBJECTIVE	RATINGS				NEW INVESTORS	
Fund Name	Ticker Symbol	Traded On	Fund Type	Category and (Prospectus Objective)	Overall Rating	Reward Rating	Risk Rating	Recent Up/ Downgrade	Open to New Investors	Telephone
Pioneer Dynamic Credit Fund Class Y	RCRYX	NAS CM	Open End	Fixed Inc Misc (Income)	D	D	D+	Down	Y	617-742-7825
Pioneer Floating Rate Fund Class A	FLARX	NAS CM	Open End	US Fixed Inc (Income)	D	D	C-	Down	Y	617-742-7825
Pioneer Floating Rate Fund Class C	FLRCX	NAS CM	Open End	US Fixed Inc (Income)	D	D	C-	Down	Y	617-742-7825
Pioneer Floating Rate Fund Class Y	FLYRX	NAS CM	Open End	US Fixed Inc (Income)	D+	D	C-	Down	Y	617-742-7825
Pioneer Floating Rate Trust	PHD	NYSE	Closed End	US Fixed Inc (Corp Bond - High Yield)	D	D	D	Down	Y	844-693-6546
Pioneer Global High Yield Fund Class A	PGHYX	NAS CM	Open End	Global Fixed Inc (Corp Bond - High Yield)	D	D	D	Down	Y	617-742-7825
Pioneer Global High Yield Fund Class C	PGYCX	NAS CM	Open End	Global Fixed Inc (Corp Bond - High Yield)	D	D	D	Down	Y	617-742-7825
Pioneer Global High Yield Fund Class Y	GHYYX	NAS CM	Open End	Global Fixed Inc (Corp Bond - High Yield)	D	D	D+	Down	Y	617-742-7825
Pioneer Global Multisector Income Fund Class A	PGABX	NAS CM	Open End	Global Fixed Inc (Worldwide Bond)	D	D	C-	Down	Y	617-742-7825
Pioneer Global Multisector Income Fund Class C	PGCBX	NAS CM	Open End	Global Fixed Inc (Worldwide Bond)	D	D	C-	Down	Y	617-742-7825
Pioneer Global Multisector Income Fund Class Y	PGYBX	NAS CM	Open End	Global Fixed Inc (Worldwide Bond)	D+	D	C-	Down	Y	617-742-7825
Pioneer High Income Municipal Fund Class A	PIMAX	NAS CM	Open End	US Muni Fixed Inc (Muni Bond - Natl)	C-	D+	C	Down	Y	617-742-7825
Pioneer High Income Municipal Fund Class C	HICMX	NAS CM	Open End	US Muni Fixed Inc (Muni Bond - Natl)	C-	D+	C	Down	Y	617-742-7825
Pioneer High Income Municipal Fund Class Y	HIMYX	NAS CM	Open End	US Muni Fixed Inc (Muni Bond - Natl)	C-	D+	C	Down	Y	617-742-7825
Pioneer High Income Trust	PHT	NYSE	Closed End	US Fixed Inc (Corp Bond - High Yield)	D	D	D	Down	Y	844-693-6546
Pioneer High Yield Fund Class A	TAHYX	NAS CM	Open End	US Fixed Inc (Corp Bond - High Yield)	D+	D	C-	Down	Y	617-742-7825
Pioneer High Yield Fund Class C	PYICX	NAS CM	Open End	US Fixed Inc (Corp Bond - High Yield)	D	D	D+	Down	Y	617-742-7825
Pioneer High Yield Fund Class R	TYHRX	NAS CM	Open End	US Fixed Inc (Corp Bond - High Yield)	D	D	D+	Down	Y	617-742-7825
Pioneer High Yield Fund Class Y	TYHYX	NAS CM	Open End	US Fixed Inc (Corp Bond - High Yield)	D+	D	C-	Down	Y	617-742-7825
Pioneer ILS Bridge Fund	XILBX	NAS CM	Closed End	US Fixed Inc (Growth & Income)	D+	D+	C	Up	Y	
Pioneer ILS Interval Fund	XILSX	NAS CM	Closed End	US Fixed Inc (Growth & Income)	C-	C-	C		Y	617-742-7825
Pioneer Multi-Asset Ultrashort Income Fund Class A	MAFRX	NAS CM	Open End	US Fixed Inc (Income)	D+	D	C	Down	Y	617-742-7825
Pioneer Multi-Asset Ultrashort Income Fund Class C	MCFRX	NAS CM	Open End	US Fixed Inc (Income)	D+	D	C	Down	Y	617-742-7825
Pioneer Multi-Asset Ultrashort Income Fund Class C2	MAUCX	NAS CM	Open End	US Fixed Inc (Income)	D+	D	C	Down	Y	617-742-7825
Pioneer Multi-Asset Ultrashort Income Fund Class K	MAUKX	NAS CM	Open End	US Fixed Inc (Income)	D+	D	C	Down	Y	617-742-7825
Pioneer Multi-Asset Ultrashort Income Fund Class Y	MYFRX	NAS CM	Open End	US Fixed Inc (Income)	D+	D	C	Down	Y	617-742-7825
Pioneer Municipal High Income Advantage Trust	MAV	NYSE	Closed End	US Muni Fixed Inc (Muni Bond - Natl)	C-	C	C-	Down	Y	844-693-6546
Pioneer Municipal High Income Trust	MHI	NYSE	Closed End	US Muni Fixed Inc (Muni Bond - Natl)	C-	C-	C-		Y	844-693-6546
Pioneer Securitized Income Fund			Closed End	US Fixed Inc (Income)	U	U	U		Y	
Pioneer Short Term Income Fund Class A	STABX	NAS CM	Open End	US Fixed Inc (Income)	D	D	C-	Down	Y	617-742-7825
Pioneer Short Term Income Fund Class C	PSHCX	NAS CM	Open End	US Fixed Inc (Income)	D	D	C-	Down	Y	617-742-7825
Pioneer Short Term Income Fund Class C2	STIIX	NAS CM	Open End	US Fixed Inc (Income)	D	D	C-	Down	Y	617-742-7825
Pioneer Short Term Income Fund Class K	STIKX	NAS CM	Open End	US Fixed Inc (Income)	D+	D	C-	Down	Y	617-742-7825
Pioneer Short Term Income Fund Class Y	PSHYX	NAS CM	Open End	US Fixed Inc (Income)	D+	D	C-	Down	Y	617-742-7825
Pioneer Strategic Income Fund Class A	PSRAX	NAS CM	Open End	US Fixed Inc (Multisector Bond)	C-	D+	C		Y	617-742-7825
Pioneer Strategic Income Fund Class C	PSRCX	NAS CM	Open End	US Fixed Inc (Multisector Bond)	C-	D+	C		Y	617-742-7825
Pioneer Strategic Income Fund Class K	STRKX	NAS CM	Open End	US Fixed Inc (Multisector Bond)	C-	D+	C		Y	617-742-7825
Pioneer Strategic Income Fund Class R	STIRX	NAS CM	Open End	US Fixed Inc (Multisector Bond)	C-	D+	C		Y	617-742-7825
Pioneer Strategic Income Fund Class Y	STRYX	NAS CM	Open End	US Fixed Inc (Multisector Bond)	C-	D+	C		Y	617-742-7825
Pioneer U.S. Government Money Market Fund Class A	PMTXX	NAS CM	Money Mkt	US Money Mkt (Money Mkt - Govt)	C	C-	C+		Y	617-742-7825
Pioneer U.S. Government Money Market Fund Class R	PRXXX	NAS CM	Money Mkt	US Money Mkt (Money Mkt - Govt)	C	C-	C		Y	617-742-7825
Pioneer U.S. Government Money Market Fund Class Y	PRYXX	NAS CM	Money Mkt	US Money Mkt (Money Mkt - Govt)	C	C-	C		Y	617-742-7825
PMC Core Fixed Income Fund	PMFIX	NAS CM	Open End	US Fixed Inc (Income)	B-	C+	B	Up	Y	
PMC Core Fixed Income Fund Institutional Class Shares	PMFQX	NAS CM	Open End	US Fixed Inc (Income)	B-	C+	B	Up	Y	
Power Floating Rate Index Fund Class A	FLOAX	NAS CM	Open End	US Fixed Inc (Growth & Income)	D+	D	C	Down	Y	877-779-7462
Power Floating Rate Index Fund Class C	FLOCX	NAS CM	Open End	US Fixed Inc (Growth & Income)	D+	D	C	Down	Y	877-779-7462
Power Floating Rate Index Fund Class I	FLOTX	NAS CM	Open End	US Fixed Inc (Growth & Income)	D+	D	C	Down	Y	877-779-7462
Power Income Fund Class A	PWRAX	NAS CM	Open End	US Fixed Inc (Income)	D	D	C-	Down	Y	877-779-7462
Power Income Fund Class C	PWRCX	NAS CM	Open End	US Fixed Inc (Income)	D	D	D+	Down	Y	877-779-7462
Power Income Fund Class I	PWRIX	NAS CM	Open End	US Fixed Inc (Income)	D	D	C-	Down	Y	877-779-7462
PPM Core Plus Fixed Income Fund Institutional Shares	PKPIX	NAS CM	Open End	US Fixed Inc (Growth & Income)	C-	D+	B	Up	Y	844-446-4776
PPM Floating Rate Income Fund Institutional Shares	PKFIX	NAS CM	Open End	US Fixed Inc (Income)	D	D	C-	Down	Y	844-446-4776

★Expanded analysis of this fund is included in Section II.

TOTAL RETURNS & PERFORMANCE									ASSETS		ASSET ALLOCATION & TURNOVER							MINIMUMS		FEES		
3-Month Total Return	6-Month Total Return	1-Year Total Return	3-Year Total Return	5-Year Total Return	Dividend Yield (TTM)	Expense Ratio	3-Yr Std Deviation	Effective Duration	NAV	Total Assets (MIL)	%Cash	%Government Bonds	%Municipal Bonds	%Corporate Bonds	%Other	Turnover Ratio	Average Coupon Rate	Min Initial Investment	Min Additional Investment	Front End Fee (%)	Back End Fee (%)	Inception Date
9.87	-6.05	-4.00	2.14	14.39	4.92	0.92	9.9	3.29	8.47	116.6	3	7	0	53	0	49	5.13	5,000,000				Apr-11
7.40	-5.90	-4.04	2.19	8.86	4.82	1.13	7.72	1.19	6.11	308.4	6	0	0	93	1	13	4.14	1,000	100	4.50		Feb-07
7.33	-5.67	-4.00	0.57	5.58	3.96	1.83	7.49	1.19	6.16	308.4	6	0	0	93	1	13	4.14	1,000	500		1.00	Feb-07
7.61	-5.09	-3.04	3.90	11.46	5.18	0.77	7.47	1.19	6.17	308.4	6	0	0	93	1	13	4.14	5,000,000				Feb-07
13.19	-10.52	-7.88	-0.53	8.81	7.33	0	13.07	1.44	10.43	252.3	-1	0	0	97	0	48	5.25					Dec-04
14.86	-9.59	-6.39	0.69	9.89	6.09	1.17	13.12	3.72	7.7	216.4	9	7	0	83	2	54	6.50	1,000	100	4.50		Aug-01
14.77	-9.98	-7.14	-1.47	6.03	5.11	1.9	13.19	3.72	7.69	216.4	9	7	0	83	2	54	6.50	1,000	500		1.00	Nov-03
15.03	-9.48	-6.24	1.45	11.30	6.39	0.92	13.18	3.72	7.56	216.4	9	7	0	83	2	54	6.50	5,000,000				Dec-05
9.61	-2.81	-1.41	1.30	8.72	2.82	1.04	7.81	6.30	9.97	37.1	9	26	0	47	0	16	4.25	1,000	100	4.50		Dec-07
9.37	-3.09	-2.20	-1.14	4.16	1.96	1.94	7.76	6.30	10	37.1	9	26	0	47	0	16	4.25	1,000	500		1.00	Dec-07
9.71	-2.56	-1.13	2.03	10.03	3.08	0.79	7.78	6.30	10.06	37.1	9	26	0	47	0	16	4.25	5,000,000				Dec-07
2.54	-2.82	0.33	13.29	27.12	4.56	0.83	6.25	6.49	7.15	1,541	3	0	97	1	0	20	5.64	1,000	100	4.50		Oct-06
2.49	-3.06	-0.28	10.88	22.53	3.75	1.61	6.25	6.49	7.16	1,541	3	0	97	1	0	20	5.64	1,000	500		1.00	Oct-06
2.77	-2.62	0.54	14.19	28.42	4.84	0.55	6.27	6.49	7.06	1,541	3	0	97	1	0	20	5.64	5,000,000				Oct-06
16.86	-14.89	-9.98	-1.99	10.29	9.89	0	17.01		8.36	239.4	4	1	0	91	0	36	7.20					Apr-02
10.83	-8.12	-3.85	4.02	13.97	5.63	1.14	10.6	3.57	8.71	628.4	1	5	0	94	0	59	5.89	1,000	100	4.50		Feb-98
10.55	-8.44	-4.51	1.68	9.93	4.78	1.86	10.58	3.57	8.9	628.4	1	5	0	94	0	59	5.89	1,000	500		1.00	Feb-98
10.60	-8.16	-4.18	2.86	11.98	5.13	1.5	10.48	3.57	9.88	628.4	1	5	0	94	0	59	5.89	0				Apr-03
10.89	-7.97	-3.57	4.92	15.64	5.94	0.85	10.58	3.57	8.72	628.4	1	5	0	94	0	59	5.89	5,000,000				Feb-98
0.00	0.00	0.00			0	1.95			10	--								1,000,000				Sep-18
1.06	2.52	4.95	-6.67	12.26	6.51	1.95	6.39		8.53	--	10				5	50		1,000,000				Dec-14
3.42	-2.84	-1.56	2.68	5.83	2.76	0.59	3.97	0.37	9.53	4,938	8	6	0	27	0	100	2.27	1,000	100	2.50		Apr-11
3.34	-2.80	-1.67	1.89	4.37	2.42	0.91	3.86	0.37	9.54	4,938	8	6	0	27	0	100	2.27	1,000	500			Apr-11
3.35	-2.79	-1.66	1.91	4.48	2.43	0.91	3.86	0.37	9.54	4,938	8	6	0	27	0	100	2.27	1,000	500		1.00	Aug-13
3.47	-2.53	-1.13	3.57	7.21	2.98	0.37	3.85	0.37	9.56	4,938	8	6	0	27	0	100	2.27	5,000,000				Dec-12
3.45	-2.57	-1.21	3.24	6.78	2.91	0.45	3.85	0.37	9.55	4,938	8	6	0	27	0	100	2.27	5,000,000				Apr-11
3.24	2.48	5.83	15.63	29.63	3.8	0	5.65		12.07	286.1	2	0	98	0	0	11	5.26					Oct-03
2.37	1.69	4.51	15.87	27.22	4.38		5.69		12.92	292.2	2	0	98	0	0	16	5.20					Jul-03
27.42	-13.51					2.12			8.55	--								1,000,000				Dec-19
4.80	-3.53	-2.15	2.50	5.64	3.18	0.83	5.51	1.83	9.03	505.4	4	6	0	33	0	84	3.29	1,000	100	2.50		Jul-04
4.85	-3.22	-2.05	2.14	4.76	2.94	1.07	5.4	1.83	9.05	505.4	4	6	0	33	0	84	3.29	1,000	500		1.00	Jul-04
4.85	-3.22	-1.96	2.24	4.89	2.91	1.09	5.34	1.83	9.06	505.4	4	6	0	33	0	84	3.29	1,000	500		1.00	Aug-13
5.10	-2.83	-1.28	4.11	7.86	3.52	0.46	5.42	1.83	9.09	505.4	4	6	0	33	0	84	3.29	5,000,000				Dec-14
5.00	-2.95	-1.40	3.81	7.44	3.53	0.46	5.4	1.83	9.05	505.4	4	6	0	33	0	84	3.29	5,000,000				Jul-04
11.48	-2.33	0.91	7.51	17.01	3.15	1.1	8.86	4.13	10.58	4,199	4	10	0	44	2	53	4.74	1,000	100	4.50		Apr-99
11.32	-2.65	0.31	5.40	13.23	2.48	1.74	8.89	4.13	10.35	4,199	4	10	0	44	2	53	4.74	1,000	500		1.00	Apr-99
11.58	-2.10	1.38	8.93	19.58	3.63	0.63	8.84	4.13	10.6	4,199	4	10	0	44	2	53	4.74	5,000,000				Dec-12
11.42	-2.51	0.64	6.52	15.18	2.84	1.39	8.89	4.13	10.76	4,199	4	10	0	44	2	53	4.74	0				Apr-03
11.57	-2.16	1.36	8.59	18.92	3.52	0.73	8.86	4.13	10.58	4,199	4	10	0	44	2	53	4.74	5,000,000				Sep-04
0.00	0.19	0.82	3.14	3.22	0.95	0.84	0.17		1	301.4	59	41	0	0	0			1,000	100			Jun-87
0.00	0.11	0.51	2.02	1.38	0.65	1.12			1	301.4	59	41	0	0	0			0				Aug-17
0.00	0.21	0.91	3.54	3.66	1.1	0.52	0.17		1	301.4	59	41	0	0	0			5,000,000				Sep-05
6.18	5.75	8.22	15.19	20.82	2.22	1.01	3.97		18.2	380.6	-13	29	1	32	0	144	3.50	1,000	50			Sep-07
6.26	5.88	8.48	15.40	21.04		0.76	3.99		18.16	380.6	-13	29	1	32	0	144	3.50	1,000	50			Jul-19
-0.21	-3.34	-2.23			2.99	1.88		1.87	9.53	58.6	3	96	0	0	0	209	1.86	1,000	100	5.00		Dec-17
-0.42	-3.68	-2.94			2.24	2.63		1.87	9.42	58.6	3	96	0	0	0	209	1.86	1,000	100			Dec-17
-0.09	-3.20	-2.02			3.74	1.63		1.87	9.51	58.6	3	96	0	0	0	209	1.86	100,000				Dec-17
1.54	-8.24	-5.91	-1.59	4.68	1.93	1.91	5.74	5.52	9.22	92.2	62	18	5	9	0	175	2.89	1,000	100	5.00		Sep-10
1.33	-8.50	-6.50	-3.70	0.81	0.72	2.66	5.71	5.52	9.13	92.2	62	18	5	9	0	175	2.89	1,000	100			Nov-14
1.65	-7.99	-5.53	-0.74	6.05	2.76	1.66	5.71	5.52	9.2	92.2	62	18	5	9	0	175	2.89	100,000				Sep-10
5.86	6.09	8.98			2.74	0.5		5.68	10.88	54.3	3	11	0	45	0	108	3.59	1,000,000				Jul-18
7.86	-5.07	-2.54			4.48	0.76			9.08	51.0	4	0	0	95	0	56	4.37	1,000,000				May-18

	MARKET		FUND TYPE, CATEGORY & OBJECTIVE		RATINGS				NEW INVESTORS	
Fund Name	Ticker Symbol	Traded On	Fund Type	Category and (Prospectus Objective)	Overall Rating	Reward Rating	Risk Rating	Recent Up/ Downgrade	Open to New Investors	Telephone
PPM High Yield Core Fund Institutional Shares	PKHIX	NAS CM	Open End	US Fixed Inc (Corp Bond - High Yield)	D	D	D+	Down	Y	844-446-4776
Praxis Impact Bond Fund Class A	MIIAX	NAS CM	Open End	US Fixed Inc (Income)	B	C+	B+	Up	Y	
Praxis Impact Bond Fund Class I	MIIIX	NAS CM	Open End	US Fixed Inc (Income)	B	C+	B+	Up	Y	
Principal Bond Market Index Fund Class J	PBIJX	NAS CM	Open End	US Fixed Inc (Income)	B	B-	B	Up	Y	800-787-1621
Principal Bond Market Index Fund R-1 Class	PBIMX	NAS CM	Open End	US Fixed Inc (Income)	B-	C+	B		Y	800-787-1621
Principal Bond Market Index Fund R-2 Class	PBINX	NAS CM	Open End	US Fixed Inc (Income)	B-	C+	B		Y	800-787-1621
Principal Bond Market Index Fund R-3 Class	PBOIX	NAS CM	Open End	US Fixed Inc (Income)	B	C+	B	Up	Y	800-787-1621
Principal Bond Market Index Fund R-4 Class	PBIPX	NAS CM	Open End	US Fixed Inc (Income)	B	B-	B	Up	Y	800-787-1621
Principal Bond Market Index Fund R-5 Class	PBIQX	NAS CM	Open End	US Fixed Inc (Income)	B	B-	B	Up	Y	800-787-1621
Principal Bond Market Index Institutional Class	PNIIX	NAS CM	Open End	US Fixed Inc (Income)	B	B-	B+		Y	800-787-1621
Principal California Municipal Fund Class A	SRCMX	NAS CM	Open End	US Muni Fixed Inc (Muni Bond - Single State)	C	C-	C+		Y	800-787-1621
Principal California Municipal Fund Class C	SRCCX	NAS CM	Open End	US Muni Fixed Inc (Muni Bond - Single State)	C	C-	C		Y	800-787-1621
Principal California Municipal Fund Institutional Class	PCMFX	NAS CM	Open End	US Muni Fixed Inc (Muni Bond - Single State)	C	C-	C+		Y	800-787-1621
Principal Core Fixed Income Fund Class A	CMPIX	NAS CM	Open End	US Fixed Inc (Corp Bond - General)	B	C+	B+	Up	Y	800-787-1621
Principal Core Fixed Income Fund Class C	CNMCX	NAS CM	Open End	US Fixed Inc (Corp Bond - General)	B-	C	B	Up	Y	800-787-1621
Principal Core Fixed Income Fund Class J	PIOJX	NAS CM	Open End	US Fixed Inc (Corp Bond - General)	B	C+	B+	Up	Y	800-787-1621
Principal Core Fixed Income Fund Class R-6	PICNX	NAS CM	Open End	US Fixed Inc (Corp Bond - General)	B	C+	B+	Up	Y	800-787-1621
Principal Core Fixed Income Fund Institutional Class	PIOIX	NAS CM	Open End	US Fixed Inc (Corp Bond - General)	B	C+	B+	Up	Y	800-787-1621
Principal Core Fixed Income Fund R-1 Class	PIOMX	NAS CM	Open End	US Fixed Inc (Corp Bond - General)	B-	C+	B+	Up	Y	800-787-1621
Principal Core Fixed Income Fund R-2 Class	PIONX	NAS CM	Open End	US Fixed Inc (Corp Bond - General)	B-	C+	B+	Up	Y	800-787-1621
Principal Core Fixed Income Fund R-3 Class	PIOOX	NAS CM	Open End	US Fixed Inc (Corp Bond - General)	B-	C+	B+	Up	Y	800-787-1621
Principal Core Fixed Income Fund R-4 Class	PIOPX	NAS CM	Open End	US Fixed Inc (Corp Bond - General)	B	C+	B+	Up	Y	800-787-1621
Principal Core Fixed Income Fund R-5 Class	PIOQX	NAS CM	Open End	US Fixed Inc (Corp Bond - General)	B	C+	B+	Up	Y	800-787-1621
Principal Core Plus Bond Fund Class A	PRBDX	NAS CM	Open End	US Fixed Inc (Govt Bond - Mortgage)	B	C+	B+	Up	Y	800-787-1621
Principal Core Plus Bond Fund Class J	PBMJX	NAS CM	Open End	US Fixed Inc (Govt Bond - Mortgage)	B	C+	B+	Up	Y	800-787-1621
Principal Core Plus Bond Fund Institutional Class	PMSIX	NAS CM	Open End	US Fixed Inc (Govt Bond - Mortgage)	B	C+	B+	Up	Y	800-787-1621
Principal Core Plus Bond Fund R-1 Class	PBOMX	NAS CM	Open End	US Fixed Inc (Govt Bond - Mortgage)	B-	C+	B	Up	Y	800-787-1621
Principal Core Plus Bond Fund R-2 Class	PBMNX	NAS CM	Open End	US Fixed Inc (Govt Bond - Mortgage)	B-	C+	B	Up	Y	800-787-1621
Principal Core Plus Bond Fund R-3 Class	PBMMX	NAS CM	Open End	US Fixed Inc (Govt Bond - Mortgage)	B	C+	B+	Up	Y	800-787-1621
Principal Core Plus Bond Fund R-4 Class	PBMSX	NAS CM	Open End	US Fixed Inc (Govt Bond - Mortgage)	B	C+	B+	Up	Y	800-787-1621
Principal Core Plus Bond Fund R-5 Class	PBMPX	NAS CM	Open End	US Fixed Inc (Govt Bond - Mortgage)	B	C+	B+	Up	Y	800-787-1621
Principal Finisterre Unconstrained Emerg Mkts Bond Cl A	PFUEX	NAS CM	Open End	Emerg Mkts Fixed Inc (Growth & Income)	C	C-	C+		Y	800-787-1621
Principal Finisterre Unconstrained Emerg Mkts Bond Cl Inst	PFUMX	NAS CM	Open End	Emerg Mkts Fixed Inc (Growth & Income)	C	C-	C+		Y	800-787-1621
Principal Government & High Quality Bond Fund Class A	CMPGX	NAS CM	Open End	US Fixed Inc (Govt Bond - General)	C+	C	B-		Y	800-787-1621
Principal Government & High Quality Bond Fund Class C	CCUGX	NAS CM	Open End	US Fixed Inc (Govt Bond - General)	C	C	B-		Y	800-787-1621
Principal Government & High Quality Bond Fund Class J	PMRJX	NAS CM	Open End	US Fixed Inc (Govt Bond - General)	C	C	C+		Y	800-787-1621
Principal Govt & High Quality Bond Institutional Cl	PMRIX	NAS CM	Open End	US Fixed Inc (Govt Bond - General)	C+	C	B-		Y	800-787-1621
Principal Government & High Quality Bond Fund R-1 Class	PMGRX	NAS CM	Open End	US Fixed Inc (Govt Bond - General)	C	C	B-		Y	800-787-1621
Principal Government & High Quality Bond Fund R-2 Class	PFMRX	NAS CM	Open End	US Fixed Inc (Govt Bond - General)	C	C	B-	Down	Y	800-787-1621
Principal Government & High Quality Bond Fund R-3 Class	PRCMX	NAS CM	Open End	US Fixed Inc (Govt Bond - General)	C	C	C+		Y	800-787-1621
Principal Government & High Quality Bond Fund R-4 Class	PMRDX	NAS CM	Open End	US Fixed Inc (Govt Bond - General)	C	C	B-	Down	Y	800-787-1621
Principal Government & High Quality Bond Fund R-5 Class	PMREX	NAS CM	Open End	US Fixed Inc (Govt Bond - General)	C	C	B-	Down	Y	800-787-1621
Principal Government Money Market Fund Institutional	PGVXX	NAS CM	Money Mkt	US Money Mkt (Money Mkt - Govt)	U	U	U		Y	800-787-1621
Principal High Income Fund Class A	PYHAX	NAS CM	Open End	US Fixed Inc (Corp Bond - High Yield)	D+	D	C-	Down	Y	800-787-1621
Principal High Income Fund Class Institutional	PYHIX	NAS CM	Open End	US Fixed Inc (Corp Bond - High Yield)	D+	D	C-	Down	Y	800-787-1621
Principal High Yield Fund Class A	CPHYX	NAS CM	Open End	US Fixed Inc (Corp Bond - High Yield)	C-	D+	C		Y	800-787-1621
Principal High Yield Fund Class C	CCHIX	NAS CM	Open End	US Fixed Inc (Corp Bond - High Yield)	D+	D	C	Down	Y	800-787-1621
Principal High Yield Fund Class R-6	PHYFX	NAS CM	Open End	US Fixed Inc (Corp Bond - High Yield)	C-	D+	C		Y	800-787-1621
Principal High Yield Fund Institutional Class	PHYTX	NAS CM	Open End	US Fixed Inc (Corp Bond - High Yield)	C-	D+	C		Y	800-787-1621
Principal Inflation Protection Fund Class A	PITAX	NAS CM	Open End	US Fixed Inc (Income)	B-	C+	B+	Up	Y	800-787-1621
Principal Inflation Protection Fund Class J	PIPJX	NAS CM	Open End	US Fixed Inc (Income)	B-	C+	B+	Up	Y	800-787-1621
Principal Inflation Protection Fund Institutional Class	PIPIX	NAS CM	Open End	US Fixed Inc (Income)	B	C+	B+	Up	Y	800-787-1621

★Expanded analysis of this fund is included in Section II.

TOTAL RETURNS & PERFORMANCE									ASSETS		ASSET ALLOCATION & TURNOVER							MINIMUMS		FEES		
3-Month Total Return	6-Month Total Return	1-Year Total Return	3-Year Total Return	5-Year Total Return	Dividend Yield (TTM)	Expense Ratio	3-Yr Std Deviation	Effective Duration	NAV	Total Assets (MIL)	%Cash	%Government Bonds	%Municipal Bonds	%Corporate Bonds	%Other	Turnover Ratio	Average Coupon Rate	Min Initial Investment	Min Additional Investment	Front End Fee (%)	Back End Fee (%)	Inception Date
8.47	-5.87	-2.17			5.55	0.79		4.28	9.25	52.6	3	0	0	97	0	78	5.86	1,000,000				Jul-18
4.00	6.00	8.24	14.72	20.80	2.02	0.95	3.34	5.24	11.2	610.4	4	22	1	48	0	18	3.56	2,500	100	3.75		May-99
4.04	6.25	8.62	16.24	23.26	2.42	0.53	3.37	5.24	11.15	610.4	4	22	1	48	0	18	3.56	100,000				May-06
2.71	5.86	8.16	14.47	19.40	1.8	0.72	3.29	5.79	11.73	2,358	1	42	1	25	0	108	3.14	1,000	100		1.00	Mar-10
2.52	5.65	7.76	13.18	17.03	1.11	1.02	3.29	5.79	11.77	2,358	1	42	1	25	0	108	3.14	0				Dec-09
2.53	5.68	7.86	13.56	17.74	1.7	0.89	3.28	5.79	11.72	2,358	1	42	1	25	0	108	3.14	0				Dec-09
2.62	5.87	8.17	14.22	18.89	1.71	0.71	3.27	5.79	11.72	2,358	1	42	1	25	0	108	3.14	0				Dec-09
2.69	5.91	8.35	15.18	20.29	1.4	0.52	3.23	5.79	11.82	2,358	1	42	1	25	0	108	3.14	0				Dec-09
2.70	6.02	8.50	15.31	20.75	2.05	0.4	3.24	5.79	11.79	2,358	1	42	1	25	0	108	3.14	0				Dec-09
2.74	6.12	8.67	16.21	22.32	2.28	0.14	3.27	5.79	11.96	2,358	1	42	1	25	0	108	3.14	0				Dec-09
3.47	0.49	2.97	11.42	21.14	2.19	0.81	5.46	5.70	10.76	609.0	2	0	98	0	0	42	4.82	1,000	100	3.75		Jul-89
3.25	0.18	2.21	8.65	16.23	1.34	1.65	5.46	5.70	10.79	609.0	2	0	98	0	0	42	4.82	1,000	100		1.00	Mar-02
3.53	0.62	3.24	12.28	22.66	2.45	0.54	5.47	5.70	10.77	609.0	2	0	98	0	0	42	4.82	0				Feb-15
5.87	5.28	8.06	15.97	22.99	2.4	0.89	4.05	5.96	10.15	8,033	1	14	0	60	0	20	3.34	1,000	100	2.25		Dec-75
5.61	4.92	7.22	13.29	18.18	1.57	1.72	4.04	5.96	10.22	8,033	1	14	0	60	0	20	3.34	1,000	100		1.00	Mar-02
5.78	5.34	8.05	16.37	23.68	2.5	0.81	4.02	5.96	10.17	8,033	1	14	0	60	0	20	3.34	1,000	100		1.00	Sep-09
5.96	5.47	8.47	17.42	25.16	2.78	0.49	4.06	5.96	10.17	8,033	1	14	0	60	0	20	3.34	0				Nov-14
5.92	5.40	8.33	17.05	24.94	2.66	0.59	4.07	5.96	10.18	8,033	1	14	0	60	0	20	3.34	0				Mar-98
5.61	5.01	7.40	14.24	19.98	1.92	1.37	3.98	5.96	10.18	8,033	1	14	0	60	0	20	3.34	0				Mar-10
5.74	5.17	7.64	14.78	20.85	2.04	1.24	4.03	5.96	10.2	8,033	1	14	0	60	0	20	3.34	0				Mar-10
5.79	5.16	7.83	15.39	21.92	2.22	1.06	4.05	5.96	10.2	8,033	1	14	0	60	0	20	3.34	0				Mar-10
5.74	5.26	8.04	15.94	22.97	2.4	0.87	3.98	5.96	10.19	8,033	1	14	0	60	0	20	3.34	0				Mar-10
5.78	5.33	8.19	16.40	23.77	2.53	0.75	4	5.96	10.17	8,033	1	14	0	60	0	20	3.34	0				Mar-10
5.34	5.78	8.23	15.29	22.21	3.07	0.89	3.76	6.03	11.53	606.2	-7	19	0	41	0	139	3.78	1,000	100	3.75		Jun-05
5.31	5.75	8.16	15.25	22.36	3.04	0.92	3.77	6.03	11.61	606.2	-7	19	0	41	0	139	3.78	1,000	100		1.00	Mar-01
5.33	5.95	8.60	16.55	24.61	3.41	0.47	3.77	6.03	11.52	606.2	-7	19	0	41	0	139	3.78	0				Mar-01
5.21	5.53	7.71	13.61	19.36	2.6	1.34	3.78	6.03	11.52	606.2	-7	19	0	41	0	139	3.78	0				Nov-04
5.21	5.57	7.75	14.03	20.08	2.77	1.21	3.74	6.03	11.39	606.2	-7	19	0	41	0	139	3.78	0				Dec-00
5.33	5.73	8.00	14.77	21.26	2.93	1.03	3.8	6.03	11.45	606.2	-7	19	0	41	0	139	3.78	0				Dec-00
5.26	5.79	8.21	15.37	22.32	3.04	0.84	3.77	6.03	11.69	606.2	-7	19	0	41	0	139	3.78	0				Dec-00
5.31	5.78	8.32	15.71	23.12	3.22	0.72	3.71	6.03	11.46	606.2	-7	19	0	41	0	139	3.78	0				Dec-00
9.59	-0.71	4.22	16.41		3.36	1.2	7.4	4.80	10.21	208.6	-52	57	0	8	0	313	4.01	1,000	100	3.75		Jul-16
9.76	-0.54	4.55	17.63		3.68	0.85	7.43	4.80	10.25	208.6	-52	57	0	8	0	313	4.01	0				Jul-16
1.46	2.07	3.90	9.40	12.32	2.35	0.83	2.37	2.65	10.6	1,675	15	1	0	0	0	23	3.44	1,000	100	2.25		May-84
1.35	1.65	3.16	6.78	7.93	1.55	1.63	2.38	2.65	10.6	1,675	15	1	0	0	0	23	3.44	1,000	100		1.00	Mar-02
1.54	2.04	3.95	9.26	12.23	2.3	0.91	2.37	2.65	10.63	1,675	15	1	0	0	0	23	3.44	1,000	100		1.00	Dec-08
1.62	2.20	4.29	10.32	13.98	2.63	0.53	2.37	2.65	10.62	1,675	15	1	0	0	0	23	3.44	0				Mar-98
1.43	1.82	3.50	7.84	9.74	1.88	1.29	2.42	2.65	10.63	1,675	15	1	0	0	0	23	3.44	0				Dec-08
1.37	1.88	3.54	8.16	10.45	2.01	1.16	2.41	2.65	10.62	1,675	15	1	0	0	0	23	3.44	0				Dec-08
1.51	2.07	3.82	8.85	11.45	2.18	0.98	2.45	2.65	10.63	1,675	15	1	0	0	0	23	3.44	0				Dec-08
1.46	2.06	3.91	9.46	12.50	2.37	0.79	2.34	2.65	10.63	1,675	15	1	0	0	0	23	3.44	0				Dec-08
1.58	2.22	4.14	9.95	13.28	2.49	0.67	2.41	2.65	10.64	1,675	15	1	0	0	0	23	3.44	0				Dec-08
0.00	0.00	0.00			0	0.15				--	97	0	0	3	0	0		0				Dec-17
8.36	-5.54	-3.24	3.43	12.83	6.49	1.06	8.54	4.01	8.66	2,745	5	0	0	95	0	57	6.32	1,000	100	3.75		Mar-13
8.46	-5.32	-2.80	4.74	15.41	6.95	0.61	8.58	4.01	8.67	2,745	5	0	0	95	0	57	6.32	0				Dec-04
8.71	-4.33	-1.46	6.48	19.56	5.68	0.94	8.18	3.61	6.74	2,933	6	2	0	91	0	50	5.94	1,000	100	3.75		Apr-98
8.40	-4.77	-2.16	4.13	15.22	4.85	1.67	8.12	3.61	6.82	2,933	6	2	0	91	0	50	5.94	1,000	100		1.00	Mar-02
8.89	-4.17	-0.91	7.84	21.15	6.16	0.52	8.16	3.61	6.69	2,933	6	2	0	91	0	50	5.94	0				Nov-16
8.86	-4.21	-1.14	7.56	21.37	6.07	0.61	8.19	3.61	6.69	2,933	6	2	0	91	0	50	5.94	0				Jul-98
4.58	4.98	7.11	12.53	14.75	1.4	0.9	3.78	7.63	8.89	1,608	38	50	0	0	0	68	1.13	1,000	100	3.75		Jun-05
4.47	4.85	6.77	11.69	13.38	1.23	1.15	3.72	7.63	8.64	1,608	38	50	0	0	0	68	1.13	1,000	100		1.00	Dec-04
4.72	5.23	7.60	14.34	17.69	1.85	0.39	3.79	7.63	9.09	1,608	38	50	0	0	0	68	1.13	0				Dec-04

	MARKET		FUND TYPE, CATEGORY & OBJECTIVE		RATINGS				NEW INVESTORS	
Fund Name	Ticker Symbol	Traded On	Fund Type	Category and (Prospectus Objective)	Overall Rating	Reward Rating	Risk Rating	Recent Up/ Downgrade	Open to New Investors	Telephone
Principal Inflation Protection Fund R-1 Class	PISPX	NAS CM	Open End	US Fixed Inc (Income)	B-	C	B	Up	Y	800-787-1621
Principal Inflation Protection Fund R-2 Class	PBSAX	NAS CM	Open End	US Fixed Inc (Income)	B-	C+	B+	Up	Y	800-787-1621
Principal Inflation Protection Fund R-3 Class	PIFPX	NAS CM	Open End	US Fixed Inc (Income)	B-	C+	B+	Up	Y	800-787-1621
Principal Inflation Protection Fund R-4 Class	PIFSX	NAS CM	Open End	US Fixed Inc (Income)	B-	C+	B+	Up	Y	800-787-1621
Principal Inflation Protection Fund R-5 Class	PBPPX	NAS CM	Open End	US Fixed Inc (Income)	B	C+	B+	Up	Y	800-787-1621
Principal Money Market Fund Class A	PCSXX	NAS CM	Money Mkt	US Money Mkt (Money Mkt - Taxable)	C	C	C+		Y	800-787-1621
Principal Money Market Fund Class J	PMJXX	NAS CM	Money Mkt	US Money Mkt (Money Mkt - Taxable)	C	C-	C+		Y	800-787-1621
Principal Opportunistic Municipal Fund Class A	PMOAX	NAS CM	Open End	US Muni Fixed Inc (Muni Bond - Natl)	C-	D+	C	Down	Y	800-787-1621
Principal Opportunistic Municipal Fund Institutional Class	POMFX	NAS CM	Open End	US Muni Fixed Inc (Muni Bond - Natl)	C-	D+	C	Down	Y	800-787-1621
Principal Short-Term Income Fund Class A	SRHQX	NAS CM	Open End	US Fixed Inc (Corp Bond - High Quality)	C	C	B-		Y	800-787-1621
Principal Short-Term Income Fund Class C	STCCX	NAS CM	Open End	US Fixed Inc (Corp Bond - High Quality)	C	C	B-		Y	800-787-1621
Principal Short-Term Income Fund Class J	PSJIX	NAS CM	Open End	US Fixed Inc (Corp Bond - High Quality)	C	C	B-		Y	800-787-1621
Principal Short-Term Income Fund Institutional Class	PSHIX	NAS CM	Open End	US Fixed Inc (Corp Bond - High Quality)	C+	C	B-	Up	Y	800-787-1621
Principal Short-Term Income Fund R-1 Class	PSIMX	NAS CM	Open End	US Fixed Inc (Corp Bond - High Quality)	C	C	C+		Y	800-787-1621
Principal Short-Term Income Fund R-2 Class	PSINX	NAS CM	Open End	US Fixed Inc (Corp Bond - High Quality)	C	C	C+		Y	800-787-1621
Principal Short-Term Income Fund R-3 Class	PSIOX	NAS CM	Open End	US Fixed Inc (Corp Bond - High Quality)	C	C	B-		Y	800-787-1621
Principal Short-Term Income Fund R-4 Class	PSIPX	NAS CM	Open End	US Fixed Inc (Corp Bond - High Quality)	C	C	B-		Y	800-787-1621
Principal Short-Term Income Fund R-5 Class	PSIQX	NAS CM	Open End	US Fixed Inc (Corp Bond - High Quality)	C	C	B-		Y	800-787-1621
Principal Street High Income Muni Fund Institutional Class	GSTAX	NAS CM	Open End	US Muni Fixed Inc (Growth & Income)	D	D	D+	Down	Y	
Principal Street High Income Municipal Fund Investor Class	GSTEX	NAS CM	Open End	US Muni Fixed Inc (Growth & Income)	D	D	D+		Y	
Principal Tax-Exempt Bond Fund Class A	PTEAX	NAS CM	Open End	US Muni Fixed Inc (Muni Bond - Natl)	C	C-	C		Y	800-787-1621
Principal Tax-Exempt Bond Fund Class C	PTBCX	NAS CM	Open End	US Muni Fixed Inc (Muni Bond - Natl)	C-	D+	C	Down	Y	800-787-1621
Principal Tax-Exempt Bond Fund Institutional Class	PITEX	NAS CM	Open End	US Muni Fixed Inc (Muni Bond - Natl)	C	C-	C+		Y	800-787-1621
Priority Income Fund, Inc. Class I			Closed End	US Fixed Inc (Income)	U	U	U		Y	
Priority Income Fund, Inc. Class R			Closed End	US Fixed Inc (Income)	U	U	U		Y	
Priority Income Fund, Inc. Class RIA			Closed End	US Fixed Inc (Income)	U	U	U		Y	
ProFunds Falling U.S. Dollar Fund Investor Class	FDPIX	NAS CM	Open End	Currency (Income)	D	D	C-		Y	614-470-8626
ProFunds Falling U.S. Dollar Fund Service Class	FDPSX	NAS CM	Open End	Currency (Income)	D	D-	D+		Y	614-470-8626
ProFunds Government Money Market ProFund Investor Class	MPIXX	NAS CM	Money Mkt	US Money Mkt (Money Mkt - Govt)	C-	C-	C		Y	614-470-8626
ProFunds Government Money Market ProFund Service Class	MPSXX	NAS CM	Money Mkt	US Money Mkt (Money Mkt - Govt)	C-	C-	C		Y	614-470-8626
ProFunds Rising U.S. Dollar Fund Investor Class	RDPIX	NAS CM	Open End	Currency (Income)	C	C-	C+	Down	Y	614-470-8626
ProFunds Rising U.S. Dollar Fund Service Class	RDPSX	NAS CM	Open End	Currency (Income)	C	C-	C		Y	614-470-8626
Putnam AMT-Free Municipal Fund Class A	PPNAX	NAS CM	Open End	US Muni Fixed Inc (Muni Bond - Natl)	C	C-	C+		Y	617-292-1000
Putnam AMT-Free Municipal Fund Class B	PTFIX	NAS CM	Open End	US Muni Fixed Inc (Muni Bond - Natl)	C	C-	C+		Y	617-292-1000
Putnam AMT-Free Municipal Fund Class C	PAMTX	NAS CM	Open End	US Muni Fixed Inc (Muni Bond - Natl)	C	C-	C		Y	617-292-1000
Putnam AMT-Free Municipal Fund Class R6	PAMLX	NAS CM	Open End	US Muni Fixed Inc (Muni Bond - Natl)	C	C-	C+		Y	617-292-1000
Putnam AMT-Free Municipal Fund Class Y	PAMYX	NAS CM	Open End	US Muni Fixed Inc (Muni Bond - Natl)	C	C-	B-		Y	617-292-1000
Putnam California Tax Exempt Income Fund Class A	PCTEX	NAS CM	Open End	US Muni Fixed Inc (Muni Bond - Single State)	C	C-	B-		Y	617-292-1000
Putnam California Tax Exempt Income Fund Class B	PCTBX	NAS CM	Open End	US Muni Fixed Inc (Muni Bond - Single State)	C	C-	B-			617-292-1000
Putnam California Tax Exempt Income Fund Class C	PCTCX	NAS CM	Open End	US Muni Fixed Inc (Muni Bond - Single State)	C	C-	C+		Y	617-292-1000
Putnam California Tax Exempt Income Fund Class R6	PCLGX	NAS CM	Open End	US Muni Fixed Inc (Muni Bond - Single State)	C	C-	B-		Y	617-292-1000
Putnam California Tax Exempt Income Fund Class Y	PCIYX	NAS CM	Open End	US Muni Fixed Inc (Muni Bond - Single State)	C	C-	B		Y	617-292-1000
Putnam Diversified Income Trust Class A	PDINX	NAS CM	Open End	Fixed Inc Misc (Income)	D+	D	C-	Down	Y	617-292-1000
Putnam Diversified Income Trust Class B	PSIBX	NAS CM	Open End	Fixed Inc Misc (Income)	D	D	D+	Down	Y	617-292-1000
Putnam Diversified Income Trust Class C	PDVCX	NAS CM	Open End	Fixed Inc Misc (Income)	D	D	D+	Down	Y	617-292-1000
Putnam Diversified Income Trust Class M	PDVMX	NAS CM	Open End	Fixed Inc Misc (Income)	D+	D	C-	Down	Y	617-292-1000
Putnam Diversified Income Trust Class R	PDVRX	NAS CM	Open End	Fixed Inc Misc (Income)	D+	D	C-	Down	Y	617-292-1000
Putnam Diversified Income Trust Class R6	PDVGX	NAS CM	Open End	Fixed Inc Misc (Income)	D+	D	C-	Down	Y	617-292-1000
Putnam Diversified Income Trust Class Y	PDVYX	NAS CM	Open End	Fixed Inc Misc (Income)	D+	D	C-	Down	Y	617-292-1000
Putnam Fixed Income Absolute Return Fund Class A	PTRNX	NAS CM	Open End	Fixed Inc Misc (Income)	C-	D+	C	Down	Y	617-292-1000
Putnam Fixed Income Absolute Return Fund Class B	PTRBX	NAS CM	Open End	Fixed Inc Misc (Income)	C-	D+	C	Down	Y	617-292-1000
Putnam Fixed Income Absolute Return Fund Class C	PTRGX	NAS CM	Open End	Fixed Inc Misc (Income)	C-	D+	C		Y	617-292-1000

★ Expanded analysis of this fund is included in Section II.

TOTAL RETURNS & PERFORMANCE									ASSETS		ASSET ALLOCATION & TURNOVER							MINIMUMS		FEES		
3-Month Total Return	6-Month Total Return	1-Year Total Return	3-Year Total Return	5-Year Total Return	Dividend Yield (TTM)	Expense Ratio	3-Yr Std Deviation	Effective Duration	NAV	Total Assets (MIL)	%Cash	%Government Bonds	%Municipal Bonds	%Corporate Bonds	%Other	Turnover Ratio	Average Coupon Rate	Min Initial Investment	Min Additional Investment	Front End Fee (%)	Back End Fee (%)	Inception Date
4.43	4.82	6.73	11.35	12.56	1.18	1.27	3.76	7.63	8.47	1,608	38	50	0	0	0	68	1.13	0				Dec-04
4.52	4.90	6.86	11.85	13.45	1.27	1.14	3.77	7.63	8.55	1,608	38	50	0	0	0	68	1.13	0				Dec-04
4.57	4.97	7.13	12.35	14.45	1.39	0.96	3.79	7.63	8.68	1,608	38	50	0	0	0	68	1.13	0				Dec-04
4.51	4.94	7.17	12.91	15.38	1.56	0.77	3.8	7.63	8.8	1,608	38	50	0	0	0	68	1.13	0				Dec-04
4.70	5.16	7.42	13.49	16.15	1.64	0.65	3.82	7.63	8.91	1,608	38	50	0	0	0	68	1.13	0				Dec-04
0.08	0.37	1.19	4.27	4.54	1.36	0.51	0.15		1	737.4	93	0	2	0	2	0		1,000	100			Jun-05
0.08	0.36	1.13	4.04	4.27	1.28	0.61	0.14		1	737.4	93	0	2	0	2	0		1,000	100		1.00	Mar-01
5.60	-2.52	0.50	14.12	26.04	3.58	0.96	8.19	7.47	10.71	124.6	-1	0	100	0	0	66	5.38	1,000	100	3.75		Jun-12
5.57	-2.47	0.78	14.94	27.72	3.87	0.68	8.23	7.47	10.71	124.6	-1	0	100	0	0	66	5.38	0				Mar-15
3.36	2.84	4.18	9.00	12.77	1.96	0.69	1.91	1.99	12.53	5,317	3	17	0	52	0	52	2.67	1,000	100	2.25		Nov-93
3.14	2.39	3.26	6.11	7.83	1.08	1.59	1.92	1.99	12.54	5,317	3	17	0	52	0	52	2.67	1,000	100		1.00	Mar-02
3.37	2.77	4.13	8.99	12.84	1.99	0.7	1.94	1.99	12.52	5,317	3	17	0	52	0	52	2.67	1,000	100		1.00	Jul-10
3.43	2.88	4.36	9.74	14.20	2.21	0.43	1.94	1.99	12.52	5,317	3	17	0	52	0	52	2.67	0				Jul-96
3.21	2.53	3.55	7.03	9.38	1.37	1.29	1.9	1.99	12.53	5,317	3	17	0	52	0	52	2.67	0				Jul-10
3.24	2.52	3.60	7.36	10.01	1.49	1.16	1.96	1.99	12.52	5,317	3	17	0	52	0	52	2.67	0				Jul-10
3.29	2.61	3.79	7.94	11.08	1.67	0.98	1.93	1.99	12.53	5,317	3	17	0	52	0	52	2.67	0				Jul-10
3.34	2.70	3.99	8.56	12.07	1.86	0.79	1.94	1.99	12.52	5,317	3	17	0	52	0	52	2.67	0				Jul-10
3.36	2.76	4.11	8.94	12.72	1.97	0.67	1.94	1.99	12.53	5,317	3	17	0	52	0	52	2.67	0				Jul-10
1.81	-9.41	-6.30			6.41	0.75			9.01	173.8	1	0	95	5	0		7.15	25,000	1,000			Sep-17
0.77	-10.44	-7.60				1.25			9.07	173.8	1	0	95	5	0		7.15	25,000	1,000			Mar-20
3.82	-0.51	2.04	11.47	18.80	2.57	0.86	6.08	6.22	7.32	610.9	0	0	100	0	0	64	4.86	1,000	100	3.75		Jan-77
3.74	-0.78	1.35	8.88	14.14	1.73	1.67	6.13	6.22	7.35	610.9	0	0	100	0	0	64	4.86	1,000	100		1.00	Mar-02
4.02	-0.38	2.45	12.50	20.36	2.84	0.59	6.13	6.22	7.33	610.9	0	0	100	0	0	64	4.86	0				May-15
8.32	44.63					8.56				--						1		1,000	500			May-13
8.32	44.63					10.88				--						1		1,000	500			May-13
8.32	44.63					8.56				--						1		1,000	500			May-13
0.89	-2.29	-3.13	-8.57	-12.47	0	1.78	4.91		15.78	0.83	93	0	0	7	0	1,298		15,000				Feb-05
0.55	-2.88	-4.16	-11.21	-16.58	0	2.78	4.92		14.49	0.83	93	0	0	7	0	1,298		15,000				Feb-05
0.00	0.00	0.00	0.00	0.00	0	1.19	0		1	280.6	100	0	0	0	0	0		15,000				Nov-97
0.00	0.00	0.00	0.00	0.00	0	2.19	0		1	280.6	100	0	0	0	0	0		15,000				Nov-97
-1.91	0.44	1.06	5.33	2.15	0.26	1.78	4.94		29.23	11.5	92	0	0	8	0	1,297		15,000				Feb-05
-2.15	0.00	0.07	2.25	-2.79	0	2.78	4.95		25.85	11.5	92	0	0	8	0	1,297		15,000				Feb-05
2.25	0.20	2.73	11.62	17.99	2.46	0.81	4.87	7.91	15.04	274.8	1	0	99	0	0	38	4.52	0		4.00	1.00	Sep-93
2.09	-0.09	2.10	9.62	14.45	1.83	1.43	4.87	7.91	15.06	274.8	1	0	99	0	0	38	4.52	0			5.00	Sep-85
2.12	-0.10	1.95	9.13	13.59	1.68	1.58	4.9	7.91	15.09	274.8	1	0	99	0	0	38	4.52	0			1.00	Jul-99
2.37	0.38	3.03	11.66	16.58	2.69	0.57	4.9	7.91	15.06	274.8	1	0	99	0	0	38	4.52	0				May-18
2.30	0.31	2.95	12.37	19.34	2.68	0.58	4.87	7.91	15.05	274.8	1	0	99	0	0	38	4.52	0				Jan-08
3.46	1.41	4.03	12.73	20.64	2.52	0.72	4.84	8.15	8.2	1,145	0	0	99	0	0	41	4.53	0		4.00	1.00	Apr-83
3.31	0.98	3.38	10.63	16.91	1.89	1.36	4.84	8.15	8.19	1,145	0	0	99	0	0	41	4.53	0			5.00	Jan-93
3.24	0.89	3.20	10.04	16.03	1.72	1.51	4.85	8.15	8.25	1,145	0	0	99	0	0	41	4.53	0			1.00	Jul-99
3.50	1.40	4.25	13.17	21.11	2.74	0.51	4.82	8.15	8.23	1,145	0	0	99	0	0	41	4.53	0				May-18
3.50	1.39	4.11	13.41	21.87	2.72	0.51	4.84	8.15	8.22	1,145	0	0	99	0	0	41	4.53	0				Jan-08
7.10	-7.75	-3.71	5.03	10.93	4.47	0.98	8.65	3.04	6.43	3,236	121	19	0	11	-3	701	4.42	0		4.00		Oct-88
6.99	-8.05	-4.47	2.57	6.78	3.7	1.73	8.66	3.04	6.35	3,236	121	19	0	11	-3	701	4.42	0			5.00	Mar-93
6.90	-8.10	-4.49	2.54	6.78	3.75	1.73	8.64	3.04	6.29	3,236	121	19	0	11	-3	701	4.42	0			1.00	Feb-99
7.05	-8.00	-3.98	4.20	9.40	4.36	1.23	8.65	3.04	6.28	3,236	121	19	0	11	-3	701	4.42	0		3.25		Dec-94
7.17	-7.94	-3.96	4.14	9.56	4.31	1.23	8.78	3.04	6.33	3,236	121	19	0	11	-3	701	4.42	0				Dec-03
7.12	-7.80	-3.55	5.88	12.66	4.9	0.64	8.68	3.04	6.35	3,236	121	19	0	11	-3	701	4.42	0				Nov-13
7.07	-7.74	-3.54	5.67	12.20	4.78	0.73	8.64	3.04	6.35	3,236	121	19	0	11	-3	701	4.42	0				Jul-96
4.83	-3.07	0.34	7.76	12.43	4.23	0.87	5.01	1.44	9.36	505.4	34	7	0	23	7	632	3.91	0		2.25		Dec-08
4.78	-3.20	0.09	7.04	11.21	3.98	1.07	5.04	1.44	9.33	505.4	34	7	0	23	7	632	3.91	0			1.00	Dec-08
4.66	-3.46	-0.53	5.28	8.26	3.43	1.62	5.06	1.44	9.32	505.4	34	7	0	23	7	632	3.91	0			1.00	Dec-08

	MARKET			FUND TYPE, CATEGORY & OBJECTIVE	RATINGS				NEW INVESTORS	
Fund Name	Ticker Symbol	Traded On	Fund Type	Category and (Prospectus Objective)	Overall Rating	Reward Rating	Risk Rating	Recent Up/ Downgrade	Open to New Investors	Telephone
Putnam Fixed Income Absolute Return Fund Class P			Open End	Fixed Inc Misc (Income)	C-	D+	C	Down		617-292-1000
Putnam Fixed Income Absolute Return Fund Class R	PTRKX	NAS CM	Open End	Fixed Inc Misc (Income)	C-	D+	C	Down	Y	617-292-1000
Putnam Fixed Income Absolute Return Fund Class R6	PTREX	NAS CM	Open End	Fixed Inc Misc (Income)	C-	D+	C	Down	Y	617-292-1000
Putnam Fixed Income Absolute Return Fund Class Y	PYTRX	NAS CM	Open End	Fixed Inc Misc (Income)	C-	D+	C	Down	Y	617-292-1000
Putnam Floating Rate Income Fund Class A	PFLRX	NAS CM	Open End	US Fixed Inc (Income)	D+	D	C-	Down	Y	617-292-1000
Putnam Floating Rate Income Fund Class B	PFRBX	NAS CM	Open End	US Fixed Inc (Income)	D+	D	C-	Down	Y	617-292-1000
Putnam Floating Rate Income Fund Class C	PFICX	NAS CM	Open End	US Fixed Inc (Income)	D	D	C-	Down	Y	617-292-1000
Putnam Floating Rate Income Fund Class R	PFLLX	NAS CM	Open End	US Fixed Inc (Income)	D+	D	C-	Down	Y	617-292-1000
Putnam Floating Rate Income Fund Class R6 Shares	PFRZX	NAS CM	Open End	US Fixed Inc (Income)	D+	D	C-	Down	Y	617-292-1000
Putnam Floating Rate Income Fund Class Y	PFRYX	NAS CM	Open End	US Fixed Inc (Income)	D+	D	C-	Down	Y	617-292-1000
Putnam Global Income Trust Class A	PGGIX	NAS CM	Open End	Global Fixed Inc (Worldwide Bond)	C	C-	C+		Y	617-292-1000
Putnam Global Income Trust Class B	PGLBX	NAS CM	Open End	Global Fixed Inc (Worldwide Bond)	C	C-	C		Y	617-292-1000
Putnam Global Income Trust Class C	PGGLX	NAS CM	Open End	Global Fixed Inc (Worldwide Bond)	C	C-	C		Y	617-292-1000
Putnam Global Income Trust Class R	PGBRX	NAS CM	Open End	Global Fixed Inc (Worldwide Bond)	C	C-	C+		Y	617-292-1000
Putnam Global Income Trust Class R5	PGGDX	NAS CM	Open End	Global Fixed Inc (Worldwide Bond)	C	C-	C+		Y	617-292-1000
Putnam Global Income Trust Class R6	PGGEX	NAS CM	Open End	Global Fixed Inc (Worldwide Bond)	C	C-	C+		Y	617-292-1000
Putnam Global Income Trust Class Y	PGGYX	NAS CM	Open End	Global Fixed Inc (Worldwide Bond)	C	C-	C+		Y	617-292-1000
Putnam Government Money Market Fund Class A	PGDXX	NAS CM	Money Mkt	US Money Mkt (Money Mkt - Govt)	C	C	C+		Y	617-292-1000
Putnam Government Money Market Fund Class B	PGBXX	NAS CM	Money Mkt	US Money Mkt (Money Mkt - Govt)	C	C	C+		Y	617-292-1000
Putnam Government Money Market Fund Class C	PGEXX	NAS CM	Money Mkt	US Money Mkt (Money Mkt - Govt)	C	C	C+		Y	617-292-1000
Putnam Government Money Market Fund Class G	PGGXX	NAS CM	Money Mkt	US Money Mkt (Money Mkt - Govt)	C	C-	C+			617-292-1000
Putnam Government Money Market Fund Class I	PGKXX	NAS CM	Money Mkt	US Money Mkt (Money Mkt - Govt)	C	C-	C+		Y	617-292-1000
Putnam Government Money Market Fund Class P	PGLXX	NAS CM	Money Mkt	US Money Mkt (Money Mkt - Govt)	C	C-	C+			617-292-1000
Putnam Government Money Market Fund Class R	PGRXX	NAS CM	Money Mkt	US Money Mkt (Money Mkt - Govt)	C	C	C+		Y	617-292-1000
Putnam High Yield Fund Class A	PHYIX	NAS CM	Open End	US Fixed Inc (Corp Bond - High Yield)	C-	D+	C		Y	617-292-1000
Putnam High Yield Fund Class B	PHYBX	NAS CM	Open End	US Fixed Inc (Corp Bond - High Yield)	C-	D+	C		Y	617-292-1000
Putnam High Yield Fund Class C	PHYLX	NAS CM	Open End	US Fixed Inc (Corp Bond - High Yield)	C-	D+	C		Y	617-292-1000
Putnam High Yield Fund Class M	PHYMX	NAS CM	Open End	US Fixed Inc (Corp Bond - High Yield)	C-	D+	C		Y	617-292-1000
Putnam High Yield Fund Class R	PFJAX	NAS CM	Open End	US Fixed Inc (Corp Bond - High Yield)	C-	D+	C		Y	617-292-1000
Putnam High Yield Fund Class R6 Shares	PHYUX	NAS CM	Open End	US Fixed Inc (Corp Bond - High Yield)	C-	D+	C		Y	617-292-1000
Putnam High Yield Fund Class Y	PHAYX	NAS CM	Open End	US Fixed Inc (Corp Bond - High Yield)	C-	D+	C		Y	617-292-1000
Putnam Income Fund Class A	PINCX	NAS CM	Open End	US Fixed Inc (Income)	B-	C	B+	Up	Y	617-292-1000
Putnam Income Fund Class B	PNCBX	NAS CM	Open End	US Fixed Inc (Income)	C+	C	B		Y	617-292-1000
Putnam Income Fund Class C	PUICX	NAS CM	Open End	US Fixed Inc (Income)	C+	C	B		Y	617-292-1000
Putnam Income Fund Class M	PNCMX	NAS CM	Open End	US Fixed Inc (Income)	C+	C	B+		Y	617-292-1000
Putnam Income Fund Class R	PIFRX	NAS CM	Open End	US Fixed Inc (Income)	B-	C	B+	Up	Y	617-292-1000
Putnam Income Fund Class R5	PINFX	NAS CM	Open End	US Fixed Inc (Income)	B-	C	B+	Up	Y	617-292-1000
Putnam Income Fund Class R6	PINHX	NAS CM	Open End	US Fixed Inc (Income)	B-	C	B+	Up	Y	617-292-1000
Putnam Income Fund Class Y	PNCYX	NAS CM	Open End	US Fixed Inc (Income)	B-	C	B+	Up	Y	617-292-1000
Putnam Intermediate-Term Municipal Income Fund Class A	PIMEX	NAS CM	Open End	US Muni Fixed Inc (Muni Bond - Natl)	C	C	B-		Y	617-292-1000
Putnam Intermediate-Term Municipal Income Fund Class B	PIMBX	NAS CM	Open End	US Muni Fixed Inc (Muni Bond - Natl)	C	C-	B-		Y	617-292-1000
Putnam Intermediate-Term Municipal Income Fund Class C	PIMFX	NAS CM	Open End	US Muni Fixed Inc (Muni Bond - Natl)	C	C-	B-		Y	617-292-1000
Putnam Intermediate-Term Muni Income Fund Class R6 Shares	PIMRX	NAS CM	Open End	US Muni Fixed Inc (Muni Bond - Natl)	C	C	B		Y	617-292-1000
Putnam Intermediate-Term Municipal Income Fund Class Y	PIMYX	NAS CM	Open End	US Muni Fixed Inc (Muni Bond - Natl)	C	C	B		Y	617-292-1000
Putnam Managed Municipal Income Trust	PMM	NYSE	Closed End	US Muni Fixed Inc (Muni Bond - Natl)	C-	D+	C	Down	Y	617-292-1000
Putnam Massachusetts Tax Exempt Income Fund Class A	PXMAX	NAS CM	Open End	US Muni Fixed Inc (Muni Bond - Single State)	C	C	B-		Y	617-292-1000
Putnam Massachusetts Tax Exempt Income Fund Class B	PMABX	NAS CM	Open End	US Muni Fixed Inc (Muni Bond - Single State)	C	C-	B-		Y	617-292-1000
Putnam Massachusetts Tax Exempt Income Fund Class C	PMMCX	NAS CM	Open End	US Muni Fixed Inc (Muni Bond - Single State)	C	C-	B-		Y	617-292-1000
Putnam Massachusetts Tax Exempt Income Cl R6 Shares	PMATX	NAS CM	Open End	US Muni Fixed Inc (Muni Bond - Single State)	C	C	B-		Y	617-292-1000
Putnam Massachusetts Tax Exempt Income Fund Class Y	PMAYX	NAS CM	Open End	US Muni Fixed Inc (Muni Bond - Single State)	C	C	B		Y	617-292-1000
Putnam Master Intermediate Income Trust	PIM	NYSE	Closed End	US Fixed Inc (Multisector Bond)	D+	D	C-	Down	Y	617-292-1000
Putnam Minnesota Tax Exempt Income Fund Class A	PXMNX	NAS CM	Open End	US Muni Fixed Inc (Muni Bond - Single State)	C	C	B-		Y	617-292-1000

★ Expanded analysis of this fund is included in Section II.

TOTAL RETURNS & PERFORMANCE									ASSETS		ASSET ALLOCATION & TURNOVER							MINIMUMS		FEES		
3-Month Total Return	6-Month Total Return	1-Year Total Return	3-Year Total Return	5-Year Total Return	Dividend Yield (TTM)	Expense Ratio	3-Yr Std Deviation	Effective Duration	NAV	Total Assets (MIL)	%Cash	%Government Bonds	%Municipal Bonds	%Corporate Bonds	%Other	Turnover Ratio	Average Coupon Rate	Min Initial Investment	Min Additional Investment	Front End Fee (%)	Back End Fee (%)	Inception Date
4.55	-3.34	0.16	8.26	13.48	4.47	0.62	5.06	1.44	9.39	505.4	34	7	0	23	7	632	3.91	0				Aug-16
4.85	-3.18	0.09	6.95	11.03	3.95	1.12	5.08	1.44	9.41	505.4	34	7	0	23	7	632	3.91	0				Dec-08
4.88	-3.04	0.48	8.59	13.86	4.47	0.62	5.07	1.44	9.39	505.4	34	7	0	23	7	632	3.91	0				Jul-12
5.01	-2.94	0.59	8.63	13.90	4.48	0.62	5.11	1.44	9.37	505.4	34	7	0	23	7	632	3.91	0				Dec-08
7.42	-5.13	-3.01	3.83	9.93	4.44	1.03	7.56	-0.13	7.86	326.7	8	0	1	92	0	33	4.13	0		2.25	1.00	Aug-04
7.24	-5.23	-3.21	3.19	8.70	4.22	1.23	7.54	-0.13	7.85	326.7	8	0	1	92	0	33	4.13	0			1.00	Sep-04
7.09	-5.50	-3.74	1.51	5.87	3.65	1.78	7.51	-0.13	7.85	326.7	8	0	1	92	0	33	4.13	0			1.00	Sep-04
7.36	-5.14	-3.13	3.17	8.56	4.17	1.28	7.56	-0.13	7.86	326.7	8	0	1	92	0	33	4.13	0				Sep-04
7.37	-4.97	-2.68	4.45	10.59	4.79	0.68	7.54	-0.13	7.86	326.7	8	0	1	92	0	33	4.13	0				May-18
7.34	-5.12	-2.76	4.48	11.18	4.7	0.78	7.55	-0.13	7.86	326.7	8	0	1	92	0	33	4.13	0				Oct-05
5.24	-0.31	1.86	9.13	15.73	1.99	1.22	5.19	6.52	12.22	240.0	-2	38	0	21	1	408	3.42	0		4.00		Jun-87
5.06	-0.70	1.15	6.67	11.45	1.2	1.97	5.2	6.52	12.16	240.0	-2	38	0	21	1	408	3.42	0			5.00	Feb-94
5.07	-0.68	1.11	6.72	11.52	1.24	1.97	5.21	6.52	12.16	240.0	-2	38	0	21	1	408	3.42	0			1.00	Jul-99
5.27	-0.41	1.70	8.43	14.45	1.74	1.47	5.23	6.52	12.22	240.0	-2	38	0	21	1	408	3.42	0				Dec-03
5.42	-0.14	2.28	10.29	17.72	2.33	0.86	5.18	6.52	12.22	240.0	-2	38	0	21	1	408	3.42	0				Jul-12
5.35	-0.10	2.36	10.52	18.21	2.4	0.79	5.18	6.52	12.22	240.0	-2	38	0	21	1	408	3.42	0				Jul-12
5.40	-0.17	2.23	10.06	17.31	2.27	0.97	5.22	6.52	12.22	240.0	-2	38	0	21	1	408	3.42	0				Oct-05
0.00	0.21	0.93	3.44		1.07	0.62	0.17		1	198.0	73	27	0	0	0			0			1.00	Apr-16
0.00	0.21	0.93	3.44		1.07	0.62	0.17		1	198.0	73	27	0	0	0			0			5.00	Jun-16
0.00	0.20	0.92	3.43		1.07	0.62	0.17		1	198.0	73	27	0	0	0			0			1.00	Jun-16
0.00	0.25	1.04	3.89		1.2	0.45	0.18		1	198.0	73	27	0	0	0			0				Aug-16
0.00	0.24	1.03	3.89		1.2	0.45	0.18		1	198.0	73	27	0	0	0			5,000,000				Apr-16
0.00	0.24	1.03	3.89		1.2	0.45	0.18		1	198.0	73	27	0	0	0			0				Apr-16
0.00	0.22	0.93	3.44		1.07	0.62	0.17		1	198.0	73	27	0	0	0			0				Jun-16
9.73	-4.27	-0.70	8.17	19.17	5.27	1.02	8.77	4.11	5.48	1,280	7	0	0	93	0	37	6.11	0		4.00	1.00	Mar-86
9.41	-4.77	-1.66	5.55	14.46	4.65	1.77	8.8	4.11	5.32	1,280	7	0	0	93	0	37	6.11	0			5.00	May-94
9.68	-4.63	-1.49	5.79	14.63	4.68	1.77	8.84	4.11	5.29	1,280	7	0	0	93	0	37	6.11	0			1.00	Mar-07
9.73	-4.40	-1.09	7.34	17.57	5.07	1.27	8.82	4.11	5.45	1,280	7	0	0	93	0	37	6.11	0		3.25		Dec-94
9.73	-4.40	-1.11	7.32	17.58	5.06	1.27	8.84	4.11	5.45	1,280	7	0	0	93	0	37	6.11	0				Mar-07
9.90	-4.01	-0.42	8.94	20.02	5.4	0.66	8.83	4.11	5.79	1,280	7	0	0	93	0	37	6.11	0				May-18
9.82	-4.11	-0.62	8.92	20.55	5.18	0.77	8.79	4.11	5.8	1,280	7	0	0	93	0	37	6.11	0				Dec-98
4.16	3.34	6.88	17.78	21.65	3.03	0.74	4.22	5.40	7.28	3,578	17	24	0	17	-3	820	3.81	0		4.00		Nov-54
4.01	2.99	6.17	15.12	17.19	2.34	1.49	4.2	5.40	7.19	3,578	17	24	0	17	-3	820	3.81	0			5.00	Mar-93
4.00	2.98	6.15	15.06	17.28	2.34	1.49	4.14	5.40	7.21	3,578	17	24	0	17	-3	820	3.81	0			1.00	Jul-99
3.93	3.03	6.56	16.81	20.13	2.92	0.99	4.13	5.40	7.06	3,578	17	24	0	17	-3	820	3.81	0		3.25		Dec-94
4.13	3.10	6.68	17.00	20.19	2.82	0.99	4.22	5.40	7.21	3,578	17	24	0	17	-3	820	3.81	0				Jan-03
4.19	3.47	7.29	18.76	23.62	3.32	0.45	4.12	5.40	7.37	3,578	17	24	0	17	-3	820	3.81	0				Jul-12
4.17	3.45	7.25	18.99	23.86	3.3	0.38	4.19	5.40	7.42	3,578	17	24	0	17	-3	820	3.81	0				Jul-12
4.29	3.40	7.29	18.66	23.22	3.19	0.49	4.17	5.40	7.42	3,578	17	24	0	17	-3	820	3.81	0				Jun-94
2.21	1.76	3.79	10.79	15.68	1.75	0.89	3.38	6.05	10.63	12.6	4	0	96	0	0	63	4.39	0		4.00	1.00	Mar-13
2.06	1.56	3.18	8.95	12.41	1.16	1.49	3.39	6.05	10.63	12.6	4	0	96	0	0	63	4.39	0			5.00	Mar-13
1.94	1.40	2.93	8.37	11.49	1.02	1.64	3.39	6.05	10.63	12.6	4	0	96	0	0	63	4.39	0			1.00	Mar-13
2.28	1.92	4.11	11.74	17.27	2.06	0.57	3.38	6.05	10.63	12.6	4	0	96	0	0	63	4.39	0				May-18
2.27	1.89	4.04	11.64	17.16	2	0.64	3.39	6.05	10.63	12.6	4	0	96	0	0	63	4.39	0				Mar-13
5.18	-1.60	1.60	14.80	27.51	5.09		8.09	7.59	7.82	368.6	4	0	96	0	0	36	5.25					Feb-89
2.27	1.56	3.66	11.05	17.63	2.35	0.8	3.93	6.81	9.83	281.0	2	0	98	0	0	22	4.75	0		4.00	1.00	Oct-89
2.13	1.26	3.03	8.91	13.95	1.72	1.42	4.02	6.81	9.82	281.0	2	0	98	0	0	22	4.75	0			5.00	Jul-93
2.08	1.19	2.88	8.51	13.17	1.58	1.57	3.91	6.81	9.85	281.0	2	0	98	0	0	22	4.75	0			1.00	Aug-03
2.43	1.78	3.90	11.63	18.25	2.58	0.56	4	6.81	9.86	281.0	2	0	98	0	0	22	4.75	0				May-18
2.32	1.67	3.89	11.77	18.91	2.57	0.57	3.91	6.81	9.86	281.0	2	0	98	0	0	22	4.75	0				Jan-08
7.08	-7.73	-3.45	5.90	13.83	4.56		8.99	2.67	4.33	219.1	61	12	0	16	-3	899	4.15					Apr-88
2.19	1.52	3.52	10.72	16.46	2.14	0.87	3.59	6.35	9.51	135.1	1	0	99	0	0	19	4.52	0		4.00	1.00	Oct-89

Fund Name	Ticker Symbol	Traded On	Fund Type	Category and (Prospectus Objective)	Overall Rating	Reward Rating	Risk Rating	Recent Up/ Downgrade	Open to New Investors	Telephone
	MARKET		FUND TYPE, CATEGORY & OBJECTIVE		RATINGS				NEW INVESTORS	
Putnam Minnesota Tax Exempt Income Fund Class B	PMTBX	NAS CM	Open End	US Muni Fixed Inc (Muni Bond - Single State)	C	C-	B-		Y	617-292-1000
Putnam Minnesota Tax Exempt Income Fund Class C	PMOCX	NAS CM	Open End	US Muni Fixed Inc (Muni Bond - Single State)	C	C-	B-		Y	617-292-1000
Putnam Minnesota Tax Exempt Income Fund Class R6	PMVTX	NAS CM	Open End	US Muni Fixed Inc (Muni Bond - Single State)	C	C	B		Y	617-292-1000
Putnam Minnesota Tax Exempt Income Fund Class Y	PMNYX	NAS CM	Open End	US Muni Fixed Inc (Muni Bond - Single State)	C	C	B		Y	617-292-1000
Putnam Money Market Fund Class A	PDDXX	NAS CM	Money Mkt	US Money Mkt (Money Mkt - Taxable)	C	C-	C+		Y	617-292-1000
Putnam Money Market Fund Class B	PTBXX	NAS CM	Money Mkt	US Money Mkt (Money Mkt - Taxable)	C	C-	C+		Y	617-292-1000
Putnam Money Market Fund Class C	PFCXX	NAS CM	Money Mkt	US Money Mkt (Money Mkt - Taxable)	C	C-	C+		Y	617-292-1000
Putnam Money Market Fund Class R	PURXX	NAS CM	Money Mkt	US Money Mkt (Money Mkt - Taxable)	C	C-	C+		Y	617-292-1000
Putnam Mortgage Opportunities Fund Class A Shares	PMORX	NAS CM	Open End	Fixed Inc Misc (Income)	D	D	D+	Down	Y	617-292-1000
Putnam Mortgage Opportunities Fund Class C Shares	PMOZX	NAS CM	Open End	Fixed Inc Misc (Income)	D	D	D+	Down	Y	617-292-1000
Putnam Mortgage Opportunities Fund Class I	PMOTX	NAS CM	Open End	Fixed Inc Misc (Income)	D	D	D+	Down	Y	617-292-1000
Putnam Mortgage Opportunities Fund Class Y Shares	PMOYX	NAS CM	Open End	Fixed Inc Misc (Income)	D	D	D+	Down	Y	617-292-1000
Putnam Mortgage Securities Fund Class A	PGSIX	NAS CM	Open End	US Fixed Inc (Govt Bond - Mortgage)	D+	D+	C	Down	Y	617-292-1000
Putnam Mortgage Securities Fund Class B	PGSBX	NAS CM	Open End	US Fixed Inc (Govt Bond - Mortgage)	D+	D+	C-	Down	Y	617-292-1000
Putnam Mortgage Securities Fund Class C	PGVCX	NAS CM	Open End	US Fixed Inc (Govt Bond - Mortgage)	D+	D+	C-	Down	Y	617-292-1000
Putnam Mortgage Securities Fund Class R	PGVRX	NAS CM	Open End	US Fixed Inc (Govt Bond - Mortgage)	D+	D+	C-	Down	Y	617-292-1000
Putnam Mortgage Securities Fund Class R6	POLYX	NAS CM	Open End	US Fixed Inc (Govt Bond - Mortgage)	D+	D+	C	Down	Y	617-292-1000
Putnam Mortgage Securities Fund Class Y	PUSYX	NAS CM	Open End	US Fixed Inc (Govt Bond - Mortgage)	D+	D+	C	Down	Y	617-292-1000
Putnam Municipal Opportunities Trust	PMO	NYSE	Closed End	US Muni Fixed Inc (Muni Bond - Natl)	C-	C-	C-	Down	Y	617-292-1000
Putnam New Jersey Tax Exempt Income Fund Class A	PTNJX	NAS CM	Open End	US Muni Fixed Inc (Muni Bond - Single State)	C	C-	C+		Y	617-292-1000
Putnam New Jersey Tax Exempt Income Fund Class B	PNJBX	NAS CM	Open End	US Muni Fixed Inc (Muni Bond - Single State)	C	C-	C		Y	617-292-1000
Putnam New Jersey Tax Exempt Income Fund Class C	PNJCX	NAS CM	Open End	US Muni Fixed Inc (Muni Bond - Single State)	C	C-	C		Y	617-292-1000
Putnam New Jersey Tax Exempt Income Fund Class R6	PNJRX	NAS CM	Open End	US Muni Fixed Inc (Muni Bond - Single State)	C	C-	C+		Y	617-292-1000
Putnam New Jersey Tax Exempt Income Fund Class Y	PNJYX	NAS CM	Open End	US Muni Fixed Inc (Muni Bond - Single State)	C	C-	C+		Y	617-292-1000
Putnam New York Tax Exempt Income Fund Class A	PTEIX	NAS CM	Open End	US Muni Fixed Inc (Muni Bond - Single State)	C	C-	C+		Y	617-292-1000
Putnam New York Tax Exempt Income Fund Class B	PEIBX	NAS CM	Open End	US Muni Fixed Inc (Muni Bond - Single State)	C	C-	C+		Y	617-292-1000
Putnam New York Tax Exempt Income Fund Class C	PNNCX	NAS CM	Open End	US Muni Fixed Inc (Muni Bond - Single State)	C	C-	C		Y	617-292-1000
Putnam New York Tax Exempt Income Fund Class R6	PNYRX	NAS CM	Open End	US Muni Fixed Inc (Muni Bond - Single State)	C	C-	C+		Y	617-292-1000
Putnam New York Tax Exempt Income Fund Class Y	PNYYX	NAS CM	Open End	US Muni Fixed Inc (Muni Bond - Single State)	C	C-	C+		Y	617-292-1000
Putnam Ohio Tax Exempt Income Fund Class A	PXOHX	NAS CM	Open End	US Muni Fixed Inc (Muni Bond - Single State)	C	C-	B-		Y	617-292-1000
Putnam Ohio Tax Exempt Income Fund Class B	POXBX	NAS CM	Open End	US Muni Fixed Inc (Muni Bond - Single State)	C	C-	C+		Y	617-292-1000
Putnam Ohio Tax Exempt Income Fund Class C	POOCX	NAS CM	Open End	US Muni Fixed Inc (Muni Bond - Single State)	C	C-	C+		Y	617-292-1000
Putnam Ohio Tax Exempt Income Fund Class R6	POHRX	NAS CM	Open End	US Muni Fixed Inc (Muni Bond - Single State)	C	C	B-		Y	617-292-1000
Putnam Ohio Tax Exempt Income Fund Class Y	POTYX	NAS CM	Open End	US Muni Fixed Inc (Muni Bond - Single State)	C	C	B-		Y	617-292-1000
Putnam Pennsylvania Tax Exempt Income Fund Class A	PTEPX	NAS CM	Open End	US Muni Fixed Inc (Muni Bond - Single State)	C	C	B-		Y	617-292-1000
Putnam Pennsylvania Tax Exempt Income Fund Class B	PPNBX	NAS CM	Open End	US Muni Fixed Inc (Muni Bond - Single State)	C	C-	B-		Y	617-292-1000
Putnam Pennsylvania Tax Exempt Income Fund Class C	PPNCX	NAS CM	Open End	US Muni Fixed Inc (Muni Bond - Single State)	C	C-	B-		Y	617-292-1000
Putnam Pennsylvania Tax Exempt Income Fund Class R6	PPTRX	NAS CM	Open End	US Muni Fixed Inc (Muni Bond - Single State)	C	C	B		Y	617-292-1000
Putnam Pennsylvania Tax Exempt Income Fund Class Y	PPTYX	NAS CM	Open End	US Muni Fixed Inc (Muni Bond - Single State)	C	C	B		Y	617-292-1000
Putnam Premier Income Trust	PPT	NYSE	Closed End	Fixed Inc Misc (Multisector Bond)	D+	D	C-	Down	Y	617-292-1000
Putnam Short Duration Bond Fund Class A	PARTX	NAS CM	Open End	US Fixed Inc (Income)	C	C-	C+		Y	617-292-1000
Putnam Short Duration Bond Fund Class B	PARPX	NAS CM	Open End	US Fixed Inc (Income)	C	C-	C+		Y	617-292-1000
Putnam Short Duration Bond Fund Class C	PARQX	NAS CM	Open End	US Fixed Inc (Income)	C	C-	C+		Y	617-292-1000
Putnam Short Duration Bond Fund Class R	PRARX	NAS CM	Open End	US Fixed Inc (Income)	C	C-	C+		Y	617-292-1000
Putnam Short Duration Bond Fund Class R6	PRREX	NAS CM	Open End	US Fixed Inc (Income)	C	C-	C+		Y	617-292-1000
Putnam Short Duration Bond Fund Class Y	PARYX	NAS CM	Open End	US Fixed Inc (Income)	C	C-	C+		Y	617-292-1000
Putnam Short-Term Municipal Income Fund Class A	PSMEX	NAS CM	Open End	US Muni Fixed Inc (Income)	C	C-	C+		Y	617-292-1000
Putnam Short-Term Municipal Income Fund Class B	PSMFX	NAS CM	Open End	US Muni Fixed Inc (Income)	C	C-	C+		Y	617-292-1000
Putnam Short-Term Municipal Income Fund Class C	PSMTX	NAS CM	Open End	US Muni Fixed Inc (Income)	C	C-	C		Y	617-292-1000
Putnam Short-Term Municipal Income Fund Class R6 Shares	PYSTX	NAS CM	Open End	US Muni Fixed Inc (Income)	C	C-	C+		Y	617-292-1000
Putnam Short-Term Municipal Income Fund Class Y	PSMYX	NAS CM	Open End	US Muni Fixed Inc (Income)	C	C-	C+		Y	617-292-1000
Putnam Tax Exempt Income Fund Class A	PTAEX	NAS CM	Open End	US Muni Fixed Inc (Muni Bond - Natl)	C	C-	C+		Y	617-292-1000

★ Expanded analysis of this fund is included in Section II.

TOTAL RETURNS & PERFORMANCE									ASSETS		ASSET ALLOCATION & TURNOVER							MINIMUMS		FEES		
3-Month Total Return	6-Month Total Return	1-Year Total Return	3-Year Total Return	5-Year Total Return	Dividend Yield (TTM)	Expense Ratio	3-Yr Std Deviation	Effective Duration	NAV	Total Assets (MIL)	%Cash	%Government Bonds	%Municipal Bonds	%Corporate Bonds	%Other	Turnover Ratio	Average Coupon Rate	Min Initial Investment	Min Additional Investment	Front End Fee (%)	Back End Fee (%)	Inception Date
1.94	1.10	2.78	8.47	12.84	1.52	1.49	3.6	6.35	9.47	135.1	1	0	99	0	0	19	4.52	0			5.00	Jul-93
2.01	1.14	2.74	8.10	11.98	1.37	1.64	3.6	6.35	9.49	135.1	1	0	99	0	0	19	4.52	0			1.00	Oct-06
2.25	1.54	3.67	11.32	17.09	2.4	0.61	3.64	6.35	9.53	135.1	1	0	99	0	0	19	4.52	0				May-18
2.24	1.52	3.64	11.34	17.65	2.37	0.64	3.63	6.35	9.52	135.1	1	0	99	0	0	19	4.52	0				Jan-08
0.05	0.34	1.19	4.32	4.61	1.35	0.48	0.16		1	850.8	96	3	0	1	0			0			1.00	Oct-76
0.05	0.33	1.19	4.32	4.48	1.35	0.48	0.16		1	850.8	96	3	0	1	0			0			5.00	Apr-92
0.05	0.34	1.20	4.31	4.48	1.35	0.48	0.16		1	850.8	96	3	0	1	0			0			1.00	Feb-99
0.05	0.34	1.19	4.32	4.48	1.35	0.48	0.16		1	850.8	96	3	0	1	0			0				Jan-03
3.74	-10.06	-5.33	4.40	10.97		0.87	8.53	0.81	9.27	254.8	206	2	0	0	-13	1,012	4.30	0		4.00		Jun-19
3.43	-10.39	-6.01	2.12	6.94		1.62	8.54	0.81	9.27	254.8	206	2	0	0	-13	1,012	4.30	0			1.00	Jun-19
3.71	-9.91	-5.00	5.30	12.47	8.02	0.48	8.51	0.81	9.28	254.8	206	2	0	0	-13	1,012	4.30	5,000,000				Apr-15
3.81	-9.94	-5.08	5.20	12.38		0.62	8.57	0.81	9.28	254.8	206	2	0	0	-13	1,012	4.30	0				Jun-19
3.70	-5.52	-0.60	5.98	6.10	4.92	0.75	6.78	1.01	12.08	787.7	171	2	0	0	-5	1,089	4.24	0		4.00		Feb-84
3.50	-5.86	-1.32	3.66	2.24	4.08	1.5	6.76	1.01	12.02	787.7	171	2	0	0	-5	1,089	4.24	0			5.00	Apr-92
3.54	-5.85	-1.29	3.61	2.16	4.14	1.5	6.76	1.01	11.96	787.7	171	2	0	0	-5	1,089	4.24	0			1.00	Jul-99
3.59	-5.63	-0.88	5.12	4.65	4.68	1	6.76	1.01	11.94	787.7	171	2	0	0	-5	1,089	4.24	0				Jan-03
3.84	-5.32	-0.23	6.85	6.96	5.38	0.37	6.76	1.01	11.94	787.7	171	2	0	0	-5	1,089	4.24	0				Apr-18
3.81	-5.38	-0.34	6.74	7.36	5.27	0.5	6.76	1.01	11.93	787.7	171	2	0	0	-5	1,089	4.24	0				Apr-94
4.51	0.81	3.88	18.17	30.76	4.88	0	7.18	7.58	13.39	445.8	1	0	98	0	0	48	5.05					May-93
2.37	-0.02	2.07	11.11	17.92	2.69	0.8	4.6	6.53	9.32	162.0	2	0	98	0	0	11	4.69	0		4.00	1.00	Feb-90
2.11	-0.33	1.44	8.95	14.21	2.06	1.43	4.6	6.53	9.3	162.0	2	0	98	0	0	11	4.69	0			5.00	Jan-93
2.19	-0.40	1.29	8.57	13.45	1.91	1.58	4.6	6.53	9.33	162.0	2	0	98	0	0	11	4.69	0			1.00	Oct-06
2.32	0.08	2.31	11.58	18.42	2.94	0.57	4.6	6.53	9.33	162.0	2	0	98	0	0	11	4.69	0				May-18
2.43	0.08	2.29	11.83	19.21	2.92	0.58	4.59	6.53	9.34	162.0	2	0	98	0	0	11	4.69	0				Jan-08
2.22	0.24	2.56	10.10	17.27	2.5	0.78	4.71	8.15	8.65	982.2	1	0	98	0	0	26	4.75	0		4.00	1.00	Sep-83
2.07	-0.05	1.93	8.07	13.69	1.86	1.38	4.71	8.15	8.63	982.2	1	0	98	0	0	26	4.75	0			5.00	Jan-93
2.03	-0.13	1.78	7.58	12.81	1.71	1.53	4.73	8.15	8.65	982.2	1	0	98	0	0	26	4.75	0			1.00	Jul-99
2.27	0.24	2.67	10.49	17.68	2.73	0.52	4.7	8.15	8.65	982.2	1	0	98	0	0	26	4.75	0				May-18
2.27	0.23	2.66	10.82	18.56	2.72	0.53	4.7	8.15	8.65	982.2	1	0	98	0	0	26	4.75	0				Jan-08
1.99	1.13	3.07	10.26	16.39	2.43	0.84	3.82	6.78	9.15	111.0	3	0	97	0	0		4.58	0		4.00	1.00	Oct-89
1.84	0.83	2.55	8.23	12.84	1.81	1.47	3.76	6.78	9.14	111.0	3	0	97	0	0		4.58	0			5.00	Jul-93
1.80	0.75	2.29	7.74	11.98	1.66	1.62	3.82	6.78	9.15	111.0	3	0	97	0	0		4.58	0			1.00	Oct-06
2.05	1.26	3.44	10.94	17.10	2.68	0.59	3.84	6.78	9.17	111.0	3	0	97	0	0		4.58	0				May-18
2.16	1.35	3.41	11.11	17.81	2.66	0.62	3.79	6.78	9.16	111.0	3	0	97	0	0		4.58	0				Jan-08
1.96	1.48	3.68	11.54	17.97	2.5	0.83	3.9	7.20	9.32	149.6	1	0	99	0	0	12	4.57	0		4.00	1.00	Jul-89
1.93	1.18	3.05	9.50	14.27	1.88	1.45	3.91	7.20	9.3	149.6	1	0	99	0	0	12	4.57	0			5.00	Jul-93
1.78	1.10	2.89	9.01	13.41	1.72	1.6	3.9	7.20	9.32	149.6	1	0	99	0	0	12	4.57	0			1.00	Oct-06
2.13	1.71	4.04	12.14	18.60	2.75	0.57	3.9	7.20	9.34	149.6	1	0	99	0	0	12	4.57	0				May-18
2.02	1.59	3.91	12.29	19.30	2.73	0.6	3.9	7.20	9.33	149.6	1	0	99	0	0	12	4.57	0				Jan-08
7.65	-8.56	-3.88	6.38	14.39	7.79		9.57		4.79	489.3	64	12	0	17	2	854	4.29					Feb-88
4.29	1.37	2.60	9.51	13.00	2.51	0.63	2.92	1.81	10.17	1,510	16	0	0	51	0	18	3.39	0		2.25		Dec-08
4.24	1.27	2.40	8.83	11.92	2.31	0.83	2.84	1.81	10.16	1,510	16	0	0	51	0	18	3.39	0			1.00	Dec-08
4.12	0.90	1.85	6.99	8.83	1.76	1.38	2.92	1.81	10.15	1,510	16	0	0	51	0	18	3.39	0			1.00	Dec-08
4.21	1.25	2.35	8.58	11.57	2.26	0.88	2.9	1.81	10.22	1,510	16	0	0	51	0	18	3.39	0				Dec-08
4.33	1.39	2.85	10.23	14.46	2.75	0.38	2.91	1.81	10.22	1,510	16	0	0	51	0	18	3.39	0				Jul-12
4.34	1.49	2.85	10.37	14.50	2.76	0.38	2.84	1.81	10.19	1,510	16	0	0	51	0	18	3.39	0				Dec-08
1.10	0.77	1.70	5.31	6.68	1.54	0.6	1.28	1.66	10.09	37.6	4	0	95	0	0	83	3.30	0		2.25	1.00	Mar-13
1.05	0.67	1.49	4.67	5.72	1.33	0.8	1.29	1.66	10.09	37.6	4	0	95	0	0	83	3.30	0			1.00	Mar-13
0.91	0.40	0.95	2.98	3.21	0.8	1.35	1.22	1.66	10.09	37.6	4	0	95	0	0	83	3.30	0			1.00	Mar-13
1.17	0.90	1.96	6.20	8.23	1.8	0.33	1.22	1.66	10.09	37.6	4	0	95	0	0	83	3.30	0				May-18
1.16	0.89	1.95	6.09	8.13	1.79	0.35	1.29	1.66	10.09	37.6	4	0	95	0	0	83	3.30	0				Mar-13
2.85	0.25	2.78	11.90	19.27	2.6	0.78	5.06	7.79	8.59	901.9	0	0	100	0	0	63	4.40	0		4.00	1.00	Dec-76

	MARKET			FUND TYPE, CATEGORY & OBJECTIVE	RATINGS				NEW INVESTORS	
Fund Name	Ticker Symbol	Traded On	Fund Type	Category and (Prospectus Objective)	Overall Rating	Reward Rating	Risk Rating	Recent Up/ Downgrade	Open to New Investors	Telephone
Putnam Tax Exempt Income Fund Class B	PTBEX	NAS CM	Open End	US Muni Fixed Inc (Muni Bond - Natl)	C	C-	C+			617-292-1000
Putnam Tax Exempt Income Fund Class C	PTECX	NAS CM	Open End	US Muni Fixed Inc (Muni Bond - Natl)	C	C-	C		Y	617-292-1000
Putnam Tax Exempt Income Fund Class R6 Shares	PEXTX	NAS CM	Open End	US Muni Fixed Inc (Muni Bond - Natl)	C	C-	C+		Y	617-292-1000
Putnam Tax Exempt Income Fund Class Y	PTEYX	NAS CM	Open End	US Muni Fixed Inc (Muni Bond - Natl)	C	C-	B-		Y	617-292-1000
Putnam Tax Free High Yield Fund Class R6 Shares	PTFRX	NAS CM	Open End	US Muni Fixed Inc (Muni Bond - Natl)	C-	D+	C	Down	Y	617-292-1000
Putnam Tax-Free High Yield Fund Class A	PTHAX	NAS CM	Open End	US Muni Fixed Inc (Muni Bond - Natl)	C-	D+	C	Down	Y	617-292-1000
Putnam Tax-Free High Yield Fund Class B	PTHYX	NAS CM	Open End	US Muni Fixed Inc (Muni Bond - Natl)	C-	D+	C	Down		617-292-1000
Putnam Tax-Free High Yield Fund Class C	PTCCX	NAS CM	Open End	US Muni Fixed Inc (Muni Bond - Natl)	C-	D+	C	Down	Y	617-292-1000
Putnam Tax-Free High Yield Fund Class Y	PTFYX	NAS CM	Open End	US Muni Fixed Inc (Muni Bond - Natl)	C-	D+	C	Down	Y	617-292-1000
Putnam Ultra Short Duration Income Fund Class A	PSDTX	NAS CM	Open End	US Fixed Inc (Income)	C	C-	C+		Y	617-292-1000
Putnam Ultra Short Duration Income Fund Class B	PSDBX	NAS CM	Open End	US Fixed Inc (Income)	C	C-	C+		Y	617-292-1000
Putnam Ultra Short Duration Income Fund Class C	PSDLX	NAS CM	Open End	US Fixed Inc (Income)	C	C-	C+		Y	617-292-1000
Putnam Ultra Short Duration Income Fund Class N	PSDNX	NAS CM	Open End	US Fixed Inc (Income)	C	C-	C+		Y	617-292-1000
Putnam Ultra Short Duration Income Fund Class R	PSDRX	NAS CM	Open End	US Fixed Inc (Income)	C	C-	C+		Y	617-292-1000
Putnam Ultra Short Duration Income Fund Class R6	PSDQX	NAS CM	Open End	US Fixed Inc (Income)	C	C-	B-		Y	617-292-1000
Putnam Ultra Short Duration Income Fund Class Y	PSDYX	NAS CM	Open End	US Fixed Inc (Income)	C	C-	C+		Y	617-292-1000
Quantified Managed Income Fund Advisor Class	QBDAX	NAS CM	Open End	US Fixed Inc (Income)	D	D	C-	Down	Y	
Quantified Managed Income Fund Investor Class	QBDSX	NAS CM	Open End	US Fixed Inc (Income)	D+	D+	C-	Down	Y	
Quantified Tactical Fixed Income Investor Cl Shares	QFITX	NAS CM	Open End	Fixed Inc Misc (Growth & Income)	U	U	U		Y	
Rational Special Situations Income Fund Class A Shares	RFXAX	NAS CM	Open End	US Fixed Inc (Income)	U	U	U		Y	800-253-0412
Rational Special Situations Income Fund Class C Shares	RFXCX	NAS CM	Open End	US Fixed Inc (Income)	U	U	U		Y	800-253-0412
Rational Special Situations Income Institutional Shares	RFXIX	NAS CM	Open End	US Fixed Inc (Income)	U	U	U		Y	800-253-0412
RBB Free Market Fixed Income Fund Institutional Class	FMFIX	NAS CM	Open End	US Fixed Inc (Corp Bond - General)	C+	C	B-	Up	Y	
RBC BlueBay Emerging Market Debt Fund Class A	RESAX	NAS CM	Open End	Emerg Mkts Fixed Inc (Growth & Income)	D+	D+	C-	Down	Y	800-422-2766
RBC BlueBay Emerging Market Debt Fund Class I	RBESX	NAS CM	Open End	Emerg Mkts Fixed Inc (Growth & Income)	D+	D+	C-	Down	Y	800-422-2766
RBC BlueBay Emerging Market Debt Fund Class R6	RBERX	NAS CM	Open End	Emerg Mkts Fixed Inc (Growth & Income)	D+	D+	C-	Down	Y	800-422-2766
RBC BlueBay Global Bond Fund Class A	RGBAX	NAS CM	Open End	Global Fixed Inc (Growth & Income)	C	C	B-		Y	800-422-2766
RBC BlueBay Global Bond Fund Class I	RBTRX	NAS CM	Open End	Global Fixed Inc (Growth & Income)	C	C	B-		Y	800-422-2766
RBC BlueBay Global Bond Fund Class R6	RBDRX	NAS CM	Open End	Global Fixed Inc (Growth & Income)	C	C	B-		Y	800-422-2766
RBC BlueBay High Yield Bond Fund Class A	RHYAX	NAS CM	Open End	US Fixed Inc (Corp Bond - High Yield)	C	C-	C		Y	800-422-2766
RBC BlueBay High Yield Bond Fund Class I	RGHYX	NAS CM	Open End	US Fixed Inc (Corp Bond - High Yield)	C	C-	B-		Y	800-422-2766
RBC Impact Bond Fund Class A	RIBAX	NAS CM	Open End	US Fixed Inc (Corp Bond - General)	C	C	B		Y	800-422-2766
RBC Impact Bond Fund Class I	RIBIX	NAS CM	Open End	US Fixed Inc (Corp Bond - General)	C	C	B		Y	800-422-2766
RBC Impact Bond Fund Class R6	RIBRX	NAS CM	Open End	US Fixed Inc (Corp Bond - General)	C	C	B		Y	800-422-2766
RBC Short Duration Fixed Income Fund Class A	RSHFX	NAS CM	Open End	US Fixed Inc (Income)	C	C-	C+		Y	800-422-2766
RBC Short Duration Fixed Income Fund Class I	RSDIX	NAS CM	Open End	US Fixed Inc (Income)	C	C	C+		Y	800-422-2766
RBC Ultra-Short Fixed Income Fund Class A	RULFX	NAS CM	Open End	US Fixed Inc (Income)	C	C-	C+		Y	800-422-2766
RBC Ultra-Short Fixed Income Fund Class I	RUSIX	NAS CM	Open End	US Fixed Inc (Income)	C	C-	C+		Y	800-422-2766
Red Cedar Short Term Bond Fund Institutional Class	RCSTX	NAS CM	Open End	US Fixed Inc (Multisector Bond)	U	U	U		Y	888-626-2575
Redwood Managed Municipal Income Fund Class I	RWMIX	NAS CM	Open End	US Muni Fixed Inc (Muni Bond - Natl)	C-	D+	C	Down	Y	
Redwood Managed Municipal Income Fund Class N	RWMNX	NAS CM	Open End	US Muni Fixed Inc (Muni Bond - Natl)	C-	D+	C	Down	Y	
Redwood Managed Volatility Fund Class I	RWDIX	NAS CM	Open End	Fixed Inc Misc (Growth & Income)	D+	D	C-	Down	Y	
Redwood Managed Volatility Fund Class N	RWDNX	NAS CM	Open End	Fixed Inc Misc (Growth & Income)	D+	D	C-	Down	Y	
Redwood Managed Volatility Fund Class Y	RWDYX	NAS CM	Open End	Fixed Inc Misc (Growth & Income)	D+	D	C-	Down	Y	
Resource Credit Income Fund Class A	RCIAX	NAS CM	Closed End	Fixed Inc Misc (Income)	D	D	D+	Down	Y	855-747-9559
Resource Credit Income Fund Class C	RCICX	NAS CM	Closed End	Fixed Inc Misc (Income)	D	D	D	Down	Y	855-747-9559
Resource Credit Income Fund Class I	RCIIX	NAS CM	Closed End	Fixed Inc Misc (Income)	D	D	D+	Down	Y	855-747-9559
Resource Credit Income Fund Class W	RCIWX	NAS CM	Closed End	Fixed Inc Misc (Income)	D	D	D+	Down	Y	855-747-9559
Rimrock Core Bond Fund	RMRKX	NAS CM	Open End	US Fixed Inc (Income)	U	U	U		Y	949-381-7800
River Canyon Total Return Bond Fund Institutional Shares	RCTIX	NAS CM	Open End	US Fixed Inc (Growth & Income)	C	C-	B-		Y	
RiverNorth Doubleline Strategic Income Fund Class I	RNSIX	NAS CM	Open End	US Fixed Inc (Multisector Bond)	C	C-	C			312-832-1440
RiverNorth Doubleline Strategic Income Fund Class R	RNDLX	NAS CM	Open End	US Fixed Inc (Multisector Bond)	C-	D+	C	Down		312-832-1440

★Expanded analysis of this fund is included in Section II.

TOTAL RETURNS & PERFORMANCE									ASSETS		ASSET ALLOCATION & TURNOVER							MINIMUMS		FEES		
3-Month Total Return	6-Month Total Return	1-Year Total Return	3-Year Total Return	5-Year Total Return	Dividend Yield (TTM)	Expense Ratio	3-Yr Std Deviation	Effective Duration	NAV	Total Assets (MIL)	%Cash	%Government Bonds	%Municipal Bonds	%Corporate Bonds	%Other	Turnover Ratio	Average Coupon Rate	Min Initial Investment	Min Additional Investment	Front End Fee (%)	Back End Fee (%)	Inception Date
2.80	0.04	2.24	9.90	15.54	1.95	1.41	4.97	7.79	8.6	901.9	0	0	100	0	0	63	4.40	0			5.00	Jan-93
2.75	-0.02	2.08	9.39	14.77	1.8	1.56	5.09	7.79	8.62	901.9	0	0	100	0	0	63	4.40	0			1.00	Jul-99
2.91	0.37	3.02	12.46	19.88	2.84	0.54	5.05	7.79	8.61	901.9	0	0	100	0	0	63	4.40	0				May-18
3.02	0.47	3.11	12.72	20.65	2.82	0.56	5.09	7.79	8.62	901.9	0	0	100	0	0	63	4.40	0				Jan-08
4.15	-2.01	1.10	11.93	21.02	3.82	0.59	7	7.94	12.43	795.3	2	0	98	0	0	47	4.94	0				May-18
4.02	-2.14	0.85	12.02	22.55	3.56	0.84	7.02	7.94	12.37	795.3	2	0	98	0	0	47	4.94	0		4.00	1.00	Sep-93
3.90	-2.40	0.26	9.98	18.92	2.86	1.46	7.02	7.94	12.41	795.3	2	0	98	0	0	47	4.94	0			5.00	Sep-85
3.86	-2.47	0.04	9.49	17.94	2.7	1.61	7.02	7.94	12.41	795.3	2	0	98	0	0	47	4.94	0			1.00	Feb-99
4.14	-2.02	1.08	12.84	24.07	3.79	0.61	7.05	7.94	12.43	795.3	2	0	98	0	0	47	4.94	0				Jan-08
2.32	0.94	2.05	6.31	8.19	1.98	0.4	1.36	0.26	10.07	15,104	31	1	0	55	2	27	1.93	0		4.00	1.00	Oct-11
2.23	0.74	1.65	5.06	6.07	1.59	0.8	1.36	0.26	10.06	15,104	31	1	0	55	2	27	1.93	0			5.00	Oct-11
2.23	0.74	1.65	5.06	6.07	1.59	0.8	1.36	0.26	10.06	15,104	31	1	0	55	2	27	1.93	0			1.00	Oct-11
2.24	0.81	1.86	5.81	7.21	1.83	0.55	1.37	0.26	10.06	15,104	31	1	0	55	2	27	1.93	50,000		1.50	0.25	Nov-18
2.23	0.74	1.65	5.06	6.07	1.59	0.8	1.37	0.26	10.06	15,104	31	1	0	55	2	27	1.93	0				Oct-11
2.34	1.09	2.26	6.65	8.76	2.09	0.29	1.32	0.26	10.09	15,104	31	1	0	55	2	27	1.93	0				Jul-12
2.34	0.98	2.15	6.62	8.72	2.08	0.3	1.36	0.26	10.08	15,104	31	1	0	55	2	27	1.93	0				Oct-11
1.56	-8.01	-5.95	-1.62	4.99	0.21	2.28	6.34	5.33	9.07	60.1	16	37	9	16	0	638	3.46	10,000	1,000			Mar-16
1.68	-7.75	-5.38	0.34	8.66	1.79	1.68	6.32	5.33	9.04	60.1	16	37	9	16	0	638	3.46	10,000	1,000			Aug-13
-0.90	10.38					1.77		1.17	10.95	70.2	90	3	0	7	0		2.76	10,000	1,000			Sep-19
6.80	-0.73					2.01			19.46	248.7	10	0	0	0	0		3.25	1,000	50	4.75		Jul-19
6.58	-1.14					2.76			19.42	248.7	10	0	0	0	0		3.25	1,000	50		1.00	Jul-19
6.85	-0.63					1.76			19.48	248.7	10	0	0	0	0		3.25	1,000	500			Jul-19
2.41	2.27	3.58	8.09	10.41	1.57	0.67	1.8	3.84	10.56	2,294	24	34	0	32	0	3	2.49	0				Dec-07
14.78	-4.28	-1.40	9.16	18.85	6.78	1.12	12.17	7.00	9.47	20.0	15	50	0	11	-6	236	5.65	2,500	100	4.25		Nov-13
14.86	-4.01	-1.06	10.14	20.39	7.01	0.87	12.1	7.00	9.58	20.0	15	50	0	11	-6	236	5.65	1,000,000	10,000			Nov-11
14.79	-4.08	-0.99	10.27	20.53	7.05	0.82	12.1	7.00	9.62	20.0	15	50	0	11	-6	236	5.65	1,000,000				Dec-16
3.70	1.29	2.86	11.49	16.27		0.79	5.75		9.66	27.8	10	37	0	9	0	232	2.81	2,500		4.25		Jan-20
3.76	1.32	3.02	12.22	17.62	3.7	0.54	5.75		9.65	27.8	10	37	0	9	0	232	2.81	1,000,000				Dec-14
3.66	1.33	3.05	12.31	17.71	3.72	0.49	5.68		9.65	27.8	10	37	0	9	0	232	2.81	1,000,000				Dec-16
6.97	-1.78	3.53	15.33	26.81	5.55	0.83	6.3	4.22	10.16	82.9	7	0	0	88	0	143	6.04	2,500	100	4.25		Nov-13
6.97	-1.69	3.71	16.23	28.64	5.74	0.58	6.25	4.22	10.23	82.9	7	0	0	88	0	143	6.04	1,000,000	10,000			Nov-11
2.55	6.36	8.65				0.72		5.58	10.55	35.5	4	10	17	29	0	175	3.23	2,500		3.75		Jan-20
2.62	6.40	8.70			2.39	0.47		5.58	10.55	35.5	4	10	17	29	0	175	3.23	1,000,000				Dec-17
2.63	6.42	8.84			2.43	0.42		5.58	10.56	35.5	4	10	17	29	0	175	3.23	1,000,000				Dec-17
4.84	1.76	3.54	8.94	13.10	2.38	0.45	3.14	1.84	10.15	58.7	4	0	0	71	0	33	3.30	1,000				Mar-14
4.77	1.83	3.56	9.15	13.66	2.49	0.35	3.07	1.84	10.14	58.7	4	0	0	71	0	33	3.30	10,000				Dec-13
4.25	0.90	2.42	7.44	11.10	2.41	0.38	2.83	0.94	9.94	46.2	19	0	0	54	0	93	3.16	1,000				Mar-14
4.28	1.07	2.62	7.84	11.53	2.5	0.28	2.76	0.94	9.93	46.2	19	0	0	54	0	93	3.16	10,000				Dec-13
2.77	2.85					0.45			10.18	106.3								10,000	100			Nov-19
-0.69	-4.72	-1.88	8.45		3.05	1.66	6.06	8.41	15.4	161.4	1	0	95	1	1	7	6.08	10,000	1,000			Mar-17
-1.23	-5.31	-2.64	7.11		0.82	1.91	6.06	8.41	16	161.4	1	0	95	1	1	7	6.08	10,000	1,000			Mar-17
-1.74	-7.01	-4.32	1.31	15.08	2.89	1.58	4.54		14.2	352.3	48	0	0	0	48	2	5.00	10,000	1,000			Dec-13
-1.76	-7.09	-4.46	0.64	13.69	1.51	1.84	4.53		14.4	352.3	48	0	0	0	48	2	5.00	10,000	500			Dec-13
-1.66	-6.95	-4.22	1.59	15.48	2.87	1.49	4.53		14.32	352.3	48	0	0	0	48	2	5.00	20,000,000	1,000			Dec-13
7.41	-10.82	-7.97	3.09	25.00	8.99	2.63	10.58		9.28	--	-6	0	0	96	30		7.75	2,500	1,000	6.50		Apr-15
7.26	-11.10	-8.67	0.86	22.69	8.13	3.38	10.57		9.39	--	-6	0	0	96	30		7.75	2,500	1,000	1.50		Apr-15
7.47	-10.68	-7.78	3.92	26.47	9.29	2.38	10.58		9.3	--	-6	0	0	96	30		7.75	5,000,000	100			Apr-15
7.41	-10.74	-7.97	3.19	24.65	8.99	4.09	10.57		9.28	--	-6	0	0	96	30		7.75	2,500	1,000			Apr-15
4.96	3.25	6.84				0.65			10.29	5.5	2	3	0	15	0		3.45	5,000				Jul-19
5.30	-0.44	1.89	17.29	32.15	3.08	0.7	5.97	1.33	10.67	124.6	20	0	8	0	0	30	3.88	100,000	10,000			Dec-14
7.23	-0.92	2.01	10.56	22.83	4.96	1.65	6.45		10.02	1,754	18	12	2	26	0	60	4.65	100,000	100			Dec-10
7.14	-1.04	1.75	9.71	21.37	4.69	1.9	6.45		10.04	1,754	18	12	2	26	0	60	4.65	5,000	100			Dec-10

Fund Name	Ticker Symbol	Traded On	Fund Type	Category and (Prospectus Objective)	Overall Rating	Reward Rating	Risk Rating	Recent Up/ Downgrade	Open to New Investors	Telephone
	MARKET		FUND TYPE, CATEGORY & OBJECTIVE		RATINGS				NEW INVESTORS	
RiverNorth Flexible Municipal Income	RFM	NYSE	Closed End	Fixed Inc Misc (Income)	U	U	U		Y	312-832-1440
RiverNorth Managed Duration Muni Inc Fd	RMM	NYSE	Closed End	US Muni Fixed Inc (Income)	U	U	U		Y	312-832-1440
RiverNorth Marketplace Lending Corp	RSF	NYSE	Closed End	US Fixed Inc (Income)	D	D-	D+	Down	Y	312-832-1440
RiverNorth Opportunistic Municipal Income Fund, Inc.	RMI	NYSE	Closed End	US Muni Fixed Inc (Income)	D+	D+	C-	Up	Y	312-832-1440
RiverNorth/Oaktree High Income Fund Class I	RNHIX	NAS CM	Open End	US Fixed Inc (Multisector Bond)	D+	D	C-	Down	Y	312-832-1440
RiverNorth/Oaktree High Income Fund Class R	RNOTX	NAS CM	Open End	US Fixed Inc (Multisector Bond)	D+	D	C-	Down	Y	312-832-1440
RiverPark Floating Rate CMBS Institutional Cl Shares	RCRIX	NAS CM	Open End	US Fixed Inc (Growth & Income)	D	D	D	Down	Y	888-564-4517
RiverPark Floating Rate CMBS Fund Retail Class Shares	RCRFX	NAS CM	Open End	US Fixed Inc (Growth & Income)	D	D	D	Down	Y	888-564-4517
RiverPark Short Term High Yield Fund Class Institutional	RPHIX	NAS CM	Open End	US Fixed Inc (Growth)	C	C-	C+			888-564-4517
RiverPark Short Term High Yield Fund Class Retail	RPHYX	NAS CM	Open End	US Fixed Inc (Growth)	C	C-	C+			888-564-4517
RiverPark Strategic Income Fund Institutional Class	RSIIX	NAS CM	Open End	US Fixed Inc (Income)	D	D	C-	Down	Y	888-564-4517
RiverPark Strategic Income Fund Retail Class	RSIVX	NAS CM	Open End	US Fixed Inc (Income)	D	D	C-	Down	Y	888-564-4517
Robinson Opportunistic Income Fund Class A Shares	RBNAX	NAS CM	Open End	US Fixed Inc (Growth & Income)	D	D	D	Down	Y	800-207-7108
Robinson Opportunistic Income Fund Class C Shares	RBNCX	NAS CM	Open End	US Fixed Inc (Growth & Income)	D	D	D	Down	Y	800-207-7108
Robinson Opportunistic Income Institutional Cl Shares	RBNNX	NAS CM	Open End	US Fixed Inc (Growth & Income)	D	D	D	Down	Y	800-207-7108
Robinson Tax Advantaged Income Fund Class A	ROBAX	NAS CM	Open End	Fixed Inc Misc (Growth & Income)	D	D	D+	Down	Y	800-207-7108
Robinson Tax Advantaged Income Fund Class C	ROBCX	NAS CM	Open End	Fixed Inc Misc (Growth & Income)	D	D	D+	Down	Y	800-207-7108
Robinson Tax Advantaged Income Fund Institutional Class	ROBNX	NAS CM	Open End	Fixed Inc Misc (Growth & Income)	D	D	D+	Down	Y	800-207-7108
Rockefeller Core Taxable Bond Fund Institutional Class	RCFIX	NAS CM	Open End	US Fixed Inc (Income)	B	B-	B+		Y	
Rockefeller Intermed Tax Exempt Natl Bond Inst Cl	RCTEX	NAS CM	Open End	US Muni Fixed Inc (Income)	C+	C	B	Up	Y	
Rockefeller Intermed Tax Exempt New York Bond Inst Cl	RCNYX	NAS CM	Open End	US Muni Fixed Inc (Income)	C	C-	B-		Y	
Russell Investments Investment Grade Bond Fund Class A	RFAAX	NAS CM	Open End	US Fixed Inc (Multisector Bond)	B-	C+	B	Up	Y	800-426-7969
Russell Investments Investment Grade Bond Fund Class C	RFACX	NAS CM	Open End	US Fixed Inc (Multisector Bond)	C+	C+	B	Up	Y	800-426-7969
Russell Investments Investment Grade Bond Fund Class E	RFAEX	NAS CM	Open End	US Fixed Inc (Multisector Bond)	B-	C+	B	Up	Y	800-426-7969
Russell Investments Investment Grade Bond Fund Class M	RIWTX	NAS CM	Open End	US Fixed Inc (Multisector Bond)	B-	C+	B	Up	Y	800-426-7969
Russell Investments Investment Grade Bond Fund Class R6	RIGRX	NAS CM	Open End	US Fixed Inc (Multisector Bond)	B-	C+	B	Up	Y	800-426-7969
Russell Investments Investment Grade Bond Fund Class S	RFATX	NAS CM	Open End	US Fixed Inc (Multisector Bond)	B-	C+	B	Up	Y	800-426-7969
Russell Investments Investment Grade Bond Fund Class Y	RFAYX	NAS CM	Open End	US Fixed Inc (Multisector Bond)	B-	C+	B+	Up	Y	800-426-7969
Russell Investments Multifactor Bond Fund Class Y	RMHYX	NAS CM	Open End	US Fixed Inc (Growth & Income)	U	U	U		Y	800-426-7969
Russell Investments Opportunistic Credit Fund Class A	RGCAX	NAS CM	Open End	US Fixed Inc (Worldwide Bond)	D+	D	C-	Down	Y	800-426-7969
Russell Investments Opportunistic Credit Fund Class C	RGCCX	NAS CM	Open End	US Fixed Inc (Worldwide Bond)	D	D	C-	Down	Y	800-426-7969
Russell Investments Opportunistic Credit Fund Class E	RCCEX	NAS CM	Open End	US Fixed Inc (Worldwide Bond)	D+	D	C-	Down	Y	800-426-7969
Russell Investments Opportunistic Credit Fund Class M	RGOTX	NAS CM	Open End	US Fixed Inc (Worldwide Bond)	D+	D	C-	Down	Y	800-426-7969
Russell Investments Opportunistic Credit Fund Class S	RGCSX	NAS CM	Open End	US Fixed Inc (Worldwide Bond)	D+	D	C-	Down	Y	800-426-7969
Russell Investments Opportunistic Credit Fund Class Y	RGCYX	NAS CM	Open End	US Fixed Inc (Worldwide Bond)	D+	D	C-	Down	Y	800-426-7969
Russell Investments Short Duration Bond Fund Class A	RSBTX	NAS CM	Open End	US Fixed Inc (Multisector Bond)	C+	C	B-	Up	Y	800-426-7969
Russell Investments Short Duration Bond Fund Class C	RSBCX	NAS CM	Open End	US Fixed Inc (Multisector Bond)	C	C	B-		Y	800-426-7969
Russell Investments Short Duration Bond Fund Class E	RSBEX	NAS CM	Open End	US Fixed Inc (Multisector Bond)	C+	C	B-	Up	Y	800-426-7969
Russell Investments Short Duration Bond Fund Class M	RSDTX	NAS CM	Open End	US Fixed Inc (Multisector Bond)	C+	C	B	Up	Y	800-426-7969
Russell Investments Short Duration Bond Fund Class R6	RDBRX	NAS CM	Open End	US Fixed Inc (Multisector Bond)	C+	C	B	Up	Y	800-426-7969
Russell Investments Short Duration Bond Fund Class S	RFBSX	NAS CM	Open End	US Fixed Inc (Multisector Bond)	C+	C	B	Up	Y	800-426-7969
Russell Investments Short Duration Bond Fund Class Y	RSBYX	NAS CM	Open End	US Fixed Inc (Multisector Bond)	C+	C	B	Up	Y	800-426-7969
Russell Investments Strategic Bond Fund Class A	RFDAX	NAS CM	Open End	US Fixed Inc (Multisector Bond)	B-	C+	B	Up	Y	800-426-7969
Russell Investments Strategic Bond Fund Class C	RFCCX	NAS CM	Open End	US Fixed Inc (Multisector Bond)	C+	C+	B	Up	Y	800-426-7969
Russell Investments Strategic Bond Fund Class E	RFCEX	NAS CM	Open End	US Fixed Inc (Multisector Bond)	B-	C+	B	Up	Y	800-426-7969
Russell Investments Strategic Bond Fund Class M	RSYTX	NAS CM	Open End	US Fixed Inc (Multisector Bond)	B-	C+	B	Up	Y	800-426-7969
Russell Investments Strategic Bond Fund Class R6	RSBRX	NAS CM	Open End	US Fixed Inc (Multisector Bond)	B-	C+	B	Up	Y	800-426-7969
Russell Investments Strategic Bond Fund Class S	RFCTX	NAS CM	Open End	US Fixed Inc (Multisector Bond)	B-	C+	B	Up	Y	800-426-7969
Russell Investments Strategic Bond Fund Class Y	RFCYX	NAS CM	Open End	US Fixed Inc (Multisector Bond)	B-	C+	B	Up	Y	800-426-7969
Russell Investments Tax-Exempt Bond Fund Class A	RTEAX	NAS CM	Open End	US Muni Fixed Inc (Muni Bond - Natl)	C	C-	C+		Y	800-426-7969
Russell Investments Tax-Exempt Bond Fund Class C	RTECX	NAS CM	Open End	US Muni Fixed Inc (Muni Bond - Natl)	C	C-	C		Y	800-426-7969
Russell Investments Tax-Exempt Bond Fund Class E	RTBEX	NAS CM	Open End	US Muni Fixed Inc (Muni Bond - Natl)	C	C-	C+		Y	800-426-7969

★Expanded analysis of this fund is included in Section II.

TOTAL RETURNS & PERFORMANCE									ASSETS		ASSET ALLOCATION & TURNOVER							MINIMUMS		FEES		
3-Month Total Return	6-Month Total Return	1-Year Total Return	3-Year Total Return	5-Year Total Return	Dividend Yield (TTM)	Expense Ratio	3-Yr Std Deviation	Effective Duration	NAV	Total Assets (MIL)	%Cash	%Government Bonds	%Municipal Bonds	%Corporate Bonds	%Other	Turnover Ratio	Average Coupon Rate	Min Initial Investment	Min Additional Investment	Front End Fee (%)	Back End Fee (%)	Inception Date
7.58						2.18			21.55	117.1												Mar-20
5.00	-8.49					4.07			18.1	324.9	-3	4	91	1	0		4.92					Jul-19
-4.77	-8.31	-8.52	-5.37		12.24	2.99	3.45		17.44	102.8	27	0	0	9	46	47	3.19					Sep-16
4.90	-1.85	2.81			4.98	3.01			22.24	140.8	0	1	95	0	0	4	5.15					Oct-18
8.97	-5.62	-2.79	4.28	16.75	5.26	1.85	8.53		8.84	45.8	3	1	0	76	0	52	4.88	100,000	100			Dec-12
8.92	-5.74	-3.03	3.49	15.29	5	2.1	8.54		8.83	45.8	3	1	0	76	0	52	4.88	5,000	100			Dec-12
15.41	-9.54	-8.24	-1.39		3.7	0.85	14.02	0.13	8.87	257.0	1	0	0	0	0	87	3.19	50,000				Sep-16
15.37	-9.66	-8.57	-1.88		3.42	1.2	14.04	0.13	8.86	257.0	1	0	0	0	0	87	3.19	1,000	100			Nov-18
1.16	0.48	0.82	6.98	12.13	2.52	0.88	0.97	0.44	9.65	628.2	25	0	5	69	0	112	5.18	100,000	100			Sep-10
1.21	0.46	0.66	6.08	10.64	2.27	1.18	1.04	0.44	9.61	628.2	25	0	5	69	0	112	5.18	1,000	100			Sep-10
9.82	-4.29	-3.95	1.78	10.13	5.6	1.12	7.93	2.32	8.42	180.7	15	0	0	82	0	39	6.38	50,000				Sep-13
9.90	-4.31	-4.09	1.21	8.86	5.32	1.33	7.96	2.32	8.42	180.7	15	0	0	82	0	39	6.38	1,000	100			Sep-13
6.36	-17.27	-13.56	-9.27		7.14	3.43	13.1	4.39	8.27	19.5	-8	17	1	62	8	114	5.43	2,500	100	4.25		Dec-15
6.17	-17.63	-14.16	-11.25		6.27	4.18	13.07	4.39	8.25	19.5	-8	17	1	62	8	114	5.43	2,500	100		1.00	Dec-15
6.43	-17.16	-13.33	-8.56		7.45	3.18	13.1	4.39	8.27	19.5	-8	17	1	62	8	114	5.43	1,000,000	100,000			Dec-15
3.43	-8.46	-5.30	-1.25	10.53	3.12	2.98	9.45	8.27	8.68	259.6	4	0	93	0	1	78	5.44	2,500	100	3.75		Sep-14
3.36	-8.72	-5.92	-3.37	6.52	2.31	3.73	9.41	8.27	8.68	259.6	4	0	93	0	1	78	5.44	2,500	100		1.00	Sep-14
3.62	-8.25	-4.96	-0.49	11.92	3.4	2.73	9.36	8.27	8.68	259.6	4	0	93	0	1	78	5.44	1,000,000	100,000			Sep-14
2.66	6.56	8.70	16.53	23.05	2.32	0.67	3.28		10.843	73.1	1	23	19	19	0	99	3.39	1,000,000	10,000			Dec-13
2.60	2.57	4.21	10.01	13.33	1.55	0.63	3.48		10.5703	102.6	0	0	100	0	0	64	4.40	1,000,000	10,000			Dec-13
2.02	1.46	2.91	8.36	11.00	1.31	0.73	3.76		10.4243	47.9	0	0	100	0	0	69	4.68	1,000,000	10,000			Dec-13
5.52	6.03	8.47	14.86	21.34	2.67	0.77	4.23	6.18	22.97	776.8	14	16	0	27	0	68	2.93	0		3.75		May-10
5.33	5.65	7.67	12.32	16.88	1.97	1.52	4.21	6.18	22.74	776.8	14	16	0	27	0	68	2.93	0				Oct-07
5.51	6.02	8.47	14.86	21.32	2.66	0.77	4.23	6.18	22.97	776.8	14	16	0	27	0	68	2.93	0				May-99
5.63	6.24	8.91	16.20	22.87	3.04	0.38	4.22	6.18	22.94	776.8	14	16	0	27	0	68	2.93	0				Mar-17
5.61	6.27	8.95	16.33	23.46	3.06	0.35	4.22	6.18	23.03	776.8	14	16	0	27	0	68	2.93	0				Mar-16
5.60	6.20	8.79	15.85	23.00	2.94	0.48	4.24	6.18	22.94	776.8	14	16	0	27	0	68	2.93	0				Oct-07
5.63	6.30	8.99	16.39	24.05	3.09	0.32	4.21	6.18	22.99	776.8	14	16	0	27	0	68	2.93	10,000,000				Mar-00
4.72	4.42					0.26			10.36	74.6	58	22	0	28	0		2.86	10,000,000				Nov-19
9.99	-5.31	-3.00	4.14	18.05	5.66	1.17	9.46	5.58	8.79	572.7	10	11	0	48	1	65	4.91	0		3.75		Sep-10
9.86	-5.63	-3.64	1.87	13.76	4.9	1.92	9.41	5.58	8.73	572.7	10	11	0	48	1	65	4.91	0				Sep-10
10.07	-5.28	-2.90	4.18	18.10	5.62	1.17	9.44	5.58	8.84	572.7	10	11	0	48	1	65	4.91	0				Sep-10
10.17	-5.08	-2.58	5.18	20.02	5.97	0.87	9.46	5.58	8.83	572.7	10	11	0	48	1	65	4.91	0				Mar-17
10.15	-5.20	-2.74	5.01	19.54	5.91	0.92	9.48	5.58	8.83	572.7	10	11	0	48	1	65	4.91	0				Sep-10
10.05	-5.18	-2.67	5.03	19.85	6	0.84	9.46	5.58	8.82	572.7	10	11	0	48	1	65	4.91	10,000,000				Sep-10
3.27	3.33	4.57	9.26	12.22	2.26	0.84	1.64	2.40	19.72	430.8	9	9	0	58	0	99	2.74	0		3.75		Mar-07
3.12	2.97	3.74	6.82	8.08	1.55	1.59	1.65	2.40	19.53	430.8	9	9	0	58	0	99	2.74	0				Mar-99
3.25	3.32	4.55	9.23	12.18	2.24	0.84	1.63	2.40	19.78	430.8	9	9	0	58	0	99	2.74	0				Feb-99
3.40	3.50	4.88	10.27	13.91	2.55	0.54	1.66	2.40	19.75	430.8	9	9	0	58	0	99	2.74	0				Mar-17
3.34	3.44	4.82	10.20	13.89	2.55	0.54	1.65	2.40	19.77	430.8	9	9	0	58	0	99	2.74	0				Mar-16
3.33	3.48	4.83	10.05	13.66	2.5	0.59	1.63	2.40	19.74	430.8	9	9	0	58	0	99	2.74	0				Oct-81
3.40	3.51	4.91	10.35	14.08	2.58	0.51	1.68	2.40	19.75	430.8	9	9	0	58	0	99	2.74	10,000,000				Sep-08
6.44	5.13	7.79	14.57	21.50	2.14	0.85	4.7	6.74	11.59	3,266	12	25	0	27	0	112	2.96	0		3.75		Sep-08
6.98	5.36	7.63	12.64	17.81	2.03	1.6	4.84	6.74	11.53	3,266	12	25	0	27	0	112	2.96	0				Sep-08
6.50	5.18	7.76	14.60	21.60	2.16	0.85	4.68	6.74	11.5	3,266	12	25	0	27	0	112	2.96	0				May-99
6.61	5.35	8.15	15.79	23.04	2.49	0.48	4.68	6.74	11.64	3,266	12	25	0	27	0	112	2.96	0				Mar-17
6.60	5.33	8.17	15.81	23.65	2.53	0.47	4.7	6.74	11.5	3,266	12	25	0	27	0	112	2.96	0				Mar-16
6.57	5.21	8.03	15.55	23.23	2.39	0.58	4.72	6.74	11.65	3,266	12	25	0	27	0	112	2.96	0				Sep-08
6.61	5.35	8.21	15.92	24.09	2.56	0.44	4.66	6.74	11.48	3,266	12	25	0	27	0	112	2.96	10,000,000				Jun-05
2.27	0.19	2.17	9.81	15.88	2.47	0.81	4	4.73	23.55	3,044	2	0	98	0	0	35	4.42	0		3.75		Jun-10
2.14	-0.12	1.46	7.51	11.88	1.76	1.52	4.01	4.73	23.41	3,044	2	0	98	0	0	35	4.42	0				Mar-99
2.31	0.24	2.19	9.94	16.06	2.5	0.77	4.04	4.73	23.55	3,044	2	0	98	0	0	35	4.42	0				May-99

	MARKET			FUND TYPE, CATEGORY & OBJECTIVE	RATINGS				NEW INVESTORS	
Fund Name	Ticker Symbol	Traded On	Fund Type	Category and (Prospectus Objective)	Overall Rating	Reward Rating	Risk Rating	Recent Up/ Downgrade	Open to New Investors	Telephone
Russell Investments Tax-Exempt Bond Fund Class M	RBCUX	NAS CM	Open End	US Muni Fixed Inc (Muni Bond - Natl)	C	C-	B-		Y	800-426-7969
Russell Investments Tax-Exempt Bond Fund Class S	RLVSX	NAS CM	Open End	US Muni Fixed Inc (Muni Bond - Natl)	C	C-	B-		Y	800-426-7969
Russell Investments Tax-Exempt High Yield Bond Cl A	RTHAX	NAS CM	Open End	US Muni Fixed Inc (Muni Bond - Natl)	C-	D+	C	Down	Y	800-426-7969
Russell Investments Tax-Exempt High Yield Bond Cl C	RTHCX	NAS CM	Open End	US Muni Fixed Inc (Muni Bond - Natl)	C-	D+	C	Down	Y	800-426-7969
Russell Investments Tax-Exempt High Yield Bond Cl E	RTHEX	NAS CM	Open End	US Muni Fixed Inc (Muni Bond - Natl)	C-	D+	C	Down	Y	800-426-7969
Russell Investments Tax-Exempt High Yield Bond Cl M	RHYTX	NAS CM	Open End	US Muni Fixed Inc (Muni Bond - Natl)	C-	D+	C	Down	Y	800-426-7969
Russell Investments Tax-Exempt High Yield Bond Cl S	RTHSX	NAS CM	Open End	US Muni Fixed Inc (Muni Bond - Natl)	C-	D+	C	Down	Y	800-426-7969
Russell Investments Unconstrained Total Return Cl A	RUTAX	NAS CM	Open End	Fixed Inc Misc (Growth & Income)	D	D	C-	Down	Y	800-426-7969
Russell Investments Unconstrained Total Return Cl C	RUTCX	NAS CM	Open End	Fixed Inc Misc (Growth & Income)	D	D	C-	Down	Y	800-426-7969
Russell Investments Unconstrained Total Return Cl M	RUCTX	NAS CM	Open End	Fixed Inc Misc (Growth & Income)	D+	D	C-	Down	Y	800-426-7969
Russell Investments Unconstrained Total Return Cl S	RUTSX	NAS CM	Open End	Fixed Inc Misc (Growth & Income)	D+	D	C-	Down	Y	800-426-7969
Russell Investments Unconstrained Total Return Cl Y	RUTYX	NAS CM	Open End	Fixed Inc Misc (Growth & Income)	D+	D	C-	Down		800-426-7969
Ryan Labs Core Bond Fund	RLCBX	NAS CM	Open End	US Fixed Inc (Growth & Income)	B-	C	B+	Up	Y	212-635-2300
Ryan Labs Long Credit Fund	RLLCX	NAS CM	Open End	US Fixed Inc (Growth & Income)	B-	C+	B	Up	Y	212-635-2300
Rydex Emerging Markets Bond Strategy Fund A-Class	RYIEX	NAS CM	Open End	Emerg Mkts Fixed Inc (Growth & Income)	D+	D	C	Down	Y	800-820-0888
Rydex Emerging Markets Bond Strategy Fund C-Class	RYFTX	NAS CM	Open End	Emerg Mkts Fixed Inc (Growth & Income)	D+	D	C-	Down	Y	800-820-0888
Rydex Emerging Markets Bond Strategy Fund H-Class	RYGTX	NAS CM	Open End	Emerg Mkts Fixed Inc (Growth & Income)	D+	D	C	Down	Y	800-820-0888
Rydex High Yield Strategy Fund Class A	RYHDX	NAS CM	Open End	US Fixed Inc (Corp Bond - High Yield)	D+	D+	C-	Down	Y	800-820-0888
Rydex High Yield Strategy Fund Class C	RYHHX	NAS CM	Open End	US Fixed Inc (Corp Bond - High Yield)	D+	D+	C-	Down	Y	800-820-0888
Rydex High Yield Strategy Fund Class H	RYHGX	NAS CM	Open End	US Fixed Inc (Corp Bond - High Yield)	D+	D+	C-	Down	Y	800-820-0888
Rydex U.S. Government Money Market Fund Money Market Class	RYFXX	NAS CM	Money Mkt	US Money Mkt (Money Mkt - Govt)	C	C-	C		Y	800-820-0888
SA Global Fixed Income Fund Investor Class	SAXIX	NAS CM	Open End	Global Fixed Inc (Income)	C	C-	C+		Y	
SA Global Fixed Income Fund Select Class	SAFLX	NAS CM	Open End	Global Fixed Inc (Income)	C	C-	C+		Y	
SA U.S. Fixed Income Fund Investor Class	SAUFX	NAS CM	Open End	US Fixed Inc (Income)	C	C-	C+		Y	
SA U.S. Fixed Income Fund Select Class	SAULX	NAS CM	Open End	US Fixed Inc (Income)	C	C-	C+		Y	
Sanford C. Bernstein California Municipal Portfolio	SNCAX	NAS CM	Open End	US Muni Fixed Inc (Muni Bond - Single State)	C	C-	C+		Y	212-969-1000
Sanford C. Bernstein Intermediate Duration Portfolio	SNIDX	NAS CM	Open End	US Fixed Inc (Corp Bond - High Quality)	B-	C	B	Up	Y	212-969-1000
Sanford C. Bernstein New York Municipal Portfolio	SNNYX	NAS CM	Open End	US Muni Fixed Inc (Muni Bond - Single State)	C	C-	C		Y	212-969-1000
Saratoga Investment Quality Bond Portfolio Class A	SQBAX	NAS CM	Open End	US Fixed Inc (Corp Bond - High Quality)	C	C	B-		Y	800-807-3863
Saratoga Investment Quality Bond Portfolio Class C	SQBCX	NAS CM	Open End	US Fixed Inc (Corp Bond - High Quality)	C	C	C+		Y	800-807-3863
Saratoga Investment Quality Bond Portfolio Class I	SIBPX	NAS CM	Open End	US Fixed Inc (Corp Bond - High Quality)	C+	C	B-	Up	Y	800-807-3863
Saratoga Municipal Bond Portfolio Fund Class A	SMBAX	NAS CM	Open End	US Muni Fixed Inc (Muni Bond - Natl)	D+	D	C		Y	800-807-3863
Saratoga Municipal Bond Portfolio Fund Class C	SMBCX	NAS CM	Open End	US Muni Fixed Inc (Muni Bond - Natl)	C-	D+	C	Up	Y	800-807-3863
Saratoga Municipal Bond Portfolio Fund Class Institutional	SMBPX	NAS CM	Open End	US Muni Fixed Inc (Muni Bond - Natl)	C-	D+	C		Y	800-807-3863
Saratoga U.S. Government Money Market Portfolio Class A	SGAXX	NAS CM	Money Mkt	US Money Mkt (Money Mkt - Govt)	C	C-	C		Y	800-807-3863
Saratoga U.S. Government Money Market Portfolio Class C	SZCXX	NAS CM	Money Mkt	US Money Mkt (Money Mkt - Govt)	C-	C-	C		Y	800-807-3863
Saratoga U.S. Government Money Market Portfolio Class I	SGMXX	NAS CM	Money Mkt	US Money Mkt (Money Mkt - Govt)	C	C-	C		Y	800-807-3863
Saturna Sustainable Bond Fund	SEBFX	NAS CM	Open End	Global Fixed Inc (Corp Bond - High Quality)	C	C	C+		Y	
Schroder Core Bond Fund R6 Shares	SCBRX	NAS CM	Open End	US Fixed Inc (Govt Bond - General)	C	C	B		Y	800-464-3108
Schroder Long Duration Inv-Grade Bond Investor Shares	STWLX	NAS CM	Open End	US Fixed Inc (Income)	B	B	B		Y	800-464-3108
Schroder Total Return Fixed Income Fund Class Investor	SBBIX	NAS CM	Open End	US Fixed Inc (Multisector Bond)	B	B-	B	Up	Y	800-464-3108
Schwab AMT Tax-Free Money Fund™ - Investor Shares	SWWXX	NAS CM	Money Mkt	US Money Mkt (Money Mkt - Fed Tax Exmpt)	C	C-	C+		Y	877-824-5615
Schwab California Municipal Money Fund™ - Investor Shares	SWKXX	NAS CM	Money Mkt	US Money Mkt (Money Mkt - Single State)	C	C-	C		Y	877-824-5615
Schwab California Tax-Free Bond Fund™	SWCAX	NAS CM	Open End	US Muni Fixed Inc (Muni Bond - Single State)	C	C	B-		Y	877-824-5615
Schwab Government Money Fund™	SWGXX	NAS CM	Money Mkt	US Money Mkt (Money Mkt - Govt)	C	C-	C+		Y	877-824-5615
Schwab Government Money Fund™ - Investor Shares	SNVXX	NAS CM	Money Mkt	US Money Mkt (Money Mkt - Govt)	C	C-	C+		Y	877-824-5615
Schwab Municipal Money Fund™ - Investor Shares	SWTXX	NAS CM	Money Mkt	US Money Mkt (Money Mkt - Fed Tax Exmpt)	C	C-	C+		Y	877-824-5615
Schwab Municipal Money Fund™ - Ultra Shares	SWOXX	NAS CM	Money Mkt	US Money Mkt (Money Mkt - Fed Tax Exmpt)	C	C-	C+		Y	877-824-5615
Schwab New York Municipal Money Fund™ - Investor Shares	SWYXX	NAS CM	Money Mkt	US Money Mkt (Money Mkt - Single State)	C	C-	C+		Y	877-824-5615
Schwab Retirement Government Money Fund	SNRXX	NAS CM	Money Mkt	US Money Mkt (Money Mkt - Govt)	C	C-	C+		Y	877-824-5615
Schwab Short-Term Bond Index Fund	SWSBX	NAS CM	Open End	US Fixed Inc (Multisector Bond)	B-	C	B	Up	Y	877-824-5615
Schwab Tax-Free Bond Fund™	SWNTX	NAS CM	Open End	US Muni Fixed Inc (Muni Bond - Natl)	C	C	B-		Y	877-824-5615

★Expanded analysis of this fund is included in Section II.

TOTAL RETURNS & PERFORMANCE									ASSETS		ASSET ALLOCATION & TURNOVER							MINIMUMS		FEES		
3-Month Total Return	6-Month Total Return	1-Year Total Return	3-Year Total Return	5-Year Total Return	Dividend Yield (TTM)	Expense Ratio	3-Yr Std Deviation	Effective Duration	NAV	Total Assets (MIL)	%Cash	%Government Bonds	%Municipal Bonds	%Corporate Bonds	%Other	Turnover Ratio	Average Coupon Rate	Min Initial Investment	Min Additional Investment	Front End Fee (%)	Back End Fee (%)	Inception Date
2.42	0.43	2.57	11.19	17.97	2.88	0.42	4.02	4.73	23.47	3,044	2	0	98	0	0	35	4.42	0				Mar-17
2.35	0.35	2.47	10.81	17.59	2.78	0.52	4.01	4.73	23.46	3,044	2	0	98	0	0	35	4.42	0				Sep-85
3.45	-2.49	0.37	13.46	27.85	3.58	0.89	6.74	6.82	10.58	951.0	1	1	98	0	0	35	4.59	0		3.75		Jun-15
3.26	-2.87	-0.34	11.01	23.27	2.82	1.64	6.72	6.82	10.56	951.0	1	1	98	0	0	35	4.59	0				Jun-15
3.50	-2.50	0.47	13.61	28.02	3.27	0.89	6.74	6.82	10.66	951.0	1	1	98	0	0	35	4.59	0				Jun-15
3.54	-2.37	0.72	14.65	29.87	3.95	0.54	6.72	6.82	10.58	951.0	1	1	98	0	0	35	4.59	0				Mar-17
3.51	-2.40	0.62	14.40	29.55	3.84	0.64	6.69	6.82	10.59	951.0	1	1	98	0	0	35	4.59	0				Jun-15
4.10	-6.02	-3.64	0.89		3.3	1.14	5.89	0.60	9.28	680.0	39	34	0	25	0	166	2.58	0		3.75		Sep-16
3.88	-6.34	-4.37	-1.32		2.62	1.89	5.84	0.60	9.24	680.0	39	34	0	25	0	166	2.58	0				Sep-16
4.21	-5.88	-3.29	1.89		3.69	0.79	5.9	0.60	9.28	680.0	39	34	0	25	0	166	2.58	0				Mar-17
4.18	-5.81	-3.39	1.70		3.57	0.89	5.88	0.60	9.29	680.0	39	34	0	25	0	166	2.58	0				Sep-16
4.23	-5.83	-3.19	2.26		3.79	0.69	5.9	0.60	9.29	680.0	39	34	0	25	0	166	2.58	10,000,000				Sep-16
5.66	5.65	8.58	17.40	24.86	2.96	0.4	4.14		10.59	69.6	1	8	0	31	0	39	3.68	1,000,000				Dec-14
13.57	9.02	16.68	31.27		3.14	0.5	10.17		11.76	90.7	1	6	3	90	0	179	4.29	1,000,000				Nov-15
9.90	-3.48	-2.35	4.34	16.76	3.27	1.66	9.2		70.26	1.9	111	0	0	0	-10	733		2,500		4.75		Oct-13
9.71	-3.83	-3.10	2.01	12.06	3.48	2.37	9.2		65.63	1.9	111	0	0	0	-10	733		2,500			1.00	Oct-13
9.92	-3.51	-2.39	4.31	16.65	3.29	1.7	9.21		69.8	1.9	111	0	0	0	-10	733		2,500				Oct-13
3.12	-9.34	-6.31	4.93	17.88	4.8	1.62	8.15		22.42	87.1	64	28	0	3	-3	21	1.05	2,500		4.75		Apr-07
2.98	-9.66	-7.00	2.68	13.66	5.57	2.36	8.17		19.35	87.1	64	28	0	3	-3	21	1.05	2,500			1.00	Apr-07
3.22	-9.27	-6.19	4.98	17.75	4.81	1.61	8.17		22.41	87.1	64	28	0	3	-3	21	1.05	2,500				Apr-07
0.00	0.12	0.62	2.32	2.33	0.73	1.05	0.14		1	274.5	29	71	0	0	0			0				Dec-93
0.82	0.67	1.35	5.46	7.77	2.44	0.73	1.12	1.83	9.42	696.1	17	49	0	34	0	75	1.05	0				Jul-99
0.77	0.74	1.55	6.11	8.44	2.64	0.51	1.13	1.83	9.38	696.1	17	49	0	34	0	75	1.05	100,000				Jul-17
0.63	0.70	1.52	4.21	4.98	1.7	0.64	0.52	0.12	10.17	541.4	44	31	0	25	0	88	1.63	0				Apr-07
0.58	0.66	1.60	4.71	5.48	1.88	0.41	0.54	0.12	10.16	541.4	44	31	0	25	0	88	1.63	100,000				Jul-17
3.14	0.68	2.11	7.58	12.20	2.05	0.55	3.52	4.22	14.42	1,357	2	0	98	0	0	24	4.86	25,000				Aug-90
4.88	4.69	7.18	14.59	23.33	2.87	0.57	3.89	6.50	13.92	3,490	-45	47	0	19	0	62	3.00	25,000				Jan-89
2.39	-0.12	1.20	6.60	11.87	2.24	0.53	3.75	4.75	14.01	1,743	0	0	99	0	0	18	4.87	25,000				Jan-89
1.88	2.92	3.51	5.31	6.44	0.68	1.7	1.46	3.36	9.75	5.0	4	69	0	27	0	11	2.40	250		5.75		Feb-06
1.79	2.67	2.95	4.16	4.67	0.22	2.42	1.51	3.36	9.74	5.0	4	69	0	27	0	11	2.40	250			1.00	Jan-99
2.08	3.22	4.10	6.55	8.35	1.05	1.37	1.52	3.36	9.78	5.0	4	69	0	27	0	11	2.40	250				Sep-94
1.15	0.38	0.54	-1.30	-0.83	0.1	3.07	1.62	2.11	8.95	0.64	15	0	85	11	1	2	3.80	250		5.75		Feb-06
1.14	0.49	0.87	-1.03	-0.71	0.1	4.12	1.65	2.11	9.03	0.64	15	0	85	11	1	2	3.80	250			1.00	Jan-99
1.14	0.38	0.65	-0.33	0.67	0.1	3.02	1.65	2.11	9.04	0.64	15	0	85	11	1	2	3.80	250				Sep-94
0.00	0.00	0.14	1.08	1.12	0.2	1.64	0.09		1	6.0	100	0	0	0	0			0		5.75		Feb-06
0.00	0.00	0.02	0.47	0.49	0.03	2.21	0.05		1	6.0	100	0	0	0	0			0			1.00	Jan-99
0.00	0.03	0.35	1.60	1.62	0.44	1.24	0.13		1	6.0	100	0	0	0	0			0				Sep-94
4.01	2.02	3.55	6.62	13.88	1.92	0.65	3.47	4.60	9.86	27.2	3	40	0	58	0	38	4.08	1,000	25			Mar-15
4.74	7.79	10.41			2.58	0.32			10.83	70.7	1	24	2	47	0	134	3.15	1,000,000				Jan-18
7.21	15.54	21.93	36.20	54.84	2.56	0.32	8.88		10.61	124.6	3	43	5	44	0	73	3.82	250,000	1,000			Oct-11
6.03	7.30	10.08	17.48	23.30	2.73	0.4	3.76		10.63	43.2	1	31	2	36	0	92	3.45	250,000	1,000			Dec-04
0.05	0.33	0.85	3.04	3.37	1.01	0.35	0.12		1	1,188	30	0	70	0	0			0				Nov-06
0.06	0.31	0.78	2.80	3.12	0.92	0.35	0.1		1	5,503	35	0	65	0	0			0				Oct-95
2.33	1.48	3.28	10.28	16.40	2.06	0.49	3.52	5.42	12.14	460.2	2	0	98	0	0	75	4.42	0				Feb-92
0.00	0.22	0.96	3.37	3.42	1.19	0.57	0.17		1	35,236	63	34	3	0	0			0				Jan-90
0.01	0.28	1.14	4.10	4.31	1.4	0.35	0.18		1	35,236	63	34	3	0	0			0				Jan-15
0.06	0.34	0.87	3.00	3.34	1.02	0.34	0.11		1	15,249	36	0	64	0	0			0				Jul-95
0.09	0.41	1.02	3.47	4.08	1.17	0.19	0.11		1	15,249	36	0	64	0	0			1,000,000	1			Jun-03
0.04	0.33	0.84	3.07	3.41	1	0.35	0.13		1	1,037	26	0	74	0	0			0				Jul-95
0.06	0.38	1.31	4.65		1.57	0.19	0.17		1	2,481	58	38	4	0	0			1,000,000	1			May-16
1.61	3.87	5.39	10.56		2.16	0.06	1.53	2.67	10.38	1,221	1	73	0	26	0	46	2.34	0				Feb-17
2.06	1.41	3.34	10.33	16.27	2.21	0.49	3.72	5.47	12.01	739.7	1	0	99	0	0	129	4.33	0				Sep-92

Fund Name	Ticker Symbol	Traded On	Fund Type	Category and (Prospectus Objective)	Overall Rating	Reward Rating	Risk Rating	Recent Up/ Downgrade	Open to New Investors	Telephone
	MARKET		FUND TYPE, CATEGORY & OBJECTIVE		RATINGS				NEW INVESTORS	
Schwab Treasury Obligations Money Fund™ - Investor Shares	SNOXX	NAS CM	Money Mkt	US Money Mkt (Money Mkt - Treasury)	C	C-	C+			877-824-5615
Schwab U.S. Aggregate Bond Index Fund	SWAGX	NAS CM	Open End	US Fixed Inc (Multisector Bond)	B	B-	B+	Up	Y	877-824-5615
Schwab U.S. Treasury Money Fund™ Investor Shares	SNSXX	NAS CM	Money Mkt	US Money Mkt (Money Mkt - Treasury)	C	C	C+		Y	877-824-5615
★ Schwab Value Advantage Money Fund® Investor Shares	SWVXX	NAS CM	Money Mkt	US Money Mkt (Money Mkt - Taxable)	C	C-	C+		Y	877-824-5615
Schwab Value Advantage Money Fund® Ultra Shares	SNAXX	NAS CM	Money Mkt	US Money Mkt (Money Mkt - Taxable)	C	C-	C+		Y	877-824-5615
Schwab Variable Share Price Money Fund™ Ultra Shares	SVUXX	NAS CM	Money Mkt	US Money Mkt (Money Mkt - Taxable)	C	C-	C+		Y	877-824-5615
Schwab® Treasury Inflation Protected Securities Index Fund	SWRSX	NAS CM	Open End	US Fixed Inc (Income)	B	B-	A-	Up	Y	877-824-5615
Segall Bryant & Hamill Colorado Tax Free Institutional Cl	WICOX	NAS CM	Open End	US Muni Fixed Inc (Muni Bond - Single State)	C+	C	B	Up	Y	312-474-1222
Segall Bryant & Hamill Colorado Tax Free Fund Retail Class	WTCOX	NAS CM	Open End	US Muni Fixed Inc (Muni Bond - Single State)	C	C	B		Y	312-474-1222
Segall Bryant & Hamill Muni Opportunities Institutional Cl	WITAX	NAS CM	Open End	US Muni Fixed Inc (Muni Bond - Natl)	C+	C	B		Y	312-474-1222
Segall Bryant & Hamill Muni Opportunities Retail Cl	WTTAX	NAS CM	Open End	US Muni Fixed Inc (Muni Bond - Natl)	C+	C	B		Y	312-474-1222
Segall Bryant & Hamill Plus Bond Fund Institutional Class	WIIBX	NAS CM	Open End	US Fixed Inc (Corp Bond - High Quality)	B	C+	B+	Up	Y	312-474-1222
Segall Bryant & Hamill Plus Bond Fund Retail Class	WTIBX	NAS CM	Open End	US Fixed Inc (Corp Bond - High Quality)	B	C+	B+	Up	Y	312-474-1222
Segall Bryant & Hamill Quality High Yield Institutional Cl	WILTX	NAS CM	Open End	US Fixed Inc (Corp Bond - High Yield)	C	C-	C+		Y	312-474-1222
Segall Bryant & Hamill Quality High Yield Retail Cl	WTLTX	NAS CM	Open End	US Fixed Inc (Corp Bond - High Yield)	C	C-	C+	Up	Y	312-474-1222
Segall Bryant & Hamill Short Term Plus Fund Institutional	SBAPX	NAS CM	Open End	US Fixed Inc (Growth & Income)	D	D+	C		Y	312-474-1222
Segall Bryant & Hamill Short Term Plus Fund Retail	SBHPX	NAS CM	Open End	US Fixed Inc (Growth & Income)	D	D+	C		Y	312-474-1222
SEI Asset Allocation Trust Defensive Strategy Fund Class F	SNSAX	NAS CM	Open End	Cautious Allocation (Growth & Income)	C	C-	C+		Y	800-342-5734
SEI Asset Allocation Trust Defensive Strategy Fund Class I	SEDIX	NAS CM	Open End	Cautious Allocation (Growth & Income)	C	C-	C+		Y	800-342-5734
SEI Catholic Values Trust Catholic Values Fixed Inc Cl F	CFVAX	NAS CM	Open End	US Fixed Inc (Income)	B	C+	B+	Up	Y	800-342-5734
SEI Catholic Values Trust Catholic Values Fixed Inc Cl Y	CFVYX	NAS CM	Open End	US Fixed Inc (Income)	B	C+	B+	Up	Y	800-342-5734
SEI Daily Income Trust GNMA Fund Class F	SEGMX	NAS CM	Open End	US Fixed Inc (Govt Bond - Mortgage)	C+	C+	B-		Y	800-342-5734
SEI Daily Income Trust GNMA Fund Class Y	SGMYX	NAS CM	Open End	US Fixed Inc (Govt Bond - Mortgage)	C+	C+	B-		Y	800-342-5734
SEI Daily Income Trust Government Fund Class CAA	GFAXX	NAS CM	Money Mkt	US Money Mkt (Money Mkt - Govt)	C	C-	C+		Y	800-342-5734
SEI Daily Income Trust Government Fund Class F	SEOXX	NAS CM	Money Mkt	US Money Mkt (Money Mkt - Govt)	C	C-	C+		Y	800-342-5734
SEI Daily Income Trust Government II Fund Class F	TCGXX	NAS CM	Money Mkt	US Money Mkt (Money Mkt - Govt)	C	C-	C+		Y	800-342-5734
SEI Daily Income Trust Short-Duration Govt Fund Class F	TCSGX	NAS CM	Open End	US Fixed Inc (Govt Bond - General)	C+	C	B	Up	Y	800-342-5734
SEI Daily Income Trust Short-Duration Govt Fund Class Y	SDGFX	NAS CM	Open End	US Fixed Inc (Govt Bond - General)	C+	C	B	Up	Y	800-342-5734
SEI Daily Income Trust Treasury II Fund Class F	SCPXX	NAS CM	Money Mkt	US Money Mkt (Money Mkt - Treasury)	C	C-	C+		Y	800-342-5734
SEI Daily Income Trust Ultra Short Duration Bond Cl F	SECPX	NAS CM	Open End	US Fixed Inc (Corp Bond - General)	C	C-	C+		Y	800-342-5734
SEI Daily Income Trust Ultra Short Duration Bond Cl Y	SECYX	NAS CM	Open End	US Fixed Inc (Corp Bond - General)	C	C	C+		Y	800-342-5734
SEI Institutional InterNatl Trust Emerg Mkts Debt Cl F	SITEX	NAS CM	Open End	Emerg Mkts Fixed Inc (Worldwide Bond)	D	D	D+	Down	Y	800-342-5734
SEI Institutional InterNatl Trust Emerg Mkts Debt Cl Y	SIEDX	NAS CM	Open End	Emerg Mkts Fixed Inc (Worldwide Bond)	D	D	C-	Down	Y	800-342-5734
SEI Inst InterNatl Trust InterNatl Fixed Income Cl F	SEFIX	NAS CM	Open End	Global Fixed Inc (Worldwide Bond)	C	C	B		Y	800-342-5734
SEI Inst InterNatl Trust InterNatl Fixed Income Cl Y	SIFIX	NAS CM	Open End	Global Fixed Inc (Worldwide Bond)	C	C	B-		Y	800-342-5734
SEI Institutional Investments Trust Core Fixed Income Cl A	SCOAX	NAS CM	Open End	US Fixed Inc (Income)	B	B-	B+	Up	Y	800-342-5734
SEI Institutional Investments Trust Emerg Mkts Debt Cl A	SEDAX	NAS CM	Open End	Emerg Mkts Fixed Inc (Diversified Emerg Mkts)	D+	D	C-	Down	Y	800-342-5734
SEI Institutional Investments Trust High Yield Bond Cl A	SGYAX	NAS CM	Open End	US Fixed Inc (Income)	D	D	D+	Down	Y	800-342-5734
SEI Inst Inv Trust Intermed Duration Credit Cl A	SIDCX	NAS CM	Open End	US Fixed Inc (Corp Bond - General)	B	C+	B+	Up	Y	800-342-5734
SEI Inst Inv Trust Limited Duration Bond Cl A	SLDBX	NAS CM	Open End	US Fixed Inc (Income)	C+	C	B	Up	Y	800-342-5734
SEI Inst Inv Trust Long Duration Credit Cl A	SLDAX	NAS CM	Open End	US Fixed Inc (Corp Bond - High Quality)	B	B	B	Up	Y	800-342-5734
SEI Institutional Investments Trust Long Duration Cl A	LDRAX	NAS CM	Open End	US Fixed Inc (Income)	B	B	B		Y	800-342-5734
SEI Inst Inv Trust Multi-Asset Real Return Cl A	SEIAX	NAS CM	Open End	Cautious Allocation (Growth & Income)	D	D	C-	Down	Y	800-342-5734
SEI Institutional Investments Trust Opportunistic Income A	ENIAX	NAS CM	Open End	US Fixed Inc (Income)	C-	D+	C		Y	800-342-5734
SEI Institutional Investments Trust Real Return Cl A	RRPAX	NAS CM	Open End	US Fixed Inc (Growth & Income)	C+	C	B	Up	Y	800-342-5734
SEI Inst Inv Trust Ultra Short Duration Bond Cl A	SUSAX	NAS CM	Open End	US Fixed Inc (Income)	C	C	B-		Y	800-342-5734
SEI Institutional Managed Trust Conservative Income Cl F	COIAX	NAS CM	Open End	US Fixed Inc (Income)	C	C-	C+		Y	800-342-5734
SEI Institutional Managed Trust Conservative Income Cl Y	COIYX	NAS CM	Open End	US Fixed Inc (Income)	C	C-	C+		Y	800-342-5734
SEI Institutional Managed Trust Core Fixed Income Cl F	TRLVX	NAS CM	Open End	US Fixed Inc (Corp Bond - High Quality)	B	C+	B+	Up	Y	800-342-5734
SEI Institutional Managed Trust Core Fixed Income Cl I	SCXIX	NAS CM	Open End	US Fixed Inc (Corp Bond - High Quality)	B	C+	B+	Up	Y	800-342-5734
SEI Institutional Managed Trust Core Fixed Income Cl Y	SCFYX	NAS CM	Open End	US Fixed Inc (Corp Bond - High Quality)	B	C+	B+	Up	Y	800-342-5734
SEI Institutional Managed Trust High Yield Bond Cl F	SHYAX	NAS CM	Open End	US Fixed Inc (Corp Bond - High Yield)	D	D	D+	Down	Y	800-342-5734

★ Expanded analysis of this fund is included in Section II.

TOTAL RETURNS & PERFORMANCE									ASSETS		ASSET ALLOCATION & TURNOVER							MINIMUMS		FEES		
3-Month Total Return	6-Month Total Return	1-Year Total Return	3-Year Total Return	5-Year Total Return	Dividend Yield (TTM)	Expense Ratio	3-Yr Std Deviation	Effective Duration	NAV	Total Assets (MIL)	%Cash	%Government Bonds	%Municipal Bonds	%Corporate Bonds	%Other	Turnover Ratio	Average Coupon Rate	Min Initial Investment	Min Additional Investment	Front End Fee (%)	Back End Fee (%)	Inception Date
0.00	0.25	1.10	4.08	4.35	1.36	0.35	0.17		1	13,549	70	30	0	0	0			0				Apr-12
2.78	6.07	8.73	16.50		2.64	0.04	3.24	5.79	10.81	4,017	6	40	1	26	0	91	3.14	0				Feb-17
0.00	0.27	1.09	3.80	3.88	1.33	0.35			1	20,404	73	27	0	0	0			0				Jan-18
0.08	0.41	1.33	4.82	5.43	1.6	0.34	0.16		1	115,358	97	0	0	3	0			0				Apr-92
0.12	0.48	1.49	5.31	6.29	1.75	0.19	0.16		1	115,358	97	0	0	3	0			1,000,000	1			Sep-06
0.17	0.49	1.49	5.31		1.73	0.19	0.17		1.0006	4,520	98	0	1	1	0			1,000,000	1			Feb-16
4.19	5.95	8.45	15.72	20.22	2.1	0.05	3.7		11.93	1,158	0	100	0	0	0	25	0.77	0				Mar-06
2.15	1.91	3.98	12.00	18.95	2.98	0.5	3.52		11.78	406.2	5	0	95	0	0	30	4.60	250,000				Apr-16
2.12	1.85	3.77	11.54	18.28	2.86	0.65	3.51		11.74	406.2	5	0	95	0	0	30	4.60	2,500	25			May-91
3.05	2.68	5.05	15.41		3.2	0.5	3.36		10.8	99.0	10	0	87	2	0	114	4.46	250,000				Dec-16
2.91	2.59	4.88	14.86		3.03	0.65	3.34		10.79	99.0	10	0	87	2	0	114	4.46	2,500	25			Dec-16
5.21	5.52	8.02	16.94	25.67	3.13	0.4	3.86		11.11	1,020	2	13	10	45	0	52	3.98	250,000				Sep-07
5.20	5.47	7.96	16.44	24.79	2.94	0.55	3.9		11.22	1,020	2	13	10	45	0	52	3.98	2,500	25			Jun-88
9.11	-1.00	2.29	11.20	26.60	4.34	0.7	6.92	3.49	8.59	62.3	5	0	0	94	0	41	5.21	250,000				Sep-07
9.11	-1.16	2.02	10.64	25.31	4.17	0.85	7.03	3.49	8.68	62.3	5	0	0	94	0	41	5.21	2,500	25			Jun-88
3.41	0.78	2.12			2.28	0.4			10.09	10.3	14	4	4	75	0	32	3.51	250,000				Dec-18
3.41	0.66	1.99			2.25	0.49			10.08	10.3	14	4	4	75	0	32	3.51	2,500	25			Dec-18
2.78	0.00	1.84	7.51	10.72	2.35	0.67	2.38		9.96	30.8	36	31	0	5	1		2.36	100,000	1,000			Nov-03
2.77	-0.15	1.63	6.70	9.23	2.15	0.92	2.4		9.78	30.8	36	31	0	5	1		2.36	100,000	1,000			Nov-03
5.90	5.53	8.24	16.69	25.36	2.51	0.71	4.14		10.72	162.5	1	21	1	43	0		3.60	500	100			Apr-15
5.82	5.47	8.24	16.91	25.91	2.61	0.61	4.1		10.72	162.5	1	21	1	43	0		3.60	500	100			May-15
0.63	3.32	4.55	10.42	14.56	2.55	0.58	2.14		10.63	72.4	4	2	0	0	0	225	3.58	0				Mar-87
0.68	3.44	4.80	11.26	15.75	2.8	0.33	2.14		10.63	72.4	4	2	0	0	0	225	3.58	100,000	1,000			Oct-15
0.06	0.37	1.29	4.49	4.93	1.42	0.2	0.17		1	12,011	74	26	0	0	0			0				Nov-15
0.02	0.33	1.24	4.45	4.89	1.42	0.2	0.17		1	12,011	74	26	0	0	0			0				Oct-95
0.04	0.36	1.27	4.57	5.01	1.45	0.2	0.17		1	2,828	75	25	0	0	0			0				Dec-85
0.46	3.14	4.08	7.49	9.27	1.68	0.48	1.09		10.59	823.4	7	36	0	0	0		2.59	0				Feb-87
0.51	3.22	4.23	8.07	9.99	1.83	0.33	1.11		10.59	823.4	7	36	0	0	0		2.59	100,000	1,000			Dec-14
0.03	0.34	1.24	4.52	4.90	1.44	0.2	0.17		1	479.1	80	20	0	0	0			0				Jul-89
2.68	1.01	2.23	6.75	9.35	2.24	0.38	1.69		9.36	307.3	9	13	3	30	0		2.24	0				Sep-93
2.70	1.05	2.31	6.89	9.76	2.32	0.3	1.75		9.36	307.3	9	13	3	30	0		2.24	100,000	1,000			Aug-15
12.67	-6.16	-3.13	2.51	13.03	2.09	1.36	12.61		9.64	1,452	5	85	0	10	-1	114	6.29	100,000	1,000			Jun-97
12.77	-6.00	-2.87	3.28	14.57	2.36	1.11	12.61		9.63	1,452	5	85	0	10	-1	114	6.29	100,000	1,000			Dec-14
2.06	1.26	2.24	11.51	19.11	2.51	1.02	2.99		10.39	510.3	2	76	0	14	0	58	2.46	100,000	1,000			Sep-93
2.16	1.46	2.49	12.27	20.46	2.75	0.77	3		10.4	510.3	2	76	0	14	0	58	2.46	100,000	1,000			Oct-15
4.64	6.79	9.87	19.00	27.40	2.82	0.12	3.54		11.05	7,441	5	28	0	29	0	368	3.29	100,000	1,000			Jun-96
12.82	-5.79	-2.32	5.16	18.18	3.6	0.42	12.59		9.59	2,075	5	85	0	10	0	96	6.28	100,000	1,000			Dec-05
9.28	-7.63	-4.52	6.22	20.96	6.98	0.29	10.04		7.8	2,282	2	0	0	91	0	60	6.37	100,000	1,000			Dec-05
7.14	6.69	10.75	20.58	32.39	2.91	0.15	5.04		11.04	3,285	2	6	2	88	0	122	3.60	100,000	1,000			Mar-15
2.01	2.86	4.18	9.25	12.22	2.34	0.11	1.03		10.17	1,294	2	21	4	25	0	155	2.27	100,000	1,000			Jul-14
9.28	10.37	17.32	32.12	56.60	3.24	0.15	8.94		12.14	4,084	1	5	6	88	0	77	4.54	100,000	1,000			Jun-12
8.52	12.76	19.90	35.97	59.25	3.14	0.15	8.84		9.74	1,295	1	28	5	65	0	102	4.43	100,000	1,000			Apr-04
4.65	-5.72	-3.59	-0.92	-4.70	2.27	1	5.42		7.41	757.8	-62	72	0	14	36	22	1.56	100,000	1,000			Jul-11
6.67	-1.54	0.42	7.97	14.37	4.47	0.24	5.48		7.95	993.6	7	1	1	34	0	26	3.08	100,000	1,000			Dec-06
2.94	2.19	3.65	8.32	10.45	2.53	0.02	1.92		9.76	295.8	0	100	0	0	0	40	0.41	100,000	1,000			Dec-06
2.58	1.25	2.59	7.70	10.79	2.52	0.12	1.63		10.02	572.6	11	24	0	28	0	75	2.37	100,000	1,000			Feb-11
0.14	0.49	1.50	5.21		1.66	0.3	0.15		10	319.7	98	0	0	1	0			100,000	1,000			Apr-16
0.16	0.54	1.60	5.53		1.76	0.2	0.15		10	319.7	98	0	0	1	0			100,000	1,000			Apr-16
4.76	6.14	9.06	16.97	24.77	2.5	0.66	3.66		12.07	4,206	6	31	0	28	-2	387	3.32	100,000	1,000			May-87
4.71	5.97	8.81	16.19	23.28	2.35	0.88	3.71		12.05	4,206	6	31	0	28	-2	387	3.32	100,000	1,000			Aug-01
4.81	6.25	9.28	17.89	26.38	2.7	0.41	3.64		12.08	4,206	6	31	0	28	-2	387	3.32	100,000	1,000			Jun-15
8.76	-8.20	-5.28	4.07	17.47	6.18	0.89	9.99		6.2	1,449	5	0	0	89	0	69	6.54	100,000	1,000			Jan-95

	MARKET		FUND TYPE, CATEGORY & OBJECTIVE		RATINGS				NEW INVESTORS	
Fund Name	Ticker Symbol	Traded On	Fund Type	Category and (Prospectus Objective)	Overall Rating	Reward Rating	Risk Rating	Recent Up/ Downgrade	Open to New Investors	Telephone
SEI Institutional Managed Trust High Yield Bond Cl I	SEIYX	NAS CM	Open End	US Fixed Inc (Corp Bond - High Yield)	D	D	D+	Down	Y	800-342-5734
SEI Institutional Managed Trust High Yield Bond Cl Y	SIYYX	NAS CM	Open End	US Fixed Inc (Corp Bond - High Yield)	D	D	D+	Down	Y	800-342-5734
SEI Institutional Managed Trust Real Return Fund Class F	SRAAX	NAS CM	Open End	US Fixed Inc (Income)	C	C	B-		Y	800-342-5734
SEI Institutional Managed Trust Real Return Fund Class Y	SRYRX	NAS CM	Open End	US Fixed Inc (Income)	C	C	B-		Y	800-342-5734
SEI Inst Managed Trust Tax-Free Conservative Income Cl F	TFCAX	NAS CM	Open End	US Muni Fixed Inc (Income)	C	C-	C+		Y	800-342-5734
SEI Inst Managed Trust Tax-Free Conservative Income Cl Y	TFCYX	NAS CM	Open End	US Muni Fixed Inc (Income)	C	C-	C+		Y	800-342-5734
SEI Tax Exempt Trust California Muni Bond Fund Class F	SBDAX	NAS CM	Open End	US Muni Fixed Inc (Muni Bond - Single State)	C	C	B-		Y	800-342-5734
SEI Tax Exempt Trust California Muni Bond Fund Class Y	SCYYX	NAS CM	Open End	US Muni Fixed Inc (Muni Bond - Single State)	C	C	B-		Y	800-342-5734
SEI Tax Exempt Trust Intermediate-Term Muni Fund Class F	SEIMX	NAS CM	Open End	US Muni Fixed Inc (Muni Bond - Natl)	C	C-	B-		Y	800-342-5734
SEI Tax Exempt Trust Intermediate-Term Muni Fund Class Y	SINYX	NAS CM	Open End	US Muni Fixed Inc (Muni Bond - Natl)	C	C-	B-		Y	800-342-5734
SEI Tax Exempt Trust Massachusetts Muni Bond Fund Class F	SMAAX	NAS CM	Open End	US Muni Fixed Inc (Muni Bond - Single State)	C	C	B-		Y	800-342-5734
SEI Tax Exempt Trust New Jersey Muni Bond Fund Class F	SENJX	NAS CM	Open End	US Muni Fixed Inc (Muni Bond - Single State)	C	C	B-		Y	800-342-5734
SEI Tax Exempt Trust New York Municipal Bond Fund Class F	SENYX	NAS CM	Open End	US Muni Fixed Inc (Muni Bond - Single State)	C	C-	C+		Y	800-342-5734
SEI Tax Exempt Trust Pennsylvania Muni Bond Fund Class F	SEPAX	NAS CM	Open End	US Muni Fixed Inc (Muni Bond - Single State)	C+	C	B	Up	Y	800-342-5734
SEI Tax Exempt Trust Short Duration Municipal Fund Class F	SUMAX	NAS CM	Open End	US Muni Fixed Inc (Money Mkt - Fed Tax Exmpt)	C	C-	C+		Y	800-342-5734
SEI Tax Exempt Trust Short Duration Municipal Fund Class Y	SHYMX	NAS CM	Open End	US Muni Fixed Inc (Money Mkt - Fed Tax Exmpt)	C	C-	C+		Y	800-342-5734
SEI Tax Exempt Trust Tax-Advantaged Income Fund Class F	SEATX	NAS CM	Open End	US Fixed Inc (Income)	C	C-	C+		Y	800-342-5734
SEI Tax Exempt Trust Tax-Advantaged Income Fund Class Y	STAYX	NAS CM	Open End	US Fixed Inc (Income)	C	C-	C+		Y	800-342-5734
SEI Tax-Exempt Trust Massachusetts Muni Bond Fund Class Y	SMSYX	NAS CM	Open End	US Muni Fixed Inc (Muni Bond - Single State)	C+	C	B-	Up	Y	800-342-5734
SEI Tax-Exempt Trust New Jersey Muni Bond Fund Class Y	SNJYX	NAS CM	Open End	US Muni Fixed Inc (Muni Bond - Single State)	C	C	B-		Y	800-342-5734
SEI Tax-Exempt Trust New York Municipal Bond Fund Class Y	SNYYX	NAS CM	Open End	US Muni Fixed Inc (Muni Bond - Single State)	C	C-	C+		Y	800-342-5734
SEI Tax-Exempt Trust Pennsylvania Muni Bond Fund Class Y	SPAYX	NAS CM	Open End	US Muni Fixed Inc (Muni Bond - Single State)	C+	C	B	Up	Y	800-342-5734
Semper MBS Total Return Fund Class A	SEMOX	NAS CM	Open End	Fixed Inc Misc (Govt Bond - Mortgage)	D	D-	D	Down	Y	877-828-8210
Semper MBS Total Return Fund Institutional Shares	SEMMX	NAS CM	Open End	Fixed Inc Misc (Govt Bond - Mortgage)	D	D-	D	Down	Y	877-828-8210
Semper MBS Total Return Fund Investor Shares	SEMPX	NAS CM	Open End	Fixed Inc Misc (Govt Bond - Mortgage)	D	D-	D	Down	Y	877-828-8210
Semper Short Duration Fund Institutional Shares	SEMIX	NAS CM	Open End	US Fixed Inc (Income)	D	D	C-	Down	Y	877-828-8210
Semper Short Duration Fund Investor Shares	SEMRX	NAS CM	Open End	US Fixed Inc (Income)	D	D	C-	Down	Y	877-828-8210
Sextant Bond Income Fund	SBIFX	NAS CM	Open End	US Fixed Inc (Corp Bond - High Quality)	B	C+	B+	Up	Y	
Sextant Short-Term Bond Fund	STBFX	NAS CM	Open End	US Fixed Inc (Corp Bond - High Quality)	C	C	B-		Y	
Shelton Capital Mgmt The U.S. Treas Trust Dir Shares	UTSXX	NAS CM	Money Mkt	US Money Mkt (Money Mkt - Treasury)	C	C-	C+		Y	800-955-9988
Shelton Capital Management U.S. Govt Securities Cl K	CAUKX	NAS CM	Open End	US Fixed Inc (Govt Bond - General)	B-	C+	B		Y	800-955-9988
Shelton Capital Mgmt U.S. Govt Securities Direct Shares	CAUSX	NAS CM	Open End	US Fixed Inc (Govt Bond - General)	B-	C+	B		Y	800-955-9988
Shenkman Capital Floating Rate High Income Fund Class F	SFHFX	NAS CM	Open End	US Fixed Inc (Income)	D+	D	C-	Down	Y	
Shenkman Capital Floating Rate High Income Inst Cl	SFHIX	NAS CM	Open End	US Fixed Inc (Income)	D+	D	C-	Down	Y	
Shenkman Capital Short Duration High Income Fund Class A	SCFAX	NAS CM	Open End	US Fixed Inc (Corp Bond - High Yield)	C	C-	C		Y	
Shenkman Capital Short Duration High Income Fund Class C	SCFCX	NAS CM	Open End	US Fixed Inc (Corp Bond - High Yield)	C-	D+	C		Y	
Shenkman Capital Short Duration High Income Fund Class F	SCFFX	NAS CM	Open End	US Fixed Inc (Corp Bond - High Yield)	C	C-	C		Y	
Shenkman Capital Short Duration High Income Inst Cl	SCFIX	NAS CM	Open End	US Fixed Inc (Corp Bond - High Yield)	C	C-	C		Y	
Sierra Tactical All Asset Fund Class A	SIRAX	NAS CM	Open End	US Fixed Inc (Growth & Income)	C	C-	C		Y	
Sierra Tactical All Asset Fund Class A1	SIRZX	NAS CM	Open End	US Fixed Inc (Growth & Income)	C	C-	C		Y	
Sierra Tactical All Asset Fund Class C	SIRCX	NAS CM	Open End	US Fixed Inc (Growth & Income)	C-	C-	C	Down	Y	
Sierra Tactical All Asset Fund Class I1	SIRJX	NAS CM	Open End	US Fixed Inc (Growth & Income)	C	C-	C		Y	
Sierra Tactical All Asset Fund Institutional Class	SIRRX	NAS CM	Open End	US Fixed Inc (Growth & Income)	C	C-	C		Y	
Sierra Tactical All Asset Fund Investor Class	SIRIX	NAS CM	Open End	US Fixed Inc (Growth & Income)	C	C-	C		Y	
Sierra Tactical Bond Fund Class A Shares	STBKX	NAS CM	Open End	Fixed Inc Misc (Income)	U	U	U		Y	
Sierra Tactical Bond Fund Class C Shares	STBDX	NAS CM	Open End	Fixed Inc Misc (Income)	U	U	U		Y	
Sierra Tactical Bond Fund Instl Class Shares	STBJX	NAS CM	Open End	Fixed Inc Misc (Income)	U	U	U		Y	
Sierra Tactical Bond Fund Investor Class Shares	STBNX	NAS CM	Open End	Fixed Inc Misc (Income)	U	U	U		Y	
Sierra Tactical Core Income Fund Class A	SSIZX	NAS CM	Open End	Fixed Inc Misc (Income)	C	C-	C		Y	
Sierra Tactical Core Income Fund Class C	SSICX	NAS CM	Open End	Fixed Inc Misc (Income)	C	C-	C		Y	
Sierra Tactical Core Income Fund Institutional Class	SSIRX	NAS CM	Open End	Fixed Inc Misc (Income)	C	C-	C+		Y	
Sierra Tactical Core Income Fund Investor Class	SSIIX	NAS CM	Open End	Fixed Inc Misc (Income)	C	C-	C		Y	

★Expanded analysis of this fund is included in Section II.

TOTAL RETURNS & PERFORMANCE									ASSETS		ASSET ALLOCATION & TURNOVER							MINIMUMS		FEES		
3-Month Total Return	6-Month Total Return	1-Year Total Return	3-Year Total Return	5-Year Total Return	Dividend Yield (TTM)	Expense Ratio	3-Yr Std Deviation	Effective Duration	NAV	Total Assets (MIL)	%Cash	%Government Bonds	%Municipal Bonds	%Corporate Bonds	%Other	Turnover Ratio	Average Coupon Rate	Min Initial Investment	Min Additional Investment	Front End Fee (%)	Back End Fee (%)	Inception Date
8.62	-8.25	-5.55	3.38	16.05	5.96	1.12	10		5.97	1,449	5	0	0	89	0	69	6.54	100,000	1,000			Oct-07
8.81	-8.09	-5.05	4.96	18.91	6.44	0.64	10.01		6.2	1,449	5	0	0	89	0	69	6.54	100,000	1,000			Dec-14
2.72	1.90	3.20	6.98	8.28	1.95	0.45	1.89		10.21	261.1	1	99	0	0	0	34	0.42	100,000	1,000			Jul-09
2.74	2.02	3.26	7.27	8.85	2.01	0.35	1.89		10.25	261.1	1	99	0	0	0	34	0.42	100,000	1,000			Dec-14
0.11	0.36	0.95	3.17		1.06	0.3	0.09		10	193.0	35	0	65	0	0		0.28	100,000	1,000			Apr-16
0.13	0.41	1.04	3.47		1.16	0.2	0.09		10	193.0	35	0	65	0	0		0.28	100,000	1,000			Apr-16
3.16	1.51	2.94	8.56	14.00	1.65	0.6	3.9		11.07	327.6	0	0	100	0	0	16	4.81	100,000	1,000			Aug-98
3.10	1.48	2.99	9.04	14.65	1.79	0.45	3.95		11.06	327.6	0	0	100	0	0	16	4.81	100,000	1,000			Oct-15
2.93	1.18	3.06	10.39	17.25	2.31	0.63	4.22		11.96	2,003	1	0	99	0	0	17	4.89	100,000	1,000			Sep-89
2.99	1.30	3.31	11.22	18.77	2.56	0.38	4.22		11.97	2,003	1	0	99	0	0	17	4.89	100,000	1,000			Apr-15
2.77	2.00	3.56	9.06	14.76	1.49	0.63	3.75		10.96	77.8	1	0	99	0	0	15	5.00	100,000	1,000			Aug-98
2.24	1.27	2.67	8.89	14.69	1.91	0.6	3.28		10.67	114.2	1	0	99	0	0	16	4.88	100,000	1,000			Aug-98
2.04	0.87	2.08	7.29	13.05	1.66	0.6	3.67		10.96	180.6	1	0	99	0	0	11	4.96	100,000	1,000			Aug-98
2.47	2.26	4.01	10.51	16.13	1.71	0.63	3.58		11.23	171.9	1	0	99	0	0	14	4.87	100,000	1,000			Aug-98
1.25	0.76	1.52	4.25	4.95	1.28	0.63	1.07		10.09	1,277	6	0	94	0	0	53	2.70	100,000	1,000			Nov-03
1.22	0.79	1.67	4.93	6.14	1.54	0.38	1		10.08	1,277	6	0	94	0	0	53	2.70	100,000	1,000			Apr-15
4.73	-0.87	2.56	12.25	26.94	3.97	0.86	5.82		10.15	1,222	5	0	75	20	0	40	5.33	100,000	1,000			Sep-07
4.79	-0.85	2.81	13.08	28.48	4.23	0.61	5.82		10.14	1,222	5	0	75	20	0	40	5.33	100,000	1,000			Apr-15
2.81	2.08	3.72	9.57	15.43	1.64	0.48	3.77		10.94	77.8	1	0	99	0	0	15	5.00	100,000	1,000			Oct-15
2.28	1.25	2.72	9.27	15.33	2.06	0.45	3.28		10.66	114.2	1	0	99	0	0	16	4.88	100,000	1,000			Oct-15
2.17	0.94	2.33	7.89	13.80	1.81	0.45	3.72		10.95	180.6	1	0	99	0	0	11	4.96	100,000	1,000			Oct-15
2.50	2.33	4.16	11.01	16.93	1.85	0.48	3.56		11.23	171.9	1	0	99	0	0	14	4.87	100,000	1,000			Oct-15
7.21	-14.98	-13.65	-5.48	2.24	5.56	1.02	13.12	1.79	8.66	1,057	-1	0	0	1	0	118	3.34	1,000	100	2.00		Dec-15
7.29	-15.07	-13.62	-5.06	3.14	5.89	0.77	13.22	1.79	8.64	1,057	-1	0	0	1	0	118	3.34	1,000,000	1,000			Jul-13
7.08	-15.00	-13.75	-5.60	1.96	5.56	1.02	13.12	1.79	8.65	1,057	-1	0	0	1	0	118	3.34	2,500	1,000			Jul-13
6.56	-4.20	-2.77	2.81	7.55	2.99	0.61	6.65	1.17	9.36	410.2	7	0	0	1	0	131	3.14	1,000,000	1,000			Dec-10
6.61	-4.21	-2.91	2.21	6.37	2.72	0.86	6.66	1.17	9.37	410.2	7	0	0	1	0	131	3.14	2,500	1,000			Dec-10
5.34	6.86	9.64	18.72	27.05	2.7	0.65	4.83	8.28	5.59	13.5	11	27	5	57	0	32	5.05	1,000	25			Mar-93
2.98	2.83	3.94	7.92	10.64	1.72	0.6	1.86	2.18	5.18	11.5	9	21	0	70	0	32	2.99	1,000	25			Sep-95
0.01	0.24	0.95	3.47	3.47	1.09	0.55	0.17		1	35.7	85	15	0	0	0			1,000	100			Apr-89
-0.03	5.74	6.55	9.85	11.08	0.82	1.26	2.99	4.82	10.99	24.3	1	96	0	0	0	8	2.81	1,000	100			Oct-03
0.09	6.01	7.06	11.62	13.93	1.27	0.76	3.06	4.82	10.97	24.3	1	96	0	0	0	8	2.81	1,000	100			Dec-85
8.48	-4.57	-1.72	6.27	12.92	5.27	0.65	7.8	0.28	8.98	214.2	2	0	0	98	0	28	4.86	1,000	100			Mar-17
8.51	-4.65	-1.69	6.26	13.04	5.29	0.55	7.85	0.28	8.98	214.2	2	0	0	98	0	28	4.86	1,000,000	100,000			Oct-14
4.17	-1.25	0.66	7.60	13.00	3.34	1	3.75	1.65	9.79	616.6	8	0	0	92	0	77	5.87	1,000	100	3.00		Oct-12
4.00	-1.62	-0.08	5.24	8.84	2.6	1.75	3.76	1.65	9.76	616.6	8	0	0	92	0	77	5.87	1,000	100		1.00	Jan-14
4.25	-1.14	1.00	8.36	14.34	3.57	0.75	3.72	1.65	9.77	616.6	8	0	0	92	0	77	5.87	1,000	100			May-13
4.27	-1.09	1.08	8.73	14.82	3.65	0.65	3.72	1.65	9.78	616.6	8	0	0	92	0	77	5.87	1,000,000	100,000			Oct-12
2.52	-0.92	0.89	6.50	12.06	2	2.4	3.98	8.68	22.96	631.9	36	30	20	2	2	320	3.63	10,000	1,000	5.75		Dec-07
2.45	-0.99	0.73	6.01	11.20	1.83	2.55	3.93	8.68	23.2	631.9	36	30	20	2	2	320	3.63	10,000	1,000	5.75		Jun-12
2.28	-1.29	0.13	4.10	7.90	1.29	3.15	3.97	8.68	23.12	631.9	36	30	20	2	2	320	3.63	10,000	1,000			Feb-10
2.46	-1.00	0.76	6.04	11.23	1.82	2.55	3.97	8.68	23.11	631.9	36	30	20	2	2	320	3.63	10,000	1,000			Jun-12
2.56	-0.81	1.16	7.27	13.44	2.27	2.15	3.97	8.68	22.76	631.9	36	30	20	2	2	320	3.63	100,000	1,000			Dec-07
2.48	-0.88	0.80	6.40	11.95	2	2.4	3.96	8.68	22.91	631.9	36	30	20	2	2	320	3.63	10,000	1,000			Dec-07
1.85	8.91					2.09		18.93	27.26	694.2	3	97	0	0	0		2.96	10,000	1,000	5.75		Oct-19
1.64	8.59					2.84		18.93	27.24	694.2	3	97	0	0	0		2.96	10,000	1,000		1.00	Oct-19
1.89	9.05					1.84		18.93	27.27	694.2	3	97	0	0	0		2.96	10,000	1,000			Oct-19
1.81	8.83					2.24		18.93	27.26	694.2	3	97	0	0	0		2.96	10,000	1,000			Oct-19
2.36	-0.82	1.33	7.97	17.03	2.61	2.01	3.46	9.03	21.17	1,534	44	34	15	1	0	221	3.42	10,000	1,000	5.75		Dec-11
2.23	-1.10	0.75	6.07	13.56	2.04	2.61	3.49	9.03	21.11	1,534	44	34	15	1	0	221	3.42	10,000	1,000			Dec-11
2.47	-0.63	1.73	9.25	19.10	3.02	1.62	3.48	9.03	21.07	1,534	44	34	15	1	0	221	3.42	100,000				Dec-11
2.36	-0.82	1.32	7.94	17.00	2.6	2.01	3.48	9.03	21.2	1,534	44	34	15	1	0	221	3.42	10,000	1,000			Dec-11

Fund Name	Ticker Symbol	Traded On	Fund Type	Category and (Prospectus Objective)	Overall Rating	Reward Rating	Risk Rating	Recent Up/ Downgrade	Open to New Investors	Telephone
Sierra Tactical Municipal Fund Class A Shares	STMKX	NAS CM	Open End	US Muni Fixed Inc (Muni Bond - Natl)	D	D	C		Y	
Sierra Tactical Municipal Fund Class C Shares	STMHX	NAS CM	Open End	US Muni Fixed Inc (Muni Bond - Natl)	D	D	C-		Y	
Sierra Tactical Municipal Fund Class Class Special Shares	STMYX	NAS CM	Open End	US Muni Fixed Inc (Muni Bond - Natl)	D	D	C		Y	
Sierra Tactical Municipal Fund Institutional Shares	STMEX	NAS CM	Open End	US Muni Fixed Inc (Muni Bond - Natl)	D	D	C		Y	
Sierra Tactical Municipal Fund Investor Shares	STMNX	NAS CM	Open End	US Muni Fixed Inc (Muni Bond - Natl)	D	D	C		Y	
SIM Income Fund Class Z Shares	SIMZX	NAS CM	Open End	US Fixed Inc (Income)	D	D	C		Y	888-802-0427
Sit Minnesota Tax-Free Income Fund	SMTFX	NAS CM	Open End	US Muni Fixed Inc (Muni Bond - Single State)	C	C-	C+		Y	800-332-5580
Sit Quality Income Fund	SQIFX	NAS CM	Open End	US Fixed Inc (Income)	C	C-	B-		Y	800-332-5580
Sit Tax-Free Income Fund	SNTIX	NAS CM	Open End	US Muni Fixed Inc (Muni Bond - Natl)	C	C-	C+		Y	800-332-5580
Sit U.S. Government Securities Fund	SNGVX	NAS CM	Open End	US Fixed Inc (Govt Bond - General)	C+	C	B		Y	800-332-5580
Sit U.S. Government Securities Fund - Class Y	SNGYX	NAS CM	Open End	US Fixed Inc (Govt Bond - General)	C+	C	B		Y	800-332-5580
Spectrum Low Volatility Fund Investor Class	SVARX	NAS CM	Open End	Fixed Inc Misc (Growth & Income)	B	B	A-		Y	
Spirit of America Income Fund Class A	SOAIX	NAS CM	Open End	US Fixed Inc (Income)	C	C-	C+		Y	
Spirit of America Income Fund Class C	SACTX	NAS CM	Open End	US Fixed Inc (Income)	C	C-	C+		Y	
Spirit of America Income Fund Institutional Shares	SOITX	NAS CM	Open End	US Fixed Inc (Income)	C	C-	C+		Y	
Spirit of America Municipal Tax Free Bond Fund Class A	SOAMX	NAS CM	Open End	US Muni Fixed Inc (Muni Bond - Natl)	C	C	B-		Y	
Spirit of America Municipal Tax Free Bond Fund Class C	SACFX	NAS CM	Open End	US Muni Fixed Inc (Muni Bond - Natl)	C	C-	C+		Y	
Spirit of America Muni Tax Free Bond Institutional Shares	SOIMX	NAS CM	Open End	US Muni Fixed Inc (Muni Bond - Natl)	C	C	B-		Y	
State Farm Interim Fund	SFITX	NAS CM	Open End	US Fixed Inc (Corp Bond - High Quality)	B-	C+	B	Up	Y	
State Farm Municipal Bond Fund	SFBDX	NAS CM	Open End	US Muni Fixed Inc (Muni Bond - Natl)	B-	C	B	Up	Y	
State Street Active Core Bond Fund Investment Class	SSFIX	NAS CM	Open End	US Fixed Inc (Income)	B	C+	B+	Up	Y	617-664-7338
State Street Active Core Bond Fund Service Class	SSFSX	NAS CM	Open End	US Fixed Inc (Income)	B	C+	B+	Up	Y	617-664-7338
State Street Aggregate Bond Index Fund Class A	SSFCX	NAS CM	Open End	US Fixed Inc (Growth & Income)	B	B-	B	Up	Y	617-664-7338
State Street Aggregate Bond Index Fund Class I	SSFDX	NAS CM	Open End	US Fixed Inc (Growth & Income)	B	B-	B+	Up	Y	617-664-7338
State Street Aggregate Bond Index Fund Class K	SSFEX	NAS CM	Open End	US Fixed Inc (Growth & Income)	B	B-	B+		Y	617-664-7338
State Street Aggregate Bond Index Portfolio	SSAFX	NAS CM	Open End	US Fixed Inc (Growth & Income)	B	B-	B+		Y	617-664-7338
State Street ESG Liquid Reserves Fund Institutional Class	ELFXX	NAS CM	Money Mkt	US Money Mkt (Money Mkt - General)	U	U	U		Y	617-664-7338
State Street ESG Liquid Reserves Fund Investor Class	ENVXX	NAS CM	Money Mkt	US Money Mkt (Money Mkt - General)	U	U	U		Y	617-664-7338
State Street ESG Liquid Reserves Fund Premier Class	ELRXX	NAS CM	Money Mkt	US Money Mkt (Money Mkt - General)	U	U	U		Y	617-664-7338
State Street Institutional Liquid Reserves Admin Cl	SSYXX	NAS CM	Money Mkt	US Money Mkt (Money Mkt - General)	C	C-	C+		Y	617-664-7338
State Street Inst Liquid Reserves Inst Cl	SSHXX	NAS CM	Money Mkt	US Money Mkt (Money Mkt - General)	C	C-	C+		Y	617-664-7338
State Street Institutional Liquid Reserves Investment Cl	SSVXX	NAS CM	Money Mkt	US Money Mkt (Money Mkt - General)	C	C	C+		Y	617-664-7338
State Street Institutional Liquid Reserves Investor Cl	SSZXX	NAS CM	Money Mkt	US Money Mkt (Money Mkt - General)	C	C-	C+		Y	617-664-7338
State Street Institutional Liquid Reserves Premier Cl	SSIXX	NAS CM	Money Mkt	US Money Mkt (Money Mkt - General)	C	C-	C+		Y	617-664-7338
State Street Institutional Liquid Reserves Trust Cl	TILXX	NAS CM	Money Mkt	US Money Mkt (Money Mkt - General)	C	C-	C+		Y	617-664-7338
State Street Institutional Treasury Money Mkt Admin Cl	SSKXX	NAS CM	Money Mkt	US Money Mkt (Money Mkt - Treasury)	C	C-	C+		Y	617-664-7338
State Street Inst Treas Money Mkt Inst Cl	SSJXX	NAS CM	Money Mkt	US Money Mkt (Money Mkt - Treasury)	C	C-	C+		Y	617-664-7338
State Street Inst Treas Money Mkt Inv Cl	TRVXX	NAS CM	Money Mkt	US Money Mkt (Money Mkt - Treasury)	C	C-	C		Y	617-664-7338
State Street Institutional Treasury Money Mkt Investor Cl	SSNXX	NAS CM	Money Mkt	US Money Mkt (Money Mkt - Treasury)	C	C-	C+		Y	617-664-7338
State Street Institutional Treasury Money Mkt Premier Cl	TRIXX	NAS CM	Money Mkt	US Money Mkt (Money Mkt - Treasury)	C	C-	C+		Y	617-664-7338
State Street Inst Treas Plus Money Mkt Admin Cl	SSQXX	NAS CM	Money Mkt	US Money Mkt (Money Mkt - Treasury)	C	C-	C+		Y	617-664-7338
State Street Inst Treas Plus Money Mkt Inst Cl	SAJXX	NAS CM	Money Mkt	US Money Mkt (Money Mkt - Treasury)	C	C-	C+		Y	617-664-7338
State Street Inst Treas Plus Money Mkt Inv Cl	TPVXX	NAS CM	Money Mkt	US Money Mkt (Money Mkt - Treasury)	C	C-	C+		Y	617-664-7338
State Street Inst Treas Plus Money Mkt Investor Cl	SAEXX	NAS CM	Money Mkt	US Money Mkt (Money Mkt - Treasury)	C	C-	C+		Y	617-664-7338
State Street Inst Treas Plus Money Mkt Trust Cl	TPLXX	NAS CM	Money Mkt	US Money Mkt (Money Mkt - Treasury)	C	C-	C+		Y	617-664-7338
★ State Street Institutional U.S. Govt Money Mkt Admin Cl	SALXX	NAS CM	Money Mkt	US Money Mkt (Money Mkt - Govt)	C	C-	C+		Y	617-664-7338
State Street Institutional U.S. Govt Money Mkt Cl G	SSOXX	NAS CM	Money Mkt	US Money Mkt (Money Mkt - Govt)	C	C	B-		Y	617-664-7338
State Street Institutional U.S. Govt Money Mkt Cl M	GOMXX	NAS CM	Money Mkt	US Money Mkt (Money Mkt - Govt)	U	U	U		Y	617-664-7338
State Street Inst U.S. Govt Money Mkt Inst Cl	SAHXX	NAS CM	Money Mkt	US Money Mkt (Money Mkt - Govt)	C	C-	C+		Y	617-664-7338
State Street Inst U.S. Govt Money Mkt Inv Cl	GVVXX	NAS CM	Money Mkt	US Money Mkt (Money Mkt - Govt)	C	C-	C+		Y	617-664-7338
State Street Institutional U.S. Govt Money Mkt Investor Cl	SAMXX	NAS CM	Money Mkt	US Money Mkt (Money Mkt - Govt)	C	C-	C+		Y	617-664-7338
State Street Institutional U.S. Govt Money Mkt Premier Cl	GVMXX	NAS CM	Money Mkt	US Money Mkt (Money Mkt - Govt)	C	C-	C+		Y	617-664-7338

★ Expanded analysis of this fund is included in Section II.

TOTAL RETURNS & PERFORMANCE									ASSETS		ASSET ALLOCATION & TURNOVER							MINIMUMS		FEES		
3-Month Total Return	6-Month Total Return	1-Year Total Return	3-Year Total Return	5-Year Total Return	Dividend Yield (TTM)	Expense Ratio	3-Yr Std Deviation	Effective Duration	NAV	Total Assets (MIL)	%Cash	%Government Bonds	%Municipal Bonds	%Corporate Bonds	%Other	Turnover Ratio	Average Coupon Rate	Min Initial Investment	Min Additional Investment	Front End Fee (%)	Back End Fee (%)	Inception Date
3.62	-1.34	0.95			2.2	1.82		5.63	25.76	196.4	53	0	46	0	2	26	4.82	10,000	1,000	5.75		Dec-18
3.40	-1.68	0.32				2.57		5.63	25.64	196.4	53	0	46	0	2	26	4.82	10,000	1,000			Sep-19
3.67	-1.12	1.29			2.56	1.51		5.63	25.72	196.4	53	0	46	0	2	26	4.82	10,000	1,000			Dec-18
3.66	-1.20	1.20			2.52	1.57		5.63	25.68	196.4	53	0	46	0	2	26	4.82	10,000	1,000			Dec-18
3.56	-1.42	0.77			1.71	1.97		5.63	25.76	196.4	53	0	46	0	2	26	4.82	10,000	1,000			Dec-18
1.09	-1.64	-0.89			0.69	2.32		4.17	10.15	9.4	39	32	0	26	0		2.88	500	500			Dec-18
2.14	-0.13	1.81	10.30	17.64	2.9	0.82	4.2	5.60	10.51	622.8	1	0	99	0	0	10	4.36	5,000	100			Dec-93
1.51	1.57	2.82	6.14	7.42	1.64	0.91	1.07	1.70	9.94	93.9	28	9	11	12	0	118	3.74	5,000	100			Dec-12
1.98	-0.40	1.67	11.21	21.94	3	0.89	4.53	6.00	9.68	310.3	2	0	97	0	0	14	4.55	5,000	100			Sep-88
0.43	3.58	4.31	9.57	11.86	1.92	0.8	1.49	3.00	11.26	442.0	2	4	0	0	0	30	6.38	5,000	100			Jun-87
0.49	3.69	4.43	9.68	11.98		0.55	1.5	3.00	11.26	442.0	2	4	0	0	0	30	6.38	1,000,000	100			Jan-20
8.83	10.57	12.13	23.07	49.35	2.75	2.95	4.03	2.14	23.53	108.4	73	0	0	28	-2	675	5.75	1,000	500			Dec-13
5.21	-0.69	2.45	13.43	25.36	4.37	1.11	6.03	6.67	11.87	127.5	5	0	70	24	0	3	6.29	500	50	4.75		Dec-08
4.94	-1.13	1.61	10.84	20.46	3.6	1.86	6.03	6.67	11.87	127.5	5	0	70	24	0	3	6.29	500	50		1.00	Mar-16
5.41	-0.50	2.64	13.65	25.60		0.86	6.03	6.67	11.91	127.5	5	0	70	24	0	3	6.29	100,000	10,000			May-20
1.31	1.36	2.91	9.36	17.79	2.81	0.92	2.64	4.33	9.47	67.1	1	0	99	0	0	6	4.63	500	50	4.75		Feb-08
1.43	1.16	2.27	6.85	12.85	1.96	1.77	2.62	4.33	9.45	67.1	1	0	99	0	0	6	4.63	500	50		1.00	Mar-16
1.55	1.59	3.15	9.61	18.06		0.77	2.64	4.33	9.45	67.1	1	0	99	0	0	6	4.63	100,000	10,000			May-20
0.22	3.92	5.13	9.70	11.36	1.59	0.18	1.81	2.57	10.42	434.6	8	92	0	0	0	20	1.97	250	50			Nov-77
2.34	3.36	5.25	12.49	18.77	2.57	0.16	2.85	4.47	9	713.6	1	0	99	0	0	14	3.82	250	50			Nov-77
4.46	5.35	7.97	15.85	24.09	2.8	0.26	3.32		9.86	117.5	14	33	0	26	0	438	3.08	5,000,000				Nov-97
4.16	4.98	9.18	16.53	24.16	3.82	0.51	3.35		10.12	117.5	14	33	0	26	0	438	3.08	5,000,000				Sep-05
3.03	6.18	8.53	15.51	21.19	2.3	0.48	3.31	5.75	106.35	294.5	2	42	1	26	0	69	3.14	2,000		3.75		Sep-14
3.15	6.37	8.82	16.52	22.99	2.6	0.23	3.32	5.75	106.09	294.5	2	42	1	26	0	69	3.14	0				Sep-14
3.11	6.47	9.06	16.78	23.17	2.7	0.03	3.36	5.75	106.09	294.5	2	42	1	26	0	69	3.14	0				Sep-14
2.93	6.24	8.86	16.71	23.29	2.57	0.03	3.35	6.02	107.88	513.8	3	41	1	27	0	90	3.13	0				Sep-14
0.25	0.50					0.15			1.0004	623.7	100	0	0	0	0			25,000,000				Dec-19
0.23	0.48					0.2			1.0004	623.7	100	0	0	0	0			10,000,000				Dec-19
0.25	0.51					0.12			1.0003	623.7	100	0	0	0	0			25,000,000				Dec-19
0.19	0.40	1.31	4.75	5.46	1.46	0.37	0.19		1.0003	17,012	96	0	0	1	0			1,000				Aug-16
0.26	0.53	1.54	5.51	6.52	1.68	0.15			1.0005	17,012	96	0	0	1	0			25,000,000				Jul-18
0.18	0.39	1.26	4.53	4.91	1.41	0.47	0.19		1.0004	17,012	96	0	0	1	0			250				Oct-07
0.24	0.50	1.50	5.34	6.35	1.63	0.2			1.0004	17,012	96	0	0	1	0			10,000,000				Jul-17
0.25	0.52	1.56	5.54	6.56	1.71	0.12	0.19		1.0004	17,012	96	0	0	1	0			250,000,000				Aug-04
0.24	0.51	1.50	5.36	6.29	1.65	0.18	0.19		1.0004	17,012	96	0	0	1	0			15,000,000				Aug-16
0.00	0.29	1.10	4.24	4.61	1.26	0.37			1	19,994	100	0	0	0	0			1,000				Jul-18
0.04	0.37	1.30	4.72	5.19	1.47	0.15			1	19,994	100	0	0	0	0			25,000,000				Jul-18
0.00	0.26	1.04	3.76	3.86	1.2	0.42	0.17		1	19,994	100	0	0	0	0			250				Oct-07
0.03	0.35	1.25	4.52	4.97	1.42	0.2	0.17		1	19,994	100	0	0	0	0			10,000,000				Dec-16
0.05	0.38	1.32	4.78	5.25	1.5	0.12	0.17		1	19,994	100	0	0	0	0			250,000,000				Oct-07
0.00	0.26	1.09	3.90	4.01	1.25	0.37			1	6,134	100	0	0	0	0			1,000				Jul-18
0.04	0.35	1.29	4.31	4.41	1.46	0.15			1	6,134	100	0	0	0	0			2,000	100			Jul-18
0.00	0.24	1.02	3.81	3.92	1.19	0.47	0.18		1	6,134	100	0	0	0	0			250				Oct-07
0.02	0.33	1.23	4.53	4.81	1.41	0.2	0.18		1	6,134	100	0	0	0	0			10,000,000				Oct-16
0.03	0.34	1.26	4.61	4.93	1.43	0.18	0.18		1	6,134	100	0	0	0	0			15,000,000				Aug-16
0.00	0.26	1.10	4.06	4.25	1.26	0.37	0.18		1	104,933	100	0	0	0	0			1,000				Aug-16
0.05	0.38	1.37	4.94	5.57	1.54	0.08	0.18		1	104,933	100	0	0	0	0			1 Billion				Oct-14
0.45	0.87	1.46	2.05	2.05	1.41	0.1				48,435	58	36	0	0	3			750,000,000				Nov-16
0.03	0.35	1.28	4.33	4.47	1.44	0.15			1	104,933	100	0	0	0	0			2,000	100			Jan-18
0.00	0.25	1.04	3.80	3.94	1.2	0.47	0.17		1	104,933	100	0	0	0	0			250				Oct-07
0.02	0.33	1.25	4.57	4.94	1.42	0.2	0.18		1	104,933	100	0	0	0	0			10,000,000				Mar-16
0.03	0.35	1.32	4.81	5.38	1.5	0.12	0.18		1	104,933	100	0	0	0	0			250,000,000				Oct-07

	MARKET		FUND TYPE, CATEGORY & OBJECTIVE		RATINGS				NEW INVESTORS	
Fund Name	Ticker Symbol	Traded On	Fund Type	Category and (Prospectus Objective)	Overall Rating	Reward Rating	Risk Rating	Recent Up/ Downgrade	Open to New Investors	Telephone
State Street Treasury Obligations Money Market Fund	TAQXX	NAS CM	Money Mkt	US Money Mkt (Money Mkt - Treasury)	U	U	U		Y	617-664-7338
Sterling Capital Corporate Fund Class A Shares	SCCMX	NAS CM	Open End	US Fixed Inc (Income)	C+	C	B	Up	Y	800-228-1872
Sterling Capital Corporate Fund Class C Shares	SCCNX	NAS CM	Open End	US Fixed Inc (Income)	C	C	B-		Y	800-228-1872
Sterling Capital Corporate Fund Institutional shares	SCCPX	NAS CM	Open End	US Fixed Inc (Income)	C+	C	B	Up	Y	800-228-1872
Sterling Capital Intermediate U.S. Government Fund Class A	BGVAX	NAS CM	Open End	US Fixed Inc (Govt Bond - General)	B-	C+	B	Up	Y	800-228-1872
Sterling Capital Intermediate U.S. Government Fund Class C	BIUCX	NAS CM	Open End	US Fixed Inc (Govt Bond - General)	C+	C	B-		Y	800-228-1872
Sterling Capital Intermed U.S. Govt Inst Shares	BBGVX	NAS CM	Open End	US Fixed Inc (Govt Bond - General)	B-	C+	B		Y	800-228-1872
Sterling Capital Kentucky Intermediate Tax-Free C Shares	BKCAX	NAS CM	Open End	US Muni Fixed Inc (Muni Bond - Single State)	C	C	B-		Y	800-228-1872
Sterling Capital Kentucky Intermediate Tax-Free Cl A	BKTAX	NAS CM	Open End	US Muni Fixed Inc (Muni Bond - Single State)	C	C	B-		Y	800-228-1872
Sterling Capital Kentucky Intermed Tax-Free Inst Shares	BKITX	NAS CM	Open End	US Muni Fixed Inc (Muni Bond - Single State)	C+	C	B	Up	Y	800-228-1872
Sterling Capital Maryland Intermediate Tax-Free C Shares	BMDCX	NAS CM	Open End	US Muni Fixed Inc (Muni Bond - Single State)	C	C	C+		Y	800-228-1872
Sterling Capital Maryland Intermediate Tax-Free Cl A	BMAAX	NAS CM	Open End	US Muni Fixed Inc (Muni Bond - Single State)	C	C	B-		Y	800-228-1872
Sterling Capital Maryland Intermed Tax-Free Inst Shares	BMAIX	NAS CM	Open End	US Muni Fixed Inc (Muni Bond - Single State)	C+	C	B-	Up	Y	800-228-1872
Sterling Capital North Carolina Intermed Tax-Free C Shares	BBNCX	NAS CM	Open End	US Muni Fixed Inc (Muni Bond - Single State)	C	C	B-		Y	800-228-1872
Sterling Capital North Carolina Intermediate Tax-Free Cl A	BNCAX	NAS CM	Open End	US Muni Fixed Inc (Muni Bond - Single State)	C+	C	B	Up	Y	800-228-1872
Sterling Capital SC Intermed Tax-Free Inst Shares	BBNTX	NAS CM	Open End	US Muni Fixed Inc (Muni Bond - Single State)	C+	C	B	Up	Y	800-228-1872
Sterling Capital Quality Income Fund Class A Shares	SCSSX	NAS CM	Open End	US Fixed Inc (Income)	B-	C	B	Up	Y	800-228-1872
Sterling Capital Quality Income Fund Class C Shares	SCSTX	NAS CM	Open End	US Fixed Inc (Income)	C+	C	B	Up	Y	800-228-1872
Sterling Capital Quality Income Fund Institutional Shares	SCSPX	NAS CM	Open End	US Fixed Inc (Income)	B-	C	B	Up	Y	800-228-1872
Sterling Capital Short Duration Bond Fund Class A	BSGAX	NAS CM	Open End	US Fixed Inc (Growth & Income)	C	C	B-		Y	800-228-1872
Sterling Capital Short Duration Bond Fund Class C	BBSCX	NAS CM	Open End	US Fixed Inc (Growth & Income)	C	C	C+		Y	800-228-1872
Sterling Capital Short Duration Bond Fund Class I	BBSGX	NAS CM	Open End	US Fixed Inc (Growth & Income)	C	C	B-		Y	800-228-1872
Sterling Capital South Carolina Intermediate Tax Free Cl A	BASCX	NAS CM	Open End	US Muni Fixed Inc (Muni Bond - Single State)	C+	C	B-	Up	Y	800-228-1872
Sterling Capital SC Intermed Tax Free Inst Shares	BSCIX	NAS CM	Open End	US Muni Fixed Inc (Muni Bond - Single State)	C+	C	B	Up	Y	800-228-1872
Sterling Capital South Carolina Intermed Tax-Free C Shares	BSCCX	NAS CM	Open End	US Muni Fixed Inc (Muni Bond - Single State)	C	C	C+		Y	800-228-1872
Sterling Capital Total Return Bond Fund Class A	BICAX	NAS CM	Open End	US Fixed Inc (Growth & Income)	B	C+	B+	Up	Y	800-228-1872
Sterling Capital Total Return Bond Fund Class C	BICCX	NAS CM	Open End	US Fixed Inc (Growth & Income)	B-	C+	B	Up	Y	800-228-1872
Sterling Capital Total Return Bond Fund Class R	BICRX	NAS CM	Open End	US Fixed Inc (Growth & Income)	B-	C+	B+	Up	Y	800-228-1872
Sterling Capital Total Return Bond Fund Class R6	STRDX	NAS CM	Open End	US Fixed Inc (Growth & Income)	B	C+	B+	Up	Y	800-228-1872
Sterling Capital Total Return Bond Institutional Shares	BIBTX	NAS CM	Open End	US Fixed Inc (Growth & Income)	B	C+	B+	Up	Y	800-228-1872
Sterling Capital Ultra Short Bond Fund Class A Shares	BUSRX	NAS CM	Open End	US Fixed Inc (Growth & Income)	C	C-	C+		Y	800-228-1872
Sterling Capital Ultra Short Bond Institutional Shares	BUSIX	NAS CM	Open End	US Fixed Inc (Growth & Income)	C	C-	B-		Y	800-228-1872
Sterling Capital Virginia Intermediate Tax-Free C Shares	BVACX	NAS CM	Open End	US Muni Fixed Inc (Muni Bond - Single State)	C	C	B-		Y	800-228-1872
Sterling Capital Virginia Intermediate Tax-Free Cl A	BVAAX	NAS CM	Open End	US Muni Fixed Inc (Muni Bond - Single State)	C+	C	B	Up	Y	800-228-1872
Sterling Capital Virginia Intermed Tax-Free Inst Shares	BVATX	NAS CM	Open End	US Muni Fixed Inc (Muni Bond - Single State)	C+	C	B	Up	Y	800-228-1872
Sterling Capital West Virginia Intermed Tax-Free C Shares	BWVCX	NAS CM	Open End	US Muni Fixed Inc (Muni Bond - Single State)	C	C	B-		Y	800-228-1872
Sterling Capital West Virginia Intermediate Tax-Free Cl A	BWVAX	NAS CM	Open End	US Muni Fixed Inc (Muni Bond - Single State)	C+	C	B	Up	Y	800-228-1872
Sterling Capital West Virginia Intermed Tax-Free Inst Cl	OWVAX	NAS CM	Open End	US Muni Fixed Inc (Muni Bond - Single State)	C+	C	B	Up	Y	800-228-1872
Stone Harbor Emerg Mkts Corp Debt Fund Institutional Class	SHCDX	NAS CM	Open End	Emerg Mkts Fixed Inc (Diversified Emerg Mkts)	D+	D	C-	Down	Y	323-277-2777
Stone Harbor Emerg Mkts Debt Allocation Inst Cl Shares	SHADX	NAS CM	Open End	Emerg Mkts Fixed Inc (Diversified Emerg Mkts)	D	D	D+	Down	Y	323-277-2777
Stone Harbor Emerg Mkts Debt Fund Institutional Class	SHMDX	NAS CM	Open End	Emerg Mkts Fixed Inc (Diversified Emerg Mkts)	D	D	D+	Down	Y	323-277-2777
Stone Harbor Emerging Markets Income Fund	EDF	NYSE	Closed End	Emerg Mkts Fixed Inc (Worldwide Bond)	D-	D-	D	Down	Y	212-548-1200
Stone Harbor Emerging Markets Total Income Fund	EDI	NYSE	Closed End	Emerg Mkts Fixed Inc (Growth & Income)	D-	D-	D	Down	Y	212-548-1200
Stone Harbor High Yield Bond Fund Institutional Class	SHHYX	NAS CM	Open End	US Fixed Inc (Corp Bond - High Yield)	C-	D+	C		Y	323-277-2777
Stone Harbor Investment Grade Fund Institutional Class	SHIGX	NAS CM	Open End	US Fixed Inc (Growth & Income)	B-	C	B	Up	Y	323-277-2777
Stone Harbor Local Markets Fund Institutional Class	SHLMX	NAS CM	Open End	Emerg Mkts Fixed Inc (Growth & Income)	D	D	D+	Down	Y	323-277-2777
Stone Harbor Strategic Income Fund Institutional Class	SHSIX	NAS CM	Open End	US Fixed Inc (Growth & Income)	C-	D+	C		Y	323-277-2777
Strategic Advisers® Core Income Fund	FPCIX	NAS CM	Open End	US Fixed Inc (Income)	B	C+	B+	Up	Y	617-563-7000
Strategic Advisers® Fidelity® Core Income Fund	FIWGX	NAS CM	Open End	US Fixed Inc (Income)	D+	D+	B	Up	Y	617-563-7000
Strategic Advisers® Income Opportunities Fund	FPIOX	NAS CM	Open End	US Fixed Inc (Income)	C-	D+	C		Y	617-563-7000
Strategic Advisers® Short Duration Fund	FAUDX	NAS CM	Open End	US Fixed Inc (Growth & Income)	C	C	B-		Y	617-563-7000
Strategic Advisers® Tax-Sensitive Short Duration Fund	FGNSX	NAS CM	Open End	US Muni Fixed Inc (Income)	C	C-	C+		Y	617-563-7000

★ Expanded analysis of this fund is included in Section II.

TOTAL RETURNS & PERFORMANCE									ASSETS		ASSET ALLOCATION & TURNOVER							MINIMUMS		FEES		
3-Month Total Return	6-Month Total Return	1-Year Total Return	3-Year Total Return	5-Year Total Return	Dividend Yield (TTM)	Expense Ratio	3-Yr Std Deviation	Effective Duration	NAV	Total Assets (MIL)	%Cash	%Government Bonds	%Municipal Bonds	%Corporate Bonds	%Other	Turnover Ratio	Average Coupon Rate	Min Initial Investment	Min Additional Investment	Front End Fee (%)	Back End Fee (%)	Inception Date
0.15	0.28					0.1				2,998								1 Billion				Oct-17
9.29	3.04	5.91	13.91	21.80	2.61	0.9	5.96	4.24	10.61	20.1	2	0	0	97	0		3.98	1,000	0	2.00		Feb-13
9.01	2.57	5.16	11.48	17.35	1.9	1.65	5.91	4.24	10.59	20.1	2	0	0	97	0		3.98	1,000	0		1.00	Feb-13
9.35	3.17	6.28	14.76	23.32	2.86	0.65	5.94	4.24	10.61	20.1	2	0	0	97	0		3.98	1,000,000	0			Jun-11
0.78	4.30	5.61	10.12	12.09	2.47	0.75	2.4	3.53	10.15	13.2	3	32	3	0	0		3.89	1,000	0	2.00		Oct-92
0.50	3.92	4.73	7.69	7.88	1.74	1.5	2.46	3.53	10.13	13.2	3	32	3	0	0		3.89	1,000	0		1.00	Feb-01
0.84	4.42	5.87	10.95	13.39	2.72	0.5	2.39	3.53	10.16	13.2	3	32	3	0	0		3.89	1,000,000	0			Oct-92
1.89	1.95	3.22	6.89	10.43	1.07	1.71	3.03	4.73	10.46	11.8	5	0	95	0	0		4.65	1,000	0		1.00	Feb-12
1.93	2.23	3.79	8.52	13.64	1.6	0.96	3.07	4.73	10.45	11.8	5	0	95	0	0		4.65	1,000	0	2.00		Feb-03
1.99	2.26	4.05	9.33	14.96	1.85	0.71	3.06	4.73	10.43	11.8	5	0	95	0	0		4.65	1,000,000	0			Feb-03
1.77	1.91	3.09	6.05	9.30	0.93	1.69	3.15	4.82	11.05	12.5	5	0	95	0	0	21	4.71	1,000	0		1.00	Feb-12
1.95	2.28	3.85	8.46	13.56	1.67	0.94	3.1	4.82	11.05	12.5	5	0	95	0	0	21	4.71	1,000	0	2.00		Feb-03
2.01	2.41	4.20	9.37	14.98	1.91	0.69	3.11	4.82	11.07	12.5	5	0	95	0	0	21	4.71	1,000,000	0			Feb-03
2.12	2.12	3.38	6.92	10.09	1.08	1.55	3.18	4.96	11.07	170.8	6	0	94	0	0	5	4.95	1,000	0		1.00	Feb-12
2.31	2.59	4.15	9.34	14.38	1.82	0.8	3.14	4.96	11.08	170.8	6	0	94	0	0	5	4.95	1,000	0	2.00		Oct-92
2.37	2.71	4.41	10.16	15.82	2.07	0.55	3.14	4.96	11.08	170.8	6	0	94	0	0	5	4.95	1,000,000	0			Oct-92
2.08	3.34	4.91	11.92	17.49	2.55	0.85	2.48	2.93	10.23	37.1	1	0	0	1	0	13	3.65	1,000	0	2.00		Feb-13
1.91	2.99	4.28	9.47	13.33	1.85	1.6	2.5	2.93	10.23	37.1	1	0	0	1	0	13	3.65	1,000	0		1.00	Feb-13
2.14	3.46	5.28	12.74	19.06	2.81	0.6	2.48	2.93	10.25	37.1	1	0	0	1	0	13	3.65	1,000,000	0			Jun-11
3.88	2.43	3.96	8.60	11.47	2.43	0.68	2.15	1.81	8.76	170.5	1	2	10	58	0	30	3.06	1,000	0	2.00		Nov-92
3.69	2.17	3.19	6.19	7.38	1.68	1.43	2.17	1.81	8.76	170.5	1	2	10	58	0	30	3.06	1,000	0		1.00	Feb-12
3.94	2.56	4.21	9.42	12.86	2.67	0.43	2.15	1.81	8.76	170.5	1	2	10	58	0	30	3.06	1,000,000	0			Nov-92
2.21	2.58	4.07	9.10	14.16	1.79	0.81	3.11	4.57	11.45	83.2	3	0	97	0	0	0	4.84	1,000	0	2.00		Oct-97
2.29	2.62	4.25	9.84	15.63	2.04	0.56	3.09	4.57	11.37	83.2	3	0	97	0	0	0	4.84	1,000,000	0			Oct-97
2.03	2.11	3.21	6.58	9.88	1.05	1.56	3.13	4.57	11.44	83.2	3	0	97	0	0	0	4.84	1,000	0		1.00	Feb-12
5.10	5.68	8.14	16.35	24.15	2.64	0.7	3.75	5.39	11.29	1,637	2	1	4	44	0	62	3.65	1,000	0	5.75		Dec-99
4.90	5.38	7.33	13.76	19.58	1.9	1.45	3.75	5.39	11.31	1,637	2	1	4	44	0	62	3.65	1,000	0		1.00	Feb-01
5.05	5.56	7.90	15.53	22.69	2.39	0.95	3.76	5.39	11.25	1,637	2	1	4	44	0	62	3.65	1,000	0			Feb-10
5.09	5.85	8.41	17.38	25.87	2.97	0.35	3.77	5.39	11.29	1,637	2	1	4	44	0	62	3.65	0				Feb-18
5.06	5.80	8.31	17.11	25.58	2.88	0.45	3.76	5.39	11.29	1,637	2	1	4	44	0	62	3.65	1,000,000	0			Dec-99
2.50	1.12	2.24	6.00	7.85	2.09	0.7	1.48	0.70	9.8	23.7	18	0	0	55	0	75	3.06	1,000	0	0.50		Nov-12
2.56	1.23	2.48	6.89	9.41	2.33	0.45	1.45	0.70	9.81	23.7	18	0	0	55	0	75	3.06	1,000,000	0			Nov-12
2.39	2.40	3.72	7.28	10.25	1	1.56	3.2	4.79	12.19	78.6	3	0	97	0	0	21	4.84	1,000	0		1.00	Feb-12
2.58	2.78	4.49	9.62	14.45	1.74	0.81	3.21	4.79	12.19	78.6	3	0	97	0	0	21	4.84	1,000	0	2.00		May-99
2.65	2.90	4.75	10.54	15.98	1.98	0.56	3.21	4.79	12.19	78.6	3	0	97	0	0	21	4.84	1,000,000	0			May-99
1.85	2.14	3.41	7.01	10.82	1.22	1.56	3.1	4.75	10.27	86.6	3	0	97	0	0	18	4.80	1,000	0		1.00	Feb-12
2.03	2.52	4.08	9.32	14.93	1.96	0.81	3.16	4.75	10.26	86.6	3	0	97	0	0	18	4.80	1,000	0	2.00		Dec-93
2.19	2.74	4.43	10.25	16.48	2.21	0.56	3.14	4.75	10.28	86.6	3	0	97	0	0	18	4.80	1,000,000	0			Dec-93
20.04	-4.10	-0.66	8.26	21.10	5.27	1.01	13.8	4.72	8.55	5.7	1	5	0	93	0	63	6.17	1,000,000	250,000			Jun-11
15.30	-5.22	-2.56	2.53	14.16	2.9	0.85	13.6	6.54	8.89	31.4	6	74	0	10	0	38	6.59	1,000,000	250,000			Oct-14
18.89	-3.41	-1.43	6.91	25.16	6.05	0.72	14.46	7.32	9.41	1,117	4	69	0	18	0	104	6.32	1,000,000	250,000			Aug-07
31.88	-17.66	-17.47	-18.63	-0.67	11.1	1.45	26.88		6.66	102.2	-31	62	0	20	0	107	8.11					Dec-10
32.09	-19.11	-19.01	-19.78	-4.64	11.09	2.66	27.3		7.62	69.4	-36	65	0	16	0	89	7.88					Oct-12
8.57	-3.98	-1.77	7.69	17.36	5.71	0.66	7.98	3.22	7.53	65.4	3	0	0	97	0	54	5.58	1,000,000	250,000			Aug-07
5.58	4.47	6.96	13.65	21.01	1.93	0.51	4.03	5.08	10.94	11.1	6	18	0	35	0	49	3.23	1,000,000	250,000			Dec-13
11.02	-7.82	-4.56	-2.33	4.56	0.12	0.91	13.93	5.83	8.36	329.7	3	82	0	3	0	101	6.79	1,000,000	250,000			Jun-10
11.71	-1.50	0.33	6.83	16.40	3.18	0.7	7.6	2.14	9.31	30.7	4	26	0	47	0	8	4.91	1,000,000	250,000			Dec-13
5.21	5.70	8.35	16.86	25.69	3.03	0.44	3.72		11.27	40,847	-8	24	0	25	1	65	3.54	0				Sep-07
5.16	6.41	9.02			2.69	0.28		6.99	11.07	24,699	8	24	0	37	0	124	3.56	0				Oct-18
9.73	-5.10	-1.51	8.38	20.32	5.91	0.73	9.13	3.55	8.85	2,444	6	1	0	92	-1	40	6.16	0				Sep-07
2.98	1.56	2.88	7.41	10.19	2.28	0.42	1.69	0.95	10.12	8,040	15	15	1	42	2	33	2.37	0				Dec-11
0.70	0.69	1.55			1.58	0.11			10.03	3,368	27	0	73	0	0	57	2.75	0				Dec-17

	MARKET			FUND TYPE, CATEGORY & OBJECTIVE	RATINGS				NEW INVESTORS	
Fund Name	Ticker Symbol	Traded On	Fund Type	Category and (Prospectus Objective)	Overall Rating	Reward Rating	Risk Rating	Recent Up/ Downgrade	Open to New Investors	Telephone
Symmetry Panoramic Global Fixed Income Fund Class I Shares	SPGBX	NAS CM	Open End	Global Fixed Inc (Growth & Income)	D+	D+	B	Up	Y	800-786-3309
Symmetry Panoramic Muni Fixed Income Fund Class I Shares	SPMFX	NAS CM	Open End	US Muni Fixed Inc (Muni Bond - Natl)	D+	D+	C+	Up	Y	800-786-3309
Symmetry Panoramic US Fixed Income Fund Class I Shares	SPUBX	NAS CM	Open End	US Fixed Inc (Income)	D+	D+	B	Up	Y	800-786-3309
T. Rowe Price California Tax Free Bond Fund I Class	TCFEX	NAS CM	Open End	US Muni Fixed Inc (Muni Bond - Single State)	C	C-	C+		Y	410-345-2000
T. Rowe Price California Tax-Free Bond Fund	PRXCX	NAS CM	Open End	US Muni Fixed Inc (Muni Bond - Single State)	C	C-	C+		Y	410-345-2000
T. Rowe Price California Tax-Free Money Fund	PCTXX	NAS CM	Money Mkt	US Money Mkt (Money Mkt - Single State)	C	C-	C		Y	410-345-2000
T. Rowe Price California Tax-Free Money Fund I Class	TCBXX	NAS CM	Money Mkt	US Money Mkt (Money Mkt - Single State)	C	C-	C+		Y	410-345-2000
T. Rowe Price Cash Reserves Fund	TSCXX	NAS CM	Money Mkt	US Money Mkt (Money Mkt - Taxable)	C	C-	C+		Y	410-345-2000
T. Rowe Price Corporate Income Fund	PRPIX	NAS CM	Open End	US Fixed Inc (Corp Bond - General)	C	C-	B-		Y	410-345-2000
T. Rowe Price Corporate Income Fund I Class	TICCX	NAS CM	Open End	US Fixed Inc (Corp Bond - General)	C	C-	B-		Y	410-345-2000
T. Rowe Price Credit Opportunities Fund, Inc.	PRCPX	NAS CM	Open End	US Fixed Inc (Growth & Income)	C-	D+	C		Y	410-345-2000
T. Rowe Price Credit Opportunities Fund Advisor Cl	PAOPX	NAS CM	Open End	US Fixed Inc (Growth & Income)	C-	D+	C		Y	410-345-2000
T. Rowe Price Credit Opportunities Fund, Inc. I Class	TCRRX	NAS CM	Open End	US Fixed Inc (Growth & Income)	C-	D+	C		Y	410-345-2000
T. Rowe Price Dynamic Credit Fund	RPIDX	NAS CM	Open End	Fixed Inc Misc (Growth & Income)	D	D	D+		Y	410-345-2000
T. Rowe Price Dynamic Credit Fund I Class	RPELX	NAS CM	Open End	Fixed Inc Misc (Growth & Income)	D	D	D+		Y	410-345-2000
T. Rowe Price Dynamic Global Bond Fund Advisor Class	PAIEX	NAS CM	Open End	Fixed Inc Misc (Income)	C+	C	B	Up	Y	410-345-2000
T. Rowe Price Dynamic Global Bond Fund I Class	RPEIX	NAS CM	Open End	Fixed Inc Misc (Income)	C+	C	B	Up	Y	410-345-2000
T. Rowe Price Dynamic Global Bond Fund Investor Class	RPIEX	NAS CM	Open End	Fixed Inc Misc (Income)	C+	C	B	Up	Y	410-345-2000
T. Rowe Price Dynamic Global Bond Fund Z Class	TRDZX	NAS CM	Open End	Fixed Inc Misc (Income)	C+	C	B			410-345-2000
T. Rowe Price Emerging Markets Bond Fund	PREMX	NAS CM	Open End	Emerg Mkts Fixed Inc (Worldwide Bond)	D	D	D+	Down	Y	410-345-2000
T. Rowe Price Emerging Markets Bond Fund Advisor Class	PAIKX	NAS CM	Open End	Emerg Mkts Fixed Inc (Worldwide Bond)	D	D	D+	Down	Y	410-345-2000
T. Rowe Price Emerging Markets Bond Fund I Class	PRXIX	NAS CM	Open End	Emerg Mkts Fixed Inc (Worldwide Bond)	D	D	D+	Down	Y	410-345-2000
T. Rowe Price Emerging Markets Bond Fund Z Class	TREZX	NAS CM	Open End	Emerg Mkts Fixed Inc (Worldwide Bond)	D	D	D+			410-345-2000
T. Rowe Price Emerging Markets Corporate Bond Fund	TRECX	NAS CM	Open End	Emerg Mkts Fixed Inc (Income)	C-	D+	C	Down	Y	410-345-2000
T. Rowe Price Emerg Mkts Corp Bond Fund Advisor Class	PACEX	NAS CM	Open End	Emerg Mkts Fixed Inc (Income)	C-	D+	C	Down	Y	410-345-2000
T. Rowe Price Emerging Markets Corporate Bond Fund I Class	TECIX	NAS CM	Open End	Emerg Mkts Fixed Inc (Income)	C-	D+	C	Down	Y	410-345-2000
T. Rowe Price Emerging Markets Local Currency Bond Fund	PRELX	NAS CM	Open End	Emerg Mkts Fixed Inc (Growth & Income)	D	D	C-	Down	Y	410-345-2000
T. Rowe Price Emerg Mkts Local Currency Bond Advisor Cl	PAELX	NAS CM	Open End	Emerg Mkts Fixed Inc (Growth & Income)	D	D	D+	Down	Y	410-345-2000
T. Rowe Price Emerg Mkts Local Currency Bond Fund I Class	TEIMX	NAS CM	Open End	Emerg Mkts Fixed Inc (Growth & Income)	D	D	C-	Down	Y	410-345-2000
T. Rowe Price Floating Rate Fund	PRFRX	NAS CM	Open End	US Fixed Inc (Growth & Income)	D+	D	C	Down	Y	410-345-2000
T. Rowe Price Floating Rate Fund Advisor Class	PAFRX	NAS CM	Open End	US Fixed Inc (Growth & Income)	D+	D	C	Down	Y	410-345-2000
T. Rowe Price Floating Rate Fund I Class	TFAIX	NAS CM	Open End	US Fixed Inc (Growth & Income)	C-	D+	C		Y	410-345-2000
T. Rowe Price Floating Rate Fund Z Class	TRIZX	NAS CM	Open End	US Fixed Inc (Growth & Income)	D+	D	C			410-345-2000
T. Rowe Price Georgia Tax Free Bond Fund I Class	TBGAX	NAS CM	Open End	US Muni Fixed Inc (Muni Bond - Single State)	C	C-	B-		Y	410-345-2000
T. Rowe Price Georgia Tax-Free Bond Fund	GTFBX	NAS CM	Open End	US Muni Fixed Inc (Muni Bond - Single State)	C	C-	B-		Y	410-345-2000
T. Rowe Price Global High Income Bond Fund	RPIHX	NAS CM	Open End	Global Fixed Inc (Corp Bond - High Yield)	C-	D+	C		Y	410-345-2000
T. Rowe Price Global High Income Bond Fund Advisor Class	PAIHX	NAS CM	Open End	Global Fixed Inc (Corp Bond - High Yield)	C-	D+	C		Y	410-345-2000
T. Rowe Price Global High Income Bond Fund I Class	RPOIX	NAS CM	Open End	Global Fixed Inc (Corp Bond - High Yield)	C-	D+	C		Y	410-345-2000
T. Rowe Price Global Multi-Sector Bond Fund Advisor Class	PRSAX	NAS CM	Open End	Global Fixed Inc (Multisector Bond)	C	C-	C+		Y	410-345-2000
T. Rowe Price Global Multi-Sector Bond Fund I Class	PGMSX	NAS CM	Open End	Global Fixed Inc (Multisector Bond)	C	C-	B-		Y	410-345-2000
T. Rowe Price Global Multi-Sector Bond Fund Investor Class	PRSNX	NAS CM	Open End	Global Fixed Inc (Multisector Bond)	C	C-	C+		Y	410-345-2000
T. Rowe Price GNMA Fund	PRGMX	NAS CM	Open End	US Fixed Inc (Govt Bond - Mortgage)	C+	C+	B-		Y	410-345-2000
T. Rowe Price GNMA Fund I Class	PRXAX	NAS CM	Open End	US Fixed Inc (Govt Bond - Mortgage)	C+	C+	B-		Y	410-345-2000
T. Rowe Price Government Money Fund	PRRXX	NAS CM	Money Mkt	US Money Mkt (Money Mkt - Taxable)	C	C-	C+		Y	410-345-2000
T. Rowe Price Government Money Fund I Class	TTGXX	NAS CM	Money Mkt	US Money Mkt (Money Mkt - Taxable)	C	C-	C+		Y	410-345-2000
T. Rowe Price High Yield Fund	PRHYX	NAS CM	Open End	US Fixed Inc (Corp Bond - High Yield)	C-	D+	C			410-345-2000
T. Rowe Price High Yield Fund Advisor Class	PAHIX	NAS CM	Open End	US Fixed Inc (Corp Bond - High Yield)	C-	D+	C			410-345-2000
T. Rowe Price High Yield Fund I Class	PRHIX	NAS CM	Open End	US Fixed Inc (Corp Bond - High Yield)	C-	D+	C		Y	410-345-2000
T. Rowe Price High Yield Fund Z Class	TRKZX	NAS CM	Open End	US Fixed Inc (Corp Bond - High Yield)	C-	D+	C			410-345-2000
T. Rowe Price Inflation Protected Bond Fund	PRIPX	NAS CM	Open End	US Fixed Inc (Govt Bond - Treasury)	B	B-	A-	Up	Y	410-345-2000
T. Rowe Price Inflation Protected Bond Fund I Class	TIIPX	NAS CM	Open End	US Fixed Inc (Govt Bond - Treasury)	B	B-	A-	Up	Y	410-345-2000
T. Rowe Price Institutional Cash Reserves Fund	ICFXX	NAS CM	Money Mkt	US Money Mkt (Money Mkt - Taxable)	C	C	B-		Y	410-345-2000

★ Expanded analysis of this fund is included in Section II.

TOTAL RETURNS & PERFORMANCE									ASSETS		ASSET ALLOCATION & TURNOVER							MINIMUMS		FEES		
3-Month Total Return	6-Month Total Return	1-Year Total Return	3-Year Total Return	5-Year Total Return	Dividend Yield (TTM)	Expense Ratio	3-Yr Std Deviation	Effective Duration	NAV	Total Assets (MIL)	%Cash	%Government Bonds	%Municipal Bonds	%Corporate Bonds	%Other	Turnover Ratio	Average Coupon Rate	Min Initial Investment	Min Additional Investment	Front End Fee (%)	Back End Fee (%)	Inception Date
2.36	3.95	5.78			2.41	0.51		6.88	10.86	417.0	3	58	0	19	0		2.56	1,000	100			Nov-18
1.19	1.22	1.90			0.9	0.62		1.97	10.29	24.1	22	0	78	0	0		4.68	1,000	100			Nov-18
2.31	4.73	6.43			1.92	0.47		4.31	10.91	261.0	2	60	0	25	0		2.78	1,000	100			Nov-18
2.13	0.32	2.53	10.69	19.35	3.01	0.44	4.31	6.04	11.61	678.6	0	0	100	0	0	8	4.96	1,000,000				Jul-17
2.10	0.28	2.52	10.45	19.10	2.91	0.54	4.33	6.04	11.62	678.6	0	0	100	0	0	8	4.96	2,500	100			Sep-86
0.02	0.21	0.53	1.95	2.12	0.6	0.55	0.09		1	71.6	19	0	81	0	0			2,500	100			Sep-86
0.01	0.27	0.70	2.55	2.73	0.79	0.33			1	71.6	19	0	81	0	0			1,000,000				Jul-17
0.16	0.50	1.38	4.63	5.04	1.51	0.45	0.14		1	3,948	68	6	21	4	0	0		2,500	100			Oct-93
9.94	2.71	7.95	16.78	27.91	3.35	0.61	7.63	8.45	10.02	735.1	1	5	1	83	0	114	4.11	2,500	100			Oct-95
9.97	2.77	8.07	17.33	28.73	3.47	0.49	7.64	8.45	10.03	735.1	1	5	1	83	0	114	4.11	1,000,000				Dec-15
11.47	-4.03	-0.53	9.90	20.83	5.31	0.92	9.19	3.26	8.15	64.7	4	0	0	95	0	53	6.67	2,500	100			Apr-14
11.47	-4.09	-0.64	9.56	20.10	5.21	1.02	9.21	3.26	8.13	64.7	4	0	0	95	0	53	6.67	0				Apr-14
11.55	-3.92	-0.29	10.58	21.72	5.57	0.66	9.2	3.26	8.14	64.7	4	0	0	95	0	53	6.67	1,000,000				Nov-16
10.20	-6.40	-3.71			3.91	0.64		4.97	9.36	34.0	7	5	4	60	0	312	4.90	2,500	100			Jan-19
10.33	-6.47	-3.68			3.94	0.61		4.97	9.36	34.0	7	5	4	60	0	312	4.90	1,000,000				Jan-19
2.57	5.75	5.28	5.49	9.74	1.99	0.9	3.54	6.05	9.65	3,963	7	61	0	24	0	188	4.52	2,500	100			Jan-15
2.66	5.84	5.69	6.57	11.62	2.37	0.51	3.55	6.05	9.66	3,963	7	61	0	24	0	188	4.52	1,000,000				Aug-15
2.62	5.75	5.53	6.18	10.99	2.23	0.65	3.54	6.05	9.66	3,963	7	61	0	24	0	188	4.52	2,500	100			Jan-15
2.79	5.93	5.71	6.36	11.18		0	3.55	6.05	9.66	3,963	7	61	0	24	0	188	4.52	0				Mar-20
11.86	-5.97	-5.20	-0.47	20.02	5.65	0.9	12.29	7.12	10.67	4,832	3	68	0	29	0	43	6.26	2,500	100			Dec-94
11.79	-6.11	-5.48	-1.35	18.30	5.33	1.2	12.3	7.12	10.67	4,832	3	68	0	29	0	43	6.26	2,500	100			Aug-15
11.92	-5.91	-5.08	-0.11	20.70	5.8	0.77	12.32	7.12	10.66	4,832	3	68	0	29	0	43	6.26	1,000,000				Aug-15
12.22	-5.68	-4.90	-0.15	20.40		0	12.31	7.12	10.68	4,832	3	68	0	29	0	43	6.26	0				Mar-20
12.78	-2.25	1.29	12.38	27.18	4.63	0.97	9.79	5.84	10.32	304.7	2	4	0	93	0	53	5.63	2,500	100			May-12
12.70	-2.39	1.00	11.70	26.29	4.33	1.25	9.82	5.84	10.32	304.7	2	4	0	93	0	53	5.63	2,500	100			May-12
12.80	-2.09	1.43	13.20	28.70	4.77	0.84	9.77	5.84	10.33	304.7	2	4	0	93	0	53	5.63	1,000,000				Dec-15
11.48	-6.96	-3.38	1.63	11.26	5.37	0.94	13.15	5.63	5.89	551.5	11	86	0	2	0	50	6.17	2,500	100			May-11
11.44	-7.09	-3.81	0.62	9.87	5.08	1.2	13.18	5.63	5.88	551.5	11	86	0	2	0	50	6.17	2,500	100			May-11
11.72	-6.73	-3.23	2.22	12.24	5.52	0.79	13.23	5.63	5.9	551.5	11	86	0	2	0	50	6.17	1,000,000				Dec-15
7.46	-4.52	-1.87	5.40	13.05	4.68	0.76	7.18	0.77	9.09	2,019	9	0	0	91	0	57	4.72	2,500	100			Jul-11
7.51	-4.61	-2.07	4.87	12.31	4.46	0.98	7.25	0.77	9.11	2,019	9	0	0	91	0	57	4.72	0				Jul-11
7.61	-4.46	-1.74	5.81	13.55	4.81	0.64	7.21	0.77	9.1	2,019	9	0	0	91	0	57	4.72	1,000,000				Nov-16
7.66	-4.34	-1.68	5.60	13.26		0.02	7.21	0.77	9.09	2,019	9	0	0	91	0	57	4.72	0				Mar-20
2.29	1.17	3.31	10.99	17.92	2.61	0.44	3.99	6.06	11.72	433.4	0	0	100	0	0	8	4.83	1,000,000				Jul-17
2.34	1.20	3.28	10.69	17.60	2.5	0.56	4.04	6.06	11.73	433.4	0	0	100	0	0	8	4.83	2,500	100			Mar-93
14.11	-4.83	-0.66	10.54	26.57	5.92	0.79	10.86	3.81	9.4	162.1	3	0	0	97	0	70	6.45	2,500	100			Jan-15
13.91	-5.02	-0.87	9.71	25.18	5.7	1	10.8	3.81	9.4	162.1	3	0	0	97	0	70	6.45	2,500	100			Jan-15
14.03	-4.77	-0.52	11.01	27.30	6.08	0.64	10.8	3.81	9.39	162.1	3	0	0	97	0	70	6.45	1,000,000				Aug-15
10.18	0.24	3.39	12.68	23.88	3	0.95	6.82	5.23	11.35	1,119	4	31	1	41	0	124	4.41	0				Dec-08
10.31	0.46	3.85	14.20	26.62	3.45	0.5	6.81	5.23	11.34	1,119	4	31	1	41	0	124	4.41	1,000,000				Mar-16
10.26	0.37	3.69	13.73	25.70	3.3	0.69	6.8	5.23	11.34	1,119	4	31	1	41	0	124	4.41	2,500	100			Dec-08
0.78	3.75	5.40	10.27	13.97	2.03	0.59	1.87	1.50	9.45	1,245	4	0	0	0	0	509	3.99	2,500	100			Nov-85
0.82	3.81	5.52	10.61	14.34	2.14	0.49	1.89	1.50	9.45	1,245	4	0	0	0	0	509	3.99	1,000,000				May-17
0.01	0.26	1.10	4.04	4.21	1.27	0.38	0.18		1	9,563	59	41	0	0	0	0		2,500	100			Jan-76
0.02	0.30	1.21	4.38	4.57	1.37	0.26	0.18		1	9,563	59	41	0	0	0	0		1,000,000				May-17
10.07	-4.76	-0.98	8.42	21.22	5.67	0.71	8.88	3.81	6.19	7,843	3	0	0	97	0	61	6.57	2,500	100			Dec-84
10.21	-4.75	-1.11	7.70	19.88	5.39	1	8.94	3.81	6.18	7,843	3	0	0	97	0	61	6.57	2,500	100			Mar-00
10.28	-4.55	-0.71	8.98	22.14	5.79	0.6	8.88	3.81	6.2	7,843	3	0	0	97	0	61	6.57	1,000,000				Aug-15
10.44	-4.44	-0.64	8.79	21.64		0	8.9	3.81	6.2	7,843	3	0	0	97	0	61	6.57	0				Mar-20
4.33	6.12	8.49	16.10	19.39	0.63	0.41	3.6	6.89	12.75	389.5	4	82	0	6	0	112	0.94	2,500	100			Oct-02
4.45	6.20	8.75	16.81	20.35	0.8	0.22	3.61	6.89	12.79	389.5	4	82	0	6	0	112	0.94	1,000,000				Dec-15
0.30	0.68	1.66	5.30		1.66	0.25	0.16		1	20.6	64	0	32	0	0	0		1,000,000				Sep-16

	MARKET			FUND TYPE, CATEGORY & OBJECTIVE	RATINGS				NEW INVESTORS	
Fund Name	Ticker Symbol	Traded On	Fund Type	Category and (Prospectus Objective)	Overall Rating	Reward Rating	Risk Rating	Recent Up/ Downgrade	Open to New Investors	Telephone
T. Rowe Price Institutional Core Plus Fund	TICPX	NAS CM	Open End	US Fixed Inc (Income)	C+	C	B	Up	Y	410-345-2000
T. Rowe Price Institutional Emerging Markets Bond Fund	TREBX	NAS CM	Open End	Emerg Mkts Fixed Inc (Growth & Income)	D	D	D+	Down	Y	410-345-2000
T. Rowe Price Institutional Floating Rate Fund	RPIFX	NAS CM	Open End	US Fixed Inc (Growth & Income)	C-	D+	C		Y	410-345-2000
T. Rowe Price Institutional Floating Rate Fund Class F	PFFRX	NAS CM	Open End	US Fixed Inc (Growth & Income)	C-	D+	C		Y	410-345-2000
T. Rowe Price Institutional Floating Rate Fund Z Class			Open End	US Fixed Inc (Growth & Income)	C-	D+	C		Y	410-345-2000
T. Rowe Price Institutional High Yield Fund	TRHYX	NAS CM	Open End	US Fixed Inc (Corp Bond - High Yield)	C-	D+	C			410-345-2000
T. Rowe Price Institutional High Yield Fund Z Class			Open End	US Fixed Inc (Corp Bond - High Yield)	C-	D+	C		Y	410-345-2000
T. Rowe Price Institutional Long Duration Credit Fund	RPLCX	NAS CM	Open End	US Fixed Inc (Corp Bond - General)	B-	C+	B		Y	410-345-2000
T. Rowe Price Intermediate Tax-Free High Yield Fund	PRIHX	NAS CM	Open End	US Muni Fixed Inc (Income)	C-	D+	C	Down	Y	410-345-2000
T. Rowe Price Intermediate Tax-Free High Yield I Cl	TFHAX	NAS CM	Open End	US Muni Fixed Inc (Income)	C-	D+	C	Down	Y	410-345-2000
T. Rowe Price Intermed Tax-Free High Yield Fund-Advisor Cl	PRAHX	NAS CM	Open End	US Muni Fixed Inc (Income)	C-	D+	C	Down	Y	410-345-2000
T. Rowe Price International Bond Fund	RPIBX	NAS CM	Open End	Global Fixed Inc (Worldwide Bond)	C	C-	C		Y	410-345-2000
T. Rowe Price International Bond Fund (USD Hedged)	TNIBX	NAS CM	Open End	Global Fixed Inc (Worldwide Bond)	C	C-	B-		Y	410-345-2000
T. Rowe Price InterNatl Bond (USD Hedged) Advisor Cl	TTABX	NAS CM	Open End	Global Fixed Inc (Worldwide Bond)	C	C-	B-		Y	410-345-2000
T. Rowe Price International Bond Fund (USD Hedged) I Class	TNBMX	NAS CM	Open End	Global Fixed Inc (Worldwide Bond)	C	C	B-		Y	410-345-2000
T. Rowe Price International Bond Fund (USD Hedged) Z Class	TRMZX	NAS CM	Open End	Global Fixed Inc (Worldwide Bond)	C	C	B-			410-345-2000
T. Rowe Price International Bond Fund Advisor Class	PAIBX	NAS CM	Open End	Global Fixed Inc (Worldwide Bond)	C	C-	C	Up	Y	410-345-2000
T. Rowe Price International Bond Fund I Class	RPISX	NAS CM	Open End	Global Fixed Inc (Worldwide Bond)	C	C-	C		Y	410-345-2000
T. Rowe Price International Bond Fund Z Class	TRLZX	NAS CM	Open End	Global Fixed Inc (Worldwide Bond)	C	C-	C			410-345-2000
T. Rowe Price Limited Duration Inflation Focused Bond Fund	TRBFX	NAS CM	Open End	US Fixed Inc (Income)	C	C	B-		Y	410-345-2000
T. Rowe Price Limited Duration Inflation Focused Bond I Cl	TRLDX	NAS CM	Open End	US Fixed Inc (Income)	C	C	B-		Y	410-345-2000
T. Rowe Price Limited Duration Inflation Focused Bond Z Cl	TRPZX	NAS CM	Open End	US Fixed Inc (Income)	C	C	B-			410-345-2000
T. Rowe Price Maryland Short-Term Tax-Free Bond Fund	PRMDX	NAS CM	Open End	US Muni Fixed Inc (Muni Bond - Single State)	C	C-	C		Y	410-345-2000
T. Rowe Price Maryland Short-Term Tax-Free Bond I Cl	TRMUX	NAS CM	Open End	US Muni Fixed Inc (Muni Bond - Single State)	C	C-	C		Y	410-345-2000
T. Rowe Price Maryland Tax Free Bond Fund I Class	TFBIX	NAS CM	Open End	US Muni Fixed Inc (Muni Bond - Single State)	C	C-	C+		Y	410-345-2000
T. Rowe Price Maryland Tax-Free Bond Fund	MDXBX	NAS CM	Open End	US Muni Fixed Inc (Muni Bond - Single State)	C	C-	C+		Y	410-345-2000
T. Rowe Price Maryland Tax-Free Money Fund	TMDXX	NAS CM	Money Mkt	US Money Mkt (Money Mkt - Single State)	C	C-	C		Y	410-345-2000
T. Rowe Price Maryland Tax-Free Money Fund I Class	TWNXX	NAS CM	Money Mkt	US Money Mkt (Money Mkt - Single State)	C	C-	C+		Y	410-345-2000
T. Rowe Price New Income Fund	PRCIX	NAS CM	Open End	US Fixed Inc (Income)	C+	C	B	Up	Y	410-345-2000
T. Rowe Price New Income Fund Advisor Class	PANIX	NAS CM	Open End	US Fixed Inc (Income)	C	C	B		Y	410-345-2000
T. Rowe Price New Income Fund I Class	PRXEX	NAS CM	Open End	US Fixed Inc (Income)	C+	C	B	Up	Y	410-345-2000
T. Rowe Price New Income Fund R Class	RRNIX	NAS CM	Open End	US Fixed Inc (Income)	C	C	B-		Y	410-345-2000
T. Rowe Price New Income Fund Z Class	TRVZX	NAS CM	Open End	US Fixed Inc (Income)	C+	C	B			410-345-2000
T. Rowe Price New Jersey Tax Free Bond Fund I Class	TRJIX	NAS CM	Open End	US Muni Fixed Inc (Muni Bond - Single State)	C	C-	C+		Y	410-345-2000
T. Rowe Price New Jersey Tax-Free Bond Fund	NJTFX	NAS CM	Open End	US Muni Fixed Inc (Muni Bond - Single State)	C	C-	C+		Y	410-345-2000
T. Rowe Price New York Tax Free Bond Fund I Class	TRYIX	NAS CM	Open End	US Muni Fixed Inc (Muni Bond - Single State)	C	C-	C+		Y	410-345-2000
T. Rowe Price New York Tax-Free Bond Fund	PRNYX	NAS CM	Open End	US Muni Fixed Inc (Muni Bond - Single State)	C	C-	C+		Y	410-345-2000
T. Rowe Price New York Tax-Free Money Fund I Class	TRNXX	NAS CM	Money Mkt	US Money Mkt (Money Mkt - Single State)	C	C-	C+		Y	410-345-2000
T. Rowe Price Short-Term Bond Fund	PRWBX	NAS CM	Open End	US Fixed Inc (Multisector Bond)	C	C	B-		Y	410-345-2000
T. Rowe Price Short-Term Bond Fund Advisor Class	PASHX	NAS CM	Open End	US Fixed Inc (Multisector Bond)	C	C	B-		Y	410-345-2000
T. Rowe Price Short-Term Bond Fund I Class	TBSIX	NAS CM	Open End	US Fixed Inc (Multisector Bond)	C	C	B-		Y	410-345-2000
T. Rowe Price Spectrum Income Fund	RPSIX	NAS CM	Open End	US Fixed Inc (Multisector Bond)	C	C-	C		Y	410-345-2000
T. Rowe Price State Tax-Free Inc Trust NY Tax-Free Money F	NYTXX	NAS CM	Money Mkt	US Money Mkt (Money Mkt - Single State)	C	C-	C		Y	410-345-2000
T. Rowe Price Summit Municipal Income Fund Advisor Class	PAIMX	NAS CM	Open End	US Muni Fixed Inc (Muni Bond - Natl)	C	C-	C+		Y	410-345-2000
T. Rowe Price Summit Municipal Income Fund I Class	PRIMX	NAS CM	Open End	US Muni Fixed Inc (Muni Bond - Natl)	C	C-	C+		Y	410-345-2000
T. Rowe Price Summit Municipal Income Fund Investor Class	PRINX	NAS CM	Open End	US Muni Fixed Inc (Muni Bond - Natl)	C	C-	C+		Y	410-345-2000
T. Rowe Price Summit Muni Intermediate Fund Advisor Class	PAIFX	NAS CM	Open End	US Muni Fixed Inc (Muni Bond - Natl)	C	C-	B-		Y	410-345-2000
T. Rowe Price Summit Municipal Intermediate Fund I Class	PRTMX	NAS CM	Open End	US Muni Fixed Inc (Muni Bond - Natl)	C	C	B-		Y	410-345-2000
T. Rowe Price Summit Muni Intermediate Fund Investor Class	PRSMX	NAS CM	Open End	US Muni Fixed Inc (Muni Bond - Natl)	C	C	B-		Y	410-345-2000
T. Rowe Price Summit Municipal Money Market Fund	TRSXX	NAS CM	Money Mkt	US Money Mkt (Money Mkt - Fed Tax Exmpt)	C	C-	C		Y	410-345-2000
T. Rowe Price Tax Free High Yield Fund Advisor Class	PATFX	NAS CM	Open End	US Muni Fixed Inc (Muni Bond - Natl)	C-	D+	C	Down	Y	410-345-2000
T. Rowe Price Tax Free High Yield Fund I Class	PTYIX	NAS CM	Open End	US Muni Fixed Inc (Muni Bond - Natl)	C-	D+	C	Down	Y	410-345-2000

★Expanded analysis of this fund is included in Section II.

TOTAL RETURNS & PERFORMANCE									ASSETS		ASSET ALLOCATION & TURNOVER							MINIMUMS		FEES		
3-Month Total Return	6-Month Total Return	1-Year Total Return	3-Year Total Return	5-Year Total Return	Dividend Yield (TTM)	Expense Ratio	3-Yr Std Deviation	Effective Duration	NAV	Total Assets (MIL)	%Cash	%Government Bonds	%Municipal Bonds	%Corporate Bonds	%Other	Turnover Ratio	Average Coupon Rate	Min Initial Investment	Min Additional Investment	Front End Fee (%)	Back End Fee (%)	Inception Date
6.60	3.53	6.24	14.77	22.75	2.88	0.4	4.85	5.74	10.85	442.7	2	18	1	37	0	95	3.84	1,000,000				Nov-04
12.66	-5.64	-4.48	3.30	25.72	5.91	0.7	12.34	6.88	7.89	414.2	3	71	0	26	0	45	6.33	1,000,000				Nov-06
8.16	-4.03	-1.12	6.96	15.39	4.99	0.58	7.36	0.77	9.28	2,740	6	0	0	94	0	59	4.83	1,000,000				Jan-08
8.13	-3.99	-1.24	6.67	14.68	4.87	0.7	7.29	0.77	9.28	2,740	6	0	0	94	0	59	4.83	2,500				Aug-10
8.14	-4.05	-1.14	6.94	15.37		0.03	7.34	0.77	9.28	2,740	6	0	0	94	0	59	4.83	0				Mar-20
10.10	-4.89	-0.94	8.91	22.54	5.91	0.5	8.98	3.80	8.22	1,534	6	0	0	94	0	62	6.60	1,000,000				May-02
10.17	-4.83	-0.89	8.97	22.61		0	8.96	3.80	8.22	1,534	6	0	0	94	0	62	6.60	0				Mar-20
11.42	8.85	16.69	31.95	53.64	3.58	0.45	9.95	14.40	11.29	24.0	2	2	11	86	0	51	4.77	1,000,000				Jun-13
2.50	-1.91	0.25	8.65	16.94	2.98	0.61	4.59	4.19	10.27	59.7	0	0	100	0	0	11	4.93	2,500	100			Jul-14
2.62	-1.89	0.30	8.92	17.23	3.04	0.54	4.6	4.19	10.27	59.7	0	0	100	0	0	11	4.93	1,000,000				Jul-17
2.54	-1.94	0.00	8.14	16.04	2.72	0.85	4.64	4.19	10.27	59.7	0	0	100	0	0	11	4.93	2,500	100			Jul-14
5.86	0.31	1.70	8.04	17.15	1.76	0.7	6.26	7.96	8.97	1,005	8	73	0	17	0	26	3.20	2,500	100			Sep-86
4.58	1.75	3.89			1.61	0.64		8.16	10.08	5,507	10	72	0	17	0	31	3.28	2,500	100			Sep-17
4.50	1.48	3.44			1.27	0.99		8.16	10.07	5,507	10	72	0	17	0	31	3.28	2,500	100			Sep-17
4.62	1.72	3.93			1.75	0.51		8.16	10.08	5,507	10	72	0	17	0	31	3.28	1,000,000				Sep-17
4.85	1.95	4.17				0		8.16	10.09	5,507	10	72	0	17	0	31	3.28	0				Mar-20
5.65	0.17	1.36	7.15	15.53	1.47	1.06	6.26	7.96	8.99	1,005	8	73	0	17	0	26	3.20	2,500	100			Mar-00
5.90	0.40	1.88	8.63	18.09	1.93	0.54	6.27	7.96	8.99	1,005	8	73	0	17	0	26	3.20	1,000,000				Aug-15
6.05	0.49	1.89	8.23	17.36		0	6.27	7.96	8.97	1,005	8	73	0	17	0	26	3.20	0				Mar-20
3.64	1.56	3.00	7.82	9.22	0.79	0.38	2.39	2.43	5.07	7,504	3	67	0	13	0	125	1.15	2,500	100			Sep-06
3.67	1.83	3.33	8.35	9.98	0.93	0.26	2.43	2.43	5.09	7,504	3	67	0	13	0	125	1.15	1,000,000				Sep-15
3.75	1.66	3.11	7.93	9.34		0	2.37	2.43	5.07	7,504	3	67	0	13	0	125	1.15	0				Mar-20
0.50	0.23	0.89	3.42	4.98	1.29	0.54	1.37	1.76	5.2	152.9	2	0	98	0	0	30	4.68	2,500	100			Jan-93
0.71	0.28	1.18	3.91	5.47	1.39	0.44	1.37	1.76	5.22	152.9	2	0	98	0	0	30	4.68	1,000,000				Jul-17
1.26	0.10	2.28	10.03	17.78	2.89	0.41	4.01	5.79	10.83	2,449	0	0	100	0	0	4	4.85	1,000,000				Jul-17
1.24	0.06	2.11	9.79	17.53	2.81	0.48	4.06	5.79	10.82	2,449	0	0	100	0	0	4	4.85	2,500	100			Mar-87
0.03	0.33	0.82	2.68	2.78	0.91	0.41	0.12		1	112.0	4	0	96	0	0			2,500	100			Mar-01
0.02	0.35	0.88	2.91	3.02	0.99	0.33			1	112.0	4	0	96	0	0			1,000,000				Jul-17
5.69	2.57	5.22	12.87	19.43	2.76	0.5	4.81	6.04	9.83	21,822	2	18	0	37	0	139	3.40	2,500	100			Aug-73
5.62	2.41	4.89	11.85	17.81	2.44	0.83	4.81	6.04	9.81	21,822	2	18	0	37	0	139	3.40	0				Sep-02
5.72	2.63	5.35	13.43	20.23	2.89	0.38	4.79	6.04	9.83	21,822	2	18	0	37	0	139	3.40	1,000,000				Aug-15
5.53	2.25	4.55	10.75	16.00	2.13	1.15	4.78	6.04	9.83	21,822	2	18	0	37	0	139	3.40	0				Sep-02
5.82	2.70	5.35	13.01	19.58		0	4.82	6.04	9.83	21,822	2	18	0	37	0	139	3.40	0				Mar-20
2.04	0.23	2.27	10.93	19.16	2.91	0.44	4.25	5.89	12.14	425.5	1	0	99	0	0	8	4.96	1,000,000				Jul-17
2.00	0.25	2.15	10.64	18.85	2.78	0.55	4.25	5.89	12.15	425.5	1	0	99	0	0	8	4.96	2,500	100			Apr-91
1.40	0.37	2.27	9.49	17.62	2.92	0.44	4.1	6.02	11.62	488.7	0	0	100	0	0	10	4.93	1,000,000				Jul-17
1.46	0.33	2.27	9.31	17.43	2.84	0.53	4.14	6.02	11.64	488.7	0	0	100	0	0	10	4.93	2,500	100			Aug-86
0.01	0.31	0.81	2.84	3.01	0.91	0.33			1	64.3	8	0	92	0	0			1,000,000				Jul-17
4.19	2.78	4.26	8.96	11.78	2.33	0.44	2.26	2.07	4.81	5,259	4	8	0	50	0	53	3.05	2,500	100			Mar-84
4.11	2.40	3.92	7.99	10.11	2.04	0.77	2.25	2.07	4.81	5,259	4	8	0	50	0	53	3.05	0				Dec-04
4.22	2.83	4.14	9.29	12.52	2.42	0.35	2.3	2.07	4.81	5,259	4	8	0	50	0	53	3.05	1,000,000				Dec-15
7.99	-2.05	1.26	9.43	20.64	3.36	0.63	6.4	5.11	12.27	6,286	5	30	0	41	0	24	4.65	2,500	100			Jun-90
0.02	0.25	0.63	2.24	2.40	0.72	0.55	0.11		1	64.3	8	0	92	0	0			2,500	100			Aug-86
2.68	0.00	2.12	10.10	18.05	2.6	0.75	5.01	6.75	12.04	2,290	0	0	100	0	0	9	4.96	0				Aug-12
2.68	0.17	2.49	11.07	19.71	2.97	0.39	5.04	6.75	12.04	2,290	0	0	100	0	0	9	4.96	1,000,000				Mar-19
2.74	0.12	2.37	10.92	19.54	2.85	0.5	5.05	6.75	12.04	2,290	0	0	100	0	0	9	4.96	25,000	1,000			Oct-93
2.56	1.38	2.99	9.39	15.42	2.14	0.75	3.52	4.70	12.17	5,605	0	0	100	0	0	9	4.96	0				Aug-12
2.65	1.57	3.37	10.38	17.04	2.52	0.38	3.53	4.70	12.17	5,605	0	0	100	0	0	9	4.96	1,000,000				Mar-19
2.62	1.51	3.24	10.21	16.86	2.39	0.5	3.54	4.70	12.18	5,605	0	0	100	0	0	9	4.96	25,000	1,000			Oct-93
0.02	0.27	0.75	2.65	2.93	0.84	0.45	0.1		1	144.1	23	0	77	0	0			25,000	1,000			Oct-93
3.10	-3.28	-0.77	8.22	18.63	3.39	0.92	6.58	6.85	11.81	4,520	0	0	100	0	0	5	5.14	2,500	100			Aug-12
3.22	-3.12	-0.36	9.63	20.41	3.87	0.51	6.63	6.85	11.74	4,520	0	0	100	0	0	5	5.14	1,000,000				Nov-16

	MARKET			FUND TYPE, CATEGORY & OBJECTIVE	RATINGS				NEW INVESTORS	
Fund Name	Ticker Symbol	Traded On	Fund Type	Category and (Prospectus Objective)	Overall Rating	Reward Rating	Risk Rating	Recent Up/ Downgrade	Open to New Investors	Telephone
T. Rowe Price Tax Free Income Fund I Class	TFILX	NAS CM	Open End	US Muni Fixed Inc (Muni Bond - Natl)	C	C-	C+		Y	410-345-2000
T. Rowe Price Tax Free Short/Intermediate Advisor Cl	PATIX	NAS CM	Open End	US Muni Fixed Inc (Muni Bond - Natl)	C	C	C+		Y	410-345-2000
T. Rowe Price Tax Free Short-Intermediate Fund I Class	TTSIX	NAS CM	Open End	US Muni Fixed Inc (Muni Bond - Natl)	C	C	B-		Y	410-345-2000
T. Rowe Price Tax-Exempt Money Fund	PTEXX	NAS CM	Money Mkt	US Money Mkt (Money Mkt - Fed Tax Exmpt)	C	C-	C		Y	410-345-2000
T. Rowe Price Tax-Exempt Money Fund I Class	TERXX	NAS CM	Money Mkt	US Money Mkt (Money Mkt - Fed Tax Exmpt)	C	C-	C+		Y	410-345-2000
T. Rowe Price Tax-Free High Yield Fund	PRFHX	NAS CM	Open End	US Muni Fixed Inc (Muni Bond - Natl)	C-	D+	C	Down	Y	410-345-2000
T. Rowe Price Tax-Free Income Fund	PRTAX	NAS CM	Open End	US Muni Fixed Inc (Muni Bond - Natl)	C	C-	C+		Y	410-345-2000
T. Rowe Price Tax-Free Income Fund Advisor Class	PATAX	NAS CM	Open End	US Muni Fixed Inc (Muni Bond - Natl)	C	C-	C+		Y	410-345-2000
T. Rowe Price Tax-Free Short-Intermediate Fund	PRFSX	NAS CM	Open End	US Muni Fixed Inc (Muni Bond - Natl)	C	C	C+		Y	410-345-2000
T. Rowe Price Total Return Fund	PTTFX	NAS CM	Open End	US Fixed Inc (Multisector Bond)	C+	C	B	Up	Y	410-345-2000
T. Rowe Price Total Return Fund Advisor Class	PTATX	NAS CM	Open End	US Fixed Inc (Multisector Bond)	C+	C	B	Up	Y	410-345-2000
T. Rowe Price Total Return Fund I Class	PTKIX	NAS CM	Open End	US Fixed Inc (Multisector Bond)	C+	C	B	Up	Y	410-345-2000
T. Rowe Price U.S. Bond Enhanced Index Fund	PBDIX	NAS CM	Open End	US Fixed Inc (Corp Bond - General)	B	C+	B+	Up	Y	410-345-2000
T. Rowe Price U.S. High Yield Fund	TUHYX	NAS CM	Open End	US Fixed Inc (Corp Bond - High Yield)	C-	D+	C			410-345-2000
T. Rowe Price U.S. High Yield Fund Advisor Class	TUHAX	NAS CM	Open End	US Fixed Inc (Corp Bond - High Yield)	C-	D+	C		Y	410-345-2000
T. Rowe Price U.S. High Yield Fund I Class	TUHIX	NAS CM	Open End	US Fixed Inc (Corp Bond - High Yield)	C-	D+	C		Y	410-345-2000
T. Rowe Price U.S. Treasury Intermediate Fund	PRTIX	NAS CM	Open End	US Fixed Inc (Govt Bond - Treasury)	B	B	B		Y	410-345-2000
T. Rowe Price U.S. Treasury Intermediate Fund I Class	PRKIX	NAS CM	Open End	US Fixed Inc (Govt Bond - Treasury)	B	B	B		Y	410-345-2000
T. Rowe Price U.S. Treasury Long Term Fund I Class	PRUUX	NAS CM	Open End	US Fixed Inc (Govt Bond - Treasury)	B	B	B		Y	410-345-2000
T. Rowe Price U.S. Treasury Long Term Fund Z Class	TRZUX	NAS CM	Open End	US Fixed Inc (Govt Bond - Treasury)	B	B	B			410-345-2000
T. Rowe Price U.S. Treasury Long-Term Fund	PRULX	NAS CM	Open End	US Fixed Inc (Govt Bond - Treasury)	B	B	B		Y	410-345-2000
T. Rowe Price U.S. Treasury Money Fund	PRTXX	NAS CM	Money Mkt	US Money Mkt (Money Mkt - Treasury)	C	C-	C+		Y	410-345-2000
T. Rowe Price U.S. Treasury Money Fund I Class	TRGXX	NAS CM	Money Mkt	US Money Mkt (Money Mkt - Treasury)	C	C-	C+		Y	410-345-2000
T. Rowe Price U.S. Treasury Money Fund Z Class	TRZXX	NAS CM	Money Mkt	US Money Mkt (Money Mkt - Treasury)	C	C-	C+			410-345-2000
T. Rowe Price Ultra Short-Term Bond Fund	TRBUX	NAS CM	Open End	US Fixed Inc (Multisector Bond)	C	C	B-		Y	410-345-2000
T. Rowe Price Ultra Short-Term Bond Fund I Class	TRSTX	NAS CM	Open End	US Fixed Inc (Multisector Bond)	C	C	B-		Y	410-345-2000
T. Rowe Price Virginia Tax Free Bond Fund I Class	TFBVX	NAS CM	Open End	US Muni Fixed Inc (Muni Bond - Single State)	C	C-	B-		Y	410-345-2000
T. Rowe Price Virginia Tax-Free Bond Fund	PRVAX	NAS CM	Open End	US Muni Fixed Inc (Muni Bond - Single State)	C	C-	B-		Y	410-345-2000
Tactical Multi-Purpose Fund	TMPFX	NAS CM	Open End	Multialternative (Growth & Income)	C-	D+	C		Y	415-851-3334
TCW Core Fixed Income Fund Class Institutional	TGCFX	NAS CM	Open End	US Fixed Inc (Multisector Bond)	B	B-	B+	Up	Y	213-244-0000
TCW Core Fixed Income Fund Class N	TGFNX	NAS CM	Open End	US Fixed Inc (Multisector Bond)	B	B-	B	Up	Y	213-244-0000
TCW Core Fixed Income Fund Class Plan	TGCPX	NAS CM	Open End	US Fixed Inc (Multisector Bond)	B	B-	B+		Y	213-244-0000
TCW Emerging Markets Income Fund Class Institutional	TGEIX	NAS CM	Open End	Emerg Mkts Fixed Inc (Diversified Emerg Mkts)	D	D	D+	Down	Y	213-244-0000
TCW Emerging Markets Income Fund Class N	TGINX	NAS CM	Open End	Emerg Mkts Fixed Inc (Diversified Emerg Mkts)	D	D	D+	Down	Y	213-244-0000
TCW Emerging Markets Income Fund Class Plan	TGEPX	NAS CM	Open End	Emerg Mkts Fixed Inc (Diversified Emerg Mkts)	D	D	D+		Y	213-244-0000
TCW Emerging Markets Local Currency Income Fund Class I	TGWIX	NAS CM	Open End	Emerg Mkts Fixed Inc (Diversified Emerg Mkts)	D	D	D+	Down	Y	213-244-0000
TCW Emerging Markets Local Currency Income Fund Class N	TGWNX	NAS CM	Open End	Emerg Mkts Fixed Inc (Diversified Emerg Mkts)	D	D	D+	Down	Y	213-244-0000
TCW Global Bond Fund Class I	TGGBX	NAS CM	Open End	Global Fixed Inc (Worldwide Bond)	C+	C	B	Up	Y	213-244-0000
TCW Global Bond Fund Class N	TGGFX	NAS CM	Open End	Global Fixed Inc (Worldwide Bond)	C+	C	B	Up	Y	213-244-0000
TCW High Yield Bond Fund Class Institutional	TGHYX	NAS CM	Open End	US Fixed Inc (Corp Bond - High Yield)	B-	C	B	Up	Y	213-244-0000
TCW High Yield Bond Fund Class N	TGHNX	NAS CM	Open End	US Fixed Inc (Corp Bond - High Yield)	C+	C	B	Up	Y	213-244-0000
TCW Short Term Bond Fund Class Institutional	TGSMX	NAS CM	Open End	US Fixed Inc (Multisector Bond)	C	C-	B-		Y	213-244-0000
TCW Strategic Income	TSI	NYSE	Closed End	US Fixed Inc (Multisector Bond)	C	C-	C+		Y	213-244-0000
TCW Total Return Bond Fund Class I	TGLMX	NAS CM	Open End	US Fixed Inc (Multisector Bond)	B	B-	B+		Y	213-244-0000
TCW Total Return Bond Fund Class N	TGMNX	NAS CM	Open End	US Fixed Inc (Multisector Bond)	B	B-	B+	Up	Y	213-244-0000
TCW Total Return Bond Fund Class Plan	TGLSX	NAS CM	Open End	US Fixed Inc (Multisector Bond)	B	B-	B+		Y	213-244-0000
Templeton Emerging Markets Bond Fund Advisor Class	FEMZX	NAS CM	Open End	Emerg Mkts Fixed Inc (Diversified Emerg Mkts)	D	D	D+	Down	Y	650-312-2000
Templeton Emerging Markets Bond Fund Class A	FEMGX	NAS CM	Open End	Emerg Mkts Fixed Inc (Diversified Emerg Mkts)	D	D	D+	Down	Y	650-312-2000
Templeton Emerging Markets Bond Fund Class C	FEMHX	NAS CM	Open End	Emerg Mkts Fixed Inc (Diversified Emerg Mkts)	D	D	D+	Down	Y	650-312-2000
Templeton Emerging Markets Bond Fund Class R			Open End	Emerg Mkts Fixed Inc (Diversified Emerg Mkts)	D	D	D+	Down	Y	650-312-2000
Templeton Emerging Markets Bond Fund Class R6	FEMRX	NAS CM	Open End	Emerg Mkts Fixed Inc (Diversified Emerg Mkts)	D	D	D+	Down	Y	650-312-2000
Templeton Emerging Markets Income Fund	TEI	NYSE	Closed End	Emerg Mkts Fixed Inc (Worldwide Bond)	D	D	D		Y	

★ Expanded analysis of this fund is included in Section II.

TOTAL RETURNS & PERFORMANCE									ASSETS		ASSET ALLOCATION & TURNOVER							MINIMUMS		FEES		
3-Month Total Return	6-Month Total Return	1-Year Total Return	3-Year Total Return	5-Year Total Return	Dividend Yield (TTM)	Expense Ratio	3-Yr Std Deviation	Effective Duration	NAV	Total Assets (MIL)	%Cash	%Government Bonds	%Municipal Bonds	%Corporate Bonds	%Other	Turnover Ratio	Average Coupon Rate	Min Initial Investment	Min Additional Investment	Front End Fee (%)	Back End Fee (%)	Inception Date
2.17	0.35	2.59	10.73	18.07	3.27	0.45	4.54	6.44	10.13	2,575	0	0	100	0	0	11	4.98	1,000,000				Jul-17
2.09	1.50	2.33	5.33	7.45	1.26	0.82	2.1	2.76	5.69	1,930	1	0	99	0	0	17	4.83	2,500	100			Aug-12
2.37	1.70	2.93	6.82	9.79	1.66	0.41	2.12	2.76	5.71	1,930	1	0	99	0	0	17	4.83	1,000,000				Nov-16
0.02	0.28	0.75	2.73	2.96	0.85	0.4	0.11		1	394.4	22	0	78	0	0			2,500	100			Apr-81
0.02	0.32	0.83	2.95	3.18	0.94	0.33			1	394.4	22	0	78	0	0			1,000,000				Jul-17
3.28	-3.08	-0.37	9.39	20.08	3.77	0.62	6.6	6.85	11.75	4,520	0	0	100	0	0	5	5.14	2,500	100			Mar-85
2.15	0.31	2.52	10.47	17.80	3.19	0.54	4.56	6.44	10.13	2,575	0	0	100	0	0	11	4.98	2,500	100			Oct-76
2.08	0.15	2.19	9.43	16.01	2.87	0.87	4.48	6.44	10.14	2,575	0	0	100	0	0	11	4.98	2,500	100			Sep-02
2.17	1.65	2.64	6.30	9.21	1.56	0.52	2.08	2.76	5.7	1,930	1	0	99	0	0	17	4.83	2,500	100			Dec-83
6.60	3.44	6.80	16.14		3.31	0.53	4.66	5.55	10.39	107.2	4	17	1	29	0	348	3.82	2,500	100			Nov-16
6.52	3.29	6.49	15.13		3.02	0.82	4.65	5.55	10.39	107.2	4	17	1	29	0	348	3.82	2,500	100			Nov-16
6.62	3.49	6.92	16.64		3.42	0.42	4.65	5.55	10.4	107.2	4	17	1	29	0	348	3.82	1,000,000				Nov-16
3.95	6.31	8.83	16.74	24.03	2.65	0.3	3.6	5.73	11.8	1,369	3	24	3	31	0	50	3.46	2,500	100			Nov-00
12.51	-3.80	1.29	10.99	28.59	5.81	0.8	10.27	3.97	9.35	335.4	2	0	0	98	0	134	6.57	2,500	100			May-17
12.48	-3.87	1.14	10.37	27.30	5.66	0.95	10.28	3.97	9.34	335.4	2	0	0	98	0	134	6.57	2,500	100	4.75		Apr-13
12.60	-3.66	1.53	11.47	29.15	5.97	0.64	10.27	3.97	9.31	335.4	2	0	0	98	0	134	6.57	1,000,000				Apr-13
0.73	8.30	9.55	16.28	20.10	1.51	0.36	3.99	5.73	6.34	1,112	6	87	0	0	0	98	2.03	2,500	100			Sep-89
0.77	8.20	9.52	16.60	20.23	1.64	0.2	3.88	5.73	6.33	1,112	6	87	0	0	0	98	2.03	1,000,000				May-17
0.29	21.82	26.15	40.44	56.46	1.91	0.16	12.08	19.11	15.4	2,771	3	86	0	0	0	59	2.81	1,000,000				May-17
0.40	21.91	26.15	40.07	56.01		0	12.08	19.11	15.41	2,771	3	86	0	0	0	59	2.81	0				Mar-20
0.25	21.74	25.97	39.86	55.78	1.78	0.3	12.08	19.11	15.4	2,771	3	86	0	0	0	59	2.81	2,500	100			Sep-89
0.00	0.26	1.10	4.03	4.20	1.26	0.37	0.18		1	10,462	73	27	0	0	0	0		2,500	100			Jun-82
0.00	0.27	1.15	4.28	4.46	1.32	0.3	0.18		1	10,462	73	27	0	0	0	0		1,000,000				May-17
0.07	0.34	1.18	4.10	4.28		0			1	10,462	73	27	0	0	0	0		0				Mar-20
3.36	1.64	2.94	8.18	11.45	2.38	0.32	1.81	1.00	5.06	2,132	16	1	0	50	0	40	2.91	2,500	100			Dec-12
3.59	1.70	3.05	8.51	11.80	2.48	0.25	1.95	1.00	5.07	2,132	16	1	0	50	0	40	2.91	1,000,000				Jul-17
2.78	1.58	3.70	11.32	19.11	2.76	0.41	4.13	6.36	12.2	1,472	0	0	100	0	0	10	4.80	1,000,000				Jul-17
2.75	1.54	3.60	11.02	18.78	2.66	0.51	4.12	6.36	12.2	1,472	0	0	100	0	0	10	4.80	2,500	100			Apr-91
-0.30	-0.20	0.00	-0.50		0	1	0.2		9.94	0.02	100	0	0	0	0	0		0				Mar-17
3.68	6.64	9.28	17.38	23.18	2.4	0.49	3.38	5.18	11.96	1,444	18	16	1	24	0	215	3.00	2,000	250			Feb-93
3.64	6.54	9.05	16.62	21.71	2.18	0.7	3.39	5.18	11.93	1,444	18	16	1	24	0	215	3.00	2,000	250			Feb-99
3.77	6.86	9.50	17.62	23.43		0.44	3.33	5.18	12.01	1,444	18	16	1	24	0	215	3.00	25,000,000	50,000			Feb-20
16.13	-6.19	-3.59	6.87	27.02	5.14	0.85	13.54	7.39	7.76	5,765	3	69	0	28	0	136	5.81	2,000	250			May-98
16.04	-6.23	-3.70	6.13	25.46	4.87	0.95	13.49	7.39	10	5,765	3	69	0	28	0	136	5.81	2,000	250			Feb-04
15.64	-6.50	-3.91	6.52	26.60		0.77	13.48	7.39	7.76	5,765	3	69	0	28	0	136	5.81	25,000,000	50,000			Feb-20
10.54	-8.26	-5.10	-0.14	9.76	1.49	0.85	13.05	5.81	8.49	219.2	4	96	0	0	0	128	6.84	2,000	250			Dec-10
10.43	-8.28	-5.23	-0.27	9.63	1.49	0.9	13	5.81	8.47	219.2	4	96	0	0	0	128	6.84	2,000	250			Dec-10
5.61	3.81	5.50	12.95	18.90	1.14	0.62	4.39	7.41	10.35	18.7	4	42	1	27	0	83	3.08	2,000	250			Nov-11
5.61	3.81	5.45	12.82	18.76	1.08	0.72	4.37	7.41	10.35	18.7	4	42	1	27	0	83	3.08	2,000	250			Nov-11
8.84	1.44	4.97	16.92	29.83	4.26	0.55	6.18	3.45	6.48	38.7	10	3	0	81	0	122	4.88	2,000	250			Feb-93
8.72	1.32	4.73	16.13	28.15	4.04	0.8	6.15	3.45	6.52	38.7	10	3	0	81	0	122	4.88	2,000	250			Feb-99
1.11	0.87	2.09	6.76	8.23	2.95	0.44	0.9	0.44	8.58	14.7	58	12	0	12	0	248	2.20	2,000	250			Feb-93
8.36	1.03	3.42	14.90	25.25	6.22		5.52		5.62	267.0	2	3	3	32	0	35	3.53					Mar-87
3.00	7.15	9.24	17.28	22.82	3.8	0.49	3.54	4.95	10.49	6,584	8	7	0	0	0	178	2.95	2,000	250			Jun-93
2.95	7.03	8.99	16.20	21.10	3.55	0.7	3.53	4.95	10.81	6,584	8	7	0	0	0	178	2.95	2,000	250			Feb-99
2.91	7.08	9.17	17.21	22.75		0.44	3.53	4.95	10.51	6,584	8	7	0	0	0	178	2.95	25,000,000	50,000			Feb-20
1.10	-6.83	-9.98	-6.01	9.23	8.02	1.01	9.83	1.00	6.89	26.7	42	54	0	2	2	24	8.96	100,000				Apr-13
1.04	-7.09	-10.25	-6.88	7.96	7.78	1.26	9.88	1.00	6.86	26.7	42	54	0	2	2	24	8.96	1,000		3.75		Apr-13
0.94	-7.28	-10.64	-8.01	5.55	7.3	1.66	9.8	1.00	6.85	26.7	42	54	0	2	2	24	8.96	1,000			1.00	Apr-13
1.04	-7.07	-10.21	-6.92	7.39	7.78	1.51	9.87	1.00	6.87	26.7	42	54	0	2	2	24	8.96	1,000				Apr-13
1.13	-6.90	-9.90	-5.86	9.62	8.18	0.88	9.88	1.00	6.87	26.7	42	54	0	2	2	24	8.96	1,000,000				May-13
3.71	-7.90	-12.19	-12.53	1.67	7.19		10.23		9.01	426.7	27	33	0	3	0	28	5.85					Sep-93

	MARKET		FUND TYPE, CATEGORY & OBJECTIVE		RATINGS				NEW INVESTORS	
Fund Name	Ticker Symbol	Traded On	Fund Type	Category and (Prospectus Objective)	Overall Rating	Reward Rating	Risk Rating	Recent Up/ Downgrade	Open to New Investors	Telephone
Templeton Global Bond Fund Advisor Class	TGBAX	NAS CM	Open End	Fixed Inc Misc (Worldwide Bond)	D	D	C-	Down	Y	650-312-2000
Templeton Global Bond Fund Class A	TPINX	NAS CM	Open End	Fixed Inc Misc (Worldwide Bond)	D	D	C-	Down	Y	650-312-2000
Templeton Global Bond Fund Class C	TEGBX	NAS CM	Open End	Fixed Inc Misc (Worldwide Bond)	D	D	C-	Down	Y	650-312-2000
Templeton Global Bond Fund Class R	FGBRX	NAS CM	Open End	Fixed Inc Misc (Worldwide Bond)	D	D	C-	Down	Y	650-312-2000
Templeton Global Bond Fund Class R6	FBNRX	NAS CM	Open End	Fixed Inc Misc (Worldwide Bond)	D	D	C-	Down	Y	650-312-2000
Templeton Global Income Fund	GIM	NYSE	Closed End	Global Fixed Inc (Worldwide Bond)	D	D	C-	Down	Y	954-527-7500
Templeton Global Total Return Fund Advisor Class	TTRZX	NAS CM	Open End	Fixed Inc Misc (Worldwide Bond)	D	D	C-	Down	Y	650-312-2000
Templeton Global Total Return Fund Class A	TGTRX	NAS CM	Open End	Fixed Inc Misc (Worldwide Bond)	D	D	C-	Down	Y	650-312-2000
Templeton Global Total Return Fund Class C	TTRCX	NAS CM	Open End	Fixed Inc Misc (Worldwide Bond)	D	D	C-	Down	Y	650-312-2000
Templeton Global Total Return Fund Class R	FRRGX	NAS CM	Open End	Fixed Inc Misc (Worldwide Bond)	D	D	C-	Down	Y	650-312-2000
Templeton Global Total Return Fund Class R6	FTTRX	NAS CM	Open End	Fixed Inc Misc (Worldwide Bond)	D	D	C-	Down	Y	650-312-2000
Templeton International Bond Fund Advisor Class	FIBZX	NAS CM	Open End	Fixed Inc Misc (Worldwide Bond)	D	D	C-	Down	Y	650-312-2000
Templeton International Bond Fund Class A	TBOAX	NAS CM	Open End	Fixed Inc Misc (Worldwide Bond)	D	D	C-	Down	Y	650-312-2000
Templeton International Bond Fund Class C	FCNBX	NAS CM	Open End	Fixed Inc Misc (Worldwide Bond)	D	D-	C-	Down	Y	650-312-2000
Templeton International Bond Fund Class R			Open End	Fixed Inc Misc (Worldwide Bond)	D	D	C-	Down	Y	650-312-2000
Templeton International Bond Fund Class R6	FIBQX	NAS CM	Open End	Fixed Inc Misc (Worldwide Bond)	D	D	C-	Down	Y	650-312-2000
The Community Development Fund Class A	CDCDX	NAS CM	Open End	US Fixed Inc (Income)	C+	C	B-		Y	305-663-0100
The Hartford Strategic Income Fund Class A	HSNAX	NAS CM	Open End	US Fixed Inc (Multisector Bond)	C	C	B		Y	888-843-7824
The Hartford Strategic Income Fund Class C	HSNCX	NAS CM	Open End	US Fixed Inc (Multisector Bond)	C	C-	B-		Y	888-843-7824
The Hartford Strategic Income Fund Class F	HSNFX	NAS CM	Open End	US Fixed Inc (Multisector Bond)	C	C	B		Y	888-843-7824
The Hartford Strategic Income Fund Class I	HSNIX	NAS CM	Open End	US Fixed Inc (Multisector Bond)	C	C	B		Y	888-843-7824
The Hartford Strategic Income Fund Class R3	HSNRX	NAS CM	Open End	US Fixed Inc (Multisector Bond)	C	C-	B-		Y	888-843-7824
The Hartford Strategic Income Fund Class R4	HSNSX	NAS CM	Open End	US Fixed Inc (Multisector Bond)	C	C-	B		Y	888-843-7824
The Hartford Strategic Income Fund Class R5	HSNTX	NAS CM	Open End	US Fixed Inc (Multisector Bond)	C	C	B		Y	888-843-7824
The Hartford Strategic Income Fund Class R6	HSNVX	NAS CM	Open End	US Fixed Inc (Multisector Bond)	C	C	B		Y	888-843-7824
The Hartford Strategic Income Fund Class Y	HSNYX	NAS CM	Open End	US Fixed Inc (Multisector Bond)	C	C	B		Y	888-843-7824
The Hartford Total Return Bond Fund Class A	ITBAX	NAS CM	Open End	US Fixed Inc (Multisector Bond)	B	C+	B+	Up	Y	888-843-7824
The Hartford Total Return Bond Fund Class C	HABCX	NAS CM	Open End	US Fixed Inc (Multisector Bond)	B-	C+	B	Up	Y	888-843-7824
The Hartford Total Return Bond Fund Class F	ITBFX	NAS CM	Open End	US Fixed Inc (Multisector Bond)	B	C+	B+	Up	Y	888-843-7824
The Hartford Total Return Bond Fund Class I	ITBIX	NAS CM	Open End	US Fixed Inc (Multisector Bond)	B	C+	B+	Up	Y	888-843-7824
The Hartford Total Return Bond Fund Class R3	ITBRX	NAS CM	Open End	US Fixed Inc (Multisector Bond)	B-	C+	B+	Up	Y	888-843-7824
The Hartford Total Return Bond Fund Class R4	ITBUX	NAS CM	Open End	US Fixed Inc (Multisector Bond)	B	C+	B+	Up	Y	888-843-7824
The Hartford Total Return Bond Fund Class R5	ITBTX	NAS CM	Open End	US Fixed Inc (Multisector Bond)	B	C+	B+	Up	Y	888-843-7824
The Hartford Total Return Bond Fund Class R6	ITBVX	NAS CM	Open End	US Fixed Inc (Multisector Bond)	B	C+	B+	Up	Y	888-843-7824
The Hartford Total Return Bond Fund Class Y	HABYX	NAS CM	Open End	US Fixed Inc (Multisector Bond)	B	C+	B+	Up	Y	888-843-7824
The Hartford World Bond Fund Class A	HWDAX	NAS CM	Open End	Global Fixed Inc (Worldwide Bond)	C	C	C+		Y	888-843-7824
The Hartford World Bond Fund Class C	HWDCX	NAS CM	Open End	Global Fixed Inc (Worldwide Bond)	C	C-	C+		Y	888-843-7824
The Hartford World Bond Fund Class F	HWDFX	NAS CM	Open End	Global Fixed Inc (Worldwide Bond)	C	C	C+		Y	888-843-7824
The Hartford World Bond Fund Class I	HWDIX	NAS CM	Open End	Global Fixed Inc (Worldwide Bond)	C	C	C+		Y	888-843-7824
The Hartford World Bond Fund Class R3	HWDRX	NAS CM	Open End	Global Fixed Inc (Worldwide Bond)	C	C	C+		Y	888-843-7824
The Hartford World Bond Fund Class R4	HWDSX	NAS CM	Open End	Global Fixed Inc (Worldwide Bond)	C	C	C+		Y	888-843-7824
The Hartford World Bond Fund Class R5	HWDTX	NAS CM	Open End	Global Fixed Inc (Worldwide Bond)	C	C	C+		Y	888-843-7824
The Hartford World Bond Fund Class R6	HWDVX	NAS CM	Open End	Global Fixed Inc (Worldwide Bond)	C	C	C+		Y	888-843-7824
The Hartford World Bond Fund Class Y	HWDYX	NAS CM	Open End	Global Fixed Inc (Worldwide Bond)	C	C	C+		Y	888-843-7824
Thompson Bond Fund	THOPX	NAS CM	Open End	US Fixed Inc (Income)	D	D	C-	Down	Y	
Thornburg California Limited Term Municipal Fund Class A	LTCAX	NAS CM	Open End	US Muni Fixed Inc (Muni Bond - Single State)	C	C-	C+		Y	800-847-0200
Thornburg California Limited Term Municipal Fund Class C	LTCCX	NAS CM	Open End	US Muni Fixed Inc (Muni Bond - Single State)	C	C-	C		Y	800-847-0200
Thornburg California Limited Term Municipal Fund Class I	LTCIX	NAS CM	Open End	US Muni Fixed Inc (Muni Bond - Single State)	C	C	C+		Y	800-847-0200
Thornburg Capital Management Fund			Open End	US Fixed Inc (Income)	C	C-	C+		Y	800-847-0200
Thornburg Intermediate Municipal Fund Class A	THIMX	NAS CM	Open End	US Muni Fixed Inc (Muni Bond - Natl)	C	C-	C+		Y	800-847-0200
Thornburg Intermediate Municipal Fund Class C	THMCX	NAS CM	Open End	US Muni Fixed Inc (Muni Bond - Natl)	C	C-	C+		Y	800-847-0200
Thornburg Intermediate Municipal Fund Class I	THMIX	NAS CM	Open End	US Muni Fixed Inc (Muni Bond - Natl)	C	C-	B-		Y	800-847-0200

★ Expanded analysis of this fund is included in Section II.

TOTAL RETURNS & PERFORMANCE									ASSETS		ASSET ALLOCATION & TURNOVER							MINIMUMS		FEES		
3-Month Total Return	6-Month Total Return	1-Year Total Return	3-Year Total Return	5-Year Total Return	Dividend Yield (TTM)	Expense Ratio	3-Yr Std Deviation	Effective Duration	NAV	Total Assets (MIL)	%Cash	%Government Bonds	%Municipal Bonds	%Corporate Bonds	%Other	Turnover Ratio	Average Coupon Rate	Min Initial Investment	Min Additional Investment	Front End Fee (%)	Back End Fee (%)	Inception Date
0.09	-4.33	-6.50	-2.73	2.49	6.09	0.67	6.24	2.06	9.96	20,603	24	75	0	0	3	33	5.18	100,000				Jan-97
0.13	-4.43	-6.70	-3.44	1.21	5.8	0.92	6.29	2.06	10.01	20,603	24	75	0	0	3	33	5.18	1,000		3.75		Sep-86
0.03	-4.61	-7.06	-4.51	-0.71	5.35	1.32	6.27	2.06	10.04	20,603	24	75	0	0	3	33	5.18	1,000			1.00	May-95
0.07	-4.55	-6.93	-4.08	0.04	5.53	1.17	6.29	2.06	10.01	20,603	24	75	0	0	3	33	5.18	1,000				Feb-09
0.13	-4.27	-6.37	-2.33	3.23	6.23	0.56	6.25	2.06	9.96	20,603	24	75	0	0	3	33	5.18	1,000,000				May-13
-0.92	-5.88	-7.89	-2.94	-0.02	5.36		6.29		6.23	842.4	69	20	0	0	0	22	5.46					Mar-88
0.32	-5.87	-7.50	-2.47	4.18	6.61	0.76	6.65	1.83	10.2	3,024	24	74	0	0	4	28	5.98	100,000				Sep-08
0.16	-6.00	-7.75	-3.20	2.81	6.35	1.01	6.64	1.83	10.18	3,024	24	74	0	0	4	28	5.98	1,000		3.75		Sep-08
0.16	-6.10	-8.12	-4.28	0.86	5.93	1.41	6.57	1.83	10.17	3,024	24	74	0	0	4	28	5.98	1,000			1.00	Sep-08
0.19	-6.12	-7.98	-3.93	1.61	6.08	1.26	6.67	1.83	10.19	3,024	24	74	0	0	4	28	5.98	1,000				Sep-08
0.36	-5.81	-7.40	-2.12	4.74	6.74	0.66	6.66	1.83	10.19	3,024	24	74	0	0	4	28	5.98	1,000,000				May-13
-1.47	-5.38	-6.97	-1.80	4.20	5.17	0.84	5.51	1.40	9.15	401.5	47	52	0	0	2	24	4.73	100,000				Dec-07
-1.53	-5.51	-7.21	-2.55	2.93	4.91	1.09	5.49	1.40	9.14	401.5	47	52	0	0	2	24	4.73	1,000		3.75		Dec-07
-1.74	-5.69	-7.57	-3.71	0.87	4.48	1.49	5.49	1.40	9.15	401.5	47	52	0	0	2	24	4.73	1,000			1.00	Dec-07
-1.60	-5.54	-7.38	-3.17	1.58	4.63	1.34	5.45	1.40	9.14	401.5	47	52	0	0	2	24	4.73	1,000				Dec-07
-1.44	-5.32	-6.83	-1.39	4.64	5.32	0.71	5.51	1.40	9.15	401.5	47	52	0	0	2	24	4.73	1,000,000				Aug-17
1.29	3.80	5.16	9.81		1.7	1	2.38		10.04	64.0	17	11	1	0	0	14	3.09	1,000,000				Apr-16
12.33	3.39	6.42	16.14	30.51	3.98	0.95	7.35	5.40	8.82	973.5	5	40	1	38	0	74	3.68	2,000	50	4.50		May-07
12.15	2.96	5.62	13.59	25.72	3.13	1.7	7.38	5.40	8.88	973.5	5	40	1	38	0	74	3.68	2,000	50		1.00	May-07
12.41	3.46	6.82	17.41	32.47	4.35	0.6	7.37	5.40	8.84	973.5	5	40	1	38	0	74	3.68	1,000,000				Feb-17
12.52	3.55	6.73	17.06	32.19	4.27	0.7	7.37	5.40	8.85	973.5	5	40	1	38	0	74	3.68	2,000	50			May-07
12.27	3.12	6.09	15.08	28.53	3.67	1.25	7.4	5.40	8.8	973.5	5	40	1	38	0	74	3.68	0				Sep-11
12.36	3.29	6.44	16.04	30.51	3.98	0.95	7.39	5.40	8.81	973.5	5	40	1	38	0	74	3.68	0				Sep-11
12.44	3.56	6.78	17.28	32.64	4.32	0.65	7.33	5.40	8.81	973.5	5	40	1	38	0	74	3.68	0				Sep-11
12.45	3.59	6.84	17.46	33.00	4.37	0.6	7.33	5.40	8.81	973.5	5	40	1	38	0	74	3.68	0				Nov-14
12.46	3.46	6.65	17.22	32.79	4.3	0.69	7.34	5.40	8.8	973.5	5	40	1	38	0	74	3.68	250,000				Aug-07
5.80	5.63	8.59	16.58	24.57	2.55	0.74	3.83	5.81	11.09	2,446	2	21	1	27	0	71	3.15	2,000	50	4.50		Jul-96
5.63	5.26	7.74	13.91	19.95	1.75	1.53	3.84	5.81	11.22	2,446	2	21	1	27	0	71	3.15	2,000	50		1.00	Jul-98
5.94	5.76	9.00	17.92	27.01	3.25	0.35	3.8	5.81	10.99	2,446	2	21	1	27	0	71	3.15	1,000,000				Feb-17
5.99	5.80	8.97	17.64	26.40	3.16	0.46	3.87	5.81	11.06	2,446	2	21	1	27	0	71	3.15	2,000	50			Aug-06
5.77	5.44	8.23	15.42	22.66	2.19	1.07	3.8	5.81	11.4	2,446	2	21	1	27	0	71	3.15	0				Dec-06
5.88	5.62	8.60	16.48	24.46	2.48	0.76	3.86	5.81	11.3	2,446	2	21	1	27	0	71	3.15	0				Dec-06
5.90	5.71	9.22	17.80	26.74	3	0.47	3.82	5.81	11.23	2,446	2	21	1	27	0	71	3.15	0				Dec-06
5.86	5.80	8.91	17.79	26.88	3.24	0.35	3.81	5.81	11.14	2,446	2	21	1	27	0	71	3.15	0				Nov-14
5.84	5.76	8.87	17.68	26.75	3.13	0.46	3.8	5.81	11.16	2,446	2	21	1	27	0	71	3.15	250,000				Jul-96
2.02	-0.14	0.42	8.54	11.57	2.22	1.03	2.45	3.59	10.47	4,867	17	55	0	14	0	93	2.00	2,000	50	4.50		May-11
1.88	-0.38	-0.28	6.22	7.69	1.55	1.76	2.39	3.59	10.26	4,867	17	55	0	14	0	93	2.00	2,000	50		1.00	May-11
2.11	0.04	0.80	9.72	13.45	2.57	0.65	2.45	3.59	10.56	4,867	17	55	0	14	0	93	2.00	1,000,000				Feb-17
2.08	0.09	0.70	9.51	13.13	2.48	0.75	2.38	3.59	10.55	4,867	17	55	0	14	0	93	2.00	2,000	50			May-11
1.95	-0.21	0.06	7.56	9.89	1.89	1.37	2.42	3.59	10.41	4,867	17	55	0	14	0	93	2.00	0				May-11
2.01	-0.13	0.44	8.52	11.55	2.33	1.07	2.42	3.59	10.47	4,867	17	55	0	14	0	93	2.00	0				May-11
2.08	0.00	0.67	9.47	13.22	2.46	0.77	2.44	3.59	10.55	4,867	17	55	0	14	0	93	2.00	0				May-11
2.10	0.14	0.80	9.80	13.72	2.57	0.65	2.39	3.59	10.59	4,867	17	55	0	14	0	93	2.00	0				Nov-14
2.08	0.00	0.71	9.54	13.46	2.49	0.74	2.42	3.59	10.58	4,867	17	55	0	14	0	93	2.00	250,000				May-11
2.92	-6.85	-4.64	1.46	11.07	3.92	0.71	6.16	2.21	10.45	2,828	8	0	1	65	0	53	4.78	250	50			Feb-92
1.59	0.93	1.80	4.57	7.59	1.47	0.74	2.1	2.79	13.76	531.0	6	0	94	0	0	18	4.19	5,000	100	1.50		Feb-87
1.52	0.79	1.51	3.71	6.19	1.18	1.02	2.1	2.79	13.77	531.0	6	0	94	0	0	18	4.19	5,000	100		0.50	Sep-94
1.65	1.05	2.05	5.38	9.09	1.71	0.49	2.09	2.79	13.77	531.0	6	0	94	0	0	18	4.19	2,500,000	100			Apr-97
0.14	0.58	1.63	5.70		1.81	0.03	0.16		10	1,006	91	0	9	0	0	0	0.06	0				Jul-15
2.20	1.18	2.77	8.66	13.72	2.5	0.77	3.37	5.51	14.29	1,019	0	0	100	0	0	16	4.88	5,000	100	2.00		Jul-91
2.03	0.93	2.33	7.45	11.82	2.13	1.14	3.39	5.51	14.3	1,019	0	0	100	0	0	16	4.88	5,000	100		0.60	Sep-94
2.26	1.30	3.03	9.49	15.27	2.75	0.53	3.41	5.51	14.27	1,019	0	0	100	0	0	16	4.88	2,500,000	100			Jul-96

Fund Name	MARKET Ticker Symbol	Traded On	FUND TYPE, CATEGORY & OBJECTIVE Fund Type	Category and (Prospectus Objective)	RATINGS Overall Rating	Reward Rating	Risk Rating	Recent Up/ Downgrade	NEW INVESTORS Open to New Investors	Telephone
Thornburg Limited Term Income Fund Class A	THIFX	NAS CM	Open End	US Fixed Inc (Corp Bond - General)	B-	C	B+	Up	Y	800-847-0200
Thornburg Limited Term Income Fund Class C	THICX	NAS CM	Open End	US Fixed Inc (Corp Bond - General)	B-	C	B	Up	Y	800-847-0200
Thornburg Limited Term Income Fund Class I	THIIX	NAS CM	Open End	US Fixed Inc (Corp Bond - General)	B-	C	B+	Up	Y	800-847-0200
Thornburg Limited Term Income Fund Class R3	THIRX	NAS CM	Open End	US Fixed Inc (Corp Bond - General)	C+	C	B-	Up	Y	800-847-0200
Thornburg Limited Term Income Fund Class R4	THRIX	NAS CM	Open End	US Fixed Inc (Corp Bond - General)	C+	C	B-	Up	Y	800-847-0200
Thornburg Limited Term Income Fund Class R5	THRRX	NAS CM	Open End	US Fixed Inc (Corp Bond - General)	C+	C	B	Up	Y	800-847-0200
Thornburg Limited Term Income Fund Class R6	THRLX	NAS CM	Open End	US Fixed Inc (Corp Bond - General)	C+	C	B	Up	Y	800-847-0200
Thornburg Limited Term Municipal Fund Class A	LTMFX	NAS CM	Open End	US Muni Fixed Inc (Muni Bond - Natl)	C	C	C+		Y	800-847-0200
Thornburg Limited Term Municipal Fund Class C	LTMCX	NAS CM	Open End	US Muni Fixed Inc (Muni Bond - Natl)	C	C	C+		Y	800-847-0200
Thornburg Limited Term Municipal Fund Class I	LTMIX	NAS CM	Open End	US Muni Fixed Inc (Muni Bond - Natl)	C	C	B-		Y	800-847-0200
Thornburg Limited Term U.S. Government Fund Class A	LTUSX	NAS CM	Open End	US Fixed Inc (Govt Bond - General)	C+	C	B	Up	Y	800-847-0200
Thornburg Limited Term U.S. Government Fund Class C	LTUCX	NAS CM	Open End	US Fixed Inc (Govt Bond - General)	C+	C	B	Up	Y	800-847-0200
Thornburg Limited Term U.S. Government Fund Class I	LTUIX	NAS CM	Open End	US Fixed Inc (Govt Bond - General)	C+	C	B		Y	800-847-0200
Thornburg Limited Term U.S. Government Fund Class R3	LTURX	NAS CM	Open End	US Fixed Inc (Govt Bond - General)	C+	C	B	Up	Y	800-847-0200
Thornburg Limited Term U.S. Government Fund Class R4	LTUGX	NAS CM	Open End	US Fixed Inc (Govt Bond - General)	C+	C	B	Up	Y	800-847-0200
Thornburg Limited Term U.S. Government Fund Class R5	LTGRX	NAS CM	Open End	US Fixed Inc (Govt Bond - General)	C+	C	B		Y	800-847-0200
Thornburg Low Duration Income Fund Class A	TLDAX	NAS CM	Open End	US Fixed Inc (Muni Bond - Natl)	C	C-	B-		Y	800-847-0200
Thornburg Low Duration Income Fund Class I	TLDIX	NAS CM	Open End	US Fixed Inc (Muni Bond - Natl)	C	C	B-		Y	800-847-0200
Thornburg New Mexico Intermediate Municipal Fund Class A	THNMX	NAS CM	Open End	US Muni Fixed Inc (Muni Bond - Single State)	C	C	B-		Y	800-847-0200
Thornburg New Mexico Intermediate Municipal Fund Class D	THNDX	NAS CM	Open End	US Muni Fixed Inc (Muni Bond - Single State)	C	C-	C+		Y	800-847-0200
Thornburg New Mexico Intermediate Municipal Fund Class I	THNIX	NAS CM	Open End	US Muni Fixed Inc (Muni Bond - Single State)	C	C	B-		Y	800-847-0200
Thornburg New York Intermediate Municipal Fund Class A	THNYX	NAS CM	Open End	US Muni Fixed Inc (Muni Bond - Single State)	C	C-	C+		Y	800-847-0200
Thornburg New York Intermediate Municipal Fund Class I	TNYIX	NAS CM	Open End	US Muni Fixed Inc (Muni Bond - Single State)	C	C-	B-		Y	800-847-0200
Thornburg Short Duration Municipal Fund Class A	TLMAX	NAS CM	Open End	US Muni Fixed Inc (Muni Bond - Natl)	C	C-	C		Y	800-847-0200
Thornburg Short Duration Municipal Fund Class I	TLMIX	NAS CM	Open End	US Muni Fixed Inc (Muni Bond - Natl)	C	C-	C		Y	800-847-0200
Thornburg Strategic Income Fund Class A	TSIAX	NAS CM	Open End	US Fixed Inc (Income)	C	C-	B-		Y	800-847-0200
Thornburg Strategic Income Fund Class C	TSICX	NAS CM	Open End	US Fixed Inc (Income)	C	C-	C+		Y	800-847-0200
Thornburg Strategic Income Fund Class I	TSIIX	NAS CM	Open End	US Fixed Inc (Income)	C	C-	B-		Y	800-847-0200
Thornburg Strategic Income Fund Class R3	TSIRX	NAS CM	Open End	US Fixed Inc (Income)	C	C-	B-		Y	800-847-0200
Thornburg Strategic Income Fund Class R4	TSRIX	NAS CM	Open End	US Fixed Inc (Income)	C	C-	B-		Y	800-847-0200
Thornburg Strategic Income Fund Class R5	TSRRX	NAS CM	Open End	US Fixed Inc (Income)	C	C-	B-		Y	800-847-0200
Thornburg Strategic Income Fund Class R6	TSRSX	NAS CM	Open End	US Fixed Inc (Income)	C	C	B-		Y	800-847-0200
Thornburg Strategic Municipal Income Fund Class A	TSSAX	NAS CM	Open End	US Muni Fixed Inc (Muni Bond - Natl)	C	C-	C+		Y	800-847-0200
Thornburg Strategic Municipal Income Fund Class C	TSSCX	NAS CM	Open End	US Muni Fixed Inc (Muni Bond - Natl)	C	C-	C		Y	800-847-0200
Thornburg Strategic Municipal Income Fund Class I	TSSIX	NAS CM	Open End	US Muni Fixed Inc (Muni Bond - Natl)	C	C-	C+		Y	800-847-0200
Thrivent Church Loan and Income Fund Class S Shares	XCLIX	NAS CM	Closed End	US Fixed Inc (Income)	D+	D+	B	Up	Y	
Thrivent Government Bond Class A	TBFAX	NAS CM	Open End	US Fixed Inc (Govt Bond - General)	B	B-	B	Up		
Thrivent Government Bond Portfolio			Open End	US Fixed Inc (Corp Bond - General)	U	U	U		Y	
Thrivent Government Bond S Class	TBFIX	NAS CM	Open End	US Fixed Inc (Govt Bond - General)	B	B-	B		Y	
Thrivent High Income Municipal Bond Fund Class S	THMBX	NAS CM	Open End	US Muni Fixed Inc (Muni Bond - Natl)	D+	D	C-	Down	Y	
Thrivent High Yield Fund Class A	LBHYX	NAS CM	Open End	US Fixed Inc (Corp Bond - High Yield)	D+	D+	C-	Down	Y	
Thrivent High Yield Fund Class S	LBHIX	NAS CM	Open End	US Fixed Inc (Corp Bond - High Yield)	D+	D+	C-	Down	Y	
Thrivent High Yield Portfolio			Open End	High Yield Fixed Inc (Corp Bond - High Yield)	U	U	U		Y	
Thrivent Income Fund Class A	LUBIX	NAS CM	Open End	US Fixed Inc (Income)	B-	C+	B	Up	Y	
Thrivent Income Fund Class S	LBIIX	NAS CM	Open End	US Fixed Inc (Income)	B-	C+	B+	Up	Y	
Thrivent Income Portfolio			Open End	US Fixed Inc (Corp Bond - General)	U	U	U		Y	
Thrivent Limited Maturity Bond Fund Class A	LBLAX	NAS CM	Open End	US Fixed Inc (Income)	C	C-	C+		Y	
Thrivent Limited Maturity Bond Fund Class S	THLIX	NAS CM	Open End	US Fixed Inc (Income)	C	C	C+		Y	
Thrivent Limited Maturity Bond Portfolio			Open End	US Fixed Inc (Corp Bond - High Yield)	U	U	U		Y	
Thrivent Money Market Fund Class A	AMMXX	NAS CM	Money Mkt	US Money Mkt (Money Mkt - Taxable)	C	C-	C+		Y	
Thrivent Money Market Fund Class S	AALXX	NAS CM	Money Mkt	US Money Mkt (Money Mkt - Taxable)	C	C-	C+		Y	
Thrivent Money Market Portfolio			Money Mkt	US Money Mkt (Money Mkt - Govt)	C	C-	C+		Y	

★Expanded analysis of this fund is included in Section II.

TOTAL RETURNS & PERFORMANCE									ASSETS		ASSET ALLOCATION & TURNOVER							MINIMUMS		FEES		
3-Month Total Return	6-Month Total Return	1-Year Total Return	3-Year Total Return	5-Year Total Return	Dividend Yield (TTM)	Expense Ratio	3-Yr Std Deviation	Effective Duration	NAV	Total Assets (MIL)	%Cash	%Government Bonds	%Municipal Bonds	%Corporate Bonds	%Other	Turnover Ratio	Average Coupon Rate	Min Initial Investment	Min Additional Investment	Front End Fee (%)	Back End Fee (%)	Inception Date
5.70	4.99	6.65	12.46	17.42	2.2	0.81	2.68	2.99	14.02	6,462	8	10	2	41	0	43	3.05	5,000	100	1.50		Oct-92
5.73	4.88	6.41	11.74	16.17	1.97	1.02	2.74	2.99	14	6,462	8	10	2	41	0	43	3.05	5,000	100		0.50	Sep-94
5.86	5.14	7.01	13.59	19.47	2.47	0.49	2.7	2.99	14.03	6,462	8	10	2	41	0	43	3.05	2,500,000	100			Jul-96
5.65	4.88	6.40	11.87	16.54	1.98	0.99	2.68	2.99	14.03	6,462	8	10	2	41	0	43	3.05	0				Jul-03
5.74	4.89	6.48	11.95	16.63	1.98	0.99	2.69	2.99	14.02	6,462	8	10	2	41	0	43	3.05	0				Feb-14
5.87	5.15	6.94	13.25	18.79	2.47	0.49	2.75	2.99	14.02	6,462	8	10	2	41	0	43	3.05	0				May-12
5.87	5.17	7.00	13.96	19.35	2.54	0.42	2.74	2.99	14.05	6,462	8	10	2	41	0	43	3.05	0				Apr-17
1.88	1.54	2.64	6.36	9.69	1.72	0.69	2.11	3.02	14.59	5,512	3	0	97	0	0	21	4.41	5,000	100	1.50		Sep-84
1.88	1.47	2.44	5.72	8.51	1.47	0.94	2.11	3.02	14.61	5,512	3	0	97	0	0	21	4.41	5,000	100		0.50	Sep-94
2.00	1.79	2.94	7.33	11.37	1.96	0.45	2.1	3.02	14.59	5,512	3	0	97	0	0	21	4.41	2,500,000	100			Jul-96
1.53	3.44	4.38	8.16	9.73	1.7	0.9	1.59	2.39	13.39	318.3	10	16	0	5	0	29	2.85	5,000	100	1.50		Nov-87
1.46	3.28	4.05	7.12	8.07	1.41	1.24	1.62	2.39	13.47	318.3	10	16	0	5	0	29	2.85	5,000	100		0.50	Sep-94
1.61	3.59	4.68	9.12	11.44	1.99	0.62	1.58	2.39	13.39	318.3	10	16	0	5	0	29	2.85	2,500,000	100			Jul-96
1.52	3.39	4.27	7.90	9.33	1.61	0.99	1.62	2.39	13.4	318.3	10	16	0	5	0	29	2.85	0				Jul-03
1.52	3.39	4.27	7.88	9.30	1.61	0.99	1.62	2.39	13.39	318.3	10	16	0	5	0	29	2.85	0				Feb-14
1.49	3.44	4.50	8.83	11.05	1.92	0.67	1.59	2.39	13.4	318.3	10	16	0	5	0	29	2.85	0				May-12
3.65	1.92	3.16	7.61	10.23	2.18	0.7	2.04	0.96	12.56	27.2	8	2	3	26	0	80	2.83	5,000	100	1.50		Dec-13
3.75	2.16	3.42	8.40	11.35	2.38	0.5	2.04	0.96	12.55	27.2	8	2	3	26	0	80	2.83	2,500,000	100			Dec-13
2.03	1.78	3.26	7.97	11.99	2.09	0.97	2.58	5.14	13.44	158.9	6	0	94	0	0	17	4.78	5,000	100	2.00		Jun-91
1.97	1.57	2.90	7.04	10.61	1.81	1.25	2.65	5.14	13.44	158.9	6	0	94	0	0	17	4.78	5,000	100			Jun-99
2.11	1.86	3.56	8.95	13.76	2.38	0.67	2.63	5.14	13.43	158.9	6	0	94	0	0	17	4.78	2,500,000	100			Feb-07
1.91	1.39	2.55	6.79	11.29	2.11	0.99	3.14	5.87	12.97	48.0	1	0	99	0	0	18	4.79	5,000	100	2.00		Sep-97
1.99	1.55	2.87	7.82	13.09	2.43	0.67	3.15	5.87	12.97	48.0	1	0	99	0	0	18	4.79	2,500,000	100			Feb-10
0.91	0.39	0.97	3.36	4.37	1.17	0.7	1.04	1.09	12.35	123.0	10	0	90	0	0	34	3.26	5,000	100	1.50		Dec-13
0.88	0.41	1.17	3.90	5.32	1.37	0.5	1.05	1.09	12.34	123.0	10	0	90	0	0	34	3.26	2,500,000	100			Dec-13
7.97	1.80	4.10	11.79	21.04	3.26	1.05	4.74	2.52	11.98	1,750	7	1	2	60	0	32	4.25	5,000	100	4.50		Dec-07
7.78	1.51	3.32	9.39	17.11	2.49	1.8	4.74	2.52	11.96	1,750	7	1	2	60	0	32	4.25	5,000	100		1.00	Dec-07
8.01	2.00	4.33	13.05	23.30	3.65	0.6	4.71	2.52	11.94	1,750	7	1	2	60	0	32	4.25	2,500,000	100			Dec-07
7.83	1.68	3.75	11.20	20.28	3	1.25	4.71	2.52	11.96	1,750	7	1	2	60	0	32	4.25	0				May-12
7.84	1.68	3.67	10.99	20.15	3.01	1.25	4.74	2.52	11.95	1,750	7	1	2	60	0	32	4.25	0				Feb-14
8.01	2.00	4.42	13.18	23.29	3.66	0.6	4.71	2.52	11.95	1,750	7	1	2	60	0	32	4.25	0				May-12
8.01	2.04	4.48	13.74	24.49	3.72	0.53	4.71	2.52	11.98	1,750	7	1	2	60	0	32	4.25	0				Apr-17
2.19	0.54	2.17	8.63	13.99	2.54	0.81	3.61	5.53	15.19	292.5	1	0	99	0	0	20	4.51	5,000	100	2.00		Apr-09
2.07	0.38	1.69	7.09	11.62	2.07	1.28	3.58	5.53	15.21	292.5	1	0	99	0	0	20	4.51	5,000	100		0.60	Apr-09
2.31	0.72	2.39	9.35	15.41	2.77	0.59	3.59	5.53	15.21	292.5	1	0	99	0	0	20	4.51	2,500,000	100			Apr-09
3.03	4.34	6.84			3.07	1			10.87	--						447		2,000	50			Sep-18
0.77	7.03	8.23	13.92	18.14	1.63	0.85	3.3	6.00	10.62	68.5	-6	52	0	2	19	274	2.59	2,000	50	2.00		Feb-10
0.26	-1.18	-1.40	3.10	10.85	1.89	0.45	2.87	5.60		188.6	8	43	0	1	0	422	2.62	0				Jun-95
0.89	7.19	8.43	14.26	18.85	1.72	0.75	3.29	6.00	10.63	68.5	-6	52	0	2	19	274	2.59	2,000	50			Feb-10
3.97	-3.82	-1.06			3.08	0.6			10.12	16.4	6	0	94	0	0	93	4.89	2,000	50			Feb-18
8.30	-6.50	-3.29	5.43	16.34	5.47	0.8	8.74	4.30	4.37	774.5	3	0	0	96	0	42	5.78	2,000	50	4.50		Apr-87
8.37	-6.37	-3.23	6.20	17.58	5.75	0.54	8.76	4.30	4.37	774.5	3	0	0	96	0	42	5.78	2,000	50			Oct-97
1.20	0.21	3.33	13.79	27.13	5.33	0.45	4.86	4.00		834.2	5	1	0	94	0	50	6.08	0				Nov-87
8.78	5.71	9.44	19.18	30.16	2.7	0.77	5.63	7.10	9.92	961.6	-2	11	0	80	8	99	3.79	2,000	50	4.50		Jun-72
8.87	5.87	9.77	20.16	32.09	2.99	0.46	5.69	7.10	9.91	961.6	-2	11	0	80	8	99	3.79	2,000	50			Oct-97
-0.34	-2.37	-0.95	8.26	19.04	3.25	0.44	3.49	6.40		1,481	10	7	0	73	0	105	4.33	0				Jan-87
4.82	2.03	3.24	8.28	12.22	2.29	0.61	2.76	1.70	12.63	1,117	10	18	0	33	0	109	2.96	2,000	100	4.50		Oct-99
4.78	2.04	3.42	8.88	13.22	2.46	0.43	2.76	1.70	12.62	1,117	10	18	0	33	0	109	2.96	2,000	50			Oct-99
0.42	0.33	1.37	5.41	9.10	1.99	0.45	0.86	1.60		902.4	5	30	0	33	0	64	2.79	0				Nov-01
0.02	0.29	1.09	3.58	3.58	1.26	0.49	0.2		1	771.0	37	62	0	1	0		0.40	2,000	100	4.50		Mar-88
0.03	0.32	1.16	4.06	4.18	1.33	0.4	0.17		1	771.0	37	62	0	1	0		0.40	2,000	50			Dec-97
0.01	0.29	1.11	3.91	4.06	1.27	0.45	0.18		1	296.0	45	55	0	0	0		0.41	0				Jan-87

Fund Name	Ticker Symbol	Traded On	Fund Type	Category and (Prospectus Objective)	Overall Rating	Reward Rating	Risk Rating	Recent Up/ Downgrade	Open to New Investors	Telephone
	MARKET			FUND TYPE, CATEGORY & OBJECTIVE	RATINGS				NEW INVESTORS	
Thrivent Multidimensional Income Fund Class S	TMLDX	NAS CM	Open End	Cautious Allocation (Income)	D+	D	C-	Down	Y	
Thrivent Municipal Bond Fund Class A	AAMBX	NAS CM	Open End	US Muni Fixed Inc (Muni Bond - Natl)	C	C-	B-		Y	
Thrivent Municipal Bond Fund Class S	TMBIX	NAS CM	Open End	US Muni Fixed Inc (Muni Bond - Natl)	C	C-	B-		Y	
Thrivent Opportunity Income Plus Fund Class A	AAINX	NAS CM	Open End	US Fixed Inc (Income)	C-	D+	C		Y	
Thrivent Opportunity Income Plus Fund Class S	IIINX	NAS CM	Open End	US Fixed Inc (Income)	C-	D+	C	Down	Y	
Thrivent Opportunity Income Plus Portfolio			Open End	US Fixed Inc (Growth & Income)	U	U	U		Y	
TIAA-CREF 5-15 Year Laddered Tax-Exempt Bond Advisor Cl	TIXHX	NAS CM	Open End	US Muni Fixed Inc (Income)	C	C-	C+		Y	877-518-9161
TIAA-CREF 5-15 Year Laddered Tax-Exempt Bond Inst Cl	TITIX	NAS CM	Open End	US Muni Fixed Inc (Income)	C	C-	C+		Y	877-518-9161
TIAA-CREF 5-15 Year Laddered Tax-Exempt Bond Retail Cl	TIXRX	NAS CM	Open End	US Muni Fixed Inc (Income)	C	C-	C+		Y	877-518-9161
TIAA-CREF Bond Index Fund Advisor Class	TBIAX	NAS CM	Open End	US Fixed Inc (Multisector Bond)	B	B-	B	Up	Y	877-518-9161
TIAA-CREF Bond Index Fund Class W	TBIWX	NAS CM	Open End	US Fixed Inc (Multisector Bond)	B	B-	B+		Y	877-518-9161
TIAA-CREF Bond Index Fund Institutional Class	TBIIX	NAS CM	Open End	US Fixed Inc (Multisector Bond)	B	B-	B+		Y	877-518-9161
TIAA-CREF Bond Index Fund Premier Class	TBIPX	NAS CM	Open End	US Fixed Inc (Multisector Bond)	B	B-	B	Up	Y	877-518-9161
TIAA-CREF Bond Index Fund Retail Class	TBILX	NAS CM	Open End	US Fixed Inc (Multisector Bond)	B	B-	B	Up	Y	877-518-9161
TIAA-CREF Bond Index Fund Retirement Class	TBIRX	NAS CM	Open End	US Fixed Inc (Multisector Bond)	B	B-	B	Up	Y	877-518-9161
TIAA-CREF Core Bond Fund Advisor Class	TIBHX	NAS CM	Open End	US Fixed Inc (Income)	B-	C	B+	Up	Y	877-518-9161
TIAA-CREF Core Bond Fund Class W	TBBWX	NAS CM	Open End	US Fixed Inc (Income)	B-	C	B+	Up	Y	877-518-9161
TIAA-CREF Core Bond Fund Institutional Class	TIBDX	NAS CM	Open End	US Fixed Inc (Income)	B-	C	B+	Up	Y	877-518-9161
TIAA-CREF Core Bond Fund Premier Class	TIDPX	NAS CM	Open End	US Fixed Inc (Income)	B-	C	B	Up	Y	877-518-9161
TIAA-CREF Core Bond Fund Retail Class	TIORX	NAS CM	Open End	US Fixed Inc (Income)	B-	C	B	Up	Y	877-518-9161
TIAA-CREF Core Bond Fund Retirement Class	TIDRX	NAS CM	Open End	US Fixed Inc (Income)	B-	C	B	Up	Y	877-518-9161
TIAA-CREF Core Impact Bond Fund Advisor Class	TSBHX	NAS CM	Open End	US Fixed Inc (Income)	B-	C	B+	Up	Y	877-518-9161
TIAA-CREF Core Impact Bond Fund Institutional Class	TSBIX	NAS CM	Open End	US Fixed Inc (Income)	B-	C	B+	Up	Y	877-518-9161
TIAA-CREF Core Impact Bond Fund Premier Class	TSBPX	NAS CM	Open End	US Fixed Inc (Income)	B-	C	B+	Up	Y	877-518-9161
TIAA-CREF Core Impact Bond Fund Retail Class	TSBRX	NAS CM	Open End	US Fixed Inc (Income)	B-	C	B	Up	Y	877-518-9161
TIAA-CREF Core Impact Bond Fund Retirement Class	TSBBX	NAS CM	Open End	US Fixed Inc (Income)	B-	C	B	Up	Y	877-518-9161
TIAA-CREF Core Plus Bond Fund Advisor Class	TCBHX	NAS CM	Open End	US Fixed Inc (Income)	C+	C	B	Up	Y	877-518-9161
TIAA-CREF Core Plus Bond Fund Class W	TCBWX	NAS CM	Open End	US Fixed Inc (Income)	B-	C	B	Up	Y	877-518-9161
TIAA-CREF Core Plus Bond Fund Institutional Class	TIBFX	NAS CM	Open End	US Fixed Inc (Income)	C+	C	B	Up	Y	877-518-9161
TIAA-CREF Core Plus Bond Fund Premier Class	TBPPX	NAS CM	Open End	US Fixed Inc (Income)	C+	C	B	Up	Y	877-518-9161
TIAA-CREF Core Plus Bond Fund Retail Class	TCBPX	NAS CM	Open End	US Fixed Inc (Income)	C+	C	B	Up	Y	877-518-9161
TIAA-CREF Core Plus Bond Fund Retirement Class	TCBRX	NAS CM	Open End	US Fixed Inc (Income)	C+	C	B	Up	Y	877-518-9161
TIAA-CREF Emerging Markets Debt Fund Advisor Class	TEDHX	NAS CM	Open End	Emerg Mkts Fixed Inc (Growth)	D+	D+	C-	Down	Y	877-518-9161
TIAA-CREF Emerging Markets Debt Fund Class W	TEDVX	NAS CM	Open End	Emerg Mkts Fixed Inc (Growth)	D+	D+	C-	Down	Y	877-518-9161
TIAA-CREF Emerging Markets Debt Fund Institutional Class	TEDNX	NAS CM	Open End	Emerg Mkts Fixed Inc (Growth)	D+	D+	C-	Down	Y	877-518-9161
TIAA-CREF Emerging Markets Debt Fund Premier Class	TEDPX	NAS CM	Open End	Emerg Mkts Fixed Inc (Growth)	D+	D+	C-	Down	Y	877-518-9161
TIAA-CREF Emerging Markets Debt Fund Retail Class	TEDLX	NAS CM	Open End	Emerg Mkts Fixed Inc (Growth)	D+	D+	C-	Down	Y	877-518-9161
TIAA-CREF Emerging Markets Debt Fund Retirement Class	TEDTX	NAS CM	Open End	Emerg Mkts Fixed Inc (Growth)	D+	D+	C-	Down	Y	877-518-9161
TIAA-CREF Green Bond Fund Advisor Class	TGRKX	NAS CM	Open End	US Fixed Inc (Corp Bond - General)	D+	D+	B-	Up	Y	877-518-9161
TIAA-CREF Green Bond Fund Institutional Class	TGRNX	NAS CM	Open End	US Fixed Inc (Corp Bond - General)	D+	D+	B-	Up	Y	877-518-9161
TIAA-CREF Green Bond Fund Premier Class	TGRLX	NAS CM	Open End	US Fixed Inc (Corp Bond - General)	D+	D+	B-	Up	Y	877-518-9161
TIAA-CREF Green Bond Fund Retail Class	TGROX	NAS CM	Open End	US Fixed Inc (Corp Bond - General)	D+	D+	B-	Up	Y	877-518-9161
TIAA-CREF Green Bond Fund Retirement Class	TGRMX	NAS CM	Open End	US Fixed Inc (Corp Bond - General)	D+	D+	B-	Up	Y	877-518-9161
TIAA-CREF High Yield Fund Advisor Class	TIHHX	NAS CM	Open End	US Fixed Inc (Corp Bond - High Yield)	C-	D+	C		Y	877-518-9161
TIAA-CREF High Yield Fund Class W	TIHWX	NAS CM	Open End	US Fixed Inc (Corp Bond - High Yield)	C-	D+	C		Y	877-518-9161
TIAA-CREF High-Yield Fund Institutional Class	TIHYX	NAS CM	Open End	US Fixed Inc (Corp Bond - High Yield)	C-	D+	C		Y	877-518-9161
TIAA-CREF High-Yield Fund Premier Class	TIHPX	NAS CM	Open End	US Fixed Inc (Corp Bond - High Yield)	C-	D+	C		Y	877-518-9161
TIAA-CREF High-Yield Fund Retail Class	TIYRX	NAS CM	Open End	US Fixed Inc (Corp Bond - High Yield)	C-	D+	C		Y	877-518-9161
TIAA-CREF High-Yield Fund Retirement Class	TIHRX	NAS CM	Open End	US Fixed Inc (Corp Bond - High Yield)	C-	D+	C		Y	877-518-9161
TIAA-CREF Inflation Linked Bond Fund Premier Class	TIKPX	NAS CM	Open End	US Fixed Inc (Income)	B-	C	B	Up	Y	877-518-9161
TIAA-CREF Inflation-Linked Bond Fund Advisor Class	TIIHX	NAS CM	Open End	US Fixed Inc (Income)	B-	C	B	Up	Y	877-518-9161
TIAA-CREF Inflation-Linked Bond Fund Class W	TIIWX	NAS CM	Open End	US Fixed Inc (Income)	B-	C	B+	Up	Y	877-518-9161

★ Expanded analysis of this fund is included in Section II.

TOTAL RETURNS & PERFORMANCE									ASSETS		ASSET ALLOCATION & TURNOVER							MINIMUMS		FEES		
3-Month Total Return	6-Month Total Return	1-Year Total Return	3-Year Total Return	5-Year Total Return	Dividend Yield (TTM)	Expense Ratio	3-Yr Std Deviation	Effective Duration	NAV	Total Assets (MIL)	%Cash	%Government Bonds	%Municipal Bonds	%Corporate Bonds	%Other	Turnover Ratio	Average Coupon Rate	Min Initial Investment	Min Additional Investment	Front End Fee (%)	Back End Fee (%)	Inception Date
9.98	-6.27	-2.17	4.88		4.6	1.14	9.88	4.40	9.22	24.9	5	7	0	81	11	96	5.21	2,000	50			Feb-17
2.25	1.20	3.27	10.18	17.08	3.02	0.75	4.2		11.42	1,514	1	0	99	0	0	31	5.05	2,000	50	4.50		Dec-76
2.30	1.30	3.48	10.89	18.41	3.21	0.55	4.2		11.42	1,514	1	0	99	0	0	31	5.05	2,000	50			Oct-97
6.56	-1.82	-0.04	7.02	15.32	3.6	0.92	5.53	3.10	9.83	744.2	6	0	0	54	14	186	3.85	2,000	50	4.50		Jul-87
6.63	-1.68	0.22	7.85	16.75	3.88	0.65	5.53	3.10	9.83	744.2	6	0	0	54	14	186	3.85	2,000	50			Dec-97
0.00	-0.45	1.27	8.78	16.16	3.39	0.69	2.2	3.10		178.8	5	4	0	54	15	218	4.25	0				Apr-03
2.66	0.30	2.44	11.30	16.98	2.38	0.41	4.6	5.40	10.72	270.6	3	0	97	0	0	21	4.79	0				Dec-15
2.78	0.44	2.62	11.56	17.31	2.46	0.3	4.62	5.40	10.73	270.6	3	0	97	0	0	21	4.79	2,000,000	1,000			Mar-06
2.71	0.21	2.34	10.64	15.59	2.18	0.59	4.6	5.40	10.74	270.6	3	0	97	0	0	21	4.79	2,500	100			Mar-06
2.75	6.16	8.55	15.92	22.47	2.36	0.22	3.3	5.80	11.66	17,355	2	42	1	26	-1	32	3.08	0				Dec-15
2.81	6.27	8.78	16.53	23.33	2.57	0	3.26	5.80	11.66	17,355	2	42	1	26	-1	32	3.08	0				Sep-18
2.78	6.21	8.66	16.31	23.09	2.46	0.11	3.25	5.80	11.66	17,355	2	42	1	26	-1	32	3.08	10,000,000	1,000			Sep-09
2.83	6.13	8.50	15.89	22.18	2.31	0.26	3.29	5.80	11.66	17,355	2	42	1	26	-1	32	3.08	0				Sep-09
2.79	6.14	8.42	15.30	21.11	2.15	0.44	3.32	5.80	11.67	17,355	2	42	1	26	-1	32	3.08	2,500	100			Sep-09
2.80	6.17	8.49	15.54	21.56	2.22	0.36	3.32	5.80	11.67	17,355	2	42	1	26	-1	32	3.08	0				Sep-09
5.60	4.61	7.26	15.41	24.55	2.57	0.44	4.17	5.57	11.01	6,891	5	16	4	42	-2	133	3.40	0				Dec-15
5.72	4.83	7.63	16.30	25.59	3	0	4.21	5.57	11	6,891	5	16	4	42	-2	133	3.40	0				Sep-18
5.64	4.68	7.41	15.70	24.94	2.71	0.3	4.17	5.57	11	6,891	5	16	4	42	-2	133	3.40	2,000,000	1,000			Jul-99
5.60	4.70	7.25	15.28	24.12	2.56	0.45	4.18	5.57	11.01	6,891	5	16	4	42	-2	133	3.40	0				Sep-09
5.48	4.57	7.02	14.69	23.18	2.42	0.6	4.16	5.57	11.19	6,891	5	16	4	42	-2	133	3.40	2,500	100			Mar-06
5.49	4.59	7.06	14.83	23.45	2.46	0.55	4.18	5.57	11.2	6,891	5	16	4	42	-2	133	3.40	0				Mar-06
5.09	4.24	6.82	15.45	23.60	2.48	0.44	4.28	5.93	10.89	5,171	4	20	8	44	-1	115	3.06	0				Dec-15
5.12	4.29	6.92	15.60	24.02	2.58	0.37	4.33	5.93	10.88	5,171	4	20	8	44	-1	115	3.06	2,000,000	1,000			Sep-12
5.07	4.20	6.73	15.13	23.14	2.41	0.55	4.28	5.93	10.89	5,171	4	20	8	44	-1	115	3.06	0				Sep-12
5.15	4.26	6.74	14.77	22.47	2.31	0.65	4.36	5.93	10.88	5,171	4	20	8	44	-1	115	3.06	2,500	100			Sep-12
5.06	4.17	6.66	14.75	22.49	2.33	0.62	4.36	5.93	10.88	5,171	4	20	8	44	-1	115	3.06	0				Sep-12
6.06	3.64	6.36	14.91	23.81	2.85	0.35	4.51	5.32	10.94	4,772	3	13	5	41	1	94	3.71	0				Dec-15
6.16	3.84	6.76	15.73	24.84	3.22	0	4.54	5.32	10.93	4,772	3	13	5	41	1	94	3.71	0				Sep-18
6.08	3.68	6.44	15.12	24.19	2.92	0.3	4.52	5.32	10.93	4,772	3	13	5	41	1	94	3.71	2,000,000	1,000			Mar-06
6.05	3.61	6.29	14.61	23.38	2.77	0.45	4.52	5.32	10.93	4,772	3	13	5	41	1	94	3.71	0				Sep-09
5.99	3.52	6.11	13.94	22.25	2.62	0.62	4.51	5.32	10.95	4,772	3	13	5	41	1	94	3.71	2,500	100			Mar-06
5.91	3.55	6.18	14.15	22.65	2.68	0.55	4.45	5.32	10.94	4,772	3	13	5	41	1	94	3.71	0				Mar-06
16.48	-4.71	-0.92	10.84	31.07	5.92	0.71	13.23	6.55	9.46	459.6	2	54	0	44	4	78	6.07	0				Dec-15
16.59	-4.46	-0.30	12.13	32.60	6.69	0	13.18	6.55	9.43	459.6	2	54	0	44	4	78	6.07	0				Sep-18
16.43	-4.78	-0.94	10.88	31.11	6.01	0.63	13.19	6.55	9.43	459.6	2	54	0	44	4	78	6.07	2,000,000	1,000			Sep-14
16.38	-4.77	-1.10	10.40	30.04	5.76	0.79	13.19	6.55	9.43	459.6	2	54	0	44	4	78	6.07	0				Sep-14
16.22	-4.95	-1.26	9.73	29.05	5.69	0.92	13.19	6.55	9.42	459.6	2	54	0	44	4	78	6.07	2,500	100			Sep-14
16.37	-4.81	-1.10	10.06	29.68	5.74	0.88	13.22	6.55	9.43	459.6	2	54	0	44	4	78	6.07	0				Sep-14
7.38	4.78	7.27			3.02	0.53		5.82	10.9	36.1	5	14	13	48	0	37	3.38	0				Nov-18
7.39	4.78	7.27			3.02	0.45		5.82	10.9	36.1	5	14	13	48	0	37	3.38	2,000,000	1,000			Nov-18
7.36	4.71	7.13			2.88	0.6		5.82	10.9	36.1	5	14	13	48	0	37	3.38	0				Nov-18
7.31	4.64	6.98			2.75	0.8		5.82	10.9	36.1	5	14	13	48	0	37	3.38	2,500	100			Nov-18
7.36	4.71	7.11			2.87	0.7		5.82	10.9	36.1	5	14	13	48	0	37	3.38	0				Nov-18
8.57	-6.96	-3.24	7.22	20.46	5.78	0.47	9.29	3.50	8.94	3,534	3	0	0	97	2	42	6.00	0				Dec-15
8.68	-6.73	-2.79	8.25	21.88	6.27	0	9.28	3.50	8.95	3,534	3	0	0	97	2	42	6.00	0				Sep-18
8.59	-6.90	-3.13	7.59	21.14	5.9	0.36	9.28	3.50	8.95	3,534	3	0	0	97	2	42	6.00	2,000,000	1,000			Mar-06
8.55	-6.95	-3.25	7.23	20.25	5.75	0.51	9.28	3.50	8.96	3,534	3	0	0	97	2	42	6.00	0				Sep-09
8.61	-6.99	-3.36	6.75	19.55	5.61	0.63	9.33	3.50	8.99	3,534	3	0	0	97	2	42	6.00	2,500	100			Mar-06
8.52	-7.01	-3.37	6.79	19.64	5.64	0.61	9.31	3.50	8.95	3,534	3	0	0	97	2	42	6.00	0				Mar-06
3.59	4.05	5.60	11.31	14.13	1.83	0.41	2.64	4.96	11.91	3,541	1	98	0	0	0	26	0.93	0				Sep-09
3.50	4.07	5.56	11.37	14.54	1.94	0.36	2.6	4.96	11.93	3,541	1	98	0	0	0	26	0.93	0				Dec-15
3.67	4.24	6.00	12.24	15.47	2.3	0	2.63	4.96	11.93	3,541	1	98	0	0	0	26	0.93	0				Sep-18

	MARKET			FUND TYPE, CATEGORY & OBJECTIVE	RATINGS				NEW INVESTORS	
Fund Name	Ticker Symbol	Traded On	Fund Type	Category and (Prospectus Objective)	Overall Rating	Reward Rating	Risk Rating	Recent Up/ Downgrade	Open to New Investors	Telephone
TIAA-CREF Inflation-Linked Bond Fund Institutional Class	TIILX	NAS CM	Open End	US Fixed Inc (Income)	B-	C	B+	Up	Y	877-518-9161
TIAA-CREF Inflation-Linked Bond Fund Retail Class	TCILX	NAS CM	Open End	US Fixed Inc (Income)	C+	C	B	Up	Y	877-518-9161
TIAA-CREF Inflation-Linked Bond Fund Retirement Class	TIKRX	NAS CM	Open End	US Fixed Inc (Income)	B-	C	B	Up	Y	877-518-9161
TIAA-CREF International Bond Fund Advisor Class	TIBNX	NAS CM	Open End	Global Fixed Inc (Worldwide Bond)	C	C	B		Y	877-518-9161
TIAA-CREF International Bond Fund Class W	TIBUX	NAS CM	Open End	Global Fixed Inc (Worldwide Bond)	C	C	B		Y	877-518-9161
TIAA-CREF International Bond Fund Institutional Class	TIBWX	NAS CM	Open End	Global Fixed Inc (Worldwide Bond)	C	C-	B		Y	877-518-9161
TIAA-CREF International Bond Fund Premier Class	TIBLX	NAS CM	Open End	Global Fixed Inc (Worldwide Bond)	C	C-	B-		Y	877-518-9161
TIAA-CREF International Bond Fund Retail Class	TIBEX	NAS CM	Open End	Global Fixed Inc (Worldwide Bond)	C	C-	B-		Y	877-518-9161
TIAA-CREF International Bond Fund Retirement Class	TIBVX	NAS CM	Open End	Global Fixed Inc (Worldwide Bond)	C	C-	B-		Y	877-518-9161
TIAA-CREF Money Market Fund Advisor Class	TMHXX	NAS CM	Money Mkt	US Money Mkt (Money Mkt - General)	C	C-	C+		Y	877-518-9161
TIAA-CREF Money Market Fund Institutional Class	TCIXX	NAS CM	Money Mkt	US Money Mkt (Money Mkt - General)	C	C-	C+		Y	877-518-9161
TIAA-CREF Money Market Fund Premier Class	TPPXX	NAS CM	Money Mkt	US Money Mkt (Money Mkt - General)	C	C	C+		Y	877-518-9161
TIAA-CREF Money Market Fund Retail Class	TIRXX	NAS CM	Money Mkt	US Money Mkt (Money Mkt - General)	C	C-	C+		Y	877-518-9161
TIAA-CREF Money Market Fund Retirement Class	TIEXX	NAS CM	Money Mkt	US Money Mkt (Money Mkt - General)	C	C-	C+		Y	877-518-9161
TIAA-CREF Short Duration Impact Bond Fund Advisor Class	TSDHX	NAS CM	Open End	US Fixed Inc (Corp Bond - General)	D+	D+	C+	Up	Y	877-518-9161
TIAA-CREF Short Duration Impact Bond Institutional Cl	TSDJX	NAS CM	Open End	US Fixed Inc (Corp Bond - General)	D+	D+	C+	Up	Y	877-518-9161
TIAA-CREF Short Duration Impact Bond Fund Premier Class	TSDFX	NAS CM	Open End	US Fixed Inc (Corp Bond - General)	D+	D+	C+	Up	Y	877-518-9161
TIAA-CREF Short Duration Impact Bond Fund Retail Class	TSDBX	NAS CM	Open End	US Fixed Inc (Corp Bond - General)	D+	D+	C+	Up	Y	877-518-9161
TIAA-CREF Short Duration Impact Bond Fund Retirement Class	TSDDX	NAS CM	Open End	US Fixed Inc (Corp Bond - General)	D+	D+	C+	Up	Y	877-518-9161
TIAA-CREF Short Term Bond Fund Advisor Class	TCTHX	NAS CM	Open End	US Fixed Inc (Income)	C	C	B-		Y	877-518-9161
TIAA-CREF Short Term Bond Fund Class W	TCTWX	NAS CM	Open End	US Fixed Inc (Income)	C	C	B-		Y	877-518-9161
TIAA-CREF Short-Term Bond Fund Institutional Class	TISIX	NAS CM	Open End	US Fixed Inc (Income)	C	C	B-		Y	877-518-9161
TIAA-CREF Short-Term Bond Fund Premier Class	TSTPX	NAS CM	Open End	US Fixed Inc (Income)	C	C	B-		Y	877-518-9161
TIAA-CREF Short-Term Bond Fund Retail Class	TCTRX	NAS CM	Open End	US Fixed Inc (Income)	C	C	B-		Y	877-518-9161
TIAA-CREF Short-Term Bond Fund Retirement Class	TISRX	NAS CM	Open End	US Fixed Inc (Income)	C	C	B-		Y	877-518-9161
TIAA-CREF Short-Term Bond Index Fund Advisor Class	TTBHX	NAS CM	Open End	US Fixed Inc (Income)	C+	C	B	Up	Y	877-518-9161
TIAA-CREF Short-Term Bond Index Fund Class W	TTBWX	NAS CM	Open End	US Fixed Inc (Income)	C+	C	B		Y	877-518-9161
TIAA-CREF Short-Term Bond Index Fund Institutional Class	TNSHX	NAS CM	Open End	US Fixed Inc (Income)	C+	C	B		Y	877-518-9161
TIAA-CREF Short-Term Bond Index Fund Premier Class	TPSHX	NAS CM	Open End	US Fixed Inc (Income)	C+	C	B	Up	Y	877-518-9161
TIAA-CREF Short-Term Bond Index Fund Retail Class	TRSHX	NAS CM	Open End	US Fixed Inc (Income)	C+	C	B	Up	Y	877-518-9161
TIAA-CREF Short-Term Bond Index Fund Retirement Class	TESHX	NAS CM	Open End	US Fixed Inc (Income)	C+	C	B	Up	Y	877-518-9161
Timothy Plan Fixed Income Fund Class A	TFIAX	NAS CM	Open End	US Fixed Inc (Multisector Bond)	B-	C+	B	Up	Y	800-662-0201
Timothy Plan Fixed Income Fund Class C	TFICX	NAS CM	Open End	US Fixed Inc (Multisector Bond)	C+	C	B-		Y	800-662-0201
Timothy Plan Fixed Income Fund Class I	TPFIX	NAS CM	Open End	US Fixed Inc (Multisector Bond)	B-	C+	B	Up	Y	800-662-0201
Timothy Plan High Yield Bond Fund Class A	TPHAX	NAS CM	Open End	US Fixed Inc (Corp Bond - High Yield)	C-	D+	C		Y	800-662-0201
Timothy Plan High Yield Bond Fund Class C	TPHCX	NAS CM	Open End	US Fixed Inc (Corp Bond - High Yield)	C-	D+	C		Y	800-662-0201
Timothy Plan High Yield Bond Fund Class I	TPHIX	NAS CM	Open End	US Fixed Inc (Corp Bond - High Yield)	C-	D+	C		Y	800-662-0201
Toews Tactical Income Fund	THHYX	NAS CM	Open End	US Fixed Inc (Corp Bond - High Yield)	C	C-	C+	Down	Y	
Toews Unconstrained Income Fund	TUIFX	NAS CM	Open End	Fixed Inc Misc (Growth & Income)	C-	C-	C	Down	Y	
Tortoise Tax-Advd Social Infrastructure Fund, Inc Inst Cl	TSIFX	NAS CM	Closed End	US Muni Fixed Inc (Growth & Income)	C-	D+	C		Y	913-981-1020
Touchstone Active Bond Fund Class Institutional	TOBIX	NAS CM	Open End	US Fixed Inc (Multisector Bond)	B-	C	B	Up	Y	800-543-0407
Touchstone Credit Opportunities II Fund A	TMARX	NAS CM	Open End	Fixed Inc Misc (Growth & Income)	D+	D	C-	Down	Y	800-543-0407
Touchstone Credit Opportunities II Institutional Cl	TARBX	NAS CM	Open End	Fixed Inc Misc (Growth & Income)	D+	D	C-	Down	Y	800-543-0407
Touchstone Credit Opportunities II Fund Y	TMAYX	NAS CM	Open End	Fixed Inc Misc (Growth & Income)	D+	D	C-	Down	Y	800-543-0407
Touchstone Flexible Income Fund Class A	FFSAX	NAS CM	Open End	US Fixed Inc (Income)	C	C	B-		Y	800-543-0407
Touchstone Flexible Income Fund Class Y	MXIIX	NAS CM	Open End	US Fixed Inc (Income)	C	C	B-		Y	800-543-0407
Touchstone Flexible Income Fund Institutional Class	TFSLX	NAS CM	Open End	US Fixed Inc (Income)	C	C	B-		Y	800-543-0407
Touchstone High Yield Fund Class A	THYAX	NAS CM	Open End	US Fixed Inc (Corp Bond - High Yield)	D+	D+	C-	Down	Y	800-543-0407
Touchstone High Yield Fund Class Institutional	THIYX	NAS CM	Open End	US Fixed Inc (Corp Bond - High Yield)	D+	D+	C-	Down	Y	800-543-0407
Touchstone High Yield Fund Class Y	THYYX	NAS CM	Open End	US Fixed Inc (Corp Bond - High Yield)	D+	D+	C-	Down	Y	800-543-0407
Touchstone Impact Bond Fund Class A	TCPAX	NAS CM	Open End	US Fixed Inc (Multisector Bond)	B-	C+	B+	Up	Y	800-543-0407
Touchstone Impact Bond Fund Class Y	TCPYX	NAS CM	Open End	US Fixed Inc (Multisector Bond)	B-	C+	B+	Up	Y	800-543-0407

★Expanded analysis of this fund is included in Section II.

TOTAL RETURNS & PERFORMANCE									ASSETS		ASSET ALLOCATION & TURNOVER							MINIMUMS		FEES		
3-Month Total Return	6-Month Total Return	1-Year Total Return	3-Year Total Return	5-Year Total Return	Dividend Yield (TTM)	Expense Ratio	3-Yr Std Deviation	Effective Duration	NAV	Total Assets (MIL)	%Cash	%Government Bonds	%Municipal Bonds	%Corporate Bonds	%Other	Turnover Ratio	Average Coupon Rate	Min Initial Investment	Min Additional Investment	Front End Fee (%)	Back End Fee (%)	Inception Date
3.61	4.12	5.75	11.77	14.99	2.01	0.26	2.62	4.96	11.93	3,541	1	98	0	0	0	26	0.93	2,000,000	1,000			Oct-02
3.54	4.06	5.48	10.70	13.23	1.69	0.58	2.58	4.96	11.63	3,541	1	98	0	0	0	26	0.93	2,500	100			Oct-02
3.52	3.96	5.44	10.97	13.53	1.69	0.51	2.63	4.96	12.02	3,541	1	98	0	0	0	26	0.93	0				Mar-06
4.14	0.90	3.03	14.28		5.39	0.7	4.19	7.52	10.06	394.4	2	79	0	19	3	51	2.43	0				Aug-16
4.23	1.20	3.64	15.69		6.02	0	4.2	7.52	10.09	394.4	2	79	0	19	3	51	2.43	0				Sep-18
4.03	0.90	2.92	14.46		5.4	0.6	4.19	7.52	10.06	394.4	2	79	0	19	3	51	2.43	2,000,000	1,000			Aug-16
4.11	0.89	2.81	13.89		5.2	0.75	4.19	7.52	10.12	394.4	2	79	0	19	3	51	2.43	0				Aug-16
4.03	0.70	2.59	13.10		5.04	0.95	4.21	7.52	10.05	394.4	2	79	0	19	3	51	2.43	2,500	100			Aug-16
4.03	0.80	2.79	13.58		5.16	0.85	4.12	7.52	10.05	394.4	2	79	0	19	3	51	2.43	0				Aug-16
0.06	0.46	1.36	4.80	5.33	1.54	0.24	0.16		1	2,267	57	43	0	0	0			0				Dec-15
0.06	0.40	1.35	4.78	5.40	1.53	0.14	0.17		1	2,267	57	43	0	0	0			2,000,000	1,000			Jul-99
0.04	0.34	1.21	4.33	4.66	1.39	0.29	0.17		1	2,267	57	43	0	0	0			0				Sep-09
0.01	0.27	1.05	3.79	3.90	1.21	0.48	0.17		1	2,267	57	43	0	0	0			2,500	100			Mar-06
0.03	0.33	1.21	4.23	4.44	1.39	0.39	0.18		1	2,267	57	43	0	0	0			0				Mar-06
4.56	2.32	3.87			2.65	0.43			10.25	30.0	6	23	7	46	0	103	2.78	0				Nov-18
4.56	2.32	3.98			2.66	0.35			10.25	30.0	6	23	7	46	0	103	2.78	2,000,000	1,000			Nov-18
4.52	2.24	3.72			2.51	0.5			10.25	30.0	6	23	7	46	0	103	2.78	0				Nov-18
4.49	2.17	3.59			2.27	0.7			10.25	30.0	6	23	7	46	0	103	2.78	2,500	100			Nov-18
4.49	2.10	3.62			2.41	0.6			10.25	30.0	6	23	7	46	0	103	2.78	0				Nov-18
2.83	1.93	3.23	8.40	12.25	2.4	0.4	1.84	2.05	10.45	1,894	4	35	2	28	0	139	2.54	0				Dec-15
2.82	2.01	3.48	9.14	13.06	2.75	0	1.84	2.05	10.45	1,894	4	35	2	28	0	139	2.54	0				Sep-18
2.75	1.97	3.21	8.63	12.54	2.48	0.27	1.84	2.05	10.45	1,894	4	35	2	28	0	139	2.54	2,000,000	1,000			Mar-06
2.71	1.80	3.05	8.14	11.70	2.33	0.42	1.84	2.05	10.46	1,894	4	35	2	28	0	139	2.54	0				Sep-09
2.67	1.82	2.90	7.65	10.84	2.19	0.58	1.78	2.05	10.46	1,894	4	35	2	28	0	139	2.54	2,500	100			Mar-06
2.68	1.74	2.95	7.82	11.14	2.23	0.52	1.85	2.05	10.46	1,894	4	35	2	28	0	139	2.54	0				Mar-06
1.10	2.78	3.96	7.96		1.95	0.26	1.04	1.83	10.19	742.9	2	74	0	24	-1	66	2.19	0				Dec-15
1.16	2.92	4.34	8.68		2.21	0	1.03	1.83	10.19	742.9	2	74	0	24	-1	66	2.19	0				Sep-18
1.13	2.86	4.22	8.45		2.09	0.12	1.02	1.83	10.19	742.9	2	74	0	24	-1	66	2.19	10,000,000	1,000			Aug-15
1.19	2.89	4.06	8.07		1.95	0.27	1.06	1.83	10.19	742.9	2	74	0	24	-1	66	2.19	0				Aug-15
1.05	2.78	3.85	7.44		1.73	0.44	1.04	1.83	10.19	742.9	2	74	0	24	-1	66	2.19	2,500	100			Aug-15
1.07	2.73	3.96	7.65		1.85	0.37	1.02	1.83	10.19	742.9	2	74	0	24	-1	66	2.19	0				Aug-15
2.58	5.36	6.84	11.37	14.82	1.55	1.31	2.76		10.82	104.8	3	47	0	23	0	53	3.13	1,000		4.50		Jul-99
2.40	4.96	6.09	8.88	10.63	0.99	2.06	2.7		10.4	104.8	3	47	0	23	0	53	3.13	1,000			1.00	Feb-04
2.65	5.54	7.16	12.29	16.45	1.77	1.06	2.73		10.75	104.8	3	47	0	23	0	53	3.13	100,000	25,000			Aug-13
13.59	-4.24	0.47	8.86	19.29	4.46	1.35	10.38		8.96	73.9	7	0	0	93	0	75	5.85	1,000		4.50		May-07
13.43	-4.62	-0.25	6.47	14.83	3.54	2.1	10.4		9.1	73.9	7	0	0	93	0	75	5.85	1,000			1.00	May-07
13.66	-4.11	0.73	9.73	20.78	4.72	1.1	10.4		8.96	73.9	7	0	0	93	0	75	5.85	100,000	25,000			Aug-13
-0.40	-1.09	0.12	5.74	18.61	3.27	1.53	3.4		10.6	607.9	0	0	0	100	0	623	1.55	10,000	100			Jun-10
0.26	-1.60	-0.46	2.09	10.94	2.27	1.48	3.28		9.79	60.6	0	8	0	92	0	666	1.49	10,000	100			Aug-13
3.03	0.24	1.62			5.01	1.5			9.63	--	0	0	100	0	0	25	6.71	2,500	100			Mar-18
7.81	5.29	8.02	16.02	24.35	2.83	0.57	4.81	6.30	11.06	332.4	5	22	0	38	0	235	3.61	500,000	50			Apr-12
10.89	-7.08	-3.59	6.55		5.96	1.19	10.41	3.80	9.13	84.1	3	0	0	88	0	28	6.20	2,500	50	5.00		Aug-15
10.90	-6.96	-3.27	7.62		6.23	0.84	10.39	3.80	9.3	84.1	3	0	0	88	0	28	6.20	500,000	50			Aug-15
10.82	-6.97	-3.41	7.35		6.15	0.94	10.38	3.80	9.24	84.1	3	0	0	88	0	28	6.20	2,500	50			Aug-15
8.30	0.88	2.54	9.55	20.61	3.22	1.09	5.89	3.20	10.79	659.6	9	12	1	50	0	136	3.50	2,500	50	2.00		Apr-04
8.35	0.91	2.70	10.25	22.18	3.46	0.84	5.88	3.20	10.82	659.6	9	12	1	50	0	136	3.50	2,500	50			Sep-98
8.38	0.96	2.80	10.58	22.68	3.56	0.74	5.93	3.20	10.81	659.6	9	12	1	50	0	136	3.50	500,000	50			Sep-12
8.72	-6.27	-3.50	5.95	13.66	5.34	1.05	8.89	4.26	7.62	205.9	2	0	0	98	0	63	5.78	2,500	50	2.00		May-00
8.88	-6.11	-3.21	7.04	15.62	5.65	0.72	8.9	4.26	7.84	205.9	2	0	0	98	0	63	5.78	500,000	50			Jan-12
8.85	-6.13	-3.16	6.81	15.32	5.57	0.8	8.89	4.26	7.85	205.9	2	0	0	98	0	63	5.78	2,500	50			Feb-07
3.52	4.91	6.96	14.02	20.05	2.08	0.86	3.91	6.10	10.74	344.8	3	29	8	27	0	22	3.75	2,500	50	2.00		Aug-10
3.48	4.92	7.22	14.86	21.39	2.31	0.61	3.92	6.10	10.75	344.8	3	29	8	27	0	22	3.75	2,500	50			Nov-91

	MARKET		FUND TYPE, CATEGORY & OBJECTIVE		RATINGS				NEW INVESTORS	
Fund Name	Ticker Symbol	Traded On	Fund Type	Category and (Prospectus Objective)	Overall Rating	Reward Rating	Risk Rating	Recent Up/ Downgrade	Open to New Investors	Telephone
Touchstone Impact Bond Fund Institutional Class	TCPNX	NAS CM	Open End	US Fixed Inc (Multisector Bond)	B-	C+	B+	Up	Y	800-543-0407
Touchstone Ohio Tax-Free Bond Fund Class A	TOHAX	NAS CM	Open End	US Muni Fixed Inc (Muni Bond - Single State)	C+	C	B	Up	Y	800-543-0407
Touchstone Ohio Tax-Free Bond Fund Class Y	TOHYX	NAS CM	Open End	US Muni Fixed Inc (Muni Bond - Single State)	C+	C	B	Up	Y	800-543-0407
Touchstone Ohio Tax-Free Bond Fund Institutional Class	TOHIX	NAS CM	Open End	US Muni Fixed Inc (Muni Bond - Single State)	C+	C	B	Up	Y	800-543-0407
Touchstone Ultra Short Duration Fixed Income Fund Class A	TSDAX	NAS CM	Open End	US Fixed Inc (Multisector Bond)	C	C-	C		Y	800-543-0407
Touchstone Ultra Short Duration Fixed Income Fund Class S	SSSGX	NAS CM	Open End	US Fixed Inc (Multisector Bond)	C	C-	C		Y	800-543-0407
Touchstone Ultra Short Duration Fixed Income Fund Class Y	TSYYX	NAS CM	Open End	US Fixed Inc (Multisector Bond)	C	C-	C+		Y	800-543-0407
Touchstone Ultra Short Duration Fixed Income Fund Class Z	TSDOX	NAS CM	Open End	US Fixed Inc (Multisector Bond)	C	C-	C		Y	800-543-0407
Touchstone Ultra Short Duration Fixed Income Inst Cl	TSDIX	NAS CM	Open End	US Fixed Inc (Multisector Bond)	C	C-	C+		Y	800-543-0407
Transamerica Asset Allocation Short Horizon R	TSHRX	NAS CM	Open End	US Fixed Inc (Asset Allocation)	C	C	B		Y	888-233-4339
Transamerica Asset Allocation Short Horizon R4	TSHFX	NAS CM	Open End	US Fixed Inc (Asset Allocation)	C+	C	B	Up	Y	888-233-4339
Transamerica Bond Class A	IDITX	NAS CM	Open End	US Fixed Inc (Income)	C	C	B-		Y	888-233-4339
Transamerica Bond Class C	IFLLX	NAS CM	Open End	US Fixed Inc (Income)	C	C-	B-		Y	888-233-4339
Transamerica Bond Class I	TFXIX	NAS CM	Open End	US Fixed Inc (Income)	C+	C	B	Up	Y	888-233-4339
Transamerica Bond Class I2			Open End	US Fixed Inc (Income)	C+	C	B	Up	Y	888-233-4339
Transamerica Bond Class R6	TAFLX	NAS CM	Open End	US Fixed Inc (Income)	C+	C	B	Up	Y	888-233-4339
Transamerica Core Bond Fund Class I2			Open End	US Fixed Inc (Multisector Bond)	B	C+	B+	Up	Y	888-233-4339
Transamerica Emerging Markets Debt Fund Class A	EMTAX	NAS CM	Open End	Emerg Mkts Fixed Inc (Diversified Emerg Mkts)	D	D	C-	Down	Y	888-233-4339
Transamerica Emerging Markets Debt Fund Class C	EMTCX	NAS CM	Open End	Emerg Mkts Fixed Inc (Diversified Emerg Mkts)	D	D	C-	Down	Y	888-233-4339
Transamerica Emerging Markets Debt Fund Class I	EMTIX	NAS CM	Open End	Emerg Mkts Fixed Inc (Diversified Emerg Mkts)	D+	D	C-	Down	Y	888-233-4339
Transamerica Emerging Markets Debt Fund Class I2			Open End	Emerg Mkts Fixed Inc (Diversified Emerg Mkts)	D+	D	C-	Down	Y	888-233-4339
Transamerica Emerging Markets Debt Fund Class R6	TAEDX	NAS CM	Open End	Emerg Mkts Fixed Inc (Diversified Emerg Mkts)	D+	D	C-	Down	Y	888-233-4339
Transamerica Floating Rate Fund Class A	TFLAX	NAS CM	Open End	US Fixed Inc (Income)	D+	D	C-	Down	Y	888-233-4339
Transamerica Floating Rate Fund Class C	TFLCX	NAS CM	Open End	US Fixed Inc (Income)	D	D	C-	Down	Y	888-233-4339
Transamerica Floating Rate Fund Class I	TFLIX	NAS CM	Open End	US Fixed Inc (Income)	D+	D	C-	Down	Y	888-233-4339
Transamerica Floating Rate Fund Class I2			Open End	US Fixed Inc (Income)	D+	D	C-	Down	Y	888-233-4339
Transamerica Government Money Market Class I3	TGTXX	NAS CM	Money Mkt	US Money Mkt (Money Mkt - Govt)	C	C-	C+		Y	888-233-4339
Transamerica Government Money Market Class R2	TGRXX	NAS CM	Money Mkt	US Money Mkt (Money Mkt - Govt)	C	C-	C		Y	888-233-4339
Transamerica Government Money Market Class R4	TFGXX	NAS CM	Money Mkt	US Money Mkt (Money Mkt - Govt)	C	C-	C		Y	888-233-4339
Transamerica Government Money Market Fund Class A	IATXX	NAS CM	Money Mkt	US Money Mkt (Money Mkt - Govt)	C	C-	C		Y	888-233-4339
Transamerica Government Money Market Fund Class C	IMLXX	NAS CM	Money Mkt	US Money Mkt (Money Mkt - Govt)	C	C-	C+	Up	Y	888-233-4339
Transamerica Government Money Market Fund Class I	TAMXX	NAS CM	Money Mkt	US Money Mkt (Money Mkt - Govt)	C	C-	C		Y	888-233-4339
Transamerica Government Money Market Fund Class I2			Money Mkt	US Money Mkt (Money Mkt - Govt)	C	C-	C		Y	888-233-4339
Transamerica High Quality Bond I3	TBDTX	NAS CM	Open End	US Fixed Inc (Corp Bond - High Quality)	C	C-	C+		Y	888-233-4339
Transamerica High Quality Bond R	TBDRX	NAS CM	Open End	US Fixed Inc (Corp Bond - High Quality)	C	C-	C		Y	888-233-4339
Transamerica High Quality Bond R4	TBDFX	NAS CM	Open End	US Fixed Inc (Corp Bond - High Quality)	C	C-	C+		Y	888-233-4339
Transamerica High Yield Bond A	IHIYX	NAS CM	Open End	US Fixed Inc (Corp Bond - High Yield)	D+	D	C-	Down	Y	888-233-4339
Transamerica High Yield Bond C	INCLX	NAS CM	Open End	US Fixed Inc (Corp Bond - High Yield)	D	D	D+	Down	Y	888-233-4339
Transamerica High Yield Bond I	TDHIX	NAS CM	Open End	US Fixed Inc (Corp Bond - High Yield)	D+	D	C-	Down	Y	888-233-4339
Transamerica High Yield Bond I2			Open End	US Fixed Inc (Corp Bond - High Yield)	D+	D	C-	Down	Y	888-233-4339
Transamerica High Yield Bond I3	TAHTX	NAS CM	Open End	US Fixed Inc (Corp Bond - High Yield)	D+	D	C-	Down	Y	888-233-4339
Transamerica High Yield Bond R	TAHRX	NAS CM	Open End	US Fixed Inc (Corp Bond - High Yield)	D+	D	C-	Down	Y	888-233-4339
Transamerica High Yield Bond R4	TAHFX	NAS CM	Open End	US Fixed Inc (Corp Bond - High Yield)	D+	D	C-	Down	Y	888-233-4339
Transamerica High Yield Bond R6	TAHBX	NAS CM	Open End	US Fixed Inc (Corp Bond - High Yield)	D+	D	C-	Down	Y	888-233-4339
Transamerica High Yield Muni Class A	THAYX	NAS CM	Open End	US Muni Fixed Inc (Muni Bond - Natl)	C-	D+	C	Down	Y	888-233-4339
Transamerica High Yield Muni Class C	THCYX	NAS CM	Open End	US Muni Fixed Inc (Muni Bond - Natl)	C-	D+	C	Down	Y	888-233-4339
Transamerica High Yield Muni Class I	THYIX	NAS CM	Open End	US Muni Fixed Inc (Muni Bond - Natl)	C-	D+	C	Down	Y	888-233-4339
Transamerica High Yield Muni I2	THYTX	NAS CM	Open End	US Muni Fixed Inc (Muni Bond - Natl)	C-	D+	C	Down	Y	888-233-4339
Transamerica Inflation Opportunities Fund Class A	TIOAX	NAS CM	Open End	US Fixed Inc (Growth & Income)	C+	C	B	Up	Y	888-233-4339
Transamerica Inflation Opportunities Fund Class C	TIOCX	NAS CM	Open End	US Fixed Inc (Growth & Income)	C	C	B-		Y	888-233-4339
Transamerica Inflation Opportunities Fund Class I	ITIOX	NAS CM	Open End	US Fixed Inc (Growth & Income)	C+	C	B	Up	Y	888-233-4339
Transamerica Inflation Opportunities Fund Class I2			Open End	US Fixed Inc (Growth & Income)	C+	C	B	Up	Y	888-233-4339

★Expanded analysis of this fund is included in Section II.

TOTAL RETURNS & PERFORMANCE									ASSETS		ASSET ALLOCATION & TURNOVER							MINIMUMS		FEES		
3-Month Total Return	6-Month Total Return	1-Year Total Return	3-Year Total Return	5-Year Total Return	Dividend Yield (TTM)	Expense Ratio	3-Yr Std Deviation	Effective Duration	NAV	Total Assets (ML)	%Cash	%Government Bonds	%Municipal Bonds	%Corporate Bonds	%Other	Turnover Ratio	Average Coupon Rate	Min Initial Investment	Min Additional Investment	Front End Fee (%)	Back End Fee (%)	Inception Date
3.50	4.98	7.32	15.20	22.18	2.41	0.51	3.92	6.10	10.75	344.8	3	29	8	27	0	22	3.75	500,000	50			Aug-11
1.98	2.43	4.34	11.29	17.22	2.52	0.85	3.24	5.60	11.83	48.7	0	0	100	0	0	53	4.71	2,500	50	2.00		Apr-85
2.04	2.64	4.69	12.22	18.52	2.76	0.6	3.26	5.60	11.85	48.7	0	0	100	0	0	53	4.71	2,500	50			Aug-16
1.97	2.58	4.56	12.26	18.57	2.81	0.55	3.23	5.60	11.84	48.7	0	0	100	0	0	53	4.71	500,000	50			Aug-16
2.46	-0.08	1.12	5.40	7.67	2.32	0.69	1.97	0.55	9.18	930.6	12	0	2	25	0	91	3.08	2,500	50	2.00		Apr-12
2.40	-0.20	0.87	4.63	6.35	2.07	0.94	1.92	0.55	9.18	930.6	12	0	2	25	0	91	3.08	1,000	50			Oct-17
2.63	0.13	1.47	6.30	9.14	2.57	0.44	1.98	0.55	9.19	930.6	12	0	2	25	0	91	3.08	2,500	50			Apr-12
2.46	-0.08	1.12	5.41	7.67	2.33	0.69	1.97	0.55	9.18	930.6	12	0	2	25	0	91	3.08	2,500	50			Mar-94
2.65	0.15	1.41	6.35	9.30	2.62	0.39	1.99	0.55	9.18	930.6	12	0	2	25	0	91	3.08	500,000	50			Apr-12
6.83	2.27	5.04	12.28	18.55	2.26	1.08	4.65	5.17	10.4	126.7	9	28	0	32	0	26	3.22	0				May-17
6.89	2.41	5.30	13.08	20.00	2.5	0.83	4.64	5.17	10.4	126.7	9	28	0	32	0	26	3.22	5,000				Sep-00
6.96	2.41	4.87	12.52	20.93	2.81	0.94	5.06	5.43	9.5	1,553	6	13	0	47	0	50	3.87	1,000	50	4.75		Jun-87
6.61	1.99	4.12	10.30	16.91	2.19	1.56	5.02	5.43	9.43	1,553	6	13	0	47	0	50	3.87	1,000	50		1.00	Nov-02
6.94	2.49	5.17	13.83	23.00	3.21	0.5	5.04	5.43	9.51	1,553	6	13	0	47	0	50	3.87	1,000,000				Nov-09
6.95	2.64	5.34	14.04	23.49	3.25	0.47	5.02	5.43	9.52	1,553	6	13	0	47	0	50	3.87	0				Nov-04
6.95	2.52	5.22	13.95	23.38	3.26	0.48	5.08	5.43	9.51	1,553	6	13	0	47	0	50	3.87	0				May-15
3.85	5.80	8.36	16.48	23.09	2.85	0.47	3.58		10.62	1,003	4	24	1	25	0	13	3.60	0				Jul-09
14.86	-3.74	-0.93	5.45	21.56	4.88	1.18	12.68	6.02	10.12	391.0	4	64	0	31	0	255	6.19	1,000	50	4.75		Aug-11
14.62	-4.16	-1.63	3.26	17.28	4.15	1.88	12.68	6.02	10.03	391.0	4	64	0	31	0	255	6.19	1,000	50		1.00	Aug-11
14.91	-3.60	-0.64	6.63	23.69	5.27	0.8	12.67	6.02	10.17	391.0	4	64	0	31	0	255	6.19	1,000,000				Aug-11
14.91	-3.56	-0.55	7.00	24.34	5.38	0.7	12.72	6.02	10.17	391.0	4	64	0	31	0	255	6.19	0				Aug-11
15.04	-3.56	-0.46	7.01	24.36	5.38	0.7	12.7	6.02	10.17	391.0	4	64	0	31	0	255	6.19	0				May-15
8.49	-4.86	-3.61	3.20	12.01	4.79	1.05	8.24	0.75	9	86.8	9	0	0	91	0	23	1.20	1,000	50	4.75		Oct-13
8.29	-5.31	-4.43	0.91	7.88	4	1.8	8.26	0.75	9	86.8	9	0	0	91	0	23	1.20	1,000	50		1.00	Oct-13
8.58	-4.87	-3.51	3.82	12.86	5.06	0.8	8.3	0.75	8.96	86.8	9	0	0	91	0	23	1.20	1,000,000				Oct-13
8.56	-4.73	-3.46	4.07	13.73	5.07	0.72	8.2	0.75	9	86.8	9	0	0	91	0	23	1.20	0				Oct-13
0.04	0.34	1.23	4.37	4.42	1.38	0.3	0.17		1	1,427	71	28	0	0	0			0				May-17
0.01	0.19	0.83	2.84	2.84	0.76	0.8	0.17		1	1,427	71	28	0	0	0			0				Jan-94
0.05	0.30	1.08	3.63	3.63	1.2	0.5	0.19		1	1,427	71	28	0	0	0			5,000				Sep-00
0.05	0.33	1.01	2.62	2.63	1.11	0.72	0.23		1	1,427	71	28	0	0	0			1,000	50			Mar-02
1.62	1.66	1.95	2.29	2.31	1.75	1.48	0.75		1	1,427	71	28	0	0	0			1,000	50		1.00	Nov-02
0.02	0.27	1.07	3.35	3.36	1.21	0.48	0.23		1	1,427	71	28	0	0	0			1,000,000				Nov-09
0.05	0.34	1.23	2.01	2.02	1.38	0.3	0.25		1	1,427	71	28	0	0	0			0				Nov-05
4.59	1.10	2.61	7.74	9.86	3.49	0.45	3.28	1.77	9.88	176.2	2	6	0	35	0	69	2.80	0				Sep-00
4.45	0.85	2.10	6.21	7.36	2.99	0.94	3.25	1.77	9.91	176.2	2	6	0	35	0	69	2.80	0				Apr-17
4.56	1.01	2.42	7.02	9.19	3.29	0.65	3.29	1.77	9.88	176.2	2	6	0	35	0	69	2.80	5,000				Sep-00
8.97	-7.55	-3.89	3.90	15.73	5.5	1.06	9.46	3.92	8.25	1,883	5	0	0	95	0	38	6.04	1,000	50	4.75		Jun-85
8.96	-7.80	-4.46	1.81	11.97	4.77	1.74	9.52	3.92	8.22	1,883	5	0	0	95	0	38	6.04	1,000	50		1.00	Nov-02
9.43	-7.06	-3.13	5.14	17.75	5.89	0.63	9.48	3.92	8.33	1,883	5	0	0	95	0	38	6.04	1,000,000				Nov-09
9.16	-7.22	-3.35	5.22	18.32	5.98	0.6	9.44	3.92	8.34	1,883	5	0	0	95	0	38	6.04	0				Nov-04
9.28	-7.24	-3.37	5.25	16.43	5.97	0.6	9.49	3.92	8.34	1,883	5	0	0	95	0	38	6.04	0				Jun-85
9.15	-7.47	-3.84	3.72	13.60	5.46	1.1	9.49	3.92	8.34	1,883	5	0	0	95	0	38	6.04	0				Mar-17
9.22	-7.35	-3.60	4.47	14.99	5.72	0.85	9.49	3.92	8.34	1,883	5	0	0	95	0	38	6.04	5,000				Mar-17
9.28	-7.24	-3.37	5.24	18.21	5.97	0.6	9.5	3.92	8.34	1,883	5	0	0	95	0	38	6.04	0				May-15
4.61	-2.50	0.52	11.04	23.53	3.95	0.92	6.84	6.82	11.47	83.3	2	0	97	1	0	54	5.04	1,000	50	3.25		Jul-13
4.46	-2.78	-0.07	9.08	19.95	3.32	1.52	6.82	6.82	11.48	83.3	2	0	97	1	0	54	5.04	1,000	50		1.00	Jul-13
4.75	-2.67	0.41	11.17	24.23	4.12	0.77	6.96	6.82	11.46	83.3	2	0	97	1	0	54	5.04	1,000,000				Jul-13
4.67	-2.45	0.68	11.66	24.34	4.21	0.74	6.87	6.82	11.48	83.3	2	0	97	1	0	54	5.04	0				Sep-16
5.78	3.09	5.56	11.79	15.09	1.19	1	4.52	8.05	10.56	101.2	4	72	0	23	0	23	1.96	1,000	50	4.75		Mar-14
5.64	2.73	4.73	9.36	10.95	0.65	1.75	4.53	8.05	10.32	101.2	4	72	0	23	0	23	1.96	1,000	50		1.00	Mar-14
5.87	3.24	5.73	12.58	16.48	1.4	0.75	4.49	8.05	10.63	101.2	4	72	0	23	0	23	1.96	1,000,000				Mar-14
5.75	3.14	5.74	12.76	16.84	1.41	0.71	4.49	8.05	10.65	101.2	4	72	0	23	0	23	1.96	0				Mar-14

Fund Name	Ticker Symbol	Traded On	Fund Type	Category and (Prospectus Objective)	Overall Rating	Reward Rating	Risk Rating	Recent Up/ Downgrade	Open to New Investors	Telephone
	MARKET			FUND TYPE, CATEGORY & OBJECTIVE	RATINGS				NEW INVESTORS	
Transamerica Inflation Opportunities Fund Class R6	RTIOX	NAS CM	Open End	US Fixed Inc (Growth & Income)	C+	C	B	Up	Y	888-233-4339
Transamerica Inflation-Protected Securities I3	TPRTX	NAS CM	Open End	US Fixed Inc (Govt Bond - General)	B-	C+	B+	Up	Y	888-233-4339
Transamerica Inflation-Protected Securities R	TPRRX	NAS CM	Open End	US Fixed Inc (Govt Bond - General)	B-	C	B+	Up	Y	888-233-4339
Transamerica Inflation-Protected Securities R4	TPRFX	NAS CM	Open End	US Fixed Inc (Govt Bond - General)	B-	C+	B+	Up	Y	888-233-4339
Transamerica Intermediate Bond I2			Open End	US Fixed Inc (Income)	B-	C+	B+	Up	Y	888-233-4339
Transamerica Intermediate Bond I3	TMBTX	NAS CM	Open End	US Fixed Inc (Income)	B-	C+	B+	Up	Y	888-233-4339
Transamerica Intermediate Bond R	TMBRX	NAS CM	Open End	US Fixed Inc (Income)	B-	C+	B	Up	Y	888-233-4339
Transamerica Intermediate Bond R4	TMBFX	NAS CM	Open End	US Fixed Inc (Income)	B-	C+	B+	Up	Y	888-233-4339
Transamerica Intermediate Muni Class A	TAMUX	NAS CM	Open End	US Muni Fixed Inc (Muni Bond - Natl)	C	C	B-		Y	888-233-4339
Transamerica Intermediate Muni Class C	TCMUX	NAS CM	Open End	US Muni Fixed Inc (Muni Bond - Natl)	C	C-	B-		Y	888-233-4339
Transamerica Intermediate Muni Class I	TIMUX	NAS CM	Open End	US Muni Fixed Inc (Muni Bond - Natl)	C	C	B-		Y	888-233-4339
Transamerica Intermediate Muni I2	TIMTX	NAS CM	Open End	US Muni Fixed Inc (Muni Bond - Natl)	C	C	B		Y	888-233-4339
Transamerica Short-Term Bond Fund Class A	ITAAX	NAS CM	Open End	US Fixed Inc (Income)	C	C-	C		Y	888-233-4339
Transamerica Short-Term Bond Fund Class C	ITACX	NAS CM	Open End	US Fixed Inc (Income)	C-	D+	C		Y	888-233-4339
Transamerica Short-Term Bond Fund Class I	TSTIX	NAS CM	Open End	US Fixed Inc (Income)	C	C-	C		Y	888-233-4339
Transamerica Short-Term Bond Fund Class I2			Open End	US Fixed Inc (Income)	C	C-	C		Y	888-233-4339
Transamerica Short-Term Bond Fund Class R6	TASTX	NAS CM	Open End	US Fixed Inc (Income)	C	C-	C		Y	888-233-4339
Transamerica Total Return Fund Class I2			Open End	US Fixed Inc (Growth & Income)	B	C+	B+	Up	Y	888-233-4339
Transamerica Unconstrained Bond Class I	TUNIX	NAS CM	Open End	Fixed Inc Misc (Worldwide Bond)	D+	D	C	Down	Y	888-233-4339
Transamerica Unconstrained Bond Class I2			Open End	Fixed Inc Misc (Worldwide Bond)	C-	D+	C		Y	888-233-4339
TransWestern Institutional Short Duration Govt Bond Fund	TWSGX	NAS CM	Open End	US Fixed Inc (Income)	C	C	B-		Y	
Tributary Income Fund Class Institutional Plus	FOIPX	NAS CM	Open End	US Fixed Inc (Corp Bond - General)	B	C+	B+	Up	Y	
Tributary Income Fund Institutional Class	FOINX	NAS CM	Open End	US Fixed Inc (Corp Bond - General)	B	C+	B+	Up	Y	
Tributary Nebraska Tax-Free Fund Institutional Plus Class	FONPX	NAS CM	Open End	US Muni Fixed Inc (Muni Bond - Single State)	C+	C	B	Up	Y	
Tributary Short/Intermediate Bond Cl Institutional Plus	FOSPX	NAS CM	Open End	US Fixed Inc (Corp Bond - General)	C+	C	B	Up	Y	
Tributary Short-Intermediate Bond Fund Institutional Class	FOSIX	NAS CM	Open End	US Fixed Inc (Corp Bond - General)	C+	C	B-	Up	Y	
Trust For Credit Unions Short Duration Port Inv Shares	TCUEX	NAS CM	Open End	US Fixed Inc (Govt Bond - Mortgage)	C+	C	B		Y	
Trust For Credit Unions Short Duration Portfol TCU Shares	TCUDX	NAS CM	Open End	US Fixed Inc (Govt Bond - Mortgage)	C+	C	B		Y	
Trust For Credit Unions Ultra-Short Duration Port Inv Sh	TCUYX	NAS CM	Open End	US Fixed Inc (Govt Bond - General)	C	C-	C+		Y	
Trust For Credit Unions Ultra-Short Duration Port TCU Sh	TCUUX	NAS CM	Open End	US Fixed Inc (Govt Bond - General)	C	C-	C+		Y	
U.S. Global Investors Near-Term Tax Free Fund	NEARX	NAS CM	Open End	US Muni Fixed Inc (Muni Bond - Natl)	C	C	C+		Y	800-873-8637
U.S. Global Investors U.S. Govt Ultra-Short Bond Fund	UGSDX	NAS CM	Open End	US Fixed Inc (Govt Bond - General)	C	C-	C+		Y	800-873-8637
UBS Liquid Assets Government Fund			Money Mkt	US Money Mkt (Money Mkt - Govt)	C	C	C+		Y	212-882-5586
UBS Municipal Bond Fund Class A	UMBAX	NAS CM	Open End	US Muni Fixed Inc (Muni Bond - Natl)	C	C	B		Y	212-882-5586
UBS Municipal Bond Fund Class P	UMBPX	NAS CM	Open End	US Muni Fixed Inc (Muni Bond - Natl)	C+	C	B	Up	Y	212-882-5586
UBS Prime Investor Fund	UPIXX	NAS CM	Money Mkt	US Money Mkt (Money Mkt - Taxable)	C	C-	C+		Y	212-882-5586
UBS Prime Preferred Fund	UPPXX	NAS CM	Money Mkt	US Money Mkt (Money Mkt - Taxable)	C	C-	C+		Y	212-882-5586
UBS Prime Reserves Fund	UPRXX	NAS CM	Money Mkt	US Money Mkt (Money Mkt - Taxable)	C	C-	C+		Y	212-882-5586
UBS RMA Government Money Market Fund	RMGXX	NAS CM	Money Mkt	US Money Mkt (Money Mkt - Govt)	C	C-	C+		Y	212-882-5586
UBS Select ESG Prime Institutional Fund	SGIXX	NAS CM	Money Mkt	US Money Mkt (Money Mkt - General)	U	U	U		Y	212-882-5586
UBS Select ESG Prime Investor Fund	SEIXX	NAS CM	Money Mkt	US Money Mkt (Money Mkt - General)	U	U	U		Y	212-882-5586
UBS Select ESG Prime Preferred Fund	SSPXX	NAS CM	Money Mkt	US Money Mkt (Money Mkt - General)	U	U	U		Y	212-882-5586
UBS Select Government Institutional Fund	SEGXX	NAS CM	Money Mkt	US Money Mkt (Money Mkt - Govt)	C	C-	C+		Y	212-882-5586
UBS Select Government Investor Fund	SGEXX	NAS CM	Money Mkt	US Money Mkt (Money Mkt - Govt)	C	C-	C+		Y	212-882-5586
UBS Select Government Preferred Fund	SGPXX	NAS CM	Money Mkt	US Money Mkt (Money Mkt - Govt)	C	C-	C+		Y	212-882-5586
UBS Select Prime Fund Class Institutional	SELXX	NAS CM	Money Mkt	US Money Mkt (Money Mkt - General)	C	C-	C+		Y	212-882-5586
UBS Select Prime Investor Fund	SPIXX	NAS CM	Money Mkt	US Money Mkt (Money Mkt - General)	C	C-	C+		Y	212-882-5586
UBS Select Prime Preferred Fund	SPPXX	NAS CM	Money Mkt	US Money Mkt (Money Mkt - General)	C	C-	C+		Y	212-882-5586
UBS Select Treasury Institutional Fund	SETXX	NAS CM	Money Mkt	US Money Mkt (Money Mkt - Govt)	C	C-	C+		Y	212-882-5586
UBS Select Treasury Investor Fund	STRXX	NAS CM	Money Mkt	US Money Mkt (Money Mkt - Treasury)	C	C-	C+		Y	212-882-5586
UBS Select Treasury Preferred Fund	STPXX	NAS CM	Money Mkt	US Money Mkt (Money Mkt - Treasury)	C	C-	C+		Y	212-882-5586
UBS Sustainable Development Bank Bond Fund Class P	UDBPX	NAS CM	Open End	Global Fixed Inc (Income)	D+	D+	B+	Up	Y	212-882-5586

★ Expanded analysis of this fund is included in Section II.

TOTAL RETURNS & PERFORMANCE									ASSETS		ASSET ALLOCATION & TURNOVER							MINIMUMS		FEES		
3-Month Total Return	6-Month Total Return	1-Year Total Return	3-Year Total Return	5-Year Total Return	Dividend Yield (TTM)	Expense Ratio	3-Yr Std Deviation	Effective Duration	NAV	Total Assets (MIL)	%Cash	%Government Bonds	%Municipal Bonds	%Corporate Bonds	%Other	Turnover Ratio	Average Coupon Rate	Min Initial Investment	Min Additional Investment	Front End Fee (%)	Back End Fee (%)	Inception Date
5.85	3.24	5.84	12.87	16.72	1.41	0.71	4.49	8.05	10.66	101.2	4	72	0	23	0	23	1.96	0				Jul-16
4.72	4.78	7.10	14.40	16.93	1.89	0.49	3.89	7.79	10.65	109.8	3	88	0	8	0	14	1.39	0				Apr-17
4.61	4.56	6.59	12.84	14.62	1.39	1	3.86	7.79	10.66	109.8	3	88	0	8	0	14	1.39	0				Apr-17
4.71	4.74	6.92	13.85	16.30	1.63	0.65	3.93	7.79	10.67	109.8	3	88	0	8	0	14	1.39	5,000				Sep-00
4.29	5.37	8.02	15.64	23.09	2.55	0.42	3.8	5.81	10.86	1,879	15	20	1	30	0	49	3.47	0				Mar-14
4.29	5.36	8.00	15.72	23.42	2.54	0.42	3.82	5.81	10.88	1,879	15	20	1	30	0	49	3.47	0				Sep-00
4.14	5.18	7.49	13.99	20.42	2.09	0.91	3.77	5.81	10.89	1,879	15	20	1	30	0	49	3.47	0				Mar-17
4.23	5.24	7.76	14.89	16.07	2.32	0.65	3.8	5.81	10.88	1,879	15	20	1	30	0	49	3.47	5,000				Sep-00
2.32	1.20	3.31	11.61	19.97	2.44	0.69	4.02	5.52	11.8	1,973	6	0	94	0	0	14	4.19	1,000	50	3.25		Oct-12
2.17	0.89	2.68	9.48	16.35	1.82	1.31	4.05	5.52	11.77	1,973	6	0	94	0	0	14	4.19	1,000	50		1.00	Oct-12
2.36	1.19	3.38	11.89	20.43	2.59	0.49	4.07	5.52	11.84	1,973	6	0	94	0	0	14	4.19	1,000,000				Oct-12
2.37	1.30	3.52	12.29	20.91	2.64	0.49	4.07	5.52	11.85	1,973	6	0	94	0	0	14	4.19	0				Sep-16
6.01	0.81	2.35	7.47	11.84	2.41	0.73	4.14	1.74	10.25	2,985	4	0	0	61	0	61	3.25	1,000	50	2.50		Nov-07
5.82	0.42	1.56	5.00	7.54	1.61	1.52	4.17	1.74	10.23	2,985	4	0	0	61	0	61	3.25	1,000	50		1.00	Nov-07
6.05	1.01	2.66	8.25	13.14	2.6	0.53	4.1	1.74	10.08	2,985	4	0	0	61	0	61	3.25	1,000,000				Nov-09
6.08	1.06	2.76	8.56	13.61	2.7	0.43	4.11	1.74	10.07	2,985	4	0	0	61	0	61	3.25	0				Nov-04
6.08	0.96	2.76	8.59	13.66	2.71	0.43	4.16	1.74	10.07	2,985	4	0	0	61	0	61	3.25	0				May-15
4.20	6.01	8.56	15.72	23.83	2.57	0.68	3.5		10.91	600.7	-2	46	0	26	0	32	2.87	0				Nov-05
8.74	-1.61	0.34	5.10	13.88	3.48	0.83	6.75	1.67	9.6	1,487	20	3	0	78	0	87	4.10	1,000,000				Dec-14
8.69	-1.66	0.45	5.47	14.56	3.58	0.73	6.76	1.67	9.57	1,487	20	3	0	78	0	87	4.10	0				Dec-14
0.75	1.84	2.95	7.26	9.30	1.98	0.65	1.08		9.8	331.8	35	9	0	0	0	431	3.44	2,000,000	500,000			Jan-11
3.31	5.60	7.78	16.12	23.62	2.72	0.55	3.34	5.94	10.95	218.0	1	18	2	29	0		3.66	5,000,000	50			Oct-11
3.27	5.50	7.59	15.49	22.69	2.54	0.73	3.35	5.94	10.95	218.0	1	18	2	29	0		3.66	1,000	50			Mar-01
2.28	2.76	4.46	10.60		1.95	0.45	2.72	4.41	9.91	76.2	2	0	98	0	0		3.94	5,000,000	50			Dec-15
2.83	2.88	4.18	9.28	13.40	2.3	0.52	1.64	2.28	9.54	201.5	2	23	1	34	0		2.95	5,000,000	50			Oct-11
2.79	2.79	4.00	8.60	12.23	2.12	0.74	1.67	2.28	9.51	201.5	2	23	1	34	0		2.95	1,000	50			Dec-92
1.48	3.32	4.70	9.35	10.16	2.31	0.35	1.27		9.9	561.3	13	0	0	9	0	60	3.00	0				Nov-12
1.38	3.23	4.52	9.32	10.16	2.34	0.33	1.22		9.89	561.3	13	0	0	9	0	60	3.00	0				Oct-92
1.22	1.03	2.07	5.23	5.65	2.01	0.36	0.64		9.41	1,012	30	0	0	8	0	60	1.61	0				Nov-12
1.23	1.04	2.10	5.30	5.82	2.04	0.33	0.64		9.41	1,012	30	0	0	8	0	60	1.61	0				Jul-91
1.18	1.50	2.63	4.62	6.39	1.26	0.45	1.9		2.24	40.7	3	0	97	0	0	35	4.31	5,000	100			Dec-90
0.09	0.32	1.02	3.41	4.42	1.11	1	0.42		2	42.6	31	69	0	0	0	97	1.36	5,000	100			Dec-13
0.09	0.44	1.40	5.02	5.75	1.57	0.08	0.17		1	1,023	60	40	0	0	0			5,000				Feb-00
2.25	2.01	3.87	11.47	18.87	1.67	0.65	4.2	5.73	10.84	116.6	1	0	99	0	0	31	4.82	1,000	100	2.25		Nov-14
2.41	2.24	4.24	12.43	20.38	1.92	0.4	4.21	5.73	10.84	116.6	1	0	99	0	0	31	4.82	2,000,000	100			Nov-14
0.04	0.33	1.18	4.36		1.36	0.5	0.16		1	2,534	100	0	0	0	0			1,000				Jan-16
0.12	0.49	1.50	5.33		1.67	0.14	0.16		1	1,410	100	0	0	0	0			50,000,000				Jan-16
0.11	0.46	1.46	5.20		1.63	0.18	0.16		1	4,493	100	0	0	0	0			1,000,000				Jan-16
0.00	0.17	0.95	3.64		1.08	0.49	0.17		1	787.0	100	0	0	0	0			5,000				Jun-16
0.19						0.18			1.0005	60.1	100	0	0	0	0			1,000,000				Jan-20
0.12						0.5			1.0005	25.1	100	0	0	0	0			1,000				Jan-20
0.21						0.14			1.0006	5.8	100	0	0	0	0			99,000,000				Jan-20
0.03	0.34	1.28	4.61		1.45	0.18	0.18		1	5,101	100	0	0	0	0			1,000,000				Jul-16
0.00	0.25	1.03	3.81		1.2	0.5	0.17		1	1,102	100	0	0	0	0			1,000				Aug-16
0.04	0.37	1.31	4.73		1.49	0.14	0.18		1	8,339	100	0	0	0	0			50,000,000				Jun-16
0.17	0.49	1.48	5.40	6.38	1.64	0.18	0.16		1.0004	10,498	100	0	0	0	0			1,000,000				Aug-98
0.11	0.37	1.23	4.50	4.93	1.37	0.5	0.16		1.0005	3,935	100	0	0	0	0			1,000				Aug-08
0.18	0.51	1.52	5.52	6.67	1.68	0.14	0.16		1.0004	2,739	100	0	0	0	0			99,000,000				Aug-07
0.03	0.32	1.25	4.57	5.06	1.42	0.18	0.18		1	14,614	100	0	0	0	0			1,000,000				Mar-04
0.00	0.22	1.01	3.77	3.93	1.17	0.5	0.17		1	2,329	100	0	0	0	0			1,000				Aug-07
0.04	0.35	1.29	4.69	5.25	1.46	0.14	0.18		1	17,886	100	0	0	0	0			50,000,000				Aug-07
1.15	6.71	8.12			1.95	0.25		5.01	11.17	36.5	2	98	0	0	0	20	2.33	2,000,000	100			Oct-18

Fund Name	Ticker Symbol	Traded On	Fund Type	Category and (Prospectus Objective)	Overall Rating	Reward Rating	Risk Rating	Recent Up/ Downgrade	Open to New Investors	Telephone
	MARKET		FUND TYPE, CATEGORY & OBJECTIVE		RATINGS				NEW INVESTORS	
UBS Tax-Free Investor Fund	SFRXX	NAS CM	Money Mkt	US Money Mkt (Money Mkt - Fed Tax Exmpt)	C	C-	C+		Y	212-882-5586
UBS Tax-Free Preferred Fund	SFPXX	NAS CM	Money Mkt	US Money Mkt (Money Mkt - Fed Tax Exmpt)	C	C-	C+		Y	212-882-5586
UBS Tax-Free Reserves Fund	STFXX	NAS CM	Money Mkt	US Money Mkt (Money Mkt - Fed Tax Exmpt)	C	C-	C		Y	212-882-5586
UBS Total Return Bond Fund Class A	UTBAX	NAS CM	Open End	US Fixed Inc (Growth & Income)	C+	C	B		Y	212-882-5586
UBS Total Return Bond Fund Class P	UTBPX	NAS CM	Open End	US Fixed Inc (Growth & Income)	C+	C	B		Y	212-882-5586
UBS Ultra Short Income Fund Class A	USIAX	NAS CM	Open End	US Fixed Inc (Income)	C	D+	C+	Up	Y	212-882-5586
UBS Ultra Short Income Fund Class I	USDIX	NAS CM	Open End	US Fixed Inc (Income)	C	D+	C+	Up	Y	212-882-5586
UBS Ultra Short Income Fund Class P	USIPX	NAS CM	Open End	US Fixed Inc (Income)	C	D+	C+	Up	Y	212-882-5586
US Government Money Market Fund RBC Institutional Class 1	TUGXX	NAS CM	Money Mkt	US Money Mkt (Money Mkt - Govt)	C	C-	C+			800-422-2766
US Government Money Market Fund RBC Institutional Class 2	TIMXX	NAS CM	Money Mkt	US Money Mkt (Money Mkt - Govt)	C	C-	C+			800-422-2766
US Government Money Market Fund RBC Investor Class	TUIXX	NAS CM	Money Mkt	US Money Mkt (Money Mkt - Govt)	C	C-	C+			800-422-2766
USAA California Bond Fund	USCBX	NAS CM	Open End	US Muni Fixed Inc (Muni Bond - Single State)	C	C	B		Y	210-694-9700
USAA California Bond Fund A Shares	UXABX	NAS CM	Open End	US Muni Fixed Inc (Muni Bond - Single State)	C	C	B-		Y	210-694-9700
USAA Government Securities Fund	USGNX	NAS CM	Open End	US Fixed Inc (Govt Bond - General)	B-	C+	B		Y	210-694-9700
USAA Government Securities Fund A Shares	UAGNX	NAS CM	Open End	US Fixed Inc (Govt Bond - General)	B-	C+	B	Up	Y	210-694-9700
USAA Government Securities Fund Institutional Shares	UIGSX	NAS CM	Open End	US Fixed Inc (Govt Bond - General)	B-	C+	B		Y	210-694-9700
USAA Government Securities Fund R6 Shares	URGSX	NAS CM	Open End	US Fixed Inc (Govt Bond - General)	B-	C+	B	Up	Y	210-694-9700
USAA High Income Fund	USHYX	NAS CM	Open End	US Fixed Inc (Corp Bond - High Yield)	D	D	D+	Down	Y	210-694-9700
USAA High Income Fund A Shares	UHYOX	NAS CM	Open End	US Fixed Inc (Corp Bond - High Yield)	D	D	D+	Down	Y	210-694-9700
USAA High Income Fund Institutional Shares	UIHIX	NAS CM	Open End	US Fixed Inc (Corp Bond - High Yield)	D	D	D+	Down	Y	210-694-9700
USAA High Income Fund R6 Shares	URHIX	NAS CM	Open End	US Fixed Inc (Corp Bond - High Yield)	D	D	D+	Down	Y	210-694-9700
USAA Income Fund	USAIX	NAS CM	Open End	US Fixed Inc (Income)	C+	C	B	Up	Y	210-694-9700
USAA Income Fund A Shares	UINCX	NAS CM	Open End	US Fixed Inc (Income)	C+	C	B	Up	Y	210-694-9700
USAA Income Fund Institutional Shares	UIINX	NAS CM	Open End	US Fixed Inc (Income)	C+	C	B	Up	Y	210-694-9700
USAA Income Fund R6 Shares	URIFX	NAS CM	Open End	US Fixed Inc (Income)	C+	C	B	Up	Y	210-694-9700
USAA Intermediate Term Bond Fund R6 Shares	URIBX	NAS CM	Open End	US Fixed Inc (Corp Bond - General)	C+	C	B	Up	Y	210-694-9700
USAA Intermediate-Term Bond Fund	USIBX	NAS CM	Open End	US Fixed Inc (Corp Bond - General)	C+	C	B	Up	Y	210-694-9700
USAA Intermediate-Term Bond Fund A Shares	UITBX	NAS CM	Open End	US Fixed Inc (Corp Bond - General)	C+	C	B	Up	Y	210-694-9700
USAA Intermediate-Term Bond Fund Institutional Shares	UIITX	NAS CM	Open End	US Fixed Inc (Corp Bond - General)	C+	C	B	Up	Y	210-694-9700
USAA Money Market Fund	USAXX	NAS CM	Money Mkt	US Money Mkt (Money Mkt - Taxable)	C	C-	C+		Y	210-694-9700
USAA New York Bond Fund	USNYX	NAS CM	Open End	US Muni Fixed Inc (Muni Bond - Single State)	C	C-	C+		Y	210-694-9700
USAA New York Bond Fund A Shares	UNYBX	NAS CM	Open End	US Muni Fixed Inc (Muni Bond - Single State)	C	C-	C+		Y	210-694-9700
USAA Short Term Bond Fund R6 Shares	URSBX	NAS CM	Open End	US Fixed Inc (Corp Bond - General)	C	C-	C+		Y	210-694-9700
USAA Short-Term Bond Fund	USSBX	NAS CM	Open End	US Fixed Inc (Corp Bond - General)	C	C-	C+		Y	210-694-9700
USAA Short-Term Bond Fund A Shares	UASBX	NAS CM	Open End	US Fixed Inc (Corp Bond - General)	C	C-	C+		Y	210-694-9700
USAA Short-Term Bond Fund Institutional Shares	UISBX	NAS CM	Open End	US Fixed Inc (Corp Bond - General)	C	C-	C+		Y	210-694-9700
USAA Tax Exempt Intermediate-Term Fund	USATX	NAS CM	Open End	US Muni Fixed Inc (Muni Bond - Natl)	C	C-	B-		Y	210-694-9700
USAA Tax Exempt Intermediate-Term Fund A Shares	UTEIX	NAS CM	Open End	US Muni Fixed Inc (Muni Bond - Natl)	C	C-	B-		Y	210-694-9700
USAA Tax Exempt Long-Term Fund	USTEX	NAS CM	Open End	US Muni Fixed Inc (Muni Bond - Natl)	C	C-	B-		Y	210-694-9700
USAA Tax Exempt Long-Term Fund A Shares	UTELX	NAS CM	Open End	US Muni Fixed Inc (Muni Bond - Natl)	C	C-	C+		Y	210-694-9700
USAA Tax Exempt Short-Term Fund	USSTX	NAS CM	Open End	US Muni Fixed Inc (Muni Bond - Natl)	C	C-	C+		Y	210-694-9700
USAA Tax Exempt Short-Term Fund A Shares	UTESX	NAS CM	Open End	US Muni Fixed Inc (Muni Bond - Natl)	C	C-	C		Y	210-694-9700
USAA Tax-Exempt Money Market Fund	USEXX	NAS CM	Money Mkt	US Money Mkt (Money Mkt - Fed Tax Exmpt)	C	C-	C+		Y	210-694-9700
USAA Treasury Money Market Trust	UATXX	NAS CM	Money Mkt	US Money Mkt (Money Mkt - Treasury)	C	C-	C+		Y	210-694-9700
USAA Ultra Short-Term Bond Fund Institutional Shares	UUSIX	NAS CM	Open End	US Fixed Inc (Corp Bond - General)	C-	D+	C	Down	Y	210-694-9700
USAA Ultra Short-Term Bond Fund R6 Shares	URUSX	NAS CM	Open End	US Fixed Inc (Corp Bond - General)	C-	D+	C	Down	Y	210-694-9700
USAA Ultra Short-Term Bond Fund Shares	UUSTX	NAS CM	Open End	US Fixed Inc (Corp Bond - General)	C-	D+	C	Down	Y	210-694-9700
USAA Virginia Bond Fund	USVAX	NAS CM	Open End	US Muni Fixed Inc (Muni Bond - Single State)	C	C-	B-		Y	210-694-9700
USAA Virginia Bond Fund A Shares	UVABX	NAS CM	Open End	US Muni Fixed Inc (Muni Bond - Single State)	C	C-	B-		Y	210-694-9700
VALIC Company I Capital Conservation Fund	VCCCX	NAS CM	Open End	US Fixed Inc (Growth & Income)	B	C+	B	Up	Y	
VALIC Company I Government Money Market I Fund	VCIXX	NAS CM	Money Mkt	US Money Mkt (Money Mkt - Govt)	C	C-	C+		Y	
VALIC Company I Government Securities Fund	VCGSX	NAS CM	Open End	US Fixed Inc (Govt Bond - General)	B	B-	B	Up	Y	

★Expanded analysis of this fund is included in Section II.

TOTAL RETURNS & PERFORMANCE									ASSETS		ASSET ALLOCATION & TURNOVER							MINIMUMS		FEES		
3-Month Total Return	6-Month Total Return	1-Year Total Return	3-Year Total Return	5-Year Total Return	Dividend Yield (TTM)	Expense Ratio	3-Yr Std Deviation	Effective Duration	NAV	Total Assets (MIL)	%Cash	%Government Bonds	%Municipal Bonds	%Corporate Bonds	%Other	Turnover Ratio	Average Coupon Rate	Min Initial Investment	Min Additional Investment	Front End Fee (%)	Back End Fee (%)	Inception Date
0.00	0.25	0.68	2.43	2.65	0.79	0.5	0.11		1	250.7	100	0	0	0	0			1,000				Aug-07
0.02	0.34	0.92	3.32	3.90	1.07	0.14	0.12		1	269.6	100	0	0	0	0			50,000,000				Aug-07
0.01	0.32	0.90	3.20	3.73	1.03	0.18	0.12		1	1,604	100	0	0	0	0			1,000,000				Aug-07
4.64	3.28	6.41	13.17	15.18	2.39	0.75	4.47	6.16	15.67	37.5	7	24	1	25	0	234	3.80	1,000	100	3.75		Sep-16
4.78	3.41	6.67	14.07	16.68	2.63	0.5	4.51	6.16	15.68	37.5	7	24	1	25	0	234	3.80	2,000,000	100			Dec-72
1.70	0.61	1.69			1.93	0.35		0.18	10	2,291	35	0	0	50	0	12	2.10	1,000				May-18
1.73	0.57	1.82			2.05	0.23		0.18	9.99	2,291	35	0	0	50	0	12	2.10	10,000,000				May-18
1.73	0.67	1.80			2.03	0.25		0.18	9.99	2,291	35	0	0	50	0	12	2.10	1,000				May-18
0.04	0.38	1.33	4.69	5.31	1.51	0.19	0.18		1	21,991	56	31	13	0	0			10,000,000				Nov-91
0.01	0.32	1.21	4.35	4.81	1.38	0.29	0.18		1	21,991	56	31	13	0	0			1,000,000				Nov-08
0.00	0.12	0.64	2.32	2.34	0.77	1	0.15		1	21,991	56	31	13	0	0			0				Nov-08
2.15	1.18	3.59	12.24	19.89	2.59	0.54	4.05	5.81	11.34	668.3	0	0	100	0	0	33	4.16	3,000	50			Aug-89
2.09	1.05	3.42	11.43	18.45	2.34	0.8	4.04	5.81	11.33	668.3	0	0	100	0	0	33	4.16	3,000				Aug-10
1.57	4.75	6.15	11.86	15.11	2.35	0.46	2.42	3.42	10.24	1,014	2	26	4	0	0	9	3.12	3,000	50			Feb-91
1.38	4.58	5.71	10.78	13.42	2.03	0.75	2.4	3.42	10.23	1,014	2	26	4	0	0	9	3.12	3,000				Aug-10
1.58	4.78	6.23	12.14	15.54	2.42	0.37	2.4	3.42	10.24	1,014	2	26	4	0	0	9	3.12	1,000,000				Aug-15
1.48	4.79	6.12	12.11	15.45	2.42	0.35	2.38	3.42	10.23	1,014	2	26	4	0	0	9	3.12	0				Dec-16
10.43	-7.59	-4.53	3.49	15.47	6.22	0.84	10.55	4.37	7.13	1,791	2	1	0	96	0	31	6.32	3,000	50			Aug-99
10.34	-7.65	-4.69	2.94	14.29	6.03	1.02	10.52	4.37	7.15	1,791	2	1	0	96	0	31	6.32	3,000				Aug-10
10.47	-7.67	-4.46	3.62	15.98	6.32	0.75	10.62	4.37	7.12	1,791	2	1	0	96	0	31	6.32	1,000,000				Aug-08
10.49	-7.64	-4.51	3.92	16.05	6.4	0.67	10.58	4.37	7.12	1,791	2	1	0	96	0	31	6.32	0				Dec-16
7.21	3.45	6.83	15.54	25.99	3.03	0.52	5.54	5.87	13.68	8,180	3	8	8	60	0		3.91	3,000	50			Mar-74
7.16	3.33	6.59	14.82	24.58	2.8	0.77	5.54	5.87	13.65	8,180	3	8	8	60	0		3.91	3,000				Aug-10
7.31	3.55	6.97	15.86	26.43	3.08	0.46	5.59	5.87	13.68	8,180	3	8	8	60	0		3.91	1,000,000				Aug-08
7.33	3.51	7.05	16.15	26.62	3.14	0.39	5.57	5.87	13.68	8,180	3	8	8	60	0		3.91	0				Dec-16
7.92	3.97	7.34	16.96	27.53	3.53	0.39	5.52	5.50	11	3,732	3	9	4	52	0	35	3.86	0				Dec-16
7.87	3.87	7.13	16.27	26.63	3.34	0.59	5.5	5.50	11	3,732	3	9	4	52	0	35	3.86	3,000	50			Aug-99
7.81	3.73	6.84	15.32	24.86	3.07	0.87	5.51	5.50	10.99	3,732	3	9	4	52	0	35	3.86	3,000				Aug-10
7.89	3.90	7.20	16.50	27.07	3.4	0.52	5.51	5.50	11	3,732	3	9	4	52	0	35	3.86	1,000,000				Aug-08
0.06	0.37	1.19	4.23	4.51	1.35	0.62	0.16		1	2,440	75	0	17	9	0			1,000	50			Jan-81
1.96	0.30	2.55	9.98	17.27	3.19	0.65	4.5	6.08	11.94	215.3	5	0	95	0	0	18	4.54	3,000	50			Oct-90
1.90	0.17	2.31	9.18	15.93	2.95	0.9	4.48	6.08	11.91	215.3	5	0	95	0	0	18	4.54	3,000				Aug-10
4.97	1.37	3.11	8.84	13.62	2.93	0.39	3.18	1.95	9.23	2,808	9	4	7	50	0	48	3.48	0				Dec-16
4.94	1.31	2.98	8.40	12.90	2.8	0.53	3.21	1.95	9.23	2,808	9	4	7	50	0	48	3.48	3,000	50			Jun-93
4.88	1.20	2.77	7.74	11.69	2.6	0.73	3.2	1.95	9.23	2,808	9	4	7	50	0	48	3.48	3,000				Aug-10
4.97	1.36	3.08	8.62	13.36	2.9	0.43	3.19	1.95	9.22	2,808	9	4	7	50	0	48	3.48	1,000,000				Aug-08
2.53	0.89	2.99	11.92	18.40	2.85	0.48	4.12	4.88	13.57	4,751	0	0	100	0	0	26	4.38	3,000	50			Mar-82
2.46	0.75	2.71	11.11	16.89	2.58	0.75	4.14	4.88	13.57	4,751	0	0	100	0	0	26	4.38	3,000				Aug-10
2.23	0.54	2.91	11.52	19.75	3.39	0.48	4.82	6.46	13.4	2,354	1	0	99	0	0	13	4.69	3,000	50			Mar-82
2.25	0.51	2.76	10.88	18.31	3.17	0.7	4.79	6.46	13.39	2,354	1	0	99	0	0	13	4.69	3,000				Aug-10
2.13	0.55	1.58	5.60	7.35	1.71	0.51	1.94	2.03	10.5	1,254	7	0	93	0	0	31	2.73	3,000	50			Mar-82
1.97	0.43	1.24	4.80	6.07	1.47	0.75	1.95	2.03	10.51	1,254	7	0	93	0	0	31	2.73	3,000				Aug-10
0.05	0.35	0.79	2.60	2.95	0.87	0.56	0.12		1	672.1	14	0	86	0	0			3,000	50			Feb-84
0.01	0.26	1.08	4.02	4.16	1.22	0.35	0.17		1	545.2	97	3	0	0	0			3,000	50			Feb-91
5.36	-0.28	1.39	6.35	8.27	2.7	0.55	3.85	0.96	9.9	237.1	5	0	3	60	0	59	3.26	1,000,000				Jul-13
5.40	-0.20	1.65	6.86	9.07	2.86	0.39	3.84	0.96	9.9	237.1	5	0	3	60	0	59	3.26	0				Mar-17
5.34	-0.29	1.45	6.20	8.24	2.65	0.59	3.85	0.96	9.9	237.1	5	0	3	60	0	59	3.26	3,000	50			Oct-10
2.32	1.12	3.10	10.29	17.66	2.68	0.54	3.7	5.39	11.45	706.4	0	0	100	0	0	9	4.10	3,000	50			Oct-90
2.35	0.98	2.92	9.53	16.30	2.43	0.8	3.7	5.39	11.45	706.4	0	0	100	0	0	9	4.10	3,000				Aug-10
3.82	5.98	9.05	16.25	22.58	3.05	0.64	3.39	5.59	10.59	277.3	5	22	0	31	0	72	3.40	0				Jan-86
0.00	0.21	0.93	3.51	3.63	1.09	0.51	0.17		1	413.0	70	30	0	0	0			0				Jan-86
0.98	6.34	8.04	14.16	18.90	2.27	0.67	3.32	5.73	11.25	148.5	5	31	0	4	0	17	3.07	0				Jan-86

	MARKET		FUND TYPE, CATEGORY & OBJECTIVE		RATINGS				NEW INVESTORS	
Fund Name	Ticker Symbol	Traded On	Fund Type	Category and (Prospectus Objective)	Overall Rating	Reward Rating	Risk Rating	Recent Up/ Downgrade	Open to New Investors	Telephone
VALIC Company I Inflation Protected Fund	VCTPX	NAS CM	Open End	US Fixed Inc (Worldwide Bond)	C+	C	B	Up	Y	
VALIC Company I International Government Bond Fund	VCIFX	NAS CM	Open End	Global Fixed Inc (Govt Bond - General)	C	C-	C+		Y	
VALIC Company II Core Bond Fund	VCCBX	NAS CM	Open End	US Fixed Inc (Corp Bond - General)	B-	C+	B+	Up	Y	
VALIC Company II Government Money Market II Fund	VIIXX	NAS CM	Money Mkt	US Money Mkt (Money Mkt - Govt)	C	C-	C+		Y	
VALIC Company II High Yield Bond Fund	VCHYX	NAS CM	Open End	US Fixed Inc (Corp Bond - High Yield)	C-	D+	C		Y	
VALIC Company II Strategic Bond Fund	VCSBX	NAS CM	Open End	US Fixed Inc (Multisector Bond)	C	C-	B-		Y	
Value Line Core Bond Fund	VAGIX	NAS CM	Open End	US Fixed Inc (Income)	B-	C	B	Up	Y	800-243-2729
Value Line Tax-Exempt Fund	VLHYX	NAS CM	Open End	US Muni Fixed Inc (Muni Bond - Natl)	C	C	B-		Y	800-243-2729
VanEck Emerging Markets Bond Fund Class A	EMBAX	NAS CM	Open End	Emerg Mkts Fixed Inc (Growth & Income)	D	D	D+	Down	Y	800-826-1115
VanEck Emerging Markets Bond Fund Class C	EMBCX	NAS CM	Open End	Emerg Mkts Fixed Inc (Growth & Income)	D	D	D+	Down	Y	800-826-1115
VanEck Emerging Markets Bond Fund Class I	EMBUX	NAS CM	Open End	Emerg Mkts Fixed Inc (Growth & Income)	D	D	D+	Down	Y	800-826-1115
VanEck Emerging Markets Bond Fund Class Y	EMBYX	NAS CM	Open End	Emerg Mkts Fixed Inc (Growth & Income)	D	D	D+	Down	Y	800-826-1115
Vanguard California Intermed-Term Tax-Ex Admiral Shares	VCADX	NAS CM	Open End	US Muni Fixed Inc (Muni Bond - Single State)	C+	C	B	Up	Y	877-662-7447
Vanguard California Intermed-Term Tax-Ex Investor Shares	VCAIX	NAS CM	Open End	US Muni Fixed Inc (Muni Bond - Single State)	C+	C	B	Up	Y	877-662-7447
Vanguard California Long-Term Tax-Exempt Admiral Shares	VCLAX	NAS CM	Open End	US Muni Fixed Inc (Muni Bond - Single State)	C+	C	B		Y	877-662-7447
Vanguard California Long-Term Tax-Exempt Investor Shares	VCITX	NAS CM	Open End	US Muni Fixed Inc (Muni Bond - Single State)	C+	C	B		Y	877-662-7447
Vanguard California Muni Money Mkt Fund Investor Shares	VCTXX	NAS CM	Money Mkt	US Money Mkt (Money Mkt - Single State)	C	C-	C+		Y	877-662-7447
Vanguard Core Bond Fund Admiral Shares	VCOBX	NAS CM	Open End	US Fixed Inc (Income)	B	B-	B+		Y	877-662-7447
Vanguard Core Bond Fund Investor Shares	VCORX	NAS CM	Open End	US Fixed Inc (Income)	B	B-	B+		Y	877-662-7447
Vanguard Emerging Markets Bond Fund Admiral Shares	VEGBX	NAS CM	Open End	Emerg Mkts Fixed Inc (Income)	C	C-	B		Y	877-662-7447
Vanguard Emerging Markets Bond Fund Investor Shares	VEMBX	NAS CM	Open End	Emerg Mkts Fixed Inc (Income)	C	C-	B		Y	877-662-7447
Vanguard Emerg Mkts Govt Bond Index Fund Admiral Shares	VGAVX	NAS CM	Open End	Emerg Mkts Fixed Inc (Govt Bond - General)	C-	D+	C	Down	Y	877-662-7447
Vanguard Emerg Mkts Govt Bond Ind Institutional Shares	VGIVX	NAS CM	Open End	Emerg Mkts Fixed Inc (Govt Bond - General)	C-	D+	C	Down	Y	877-662-7447
Vanguard Extended Duration Treas Ind Inst Plus Shares	VEDIX	NAS CM	Open End	US Fixed Inc (Govt Bond - Treasury)	B	B	B		Y	877-662-7447
Vanguard Extended Duration Treas Ind Inst Shares	VEDTX	NAS CM	Open End	US Fixed Inc (Govt Bond - Treasury)	B	B	B		Y	877-662-7447
★ Vanguard Federal Money Market Fund Investor Shares	VMFXX	NAS CM	Money Mkt	US Money Mkt (Money Mkt - Govt)	C	C-	C+			877-662-7447
Vanguard Global Credit Bond Fund Admiral Shares	VGCAX	NAS CM	Open End	Global Fixed Inc (Income)	D+	D+	B	Up	Y	877-662-7447
Vanguard Global Credit Bond Fund Investor Shares	VGCIX	NAS CM	Open End	Global Fixed Inc (Income)	D+	D+	B	Up	Y	877-662-7447
Vanguard GNMA Fund Admiral Shares	VFIJX	NAS CM	Open End	US Fixed Inc (Govt Bond - Mortgage)	B-	C+	B	Up	Y	877-662-7447
Vanguard GNMA Fund Investor Shares	VFIIX	NAS CM	Open End	US Fixed Inc (Govt Bond - Mortgage)	B-	C+	B	Up	Y	877-662-7447
Vanguard High-Yield Corporate Fund Admiral Shares	VWEAX	NAS CM	Open End	US Fixed Inc (Corp Bond - High Yield)	C-	D+	C	Down	Y	877-662-7447
Vanguard High-Yield Corporate Fund Investor Shares	VWEHX	NAS CM	Open End	US Fixed Inc (Corp Bond - High Yield)	C-	D+	C	Down	Y	877-662-7447
Vanguard High-Yield Tax-Exempt Fund	VWAHX	NAS CM	Open End	US Muni Fixed Inc (Muni Bond - Natl)	C	C-	B-	Down	Y	877-662-7447
Vanguard High-Yield Tax-Exempt Fund Admiral Shares	VWALX	NAS CM	Open End	US Muni Fixed Inc (Muni Bond - Natl)	C	C-	B-	Down	Y	877-662-7447
Vanguard Inflation-Protected Securities Admiral Shares	VAIPX	NAS CM	Open End	US Fixed Inc (Govt Bond - Treasury)	B	B-	A-	Up	Y	877-662-7447
Vanguard Inflation-Protected Securities Inst Shares	VIPIX	NAS CM	Open End	US Fixed Inc (Govt Bond - Treasury)	B	B-	A-	Up	Y	877-662-7447
Vanguard Inflation-Protected Securities Investor Shares	VIPSX	NAS CM	Open End	US Fixed Inc (Govt Bond - Treasury)	B	C+	B+	Up	Y	877-662-7447
Vanguard Inst Intermed-Term Bond Inst Plus Shares	VIITX	NAS CM	Open End	US Fixed Inc (Income)	B-	C+	B	Up	Y	877-662-7447
Vanguard Inst Short-Term Bond Inst Plus Shares	VISTX	NAS CM	Open End	US Fixed Inc (Income)	C+	C	B	Up	Y	877-662-7447
Vanguard Instl Total Bond Market Index Trust	VTBSX	NAS CM	Open End	US Fixed Inc (Income)	B	B-	B+		Y	877-662-7447
Vanguard Intermediate-Term Bond Index Fund Admiral Shares	VBILX	NAS CM	Open End	US Fixed Inc (Income)	B	B-	B	Up	Y	877-662-7447
Vanguard Intermed-Term Bond Ind Inst Plus Shares	VBIUX	NAS CM	Open End	US Fixed Inc (Income)	B	B-	B	Up	Y	877-662-7447
Vanguard Intermediate-Term Bond Ind Institutional Shares	VBIMX	NAS CM	Open End	US Fixed Inc (Income)	B	B-	B	Up	Y	877-662-7447
Vanguard Intermediate-Term Bond Index Fund Investor Shares	VBIIX	NAS CM	Open End	US Fixed Inc (Income)	B	B-	B	Up	Y	877-662-7447
Vanguard Intermediate-Term Corp Bond Ind Admiral Shares	VICSX	NAS CM	Open End	US Fixed Inc (Corp Bond - General)	B-	C	B	Up	Y	877-662-7447
Vanguard Intermed-Term Corp Bond Ind Inst Shares	VICBX	NAS CM	Open End	US Fixed Inc (Corp Bond - General)	B-	C	B	Up	Y	877-662-7447
Vanguard Intermediate-Term Investment-Grade Admiral Shares	VFIDX	NAS CM	Open End	US Fixed Inc (Corp Bond - General)	B-	C+	B	Up	Y	877-662-7447
Vanguard Intermed-Term Inv-Grade Investor Shares	VFICX	NAS CM	Open End	US Fixed Inc (Corp Bond - General)	B-	C+	B	Up	Y	877-662-7447
★ Vanguard Intermediate-Term Tax-Exempt Fund Admiral Shares	VWIUX	NAS CM	Open End	US Muni Fixed Inc (Muni Bond - Natl)	C+	C	B	Up	Y	877-662-7447
★ Vanguard Intermediate-Term Tax-Exempt Fund Investor Shares	VWITX	NAS CM	Open End	US Muni Fixed Inc (Muni Bond - Natl)	C+	C	B	Up	Y	877-662-7447
Vanguard Intermediate-Term Treasury Fund Admiral Shares	VFIUX	NAS CM	Open End	US Fixed Inc (Govt Bond - Treasury)	B	B	B		Y	877-662-7447
Vanguard Intermediate-Term Treasury Fund Investor Shares	VFITX	NAS CM	Open End	US Fixed Inc (Govt Bond - Treasury)	B	B	B		Y	877-662-7447

★Expanded analysis of this fund is included in Section II.

TOTAL RETURNS & PERFORMANCE									ASSETS		ASSET ALLOCATION & TURNOVER							MINIMUMS		FEES		
3-Month Total Return	6-Month Total Return	1-Year Total Return	3-Year Total Return	5-Year Total Return	Dividend Yield (TTM)	Expense Ratio	3-Yr Std Deviation	Effective Duration	NAV	Total Assets (MIL)	%Cash	%Government Bonds	%Municipal Bonds	%Corporate Bonds	%Other	Turnover Ratio	Average Coupon Rate	Min Initial Investment	Min Additional Investment	Front End Fee (%)	Back End Fee (%)	Inception Date
6.93	3.27	5.67	12.20	16.87	2.36	0.56	4.73	7.27	11.56	764.6	4	73	0	21	0	42	2.21	0				Dec-04
7.42	2.67	4.45	10.94	20.61	1.72	0.65	5.85	8.32	12.45	174.0	1	93	0	5	0	94	3.87	0				Oct-91
4.88	4.97	8.15	15.61	22.86	1.96	0.77	3.63	5.53	11.76	1,591	2	13	0	42	0	97	3.76	0				Sep-98
0.00	0.20	0.91	3.39	3.49	1.06	0.55	0.16		1	134.5	78	22	0	0	0			0				Sep-98
10.03	-4.41	-0.26	9.68	21.85	4.67	0.93	9.02	4.27	7.04	488.4	2	0	0	98	0	34	5.55	0				Sep-98
7.63	1.07	3.87	11.38	21.82	3.48	0.87	5.54	4.59	11.06	835.9	3	14	0	55	0	95	4.38	0				Sep-98
3.75	4.40	6.81	13.11	18.98	2.18	0.9	3.69	5.82	15.77	54.5	7	23	4	32	0	39	3.39	1,000				Feb-86
1.81	1.54	3.25	9.10	14.86	2.55	0.87	3.5	4.77	9.97	49.8	3	0	97	0	0	15	4.70	1,000				Mar-84
22.08	-2.35	-0.35	7.09	10.38	9.78	1.26	15.36		6	23.5	1	79	0	20	0	302	8.00	1,000	100	5.75		Jul-12
-17.69	-13.89	-12.64	-9.66	-13.42	9.39	1.96	14.19			23.5	1	79	0	20	0	302	8.00	1,000	100		1.00	Jul-12
22.26	-2.16	0.00	8.21	12.10	10.18	0.96	15.37		6.09	23.5	1	79	0	20	0	302	8.00	1,000,000		0.00		Jul-12
22.18	-2.21	0.03	7.98	11.58	10.39	1.02	15.35		6.05	23.5	1	79	0	20	0	302	8.00	1,000	100	0.00		Jul-12
2.59	2.09	4.13	12.02	19.58	2.42	0.09	3.56	4.76	12.2	16,377	1	0	99	0	0	9	4.58	50,000	1			Nov-01
2.57	2.05	4.05	11.75	19.05	2.34	0.17	3.56	4.76	12.2	16,377	1	0	99	0	0	9	4.58	3,000	1			Mar-94
2.63	2.19	4.85	14.86	25.23	2.86	0.09	4.46	6.23	12.64	5,003	1	0	99	0	0	11	4.59	50,000	1			Nov-01
2.61	2.15	4.77	14.58	24.68	2.78	0.17	4.46	6.23	12.64	5,003	1	0	99	0	0	11	4.59	3,000	1			Apr-86
0.09	0.37	0.92	3.25	3.87	1.02	0.16	0.09		1	5,442	32	0	68	0	0			3,000	1			Jun-87
4.45	7.71	10.38	18.58		2.57	0.1	3.52	6.04	21.69	1,912	0	28	0	30	0	406	3.33	50,000	1			Mar-16
4.46	7.62	10.26	18.16		2.42	0.25	3.54	6.04	10.85	1,912	0	28	0	30	0	406	3.33	3,000	1			Mar-16
16.14	4.22	7.96	28.65		3.78	0.45	9.82		26.59	516.4	1	85	0	14	0	272	5.40	50,000	1			Dec-17
16.12	4.16	7.83	28.18		3.64	0.6	9.83		11.43	516.4	1	85	0	14	0	272	5.40	3,000	1			Mar-16
11.66	-2.43	0.65	11.17	27.75	4.95	0.25	9.62	7.33	19.41	1,853	0	89	0	11	0	48	5.34	3,000	1			May-13
11.62	-2.44	0.68	11.21	27.80	4.97	0.23	9.62	7.33	31.13	1,853	0	89	0	11	0	48	5.34	5,000,000	1			Feb-15
-0.86	28.60	34.89	54.64	84.93	2.03	0.04	17.07	24.50	124.93	3,288	0	100	0	0	0	20		100,000,000	1			Aug-13
-0.86	28.58	34.86	54.54	84.76	2.01	0.06	17.06	24.50	49.77	3,288	0	100	0	0	0	20		5,000,000	1			Nov-07
0.08	0.43	1.39	4.92	5.60	1.56	0.11	0.17		1	191,650	61	39	0	0	0			3,000	1			Jul-81
8.53	4.70	8.45			3.34	0.25			22.12	199.8	1	14	0	81	0	284	3.36	50,000	1			Nov-18
8.53	4.67	8.31			3.25	0.35			11.06	199.8	1	14	0	81	0	284	3.36	3,000	1			Nov-18
0.51	3.52	5.50	11.66	16.75	2.52	0.11	2.18	1.00	10.8	25,945	5	0	0	0	0	616	3.58	50,000	1			Feb-01
0.49	3.47	5.39	11.33	16.17	2.42	0.21	2.18	1.00	10.8	25,945	5	0	0	0	0	616	3.58	3,000	1			Jun-80
8.02	-3.41	0.68	11.07	25.35	5.44	0.13	7.9	4.00	5.61	24,635	2	5	0	93	0	28	5.36	50,000	1			Nov-01
7.99	-3.46	0.58	10.74	24.73	5.33	0.23	7.9	4.00	5.61	24,635	2	5	0	93	0	28	5.36	3,000	1			Dec-78
3.04	0.24	2.98	14.61	25.58	3.36	0.17	5.38	6.42	11.58	14,624	0	0	100	0	2	16	4.92	3,000	1			Dec-78
3.06	0.27	3.06	14.89	26.13	3.44	0.09	5.39	6.42	11.58	14,624	0	0	100	0	2	16	4.92	50,000	1			Nov-01
4.13	5.99	8.21	15.30	20.13	2.23	0.1	3.51	7.86	27.42	29,558	1	99	0	0	0	26	0.81	50,000	1			Jun-05
4.10	6.02	8.22	15.38	20.35	2.25	0.07	3.5	7.86	11.17	29,558	1	99	0	0	0	26	0.81	5,000,000	1			Dec-03
4.17	6.00	8.16	15.00	19.56	2.13	0.2	3.52	7.86	13.97	29,558	1	99	0	0	0	26	0.81	3,000				Jun-00
2.36	5.04	6.92	13.39	18.53	2.37	0.02	2.09		24.29	28,687	1	20	0	26	0	323	2.86	10,000,000	1			Jun-15
2.88	2.97	4.39	9.73	12.90	2.54	0.02	1.45		14.05	7,486						83		10,000,000	1			Jun-15
2.98	6.36	8.98	17.02	24.02	2.56	0.01	3.32	6.21	11.61	269,048	3	44	1	28	0	31	3.12	3 Billion	1			Jun-16
4.65	7.89	10.38	19.73	28.15	2.51	0.07	4.01	6.38	12.59	35,623	1	54	0	44	0	50	2.89	3,000	1			Nov-01
4.65	7.91	10.41	19.84	28.36	2.53	0.04	4.03	6.38	12.59	35,623	1	54	0	44	0	50	2.89	100,000,000	1			Nov-11
4.65	7.90	10.40	19.80	28.29	2.53	0.05	4.03	6.38	12.59	35,623	1	54	0	44	0	50	2.89	5,000,000	1			Jan-06
4.63	7.85	10.29	19.45	27.67	2.43	0.15	4.01	6.38	12.59	35,623	1	54	0	44	0	50	2.89	3,000	1			Mar-94
9.63	5.25	8.98	19.94	31.97	3.15	0.07	6.32	6.17	25.49	31,474	0	0	0	99	0	59	3.69	3,000	1			Mar-10
9.63	5.30	9.03	20.02	32.12	3.17	0.05	6.33	6.17	31.5	31,474	0	0	0	99	0	59	3.69	5,000,000	1			Nov-09
7.30	6.78	9.60	18.95	28.80	2.84	0.1	4.4	5.44	10.52	33,415	0	11	0	70	0	114	3.32	50,000	1			Feb-01
7.27	6.72	9.49	18.60	28.16	2.74	0.2	4.4	5.44	10.52	33,415	0	11	0	70	0	114	3.32	3,000	1			Nov-93
2.65	2.16	4.14	12.11	19.61	2.57	0.09	3.58	4.78	14.6	73,170	1	0	99	0	0	8	4.70	50,000	1			Feb-01
2.63	2.11	4.06	11.83	19.09	2.49	0.17	3.58	4.78	14.6	73,170	1	0	99	0	0	8	4.70	3,000	1			Sep-77
1.21	8.05	9.39	16.18	21.06	1.91	0.1	3.59	5.17	12.16	7,317	1	91	0	0	0	214	2.28	50,000	1			Feb-01
1.18	7.99	9.28	15.83	20.46	1.82	0.2	3.59	5.17	12.16	7,317	1	91	0	0	0	214	2.28	3,000	1			Oct-91

	MARKET			FUND TYPE, CATEGORY & OBJECTIVE	RATINGS				NEW INVESTORS	
Fund Name	Ticker Symbol	Traded On	Fund Type	Category and (Prospectus Objective)	Overall Rating	Reward Rating	Risk Rating	Recent Up/ Downgrade	Open to New Investors	Telephone
Vanguard Intermediate-Term Treasury Ind Admiral Shares	VSIGX	NAS CM	Open End	US Fixed Inc (Govt Bond - General)	B	B	B		Y	877-662-7447
Vanguard Intermed-Term Treas Ind Inst Shares	VIIGX	NAS CM	Open End	US Fixed Inc (Govt Bond - General)	B	B	B		Y	877-662-7447
Vanguard Limited-Term Tax-Exempt Fund	VMLTX	NAS CM	Open End	US Muni Fixed Inc (Muni Bond - Natl)	C	C	B-		Y	877-662-7447
Vanguard Limited-Term Tax-Exempt Fund Admiral Shares	VMLUX	NAS CM	Open End	US Muni Fixed Inc (Muni Bond - Natl)	C	C	B-		Y	877-662-7447
Vanguard Long-Term Bond Index Fund Admiral Shares	VBLAX	NAS CM	Open End	US Fixed Inc (Income)	B	B	B		Y	877-662-7447
Vanguard Long-Term Bond Ind Institutional Plus Shares	VBLIX	NAS CM	Open End	US Fixed Inc (Income)	B	B	B		Y	877-662-7447
Vanguard Long-Term Bond Index Fund Institutional Shares	VBLLX	NAS CM	Open End	US Fixed Inc (Income)	B	B	B		Y	877-662-7447
Vanguard Long-Term Corp Bond Index Fund Admiral Shares	VLTCX	NAS CM	Open End	US Fixed Inc (Corp Bond - General)	C+	C	B		Y	877-662-7447
Vanguard Long-Term Corp Bond Ind Institutional Shares	VLCIX	NAS CM	Open End	US Fixed Inc (Corp Bond - General)	C+	C	B		Y	877-662-7447
Vanguard Long-Term Investment-Grade Fund Admiral Shares	VWETX	NAS CM	Open End	US Fixed Inc (Corp Bond - High Quality)	B	B	B	Up	Y	877-662-7447
Vanguard Long-Term Investment-Grade Fund Investor Shares	VWESX	NAS CM	Open End	US Fixed Inc (Corp Bond - High Quality)	B	B	B	Up	Y	877-662-7447
Vanguard Long-Term Tax-Exempt Fund	VWLTX	NAS CM	Open End	US Muni Fixed Inc (Muni Bond - Natl)	C+	C	B		Y	877-662-7447
Vanguard Long-Term Tax-Exempt Fund Admiral Shares	VWLUX	NAS CM	Open End	US Muni Fixed Inc (Muni Bond - Natl)	C+	C	B		Y	877-662-7447
Vanguard Long-Term Treasury Fund Admiral Shares	VUSUX	NAS CM	Open End	US Fixed Inc (Govt Bond - Treasury)	B	B	B		Y	877-662-7447
Vanguard Long-Term Treasury Fund Investor Shares	VUSTX	NAS CM	Open End	US Fixed Inc (Govt Bond - Treasury)	B	B	B		Y	877-662-7447
Vanguard Long-Term Treasury Index Fund Admiral Shares	VLGSX	NAS CM	Open End	US Fixed Inc (Govt Bond - General)	B	B	B		Y	877-662-7447
Vanguard Long-Term Treasury Ind Institutional Shares	VLGIX	NAS CM	Open End	US Fixed Inc (Govt Bond - General)	B	B	B		Y	877-662-7447
Vanguard Massachusetts Tax-Exempt Fund Investor Shares	VMATX	NAS CM	Open End	US Muni Fixed Inc (Muni Bond - Single State)	C+	C	B		Y	877-662-7447
Vanguard Mortgage-Backed Securities Ind Admiral Shares	VMBSX	NAS CM	Open End	US Fixed Inc (Govt Bond - Mortgage)	B-	C+	B	Up	Y	877-662-7447
Vanguard Mortgage-Backed Securities Ind Inst Shares	VMBIX	NAS CM	Open End	US Fixed Inc (Govt Bond - Mortgage)	B-	C+	B	Up	Y	877-662-7447
Vanguard Municipal Money Market Fund Investor Shares	VMSXX	NAS CM	Money Mkt	US Money Mkt (Money Mkt - Fed Tax Exmpt)	C	C-	C+		Y	877-662-7447
Vanguard New Jersey Long-Term Tax-Exempt Admiral Shares	VNJUX	NAS CM	Open End	US Muni Fixed Inc (Muni Bond - Single State)	C	C-	B-	Down	Y	877-662-7447
Vanguard New Jersey Long-Term Tax-Exempt Investor Shares	VNJTX	NAS CM	Open End	US Muni Fixed Inc (Muni Bond - Single State)	C	C-	B-	Down	Y	877-662-7447
Vanguard New Jersey Muni Money Mkt Fund Investor Shares	VNJXX	NAS CM	Money Mkt	US Money Mkt (Money Mkt - Single State)	C	C-	C+		Y	877-662-7447
Vanguard New York Long-Term Tax-Exempt Fund Admiral Shares	VNYUX	NAS CM	Open End	US Muni Fixed Inc (Muni Bond - Single State)	C	C	B	Down	Y	877-662-7447
Vanguard New York Long-Term Tax-Exempt Investor Shares	VNYTX	NAS CM	Open End	US Muni Fixed Inc (Muni Bond - Single State)	C	C	B		Y	877-662-7447
Vanguard New York Muni Money Mkt Fund Investor Shares	VYFXX	NAS CM	Money Mkt	US Money Mkt (Money Mkt - Single State)	C	C-	C+		Y	877-662-7447
Vanguard Ohio Long-Term Tax-Exempt Fund	VOHIX	NAS CM	Open End	US Muni Fixed Inc (Muni Bond - Single State)	B-	C	B	Up	Y	877-662-7447
Vanguard Pennsylvania Long-Term Tax-Exempt Admiral Shares	VPALX	NAS CM	Open End	US Muni Fixed Inc (Muni Bond - Single State)	C+	C	B		Y	877-662-7447
Vanguard Pennsylvania Long-Term Tax-Exempt Investor Shares	VPAIX	NAS CM	Open End	US Muni Fixed Inc (Muni Bond - Single State)	C+	C	B		Y	877-662-7447
Vanguard Pennsylvania Muni Money Mkt Fund Investor Shares	VPTXX	NAS CM	Money Mkt	US Money Mkt (Money Mkt - Single State)	C	C-	C+		Y	877-662-7447
Vanguard Prime Money Market Fund Admiral Shares	VMRXX	NAS CM	Money Mkt	US Money Mkt (Money Mkt - Taxable)	C	C-	C+		Y	877-662-7447
★ Vanguard Prime Money Market Fund Investor Shares	VMMXX	NAS CM	Money Mkt	US Money Mkt (Money Mkt - Taxable)	C	C-	C+		Y	877-662-7447
★ Vanguard Short-Term Bond Index Fund Admiral Shares	VBIRX	NAS CM	Open End	US Fixed Inc (Income)	B-	C	B	Up	Y	877-662-7447
Vanguard Short-Term Bond Ind Institutional Plus Shares	VBIPX	NAS CM	Open End	US Fixed Inc (Income)	B-	C+	B	Up	Y	877-662-7447
Vanguard Short-Term Bond Index Fund Institutional Shares	VBITX	NAS CM	Open End	US Fixed Inc (Income)	B-	C	B	Up	Y	877-662-7447
★ Vanguard Short-Term Bond Index Fund Investor Shares	VBISX	NAS CM	Open End	US Fixed Inc (Income)	B-	C	B	Up	Y	877-662-7447
Vanguard Short-Term Corp Bond Index Fund Admiral Shares	VSCSX	NAS CM	Open End	US Fixed Inc (Corp Bond - General)	C	C	B-		Y	877-662-7447
Vanguard Short-Term Corp Bond Ind Institutional Shares	VSTBX	NAS CM	Open End	US Fixed Inc (Corp Bond - General)	C	C	B-		Y	877-662-7447
Vanguard Short-Term Federal Fund Admiral Shares	VSGDX	NAS CM	Open End	US Fixed Inc (Govt Bond - General)	B-	C	B	Up	Y	877-662-7447
Vanguard Short-Term Federal Fund Investor Shares	VSGBX	NAS CM	Open End	US Fixed Inc (Govt Bond - General)	C+	C	B		Y	877-662-7447
Vanguard Short-Term Inflat-Protect Sec Ind Admiral Shares	VTAPX	NAS CM	Open End	US Fixed Inc (Govt Bond - Treasury)	C	C	B		Y	877-662-7447
Vanguard Short-Term Inflat-Protect Sec Ind Inst Shares	VTSPX	NAS CM	Open End	US Fixed Inc (Govt Bond - Treasury)	C	C	B		Y	877-662-7447
Vanguard Short-Term Inflat-Protect Sec Ind Investor Shares	VTIPX	NAS CM	Open End	US Fixed Inc (Govt Bond - Treasury)	C	C	B-		Y	877-662-7447
★ Vanguard Short-Term Investment-Grade Fund Admiral Shares	VFSUX	NAS CM	Open End	US Fixed Inc (Income)	C	C	B-		Y	877-662-7447
Vanguard Short-Term Investment-Grade Institutional Shares	VFSIX	NAS CM	Open End	US Fixed Inc (Income)	C	C	B-		Y	877-662-7447
★ Vanguard Short-Term Investment-Grade Fund Investor Shares	VFSTX	NAS CM	Open End	US Fixed Inc (Income)	C+	C	B	Up	Y	877-662-7447
Vanguard Short-Term Tax-Exempt Fund	VWSTX	NAS CM	Open End	US Muni Fixed Inc (Muni Bond - Natl)	C	C-	C+		Y	877-662-7447
Vanguard Short-Term Tax-Exempt Fund Class Admiral	VWSUX	NAS CM	Open End	US Muni Fixed Inc (Muni Bond - Natl)	C	C-	C+		Y	877-662-7447
Vanguard Short-Term Treasury Fund Admiral Shares	VFIRX	NAS CM	Open End	US Fixed Inc (Govt Bond - Treasury)	C+	C	B		Y	877-662-7447
Vanguard Short-Term Treasury Fund Investor Shares	VFISX	NAS CM	Open End	US Fixed Inc (Govt Bond - Treasury)	C+	C	B		Y	877-662-7447
Vanguard Short-Term Treasury Index Fund Admiral Shares	VSBSX	NAS CM	Open End	US Fixed Inc (Govt Bond - General)	C+	C	B		Y	877-662-7447

★ Expanded analysis of this fund is included in Section II.

TOTAL RETURNS & PERFORMANCE									ASSETS		ASSET ALLOCATION & TURNOVER							MINIMUMS		FEES		
3-Month Total Return	6-Month Total Return	1-Year Total Return	3-Year Total Return	5-Year Total Return	Dividend Yield (TTM)	Expense Ratio	3-Yr Std Deviation	Effective Duration	NAV	Total Assets (MIL)	%Cash	%Government Bonds	%Municipal Bonds	%Corporate Bonds	%Other	Turnover Ratio	Average Coupon Rate	Min Initial Investment	Min Additional Investment	Front End Fee (%)	Back End Fee (%)	Inception Date
0.72	7.88	9.24	16.03	20.66	1.91	0.07	3.62	5.24	23.81	10,255	1	99	0	0	0	29	2.17	3,000	1			Aug-10
0.76	7.88	9.29	16.07	20.81	1.93	0.05	3.62	5.24	29.55	10,255	1	99	0	0	0	29	2.17	5,000,000	1			Mar-10
2.25	1.68	2.89	7.49	10.64	1.8	0.17	1.94	2.66	11.17	29,516	1	0	99	0	0	21	4.27	3,000	1			Aug-87
2.27	1.72	2.97	7.76	11.13	1.88	0.09	1.94	2.66	11.17	29,516	1	0	99	0	0	21	4.27	50,000	1			Feb-01
6.34	13.06	19.10	34.24	55.55	3.07	0.07	8.94	16.04	16.86	12,388	1	44	3	52	0	33	4.15	3,000	1			Feb-19
6.35	13.08	19.13	34.31	55.69	3.1	0.04	8.96	16.04	16.86	12,388	1	44	3	52	0	33	4.15	100,000,000	1			Oct-11
6.35	13.07	19.12	34.27	55.60	3.09	0.05	8.96	16.04	16.86	12,388	1	44	3	52	0	33	4.15	5,000,000	1			Feb-06
11.26	6.49	13.60	28.61	53.30	3.7	0.07	10.11	14.17	28.31	4,317	0	0	0	100	0	47	4.77	3,000	1			Jan-10
11.27	6.53	13.62	28.67	53.42	3.72	0.05	10.12	14.17	35.13	4,317	0	0	0	100	0	47	4.77	5,000,000	1			Nov-09
8.33	10.56	16.75	32.11	57.28	3.4	0.12	8.83	14.18	11.83	19,772	5	6	10	77	0	34	4.51	50,000	1			Feb-01
8.30	10.50	16.63	31.72	56.50	3.3	0.22	8.83	14.18	11.83	19,772	5	6	10	77	0	34	4.51	3,000	1			Jul-73
2.78	2.23	4.77	14.83	24.89	3.02	0.17	4.5	6.05	11.99	14,189	0	0	100	0	3	16	4.78	3,000	1			Sep-77
2.80	2.27	4.85	15.11	25.44	3.1	0.09	4.5	6.05	11.99	14,189	0	0	100	0	3	16	4.78	50,000	1			Feb-01
0.53	21.50	25.75	40.11	57.81	2.09	0.1	11.97	18.33	15.65	4,647	3	93	0	0	0	96	3.16	50,000	1			Feb-01
0.50	21.44	25.63	39.69	57.03	2	0.2	11.98	18.33	15.65	4,647	3	93	0	0	0	96	3.16	3,000	1			May-86
0.36	21.27	25.62	40.10	57.73	1.97	0.07	11.94	18.58	33.61	4,711	1	99	0	0	0	16	3.07	3,000	1			Mar-10
0.36	21.30	25.60	40.16	57.90	1.98	0.05	11.96	18.58	42.66	4,711	1	99	0	0	0	16	3.07	5,000,000	1			Nov-09
2.73	2.74	5.31	14.85	23.62	2.64	0.13	4.4	6.01	11.26	2,252	0	0	100	0	0	31	4.57	3,000	1			Dec-98
0.17	3.39	5.58	11.79	16.45	2.42	0.07	2.23	3.44	21.74	12,529	9	0	0	0	0	190	3.49	3,000	1			Dec-09
0.15	3.36	5.56	11.82	16.50	2.44	0.05	2.22	3.44	29.45	12,529	9	0	0	0	0	190	3.49	5,000,000	1			Oct-13
0.12	0.46	1.08	3.63	4.32	1.19	0.15	0.11		1	18,187	26	0	74	0	0			3,000	1			Jun-80
2.45	0.27	2.97	15.83	26.87	3.29	0.09	5.21	6.20	12.28	2,363	0	0	100	0	0	12	4.57	50,000	1			May-01
2.43	0.23	2.89	15.55	26.31	3.2	0.17	5.21	6.20	12.28	2,363	0	0	100	0	0	12	4.57	3,000	1			Feb-88
0.11	0.41	0.95	3.36	3.95	1.06	0.16	0.1		1	1,276	13	0	86	0	8			3,000	1			Feb-88
2.06	1.59	3.97	13.15	22.94	2.94	0.09	4.52	6.01	12	4,959	0	0	100	0	0	15	4.61	50,000	1			May-01
2.04	1.55	3.89	12.87	22.40	2.86	0.17	4.52	6.01	12	4,959	0	0	100	0	0	15	4.61	3,000	1			Apr-86
0.10	0.44	1.03	3.51	4.15	1.14	0.16	0.11		1	2,961	19	0	81	0	0			3,000	1			Sep-97
2.80	3.36	5.84	15.73	26.09	2.83	0.13	4.03	6.24	13.06	1,435	0	0	100	0	0	26	4.45	3,000	1			Jun-90
1.78	2.22	4.75	15.75	25.83	3.14	0.09	4.25	6.20	11.94	3,983	0	0	100	0	0	9	4.57	50,000	1			May-01
1.76	2.18	4.67	15.47	25.28	3.06	0.17	4.25	6.20	11.94	3,983	0	0	100	0	0	9	4.57	3,000	1			Apr-86
0.08	0.42	1.00	3.42	4.03	1.12	0.16	0.12		1	1,927	7	0	93	0	0			3,000	1			Jun-88
0.14	0.54	1.57	5.55	6.71	1.74	0.1	0.16		1	127,205	84	15	1	2	0	37		5,000,000	1			Oct-89
0.12	0.51	1.51	5.36	6.38	1.68	0.16	0.16		1	127,205	84	15	1	2	0	37		3,000	1			Jun-75
1.77	4.05	5.41	10.66	13.72	2.11	0.07	1.52	2.66	10.89	52,731	1	73	0	27	0	44	2.31	3,000	1			Nov-01
1.78	4.06	5.44	10.76	13.90	2.14	0.04	1.52	2.66	10.89	52,731	1	73	0	27	0	44	2.31	100,000,000	1			Sep-11
1.78	4.06	5.43	10.73	13.84	2.13	0.05	1.52	2.66	10.89	52,731	1	73	0	27	0	44	2.31	5,000,000	1			Sep-11
1.75	4.00	5.33	10.40	13.28	2.03	0.15	1.52	2.66	10.89	52,731	1	73	0	27	0	44	2.31	3,000	1			Mar-94
5.54	3.03	5.14	11.73	17.17	2.74	0.07	3.34	2.62	22.41	32,476	0	0	0	100	0	51	3.32	3,000	1			Nov-10
5.57	3.06	5.18	11.85	17.33	2.76	0.05	3.33	2.62	27.44	32,476	0	0	0	100	0	51	3.32	5,000,000	1			Nov-09
1.03	3.56	4.87	9.55	11.97	2.13	0.1	1.37	2.20	11.01	6,215	6	35	0	0	0	499	2.55	50,000	1			Feb-01
1.00	3.51	4.77	9.22	11.41	2.04	0.2	1.37	2.20	11.01	6,215	6	35	0	0	0	499	2.55	3,000	1			Dec-87
2.61	1.86	3.37	8.06	10.18	1.92	0.06	1.64	2.55	25.15	32,438	5	95	0	0	0	26	0.44	3,000	1			Oct-12
2.60	1.90	3.38	8.10	10.31	1.93	0.04	1.64	2.55	25.17	32,438	5	95	0	0	0	26	0.44	5,000,000	1			Oct-12
2.61	1.82	3.29	7.81	9.69	1.86	0.14	1.63	2.55	25.11	32,438	5	95	0	0	0	26	0.44	3,000	1			Oct-12
4.83	3.26	5.03	10.94	16.16	2.74	0.1	2.73	2.45	10.94	60,817	3	9	0	65	0	76	3.18	50,000	1			Feb-01
4.84	3.27	5.06	11.04	16.33	2.77	0.07	2.73	2.45	10.94	60,817	3	9	0	65	0	76	3.18	5,000,000	1			Sep-97
4.81	3.20	4.93	10.61	15.58	2.64	0.2	2.72	2.45	10.94	60,817	3	9	0	65	0	76	3.18	3,000	1			Oct-82
1.27	1.15	2.05	5.24	7.00	1.51	0.17	0.88	1.32	15.92	16,921	4	0	96	0	1	34	3.57	3,000	1			Sep-77
1.29	1.19	2.13	5.51	7.47	1.59	0.09	0.88	1.32	15.92	16,921	4	0	96	0	1	34	3.57	50,000	1			Feb-01
0.71	3.43	4.48	8.70	10.54	1.85	0.1	1.37	2.21	10.89	9,532	3	86	0	0	0	340	1.73	50,000	1			Feb-01
0.69	3.38	4.37	8.38	9.99	1.75	0.2	1.37	2.21	10.89	9,532	3	86	0	0	0	340	1.73	3,000	1			Oct-91
0.29	2.97	4.14	8.12	9.40	1.89	0.07	1.22	1.89	20.73	12,354	0	100	0	0	0	55	1.59	3,000	1			Dec-09

	MARKET			FUND TYPE, CATEGORY & OBJECTIVE	RATINGS				NEW INVESTORS	
Fund Name	Ticker Symbol	Traded On	Fund Type	Category and (Prospectus Objective)	Overall Rating	Reward Rating	Risk Rating	Recent Up/ Downgrade	Open to New Investors	Telephone
Vanguard Short-Term Treasury Ind Institutional Shares	**VSBIX**	NAS CM	Open End	US Fixed Inc (Govt Bond - General)	C+	C	B		Y	877-662-7447
Vanguard Tax-Exempt Bond Fund Admiral Shares	**VTEAX**	NAS CM	Open End	US Muni Fixed Inc (Muni Bond - Natl)	C+	C	B	Up	Y	877-662-7447
Vanguard Total Bond Market II Ind Institutional Shares	**VTBNX**	NAS CM	Open End	US Fixed Inc (Income)	B	C+	B+		Y	877-662-7447
★ Vanguard Total Bond Market II Index Fund Investor Shares	**VTBIX**	NAS CM	Open End	US Fixed Inc (Income)	B	C+	B+		Y	877-662-7447
★ Vanguard Total Bond Market Index Fund Admiral Shares	**VBTLX**	NAS CM	Open End	US Fixed Inc (Income)	B	B-	B+		Y	877-662-7447
Vanguard Total Bond Market Ind Institutional Plus Shares	**VBMPX**	NAS CM	Open End	US Fixed Inc (Income)	B	B-	B+		Y	877-662-7447
Vanguard Total Bond Market Index Fund Institutional Shares	**VBTIX**	NAS CM	Open End	US Fixed Inc (Income)	B	B-	B+		Y	877-662-7447
★ Vanguard Total Bond Market Index Fund Investor Shares	**VBMFX**	NAS CM	Open End	US Fixed Inc (Income)	B	B-	B+		Y	877-662-7447
★ Vanguard Total InterNatl Bond Index Fund Admiral™ Shares	**VTABX**	NAS CM	Open End	Global Fixed Inc (Worldwide Bond)	B-	C	B+	Up	Y	877-662-7447
Vanguard Total InterNatl Bond Ind Inst Select Shares	**VSIBX**	NAS CM	Open End	Global Fixed Inc (Worldwide Bond)	B-	C	B+	Up	Y	877-662-7447
Vanguard Total InterNatl Bond Ind Institutional Shares	**VTIFX**	NAS CM	Open End	Global Fixed Inc (Worldwide Bond)	B-	C	B+	Up	Y	877-662-7447
★ Vanguard Total InterNatl Bond Index Fund Investor Shares	**VTIBX**	NAS CM	Open End	Global Fixed Inc (Worldwide Bond)	B-	C	B	Up	Y	877-662-7447
Vanguard Treasury Money Market Fund Investor Shares	**VUSXX**	NAS CM	Money Mkt	US Money Mkt (Money Mkt - Treasury)	C	C-	C+			877-662-7447
Vanguard Ultra-Short-Term Bond Fund Admiral Shares	**VUSFX**	NAS CM	Open End	US Fixed Inc (Income)	C	C	B-		Y	877-662-7447
Vanguard Ultra-Short-Term Bond Fund Investor Shares	**VUBFX**	NAS CM	Open End	US Fixed Inc (Income)	C	C-	B-		Y	877-662-7447
Vertical Capital Income Fund	**VCIF**	NYSE	Closed End	US Fixed Inc (Income)	C	C	C-		Y	866-224-8867
Victory Floating Rate Fund Class A	**RSFLX**	NAS CM	Open End	US Fixed Inc (Income)	D+	D	C-	Down	Y	210-694-9700
Victory Floating Rate Fund Class C	**RSFCX**	NAS CM	Open End	US Fixed Inc (Income)	D	D	C-	Down	Y	210-694-9700
Victory Floating Rate Fund Class R	**RSFKX**	NAS CM	Open End	US Fixed Inc (Income)	D+	D	C-	Down	Y	210-694-9700
Victory Floating Rate Fund Class Y	**RSFYX**	NAS CM	Open End	US Fixed Inc (Income)	D+	D	C-	Down	Y	210-694-9700
Victory High Income Municipal Bond Fund Class A	**RSHMX**	NAS CM	Open End	US Muni Fixed Inc (Corp Bond - High Yield)	C	C-	C+		Y	210-694-9700
Victory High Income Municipal Bond Fund Class C	**RSHCX**	NAS CM	Open End	US Muni Fixed Inc (Corp Bond - High Yield)	C-	D+	C	Down	Y	210-694-9700
Victory High Income Municipal Bond Fund Class Y	**RHMYX**	NAS CM	Open End	US Muni Fixed Inc (Corp Bond - High Yield)	C	C-	C+		Y	210-694-9700
Victory High Yield Fund Class A	**GUHYX**	NAS CM	Open End	US Fixed Inc (Corp Bond - High Yield)	C-	D+	C	Down	Y	210-694-9700
Victory High Yield Fund Class C	**RHYCX**	NAS CM	Open End	US Fixed Inc (Corp Bond - High Yield)	C-	D+	C		Y	210-694-9700
Victory High Yield Fund Class R	**RHYKX**	NAS CM	Open End	US Fixed Inc (Corp Bond - High Yield)	C-	D+	C	Down	Y	210-694-9700
Victory High Yield Fund Class Y	**RSYYX**	NAS CM	Open End	US Fixed Inc (Corp Bond - High Yield)	D+	D+	C-	Down	Y	210-694-9700
Victory INCORE Fund for Income Class A	**IPFIX**	NAS CM	Open End	US Fixed Inc (Income)	C+	C	B		Y	210-694-9700
Victory INCORE Fund for Income Class C	**VFFCX**	NAS CM	Open End	US Fixed Inc (Income)	C+	C	B-	Up	Y	210-694-9700
Victory INCORE Fund for Income Class I	**VFFIX**	NAS CM	Open End	US Fixed Inc (Income)	C+	C	B		Y	210-694-9700
Victory INCORE Fund for Income Class R	**GGIFX**	NAS CM	Open End	US Fixed Inc (Income)	C+	C	B		Y	210-694-9700
Victory INCORE Fund for Income Class R6	**VFFRX**	NAS CM	Open End	US Fixed Inc (Income)	C+	C	B		Y	210-694-9700
Victory INCORE Fund for Income Class Y	**VFFYX**	NAS CM	Open End	US Fixed Inc (Income)	C+	C	B		Y	210-694-9700
Victory INCORE Investment Quality Bond Fund Class A	**GUIQX**	NAS CM	Open End	US Fixed Inc (Corp Bond - General)	B-	C+	B	Up	Y	210-694-9700
Victory INCORE Investment Quality Bond Fund Class C	**RIQCX**	NAS CM	Open End	US Fixed Inc (Corp Bond - General)	C+	C	B	Up	Y	210-694-9700
Victory INCORE Investment Quality Bond Fund Class R	**RIQKX**	NAS CM	Open End	US Fixed Inc (Corp Bond - General)	B-	C	B	Up	Y	210-694-9700
Victory INCORE Investment Quality Bond Fund Class Y	**RSQYX**	NAS CM	Open End	US Fixed Inc (Corp Bond - General)	B-	C+	B+	Up	Y	210-694-9700
Victory INCORE Low Duration Bond Fund Class A	**RLDAX**	NAS CM	Open End	US Fixed Inc (Growth & Income)	C	C	B-		Y	210-694-9700
Victory INCORE Low Duration Bond Fund Class C	**RLDCX**	NAS CM	Open End	US Fixed Inc (Growth & Income)	C	C	C+		Y	210-694-9700
Victory INCORE Low Duration Bond Fund Class R	**RLDKX**	NAS CM	Open End	US Fixed Inc (Growth & Income)	C	C	B-		Y	210-694-9700
Victory INCORE Low Duration Bond Fund Class Y	**RSDYX**	NAS CM	Open End	US Fixed Inc (Growth & Income)	C	C	B-		Y	210-694-9700
Victory INCORE Total Return Bond Fund Class A	**MUCAX**	NAS CM	Open End	US Fixed Inc (Multisector Bond)	B-	C+	B	Up	Y	210-694-9700
Victory INCORE Total Return Bond Fund Class C	**MUCCX**	NAS CM	Open End	US Fixed Inc (Multisector Bond)	C+	C	B	Up	Y	210-694-9700
Victory INCORE Total Return Bond Fund Class R6	**MUCRX**	NAS CM	Open End	US Fixed Inc (Multisector Bond)	B-	C+	B+	Up	Y	210-694-9700
Victory INCORE Total Return Bond Fund Class Y	**MUCYX**	NAS CM	Open End	US Fixed Inc (Multisector Bond)	B-	C+	B+	Up	Y	210-694-9700
Victory Strategic Income Fund Class A	**RSIAX**	NAS CM	Open End	US Fixed Inc (Multisector Bond)	B-	C	B+	Up	Y	210-694-9700
Victory Strategic Income Fund Class C	**RSICX**	NAS CM	Open End	US Fixed Inc (Multisector Bond)	B-	C	B	Up	Y	210-694-9700
Victory Strategic Income Fund Class R	**RINKX**	NAS CM	Open End	US Fixed Inc (Multisector Bond)	B-	C	B+	Up	Y	210-694-9700
Victory Strategic Income Fund Class Y	**RSRYX**	NAS CM	Open End	US Fixed Inc (Multisector Bond)	B-	C	B+	Up	Y	210-694-9700
Victory Tax-Exempt Fund Class A	**GUTEX**	NAS CM	Open End	US Muni Fixed Inc (Muni Bond - Natl)	C	C-	C+	Down	Y	210-694-9700
Victory Tax-Exempt Fund Class C	**RETCX**	NAS CM	Open End	US Muni Fixed Inc (Muni Bond - Natl)	C	C-	C		Y	210-694-9700
Victory Tax-Exempt Fund Class Y	**RSTYX**	NAS CM	Open End	US Muni Fixed Inc (Muni Bond - Natl)	C	C-	C+	Down	Y	210-694-9700

★ Expanded analysis of this fund is included in Section II.

TOTAL RETURNS & PERFORMANCE									ASSETS		ASSET ALLOCATION & TURNOVER							MINIMUMS		FEES		
3-Month Total Return	6-Month Total Return	1-Year Total Return	3-Year Total Return	5-Year Total Return	Dividend Yield (TTM)	Expense Ratio	3-Yr Std Deviation	Effective Duration	NAV	Total Assets (MIL)	%Cash	%Government Bonds	%Municipal Bonds	%Corporate Bonds	%Other	Turnover Ratio	Average Coupon Rate	Min Initial Investment	Min Additional Investment	Front End Fee (%)	Back End Fee (%)	Inception Date
0.26	3.00	4.13	8.16	9.48	1.91	0.05	1.25	1.89	26.04	12,354	0	100	0	0	0	55	1.59	5,000,000	1			Aug-10
2.46	2.04	4.26	12.60		2.18	0.09	3.84	5.22	21.61	7,956	3	0	97	0	0	18	4.84	3,000	1			Aug-15
2.89	5.99	8.62	16.54	23.55	2.56	0.02	3.38	6.19	11.53	185,732	4	43	1	28	0	66	3.02	5,000,000				Feb-09
2.87	5.96	8.54	16.30	23.12	2.49	0.09	3.38	6.19	11.53	185,732	4	43	1	28	0	66	3.02	0				Jan-09
2.97	6.34	8.94	16.88	23.94	2.52	0.05	3.32	6.21	11.61	269,048	3	44	1	28	0	31	3.12	3,000	1			Nov-01
2.97	6.35	8.96	16.96	24.08	2.54	0.03	3.32	6.21	11.61	269,048	3	44	1	28	0	31	3.12	100,000,000	1			Feb-10
2.97	6.35	8.96	16.93	24.02	2.53	0.04	3.32	6.21	11.61	269,048	3	44	1	28	0	31	3.12	5,000,000	1			Sep-95
2.94	6.29	8.83	16.54	23.35	2.42	0.15	3.32	6.21	11.61	269,048	3	44	1	28	0	31	3.12	3,000	1			Dec-86
2.19	2.34	3.85	15.65	24.39	3.28	0.11	3.11	8.25	23.04	142,843	1	79	0	15	0	26	2.09	3,000	1			May-13
2.20	2.45	3.98	16.16	25.06	0	0.03	3.1	8.25	118.15	142,843	1	79	0	15	0	26	2.09	3 Billion	1			Mar-16
2.20	2.36	3.90	15.79	24.64	3.32	0.07	3.12	8.25	34.57	142,843	1	79	0	15	0	26	2.09	5,000,000	1			May-13
2.18	2.32	3.83	15.61	24.17	3.26	0.13	3.15	8.25	11.52	142,843	1	79	0	15	0	26	2.09	3,000	1			May-13
0.08	0.44	1.39	4.94	5.53	1.57	0.09	0.16		1	41,350	72	28	0	0	0			50,000	1			Dec-92
1.77	1.33	2.66	7.68	10.00	2.48	0.1	0.92	0.88	20.11	7,316	8	7	1	37	0	70	2.89	50,000	1			Feb-15
1.75	1.22	2.50	7.27	9.49	2.38	0.2	0.95	0.88	10.05	7,316	8	7	1	37	0	70	2.89	3,000	1			Feb-15
0.00	0.00	0.98	11.26	37.84	4	2.5	4.14		12.291	127.6						7						Dec-11
10.79	-5.44	-2.32	6.31	14.62	6.25	1	9.52	0.46	8.65	485.2	5	0	0	95	0	35		2,500	50	2.00		Dec-09
10.70	-5.71	-3.08	3.84	10.30	5.46	1.8	9.51	0.46	8.66	485.2	5	0	0	95	0	35		2,500	50	2.00	1.00	Dec-09
10.78	-5.59	-2.84	4.59	11.62	5.71	1.56	9.54	0.46	8.65	485.2	5	0	0	95	0	35		0		2.00		Dec-09
10.97	-5.33	-2.11	7.00	15.99	6.47	0.78	9.54	0.46	8.66	485.2	5	0	0	95	0	35		1,000,000		2.00		Dec-09
3.14	-0.16	2.45	12.86	20.44	3.89	0.8	6.01	6.94	10.53	37.4	2	0	98	0	0	49	5.33	2,500	50	2.00		Dec-09
2.94	-0.54	1.67	10.29	15.92	3.09	1.57	6.02	6.94	10.53	37.4	2	0	98	0	0	49	5.33	2,500	50	2.00	1.00	Dec-09
3.20	-0.05	2.69	13.65	21.85	4.13	0.57	6.03	6.94	10.53	37.4	2	0	98	0	0	49	5.33	1,000,000		2.00		Dec-09
9.45	-5.87	-1.28	13.47	26.28	6.1	1	9.62	3.19	6.15	185.3	6	0	0	94	0	87	7.16	2,500	50	2.00		Sep-98
9.25	-6.33	-1.97	10.95	21.95	5.34	1.7	9.6	3.19	6.16	185.3	6	0	0	94	0	87	7.16	2,500	50	2.00	1.00	Aug-00
9.35	-6.16	-1.59	12.07	23.84	5.75	1.33	9.66	3.19	6.16	185.3	6	0	0	94	0	87	7.16	0		2.00		May-01
9.56	-5.79	-0.90	14.35	28.07	6.38	0.76	9.59	3.19	6.12	185.3	6	0	0	94	0	87	7.16	1,000,000		2.00		May-09
0.20	3.16	3.64	7.88	9.03	4.71	0.91	1.69	2.92	8.56	905.6	14	10	0	0	0	29	7.04	2,500	50	2.00		Mar-99
0.00	2.69	2.75	5.22	4.83	3.98	1.71	1.69	2.92	8.47	905.6	14	10	0	0	0	29	7.04	2,500	50		1.00	Mar-02
0.26	3.17	3.79	8.64	10.52	4.96	0.64	1.75	2.92	8.55	905.6	14	10	0	0	0	29	7.04	2,000,000				Mar-11
0.08	3.03	3.52	7.76	9.01	4.7	0.91	1.7	2.92	8.56	905.6	14	10	0	0	0	29	7.04	0				Sep-87
0.27	3.19	3.82	8.68	10.56	4.99	0.63	1.7	2.92	8.54	905.6	14	10	0	0	0	29	7.04	0				Mar-15
0.25	3.26	3.85	8.54	10.13	4.9	0.71	1.7	2.92	8.56	905.6	14	10	0	0	0	29	7.04	1,000,000				Jan-13
3.94	5.18	7.96	13.58	20.03	2.27	0.9	3.51		10.11	31.1	7	18	0	36	0	92	3.57	2,500	50	2.00		Feb-93
3.82	4.72	7.13	10.65	14.94	1.41	1.77	3.57		10.11	31.1	7	18	0	36	0	92	3.57	2,500	50		1.00	Aug-00
3.93	4.95	7.61	12.23	17.67	1.86	1.3	3.59		10.14	31.1	7	18	0	36	0	92	3.57	0				May-01
4.01	5.31	8.24	14.43	21.50	2.51	0.66	3.51		10.1	31.1	7	18	0	36	0	92	3.57	1,000,000				May-09
3.51	2.36	3.56	7.24	9.59	2.11	0.85	1.92		10.13	254.6	3	33	0	38	0	50	3.00	2,500	50	2.00		Jul-03
3.31	1.96	2.76	4.88	5.52	1.33	1.62	1.93		10.13	254.6	3	33	0	38	0	50	3.00	2,500	50		1.00	Jul-03
3.40	2.14	3.12	5.99	7.42	1.68	1.27	1.91		10.13	254.6	3	33	0	38	0	50	3.00	0				Jul-03
3.67	2.57	3.80	8.10	10.97	2.34	0.62	1.94		10.14	254.6	3	33	0	38	0	50	3.00	1,000,000				May-09
3.99	5.10	7.68	13.22	18.63	2.48	0.85	3.59		9.91	70.5	8	18	0	33	0	150	3.57	2,500	250	2.00		Dec-92
3.87	4.70	6.86	10.88	14.33	1.77	1.6	3.57		9.99	70.5	8	18	0	33	0	150	3.57	2,500	250		1.00	Mar-96
4.15	5.22	8.05	14.33	20.22	2.71	0.57	3.6		9.94	70.5	8	18	0	33	0	150	3.57	0				Mar-15
4.15	5.32	8.03	14.23	20.21	2.69	0.6	3.63		9.94	70.5	8	18	0	33	0	150	3.57	1,000,000				Nov-91
4.41	4.46	6.60	15.99	24.49	2.07	0.96	3.74	5.06	10.73	70.3	3	62	0	28	0	106	2.56	2,500	50	2.00		Dec-09
4.19	4.03	5.69	13.28	19.67	1.27	1.75	3.79	5.06	10.78	70.3	3	62	0	28	0	106	2.56	2,500	50	2.00	1.00	Dec-09
4.19	4.14	6.02	14.53	21.95	1.66	1.35	3.76	5.06	10.78	70.3	3	62	0	28	0	106	2.56	0		2.00		Dec-09
4.39	4.60	6.87	16.85	25.96	2.29	0.75	3.75	5.06	10.67	70.3	3	62	0	28	0	106	2.56	1,000,000		2.00		Dec-09
3.20	-0.10	2.90	13.77	19.72	3.42	0.8	6.22	7.67	9.67	59.0	3	0	97	0	0	64	5.02	2,500	50	2.00		Feb-93
2.99	-0.50	2.18	11.08	15.14	2.59	1.6	6.22	7.67	9.67	59.0	3	0	97	0	0	64	5.02	2,500	50	2.00	1.00	Aug-00
3.22	-0.04	3.12	14.27	20.50	3.53	0.69	6.22	7.67	9.67	59.0	3	0	97	0	0	64	5.02	1,000,000		2.00		May-09

Fund Name	Ticker Symbol	Traded On	Fund Type	Category and (Prospectus Objective)	Overall Rating	Reward Rating	Risk Rating	Recent Up/ Downgrade	Open to New Investors	Telephone
	MARKET			FUND TYPE, CATEGORY & OBJECTIVE	RATINGS				NEW INVESTORS	
Viking Tax-Free Fund For Montana Class A	VMTTX	NAS CM	Open End	US Muni Fixed Inc (Muni Bond - Single State)	C	C	B-		Y	800-276-1262
Viking Tax-Free Fund For Montana Class I	VMTIX	NAS CM	Open End	US Muni Fixed Inc (Muni Bond - Single State)	C+	C	B	Up	Y	800-276-1262
Viking Tax-Free Fund for North Dakota Class A	VNDFX	NAS CM	Open End	US Muni Fixed Inc (Muni Bond - Single State)	C	C	B-		Y	800-276-1262
Viking Tax-Free Fund for North Dakota Class I	VNDIX	NAS CM	Open End	US Muni Fixed Inc (Muni Bond - Single State)	C	C	B-		Y	800-276-1262
Virtus Global Multi-Sector Income Fund	VGI	NYSE	Closed End	Global Fixed Inc (Income)	D	D	D+	Down	Y	
Virtus Newfleet Core Plus Bond Fund Class A	SAVAX	NAS CM	Open End	US Fixed Inc (Multisector Bond)	C+	C	B	Up	Y	800-243-1574
Virtus Newfleet Core Plus Bond Fund Class C	SAVCX	NAS CM	Open End	US Fixed Inc (Multisector Bond)	C	C	B-		Y	800-243-1574
Virtus Newfleet Core Plus Bond Fund Class I	SAVYX	NAS CM	Open End	US Fixed Inc (Multisector Bond)	C+	C	B	Up	Y	800-243-1574
Virtus Newfleet Core Plus Bond Fund Class R6	VBFRX	NAS CM	Open End	US Fixed Inc (Multisector Bond)	C+	C	B	Up	Y	800-243-1574
Virtus Newfleet High Yield Fund Class A	PHCHX	NAS CM	Open End	US Fixed Inc (Corp Bond - High Yield)	C-	D+	C		Y	800-243-1574
Virtus Newfleet High Yield Fund Class C	PGHCX	NAS CM	Open End	US Fixed Inc (Corp Bond - High Yield)	D+	D	C	Down	Y	800-243-1574
Virtus Newfleet High Yield Fund Class I	PHCIX	NAS CM	Open End	US Fixed Inc (Corp Bond - High Yield)	C-	D+	C		Y	800-243-1574
Virtus Newfleet High Yield Fund Class R6	VRHYX	NAS CM	Open End	US Fixed Inc (Corp Bond - High Yield)	C-	D+	C		Y	800-243-1574
Virtus Newfleet Low Duration Core Plus Bond Fund Class A	HIMZX	NAS CM	Open End	US Fixed Inc (Corp Bond - General)	C	C-	C+		Y	800-243-1574
Virtus Newfleet Low Duration Core Plus Bond Fund Class C	PCMZX	NAS CM	Open End	US Fixed Inc (Corp Bond - General)	C	C-	C		Y	800-243-1574
Virtus Newfleet Low Duration Core Plus Bond Fund Class I	HIBIX	NAS CM	Open End	US Fixed Inc (Corp Bond - General)	C	C-	C+		Y	800-243-1574
Virtus Newfleet Low Duration Core Plus Bond Fund Class R6	VLDRX	NAS CM	Open End	US Fixed Inc (Corp Bond - General)	C	C-	C+		Y	800-243-1574
Virtus Newfleet Multi-Sector Intermediate Bond Cl A	NAMFX	NAS CM	Open End	US Fixed Inc (Multisector Bond)	C-	D+	C		Y	800-243-1574
Virtus Newfleet Multi-Sector Intermediate Bond Cl C	NCMFX	NAS CM	Open End	US Fixed Inc (Multisector Bond)	C-	D+	C		Y	800-243-1574
Virtus Newfleet Multi-Sector Intermediate Bond Cl I	VMFIX	NAS CM	Open End	US Fixed Inc (Multisector Bond)	C-	D+	C	Down	Y	800-243-1574
Virtus Newfleet Multi-Sector Intermediate Bond Cl R6	VMFRX	NAS CM	Open End	US Fixed Inc (Multisector Bond)	C-	D+	C	Down	Y	800-243-1574
Virtus Newfleet Multi-Sector Short Term Bond Fund Class A	NARAX	NAS CM	Open End	US Fixed Inc (Multisector Bond)	C-	D+	C	Down	Y	800-243-1574
Virtus Newfleet Multi-Sector Short Term Bond Fund Class C	PSTCX	NAS CM	Open End	US Fixed Inc (Multisector Bond)	C-	D+	C		Y	800-243-1574
Virtus Newfleet Multi-Sector Short Term Bond Fund Class C1	PMSTX	NAS CM	Open End	US Fixed Inc (Multisector Bond)	C-	D+	C		Y	800-243-1574
Virtus Newfleet Multi-Sector Short Term Bond Fund Class I	PIMSX	NAS CM	Open End	US Fixed Inc (Multisector Bond)	C	C-	C		Y	800-243-1574
Virtus Newfleet Multi-Sector Short Term Bond Fund Class R6	VMSSX	NAS CM	Open End	US Fixed Inc (Multisector Bond)	C	C-	C		Y	800-243-1574
Virtus Newfleet Senior Floating Rate Fund Class A	PSFRX	NAS CM	Open End	US Fixed Inc (Growth & Income)	D	D	D+	Down	Y	800-243-1574
Virtus Newfleet Senior Floating Rate Fund Class C	PFSRX	NAS CM	Open End	US Fixed Inc (Growth & Income)	D	D	D+	Down	Y	800-243-1574
Virtus Newfleet Senior Floating Rate Fund Class I	PSFIX	NAS CM	Open End	US Fixed Inc (Growth & Income)	D	D	C-	Down	Y	800-243-1574
Virtus Newfleet Senior Floating Rate Fund Class R6	VRSFX	NAS CM	Open End	US Fixed Inc (Growth & Income)	D	D	C-	Down	Y	800-243-1574
Virtus Newfleet Tax-Exempt Bond Fund Class A	HXBZX	NAS CM	Open End	US Muni Fixed Inc (Muni Bond - Natl)	C	C	B-		Y	800-243-1574
Virtus Newfleet Tax-Exempt Bond Fund Class C	PXCZX	NAS CM	Open End	US Muni Fixed Inc (Muni Bond - Natl)	C	C-	C+		Y	800-243-1574
Virtus Newfleet Tax-Exempt Bond Fund Class I	HXBIX	NAS CM	Open End	US Muni Fixed Inc (Muni Bond - Natl)	C	C	B-		Y	800-243-1574
Virtus Seix Core Bond Fund Class A	STGIX	NAS CM	Open End	US Fixed Inc (Multisector Bond)	B	B-	B	Up	Y	800-243-1574
Virtus Seix Core Bond Fund Class I	STIGX	NAS CM	Open End	US Fixed Inc (Multisector Bond)	B	B	B		Y	800-243-1574
Virtus Seix Core Bond Fund Class R6	STGZX	NAS CM	Open End	US Fixed Inc (Multisector Bond)	B	B	B		Y	800-243-1574
Virtus Seix Corporate Bond Fund Class A	SAINX	NAS CM	Open End	US Fixed Inc (Income)	B	B	B	Up	Y	800-243-1574
Virtus Seix Corporate Bond Fund Class C	STIFX	NAS CM	Open End	US Fixed Inc (Income)	B	B	B	Up	Y	800-243-1574
Virtus Seix Corporate Bond Fund Class I	STICX	NAS CM	Open End	US Fixed Inc (Income)	B	B	B	Up	Y	800-243-1574
Virtus Seix Floating Rate High Income Fund Class A	SFRAX	NAS CM	Open End	US Fixed Inc (Income)	D	D	C-	Down	Y	800-243-1574
Virtus Seix Floating Rate High Income Fund Class C	SFRCX	NAS CM	Open End	US Fixed Inc (Income)	D	D	D+	Down	Y	800-243-1574
Virtus Seix Floating Rate High Income Fund Class I	SAMBX	NAS CM	Open End	US Fixed Inc (Income)	D	D	C-	Down	Y	800-243-1574
Virtus Seix Floating Rate High Income Fund Class R6	SFRZX	NAS CM	Open End	US Fixed Inc (Income)	D	D	C-	Down	Y	800-243-1574
Virtus Seix High Grade Municipal Bond Fund Class A	SFLTX	NAS CM	Open End	US Muni Fixed Inc (Muni Bond - Natl)	B-	C	B+	Up	Y	800-243-1574
Virtus Seix High Grade Municipal Bond Fund Class I	SCFTX	NAS CM	Open End	US Muni Fixed Inc (Muni Bond - Natl)	B-	C	B+	Up	Y	800-243-1574
Virtus Seix High Income Fund Class A	SAHIX	NAS CM	Open End	US Fixed Inc (Corp Bond - High Yield)	D+	D	C-	Down	Y	800-243-1574
Virtus Seix High Income Fund Class I	STHTX	NAS CM	Open End	US Fixed Inc (Corp Bond - High Yield)	D+	D	C-	Down	Y	800-243-1574
Virtus Seix High Income Fund Class R6	STHZX	NAS CM	Open End	US Fixed Inc (Corp Bond - High Yield)	D+	D	C-	Down	Y	800-243-1574
Virtus Seix High Yield Fund Class A	HYPSX	NAS CM	Open End	US Fixed Inc (Corp Bond - High Yield)	C	D+	C+	Up	Y	800-243-1574
Virtus Seix High Yield Fund Class I	SAMHX	NAS CM	Open End	US Fixed Inc (Corp Bond - High Yield)	C	C-	C+		Y	800-243-1574
Virtus Seix High Yield Fund Class R6	HYIZX	NAS CM	Open End	US Fixed Inc (Corp Bond - High Yield)	C	C-	C+		Y	800-243-1574
Virtus Seix Investment Grade Tax-Exempt Bond Fund Class A	SISIX	NAS CM	Open End	US Muni Fixed Inc (Muni Bond - Natl)	B-	C	B	Up	Y	800-243-1574

★Expanded analysis of this fund is included in Section II.

TOTAL RETURNS & PERFORMANCE									ASSETS		ASSET ALLOCATION & TURNOVER							MINIMUMS		FEES		
3-Month Total Return	6-Month Total Return	1-Year Total Return	3-Year Total Return	5-Year Total Return	Dividend Yield (TTM)	Expense Ratio	3-Yr Std Deviation	Effective Duration	NAV	Total Assets (MIL)	%Cash	%Government Bonds	%Municipal Bonds	%Corporate Bonds	%Other	Turnover Ratio	Average Coupon Rate	Min Initial Investment	Min Additional Investment	Front End Fee (%)	Back End Fee (%)	Inception Date
1.29	1.73	3.13	9.06	14.60	2.25	0.98	3.01		10.23	81.6	0	0	100	0	0	20	4.35	1,000	50	2.50		Aug-99
1.25	1.85	3.39	9.88	15.71	2.5	0.73	2.99		10.23	81.6	0	0	100	0	0	20	4.35	1,000	50			Aug-16
0.82	1.20	2.61	7.77	13.39	2.34	0.98	2.6		10.31	30.1	0	0	100	0	0	23	4.01	1,000	50	2.50		Aug-99
0.98	1.32	2.86	8.58	14.59	2.59	0.73	2.53		10.32	30.1	0	0	100	0	0	23	4.01	1,000	50			Aug-16
14.83	-4.27	-0.54	-1.50	17.66	4.88	2.24	12.76	5.49	11.99	132.1	0	23	1	54	0	45	5.22					Feb-12
6.74	3.14	6.03	14.01	21.99	2.76	0.8	4.95	5.12	11.69	101.5	6	18	2	39	0	59	3.78	2,500	100	3.75		Jul-98
6.50	2.80	5.32	11.49	17.50	2.02	1.55	4.92	5.12	11.42	101.5	6	18	2	39	0	59	3.78	2,500	100		1.00	Jul-98
6.79	3.23	6.33	14.78	23.51	3	0.55	4.93	5.12	11.88	101.5	6	18	2	39	0	59	3.78	100,000				Mar-96
6.82	3.38	6.45	15.26	23.94	3.12	0.43	4.94	5.12	11.89	101.5	6	18	2	39	0	59	3.78	0				Nov-16
11.12	-4.87	-0.85	7.59	19.64	5.7	1.01	9.76	4.04	3.86	55.1	6	0	0	92	0	59	6.16	2,500	100	3.75		Jul-80
10.80	-5.35	-1.70	5.07	15.32	4.92	1.76	9.66	4.04	3.79	55.1	6	0	0	92	0	59	6.16	2,500	100		1.00	Feb-98
10.87	-4.98	-0.85	8.12	21.13	5.95	0.76	9.62	4.04	3.86	55.1	6	0	0	92	0	59	6.16	100,000				Aug-12
10.89	-4.95	-0.79	8.56	20.64	6.03	0.7	9.59	4.04	3.86	55.1	6	0	0	92	0	59	6.16	0				Nov-16
4.98	1.22	2.60	7.87	11.89	2.46	0.75	3.38	2.01	10.85	459.5	5	4	0	24	0	45	3.34	2,500	100	2.25		Jul-99
4.79	0.84	1.84	5.49	7.69	1.71	1.5	3.37	2.01	10.85	459.5	5	4	0	24	0	45	3.34	2,500	100		1.00	Jun-06
5.05	1.34	2.85	8.68	13.29	2.71	0.5	3.38	2.01	10.85	459.5	5	4	0	24	0	45	3.34	100,000				Feb-96
5.07	1.28	2.92	8.80	13.41	2.78	0.43	3.37	2.01	10.85	459.5	5	4	0	24	0	45	3.34	2,500,000				Dec-18
9.61	-2.00	0.81	7.75	19.36	4.07	0.99	7.96	4.24	9.83	347.9	8	9	1	56	0	81	4.91	2,500	100	3.75		Dec-89
9.54	-2.33	0.15	5.41	15.03	3.25	1.74	8	4.24	9.94	347.9	8	9	1	56	0	81	4.91	2,500	100		1.00	Oct-97
9.82	-1.84	1.13	8.63	21.05	4.4	0.74	7.96	4.24	9.83	347.9	8	9	1	56	0	81	4.91	100,000				Oct-09
9.91	-1.74	1.33	9.03	21.68	4.39	0.6	8.02	4.24	9.86	347.9	8	9	1	56	0	81	4.91	0				Nov-14
6.10	0.24	1.68	6.88	13.32	3.01	0.98	4.4	2.33	4.66	5,738	6	6	0	36	0	58	3.79	2,500	100	2.25		Jul-92
5.96	0.13	1.42	6.03	11.77	2.73	1.21	4.45	2.33	4.72	5,738	6	6	0	36	0	58	3.79	2,500	100			Oct-97
5.84	-0.11	0.92	4.47	9.07	2.23	1.72	4.44	2.33	4.71	5,738	6	6	0	36	0	58	3.79	2,500	100		1.00	Jun-03
6.15	0.37	2.15	7.70	14.75	3.27	0.72	4.35	2.33	4.67	5,738	6	6	0	36	0	58	3.79	100,000				Jun-08
6.17	0.41	2.22	8.16	14.87	3.33	0.55	4.38	2.33	4.67	5,738	6	6	0	36	0	58	3.79	0				Nov-16
9.31	-6.94	-4.70	1.17	7.52	5	1.11	9.34	0.50	8.32	185.8	12	0	0	88	0	24	4.81	2,500	100	2.75		Jan-08
9.14	-7.35	-5.36	-1.02	3.60	4.24	1.86	9.38	0.50	8.33	185.8	12	0	0	88	0	24	4.81	2,500	100		1.00	Jan-08
9.43	-6.81	-4.44	1.95	8.89	5.29	0.86	9.4	0.50	8.31	185.8	12	0	0	88	0	24	4.81	100,000				Jan-08
9.50	-6.82	-4.39	2.36	9.37	5.47	0.72	9.41	0.50	8.31	185.8	12	0	0	88	0	24	4.81	0				Nov-16
2.04	1.23	3.11	9.85	15.70	2.22	0.86	3.62	4.72	11.35	114.6	6	0	94	0	0	4	4.96	2,500	100	2.75		Jan-01
1.86	0.86	2.35	7.42	11.38	1.48	1.61	3.67	4.72	11.35	114.6	6	0	94	0	0	4	4.96	2,500	100		1.00	Jun-06
2.10	1.35	3.37	10.67	17.18	2.47	0.61	3.62	4.72	11.35	114.6	6	0	94	0	0	4	4.96	100,000				Feb-96
2.73	7.22	9.45	15.81	22.29	1.56	0.64	3.3	5.69	11.62	142.7	24	29	0	18	0	197	2.88	2,500	100	3.75		Jun-92
2.68	7.29	9.50	16.29	23.05	1.69	0.5	3.32	5.69	11.62	142.7	24	29	0	18	0	197	2.88	100,000				Jul-92
2.80	7.46	9.75	16.86	23.94	1.82	0.36	3.31	5.69	11.63	142.7	24	29	0	18	0	197	2.88	2,500,000				Aug-15
10.12	9.28	13.02	20.98	34.80	2.04	0.95	5.71	8.36	9.68	55.3	5	1	0	88	0	118	3.95	2,500	100	3.75		Oct-03
9.97	8.95	12.18	18.42	30.17	1.29	1.65	5.68	8.36	9.64	55.3	5	1	0	88	0	118	3.95	2,500	100		1.00	Nov-01
10.24	9.46	13.36	21.80	36.42	2.27	0.7	5.72	8.36	9.63	55.3	5	1	0	88	0	118	3.95	100,000				Nov-01
8.91	-5.77	-4.50	1.95	9.56	4.83	0.93	8.2	0.24	7.76	2,142	2	0	0	96	1	17	4.43	2,500	100	2.75		May-06
8.61	-6.04	-5.05	0.19	6.41	4.21	1.52	8.18	0.24	7.76	2,142	2	0	0	96	1	17	4.43	2,500	100		1.00	Aug-07
8.84	-5.62	-4.19	2.93	11.27	5.17	0.62	8.12	0.24	7.76	2,142	2	0	0	96	1	17	4.43	100,000				Mar-06
8.87	-5.57	-4.10	3.24	11.85	5.28	0.52	8.18	0.24	7.76	2,142	2	0	0	96	1	17	4.43	2,500,000				Feb-15
3.26	3.65	6.02	14.46	23.10	1.34	0.78	4.24	5.49	12.42	67.6	6	0	92	0	0	233	4.88	2,500	100	2.75		Jan-94
3.30	3.72	6.26	15.06	24.01	1.48	0.63	4.2	5.49	12.42	67.6	6	0	92	0	0	233	4.88	100,000				Jan-94
11.33	-4.45	-1.94	6.95	18.59	5.28	0.93	9.43	4.08	5.9	200.2	1	0	0	97	0	113	6.42	2,500	100	3.75		Oct-03
11.42	-4.34	-1.70	7.70	19.98	5.54	0.68	9.45	4.08	5.89	200.2	1	0	0	97	0	113	6.42	100,000				Oct-01
11.46	-4.14	-1.60	8.15	20.87	5.64	0.59	9.42	4.08	5.89	200.2	1	0	0	97	0	113	6.42	2,500,000				Aug-14
10.56	-0.92	2.31	12.44	21.92	4.57	0.82	7.64	4.07	7.93	322.0	2	0	0	97	0	98	5.98	2,500	100	3.75		Dec-01
10.51	-0.98	2.44	13.03	23.12	4.77	0.64	7.63	4.07	8.13	322.0	2	0	0	97	0	98	5.98	100,000				Dec-00
10.56	-0.91	2.56	13.38	23.47	4.88	0.53	7.64	4.07	8.13	322.0	2	0	0	97	0	98	5.98	2,500,000				Aug-16
3.04	3.22	5.24	11.87	17.88	1.18	0.74	3.61	4.98	12.04	288.5	3	0	94	0	0	203	4.96	2,500	100	2.75		Jun-92

	MARKET		FUND TYPE, CATEGORY & OBJECTIVE		RATINGS				NEW INVESTORS	
Fund Name	Ticker Symbol	Traded On	Fund Type	Category and (Prospectus Objective)	Overall Rating	Reward Rating	Risk Rating	Recent Up/ Downgrade	Open to New Investors	Telephone
Virtus Seix Investment Grade Tax-Exempt Bond Fund Class I	STTBX	NAS CM	Open End	US Muni Fixed Inc (Muni Bond - Natl)	B-	C	B	Up	Y	800-243-1574
Virtus Seix Short-Term Bond Fund Class A	STSBX	NAS CM	Open End	US Fixed Inc (Income)	C+	C	B	Up	Y	800-243-1574
Virtus Seix Short-Term Bond Fund Class C	SCBSX	NAS CM	Open End	US Fixed Inc (Income)	C	C	B-		Y	800-243-1574
Virtus Seix Short-Term Bond Fund Class I	SSBTX	NAS CM	Open End	US Fixed Inc (Income)	C+	C	B	Up	Y	800-243-1574
Virtus Seix Short-Term Municipal Bond Fund Class A	SMMAX	NAS CM	Open End	US Muni Fixed Inc (Muni Bond - Natl)	C	C	B-		Y	800-243-1574
Virtus Seix Short-Term Municipal Bond Fund Class I	CMDTX	NAS CM	Open End	US Muni Fixed Inc (Muni Bond - Natl)	C	C	B-		Y	800-243-1574
Virtus Seix Total Return Bond Fund Class A	CBPSX	NAS CM	Open End	US Fixed Inc (Multisector Bond)	B	B	B	Up	Y	800-243-1574
Virtus Seix Total Return Bond Fund Class I	SAMFX	NAS CM	Open End	US Fixed Inc (Multisector Bond)	B	B	B	Up	Y	800-243-1574
Virtus Seix Total Return Bond Fund Class R6	SAMZX	NAS CM	Open End	US Fixed Inc (Multisector Bond)	B	B	B	Up	Y	800-243-1574
Virtus Seix U.S. Govt Securities Ultra-Short Bond Cl A	SSAGX	NAS CM	Open End	US Fixed Inc (Govt Bond - General)	C	C-	C+		Y	800-243-1574
Virtus Seix U.S. Govt Securities Ultra-Short Bond Cl I	SIGVX	NAS CM	Open End	US Fixed Inc (Govt Bond - General)	C	C-	C+		Y	800-243-1574
Virtus Seix U.S. Govt Securities Ultra-Short Bond Cl R6	SIGZX	NAS CM	Open End	US Fixed Inc (Govt Bond - General)	C	C-	B-		Y	800-243-1574
Virtus Seix U.S. Mortgage Fund Class A	SLTMX	NAS CM	Open End	US Fixed Inc (Govt Bond - Mortgage)	C+	C+	B-		Y	800-243-1574
Virtus Seix U.S. Mortgage Fund Class C	SCLFX	NAS CM	Open End	US Fixed Inc (Govt Bond - Mortgage)	C+	C	B-		Y	800-243-1574
Virtus Seix U.S. Mortgage Fund Class I	SLMTX	NAS CM	Open End	US Fixed Inc (Govt Bond - Mortgage)	C+	C+	B-		Y	800-243-1574
Virtus Seix Ultra-Short Bond Fund Class A	SASSX	NAS CM	Open End	US Fixed Inc (Govt Bond - Treasury)	C	C-	C+		Y	800-243-1574
Virtus Seix Ultra-Short Bond Fund Class I	SISSX	NAS CM	Open End	US Fixed Inc (Govt Bond - Treasury)	C	C-	C+		Y	800-243-1574
Voya Diversified Emerging Markets Debt Fund Class A	IADEX	NAS CM	Open End	Emerg Mkts Fixed Inc (Diversified Emerg Mkts)	D+	D+	C-	Down	Y	800-366-0066
Voya Diversified Emerging Markets Debt Fund Class C	ICDEX	NAS CM	Open End	Emerg Mkts Fixed Inc (Diversified Emerg Mkts)	D	D	C-	Down	Y	800-366-0066
Voya Diversified Emerging Markets Debt Fund Class I	IIDEX	NAS CM	Open End	Emerg Mkts Fixed Inc (Diversified Emerg Mkts)	C-	D+	C	Down	Y	800-366-0066
Voya Diversified Emerging Markets Debt Fund Class W	IWDEX	NAS CM	Open End	Emerg Mkts Fixed Inc (Diversified Emerg Mkts)	D+	D+	C-	Down	Y	800-366-0066
Voya Emerging Markets Corporate Debt Fund Class P	IMCDX	NAS CM	Open End	Emerg Mkts Fixed Inc (Corp Bond - General)	C	C-	C+		Y	800-366-0066
Voya Emerging Markets Hard Currency Debt Fund A	VMHAX	NAS CM	Open End	Emerg Mkts Fixed Inc (Govt Bond - General)	C-	D+	C		Y	800-366-0066
Voya Emerging Markets Hard Currency Debt Fund Class P	IHCSX	NAS CM	Open End	Emerg Mkts Fixed Inc (Govt Bond - General)	C-	D+	C	Down	Y	800-366-0066
Voya Emerging Markets Hard Currency Debt Fund I	VEMHX	NAS CM	Open End	Emerg Mkts Fixed Inc (Govt Bond - General)	C-	D+	C		Y	800-366-0066
Voya Emerging Markets Hard Currency Debt Fund W	VEMWX	NAS CM	Open End	Emerg Mkts Fixed Inc (Govt Bond - General)	C-	D+	C		Y	800-366-0066
Voya Emerging Markets Local Currency Debt Fund Class P	ILCDX	NAS CM	Open End	Emerg Mkts Fixed Inc (Govt Bond - General)	D	D	D+	Down	Y	800-366-0066
Voya Floating Rate Fund Class A	IFRAX	NAS CM	Open End	US Fixed Inc (Income)	D	D	D+	Down	Y	800-366-0066
Voya Floating Rate Fund Class C	IFRCX	NAS CM	Open End	US Fixed Inc (Income)	D	D	D+	Down	Y	800-366-0066
Voya Floating Rate Fund Class I	IFRIX	NAS CM	Open End	US Fixed Inc (Income)	D	D	D+	Down	Y	800-366-0066
Voya Floating Rate Fund Class P	IFRPX	NAS CM	Open End	US Fixed Inc (Income)	D	D	D+	Down	Y	800-366-0066
Voya Floating Rate Fund Class R	IFRRX	NAS CM	Open End	US Fixed Inc (Income)	D	D	D+	Down	Y	800-366-0066
Voya Floating Rate Fund Class W	IFRWX	NAS CM	Open End	US Fixed Inc (Income)	D	D	D+	Down	Y	800-366-0066
Voya Global Bond Fund Class A	INGBX	NAS CM	Open End	Global Fixed Inc (Worldwide Bond)	C	C-	C+		Y	800-366-0066
Voya Global Bond Fund Class C	IGBCX	NAS CM	Open End	Global Fixed Inc (Worldwide Bond)	C	C-	C	Up	Y	800-366-0066
Voya Global Bond Fund Class I	IGBIX	NAS CM	Open End	Global Fixed Inc (Worldwide Bond)	C	C-	C+		Y	800-366-0066
Voya Global Bond Fund Class P	IGBPX	NAS CM	Open End	Global Fixed Inc (Worldwide Bond)	C	C-	B-		Y	800-366-0066
Voya Global Bond Fund Class P3	VPGBX	NAS CM	Open End	Global Fixed Inc (Worldwide Bond)	C	C-	C+		Y	800-366-0066
Voya Global Bond Fund Class R	IGBRX	NAS CM	Open End	Global Fixed Inc (Worldwide Bond)	C	C-	C+		Y	800-366-0066
Voya Global Bond Fund Class R6	IGBZX	NAS CM	Open End	Global Fixed Inc (Worldwide Bond)	C	C-	C+		Y	800-366-0066
Voya Global Bond Fund Class W	IGBWX	NAS CM	Open End	Global Fixed Inc (Worldwide Bond)	C	C-	C+		Y	800-366-0066
Voya Global Bond Portfolio Class A	IOSAX	NAS CM	Open End	Global Fixed Inc (Worldwide Bond)	C	C-	C		Y	800-366-0066
Voya Global Bond Portfolio Class I	IOSIX	NAS CM	Open End	Global Fixed Inc (Worldwide Bond)	C	C-	C+		Y	800-366-0066
Voya Global Bond Portfolio Class S	IOSSX	NAS CM	Open End	Global Fixed Inc (Worldwide Bond)	C	C-	C		Y	800-366-0066
Voya GNMA Income Fund Class A	LEXNX	NAS CM	Open End	US Fixed Inc (Govt Bond - Mortgage)	C+	C	B		Y	800-366-0066
Voya GNMA Income Fund Class C	LEGNX	NAS CM	Open End	US Fixed Inc (Govt Bond - Mortgage)	C+	C	C+	Up	Y	800-366-0066
Voya GNMA Income Fund Class I	LEINX	NAS CM	Open End	US Fixed Inc (Govt Bond - Mortgage)	C+	C+	B-		Y	800-366-0066
Voya GNMA Income Fund Class P	VGMPX	NAS CM	Open End	US Fixed Inc (Govt Bond - Mortgage)	C+	C	B-		Y	800-366-0066
Voya GNMA Income Fund Class W	IGMWX	NAS CM	Open End	US Fixed Inc (Govt Bond - Mortgage)	C+	C+	B-		Y	800-366-0066
Voya Government Liquid Assets Portfolio Class I	IPLXX	NAS CM	Money Mkt	US Money Mkt (Money Mkt - Govt)	C	C	C+		Y	800-366-0066
Voya Government Liquid Assets Portfolio Class S	ISPXX	NAS CM	Money Mkt	US Money Mkt (Money Mkt - Govt)	C	C-	C+		Y	800-366-0066
Voya Government Liquid Assets Portfolio Class S2	ITLXX	NAS CM	Money Mkt	US Money Mkt (Money Mkt - Govt)	C	C-	C		Y	800-366-0066

★ Expanded analysis of this fund is included in Section II.

TOTAL RETURNS & PERFORMANCE									ASSETS		ASSET ALLOCATION & TURNOVER							MINIMUMS		FEES		
3-Month Total Return	6-Month Total Return	1-Year Total Return	3-Year Total Return	5-Year Total Return	Dividend Yield (TTM)	Expense Ratio	3-Yr Std Deviation	Effective Duration	NAV	Total Assets (MIL)	%Cash	%Government Bonds	%Municipal Bonds	%Corporate Bonds	%Other	Turnover Ratio	Average Coupon Rate	Min Initial Investment	Min Additional Investment	Front End Fee (%)	Back End Fee (%)	Inception Date
3.00	3.30	5.32	12.29	18.68	1.32	0.59	3.55	4.98	12.02	288.5	3	0	94	0	0	203	4.96	100,000				Oct-93
1.06	3.21	4.06	7.31	8.42	1.37	0.8	1.13	1.87	10.23	20.6	3	60	0	21	0	77	1.87	2,500	100	2.25		Mar-93
0.79	2.75	3.19	4.76	4.70	0.64	1.57	1.09	1.87	10.22	20.6	3	60	0	21	0	77	1.87	2,500	100		1.00	Jun-95
1.11	3.32	4.27	7.96	9.51	1.56	0.6	1.13	1.87	10.2	20.6	3	60	0	21	0	77	1.87	100,000				Mar-93
2.21	1.84	2.92	6.62	7.99	0.93	0.67	1.82	2.35	10.18	14.6	19	0	76	0	0	77	4.50	2,500	100	2.25		Apr-05
2.15	1.82	3.09	7.16	8.77	1.09	0.5	1.79	2.35	10.18	14.6	19	0	76	0	0	77	4.50	100,000				Mar-96
2.92	8.59	10.19	15.48	22.10	1.36	0.7	3.55	5.69	11.9	364.6	7	36	0	23	0	190	2.97	2,500	100	3.75		Oct-04
3.06	8.69	10.56	16.35	23.70	1.58	0.46	3.5	5.69	11.52	364.6	7	36	0	23	0	190	2.97	100,000				Dec-97
3.01	8.78	10.63	16.77	24.50	1.73	0.31	3.54	5.69	11.51	364.6	7	36	0	23	0	190	2.97	2,500,000				Aug-14
0.96	0.83	1.74	5.01	5.73	1.57	0.65	0.59	0.44	10.03	998.9	6	0	2	0	0	63	1.63	2,500	100			Jul-18
1.01	0.95	1.99	5.77	7.03	1.81	0.41	0.54	0.44	10.03	998.9	6	0	2	0	0	63	1.63	100,000				Apr-02
1.05	1.03	2.14	6.24	7.64	1.96	0.26	0.61	0.44	10.04	998.9	6	0	2	0	0	63	1.63	2,500,000				Aug-16
0.41	3.00	4.80	10.16	14.28	1.45	0.9	2.15	1.73	11.55	21.0	9	0	0	0	0	101	3.61	2,500	100	2.25		Jul-94
0.22	2.62	4.08	7.66	10.06	0.69	1.65	2.1	1.73	11.57	21.0	9	0	0	0	0	101	3.61	2,500	100		1.00	Jun-95
0.46	3.09	5.00	10.80	15.41	1.64	0.7	2.12	1.73	11.57	21.0	9	0	0	0	0	101	3.61	100,000				Jun-94
2.86	0.46	1.46	5.33	7.11	1.76	0.65	1.98	0.35	9.94	45.6	10	0	0	45	0	97	1.93	2,500	100			Jul-18
2.93	0.58	1.72	6.01	8.34	2.01	0.4	1.98	0.35	9.93	45.6	10	0	0	45	0	97	1.93	100,000				Apr-02
12.14	-4.29	-1.18	6.04	16.57	3.28	1.2	10.49	5.58	9.14	10.6	0	66	0	32	0	73	5.80	1,000		2.50		Nov-12
11.90	-4.69	-1.92	3.65	12.17	2.57	1.95	10.46	5.58	8.93	10.6	0	66	0	32	0	73	5.80	1,000			1.00	Nov-12
12.11	-4.18	-0.93	6.85	18.09	3.55	0.9	10.44	5.58	9.16	10.6	0	66	0	32	0	73	5.80	250,000				Nov-12
12.14	-4.19	-0.92	6.82	17.81	3.57	0.95	10.44	5.58	9.14	10.6	0	66	0	32	0	73	5.80	1,000				Nov-12
12.85	-0.49	3.52	14.88	29.64	5.28	0.1	8.98	4.25	9.86	99.0	3	22	0	75	0	50	5.20	0				Aug-12
13.98	-2.82	-0.71	8.30	26.05	4.32	1.15	11.11	6.35	9.36	158.5	-2	81	0	19	0	55	5.89	1,000		2.50		Aug-17
14.39	-2.31	0.34	11.75	30.71	5.44	0.11	11.13	6.35	9.36	158.5	-2	81	0	19	0	55	5.89	0				Aug-12
14.05	-2.68	-0.41	9.33	27.87	4.64	0.9	11.05	6.35	9.36	158.5	-2	81	0	19	0	55	5.89	250,000				Aug-17
14.18	-2.70	-0.45	9.26	27.80	4.59	0.9	11.12	6.35	9.36	158.5	-2	81	0	19	0	55	5.89	1,000				Aug-17
9.99	-8.35	-4.28	0.17	6.50	4.92	0.16	12.98	6.17	6.67	83.6	10	90	0	0	0	48	6.21	0				Aug-12
7.73	-8.22	-6.62	-1.05	4.80	5.09	1.05	9.1	0.14	8.54	621.0	4	0	0	96	0	52	4.15	1,000		2.50		Aug-10
7.40	-8.57	-7.33	-3.35	0.94	4.27	1.8	9.03	0.14	8.54	621.0	4	0	0	96	0	52	4.15	1,000			1.00	Aug-10
7.79	-8.10	-6.39	-0.38	6.27	5.36	0.8	9.1	0.14	8.54	621.0	4	0	0	96	0	52	4.15	250,000				Aug-10
7.98	-7.79	-5.74	1.64	9.77	6.12	0.12	9.09	0.14	8.53	621.0	4	0	0	96	0	52	4.15	0				Jun-13
7.67	-8.34	-6.86	-1.79	3.61	4.82	1.3	9.06	0.14	8.53	621.0	4	0	0	96	0	52	4.15	0				Aug-10
7.78	-8.10	-6.48	-0.49	6.03	5.36	0.8	9.08	0.14	8.55	621.0	4	0	0	96	0	52	4.15	1,000				Aug-10
7.98	1.04	2.14	9.96	20.25	4.52	0.91	6.3	6.92	9.55	251.8	1	35	0	25	0	247	4.36	1,000		2.50		Jun-06
7.71	0.67	1.37	7.51	15.73	3.75	1.66	6.26	6.92	9.49	251.8	1	35	0	25	0	247	4.36	1,000			1.00	Jun-06
7.96	1.16	2.38	10.72	21.82	4.77	0.66	6.24	6.92	9.5	251.8	1	35	0	25	0	247	4.36	250,000				Jun-06
8.04	1.42	2.90	12.43	24.28	5.28	0.16	6.29	6.92	9.56	251.8	1	35	0	25	0	247	4.36	0				Jun-16
8.11	1.49	3.05	12.03	23.26	5.43	0.01	6.31	6.92	9.52	251.8	1	35	0	25	0	247	4.36	0				Jun-18
7.77	0.96	1.87	9.05	18.70	4.14	1.16	6.26	6.92	9.54	251.8	1	35	0	25	0	247	4.36	0				Aug-11
7.95	1.17	2.41	10.69	21.69	4.79	0.66	6.31	6.92	9.52	251.8	1	35	0	25	0	247	4.36	1,000,000				May-13
8.04	1.19	2.44	10.85	21.81	4.65	0.66	6.3	6.92	9.35	251.8	1	35	0	25	0	247	4.36	1,000				Jun-09
6.34	-0.14	0.86	8.17	18.55	2.42	1.2	5.99	7.11	10.5	189.8	-5	39	0	24	0	228	4.52	0				Nov-04
6.46	0.12	1.38	9.78	21.59	2.93	0.7	6	7.11	10.69	189.8	-5	39	0	24	0	228	4.52	0				Nov-04
6.41	-0.09	1.04	8.97	19.99	2.67	0.95	6.02	7.11	10.67	189.8	-5	39	0	24	0	228	4.52	0				Nov-04
0.84	3.07	4.51	9.86	14.01	2.66	0.84	2.01	2.33	8.6	1,326	27	1	0	0	0	421	3.59	1,000		2.50		Aug-73
0.77	2.70	3.87	7.56	9.86	1.92	1.59	1.95	2.33	8.56	1,326	27	1	0	0	0	421	3.59	1,000			1.00	Oct-00
1.03	3.21	4.94	10.96	15.81	2.95	0.54	1.93	2.33	8.62	1,326	27	1	0	0	0	421	3.59	250,000				Jan-02
0.83	3.07	4.51	9.86	14.01		0.15	2.01	2.33	8.61	1,326	27	1	0	0	0	421	3.59	0				May-20
1.01	3.19	4.88	10.81	15.56	2.9	0.59	1.92	2.33	8.63	1,326	27	1	0	0	0	421	3.59	1,000				Dec-07
0.01	0.28	1.15	4.36	4.86	1.28	0.29	0.18		1	962.7	70	30	0	0	0	16		0				May-04
0.02	0.24	1.00	3.69	3.91	1.08	0.54	0.17		1	962.7	70	30	0	0	0	16		0				Jan-89
0.02	0.20	0.87	3.24	3.41	0.96	0.69	0.16		1	962.7	70	30	0	0	0	16		0				Sep-02

	MARKET			FUND TYPE, CATEGORY & OBJECTIVE	RATINGS				NEW INVESTORS	
Fund Name	Ticker Symbol	Traded On	Fund Type	Category and (Prospectus Objective)	Overall Rating	Reward Rating	Risk Rating	Recent Up/ Downgrade	Open to New Investors	Telephone
Voya Government Money Market Fund Class A	**VYAXX**	NAS CM	Money Mkt	US Money Mkt (Money Mkt - Govt)	**C**	C-	C+		Y	800-366-0066
Voya Government Money Market Fund Class C	**VYBXX**	NAS CM	Money Mkt	US Money Mkt (Money Mkt - Govt)	**C**	C-	C		Y	800-366-0066
Voya Government Money Market Fund Class I	**VYCXX**	NAS CM	Money Mkt	US Money Mkt (Money Mkt - Govt)	**C**	C-	C+		Y	800-366-0066
Voya Government Money Market Fund Class W	**VYGXX**	NAS CM	Money Mkt	US Money Mkt (Money Mkt - Govt)	**C**	C-	C+		Y	800-366-0066
Voya Government Money Market Portfolio Class I	**IVMXX**	NAS CM	Money Mkt	US Money Mkt (Money Mkt - Govt)	**C**	C-	C+		Y	800-366-0066
Voya Government Money Market Portfolio Class S	**IMSXX**	NAS CM	Money Mkt	US Money Mkt (Money Mkt - Govt)	**C**	C-	C		Y	800-366-0066
Voya High Yield Bond Fund Class A	**IHYAX**	NAS CM	Open End	US Fixed Inc (Corp Bond - High Yield)	**C-**	D+	C		Y	800-366-0066
Voya High Yield Bond Fund Class C	**IMYCX**	NAS CM	Open End	US Fixed Inc (Corp Bond - High Yield)	**C-**	D+	C		Y	800-366-0066
Voya High Yield Bond Fund Class I	**IHYIX**	NAS CM	Open End	US Fixed Inc (Corp Bond - High Yield)	**C-**	D+	C		Y	800-366-0066
Voya High Yield Bond Fund Class P	**IHYPX**	NAS CM	Open End	US Fixed Inc (Corp Bond - High Yield)	**C-**	D+	C	Down	Y	800-366-0066
Voya High Yield Bond Fund Class P3	**VPHYX**	NAS CM	Open End	US Fixed Inc (Corp Bond - High Yield)	**C-**	D+	C	Down	Y	800-366-0066
Voya High Yield Bond Fund Class R	**IRSTX**	NAS CM	Open End	US Fixed Inc (Corp Bond - High Yield)	**C-**	D+	C		Y	800-366-0066
Voya High Yield Bond Fund Class W	**IHYWX**	NAS CM	Open End	US Fixed Inc (Corp Bond - High Yield)	**C-**	D+	C		Y	800-366-0066
Voya High Yield Bond Fund ClassR6	**VHYRX**	NAS CM	Open End	US Fixed Inc (Corp Bond - High Yield)	**C-**	D+	C		Y	800-366-0066
Voya High Yield Portfolio Class A	**IPYAX**	NAS CM	Open End	US Fixed Inc (Corp Bond - High Yield)	**C-**	D+	C		Y	800-366-0066
Voya High Yield Portfolio Class I	**IPIMX**	NAS CM	Open End	US Fixed Inc (Corp Bond - High Yield)	**C-**	D+	C		Y	800-366-0066
Voya High Yield Portfolio Class S	**IPHYX**	NAS CM	Open End	US Fixed Inc (Corp Bond - High Yield)	**C-**	D+	C		Y	800-366-0066
Voya High Yield Portfolio Class S2	**IPYSX**	NAS CM	Open End	US Fixed Inc (Corp Bond - High Yield)	**C-**	D+	C		Y	800-366-0066
Voya Intermediate Bond Fund Class A	**IIBAX**	NAS CM	Open End	US Fixed Inc (Growth & Income)	**B-**	C	B	Up	Y	800-366-0066
Voya Intermediate Bond Fund Class C	**IICCX**	NAS CM	Open End	US Fixed Inc (Growth & Income)	**C+**	C	B	Up	Y	800-366-0066
Voya Intermediate Bond Fund Class I	**IICIX**	NAS CM	Open End	US Fixed Inc (Growth & Income)	**B-**	C	B	Up	Y	800-366-0066
Voya Intermediate Bond Fund Class P3	**VPIBX**	NAS CM	Open End	US Fixed Inc (Growth & Income)	**B-**	C	B	Up	Y	800-366-0066
Voya Intermediate Bond Fund Class R	**IIBOX**	NAS CM	Open End	US Fixed Inc (Growth & Income)	**C+**	C	B	Up	Y	800-366-0066
Voya Intermediate Bond Fund Class R6	**IIBZX**	NAS CM	Open End	US Fixed Inc (Growth & Income)	**B-**	C	B	Up	Y	800-366-0066
Voya Intermediate Bond Fund Class W	**IIBWX**	NAS CM	Open End	US Fixed Inc (Growth & Income)	**B-**	C	B	Up	Y	800-366-0066
Voya Intermediate Bond Portfolio Class A	**IIBPX**	NAS CM	Open End	US Fixed Inc (Growth & Income)	**C+**	C	B	Up	Y	800-366-0066
Voya Intermediate Bond Portfolio Class I	**IPIIX**	NAS CM	Open End	US Fixed Inc (Growth & Income)	**B-**	C	B	Up	Y	800-366-0066
Voya Intermediate Bond Portfolio Class S	**IPISX**	NAS CM	Open End	US Fixed Inc (Growth & Income)	**B-**	C	B	Up	Y	800-366-0066
Voya Intermediate Bond Portfolio Class S2	**IIBTX**	NAS CM	Open End	US Fixed Inc (Growth & Income)	**B-**	C	B	Up	Y	800-366-0066
Voya Investment Grade Credit Fund A	**VACFX**	NAS CM	Open End	US Fixed Inc (Income)	**B-**	C+	B	Up	Y	800-366-0066
Voya Investment Grade Credit Fund Class P	**IIGPX**	NAS CM	Open End	US Fixed Inc (Income)	**B-**	C+	B	Up	Y	800-366-0066
Voya Investment Grade Credit Fund Class R6	**VIGTX**	NAS CM	Open End	US Fixed Inc (Income)	**B-**	C+	B	Up	Y	800-366-0066
Voya Investment Grade Credit Fund Class SMA	**ISCFX**	NAS CM	Open End	US Fixed Inc (Income)	**B-**	C+	B	Up	Y	800-366-0066
Voya Investment Grade Credit Fund I	**VIGCX**	NAS CM	Open End	US Fixed Inc (Income)	**B-**	C+	B	Up	Y	800-366-0066
Voya Investment Grade Credit Fund W	**VIGWX**	NAS CM	Open End	US Fixed Inc (Income)	**B-**	C+	B	Up	Y	800-366-0066
Voya Limited Maturity Bond Portfolio Class A	**IMBAX**	NAS CM	Open End	US Fixed Inc (Corp Bond - General)	**C**	C	C+		Y	800-366-0066
Voya Limited Maturity Bond Portfolio Class I	**ILBPX**	NAS CM	Open End	US Fixed Inc (Corp Bond - General)	**C**	C	B-		Y	800-366-0066
Voya Limited Maturity Bond Portfolio Class S	**ILMBX**	NAS CM	Open End	US Fixed Inc (Corp Bond - General)	**C**	C	B-		Y	800-366-0066
Voya Prime Rate Trust	**PPR**	NYSE	Closed End	US Fixed Inc (Corp Bond - General)	**D**	D	D	Down	Y	
Voya Securitized Credit Fund Class A	**VCFAX**	NAS CM	Open End	US Fixed Inc (Income)	**D**	D	D+	Down	Y	800-366-0066
Voya Securitized Credit Fund Class I	**VCFIX**	NAS CM	Open End	US Fixed Inc (Income)	**D**	D	D+	Down	Y	800-366-0066
Voya Securitized Credit Fund Class P	**VSCFX**	NAS CM	Open End	US Fixed Inc (Income)	**D**	D	D+	Down	Y	800-366-0066
Voya Securitized Credit Fund W	**VSCWX**	NAS CM	Open End	US Fixed Inc (Income)	**D**	D	D+	Down	Y	800-366-0066
Voya Senior Income Fund Class A	**XSIAX**	NAS CM	Closed End	US Fixed Inc (Income)	**D**	D	D		Y	800-366-0066
Voya Senior Income Fund Class C	**XSICX**	NAS CM	Closed End	US Fixed Inc (Income)	**D**	D	D		Y	800-366-0066
Voya Senior Income Fund Class I	**XSIIX**	NAS CM	Closed End	US Fixed Inc (Income)	**D**	D	D	Down	Y	800-366-0066
Voya Senior Income Fund Class W	**XSIWX**	NAS CM	Closed End	US Fixed Inc (Income)	**D**	D	D	Down	Y	800-366-0066
Voya Short Term Bond Fund Class A	**IASBX**	NAS CM	Open End	US Fixed Inc (Growth & Income)	**C**	C-	C+		Y	800-366-0066
Voya Short Term Bond Fund Class C	**ICSBX**	NAS CM	Open End	US Fixed Inc (Growth & Income)	**C**	C-	C	Up	Y	800-366-0066
Voya Short Term Bond Fund Class I	**IISBX**	NAS CM	Open End	US Fixed Inc (Growth & Income)	**C**	C-	C+		Y	800-366-0066
Voya Short Term Bond Fund Class P2	**VSTUX**	NAS CM	Open End	US Fixed Inc (Growth & Income)	**C**	C-	C+		Y	800-366-0066
Voya Short Term Bond Fund Class P3	**VPSTX**	NAS CM	Open End	US Fixed Inc (Growth & Income)	**C**	C-	C+		Y	800-366-0066

★ Expanded analysis of this fund is included in Section II.

TOTAL RETURNS & PERFORMANCE									ASSETS		ASSET ALLOCATION & TURNOVER							MINIMUMS		FEES		
3-Month Total Return	6-Month Total Return	1-Year Total Return	3-Year Total Return	5-Year Total Return	Dividend Yield (TTM)	Expense Ratio	3-Yr Std Deviation	Effective Duration	NAV	Total Assets (MIL)	%Cash	%Government Bonds	%Municipal Bonds	%Corporate Bonds	%Other	Turnover Ratio	Average Coupon Rate	Min Initial Investment	Min Additional Investment	Front End Fee (%)	Back End Fee (%)	Inception Date
0.02	0.27	1.09	3.92	4.07	1.19	0.4	0.2		1	199.0	68	32	0	0	0	235		1,000				Apr-94
0.01	0.07	0.39	1.48	1.58	0.41	1.4	0.12		1	199.0	68	32	0	0	0	235		1,000			1.00	Jul-11
0.02	0.29	1.11	3.94	4.09	1.21	0.4	0.19		1	199.0	68	32	0	0	0	235		250,000				Jan-92
0.02	0.27	1.09	3.93	4.07	1.19	0.4	0.2		1	199.0	68	32	0	0	0	235		1,000				Jul-11
0.03	0.28	1.15	4.28	4.68	1.25	0.34	0.18		1	597.7	70	30	0	0	0	2		0				Dec-79
0.02	0.04	0.09	1.27	1.51	0.01	0.49	0.14		1	597.7	70	30	0	0	0	2		0				Mar-10
7.75	-4.71	-1.29	7.12	20.10	5.57	1.1	7.94	4.41	7.47	655.2	3	0	0	97	0	57	6.08	1,000		2.50		Dec-98
7.42	-5.07	-2.16	4.61	15.53	4.78	1.85	7.94	4.41	7.46	655.2	3	0	0	97	0	57	6.08	1,000			1.00	Dec-98
7.70	-4.56	-1.09	8.22	22.08	5.94	0.75	7.96	4.41	7.45	655.2	3	0	0	97	0	57	6.08	250,000				Jul-08
8.01	-4.23	-0.42	10.33	26.29	6.63	0.08	7.93	4.41	7.47	655.2	3	0	0	97	0	57	6.08	0				Jun-13
8.16	-4.07	-0.23	9.42	22.68	6.69	0	7.97	4.41	7.48	655.2	3	0	0	97	0	57	6.08	0				Jun-18
7.53	-4.83	-1.66	6.32	18.64	5.31	1.35	7.91	4.41	7.47	655.2	3	0	0	97	0	57	6.08	0				Jan-14
7.80	-4.58	-1.16	7.94	21.80	5.84	0.85	7.94	4.41	7.48	655.2	3	0	0	97	0	57	6.08	1,000				Jul-11
7.85	-4.52	-1.01	8.44	22.05	6	0.69	8.03	4.41	7.47	655.2	3	0	0	97	0	57	6.08	1,000,000				Aug-16
7.83	-4.94	-1.49	7.09	20.33	5.16	1.08	8.08	4.38	9.22	511.3	3	0	0	97	0	59	6.10	0				May-06
7.97	-4.56	-0.79	9.12	24.09	5.79	0.48	8.08	4.38	9.23	511.3	3	0	0	97	0	59	6.10	0				Apr-05
7.91	-4.78	-1.14	8.20	22.55	5.53	0.73	8.09	4.38	9.22	511.3	3	0	0	97	0	59	6.10	0				May-04
7.87	-4.84	-1.28	7.73	21.54	5.37	0.88	8.07	4.38	9.23	511.3	3	0	0	97	0	59	6.10	0				Dec-06
5.96	4.26	7.07	15.17	23.92	3.2	0.7	4.65	6.29	10.63	8,783	-16	25	0	28	0	253	3.73	1,000		2.50		Dec-98
5.78	3.88	6.19	12.52	19.28	2.46	1.45	4.69	6.29	10.61	8,783	-16	25	0	28	0	253	3.73	1,000			1.00	Dec-98
6.04	4.32	7.31	16.20	25.88	3.52	0.36	4.67	6.29	10.62	8,783	-16	25	0	28	0	253	3.73	250,000				Jan-02
6.13	4.60	7.78	16.82	25.70	3.87	0	4.68	6.29	10.63	8,783	-16	25	0	28	0	253	3.73	0				Jun-18
5.89	4.13	6.70	14.20	22.26	2.96	0.95	4.64	6.29	10.64	8,783	-16	25	0	28	0	253	3.73	0				Mar-04
6.05	4.44	7.45	16.51	26.11	3.56	0.31	4.65	6.29	10.63	8,783	-16	25	0	28	0	253	3.73	1,000,000				May-13
6.03	4.39	7.24	16.04	25.49	3.45	0.45	4.66	6.29	10.62	8,783	-16	25	0	28	0	253	3.73	1,000				Dec-07
5.80	4.04	6.60	14.06	22.52	2.9	1.05	4.54	6.32	13.27	3,485	-18	28	0	26	0	149	3.91	0				Dec-06
5.96	4.27	7.09	15.81	25.55	3.39	0.55	4.57	6.32	13.41	3,485	-18	28	0	26	0	149	3.91	0				May-73
5.85	4.16	6.85	14.90	24.00	3.15	0.8	4.52	6.32	13.32	3,485	-18	28	0	26	0	149	3.91	0				May-02
5.83	4.09	6.63	14.40	23.06	3	0.95	4.54	6.32	13.27	3,485	-18	28	0	26	0	149	3.91	0				Feb-09
11.02	6.48	11.12	21.54	36.33	3.08	0.9	6.94	7.85	11.69	172.0	-1	11	0	87	0	553	3.88	1,000		2.50		Aug-16
11.23	6.87	11.96	24.30	40.60	3.81	0.15	6.94	7.85	11.68	172.0	-1	11	0	87	0	553	3.88	0				Mar-13
10.98	6.62	11.32	22.53	38.14	3.34	0.63	6.92	7.85	11.69	172.0	-1	11	0	87	0	553	3.88	1,000,000				Aug-16
11.26	6.95	12.03	24.87	41.53	3.95	0	6.97	7.85	11.68	172.0	-1	11	0	87	0	553	3.88	0				Jun-07
10.98	6.61	11.40	22.44	38.03	3.32	0.65	6.88	7.85	11.69	172.0	-1	11	0	87	0	553	3.88	250,000				Aug-16
11.01	6.62	11.32	22.52	38.87	3.32	0.65	6.9	7.85	11.67	172.0	-1	11	0	87	0	553	3.88	1,000				Aug-17
2.54	1.71	2.72	6.39	7.86	1.45	0.89	1.76	1.82	10	336.5	-18	41	0	25	0	330	2.62	0				Apr-06
2.64	1.99	3.31	8.26	11.20	2.05	0.29	1.71	1.82	10.2	336.5	-18	41	0	25	0	330	2.62	0				Apr-05
2.56	1.86	3.14	7.55	9.76	1.8	0.54	1.72	1.82	10.28	336.5	-18	41	0	25	0	330	2.62	0				Jan-89
9.19	-13.39	-11.18	-5.31	2.39	6.17	2.31	12.56		4.61	681.3	0	0	0	100	0	53	1.02					May-88
6.25	-7.82	-6.16	3.93	16.01	5	1	9.1	2.56	9.26	936.6	27	9	0	0	0	30	3.68	1,000		2.50		Aug-15
6.32	-7.66	-5.94	4.76	17.78	5.36	0.68	9.14	2.56	9.27	936.6	27	9	0	0	0	30	3.68	250,000				Aug-15
6.58	-7.33	-5.31	6.77	21.40	6.07	0.05	9.1	2.56	9.31	936.6	27	9	0	0	0	30	3.68	0				Aug-14
6.30	-7.69	-5.91	4.82	19.18	5.28	0.75	9.14	2.56	9.28	936.6	27	9	0	0	0	30	3.68	1,000				Aug-17
9.97	-13.33	-11.98	-6.74	0.50	6.3	2.71	12.78	0.14	10.02	903.6	0	0	0	100	0	45	4.03	1,000		2.50		Apr-01
9.86	-13.50	-12.44	-8.06	-1.90	5.73	3.21	12.78	0.14	10	903.6	0	0	0	100	0	45	4.03	1,000			1.00	Apr-01
10.08	-13.26	-11.80	-6.06	1.76	6.61	2.46	12.79	0.14	9.98	903.6	0	0	0	100	0	45	4.03	250,000				Apr-08
10.14	-13.21	-11.75	-5.95	1.77	6.58	2.46	12.81	0.14	10.03	903.6	0	0	0	100	0	45	4.03	1,000				Apr-08
3.98	1.23	2.48	6.66	9.05	2.16	0.65	2.77	1.78	9.88	177.0	-9	27	0	34	0	192	3.16	1,000		2.50		Dec-12
3.90	0.96	1.93	4.40	5.14	1.41	1.4	2.86	1.78	9.89	177.0	-9	27	0	34	0	192	3.16	1,000			1.00	Dec-12
4.16	1.38	2.89	7.62	10.66	2.46	0.35	2.84	1.78	9.88	177.0	-9	27	0	34	0	192	3.16	250,000				Dec-12
4.23	1.53	3.00	7.74	10.79		0.15	2.83	1.78	9.88	177.0	-9	27	0	34	0	192	3.16	0				Oct-19
4.74	1.54	3.21	8.49	11.45	2.98	0	2.85	1.78	9.88	177.0	-9	27	0	34	0	192	3.16	0				Jun-18

Fund Name	MARKET Ticker Symbol	Traded On	FUND TYPE, CATEGORY & OBJECTIVE Fund Type	Category and (Prospectus Objective)	RATINGS Overall Rating	Reward Rating	Risk Rating	Recent Up/ Downgrade	NEW INVESTORS Open to New Investors	Telephone
Voya Short Term Bond Fund Class R	VSTRX	NAS CM	Open End	US Fixed Inc (Growth & Income)	C	C-	C+		Y	800-366-0066
Voya Short Term Bond Fund Class R6	IGZAX	NAS CM	Open End	US Fixed Inc (Growth & Income)	C	C-	C+		Y	800-366-0066
Voya Short Term Bond Fund Class W	IWSBX	NAS CM	Open End	US Fixed Inc (Growth & Income)	C	C-	C+		Y	800-366-0066
Voya Strategic Income Opportunities Fund Class A	ISIAX	NAS CM	Open End	Fixed Inc Misc (Income)	D+	D	C-	Down	Y	800-366-0066
Voya Strategic Income Opportunities Fund Class C	ISICX	NAS CM	Open End	Fixed Inc Misc (Income)	D+	D	C-	Down	Y	800-366-0066
Voya Strategic Income Opportunities Fund Class I	IISIX	NAS CM	Open End	Fixed Inc Misc (Income)	D+	D+	C-	Down	Y	800-366-0066
Voya Strategic Income Opportunities Fund Class P	VSTPX	NAS CM	Open End	Fixed Inc Misc (Income)	C-	D+	C	Down	Y	800-366-0066
Voya Strategic Income Opportunities Fund Class P3	VSIOX	NAS CM	Open End	Fixed Inc Misc (Income)	C-	D+	C		Y	800-366-0066
Voya Strategic Income Opportunities Fund Class R	ISIRX	NAS CM	Open End	Fixed Inc Misc (Income)	D+	D	C-	Down	Y	800-366-0066
Voya Strategic Income Opportunities Fund Class R6	VSIRX	NAS CM	Open End	Fixed Inc Misc (Income)	D+	D+	C-	Down	Y	800-366-0066
Voya Strategic Income Opportunities Fund Class W	ISIWX	NAS CM	Open End	Fixed Inc Misc (Income)	D+	D+	C-	Down	Y	800-366-0066
Voya U.S. Bond Index Portfolio Class A	ILUAX	NAS CM	Open End	US Fixed Inc (Corp Bond - General)	B-	B-	B		Y	800-366-0066
Voya U.S. Bond Index Portfolio Class I	ILBAX	NAS CM	Open End	US Fixed Inc (Corp Bond - General)	B	B-	B+	Up	Y	800-366-0066
Voya U.S. Bond Index Portfolio Class P2	VPUPX	NAS CM	Open End	US Fixed Inc (Corp Bond - General)	B	B-	B+		Y	800-366-0066
Voya U.S. Bond Index Portfolio Class S	ILABX	NAS CM	Open End	US Fixed Inc (Corp Bond - General)	B	B-	B	Up	Y	800-366-0066
Voya U.S. Bond Index Portfolio Class S2	IUSBX	NAS CM	Open End	US Fixed Inc (Corp Bond - General)	B	B-	B	Up	Y	800-366-0066
VY® BlackRock Inflation Protected Bond Portfolio Class A	IBRAX	NAS CM	Open End	US Fixed Inc (Income)	B-	C	B+	Up	Y	800-366-0066
VY® BlackRock Inflation Protected Bond Portfolio Class I	IBRIX	NAS CM	Open End	US Fixed Inc (Income)	B	C+	B+	Up	Y	800-366-0066
VY® BlackRock Inflation Protected Bond Portfolio Class S	IBRSX	NAS CM	Open End	US Fixed Inc (Income)	B-	C+	B+	Up	Y	800-366-0066
VY® BrandywineGLOBAL - Bond Portfolio	VGSBX	NAS CM	Open End	US Fixed Inc (Growth & Income)	B	B	B	Up	Y	800-366-0066
Wasatch-Hoisington U.S. Treasury Fund	WHOSX	NAS CM	Open End	US Fixed Inc (Govt Bond - Treasury)	B	B	B		Y	800-551-1700
Wasmer Schroeder High Yield Muni Fund Institutional Class	WSHYX	NAS CM	Open End	US Muni Fixed Inc (Muni Bond - Natl)	D+	D+	C-	Down	Y	216-622-0000
Wavelength Interest Rate Neutral Fund	WAVLX	NAS CM	Open End	Fixed Inc Misc (Income)	C	C-	B		Y	
Weitz Core Plus Income Fund Institutional Class	WCPBX	NAS CM	Open End	US Fixed Inc (Multisector Bond)	B-	C	B+	Up	Y	800-304-9745
Weitz Core Plus Income Fund Investor Class	WCPNX	NAS CM	Open End	US Fixed Inc (Multisector Bond)	B-	C	B	Up	Y	800-304-9745
Weitz Nebraska Tax-Free Income Fund	WNTFX	NAS CM	Open End	US Muni Fixed Inc (Muni Bond - Single State)	C	C	B-		Y	800-304-9745
Weitz Short Duration Income Fund Institutional Class	WEFIX	NAS CM	Open End	US Fixed Inc (Multisector Bond)	C	C-	C+		Y	800-304-9745
Weitz Short Duration Income Fund Investor Class	WSHNX	NAS CM	Open End	US Fixed Inc (Multisector Bond)	C	C-	C+		Y	800-304-9745
Weitz Ultra Short Government Fund Institutional Class	SAFEX	NAS CM	Open End	US Fixed Inc (Govt Bond - General)	C	C-	B-			800-304-9745
Wells Fargo 100% Treasury Money Market Fund - Class A	WFTXX	NAS CM	Money Mkt	US Money Mkt (Money Mkt - Treasury)	C	C-	C		Y	800-222-8222
Wells Fargo 100% Treasury Money Market Fund - Class Admin	WTRXX	NAS CM	Money Mkt	US Money Mkt (Money Mkt - Treasury)	C	C	C+		Y	800-222-8222
Wells Fargo 100% Treasury Money Market Fund - Class Inst	WOTXX	NAS CM	Money Mkt	US Money Mkt (Money Mkt - Treasury)	C	C-	C+		Y	800-222-8222
Wells Fargo 100% Treasury Money Market Fund - Class Svc	NWTXX	NAS CM	Money Mkt	US Money Mkt (Money Mkt - Treasury)	C	C-	C+		Y	800-222-8222
Wells Fargo 100% Treasury Money Market Fund - Class Swp			Money Mkt	US Money Mkt (Money Mkt - Treasury)	C	C-	C		Y	800-222-8222
Wells Fargo Adjustable Rate Government Fund - Class A	ESAAX	NAS CM	Open End	US Fixed Inc (Govt Bond - ARM)	C	C-	C+		Y	800-222-8222
Wells Fargo Adjustable Rate Government Fund - Class Admin	ESADX	NAS CM	Open End	US Fixed Inc (Govt Bond - ARM)	C	C-	C+		Y	800-222-8222
Wells Fargo Adjustable Rate Government Fund - Class C	ESACX	NAS CM	Open End	US Fixed Inc (Govt Bond - ARM)	C	C-	C		Y	800-222-8222
Wells Fargo Adjustable Rate Government Fund - Class Inst	EKIZX	NAS CM	Open End	US Fixed Inc (Govt Bond - ARM)	C	C-	C+		Y	800-222-8222
Wells Fargo Calif Limited-Term Tax-Free - Administrator Cl	SCTIX	NAS CM	Open End	US Muni Fixed Inc (Income)	C	C-	C+		Y	800-222-8222
Wells Fargo California Limited-Term Tax-Free - Cl A	SFCIX	NAS CM	Open End	US Muni Fixed Inc (Income)	C	C-	C		Y	800-222-8222
Wells Fargo California Limited-Term Tax-Free - Cl C	SFCCX	NAS CM	Open End	US Muni Fixed Inc (Income)	C-	D+	C	Down	Y	800-222-8222
Wells Fargo California Limited-Term Tax-Free - Inst Cl	SFCNX	NAS CM	Open End	US Muni Fixed Inc (Income)	C	C-	C+		Y	800-222-8222
Wells Fargo California Tax-Free Fund - Class A	SCTAX	NAS CM	Open End	US Muni Fixed Inc (Income)	C	C-	B-		Y	800-222-8222
Wells Fargo California Tax-Free Fund - Class Admin	SGCAX	NAS CM	Open End	US Muni Fixed Inc (Income)	C	C-	B-		Y	800-222-8222
Wells Fargo California Tax-Free Fund - Class C	SCTCX	NAS CM	Open End	US Muni Fixed Inc (Income)	C	C-	C+		Y	800-222-8222
Wells Fargo California Tax-Free Fund - Class Inst	SGTIX	NAS CM	Open End	US Muni Fixed Inc (Income)	C	C-	B-		Y	800-222-8222
Wells Fargo Cash Investment Money Market Fund - Class Inst	WFIXX	NAS CM	Money Mkt	US Money Mkt (Money Mkt - Taxable)	C	C-	C+		Y	800-222-8222
Wells Fargo Cash Investment Money Mkt Fund - Class Select	WFQXX	NAS CM	Money Mkt	US Money Mkt (Money Mkt - Taxable)	C	C-	C+		Y	800-222-8222
Wells Fargo Cash Investment Money Market Fund - Class Svc	NWIXX	NAS CM	Money Mkt	US Money Mkt (Money Mkt - Taxable)	C	C-	C+		Y	800-222-8222
Wells Fargo Cash Investment Money Market Fund -Admin	WFAXX	NAS CM	Money Mkt	US Money Mkt (Money Mkt - Taxable)	C	C-	C+		Y	800-222-8222
Wells Fargo Conservative Income Fund - Class Inst	WCIIX	NAS CM	Open End	US Fixed Inc (Income)	C	C-	B-		Y	800-222-8222
Wells Fargo Core Bond Fund - Class A	MBFAX	NAS CM	Open End	US Fixed Inc (Corp Bond - General)	B	B-	B	Up	Y	800-222-8222

★Expanded analysis of this fund is included in Section II.

TOTAL RETURNS & PERFORMANCE									ASSETS		ASSET ALLOCATION & TURNOVER							MINIMUMS		FEES		
3-Month Total Return	6-Month Total Return	1-Year Total Return	3-Year Total Return	5-Year Total Return	Dividend Yield (TTM)	Expense Ratio	3-Yr Std Deviation	Effective Duration	NAV	Total Assets (MIL)	%Cash	%Government Bonds	%Municipal Bonds	%Corporate Bonds	%Other	Turnover Ratio	Average Coupon Rate	Min Initial Investment	Min Additional Investment	Front End Fee (%)	Back End Fee (%)	Inception Date
4.01	1.21	2.43	6.20	8.11	1.91	0.9	2.84	1.78	9.91	177.0	-9	27	0	34	0	192	3.16	0				Jul-14
4.17	1.49	3.02	7.82	10.83	2.49	0.3	2.8	1.78	9.89	177.0	-9	27	0	34	0	192	3.16	1,000,000				Jul-13
4.14	1.25	2.84	7.67	10.73	2.41	0.4	2.89	1.78	9.91	177.0	-9	27	0	34	0	192	3.16	1,000				Dec-12
6.64	-4.74	-2.91	6.13	14.59	4.08	0.94	7.06	3.50	9.63	2,613	6	7	0	25	0	167	4.14	1,000		2.50		Nov-12
6.31	-5.19	-3.73	3.79	10.48	3.28	1.69	7.05	3.50	9.49	2,613	6	7	0	25	0	167	4.14	1,000			1.00	Nov-12
6.59	-4.74	-2.74	7.21	17.03	4.45	0.61	7.1	3.50	9.66	2,613	6	7	0	25	0	167	4.14	250,000				Nov-12
6.76	-4.40	-2.21	7.89	17.77	5.06	0.08	7.05	3.50	9.62	2,613	6	7	0	25	0	167	4.14	0				Feb-19
6.83	-4.33	-2.21	7.79	17.67		0	7.04	3.50	9.68	2,613	6	7	0	25	0	167	4.14	0				Aug-19
6.51	-4.91	-3.20	5.29	13.36	3.81	1.19	7.06	3.50	9.55	2,613	6	7	0	25	0	167	4.14	0				Nov-12
6.63	-4.63	-2.70	7.23	16.99	4.52	0.58	7.1	3.50	9.63	2,613	6	7	0	25	0	167	4.14	1,000,000				Oct-15
6.60	-4.73	-2.69	7.01	15.81	4.34	0.69	7.08	3.50	9.6	2,613	6	7	0	25	0	167	4.14	1,000				Nov-12
2.40	5.80	7.95	13.90	18.78	1.99	0.88	3.21	5.80	11.36	3,084	15	37	1	22	0	222	2.73	0				Mar-08
2.61	6.03	8.46	15.68	21.89	2.47	0.38	3.22	5.80	11.41	3,084	15	37	1	22	0	222	2.73	0				Mar-08
2.67	6.16	8.73	16.54	22.83	2.72	0.15	3.22	5.80	11.41	3,084	15	37	1	22	0	222	2.73	0				May-17
2.46	5.92	8.11	14.74	20.34	2.23	0.63	3.22	5.80	11.37	3,084	15	37	1	22	0	222	2.73	0				Mar-08
2.52	5.84	8.05	14.22	19.46	2.08	0.78	3.24	5.80	11.38	3,084	15	37	1	22	0	222	2.73	0				Feb-09
6.03	5.36	7.40	12.51	13.85	1.28	1.19	3.95	7.69	9.85	275.3	-4	71	0	22	0	72	1.82	0				Apr-07
6.16	5.57	7.98	14.61	17.31	1.66	0.59	3.87	7.69	10.23	275.3	-4	71	0	22	0	72	1.82	0				Apr-07
6.04	5.45	7.73	13.70	15.87	1.41	0.84	3.87	7.69	10.15	275.3	-4	71	0	22	0	72	1.82	0				Apr-07
7.60	9.03	12.01	18.72	26.21	1.76	0.58	4	7.73	11.46	291.5	9	21	0	64	0	449	3.68	0				Feb-15
-1.33	24.47	30.48	45.65	63.53	1.5	0.69	15.12	21.93	22.47	458.5	2	98	0	0	0	29	2.52	2,000	100			Dec-86
1.53	-5.85	-3.08	6.85	18.93	3.6	0.75	7.07	6.08	10.18	68.3	7	0	93	0	0	27	4.99	10,000	500			Mar-14
7.19	1.38	4.45	16.07	23.07	2.2	1.28	5.71	5.51	10.46	74.1	15	56	7	18	1	20	3.58	100,000	100			Sep-13
8.49	5.25	7.60	16.05	26.00	2.88	0.4	4.95	4.63	10.77	108.6	1	18	0	36	0	51	3.64	1,000,000	25			Jul-14
8.56	5.17	7.41	15.42	24.81	2.71	0.5	4.98	4.63	10.77	108.6	1	18	0	36	0	51	3.64	2,500	25			Jul-14
1.83	2.22	3.20	7.13	8.84	1.29	0.45	2.22	3.40	10.21	32.5	5	0	95	0	0	7	3.70	2,500	25			Dec-06
3.79	1.56	2.97	7.62	12.06	2.42	0.48	2.46	1.58	12.32	738.0	3	18	0	20	0	51	2.91	1,000,000	25			Dec-88
3.78	1.51	2.81	7.02	10.90	2.24	0.55	2.44	1.58	12.3	738.0	3	18	0	20	0	51	2.91	2,500	25			Aug-11
0.20	0.95	1.92	5.76	6.16	1.96	0.2	0.27	0.40	10.02	69.9	34	50	0	3	0	46	1.86	1,000,000	25			Aug-91
0.00	0.21	0.90	3.32	3.38	1.05	0.6	0.17		1	22,129	71	29	0	0	0			1,000	100			Dec-90
0.01	0.29	1.14	4.24	4.49	1.31	0.3	0.17		1	22,129	71	29	0	0	0			1,000,000				Jun-10
0.02	0.34	1.23	4.54	4.96	1.41	0.2	0.17		1	22,129	71	29	0	0	0			10,000,000				Oct-14
0.00	0.23	0.97	3.65	3.76	1.13	0.5	0.17		1	22,129	71	29	0	0	0			100,000				Dec-90
0.00	0.17	0.77	2.76	2.77	0.9	0.78	0.16		1	22,129	71	29	0	0	0			0				Jun-10
1.23	0.28	1.31	4.66	4.58	2.11	0.74	1.18	1.25	8.91	304.1	7	1	0	0	0	5	3.57	1,000	100	2.00		Jun-00
1.26	0.35	1.45	5.09	5.31	2.25	0.6	1.18	1.25	8.91	304.1	7	1	0	0	0	5	3.57	1,000,000				Jul-10
1.16	-0.08	0.66	2.22	0.63	1.35	1.49	1.26	1.25	8.9	304.1	7	1	0	0	0	5	3.57	1,000	100		1.00	Jun-00
1.30	0.42	1.59	5.53	6.06	2.39	0.46	1.17	1.25	8.91	304.1	7	1	0	0	0	5	3.57	1,000,000				Oct-91
1.93	0.41	1.48	5.32	8.99	1.99	0.6	2.5	2.70	10.55	532.1	1	0	99	0	0	11	4.39	1,000,000				Sep-96
1.86	0.32	1.29	4.71	7.83	1.79	0.8	2.51	2.70	10.71	532.1	1	0	99	0	0	11	4.39	1,000	100	2.00		Nov-92
1.67	-0.04	0.53	2.38	3.86	1.03	1.55	2.48	2.70	10.71	532.1	1	0	99	0	0	11	4.39	1,000	100		1.00	Aug-02
1.95	0.46	1.58	5.64	9.44	2.1	0.5	2.46	2.70	10.54	532.1	1	0	99	0	0	11	4.39	1,000,000				Oct-14
2.27	0.83	2.91	10.45	17.93	2.96	0.75	4.25	6.05	11.91	1,113	0	0	100	0	0	9	4.71	1,000	100	4.50		Oct-88
2.31	0.84	3.03	11.01	19.01	3.16	0.55	4.27	6.05	11.93	1,113	0	0	100	0	0	9	4.71	1,000,000				Dec-97
2.05	0.38	2.06	7.90	13.48	2.2	1.5	4.28	6.05	12.14	1,113	0	0	100	0	0	9	4.71	1,000	100		1.00	Jul-93
2.25	0.88	3.11	11.25	19.43	3.23	0.48	4.26	6.05	11.93	1,113	0	0	100	0	0	9	4.71	1,000,000				Oct-14
0.23	0.54	1.55	5.43	6.40	1.68	0.2	0.16		1.0009	2,026	67	9	12	12	0	0		10,000,000				Oct-87
0.24	0.58	1.61	5.65	6.78	1.75	0.13	0.16		1.001	2,026	67	9	12	12	0	0		50,000,000				Jun-07
0.15	0.41	1.26	4.49	4.95	1.38	0.45	0.16		1.001	2,026	67	9	12	12	0	0		100,000				Oct-87
0.19	0.48	1.42	5.02	5.73	1.55	0.33	0.16		1.0009	2,026	67	9	12	12	0	0		1,000,000				Jul-03
2.19	1.24	2.43	6.75	8.72	2.12	0.27	1.21	0.54	10.04	383.3	19	0	3	49	0	171	2.19	1,000,000				May-13
4.20	6.43	8.73	15.44	21.54	1.84	0.78	3.44	5.94	14.29	5,456	2	14	0	29	0	577	3.29	1,000	100	4.50		Oct-01

	MARKET			FUND TYPE, CATEGORY & OBJECTIVE	RATINGS				NEW INVESTORS	
Fund Name	Ticker Symbol	Traded On	Fund Type	Category and (Prospectus Objective)	Overall Rating	Reward Rating	Risk Rating	Recent Up/ Downgrade	Open to New Investors	Telephone
Wells Fargo Core Bond Fund - Class Admin	MNTRX	NAS CM	Open End	US Fixed Inc (Corp Bond - General)	B	B-	B	Up	Y	800-222-8222
Wells Fargo Core Bond Fund - Class C	MBFCX	NAS CM	Open End	US Fixed Inc (Corp Bond - General)	B-	C+	B	Up	Y	800-222-8222
Wells Fargo Core Bond Fund - Class Inst	MBFIX	NAS CM	Open End	US Fixed Inc (Corp Bond - General)	B	B-	B+	Up	Y	800-222-8222
Wells Fargo Core Bond Fund - Class R	WTRRX	NAS CM	Open End	US Fixed Inc (Corp Bond - General)	B	B-	B	Up	Y	800-222-8222
Wells Fargo Core Bond Fund - Class R4	MBFRX	NAS CM	Open End	US Fixed Inc (Corp Bond - General)	B	B-	B+	Up	Y	800-222-8222
Wells Fargo Core Bond Fund - Class R6	WTRIX	NAS CM	Open End	US Fixed Inc (Corp Bond - General)	B	B-	B+	Up	Y	800-222-8222
Wells Fargo Core Plus Bond Fund Class A	STYAX	NAS CM	Open End	US Fixed Inc (Multisector Bond)	B	C+	B+	Up	Y	800-222-8222
Wells Fargo Core Plus Bond Fund Class Admin	WIPDX	NAS CM	Open End	US Fixed Inc (Multisector Bond)	B	C+	B+	Up	Y	800-222-8222
Wells Fargo Core Plus Bond Fund Class C	WFIPX	NAS CM	Open End	US Fixed Inc (Multisector Bond)	B-	C+	B+	Up	Y	800-222-8222
Wells Fargo Core Plus Bond Fund Class Institutional	WIPIX	NAS CM	Open End	US Fixed Inc (Multisector Bond)	B	C+	B+	Up	Y	800-222-8222
Wells Fargo Core Plus Bond Fund Class R6	STYJX	NAS CM	Open End	US Fixed Inc (Multisector Bond)	B	C+	B+	Up	Y	800-222-8222
Wells Fargo CoreBuilder Shares Series M	WFCMX	NAS CM	Open End	US Muni Fixed Inc (Muni Bond - Natl)	C	C-	B-	Down	Y	800-222-8222
Wells Fargo Emerging Markets Bond Fund	WBEMX	NAS CM	Open End	Emerg Mkts Fixed Inc (Growth & Income)	D+	D	C-	Down	Y	800-222-8222
Wells Fargo Global Investment Grade Credit Fund Class R6	WGCRX	NAS CM	Open End	Global Fixed Inc (Growth & Income)	D	D+	C+		Y	800-222-8222
Wells Fargo Global Inv Grade Credit Inst Cl	WGCIX	NAS CM	Open End	Global Fixed Inc (Growth & Income)	D	D+	C+			800-222-8222
★ Wells Fargo Government Money Market Fund - Class A	WFGXX	NAS CM	Money Mkt	US Money Mkt (Money Mkt - Govt)	C	C-	C+		Y	800-222-8222
Wells Fargo Government Money Market Fund - Class Admin	WGAXX	NAS CM	Money Mkt	US Money Mkt (Money Mkt - Govt)	C	C-	C+		Y	800-222-8222
Wells Fargo Government Money Market Fund - Class Inst	GVIXX	NAS CM	Money Mkt	US Money Mkt (Money Mkt - Govt)	C	C-	C+		Y	800-222-8222
Wells Fargo Government Money Market Fund - Class Select	WFFXX	NAS CM	Money Mkt	US Money Mkt (Money Mkt - Govt)	C	C-	C+		Y	800-222-8222
Wells Fargo Government Money Market Fund - Class Svc	NWGXX	NAS CM	Money Mkt	US Money Mkt (Money Mkt - Govt)	C	C-	C+		Y	800-222-8222
Wells Fargo Government Securities Fund - Class A	SGVDX	NAS CM	Open End	US Fixed Inc (Govt Bond - General)	B	B-	B	Up	Y	800-222-8222
Wells Fargo Government Securities Fund - Class Admin	WGSDX	NAS CM	Open End	US Fixed Inc (Govt Bond - General)	B	B-	B+	Up	Y	800-222-8222
Wells Fargo Government Securities Fund - Class C	WGSCX	NAS CM	Open End	US Fixed Inc (Govt Bond - General)	B-	C+	B		Y	800-222-8222
Wells Fargo Government Securities Fund - Class Inst	SGVIX	NAS CM	Open End	US Fixed Inc (Govt Bond - General)	B	B-	B+		Y	800-222-8222
Wells Fargo Heritage Money Market Fund - Class Inst	SHIXX	NAS CM	Money Mkt	US Money Mkt (Money Mkt - Taxable)	C	C	C+		Y	800-222-8222
Wells Fargo Heritage Money Market Fund - Class Select	WFJXX	NAS CM	Money Mkt	US Money Mkt (Money Mkt - Taxable)	C	C-	C+		Y	800-222-8222
Wells Fargo Heritage Money Market Fund - Class Svc	WHTXX	NAS CM	Money Mkt	US Money Mkt (Money Mkt - Taxable)	C	C-	C+		Y	800-222-8222
Wells Fargo Heritage Money Market Fund -Admin	SHMXX	NAS CM	Money Mkt	US Money Mkt (Money Mkt - Taxable)	C	C-	C+		Y	800-222-8222
Wells Fargo High Yield Bond Fund - Class A	EKHAX	NAS CM	Open End	US Fixed Inc (Corp Bond - High Yield)	C-	D+	C	Down	Y	800-222-8222
Wells Fargo High Yield Bond Fund - Class Admin	EKHYX	NAS CM	Open End	US Fixed Inc (Corp Bond - High Yield)	C-	D+	C	Down	Y	800-222-8222
Wells Fargo High Yield Bond Fund - Class C	EKHCX	NAS CM	Open End	US Fixed Inc (Corp Bond - High Yield)	C-	D+	C		Y	800-222-8222
Wells Fargo High Yield Bond Fund - Class Inst	EKHIX	NAS CM	Open End	US Fixed Inc (Corp Bond - High Yield)	C	C-	C		Y	800-222-8222
Wells Fargo High Yield Corporate Bond Fund	WYCBX	NAS CM	Open End	US Fixed Inc (Corp Bond - High Yield)	D+	D	C-	Down	Y	800-222-8222
Wells Fargo High Yield Municipal Bond Fund - Class A	WHYMX	NAS CM	Open End	US Muni Fixed Inc (Muni Bond - Natl)	C-	D+	C	Down	Y	800-222-8222
Wells Fargo High Yield Municipal Bond Fund - Class Admin	WHYDX	NAS CM	Open End	US Muni Fixed Inc (Muni Bond - Natl)	C-	D+	C	Down	Y	800-222-8222
Wells Fargo High Yield Municipal Bond Fund - Class C	WHYCX	NAS CM	Open End	US Muni Fixed Inc (Muni Bond - Natl)	C-	D+	C	Down	Y	800-222-8222
Wells Fargo High Yield Municipal Bond Fund - Class Inst	WHYIX	NAS CM	Open End	US Muni Fixed Inc (Muni Bond - Natl)	C-	D+	C	Down	Y	800-222-8222
Wells Fargo High Yield Municipal Bond Fund - Class R6	EKHRX	NAS CM	Open End	US Muni Fixed Inc (Muni Bond - Natl)	C-	D+	C	Down	Y	800-222-8222
Wells Fargo Income Opportunities Fund	EAD	AMEX	Closed End	US Fixed Inc (Corp Bond - High Yield)	D+	D+	C-	Down	Y	877-709-8009
Wells Fargo Intermediate Tax/AMT-Free Fund - Class A	WFTAX	NAS CM	Open End	US Muni Fixed Inc (Muni Bond - Natl)	C	C-	B-		Y	800-222-8222
Wells Fargo Intermediate Tax/AMT-Free Fund - Class Admin	WFITX	NAS CM	Open End	US Muni Fixed Inc (Muni Bond - Natl)	C	C-	B-		Y	800-222-8222
Wells Fargo Intermediate Tax/AMT-Free Fund - Class C	WFTFX	NAS CM	Open End	US Muni Fixed Inc (Muni Bond - Natl)	C	C-	C+		Y	800-222-8222
Wells Fargo Intermediate Tax/AMT-Free Fund - Class Inst	WITIX	NAS CM	Open End	US Muni Fixed Inc (Muni Bond - Natl)	C	C	B-		Y	800-222-8222
Wells Fargo Intermediate Tax/AMT-Free Fund - Class R6	WFRTX	NAS CM	Open End	US Muni Fixed Inc (Muni Bond - Natl)	C	C	B-		Y	800-222-8222
Wells Fargo International Bond Fund - Class A	ESIYX	NAS CM	Open End	Global Fixed Inc (Worldwide Bond)	C	C-	C		Y	800-222-8222
Wells Fargo International Bond Fund - Class Admin	ESIDX	NAS CM	Open End	Global Fixed Inc (Worldwide Bond)	C	C-	C		Y	800-222-8222
Wells Fargo International Bond Fund - Class C	ESIVX	NAS CM	Open End	Global Fixed Inc (Worldwide Bond)	C	C-	C	Up	Y	800-222-8222
Wells Fargo International Bond Fund - Class Inst	ESICX	NAS CM	Open End	Global Fixed Inc (Worldwide Bond)	C	C-	C		Y	800-222-8222
Wells Fargo International Bond Fund - Class R6	ESIRX	NAS CM	Open End	Global Fixed Inc (Worldwide Bond)	C	C-	C		Y	800-222-8222
Wells Fargo International Government Bond Fund	WIGBX	NAS CM	Open End	Global Fixed Inc (Govt Bond - General)	C-	C-	C	Down	Y	800-222-8222
Wells Fargo Minnesota Tax-Free Fund - Class A	NMTFX	NAS CM	Open End	US Muni Fixed Inc (Muni Bond - Single State)	C	C-	B-		Y	800-222-8222
Wells Fargo Minnesota Tax-Free Fund - Class Admin	NWMIX	NAS CM	Open End	US Muni Fixed Inc (Muni Bond - Single State)	C	C	B-		Y	800-222-8222

★ Expanded analysis of this fund is included in Section II.

TOTAL RETURNS & PERFORMANCE									ASSETS		ASSET ALLOCATION & TURNOVER							MINIMUMS		FEES		
3-Month Total Return	6-Month Total Return	1-Year Total Return	3-Year Total Return	5-Year Total Return	Dividend Yield (TTM)	Expense Ratio	3-Yr Std Deviation	Effective Duration	NAV	Total Assets (MIL)	%Cash	%Government Bonds	%Municipal Bonds	%Corporate Bonds	%Other	Turnover Ratio	Average Coupon Rate	Min Initial Investment	Min Additional Investment	Front End Fee (%)	Back End Fee (%)	Inception Date
4.16	6.46	8.83	15.69	21.96	1.91	0.7	3.42	5.94	13.95	5,456	2	14	0	29	0	577	3.29	1,000,000				Jun-97
3.97	6.02	7.91	12.81	17.02	1.11	1.53	3.44	5.94	14.15	5,456	2	14	0	29	0	577	3.29	1,000	100		1.00	Oct-01
4.23	6.61	9.05	16.67	23.69	2.18	0.42	3.39	5.94	13.93	5,456	2	14	0	29	0	577	3.29	1,000,000				Oct-01
4.11	6.25	8.43	14.51	19.92	1.61	1.03	3.45	5.94	13.94	5,456	2	14	0	29	0	577	3.29	0				Jul-10
4.21	6.56	8.94	16.41	23.16	2.08	0.52	3.41	5.94	13.94	5,456	2	14	0	29	0	577	3.29	0				Nov-12
4.25	6.56	9.11	16.85	24.00	2.23	0.37	3.4	5.94	13.93	5,456	2	14	0	29	0	577	3.29	0				Nov-12
6.78	6.01	8.64	16.88	28.47	2.62	0.74	4	6.12	13.49	1,108	9	30	1	32	0	89	3.77	1,000	100	4.50		Jul-98
6.82	6.07	8.77	17.27	29.21	2.73	0.63	3.99	6.12	13.47	1,108	9	30	1	32	0	89	3.77	1,000,000				Jul-10
6.51	5.59	7.76	14.30	23.75	1.91	1.49	3.97	6.12	13.48	1,108	9	30	1	32	0	89	3.77	1,000	100		1.00	Jul-98
6.85	6.24	9.06	18.08	30.52	2.92	0.41	3.98	6.12	13.51	1,108	9	30	1	32	0	89	3.77	1,000,000				Jul-08
6.87	6.18	9.02	18.25	30.28	2.97	0.36	3.99	6.12	13.51	1,108	9	30	1	32	0	89	3.77	0				Oct-16
2.66	0.00	2.53	14.72	23.36	3.34	0	4.72	5.44	12.16	822.9	1	0	99	0	0	7	4.50	0				Apr-08
11.61	-3.22	-0.69			5.77	0		7.31	8.95	0.96	3	89	0	8	0	36	5.39	0				Aug-17
8.83	3.54	6.95			3.41	0.45		7.03	10.8	66.9	25	2	0	71	0	36	3.36	0				Feb-19
8.80	3.60	6.88			3.37	0.5		7.03	10.8	66.9	25	2	0	71	0	36	3.36	1,000,000				Feb-19
0.00	0.21	0.93	3.43	3.52	1.08	0.6	0.17		1	132,598	59	37	1	2	0			1,000	100			Nov-99
0.00	0.27	1.13	4.19	4.49	1.3	0.34	0.18		1	132,598	59	37	1	2	0			1,000,000				Jul-03
0.03	0.33	1.25	4.61	5.13	1.43	0.2	0.18		1	132,598	59	37	1	2	0			10,000,000				Jul-03
0.03	0.35	1.30	4.79	5.42	1.49	0.14	0.18		1	132,598	59	37	1	2	0			50,000,000				Jun-15
0.00	0.23	1.00	3.72	3.87	1.16	0.5	0.17		1	132,598	59	37	1	2	0			100,000				Nov-87
1.05	5.92	7.49	13.39	17.21	1.88	0.85	3.08	4.72	11.67	686.9	9	40	1	0	0	178	3.67	1,000	100	4.50		Aug-99
1.10	5.93	7.63	14.01	18.35	2.09	0.64	3.02	4.72	11.66	686.9	9	40	1	0	0	178	3.67	1,000,000				Apr-05
0.78	5.44	6.60	10.78	12.81	1.15	1.6	3.06	4.72	11.66	686.9	9	40	1	0	0	178	3.67	1,000	100		1.00	Dec-02
1.14	6.02	7.89	14.65	19.39	2.24	0.48	3.04	4.72	11.66	686.9	9	40	1	0	0	178	3.67	1,000,000				Aug-99
0.22	0.53	1.54	5.42	6.35	1.69	0.2	0.16		1.0006	10,239	69	11	14	7	0			10,000,000				Mar-00
0.24	0.57	1.62	5.65	6.74	1.77	0.13	0.16		1.0007	10,239	69	11	14	7	0			50,000,000				Jun-07
0.18	0.43	1.31	4.70	5.21	1.46	0.43	0.17		1.0006	10,239	69	11	14	7	0			100,000				Jun-10
0.19	0.47	1.41	5.02	5.70	1.57	0.33	0.16		1.0006	10,239	69	11	14	7	0			1,000,000				Jun-95
7.75	-3.39	0.64	7.14	22.09	4.17	0.93	7.48	3.99	3.2	336.4	1	0	0	99	0	26	5.26	1,000	100	4.50		Jan-98
7.42	-3.33	0.77	7.56	23.01	4.3	0.8	7.38	3.99	3.2	336.4	1	0	0	99	0	26	5.26	1,000,000				Apr-98
7.21	-4.05	-0.41	4.43	17.24	3.4	1.68	7.39	3.99	3.19	336.4	1	0	0	99	0	26	5.26	1,000	100		1.00	Jan-98
7.49	-3.20	0.73	8.41	24.44	4.57	0.53	7.31	3.99	3.2	336.4	1	0	0	99	0	26	5.26	1,000,000				Oct-14
7.86	-7.82	-4.39			6.29	0		3.76	8.64	0.92	2	0	0	98	0	52	5.93	0				Aug-17
2.97	-3.95	-0.90	12.95	23.03	4.3	0.8	6.58	7.31	10.44	79.8	1	0	99	0	0	20	5.19	1,000	100	4.50		Jan-13
2.99	-3.90	-0.89	13.28	23.53	4.41	0.7	6.59	7.31	10.44	79.8	1	0	99	0	0	20	5.19	1,000,000				Jan-13
2.78	-4.31	-1.73	10.45	18.52	3.5	1.55	6.58	7.31	10.44	79.8	1	0	99	0	0	20	5.19	1,000	100		1.00	Jan-13
3.03	-3.83	-0.66	13.78	24.56	4.57	0.55	6.58	7.31	10.44	79.8	1	0	99	0	0	20	5.19	1,000,000				Jan-13
3.04	-3.81	-0.70	13.89	24.68	4.63	0.5	6.59	7.31	10.44	79.8	1	0	99	0	0	20	5.19	0				Aug-18
14.62	-7.35	-3.40	9.42	27.94	8.06		12.47		8.09	492.2	2	0	0	98	0	16	5.56					Feb-03
2.20	1.06	2.70	9.68	14.89	2.19	0.7	3.48	4.34	11.72	2,669	1	0	99	0	0	14	4.47	1,000	100	3.00		Jul-07
2.22	1.11	2.80	10.01	15.45	2.29	0.6	3.45	4.34	11.73	2,669	1	0	99	0	0	14	4.47	1,000,000				Mar-08
2.00	0.69	1.93	7.25	10.67	1.44	1.45	3.47	4.34	11.72	2,669	1	0	99	0	0	14	4.47	1,000	100		1.00	Jul-07
2.25	1.18	2.95	10.59	16.33	2.44	0.45	3.46	4.34	11.74	2,669	1	0	99	0	0	14	4.47	1,000,000				Mar-08
2.35	1.21	3.00	10.37	15.61	2.49	0.4	3.43	4.34	11.74	2,669	1	0	99	0	0	14	4.47	0				Aug-18
5.02	0.37	1.71	5.85	11.36	0	1.03	6.51	6.33	10.66	84.2	14	50	0	8	0	129	3.58	1,000	100	4.50		Sep-03
4.97	0.46	1.89	6.42	12.39	0	0.85	6.49	6.33	10.76	84.2	14	50	0	8	0	129	3.58	1,000,000				Jul-10
4.86	0.09	1.09	3.57	7.41	0	1.78	6.49	6.33	10.13	84.2	14	50	0	8	0	129	3.58	1,000	100		1.00	Sep-03
5.12	0.55	2.06	6.87	13.29	0	0.7	6.49	6.33	10.88	84.2	14	50	0	8	0	129	3.58	1,000,000				Dec-93
5.19	0.64	2.14	7.15	13.57	0	0.65	6.51	6.33	10.93	84.2	14	50	0	8	0	129	3.58	0				Nov-12
3.70	-0.29	1.13			1.27	0		7.82	10.08	1.0	24	76	0	0	0	291	1.95	0				Oct-17
2.20	1.28	2.97	9.43	15.21	2.14	0.85	3.31	4.94	10.86	171.6	0	0	100	0	0	18	4.69	1,000	100	4.50		Jan-88
2.26	1.41	3.32	10.24	16.75	2.39	0.6	3.25	4.94	10.86	171.6	0	0	100	0	0	18	4.69	1,000,000				Aug-93

	MARKET		FUND TYPE, CATEGORY & OBJECTIVE		RATINGS				NEW INVESTORS	
Fund Name	Ticker Symbol	Traded On	Fund Type	Category and (Prospectus Objective)	Overall Rating	Reward Rating	Risk Rating	Recent Up/ Downgrade	Open to New Investors	Telephone
Wells Fargo Minnesota Tax-Free Fund - Class C	WMTCX	NAS CM	Open End	US Muni Fixed Inc (Muni Bond - Single State)	C	C-	C+		Y	800-222-8222
Wells Fargo Minnesota Tax-Free Fund Institutional Class	WMTIX	NAS CM	Open End	US Muni Fixed Inc (Muni Bond - Single State)	C	C	B-		Y	800-222-8222
Wells Fargo Money Market Fund - Class A	STGXX	NAS CM	Money Mkt	US Money Mkt (Money Mkt - Taxable)	C	C-	C+		Y	800-222-8222
Wells Fargo Money Market Fund - Class C			Money Mkt	US Money Mkt (Money Mkt - Taxable)	C	C-	C		Y	800-222-8222
Wells Fargo Money Market Fund - Class Premier	WMPXX	NAS CM	Money Mkt	US Money Mkt (Money Mkt - Taxable)	C	C-	C+		Y	800-222-8222
Wells Fargo Money Market Fund - Class Service	WMOXX	NAS CM	Money Mkt	US Money Mkt (Money Mkt - Taxable)	C	C-	C+		Y	800-222-8222
Wells Fargo Multi-Sector Income Fund	ERC	AMEX	Closed End	US Fixed Inc (Multisector Bond)	D+	D	C-	Down	Y	877-709-8009
Wells Fargo Municipal Bond Fund - Class A	WMFAX	NAS CM	Open End	US Muni Fixed Inc (Muni Bond - Natl)	C	C-	B-		Y	800-222-8222
Wells Fargo Municipal Bond Fund - Class Admin	WMFDX	NAS CM	Open End	US Muni Fixed Inc (Muni Bond - Natl)	C	C-	B-		Y	800-222-8222
Wells Fargo Municipal Bond Fund - Class C	WMFCX	NAS CM	Open End	US Muni Fixed Inc (Muni Bond - Natl)	C	C-	C+		Y	800-222-8222
Wells Fargo Municipal Bond Fund - Class Inst	WMBIX	NAS CM	Open End	US Muni Fixed Inc (Muni Bond - Natl)	C	C-	B-		Y	800-222-8222
Wells Fargo Municipal Bond Fund - Class R6	WMBRX	NAS CM	Open End	US Muni Fixed Inc (Muni Bond - Natl)	C	C-	B-		Y	800-222-8222
Wells Fargo Muni Cash Management Money Mkt - Cl Admin	WUCXX	NAS CM	Money Mkt	US Money Mkt (Money Mkt - Fed Tax Exmpt)	C	C-	C+		Y	800-222-8222
Wells Fargo Muni Cash Management Money Mkt - Cl Inst	EMMXX	NAS CM	Money Mkt	US Money Mkt (Money Mkt - Fed Tax Exmpt)	C	C-	C+		Y	800-222-8222
Wells Fargo Muni Cash Management Money Mkt - Cl Svc	EISXX	NAS CM	Money Mkt	US Money Mkt (Money Mkt - Fed Tax Exmpt)	C	C-	C+		Y	800-222-8222
Wells Fargo Muni Sustainability Fund Administrator Class	WMSDX	NAS CM	Open End	US Muni Fixed Inc (Income)	U	U	U		Y	800-222-8222
Wells Fargo Municipal Sustainability Fund Class A	WMSAX	NAS CM	Open End	US Muni Fixed Inc (Income)	U	U	U		Y	800-222-8222
Wells Fargo Municipal Sustainability Fund Class C	WMSCX	NAS CM	Open End	US Muni Fixed Inc (Income)	U	U	U		Y	800-222-8222
Wells Fargo Municipal Sustainability Fund Class R6	WMSRX	NAS CM	Open End	US Muni Fixed Inc (Income)	U	U	U		Y	800-222-8222
Wells Fargo Muni Sustainability Fund Institutional Class	WMSIX	NAS CM	Open End	US Muni Fixed Inc (Income)	U	U	U		Y	800-222-8222
Wells Fargo National Tax-Free Money Market Fund - Class A	NWMXX	NAS CM	Money Mkt	US Money Mkt (Money Mkt - Fed Tax Exmpt)	C	C-	C		Y	800-222-8222
Wells Fargo Natl Tax-Free Money Mkt Fund - Class Admin	WNTXX	NAS CM	Money Mkt	US Money Mkt (Money Mkt - Fed Tax Exmpt)	C	C-	C		Y	800-222-8222
Wells Fargo Natl Tax-Free Money Mkt Fund - Class Svc	MMIXX	NAS CM	Money Mkt	US Money Mkt (Money Mkt - Fed Tax Exmpt)	C	C-	C+		Y	800-222-8222
Wells Fargo Natl Tax-Free Money Mkt Fund - Premier Class	WFNXX	NAS CM	Money Mkt	US Money Mkt (Money Mkt - Fed Tax Exmpt)	C	C-	C+		Y	800-222-8222
Wells Fargo Pennsylvania Tax-Free Fund - Class A	EKVAX	NAS CM	Open End	US Muni Fixed Inc (Muni Bond - Single State)	C	C-	B-		Y	800-222-8222
Wells Fargo Pennsylvania Tax-Free Fund - Class C	EKVCX	NAS CM	Open End	US Muni Fixed Inc (Muni Bond - Single State)	C	C-	C+		Y	800-222-8222
Wells Fargo Pennsylvania Tax-Free Fund - Class Inst	EKVYX	NAS CM	Open End	US Muni Fixed Inc (Muni Bond - Single State)	C	C	B-		Y	800-222-8222
Wells Fargo Real Return Fund - Class A	IPBAX	NAS CM	Open End	US Fixed Inc (Corp Bond - High Quality)	C+	C	B	Up	Y	800-222-8222
Wells Fargo Real Return Fund - Class Admin	IPBIX	NAS CM	Open End	US Fixed Inc (Corp Bond - High Quality)	C+	C	B	Up	Y	800-222-8222
Wells Fargo Real Return Fund - Class C	IPBCX	NAS CM	Open End	US Fixed Inc (Corp Bond - High Quality)	C	C	B-		Y	800-222-8222
Wells Fargo Real Return Fund - Institutional Class	IPBNX	NAS CM	Open End	US Fixed Inc (Corp Bond - High Quality)	C+	C	B	Up	Y	800-222-8222
Wells Fargo Real Return Fund Class R6	IPBJX	NAS CM	Open End	US Fixed Inc (Corp Bond - High Quality)	C+	C	B	Up	Y	800-222-8222
Wells Fargo Short Duration Government Bond Fund - Class A	MSDAX	NAS CM	Open End	US Fixed Inc (Govt Bond - General)	C+	C	B	Up	Y	800-222-8222
Wells Fargo Short Duration Govt Bond Fund - Class Admin	MNSGX	NAS CM	Open End	US Fixed Inc (Govt Bond - General)	C+	C	B	Up	Y	800-222-8222
Wells Fargo Short Duration Government Bond Fund - Class C	MSDCX	NAS CM	Open End	US Fixed Inc (Govt Bond - General)	C	C	B-		Y	800-222-8222
Wells Fargo Short Duration Govt Bond Fund - Class Inst	WSGIX	NAS CM	Open End	US Fixed Inc (Govt Bond - General)	C+	C	B	Up	Y	800-222-8222
Wells Fargo Short Duration Government Bond Fund - Class R6	MSDRX	NAS CM	Open End	US Fixed Inc (Govt Bond - General)	C+	C	B		Y	800-222-8222
Wells Fargo Short-Term Bond Fund - Class A	SSTVX	NAS CM	Open End	US Fixed Inc (Corp Bond - General)	C	C	B-		Y	800-222-8222
Wells Fargo Short-Term Bond Fund - Class C	WFSHX	NAS CM	Open End	US Fixed Inc (Corp Bond - General)	C	C	C+		Y	800-222-8222
Wells Fargo Short-Term Bond Fund - Class Inst	SSHIX	NAS CM	Open End	US Fixed Inc (Corp Bond - General)	C	C	B-		Y	800-222-8222
Wells Fargo Short-Term Bond Fund - Class R6	SSTYX	NAS CM	Open End	US Fixed Inc (Corp Bond - General)	C	C	B-		Y	800-222-8222
Wells Fargo Short-Term High Yield Bond Fund - Class A	SSTHX	NAS CM	Open End	US Fixed Inc (Corp Bond - High Yield)	C	C-	C	Up	Y	800-222-8222
Wells Fargo Short-Term High Yield Bond Fund - Class Admin	WDHYX	NAS CM	Open End	US Fixed Inc (Corp Bond - High Yield)	C	C-	C	Up	Y	800-222-8222
Wells Fargo Short-Term High Yield Bond Fund - Class C	WFHYX	NAS CM	Open End	US Fixed Inc (Corp Bond - High Yield)	C-	D+	C		Y	800-222-8222
Wells Fargo Short-Term High Yield Bond Fund - Class Inst	STYIX	NAS CM	Open End	US Fixed Inc (Corp Bond - High Yield)	C	C-	C		Y	800-222-8222
Wells Fargo Short-Term Municipal Bond Fund - Class A	WSMAX	NAS CM	Open End	US Muni Fixed Inc (Muni Bond - Natl)	C	C-	C+		Y	800-222-8222
Wells Fargo Short-Term Municipal Bond Fund - Class Admin	WSTMX	NAS CM	Open End	US Muni Fixed Inc (Muni Bond - Natl)	C	C-	C+		Y	800-222-8222
Wells Fargo Short-Term Municipal Bond Fund - Class C	WSSCX	NAS CM	Open End	US Muni Fixed Inc (Muni Bond - Natl)	C	C-	C		Y	800-222-8222
Wells Fargo Short-Term Municipal Bond Fund - Class Inst	WSBIX	NAS CM	Open End	US Muni Fixed Inc (Muni Bond - Natl)	C	C-	C+		Y	800-222-8222
Wells Fargo Short-Term Municipal Bond Fund -Class R6	WSSRX	NAS CM	Open End	US Muni Fixed Inc (Muni Bond - Natl)	C	C-	C+		Y	800-222-8222
Wells Fargo Strategic Income Fund - Class A	WSIAX	NAS CM	Open End	Fixed Inc Misc (Income)	C-	D+	C	Down	Y	800-222-8222
Wells Fargo Strategic Income Fund - Class Admin	WSIDX	NAS CM	Open End	Fixed Inc Misc (Income)	C	D+	C		Y	800-222-8222

★ Expanded analysis of this fund is included in Section II.

TOTAL RETURNS & PERFORMANCE									ASSETS		ASSET ALLOCATION & TURNOVER							MINIMUMS		FEES		
3-Month Total Return	6-Month Total Return	1-Year Total Return	3-Year Total Return	5-Year Total Return	Dividend Yield (TTM)	Expense Ratio	3-Yr Std Deviation	Effective Duration	NAV	Total Assets (MIL)	%Cash	%Government Bonds	%Municipal Bonds	%Corporate Bonds	%Other	Turnover Ratio	Average Coupon Rate	Min Initial Investment	Min Additional Investment	Front End Fee (%)	Back End Fee (%)	Inception Date
2.01	0.91	2.21	7.01	10.98	1.39	1.6	3.31	4.94	10.86	171.6	0	0	100	0	0	18	4.69	1,000	100		1.00	Apr-05
2.28	1.45	3.40	10.51	16.68	2.47	0.52	3.24	4.94	10.87	171.6	0	0	100	0	0	18	4.69	1,000,000				Nov-16
0.07	0.37	1.16	4.14	4.39	1.33	0.6	0.15		1	4,650	72	9	14	4	0			1,000	100			Jul-92
0.00	0.11	0.54	1.95	1.97	0.64	1.35	0.14		1	4,650	72	9	14	4	0			1,000	100		1.00	Jun-10
0.18	0.60	1.62	5.49	6.22	1.78	0.2	0.15		1	4,650	72	9	14	4	0			10,000,000				Apr-16
0.10	0.42	1.27	4.49	4.86	1.43	0.5	0.15		1	4,650	72	9	14	4	0			100,000				Jun-10
13.64	-7.48	-3.66	7.62	22.76	6.8		12.03		11.85	360.2	2	23	0	70	0	26	5.18					Jun-03
2.24	0.43	2.52	12.26	20.97	2.44	0.75	4.26	5.33	10.55	5,407	1	0	99	0	0	20	4.44	1,000	100	4.50		Apr-05
2.27	0.59	2.67	12.87	21.87	2.59	0.6	4.21	5.33	10.56	5,407	1	0	99	0	0	20	4.44	1,000,000				Apr-05
2.05	0.05	1.76	9.88	16.52	1.68	1.5	4.21	5.33	10.55	5,407	1	0	99	0	0	20	4.44	1,000	100		1.00	Apr-05
2.31	0.58	2.83	13.37	22.75	2.75	0.45	4.26	5.33	10.55	5,407	1	0	99	0	0	20	4.44	1,000,000				Mar-08
2.32	0.70	2.98	13.29	22.33	2.8	0.4	4.24	5.33	10.56	5,407	1	0	99	0	0	20	4.44	0				Aug-18
0.05	0.38	0.94	3.38	4.01	1.11	0.3	0.11		1.0003	225.7	4	0	96	0	0			1,000,000				Jul-10
0.08	0.42	1.05	3.69	4.45	1.21	0.2	0.11		1.0003	225.7	4	0	96	0	0			10,000,000				Nov-96
0.04	0.34	0.83	2.95	3.39	0.98	0.45	0.11		1.0003	225.7	4	0	96	0	0			100,000				Nov-96
2.12						0.6		5.69	20.35	25.3	3	0	97	0	0		4.27	1,000,000				Feb-20
2.08						0.75		5.69	20.35	25.3	3	0	97	0	0		4.27	1,000	100	4.50		Feb-20
1.89						1.5		5.69	20.35	25.3	3	0	97	0	0		4.27	1,000	100		1.00	Feb-20
2.17						0.4		5.69	20.35	25.3	3	0	97	0	0		4.27	0				Feb-20
2.16						0.45		5.69	20.35	25.3	3	0	97	0	0		4.27	1,000,000				Feb-20
0.02	0.27	0.68	2.35	2.57	0.79	0.6	0.11		1	1,212	10	0	90	0	0			1,000	100			Jan-88
0.05	0.37	0.93	3.25	3.83	1.06	0.3	0.12		1	1,212	10	0	90	0	0			1,000,000				Apr-05
0.03	0.31	0.81	2.81	3.19	0.92	0.45	0.12		1	1,212	10	0	90	0	0			100,000				Jan-88
0.07	0.41	1.03	3.57	4.27	1.16	0.2	0.12		1	1,212	10	0	90	0	0			10,000,000				Jan-88
1.62	0.78	2.54	10.55	17.09	2.94	0.74	3.43	4.67	11.75	130.1	1	0	99	0	0	9	4.86	1,000	100	4.50		Dec-90
1.44	0.41	1.78	8.10	12.79	2.18	1.49	3.43	4.67	11.73	130.1	1	0	99	0	0	9	4.86	1,000	100		1.00	Feb-93
1.68	0.91	2.80	11.37	18.56	3.19	0.49	3.43	4.67	11.75	130.1	1	0	99	0	0	9	4.86	1,000,000				Nov-97
6.13	2.38	5.09	11.61	16.28	2.03	0.78	4.69	6.37	10.32	57.3	1	78	0	20	0	39	1.74	1,000	100	4.50		Feb-03
6.16	2.47	5.27	12.30	17.55	2.06	0.6	4.7	6.37	10.48	57.3	1	78	0	20	0	39	1.74	1,000,000				Feb-03
5.80	1.97	4.24	9.14	11.87	1.31	1.53	4.67	6.37	10.14	57.3	1	78	0	20	0	39	1.74	1,000	100		1.00	Feb-03
6.12	2.58	5.35	12.76	18.11	2.33	0.45	4.67	6.37	10.43	57.3	1	78	0	20	0	39	1.74	1,000,000				Oct-16
6.24	2.60	5.51	12.93	18.35	2.38	0.4	4.67	6.37	10.43	57.3	1	78	0	20	0	39	1.74	0				Oct-16
1.13	2.94	3.92	6.94	8.14	2.23	0.78	1.12	1.75	9.86	601.4	2	36	0	0	0	635	3.11	1,000	100	2.00		Mar-96
1.17	3.03	4.11	7.52	9.12	2.41	0.6	1.1	1.75	9.88	601.4	2	36	0	0	0	635	3.11	1,000,000				Dec-92
1.05	2.56	3.15	4.57	4.17	1.49	1.53	1.13	1.75	9.88	601.4	2	36	0	0	0	635	3.11	1,000	100		1.00	May-02
1.32	3.23	4.29	8.20	10.10	2.59	0.42	1.15	1.75	9.88	601.4	2	36	0	0	0	635	3.11	1,000,000				Apr-05
1.33	3.14	4.34	8.36	10.49	2.64	0.37	1.12	1.75	9.9	601.4	2	36	0	0	0	635	3.11	0				Nov-12
4.56	3.11	4.53	9.11	12.00	2.21	0.72	2.31	1.92	9	422.5	4	30	1	38	0	43	3.02	1,000	100	2.00		Aug-99
4.37	2.72	3.75	6.70	8.01	1.46	1.47	2.31	1.92	8.99	422.5	4	30	1	38	0	43	3.02	1,000	100		1.00	Mar-08
4.51	3.24	4.68	9.98	13.43	2.47	0.45	2.23	1.92	9	422.5	4	30	1	38	0	43	3.02	1,000,000				Aug-99
4.53	3.15	4.74	9.96	13.42	2.52	0.4	2.23	1.92	8.99	422.5	4	30	1	38	0	43	3.02	0				Jul-18
5.38	-0.85	1.23	7.31	13.13	3.27	0.82	4.02	1.62	7.89	732.4	3	0	0	97	0	44	4.44	1,000	100	3.00		Feb-00
5.42	-0.78	1.38	7.82	14.16	3.43	0.66	4.02	1.62	7.89	732.4	3	0	0	97	0	44	4.44	1,000,000				Jul-10
5.18	-1.22	0.47	4.93	8.97	2.51	1.57	4.07	1.62	7.89	732.4	3	0	0	97	0	44	4.44	1,000	100		1.00	Mar-08
5.46	-0.71	1.53	8.30	15.02	3.58	0.51	4.02	1.62	7.88	732.4	3	0	0	97	0	44	4.44	1,000,000				Nov-12
1.55	0.57	1.46	5.27	7.09	1.5	0.63	1.42	1.62	9.92	3,274	2	0	98	0	0	33	3.03	1,000	100	2.00		Jul-08
1.45	0.48	1.38	5.25	6.93	1.53	0.6	1.4	1.62	9.92	3,274	2	0	98	0	0	33	3.03	1,000,000				Jul-10
1.35	0.20	0.70	2.93	3.05	0.75	1.38	1.42	1.62	9.92	3,274	2	0	98	0	0	33	3.03	1,000	100		1.00	Jan-03
1.60	0.68	1.68	5.99	8.31	1.73	0.4	1.41	1.62	9.94	3,274	2	0	98	0	0	33	3.03	1,000,000				Mar-08
1.61	0.71	1.73	4.88	5.00	1.78	0.35	1.43	1.62	9.94	3,274	2	0	98	0	0	33	3.03	0				Aug-18
9.21	-0.23	2.24	9.71	14.46	2.71	0.92	6.24	2.83	9.48	141.6	34	21	0	32	5	116	4.24	1,000	100	4.00		Jan-13
9.28	0.00	2.51	10.28	15.08	2.6	0.77	6.2	2.83	9.55	141.6	34	21	0	32	5	116	4.24	1,000,000				Jan-13

	MARKET		FUND TYPE, CATEGORY & OBJECTIVE		RATINGS				NEW INVESTORS	
Fund Name	Ticker Symbol	Traded On	Fund Type	Category and (Prospectus Objective)	Overall Rating	Reward Rating	Risk Rating	Recent Up/ Downgrade	Open to New Investors	Telephone
Wells Fargo Strategic Income Fund - Class C	WSICX	NAS CM	Open End	Fixed Inc Misc (Income)	C-	D+	C		Y	800-222-8222
Wells Fargo Strategic Income Fund - Class Inst	WSINX	NAS CM	Open End	Fixed Inc Misc (Income)	C	C-	C+		Y	800-222-8222
Wells Fargo Strategic Municipal Bond Fund - Class A	VMPAX	NAS CM	Open End	US Muni Fixed Inc (Muni Bond - Natl)	C	C-	C+		Y	800-222-8222
Wells Fargo Strategic Municipal Bond Fund - Class Admin	VMPYX	NAS CM	Open End	US Muni Fixed Inc (Muni Bond - Natl)	C	C-	B-		Y	800-222-8222
Wells Fargo Strategic Municipal Bond Fund - Class C	DHICX	NAS CM	Open End	US Muni Fixed Inc (Muni Bond - Natl)	C	C-	C+		Y	800-222-8222
Wells Fargo Strategic Municipal Bond Fund - Class Inst	STRIX	NAS CM	Open End	US Muni Fixed Inc (Muni Bond - Natl)	C	C-	C+		Y	800-222-8222
Wells Fargo Strategic Municipal Bond Fund - Class R6	VMPRX	NAS CM	Open End	US Muni Fixed Inc (Muni Bond - Natl)	C	C-	C+		Y	800-222-8222
Wells Fargo Treasury Plus Money Market Fund - Class A	PIVXX	NAS CM	Money Mkt	US Money Mkt (Money Mkt - Treasury)	C	C-	C+		Y	800-222-8222
Wells Fargo Treasury Plus Money Market Fund - Class Admin	WTPXX	NAS CM	Money Mkt	US Money Mkt (Money Mkt - Treasury)	C	C-	C+		Y	800-222-8222
Wells Fargo Treasury Plus Money Market Fund - Class Inst	PISXX	NAS CM	Money Mkt	US Money Mkt (Money Mkt - Treasury)	C	C-	C+		Y	800-222-8222
Wells Fargo Treasury Plus Money Market Fund - Class Svc	PRVXX	NAS CM	Money Mkt	US Money Mkt (Money Mkt - Treasury)	C	C-	C+		Y	800-222-8222
Wells Fargo Treasury Plus Money Market Fund Select Class	WTLXX	NAS CM	Money Mkt	US Money Mkt (Money Mkt - Treasury)	C	C-	C+		Y	800-222-8222
Wells Fargo U.S. Core Bond Fund	WUSBX	NAS CM	Open End	US Fixed Inc (Income)	C+	C	B		Y	800-222-8222
Wells Fargo Ultra Short-Term Income Fund - Class A	SADAX	NAS CM	Open End	US Fixed Inc (Corp Bond - General)	C	C-	C+		Y	800-222-8222
Wells Fargo Ultra Short-Term Income Fund - Class Admin	WUSDX	NAS CM	Open End	US Fixed Inc (Corp Bond - General)	C	C	C+		Y	800-222-8222
Wells Fargo Ultra Short-Term Income Fund - Class C	WUSTX	NAS CM	Open End	US Fixed Inc (Corp Bond - General)	C	C-	C	Up	Y	800-222-8222
Wells Fargo Ultra Short-Term Income Fund - Class Inst	SADIX	NAS CM	Open End	US Fixed Inc (Corp Bond - General)	C	C	C+		Y	800-222-8222
Wells Fargo Ultra Short-Term Muni Income Fund - Class A	SMAVX	NAS CM	Open End	US Muni Fixed Inc (Muni Bond - Natl)	C	C-	C+		Y	800-222-8222
Wells Fargo Ultra Short-Term Muni Income - Cl Admin	WUSMX	NAS CM	Open End	US Muni Fixed Inc (Muni Bond - Natl)	C	C-	C+		Y	800-222-8222
Wells Fargo Ultra Short-Term Muni Income Fund - Class C	WFUSX	NAS CM	Open End	US Muni Fixed Inc (Muni Bond - Natl)	C	C-	C	Up	Y	800-222-8222
Wells Fargo Ultra Short-Term Muni Income Fund - Class Inst	SMAIX	NAS CM	Open End	US Muni Fixed Inc (Muni Bond - Natl)	C	C-	C+		Y	800-222-8222
Wells Fargo Ultra Short-Term Muni Income Fund - Class R6	WUSRX	NAS CM	Open End	US Muni Fixed Inc (Muni Bond - Natl)	C	C-	C+		Y	800-222-8222
Wells Fargo Wisconsin Tax-Free Fund - Class A	WWTFX	NAS CM	Open End	US Muni Fixed Inc (Muni Bond - Single State)	C	C	B		Y	800-222-8222
Wells Fargo Wisconsin Tax-Free Fund - Class C	WWTCX	NAS CM	Open End	US Muni Fixed Inc (Muni Bond - Single State)	C	C-	B-		Y	800-222-8222
Wells Fargo Wisconsin Tax-Free Fund Institutional Class	WWTIX	NAS CM	Open End	US Muni Fixed Inc (Muni Bond - Single State)	C	C	B		Y	800-222-8222
WesMark Government Bond Fund	WMBDX	NAS CM	Open End	US Fixed Inc (Corp Bond - General)	C+	C	B-		Y	800-861-1013
WesMark West Virginia Municipal Bond Fund	WMKMX	NAS CM	Open End	US Muni Fixed Inc (Muni Bond - Single State)	C+	C	B	Up	Y	800-861-1013
Western Asset California Municipals Fund Class A	SHRCX	NAS CM	Open End	US Muni Fixed Inc (Muni Bond - Single State)	C	C-	C+		Y	877-721-1926
Western Asset California Municipals Fund Class C	SCACX	NAS CM	Open End	US Muni Fixed Inc (Muni Bond - Single State)	C	C-	C		Y	877-721-1926
Western Asset California Municipals Fund Class I	LMCUX	NAS CM	Open End	US Muni Fixed Inc (Muni Bond - Single State)	C	C-	C+		Y	877-721-1926
Western Asset California Municipals Fund Class IS	SHRSX	NAS CM	Open End	US Muni Fixed Inc (Muni Bond - Single State)	C	C-	C+		Y	877-721-1926
Western Asset Core Bond Fund Class A	WABAX	NAS CM	Open End	US Fixed Inc (Corp Bond - General)	B	C+	B+	Up	Y	877-721-1926
Western Asset Core Bond Fund Class C	WABCX	NAS CM	Open End	US Fixed Inc (Corp Bond - General)	B-	C+	B	Up	Y	877-721-1926
Western Asset Core Bond Fund Class C1	LWACX	NAS CM	Open End	US Fixed Inc (Corp Bond - General)	B-	C+	B+	Up	Y	877-721-1926
Western Asset Core Bond Fund Class FI	WAPIX	NAS CM	Open End	US Fixed Inc (Corp Bond - General)	B	C+	B+	Up	Y	877-721-1926
Western Asset Core Bond Fund Class I	WATFX	NAS CM	Open End	US Fixed Inc (Corp Bond - General)	B	C+	B+	Up	Y	877-721-1926
Western Asset Core Bond Fund Class IS	WACSX	NAS CM	Open End	US Fixed Inc (Corp Bond - General)	B	C+	B+	Up	Y	877-721-1926
Western Asset Core Bond Fund Class R	WABRX	NAS CM	Open End	US Fixed Inc (Corp Bond - General)	B-	C+	B+	Up	Y	877-721-1926
Western Asset Core Plus Bond Fund Class A	WAPAX	NAS CM	Open End	US Fixed Inc (Corp Bond - General)	B-	C	B	Up	Y	877-721-1926
Western Asset Core Plus Bond Fund Class C	WAPCX	NAS CM	Open End	US Fixed Inc (Corp Bond - General)	C+	C	B	Up	Y	877-721-1926
Western Asset Core Plus Bond Fund Class C1	LWCPX	NAS CM	Open End	US Fixed Inc (Corp Bond - General)	B-	C	B	Up	Y	877-721-1926
Western Asset Core Plus Bond Fund Class FI	WACIX	NAS CM	Open End	US Fixed Inc (Corp Bond - General)	B-	C	B	Up	Y	877-721-1926
Western Asset Core Plus Bond Fund Class I	WACPX	NAS CM	Open End	US Fixed Inc (Corp Bond - General)	B-	C	B+	Up	Y	877-721-1926
Western Asset Core Plus Bond Fund Class IS	WAPSX	NAS CM	Open End	US Fixed Inc (Corp Bond - General)	B-	C	B+	Up	Y	877-721-1926
Western Asset Core Plus Bond Fund Class R	WAPRX	NAS CM	Open End	US Fixed Inc (Corp Bond - General)	B-	C	B	Up	Y	877-721-1926
Western Asset Corporate Bond Fund Class A	SIGAX	NAS CM	Open End	US Fixed Inc (Corp Bond - General)	C+	C	B	Up	Y	877-721-1926
Western Asset Corporate Bond Fund Class C	LWBOX	NAS CM	Open End	US Fixed Inc (Corp Bond - General)	C	C	B-		Y	877-721-1926
Western Asset Corporate Bond Fund Class C1	SBILX	NAS CM	Open End	US Fixed Inc (Corp Bond - General)	C+	C	B-	Up		877-721-1926
Western Asset Corporate Bond Fund Class I	SIGYX	NAS CM	Open End	US Fixed Inc (Corp Bond - General)	C+	C	B	Up	Y	877-721-1926
Western Asset Corporate Bond Fund Class P	LCBPX	NAS CM	Open End	US Fixed Inc (Corp Bond - General)	C+	C	B	Up	Y	877-721-1926
Western Asset Corporate Loan Fund	TLI	NYSE	Closed End	US Fixed Inc (Corp Bond - High Yield)	D	D	D	Down	Y	877-721-1926
Western Asset Emerging Markets Debt Fund Class A	LWEAX	NAS CM	Open End	Emerg Mkts Fixed Inc (Growth & Income)	C-	D+	C	Down	Y	877-721-1926

★Expanded analysis of this fund is included in Section II.

TOTAL RETURNS & PERFORMANCE									ASSETS		ASSET ALLOCATION & TURNOVER							MINIMUMS		FEES		
3-Month Total Return	6-Month Total Return	1-Year Total Return	3-Year Total Return	5-Year Total Return	Dividend Yield (TTM)	Expense Ratio	3-Yr Std Deviation	Effective Duration	NAV	Total Assets (MIL)	%Cash	%Government Bonds	%Municipal Bonds	%Corporate Bonds	%Other	Turnover Ratio	Average Coupon Rate	Min Initial Investment	Min Additional Investment	Front End Fee (%)	Back End Fee (%)	Inception Date
9.02	-0.49	1.56	7.33	10.28	2.04	1.67	6.2	2.83	9.46	141.6	34	21	0	32	5	116	4.24	1,000	100		1.00	Jan-13
9.21	0.01	2.58	10.71	16.16	3.05	0.62	6.14	2.83	9.47	141.6	34	21	0	32	5	116	4.24	1,000,000				Jan-13
2.34	0.78	2.22	8.66	13.39	1.84	0.8	2.69	3.34	9.17	2,523	2	0	98	0	0	29	4.00	1,000	100	4.00		Dec-94
2.48	0.84	2.33	9.18	14.22	1.95	0.68	2.71	3.34	9.17	2,523	2	0	98	0	0	29	4.00	1,000,000				Oct-97
2.14	0.41	1.35	6.24	9.21	1.08	1.55	2.68	3.34	9.2	2,523	2	0	98	0	0	29	4.00	1,000	100		1.00	Aug-97
2.42	0.95	2.55	9.75	15.29	2.17	0.47	2.63	3.34	9.17	2,523	2	0	98	0	0	29	4.00	1,000,000				Nov-12
2.43	0.97	2.49	9.41	14.18	2.22	0.42	2.69	3.34	9.17	2,523	2	0	98	0	0	29	4.00	0				Aug-18
0.00	0.20	0.90	3.39	3.48	1.06	0.6	0.17		1	22,235	59	37	0	4	0			1,000	100			Oct-85
0.00	0.26	1.10	4.14	4.39	1.27	0.34	0.18		1	22,235	59	37	0	4	0			1,000,000				Mar-08
0.02	0.31	1.22	4.56	5.03	1.4	0.2	0.18		1	22,235	59	37	0	4	0			10,000,000				Oct-85
0.00	0.23	1.01	3.82	3.99	1.18	0.45	0.17		1	22,235	59	37	0	4	0			100,000				Oct-85
0.02	0.34	1.28	4.63	5.11	1.46	0.14			1	22,235	59	37	0	4	0			50,000,000				Mar-19
2.64	5.86	8.43			2.52	0		5.54	10.49	1.1	1	45	1	24	0	39	3.22	0				Aug-17
3.47	1.07	2.34	6.46	8.68	2.01	0.51	2.06	0.54	8.56	977.2	12	1	1	46	0	36	3.12	1,000	100	2.00		Aug-99
3.38	1.13	2.48	6.79	9.35	2.15	0.51	1.98	0.54	8.52	977.2	12	1	1	46	0	36	3.12	1,000,000				Apr-05
3.28	0.69	1.58	4.09	4.69	1.25	1.26	2.06	0.54	8.55	977.2	12	1	1	46	0	36	3.12	1,000	100		1.00	Jul-08
3.42	1.11	2.57	7.43	10.45	2.35	0.26	2	0.54	8.55	977.2	12	1	1	46	0	36	3.12	1,000,000				Aug-99
0.59	0.49	1.12	3.66	4.25	1.27	0.5	0.58	0.67	9.59	1,739	5	0	95	0	0	55	2.11	1,000	100	2.00		Oct-00
0.60	0.51	1.18	3.87	4.60	1.34	0.5	0.54	0.67	9.59	1,739	5	0	95	0	0	55	2.11	1,000,000				Jul-10
0.41	0.00	0.25	1.29	0.35	0.51	1.25	0.59	0.67	9.41	1,739	5	0	95	0	0	55	2.11	1,000	100		1.00	Mar-08
0.66	0.52	1.41	4.48	5.82	1.57	0.25	0.53	0.67	9.59	1,739	5	0	95	0	0	55	2.11	1,000,000				Jul-00
0.67	0.65	1.46	4.46	5.80	1.62	0.2	0.6	0.67	9.59	1,739	5	0	95	0	0	55	2.11	0				Aug-18
1.34	1.15	3.03	10.67	16.25	2.29	0.7	2.67	4.47	11.12	151.4	1	0	99	0	0	8	3.89	1,000	100	4.50		Mar-08
1.14	0.77	2.26	8.22	11.98	1.53	1.45	2.67	4.47	11.12	151.4	1	0	99	0	0	8	3.89	1,000	100		1.00	Dec-02
1.28	1.23	3.11	11.26	15.85	2.46	0.52	2.68	4.47	11.12	151.4	1	0	99	0	0	8	3.89	1,000,000				Oct-16
0.50	3.25	4.13	9.33	12.53	2.05	1.01	2.48		10.15	220.3	-5	5	23	0	0	37	3.45	1,000	100			Apr-98
1.76	2.16	3.46	8.87	14.52	1.87	1.08	2.45		10.8	117.1	2	0	98	0	0	9	3.94	1,000	100			Apr-97
3.15	-0.01	2.27	10.09	16.45	2.96	0.79	5	5.89	15.71	406.1	-2	0	100	0	0	31	5.01	1,000	50	4.25		Apr-84
3.01	-0.34	1.70	8.21	13.18	2.39	1.34	5	5.89	15.66	406.1	-2	0	100	0	0	31	5.01	1,000	50		1.00	Nov-94
3.19	0.06	2.43	10.67	17.35	3.13	0.6	5	5.89	15.71	406.1	-2	0	100	0	0	31	5.01	1,000,000				Mar-07
3.20	0.02	2.38	10.21	16.58		0.55	5.02	5.89	15.7	406.1	-2	0	100	0	0	31	5.01	1,000,000				Aug-19
5.54	5.22	8.20	16.73	25.84	2.28	0.82	3.75	5.53	13.55	15,751	-3	21	0	25	0	125	3.46	1,000	50	4.25		Apr-12
5.36	4.86	7.37	14.30	21.55	1.6	1.52	3.76	5.53	13.55	15,751	-3	21	0	25	0	125	3.46	1,000	50		1.00	Apr-12
5.50	5.06	7.78	15.48	23.56	1.91	1.19	3.77	5.53	13.57	15,751	-3	21	0	25	0	125	3.46	1,000	50		1.00	Oct-12
5.62	5.22	8.21	16.77	25.98	2.29	0.81	3.76	5.53	13.56	15,751	-3	21	0	25	0	125	3.46	0				Jul-99
5.63	5.40	8.51	18.02	28.23	2.63	0.45	3.78	5.53	13.55	15,751	-3	21	0	25	0	125	3.46	1,000,000				Sep-90
5.72	5.41	8.61	18.11	28.37	2.66	0.42	3.78	5.53	13.57	15,751	-3	21	0	25	0	125	3.46	1,000,000				Aug-08
5.53	5.13	7.86	15.67	24.01	1.98	1.13	3.78	5.53	13.57	15,751	-3	21	0	25	0	125	3.46	0				Apr-12
6.39	3.91	7.79	16.40	28.43	3.03	0.82	4.93	6.53	12.27	32,923	2	15	0	24	0	122	3.88	1,000	50	4.25		Apr-12
6.29	3.64	7.04	13.99	24.03	2.35	1.52	4.97	6.53	12.29	32,923	2	15	0	24	0	122	3.88	1,000	50		1.00	Apr-12
6.34	3.75	7.48	15.18	26.05	2.67	1.2	4.95	6.53	12.28	32,923	2	15	0	24	0	122	3.88	1,000	50		1.00	Oct-12
6.47	3.99	7.88	16.47	28.42	3.03	0.82	4.94	6.53	12.29	32,923	2	15	0	24	0	122	3.88	0				Jan-02
6.57	4.18	8.27	17.78	30.93	3.39	0.45	4.95	6.53	12.29	32,923	2	15	0	24	0	122	3.88	1,000,000				Jul-98
6.58	4.20	8.21	17.79	31.00	3.41	0.42	4.97	6.53	12.28	32,923	2	15	0	24	0	122	3.88	1,000,000				Aug-08
6.40	3.84	7.55	15.43	26.66	2.73	1.12	4.92	6.53	12.27	32,923	2	15	0	24	0	122	3.88	0				Apr-12
12.34	4.08	7.57	17.98	32.32	3.46	0.93	8.19	7.17	13.2	836.6	1	2	1	93	0	84	4.49	1,000	50	4.25		Nov-92
12.16	3.74	6.95	15.62	27.91	2.81	1.59	8.19	7.17	13.2	836.6	1	2	1	93	0	84	4.49	1,000	50		1.00	Aug-12
12.29	3.86	7.22	16.59	29.55	3.11	1.37	8.21	7.17	13.12	836.6	1	2	1	93	0	84	4.49	1,000	50		1.00	Feb-93
12.44	4.27	7.95	19.13	34.47	3.8	0.55	8.18	7.17	13.2	836.6	1	2	1	93	0	84	4.49	1,000,000				Feb-96
12.30	3.99	7.48	17.38	31.25	3.29	1.1	8.2	7.17	13.19	836.6	1	2	1	93	0	84	4.49	0	50			Jul-09
12.16	-11.94	-9.74	-2.96	4.09	8.43	0	13.51		9.15	89.6	-46	0	0	93	0	122	5.06					Nov-98
12.29	-0.83	2.09	8.86	23.44	3.26	1.1	10.11	8.97	4.84	32.5	8	49	0	26	0	47	5.58	1,000	50	4.25		Jan-10

	MARKET		FUND TYPE, CATEGORY & OBJECTIVE		RATINGS				NEW INVESTORS	
Fund Name	Ticker Symbol	Traded On	Fund Type	Category and (Prospectus Objective)	Overall Rating	Reward Rating	Risk Rating	Recent Up/ Downgrade	Open to New Investors	Telephone
Western Asset Emerging Markets Debt Fund Class A2	WEMDX	NAS CM	Open End	Emerg Mkts Fixed Inc (Growth & Income)	C-	D+	C	Down	Y	877-721-1926
Western Asset Emerging Markets Debt Fund Class C	WAEOX	NAS CM	Open End	Emerg Mkts Fixed Inc (Growth & Income)	C-	D+	C	Down	Y	877-721-1926
Western Asset Emerging Markets Debt Fund Class FI	LMWDX	NAS CM	Open End	Emerg Mkts Fixed Inc (Growth & Income)	C-	D+	C	Down	Y	877-721-1926
Western Asset Emerging Markets Debt Fund Class I	SEMDX	NAS CM	Open End	Emerg Mkts Fixed Inc (Growth & Income)	C-	D+	C	Down	Y	877-721-1926
Western Asset Emerging Markets Debt Fund Class IS	LWISX	NAS CM	Open End	Emerg Mkts Fixed Inc (Growth & Income)	C-	C-	C	Down	Y	877-721-1926
Western Asset Emerging Markets Debt Fund Inc	EMD	NYSE	Closed End	Emerg Mkts Fixed Inc (Worldwide Bond)	D	D	D+	Down	Y	877-721-1926
Western Asset Global Corporate Defined Opportunity Fund	GDO	NYSE	Closed End	Global Fixed Inc (World Stock)	D+	D+	C-	Down	Y	877-721-1926
Western Asset Global High Income Fund	EHI	NYSE	Closed End	US Fixed Inc (Multisector Bond)	D+	D+	C-	Down	Y	877-721-1926
Western Asset Global High Yield Bond Fund Class A	SAHYX	NAS CM	Open End	Global Fixed Inc (Corp Bond - High Yield)	C-	D+	C		Y	877-721-1926
Western Asset Global High Yield Bond Fund Class C	LWGOX	NAS CM	Open End	Global Fixed Inc (Corp Bond - High Yield)	C-	D+	C		Y	877-721-1926
Western Asset Global High Yield Bond Fund Class C1	SHYCX	NAS CM	Open End	Global Fixed Inc (Corp Bond - High Yield)	C-	D+	C			877-721-1926
Western Asset Global High Yield Bond Fund Class I	SHYOX	NAS CM	Open End	Global Fixed Inc (Corp Bond - High Yield)	C-	D+	C		Y	877-721-1926
Western Asset Global High Yield Bond Fund Class IS	LWGSX	NAS CM	Open End	Global Fixed Inc (Corp Bond - High Yield)	C-	D+	C		Y	877-721-1926
Western Asset Government Reserves Class A	SMGXX	NAS CM	Money Mkt	US Money Mkt (Money Mkt - Govt)	C	C-	C+		Y	877-721-1926
Western Asset Government Reserves Class A2	SMTXX	NAS CM	Money Mkt	US Money Mkt (Money Mkt - Govt)	C	C-	C+		Y	877-721-1926
Western Asset Government Reserves Service Shares	LGSXX	NAS CM	Money Mkt	US Money Mkt (Money Mkt - Govt)	C	C-	C		Y	877-721-1926
Western Asset High Income Fund II	HIX	NYSE	Closed End	US Fixed Inc (Corp Bond - High Yield)	D+	D+	C-	Down	Y	877-721-1926
Western Asset High Income Opportunity Fund Inc.	HIO	NYSE	Closed End	US Fixed Inc (Corp Bond - High Yield)	C-	D+	C		Y	877-721-1926
Western Asset High Yield Defined Opportunity Fund	HYI	NYSE	Closed End	US Fixed Inc (Corp Bond - High Yield)	D+	D+	C-	Down	Y	877-721-1926
Western Asset High Yield Fund Class A	WAYAX	NAS CM	Open End	US Fixed Inc (Corp Bond - High Yield)	C-	D+	C		Y	877-721-1926
Western Asset High Yield Fund Class A2	WHAYX	NAS CM	Open End	US Fixed Inc (Corp Bond - High Yield)	C-	D+	C		Y	877-721-1926
Western Asset High Yield Fund Class C	WAYCX	NAS CM	Open End	US Fixed Inc (Corp Bond - High Yield)	D+	D	C-	Down	Y	877-721-1926
Western Asset High Yield Fund Class I	WAHYX	NAS CM	Open End	US Fixed Inc (Corp Bond - High Yield)	C-	D+	C		Y	877-721-1926
Western Asset High Yield Fund Class IS	WAHSX	NAS CM	Open End	US Fixed Inc (Corp Bond - High Yield)	C-	D+	C		Y	877-721-1926
Western Asset High Yield Fund Class R	WAYRX	NAS CM	Open End	US Fixed Inc (Corp Bond - High Yield)	D+	D+	C-	Down	Y	877-721-1926
Western Asset Income Fund Class A	SDSAX	NAS CM	Open End	US Fixed Inc (Multisector Bond)	D+	D	C-	Down	Y	877-721-1926
Western Asset Income Fund Class C	LWSIX	NAS CM	Open End	US Fixed Inc (Multisector Bond)	D+	D	C-	Down	Y	877-721-1926
Western Asset Income Fund Class C1	SDSIX	NAS CM	Open End	US Fixed Inc (Multisector Bond)	D+	D	C-	Down		877-721-1926
Western Asset Income Fund Class I	SDSYX	NAS CM	Open End	US Fixed Inc (Multisector Bond)	D+	D+	C-	Down	Y	877-721-1926
Western Asset Income Fund Class IS	WAGIX	NAS CM	Open End	US Fixed Inc (Multisector Bond)	C-	D+	C		Y	877-721-1926
Western Asset Inflation Indexed Plus Bond Fund Class A	WAFAX	NAS CM	Open End	US Fixed Inc (Govt Bond - Treasury)	B-	C	B+	Up	Y	877-721-1926
Western Asset Inflation Indexed Plus Bond Fund Class C	WAFCX	NAS CM	Open End	US Fixed Inc (Govt Bond - Treasury)	C+	C	B	Up	Y	877-721-1926
Western Asset Inflation Indexed Plus Bond Fund Class C1	LWICX	NAS CM	Open End	US Fixed Inc (Govt Bond - Treasury)	B-	C	B	Up	Y	877-721-1926
Western Asset Inflation Indexed Plus Bond Fund Class FI	WATPX	NAS CM	Open End	US Fixed Inc (Govt Bond - Treasury)	B-	C	B+	Up	Y	877-721-1926
Western Asset Inflation Indexed Plus Bond Fund Class I	WAIIX	NAS CM	Open End	US Fixed Inc (Govt Bond - Treasury)	B-	C+	B+	Up	Y	877-721-1926
Western Asset Inflation Indexed Plus Bond Fund Class IS	WAFSX	NAS CM	Open End	US Fixed Inc (Govt Bond - Treasury)	B-	C+	B+	Up	Y	877-721-1926
Western Asset Inflation Indexed Plus Bond Fund Class R	WAFRX	NAS CM	Open End	US Fixed Inc (Govt Bond - Treasury)	B-	C	B	Up	Y	877-721-1926
Western Asset Inflation-Linked Income Fd	WIA	NYSE	Closed End	US Fixed Inc (Govt Bond - Treasury)	C-	C-	C-		Y	877-721-1926
Western Asset Infl-Linked Opps & Inc Fd	WIW	NYSE	Closed End	US Fixed Inc (Govt Bond - Treasury)	C	C-	C+		Y	877-721-1926
Western Asset Institutional Government Reserves Class L	LWPXX	NAS CM	Money Mkt	US Money Mkt (Money Mkt - Govt)	C	C-	C+		Y	877-721-1926
Western Asset Inst Govt Reserves Inst Shares	INGXX	NAS CM	Money Mkt	US Money Mkt (Money Mkt - Govt)	C	C-	C+		Y	877-721-1926
Western Asset Institutional Govt Reserves Investors Shares	LGRXX	NAS CM	Money Mkt	US Money Mkt (Money Mkt - Govt)	C	C-	C+		Y	877-721-1926
Western Asset Institutional Liquid Reserves Institutional	CILXX	NAS CM	Money Mkt	US Money Mkt (Money Mkt - Taxable)	C	C-	C+		Y	877-721-1926
Western Asset Institutional Liquid Reserves Investors	LLRXX	NAS CM	Money Mkt	US Money Mkt (Money Mkt - Taxable)	C	C-	C+		Y	877-721-1926
Western Asset Inst U.S. Treas Oblig Money Mkt Admin Shares	LAOXX	NAS CM	Money Mkt	US Money Mkt (Money Mkt - Treasury)	C	C-	C+		Y	877-721-1926
Western Asset Inst U.S. Treas Oblig Money Mkt Inst Shares	LUIXX	NAS CM	Money Mkt	US Money Mkt (Money Mkt - Treasury)	C	C-	C+		Y	877-721-1926
Western Asset Inst U.S. Treas Oblig Money Mkt Inv Shares	LAIXX	NAS CM	Money Mkt	US Money Mkt (Money Mkt - Treasury)	C	C-	C+		Y	877-721-1926
Western Asset Inst U.S. Treas Reserves Inst Shares	CIIXX	NAS CM	Money Mkt	US Money Mkt (Money Mkt - Treasury)	C	C-	C+		Y	877-721-1926
Western Asset Inst U.S. Treas Reserves Investors Shares	LTRXX	NAS CM	Money Mkt	US Money Mkt (Money Mkt - Treasury)	C	C-	C+		Y	877-721-1926
Western Asset Intermediate Bond Fund Class A	WATAX	NAS CM	Open End	US Fixed Inc (Corp Bond - General)	B-	C	B	Up	Y	877-721-1926
Western Asset Intermediate Bond Fund Class C	WATCX	NAS CM	Open End	US Fixed Inc (Corp Bond - General)	C+	C	B	Up	Y	877-721-1926
Western Asset Intermediate Bond Fund Class I	WATIX	NAS CM	Open End	US Fixed Inc (Corp Bond - General)	B-	C+	B+	Up	Y	877-721-1926

★ Expanded analysis of this fund is included in Section II.

TOTAL RETURNS & PERFORMANCE									ASSETS		ASSET ALLOCATION & TURNOVER							MINIMUMS		FEES		
3-Month Total Return	6-Month Total Return	1-Year Total Return	3-Year Total Return	5-Year Total Return	Dividend Yield (TTM)	Expense Ratio	3-Yr Std Deviation	Effective Duration	NAV	Total Assets (MIL)	%Cash	%Government Bonds	%Municipal Bonds	%Corporate Bonds	%Other	Turnover Ratio	Average Coupon Rate	Min Initial Investment	Min Additional Investment	Front End Fee (%)	Back End Fee (%)	Inception Date
12.32	-0.84	2.08	8.78	23.43	3.24	1.3	10.12	8.97	4.83	32.5	8	49	0	26	0	47	5.58	1,000	50	4.25		Sep-13
12.32	-1.12	1.38	6.29	19.05	2.38	1.85	10.22	8.97	4.83	32.5	8	49	0	26	0	47	5.58	1,000	50		1.00	Aug-12
12.47	-0.89	1.97	11.55	29.64	3.12	1.1	10.09	8.97	4.87	32.5	8	49	0	26	0	47	5.58	0				Dec-11
12.55	-0.56	2.49	9.87	25.54	3.5	0.8	10.12	8.97	4.84	32.5	8	49	0	26	0	47	5.58	1,000,000				Oct-96
12.61	-0.53	2.58	10.11	26.07	3.61	0.7	10.2	8.97	4.82	32.5	8	49	0	26	0	47	5.58	1,000,000				Jan-13
17.31	-5.17	-4.02	2.67	17.74	7.03		14.52	6.02	14.32	837.7	-5	53	0	27	0	29	6.10					Dec-03
14.80	-2.95	1.50	12.12	27.11	6.5	1.2	11.24	4.42	17.41	256.4	-41	11	0	80	0	52	5.23					Nov-09
15.73	-5.85	-2.81	9.09	25.09	7.45		13.07	4.35	9.87	430.0	-5	25	0	72	0	89	5.82					Jul-03
10.75	-2.86	-1.07	8.50	20.26	5.5	1.15	9.09	3.57	5.97	228.5	3	24	0	69	0	70	5.35	1,000	50	4.25		Feb-95
10.52	-3.22	-1.79	6.17	16.04	4.74	1.88	9.1	3.57	5.98	228.5	3	24	0	69	0	70	5.35	1,000	50		1.00	Aug-12
10.50	-3.21	-1.60	6.89	17.35	5.04	1.63	9.18	3.57	6.03	228.5	3	24	0	69	0	70	5.35	1,000	50		1.00	Feb-95
10.84	-2.75	-0.82	9.31	21.56	5.77	0.9	9.23	3.57	5.96	228.5	3	24	0	69	0	70	5.35	1,000,000				Feb-95
10.66	-2.70	-0.73	9.61	22.14	5.86	0.8	9.11	3.57	5.96	228.5	3	24	0	69	0	70	5.35	1,000,000				Aug-12
0.00	0.20	0.91	3.41	3.52	1.07	0.6	0.17		1	1,611	50	48	0	0	0			1,000	50			Jan-91
0.00	0.16	0.77	3.04	3.13	0.91	0.8	0.17		1	1,611	50	48	0	0	0			1,000	50			May-16
0.00	0.12	0.63	2.30	1.78	0.75	1	0.15		1	1,611	50	48	0	0	0			0				Nov-16
15.64	-7.02	-3.89	8.02	22.88	7.94		13.42	4.07	6.6	550.1	-40	11	0	85	0	66	5.99					May-98
11.02	-3.92	-0.72	10.69	21.91	7.05		9.46	4.32	5.14	647.8	3	4	0	92	0	83	6.36					Oct-93
11.33	-6.40	-3.23	8.43	20.16	7.48	0.9	10.56	3.97	14.86	335.6	1	6	0	90	0	89	6.58					Oct-10
10.88	-5.09	-1.85	7.95	16.99	5.63	1.05	9.97	4.17	7.46	211.1	3	1	0	90	0	71	6.27	1,000	50	4.25		Apr-12
10.91	-5.06	-1.80	7.81	16.93	5.69	1.01	9.96	4.17	7.46	211.1	3	1	0	90	0	71	6.27	1,000	50	4.25		Aug-14
10.62	-5.39	-2.53	5.34	12.60	4.85	1.79	9.89	4.17	7.39	211.1	3	1	0	90	0	71	6.27	1,000	50		1.00	Apr-12
10.90	-4.88	-1.49	8.67	18.55	5.95	0.76	9.87	4.17	7.4	211.1	3	1	0	90	0	71	6.27	1,000,000				Sep-01
10.92	-4.98	-1.57	8.75	18.72	6.02	0.66	9.94	4.17	7.51	211.1	3	1	0	90	0	71	6.27	1,000,000				Aug-08
10.89	-5.15	-2.06	6.79	15.28	5.33	1.31	9.94	4.17	7.41	211.1	3	1	0	90	0	71	6.27	0				Apr-12
9.83	-5.14	-1.82	5.74	17.15	5.84	1	9.22	3.98	5.75	493.0	4	8	0	36	0	54	5.30	1,000	50	4.25		Nov-92
9.44	-5.49	-2.54	3.48	13.01	5.07	1.71	9.13	3.98	5.74	493.0	4	8	0	36	0	54	5.30	1,000	50		1.00	Aug-12
9.56	-5.41	-2.31	4.40	14.75	5.45	1.39	9.12	3.98	5.75	493.0	4	8	0	36	0	54	5.30	1,000	50		1.00	Mar-93
9.86	-4.96	-1.49	6.75	18.94	6.16	0.7	9.15	3.98	5.78	493.0	4	8	0	36	0	54	5.30	1,000,000				Oct-95
9.89	-4.92	-1.40	6.87	19.42	6.25	0.6	9.19	3.98	5.78	493.0	4	8	0	36	0	54	5.30	1,000,000				Oct-14
5.27	4.04	6.92	13.46	14.83	2.01	0.71	4.53	7.92	11.77	453.7	1	94	0	5	0	60	1.66	1,000	50	4.25		Apr-12
5.04	3.69	6.22	11.30	11.08	1.28	1.38	4.53	7.92	11.45	453.7	1	94	0	5	0	60	1.66	1,000	50		1.00	Apr-12
5.05	3.65	6.48	11.99	12.20	0.97	1.21	4.52	7.92	11.64	453.7	1	94	0	5	0	60	1.66	1,000	50			Oct-12
5.22	4.01	6.98	13.58	14.83	2.1	0.64	4.49	7.92	11.69	453.7	1	94	0	5	0	60	1.66	0				Jun-07
5.40	4.20	7.36	14.75	16.64	2.46	0.36	4.54	7.92	11.89	453.7	1	94	0	5	0	60	1.66	1,000,000				Mar-01
5.37	4.21	7.38	14.98	17.31	2.53	0.27	4.55	7.92	11.95	453.7	1	94	0	5	0	60	1.66	1,000,000				Dec-08
5.16	3.82	6.51	12.36	12.74	1.6	1.05	4.57	7.92	11.61	453.7	1	94	0	5	0	60	1.66	0				Apr-12
11.14	-0.44	3.48	15.05	19.89	3.19		7.84		13.28	377.8	-48	68	0	6	1	38	2.13					Sep-03
11.48	-1.54	2.07	12.43	16.78	3.49		8.32		12.7	757.5	-48	70	0	7	1	35	2.39					Feb-04
0.02	0.32	1.24	4.57	5.04	1.42	0.2	0.18		1	12,080	50	48	0	0	0			1,000,000	50			Aug-16
0.03	0.33	1.26	4.68	5.33	1.44	0.18	0.18		1	12,080	50	48	0	0	0			1,000,000	50			Jun-95
0.01	0.31	1.21	4.53	5.06	1.39	0.23	0.18		1	12,080	50	48	0	0	0			1,000,000	50			Sep-13
0.19	0.59	1.59	5.49	6.65	1.71	0.18	0.16		1.001	4,354	89	10	0	0	0			1,000,000	50			Oct-92
0.16	0.56	1.55	5.33	6.38	1.66	0.23	0.16		1.0009	4,354	89	10	0	0	0			1,000,000	50			Sep-13
0.00	0.25	1.06	4.00	4.24	1.23	0.4	0.18		1	1,013	75	25	0	0	0			1,000,000	50			Jun-14
0.00	0.29	1.20	4.53	5.12	1.38	0.18	0.18		1	1,013	75	25	0	0	0			1,000,000	50			Sep-13
0.00	0.27	1.15	4.38	4.82	1.34	0.23	0.18		1	1,013	75	25	0	0	0			1,000,000	50			Sep-13
0.03	0.34	1.24	4.59	5.08	1.42	0.18	0.17		1	10,809	64	34	0	0	0			1,000,000	50			Oct-92
0.01	0.32	1.19	4.44	4.84	1.37	0.23	0.17		1	10,809	64	34	0	0	0			1,000,000	50			Sep-13
5.19	4.03	6.12	12.85	19.73	2.14	0.85	3.18	4.23	11.48	1,107	0	35	0	33	0	94	3.30	1,000	50	4.25		Apr-12
5.09	3.67	5.52	10.94	15.87	1.49	1.57	3.2	4.23	11.51	1,107	0	35	0	33	0	94	3.30	1,000	50		1.00	Apr-12
5.27	4.20	6.48	14.33	22.08	2.46	0.54	3.18	4.23	11.49	1,107	0	35	0	33	0	94	3.30	1,000,000				Jul-94

Fund Name	MARKET Ticker Symbol	Traded On	FUND TYPE, CATEGORY & OBJECTIVE Fund Type	Category and (Prospectus Objective)	RATINGS Overall Rating	Reward Rating	Risk Rating	Recent Up/ Downgrade	NEW INVESTORS Open to New Investors	Telephone
Western Asset Intermediate Bond Fund Class IS	WABSX	NAS CM	Open End	US Fixed Inc (Corp Bond - General)	B-	C+	B+	Up	Y	877-721-1926
Western Asset Intermediate Bond Fund Class R	WATRX	NAS CM	Open End	US Fixed Inc (Corp Bond - General)	B-	C	B	Up	Y	877-721-1926
Western Asset Intermediate Maturity California Munis Cl A	ITCAX	NAS CM	Open End	US Muni Fixed Inc (Muni Bond - Single State)	C-	D+	C	Down	Y	877-721-1926
Western Asset Intermediate Maturity California Munis Cl C	SIMLX	NAS CM	Open End	US Muni Fixed Inc (Muni Bond - Single State)	C-	D+	C	Down	Y	877-721-1926
Western Asset Intermediate Maturity California Munis Cl I	SICYX	NAS CM	Open End	US Muni Fixed Inc (Muni Bond - Single State)	C-	D+	C	Down	Y	877-721-1926
Western Asset Intermediate Maturity New York Munis Cl A	IMNYX	NAS CM	Open End	US Muni Fixed Inc (Muni Bond - Single State)	C	C-	C		Y	877-721-1926
Western Asset Intermediate Maturity New York Munis Cl C	SINLX	NAS CM	Open End	US Muni Fixed Inc (Muni Bond - Single State)	C-	D+	C	Down	Y	877-721-1926
Western Asset Intermediate Maturity New York Munis Cl I	LMIIX	NAS CM	Open End	US Muni Fixed Inc (Muni Bond - Single State)	C	C-	C		Y	877-721-1926
Western Asset Intermediate Municipal Fund	SBI	NYSE	Closed End	US Muni Fixed Inc (Muni Bond - Natl)	D+	D+	C-	Down	Y	877-721-1926
Western Asset Intermediate-Term Municipals Fund Class A	SBLTX	NAS CM	Open End	US Muni Fixed Inc (Muni Bond - Natl)	C-	D+	C	Down	Y	877-721-1926
Western Asset Intermediate-Term Municipals Fund Class C	SMLLX	NAS CM	Open End	US Muni Fixed Inc (Muni Bond - Natl)	C-	D+	C	Down	Y	877-721-1926
Western Asset Intermediate-Term Municipals Fund Class I	SBTYX	NAS CM	Open End	US Muni Fixed Inc (Muni Bond - Natl)	C	C-	C		Y	877-721-1926
Western Asset Intermediate-Term Municipals Fund Class IS	SMLSX	NAS CM	Open End	US Muni Fixed Inc (Muni Bond - Natl)	C	C-	C		Y	877-721-1926
Western Asset Inv Grade Income Fund Inc	PAI	NYSE	Closed End	US Fixed Inc (Corp Bond - General)	C-	C-	C-		Y	
Western Asset Inv Grade Defined Opportunity Trust Inc.	IGI	NYSE	Closed End	US Fixed Inc (Corp Bond - High Quality)	C-	C-	C-		Y	877-721-1926
Western Asset Macro Opportunities Fund Class A	LAAAX	NAS CM	Open End	Fixed Inc Misc (Growth)	C-	C-	C	Down	Y	877-721-1926
Western Asset Macro Opportunities Fund Class A2	LAATX	NAS CM	Open End	Fixed Inc Misc (Growth)	C-	C-	C	Down	Y	877-721-1926
Western Asset Macro Opportunities Fund Class C	LAACX	NAS CM	Open End	Fixed Inc Misc (Growth)	C-	C-	C	Down	Y	877-721-1926
Western Asset Macro Opportunities Fund Class FI	LAFIX	NAS CM	Open End	Fixed Inc Misc (Growth)	C-	C-	C	Down	Y	877-721-1926
Western Asset Macro Opportunities Fund Class I	LAOIX	NAS CM	Open End	Fixed Inc Misc (Growth)	C-	C-	C	Down	Y	877-721-1926
Western Asset Macro Opportunities Fund Class IS	LAOSX	NAS CM	Open End	Fixed Inc Misc (Growth)	C-	C-	C	Down	Y	877-721-1926
Western Asset Managed Municipals Fund Class 1	SMMOX	NAS CM	Open End	US Muni Fixed Inc (Muni Bond - Natl)	C-	D+	C	Down		877-721-1926
Western Asset Managed Municipals Fund Class A	SHMMX	NAS CM	Open End	US Muni Fixed Inc (Muni Bond - Natl)	C-	D+	C	Down	Y	877-721-1926
Western Asset Managed Municipals Fund Class C	SMMCX	NAS CM	Open End	US Muni Fixed Inc (Muni Bond - Natl)	C-	D+	C	Down	Y	877-721-1926
Western Asset Managed Municipals Fund Class I	SMMYX	NAS CM	Open End	US Muni Fixed Inc (Muni Bond - Natl)	C-	D+	C	Down	Y	877-721-1926
Western Asset Managed Municipals Fund Class IS	SSMMX	NAS CM	Open End	US Muni Fixed Inc (Muni Bond - Natl)	C-	D+	C	Down	Y	877-721-1926
Western Asset Managed Municipals Portfolio	MMU	NYSE	Closed End	US Muni Fixed Inc (Muni Bond - Natl)	C-	D+	C		Y	877-721-1926
Western Asset Massachusetts Municipals Fund Class A	SLMMX	NAS CM	Open End	US Muni Fixed Inc (Muni Bond - Single State)	C	C-	C+		Y	877-721-1926
Western Asset Massachusetts Municipals Fund Class C	SMALX	NAS CM	Open End	US Muni Fixed Inc (Muni Bond - Single State)	C	C-	C+		Y	877-721-1926
Western Asset Massachusetts Municipals Fund Class I	LHMIX	NAS CM	Open End	US Muni Fixed Inc (Muni Bond - Single State)	C	C-	C+		Y	877-721-1926
Western Asset Middle Market Debt Fund Inc.	XWAMX	NAS CM	Closed End	US Fixed Inc (Income)	D	D	D	Down	Y	877-721-1926
Western Asset Middle Market Income Fund Inc.	XWMFX	NAS CM	Closed End	US Fixed Inc (Income)	D	D-	D	Down	Y	877-721-1926
Western Asset Mortgage Defined Opportunity Fund Inc.	DMO	NYSE	Closed End	US Fixed Inc (Govt Bond - Mortgage)	D-	D-	D	Down	Y	877-721-1926
Western Asset Mortgage Total Return Fund Class 1	SGVSX	NAS CM	Open End	US Fixed Inc (Govt Bond - Mortgage)	C	C-	C+			877-721-1926
Western Asset Mortgage Total Return Fund Class A	SGVAX	NAS CM	Open End	US Fixed Inc (Govt Bond - Mortgage)	C	C-	C+		Y	877-721-1926
Western Asset Mortgage Total Return Fund Class C	LWMSX	NAS CM	Open End	US Fixed Inc (Govt Bond - Mortgage)	C	C-	C		Y	877-721-1926
Western Asset Mortgage Total Return Fund Class C1	SGSLX	NAS CM	Open End	US Fixed Inc (Govt Bond - Mortgage)	C	C-	C+			877-721-1926
Western Asset Mortgage Total Return Fund Class I	SGSYX	NAS CM	Open End	US Fixed Inc (Govt Bond - Mortgage)	C	C-	C+		Y	877-721-1926
Western Asset Mortgage Total Return Fund Class IS	LMBSX	NAS CM	Open End	US Fixed Inc (Govt Bond - Mortgage)	C	C-	C+		Y	877-721-1926
Western Asset Municipal Defined Opportunity Trust, Inc.	MTT	NYSE	Closed End	US Muni Fixed Inc (Muni Bond - Natl)	D+	D+	C-	Down	Y	877-721-1926
Western Asset Municipal High Income Fund Inc	MHF	NYSE	Closed End	US Muni Fixed Inc (Muni Bond - Natl)	D+	D+	C-	Down	Y	
Western Asset Municipal Partners Fund Inc	MNP	NYSE	Closed End	US Muni Fixed Inc (Muni Bond - Natl)	D+	D+	C-	Down	Y	877-721-1926
Western Asset New Jersey Municipals Fund Class A	SHNJX	NAS CM	Open End	US Muni Fixed Inc (Muni Bond - Single State)	C-	D+	C	Down	Y	877-721-1926
Western Asset New Jersey Municipals Fund Class C	SNJLX	NAS CM	Open End	US Muni Fixed Inc (Muni Bond - Single State)	C-	D+	C	Down	Y	877-721-1926
Western Asset New Jersey Municipals Fund Class I	LNJIX	NAS CM	Open End	US Muni Fixed Inc (Muni Bond - Single State)	C-	D+	C	Down	Y	877-721-1926
Western Asset New York Municipals Fund Class A	SBNYX	NAS CM	Open End	US Muni Fixed Inc (Muni Bond - Single State)	C	C-	C+		Y	877-721-1926
Western Asset New York Municipals Fund Class C	SBYLX	NAS CM	Open End	US Muni Fixed Inc (Muni Bond - Single State)	C	C-	C+		Y	877-721-1926
Western Asset New York Municipals Fund Class I	SNPYX	NAS CM	Open End	US Muni Fixed Inc (Muni Bond - Single State)	C	C-	C+		Y	877-721-1926
Western Asset New York Tax Free Money Market Fund Class A	LNAXX	NAS CM	Money Mkt	US Money Mkt (Money Mkt - Single State)	C	C-	C		Y	877-721-1926
Western Asset New York Tax Free Money Market Fund Class N	CIYXX	NAS CM	Money Mkt	US Money Mkt (Money Mkt - Single State)	C	C-	C		Y	877-721-1926
Western Asset Oregon Municipals Fund Class A	SHORX	NAS CM	Open End	US Muni Fixed Inc (Muni Bond - Single State)	C	C	B-		Y	877-721-1926
Western Asset Oregon Municipals Fund Class C	SORLX	NAS CM	Open End	US Muni Fixed Inc (Muni Bond - Single State)	C	C-	B-		Y	877-721-1926

★ Expanded analysis of this fund is included in Section II.

TOTAL RETURNS & PERFORMANCE									ASSETS		ASSET ALLOCATION & TURNOVER							MINIMUMS		FEES		
3-Month Total Return	6-Month Total Return	1-Year Total Return	3-Year Total Return	5-Year Total Return	Dividend Yield (TTM)	Expense Ratio	3-Yr Std Deviation	Effective Duration	NAV	Total Assets (MIL)	%Cash	%Government Bonds	%Municipal Bonds	%Corporate Bonds	%Other	Turnover Ratio	Average Coupon Rate	Min Initial Investment	Min Additional Investment	Front End Fee (%)	Back End Fee (%)	Inception Date
5.39	4.26	6.59	14.62	22.64	2.57	0.45	3.2	4.23	11.5	1,107	0	35	0	33	0	94	3.30	1,000,000				Oct-08
5.21	3.90	5.94	12.35	18.44	1.88	1.15	3.2	4.23	11.5	1,107	0	35	0	33	0	94	3.30	0				Apr-12
2.86	-1.08	0.54	7.05	11.84	2.16	0.75	4.95	4.20	8.73	167.2	-3	0	100	0	0	33	4.51	1,000	50	2.25		Dec-91
2.71	-1.49	-0.04	5.02	8.42	1.55	1.35	4.93	4.20	8.71	167.2	-3	0	100	0	0	33	4.51	1,000	50			Jul-02
2.89	-1.00	0.70	7.53	12.69	2.32	0.6	4.95	4.20	8.76	167.2	-3	0	100	0	0	33	4.51	1,000,000				Sep-95
1.84	-0.50	1.08	7.37	10.85	2.51	0.75	4.05	4.10	8.59	159.8	-2	0	100	0	0	31	4.56	1,000	50	2.25		Dec-91
1.69	-0.79	0.37	5.34	7.49	1.89	1.35	4.06	4.10	8.59	159.8	-2	0	100	0	0	31	4.56	1,000	50			Jul-02
1.88	-0.43	1.11	7.72	11.54	2.66	0.6	4.06	4.10	8.57	159.8	-2	0	100	0	0	31	4.56	1,000,000				Apr-08
4.05	-1.02	1.02	8.63	16.54	3.13		6.36	4.91	10	137.9	-1	0	100	0	0	18	4.89					Mar-92
2.92	-0.29	1.42	8.03	13.23	2.78	0.61	4.66	4.57	6.35	2,385	0	0	100	0	0	32	4.74	1,000	50	2.25		Nov-88
2.76	-0.56	0.84	6.14	10.04	2.19	1.19	4.65	4.57	6.36	2,385	0	0	100	0	0	32	4.74	1,000	50			Dec-01
2.96	-0.21	1.58	8.52	14.10	2.95	0.43	4.67	4.57	6.35	2,385	0	0	100	0	0	32	4.74	1,000,000				Sep-07
3.14	-0.18	1.80	8.62	13.85	3.01	0.38	4.71	4.57	6.36	2,385	0	0	100	0	0	32	4.74	1,000,000				Sep-18
13.08	1.05	5.52	16.24	33.73	4.46		9.46	7.43	15.31	142.4	1	4	1	93	0	66	5.61					Mar-73
12.92	1.69	6.10	16.77	32.12	1.99	0.85	9.19	7.56	21.1	224.3	0	1	1	97	0	56	5.54					Jun-09
12.90	-3.23	3.35	9.64	28.94	5.08	1.57	10.46	-2.18	10.76	1,431	19	20	0	18	0	165	5.40	1,000	50	4.25		Aug-13
12.80	-3.26	3.27	9.56	29.21	5.1	1.59	10.42	-2.18	10.66	1,431	19	20	0	18	0	165	5.40	1,000	50	4.25		Dec-16
12.60	-3.62	2.52	7.30	24.52	4.36	2.29	10.45	-2.18	10.63	1,431	19	20	0	18	0	165	5.40	1,000	50		1.00	Aug-13
12.80	-3.32	3.23	9.50	28.77	5.06	1.61	10.45	-2.18	10.75	1,431	19	20	0	18	0	165	5.40	0				Aug-13
12.91	-3.15	3.53	10.55	30.84	5.35	1.3	10.46	-2.18	10.75	1,431	19	20	0	18	0	165	5.40	1,000,000				Aug-13
12.99	-3.05	3.61	10.91	31.44	5.42	1.21	10.46	-2.18	10.78	1,431	19	20	0	18	0	165	5.40	1,000,000				Aug-13
3.68	-0.55	1.65	9.76	16.60	3.23	0.51	5.55	5.74	16.02	4,295	-1	0	100	0	0	31	4.91	0				Sep-00
3.63	-0.61	1.51	9.32	15.91	3.09	0.65	5.57	5.74	16.07	4,295	-1	0	100	0	0	31	4.91	1,000	50	4.25		Mar-81
3.49	-0.87	0.96	7.52	12.75	2.51	1.2	5.57	5.74	16.08	4,295	-1	0	100	0	0	31	4.91	1,000	50		1.00	Nov-94
3.68	-0.51	1.70	9.82	16.65	3.27	0.45	5.56	5.74	16.1	4,295	-1	0	100	0	0	31	4.91	1,000,000				Apr-95
3.62	-0.56	1.67	9.79	16.40	3.31	0.42	5.56	5.74	16.09	4,295	-1	0	100	0	0	31	4.91	1,000,000				Mar-18
5.61	-1.01	1.75	11.75	21.94	4.57		7.82	6.82	13.39	565.5	0	0	100	0	0	21	5.02					Jun-92
1.47	0.17	1.99	8.94	15.01	2.64	0.75	4.46	5.59	12.68	94.7	0	0	100	0	0	15	4.82	1,000	50	4.25		Dec-87
1.34	-0.10	1.35	7.25	11.99	2.08	1.3	4.43	5.59	12.67	94.7	0	0	100	0	0	15	4.82	1,000	50		1.00	Nov-94
1.51	0.24	2.14	9.60	15.97	2.79	0.6	4.46	5.59	12.69	94.7	0	0	100	0	0	15	4.82	1,000,000				Jun-08
10.39	-11.75	-10.34	-0.05	8.86	9.51	1.38	12.18		593.15	--	-20	0	0	99	0	33	8.30	25		2.50		Dec-12
11.41	-15.96	-15.64	-3.99	7.60	10.8	2.12	14.54		579.46	--	-1	0	0	97	0	29	8.41	0		3.00		Aug-14
16.49	-23.56	-20.69	0.06	16.79	4.96	2.23	21.48		14.08	50.2	-44	0	0	0	0	17	4.96					Feb-10
3.05	0.26	2.03	11.11	16.21	4.21	0.67	3.67	2.20	10.23	979.4	0	0	0	1	0	74	3.90	0				Sep-00
2.99	0.03	1.65	10.08	14.51	3.93	0.95	3.67	2.20	10.21	979.4	0	0	0	1	0	74	3.90	1,000	50	4.25		Nov-92
2.82	-0.30	0.95	7.92	10.70	3.22	1.64	3.63	2.20	10.21	979.4	0	0	0	1	0	74	3.90	1,000	50		1.00	Aug-12
2.86	-0.22	1.29	8.75	12.16	3.56	1.36	3.66	2.20	10.22	979.4	0	0	0	1	0	74	3.90	1,000	50		1.00	Feb-93
3.06	0.18	1.94	11.18	16.23	4.21	0.67	3.61	2.20	10.26	979.4	0	0	0	1	0	74	3.90	1,000,000				Feb-96
3.08	0.23	2.05	11.50	16.45	4.32	0.56	3.64	2.20	10.27	979.4	0	0	0	1	0	74	3.90	1,000,000				Jun-16
4.41	-1.06	1.12	9.23	13.87	2.21	0.84	6.15	6.74	20.53	244.9	0	0	100	0	0	33	4.79					Mar-09
3.62	-1.25	1.38	10.03	18.91	3.94		5.62	7.31	7.78	164.2	0	0	100	0	0	16	5.25					Nov-88
5.07	-0.81	1.78	11.93	22.51	3.91	0.97	7.73	6.66	16.16	152.9	-1	0	100	0	0	19	4.98					Jan-93
2.60	-1.75	0.20	8.57	14.51	2.99	0.83	5.71	6.19	12.06	170.4	0	0	100	0	0	22	4.97	1,000	50	4.25		Apr-88
2.45	-2.01	-0.34	6.78	11.27	2.41	1.39	5.74	6.19	12.06	170.4	0	0	100	0	0	22	4.97	1,000	50		1.00	Dec-94
2.65	-1.64	0.42	9.26	15.62	3.22	0.6	5.71	6.19	12.07	170.4	0	0	100	0	0	22	4.97	1,000,000				Oct-07
2.17	0.42	2.49	9.76	14.66	3.12	0.76	4.24	5.44	13.11	540.1	-1	0	100	0	0	21	4.92	1,000	50	4.25		Jan-87
2.03	0.15	1.91	7.91	11.44	2.54	1.33	4.24	5.44	13.1	540.1	-1	0	100	0	0	21	4.92	1,000	50		1.00	Jan-93
2.22	0.50	2.65	10.28	15.49	3.28	0.6	4.24	5.44	13.1	540.1	-1	0	100	0	0	21	4.92	1,000,000				Jan-01
0.01	0.27	0.63	2.15	2.29	0.73	0.6	0.12		1	115.1	3	0	97	0	0			1,000	50			Mar-11
0.02	0.23	0.51	1.72	1.79	0.6	0.75	0.12		1	115.1	3	0	97	0	0			0				Nov-85
2.25	1.68	3.60	10.98	15.64	2.17	0.75	4.16	5.57	10.48	64.9	0	0	100	0	0	17	4.84	1,000	50	4.25		May-94
2.13	1.41	3.04	9.18	12.53	1.62	1.3	4.16	5.57	10.43	64.9	0	0	100	0	0	17	4.84	1,000	50		1.00	May-95

	MARKET			FUND TYPE, CATEGORY & OBJECTIVE	RATINGS				NEW INVESTORS	
Fund Name	Ticker Symbol	Traded On	Fund Type	Category and (Prospectus Objective)	Overall Rating	Reward Rating	Risk Rating	Recent Up/ Downgrade	Open to New Investors	Telephone
Western Asset Oregon Municipals Fund Class I	LMOOX	NAS CM	Open End	US Muni Fixed Inc (Muni Bond - Single State)	C	C	B		Y	877-721-1926
Western Asset Pennsylvania Municipals Fund Class A	SBPAX	NAS CM	Open End	US Muni Fixed Inc (Muni Bond - Single State)	C	C-	B-		Y	877-721-1926
Western Asset Pennsylvania Municipals Fund Class C	SPALX	NAS CM	Open End	US Muni Fixed Inc (Muni Bond - Single State)	C	C-	C+		Y	877-721-1926
Western Asset Pennsylvania Municipals Fund Class I	LPPIX	NAS CM	Open End	US Muni Fixed Inc (Muni Bond - Single State)	C	C-	B-		Y	877-721-1926
Western Asset Premier Bond Fund	WEA	NYSE	Closed End	US Fixed Inc (Multisector Bond)	D+	D+	C-	Down	Y	877-721-1926
Western Asset Premier Inst Govt Reserves Capital Shares	WABXX	NAS CM	Money Mkt	US Money Mkt (Money Mkt - Govt)	U	U	U		Y	877-721-1926
Western Asset Premier Inst Govt Reserves Preferred Shares	WACXX	NAS CM	Money Mkt	US Money Mkt (Money Mkt - Govt)	U	U	U		Y	877-721-1926
Western Asset Premier Inst Liquid Reserves Capital Shares	WAAXX	NAS CM	Money Mkt	US Money Mkt (Money Mkt - General)	U	U	U		Y	877-721-1926
Western Asset Premier Inst U.S. Treas Res Capital Shares	WADXX	NAS CM	Money Mkt	US Money Mkt (Money Mkt - Treasury)	U	U	U		Y	877-721-1926
Western Asset Premier Inst U.S. Treas Res Preferred Shares	WAEXX	NAS CM	Money Mkt	US Money Mkt (Money Mkt - Treasury)	U	U	U		Y	877-721-1926
Western Asset Premium Liquid Reserves Class A	CIPXX	NAS CM	Money Mkt	US Money Mkt (Money Mkt - Taxable)	C	C-	C+		Y	877-721-1926
Western Asset Premium U.S. Treasury Reserves Class A	CIMXX	NAS CM	Money Mkt	US Money Mkt (Money Mkt - Treasury)	C	C-	C+		Y	877-721-1926
Western Asset Select Tax Free Reserves Investor Shares	LTFXX	NAS CM	Money Mkt	US Money Mkt (Money Mkt - Fed Tax Exmpt)	C	C-	C+		Y	877-721-1926
Western Asset Select Tax Free Reserves Select Shares	CIFXX	NAS CM	Money Mkt	US Money Mkt (Money Mkt - Fed Tax Exmpt)	C	C-	C+		Y	877-721-1926
Western Asset Short Duration High Income Fund Class A	SHIAX	NAS CM	Open End	US Fixed Inc (Corp Bond - High Yield)	D+	D	C-	Down	Y	877-721-1926
Western Asset Short Duration High Income Fund Class C	LWHIX	NAS CM	Open End	US Fixed Inc (Corp Bond - High Yield)	D	D	C-	Down	Y	877-721-1926
Western Asset Short Duration High Income Fund Class C1	SHICX	NAS CM	Open End	US Fixed Inc (Corp Bond - High Yield)	D+	D	C-	Down		877-721-1926
Western Asset Short Duration High Income Fund Class I	SHIYX	NAS CM	Open End	US Fixed Inc (Corp Bond - High Yield)	D+	D	C-	Down	Y	877-721-1926
Western Asset Short Duration High Income Fund Class R	LWSRX	NAS CM	Open End	US Fixed Inc (Corp Bond - High Yield)	D+	D	C-	Down	Y	877-721-1926
Western Asset Short Duration Municipal Income Fund Class A	SHDAX	NAS CM	Open End	US Muni Fixed Inc (Muni Bond - Natl)	C	C-	C+		Y	877-721-1926
Western Asset Short Duration Muni Income Fund Class A2	SHDQX	NAS CM	Open End	US Muni Fixed Inc (Muni Bond - Natl)	C	C-	C		Y	877-721-1926
Western Asset Short Duration Municipal Income Fund Class C	SHDLX	NAS CM	Open End	US Muni Fixed Inc (Muni Bond - Natl)	C	C-	C		Y	877-721-1926
Western Asset Short Duration Municipal Income Fund Class I	SMDYX	NAS CM	Open End	US Muni Fixed Inc (Muni Bond - Natl)	C	C-	C+		Y	877-721-1926
Western Asset Short Duration Muni Income Fund Class IS	SHDSX	NAS CM	Open End	US Muni Fixed Inc (Muni Bond - Natl)	C	C-	C+		Y	877-721-1926
Western Asset Short-Term Bond Fund Class A	SBSTX	NAS CM	Open End	US Fixed Inc (Corp Bond - General)	C	C	B-		Y	877-721-1926
Western Asset Short-Term Bond Fund Class C	LWSOX	NAS CM	Open End	US Fixed Inc (Corp Bond - General)	C	C	B-		Y	877-721-1926
Western Asset Short-Term Bond Fund Class C1	SSTLX	NAS CM	Open End	US Fixed Inc (Corp Bond - General)	C	C	C+			877-721-1926
Western Asset Short-Term Bond Fund Class I	SBSYX	NAS CM	Open End	US Fixed Inc (Corp Bond - General)	C	C	B-		Y	877-721-1926
Western Asset Short-Term Bond Fund Class IS	LWSTX	NAS CM	Open End	US Fixed Inc (Corp Bond - General)	C	C	B-		Y	877-721-1926
Western Asset Short-Term Bond Fund Class R	LWARX	NAS CM	Open End	US Fixed Inc (Corp Bond - General)	C	C	C+		Y	877-721-1926
Western Asset SMASh Series C Fund	LMLCX	NAS CM	Open End	US Fixed Inc (Growth & Income)	C-	D+	C		Y	877-721-1926
Western Asset SMASh Series EC Fund	LMECX	NAS CM	Open End	US Fixed Inc (Growth & Income)	D+	D+	C-	Down	Y	877-721-1926
Western Asset SMASh Series M Fund	LMSMX	NAS CM	Open End	US Fixed Inc (Growth & Income)	B	B-	B+		Y	877-721-1926
Western Asset Tax Free Reserves Class A	LWAXX	NAS CM	Money Mkt	US Money Mkt (Money Mkt - Fed Tax Exmpt)	C	C-	C		Y	877-721-1926
Western Asset Tax Free Reserves Class N	CIXXX	NAS CM	Money Mkt	US Money Mkt (Money Mkt - Fed Tax Exmpt)	C	C-	C		Y	877-721-1926
Western Asset Total Return Unconstrained Fund Class A	WAUAX	NAS CM	Open End	Fixed Inc Misc (Growth & Income)	C-	D+	C	Down	Y	877-721-1926
Western Asset Total Return Unconstrained Fund Class A2	WRTUX	NAS CM	Open End	Fixed Inc Misc (Growth & Income)	C-	D+	C	Down	Y	877-721-1926
Western Asset Total Return Unconstrained Fund Class C	WAUCX	NAS CM	Open End	Fixed Inc Misc (Growth & Income)	C-	D+	C		Y	877-721-1926
Western Asset Total Return Unconstrained Fund Class FI	WARIX	NAS CM	Open End	Fixed Inc Misc (Growth & Income)	C-	D+	C	Down	Y	877-721-1926
Western Asset Total Return Unconstrained Fund Class I	WAARX	NAS CM	Open End	Fixed Inc Misc (Growth & Income)	C-	C-	C	Down	Y	877-721-1926
Western Asset Total Return Unconstrained Fund Class IS	WAASX	NAS CM	Open End	Fixed Inc Misc (Growth & Income)	C	C-	C		Y	877-721-1926
Western Asset Total Return Unconstrained Fund Class R	WAURX	NAS CM	Open End	Fixed Inc Misc (Growth & Income)	C-	D+	C	Down	Y	877-721-1926
Western Asset U.S. Treasury Reserves Class N	CISXX	NAS CM	Money Mkt	US Money Mkt (Money Mkt - Treasury)	C	C-	C		Y	877-721-1926
Western Asset U.S. Treasury Reserves Service Shares	LTSXX	NAS CM	Money Mkt	US Money Mkt (Money Mkt - Treasury)	C	C-	C		Y	877-721-1926
Western Asset Ultra-Short Income Fund Class A	ARMZX	NAS CM	Open End	US Fixed Inc (Govt Bond - ARM)	C-	D+	C	Down	Y	877-721-1926
Western Asset Ultra-Short Income Fund Class C	LWAIX	NAS CM	Open End	US Fixed Inc (Govt Bond - ARM)	C	C-	C+	Up	Y	877-721-1926
Western Asset Ultra-Short Income Fund Class C1	ARMGX	NAS CM	Open End	US Fixed Inc (Govt Bond - ARM)	C-	D+	C			877-721-1926
Western Asset Ultra-Short Income Fund Class I	SBAYX	NAS CM	Open End	US Fixed Inc (Govt Bond - ARM)	C-	D+	C	Down	Y	877-721-1926
Western Asset Ultra-Short Income Fund Class IS	ARMLX	NAS CM	Open End	US Fixed Inc (Govt Bond - ARM)	C	C-	C		Y	877-721-1926
Western Asset Variable Rate Strategic Fund Inc	GFY	NYSE	Closed End	US Fixed Inc (Corp Bond - General)	D	D	D+	Down	Y	877-721-1926
Westwood High Income Fund A Class	WSDAX	NAS CM	Open End	US Fixed Inc (Corp Bond - High Yield)	C	D+	C+	Up	Y	
Westwood High Income Fund C Class Shares	WWHCX	NAS CM	Open End	US Fixed Inc (Corp Bond - High Yield)	C-	D+	C		Y	

★Expanded analysis of this fund is included in Section II.

TOTAL RETURNS & PERFORMANCE									ASSETS		ASSET ALLOCATION & TURNOVER							MINIMUMS		FEES		
3-Month Total Return	6-Month Total Return	1-Year Total Return	3-Year Total Return	5-Year Total Return	Dividend Yield (TTM)	Expense Ratio	3-Yr Std Deviation	Effective Duration	NAV	Total Assets (MIL)	%Cash	%Government Bonds	%Municipal Bonds	%Corporate Bonds	%Other	Turnover Ratio	Average Coupon Rate	Min Initial Investment	Min Additional Investment	Front End Fee (%)	Back End Fee (%)	Inception Date
2.19	1.66	3.65	11.48	16.42	2.32	0.6	4.05	5.57	10.48	64.9	0	0	100	0	0	17	4.84	1,000,000				Sep-07
1.49	0.64	2.54	10.36	17.33	2.69	0.78	3.96	5.87	12.91	166.1	0	0	100	0	0	21	4.85	1,000	50	4.25		Apr-94
1.35	0.37	1.99	8.57	14.14	2.14	1.33	3.94	5.87	12.86	166.1	0	0	100	0	0	21	4.85	1,000	50		1.00	Apr-94
1.54	0.80	2.72	10.93	18.21	2.88	0.6	3.95	5.87	12.91	166.1	0	0	100	0	0	21	4.85	1,000,000				Feb-08
15.08	-3.57	1.03	12.96	31.78	5.62		11.83	4.58	13.72	160.4	-41	9	0	84	0	47	5.27					Mar-02
0.04	0.37					0.12			1	1,161	100	0	0	0	0			200,000,000				Oct-19
0.03	0.35					0.14			1	1,161	100	0	0	0	0			0				Oct-19
0.19	0.63					0.12			1.0006	0.10	100	0	0	0	0			200,000,000				Oct-19
0.04	0.37					0.12			1	171.9	100	0	0	0	0			0				Oct-19
0.04	0.37					0.14			1	171.9	100	0	0	0	0			200,000,000				Oct-19
0.11	0.45	1.31	4.59	5.25	1.43	0.45	0.16		1.0009	14.1	89	10	0	0	0			100,000	50			May-90
0.00	0.24	1.01	3.81	4.02	1.18	0.45	0.17		1	172.8	64	34	0	0	0			100,000	50			Mar-91
0.02	0.35	0.91	3.24	3.79	1.05	0.23	0.12		1	256.1	5	0	95	0	0			1,000,000	50			Dec-13
0.03	0.37	0.96	3.38	4.01	1.09	0.18	0.12		1	256.1	5	0	95	0	0			1,000,000	50			May-97
10.77	-5.97	-3.41	5.68	9.39	5.85	1	9.67	2.46	4.83	329.7	1	1	0	86	0	73	5.95	1,000	50	2.25		Nov-92
10.57	-6.32	-4.11	3.44	5.58	5.07	1.71	9.66	2.46	4.83	329.7	1	1	0	86	0	73	5.95	1,000	50		1.00	Aug-12
10.65	-6.26	-3.91	4.29	7.13	5.45	1.41	9.7	2.46	4.85	329.7	1	1	0	86	0	73	5.95	1,000	50		1.00	Aug-94
10.79	-5.82	-3.13	6.60	10.99	6.13	0.72	9.64	2.46	4.85	329.7	1	1	0	86	0	73	5.95	1,000,000				Feb-96
10.43	-6.35	-3.99	4.43	7.39	5.43	1.4	9.63	2.46	4.82	329.7	1	1	0	86	0	73	5.95	0				Jan-14
2.15	0.77	1.79	5.51	6.99	1.63	0.55	2	2.14	5.13	803.1	-2	0	100	0	0	47	3.28	1,000	50	2.25		Mar-03
2.14	0.76	1.73	5.07	6.12	1.55	0.69	1.91	2.14	5.13	803.1	-2	0	100	0	0	47	3.28	1,000	50	2.25		Feb-15
2.06	0.60	1.46	4.45	5.17	1.29	0.9	2	2.14	5.13	803.1	-2	0	100	0	0	47	3.28	1,000	50			Mar-03
2.19	0.84	1.95	5.96	7.60	1.78	0.4	1.92	2.14	5.13	803.1	-2	0	100	0	0	47	3.28	1,000,000				Nov-03
2.20	0.87	2.00	6.09	7.58	1.84	0.34	2	2.14	5.13	803.1	-2	0	100	0	0	47	3.28	1,000,000				Sep-17
3.38	1.84	3.10	8.47	11.64	2.36	0.75	2.12	2.19	3.93	765.2	10	22	0	35	0	41	2.93	1,000	50	2.25		Nov-91
3.20	1.73	2.34	6.06	7.57	1.61	1.5	2.21	2.19	3.93	765.2	10	22	0	35	0	41	2.93	1,000	50		1.00	Aug-12
3.04	1.69	2.87	7.71	10.26	2.15	0.98	2.01	2.19	3.93	765.2	10	22	0	35	0	41	2.93	1,000	50			Aug-02
3.44	1.95	3.35	9.25	13.32	2.61	0.5	2.13	2.19	3.93	765.2	10	22	0	35	0	41	2.93	1,000,000				Feb-96
3.47	2.00	3.45	9.57	13.50	2.71	0.4	2.18	2.19	3.93	765.2	10	22	0	35	0	41	2.93	1,000,000				Oct-12
3.29	1.66	2.75	7.59	9.97	2.01	1.1	2.24	2.19	3.93	765.2	10	22	0	35	0	41	2.93	0				Jan-14
11.65	-4.14	0.90	10.46	20.63	4.32	0	9.33		9.32	1,850	-67	15	0	32	37	15		0	0			Dec-06
8.91	-8.35	-1.61	8.62	28.84	7.09	0	11.71		8.5	2,702	-67	44	0	6	0	31		0	0			Dec-06
0.31	3.43	5.59	15.29	30.88	2.77	0	3.63		11.01	2,385	-221	83	0	0	-16	303		0	0			Dec-06
0.00	0.25	0.61	2.15	2.31	0.72	0.6	0.12		1	79.6	5	0	95	0	0			1,000	50			Aug-10
0.00	0.21	0.50	1.72	1.80	0.59	0.75	0.11		1	79.6	5	0	95	0	0			0				Sep-84
7.82	-1.81	1.44	5.79	15.39	3.62	1.1	6.21	0.15	10.17	1,279	5	33	0	20	0	49	4.23	1,000	50	4.25		Apr-12
7.77	-1.87	1.47	5.58	14.69	3.56	1.14	6.18	0.15	10.17	1,279	5	33	0	20	0	49	4.23	1,000	50	4.25		May-14
7.54	-2.15	0.77	3.59	11.65	2.93	1.76	6.18	0.15	10.16	1,279	5	33	0	20	0	49	4.23	1,000	50		1.00	Apr-12
7.73	-1.81	1.48	5.82	15.60	3.67	1.02	6.17	0.15	10.15	1,279	5	33	0	20	0	49	4.23	0				Sep-06
7.92	-1.64	1.91	6.94	17.41	4	0.73	6.18	0.15	10.17	1,279	5	33	0	20	0	49	4.23	1,000,000				Jul-06
7.84	-1.60	1.90	7.23	18.01	4.08	0.65	6.17	0.15	10.15	1,279	5	33	0	20	0	49	4.23	1,000,000				Aug-08
7.75	-1.84	1.30	5.13	14.28	3.37	1.33	6.15	0.15	10.18	1,279	5	33	0	20	0	49	4.23	0				Apr-12
0.00	0.20	0.90	3.39	3.49	1.06	0.6	0.16		1	259.0	64	34	0	0	0			0				May-91
0.00	0.11	0.61	2.31	2.30	0.73	1	0.15		1	259.0	64	34	0	0	0			0				Aug-15
4.62	-0.37	0.95	6.41	11.19	2.65	0.65	3.34	0.61	8.97	207.2	2	0	0	34	0	32	2.56	1,000	50	2.25		Apr-97
4.61	0.90	1.73	5.64	8.63	1.83	1.54	2.73	0.61	9.08	207.2	2	0	0	34	0	32	2.56	1,000	50		1.00	Aug-12
4.48	-0.67	0.23	4.61	7.98	2.15	1.31	3.35	0.61	8.89	207.2	2	0	0	34	0	32	2.56	1,000	50			Jun-92
4.71	-0.14	1.19	7.28	12.42	2.9	0.38	3.34	0.61	8.94	207.2	2	0	0	34	0	32	2.56	1,000,000				Oct-02
4.70	-0.22	1.37	7.52	12.87	2.97	0.35	3.34	0.61	8.97	207.2	2	0	0	34	0	32	2.56	1,000,000				Jan-14
9.18	-5.13	-3.49	5.84	17.48	4.71		8.29	0.81	16.41	75.1	-22	3	0	38	0	21	3.57					Oct-04
12.46	0.12	3.15	11.30	18.46	3.87	0.73	7.62		9.22	54.6	7	19	0	63	0	59	4.44	1,000		3.00		Jun-13
12.59	0.08	2.67	8.89	14.18		1.48	7.6		9.18	54.6	7	19	0	63	0	59	4.44	1,000			1.00	Mar-20

	MARKET			FUND TYPE, CATEGORY & OBJECTIVE	RATINGS				NEW INVESTORS	
Fund Name	Ticker Symbol	Traded On	Fund Type	Category and (Prospectus Objective)	Overall Rating	Reward Rating	Risk Rating	Recent Up/ Downgrade	Open to New Investors	Telephone
Westwood High Income Fund Institutional Class	WHGHX	NAS CM	Open End	US Fixed Inc (Corp Bond - High Yield)	C-	D+	C		Y	
William Blair Bond Fund Class I	WBFIX	NAS CM	Open End	US Fixed Inc (Income)	B-	C	B+	Up	Y	312-364-5409
William Blair Bond Fund Class N	WBBNX	NAS CM	Open End	US Fixed Inc (Income)	B-	C	B	Up	Y	312-364-5409
William Blair Bond Fund R6 Class	BBFIX	NAS CM	Open End	US Fixed Inc (Income)	B-	C	B+	Up	Y	312-364-5409
William Blair Income Fund Class I	BIFIX	NAS CM	Open End	US Fixed Inc (Corp Bond - High Quality)	C+	C	B	Up	Y	312-364-5409
William Blair Income Fund Class N	WBRRX	NAS CM	Open End	US Fixed Inc (Corp Bond - High Quality)	C+	C	B	Up	Y	312-364-5409
William Blair Income Fund Class R6	BIFJX	NAS CM	Open End	US Fixed Inc (Corp Bond - High Quality)	C+	C	B	Up	Y	312-364-5409
William Blair Low Duration Fund Class I	WBLIX	NAS CM	Open End	US Fixed Inc (Growth & Income)	C	C	B-		Y	312-364-5409
William Blair Low Duration Fund Class N	WBLNX	NAS CM	Open End	US Fixed Inc (Growth & Income)	C	C	B-		Y	312-364-5409
William Blair Low Duration Fund R6 Class	WBLJX	NAS CM	Open End	US Fixed Inc (Growth & Income)	C	C	B-		Y	312-364-5409
Wilmington Broad Market Bond Fund Class A	WABMX	NAS CM	Open End	US Fixed Inc (Corp Bond - General)	B-	C+	B	Up	Y	800-836-2211
Wilmington Broad Market Bond Fund Institutional Class	WIBMX	NAS CM	Open End	US Fixed Inc (Corp Bond - General)	B	C+	B+	Up	Y	800-836-2211
Wilmington Intermediate-Term Bond Fund Class A	WIBAX	NAS CM	Open End	US Fixed Inc (Income)	B-	C+	B	Up	Y	800-836-2211
Wilmington Intermediate-Term Bond Fund Institutional Class	WIBIX	NAS CM	Open End	US Fixed Inc (Income)	B-	C+	B	Up	Y	800-836-2211
Wilmington Municipal Bond Fund Class A	WTABX	NAS CM	Open End	US Muni Fixed Inc (Muni Bond - Natl)	C	C-	C+		Y	800-836-2211
Wilmington Municipal Bond Fund Class Institutional	WTAIX	NAS CM	Open End	US Muni Fixed Inc (Muni Bond - Natl)	C	C-	C+		Y	800-836-2211
Wilmington New York Municipal Bond Fund Class A	WNYAX	NAS CM	Open End	US Muni Fixed Inc (Muni Bond - Single State)	C	C-	C+		Y	800-836-2211
Wilmington New York Muni Bond Fund Institutional Class	WNYIX	NAS CM	Open End	US Muni Fixed Inc (Muni Bond - Single State)	C	C-	C+		Y	800-836-2211
Wilmington Short-Term Bond Fund Class A	WSBAX	NAS CM	Open End	US Fixed Inc (Corp Bond - General)	C	C	B-		Y	800-836-2211
Wilmington Short-Term Bond Fund Institutional Class	WISBX	NAS CM	Open End	US Fixed Inc (Corp Bond - General)	C+	C	B	Up	Y	800-836-2211
Wilmington U.S. Govt Money Mkt Administrative Class	WAGXX	NAS CM	Money Mkt	US Money Mkt (Money Mkt - Govt)	C	C-	C			800-836-2211
Wilmington U.S. Govt Money Mkt Fund Institutional Class	WGOXX	NAS CM	Money Mkt	US Money Mkt (Money Mkt - Govt)	C	C	C+		Y	800-836-2211
Wilmington U.S. Government Money Market Fund Select Class	WGEXX	NAS CM	Money Mkt	US Money Mkt (Money Mkt - Govt)	C	C-	C+			800-836-2211
Wilmington U.S. Government Money Market Fund Service Class	WGSXX	NAS CM	Money Mkt	US Money Mkt (Money Mkt - Govt)	C	C-	C+			800-836-2211
Wilmington U.S. Treasury Money Mkt Administrative Cl	WTAXX	NAS CM	Money Mkt	US Money Mkt (Money Mkt - Govt)	C	C-	C+			800-836-2211
Wilmington U.S. Treasury Money Mkt Institutional Cl	WTIXX	NAS CM	Money Mkt	US Money Mkt (Money Mkt - Govt)	C	C	C+		Y	800-836-2211
Wilmington U.S. Treasury Money Market Fund Select Class	WTEXX	NAS CM	Money Mkt	US Money Mkt (Money Mkt - Govt)	C	C-	C+			800-836-2211
Wilmington U.S. Treasury Money Market Fund Service Class	WTSXX	NAS CM	Money Mkt	US Money Mkt (Money Mkt - Govt)	C	C-	C+			800-836-2211
Wilshire Income Opportunities Fund Institutional Class	WIOPX	NAS CM	Open End	US Fixed Inc (Income)	C-	D+	C	Down	Y	888-200-6796
Wilshire Income Opportunities Fund Investment Class	WIORX	NAS CM	Open End	US Fixed Inc (Income)	C-	D+	C	Down	Y	888-200-6796
WP Income Plus Fund Institutional Class	WPINX	NAS CM	Open End	US Fixed Inc (Income)	D-	E+	D-	Down	Y	800-950-9112
WSTCM Credit Select Risk - Managed Institutional Shares	WAMIX	NAS CM	Open End	Fixed Inc Misc (Growth & Income)	C	C	B-		Y	865-243-8000
WSTCM Credit Select Risk - Managed Fund Investor Shares	WAMBX	NAS CM	Open End	Fixed Inc Misc (Growth & Income)	C	C	B-		Y	865-243-8000
XAI Octagon Floating Rate & Alternative Income Term Trust	XFLT	NYSE	Closed End	US Fixed Inc (Income)	D	D	D-		Y	
Yorktown Short Term Bond Fund Class A	APIMX	NAS CM	Open End	US Fixed Inc (Growth & Income)	C	C-	C		Y	800-544-6060
Yorktown Short Term Bond Fund Class Institutional	APIBX	NAS CM	Open End	US Fixed Inc (Growth & Income)	C	C-	C		Y	800-544-6060
Yorktown Short Term Bond Fund Class L	AFMMX	NAS CM	Open End	US Fixed Inc (Growth & Income)	C-	D+	C		Y	800-544-6060
Zeo Short Duration Income Fund Class I	ZEOIX	NAS CM	Open End	US Fixed Inc (Income)	D+	D	C-	Down	Y	
Zeo Sustainable Credit Fund Class I	ZSRIX	NAS CM	Open End	US Fixed Inc (Income)	D	D	D		Y	
Ziegler Senior Floating Rate Fund Class A	ZFLAX	NAS CM	Open End	US Fixed Inc (Growth & Income)	D+	D	C	Down	Y	877-568-7633
Ziegler Senior Floating Rate Fund Class C	ZFLCX	NAS CM	Open End	US Fixed Inc (Growth & Income)	D+	D	C-	Down	Y	877-568-7633
Ziegler Senior Floating Rate Fund Institutional Class	ZFLIX	NAS CM	Open End	US Fixed Inc (Growth & Income)	D+	D	C	Down	Y	877-568-7633

★ Expanded analysis of this fund is included in Section II.

TOTAL RETURNS & PERFORMANCE									ASSETS		ASSET ALLOCATION & TURNOVER							MINIMUMS		FEES		
3-Month Total Return	6-Month Total Return	1-Year Total Return	3-Year Total Return	5-Year Total Return	Dividend Yield (TTM)	Expense Ratio	3-Yr Std Deviation	Effective Duration	NAV	Total Assets (MIL)	%Cash	%Government Bonds	%Municipal Bonds	%Corporate Bonds	%Other	Turnover Ratio	Average Coupon Rate	Min Initial Investment	Min Additional Investment	Front End Fee (%)	Back End Fee (%)	Inception Date
12.59	0.33	3.43	11.91	19.70	4.26	0.67	7.56		9.18	54.6	7	19	0	63	0	59	4.44	100,000				Dec-11
5.34	4.26	7.28	15.42	22.96	3.89	0.45	4.13	6.01	10.54	271.0	2	4	0	39	0	58	5.24	500,000				May-07
5.35	4.26	7.19	14.93	21.89	3.74	0.6	4.16	6.01	10.66	271.0	2	4	0	39	0	58	5.24	2,500	1,000			May-07
5.46	4.29	7.33	15.74	23.46	3.94	0.4	4.17	6.01	10.54	271.0	2	4	0	39	0	58	5.24	1,000,000				May-07
3.16	3.19	4.84	9.54	13.65	3.36	0.7	2.29	3.26	8.65	51.3	2	5	0	27	0	114	4.83	500,000				Oct-99
3.11	3.11	4.55	8.82	12.25	3.21	0.85	2.26	3.26	8.7	51.3	2	5	0	27	0	114	4.83	2,500	1,000			Oct-90
3.17	3.22	4.89	9.19	12.63	3.41	0.65	2.26	3.26	8.65	51.3	2	5	0	27	0	114	4.83	1,000,000				May-19
1.46	1.90	2.76	7.33	9.08	3.62	0.4	1.12	0.95	8.69	87.2	8	5	0	23	0	183	4.57	500,000				Dec-09
1.42	1.82	2.72	6.82	8.18	3.47	0.55	1.15	0.95	8.7	87.2	8	5	0	23	0	183	4.57	2,500	1,000			Dec-09
1.36	1.81	2.81	7.34	9.29	3.67	0.35	1.12	0.95	8.69	87.2	8	5	0	23	0	183	4.57	1,000,000				Dec-09
3.45	5.55	7.88	14.01	19.58	2.09	0.84	3.19	5.85	10.5	545.4	6	28	0	40	0	36	3.29	1,000	25	4.50		Jul-93
3.69	5.81	8.34	15.31	21.65	2.42	0.49	3.26	5.85	10.33	545.4	6	28	0	40	0	36	3.29	100,000	25			Jul-93
4.56	5.16	6.77	12.25	15.68	1.85	0.84	2.78	3.96	10.4	49.7	4	31	0	64	0	25	3.01	1,000	25	4.50		Aug-03
4.54	5.21	6.98	13.29	17.52	2.14	0.49	2.81	3.96	10.4	49.7	4	31	0	64	0	25	3.01	100,000	25			Nov-96
2.44	-0.10	1.65	8.11	13.98	1.88	0.74	4.63	4.80	13.2	353.9	5	0	95	0	0	83	4.70	1,000	25	4.50		Dec-05
2.43	-0.05	1.90	8.84	15.34	2.13	0.49	4.56	4.80	13.2	353.9	5	0	95	0	0	83	4.70	100,000	25			Nov-93
1.69	-0.07	1.23	6.75	12.27	1.42	0.83	3.97	4.79	10.51	64.4	3	0	97	0	0	45	4.58	1,000	25	4.50		Sep-93
1.85	0.04	1.48	7.55	13.78	1.67	0.58	4.03	4.79	10.52	64.4	3	0	97	0	0	45	4.58	100,000	25			Aug-03
1.77	2.30	3.56	7.35	9.13	1.75	0.73	1.15	1.76	10.2	48.3	23	35	0	37	0	67	2.80	1,000	25	1.75		Aug-03
1.83	2.44	3.84	8.17	10.52	2.01	0.48	1.15	1.76	10.2	48.3	23	35	0	37	0	67	2.80	100,000	25			Apr-96
0.00	0.19	0.89	3.32	3.42	1.05	0.62	0.17		1	8,634	72	28	0	0	0			1,000	25			Jul-95
0.02	0.30	1.18	4.34	4.63	1.36	0.27	0.17		1	8,634	72	28	0	0	0			5,000,000	25			Mar-12
0.02	0.27	1.10	4.05	4.28	1.27	0.37	0.17		1	8,634	72	28	0	0	0			100,000	25			Jun-93
0.00	0.16	0.79	2.90	2.94	0.93	0.77	0.16		1	8,634	72	28	0	0	0			0	0			Jul-97
0.00	0.19	0.89	3.32	3.41	1.04	0.6	0.16		1	1,370	73	27	0	0	0			1,000	25			Aug-03
0.02	0.29	1.06	4.03	4.25		0.25			1	1,370	73	27	0	0	0			1,000,000	25			Oct-19
0.02	0.27	1.09	4.05	4.27	1.26	0.35	0.17		1	1,370	73	27	0	0	0			100,000	25			Jun-88
0.00	0.16	0.77	2.91	2.94	0.92	0.75	0.16		1	1,370	73	27	0	0	0			0	0			Jun-98
5.73	-2.89	-0.79	8.42		5.4	0.92	6.27		9.96	281.9	-7	23	0	22	0	89	3.81	250,000	100,000			Mar-16
5.70	-2.96	-1.02	7.72		4.99	1.18	6.28		10.01	281.9	-7	23	0	22	0	89	3.81	2,500	100			Mar-16
-7.29	-53.18	-51.90	-48.72		5.49	3.54	28.97	4.04	5.15	5.1	65	0	0	44	0	2	6.02	2,000	100			Dec-15
3.05	2.01	3.78	8.33	23.76	4.31	1.54	2.71	6.76	10.12	45.7	84	12	0	2	0	524	2.94	100,000	1,000			Sep-14
2.95	1.81	3.51	7.49	22.34	3.75	1.75	2.76	6.76	10.11	45.7	84	12	0	2	0	524	2.94	1,000	250			Sep-14
26.02	-20.84	-25.54			16.25	4.24			5.87	67.8	-45	0	0	53	0	94	8.38					Sep-17
4.29	0.08	1.69	7.21	12.16	2.56	0.89	3.54		3.91	465.7	1	0	0	63	0	62	3.69	1,000	100	2.25		Jul-97
4.27	-0.16	1.58	7.11	12.02	2.4	0.89	3.71		4.17	465.7	1	0	0	63	0	62	3.69	1,000,000	100,000			May-13
3.96	-0.59	0.67	3.95	6.59	1.88	1.54	3.67		3.55	465.7	1	0	0	63	0	62	3.69	1,000	100			Jul-04
6.59	-4.84	-2.77	3.40	8.73	4.34	1.03	6.87	1.77	9.3	300.3	12	0	0	88	0	135	6.06	5,000	1,000			May-11
5.44	-6.23	-5.02			2.69	1.25			9.25	10.8	16	0	0	84	0		5.94	5,000	1,000			May-19
8.54	-3.54	-1.76	6.62		5.11	1	7.42		23.75	75.0	2	0	0	98	0	61	4.97	1,000	100	4.25		Apr-16
8.30	-4.20	-2.83	3.86		4.35	1.75	7.54		23.61	75.0	2	0	0	98	0	61	4.97	1,000	100		1.00	Apr-16
8.58	-3.70	-1.84	7.07		5.39	0.75	7.54		23.69	75.0	2	0	0	98	0	61	4.97	1,000,000				Apr-16

Section II: Analysis of 100 Largest Bond & Money Market Mutual Funds

Detailed analysis of the 100 Largest Bond & Money Market Mutual Funds. Funds are listed by their Asset Size.

Section II: Contents

This section contains an expanded analysis of the 100 Largest Bond & Money Market Mutual Funds, with current and historical Weiss Investment Ratings, key rating factors, summary financial data and performance charts. Funds are listed by their Asset Size.

TOP ROW

Fund Name
Describes the fund's assets, regions of investments and investment strategies. Many funds have similar names, so you want to make sure the fund you look up is really the one you are interested in evaluating.

Overall Rating
The Weiss rating measured on a scale from A to E based on each fund's risk and performance. See the preceding section, "What Our Ratings Mean," for an explanation of each letter grade rating.

BUY-HOLD-SELL Indicator
Funds that are rated in the A or B range are, in our opinion, a potential BUY. Funds in the C range will indicate a HOLD status. Funds in the D or E range will indicate a SELL status.

Ticker Symbol
An arrangement of characters (usually letters) representing a particular security listed on an exchange or otherwise traded publicly. When a company issues securities to the public marketplace, it selects an available ticker symbol for its securities which investors use to place trade orders. Every listed security has a unique ticker symbol, facilitating the vast array of trade orders that flow through the financial markets every day. If a ticker symbol is not assigned to a particular fund, the International Securities Identification Number (ISIN) is displayed.

Traded On (Exchange)
The stock exchange on which the fund is listed. The core function of a stock exchange is to ensure fair and orderly trading, as well as efficient dissemination of price information. Exchanges such as: NYSE (New York Stock Exchange), AMEX (American Stock Exchange), NNM (NASDAQ National Market), and NASQ (NASDAQ Small Cap) give companies, governments and other groups a platform to sell securities to the investing public.

NAV (Net Asset Value)
A fund's price per share. The value is calculated by dividing the total value of all the securities in the portfolio, less any liabilities, by the number of fund shares outstanding.

Total Assets ($)
The total of all assets listed on the institution's balance sheet. This figure primarily consists of loans, investments, and fixed assets. Total Assets are displayed in dollars.

Dividend Yield (TTM)

Trailing twelve months dividends paid out relative to the share price. Expressed as a percentage and measures how much cash flow an investor is getting for each invested dollar. **Trailing Twelve Months (TTM)** is a representation of a fund's financial performance over the most recent 12 months. TTM uses the latest available financial data from a company's interim, quarterly or annual reports.

Turnover Ratio

The percentage of a mutual fund or other investment vehicle's holdings that have been replaced with other holdings in a given year. Generally, low turnover ratio is favorable, because high turnover equates to higher brokerage transaction fees, which reduce fund returns.

Expense Ratio

A measure of what it costs an investment company to operate a mutual fund. An expense ratio is determined through an annual calculation, where a fund's operating expenses are divided by the average dollar value of its assets under management. Operating expenses may include money spent on administration and management of the fund, advertising, etc. An expense ratio of 1 percent per annum means that each year 1 percent of the fund's total assets will be used to cover expenses.

LEFT COLUMN

<u>Ratings</u>

Reward Rating

This is based on the total return over a period of up to five years, including net asset value and price growth. The total return figure is stated net of the expenses and fees charged by the fund. Based on proprietary modeling the individual components of the risk and reward ratings are calculated and weighted and the final rating is generated.

Risk Rating

This is includes the risk ratings of component stocks where applicable and also includes the financial stability of the fund, turnover where applicable, together with the level of volatility as measured by the fund's daily returns over a period of up to five years. Funds with greater stability are considered less risky and receive a higher risk rating. Funds with greater volatility are considered riskier, and will receive a lower risk rating. In addition to considering the fund's volatility, the risk rating also considers an assessment of the valuation and quality of a fund's holdings.

Recent Upgrade/Downgrade

An "Up" or "Down" indicates that the Weiss Mutual Fund rating has changed since the publication of the last print edition. If a fund has had a rating change since March 31, 2020, the change is identified with an "Up" or "Down."

Fund Information

Fund Type
Describes the fund's assets, regions of investments and investment strategies.

Open End Fund
A type of mutual fund that does not have restrictions on the amount of shares the fund will issue. If demand is high enough, the fund will continue to issue shares no matter how many investors there are. Open-end funds also buy back shares when investors wish to sell.

Closed End Fund
They are launched through an Initial Public Offering in order to raise money and then trade in the open market just like a stock or an ETF. They only issue a set amount of shares and, although their value is also based on the Net Asset Value, the actual price of the fund is affected by supply and demand, allowing it to trade at prices above or below its real value.

Money Market Fund
Mutual fund that invests primarily in low-risk, short-term investments such as treasury bills, government securities, certificates of deposit and other highly liquid, safe securities.

Category
Identifies funds according to their actual investment styles as measured by their portfolio holdings. This categorization allows investors to spread their money around in a mix of funds with a variety of risk and return characteristics.

Sub-Category
A subdivision of funds, usually with common characteristics as the category.

Prospectus Objective
Gives a general idea of a fund's overall investment approach and goals.

Inception Date
The date on which the fund began its operations. The commencement date indicates when a fund began investing in the market. Many investors prefer funds with longer operating histories. Funds with longer histories have longer track records and can thereby provide investors with a more long-standing picture of their performance.

Open to New Investments
Indicates whether the fund accepts investments from those who are not existing investors. A “Y” in this column identifies that the fund accepts new investors. No data in this column indicates that the fund is closed to new investors. The fund may be closed to new investors because the fund's asset base is getting too large to effectively execute its investing style. Although, the fund may be closed, in most cases, existing investors are able to add to their holdings.

Minimum Initial Investment
The smallest investment amount a fund will accept to establish a new account. This amount could be $0 or any other number set by the fund.

Minimum Subsequent Investment
The smallest additional investment amount a fund will accept in an existing account.

Front End Fee
A commission or sales charge applied at the time of the initial purchase of an investment. The fee percentage is generally based on the amount of the investment. Larger investments, both initial and cumulative, generally receive percentage discounts based on the dollar value invested. Fees are displayed as a percent.

Back End Fee
A fee that investors pay when withdrawing money from an investment within a specified number of years, usually five to 10 years. The back-end load is designed to discourage withdrawals and typically declines for each year that a shareholder remains in a fund. The fee is a percentage of the value of the share being sold. Fees are displayed as a percent.

Total Returns (%)

3-Month Total Return
The rate of return on an investment over three months that includes interest, capital gains, dividends and distributions realized.

6-Month Total Return
The rate of return on an investment over six months that includes interest, capital gains, dividends and distributions realized.

1-Year Total Return
The rate of return on an investment over one year that includes interest, capital gains, dividends and distributions realized.

3-Year Total Return
The rate of return on an investment over three years that includes interest, capital gains, dividends and distributions realized.

5-Year Total Return
The rate of return on an investment over five years that includes interest, capital gains, dividends and distributions realized.

3-Year Standard Deviation

A statistical measurement of dispersion about an average, which depicts how widely the returns varied over the past three years. Investors use the standard deviation of historical performance to try to predict the range of returns that are most likely for a given fund. When a fund has a high standard deviation, the predicted range of performance is wide, implying greater volatility. Standard deviation is most appropriate for measuring risk if it is for a fund that is an investor's only holding. The figure cannot be combined for more than one fund because the standard deviation for a portfolio of multiple funds is a function of not only the individual standard deviations, but also of the degree of correlation among the funds' returns. If a fund's returns follow a normal distribution, then approximately 68 percent of the time they will fall within one standard deviation of the mean return for the fund, and 95 percent of the time within two standard deviations.

Effective Duration

Effective duration for all long fixed income positions in a portfolio. This value gives a better estimation of how the price of bonds with embedded options, which are common in many mutual funds, will change as a result of changes in interest rates. Effective duration takes into account expected mortgage prepayment or the likelihood that embedded options will be exercised if a fund holds futures, other derivative securities, or other funds as assets, the aggregate effective duration should include the weighted impact of those exposures.

Average Coupon Rate

The annual interest rate of a debt/bond security that the issuer promises to pay to the holder until maturity.

Company Information

Provider

The legal company that issues the fund.

Manager/Tenure (Years)

The name of the manager and the number of years spent managing the fund.

Website

The company's web address.

Address

The company's street address.

Phone Number

The company's phone number.

RIGHT COLUMN

Performance Chart
A graphical representation of the fund's total returns over the past year.

Ratings History

Indicates the fund's Overall, Risk and Reward Ratings for the previous five years. Ratings are listed as of June 30, 2020 (Q2-20), December 31, 2019 (Q4-19), December 31, 2018 (Q4-18), December 31, 2017 (Q4-17), and December 31, 2016 (Q4-16).

Overall Rating
The Weiss rating measured on a scale from A to E based on each fund's risk and performance. See the preceding section, "What Our Ratings Mean," for an explanation of each letter grade rating.

Risk Rating
This is includes the risk ratings of component stocks where applicable and also includes the financial stability of the fund, turnover where applicable, together with the level of volatility as measured by the fund's daily returns over a period of up to five years. Funds with greater stability are considered less risky and receive a higher risk rating. Funds with greater volatility are considered riskier, and will receive a lower risk rating. In addition to considering the fund's volatility, the risk rating also considers an assessment of the valuation and quality of a fund's holdings.

Reward Rating
This is based on the total return over a period of up to five years, including net asset value and price growth. The total return figure is stated net of the expenses and fees charged by the fund. Based on proprietary modeling the individual components of the risk and reward ratings are calculated and weighted and the final rating is generated.

Asset & Performance History

Indicates the fund's NAV (Net Asset Value) and 1-Year Total Return for the previous 6 years.

NAV (Net Asset Value)
A fund's price per share. The value is calculated by dividing the total value of all the securities in the portfolio, less any liabilities, by the number of fund shares outstanding.

1-Year Total Return
The rate of return on an investment over one year that includes interest, capital gains, dividends and distributions realized.

Total Assets ($)
The total of all assets listed on the institution's balance sheet. This figure primarily consists of loans, investments, and fixed assets. Total Assets are displayed in dollars.

Asset Allocation

Indicates the percentage of assets in each category. Used as an investment strategy that attempts to balance risk versus reward by adjusting the percentage of each asset in an investment portfolio according to the investor's risk tolerance, goals and investment time frame. Allocation percentages may not add up to 100%. Negative values reflect short positions.

%Cash

The percentage of the fund's assets invested in short-term obligations, usually less than 90 days, that provide a return in the form of interest payments. This type of investment generally offers a low return compared to other investments but has a low risk level.

%Government Bonds

The percentage of the fund's assets invested in government bonds. A government bond is issued by a national government.

%Municipal Bonds

The percentage of the fund's assets invested in municipal bonds. A municipal bond is issued by or on behalf of a local authority.

%Corporate Bonds

The percentage of the fund's assets invested in corporate bonds. A corporate bond is issued by a corporation.

%Other

The percentage of the fund's assets invested in other financial instruments.

Services Offered

Services offered by the fund provider. Such services can include:

Systematic Withdrawal Plan

A plan offered by mutual funds that pays specific amounts to shareholders at predetermined intervals.

Institutional Only

This indicates if the fund is offered to institutional clients only (pension funds, mutual funds, money managers, insurance companies, investment banks, commercial trusts, endowment funds, hedge funds, and some hedge fund investors).

Phone Exchange

This indicates that investors can move money between different funds within the same fund family over the phone.

Wire Redemption

This indicates whether or not investors can redeem electronically.

Qualified Investment

Under a qualified plan, an investor may invest in the variable annuity with pretax dollars through an employee pension plan, such as a 401(k) or 403(b). Money builds up on a tax-deferred basis, and when the qualified investor makes a withdrawal or annuitizes, all contributions received are taxable income.

Investment Strategy

A set of rules, behaviors or procedures, designed to guide an investor's selection of an investment portfolio. Individuals have different profit objectives, and their individual skills make different tactics and strategies appropriate.

Top Holdings

The highest amount of publicly traded assets held by a fund. These publicly traded assets may include company stock, mutual funds or other investment vehicles.

Vanguard Total Bond Market Index Fund Investor Shares — B BUY

Ticker	Traded On	NAV	Total Assets ($)	Dividend Yield (TTM)	Turnover Ratio	Expense Ratio
VBMFX	NAS CM	11.61	$269,048,000,000	2.42	31	0.15

Ratings

Reward	B-
Risk	B+
Recent Upgrade/Downgrade	

Fund Information

Fund Type	Open End
Category	US Fixed Inc
Sub-Category	Intermediate Core Bond
Prospectus Objective	Income
Inception Date	Dec-86
Open to New Investments	Y
Minimum Initial Investment	3,000
Minimum Subsequent Investment	1
Front End Fee	
Back End Fee	

Total Returns (%)

3-Month	6-Month	1-Year	3-Year	5-Year
2.94	6.29	8.83	16.54	23.35

3-Year Standard Deviation	3.32
Effective Duration	6.21
Average Coupon Rate	3.12

Company Information

Provider	Vanguard
Manager/Tenure	Joshua C. Barrickman (7)
Website	http://www.vanguard.com
Address	Vanguard 100 Vanguard Boulevard Malvern PA 19355 United States
Phone Number	877-662-7447

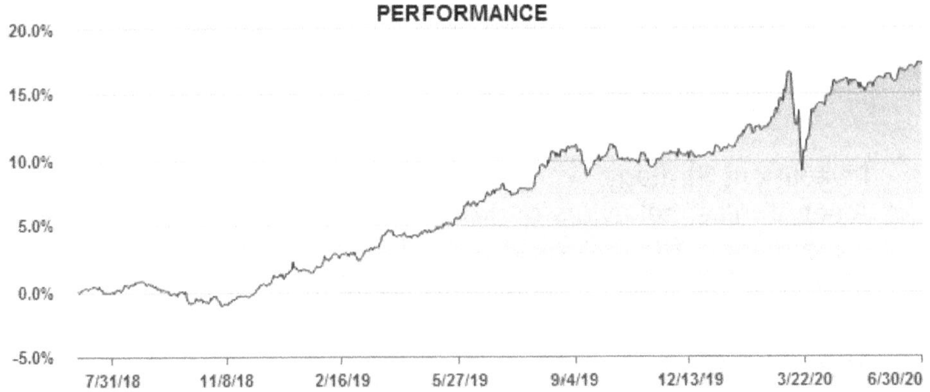

Ratings History

Date	Overall Rating	Risk Rating	Reward Rating
Q2-20	BB+	B-	2019
Q4-19	C	B	C
Q4-18	C-	C+	D+
Q4-17	B-	B+	C
Q4-16	C	C	C

Asset & Performance History

Date	NAV	1-Year Total Return
11.05	8.59	Cash
2018	10.45	-0.15
2017	10.75	3.43
2016	10.65	2.48
2015	10.64	0.29
2014	10.87	5.75

Total Assets: $269,048,000,000

Asset Allocation

Asset	%
3%	
Bonds	96%
Govt Bond	44%
Muni Bond	1%
Corp Bond	28%
Other	0%

Services Offered: Systematic Withdrawal Plan, Automatic Investment Plan, Phone Exchange, Wire Redemption

Investment Strategy: The investment seeks the performance of Bloomberg Barclays U.S. Aggregate Float Adjusted Index. Bloomberg Barclays U.S. Aggregate Float Adjusted Index measures the performance of a wide spectrum of public, investment-grade, taxable, fixed income securities in the United States-including government, corporate, and international dollar-denominated bonds, as well as mortgage-backed and asset-backed securities-all with maturities of more than 1 year. All of its investments will be selected through the sampling process, and at least 80% of its assets will be invested in bonds held in the index. **Top Holdings:** Federal National Mortgage Association 3% United States Treasury Notes 2.88% United States Treasury Notes 2.12% United States Treasury Notes 2% United States Treasury Notes 1.5%

Vanguard Total Bond Market Index Fund Admiral Shares — B BUY

Ticker	Traded On	NAV	Total Assets ($)	Dividend Yield (TTM)	Turnover Ratio	Expense Ratio
VBTLX	NAS CM	11.61	$269,048,000,000	2.52	31	0.05

Ratings

Reward	B-
Risk	B+
Recent Upgrade/Downgrade	

Fund Information

Fund Type	Open End
Category	US Fixed Inc
Sub-Category	Intermediate Core Bond
Prospectus Objective	Income
Inception Date	Nov-01
Open to New Investments	Y
Minimum Initial Investment	3,000
Minimum Subsequent Investment	1
Front End Fee	
Back End Fee	

Total Returns (%)

3-Month	6-Month	1-Year	3-Year	5-Year
2.97	6.34	8.94	16.88	23.94

3-Year Standard Deviation	3.32
Effective Duration	6.21
Average Coupon Rate	3.12

Company Information

Provider	Vanguard
Manager/Tenure	Joshua C. Barrickman (7)
Website	http://www.vanguard.com
Address	Vanguard 100 Vanguard Boulevard Malvern PA 19355 United States
Phone Number	877-662-7447

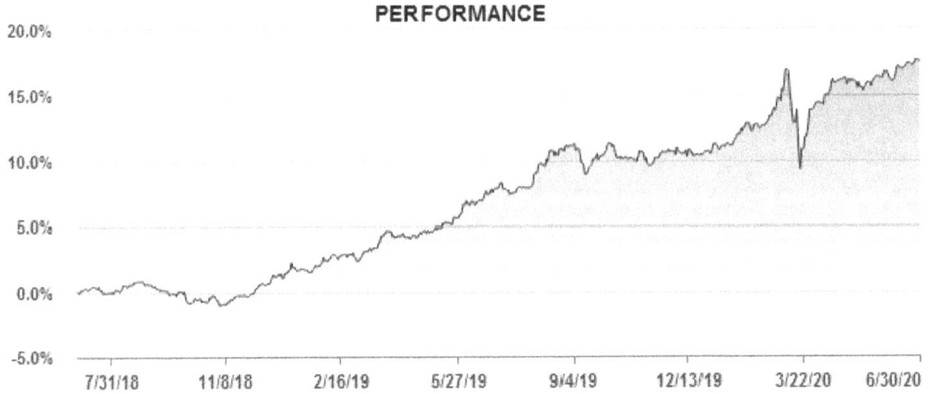

Ratings History

Date	Overall Rating	Risk Rating	Reward Rating
Q2-20	BB+	B-	2019
Q4-19	C+	B	C
Q4-18	C	C+	D+
Q4-17	B-	A-	C
Q4-16	C	B-	C

Asset & Performance History

Date	NAV	1-Year Total Return
11.05	8.69	Cash
2018	10.45	-0.05
2017	10.75	3.53
2016	10.65	2.58
2015	10.64	0.39
2014	10.87	5.89

Total Assets: $269,048,000,000

Asset Allocation

Asset	%
3%	
Bonds	96%
Govt Bond	44%
Muni Bond	1%
Corp Bond	28%
Other	0%

Services Offered: Systematic Withdrawal Plan, Automatic Investment Plan, Phone Exchange, Wire Redemption

Investment Strategy: The investment seeks the performance of Bloomberg Barclays U.S. Aggregate Float Adjusted Index. Bloomberg Barclays U.S. Aggregate Float Adjusted Index measures the performance of a wide spectrum of public, investment-grade, taxable, fixed income securities in the United States-including government, corporate, and international dollar-denominated bonds, as well as mortgage-backed and asset-backed securities-all with maturities of more than 1 year. All of its investments will be selected through the sampling process, and at least 80% of its assets will be invested in bonds held in the index. **Top Holdings:** Federal National Mortgage Association 3% United States Treasury Notes 2.88% United States Treasury Notes 2.12% United States Treasury Notes 2% United States Treasury Notes 1.5%

Goldman Sachs Financial Square Government Fund A Shares — C HOLD

Ticker	Traded On	NAV	Total Assets ($)	Dividend Yield (TTM)	Turnover Ratio	Expense Ratio
FSOXX	NAS CM	1	$225,345,000,000	1.25		0.43

Ratings

Reward	C-
Risk	C+
Recent Upgrade/Downgrade	

Fund Information

Fund Type	Money Mkt
Category	US Money Mkt
Sub-Category	Money Mkt-Taxable
Prospectus Objective	Money Mkt - Govt
Inception Date	Feb-16
Open to New Investments	Y
Minimum Initial Investment	1,000
Minimum Subsequent Investment	
Front End Fee	
Back End Fee	

Total Returns (%)

3-Month	6-Month	1-Year	3-Year	5-Year
0.00	0.25	1.07	4.01	4.09

3-Year Standard Deviation	0.17
Effective Duration	
Average Coupon Rate	

Company Information

Provider	Goldman Sachs
Manager/Tenure	Management Team (27)
Website	http://www.gsamfunds.com
Address	Goldman Sachs 200 West Stree New York NY 10282 United States
Phone Number	800-526-7384

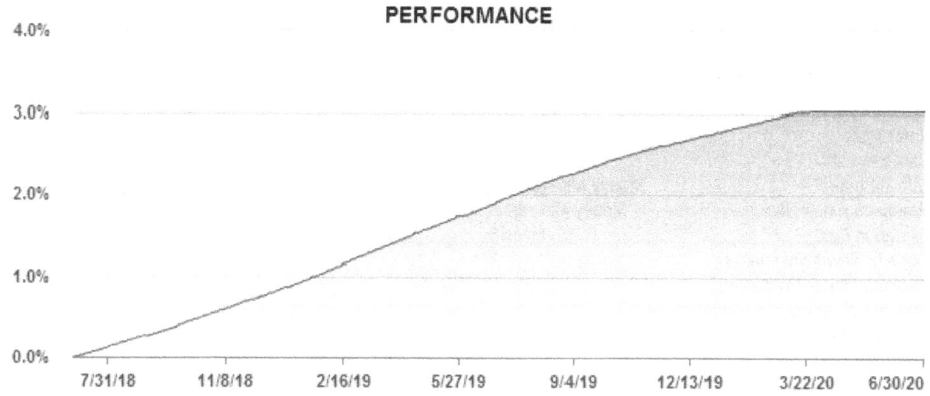

Ratings History

Date	Overall Rating	Risk Rating	Reward Rating
Q2-20	CC+	C-	2019
Q4-19	C	C+	C
Q4-18	C	C+	C-
Q4-17	C	C	C-
Q4-16	C-	C	D+

Asset & Performance History

Date	NAV	1-Year Total Return
1	1.86	Cash
2018	1	1.49
2017	1	0.51
2016	1	0.03
2015		-0.22
2014		-0.23

Total Assets: $225,345,000,000

Asset Allocation

Asset	%
77%	
Bonds	22%
Govt Bond	22%
Muni Bond	0%
Corp Bond	1%
Other	0%

Services Offered: Systematic Withdrawal Plan, Automatic Investment Plan, Qualified Investment, Wire Redemption, Retirement Investment

Investment Strategy: The investment seeks to maximize current income to the extent consistent with the preservation of capital and the maintenance of liquidity by investing exclusively in high quality money market instruments. The fund pursues its investment objective by investing only in "government securities," as such term is defined in or interpreted under the Investment Company Act of 1940, as amended ("Investment Company Act"), and repurchase agreements collateralized by such securities. "Government securities" generally are securities issued or guaranteed by the United States or certain U.S. government agencies or instrumentalities ("U.S. government securities"). **Top Holdings:** United States Treasury Bills 0% United States Treasury Bills 0% United States Treasury Bills 0% Sumitbc 0.04 05/01/20 Ja3 0.03833 05/01/20

Goldman Sachs Financial Square Government Fund C Shares — C HOLD

Ticker	Traded On	NAV	Total Assets ($)	Dividend Yield (TTM)	Turnover Ratio	Expense Ratio
FSGXX	NAS CM	1	$225,345,000,000	0.65		1.18

Ratings

Reward	C-
Risk	C
Recent Upgrade/Downgrade	

Fund Information

Fund Type	Money Mkt
Category	US Money Mkt
Sub-Category	Money Mkt-Taxable
Prospectus Objective	Money Mkt - Govt
Inception Date	Feb-16
Open to New Investments	Y
Minimum Initial Investment	1,000
Minimum Subsequent Investment	
Front End Fee	
Back End Fee	1.00

Total Returns (%)

3-Month	6-Month	1-Year	3-Year	5-Year
0.00	0.09	0.53	1.94	1.51

3-Year Standard Deviation	0.14
Effective Duration	
Average Coupon Rate	

Company Information

Provider	Goldman Sachs
Manager/Tenure	Management Team (27)
Website	http://www.gsamfunds.com
Address	Goldman Sachs 200 West Stree New York NY 10282 United States
Phone Number	800-526-7384

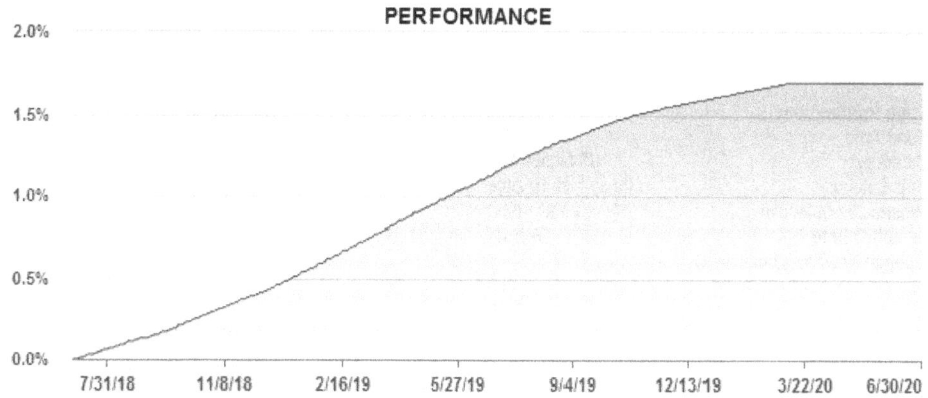

Ratings History

Date	Overall Rating	Risk Rating	Reward Rating
Q2-20	CC	C-	2019
Q4-19	C	C+	C-
Q4-18	C	C+	C-
Q4-17	C-	C	D+
Q4-16	D+	C	D

Asset & Performance History

Date	NAV	1-Year Total Return
1	1.1	Cash
2018	1	0.72
2017	1	0
2016	1	-0.07
2015		-0.71
2014		-0.73

Total Assets: $225,345,000,000

Asset Allocation

Asset	%
77%	
Bonds	22%
Govt Bond	22%
Muni Bond	0%
Corp Bond	1%
Other	0%

Services Offered: Systematic Withdrawal Plan, Automatic Investment Plan, Qualified Investment, Wire Redemption, Retirement Investment

Investment Strategy: The investment seeks to maximize current income to the extent consistent with the preservation of capital and the maintenance of liquidity by investing exclusively in high quality money market instruments. The fund pursues its investment objective by investing only in "government securities," as such term is defined in or interpreted under the Investment Company Act of 1940, as amended ("Investment Company Act"), and repurchase agreements collateralized by such securities. "Government securities" generally are securities issued or guaranteed by the United States or certain U.S. government agencies or instrumentalities ("U.S. government securities"). **Top Holdings:** United States Treasury Bills 0% United States Treasury Bills 0% United States Treasury Bills 0% Sumitbc 0.04 05/01/20 Ja3 0.03833 05/01/20

JPMorgan U.S. Government Money Market Fund E*TRADE Class — C HOLD

Ticker	Traded On	NAV	Total Assets ($)	Dividend Yield (TTM)	Turnover Ratio	Expense Ratio
JUSXX	NAS CM		$218,802,000,000	0.76		1

Ratings

Reward	C-
Risk	C
Recent Upgrade/Downgrade	

Fund Information

Fund Type	Money Mkt
Category	US Money Mkt
Sub-Category	Money Mkt-Taxable
Prospectus Objective	Money Mkt - Govt
Inception Date	Mar-16
Open to New Investments	Y
Minimum Initial Investment	0
Minimum Subsequent Investment	
Front End Fee	
Back End Fee	

Total Returns (%)

3-Month	6-Month	1-Year	3-Year	5-Year
	0.18	0.76	2.31	1.89

3-Year Standard Deviation	0.15
Effective Duration	
Average Coupon Rate	

Company Information

Provider	JPMorgan
Manager/Tenure	Management Team (10)
Website	http://www.jpmorganfunds.com
Address	JPMorgan 270 Park Avenue New York NY 10017-2070 United States
Phone Number	800-480-4111

PERFORMANCE

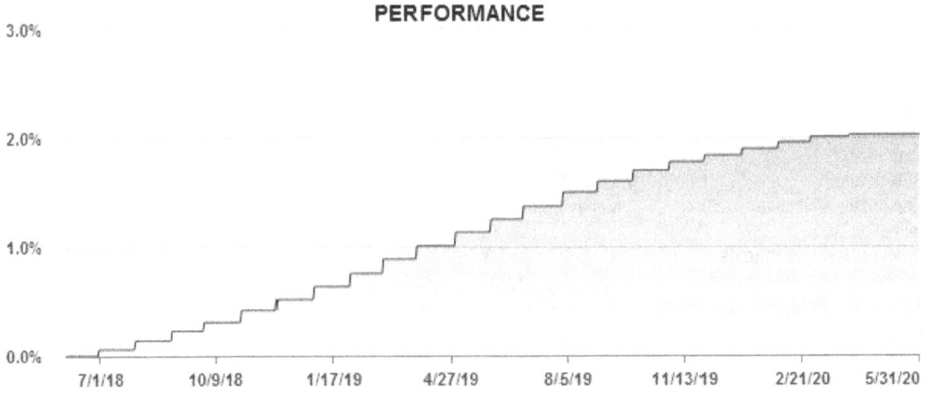

Ratings History

Date	Overall Rating	Risk Rating	Reward Rating
Q2-20	CC	C-	2019
Q4-19	C	C	C-
Q4-18	C-	C	C-
Q4-17	C-	C	D+
Q4-16	C-	C	D

Asset & Performance History

Date	NAV	1-Year Total Return
1	1.35	Cash
2018	1	0.36
2017	1	0
2016	1	-0.51
2015		-0.58
2014		-0.58

Total Assets: $218,802,000,000

Asset Allocation

Asset	%
65%	
Bonds	34%
Govt Bond	33%
Muni Bond	0%
Corp Bond	1%
Other	0%

Services Offered: Qualified Investment, Phone Exchange, Wire Redemption

Investment Strategy: The investment seeks high current income with liquidity and stability of principal. The fund normally invests its assets exclusively in debt securities issued or guaranteed by the U.S. government, or by U.S. government agencies or instrumentalities or GSEs, and repurchase agreements fully collateralized by U.S. Treasury and U.S. government securities. The dollar-weighted average maturity of the fund will be 60 days or less and the dollar-weighted average life to maturity will be 120 days or less. It may invest significantly in securities with floating or variable rates of interest. Their yields will vary as interest rates change. **Top Holdings:** National Securities Clearing Corporation 0% Goldman Sachs & Co. Llc Daiwa Capital Markets America. Inc. Sumitomo Mitsui Banking Corp. United States Treasury Bills 0%

JPMorgan U.S. Government Money Market Fund Morgan Class — C HOLD

Ticker	Traded On	NAV	Total Assets ($)	Dividend Yield (TTM)	Turnover Ratio	Expense Ratio
MJGXX	NAS CM	1	$218,802,000,000	1.09		0.59

Ratings

Reward	C-
Risk	C+
Recent Upgrade/Downgrade	

Fund Information

Fund Type	Money Mkt
Category	US Money Mkt
Sub-Category	Money Mkt-Taxable
Prospectus Objective	Money Mkt - Govt
Inception Date	Feb-05
Open to New Investments	Y
Minimum Initial Investment	1,000
Minimum Subsequent Investment	50
Front End Fee	
Back End Fee	

Total Returns (%)

3-Month	6-Month	1-Year	3-Year	5-Year
0.00	0.21	0.94	3.48	3.60

3-Year Standard Deviation	0.17
Effective Duration	
Average Coupon Rate	

Company Information

Provider	JPMorgan
Manager/Tenure	Management Team (10)
Website	http://www.jpmorganfunds.com
Address	JPMorgan 270 Park Avenue New York NY 10017-2070 United States
Phone Number	800-480-4111

PERFORMANCE

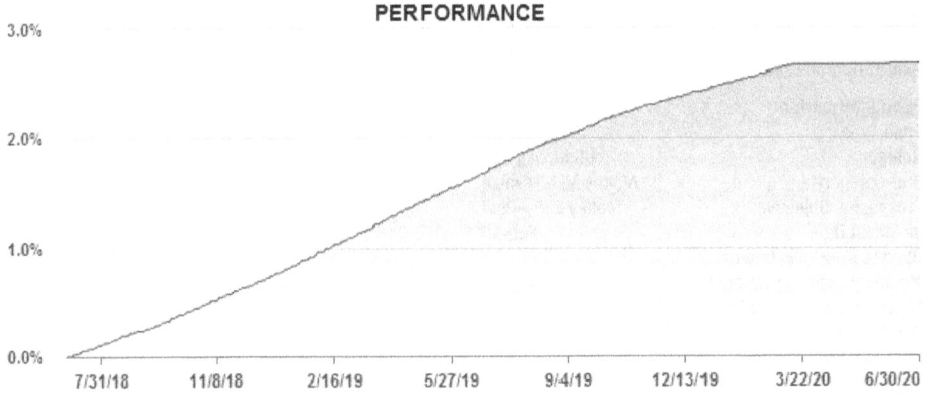

Ratings History

Date	Overall Rating	Risk Rating	Reward Rating
Q2-20	CC+	C-	2019
Q4-19	C	C	C-
Q4-18	C	C	C-
Q4-17	C	C	C-
Q4-16	C-	C	C-

Asset & Performance History

Date	NAV	1-Year Total Return
1	1.66	Cash
2018	1	1.3
2017	1	0.34
2016	1	0.01
2015	1	0
2014	1	0

Total Assets: $218,802,000,000

Asset Allocation

Asset	%
65%	
Bonds	34%
Govt Bond	33%
Muni Bond	0%
Corp Bond	1%
Other	0%

Services Offered: Systematic Withdrawal Plan, Automatic Investment Plan, Qualified Investment, Phone Exchange, Wire Redemption

Investment Strategy: The investment seeks high current income with liquidity and stability of principal. The fund normally invests its assets exclusively in debt securities issued or guaranteed by the U.S. government, or by U.S. government agencies or instrumentalities or GSEs, and repurchase agreements fully collateralized by U.S. Treasury and U.S. government securities. The dollar-weighted average maturity of the fund will be 60 days or less and the dollar-weighted average life to maturity will be 120 days or less. It may invest significantly in securities with floating or variable rates of interest. Their yields will vary as interest rates change. **Top Holdings:** National Securities Clearing Corporation 0% Goldman Sachs & Co. Llc Daiwa Capital Markets America. Inc. Sumitomo Mitsui Banking Corp. United States Treasury Bills 0%

Fidelity® Government Cash Reserves C HOLD

Ticker	Traded On	NAV	Total Assets ($)	Dividend Yield (TTM)	Turnover Ratio	Expense Ratio
FDRXX	NAS CM	1	$201,168,000,000	1.28	0	0.38

Ratings

Reward	C-
Risk	C+
Recent Upgrade/Downgrade	

Fund Information

Fund Type	Money Mkt
Category	US Money Mkt
Sub-Category	Money Mkt-Taxable
Prospectus Objective	Money Mkt - Taxable
Inception Date	May-79
Open to New Investments	Y
Minimum Initial Investment	0
Minimum Subsequent Investment	
Front End Fee	
Back End Fee	

Total Returns (%)

3-Month	6-Month	1-Year	3-Year	5-Year
0.00	0.26	1.10	4.11	4.40

3-Year Standard Deviation	0.18
Effective Duration	
Average Coupon Rate	

Company Information

Provider	Fidelity Investments
Manager/Tenure	Management Team (13)
Website	http://www.institutional.fidelity.com
Address	Fidelity Investments 82 Devonshire Street Boston MA 2109 United States
Phone Number	617-563-7000

PERFORMANCE

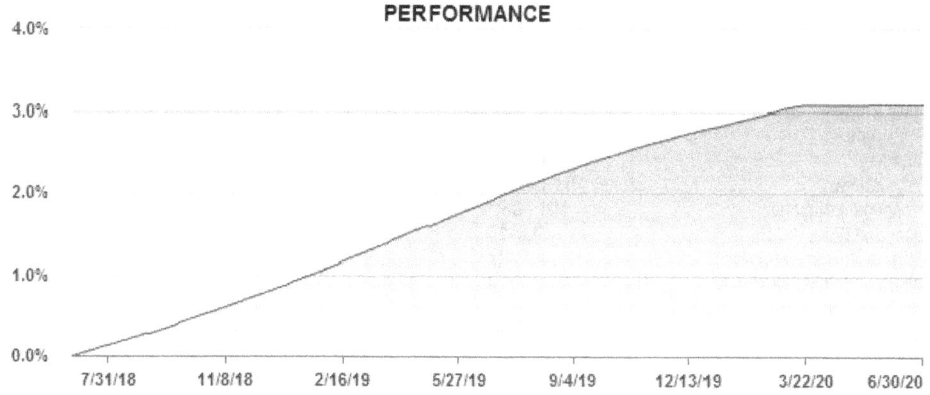

Ratings History

Date	Overall Rating	Risk Rating	Reward Rating
Q2-20	CC+	C-	2019
Q4-19	C	C+	C-
Q4-18	C	C+	C-
Q4-17	C	C+	C-
Q4-16	C	C+	C-

Asset & Performance History

Date	NAV	1-Year Total Return
1	1.89	Cash
2018	1	1.49
2017	1	0.55
2016	1	0.09
2015	1	0
2014	1	0

Total Assets: $201,168,000,000

Asset Allocation

Asset	%
63%	
Bonds	36%
Govt Bond	36%
Muni Bond	0%
Corp Bond	1%
Other	0%

Services Offered: Qualified Investment, Phone Exchange, Wire Redemption, Retirement Investment

Investment Strategy: The investment seeks as high a level of current income as is consistent with the preservation of capital and liquidity. The fund invests in U.S. government securities issued by entities that are chartered or sponsored by Congress but whose securities are neither issued nor guaranteed by the U.S. Treasury, and invests in compliance with industry-standard regulatory requirements for money market funds for the quality, maturity, liquidity, and diversification of investments. The adviser normally invests at least 80% of the fund's total assets in U.S. government securities and repurchase agreements for those securities. **Top Holdings:** Barclays Bank Plc Barclays Bank Plc, 0.04% Sumitomo Mitsui Bk Corp (Repo) In A Joint Trading Account With Sumitomo Mit Fixed Income Clearing Corp. - Ssb Fixed Income Clearing Corp. - Ssb, 0.04% Rbc Financial Group Rbc Financial Group, 0.18% United States Treasury Bills

Vanguard Federal Money Market Fund Investor Shares C HOLD

Ticker	Traded On	NAV	Total Assets ($)	Dividend Yield (TTM)	Turnover Ratio	Expense Ratio
VMFXX	NAS CM	1	$191,650,000,000	1.56		0.11

Ratings

Reward	C-
Risk	C+
Recent Upgrade/Downgrade	

Fund Information

Fund Type	Money Mkt
Category	US Money Mkt
Sub-Category	Money Mkt-Taxable
Prospectus Objective	Money Mkt - Govt
Inception Date	Jul-81
Open to New Investments	
Minimum Initial Investment	3,000
Minimum Subsequent Investment	1
Front End Fee	
Back End Fee	

Total Returns (%)

3-Month	6-Month	1-Year	3-Year	5-Year
0.08	0.43	1.39	4.92	5.60

3-Year Standard Deviation	0.17
Effective Duration	
Average Coupon Rate	

Company Information

Provider	Vanguard
Manager/Tenure	John C. Lanius (12)
Website	http://www.vanguard.com
Address	Vanguard 100 Vanguard Boulevard Malvern PA 19355 United States
Phone Number	877-662-7447

PERFORMANCE

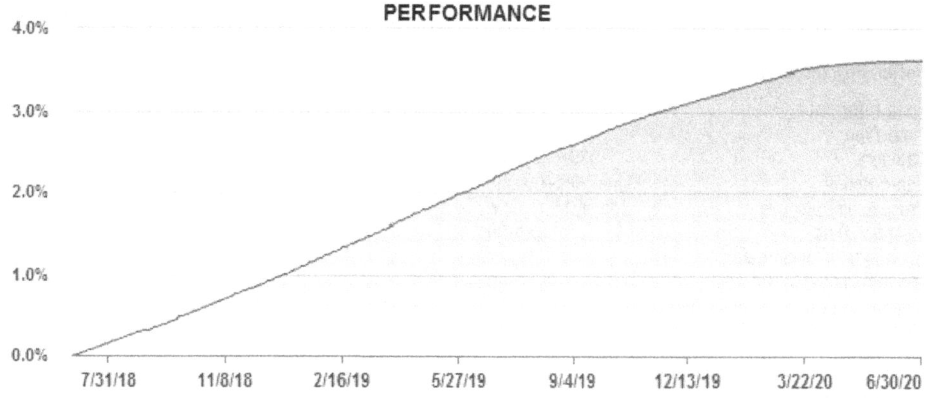

Ratings History

Date	Overall Rating	Risk Rating	Reward Rating
Q2-20	CC+	C-	2019
Q4-19	C	C+	C-
Q4-18	C	B-	C-
Q4-17	C	B-	C-
Q4-16	C	C+	C-

Asset & Performance History

Date	NAV	1-Year Total Return
1	2.13	Cash
2018	1	1.76
2017	1	0.8
2016	1	0.3
2015	1	0.03
2014	1	0

Total Assets: $191,650,000,000

Asset Allocation

Asset	%
61%	
Bonds	39%
Govt Bond	39%
Muni Bond	0%
Corp Bond	0%
Other	0%

Services Offered: Systematic Withdrawal Plan, Automatic Investment Plan, Phone Exchange, Wire Redemption

Investment Strategy: The investment seeks to provide current income while maintaining liquidity and a stable share price of $1. The fund invests primarily in high-quality, short-term money market instruments. Under normal circumstances, at least 80% of the fund's assets are invested in securities issued by the U.S. government and its agencies and instrumentalities. It maintains a dollar-weighted average maturity of 60 days or less and a dollar-weighted average life of 120 days or less. The fund generally invests 100% of its assets in government securities and therefore will satisfy the 99.5% requirement for designation as a government money market fund. **Top Holdings:** Sumitomo Mitsui Banking Corp (New York Branch) Sumitomo Mitsui Banking Corp United States Treasury Notes United States Treasury Notes United States Treasury Bills Federal Home Loan Banks

Fidelity® Government Money Market Fund Daily Money Class — C HOLD

Ticker	Traded On	NAV	Total Assets ($)	Dividend Yield (TTM)	Turnover Ratio	Expense Ratio
FZBXX	NAS CM	1	$189,478,000,000	1.01	0	0.7

Ratings

Reward	C-
Risk	C+
Recent Upgrade/Downgrade	

Fund Information

Fund Type	Money Mkt
Category	US Money Mkt
Sub-Category	Money Mkt-Taxable
Prospectus Objective	Money Mkt - Govt
Inception Date	Apr-15
Open to New Investments	Y
Minimum Initial Investment	0
Minimum Subsequent Investment	
Front End Fee	
Back End Fee	

Total Returns (%)

3-Month	6-Month	1-Year	3-Year	5-Year
0.00	0.19	0.85	3.17	3.24

3-Year Standard Deviation	0.16
Effective Duration	
Average Coupon Rate	

Company Information

Provider	Fidelity Investments
Manager/Tenure	Management Team (12)
Website	http://www.institutional.fidelity.com
Address	Fidelity Investments 82 Devonshire Street Boston MA 2109 United States
Phone Number	617-563-7000

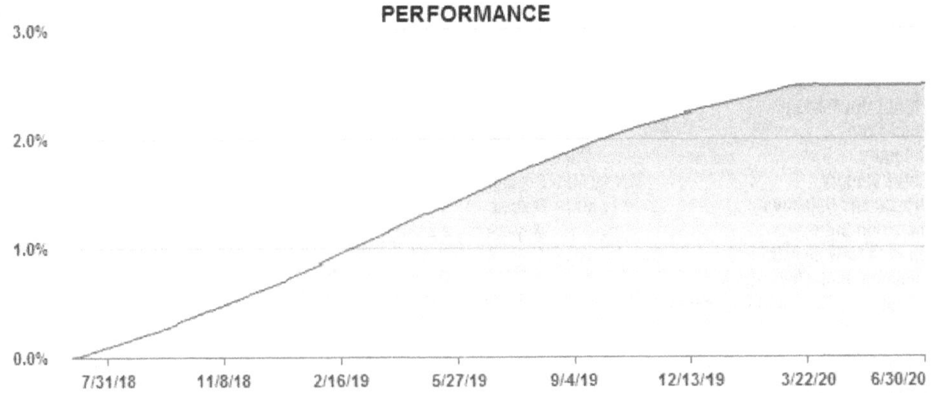

Ratings History

Date	Overall Rating	Risk Rating	Reward Rating
Q2-20	CC+	C-	2019
Q4-19	C	C+	C-
Q4-18	C	C	C-
Q4-17	C	C	C-
Q4-16	C-	C	C-

Asset & Performance History

Date	NAV	1-Year Total Return
1	1.55	Cash
2018	1	1.17
2017	1	0.22
2016	1	0
2015	1	-0.06
2014		-0.23

Total Assets: $189,478,000,000

Asset Allocation

Asset	%
65%	
Bonds	34%
Govt Bond	34%
Muni Bond	0%
Corp Bond	1%
Other	0%

Services Offered: Systematic Withdrawal Plan, Automatic Investment Plan, Qualified Investment, Phone Exchange, Wire Redemption, Retirement Investment

Investment Strategy: The investment seeks as high a level of current income as is consistent with preservation of capital and liquidity. The fund normally invests at least 99.5% of its total assets in cash, U.S. government securities and/or repurchase agreements that are collateralized fully (i.e., collateralized by cash or government securities). It normally invests at least 80% of its assets in U.S. government securities and repurchase agreements for those securities. The fund invests in U.S. government securities issued by entities that are chartered or sponsored by Congress, but whose securities are neither issued nor guaranteed by the U.S. Treasury. **Top Holdings:** Barclays Bank Plc Barclays Bank Plc, 0.04% Sumitomo Mitsui Bk Corp (Repo) In A Joint Trading Account With Sumitomo Mit Fixed Income Clearing Corp. - Ssb Fixed Income Clearing Corp. - Ssb, 0.04% Rbc Financial Group Rbc Financial Group, 0.18% Jp Morgan Secs Llc In A Joint Trading Account With Jp Morgan Secs Llc At 0.

Fidelity® Government Money Market Fund — C HOLD

Ticker	Traded On	NAV	Total Assets ($)	Dividend Yield (TTM)	Turnover Ratio	Expense Ratio
SPAXX	NAS CM	1	$189,478,000,000	1.23	0	0.42

Ratings

Reward	C-
Risk	C+
Recent Upgrade/Downgrade	

Fund Information

Fund Type	Money Mkt
Category	US Money Mkt
Sub-Category	Money Mkt-Taxable
Prospectus Objective	Money Mkt - Govt
Inception Date	Feb-90
Open to New Investments	Y
Minimum Initial Investment	0
Minimum Subsequent Investment	
Front End Fee	
Back End Fee	

Total Returns (%)

3-Month	6-Month	1-Year	3-Year	5-Year
0.00	0.25	1.06	3.96	4.18

3-Year Standard Deviation	0.17
Effective Duration	
Average Coupon Rate	

Company Information

Provider	Fidelity Investments
Manager/Tenure	Management Team (12)
Website	http://www.institutional.fidelity.com
Address	Fidelity Investments 82 Devonshire Street Boston MA 2109 United States
Phone Number	617-563-7000

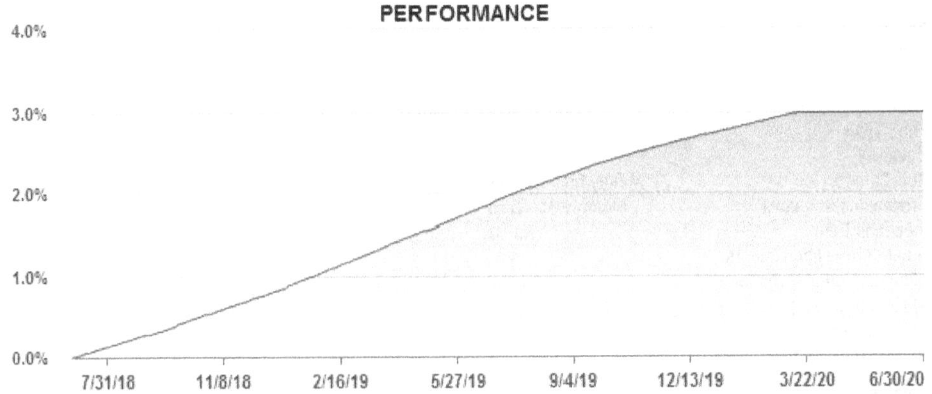

Ratings History

Date	Overall Rating	Risk Rating	Reward Rating
Q2-20	CC+	C-	2019
Q4-19	C	C+	C-
Q4-18	C	C+	C-
Q4-17	C	C+	C-
Q4-16	C-	C	C-

Asset & Performance History

Date	NAV	1-Year Total Return
1	1.84	Cash
2018	1	1.44
2017	1	0.49
2016	1	0.04
2015	1	0
2014	1	0

Total Assets: $189,478,000,000

Asset Allocation

Asset	%
65%	
Bonds	34%
Govt Bond	34%
Muni Bond	0%
Corp Bond	1%
Other	0%

Services Offered: Systematic Withdrawal Plan, Automatic Investment Plan, Qualified Investment, Phone Exchange, Wire Redemption, Retirement Investment

Investment Strategy: The investment seeks as high a level of current income as is consistent with preservation of capital and liquidity. The fund normally invests at least 99.5% of its total assets in cash, U.S. government securities and/or repurchase agreements that are collateralized fully (i.e., collateralized by cash or government securities). It normally invests at least 80% of its assets in U.S. government securities and repurchase agreements for those securities. The fund invests in U.S. government securities issued by entities that are chartered or sponsored by Congress, but whose securities are neither issued nor guaranteed by the U.S. Treasury. **Top Holdings:** Barclays Bank Plc Barclays Bank Plc, 0.04% Sumitomo Mitsui Bk Corp (Repo) In A Joint Trading Account With Sumitomo Mit Fixed Income Clearing Corp. - Ssb Fixed Income Clearing Corp. - Ssb, 0.04% Rbc Financial Group Rbc Financial Group, 0.18% Jp Morgan Secs Llc In A Joint Trading Account With Jp Morgan Secs Llc At 0.

Fidelity® Government Money Market Fund Capital Reserves Class — C HOLD

Ticker	Traded On	NAV	Total Assets ($)	Dividend Yield (TTM)	Turnover Ratio	Expense Ratio
FZAXX	NAS CM	1	$189,478,000,000	0.81	0	0.95

Ratings

Reward	C-
Risk	C+
Recent Upgrade/Downgrade	

Fund Information

Fund Type	Money Mkt
Category	US Money Mkt
Sub-Category	Money Mkt-Taxable
Prospectus Objective	Money Mkt - Govt
Inception Date	Apr-15
Open to New Investments	Y
Minimum Initial Investment	0
Minimum Subsequent Investment	
Front End Fee	
Back End Fee	

Total Returns (%)

3-Month	6-Month	1-Year	3-Year	5-Year
0.00	0.13	0.68	2.48	2.51

3-Year Standard Deviation	0.16
Effective Duration	
Average Coupon Rate	

Company Information

Provider	Fidelity Investments
Manager/Tenure	Management Team (12)
Website	http://www.institutional.fidelity.com
Address	Fidelity Investments 82 Devonshire Street Boston MA 2109 United States
Phone Number	617-563-7000

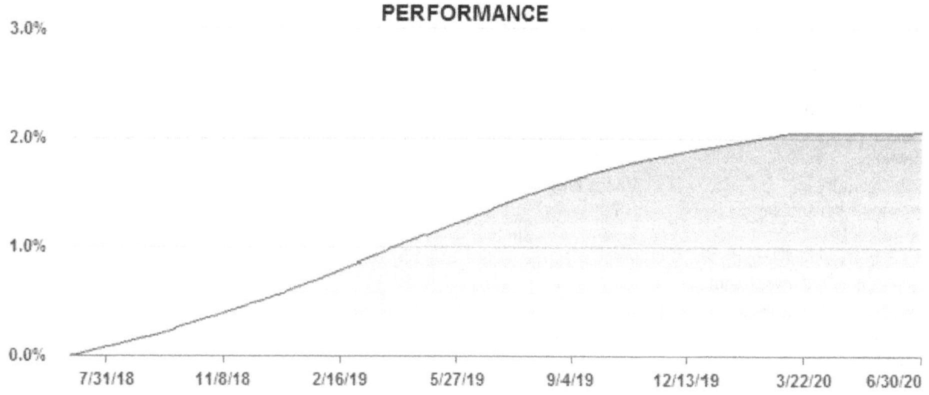

Ratings History

Date	Overall Rating	Risk Rating	Reward Rating
Q2-20	CC+	C-	2019
Q4-19	C	C	C-
Q4-18	C	C+	C-
Q4-17	C-	C	C-
Q4-16	C-	C	D+

Asset & Performance History

Date	NAV	1-Year Total Return
1	1.31	Cash
2018	1	0.91
2017	1	0.07
2016	1	0
2015	1	-0.14
2014		-0.48

Total Assets: $189,478,000,000

Asset Allocation

Asset	%
65%	
Bonds	34%
Govt Bond	34%
Muni Bond	0%
Corp Bond	1%
Other	0%

Services Offered: Systematic Withdrawal Plan, Automatic Investment Plan, Qualified Investment, Phone Exchange, Wire Redemption, Retirement Investment

Investment Strategy: The investment seeks as high a level of current income as is consistent with preservation of capital and liquidity. The fund normally invests at least 99.5% of its total assets in cash, U.S. government securities and/or repurchase agreements that are collateralized fully (i.e., collateralized by cash or government securities). It normally invests at least 80% of its assets in U.S. government securities and repurchase agreements for those securities. The fund invests in U.S. government securities issued by entities that are chartered or sponsored by Congress, but whose securities are neither issued nor guaranteed by the U.S. Treasury. **Top Holdings:** Barclays Bank Plc Barclays Bank Plc, 0.04% Sumitomo Mitsui Bk Corp (Repo) In A Joint Trading Account With Sumitomo Mit Fixed Income Clearing Corp. - Ssb Fixed Income Clearing Corp. - Ssb, 0.04% Rbc Financial Group Rbc Financial Group, 0.18% Jp Morgan Secs Llc In A Joint Trading Account With Jp Morgan Secs Llc At 0.

Fidelity® Government Money Market Fund Advisor M Class — C HOLD

Ticker	Traded On	NAV	Total Assets ($)	Dividend Yield (TTM)	Turnover Ratio	Expense Ratio
FZGXX	NAS CM	1	$189,478,000,000	1.02	0	0.7

Ratings

Reward	C-
Risk	C+
Recent Upgrade/Downgrade	

Fund Information

Fund Type	Money Mkt
Category	US Money Mkt
Sub-Category	Money Mkt-Taxable
Prospectus Objective	Money Mkt - Govt
Inception Date	Jul-17
Open to New Investments	Y
Minimum Initial Investment	0
Minimum Subsequent Investment	
Front End Fee	
Back End Fee	

Total Returns (%)

3-Month	6-Month	1-Year	3-Year	5-Year
0.00	0.19	0.86	3.20	2.91

3-Year Standard Deviation	
Effective Duration	
Average Coupon Rate	

Company Information

Provider	Fidelity Investments
Manager/Tenure	Management Team (12)
Website	http://www.institutional.fidelity.com
Address	Fidelity Investments 82 Devonshire Street Boston MA 2109 United States
Phone Number	617-563-7000

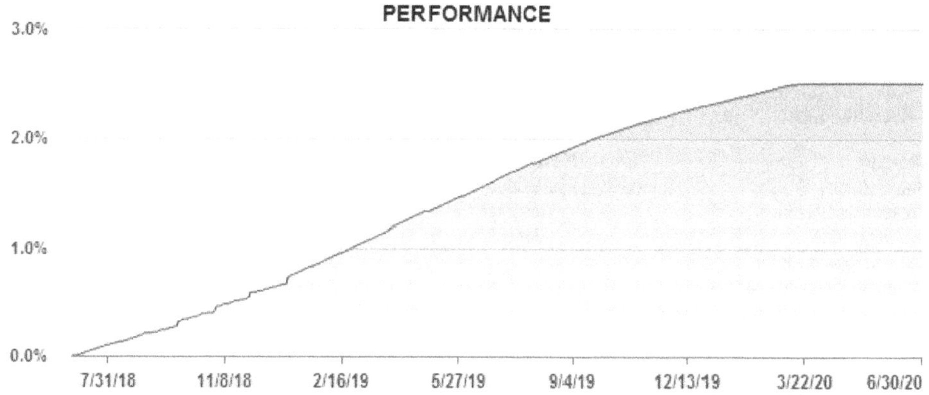

Ratings History

Date	Overall Rating	Risk Rating	Reward Rating
Q2-20	CC+	C-	2019
Q4-19	C	C+	C-
Q4-18	C	C	C-
Q4-17	C-	C	C-
Q4-16			

Asset & Performance History

Date	NAV	1-Year Total Return
1	1.56	Cash
2018	1	1.12
2017	1	0.23
2016		
2015		
2014		

Total Assets: $189,478,000,000

Asset Allocation

Asset	%
65%	
Bonds	34%
Govt Bond	34%
Muni Bond	0%
Corp Bond	1%
Other	0%

Services Offered: Automatic Investment Plan, Phone Exchange, Retirement Investment

Investment Strategy: The investment seeks as high a level of current income as is consistent with preservation of capital and liquidity. The fund normally invests at least 99.5% of its total assets in cash, U.S. government securities and/or repurchase agreements that are collateralized fully (i.e., collateralized by cash or government securities). It normally invests at least 80% of its assets in U.S. government securities and repurchase agreements for those securities. The fund invests in U.S. government securities issued by entities that are chartered or sponsored by Congress, but whose securities are neither issued nor guaranteed by the U.S. Treasury. **Top Holdings:** Barclays Bank Plc Barclays Bank Plc, 0.04% Sumitomo Mitsui Bk Corp (Repo) In A Joint Trading Account With Sumitomo Mit Fixed Income Clearing Corp. - Ssb Fixed Income Clearing Corp. - Ssb, 0.04% Rbc Financial Group Rbc Financial Group, 0.18% Jp Morgan Secs Llc In A Joint Trading Account With Jp Morgan Secs Llc At 0.

Fidelity® Government Money Market Fund Class K6 — C HOLD

Ticker	Traded On	NAV	Total Assets ($)	Dividend Yield (TTM)	Turnover Ratio	Expense Ratio
FNBXX	NAS CM	1	$189,478,000,000	1.39	0	0.25

Ratings

Reward	C-
Risk	C
Recent Upgrade/Downgrade	

Fund Information

Fund Type	Money Mkt
Category	US Money Mkt
Sub-Category	Money Mkt-Taxable
Prospectus Objective	Money Mkt - Govt
Inception Date	Jan-18
Open to New Investments	Y
Minimum Initial Investment	0
Minimum Subsequent Investment	
Front End Fee	
Back End Fee	

Total Returns (%)

3-Month	6-Month	1-Year	3-Year	5-Year
0.01	0.31	1.20	4.37	4.58

3-Year Standard Deviation	
Effective Duration	
Average Coupon Rate	

Company Information

Provider	Fidelity Investments
Manager/Tenure	Management Team (12)
Website	http://www.institutional.fidelity.com
Address	Fidelity Investments 82 Devonshire Street Boston MA 2109 United States
Phone Number	617-563-7000

PERFORMANCE

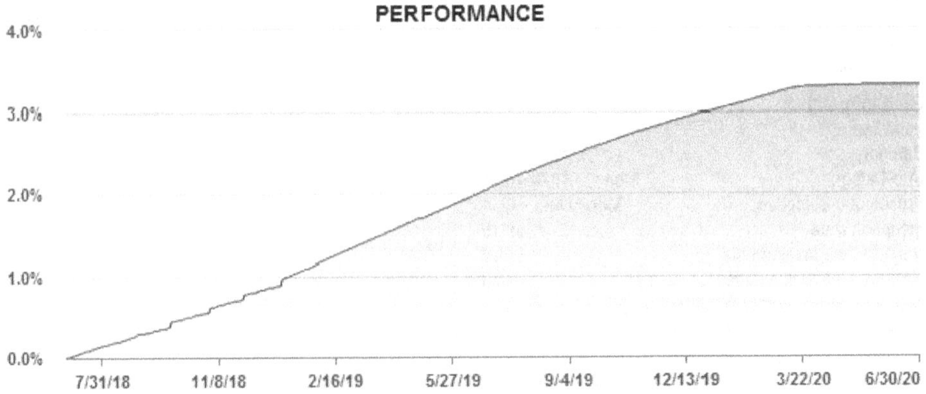

Ratings History

Date	Overall Rating	Risk Rating	Reward Rating
Q2-20	CC	C-	2019
Q4-19	C	C+	C-
Q4-18	C	C+	C-
Q4-17			
Q4-16			

Asset & Performance History

Date	NAV	1-Year Total Return
1	2.01	Cash
2018	1	1.55
2017		
2016		
2015		
2014		

Total Assets: $189,478,000,000

Asset Allocation

Asset	%
65%	
Bonds	34%
Govt Bond	34%
Muni Bond	0%
Corp Bond	1%
Other	0%

Services Offered: Qualified Investment, Phone Exchange

Investment Strategy: The investment seeks as high a level of current income as is consistent with preservation of capital and liquidity. The fund normally invests at least 99.5% of its total assets in cash, U.S. government securities and/or repurchase agreements that are collateralized fully (i.e., collateralized by cash or government securities). It normally invests at least 80% of its assets in U.S. government securities and repurchase agreements for those securities. The fund invests in U.S. government securities issued by entities that are chartered or sponsored by Congress, but whose securities are neither issued nor guaranteed by the U.S. Treasury. **Top Holdings:** Barclays Bank Plc Barclays Bank Plc, 0.04% Sumitomo Mitsui Bk Corp (Repo) In A Joint Trading Account With Sumitomo Mit Fixed Income Clearing Corp. - Ssb Fixed Income Clearing Corp. - Ssb, 0.04% Rbc Financial Group Rbc Financial Group, 0.18% Jp Morgan Secs Llc In A Joint Trading Account With Jp Morgan Secs Llc At 0.

Vanguard Total Bond Market II Index Fund Investor Shares — B BUY

Ticker	Traded On	NAV	Total Assets ($)	Dividend Yield (TTM)	Turnover Ratio	Expense Ratio
VTBIX	NAS CM	11.53	$185,732,000,000	2.49	66	0.09

Ratings

Reward	C+
Risk	B+
Recent Upgrade/Downgrade	

Fund Information

Fund Type	Open End
Category	US Fixed Inc
Sub-Category	Intermediate Core Bond
Prospectus Objective	Income
Inception Date	Jan-09
Open to New Investments	Y
Minimum Initial Investment	0
Minimum Subsequent Investment	
Front End Fee	
Back End Fee	

Total Returns (%)

3-Month	6-Month	1-Year	3-Year	5-Year
2.87	5.96	8.54	16.30	23.12

3-Year Standard Deviation	3.38
Effective Duration	6.19
Average Coupon Rate	3.02

Company Information

Provider	Vanguard
Manager/Tenure	Joshua C. Barrickman (10)
Website	http://www.vanguard.com
Address	Vanguard 100 Vanguard Boulevard Malvern PA 19355 United States
Phone Number	877-662-7447

PERFORMANCE

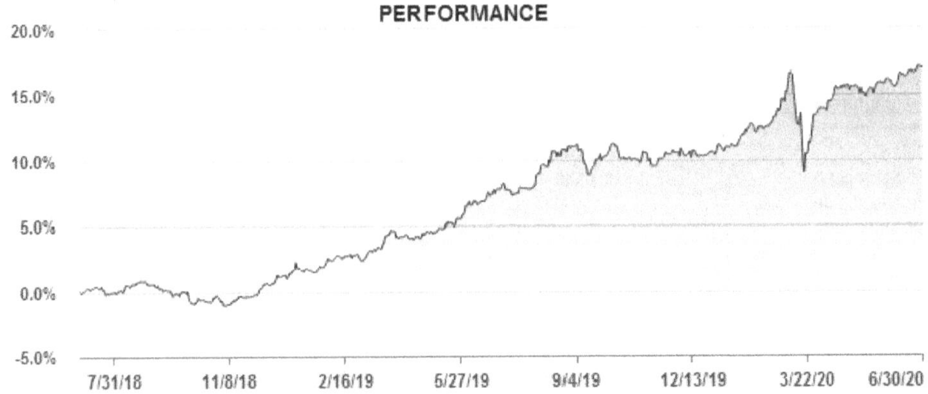

Ratings History

Date	Overall Rating	Risk Rating	Reward Rating
Q2-20	BB+	C+	2019
Q4-19	C	B	C
Q4-18	C-	C+	D+
Q4-17	B-	B+	C
Q4-16	C	C	C

Asset & Performance History

Date	NAV	1-Year Total Return
11.01	8.6	Cash
2018	10.42	-0.12
2017	10.72	3.48
2016	10.61	2.42
2015	10.6	0.27
2014	10.84	5.93

Total Assets: $185,732,000,000

Asset Allocation

Asset	%
4%	
Bonds	95%
Govt Bond	43%
Muni Bond	1%
Corp Bond	28%
Other	0%

Services Offered: Qualified Investment, Phone Exchange, Wire Redemption

Investment Strategy: The investment seeks to track the performance of the Bloomberg Barclays U.S. Aggregate Float Adjusted Index. The fund employs an indexing investment approach designed to track the performance of the Bloomberg Barclays U.S. Aggregate Float Adjusted Index. It invests by sampling the index, meaning that it holds a broadly diversified collection of securities that, in the aggregate, approximates the full index in terms of key risk factors and other characteristics. The fund invests at least 80% of its assets in bonds held in the index. **Top Holdings:** United States Treasury Notes 0.38% United States Treasury Notes 1.5% United States Treasury Bonds 2% United States Treasury Notes 0.62% United States Treasury Notes 0.5%

BlackRock Liquidity Funds FedFund Cash Management Shares C HOLD

Ticker	Traded On	NAV	Total Assets ($)	Dividend Yield (TTM)	Turnover Ratio	Expense Ratio
BFFXX	NAS CM	1	$168,607,000,000	1.03	0	0.67

Ratings

Reward	C-
Risk	C+
Recent Upgrade/Downgrade	

Fund Information

Fund Type	Money Mkt
Category	US Money Mkt
Sub-Category	Money Mkt-Taxable
Prospectus Objective	Money Mkt - Govt
Inception Date	Aug-08
Open to New Investments	Y
Minimum Initial Investment	5,000
Minimum Subsequent Investment	
Front End Fee	
Back End Fee	

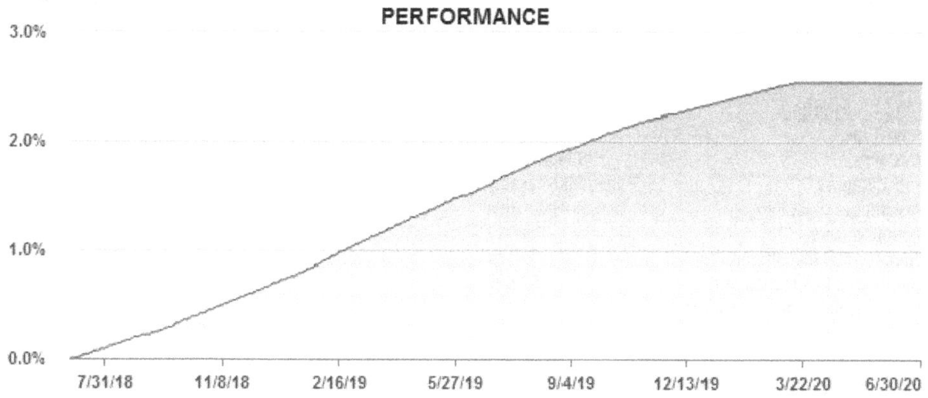

Total Returns (%)

3-Month	6-Month	1-Year	3-Year	5-Year
0.00	0.19	0.88	3.26	3.38

3-Year Standard Deviation	0.16
Effective Duration	
Average Coupon Rate	

Company Information

Provider	BlackRock
Manager/Tenure	Management Team (14)
Website	http://www.blackrock.com
Address	BlackRock Funds Providence RI 02940-8019 United States
Phone Number	800-441-7762

Ratings History

Date	Overall Rating	Risk Rating	Reward Rating
Q2-20	CC+	C-	2019
Q4-19	C	C+	C-
Q4-18	C	C+	C-
Q4-17	C	C	C-
Q4-16			

Asset & Performance History

Date	NAV	1-Year Total Return
1	1.59	Cash
2018	1	1.21
2017	1	0.27
2016	1	
2015	1	0.01
2014	1	0

Total Assets: $168,607,000,000

Asset Allocation

Asset	%
71%	
Bonds	29%
Govt Bond	28%
Muni Bond	0%
Corp Bond	0%
Other	0%

Services Offered: Qualified Investment, Wire Redemption

Investment Strategy: The investment seeks current income as is consistent with liquidity and stability of principal. The fund invests at least 99.5% of its total assets in cash, U.S. Treasury bills, notes and other obligations issued or guaranteed as to principal and interest by the U.S. government, its agencies or instrumentalities, and repurchase agreements secured by such obligations or cash. It invests in securities maturing in 397 days or less (with certain exceptions) and the portfolio will have a dollar-weighted average maturity of 60 days or less and a dollar-weighted average life of 120 days or less. **Top Holdings:** Usd Cash(Committed) Tri-Party J.P. Morgan Securities L Tri-Party Citigroup Global Markets Tri-Party Hsbc Securities (Usa) In Tri-Party Ficc - The Bank Of New Y

BlackRock Liquidity Funds FedFund Cash Reserve Shares C HOLD

Ticker	Traded On	NAV	Total Assets ($)	Dividend Yield (TTM)	Turnover Ratio	Expense Ratio
BFRXX	NAS CM	1	$168,607,000,000	1.11	0	0.57

Ratings

Reward	C-
Risk	C+
Recent Upgrade/Downgrade	

Fund Information

Fund Type	Money Mkt
Category	US Money Mkt
Sub-Category	Money Mkt-Taxable
Prospectus Objective	Money Mkt - Govt
Inception Date	Apr-03
Open to New Investments	Y
Minimum Initial Investment	5,000
Minimum Subsequent Investment	
Front End Fee	
Back End Fee	

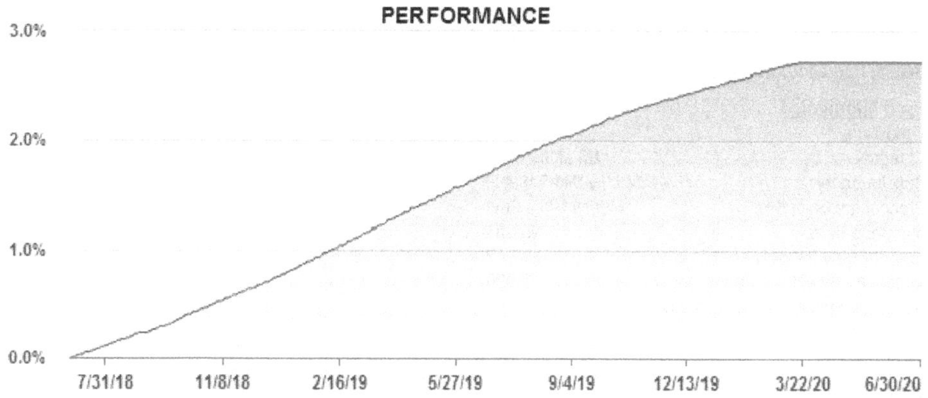

Total Returns (%)

3-Month	6-Month	1-Year	3-Year	5-Year
0.00	0.21	0.95	3.55	3.70

3-Year Standard Deviation	0.17
Effective Duration	
Average Coupon Rate	

Company Information

Provider	BlackRock
Manager/Tenure	Management Team (14)
Website	http://www.blackrock.com
Address	BlackRock Funds Providence RI 02940-8019 United States
Phone Number	800-441-7762

Ratings History

Date	Overall Rating	Risk Rating	Reward Rating
Q2-20	CC+	C-	2019
Q4-19	C	C+	C-
Q4-18			
Q4-17			
Q4-16			

Asset & Performance History

Date	NAV	1-Year Total Return
1	1.69	Cash
2018	1	
2017	1	
2016	1	
2015	1	
2014	1	

Total Assets: $168,607,000,000

Asset Allocation

Asset	%
71%	
Bonds	29%
Govt Bond	28%
Muni Bond	0%
Corp Bond	0%
Other	0%

Services Offered: Qualified Investment, Wire Redemption

Investment Strategy: The investment seeks current income as is consistent with liquidity and stability of principal. The fund invests at least 99.5% of its total assets in cash, U.S. Treasury bills, notes and other obligations issued or guaranteed as to principal and interest by the U.S. government, its agencies or instrumentalities, and repurchase agreements secured by such obligations or cash. It invests in securities maturing in 397 days or less (with certain exceptions) and the portfolio will have a dollar-weighted average maturity of 60 days or less and a dollar-weighted average life of 120 days or less. **Top Holdings:** Usd Cash(Committed) Tri-Party J.P. Morgan Securities L Tri-Party Citigroup Global Markets Tri-Party Hsbc Securities (Usa) In Tri-Party Ficc - The Bank Of New Y

BlackRock Liquidity FedFund Fund Capital — C HOLD

Ticker	Traded On	NAV	Total Assets ($)	Dividend Yield (TTM)	Turnover Ratio	Expense Ratio
		1	$168,607,000,000	1.43	0	0.22

Ratings

Reward	C-
Risk	C+
Recent Upgrade/Downgrade	

Fund Information

Fund Type	Money Mkt
Category	US Money Mkt
Sub-Category	Money Mkt-Taxable
Prospectus Objective	Money Mkt - Govt
Inception Date	Nov-17
Open to New Investments	Y
Minimum Initial Investment	50,000
Minimum Subsequent Investment	
Front End Fee	
Back End Fee	

Total Returns (%)

3-Month	6-Month	1-Year	3-Year	5-Year
0.02	0.32	1.25	4.62	5.24

3-Year Standard Deviation	
Effective Duration	
Average Coupon Rate	

Company Information

Provider	BlackRock
Manager/Tenure	Management Team (14)
Website	http://www.blackrock.com
Address	BlackRock Funds Providence RI 02940-8019 United States
Phone Number	800-441-7762

Performance Chart Unavailable

Ratings History

Date	Overall Rating	Risk Rating	Reward Rating
Q2-20	CC+	C-	2019
Q4-19	C	B-	C
Q4-18			
Q4-17			
Q4-16			

Asset & Performance History

Date	NAV	1-Year Total Return
1	2.06	Cash
2018	1	
2017	1	
2016		
2015		
2014		

Total Assets: $168,607,000,000

Asset Allocation

Asset	%
71%	
Bonds	29%
Govt Bond	28%
Muni Bond	0%
Corp Bond	0%
Other	0%

Services Offered: Qualified Investment

Investment Strategy: The investment seeks current income as is consistent with liquidity and stability of principal. The fund invests at least 99.5% of its total assets in cash, U.S. Treasury bills, notes and other obligations issued or guaranteed as to principal and interest by the U.S. government, its agencies or instrumentalities, and repurchase agreements secured by such obligations or cash. It invests in securities maturing in 397 days or less (with certain exceptions) and the portfolio will have a dollar-weighted average maturity of 60 days or less and a dollar-weighted average life of 120 days or less. **Top Holdings:** Usd Cash(Committed) Tri-Party J.P. Morgan Securities L Tri-Party Citigroup Global Markets Tri-Party Hsbc Securities (Usa) In Tri-Party Ficc - The Bank Of New Y

BlackRock Liquidity Funds FedFund Administration Shares — C HOLD

Ticker	Traded On	NAV	Total Assets ($)	Dividend Yield (TTM)	Turnover Ratio	Expense Ratio
BLFXX	NAS CM	1	$168,607,000,000	1.38	0	0.27

Ratings

Reward	C-
Risk	C+
Recent Upgrade/Downgrade	

Fund Information

Fund Type	Money Mkt
Category	US Money Mkt
Sub-Category	Money Mkt-Taxable
Prospectus Objective	Money Mkt - Govt
Inception Date	Nov-04
Open to New Investments	Y
Minimum Initial Investment	5,000
Minimum Subsequent Investment	
Front End Fee	
Back End Fee	

Total Returns (%)

3-Month	6-Month	1-Year	3-Year	5-Year
0.01	0.30	1.19	4.42	4.88

3-Year Standard Deviation	0.17
Effective Duration	
Average Coupon Rate	

Company Information

Provider	BlackRock
Manager/Tenure	Management Team (14)
Website	http://www.blackrock.com
Address	BlackRock Funds Providence RI 02940-8019 United States
Phone Number	800-441-7762

PERFORMANCE

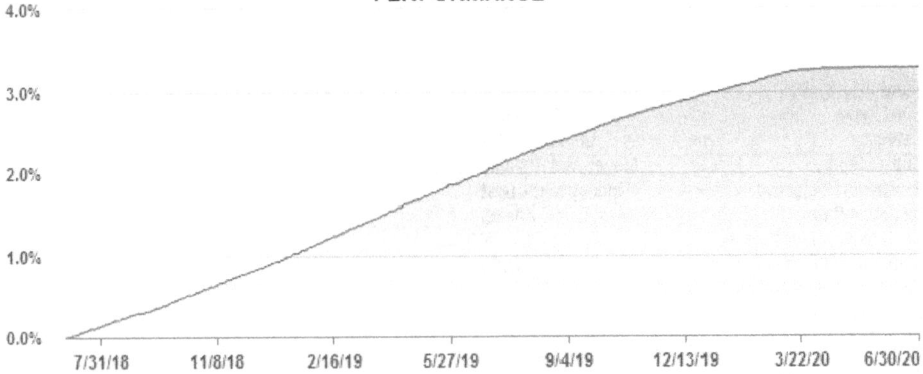

Ratings History

Date	Overall Rating	Risk Rating	Reward Rating
Q2-20	CC+	C-	2019
Q4-19	C	C+	C
Q4-18	C	C+	C-
Q4-17	C	B-	C-
Q4-16	C	C	C-

Asset & Performance History

Date	NAV	1-Year Total Return
1	1.99	Cash
2018	1	1.61
2017	1	0.68
2016	1	0.17
2015	1	0.01
2014	1	0

Total Assets: $168,607,000,000

Asset Allocation

Asset	%
71%	
Bonds	29%
Govt Bond	28%
Muni Bond	0%
Corp Bond	0%
Other	0%

Services Offered: Qualified Investment, Wire Redemption

Investment Strategy: The investment seeks current income as is consistent with liquidity and stability of principal. The fund invests at least 99.5% of its total assets in cash, U.S. Treasury bills, notes and other obligations issued or guaranteed as to principal and interest by the U.S. government, its agencies or instrumentalities, and repurchase agreements secured by such obligations or cash. It invests in securities maturing in 397 days or less (with certain exceptions) and the portfolio will have a dollar-weighted average maturity of 60 days or less and a dollar-weighted average life of 120 days or less. **Top Holdings:** Usd Cash(Committed) Tri-Party J.P. Morgan Securities L Tri-Party Citigroup Global Markets Tri-Party Hsbc Securities (Usa) In Tri-Party Ficc - The Bank Of New Y

BlackRock Liquidity Funds FedFund Select Shares — C HOLD

Ticker	Traded On	NAV	Total Assets ($)	Dividend Yield (TTM)	Turnover Ratio	Expense Ratio
BFBXX	NAS CM	1	$168,607,000,000	0.77	0	1

Ratings

Reward	C-
Risk	C
Recent Upgrade/Downgrade	

Fund Information

Fund Type	Money Mkt
Category	US Money Mkt
Sub-Category	Money Mkt-Taxable
Prospectus Objective	Money Mkt - Govt
Inception Date	May-02
Open to New Investments	Y
Minimum Initial Investment	0
Minimum Subsequent Investment	
Front End Fee	
Back End Fee	

Total Returns (%)

3-Month	6-Month	1-Year	3-Year	5-Year
0.00	0.12	0.64	2.33	2.38

3-Year Standard Deviation	0.15
Effective Duration	
Average Coupon Rate	

Company Information

Provider	BlackRock
Manager/Tenure	Management Team (14)
Website	http://www.blackrock.com
Address	BlackRock Funds Providence RI 02940-8019 United States
Phone Number	800-441-7762

PERFORMANCE

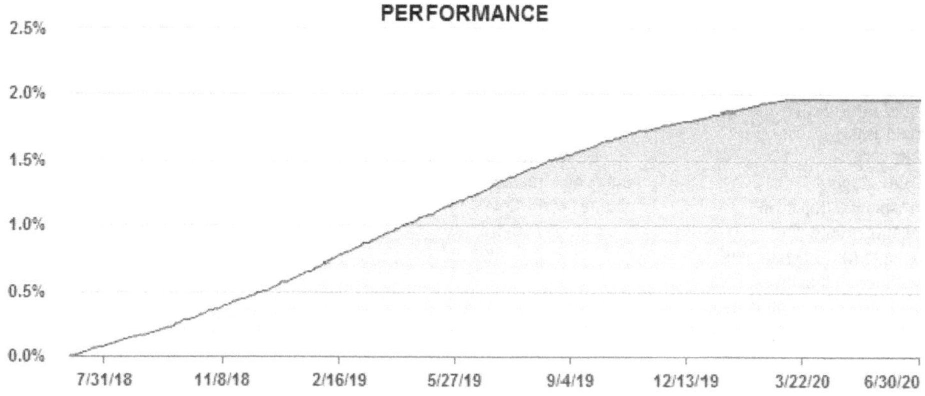

Ratings History

Date	Overall Rating	Risk Rating	Reward Rating
Q2-20	CC	C-	2019
Q4-19	C	C	C-
Q4-18	C	C	C-
Q4-17	C-	C	C-
Q4-16	C-	C	C-

Asset & Performance History

Date	NAV	1-Year Total Return
1	1.25	Cash
2018	1	0.88
2017	1	0.05
2016	1	0.03
2015	1	0.01
2014	1	0

Total Assets: $168,607,000,000

Asset Allocation

Asset	%
71%	
Bonds	29%
Govt Bond	28%
Muni Bond	0%
Corp Bond	0%
Other	0%

Services Offered: Qualified Investment, Wire Redemption

Investment Strategy: The investment seeks current income as is consistent with liquidity and stability of principal. The fund invests at least 99.5% of its total assets in cash, U.S. Treasury bills, notes and other obligations issued or guaranteed as to principal and interest by the U.S. government, its agencies or instrumentalities, and repurchase agreements secured by such obligations or cash. It invests in securities maturing in 397 days or less (with certain exceptions) and the portfolio will have a dollar-weighted average maturity of 60 days or less and a dollar-weighted average life of 120 days or less. **Top Holdings:** Usd Cash(Committed) Tri-Party J.P. Morgan Securities L Tri-Party Citigroup Global Markets Tri-Party Hsbc Securities (Usa) In Tri-Party Ficc - The Bank Of New Y

BlackRock Liquidity Funds FedFund Dollar Shares — C HOLD

Ticker	Traded On	NAV	Total Assets ($)	Dividend Yield (TTM)	Turnover Ratio	Expense Ratio
TDDXX	NAS CM	1	$168,607,000,000	1.23	0	0.42

Ratings

Reward	C-
Risk	C+
Recent Upgrade/Downgrade	

Fund Information

Fund Type	Money Mkt
Category	US Money Mkt
Sub-Category	Money Mkt-Taxable
Prospectus Objective	Money Mkt - Govt
Inception Date	Mar-84
Open to New Investments	Y
Minimum Initial Investment	5,000
Minimum Subsequent Investment	
Front End Fee	
Back End Fee	

Total Returns (%)

3-Month	6-Month	1-Year	3-Year	5-Year
0.00	0.25	1.06	4.01	4.25

3-Year Standard Deviation	0.18
Effective Duration	
Average Coupon Rate	

Company Information

Provider	BlackRock
Manager/Tenure	Management Team (14)
Website	http://www.blackrock.com
Address	BlackRock Funds Providence RI 02940-8019 United States
Phone Number	800-441-7762

PERFORMANCE

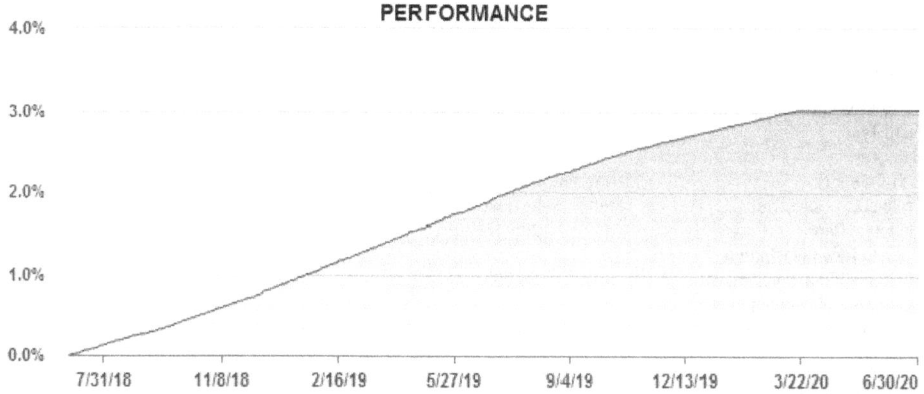

Ratings History

Date	Overall Rating	Risk Rating	Reward Rating
Q2-20	CC+	C-	2019
Q4-19	C	C+	C-
Q4-18	C	C+	C-
Q4-17	C	C+	C-
Q4-16	C-	C	C-

Asset & Performance History

Date	NAV	1-Year Total Return
1	1.84	Cash
2018	1	1.49
2017	1	0.52
2016	1	0.05
2015	1	0.01
2014	1	0.01

Total Assets: $168,607,000,000

Asset Allocation

Asset	%
71%	
Bonds	29%
Govt Bond	28%
Muni Bond	0%
Corp Bond	0%
Other	0%

Services Offered: Qualified Investment, Wire Redemption

Investment Strategy: The investment seeks current income as is consistent with liquidity and stability of principal. The fund invests at least 99.5% of its total assets in cash, U.S. Treasury bills, notes and other obligations issued or guaranteed as to principal and interest by the U.S. government, its agencies or instrumentalities, and repurchase agreements secured by such obligations or cash. It invests in securities maturing in 397 days or less (with certain exceptions) and the portfolio will have a dollar-weighted average maturity of 60 days or less and a dollar-weighted average life of 120 days or less. **Top Holdings:** Usd Cash(Committed) Tri-Party J.P. Morgan Securities L Tri-Party Citigroup Global Markets Tri-Party Hsbc Securities (Usa) In Tri-Party Ficc - The Bank Of New Y

Federated Hermes Govt Obl Select

C HOLD

Ticker	Traded On	NAV	Total Assets ($)	Dividend Yield (TTM)	Turnover Ratio	Expense Ratio
GRTXX	NAS CM	1	$155,932,000,000	1.31		0.17

Ratings

Reward	C
Risk	C+
Recent Upgrade/Downgrade	

Fund Information

Fund Type	Money Mkt
Category	US Money Mkt
Sub-Category	Money Mkt-Taxable
Prospectus Objective	Money Mkt - Govt
Inception Date	Feb-16
Open to New Investments	Y
Minimum Initial Investment	0
Minimum Subsequent Investment	
Front End Fee	
Back End Fee	

Total Returns (%)

3-Month	6-Month	1-Year	3-Year	5-Year
0.04	0.36	1.22	2.67	2.73

3-Year Standard Deviation	0.18
Effective Duration	
Average Coupon Rate	

Company Information

Provider	Federated
Manager/Tenure	Management Team (16)
Website	http://www.federatedinvestors.com
Address	Federated Investors Funds 4000 Ericsson Drive Warrendale PA 15086-7561 United States
Phone Number	800-341-7400

PERFORMANCE

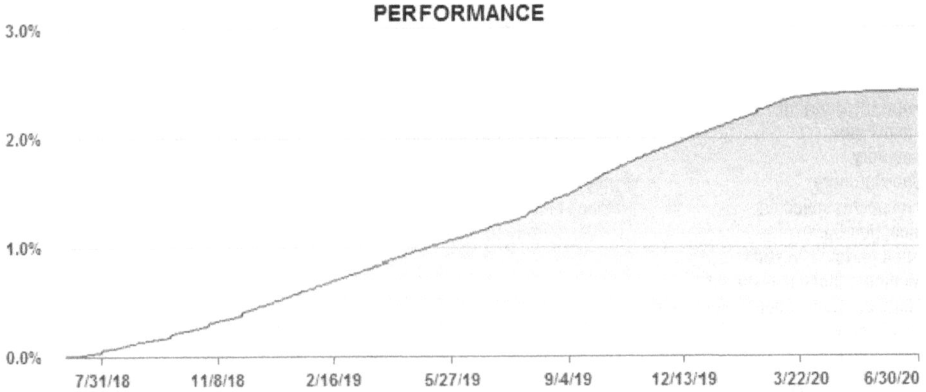

Ratings History

Date	Overall Rating	Risk Rating	Reward Rating
Q2-20	CC+	C	2019
Q4-19	C	C+	C-
Q4-18	C	C+	C-
Q4-17	C-	C	D+
Q4-16	C-	C	D

Asset & Performance History

Date	NAV	1-Year Total Return
1	1.51	Cash
2018	1	0.7
2017	1	0.01
2016	1	-0.04
2015		-0.47
2014		-0.48

Total Assets: $155,932,000,000

Asset Allocation

Asset	%
66%	
Bonds	34%
Govt Bond	34%
Muni Bond	0%
Corp Bond	0%
Other	0%

Services Offered: Systematic Withdrawal Plan, Automatic Investment Plan, Qualified Investment, Wire Redemption, Retirement Investment

Investment Strategy: The investment seeks to provide current income consistent with stability of principal. The fund invests in a portfolio of U.S. Treasury and government securities maturing in 397 days or less and repurchase agreements collateralized fully by U.S. Treasury and government securities. The fund will operate as a "government money market fund," as such term is defined in or interpreted under Rule 2a-7 under the Investment Company Act of 1940. **Top Holdings:** Frbnybo Prime 1 Frbnybo Prime 1 Usd Ficcjpm 1 Ficc Jpm 1 Ss Ficc P Repo 1 Repo Anz Prime Repo 1 Anz Prime Rep 1

Federated Hermes Govt Obl Cash II

C HOLD

Ticker	Traded On	NAV	Total Assets ($)	Dividend Yield (TTM)	Turnover Ratio	Expense Ratio
GFYXX	NAS CM	1	$155,932,000,000	0.89		0.85

Ratings

Reward	C-
Risk	C
Recent Upgrade/Downgrade	

Fund Information

Fund Type	Money Mkt
Category	US Money Mkt
Sub-Category	Money Mkt-Taxable
Prospectus Objective	Money Mkt - Govt
Inception Date	Jun-15
Open to New Investments	Y
Minimum Initial Investment	25,000
Minimum Subsequent Investment	
Front End Fee	
Back End Fee	

Total Returns (%)

3-Month	6-Month	1-Year	3-Year	5-Year
0.00	0.16	0.76	2.77	2.81

3-Year Standard Deviation	0.16
Effective Duration	
Average Coupon Rate	

Company Information

Provider	Federated
Manager/Tenure	Management Team (16)
Website	http://www.federatedinvestors.com
Address	Federated Investors Funds 4000 Ericsson Drive Warrendale PA 15086-7561 United States
Phone Number	800-341-7400

PERFORMANCE

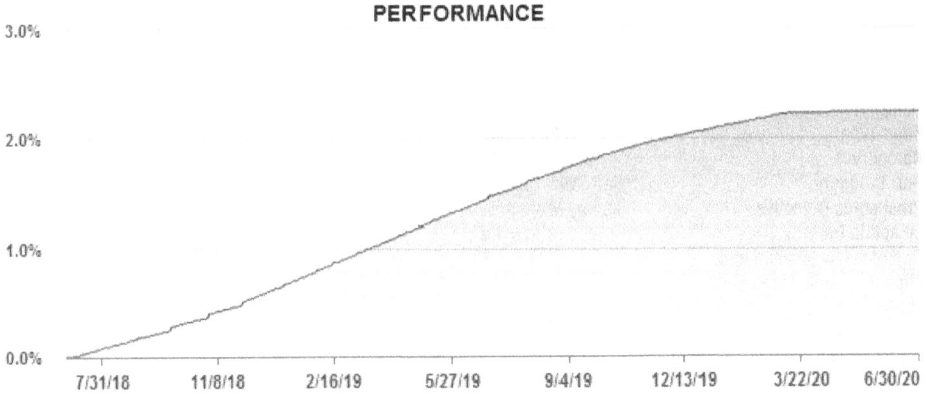

Ratings History

Date	Overall Rating	Risk Rating	Reward Rating
Q2-20	CC	C-	2019
Q4-19	C	C+	C-
Q4-18	C	C+	C-
Q4-17	C-	C	C-
Q4-16	C-	C	D+

Asset & Performance History

Date	NAV	1-Year Total Return
1	1.41	Cash
2018	1	0.98
2017	1	0.13
2016	1	0
2015	1	-0.15
2014		-0.33

Total Assets: $155,932,000,000

Asset Allocation

Asset	%
66%	
Bonds	34%
Govt Bond	34%
Muni Bond	0%
Corp Bond	0%
Other	0%

Services Offered: Systematic Withdrawal Plan, Automatic Investment Plan, Qualified Investment, Phone Exchange, Wire Redemption, Retirement Investment

Investment Strategy: The investment seeks to provide current income consistent with stability of principal. The fund invests in a portfolio of U.S. Treasury and government securities maturing in 397 days or less and repurchase agreements collateralized fully by U.S. Treasury and government securities. The fund will operate as a "government money market fund," as such term is defined in or interpreted under Rule 2a-7 under the Investment Company Act of 1940. **Top Holdings:** Frbnybo Prime 1 Frbnybo Prime 1 Usd Ficcjpm 1 Ficc Jpm 1 Ss Ficc P Repo 1 Repo Anz Prime Repo 1 Anz Prime Rep 1

Federated Hermes Govt Obl Cash Srs — C HOLD

Ticker	Traded On	NAV	Total Assets ($)	Dividend Yield (TTM)	Turnover Ratio	Expense Ratio
GFSXX	NAS CM	1	$155,932,000,000	0.78		1.05

Ratings

Reward	C-
Risk	C
Recent Upgrade/Downgrade	

Fund Information

Fund Type	Money Mkt
Category	US Money Mkt
Sub-Category	Money Mkt-Taxable
Prospectus Objective	Money Mkt - Govt
Inception Date	Jun-15
Open to New Investments	Y
Minimum Initial Investment	10,000
Minimum Subsequent Investment	250
Front End Fee	
Back End Fee	

Total Returns (%)

3-Month	6-Month	1-Year	3-Year	5-Year
0.00	0.12	0.65	2.28	2.31

3-Year Standard Deviation	0.16
Effective Duration	
Average Coupon Rate	

Company Information

Provider	Federated
Manager/Tenure	Management Team (16)
Website	http://www.federatedinvestors.com
Address	Federated Investors Funds 4000 Ericsson Drive Warrendale PA 15086-7561 United States
Phone Number	800-341-7400

PERFORMANCE

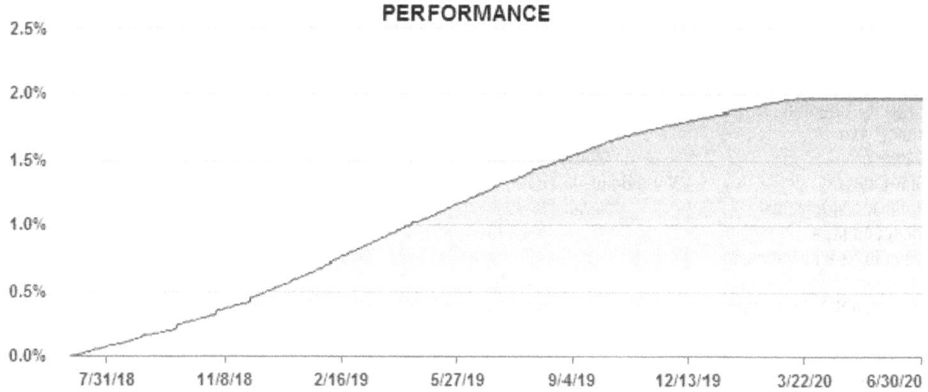

Ratings History

Date	Overall Rating	Risk Rating	Reward Rating
Q2-20	CC	C-	2019
Q4-19	C	C	C-
Q4-18	C	C+	C-
Q4-17	C-	C	C-
Q4-16	C-	C	D+

Asset & Performance History

Date	NAV	1-Year Total Return
1	1.25	Cash
2018	1	0.8
2017	1	0.02
2016	1	0
2015	1	-0.27
2014		-0.58

Total Assets: $155,932,000,000

Asset Allocation

Asset	%
66%	
Bonds	34%
Govt Bond	34%
Muni Bond	0%
Corp Bond	0%
Other	0%

Services Offered: Systematic Withdrawal Plan, Automatic Investment Plan, Qualified Investment, Phone Exchange, Wire Redemption

Investment Strategy: The investment seeks to provide current income consistent with stability of principal. The fund invests in a portfolio of U.S. Treasury and government securities maturing in 397 days or less and repurchase agreements collateralized fully by U.S. Treasury and government securities. The fund will operate as a "government money market fund," as such term is defined in or interpreted under Rule 2a-7 under the Investment Company Act of 1940. **Top Holdings:** Frbnybo Prime 1 Frbnybo Prime 1 Usd Ficcjpm 1 Ficc Jpm 1 Ss Ficc P Repo 1 Repo Anz Prime Repo 1 Anz Prime Rep 1

Vanguard Total International Bond Index Fund Investor Shares — B- BUY

Ticker	Traded On	NAV	Total Assets ($)	Dividend Yield (TTM)	Turnover Ratio	Expense Ratio
VTIBX	NAS CM	11.52	$142,843,000,000	3.26	26	0.13

Ratings

Reward	C
Risk	B
Recent Upgrade/Downgrade	Up

Fund Information

Fund Type	Open End
Category	Global Fixed Inc
Sub-Category	World Bond-USD Hedged
Prospectus Objective	Worldwide Bond
Inception Date	May-13
Open to New Investments	Y
Minimum Initial Investment	3,000
Minimum Subsequent Investment	1
Front End Fee	
Back End Fee	

Total Returns (%)

3-Month	6-Month	1-Year	3-Year	5-Year
2.18	2.32	3.83	15.61	24.17

3-Year Standard Deviation	3.15
Effective Duration	8.25
Average Coupon Rate	2.09

Company Information

Provider	Vanguard
Manager/Tenure	Joshua C. Barrickman (7)
Website	http://www.vanguard.com
Address	Vanguard 100 Vanguard Boulevard Malvern PA 19355 United States
Phone Number	877-662-7447

PERFORMANCE

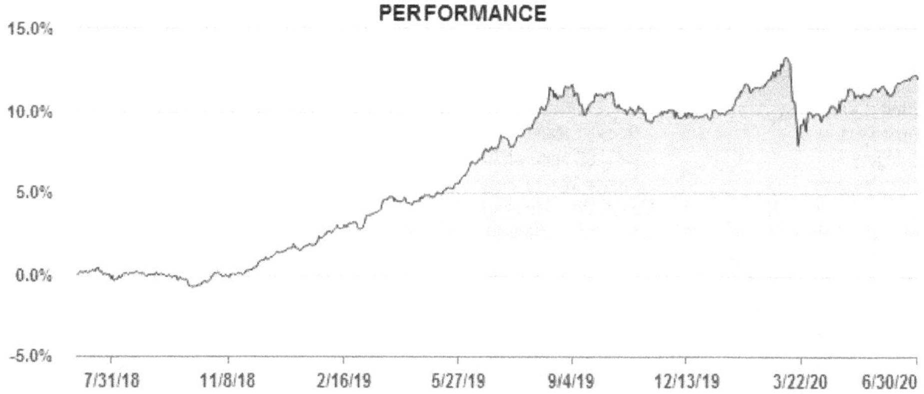

Ratings History

Date	Overall Rating	Risk Rating	Reward Rating
Q2-20	B-B	C	2019
Q4-19	C+	B+	C
Q4-18	C+	B	C
Q4-17	B-	A-	C
Q4-16	B-	A-	C

Asset & Performance History

Date	NAV	1-Year Total Return
11.31	7.75	Cash
2018	10.85	2.9
2017	10.86	2.31
2016	10.84	4.66
2015	10.55	1.03
2014	10.61	8.82

Total Assets: $142,843,000,000

Asset Allocation

Asset	%
1%	
Bonds	98%
Govt Bond	79%
Muni Bond	0%
Corp Bond	15%
Other	0%

Services Offered: Systematic Withdrawal Plan, Automatic Investment Plan, Phone Exchange, Wire Redemption

Investment Strategy: The investment seeks to track the performance of a benchmark index that measures the investment return of non-U.S. dollar-denominated investment-grade bonds. The fund employs an indexing investment approach designed to track the performance of the Bloomberg Barclays Global Aggregate ex-USD Float Adjusted RIC Capped Index (USD Hedged). This index provides a broad-based measure of the global, investment-grade, fixed-rate debt markets. It is non-diversified. **Top Holdings:** Pfandbriefzentrale der schweizerischen Kantonalbanken AG 0.5% United Kingdom of Great Britain and Northern Ireland 1.625% Germany (Federal Republic Of) 0% Italy (Republic Of) 3% Ireland (Republic Of) 0.9%

Vanguard Total International Bond Index Fund Admiral™ Shares B- BUY

Ticker	Traded On	NAV	Total Assets ($)	Dividend Yield (TTM)	Turnover Ratio	Expense Ratio
VTABX	NAS CM	23.04	$142,843,000,000	3.28	26	0.11

Ratings

Reward	C
Risk	B+
Recent Upgrade/Downgrade	Up

Fund Information

Fund Type	Open End
Category	Global Fixed Inc
Sub-Category	World Bond-USD Hedged
Prospectus Objective	Worldwide Bond
Inception Date	May-13
Open to New Investments	Y
Minimum Initial Investment	3,000
Minimum Subsequent Investment	1
Front End Fee	
Back End Fee	

Total Returns (%)

3-Month	6-Month	1-Year	3-Year	5-Year
2.19	2.34	3.85	15.65	24.39

3-Year Standard Deviation	3.11
Effective Duration	8.25
Average Coupon Rate	2.09

Company Information

Provider	Vanguard
Manager/Tenure	Joshua C. Barrickman (7)
Website	http://www.vanguard.com
Address	Vanguard 100 Vanguard Boulevard Malvern PA 19355 United States
Phone Number	877-662-7447

PERFORMANCE

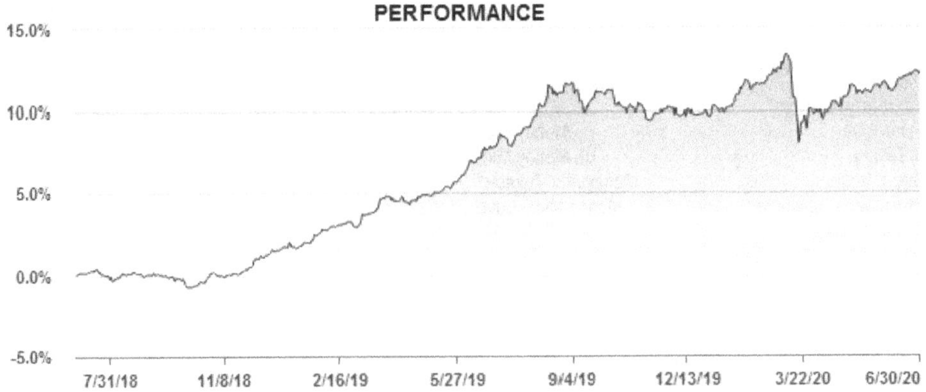

Ratings History

Date	Overall Rating	Risk Rating	Reward Rating
Q2-20	B-B+	C	2019
Q4-19	C+	B+	C
Q4-18	C+	B	C
Q4-17	B	A	C
Q4-16	B-	B+	C

Asset & Performance History

Date	NAV	1-Year Total Return
22.62	7.87	Cash
2018	21.68	2.97
2017	21.7	2.39
2016	21.67	4.65
2015	21.1	1.06
2014	21.22	8.82

Total Assets: $142,843,000,000

Asset Allocation

Asset	%
1%	
Bonds	98%
Govt Bond	79%
Muni Bond	0%
Corp Bond	15%
Other	0%

Services Offered: Systematic Withdrawal Plan, Automatic Investment Plan, Phone Exchange, Wire Redemption

Investment Strategy: The investment seeks to track the performance of a benchmark index that measures the investment return of non-U.S. dollar-denominated investment-grade bonds. The fund employs an indexing investment approach designed to track the performance of the Bloomberg Barclays Global Aggregate ex-USD Float Adjusted RIC Capped Index (USD Hedged). This index provides a broad-based measure of the global, investment-grade, fixed-rate debt markets. It is non-diversified. **Top Holdings:** Pfandbriefzentrale der schweizerischen Kantonalbanken AG 0.5% United Kingdom of Great Britain and Northern Ireland 1.625% Germany (Federal Republic Of) 0% Italy (Republic Of) 3% Ireland (Republic Of) 0.9%

JPMorgan 100% U.S. Treasury Securities Money Market Fund Morgan Class C HOLD

Ticker	Traded On	NAV	Total Assets ($)	Dividend Yield (TTM)	Turnover Ratio	Expense Ratio
HTSXX	NAS CM	1	$139,126,000,000	1.05		0.59

Ratings

Reward	C-
Risk	C+
Recent Upgrade/Downgrade	

Fund Information

Fund Type	Money Mkt
Category	US Money Mkt
Sub-Category	Money Mkt-Taxable
Prospectus Objective	Money Mkt - Treasury
Inception Date	Nov-91
Open to New Investments	Y
Minimum Initial Investment	1,000
Minimum Subsequent Investment	50
Front End Fee	
Back End Fee	

Total Returns (%)

3-Month	6-Month	1-Year	3-Year	5-Year
0.00	0.21	0.90	3.41	3.48

3-Year Standard Deviation	0.16
Effective Duration	
Average Coupon Rate	

Company Information

Provider	JPMorgan
Manager/Tenure	Management Team (15)
Website	http://www.jpmorganfunds.com
Address	JPMorgan 270 Park Avenue New York NY 10017-2070 United States
Phone Number	800-480-4111

PERFORMANCE

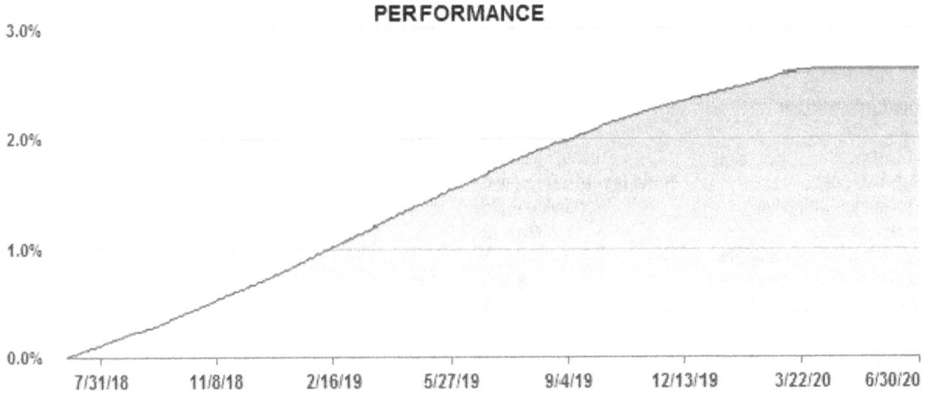

Ratings History

Date	Overall Rating	Risk Rating	Reward Rating
Q2-20	CC+	C-	2019
Q4-19	C	C+	C-
Q4-18	C	C+	C-
Q4-17	C	B-	C-
Q4-16	C-	C	C-

Asset & Performance History

Date	NAV	1-Year Total Return
1	1.62	Cash
2018	1	1.28
2017	1	0.32
2016	1	0
2015	1	0
2014	1	0

Total Assets: $139,126,000,000

Asset Allocation

Asset	%
71%	
Bonds	29%
Govt Bond	29%
Muni Bond	0%
Corp Bond	0%
Other	0%

Services Offered: Systematic Withdrawal Plan, Automatic Investment Plan, Qualified Investment, Phone Exchange, Wire Redemption

Investment Strategy: The investment seeks to provide the highest possible level of current income while still maintaining liquidity and providing maximum safety of principal. The fund normally invests its assets exclusively in obligations of the U.S. Treasury, including Treasury bills, bonds and notes. It does not buy securities issued or guaranteed by agencies of the U.S. government. The fund's adviser seeks to develop an appropriate portfolio by considering the differences in yields among securities of different maturities and issue dates. **Top Holdings:** United States Treasury Notes 0.26% United States Treasury Bills 0% United States Treasury Bills 0% United States Treasury Bills 0% United States Treasury Notes 0.24%

Wells Fargo Government Money Market Fund - Class A — C HOLD

Ticker	Traded On	NAV	Total Assets ($)	Dividend Yield (TTM)	Turnover Ratio	Expense Ratio
WFGXX	NAS CM	1	$132,598,000,000	1.08		0.6

Ratings

Reward	C-
Risk	C+
Recent Upgrade/Downgrade	

Fund Information

Fund Type	Money Mkt
Category	US Money Mkt
Sub-Category	Money Mkt-Taxable
Prospectus Objective	Money Mkt - Govt
Inception Date	Nov-99
Open to New Investments	Y
Minimum Initial Investment	1,000
Minimum Subsequent Investment	100
Front End Fee	
Back End Fee	

Total Returns (%)

3-Month	6-Month	1-Year	3-Year	5-Year
0.00	0.21	0.93	3.43	3.52

3-Year Standard Deviation	0.17
Effective Duration	
Average Coupon Rate	

Company Information

Provider	Wells Fargo Funds
Manager/Tenure	Management Team (12)
Website	http://https://www.wellsfargofunds.com/
Address	Wells Fargo Funds 525 Market Street San Francisco CA 94105 United States
Phone Number	800-222-8222

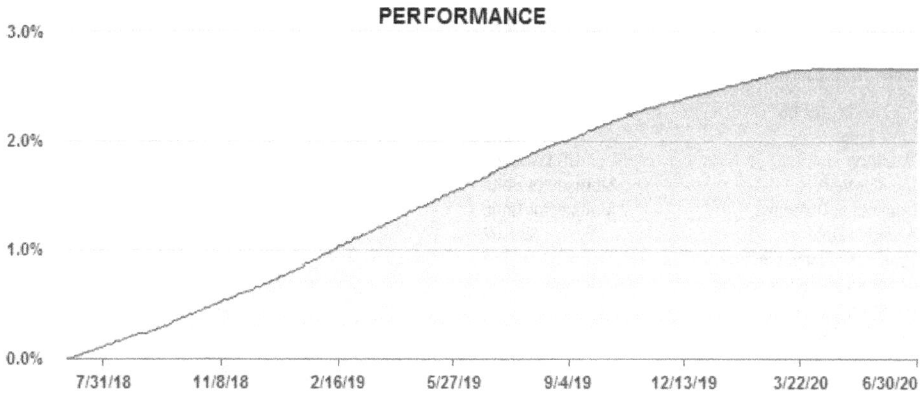

Ratings History

Date	Overall Rating	Risk Rating	Reward Rating
Q2-20	CC+	C-	2019
Q4-19	C	C+	C-
Q4-18	C	C+	C-
Q4-17	C	C	C-
Q4-16	C-	C	C-

Asset & Performance History

Date	NAV	1-Year Total Return
1	1.64	Cash
2018	1	1.26
2017	1	0.31
2016	1	0.01
2015	1	0
2014	1	0

Total Assets: $132,598,000,000

Asset Allocation

Asset	%
59%	
Bonds	39%
Govt Bond	37%
Muni Bond	1%
Corp Bond	2%
Other	0%

Services Offered: Systematic Withdrawal Plan, Automatic Investment Plan, Phone Exchange, Wire Redemption, Retirement Investment

Investment Strategy: The investment seeks current income, while preserving capital and liquidity. Under normal circumstances, the fund invests exclusively in high-quality, short-term, U.S. dollar-denominated money market instruments that consist of U.S. government obligations and repurchase agreements collateralized by U.S. government obligations. These investments may have fixed, floating, or variable rates of interest. The security selection is based on several factors, including credit quality, yield and maturity, while taking into account the fund's overall level of liquidity and weighted average maturity. **Top Holdings:** National Securities Clearing Corporation 0% Deutsche Bank Securities Repo Mbs Db 3 Rbc Dominion Repo Repo Bnp Repo Nomura Tri Party Repo

Vanguard Prime Money Market Fund Investor Shares — C HOLD

Ticker	Traded On	NAV	Total Assets ($)	Dividend Yield (TTM)	Turnover Ratio	Expense Ratio
VMMXX	NAS CM	1	$127,205,000,000	1.68	37	0.16

Ratings

Reward	C-
Risk	C+
Recent Upgrade/Downgrade	

Fund Information

Fund Type	Money Mkt
Category	US Money Mkt
Sub-Category	Prime Money Mkt
Prospectus Objective	Money Mkt - Taxable
Inception Date	Jun-75
Open to New Investments	Y
Minimum Initial Investment	3,000
Minimum Subsequent Investment	1
Front End Fee	
Back End Fee	

Total Returns (%)

3-Month	6-Month	1-Year	3-Year	5-Year
0.12	0.51	1.51	5.36	6.38

3-Year Standard Deviation	0.16
Effective Duration	
Average Coupon Rate	

Company Information

Provider	Vanguard
Manager/Tenure	Nafis T. Smith (2)
Website	http://www.vanguard.com
Address	Vanguard 100 Vanguard Boulevard Malvern PA 19355 United States
Phone Number	877-662-7447

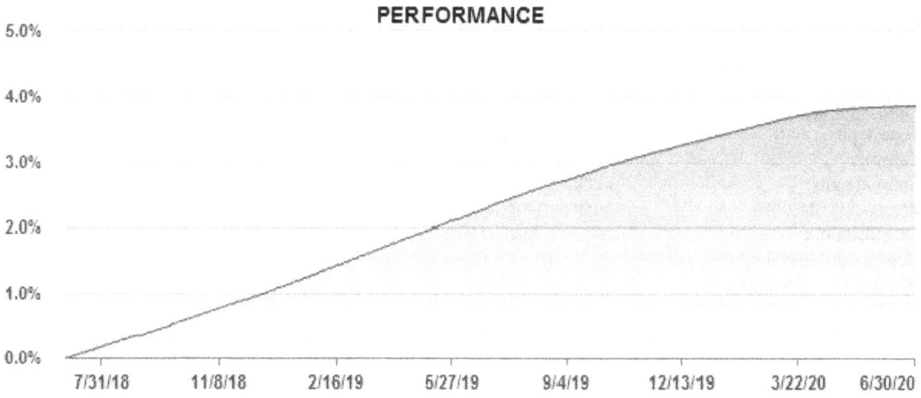

Ratings History

Date	Overall Rating	Risk Rating	Reward Rating
Q2-20	CC+	C-	2019
Q4-19	C	C+	C-
Q4-18	C	B-	C-
Q4-17	C	B-	C-
Q4-16	C	B-	C-

Asset & Performance History

Date	NAV	1-Year Total Return
1	2.22	Cash
2018	1	1.93
2017	1	1.01
2016	1	0.49
2015	1	0.04
2014	1	0.01

Total Assets: $127,205,000,000

Asset Allocation

Asset	%
84%	
Bonds	16%
Govt Bond	15%
Muni Bond	1%
Corp Bond	2%
Other	0%

Services Offered: Systematic Withdrawal Plan, Automatic Investment Plan, Phone Exchange, Wire Redemption

Investment Strategy: The investment seeks to provide current income while maintaining liquidity and a stable share price of $1. The fund invests primarily in high-quality, short-term money market instruments, including certificates of deposit, banker's acceptances, commercial paper, Eurodollar and Yankee obligations, and other money market securities. To be considered high quality, a security must be determined by Vanguard to present minimal credit risk based in part on a consideration of maturity, portfolio diversification, portfolio liquidity, and credit quality. The fund invests more than 25% of its assets in securities issued by companies in the financial services industry. **Top Holdings:** United States Treasury Bills 0.29% United States Treasury Bills 0.16% United States Treasury Bills 0.01% Ing Bank Nv Cd United States Treasury Bills 0.18%

PIMCO Income Fund Class R — C- HOLD

Ticker	Traded On	NAV	Total Assets ($)	Dividend Yield (TTM)	Turnover Ratio	Expense Ratio
PONRX	NAS CM	11.5	$116,854,000,000	5.49	421	1.7

Ratings

Reward	D+
Risk	C
Recent Upgrade/Downgrade	Down

Fund Information

Fund Type	Open End
Category	US Fixed Inc
Sub-Category	Multisector Bond
Prospectus Objective	Multisector Bond
Inception Date	Mar-07
Open to New Investments	Y
Minimum Initial Investment	0
Minimum Subsequent Investment	
Front End Fee	
Back End Fee	

Total Returns (%)

3-Month	6-Month	1-Year	3-Year	5-Year
6.29	-2.01	-0.06	8.13	21.60

3-Year Standard Deviation	5.45
Effective Duration	0.77
Average Coupon Rate	3.22

Company Information

Provider	PIMCO
Manager/Tenure	Daniel J. Ivascyn (13), Alfred T. Murata (7), Joshua Anderson (1)
Website	http://www.pimco.com
Address	PIMCO 840 Newport Center Drive, Suite 100 Newport Beach CA 92660 United States
Phone Number	866-746-2602

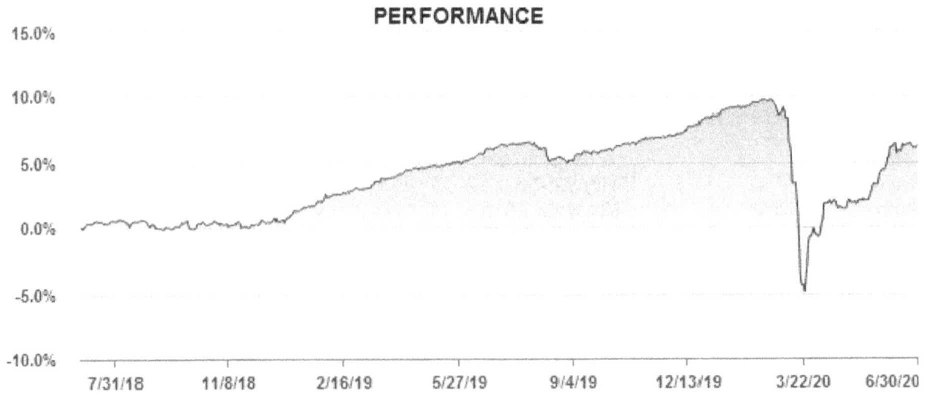

Ratings History

Date	Overall Rating	Risk Rating	Reward Rating
Q2-20	C-C	D+	2019
Q4-19	C+	B	C
Q4-18	C	B	C-
Q4-17	B	A	C+
Q4-16	B	A	C+

Asset & Performance History

Date	NAV	1-Year Total Return
12.04	7.32	Cash
2018	11.81	-0.07
2017	12.41	7.85
2016	12.06	7.96
2015	11.73	1.95
2014	12.33	6.56

Total Assets: $116,854,000,000

Asset Allocation

Asset	%
-26%	
Bonds	121%
Govt Bond	25%
Muni Bond	0%
Corp Bond	7%
Other	0%

Services Offered: Systematic Withdrawal Plan, Automatic Investment Plan, Qualified Investment, Phone Exchange, Wire Redemption

Investment Strategy: The investment seeks to maximize current income; long-term capital appreciation is a secondary objective. The fund invests at least 65% of its total assets in a multi-sector portfolio of Fixed Income Instruments of varying maturities, which may be represented by forwards or derivatives such as options, futures contracts or swap agreements. It may invest up to 50% of its total assets in high yield securities rated below investment grade by Moody's, S&P or Fitch, or if unrated, as determined by PIMCO. **Top Holdings:** Irs Usd 1.40000 06/19/20-4y Cme Irs Eur -0.33000 03/18/20-2y Lch Irs Jpy 0.45000 03/20/19-10y Lch Federal National Mortgage Association 3% Cirs Usd 4y Mat 3.85/2.00% M 7/2020 Dub

PIMCO Income Fund Class A — C- HOLD

Ticker	Traded On	NAV	Total Assets ($)	Dividend Yield (TTM)	Turnover Ratio	Expense Ratio
PONAX	NAS CM	11.5	$116,854,000,000	5.75	421	1.45

Ratings

Reward	D+
Risk	C
Recent Upgrade/Downgrade	Down

Fund Information

Fund Type	Open End
Category	US Fixed Inc
Sub-Category	Multisector Bond
Prospectus Objective	Multisector Bond
Inception Date	Mar-07
Open to New Investments	Y
Minimum Initial Investment	1,000
Minimum Subsequent Investment	50
Front End Fee	3.75
Back End Fee	

Total Returns (%)

3-Month	6-Month	1-Year	3-Year	5-Year
6.35	-1.89	0.18	8.95	23.13

3-Year Standard Deviation	5.45
Effective Duration	0.77
Average Coupon Rate	3.22

Company Information

Provider	PIMCO
Manager/Tenure	Daniel J. Ivascyn (13), Alfred T. Murata (7), Joshua Anderson (1)
Website	http://www.pimco.com
Address	PIMCO 840 Newport Center Drive, Suite 100 Newport Beach CA 92660 United States
Phone Number	866-746-2602

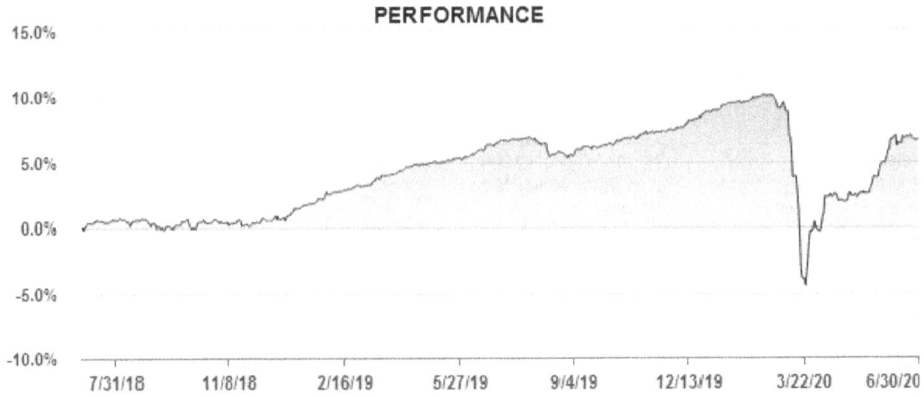

Ratings History

Date	Overall Rating	Risk Rating	Reward Rating
Q2-20	C-C	D+	2019
Q4-19	C+	B	C
Q4-18	C+	B	C
Q4-17	B	A	C+
Q4-16	B	A	C+

Asset & Performance History

Date	NAV	1-Year Total Return
12.04	7.59	Cash
2018	11.81	0.17
2017	12.41	8.11
2016	12.06	8.23
2015	11.73	2.22
2014	12.33	6.79

Total Assets: $116,854,000,000

Asset Allocation

Asset	%
-26%	
Bonds	121%
Govt Bond	25%
Muni Bond	0%
Corp Bond	7%
Other	0%

Services Offered: Systematic Withdrawal Plan, Automatic Investment Plan, Phone Exchange, Wire Redemption, Retirement Investment

Investment Strategy: The investment seeks to maximize current income; long-term capital appreciation is a secondary objective. The fund invests at least 65% of its total assets in a multi-sector portfolio of Fixed Income Instruments of varying maturities, which may be represented by forwards or derivatives such as options, futures contracts or swap agreements. It may invest up to 50% of its total assets in high yield securities rated below investment grade by Moody's, S&P or Fitch, or if unrated, as determined by PIMCO. **Top Holdings:** Irs Usd 1.40000 06/19/20-4y Cme Irs Eur -0.33000 03/18/20-2y Lch Irs Jpy 0.45000 03/20/19-10y Lch Federal National Mortgage Association 3% Cirs Usd 4y Mat 3.85/2.00% M 7/2020 Dub

PIMCO Income Fund Class C — C- HOLD

Ticker	Traded On	NAV	Total Assets ($)	Dividend Yield (TTM)	Turnover Ratio	Expense Ratio
PONCX	NAS CM	11.5	$116,854,000,000	4.96	421	2.2

Ratings

Reward	D+
Risk	C
Recent Upgrade/Downgrade	Down

Fund Information

Fund Type	Open End
Category	US Fixed Inc
Sub-Category	Multisector Bond
Prospectus Objective	Multisector Bond
Inception Date	Mar-07
Open to New Investments	Y
Minimum Initial Investment	1,000
Minimum Subsequent Investment	50
Front End Fee	
Back End Fee	1.00

Total Returns (%)

3-Month	6-Month	1-Year	3-Year	5-Year
6.16	-2.26	-0.56	6.53	18.61

3-Year Standard Deviation	5.45
Effective Duration	0.77
Average Coupon Rate	3.22

Company Information

Provider	PIMCO
Manager/Tenure	Daniel J. Ivascyn (13), Alfred T. Murata (7), Joshua Anderson (1)
Website	http://www.pimco.com
Address	PIMCO 840 Newport Center Drive, Suite 100 Newport Beach CA 92660 United States
Phone Number	866-746-2602

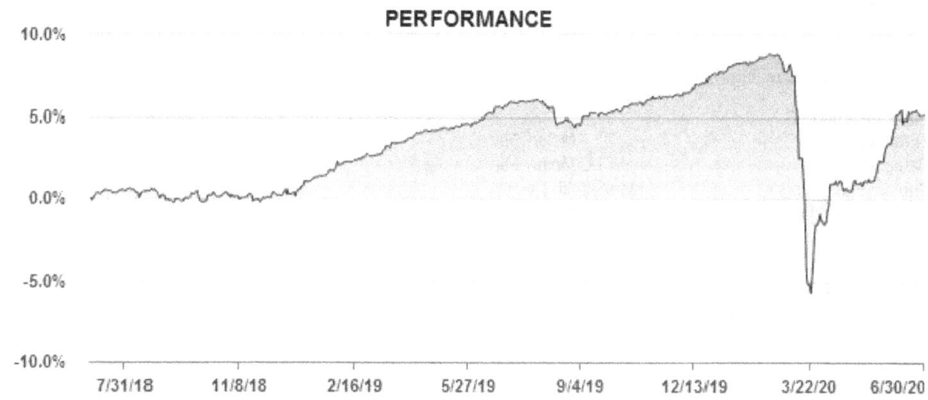

Ratings History

Date	Overall Rating	Risk Rating	Reward Rating
Q2-20	C-C	D+	2019
Q4-19	C+	B	C
Q4-18	C	B	C-
Q4-17	B	A	C+
Q4-16	B	A-	C+

Asset & Performance History

Date	NAV	1-Year Total Return
12.04	6.8	Cash
2018	11.81	-0.57
2017	12.41	7.32
2016	12.06	7.45
2015	11.73	1.42
2014	12.33	6.11

Total Assets: $116,854,000,000

Asset Allocation

Asset	%
-26%	
Bonds	121%
Govt Bond	25%
Muni Bond	0%
Corp Bond	7%
Other	0%

Services Offered: Systematic Withdrawal Plan, Automatic Investment Plan, Phone Exchange, Wire Redemption, Retirement Investment

Investment Strategy: The investment seeks to maximize current income; long-term capital appreciation is a secondary objective. The fund invests at least 65% of its total assets in a multi-sector portfolio of Fixed Income Instruments of varying maturities, which may be represented by forwards or derivatives such as options, futures contracts or swap agreements. It may invest up to 50% of its total assets in high yield securities rated below investment grade by Moody's, S&P or Fitch, or if unrated, as determined by PIMCO. **Top Holdings:** Irs Usd 1.40000 06/19/20-4y Cme Irs Eur -0.33000 03/18/20-2y Lch Irs Jpy 0.45000 03/20/19-10y Lch Federal National Mortgage Association 3% Cirs Usd 4y Mat 3.85/2.00% M 7/2020 Dub

Schwab Value Advantage Money Fund® Investor Shares — C HOLD

Ticker	Traded On	NAV	Total Assets ($)	Dividend Yield (TTM)	Turnover Ratio	Expense Ratio
SWVXX	NAS CM	1	$115,358,000,000	1.6		0.34

Ratings

Reward	C-
Risk	C+
Recent Upgrade/Downgrade	

Fund Information

Fund Type	Money Mkt
Category	US Money Mkt
Sub-Category	Prime Money Mkt
Prospectus Objective	Money Mkt - Taxable
Inception Date	Apr-92
Open to New Investments	Y
Minimum Initial Investment	0
Minimum Subsequent Investment	
Front End Fee	
Back End Fee	

Total Returns (%)

3-Month	6-Month	1-Year	3-Year	5-Year
0.08	0.41	1.33	4.82	5.43

3-Year Standard Deviation	0.16
Effective Duration	
Average Coupon Rate	

Company Information

Provider	Schwab Funds
Manager/Tenure	Management Team (13)
Website	http://www.schwabfunds.com
Address	Schwab Funds 101 Montgomery Street San Francisco CA 94104 United States
Phone Number	877-824-5615

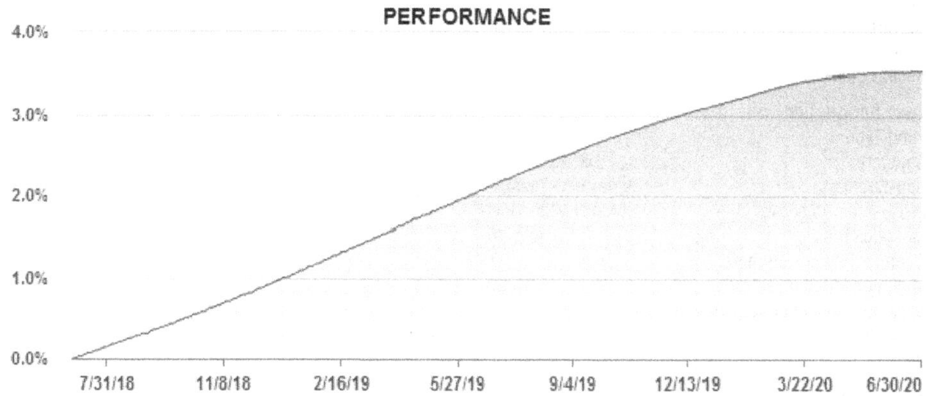

Ratings History

Date	Overall Rating	Risk Rating	Reward Rating
Q2-20	CC+	C-	2019
Q4-19	C	C+	C-
Q4-18	C	B-	C-
Q4-17	C	B-	C-
Q4-16	C	C	C-

Asset & Performance History

Date	NAV	1-Year Total Return
1	2.06	Cash
2018	1	1.77
2017	1	0.8
2016	1	0.24
2015	1	0.01
2014	1	0.01

Total Assets: $115,358,000,000

Asset Allocation

Asset	%
97%	
Bonds	3%
Govt Bond	0%
Muni Bond	0%
Corp Bond	3%
Other	0%

Services Offered: Qualified Investment, Phone Exchange, Wire Redemption, Retirement Investment

Investment Strategy: The investment seeks the highest current income consistent with stability of capital and liquidity. The fund invests in high-quality short-term money market investments issued by U.S. and foreign issuers, such as: commercial paper, including asset-backed commercial paper; promissory notes; certificates of deposit and time deposits; variable- and floating-rate debt securities; bank notes and bankers' acceptances; repurchase agreements; obligations that are issued by the U.S. government, its agencies or instrumentalities. All of these investments will be denominated in U.S. dollars, including those that are issued by foreign issuers. **Top Holdings:** Tri-Party Ficc Bny/Xiss/Ficc Repo - 01apr20 Tri-Party Royal Bank Of Canada Repo - 01apr20 Tri-Party Royal Bank Of Canada Repo - 21apr20 Tri-Party Bnp Paribas Sa/Xiss/ Repo - 01apr20 Tri-Party Barclays Bank Plc/Xi Repo - 01apr20

Morgan Stanley Institutional Liquidity Government Portfolio Select Class — C HOLD

Ticker	Traded On	NAV	Total Assets ($)	Dividend Yield (TTM)	Turnover Ratio	Expense Ratio
MSDXX	NAS CM	1	$109,097,000,000	0.77		1

Ratings

Reward	C-
Risk	C
Recent Upgrade/Downgrade	

Fund Information

Fund Type	Money Mkt
Category	US Money Mkt
Sub-Category	Money Mkt-Taxable
Prospectus Objective	Money Mkt - General
Inception Date	Mar-16
Open to New Investments	Y
Minimum Initial Investment	0
Minimum Subsequent Investment	
Front End Fee	
Back End Fee	

Total Returns (%)

3-Month	6-Month	1-Year	3-Year	5-Year
0.00	0.12	0.64	2.41	2.09

3-Year Standard Deviation	0.16
Effective Duration	
Average Coupon Rate	

Company Information

Provider	Morgan Stanley
Manager/Tenure	Management Team (15)
Website	http://www.morganstanley.com
Address	Morgan Stanley 1221 Avenue of the Americas New York NY 10020 United States
Phone Number	855-332-5306

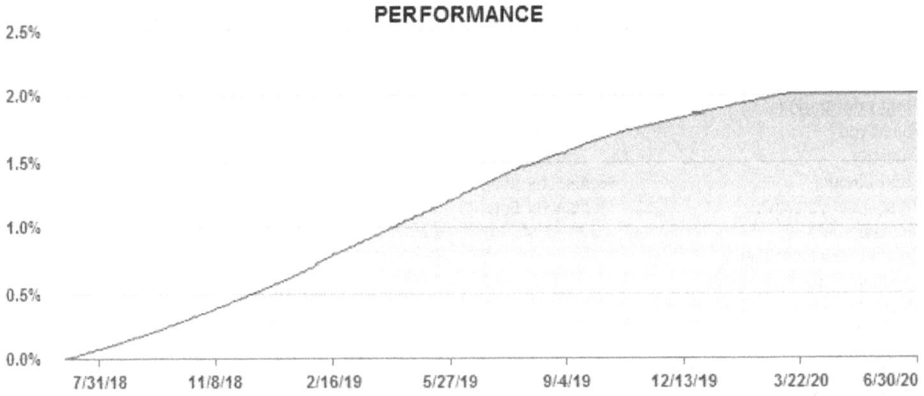

Ratings History

Date	Overall Rating	Risk Rating	Reward Rating
Q2-20	CC	C-	2019
Q4-19	C	C	C-
Q4-18	C	C+	C-
Q4-17	C-	C	D+
Q4-16	C-	C	D

Asset & Performance History

Date	NAV	1-Year Total Return
1	1.27	Cash
2018	1	0.9
2017	1	0.06
2016	1	-0.07
2015		-0.5
2014		-0.5

Total Assets: $109,097,000,000

Asset Allocation

Asset	%
66%	
Bonds	34%
Govt Bond	34%
Muni Bond	0%
Corp Bond	0%
Other	0%

Services Offered: Qualified Investment, Phone Exchange, Wire Redemption

Investment Strategy: The investment seeks preservation of capital, daily liquidity and maximum current income. The portfolio has adopted a policy to invest exclusively in obligations issued or guaranteed by the U.S. government and its agencies and instrumentalities and in repurchase agreements collateralized by such securities in order to qualify as a "government money market fund" under federal regulations. A "government money market fund" is a money market fund that invests at least 99.5% of its total assets in cash, securities issued or guaranteed by the United States or certain U.S. government agencies or instrumentalities and/or repurchase agreements. **Top Holdings:** Fixed Income Clearing Corp:0.0 Repo - 01jun20 Jp Morgan Securities Llc:0.000 Repo - 30dec50 United States Treasury Bills 0.01% Federal Home Loan Banks 0.01% Daiwa Capital Markets America Repo - 01jun20

State Street Institutional U.S. Government Money Market Fund Administration Class — C HOLD

Ticker	Traded On	NAV	Total Assets ($)	Dividend Yield (TTM)	Turnover Ratio	Expense Ratio
SALXX	NAS CM	1	$104,933,000,000	1.26		0.37

Ratings

Reward	C-
Risk	C+
Recent Upgrade/Downgrade	

Fund Information

Fund Type	Money Mkt
Category	US Money Mkt
Sub-Category	Money Mkt-Taxable
Prospectus Objective	Money Mkt - Govt
Inception Date	Aug-16
Open to New Investments	Y
Minimum Initial Investment	1,000
Minimum Subsequent Investment	
Front End Fee	
Back End Fee	

Total Returns (%)

3-Month	6-Month	1-Year	3-Year	5-Year
0.00	0.26	1.10	4.06	4.25

3-Year Standard Deviation	0.18
Effective Duration	
Average Coupon Rate	

Company Information

Provider	State Street Global Advisors
Manager/Tenure	Management Team (12)
Website	http://www.ssga.com
Address	State Street Global Advisors One Iron Street Boston MA 02210 United States
Phone Number	617-664-7338

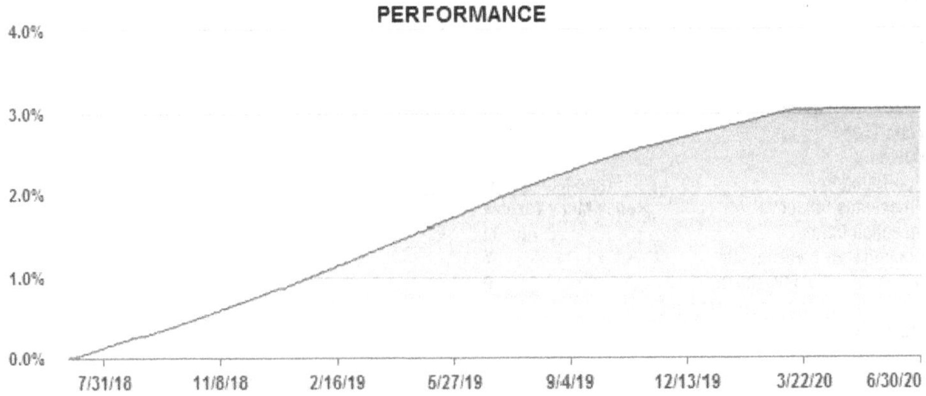

Ratings History

Date	Overall Rating	Risk Rating	Reward Rating
Q2-20	CC+	C-	2019
Q4-19	C	C+	C
Q4-18	C	C+	C-
Q4-17	C	C	C-
Q4-16	C-	C	C-

Asset & Performance History

Date	NAV	1-Year Total Return
1	1.9	Cash
2018	1	1.49
2017	1	0.46
2016	1	0.01
2015		0
2014		0

Total Assets: $104,933,000,000

Asset Allocation

Asset	%
100%	
Bonds	0%
Govt Bond	0%
Muni Bond	0%
Corp Bond	0%
Other	0%

Services Offered: Systematic Withdrawal Plan, Automatic Investment Plan, Phone Exchange, Wire Redemption

Investment Strategy: The investment seeks to maximize current income, to the extent consistent with the preservation of capital and liquidity and the maintenance of a stable $1.00 per share net asset value. The fund invests only in obligations issued or guaranteed as to principal and/or interest, as applicable, by the U.S. government or its agencies and instrumentalities, as well as repurchase agreements secured by such instruments. The manager follows a disciplined investment process that attempts to provide stability of principal, liquidity and current income, by investing in U.S. government securities. **Top Holdings:** State Street U.S. Government Money Market Portfolio Agreement With Barclays Capital, Inc. And Bank Of New York Mellon (Tri-Part U.S. Treasury Note, 3 Month Usd Mmy 0.03% Agreement With Citigroup Global Markets, Inc. And Bank Of New York Mellon (U.S. Treasury Note, 3 Month Usd Mmy 0.06%

BlackRock Liquidity T-Fund Capital Shares — C HOLD

Ticker	Traded On	NAV	Total Assets ($)	Dividend Yield (TTM)	Turnover Ratio	Expense Ratio
BCHXX	NAS CM	1	$85,954,131,860	1.4	0	0.22

Ratings

Reward	C-
Risk	C+
Recent Upgrade/Downgrade	

Fund Information

Fund Type	Money Mkt
Category	US Money Mkt
Sub-Category	Money Mkt-Taxable
Prospectus Objective	Money Mkt - Treasury
Inception Date	Nov-17
Open to New Investments	Y
Minimum Initial Investment	50,000
Minimum Subsequent Investment	
Front End Fee	
Back End Fee	

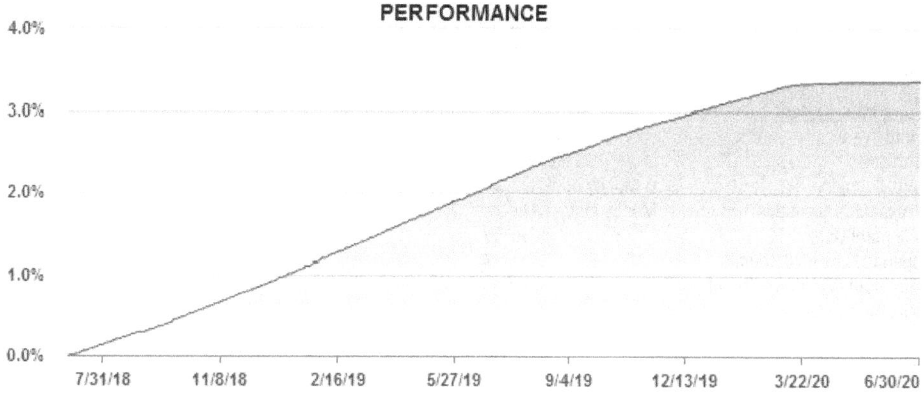

Total Returns (%)

3-Month	6-Month	1-Year	3-Year	5-Year
0.02	0.31	1.22	4.57	5.10

3-Year Standard Deviation	
Effective Duration	
Average Coupon Rate	

Ratings History

Date	Overall Rating	Risk Rating	Reward Rating
Q2-20	CC+	C-	2019
Q4-19	C	C+	C
Q4-18	C	C+	C-
Q4-17	U		
Q4-16			

Asset & Performance History

Date	NAV	1-Year Total Return
1	2.04	Cash
2018	1	1.66
2017	1	0.65
2016	1	
2015	1	
2014	1	

Total Assets: $85,954,131,860

Asset Allocation

Asset	%
64%	
Bonds	36%
Govt Bond	36%
Muni Bond	0%
Corp Bond	0%
Other	0%

Company Information

Provider	BlackRock
Manager/Tenure	Management Team (14)
Website	http://www.blackrock.com
Address	BlackRock Funds Providence RI 02940-8019 United States
Phone Number	800-441-7762

Services Offered: Qualified Investment

Investment Strategy: The investment seeks current income as is consistent with liquidity and stability of principal. The fund invests at least 99.5% of its total assets in cash, U.S. Treasury bills, notes and other obligations issued or guaranteed as to principal and interest by the U.S. Treasury, and repurchase agreements secured by such obligations or cash. It invests in securities maturing in 397 days or less (with certain exceptions) and the portfolio will have a dollar-weighted average maturity of 60 days or less and a dollar-weighted average life of 120 days or less. **Top Holdings:** Usd Cash(Committed) Tri-Party Barclays Bank Plc Tri-Party Bnp Paribas United States Treasury Bills United States Treasury Notes 0.34%

BlackRock Liquidity Funds T-Fund Select Shares — C HOLD

Ticker	Traded On	NAV	Total Assets ($)	Dividend Yield (TTM)	Turnover Ratio	Expense Ratio
BSLXX	NAS CM	1	$85,954,131,860	0.75	0	1

Ratings

Reward	C-
Risk	C
Recent Upgrade/Downgrade	

Fund Information

Fund Type	Money Mkt
Category	US Money Mkt
Sub-Category	Money Mkt-Taxable
Prospectus Objective	Money Mkt - Treasury
Inception Date	Mar-08
Open to New Investments	Y
Minimum Initial Investment	0
Minimum Subsequent Investment	
Front End Fee	
Back End Fee	

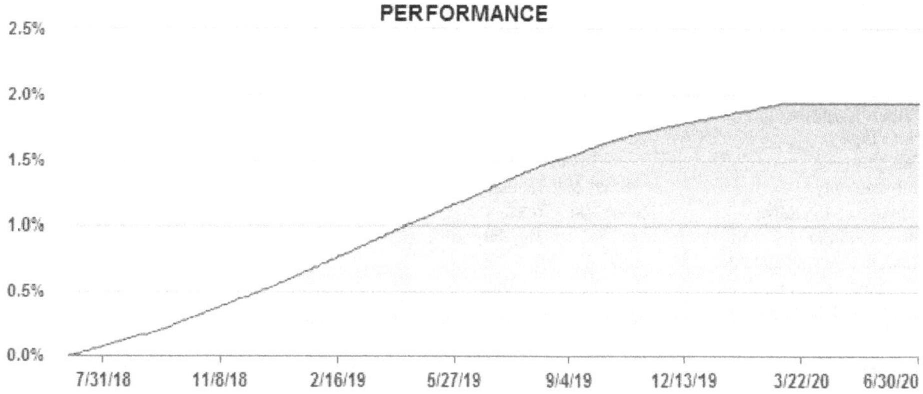

Total Returns (%)

3-Month	6-Month	1-Year	3-Year	5-Year
0.00	0.11	0.62	2.30	2.31

3-Year Standard Deviation	0.15
Effective Duration	
Average Coupon Rate	

Ratings History

Date	Overall Rating	Risk Rating	Reward Rating
Q2-20	CC	C-	2019
Q4-19	C	C	C-
Q4-18	C	C	C-
Q4-17	C-	C	C-
Q4-16	C-	C	C-

Asset & Performance History

Date	NAV	1-Year Total Return
1	1.24	Cash
2018	1	0.87
2017	1	0.04
2016	1	0
2015	1	0
2014	1	0

Total Assets: $85,954,131,860

Asset Allocation

Asset	%
64%	
Bonds	36%
Govt Bond	36%
Muni Bond	0%
Corp Bond	0%
Other	0%

Company Information

Provider	BlackRock
Manager/Tenure	Management Team (14)
Website	http://www.blackrock.com
Address	BlackRock Funds Providence RI 02940-8019 United States
Phone Number	800-441-7762

Services Offered: Qualified Investment, Wire Redemption

Investment Strategy: The investment seeks current income as is consistent with liquidity and stability of principal. The fund invests at least 99.5% of its total assets in cash, U.S. Treasury bills, notes and other obligations issued or guaranteed as to principal and interest by the U.S. Treasury, and repurchase agreements secured by such obligations or cash. It invests in securities maturing in 397 days or less (with certain exceptions) and the portfolio will have a dollar-weighted average maturity of 60 days or less and a dollar-weighted average life of 120 days or less. **Top Holdings:** Usd Cash(Committed) Tri-Party Barclays Bank Plc Tri-Party Bnp Paribas United States Treasury Bills United States Treasury Notes 0.34%

BlackRock Liquidity Funds T-Fund Dollar Shares — C HOLD

Ticker	Traded On	NAV	Total Assets ($)	Dividend Yield (TTM)	Turnover Ratio	Expense Ratio
TFEXX	NAS CM	1	$85,954,131,860	1.21	0	0.42

Ratings

Reward	C-
Risk	C+
Recent Upgrade/Downgrade	

Fund Information

Fund Type	Money Mkt
Category	US Money Mkt
Sub-Category	Money Mkt-Taxable
Prospectus Objective	Money Mkt - Treasury
Inception Date	Jan-86
Open to New Investments	Y
Minimum Initial Investment	5,000
Minimum Subsequent Investment	
Front End Fee	
Back End Fee	

Total Returns (%)

3-Month	6-Month	1-Year	3-Year	5-Year
0.00	0.24	1.04	3.93	4.12

3-Year Standard Deviation	0.17
Effective Duration	
Average Coupon Rate	

Company Information

Provider	BlackRock
Manager/Tenure	Management Team (14)
Website	http://www.blackrock.com
Address	BlackRock Funds Providence RI 02940-8019 United States
Phone Number	800-441-7762

PERFORMANCE

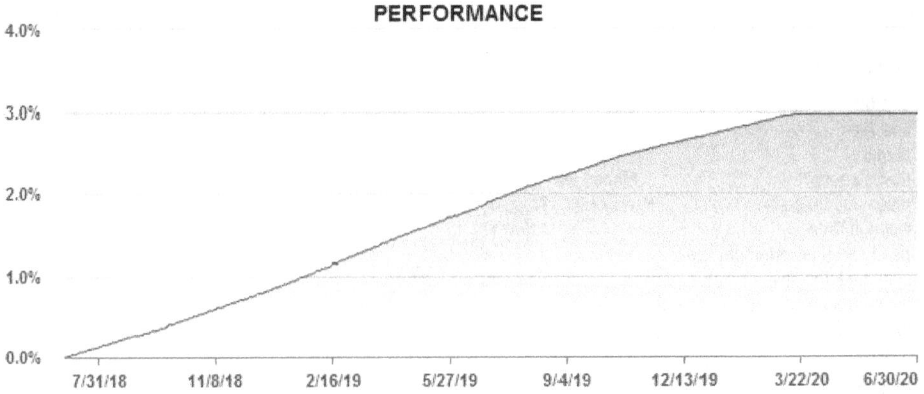

Ratings History

Date	Overall Rating	Risk Rating	Reward Rating
Q2-20	CC+	C-	2019
Q4-19	C	C+	C-
Q4-18	C	C+	C-
Q4-17	C	C	C-
Q4-16	C-	C	C-

Asset & Performance History

Date	NAV	1-Year Total Return
1	1.82	Cash
2018	1	1.46
2017	1	0.49
2016	1	0.02
2015	1	0.01
2014	1	0.01

Total Assets: $85,954,131,860

Asset Allocation

Asset	%
64%	
Bonds	36%
Govt Bond	36%
Muni Bond	0%
Corp Bond	0%
Other	0%

Services Offered: Qualified Investment, Wire Redemption

Investment Strategy: The investment seeks current income as is consistent with liquidity and stability of principal. The fund invests at least 99.5% of its total assets in cash, U.S. Treasury bills, notes and other obligations issued or guaranteed as to principal and interest by the U.S. Treasury, and repurchase agreements secured by such obligations or cash. It invests in securities maturing in 397 days or less (with certain exceptions) and the portfolio will have a dollar-weighted average maturity of 60 days or less and a dollar-weighted average life of 120 days or less. **Top Holdings:** Usd Cash(Committed) Tri-Party Barclays Bank Plc Tri-Party Bnp Paribas United States Treasury Bills United States Treasury Notes 0.34%

BlackRock Liquidity Funds T-Fund Cash Management Shares — C HOLD

Ticker	Traded On	NAV	Total Assets ($)	Dividend Yield (TTM)	Turnover Ratio	Expense Ratio
BPTXX	NAS CM	1	$85,954,131,860	1.01	0	0.67

Ratings

Reward	C-
Risk	C+
Recent Upgrade/Downgrade	

Fund Information

Fund Type	Money Mkt
Category	US Money Mkt
Sub-Category	Money Mkt-Taxable
Prospectus Objective	Money Mkt - Treasury
Inception Date	May-99
Open to New Investments	Y
Minimum Initial Investment	5,000
Minimum Subsequent Investment	
Front End Fee	
Back End Fee	

Total Returns (%)

3-Month	6-Month	1-Year	3-Year	5-Year
0.00	0.18	0.86	3.24	3.31

3-Year Standard Deviation	0.16
Effective Duration	
Average Coupon Rate	

Company Information

Provider	BlackRock
Manager/Tenure	Management Team (14)
Website	http://www.blackrock.com
Address	BlackRock Funds Providence RI 02940-8019 United States
Phone Number	800-441-7762

PERFORMANCE

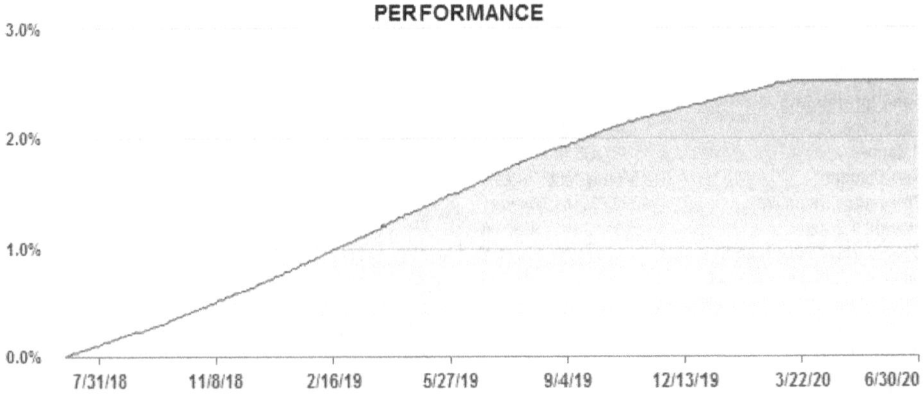

Ratings History

Date	Overall Rating	Risk Rating	Reward Rating
Q2-20	CC+	C-	2019
Q4-19	C	C+	C-
Q4-18	C	C	C-
Q4-17	C	C	C-
Q4-16	C-	C	C-

Asset & Performance History

Date	NAV	1-Year Total Return
1	1.57	Cash
2018	1	1.22
2017	1	0.26
2016	1	0.01
2015	1	0.01
2014	1	0.01

Total Assets: $85,954,131,860

Asset Allocation

Asset	%
64%	
Bonds	36%
Govt Bond	36%
Muni Bond	0%
Corp Bond	0%
Other	0%

Services Offered: Qualified Investment, Wire Redemption

Investment Strategy: The investment seeks current income as is consistent with liquidity and stability of principal. The fund invests at least 99.5% of its total assets in cash, U.S. Treasury bills, notes and other obligations issued or guaranteed as to principal and interest by the U.S. Treasury, and repurchase agreements secured by such obligations or cash. It invests in securities maturing in 397 days or less (with certain exceptions) and the portfolio will have a dollar-weighted average maturity of 60 days or less and a dollar-weighted average life of 120 days or less. **Top Holdings:** Usd Cash(Committed) Tri-Party Barclays Bank Plc Tri-Party Bnp Paribas United States Treasury Bills United States Treasury Notes 0.34%

BlackRock Liquidity Funds T-Fund Administration Shares

C HOLD

Ticker	Traded On	NAV	Total Assets ($)	Dividend Yield (TTM)	Turnover Ratio	Expense Ratio
BTAXX	NAS CM	1	$85,954,131,860	1.34	0	0.27

Ratings

Reward	C-
Risk	C+
Recent Upgrade/Downgrade	

Fund Information

Fund Type	Money Mkt
Category	US Money Mkt
Sub-Category	Money Mkt-Taxable
Prospectus Objective	Money Mkt - Treasury
Inception Date	Apr-02
Open to New Investments	Y
Minimum Initial Investment	5,000
Minimum Subsequent Investment	
Front End Fee	
Back End Fee	

Total Returns (%)

3-Month	6-Month	1-Year	3-Year	5-Year
0.00	0.29	1.16	4.37	4.73

3-Year Standard Deviation	0.18
Effective Duration	
Average Coupon Rate	

Company Information

Provider	BlackRock
Manager/Tenure	Management Team (14)
Website	http://www.blackrock.com
Address	BlackRock Funds Providence RI 02940-8019 United States
Phone Number	800-441-7762

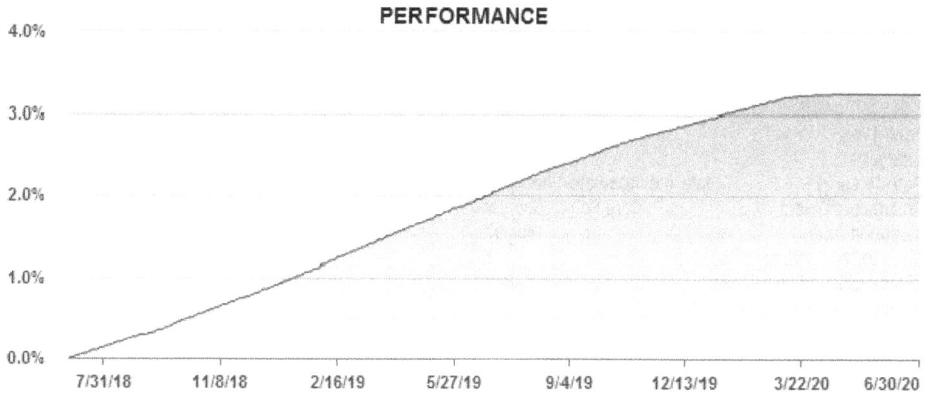

Ratings History

Date	Overall Rating	Risk Rating	Reward Rating
Q2-20	CC+	C-	2019
Q4-19	C	C+	C-
Q4-18	C	B-	C
Q4-17	C	C+	C-
Q4-16	C	C	C-

Asset & Performance History

Date	NAV	1-Year Total Return
1	1.97	Cash
2018	1	1.61
2017	1	0.65
2016	1	0.1
2015	1	0.01
2014	1	0.01

Total Assets: $85,954,131,860

Asset Allocation

Asset	%
64%	
Bonds	36%
Govt Bond	36%
Muni Bond	0%
Corp Bond	0%
Other	0%

Services Offered: Qualified Investment, Wire Redemption

Investment Strategy: The investment seeks current income as is consistent with liquidity and stability of principal. The fund invests at least 99.5% of its total assets in cash, U.S. Treasury bills, notes and other obligations issued or guaranteed as to principal and interest by the U.S. Treasury, and repurchase agreements secured by such obligations or cash. It invests in securities maturing in 397 days or less (with certain exceptions) and the portfolio will have a dollar-weighted average maturity of 60 days or less and a dollar-weighted average life of 120 days or less. **Top Holdings:** Usd Cash(Committed) Tri-Party Barclays Bank Plc Tri-Party Bnp Paribas United States Treasury Bills United States Treasury Notes 0.34%

Northern Institutional Treasury Portfolio Premier Shares

C HOLD

Ticker	Traded On	NAV	Total Assets ($)	Dividend Yield (TTM)	Turnover Ratio	Expense Ratio
NTPXX	NAS CM	1	$84,261,857,566	1.46		0.2

Ratings

Reward	C-
Risk	C+
Recent Upgrade/Downgrade	

Fund Information

Fund Type	Money Mkt
Category	US Money Mkt
Sub-Category	Money Mkt-Taxable
Prospectus Objective	Money Mkt - Treasury
Inception Date	Aug-16
Open to New Investments	Y
Minimum Initial Investment	0
Minimum Subsequent Investment	
Front End Fee	
Back End Fee	

Total Returns (%)

3-Month	6-Month	1-Year	3-Year	5-Year
0.04	0.35	1.29	4.61	5.14

3-Year Standard Deviation	0.17
Effective Duration	
Average Coupon Rate	

Company Information

Provider	Northern Funds
Manager/Tenure	Management Team (11)
Website	http://www.northernfunds.com
Address	Northern Funds 50 South Lasalle Chicago IL 60603 United States
Phone Number	800-595-9111

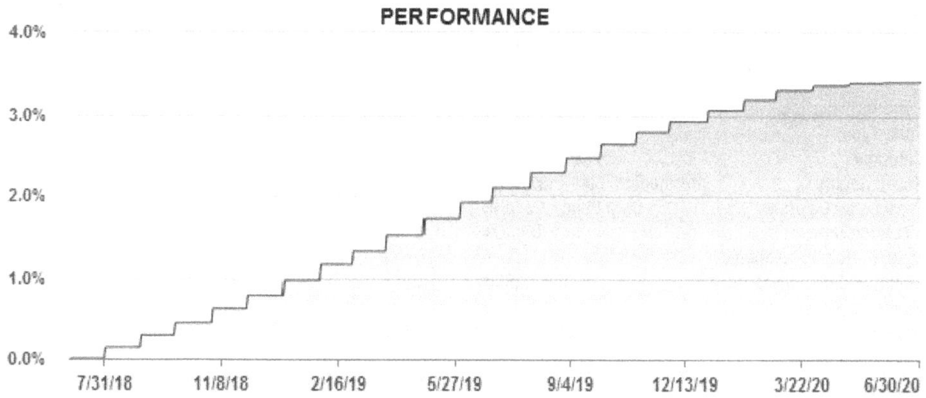

Ratings History

Date	Overall Rating	Risk Rating	Reward Rating
Q2-20	CC+	C-	2019
Q4-19	C	C+	C-
Q4-18	C	C+	C-
Q4-17	C	B	C-
Q4-16	C	C	C-

Asset & Performance History

Date	NAV	1-Year Total Return
1	1.93	Cash
2018	1	1.48
2017	1	0.61
2016	1	0.24
2015		0.01
2014		0.01

Total Assets: $84,261,857,566

Asset Allocation

Asset	%
70%	
Bonds	30%
Govt Bond	29%
Muni Bond	0%
Corp Bond	0%
Other	0%

Services Offered: Qualified Investment, Phone Exchange, Wire Redemption

Investment Strategy: The investment seeks to maximize current income to the extent consistent with the preservation of capital and maintenance of liquidity by investing its net assets, exclusively in U.S. Treasury securities and related repurchase agreements and other securities. The fund seeks to achieve its objective by investing, under normal circumstances, its total assets exclusively in: Cash; Short-term bills, notes and other obligations issued or guaranteed by the U.S. Treasury ("Treasury Obligations"); and Repurchase agreements collateralized fully by cash or Treasury Obligations. **Top Holdings:** National Securities Clearing Corporation 0% Triparty Jp Morgan Securities Llc United States Treasury Notes 0.24% Triparty Bnp Paribas Sa United States Treasury Notes 0.34%

Metropolitan West Total Return Bond Fund Class M

B BUY

Ticker	Traded On	NAV	Total Assets ($)	Dividend Yield (TTM)	Turnover Ratio	Expense Ratio
MWTRX	NAS CM	11.52	$83,642,327,136	2.12	405	0.67

Ratings

Reward	B-
Risk	B+
Recent Upgrade/Downgrade	Up

Fund Information

Fund Type	Open End
Category	US Fixed Inc
Sub-Category	Intermediate Core-Plus Bond
Prospectus Objective	Corp Bond - General
Inception Date	Mar-97
Open to New Investments	Y
Minimum Initial Investment	5,000
Minimum Subsequent Investment	0
Front End Fee	
Back End Fee	

Total Returns (%)

3-Month	6-Month	1-Year	3-Year	5-Year
4.00	6.26	8.92	16.83	22.65

3-Year Standard Deviation	3.43
Effective Duration	5.32
Average Coupon Rate	3.04

Company Information

Provider	Metropolitan West Funds
Manager/Tenure	Stephen M. Kane (23), Laird R. Landmann (23), Tad Rivelle (23), 1 oth
Website	http://www.mwamllc.com
Address	METROPOLITAN WEST ASSET MANAGEMENT 865 S. FIGUEROA STREET, SUITE 2100 LOS ANGELES CA 90017 United States
Phone Number	800-241-4671

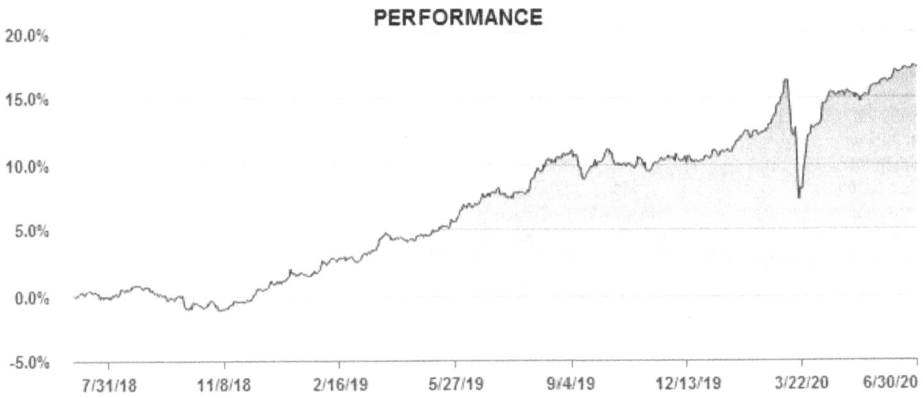

Ratings History

Date	Overall Rating	Risk Rating	Reward Rating
Q2-20	BB+	B-	2019
Q4-19	C	B	C
Q4-18	C-	C+	D+
Q4-17	B-	B+	C
Q4-16	C	C	C

Asset & Performance History

Date	NAV	1-Year Total Return
10.94	8.92	Cash
2018	10.39	-0.06
2017	10.66	3.07
2016	10.54	2.33
2015	10.62	-0.04
2014	10.91	5.83

Total Assets: $83,642,327,136

Asset Allocation

Asset	%
2%	
Bonds	98%
Govt Bond	18%
Muni Bond	1%
Corp Bond	30%
Other	0%

Services Offered: Systematic Withdrawal Plan, Automatic Investment Plan, Phone Exchange, Wire Redemption, Retirement Investment

Investment Strategy: The investment seeks to maximize long-term total return. The fund pursues its objective by investing, under normal circumstances, at least 80% of its net assets in investment grade fixed income securities or unrated securities determined by the Adviser to be of comparable quality. Up to 20% of the fund's net assets may be invested in securities rated below investment grade or unrated securities determined by the Adviser to be of comparable quality. The fund also invests at least 80% of its net assets plus borrowings for investment purposes in fixed income securities it regards as bonds. **Top Holdings:** United States Treasury Notes 0.5% Federal National Mortgage Association 3% Federal National Mortgage Association 2.5% Federal National Mortgage Association 3% Federal National Mortgage Association 2.5%

Metropolitan West Total Return Bond Fund Administrative Class

B BUY

Ticker	Traded On	NAV	Total Assets ($)	Dividend Yield (TTM)	Turnover Ratio	Expense Ratio
MWTNX	NAS CM	11.53	$83,642,327,136	2.01	405	0.78

Ratings

Reward	B-
Risk	B
Recent Upgrade/Downgrade	Up

Fund Information

Fund Type	Open End
Category	US Fixed Inc
Sub-Category	Intermediate Core-Plus Bond
Prospectus Objective	Corp Bond - General
Inception Date	Dec-09
Open to New Investments	Y
Minimum Initial Investment	2,500
Minimum Subsequent Investment	0
Front End Fee	
Back End Fee	

Total Returns (%)

3-Month	6-Month	1-Year	3-Year	5-Year
3.97	6.30	8.79	16.54	21.95

3-Year Standard Deviation	3.48
Effective Duration	5.32
Average Coupon Rate	3.04

Company Information

Provider	Metropolitan West Funds
Manager/Tenure	Stephen M. Kane (23), Laird R. Landmann (23), Tad Rivelle (23), 1 oth
Website	http://www.mwamllc.com
Address	METROPOLITAN WEST ASSET MANAGEMENT 865 S. FIGUEROA STREET, SUITE 2100 LOS ANGELES CA 90017 United States
Phone Number	800-241-4671

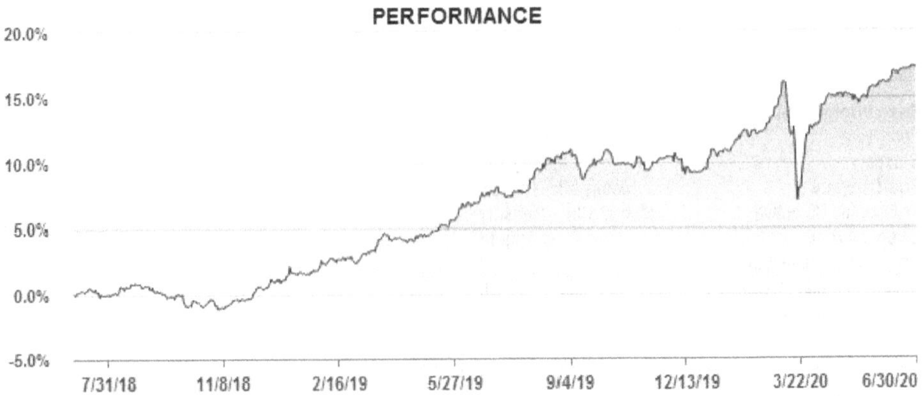

Ratings History

Date	Overall Rating	Risk Rating	Reward Rating
Q2-20	BB	B-	2019
Q4-19	C	B	C
Q4-18	C-	C+	D+
Q4-17	B-	B+	C
Q4-16	C+	B	C

Asset & Performance History

Date	NAV	1-Year Total Return
10.94	8.69	Cash
2018	10.4	-0.16
2017	10.67	3.06
2016	10.54	2.09
2015	10.63	-0.06
2014	10.91	5.67

Total Assets: $83,642,327,136

Asset Allocation

Asset	%
2%	
Bonds	98%
Govt Bond	18%
Muni Bond	1%
Corp Bond	30%
Other	0%

Services Offered: Systematic Withdrawal Plan, Phone Exchange, Wire Redemption, Retirement Investment

Investment Strategy: The investment seeks to maximize long-term total return. The fund pursues its objective by investing, under normal circumstances, at least 80% of its net assets in investment grade fixed income securities or unrated securities determined by the Adviser to be of comparable quality. Up to 20% of the fund's net assets may be invested in securities rated below investment grade or unrated securities determined by the Adviser to be of comparable quality. The fund also invests at least 80% of its net assets plus borrowings for investment purposes in fixed income securities it regards as bonds. **Top Holdings:** United States Treasury Notes 0.5% Federal National Mortgage Association 3% Federal National Mortgage Association 2.5% Federal National Mortgage Association 3% Federal National Mortgage Association 2.5%

Vanguard Intermediate-Term Tax-Exempt Fund Admiral Shares — C+ HOLD

Ticker	Traded On	NAV	Total Assets ($)	Dividend Yield (TTM)	Turnover Ratio	Expense Ratio
VWIUX	NAS CM	14.6	$73,170,471,804	2.57	8	0.09

Ratings

Reward	C
Risk	B
Recent Upgrade/Downgrade	Up

Fund Information

Fund Type	Open End
Category	US Muni Fixed Inc
Sub-Category	Muni Natl Interm
Prospectus Objective	Muni Bond - Natl
Inception Date	Feb-01
Open to New Investments	Y
Minimum Initial Investment	50,000
Minimum Subsequent Investment	1
Front End Fee	
Back End Fee	

Total Returns (%)

3-Month	6-Month	1-Year	3-Year	5-Year
2.65	2.16	4.14	12.11	19.61

3-Year Standard Deviation	3.58
Effective Duration	4.78
Average Coupon Rate	4.70

Company Information

Provider	Vanguard
Manager/Tenure	James M. D'Arcy (6)
Website	http://www.vanguard.com
Address	Vanguard 100 Vanguard Boulevard Malvern PA 19355 United States
Phone Number	877-662-7447

Ratings History

Date	Overall Rating	Risk Rating	Reward Rating
Q2-20	C+B	C	2019
Q4-19	C+	B	C
Q4-18	C	C+	C-
Q4-17	B-	B+	C
Q4-16	C	C	C

Asset & Performance History

Date	NAV	1-Year Total Return
14.47	6.85	Cash
2018	13.91	1.3
2017	14.13	4.61
2016	13.89	0.16
2015	14.26	2.94
2014	14.27	7.33

Total Assets: $73,170,471,804

Asset Allocation

Asset	%
1%	
Bonds	99%
Govt Bond	0%
Muni Bond	99%
Corp Bond	0%
Other	0%

Services Offered: Systematic Withdrawal Plan, Automatic Investment Plan, Phone Exchange, Wire Redemption

Investment Strategy: The investment seeks a moderate and sustainable level of current income that is exempt from federal personal income taxes. The fund has no limitations on the maturity of individual securities but is expected to maintain a dollar-weighted average maturity of 6 to 12 years. At least 75% of the securities held by the fund are municipal bonds in the top three credit-rating categories as determined by a nationally recognized statistical rating organization (NRSRO) or, if unrated, determined to be of comparable quality by the advisor. **Top Holdings:** SOUTHEAST ALA GAS SUPPLY DIST GAS SUPPLY REV 4% METROPOLITAN TRANSN AUTH N Y REV 5% KENTUCKY INC KY PUB ENERGY AUTH GAS SUPLLY REV 4% MAIN STR NAT GAS INC GA GAS SUPPLY REV 4% METROPOLITAN TRANSN AUTH N Y REV 5%

Vanguard Intermediate-Term Tax-Exempt Fund Investor Shares — C+ HOLD

Ticker	Traded On	NAV	Total Assets ($)	Dividend Yield (TTM)	Turnover Ratio	Expense Ratio
VWITX	NAS CM	14.6	$73,170,471,804	2.49	8	0.17

Ratings

Reward	C
Risk	B
Recent Upgrade/Downgrade	Up

Fund Information

Fund Type	Open End
Category	US Muni Fixed Inc
Sub-Category	Muni Natl Interm
Prospectus Objective	Muni Bond - Natl
Inception Date	Sep-77
Open to New Investments	Y
Minimum Initial Investment	3,000
Minimum Subsequent Investment	1
Front End Fee	
Back End Fee	

Total Returns (%)

3-Month	6-Month	1-Year	3-Year	5-Year
2.63	2.11	4.06	11.83	19.09

3-Year Standard Deviation	3.58
Effective Duration	4.78
Average Coupon Rate	4.70

Company Information

Provider	Vanguard
Manager/Tenure	James M. D'Arcy (6)
Website	http://www.vanguard.com
Address	Vanguard 100 Vanguard Boulevard Malvern PA 19355 United States
Phone Number	877-662-7447

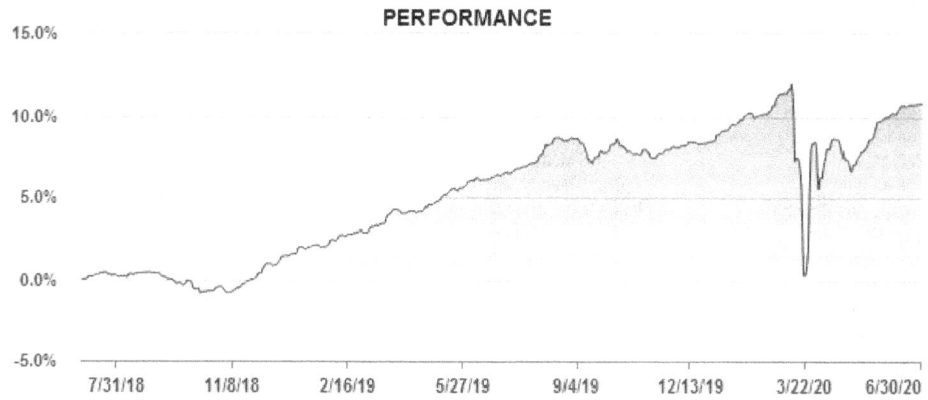

Ratings History

Date	Overall Rating	Risk Rating	Reward Rating
Q2-20	C+B	C	2019
Q4-19	C+	B	C
Q4-18	C	C+	C-
Q4-17	B-	B+	C
Q4-16	C	C	C

Asset & Performance History

Date	NAV	1-Year Total Return
14.47	6.76	Cash
2018	13.91	1.22
2017	14.13	4.51
2016	13.89	0.06
2015	14.26	2.85
2014	14.27	7.24

Total Assets: $73,170,471,804

Asset Allocation

Asset	%
1%	
Bonds	99%
Govt Bond	0%
Muni Bond	99%
Corp Bond	0%
Other	0%

Services Offered: Systematic Withdrawal Plan, Automatic Investment Plan, Phone Exchange, Wire Redemption

Investment Strategy: The investment seeks a moderate and sustainable level of current income that is exempt from federal personal income taxes. The fund has no limitations on the maturity of individual securities but is expected to maintain a dollar-weighted average maturity of 6 to 12 years. At least 75% of the securities held by the fund are municipal bonds in the top three credit-rating categories as determined by a nationally recognized statistical rating organization (NRSRO) or, if unrated, determined to be of comparable quality by the advisor. **Top Holdings:** SOUTHEAST ALA GAS SUPPLY DIST GAS SUPPLY REV 4% METROPOLITAN TRANSN AUTH N Y REV 5% KENTUCKY INC KY PUB ENERGY AUTH GAS SUPLLY REV 4% MAIN STR NAT GAS INC GA GAS SUPPLY REV 4% METROPOLITAN TRANSN AUTH N Y REV 5%

JPMorgan Prime Money Market Fund Class C — C HOLD

Ticker	Traded On	NAV	Total Assets ($)	Dividend Yield (TTM)	Turnover Ratio	Expense Ratio
JXCXX	NAS CM	1.0009	$70,465,213,394	1.03		0.97

Ratings

Reward	C-
Risk	C+
Recent Upgrade/Downgrade	

Fund Information

Fund Type	Money Mkt
Category	US Money Mkt
Sub-Category	Prime Money Mkt
Prospectus Objective	Money Mkt - Taxable
Inception Date	May-98
Open to New Investments	Y
Minimum Initial Investment	1,000
Minimum Subsequent Investment	50
Front End Fee	
Back End Fee	1.00

Total Returns (%)

3-Month	6-Month	1-Year	3-Year	5-Year
0.12	0.33	0.94	3.23	3.38

3-Year Standard Deviation	0.15
Effective Duration	
Average Coupon Rate	

Company Information

Provider	JPMorgan
Manager/Tenure	Management Team (18)
Website	http://www.jpmorganfunds.com
Address	JPMorgan 270 Park Avenue New York NY 10017-2070 United States
Phone Number	800-480-4111

PERFORMANCE

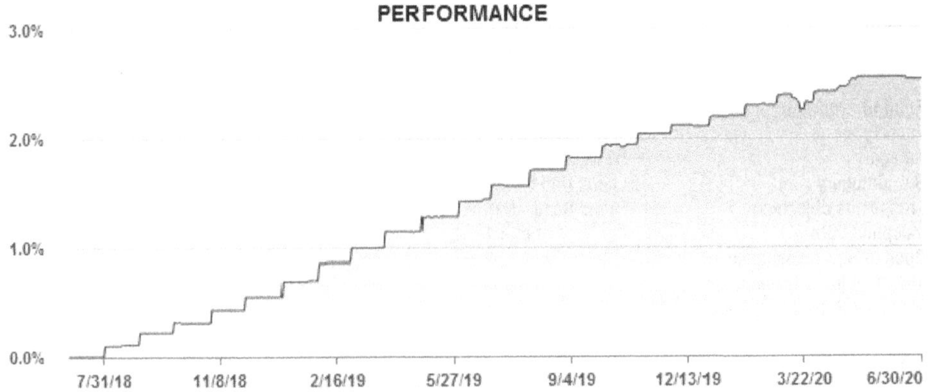

Ratings History

Date	Overall Rating	Risk Rating	Reward Rating
Q2-20	CC+	C-	2019
Q4-19	C	C+	C-
Q4-18	C	C+	C-
Q4-17	C	C+	C-
Q4-16	C-	C	C-

Asset & Performance History

Date	NAV	1-Year Total Return
1	1.41	Cash
2018	1	1.03
2017	1	0.17
2016	1	0.01
2015	1	0
2014	1	0.01

Total Assets: $70,465,213,394

Asset Allocation

Asset	%
91%	
Bonds	8%
Govt Bond	4%
Muni Bond	0%
Corp Bond	3%
Other	0%

Services Offered: Systematic Withdrawal Plan, Automatic Investment Plan, Qualified Investment, Phone Exchange, Wire Redemption

Investment Strategy: The investment seeks current income while seeking to maintain liquidity and a low volatility of principal. The fund invests in high quality, short-term money market instruments which are issued and payable in U.S. dollars. It will invest at least 25% of its total assets in securities issued by companies in the banking industry. The fund may, however, invest less than 25% of its total assets in this industry as a temporary defensive measure. It may invest significantly in securities with floating or variable rates of interest. **Top Holdings:** National Securities Clearing Corporation 0% Kbc Bank Nv Mizuho Bank Ltd. Societe Generale Sa Mizuho Bank Ltd.

JPMorgan Prime Money Market Fund Morgan Class — C HOLD

Ticker	Traded On	NAV	Total Assets ($)	Dividend Yield (TTM)	Turnover Ratio	Expense Ratio
VMVXX	NAS CM	1.0015	$70,465,213,394	1.39		0.52

Ratings

Reward	C-
Risk	C+
Recent Upgrade/Downgrade	

Fund Information

Fund Type	Money Mkt
Category	US Money Mkt
Sub-Category	Prime Money Mkt
Prospectus Objective	Money Mkt - Taxable
Inception Date	Oct-98
Open to New Investments	Y
Minimum Initial Investment	1,000
Minimum Subsequent Investment	50
Front End Fee	
Back End Fee	

Total Returns (%)

3-Month	6-Month	1-Year	3-Year	5-Year
0.17	0.47	1.32	4.59	5.09

3-Year Standard Deviation	0.16
Effective Duration	
Average Coupon Rate	

Company Information

Provider	JPMorgan
Manager/Tenure	Management Team (18)
Website	http://www.jpmorganfunds.com
Address	JPMorgan 270 Park Avenue New York NY 10017-2070 United States
Phone Number	800-480-4111

PERFORMANCE

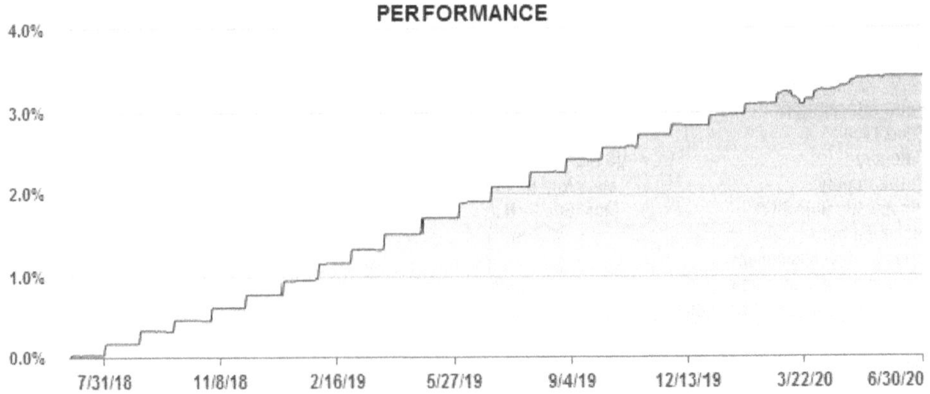

Ratings History

Date	Overall Rating	Risk Rating	Reward Rating
Q2-20	CC+	C-	2019
Q4-19	C	C+	C-
Q4-18	C	C+	C-
Q4-17	C	C	C-
Q4-16	C	C	C-

Asset & Performance History

Date	NAV	1-Year Total Return
1	1.86	Cash
2018	1	1.44
2017	1	0.47
2016	1	0.14
2015	1	0
2014	1	0.01

Total Assets: $70,465,213,394

Asset Allocation

Asset	%
91%	
Bonds	8%
Govt Bond	4%
Muni Bond	0%
Corp Bond	3%
Other	0%

Services Offered: Systematic Withdrawal Plan, Automatic Investment Plan, Qualified Investment, Phone Exchange, Wire Redemption

Investment Strategy: The investment seeks current income while seeking to maintain liquidity and a low volatility of principal. The fund invests in high quality, short-term money market instruments which are issued and payable in U.S. dollars. It will invest at least 25% of its total assets in securities issued by companies in the banking industry. The fund may, however, invest less than 25% of its total assets in this industry as a temporary defensive measure. It may invest significantly in securities with floating or variable rates of interest. **Top Holdings:** National Securities Clearing Corporation 0% Kbc Bank Nv Mizuho Bank Ltd. Societe Generale Sa Mizuho Bank Ltd.

BlackRock Liquidity Funds Treasury Trust Fund Administration Shares — C HOLD

Ticker	Traded On	NAV	Total Assets ($)	Dividend Yield (TTM)	Turnover Ratio	Expense Ratio
BITXX	NAS CM	1	$68,610,561,086	1.34	0	0.27

Ratings

Reward	C-
Risk	C+
Recent Upgrade/Downgrade	

Fund Information

Fund Type	Money Mkt
Category	US Money Mkt
Sub-Category	Money Mkt-Taxable
Prospectus Objective	Money Mkt - Treasury
Inception Date	May-02
Open to New Investments	Y
Minimum Initial Investment	5,000
Minimum Subsequent Investment	
Front End Fee	
Back End Fee	

Total Returns (%)

3-Month	6-Month	1-Year	3-Year	5-Year
0.02	0.32	1.17	4.34	4.65

3-Year Standard Deviation	0.17
Effective Duration	
Average Coupon Rate	

Company Information

Provider	BlackRock
Manager/Tenure	Management Team (14)
Website	http://www.blackrock.com
Address	BlackRock Funds Providence RI 02940-8019 United States
Phone Number	800-441-7762

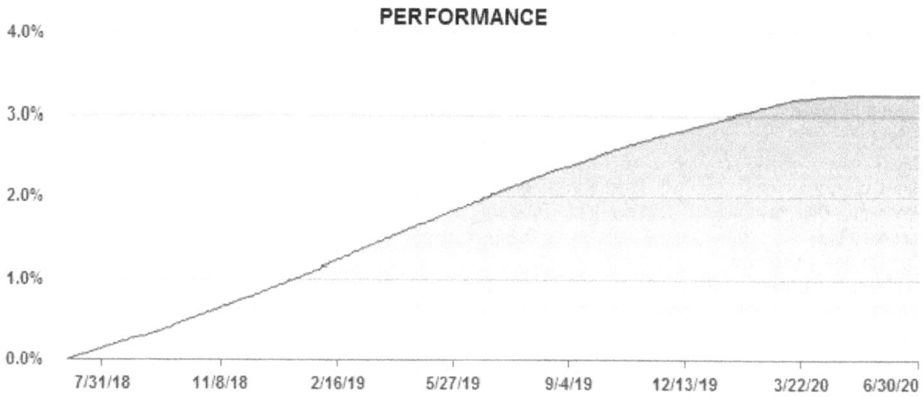

Ratings History

Date	Overall Rating	Risk Rating	Reward Rating
Q2-20	CC+	C-	2019
Q4-19	C	C+	C-
Q4-18	C	C+	C-
Q4-17	C	C	C-
Q4-16	C-	C	C-

Asset & Performance History

Date	NAV	1-Year Total Return
1	1.94	Cash
2018	1	1.6
2017	1	0.62
2016	1	0.07
2015	1	0
2014	1	0

Total Assets: $68,610,561,086

Asset Allocation

Asset	%
72%	
Bonds	28%
Govt Bond	25%
Muni Bond	0%
Corp Bond	0%
Other	0%

Services Offered: Qualified Investment, Wire Redemption

Investment Strategy: The investment seeks current income as is consistent with liquidity and stability of principal. The fund invests 100% of its total assets in cash, U.S. Treasury bills, notes and other obligations issued or guaranteed as to principal and interest by the U.S. Treasury. It invests in securities maturing in 397 days or less (with certain exceptions) and the portfolio will have a dollar-weighted average maturity of 60 days or less and a dollar-weighted average life of 120 days or less. **Top Holdings:** Usd Cash(Committed) Cash United States Treasury Bills United States Treasury Notes 0.24% United States Treasury Notes 0.34%

BlackRock Liquidity Funds Treasury Trust Fund Dollar Shares — C HOLD

Ticker	Traded On	NAV	Total Assets ($)	Dividend Yield (TTM)	Turnover Ratio	Expense Ratio
TTDXX	NAS CM	1	$68,610,561,086	1.22	0	0.42

Ratings

Reward	C-
Risk	C+
Recent Upgrade/Downgrade	

Fund Information

Fund Type	Money Mkt
Category	US Money Mkt
Sub-Category	Money Mkt-Taxable
Prospectus Objective	Money Mkt - Treasury
Inception Date	Jun-89
Open to New Investments	Y
Minimum Initial Investment	5,000
Minimum Subsequent Investment	
Front End Fee	
Back End Fee	

Total Returns (%)

3-Month	6-Month	1-Year	3-Year	5-Year
0.01	0.27	1.05	3.99	4.16

3-Year Standard Deviation	0.18
Effective Duration	
Average Coupon Rate	

Company Information

Provider	BlackRock
Manager/Tenure	Management Team (14)
Website	http://www.blackrock.com
Address	BlackRock Funds Providence RI 02940-8019 United States
Phone Number	800-441-7762

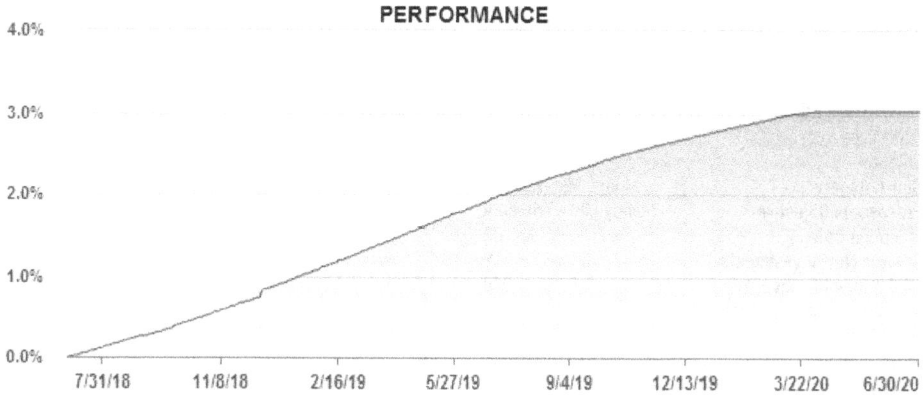

Ratings History

Date	Overall Rating	Risk Rating	Reward Rating
Q2-20	CC+	C-	2019
Q4-19	C	C+	C-
Q4-18	C	C+	C-
Q4-17	C	C+	C-
Q4-16	C-	C	C-

Asset & Performance History

Date	NAV	1-Year Total Return
1	1.81	Cash
2018	1	1.51
2017	1	0.47
2016	1	0.01
2015	1	0
2014	1	0

Total Assets: $68,610,561,086

Asset Allocation

Asset	%
72%	
Bonds	28%
Govt Bond	25%
Muni Bond	0%
Corp Bond	0%
Other	0%

Services Offered: Qualified Investment, Wire Redemption

Investment Strategy: The investment seeks current income as is consistent with liquidity and stability of principal. The fund invests 100% of its total assets in cash, U.S. Treasury bills, notes and other obligations issued or guaranteed as to principal and interest by the U.S. Treasury. It invests in securities maturing in 397 days or less (with certain exceptions) and the portfolio will have a dollar-weighted average maturity of 60 days or less and a dollar-weighted average life of 120 days or less. **Top Holdings:** Usd Cash(Committed) Cash United States Treasury Bills United States Treasury Notes 0.24% United States Treasury Notes 0.34%

BlackRock Liquidity Funds Treasury Trust Fund Select Shares C HOLD

Ticker	Traded On	NAV	Total Assets ($)	Dividend Yield (TTM)	Turnover Ratio	Expense Ratio
TSLXX	NAS CM	1	$68,610,561,086	0.72	0	1

Ratings

Reward	C-
Risk	C
Recent Upgrade/Downgrade	

Fund Information

Fund Type	Money Mkt
Category	US Money Mkt
Sub-Category	Money Mkt-Taxable
Prospectus Objective	Money Mkt - Treasury
Inception Date	Oct-15
Open to New Investments	Y
Minimum Initial Investment	0
Minimum Subsequent Investment	
Front End Fee	
Back End Fee	

Total Returns (%)

3-Month	6-Month	1-Year	3-Year	5-Year
0.00	0.11	0.60	2.24	2.14

3-Year Standard Deviation	0.15
Effective Duration	
Average Coupon Rate	

Company Information

Provider	BlackRock
Manager/Tenure	Management Team (14)
Website	http://www.blackrock.com
Address	BlackRock Funds Providence RI 02940-8019 United States
Phone Number	800-441-7762

PERFORMANCE

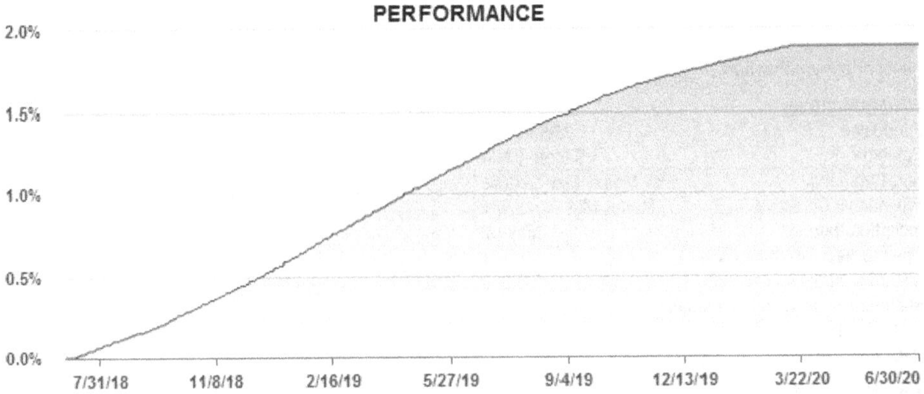

Ratings History

Date	Overall Rating	Risk Rating	Reward Rating
Q2-20	CC	C-	2019
Q4-19	C	C	C-
Q4-18	C	C+	C-
Q4-17	C-	C	C-
Q4-16	C-	C	D+

Asset & Performance History

Date	NAV	1-Year Total Return
1	1.19	Cash
2018	1	0.86
2017	1	0.03
2016	1	0
2015	1	-0.27
2014		-0.34

Total Assets: $68,610,561,086

Asset Allocation

Asset	%
72%	
Bonds	28%
Govt Bond	25%
Muni Bond	0%
Corp Bond	0%
Other	0%

Services Offered: Qualified Investment, Wire Redemption

Investment Strategy: The investment seeks current income as is consistent with liquidity and stability of principal. The fund invests 100% of its total assets in cash, U.S. Treasury bills, notes and other obligations issued or guaranteed as to principal and interest by the U.S. Treasury. It invests in securities maturing in 397 days or less (with certain exceptions) and the portfolio will have a dollar-weighted average maturity of 60 days or less and a dollar-weighted average life of 120 days or less. **Top Holdings:** Usd Cash(Committed) Cash United States Treasury Bills United States Treasury Notes 0.24% United States Treasury Notes 0.34%

BlackRock Liquidity Funds Treasury Trust Fund Cash Reserve Shares C HOLD

Ticker	Traded On	NAV	Total Assets ($)	Dividend Yield (TTM)	Turnover Ratio	Expense Ratio
BTFXX	NAS CM	1	$68,610,561,086	1.07	0	0.57

Ratings

Reward	C
Risk	C+
Recent Upgrade/Downgrade	

Fund Information

Fund Type	Money Mkt
Category	US Money Mkt
Sub-Category	Money Mkt-Taxable
Prospectus Objective	Money Mkt - Treasury
Inception Date	Jan-03
Open to New Investments	Y
Minimum Initial Investment	5,000
Minimum Subsequent Investment	
Front End Fee	
Back End Fee	

Total Returns (%)

3-Month	6-Month	1-Year	3-Year	5-Year
0.00	0.21	0.91	3.45	3.53

3-Year Standard Deviation	0.16
Effective Duration	
Average Coupon Rate	

Company Information

Provider	BlackRock
Manager/Tenure	Management Team (14)
Website	http://www.blackrock.com
Address	BlackRock Funds Providence RI 02940-8019 United States
Phone Number	800-441-7762

PERFORMANCE

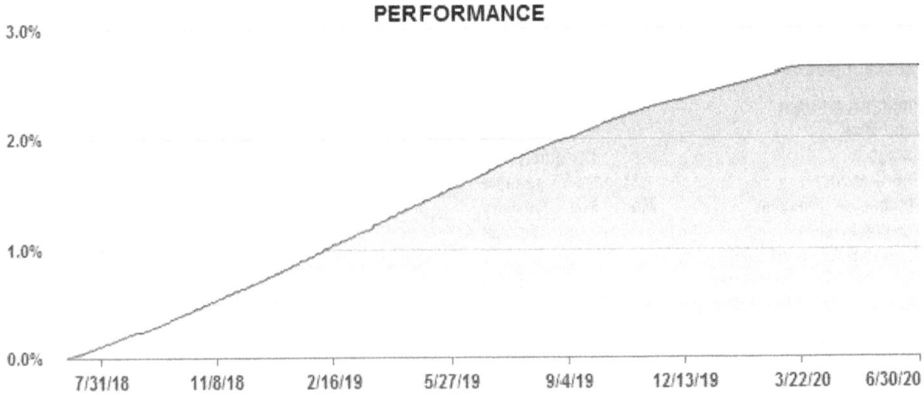

Ratings History

Date	Overall Rating	Risk Rating	Reward Rating
Q2-20	CC+	C	2019
Q4-19	C	C	C-
Q4-18	C	C	C-
Q4-17			
Q4-16			

Asset & Performance History

Date	NAV	1-Year Total Return
1	1.63	Cash
2018	1	1.3
2017	1	
2016	1	
2015	1	
2014	1	

Total Assets: $68,610,561,086

Asset Allocation

Asset	%
72%	
Bonds	28%
Govt Bond	25%
Muni Bond	0%
Corp Bond	0%
Other	0%

Services Offered: Qualified Investment, Wire Redemption

Investment Strategy: The investment seeks current income as is consistent with liquidity and stability of principal. The fund invests 100% of its total assets in cash, U.S. Treasury bills, notes and other obligations issued or guaranteed as to principal and interest by the U.S. Treasury. It invests in securities maturing in 397 days or less (with certain exceptions) and the portfolio will have a dollar-weighted average maturity of 60 days or less and a dollar-weighted average life of 120 days or less. **Top Holdings:** Usd Cash(Committed) Cash United States Treasury Bills United States Treasury Notes 0.24% United States Treasury Notes 0.34%

PIMCO Total Return Fund Class A

B BUY

Ticker	Traded On	NAV	Total Assets ($)	Dividend Yield (TTM)	Turnover Ratio	Expense Ratio
PTTAX	NAS CM	10.83	$67,969,618,126	3.08	554	1.05

Ratings

Reward	C+
Risk	B+
Recent Upgrade/Downgrade	Up

Fund Information

Fund Type	Open End
Category	US Fixed Inc
Sub-Category	Intermediate Core-Plus Bond
Prospectus Objective	Growth & Income
Inception Date	Jan-97
Open to New Investments	Y
Minimum Initial Investment	1,000
Minimum Subsequent Investment	50
Front End Fee	3.75
Back End Fee	

Total Returns (%)

3-Month	6-Month	1-Year	3-Year	5-Year
3.78	5.97	8.16	15.27	22.11

3-Year Standard Deviation	3.38
Effective Duration	6.57
Average Coupon Rate	3.67

Company Information

Provider	PIMCO
Manager/Tenure	Mark R. Kiesel (5), Scott A. Mather (5), Mohit Mittal (0)
Website	http://www.pimco.com
Address	PIMCO 840 Newport Center Drive, Suite 100 Newport Beach CA 92660 United States
Phone Number	866-746-2602

Ratings History

Date	Overall Rating	Risk Rating	Reward Rating
Q2-20	BB+	C+	2019
Q4-19	C	B-	C
Q4-18	C	C+	D+
Q4-17	B-	B+	C
Q4-16	C	C	C

Asset & Performance History

Date	NAV	1-Year Total Return
10.34	7.87	Cash
2018	9.93	-0.59
2017	10.27	4.71
2016	10.03	2.17
2015	10.07	0.33
2014	10.66	4.28

Total Assets: $67,969,618,126

Asset Allocation

Asset	%
-54%	
Bonds	144%
Govt Bond	34%
Muni Bond	0%
Corp Bond	16%
Other	7%

Services Offered: Systematic Withdrawal Plan, Automatic Investment Plan, Phone Exchange, Wire Redemption, Retirement Investment

Investment Strategy: The investment seeks maximum total return, consistent with preservation of capital and prudent investment management. The fund invests at least 65% of its total assets in a diversified portfolio of Fixed Income Instruments of varying maturities, which may be represented by forwards or derivatives such as options, futures contracts, or swap agreements. It invests primarily in investment-grade debt securities, but may invest up to 20% of its total assets in high yield securities. It may invest up to 30% of its total assets in securities denominated in foreign currencies, and may invest beyond this limit in U.S. dollar-denominated securities of foreign issuers. **Top Holdings:** 5 Year Treasury Note Future Mar 20 Fin Fut Eur-Bund 10yr Eux 03/06/20 Federal National Mortgage Association 3% Pimco Fds Fin Fut Eux Euro-Btp 03/06/20

PIMCO Total Return Fund Class C

B- BUY

Ticker	Traded On	NAV	Total Assets ($)	Dividend Yield (TTM)	Turnover Ratio	Expense Ratio
PTTCX	NAS CM	10.83	$67,969,618,126	2.35	554	1.8

Ratings

Reward	C+
Risk	B
Recent Upgrade/Downgrade	Up

Fund Information

Fund Type	Open End
Category	US Fixed Inc
Sub-Category	Intermediate Core-Plus Bond
Prospectus Objective	Growth & Income
Inception Date	Jan-97
Open to New Investments	Y
Minimum Initial Investment	1,000
Minimum Subsequent Investment	50
Front End Fee	
Back End Fee	1.00

Total Returns (%)

3-Month	6-Month	1-Year	3-Year	5-Year
3.59	5.58	7.36	12.66	17.57

3-Year Standard Deviation	3.38
Effective Duration	6.57
Average Coupon Rate	3.67

Company Information

Provider	PIMCO
Manager/Tenure	Mark R. Kiesel (5), Scott A. Mather (5), Mohit Mittal (0)
Website	http://www.pimco.com
Address	PIMCO 840 Newport Center Drive, Suite 100 Newport Beach CA 92660 United States
Phone Number	866-746-2602

Ratings History

Date	Overall Rating	Risk Rating	Reward Rating
Q2-20	B-B	C+	2019
Q4-19	C	B-	C
Q4-18	C-	C	D+
Q4-17	C+	B+	C
Q4-16	C	C	C-

Asset & Performance History

Date	NAV	1-Year Total Return
10.34	7.07	Cash
2018	9.93	-1.37
2017	10.27	3.93
2016	10.03	1.42
2015	10.07	-0.4
2014	10.66	3.51

Total Assets: $67,969,618,126

Asset Allocation

Asset	%
-54%	
Bonds	144%
Govt Bond	34%
Muni Bond	0%
Corp Bond	16%
Other	7%

Services Offered: Systematic Withdrawal Plan, Automatic Investment Plan, Phone Exchange, Wire Redemption, Retirement Investment

Investment Strategy: The investment seeks maximum total return, consistent with preservation of capital and prudent investment management. The fund invests at least 65% of its total assets in a diversified portfolio of Fixed Income Instruments of varying maturities, which may be represented by forwards or derivatives such as options, futures contracts, or swap agreements. It invests primarily in investment-grade debt securities, but may invest up to 20% of its total assets in high yield securities. It may invest up to 30% of its total assets in securities denominated in foreign currencies, and may invest beyond this limit in U.S. dollar-denominated securities of foreign issuers. **Top Holdings:** 5 Year Treasury Note Future Mar 20 Fin Fut Eur-Bund 10yr Eux 03/06/20 Federal National Mortgage Association 3% Pimco Fds Fin Fut Eux Euro-Btp 03/06/20

PIMCO Total Return Fund Class R — B BUY

Ticker	Traded On	NAV	Total Assets ($)	Dividend Yield (TTM)	Turnover Ratio	Expense Ratio
PTRRX	NAS CM	10.83	$67,969,618,126	2.84	554	1.3

Ratings

Reward	C+
Risk	B+
Recent Upgrade/Downgrade	Up

Fund Information

Fund Type	Open End
Category	US Fixed Inc
Sub-Category	Intermediate Core-Plus Bond
Prospectus Objective	Growth & Income
Inception Date	Dec-02
Open to New Investments	Y
Minimum Initial Investment	0
Minimum Subsequent Investment	
Front End Fee	
Back End Fee	

Total Returns (%)

3-Month	6-Month	1-Year	3-Year	5-Year
3.72	5.84	7.90	14.36	20.53

3-Year Standard Deviation	3.38
Effective Duration	6.57
Average Coupon Rate	3.67

Company Information

Provider	PIMCO
Manager/Tenure	Mark R. Kiesel (5), Scott A. Mather (5), Mohit Mittal (0)
Website	http://www.pimco.com
Address	PIMCO 840 Newport Center Drive, Suite 100 Newport Beach CA 92660 United States
Phone Number	866-746-2602

PERFORMANCE

Ratings History

Date	Overall Rating	Risk Rating	Reward Rating
Q2-20	BB+	C+	2019
Q4-19	C	B-	C
Q4-18	C-	C+	D+
Q4-17	B-	B+	C
Q4-16	C+	B	C

Asset & Performance History

Date	NAV	1-Year Total Return
10.34	7.6	Cash
2018	9.93	-0.88
2017	10.27	4.44
2016	10.03	1.92
2015	10.07	0.08
2014	10.66	4.02

Total Assets: $67,969,618,126

Asset Allocation

Asset	%
-54%	
Bonds	144%
Govt Bond	34%
Muni Bond	0%
Corp Bond	16%
Other	7%

Services Offered: Systematic Withdrawal Plan, Automatic Investment Plan, Qualified Investment, Phone Exchange, Wire Redemption

Investment Strategy: The investment seeks maximum total return, consistent with preservation of capital and prudent investment management. The fund invests at least 65% of its total assets in a diversified portfolio of Fixed Income Instruments of varying maturities, which may be represented by forwards or derivatives such as options, futures contracts, or swap agreements. It invests primarily in investment-grade debt securities, but may invest up to 20% of its total assets in high yield securities. It may invest up to 30% of its total assets in securities denominated in foreign currencies, and may invest beyond this limit in U.S. dollar-denominated securities of foreign issuers. **Top Holdings:** 5 Year Treasury Note Future Mar 20 Fin Fut Eur-Bund 10yr Eux 03/06/20 Federal National Mortgage Association 3% Pimco Fds Fin Fut Eux Euro-Btp 03/06/20

First American Government Obligations Fund Class P — C HOLD

Ticker	Traded On	NAV	Total Assets ($)	Dividend Yield (TTM)	Turnover Ratio	Expense Ratio
FPPXX	NAS CM	1	$66,790,279,851	1.48		0.18

Ratings

Reward	C-
Risk	C+
Recent Upgrade/Downgrade	

Fund Information

Fund Type	Money Mkt
Category	US Money Mkt
Sub-Category	Money Mkt-Taxable
Prospectus Objective	Money Mkt - Govt
Inception Date	Dec-17
Open to New Investments	Y
Minimum Initial Investment	0
Minimum Subsequent Investment	
Front End Fee	
Back End Fee	

Total Returns (%)

3-Month	6-Month	1-Year	3-Year	5-Year
0.03	0.35	1.30	4.58	4.76

3-Year Standard Deviation	
Effective Duration	
Average Coupon Rate	

Company Information

Provider	First American
Manager/Tenure	Management Team (17)
Website	http://www.firstamericanfunds.com
Address	First American 800 Nicollet Mall Minneapolis MN 55402 United States
Phone Number	800-677-3863

PERFORMANCE

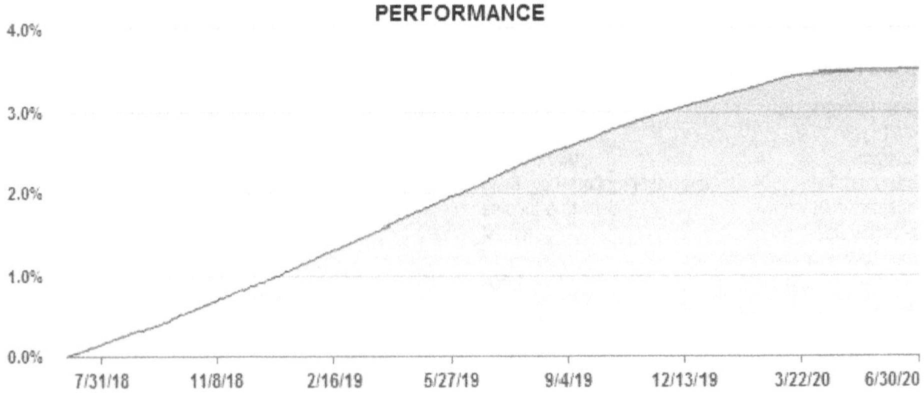

Ratings History

Date	Overall Rating	Risk Rating	Reward Rating
Q2-20	CC+	C-	2019
Q4-19	C	C+	C
Q4-18	C	C+	C-
Q4-17	U		
Q4-16			

Asset & Performance History

Date	NAV	1-Year Total Return
1	2.1	Cash
2018	1	1.7
2017	1	0.47
2016		
2015		
2014		

Total Assets: $66,790,279,851

Asset Allocation

Asset	%
70%	
Bonds	30%
Govt Bond	30%
Muni Bond	0%
Corp Bond	0%
Other	0%

Services Offered: Qualified Investment, Phone Exchange, Wire Redemption

Investment Strategy: The investment seeks maximum current income to the extent consistent with the preservation of capital and maintenance of liquidity. The fund invests exclusively in short-term U.S. government securities, including repurchase agreements secured by U.S. government securities. U.S. government securities are bonds or other debt obligations issued or guaranteed as to principal and interest by the U.S. government or one of its agencies or instrumentalities. U.S. Treasury securities and some obligations of U.S. government agencies and instrumentalities are supported by the full faith and credit of the U.S. government. **Top Holdings:** Federal Reserve Bank Of New York Repo 0.0% 4/1/2020 State Street Ficc Repo 0.01% 4/1/2020 Bank Of New York Ficc Repo 0.01% 4/1/2020 Bnp Paribas Sa Ficc Repodvp 0.01% 4/1/2020 Multi Societe Generale Sa Repo 0.1% 4/7/2020

First American Government Obligations Fund Class U — C HOLD

Ticker	Traded On	NAV	Total Assets ($)	Dividend Yield (TTM)	Turnover Ratio	Expense Ratio
FGUXX	NAS CM	1	$66,790,279,851	1.51		0.12

Ratings

Reward	C-
Risk	C+
Recent Upgrade/Downgrade	

Fund Information

Fund Type	Money Mkt
Category	US Money Mkt
Sub-Category	Money Mkt-Taxable
Prospectus Objective	Money Mkt - Govt
Inception Date	Feb-18
Open to New Investments	Y
Minimum Initial Investment	0
Minimum Subsequent Investment	
Front End Fee	
Back End Fee	

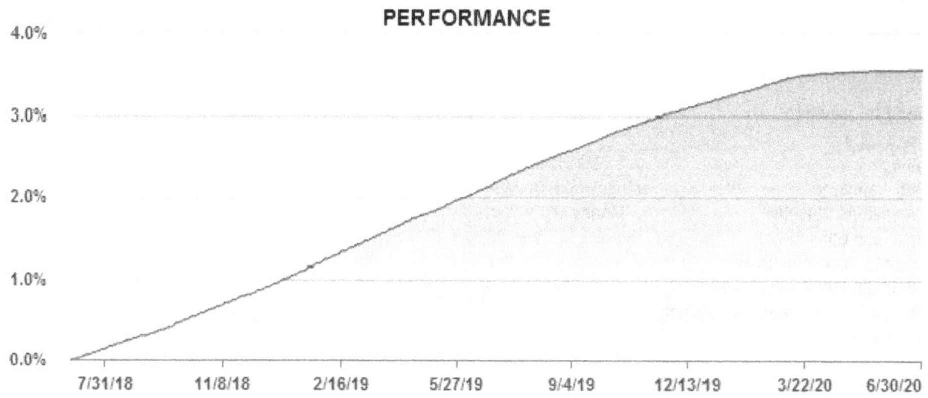

Total Returns (%)

3-Month	6-Month	1-Year	3-Year	5-Year
0.04	0.37	1.33	4.62	4.79

3-Year Standard Deviation	
Effective Duration	
Average Coupon Rate	

Ratings History

Date	Overall Rating	Risk Rating	Reward Rating
Q2-20	CC+	C-	2019
Q4-19	C	C+	C
Q4-18	C	C+	C-
Q4-17			
Q4-16			

Asset & Performance History

Date	NAV	1-Year Total Return
1	2.12	Cash
2018	1	1.51
2017		
2016		
2015		
2014		

Total Assets: $66,790,279,851

Asset Allocation

Asset	%
70%	
Bonds	30%
Govt Bond	30%
Muni Bond	0%
Corp Bond	0%
Other	0%

Company Information

Provider	First American
Manager/Tenure	Management Team (17)
Website	http://www.firstamericanfunds.com
Address	First American 800 Nicollet Mall Minneapolis MN 55402 United States
Phone Number	800-677-3863

Services Offered: Qualified Investment, Wire Redemption

Investment Strategy: The investment seeks maximum current income to the extent consistent with the preservation of capital and maintenance of liquidity. The fund invests exclusively in short-term U.S. government securities, including repurchase agreements secured by U.S. government securities. U.S. government securities are bonds or other debt obligations issued or guaranteed as to principal and interest by the U.S. government or one of its agencies or instrumentalities. U.S. Treasury securities and some obligations of U.S. government agencies and instrumentalities are supported by the full faith and credit of the U.S. government. **Top Holdings:** Federal Reserve Bank Of New York Repo 0.0% 4/1/2020 State Street Ficc Repo 0.01% 4/1/2020 Bank Of New York Ficc Repo 0.01% 4/1/2020 Bnp Paribas Sa Ficc Repodvp 0.01% 4/1/2020 Multi Societe Generale Sa Repo 0.1% 4/7/2020

First American Government Obligations Fund Class A — C HOLD

Ticker	Traded On	NAV	Total Assets ($)	Dividend Yield (TTM)	Turnover Ratio	Expense Ratio
FAAXX	NAS CM	1	$66,790,279,851	0.95		0.75

Ratings

Reward	C-
Risk	C+
Recent Upgrade/Downgrade	

Fund Information

Fund Type	Money Mkt
Category	US Money Mkt
Sub-Category	Money Mkt-Taxable
Prospectus Objective	Money Mkt - Govt
Inception Date	Sep-01
Open to New Investments	Y
Minimum Initial Investment	1,000
Minimum Subsequent Investment	
Front End Fee	
Back End Fee	

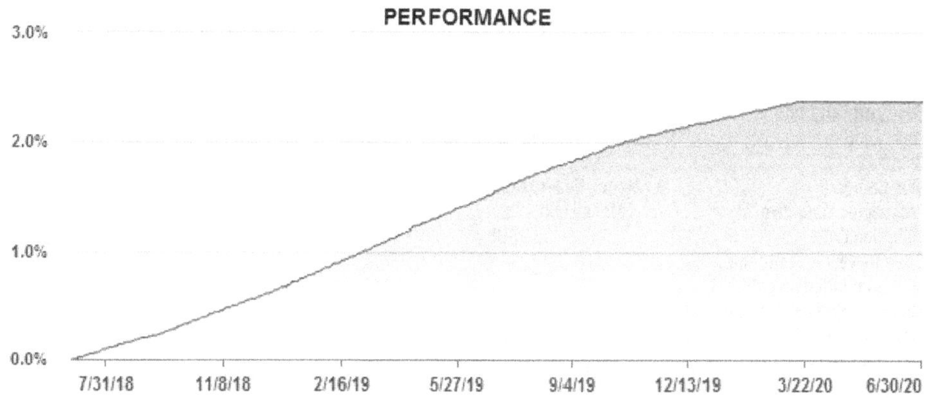

Total Returns (%)

3-Month	6-Month	1-Year	3-Year	5-Year
0.00	0.17	0.81	3.00	3.04

3-Year Standard Deviation	0.16
Effective Duration	
Average Coupon Rate	

Ratings History

Date	Overall Rating	Risk Rating	Reward Rating
Q2-20	CC+	C-	2019
Q4-19	C	C	C-
Q4-18	C	C	C-
Q4-17	C	C	C-
Q4-16	C-	C	C-

Asset & Performance History

Date	NAV	1-Year Total Return
1	1.49	Cash
2018	1	1.1
2017	1	0.19
2016	1	0
2015	1	0
2014	1	0

Total Assets: $66,790,279,851

Asset Allocation

Asset	%
70%	
Bonds	30%
Govt Bond	30%
Muni Bond	0%
Corp Bond	0%
Other	0%

Company Information

Provider	First American
Manager/Tenure	Management Team (17)
Website	http://www.firstamericanfunds.com
Address	First American 800 Nicollet Mall Minneapolis MN 55402 United States
Phone Number	800-677-3863

Services Offered: Systematic Withdrawal Plan, Automatic Investment Plan, Qualified Investment, Phone Exchange, Wire Redemption

Investment Strategy: The investment seeks maximum current income to the extent consistent with the preservation of capital and maintenance of liquidity. The fund invests exclusively in short-term U.S. government securities, including repurchase agreements secured by U.S. government securities. U.S. government securities are bonds or other debt obligations issued or guaranteed as to principal and interest by the U.S. government or one of its agencies or instrumentalities. U.S. Treasury securities and some obligations of U.S. government agencies and instrumentalities are supported by the full faith and credit of the U.S. government. **Top Holdings:** Federal Reserve Bank Of New York Repo 0.0% 4/1/2020 State Street Ficc Repo 0.01% 4/1/2020 Bank Of New York Ficc Repo 0.01% 4/1/2020 Bnp Paribas Sa Ficc Repodvp 0.01% 4/1/2020 Multi Societe Generale Sa Repo 0.1% 4/7/2020

First American Government Obligations Fund Class Y — C HOLD

Ticker	Traded On	NAV	Total Assets ($)	Dividend Yield (TTM)	Turnover Ratio	Expense Ratio
FGVXX	NAS CM	1	$66,790,279,851	1.2		0.45

Ratings

Reward	C-
Risk	C+
Recent Upgrade/Downgrade	

Fund Information

Fund Type	Money Mkt
Category	US Money Mkt
Sub-Category	Money Mkt-Taxable
Prospectus Objective	Money Mkt - Govt
Inception Date	Mar-90
Open to New Investments	Y
Minimum Initial Investment	0
Minimum Subsequent Investment	
Front End Fee	
Back End Fee	

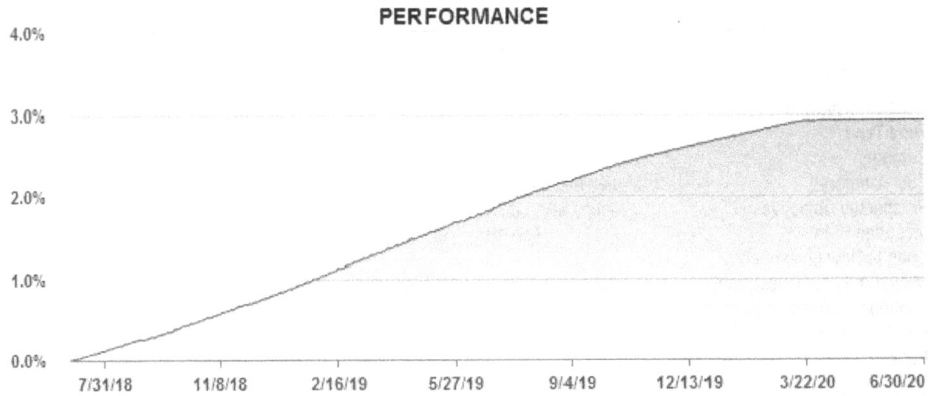

Total Returns (%)

3-Month	6-Month	1-Year	3-Year	5-Year
0.00	0.24	1.03	3.85	4.02

3-Year Standard Deviation	0.17
Effective Duration	
Average Coupon Rate	

Company Information

Provider	First American
Manager/Tenure	Management Team (17)
Website	http://www.firstamericanfunds.com
Address	First American 800 Nicollet Mall Minneapolis MN 55402 United States
Phone Number	800-677-3863

Ratings History

Date	Overall Rating	Risk Rating	Reward Rating
Q2-20	CC+	C-	2019
Q4-19	C	C+	C-
Q4-18	C	C+	C-
Q4-17	C	C+	C-
Q4-16	C-	C	C-

Asset & Performance History

Date	NAV	1-Year Total Return
1	1.8	Cash
2018	1	1.41
2017	1	0.47
2016	1	0
2015	1	0
2014	1	0

Total Assets: $66,790,279,851

Asset Allocation

Asset	%
70%	
Bonds	30%
Govt Bond	30%
Muni Bond	0%
Corp Bond	0%
Other	0%

Services Offered: Qualified Investment, Phone Exchange, Wire Redemption

Investment Strategy: The investment seeks maximum current income to the extent consistent with the preservation of capital and maintenance of liquidity. The fund invests exclusively in short-term U.S. government securities, including repurchase agreements secured by U.S. government securities. U.S. government securities are bonds or other debt obligations issued or guaranteed as to principal and interest by the U.S. government or one of its agencies or instrumentalities. U.S. Treasury securities and some obligations of U.S. government agencies and instrumentalities are supported by the full faith and credit of the U.S. government. **Top Holdings:** Federal Reserve Bank Of New York Repo 0.0% 4/1/2020 State Street Ficc Repo 0.01% 4/1/2020 Bank Of New York Ficc Repo 0.01% 4/1/2020 Bnp Paribas Sa Ficc Repodvp 0.01% 4/1/2020 Multi Societe Generale Sa Repo 0.1% 4/7/2020

First American Government Obligations Fund Class D — C HOLD

Ticker	Traded On	NAV	Total Assets ($)	Dividend Yield (TTM)	Turnover Ratio	Expense Ratio
FGDXX	NAS CM	1	$66,790,279,851	1.08		0.6

Ratings

Reward	C-
Risk	C
Recent Upgrade/Downgrade	

Fund Information

Fund Type	Money Mkt
Category	US Money Mkt
Sub-Category	Money Mkt-Taxable
Prospectus Objective	Money Mkt - Govt
Inception Date	Jan-95
Open to New Investments	Y
Minimum Initial Investment	0
Minimum Subsequent Investment	
Front End Fee	
Back End Fee	

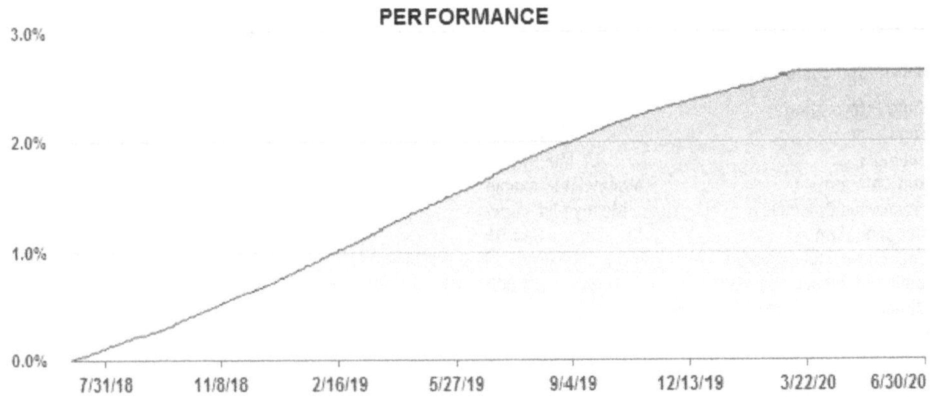

Total Returns (%)

3-Month	6-Month	1-Year	3-Year	5-Year
0.00	0.21	0.92	3.42	3.51

3-Year Standard Deviation	0.17
Effective Duration	
Average Coupon Rate	

Company Information

Provider	First American
Manager/Tenure	Management Team (17)
Website	http://www.firstamericanfunds.com
Address	First American 800 Nicollet Mall Minneapolis MN 55402 United States
Phone Number	800-677-3863

Ratings History

Date	Overall Rating	Risk Rating	Reward Rating
Q2-20	CC	C-	2019
Q4-19	C	C+	C-
Q4-18	C	C+	C-
Q4-17	C	C	C-
Q4-16	C-	C	C-

Asset & Performance History

Date	NAV	1-Year Total Return
1	1.64	Cash
2018	1	1.25
2017	1	0.32
2016	1	0
2015	1	0
2014	1	0

Total Assets: $66,790,279,851

Asset Allocation

Asset	%
70%	
Bonds	30%
Govt Bond	30%
Muni Bond	0%
Corp Bond	0%
Other	0%

Services Offered: Qualified Investment, Phone Exchange, Wire Redemption

Investment Strategy: The investment seeks maximum current income to the extent consistent with the preservation of capital and maintenance of liquidity. The fund invests exclusively in short-term U.S. government securities, including repurchase agreements secured by U.S. government securities. U.S. government securities are bonds or other debt obligations issued or guaranteed as to principal and interest by the U.S. government or one of its agencies or instrumentalities. U.S. Treasury securities and some obligations of U.S. government agencies and instrumentalities are supported by the full faith and credit of the U.S. government. **Top Holdings:** Federal Reserve Bank Of New York Repo 0.0% 4/1/2020 State Street Ficc Repo 0.01% 4/1/2020 Bank Of New York Ficc Repo 0.01% 4/1/2020 Bnp Paribas Sa Ficc Repodvp 0.01% 4/1/2020 Multi Societe Generale Sa Repo 0.1% 4/7/2020

Dodge & Cox Income Fund

B BUY

Ticker	Traded On	NAV	Total Assets ($)	Dividend Yield (TTM)	Turnover Ratio	Expense Ratio
DODIX	NAS CM	14.53	$63,192,001,981	2.87	49	0.42

Ratings

Reward	C+
Risk	B+
Recent Upgrade/Downgrade	Up

Fund Information

Fund Type	Open End
Category	US Fixed Inc
Sub-Category	Intermediate Core-Plus Bond
Prospectus Objective	Income
Inception Date	Jan-89
Open to New Investments	Y
Minimum Initial Investment	2,500
Minimum Subsequent Investment	100
Front End Fee	
Back End Fee	

Total Returns (%)

3-Month	6-Month	1-Year	3-Year	5-Year
6.01	5.27	8.38	17.02	26.26

3-Year Standard Deviation	3.41
Effective Duration	4.20
Average Coupon Rate	4.21

Company Information

Provider	Dodge & Cox
Manager/Tenure	Dana M. Emery (31), Thomas S. Dugan (26), Larissa K. Roesch (22), 6 others
Website	http://www.dodgeandcox.com
Address	Dodge and Cox 555 California Street, 40th Floor San Francisco CA 94104 United States
Phone Number	415-981-1710

PERFORMANCE

Ratings History

Date	Overall Rating	Risk Rating	Reward Rating
Q2-20	BB+	C+	2019
Q4-19	C+	B	C
Q4-18	C	B	C-
Q4-17	B-	A-	C
Q4-16	C+	B	C

Asset & Performance History

Date	NAV	1-Year Total Return
14.03	9.75	Cash
2018	13.26	-0.32
2017	13.76	4.36
2016	13.59	5.61
2015	13.29	-0.58
2014	13.78	5.48

Total Assets: $63,192,001,981

Asset Allocation

Asset	%
2%	
Bonds	96%
Govt Bond	9%
Muni Bond	3%
Corp Bond	39%
Other	0%

Services Offered: Systematic Withdrawal Plan, Automatic Investment Plan, Phone Exchange, Wire Redemption, Retirement Investment

Investment Strategy: The investment seeks a high and stable rate of current income, consistent with long-term preservation of capital. The fund invests in a diversified portfolio of bonds and other debt securities. Under normal circumstances, the fund will invest at least 80% of its total assets in (1) investment-grade debt securities and (2) cash equivalents. "Investment grade" means securities rated Baa3 or higher by Moody's Investors Service, or BBB- or higher by Standard & Poor's Ratings Group or Fitch Ratings, or equivalently rated by any nationally recognized statistical rating organization, or, if unrated, deemed to be of similar quality by Dodge & Cox. **Top Holdings:** Federal National Mortgage Association 3.5% United States Treasury Notes 2.5% Federal National Mortgage Association 3.5% United States Treasury Notes 0.12% Fnma Pass-Thru I 4.5%

Vanguard Short-Term Investment-Grade Fund Admiral Shares

C HOLD

Ticker	Traded On	NAV	Total Assets ($)	Dividend Yield (TTM)	Turnover Ratio	Expense Ratio
VFSUX	NAS CM	10.94	$60,816,651,019	2.74	76	0.1

Ratings

Reward	C
Risk	B-
Recent Upgrade/Downgrade	

Fund Information

Fund Type	Open End
Category	US Fixed Inc
Sub-Category	Short-Term Bond
Prospectus Objective	Income
Inception Date	Feb-01
Open to New Investments	Y
Minimum Initial Investment	50,000
Minimum Subsequent Investment	1
Front End Fee	
Back End Fee	

Total Returns (%)

3-Month	6-Month	1-Year	3-Year	5-Year
4.83	3.26	5.03	10.94	16.16

3-Year Standard Deviation	2.73
Effective Duration	2.45
Average Coupon Rate	3.18

Company Information

Provider	Vanguard
Manager/Tenure	Samuel C. Martinez (2), Daniel Shaykevich (2), Arvind Narayanan (0)
Website	http://www.vanguard.com
Address	Vanguard 100 Vanguard Boulevard Malvern PA 19355 United States
Phone Number	877-662-7447

PERFORMANCE

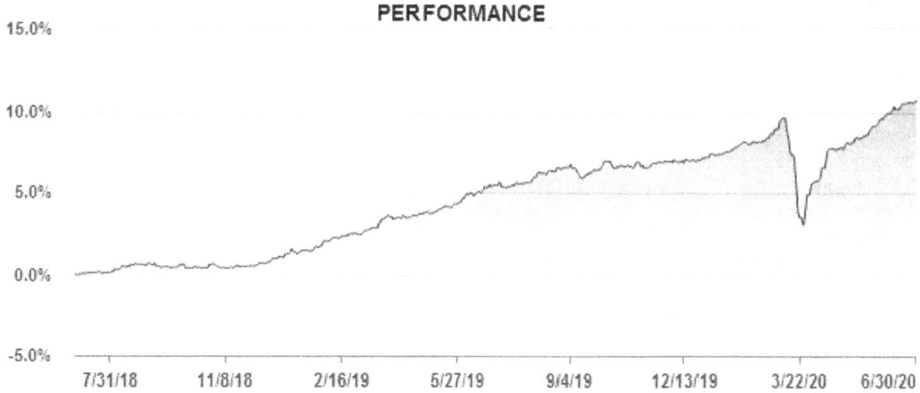

Ratings History

Date	Overall Rating	Risk Rating	Reward Rating
Q2-20	CB-	C	2019
Q4-19	C	B	C
Q4-18	C	B-	C
Q4-17	B	A+	C
Q4-16	C	B-	C

Asset & Performance History

Date	NAV	1-Year Total Return
10.73	5.82	Cash
2018	10.44	0.93
2017	10.63	2.1
2016	10.63	2.81
2015	10.56	1.12
2014	10.66	1.86

Total Assets: $60,816,651,019

Asset Allocation

Asset	%
3%	
Bonds	94%
Govt Bond	9%
Muni Bond	0%
Corp Bond	65%
Other	0%

Services Offered: Systematic Withdrawal Plan, Automatic Investment Plan, Phone Exchange, Wire Redemption

Investment Strategy: The investment seeks to provide current income while maintaining limited price volatility. The fund invests in a variety of high-quality and, to a lesser extent, medium-quality fixed income securities, at least 80% of which will be short- and intermediate-term investment-grade securities. High-quality fixed income securities are those rated the equivalent of A3 or better; medium-quality fixed income securities are those rated the equivalent of Baa1, Baa2, or Baa3. **Top Holdings:** United States Treasury Notes 1.12% United States Treasury Notes 0.5% United States Treasury Notes 1.38% CVS Health Corp 3.7% United States Treasury Notes 1.88%

Vanguard Short-Term Investment-Grade Fund Investor Shares C+ HOLD

Ticker	Traded On	NAV	Total Assets ($)	Dividend Yield (TTM)	Turnover Ratio	Expense Ratio
VFSTX	NAS CM	10.94	$60,816,651,019	2.64	76	0.2

Ratings

Reward	C
Risk	B
Recent Upgrade/Downgrade	Up

Fund Information

Fund Type	Open End
Category	US Fixed Inc
Sub-Category	Short-Term Bond
Prospectus Objective	Income
Inception Date	Oct-82
Open to New Investments	Y
Minimum Initial Investment	3,000
Minimum Subsequent Investment	1
Front End Fee	
Back End Fee	

Total Returns (%)

3-Month	6-Month	1-Year	3-Year	5-Year
4.81	3.20	4.93	10.61	15.58

3-Year Standard Deviation	2.72
Effective Duration	2.45
Average Coupon Rate	3.18

Company Information

Provider	Vanguard
Manager/Tenure	Samuel C. Martinez (2), Daniel Shaykevich (2), Arvind Narayanan (0)
Website	http://www.vanguard.com
Address	Vanguard 100 Vanguard Boulevard Malvern PA 19355 United States
Phone Number	877-662-7447

PERFORMANCE

Ratings History

Date	Overall Rating	Risk Rating	Reward Rating
Q2-20	C+B	C	2019
Q4-19	C	B-	C
Q4-18	C	B-	C-
Q4-17	B	A+	C
Q4-16	C	B-	C

Asset & Performance History

Date	NAV	1-Year Total Return
10.73	5.71	Cash
2018	10.44	0.84
2017	10.63	2
2016	10.63	2.7
2015	10.56	1.02
2014	10.66	1.76

Total Assets: $60,816,651,019

Asset Allocation

Asset	%
3%	
Bonds	94%
Govt Bond	9%
Muni Bond	0%
Corp Bond	65%
Other	0%

Services Offered: Systematic Withdrawal Plan, Automatic Investment Plan, Phone Exchange, Wire Redemption

Investment Strategy: The investment seeks to provide current income while maintaining limited price volatility. The fund invests in a variety of high-quality and, to a lesser extent, medium-quality fixed income securities, at least 80% of which will be short- and intermediate-term investment-grade securities. High-quality fixed income securities are those rated the equivalent of A3 or better; medium-quality fixed income securities are those rated the equivalent of Baa1, Baa2, or Baa3. **Top Holdings:** United States Treasury Notes 1.12% United States Treasury Notes 0.5% United States Treasury Notes 1.38% CVS Health Corp 3.7% United States Treasury Notes 1.88%

American Funds The Bond Fund of America® Class R-5E B BUY

Ticker	Traded On	NAV	Total Assets ($)	Dividend Yield (TTM)	Turnover Ratio	Expense Ratio
RBFHX	NAS CM	13.99	$56,642,147,665	2.36	286	0.37

Ratings

Reward	B
Risk	B
Recent Upgrade/Downgrade	

Fund Information

Fund Type	Open End
Category	US Fixed Inc
Sub-Category	Intermediate Core Bond
Prospectus Objective	Income
Inception Date	Nov-15
Open to New Investments	Y
Minimum Initial Investment	250
Minimum Subsequent Investment	50
Front End Fee	
Back End Fee	

Total Returns (%)

3-Month	6-Month	1-Year	3-Year	5-Year
4.17	8.16	10.44	18.10	25.51

3-Year Standard Deviation	3.12
Effective Duration	6.27
Average Coupon Rate	3.09

Company Information

Provider	American Funds
Manager/Tenure	David A. Hoag (11), Robert H. Neithart (11), Fergus N. MacDonald (4), 3 others
Website	http://www.americanfunds.com
Address	American Funds 333 South Hope Street Los Angeles CA 90071-1406 United States
Phone Number	800-421-4225

PERFORMANCE

Ratings History

Date	Overall Rating	Risk Rating	Reward Rating
Q2-20	BB	B	2019
Q4-19	C	B-	C
Q4-18	C	C+	D+
Q4-17	B-	A-	C
Q4-16	C	C	C

Asset & Performance History

Date	NAV	1-Year Total Return
13.09	8.25	Cash
2018	12.57	0.08
2017	12.89	3.39
2016	12.72	2.89
2015	12.59	0.25
2014		5.53

Total Assets: $56,642,147,665

Asset Allocation

Asset	%
7%	
Bonds	92%
Govt Bond	30%
Muni Bond	1%
Corp Bond	28%
Other	0%

Services Offered: Automatic Investment Plan, Qualified Investment, Phone Exchange

Investment Strategy: The investment seeks to provide as high a level of current income as is consistent with the preservation of capital. The fund normally invests at least 80% of its assets in bonds and other debt securities. It invests a majority of its assets in debt securities rated A3 or better or A- or better. It may invest in debt securities and mortgage-backed securities issued by government-sponsored entities and federal agencies and instrumentalities that are not backed by the full faith and credit of the U.S. government. **Top Holdings:** Federal National Mortgage Association 3.5% Federal National Mortgage Association 3% United States Treasury Notes 2.75% Government National Mortgage Association 3.5% Federal National Mortgage Association 2%

American Funds The Bond Fund of America® Class A — B BUY

Ticker	Traded On	NAV	Total Assets ($)	Dividend Yield (TTM)	Turnover Ratio	Expense Ratio
ABNDX	NAS CM	13.99	$56,642,147,665	2.15	286	0.61

Ratings

Reward	B
Risk	B
Recent Upgrade/Downgrade	

Fund Information

Fund Type	Open End
Category	US Fixed Inc
Sub-Category	Intermediate Core Bond
Prospectus Objective	Income
Inception Date	May-74
Open to New Investments	Y
Minimum Initial Investment	250
Minimum Subsequent Investment	50
Front End Fee	3.75
Back End Fee	

Total Returns (%)

3-Month	6-Month	1-Year	3-Year	5-Year
4.12	8.05	10.20	17.38	24.42

3-Year Standard Deviation	3.11
Effective Duration	6.27
Average Coupon Rate	3.09

Company Information

Provider	American Funds
Manager/Tenure	David A. Hoag (11), Robert H. Neithart (11), Fergus N. MacDonald (4), 3 others
Website	http://www.americanfunds.com
Address	American Funds 333 South Hope Street Los Angeles CA 90071-1406 United States
Phone Number	800-421-4225

PERFORMANCE

Ratings History

Date	Overall Rating	Risk Rating	Reward Rating
Q2-20	BB	B	2019
Q4-19	C	B-	C
Q4-18	C-	C+	D+
Q4-17	B-	A-	C
Q4-16	C	B-	C

Asset & Performance History

Date	NAV	1-Year Total Return
13.09	8.01	Cash
2018	12.57	-0.12
2017	12.89	3.21
2016	12.72	2.74
2015	12.59	0.23
2014	12.81	5.53

Total Assets: $56,642,147,665

Asset Allocation

Asset	%
7%	
Bonds	92%
Govt Bond	30%
Muni Bond	1%
Corp Bond	28%
Other	0%

Services Offered: Systematic Withdrawal Plan, Automatic Investment Plan, Phone Exchange, Retirement Investment

Investment Strategy: The investment seeks to provide as high a level of current income as is consistent with the preservation of capital. The fund normally invests at least 80% of its assets in bonds and other debt securities. It invests a majority of its assets in debt securities rated A3 or better or A- or better. It may invest in debt securities and mortgage-backed securities issued by government-sponsored entities and federal agencies and instrumentalities that are not backed by the full faith and credit of the U.S. government. **Top Holdings:** Federal National Mortgage Association 3.5% Federal National Mortgage Association 3% United States Treasury Notes 2.75% Government National Mortgage Association 3.5% Federal National Mortgage Association 2%

American Funds The Bond Fund of America® Class F-2 — B BUY

Ticker	Traded On	NAV	Total Assets ($)	Dividend Yield (TTM)	Turnover Ratio	Expense Ratio
ABNFX	NAS CM	13.99	$56,642,147,665	2.39	286	0.34

Ratings

Reward	B
Risk	B+
Recent Upgrade/Downgrade	

Fund Information

Fund Type	Open End
Category	US Fixed Inc
Sub-Category	Intermediate Core Bond
Prospectus Objective	Income
Inception Date	Aug-08
Open to New Investments	Y
Minimum Initial Investment	250
Minimum Subsequent Investment	50
Front End Fee	
Back End Fee	

Total Returns (%)

3-Month	6-Month	1-Year	3-Year	5-Year
4.18	8.18	10.48	18.29	26.00

3-Year Standard Deviation	3.11
Effective Duration	6.27
Average Coupon Rate	3.09

Company Information

Provider	American Funds
Manager/Tenure	David A. Hoag (11), Robert H. Neithart (11), Fergus N. MacDonald (4), 3 others
Website	http://www.americanfunds.com
Address	American Funds 333 South Hope Street Los Angeles CA 90071-1406 United States
Phone Number	800-421-4225

PERFORMANCE

Ratings History

Date	Overall Rating	Risk Rating	Reward Rating
Q2-20	BB+	B	2019
Q4-19	C	B-	C
Q4-18	C	C+	D+
Q4-17	B-	A-	C
Q4-16	C	C	C

Asset & Performance History

Date	NAV	1-Year Total Return
13.09	8.28	Cash
2018	12.57	0.14
2017	12.89	3.47
2016	12.72	2.99
2015	12.59	0.46
2014	12.81	5.81

Total Assets: $56,642,147,665

Asset Allocation

Asset	%
7%	
Bonds	92%
Govt Bond	30%
Muni Bond	1%
Corp Bond	28%
Other	0%

Services Offered: Systematic Withdrawal Plan, Automatic Investment Plan, Qualified Investment, Phone Exchange, Retirement Investment

Investment Strategy: The investment seeks to provide as high a level of current income as is consistent with the preservation of capital. The fund normally invests at least 80% of its assets in bonds and other debt securities. It invests a majority of its assets in debt securities rated A3 or better or A- or better. It may invest in debt securities and mortgage-backed securities issued by government-sponsored entities and federal agencies and instrumentalities that are not backed by the full faith and credit of the U.S. government. **Top Holdings:** Federal National Mortgage Association 3.5% Federal National Mortgage Association 3% United States Treasury Notes 2.75% Government National Mortgage Association 3.5% Federal National Mortgage Association 2%

American Funds The Bond Fund of America® Class F-1 — B BUY

Ticker	Traded On	NAV	Total Assets ($)	Dividend Yield (TTM)	Turnover Ratio	Expense Ratio
BFAFX	NAS CM	13.99	$56,642,147,665	2.12	286	0.63

Ratings

Reward	B
Risk	B
Recent Upgrade/Downgrade	Up

Fund Information

Fund Type	Open End
Category	US Fixed Inc
Sub-Category	Intermediate Core Bond
Prospectus Objective	Income
Inception Date	Mar-01
Open to New Investments	Y
Minimum Initial Investment	250
Minimum Subsequent Investment	50
Front End Fee	
Back End Fee	

Total Returns (%)

3-Month	6-Month	1-Year	3-Year	5-Year
4.11	8.03	10.17	17.23	24.17

3-Year Standard Deviation	3.11
Effective Duration	6.27
Average Coupon Rate	3.09

Company Information

Provider	American Funds
Manager/Tenure	David A. Hoag (11), Robert H. Neithart (11), Fergus N. MacDonald (4), 3 others
Website	http://www.americanfunds.com
Address	American Funds 333 South Hope Street Los Angeles CA 90071-1406 United States
Phone Number	800-421-4225

PERFORMANCE

Ratings History

Date	Overall Rating	Risk Rating	Reward Rating
Q2-20	BB	B	2019
Q4-19	C	B-	C
Q4-18	C-	C+	D
Q4-17	B-	A-	C
Q4-16	C	C	C

Asset & Performance History

Date	NAV	1-Year Total Return
13.09	7.97	Cash
2018	12.57	-0.17
2017	12.89	3.16
2016	12.72	2.7
2015	12.59	0.2
2014	12.81	5.53

Total Assets: $56,642,147,665

Asset Allocation

Asset	%
7%	
Bonds	92%
Govt Bond	30%
Muni Bond	1%
Corp Bond	28%
Other	0%

Services Offered: Systematic Withdrawal Plan, Automatic Investment Plan, Qualified Investment, Phone Exchange, Retirement Investment

Investment Strategy: The investment seeks to provide as high a level of current income as is consistent with the preservation of capital. The fund normally invests at least 80% of its assets in bonds and other debt securities. It invests a majority of its assets in debt securities rated A3 or better or A- or better. It may invest in debt securities and mortgage-backed securities issued by government-sponsored entities and federal agencies and instrumentalities that are not backed by the full faith and credit of the U.S. government. **Top Holdings:** Federal National Mortgage Association 3.5% Federal National Mortgage Association 3% United States Treasury Notes 2.75% Government National Mortgage Association 3.5% Federal National Mortgage Association 2%

American Funds The Bond Fund of America® Class 529-C — B BUY

Ticker	Traded On	NAV	Total Assets ($)	Dividend Yield (TTM)	Turnover Ratio	Expense Ratio
CFACX	NAS CM	13.99	$56,642,147,665	1.4	286	1.41

Ratings

Reward	B-
Risk	B
Recent Upgrade/Downgrade	Up

Fund Information

Fund Type	Open End
Category	US Fixed Inc
Sub-Category	Intermediate Core Bond
Prospectus Objective	Income
Inception Date	Feb-02
Open to New Investments	Y
Minimum Initial Investment	250
Minimum Subsequent Investment	50
Front End Fee	
Back End Fee	1.00

Total Returns (%)

3-Month	6-Month	1-Year	3-Year	5-Year
3.91	7.63	9.35	14.56	19.40

3-Year Standard Deviation	3.11
Effective Duration	6.27
Average Coupon Rate	3.09

Company Information

Provider	American Funds
Manager/Tenure	David A. Hoag (11), Robert H. Neithart (11), Fergus N. MacDonald (4), 3 others
Website	http://www.americanfunds.com
Address	American Funds 333 South Hope Street Los Angeles CA 90071-1406 United States
Phone Number	800-421-4225

PERFORMANCE

Ratings History

Date	Overall Rating	Risk Rating	Reward Rating
Q2-20	BB	B-	2019
Q4-19	C	B-	C
Q4-18	D+	C	D
Q4-17	C	B-	C
Q4-16	C+	B	C

Asset & Performance History

Date	NAV	1-Year Total Return
13.09	7.16	Cash
2018	12.57	-0.94
2017	12.89	2.35
2016	12.72	1.88
2015	12.59	-0.62
2014	12.81	4.63

Total Assets: $56,642,147,665

Asset Allocation

Asset	%
7%	
Bonds	92%
Govt Bond	30%
Muni Bond	1%
Corp Bond	28%
Other	0%

Services Offered: Systematic Withdrawal Plan, Automatic Investment Plan, Qualified Investment, Phone Exchange, Retirement Investment

Investment Strategy: The investment seeks to provide as high a level of current income as is consistent with the preservation of capital. The fund normally invests at least 80% of its assets in bonds and other debt securities. It invests a majority of its assets in debt securities rated A3 or better or A- or better. It may invest in debt securities and mortgage-backed securities issued by government-sponsored entities and federal agencies and instrumentalities that are not backed by the full faith and credit of the U.S. government. **Top Holdings:** Federal National Mortgage Association 3.5% Federal National Mortgage Association 3% United States Treasury Notes 2.75% Government National Mortgage Association 3.5% Federal National Mortgage Association 2%

American Funds The Bond Fund of America® Class 529-A — B BUY

Ticker	Traded On	NAV	Total Assets ($)	Dividend Yield (TTM)	Turnover Ratio	Expense Ratio
CFAAX	NAS CM	13.99	$56,642,147,665	2.1	286	0.65

Ratings

Reward	B
Risk	B
Recent Upgrade/Downgrade	Up

Fund Information

Fund Type	Open End
Category	US Fixed Inc
Sub-Category	Intermediate Core Bond
Prospectus Objective	Income
Inception Date	Feb-02
Open to New Investments	Y
Minimum Initial Investment	250
Minimum Subsequent Investment	50
Front End Fee	3.75
Back End Fee	

Total Returns (%)

3-Month	6-Month	1-Year	3-Year	5-Year
4.10	8.02	10.15	17.14	23.95

3-Year Standard Deviation	3.11
Effective Duration	6.27
Average Coupon Rate	3.09

Company Information

Provider	American Funds
Manager/Tenure	David A. Hoag (11), Robert H. Neithart (11), Fergus N. MacDonald (4), 3 others
Website	http://www.americanfunds.com
Address	American Funds 333 South Hope Street Los Angeles CA 90071-1406 United States
Phone Number	800-421-4225

Ratings History

Date	Overall Rating	Risk Rating	Reward Rating
Q2-20	BB	B	2019
Q4-19	C	B-	C
Q4-18	C-	C+	D
Q4-17	B-	B+	C
Q4-16	C	C	C

Asset & Performance History

Date	NAV	1-Year Total Return
13.09	7.94	Cash
2018	12.57	-0.2
2017	12.89	3.13
2016	12.72	2.65
2015	12.59	0.13
2014	12.81	5.43

Total Assets: $56,642,147,665

Asset Allocation

Asset	%
7%	
Bonds	92%
Govt Bond	30%
Muni Bond	1%
Corp Bond	28%
Other	0%

Services Offered: Systematic Withdrawal Plan, Automatic Investment Plan, Qualified Investment, Phone Exchange, Retirement Investment

Investment Strategy: The investment seeks to provide as high a level of current income as is consistent with the preservation of capital. The fund normally invests at least 80% of its assets in bonds and other debt securities. It invests a majority of its assets in debt securities rated A3 or better or A- or better. It may invest in debt securities and mortgage-backed securities issued by government-sponsored entities and federal agencies and instrumentalities that are not backed by the full faith and credit of the U.S. government. **Top Holdings:** Federal National Mortgage Association 3.5% Federal National Mortgage Association 3% United States Treasury Notes 2.75% Government National Mortgage Association 3.5% Federal National Mortgage Association 2%

American Funds The Bond Fund of America® Class R-3 — B BUY

Ticker	Traded On	NAV	Total Assets ($)	Dividend Yield (TTM)	Turnover Ratio	Expense Ratio
RBFCX	NAS CM	13.99	$56,642,147,665	1.87	286	0.89

Ratings

Reward	B
Risk	B
Recent Upgrade/Downgrade	Up

Fund Information

Fund Type	Open End
Category	US Fixed Inc
Sub-Category	Intermediate Core Bond
Prospectus Objective	Income
Inception Date	Jun-02
Open to New Investments	Y
Minimum Initial Investment	250
Minimum Subsequent Investment	50
Front End Fee	
Back End Fee	

Total Returns (%)

3-Month	6-Month	1-Year	3-Year	5-Year
4.04	7.89	9.89	16.33	22.55

3-Year Standard Deviation	3.11
Effective Duration	6.27
Average Coupon Rate	3.09

Company Information

Provider	American Funds
Manager/Tenure	David A. Hoag (11), Robert H. Neithart (11), Fergus N. MacDonald (4), 3 others
Website	http://www.americanfunds.com
Address	American Funds 333 South Hope Street Los Angeles CA 90071-1406 United States
Phone Number	800-421-4225

Ratings History

Date	Overall Rating	Risk Rating	Reward Rating
Q2-20	BB	B	2019
Q4-19	C	B-	C
Q4-18	C-	C	D
Q4-17	C+	B+	C
Q4-16	C	C	C

Asset & Performance History

Date	NAV	1-Year Total Return
13.09	7.69	Cash
2018	12.57	-0.43
2017	12.89	2.9
2016	12.72	2.43
2015	12.59	-0.07
2014	12.81	5.2

Total Assets: $56,642,147,665

Asset Allocation

Asset	%
7%	
Bonds	92%
Govt Bond	30%
Muni Bond	1%
Corp Bond	28%
Other	0%

Services Offered: Automatic Investment Plan, Qualified Investment, Phone Exchange

Investment Strategy: The investment seeks to provide as high a level of current income as is consistent with the preservation of capital. The fund normally invests at least 80% of its assets in bonds and other debt securities. It invests a majority of its assets in debt securities rated A3 or better or A- or better. It may invest in debt securities and mortgage-backed securities issued by government-sponsored entities and federal agencies and instrumentalities that are not backed by the full faith and credit of the U.S. government. **Top Holdings:** Federal National Mortgage Association 3.5% Federal National Mortgage Association 3% United States Treasury Notes 2.75% Government National Mortgage Association 3.5% Federal National Mortgage Association 2%

American Funds The Bond Fund of America® Class R-1 — B BUY

Ticker	Traded On	NAV	Total Assets ($)	Dividend Yield (TTM)	Turnover Ratio	Expense Ratio
RBFAX	NAS CM	13.99	$56,642,147,665	1.43	286	1.35

Ratings

Reward	B-
Risk	B
Recent Upgrade/Downgrade	Up

Fund Information

Fund Type	Open End
Category	US Fixed Inc
Sub-Category	Intermediate Core Bond
Prospectus Objective	Income
Inception Date	Jun-02
Open to New Investments	Y
Minimum Initial Investment	250
Minimum Subsequent Investment	50
Front End Fee	
Back End Fee	

Total Returns (%)

3-Month	6-Month	1-Year	3-Year	5-Year
3.92	7.64	9.38	14.74	19.79

3-Year Standard Deviation	3.11
Effective Duration	6.27
Average Coupon Rate	3.09

Company Information

Provider	American Funds
Manager/Tenure	David A. Hoag (11), Robert H. Neithart (11), Fergus N. MacDonald (4), 3 others
Website	http://www.americanfunds.com
Address	American Funds 333 South Hope Street Los Angeles CA 90071-1406 United States
Phone Number	800-421-4225

Ratings History

Date	Overall Rating	Risk Rating	Reward Rating
Q2-20	BB	B-	2019
Q4-19	C	B-	C
Q4-18	D+	C	D
Q4-17	C	B-	C
Q4-16	C+	B	C

Asset & Performance History

Date	NAV	1-Year Total Return
13.09	7.21	Cash
2018	12.57	-0.89
2017	12.89	2.42
2016	12.72	1.96
2015	12.59	-0.52
2014	12.81	4.75

Total Assets: $56,642,147,665

Asset Allocation

Asset	%
7%	
Bonds	92%
Govt Bond	30%
Muni Bond	1%
Corp Bond	28%
Other	0%

Services Offered: Automatic Investment Plan, Qualified Investment, Phone Exchange

Investment Strategy: The investment seeks to provide as high a level of current income as is consistent with the preservation of capital. The fund normally invests at least 80% of its assets in bonds and other debt securities. It invests a majority of its assets in debt securities rated A3 or better or A- or better. It may invest in debt securities and mortgage-backed securities issued by government-sponsored entities and federal agencies and instrumentalities that are not backed by the full faith and credit of the U.S. government. **Top Holdings:** Federal National Mortgage Association 3.5% Federal National Mortgage Association 3% United States Treasury Notes 2.75% Government National Mortgage Association 3.5% Federal National Mortgage Association 2%

American Funds The Bond Fund of America® Class R-6 — B BUY

Ticker	Traded On	NAV	Total Assets ($)	Dividend Yield (TTM)	Turnover Ratio	Expense Ratio
RBFGX	NAS CM	13.99	$56,642,147,665	2.5	286	0.23

Ratings

Reward	B
Risk	B
Recent Upgrade/Downgrade	Up

Fund Information

Fund Type	Open End
Category	US Fixed Inc
Sub-Category	Intermediate Core Bond
Prospectus Objective	Income
Inception Date	May-09
Open to New Investments	Y
Minimum Initial Investment	250
Minimum Subsequent Investment	50
Front End Fee	
Back End Fee	

Total Returns (%)

3-Month	6-Month	1-Year	3-Year	5-Year
4.21	8.24	10.60	18.64	26.64

3-Year Standard Deviation	3.11
Effective Duration	6.27
Average Coupon Rate	3.09

Company Information

Provider	American Funds
Manager/Tenure	David A. Hoag (11), Robert H. Neithart (11), Fergus N. MacDonald (4), 3 others
Website	http://www.americanfunds.com
Address	American Funds 333 South Hope Street Los Angeles CA 90071-1406 United States
Phone Number	800-421-4225

Ratings History

Date	Overall Rating	Risk Rating	Reward Rating
Q2-20	BB	B	2019
Q4-19	C	B-	C
Q4-18	C	C+	D+
Q4-17	B-	A-	C
Q4-16	C	C	C

Asset & Performance History

Date	NAV	1-Year Total Return
13.09	8.4	Cash
2018	12.57	0.22
2017	12.89	3.57
2016	12.72	3.1
2015	12.59	0.58
2014	12.81	5.91

Total Assets: $56,642,147,665

Asset Allocation

Asset	%
7%	
Bonds	92%
Govt Bond	30%
Muni Bond	1%
Corp Bond	28%
Other	0%

Services Offered: Automatic Investment Plan, Qualified Investment, Phone Exchange

Investment Strategy: The investment seeks to provide as high a level of current income as is consistent with the preservation of capital. The fund normally invests at least 80% of its assets in bonds and other debt securities. It invests a majority of its assets in debt securities rated A3 or better or A- or better. It may invest in debt securities and mortgage-backed securities issued by government-sponsored entities and federal agencies and instrumentalities that are not backed by the full faith and credit of the U.S. government. **Top Holdings:** Federal National Mortgage Association 3.5% Federal National Mortgage Association 3% United States Treasury Notes 2.75% Government National Mortgage Association 3.5% Federal National Mortgage Association 2%

American Funds The Bond Fund of America® Class R-4 B BUY

Ticker	Traded On	NAV	Total Assets ($)	Dividend Yield (TTM)	Turnover Ratio	Expense Ratio
RBFEX	NAS CM	13.99	$56,642,147,665	2.16	286	0.58

Ratings

Reward	B
Risk	B
Recent Upgrade/Downgrade	

Fund Information

Fund Type	Open End
Category	US Fixed Inc
Sub-Category	Intermediate Core Bond
Prospectus Objective	Income
Inception Date	May-02
Open to New Investments	Y
Minimum Initial Investment	250
Minimum Subsequent Investment	50
Front End Fee	
Back End Fee	

Total Returns (%)

3-Month	6-Month	1-Year	3-Year	5-Year
4.12	8.06	10.22	17.40	24.45

3-Year Standard Deviation	3.11
Effective Duration	6.27
Average Coupon Rate	3.09

Company Information

Provider	American Funds
Manager/Tenure	David A. Hoag (11), Robert H. Neithart (11), Fergus N. MacDonald (4), 3 others
Website	http://www.americanfunds.com
Address	American Funds 333 South Hope Street Los Angeles CA 90071-1406 United States
Phone Number	800-421-4225

PERFORMANCE

Ratings History

Date	Overall Rating	Risk Rating	Reward Rating
Q2-20	BB	B	2019
Q4-19	C	B-	C
Q4-18	C-	C+	D+
Q4-17	B-	A-	C
Q4-16	C	C	C

Asset & Performance History

Date	NAV	1-Year Total Return
13.09	8.02	Cash
2018	12.57	-0.12
2017	12.89	3.21
2016	12.72	2.74
2015	12.59	0.24
2014	12.81	5.54

Total Assets: $56,642,147,665

Asset Allocation

Asset	%
7%	
Bonds	92%
Govt Bond	30%
Muni Bond	1%
Corp Bond	28%
Other	0%

Services Offered: Automatic Investment Plan, Qualified Investment, Phone Exchange

Investment Strategy: The investment seeks to provide as high a level of current income as is consistent with the preservation of capital. The fund normally invests at least 80% of its assets in bonds and other debt securities. It invests a majority of its assets in debt securities rated A3 or better or A- or better. It may invest in debt securities and mortgage-backed securities issued by government-sponsored entities and federal agencies and instrumentalities that are not backed by the full faith and credit of the U.S. government. **Top Holdings:** Federal National Mortgage Association 3.5% Federal National Mortgage Association 3% United States Treasury Notes 2.75% Government National Mortgage Association 3.5% Federal National Mortgage Association 2%

American Funds The Bond Fund of America® Class C B BUY

Ticker	Traded On	NAV	Total Assets ($)	Dividend Yield (TTM)	Turnover Ratio	Expense Ratio
BFACX	NAS CM	13.99	$56,642,147,665	1.44	286	1.36

Ratings

Reward	B-
Risk	B
Recent Upgrade/Downgrade	Up

Fund Information

Fund Type	Open End
Category	US Fixed Inc
Sub-Category	Intermediate Core Bond
Prospectus Objective	Income
Inception Date	Mar-01
Open to New Investments	Y
Minimum Initial Investment	250
Minimum Subsequent Investment	50
Front End Fee	
Back End Fee	1.00

Total Returns (%)

3-Month	6-Month	1-Year	3-Year	5-Year
3.93	7.65	9.39	14.71	19.67

3-Year Standard Deviation	3.11
Effective Duration	6.27
Average Coupon Rate	3.09

Company Information

Provider	American Funds
Manager/Tenure	David A. Hoag (11), Robert H. Neithart (11), Fergus N. MacDonald (4), 3 others
Website	http://www.americanfunds.com
Address	American Funds 333 South Hope Street Los Angeles CA 90071-1406 United States
Phone Number	800-421-4225

PERFORMANCE

Ratings History

Date	Overall Rating	Risk Rating	Reward Rating
Q2-20	BB	B-	2019
Q4-19	C	B-	C
Q4-18	D+	C	D
Q4-17	C	B-	C
Q4-16	C+	B	C

Asset & Performance History

Date	NAV	1-Year Total Return
13.09	7.2	Cash
2018	12.57	-0.9
2017	12.89	2.4
2016	12.72	1.93
2015	12.59	-0.55
2014	12.81	4.7

Total Assets: $56,642,147,665

Asset Allocation

Asset	%
7%	
Bonds	92%
Govt Bond	30%
Muni Bond	1%
Corp Bond	28%
Other	0%

Services Offered: Systematic Withdrawal Plan, Automatic Investment Plan, Phone Exchange, Retirement Investment

Investment Strategy: The investment seeks to provide as high a level of current income as is consistent with the preservation of capital. The fund normally invests at least 80% of its assets in bonds and other debt securities. It invests a majority of its assets in debt securities rated A3 or better or A- or better. It may invest in debt securities and mortgage-backed securities issued by government-sponsored entities and federal agencies and instrumentalities that are not backed by the full faith and credit of the U.S. government. **Top Holdings:** Federal National Mortgage Association 3.5% Federal National Mortgage Association 3% United States Treasury Notes 2.75% Government National Mortgage Association 3.5% Federal National Mortgage Association 2%

American Funds The Bond Fund of America® Class R-2E B BUY

Ticker	Traded On	NAV	Total Assets ($)	Dividend Yield (TTM)	Turnover Ratio	Expense Ratio
RBEBX	NAS CM	13.99	$56,642,147,665	1.73	286	1.04

Ratings

Reward	B
Risk	B
Recent Upgrade/Downgrade	Up

Fund Information

Fund Type	Open End
Category	US Fixed Inc
Sub-Category	Intermediate Core Bond
Prospectus Objective	Income
Inception Date	Aug-14
Open to New Investments	Y
Minimum Initial Investment	250
Minimum Subsequent Investment	50
Front End Fee	
Back End Fee	

Total Returns (%)

3-Month	6-Month	1-Year	3-Year	5-Year
4.01	7.81	9.72	15.80	21.81

3-Year Standard Deviation	3.11
Effective Duration	6.27
Average Coupon Rate	3.09

Company Information

Provider	American Funds
Manager/Tenure	David A. Hoag (11), Robert H. Neithart (11), Fergus N. MacDonald (4), 3 others
Website	http://www.americanfunds.com
Address	American Funds 333 South Hope Street Los Angeles CA 90071-1406 United States
Phone Number	800-421-4225

Ratings History

Date	Overall Rating	Risk Rating	Reward Rating
Q2-20	BB	B	2019
Q4-19	C	B-	C
Q4-18	C-	C	D
Q4-17	C+	B	C
Q4-16	C	C	C

Asset & Performance History

Date	NAV	1-Year Total Return
13.09	7.53	Cash
2018	12.57	-0.58
2017	12.89	2.74
2016	12.72	2.31
2015	12.59	-0.07
2014	12.81	5.32

Total Assets: $56,642,147,665
Asset Allocation

Asset	%
7%	
Bonds	92%
Govt Bond	30%
Muni Bond	1%
Corp Bond	28%
Other	0%

Services Offered: Automatic Investment Plan, Qualified Investment, Phone Exchange

Investment Strategy: The investment seeks to provide as high a level of current income as is consistent with the preservation of capital. The fund normally invests at least 80% of its assets in bonds and other debt securities. It invests a majority of its assets in debt securities rated A3 or better or A- or better. It may invest in debt securities and mortgage-backed securities issued by government-sponsored entities and federal agencies and instrumentalities that are not backed by the full faith and credit of the U.S. government. **Top Holdings:** Federal National Mortgage Association 3.5% Federal National Mortgage Association 3% United States Treasury Notes 2.75% Government National Mortgage Association 3.5% Federal National Mortgage Association 2%

American Funds The Bond Fund of America® Class 529-F B BUY

Ticker	Traded On	NAV	Total Assets ($)	Dividend Yield (TTM)	Turnover Ratio	Expense Ratio
CFAFX	NAS CM	13.99	$56,642,147,665	2.33	286	0.41

Ratings

Reward	B
Risk	B
Recent Upgrade/Downgrade	

Fund Information

Fund Type	Open End
Category	US Fixed Inc
Sub-Category	Intermediate Core Bond
Prospectus Objective	Income
Inception Date	Sep-02
Open to New Investments	Y
Minimum Initial Investment	250
Minimum Subsequent Investment	50
Front End Fee	
Back End Fee	

Total Returns (%)

3-Month	6-Month	1-Year	3-Year	5-Year
4.17	8.15	10.41	17.98	25.41

3-Year Standard Deviation	3.11
Effective Duration	6.27
Average Coupon Rate	3.09

Company Information

Provider	American Funds
Manager/Tenure	David A. Hoag (11), Robert H. Neithart (11), Fergus N. MacDonald (4), 3 others
Website	http://www.americanfunds.com
Address	American Funds 333 South Hope Street Los Angeles CA 90071-1406 United States
Phone Number	800-421-4225

Ratings History

Date	Overall Rating	Risk Rating	Reward Rating
Q2-20	BB	B	2019
Q4-19	C	B-	C
Q4-18	C	C+	D+
Q4-17	B-	A-	C
Q4-16	C	C	C

Asset & Performance History

Date	NAV	1-Year Total Return
13.09	8.2	Cash
2018	12.57	0.03
2017	12.89	3.37
2016	12.72	2.89
2015	12.59	0.36
2014	12.81	5.68

Total Assets: $56,642,147,665
Asset Allocation

Asset	%
7%	
Bonds	92%
Govt Bond	30%
Muni Bond	1%
Corp Bond	28%
Other	0%

Services Offered: Systematic Withdrawal Plan, Automatic Investment Plan, Qualified Investment, Phone Exchange, Retirement Investment

Investment Strategy: The investment seeks to provide as high a level of current income as is consistent with the preservation of capital. The fund normally invests at least 80% of its assets in bonds and other debt securities. It invests a majority of its assets in debt securities rated A3 or better or A- or better. It may invest in debt securities and mortgage-backed securities issued by government-sponsored entities and federal agencies and instrumentalities that are not backed by the full faith and credit of the U.S. government. **Top Holdings:** Federal National Mortgage Association 3.5% Federal National Mortgage Association 3% United States Treasury Notes 2.75% Government National Mortgage Association 3.5% Federal National Mortgage Association 2%

American Funds The Bond Fund of America® Class R-5 — B BUY

Ticker	Traded On	NAV	Total Assets ($)	Dividend Yield (TTM)	Turnover Ratio	Expense Ratio
RBFFX	NAS CM	13.99	$56,642,147,665	2.45	286	0.28

Ratings

Reward	B
Risk	B+
Recent Upgrade/Downgrade	

Fund Information

Fund Type	Open End
Category	US Fixed Inc
Sub-Category	Intermediate Core Bond
Prospectus Objective	Income
Inception Date	May-02
Open to New Investments	Y
Minimum Initial Investment	250
Minimum Subsequent Investment	50
Front End Fee	
Back End Fee	

Total Returns (%)

3-Month	6-Month	1-Year	3-Year	5-Year
4.20	8.21	10.55	18.45	26.31

3-Year Standard Deviation	3.11
Effective Duration	6.27
Average Coupon Rate	3.09

Company Information

Provider	American Funds
Manager/Tenure	David A. Hoag (11), Robert H. Neithart (11), Fergus N. MacDonald (4), 3 others
Website	http://www.americanfunds.com
Address	American Funds 333 South Hope Street Los Angeles CA 90071-1406 United States
Phone Number	800-421-4225

Ratings History

Date	Overall Rating	Risk Rating	Reward Rating
Q2-20	BB+	B	2019
Q4-19	C	B	C
Q4-18	C	C+	D+
Q4-17	B-	A-	C
Q4-16	C	C	C

Asset & Performance History

Date	NAV	1-Year Total Return
13.09	8.34	Cash
2018	12.57	0.16
2017	12.89	3.52
2016	12.72	3.05
2015	12.59	0.53
2014	12.81	5.86

Total Assets: $56,642,147,665

Asset Allocation

Asset	%
7%	
Bonds	92%
Govt Bond	30%
Muni Bond	1%
Corp Bond	28%
Other	0%

Services Offered: Automatic Investment Plan, Qualified Investment, Phone Exchange

Investment Strategy: The investment seeks to provide as high a level of current income as is consistent with the preservation of capital. The fund normally invests at least 80% of its assets in bonds and other debt securities. It invests a majority of its assets in debt securities rated A3 or better or A- or better. It may invest in debt securities and mortgage-backed securities issued by government-sponsored entities and federal agencies and instrumentalities that are not backed by the full faith and credit of the U.S. government. **Top Holdings:** Federal National Mortgage Association 3.5% Federal National Mortgage Association 3% United States Treasury Notes 2.75% Government National Mortgage Association 3.5% Federal National Mortgage Association 2%

American Funds The Bond Fund of America® Class R-2 — B BUY

Ticker	Traded On	NAV	Total Assets ($)	Dividend Yield (TTM)	Turnover Ratio	Expense Ratio
RBFBX	NAS CM	13.99	$56,642,147,665	1.44	286	1.34

Ratings

Reward	B-
Risk	B
Recent Upgrade/Downgrade	Up

Fund Information

Fund Type	Open End
Category	US Fixed Inc
Sub-Category	Intermediate Core Bond
Prospectus Objective	Income
Inception Date	May-02
Open to New Investments	Y
Minimum Initial Investment	250
Minimum Subsequent Investment	50
Front End Fee	
Back End Fee	

Total Returns (%)

3-Month	6-Month	1-Year	3-Year	5-Year
3.93	7.66	9.39	14.78	19.85

3-Year Standard Deviation	3.11
Effective Duration	6.27
Average Coupon Rate	3.09

Company Information

Provider	American Funds
Manager/Tenure	David A. Hoag (11), Robert H. Neithart (11), Fergus N. MacDonald (4), 3 others
Website	http://www.americanfunds.com
Address	American Funds 333 South Hope Street Los Angeles CA 90071-1406 United States
Phone Number	800-421-4225

Ratings History

Date	Overall Rating	Risk Rating	Reward Rating
Q2-20	BB	B-	2019
Q4-19	C	B-	C
Q4-18	D+	C	D
Q4-17	C	B-	C
Q4-16	C	C	C

Asset & Performance History

Date	NAV	1-Year Total Return
13.09	7.21	Cash
2018	12.57	-0.88
2017	12.89	2.44
2016	12.72	1.98
2015	12.59	-0.5
2014	12.81	4.72

Total Assets: $56,642,147,665

Asset Allocation

Asset	%
7%	
Bonds	92%
Govt Bond	30%
Muni Bond	1%
Corp Bond	28%
Other	0%

Services Offered: Automatic Investment Plan, Qualified Investment, Phone Exchange

Investment Strategy: The investment seeks to provide as high a level of current income as is consistent with the preservation of capital. The fund normally invests at least 80% of its assets in bonds and other debt securities. It invests a majority of its assets in debt securities rated A3 or better or A- or better. It may invest in debt securities and mortgage-backed securities issued by government-sponsored entities and federal agencies and instrumentalities that are not backed by the full faith and credit of the U.S. government. **Top Holdings:** Federal National Mortgage Association 3.5% Federal National Mortgage Association 3% United States Treasury Notes 2.75% Government National Mortgage Association 3.5% Federal National Mortgage Association 2%

American Funds The Bond Fund of America® Class 529-E — B BUY

Ticker	Traded On	NAV	Total Assets ($)	Dividend Yield (TTM)	Turnover Ratio	Expense Ratio
CFAEX	NAS CM	13.99	$56,642,147,665	1.93	286	0.85

Ratings

Reward	B
Risk	B
Recent Upgrade/Downgrade	Up

Fund Information

Fund Type	Open End
Category	US Fixed Inc
Sub-Category	Intermediate Core Bond
Prospectus Objective	Income
Inception Date	Mar-02
Open to New Investments	Y
Minimum Initial Investment	250
Minimum Subsequent Investment	50
Front End Fee	
Back End Fee	

Total Returns (%)

3-Month	6-Month	1-Year	3-Year	5-Year
4.06	7.92	9.95	16.48	22.75

3-Year Standard Deviation	3.11
Effective Duration	6.27
Average Coupon Rate	3.09

Company Information

Provider	American Funds
Manager/Tenure	David A. Hoag (11), Robert H. Neithart (11), Fergus N. MacDonald (4), 3 others
Website	http://www.americanfunds.com
Address	American Funds 333 South Hope Street Los Angeles CA 90071-1406 United States
Phone Number	800-421-4225

PERFORMANCE

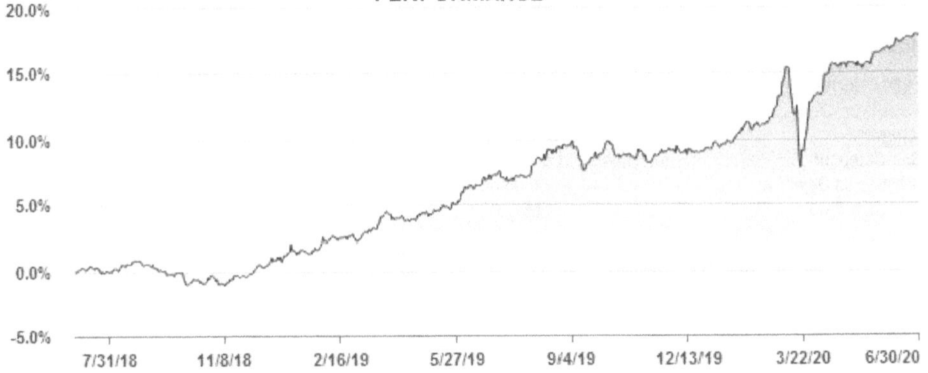

Ratings History

Date	Overall Rating	Risk Rating	Reward Rating
Q2-20	BB	B	2019
Q4-19	C	B-	C
Q4-18	C-	C	D
Q4-17	C+	B+	C
Q4-16	C	C	C

Asset & Performance History

Date	NAV	1-Year Total Return
13.09	7.74	Cash
2018	12.57	-0.39
2017	12.89	2.93
2016	12.72	2.44
2015	12.59	-0.07
2014	12.81	5.2

Total Assets: $56,642,147,665

Asset Allocation

Asset	%
7%	
Bonds	92%
Govt Bond	30%
Muni Bond	1%
Corp Bond	28%
Other	0%

Services Offered: Systematic Withdrawal Plan, Automatic Investment Plan, Qualified Investment, Phone Exchange, Retirement Investment

Investment Strategy: The investment seeks to provide as high a level of current income as is consistent with the preservation of capital. The fund normally invests at least 80% of its assets in bonds and other debt securities. It invests a majority of its assets in debt securities rated A3 or better or A- or better. It may invest in debt securities and mortgage-backed securities issued by government-sponsored entities and federal agencies and instrumentalities that are not backed by the full faith and credit of the U.S. government. **Top Holdings:** Federal National Mortgage Association 3.5% Federal National Mortgage Association 3% United States Treasury Notes 2.75% Government National Mortgage Association 3.5% Federal National Mortgage Association 2%

Fidelity® Money Market Fund — C HOLD

Ticker	Traded On	NAV	Total Assets ($)	Dividend Yield (TTM)	Turnover Ratio	Expense Ratio
SPRXX	NAS CM	1	$56,039,147,525	1.42		0.42

Ratings

Reward	C-
Risk	C+
Recent Upgrade/Downgrade	

Fund Information

Fund Type	Money Mkt
Category	US Money Mkt
Sub-Category	Prime Money Mkt
Prospectus Objective	Money Mkt - Taxable
Inception Date	Jan-89
Open to New Investments	Y
Minimum Initial Investment	0
Minimum Subsequent Investment	
Front End Fee	
Back End Fee	

Total Returns (%)

3-Month	6-Month	1-Year	3-Year	5-Year
0.04	0.35	1.24	4.69	5.47

3-Year Standard Deviation	0.16
Effective Duration	
Average Coupon Rate	

Company Information

Provider	Fidelity Investments
Manager/Tenure	Management Team (12)
Website	http://www.institutional.fidelity.com
Address	Fidelity Investments 82 Devonshire Street Boston MA 2109 United States
Phone Number	617-563-7000

PERFORMANCE

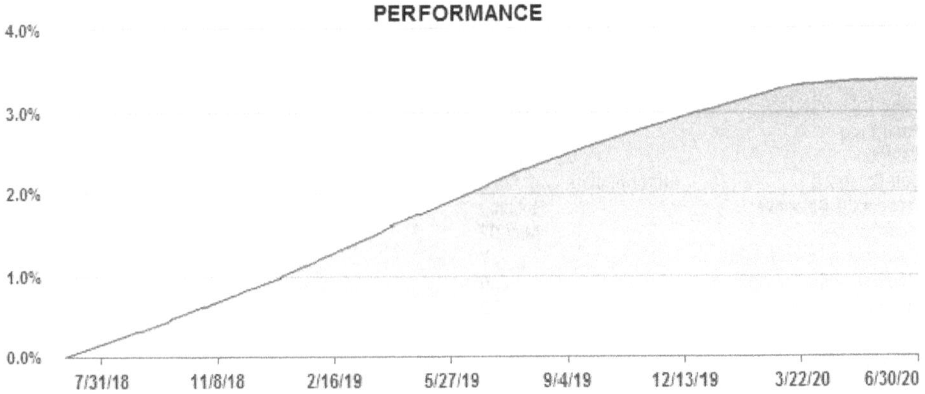

Ratings History

Date	Overall Rating	Risk Rating	Reward Rating
Q2-20	CC+	C-	2019
Q4-19	C	C+	C-
Q4-18	C	C+	C-
Q4-17	C	C+	C-
Q4-16	C	C+	C-

Asset & Performance History

Date	NAV	1-Year Total Return
1	2	Cash
2018	1	1.72
2017	1	0.87
2016	1	0.35
2015	1	0.01
2014	1	0.01

Total Assets: $56,039,147,525

Asset Allocation

Asset	%
89%	
Bonds	11%
Govt Bond	10%
Muni Bond	0%
Corp Bond	0%
Other	0%

Services Offered: Systematic Withdrawal Plan, Automatic Investment Plan, Qualified Investment, Phone Exchange, Wire Redemption, Retirement Investment

Investment Strategy: The investment seeks as high a level of current income as is consistent with preservation of capital and liquidity. The fund invests in U.S. dollar-denominated money market securities of domestic and foreign issuers and repurchase agreements. It invests more than 25% of total assets in the financial services industries. The fund invests in compliance with industry-standard regulatory requirements for money market funds for the quality, maturity, liquidity, and diversification of investments. **Top Holdings:** Barclays Bank Plc Barclays Bank Plc, 0.18% Sumitomo Mitsui Bk Corp (Repo) In A Joint Trading Account With Sumitomo Mit Landesbank Baden Wurttemberg New York Branch Smbc Nikko Securities America, Inc. Smbc Nikko Securities America, Inc., 0. Mizuho Bank Ltd. Mizuho Bank Ltd., 0.06%

PGIM Total Return Bond Fund -Class A C+ HOLD

Ticker	Traded On	NAV	Total Assets ($)	Dividend Yield (TTM)	Turnover Ratio	Expense Ratio
PDBAX	NAS CM	14.75	$55,452,600,377	3.08	45	0.76

Ratings

Reward	C
Risk	B
Recent Upgrade/Downgrade	

Fund Information

Fund Type	Open End
Category	US Fixed Inc
Sub-Category	Intermediate Core-Plus Bond
Prospectus Objective	Multisector Bond
Inception Date	Jan-95
Open to New Investments	Y
Minimum Initial Investment	1,000
Minimum Subsequent Investment	100
Front End Fee	3.25
Back End Fee	

Total Returns (%)

3-Month	6-Month	1-Year	3-Year	5-Year
6.66	3.54	6.55	16.15	26.33

3-Year Standard Deviation	5.49
Effective Duration	6.01
Average Coupon Rate	3.83

Company Information

Provider	PGIM Funds (Prudential)
Manager/Tenure	Robert Tipp (17), Michael J. Collins (10), Richard Piccirillo (7), 1 other
Website	http://www.pgiminvestments.com
Address	PGIM Funds (Prudential) PO Box 9658 Providence RI 02940 United States
Phone Number	800-225-1852

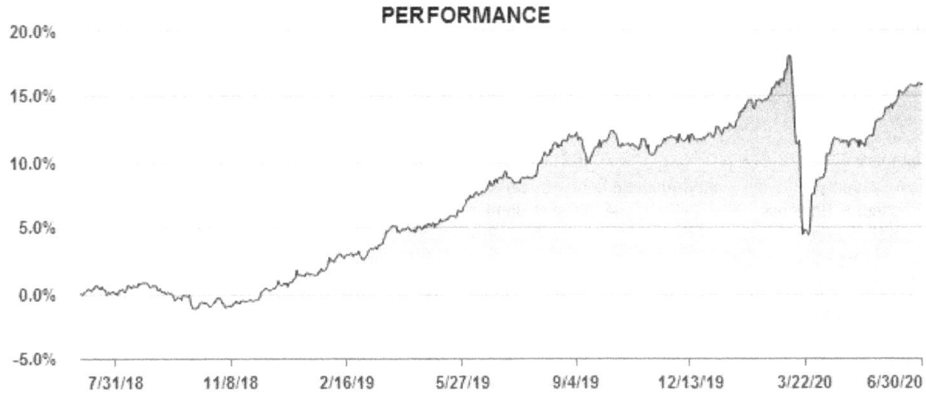

Ratings History

Date	Overall Rating	Risk Rating	Reward Rating
Q2-20	C+B	C	2019
Q4-19	C+	B	C
Q4-18	C	C+	D+
Q4-17	B-	B+	C
Q4-16	C+	B	C

Asset & Performance History

Date	NAV	1-Year Total Return
14.45	10.68	Cash
2018	13.96	-0.97
2017	14.63	6.3
2016	14.13	4.53
2015	14.01	-0.29
2014	14.46	6.77

Total Assets: $55,452,600,377

Asset Allocation

Asset	%
4%	
Bonds	95%
Govt Bond	18%
Muni Bond	1%
Corp Bond	29%
Other	0%

Services Offered: Systematic Withdrawal Plan, Automatic Investment Plan, Phone Exchange, Retirement Investment

Investment Strategy: The investment seeks total return. The fund will seek to achieve its objective through a mix of current income and capital appreciation as determined by the fund's subadviser. It invests, under normal circumstances, at least 80% of the fund's investable assets in bonds. For purposes of this policy, bonds include all fixed income securities, other than preferred stock, with a maturity at date of issue of greater than one year. The fund may invest up to 30% of its investable assets in speculative, high risk, below investment-grade securities having a rating of not lower than CCC. It may invest up to 30% of its investable assets in foreign debt securities. **Top Holdings:** United States Treasury Bonds 3.38% Portugal (Republic Of) 5.12% Ultra US Treasury Bond Future June 20 Bvrt_19-1f Republika Slovenija 5.25%

PGIM Total Return Bond Fund -Class B C HOLD

Ticker	Traded On	NAV	Total Assets ($)	Dividend Yield (TTM)	Turnover Ratio	Expense Ratio
PRDBX	NAS CM		$55,452,600,377	2.6	45	1.26

Ratings

Reward	C
Risk	B
Recent Upgrade/Downgrade	

Fund Information

Fund Type	Open End
Category	US Fixed Inc
Sub-Category	Intermediate Core-Plus Bond
Prospectus Objective	Multisector Bond
Inception Date	Jan-95
Open to New Investments	
Minimum Initial Investment	2,500
Minimum Subsequent Investment	100
Front End Fee	
Back End Fee	5.00

Total Returns (%)

3-Month	6-Month	1-Year	3-Year	5-Year
7.70	3.15	6.10	14.38	22.89

3-Year Standard Deviation	5.46
Effective Duration	6.01
Average Coupon Rate	3.83

Company Information

Provider	PGIM Funds (Prudential)
Manager/Tenure	Robert Tipp (17), Michael J. Collins (10), Richard Piccirillo (7), 1 other
Website	http://www.pgiminvestments.com
Address	PGIM Funds (Prudential) PO Box 9658 Providence RI 02940 United States
Phone Number	800-225-1852

Ratings History

Date	Overall Rating	Risk Rating	Reward Rating
Q2-20	CB	C	2019
Q4-19	C+	B	C
Q4-18	C-	C+	D+
Q4-17	B-	B+	C
Q4-16	C+	B	C

Asset & Performance History

Date	NAV	1-Year Total Return
14.45	10.14	Cash
2018	13.96	-1.4
2017	14.62	5.78
2016	14.12	3.94
2015	14.01	-0.8
2014	14.46	6.24

Total Assets: $55,452,600,377

Asset Allocation

Asset	%
4%	
Bonds	95%
Govt Bond	18%
Muni Bond	1%
Corp Bond	29%
Other	0%

Services Offered: Systematic Withdrawal Plan, Automatic Investment Plan, Phone Exchange, Retirement Investment

Investment Strategy: The investment seeks total return. The fund will seek to achieve its objective through a mix of current income and capital appreciation as determined by the fund's subadviser. It invests, under normal circumstances, at least 80% of the fund's investable assets in bonds. For purposes of this policy, bonds include all fixed income securities, other than preferred stock, with a maturity at date of issue of greater than one year. The fund may invest up to 30% of its investable assets in speculative, high risk, below investment-grade securities having a rating of not lower than CCC. It may invest up to 30% of its investable assets in foreign debt securities. **Top Holdings:** United States Treasury Bonds 3.38% Portugal (Republic Of) 5.12% Ultra US Treasury Bond Future June 20 Bvrt_19-1f Republika Slovenija 5.25%

PGIM Total Return Bond Fund -Class R2

C+ HOLD

Ticker	Traded On	NAV	Total Assets ($)	Dividend Yield (TTM)	Turnover Ratio	Expense Ratio
PDBRX	NAS CM	14.71	$55,452,600,377	2.96	45	0.89

Ratings

Reward	C
Risk	B
Recent Upgrade/Downgrade	Up

Fund Information

Fund Type	Open End
Category	US Fixed Inc
Sub-Category	Intermediate Core-Plus Bond
Prospectus Objective	Multisector Bond
Inception Date	Dec-17
Open to New Investments	Y
Minimum Initial Investment	0
Minimum Subsequent Investment	
Front End Fee	
Back End Fee	

Total Returns (%)

3-Month	6-Month	1-Year	3-Year	5-Year
6.56	3.48	6.42	15.79	25.94

3-Year Standard Deviation	5.46
Effective Duration	6.01
Average Coupon Rate	3.83

Company Information

Provider	PGIM Funds (Prudential)
Manager/Tenure	Robert Tipp (17), Michael J. Collins (10), Richard Piccirillo (7), 1 other
Website	http://www.pgiminvestments.com
Address	PGIM Funds (Prudential) PO Box 9658 Providence RI 02940 United States
Phone Number	800-225-1852

PERFORMANCE

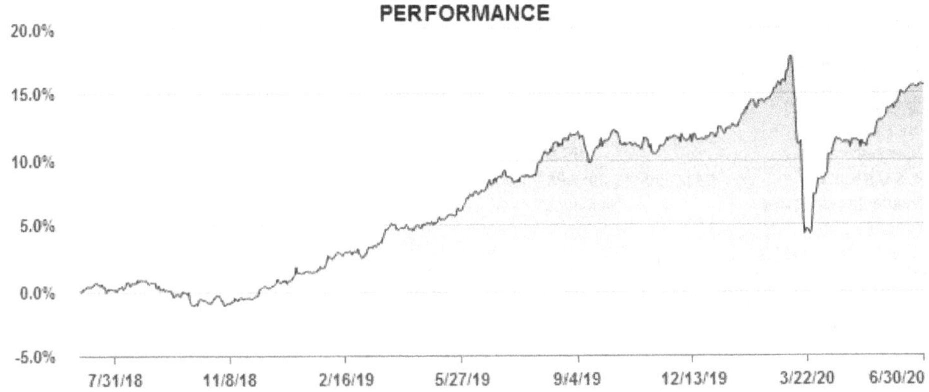

Ratings History

Date	Overall Rating	Risk Rating	Reward Rating
Q2-20	C+B	C	2019
Q4-19	C+	B	C
Q4-18	C	C+	D+
Q4-17			
Q4-16			

Asset & Performance History

Date	NAV	1-Year Total Return
14.41	10.47	Cash
2018	13.93	-1.04
2017	14.59	
2016		
2015		
2014		

Total Assets: $55,452,600,377

Asset Allocation

Asset	%
4%	
Bonds	95%
Govt Bond	18%
Muni Bond	1%
Corp Bond	29%
Other	0%

Services Offered: Qualified Investment

Investment Strategy: The investment seeks total return. The fund will seek to achieve its objective through a mix of current income and capital appreciation as determined by the fund's subadviser. It invests, under normal circumstances, at least 80% of the fund's investable assets in bonds. For purposes of this policy, bonds include all fixed income securities, other than preferred stock, with a maturity at date of issue of greater than one year. The fund may invest up to 30% of its investable assets in speculative, high risk, below investment-grade securities having a rating of not lower than CCC. It may invest up to 30% of its investable assets in foreign debt securities. **Top Holdings:** United States Treasury Bonds 3.38% Portugal (Republic Of) 5.12% Ultra US Treasury Bond Future June 20 Bvrt_19-1f Republika Slovenija 5.25%

PGIM Total Return Bond Fund -Class R4

C+ HOLD

Ticker	Traded On	NAV	Total Assets ($)	Dividend Yield (TTM)	Turnover Ratio	Expense Ratio
PDBSX	NAS CM	14.71	$55,452,600,377	3.21	45	0.64

Ratings

Reward	C
Risk	B
Recent Upgrade/Downgrade	

Fund Information

Fund Type	Open End
Category	US Fixed Inc
Sub-Category	Intermediate Core-Plus Bond
Prospectus Objective	Multisector Bond
Inception Date	Dec-17
Open to New Investments	Y
Minimum Initial Investment	0
Minimum Subsequent Investment	
Front End Fee	
Back End Fee	

Total Returns (%)

3-Month	6-Month	1-Year	3-Year	5-Year
6.62	3.54	6.69	16.52	26.72

3-Year Standard Deviation	5.47
Effective Duration	6.01
Average Coupon Rate	3.83

Company Information

Provider	PGIM Funds (Prudential)
Manager/Tenure	Robert Tipp (17), Michael J. Collins (10), Richard Piccirillo (7), 1 other
Website	http://www.pgiminvestments.com
Address	PGIM Funds (Prudential) PO Box 9658 Providence RI 02940 United States
Phone Number	800-225-1852

PERFORMANCE

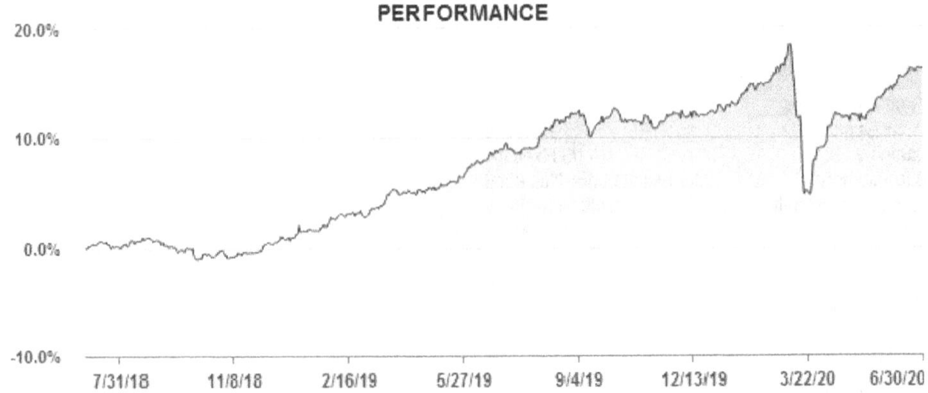

Ratings History

Date	Overall Rating	Risk Rating	Reward Rating
Q2-20	C+B	C	2019
Q4-19	C+	B	C
Q4-18	C	C+	D+
Q4-17			
Q4-16			

Asset & Performance History

Date	NAV	1-Year Total Return
14.42	10.83	Cash
2018	13.93	-0.8
2017	14.59	
2016		
2015		
2014		

Total Assets: $55,452,600,377

Asset Allocation

Asset	%
4%	
Bonds	95%
Govt Bond	18%
Muni Bond	1%
Corp Bond	29%
Other	0%

Services Offered: Qualified Investment

Investment Strategy: The investment seeks total return. The fund will seek to achieve its objective through a mix of current income and capital appreciation as determined by the fund's subadviser. It invests, under normal circumstances, at least 80% of the fund's investable assets in bonds. For purposes of this policy, bonds include all fixed income securities, other than preferred stock, with a maturity at date of issue of greater than one year. The fund may invest up to 30% of its investable assets in speculative, high risk, below investment-grade securities having a rating of not lower than CCC. It may invest up to 30% of its investable assets in foreign debt securities. **Top Holdings:** United States Treasury Bonds 3.38% Portugal (Republic Of) 5.12% Ultra US Treasury Bond Future June 20 Bvrt_19-1f Republika Slovenija 5.25%

PGIM Total Return Bond Fund -Class C **C+ HOLD**

Ticker	Traded On	NAV	Total Assets ($)	Dividend Yield (TTM)	Turnover Ratio	Expense Ratio
PDBCX	NAS CM	14.73	$55,452,600,377	2.39	45	1.48

Ratings

Reward	C
Risk	B
Recent Upgrade/Downgrade	Up

Fund Information

Fund Type	Open End
Category	US Fixed Inc
Sub-Category	Intermediate Core-Plus Bond
Prospectus Objective	Multisector Bond
Inception Date	Jan-95
Open to New Investments	Y
Minimum Initial Investment	1,000
Minimum Subsequent Investment	100
Front End Fee	
Back End Fee	1.00

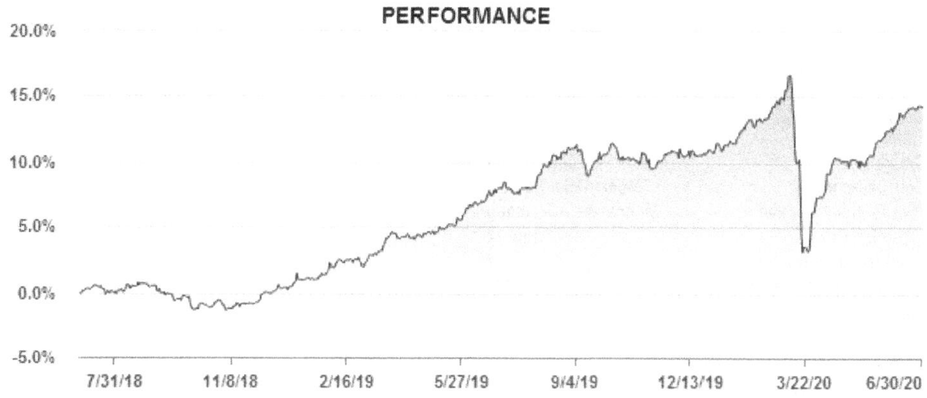

Total Returns (%)

3-Month	6-Month	1-Year	3-Year	5-Year
6.40	3.11	5.80	13.65	21.69

3-Year Standard Deviation	5.47
Effective Duration	6.01
Average Coupon Rate	3.83

Ratings History

Date	Overall Rating	Risk Rating	Reward Rating
Q2-20	C+B	C	2019
Q4-19	C	B-	C
Q4-18	C-	C	D+
Q4-17	B-	B+	C
Q4-16	C+	B	C

Asset & Performance History

Date	NAV	1-Year Total Return
14.44	9.9	Cash
2018	13.95	-1.64
2017	14.61	5.53
2016	14.11	3.68
2015	14	-1.04
2014	14.45	5.98

Total Assets: $55,452,600,377

Asset Allocation

Asset	%
4%	
Bonds	95%
Govt Bond	18%
Muni Bond	1%
Corp Bond	29%
Other	0%

Company Information

Provider	PGIM Funds (Prudential)
Manager/Tenure	Robert Tipp (17), Michael J. Collins (10), Richard Piccirillo (7), 1 other
Website	http://www.pgiminvestments.com
Address	PGIM Funds (Prudential) PO Box 9658 Providence RI 02940 United States
Phone Number	800-225-1852

Services Offered: Systematic Withdrawal Plan, Automatic Investment Plan, Phone Exchange, Retirement Investment

Investment Strategy: The investment seeks total return. The fund will seek to achieve its objective through a mix of current income and capital appreciation as determined by the fund's subadviser. It invests, under normal circumstances, at least 80% of the fund's investable assets in bonds. For purposes of this policy, bonds include all fixed income securities, other than preferred stock, with a maturity at date of issue of greater than one year. The fund may invest up to 30% of its investable assets in speculative, high risk, below investment-grade securities having a rating of not lower than CCC. It may invest up to 30% of its investable assets in foreign debt securities. **Top Holdings:** United States Treasury Bonds 3.38% Portugal (Republic Of) 5.12% Ultra US Treasury Bond Future June 20 Bvrt_19-1f Republika Slovenija 5.25%

PGIM Total Return Bond Fund -Class R **C+ HOLD**

Ticker	Traded On	NAV	Total Assets ($)	Dividend Yield (TTM)	Turnover Ratio	Expense Ratio
DTBRX	NAS CM	14.77	$55,452,600,377	2.84	45	1.01

Ratings

Reward	C
Risk	B
Recent Upgrade/Downgrade	Up

Fund Information

Fund Type	Open End
Category	US Fixed Inc
Sub-Category	Intermediate Core-Plus Bond
Prospectus Objective	Multisector Bond
Inception Date	Jan-08
Open to New Investments	Y
Minimum Initial Investment	0
Minimum Subsequent Investment	
Front End Fee	
Back End Fee	

Total Returns (%)

3-Month	6-Month	1-Year	3-Year	5-Year
6.51	3.34	6.28	15.27	24.65

3-Year Standard Deviation	5.46
Effective Duration	6.01
Average Coupon Rate	3.83

Ratings History

Date	Overall Rating	Risk Rating	Reward Rating
Q2-20	C+B	C	2019
Q4-19	C+	B	C
Q4-18	C	C+	D+
Q4-17	B-	B+	C
Q4-16	C+	B	C

Asset & Performance History

Date	NAV	1-Year Total Return
14.48	10.39	Cash
2018	13.99	-1.16
2017	14.65	6.03
2016	14.15	4.19
2015	14.04	-0.46
2014	14.48	6.49

Total Assets: $55,452,600,377

Asset Allocation

Asset	%
4%	
Bonds	95%
Govt Bond	18%
Muni Bond	1%
Corp Bond	29%
Other	0%

Company Information

Provider	PGIM Funds (Prudential)
Manager/Tenure	Robert Tipp (17), Michael J. Collins (10), Richard Piccirillo (7), 1 other
Website	http://www.pgiminvestments.com
Address	PGIM Funds (Prudential) PO Box 9658 Providence RI 02940 United States
Phone Number	800-225-1852

Services Offered: Qualified Investment, Phone Exchange

Investment Strategy: The investment seeks total return. The fund will seek to achieve its objective through a mix of current income and capital appreciation as determined by the fund's subadviser. It invests, under normal circumstances, at least 80% of the fund's investable assets in bonds. For purposes of this policy, bonds include all fixed income securities, other than preferred stock, with a maturity at date of issue of greater than one year. The fund may invest up to 30% of its investable assets in speculative, high risk, below investment-grade securities having a rating of not lower than CCC. It may invest up to 30% of its investable assets in foreign debt securities. **Top Holdings:** United States Treasury Bonds 3.38% Portugal (Republic Of) 5.12% Ultra US Treasury Bond Future June 20 Bvrt_19-1f Republika Slovenija 5.25%

Federated Hermes Treasury Obl Automated — C HOLD

Ticker	Traded On	NAV	Total Assets ($)	Dividend Yield (TTM)	Turnover Ratio	Expense Ratio
TOAXX	NAS CM	1	$54,380,909,203	1.16		0.55

Ratings

Reward	C-
Risk	C+
Recent Upgrade/Downgrade	

Fund Information

Fund Type	Money Mkt
Category	US Money Mkt
Sub-Category	Money Mkt-Taxable
Prospectus Objective	Money Mkt - Treasury
Inception Date	Jun-14
Open to New Investments	Y
Minimum Initial Investment	25,000
Minimum Subsequent Investment	
Front End Fee	
Back End Fee	

Total Returns (%)

3-Month	6-Month	1-Year	3-Year	5-Year
0.00	0.23	1.00	3.84	3.97

3-Year Standard Deviation	0.17
Effective Duration	
Average Coupon Rate	

Company Information

Provider	Federated
Manager/Tenure	Management Team (13)
Website	http://www.federatedinvestors.com
Address	Federated Investors Funds 4000 Ericsson Drive Warrendale PA 15086-7561 United States
Phone Number	800-341-7400

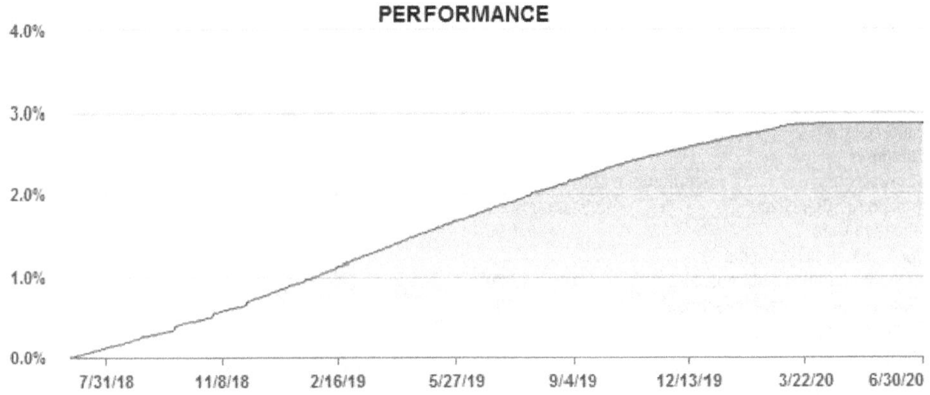

Ratings History

Date	Overall Rating	Risk Rating	Reward Rating
Q2-20	CC+	C-	2019
Q4-19	C	C+	C
Q4-18	C	C+	C-
Q4-17	C	C	C-
Q4-16	C-	C	C-

Asset & Performance History

Date	NAV	1-Year Total Return
1	1.74	Cash
2018	1	1.38
2017	1	0.45
2016	1	0
2015	1	0
2014	1	0.01

Total Assets: $54,380,909,203

Asset Allocation

Asset	%
75%	
Bonds	25%
Govt Bond	25%
Muni Bond	0%
Corp Bond	0%
Other	0%

Services Offered: Systematic Withdrawal Plan, Automatic Investment Plan, Qualified Investment, Phone Exchange, Wire Redemption, Retirement Investment

Investment Strategy: The investment seeks to provide current income consistent with stability of principal. The fund invests in a portfolio of U.S. Treasury securities maturing in 397 days or less and repurchase agreements collateralized fully by U.S. Treasury securities. It will invest its assets so that at least 80% of its net assets (plus any borrowings for investment purposes) are invested in Treasury investments. The fund may also hold cash. **Top Holdings:** Sumitomo 4 Repo Frbnybo Prime 1 Frbnybo Prime 1 Nab P Repo 1 Repo Ss Ficc P Repo 1 Repo Ficcjpm 1 Ficc Jpm 1

Vanguard Short-Term Bond Index Fund Admiral Shares — B- BUY

Ticker	Traded On	NAV	Total Assets ($)	Dividend Yield (TTM)	Turnover Ratio	Expense Ratio
VBIRX	NAS CM	10.89	$52,730,821,140	2.11	44	0.07

Ratings

Reward	C
Risk	B
Recent Upgrade/Downgrade	Up

Fund Information

Fund Type	Open End
Category	US Fixed Inc
Sub-Category	Short-Term Bond
Prospectus Objective	Income
Inception Date	Nov-01
Open to New Investments	Y
Minimum Initial Investment	3,000
Minimum Subsequent Investment	1
Front End Fee	
Back End Fee	

Total Returns (%)

3-Month	6-Month	1-Year	3-Year	5-Year
1.77	4.05	5.41	10.66	13.72

3-Year Standard Deviation	1.52
Effective Duration	2.66
Average Coupon Rate	2.31

Company Information

Provider	Vanguard
Manager/Tenure	Joshua C. Barrickman (7)
Website	http://www.vanguard.com
Address	Vanguard 100 Vanguard Boulevard Malvern PA 19355 United States
Phone Number	877-662-7447

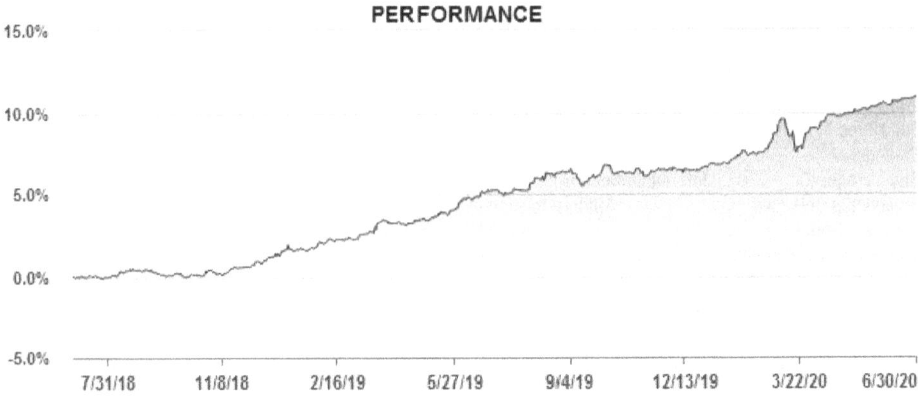

Ratings History

Date	Overall Rating	Risk Rating	Reward Rating
Q2-20	B-B	C	2019
Q4-19	C	B-	C
Q4-18	C	C+	D+
Q4-17	C	B	C
Q4-16	C	B-	C

Asset & Performance History

Date	NAV	1-Year Total Return
10.57	4.84	Cash
2018	10.31	1.33
2017	10.38	1.16
2016	10.43	1.48
2015	10.43	0.92
2014	10.48	1.25

Total Assets: $52,730,821,140

Asset Allocation

Asset	%
1%	
Bonds	98%
Govt Bond	73%
Muni Bond	0%
Corp Bond	27%
Other	0%

Services Offered: Systematic Withdrawal Plan, Automatic Investment Plan, Phone Exchange, Wire Redemption

Investment Strategy: The investment seeks to track the performance of Bloomberg Barclays U.S. 1-5 Year Government/Credit Float Adjusted Index. Bloomberg Barclays U.S. 1-5 Year Government/Credit Float Adjusted Index includes all medium and larger issues of U.S. government, investment-grade corporate, and investment-grade international dollar-denominated bonds that have maturities between 1 and 5 years and are publicly issued. All of its investments will be selected through the sampling process, and at least 80% of its assets will be invested in bonds held in the index. **Top Holdings:** United States Treasury Notes 1.25% United States Treasury Notes 0.38% United States Treasury Notes 0.25% United States Treasury Notes 1.12% United States Treasury Notes 2.62%

Vanguard Short-Term Bond Index Fund Investor Shares — B- BUY

Ticker	Traded On	NAV	Total Assets ($)	Dividend Yield (TTM)	Turnover Ratio	Expense Ratio
VBISX	NAS CM	10.89	$52,730,821,140	2.03	44	0.15

Ratings

Reward	C
Risk	B
Recent Upgrade/Downgrade	Up

Fund Information

Fund Type	Open End
Category	US Fixed Inc
Sub-Category	Short-Term Bond
Prospectus Objective	Income
Inception Date	Mar-94
Open to New Investments	Y
Minimum Initial Investment	3,000
Minimum Subsequent Investment	1
Front End Fee	
Back End Fee	

Total Returns (%)

3-Month	6-Month	1-Year	3-Year	5-Year
1.75	4.00	5.33	10.40	13.28

3-Year Standard Deviation	1.52
Effective Duration	2.66
Average Coupon Rate	2.31

Ratings History

Date	Overall Rating	Risk Rating	Reward Rating
Q2-20	B-B	C	2019
Q4-19	C	B-	C
Q4-18	C	C+	D+
Q4-17	C	B-	C
Q4-16	C+	B	C

Asset & Performance History

Date	NAV	1-Year Total Return
10.57	4.76	Cash
2018	10.31	1.24
2017	10.38	1.08
2016	10.43	1.4
2015	10.43	0.85
2014	10.48	1.15

Total Assets: $52,730,821,140

Asset Allocation

Asset	%
1%	
Bonds	98%
Govt Bond	73%
Muni Bond	0%
Corp Bond	27%
Other	0%

Company Information

Provider	Vanguard
Manager/Tenure	Joshua C. Barrickman (7)
Website	http://www.vanguard.com
Address	Vanguard 100 Vanguard Boulevard Malvern PA 19355 United States
Phone Number	877-662-7447

Services Offered: Systematic Withdrawal Plan, Automatic Investment Plan, Phone Exchange, Wire Redemption

Investment Strategy: The investment seeks to track the performance of Bloomberg Barclays U.S. 1-5 Year Government/Credit Float Adjusted Index. Bloomberg Barclays U.S. 1-5 Year Government/Credit Float Adjusted Index includes all medium and larger issues of U.S. government, investment-grade corporate, and investment-grade international dollar-denominated bonds that have maturities between 1 and 5 years and are publicly issued. All of its investments will be selected through the sampling process, and at least 80% of its assets will be invested in bonds held in the index. **Top Holdings:** United States Treasury Notes 1.25% United States Treasury Notes 0.38% United States Treasury Notes 0.25% United States Treasury Notes 1.12% United States Treasury Notes 2.62%

Morgan Stanley Institutional Liquidity Treasury Securities Portfolio Select Class — C HOLD

Ticker	Traded On	NAV	Total Assets ($)	Dividend Yield (TTM)	Turnover Ratio	Expense Ratio
MSEXX	NAS CM	1	$51,700,969,068	0.72		1

Ratings

Reward	C-
Risk	C
Recent Upgrade/Downgrade	

Fund Information

Fund Type	Money Mkt
Category	US Money Mkt
Sub-Category	Money Mkt-Taxable
Prospectus Objective	Money Mkt - General
Inception Date	Mar-16
Open to New Investments	Y
Minimum Initial Investment	0
Minimum Subsequent Investment	
Front End Fee	
Back End Fee	

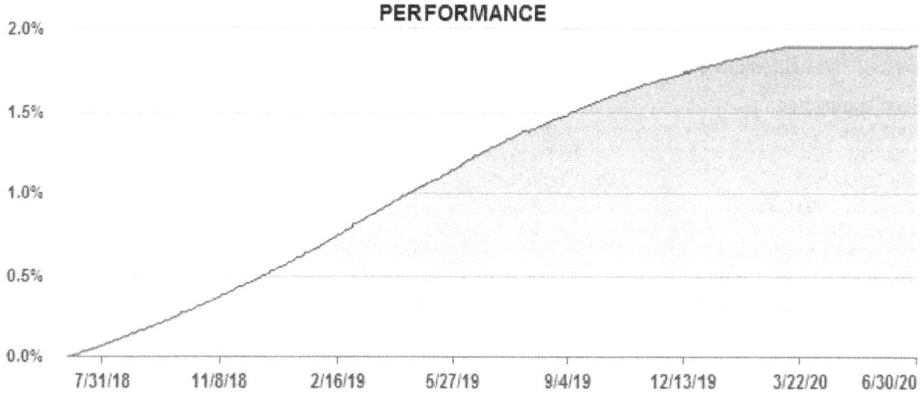

Total Returns (%)

3-Month	6-Month	1-Year	3-Year	5-Year
0.00	0.12	0.60	2.26	1.90

3-Year Standard Deviation	0.15
Effective Duration	
Average Coupon Rate	

Ratings History

Date	Overall Rating	Risk Rating	Reward Rating
Q2-20	CC	C-	2019
Q4-19	C	C	C-
Q4-18	C	C+	C-
Q4-17	C-	C	D+
Q4-16	C-	C	D

Asset & Performance History

Date	NAV	1-Year Total Return
1	1.19	Cash
2018	1	0.86
2017	1	0.06
2016	1	-0.09
2015		-0.53
2014		-0.54

Total Assets: $51,700,969,068

Asset Allocation

Asset	%
71%	
Bonds	29%
Govt Bond	29%
Muni Bond	0%
Corp Bond	0%
Other	0%

Company Information

Provider	Morgan Stanley
Manager/Tenure	Management Team (11)
Website	http://www.morganstanley.com
Address	Morgan Stanley 1221 Avenue of the Americas New York NY 10020 United States
Phone Number	855-332-5306

Services Offered: Qualified Investment, Phone Exchange, Wire Redemption

Investment Strategy: The investment seeks preservation of capital, daily liquidity and maximum current income. The Portfolio has adopted a policy to invest exclusively in U.S. Treasury obligations, which are backed by the full faith and credit of the United States, in order to qualify as a "government money market fund" under federal regulations. A "government money market fund" is a money market fund that invests at least 99.5% of its total assets in cash, securities issued or guaranteed by the United States or certain U.S. government agencies or instrumentalities and/or repurchase agreements that are collateralized fully by the foregoing. **Top Holdings:** United States Treasury Notes 0.25% United States Treasury Notes 0.18% United States Treasury Bills 0.01% United States Treasury Bills 0.01% United States Treasury Notes 0.43%

Lord Abbett Short Duration Income Fund Class A — C HOLD

Ticker	Traded On	NAV	Total Assets ($)	Dividend Yield (TTM)	Turnover Ratio	Expense Ratio
LALDX	NAS CM	4.15	$51,495,822,734	3.42	57	0.6

Ratings

Reward	C-
Risk	C
Recent Upgrade/Downgrade	

Fund Information

Fund Type	Open End
Category	US Fixed Inc
Sub-Category	Short-Term Bond
Prospectus Objective	Income
Inception Date	Nov-93
Open to New Investments	Y
Minimum Initial Investment	1,500
Minimum Subsequent Investment	
Front End Fee	2.25
Back End Fee	

Total Returns (%)

3-Month	6-Month	1-Year	3-Year	5-Year
5.88	0.14	1.62	7.78	12.75

3-Year Standard Deviation	4.31
Effective Duration	1.58
Average Coupon Rate	3.42

Company Information

Provider	Lord Abbett
Manager/Tenure	Robert A. Lee (21), Andrew H. O'Brien (12), Kewjin Yuoh (8), 1 other
Website	http://www.lordabbett.com
Address	Lord Abbett 90 Hudson Street Jersey City NJ 7302 United States
Phone Number	201-827-2000

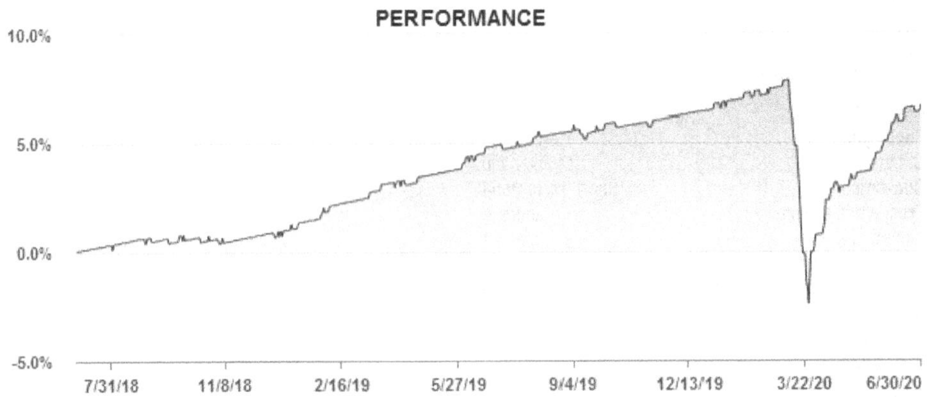

Ratings History

Date	Overall Rating	Risk Rating	Reward Rating
Q2-20	CC	C-	2019
Q4-19	C	B-	C
Q4-18	C+	B	C
Q4-17	B-	A-	C
Q4-16	C	C+	C

Asset & Performance History

Date	NAV	1-Year Total Return
4.21	5.42	Cash
2018	4.14	1.23
2017	4.25	2.26
2016	4.31	4.02
2015	4.31	0.43
2014	4.46	1.73

Total Assets: $51,495,822,734

Asset Allocation

Asset	%
3%	
Bonds	96%
Govt Bond	4%
Muni Bond	0%
Corp Bond	51%
Other	0%

Services Offered: Systematic Withdrawal Plan, Automatic Investment Plan, Phone Exchange, Wire Redemption, Retirement Investment

Investment Strategy: The investment seeks a high level of income consistent with preservation of capital. The fund invests primarily in various types of short duration debt (or fixed income) securities. It invests at least 65% of its net assets in investment grade debt securities including corporate debt securities of U.S. issuers; corporate debt securities of non-U.S. (including emerging market) issuers that are denominated in U.S. dollars; mortgage backed, mortgage-related, and other asset-backed securities; and securities issued or guaranteed by the U.S. government, its agencies and instrumentalities; and inflation-linked investments. **Top Holdings:** Boeing Co BX COMMERCIAL MORTGAGE TRUST 1.62% AT&T Inc 3.07% Dbwf 2018-Amxp Mortgage Trust 3.75% Abe Investment Holdings, Inc.

Lord Abbett Short Duration Income Fund Class F — C HOLD

Ticker	Traded On	NAV	Total Assets ($)	Dividend Yield (TTM)	Turnover Ratio	Expense Ratio
LDLFX	NAS CM	4.14	$51,495,822,734	3.52	57	0.5

Ratings

Reward	C-
Risk	C
Recent Upgrade/Downgrade	

Fund Information

Fund Type	Open End
Category	US Fixed Inc
Sub-Category	Short-Term Bond
Prospectus Objective	Income
Inception Date	Sep-07
Open to New Investments	Y
Minimum Initial Investment	0
Minimum Subsequent Investment	
Front End Fee	
Back End Fee	

Total Returns (%)

3-Month	6-Month	1-Year	3-Year	5-Year
5.65	-0.05	1.72	7.83	13.02

3-Year Standard Deviation	4.27
Effective Duration	1.58
Average Coupon Rate	3.42

Company Information

Provider	Lord Abbett
Manager/Tenure	Robert A. Lee (21), Andrew H. O'Brien (12), Kewjin Yuoh (8), 1 other
Website	http://www.lordabbett.com
Address	Lord Abbett 90 Hudson Street Jersey City NJ 7302 United States
Phone Number	201-827-2000

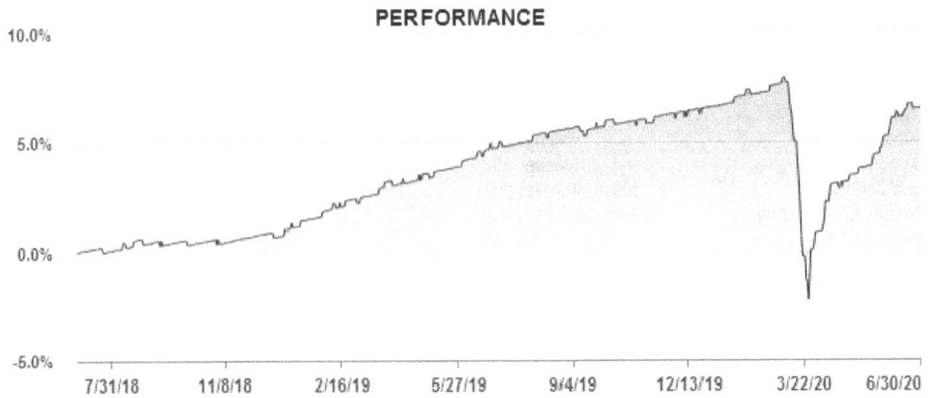

Ratings History

Date	Overall Rating	Risk Rating	Reward Rating
Q2-20	CC	C-	2019
Q4-19	C	B	C
Q4-18	C+	B	C
Q4-17	B-	A-	C
Q4-16	C	C+	C

Asset & Performance History

Date	NAV	1-Year Total Return
4.21	5.52	Cash
2018	4.14	1.31
2017	4.25	2.59
2016	4.3	3.88
2015	4.31	0.75
2014	4.45	1.6

Total Assets: $51,495,822,734

Asset Allocation

Asset	%
3%	
Bonds	96%
Govt Bond	4%
Muni Bond	0%
Corp Bond	51%
Other	0%

Services Offered: Systematic Withdrawal Plan, Qualified Investment, Phone Exchange, Wire Redemption

Investment Strategy: The investment seeks a high level of income consistent with preservation of capital. The fund invests primarily in various types of short duration debt (or fixed income) securities. It invests at least 65% of its net assets in investment grade debt securities including corporate debt securities of U.S. issuers; corporate debt securities of non-U.S. (including emerging market) issuers that are denominated in U.S. dollars; mortgage backed, mortgage-related, and other asset-backed securities; and securities issued or guaranteed by the U.S. government, its agencies and instrumentalities; and inflation-linked investments. **Top Holdings:** Boeing Co BX COMMERCIAL MORTGAGE TRUST 1.62% AT&T Inc 3.07% Dbwf 2018-Amxp Mortgage Trust 3.75% Abe Investment Holdings, Inc.

Lord Abbett Short Duration Income Fund Class R5 — C HOLD

Ticker	Traded On	NAV	Total Assets ($)	Dividend Yield (TTM)	Turnover Ratio	Expense Ratio
LDLTX	NAS CM	4.14	$51,495,822,734	3.62	57	0.4

Ratings

Reward	C-
Risk	C
Recent Upgrade/Downgrade	

Fund Information

Fund Type	Open End
Category	US Fixed Inc
Sub-Category	Short-Term Bond
Prospectus Objective	Income
Inception Date	Jun-15
Open to New Investments	Y
Minimum Initial Investment	0
Minimum Subsequent Investment	
Front End Fee	
Back End Fee	

Total Returns (%)

3-Month	6-Month	1-Year	3-Year	5-Year
5.67	0.22	1.81	8.44	13.62

3-Year Standard Deviation	4.29
Effective Duration	1.58
Average Coupon Rate	3.42

Company Information

Provider	Lord Abbett
Manager/Tenure	Robert A. Lee (21), Andrew H. O'Brien (12), Kewjin Yuoh (8), 1 other
Website	http://www.lordabbett.com
Address	Lord Abbett 90 Hudson Street Jersey City NJ 7302 United States
Phone Number	201-827-2000

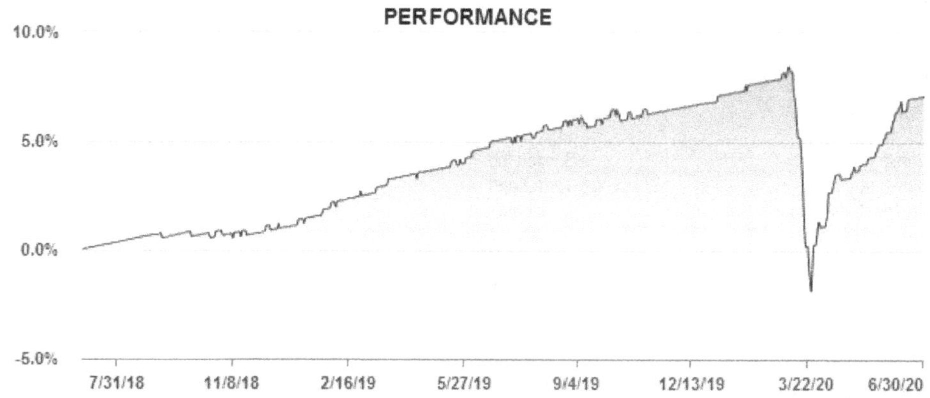

Ratings History

Date	Overall Rating	Risk Rating	Reward Rating
Q2-20	CC	C-	2019
Q4-19	C	B	C
Q4-18	C+	B	C
Q4-17	B-	A-	C
Q4-16	C	C+	C

Asset & Performance History

Date	NAV	1-Year Total Return
4.2	5.64	Cash
2018	4.13	1.42
2017	4.24	2.46
2016	4.3	3.99
2015	4.31	0.75
2014		1.73

Total Assets: $51,495,822,734

Asset Allocation

Asset	%
3%	
Bonds	96%
Govt Bond	4%
Muni Bond	0%
Corp Bond	51%
Other	0%

Services Offered: Systematic Withdrawal Plan, Qualified Investment, Phone Exchange, Wire Redemption

Investment Strategy: The investment seeks a high level of income consistent with preservation of capital. The fund invests primarily in various types of short duration debt (or fixed income) securities. It invests at least 65% of its net assets in investment grade debt securities including corporate debt securities of U.S. issuers; corporate debt securities of non-U.S. (including emerging market) issuers that are denominated in U.S. dollars; mortgage backed, mortgage-related, and other asset-backed securities; and securities issued or guaranteed by the U.S. government, its agencies and instrumentalities; and inflation-linked investments. **Top Holdings:** Boeing Co BX COMMERCIAL MORTGAGE TRUST 1.62% AT&T Inc 3.07% Dbwf 2018-Amxp Mortgage Trust 3.75% Abe Investment Holdings, Inc.

Lord Abbett Short Duration Income Fund Class R3 — C- HOLD

Ticker	Traded On	NAV	Total Assets ($)	Dividend Yield (TTM)	Turnover Ratio	Expense Ratio
LDLRX	NAS CM	4.15	$51,495,822,734	3.12	57	0.9

Ratings

Reward	D+
Risk	C
Recent Upgrade/Downgrade	Down

Fund Information

Fund Type	Open End
Category	US Fixed Inc
Sub-Category	Short-Term Bond
Prospectus Objective	Income
Inception Date	Jul-09
Open to New Investments	Y
Minimum Initial Investment	0
Minimum Subsequent Investment	
Front End Fee	
Back End Fee	

Total Returns (%)

3-Month	6-Month	1-Year	3-Year	5-Year
5.53	0.00	1.32	6.59	10.87

3-Year Standard Deviation	4.25
Effective Duration	1.58
Average Coupon Rate	3.42

Company Information

Provider	Lord Abbett
Manager/Tenure	Robert A. Lee (21), Andrew H. O'Brien (12), Kewjin Yuoh (8), 1 other
Website	http://www.lordabbett.com
Address	Lord Abbett 90 Hudson Street Jersey City NJ 7302 United States
Phone Number	201-827-2000

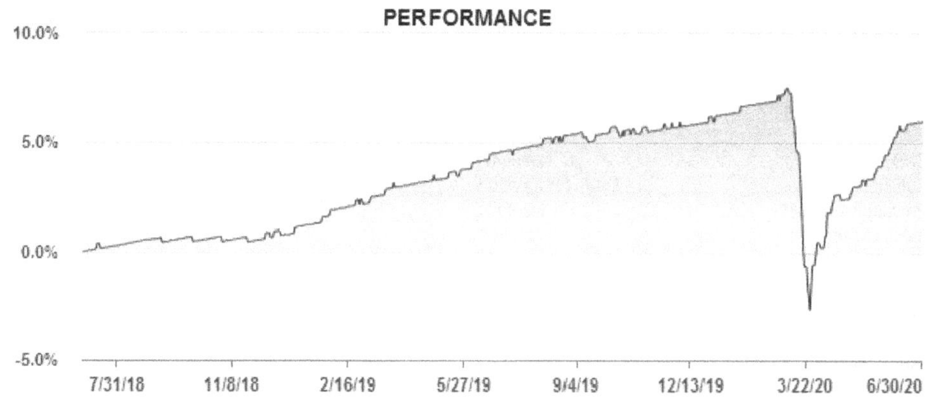

Ratings History

Date	Overall Rating	Risk Rating	Reward Rating
Q2-20	C-C	D+	2019
Q4-19	C	B-	C
Q4-18	C	B	C
Q4-17	B-	B+	C
Q4-16	C	C	C

Asset & Performance History

Date	NAV	1-Year Total Return
4.21	4.86	Cash
2018	4.15	1.16
2017	4.25	1.96
2016	4.31	3.49
2015	4.32	0.37
2014	4.46	1.21

Total Assets: $51,495,822,734

Asset Allocation

Asset	%
3%	
Bonds	96%
Govt Bond	4%
Muni Bond	0%
Corp Bond	51%
Other	0%

Services Offered: Systematic Withdrawal Plan, Qualified Investment, Phone Exchange, Wire Redemption

Investment Strategy: The investment seeks a high level of income consistent with preservation of capital. The fund invests primarily in various types of short duration debt (or fixed income) securities. It invests at least 65% of its net assets in investment grade debt securities including corporate debt securities of U.S. issuers; corporate debt securities of non-U.S. (including emerging market) issuers that are denominated in U.S. dollars; mortgage backed, mortgage-related, and other asset-backed securities; and securities issued or guaranteed by the U.S. government, its agencies and instrumentalities; and inflation-linked investments. **Top Holdings:** Boeing Co BX COMMERCIAL MORTGAGE TRUST 1.62% AT&T Inc 3.07% Dbwf 2018-Amxp Mortgage Trust 3.75% Abe Investment Holdings, Inc.

Lord Abbett Short Duration Income Fund Class F3 — C HOLD

Ticker	Traded On	NAV	Total Assets ($)	Dividend Yield (TTM)	Turnover Ratio	Expense Ratio
LOLDX	NAS CM	4.15	$51,495,822,734	3.68	57	0.34

Ratings

Reward	C-
Risk	C
Recent Upgrade/Downgrade	

Fund Information

Fund Type	Open End
Category	US Fixed Inc
Sub-Category	Short-Term Bond
Prospectus Objective	Income
Inception Date	Apr-17
Open to New Investments	Y
Minimum Initial Investment	0
Minimum Subsequent Investment	
Front End Fee	
Back End Fee	

Total Returns (%)

3-Month	6-Month	1-Year	3-Year	5-Year
5.68	0.02	1.88	8.60	13.66

3-Year Standard Deviation	4.24
Effective Duration	1.58
Average Coupon Rate	3.42

Company Information

Provider	Lord Abbett
Manager/Tenure	Robert A. Lee (21), Andrew H. O'Brien (12), Kewjin Yuoh (8), 1 other
Website	http://www.lordabbett.com
Address	Lord Abbett 90 Hudson Street Jersey City NJ 7302 United States
Phone Number	201-827-2000

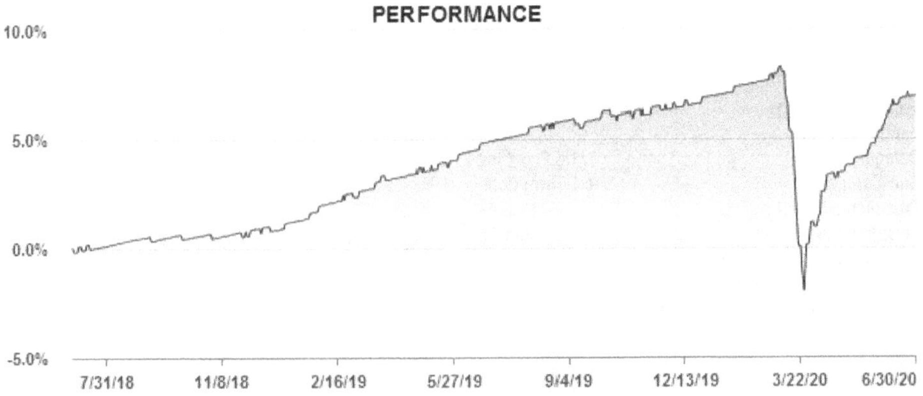

Ratings History

Date	Overall Rating	Risk Rating	Reward Rating
Q2-20	CC	C-	2019
Q4-19	C+	B	C
Q4-18	C+	B	C
Q4-17	B-	A-	C
Q4-16			

Asset & Performance History

Date	NAV	1-Year Total Return
4.22	5.69	Cash
2018	4.15	1.71
2017	4.25	2.13
2016		
2015		0.43
2014		1.73

Total Assets: $51,495,822,734

Asset Allocation

Asset	%
3%	
Bonds	96%
Govt Bond	4%
Muni Bond	0%
Corp Bond	51%
Other	0%

Services Offered: Qualified Investment, Phone Exchange, Wire Redemption

Investment Strategy: The investment seeks a high level of income consistent with preservation of capital. The fund invests primarily in various types of short duration debt (or fixed income) securities. It invests at least 65% of its net assets in investment grade debt securities including corporate debt securities of U.S. issuers; corporate debt securities of non-U.S. (including emerging market) issuers that are denominated in U.S. dollars; mortgage backed, mortgage-related, and other asset-backed securities; and securities issued or guaranteed by the U.S. government, its agencies and instrumentalities; and inflation-linked investments. **Top Holdings:** Boeing Co BX COMMERCIAL MORTGAGE TRUST 1.62% AT&T Inc 3.07% Dbwf 2018-Amxp Mortgage Trust 3.75% Abe Investment Holdings, Inc.

Lord Abbett Short Duration Income Fund Class C — C- HOLD

Ticker	Traded On	NAV	Total Assets ($)	Dividend Yield (TTM)	Turnover Ratio	Expense Ratio
LDLAX	NAS CM	4.17	$51,495,822,734	2.78	57	1.22

Ratings

Reward	D+
Risk	C
Recent Upgrade/Downgrade	

Fund Information

Fund Type	Open End
Category	US Fixed Inc
Sub-Category	Short-Term Bond
Prospectus Objective	Income
Inception Date	Jul-96
Open to New Investments	Y
Minimum Initial Investment	1,500
Minimum Subsequent Investment	
Front End Fee	
Back End Fee	1.00

Total Returns (%)

3-Month	6-Month	1-Year	3-Year	5-Year
5.42	-0.40	0.99	5.54	9.04

3-Year Standard Deviation	4.21
Effective Duration	1.58
Average Coupon Rate	3.42

Company Information

Provider	Lord Abbett
Manager/Tenure	Robert A. Lee (21), Andrew H. O'Brien (12), Kewjin Yuoh (8), 1 other
Website	http://www.lordabbett.com
Address	Lord Abbett 90 Hudson Street Jersey City NJ 7302 United States
Phone Number	201-827-2000

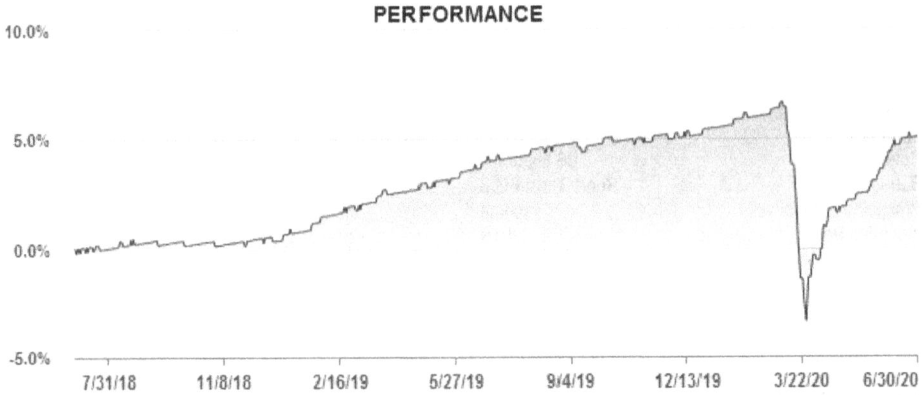

Ratings History

Date	Overall Rating	Risk Rating	Reward Rating
Q2-20	C-C	D+	2019
Q4-19	C	B-	C
Q4-18	C	B-	C-
Q4-17	C+	B+	C
Q4-16	C	C	C

Asset & Performance History

Date	NAV	1-Year Total Return
4.24	4.75	Cash
2018	4.17	0.6
2017	4.28	1.86
2016	4.33	3.13
2015	4.34	-0.18
2014	4.49	1.07

Total Assets: $51,495,822,734

Asset Allocation

Asset	%
3%	
Bonds	96%
Govt Bond	4%
Muni Bond	0%
Corp Bond	51%
Other	0%

Services Offered: Systematic Withdrawal Plan, Automatic Investment Plan, Phone Exchange, Wire Redemption, Retirement Investment

Investment Strategy: The investment seeks a high level of income consistent with preservation of capital. The fund invests primarily in various types of short duration debt (or fixed income) securities. It invests at least 65% of its net assets in investment grade debt securities including corporate debt securities of U.S. issuers; corporate debt securities of non-U.S. (including emerging market) issuers that are denominated in U.S. dollars; mortgage backed, mortgage-related, and other asset-backed securities; and securities issued or guaranteed by the U.S. government, its agencies and instrumentalities; and inflation-linked investments. **Top Holdings:** Boeing Co BX COMMERCIAL MORTGAGE TRUST 1.62% AT&T Inc 3.07% Dbwf 2018-Amxp Mortgage Trust 3.75% Abe Investment Holdings, Inc.

Lord Abbett Short Duration Income Fund Class R2 — C- HOLD

Ticker	Traded On	NAV	Total Assets ($)	Dividend Yield (TTM)	Turnover Ratio	Expense Ratio
LDLQX	NAS CM	4.15	$51,495,822,734	3.02	57	1

Ratings

Reward	D+
Risk	C
Recent Upgrade/Downgrade	Down

Fund Information

Fund Type	Open End
Category	US Fixed Inc
Sub-Category	Short-Term Bond
Prospectus Objective	Income
Inception Date	Jul-09
Open to New Investments	Y
Minimum Initial Investment	0
Minimum Subsequent Investment	
Front End Fee	
Back End Fee	

Total Returns (%)

3-Month	6-Month	1-Year	3-Year	5-Year
5.51	-0.05	1.22	6.51	10.55

3-Year Standard Deviation	4.27
Effective Duration	1.58
Average Coupon Rate	3.42

Company Information

Provider	Lord Abbett
Manager/Tenure	Robert A. Lee (21), Andrew H. O'Brien (12), Kewjin Yuoh (8), 1 other
Website	http://www.lordabbett.com
Address	Lord Abbett 90 Hudson Street Jersey City NJ 7302 United States
Phone Number	201-827-2000

PERFORMANCE

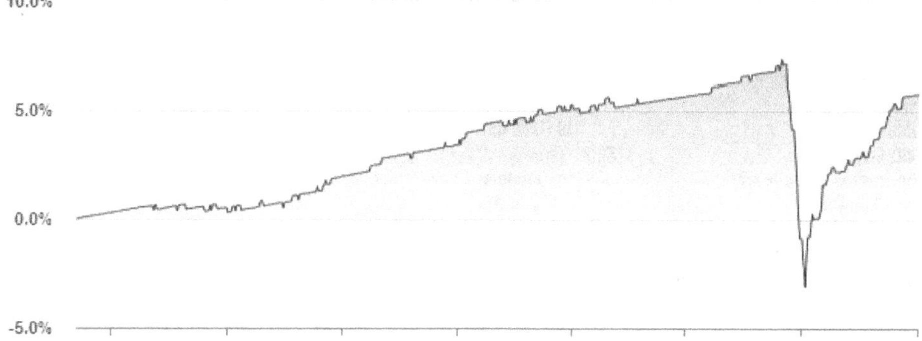

Ratings History

Date	Overall Rating	Risk Rating	Reward Rating
Q2-20	C-C	D+	2019
Q4-19	C	B-	C
Q4-18	C	B-	C
Q4-17	B-	B+	C
Q4-16	C+	B-	C

Asset & Performance History

Date	NAV	1-Year Total Return
4.21	5.01	Cash
2018	4.14	0.81
2017	4.25	1.85
2016	4.31	3.61
2015	4.31	0.03
2014	4.46	1.33

Total Assets: $51,495,822,734

Asset Allocation

Asset	%
3%	
Bonds	96%
Govt Bond	4%
Muni Bond	0%
Corp Bond	51%
Other	0%

Services Offered: Systematic Withdrawal Plan, Qualified Investment, Phone Exchange, Wire Redemption

Investment Strategy: The investment seeks a high level of income consistent with preservation of capital. The fund invests primarily in various types of short duration debt (or fixed income) securities. It invests at least 65% of its net assets in investment grade debt securities including corporate debt securities of U.S. issuers; corporate debt securities of non-U.S. (including emerging market) issuers that are denominated in U.S. dollars; mortgage backed, mortgage-related, and other asset-backed securities; and securities issued or guaranteed by the U.S. government, its agencies and instrumentalities; and inflation-linked investments. **Top Holdings:** Boeing Co BX COMMERCIAL MORTGAGE TRUST 1.62% AT&T Inc 3.07% Dbwf 2018-Amxp Mortgage Trust 3.75% Abe Investment Holdings, Inc.

Lord Abbett Short Duration Income Fund Class R4 — C HOLD

Ticker	Traded On	NAV	Total Assets ($)	Dividend Yield (TTM)	Turnover Ratio	Expense Ratio
LDLKX	NAS CM	4.15	$51,495,822,734	3.36	57	0.65

Ratings

Reward	C-
Risk	C
Recent Upgrade/Downgrade	

Fund Information

Fund Type	Open End
Category	US Fixed Inc
Sub-Category	Short-Term Bond
Prospectus Objective	Income
Inception Date	Jun-15
Open to New Investments	Y
Minimum Initial Investment	0
Minimum Subsequent Investment	
Front End Fee	
Back End Fee	

Total Returns (%)

3-Month	6-Month	1-Year	3-Year	5-Year
5.60	-0.12	1.57	7.39	12.24

3-Year Standard Deviation	4.27
Effective Duration	1.58
Average Coupon Rate	3.42

Company Information

Provider	Lord Abbett
Manager/Tenure	Robert A. Lee (21), Andrew H. O'Brien (12), Kewjin Yuoh (8), 1 other
Website	http://www.lordabbett.com
Address	Lord Abbett 90 Hudson Street Jersey City NJ 7302 United States
Phone Number	201-827-2000

PERFORMANCE

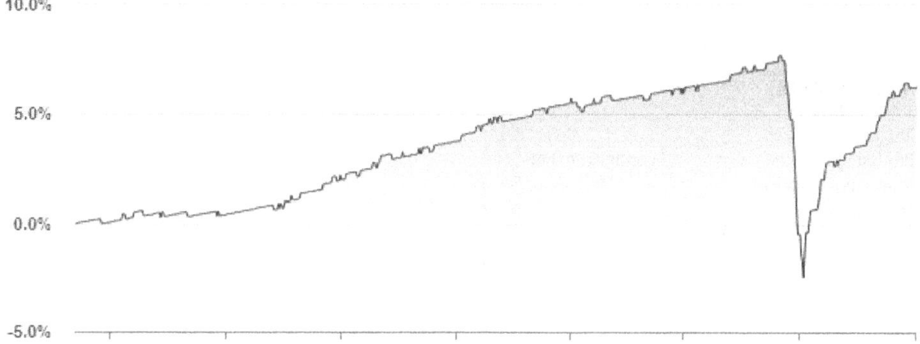

Ratings History

Date	Overall Rating	Risk Rating	Reward Rating
Q2-20	CC	C-	2019
Q4-19	C	B-	C
Q4-18	C	B	C
Q4-17	B-	A-	C
Q4-16	C	C+	C

Asset & Performance History

Date	NAV	1-Year Total Return
4.22	5.37	Cash
2018	4.15	1.19
2017	4.26	2.45
2016	4.31	3.73
2015	4.32	0.62
2014		1.67

Total Assets: $51,495,822,734

Asset Allocation

Asset	%
3%	
Bonds	96%
Govt Bond	4%
Muni Bond	0%
Corp Bond	51%
Other	0%

Services Offered: Systematic Withdrawal Plan, Qualified Investment, Phone Exchange, Wire Redemption

Investment Strategy: The investment seeks a high level of income consistent with preservation of capital. The fund invests primarily in various types of short duration debt (or fixed income) securities. It invests at least 65% of its net assets in investment grade debt securities including corporate debt securities of U.S. issuers; corporate debt securities of non-U.S. (including emerging market) issuers that are denominated in U.S. dollars; mortgage backed, mortgage-related, and other asset-backed securities; and securities issued or guaranteed by the U.S. government, its agencies and instrumentalities; and inflation-linked investments. **Top Holdings:** Boeing Co BX COMMERCIAL MORTGAGE TRUST 1.62% AT&T Inc 3.07% Dbwf 2018-Amxp Mortgage Trust 3.75% Abe Investment Holdings, Inc.

Lord Abbett Short Duration Income Fund Class R6 — C HOLD

Ticker	Traded On	NAV	Total Assets ($)	Dividend Yield (TTM)	Turnover Ratio	Expense Ratio
LDLVX	NAS CM	4.14	$51,495,822,734	3.68	57	0.34

Ratings

Reward	C-
Risk	C
Recent Upgrade/Downgrade	

Fund Information

Fund Type	Open End
Category	US Fixed Inc
Sub-Category	Short-Term Bond
Prospectus Objective	Income
Inception Date	Jun-15
Open to New Investments	Y
Minimum Initial Investment	0
Minimum Subsequent Investment	
Front End Fee	
Back End Fee	

Total Returns (%)

3-Month	6-Month	1-Year	3-Year	5-Year
5.69	0.02	1.88	8.37	13.98

3-Year Standard Deviation	4.27
Effective Duration	1.58
Average Coupon Rate	3.42

Company Information

Provider	Lord Abbett
Manager/Tenure	Robert A. Lee (21), Andrew H. O'Brien (12), Kewjin Yuoh (8), 1 other
Website	http://www.lordabbett.com
Address	Lord Abbett 90 Hudson Street Jersey City NJ 7302 United States
Phone Number	201-827-2000

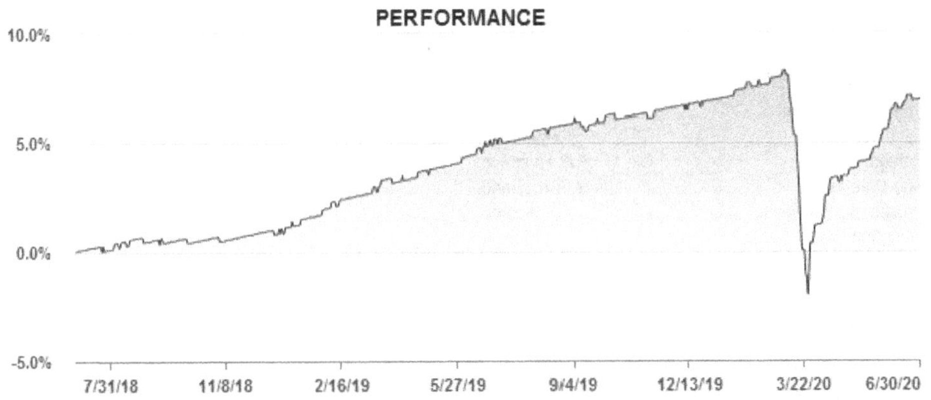

Ratings History

Date	Overall Rating	Risk Rating	Reward Rating
Q2-20	CC	C-	2019
Q4-19	C+	B	C
Q4-18	C+	B	C
Q4-17	B	A	C
Q4-16	C	C+	C

Asset & Performance History

Date	NAV	1-Year Total Return
4.21	5.7	Cash
2018	4.14	1.48
2017	4.25	2.52
2016	4.31	4.31
2015	4.31	0.79
2014		1.73

Total Assets: $51,495,822,734

Asset Allocation

Asset	%
3%	
Bonds	96%
Govt Bond	4%
Muni Bond	0%
Corp Bond	51%
Other	0%

Services Offered: Systematic Withdrawal Plan, Qualified Investment, Phone Exchange, Wire Redemption

Investment Strategy: The investment seeks a high level of income consistent with preservation of capital. The fund invests primarily in various types of short duration debt (or fixed income) securities. It invests at least 65% of its net assets in investment grade debt securities including corporate debt securities of U.S. issuers; corporate debt securities of non-U.S. (including emerging market) issuers that are denominated in U.S. dollars; mortgage backed, mortgage-related, and other asset-backed securities; and securities issued or guaranteed by the U.S. government, its agencies and instrumentalities; and inflation-linked investments. **Top Holdings:** Boeing Co BX COMMERCIAL MORTGAGE TRUST 1.62% AT&T Inc 3.07% Dbwf 2018-Amxp Mortgage Trust 3.75% Abe Investment Holdings, Inc.

Fidelity® U.S. Bond Index Fund — B BUY

Ticker	Traded On	NAV	Total Assets ($)	Dividend Yield (TTM)	Turnover Ratio	Expense Ratio
FXNAX	NAS CM	12.54	$50,694,291,205	2.46	35	0.03

Ratings

Reward	B-
Risk	B+
Recent Upgrade/Downgrade	

Fund Information

Fund Type	Open End
Category	US Fixed Inc
Sub-Category	Intermediate Core Bond
Prospectus Objective	Multisector Bond
Inception Date	May-11
Open to New Investments	Y
Minimum Initial Investment	0
Minimum Subsequent Investment	
Front End Fee	
Back End Fee	

Total Returns (%)

3-Month	6-Month	1-Year	3-Year	5-Year
2.77	6.54	9.01	17.02	23.88

3-Year Standard Deviation	3.29
Effective Duration	5.48
Average Coupon Rate	3.06

Company Information

Provider	Fidelity Investments
Manager/Tenure	Brandon Bettencourt (6), Jay Small (5)
Website	http://www.institutional.fidelity.com
Address	Fidelity Investments 82 Devonshire Street Boston MA 2109 United States
Phone Number	617-563-7000

Ratings History

Date	Overall Rating	Risk Rating	Reward Rating
Q2-20	BB+	B-	2019
Q4-19	C	B	C
Q4-18	C-	C+	D+
Q4-17	B-	B+	C
Q4-16	C	B-	C

Asset & Performance History

Date	NAV	1-Year Total Return
11.91	8.46	Cash
2018	11.28	-0.01
2017	11.59	3.46
2016	11.49	2.48
2015	11.49	0.62
2014	11.73	5.97

Total Assets: $50,694,291,205

Asset Allocation

Asset	%
3%	
Bonds	96%
Govt Bond	45%
Muni Bond	0%
Corp Bond	24%
Other	0%

Services Offered: Systematic Withdrawal Plan, Automatic Investment Plan, Qualified Investment, Phone Exchange, Wire Redemption, Retirement Investment

Investment Strategy: The investment seeks to provide investment results that correspond to the aggregate price and interest performance of the debt securities in the Bloomberg Barclays U.S. Aggregate Bond Index. The fund normally invests at least 80% of the fund's assets in bonds included in the Bloomberg Barclays U.S. Aggregate Bond Index. Its manager uses statistical sampling techniques based on duration, maturity, interest rate sensitivity, security structure, and credit quality to attempt to replicate the returns of the Bloomberg Barclays U.S. Aggregate Bond Index using a smaller number of securities. The fund invests in Fidelity's central funds. **Top Holdings:** Fannie Mae 3% 30 Year Fannie Mae 3.5% 30 Year Ginnie Mae 3.5% 30 Year Fannie Mae 4% 30 Year Freddie Mac 3.5% 30 Year

DoubleLine Total Return Bond Fund Class R6 — C HOLD

Ticker	Traded On	NAV	Total Assets ($)	Dividend Yield (TTM)	Turnover Ratio	Expense Ratio
DDTRX	NAS CM	10.72	$50,032,252,577		31	0.43

Ratings

Reward	C
Risk	C+
Recent Upgrade/Downgrade	

Fund Information

Fund Type	Open End
Category	US Fixed Inc
Sub-Category	Intermediate Core-Plus Bond
Prospectus Objective	Govt Bond - General
Inception Date	Jul-19
Open to New Investments	Y
Minimum Initial Investment	0
Minimum Subsequent Investment	
Front End Fee	
Back End Fee	

Total Returns (%)

3-Month	6-Month	1-Year	3-Year	5-Year
3.42	2.55	4.19	11.98	18.96

3-Year Standard Deviation	3.44
Effective Duration	3.23
Average Coupon Rate	3.23

Ratings History

Date	Overall Rating	Risk Rating	Reward Rating
Q2-20	CC+	C	2019
Q4-19	C	B	C
Q4-18			
Q4-17			
Q4-16			

Asset & Performance History

Date	NAV	1-Year Total Return
10.64	5.93	Cash
2018		
2017		
2016		
2015		
2014		

Total Assets: $50,032,252,577

Asset Allocation

Asset	%
0%	
Bonds	100%
Govt Bond	11%
Muni Bond	0%
Corp Bond	1%
Other	0%

Company Information

Provider	DoubleLine
Manager/Tenure	Jeffrey E. Gundlach (10), Andrew Hsu (0)
Website	http://www.doublelinefunds.com
Address	DoubleLine 333 South Grand Avenue Los Angeles CA 90071 United States
Phone Number	877-354-6311

Services Offered: Systematic Withdrawal Plan, Automatic Investment Plan, Qualified Investment, Phone Exchange, Wire Redemption

Investment Strategy: The investment seeks to maximize total return. The advisor intends to invest at least 80% of the fund's net assets (plus the amount of borrowings for investment purposes) in bonds. Bonds include bonds, debt securities, and other fixed income instruments issued by governmental or private-sector entities. Under normal circumstances, the advisor intends to invest more than 50% of the fund's net assets in residential and commercial mortgage-backed securities. **Top Holdings:** 10 Year Treasury Note Future June 20 United States Treasury Notes 1.75% United States Treasury Notes 1.5% United States Treasury Notes 2.38% United States Treasury Notes 3.13%

DoubleLine Total Return Bond Fund Class N — C HOLD

Ticker	Traded On	NAV	Total Assets ($)	Dividend Yield (TTM)	Turnover Ratio	Expense Ratio
DLTNX	NAS CM	10.71	$50,032,252,577	3.36	31	0.73

Ratings

Reward	C
Risk	B-
Recent Upgrade/Downgrade	

Fund Information

Fund Type	Open End
Category	US Fixed Inc
Sub-Category	Intermediate Core-Plus Bond
Prospectus Objective	Govt Bond - General
Inception Date	Apr-10
Open to New Investments	Y
Minimum Initial Investment	2,000
Minimum Subsequent Investment	100
Front End Fee	
Back End Fee	

Total Returns (%)

3-Month	6-Month	1-Year	3-Year	5-Year
3.24	2.40	3.78	10.99	17.32

3-Year Standard Deviation	3.4
Effective Duration	3.23
Average Coupon Rate	3.23

Ratings History

Date	Overall Rating	Risk Rating	Reward Rating
Q2-20	CB-	C	2019
Q4-19	C+	B	C
Q4-18	C	B-	C-
Q4-17	B	A+	C
Q4-16	C	B-	C

Asset & Performance History

Date	NAV	1-Year Total Return
10.63	5.64	Cash
2018	10.41	1.49
2017	10.62	3.43
2016	10.62	1.91
2015	10.78	2.06
2014	10.97	6.47

Total Assets: $50,032,252,577

Asset Allocation

Asset	%
0%	
Bonds	100%
Govt Bond	11%
Muni Bond	0%
Corp Bond	1%
Other	0%

Company Information

Provider	DoubleLine
Manager/Tenure	Jeffrey E. Gundlach (10), Andrew Hsu (0)
Website	http://www.doublelinefunds.com
Address	DoubleLine 333 South Grand Avenue Los Angeles CA 90071 United States
Phone Number	877-354-6311

Services Offered: Systematic Withdrawal Plan, Automatic Investment Plan, Phone Exchange, Wire Redemption, Retirement Investment

Investment Strategy: The investment seeks to maximize total return. The advisor intends to invest at least 80% of the fund's net assets (plus the amount of borrowings for investment purposes) in bonds. Bonds include bonds, debt securities, and other fixed income instruments issued by governmental or private-sector entities. Under normal circumstances, the advisor intends to invest more than 50% of the fund's net assets in residential and commercial mortgage-backed securities. **Top Holdings:** 10 Year Treasury Note Future June 20 United States Treasury Notes 1.75% United States Treasury Notes 1.5% United States Treasury Notes 2.38% United States Treasury Notes 3.13%

Section III:
Best All-Around Bond & Money Market Mutual Funds

Investment Ratings and analysis of the Best All-Around Bond & Money Market Mutual Funds. Funds are listed in order by their dividend yield and overall rating.

Section III: Contents

This section contains Weiss Investment Ratings, key rating factors, and summary financial data for our selections for "Best All-Around Bond & Money Market Mutual Funds." We have selected what we believe provides a better return for those funds with over $1 billion in assets and with a maximum initial investment of $5,000 or less required. Funds are listed in order by their dividend yield and overall rating.

Fund Name

Describes the fund's assets, regions of investments and investment strategies. Many funds have similar names, so you want to make sure the fund you look up is really the one you are interested in evaluating.

Ticker Symbol

An arrangement of characters (usually letters) representing a particular security listed on an exchange or otherwise traded publicly. When a company issues securities to the public marketplace, it selects an available ticker symbol for its securities which investors use to place trade orders. Every listed security has a unique ticker symbol, facilitating the vast array of trade orders that flow through the financial markets every day. If a ticker symbol is not assigned to a particular fund, the International Securities Identification Number (ISIN) is displayed.

RATINGS

Overall Rating

The Weiss rating measured on a scale from A to E based on each fund's risk and performance. See the preceding section, "What Our Ratings Mean," for an explanation of each letter grade rating.

Reward Rating

This is based on the total return over a period of up to five years, including net asset value and price growth. The total return figure is stated net of the expenses and fees charged by the fund. Based on proprietary modeling the individual components of the risk and reward ratings are calculated and weighted and the final rating is generated.

Risk Rating

This is includes the risk ratings of component stocks where applicable and also includes the financial stability of the fund, turnover where applicable, together with the level of volatility as measured by the fund's daily returns over a period of up to five years. Funds with greater stability are considered less risky and receive a higher risk rating. Funds with greater volatility are considered riskier, and will receive a lower risk rating. In addition to considering the fund's volatility, the risk rating also considers an assessment of the valuation and quality of a fund's holdings.

Recent Upgrade/Downgrade

An "Up" or "Down" indicates that the Weiss Mutual Fund rating has changed since the publication of the last print edition. If a fund has had a rating change since March 31, 2020, the change is identified with an "Up" or "Down."

TOTAL RETURNS & PERFORMANCE

3-Month Total Return
The rate of return on an investment over three months that includes interest, capital gains, dividends and distributions realized.

6-Month Total Return
The rate of return on an investment over six months that includes interest, capital gains, dividends and distributions realized.

1-Year Total Return
The rate of return on an investment over one year that includes interest, capital gains, dividends and distributions realized.

3-Year Total Return
The rate of return on an investment over three years that includes interest, capital gains, dividends and distributions realized.

Dividend Yield (TTM)
Trailing twelve months dividends paid out relative to the share price. Expressed as a percentage and measures how much cash flow an investor is getting for each invested dollar. **Trailing Twelve Months** (TTM) is a representation of a fund's financial performance over the most recent 12 months. TTM uses the latest available financial data from a company's interim, quarterly or annual reports.

ASSETS

NAV (Net Asset Value)
A fund's price per share. The value is calculated by dividing the total value of all the securities in the portfolio, less any liabilities, by the number of fund shares outstanding.

Total Assets (MIL)
The total of all assets listed on the institution's balance sheet. This figure primarily consists of loans, investments, and fixed assets. Total Assets are displayed in millions.

NEW INVESTORS

Telephone
The company's phone number.

Open to New Investors
Indicates whether the fund accepts investments from those who are not existing investors. A "Y" in this column identifies that the fund accepts new investors. No data in this column indicates that the fund is closed to new investors. The fund may be closed to new investors because the fund's asset base is getting too large to effectively execute its investing style. Although, the fund may be closed, in most cases, existing investors are able to add to their holdings.

		RATINGS				TOTAL RETURNS & PERFORMANCE					ASSETS		NEW INVESTORS	
Fund Name	Ticker Symbol	Overall Rating	Reward Rating	Risk Rating	Recent Up/ Downgrade	3-Month Total Return	6-Month Total Return	1-Year Total Return	3-Year Total Return	Dividend Yield (TTM)	NAV	Total Assets (MIL)	Telephone	Open to New Investors
PGIM High Yield Fund- Class R6	PHYQX	C-	D+	C	Down	10.47	-5.17	-0.85	11.73	6.8	5.12	15,592	800-225-1852	Y
PGIM High Yield Fund- Class Z	PHYZX	C-	D+	C		10.63	-5.04	-0.79	11.30	6.65	5.14	15,592	800-225-1852	Y
PGIM High Yield Fund- Class R4	PHYGX	C-	D+	C		10.61	-5.10	-0.92	10.59	6.53	5.13	15,592	800-225-1852	Y
MainStay MacKay High Yield Corporate Bond Fund Class R6	MHYSX	C-	D+	C		9.56	-4.19	-0.37	10.03	6.48	5.26	10,964	800-624-6782	Y
PGIM High Yield Fund- Class A	PBHAX	C-	D+	C		10.36	-5.36	-1.25	10.41	6.37	5.12	15,592	800-225-1852	Y
TIAA-CREF High Yield Fund Class W	TIHWX	C-	D+	C		8.68	-6.73	-2.79	8.25	6.27	8.95	3,534	877-518-9161	Y
MainStay MacKay High Yield Corporate Bond Fund Class R1	MHHRX	C-	D+	C		9.49	-4.31	-0.62	9.22	6.23	5.26	10,964	800-624-6782	Y
Goldman Sachs High Yield Fund Class P	GGMPX	C-	D+	C		10.18	-5.50	-1.54	7.23	6.2	5.96	1,945	800-526-7384	Y
Principal High Yield Fund Class R-6	PHYFX	C-	D+	C		8.89	-4.17	-0.91	7.84	6.16	6.69	2,933	800-787-1621	Y
Goldman Sachs High Yield Fund Investor Shares	GSHTX	C-	D+	C		10.37	-5.37	-1.44	7.09	6.16	5.96	1,945	800-526-7384	Y
Principal High Yield Fund Institutional Class	PHYTX	C-	D+	C		8.86	-4.21	-1.14	7.56	6.07	6.69	2,933	800-787-1621	Y
Federated Hermes Institutional High Yield Bond Cl R6	FIHLX	C-	D+	C		9.40	-3.83	0.07	9.58	5.98	9.29	7,903	800-341-7400	Y
Strategic Advisers® Income Opportunities Fund	FPIOX	C-	D+	C		9.73	-5.10	-1.51	8.38	5.91	8.85	2,444	617-563-7000	Y
TIAA-CREF High Yield Fund Advisor Class	TIHHX	C-	D+	C		8.57	-6.96	-3.24	7.22	5.78	8.94	3,534	877-518-9161	Y
TIAA-CREF High-Yield Fund Premier Class	TIHPX	C-	D+	C		8.55	-6.95	-3.25	7.23	5.75	8.96	3,534	877-518-9161	Y
MFS High Yield Pooled Portfolio Fund Shares	HYPPX	C-	D+	C	Down	7.62	-4.22	0.28	10.57	5.72	8.73	1,180	877-960-6077	Y
Neuberger Berman High Income Bond Fund Class R6	NRHIX	C-	D+	C		10.08	-4.71	-0.85	8.07	5.7	8.04	1,758	212-476-9000	Y
Franklin High Income Fund Class A1	FHAIX	C-	D+	C		8.79	-3.88	-0.72	8.21	5.69	1.74	2,757	650-312-2000	Y
PGIM Short Duration High Yield Income Fund- Class R6	HYSQX	C-	D+	C		9.16	-3.76	-0.42	10.53	5.69	8.47	2,874	800-225-1852	Y
PGIM Short Duration High Yield Income Fund- Class Z	HYSZX	C-	D+	C		9.15	-3.78	-0.35	10.37	5.64	8.47	2,874	800-225-1852	Y
TIAA-CREF High-Yield Fund Retirement Class	TIHRX	C-	D+	C		8.52	-7.01	-3.37	6.79	5.64	8.95	3,534	877-518-9161	Y
TIAA-CREF High-Yield Fund Retail Class	TIYRX	C-	D+	C		8.61	-6.99	-3.36	6.75	5.61	8.99	3,534	877-518-9161	Y
Putnam High Yield Fund Class R6 Shares	PHYUX	C-	D+	C		9.90	-4.01	-0.42	8.94	5.4	5.79	1,280	617-292-1000	Y
Columbia High Yield Bond Fund Institutional 2 Class	RSHRX	C-	D+	C	Down	9.14	-4.19	0.67	9.59	5.39	2.79	1,332	800-345-6611	Y
Vanguard High-Yield Corporate Fund Investor Shares	VWEHX	C-	D+	C	Down	7.99	-3.46	0.58	10.74	5.33	5.61	24,635	877-662-7447	Y
Columbia High Yield Bond Fund Advisor Class	CYLRX	C-	D+	C		9.06	-4.50	0.29	9.04	5.33	2.81	1,332	800-345-6611	Y
Columbia High Yield Bond Fund Institutional Class	CHYZX	C-	D+	C		9.12	-4.54	0.26	9.35	5.31	2.79	1,332	800-345-6611	Y
Putnam High Yield Fund Class Y	PHAYX	C-	D+	C		9.82	-4.11	-0.62	8.92	5.18	5.8	1,280	617-292-1000	Y
MFS High Income Fund Class R6	MHIKX	C-	D+	C	Down	7.25	-3.94	0.16	9.19	5.16	3.24	1,623	877-960-6077	Y
JPMorgan Income Fund Class A	JGIAX	C-	D+	C	Down	8.81	-3.69	-0.64	10.82	5.14	9.06	5,716	800-480-4111	Y
Voya Strategic Income Opportunities Fund Class P	VSTPX	C-	D+	C	Down	6.76	-4.40	-2.21	7.89	5.06	9.62	2,613	800-366-0066	Y
MFS High Income Fund Class R4	MHIJX	C-	D+	C	Down	7.20	-3.70	0.35	9.16	5.05	3.25	1,623	877-960-6077	Y
MFS High Income Fund Class I	MHIIX	C-	D+	C	Down	6.89	-4.01	0.03	8.81	5.05	3.23	1,623	877-960-6077	Y
Columbia Income Opportunities Fund Institutional 2 Class	CEPRX	C-	D+	C		8.57	-6.10	-1.83	7.16	5.04	9.28	1,502	800-345-6611	Y
Columbia Income Opportunities Fund Institutional Class	CIOZX	C-	D+	C		8.43	-6.24	-1.90	6.92	4.97	9.27	1,502	800-345-6611	Y
Columbia Income Opportunities Fund Advisor Class	CPPRX	C-	D+	C		8.42	-6.23	-1.90	6.92	4.97	9.28	1,502	800-345-6611	Y
Pacific Funds Floating Rate Income Fund Class P Shares		C-	D+	C		6.83	-4.27	-1.82	6.43	4.94	9.32	1,332	800-722-2333	Y
T. Rowe Price Institutional Floating Rate Fund Class F	PFFRX	C-	D+	C		8.13	-3.99	-1.24	6.67	4.87	9.28	2,740	410-345-2000	Y
Janus Henderson Multi-Sector Income Fund Class D	JMUDX	C-	D+	C	Down	9.56	-2.80	0.85	11.63	4.7	9.47	2,348	877-335-2687	Y
PGIM Strategic Bond Fund- Class R6	PUCQX	C	C-	C		10.17	-1.87	2.03	16.36	4.54	10.06	1,375	800-225-1852	Y
PGIM Strategic Bond Fund- Class Z	PUCZX	C	C-	C		10.17	-1.89	2.00	16.15	4.52	10.05	1,375	800-225-1852	Y
BlackRock Allocation Target Shares Series A Portfolio	BATAX	C-	D+	C	Down	8.54	-1.22	0.58	11.37	4.52	9.73	1,084	800-441-7762	Y
Neuberger Berman Strategic Income Fund Class R6	NRSIX	C-	D+	C		11.09	-0.68	2.04	9.70	4.22	10.78	2,663	212-476-9000	Y
Columbia Strategic Income Fund Institutional 2 Class	CTIVX	C-	D+	C	Down	10.31	-0.74	1.79	11.04	4.1	5.8	4,920	800-345-6611	Y
Columbia Strategic Income Fund Advisor Class	CMNRX	C-	D+	C	Down	10.32	-0.76	1.92	10.91	4.07	5.79	4,920	800-345-6611	Y
Columbia Strategic Income Fund Institutional Class	LSIZX	C-	D+	C	Down	10.31	-0.76	1.92	10.90	4.06	5.8	4,920	800-345-6611	Y
Invesco Quality Income Fund Class Y	VUSIX	C+	C	B	Up	2.70	3.28	5.16	10.87	3.93	11.92	1,624	800-659-1005	Y
Nuveen Short Duration High Yield Muni Bond Fund Class A	NVHAX	C-	D+	C	Down	2.30	-4.23	-1.97	10.32	3.82	9.9	4,513	312-917-8146	Y
Invesco Oppenheimer Rochester Limited Term NY Muni Cl R6	IORMX	C	C-	C+		1.78	0.27	2.09	13.69	3.78	3.02	1,685	800-659-1005	Y
Invesco Oppenheimer Rochester® Limited Term NY Muni Cl Y	LTBYX	C	C-	C+		2.10	0.58	2.72	14.55	3.74	3.03	1,685	800-659-1005	Y
Thornburg Strategic Income Fund Class R6	TSRSX	C	C	B-		8.01	2.04	4.48	13.74	3.72	11.98	1,750	800-847-0200	Y
Invesco Quality Income Fund Class A	VKMGX	C+	C	B-	Up	2.56	3.16	4.82	10.07	3.69	11.87	1,624	800-659-1005	Y

		RATINGS				TOTAL RETURNS & PERFORMANCE					ASSETS		NEW INVESTORS	
Fund Name	Ticker Symbol	Overall Rating	Reward Rating	Risk Rating	Recent Up/ Downgrade	3-Month Total Return	6-Month Total Return	1-Year Total Return	3-Year Total Return	Dividend Yield (TTM)	NAV	Total Assets (MIL)	Telephone	Open to New Investors
PGIM Short Duration Multi-Sector Bond Fund- Class R6	SDMQX	C	C-	C+		5.18	0.34	2.41	9.66	3.69	9.47	1,989	800-225-1852	Y
Lord Abbett Short Duration Income Fund Class F3	LOLDX	C	C-	C		5.68	0.02	1.88	8.60	3.68	4.15	51,496	201-827-2000	Y
Lord Abbett Short Duration Income Fund Class R6	LDLVX	C	C-	C		5.69	0.02	1.88	8.37	3.68	4.14	51,496	201-827-2000	Y
Thornburg Strategic Income Fund Class R5	TSRRX	C	C-	B-		8.01	2.00	4.42	13.18	3.66	11.95	1,750	800-847-0200	Y
Goldman Sachs Strategic Income Fund Class P	GSOPX	C	D+	C	Up	9.48	1.24	2.37	3.70	3.63	9.18	1,064	800-526-7384	Y
Lord Abbett Short Duration Income Fund Class R5	LDLTX	C	C-	C		5.67	0.22	1.81	8.44	3.62	4.14	51,496	201-827-2000	Y
Columbia Short Term Bond Fund Institutional 2 Class	CCBRX	C	C-	C		6.39	0.35	1.90	6.72	3.61	9.88	1,042	800-345-6611	Y
Columbia Mortgage Opportunities Fund Institutional 2 Class	CLMVX	C-	D+	C	Down	8.85	-1.09	0.70	15.41	3.61	9.8	1,452	800-345-6611	Y
PGIM Short Duration Multi-Sector Bond Fund- Class Z	SDMZX	C	C-	C+		5.15	0.31	2.32	9.40	3.59	9.5	1,989	800-225-1852	Y
Transamerica Unconstrained Bond Class I2		C-	D+	C		8.69	-1.66	0.45	5.47	3.58	9.57	1,487	888-233-4339	Y
Columbia Mortgage Opportunities Fund Advisor Class	CLMFX	C-	D+	C	Down	8.72	-1.21	0.65	15.25	3.56	9.8	1,452	800-345-6611	Y
Columbia Mortgage Opportunities Fund Institutional Class	CLMZX	C-	D+	C	Down	8.83	-1.11	0.76	15.36	3.56	9.81	1,452	800-345-6611	Y
Columbia Short Term Bond Fund Advisor Class	CMDRX	C	C-	C		6.47	0.42	1.92	6.54	3.53	9.9	1,042	800-345-6611	Y
Columbia Short Term Bond Fund Institutional Class	NSTMX	C-	D+	C	Down	6.47	0.41	1.92	6.54	3.53	9.9	1,042	800-345-6611	Y
Lord Abbett Short Duration Income Fund Class F	LDLFX	C	C-	C		5.65	-0.05	1.72	7.83	3.52	4.14	51,496	201-827-2000	Y
Goldman Sachs Strategic Income Fund Investor Class	GZIRX	C-	D+	C		5.16	-2.77	-1.74	-0.63	3.52	9.2	1,064	800-526-7384	Y
Lord Abbett Short Duration Income Fund Class A	LALDX	C	C-	C		5.88	0.14	1.62	7.78	3.42	4.15	51,496	201-827-2000	Y
DoubleLine Total Return Bond Fund Class N	DLTNX	C	C	B-		3.24	2.40	3.78	10.99	3.36	10.71	50,032	877-354-6311	Y
Lord Abbett Short Duration Income Fund Class R4	LDLKX	C	C-	C		5.60	-0.12	1.57	7.39	3.36	4.15	51,496	201-827-2000	Y
PGIM Short Duration Multi-Sector Bond Fund- Class A	SDMAX	C	C-	C		4.98	0.07	1.95	8.48	3.33	9.46	1,989	800-225-1852	Y
Virtus Newfleet Multi-Sector Short Term Bond Fund Class R6	VMSSX	C	C-	C		6.17	0.41	2.22	8.16	3.33	4.67	5,738	800-243-1574	Y
BlackRock Allocation Target Shares Series M Portfolio	BRAMX	B-	C+	B+	Up	2.37	3.72	6.00	13.51	3.27	9.96	1,017	800-441-7762	Y
Columbia Short Term Bond Fund Class A	NSTRX	C-	D+	C		6.40	0.29	1.57	5.75	3.27	9.91	1,042	800-345-6611	Y
Franklin Low Duration Total Return Fund Class A	FLDAX	C-	D+	C		6.07	-0.76	0.32	4.45	3.27	9.44	3,058	650-312-2000	Y
Franklin Pennsylvania Tax-Free Income Fund Class R6	FRPRX	C	C	B-		1.35	1.41	3.04	9.65	3.16	9.91	1,081	650-312-2000	Y
Columbia Intermediate Muni Bond Fund Institutional 3 Class	CIMYX	C	C-	C+		2.03	0.56	2.54	9.79	3.13	10.46	1,138	800-345-6611	Y
Loomis Sayles Investment Grade Bond Fund Class A	LIGRX	B-	C	B+	Up	8.54	5.47	8.14	15.95	3.09	11.7	5,463	800-862-4863	Y
DoubleLine Core Fixed Income Fund Class N	DLFNX	C	C-	B-		5.34	1.71	3.61	10.96	3.08	11.1	11,587	877-354-6311	Y
John Hancock Income Fund Class R5	JSNVX	C	C-	B-		6.16	0.54	3.82	9.67	3.04	6.43	1,776	800-225-5291	Y
Franklin U.S. Government Securities Fund Class R6	FGORX	C+	C+	B-		0.56	3.34	4.96	10.53	3.02	6.17	4,905	650-312-2000	Y
Franklin Pennsylvania Tax-Free Income Fund Class A1	FRPAX	C	C-	B-		1.42	1.45	3.00	9.24	3.02	9.9	1,081	650-312-2000	Y
Hartford Short Duration Fund Class R6	HSDVX	C	C-	B-		5.87	1.10	3.16	8.79	3.02	9.85	1,414	888-843-7824	Y
Columbia Intermediate Municipal Bond Fund Advisor Class	CIMRX	C	C-	C+		2.00	0.50	2.42	9.41	3.02	10.44	1,138	800-345-6611	Y
Columbia Intermediate Muni Bond Fund Institutional Class	SETMX	C	C-	C+		2.00	0.50	2.42	9.41	3.02	10.45	1,138	800-345-6611	Y
JNL/PIMCO Income Fund Class I		C-	D+	C	Down	5.44	-1.13	0.32		2.95	10.45	1,548		Y

Section IV:
High Performance Bond & Money Market Mutual Funds

Investment Ratings and analysis our selections for High Performance Bond & Money Market Mutual Funds.   Funds are listed in order by their five-year total return and overall rating.

Section IV: Contents

This section contains Weiss Investment Ratings, key rating factors, and summary financial data for our selections for "High Performance Bond & Money Market Mutual Funds." If your priority is to achieve the highest return, balanced with the amount of risk we have chosen the top mutual funds with the best financial performance. Not just "Buy" rated these funds have hit our demanding criteria of being in the top 25% of total returns for funds over a number of time-periods. Keep in mind that past performance alone is not always a guide to future performance. Funds are listed in order by their five-year total return and overall rating.

Fund Name

Describes the fund's assets, regions of investments and investment strategies. Many funds have similar names, so you want to make sure the fund you look up is really the one you are interested in evaluating.

Ticker Symbol

An arrangement of characters (usually letters) representing a particular security listed on an exchange or otherwise traded publicly. When a company issues securities to the public marketplace, it selects an available ticker symbol for its securities which investors use to place trade orders. Every listed security has a unique ticker symbol, facilitating the vast array of trade orders that flow through the financial markets every day. If a ticker symbol is not assigned to a particular fund, the International Securities Identification Number (ISIN) is displayed.

RATINGS

Overall Rating

The Weiss rating measured on a scale from A to E based on each fund's risk and performance. See the preceding section, "What Our Ratings Mean," for an explanation of each letter grade rating.

Reward Rating

This is based on the total return over a period of up to five years, including net asset value and price growth. The total return figure is stated net of the expenses and fees charged by the fund. Based on proprietary modeling the individual components of the risk and reward ratings are calculated and weighted and the final rating is generated.

Risk Rating

This is includes the risk ratings of component stocks where applicable and also includes the financial stability of the fund, turnover where applicable, together with the level of volatility as measured by the fund's daily returns over a period of up to five years. Funds with greater stability are considered less risky and receive a higher risk rating. Funds with greater volatility are considered riskier, and will receive a lower risk rating. In addition to considering the fund's volatility, the risk rating also considers an assessment of the valuation and quality of a fund's holdings.

Recent Upgrade/Downgrade
An "Up" or "Down" indicates that the Weiss Mutual Fund rating has changed since the publication of the last print edition. If a fund has had a rating change since March 31, 2020, the change is identified with an "Up" or "Down."

TOTAL RETURNS & PERFORMANCE

3-Month Total Return
The rate of return on an investment over three months that includes interest, capital gains, dividends and distributions realized.

6-Month Total Return
The rate of return on an investment over six months that includes interest, capital gains, dividends and distributions realized.

1-Year Total Return
The rate of return on an investment over one year that includes interest, capital gains, dividends and distributions realized.

3-Year Total Return
The rate of return on an investment over three years that includes interest, capital gains, dividends and distributions realized.

5-Year Total Return
The rate of return on an investment over five years that includes interest, capital gains, dividends and distributions realized.

ASSETS

NAV (Net Asset Value)
A fund's price per share. The value is calculated by dividing the total value of all the securities in the portfolio, less any liabilities, by the number of fund shares outstanding.

Total Assets (MIL)
The total of all assets listed on the institution's balance sheet. This figure primarily consists of loans, investments, and fixed assets. Total Assets are displayed in millions.

NEW INVESTORS

Telephone
The company's phone number.

Open to New Investors
Indicates whether the fund accepts investments from those who are not existing investors. A "Y" in this column identifies that the fund accepts new investors. No data in this column indicates that the fund is closed to new investors. The fund may be closed to new investors because the fund's asset base is getting too large to effectively execute its investing style. Although, the fund may be closed, in most cases, existing investors are able to add to their holdings.

		RATINGS				TOTAL RETURNS & PERFORMANCE					ASSETS		NEW INVESTORS	
Fund Name	Ticker Symbol	Overall Rating	Reward Rating	Risk Rating	Recent Up/ Downgrade	3-Month Total Return	6-Month Total Return	1-Year Total Return	3-Year Total Return	5-Year Total Return	NAV	Total Assets (MIL)	Telephone	Open to New Investors
PIMCO Long Duration Total Return Fund Class A	PLRAX	B	B	B	Up	7.50	12.96	18.63	33.24	54.74	11.9	3,411	866-746-2602	Y
PIMCO Long-Term U.S. Government Fund Class A	PFGAX	B	B	B		0.54	21.45	25.44	37.41	53.29	7.88	1,018	866-746-2602	Y
PIMCO Long Duration Total Return Fund Class C	PLRCX	B	B	B	Up	7.30	12.54	17.76	30.29	49.08	11.9	3,411	866-746-2602	Y
PIMCO Long-Term U.S. Government Fund Class C	PFGCX	B	B	B		0.35	21.02	24.52	34.38	47.69	7.88	1,018	866-746-2602	Y
Invesco Oppenheimer Rochester High Yield Muni Fund Class C	ORNCX	C	C-	C+		5.10	-1.21	2.45	18.80	41.07	7.6	6,492	800-659-1005	Y
MFS Corporate Bond Fund Class R6	MFBKX	B-	C+	B	Up	9.92	6.04	10.49	21.04	33.76	15.36	5,159	877-960-6077	Y
Invesco Corporate Bond Fund Class Y	ACCHX	C	C	B		10.14	3.53	8.44	18.21	33.47	7.74	2,120	800-659-1005	Y
MFS Corporate Bond Fund Class R4	MFBJX	B-	C+	B	Up	9.88	6.05	10.38	20.75	33.16	15.38	5,159	877-960-6077	Y
MFS Corporate Bond Fund Class I	MBDIX	B-	C+	B	Up	9.89	5.99	10.39	20.68	33.09	15.36	5,159	877-960-6077	Y
Invesco Corporate Bond Fund Class A	ACCBX	C	C	B-		10.24	3.54	8.32	17.33	31.83	7.73	2,120	800-659-1005	Y
Delaware Corporate Bond Fund Institutional Class	DGCIX	B-	C	B	Up	10.52	5.04	9.53	20.45	31.46	6.31	1,096		Y
Delaware Corporate Bond Fund Class A	DGCAX	B-	C	B	Up	10.45	4.91	9.27	19.56	29.84	6.31	1,096		Y
PIMCO Investment Grade Credit Bond Fund Class A	PBDAX	C	C-	B-		8.47	1.83	6.08	16.32	29.43	10.94	17,737	866-746-2602	Y
Delaware Corporate Bond Fund Class R	DGCRX	C+	C	B	Up	10.37	4.78	8.99	18.66	28.22	6.32	1,096		Y
Eaton Vance Emerging Markets Local Income Fund Class A	EEIAX	C-	C-	C-	Down	14.13	-4.48	4.25	12.05	27.57	5.16	1,143		Y
PIMCO Emerging Markets Bond Fund Class A	PAEMX	C-	D+	C	Down	11.74	-2.85	0.44	9.88	25.89	10.18	2,189	866-746-2602	Y
Pioneer AMT-Free Municipal Fund Class A	PBMFX	B-	C	B	Up	2.71	3.21	6.70	15.61	25.84	15.47	1,301	617-742-7825	Y
Federated Hermes Institutional High Yield Bond Cl R6	FIHLX	C-	D+	C		9.40	-3.83	0.07	9.58	25.82	9.29	7,903	800-341-7400	Y
Mercer Core Fixed Income Fund Class Y3	MCFIX	B	C+	B+	Up	4.58	6.30	9.36	17.72	25.50	10.96	1,025		Y
MFS Emerging Markets Debt Fund Class R6	MEDHX	C-	D+	C	Down	11.97	-1.17	1.77	11.16	25.21	14.38	5,943	877-960-6077	Y
Delaware Corporate Bond Fund Class C	DGCCX	C+	C	B	Up	10.26	4.54	8.47	16.92	25.10	6.31	1,096		Y
MFS Emerging Markets Debt Fund Class R4	MEDGX	C-	D+	C	Down	12.01	-1.15	1.74	10.94	24.72	14.4	5,943	877-960-6077	Y
MFS Emerging Markets Debt Fund Class I	MEDIX	C-	D+	C	Down	11.96	-1.23	1.73	10.85	24.63	14.35	5,943	877-960-6077	Y
AB Income Fund Advisor Class	ACGYX	C	C-	C+		7.69	1.18	4.56	12.04	23.38	7.93	4,321	212-969-1000	Y
Eaton Vance Emerging Markets Local Income Fund Class C	EEICX	C-	C-	C-	Down	14.03	-4.88	3.58	9.73	23.24	5.22	1,143		Y
MFS Emerging Markets Debt Fund Class A	MEDAX	C-	D+	C	Down	11.87	-1.34	1.42	10.12	23.19	14.39	5,943	877-960-6077	Y
MFS Emerging Markets Debt Fund Class R3	MEDFX	C-	D+	C	Down	11.94	-1.28	1.48	10.12	23.18	14.4	5,943	877-960-6077	Y
Columbia High Yield Bond Fund Institutional 2 Class	RSHRX	C-	D+	C	Down	9.14	-4.19	0.67	9.59	22.84	2.79	1,332	800-345-6611	Y
MFS High Income Fund Class R6	MHIKX	C-	D+	C	Down	7.25	-3.94	0.16	9.19	21.66	3.24	1,623	877-960-6077	Y
MFS Emerging Markets Debt Fund Class R2	MEDEX	C-	D+	C	Down	11.92	-1.39	1.24	9.31	21.66	14.45	5,943	877-960-6077	Y
MFS High Income Fund Class R4	MHIJX	C-	D+	C	Down	7.20	-3.70	0.35	9.16	21.39	3.25	1,623	877-960-6077	Y
Pioneer AMT-Free Municipal Fund Class C	MNBCX	C+	C	B	Up	2.47	2.77	5.87	12.94	21.15	15.33	1,301	617-742-7825	Y
MFS High Income Fund Class I	MHIIX	C-	D+	C	Down	6.89	-4.01	0.03	8.81	20.64	3.23	1,623	877-960-6077	Y
MFS High Income Fund Class R3	MHIHX	C-	D+	C	Down	7.15	-4.11	0.08	8.33	19.52	3.24	1,623	877-960-6077	Y
MFS Emerging Markets Debt Fund Class B	MEDBX	C-	D+	C	Down	11.70	-1.70	0.67	7.62	18.68	14.45	5,943	877-960-6077	Y
MFS Emerging Markets Debt Fund Class R1	MEDDX	C-	D+	C	Down	11.70	-1.70	0.67	7.62	18.59	14.45	5,943	877-960-6077	Y
MFS Emerging Markets Debt Fund Class C	MEDCX	C-	D+	C	Down	11.71	-1.71	0.67	7.61	18.59	14.43	5,943	877-960-6077	Y
John Hancock Funds Strategic Income Opportunities Cl NAV	JHSEX	C	C-	C		7.16	-0.31	2.58	7.13	16.03	10.56	4,494	800-225-5291	Y
John Hancock Funds Strategic Income Opportunities Cl A	JIPAX	C	C-	C	Up	7.14	-0.43	2.14	5.90	13.62	10.57	4,494	800-225-5291	Y
John Hancock Funds Strategic Income Opportunities Cl R2	JIPPX	C	C-	C	Up	7.11	-0.47	2.06	5.63	13.13	10.58	4,494	800-225-5291	Y
Fidelity Advisor® Short-Term Bond Fund Class I	FBNIX	C+	C	B-	Up	2.97	2.74	4.09	8.45	11.03	8.86	5,482	617-563-7000	Y
Fidelity Advisor® Short-Term Bond Fund Class A	FBNAX	C	C	B-		2.93	2.66	3.94	7.97	10.22	8.86	5,482	617-563-7000	Y
Fidelity Advisor® Short-Term Bond Fund Class M	FBNTX	C	C	B-		2.93	2.66	3.93	7.94	10.16	8.86	5,482	617-563-7000	Y
Fidelity Advisor® Short-Term Bond Fund Class C	FANCX	C	C	B-		2.59	2.23	2.94	5.11	5.55	8.85	5,482	617-563-7000	Y

Section V:
Low Volatility Bond & Money Market Mutual Funds

Investment Ratings and analysis of Low Volatility Bond & Money Market Mutual Funds. Funds are listed in order by their lowest volatility (Beta) and overall rating.

Section V: Contents

This section contains Weiss Investment Ratings, key rating factors, and summary financial data for our selections for "Low Volatility Bond & Money Market Mutual Funds". If ultimate safety is your top priority, the top recommended mutual funds with the lowest volatility may be your best bet. These funds may have lower performance ratings than some other funds, but can provide a safe place for your savings. Funds are listed in order by their lowest volatility (Beta) and overall rating.

Fund Name
Describes the fund's assets, regions of investments and investment strategies. Many funds have similar names, so you want to make sure the fund you look up is really the one you are interested in evaluating.

Ticker Symbol
An arrangement of characters (usually letters) representing a particular security listed on an exchange or otherwise traded publicly. When a company issues securities to the public marketplace, it selects an available ticker symbol for its securities which investors use to place trade orders. Every listed security has a unique ticker symbol, facilitating the vast array of trade orders that flow through the financial markets every day. If a ticker symbol is not assigned to a particular fund, the International Securities Identification Number (ISIN) is displayed.

RATINGS

Overall Rating
The Weiss rating measured on a scale from A to E based on each fund's risk and performance. See the preceding section, "What Our Ratings Mean," for an explanation of each letter grade rating.

Reward Rating
This is based on the total return over a period of up to five years, including net asset value and price growth. The total return figure is stated net of the expenses and fees charged by the fund. Based on proprietary modeling the individual components of the risk and reward ratings are calculated and weighted and the final rating is generated.

Risk Rating
This is includes the risk ratings of component stocks where applicable and also includes the financial stability of the fund, turnover where applicable, together with the level of volatility as measured by the fund's daily returns over a period of up to five years. Funds with greater stability are considered less risky and receive a higher risk rating. Funds with greater volatility are considered riskier, and will receive a lower risk rating. In addition to considering the fund's volatility, the risk rating also considers an assessment of the valuation and quality of a fund's holdings.

Recent Upgrade/Downgrade
An "Up" or "Down" indicates that the Weiss Mutual Fund rating has changed since the publication of the last print edition. If a fund has had a rating change since March 31, 2020, the change is identified with an "Up" or "Down."

TOTAL RETURNS & PERFORMANCE

3-Month Total Return
The rate of return on an investment over three months that includes interest, capital gains, dividends and distributions realized.

6-Month Total Return
The rate of return on an investment over six months that includes interest, capital gains, dividends and distributions realized.

1-Year Total Return
The rate of return on an investment over one year that includes interest, capital gains, dividends and distributions realized.

3-Year Total Return
The rate of return on an investment over three years that includes interest, capital gains, dividends and distributions realized.

3-Year Beta
A three year measure of volatility, or systematic risk, of a security in comparison to the market as a whole. A beta of less than 1 means that the security will be less volatile than the market, a beta larger than 1 means more volatility. Beta value cannot be calculated if less than 24 months of pricing is available.

ASSETS

NAV (Net Asset Value)
A fund's price per share. The value is calculated by dividing the total value of all the securities in the portfolio, less any liabilities, by the number of fund shares outstanding.

Total Assets (MIL)
The total of all assets listed on the institution's balance sheet. This figure primarily consists of loans, investments, and fixed assets. Total Assets are displayed in millions.

NEW INVESTORS

Telephone
The company's phone number.

Open to New Investors
Indicates whether the fund accepts investments from those who are not existing investors. A "Y" in this column identifies that the fund accepts new investors. No data in this column indicates that the fund is closed to new investors. The fund may be closed to new investors because the fund's asset base is getting too large to effectively execute its investing style. Although, the fund may be closed, in most cases, existing investors are able to add to their holdings.

		RATINGS				TOTAL RETURNS & PERFORMANCE					ASSETS		NEW INVESTORS	
Fund Name	Ticker Symbol	Overall Rating	Reward Rating	Risk Rating	Recent Up/ Downgrade	3-Month Total Return	6-Month Total Return	1-Year Total Return	3-Year Total Return	3-Year Beta	NAV	Total Assets (MIL)	Telephone	Open to New Investors
Invesco Oppenheimer Total Return Bond Fund Class Y	OPBYX	B	C+	B+	Up	5.84	7.14	9.94	18.58	0.56	7.33	1,856	800-659-1005	Y
Invesco Oppenheimer Total Return Bond Fund Class R	OPBNX	B	C+	B	Up	5.80	6.79	9.26	16.41	0.57	7.37	1,856	800-659-1005	Y
Invesco Oppenheimer Total Return Bond Fund Class C	OPBCX	B-	C+	B	Up	5.67	6.67	8.71	14.67	0.57	7.38	1,856	800-659-1005	Y
Invesco Oppenheimer Total Return Bond Fund Class A	OPIGX	B	C+	B+	Up	5.73	6.94	9.58	17.47	0.58	7.37	1,856	800-659-1005	Y
American Funds Strategic Bond Fund Class R-2E	RANHX	B	B	B+		6.21	14.35	15.41	24.11	0.71	11.69	2,132	800-421-4225	Y
American Funds Strategic Bond Fund Class R-2	RANBX	B	B	B		6.11	14.14	15.05	22.11	0.72	11.65	2,132	800-421-4225	Y
American Funds Strategic Bond Fund Class F-2	ANBFX	B	B	B	Up	6.41	14.67	16.14	25.74	0.72	11.7	2,132	800-421-4225	Y
American Funds Strategic Bond Fund Class R-6	RANGX	B	B	B+		6.51	14.80	16.34	26.05	0.73	11.71	2,132	800-421-4225	Y
American Funds Strategic Bond Fund Class F-1	ANBEX	B	B	B+		6.30	14.52	15.84	24.56	0.73	11.68	2,132	800-421-4225	Y
American Funds Strategic Bond Fund Class 529-C	CANCX	B	B	B		6.17	14.16	15.02	21.73	0.73	11.64	2,132	800-421-4225	Y
American Funds Strategic Bond Fund Class R-4	RANEX	B	B	B	Up	6.35	14.56	15.92	24.83	0.73	11.69	2,132	800-421-4225	Y
American Funds Strategic Bond Fund Class A	ANBAX	B	B	B+		6.34	14.52	15.83	24.71	0.74	11.69	2,132	800-421-4225	Y
American Funds Strategic Bond Fund Class R-1	RANAX	B	B	B		6.23	14.17	15.11	22.29	0.74	11.68	2,132	800-421-4225	Y
American Funds Strategic Bond Fund Class R-5	RANFX	B	B	B	Up	6.41	14.68	16.19	25.77	0.74	11.7	2,132	800-421-4225	Y
American Funds Strategic Bond Fund Class 529-F-1	CANFX	B	B	B	Up	6.39	14.64	16.10	25.40	0.74	11.69	2,132	800-421-4225	Y
American Funds Strategic Bond Fund Class R-5E	RANJX	B	B	B	Up	6.39	14.64	16.09	25.57	0.74	11.7	2,132	800-421-4225	Y
American Funds Strategic Bond Fund Class 529-A	CANAX	B	B	B	Up	6.34	14.54	15.85	24.54	0.74	11.68	2,132	800-421-4225	Y
American Funds Strategic Bond Fund Class R-3	RANCX	B	B	B	Up	6.29	14.41	15.60	23.84	0.74	11.68	2,132	800-421-4225	Y
American Funds Strategic Bond Fund Class 529-E	CANEX	B	B	B	Up	6.29	14.40	15.59	23.87	0.74	11.69	2,132	800-421-4225	Y
American Funds Strategic Bond Fund Class C	ANBCX	B	B	B	Up	6.13	14.06	14.95	21.85	0.74	11.63	2,132	800-421-4225	Y
JNL/JPMorgan U.S. Government & Quality Bond Fund Class I		B	B-	B+		1.40	6.51	8.33	15.55	0.75	15.2	2,169		Y
JNL/JPMorgan U.S. Government & Quality Bond Fund Class A		B	B-	B+	Up	1.40	6.43	8.11	14.57	0.75	14.39	2,169		Y
Guggenheim Investment Grade Bond Fund Class P	SIUPX	B	B-	A-	Up	5.38	8.64	9.72	17.01	0.76	20.15	1,078	212-518-9290	Y
Guggenheim Total Return Bond Fund Class P	GIBLX	B	B-	A-	Up	5.65	8.80	9.88	16.87	0.77	29.14	16,534	212-518-9290	Y
American Funds Inflation Linked Bond Fund Class 529-F-1	CNLFX	B	B	B+	Up	5.25	9.51	11.21	18.11	0.78	10.82	6,297	800-421-4225	Y
American Funds Inflation Linked Bond Fund Class A	BFIAX	B	B	B+	Up	5.16	9.43	10.91	17.41	0.78	10.79	6,297	800-421-4225	Y
American Funds Inflation Linked Bond Fund Class R-4	RILDX	B	B	B+	Up	5.17	9.44	11.03	17.37	0.78	10.78	6,297	800-421-4225	Y
American Funds Inflation Linked Bond Fund Class 529-E	CNLEX	B	B	B+	Up	5.19	9.36	10.75	16.58	0.78	10.74	6,297	800-421-4225	Y
American Funds Inflation Linked Bond Fund Class R-3	RILCX	B	B	B+	Up	5.10	9.28	10.69	16.38	0.78	10.71	6,297	800-421-4225	Y
American Funds Inflation Linked Bond Fund Class 529-C	CNLCX	B	B-	B	Up	4.99	9.05	10.17	14.85	0.78	10.72	6,297	800-421-4225	Y
American Funds Inflation Linked Bond Fund Class R-1	RILAX	B	B-	B	Up	4.98	9.03	10.22	14.78	0.78	10.74	6,297	800-421-4225	Y
JPMorgan Government Bond Fund Class R2	JGBZX	B-	B-	B		0.79	6.31	7.72	13.20	0.78	11.34	3,245	800-480-4111	Y
American Funds Inflation Linked Bond Fund Class R-5	RILEX	B	B	B+	Up	5.24	9.60	11.35	18.54	0.79	10.84	6,297	800-421-4225	Y
American Funds Inflation Linked Bond Fund Class R-6	RILFX	B	B	B+	Up	5.34	9.59	11.39	18.66	0.79	10.85	6,297	800-421-4225	Y
American Funds Inflation Linked Bond Fund Class F-2	BFIGX	B	B	B+	Up	5.24	9.60	11.38	18.34	0.79	10.84	6,297	800-421-4225	Y
American Funds Inflation Linked Bond Fund Class R-5E	RILHX	B	B	B+	Up	5.26	9.53	11.23	18.18	0.79	10.8	6,297	800-421-4225	Y
American Funds Corporate Bond Fund Class R-5	RCBEX	B	B	B+	Up	9.25	9.60	13.60	24.58	0.79	11.69	1,181	800-421-4225	Y
American Funds Corporate Bond Fund Class R-5E	RCBHX	B	B	B+	Up	9.22	9.54	13.48	24.36	0.79	11.69	1,181	800-421-4225	Y
American Funds Corporate Bond Fund Class R-6	RCBFX	B	B	B+	Up	9.26	9.62	13.65	24.71	0.79	11.69	1,181	800-421-4225	Y
American Funds Corporate Bond Fund Class F-2	BFCGX	B	B	B+	Up	9.23	9.57	13.54	24.39	0.79	11.69	1,181	800-421-4225	Y
American Funds Corporate Bond Fund Class 529-F-1	COBFX	B	B	B+	Up	9.22	9.54	13.47	24.15	0.79	11.69	1,181	800-421-4225	Y
American Funds Corporate Bond Fund Class R-4	RCBDX	B	B	B	Up	9.17	9.44	13.26	23.47	0.79	11.69	1,181	800-421-4225	Y
American Funds Corporate Bond Fund Class F-1	BFCFX	B	B	B	Up	9.16	9.43	13.23	23.36	0.79	11.69	1,181	800-421-4225	Y
American Funds Corporate Bond Fund Class A	BFCAX	B	B	B	Up	9.15	9.41	13.20	23.41	0.79	11.69	1,181	800-421-4225	Y
American Funds Corporate Bond Fund Class 529-A	COBAX	B	B	B	Up	9.15	9.42	13.20	23.30	0.79	11.69	1,181	800-421-4225	Y
American Funds Corporate Bond Fund Class R-2E	RCBGX	B	B	B	Up	9.05	9.20	12.78	22.28	0.79	11.69	1,181	800-421-4225	Y
American Funds Corporate Bond Fund Class 529-E	COBEX	B	B	B	Up	9.10	9.31	13.00	22.60	0.79	11.69	1,181	800-421-4225	Y
American Funds Corporate Bond Fund Class R-3	RCBCX	B	B	B	Up	9.09	9.28	12.93	22.43	0.79	11.69	1,181	800-421-4225	Y
American Funds Corporate Bond Fund Class R-1	RCBAX	B	B	B	Up	8.99	9.09	12.52	21.17	0.79	11.69	1,181	800-421-4225	Y
American Funds Corporate Bond Fund Class R-2	RCBBX	B	B	B	Up	8.98	9.05	12.45	20.87	0.79	11.69	1,181	800-421-4225	Y
American Funds Corporate Bond Fund Class C	BFCCX	B	B	B	Up	8.96	9.03	12.42	20.70	0.79	11.69	1,181	800-421-4225	Y
American Funds Corporate Bond Fund Class 529-C	COBCX	B	B	B	Up	8.95	9.00	12.36	20.50	0.79	11.69	1,181	800-421-4225	Y

		RATINGS				TOTAL RETURNS & PERFORMANCE					ASSETS		NEW INVESTORS	
Fund Name	Ticker Symbol	Overall Rating	Reward Rating	Risk Rating	Recent Up/ Downgrade	3-Month Total Return	6-Month Total Return	1-Year Total Return	3-Year Total Return	3-Year Beta	NAV	Total Assets (MIL)	Telephone	Open to New Investors
American Funds Inflation Linked Bond Fund Class R-2E	RILGX	B	B	B	Up	5.07	9.23	10.50	15.81	0.79	10.76	6,297	800-421-4225	Y
JPMorgan Government Bond Fund Class R4	OGGQX	B	B-	B		0.83	6.58	8.26	14.93	0.79	11.34	3,245	800-480-4111	Y
American Funds Inflation Linked Bond Fund Class R-2	RILBX	B	B-	B	Up	4.94	9.03	10.20	14.85	0.79	10.62	6,297	800-421-4225	Y
JPMorgan Government Bond Fund Class R3	OGGPX	B	B-	B	Up	0.77	6.44	7.99	14.07	0.79	11.34	3,245	800-480-4111	Y
American Funds Inflation Linked Bond Fund Class C	BFICX	B	B-	B	Up	5.09	9.05	10.32	14.89	0.79	10.72	6,297	800-421-4225	Y
JPMorgan Government Bond Fund Class A	OGGAX	B	B-	B	Up	0.87	6.49	8.08	14.37	0.79	11.35	3,245	800-480-4111	Y
JPMorgan Government Bond Fund Class C	OGVCX	B-	B-	B		0.65	6.11	7.38	12.26	0.79	11.31	3,245	800-480-4111	Y
American Funds Inflation Linked Bond Fund Class 529-A	CNLAX	B	B	B+	Up	5.16	9.43	10.92	17.35	0.8	10.79	6,297	800-421-4225	Y
American Funds Inflation Linked Bond Fund Class F-1	BFIFX	B	B	B+	Up	5.16	9.42	10.98	17.37	0.8	10.8	6,297	800-421-4225	Y
JPMorgan Mortgage-Backed Securities Fund Class A	OMBAX	B-	C	B	Up	2.78	3.63	5.40	12.89	0.8	11.9	2,998	800-480-4111	Y
Franklin Ohio Tax-Free Income Fund Class R6	FKTOX	B-	C	B	Up	2.01	2.82	4.91	12.99	0.8	13.07	1,593	650-312-2000	Y
Fidelity® GNMA Fund	FGMNX	B-	C+	B	Up	1.02	3.20	4.77	10.59	0.85	11.8	4,204	617-563-7000	Y
Fidelity Advisor® Government Income Fund Class Z	FIKPX	B	B	B		0.45	7.43	9.14	15.58	0.87	11.2	4,665	617-563-7000	Y
Fidelity® Government Income Fund	FGOVX	B	B	B		0.51	7.40	9.06	15.45	0.87	11.18	4,665	617-563-7000	Y
Fidelity Advisor® Government Income Fund Class A	FVIAX	B	B	B		0.34	7.12	8.60	14.21	0.87	11.19	4,665	617-563-7000	Y
Loomis Sayles Investment Grade Bond Fund Admin Class	LIGAX	B-	C	B	Up	8.50	5.36	7.89	15.22	0.87	11.67	5,463	800-862-4863	Y
Fidelity Advisor® Government Income Fund Class I	FVIIX	B	B	B		0.41	7.37	8.91	15.30	0.88	11.19	4,665	617-563-7000	Y
Fidelity Advisor® Government Income Fund Class M	FVITX	B	B	B		0.35	7.23	8.62	14.37	0.88	11.19	4,665	617-563-7000	Y
BMO Core Plus Bond Fund Class Y	MCYBX	B-	C+	B+	Up	4.71	4.62	7.27	14.75	0.88	12.29	1,117	800-236-3863	Y
BMO Core Plus Bond Fund Class A	BATCX	B-	C+	B+	Up	4.62	4.54	7.28	14.66	0.88	12.28	1,117	800-236-3863	Y
Federated Hermes Total Return Bond Fund Class R6 Shares	FTRLX	B	C+	B+	Up	5.61	5.56	8.29	16.63	0.89	11.51	8,906	800-341-7400	Y
BlackRock Allocation Target Shares Series M Portfolio	BRAMX	B-	C+	B+	Up	2.37	3.72	6.00	13.51	0.89	9.96	1,017	800-441-7762	Y
Fidelity Advisor® Government Income Fund Class C	FVICX	B-	B-	B		0.18	6.84	7.82	11.77	0.89	11.19	4,665	617-563-7000	Y
American Funds Preservation Portfolio Class 529-A	CPPAX	B-	C+	B	Up	1.94	4.74	5.64	9.74	0.89	10.37	2,119	800-421-4225	Y
Federated Hermes Total Return Bond Fund Class R Shares	FTRKX	B-	C+	B	Up	5.32	5.08	7.50	14.02	0.9	11.51	8,906	800-341-7400	Y
American Funds Preservation Portfolio Class R-6	RPPGX	B-	C+	B	Up	2.03	4.90	6.01	10.96	0.9	10.38	2,119	800-421-4225	Y
American Funds Preservation Portfolio Class R-5	RPPFX	B-	C+	B	Up	2.02	4.88	5.96	10.79	0.9	10.38	2,119	800-421-4225	Y
American Funds Preservation Portfolio Class R-4	RPPEX	B-	C+	B	Up	1.95	4.75	5.66	9.87	0.9	10.38	2,119	800-421-4225	Y
American Funds Preservation Portfolio Class F-1	PPVFX	B-	C+	B	Up	1.85	4.65	5.54	9.77	0.9	10.37	2,119	800-421-4225	Y
American Funds Intermediate Bond of America® Cl R-6	RBOGX	B-	C+	B	Up	2.53	6.06	7.25	12.75	0.91	14.13	23,949	800-421-4225	Y
American Funds Intermediate Bond Fund of America® Class A	AIBAX	B-	C+	B	Up	2.50	5.91	6.89	11.59	0.91	14.14	23,949	800-421-4225	Y
American Funds Intermediate Bond of America® Cl F-2	IBAFX	B-	C+	B	Up	2.57	6.07	7.21	12.46	0.91	14.14	23,949	800-421-4225	Y
American Funds Intermediate Bond of America® Cl R-5E	RBOHX	B-	C+	B	Up	2.57	6.05	7.16	12.40	0.91	14.14	23,949	800-421-4225	Y
American Funds Intermediate Bond of America® Cl 529-A	CBOAX	B-	C+	B	Up	2.50	5.92	6.89	11.44	0.91	14.14	23,949	800-421-4225	Y
American Funds Intermediate Bond of America® Cl 529-F	CBOFX	B-	C+	B	Up	2.56	6.04	7.15	12.24	0.91	14.14	23,949	800-421-4225	Y
American Funds Intermediate Bond of America® Cl 529-E	CBOEX	B-	C+	B	Up	2.45	5.82	6.70	10.83	0.91	14.14	23,949	800-421-4225	Y
American Funds Intermediate Bond of America® Cl R-3	RBOCX	B-	C+	B	Up	2.44	5.79	6.63	10.64	0.91	14.14	23,949	800-421-4225	Y
MFS Government Securities Fund Class I	MGSIX	B	B-	B	Up	1.14	6.24	7.92	14.35	0.92	10.44	2,270	877-960-6077	Y
DFA Diversified Fixed Income PortfolioInstitutional Class	DFXIX	B-	C+	B		1.25	5.53	6.87	12.85	0.92	10.39	1,177	512-306-7400	Y
American Funds Intermediate Bond of America® Cl R-5	RBOFX	B-	C+	B	Up	2.59	6.10	7.27	12.65	0.92	14.14	23,949	800-421-4225	Y
American Funds Intermediate Bond of America® Cl R-4	RBOEX	B-	C+	B	Up	2.52	5.95	6.95	11.65	0.92	14.14	23,949	800-421-4225	Y
American Funds Intermediate Bond of America® Cl F-1	IBFFX	B-	C+	B	Up	2.50	5.92	6.90	11.47	0.92	14.14	23,949	800-421-4225	Y
American Funds Preservation Portfolio Class F-2	PPEFX	B-	C+	B	Up	1.91	4.87	5.82	10.66	0.92	10.37	2,119	800-421-4225	Y
American Funds Preservation Portfolio Class 529-F-1	CPPFX	B-	C+	B	Up	2.00	4.85	5.78	10.52	0.92	10.37	2,119	800-421-4225	Y
American Funds Preservation Portfolio Class A	PPVAX	B-	C+	B	Up	1.84	4.74	5.53	9.76	0.92	10.37	2,119	800-421-4225	Y
American Funds The Bond Fund of America® Class R-5	RBFFX	B	B	B+		4.20	8.21	10.55	18.45	0.93	13.99	56,642	800-421-4225	Y
American Funds The Bond Fund of America® Class F-2	ABNFX	B	B	B+		4.18	8.18	10.48	18.29	0.93	13.99	56,642	800-421-4225	Y
American Funds The Bond Fund of America® Class 529-F	CFAFX	B	B	B		4.17	8.15	10.41	17.98	0.93	13.99	56,642	800-421-4225	Y
American Funds The Bond Fund of America® Class R-5E	RBFHX	B	B	B		4.17	8.16	10.44	18.10	0.93	13.99	56,642	800-421-4225	Y
American Funds The Bond Fund of America® Class A	ABNDX	B	B	B		4.12	8.05	10.20	17.38	0.93	13.99	56,642	800-421-4225	Y
American Funds The Bond Fund of America® Class R-4	RBFEX	B	B	B		4.12	8.06	10.22	17.40	0.93	13.99	56,642	800-421-4225	Y
American Funds The Bond Fund of America® Class F-1	BFAFX	B	B	B	Up	4.11	8.03	10.17	17.23	0.93	13.99	56,642	800-421-4225	Y

		RATINGS				TOTAL RETURNS & PERFORMANCE					ASSETS		NEW INVESTORS	
Fund Name	Ticker Symbol	Overall Rating	Reward Rating	Risk Rating	Recent Up/ Downgrade	3-Month Total Return	6-Month Total Return	1-Year Total Return	3-Year Total Return	3-Year Beta	NAV	Total Assets (MIL.)	Telephone	Open to New Investors
American Funds The Bond Fund of America® Class 529-A	CFAAX	B	B	B	Up	4.10	8.02	10.15	17.14	0.93	13.99	56,642	800-421-4225	Y
American Funds The Bond Fund of America® Class 529-E	CFAEX	B	B	B	Up	4.06	7.92	9.95	16.48	0.93	13.99	56,642	800-421-4225	Y
American Funds The Bond Fund of America® Class R-3	RBFCX	B	B	B	Up	4.04	7.89	9.89	16.33	0.93	13.99	56,642	800-421-4225	Y
American Funds The Bond Fund of America® Class R-2E	RBEBX	B	B	B	Up	4.01	7.81	9.72	15.80	0.93	13.99	56,642	800-421-4225	Y
American Funds The Bond Fund of America® Class R-6	RBFGX	B	B	B	Up	4.21	8.24	10.60	18.64	0.93	13.99	56,642	800-421-4225	Y
MFS Government Securities Fund Class R4	MFGJX	B	B-	B	Up	1.04	6.23	7.91	14.34	0.93	10.45	2,270	877-960-6077	Y
American Funds The Bond Fund of America® Class R-2	RBFBX	B	B-	B	Up	3.93	7.66	9.39	14.78	0.93	13.99	56,642	800-421-4225	Y
American Funds The Bond Fund of America® Class R-1	RBFAX	B	B-	B	Up	3.92	7.64	9.38	14.74	0.93	13.99	56,642	800-421-4225	Y
American Funds The Bond Fund of America® Class C	BFACX	B	B-	B	Up	3.93	7.65	9.39	14.71	0.93	13.99	56,642	800-421-4225	Y
American Funds The Bond Fund of America® Class 529-C	CFACX	B	B-	B	Up	3.91	7.63	9.35	14.56	0.93	13.99	56,642	800-421-4225	Y
MFS Government Securities Fund Class R3	MFGHX	B	B-	B	Up	1.08	6.21	7.76	13.49	0.93	10.45	2,270	877-960-6077	Y
KP Fixed Income Fund Institutional Shares	KPFIX	B-	C	B+	Up	5.32	4.49	7.30	15.58	0.93	10.69	2,255		Y
MFS Government Securities Fund Class B	MFGBX	B-	C+	B		0.89	5.83	6.97	10.99	0.93	10.44	2,270	877-960-6077	Y
MFS Government Securities Fund Class C	MFGDX	B-	C+	B		0.89	5.81	6.95	10.97	0.93	10.47	2,270	877-960-6077	Y
MFS Government Securities Fund Class R1	MFGGX	B-	C+	B		0.89	5.83	6.97	10.99	0.93	10.44	2,270	877-960-6077	Y
American Funds Preservation Portfolio Class ABLE-A	CPPGX	B-	C+	B	Up	1.84	4.74	5.64	9.76	0.93	10.37	2,119	800-421-4225	Y
MFS Government Securities Fund Class R6	MFGKX	B	B-	B		1.07	6.29	8.02	14.71	0.94	10.44	2,270	877-960-6077	Y
Optimum Fixed Income Fund Institutional Class	OIFIX	B	C+	B+	Up	5.27	5.60	7.67	15.56	0.94	10.17	2,575		Y
MFS Government Securities Fund Class A	MFGSX	B	B-	B	Up	0.98	6.10	7.65	13.49	0.94	10.45	2,270	877-960-6077	Y
MFS Government Securities Fund Class R2	MGVSX	B-	B-	B		0.92	5.98	7.39	12.66	0.94	10.44	2,270	877-960-6077	Y
American Funds Preservation Portfolio Class R-5E	RGMFX	B-	C+	B	Up	1.90	4.84	5.75	10.55	0.94	10.38	2,119	800-421-4225	Y
Optimum Fixed Income Fund Class C	OCFIX	B-	C+	B	Up	4.96	4.96	6.57	12.14	0.94	10.15	2,575		Y
Fidelity® Inflation-Protected Bond Index Fund	FIPDX	B	B-	A-	Up	4.17	6.13	8.42	15.85	0.95	10.68	7,433	617-563-7000	Y
Fidelity Advisor® Total Bond Fund Class Z	FBKWX	B	C+	B+	Up	5.91	5.47	8.29	17.07	0.95	11.33	28,185	617-563-7000	Y
Optimum Fixed Income Fund Class A	OAFIX	B	C+	B+	Up	5.17	5.38	7.38	14.65	0.95	10.17	2,575		Y
Fidelity Advisor® Total Bond Fund Class A	FEPAX	B-	C+	B+	Up	5.80	5.25	7.86	15.69	0.95	11.35	28,185	617-563-7000	Y
VALIC Company II Core Bond Fund	VCCBX	B-	C+	B+	Up	4.88	4.97	8.15	15.61	0.95	11.76	1,591		Y
JNL/PIMCO Investment Grade Credit Bond I		B-	C+	B+	Up	8.53	5.61	9.79	21.09	0.95	12.97	1,580		Y
JNL/PIMCO Investment Grade Credit Bond A		B-	C+	B	Up	8.38	5.38	9.46	20.06	0.95	12.92	1,580		Y
TIAA-CREF Inflation-Linked Bond Fund Advisor Class	TIIHX	B-	C	B	Up	3.50	4.07	5.56	11.37	0.95	11.93	3,541	877-518-9161	Y
Pacific Funds Core Income Fund Class A	PLIAX	B-	C	B	Up	6.73	3.95	7.00	15.37	0.95	11.25	1,032	800-722-2333	Y
Fidelity® Total Bond Fund	FTBFX	B	C+	B+	Up	5.88	5.32	8.08	16.64	0.96	11.34	28,185	617-563-7000	Y
Fidelity Advisor® Total Bond Fund Class I	FEPIX	B	C+	B+	Up	5.97	5.39	8.14	16.59	0.96	11.33	28,185	617-563-7000	Y
Fidelity Advisor® Total Bond Fund Class M	FEPTX	B-	C+	B+	Up	5.81	5.26	7.87	15.70	0.96	11.33	28,185	617-563-7000	Y
TIAA-CREF Inflation-Linked Bond Fund Class W	TIIWX	B-	C	B+	Up	3.67	4.24	6.00	12.24	0.96	11.93	3,541	877-518-9161	Y
TIAA-CREF Inflation Linked Bond Fund Premier Class	TIKPX	B-	C	B	Up	3.59	4.05	5.60	11.31	0.96	11.91	3,541	877-518-9161	Y
TIAA-CREF Inflation-Linked Bond Fund Retirement Class	TIKRX	B-	C	B	Up	3.52	3.96	5.44	10.97	0.96	12.02	3,541	877-518-9161	Y
Fidelity Advisor® Total Bond Fund Class C	FCEPX	B-	C	B	Up	5.60	4.76	6.95	12.97	0.96	11.35	28,185	617-563-7000	Y
American Century Ginnie Mae Fund R5 Class	AGMNX	B-	C+	B-	Up	0.83	3.52	5.38	11.58	0.96	10.78	1,042	800-444-4015	Y
JNL/PPM America Total Return Fund Class A		B	B-	B+	Up	5.97	6.30	9.05	17.48	0.97	13.49	1,548		Y
PIMCO Total Return Fund Class A	PTTAX	B	C+	B+	Up	3.78	5.97	8.16	15.27	0.97	10.83	67,970	866-746-2602	Y
PIMCO Total Return Fund Class R	PTRRX	B	C+	B+	Up	3.72	5.84	7.90	14.36	0.97	10.83	67,970	866-746-2602	Y
GE RSP Income Fund	GESLX	B	C+	B+	Up	4.79	5.22	7.94	15.78	0.97	12.29	2,057	617-664-7338	Y
Voya U.S. Bond Index Portfolio Class A	ILUAX	B-	B-	B		2.40	5.80	7.95	13.90	0.97	11.36	3,084	800-366-0066	Y
PIMCO Total Return Fund Class C	PTTCX	B-	C+	B	Up	3.59	5.58	7.36	12.66	0.97	10.83	67,970	866-746-2602	Y
Pacific Funds Core Income Class P		B-	C	B	Up	6.88	4.18	7.39	16.43	0.97	11.3	1,032	800-722-2333	Y
Pacific Funds Core Income Fund Advisor Class	PLIDX	B-	C	B	Up	6.90	4.19	7.40	16.47	0.97	11.28	1,032	800-722-2333	Y
Schwab Short-Term Bond Index Fund	SWSBX	B-	C	B	Up	1.61	3.87	5.39	10.56	0.97	10.38	1,221	877-824-5615	Y
JNL/PPM America Total Return Fund Class I		B	B-	B+	Up	6.03	6.54	9.38	18.57	0.98	13.52	1,548		Y
BNY Mellon Bond Market Index Fund - Class I	DBIRX	B	B-	B+		2.64	6.24	8.73	16.38	0.98	11.09	1,118		Y
Voya U.S. Bond Index Portfolio Class P2	VPUPX	B	B-	B+		2.67	6.16	8.73	16.54	0.98	11.41	3,084	800-366-0066	Y
Harbor Bond Fund Institutional Class	HABDX	B	C+	B+	Up	4.20	6.19	8.54	16.82	0.98	12.29	1,903	800-422-1050	Y

Fund Name	Ticker Symbol	RATINGS: Overall Rating	Reward Rating	Risk Rating	Recent Up/ Downgrade	TOTAL RETURNS & PERFORMANCE: 3-Month Total Return	6-Month Total Return	1-Year Total Return	3-Year Total Return	3-Year Beta	ASSETS: NAV	Total Assets (MIL)	NEW INVESTORS: Telephone	Open to New Investors
Voya U.S. Bond Index Portfolio Class I	ILBAX	B	B-	B+	Up	2.61	6.03	8.46	15.68	0.98	11.41	3,084	800-366-0066	Y
Voya U.S. Bond Index Portfolio Class S	ILABX	B	B-	B	Up	2.46	5.92	8.11	14.74	0.98	11.37	3,084	800-366-0066	Y
Principal Bond Market Index Fund R-5 Class	PBIQX	B	B-	B	Up	2.70	6.02	8.50	15.31	0.98	11.79	2,358	800-787-1621	Y
JNL/Mellon Bond Index Fund Class A		B	B-	B	Up	2.65	5.97	8.13	14.78	0.98	12.78	1,295		Y
Principal Bond Market Index Fund R-4 Class	PBIPX	B	B-	B	Up	2.69	5.91	8.35	15.18	0.98	11.82	2,358	800-787-1621	Y
Voya U.S. Bond Index Portfolio Class S2	IUSBX	B	B-	B	Up	2.52	5.84	8.05	14.22	0.98	11.38	3,084	800-366-0066	Y
PIMCO Fixed Income SHares: Series C	FXICX	B-	C	B+	Up	6.68	5.03	7.73	17.23	0.98	10.77	1,462	866-746-2602	Y
Schwab® Treasury Inflation Protected Securities Index Fund	SWRSX	B	B-	A-	Up	4.19	5.95	8.45	15.72	0.99	11.93	1,158	877-824-5615	Y
Fidelity Advisor® Investment Grade Bond Fund Class A	FGBAX	B	B-	B+	Up	5.52	7.33	9.96	18.18	0.99	8.7	7,365	617-563-7000	Y
DFA Inflation-Protected Securities Portfol Inst Cl	DIPSX	B	B-	B+	Up	4.58	6.32	8.04	16.21	0.99	12.78	5,056	512-306-7400	Y
TIAA-CREF Bond Index Fund Class W	TBIWX	B	B-	B+		2.81	6.27	8.78	16.53	0.99	11.66	17,355	877-518-9161	Y
PIMCO Real Return Fund Class A	PRTNX	B	C+	B+	Up	5.27	5.98	8.12	14.20	0.99	11.85	9,094	866-746-2602	Y
Schwab U.S. Aggregate Bond Index Fund	SWAGX	B	B-	B+	Up	2.78	6.07	8.73	16.50	0.99	10.81	4,017	877-824-5615	Y
JNL/Mellon Bond Index Fund Class I		B	B-	B	Up	2.70	6.06	8.52	15.87	0.99	13.29	1,295		Y
iShares U.S. Aggregate Bond Index Fund Investor A Shares	BMOAX	B	B-	B	Up	2.84	6.15	8.69	15.76	0.99	10.9	2,215	800-441-7762	Y
Wells Fargo Core Plus Bond Fund Class A	STYAX	B	C+	B+	Up	6.78	6.01	8.64	16.88	0.99	13.49	1,108	800-222-8222	Y
Great-West Bond Index Fund Investor Class	MXBIX	B	B-	B	Up	2.68	6.12	8.42	15.31	0.99	15.31	1,366		Y
PIMCO Real Return Fund Class R	PRRRX	B	C+	B+	Up	5.21	5.85	7.85	13.35	0.99	11.85	9,094	866-746-2602	Y
The Hartford Total Return Bond Fund Class R5	ITBTX	B	C+	B+	Up	5.90	5.71	9.22	17.80	0.99	11.23	2,446	888-843-7824	Y
Bridge Builder Core Plus Bond Fund	BBCPX	B	C+	B+	Up	5.69	5.58	7.91	17.48	0.99	10.56	18,564		Y
Principal Bond Market Index Fund R-3 Class	PBOIX	B	C+	B	Up	2.62	5.87	8.17	14.22	0.99	11.72	2,358	800-787-1621	Y
The Hartford Total Return Bond Fund Class R3	ITBRX	B-	C+	B+	Up	5.77	5.44	8.23	15.42	0.99	11.4	2,446	888-843-7824	Y
PIMCO Real Return Fund Class C	PRTCX	B-	C+	B+	Up	5.14	5.72	7.58	12.51	0.99	11.85	9,094	866-746-2602	Y
Wells Fargo Core Plus Bond Fund Class C	WFIPX	B-	C+	B+	Up	6.51	5.59	7.76	14.30	0.99	13.48	1,108	800-222-8222	Y
Principal Inflation Protection Fund Class J	PIPJX	B-	C+	B+	Up	4.47	4.85	6.77	11.69	0.99	8.64	1,608	800-787-1621	Y
Putnam Income Fund Class R5	PINFX	B-	C	B+	Up	4.19	3.47	7.29	18.76	0.99	7.37	3,578	617-292-1000	Y
Putnam Income Fund Class Y	PNCYX	B-	C	B+	Up	4.29	3.40	7.29	18.66	0.99	7.42	3,578	617-292-1000	Y
Putnam Income Fund Class R	PIFRX	B-	C	B+	Up	4.13	3.10	6.68	17.00	0.99	7.21	3,578	617-292-1000	Y
Columbia U.S. Treasury Index Fund Institutional 2 Class	CUTRX	B	B	B		0.48	8.60	10.38	16.86	1	12.22	1,134	800-345-6611	Y
Fidelity® Investment Grade Bond Fund	FBNDX	B	B-	B+	Up	5.72	7.49	10.29	19.29	1	8.71	7,365	617-563-7000	Y
Fidelity Advisor® Investment Grade Bond Fund Class Z	FIKQX	B	B-	B+	Up	5.61	7.53	10.38	19.27	1	8.72	7,365	617-563-7000	Y
Fidelity® U.S. Bond Index Fund	FXNAX	B	B-	B+		2.77	6.54	9.01	17.02	1	12.54	50,694	617-563-7000	Y
Principal Bond Market Index Institutional Class	PNIIX	B	B-	B+		2.74	6.12	8.67	16.21	1	11.96	2,358	800-787-1621	Y
Wells Fargo Core Plus Bond Fund Class R6	STYJX	B	C+	B+	Up	6.87	6.18	9.02	18.25	1	13.51	1,108	800-222-8222	Y
TIAA-CREF Bond Index Fund Premier Class	TBIPX	B	B-	B	Up	2.83	6.13	8.50	15.89	1	11.66	17,355	877-518-9161	Y
Principal Inflation Protection Fund Institutional Class	PIPIX	B	C+	B+	Up	4.72	5.23	7.60	14.34	1	9.09	1,608	800-787-1621	Y
iShares U.S. Aggregate Bond Index Fund Investor P Shares	BMOPX	B	B-	B	Up	2.84	6.16	8.72	15.75	1	10.9	2,215	800-441-7762	Y
TIAA-CREF Bond Index Fund Advisor Class	TBIAX	B	B-	B	Up	2.75	6.16	8.55	15.92	1	11.66	17,355	877-518-9161	Y
Vanguard Total Bond Market II Index Fund Investor Shares	VTBIX	B	C+	B+		2.87	5.96	8.54	16.30	1	11.53	185,732	877-662-7447	Y
The Hartford Total Return Bond Fund Class R6	ITBVX	B	C+	B+	Up	5.86	5.80	8.91	17.79	1	11.14	2,446	888-843-7824	Y
Principal Bond Market Index Fund Class J	PBIJX	B	B-	B	Up	2.71	5.86	8.16	14.47	1	11.73	2,358	800-787-1621	Y
The Hartford Total Return Bond Fund Class R4	ITBUX	B	C+	B+	Up	5.88	5.62	8.60	16.48	1	11.3	2,446	888-843-7824	Y
Principal Core Fixed Income Fund R-4 Class	PIOPX	B	C+	B+	Up	5.74	5.26	8.04	15.94	1	10.19	8,033	800-787-1621	Y
Principal Core Fixed Income Fund R-3 Class	PIOOX	B-	C+	B+	Up	5.79	5.16	7.83	15.39	1	10.2	8,033	800-787-1621	Y
Lord Abbett Core Fixed Income Fund Class R5	LCRTX	B-	C+	B+	Up	3.66	5.40	7.52	14.93	1	11.52	1,929	201-827-2000	Y
Principal Inflation Protection Fund Class A	PITAX	B-	C+	B+	Up	4.58	4.98	7.11	12.53	1	8.89	1,608	800-787-1621	Y
Principal Bond Market Index Fund R-2 Class	PBINX	B-	C+	B		2.53	5.68	7.86	13.56	1	11.72	2,358	800-787-1621	Y
JPMorgan Core Plus Bond Fund Class R5	JCPYX	B-	C	B+	Up	3.92	4.66	6.84	15.33	1	8.71	14,071	800-480-4111	Y
Lord Abbett Core Fixed Income Fund Class R4	LCRSX	B-	C+	B	Up	3.60	5.37	7.36	14.08	1	11.52	1,929	201-827-2000	Y
Principal Inflation Protection Fund R-2 Class	PBSAX	B-	C+	B+	Up	4.52	4.90	6.86	11.85	1	8.55	1,608	800-787-1621	Y
Principal Core Fixed Income Fund R-1 Class	PIOMX	B-	C+	B+	Up	5.61	5.01	7.40	14.24	1	10.18	8,033	800-787-1621	Y
Principal Bond Market Index Fund R-1 Class	PBIMX	B-	C+	B		2.52	5.65	7.76	13.18	1	11.77	2,358	800-787-1621	Y

Fund Name	Ticker Symbol	RATINGS: Overall Rating	Reward Rating	Risk Rating	Recent Up/ Downgrade	TOTAL RETURNS & PERFORMANCE: 3-Month Total Return	6-Month Total Return	1-Year Total Return	3-Year Total Return	3-Year Beta	ASSETS: NAV	Total Assets (MIL)	NEW INVESTORS: Telephone	Open to New Investors
JPMorgan Core Plus Bond Fund Class R4	JCPQX	B-	C	B+	Up	3.88	4.58	6.56	14.82	1	8.7	14,071	800-480-4111	Y
Great-West Bond Index Fund Institutional Class	MXCOX	B-	B-	B		2.67	6.26	8.76	16.57	1	10.47	1,366		Y
PIMCO GNMA and Government Securities Fund Class A	PAGNX	B-	C+	B	Up	1.55	4.13	6.17	11.79	1	11.43	1,737	866-746-2602	Y
Principal Inflation Protection Fund R-1 Class	PISPX	B-	C	B	Up	4.43	4.82	6.73	11.35	1	8.47	1,608	800-787-1621	Y
BNY Mellon Core Plus Fund Class C	DCPCX	B-	C	B	Up	6.57	4.60	7.26	14.91	1	10.88	1,182		Y
JPMorgan Core Plus Bond Fund Class R3	JCPPX	B-	C	B	Up	3.82	4.45	6.42	13.96	1	8.7	14,071	800-480-4111	Y
Lord Abbett Core Fixed Income Fund Class R3	LCRRX	B-	C+	B	Up	3.53	5.14	6.99	13.13	1	11.52	1,929	201-827-2000	Y
Lord Abbett Core Fixed Income Fund Class R2	LCRQX	B-	C+	B	Up	3.51	5.09	6.89	12.79	1	11.52	1,929	201-827-2000	Y
Putnam Income Fund Class R6	PINHX	B-	C	B+	Up	4.17	3.45	7.25	18.99	1	7.42	3,578	617-292-1000	Y
Putnam Income Fund Class A	PINCX	B-	C	B+	Up	4.16	3.34	6.88	17.78	1	7.28	3,578	617-292-1000	Y
JPMorgan Core Plus Bond Fund Class R2	JCPZX	B-	C	B	Up	3.75	4.32	6.14	13.21	1	8.71	14,071	800-480-4111	Y

Section VI:
BUY Rated Bond & Money Market Mutual Funds by Category

Investment Ratings and analysis for BUY Rated Bond & Money Market Mutual Funds by Category. Within category, funds are listed in alphabetical order.

Section VI: Contents

This section contains Weiss Investment Ratings, key rating factors, and summary financial data for BUY Rated Bond & Money Market Mutual Funds by Category. Within category, funds are listed in alphabetical order.

Fund Name
Describes the fund's assets, regions of investments and investment strategies. Many funds have similar names, so you want to make sure the fund you look up is really the one you are interested in evaluating.

Ticker Symbol
An arrangement of characters (usually letters) representing a particular security listed on an exchange or otherwise traded publicly. When a company issues securities to the public marketplace, it selects an available ticker symbol for its securities which investors use to place trade orders. Every listed security has a unique ticker symbol, facilitating the vast array of trade orders that flow through the financial markets every day. If a ticker symbol is not assigned to a particular fund, the International Securities Identification Number (ISIN) is displayed.

RATINGS

Overall Rating
The Weiss rating measured on a scale from A to E based on each fund's risk and performance. See the preceding section, "What Our Ratings Mean," for an explanation of each letter grade rating.

Reward Rating
This is based on the total return over a period of up to five years, including net asset value and price growth. The total return figure is stated net of the expenses and fees charged by the fund. Based on proprietary modeling the individual components of the risk and reward ratings are calculated and weighted and the final rating is generated.

Risk Rating
This is includes the risk ratings of component stocks where applicable and also includes the financial stability of the fund, turnover where applicable, together with the level of volatility as measured by the fund's daily returns over a period of up to five years. Funds with greater stability are considered less risky and receive a higher risk rating. Funds with greater volatility are considered riskier, and will receive a lower risk rating. In addition to considering the fund's volatility, the risk rating also considers an assessment of the valuation and quality of a fund's holdings.

Recent Upgrade/Downgrade
An "Up" or "Down" indicates that the Weiss Mutual Fund rating has changed since the publication of the last print edition. If a fund has had a rating change since March 31, 2020, the change is identified with an "Up" or "Down."

TOTAL RETURNS & PERFORMANCE

3-Month Total Return
The rate of return on an investment over three months that includes interest, capital gains, dividends and distributions realized.

6-Month Total Return
The rate of return on an investment over six months that includes interest, capital gains, dividends and distributions realized.

1-Year Total Return
The rate of return on an investment over one year that includes interest, capital gains, dividends and distributions realized.

3-Year Total Return
The rate of return on an investment over three years that includes interest, capital gains, dividends and distributions realized.

5-Year Total Return
The rate of return on an investment over five years that includes interest, capital gains, dividends and distributions realized.

ASSETS

NAV (Net Asset Value)
A fund's price per share. The value is calculated by dividing the total value of all the securities in the portfolio, less any liabilities, by the number of fund shares outstanding.

Total Assets (MIL)
The total of all assets listed on the institution's balance sheet. This figure primarily consists of loans, investments, and fixed assets. Total Assets are displayed in millions.

NEW INVESTORS

Telephone
The company's phone number.

Open to New Investors
Indicates whether the fund accepts investments from those who are not existing investors. A "Y" in this column identifies that the fund accepts new investors. No data in this column indicates that the fund is closed to new investors. The fund may be closed to new investors because the fund's asset base is getting too large to effectively execute its investing style. Although, the fund may be closed, in most cases, existing investors are able to add to their holdings.

Category: Fixed Income Miscellaneous

Fund Name	Ticker Symbol	Overall Rating	Reward Rating	Risk Rating	Recent Up/ Downgrade	3-Month Total Return	6-Month Total Return	1-Year Total Return	3-Year Total Return	5-Year Total Return	NAV	Total Assets (MIL)	Telephone	Open to New Investors
		RATINGS				TOTAL RETURNS & PERFORMANCE					ASSETS		NEW INVESTORS	
1290 Diversified Bond Fund Class A	TNUAX	B-	C	B+	Up	11.18	5.68	8.34	20.24	27.57	10.5248	110.0	212-554-1234	Y
1290 Diversified Bond Fund Class I	TNUIX	B-	C	B+	Up	11.29	5.89	8.67	21.29	29.33	10.5614	110.0	212-554-1234	Y
1290 Diversified Bond Fund Class R	TNURX	B-	C	B	Up	11.20	5.66	8.11	19.54	26.20	10.5071	110.0	212-554-1234	Y
Carillon Reams Unconstrained Bond Fund Class A	SUBDX	B-	C	B	Up	8.23	5.62	7.71	12.55	19.29	12.62	880.2	800-421-4184	Y
Carillon Reams Unconstrained Bond Fund Class I	SUBFX	B-	C+	B+	Up	8.39	5.83	8.16	13.47	20.87	12.62	880.2	800-421-4184	Y
Carillon Reams Unconstrained Bond Fund Class R-3	SUBRX	B-	C	B	Up	8.16	5.51	7.53	11.59	17.69	12.61	880.2	800-421-4184	Y
Carillon Reams Unconstrained Bond Fund Class R-5	SUBSX	B-	C+	B+	Up	8.39	5.83	8.16	13.47	20.87	12.62	880.2	800-421-4184	Y
Carillon Reams Unconstrained Bond Fund Class R-6	SUBTX	B-	C+	B+	Up	8.42	5.88	8.26	13.76	21.18	12.62	880.2	800-421-4184	Y
Carillon Reams Unconstrained Bond Fund Class Y	SUBYX	B-	C	B	Up	8.26	5.67	7.81	12.48	19.14	12.68	880.2	800-421-4184	Y
Catalyst/Stone Beach Income Opportunity Fund Class A	IOXAX	B-	C	A-		1.72	4.09	6.77	13.81	16.06	9.63	27.0	866-447-4228	Y
Catalyst/Stone Beach Income Opportunity Fund Class C	IOXCX	B-	C	涿		1.55	3.76	6.01	11.44	11.75	9.6	27.0	866-447-4228	Y
Catalyst/Stone Beach Income Opportunity Fund Class I	IOXIX	B	C	A-	Up	1.78	4.22	7.04	14.33	17.25	9.6	27.0	866-447-4228	Y
Navigator Tactical Fixed Income Fund Class I	NTBIX	B-	C	B	Up	6.37	2.11	5.75	12.84	33.85	10.53	5,572		Y
Spectrum Low Volatility Fund Investor Class	SVARX	B	B	A-		8.83	10.57	12.13	23.07	49.35	23.53	108.4		Y

Category: Global Fixed Income

Fund Name	Ticker Symbol	Overall Rating	Reward Rating	Risk Rating	Recent Up/ Downgrade	3-Month Total Return	6-Month Total Return	1-Year Total Return	3-Year Total Return	5-Year Total Return	NAV	Total Assets (MIL)	Telephone	Open to New Investors
		RATINGS				TOTAL RETURNS & PERFORMANCE					ASSETS		NEW INVESTORS	
DFA World ex U.S. Govt Fixed Income Portfol Inst Cl Shares	DWFIX	B-	C	B+		2.39	4.29	4.86	19.40	30.26	10.68	1,500	512-306-7400	Y
Goldman Sachs Global Core Fixed Income Fund Class A Shares	GSGIX	B	C+	B+	Up	4.57	4.47	6.24	14.66	21.62	13.36	675.3	800-526-7384	Y
Goldman Sachs Global Core Fixed Income Fund Class P	GGXPX	B	C+	B+	Up	4.65	4.63	6.59	15.45	21.66	13.35	675.3	800-526-7384	Y
Goldman Sachs Global Core Fixed Income Cl R6 Shares	GBIUX	B	C+	B+	Up	4.73	4.72	6.59	15.93	23.76	13.34	675.3	800-526-7384	Y
Goldman Sachs Global Core Fixed Income Inst Shares	GSGLX	B	C+	B+	Up	4.65	4.63	6.58	15.81	23.67	13.34	675.3	800-526-7384	Y
Goldman Sachs Global Core Fixed Income Investor Shares	GBIRX	B	C+	B+	Up	4.73	4.61	6.52	15.55	23.23	13.31	675.3	800-526-7384	Y
Goldman Sachs Global Core Fixed Income Fund Service Shares	GGISX	B-	C+	B+	Up	4.55	4.40	6.08	14.17	20.31	13.26	675.3	800-526-7384	Y
Janus Henderson Developed World Bond Fund Class A	HFAAX	B-	C	B+	Up	6.80	3.87	5.95	16.20	28.88	9.94	1,504	877-335-2687	Y
Janus Henderson Developed World Bond Fund Class D	HFADX	B-	C	B+	Up	6.86	3.98	6.05	16.84	29.59	9.93	1,504	877-335-2687	Y
Janus Henderson Developed World Bond Fund Class I	HFAIX	B-	C	B+	Up	6.90	4.02	6.24	17.12	30.57	9.91	1,504	877-335-2687	Y
Janus Henderson Developed World Bond Fund Class N	HFARX	B-	C	B+	Up	6.91	4.05	6.20	17.21	30.67	9.91	1,504	877-335-2687	Y
Janus Henderson Developed World Bond Fund Class S	HFASX	B-	C	B	Up	6.76	3.78	5.82	15.81	28.46	9.93	1,504	877-335-2687	Y
Janus Henderson Developed World Bond Fund Class T	HFATX	B-	C	B+	Up	6.82	3.91	6.05	16.81	29.57	9.93	1,504	877-335-2687	Y
Janus Henderson Global Bond Fund Class A	JGBAX	B-	C+	B	Up	3.79	5.47	6.52	11.41	15.34	10.1	219.3	877-335-2687	Y
Janus Henderson Global Bond Fund Class D	JGBDX	B-	C+	B	Up	3.85	5.59	6.75	12.11	16.38	10.09	219.3	877-335-2687	Y
Janus Henderson Global Bond Fund Class I	JGBIX	B-	C+	B	Up	3.86	5.61	6.79	12.28	16.69	10.09	219.3	877-335-2687	Y
Janus Henderson Global Bond Fund Class N	JGLNX	B-	C+	B	Up	3.99	5.66	6.90	12.73	17.38	10.09	219.3	877-335-2687	Y
Janus Henderson Global Bond Fund Class S	JGBSX	B-	C+	B	Up	3.74	5.38	6.24	11.09	15.04	10.1	219.3	877-335-2687	Y
Janus Henderson Global Bond Fund Class T	JHBTX	B-	C+	B	Up	3.81	5.53	6.64	11.92	15.87	10.1	219.3	877-335-2687	Y
John Hancock Funds II Opportunistic Fixed Income Cl 1	JIGDX	B-	C+	B	Up	8.52	5.22	6.68	14.06	24.66	13.49	67.4	800-225-5291	Y
Vanguard Total InterNatl Bond Index Fund Admiral™ Shares	VTABX	B-	C	B+	Up	2.19	2.34	3.85	15.65	24.39	23.04	142,843	877-662-7447	Y
Vanguard Total InterNatl Bond Ind Inst Select Shares	VSIBX	B-	C	B+	Up	2.20	2.45	3.98	16.16	25.06	118.15	142,843	877-662-7447	Y
Vanguard Total InterNatl Bond Ind Institutional Shares	VTIFX	B-	C	B+	Up	2.20	2.36	3.90	15.79	24.64	34.57	142,843	877-662-7447	Y
Vanguard Total InterNatl Bond Index Fund Investor Shares	VTIBX	B-	C	B	Up	2.18	2.32	3.83	15.61	24.17	11.52	142,843	877-662-7447	Y

Category: US Fixed Income

Fund Name	Ticker Symbol	Overall Rating	Reward Rating	Risk Rating	Recent Up/ Downgrade	3-Month Total Return	6-Month Total Return	1-Year Total Return	3-Year Total Return	5-Year Total Return	NAV	Total Assets (MIL)	Telephone	Open to New Investors
		RATINGS				TOTAL RETURNS & PERFORMANCE					ASSETS		NEW INVESTORS	
AB Intermediate Duration Portfolio Advisor Class	IDPYX	B-	C	B	Up	4.84	4.37	6.09	13.42	22.07	13.92	3,490	212-969-1000	Y
AB Intermediate Duration Portfolio Class Z	IDPZX	B-	C	B	Up	4.91	4.66	6.93	14.32	23.04	13.92	3,490	212-969-1000	Y
Aberdeen Total Return Bond Fund Class A	BJBGX	B	B-	B+	Up	6.14	7.37	9.88	17.21	25.07	14.38	192.3	866-667-9231	Y
Aberdeen Total Return Bond Fund Class I	JBGIX	B	B-	B+	Up	6.25	7.59	10.19	18.16	26.67	14.14	192.3	866-667-9231	Y
AIG U.S. Government Securities Fund Class A	SGTAX	B	B-	B	Up	0.24	7.19	8.32	12.67	12.20	9.81	136.5	800-858-8850	Y
AIG U.S. Government Securities Fund Class C	NASBX	B-	C+	B		0.08	6.74	7.64	10.41	8.52	9.8	136.5	800-858-8850	Y
American Century Core Plus Fund Class A	ACCQX	B-	C	B	Up	4.55	3.82	5.90	12.50	19.77	11.23	148.3	800-444-4015	Y
American Century Core Plus Fund I Class	ACCTX	B-	C	B	Up	4.64	3.99	6.27	13.78	21.75	11.23	148.3	800-444-4015	Y
American Century Core Plus Fund Investor Class	ACCNX	B-	C	B	Up	4.61	3.94	6.16	13.42	21.26	11.23	148.3	800-444-4015	Y
American Century Core Plus Fund R5 Class	ACCUX	B-	C	B	Up	4.67	3.95	6.37	14.02	22.36	11.22	148.3	800-444-4015	Y
American Century Diversified Bond Fund A Class	ADFAX	B-	C+	B	Up	3.88	5.75	7.81	13.31	19.32	11.5	2,349	800-444-4015	Y
American Century Diversified Bond Fund I Class	ACBPX	B	C+	B+	Up	3.89	5.98	8.28	14.78	21.96	11.5	2,349	800-444-4015	Y
American Century Diversified Bond Fund Investor Class	ADFIX	B	C+	B	Up	3.94	5.88	8.17	14.12	20.78	11.5	2,349	800-444-4015	Y
American Century Diversified Bond Fund R Class	ADVRX	B-	C+	B	Up	3.81	5.63	7.64	12.50	17.88	11.5	2,349	800-444-4015	Y
American Century Diversified Bond Fund R5 Class	ADRVX	B	C+	B+	Up	3.98	5.98	8.28	14.80	21.99	11.5	2,349	800-444-4015	Y
American Century Diversified Bond Fund R6 Class	ADDVX	B	C+	B+	Up	3.99	6.00	8.43	15.05	22.36	11.51	2,349	800-444-4015	Y
American Century Diversified Bond Fund Y Class	ADVYX	B	C+	B+	Up	3.90	6.00	8.31	14.88	22.07	11.5	2,349	800-444-4015	Y
American Century Ginnie Mae Fund R5 Class	AGMNX	B-	C+	B-	Up	0.83	3.52	5.38	11.58	14.95	10.78	1,042	800-444-4015	Y
American Century Government Bond Fund A Class	ABTAX	B	B-	B	Up	0.66	6.32	7.75	13.50	16.80	11.72	898.1	800-444-4015	Y
American Century Government Bond Fund C Class	ABTCX	B-	C+	B		0.48	5.94	7.06	11.00	12.53	11.72	898.1	800-444-4015	Y
American Century Government Bond Fund I Class	ABHTX	B	B-	B		0.74	6.50	8.22	14.59	18.63	11.71	898.1	800-444-4015	Y
American Century Government Bond Fund Investor Class	CPTNX	B	B-	B		0.63	6.44	8.01	14.35	18.26	11.72	898.1	800-444-4015	Y
American Century Government Bond Fund R Class	ABTRX	B	B-	B	Up	0.60	6.19	7.58	12.66	15.36	11.72	898.1	800-444-4015	Y
American Century Government Bond Fund R5 Class	ABTIX	B	B-	B+		0.76	6.55	8.32	15.03	19.44	11.72	898.1	800-444-4015	Y
American Century Inflation Adjusted Bond Fund A Class	AIAVX	B-	C+	B+	Up	4.89	4.98	6.65	12.08	15.95	12.05	2,414	800-444-4015	Y
American Century Inflation Adjusted Bond Fund I Class	AIAHX	B-	C+	B+	Up	4.96	5.14	7.02	13.15	17.67	12.06	2,414	800-444-4015	Y
American Century Inflation Adjusted Bond Investor Cl	ACITX	B-	C+	B+	Up	4.90	5.08	7.00	12.90	17.38	12.08	2,414	800-444-4015	Y
American Century Inflation Adjusted Bond Fund R Class	AIARX	B-	C	B	Up	4.74	4.83	6.35	11.18	14.42	12.11	2,414	800-444-4015	Y
American Century Inflation Adjusted Bond Fund R5 Class	AIANX	B	C+	B+	Up	5.00	5.19	7.22	13.59	18.59	12.07	2,414	800-444-4015	Y
American Century Inflation Adjusted Bond Fund Y Class	AIAYX	B-	C+	B+	Up	4.92	5.19	7.13	13.49	18.05	12.06	2,414	800-444-4015	Y
American Century Inflation-Adjusted Bond Fund G Class	AINGX	B	C+	B+	Up	5.04	5.31	7.49	14.41	18.96	12.07	2,414	800-444-4015	Y
American Century Inflation-Adjusted Bond Fund R6 Class	AIADX	B	C+	B+	Up	5.03	5.21	7.27	13.67	18.18	12.06	2,414	800-444-4015	Y
American Century NT Diversified Bond Fund G Class	ACLDX	B	C+	B+	Up	3.63	6.24	8.75	16.21	23.41	11.5	2,213	800-444-4015	Y
American Century Zero Coupon 2025 Fund Advisor Class	ACTVX	B	B	B		1.71	8.25	9.25	15.65	23.87	109.27	140.0	800-444-4015	Y
American Century Zero Coupon 2025 Fund Investor Class	BTTRX	B	B	B		1.78	8.38	9.51	16.51	25.42	115.41	140.0	800-444-4015	Y
American Funds College Enrollment Fund Class 529-A	CENAX	B-	C+	B	Up	1.66	4.86	5.77	9.79	12.69	10.35	1,113	800-421-4225	Y
American Funds College Enrollment Fund Class 529-E	CENEX	B-	C	B	Up	1.57	4.66	5.52	9.07	11.57	10.32	1,113	800-421-4225	Y
American Funds College Enrollment Fund Class 529-F-1	CENFX	B-	C+	B	Up	1.66	4.95	6.02	10.52	14.04	10.38	1,113	800-421-4225	Y
American Funds Corporate Bond Fund Class 529-A	COBAX	B	B	B	Up	9.15	9.42	13.20	23.30	37.84	11.69	1,181	800-421-4225	Y
American Funds Corporate Bond Fund Class 529-C	COBCX	B	B	B	Up	8.95	9.00	12.36	20.50	32.89	11.69	1,181	800-421-4225	Y
American Funds Corporate Bond Fund Class 529-E	COBEX	B	B	B	Up	9.10	9.31	13.00	22.60	36.63	11.69	1,181	800-421-4225	Y
American Funds Corporate Bond Fund Class 529-F-1	COBFX	B	B	B+	Up	9.22	9.54	13.47	24.15	39.16	11.69	1,181	800-421-4225	Y
American Funds Corporate Bond Fund Class A	BFCAX	B	B	B	Up	9.15	9.41	13.20	23.41	38.09	11.69	1,181	800-421-4225	Y
American Funds Corporate Bond Fund Class C	BFCCX	B	B	B	Up	8.96	9.03	12.42	20.70	33.14	11.69	1,181	800-421-4225	Y
American Funds Corporate Bond Fund Class F-1	BFCFX	B	B	B	Up	9.16	9.43	13.23	23.36	37.97	11.69	1,181	800-421-4225	Y
American Funds Corporate Bond Fund Class F-2	BFCGX	B	B	B+	Up	9.23	9.57	13.54	24.39	39.49	11.69	1,181	800-421-4225	Y
American Funds Corporate Bond Fund Class F-3	CFBFX	B	B	B+	Up	9.26	9.62	13.65	24.75	39.79	11.69	1,181	800-421-4225	Y
American Funds Corporate Bond Fund Class R-1	RCBAX	B	B	B	Up	8.99	9.09	12.52	21.17	34.52	11.69	1,181	800-421-4225	Y
American Funds Corporate Bond Fund Class R-2	RCBBX	B	B	B	Up	8.98	9.05	12.45	20.87	34.17	11.69	1,181	800-421-4225	Y
American Funds Corporate Bond Fund Class R-2E	RCBGX	B	B	B	Up	9.05	9.20	12.78	22.28	36.71	11.69	1,181	800-421-4225	Y
American Funds Corporate Bond Fund Class R-3	RCBCX	B	B	B	Up	9.09	9.28	12.93	22.43	36.60	11.69	1,181	800-421-4225	Y
American Funds Corporate Bond Fund Class R-4	RCBDX	B	B	B	Up	9.17	9.44	13.26	23.47	38.32	11.69	1,181	800-421-4225	Y

Category: US Fixed Income (con't)

Fund Name	Ticker Symbol	RATINGS				TOTAL RETURNS & PERFORMANCE					ASSETS		NEW INVESTORS	
		Overall Rating	Reward Rating	Risk Rating	Recent Up/ Downgrade	3-Month Total Return	6-Month Total Return	1-Year Total Return	3-Year Total Return	5-Year Total Return	NAV	Total Assets (MIL)	Telephone	Open to New Investors
American Funds Corporate Bond Fund Class R-5	RCBEX	B	B	B+	Up	9.25	9.60	13.60	24.58	39.71	11.69	1,181	800-421-4225	Y
American Funds Corporate Bond Fund Class R-5E	RCBHX	B	B	B+	Up	9.22	9.54	13.48	24.36	39.52	11.69	1,181	800-421-4225	Y
American Funds Corporate Bond Fund Class R-6	RCBFX	B	B	B+	Up	9.26	9.62	13.65	24.71	39.79	11.69	1,181	800-421-4225	Y
American Funds Inflation Linked Bond Fund Class 529-A	CNLAX	B	B	B+	Up	5.16	9.43	10.92	17.35	21.92	10.79	6,297	800-421-4225	Y
American Funds Inflation Linked Bond Fund Class 529-C	CNLCX	B	B-	B	Up	4.99	9.05	10.17	14.85	17.22	10.72	6,297	800-421-4225	Y
American Funds Inflation Linked Bond Fund Class 529-E	CNLEX	B	B	B+	Up	5.19	9.36	10.75	16.58	20.30	10.74	6,297	800-421-4225	Y
American Funds Inflation Linked Bond Fund Class 529-F-1	CNLFX	B	B	B+	Up	5.25	9.51	11.21	18.11	22.88	10.82	6,297	800-421-4225	Y
American Funds Inflation Linked Bond Fund Class A	BFIAX	B	B	B+	Up	5.16	9.43	10.91	17.41	21.73	10.79	6,297	800-421-4225	Y
American Funds Inflation Linked Bond Fund Class C	BFICX	B	B-	B	Up	5.09	9.05	10.32	14.89	17.46	10.72	6,297	800-421-4225	Y
American Funds Inflation Linked Bond Fund Class F-1	BFIFX	B	B	B+	Up	5.16	9.42	10.98	17.37	21.71	10.8	6,297	800-421-4225	Y
American Funds Inflation Linked Bond Fund Class F-2	BFIGX	B	B	B+	Up	5.24	9.60	11.38	18.34	23.38	10.84	6,297	800-421-4225	Y
American Funds Inflation Linked Bond Fund Class F-3	FILBX	B	B	B+	Up	5.35	9.62	11.41	18.68	23.18	10.82	6,297	800-421-4225	Y
American Funds Inflation Linked Bond Fund Class R-1	RILAX	B	B-	B	Up	4.98	9.03	10.22	14.78	17.31	10.74	6,297	800-421-4225	Y
American Funds Inflation Linked Bond Fund Class R-2	RILBX	B	B-	B	Up	4.94	9.03	10.20	14.85	17.25	10.62	6,297	800-421-4225	Y
American Funds Inflation Linked Bond Fund Class R-2E	RILGX	B	B	B	Up	5.07	9.23	10.50	15.81	19.80	10.76	6,297	800-421-4225	Y
American Funds Inflation Linked Bond Fund Class R-3	RILCX	B	B	B+	Up	5.10	9.28	10.69	16.38	19.97	10.71	6,297	800-421-4225	Y
American Funds Inflation Linked Bond Fund Class R-4	RILDX	B	B	B+	Up	5.17	9.44	11.03	17.37	21.75	10.78	6,297	800-421-4225	Y
American Funds Inflation Linked Bond Fund Class R-5	RILEX	B	B	B+	Up	5.24	9.60	11.35	18.54	23.62	10.84	6,297	800-421-4225	Y
American Funds Inflation Linked Bond Fund Class R-5E	RILHX	B	B	B+	Up	5.26	9.53	11.23	18.18	22.97	10.8	6,297	800-421-4225	Y
American Funds Inflation Linked Bond Fund Class R-6	RILFX	B	B	B+	Up	5.34	9.59	11.39	18.66	23.93	10.85	6,297	800-421-4225	Y
American Funds Intermediate Bond of America® Cl 529-A	CBOAX	B-	C+	B	Up	2.50	5.92	6.89	11.44	14.18	14.14	23,949	800-421-4225	Y
American Funds Intermediate Bond of America® Cl 529-E	CBOEX	B-	C+	B	Up	2.45	5.82	6.70	10.83	13.10	14.14	23,949	800-421-4225	Y
American Funds Intermediate Bond of America® Cl 529-F	CBOFX	B-	C+	B	Up	2.56	6.04	7.15	12.24	15.53	14.14	23,949	800-421-4225	Y
American Funds Intermediate Bond Fund of America® Class A	AIBAX	B-	C+	B	Up	2.50	5.91	6.89	11.59	14.53	14.14	23,949	800-421-4225	Y
American Funds Intermediate Bond of America® Cl F-1	IBFFX	B-	C+	B	Up	2.50	5.92	6.90	11.47	14.27	14.14	23,949	800-421-4225	Y
American Funds Intermediate Bond of America® Cl F-2	IBAFX	B-	C+	B	Up	2.57	6.07	7.21	12.46	15.94	14.14	23,949	800-421-4225	Y
American Funds Intermediate Bond of America® Cl F-3	IFBFX	B-	C+	B	Up	2.53	6.05	7.25	12.73	15.84	14.13	23,949	800-421-4225	Y
American Funds Intermediate Bond of America® Cl R-3	RBOCX	B-	C+	B	Up	2.44	5.79	6.63	10.64	12.83	14.14	23,949	800-421-4225	Y
American Funds Intermediate Bond of America® Cl R-4	RBOEX	B-	C+	B	Up	2.52	5.95	6.95	11.65	14.55	14.14	23,949	800-421-4225	Y
American Funds Intermediate Bond of America® Cl R-5	RBOFX	B-	C+	B	Up	2.59	6.10	7.27	12.65	16.27	14.14	23,949	800-421-4225	Y
American Funds Intermediate Bond of America® Cl R-5E	RBOHX	B-	C+	B	Up	2.57	6.05	7.16	12.40	15.69	14.14	23,949	800-421-4225	Y
American Funds Intermediate Bond of America® Cl R-6	RBOGX	B-	C+	B	Up	2.53	6.06	7.25	12.75	16.51	14.13	23,949	800-421-4225	Y
American Funds Mortgage Fund® Class 529-A	CMFAX	B-	C+	B	Up	1.31	5.69	6.80	11.00	16.44	10.56	7,229	800-421-4225	Y
American Funds Mortgage Fund® Class 529-E	CMFEX	B-	C+	B	Up	1.16	5.48	6.60	10.32	15.15	10.56	7,229	800-421-4225	Y
American Funds Mortgage Fund® Class 529-F-1	CMFFX	B-	B-	B		1.37	5.71	7.06	11.78	17.74	10.56	7,229	800-421-4225	Y
American Funds Mortgage Fund® Class A	MFAAX	B-	C+	B	Up	1.31	5.71	6.85	11.31	16.92	10.57	7,229	800-421-4225	Y
American Funds Mortgage Fund® Class F-1	MFAEX	B-	C+	B	Up	1.32	5.72	6.88	11.20	16.90	10.57	7,229	800-421-4225	Y
American Funds Mortgage Fund® Class F-2	MFAFX	B-	B-	B		1.39	5.86	7.17	12.14	18.52	10.57	7,229	800-421-4225	Y
American Funds Mortgage Fund® Class F-3	AFFMX	B	B-	B	Up	1.42	5.92	7.28	12.49	19.14	10.57	7,229	800-421-4225	Y
American Funds Mortgage Fund® Class R-2E	RMBEX	B-	C+	B	Up	1.22	5.52	6.45	9.90	15.16	10.55	7,229	800-421-4225	Y
American Funds Mortgage Fund® Class R-3	RMACX	B-	C+	B	Up	1.25	5.58	6.56	10.08	14.86	10.55	7,229	800-421-4225	Y
American Funds Mortgage Fund® Class R-4	RMAEX	B-	C+	B	Up	1.33	5.73	6.89	11.28	17.05	10.57	7,229	800-421-4225	Y
American Funds Mortgage Fund® Class R-5	RMAFX	B-	B-	B	Up	1.40	5.88	7.20	12.28	18.75	10.57	7,229	800-421-4225	Y
American Funds Mortgage Fund® Class R-5E	RMAHX	B-	B-	B		1.37	5.73	7.11	12.06	18.40	10.56	7,229	800-421-4225	Y
American Funds Mortgage Fund® Class R-6	RMAGX	B-	B-	B	Up	1.42	5.92	7.29	12.51	19.17	10.57	7,229	800-421-4225	Y
American Funds Preservation Portfolio Class 529-A	CPPAX	B-	C+	B	Up	1.94	4.74	5.64	9.74	12.39	10.37	2,119	800-421-4225	Y
American Funds Preservation Portfolio Class 529-F-1	CPPFX	B-	C+	B	Up	2.00	4.85	5.78	10.52	13.60	10.37	2,119	800-421-4225	Y
American Funds Preservation Portfolio Class A	PPVAX	B-	C+	B	Up	1.84	4.74	5.53	9.76	12.40	10.37	2,119	800-421-4225	Y
American Funds Preservation Portfolio Class ABLE-A	CPPGX	B-	C+	B	Up	1.84	4.74	5.64	9.76	12.53	10.37	2,119	800-421-4225	Y
American Funds Preservation Portfolio Class F-1	PPVFX	B-	C+	B	Up	1.85	4.65	5.54	9.77	12.39	10.37	2,119	800-421-4225	Y
American Funds Preservation Portfolio Class F-2	PPEFX	B-	C+	B	Up	1.91	4.87	5.82	10.66	13.90	10.37	2,119	800-421-4225	Y
American Funds Preservation Portfolio Class F-3	PPFFX	B-	C+	B	Up	2.03	4.91	6.02	10.99	14.37	10.37	2,119	800-421-4225	Y

Category: US Fixed Income (con't)

Fund Name	Ticker Symbol	RATINGS: Overall Rating	Reward Rating	Risk Rating	Recent Up/ Downgrade	TOTAL RETURNS & PERFORMANCE: 3-Month Total Return	6-Month Total Return	1-Year Total Return	3-Year Total Return	5-Year Total Return	ASSETS: NAV	Total Assets (MIL)	NEW INVESTORS: Telephone	Open to New Investors
American Funds Preservation Portfolio Class R-4	RPPEX	B-	C+	B	Up	1.95	4.75	5.66	9.87	12.67	10.38	2,119	800-421-4225	Y
American Funds Preservation Portfolio Class R-5	RPPFX	B-	C+	B	Up	2.02	4.88	5.96	10.79	14.26	10.38	2,119	800-421-4225	Y
American Funds Preservation Portfolio Class R-5E	RGMFX	B-	C+	B	Up	1.90	4.84	5.75	10.55	13.83	10.38	2,119	800-421-4225	Y
American Funds Preservation Portfolio Class R-6	RPPGX	B-	C+	B	Up	2.03	4.90	6.01	10.96	14.56	10.38	2,119	800-421-4225	Y
American Funds Strategic Bond Fund Class 529-A	CANAX	B	B	B	Up	6.34	14.54	15.85	24.54		11.68	2,132	800-421-4225	Y
American Funds Strategic Bond Fund Class 529-C	CANCX	B	B	B		6.17	14.16	15.02	21.73		11.64	2,132	800-421-4225	Y
American Funds Strategic Bond Fund Class 529-E	CANEX	B	B	B	Up	6.29	14.40	15.59	23.87		11.69	2,132	800-421-4225	Y
American Funds Strategic Bond Fund Class 529-F-1	CANFX	B	B	B	Up	6.39	14.64	16.10	25.40		11.69	2,132	800-421-4225	Y
American Funds Strategic Bond Fund Class A	ANBAX	B	B	B+		6.34	14.52	15.83	24.71		11.69	2,132	800-421-4225	Y
American Funds Strategic Bond Fund Class C	ANBCX	B	B	B	Up	6.13	14.06	14.95	21.85		11.63	2,132	800-421-4225	Y
American Funds Strategic Bond Fund Class F-1	ANBEX	B	B	B+		6.30	14.52	15.84	24.56		11.68	2,132	800-421-4225	Y
American Funds Strategic Bond Fund Class F-2	ANBFX	B	B	B	Up	6.41	14.67	16.14	25.74		11.7	2,132	800-421-4225	Y
American Funds Strategic Bond Fund Class F-3	ANBGX	B	B	B	Up	6.43	14.72	16.26	25.97		11.69	2,132	800-421-4225	Y
American Funds Strategic Bond Fund Class R-1	RANAX	B	B	B		6.23	14.17	15.11	22.29		11.68	2,132	800-421-4225	Y
American Funds Strategic Bond Fund Class R-2	RANBX	B	B	B		6.11	14.14	15.05	22.11		11.65	2,132	800-421-4225	Y
American Funds Strategic Bond Fund Class R-2E	RANHX	B	B	B+		6.21	14.35	15.41	24.11		11.69	2,132	800-421-4225	Y
American Funds Strategic Bond Fund Class R-3	RANCX	B	B	B	Up	6.29	14.41	15.60	23.84		11.68	2,132	800-421-4225	Y
American Funds Strategic Bond Fund Class R-4	RANEX	B	B	B	Up	6.35	14.56	15.92	24.83		11.69	2,132	800-421-4225	Y
American Funds Strategic Bond Fund Class R-5	RANFX	B	B	B	Up	6.41	14.68	16.19	25.77		11.7	2,132	800-421-4225	Y
American Funds Strategic Bond Fund Class R-5E	RANJX	B	B	B	Up	6.39	14.64	16.09	25.57		11.7	2,132	800-421-4225	Y
American Funds Strategic Bond Fund Class R-6	RANGX	B	B	B+		6.51	14.80	16.34	26.05		11.71	2,132	800-421-4225	Y
American Funds The Bond Fund of America® Class 529-A	CFAAX	B	B	B	Up	4.10	8.02	10.15	17.14	23.95	13.99	56,642	800-421-4225	Y
American Funds The Bond Fund of America® Class 529-C	CFACX	B	B-	B	Up	3.91	7.63	9.35	14.56	19.40	13.99	56,642	800-421-4225	Y
American Funds The Bond Fund of America® Class 529-E	CFAEX	B	B	B	Up	4.06	7.92	9.95	16.48	22.75	13.99	56,642	800-421-4225	Y
American Funds The Bond Fund of America® Class 529-F	CFAFX	B	B	B		4.17	8.15	10.41	17.98	25.41	13.99	56,642	800-421-4225	Y
American Funds The Bond Fund of America® Class A	ABNDX	B	B	B		4.12	8.05	10.20	17.38	24.42	13.99	56,642	800-421-4225	Y
American Funds The Bond Fund of America® Class C	BFACX	B	B-	B	Up	3.93	7.65	9.39	14.71	19.67	13.99	56,642	800-421-4225	Y
American Funds The Bond Fund of America® Class F-1	BFAFX	B	B	B	Up	4.11	8.03	10.17	17.23	24.17	13.99	56,642	800-421-4225	Y
American Funds The Bond Fund of America® Class F-2	ABNFX	B	B	B+		4.18	8.18	10.48	18.29	26.00	13.99	56,642	800-421-4225	Y
American Funds The Bond Fund of America® Class F-3	BFFAX	B	B	B+		4.21	8.24	10.60	18.60	25.89	13.99	56,642	800-421-4225	Y
American Funds The Bond Fund of America® Class R-1	RBFAX	B	B-	B	Up	3.92	7.64	9.38	14.74	19.79	13.99	56,642	800-421-4225	Y
American Funds The Bond Fund of America® Class R-2	RBFBX	B	B-	B	Up	3.93	7.66	9.39	14.78	19.85	13.99	56,642	800-421-4225	Y
American Funds The Bond Fund of America® Class R-2E	RBEBX	B	B	B	Up	4.01	7.81	9.72	15.80	21.81	13.99	56,642	800-421-4225	Y
American Funds The Bond Fund of America® Class R-3	RBFCX	B	B	B	Up	4.04	7.89	9.89	16.33	22.55	13.99	56,642	800-421-4225	Y
American Funds The Bond Fund of America® Class R-4	RBFEX	B	B	B		4.12	8.06	10.22	17.40	24.45	13.99	56,642	800-421-4225	Y
American Funds The Bond Fund of America® Class R-5	RBFFX	B	B	B+		4.20	8.21	10.55	18.45	26.31	13.99	56,642	800-421-4225	Y
American Funds The Bond Fund of America® Class R-5E	RBFHX	B	B	B		4.17	8.16	10.44	18.10	25.51	13.99	56,642	800-421-4225	Y
American Funds The Bond Fund of America® Class R-6	RBFGX	B	B	B	Up	4.21	8.24	10.60	18.64	26.64	13.99	56,642	800-421-4225	Y
American Funds U.S. Govt Securities Fund® Class 529-A	CGTAX	B	B	B		0.97	8.80	9.86	14.89	19.07	14.91	17,998	800-421-4225	Y
American Funds U.S. Govt Securities Fund® Class 529-C	CGTCX	B-	B-	B		0.74	8.39	8.98	12.32	14.69	14.85	17,998	800-421-4225	Y
American Funds U.S. Govt Securities Fund® Class 529-E	CGTEX	B	B	B	Up	0.91	8.69	9.63	14.16	17.77	14.91	17,998	800-421-4225	Y
American Funds U.S. Govt Securities Fund® Class 529-F-1	CGTFX	B	B	B		1.02	8.92	10.11	15.69	20.42	14.91	17,998	800-421-4225	Y
American Funds U.S. Government Securities Fund® Class A	AMUSX	B	B	B		0.96	8.79	9.84	14.91	19.34	14.91	17,998	800-421-4225	Y
American Funds U.S. Government Securities Fund® Class C	UGSCX	B-	B-	B		0.81	8.39	9.07	12.46	14.91	14.87	17,998	800-421-4225	Y
American Funds U.S. Government Securities Fund® Class F-1	UGSFX	B	B	B		0.97	8.81	9.89	15.03	19.34	14.91	17,998	800-421-4225	Y
American Funds U.S. Government Securities Fund® Class F-2	GVTFX	B	B	B		1.04	8.96	10.19	15.89	20.95	14.91	17,998	800-421-4225	Y
American Funds U.S. Government Securities Fund® Class F-3	USGFX	B	B	B		1.07	8.94	10.23	16.26	20.91	14.91	17,998	800-421-4225	Y
American Funds U.S. Government Securities Fund® Class R-1	RGVAX	B-	B-	B		0.75	8.39	9.08	12.44	15.02	14.87	17,998	800-421-4225	Y
American Funds U.S. Government Securities Fund® Class R-2	RGVBX	B	B-	B	Up	0.82	8.41	9.09	12.59	15.13	14.87	17,998	800-421-4225	Y
American Funds U.S. Government Securities Fund® Class R-2E	RGEVX	B	B-	B	Up	0.87	8.59	9.43	13.52	17.03	14.91	17,998	800-421-4225	Y
American Funds U.S. Government Securities Fund® Class R-3	RGVCX	B	B	B	Up	0.84	8.59	9.51	13.94	17.51	14.9	17,998	800-421-4225	Y
American Funds U.S. Government Securities Fund® Class R-4	RGVEX	B	B	B		0.98	8.75	9.85	15.05	19.52	14.91	17,998	800-421-4225	Y

Category: US Fixed Income (con't)

Fund Name	Ticker Symbol	RATINGS: Overall Rating	Reward Rating	Risk Rating	Recent Up/ Downgrade	TOTAL RETURNS & PERFORMANCE: 3-Month Total Return	6-Month Total Return	1-Year Total Return	3-Year Total Return	5-Year Total Return	ASSETS: NAV	Total Assets (MIL)	NEW INVESTORS: Telephone	Open to New Investors
American Funds U.S. Government Securities Fund® Class R-5	RGVFX	B		B		1.06	8.91	10.17	16.08	21.29	14.91	17,998	800-421-4225	Y
American Funds U.S. Government Securities Fund® Class R-5E	RGVJX	B	B	B		1.03	8.87	10.07	15.81	20.58	14.9	17,998	800-421-4225	Y
American Funds U.S. Government Securities Fund® Class R-6	RGVGX	B	B	B		1.07	9.02	10.31	16.36	21.64	14.91	17,998	800-421-4225	Y
AMG GW&K Core Bond ESG Fund - Class I	MBDFX	B-	C+	B	Up	4.99	5.36	8.20	15.85	22.59	10.94	210.6	800-835-3879	Y
AMG GW&K Core Bond ESG Fund - Class N	MBGVX	B-	C+	B	Up	4.91	5.09	7.76	14.72	20.46	10.93	210.6	800-835-3879	Y
AMG GW&K Core Bond ESG Fund - Class Z	MBDLX	B-	C+	B+	Up	5.01	5.40	8.29	16.02	22.93	10.93	210.6	800-835-3879	Y
AMG GW&K Enhanced Core Bond ESG Fund - Class I	MFDSX	B-	C+	B	Up	5.61	5.42	8.47	16.52	20.36	10.62	34.6	800-835-3879	Y
AMG GW&K Enhanced Core Bond ESG Fund - Class N	MFDAX	B-	C+	B	Up	5.68	5.45	8.30	16.06	19.47	10.59	34.6	800-835-3879	Y
AMG GW&K Enhanced Core Bond ESG Fund - Class Z	MFDYX	B-	C+	B+	Up	5.63	5.56	8.54	16.87	20.92	10.62	34.6	800-835-3879	Y
Baird Aggregate Bond Fund Class Institutional	BAGIX	B	C+	B+	Up	4.78	6.35	9.34	17.76	26.34	11.78	25,882	800-792-2473	Y
Baird Aggregate Bond Fund Class Investor	BAGSX	B	C+	B+	Up	4.72	6.27	9.01	16.84	24.70	12.2	25,882	800-792-2473	Y
Baird Core Plus Bond Fund Class Institutional	BCOIX	B	C+	B+	Up	5.75	5.79	8.92	17.76	27.38	12.07	26,008	800-792-2473	Y
Baird Core Plus Bond Fund Class Investor	BCOSX	B	C+	B+	Up	5.70	5.68	8.62	16.78	25.66	12.59	26,008	800-792-2473	Y
Baird Intermediate Bond Fund Class Institutional	BIMIX	B	C+	B+	Up	4.40	5.55	7.50	14.45	20.39	11.76	4,546	800-792-2473	Y
Baird Intermediate Bond Fund Class Investor	BIMSX	B-	C+	B+	Up	4.39	5.43	7.33	13.67	18.93	12.32	4,546	800-792-2473	Y
Bernstein Intermediate Duration Institutional Portfolio	SIIDX	B-	C+	B+	Up	5.32	5.19	7.75	15.36	24.36	15.92	837.8	212-969-1000	Y
Bishop Street High Grade Income Fund Class Institutional	BSHGX	B	B-	B	Up	3.60	6.24	8.84	15.69	21.44	10.41	34.2		Y
BlackRock Allocation Target Shares Series C Portfolio	BRACX	B-	C+	B+	Up	8.83	6.50	10.94	21.87	33.98	11.33	509.6	800-441-7762	Y
BlackRock Allocation Target Shares Series M Portfolio	BRAMX	B-	C+	B+	Up	2.37	3.72	6.00	13.51	19.37	9.96	1,017	800-441-7762	Y
BlackRock Core Bond Portfolio Class K	CCBBX	B-	C+	B	Up	5.11	5.72	8.69	16.77	23.54	10.39	4,127	800-441-7762	Y
BlackRock Core Bond Portfolio Class R Shares	BCBRX	B-	C+	B	Up	4.97	5.44	8.11	14.87	20.07	10.38	4,127	800-441-7762	Y
BlackRock Core Bond Portfolio Institutional Shares	BFMCX	B-	C+	B	Up	5.11	5.71	8.66	16.50	23.26	10.36	4,127	800-441-7762	Y
BlackRock Core Bond Portfolio Investor A Shares	BCBAX	B-	C+	B	Up	5.04	5.57	8.27	15.63	21.47	10.37	4,127	800-441-7762	Y
BlackRock Core Bond Portfolio Investor C Shares	BCBCX	B-	C+	B	Up	4.86	5.20	7.49	13.10	17.06	10.33	4,127	800-441-7762	Y
BlackRock Core Bond Portfolio Service Shares	CMCBX	B-	C+	B	Up	5.04	5.58	8.28	15.63	21.61	10.36	4,127	800-441-7762	Y
BlackRock CoreAlpha Bond Fund Class K	BCRKX	B	C+	B+	Up	5.45	6.48	9.22	18.71	25.69	11.09	1,675	800-441-7762	Y
BlackRock CoreAlpha Bond Fund Institutional Shares	BCRIX	B	C+	B+	Up	5.54	6.45	9.17	18.55	25.43	11.09	1,675	800-441-7762	Y
BlackRock CoreAlpha Bond Fund Investor A Shares	BCRAX	B	C+	B+	Up	5.47	6.32	8.90	17.51	23.35	11.09	1,675	800-441-7762	Y
BlackRock CoreAlpha Bond Fund Investor C Shares	BCRCX	B-	C+	B	Up	5.18	5.93	8.10	14.89	18.93	11.09	1,675	800-441-7762	Y
BlackRock GNMA Portfolio Class K	BBGPX	B-	C+	B-	Up	1.55	3.51	5.49	11.66	15.70	9.55	559.1	800-441-7762	Y
BlackRock GNMA Portfolio Institutional Shares	BGNIX	B-	C+	B	Up	1.53	3.48	5.43	11.37	15.33	9.58	559.1	800-441-7762	Y
BlackRock GNMA Portfolio Investor A Shares	BGPAX	B-	C+	B	Up	1.47	3.35	5.16	10.55	13.79	9.62	559.1	800-441-7762	Y
BlackRock GNMA Portfolio Service Shares	BGPSX	B-	C+	B	Up	1.36	3.36	5.17	10.55	13.76	9.56	559.1	800-441-7762	Y
BlackRock Inflation Protected Bond Fund Class K	BPLBX	B	C+	A-	Up	5.35	6.08	8.64	15.24	18.95	11.24	1,814	800-441-7762	Y
BlackRock Inflation Protected Bond Institutional Shares	BPRIX	B	C+	A-	Up	5.37	6.08	8.70	15.11	18.64	11.42	1,814	800-441-7762	Y
BlackRock Inflation Protected Bond Fund Investor A Shares	BPRAX	B	C+	B+	Up	5.28	6.01	8.40	14.28	17.03	11.13	1,814	800-441-7762	Y
BlackRock Inflation Protected Bond Fund Investor C Shares	BPRCX	B-	C+	B	Up	5.11	5.56	7.63	11.74	12.80	10.69	1,814	800-441-7762	Y
BlackRock Inflation Protected Bond Fund Service Shares	BPRSX	B	C+	B+	Up	5.32	5.95	8.42	14.29	17.05	11.25	1,814	800-441-7762	Y
BlackRock Systematic ESG Bond Fund Class K	BIAKX	B	B-	B	Up	3.47	7.00	9.61	17.78		10.65	49.8	800-441-7762	Y
BlackRock Systematic ESG Bond Fund Institutional	BIIIX	B	B-	B	Up	3.46	6.98	9.57	17.65		10.65	49.8	800-441-7762	Y
BlackRock Systematic ESG Bond Fund Investor A	BIAAX	B	B-	B	Up	3.39	6.84	9.29	16.73		10.65	49.8	800-441-7762	Y
BlackRock Systematic ESG Bond Fund Investor C	BIACX	B-	B-	B		3.20	6.45	8.48	14.15		10.65	49.8	800-441-7762	Y
BlackRock Total Return Fund Class K Shares	MPHQX	B-	C+	B+	Up	5.64	5.12	8.02	16.19	24.29	12.39	17,266	800-441-7762	Y
BlackRock Total Return Fund Class R Shares	MRCBX	B-	C+	B	Up	5.47	4.78	7.40	13.93	20.33	12.4	17,266	800-441-7762	Y
BlackRock Total Return Fund Institutional Shares	MAHQX	B-	C+	B+	Up	5.62	5.09	7.94	15.96	23.89	12.39	17,266	800-441-7762	Y
BlackRock Total Return Fund Investor A Shares	MDHQX	B-	C+	B	Up	5.63	4.92	7.67	14.80	21.83	12.4	17,266	800-441-7762	Y
BlackRock Total Return Fund Investor A1 Shares	MEHQX	B-	C+	B+	Up	5.68	5.01	7.87	15.45	22.98	12.39	17,266	800-441-7762	
BlackRock Total Return Fund Investor C Shares	MFHQX	B-	C	B	Up	5.45	4.57	6.96	12.55	17.90	12.39	17,266	800-441-7762	Y
BlackRock Total Return Fund Service Shares	MSHQX	B-	C+	B	Up	5.63	5.02	7.71	15.01	22.08	12.4	17,266	800-441-7762	Y
BlackRock U.S. Government Bond Portfolio Class K	BIGLX	B	B-	B		1.29	6.16	8.26	14.45	19.22	11.11	818.1	800-441-7762	Y
BlackRock U.S. Government Bond Portfolio Class R	BGBRX	B	B-	B	Up	1.15	5.96	7.75	12.71	16.11	11.14	818.1	800-441-7762	Y
BlackRock U.S. Govt Bond Portfolio Institutional Shares	PNIGX	B	B-	B		1.28	6.13	8.20	14.31	19.08	11.11	818.1	800-441-7762	Y

Category: US Fixed Income (con't)

Fund Name	Ticker Symbol	Overall Rating	Reward Rating	Risk Rating	Recent Up/ Downgrade	3-Month Total Return	6-Month Total Return	1-Year Total Return	3-Year Total Return	5-Year Total Return	NAV	Total Assets (MIL)	Telephone	Open to New Investors
		RATINGS				TOTAL RETURNS & PERFORMANCE					ASSETS		NEW INVESTORS	
BlackRock U.S. Government Bond Portfolio Investor A Shares	CIGAX	B	B-	B	Up	1.21	6.09	7.92	13.56	17.60	11.14	818.1	800-441-7762	Y
BlackRock U.S. Government Bond Portfolio Investor C Shares	BIGCX	B-	C+	B		1.03	5.71	7.13	11.06	13.15	11.12	818.1	800-441-7762	Y
BlackRock U.S. Government Bond Portfolio Service Shares	PIGSX	B	B-	B	Up	1.21	6.01	7.84	13.48	17.71	11.1	818.1	800-441-7762	Y
BMO Core Plus Bond Fund Class A	BATCX	B-	C+	B+	Up	4.62	4.54	7.28	14.66	23.62	12.28	1,117	800-236-3863	Y
BMO Core Plus Bond Fund Class I	MCBIX	B-	C+	B+	Up	4.78	4.75	7.54	15.61	25.16	12.28	1,117	800-236-3863	Y
BMO Core Plus Bond Fund Class Y	MCYBX	B-	C+	B+	Up	4.71	4.62	7.27	14.75	23.71	12.29	1,117	800-236-3863	Y
BNY Mellon Bond Fund Class Investor	MIBDX	B	C+	B+	Up	3.93	5.58	7.99	15.19	21.42	13.51	1,201	800-645-6561	Y
BNY Mellon Bond Fund Class M	MPBFX	B	C+	B+	Up	3.99	5.71	8.26	16.07	22.97	13.54	1,201	800-645-6561	Y
BNY Mellon Bond Market Index Fund - Class I	DBIRX	B	B-	B+		2.64	6.24	8.73	16.38	22.84	11.09	1,118		Y
BNY Mellon Bond Market Index Fund - Investor Shares	DBMIX	B	B-	B	Up	2.57	6.21	8.46	15.62	21.33	11.09	1,118		Y
BNY Mellon Core Plus Fund Class A	DCPAX	B-	C+	B+	Up	6.78	4.99	7.97	17.43	27.02	10.87	1,182		Y
BNY Mellon Core Plus Fund Class C	DCPCX	B-	C	B	Up	6.57	4.60	7.26	14.91	22.45	10.88	1,182		Y
BNY Mellon Core Plus Fund Class I	DCPIX	B-	C+	B+	Up	6.84	5.12	8.23	18.15	27.80	10.87	1,182		Y
BNY Mellon Core Plus Fund Class Y	DCPYX	B-	C+	B+	Up	6.95	5.24	8.48	18.26	27.91	10.88	1,182		Y
BNY Mellon Inflation Adjusted Securities Fund Class I	DIASX	B-	C	B	Up	3.53	3.88	5.27	10.65	13.49	13.17	69.1		Y
BNY Mellon Inflation Adjusted Securities Fund Class Y	DAIYX	B-	C	B	Up	3.46	3.91	5.34	10.86	13.88	13.18	69.1		Y
BNY Mellon Intermediate Bond Fund Class M	MPIBX	B-	C	B	Up	3.35	3.89	5.56	10.94	15.18	13.03	949.8	800-645-6561	Y
Brandes Core Plus Fixed Income Fund Class I	BCPIX	B-	C+	B	Up	2.42	4.35	5.75	11.33	17.96	9.52	86.5	800-331-2979	Y
Brandes Core Plus Fixed Income Fund Class R6	BCPRX	B-	C+	B+	Up	2.53	4.57	6.26	13.27	20.02	9.52	86.5	800-331-2979	Y
BrandywineGLOBAL - Global Flexible Income Fund Class A	LFLAX	B-	C+	B+	Up	6.54	5.77	8.08	17.70	30.77	10.46	15.9	877-721-1926	Y
BrandywineGLOBAL - Global Flexible Income Fund Class I	LFLIX	B	C+	B+	Up	6.45	5.68	8.25	18.43	32.34	10.46	15.9	877-721-1926	Y
BrandywineGLOBAL - Global Flexible Income Fund Class IS	LFLSX	B	C+	B+	Up	6.55	5.80	8.28	18.53	32.64	10.47	15.9	877-721-1926	Y
Bridge Builder Core Bond Fund	BBTBX	B	C+	B+	Up	4.44	6.23	8.98	17.73	26.05	10.91	13,593		Y
Bridge Builder Core Plus Bond Fund	BBCPX	B	C+	B+	Up	5.69	5.58	7.91	17.48	24.02	10.56	18,564		Y
Calamos Total Return Bond Fund Class A	CTRAX	B-	C+	B	Up	3.56	4.69	6.97	13.42	20.17	10.86	78.6	800-582-6959	Y
Calamos Total Return Bond Fund Class I	CTRIX	B-	C+	B	Up	3.62	4.82	7.23	14.27	21.79	10.86	78.6	800-582-6959	Y
Calvert Long-Term Income Fund Class A	CLDAX	B-	C+	B		9.95	8.02	14.21	26.89	45.20	19.64	92.6	202-238-2200	Y
Calvert Long-Term Income Fund Class I	CLDIX	B-	C+	B		10.01	8.15	14.49	27.97	48.06	19.66	92.6	202-238-2200	Y
Capital Group Core Bond Fund	CCBPX	B-	C+	B	Up	2.74	5.76	7.17	12.91	17.15	10.71	525.4	213-486-9257	Y
Carillon Reams Core Bond Fund Class A	CRCBX	B	B	B+		6.34	12.62	14.83	23.54	29.84	13.07	246.3	800-421-4184	Y
Carillon Reams Core Bond Fund Class C	CRCDX	B	B	B	Up	6.17	12.22	13.98	20.81	25.09	13.06	246.3	800-421-4184	Y
Carillon Reams Core Bond Fund Class I	SCCIX	B	B	B+		6.52	12.88	15.32	25.01	32.04	13.09	246.3	800-421-4184	Y
Carillon Reams Core Bond Fund Class R-3	CRCQX	B	B	B+	Up	6.26	12.49	14.55	22.63	28.24	13.08	246.3	800-421-4184	Y
Carillon Reams Core Bond Fund Class R-5	CRCSX	B	B	B+		6.40	12.74	15.21	24.69	31.70	13.09	246.3	800-421-4184	Y
Carillon Reams Core Bond Fund Class R-6	CRCUX	B	B	B+		6.43	12.88	15.31	25.01	32.04	13.09	246.3	800-421-4184	Y
Carillon Reams Core Bond Fund Class Y	SCCYX	B	B	B+		6.35	12.63	14.82	23.48	29.47	13.08	246.3	800-421-4184	Y
Carillon Reams Core Plus Bond Fund Class A	SCPDX	B	B	B+	Up	8.58	12.27	14.56	22.90	29.22	36.15	754.8	800-421-4184	Y
Carillon Reams Core Plus Bond Fund Class C	SCPEX	B	B	B	Up	8.51	11.99	13.85	20.30	24.62	36.16	754.8	800-421-4184	Y
Carillon Reams Core Plus Bond Fund Class I	SCPZX	B	B	B+	Up	8.79	12.61	15.17	24.43	31.49	36.23	754.8	800-421-4184	Y
Carillon Reams Core Plus Bond Fund Class R-3	SCPUX	B	B	B	Up	8.68	12.32	14.46	22.17	27.81	36.22	754.8	800-421-4184	Y
Carillon Reams Core Plus Bond Fund Class R-5	SCPVX	B	B	B+	Up	8.82	12.60	15.10	24.15	31.19	36.24	754.8	800-421-4184	Y
Carillon Reams Core Plus Bond Fund Class R-6	SCPWX	B	B	B+	Up	8.82	12.64	15.20	24.47	31.52	36.24	754.8	800-421-4184	Y
Carillon Reams Core Plus Bond Fund Class Y	SCPYX	B	B	B+	Up	8.71	12.43	14.71	22.95	28.95	36.2	754.8	800-421-4184	Y
Cavanal Hill Bond Fund Class A	AABOX	B-	C+	B	Up	2.90	5.13	7.29	13.65	17.52	10.07	92.8		Y
Cavanal Hill Bond Fund Institutional Class	AIBNX	B-	C+	B+		2.86	5.16	7.46	14.40	18.76	10.04	92.8		Y
Cavanal Hill Bond Fund Investor Class	APBDX	B-	C+	B	Up	2.90	5.13	7.17	13.47	17.54	10.07	92.8		Y
City Natl Rochdale Intermed Fixed Income Inst Cl	CNRIX	B-	C	B	Up	5.36	5.14	7.08	13.07	19.44	27.46	110.9		Y
Columbia Bond Fund Advisor Class	CNDRX	B-	C	B	Up	7.18	5.39	7.86	16.04	24.62	8.99	438.1	800-345-6611	Y
Columbia Bond Fund Class A	CNDAX	B-	C	B	Up	7.11	5.25	7.71	15.17	23.07	9	438.1	800-345-6611	Y
Columbia Bond Fund Class V	CNDTX	B-	C	B	Up	7.15	5.19	7.70	15.53	23.56	8.98	438.1	800-345-6611	
Columbia Bond Fund Institutional 2 Class	CNFRX	B-	C	B+	Up	7.22	5.44	7.96	16.40	25.14	8.97	438.1	800-345-6611	Y
Columbia Bond Fund Institutional 3 Class	CBFYX	B-	C	B+	Up	7.32	5.45	8.12	16.68	25.69	9.02	438.1	800-345-6611	Y

Category: US Fixed Income (con't)

Fund Name	Ticker Symbol	RATINGS: Overall Rating	Reward Rating	Risk Rating	Recent Up/ Downgrade	TOTAL RETURNS & PERFORMANCE: 3-Month Total Return	6-Month Total Return	1-Year Total Return	3-Year Total Return	5-Year Total Return	ASSETS: NAV	Total Assets (MIL)	NEW INVESTORS: Telephone	Open to New Investors
Columbia Bond Fund Institutional Class	UMMGX	B-	C	B	Up	7.17	5.38	7.98	16.02	24.60	9	438.1	800-345-6611	Y
Columbia Corporate Income Fund Advisor Class	CIFRX	B-	C+	B	Up	10.31	5.52	9.97	20.22	32.02	11.18	1,124	800-345-6611	Y
Columbia Corporate Income Fund Class A	LIIAX	B-	C+	B	Up	10.13	5.28	9.69	19.32	30.37	11.19	1,124	800-345-6611	Y
Columbia Corporate Income Fund Class C	CIOCX	B-	C+	B	Up	10.08	5.07	9.04	17.20	26.53	11.19	1,124	800-345-6611	Y
Columbia Corporate Income Fund Institutional 2 Class	CPIRX	B-	C+	B	Up	10.34	5.57	10.08	20.69	32.83	11.18	1,124	800-345-6611	Y
Columbia Corporate Income Fund Institutional 3 Class	CRIYX	B-	C+	B	Up	10.35	5.59	10.14	20.76	33.03	11.19	1,124	800-345-6611	Y
Columbia Corporate Income Fund Institutional Class	SRINX	B-	C+	B	Up	10.20	5.51	9.96	20.21	32.00	11.19	1,124	800-345-6611	Y
Columbia Total Return Bond Fund Advisor Class	CBNRX	B-	C	B+	Up	9.10	6.33	8.70	18.07	27.64	9.67	2,186	800-345-6611	Y
Columbia Total Return Bond Fund Class A	LIBAX	B-	C	B+	Up	9.02	6.30	8.42	17.18	26.04	9.68	2,186	800-345-6611	Y
Columbia Total Return Bond Fund Class R	CIBRX	B-	C	B	Up	8.96	6.06	8.15	16.31	24.48	9.68	2,186	800-345-6611	Y
Columbia Total Return Bond Fund Institutional 2 Class	CTBRX	B-	C	B+	Up	9.12	6.48	8.78	18.32	28.06	9.67	2,186	800-345-6611	Y
Columbia Total Return Bond Fund Institutional 3 Class	CTBYX	B-	C	B+	Up	9.23	6.49	8.94	18.60	28.50	9.69	2,186	800-345-6611	Y
Columbia Total Return Bond Fund Institutional Class	SRBFX	B-	C	B+	Up	9.09	6.32	8.69	18.05	27.62	9.68	2,186	800-345-6611	Y
Columbia U.S. Treasury Index Fund Class A	LUTAX	B	B	B		0.44	8.50	10.20	16.31	20.33	12.24	1,134	800-345-6611	Y
Columbia U.S. Treasury Index Fund Class C	LUTCX	B	B	B		0.27	8.13	9.53	13.91	16.32	12.24	1,134	800-345-6611	Y
Columbia U.S. Treasury Index Fund Institutional 2 Class	CUTRX	B	B	B		0.48	8.60	10.38	16.86	21.37	12.22	1,134	800-345-6611	Y
Columbia U.S. Treasury Index Fund Institutional 3 Class	CUTYX	B	B	B		0.48	8.63	10.49	16.97	21.36	12.32	1,134	800-345-6611	Y
Columbia U.S. Treasury Index Fund Institutional Class	IUTIX	B	B	B		0.48	8.58	10.45	16.93	21.44	12.25	1,134	800-345-6611	Y
Commerce Bond Fund	CFBNX	B-	C	B	Up	5.54	3.96	6.44	14.57	22.65	20.84	1,233		Y
Crossmark Steward Select Bond Fund Class Institutional	SEACX	B-	C	B	Up	4.17	3.69	5.94	11.19	16.01	25.47	153.3	800-262-6631	Y
Delaware Corporate Bond Fund Class A	DGCAX	B-	C	B	Up	10.45	4.91	9.27	19.56	29.84	6.31	1,096		Y
Delaware Corporate Bond Fund Class R6	DGCZX	B-	C	B	Up	10.54	5.08	9.64	20.60	31.63	6.31	1,096		Y
Delaware Corporate Bond Fund Institutional Class	DGCIX	B-	C	B	Up	10.52	5.04	9.53	20.45	31.46	6.31	1,096		Y
Delaware Diversified Income Fund Class A	DPDFX	B-	C+	B+	Up	6.72	5.07	7.80	15.67	22.50	9.13	3,446		Y
Delaware Diversified Income Fund Class C	DPCFX	B-	C	B	Up	6.53	4.70	7.01	13.13	18.03	9.13	3,446		Y
Delaware Diversified Income Fund Class R	DPRFX	B-	C+	B+	Up	6.54	4.96	7.42	14.82	20.85	9.12	3,446		Y
Delaware Diversified Income Fund Class R6	DPZRX	B-	C+	B+	Up	6.79	5.36	8.14	16.94	24.06	9.14	3,446		Y
Delaware Diversified Income Fund Institutional Class	DPFFX	B-	C+	B+	Up	6.77	5.31	8.05	16.66	24.02	9.14	3,446		Y
Delaware Investment Grade Fund Class R6	FIIKX	B-	C	B	Up	11.15	4.91	8.68	18.79	28.38	9.94	290.5		Y
Delaware Investment Grade Fund Institutional Class	FIIJX	B-	C	B	Up	11.11	4.75	8.66	18.53	27.72	9.96	290.5		Y
DFA Diversified Fixed Income PortfolioInstitutional Class	DFXIX	B-	C+	B		1.25	5.53	6.87	12.85		10.39	1,177	512-306-7400	Y
DFA Inflation-Protected Securities Portfol Inst Cl	DIPSX	B	B-	B+	Up	4.58	6.32	8.04	16.21	21.12	12.78	5,056	512-306-7400	Y
DFA Intermed Govt Fixed Income Portfol Inst Cl	DFIGX	B	B	B		0.97	9.62	11.14	18.72	24.29	13.88	5,344	512-306-7400	Y
DFA Intermed-Term Extended Quality Portfol Inst Cl Shares	DFTEX	B-	C	B	Up	8.77	6.00	9.68	19.81	31.25	11.74	1,870	512-306-7400	Y
DFA Investment Grade Portfolio Institutional Class Shares	DFAPX	B	B-	B	Up	4.90	7.34	9.88	18.64	26.49	11.97	9,643	512-306-7400	Y
DFA LTIP Portfolio Institutional Class	DRXIX	B	B	B		6.53	18.63	26.74	40.45	54.16	11.9	240.5	512-306-7400	Y
DFA Social Fixed Income Portfolio Institutional Class	DSFIX	B	B-	B	Up	4.92	7.42	9.81	18.49		10.89	373.1	512-306-7400	Y
Diamond Hill Core Bond Fund Class A	DHRAX	B	C+	B+	Up	4.02	6.15	8.11	17.04		10.7	200.3	888-226-5595	Y
Diamond Hill Core Bond Fund Class I	DHRIX	B	C+	A-	Up	4.09	6.30	8.41	17.97		10.7	200.3	888-226-5595	Y
Diamond Hill Core Bond Fund Class Y	DHRYX	B	C+	A-	Up	4.12	6.35	8.53	18.40		10.71	200.3	888-226-5595	Y
Dodge & Cox Income Fund	DODIX	B	C+	B+	Up	6.01	5.27	8.38	17.02	26.26	14.53	63,192	415-981-1710	Y
Domini Impact Bond Fund Institutional Shares	DSBIX	B	B-	B+	Up	4.91	7.07	9.93	18.24	27.15	12.2	182.0	800-582-6757	Y
Domini Impact Bond Fund Investor Shares	DSBFX	B	B-	B+	Up	4.81	6.88	9.65	17.18	25.40	12.28	182.0	800-582-6757	Y
DoubleLine Long Duration Total Return Bond Fund Class I	DBLDX	B	B	B		1.14	17.14	20.17	31.91	45.98	11.82	105.2	877-354-6311	Y
DoubleLine Long Duration Total Return Bond Fund Class N	DLLDX	B	B	B-		0.99	16.90	19.77	30.82	44.05	11.81	105.2	877-354-6311	Y
DWS Total Return Bond Fund - Class A	SZIAX	B-	C	B	Up	5.79	4.65	6.41	14.45	22.33	11.24	442.4		Y
DWS Total Return Bond Fund - Class Inst	SZIIX	B-	C	B+	Up	5.97	4.89	6.70	15.44	23.91	11.2	442.4		Y
DWS Total Return Bond Fund - Class R	SZIRX	B-	C	B	Up	5.72	4.52	6.15	13.60	20.82	11.24	442.4		Y
DWS Total Return Bond Fund - Class S	SCSBX	B-	C	B+	Up	5.86	4.78	6.68	15.32	23.87	11.24	442.4		Y
DWS Total Return Bond Fund Class R6	SZIWX	B-	C	B+	Up	5.78	4.70	6.69	15.32	23.88	11.19	442.4		Y
Elfun Income Fund	EINFX	B-	C+	B+	Up	4.76	5.11	7.82	15.65	23.68	12.16	239.3	617-664-7338	Y
FCI Bond Fund	FCIZX	B-	C+	B	Up	4.71	5.00	6.94	13.08	18.00	11.03	37.8		Y

Category: US Fixed Income (con't)

		RATINGS				TOTAL RETURNS & PERFORMANCE					ASSETS		NEW INVESTORS	
Fund Name	Ticker Symbol	Overall Rating	Reward Rating	Risk Rating	Recent Up/ Downgrade	3-Month Total Return	6-Month Total Return	1-Year Total Return	3-Year Total Return	5-Year Total Return	NAV	Total Assets (MIL)	Telephone	Open to New Investors
Federated Govt Income Securities Fund Institutional Shares	GISIX	B-	C+	B		1.00	5.31	6.85	12.09	15.44	9.24	157.1	800-341-7400	Y
Federated Hermes Corporate Bond Strategy Portfolio	FCSPX	B-	C	B	Up	11.66	5.38	10.44	23.06	38.35	11.87	110.3	800-341-7400	Y
Federated Hermes Govt Income Fund Institutional Shares	FICMX	B-	C+	B	Up	1.25	3.40	5.46	10.87	14.57	10.51	276.0	800-341-7400	Y
Federated Hermes Government Income Fund Service Shares	FITSX	B-	C	B	Up	1.20	3.30	5.25	10.21	13.43	10.51	276.0	800-341-7400	Y
Federated Hermes Govt Income Securities Class C Shares	FGOCX	B-	C+	B	Up	0.78	4.94	6.06	9.42	11.35	9.27	157.1	800-341-7400	Y
Federated Hermes Govt Income Securities Inc Class A Shares	FGOAX	B-	C+	B		0.98	5.34	6.87	11.96	15.68	9.26	157.1	800-341-7400	Y
Federated Hermes Govt Income Securities Inc Class F Shares	FGOIX	B-	C+	B		0.99	5.23	6.89	12.00	15.74	9.24	157.1	800-341-7400	Y
Federated Hermes Intermed Corp Bond Inst Shares	FIIFX	B-	C	B	Up	7.84	4.05	7.12	14.89	22.43	9.6	154.1	800-341-7400	Y
Federated Hermes Mortgage Strategy Portfolio	FMBPX	B-	C+	B	Up	1.24	3.94	5.98	12.98	19.00	10.23	133.8	800-341-7400	Y
Federated Hermes Real Return Bond Fund Class A Shares	RRFAX	B	C+	A-	Up	4.38	5.33	7.46	15.02	17.48	11.19	45.9	800-341-7400	Y
Federated Hermes Real Return Bond Fund Class C Shares	RRFCX	B-	C+	B+	Up	4.17	4.97	6.61	12.36	13.14	10.98	45.9	800-341-7400	Y
Federated Hermes Real Return Bond Institutional Shares	RRFIX	B	C+	A-	Up	4.35	5.46	7.71	15.84	19.00	11.26	45.9	800-341-7400	Y
Federated Hermes Short-Intermed Govt Inst Shares	FIGTX	B-	C+	B		0.58	5.54	6.50	10.93	12.30	11.4	289.3	800-341-7400	Y
Federated Hermes Short-Intermediate Govt Service Shares	FIGIX	B-	C+	B	Up	0.53	5.42	6.25	10.17	11.12	11.4	289.3	800-341-7400	Y
Federated Hermes Total Return Bond Fund Class A Shares	TLRAX	B-	C+	B+	Up	5.46	5.18	7.69	14.70	22.19	11.51	8,906	800-341-7400	Y
Federated Hermes Total Return Bond Fund Class B Shares	TLRBX	B-	C+	B	Up	5.32	4.98	7.12	12.86	18.80	11.51	8,906	800-341-7400	Y
Federated Hermes Total Return Bond Fund Class C Shares	TLRCX	B-	C+	B	Up	5.33	4.92	7.16	12.98	19.01	11.51	8,906	800-341-7400	Y
Federated Hermes Total Return Bond Fund Class R Shares	FTRKX	B-	C+	B	Up	5.32	5.08	7.50	14.02	21.05	11.51	8,906	800-341-7400	Y
Federated Hermes Total Return Bond Fund Class R6 Shares	FTRLX	B	C+	B+	Up	5.61	5.56	8.29	16.63	25.52	11.51	8,906	800-341-7400	Y
Federated Hermes Total Return Bond Institutional Shares	FTRBX	B	C+	B+	Up	5.51	5.46	8.28	16.49	25.46	11.51	8,906	800-341-7400	Y
Federated Hermes Total Return Bond Fund Service Shares	FTRFX	B	C+	B+	Up	5.43	5.31	7.96	15.46	23.60	11.51	8,906	800-341-7400	Y
Federated Hermes Total Return Govt Bond Fund Class R6	FTGLX	B	B	B+		0.65	8.38	10.12	17.35	22.08	11.82	467.7	800-341-7400	Y
Federated Hermes Total Return Govt Bond Inst Shares	FTRGX	B	B	B+		0.56	8.37	10.11	17.21	22.03	11.82	467.7	800-341-7400	Y
Federated Hermes Total Return Govt Bond Service Shares	FTGSX	B	B	B		0.56	8.19	9.74	16.03	19.98	11.82	467.7	800-341-7400	Y
Fidelity Advisor® Corporate Bond Fund Class A	FCBAX	B-	C	B	Up	10.15	5.76	9.70	19.87	31.53	12.68	2,855	617-563-7000	Y
Fidelity Advisor® Corporate Bond Fund Class C	FCCCX	B-	C	B	Up	9.85	5.27	8.78	17.07	26.54	12.67	2,855	617-563-7000	Y
Fidelity Advisor® Corporate Bond Fund Class M	FCBTX	B-	C	B	Up	10.13	5.73	9.64	19.61	31.03	12.68	2,855	617-563-7000	Y
Fidelity Advisor® Corporate Bond Fund Class Z	FIKOX	B-	C	B	Up	10.17	5.89	10.06	21.08	33.62	12.67	2,855	617-563-7000	Y
Fidelity Advisor® Corporate Bond Fund I Class	FCBIX	B-	C	B	Up	10.22	5.90	10.00	20.90	33.42	12.68	2,855	617-563-7000	Y
Fidelity Advisor® Government Income Fund Class A	FVIAX	B	B	B		0.34	7.12	8.60	14.21	17.75	11.19	4,665	617-563-7000	Y
Fidelity Advisor® Government Income Fund Class C	FVICX	B-	B-	B		0.18	6.84	7.82	11.77	13.46	11.19	4,665	617-563-7000	Y
Fidelity Advisor® Government Income Fund Class I	FVIIX	B	B	B		0.41	7.37	8.91	15.30	19.39	11.19	4,665	617-563-7000	Y
Fidelity Advisor® Government Income Fund Class M	FVITX	B	B	B		0.35	7.23	8.62	14.37	17.92	11.19	4,665	617-563-7000	Y
Fidelity Advisor® Government Income Fund Class Z	FIKPX	B	B	B		0.45	7.43	9.14	15.58	19.91	11.2	4,665	617-563-7000	Y
Fidelity Advisor® Investment Grade Bond Fund Class A	FGBAX	B	B-	B+	Up	5.52	7.33	9.96	18.18	25.11	8.7	7,365	617-563-7000	Y
Fidelity Advisor® Investment Grade Bond Fund Class C	FGBCX	B-	B-	B	Up	5.31	6.91	9.11	15.47	20.40	8.71	7,365	617-563-7000	Y
Fidelity Advisor® Investment Grade Bond Fund Class I	FGBPX	B	B-	B+	Up	5.58	7.47	10.12	18.98	26.80	8.71	7,365	617-563-7000	Y
Fidelity Advisor® Investment Grade Bond Fund Class M	FGBTX	B	B-	B+	Up	5.52	7.34	9.83	18.00	24.99	8.7	7,365	617-563-7000	Y
Fidelity Advisor® Investment Grade Bond Fund Class Z	FIKQX	B	B-	B+	Up	5.61	7.53	10.38	19.27	27.08	8.72	7,365	617-563-7000	Y
Fidelity Advisor® Mortgage Securities Fund Class A	FMGAX	B-	C+	B	Up	1.19	3.31	5.11	10.85	15.18	11.62	870.3	617-563-7000	Y
Fidelity Advisor® Mortgage Securities Fund Class M	FMSAX	B-	C+	B	Up	1.19	3.30	5.10	10.81	15.13	11.64	870.3	617-563-7000	Y
Fidelity Advisor® Mortgage Securities Fund Class Z	FIKUX	B-	C+	B	Up	1.22	3.54	5.47	12.19	17.47	11.61	870.3	617-563-7000	Y
Fidelity Advisor® Total Bond Fund Class A	FEPAX	B-	C+	B+	Up	5.80	5.25	7.86	15.69	24.09	11.35	28,185	617-563-7000	Y
Fidelity Advisor® Total Bond Fund Class C	FCEPX	B-	C	B	Up	5.60	4.76	6.95	12.97	19.44	11.35	28,185	617-563-7000	Y
Fidelity Advisor® Total Bond Fund Class I	FEPIX	B	C+	B+	Up	5.97	5.39	8.14	16.59	25.68	11.33	28,185	617-563-7000	Y
Fidelity Advisor® Total Bond Fund Class M	FEPTX	B-	C+	B+	Up	5.81	5.26	7.87	15.70	24.06	11.33	28,185	617-563-7000	Y
Fidelity Advisor® Total Bond Fund Class Z	FBKWX	B	C+	B+	Up	5.91	5.47	8.29	17.07	26.55	11.33	28,185	617-563-7000	Y
Fidelity® Corporate Bond Fund	FCBFX	B-	C	B	Up	10.24	5.93	10.05	21.07	33.74	12.68	2,855	617-563-7000	Y
Fidelity® Flex Core Bond Fund	FLXCX	B	C+	B+	Up	6.92	6.54	9.60	19.10		10.87	63.5	617-563-7000	Y
Fidelity® Flex Inflation-Protected Bond Index Fund	FBUIX	B	B-	A-	Up	4.06	6.07	8.38	15.87		10.99	6.5	617-563-7000	Y
Fidelity® Flex U.S. Bond Index Fund	FIBUX	B-	B-	B	Up	2.89	6.52	9.01	17.03		10.95	477.1	617-563-7000	Y
Fidelity® GNMA Fund	FGMNX	B-	C+	B	Up	1.02	3.20	4.77	10.59	14.98	11.8	4,204	617-563-7000	Y

Category: US Fixed Income (con't)

Fund Name	Ticker Symbol	RATINGS: Overall Rating	Reward Rating	Risk Rating	Recent Up/ Downgrade	TOTAL RETURNS & PERFORMANCE: 3-Month Total Return	6-Month Total Return	1-Year Total Return	3-Year Total Return	5-Year Total Return	ASSETS: NAV	Total Assets (MIL)	NEW INVESTORS: Telephone	Open to New Investors
Fidelity® Government Income Fund	FGOVX	B	B	B		0.51	7.40	9.06	15.45	19.77	11.18	4,665	617-563-7000	Y
Fidelity® Inflation-Protected Bond Index Fund	FIPDX	B	B-	A-	Up	4.17	6.13	8.42	15.85	20.72	10.68	7,433	617-563-7000	Y
Fidelity® Intermediate Bond Fund	FTHRX	B-	C+	B	Up	4.65	4.97	6.95	13.50	19.11	11.49	2,860	617-563-7000	Y
Fidelity® Intermediate Government Income Fund	FSTGX	B-	C+	B		0.48	5.74	6.75	11.96	14.49	11.16	578.1	617-563-7000	Y
Fidelity® Intermediate Treasury Bond Index Fund	FUAMX	B	B	B		0.74	9.71	11.25	19.05	24.88	12.04	3,960	617-563-7000	Y
Fidelity® Investment Grade Bond Fund	FBNDX	B	B-	B+	Up	5.72	7.49	10.29	19.29	27.09	8.71	7,365	617-563-7000	Y
Fidelity® Limited Term Government Fund	FFXSX	B-	C	B	Up	0.34	4.05	4.99	8.94	10.34	10.37	469.4	617-563-7000	Y
Fidelity® Long-Term Treasury Bond Index Fund	FNBGX	B	B	B		-0.54	21.58	25.69	40.23	57.64	16.96	2,895	617-563-7000	Y
Fidelity® Mortgage Securities Fund	FMSFX	B-	C+	B		1.28	3.48	5.46	11.99	17.26	11.65	870.3	617-563-7000	Y
Fidelity® SAI Long-Term Treasury Bond Index Fund	FBLTX	B	B	B		-0.60	22.13	26.43	41.88		13.3	1,108	617-563-7000	Y
Fidelity® SAI U.S. Treasury Bond Index Fund	FUTBX	B	B	B		0.26	8.82	10.51	17.56		10.88	3,961	617-563-7000	Y
Fidelity® Series Inflation-Protected Bond Index Fund	FSIPX	B-	C	B+	Up	3.72	4.11	5.84	12.31	15.68	10.45	11,830	617-563-7000	
Fidelity® Series Investment Grade Bond Fund	FSIGX	B	C+	B+	Up	5.94	6.32	9.26	18.53	27.13	12.13	32,265	617-563-7000	
Fidelity® Series Long-Term Treasury Bond Index Fund	FTLTX	B	B	B		-0.54	21.34	25.52	40.11		10.39	6,050	617-563-7000	Y
Fidelity® Short-Term Treasury Bond Index Fund	FUMBX	B-	C+	B	Up	0.23	4.20	5.37	10.04	11.98	10.89	3,467	617-563-7000	Y
Fidelity® Total Bond Fund	FTBFX	B	C+	B+	Up	5.88	5.32	8.08	16.64	25.86	11.34	28,185	617-563-7000	Y
Fidelity® U.S. Bond Index Fund	FXNAX	B	B-	B+		2.77	6.54	9.01	17.02	23.88	12.54	50,694	617-563-7000	Y
GE RSP Income Fund	GESLX	B	C+	B+	Up	4.79	5.22	7.94	15.78	23.76	12.29	2,057	617-664-7338	Y
Glenmede Fund Core Fixed Income Portfolio	GTCGX	B	B-	B		1.83	6.13	8.45	15.17	20.50	11.81	474.5	800-442-8299	Y
GMO Asset Allocation Bond Fund Class III	GMOBX	B	B-	A-	Up	4.18	6.36	8.03	17.23	13.75	23.38	171.7	617-330-7500	Y
GMO Asset Allocation Bond Fund Class VI	GABFX	B	B-	A-	Up	4.22	6.44	8.17	17.56	14.27	23.45	171.7	617-330-7500	Y
GMO Core Plus Bond Fund Class III	GUGAX	B	C+	B+	Up	4.47	5.83	8.37	20.01	25.32	22.66	411.1	617-330-7500	Y
GMO Core Plus Bond Fund Class IV	GPBFX	B	C+	B+	Up	4.45	5.86	8.39	20.22	25.68	22.73	411.1	617-330-7500	Y
Goldman Sachs Bond Fund Class A Shares	GSFAX	B-	B-	B	Up	5.86	5.73	8.24	14.70	21.76	10.98	462.1	800-526-7384	Y
Goldman Sachs Bond Fund Class C Shares	GSFCX	B-	C+	B	Up	5.67	5.35	7.45	12.17	17.32	10.97	462.1	800-526-7384	Y
Goldman Sachs Bond Fund Class P	GMVPX	B	B-	B	Up	5.95	5.81	8.52	15.86	23.71	10.98	462.1	800-526-7384	Y
Goldman Sachs Bond Fund Class R Shares	GSNRX	B-	C+	B	Up	5.80	5.61	7.98	13.96	20.27	10.97	462.1	800-526-7384	Y
Goldman Sachs Bond Fund Class R6 Shares	GSFUX	B	B-	B	Up	5.95	5.81	8.52	15.91	23.76	10.98	462.1	800-526-7384	Y
Goldman Sachs Bond Fund Institutional Shares	GSNIX	B	B-	B	Up	5.95	5.91	8.60	15.98	23.84	10.98	462.1	800-526-7384	Y
Goldman Sachs Bond Fund Investor Shares	GSNTX	B-	B-	B	Up	5.94	5.77	8.42	15.58	23.32	10.94	462.1	800-526-7384	Y
Goldman Sachs Bond Fund Service Shares	GSNSX	B-	B-	B	Up	5.82	5.65	8.07	14.26	20.81	10.98	462.1	800-526-7384	Y
Goldman Sachs Core Fixed Income Fund Class A	GCFIX	B	B-	B	Up	5.09	6.51	9.05	16.60	23.22	11.32	1,530	800-526-7384	Y
Goldman Sachs Core Fixed Income Fund Class C	GCFCX	B-	B-	B	Up	4.97	6.18	8.31	13.97	18.76	11.38	1,530	800-526-7384	Y
Goldman Sachs Core Fixed Income Fund Class P	GAKPX	B	B-	B	Up	5.16	6.66	9.39	17.74	25.38	11.39	1,530	800-526-7384	Y
Goldman Sachs Core Fixed Income Fund Class R6	GCFUX	B	B-	B	Up	5.26	6.76	9.50	17.89	25.53	11.38	1,530	800-526-7384	Y
Goldman Sachs Core Fixed Income Fund Institutional Class	GSFIX	B	B-	B	Up	5.26	6.76	9.49	17.74	25.38	11.37	1,530	800-526-7384	Y
Goldman Sachs Core Fixed Income Fund Service Class	GSCSX	B	B-	B	Up	5.03	6.50	8.95	16.00	22.19	11.37	1,530	800-526-7384	Y
Goldman Sachs Core Fixed-Income Fund Class R	GDFRX	B	B-	B	Up	5.12	6.47	8.88	15.72	21.68	11.33	1,530	800-526-7384	Y
Goldman Sachs Core Fixed-Income Fund Investor Class	GDFTX	B	B-	B	Up	5.15	6.73	9.42	17.46	24.74	11.33	1,530	800-526-7384	Y
Goldman Sachs Government Income Fund Class A	GSGOX	B	B-	B	Up	1.04	6.01	7.54	12.83	16.46	15.68	369.9	800-526-7384	Y
Goldman Sachs Government Income Fund Class C	GSOCX	B-	C+	B		0.79	5.62	6.74	10.34	12.19	15.68	369.9	800-526-7384	Y
Goldman Sachs Government Income Fund Class P	GGTPX	B	B-	B	Up	1.12	6.12	7.89	13.67	17.32	15.65	369.9	800-526-7384	Y
Goldman Sachs Government Income Fund Class R	GSORX	B-	B-	B		0.92	5.82	7.28	12.01	15.03	15.66	369.9	800-526-7384	Y
Goldman Sachs Government Income Fund Class R6	GSOUX	B	B-	B	Up	1.06	6.12	7.82	14.00	18.39	15.65	369.9	800-526-7384	Y
Goldman Sachs Government Income Fund Institutional Class	GSOIX	B	B-	B+	Up	1.06	6.11	7.81	13.97	18.35	15.65	369.9	800-526-7384	Y
Goldman Sachs Government Income Fund Investor Class	GSOTX	B	B-	B	Up	1.04	6.07	7.73	13.68	17.92	15.67	369.9	800-526-7384	Y
Goldman Sachs Government Income Fund Service Class	GSOSX	B-	B-	B		0.93	5.86	7.28	12.21	15.45	15.63	369.9	800-526-7384	Y
Goldman Sachs Inflation Protected Securities Cl A Shares	GSAPX	B	C+	B+	Up	4.12	5.46	7.76	13.78	17.65	11.16	373.3	800-526-7384	Y
Goldman Sachs Inflation Protected Securities Cl C Shares	GSCFX	B-	C+	B	Up	3.89	5.01	6.89	11.21	13.32	10.95	373.3	800-526-7384	Y
Goldman Sachs Inflation Protected Securities Fund Class P	GGJPX	B	C+	A-	Up	4.15	5.66	8.12	14.91	19.70	11.3	373.3	800-526-7384	Y
Goldman Sachs Inflation Protected Securities Cl R Shares	GSRPX	B-	C+	B+	Up	4.03	5.31	7.41	12.87	16.18	11.1	373.3	800-526-7384	Y
Goldman Sachs Inflation Protected Securities Cl R6 Shares	GSRUX	B	C+	A-	Up	4.25	5.66	8.13	15.04	19.76	11.3	373.3	800-526-7384	Y

Category: US Fixed Income (con't)

Fund Name	Ticker Symbol	Overall Rating	Reward Rating	Risk Rating	Recent Up/ Downgrade	3-Month Total Return	6-Month Total Return	1-Year Total Return	3-Year Total Return	5-Year Total Return	NAV	Total Assets (MIL)	Telephone	Open to New Investors
		RATINGS				TOTAL RETURNS & PERFORMANCE					ASSETS		NEW INVESTORS	
Goldman Sachs Inflation Protected Securities Inst Shares	GSIPX	B	C+	A-	Up	4.15	5.56	8.01	14.88	19.66	11.3	373.3	800-526-7384	Y
Goldman Sachs Inflation Protected Sec Investor Shares	GSTPX	B	C+	A-	Up	4.16	5.56	7.98	14.58	19.12	11.23	373.3	800-526-7384	Y
Goldman Sachs U.S. Mortgages Fund Class P	GSBPX	B-	C+	B	Up	2.31	3.91	6.09	12.10	16.94	10.74	360.2	800-526-7384	Y
Goldman Sachs U.S. Mortgages Fund Class R6 Shares	GGIUX	B-	C+	B	Up	2.41	4.01	6.09	12.12	17.10	10.75	360.2	800-526-7384	Y
Goldman Sachs U.S. Mortgages Cl Sep Account Inst Shares	GSUPX	B-	C+	B	Up	2.41	3.92	6.09	12.12	16.96	10.72	360.2	800-526-7384	Y
Great-West Bond Index Fund Class L	MXBJX	B	B-	B	Up	2.64	6.00	8.15	14.49	19.57	9.53	1,366		Y
Great-West Bond Index Fund Institutional Class	MXCOX	B-	B-	B		2.67	6.26	8.76	16.57	23.12	10.47	1,366		Y
Great-West Bond Index Fund Investor Class	MXBIX	B	B-	B	Up	2.68	6.12	8.42	15.31	21.03	15.31	1,366		Y
Great-West Core Bond Fund Institutional Class	MXIUX	B	C+	B+	Up	4.86	5.85	8.46	17.25	25.22	10.49	431.7		Y
Great-West Core Bond Fund Investor Class	MXFDX	B	C+	B+	Up	4.66	5.59	8.10	15.94	22.93	11.54	431.7		Y
Great-West U.S. Govt Securities Fund Institutional Class	MXDQX	B	B-	B+		0.96	6.29	7.98	15.19	20.04	10.14	361.6		Y
Great-West U.S. Government Securities Fund Investor Class	MXGMX	B	B-	B+	Up	0.88	6.03	7.64	13.95	18.07	12.97	361.6		Y
Guggenheim Investment Grade Bond Fund Class A	SIUSX	B	B-	A-	Up	5.44	8.71	9.79	17.05	27.98	20.14	1,078	212-518-9290	Y
Guggenheim Investment Grade Bond Fund Class C	SDICX	B	C+	A-	Up	5.22	8.30	8.96	14.50	23.30	20.05	1,078	212-518-9290	Y
Guggenheim Investment Grade Bond Fund Class P	SIUPX	B	B-	A-	Up	5.38	8.64	9.72	17.01	27.97	20.15	1,078	212-518-9290	Y
Guggenheim Investment Grade Bond Fund Institutional Class	GIUSX	B	B-	A-	Up	5.47	8.87	10.06	18.06	29.77	20.11	1,078	212-518-9290	Y
Guggenheim Total Return Bond Fund Class A	GIBAX	B	B-	A-	Up	5.62	8.76	9.84	16.83	28.59	29.15	16,534	212-518-9290	Y
Guggenheim Total Return Bond Fund Class C	GIBCX	B	C+	A-	Up	5.46	8.40	9.06	14.29	23.95	29.16	16,534	212-518-9290	Y
Guggenheim Total Return Bond Fund Class P	GIBLX	B	B-	A-	Up	5.65	8.80	9.88	16.87	28.78	29.14	16,534	212-518-9290	Y
Guggenheim Total Return Bond Fund Class R6	GIBRX	B	B-	A-	Up	5.68	8.90	10.14	17.89	30.66	29.19	16,534	212-518-9290	Y
Guggenheim Total Return Bond Fund Institutional Class	GIBIX	B	B-	A-	Up	5.68	8.94	10.19	17.91	30.67	29.18	16,534	212-518-9290	Y
GuideMark® Core Fixed Income Fund Service Shares	GMCOX	B-	B-	B	Up	4.43	6.41	8.77	14.70	20.49	10.196	139.3	603-888-5500	Y
GuideStone Funds Extended-Duration Bond Institutional Cl	GEDYX	B	B-	B+	Up	5.55	8.49	12.65	24.00	41.83	19.45	276.7	214-720-1171	Y
GuideStone Funds Extended-Duration Bond Investor Cl	GEDZX	B	B-	B+	Up	5.53	8.41	12.41	23.06	40.03	19.46	276.7	214-720-1171	Y
GuideStone Funds Medium-Duration Bond Institutional Cl	GMDYX	B	C+	B+	Up	5.40	6.15	9.31	17.54	25.35	15.79	1,756	214-720-1171	Y
GuideStone Funds Medium-Duration Bond Fund Investor Class	GMDZX	B	C+	B+	Up	5.33	5.96	8.95	16.60	23.58	15.79	1,756	214-720-1171	Y
Harbor Bond Fund Administrative Class	HRBDX	B	C+	B+	Up	4.22	6.05	8.32	15.91	22.95	12.31	1,903	800-422-1050	Y
Harbor Bond Fund Institutional Class	HABDX	B	C+	B+	Up	4.20	6.19	8.54	16.82	24.45	12.29	1,903	800-422-1050	Y
Harbor Bond Fund Retirement Class	HBFRX	B	C+	B+	Up	4.22	6.24	8.64	16.92	24.56	12.28	1,903	800-422-1050	Y
Hartford Quality Bond Fund Class A	HQBAX	B	B-	B+	Up	2.51	6.24	8.25	14.47	19.83	10.65	140.3	888-843-7824	Y
Hartford Quality Bond Fund Class C	HQBCX	B-	C+	B		2.20	5.85	7.47	11.80	15.20	10.57	140.3	888-843-7824	Y
Hartford Quality Bond Fund Class F	HQBFX	B	B-	B+	Up	2.58	6.43	8.62	15.77	21.80	10.6	140.3	888-843-7824	Y
Hartford Quality Bond Fund Class I	HQBIX	B	B-	B+	Up	2.57	6.40	8.62	15.38	21.35	10.61	140.3	888-843-7824	Y
Hartford Quality Bond Fund Class R3	HQBRX	B-	C+	B		2.36	6.12	7.74	13.18	18.23	10.63	140.3	888-843-7824	Y
Hartford Quality Bond Fund Class R4	HQBSX	B	B-	B+	Up	2.54	6.44	8.50	15.11	21.16	10.64	140.3	888-843-7824	Y
Hartford Quality Bond Fund Class R5	HQBTX	B	B-	B+	Up	2.55	6.47	8.52	15.47	22.17	10.63	140.3	888-843-7824	Y
Hartford Quality Bond Fund Class Y	HQBYX	B	B-	B+	Up	2.55	6.44	8.88	15.86	22.07	10.68	140.3	888-843-7824	Y
Hartford Schroders Tax-Aware Bond Fund Class A	STWVX	B-	C	B+	Up	3.98	3.64	5.28	13.27	21.99	11.41	395.3	888-843-7824	Y
Hartford Schroders Tax-Aware Bond Fund Class F	HFKFX	B-	C	B+	Up	3.95	3.77	5.55	14.03	23.48	11.42	395.3	888-843-7824	Y
Hartford Schroders Tax-Aware Bond Fund Class I	STWTX	B-	C	B+	Up	4.04	3.85	5.52	14.01	23.46	11.42	395.3	888-843-7824	Y
Hartford Schroders Tax-Aware Bond Fund Class SDR	HFKVX	B-	C	B+	Up	3.96	3.78	5.56	14.07	23.52	11.41	395.3	888-843-7824	Y
Hartford Schroders Tax-Aware Bond Fund Class Y	HFKYX	B-	C	B+	Up	3.92	3.72	5.43	13.83	23.37	11.42	395.3	888-843-7824	Y
Hartford Total Return Bond HLS Fund Class IA	HIABX	B-	C+	B+	Up	6.53	5.41	8.85	17.74	27.05	12.06	1,998	888-843-7824	Y
Hartford Total Return Bond HLS Fund Class IB	HBNBX	B-	C+	B+	Up	6.48	5.27	8.52	16.78	25.53	11.98	1,998	888-843-7824	Y
Hartford U.S. Government Securities HLS Fund Class IA	HAUSX	B-	C+	B		1.68	5.33	6.58	11.61	15.88	10.86	335.5	888-843-7824	Y
Hartford U.S. Government Securities HLS Fund Class IB	HBUSX	B-	C+	B	Up	1.59	5.24	6.30	10.76	14.45	10.84	335.5	888-843-7824	Y
Homestead Funds Short-Term Bond Fund	HOSBX	B-	C	B	Up	2.84	4.14	5.20	10.51	13.91	5.41	533.6		Y
Invesco Core Plus Bond Fund Class R6	CPBFX	B-	C	B	Up	7.45	4.96	8.48	16.04	27.30	11.41	4,582	800-659-1005	Y
Invesco Core Plus Bond Fund Class Y	CPBYX	B-	C	B	Up	7.52	4.92	8.41	15.92	26.83	11.43	4,582	800-659-1005	Y
Invesco Core Plus Bond Fund R5 Class	CPIIX	B-	C	B	Up	7.43	4.93	8.42	15.84	26.91	11.41	4,582	800-659-1005	Y
Invesco Intermediate Bond Factor Fund Class A	OFIAX	B-	C+	B	Up	4.77	4.67	7.56	14.04	23.80	11.38	192.8	800-659-1005	Y
Invesco Intermediate Bond Factor Fund Class R	OFINX	B-	C	B	Up	4.61	4.51	7.13	12.94	22.00	11.38	192.8	800-659-1005	Y

Category: US Fixed Income (con't)

Fund Name	Ticker Symbol	RATINGS: Overall Rating	Reward Rating	Risk Rating	Recent Up/ Downgrade	TOTAL RETURNS & PERFORMANCE: 3-Month Total Return	6-Month Total Return	1-Year Total Return	3-Year Total Return	5-Year Total Return	ASSETS: NAV	Total Assets (MIL)	NEW INVESTORS: Telephone	Open to New Investors
Invesco Intermediate Bond Factor Fund Class R5	IOTEX	B-	C+	B	Up	4.84	4.80	7.78	14.85	25.31	11.38	192.8	800-659-1005	Y
Invesco Intermediate Bond Factor Fund Class R6	OFIIX	B-	C+	B	Up	4.84	4.81	7.89	15.39	26.37	11.38	192.8	800-659-1005	Y
Invesco Intermediate Bond Factor Fund Class Y	OFIYX	B-	C+	B	Up	4.74	4.81	7.93	15.02	25.49	11.37	192.8	800-659-1005	Y
Invesco Oppenheimer Total Return Bond Fund Class A	OPIGX	B	C+	B+	Up	5.73	6.94	9.58	17.47	24.81	7.37	1,856	800-659-1005	Y
Invesco Oppenheimer Total Return Bond Fund Class C	OPBCX	B-	C+	B	Up	5.67	6.67	8.71	14.67	20.06	7.38	1,856	800-659-1005	Y
Invesco Oppenheimer Total Return Bond Fund Class R	OPBNX	B	C+	B	Up	5.80	6.79	9.26	16.41	23.10	7.37	1,856	800-659-1005	Y
Invesco Oppenheimer Total Return Bond Fund Class R5	TRTMX	B	C+	B+	Up	5.81	7.11	9.90	17.85	25.22	7.37	1,856	800-659-1005	Y
Invesco Oppenheimer Total Return Bond Fund Class R6	OPBIX	B	C+	B+	Up	5.84	7.15	9.83	18.75	27.05	7.36	1,856	800-659-1005	Y
Invesco Oppenheimer Total Return Bond Fund Class Y	OPBYX	B	C+	B+	Up	5.84	7.14	9.94	18.58	26.83	7.33	1,856	800-659-1005	Y
iShares U.S. Aggregate Bond Index Fund Class K	WFBIX	B	B-	B+		2.91	6.30	9.01	16.79	23.54	10.91	2,215	800-441-7762	Y
iShares U.S. Aggregate Bond Ind Institutional Shares	BMOIX	B	B-	B+		2.90	6.28	8.97	16.51	23.13	10.9	2,215	800-441-7762	Y
iShares U.S. Aggregate Bond Index Fund Investor A Shares	BMOAX	B	B-	B	Up	2.84	6.15	8.69	15.76	21.63	10.9	2,215	800-441-7762	Y
iShares U.S. Aggregate Bond Index Fund Investor P Shares	BMOPX	B	B-	B	Up	2.84	6.16	8.72	15.75	21.84	10.9	2,215	800-441-7762	Y
Ivy Corporate Bond Fund Class A	IBJAX	B-	C+	B	Up	9.12	6.05	9.52	17.63	26.03	6.83	856.7		Y
Ivy Corporate Bond Fund Class I	IBJIX	B-	C+	B	Up	9.20	6.05	9.69	18.74	27.96	6.83	856.7		Y
Ivy Corporate Bond Fund Class N	IBJNX	B-	C+	B	Up	9.24	6.29	10.01	19.30	27.83	6.83	856.7		Y
Ivy Corporate Bond Fund Class Y	IBJYX	B-	C+	B	Up	9.15	6.10	9.59	18.05	26.49	6.83	856.7		
Ivy Government Securities Fund Class A	IGJAX	B-	C+	B		0.32	5.56	6.54	11.27	14.36	5.8	355.6		Y
Ivy Government Securities Fund Class I	IGJIX	B-	B-	B		0.38	5.69	6.82	12.16	15.97	5.8	355.6		Y
Ivy Government Securities Fund Class N	IGJNX	B-	B-	B		0.41	5.74	6.94	12.47	15.60	5.8	355.6		Y
Janus Henderson Flexible Bond Fund Class A	JDFAX	B-	C+	B	Up	6.82	6.73	9.89	16.05	21.35	11.14	3,779	877-335-2687	Y
Janus Henderson Flexible Bond Fund Class C	JFICX	B-	C+	B	Up	6.55	6.40	9.11	13.96	17.57	11.14	3,779	877-335-2687	Y
Janus Henderson Flexible Bond Fund Class D	JANFX	B	C+	B+	Up	6.90	6.88	10.21	17.11	23.01	11.14	3,779	877-335-2687	
Janus Henderson Flexible Bond Fund Class I	JFLEX	B	C+	B+	Up	6.81	6.92	10.18	17.40	23.42	11.14	3,779	877-335-2687	Y
Janus Henderson Flexible Bond Fund Class N	JDFNX	B	C+	B+	Up	6.93	7.06	10.37	17.64	24.08	11.14	3,779	877-335-2687	Y
Janus Henderson Flexible Bond Fund Class R	JDFRX	B-	C+	B	Up	6.63	6.56	9.44	15.02	19.39	11.14	3,779	877-335-2687	Y
Janus Henderson Flexible Bond Fund Class S	JADFX	B-	C+	B	Up	6.70	6.69	9.71	15.88	20.90	11.14	3,779	877-335-2687	Y
Janus Henderson Flexible Bond Fund Class T	JAFIX	B	C+	B	Up	6.87	6.83	10.10	16.80	22.60	11.14	3,779	877-335-2687	Y
Janus Henderson VIT Flexible Bond Portfol Inst Cl	JAFLX	B	C+	B	Up	6.81	6.72	10.00	16.94	22.85	12.46	557.9	877-335-2687	Y
Janus Henderson VIT Flexible Bond Portfolio Service Class		B-	C+	B	Up	6.70	6.62	9.68	16.07	21.35	13.65	557.9	877-335-2687	Y
JNL/Fidelity Inst Asset Management® Total Bond Cl A		B-	C	B	Up	5.88	4.82	7.30	13.24	19.58	12.59	1,122		Y
JNL/Fidelity Inst Asset Management® Total Bond Cl I		B-	C+	B	Up	6.02	4.98	7.65	14.23	21.11	12.85	1,122		Y
JNL/JPMorgan U.S. Government & Quality Bond Fund Class A		B	B-	B+	Up	1.40	6.43	8.11	14.57	18.98	14.39	2,169		Y
JNL/JPMorgan U.S. Government & Quality Bond Fund Class I		B	B-	B+		1.40	6.51	8.33	15.55	20.44	15.2	2,169		Y
JNL/Mellon Bond Index Fund Class A		B	B-	B	Up	2.65	5.97	8.13	14.78	20.17	12.78	1,295		Y
JNL/Mellon Bond Index Fund Class I		B	B-	B	Up	2.70	6.06	8.52	15.87	21.73	13.29	1,295		Y
JNL/PIMCO Investment Grade Credit Bond A		B-	C+	B	Up	8.38	5.38	9.46	20.06	32.21	12.92	1,580		Y
JNL/PIMCO Investment Grade Credit Bond I		B-	C+	B+	Up	8.53	5.61	9.79	21.09	33.34	12.97	1,580		Y
JNL/PIMCO Real Return Fund Class A		B	C+	B+	Up	5.63	5.63	7.90	14.11	18.29	11.06	1,335		Y
JNL/PIMCO Real Return Fund Class I		B	C+	B+	Up	5.74	5.84	8.29	15.10	19.83	11.23	1,335		Y
JNL/PPM America Total Return Fund Class A		B	B-	B+	Up	5.97	6.30	9.05	17.48	25.81	13.49	1,548		Y
JNL/PPM America Total Return Fund Class I		B	B-	B+	Up	6.03	6.54	9.38	18.57	26.98	13.52	1,548		Y
John Hancock Bond Fund Class A	JHNBX	B-	C	B	Up	5.96	4.56	7.31	15.44	23.87	16.58	18,214	800-225-5291	Y
John Hancock Bond Fund Class I	JHBIX	B-	C	B+	Up	6.04	4.64	7.56	16.45	25.74	16.58	18,214	800-225-5291	Y
John Hancock Bond Fund Class NAV		B-	C	B+	Up	6.08	4.72	7.70	16.88	26.43	16.6	18,214	800-225-5291	Y
John Hancock Bond Fund Class R2	JHRBX	B-	C	B	Up	6.00	4.51	7.22	15.10	23.26	16.6	18,214	800-225-5291	Y
John Hancock Bond Fund Class R4	JBFRX	B-	C	B+	Up	6.00	4.57	7.42	15.97	24.96	16.6	18,214	800-225-5291	Y
John Hancock Bond Fund Class R6	JHBSX	B-	C	B+	Up	6.13	4.76	7.74	16.82	26.50	16.61	18,214	800-225-5291	Y
John Hancock ESG Core Bond Fund Class A	JBOAX	B-	C+	B	Up	2.92	5.16	6.64	11.80		10.69	64.6	800-225-5291	Y
John Hancock ESG Core Bond Fund Class I	JBOIX	B-	C+	B	Up	2.97	5.26	6.89	12.60		10.69	64.6	800-225-5291	Y
John Hancock ESG Core Bond Fund Class R6	JBORX	B-	C+	B	Up	2.99	5.31	7.00	12.95		10.69	64.6	800-225-5291	Y
John Hancock Funds II Core Bond Fund Class 1	JICDX	B	B-	B	Up	4.28	6.28	8.66	15.57	21.84	13.83	2,621	800-225-5291	Y

Category: US Fixed Income (con't)

Fund Name	Ticker Symbol	RATINGS				TOTAL RETURNS & PERFORMANCE					ASSETS		NEW INVESTORS	
		Overall Rating	Reward Rating	Risk Rating	Recent Up/ Downgrade	3-Month Total Return	6-Month Total Return	1-Year Total Return	3-Year Total Return	5-Year Total Return	NAV	Total Assets (MIL.)	Telephone	Open to New Investors
John Hancock Funds II Core Bond Fund Class NAV	JHCDX	B	B-	B	Up	4.30	6.32	8.81	15.77	22.09	13.81	2,621	800-225-5291	Y
John Hancock Government Income Fund Class A	JHGIX	B	B	B		0.39	7.50	8.95	14.19	17.28	10.07	316.5	800-225-5291	Y
John Hancock Government Income Fund Class B	TSGIX	B-	C+	B		0.20	7.08	7.99	11.41	12.78	10.06	316.5	800-225-5291	
John Hancock Government Income Fund Class C	TCGIX	B-	C+	B		0.20	7.19	8.10	11.53	12.78	10.07	316.5	800-225-5291	Y
John Hancock Government Income Fund Class I	JGIFX	B	B	B		0.54	7.71	9.17	14.88	17.30	10.08	316.5	800-225-5291	Y
John Hancock Government Income Fund Class R6	JTSRX	B	B	B		0.57	7.77	9.28	15.04	16.46	10.08	316.5	800-225-5291	Y
John Hancock Investment Grade Bond Fund Class A	TAUSX	B-	C+	B+	Up	4.91	5.65	8.09	15.53	22.36	11.15	2,069	800-225-5291	Y
John Hancock Investment Grade Bond Fund Class B	TSUSX	B-	C+	B	Up	4.72	5.26	7.29	12.98	17.88	11.15	2,069	800-225-5291	
John Hancock Investment Grade Bond Fund Class C	TCUSX	B-	C+	B	Up	4.72	5.26	7.29	12.98	17.88	11.15	2,069	800-225-5291	Y
John Hancock Investment Grade Bond Fund Class I	TIUSX	B	C+	B+	Up	4.88	5.78	8.25	16.38	23.90	11.15	2,069	800-225-5291	Y
John Hancock Investment Grade Bond Fund Class R2	JIGBX	B-	C+	B+	Up	4.87	5.58	7.96	15.03	21.79	11.15	2,069	800-225-5291	Y
John Hancock Investment Grade Bond Fund Class R4	JIGMX	B	C+	B+	Up	4.84	5.71	8.10	15.92	23.18	11.15	2,069	800-225-5291	Y
John Hancock Investment Grade Bond Fund Class R6	JIGEX	B	C+	B+	Up	4.91	5.84	8.37	16.75	24.59	11.15	2,069	800-225-5291	Y
Johnson Fixed Income Fund	JFINX	B	B-	B+	Up	3.07	7.31	9.58	16.88	23.81	18.48	872.3		Y
Johnson Institutional Core Bond Fund	JIBFX	B	B	B+		3.31	8.53	11.06	20.02	28.46	17.61	328.0		Y
Johnson Institutional Core Bond Fund Class F	JIMFX	B	B	B+		3.27	8.51	10.82	18.92	26.65	17.73	328.0		Y
Johnson Institutional Intermediate Bond Fund	JIBEX	B	B-	B+	Up	3.19	6.00	8.13	15.73	22.58	16.75	160.7		Y
Johnson Institutional Intermediate Bond Fund Class F	JIMEX	B	C+	B+	Up	3.18	5.90	7.94	14.81	21.00	16.89	160.7		Y
JPMorgan Core Bond Fund Class A	PGBOX	B	C+	B+	Up	3.41	5.74	8.01	15.45	21.58	12.37	33,035	800-480-4111	Y
JPMorgan Core Bond Fund Class C	OBOCX	B-	C+	B	Up	3.23	5.47	7.30	13.43	17.95	12.46	33,035	800-480-4111	Y
JPMorgan Core Bond Fund Class I	WOBDX	B	C+	B+	Up	3.39	5.87	8.29	16.34	23.02	12.36	33,035	800-480-4111	Y
JPMorgan Core Bond Fund Class R2	JCBZX	B-	C+	B	Up	3.24	5.56	7.55	14.27	19.76	12.35	33,035	800-480-4111	Y
JPMorgan Core Bond Fund Class R3	JCBPX	B	C+	B+	Up	3.32	5.62	7.85	15.10	20.89	12.33	33,035	800-480-4111	Y
JPMorgan Core Bond Fund Class R4	JCBQX	B	C+	B+	Up	3.38	5.79	8.15	15.98	22.44	12.35	33,035	800-480-4111	Y
JPMorgan Core Bond Fund Class R5	JCBRX	B	C+	B+	Up	3.49	5.91	8.36	16.53	23.50	12.35	33,035	800-480-4111	Y
JPMorgan Core Bond Fund Class R6	JCBUX	B	C+	B+	Up	3.51	5.94	8.44	16.94	24.16	12.38	33,035	800-480-4111	Y
JPMorgan Core Plus Bond Fund Class A	ONIAX	B-	C	B+	Up	3.85	4.52	6.57	14.45	21.77	8.71	14,071	800-480-4111	Y
JPMorgan Core Plus Bond Fund Class I	HLIPX	B-	C	B+	Up	3.92	4.68	6.88	15.45	23.54	8.71	14,071	800-480-4111	Y
JPMorgan Core Plus Bond Fund Class R2	JCPZX	B-	C	B	Up	3.75	4.32	6.14	13.21	19.47	8.71	14,071	800-480-4111	Y
JPMorgan Core Plus Bond Fund Class R3	JCPPX	B-	C	B	Up	3.82	4.45	6.42	13.96	21.08	8.7	14,071	800-480-4111	Y
JPMorgan Core Plus Bond Fund Class R4	JCPQX	B-	C	B+	Up	3.88	4.58	6.56	14.82	22.54	8.7	14,071	800-480-4111	Y
JPMorgan Core Plus Bond Fund Class R5	JCPYX	B-	C	B+	Up	3.92	4.66	6.84	15.33	23.37	8.71	14,071	800-480-4111	Y
JPMorgan Core Plus Bond Fund Class R6	JCPUX	B-	C	B+	Up	3.94	4.70	6.94	15.79	24.04	8.72	14,071	800-480-4111	Y
JPMorgan Corporate Bond Fund Class A	CBRAX	B-	C	B	Up	8.54	4.79	8.91	20.44	33.02	10.66	2,630	800-480-4111	Y
JPMorgan Corporate Bond Fund Class C	CBRCX	B-	C	B	Up	8.42	4.64	8.50	18.72	29.79	10.65	2,630	800-480-4111	Y
JPMorgan Corporate Bond Fund Class I	CBFSX	B-	C	B	Up	8.59	4.91	9.28	21.33	34.81	10.68	2,630	800-480-4111	Y
JPMorgan Corporate Bond Fund Class R6	CBFVX	B-	C	B	Up	8.72	5.06	9.38	21.80	35.61	10.69	2,630	800-480-4111	Y
JPMorgan Government Bond Fund Class A	OGGAX	B	B-	B	Up	0.87	6.49	8.08	14.37	18.41	11.35	3,245	800-480-4111	Y
JPMorgan Government Bond Fund Class C	OGVCX	B-	B-	B		0.65	6.11	7.38	12.26	14.68	11.31	3,245	800-480-4111	Y
JPMorgan Government Bond Fund Class I	HLGAX	B	B-	B		0.85	6.64	8.38	15.32	19.96	11.34	3,245	800-480-4111	Y
JPMorgan Government Bond Fund Class R2	JGBZX	B-	B-	B		0.79	6.31	7.72	13.20	16.61	11.34	3,245	800-480-4111	Y
JPMorgan Government Bond Fund Class R3	OGGPX	B	B-	B	Up	0.77	6.44	7.99	14.07	17.97	11.34	3,245	800-480-4111	Y
JPMorgan Government Bond Fund Class R4	OGGQX	B	B-	B		0.83	6.58	8.26	14.93	19.40	11.34	3,245	800-480-4111	Y
JPMorgan Government Bond Fund Class R6	OGGYX	B	B-	B+		0.89	6.70	8.53	15.77	20.66	11.34	3,245	800-480-4111	Y
JPMorgan Insurance Trust Core Bond Portfolio Class 1		B-	C+	B+		3.45	5.57	7.97	15.63	21.85	11.63	460.2	800-480-4111	Y
JPMorgan Insurance Trust Core Bond Portfolio Class 2		B-	C+	B+	Up	3.42	5.56	7.70	14.78	20.41	11.49	460.2	800-480-4111	Y
JPMorgan Mortgage-Backed Securities Fund Class A	OMBAX	B-	C	B	Up	2.78	3.63	5.40	12.89	18.40	11.9	2,998	800-480-4111	Y
JPMorgan Mortgage-Backed Securities Fund Class I	OMBIX	B-	C	B+	Up	2.92	3.78	5.73	13.74	19.94	11.58	2,998	800-480-4111	Y
JPMorgan Mortgage-Backed Securities Fund Class R6	JMBUX	B-	C	B+	Up	2.87	3.76	5.80	14.15	20.77	11.57	2,998	800-480-4111	Y
JPMorgan Total Return Fund Class A Shares	JMTAX	B	C+	B+	Up	4.43	5.35	7.88	15.74	24.27	10.68	501.5	800-480-4111	Y
JPMorgan Total Return Fund Class C Shares	JMTCX	B-	C+	B	Up	4.27	5.02	7.10	13.54	20.28	10.65	501.5	800-480-4111	Y
JPMorgan Total Return Fund Class I Shares	JMTSX	B	C+	B+	Up	4.54	5.47	7.95	16.16	24.96	10.71	501.5	800-480-4111	Y

Category: US Fixed Income (con't)

		RATINGS				TOTAL RETURNS & PERFORMANCE					ASSETS		NEW INVESTORS	
Fund Name	Ticker Symbol	Overall Rating	Reward Rating	Risk Rating	Recent Up/ Downgrade	3-Month Total Return	6-Month Total Return	1-Year Total Return	3-Year Total Return	5-Year Total Return	NAV	Total Assets (MIL)	Telephone	Open to New Investors
JPMorgan Total Return Fund Class R2 Shares	JMTTX	B-	C+	B	Up	4.38	5.15	7.29	14.04	21.15	10.7	501.5	800-480-4111	Y
JPMorgan Total Return Fund Class R5 Shares	JMTRX	B	C+	B+	Up	4.46	5.43	7.97	16.40	25.42	10.7	501.5	800-480-4111	Y
JPMorgan Total Return Fund Class R6 Shares	JMTIX	B	C+	B+	Up	4.58	5.56	8.13	16.58	25.76	10.7	501.5	800-480-4111	Y
Knights of Columbus Core Bond Fund Class S Shares	KCCSX	B-	C	B	Up	4.43	3.71	6.74	14.57	22.67	10.5	104.2	203-772-2130	Y
Knights of Columbus Core Bond Fund I Shares	KCCIX	B-	C	B	Up	4.45	3.76	6.84	14.78	23.09	10.51	104.2	203-772-2130	Y
KP Fixed Income Fund Institutional Shares	KPFIX	B-	C	B+	Up	5.32	4.49	7.30	15.58	23.67	10.69	2,255		Y
Loomis Sayles Core Plus Bond Fund Class A	NEFRX	B	C+	B+	Up	5.14	6.63	9.11	17.13	25.20	13.94	8,216	800-862-4863	Y
Loomis Sayles Core Plus Bond Fund Class C	NECRX	B	C+	B+	Up	4.94	6.32	8.36	14.58	20.69	13.95	8,216	800-862-4863	Y
Loomis Sayles Core Plus Bond Fund Class N	NERNX	B	B-	B+	Up	5.26	6.90	9.55	18.34	27.51	14.07	8,216	800-862-4863	Y
Loomis Sayles Core Plus Bond Fund Class Y	NERYX	B	C+	B+	Up	5.24	6.86	9.46	18.04	26.85	14.06	8,216	800-862-4863	Y
Loomis Sayles Inflation Protected Securities Cl Inst	LSGSX	B	B	A-	Up	5.23	8.10	10.29	17.80	22.31	11.45	64.8	800-633-3330	Y
Loomis Sayles Inflation Protected Securities Fund Class N	LIPNX	B	B	A-	Up	5.23	8.10	10.43	18.06	22.61	11.46	64.8	800-633-3330	Y
Loomis Sayles Inflation Protected Securities Retail Cl	LIPRX	B	B	A-	Up	5.24	8.01	10.19	17.09	20.74	11.44	64.8	800-633-3330	Y
Loomis Sayles Intermediate Duration Bond Fund A Class	LSDRX	B-	C+	B	Up	5.05	5.46	7.42	14.15	18.99	10.91	277.6	800-862-4863	Y
Loomis Sayles Intermediate Duration Bond Fund Class N	LSDNX	B-	C+	B+	Up	5.13	5.62	7.74	15.10	20.47	10.9	277.6	800-862-4863	Y
Loomis Sayles Intermediate Duration Bond Fund Y Class	LSDIX	B-	C+	B+	Up	5.02	5.50	7.69	15.02	20.39	10.9	277.6	800-862-4863	Y
Loomis Sayles Investment Grade Bond Fund Admin Class	LIGAX	B-	C	B	Up	8.50	5.36	7.89	15.22	23.69	11.67	5,463	800-862-4863	Y
Loomis Sayles Investment Grade Bond Fund Class A	LIGRX	B-	C	B+	Up	8.54	5.47	8.14	15.95	24.97	11.7	5,463	800-862-4863	Y
Loomis Sayles Investment Grade Bond Fund Class N	LGBNX	B-	C	B+	Up	8.62	5.62	8.46	17.01	27.18	11.7	5,463	800-862-4863	Y
Loomis Sayles Investment Grade Bond Fund Class Y	LSIIX	B-	C	B+	Up	8.60	5.59	8.40	16.90	26.63	11.71	5,463	800-862-4863	Y
Lord Abbett Core Fixed Income Fund Class A	LCRAX	B-	C+	B	Up	3.61	5.30	7.31	14.24	20.06	11.52	1,929	201-827-2000	Y
Lord Abbett Core Fixed Income Fund Class C	LCRCX	B-	C	B	Up	3.46	4.99	6.68	12.18	16.44	11.47	1,929	201-827-2000	Y
Lord Abbett Core Fixed Income Fund Class F	LCRFX	B-	C+	B+	Up	3.63	5.44	7.51	14.58	20.64	11.52	1,929	201-827-2000	Y
Lord Abbett Core Fixed Income Fund Class F3	LCROX	B	C+	B+	Up	3.68	5.42	7.59	15.21	21.57	11.52	1,929	201-827-2000	Y
Lord Abbett Core Fixed Income Fund Class I	LCRYX	B-	C+	B+	Up	3.66	5.51	7.65	15.02	21.35	11.52	1,929	201-827-2000	Y
Lord Abbett Core Fixed Income Fund Class P	LCRPX	B	C+	B+	Up	3.96	5.90	8.44	17.65	23.46	11.75	1,929	201-827-2000	
Lord Abbett Core Fixed Income Fund Class R2	LCRQX	B-	C+	B	Up	3.51	5.09	6.89	12.79	17.70	11.52	1,929	201-827-2000	Y
Lord Abbett Core Fixed Income Fund Class R3	LCRRX	B-	C+	B	Up	3.53	5.14	6.99	13.13	18.31	11.52	1,929	201-827-2000	Y
Lord Abbett Core Fixed Income Fund Class R4	LCRSX	B-	C+	B	Up	3.60	5.37	7.36	14.08	19.82	11.52	1,929	201-827-2000	Y
Lord Abbett Core Fixed Income Fund Class R5	LCRTX	B-	C+	B+	Up	3.66	5.40	7.52	14.93	21.34	11.52	1,929	201-827-2000	Y
Lord Abbett Core Fixed Income Fund Class R6	LCRVX	B	C+	B+	Up	3.68	5.53	7.70	15.22	21.87	11.52	1,929	201-827-2000	Y
Macquarie Pooled Trust Core Plus Bond Portfolio	DCPFX	B	C+	B+	Up	6.96	5.47	8.45	17.06	24.24	10.59	140.0	215-255-2300	Y
Madison Core Bond Fund Class A	MBOAX	B	B-	B	Up	4.57	6.64	8.82	15.55	22.01	10.77	120.1	800-767-0300	Y
Madison Core Bond Fund Class B	MBOBX	B-	C+	B	Up	4.37	6.12	8.00	12.87	17.53	10.78	120.1	800-767-0300	Y
Madison Core Bond Fund Class Y	MBOYX	B	B-	B+	Up	4.66	6.81	9.17	16.40	23.60	10.71	120.1	800-767-0300	Y
Madison Corporate Bond Fund Class Y	COINX	B-	C+	B	Up	11.42	5.85	10.04	20.03	31.35	12.57	14.2	800-767-0300	Y
MainStay MacKay Total Return Bond Fund Class A	MTMAX	B-	C+	B	Up	5.94	5.18	7.99	14.55	21.62	11.28	1,323	800-624-6782	Y
MainStay MacKay Total Return Bond Fund Class I	MTMIX	B-	C+	B+	Up	5.90	5.31	8.28	15.53	23.66	11.28	1,323	800-624-6782	Y
MainStay MacKay Total Return Bond Fund Class R1	MTMRX	B-	C+	B	Up	5.98	5.26	8.16	15.17	23.03	11.28	1,323	800-624-6782	Y
MainStay MacKay Total Return Bond Fund Class R2	MTRTX	B-	C+	B	Up	5.82	5.13	7.81	14.23	21.29	11.27	1,323	800-624-6782	Y
MainStay MacKay Total Return Bond Fund Class R3	MTRVX	B-	C+	B	Up	5.85	5.00	7.64	13.48	20.07	11.28	1,323	800-624-6782	Y
MainStay MacKay Total Return Bond Fund Class R6	MTRDX	B-	C+	B+	Up	6.02	5.34	8.35	15.79	24.08	11.28	1,323	800-624-6782	Y
MainStay MacKay Total Return Bond Fund Investor Class	MTMNX	B-	C+	B	Up	5.85	5.04	7.74	13.93	21.12	11.34	1,323	800-624-6782	Y
Manning & Napier Core Bond Series Class I	EXCIX	B	C+	B	Up	4.14	6.07	8.47	15.43	21.53	10.58	315.6	585-325-6880	Y
Manning & Napier Core Bond Series Class S	EXCRX	B-	C+	B	Up	4.03	5.86	8.25	14.62	20.02	11.5	315.6	585-325-6880	Y
Manning & Napier Core Bond Series Class W	MCBWX	B	C+	B	Up	4.13	6.17	8.87	15.52	20.97	11.49	315.6	585-325-6880	Y
Manning & Napier Core Bond Series Class Z	MCBZX	B-	C+	B	Up	4.14	6.09	8.62	15.24	20.68	10.6	315.6	585-325-6880	Y
Manor Investment Funds Bond Fund	MNRBX	B-	C+	B		0.26	6.74	7.66	11.54	10.21	11.24	1.5		Y
MassMutual Prem Inflat-Protect & Income Administrative Cl	MIPLX	B-	C	B+	Up	6.04	4.93	7.21	13.71	18.78	11.05	323.4		Y
MassMutual Premier Inflation-Protected & Income Cl A	MPSAX	B-	C	B	Up	6.00	4.76	6.85	12.86	17.27	10.77	323.4		Y
MassMutual Premier Inflation-Protected & Income Cl I	MIPZX	B-	C	B+	Up	6.19	5.17	7.60	14.89	20.61	10.97	323.4		Y
MassMutual Premier Inflation-Protected & Income Cl R3	MIPNX	B-	C	B	Up	6.03	4.78	6.82	12.53	16.53	10.72	323.4		Y

Category: US Fixed Income (con't)

Fund Name	Ticker Symbol	RATINGS: Overall Rating	Reward Rating	Risk Rating	Recent Up/ Downgrade	TOTAL RETURNS & PERFORMANCE: 3-Month Total Return	6-Month Total Return	1-Year Total Return	3-Year Total Return	5-Year Total Return	NAV	ASSETS: Total Assets (MIL)	NEW INVESTORS: Telephone	Open to New Investors
MassMutual Premier Inflation-Protected & Income Cl R4	MIPRX	B-	C	B	Up	6.14	4.89	7.13	13.32	18.09	10.71	323.4		Y
MassMutual Premier Inflation-Protected & Income Cl R5	MIPSX	B-	C	B+	Up	6.19	4.97	7.40	14.43	19.99	10.97	323.4		Y
MassMutual Premier Inflation-Protected & Income Service Cl	MIPYX	B-	C	B+	Up	6.21	4.98	7.40	14.19	19.39	10.94	323.4		Y
MassMutual Select Total Return Bond Administrative Cl	MSPLX	B	B-	B+	Up	3.90	6.19	8.71	16.42	22.71	10.63	882.0		Y
MassMutual Select Total Return Bond Fund Class A	MPTRX	B	C+	B	Up	3.82	6.00	8.47	15.57	21.24	10.59	882.0		Y
MassMutual Select Total Return Bond Fund Class I	MSPZX	B	B-	B+	Up	3.99	6.38	9.09	17.56	24.61	10.66	882.0		Y
MassMutual Select Total Return Bond Fund Class R3	MSPNX	B	C+	B	Up	3.81	5.99	8.35	15.07	20.38	10.61	882.0		Y
MassMutual Select Total Return Bond Fund Class R4	MSPGX	B	B-	B	Up	3.88	6.15	8.55	15.97	21.91	10.7	882.0		Y
MassMutual Select Total Return Bond Fund Class R5	MSPSX	B	B-	B+	Up	4.00	6.39	8.97	17.28	24.07	10.65	882.0		Y
MassMutual Select Total Return Bond Fund Service Class	MSPHX	B	B-	B+	Up	3.98	6.36	8.85	16.87	23.42	10.69	882.0		Y
Meeder Total Return Bond Fund Adviser Class	BNDAX	B-	C	B	Up	4.24	4.37	6.09	11.77	18.15	9.79	62.0		Y
Meeder Total Return Bond Fund Institutional Class	BNDIX	B-	C	B	Up	4.23	4.38	6.12	12.30	18.68	9.79	62.0		Y
Mercer Core Fixed Income Fund Class Y3	MCFIX	B	C+	B+	Up	4.58	6.30	9.36	17.72	25.50	10.96	1,025		Y
MetLife Core Plus Fund I Class	LPCIX	B	C+	B+	Up	4.82	5.60	8.40	16.81	26.05	10.41	49.3		Y
Metropolitan West High Yield Bond Fund Class Institutional	MWHIX	B-	C	B	Up	8.65	2.42	5.30	16.67	27.85	9.96	565.3	800-241-4671	Y
Metropolitan West High Yield Bond Fund Class M	MWHYX	B-	C	B	Up	8.58	2.39	5.14	15.92	26.39	9.97	565.3	800-241-4671	Y
Metropolitan West Intermediate Bond Cl Institutional	MWIIX	B-	C+	B+	Up	3.84	5.23	6.97	13.89	18.01	11.01	740.2	800-241-4671	Y
Metropolitan West Intermediate Bond Fund Class M	MWIMX	B-	C+	B	Up	3.88	5.21	6.84	13.22	16.73	11.02	740.2	800-241-4671	Y
Metropolitan West Total Return Bond Administrative Cl	MWTNX	B	B-	B	Up	3.97	6.30	8.79	16.54	21.95	11.53	83,642	800-241-4671	Y
Metropolitan West Total Return Bond Fund Class I	MWTIX	B	B-	B+	Up	4.06	6.48	9.16	17.73	24.04	11.52	83,642	800-241-4671	Y
Metropolitan West Total Return Bond Fund Class I-2	MWTTX	B	B-	B+		4.07	6.34	8.99	16.91	22.73	11.52	83,642	800-241-4671	Y
Metropolitan West Total Return Bond Fund Class M	MWTRX	B	B-	B+	Up	4.00	6.26	8.92	16.83	22.65	11.52	83,642	800-241-4671	Y
Metropolitan West Total Return Bond Fund Plan Class	MWTSX	B	B-	B+	Up	4.11	6.46	9.27	17.94	24.54	10.84	83,642	800-241-4671	Y
MFS Corporate Bond Fund Class A	MFBFX	B-	C+	B	Up	9.82	5.86	10.04	19.78	31.53	15.37	5,159	877-960-6077	Y
MFS Corporate Bond Fund Class B	MFBBX	B-	C	B	Up	9.56	5.48	9.25	17.16	26.76	15.34	5,159	877-960-6077	Y
MFS Corporate Bond Fund Class C	MFBCX	B-	C	B	Up	9.58	5.48	9.26	17.09	26.68	15.32	5,159	877-960-6077	Y
MFS Corporate Bond Fund Class I	MBDIX	B-	C+	B	Up	9.89	5.99	10.39	20.68	33.09	15.36	5,159	877-960-6077	Y
MFS Corporate Bond Fund Class R1	MFBGX	B-	C+	B	Up	9.64	5.55	9.32	17.16	26.76	15.34	5,159	877-960-6077	Y
MFS Corporate Bond Fund Class R2	MBRRX	B-	C+	B	Up	9.68	5.73	9.77	18.90	29.91	15.37	5,159	877-960-6077	Y
MFS Corporate Bond Fund Class R3	MFBHX	B-	C+	B	Up	9.82	5.86	10.04	19.78	31.53	15.37	5,159	877-960-6077	Y
MFS Corporate Bond Fund Class R4	MFBJX	B-	C+	B	Up	9.88	6.05	10.38	20.75	33.16	15.38	5,159	877-960-6077	Y
MFS Corporate Bond Fund Class R6	MFBKX	B-	C+	B	Up	9.92	6.04	10.49	21.04	33.76	15.36	5,159	877-960-6077	Y
MFS Government Securities Fund Class A	MFGSX	B	B-	B	Up	0.98	6.10	7.65	13.49	16.55	10.45	2,270	877-960-6077	Y
MFS Government Securities Fund Class B	MFGBX	B-	C+	B		0.89	5.83	6.97	10.99	12.29	10.44	2,270	877-960-6077	Y
MFS Government Securities Fund Class C	MFGDX	B-	C+	B		0.89	5.81	6.95	10.97	12.27	10.47	2,270	877-960-6077	Y
MFS Government Securities Fund Class I	MGSIX	B	B-	B	Up	1.14	6.24	7.92	14.35	17.90	10.44	2,270	877-960-6077	Y
MFS Government Securities Fund Class R1	MFGGX	B-	C+	B		0.89	5.83	6.97	10.99	12.29	10.44	2,270	877-960-6077	Y
MFS Government Securities Fund Class R2	MGVSX	B-	B-	B		0.92	5.98	7.39	12.66	15.12	10.44	2,270	877-960-6077	Y
MFS Government Securities Fund Class R3	MFGHX	B	B-	B	Up	1.08	6.21	7.76	13.49	16.55	10.45	2,270	877-960-6077	Y
MFS Government Securities Fund Class R4	MFGJX	B	B-	B	Up	1.04	6.23	7.91	14.34	18.01	10.45	2,270	877-960-6077	Y
MFS Government Securities Fund Class R6	MFGKX	B	B-	B		1.07	6.29	8.02	14.71	18.67	10.44	2,270	877-960-6077	Y
MFS Inflation-Adjusted Bond Fund Class A	MIAAX	B	C+	B+	Up	4.07	5.71	7.79	13.95	16.96	10.95	1,174	877-960-6077	Y
MFS Inflation-Adjusted Bond Fund Class B	MIABX	B-	C+	B	Up	3.86	5.41	6.99	11.42	12.74	10.9	1,174	877-960-6077	Y
MFS Inflation-Adjusted Bond Fund Class C	MIACX	B-	C+	B	Up	3.84	5.27	6.79	11.10	12.09	10.9	1,174	877-960-6077	Y
MFS Inflation-Adjusted Bond Fund Class I	MIAIX	B	C+	B+	Up	4.09	5.87	7.93	14.44	17.80	10.96	1,174	877-960-6077	Y
MFS Inflation-Adjusted Bond Fund Class R2	MIATX	B-	C+	B+	Up	3.92	5.57	7.36	12.81	14.91	10.93	1,174	877-960-6077	Y
MFS Inflation-Adjusted Bond Fund Class R3	MIAHX	B	C+	B+	Up	4.05	5.77	7.69	13.62	16.40	10.95	1,174	877-960-6077	Y
MFS Inflation-Adjusted Bond Fund Class R4	MIAJX	B	C+	B+	Up	4.09	5.88	7.94	14.34	17.81	10.95	1,174	877-960-6077	Y
MFS Inflation-Adjusted Bond Fund Class R6	MIAKX	B	C+	B+	Up	4.19	6.00	8.10	14.82	18.39	10.99	1,174	877-960-6077	Y
MFS Total Return Bond Fund Class 529A	EARBX	B-	C	B	Up	6.36	4.81	7.55	15.24	22.24	11.37	6,991	877-960-6077	Y
MFS Total Return Bond Fund Class A	MRBFX	B-	C	B	Up	6.26	4.82	7.57	15.32	22.29	11.38	6,991	877-960-6077	Y
MFS Total Return Bond Fund Class I	MRBIX	B-	C	B	Up	6.39	4.99	7.72	15.82	23.31	11.39	6,991	877-960-6077	Y

Category: US Fixed Income (con't)

		RATINGS				TOTAL RETURNS & PERFORMANCE					ASSETS		NEW INVESTORS	
Fund Name	Ticker Symbol	Overall Rating	Reward Rating	Risk Rating	Recent Up/ Downgrade	3-Month Total Return	6-Month Total Return	1-Year Total Return	3-Year Total Return	5-Year Total Return	NAV	Total Assets (MIL)	Telephone	Open to New Investors
MFS Total Return Bond Fund Class R2	MRRRX	B-	C	B	Up	6.17	4.64	7.20	14.12	20.29	11.38	6,991	877-960-6077	Y
MFS Total Return Bond Fund Class R3	MRBHX	B-	C	B	Up	6.23	4.77	7.46	14.97	21.80	11.38	6,991	877-960-6077	Y
MFS Total Return Bond Fund Class R4	MRBJX	B-	C	B	Up	6.39	4.99	7.72	15.82	23.31	11.39	6,991	877-960-6077	Y
MFS Total Return Bond Fund Class R6	MRBKX	B-	C	B+	Up	6.42	5.04	7.83	16.18	23.97	11.39	6,991	877-960-6077	Y
MFS® Government Markets Income	MGF	B-	B-	C+	Up	2.67	6.99	8.88	15.79	20.57	4.85	158.1	877-960-6077	Y
Morgan Stanley Inst Trust Core Plus Fixed Inc Port Cl Inst	MPFIX	B-	C	B	Up	6.42	4.01	7.05	17.14	36.65	11.79	808.1	855-332-5306	Y
Morgan Stanley Inst Trust Core Plus Fixed Inc Port Cl IS	MPLRX	B-	C	B	Up	6.34	4.04	7.02	17.16	36.67	11.78	808.1	855-332-5306	Y
Morgan Stanley Pathway Funds Core Fixed Income Fund	TIIUX	B	C+	B+	Up	4.96	5.70	8.88	16.73	24.56	8.7	965.4	855-332-5306	Y
Morgan Stanley Pathway Funds Inflation-Linked Fixed Inc Fu	TILUX	B	B-	B+	Up	6.17	6.70	8.79	15.35		10.7	150.4	855-332-5306	Y
Morgan Stanley U.S. Government Securities Trust Class A	USGAX	B-	C+	B		2.33	4.93	6.61	12.56	18.65	8.99	400.6	855-332-5306	Y
Morgan Stanley U.S. Government Securities Trust Class I	USGDX	B	C+	B+	Up	2.41	5.09	7.07	13.83	20.47	9	400.6	855-332-5306	Y
Morgan Stanley U.S. Government Securities Trust Class L	USGCX	B-	C+	B		2.23	4.72	6.27	11.71	16.77	9.06	400.6	855-332-5306	
Multi-Manager Total Return Bond Strategies Inst 3 Cl	CTREX	B-	C+	B	Up	5.68	5.26	8.16	15.06	22.35	10.65	8,344	800-345-6611	Y
Multi-Manager Total Return Bond Strategies Inst Cl	CTRZX	B-	C	B	Up	5.69	5.15	8.05	14.95	22.23	10.63	8,344	800-345-6611	Y
Mutual of America Institutional Funds Inc Bond Fund	MABOX	B	B-	B+		1.67	6.66	8.55	15.73	23.69	10.5354	25.0		Y
Nationwide Bond Fund Class A	NBDAX	B-	C+	B+	Up	4.12	4.96	7.08	15.22	21.96	10.3	373.5	800-848-0920	Y
Nationwide Bond Fund Class R	GBDRX	B-	C	B	Up	4.01	4.75	6.85	14.17	19.91	10.31	373.5	800-848-0920	Y
Nationwide Bond Fund Class R6	NWIBX	B-	C+	B+	Up	4.18	5.10	7.47	16.18	23.69	10.32	373.5	800-848-0920	Y
Nationwide Bond Fund Institutional Service Class	MUIBX	B-	C+	B+	Up	4.06	5.06	7.29	15.84	23.21	10.31	373.5	800-848-0920	Y
Nationwide Bond Index Fund Class A	GBIAX	B	C+	B	Up	2.63	5.62	7.95	14.29	19.56	11.82	909.3	800-848-0920	Y
Nationwide Bond Index Fund Class C	GBICX	B-	C+	B		2.46	5.27	7.22	11.98	15.60	11.82	909.3	800-848-0920	Y
Nationwide Bond Index Fund Class R6	GBXIX	B	C+	B+		2.75	5.85	8.41	15.75	22.09	11.8	909.3	800-848-0920	Y
Nationwide Bond Index Fund Institutional Service Class	NWXOX	B-	C+	B	Up	2.77	5.72	8.15	15.07	21.18	11.8	909.3	800-848-0920	Y
Nationwide Core Plus Bond Fund Class A	NWCPX	B-	C+	B+	Up	5.77	4.89	7.30	14.51	22.39	10.76	1,108	800-848-0920	Y
Nationwide Core Plus Bond Fund Class R6	NWCIX	B-	C+	B+	Up	5.85	5.06	7.77	15.73	24.70	10.77	1,108	800-848-0920	Y
Nationwide Core Plus Bond Fund Institutional Service Class	NWCSX	B-	C+	B+	Up	5.83	5.02	7.57	15.37	23.97	10.77	1,108	800-848-0920	Y
Nationwide Inflation-Protected Securities Fund Class A	NIFAX	B	C+	B+	Up	4.26	5.63	7.93	14.09	17.87	10.51	242.9	800-848-0920	Y
Nationwide Inflation-Protected Securities Fund Class R6	NIFIX	B	C+	A-	Up	4.22	5.72	8.21	15.05	19.40	10.58	242.9	800-848-0920	Y
Nationwide Inflation-Protected Securities Inst Service Cl	NWXNX	B	C+	B+	Up	4.29	5.74	8.19	14.78	18.91	10.58	242.9	800-848-0920	Y
Nationwide Loomis Core Bond Fund Class A	NWJGX	B-	C+	B	Up	4.84	6.27	9.00	16.55	23.14	11.52	516.1	800-848-0920	Y
Nationwide Loomis Core Bond Fund Class C	NWJHX	B-	C+	B	Up	4.64	5.95	8.53	15.02	20.53	11.45	516.1	800-848-0920	Y
Nationwide Loomis Core Bond Fund Class R6	NWJIX	B	C+	B+	Up	4.92	6.41	9.39	17.77	25.28	11.74	516.1	800-848-0920	Y
Nationwide Loomis Core Bond Institutional Service Cl	NWJJX	B-	C+	B	Up	4.85	6.28	9.02	16.78	23.79	11.74	516.1	800-848-0920	Y
Neuberger Berman Core Bond Fund Class A	NCRAX	B-	C+	B	Up	5.54	6.23	8.44	15.11	21.25	10.94	413.4	212-476-9000	Y
Neuberger Berman Core Bond Fund Class C	NCRCX	B-	C+	B	Up	5.24	5.84	7.64	12.55	16.80	10.95	413.4	212-476-9000	Y
Neuberger Berman Core Bond Fund Class R6	NRCRX	B	C+	B+	Up	5.65	6.47	9.07	16.74	23.83	10.98	413.4	212-476-9000	Y
Neuberger Berman Core Bond Fund Institutional Class	NCRLX	B	C+	B+	Up	5.62	6.42	8.85	16.58	23.66	10.98	413.4	212-476-9000	Y
Neuberger Berman Core Bond Fund Investor Class	NCRIX	B-	C+	B	Up	5.43	6.22	8.33	15.10	21.12	10.95	413.4	212-476-9000	
New Covenant Income Fund	NCICX	B-	C	B	Up	3.99	3.94	5.89	12.09	17.15	24.32	328.0		Y
North Country Intermediate Bond Fund	NCBDX	B-	C+	B	Up	4.45	4.44	6.73	13.29	18.07	10.93	83.5		Y
North Square Strategic Income Fund I	ADVNX	B	C+	B+	Up	6.66	4.52	8.07	14.56	24.32	9.8163	65.7	855-551-5521	Y
Northern Bond Index Fund	NOBOX	B	B-	B+		2.69	6.06	8.73	16.41	23.05	11.28	3,094	800-595-9111	Y
Northern Core Bond Fund	NOCBX	B-	C+	B+	Up	4.65	5.08	8.05	15.72	21.94	10.9	195.9	800-595-9111	Y
Northern Fixed Income Fund	NOFIX	B-	C	B	Up	5.27	4.35	7.27	15.07	21.77	10.65	831.3	800-595-9111	Y
Northern Short-Intermediate U.S. Government Fund	NSIUX	B-	C	B	Up	0.49	3.88	4.99	8.66	9.65	10.1	73.0	800-595-9111	Y
Northern U.S. Government Fund	NOUGX	B-	C+	B		0.71	5.58	6.94	11.82	13.82	10.23	44.3	800-595-9111	Y
Northern U.S. Treasury Index Fund	BTIAX	B	B	B		0.21	8.62	10.49	17.07	21.51	23.75	115.8	800-595-9111	Y
Old Westbury Fixed Income Fund	OWFIX	B-	C+	B		1.71	5.58	7.23	13.03	15.68	11.88	1,553	212-708-9100	Y
Optimum Fixed Income Fund Class A	OAFIX	B	C+	B+	Up	5.17	5.38	7.38	14.65	20.31	10.17	2,575		Y
Optimum Fixed Income Fund Class C	OCFIX	B-	C+	B	Up	4.96	4.96	6.57	12.14	15.92	10.15	2,575		Y
Optimum Fixed Income Fund Institutional Class	OIFIX	B	C+	B+	Up	5.27	5.60	7.67	15.56	21.77	10.17	2,575		Y
PACE Intermediate Fixed Income Investments Class A	PIFAX	B-	C+	B	Up	4.35	5.94	8.14	14.54	18.93	13.16	336.7	212-882-5586	Y

Category: US Fixed Income (con't)

Fund Name	Ticker Symbol	RATINGS: Overall Rating	Reward Rating	Risk Rating	Recent Up/ Downgrade	TOTAL RETURNS & PERFORMANCE: 3-Month Total Return	6-Month Total Return	1-Year Total Return	3-Year Total Return	5-Year Total Return	ASSETS: NAV	Total Assets (MIL)	NEW INVESTORS: Telephone	Open to New Investors
PACE Intermediate Fixed Income Investments Class P	PCIFX	B	C+	B	Up	4.41	5.98	8.32	15.38	20.41	13.16	336.7	212-882-5586	Y
PACE Intermediate Fixed Income Investments Class Y	PIFYX	B	C+	B	Up	4.41	6.07	8.41	15.39	20.42	13.16	336.7	212-882-5586	Y
PACE Mortgage-Backed Securities Fixed Income Inv Cl A	PFXAX	B-	C+	B	Up	2.53	3.77	5.66	11.40	16.21	13	335.3	212-882-5586	Y
PACE Mortgage-Backed Securities Fixed Income Inv Cl P	PCGTX	B-	C+	B	Up	2.67	3.90	6.01	12.24	17.66	13.01	335.3	212-882-5586	Y
PACE Mortgage-Backed Securities Fixed Income Inv Cl Y	PFXYX	B-	C+	B	Up	2.67	3.90	6.01	12.24	17.76	13.01	335.3	212-882-5586	Y
PACE Strategic Fixed Income Investments Class A	PBNAX	B-	C+	B+	Up	5.38	5.46	8.17	16.13	24.61	14.61	708.9	212-882-5586	Y
PACE Strategic Fixed Income Investments Class P	PCSIX	B-	C+	B+	Up	5.37	5.59	8.37	16.93	26.14	14.6	708.9	212-882-5586	Y
PACE Strategic Fixed Income Investments Class Y	PSFYX	B-	C+	B+	Up	5.38	5.60	8.39	16.96	26.00	14.58	708.9	212-882-5586	Y
Pacific Funds Core Income Class P		B-	C	B	Up	6.88	4.18	7.39	16.43	24.20	11.3	1,032	800-722-2333	Y
Pacific Funds Core Income Fund Advisor Class	PLIDX	B-	C	B	Up	6.90	4.19	7.40	16.47	24.23	11.28	1,032	800-722-2333	Y
Pacific Funds Core Income Fund Class A	PLIAX	B-	C	B	Up	6.73	3.95	7.00	15.37	22.42	11.25	1,032	800-722-2333	Y
Pacific Funds Core Income Fund Class I	PLIIX	B-	C	B	Up	6.81	4.10	7.31	16.39	24.36	11.26	1,032	800-722-2333	Y
Parnassus Fixed Income Fund	PRFIX	B	B-	B	Up	3.19	6.65	8.87	16.42	23.29	18.03	293.1	999-350-5	Y
Parnassus Fixed Income Fund Institutional Shares	PFPLX	B	B-	B	Up	3.30	6.82	9.11	17.27	24.54	18.03	293.1	999-350-5	Y
Pax Core Bond Fund Individual Investor Class	PAXBX	B-	C+	B		3.34	5.59	7.86	14.32		10.76	687.0	800-767-1729	Y
Pax Core Bond Fund Institutional Class	PXBIX	B-	C+	B		3.40	5.72	8.13	15.17		10.76	687.0	800-767-1729	Y
Payden GNMA Fund Investor Class	PYGNX	B-	C+	B	Up	0.73	3.86	5.35	10.90	14.77	9.57	123.1	614-470-8006	Y
PF Inflation Managed Fund Class P		B	C+	B+	Up	6.02	5.90	8.43	15.55	18.90	9.68	21.5	800-722-2333	Y
PF Managed Bond Fund Class P		B	C+	B+	Up	5.53	6.39	9.18	17.64	29.06	11.64	403.5	800-722-2333	Y
PGIM Core Bond Fund- Class A	TPCAX	B-	C+	B	Up	5.12	5.36	7.92	15.30	22.62	10.61	1,094	800-225-1852	Y
PGIM Core Bond Fund- Class R	TPCRX	B-	C+	B	Up	5.06	5.22	7.76	14.44	21.16	10.61	1,094	800-225-1852	Y
PGIM Core Bond Fund- Class R6	TPCQX	B-	C+	B+	Up	5.11	5.55	8.31	16.40	24.52	10.61	1,094	800-225-1852	Y
PGIM Core Bond Fund- Class Z	TAIBX	B-	C+	B+	Up	5.22	5.54	8.28	16.26	24.31	10.61	1,094	800-225-1852	Y
PGIM Core Conservative Bond Fund-Class R6	PQCNX	B	C+	B	Up	3.08	5.67	8.22	15.14		10.67	51.4	800-225-1852	Y
PGIM Government Income Fund- Class A	PGVAX	B-	B-	B		0.85	5.60	7.18	12.38	16.55	10.13	778.1	800-225-1852	Y
PGIM Government Income Fund- Class C	PRICX	B-	C+	B	Up	0.76	5.32	6.33	9.75	12.12	10.16	778.1	800-225-1852	Y
PGIM Government Income Fund- Class R	JDRVX	B-	C+	B		0.87	5.55	6.87	11.46	15.00	10.15	778.1	800-225-1852	Y
PGIM Government Income Fund- Class R6	PGIQX	B	B-	B	Up	1.06	5.95	7.69	14.04	17.65	10.11	778.1	800-225-1852	Y
PGIM Government Income Fund- Class Z	PGVZX	B	B-	B	Up	0.96	5.84	7.63	13.58	18.37	10.11	778.1	800-225-1852	Y
PGIM TIPS Fund- Class R6	PQTSX	B	C+	B+	Up	3.97	5.55	7.97	14.48		10.44	39.0	800-225-1852	Y
PIA MBS Bond Fund	PMTGX	B-	C+	B-	Up	0.29	3.27	5.16	11.34	16.08	9.76	70.2	800-251-1970	Y
PIMCO Extended Duration Fund Class I-2	PEDPX	B	B	B		-0.76	29.10	34.88	53.43	82.63	10.93	1,387	866-746-2602	Y
PIMCO Extended Duration Fund Institutional Class	PEDIX	B	B	B		-0.73	29.16	35.02	53.89	83.55	10.93	1,387	866-746-2602	Y
PIMCO Fixed Income SHares: Series C	FXICX	B-	C	B+	Up	6.68	5.03	7.73	17.23	21.39	10.77	1,462	866-746-2602	Y
PIMCO Fixed Income SHares: Series R	FXIRX	B	B	A-	Up	7.16	8.42	11.44	21.38	25.64	10.11	128.0	866-746-2602	Y
PIMCO GNMA and Government Securities Fund Class A	PAGNX	B-	C+	B	Up	1.55	4.13	6.17	11.79	15.58	11.43	1,737	866-746-2602	Y
PIMCO GNMA and Government Securities Fund Class I-2	PPGNX	B-	C+	B	Up	1.62	4.29	6.49	12.79	17.32	11.43	1,737	866-746-2602	Y
PIMCO GNMA and Government Securities Fund Class I-3	PANNX	B-	C+	B	Up	1.61	4.26	6.44	12.54	16.83	11.43	1,737	866-746-2602	Y
PIMCO GNMA & Govt Securities Fund Institutional Class	PDMIX	B-	B-	B	Up	1.65	4.34	6.59	13.13	17.91	11.43	1,737	866-746-2602	Y
PIMCO Long Duration Total Return Fund Class A	PLRAX	B	B	B	Up	7.50	12.96	18.63	33.24	54.74	11.9	3,411	866-746-2602	Y
PIMCO Long Duration Total Return Fund Class C	PLRCX	B	B	B	Up	7.30	12.54	17.76	30.29	49.08	11.9	3,411	866-746-2602	Y
PIMCO Long Duration Total Return Fund Class I-2	PLRPX	B	B	B		7.58	13.12	18.97	34.39	57.02	11.9	3,411	866-746-2602	Y
PIMCO Long Duration Total Return Fund Institutional Class	PLRIX	B	B	B		7.60	13.17	19.09	34.79	57.80	11.9	3,411	866-746-2602	Y
PIMCO Long-Term Real Return Fund Class I-2	PRTPX	B	B	B+		8.07	16.91	23.62	35.73	44.84	10.13	984.7	866-746-2602	Y
PIMCO Long-Term Real Return Fund Institutional Class	PRAIX	B	B	B+		8.09	16.97	23.74	36.14	45.56	10.13	984.7	866-746-2602	Y
PIMCO Long-Term U.S. Government Fund Administrative Class	PLGBX	B	B	B		0.56	21.51	25.56	37.81	54.04	7.88	1,018	866-746-2602	Y
PIMCO Long-Term U.S. Government Fund Class A	PFGAX	B	B	B		0.54	21.45	25.44	37.41	53.29	7.88	1,018	866-746-2602	Y
PIMCO Long-Term U.S. Government Fund Class C	PFGCX	B	B	B		0.35	21.02	24.52	34.38	47.69	7.88	1,018	866-746-2602	Y
PIMCO Long-Term U.S. Government Fund Class I-2	PLTPX	B	B	B		0.60	21.60	25.74	38.42	55.19	7.88	1,018	866-746-2602	Y
PIMCO Long-Term U.S. Government Fund Institutional Class	PGOVX	B	B	B		0.63	21.66	25.87	38.84	55.97	7.88	1,018	866-746-2602	Y
PIMCO Moderate Duration Fund Class I-2	PMOPX	B-	C+	B	Up	3.83	5.91	7.50	13.85	19.11	10.85	1,427	866-746-2602	Y
PIMCO Moderate Duration Fund Institutional Class	PMDRX	B	C+	B+	Up	3.86	5.96	7.61	14.19	19.71	10.85	1,427	866-746-2602	Y

Category: US Fixed Income (con't)

Fund Name	Ticker Symbol	RATINGS Overall Rating	Reward Rating	Risk Rating	Recent Up/ Downgrade	TOTAL RETURNS & PERFORMANCE 3-Month Total Return	6-Month Total Return	1-Year Total Return	3-Year Total Return	5-Year Total Return	ASSETS NAV	Total Assets (MIL)	NEW INVESTORS Telephone	Open to New Investors
PIMCO Mortgage-Backed Securities Fund Class A	PMRAX	B-	C	B	Up	2.24	2.81	4.56	11.66	18.35	10.72	180.9	866-746-2602	Y
PIMCO Mortgage-Backed Securities Fund Class I-2	PMRPX	B-	C	B	Up	2.32	2.96	4.87	12.67	20.14	10.72	180.9	866-746-2602	Y
PIMCO Mortgage-Backed Securities Fund Class I-3	PSANX	B-	C	B	Up	2.31	2.94	4.83	12.45	19.67	10.72	180.9	866-746-2602	Y
PIMCO Mortgage-Backed Securities Fund Institutional Class	PTRIX	B-	C	B+	Up	2.34	3.01	4.98	13.00	20.74	10.72	180.9	866-746-2602	Y
PIMCO Real Return Fund Administrative Class	PARRX	B	C+	B+	Up	5.31	6.06	8.28	14.71	18.82	11.85	9,094	866-746-2602	Y
PIMCO Real Return Fund Class A	PRTNX	B	C+	B+	Up	5.27	5.98	8.12	14.20	17.94	11.85	9,094	866-746-2602	Y
PIMCO Real Return Fund Class C	PRTCX	B-	C+	B+	Up	5.14	5.72	7.58	12.51	15.03	11.85	9,094	866-746-2602	Y
PIMCO Real Return Fund Class I-2	PRLPX	B	C+	B+	Up	5.35	6.14	8.44	15.22	19.71	11.85	9,094	866-746-2602	Y
PIMCO Real Return Fund Class R	PRRRX	B	C+	B+	Up	5.21	5.85	7.85	13.35	16.48	11.85	9,094	866-746-2602	Y
PIMCO Real Return Fund I-3	PRNPX	B	C+	B+	Up	5.34	6.11	8.39	15.00	19.24	11.85	9,094	866-746-2602	Y
PIMCO Real Return Fund Institutional Class	PRRIX	B	C+	B+	Up	5.38	6.19	8.55	15.57	20.31	11.85	9,094	866-746-2602	Y
PIMCO Total Return ESG Fund Administrative Class	PRFAX	B	C+	B+	Up	4.05	5.69	8.13	15.16	21.64	9.7	1,542	866-746-2602	Y
PIMCO Total Return ESG Fund Class A	PTGAX	B-	C+	B+	Up	4.01	5.61	7.98	14.65	20.74	9.7	1,542	866-746-2602	Y
PIMCO Total Return ESG Fund Class C	PTGCX	B-	C+	B	Up	3.94	5.34	7.30	12.26	16.47	9.7	1,542	866-746-2602	Y
PIMCO Total Return ESG Fund Class I-2	PRAPX	B	C+	B+	Up	4.20	5.87	8.41	15.80	22.68	9.7	1,542	866-746-2602	Y
PIMCO Total Return ESG Fund Institutional Class	PTSAX	B	C+	B+	Up	4.11	5.82	8.40	16.03	23.17	9.7	1,542	866-746-2602	Y
PIMCO Total Return Fund Administrative Class	PTRAX	B	C+	B+	Up	3.81	6.02	8.26	15.59	22.79	10.83	67,970	866-746-2602	Y
PIMCO Total Return Fund Class A	PTTAX	B	C+	B+	Up	3.78	5.97	8.16	15.27	22.11	10.83	67,970	866-746-2602	Y
PIMCO Total Return Fund Class C	PTTCX	B-	C+	B	Up	3.59	5.58	7.36	12.66	17.57	10.83	67,970	866-746-2602	Y
PIMCO Total Return Fund Class I-2	PTTPX	B	C+	B+	Up	3.85	6.09	8.42	16.11	23.71	10.83	67,970	866-746-2602	Y
PIMCO Total Return Fund Class R	PTRRX	B	C+	B+	Up	3.72	5.84	7.90	14.36	20.53	10.83	67,970	866-746-2602	Y
PIMCO Total Return Fund I-3	PTTNX	B	C+	B+	Up	3.83	6.07	8.37	15.90	23.24	10.83	67,970	866-746-2602	Y
PIMCO Total Return Fund Institutional Class	PTTRX	B	C+	B+	Up	3.87	6.15	8.53	16.46	24.33	10.83	67,970	866-746-2602	Y
PIMCO Total Return Fund IV Class A	PTUZX	B-	C	B	Up	3.50	4.45	7.05	14.42	20.89	11.17	438.8	866-746-2602	Y
PIMCO Total Return Fund IV Institutional Class	PTUIX	B-	C	B+	Up	3.59	4.62	7.42	15.61	23.01	11.17	438.8	866-746-2602	Y
PIMCO Total Return II Fund Administrative Class	PRADX	B	C+	B+	Up	3.63	6.26	8.39	16.69	24.13	10.29	577.6	866-746-2602	Y
PIMCO Total Return II Fund Class I-2	PMTPX	B	C+	B+	Up	3.67	6.34	8.55	17.20	25.05	10.29	577.6	866-746-2602	Y
PIMCO Total Return II Fund Institutional Class	PMBIX	B	C+	B+	Up	3.70	6.39	8.66	17.56	25.68	10.29	577.6	866-746-2602	Y
PMC Core Fixed Income Fund	PMFIX	B-	C+	B	Up	6.18	5.75	8.22	15.19	20.82	18.2	380.6		Y
PMC Core Fixed Income Fund Institutional Class Shares	PMFQX	B-	C+	B	Up	6.26	5.88	8.48	15.40	21.04	18.16	380.6		Y
Praxis Impact Bond Fund Class A	MIIAX	B	C+	B+	Up	4.00	6.00	8.24	14.72	20.80	11.2	610.4		Y
Praxis Impact Bond Fund Class I	MIIIX	B	C+	B+	Up	4.04	6.25	8.62	16.24	23.26	11.15	610.4		Y
Principal Bond Market Index Fund Class J	PBIJX	B	B-	B	Up	2.71	5.86	8.16	14.47	19.40	11.73	2,358	800-787-1621	Y
Principal Bond Market Index Fund R-1 Class	PBIMX	B-	C+	B		2.52	5.65	7.76	13.18	17.03	11.77	2,358	800-787-1621	Y
Principal Bond Market Index Fund R-2 Class	PBINX	B-	C+	B		2.53	5.68	7.86	13.56	17.74	11.72	2,358	800-787-1621	Y
Principal Bond Market Index Fund R-3 Class	PBOIX	B	C+	B	Up	2.62	5.87	8.17	14.22	18.89	11.72	2,358	800-787-1621	Y
Principal Bond Market Index Fund R-4 Class	PBIPX	B	B-	B	Up	2.69	5.91	8.35	15.18	20.29	11.82	2,358	800-787-1621	Y
Principal Bond Market Index Fund R-5 Class	PBIQX	B	B-	B	Up	2.70	6.02	8.50	15.31	20.75	11.79	2,358	800-787-1621	Y
Principal Bond Market Index Institutional Class	PNIIX	B	B-	B+		2.74	6.12	8.67	16.21	22.32	11.96	2,358	800-787-1621	Y
Principal Core Fixed Income Fund Class A	CMPIX	B	C+	B+	Up	5.87	5.28	8.06	15.97	22.99	10.15	8,033	800-787-1621	Y
Principal Core Fixed Income Fund Class C	CNMCX	B-	C	B	Up	5.61	4.92	7.22	13.29	18.18	10.22	8,033	800-787-1621	Y
Principal Core Fixed Income Fund Class J	PIOJX	B	C+	B+	Up	5.78	5.34	8.05	16.37	23.68	10.17	8,033	800-787-1621	Y
Principal Core Fixed Income Fund Class R-6	PICNX	B	C+	B+	Up	5.96	5.47	8.47	17.42	25.16	10.17	8,033	800-787-1621	Y
Principal Core Fixed Income Fund Institutional Class	PIOIX	B	C+	B+	Up	5.92	5.40	8.33	17.05	24.94	10.18	8,033	800-787-1621	Y
Principal Core Fixed Income Fund R-1 Class	PIOMX	B-	C+	B+	Up	5.61	5.01	7.40	14.24	19.98	10.18	8,033	800-787-1621	Y
Principal Core Fixed Income Fund R-2 Class	PIONX	B-	C+	B+	Up	5.74	5.17	7.64	14.78	20.85	10.2	8,033	800-787-1621	Y
Principal Core Fixed Income Fund R-3 Class	PIOOX	B-	C+	B+	Up	5.79	5.16	7.83	15.39	21.92	10.2	8,033	800-787-1621	Y
Principal Core Fixed Income Fund R-4 Class	PIOPX	B	C+	B+	Up	5.74	5.26	8.04	15.94	22.97	10.19	8,033	800-787-1621	Y
Principal Core Fixed Income Fund R-5 Class	PIOQX	B	C+	B+	Up	5.78	5.33	8.19	16.40	23.77	10.17	8,033	800-787-1621	Y
Principal Core Plus Bond Fund Class A	PRBDX	B	C+	B+	Up	5.34	5.78	8.23	15.29	22.21	11.53	606.2	800-787-1621	Y
Principal Core Plus Bond Fund Class J	PBMJX	B	C+	B+	Up	5.31	5.75	8.16	15.25	22.36	11.61	606.2	800-787-1621	Y
Principal Core Plus Bond Fund Institutional Class	PMSIX	B	C+	B+	Up	5.33	5.95	8.60	16.55	24.61	11.52	606.2	800-787-1621	Y

Category: US Fixed Income (con't)

Fund Name	Ticker Symbol	RATINGS: Overall Rating	Reward Rating	Risk Rating	Recent Up/ Downgrade	TOTAL RETURNS & PERFORMANCE: 3-Month Total Return	6-Month Total Return	1-Year Total Return	3-Year Total Return	5-Year Total Return	ASSETS: NAV	Total Assets (MIL)	NEW INVESTORS: Telephone	Open to New Investors
Principal Core Plus Bond Fund R-1 Class	PBOMX	B-	C+	B	Up	5.21	5.53	7.71	13.61	19.36	11.52	606.2	800-787-1621	Y
Principal Core Plus Bond Fund R-2 Class	PBMNX	B-	C+	B	Up	5.21	5.57	7.75	14.03	20.08	11.39	606.2	800-787-1621	Y
Principal Core Plus Bond Fund R-3 Class	PBMMX	B	C+	B+	Up	5.33	5.73	8.00	14.77	21.26	11.45	606.2	800-787-1621	Y
Principal Core Plus Bond Fund R-4 Class	PBMSX	B	C+	B+	Up	5.26	5.79	8.21	15.37	22.32	11.69	606.2	800-787-1621	Y
Principal Core Plus Bond Fund R-5 Class	PBMPX	B	C+	B+	Up	5.31	5.78	8.32	15.71	23.12	11.46	606.2	800-787-1621	Y
Principal Inflation Protection Fund Class A	PITAX	B-	C+	B+	Up	4.58	4.98	7.11	12.53	14.75	8.89	1,608	800-787-1621	Y
Principal Inflation Protection Fund Class J	PIPJX	B-	C+	B+	Up	4.47	4.85	6.77	11.69	13.38	8.64	1,608	800-787-1621	Y
Principal Inflation Protection Fund Institutional Class	PIPIX	B	C+	B+	Up	4.72	5.23	7.60	14.34	17.69	9.09	1,608	800-787-1621	Y
Principal Inflation Protection Fund R-1 Class	PISPX	B-	C	B	Up	4.43	4.82	6.73	11.35	12.56	8.47	1,608	800-787-1621	Y
Principal Inflation Protection Fund R-2 Class	PBSAX	B-	C+	B+	Up	4.52	4.90	6.86	11.85	13.45	8.55	1,608	800-787-1621	Y
Principal Inflation Protection Fund R-3 Class	PIFPX	B-	C+	B+	Up	4.57	4.97	7.13	12.35	14.45	8.68	1,608	800-787-1621	Y
Principal Inflation Protection Fund R-4 Class	PIFSX	B-	C+	B+	Up	4.51	4.94	7.17	12.91	15.38	8.8	1,608	800-787-1621	Y
Principal Inflation Protection Fund R-5 Class	PBPPX	B	C+	B+	Up	4.70	5.16	7.42	13.49	16.15	8.91	1,608	800-787-1621	Y
Putnam Income Fund Class A	PINCX	B-	C	B+	Up	4.16	3.34	6.88	17.78	21.65	7.28	3,578	617-292-1000	Y
Putnam Income Fund Class R	PIFRX	B-	C	B+	Up	4.13	3.10	6.68	17.00	20.19	7.21	3,578	617-292-1000	Y
Putnam Income Fund Class R5	PINFX	B-	C	B+	Up	4.19	3.47	7.29	18.76	23.62	7.37	3,578	617-292-1000	Y
Putnam Income Fund Class R6	PINHX	B-	C	B+	Up	4.17	3.45	7.25	18.99	23.86	7.42	3,578	617-292-1000	Y
Putnam Income Fund Class Y	PNCYX	B-	C	B+	Up	4.29	3.40	7.29	18.66	23.22	7.42	3,578	617-292-1000	Y
Rockefeller Core Taxable Bond Fund Institutional Class	RCFIX	B	B-	B+		2.66	6.56	8.70	16.53	23.05	10.843	73.1		Y
Russell Investments Investment Grade Bond Fund Class A	RFAAX	B-	C+	B	Up	5.52	6.03	8.47	14.86	21.34	22.97	776.8	800-426-7969	Y
Russell Investments Investment Grade Bond Fund Class E	RFAEX	B-	C+	B	Up	5.51	6.02	8.47	14.86	21.32	22.97	776.8	800-426-7969	Y
Russell Investments Investment Grade Bond Fund Class M	RIWTX	B-	C+	B	Up	5.63	6.24	8.91	16.20	22.87	22.94	776.8	800-426-7969	Y
Russell Investments Investment Grade Bond Fund Class R6	RIGRX	B-	C+	B	Up	5.61	6.27	8.95	16.33	23.46	23.03	776.8	800-426-7969	Y
Russell Investments Investment Grade Bond Fund Class S	RFATX	B-	C+	B	Up	5.60	6.20	8.79	15.85	23.00	22.94	776.8	800-426-7969	Y
Russell Investments Investment Grade Bond Fund Class Y	RFAYX	B-	C+	B+	Up	5.63	6.30	8.99	16.39	24.05	22.99	776.8	800-426-7969	Y
Russell Investments Strategic Bond Fund Class A	RFDAX	B-	C+	B	Up	6.44	5.13	7.79	14.57	21.50	11.59	3,266	800-426-7969	Y
Russell Investments Strategic Bond Fund Class E	RFCEX	B-	C+	B	Up	6.50	5.18	7.76	14.60	21.60	11.5	3,266	800-426-7969	Y
Russell Investments Strategic Bond Fund Class M	RSYTX	B-	C+	B	Up	6.61	5.35	8.15	15.79	23.04	11.64	3,266	800-426-7969	Y
Russell Investments Strategic Bond Fund Class R6	RSBRX	B-	C+	B	Up	6.60	5.33	8.17	15.81	23.65	11.5	3,266	800-426-7969	Y
Russell Investments Strategic Bond Fund Class S	RFCTX	B-	C+	B	Up	6.57	5.21	8.03	15.55	23.23	11.65	3,266	800-426-7969	Y
Russell Investments Strategic Bond Fund Class Y	RFCYX	B-	C+	B	Up	6.61	5.35	8.21	15.92	24.09	11.48	3,266	800-426-7969	Y
Ryan Labs Core Bond Fund	RLCBX	B-	C	B+	Up	5.66	5.65	8.58	17.40	24.86	10.59	69.6	212-635-2300	Y
Ryan Labs Long Credit Fund	RLLCX	B-	C+	B	Up	13.57	9.02	16.68	31.27		11.76	90.7	212-635-2300	Y
Sanford C. Bernstein Intermediate Duration Portfolio	SNIDX	B-	C	B	Up	4.88	4.69	7.18	14.59	23.33	13.92	3,490	212-969-1000	Y
Schroder Long Duration Inv-Grade Bond Investor Shares	STWLX	B	B	B		7.21	15.54	21.93	36.20	54.84	10.61	124.6	800-464-3108	Y
Schroder Total Return Fixed Income Fund Class Investor	SBBIX	B	B-	B	Up	6.03	7.30	10.08	17.48	23.30	10.63	43.2	800-464-3108	Y
Schwab Short-Term Bond Index Fund	SWSBX	B-	C	B	Up	1.61	3.87	5.39	10.56		10.38	1,221	877-824-5615	Y
Schwab U.S. Aggregate Bond Index Fund	SWAGX	B	B-	B+	Up	2.78	6.07	8.73	16.50		10.81	4,017	877-824-5615	Y
Schwab® Treasury Inflation Protected Securities Index Fund	SWRSX	B	B-	A-	Up	4.19	5.95	8.45	15.72	20.22	11.93	1,158	877-824-5615	Y
Segall Bryant & Hamill Plus Bond Fund Institutional Class	WIIBX	B	C+	B+	Up	5.21	5.52	8.02	16.94	25.67	11.11	1,020	312-474-1222	Y
Segall Bryant & Hamill Plus Bond Fund Retail Class	WTIBX	B	C+	B+	Up	5.20	5.47	7.96	16.44	24.79	11.22	1,020	312-474-1222	Y
SEI Catholic Values Trust Catholic Values Fixed Inc Cl F	CFVAX	B	C+	B+	Up	5.90	5.53	8.24	16.69	25.36	10.72	162.5	800-342-5734	Y
SEI Catholic Values Trust Catholic Values Fixed Inc Cl Y	CFVYX	B	C+	B+	Up	5.82	5.47	8.24	16.91	25.91	10.72	162.5	800-342-5734	Y
SEI Institutional Investments Trust Core Fixed Income Cl A	SCOAX	B	B-	B+	Up	4.64	6.79	9.87	19.00	27.40	11.05	7,441	800-342-5734	Y
SEI Inst Inv Trust Intermed Duration Credit Cl A	SIDCX	B	C+	B+	Up	7.14	6.69	10.75	20.58	32.39	11.04	3,285	800-342-5734	Y
SEI Inst Inv Trust Long Duration Credit Cl A	SLDAX	B	B	B	Up	9.28	10.37	17.32	32.12	56.60	12.14	4,084	800-342-5734	Y
SEI Institutional Investments Trust Long Duration Cl A	LDRAX	B	B	B		8.52	12.76	19.90	35.97	59.25	9.74	1,295	800-342-5734	Y
SEI Institutional Managed Trust Core Fixed Income Cl F	TRLVX	B	C+	B+	Up	4.76	6.14	9.06	16.97	24.77	12.07	4,206	800-342-5734	Y
SEI Institutional Managed Trust Core Fixed Income Cl I	SCXIX	B	C+	B+	Up	4.71	5.97	8.81	16.19	23.28	12.05	4,206	800-342-5734	Y
SEI Institutional Managed Trust Core Fixed Income Cl Y	SCFYX	B	C+	B+	Up	4.81	6.25	9.28	17.89	26.38	12.08	4,206	800-342-5734	Y
Sextant Bond Income Fund	SBIFX	B	C+	B+	Up	5.34	6.86	9.64	18.72	27.05	5.59	13.5		Y
Shelton Capital Management U.S. Govt Securities Cl K	CAUKX	B-	C+	B		-0.03	5.74	6.55	9.85	11.08	10.99	24.3	800-955-9988	Y

Category: US Fixed Income (con't)

Fund Name	Ticker Symbol	RATINGS: Overall Rating	Reward Rating	Risk Rating	Recent Up/ Downgrade	TOTAL RETURNS & PERFORMANCE: 3-Month Total Return	6-Month Total Return	1-Year Total Return	3-Year Total Return	5-Year Total Return	ASSETS: NAV	Total Assets (MIL)	NEW INVESTORS: Telephone	Open to New Investors
Shelton Capital Mgmt U.S. Govt Securities Direct Shares	CAUSX	B-	C+	B		0.09	6.01	7.06	11.62	13.93	10.97	24.3	800-955-9988	Y
State Farm Interim Fund	SFITX	B-	C+	B	Up	0.22	3.92	5.13	9.70	11.36	10.42	434.6		Y
State Street Active Core Bond Fund Investment Class	SSFIX	B	C+	B+	Up	4.46	5.35	7.97	15.85	24.09	9.86	117.5	617-664-7338	Y
State Street Active Core Bond Fund Service Class	SSFSX	B	C+	B+	Up	4.16	4.98	9.18	16.53	24.16	10.12	117.5	617-664-7338	Y
State Street Aggregate Bond Index Fund Class A	SSFCX	B	B-	B	Up	3.03	6.18	8.53	15.51	21.19	106.35	294.5	617-664-7338	Y
State Street Aggregate Bond Index Fund Class I	SSFDX	B	B-	B+	Up	3.15	6.37	8.82	16.52	22.99	106.09	294.5	617-664-7338	Y
State Street Aggregate Bond Index Fund Class K	SSFEX	B	B-	B+		3.11	6.47	9.06	16.78	23.17	106.09	294.5	617-664-7338	Y
State Street Aggregate Bond Index Portfolio	SSAFX	B	B-	B+		2.93	6.24	8.86	16.71	23.29	107.88	513.8	617-664-7338	Y
Sterling Capital Intermediate U.S. Government Fund Class A	BGVAX	B-	C+	B	Up	0.78	4.30	5.61	10.12	12.09	10.15	13.2	800-228-1872	Y
Sterling Capital Intermed U.S. Govt Inst Shares	BBGVX	B-	C+	B		0.84	4.42	5.87	10.95	13.39	10.16	13.2	800-228-1872	Y
Sterling Capital Quality Income Fund Class A Shares	SCSSX	B-	C	B	Up	2.08	3.34	4.91	11.92	17.49	10.23	37.1	800-228-1872	Y
Sterling Capital Quality Income Fund Institutional Shares	SCSPX	B-	C	B	Up	2.14	3.46	5.28	12.74	19.06	10.25	37.1	800-228-1872	Y
Sterling Capital Total Return Bond Fund Class A	BICAX	B	C+	B+	Up	5.10	5.68	8.14	16.35	24.15	11.29	1,637	800-228-1872	Y
Sterling Capital Total Return Bond Fund Class C	BICCX	B-	C+	B	Up	4.90	5.38	7.33	13.76	19.58	11.31	1,637	800-228-1872	Y
Sterling Capital Total Return Bond Fund Class R	BICRX	B-	C+	B+	Up	5.05	5.56	7.90	15.53	22.69	11.25	1,637	800-228-1872	Y
Sterling Capital Total Return Bond Fund Class R6	STRDX	B	C+	B+	Up	5.09	5.85	8.41	17.38	25.87	11.29	1,637	800-228-1872	Y
Sterling Capital Total Return Bond Institutional Shares	BIBTX	B	C+	B+	Up	5.06	5.80	8.31	17.11	25.58	11.29	1,637	800-228-1872	Y
Stone Harbor Investment Grade Fund Institutional Class	SHIGX	B-	C	B	Up	5.58	4.47	6.96	13.65	21.01	10.94	11.1	323-277-2777	Y
Strategic Advisers® Core Income Fund	FPCIX	B	C+	B+	Up	5.21	5.70	8.35	16.86	25.69	11.27	40,847	617-563-7000	Y
T. Rowe Price Inflation Protected Bond Fund	PRIPX	B	B-	A-	Up	4.33	6.12	8.49	16.10	19.39	12.75	389.5	410-345-2000	Y
T. Rowe Price Inflation Protected Bond Fund I Class	TIIPX	B	B-	A-	Up	4.45	6.20	8.75	16.81	20.35	12.79	389.5	410-345-2000	Y
T. Rowe Price Institutional Long Duration Credit Fund	RPLCX	B-	C+	B		11.42	8.85	16.69	31.95	53.64	11.29	24.0	410-345-2000	Y
T. Rowe Price U.S. Bond Enhanced Index Fund	PBDIX	B	C+	B+	Up	3.95	6.31	8.83	16.74	24.03	11.8	1,369	410-345-2000	Y
T. Rowe Price U.S. Treasury Intermediate Fund	PRTIX	B	B	B		0.73	8.30	9.55	16.28	20.10	6.34	1,112	410-345-2000	Y
T. Rowe Price U.S. Treasury Intermediate Fund I Class	PRKIX	B	B	B		0.77	8.20	9.52	16.60	20.23	6.33	1,112	410-345-2000	Y
T. Rowe Price U.S. Treasury Long Term Fund I Class	PRUUX	B	B	B		0.29	21.82	26.15	40.44	56.46	15.4	2,771	410-345-2000	Y
T. Rowe Price U.S. Treasury Long Term Fund Z Class	TRZUX	B	B	B		0.40	21.91	26.15	40.07	56.01	15.41	2,771	410-345-2000	
T. Rowe Price U.S. Treasury Long-Term Fund	PRULX	B	B	B		0.25	21.74	25.97	39.86	55.78	15.4	2,771	410-345-2000	Y
TCW Core Fixed Income Fund Class Institutional	TGCFX	B	B-	B+	Up	3.68	6.64	9.28	17.38	23.18	11.96	1,444	213-244-0000	Y
TCW Core Fixed Income Fund Class N	TGFNX	B	B-	B	Up	3.64	6.54	9.05	16.62	21.71	11.93	1,444	213-244-0000	Y
TCW Core Fixed Income Fund Class Plan	TGCPX	B	B-	B+		3.77	6.86	9.50	17.62	23.43	12.01	1,444	213-244-0000	Y
TCW High Yield Bond Fund Class Institutional	TGHYX	B-	C	B	Up	8.84	1.44	4.97	16.92	29.83	6.48	38.7	213-244-0000	Y
TCW Total Return Bond Fund Class I	TGLMX	B	B-	B+		3.00	7.15	9.24	17.28	22.82	10.49	6,584	213-244-0000	Y
TCW Total Return Bond Fund Class N	TGMNX	B	B-	B+	Up	2.95	7.03	8.99	16.20	21.10	10.81	6,584	213-244-0000	Y
TCW Total Return Bond Fund Class Plan	TGLSX	B	B-	B+		2.91	7.08	9.17	17.21	22.75	10.51	6,584	213-244-0000	Y
The Hartford Total Return Bond Fund Class A	ITBAX	B	C+	B+	Up	5.80	5.63	8.59	16.58	24.57	11.09	2,446	888-843-7824	Y
The Hartford Total Return Bond Fund Class C	HABCX	B-	C+	B	Up	5.63	5.26	7.74	13.91	19.95	11.22	2,446	888-843-7824	Y
The Hartford Total Return Bond Fund Class F	ITBFX	B	C+	B+	Up	5.94	5.76	9.00	17.92	27.01	10.99	2,446	888-843-7824	Y
The Hartford Total Return Bond Fund Class I	ITBIX	B	C+	B+	Up	5.99	5.80	8.97	17.64	26.40	11.06	2,446	888-843-7824	Y
The Hartford Total Return Bond Fund Class R3	ITBRX	B-	C+	B+	Up	5.77	5.44	8.23	15.42	22.66	11.4	2,446	888-843-7824	Y
The Hartford Total Return Bond Fund Class R4	ITBUX	B	C+	B+	Up	5.88	5.62	8.60	16.48	24.46	11.3	2,446	888-843-7824	Y
The Hartford Total Return Bond Fund Class R5	ITBTX	B	C+	B+	Up	5.90	5.71	9.22	17.80	26.74	11.23	2,446	888-843-7824	Y
The Hartford Total Return Bond Fund Class R6	ITBVX	B	C+	B+	Up	5.86	5.80	8.91	17.79	26.88	11.14	2,446	888-843-7824	Y
The Hartford Total Return Bond Fund Class Y	HABYX	B	C+	B+	Up	5.84	5.76	8.87	17.68	26.75	11.16	2,446	888-843-7824	Y
Thornburg Limited Term Income Fund Class A	THIFX	B-	C	B+	Up	5.70	4.99	6.65	12.46	17.42	14.02	6,462	800-847-0200	Y
Thornburg Limited Term Income Fund Class C	THICX	B-	C	B	Up	5.73	4.88	6.41	11.74	16.17	14	6,462	800-847-0200	Y
Thornburg Limited Term Income Fund Class I	THIIX	B-	C	B+	Up	5.86	5.14	7.01	13.59	19.47	14.03	6,462	800-847-0200	Y
Thrivent Government Bond Class A	TBFAX	B	B-	B	Up	0.77	7.03	8.23	13.92	18.14	10.62	68.5		
Thrivent Government Bond S Class	TBFIX	B	B-	B		0.89	7.19	8.43	14.26	18.85	10.63	68.5		Y
Thrivent Income Fund Class A	LUBIX	B-	C+	B	Up	8.78	5.71	9.44	19.18	30.16	9.92	961.6		Y
Thrivent Income Fund Class S	LBIIX	B-	C+	B+	Up	8.87	5.87	9.77	20.16	32.09	9.91	961.6		Y
TIAA-CREF Bond Index Fund Advisor Class	TBIAX	B	B-	B	Up	2.75	6.16	8.55	15.92	22.47	11.66	17,355	877-518-9161	Y

Category: US Fixed Income (con't)

Fund Name	Ticker Symbol	RATINGS Overall Rating	Reward Rating	Risk Rating	Recent Up/ Downgrade	TOTAL RETURNS & PERFORMANCE 3-Month Total Return	6-Month Total Return	1-Year Total Return	3-Year Total Return	5-Year Total Return	ASSETS NAV	Total Assets (MIL)	NEW INVESTORS Telephone	Open to New Investors
TIAA-CREF Bond Index Fund Class W	TBIWX	B	B-	B+		2.81	6.27	8.78	16.53	23.33	11.66	17,355	877-518-9161	Y
TIAA-CREF Bond Index Fund Institutional Class	TBIIX	B	B-	B+		2.78	6.21	8.66	16.31	23.09	11.66	17,355	877-518-9161	Y
TIAA-CREF Bond Index Fund Premier Class	TBIPX	B	B-	B	Up	2.83	6.13	8.50	15.89	22.18	11.66	17,355	877-518-9161	Y
TIAA-CREF Bond Index Fund Retail Class	TBILX	B	B-	B	Up	2.79	6.14	8.42	15.30	21.11	11.67	17,355	877-518-9161	Y
TIAA-CREF Bond Index Fund Retirement Class	TBIRX	B	B-	B	Up	2.80	6.17	8.49	15.54	21.56	11.67	17,355	877-518-9161	Y
TIAA-CREF Core Bond Fund Advisor Class	TIBHX	B-	C	B+	Up	5.60	4.61	7.26	15.41	24.55	11.01	6,891	877-518-9161	Y
TIAA-CREF Core Bond Fund Class W	TBBWX	B-	C	B+	Up	5.72	4.83	7.63	16.30	25.59	11	6,891	877-518-9161	Y
TIAA-CREF Core Bond Fund Institutional Class	TIBDX	B-	C	B+	Up	5.64	4.68	7.41	15.70	24.94	11	6,891	877-518-9161	Y
TIAA-CREF Core Bond Fund Premier Class	TIDPX	B-	C	B	Up	5.60	4.70	7.25	15.28	24.12	11.01	6,891	877-518-9161	Y
TIAA-CREF Core Bond Fund Retail Class	TIORX	B-	C	B	Up	5.48	4.57	7.02	14.69	23.18	11.19	6,891	877-518-9161	Y
TIAA-CREF Core Bond Fund Retirement Class	TIDRX	B-	C	B	Up	5.49	4.59	7.06	14.83	23.45	11.2	6,891	877-518-9161	Y
TIAA-CREF Core Impact Bond Fund Advisor Class	TSBHX	B-	C	B+	Up	5.09	4.24	6.82	15.45	23.60	10.89	5,171	877-518-9161	Y
TIAA-CREF Core Impact Bond Fund Institutional Class	TSBIX	B-	C	B+	Up	5.12	4.29	6.92	15.60	24.02	10.88	5,171	877-518-9161	Y
TIAA-CREF Core Impact Bond Fund Premier Class	TSBPX	B-	C	B+	Up	5.07	4.20	6.73	15.13	23.14	10.89	5,171	877-518-9161	Y
TIAA-CREF Core Impact Bond Fund Retail Class	TSBRX	B-	C	B	Up	5.15	4.26	6.74	14.77	22.47	10.88	5,171	877-518-9161	Y
TIAA-CREF Core Impact Bond Fund Retirement Class	TSBBX	B-	C	B	Up	5.06	4.17	6.66	14.75	22.49	10.88	5,171	877-518-9161	Y
TIAA-CREF Core Plus Bond Fund Class W	TCBWX	B-	C	B	Up	6.16	3.84	6.76	15.73	24.84	10.93	4,772	877-518-9161	Y
TIAA-CREF Inflation Linked Bond Fund Premier Class	TIKPX	B-	C	B	Up	3.59	4.05	5.60	11.31	14.13	11.91	3,541	877-518-9161	Y
TIAA-CREF Inflation-Linked Bond Fund Advisor Class	TIIHX	B-	C	B	Up	3.50	4.07	5.56	11.37	14.54	11.93	3,541	877-518-9161	Y
TIAA-CREF Inflation-Linked Bond Fund Class W	TIIWX	B-	C	B+	Up	3.67	4.24	6.00	12.24	15.47	11.93	3,541	877-518-9161	Y
TIAA-CREF Inflation-Linked Bond Fund Institutional Class	TIILX	B-	C	B+	Up	3.61	4.12	5.75	11.77	14.99	11.93	3,541	877-518-9161	Y
TIAA-CREF Inflation-Linked Bond Fund Retirement Class	TIKRX	B-	C	B	Up	3.52	3.96	5.44	10.97	13.53	12.02	3,541	877-518-9161	Y
Timothy Plan Fixed Income Fund Class A	TFIAX	B-	C+	B	Up	2.58	5.36	6.84	11.37	14.82	10.82	104.8	800-662-0201	Y
Timothy Plan Fixed Income Fund Class I	TPFIX	B-	C+	B	Up	2.65	5.54	7.16	12.29	16.45	10.75	104.8	800-662-0201	Y
Touchstone Active Bond Fund Class Institutional	TOBIX	B-	C	B	Up	7.81	5.29	8.02	16.02	24.35	11.06	332.4	800-543-0407	Y
Touchstone Impact Bond Fund Class A	TCPAX	B-	C+	B+	Up	3.52	4.91	6.96	14.02	20.05	10.74	344.8	800-543-0407	Y
Touchstone Impact Bond Fund Class Y	TCPYX	B-	C+	B+	Up	3.48	4.92	7.22	14.86	21.39	10.75	344.8	800-543-0407	Y
Touchstone Impact Bond Fund Institutional Class	TCPNX	B-	C+	B+	Up	3.50	4.98	7.32	15.20	22.18	10.75	344.8	800-543-0407	Y
Transamerica Core Bond Fund Class I2		B	C+	B+	Up	3.85	5.80	8.36	16.48	23.09	10.62	1,003	888-233-4339	Y
Transamerica Inflation-Protected Securities I3	TPRTX	B-	C+	B+	Up	4.72	4.78	7.10	14.40	16.93	10.65	109.8	888-233-4339	Y
Transamerica Inflation-Protected Securities R	TPRRX	B-	C	B+	Up	4.61	4.56	6.59	12.84	14.62	10.66	109.8	888-233-4339	Y
Transamerica Inflation-Protected Securities R4	TPRFX	B-	C+	B+	Up	4.71	4.74	6.92	13.85	16.30	10.67	109.8	888-233-4339	Y
Transamerica Intermediate Bond I2		B-	C+	B+	Up	4.29	5.37	8.02	15.64	23.09	10.86	1,879	888-233-4339	Y
Transamerica Intermediate Bond I3	TMBTX	B-	C+	B+	Up	4.29	5.36	8.00	15.72	23.42	10.88	1,879	888-233-4339	Y
Transamerica Intermediate Bond R	TMBRX	B-	C+	B	Up	4.14	5.18	7.49	13.99	20.42	10.89	1,879	888-233-4339	Y
Transamerica Intermediate Bond R4	TMBFX	B-	C+	B+	Up	4.23	5.24	7.76	14.89	16.07	10.88	1,879	888-233-4339	Y
Transamerica Total Return Fund Class I2		B	C+	B+	Up	4.20	6.01	8.56	15.72	23.83	10.91	600.7	888-233-4339	Y
Tributary Income Fund Class Institutional Plus	FOIPX	B	C+	B+	Up	3.31	5.60	7.78	16.12	23.62	10.95	218.0		Y
Tributary Income Fund Institutional Class	FOINX	B	C+	B+	Up	3.27	5.50	7.59	15.49	22.69	10.95	218.0		Y
USAA Government Securities Fund	USGNX	B-	C+	B		1.57	4.75	6.15	11.86	15.11	10.24	1,014	210-694-9700	Y
USAA Government Securities Fund A Shares	UAGNX	B-	C+	B	Up	1.38	4.58	5.71	10.78	13.42	10.23	1,014	210-694-9700	Y
USAA Government Securities Fund Institutional Shares	UIGSX	B-	C+	B		1.58	4.78	6.23	12.14	15.54	10.24	1,014	210-694-9700	Y
USAA Government Securities Fund R6 Shares	URGSX	B-	C+	B	Up	1.48	4.79	6.12	12.11	15.45	10.23	1,014	210-694-9700	Y
VALIC Company I Capital Conservation Fund	VCCCX	B	C+	B	Up	3.82	5.98	9.05	16.25	22.58	10.59	277.3		Y
VALIC Company I Government Securities Fund	VCGSX	B	B-	B	Up	0.98	6.34	8.04	14.16	18.90	11.25	148.5		Y
VALIC Company II Core Bond Fund	VCCBX	B-	C+	B+	Up	4.88	4.97	8.15	15.61	22.86	11.76	1,591		Y
Value Line Core Bond Fund	VAGIX	B-	C	B	Up	3.75	4.40	6.81	13.11	18.98	15.77	54.5	800-243-2729	Y
Vanguard Core Bond Fund Admiral Shares	VCOBX	B	B-	B+		4.45	7.71	10.38	18.58		21.69	1,912	877-662-7447	Y
Vanguard Core Bond Fund Investor Shares	VCORX	B	B-	B+		4.46	7.62	10.26	18.16		10.85	1,912	877-662-7447	Y
Vanguard Extended Duration Treas Ind Inst Plus Shares	VEDIX	B	B	B		-0.86	28.60	34.89	54.64	84.93	124.93	3,288	877-662-7447	Y
Vanguard Extended Duration Treas Ind Inst Shares	VEDTX	B	B	B		-0.86	28.58	34.86	54.54	84.76	49.77	3,288	877-662-7447	Y
Vanguard GNMA Fund Admiral Shares	VFIJX	B-	C+	B	Up	0.51	3.52	5.50	11.66	16.75	10.8	25,945	877-662-7447	Y

Category: US Fixed Income (con't)

Fund Name	Ticker Symbol	RATINGS: Overall Rating	RATINGS: Reward Rating	RATINGS: Risk Rating	RATINGS: Recent Up/ Downgrade	TOTAL RETURNS & PERFORMANCE: 3-Month Total Return	6-Month Total Return	1-Year Total Return	3-Year Total Return	5-Year Total Return	NAV	ASSETS: Total Assets (MIL)	NEW INVESTORS: Telephone	Open to New Investors
Vanguard GNMA Fund Investor Shares	VFIIX	B-	C+	B	Up	0.49	3.47	5.39	11.33	16.17	10.8	25,945	877-662-7447	Y
Vanguard Inflation-Protected Securities Admiral Shares	VAIPX	B	B-	A-	Up	4.13	5.99	8.21	15.30	20.13	27.42	29,558	877-662-7447	Y
Vanguard Inflation-Protected Securities Inst Shares	VIPIX	B	B-	A-	Up	4.10	6.02	8.22	15.38	20.35	11.17	29,558	877-662-7447	Y
Vanguard Inflation-Protected Securities Investor Shares	VIPSX	B	C+	B+	Up	4.17	6.00	8.16	15.00	19.56	13.97	29,558	877-662-7447	Y
Vanguard Inst Intermed-Term Bond Inst Plus Shares	VIITX	B-	C+	B	Up	2.36	5.04	6.92	13.39	18.53	24.29	28,687	877-662-7447	Y
Vanguard Instl Total Bond Market Index Trust	VTBSX	B	B-	B+		2.98	6.36	8.98	17.02	24.02	11.61	269,048	877-662-7447	Y
Vanguard Intermediate-Term Bond Index Fund Admiral Shares	VBILX	B	B-	B	Up	4.65	7.89	10.38	19.73	28.15	12.59	35,623	877-662-7447	Y
Vanguard Intermed-Term Bond Ind Inst Plus Shares	VBIUX	B	B-	B	Up	4.65	7.91	10.41	19.84	28.36	12.59	35,623	877-662-7447	Y
Vanguard Intermediate-Term Bond Ind Institutional Shares	VBIMX	B	B-	B	Up	4.65	7.90	10.40	19.80	28.29	12.59	35,623	877-662-7447	Y
Vanguard Intermediate-Term Bond Index Fund Investor Shares	VBIIX	B	B-	B	Up	4.63	7.85	10.29	19.45	27.67	12.59	35,623	877-662-7447	Y
Vanguard Intermediate-Term Corp Bond Ind Admiral Shares	VICSX	B-	C	B	Up	9.63	5.25	8.98	19.94	31.97	25.49	31,474	877-662-7447	Y
Vanguard Intermed-Term Corp Bond Ind Inst Shares	VICBX	B-	C	B	Up	9.63	5.30	9.03	20.02	32.12	31.5	31,474	877-662-7447	Y
Vanguard Intermediate-Term Investment-Grade Admiral Shares	VFIDX	B-	C+	B	Up	7.30	6.78	9.60	18.95	28.80	10.52	33,415	877-662-7447	Y
Vanguard Intermed-Term Inv-Grade Investor Shares	VFICX	B-	C+	B	Up	7.27	6.72	9.49	18.60	28.16	10.52	33,415	877-662-7447	Y
Vanguard Intermediate-Term Treasury Fund Admiral Shares	VFIUX	B	B	B		1.21	8.05	9.39	16.18	21.06	12.16	7,317	877-662-7447	Y
Vanguard Intermediate-Term Treasury Fund Investor Shares	VFITX	B	B	B		1.18	7.99	9.28	15.83	20.46	12.16	7,317	877-662-7447	Y
Vanguard Intermediate-Term Treasury Ind Admiral Shares	VSIGX	B	B	B		0.72	7.88	9.24	16.03	20.66	23.81	10,255	877-662-7447	Y
Vanguard Intermed-Term Treas Ind Inst Shares	VIIGX	B	B	B		0.76	7.88	9.29	16.07	20.81	29.55	10,255	877-662-7447	Y
Vanguard Long-Term Bond Index Fund Admiral Shares	VBLAX	B	B	B		6.34	13.06	19.10	34.24	55.55	16.86	12,388	877-662-7447	Y
Vanguard Long-Term Bond Ind Institutional Plus Shares	VBLIX	B	B	B		6.35	13.08	19.13	34.31	55.69	16.86	12,388	877-662-7447	Y
Vanguard Long-Term Bond Index Fund Institutional Shares	VBLLX	B	B	B		6.35	13.07	19.12	34.27	55.60	16.86	12,388	877-662-7447	Y
Vanguard Long-Term Investment-Grade Fund Admiral Shares	VWETX	B	B	B	Up	8.33	10.56	16.75	32.11	57.28	11.83	19,772	877-662-7447	Y
Vanguard Long-Term Investment-Grade Fund Investor Shares	VWESX	B	B	B	Up	8.30	10.50	16.63	31.72	56.50	11.83	19,772	877-662-7447	Y
Vanguard Long-Term Treasury Fund Admiral Shares	VUSUX	B	B	B		0.53	21.50	25.75	40.11	57.81	15.65	4,647	877-662-7447	Y
Vanguard Long-Term Treasury Fund Investor Shares	VUSTX	B	B	B		0.50	21.44	25.63	39.69	57.03	15.65	4,647	877-662-7447	Y
Vanguard Long-Term Treasury Index Fund Admiral Shares	VLGSX	B	B	B		0.36	21.27	25.62	40.10	57.73	33.61	4,711	877-662-7447	Y
Vanguard Long-Term Treasury Ind Institutional Shares	VLGIX	B	B	B		0.36	21.30	25.60	40.16	57.90	42.66	4,711	877-662-7447	Y
Vanguard Mortgage-Backed Securities Ind Admiral Shares	VMBSX	B-	C+	B	Up	0.17	3.39	5.58	11.79	16.45	21.74	12,529	877-662-7447	Y
Vanguard Mortgage-Backed Securities Ind Inst Shares	VMBIX	B-	C+	B	Up	0.15	3.36	5.56	11.82	16.50	29.45	12,529	877-662-7447	Y
Vanguard Short-Term Bond Index Fund Admiral Shares	VBIRX	B-	C	B	Up	1.77	4.05	5.41	10.66	13.72	10.89	52,731	877-662-7447	Y
Vanguard Short-Term Bond Ind Institutional Plus Shares	VBIPX	B-	C+	B	Up	1.78	4.06	5.44	10.76	13.90	10.89	52,731	877-662-7447	Y
Vanguard Short-Term Bond Index Fund Institutional Shares	VBITX	B-	C	B	Up	1.78	4.06	5.43	10.73	13.84	10.89	52,731	877-662-7447	Y
Vanguard Short-Term Bond Index Fund Investor Shares	VBISX	B-	C	B	Up	1.75	4.00	5.33	10.40	13.28	10.89	52,731	877-662-7447	Y
Vanguard Short-Term Federal Fund Admiral Shares	VSGDX	B-	C	B	Up	1.03	3.56	4.87	9.55	11.97	11.01	6,215	877-662-7447	Y
Vanguard Total Bond Market II Ind Institutional Shares	VTBNX	B	C+	B+		2.89	5.99	8.62	16.54	23.55	11.53	185,732	877-662-7447	Y
Vanguard Total Bond Market II Index Fund Investor Shares	VTBIX	B	C+	B+		2.87	5.96	8.54	16.30	23.12	11.53	185,732	877-662-7447	Y
Vanguard Total Bond Market Index Fund Admiral Shares	VBTLX	B	B-	B+		2.97	6.34	8.94	16.88	23.94	11.61	269,048	877-662-7447	Y
Vanguard Total Bond Market Ind Institutional Plus Shares	VBMPX	B	B-	B+		2.97	6.35	8.96	16.96	24.08	11.61	269,048	877-662-7447	Y
Vanguard Total Bond Market Index Fund Institutional Shares	VBTIX	B	B-	B+		2.97	6.35	8.96	16.93	24.02	11.61	269,048	877-662-7447	Y
Vanguard Total Bond Market Index Fund Investor Shares	VBMFX	B	B-	B+		2.94	6.29	8.83	16.54	23.35	11.61	269,048	877-662-7447	Y
Victory INCORE Investment Quality Bond Fund Class A	GUIQX	B-	C+	B	Up	3.94	5.18	7.96	13.58	20.03	10.11	31.1	210-694-9700	Y
Victory INCORE Investment Quality Bond Fund Class R	RIQKX	B-	C	B	Up	3.93	4.95	7.61	12.23	17.67	10.14	31.1	210-694-9700	Y
Victory INCORE Investment Quality Bond Fund Class Y	RSQYX	B-	C+	B+	Up	4.01	5.31	8.24	14.43	21.50	10.1	31.1	210-694-9700	Y
Victory INCORE Total Return Bond Fund Class A	MUCAX	B-	C+	B	Up	3.99	5.10	7.68	13.22	18.63	9.91	70.5	210-694-9700	Y
Victory INCORE Total Return Bond Fund Class R6	MUCRX	B-	C+	B+	Up	4.15	5.22	8.05	14.33	20.22	9.94	70.5	210-694-9700	Y
Victory INCORE Total Return Bond Fund Class Y	MUCYX	B-	C+	B+	Up	4.15	5.32	8.03	14.23	20.21	9.94	70.5	210-694-9700	Y
Victory Strategic Income Fund Class A	RSIAX	B-	C	B+	Up	4.41	4.46	6.60	15.99	24.49	10.73	70.3	210-694-9700	Y
Victory Strategic Income Fund Class C	RSICX	B-	C	B	Up	4.19	4.03	5.69	13.28	19.67	10.78	70.3	210-694-9700	Y
Victory Strategic Income Fund Class R	RINKX	B-	C	B+	Up	4.19	4.14	6.02	14.53	21.95	10.78	70.3	210-694-9700	Y
Victory Strategic Income Fund Class Y	RSRYX	B-	C	B+	Up	4.39	4.60	6.87	16.85	25.96	10.67	70.3	210-694-9700	Y
Virtus Seix Core Bond Fund Class A	STGIX	B	B-	B	Up	2.73	7.22	9.45	15.81	22.29	11.62	142.7	800-243-1574	Y
Virtus Seix Core Bond Fund Class I	STIGX	B	B	B		2.68	7.29	9.50	16.29	23.05	11.62	142.7	800-243-1574	Y

Category: US Fixed Income (con't)

		RATINGS				TOTAL RETURNS & PERFORMANCE					ASSETS		NEW INVESTORS	
Fund Name	Ticker Symbol	Overall Rating	Reward Rating	Risk Rating	Recent Up/ Downgrade	3-Month Total Return	6-Month Total Return	1-Year Total Return	3-Year Total Return	5-Year Total Return	NAV	Total Assets (MIL)	Telephone	Open to New Investors
Virtus Seix Core Bond Fund Class R6	STGZX	B	B	B		2.80	7.46	9.75	16.86	23.94	11.63	142.7	800-243-1574	Y
Virtus Seix Corporate Bond Fund Class A	SAINX	B	B	B	Up	10.12	9.28	13.02	20.98	34.80	9.68	55.3	800-243-1574	Y
Virtus Seix Corporate Bond Fund Class C	STIFX	B	B	B	Up	9.97	8.95	12.18	18.42	30.17	9.64	55.3	800-243-1574	Y
Virtus Seix Corporate Bond Fund Class I	STICX	B	B	B	Up	10.24	9.46	13.36	21.80	36.42	9.63	55.3	800-243-1574	Y
Virtus Seix Total Return Bond Fund Class A	CBPSX	B	B	B	Up	2.92	8.59	10.19	15.48	22.10	11.9	364.6	800-243-1574	Y
Virtus Seix Total Return Bond Fund Class I	SAMFX	B	B	B	Up	3.06	8.69	10.56	16.35	23.70	11.52	364.6	800-243-1574	Y
Virtus Seix Total Return Bond Fund Class R6	SAMZX	B	B	B	Up	3.01	8.78	10.63	16.77	24.50	11.51	364.6	800-243-1574	Y
Voya Intermediate Bond Fund Class A	IIBAX	B-	C	B	Up	5.96	4.26	7.07	15.17	23.92	10.63	8,783	800-366-0066	Y
Voya Intermediate Bond Fund Class I	IICIX	B-	C	B	Up	6.04	4.32	7.31	16.20	25.88	10.62	8,783	800-366-0066	Y
Voya Intermediate Bond Fund Class P3	VPIBX	B-	C	B	Up	6.13	4.60	7.78	16.82	25.70	10.63	8,783	800-366-0066	Y
Voya Intermediate Bond Fund Class R6	IIBZX	B-	C	B	Up	6.05	4.44	7.45	16.51	26.11	10.63	8,783	800-366-0066	Y
Voya Intermediate Bond Fund Class W	IIBWX	B-	C	B	Up	6.03	4.39	7.24	16.04	25.49	10.62	8,783	800-366-0066	Y
Voya Intermediate Bond Portfolio Class I	IPIIX	B-	C	B	Up	5.96	4.27	7.09	15.81	25.55	13.41	3,485	800-366-0066	Y
Voya Intermediate Bond Portfolio Class S	IPISX	B-	C	B	Up	5.85	4.16	6.85	14.90	24.00	13.32	3,485	800-366-0066	Y
Voya Intermediate Bond Portfolio Class S2	IIBTX	B-	C	B	Up	5.83	4.09	6.63	14.40	23.06	13.27	3,485	800-366-0066	Y
Voya Investment Grade Credit Fund A	VACFX	B-	C+	B	Up	11.02	6.48	11.12	21.54	36.33	11.69	172.0	800-366-0066	Y
Voya Investment Grade Credit Fund Class P	IIGPX	B-	C+	B	Up	11.23	6.87	11.96	24.30	40.60	11.68	172.0	800-366-0066	Y
Voya Investment Grade Credit Fund Class R6	VIGTX	B-	C+	B	Up	10.98	6.62	11.32	22.53	38.14	11.69	172.0	800-366-0066	Y
Voya Investment Grade Credit Fund Class SMA	ISCFX	B-	C+	B	Up	11.26	6.95	12.03	24.87	41.53	11.68	172.0	800-366-0066	Y
Voya Investment Grade Credit Fund I	VIGCX	B-	C+	B	Up	10.98	6.61	11.40	22.44	38.03	11.69	172.0	800-366-0066	Y
Voya Investment Grade Credit Fund W	VIGWX	B-	C+	B	Up	11.01	6.62	11.32	22.52	38.87	11.67	172.0	800-366-0066	Y
Voya U.S. Bond Index Portfolio Class A	ILUAX	B-	B-	B		2.40	5.80	7.95	13.90	18.78	11.36	3,084	800-366-0066	Y
Voya U.S. Bond Index Portfolio Class I	ILBAX	B	B-	B+	Up	2.61	6.03	8.46	15.68	21.89	11.41	3,084	800-366-0066	Y
Voya U.S. Bond Index Portfolio Class P2	VPUPX	B	B-	B+		2.67	6.16	8.73	16.54	22.83	11.41	3,084	800-366-0066	Y
Voya U.S. Bond Index Portfolio Class S	ILABX	B	B-	B	Up	2.46	5.92	8.11	14.74	20.34	11.37	3,084	800-366-0066	Y
Voya U.S. Bond Index Portfolio Class S2	IUSBX	B	B-	B	Up	2.52	5.84	8.05	14.22	19.46	11.38	3,084	800-366-0066	Y
VY® BlackRock Inflation Protected Bond Portfolio Class A	IBRAX	B-	C	B+	Up	6.03	5.36	7.40	12.51	13.85	9.85	275.3	800-366-0066	Y
VY® BlackRock Inflation Protected Bond Portfolio Class I	IBRIX	B	C+	B+	Up	6.16	5.57	7.98	14.61	17.31	10.23	275.3	800-366-0066	Y
VY® BlackRock Inflation Protected Bond Portfolio Class S	IBRSX	B-	C+	B+	Up	6.04	5.45	7.73	13.70	15.87	10.15	275.3	800-366-0066	Y
VY® BrandywineGLOBAL - Bond Portfolio	VGSBX	B	B	B	Up	7.60	9.03	12.01	18.72	26.21	11.46	291.5	800-366-0066	Y
Wasatch-Hoisington U.S. Treasury Fund	WHOSX	B	B	B		-1.33	24.47	30.48	45.65	63.53	22.47	458.5	800-551-1700	Y
Weitz Core Plus Income Fund Institutional Class	WCPBX	B-	C	B+	Up	8.49	5.25	7.60	16.05	26.00	10.77	108.6	800-304-9745	Y
Weitz Core Plus Income Fund Investor Class	WCPNX	B-	C	B	Up	8.56	5.17	7.41	15.42	24.81	10.77	108.6	800-304-9745	Y
Wells Fargo Core Bond Fund - Class A	MBFAX	B	B-	B	Up	4.20	6.43	8.73	15.44	21.54	14.29	5,456	800-222-8222	Y
Wells Fargo Core Bond Fund - Class Admin	MNTRX	B	B-	B	Up	4.16	6.46	8.83	15.69	21.96	13.95	5,456	800-222-8222	Y
Wells Fargo Core Bond Fund - Class C	MBFCX	B-	C+	B	Up	3.97	6.02	7.91	12.81	17.02	14.15	5,456	800-222-8222	Y
Wells Fargo Core Bond Fund - Class Inst	MBFIX	B	B-	B+	Up	4.23	6.61	9.05	16.67	23.69	13.93	5,456	800-222-8222	Y
Wells Fargo Core Bond Fund - Class R	WTRRX	B	B-	B	Up	4.11	6.25	8.43	14.51	19.92	13.94	5,456	800-222-8222	Y
Wells Fargo Core Bond Fund - Class R4	MBFRX	B	B-	B+	Up	4.21	6.56	8.94	16.41	23.16	13.94	5,456	800-222-8222	Y
Wells Fargo Core Bond Fund - Class R6	WTRIX	B	B-	B+	Up	4.25	6.56	9.11	16.85	24.00	13.93	5,456	800-222-8222	Y
Wells Fargo Core Plus Bond Fund Class A	STYAX	B	C+	B+	Up	6.78	6.01	8.64	16.88	28.47	13.49	1,108	800-222-8222	Y
Wells Fargo Core Plus Bond Fund Class Admin	WIPDX	B	C+	B+	Up	6.82	6.07	8.77	17.27	29.21	13.47	1,108	800-222-8222	Y
Wells Fargo Core Plus Bond Fund Class C	WFIPX	B-	C+	B+	Up	6.51	5.59	7.76	14.30	23.75	13.48	1,108	800-222-8222	Y
Wells Fargo Core Plus Bond Fund Class Institutional	WIPIX	B	C+	B+	Up	6.85	6.24	9.06	18.08	30.52	13.51	1,108	800-222-8222	Y
Wells Fargo Core Plus Bond Fund Class R6	STYJX	B	C+	B+	Up	6.87	6.18	9.02	18.25	30.28	13.51	1,108	800-222-8222	Y
Wells Fargo Government Securities Fund - Class A	SGVDX	B	B-	B	Up	1.05	5.92	7.49	13.39	17.21	11.67	686.9	800-222-8222	Y
Wells Fargo Government Securities Fund - Class Admin	WGSDX	B	B-	B+	Up	1.10	5.93	7.63	14.01	18.35	11.66	686.9	800-222-8222	Y
Wells Fargo Government Securities Fund - Class C	WGSCX	B-	C+	B		0.78	5.44	6.60	10.78	12.81	11.66	686.9	800-222-8222	Y
Wells Fargo Government Securities Fund - Class Inst	SGVIX	B	B-	B+		1.14	6.02	7.89	14.65	19.39	11.66	686.9	800-222-8222	Y
Western Asset Core Bond Fund Class A	WABAX	B	C+	B+	Up	5.54	5.22	8.20	16.73	25.84	13.55	15,751	877-721-1926	Y
Western Asset Core Bond Fund Class C	WABCX	B-	C+	B	Up	5.36	4.86	7.37	14.30	21.55	13.55	15,751	877-721-1926	Y
Western Asset Core Bond Fund Class C1	LWACX	B-	C+	B+	Up	5.50	5.06	7.78	15.48	23.56	13.57	15,751	877-721-1926	Y

Category: US Fixed Income (con't)

		RATINGS				TOTAL RETURNS & PERFORMANCE					ASSETS		NEW INVESTORS	
Fund Name	Ticker Symbol	Overall Rating	Reward Rating	Risk Rating	Recent Up/ Downgrade	3-Month Total Return	6-Month Total Return	1-Year Total Return	3-Year Total Return	5-Year Total Return	NAV	Total Assets (MIL)	Telephone	Open to New Investors
Western Asset Core Bond Fund Class FI	WAPIX	B	C+	B+	Up	5.62	5.22	8.21	16.77	25.98	13.56	15,751	877-721-1926	Y
Western Asset Core Bond Fund Class I	WATFX	B	C+	B+	Up	5.63	5.40	8.51	18.02	28.23	13.55	15,751	877-721-1926	Y
Western Asset Core Bond Fund Class IS	WACSX	B	C+	B+	Up	5.72	5.41	8.61	18.11	28.37	13.57	15,751	877-721-1926	Y
Western Asset Core Bond Fund Class R	WABRX	B-	C+	B+	Up	5.53	5.13	7.86	15.67	24.01	13.57	15,751	877-721-1926	Y
Western Asset Core Plus Bond Fund Class A	WAPAX	B-	C	B	Up	6.39	3.91	7.79	16.40	28.43	12.27	32,923	877-721-1926	Y
Western Asset Core Plus Bond Fund Class C1	LWCPX	B-	C	B	Up	6.34	3.75	7.48	15.18	26.05	12.28	32,923	877-721-1926	Y
Western Asset Core Plus Bond Fund Class FI	WACIX	B-	C	B	Up	6.47	3.99	7.88	16.47	28.42	12.29	32,923	877-721-1926	Y
Western Asset Core Plus Bond Fund Class I	WACPX	B-	C	B+	Up	6.57	4.18	8.27	17.78	30.93	12.29	32,923	877-721-1926	Y
Western Asset Core Plus Bond Fund Class IS	WAPSX	B-	C	B+	Up	6.58	4.20	8.21	17.79	31.00	12.28	32,923	877-721-1926	Y
Western Asset Core Plus Bond Fund Class R	WAPRX	B-	C	B	Up	6.40	3.84	7.55	15.43	26.66	12.27	32,923	877-721-1926	Y
Western Asset Inflation Indexed Plus Bond Fund Class A	WAFAX	B-	C	B+	Up	5.27	4.04	6.92	13.46	14.83	11.77	453.7	877-721-1926	Y
Western Asset Inflation Indexed Plus Bond Fund Class C1	LWICX	B-	C	B	Up	5.05	3.65	6.48	11.99	12.20	11.64	453.7	877-721-1926	Y
Western Asset Inflation Indexed Plus Bond Fund Class FI	WATPX	B-	C	B+	Up	5.22	4.01	6.98	13.58	14.83	11.69	453.7	877-721-1926	Y
Western Asset Inflation Indexed Plus Bond Fund Class I	WAIIX	B-	C+	B+	Up	5.40	4.20	7.36	14.75	16.64	11.89	453.7	877-721-1926	Y
Western Asset Inflation Indexed Plus Bond Fund Class IS	WAFSX	B-	C+	B+	Up	5.37	4.21	7.38	14.98	17.31	11.95	453.7	877-721-1926	Y
Western Asset Inflation Indexed Plus Bond Fund Class R	WAFRX	B-	C	B	Up	5.16	3.82	6.51	12.36	12.74	11.61	453.7	877-721-1926	Y
Western Asset Intermediate Bond Fund Class A	WATAX	B-	C	B	Up	5.19	4.03	6.12	12.85	19.73	11.48	1,107	877-721-1926	Y
Western Asset Intermediate Bond Fund Class I	WATIX	B-	C+	B+	Up	5.27	4.20	6.48	14.33	22.08	11.49	1,107	877-721-1926	Y
Western Asset Intermediate Bond Fund Class IS	WABSX	B-	C+	B+	Up	5.39	4.26	6.59	14.62	22.64	11.5	1,107	877-721-1926	Y
Western Asset Intermediate Bond Fund Class R	WATRX	B-	C	B	Up	5.21	3.90	5.94	12.35	18.44	11.5	1,107	877-721-1926	Y
Western Asset SMASh Series M Fund	LMSMX	B	B-	B+		0.31	3.43	5.59	15.29	30.88	11.01	2,385	877-721-1926	Y
William Blair Bond Fund Class I	WBFIX	B-	C	B+	Up	5.34	4.26	7.28	15.42	22.96	10.54	271.0	312-364-5409	Y
William Blair Bond Fund Class N	WBBNX	B-	C	B	Up	5.35	4.26	7.19	14.93	21.89	10.66	271.0	312-364-5409	Y
William Blair Bond Fund R6 Class	BBFIX	B-	C	B+	Up	5.46	4.29	7.33	15.74	23.46	10.54	271.0	312-364-5409	Y
Wilmington Broad Market Bond Fund Class A	WABMX	B-	C+	B	Up	3.45	5.55	7.88	14.01	19.58	10.5	545.4	800-836-2211	Y
Wilmington Broad Market Bond Fund Institutional Class	WIBMX	B	C+	B+	Up	3.69	5.81	8.34	15.31	21.65	10.33	545.4	800-836-2211	Y
Wilmington Intermediate-Term Bond Fund Class A	WIBAX	B-	C+	B	Up	4.56	5.16	6.77	12.25	15.68	10.4	49.7	800-836-2211	Y
Wilmington Intermediate-Term Bond Fund Institutional Class	WIBIX	B-	C+	B	Up	4.54	5.21	6.98	13.29	17.52	10.4	49.7	800-836-2211	Y

Category: US Municipal Fixed Income

		RATINGS				TOTAL RETURNS & PERFORMANCE					ASSETS		NEW INVESTORS	
Fund Name	Ticker Symbol	Overall Rating	Reward Rating	Risk Rating	Recent Up/ Downgrade	3-Month Total Return	6-Month Total Return	1-Year Total Return	3-Year Total Return	5-Year Total Return	NAV	Total Assets (MIL)	Telephone	Open to New Investors
Dupree Mutual Fund Alabama Tax-Free Income Fund	DUALX	B-	C	B+	Up	2.29	3.19	5.48	13.00	19.65	12.78	27.0		Y
Dupree Taxable Municipal Bond Series	DUTMX	B-	C	B+		1.99	3.48	5.28	15.16	27.31	10.4	13.4		Y
Eaton Vance Oregon Municipal Income Fund Class I	EIORX	B-	C	B	Up	2.66	3.16	5.33	12.99	22.58	8.86	138.5		Y
Franklin Ohio Tax-Free Income Fund Class Adv	FROZX	B-	C	B	Up	2.00	2.80	4.95	12.89	20.86	13.07	1,593	650-312-2000	Y
Franklin Ohio Tax-Free Income Fund Class R6	FKTOX	B-	C	B	Up	2.01	2.82	4.91	12.99	20.74	13.07	1,593	650-312-2000	Y
Nuveen Ohio Municipal Bond Fund Class I	NXOHX	B-	C	B	Up	3.63	3.43	5.47	13.94	22.77	11.92	682.1	312-917-8146	Y
Parametric TABS Short-Term Municipal Bond Fund Class I	EIBSX	B-	C	B	Up	2.54	4.38	5.58	9.61	13.42	10.92	322.2		Y
Pioneer AMT-Free Municipal Fund Class A	PBMFX	B-	C	B	Up	2.71	3.21	6.70	15.61	25.84	15.47	1,301	617-742-7825	Y
Pioneer AMT-Free Municipal Fund Class Y	PBYMX	B-	C	B	Up	2.65	3.15	6.77	16.29	27.25	15.4	1,301	617-742-7825	Y
State Farm Municipal Bond Fund	SFBDX	B-	C	B	Up	2.34	3.36	5.25	12.49	18.77	9	713.6		Y
Vanguard Ohio Long-Term Tax-Exempt Fund	VOHIX	B-	C	B	Up	2.80	3.36	5.84	15.73	26.09	13.06	1,435	877-662-7447	Y
Virtus Seix High Grade Municipal Bond Fund Class A	SFLTX	B-	C	B+	Up	3.26	3.65	6.02	14.46	23.10	12.42	67.6	800-243-1574	Y
Virtus Seix High Grade Municipal Bond Fund Class I	SCFTX	B-	C	B+	Up	3.30	3.72	6.26	15.06	24.01	12.42	67.6	800-243-1574	Y
Virtus Seix Investment Grade Tax-Exempt Bond Fund Class A	SISIX	B-	C	B	Up	3.04	3.22	5.24	11.87	17.88	12.04	288.5	800-243-1574	Y
Virtus Seix Investment Grade Tax-Exempt Bond Fund Class I	STTBX	B-	C	B	Up	3.00	3.30	5.32	12.29	18.68	12.02	288.5	800-243-1574	Y

Appendix:

Glossary

This section contains an explanation of the fields of data used throughout this guide.

1-Year Total Return
The rate of return on an investment over one year that includes interest, capital gains, dividends and distributions realized.

3-Year Total Return
The rate of return on an investment over three years that includes interest, capital gains, dividends and distributions realized.

3-Month Total Return
The rate of return on an investment over three months that includes interest, capital gains, dividends and distributions realized.

3-Year Beta
A three year measure of volatility, or systematic risk, of a security in comparison to the market as a whole. A beta of less than 1 means that the security will be less volatile than the market, a beta larger than 1 means more volatility. Beta value cannot be calculated if less than 24 months of pricing is available.

3-Year Standard Deviation
A statistical measurement of dispersion about an average, which depicts how widely the returns varied over the past three years. Investors use the standard deviation of historical performance to try to predict the range of returns that are most likely for a given fund. When a fund has a high standard deviation, the predicted range of performance is wide, implying greater volatility. Standard deviation is most appropriate for measuring risk if it is for a fund that is an investor's only holding. The figure cannot be combined for more than one fund because the standard deviation for a portfolio of multiple funds is a function of not only the individual standard deviations, but also of the degree of correlation among the funds' returns. If a fund's returns follow a normal distribution, then approximately 68 percent of the time they will fall within one standard deviation of the mean return for the fund, and 95 percent of the time within two standard deviations.

5-Year Total Return
The rate of return on an investment over five years that includes interest, capital gains, dividends and distributions realized.

6-Month Total Return
The rate of return on an investment over six months that includes interest, capital gains, dividends and distributions realized.

Address
The company's street address.

Asset & Performance History
Indicates the fund's **NAV (Net Asset Value)** and **1-Year Total Return** for the previous 6 years.

Asset Allocation
Indicates the percentage of assets in each category. Used as an investment strategy that attempts to balance risk versus reward by adjusting the percentage of each asset in an investment portfolio according to the investor's risk tolerance, goals and investment time frame. Allocation percentages may not add up to 100%. Negative values reflect short positions. See Cash, Stocks, US Stocks, Bonds, US Bonds, Other)

Average Coupon Rate
The annual interest rate of a debt/bond security that the issuer promises to pay to the holder until maturity.

Back End Fee (%)
A fee that investors pay when withdrawing money from an investment within a specified number of years, usually five to 10 years. The back-end load is designed to discourage withdrawals and typically declines for each year that a shareholder remains in a fund. The fee is a percentage of the value of the share being sold. Fees are displayed as a percent.

BUY-HOLD-SELL Indicator
Funds that are rated in the A or B range are, in our opinion, a potential BUY. Funds in the C range will indicate a HOLD status. Funds in the D or E range will indicate a SELL status.

Cash (%)
The percentage of the fund's assets invested in short-term obligations, usually less than 90 days, that provide a return in the form of interest payments. This type of investment generally offers a low return compared to other investments but has a low risk level.

Category
Identifies funds according to their actual investment styles as measured by their portfolio holdings. This categorization allows investors to spread their money around in a mix of funds with a variety of risk and return characteristics.

Class A
This class of Mutual Fund typically has a front-end sales load and a loaded fee structure. Although the fees for Class A may typically be lower, because they normally charge front end fees, your initial amount invested will be lower and your overall return will be affected. An annual asset based fee may well be levied, although this is typically lower than other classes.

Class B
This class of shares, instead of a front-end or back-end sales load normally charges fees called a contingent deferred sales charge (CDSC). This fee is paid if you sell the shares within a certain period of time and may well decline after each year. An annual asset based fee is likely to be levied. Often a Class B share will convert to Class A within a couple of years of reaching the end of the CDSC expiry at which point Class A fees will be initiated.

Class C
A C-share is a class of mutual fund with a level load. They typically don't have front-end loads, but do sometimes have back-end loads. They are usually around 1% but are sometimes eliminated after the shares are held for over a year. Annual asset based fees are normal for this class of share.

Class I
This class is sold to institutional shareholders. Also called Y-Shares, these have different fees and do not charge traditional loads.

Class R
R share funds, Also known as K shares, are for retirement accounts, and the R share class mutual funds are only available through employer-sponsored retirement plans. R share mutual funds do not have any loads, but they do have annual asset based fees typically of around 0.25% to 0.50%.

Closed End Fund
They are launched through an Initial Public Offering in order to raise money and then trade in the open market just like a stock or an ETF. They only issue a set amount of shares and, although their value is also based on the Net Asset Value (NAV), the actual price of the fund is affected by supply and demand, allowing it to trade at prices above or below its real value.

Corporate Bonds (%)
The percentage of the fund's assets invested in corporate bonds. A corporate bond is issued by a corporation. See **Asset Allocation**.

Dividend Yield (TTM)

Trailing twelve months dividends paid out relative to the share price. Expressed as a percentage and measures how much cash flow an investor is getting for each invested dollar. **Trailing Twelve Months (TTM)** is a representation of a fund's financial performance over the most recent 12 months. TTM uses the latest available financial data from a company's interim, quarterly or annual reports.

Effective Duration

Effective duration for all long fixed income positions in a portfolio. This value gives a better estimation of how the price of bonds with embedded options, which are common in many mutual funds, will change as a result of changes in interest rates. Effective duration takes into account expected mortgage prepayment or the likelihood that embedded options will be exercised if a fund holds futures, other derivative securities, or other funds as assets, the aggregate effective duration should include the weighted impact of those exposures.

Expense Ratio

A measure of what it costs an investment company to operate a mutual fund. An expense ratio is determined through an annual calculation, where a fund's operating expenses are divided by the average dollar value of its assets under management. Operating expenses may include money spent on administration and management of the fund, advertising, etc. An expense ratio of 1 percent per annum means that each year 1 percent of the fund's total assets will be used to cover expenses.

Front End Fee (%)

A commission or sales charge applied at the time of the initial purchase of an investment. The fee percentage is generally based on the amount of the investment. Larger investments, both initial and cumulative, generally receive percentage discounts based on the dollar value invested. Fees are displayed as a percent.

Fund Name

Describes the fund's assets, regions of investments and investment strategies. Many funds have similar names, so you want to make sure the fund you look up is really the one you are interested in evaluating.

Fund Type

Describes the fund's assets, regions of investments and investment strategies. (See **Open End Fund, Closed End Fund.**)

Government Bonds (%)

The percentage of the fund's assets invested in government bonds. A government bond is issued by a national government. See **Asset Allocation**.

Inception Date
The date on which the fund began its operations. The commencement date indicates when a fund began investing in the market. Many investors prefer funds with longer operating histories. Funds with longer histories have longer track records and can thereby provide investors with a more long-standing picture of their performance.

Institutional Only
This indicates if the fund is offered to institutional clients only (pension funds, mutual funds, money managers, insurance companies, investment banks, commercial trusts, endowment funds, hedge funds, and some hedge fund investors). See **Services Offered**.

Investment Strategy
A set of rules, behaviors or procedures, designed to guide an investor's selection of an investment portfolio. Individuals have different profit objectives, and their individual skills make different tactics and strategies appropriate.

Manager/Tenure (Years)
The name of the manager and the number of years spent managing the fund.

Minimum Initial Investment
The smallest investment amount a fund will accept to establish a new account. This amount could be $0 or any other number set by the fund.

Minimum Subsequent Investment
The smallest additional investment amount a fund will accept in an existing account.

Money Market Fund
Mutual fund that invests primarily in low-risk, short-term investments such as treasury bills, government securities, certificates of deposit and other highly liquid, safe securities.

Municipal Bonds (%)
The percentage of the fund's assets invested in municipal bonds. A municipal bond is issued by or on behalf of a local authority. See **Asset Allocation**.

NAV (Net Asset Value)
A fund's price per share. The value is calculated by dividing the total value of all the securities in the portfolio, less any liabilities, by the number of fund shares outstanding.

Open End Fund
A type of mutual fund that does not have restrictions on the amount of shares the fund will issue. If demand is high enough, the fund will continue to issue shares no matter how many investors there are. Open-end funds also buy back shares when investors wish to sell.

Open to New Investments
Indicates whether the fund accepts investments from those who are not existing investors. A "Y" in this column identifies that the fund accepts new investors. No data in this column indicates that the fund is closed to new investors. The fund may be closed to new investors because the fund's asset base is getting too large to effectively execute its investing style. Although, the fund may be closed, in most cases, existing investors are able to add to their holdings.

Other (%)
The percentage of the fund's assets invested in other financial instruments. See **Asset Allocation.**

Overall Rating
The Weiss rating measured on a scale from A to E based on each fund's risk and performance. See the preceding section, "What Our Ratings Mean," for an explanation of each letter grade rating.

Performance Chart
A graphical representation of the fund's total returns over the past year.

Phone Exchange
This indicates that investors can move money between different funds within the same fund family over the phone. See **Services Offered**.

Phone Number
The company's phone number.

Prospectus Objective
Gives a general idea of a fund's overall investment approach and goals.

Provider
The legal company that issues the fund.

Ratings History
Indicates the fund's Overall, Risk and Reward Ratings for the previous five years. Ratings are listed as of June 30, 2020 (Q2-20), December 31, 2019 (Q4-19), December 31, 2018 (Q4-18), December 31, 2017 (Q4-17), and December 31, 2016 (Q4-16). See **Overall Rating, Risk Rating, Reward Rating.**

Recent Upgrade/Downgrade
An "Up" or "Down" indicates that the Weiss Mutual Fund rating has changed since the publication of the last print edition. If a fund has had a rating change since March 31, 2020, the change is identified with an "Up" or "Down."

Reward Rating
This is based on the total return over a period of up to five years, including net asset value and price growth. The total return figure is stated net of the expenses and fees charged by the fund. Based on proprietary modeling the individual components of the risk and reward ratings are calculated and weighted and the final rating is generated.

Risk Rating
This is includes the risk ratings of component stocks where applicable and also includes the financial stability of the fund, turnover where applicable, together with the level of volatility as measured by the fund's daily returns over a period of up to five years. Funds with greater stability are considered less risky and receive a higher risk rating. Funds with greater volatility are considered riskier, and will receive a lower risk rating. In addition to considering the fund's volatility, the risk rating also considers an assessment of the valuation and quality of a fund's holdings.

Services Offered
Services offered by the fund provider. Such services can include:

Systematic Withdrawal Plan
A plan offered by mutual funds that pays specific amounts to shareholders at predetermined intervals.

Institutional Only
This indicates if the fund is offered to institutional clients only (pension funds, mutual funds, money managers, insurance companies, investment banks, commercial trusts, endowment funds, hedge funds, and some hedge fund investors).

Phone Exchange
This indicates that investors can move money between different funds within the same fund family over the phone.

Wire Redemption
This indicates whether or not investors can redeem electronically.

Qualified Investment
Under a qualified plan, an investor may invest in the variable annuity with pretax dollars through an employee pension plan, such as a 401(k) or 403(b). Money builds up on a tax-deferred basis, and when the qualified investor makes a withdrawal or annuitizes, all contributions received are taxable income.

Sub-Category
A subdivision of funds, usually with common characteristics as the category.

Systematic Withdrawal Plan
A plan offered by mutual funds that pays specific amounts to shareholders at predetermined intervals. See **Services Offered**.

Ticker Symbol
An arrangement of characters (usually letters) representing a particular security listed on an exchange or otherwise traded publicly. When a company issues securities to the public marketplace, it selects an available ticker symbol for its securities which investors use to place trade orders. Every listed security has a unique ticker symbol, facilitating the vast array of trade orders that flow through the financial markets every day. If a ticker symbol is not assigned to a particular fund, the International Securities Identification Number (ISIN) is displayed.

Top Holdings
The highest amount of publicly traded assets held by a fund. These publicly traded assets may include company stock, mutual funds or other investment vehicles.

Total Returns (%)
See **3-Month Total Return, 6-Month Total Return, 1-Year Total Return, 3-Year Total Return, 5-Year Total Return**.

Traded On (Exchange)
The stock exchange on which the fund is listed. The core function of a stock exchange is to ensure fair and orderly trading, as well as efficient dissemination of price information. Exchanges such as: NYSE (New York Stock Exchange), AMEX (American Stock Exchange), NNM (NASDAQ National Market), and NASQ (NASDAQ Small Cap) give companies, governments and other groups a platform to sell securities to the investing public.

Turnover Ratio
The percentage of a mutual fund or other investment vehicle's holdings that have been replaced with other holdings in a given year. Generally, low turnover ratio is favorable, because high turnover equates to higher brokerage transaction fees, which reduce fund returns.

Website
The company's web address.

Wire Redemption
This indicates whether or not investors can redeem electronically. See **Services Offered**.

This section lists all of the Providers in Section I: Index of Bond & Money Market Mutual Funds. Address, Telephone and Website are provided where available.

1290 Funds
1290 Funds 1290 Avenue of the Americas New York NY 10104 United States
212-554-1234
http://www.1290Funds.com

1919 Funds
1919 Funds P.O. Box 701 Milwaukee WI 53201-0701 United States
http://www.1919Funds.com

1WS Capital Advisors
1290 AVENUE OF THE AMERICAS, 34TH FLOOR NEW YORK NY 10104 New York NY 10104 United States

A3 Financial Investments
A3 Financial Investments 90 Madison Street, Suite 303 United States
303-997-9010
http://https://www.a3.financial/

AAAMCO
AAAMCO 1000 Brickell Avenue, Suite 500 Miami FL 33131 United States
305-379-6656
http://austinatlantic.com/

AAM
AAM 18925 Base Camp Road Monument CO 80132 United States
800-617-0004
http://www.aamlive.com/publicsite/mutual-funds

AAMA
AAMA P.O. Box 46707 Cincinnati OH 45246-0707 United States
http://www.aamafunds.com

Aberdeen
Aberdeen Asset Management 1735 Market Street 32nd Floor Philadelphia PA 19103 United States
866-667-9231
http://www.aberdeen-asset.us

Aberdeen Standard Investments Inc.
1735 Market Street 32nd Floor Philadelphia PA 19103 United States
215-405-5700
http://www.aberdeen-asset.com

ACM
ACM United States
http://www.ACM-Funds.com

Adhia
Adhia 1408 N. Westshore Blvd., Suite 805 Tampa FL 33607 United States
http://www.hewittfs.com

Advanced Series Trust
Advanced Series Trust 100 Mulberry Street,Gateway Center Three, 4th Floor Newark NJ 07102 United States
http://www.prudential.com

AdvisorOne Funds
Advisorone Funds 4020 South 147th Street Omaha NE 68137 United States
http://www.advisoronefunds.com

Advisors Preferred
Advisors Preferred United States
http://www.advisorspreferred.com

Aegon Asset Management US
Aegon Asset Management US United States

AIG
AIG Harborside Financial Center, 3200 Plaza 5 Jersey City NJ 07311 United States
800-858-8850
http://https://www.aig.com/getprospectus

AllianceBernstein
AllianceBernstein 11345 Avenue of the Americas New York NY 10105 United States
212-969-1000
http://www.abglobal.com

AllianceBernstein L.P.
1345 Avenue of the Americas New York NY 10105 United States
212-969-1000
http://www.alliancebernstein.com

Allianz Global Investors
Allianz Funds 1633 Broadway New York New York 10019 United States
800-498-5413
http://www.US.allianzGI.com

AlphaCentric Funds
17605 Wright Street Suite 2 United States
http://www.AlphaCentricFunds.com.

ALPS
ALPS 1290 Broadway, Suite 1100 Denver CO 80203 United States
866-759-5679
http://www.alpsfunds.com

Amana
Amana Bellingham WA 98227-0596 United States
888-732-6262
http://www.amanafunds.com

American Beacon
American Beacon 220 East Las Colinas Blvd., Suite 1200 Irving TX 75039 United States
800-658-5811
http://www.americanbeaconfunds.com

American Century Investments
American Century Investments P.O. Box 419200,4500 Main Street Kansas City, MO 64141 United States
800-444-4015
http://www.americancentury.com

American Funds
American Funds 333 South Hope Street Los Angeles CA 90071-1406 United States
800-421-4225
http://www.americanfunds.com

American Independence
American Independence 225 West 34th Street 9th Floor New York NY 10122 United States
http://www.americanindependence.com

AMG Funds
AMG Funds 600 Steamboat Road, Suite 300 Norwalk CT 06830 United States
800-835-3879
http://www.amgfunds.com

Amundi Pioneer Asset Management, Inc.
Amundi Pioneer Asset Management, Inc. 60 State Street Boston MA 2109 United States
http://www.pioneerinvestments.com

Anchor
Anchor 17605 Wright Street, Suite 2 Omaha NE 68130 United States
http://www.anchorcapitalfunds.com

Ancora
Ancora 2000 Auburn Drive, Suite 430 Cleveland OH 44122 United States
http://www.ancorafunds.com

Anfield
Anfield Capital Management, LLC 4695 MacArthur Court, Suite 430 Newport Beach CA 92660 United States
http://www.AnfieldFunds.com

Angel Oak
Angel Oak Funds One Buckhead Plaza, 3060 Peachtree Rd. NW, Suite 500 Atlanta GA 30305 United States
404-953-4900
http://www.angeloakcapital.com

Angel Oak Capital Advisors, LLC
3344 Peachtree RD NE Suite 1725 Atlanta GA 30326 United States
404-953-4397
http://www.angeloakcapital.com

Aperture Investors
Aperture Investors 250 West 55th Street, 30th Floor New York NY 10019 United States

Apollo Credit Management, LLC
Apollo Credit Management, LLC 9 West 57th Street, 43rd Floor New York NY 10019 United States

AQR Funds
AQR Funds Two Greewich Plaza,3rd Floor Greenwich CT 06830 United States
203-742-3600
http://www.aqrfunds.com

Aquila
Aquila 120 West 45th Street, Suite 3600 New York NY 10036 United States
800-437-1020
http://www.aquilafunds.com

Archer
Archer c/o Unified Fund Services Inc., P.O. Box 6110 Indianapolis IN 46206 United States
http://www.thearcherfunds.com

Ares Capital Corp
2000 Avenue of the Stars 12th Floor Los Angeles CA 90067 United States
310-201-4100
http://www.arespublicfunds.com

Aristotle
Aristotle P.O. Box 2175 Milwaukee WI 53201-2175 United States
http://www.aristotlefunds.com

Arrow Funds
Arrow Funds 6100 Chevy Chase Drive, Suite 100 New York MD 20707 United States
877-277-6933
http://www.arrowfunds.com

Artisan
875 E. Wisconsin Avenue, Suite 800 Milwaukee WI 53202 United States
800-344-1770
http://www.artisanfunds.com

Ascendant
Ascendant United States
http://www.ascendantfunds.com

Ashmore
Ashmore United States
866-876-8294
http://www.ashmoregroup.com/

Aspiriant
c/o UMB Fund Services, Inc. 235 West Galena Street Milwaukee WI 53212 United States
877-997-9971
http://www.aspiriantfunds.com

AXA Equitable
AXA Equitable 1290 Avenue of the Americas New York NY 10104 United States
877-222-2144
http://www.axa-equitablefunds.com

Axonic
Axonic 520 Madison Avenue New York NY 10022 United States
http://www.axoniccap.com

Axonic Capital LLC
390 Park Ave Floor 15 New York NY 10022 United States
212-259-0430
http://www.axoniccap.com

Azzad Fund
Azzad Fund United States
http://www.azzadfunds.com.

Baird
Baird 777 E. Wisconsin Avenue, Suite 2100 Milwaukee WI 53202 United States
800-792-2473
http://www.bairdfunds.com

Barings Funds
Barings 1500 Main Street, Ste. 2800 Springfield MA 01115 United States
http://www.barings.com

BBH
140 Broadway New York NY 10005 United States
800-575-1265
http://www.bbhfunds.com

Bishop Street
Bishop Street 11 Freedom Valley Drive Oaks PA 19087 United States
http://www.bishopstreetfunds.com

BlackRock
BlackRock Funds Providence RI 02940-8019 United States
800-441-7762
http://www.blackrock.com

Blackstone Group Inc
345 Park Avenue New York NY 10154 United States
http://www.blackstone.com

Bluestone Capital Partners LLC
Bluestone Capital Partners LLC 151 Calle San Francisco San Juan PR 00901-1607 United States

BMO Funds
BMO Funds Boston United States
800-236-3863
http://www.bmofunds.com

BNY Mellon
BNY Mellon 240 Greenwich Street New York NY 10286 United States
http://www.bnymellonim.com/us

BNY Mellon Funds
BNY Mellon Funds 200 Park Avenue New York NY 10166 United States
800-645-6561
http://www.bnymellon.com

Boyd Watterson
Boyd Watterson 17605 Wright Street, Suite 2 Omaha Nebraska United States
http://www.boydwattersonfunds.com

Bramshill Investments
Bramshill Investments 411 Hackensack Avenue,9th Floor Hackensack New Jersey 07601 United States
http://www.bramshillinvestments.com

Brandes
Brandes 11988 El Camino Real, Suite 500 San Diego CA 92130 United States
800-331-2979
http://www.brandesfunds.com/

Bridge Builder
Bridge Builder 615 East Michigan Street Milwaukee WI 53202 United States
http://www.bridgebuildermutualfunds.com

Brookfield Public Securities Group LLC
71 South Wacker Drive Suite 3400 Chicago IL 60606-2841 United States
312-377-8300
http://www.brookfield.com

Brown Advisory Funds
Brown Advisory Incorporated 901 S. Bond Street Suite 400 Baltimore MD 21231 United States
800-540-6807
http://www.brownadvisoryfunds.com

BTS
BTS 420 Bedford Street Lexington MA 2420 United States
877-287-9820
http://www.btsfunds.com.

Buffalo
Buffalo 55420 W. 61st Place Shawnee Mission KS 66205 United States
800-492-8332
http://www.buffalofunds.com

Calamos
Calamos 2020 Calamos Court Naperville IL 60563 United States
800-582-6959
http://www.calamos.com

Calvert Research and Management
Calvert Research and Management 1825 Connecticut Avenue NW, Suite 400 Washington DC 20009-5727 United States
202-238-2200
http://www.calvert.com

Capital Group
333 S. Hope Street Los Angeles CA 90071 United States
213-486-9257

Carillon Family of Funds
Carillon Family of Funds P.O. Box 23572 St. Petersburg FL 33742 United States
800-421-4184
http://www.carillontower.com

Catalyst Mutual Funds
Catalyst Mutual Funds 630-A Fitzwatertown Road, 2nd Floor Willow Grove PA 19090 United States
866-447-4228
http://www.catalystmutualfunds.com

Catholic Investor
Knights Of Columbus One Columbus Plaza New Haven CT 06510 United States
203-772-2130
http://www.kofcassetadvisors.org

Cavalier
Cavalier Funds Post Office Box 4365 Rocky Mount NC 27803 United States
800-773-3863
http://www.cavalierfunds.com

Cavanal Hill funds
Cavanal Hill Funds 3435 Stelzer Road Columbus OH 43219 United States
http://www.cavanalhillfunds.com

Centre Funds
Centre Funds 48 Wall Street New York NY 10005 United States
855-298-4236
http://www.centrefunds.com

Changing Parameters
Changing Parameters United States

Chartwell Investment Partners
Chartwell Investment Partners 1205 Westlakes Drive Suite 100 Berwyn PA 19312 United States
610-296-1400
http://www.chartwellip.com

CION Investments
CION Investments 3 Park Avenue,36th Floor New York NY 10016 United States
212-418-4700
http://www.cioninvestments.com

City National Rochdale
City National Rochdale c/o SEI Investments Distribution Co. Oaks PA 19456 United States
http://www.citynationalrochdalefunds.com

Cliffwater LLC
310-448-5015
http://www.cliffwater.com

CM Advisors
CM Advisors 805 Las Cimas Parkway, Suite 430 Austin TX 78746 United States
888-859-5856
http://www.cmadvisorsfunds.com

CMG
CMG 150 N. Radnor Chester Road, Suite A150 Radnor PA 19087 United States
http://www.cmgmutualfunds.com

Columbia
Liberty Financial Funds P.O. Box 8081 Boston MA 02266-8081 United States
800-345-6611
http://www.columbiathreadneedleus.com

Commerce
Commerce 11000 Walnut Street Kansas City MO 64121 United States
http://www.commercefunds.com

Community Capital Management
1830 Main Street Ste 204 Weston FL 33326 United States
877-272-1977
http://www.ccmfixedincome.com

Community Development Fund
Community Development Fund 6255 Chapman Field Drive Miami FL 33156 United States
305-663-0100
http://www.communitydevelopmentfund.com

Cornerstone
Cornerstone 74 W. Broad Street, Suite 340 Bethlehem PA 18018 United States
http://www.aicfundholdings.com

Counterpoint Mutual Funds
Counterpoint Mutual Funds 12707 High Bluff Drive, Suite 200 San Diego CA 92130 United States
http://www.counterpointmutualfunds.com

Credit Suisse (New York, NY)
Credit Suisse Eleven Madison Avenue New York NY United States
877-870-2874
http://www.credit-suisse.com/us/funds

Credit Suisse AG
Kilmore House Park Lane Dublin Ireland

CrossingBridge
CrossingBridge Funds P.O. Box 701 Milwaukee WI 53201-0701 United States
http://www.crossingbridgefunds.com

Crossmark Steward Funds
Capstone 5847 San Felipe, Suite 4100 Houston TX 77057 United States
800-262-6631
http://www.stewardmutualfunds.com.

Crow Point
Crow Point Partners, LLC 10 New Driftway, Suite 203 Scituate, MA 02066 United States
http://www.cppfunds.com

Davis Funds
Davis Funds 2949 E. Elvira Rd., Suite 101 Tucson AZ 85706 United States
800-279-0279
http://www.davisfunds.com

DDJ
DDJ 130 Turner Street, Building 3, Suite 600 Waltham MA 02543 United States
http://www.ddjfunds.com

Deer Park
Deer Park 1865 Ski Time Square, Suite 102 Steamboat Springs CO 80477 United States
888-868-9501
http://www.deerparkfund.com

Delaware Funds by Macquarie
Delaware Funds by Macquarie Philadelphia United States

Destinations Funds
Destination Funds 1277 Treat Boulevard,#200 Walnut Creek CA 94597 United States
http://www.destinationfunds.com

Destra
Destra Capital Advisors, LLC 901 Warrenville Road, Suite 15 Lisle IL 60532 United States
877-855-3434
http://destracapital.com

Deutsche Investment Management Inc
222 South Riverside Chicago IL 60606 United States

Diamond Hill Funds
Diamond Hill Funds 325 John H. Mcconnell Boulevard,Suite 200 Columbus OH 43215 United States
888-226-5595
http://www.diamond-hill.com

Dimensional Fund Advisors
Dimensional Fund Advisors 1299 Ocean Avenue, 11th Floor Santa Monica CA 90401 United States
512-306-7400
http://www.dimensional.com

Dodge & Cox
Dodge and Cox 555 California Street, 40th Floor San Francisco CA 94104 United States
415-981-1710
http://www.dodgeandcox.com

Domini
Domini 5536 Broadway, 77th Floor New York NY 10012 United States
800-582-6757
http://www.domini.com

DoubleLine
DoubleLine 333 South Grand Avenue Los Angeles CA 90071 United States
877-354-6311
http://www.doublelinefunds.com

Dreyfus
Dreyfus 144 Glenn Curtiss Blvd Uniondale NY 11556-0144 United States
800-645-6561
http://www.dreyfus.com

Duff & Phelps
55 Park Avenue Plz New York NY 100550002 United States
212-871-2549

Dunham Funds
Dunham Funds 10251 Vista Sorrento Parkway Suite 200 San Diego CA 92121 United States
800-442-4358
http://www.dunham.com

DuPont
DuPont 1007 Market Street Wilmington DE 19898 United States
888-447-0014
http://www.dupont.com

Dupree
Dupree P.O. Box 1149 Lexington KY 40588 United States
http://www.dupree-funds.com

DWS
DWS 210 West 10th Street Kansas City MO 64105-1614 United States
http://dws.com

Eagle Point Credit Management
20 Horseneck Lane Greenwich CT 06830 United States
http://eaglepointcreditcompany.com/about-us/default.aspx

Eaton Vance
P.O. Boc 43027 Providence RI 02940-3027 United States

Eaton Vance
c/o Boston Management and Research Two International Place Boston MA 02110 United States
800-836-2414
http://www.eatonvance.com

Eaton Vance Management
2 International Place Boston MA 02110 United States
617-672-8277
http://www.eatonvance.com

Edward Jones
Edward Jones 201 Progress Parkway Maryland Heights United States

Ellington Global Asset Management, LLC
53 FOREST AVENUE OLD GREENWICH CT 6870 United States

Euro Pacific Asset Management
Euro Pacific Asset Management, LLC 1201 Dove Street, Suite 370 Newport Beach CA 92660 United States
http://www.europacificfunds.com

Eventide Funds
Eventide Funds 60 State Street, Suite 700 Boston MA 2109 United States
http://www.eventidefunds.com

Fairholme
Fairholme 83 General Warren Blvd., Suite 170 Malvern PA 19355 United States
866-202-2263
http://www.fairholmefunds.com

FCI Funds
FCI Funds 2960 N. Meridian Street, Suite 300 Indianapolis IN 46208 United States
http://www.fciadvisors.com

Federated
Federated Investors Funds 4000 Ericsson Drive Warrendale PA 15086-7561 United States
800-341-7400
http://www.federatedinvestors.com

Federated Advisers
Federated Investors Tower, Pittsburgh PA 15222 United States

Fidelity Investments
Fidelity Investments 82 Devonshire Street Boston MA 2109 United States
617-563-7000
http://www.institutional.fidelity.com

First American
First American 800 Nicollet Mall Minneapolis MN 55402 United States
800-677-3863
http://www.firstamericanfunds.com

First Eagle
First Eagle 1345 Avenue of the Americas New York NY 10105 United States
800-334-2143
http://www.firsteaglefunds.com

First Investors
First Investors Life Insurance 95 Wall Street New York NY 10005 United States
800-423-4026
http://www.firstinvestors.com

First Trust
First Trust 120 E. Liberty Drive, Suite 400 Wheaton IL 60187 United States
800-621-1675
http://www.ftportfolios.com/

First Trust Advisors L.P.
First Trust Advisors L.P. 120 E. Liberty Wheaton IL 60187 United States
866-848-9727
http://www.ftportfolios.com

First Western Capital Mgt
First Western Capital Mgt 1900 Avenue of the Stars, Suite 900 Los Angeles CA 90067 United States
310-229-2940
http://www.fwcapmgmt.com

Fisher Investments
Fisher Investments 5525 NW Fisher Creek Drive Camas WA 98607 United States
415-851-3334

Forefront Income Trust
Forefront Income Trust 590 Madison Avenue, 34th Floor New York NY 10022 United States

Four Wood Capital Partners, LLC
100 Wall Street - 11th Floor New York New York 10005 United States
212-701-4500
http://fourwoodcapital.com/

FPA
FPA 111400 W. Olympic Blvd., Suite 1200 Los Angeles CA 90064 United States
800-982-4372
http://www.fpafunds.com

Franklin Advisers, Inc.
Franklin Advisers, Inc. One Franklin Parkway San Mateo CA 94403 United States

Franklin Templeton
500 East Broward Blvd Suite 2100 Ft. Lauderdale FL 33394-3091 United States
954-527-7500
http://www.franklintempleton.com

Franklin Templeton Investments
Franklin Templeton Investments One Franklin Parkway, Building 970, 1st Floor San Mateo CA 94403 United States
650-312-2000
http://www.franklintempleton.com

Freedom Funds
Freedom Funds 17th Street Suite 1000 Denver CO 80202 United States
800-572-0069

Frost Funds
Frost Funds 100 W. Houston Street, 15th Floor San Antonio TX 78205 United States
http://www.frostbank.com

FS Investments
FS 201 Rouse Boulevard Philadelphia PA 19112 United States
877-628-8575
http://www.fsinvestments.com

Fund X
c/o US Bancorp Mutual Fund Services, LLC PO Box 701 Milwaukee WI 53201 United States
866-455-3863
http://www.upgraderfunds.com

Gabelli
Gabelli 1 Corporate Center Rye NY NY United States
914-921-5135
http://www.gabelli.com

GL
GL 400 Fifth Avenue, Suite 600, Waltham, MA Waltham MA 02451 United States

Glenmede
Glenmede 11650 Market Street, Suite 1200 Philadelphia PA 19103 United States
800-442-8299
http://www.glenmede.com

GMO
GMO 40 Rowes Wharf Boston MA 02110 United States
617-330-7500
http://www.gmo.com

Goldman Sachs
Goldman Sachs 200 West Stree New York NY 10282 United States
800-526-7384
http://www.gsamfunds.com

Goldman Sachs
71 South Wacker Drive, Chicago, Illinois 60606, Chicago United States
312-362-3000
http://www.gsamfunds.com

Great Lakes Funds
Great Lakes Funds 222 South Riverside Plaza, 28th Floor, Chicago, Illinois Chicago IL 60606 United States
http://www.glafunds.com

Great-West Funds
Maxim 88525 E. Orchard Road Greenwood Village CO 80111 United States
http://www.greatwestfunds.com

Green Square Asset Management
Green Square Asset Management 6075 Poplar Avenue, Suite 221 Memphis TN 38119 United States
http://gsequityincome.com/

Griffin Capital
Griffin Capital Griffin Capital Plaza, 1520 Grand Avenue El Segundo CA 90245 United States
310-469-6100
http://www.griffincapital.com

GSO / Blackstone Debt Funds Management
GSO / Blackstone Debt Funds Management LLC 280 Park Avenue, 11th Floor New York New York 10017 United States

Guggenheim
330 Madison Avenue New York New York 10017 United States
212-739-0700
http://www.guggenheimpartners.com

Guggenheim Investments
Guggenheim Investments 330 Madison Avenue New York NY 10017 United States
212-518-9290
http://www.guggenheimpartners.com

Guggenheim Investments Asset Management
227 West Monroe Street Chicago IL 60606 United States
312-827-0100
http://www.guggenheimpartners.com

GuideMark
GuideMark 7A Greenridge Park Nashua NH 003060 United States
603-888-5500
http://www.AssetMark.com

GuidePath
GuidePath 2300 Contra Costa Blvd., Suite 600 Pleasant Hill, CA Pleasant Hill CA 94523 United States
800-664-5345
http://www.AssetMark.com

GuideStone Funds
Guidestone Funds Suite 2200 Dallas TX 75244-6152 United States
214-720-1171
http://www.guidestonefunds.org

Guinness Atkinson
Guinness Atkinson 21550 Oxnard Street, Suite 750 Woodland Hills CA 91367 United States
800-915-6566
http://www.gafunds.com

Hancock Horizon
Hancock Horizon 2600 Citiplace Drive, Suite 100 Baton Rouge LA 70808 United States
800-990-2434
http://www.hancockhorizonfunds.com

Hanlon
Hanlon 17605 Wright Street, Suite 2 Omaha NE 68130 United States
http://www.HanlonFunds.com

Harbor
Harbor 111 S. Wacker Drive, 34th Floor Chicago IL 60606 United States
800-422-1050
http://www.harborfunds.com

Hartford
not available United States

Hartford Mutual Funds
Hartford Mutual Funds United States
888-843-7824
http://www.hartfordfunds.com

Harvest Funds
112 Ballymeade Drive 4000 Park Road Wilmington DE 19810 United States
http://https://www.harvestfund.se

HC Capital Trust

Highland Capital Management Fund Advisors, L.P.
Highland Funds Asset Management, L.P. 200 Crescent Ct, Ste 700 Dallas TX 75201 United States
877-665-1287
http://www.highlandfunds.com

Highland Funds
Highland Funds 200 Crescent Court, Suite 700 Dallas TX 75201 United States
877-665-1287
http://www.highlandfunds.com

Holbrook Holdings
Holbrook Holdings 2670 NW Lovejoy Street Portland Portland 97210 United States
http://www.holbrookholdings.com/

Homestead
Homestead 4301 Wilson Blvd., IFS8-305 Arlington VA 22203 United States
http://www.homesteadfunds.com

Horizon Investments
13024 Ballantyne Corporate Place Suite 225 Charlotte NC 28277 United States
http://www.horizonmutualfunds.com

Hotchkis & Wiley
Hotchkis & Wiley 725 South Figueroa Suite 400 Los Angeles CA 90017 United States
866-493-8637
http://www.hwcm.com

HSBC
HSBC 452 Fifth Avenue, 17th Floor New York NY 10018 United States
888-936-4722
http://www.investorfunds.us.hsbc.com

ICON Funds
ICON Funds 5299 DTC Boulevard, Suite 1200 Greenwood Village CO 80111 United States
303-790-1600
http://www.iconfunds.com

iM Global Partner (US)
iM Global Partner 300 Barr Harbor Drive, Suite 720 Conshohocken PA United States
888-898-1041
http://www.imglobalpartner.com

Insight Investment
200 Park Avenue, 7th Floor New York NY 10166 United States
212-527-1800
http://www.insightinvestment.com

IntegrityVikingFunds
Integrity 1 Main Street Minot ND 58703 United States
800-276-1262
http://www.integrityvikingfunds.com

Intrepid Funds
Intrepid Funds 1400 Marsh Landing Pkwy., Suite 106 Jacksonville Beach FL 32250 United States
http://www.intrepidcapitalfunds.com

Invesco
Invesco 11 Greenway Plaza, Ste. 2500 Houston TX 77046 United States
800-659-1005
http://www.invesco.com/us

Invesco Advisers, Inc
Invesco Ltd Atlanta GA 30309 United States
404-892-0896
http://www.invesco.com

Iron Funds
Iron Funds 2960 Meridian St., Suite 300 Indianapolis IN 46208 United States
877-322-0575
http://www.ironfunds.com

Ivy Funds
Ivy Funds Inc 6300 Lamar Ave Overland Park KS 66202 United States
http://www.ivyinvestments.com

Jackson National
Jackson Natl Life Insurance Co P.O. Box 30389 Lansing MI 48909-7889 United States
http://www.jackson.com

James Alpha Advisors
James Alpha Advisors United States

Janus Henderson
Janus 151 Detroit Street Denver CO 80206 United States
877-335-2687
http://janushenderson.com

John Hancock
601 Congress Street, Boston MA 02210 United States
800-225-5291
http://jhinvestments.com

John Hancock
601 Congress Street, Boston MA 02210 United States
800-225-5913
http://jhinvestments.com

John Hancock
John Hancock PO Box 55913 Boston MA 02205-5913 United States
800-225-5913
http://jhinvestments.com

Johnson Mutual Funds
Johnson Mutual Funds 3777 West Fork Rd Cincinnati OH 45247 United States
http://www.johnsonmutualfunds.com

JPMorgan
JPMorgan 270 Park Avenue New York NY 10017-2070 United States
800-480-4111
http://www.jpmorganfunds.com

Kinetics
Kinetics 615 E. Michigan Street Milwaukee WI 53202 United States
800-930-3828
http://www.kineticsfunds.com

KKR

KKR & Co. L.P.
9 West 57th St Suite 4200 New York NY 10019 United States
212-750-8300
http://www.kkr.com

KP Funds
KP Funds One Freedome Valley Drive OAKS PA 19456 United States
http://www.kp-funds.com

Lazard
Lazard Asset Management LLC 30 Rockefeller Plaza, New York NY 10112-6300 United States
800-823-6300
http://www.lazardassetmanagement.com

LEADER
Leader 33435 Stelzer Road, Suite 110 Columbus OH 43219 United States
800-711-9164
http://www.leadercapital.com

Lebenthal
Lebenthal 225 Pictoria Drive, Suite 450 Cincinnati OH 45246 United States
http://www.dcmmutualfunds.com

LeeHawaii
LeeHawaii United States

Legg Mason
Legg Mason/Western 100 International Drive Baltimore MD 21202 United States
877-721-1926
http://www.leggmason.com

Legg Mason Partners Fund Advisor, LLC
100 International Drive Baltimore Maryland 21202 United States

Liberty Street
Liberty Street 803 W. Michigan Street Milwaukee WI 53233 United States
800-207-7108
http://www.libertystreetfunds.com

LKCM
LKCM 301 Commerce Street, Suite 1600 Fort Worth TX 76102 United States
800-688-5526
http://www.lkcm.com

Logan Circle Partners
1717 Arch Street Suite 1500 Philadelphia PA 19103 United States

Loomis Sayles Funds
Loomis Sayles Funds P.O. Box 219594 Kansas City MO 64121-9594 United States
800-633-3330
http://www.loomissayles.com

Lord Abbett
Lord Abbett 90 Hudson Street Jersey City NJ 7302 United States
201-827-2000
http://www.lordabbett.com

Macquarie Investment Management
Macquarie Investment Management 2005 Market Street, One Commerce Square Philadelphia PA 19103 United States
215-255-2300
http://macquarie.com/investment-management

Madison Funds
Madison 420 W 7th Street STE 219083 Kansas City MO 53711 United States
800-767-0300
http://www.madisonfunds.com

MainStay
MainStay 30 Hudson Street Jersey City NJ 10010 United States
800-624-6782
http://mainstayinvestments.com/

Manning & Napier
Manning Napier 290 Woodcliff Drive Fairport NY 14450 United States
585-325-6880
http://www.manning-napier.com

Manor Investment Funds
Manor Investment Funds United States
http://www.morriscapitaladvisors.com

MassMutual
MML Investment Advisers, LLC 100 Bright Meadow Blvd., Enfield CT 06082 United States
http://www.massmutual.com/funds

Matthews Asia Funds
Matthews Asia Funds Four Embarcadero Center Suite 550 San Francisco CA 94111 United States
800-789-2742
http://www.matthewsasia.com

MD Sass
MD Sass United States

Meeder Funds
Meeder Funds 6125 Memorial Dr. PO Box 7177 Dublin OH 43017 United States
http://www.meederfunds.com

Mercer Funds

Merk Funds
Merk Funds P.O. Box 588 Portland ME 4112 United States
866-637-5386
http://www.merkfund.com

Mesirow Financial
Mesirow Financial P.O. Box 219009 Kansas City MO 64121-9009 United States
http://www.mesirowfinancial.com

MetLife
Metlife One Madison Avenue New York United States
http://www.metlife.com

Metropolitan West Funds
METROPOLITAN WEST ASSET MANAGEMENT 865 S. FIGUEROA STREET, SUITE 2100 LOS ANGELES CA 90017 United States
800-241-4671
http://www.mwamllc.com

MFS
MFS 111 Huntington Avenue Boston MA 02199-7632 United States
877-960-6077
http://www.mfs.com

MH Elite
MH Elite 220 Russell Avenue Rahway NJ 7065 United States
http://www.mhelite.com

Milestone
Milestone 115 E. Putnam Avenue Greenwich NY 10701 United States
http://www.advisoronefunds.com

Miller Investment
Miller Investment 2 Deanna Drive Oxford CT 6478 United States
877-441-4434
http://www.millerconvertiblefund.com

Mondrian
Mondrian Two Commerce Square, 2001 Market Str., Suite 3810 Philadelphia PA 19103-7039 United States
888-832-4386
http://www.mondrian.com/mutualfunds

Monteagle Funds
Monteagle Funds 8000 Town Centre Drive, Suite 400 OH 44147 United States
http://www.monteaglefunds.com

Morgan Stanley
Morgan Stanley 1221 Avenue of the Americas New York NY 10020 United States
855-332-5306
http://www.morganstanley.com

Morningstar
225 North Michigan Ave Suite 400 Chicago IL 60601 United States
312-616-1620
http://www.morningstar.com

Mutual of America
Mutual of America 666 Fifth Avenue New York NY 10103 United States
http://www.mutualofamerica.com

Muzinich
Muzinich 450 Park Avenue New York NY 10022 United States
http://www.MuzinichUSFunds.com

Nationwide
Nationwide One Nationwide Plaza Columbus OH 43215 United States
800-848-0920
http://www.nationwide.com/mutualfunds

Natixis Funds
Natixis Funds 399 Boylston Street Boston MA 02116 United States
800-862-4863
http://NGAM.natixis.com

Navigator Funds
Navigator Funds United States
http://www.navigatorfund.com.

Neuberger Berman
Neuberger Berman 1290 Avenue of the Americas New York NY 10104 United States
212-476-9000
http://www.nb.com

New Covenant
New Covenant P.O. Box 701 Milwaukee WI 53201 United States
http://www.newcovenantfunds.com

New York Life Investment Management LLC
New York Life Investment Management Llc 51 Madison Avenue New York NY 10036 United States
212-938-6500
http://www.nylim.com/institutional

Nicholas
Nicholas P.O. Box 701 Milwaukee WI 53201 United States
800-544-6547
http://www.nicholasfunds.com

North Capital
315 Montgomery Street Suite 900 SAN FRANCISCO CA United States
http://www.northcapital.com

North Country Funds
Gemini Fund Services, Llc. 450 Wireless Boulevard Hauppauge NY 11788 United States
http://www.arrowfinancial.com

North Square
North Square 10 South LaSalle Street, Suite 1925 Chicago IL 60603 United States
855-551-5521
http://www.northsquareinvest.com

North Star
North Star 20 N. Wacker Drive Chicago IL 60606 United States
312-580-0
http://www.nsinvestfunds.com

Northeast Investors
Northeast Investors 100 High Street Suite 1000 Boston MA 02110 United States
855-755-6344
http://www.northeastinvestors.com

Northern Funds
Northern Funds 50 South Lasalle Chicago IL 60603 United States
800-595-9111
http://www.northernfunds.com

Nuveen
Nuveen Investment Trust John Nuveen & Co. Inc. Chicago IL 60606 United States
312-917-8146
http://www.nuveen.com

Nuveen Fund Advisors, LLC.
Nuveen Fund Advisors, Inc. 333 West Wacker Drive Chicago IL 60606 United States
312-917-8146
http://www.nuveen.com

OFS Credit Co Inc
10 S. WACKER DRIVE, SUITE 2500 Chicago 60606 United States
http://www.ofscapital.com/investments/

Old Westbury
Old Westbury 630 5Th Ave New York NY 10111 United States
212-708-9100

Osterweis
One Maritime Plaza Suite 800 San Francisco CA 94111 United States
866-236-0050
http://www.osterweis.com

Oxford Lane Capital Corp
8 Sound Shore Drive- Suite 255 Greenwich United States

Pacific Capital
Pacific Capital 305 Windmill Park Lane Mountain View CA 94043 United States
http://www.pacificcapitalfunds.com

Pacific Funds Series Trust
Pacific Funds 700 Newport Center Drive Post Offfice Box 7500 Newport Beach CA 92660 United States
800-722-2333
http://www.pacificlife.com

Palmer Square
Palmer Square 11300 Tomahawk Creek Parkway, Suite 200 Leawood KS 66211 United States
866-933-9033
http://www.palmersquarefunds.com

Parnassus
Parnassus 1 Market Street, Suite 1600 San Francisco CA 94105 United States
999-350-5
http://www.parnassus.com

Pax World
Pax World 30 Penhallow Street, Suite 400 Portsmouth NH 3801 United States
800-767-1729
http://www.paxworld.com

Paydenfunds
Paydenfunds 333 S Grand Ave, 32nd Floor Los Angeles CA 90071 United States
614-470-8006
http://www.payden.com

Penn Capital Management
Penn Capital Management United States
http://www.penncapitalfunds.com

Penn Mutual Asset Management
Penn Insurance and Annuity Co Independence Square Philadelphia 19172 United States
877--
http://www.pennmutualam.com

Permanent Portfolio
Permanent Portfolio 600 Montgomery Street, 27th Floor San Francisco CA 94111 United States
800-531-5142
http://www.permanentportfoliofunds.com

PFM Multi-Manager Series Trust
PFM Multi-Manager Series Trust One Keystone Plaza, Suite 300,North Front & Market Streets Harrisburg Pennsylvania 17101-2044 United States

PGIM Funds (Prudential)
PGIM Funds (Prudential) PO Box 9658 Providence RI 02940 United States
800-225-1852
http://www.pgiminvestments.com

PGIM Investments
Prudential Investments One Seaport Plaza New York NY 10292 United States
800-225-1852
http://www.prudentialfunds.com

PIA Mutual Funds
PIA Mutual Funds 1299 Ocean Avenue, 2nd Floor Santa Monica CA 90401 United States
800-251-1970
http://www.pacificincome.com

PIMCO
PIMCO 840 Newport Center Drive, Suite 100 Newport Beach CA 92660 United States
866-746-2602
http://www.pimco.com

Pioneer Advisors, LLC
21090 N PIMA RD Scottsdale AZ 85255 United States
844-693-6546
http://www.PioneerAdvisors.com

Pioneer Investments
Amundi Pioneer Investments 60 State Street Boston MA 02109 United States
617-742-7825
http://www.pioneerinvestments.com

PMC Funds
PMC Funds 35 E. Wacker Drive, Suite 1600 Chicago IL 60601 United States
http://www.investpmc.com

Power Mutual Funds
629 Washington Street Norwood, MA 02062 United States
877-779-7462
http://www.powermutualfunds.com/

Ppm America
PPM America 225 West Wacker Drive, Suite 1200 Chicago IL 60606 United States
844-446-4776
http://www.ppmamerica.com/ppmfunds

Praxis Mutual Funds
Praxis Mutual Funds 303 Broadway, Suite 900 Cincinnati OH 45202 United States
http://www.praxismutualfunds.com

Principal Funds
Principal Funds 430 W 7th St, Ste 219971 Kansas City MO 64105-1407 United States
800-787-1621
http://www.principalfunds.com

Priority Income Fund
10 East 40th Street, 42nd Floor New York New York NY 10016 United States
http://www.priority-incomefund.com

ProFunds
Profunds 3435 Stelzler Rd Columbus OH 43219 United States
614-470-8626
http://www.profunds.com

PT Asset Management, LLC (PTAM)
PT Asset Management, LLC (PTAM) P.O. Box 701 Milwaukee WI 53201-0701 United States
http://www.ptamfunds.com

Putnam
Putnam 100 Federal Street Boston MA 02110 United States
617-292-1000
http://www.putnam.com

Rational Funds
Rational Funds 36 North New York Avenue NY Huntington 11743 United States
800-253-0412
http://www.rationalmf.com

RBB Funds
RBB Funds 125 W. 55th Street New York NY 10019 United States
http://www.matsonmoney.com

RBC Global Asset Management.
RBC Global Asset Management 100 South Fifth Street, Suite 2300 Minneapolis MN 55402 United States
800-422-2766
http://www.rbcgam.us

Red Cedar
Red Cedar 333 Bridge Street NW, Suite 601 Grand Rapids MI 49504 United States
888-626-2575
http://www.redcedarfunds.com

Redwood
Redwood United States
http://www.redwoodmutualfund.com

Resource Real Estate
Resource Real Estate One Commerce Square 2005 Market Street, 15th Floor Philadelphia PA United States
855-747-9559
http://www.RREDIF.com

Rimrock Funds Trust
Rimrock Funds Trust 100 INNOVATION DRIVE SUITE 200 IRVINE CA 92617 United States
949-381-7800

River Canyon
United States United States

RiverNorth Capital Management, LLC
RiverNorth Capital Management, LLC 325 N. LaSalle Street, Suite 645 Chicago IL 60654 United States
312-832-1440
http://www.rivernorth.com

RiverNorth Funds
RiverNorth Funds 325 N Lasalle St. Suite 645 Chicago IL 60654 United States
312-832-1440
http://www.rivernorthfunds.com

RiverPark Funds
RiverPark Funds 156 West 56th Street, 17th Floor, New York, NY 10011 United States
888-564-4517
http://www.riverparkfunds.com

Rockefeller
Rockefeller United States
http://www.rockefellerfunds.com/

Russell
1301 Second Avenue 18th Floor Seattle 98101 United States
800-426-7969
http://https://russellinvestments.com

Ryan Labs
88 Pine St Fl 32 88 Pine Street, 32Nd Floor New York NY 100051801 United States
212-635-2300
http://www.ryanlabsfunds.com

Rydex Funds
Rydex Funds 9601 Blackwell Rd, Suite 500 Rockville MD 20850 United States
800-820-0888
http://www.guggenheiminvestments.com

SA Funds
SA Funds 3055 Olin Ave,Suite 2000 San Jose CA 95128 United States
http://www.sa-funds.net

Saratoga
Saratoga 99 Wall Street, Suite 1200 New York NY 10005 United States
800-807-3863
http://www.saratogacap.com/

Saturna Capital
Saturna Capital 1300 N. State St. Bellingham WA 98225 United States
http://www.saturna.com

Saturna Sustainable Funds
United States United States
http://www.saturnasustainable.com

Schroder
Schroders 875 Third Avenue, 22nd Floor New York NY United States
800-464-3108
http://www.schroderfunds.com/

Schwab Funds
Schwab Funds 101 Montgomery Street San Francisco CA 94104 United States
877-824-5615
http://www.schwabfunds.com

Secure Investment Management
Secure Investment Management 3067 W. Ina Rd., Suite 125 Tucson AZ 85741 United States
888-802-0427
http://www.secureinvestmentmanagement.com/

Segall Bryant & Hamill
Segall Bryant & Hamill 540 West Madison Street, Suite 1900 Chicago IL 60661-2551 United States
312-474-1222
http://sbhic.com

SEI
SEI Asset Allocation Trust 1 Freedom Valley Drive Oaks PA 19456 United States
800-342-5734
http://www.seic.com

Semper
Semper Funds P.O. Box 588 Portland ME 04112 United States
877-828-8210
http://www.sempercap.com

Sextant Mutual Funds
Sextant United States
http://www.sextantfunds.com

Shelton Capital Management
Shelton Capital Management 455 Market Street, Suite 1600 San Francisco CA 94105 United States
800-955-9988
http://www.sheltoncap.com

Shenkman Funds
Shenkman Funds United States
http://www.shenkmancapital.com/funds

Sierra Trust
Sierra Trust Funds 9301 Corbin Avenue Suite 333 Northridge CA 91328-1160 United States
http://www.SierraMutualFunds.com.

Sit
Sit 101 Sabin Street Pawtucket RI 2860 United States
800-332-5580
http://www.sitfunds.com

Spirit of America
Spirit of America 477 Jericho Turnpike Syosset NY 11791 United States

State Farm
State Farm Life Insurance Company One State Farm Plaza Bloomington IL 61710-0001 United States
http://www.statefarm.com

State Street Global Advisors
State Street Global Advisors One Iron Street Boston MA 02210 United States
617-664-7338
http://www.ssga.com

Sterling Capital Funds
434 Fayetteville Street Mall 5th Floor,434 Fayetteville Street Mall Raleigh NC 27601 United States
800-228-1872
http://www.sterlingcapitalfunds.com

Stone Harbor
5015 District Blvd Vernon CA 900582719 United States
323-277-2777
http://www.shiplp.com

Stone Harbor Investment Partners LP
10 S. Riverside Plaza Suite 875 Chicago IL 60606 United States
212-548-1200

Symmetry Partners
151 National Drive Glastonbury CT 06033 United States
800-786-3309
http://www.symmetrypartners.com

T. Rowe Price
T. Rowe Price 100 East Pratt Street Baltimore MD 21202 United States
410-345-2000
http://www.troweprice.com

TCW
TCW 865 South Figueroa Street,Suite 1800 Los Angeles CA 90017 United States
213-244-0000
http://www.tcw.com

The Pacific Financial Group
The Pacific Financial Group 777 108th Avenue NE Suite 2100 Bellevue WA 98004 United States
800-735-7199
http://www.TPFG.com

Thompson IM
Thompson IM United States
http://www.thompsonim.com

Thornburg
Thornburg Investment Management 2300 North Ridgetop Road Santa Fe NM 87506 United States
800-847-0200
http://www.thornburg.com

Thrivent
Thrivent Mutual Funds 625 Fourth Avenue South Minneapolis MN 55415 United States
http://www.thrivent.com

Thrivent Funds
Thrivent Funds 625 Fourth Avenue South Minneapolis MN 55415 United States
http://ThriventFunds.com

TIAA Investments
TIAA-CREF Funds P.O. Box 1259 Charlotte NC 28201 United States
877-518-9161
http://www.tiaa.org

Timothy Plan
Timothy Plan 1055 Maitland Center Commons Maitland FL 32759 United States
800-662-0201
http://www.timothyplan.com

Toews Funds
Toews Funds P.O. Box 446 Portland ME 04112 United States
http://www.ToewsCorp.com.

Tortoise
5100 W. 115th Place Leawood KS 66211 United States
913-981-1020

Touchstone
Touchstone 303 Broadway, Suite 1100, PO Box 5354 Cincinnati OH 45201-5354 United States
800-543-0407
http://www.touchstoneinvestments.com

Transamerica
Transamerica Funds 1801 California Street, Suite 5200 Denver CO 80202 United States
888-233-4339
http://www.transamericafunds.com

TransWestern Funds
TransWestern Funds United States
http://www.TransWesternFunds.com

Tributary Funds
Tributary Funds PO Box 219022 Kansas City MO 64121-9022 United States
http://www.tributaryfunds.com

Trust for Credit Unions
Trust for Credit Unions 4900 Sears Tower Chicago IL 60606-6303 United States
http://www.trustcu.com

U.S. Global Investors
U.S. Global Investors P.O. Box 781234 San Antonio TX 78278-1234 United States
800-873-8637
http://www.usfunds.com

UBS Asset Management
1285 Avenue of Americas New York NY 10019 United States
212-882-5586
http://www.ubs.com

VALIC
VALIC 2929 Allen Parkway Houston TX 77019 United States
http://https://www.valic.com

Value Line
Value Line 7 Times Square, Suite 1606 New York NY 10036. United States
800-243-2729
http://www.vlfunds.com

VanEck
Van Eck Associates Corporation 666 Third Avenue New York NY 10017 United States
800-826-1115
http://www.vaneck.com

Vanguard
Vanguard 100 Vanguard Boulevard Malvern PA 19355 United States
877-662-7447
http://www.vanguard.com

Vertical Capital
Vertical Capital 20 Pacifica, Suite 190, Irvine, CA Irvine CA 92618 United States
866-224-8867
http://verticalus.com/

Victory Capital
Victory Capital Management Inc. 15935 La Cantera Parkway, Building Two San Antonio TX 78256 United States
210-694-9700
http://www.vcm.com

Virtus
Virtus Opportunities Trust 101 Munson Street Greenfield MA 1301 United States
800-243-1574
http://www.virtus.com

Virtus Investment Partners Inc
PO Box 9874 Providence RI United States

Voya
Voya Investments 7337 E. Doubletree Ranch Road Scottsdale AZ 85258 United States
800-366-0066
http://www.voyainvestments.com

Voya Investments, LLC
Voya Investments, LLC 7337 East Doubletree Ranch Road Scottsdale AZ 85258 United States

Waddell & Reed
Waddell & Reed Financial Advisors 6300 Lamar Ave Overland Park KS 66202 United States
888-923-3355
http://www.waddell.com

Wasatch
Wasatch Funds Inc P.O. Box 2172 Milwaukee WI United States
800-551-1700
http://www.wasatchfunds.com

Wasmer Schroeder
1111 Superior Avenue, Suite 1100 Cleveland OH 44114 United States
216-622-0000

Wavelength Funds
c/o Ultimus Fund Distributors, LLC c/o Ultimus Fund Distributors, LLC United States
http://www.wavelengthfunds.com

Weitz
Weitz Funds 1125 South 103rd Street, Suite 200 Omaha NE 68124-1071 United States
800-304-9745
http://www.weitzfunds.com

Wells Fargo
Wells Fargo 420 MONTGOMERY STREET San Francisco NULL NULL United States
877-709-8009
http://www.wellsfargo.com/

Wells Fargo Funds
Wells Fargo Funds 525 Market Street San Francisco CA 94105 United States
800-222-8222
http://https://www.wellsfargofunds.com/

WesMark
WesMark Funds 5800 Corporate Drive Pittsburgh PA United States
800-861-1013
http://www.wesmarkfunds.com

Westwood
The WHG Funds P.O. Box 219009 Kansas City MO United States
http://www.westwoodfunds.com

Wilbanks Smith & Thomas
Wilbanks Smith & Thomas 150 West Main Street, Suite 1700 Norfolk VA 23510 United States
865-243-8000
http://www.wstamfunds.com

William Blair
The William Blair Building 150 North Riverside Plaza Chicago IL 60606 United States
312-364-5409
http://www.williamblair.com

Wilmington Funds
Wilmington Funds 100 e. Pratt Street,17th Floor Baltimore MD 21202 United States
800-836-2211
http://www.wilmingtonfunds.com

Wilshire Mutual Funds
Wilshire Mutual Funds 1299 Ocean Avenue, Suite 700 King Of Prussia PA 19406 United States
888-200-6796
http://www.advisor.wilshire.com

WP Trust
Wp Trust 129 NW 13th Street, Suite D-26 Boca Raton FL FL 33432 United States
800-950-9112

XAI Octagon FR & Alt Income Term Trust
321 NORTH CLARK STREET #2430 Chicago Illinois 60654 United States
http://xainvestments.com/funds/

Yorktown Funds
Yorktown Funds 2303 Yorktown Ave Lynchburg VA 24501 United States
800-544-6060
http://www.yorktownfunds.com

Zeo
Zeo United States
http://www.zeo.com

Ziegler
c/o U.S. Bancorp Fund Services, LLC, PO Box 701 Milwaukee WI 53201-0701 United States
877-568-7633
http://www.zcmfunds.com

Weiss Ratings Investment Series

Weiss Ratings Investment Research Guide to Stock Mutual Funds

Weiss Ratings Investment Research Guide to Stock Mutual Funds provides immediate access to Weiss' Buy-Hold-Sell Investment Ratings, key rating factors, and summary financial data for 20,000 stock mutual funds—more than any other ratings publication. This easy-to-use guide provides understandable, accurate investment ratings so investors can make informed decisions about their investment selections.

- Index of Stock Mutual Funds – with data on 20,000 funds
- Expanded Analysis of 100 Largest Stock Mutual Funds
- Best All-Around Stock Mutual Funds
- Consistent Return BUY Stock Mutual Funds
- High Performance Stock Mutual Funds
- Low Volatility Stock Mutual Funds
- BUY Rated Stock Mutual Funds by Category

Annual Subscription of 4 Quarterly Issues: $549 | Single Issue: $279

Weiss Ratings Investment Research Guide to Exchange-Traded Funds

With investing such a complex subject and the growing popularity of exchange-traded funds as a simple way to enter the markets it is no surprise that consumers need assistance. *Weiss Ratings Investment Research Guide to Exchange-Traded Funds* answers this need, by providing accurate, easy-to-understand ratings and financial data on more than 2,200 ETFs.

- Index of Exchange-Traded Funds – over 2,200 funds are included
- Expanded Analysis of All BUY Rated Exchange-Traded Funds
- Expanded Analysis of ETFs with Assets over 50 Million
- Best One-Year Return BUY Rated Exchange-Traded Funds
- Best Low Expense Exchange-Traded Funds
- BUY Rated Exchange-Traded Funds by Category

Annual Subscription of 4 Quarterly Issues: $549 | Single Issue: $279

Weiss Ratings Investment Research Guide to Stocks

Taking into account the thousands of stock options available, it is no surprise that consumers need assistance. It is a complex subject and consumers want unbiased, independent guidance in helping them find a path to investing that is focused on their needs. *Weiss Ratings Investment Research Guide to Stocks* gives investors and consumers independent, unbiased data on which stocks to consider and those that should be avoided.

- Index of Stocks – over 11,000 U.S. traded stocks are listed
- Best Performing Stocks
- High Yield BUYs
- Stocks with High Volatility
- Undervalued Stocks by Sector
- BUY Rated Stocks by Sector
- Expanded Analysis of All A Rated Stocks

Annual Subscription of 4 Quarterly Issues: $549 | Single Issue: $279